INTRODUCING: THE DIGITAL TOOL

A Digital Tool. Why?

The professional role of accountants is changing. Advances in technology have relegated the mechanical aspects of accounting to the computer. The "new accountants" are concerned about the implications of these numbers. What do they actually mean and what are their effects on the decision-making process, both from a company and individual investor perspective? To address this issue, the Tenth Edition of INTERMEDIATE ACCOUNTING features a new Digital Tool that develops the financial analysis and reporting skills students need for the new roles they will play in the workforce.

What Is It?

The DIGITAL TOOL is an electronic gateway, either through the CD-ROM or the Internet, to a comprehensive set of materials that uniquely prepares students to enter the profession as communicators, consultants, and decision-makers. It is comprised of three main components: Analyst's Toolkit, Professional Toolkit, and Student Helper Toolkit.

Contents of the Digital Tool

1. The Analyst's Toolkit
   - A Financial Statement Analysis primer that provides the theoretical background students need to develop skills
   - An annual report database of more than 30 real companies where students can develop their financial analysis and reporting skills
   - Company Web links with industry codes
   - Pre-formatted Excel worksheets for performing ratio analysis
   - Spreadsheet Tools (present value templates)
   - Additional Web links
   - Assignment material
2. The Professional Toolkit
   - Accountant's Writing Handbook that helps students effectively communicate results
   - Group activity model for instructors and students
   - Expanded discussion of ethics
   - Career and professional spotlights including salary information, a résumé builder, and related Web links
3. Student Helper Toolkit
   - 15 Web-based self-study questions for each chapter
   - Expanded discussion of International Accounting
   - Additional topics of interest and illustrations not covered in text

Checklist of key figures

PowerPoint slides for study and review for each chapter

Learning Styles Survey

Intermediate Accounting

TENTH EDITION

INTERMEDIATE ACCOUNTING

Donald E. Kieso Ph.D., C.P.A.
KPMG Peat Marwick Emeritus Professor of Accounting
Northern Illinois University
DeKalb, Illinois

Jerry J. Weygandt Ph.D., C.P.A.
Arthur Andersen Alumni Professor of Accounting
University of Wisconsin
Madison, Wisconsin

Terry D. Warfield Ph.D.
PricewaterhouseCoopers Research Scholar
University of Wisconsin
Madison, Wisconsin

John Wiley & Sons, Inc.
New York • Chichester • Weinheim
Brisbane • Singapore • Toronto

PUBLISHER: Susan Elbe
ACQUISITIONS EDITOR: Mark Bonadeo
DEVELOPMENTAL EDITOR: Ellen Ford
MEDIA EDITOR: David B. Kear
SUPPLEMENTS EDITOR: Julie Kerr
MARKETING MANAGER: Clancy Marshall
PRODUCTION SERVICES MANAGER: Jeanine Furino
PHOTO EDITOR: Nicole Horlacher
ILLUSTRATION EDITOR: Anna Melhorn
TEXT DESIGNER: Lee Goldstein
COVER DESIGNER: Carol C. Grobe
PROJECT MANAGEMENT: Elm Street Publishing Services, Inc.
COVER PHOTOS: ©James Rudnick/The Stock Market

Perspective background collage photo credits: Palm Pilot courtesy A&R Partners. Pencils ©EyeWire, Inc. Electronic Organizer and Adding Machine Tape ©CORBIS.

All "Perspectives On" and "From Classroom to Career" photographs provided courtesy of featured individuals.

This book was set in Palatino by York Graphic Services and printed and bound by Von Hoffmann Press. The cover was printed by Lehigh Press.

This book is printed on acid-free paper. ∞

0-471-36304-9
0-471-39225-1 (Wiley International Edition)
Printed in the United States of America
10 9 8 7 6 5 4 3

Dedicated to our wives,

Donna, Enid, and Mary,

and to our children,

Douglas and Debra,

Matt, Erin, and Lia,

Andrew, Lauren, and Katie,

for their

Love, Support, and Encouragement

About the Authors

Donald E. Kieso, Ph.D., C.P.A., received his bachelor's degree from Aurora University and his doctorate in accounting from the University of Illinois. He has served as chairman of the Department of Accountancy and is currently the KPMG Peat Marwick Emeritus Professor of Accountancy at Northern Illinois University. He has public accounting experience with Price Waterhouse & Co. (San Francisco and Chicago) and Arthur Andersen & Co. (Chicago) and research experience with the Research Division of the American Institute of Certified Public Accountants (New York). He has done postdoctorate work as a Visiting Scholar at the University of California at Berkeley and is a recipient of NIU's Teaching Excellence Award and four Golden Apple Teaching Awards. Professor Kieso is the author of other accounting and business books and is a member of the American Accounting Association, the American Institute of Certified Public Accountants, and the Illinois CPA Society. He has served as a member of the Board of Directors of the Illinois CPA Society, the AACSB's Accounting Accreditation Committees, the State of Illinois Comptroller's Commission, as Secretary-Treasurer of the Federation of Schools of Accountancy, and as Secretary-Treasurer of the American Accounting Association. Professor Kieso is currently serving as Chairman of the Board of Trustees and Executive Committee of Aurora University, as a member of the Boards of Directors of Castle BancGroup Inc. and the Sandwich State Bank, and as Treasurer and Director of Valley West Community Hospital. From 1989 to 1993 he served as a charter member of the national Accounting Education Change Commission. In 1988 he received the Outstanding Accounting Educator Award from the Illinois CPA Society, in 1992 he received the FSA's Joseph A. Silvoso Award of Merit and the NIU Foundation's Humanitarian Award for Service to Higher Education, and in 1995 he received a Distinguished Service Award from the Illinois CPA Society.

Jerry J. Weygandt, Ph.D., C.P.A., is Arthur Andersen Alumni Professor of Accounting at the University of Wisconsin—Madison. He holds a Ph.D. in accounting from the University of Illinois. Articles by Professor Weygandt have appeared in the *Accounting Review, Journal of Accounting Research, Accounting Horizons, Journal of Accountancy,* and other academic and professional journals. These articles have examined such financial reporting issues as accounting for price-level adjustments, pensions, convertible securities, stock option contracts, and interim reports. Professor Weygandt is author of other accounting and financial reporting books and is a member of the American Accounting Association, the American Institute of Certified Public Accountants, and the Wisconsin Society of Certified Public Accountants. He has served on numerous committees of the American Accounting Association and as a member of the editorial board of the *Accounting Review;* he also has served as President and Secretary-Treasurer of the American Accounting Association. In addition, he has been actively involved with the American Institute of Certified Public Accountants and has been a member of the Accounting Standards Executive Committee (AcSEC) of that organization. He has served on the FASB task force that examined the reporting issues related to accounting for income taxes and is presently a trustee of the Financial Accounting Foundation. Professor Weygandt has received the Chancellor's Award for Excellence in Teaching and the Beta Gamma Sigma Dean's Teaching Award. He is on the board of directors of M & I Bank of Southern Wisconsin and the Dean Foundation. Recently he received the Wisconsin Institute of CPA's Outstanding Educator's Award and the Lifetime Achievement Award.

Terry D. Warfield, Ph.D., is PricewaterhouseCoopers Research Scholar at the University of Wisconsin—Madison. He received a B.S. and M.B.A. from Indiana University and a Ph.D. in accounting from the University of Iowa. Professor Warfield's area of expertise is financial reporting, and prior to his academic career, he worked for five years in the banking industry. He served as the Academic Accounting Fellow in the Office of the Chief Accountant at the U.S. Securities and Exchange Commission in Washington, D.C., from 1995–1996. While on the staff, he worked on projects related to financial instruments and financial institutions, and he helped coordinate a symposium on intangible asset financial reporting. Professor Warfield's primary research interests concern financial accounting standards and disclosure policies. He has published scholarly articles in *The Accounting Review, Journal of Accounting and Economics, Research in Accounting Regulation,* and *Accounting Horizons,* and he has served on the editorial boards of *The Accounting Review* and *Accounting Horizons.* He has served on the Financial Accounting Standards Committee of the American Accounting Association (past Chair 1995–1996) and on the Association Council, the Nominations Committee, and the AAA-FASB Research Conference Committee. Professor Warfield has taught accounting courses at the introductory, intermediate, and graduate levels. He has received teaching awards at both the University of Iowa and the University of Wisconsin, and he was named to the Teaching Academy at the University of Wisconsin in 1995. Professor Warfield has developed and published several case studies based on his research for use in accounting classes. These cases have been selected for the AICPA Professor-Practitioner Case Development Program, and a case on hybrid securities has been published in *Issues in Accounting Education.* Professor Warfield also has developed materials on cooperative learning in accounting that have been presented at teaching workshops at the University of Wisconsin and included in instructor materials for accounting textbooks.

Preface

This edition of *Intermediate Accounting* represents an important milestone in the evolution of this textbook—the tenth edition of a text that has been a "Gateway to the Profession" for over a million students who have used its prior editions. As with the prior editions, in planning this edition we conducted extensive market research, including instructor focus groups, student focus groups, direct mail and electronic mail surveys, and one-on-one discussions with practitioners to help us focus on how the text should evolve into the next millennium.

Two themes emerged from this research. These themes confirmed development decisions made in recent editions of *Intermediate Accounting* and suggested ways that we could further enhance the usefulness of the text to students and instructors. The first theme is the continuing rapid pace of information technology and, in particular, the growth of the Internet. This continuing trend confirmed our decision to feature Intel for the specimen financial statements in the ninth edition and to continue their use in the tenth edition. Similar to *Intermediate Accounting,* Intel continues to lead its industry—one characterized by rapid-fire change and increasing diversified needs. Further support for this information technology trend is reflected in the introduction in this edition of the *Gateway to the Profession* Digital Tool.

The Digital Tool is an electronic gateway, either via the Internet or CD-ROM, to a comprehensive set of materials that supplement the already-comprehensive coverage of accounting topics in the textbook. Included are "professional tools" related to written communication, working in groups, and ethics. A financial analyst's toolkit contains a comprehensive primer on financial statement analysis and a collection of over 30 real-company financial statements that students can access for financial statement and other research. Also included are expanded discussions and illustrations for topics such as international accounting and the accounting for securitizations, and additional real-company disclosures for topics introduced in the text. We believe the *Gateway to the Profession* Digital Tool will be an invaluable resource to students that will help them get the most out of their *Intermediate Accounting* investment.

The second theme that emerged from our research is the continuing evolution of the accounting profession and accounting education away from knowledge of accounting facts to the development of skills in how to *use* accounting facts and procedures in various business contexts. This trend is reflected in the recent framework introduced by the AICPA that recommends a skill-based as opposed to a fact-based accounting curriculum and confirms the recommendations of the Accounting Education Change Commission. Accountants must act as well as think, and we believe that it is important for students to understand the how as well as the why of accounting. The content and focus of many of the elements of the *Gateway to the Profession* Digital Tool (writing, working in teams, analyst's toolkit) respond to this trend by providing an expanded set of materials that can be used to extend and apply the concepts and methods introduced within the text.

We continue to strive for a balanced discussion of conceptual and procedural presentation so that these elements are mutually reinforcing. In addition, discussions focus on explaining the rationale behind business transactions before addressing the accounting and reporting for those transactions. As in prior editions, we have thoroughly revised and updated the text to include all the latest developments in the accounting profession and practice. Benefiting from the comments and recommendations of adopters of the ninth edition, we have made significant revisions. Explanations have been expanded where necessary; complicated discussions and illustrations have been simplified; realism has been integrated to heighten interest and relevancy; and new topics and coverage have been added to maintain currency. We have deleted some ninth edition coverage from the text. To provide the instructor with no loss in material coverage and flexibility in use, discussions of less commonly used methods, more complex, or specialized topics have been moved to the Digital Tool.

NEW FEATURES

Based on extensive reviews, focus groups, and interactions with other intermediate accounting instructors and students, we have developed a number of new pedagogical features and content changes designed both to help students learn more effectively and to answer the changing needs of the course.

Digital Tool

As mentioned above, a major new resource developed for this edition is the *Gateway to the Profession* Digital Tool. The Digital Tool is an electronic gateway, either via the Internet or CD-ROM, to a comprehensive set of materials that supplement the already-comprehensive coverage of accounting topics in the textbook. When the Digital Tool icon (shown in the margin) appears in the textbook, the student is directed to expanded materials as described below. Major elements of the Digital Tool are:

Analyst's Toolkit

The Analyst's Toolkit contains the following items.

Database of Real Companies. Over 20 annual reports of well-known companies, including several international companies, are provided on the Digital Tool. These annual reports can be used in a variety of ways. For example, they can be used as illustrations of different presentations of financial information or for comparing note disclosures across companies. In addition, these reports can be used to analyze a company's financial condition and compare its prospects with other companies in the same industry. Assignment material provides some examples of different types of analysis that can be performed.

Company Web Links. Each of the companies in the database of real companies is identified by a Web address to facilitate the gathering of additional information, if desired.

Preformatted Excel Worksheets. Worksheets formatted in Excel are available for some assignments on the Digital Tool. For example, students may be asked to compute key ratios for a certain company (with a digital calculator provided), and to compare the computed ratios against those of another company. The other company's ratios are provided on a worksheet to expedite the analysis phase of the assignment.

Additional Enrichment Material. A chapter on Financial Statement Analysis is provided, with related assignment material. This chapter can also be used with the database of annual reports of real companies.

Spreadsheet Tools. Present value templates are provided which can be used to solve time value of money problems.

Additional Internet Links. A number of useful links related to financial analysis are provided to expand expertise in this area.

Professional Toolkit

Consistent with expanding beyond technical accounting knowledge, the *Gateway to the Profession* Digital Tool emphasizes certain skills necessary to become a successful accountant and financial manager.

Writing Materials. A primer on professional communications is provided that will give students a framework for writing professional materials. This primer discusses issues such as the top ten writing problems, strategies for prewriting, how to do revisions, and tips on clarity. This primer has been class tested and is effective in helping students enhance their writing skills.

Group Work Materials. Recent evaluation of accounting education has identified the need to develop more skills in group problem solving. The Digital Tool provides a second primer dealing with the role that groups play in organizations. Information on what makes a successful group, and how students can participate effectively in the group, is included.

Ethics. Expanded materials on the role of ethics in the profession are part of the Digital Tool, including references to:

- Speeches and articles on ethics in accounting.
- Codes of ethics for major professional bodies.
- Examples and additional case studies on ethics.

Career Professional Spotlights. Every student should have a good understanding of the profession that he or she is entering. Various vignettes in the Digital Tool indicate the types of work that accountants do. These vignettes are interviews with professional accountants, some well known and some only a few years out of college. Some of these interviews are included in the book but are also included, along with others that are not in the book, on the Digital Tool.

Other aspects of the spotlight on careers are also included. As part of the *Gateway to the Profession* Digital Tool, the following information is provided to help students make successful career choices:

- Salary information by region of the country.
- A résumé builder, to help students prepare a professional-looking résumé.
- Professional Web-links—important links to Web sites that can provide useful career information.

Student Helper Toolkit

Expanded Discussions and Illustrations. This section provides additional topics that are not covered in depth in the textbook. The *Gateway to the Profession* Digital Tool gives the flexibility to discuss these topics of interest in more detail.

Additional topics are as follows (with appropriate chapter linkage identified):

Chapter 3

- Presentation of worksheet using the periodic method.
- Specialized journals and methods of processing accounting data.

Chapter 6

- Present-value based measurements.

Chapter 7

- Discussion of how a four-column bank reconciliation (often referred to as the proof of cash) can be used for control purposes.
- Expanded example of transfers of receivables without recourse, with accounting entries.

Chapter 11

- Discussion of lesser-used depreciation methods, such as the retirement and replacement methods.

Chapter 17

- Comprehensive earnings per share illustration.

Chapter 18

- Illustration of accounting entries for transfers of investment securities.

Chapter 20

- Discussion of the conceptual aspects of interperiod tax allocation, including the deferred and net of tax methods.
- Discussion of accounting for intraperiod tax allocation, with examples.

Chapter 22

- Real estate leases and leveraged leases.

Chapter 24

- Discussion of the T-account method for preparing a statement of cash flows. A detailed example is provided.

Chapter 25

- Discussion of accounting for changing prices both for general and specific price level changes.
- In addition to these materials, illustrative disclosures of financial reporting practices are provided.

International Accounting. An expanded discussion of international accounting institutions, the evolution of international accounting standards, and a framework for understanding differences in accounting practice is provided. This discussion is designed to complement the international reporting problems in the textbook.

Learning Style Survey. Research on left brain/right brain differences and also on learning and personality differences suggests that each person has preferred ways to receive and communicate information. After completing this survey, students will be able to pinpoint the study aids in the text that will help them learn the material based on their particular learning styles.

In summary, the *Gateway to the Profession* Digital Tool is a comprehensive complement to the tenth edition of *Intermediate Accounting,* providing new materials as well as a new way to communicate that material. The contents of the Digital Tool will be accessible to students either on a CD-ROM or online at the Wiley Web site. In addition, the following items are provided on the Kieso web site (www.wiley.com/college/kieso).

Self-Study Multiple Choice Questions. For each chapter, 15 multiple-choice questions are provided in the Digital Tool for review purposes. In addition to the correct answer, reasons are provided as to why the answer is correct. These multiple-choice questions can be used to assess the student's understanding of the subject material covered in the course and also as a quick review of the chapter.

Checklist of Key Figures. A checklist of key figures by chapter is included.

PowerPoint Presentations. A PowerPoint presentation by chapter is provided for study and review purposes.

Calculator Solutions

Financial calculator solutions (marked with the icon shown here in the margin) are included for certain time value of money problems throughout the textbook. These solutions will help enhance student skills in using a financial calculator.

International Reporting Cases

We have extended the international coverage in the text by introducing a number of international reporting cases that are based on real companies and designed to illustrate international accounting differences. These cases illustrate the importance of adjusting international financial statements to make them comparable across countries. This emphasis reinforces the user orientation of the "Using Your Judgement" element.

ENHANCED FEATURES

We have continued and enhanced many of the features that were introduced in the ninth edition of *Intermediate Accounting*, including:

Chapter-opening Vignettes

We have updated and introduced new chapter-opening vignettes to provide an even better real-world context that helps motivate student interest in the chapter topic.

Using Your Judgment

The "Using Your Judgment" elements (Financial Reporting Problems, Financial Statement Analysis, Comparative Analysis, and Research Cases) at the end of each chapter have been revised and updated. In addition, explicit writing and group assignments have been integrated into the exercises, problems, and cases. Exercises, problems, and cases that are especially suited for group or writing assignments are identified with special icons, as shown here in the margin.

Real-World Emphasis

We believe that one of the goals of the intermediate accounting course is to orient students to the application of accounting principles and techniques in practice. Accordingly, we have continued our practice of using numerous examples from real corporations, highlighted in red, throughout the text. Illustrations and exhibits marked by the icon shown here are excerpts from actual financial statements of existing firms. In addition, the 1998 annual report of Intel Corporation, is included in Appendix 5B, and many real-company financial reports appear in the database on the Digital Tool.

Perspectives

We have retained the interviews with prominent accounting and business personalities on relevant accounting topics. These interviews give a real-world emphasis that is important for students in the intermediate accounting course who are considering choosing accounting as a career. In the tenth edition, we have updated a number of interviews from the ninth edition and added new interviews with accounting professionals as well as with young accountants who describe their transitions from school into the business world in interviews entitled "From Classroom to Career."

International Insights

International Insight paragraphs that describe or compare the accounting practices in other countries are provided in the margin. We have continued this feature to help students understand that other countries sometimes use different recognition and measurement principles to report financial information.

Streamlined Presentation

We have continued our efforts to keep the topical coverage of *Intermediate Accounting* in line with the way instructors are currently teaching the course. Accordingly, we have moved some optional topics into appendices and have omitted altogether some topics that formerly were covered in appendices, moving them to the Digital Tool. Details are noted in the list of specific content changes below.

Currency and Accuracy

Accounting continually changes as its environment changes; an up-to-date book is therefore a necessity. As in past editions, we have strived to make this edition the most up-to-date and accurate text available.

CONTENT CHANGES

The following list outlines the revisions and improvements made in chapters of the tenth edition.

Chapter 1

- New vignette.
- Updated international discussion.

Chapter 2

- Increased emphasis on fair-value accounting.
- Increased emphasis on revenue recognition.
- Revised section on materiality.

Chapter 3

- Revised discussion of inventory methods with emphasis on the perpetual inventory method.
- Simplified work sheet based on the perpetual method.
- Moved material on reversing entries to appendix.
- Discussion of subsidiary ledgers and special journals moved to the Digital Tool.
- Revised and simplified section on conversion from cash to accrual basis.
- The accounting equation has been inserted in the margin next to key journal entries in this chapter. This new feature reinforces the students' understanding of the impact of an accounting transaction on the financial statements.

Chapter 4

- New discussion and infographic that simplify the discussion related to the advantages and disadvantages of the income statement.
- New section on earnings management.
- Revised section on irregular items, emphasizing restructuring charges and reporting within the income statement.

Chapter 5

- New infographic that simplifies the discussion related to the advantages and disadvantages of the balance sheet.
- Moved discussion of subsequent events to the disclosure materials in Chapter 25.
- Introduced discussion of financial instruments.

Chapter 6

- New appendix on using a financial calculator called "Technology Tools for Time Value Problems." It illustrates how to use a financial calculator or computer spreadsheet to solve time value of money problems.
- Introduced calculator solutions for selected problems.

Chapter 7

- New vignette on sale of loans by sub-prime lenders.
- Updated discussion on control of cash and electronic commerce.
- Introduced calculator solutions.
- Additional real-company disclosures of cash and receivables.
- New graphic on impact of credit cards on bad debts.
- New discussion of allowance for loan losses used for earnings management.

Chapter 8

- New infographic on items included in inventory.
- Introduced real companies to illustrate merchandising and manufacturing inventories.

Chapter 9

- New opening vignette on inventory valuation.

Chapter 10

- New infographic on interest capitalization.
- Introduced real-company disclosure on interest capitalization.
- New infographic to summarize the accounting for exchanges.

Chapter 11

- New vignette on impairment, including discussion of international standards.
- New disclosure on impairments and property, plant, and equipment.

Chapter 12

- Revised discussion of characteristics of intangible assets.
- Expanded discussion of goodwill.
- New infographic on identifying research and development costs.
- Revised and updated discussion of start-up costs, advertising costs, and initial operating losses.
- Updated disclosures related to intangibles and research and development costs.
- Appendix updated for software costs developed or obtained for internal use.

Chapter 13

- New vignette on unearned revenues.
- New illustration summarizing payroll liabilities.
- Updated disclosures of current liabilities.

Chapter 14

- New vignette on weather bonds.
- Introduced calculator solutions.
- Updated real-company disclosure on debt extinguishment.
- Simplified discussion on the presentation and analysis of long-term debt.
- Updated real-company disclosure of long-term debt.

Chapter 15

- Updated vignette.
- New discussion on use of dividends versus treasury stock purchases.
- Revised discussion of issue costs.
- Revised discussion of debt-like preferred stock.

Chapter 16

- Updated vignette on stock splits
- Updated disclosure of the statement of stockholders' equity, including comprehensive income

Chapter 17

- Streamlined discussion of accounting for convertible debt.
- Updated discussion of preferred stock.
- Streamlined and updated discussion of political debate on stock option accounting.
- Updated real-company disclosure on stock compensation plans.
- Updated discussion in appendix on additional complications related to stock options.

Chapter 18

- New vignette on equity accounting.
- Enhanced discussion of portfolio effects of debt and equity investments.
- Moved Appendix 18A on transfers between categories to the Digital Tool.
- Moved Appendix 18B on changing from and to the equity method to Chapter 23 (*Accounting Changes*) to better illustrate these changes.
- Streamlined discussion in Appendix 18C on special issues related to investments.
- New appendix on accounting for derivatives.

Chapter 19

- New vignette on revenue recognition for Internet companies.
- Revised discussion on revenue recognition.

Chapter 20

- New vignette on management of tax costs.
- New discussion on differences between tax return and GAAP reporting.
- New real-company income tax disclosure.
- Deletion of alternative minimum tax.
- Moved discussion of intra-period tax allocation to the Digital Tool.
- Moved Appendix 20B on the conceptual aspects of inter-period tax allocation to the Digital Tool.

Chapter 21

- New vignette on wealth creation in retirement plans.
- New graphic on size of pension funds.
- Expanded discussion of trends in pensions.
- Streamlined discussion on capitalization versus non-capitalization.
- Updated discussion for new pension disclosure standard.
- Revised discussion on the Pension Reform Act and related issues.

Chapter 22

- Updated vignette on leasing.
- Streamlined discussion related to the advantages of leasing.
- Updated real-company disclosures of leases by lessees and lessors.
- Expanded discussion of rationale for sale-leaseback.

Chapter 23

- Updated discussion of motivations for changes.
- Appendix on changing from and to the equity method added.

Chapter 24

- Relocated "Usefulness of Statement of Cash Flows" section to the front of the chapter.
- Real-company disclosures used throughout the chapter.

Chapter 25

- Updated and simplified discussion of reporting for diversified companies.
- New section on subsequent events added.
- New discussion on Internet reporting.
- Updated discussion on reporting of future events.
- Updated discussion on fraudulent financial reporting and the profession's response.
- Moved the appendix "Accounting for Changing Prices" to the Digital Tool.

END-OF-CHAPTER ASSIGNMENT MATERIAL

At the end of each chapter we have provided a comprehensive set of review and homework material consisting of questions, exercises, problems, and short cases. For this edition, many of the exercises and problems have been revised or updated. In addition, the Using Your Judgment sections, which include financial reporting problems, ethics cases, financial statement analysis cases, comparative analysis cases, and research cases have all been updated. A number of international reporting cases that are based on real companies are introduced throughout the textbook. All of the assignment materials have been class tested and/or double checked for accuracy and clarity.

The questions are designed for review, self-testing, and classroom discussion purposes as well as homework assignments. Typically, a brief exercise covers one topic, an exercise one or two topics. Exercises require less time and effort to solve than problems and cases. The problems are designed to develop a professional level of achievement and are more challenging and time-consuming to solve than the exercises. Those exercises and problems that are contained in the *Excel Problems* supplements are identified by a blue computer disk icon in the margin. The cases generally require essay as opposed to quantitative solutions; they are intended to confront the student with situations calling for conceptual analysis and the exercise of judgment in identifying problems and evaluating alternatives. The Using Your Judgment assignments are designed to develop students' critical thinking, analytical, interpersonal, and communication skills.

Probably no more than one-fourth of the total exercise, problem, and case material must be used to cover the subject matter adequately; consequently, problem assignments may be varied from year to year.

COLOR DESIGN

The color coding in the design not only enlivens the textbook's appearance but, through planned and consistent usage, eases learning. Note that the financial statements are presented in beige screens with blue headers. Trial balances, work sheets, and large schedules are presented in blue screens with beige headers.

All end-of-chapter summaries and assignments (including appendices) are tabbed with a red color bar, while the five interest and annuity tables in Chapter 6 are tabbed with a blue color bar to make it easy to locate and identify them.

The color design is summarized as follows:

- The names of real-world companies in the text and illustrations are shown in red.
- Excerpts from the financial statements of real world companies are indicated by this icon .

- Other external statements have a blue heading with beige background for text.
- Internal statements show a beige heading and blue background for text.

SUPPLEMENTARY MATERIALS

Accompanying this textbook is an improved and expanded package of student learning aids and instructor teaching aids.

The *Intermediate Accounting,* 10/e, Digital Tool (CD-ROM and Web site) described in detail on pages ix–xii provides additional tools for students and instructors. Key features include:

- Analyst's Toolkit
- Professional Toolkit
- Student Helper Toolkit

Instructor Teaching Aids

Instructor's Resource System on CD-ROM

- Resource manager with friendly interface for course development and presentation.
- Includes all instructor supplements, text art, and transparencies.

Instructor's Manual: Vol. 1 Chs. 1–14
Instructor's Manual: Vol. 2 Chs. 15–25

- Lecture outlines keyed to text learning objectives
- Updated Bibliography.
- Teaching Transparency Masters.
- Section on "How to assign and evaluate ethical issues in the course."
- Sections on "How to incorporate writing" and "How to incorporate group (collaborative) work."

Solutions Manual, Vol. 1: Chs. 1–14
Solutions Manual, Vol. 2: Chs. 15–25

- Answers to all questions, brief exercises, exercises, problems, and case material provided.
- Classification Tables categorize the end-of-chapter material by topic to assist in assigning homework.
- Assignment Tables (characteristics) describe the end-of-chapter material, its difficulty level, and estimated completion time.
- All solutions triple-checked to ensure accuracy.

Test Bank, Vol. 1: Chs. 1–14
Test Bank, Vol. 2: Chs. 15–25

- Essay questions with solutions help you test students' communication skills.
- Estimated completion times facilitate test planning.
- Computations for multiple-choice problems assist you in giving partial credit.

Computerized Test Bank IBM 3.5″

- A large collection of objective questions and exercises with answers for each chapter in the text.

- Generate questions randomly or manually, and modify/customize tests with your own material.
- Create multiple versions of the same test by scrambling by type, character, number, or learning objective.

Test Preparation Service

- Simply call Wiley's Accounting Hotline (800) 541-5602 with the questions you have selected for an exam. Wiley will provide a master exam within 24 hours.

Solution Transparencies, Vol. 1: Chs. 1–14
Solution Transparencies, Vol. 2: Chs. 15–25

- Provided in organizer box with chapter file folders.
- Large, bold type size for easier class presentation.
- Provided for all exercises, problems, and cases.

PowerPoint Presentations

- Designed to enhance presentation of chapter topics and examples.
- Separate presentation for each chapter available on the Kieso Web site (www. wiley.com/college/kieso).

Teaching Transparencies

- Over 100 color figure illustrations and exhibits.
- 90% from outside the text.

Checklist of Key Figures

- Available at the Kieso Web site to both students and instructors.

Expanded Special Journal Discussion

Available under Instructor Resources at the Kieso Web site (www.wiley.com/college/kieso), this discussion includes

- Subsidiary ledgers and special journals for periodic inventory.
- Subsidiary ledgers and special journals for perpetual inventory.
- Periodic inventory method work sheet.
- Alternative treatment of prepaid expenses and unearned revenues.
- Addition problem material.

Student Learning Aids

Student Study Guide, Vol. 1: Chs. 1–14
Student Study Guide, Vol. 2: Chs. 15–25

- Chapter Learning Objectives.
- Chapter Outline—a broad overview of general chapter content with space for note-taking in class.
- Chapter Review with summary of key concepts.
- Glossary of key terms.
- Review Questions and Exercises—self-test items with supporting computations.

Workpapers, Vol. 1: Chs. 1–14
Workpapers, Vol. 2: Chs. 15–25
Electronic Working Papers. Vol. 1 Chs 1–14
Electronic Working Papers. Vol. 2 Chs 15–25

Problem Solving Survival Guide Vol. 1, Chs. 1–14
Problem Solving Survival Guide Vol. 2, Chs. 15–25

- Provides additional questions and problems to develop students' problem-solving skills.
- Explanations assist in the approach, set-up, and completion of problems.
- Tips alert students to common pitfalls and misconceptions.

Excel Problems

- Spreadsheet requirements range in difficulty (from data entry to developing spreadsheets).
- Review of intermediate accounting and Excel concepts.
- Each chapter consists of a basic tutorial, a more advanced tutorial, and two or three problems from the text.
- Each problem followed by "what-if" questions to build students' analytical skills.

Rockford Corporation: An Accounting Practice Set
Rockford Corporation: A Computerized Accounting Practice Set

- This practice set has been designed as a students' review and update of the accounting cycle and the preparation of financial statements. It is available in a print version and in a computerized version updated to a Windows platform.

ACKNOWLEDGMENTS

We thank the many users of our ninth edition who contributed to the revision through their comments and instructive criticism. Special thanks are extended to the primary reviewers of, and contributors to, our tenth edition manuscript.

Edwin Cohen
DePaul University

Judith Doing
University of Arizona

Susan Gill
Washington State University

M. Zafar Iqbal
California Polytechnic State University

Timothy Lindquist
University of Northern Iowa

Mostafa Maksy
Northeastern Illinois University

Carlton D. Stolle
Texas A&M University

Eric Sussman
University of California, Los Angeles

Diane L. Tanner
University of North Florida

Paula B. Thomas
Middle Tennessee State University

James D. Waddington, Jr.
Hawaii Pacific University

Michael Willenborg
University of Connecticut

Joni Young
University of New Mexico

Paul Zarowin
New York University

Other colleagues who have provided helpful criticisms and made valuable suggestions as members of focus groups, or as adopters and reviewers of previous editions include:

Charlene Abendroth
California State University—Hayward

Diana Adcox
University of North Florida

Noel Addy
Mississippi State University

James Bannister
University of Hartford

Kathleen Bauer
Midwestern State University

Jon A. Booker
Tennessee Technical University

John C. Borke
University of Wisconsin—Platteville

Suzanne M. Busch
California State University—Hayward

Eric Carlsen
Kean College of New Jersey

Patrick Delaney
Northern Illinois University

Dean S. Eiteman
Indiana University—Pennsylvania

Larry R. Falcetto
Emporia State University

Richard Fern
Eastern Kentucky University

Richard Fleischman
John Carroll University

Stephen L. Fogg
Temple University

Clyde Galbraith
West Chester University

Lynford E. Graham
Rutgers University

Jim Green
Arthur Andersen & Co.

Donald J. Griffin
Cayuga Community College

Marcia I. Halvorsen
University of Cincinnati

Gary Heesacker
Central Washington University

Wayne M. Higley
Buena Vista University

Geoffrey R. Horlick
St. Francis College

Cynthia Jeffrey
Iowa State University

Douglas W. Kieso
University of California—Irvine

Paul D. Kimmel
University of Wisconsin—Milwaukee

Martha King
Emporia State University

Florence Kirk
State University of New York at Oswego

Lisa Koonce
University of Texas—Austin

David B. Law
Youngstown State University

Henry Le Clerc
Suffolk Community College—Selden Campus

Barbara Leonard
Loyola University—Chicago

Tom Linsmeier
Michigan State University

Daphne Main
University of New Orleans

Danny Matthews
Midwestern State University

Robert J. Matthews
New Jersey City University

Robert Milbrath
University of Houston

John Mills
University of Nevada, Reno

Suzanne Morsfield
CUNY-Baruch College

Mohamed E. Moustafa
California State University—Long Beach

Kermit Natho
Georgia State University

Obeau S. Persons
Rider University

Robert Rambo
University of New Orleans

Jeffrey D. Ritter
St. Norbert College

James Sander
Butler University

Douglas Sharp
Wichita State University

John R. Simon
Northern Illinois University

Keith Smith
George Washington University

Pam Smith
Northern Illinois University

Billy S. Soo
Boston College

Dick Wasson
Southwestern College

Frank F. Weinberg
Golden Gate University

Shari H. Wescott
Houston Baptist University

William H. Wilson
Oregon Health University

Kenneth Wooling
Hampton University

Stephen A. Zeff
Rice University

We would also like to thank those colleagues who contributed to several of the unique features of this edition:

International Notes
Judith Ramaglia, *Pacific Lutheran University*

Ethics Cases
Bill N. Schwartz, *Virginia Commonwealth University*

Underlying Concepts
John Cheever, *California State Polytechnic University—Pomona*

Writing Assignments
Susan Smith, *Northern Illinois University*
Katherene P. Terrell and Robert L. Terrell, *University of Central Oklahoma*

Group Cases/Assignments
Katherene P. Terrell and Robert L. Terrell, *University of Central Oklahoma*

Perspectives and "From Classroom to Career" Interviews
Stuart Weiss, *Stuart Weiss Business Writing, Inc.*

Financial Analysis Cases and Problems
Martha King, *Emporia State University*
Carol M. Fischer, *University of Wisconsin—Waukesha*

Research Cases
Mark Bauman, *University of Illinois—Chicago*

Digital Tool Development
Paul Rifelj, *University of Wisconsin—Madison*
Craig Schedler, *Tucker, Anthony, Cleary, and Gull*

"Working in Teams" Materials
Edward Wertheim, *Northeastern University*

The Writing Handbook
Michelle Ephraim, *Worcester Polytechnic Institute*

Self-Test Materials
Larry Falcetto, *Emporia State University*

Practicing Accountants and Business Executives
From the field of corporate and public accounting, we owe thanks to the following practitioners for their technical advice and for consenting to interviews:

Tracy Barber
Deloitte & Touche

Ron Bernard
NFL Enterprises

Penelope Flugger
J.P. Morgan & Co.

John Gribble
PricewaterhouseCoopers

Darien Griffin
S.C. Johnson & Son Wax

Ed Jenkins
Financial Accounting Standards Board

Michael Lehman
Sun Microsystems, Inc.

Michelle Lippert
evoke.com

Sue McGrath
Vision Capital Management

David Miniken
Sweeney Conrad

Robert Sack
University of Virginia

Claire Schulte
Deloitte & Touche

Willie Sutton
Mutual Community Savings Bank—Durham, NC

Gary Valenzuela
Yahoo!

Rachel Woods
PricewaterhouseCoopers

Arthur Wyatt
Arthur Andersen & Co. and the University of Illinois—Urbana

We appreciate the exemplary support and professional commitment given us by the development, marketing, production, and editorial staffs of John Wiley & Sons, including Susan Elbe, Mark Bonadeo, Ellen Ford, Julie Kerr, Dana Bigelow, Jeanine Furino, Nicole Horlacher, Karen Kincheloe, David Kear, Hilary Newman, Anna Melhorn, and the management and staff at York Graphic Services, Inc. A special note of thanks also to Ann Torbert (editorial and content assistance) and Elm Street Publishing Services (Martha Beyerlein and Barb Lange) for facilitating the production of the manuscript. We also wish to thank Dick Wasson of Southwestern College for coordinating the efforts of the supplements authors and checkers. Finally, thanks to Lenox Softworks of Lenox, Massachusetts, for developing the format of the Digital Tool.

We appreciate the cooperation of the American Institute of Certified Public Accountants and the Financial Accounting Standards Board in permitting us to quote from their pronouncements. We thank Intel Corporation for permitting us to use its 1998 Annual Report for our specimen financial statements. We also acknowledge permission from the American Institute of Certified Public Accountants, the Institute of Management Accountants, and the Institute of Internal Auditors to adapt and use material from the Uniform CPA Examinations, the CMA Examinations, and the CIA Examinations, respectively.

If this book helps teachers instill in their students an appreciation for the challenges, worth, and limitations of accounting, if it encourages students to evaluate critically and understand financial accounting theory and practice, and if it prepares students for advanced study, professional examinations, and the successful and ethical pursuit of their careers in accounting or business, then we will have attained our objective.

Suggestions and comments from users of this book will be appreciated.

Somonauk, Illinois — **Donald E. Kieso**
Madison, Wisconsin — **Jerry J. Weygandt**
Madison, Wisconsin — **Terry D. Warfield**

Brief Contents

Contents

CHAPTER 1

Financial Accounting and Accounting Standards

Needed: Full Disclosure

Here are the opinions of some market leaders about the need for high-quality financial information:

Alan Greenspan, Chairman of the U.S. Federal Reserve: "Transparent accounting plays an important role in maintaining the vibrancy of our capital markets." Greenspan later noted that turbulence in overseas markets will not stop unless foreign regulators enforce better and clearer accounting rules.

Abby Joseph Cohen, the highly respected Goldman Sachs market strategist: "The quality of information we now receive from companies in the United States is about the best we have ever seen and dramatically exceeds that of almost any other nation."

Lawrence Summers, Secretary of the U.S. Treasury: "The single most important innovation shaping [the American capital] market was the idea of generally accepted accounting principles. We need something similar internationally."

What these individuals are saying is that the U.S. capital markets are the best in the world because U.S. financial reporting is generally considered the best in the world. Full disclosure of financial information is imperative. Without it, investors are misled; this can lead to substantial losses and collapses of capital markets.

Consider, for example, the recent Asian financial crisis, which saw stock values in Asian countries plummet. Many believe this crisis was caused because a majority of the largest banks and companies did not disclose problem loans and debt to related parties. In the United States, this information is required to be disclosed under generally accepted accounting principles. Similar to the Asian crisis, many European companies did not provide information on their exposure to loans in Asia, Latin America, and Russia, three regions of the world that have suffered significant economic hardship. As a result, many investors who purchased stock in these companies were seriously harmed.

So what should be done? Much attention is now being directed toward the development of a set of high-quality standards that can be used worldwide with some confidence. If such a goal can be achieved, a more efficient allocation of resources to all parties will occur.

LEARNING OBJECTIVES

After studying this chapter, you should be able to:

1. **Describe the essential characteristics of accounting.**
2. **Identify the major financial statements and other means of financial reporting.**
3. **Explain how accounting assists in the efficient use of scarce resources.**
4. **Identify some of the challenges facing accounting.**
5. **Identify the objectives of financial reporting.**
6. **Explain the need for accounting standards.**
7. **Identify the major policy-setting bodies and their role in the standard-setting process.**
8. **Explain the meaning of generally accepted accounting principles.**
9. **Describe the impact of user groups on the standard-setting process.**
10. **Understand issues related to ethics and financial accounting.**

PREVIEW OF CHAPTER 1

As the opening story indicates, the U.S. financial reporting system is one of the best in the world. But it will continue to be challenged as the business world experiences unprecedented change caused by globalization, deregulation, and computerization. In the middle of this changing business world, relevant and reliable information must be provided so that our capital markets work efficiently.

The purpose of this chapter is to explain the environment of financial reporting and the many factors affecting it. The content and organization of the chapter are as follows:

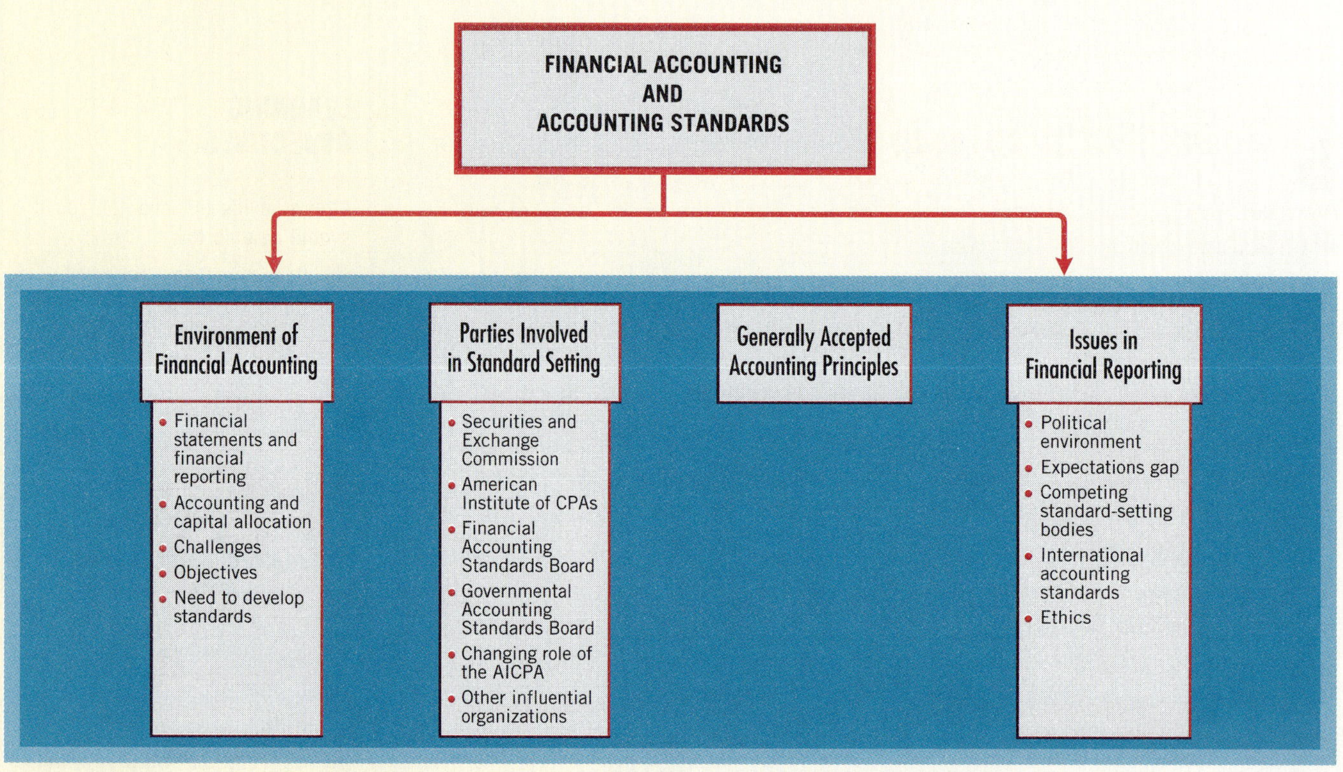

THE ENVIRONMENT OF FINANCIAL ACCOUNTING

Like other human activities and disciplines, accounting is largely a product of its environment. The environment of accounting consists of social-economic-political-legal conditions, restraints, and influences that vary from time to time. As a result, accounting objectives and practices are not the same today as they were in the past. **Accounting theory has evolved to meet changing demands and influences.**

OBJECTIVE 1
Describe the essential characteristics of accounting.

Accounting may best be defined by describing the three essential characteristics of accounting: (1) **identification, measurement, and communication of financial information about** (2) **economic entities to** (3) **interested persons**. These characteristics have described accounting for hundreds of years. Yet, in the last 30 years economic entities have increased so greatly in size and complexity, and the interested persons have increased so greatly in number and diversity, that the responsibility placed on the accounting profession is greater today than ever before.

Financial Statements and Financial Reporting

Financial accounting is the process that culminates in the preparation of financial reports on the enterprise as a whole for use by both internal and external parties. Users of these financial reports include investors, creditors, managers, unions, and government agencies. In contrast, managerial accounting is the process of identifying, measuring, analyzing, and communicating financial information needed by management to plan, evaluate, and control an organization's operations.

OBJECTIVE 2
Identify the major financial statements and other means of financial reporting.

Financial statements are the principal means through which financial information is communicated to those outside an enterprise. These statements provide the firm's history quantified in money terms. The **financial statements** most frequently provided are (1) the balance sheet, (2) the income statement, (3) the statement of cash flows, and (4) the statement of owners' or stockholders' equity. In addition, note disclosures are an integral part of each financial statement.

Some financial information is better provided, or can be provided only, by means of **financial reporting** other than formal financial statements. Examples include the president's letter or supplementary schedules in the corporate annual report, prospectuses, reports filed with government agencies, news releases, management's forecasts, and descriptions of an enterprise's social or environmental impact. Such information may be required by authoritative pronouncement, regulatory rule, or custom; or because management wishes to disclose it voluntarily. The primary focus of this textbook concerns the development of two types of financial information: (1) the basic financial statements and (2) related disclosures.

Accounting and Capital Allocation

OBJECTIVE 3
Explain how accounting assists in the efficient use of scarce resources.

Because resources are limited, people try to conserve them, to use them effectively, and to identify and encourage those who can make efficient use of them. Through an efficient use of resources, our standard of living increases.

Markets, free enterprise, and competition—not a committee of social engineers—determine whether a business is to be successful and thrive. This fact places a substantial burden on the accounting profession to measure performance accurately and fairly on a timely basis, so that the right managers and companies are able to attract investment capital. For example, accounting enables investors and creditors to compare the income and assets employed by such companies as **IBM**, **McDonald's**, **Microsoft**, and **Ford**. As a result, they can assess the relative return and risks associated with investment opportunities and thereby channel resources more effectively. This process of capital allocation works as follows:

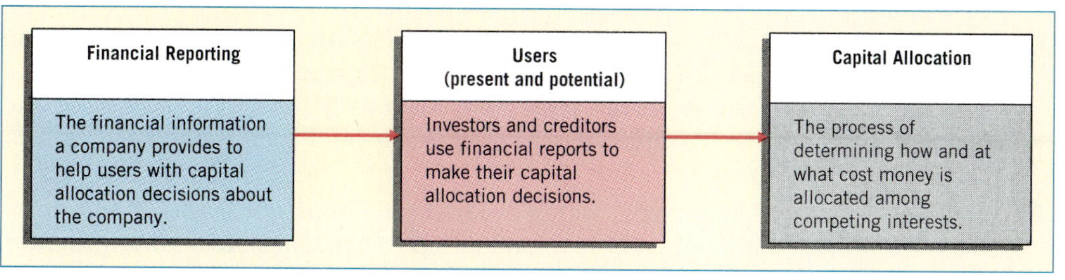

ILLUSTRATION 1-1
Capital Allocation Process

An effective process of capital allocation is critical to a healthy economy, which promotes productivity, encourages innovation, and provides an efficient and liquid market for buying and selling securities and obtaining and granting credit.[1] As indicated

[1]AICPA Special Committee on Financial Reporting, "Improving Business Reporting—A Customer Focus," *Journal of Accountancy*, Supplement, October 1994.

in our opening story, unreliable and irrelevant information leads to poor capital allocation, which adversely affects the securities markets.

The accounting numbers that are reported affect the transfer of resources among companies and individuals. Consider the following example: When companies were required to record certain retirement benefits as liabilities, **General Motors (GM)** had to record a new liability of $36 billion for health care costs, which reduced its stockholders' equity from $42 billion to $6 billion! It is no surprise that GM and many other companies resisted the new requirement and that, once it was adopted, they are now making changes to their medical benefit plans.

Accounting for investment securities provides another illustration. Prior to 1993, these securities were often carried at historical cost on the balance sheet. Under this standard, the **savings and loan (S&L) industry** reported a positive stockholders' equity of approximately $38 billion. If the S&L industry had reported the investment securities at market value, it is estimated the stockholders' equity could have been as low as a *negative* $118 billion. If Congress had known these figures, it is quite possible that the industry would not have been deregulated, and U.S. taxpayers would have been saved the cost of the eventual $200 billion bailout of the S&L industry.

The Challenges Facing Financial Accounting

OBJECTIVE 4
Identify some of the challenges facing accounting.

As indicated in the opening story, much is right about financial reporting in the United States. We presently have the most liquid, deep, secure, and efficient public capital markets of any country at any time in history. One reason for this success is that our financial statements and related disclosures have captured and organized financial information in a useful and reliable fashion. However, much still needs to be done. For example, suppose you could move to the turn of the next century, say 2100, and look back at financial reporting today. Here is what you might read:

1. ***Non-financial Measurements.*** Financial reports in the late 1990s failed to provide some key performance measures widely used by management. For example, non-financial measures such as customer satisfaction indexes, backlog information, and reject rates on goods purchased, all now used to evaluate the long-term stability of the company, were provided on an ad hoc basis, if at all.
2. ***Forward-looking Information.*** Financial reports failed to provide forward-looking information needed by present and potential investors and creditors. One individual noted that financial statements in the 1990s should have started with the phrase, "Once upon a time," to signify their use of historical cost and their accumulation of past events.
3. ***Soft Assets.*** Financial reports focused on hard assets (inventory, plant assets) but failed to provide much information on a company's soft assets (intangibles). For example, often the best assets are intangible, such as **Microsoft**'s know-how and market dominance, **Dell**'s unique marketing setup and well-trained employees, and **GAP**'s brand image.
4. ***Timeliness.*** Financial statements were prepared only quarterly, and audited financials were provided annually. Little to no real-time financial statement information was available.

We believe each of these challenges must be met for the accounting profession to continue to provide the type of information needed for an efficient capital allocation process. Already a blue-ribbon committee has suggested that in the future financial statements should include the following:[2]

[2]AICPA Special Committee on Financial Reporting, *op. cit.*

ILLUSTRATION 1-2
Financial Reporting in the Future

Financial and nonfinancial data
- Financial statements and related disclosures.
- High-level operating data and performance measurements that management uses to manage the business.

Management's analysis
- Reasons for changes in the financial, operating, and performance-related data, and the identity and past effects of key trends.

Forward-looking information
- Opportunities and risks, including those resulting from key trends.
- Management's plans, including critical success factors.
- Comparison of actual business performance to previously disclosed forward-looking information.

Information about management and shareholders
- Directors, management, compensation, major shareholders, and transactions and relationships among related parties.

Background about the company
- Broad objectives and strategies.
- Scope and description of business and properties.
- Impact of industry structure on the company.

Changes in these directions would broaden the focus from financial reporting to business reporting.

Objectives of Financial Reporting

OBJECTIVE 5
Identify the objectives of financial reporting.

In an attempt to establish a foundation for financial accounting and reporting, the accounting profession identified a set of **objectives of financial reporting by business enterprises**. Financial reporting should provide information:

(a) that is useful to present and potential investors and creditors and other users **in making rational investment, credit, and similar decisions**. The information should be comprehensible to those who have a **reasonable understanding** of business and economic activities and are willing to study the information with reasonable diligence.

(b) to help present and potential investors and creditors and other users **in assessing the amounts, timing, and uncertainty of prospective cash receipts** from dividends or interest and the proceeds from the sale, redemption, or maturity of securities or loans. Since investors' and creditors' cash flows are related to enterprise cash flows, financial reporting should provide information to help investors, creditors, and others assess the amounts, timing, and uncertainty of prospective net cash inflows to the related enterprise.

(c) about the economic resources of an enterprise, the claims to those resources (obligations of the enterprise to transfer resources to other entities and owners' equity), and the effects of transactions, events, and circumstances that change its resources and claims to those resources.[3]

INTERNATIONAL INSIGHT

The objectives of financial reporting differ across nations. Traditionally, the primary objective of accounting in many continental European nations and in Japan was conformity with the law. In contrast, Canada, the U.K., the Netherlands, and many other nations have shared the U.S. view that the primary objective is to provide information for investors. Insights into international standards and practices will be presented throughout the text.

In brief, the objectives of financial reporting are to provide (1) information that is useful in investment and credit decisions, (2) information that is useful in assessing cash flow prospects, and (3) information about enterprise resources, claims to those resources, and changes in them.

The emphasis on "assessing cash flow prospects" might lead one to suppose that the cash basis is preferred over the accrual basis of accounting. That is not the case. Information based on **accrual accounting generally provides a better indication of an**

[3]"Objectives of Financial Reporting by Business Enterprises," *Statement of Financial Accounting Concepts No. 1* (Stamford, Conn.: FASB, November 1978), pars. 5–8.

enterprise's present and continuing ability to generate favorable cash flows than does information limited to the financial effects of cash receipts and payments.[4]

Recall from your first accounting course that the objective of accrual basis accounting is to ensure that events that change an entity's financial statements are recorded in the periods in which the events occur, rather than only in the periods in which the entity receives or pays cash. Using the accrual basis to determine net income means recognizing revenues when earned rather than when cash is received, and recognizing expenses when incurred rather than when paid. Under accrual accounting, revenues, for the most part, are recognized when sales are made so they can be related to the economic environment of the period in which they occurred. Over the long run, trends in revenues are generally more meaningful than trends in cash receipts.

The Need to Develop Standards

OBJECTIVE 6
Explain the need for accounting standards.

INTERNATIONAL INSIGHT

Nations also differ in the degree to which they have developed national standards and consistent accounting practices. One indicator of the level of a nation's accounting is the nature of the accounting profession within the country. Professional accounting bodies were established in the Netherlands, the U.K., Canada, and the U.S. in the nineteenth century. In contrast, public accountancy bodies were established in Hong Kong, Singapore, and Korea only in the last half century.

The main controversy in setting accounting standards is "Whose rules should we play by, and what should they be?" The answer is not immediately clear because the users of financial accounting statements have both coinciding and conflicting needs for information of various types. To meet these needs, and to satisfy the fiduciary[5] reporting responsibility of management, a single set of **general-purpose financial statements** is prepared. These statements are expected to present fairly, clearly, and completely the financial operations of the enterprise.

As a result, the accounting profession has attempted to develop a set of standards that are generally accepted and universally practiced. Without these standards, each enterprise would have to develop its own standards, and readers of financial statements would have to familiarize themselves with every company's peculiar accounting and reporting practices. It would be almost impossible to prepare statements that could be compared.

This common set of standards and procedures are called generally accepted accounting principles (GAAP). The term "generally accepted" means either that an authoritative accounting rule-making body has established a principle of reporting in a given area or that over time a given practice has been accepted as appropriate because of its universal application.[6] Although principles and practices have provoked both debate and criticism, most members of the financial community recognize them as the standards that over time have proven to be most useful. A more extensive discussion of what constitutes GAAP is presented later in this chapter.

PARTIES INVOLVED IN STANDARD SETTING

OBJECTIVE 7
Identify the major policy-setting bodies and their role in the standard-setting process.

A number of organizations are instrumental in the development of financial accounting standards (GAAP) in the United States. The major organizations are as follows:

1. Securities and Exchange Commission (SEC)
2. American Institute of Certified Public Accountants (AICPA)
3. Financial Accounting Standards Board (FASB)
4. Governmental Accounting Standards Board (GASB)
5. Other influential organizations

---

[4]*SFAC No. 1*, p. iv. As used here, cash flow means "cash generated and used in operations." The term **cash flows** is frequently used also to include cash obtained by borrowing and used to repay borrowing, cash used for investments in resources and obtained from the disposal of investments, and cash contributed by or distributed to owners.

[5]Management's responsibility to manage assets with care and trust is its **fiduciary** responsibility.

[6]The terms **principles** and **standards** are used interchangeably in practice and throughout this textbook.

Securities and Exchange Commission (SEC)

Prior to 1900 single ownership was the predominant form of business organization in our economy. Financial reports emphasized solvency and liquidity and were limited to internal use and scrutiny by banks and other lending institutions. From 1900 to 1929, the growth of large corporations, with their absentee ownership, led to increasing investment and speculation in corporate stock. Unfortunately, after a couple of days on which stock prices dropped rapidly, both individual and institutional investors panicked, and sold over 16 million shares of stock at huge losses. The stock market crashed in 1929 and contributed to the Great Depression.

INTERNATIONAL INSIGHT

The International Organization of Securities Commissions (IOSCO) is a group of more than 100 securities regulatory agencies or securities exchanges from all over the world. IOSCO has existed since 1987. Collectively, its members represent a substantial proportion of the world's capital markets. The SEC is a member of IOSCO.

As a result of these events, the federal government established the **Securities and Exchange Commission (SEC)** to help develop and standardize financial information presented to stockholders. The SEC is a federal agency. It administers the Securities Exchange Act of 1934 and several other acts. Most companies that issue securities to the public or are listed on a stock exchange are required to file audited financial statements with the SEC. In addition, the SEC has broad powers to prescribe, in whatever detail it desires, the accounting practices and standards to be employed by companies that fall within its jurisdiction. As a result, the SEC exercises oversight over 12,000 companies that are listed on the major exchanges (such as the New York Stock Exchange and the American Stock Exchange). The SEC filing requirements[7] and accounting opinions are published in: (1) its Financial Reporting Releases (FRRs),[8] (2) Regulation S-X, which contains instructions and forms for filing financial statements, and (3) decisions on cases coming before the SEC.

Public/Private Partnership

At the time the SEC was created, no group—public or private—was issuing accounting standards. The SEC encouraged the creation of a private standard-setting body because it believed that the private sector had the resources and talent to develop appropriate accounting standards. As a result, accounting standards have generally developed in the private sector either through the American Institute of Certified Public Accountants (AICPA) or the Financial Accounting Standards Board (FASB).

The SEC has affirmed its support for the FASB by indicating that financial statements conforming to standards set by the FASB will be presumed to have substantial authoritative support. In short, the **SEC requires registrants to adhere to GAAP**. In addition, it has indicated in its reports to Congress that "it continues to believe that the initiative for establishing and improving accounting standards should remain in the private sector, subject to Commission oversight."

SEC Oversight

The SEC's partnership with the private sector has worked well. It has acted with remarkable restraint in the area of developing accounting standards. Generally, **the SEC has relied on the AICPA and FASB to regulate the accounting profession and develop and enforce accounting standards.**

Over its history, however, the SEC's involvement in the development of accounting standards has varied. In some cases the private sector has attempted to establish a

---

[7]The Securities Acts require that companies issuing securities file registration statements and periodic reports with the SEC. Most commercial and industrial companies file a *Form S-1* registration statement upon the initial issuance of securities. (Forms S-2 through S-18 are filed by companies in certain specialized industries.) *Form 10-K* is the annual report form required to be filed and *Form 10-Q* the report that must be filed for the first three quarters of each fiscal year. *Form 8-K* must be filed after the occurrence of a material event. Regulation S-K requires nonfinancial information, such as the Management's Discussion and Analysis, to be reported.

[8]Prior to 1982 these pronouncements were referred to as Accounting Series Releases (ASRs). The SEC has changed the title of new releases to better reflect their nature and to differentiate FRRs (nonenforcement, nondisciplinary type releases) from the new AAERs (accounting and auditing enforcement releases, which are disciplinary in nature).

standard, but the SEC has refused to accept it. In other cases it has prodded the private sector into taking quicker action on certain reporting problems, such as accounting for investments in debt and equity securities and the reporting of derivative instruments. In still other situations the SEC communicates problems to the FASB, responds to FASB exposure drafts, and provides the FASB with counsel and advice upon request.

The SEC has the mandate to establish accounting principles. The private sector, therefore, must listen carefully to the views of the SEC. In some sense the private sector is the formulator and the implementor of the standards.[9] The partnership appears to be a good one.

Enforcement

As indicated earlier, companies listed on a stock exchange are required to submit their financial statements to the SEC. If the SEC believes that an accounting or disclosure irregularity exists regarding the form or content of the financial statements, it sends a deficiency letter to the company. Usually these deficiency letters are resolved quickly. However, if disagreement continues, the SEC has the power to issue a "stop order," which prevents the registrant from issuing securities or trading securities on the exchanges. Criminal charges may also be brought by the Department of Justice for violations of certain laws. The SEC program, private sector initiatives, and civil and criminal litigation help to ensure the integrity of financial reporting for public companies.

American Institute of Certified Public Accountants (AICPA)

As indicated earlier, the **American Institute of Certified Public Accountants (AICPA)**, the national professional organization of practicing Certified Public Accountants (CPAs), has been vital to the development of GAAP. Various committees and boards established since the founding of the AICPA have contributed to this effort.

Committee on Accounting Procedure

At the urging of the SEC, the AICPA appointed the Committee on Accounting Procedure in 1939. The **Committee on Accounting Procedure (CAP)**, composed of practicing CPAs, issued 51 **Accounting Research Bulletins** (see list at the back of the book) dealing with a variety of timely accounting problems during the years 1939 to 1959. But this problem-by-problem approach failed to provide the structured body of accounting principles that was both needed and desired. In response, in 1959 the AICPA created the Accounting Principles Board.

Accounting Principles Board

The major purposes of the **Accounting Principles Board (APB)** were (1) to advance the written expression of accounting principles, (2) to determine appropriate practices, and (3) to narrow the areas of difference and inconsistency in practice. To achieve these objectives, its mission was to develop an overall conceptual framework to assist in the resolution of problems as they become evident and to do substantive research on individual issues before pronouncements were issued.

The Board's 18 to 21 members, selected primarily from public accounting, also included representatives from industry and the academic community. The Board's official pronouncements, called **APB Opinions**, were intended to be based mainly on re-

[9]One writer has described the relationship of the FASB and SEC and the development of financial reporting standards using the analogy of a pearl. The pearl (financial reporting standard) "is formed by the reaction of certain oysters (FASB) to an irritant (the SEC)—usually a grain of sand—that becomes embedded inside the shell. The oyster coats this grain with layers of nacre, and ultimately a pearl is formed. The pearl is a joint result of the irritant (SEC) and oyster (FASB); without both, it cannot be created." John C. Burton, "Government Regulation of Accounting and Information," *Journal of Accountancy,* June 1982.

search studies and be supported by reasons and analysis. Between its inception in 1959 and its dissolution in 1973, the APB issued 31 opinions (see complete list at the back of the book).

Unfortunately, the APB came under fire early, charged with lack of productivity and failing to act promptly to correct alleged accounting abuses. Later the APB tackled numerous thorny accounting issues, only to meet a buzz saw of industry and CPA firm opposition and occasional governmental interference. In 1971 the accounting profession's leaders, anxious to avoid governmental rule-making, appointed a Study Group on Establishment of Accounting Principles. Commonly known as the **Wheat Committee** for its chair Francis Wheat, this group was to examine the organization and operation of the APB and determine what changes would be necessary to attain better results. The Study Group's recommendations were submitted to the AICPA Council in the spring of 1972, adopted in total, and implemented by early 1973.

Financial Accounting Standards Board (FASB)

The Wheat Committee's recommendations resulted in the demise of the APB and the creation of a new standard-setting structure composed of three organizations—the Financial Accounting Foundation (FAF), the Financial Accounting Standards Board (FASB), and the Financial Accounting Standards Advisory Council (FASAC). The **Financial Accounting Foundation** selects the members of the FASB and the Advisory Council, funds their activities, and generally oversees the FASB's activities.

The major operating organization in this three-part structure is the **Financial Accounting Standards Board (FASB)**. Its mission is to establish and improve standards of financial accounting and reporting for the guidance and education of the public, which includes issuers, auditors, and users of financial information. The expectations of success and support for the new FASB were based upon several significant differences between it and its predecessor, the APB:

1. *Smaller Membership.* The FASB is composed of seven members, replacing the relatively large 18-member APB.
2. *Full-time, Remunerated Membership.* FASB members are well-paid, full-time members appointed for renewable 5-year terms, whereas the APB members were unpaid and part-time.
3. *Greater Autonomy.* The APB was a senior committee of the AICPA, whereas the FASB is not an organ of any single professional organization. It is appointed by and answerable only to the Financial Accounting Foundation.
4. *Increased Independence.* APB members retained their private positions with firms, companies, or institutions; FASB members must sever all such ties.
5. *Broader Representation.* All APB members were required to be CPAs and members of the AICPA; currently, it is not necessary to be a CPA to be a member of the FASB.

INTERNATIONAL INSIGHT

The U.S. legal system is based on English common law, whereby the government generally allows professionals to make the rules. These rules (standards) are, therefore, developed in the private sector. Conversely, some countries follow codified law, which leads to government-run accounting systems.

In addition to research help from its own staff, the FASB relies on the expertise of various task force groups formed for various projects and on the **Financial Accounting Standards Advisory Council (FASAC)**. FASAC has responsibility for consulting with the FASB on both major policy and technical issues and also for helping select task force members.

Due Process

Two basic premises of the FASB are that in establishing financial accounting standards: (1) it should be responsive to the needs and viewpoints of the entire economic community, not just the public accounting profession, and (2) it should operate in full view of the public through a "due process" system that gives interested persons ample opportunity to make their views known. To ensure the achievement of these goals, the steps shown in Illustration 1-3 are taken in the evolution of a typical FASB Statement of Financial Accounting Standards.

ILLUSTRATION 1-3
Due Process

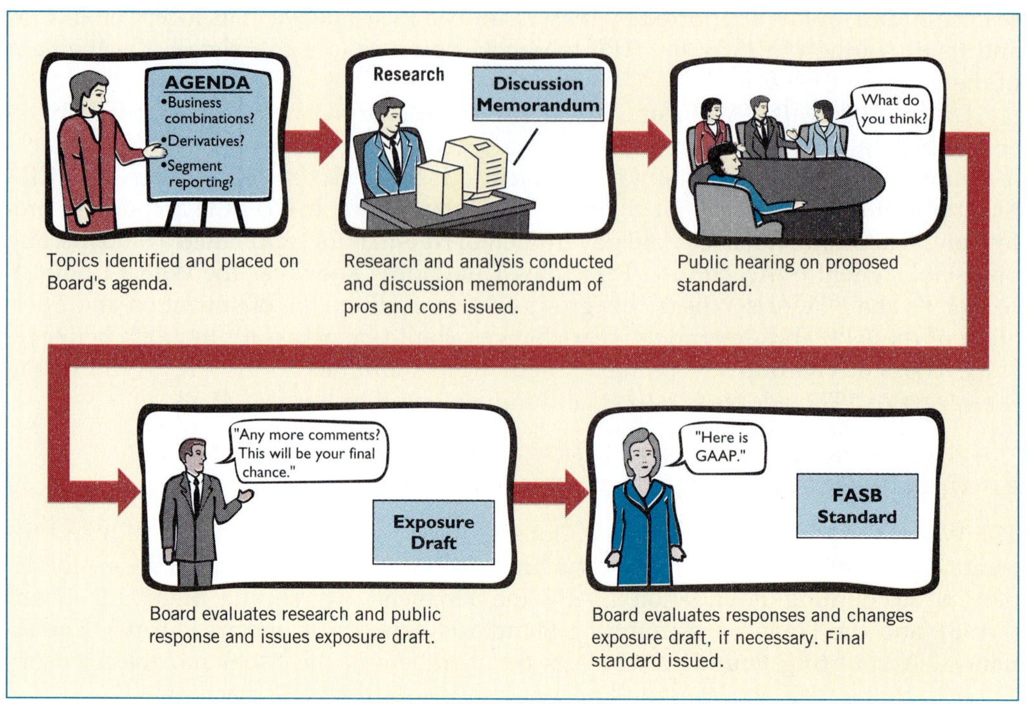

Topics identified and placed on Board's agenda.

Research and analysis conducted and discussion memorandum of pros and cons issued.

Public hearing on proposed standard.

Board evaluates research and public response and issues exposure draft.

Board evaluates responses and changes exposure draft, if necessary. Final standard issued.

The passage of a new FASB **Standards Statement** requires the support of five of the seven Board members. FASB Statements are considered GAAP and thereby binding in practice. All ARBs and APB Opinions that were in effect in 1973 when the FASB became effective continue to be effective until amended or superseded by FASB pronouncements. In recognition of possible misconceptions of the term "principles," the FASB uses the term **financial accounting standards** in its pronouncements.

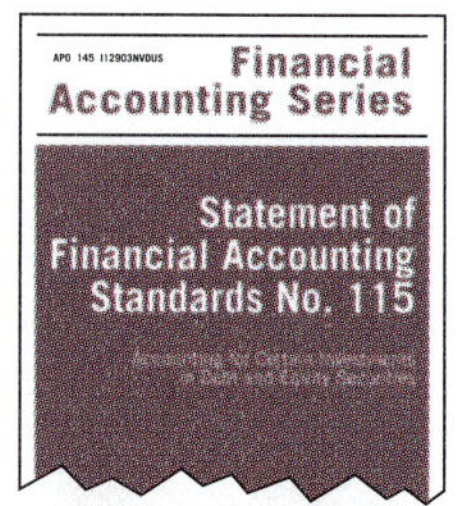

Types of Pronouncements

The major types of pronouncements that the FASB issues are:

1. Standards and Interpretations.
2. Financial Accounting Concepts.
3. Technical Bulletins.
4. Emerging Issues Task Force Statements.

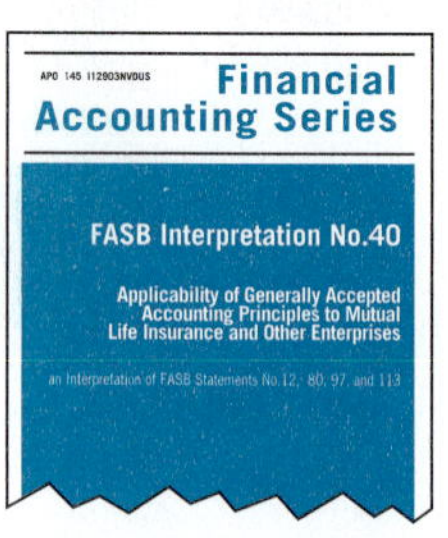

Standards and Interpretations. Financial accounting standards issued by the FASB are considered generally accepted accounting principles. In addition, the FASB also issues **interpretations** that represent modifications or extensions of existing standards. The interpretations have the same authority as standards and require the same votes for passage as standards. However, interpretations do not require the FASB to operate in full view of the public through the due process system that is required for FASB Standards. The APB also issued interpretations of APB Opinions. Both types of interpretations are now considered authoritative support for purposes of determining GAAP. Since replacing the APB, the FASB has issued 137 standards and 43 interpretations (see list at the back of the book).

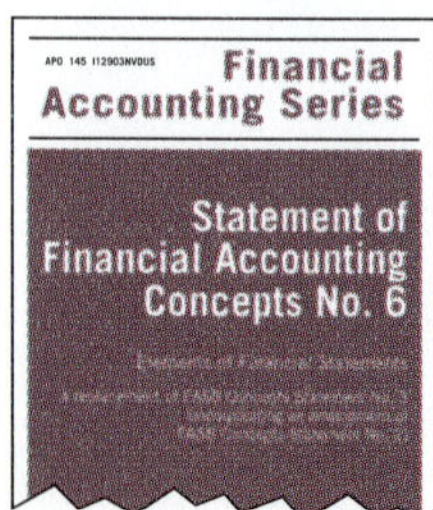

Financial Accounting Concepts. As part of a long-range effort to move away from the problem-by-problem approach, the FASB in November 1978 issued the first in a series of **Statements of Financial Accounting Concepts** (see list at the back of the book) as part of its conceptual framework project. The purpose of the series is to set forth fundamental objectives and concepts that the Board will use in developing future standards of financial accounting and reporting. They are intended to form a cohesive set of interrelated concepts, a conceptual framework, that will serve as tools for solving existing and emerging problems in a consistent manner. Unlike a Statement of Financial Accounting Standards, **a Statement of Financial Accounting Concepts does not establish GAAP.** Concepts statements, however, pass through the same due process system (discussion memo, public hearing, exposure draft, etc.) as do standards statements.

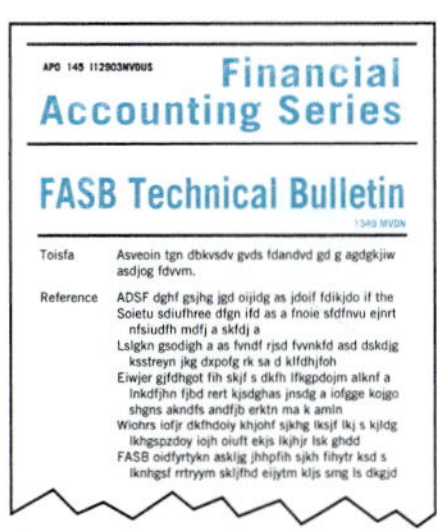

FASB Technical Bulletins. The FASB receives many requests from various sources for guidelines on implementing or applying FASB Standards or Interpretations, APB Opinions, and Accounting Research Bulletins. In addition, a strong need exists for timely guidance on financial accounting and reporting problems. For example, in one tax law change, certain income taxes that companies had accrued as liabilities were forgiven. The immediate question was: How should the forgiven taxes be reported—as a reduction of income tax expense, as a prior period adjustment, or as an extraordinary item? A technical bulletin was quickly issued that required the tax reduction be reported as a reduction of the current period's income tax expense. Note that a **technical bulletin** is issued only when (1) **it is not expected to cause a major change in accounting practice for a number of enterprises,** (2) **its cost of implementation is low,** **and** (3) **the guidance provided by the bulletin does not conflict with any broad fundamental accounting principle.**[10]

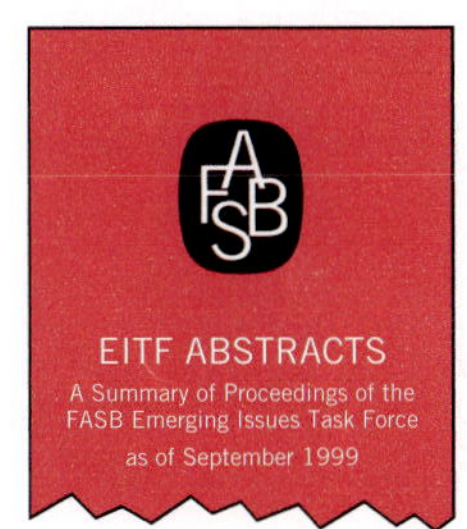

Emerging Issues Task Force Statements. In 1984 the FASB created the **Emerging Issues Task Force (EITF).** The EITF is composed of 13 members, representing CPA firms and preparers of financial statements. Also attending EITF meetings are observers from the SEC and AICPA. The purpose of the task force is to reach a consensus on how to account for new and unusual financial transactions that have the potential for creating differing financial reporting practices. Examples include how to account for pension plan terminations; how to account for revenue from barter transactions by Internet companies; and how to account for excessive amounts paid to takeover specialists.

We cannot overestimate the importance of the EITF. In one year, for example, the task force examined 61 emerging financial reporting issues and arrived at a consensus on approximately 75% of them. The SEC has indicated that it will view consensus solutions as preferred accounting and will require persuasive justification for departing from them.

The EITF helps the FASB in many ways. For example, emerging issues often attract public attention. If they are not resolved quickly, they can lead to financial crises and scandal and can undercut public confidence in current reporting practices. The next step, possible governmental intervention, would threaten the continuance of standard setting in the private sector. In addition, the EITF identifies controversial accounting problems as they arise and determines whether they can be quickly resolved or whether the FASB should become involved in solving them. In essence, it becomes a "problem filter" for the FASB. Thus, it is hoped that the FASB will be able to work on more pervasive long-term problems, while the EITF deals with short-term emerging issues.

Governmental Accounting Standards Board (GASB)

Financial statements prepared by state and local governments are not comparable with financial reports prepared by private business organizations. This lack of comparability was highlighted in the 1970s when a number of large U.S. cities such as New York and Cleveland faced potential bankruptcy. As a result, a new **Governmental Accounting Standards Board (GASB),** under the oversight of the Financial Accounting Foundation, was created in 1984 to address state and local governmental reporting issues.

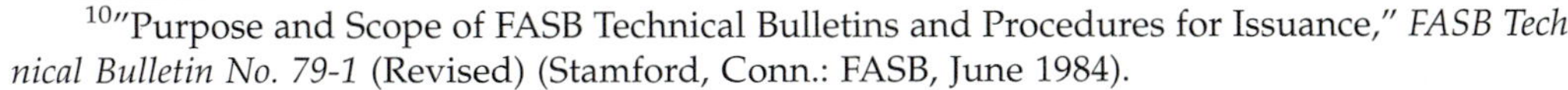

[10]"Purpose and Scope of FASB Technical Bulletins and Procedures for Issuance," *FASB Technical Bulletin No. 79-1* (Revised) (Stamford, Conn.: FASB, June 1984).

The operational structure of the GASB is similar to that of the FASB. That is, it has an advisory council called the Governmental Accounting Standards Advisory Council (GASAC), and it is assisted by its own technical staff and task forces.

The creation of GASB was controversial. Many believe that there should be only one standard-setting body—the FASB. It was hoped that partitioning standard setting between the GASB, which deals only with state and local government reporting, and the FASB, which addresses reporting for all other entities, would not lead to conflict. Since we are primarily concerned with financial reports prepared by profit-seeking organizations, this textbook will focus on standards issued by the FASB only.

The formal organizational structure as it currently exists for the development of financial reporting standards is presented in Illustration 1-4.

ILLUSTRATION 1-4
Organizational Structure for Setting Accounting Standards

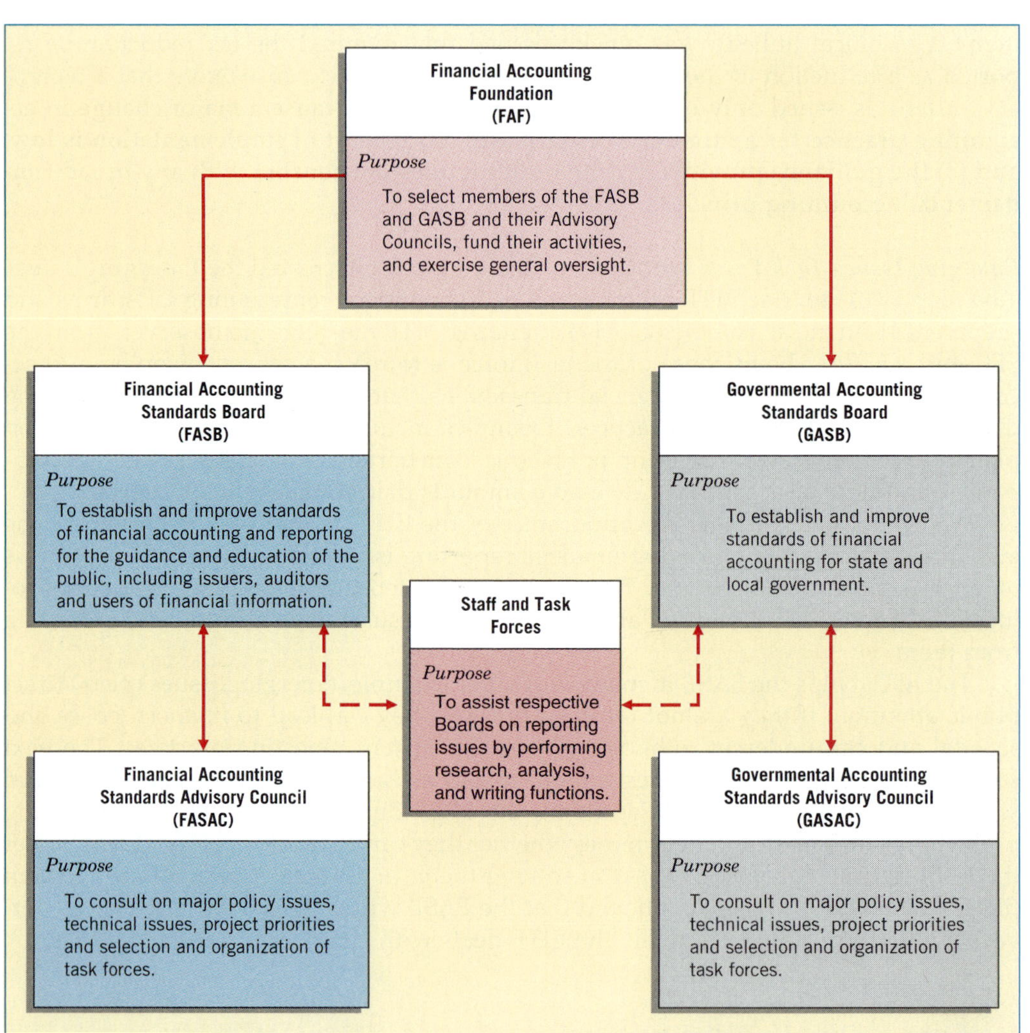

Changing Role of the AICPA

For several decades the AICPA provided the leadership in the development of accounting principles and rules; it regulated the accounting profession and developed and enforced accounting practice more than did any other professional organization. When the Accounting Principles Board was dissolved and replaced with the FASB, the AICPA established the Accounting Standards Division to act as its official voice on accounting and reporting issues.

The **Accounting Standards Executive Committee (AcSEC)** was established within the Division and was designated as the senior technical committee authorized to speak for the AICPA in the area of financial accounting and reporting. It does so through various written communications:

Audit and Accounting Guidelines summarize the accounting practices of specific industries and provide specific guidance on matters not addressed by the FASB and GASB. Examples are accounting for casinos, airlines, colleges and universities, banks, insurance companies, and many others.

Statements of Position (SOP) provide guidance on financial reporting topics until the FASB or GASB sets standards on the issue in question. SOPs may update, revise, and clarify audit and accounting guides or provide free-standing guidance.

Practice Bulletins indicate AcSEC's views on narrow financial reporting issues not considered by the FASB or GASB.

The AICPA is still the leader in developing auditing standards through its **Auditing Standards Board**, in regulating auditing practice, in developing and enforcing professional ethics, and in providing continuing professional education programs. The AICPA also develops and grades the CPA examination, which is administered in all 50 states.

Other Influential Organizations

Several other organizations also have been influential in the development of accounting theory and standard setting. Illustration 1-5 provides an overview of these organizations.

ILLUSTRATION 1-5
Overview of Other Influential Organizations

Organization	Members	Purpose
American Accounting Association	Primarily accounting academics	Furthers the development of accounting theory by encouraging and sponsoring accounting research.
Institute of Management Accountants (IMA)	Primarily internal accountants	Conducts research and provides input on cost and managerial accounting issues.
Financial Executives Institute (FEI)	Financial executives generally of large corporations (treasurers, financial vice presidents, chief financial officers)	Conducts research and makes recommendations on the impact of financial reporting at the corporate level.

In addition, the **Internal Revenue Service (IRS)**, which derives its authority from the Internal Revenue Code and its amendments and legal interpretations, constitutes one of the strongest influences on accounting practice. In an effort to lessen the impact of taxes, and to avoid keeping two sets of books, business managers frequently adopt "acceptable" accounting procedures that minimize taxable income. Because the objectives of the tax law differ from the objectives of financial accounting, however, "good tax accounting" is not necessarily "good financial accounting." As noted throughout this textbook, tax laws and "tax effects" are a pervasive influence in business decision making and on the selection of accounting methods. Differences between tax accounting and financial accounting are generally permissible; however, in the preparation of financial statements, tax considerations must give ground to the requirements of sound accounting.

GENERALLY ACCEPTED ACCOUNTING PRINCIPLES

OBJECTIVE 8
Explain the meaning of generally accepted accounting principles.

Generally accepted accounting principles are those principles that have "substantial authoritative support." The AICPA's Code of Professional Conduct requires that members prepare financial statements in accordance with generally accepted accounting principles. Specifically, Rule 203 of this Code prohibits a member from expressing an opinion that financial statements conform with GAAP if those statements contain a material departure from a generally accepted accounting principle, unless the member can demonstrate that because of unusual circumstances the financial statements would otherwise have been misleading. Failure to follow Rule 203 can lead to loss of a CPA's license to practice.

The meaning of generally accepted accounting principles is defined by *Statement on Auditing Standards (SAS) No. 69,* "The Meaning of 'Present Fairly in Conformity With Generally Accepted Accounting Principles' in the Independent Auditor's Report." **Under this standard, generally accepted accounting principles covered by Rule 203 are construed to be FASB Standards and Interpretations, APB Opinions, and AICPA Accounting Research Bulletins.**

Oftentimes, however, a specific accounting transaction occurs that is not covered by any of these documents. In this case, other authoritative literature is used. Major examples are: FASB Technical Bulletins; AICPA Industry Auditing and Accounting Guides; and Statements of Position that have been "cleared" by the FASB.[11] These documents are considered to have substantial authoritative support because the recognized professional bodies, after giving interested and affected parties the opportunity to react to exposure drafts and respond at public hearings, have voted their issuance. If these pronouncements are lacking in guidance, then other sources might be considered. The hierarchy of these sources is presented in Illustration 1-6.[12] If the accounting treatment of an event is not specified by a category (a) pronouncement, then categories (b) through (d) should be investigated. If there is a conflict between pronouncements in

ILLUSTRATION 1-6
The House of GAAP

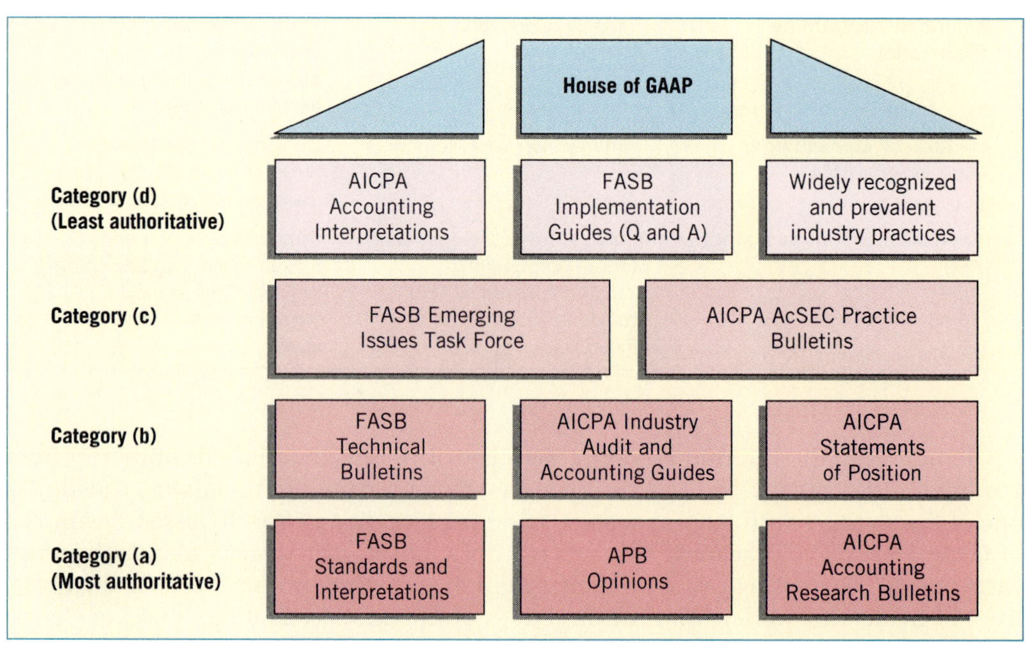

[11] *SAS No. 69* states that Audit Guides and Statements of Position are assumed to be cleared (approved) by the FASB unless the pronouncement states otherwise.

[12] See for example, "Remodeling the House of GAAP," by Douglas Sauter, *Journal of Accountancy*, July 1991, pp. 30–37.

(b) through (d), the higher category [for example (b) is higher than (c)] is to be followed.

In the event that none of these pronouncements addresses the event, the support is sought from other accounting literature. Examples of other accounting literature include FASB Concepts Statements, International Accounting Standards, and accounting articles.

ISSUES IN FINANCIAL REPORTING

Since many interests may be affected by the implementation of an accounting standard, it is not surprising that there is much discussion about who should develop these standards and to whom they should apply. Some of the major issues are discussed below.

Standard Setting in a Political Environment

Possibly the most powerful force influencing the development of accounting standards is user groups. User groups consist of the parties who are most interested in or affected by accounting standards, rules, and procedures. Like lobbyists in our state and national capitals, user groups play a significant role. **Accounting standards are as much a product of political action as they are of careful logic or empirical findings.**

OBJECTIVE 9
Describe the impact of user groups on the standard-setting process.

User groups may want particular economic events accounted for or reported in a particular way, and they fight hard to get what they want. They know that the most effective way to influence the standards that dictate accounting practice is to participate in the formulation of these standards or to try to influence or persuade the formulator of them. Therefore, the FASB has become the target of many pressures and efforts to influence changes in the existing standards and the development of new ones.[13] To top it off, these pressures have been multiplying. Some influential groups demand that the accounting profession act more quickly and decisively to solve its problems and remedy its deficiencies. Other groups resist such action, preferring to implement change more slowly, if at all. Illustration 1-7 shows the various user groups that apply pressure.

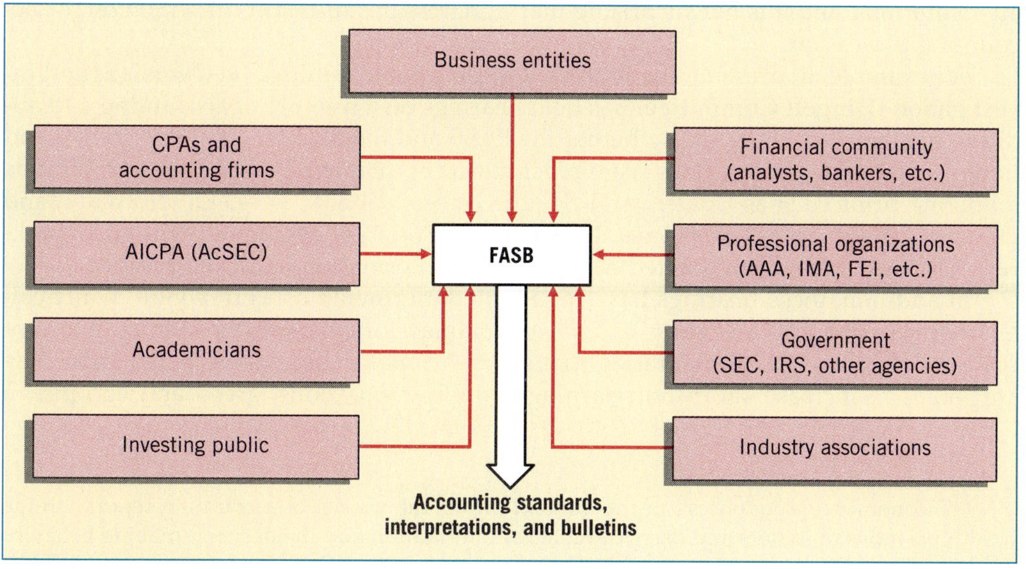

ILLUSTRATION 1-7
User Groups that Influence the Formulation of Accounting Standards

[13]All the FASB chairmen have acknowledged that many of the Board's projects, such as "Accounting for Contingencies," "Accounting for Pensions," "Statement of Cash Flows," and "Accounting for Derivatives," were targets of political pressure.

Should there be politics in setting financial accounting and reporting standards? We have politics at home; at school; at the fraternity, sorority, and dormitory; at the office; at church, temple, and mosque—politics is everywhere. The FASB does not exist in a vacuum. Standard setting is part of the real world, and it cannot escape politics and political pressures.

That is not to say that politics in standard setting is evil. Considering the **economic consequences**[14] of many accounting standards, it is not surprising that special interest groups become vocal and critical (some supporting, some opposing) when standards are being formulated. The Board must be attentive to the economic consequences of its actions. What the Board should *not* do is issue pronouncements that are primarily politically motivated. While paying attention to its constituencies, the Board should base its standards on sound research and a conceptual framework that has its foundation in economic reality. Even so, the FASB can continue to expect politics and special interest pressures, since as T. S. Eliot said, "Humankind cannot bear very much reality."

An illustration of an economic consequence issue is the turmoil caused by the FASB's standard that stock options granted to executives be charged as an expense on the income statement. The consequences of the standard, executives argued, would be disastrous. Big companies would reduce their investment in research and development and equipment. Small companies, being cash starved, would go bankrupt. They would not be able to attract top executives because stock option plans involve too high a charge to income. Employment in the United States would plummet because small companies (who create most of the job growth) would not hire additional workers. The FASB, however, noted that options are compensation, the cost of which should be recorded.

Expectations Gap

All professions have come under increasing scrutiny by the government, whether it be the investment banking profession because of insider trading, the medical profession because of high costs and Medicare or Medicaid frauds, or engineers because of their failure to consider environmental consequences in their work.

The accounting profession has not escaped criticism. Because of some well-publicized instances of corporate fraud, domestic and foreign bribery, underfunded pensions, and sudden bankruptcies, critics of the accounting profession have questioned its performance. Add to this society's general desire for more accountability from all institutions, and it is not surprising that Congress has turned its attention on the accounting profession.

For example, Representative John D. Dingell's Subcommittee on Oversight and Investigation **(Dingell Committee)** has held hearings on a number of accounting and auditing matters. One of these is whether the FASB and the SEC are issuing effective and timely standards. The hearings were precipitated by massive bankruptcies and frauds involving firms such as **Continental Illinois National Bank**, **Penn Square Bank**, and **Drysdale Government Securities, Inc.** Some in Congress contended that such bankruptcies could have been averted if more timely information had been provided.

In addition, these hearings have highlighted a growing concern about "white collar" crime in financial reporting. In some companies, for example, the culture of a company exerts pressures on operating managers "to make things look better than they are" so as to increase short-term earnings. In other situations, greed and ego play a

[14]"Economic consequences" in this context means the impact of accounting reports on the wealth positions of issuers and users of financial information and the decision-making behavior resulting from that impact. The resulting behavior of these individuals and groups could have detrimental financial effects on the providers (enterprises) of the financial information. For a more detailed discussion of this phenomenon, see Stephen A. Zeff, "The Rise of 'Economic Consequences'," *Journal of Accountancy*, December 1978, pp. 56–63. Special appreciation is extended to Professor Zeff for his insights on this chapter.

large role. For example, in one recent year the FBI investigated approximately 280 banks suspected of fraud, an increase of approximately 30% over the preceding year. It was estimated that banks lose eight times as much money to insiders as they do to "bank robbers."

The accounting profession recognizes that it must play an important role in combatting "white collar" fraud, and its response to criticisms in this area has been direct and immediate. For example, the AICPA established a new Accounting Firms Division with two sections: one for firms auditing SEC clients (called the **SEC Practice Section**) and the other for firms auditing privately owned, non-SEC clients (called the **Private Companies Section**).[15] And, to help assure the public that the SEC Practice Section is meeting its responsibilities, the AICPA established as part of this structure an independent **Public Oversight Board**. The Board, composed of distinguished individuals, has its own staff and is free to conduct its own inquiries and to report publicly as it wishes. The Private Companies Section also has its own quality control standards and peer review requirements.

More recently, the profession has issued new auditing standards on internal control, fraud and illegal acts, and auditors' communications. It has supported and begun to act on recommendations made by the **National Commission on Fraudulent Financial Reporting (the Treadway Commission)**, chaired by former SEC Commissioner James C. Treadway. And it is developing guidelines in relation to proper disclosures of reasons why auditors resign from audit engagements, particularly when there are questions about management's integrity.

But is it enough? The **expectations gap**—what the public thinks accountants should be doing and what accountants think they can do—is a difficult one to close. The instances of fraudulent reporting have caused some to question whether the profession is doing enough.[16] Although the profession can argue rightfully that they cannot be responsible for every financial catastrophe, it must continue to strive to meet the needs of society.

Competing Standard-Setting Bodies

As a prominent accountant noted, "the FASB is literally unique: it is a private sector institution performing a public function that is defined in the federal statutes." It is not surprising therefore that the right of the FASB to establish accounting standards continues to be challenged. Some of the major challenges come not only from outside the profession, but from within as well.

AICPA

The AICPA started issuing Statements of Position because it believed that more immediate guidance was needed for specific reporting problems. Although the AICPA has reduced its issuance of SOPs, it continues to be concerned about timely financial reporting. In addition, support exists within the AICPA for two sets of GAAP—one for large companies and one for small companies. Small companies complain that the detailed reporting required by GAAP is too costly and not needed by them. This is often referred to as the BIG GAAP–LITTLE GAAP issue.

---

[15]CPA firms that audit SEC registered firms must join the SEC Practice Section and therefore must comply with more comprehensive practice requirements (such as compulsory peer practice review) than those of the Private Companies Section.

[16]The accounting and auditing profession has designed a new tool to close this expectation gap in the form of a recently issued auditing standard entitled Statement on Auditing Standards (SAS) 82, *Consideration of Fraud in a Financial Statement Audit.* This recent 1997 standard "raises the bar" on the performance of financial statement audits by explicitly requiring auditors to assess the risk of material financial statement misstatement due to fraud and misappropriation of assets.

GASB

As indicated earlier, the GASB is a separate governmental accounting standards board established to regulate state and local governmental reporting. It is modeled after the FASB. The two organizations continue to debate who should set standards in certain not-for-profit accounting areas.

Congress

From time to time Congress becomes active in the standard-setting process, particularly when the issue becomes highly political. For example, Senator Joseph Lieberman (D-Connecticut) introduced legislation that would permit companies not to follow any FASB standard that requires a new expense charge for stock options. Senator Lieberman believes that a standard which results in a substantial expense for stock options would be disastrous to the national economy. Such political reaction is unfortunate and raises serious issues about who should be developing accounting standards.

Business Community

Members of the business community have registered numerous complaints about accounting standards. They contend that FASB standards are too complex and costly to implement and that some standards introduce volatility into reported income numbers. Further, they contend that standards requiring disclosures put their companies at a competitive disadvantage in world markets. As a result, this group lobbied hard—and won—for a change in the voting rules of the FASB, from a simple majority (4-3) to a supermajority (5-2). By requiring a supermajority, it is hoped that standards will be less controversial and will be issued only if truly "generally accepted." In addition, the business world argues for more representation on the FASB and the Financial Accounting Foundation.[17]

These developments are viewed by some with alarm. They believe that the supermajority will only lead to a delay in the issuances of standards. And, if the business community dominates the standard-setting process, the regulated will have too much influence on the regulations (leading to a "fox in the chicken coop" situation) and, thus, undermine the credibility of financial reports.

International Accounting Standards

In Germany, the amortization period for an intangible asset is 5 years. In the United States, a maximum period of 40 years is allowed. In Mexico, assets are adjusted for price-level changes. In the United States, assets are generally valued at historical cost. In Japan, income smoothing is permitted because firms are allowed discretionary charges to income for such items as depreciation and bad debts. In the United States, arbitrary charges to income are not permitted. These are just some of the ways in which reporting practices in the United States differ from reporting practices in other countries.

Many developing and newly industrialized nations, e.g., Nigeria, Singapore, and Malaysia, have adopted IASC standards as their national standards.

Most countries recognize the need for more uniform standards. As a result, the **International Accounting Standards Committee (IASC)** was formed in 1973—the same year the FASB was born—to attempt to narrow the areas of divergence. The objective of the IASC in terms of standard setting is "to work generally for the improvement and harmonization of regulations, accounting standards and procedures relating to the presentation of financial statements." Eliminating differences is not easy because the objectives of financial reporting in the United States often differ from those in for-

[17]To date, that argument has not prevailed. In fact, the exact opposite has occurred at the FAF. The SEC recently demanded that the FAF have more public-interest representatives on its board. The SEC argued that more individuals with a strong track record of independence and public service (free of conflicts and committed to the interests of investors) be selected. As a result of the SEC's insistence, the composition of the Foundation board has changed dramatically in favor of more "public-interest" members.

eign countries, the institutional structures are often not comparable, and strong national tendencies are pervasive. Nevertheless, much headway has been made since IASC's inception, and international standards may gradually supplant national standards.

Recently the SEC indicated that it would allow foreign companies to use IASC standards in securities offerings in the United States, if the IASC met the following three conditions:

1. The core standards must constitute a comprehensive generally accepted basis of accounting.
2. The standards must be of high quality.
3. The standards must be rigorously interpreted and applied.

These three conditions will be difficult to meet, but the IASC is making substantial progress. It is entirely possible that the SEC will accept IASC standards in the near future. Once that happens, many U.S.-based companies will petition to use IASC standards instead of U.S.-based standards. They will argue that for competitive purposes it is better that all companies follow the same standards.

Would this change be good or bad? We believe it has the potential to be both: It is good because a common set of standards is needed to measure and recognize economic events. Under international standards, users of financial information will find it easier to make comparisons among companies in different countries—for example, to compare **Ford Motor Co.** (U.S.) to **DaimlerChrysler** (Germany) to **Toyota Motor Co.** (Japan). It is bad because the United States is generally viewed as having the most rigorous and comprehensive reporting standards in the world. It is highly likely that international standards will initially not be of the same quality as U.S. standards, nor will enforcement procedures be as strong.

It should be emphasized that the United States has a major voice in how international standards are being developed. As a result, there are many similarities between IASC- and U.S.-based standards. Throughout this textbook, international considerations are presented to help you understand the international reporting environment.

INTERNATIONAL INSIGHT

The IASC recently completed work on a set of core international standards for use in cross-border offerings and listings. The SEC supports the IASC's work and has said that it would consider allowing the use of international standards by foreign issuers when they offer securities in the U.S.

Go to the Digital Tool for an expanded discussion of international accounting.

Ethics in the Environment of Financial Accounting

OBJECTIVE 10
Understand issues related to ethics and financial accounting.

Robert Sack, a commentator on the subject of accounting ethics, noted that "Based on my experience, new graduates tend to be idealistic . . . thank goodness for that! Still it is very dangerous to think that your armor is all in place and say to yourself 'I would have never given in to that.' The pressures don't explode on us; they build, and we often don't recognize them until they have us."

These observations are particularly appropriate for anyone entering the business world. In accounting, as in other areas of business, ethical dilemmas are encountered frequently. Some of these dilemmas are simple and easy to resolve. Many, however, are complex, and solutions are not obvious. Businesses' concentration on "maximizing the bottom line," "facing the challenges of competition," and "stressing short-term results" places accountants in an environment of conflict and pressure. Basic questions such as: "Is this way of communicating financial information good or bad?" "Is it right or wrong?" "What should I do in the circumstance?" cannot always be answered by simply adhering to GAAP or following the rules of the profession. Technical competence is not enough when ethical decisions are encountered.

Doing the right thing, making the right decision, is not always easy. Right is not always evident. And, the pressures "to bend the rules," "to play the game," "to just ignore it," can be considerable. For example, "Will my decision affect my job performance negatively?" "Will my superiors be upset?" "Will my colleagues be unhappy with me?" are often questions faced in making a tough ethical decision. The decision is more difficult because a public consensus has not emerged to formulate a comprehensive ethical system to provide guidelines.

This whole process of ethical sensitivity and selection among alternatives can be complicated by pressures that may take the form of time pressures, job pressures, client

Go to the Digital Tool for an expanded discussion of ethical issues in financial reporting.

pressures, personal pressures, and peer pressures. Throughout this textbook, **ethical considerations are presented for the purpose of sensitizing you** to the type of situations you may encounter in the performance of your professional responsibility.

Conclusion

The FASB is in its twenty-seventh year as this textbook is written. Will the FASB survive in its present state, or will it be restructured or changed as its predecessors were? As indicated, some people in government, some in the financial community, and some in the profession itself are continually challenging the accounting profession to assume more responsibility and to be more responsive to the needs of its constituencies.

At present, we believe that the accounting profession is reacting responsibly and effectively to remedy identified shortcomings. Because of its substantive resources and expertise, the private sector should be able to develop and maintain high standards. But it is a difficult process requiring time, logic, and diplomacy. By a judicious mix of these three ingredients, and a measure of luck, the profession may be able to continue to develop its own standards and regulate itself with minimal intervention.

KEY TERMS

- Accounting Principles Board (APB), *8*
- Accounting Research Bulletins, *8*
- accrual basis accounting, *6*
- American Institute of Certified Public Accountants (AICPA), *8*
- APB Opinions, *8*
- Auditing Standards Board, *13*
- Committee on Accounting Procedure (CAP), *8*
- Emerging Issues Task Force (EITF), *11*
- expectations gap, *17*
- financial accounting, *3*
- Financial Accounting Standards Board (FASB), *9*
- financial reporting, *3*
- financial statements, *3*
- generally accepted accounting principles (GAAP), *6*
- Governmental Accounting Standards Board (GASB), *11*
- International Accounting Standards Committee (IASC), *18*
- interpretations, *10*
- objectives of financial reporting, *5*
- Public Oversight Board, *17*
- Securities and Exchange Commission (SEC), *7*
- Standards Statement, *10*
- Statement of Financial Accounting Concepts, *10*
- technical bulletins, *11*
- Wheat Committee, *9*

SUMMARY OF LEARNING OBJECTIVES

1 Describe the essential characteristics of accounting. The essential characteristics of accounting are: (1) identification, measurement, and communication of financial information about (2) economic entities to (3) interested persons.

2 Identify the major financial statements and other means of financial reporting. The financial statements most frequently provided are (1) the balance sheet, (2) the income statement, (3) the statement of cash flows, and (4) the statement of owners' or stockholders' equity. Financial reporting other than financial statements may take various forms. Examples include the president's letter or supplementary schedules in the corporate annual report, prospectuses, reports filed with government agencies, news releases, management's forecasts, and descriptions of an enterprise's social or environmental impact.

3 Explain how accounting assists in the efficient use of scarce resources. Accounting provides reliable, relevant, and timely information to managers, investors, and creditors so that resources are allocated to the most efficient enterprises. Accounting also provides measurements of efficiency (profitability) and financial soundness.

4 Identify some of the challenges facing accounting. Financial reports fail to provide (1) some key performance measures widely used by management, (2) forward-looking information needed by investors and creditors, (3) sufficient information on a company's soft assets (intangibles), and (4) real-time financial information.

5 Identify the objectives of financial reporting. The objectives of financial reporting are to provide (1) information that is useful in investment and credit decisions, (2) information that is useful in assessing cash flow prospects, and (3) information about enterprise resources, claims to those resources, and changes in them.

6 Explain the need for accounting standards. The accounting profession has attempted to develop a set of standards that is generally accepted and universally practiced. Without this set of standards, each enterprise would have to develop its own standards, and readers of financial statements would have to familiarize themselves with every company's peculiar accounting and reporting practices. As a result, it would be almost impossible to prepare statements that could be compared.

7 Identify the major policy-setting bodies and their role in the standard-setting process. The *Securities and Exchange Commission (SEC)* is an agency of the federal government that has the broad powers to prescribe, in whatever detail it desires, the accounting standards to be employed by companies that fall within its jurisdiction. The *American Institute of Certified Public Accountants (AICPA)* issued standards through its Committee on Accounting Procedure and Accounting Principles Board. The *Financial Accounting Standards Board (FASB)* establishes and improves standards of financial accounting and reporting for the guidance and education of the public. The *Governmental Accounting Standards Board (GASB)* establishes and improves standards of financial accounting for state and local governments.

8 Explain the meaning of generally accepted accounting principles. Generally accepted accounting principles are those principles that have substantial authoritative support, such as FASB Standards and Interpretations, APB Opinions and Interpretations, AICPA Accounting Research Bulletins, and other authoritative pronouncements.

9 Describe the impact of user groups on the standard-setting process. User groups may want particular economic events accounted for or reported in a particular way, and they fight hard to get what they want. Therefore, the FASB has become the target of many pressures and efforts to influence changes in the existing standards and the development of new ones. Because of the accelerated rate of change and the increased complexity of our economy, these pressures have been multiplying. As a result, accounting standards are as much a product of political action as they are of careful logic or empirical findings.

10 Understand issues related to ethics and financial accounting. Financial accountants in the performance of their professional duties are called on for moral discernment and ethical decision making. The decision is more difficult because a public consensus has not emerged to formulate a comprehensive ethical system that provides guidelines in making ethical judgments.

QUESTIONS

1 How might accounting best be defined?

2 Differentiate broadly between financial accounting and managerial accounting.

3 Differentiate between "financial statements" and "financial reporting."

4 How does accounting help the capital allocation process?

5 What are some of the major challenges facing the accounting profession?

6 What are the major objectives of financial reporting?

7 Of what value is a common set of standards in financial accounting and reporting?

8 What is the likely limitation of "general-purpose financial statements"?

9 What are some of the developments or events that occurred between 1900 and 1930 that helped bring about changes in accounting theory or practice?

10 In what way is the Securities and Exchange Commission concerned about and supportive of accounting principles and standards?

11 What was the Committee on Accounting Procedure and what were its accomplishments and failings?

12 For what purposes did the AICPA in 1959 create the Accounting Principles Board?

13 Distinguish between Accounting Research Bulletins, Opinions of the Accounting Principles Board, and Statements of the Financial Accounting Standards Board.

14 If you had to explain or define "generally accepted accounting principles or standards," what essential characteristics would you include in your explanation?

15 In what ways was it felt that the statements issued by the Financial Accounting Standards Board would carry greater weight than the opinions issued by the Accounting Principles Board?

16 How are FASB discussion memoranda and FASB exposure drafts related to FASB "statements"?

17 Distinguish between FASB "statements of financial accounting standards" and FASB "statements of financial accounting concepts."

18 What is Rule 203 of the Code of Professional Conduct and what relationship does it have to the standard-setting process?

19 Rank from the most authoritative to the least authoritative, the following three items: FASB Technical Bulletins, AICPA Practice Bulletins, and FASB Standards.

20 The chairman of the FASB at one time noted that "the flow of standards can only be slowed if (1) producers focus less on quarterly earnings per share and tax benefits and more on quality products and (2) accountants and lawyers rely less on rules and law and more on professional judgment and conduct." Explain his comment.

21 What is the purpose of FASB Technical Bulletins? How do FASB Technical Bulletins differ from FASB Interpretations?

22 Explain the role of the Emerging Issues Task Force in establishing generally accepted accounting principles.

23 What is the purpose of the Governmental Accounting Standards Board?

24 What is AcSEC and what is its relationship to the FASB?

25 What are the sources of pressure that change and influence the development of accounting principles and standards?

26 Some individuals have indicated that the FASB must be cognizant of the economic consequences of its pronouncements. What is meant by economic consequences? What dangers exist if politics play too much of a role in the development of financial reporting standards?

27 What are some possible reasons why another organization, such as the Governmental Accounting Standards Board, should not issue financial reporting standards?

28 If you were given complete authority in the matter, how would you propose that accounting principles or standards should be developed and enforced?

29 One writer recently noted that 99.4% of all companies prepare statements that are in accordance with GAAP. Why then is there such concern about fraudulent financial reporting?

30 What is the "expectations gap"? What is the profession doing to try to close this gap?

31 A number of foreign countries often have reporting standards that differ from those in the United States. What are some of the main reasons why reporting standards are often different among countries?

32 How are financial accountants challenged in their work to make ethical decisions? Is not technical mastery of GAAP sufficient to the practice of financial accounting?

CONCEPTUAL CASES

C1-1 (Financial Accounting) Alan Rodriquez has recently completed his first year of studying accounting. His instructor for next semester has indicated that the primary focus will be the area of financial accounting.

Instructions

(a) Differentiate between financial accounting and managerial accounting.
(b) One part of financial accounting involves the preparation of financial statements. What are the financial statements most frequently provided?
(c) What is the difference between financial statements and financial reporting?

C1-2 (Objectives of Financial Reporting) Celia Cruz, a recent graduate of the local state university, is presently employed by a large manufacturing company. She has been asked by Angeles Ochoa, controller, to prepare the company's response to a current Discussion Memorandum published by the Financial Accounting Standards Board (FASB). Cruz knows that the FASB has issued six *Statements of Financial Accounting Concepts,* and she believes that these concept statements could be used to support the company's response to the Discussion Memorandum. She has prepared a rough draft of the response citing *Statement of Financial Accounting Concepts No. 1,* "Objectives of Financial Reporting by Business Enterprises."

Instructions

(a) Identify the three objectives of financial reporting as presented in *Statement of Financial Accounting Concepts No. 1 (SFAC No. 1).*
(b) Describe the level of sophistication expected of the users of financial information by *SFAC No. 1.*

(CMA adapted)

C1-3 (Accounting Numbers and the Environment) Hardly a day goes by without an article appearing on the crises affecting many of our financial institutions in the United States. It is estimated that the savings and loan (S&L) debacle ended up costing $500 billion ($2,000 for every man, woman, and child in the United States). Some argue that if the S&Ls were required to report their investments at market value instead of cost, large losses would have been reported earlier, which would have signaled regulators to close those S&Ls and, therefore, minimize the losses to American taxpayers.

Instructions

Explain how reported accounting numbers might affect an individual's perceptions and actions. Cite two examples.

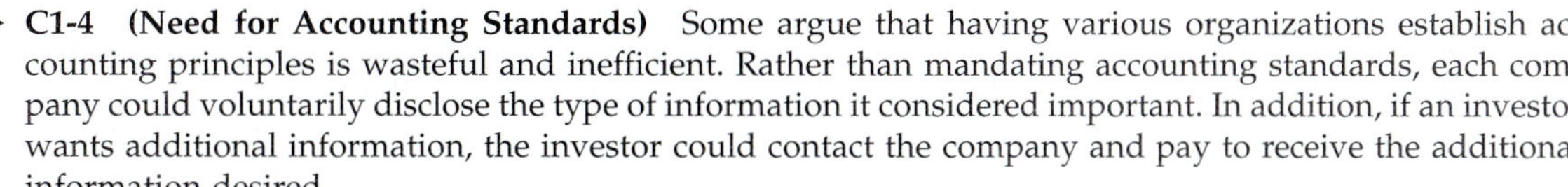

C1-4 (Need for Accounting Standards) Some argue that having various organizations establish accounting principles is wasteful and inefficient. Rather than mandating accounting standards, each company could voluntarily disclose the type of information it considered important. In addition, if an investor wants additional information, the investor could contact the company and pay to receive the additional information desired.

Instructions

Comment on the appropriateness of this viewpoint.

C1-5 (AICPA's Role in Standard Setting) One of the major groups involved in the standard-setting process is the American Institute of Certified Public Accountants. Initially it was the primary organization that established accounting principles in the United States. Subsequently it relinquished most of its power to the FASB.

Instructions

- **(a)** Identify the two committees of the AICPA that established accounting principles prior to the establishment of the FASB.
- **(b)** Speculate as to why these two organizations failed. In your answer, identify steps the FASB has taken to avoid failure.
- **(c)** What is the present role of the AICPA in the standard-setting environment?

C1-6 (FASB Role in Standard Setting) A press release announcing the appointment of the trustees of the new Financial Accounting Foundation stated that the Financial Accounting Standards Board (to be appointed by the trustees) ". . . will become the established authority for setting accounting principles under which corporations report to the shareholders and others" (AICPA news release July 20, 1972).

Instructions

- **(a)** Identify the sponsoring organization of the FASB and the process by which the FASB arrives at a decision and issues an accounting standard.
- **(b)** Indicate the major types of pronouncements issued by the FASB and the purposes of each of these pronouncements.

C1-7 (Government Role in Standard Setting) Recently an article stated "the setting of accounting standards in the United States is now about 60 years old. It is a unique process in our society, one that has undergone numerous changes over the years. The standards are established by a private sector entity that has no dominant sponsor and is not part of any professional organization or trade association. The governmental entity that provides oversight, on the other hand, is far more a friend than a competitor or an antagonist."

Instructions

Identify the governmental entity that provides oversight and indicate its role in the standard-setting process.

C1-8 (Meaning of Generally Accepted Accounting Principles) At the completion of Bloom Company's audit, the president, Judy Bloom, asks about the meaning of the phrase "in conformity with generally accepted accounting principles" that appears in your audit report on the management's financial statements. Judy observes that the meaning of the phrase must include something more and different than what she thinks of as "principles."

Instructions

- **(a)** Explain the meaning of the term "accounting principles" as used in the audit report. (Do not discuss in this part the significance of "generally accepted.")
- **(b)** President Bloom wants to know how you determine whether or not an accounting principle is generally accepted. Discuss the sources of evidence for determining whether an accounting principle has substantial authoritative support. Do not merely list the titles of publications.

C1-9 (Politicization of Standard Setting) Some accountants have said that politicization in the development and acceptance of generally accepted accounting principles (i.e., standard setting) is taking place. Some use the term "politicization" in a narrow sense to mean the influence by governmental agencies, particularly the Securities and Exchange Commission, on the development of generally accepted accounting principles. Others use it more broadly to mean the compromise that results when the bodies responsible for developing generally accepted accounting principles are pressured by interest groups (SEC, American Accounting Association, businesses through their various organizations, Institute of Management Accountants, financial analysts, bankers, lawyers, etc.).

Instructions

(a) The Committee on Accounting Procedures of the AICPA was established in the mid to late 1930s and functioned until 1959, at which time the Accounting Principles Board came into existence. In 1973, the Financial Accounting Standards Board was formed and the APB went out of existence. Do the reasons these groups were formed, their methods of operation while in existence, and the reasons for the demise of the first two indicate an increasing politicization (as the term is used in the broad sense) of accounting standard setting? Explain your answer by indicating how the CAP, the APB, and the FASB operated or operate. Cite specific developments that tend to support your answer.

(b) What arguments can be raised to support the "politicization" of accounting standard setting?

(c) What arguments can be raised against the "politicization" of accounting standard setting?

(CMA adapted)

C1-10 (Models for Setting Accounting Standards) Presented below are three models for setting accounting standards.

1. The purely political approach, where national legislative action decrees accounting standards.
2. The private, professional approach, where financial accounting standards are set and enforced by private professional actions only.
3. The public/private mixed approach, where standards are basically set by private sector bodies that behave as though they were public agencies and whose standards to a great extent are enforced through governmental agencies.

Instructions

(a) Which of these three models best describes standard setting in the United States? Comment on your answer.

(b) Why do companies, financial analysts, labor unions, industry trade associations, and others take such an active interest in standard setting?

(c) Cite an example of a group other than the FASB that attempts to establish accounting standards. Speculate as to why another group might wish to set its own standards.

C1-11 (Standard-Setting Terminology) Andrew Wyeth, an administrator at a major university, recently said, "I've got some CDs in my IRA, which I set up to beat the IRS." As elsewhere, in the world of accounting and finance, it often helps to be fluent in abbreviations and acronyms.

Instructions

Presented below is a list of common accounting acronyms. Identify the term for which each acronym stands, and provide a brief definition of each term.

(a) FEI	**(g)** FAF	**(m)** CPA
(b) IMA	**(h)** FASAC	**(n)** FASB
(c) AICPA	**(i)** FRR	**(o)** GASB
(d) CAP	**(j)** IRS	**(p)** SEC
(e) ARB	**(k)** SOP	**(q)** AAA
(f) APB	**(l)** GAAP	**(r)** IASC

C1-12 (Accounting Organizations and Documents Issued) Presented below are a number of accounting organizations and type of documents they have issued. Match the appropriate document to the organization involved. Note that more than one document may be issued by the same organization. If no document is provided for an organization, write in "0."

Organization	*Document*
1. ____ Securities and Exchange Commission	**(a)** Opinions
2. ____ Accounting Standards Executive Committee	**(b)** Practice Bulletins
3. ____ Accounting Principles Board	**(c)** Accounting Research Bulletins
4. ____ Committee on Accounting Procedure	**(d)** Financial Reporting Releases
5. ____ Financial Accounting Standards Board	**(e)** Financial Accounting Standards
	(f) Statements of Position
	(g) Technical Bulletins

C1-13 (Accounting Pronouncements) A number of authoritative pronouncements have been issued by standard-setting bodies during the last 50 years. A list is provided on the left with a description of these pronouncements on the right. Match the description to the pronouncements.

1. _____ Technical Bulletin
2. _____ Interpretations (of the Financial Accounting Standards Board)
3. _____ Statement of Financial Accounting Standards
4. _____ EITF Statements
5. _____ Opinions
6. _____ Statement of Financial Accounting Concepts

(a) Official pronouncements of the APB
(b) Sets forth fundamental objectives and concepts that will be used in developing future standards
(c) Primary document of the FASB that establishes GAAP
(d) Provides additional guidance on implementing or applying FASB Standards or Interpretations
(e) Provides guidance on how to account for new and unusual financial transactions that have the potential for creating diversity in financial reporting practices
(f) Represent extensions or modifications of existing standards

C1-14 (Issues Involving Standard Setting) There have been a number of articles on accounting matters in the financial press. Some of the comments made in these articles are presented below. Answer the related question for each comment.

(a) "In its first formal action upon commencing operations the GASB unanimously approved GASB Statement No. 1, Authoritative Status of NCGA Pronouncements and AICPA Industry Audit Guide." What is the GASB and what role does it play in the standard-setting process?

(b) Some people want the FASB to deal with emerging accounting issues more promptly. But prompt resolution of issues comes at the expense of some of the elaborate due process the FASB imposes on itself. If the FASB reduces that due process, it risks undermining the acceptance of accounting rules set by a nongovernmental standard-setting body. What is meant by "due process" and how is the profession attempting to handle the problem of providing timely guidance?

(c) Recently the FASB has published what it considers to be the mission of the FASB. It noted that one concept it will follow will be to weigh carefully the views of its constituents in developing standards. Who are the FASB's major constituents and what role do they play in the standard-setting process?

(d) "A Securities and Exchange Commission report to Congress on the accounting profession shows that the profession has taken significant strides in regulating itself." What might be some significant strides the profession has taken to regulate itself?

C1-15 (Securities and Exchange Commission) The U.S. Securities and Exchange Commission (SEC) was created in 1934 and consists of five commissioners and a large professional staff. The SEC professional staff is organized into five divisions and several principal offices. The primary objective of the SEC is to support fair securities markets. The SEC also strives to foster enlightened shareholder participation in corporate decisions of publicly traded companies. The SEC has a significant presence in financial markets, the development of accounting practices, and corporation-shareholder relations, and has the power to exert influence on entities whose actions lie within the scope of its authority.

Instructions

(a) Explain where the Securities and Exchange Commission receives its authority.

(b) Describe the official role of the Securities and Exchange Commission in the development of financial accounting theory and practices.

(c) Discuss the interrelationship between the Securities and Exchange Commission and the Financial Accounting Standards Board with respect to the development and establishment of financial accounting theory and practices.

(CMA adapted)

C1-16 (Standard-Setting Process) In 1973, the responsibility for developing and issuing rules on accounting practices was given to the Financial Accounting Foundation and, in particular, to an arm of the foundation called the Financial Accounting Standards Board (FASB). The generally accepted accounting principles established by the FASB are enunciated through a publication series entitled **Statements of Financial Accounting Standards**. These statements are issued periodically, and over 120 are currently in force. The statements have a significant influence on the way in which financial statements are prepared by U.S. corporations.

Instructions

(a) Describe the process by which a topic is selected or identified as appropriate for study by the Financial Accounting Standards Board (FASB).

(b) Once a topic is considered appropriate for consideration by the FASB, a series of steps are followed before a **Statement of Financial Accounting Standards** is issued. Describe the major steps in the process leading to the issuance of a standard.

(c) Identify at least three other organizations that influence the setting of generally accepted accounting principles (GAAP).

(CMA adapted)

C1-17 (History of Standard-Setting Organizations) Beta Alpha Psi, your university's accounting society, has decided to publish a brief pamphlet for seniors in high school, detailing the various facets of the accountancy profession. As a junior accountancy major, you have been asked to contribute an article for this publication. Your topic is the evolution of accounting standard-setting organizations in the United States.

Instructions

Write a 1–2 page article on the historical development of the organizations responsible for giving us GAAP. (The most appropriate introduction would explain the increasing need for a more standardized approach to accounting for a company's assets.)

C1-18 (Economic Consequences) Presented below are comments made in the financial press. Prepare responses to the requirements in each item.

(a) Rep. John Dingell, the ranking Democrat on the House Commerce Committee, has thrown his support behind the FASB's controversial derivatives accounting standard and encouraged the FASB to adopt the proposed rule promptly. Indicate why a member of Congress might feel obligated to comment on this proposed FASB standard.

(b) In the area of the internationalization of accounting standards, many foreign companies want to list their stock for trading in the United States while continuing to use foreign accounting standards. The New York Stock Exchange has been lobbying for more foreign listings. Explain the position of the SEC in regard to accepting international accounting standards for listings in the United States.

(c) In a strongly worded letter to Senator Lauch Faircloth (R-NC) and House Banking Committee Chairman Jim Leach (R-IA), the American Institute of Certified Public Accountants (AICPA) cautioned against government intervention in the accounting standard-setting process, warning that it had the potential of jeopardizing U.S. capital markets. Explain how government intervention could possibly affect capital markets adversely.

C1-19 (Standard-Setting Process, Economic Consequences) The following letter was sent to the SEC and the FASB by leaders of the business community.

> Dear Sirs:
>
> The FASB has been struggling with accounting for derivatives and hedging for many years. The FASB has now developed, over the last few weeks, a new approach that it proposes to adopt as a final standard. We understand that the Board intends to adopt this new approach as a final standard without exposing it for public comment and debate, despite the evident complexity of the new approach, the speed with which it has been developed and the significant changes to the exposure draft since it was released more than one year ago. Instead, the Board plans to allow only a brief review by selected parties, limited to issues of operationality and clarity, and would exclude questions as to the merits of the proposed approach.
>
> As the FASB itself has said throughout this process, its mission does not permit it to consider matters that go beyond accounting and reporting considerations. Accordingly, the FASB may not have adequately considered the wide range of concerns that have been expressed about the derivatives and hedging proposal, including concerns related to the potential impact on the capital markets, the weakening of companies' ability to manage risk, and the adverse control implications of implementing costly and complex new rules imposed at the same time as other major initiatives, including the Year 2000 issues and a single European currency. We believe that these crucial issues must be considered, if not by the FASB, then by the Securities and Exchange Commission, other regulatory agencies, or Congress.
>
> We believe it is essential that the FASB solicit all comments in order to identify and address all material issues that may exist before issuing a final standard. We understand the desire to bring this process to a prompt conclusion, but the underlying issues are so important to this nation's businesses, the customers they serve and the economy as a whole that expediency cannot be the dominant con-

sideration. As a result, we urge the FASB to expose its new proposal for public comment, following the established due process procedures that are essential to acceptance of its standards, and providing sufficient time to affected parties to understand and assess the new approach.

We also urge the SEC to study the comments received in order to assess the impact that these proposed rules may have on the capital markets, on companies' risk management practices, and on management and financial controls. These vital public policy matters deserve consideration as part of the Commission's oversight responsibilities.

We believe that these steps are essential if the FASB is to produce the best possible accounting standard while minimizing adverse economic effects and maintaining the competitiveness of U.S. businesses in the international marketplace.

Very truly yours,

(This letter was signed by the chairs of 22 of the largest U.S. companies.)

Instructions

Answer the following questions:

(a) Explain the "due process" procedures followed by the FASB in developing a financial reporting standard.

(b) What is meant by the term "economic consequences" in accounting standard setting?

(c) What economic consequences arguments are used in this letter?

(d) What do you believe is the main point of the letter?

(e) Why do you believe a copy of this letter was sent by the business community to influential members of the United States Congress?

USING YOUR JUDGMENT

FINANCIAL REPORTING PROBLEM

Kate Jackson, a new staff accountant, is confused because of the complexities involving accounting standard setting. Specifically, she is confused by the number of bodies issuing financial reporting standards of one kind or another and the level of authoritative support that can be attached to these reporting standards. Kate decides that she must review the environment in which accounting standards are set, if she is to increase her understanding of the accounting profession.

Kate recalls that during her accounting education there was a chapter or two regarding the environment of financial accounting and the development of accounting standards. However, she remembers that little emphasis was placed on these chapters by her instructor.

Instructions

(a) Help Kate by identifying key organizations involved in accounting standard setting.

(b) Kate asks for guidance regarding authoritative support. Please assist her by explaining what is meant by authoritative support.

(c) Give Kate a historical overview of how standard setting has evolved so that she will not feel that she is the only one to be confused.

(d) What authority for compliance with GAAP has existed throughout the period of standard setting?

RESEARCH CASES

Case 1

In 1994, the AICPA Special Committee on Financial Reporting issued *Improving Business Reporting—A Customer Focus* (the "Jenkins report"). The chapter includes a brief overview of the committee's findings.

Instructions

Obtain a copy of the report and use it to answer the following questions:

(a) Identify three members of the committee and their professional backgrounds.

(b) How is "business reporting" defined in the report?

(c) In what ways did the committee investigate the information needs of financial statement users?

(d) Identify two benefits and two costs of informative disclosure from the perspective of (1) the overall economy and (2) individual reporting entities and their owners.

(e) The FASB has begun to address a number of the issues raised in the Jenkins report. Obtain a recent copy of the FASB's *Financial Accounting Series Status Report* which addresses an issue from the Jenkins report. Summarize the status of the FASB's investigation of the issue.

Case 2

In the *Journal of Corporate Accounting and Finance*/Autumn 1996, an article appeared entitled "The FAF Restructuring Controversy: What Happened, and How Will It Affect the FASB."

Instructions

Read the article and answer the following questions:

(a) Explain the responsibility of the Financial Accounting Foundation.

(b) What recommendations did the FEI's Committee on Corporate Reporting make regarding the Financial Accounting Standards Board?

(c) What was the reaction of the Securities and Exchange Commission to the recommendations of the FEI Committee on Corporate Reporting?

(d) What finally happened regarding the restructuring controversy?

(e) What does this controversy indicate about the standard setting process?

Case 3

In *The Wall Street Journal,* March 21, 1996, p. C1, an article appeared entitled "Can FASB Be Considered Antibusiness?"

Instructions

Read this article and answer the following questions:

(a) Why do certain parties believe the FASB is antibusiness?

(b) What is the author's conclusion?

INTERNATIONAL REPORTING CASE

Michael Sharpe, Deputy Chairman, International Accounting Standards Committee, made the following comments before the FEI's 63rd Annual Conference: There is an irreversible movement towards the harmonization of financial reporting throughout the world. The international capital markets require an end to:

1. The confusion caused by international companies announcing different results depending on the set of accounting standards applied. Recent announcements by Daimler-Benz (now DaimlerChrysler) highlight the confusion that this causes.
2. Companies in some countries obtaining unfair commercial advantages from the use of particular national accounting standards.
3. The complications in negotiating commercial arrangements for international joint ventures caused by different accounting requirements.
4. The inefficiency of international companies having to understand and use a myriad of different accounting standards depending on the countries in which they operate and the countries in which they raise capital and debt. Executive talent is wasted on keeping up to date with numerous sets of accounting standards and the never-ending changes to them.
5. The inefficiency of investment managers, bankers, and financial analysts as they seek to compare financial reporting drawn up in accordance with different sets of accounting standards.
6. Failure of many stock exchanges and regulators to require companies subject to their jurisdiction to provide comparable, comprehensive, and transparent financial reporting frameworks giving international comparability.
7. Difficulty for developing countries and countries entering the free market economy such as China and Russia in accessing foreign capital markets because of the complexity of and differences between national standards.
8. The restriction on the mobility of financial service providers across the world as a result of different accounting standards.

Clearly the elimination of these inefficiencies by having comparable high-quality financial reporting used across the world would benefit international businesses.

Instructions

(a) What is the International Accounting Standards Committee?

(b) What stakeholders might benefit from the use of International Accounting Standards?

(c) What do you believe are some of the major obstacles to harmonization?

ETHICS CASE

When the FASB issues new standards, the implementation date is usually 12 months from date of issuance, with early implementation encouraged. Paula Popovich, controller, discusses with her financial vice president the need for early implementation of a standard which would result in a fairer presentation of the company's financial condition and earnings. When the financial vice president determines that early implementation of the standard will adversely affect the reported net income for the year, he discourages Popovich from implementing the standard until it is required.

Instructions

Answer the following questions:

(a) What, if any, is the ethical issue involved in this case?

(b) Is the financial vice president acting improperly or immorally?

(c) What does Popovich have to gain by advocacy of early implementation?

(d) Which stakeholders might be affected by the decision against early implementation?

(CMA adapted)

A visit with
Arthur R. Wyatt

Arthur Wyatt teaches financial reporting at the University of Illinois. He is a former member of the FASB and IASC. In addition, he is an expert witness on litigation matters and has been a consultant to the Securities & Exchange Commission on issues relating to international accounting standards.

PERSPECTIVES ON

International Accounting Standards

Why is there a need for international accounting standards? Let's say a London bank receives loan applications from companies in twelve different countries—and that each company prepares its financial statements in accordance with the standards in its own country. Unless the banker understood all twelve accounting standards, he or she wouldn't be able to analyze those financial statements in a knowledgeable way. What happens when a U.S. mutual fund manager who runs an international equity fund tries to read the financial statements of companies from fifty different countries? It is in the best interests of those companies to prepare their financial statements in a manner that can be clearly understood by the portfolio manager. The international standards are viewed as a vehicle to get greater comparability.

How has the advent of the European Monetary Union and the euro affected European accounting standards? The move toward making Europe a single economy has driven accounting in the same direction. There's pressure for their accounting systems to become more similar rather than employing the widely varying approaches that the different countries were using. At the same time, overall financial disclosure has improved as European companies seek capital from abroad, particularly in the United States. The same trend is occurring in Japan—better disclosure that makes things more transparent for investors. While many changes are being driven by legislative changes, the real driving forces are the capital markets. Historically, most of the capital for corporations in countries such as Germany and Japan had been provided by a limited number of banks. For decades, there wasn't a robust stock market, and there was no reason for a company to report openly on its financial affairs. All of that has changed.

Where do you think international accounting standards may be deficient? I think there are two places that cause trouble for the Securities & Exchange Commission. The first is disclosure. The extent of the disclosures required by international standards is still not sufficient to satisfy the SEC. The second is that enforcement of accounting regulation in most other countries is not as stringent as it is in the U.S. The SEC would like to have some assurance that the regulators in other countries are going to force companies to follow international standards, just as the SEC forces companies to follow the U.S. standards. The SEC is currently considering whether to permit companies' shares to trade in the United States if their financial statements are filed in accordance with international standards, not U.S. GAAP standards. My guess is that it will be another year and a half or two years before they actually move in that direction.

What recent developments in international accounting would you highlight? Right now, the International Accounting Standards Committee, based in London, is being restructured. It will be a larger board using mostly full-time professionals representing major countries around the world. They will have the authority to set standards that would have to be accepted in all countries. That requires greater funding than they currently have in place. Although there hasn't been much in the way of recent technical developments, there has been some compromise between the U.S. and European accounting representatives. Many European representatives resist the notion that the IASC would be patterned after the U.S. system. Meanwhile, the SEC has let the committee know that it is not willing to buy into international standards unless the standards setting process is independent of outside influence.

From a technical standpoint, how do international standards differ from those of the U.S.? The international standards permit real estate to be written up to appraised values periodically, which is a British practice that's probably not going to be accepted by the SEC. In addition, the international standard on business combinations does not permit pooling of interest accounting, except in extremely rare circumstances. Although the FASB is on the verge of eliminating it, the pooling of interest concept has been very popular in the United States because it has permitted companies to buy other companies and not record what they paid for them and to get the benefit of higher profits in future years. I think when the SEC agrees to buy into an international standard, it probably will agree to do so with a small number of exceptions, and they will indicate that certain practices that are permitted by international standard will not be accepted by the SEC.

However, international standards on marketable investments, pension accounting, leases, and many other issues are very similar to ours. Some differences arise not because of accounting but because a particular country's economy functions differently. For instance, in Japan, most of the pensions are sponsored by the government rather than by corporations. As a result, the Japanese standard setters did not want all of the disclosures that the U.S. standard requires. And they probably don't have as much accrual accounting in their pension area as we do. But the international standard on pensions is close to ours.

What other differences exist in financial reporting? Many other countries resist disclosure because the attitude in the corporate community is that they don't want to provide help to their competitors. In contrast, the emphasis in the United States is towards more disclosure and towards helping investors make informed decisions.

Another difference is the specificity of U.S. standards. While some alternatives are provided, such as for inventory and depreciation, we have a highly specific set of rules. In particular, many European standards provide acceptable alternatives, which was often necessary to get the standards published. Generally, however, the international standards are based on essentially the same body of principles that govern the United States. Their notion of accrual accounting is very similar, and the former practice of using reserves to smooth earnings is no longer acceptable.

Where do students typically get exposure to international accounting? It's very limited. If they do get an exposure, it's because there happens to be a professor at their school who has an interest in the area and develops a course that is offered as an elective. This year I happened to have a student from Germany who is spending a year here. Fortunately, he was willing to speak up and has commented several times that this wasn't the way they did things in Germany. And that gave me a chance to go through a discussion with the class on the difference in approach between Germany and the United States, and why it existed. But if I hadn't had him in class, that issue wouldn't have come up.

How do you see international accounting standards evolving? Once the SEC has accepted international standards, I think that you will find that the global standards-setting body will be the International Accounting Standards Committee. The FASB will still have a role, but it will deal primarily with emerging issues and matters that are primarily U.S.-oriented. And gradually the textbooks and accounting courses, instead of referring to U.S. GAAP, will refer to international standards. But this change is still years away.

CHAPTER 2

Conceptual Framework Underlying Financial Accounting

There Are Profits . . . And There Are Profits

Accounting in Hollywood affects two parties dramatically. The first is the numerous actors, writers, and producers who sign "net profit contracts" on highly successful projects but never receive a share of the profits. With the big studios' ability to allocate overhead costs creatively, "net profits" often fail to materialize. As a result, large-grossing productions like *Forrest Gump*, *Batman*, *J.F.K.*, *Alien*, *Ghostbusters*, and *Coming to America* have never produced a "net profit." Thus, several stars have brought lawsuits against the movie studios in an attempt to uncover the creative measurement of "net loss." Whether that issue will ever be resolved is anybody's guess.

Investors are another party affected by Hollywood accounting. For example, major motion picture studios have been allowed to capitalize advertising and marketing costs and amortize these costs against revenues over the life of the film. As a result, many investors have suggested that the studios' profit numbers were overstated. Under a new GAAP standard, these costs now must be amortized over no more than three months; in many cases, they have to be expensed immediately. Similarly, the costs related to abandoned projects often were allocated to overhead and spread out over the lives of the successful projects. Not anymore. These costs now must be expensed as they are incurred. Here is a rough estimate of the amounts of capitalized advertising costs some major studios will have to write off:

Studio (Parent Company)	Capitalized Advertising (in millions)
Columbia Tri-Star (Sony)	$200
Paramount (Viacom)	200
20th Century Fox (News Corp)	150

Why the more conservative approach? A lot has to do with a stricter application of the definitions of assets and expenses. While many argue that advertising and marketing costs have future service potential, difficulty in reliably measuring these benefits suggests they are not assets. Therefore, a very short amortization period or immediate charge-off is justified.

These new guidelines will not fix the problem of vanishing profits that are used to determine what film stars receive, but investors will now be better able to understand what is happening to the performance of companies in this industry.

LEARNING OBJECTIVES

After studying this chapter, you should be able to:

1. **Describe the usefulness of a conceptual framework.**
2. **Describe the FASB's efforts to construct a conceptual framework.**
3. **Understand the objectives of financial reporting.**
4. **Identify the qualitative characteristics of accounting information.**
5. **Define the basic elements of financial statements.**
6. **Describe the basic assumptions of accounting.**
7. **Explain the application of the basic principles of accounting.**
8. **Describe the impact that constraints have on reporting accounting information.**

PREVIEW OF CHAPTER 2

As indicated in the opening story about Hollywood accounting, users of financial statements need relevant and reliable information. To help develop this type of financial information, accountants use a conceptual framework that guides financial accounting and reporting. This chapter discusses the basic concepts underlying this conceptual framework. The content and organization of this chapter are as follows:

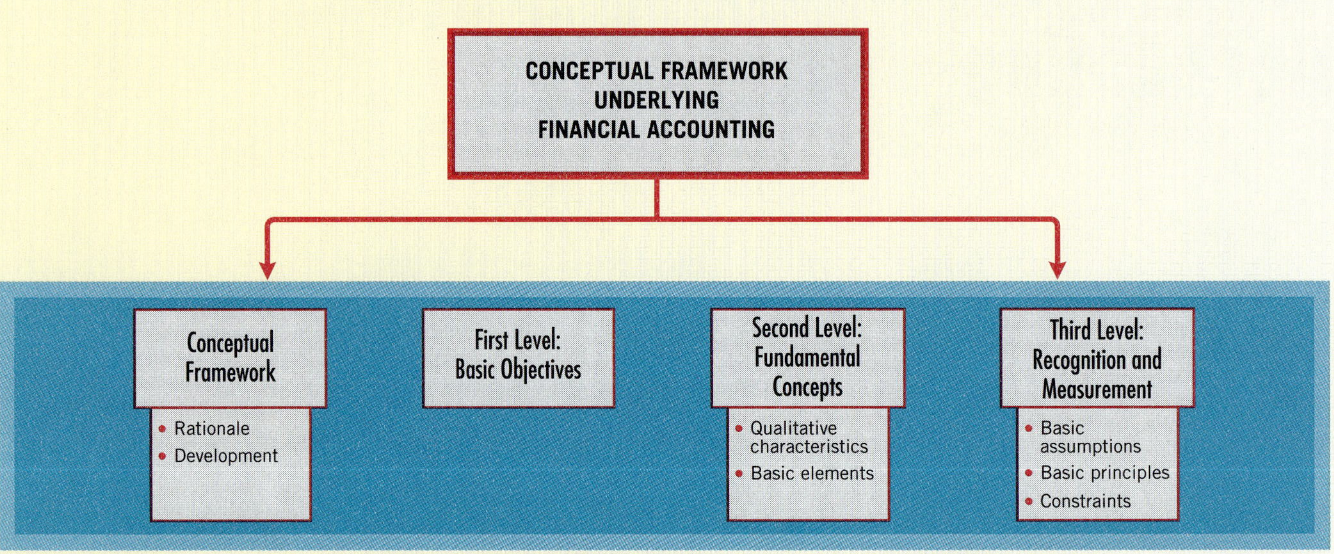

CONCEPTUAL FRAMEWORK

A **conceptual framework** is like a **constitution**: It is "a coherent system of interrelated objectives and fundamentals that can lead to consistent standards and that prescribes the nature, function, and limits of financial accounting and financial statements."[1] Many have considered the Board's real contribution—and even its continued existence—to depend on the quality and utility of the conceptual framework.

Need for Conceptual Framework

OBJECTIVE 1
Describe the usefulness of a conceptual framework.

Why is a conceptual framework necessary? First, to be useful, standard setting should build on and relate to an established body of concepts and objectives. A soundly developed conceptual framework should enable the FASB to issue more useful and consistent standards over time. **A coherent set of standards and rules should be the result**, because they would be built upon the same foundation. The framework should increase financial statement users' understanding of and confidence in financial reporting, and it should enhance comparability among companies' financial statements.

Second, new and emerging **practical problems should be more quickly solved by reference to an existing framework of basic theory**. To illustrate an emerging problem: Unique debt instruments were issued by companies in the early 1980s as a response to high interest and inflation rates. These included shared appreciation mortgages (debt in which the lender receives equity participation), zero coupon bonds (debt issued at a deep discount with no stated interest rate), and commodity-backed bonds (debt that

[1]"Conceptual Framework for Financial Accounting and Reporting: Elements of Financial Statements and Their Measurement," *FASB Discussion Memorandum* (Stamford, Conn.: FASB, 1976), page 1 of the "Scope and Implications of the Conceptual Framework Project" section.

may be repaid in a commodity). For example, **Sunshine Mining** (a silver mining company) sold two issues of bonds that it would redeem either with $1,000 in cash or with 50 ounces of silver, whichever was worth more at maturity. Both bond issues had a stated interest rate of 8.5%. At what amounts should the bonds have been recorded by Sunshine or the buyers of the bonds? What is the amount of the premium or discount on the bonds and how should it be amortized, if the bond redemption payments are to be made in silver (the future value of which was unknown at the date of issuance)?

It is difficult, if not impossible, for the FASB to prescribe the proper accounting treatment quickly for situations like this. Practicing accountants, however, must resolve such problems on a day-to-day basis. Through the exercise of good judgment and with the help of a universally accepted conceptual framework, it is hoped that practitioners will be able to dismiss certain alternatives quickly and then to focus upon a logical and acceptable treatment.

Development of Conceptual Framework

Over the years numerous organizations, committees, and interested individuals developed and published their own conceptual frameworks. But no single framework was universally accepted and relied on in practice. Perhaps the most successful was *Accounting Principles Board Statement No. 4*, "Basic Concepts and Accounting Principles Underlying Financial Statements of Business Enterprises," which described existing practice but did not prescribe what practice ought to be.[2] Recognizing the need for a generally accepted framework, the FASB in 1976 issued a massive three-part Discussion Memorandum entitled *Conceptual Framework for Financial Accounting and Reporting: Elements of Financial Statements and Their Measurement*. It set forth the major issues that must be addressed in establishing a conceptual framework that would be a basis for setting accounting standards and for resolving financial reporting controversies. Since the publication of that document, the FASB has issued six Statements of Financial Accounting Concepts that relate to financial reporting for business enterprises.[3] They are:

OBJECTIVE 2
Describe the FASB's efforts to construct a conceptual framework.

The IASC has issued a conceptual framework that is broadly consistent with that of the U.S.

1. *SFAC No. 1*, "Objectives of Financial Reporting by Business Enterprises," presents the goals and purposes of accounting.
2. *SFAC No. 2*, "Qualitative Characteristics of Accounting Information," examines the characteristics that make accounting information useful.
3. *SFAC No. 3*, "Elements of Financial Statements of Business Enterprises," provides definitions of items in financial statements, such as assets, liabilities, revenues, and expenses.
4. *SFAC No. 5*, "Recognition and Measurement in Financial Statements of Business Enterprises," sets forth fundamental recognition and measurement criteria and guidance on what information should be formally incorporated into financial statements and when.
5. *SFAC No. 6*, "Elements of Financial Statements," replaces *SFAC No. 3* and expands its scope to include not-for-profit organizations.
6. *SFAC No. 7*, "Using Cash Flow Information and Present Value in Accounting Measurements," provides a framework for using expected future cash flows and present values as a basis for measurement.

Illustration 2-1 provides an overview of the conceptual framework.[4] At the first level, the **objectives** identify the goals and purposes of accounting and are the build-

[2]"Basic Concepts and Accounting Principles Underlying Financial Statements of Business Enterprises," *APB Statement No. 4* (New York: AICPA, 1970).

[3]The FASB has also issued a Statement of Financial Accounting Concepts that relates to nonbusiness organizations: *Statement of Financial Accounting Concepts No. 4*, "Objectives of Financial Reporting by Nonbusiness Organizations" (December 1980).

[4]Adapted from William C. Norby, *The Financial Analysts Journal*, March–April 1982, p. 22.

ILLUSTRATION 2-1
Conceptual Framework for Financial Reporting

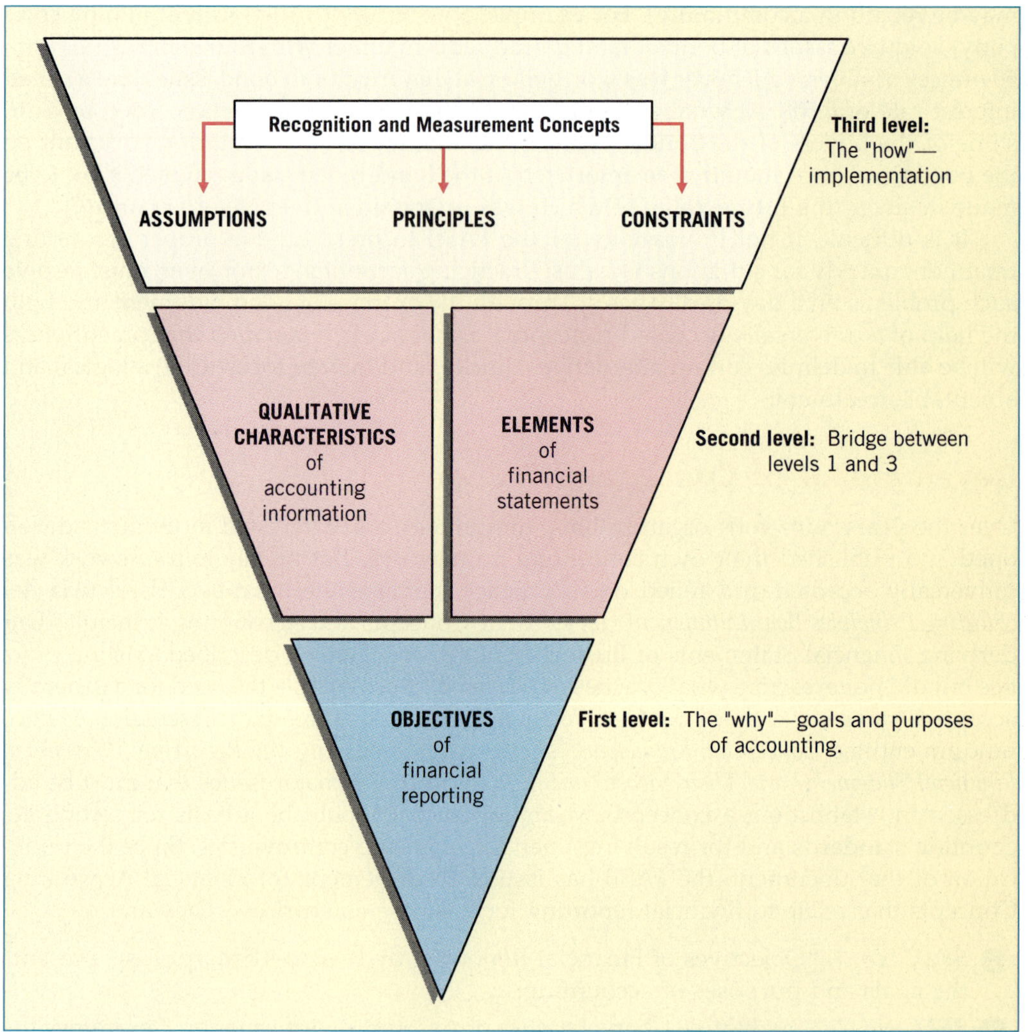

ing blocks for the conceptual framework. At the second level are the **qualitative characteristics** that make accounting information useful and the **elements** of financial statements (assets, liabilities, and so on). At the final or third level are the **measurement and recognition concepts** used in establishing and applying accounting standards. These concepts include assumptions, principles, and constraints that describe the present reporting environment.

FIRST LEVEL: BASIC OBJECTIVES

OBJECTIVE 3
Understand the objectives of financial reporting.

As we discussed in Chapter 1, the **objectives of financial reporting** are to provide information that is: (1) useful to those making investment and credit decisions who have a reasonable understanding of business and economic activities; (2) helpful to present and potential investors, creditors, and other users in assessing the amounts, timing, and uncertainty of future cash flows; and (3) about economic resources, the claims to those resources, and the changes in them.

In Sweden, the government often provides capital to businesses. Swedish financial reporting is more oriented toward helping government decision makers manage the economy.

The objectives, therefore, begin with a broad concern about information that is useful to investor and creditor decisions. That concern narrows to the investors' and creditors' interest in the prospect of receiving cash from their investments in, or loans to, business enterprises. Finally, the objectives focus on the financial statements that provide information useful in the assessment of prospective cash flows to the business enterprise, cash flows upon which investors and creditors depend.

In providing information to users of financial statements, the accounting profession relies on general-purpose financial statements. The intent of such statements is to provide the most useful information possible at minimal cost to various user groups. Underlying these objectives is the notion that users need reasonable knowledge of business and financial accounting matters to understand the information contained in financial statements. This point is important: It means that in the preparation of financial statements a level of reasonable competence on the part of users can be assumed; this has an impact on the way and the extent to which information is reported.

INTERNATIONAL INSIGHT

In Switzerland, Germany, Korea, and other nations, capital is provided to business primarily by large banks. Creditors have very close ties to firms and can obtain information directly from them. Creditors do not need to rely on publicly available information, and financial information is focused on creditor protection. This process of capital allocation, however, is starting to change.

SECOND LEVEL: FUNDAMENTAL CONCEPTS

The objectives (first level) are concerned with the goals and purposes of accounting. Later, we will discuss the ways these goals and purposes are implemented (third level). Between these two levels it is necessary to provide certain conceptual building blocks that explain the qualitative characteristics of accounting information and define the elements of financial statements. These conceptual building blocks form a bridge between the **why** of accounting (the objectives) and the **how** of accounting (recognition and measurement).

Qualitative Characteristics of Accounting Information

How does one decide whether financial reports should provide information on how much a firm's assets cost to acquire (historical cost basis) or how much they are currently worth (current value basis)? Or how does one decide whether the three main segments that constitute PepsiCo—PepsiCola, Frito Lay, and Tropicana—should be combined and shown as one company or disaggregated and reported as three separate segments for financial reporting purposes?

Choosing an acceptable accounting method, the amount and types of information to be disclosed, and the format in which information should be presented involves determining **which alternative provides the most useful information for decision making purposes (decision usefulness)**. The FASB has identified the qualitative characteristics of accounting information that distinguish better (more useful) information from inferior (less useful) information for decision making purposes.[5] In addition, the FASB has identified certain constraints (cost-benefit and materiality) as part of the conceptual framework; these are discussed later in the chapter. The characteristics may be viewed as a hierarchy, as shown in Illustration 2-2 on the next page.

OBJECTIVE 4
Identify the qualitative characteristics of accounting information.

Decision Makers (Users) and Understandability

Decision makers vary widely in the types of decisions they make, the methods of decision making they employ, the information they already possess or can obtain from other sources, and their ability to process the information. For information to be useful, there must be a connection (linkage) between these users and the decisions they make. This link, understandability, is the quality of information that permits reasonably informed users to perceive its significance. To illustrate the importance of this linkage, assume that IBM Corp. issues a three-months' earnings report (interim report) that shows interim earnings way down. This report provides relevant and reliable information for decision making purposes. Some users, upon reading the report, decide to sell their stock. Other users do not understand the report's content and significance. They are surprised when IBM declares a smaller year-end dividend and the value of the stock declines. Thus, although the information presented was highly relevant and reliable, it was useless to users who did not understand it.

[5]"Qualitative Characteristics of Accounting Information," *Statement of Financial Accounting Concepts No. 2* (Stamford, Conn.: FASB, May 1980).

ILLUSTRATION 2-2
Hierarchy of Accounting Qualities

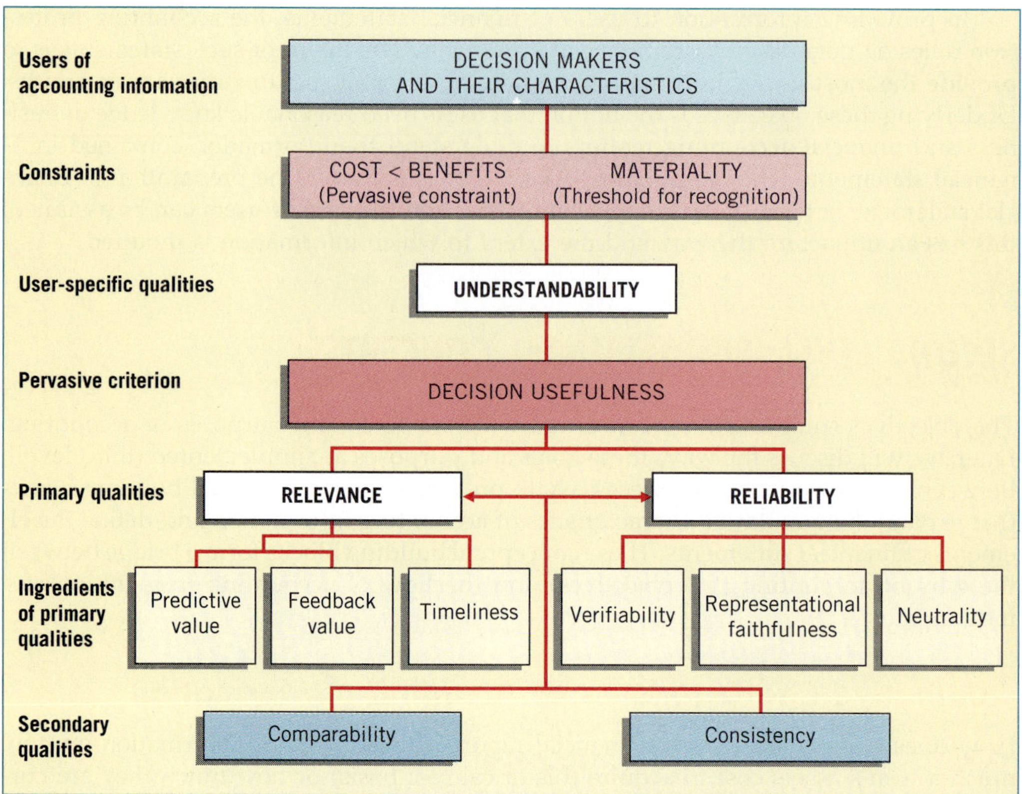

Primary Qualities: Relevance and Reliability

Relevance and reliability are the two primary qualities that make accounting information useful for decision making. As stated in FASB *Concepts Statement No. 2,* "the qualities that distinguish 'better' (more useful) information from 'inferior' (less useful) information are primarily the qualities of relevance and reliability, with some other characteristics that those qualities imply."[6]

Relevance. To be relevant, accounting information must be capable of making a difference in a decision.[7] If certain information has no bearing on a decision, it is irrelevant to that decision. Relevant information helps users make predictions about the ultimate outcome of past, present, and future events; that is, it has **predictive value**. Relevant information also helps users confirm or correct prior expectations; it has **feedback value**. For example, when **UPS (United Parcel Service)** issues an interim report, this information is considered relevant because it provides a basis for forecasting annual earnings and provides feedback on past performance. For information to be relevant, it must also be available to decision makers before it loses its capacity to influence their decisions. Thus **timeliness** is a primary ingredient. If UPS did not report its interim results until six months after the end of the period, the information would be much less useful for decision making purposes. **For information to be relevant, it should have predictive or feedback value, and it must be presented on a timely basis.**

Reliability. Accounting information is reliable to the extent that **it is verifiable, is a faithful representation, and is reasonably free of error and bias**. Reliability is a ne-

[6]Ibid., par. 15.

[7]Ibid., par. 47.

cessity for individuals who have neither the time nor the expertise to evaluate the factual content of the information.

Verifiability is demonstrated when independent measurers, using the same measurement methods, obtain similar results. For example, would several independent auditors come to the same conclusion about a set of financial statements? If outside parties using the same measurement methods arrive at different conclusions, then the statements are not verifiable. Auditors could not render an opinion on such statements.

Representational faithfulness means that the numbers and descriptions represent what really existed or happened. The accounting numbers and descriptions agree with the resources or events that these numbers and descriptions purport to represent. If **General Motors** income statement reports sales of $150 billion when it had sales of $138.2 billion, then the statements are not a faithful representation.

Neutrality means that information cannot be selected to favor one set of interested parties over another. Factual, truthful, unbiased information must be the overriding consideration. For example, **ValuJet, Inc.** should not be permitted to suppress information in the notes to its financial statements about the numerous lawsuits that have been filed against it because of airline safety issues—even though such disclosure is embarrassing and damaging to the company.

Neutrality in standard setting has come under increasing attack. Some argue that standards should not be issued if they cause undesirable economic effects on an industry or company. We disagree. Standards must be free from bias or we will no longer have credible financial statements. Without credible financial statements, individuals will no longer use this information. An analogy demonstrates the point: In the United States, we have both boxing and wrestling matches. Many individuals bet on boxing matches because such contests are assumed not to be fixed. But nobody bets on wrestling matches. Why? Because the public assumes that wrestling matches are rigged. If financial information is biased (rigged), the public will lose confidence and no longer use this information.

Secondary Qualities: Comparability and Consistency

Information about an enterprise is more useful if it can be compared with similar information about another enterprise (**comparability**) and with similar information about the same enterprise at other points in time (**consistency**).[8]

Comparability. Information that has been measured and reported in a similar manner for different enterprises is considered comparable. Comparability enables users to identify the real similarities and differences in economic phenomena because these differences and similarities have not been obscured by the use of noncomparable accounting methods. For example, the accounting for pensions is different in the United States and Japan. In the U.S., pension cost is recorded as incurred, whereas in Japan there is little or no charge to income for these costs. As a result, it is difficult to compare and evaluate the financial results of **General Motors** or **Ford** to **Nissan** or **Honda**. Also, resource allocation decisions involve evaluations of alternatives; a valid evaluation can be made only if comparable information is available.

Consistency. When an entity applies the same accounting treatment to similar events, from period to period, the entity is considered to be consistent in its use of accounting standards. It does not mean that companies cannot switch from one method of accounting to another. Companies can change methods, but the changes are restricted to

[8]As indicated in Chapter 1, the environment of accounting is continually changing; comparability and consistency are thereby made more difficult to achieve. Tax laws change, new industries (e.g., computer software) grow dramatically, new financial instruments (e.g., financial futures, collateral mortgage obligations, zero-coupon convertible bonds) are created, and mergers and divestitures occur frequently.

situations in which it can be demonstrated that the newly adopted method is preferable to the old. Then the nature and effect of the accounting change, as well as the justification for it, must be disclosed in the financial statements for the period in which the change is made.[9]

When there has been a change in accounting principles, the auditor refers to it in an explanatory paragraph of the audit report. This paragraph identifies the nature of the change and refers the reader to the note in the financial statements that discusses the change in detail.[10]

In summary, accounting reports for any given year are more useful if they can be compared with reports from other companies and with prior reports of the same entity. For example, if **Microsoft** is the only enterprise that prepares interim reports, the information is less useful because the user cannot relate it to interim reports for any other enterprise; that is, there is no comparability. Similarly, if the measurement methods used to prepare Microsoft's interim report change from one interim period to another, the information is considered less useful because the user cannot relate it to previous interim periods; that is, it lacks consistency.

Basic Elements

OBJECTIVE 5
Define the basic elements of financial statements.

An important aspect of developing any theoretical structure is the body of **basic elements** or definitions to be included in the structure. At present, accounting uses many terms that have peculiar and specific meanings. These terms constitute the language of business or the jargon of accounting.

One such term is **asset**. Is it something we own? If the answer is yes, can we assume that any leased asset would not be shown on the balance sheet? Is an asset something we have the right to use, or is it anything of value used by the enterprise to generate revenues? If the answer is yes, then why should the management of the enterprise not be considered an asset? It seems necessary, therefore, to develop basic definitions for the elements of financial statements. *Concepts Statement No. 6* defines the ten interrelated elements that are most directly related to measuring the performance and financial status of an enterprise. We list them here for review and information purposes; you need not memorize these definitions at this point. Each of these elements will be explained and examined in more detail in subsequent chapters.

ELEMENTS OF FINANCIAL STATEMENTS

ASSETS. Probable future economic benefits obtained or controlled by a particular entity as a result of past transactions or events.

LIABILITIES. Probable future sacrifices of economic benefits arising from present obligations of a particular entity to transfer assets or provide services to other entities in the future as a result of past transactions or events.

EQUITY. Residual interest in the assets of an entity that remains after deducting its liabilities. In a business enterprise, the equity is the ownership interest.

INVESTMENTS BY OWNERS. Increases in net assets of a particular enterprise resulting from transfers to it from other entities of something of value to obtain or increase ownership interests (or equity) in it. Assets are most commonly re-

[9]The AICPA Special Committee on Financial Reporting noted that users highly value consistency. They note that a change tends to destroy the comparability of data before and after the change. Some companies take the time to assist users to understand the pre- and post-change data. Generally, however, users say they lose the ability to analyze over time.

[10]"Reports on Audited Financial Statements," *Statement on Auditing Standards No. 58* (New York: AICPA, April 1988), par. 34.

ceived as investments by owners, but that which is received may also include services or satisfaction or conversion of liabilities of the enterprise.

DISTRIBUTIONS TO OWNERS. Decreases in net assets of a particular enterprise resulting from transferring assets, rendering services, or incurring liabilities by the enterprise to owners. Distributions to owners decrease ownership interests (or equity) in an enterprise.

COMPREHENSIVE INCOME. Change in equity (net assets) of an entity during a period from transactions and other events and circumstances from nonowner sources. It includes all changes in equity during a period except those resulting from investments by owners and distributions to owners.

REVENUES. Inflows or other enhancements of assets of an entity or settlement of its liabilities (or a combination of both) during a period from delivering or producing goods, rendering services, or other activities that constitute the entity's ongoing major or central operations.

EXPENSES. Outflows or other using up of assets or incurrences of liabilities (or a combination of both) during a period from delivering or producing goods, rendering services, or carrying out other activities that constitute the entity's ongoing major or central operations.

GAINS. Increases in equity (net assets) from peripheral or incidental transactions of an entity and from all other transactions and other events and circumstances affecting the entity during a period except those that result from revenues or investments by owners.

LOSSES. Decreases in equity (net assets) from peripheral or incidental transactions of an entity and from all other transactions and other events and circumstances affecting the entity during a period except those that result from expenses or distributions to owners.[11]

Two important points should be noted about these definitions. First, the term **comprehensive income** represents a relatively new concept. Comprehensive income is more inclusive than the traditional notion of net income. It includes net income and all other changes in equity exclusive of owners' investments and distributions. For example, unrealized holding gains and losses on available-for-sale securities, which are currently excluded from net income, are included under comprehensive income. The reporting of comprehensive income is discussed in Chapter 4.

Second, the FASB classifies the elements into two distinct groups. The first group of three elements—assets, liabilities, and equity—describes amounts of resources and claims to resources at a **moment in time**. The other seven elements (comprehensive income and its components—revenues, expenses, gains, and losses—as well as investments by owners and distributions to owners) describe transactions, events, and circumstances that affect an enterprise during a **period of time**. The first class—assets, liabilities, and equity—is changed by elements of the second class and at any time is the cumulative result of all changes. This interaction is referred to as "articulation." That is, key figures in one statement correspond to balances in another.

THIRD LEVEL: RECOGNITION AND MEASUREMENT CONCEPTS

The third level of the framework consists of concepts that implement the basic objectives of level one. These concepts explain which, when, and how financial elements and events should be recognized, measured, and reported by the accounting system.

[11]"Elements of Financial Statements," *Statement of Financial Accounting Concepts No. 6* (Stamford, Conn.: FASB, December 1985), pp. ix and x.

Most of them are set forth in FASB *Statement of Financial Accounting Concepts No. 5,* "Recognition and Measurement in Financial Statements of Business Enterprises." According to *SFAC No. 5,* to be recognized, an item (event or transaction) must meet the definition of an "element of financial statements" as defined in *SFAC No. 6* and must be measurable. Most aspects of current practice are consistent with this recognition and measurement concept.

The accounting profession continues to use the concepts in *SFAC No. 5* as operational guidelines. For discussion purposes, we have chosen to identify the concepts as basic assumptions, principles, and constraints. Not everyone uses this classification system, so it is best to focus your attention more on **understanding the concepts** than on how they are classified and organized. These concepts serve as guidelines in developing rational responses to controversial financial reporting issues. They have evolved over time and are fundamental to the specific accounting principles issued by the FASB and its predecessor organizations.

Basic Assumptions

OBJECTIVE 6
Describe the basic assumptions of accounting.

Four basic assumptions underlie the financial accounting structure: (1) **economic entity**, (2) **going concern**, (3) **monetary unit**, and (4) **periodicity**.

Economic Entity Assumption

The economic entity assumption means that economic activity can be identified with a particular unit of accountability. In other words, the activity of a business enterprise can be kept separate and distinct from its owners and any other business unit. For example, if the activities and elements of General Motors could not be distinguished from those of Ford or DaimlerChrysler, then it would be impossible to know which company financially outperformed the other two in recent years. If there were no meaningful way to separate all of the economic events that occur, no basis for accounting would exist.

The entity concept does not apply solely to the segregation of activities among given business enterprises. An individual, a department or division, or an entire industry could be considered a separate entity if we chose to define the unit in such a manner. Thus, **the entity concept does not necessarily refer to a legal entity**. A parent and its subsidiaries are separate **legal** entities, but merging their activities for accounting and reporting purposes does not violate the **economic entity** assumption.[12]

Going Concern Assumption

Most accounting methods are based on the going concern assumption—**that the business enterprise will have a long life**. Experience indicates that, in spite of numerous business failures, companies have a fairly high continuance rate. Although accountants do not believe that business firms will last indefinitely, they do expect them to last long enough to fulfill their objectives and commitments.

The implications of this assumption are profound. The historical cost principle would be of limited usefulness if eventual liquidation were assumed. Under a liqui-

[12]The concept of the entity is changing. For example, it is now harder to define the outer edges of companies. There are public companies with multiple public subsidiaries, each with joint ventures, licensing arrangements, and other affiliations. Increasingly, loose affiliations of enterprises in joint ventures or customer-supplier relationships are formed and dissolved in a matter of months or weeks. These "virtual companies" raise accounting issues about how to account for the entity. See Steven H. Wallman, "The Future of Accounting and Disclosure in an Evolving World: The Need for Dramatic Change," *Accounting Horizons,* September 1995.

dation approach, for example, asset values are better stated at net realizable value (sales price less costs of disposal) than at acquisition cost. **Depreciation and amortization policies are justifiable and appropriate only if we assume some permanence to the enterprise.** If a liquidation approach were adopted, the current-noncurrent classification of assets and liabilities would lose much of its significance. Labeling anything a fixed or long-term asset would be difficult to justify. Indeed, listing liabilities on the basis of priority in liquidation would be more reasonable.

The going concern assumption applies in most business situations. **Only where liquidation appears imminent is the assumption inapplicable.** In these cases a total revaluation of assets and liabilities can provide information that closely approximates the entity's net realizable value. Accounting problems related to an enterprise in liquidation are presented in advanced accounting courses.

Monetary Unit Assumption

The **monetary unit assumption** means that money is the common denominator of economic activity and provides an appropriate basis for accounting measurement and analysis. This assumption implies that the monetary unit is the most effective means of expressing to interested parties changes in capital and exchanges of goods and services. **The monetary unit is relevant, simple, universally available, understandable, and useful.** Application of this assumption depends on the even more basic assumption that quantitative data are useful in communicating economic information and in making rational economic decisions.

Due to their experiences with persistent inflation, several South American countries produce "constant currency" financial reports. Typically, a general price-level index is used to adjust for the effects of inflation.

In the United States, accountants have chosen generally to ignore the phenomenon of price-level change (inflation and deflation) by assuming that **the unit of measure—the dollar—remains reasonably stable**. This assumption about the monetary unit has been used to justify adding 1970 dollars to 2001 dollars without any adjustment. The FASB in *SFAC No. 5* indicated that it expects the dollar, unadjusted for inflation or deflation, to continue to be used to measure items recognized in financial statements. Only if circumstances change dramatically (such as if the United States were to experience high inflation similar to that in many South American countries) will the Board again consider "inflation accounting."

Go to the Digital Tool for an expanded discussion of inflation accounting approaches.

Periodicity Assumption

The most accurate way to measure the results of enterprise activity would be to measure them at the time of the enterprise's eventual liquidation. Business, government, investors, and various other user groups, however, cannot wait that long for such information. Users need to be apprised of performance and economic status on a timely basis so that they can evaluate and compare firms. Therefore, information must be reported periodically.

The **periodicity** (or **time period**) **assumption** implies that **the economic activities of an enterprise can be divided into artificial time periods**. These time periods vary, but the most common are monthly, quarterly, and yearly.

The shorter the time period, the more difficult it becomes to determine the proper net income for the period. A month's results are usually less reliable than a quarter's results, and a quarter's results are likely to be less reliable than a year's results. Investors desire and demand that information be quickly processed and disseminated; yet the quicker the information is released, the more it is subject to error. **This phenomenon provides an interesting example of the trade-off between relevance and reliability in preparing financial data.**

This problem of defining the time period is becoming more serious because product cycles are shorter and products become obsolete more quickly. Many believe that, given technology advances, more on-line, real-time financial information needs to be provided to ensure that relevant information is available.

Basic Principles of Accounting

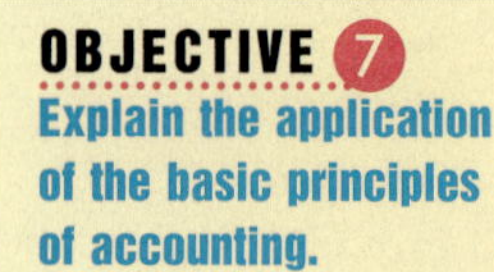

OBJECTIVE 7
Explain the application of the basic principles of accounting.

Four basic principles of accounting are used to record transactions: (1) **historical cost**, (2) **revenue recognition**, (3) **matching**, and (4) **full disclosure**.

Historical Cost Principle

GAAP requires that most assets and liabilities be accounted for and reported on the basis of acquisition price. This is often referred to as the historical cost principle.

Cost has an important advantage over other valuations: it is reliable. To illustrate the importance of this advantage, consider the problems that would arise if we adopted some other basis for keeping records. If we were to select current selling price, for instance, we might have a difficult time in attempting to establish a sales value for a given item without selling it. Every member of the accounting department might have a different opinion regarding an asset's value, and management might desire still another figure. And how often would it be necessary to establish sales value? All companies close their accounts at least annually, and some compute their net income every month. These companies would find it necessary to place a sales value on every asset each time they wished to determine income—a laborious task and one that would result in a figure of net income materially affected by opinion. Similar objections have been leveled against current cost (replacement cost, present value of future cash flows) and any other basis of valuation *except cost*.

What about liabilities? Are they accounted for on a cost basis? Yes, they are. **If we convert the term "cost" to "exchange price," we find that it applies to liabilities as well.** Liabilities, such as bonds, notes, and accounts payable, are issued by a business enterprise in exchange for assets, or perhaps services, upon which an agreed price has usually been placed. This price, established by the exchange transaction, is the "cost" of the liability and provides the figure at which it should be recorded in the accounts and reported in financial statements.

In the European Community, accounting standards are set by means of directives. The Fourth Directive permits replacement value accounting for some fixed assets. The use of replacement value requires full disclosure of its impact on the financial statements.

A recent survey of users by the AICPA's Special Committee on Financial Reporting appears to support the historical cost principle in most situations. Users indicated that historical cost provides them with a stable and consistent benchmark that they can rely on to establish historical trends. They are concerned about the subjectivity and potential volatility in reported results of a model based on some type of current value.

Users also reported that they found fair value information useful for particular types of assets and liabilities and in certain types of industries. This result is not surprising because certain assets and liabilities are already reported at current values either in the financial statements or related notes. For example, most investments in debt and equity securities are currently reported at fair value, receivables are reported at net realizable value, and inventories are reported at the lower of cost or market (usually replacement cost). At this time, certain industries, such as brokerage houses and mutual funds, prepare their basic financial statements on a fair value basis.

As indicated from the above discussion, **we presently have a "mixed attribute" system that permits the use of historical cost, fair value, lower of cost or market, and other valuation bases.** Although the historical cost principle continues to be the primary basis of valuation, recording and reporting of fair value information is increasing. Most debt and equity security investments are now reported at fair value. And the FASB requires the disclosure of the fair value of most financial instruments. It appears this trend will continue.

Revenue Recognition Principle

A crucial question for many enterprises is when revenue should be recognized. Revenue is generally recognized when (1) **realized** or **realizable** and (2) **earned**. This approach has often been referred to as the revenue recognition principle. Revenues are realized when products (goods or services), merchandise, or other assets are exchanged for cash or claims to cash. Revenues are realizable when assets received or held are readily convertible into cash or claims to cash. Assets are readily convertible when they are salable or interchangeable in an active market at readily determinable prices without significant additional cost.

In addition to the first test (realized or realizable), revenues are not recognized until earned. And revenues are considered **earned** when the entity has substantially accomplished what it must do to be entitled to the benefits represented by the revenues.[13]

Generally, an objective test—confirmation by a sale to independent interests—is used to indicate the point at which revenue is recognized. Usually, only at the date of sale is there an objective and verifiable measure of revenue—the sales price. Any basis for revenue recognition short of actual sale opens the door to wide variations in practice. To give accounting reports uniform meaning, a rule of revenue recognition comparable to the cost rule for asset valuation is essential. **Recognition at the time of sale provides a uniform and reasonable test.**

There are, however, exceptions to the rule, as shown in Illustration 2-3.

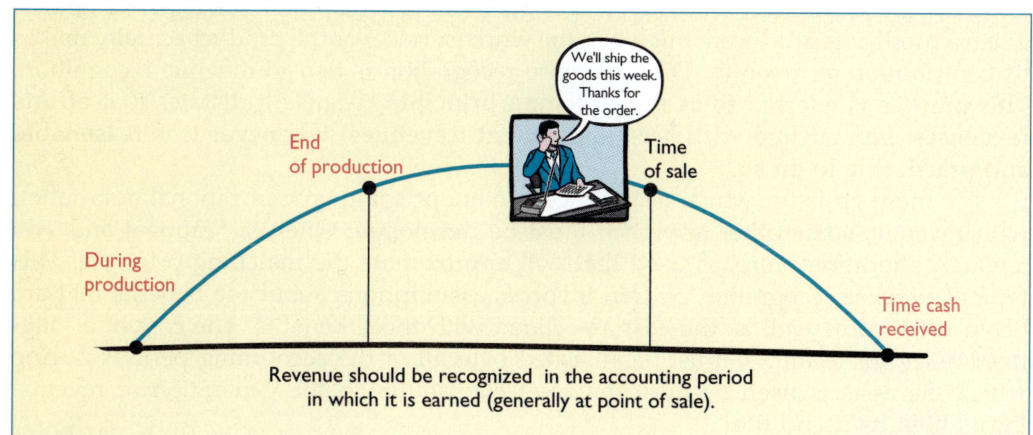

ILLUSTRATION 2-3
Timing of Revenue Recognition

During Production. **Recognition of revenue is allowed before the contract is completed in certain long-term construction contracts.** In this method revenue is recognized periodically based on the percentage of the job that has been completed instead of waiting until the entire job has been finished. Although technically a transfer of ownership has not occurred, the earning process is considered substantially completed at various stages as construction progresses. Naturally, if it is not possible to obtain dependable estimates of cost and progress, then revenue recognition is delayed until the job is completed.

End of Production. At times, **revenue might be recognized after the production cycle has ended but before the sale takes place**. This is the case where the selling price is certain as well as the amount. For instance, if products or other assets are salable in an active market at readily determinable prices without significant additional cost, then revenue can be recognized at the completion of production. An example would be the mining of certain minerals for which, once the mineral is mined, a ready market at a standard price exists. The same holds true for some artificial price supports set by the government in establishing agricultural prices.

Receipt of Cash. **Receipt of cash is another basis for revenue recognition.** The cash basis approach is used only when it is impossible to establish the revenue figure at the time of sale because of the uncertainty of collection. One form of the cash basis is the installment sales method where payment is required in periodic installments over a

[13]"Recognition and Measurement in Financial Statements of Business Enterprises," *Statement of Financial Accounting Concepts No. 5* (Stamford, Conn.: FASB, December 1984), par. 83(a) and (b).

long period of time. Its most common use is in the retail field. Farm and home equipment and furnishings are typically sold on an installment basis. The installment method is frequently justified on the basis that the risk of not collecting an account receivable is so great that the sale is not sufficient evidence for recognition to take place. In some instances, this reasoning may be valid. Generally, though, if a sale has been completed, it should be recognized; if bad debts are expected, they should be recorded as separate estimates.

Revenue, then, is recorded in the period when realized or realizable and earned. Normally, this is the date of sale. But circumstances may dictate application of the percentage-of-completion approach, the end-of-production approach, or the receipt-of-cash approach.

Matching Principle

In recognizing expenses, the approach followed is "let the expense follow the revenues." Expenses are recognized not when wages are paid, or when the work is performed, or when a product is produced, but when the work (service) or the product actually makes its contribution to revenue. Thus, expense recognition is tied to revenue recognition. This practice is referred to as the **matching principle** because it dictates that **efforts (expenses) be matched with accomplishment (revenues) whenever it is reasonable and practicable to do so.**

For those costs for which it is difficult to adopt some type of rational association with revenue, some other approach must be developed. Often, a "rational and systematic" allocation policy is used that will approximate the matching principle. This type of expense recognition pattern involves assumptions about the benefits that are being received as well as the cost associated with those benefits. The cost of a long-lived asset, for example, must be allocated over all of the accounting periods during which the asset is used because the asset contributes to the generation of revenue throughout its useful life.

Some costs are charged to the current period as expenses (or losses) simply because no connection with revenue can be determined. Examples of these types of costs are officers' salaries and other administrative expenses.

Summarizing, we might say that costs are analyzed to determine whether a relationship exists with revenue. Where this association holds, the costs are expensed and matched against the revenue in the period when the revenue is recognized. If no connection appears between costs and revenues, an allocation of cost on some systematic and rational basis might be appropriate. Where this method does not seem desirable, the cost may be expensed immediately.[14]

The problem of expense recognition is as complex as that of revenue recognition. For example, in the opening story, the main issue was whether marketing costs related to major motion pictures should be expensed immediately, amortized over a very short period of time, or amortized over the life of the picture (whatever that is). A similar issue involved the accounting for marketing costs related to **America Online (AOL)**, an interactive online consumer service company that provides its subscribers access to many electronic databases. AOL's largest expenditures are the costs of advertising and of free trials to attract subscribers. These promotions are expensive. Not too long ago, subscription acquisition costs totaled $363 million for AOL, of which only $126 million was charged to expense and the rest was recorded as an asset and amortized over two years. Conversely, **CompuServe**, a major competitor at the time, expensed these costs

[14]Costs are generally classified into two groups: **product costs and period costs. Product costs** such as material, labor, and overhead attach to the product and are carried into future periods if the revenue from the product is recognized in subsequent periods. **Period costs** such as officers' salaries and other administrative expenses are charged off immediately, even though benefits associated with these costs occur in the future, because no direct relationship between cost and revenue can be determined.

as incurred. Both companies believed they were matching costs to revenues appropriately. AOL has since changed its accounting and now expenses these costs as incurred.

The conceptual validity of the matching principle has been a subject of debate. **A major concern is that matching permits certain costs to be deferred and treated as assets on the balance sheet when in fact these costs may not have future benefits.** If abused, this principle permits the balance sheet to become a "dumping ground" for unmatched costs. In addition, there appears to be no objective definition of "systematic and rational." For example, Hartwig, Inc. purchased an asset for $100,000 that will last 5 years. Various depreciation methods (all considered systematic and rational) might be used to allocate this cost over the 5-year period. However, it is difficult to develop objective criteria to be used in determining what portion of the cost of the asset should be written off each period.[15]

Full Disclosure Principle

In deciding what information to report, the general practice of providing information that is of sufficient importance to influence the judgment and decisions of an informed user is followed. Often referred to as the **full disclosure principle**, it recognizes that the nature and amount of information included in financial reports reflects a series of judgmental trade-offs. These trade-offs strive for (1) sufficient detail to disclose matters that **make a difference** to users, yet (2) sufficient condensation to make the **information understandable**, keeping in mind costs of preparing and using it. Information about financial position, income, cash flows, and investments can be found in one of three places: (1) within the main body of financial statements, (2) in the notes to those statements, or (3) as supplementary information.

The **financial statements** are a formalized, structured means of communicating financial information. To be recognized in the main body of financial statements, **an item should meet the definition of a basic element, be measurable with sufficient certainty, and be relevant and reliable.**[16]

Disclosure is not a substitute for proper accounting. As the chief accountant of the SEC recently noted: Good disclosure does not cure bad accounting any more than an adjective or adverb can be used without—or in place of—a noun or verb. Thus, for example, cash basis accounting for cost of goods sold is misleading, even if accrual basis amounts were disclosed in the notes to the financial statements.

The **notes to financial statements** generally amplify or explain the items presented in the main body of the statements. If the information in the main body of the financial statements gives an incomplete picture of the performance and position of the enterprise, additional information that is needed to complete the picture should be included in the notes. Information in the notes does not have to be quantifiable, nor does it need to qualify as an element. Notes can be partially or totally narrative. Examples of notes are: descriptions of the accounting policies and methods used in measuring the elements reported in the statements; explanations of uncertainties and contingencies; and statistics and details too voluminous for inclusion in the statements. The notes are not only helpful but also essential to understanding the enterprise's performance and position.

Supplementary information may include details or amounts that present a different perspective from that adopted in the financial statements. It may be quantifiable information that is high in relevance but low in reliability, or information that is help-

---

[15]Some would suggest that even that procedure is nearly impossible, given that the revenue flow from any given asset is interrelated with the remaining asset structure of the enterprise. For example, see Arthur L. Thomas, "The Allocation Problem in Financial Accounting Theory," *Studies in Accounting Research No. 3* (Evanston, Ill.: American Accounting Association, 1969), and "The Allocation Problem: Part Two," *Studies in Accounting Research No. 9* (Sarasota, Fla.: American Accounting Association, 1974).

[16]*SFAC No. 5,* par. 63.

ful but not essential. One example of supplementary information is the data and schedules provided by oil and gas companies: Typically they provide information on proven reserves as well as the related discounted cash flows.

Supplementary information may also include management's explanation of the financial information and its discussion of the significance of that information. For example, during the past decade many business combinations have produced innumerable conglomerate-type business organizations and financing arrangements that demand new and peculiar accounting and reporting practices and principles. In each of these situations, the same problem must be faced: making sure that enough information is presented to ensure that the **reasonably prudent investor** will not be misled.

A classic illustration of the problem of determining adequate disclosure guidelines is the recent question on what banks should disclose about loans made for highly leveraged transactions such as leveraged buyouts. Investors want to know the percentage of a bank's loans that are of this risky type. The problem is what do we mean by "leveraged"? As one regulator noted: "If it looks leveraged, it probably is leveraged, but most of us would be hard-pressed to come up with a definition." Is a loan to a company with a debt to equity ratio of 4 to 1 highly leveraged? Or is 8 to 1 or 10 to 1 high leverage? The problem is complicated because some highly leveraged companies have cash flows that cover interest payments; therefore, they are not as risky as they might appear. In short, providing the appropriate disclosure to help investors and regulators differentiate risky from safe is difficult.

The content, arrangement, and display of financial statements, along with other facets of full disclosure, are discussed in Chapters 4, 5, 24, and 25.

Constraints

OBJECTIVE 8
Describe the impact that constraints have on reporting accounting information.

In providing information with the qualitative characteristics that make it useful, two overriding **constraints** must be considered: (1) the **cost-benefit relationship** and (2) **materiality**. Two other less dominant yet important constraints that are part of the reporting environment are **industry practices** and **conservatism**.

Cost-Benefit Relationship

Too often, users assume that information is a cost-free commodity. But preparers and providers of accounting information know that it is not. Therefore, the **cost-benefit relationship** must be considered: The costs of providing the information must be weighed against the benefits that can be derived from using the information. Standard-setting bodies and governmental agencies now use cost-benefit analysis before making their informational requirements final. In order to justify requiring a particular measurement or disclosure, the benefits perceived to be derived from it must exceed the costs perceived to be associated with it.

The following remark, made by a corporate executive about a proposed standard, was addressed to the FASB: "In all my years in the financial arena, I have never seen such an absolutely ridiculous proposal. . . . To dignify these 'actuarial' estimates by recording them as assets and liabilities would be virtually unthinkable except for the fact that the FASB has done equally stupid things in the past. . . . For God's sake, use common sense just this once."[17] Although this remark is extreme, it does indicate the frustration expressed by members of the business community about standard setting and whether the benefits of a given standard exceed the costs.

The difficulty in cost-benefit analysis is that the costs and especially the benefits are not always evident or measurable. The costs are of several kinds, including costs of collecting and processing, costs of disseminating, costs of auditing, costs of potential litigation, costs of disclosure to competitors, and costs of analysis and interpretation. Benefits accrue to preparers (in terms of greater management control and access

[17]"Decision-Usefulness: The Overriding Objective," *FASB Viewpoints,* October 19, 1983, p. 4.

to capital) and to users (in terms of allocation of resources, tax assessment, and rate regulation). But benefits are generally more difficult to quantify than are costs.

Most recently, the AICPA Special Committee on Financial Reporting submitted the following **constraints to limit the costs of reporting**:

a. Business reporting should exclude information outside of management's expertise or for which management is not the best source, such as information about competitors.

b. Management should not be required to report information that would significantly harm the company's competitive position.

c. Management should not be required to provide forecasted financial statements. Rather, management should provide information that helps users forecast for themselves the company's financial future.

d. Other than for financial statements, management need only report the information it knows. That is, management should be under no obligation to gather information it does not have, or need, to manage the business.

e. Certain elements of business reporting should be presented only if users and management agree they should be reported—a concept of flexible reporting.

f. Companies should not have to report forward-looking information unless there are effective deterrents to unwarranted litigation that discourages companies from doing so.

Materiality

The constraint of **materiality** relates to an item's impact on a firm's overall financial operations. An item is material if its inclusion or omission would influence or change the judgment of a reasonable person.[18] It is immaterial and, therefore, irrelevant if it would have no impact on a decision maker. In short, **it must make a difference** or it need not be disclosed. The point involved here is one of **relative size and importance**. If the amount involved is significant when compared with the other revenues and expenses, assets and liabilities, or net income of the entity, sound and acceptable standards should be followed. If the amount is so small that it is quite unimportant when compared with other items, application of a particular standard may be considered of less importance. It is difficult to provide firm guides in judging when a given item is or is not material because materiality varies both with relative amount and with relative importance. For example, the two sets of numbers presented below illustrate relative size.

ILLUSTRATION 2-4
Materiality Comparison

	Company A	Company B
Sales	$10,000,000	$100,000
Costs and expenses	9,000,000	90,000
Income from operations	$ 1,000,000	$ 10,000
Unusual gain	$ 20,000	$ 5,000

During the period in question, the revenues and expenses and, therefore, the net incomes of Company A and Company B have been proportional. Each has had an unusual gain. In looking at the abbreviated income figures for Company A, it does not appear significant whether the amount of the unusual gain is set out separately or

[18]*SFAC No. 2* (par. 132) sets forth the essence of materiality: "The omission or misstatement of an item in a financial report is material if, in the light of surrounding circumstances, the magnitude of the item is such that it is probable that the judgement of a reasonable person relying upon the report would have been changed or influenced by the inclusion or correction of the item." This same concept of materiality has been adopted by the auditing profession. See "Audit Risk and Materiality in Conducting an Audit," *Statement on Auditing Standards No. 47* (New York: AICPA, 1983), par. 6.

merged with the regular operating income. It is only 2% of the net income and, if merged, would not seriously distort the net income figure. Company B has had an unusual gain of only $5,000, but it is relatively much more significant than the larger gain realized by A. For Company B, an item of $5,000 amounts to 50% of its net income. Obviously, the inclusion of such an item in ordinary operating income would affect the amount of that income materially. Thus we see the importance of the **relative size** of an item in determining its materiality.

Companies and their auditors for the most part have adopted the general rule of thumb that anything under 5% of net income is considered not material. Recently the SEC has indicated that it is acceptable to use this percentage for an initial assessment of materiality, but that other factors must also be considered.[19] For example, companies can no longer fail to record items in order to meet consensus analysts' earnings numbers, preserve a positive earnings trend, convert a loss to a profit or vice versa, increase management compensation, or hide an illegal transaction like a bribe. In other words, **both quantitative and qualitative factors must be considered in determining whether an item is material.**

The SEC has also indicated that companies must consider each misstatement separately and the aggregate effect of all misstatements in determining materiality. For example, at one time, **General Dynamics** disclosed that its Resources Group had improved its earnings by $5.8 million at the same time that one of its other subsidiaries had taken write-offs of $6.7 million. Although both numbers were far larger than the $2.5 million that General Dynamics as a whole earned for the year, neither was disclosed as unusual because the net effect on earnings was considered immaterial. This practice is now prohibited because each item must be considered separately. In addition, even though an individual item may be immaterial, it may be considered material when added to other immaterial items. Such items must be disclosed.

Materiality is a factor in a great many internal accounting decisions, too. The amount of classification required in a subsidiary expense ledger, the degree of accuracy required in prorating expenses among the departments of a business, and the extent to which adjustments should be made for accrued and deferred items, are examples of judgments that should finally be determined on a basis of reasonableness and practicability, which is the materiality constraint sensibly applied. Only by **the exercise of good judgment and professional expertise** can reasonable and appropriate answers be found.

Industry Practices

INTERNATIONAL INSIGHT

In Japan, capital is also provided by very large banks. Assets are often undervalued and liabilities overvalued. These practices reduce the demand for dividends and protect creditors in event of a default.

Another practical consideration is **industry practices**. **The peculiar nature of some industries and business concerns** sometimes requires departure from basic theory. In the public utility industry, noncurrent assets are reported first on the balance sheet to highlight the industry's capital-intensive nature. Agricultural crops are often reported at market value because it is costly to develop accurate cost figures on individual crops. Such variations from basic theory are not many, yet they do exist. Whenever we find what appears to be a violation of basic accounting theory, we should determine whether it is explained by some peculiar feature of the type of business involved before we criticize the procedures followed.

Conservatism

Few conventions in accounting are as misunderstood as the constraint of conservatism. **Conservatism** means **when in doubt choose the solution that will be least likely to overstate assets and income**. Note that there is nothing in the conservatism convention urging that net assets or net income be *understated*. Unfortunately it has been interpreted by some to mean just that. All that conservatism does, properly applied, is

[19] "Materiality," *SEC Staff Accounting Bulletin No. 99* (Washington, D.C.: SEC, 1999).

provide a very reasonable guide in difficult situations: refrain from overstatement of net income and net assets. Examples of conservatism in accounting are the use of the lower of cost or market approach in valuing inventories and the rule that accrued net losses should be recognized on firm purchase commitments for goods for inventory. If the issue is in doubt, it is better to understate than overstate net income and net assets. Of course, if there is no doubt, there is no need to apply this constraint.

Summary of the Structure

Illustration 2-5 presents the conceptual framework discussed in this chapter. It is similar to Illustration 2-1, except that it provides additional information for each level. We cannot overemphasize the usefulness of this conceptual framework in helping to understand many of the problem areas that are examined in subsequent chapters.

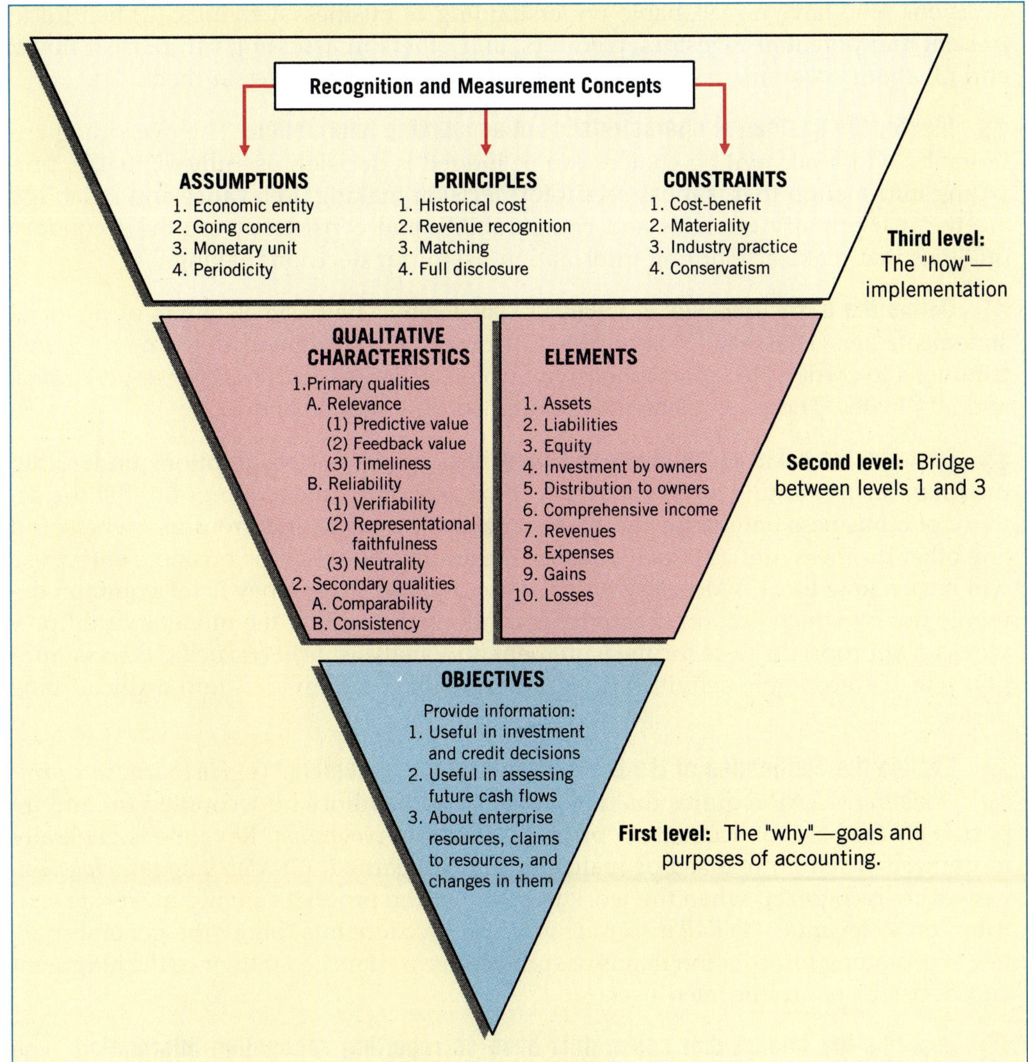

ILLUSTRATION 2-5
Conceptual Framework for Financial Reporting

KEY TERMS

assumption, *42*
comparability, *39*
comprehensive income, *41*
conceptual framework, *34*
conservatism, *50*
consistency, *39*
constraints, *48*
cost-benefit relationship, *48*
decision usefulness, *37*
earned (revenue), *45*
economic entity assumption, *42*
elements, basic, *40*
feedback value, *38*
financial statements, *47*
full disclosure principle, *47*
going concern assumption, *42*
historical cost principle, *44*
industry practices, *50*
matching principle, *46*
materiality, *49*
monetary unit assumption, *43*
neutrality, *39*
notes to financial statements, *47*
objectives of financial reporting, *36*
periodicity assumption, *43*
predictive value, *38*
principles of accounting, *44*
qualitative characteristics, *37*
realizable (revenue), *44*
realized (revenue), *44*
relevance, *38*
reliability, *38*
representational faithfulness, *39*
revenue recognition principle, *44*
supplementary information, *47*
timeliness, *38*
understandability, *37*
verifiability, *39*

SUMMARY OF LEARNING OBJECTIVES

1 **Describe the usefulness of a conceptual framework.** A conceptual framework is needed to (1) build on and relate to an established body of concepts and objectives, (2) provide a framework for solving new and emerging practical problems, (3) increase financial statement users' understanding of and confidence in financial reporting, and (4) enhance comparability among companies' financial statements.

2 **Describe the FASB's efforts to construct a conceptual framework.** The FASB has issued six Statements of Financial Accounting Concepts that relate to financial reporting for business enterprises. These concept statements provide the framework for the conceptual framework and include objectives, qualitative characteristics, and elements. In addition, measurement and recognition concepts are developed.

3 **Understand the objectives of financial reporting.** The objectives of financial reporting are to provide information that is (1) useful to those making investment and credit decisions who have a reasonable understanding of business activities; (2) helpful to present and potential investors, creditors, and others in assessing future cash flows; and (3) about economic resources and the claims to and changes in them.

4 **Identify the qualitative characteristics of accounting information.** The overriding criterion by which accounting choices can be judged is decision usefulness; that is, providing information that is most useful for decision making. Relevance and reliability are the two primary qualities and comparability and consistency are the secondary qualities that make accounting information useful for decision making.

5 **Define the basic elements of financial statements.** The basic elements of financial statements are: (1) assets, (2) liabilities, (3) equity, (4) investments by owners, (5) distributions to owners, (6) comprehensive income, (7) revenues, (8) expenses, (9) gains, and (10) losses. These ten elements are defined on pages 40 and 41.

6 **Describe the basic assumptions of accounting.** Four basic assumptions underlying the financial accounting structure are: (1) *Economic entity:* the assumption that the activity of a business enterprise can be kept separate and distinct from its owners and any other business unit. (2) *Going concern:* the assumption that the business enterprise will have a long life. (3) *Monetary unit:* the assumption that money is the common denominator by which economic activity is conducted, and that the monetary unit provides an appropriate basis for measurement and analysis. (4) *Periodicity:* the assumption that the economic activities of an enterprise can be divided into artificial time periods.

7 **Explain the application of the basic principles of accounting.** (1) *Historical cost principle:* Existing GAAP requires that most assets and liabilities be accounted for and reported on the basis of acquisition price. (2) *Revenue recognition:* Revenue is generally recognized when (a) realized or realizable and (b) earned. (3) *Matching principle:* Expenses are recognized when the work (service) or the product actually makes its contribution to revenue. (4) *Full disclosure principle:* Accountants follow the general practice of providing information that is of sufficient importance to influence the judgment and decisions of an informed user.

8 **Describe the impact that constraints have on reporting accounting information.** The constraints and their impact are: (1) *Cost-benefit relationship:* The costs of providing the information must be weighed against the benefits that can be derived from using the information. (2) *Materiality:* Sound and acceptable standards should be followed if the amount involved is significant when compared with the other revenues and expenses, assets and liabilities, or net income of the entity. (3) *Industry practices:* Follow the general practices in the firm's industry, which sometimes requires departure from basic theory. (4) *Conservatism:* When in doubt, choose the solution that will be least likely to overstate net assets and net income.

FROM CLASSROOM TO CAREER

RACHEL WOODS
is an auditor with PricewaterhouseCoopers, a "Big 5" accounting and consulting firm. She is a 1998 graduate of the University of Iowa with a major in accounting.

How did you decide on accounting as a career?

First of all, I grew up in a family that ran a small business—a convenience store and gas station. I was always interested in understanding the business beyond just handling the cash coming in the door. I thought that accounting would give me a broad and diverse background relating to the business world, and that it would open doors in finance or general management, in case I did not want to pursue a career as an accountant.

As a member of the audit staff, what is a typical engagement like for you?

When you first start an audit, you meet with the PricewaterhouseCoopers engagement team. You walk through who's responsible for what tasks, and then you sit down individually with the audit senior, and he or she will describe the different areas that you'll be working on. If you're auditing the balance sheet, for example, then you would test to see if cash, accounts receivable, inventory, and so on would require adjustment. We have audit programs that help us test account balances, but others are judgment calls. For instance, I might ask a client why accrued vacation is $50,000 at December 31, asking for the January payroll report that would substantiate it. If they actually paid out $52,000, then you have to decide if the $2,000 difference is material enough to propose an adjustment. There's a lot of testing, talking with clients—but also sitting back and thinking through the big picture.

What type of clients do you audit?

It's really varied, from manufacturing to service, not-for-profit, health care—right now I'm auditing an e-commerce client, which I find pretty exciting. There are some major issues regarding revenue recognition, but accounting standards for the Internet are in a state of flux.

What non-accounting skills have you found to be important?

Communication skills are very important. Many times I've had to speak to the controller or chief executive officer who has worked at the company for 20 years. And here I am just one year out of college, so I have to know what I'm talking about and come across in a very clear manner. Writing ability is also very important in my work because I have to document concisely the procedures.

Do you have any advice about how to deal with clients?

It seems like everyone is busy, but they do their best not to stay late and work long hours. And we come in for a few weeks out of the year and we throw off their schedules. So they have to get their day-to-day business done, but they also have us popping in and asking questions, which could create a tense environment. You have to figure out the best time to talk to them and to ask your questions concisely. Rather than ask them questions throughout the day, it's a good idea to make an appointment with them for a set time, giving them a list of questions ahead of time so they can prepare their answers. Otherwise, the meeting could be wasted with them saying, "I'll have to get back to you."

What kind of extra-curricular activities did you pursue in college?

Aside from being involved with Beta Alpha Psi, the accounting club on campus, I worked part time at the University hospital in the grant accounting area to get some real-world experience. I also played intramural volleyball, which led to my current involvement in sports with the firm.

QUESTIONS

1 What is a conceptual framework? Why is a conceptual framework necessary in financial accounting?

2 What are the primary objectives of financial reporting as indicated in *Statement of Financial Accounting Concepts No. 1?*

3 What is meant by the term "qualitative characteristics of accounting information"?

4 Briefly describe the two primary qualities of useful accounting information.

5 According to the FASB conceptual framework, the objectives of financial reporting for business enterprises are based on the needs of the users of financial statements. Explain the level of sophistication that the Board assumes about the users of financial statements.

6 What is the distinction between comparability and consistency?

7 Why is it necessary to develop a definitional framework for the basic elements of accounting?

8 Expenses, losses, and distributions to owners are all decreases in net assets. What are the distinctions among them?

9 Revenues, gains, and investments by owners are all increases in net assets. What are the distinctions among them?

10 What are the four basic assumptions that underlie the financial accounting structure?

11 The life of a business is divided into specific time periods, usually a year, to measure results of operations for each such time period and to portray financial conditions at the end of each period.

(a) This practice is based on the accounting assumption that the life of the business consists of a series of time periods and that it is possible to measure accurately the results of operations for each period. Comment on the validity and necessity of this assumption.

(b) What has been the effect of this practice on accounting? What is its relation to the accrual system? What influence has it had on accounting entries and methodology?

12 What is the basic accounting problem created by the monetary unit assumption when there is significant inflation? What appears to be the FASB position on a stable monetary unit?

13 The chairman of the board of directors of the company for which you are chief accountant has told you that he has little use for accounting figures based on cost. He believes that replacement values are of far more significance to the board of directors than "out-of-date costs." Present some arguments to convince him that accounting data should still be based on cost.

14 Develop an argument supporting the adjustment of cost figures in financial statements for general price-level changes, or at least, the preparation of supplementary statements adjusted for changes in the general price level.

15 When is revenue generally recognized? Why has the date of sale been chosen as the point at which to recognize the revenue resulting from the entire producing and selling process?

16 Magnus Eatery operates a catering service specializing in business luncheons for large corporations. Magnus requires customers to place their orders 2 weeks in advance of the scheduled events. Magnus bills its customers on the tenth day of the month following the date of service and requires that payment be made within 30 days of the billing date. Conceptually, when should Magnus recognize revenue related to its catering service?

17 What is the difference between realized and realizable? Give an example of where the concept of realizable is used to recognize revenue.

18 What is the justification for the following deviations from recognizing revenue at the time of sale?

(a) Installment sales method of recognizing revenue.

(b) Recognition of revenue at completion of production for certain agricultural products.

(c) The percentage-of-completion basis in long-term construction contracts.

19 Jane Hull Company paid $135,000 for a machine in 2001. The Accumulated Depreciation account has a balance of $46,500 at the present time. The company could sell the machine today for $150,000. The company president believes that the company has a "right to this gain." What does the president mean by this statement? Do you agree?

20 Three expense recognition methods (associating cause and effect, systematic and rational allocation, and immediate recognition) were discussed in the text under the matching principle. Indicate the basic nature of each of these types of expenses and give two examples of each.

21 *Statement of Financial Accounting Concepts No. 5* identifies four characteristics that an item must have before it is recognized in the financial statements. What are these four characteristics?

22 Briefly describe the types of information concerning financial position, income, and cash flows that might be provided: (a) within the main body of the financial statements, (b) in the notes to the financial statements, or (c) as supplementary information.

23 In January 2001, Alan Jackson Inc. doubled the amount of its outstanding stock by selling on the market an additional 10,000 shares to finance an expansion of the business. You propose that this information be shown by a footnote on the balance sheet as of December 31, 2000.

The president objects, claiming that this sale took place after December 31, 2000, and, therefore, should not be shown. Explain your position.

24 Describe the two major constraints inherent in the presentation of accounting information.

25 What are some of the costs of providing accounting information? What are some of the benefits of accounting information? Describe the cost/benefit factors that should be considered when new accounting standards are being proposed.

26 How are materiality (and immateriality) related to the proper presentation of financial statements? What factors and measures should the CPA consider in assessing the materiality of a misstatement in the presentation of a financial statement?

27 The treasurer of Joan Osborne Co. has heard that conservatism is a doctrine that is followed in accounting and, therefore, proposes that several policies be followed that are conservative in nature. State your opinion with respect to each of the policies listed below.

(a) The company gives a 2-year warranty to its customers on all products sold. The estimated warranty costs incurred from this year's sales should be entered as an expense this year instead of an expense in the period in the future when the warranty is made good.

(b) When sales are made on account, there is always uncertainty about whether the accounts are collectible. Therefore, the treasurer recommends recording the sale when the cash is received from the customers.

(c) A personal liability lawsuit is pending against the company. The treasurer believes there is an even chance that the company will lose the suit and have to pay damages of $200,000 to $300,000. The treasurer recommends that a loss be recorded and a liability created in the amount of $300,000.

(d) The inventory should be valued at "cost or market whichever is lower" because the losses from price declines should be recognized in the accounts in the period in which the price decline takes place.

BRIEF EXERCISES

BE2-1 Discuss whether the changes described in each of the cases below require recognition in the CPA's report as to consistency (assume that the amounts are material).

(a) After 3 years of computing depreciation under an accelerated method for income tax purposes and under the straight-line method for reporting purposes, the company adopted an accelerated method for reporting purposes.
(b) The company disposed of one of the two subsidiaries that had been included in its consolidated statements for prior years.
(c) The estimated remaining useful life of plant property was reduced because of obsolescence.
(d) The company is using an inventory valuation method that is different from all those used by other companies in its industry.

BE2-2 Identify which qualitative characteristic of accounting information is best described in each item below. (Do not use relevance and reliability.)

(a) The annual reports of Garbo Corp. are audited by certified public accountants.
(b) Klamoth Corp. and Kutenai, Inc. both use the FIFO cost flow assumption.
(c) Claudio Abbado Corp. has used straight-line depreciation since they began operations.
(d) Augusta Corp. issues its quarterly reports immediately after each quarter ends.

BE2-3 For each item below, indicate to which category of elements of financial statements it belongs.

(a) Retained earnings
(b) Sales
(c) Total increase in net assets from nonowner sources
(d) Inventory
(e) Depreciation
(f) Loss on sale of equipment
(g) Interest payable
(h) Dividends
(i) Gain on sale of investment
(j) Issuance of common stock

BE2-4 Identify which basic assumption of accounting is best described in each item below.

(a) The economic activities of Kristi Thomas Corp. are divided into 12-month periods for the purpose of issuing annual reports.
(b) Watson Brewer, Inc. does not adjust amounts in its financial statements for the effects of inflation.
(c) Jessi Ramsey Company reports current and noncurrent classifications in its balance sheet.
(d) The economic activities of Mallory Pike Corporation and its subsidiaries are merged for accounting and reporting purposes.

BE2-5 Identify which basic principle of accounting is best described in each item below.

(a) New Hampshire Corporation reports revenue in its income statement when it is earned instead of when the cash is collected.

(b) Vermont Enterprise recognizes depreciation expense for a machine over the five-year period during which that machine helps the company earn revenue.
(c) Massachusetts, Inc. reports information about pending lawsuits in the notes to its financial statements.
(d) Rhode Island Farms reports land on its balance sheet at the amount paid to acquire it, even though the estimated fair market value is greater.

BE2-6 Which constraints on accounting information are illustrated by the items below?

(a) Zip's Farms, Inc. reports agricultural crops on its balance sheet at market value.
(b) Crimson Tide Corporation does not accrue a contingent lawsuit gain of $650,000.
(c) Wildcat Company does not disclose any information in the notes to the financial statements unless the value of the information to financial statement users exceeds the expense of gathering it.
(d) Sun Devil Corporation expenses the cost of wastebaskets in the year they are acquired.

BE2-7 Presented below are four concepts discussed in this chapter.

(a) Periodicity assumption.
(b) Historical cost principle.
(c) Conservatism.
(d) Full disclosure principle.

Match these concepts to the following accounting practices. Each letter can be used only once.

1. __________ Preparing financial statements on a quarterly basis.
2. __________ Using the lower of cost or market method for inventory valuation.
3. __________ Recording equipment at its purchase price.
4. __________ Using notes and supplementary schedules in the financial statements.

BE2-8 Presented below are three different transactions related to materiality. Explain whether you would classify these transactions as material.

(a) Marcus Co. has reported a positive trend in earnings over the last 3 years. In the current year, it reduces its bad debt allowance to ensure another positive earnings year. The impact of this adjustment is equal to 3% of net income.
(b) Sosa Co. has an extraordinary gain of $3.1 million on the sale of plant assets and a $3.3 million loss on the sale of investments. It decides to net the gain and loss because the net effect is considered immaterial. Sosa Co.'s income for the current year was $10 million.
(c) Seliz Co. expenses all capital equipment under $25,000 on the basis that it is immaterial. The company has followed this practice for a number of years.

BE2-9 If the going concern assumption is not made in accounting, what difference does it make in the amounts shown in the financial statements for the following items?

(a) Land.
(b) Unamortized bond premium.
(c) Depreciation expense on equipment.
(d) Merchandise inventory.
(e) Prepaid insurance.

BE2-10 What accounting assumption, principle, or modifying convention does Accra Co. use in each of the situations below?

(a) Accra Co. uses the lower of cost or market basis to value inventories.
(b) Accra was involved in litigation with Kinshasa Co. over a product malfunction. This litigation is disclosed in the financial statements.
(c) Accra allocates the cost of its depreciable assets over the life it expects to receive revenue from these assets.
(d) Accra records the purchase of a new IBM PC at its cash equivalent price.

BE2-11 Explain how you would decide whether to record each of the following expenditures as an asset or an expense. Assume all items are material.

(a) Legal fees paid in connection with the purchase of land are $1,500.
(b) Benjamin Bratt, Inc. paves the driveway leading to the office building at a cost of $21,000.
(c) A meat market purchases a meat-grinding machine at a cost of $345.
(d) On June 30, Alan and Alda, medical doctors, pay six months' office rent to cover the month of June and the next five months.

(e) Tim Taylor's Hardware Company pays $9,000 in wages to laborers for construction on a building to be used in the business.

(f) Nancy Kwan's Florists pays wages of $2,100 for November to an employee who serves as driver of their delivery truck.

EXERCISES

E2-1 (Qualitative Characteristics) *SFAC No. 2* identifies the qualitative characteristics that make accounting information useful. Presented below are a number of questions related to these qualitative characteristics and underlying constraints.

1. What is the quality of information that enables users to confirm or correct prior expectations?
2. Identify the two overall or pervasive constraints developed in *SFAC No. 2.*
3. The chairman of the SEC at one time noted that "if it becomes accepted or expected that accounting principles are determined or modified in order to secure purposes other than economic measurement—we assume a grave risk that confidence in the credibility of our financial information system will be undermined." Which qualitative characteristic of accounting information should ensure that such a situation will not occur? (Do not use reliability.)
4. Billy Owens Corp. switches from FIFO to average cost to FIFO over a 2-year period. Which qualitative characteristic of accounting information is not followed?
5. Assume that the profession permits the savings and loan industry to defer losses on investments it sells, because immediate recognition of the loss may have adverse economic consequences on the industry. Which qualitative characteristic of accounting information is not followed? (Do not use relevance or reliability.)
6. What are the two primary qualities that make accounting information useful for decision making?
7. Rex Chapman, Inc. does not issue its first-quarter report until after the second quarter's results are reported. Which qualitative characteristic of accounting is not followed? (Do not use relevance.)
8. Predictive value is an ingredient of which of the two primary qualities that make accounting information useful for decision making purposes?
9. Ronald Coles, Inc. is the only company in its industry to depreciate its plant assets on a straight-line basis. Which qualitative characteristic of accounting information may not be followed? (Do not use industry practices.)
10. Jeff Malone Company has attempted to determine the replacement cost of its inventory. Three different appraisers arrive at substantially different amounts for this value. The president, nevertheless, decides to report the middle value for external reporting purposes. Which qualitative characteristic of information is lacking in these data? (Do not use reliability or representational faithfulness.)

E2-2 (Qualitative Characteristics) The qualitative characteristics that make accounting information useful for decision-making purposes are as follows:

Relevance	Timeliness	Representational faithfulness
Reliability	Verifiability	Comparability
Predictive value	Neutrality	Consistency
Feedback value		

Instructions

Identify the appropriate qualitative characteristic(s) to be used given the information provided below.

1. Qualitative characteristic being employed when companies in the same industry are using the same accounting principles.
2. Quality of information that confirms users' earlier expectations.
3. Imperative for providing comparisons of a firm from period to period.
4. Ignores the economic consequences of a standard or rule.
5. Requires a high degree of consensus among individuals on a given measurement.
6. Predictive value is an ingredient of this primary quality of information.
7. Two qualitative characteristics that are related to both relevance and reliability.
8. Neutrality is an ingredient of this primary quality of accounting information.
9. Two primary qualities that make accounting information useful for decision-making purposes.
10. Issuance of interim reports is an example of what primary ingredient of relevance?

E2-3 (Elements of Financial Statements) Ten interrelated elements that are most directly related to measuring the performance and financial status of an enterprise are provided below:

Assets	Distributions to owners	Expenses
Liabilities	Comprehensive income	Gains
Equity	Revenues	Losses
Investments by owners		

Instructions

Identify the element or elements associated with the 12 items below:

1. Arises from peripheral or incidental transactions.
2. Obligation to transfer resources arising from past transaction.
3. Increases ownership interest.
4. Declares and pays cash dividends to owners.
5. Increases in net assets in a period from nonowner sources.
6. Items characterized by service potential or future economic benefit.
7. Equals increase in assets less liabilities during the year, after adding distributions to owners and subtracting investments by owners.
8. Arises from income statement activities that constitute the entity's ongoing major or central operations.
9. Residual interest in the assets of the enterprise after deducting its liabilities.
10. Increases assets during a period through sale of product.
11. Decreases assets during the period by purchasing the company's own stock.
12. Includes all changes in equity during the period, except those resulting from investments by owners and distributions to owners.

E2-4 (Assumptions, Principles, and Constraints) Presented below are the assumptions, principles, and constraints used in this chapter:

(a) Economic entity assumption	**(e)** Historical cost principle	**(i)** Materiality
(b) Going concern assumption	**(f)** Matching principle	**(j)** Industry practices
(c) Monetary unit assumption	**(g)** Full disclosure principle	**(k)** Conservatism
(d) Periodicity assumption	**(h)** Cost-benefit relationship	

Instructions

Identify by letter the accounting assumption, principle, or constraint that describes each situation below. Do not use a letter more than once.

1. Allocates expenses to revenues in the proper period.
2. Indicates that market value changes subsequent to purchase are not recorded in the accounts. (Do not use revenue recognition principle.)
3. Ensures that all relevant financial information is reported.
4. Rationale why plant assets are not reported at liquidation value. (Do not use historical cost principle.)
5. Anticipates all losses, but reports no gains.
6. Indicates that personal and business record keeping should be separately maintained.
7. Separates financial information into time periods for reporting purposes.
8. Permits the use of market value valuation in certain specific situations.
9. Requires that information significant enough to affect the decision of reasonably informed users should be disclosed. (Do not use full disclosure principle.)
10. Assumes that the dollar is the "measuring stick" used to report on financial performance.

E2-5 (Assumptions, Principles, and Constraints) Presented below are a number of operational guidelines and practices that have developed over time.

1. Price-level changes are not recognized in the accounting records.
2. Lower of cost or market is used to value inventories.
3. Financial information is presented so that reasonably prudent investors will not be misled.
4. Intangibles are capitalized and amortized over periods benefited.
5. Repair tools are expensed when purchased.
6. Brokerage firms use market value for purposes of valuation of all marketable securities.
7. Each enterprise is kept as a unit distinct from its owner or owners.
8. All significant postbalance sheet events are reported.
9. Revenue is recorded at point of sale.

10. All important aspects of bond indentures are presented in financial statements.
11. Rationale for accrual accounting is stated.
12. The use of consolidated statements is justified.
13. Reporting must be done at defined time intervals.
14. An allowance for doubtful accounts is established.
15. All payments out of petty cash are charged to Miscellaneous Expense. (Do not use conservatism.)
16. Goodwill is recorded only at time of purchase.
17. No profits are anticipated and all possible losses are recognized.
18. A company charges its sales commission costs to expense.

Instructions

Select the assumption, principle, or constraint that most appropriately justifies these procedures and practices. (Do not use qualitative characteristics.)

E2-6 (Assumptions, Principles, and Constraints) A number of operational guidelines used by accountants are described below.

1. The treasurer of Doug Flutie Co. wishes to prepare financial statements only during downturns in their wine production, which occur periodically when the rhubarb crop fails. He states that it is at such times that the statements could be most easily prepared. In no event would more than 30 months pass without statements being prepared.
2. The Chicago Power & Light Company has purchased a large amount of property, plant, and equipment over a number of years. They have decided that because the general price level has changed materially over the years, they will issue only price-level adjusted financial statements.
3. Robert Smith Manufacturing Co. decided to manufacture its own widgets because it would be cheaper to do so than to buy them from an outside supplier. In an attempt to make their statements more comparable with those of their competitors, Robert Smith charged its inventory account for what they felt the widgets would have cost if they had been purchased from an outside supplier. (Do not use the revenue recognition principle.)
4. Flanagan's Discount Centers buys its merchandise by the truck and train-carload. Flanagan does not defer any transportation costs in computing the cost of its ending inventory. Such costs, although varying from period to period, are always material in amount.
5. Grab & Run, Inc., a fast-food company, sells franchises for $100,000, accepting a $5,000 down payment and a 50-year note for the remainder. Grab & Run promises for 3 years to assist in site selection, building, and management training. Grab & Run records the $100,000 franchise fee as revenue in the period in which the contract is signed.
6. Curtis Conway Company "faces possible expropriation (i.e., takeover) of foreign facilities and possible losses on sums owed by various customers on the verge of bankruptcy." The company president has decided that these possibilities should not be noted on the financial statements because Conway still hopes that these events will not take place.
7. Mike Singletary, manager of College Bookstore, Inc., bought a computer for his own use. He paid for the computer by writing a check on the bookstore checking account and charged the "Office Equipment" account.
8. Curtis Enis, Inc. recently completed a new 60-story office building that houses their home offices and many other tenants. All the office equipment for the building that had a per item or per unit cost of $1,000 or less was expensed as immaterial, even though the office equipment has an average life of 10 years. The total cost of such office equipment was approximately $26 million. (Do not use the matching principle.)
9. The AICPA, in an accounting guide for brokers and other dealers in securities, stated that "the trading and investment accounts . . . should be valued at market or fair value for financial reporting purposes. . . ." The brokerage firm of James and Williams, Inc. continues to value its trading and investment accounts at cost or market, whichever is lower.
10. A large lawsuit has been filed against Big Cat Corp. by Perry Co. Perry has recorded a gain and related estimated receivable equal to the possible amount it feels it might win.

Instructions

For each of the foregoing, list the assumption, principle, or constraint that has been violated. List only one term for each case.

E2-7 (Full Disclosure Principle) Presented below are a number of facts related to R. Kelly, Inc. Assume that no mention of these facts was made in the financial statements and the related notes.

(a) The company decided that, for the sake of conciseness, only net income should be reported on the income statement. Details as to revenues, cost of goods sold, and expenses were omitted.

(b) Equipment purchases of $170,000 were partly financed during the year through the issuance of a $110,000 notes payable. The company offset the equipment against the notes payable and reported plant assets at $60,000.

(c) During the year, an assistant controller for the company embezzled $15,000. R. Kelly's net income for the year was $2,300,000. Neither the assistant controller nor the money have been found.

(d) R. Kelly has reported its ending inventory at $2,100,000 in the financial statements. No other information related to inventories is presented in the financial statements and related notes.

(e) The company changed its method of depreciating equipment from the double-declining balance to the straight-line method. No mention of this change was made in the financial statements.

Instructions

Assume that you are the auditor of R. Kelly, Inc. and that you have been asked to explain the appropriate accounting and related disclosure necessary for each of these items.

E2-8 (Accounting Principles—Comprehensive) Presented below are a number of business transactions that occurred during the current year for Fresh Horses, Inc.

(a) The president of Fresh Horses, Inc. used his expense account to purchase a new Camaro solely for personal use. The following journal entry was made:

Miscellaneous Expense	29,000	
Cash		29,000

(b) Merchandise inventory that cost $620,000 is reported on the balance sheet at $690,000, the expected selling price less estimated selling costs. The following entry was made to record this increase in value:

Merchandise Inventory	70,000	
Income		70,000

(c) The company is being sued for $500,000 by a customer who claims damages for personal injury apparently caused by a defective product. Company attorneys feel extremely confident that the company will have no liability for damages resulting from the situation. Nevertheless, the company decides to make the following entry:

Loss from Lawsuit	500,000	
Liability for Lawsuit		500,000

(d) Because the general level of prices increased during the current year, Fresh Horses, Inc. determined that there was a $16,000 understatement of depreciation expense on its equipment and decided to record it in its accounts. The following entry was made:

Depreciation Expense	16,000	
Accumulated Depreciation		16,000

(e) Fresh Horses, Inc. has been concerned about whether intangible assets could generate cash in case of liquidation. As a consequence, goodwill arising from a purchase transaction during the current year and recorded at $800,000 was written off as follows:

Retained Earnings	800,000	
Goodwill		800,000

(f) Because of a "fire sale," equipment obviously worth $200,000 was acquired at a cost of $155,000. The following entry was made:

Equipment	200,000	
Cash		155,000
Income		45,000

Instructions

In each of the situations above, discuss the appropriateness of the journal entries in terms of generally accepted accounting principles.

E2-9 (Accounting Principles—Comprehensive) Presented below is information related to Garth Brooks, Inc.

(a) Depreciation expense on the building for the year was $60,000. Because the building was increasing in value during the year, the controller decided to charge the depreciation expense to retained earnings instead of to net income. The following entry is recorded.

Retained Earnings	60,000	
Accumulated Depreciation — Buildings		60,000

(b) Materials were purchased on January 1, 2001, for $120,000 and this amount was entered in the Materials account. On December 31, 2001, the materials would have cost $141,000, so the following entry is made.

Inventory	21,000	
Gain on Inventories		21,000

(c) During the year, the company purchased equipment through the issuance of common stock. The stock had a par value of $135,000 and a fair market value of $450,000. The fair market value of the equipment was not easily determinable. The company recorded this transaction as follows:

Equipment	135,000	
Common Stock		135,000

(d) During the year, the company sold certain equipment for $285,000, recognizing a gain of $69,000. Because the controller believed that new equipment would be needed in the near future, the controller decided to defer the gain and amortize it over the life of any new equipment purchased.

(e) An order for $61,500 has been received from a customer for products on hand. This order was shipped on January 9, 2002. The company made the following entry in 2001.

Accounts Receivable	61,500	
Sales		61,500

Instructions

Comment on the appropriateness of the accounting procedures followed by Garth Brooks, Inc.

CONCEPTUAL CASES

C2-1 (Conceptual Framework—General) Roger Morgan has some questions regarding the theoretical framework in which standards are set. He knows that the FASB and other predecessor organizations have attempted to develop a conceptual framework for accounting theory formulation. Yet, Roger's supervisors have indicated that these theoretical frameworks have little value in the practical sense (i.e., in the real world). Roger did notice that accounting standards seem to be established after the fact rather than before. He thought this indicated a lack of theory structure but never really questioned the process at school because he was too busy doing the homework.

Roger feels that some of his anxiety about accounting theory and accounting semantics could be alleviated by identifying the basic concepts and definitions accepted by the profession and considering them in light of his current work. By doing this, he hopes to develop an appropriate connection between theory and practice.

Instructions

(a) Help Roger recognize the purpose of and benefit of a conceptual framework.

(b) Identify any *Statements of Financial Accounting Concepts* issued by FASB that may be helpful to Roger in developing his theoretical background.

C2-2 (Conceptual Framework—General) The Financial Accounting Standards Board (FASB) has developed a conceptual framework for financial accounting and reporting. The FASB has issued seven *Statements of Financial Accounting Concepts*. These statements are intended to set forth objectives and fundamentals that will be the basis for developing financial accounting and reporting standards. The objectives identify the goals and purposes of financial reporting. The fundamentals are the underlying concepts of financial accounting—concepts that guide the selection of transactions, events, and circumstances to be accounted for; their recognition and measurement; and the means of summarizing and communicating them to interested parties.

The purpose of *Statement of Financial Accounting Concepts No. 2*, "Qualitative Characteristics of Accounting Information," is to examine the characteristics that make accounting information useful. The characteristics or qualities of information discussed in *SFAC No. 2* are the ingredients that make information useful and the qualities to be sought when accounting choices are made.

Instructions

(a) Identify and discuss the benefits that can be expected to be derived from the FASB's conceptual framework study.

(b) What is the most important quality for accounting information as identified in *Statement of Financial Accounting Concepts No. 2*? Explain why it is the most important.

(c) *Statement of Financial Accounting Concepts No. 2* describes a number of key characteristics or qualities for accounting information. Briefly discuss the importance of any three of these qualities for financial reporting purposes.

(CMA adapted)

C2-3 (Objectives of Financial Reporting) Regis Gordon and Kathy Medford are discussing various aspects of the FASB's pronouncement, *Statement of Financial Accounting Concepts No. 1*, "Objectives of Financial Reporting by Business Enterprises." Regis indicates that this pronouncement provides little, if any, guidance to the practicing professional in resolving accounting controversies. He believes that the statement provides such broad guidelines that it would be impossible to apply the objectives to present-day reporting problems. Kathy concedes this point but indicates that objectives are still needed to provide a starting point for the FASB in helping to improve financial reporting.

Instructions

(a) Indicate the basic objectives established in *Statement of Financial Accounting Concepts No. 1.*

(b) What do you think is the meaning of Kathy's statement that the FASB needs a starting point to resolve accounting controversies?

C2-4 (Qualitative Characteristics) Accounting information provides useful information about business transactions and events. Those who provide and use financial reports must often select and evaluate accounting alternatives. *FASB Statement of Financial Accounting Concepts No. 2,* "Qualitative Characteristics of Accounting Information," examines the characteristics of accounting information that make it useful for decision making. It also points out that various limitations inherent in the measurement and reporting process may necessitate trade-offs or sacrifices among the characteristics of useful information.

Instructions

(a) Describe briefly the following characteristics of useful accounting information:

(1) Relevance
(2) Reliability
(3) Understandability
(4) Comparability.
(5) Consistency.

(b) For each of the following pairs of information characteristics, give an example of a situation in which one of the characteristics may be sacrificed in return for a gain in the other:

(1) Relevance and reliability.
(2) Relevance and consistency.
(3) Comparability and consistency.
(4) Relevance and understandability.

(c) What criterion should be used to evaluate trade-offs between information characteristics?

C2-5 (Assumptions, Principles, and Constraints) You are engaged to review the accounting records of Jeremy Roenick Corporation prior to the closing of the revenue and expense accounts as of December 31, the end of the current fiscal year. The following information comes to your attention.

1. During the current year, Jeremy Roenick Corporation changed its policy in regard to expensing purchases of small tools. In the past, these purchases had always been expensed because they amounted to less than 2% of net income, but the president has decided that capitalization and subsequent depreciation should now be followed. It is expected that purchases of small tools will not fluctuate greatly from year to year.
2. Jeremy Roenick Corporation constructed a warehouse at a cost of $1,000,000. The company had been depreciating the asset on a straight-line basis over 10 years. In the current year, the controller doubled depreciation expense because the replacement cost of the warehouse had increased significantly.
3. When the balance sheet was prepared, detailed information as to the amount of cash on deposit in each of several banks was omitted. Only the total amount of cash under a caption "Cash in banks" was presented.
4. On July 15 of the current year, Jeremy Roenick Corporation purchased an undeveloped tract of land at a cost of $320,000. The company spent $80,000 in subdividing the land and getting it ready for sale. An appraisal of the property at the end of the year indicated that the land was now worth $500,000. Although none of the lots were sold, the company recognized revenue of $180,000, less related expenses of $80,000, for a net income on the project of $100,000.
5. For a number of years the company used the FIFO method for inventory valuation purposes. During the current year, the president noted that all the other companies in their industry had switched to the LIFO method. The company decided not to switch to LIFO because net income would decrease $830,000.

Instructions

State whether or not you agree with the decisions made by Jeremy Roenick Corporation. Support your answers with reference, whenever possible, to the generally accepted principles, assumptions, and constraints applicable in the circumstances.

C2-6 (Revenue Recognition and Matching Principle) After the presentation of your report on the examination of the financial statements to the board of directors of Bones Publishing Company, one of the new directors expresses surprise that the income statement assumes that an equal proportion of the revenue is earned with the publication of every issue of the company's magazine. She feels that the "crucial event" in the process of earning revenue in the magazine business is the cash sale of the subscription. She says that she does not understand why most of the revenue cannot be "recognized" in the period of the sale.

Instructions

(a) List the various accepted times for recognizing revenue in the accounts and explain when the methods are appropriate.

(b) Discuss the propriety of timing the recognition of revenue in Bones Publishing Company's account with:

(1) The cash sale of the magazine subscription.

(2) The publication of the magazine every month.

(3) Both events, by recognizing a portion of the revenue with cash sale of the magazine subscription and a portion of the revenue with the publication of the magazine every month.

C2-7 (Revenue Recognition and Matching Principle) On June 5, 2001, McCoy Corporation signed a contract with Sulu Associates under which Sulu agreed (1) to construct an office building on land owned by McCoy, (2) to accept responsibility for procuring financing for the project and finding tenants, and (3) to manage the property for 35 years. The annual net income from the project, after debt service, was to be divided equally between McCoy Corporation and Sulu Associates. Sulu was to accept its share of future net income as full payment for its services in construction, obtaining finances and tenants, and management of the project.

By May 31, 2002, the project was nearly completed and tenants had signed leases to occupy 90% of the available space at annual rentals aggregating $4,000,000. It is estimated that, after operating expenses and debt service, the annual net income will amount to $1,500,000. The management of Sulu Associates believed that (a) the economic benefit derived from the contract with McCoy should be reflected on its financial statements for the fiscal year ended May 31, 2002, and directed that revenue be accrued in an amount equal to the commercial value of the services Sulu had rendered during the year, (b) this amount be carried in contracts receivable, and (c) all related expenditures be charged against the revenue.

Instructions

(a) Explain the main difference between the economic concept of business income as reflected by Sulu's management and the measurement of income under generally accepted accounting principles.

(b) Discuss the factors to be considered in determining when revenue should be recognized for the purpose of accounting measurement of periodic income.

(c) Is the belief of Sulu's management in accordance with generally accepted accounting principles for the measurement of revenue and expense for the year ended May 31, 2002? Support your opinion by discussing the application to this case of the factors to be considered for asset measurement and revenue and expense recognition.

(AICPA adapted)

C2-8 (Matching Principle) An accountant must be familiar with the concepts involved in determining earnings of a business entity. The amount of earnings reported for a business entity is dependent on the proper recognition, in general, of revenue and expense for a given time period. In some situations, costs are recognized as expenses at the time of product sale; in other situations, guidelines have been developed for recognizing costs as expenses or losses by other criteria.

Instructions

(a) Explain the rationale for recognizing costs as expenses at the time of product sale.

(b) What is the rationale underlying the appropriateness of treating costs as expenses of a period instead of assigning the costs to an asset? Explain.

(c) In what general circumstances would it be appropriate to treat a cost as an asset instead of as an expense? Explain.

(d) Some expenses are assigned to specific accounting periods on the basis of systematic and rational allocation of asset cost. Explain the underlying rationale for recognizing expenses on the basis of systematic and rational allocation of asset cost.

(e) Identify the conditions in which it would be appropriate to treat a cost as a loss.

(AICPA adapted)

C2-9 (Matching Principle) Accountants try to prepare income statements that are as accurate as possible. A basic requirement in preparing accurate income statements is to match costs against revenues properly. Proper matching of costs against revenues requires that costs resulting from typical business operations be recognized in the period in which they expired.

Instructions

(a) List three criteria that can be used to determine whether such costs should appear as charges in the income statement for the current period.

(b) As generally presented in financial statements, the following items or procedures have been criticized as improperly matching costs with revenues. Briefly discuss each item from the viewpoint of matching costs with revenues and suggest corrective or alternative means of presenting the financial information.

(1) Receiving and handling costs.

(2) Valuation of inventories at the lower of cost or market.

(3) Cash discounts on purchases.

C2-10 (Matching Principle) Carlos Rodriguez sells and erects shell houses, that is, frame structures that are completely finished on the outside but are unfinished on the inside except for flooring, partition studding, and ceiling joists. Shell houses are sold chiefly to customers who are handy with tools and who have time to do the interior wiring, plumbing, wall completion and finishing, and other work necessary to make the shell houses livable dwellings.

Rodriguez buys shell houses from a manufacturer in unassembled packages consisting of all lumber, roofing, doors, windows, and similar materials necessary to complete a shell house. Upon commencing operations in a new area, Rodriguez buys or leases land as a site for its local warehouse, field office, and display houses. Sample display houses are erected at a total cost of $20,000 to $29,000 including the cost of the unassembled packages. The chief element of cost of the display houses is the unassembled packages, inasmuch as erection is a short, low-cost operation. Old sample models are torn down or altered into new models every 3 to 7 years. Sample display houses have little salvage value because dismantling and moving costs amount to nearly as much as the cost of an unassembled package.

Instructions

(a) A choice must be made between (1) expensing the costs of sample display houses in the periods in which the expenditure is made and (2) spreading the costs over more than one period. Discuss the advantages of each method.

(b) Would it be preferable to amortize the cost of display houses on the basis of (1) the passage of time or (2) the number of shell houses sold? Explain.

(AICPA adapted)

C2-11 (Qualitative Characteristics) Recently, your Uncle Waldo Ralph, who knows that you always have your eye out for a profitable investment, has discussed the possibility of you purchasing some corporate bonds. He suggests that you may wish to get in on the "ground floor" of this deal. The bonds being issued by the Cricket Corp. are 10-year debentures which promise a 40 percent rate of return. Cricket manufactures novelty/party items.

You have told Waldo that, unless you can take a look at Cricket's financial statements, you would not feel comfortable about such an investment. Knowing that this is the chance of a lifetime, Uncle Waldo has procured a copy of Cricket's most recent, unaudited financial statements which are a year old. These statements were prepared by Mrs. John Cricket. You peruse these statements, and they are quite impressive. The balance sheet showed a debt-to-equity ratio of .10 and, for the year shown, the company reported net income of $2,424,240.

The financial statements are not shown in comparison with amounts from other years. In addition, no significant note disclosures about inventory valuation, depreciation methods, loan agreements, etc. are available.

Instructions

Write a letter to Uncle Waldo explaining why it would be unwise to base an investment decision on the financial statements which he has provided to you. Be sure to explain why these financial statements are neither relevant nor reliable.

USING YOUR JUDGMENT

FINANCIAL REPORTING PROBLEM: INTEL CORPORATION

The financial statements of Intel are presented in Appendix 5B. Refer to these financial statements and the accompanying notes to answer the following questions.

Instructions

(a) Using the notes to the consolidated financial statements, determine Intel's revenue recognition policies regarding sales to distributors under agreements allowing price protection and/or right of return on merchandise unsold by distributors. Comment on whether Intel uses a conservative method for reporting revenue in this area.

(b) Give two examples of where historical cost information is reported on Intel's financial statements and related notes. Give two examples of the use of fair value information reported in either the financial statements or related notes.

(c) How can we determine that the accounting principles used by Intel are prepared on a basis consistent with those of last year?

(d) What is Intel's accounting policy related to advertising? What accounting principle does Intel follow regarding accounting for advertising?

FINANCIAL STATEMENT ANALYSIS CASE

Weyerhaeuser Company

Presented below is a statement that appeared about Weyerhaeuser Company in a financial magazine.

> The land and timber holdings are now carried on the company's books at a mere $422 million. The value of the timber alone is variously estimated at $3 billion to $7 billion and is rising all the time. "The understatement of the company is pretty severe," conceded Charles W. Bingham, a senior vice-president. Adds Robert L. Schuyler, another senior vice-president: "We have a whole stream of profit nobody sees and there is no way to show it on our books."

Instructions

(a) What does Schuyler mean when he says that "we have a whole stream of profit nobody sees and there is no way to show it on our books"?

(b) If the understatement of the company's assets is severe, why does accounting not report this information?

COMPARATIVE ANALYSIS CASE

The Coca-Cola Company versus PepsiCo Inc.

Instructions

Go to the Digital Tool, and use information found there to answer the following questions related to The Coca-Cola Company and PepsiCo Inc.

(a) What are the primary lines of business of these two companies as shown in their notes to the financial statements?

(b) Which company has the dominant position in beverage sales?

(c) How are inventories for these two companies valued? What cost allocation method is used to report inventory? How does their accounting for inventories affect comparability between the two companies?

(d) Which company changed its accounting policies during 1998 which affected the consistency of the financial results from the previous year? What were these changes?

RESEARCH CASES

Case 1 Retrieval of Information on Public Company

There are several commonly-available indexes which enable individuals to locate articles previously included in numerous business publications and periodicals. Articles can generally be searched by company or by subject matter. Four common indexes are *The Wall Street Journal Index, Business Abstracts* (formerly the *Business Periodical Index*), *Predicasts F&S Index,* and *ABI/Inform.*

Instructions

Use one of these resources to find an article about a company in which you are interested. Read the article and answer the following questions. (*Note:* Your library may have hard copy or CD-ROM versions of these indexes.)

(a) What is the article about?

(b) What company-specific information is included in the article?

(c) Is the article somehow related to the article you read from the previous chapter?

(d) Identify any accounting-related issues discussed in the article.

Case 2 Concepts and Quantitative Guidelines

Obtain copies of the FASB's *Statements of Financial Accounting Concepts* (SFACs) from the library and use them to answer the following questions.

(a) The textbook indicates that it is "difficult to provide firm guides in judging when a given item is or is not material." SFAC No. 2 identifies a number of examples in which specific quantitative guidelines are provided to firms. Identify two of these examples. Do you think that materiality guidelines should be quantified? Why or why not?

(b) SFAC No. 3 discusses the concept of "articulation" between financial statement elements. Briefly summarize the meaning of this term and how it relates to an entity's financial statements.

ETHICS CASE

Hinckley Nuclear Power Plant will be "mothballed" at the end of its useful life (approximately 20 years) at great expense. The matching principle requires that expenses be matched to revenue. Accountants Jana Kingston and Pete Henning argue whether it is better to allocate the expense of mothballing over the next 20 years or ignore it until mothballing occurs.

Instructions

Answer the following questions.

(a) What stakeholders should be considered?

(b) What ethical issue, if any, underlies the dispute?

(c) What alternatives should be considered?

(d) Assess the consequences of the alternatives.

(e) What decision would you recommend?

CHAPTER 3

The Accounting Information System

Needed: A Reliable Information System

Maintaining a set of accounting records is not optional. The Internal Revenue Service requires that businesses prepare and retain a set of records and documents that can be audited. The Foreign Corrupt Practices Act (federal legislation) requires public companies to " . . . make and keep books, records, and accounts, which, in reasonable detail, accurately and fairly reflect the transactions and dispositions of the assets. . . . " But beyond these two reasons, a company that does not keep an accurate record of its business transactions may lose revenue and is more likely to operate inefficiently.

Some companies are inefficient partly because of poor accounting systems. Consider, for example, the **Long Island Railroad**, once one of the nation's busiest commuter lines. The LIRR lost money because its cash position was unknown; large amounts of money owed the railroad had not been billed; some payables were erroneously paid twice; and redemptions of bonds were not recorded. Also, consider **Gould Inc.**, an electronics conglomerate, where accounting and record keeping became so chaotic that results from operations had to be restated for five of seven years.

Similarly, when the **International Gold Bullion Exchange** (IGBE), one of the largest gold and silver retailers, was forced to declare bankruptcy, its records were in such shambles that it was difficult to determine how much money it lost. The company had failed to keep track of its revenues and had written checks on uncollected funds. IGBE had even allowed its employee health insurance to lapse while continuing to collect premiums from workers. Although these situations are not common in large enterprises, they illustrate our point: accounts and detailed records must be kept by every business enterprise.

Even the use of computers is no assurance of accuracy and efficiency. "The conversion to a new system called MasterNet fouled up data processing records to the extent that **BankAmerica** is frequently unable to produce or deliver customer statements on a timely basis," said an executive at one of the country's largest banks.

LEARNING OBJECTIVES

After studying this chapter, you should be able to:

1. Understand basic accounting terminology.
2. Explain double-entry rules.
3. Identify steps in the accounting cycle.
4. Record transactions in journals, post to ledger accounts, and prepare a trial balance.
5. Explain the reasons for preparing adjusting entries.
6. Prepare closing entries.
7. Explain how inventory accounts are adjusted at year-end.
8. Prepare a 10-column work sheet.

PREVIEW OF CHAPTER 3

As the opening story indicates, a reliable information system is a necessity for all companies. The purpose of this chapter is to explain and illustrate the features of an accounting information system. The content and organization of this chapter are as follows:

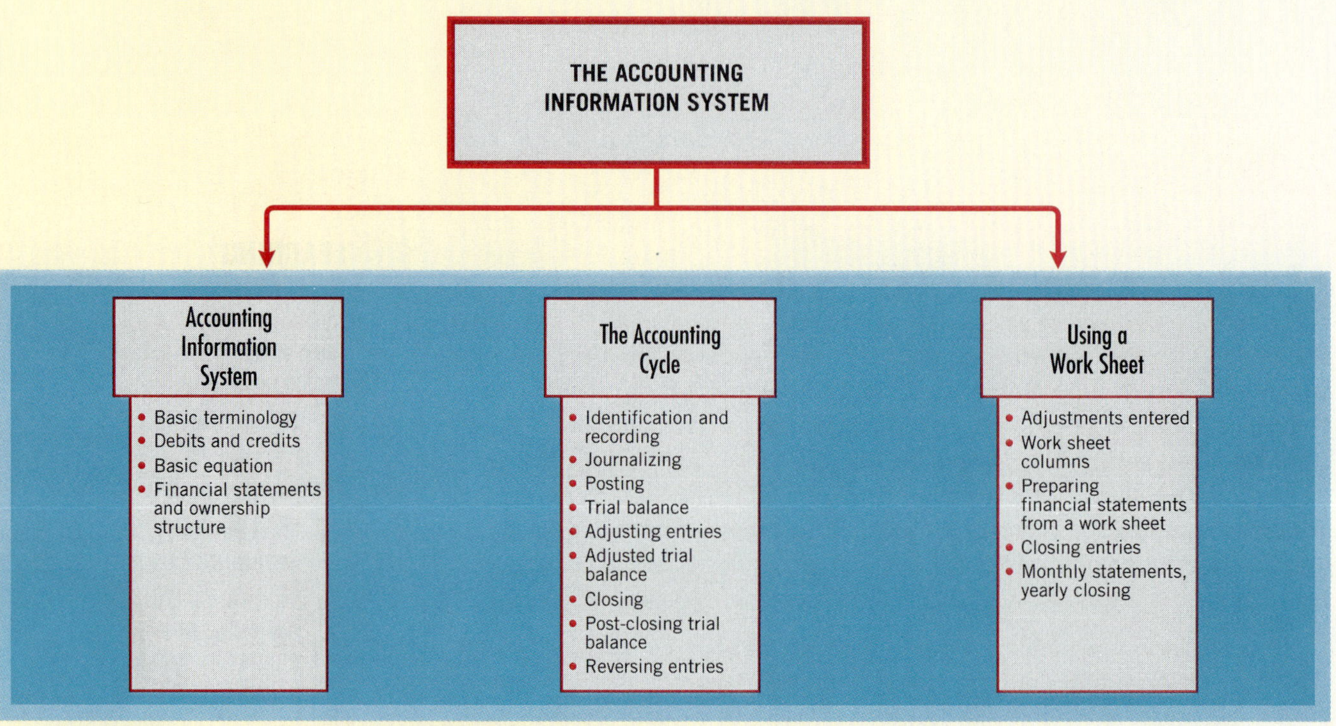

ACCOUNTING INFORMATION SYSTEM

The system of collecting and processing transaction data and disseminating financial information to interested parties is known as the accounting information system. Accounting information systems vary widely from one business to another. Factors that shape these systems are the **nature of the business** and the transactions in which it engages, the **size of the firm**, the **volume of data** to be handled, and the **informational demands** that management and others place on the system.

A good accounting information system helps management answer such questions as:

How much and what kind of debt is outstanding?

Were our sales higher this period than last?

What assets do we have?

What were our cash inflows and outflows?

Did we make a profit last period?

Are any of our product lines or divisions operating at a loss?

Can we safely increase our dividends to stockholders?

Is our rate of return on net assets increasing?

Many other questions can be answered when there is an efficient accounting system to provide the data. A well-devised accounting information system is beneficial for every business enterprise.

Basic Terminology

Financial accounting rests on a set of concepts (discussed in Chapters 1 and 2) for identifying, recording, classifying, and interpreting transactions and other events relating to enterprises. It is important to understand the **basic terminology employed in collecting accounting data**.

OBJECTIVE 1
Understand basic accounting terminology.

BASIC TERMINOLOGY

EVENT. A happening of consequence. An event generally is the source or cause of changes in assets, liabilities, and equity. Events may be external or internal.

TRANSACTION. An **external event** involving a transfer or exchange between two or more entities.

ACCOUNT. A systematic arrangement that shows the effect of transactions and other events on a specific asset or equity. A separate account is kept for each asset, liability, revenue, expense, and for capital (owners' equity).

REAL AND NOMINAL ACCOUNTS. **Real** (permanent) **accounts** are asset, liability, and equity accounts; they appear on the balance sheet. **Nominal** (temporary) **accounts** are revenue, expense, and dividend accounts; except for dividends, they appear on the income statement. Nominal accounts are periodically closed; real accounts are not.

LEDGER. The book (or computer printouts) containing the accounts. Each account usually has a separate page. A **general ledger** is a collection of all the asset, liability, owners' equity, revenue, and expense accounts. A **subsidiary ledger** contains the details related to a given general ledger account.

JOURNAL. The book of original entry where transactions and selected other events are initially recorded. Various amounts are transferred to the ledger from the book of original entry, the journal.

POSTING. The process of transferring the essential facts and figures from the book of original entry to the ledger accounts.

TRIAL BALANCE. A list of all open accounts in the ledger and their balances. A trial balance taken immediately after all adjustments have been posted is called an **adjusted trial balance**. A trial balance taken immediately after closing entries have been posted is designated as a **post-closing** or **after-closing trial balance**. A trial balance may be prepared at any time.

ADJUSTING ENTRIES. Entries made at the end of an accounting period to bring all accounts up to date on an accrual accounting basis so that correct financial statements can be prepared.

FINANCIAL STATEMENTS. Statements that reflect the collection, tabulation, and final summarization of the accounting data. Four statements are involved: (1) the **balance sheet**, which shows the financial condition of the enterprise at the end of a period, (2) the **income statement**, which measures the results of operations during the period, (3) the **statement of cash flows**, which reports the cash provided and used by operating, investing, and financing activities during the period, and (4) the **statement of retained earnings**, which reconciles the balance of the retained earnings account from the beginning to the end of the period.

CLOSING ENTRIES. The formal process by which all nominal accounts are reduced to zero and the net income or net loss is determined and transferred to an owners' equity account, also known as "closing the ledger," "closing the books," or merely "closing."

Debits and Credits

OBJECTIVE 2
Explain double-entry rules.

The terms debit and credit mean left and right, respectively. They are commonly abbreviated as Dr. for debit and Cr. for credit. These terms do not mean increase or decrease. The terms debit and credit are used repeatedly in the recording process to describe where entries are made. For example, the act of entering an amount on the left side of an account is called **debiting** the account, and making an entry on the right side is **crediting** the account. When the totals of the two sides are compared, an account will have a **debit balance** if the total of the debit amounts exceeds the credits. Conversely, an account will have a **credit balance** if the credit amounts exceed the debits.

The procedure of having debits on the left and credits on the right is an accounting custom or rule. We could function just as well if debits and credits were reversed. However, the custom of having debits on the left side of an account and credits on the right side (like the custom of driving on the right-hand side of the road) has been adopted in the United States. **This rule applies to all accounts.**

The equality of debits and credits provides the basis for the double-entry system of recording transactions (sometimes referred to as double-entry bookkeeping). Under the universally used double-entry accounting system, the dual (two-sided) effect of each transaction is recorded in appropriate accounts. This system provides a logical method for recording transactions. It also offers a means of proving the accuracy of the recorded amounts. If every transaction is recorded with equal debits and credits, then the sum of all the debits to the accounts must equal the sum of all the credits.

All asset and expense accounts are increased on the left (or debit side) and decreased on the right (or credit side). Conversely, all liability and revenue accounts are increased on the right (or credit side) and decreased on the left (or debit side). Stockholders' equity accounts, such as Common Stock and Retained Earnings, are increased on the credit side, whereas Dividends is increased on the debit side. The basic guidelines for an accounting system are presented in Illustration 3-1.

ILLUSTRATION 3-1
Double-entry (Debit and Credit) Accounting System

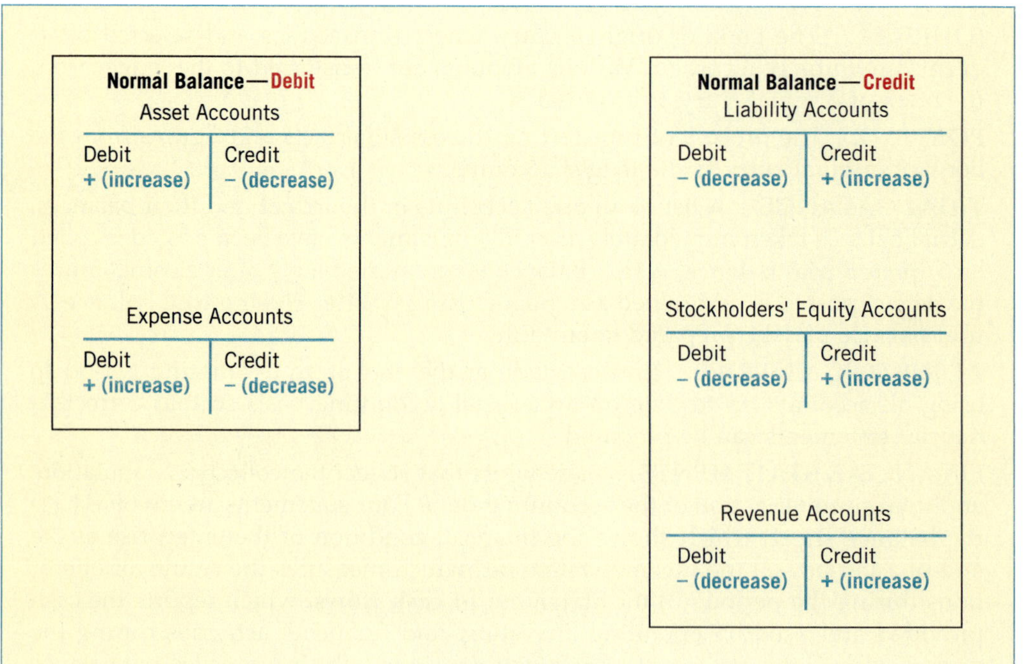

Basic Equation

In a double-entry system, for every debit there must be a credit and vice-versa. This leads us, then, to the basic equation in accounting (Illustration 3-2).

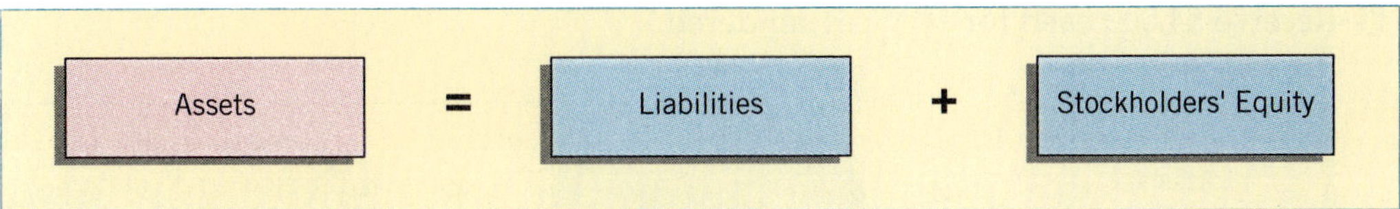

ILLUSTRATION 3-2
The Basic Accounting Equation

Illustration 3-3 expands this equation to show the accounts that comprise stockholders' equity. In addition, the debit/credit rules and effects on each type of account are illustrated. Study this diagram carefully. It will help you understand the fundamentals of the double-entry system. Like the basic equation, the expanded basic equation must be in balance (total debits equal total credits).

ILLUSTRATION 3-3
Expanded Basic Equation and Debit/Credit Rules and Effects

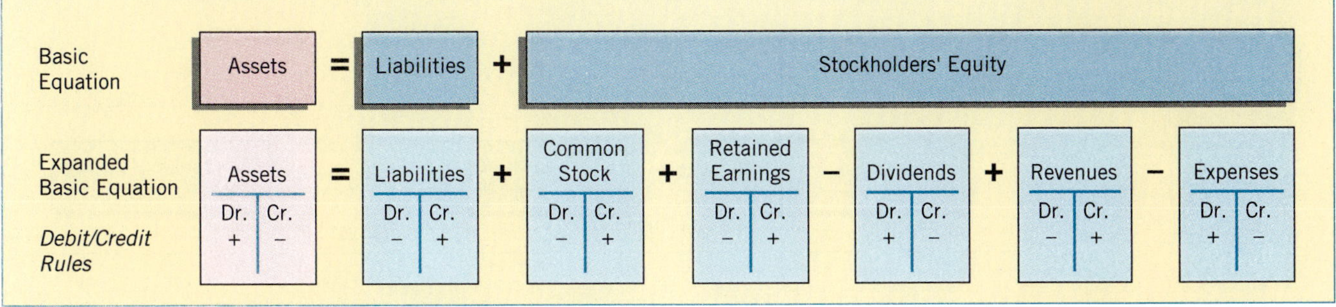

Every time a transactions occurs, the elements of the equation change, but the basic equality remains. To illustrate, here are eight different transactions for Perez Inc.

1. Owners invest $40,000 in exchange for common stock:

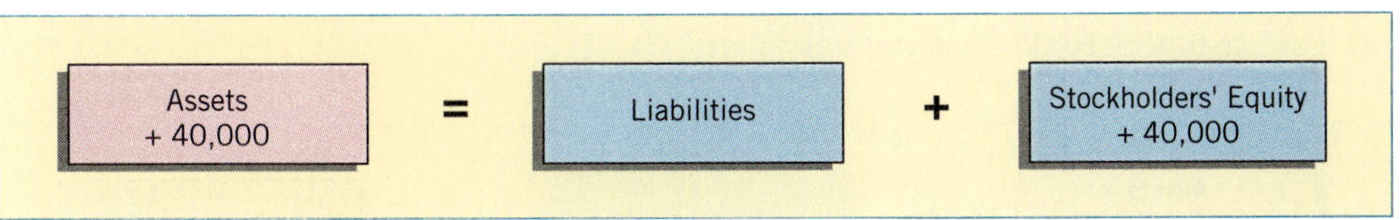

2. Disburse $600 cash for secretarial wages:

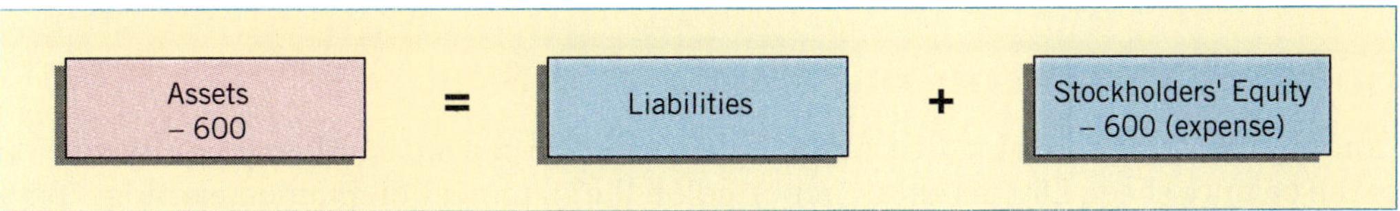

3. Purchase office equipment priced at $5,200, giving a 10% promissory note in exchange:

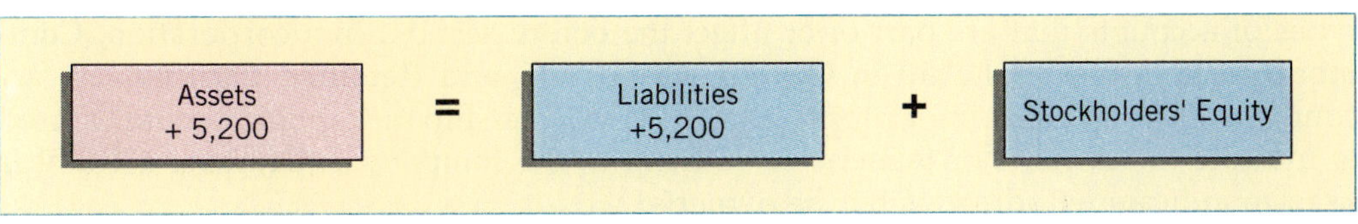

❹ Receive $4,000 cash for services rendered:

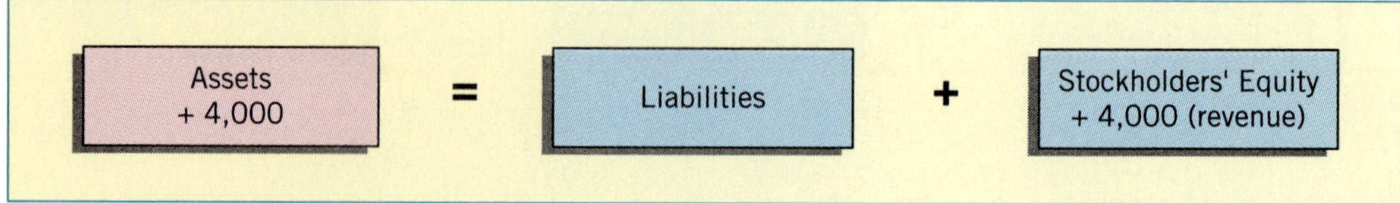

❺ Pay off a short-term liability of $7,000:

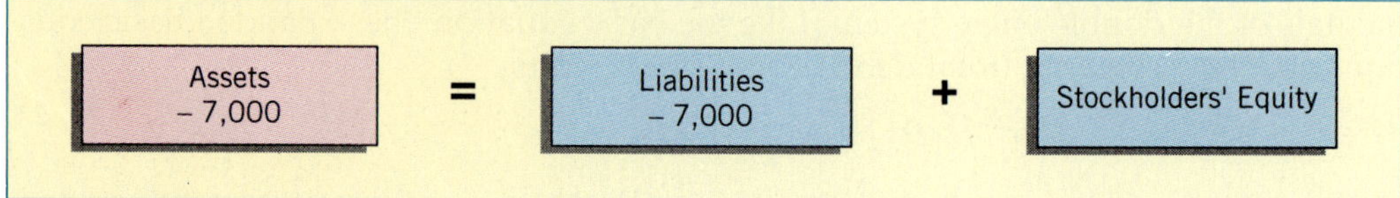

❻ Declare a cash dividend of $5,000:

Assets = Liabilities + 5,000 + Stockholders' Equity – 5,000

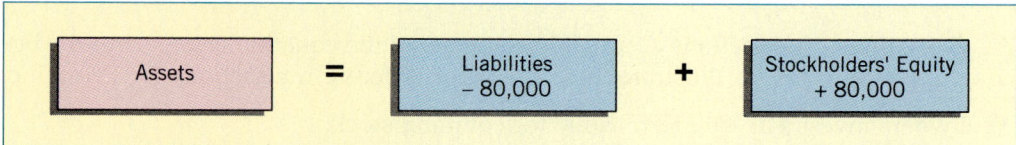

❼ Convert a long-term liability of $80,000 into common stock:

Assets = Liabilities – 80,000 + Stockholders' Equity + 80,000

❽ Pay cash of $16,000 for a delivery van:

Assets –16,000 +16,000 = Liabilities + Stockholders' Equity

Financial Statements and Ownership Structure

Common stock and retained earnings are reported in the stockholders' equity section of the balance sheet. Dividends are reported on the statement of retained earnings. Revenues and expenses are reported on the income statement. Dividends, revenues, and expenses are eventually transferred to retained earnings at the end of the period. As a result, a change in any one of these three items affects stockholders' equity. The relationships related to stockholders' equity are shown in Illustration 3-4.

The type of ownership structure employed by a business enterprise dictates the types of accounts that are part of or affect the equity section. In a corporation, **Common Stock**, **Additional Paid-in Capital**, **Dividends**, and **Retained Earnings** are accounts commonly used. In a proprietorship or partnership, a Capital account is used to indicate the owner's or owners' investment in the company. A Drawing account is used to indicate withdrawals by the owner(s).

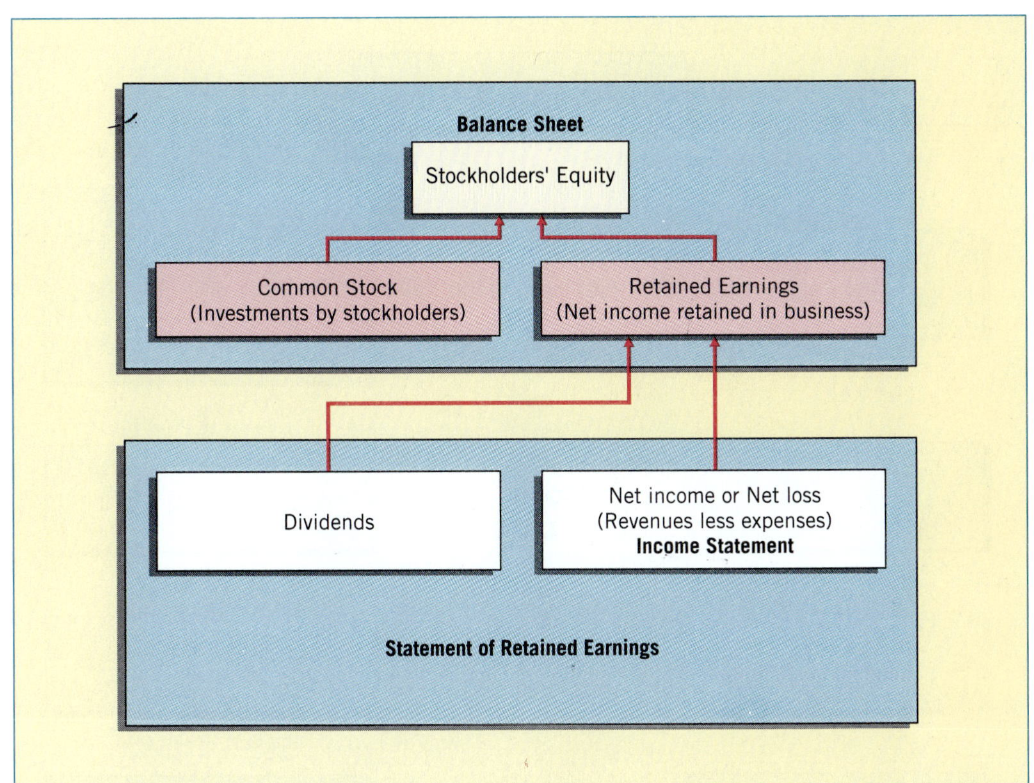

ILLUSTRATION 3-4
Financial Statements and Ownership Structure

Illustration 3-5 summarizes and relates the transactions affecting owners' equity to the nominal (temporary) and real (permanent) classifications and to the types of business ownership.

ILLUSTRATION 3-5
Effects of Transactions on Owners' Equity Accounts

		Ownership Structure			
		Proprietorships and Partnerships		Corporations	
Transactions Affecting Owners' Equity	Impact on Owners' Equity	Nominal (Temporary) Accounts	Real (Permanent) Accounts	Nominal (Temporary) Accounts	Real (Permanent) Accounts
Investment by owner(s)	Increase		Capital		Common Stock and related accounts
Revenues earned	Increase	Revenue	Capital	Revenue	Retained Earnings
Expenses incurred	Decrease	Expense		Expense	
Withdrawal by owner(s)	Decrease	Drawing		Dividends	

THE ACCOUNTING CYCLE

Illustration 3-6 flowcharts the steps in the **accounting cycle**. These are the accounting procedures normally used by enterprises to record transactions and prepare financial statements.

Identifying and Recording Transactions and Other Events

The first step in the accounting cycle is analysis of transactions and selected other events. The problem is to determine **what to record**. No simple rules exist that state whether an event should be recorded. Most agree that changes in personnel, changes in mana-

ILLUSTRATION 3-6
The Accounting Cycle

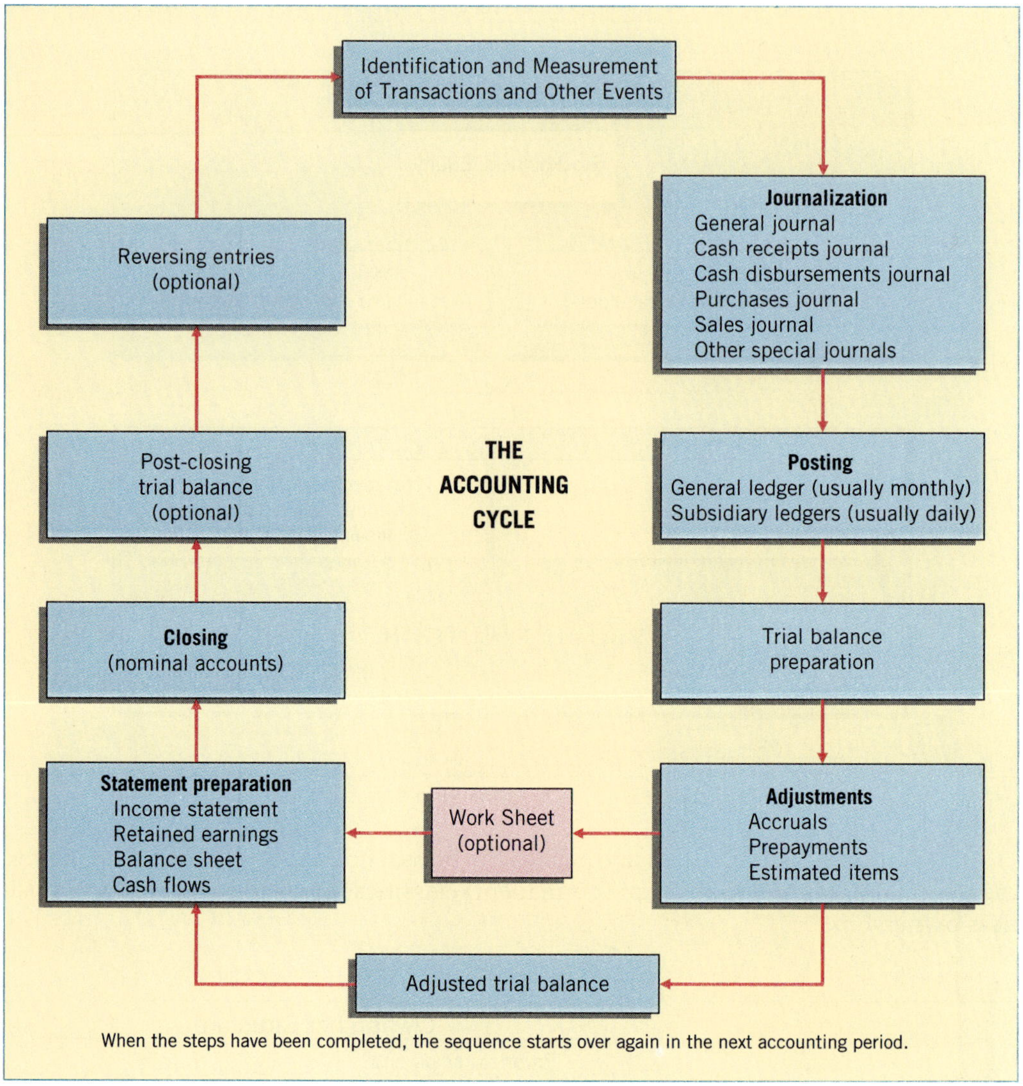

Identification and Measurement of Transactions and Other Events

Journalization
General journal
Cash receipts journal
Cash disbursements journal
Purchases journal
Sales journal
Other special journals

Posting
General ledger (usually monthly)
Subsidiary ledgers (usually daily)

Trial balance preparation

Adjustments
Accruals
Prepayments
Estimated items

Adjusted trial balance

Work Sheet (optional)

Statement preparation
Income statement
Retained earnings
Balance sheet
Cash flows

Closing (nominal accounts)

Post-closing trial balance (optional)

Reversing entries (optional)

THE ACCOUNTING CYCLE

When the steps have been completed, the sequence starts over again in the next accounting period.

gerial policies, and the value of human resources, though important, should not be recorded in the accounts. On the other hand, when the company makes a cash sale or purchase—no matter how small—it should be recorded.

The treatment relates to the accounting concepts presented in Chapter 2. **An item should be recognized in the financial statements if it is an element, is measurable, and is relevant and reliable.** Consider human resources. R.G. Barry & Co. at one time reported as supplemental data total assets of $14,055,926, including $986,094 for "net investments in human resources." AT&T and Exxon Mobil Company have also experimented with human resource accounting. Should we value employees for balance sheet and income statement purposes? Certainly skilled employees are an important asset (highly relevant), but the problems of **determining their value and measuring it reliably have not yet been solved**. Consequently, human resources are not recorded. Perhaps when measurement techniques become more sophisticated and accepted, such information will be presented, if only in supplemental form.

UNDERLYING CONCEPTS

Assets are probable economic benefits controlled by a particular entity as a result of a past transaction or event. Do human resources of a company meet this definition?

The phrase "transactions and other events and circumstances that affect a business enterprise" is used to describe the sources or causes of changes in an entity's assets, liabilities, and equity.[1] **Events** are of two types: (1) **External events** involve interaction

[1] "Elements of Financial Statements of Business Enterprises," *Statement of Financial Accounting Concepts No. 6* (Stamford, Conn.: FASB, 1985), pp. 259–60.

between an entity and its environment, such as a transaction with another entity, a change in the price of a good or service that an entity buys or sells, a flood or earthquake, or an improvement in technology by a competitor. (2) **Internal events** occur within an entity, such as using buildings and machinery in its operations or transferring or consuming raw materials in production processes.

Many events have both external and internal elements. For example, acquiring the services of employees or others involves exchange transactions, which are external events; using those services (labor), often simultaneously with their acquisition, is part of production, which is internal. Events may be initiated and controlled by an entity, such as the purchase of merchandise or the use of a machine, or they may be beyond its control, such as an interest rate change, a theft or vandalism, or the imposition of taxes.

Transactions, as particular kinds of external events, may be an exchange in which each entity both receives and sacrifices value, such as purchases and sales of goods or services. Or transactions may be transfers in one direction in which an entity incurs a liability or transfers an asset to another entity without directly receiving (or giving) value in exchange. Examples include investments by owners, distributions to owners, payment of taxes, gifts, charitable contributions, casualty losses, and thefts.

In short, as many events as possible that affect the financial position of the enterprise are recorded. Some events are omitted because of tradition and others because the problems of measuring them are too complex. The accounting profession in recent years has shown signs of breaking with age-old traditions and is more receptive than ever to accepting the challenge of measuring and reporting events and phenomena previously viewed as too complex and immeasurable.

Journalizing

Differing effects on the basic business elements (assets, liabilities, and equities) are categorized and collected in **accounts**. The **general ledger** is a collection of all the asset, liability, stockholders' equity, revenue, and expense accounts. A **"T"-account** (as shown in Illustration 3-8) is a convenient method of illustrating the effect of transactions on particular asset, liability, equity, revenue, and expense items.

In practice, transactions and selected other events are not recorded originally in the ledger because a transaction affects two or more accounts, each of which is on a different page in the ledger. To circumvent this deficiency and to have a complete record of each transaction or other event in one place, a **journal** (the book of original entry) is employed. The simplest journal form is a chronological listing of transactions and other events expressed in terms of debits and credits to particular accounts. This is called a **general journal**. It is illustrated on the next page for the following transactions.

OBJECTIVE 4
Record transactions in journals, post to ledger accounts, and prepare a trial balance.

Nov. 1 Buys a new delivery truck on account from Auto Sales Co., $22,400.
3 Receives an invoice from the *Evening Graphic* for advertising, $280.
4 Returns merchandise to Yankee Supply for credit, $175.
16 Receives a $95 debit memo from Confederate Co., indicating that freight on a purchase from Confederate Co. was prepaid but is our obligation.

Each **general journal entry** consists of four parts: (1) the accounts and amounts to be debited (Dr.), (2) the accounts and amounts to be credited (Cr.), (3) a date, and (4) an explanation. Debits are entered first, followed by the credits, which are slightly indented. The explanation is begun below the name of the last account to be credited and may take one or more lines. The "Ref." column is completed at the time the accounts are posted.

In some cases, businesses use **special journals** in addition to the general journal. Special journals summarize transactions possessing a common characteristic (e.g., cash receipts, sales, purchases, cash payments), thereby reducing the time necessary to accomplish the various bookkeeping tasks.

Go to the Digital Tool for discussion of special journals.

ILLUSTRATION 3-7
General Journal with Sample Entries

GENERAL JOURNAL Page 12

Date 2002	Account Title and Explanation	Ref.	Amount Debit	Amount Credit
Nov. 1	Delivery Equipment	8	22,400	
	Accounts Payable	34		22,400
	(Purchased delivery truck on account from Auto Sales Co.)			
3	Advertising Expenses	65	280	
	Accounts Payable	34		280
	(Received invoice for advertising from *Evening Graphic*)			
4	Accounts Payable	34	175	
	Purchase Returns	53		175
	(Returned merchandise for credit to Yankee Supply)			
16	Transportation-In	55	95	
	Accounts Payable	34		95
	(Received debit memo for freight on merchandise purchased from Confederate Co.)			

Posting

The items entered in a general journal must be transferred to the general ledger. This procedure, **posting**, is part of the summarizing and classifying process.

For example, the November 1 entry in the general journal in Illustration 3-7 showed a debit to Delivery Equipment of $22,400 and a credit to Accounts Payable of $22,400. The amount in the debit column is posted from the journal to the debit side of the ledger account (Delivery Equipment). The amount in the credit column is posted from the journal to the credit side of the ledger account (Accounts Payable).

The numbers in the "Ref." column of the general journal refer to the accounts in the ledger to which the respective items are posted. For example, the "34" placed in the column to the right of "Accounts Payable" indicates that this $22,400 item was posted to Account No. 34 in the ledger.

The posting of the general journal is completed when all of the posting reference numbers have been recorded opposite the account titles in the journal. Thus the number in the posting reference column serves two purposes: (1) to indicate the ledger account number of the account involved, and (2) to indicate that the posting has been completed for the particular item. Each business enterprise selects its own numbering system for its ledger accounts. One practice is to begin numbering with asset accounts and to follow with liabilities, owners' equity, revenue, and expense accounts, in that order.

The various ledger accounts in Illustration 3-8 are after the posting process is completed. The source of the data transferred to the ledger account is indicated by the reference GJ 12 (General Journal, page 12).

Trial Balance

A **trial balance** is a list of accounts and their balances at a given time. Customarily, a trial balance is prepared at the end of an accounting period. The accounts are listed in the order in which they appear in the ledger, with debit balances listed in the left column and credit balances in the right column. The totals of the two columns must be in agreement.

ILLUSTRATION 3-8
Ledger Accounts, in T-Account Format

Delivery Equipment — No. 8

Debit			Credit		
Nov. 1	GJ 12	22,400			

Accounts Payable — No. 34

Debit			Credit		
Nov. 4	GJ 12	175	Nov. 1	GJ 12	22,400
			3	GJ 12	280
			16	GJ 12	95

Purchase Returns — No. 53

Debit			Credit		
			Nov. 4	GJ 12	175

Transportation-In — No. 55

Debit			Credit		
Nov. 16	GJ 12	95			

Advertising Expense — No. 65

Debit			Credit		
Nov. 3	GJ 12	280			

The primary purpose of a trial balance is to prove the mathematical equality of debits and credits after posting. Under the double-entry system this equality will occur when the sum of the debit account balances equals the sum of the credit account balances. **A trial balance also uncovers errors in journalizing and posting. In addition, it is useful in the preparation of financial statements.** The procedures for preparing a trial balance consist of:

1. Listing the account titles and their balances.
2. Totaling the debit and credit columns.
3. Proving the equality of the two columns.

The trial balance prepared from the ledger of Pioneer Advertising Agency Inc. is presented below:

ILLUSTRATION 3-9
Trial Balance (Unadjusted)

PIONEER ADVERTISING AGENCY INC.
Trial Balance
October 31, 2002

	Debit	Credit
Cash	$ 80,000	
Accounts Receivable	72,000	
Advertising Supplies	25,000	
Prepaid Insurance	6,000	
Office Equipment	50,000	
Notes Payable		$ 50,000
Accounts Payable		25,000
Unearned Service Revenue		12,000
Common Stock		100,000
Dividends	5,000	
Service Revenue		100,000
Salaries Expense	40,000	
Rent Expense	9,000	
	$287,000	$287,000

Note that the total debits $287,000 equal the total credits $287,000. Account numbers to the left of the account titles in the trial balance are also often shown.

A trial balance does not prove that all transactions have been recorded or that the ledger is correct. Numerous errors may exist even though the trial balance columns agree. For example, the trial balance may balance even when (1) a transaction is not journalized, (2) a correct journal entry is not posted, (3) a journal entry is posted twice, (4) incorrect accounts are used in journalizing or posting, or (5) offsetting errors are made in recording the amount of a transaction. In other words, as long as equal debits and credits are posted, even to the wrong account or in the wrong amount, the total debits will equal the total credits.

Adjusting Entries

OBJECTIVE 5
Explain the reasons for preparing adjusting entries.

In order for revenues to be recorded in the period in which they are earned, and for expenses to be recognized in the period in which they are incurred, adjusting entries are made at the end of the accounting period. In short, **adjustments are needed to ensure that the revenue recognition and matching principles are followed**.

The use of adjusting entries makes it possible to report on the balance sheet the appropriate assets, liabilities, and owners' equity at the statement date and to report on the income statement the proper net income (or loss) for the period. However, the trial balance—the first pulling together of the transaction data—may not contain up-to-date and complete data. This is true for the following reasons:

1. Some events are not journalized daily because it is not expedient. Examples are the consumption of supplies and the earning of wages by employees.
2. Some costs are not journalized during the accounting period because these costs expire with the passage of time rather than as a result of recurring daily transactions. Examples of such costs are building and equipment deterioration and rent and insurance.
3. Some items may be unrecorded. An example is a utility service bill that will not be received until the next accounting period.

Adjusting entries are required every time financial statements are prepared. An essential starting point is an analysis of each account in the trial balance to determine whether it is complete and up-to-date for financial statement purposes. The analysis requires a thorough understanding of the company's operations and the interrelationship of accounts. The preparation of adjusting entries is often an involved process that requires the services of a skilled professional. In accumulating the adjustment data, the company may need to make inventory counts of supplies and repair parts. Also it may be desirable to prepare supporting schedules of insurance policies, rental agreements, and other contractual commitments. Adjustments are often prepared after the balance sheet date. However, the entries are dated as of the balance sheet date.

Types of Adjusting Entries

Adjusting entries can be classified as either prepayments or accruals. Each of these classes has two subcategories as shown below:

Prepayments	Accruals
1. Prepaid Expenses. Expenses paid in cash and recorded as assets before they are used or consumed.	3. Accrued Revenues. Revenues earned but not yet received in cash or recorded.
2. Unearned Revenues. Revenues received in cash and recorded as liabilities before they are earned.	4. Accrued Expenses. Expenses incurred but not yet paid in cash or recorded.

Specific examples and explanations of each type of adjustment are given in subsequent sections. Each example is based on the October 31 trial balance of Pioneer Advertising Agency Inc. (Illustration 3-9). We assume that Pioneer Advertising uses an accounting period of one month. Thus, monthly adjusting entries will be made. The entries will be dated October 31.

Adjusting Entries for Prepayments

As indicated earlier, prepayments are either prepaid expenses or unearned revenues. Adjusting entries for prepayments are required at the statement date to record the portion of the prepayment that represents the **expense incurred or the revenue earned** in the current accounting period. Assuming an adjustment is needed for both types of prepayments, the asset and liability are overstated and the related expense and revenue are understated. For example, in the trial balance, the balance in the asset Supplies shows only supplies purchased. This balance is overstated; the related expense account, Supplies Expense, is understated because the cost of supplies used has not been recognized. Thus the adjusting entry for prepayments will decrease a balance sheet account and increase an income statement account. The effects of adjusting entries for prepayments are graphically depicted in Illustration 3-10.

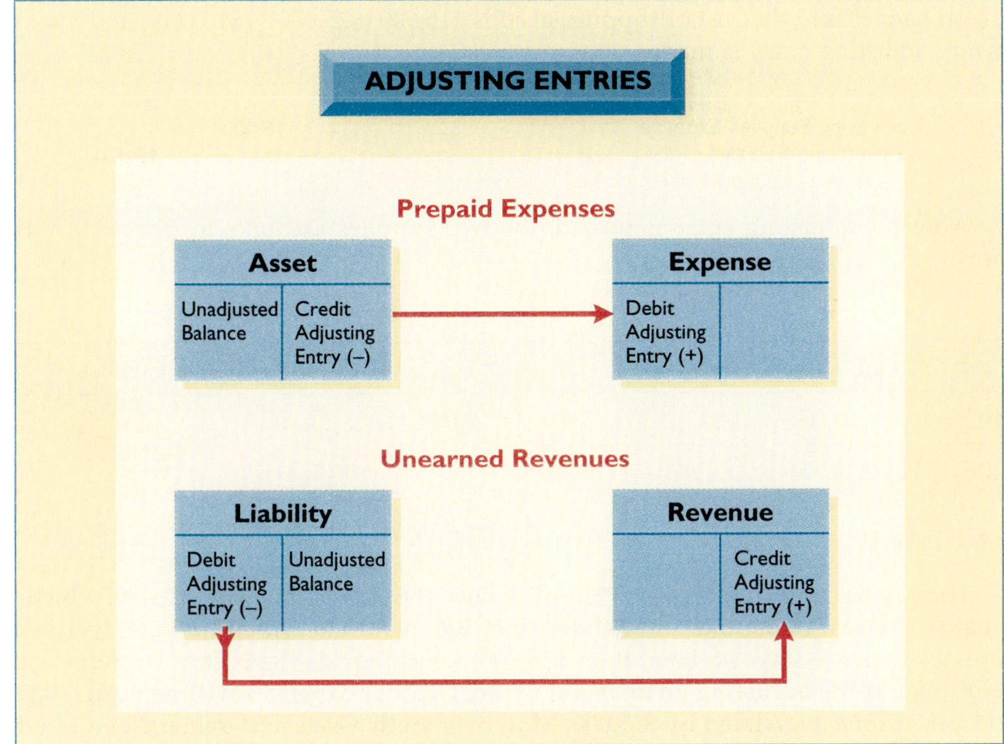

ILLUSTRATION 3-10
Adjusting Entries for Prepayments

Prepaid Expenses. As stated on page 78, expenses paid in cash and recorded as assets before they are used or consumed are identified as prepaid expenses. When a cost is incurred, an asset account is debited to show the service or benefit that will be received in the future. Prepayments often occur in regard to insurance, supplies, advertising, and rent. In addition, prepayments are made when buildings and equipment are purchased.

Prepaid expenses expire either with the passage of time (e.g., rent and insurance) or through use and consumption (e.g., supplies). The expiration of these costs does not require daily recurring entries, which would be unnecessary and impractical. Accordingly, it is customary to postpone the recognition of such cost expirations until financial statements are prepared. At each statement date, adjusting entries are made to record the expenses that apply to the current accounting period and to show the unexpired costs in the asset accounts.

Prior to adjustment, assets are overstated and expenses are understated. **Thus, the prepaid expense adjusting entry results in a debit to an expense account and a credit to an asset account.**

Supplies. Several different types of supplies are used in a business enterprise. For example, a CPA firm will have **office supplies** such as stationery, envelopes, and accounting paper. In contrast, an advertising firm will have **advertising supplies** such as graph paper, video film, and poster paper. Supplies are generally debited to an asset account when they are acquired. During the course of operations, supplies are depleted or entirely consumed. However, recognition of supplies used is deferred until the adjustment process when a physical inventory (count) of supplies is taken. The difference between the balance in the Supplies (asset) account and the cost of supplies on hand represents the supplies used (expense) for the period.

Pioneer Advertising Agency (see Illustration 3-9) purchased advertising supplies costing $25,000 on October 5. The debit was made to the asset Advertising Supplies, and this account shows a balance of $25,000 in the October 31 trial balance. An inventory count at the close of business on October 31 reveals that $10,000 of supplies are still on hand. Thus, the cost of supplies used is $15,000 ($25,000 − $10,000), and the following adjusting entry is made:

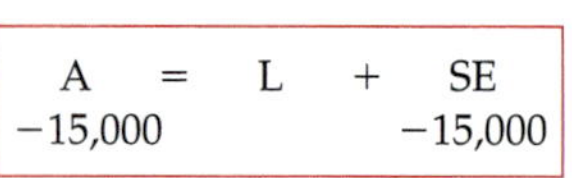

Oct. 31		
Advertising Supplies Expense	15,000	
Advertising Supplies		15,000
(To record supplies used)		

After the adjusting entry is posted, the two supplies accounts in T-account form show:

ILLUSTRATION 3-11
Supplies Accounts after Adjustment

Advertising Supplies				Advertising Supplies Expense	
10/5	25,000	10/31 Adj.	15,000	10/31 Adj. 15,000	
10/31 Bal.	10,000				

The asset account Advertising Supplies now shows a balance of $10,000, which is equal to the cost of supplies on hand at the statement date. In addition, Advertising Supplies Expense shows a balance of $15,000, which equals the cost of supplies used in October. **If the adjusting entry is not made, October expenses will be understated and net income overstated by $15,000. Moreover, both assets and owners' equity will be overstated by $15,000 on the October 31 balance sheet.**

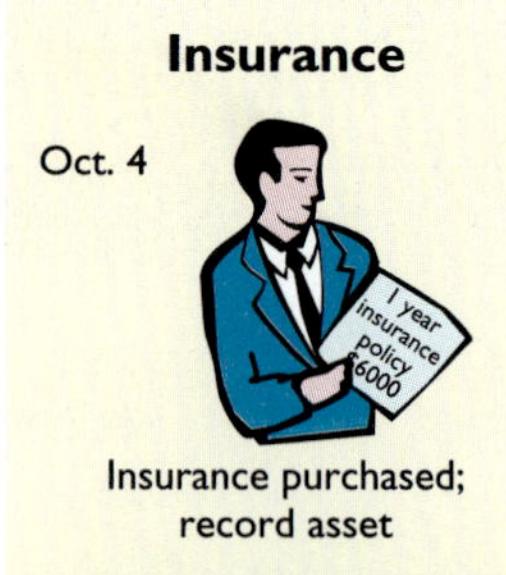

Insurance purchased;
record asset

Insurance Policy			
Oct $500	Nov $500	Dec $500	Jan $500
Feb $500	March $500	April $500	May $500
June $500	July $500	Aug $500	Sept $500
1 YEAR $6,000			

Oct. 31
Insurance expired;
record insurance expense

Insurance. Most companies have fire and theft insurance on merchandise and equipment, personal liability insurance for accidents suffered by customers, and automobile insurance on company cars and trucks. The cost of insurance protection is determined by the payment of insurance premiums. The term and coverage are specified in the insurance policy. The minimum term is usually one year, but three- to five-year terms are available and offer lower annual premiums. Insurance premiums normally are charged to the asset account Prepaid Insurance when paid. At the financial statement date it is necessary to debit Insurance Expense and credit Prepaid Insurance for the cost that has expired during the period.

On October 4, Pioneer Advertising Agency Inc. paid $6,000 for a one-year fire insurance policy. The effective date of coverage was October 1. The premium was charged to Prepaid Insurance when it was paid, and this account shows a balance of $6,000 in the October 31 trial balance. An analysis of the policy reveals that \$500 (\$6,000 ÷ 12) of insurance expires each month. Thus, the following adjusting entry is made:

Oct. 31		
Insurance Expense	500	
Prepaid Insurance		500
(To record insurance expired)		

A	=	L	+	SE
−500				−500

After the adjusting entry is posted, the accounts show:

ILLUSTRATION 3-12
Insurance Accounts after Adjustment

Prepaid Insurance			
10/4	6,000	10/31 Adj.	500
10/31 Bal.	5,500		

Insurance Expense			
10/31 Adj.	500		

The asset Prepaid Insurance shows a balance of \$5,500, which represents the unexpired cost applicable to the remaining 11 months of coverage. At the same time, the balance in Insurance Expense is equal to the insurance cost that has expired in October. **If this adjustment is not made, October expenses will be understated by \$500 and net income overstated by \$500. Moreover, both assets and owners' equity also will be overstated by \$500 on the October 31 balance sheet.**

Depreciation. A business enterprise typically owns a variety of productive facilities such as buildings, equipment, and motor vehicles. These assets provide a service for a number of years. The term of service is commonly referred to as the **useful life** of the asset. Because an asset such as a building is expected to provide service for many years, it is recorded as an asset, rather than an expense, in the year it is acquired. Such assets are recorded at cost, as required by the cost principle.

According to the matching principle, a portion of the cost of a long-lived asset should be reported as an expense during each period of the asset's useful life. **Depreciation** is the process of allocating the cost of an asset to expense over its useful life in a rational and systematic manner.

Depreciation

Oct. 1

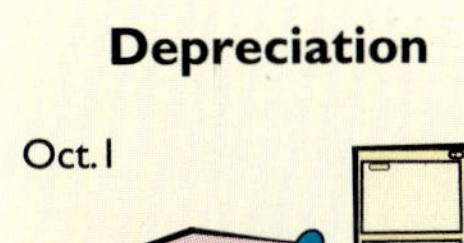

Office equipment purchased; record asset (\$50,000)

Office Equipment			
Oct \$400	Nov \$400	Dec \$400	Jan \$400
Feb \$400	March \$400	April \$400	May \$400
June \$400	July \$400	Aug \$400	Sept \$400
Depreciation = \$4,800/year			

Oct. 31
Depreciation recognized; record depreciation expense

Need for depreciation adjustment. From an accounting standpoint, the acquisition of productive facilities is viewed essentially as a long-term prepayment for services. The need for making periodic adjusting entries for depreciation is, therefore, the same as described before for other prepaid expenses; that is, to recognize the cost that has expired (expense) during the period and to report the unexpired cost (asset) at the end of the period.

In determining the useful life of a productive facility, the primary causes of depreciation are actual use, deterioration due to the elements, and obsolescence. At the time an asset is acquired, the effects of these factors cannot be known with certainty, so they must be estimated. Thus, you should recognize that depreciation is an estimate rather than a factual measurement of the cost that has expired. A common procedure in computing depreciation expense is to divide the cost of the asset by its useful life. For example, if cost is \$10,000 and useful life is expected to be 10 years, annual depreciation is \$1,000.

For Pioneer Advertising, depreciation on the office equipment is estimated to be \$4,800 a year (cost \$50,000 less salvage value \$2,000 divided by useful life of 10 years), or \$400 per month. Accordingly, depreciation for October is recognized by the following adjusting entry:

Oct. 31		
Depreciation Expense	400	
Accumulated Depreciation—Office Equipment		400
(To record monthly depreciation)		

A	=	L	+	SE
−400				−400

After the adjusting entry is posted, the accounts show:

ILLUSTRATION 3-13
Accounts after Adjustment for Depreciation

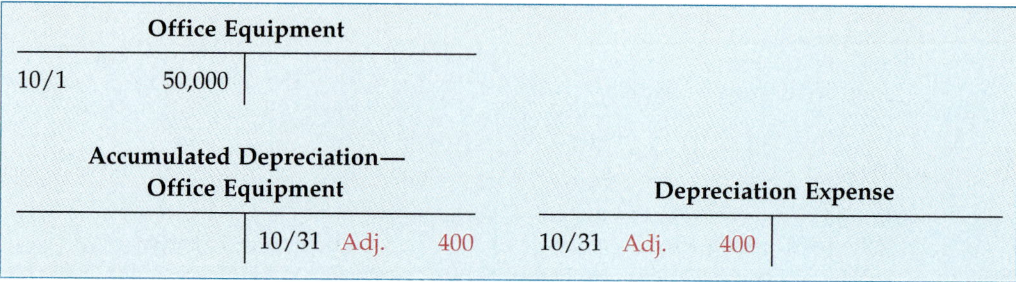

The balance in the accumulated depreciation account will increase $400 each month. Therefore, after journalizing and posting the adjusting entry at November 30, the balance will be $800.

Statement presentation. Accumulated Depreciation—Office Equipment is a contra asset account. A **contra asset account** is an account that is offset against an asset account on the balance sheet. This means that the accumulated depreciation account is offset against Office Equipment on the balance sheet and that its normal balance is a credit. This account is used instead of crediting Office Equipment in order to permit disclosure of **both the original cost** of the equipment **and the total cost that has expired to date**. In the balance sheet, Accumulated Depreciation—Office Equipment is deducted from the related asset account as follows:

ILLUSTRATION 3-14
Balance Sheet Presentation of Accumulated Depreciation

Office equipment	$50,000	
Less: Accumulated depreciation—office equipment	400	$49,600

The difference between the cost of any depreciable asset and its related accumulated depreciation is referred to as the **book value** of that asset. In Illustration 3-14, the book value of the equipment at the balance sheet date is $49,600. It is important to realize that the book value and the market value of the asset are generally two different values. The reason the two are different is that depreciation is not a matter of valuation but rather a means of cost allocation.

Note also that depreciation expense identifies that portion of the asset's cost that has expired in October. As in the case of other prepaid adjustments, the omission of this adjusting entry would cause total assets, total owners' equity, and net income to be overstated and depreciation expense to be understated.

If additional equipment is involved, such as delivery or store equipment, or if the company has buildings, depreciation expense is recorded on each of these items. Related accumulated depreciation accounts also are established. These accumulated depreciation accounts would be described in the ledger as follows: Accumulated Depreciation—Delivery Equipment; Accumulated Depreciation—Store Equipment; and Accumulated Depreciation—Buildings.

Unearned Revenues. As stated on page 78, revenues received in cash and recorded as liabilities before they are earned are called **unearned revenues**. Such items as rent, magazine subscriptions, and customer deposits for further service may result in unearned revenues. Airlines such as **United**, **American**, and **Delta** treat receipts from the sale of tickets as unearned revenue until the flight service is provided. Similarly, tuition received prior to the start of a semester is considered to be unearned revenue. Unearned revenues are the opposite of prepaid expenses. Indeed, unearned revenue on the books of one company is likely to be a prepayment on the books of the company that has made the advance payment. For example, if identical accounting periods are assumed, a landlord will have unearned rent revenue when a tenant has prepaid rent.

When the payment is received for services to be provided in a future accounting period, an unearned revenue (a liability) account should be credited to recognize the obligation that exists. Unearned revenues are subsequently earned through rendering service to a customer. During the accounting period it may not be practical to make daily recurring entries as the revenue is earned. In such cases, the recognition of earned revenue is delayed until the adjustment process. Then an adjusting entry is made to record the revenue that has been earned and to show the liability that remains. In the typical case, liabilities are overstated and revenues are understated prior to adjustment. Thus, **the adjusting entry for unearned revenues results in a debit (decrease) to a liability account and a credit (increase) to a revenue account**.

Unearned Revenues

Oct. 2

Thank you in advance for your work

I will finish by Dec. 31

$12,000

Cash is received in advance; liability is recorded

Oct. 31

Service is provided; revenue is recorded

Pioneer Advertising Agency received $12,000 on October 2 from R. Knox for advertising services expected to be completed by December 31. The payment was credited to Unearned Service Revenue, and this account shows a balance of $12,000 in the October 31 trial balance.When analysis reveals that $4,000 of these services have been earned in October, the following adjusting entry is made:

Oct. 31		
Unearned Service Revenue	4,000	
Service Revenue		4,000
(To record revenue for services provided)		

After the adjusting entry is posted, the accounts show:

ILLUSTRATION 3-15
Service Revenue Accounts after Prepayments Adjustment

Unearned Service Revenue			
10/31 Adj.	4,000	10/2	12,000
		10/31 Bal.	8,000

Service Revenue			
		10/31 Bal.	100,000
		31 Adj.	4,000

The liability Unearned Service Revenue now shows a balance of $8,000, which represents the remaining advertising services expected to be performed in the future. At the same time, Service Revenue shows total revenue earned in October of $104,000. **If this adjustment is not made, revenues and net income will be understated by $4,000 in the income statement. Moreover, liabilities will be overstated and owners' equity will be understated by $4,000 on the October 31 balance sheet.**

Adjusting Entries for Accruals

The second category of adjusting entries is **accruals**. Adjusting entries for accruals are required to record revenues earned and expenses incurred in the current accounting period that have not been recognized through daily entries. If an accrual adjustment is needed, the revenue account (and the related asset account) and/or the expense account (and the related liability account) is understated. Thus, the adjusting entry for accruals will **increase both a balance sheet and an income statement account**. Adjusting entries for accruals are graphically depicted in Illustration 3-16.

Accrued Revenues. As explained on page 78, revenues earned but not yet received in cash or recorded at the statement date are **accrued revenues**. Accrued revenues may accumulate (accrue) with the passing of time, as in the case of interest revenue and rent revenue. Or they may result from services that have been performed but neither billed nor collected, as in the case of commissions and fees. The former are unrecorded because the earning of interest and rent does not involve daily transactions; the latter may be unrecorded because only a portion of the total service has been provided.

An adjusting entry is required to show the receivable that exists at the balance sheet date and to record the revenue that has been earned during the period. Prior to ad-

ILLUSTRATION 3-16
Adjusting Entries for Accruals

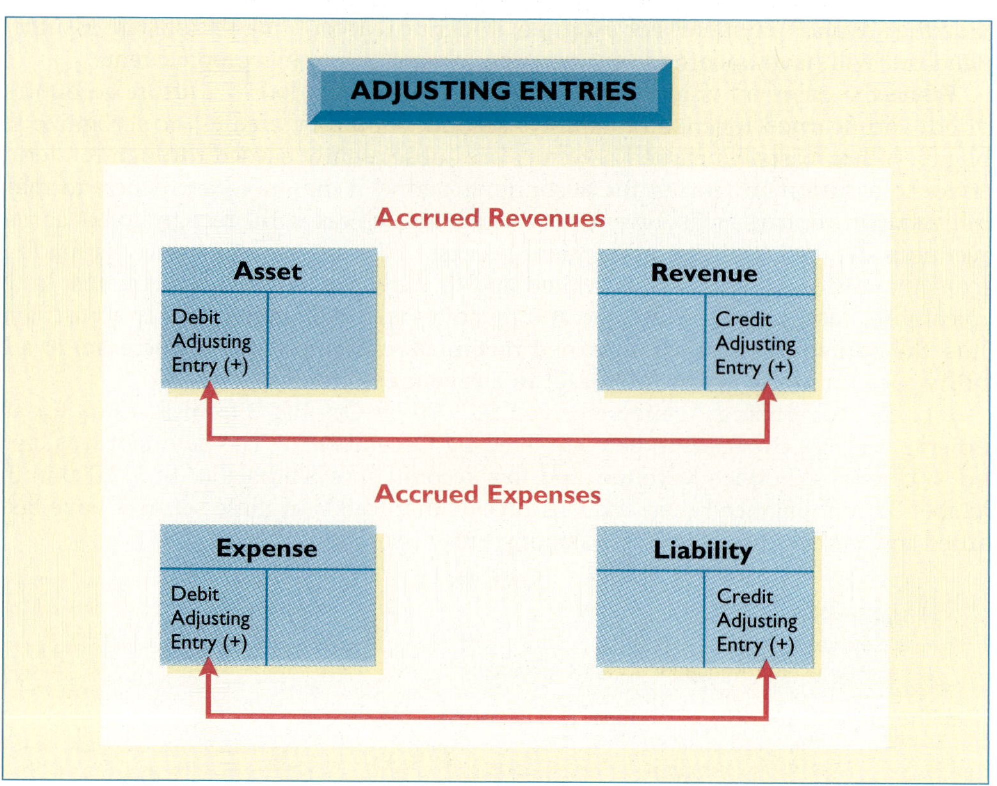

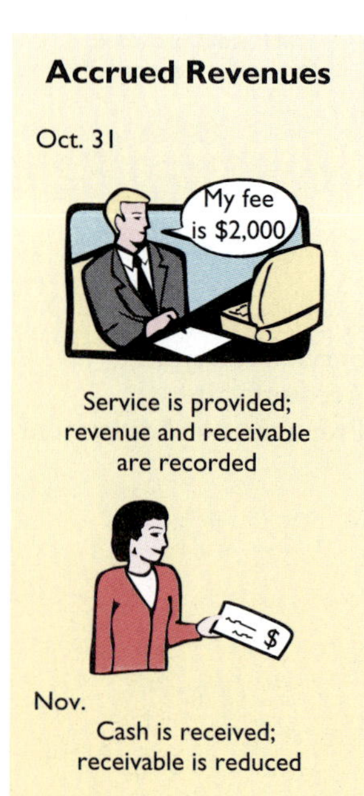

justment both assets and revenues are understated. Accordingly, **an adjusting entry for accrued revenues results in a debit (increase) to an asset account and a credit (increase) to a revenue account.**

Accrued Revenues
Oct. 31
My fee is $2,000
Service is provided; revenue and receivable are recorded
Nov.
Cash is received; receivable is reduced

In October Pioneer Advertising Agency earned $2,000 for advertising services that were not billed to clients before October 31. Because these services have not been billed, they have not been recorded. Thus, the following adjusting entry is made:

Oct. 31		
Accounts Receivable	2,000	
Service Revenue		2,000
(To record revenue for services provided)		

After the adjusting entry is posted, the accounts show:

ILLUSTRATION 3-17
Receivable and Revenue Accounts after Accrual Adjustment

Accounts Receivable

Debit		Credit
10/31	72,000	
31 Adj.	2,000	

Service Revenue

Debit	Credit	
	10/31	100,000
	31	4,000
	31 Adj.	2,000
	10/31 Bal.	106,000

The asset Accounts Receivable shows that $74,000 is owed by clients at the balance sheet date. The balance of $106,000 in Service Revenue represents the total revenue earned during the month ($100,000 + $4,000 + $2,000). **If the adjusting entry is not made, assets and owners' equity on the balance sheet, and revenues and net income on the income statement, will all be understated.**

Accrued Expenses. As indicated on page 78, expenses incurred but not yet paid or recorded at the statement date are called **accrued expenses**. Interest, rent, taxes, and salaries can be accrued expenses. Accrued expenses result from the same causes as accrued revenues. In fact, an accrued expense on the books of one company is an accrued revenue to another company. For example, the $2,000 accrual of service revenue by Pioneer is an accrued expense to the client that received the service.

Adjustments for accrued expenses are necessary to record the obligations that exist at the balance sheet date and to recognize the expenses that apply to the current accounting period. Prior to adjustment both liabilities and expenses are understated. Therefore, **the adjusting entry for accrued expenses results in a debit (increase) to an expense account and a credit (increase) to a liability account.**

Accrued Interest. Pioneer Advertising Agency signed a three-month note payable in the amount of $50,000 on October 1. The note requires interest at an annual rate of 12%. The amount of the interest accumulation is determined by three factors: (1) the face value of the note, (2) the interest rate, which is always expressed as an annual rate, and (3) the length of time the note is outstanding. In this instance, the total interest due on the $50,000 note at its due date 3 months hence is $1,500 ($50,000 × 12% × 3/12), or $500 for one month. The formula for computing interest and its application to Pioneer Advertising Agency for the month of October are shown in Illustration 3-18.

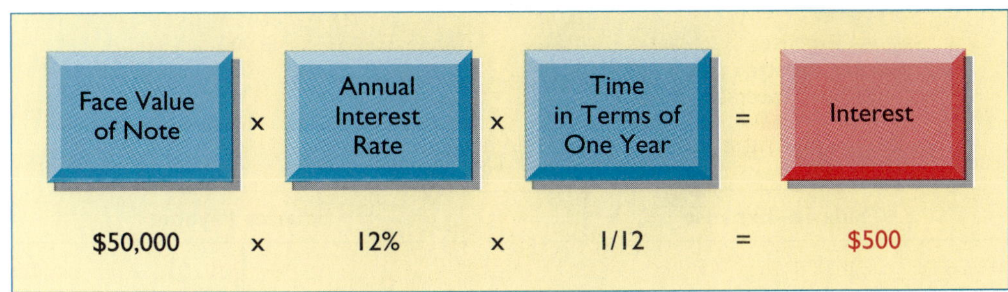

ILLUSTRATION 3-18
Formula for Computing Interest

Note that the time period is expressed as a fraction of a year. The accrued expense adjusting entry at October 31 is as follows:

	Oct. 31		
Interest Expense		500	
Interest Payable			500
(To record interest on notes payable)			

A	=	L	+	SE
		+500		−500

After this adjusting entry is posted, the accounts show:

Interest Expense			Interest Payable	
10/31	500		10/31	500

ILLUSTRATION 3-19
Interest Accounts after Adjustment

Interest Expense shows the interest charges applicable to the month of October. The amount of interest owed at the statement date is shown in Interest Payable. It will not be paid until the note comes due at the end of three months. The Interest Payable account is used instead of crediting Notes Payable to disclose the two types of obligations (interest and principal) in the accounts and statements. **If this adjusting entry is not made, liabilities and interest expense will be understated, and net income and owners' equity will be overstated.**

Accrued Salaries. Some types of expenses, such as employee salaries and commissions, are paid for after the services have been performed. At Pioneer Advertising, salaries were last paid on October 26; the next payment of salaries will not occur until November 9. As shown in the calendar on the next page, three working days remain in October (October 29–31).

At October 31, the salaries for these days represent an accrued expense and a related liability to Pioneer Advertising. The employees receive total salaries of $10,000

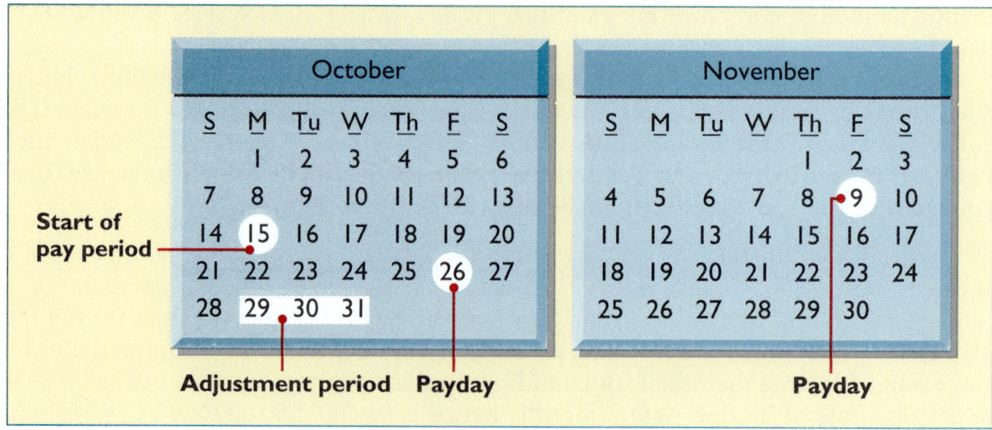

for a five-day work week, or $2,000 per day. Thus, accrued salaries at October 31 are $6,000 ($2,000 × 3), and the adjusting entry is:

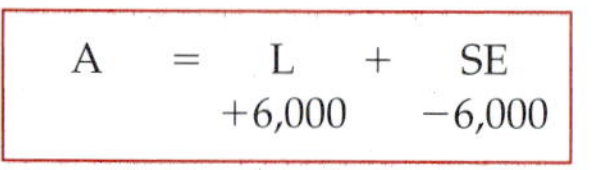

Oct. 31		
Salaries Expense	6,000	
Salaries Payable		6,000
(To record accrued salaries)		

After this adjusting entry is posted, the accounts show:

ILLUSTRATION 3-20
Salary Accounts after Adjustment

Salaries Expense				Salaries Payable			
10/26		40,000			10/31	Adj.	6,000
31	Adj.	6,000					
10/31	Bal.	46,000					

After this adjustment, the balance in Salaries Expense of $46,000 (23 days × $2,000) is the actual salary expense for October. The balance in Salaries Payable of $6,000 is the amount of the liability for salaries owed as of October 31. **If the $6,000 adjustment for salaries is not recorded, Pioneer's expenses will be understated $6,000, and its liabilities will be understated $6,000.**

At Pioneer Advertising, salaries are payable every two weeks. Consequently, the next payday is November 9, when total salaries of $20,000 will again be paid. The payment consists of $6,000 of salaries payable at October 31 plus $14,000 of salaries expense for November (7 working days as shown in the November calendar × $2,000). Therefore, the following entry is made on November 9:

A	=	L	+	SE
−20,000		−6,000		−14,000

Nov. 9		
Salaries Payable	6,000	
Salaries Expense	14,000	
Cash		20,000
(To record November 9 payroll)		

This entry eliminates the liability for Salaries Payable that was recorded in the October 31 adjusting entry and records the proper amount of Salaries Expense for the period between November 1 and November 9.

Bad Debts. Proper matching of revenues and expenses dictates recording bad debts as an expense of the period in which revenue is earned instead of the period in which the accounts or notes are written off. The proper valuation of the receivable balance also requires recognition of uncollectible, worthless receivables. Proper matching and valuation require an adjusting entry.

At the end of each period an estimate is made of the amount of current period revenue on account that will later prove to be uncollectible. The estimate is based on the amount of bad debts experienced in past years, general economic conditions, how long the receivables are past due, and other factors that indicate the element of uncollectibility. Usually it is expressed as a percent of the revenue on account for the period. Or it may be computed by adjusting the Allowance for Doubtful Accounts to a certain percent of the trade accounts receivable and trade notes receivable at the end of the period.

To illustrate, assume that experience indicates a reasonable estimate for bad debt expense for the month is $1,600. The adjusting entry for bad debts is:

Oct. 31		
Bad Debt Expense	1,600	
Allowance for Doubtful Accounts		1,600
(To record monthly bad debt expense)		

After the adjusting entry is posted, the accounts show:

ILLUSTRATION 3-21
Accounts after Adjustment for Bad Debt Expense

Accounts Receivable

Debit	Credit
10/1 72,000	
31 Adj. 2,000	

Allowance for Doubtful Accounts

Debit	Credit
	10/31 Adj. 1,600

Bad Debt Expense

Debit	Credit
10/31 Adj. 1,600	

Adjusted Trial Balance

After all adjusting entries have been journalized and posted, another trial balance is prepared from the ledger accounts. This trial balance is called an adjusted trial balance. It shows the balance of all accounts, including those that have been adjusted, at the end of the accounting period. The purpose of an adjusted trial balance is to show the effects of all financial events that have occurred during the accounting period.

ILLUSTRATION 3-22
Trial Balance (Adjusted)

PIONEER ADVERTISING AGENCY, INC.
Adjusted Trial Balance
October 31, 2002

	Debit	Credit
Cash	$ 80,000	
Accounts Receivable	74,000	
Allowance for Doubtful Accounts		$ 1,600
Advertising Supplies	10,000	
Prepaid Insurance	5,500	
Office Equipment	50,000	
Accumulated Depreciation—Office Equipment		400
Notes Payable		50,000
Accounts Payable		25,000
Interest Payable		500
Unearned Service Revenue		8,000
Salaries Payable		6,000
Common Stock		100,000
Dividends	5,000	
Service Revenue		106,000
Salaries Expense	46,000	
Advertising Supplies Expense	15,000	
Rent Expense	9,000	
Insurance Expense	500	
Interest Expense	500	
Depreciation Expense	400	
Bad Debt Expense	1,600	
	$297,500	$297,500

Closing

Basic Process

The procedure generally followed to reduce the balance of nominal (temporary) accounts to zero in order to prepare the accounts for the next period's transactions is known as the **closing process**. In the closing process all of the revenue and expense account balances (income statement items) are transferred to a clearing or suspense account called Income Summary, which is used only at the end of each accounting period (yearly). Revenues and expenses are matched in the Income Summary account, and the net result of this matching, which represents the net income or net loss for the period, is then transferred to an owners' equity account (retained earnings for a corporation and capital accounts normally for proprietorships and partnerships). All closing entries are posted to the appropriate general ledger accounts.

For example, assume that revenue accounts of Collegiate Apparel Shop have the following balances, after adjustments, at the end of the year:

Sales Revenue	$280,000
Rental Revenue	27,000
Interest Revenue	5,000

These **revenue accounts** would be closed and the balances transferred by the following closing journal entry:

Sales Revenue	280,000	
Rental Revenue	27,000	
Interest Revenue	5,000	
Income Summary		312,000
(To close revenue accounts to Income Summary)		

Assume that the expense accounts, including Cost of Goods Sold, have the following balances, after adjustments, at the end of the year:

Cost of Goods Sold	$206,000
Selling Expenses	25,000
General and Adm. Expenses	40,600
Interest Expense	4,400
Income Tax Expense	13,000

These **expense accounts** would be closed and the balances transferred through the following closing journal entry:

Income Summary	289,000	
Cost of Goods Sold		206,000
Selling Expenses		25,000
General and Adm. Expenses		40,600
Interest Expense		4,400
Income Tax Expense		13,000
(To close expense accounts to Income Summary)		

The Income Summary account now has a credit balance of $23,000 which is net income. The **net income is transferred to owners' equity** by closing the Income Summary account to Retained Earnings as follows:

A	=	L	+	SE
				−23,000
				+23,000

Income Summary	23,000	
Retained Earnings		23,000
(To close Income Summary to Retained Earnings)		

Assuming that dividends of $7,000 were declared and distributed during the year, the Dividends account is closed directly to Retained Earnings as follows:

Retained Earnings	7,000	
Dividends		7,000
(To close Dividends to Retained Earnings)		

A	=	L	+	SE
				−7,000
				+7,000

After the closing process is completed, each income statement (i.e., nominal) account is balanced out to zero and is ready for use in the next accounting period.

Illustration 3-23 shows the closing process in T-account form.

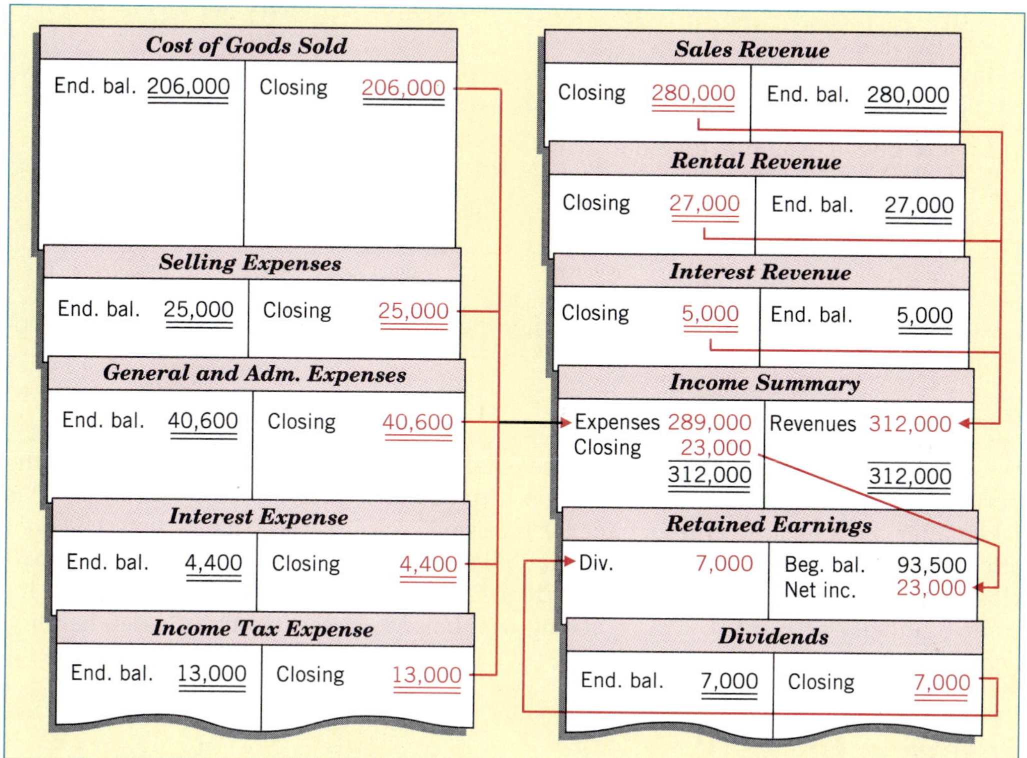

ILLUSTRATION 3-23
The Closing Process

Inventory and Cost of Goods Sold

The closing procedures illustrated above assumed the use of the perpetual inventory system. With a **perpetual inventory system**, purchases and sales are recorded directly in the inventory account as the purchases and sales occur. Therefore, the balance in the Inventory account should represent the ending inventory amount, and no adjusting entries are needed. To ensure this accuracy, a physical count of the items in the inventory is generally made annually. No Purchases account is used because the purchases are debited directly to the Inventory account. However, a Cost of Goods Sold account is used to accumulate the issuances from inventory. That is, when inventory items are sold, the cost of the sold goods is credited to Inventory and debited to Cost of Goods Sold.

OBJECTIVE 7
Explain how inventory accounts are adjusted at year-end.

With a **periodic inventory system**, a Purchases account is used, and the Inventory account is unchanged during the period. The Inventory account represents the beginning inventory amount throughout the period. At the end of the accounting period the Inventory account must be adjusted by **closing out the beginning inventory** amount and **recording the ending inventory** amount. The ending inventory is determined by physically counting the items on hand and valuing them at cost or at the lower of cost or market. Under the periodic inventory system, cost of goods sold is, therefore, determined by adding the beginning inventory together with net purchases and deducting the ending inventory.

To illustrate how cost of goods sold is computed with a periodic inventory system, assume that Collegiate Apparel Shop has a beginning inventory of $30,000; Purchases $200,000; Transportation-In $6,000; Purchase Returns and Allowances $1,000; Purchase

Discounts $3,000; and the ending inventory is $26,000. The computation of cost of goods sold is as follows:

ILLUSTRATION 3-24
Computation of Cost of Goods Sold

Beginning inventory			$ 30,000
Purchases		$200,000	
Less: Purchase returns and allowances	$1,000		
Purchase discounts	3,000	4,000	
Net purchases		196,000	
Plus: Transportation-in		6,000	
Cost of goods purchased			202,000
Cost of goods available for sale			232,000
Less: Ending inventory			26,000
Cost of goods sold			$206,000

Cost of goods sold will be the same whether the perpetual or periodic method is used.

Post-Closing Trial Balance

We already mentioned that a trial balance is taken after the regular transactions of the period have been entered and that a second trial balance (the adjusted trial balance) is taken after the adjusting entries have been posted. A third trial balance may be taken after posting the closing entries. The trial balance after closing, often called the **post-closing trial balance**, shows that equal debits and credits have been posted to the Income Summary account. The post-closing trial balance consists only of asset, liability, and owners' equity (the real) accounts.

Reversing Entries

After the financial statements have been prepared and the books have been closed, it is often helpful to reverse some of the adjusting entries before recording the regular transactions of the next period. Such entries are called reversing entries. **A reversing entry is made at the beginning of the next accounting period and is the exact opposite of the related adjusting entry made in the previous period.** The recording of reversing entries is an **optional** step in the accounting cycle that may be performed at the beginning of the next accounting period. Appendix 3B discusses reversing entries in more detail.

The Accounting Cycle Summarized

A summary of the steps in the accounting cycle shows a logical sequence of the accounting procedures used during a fiscal period:

1. Enter the transactions of the period in appropriate journals.
2. Post from the journals to the ledger (or ledgers).
3. Take an unadjusted trial balance (trial balance).
4. Prepare adjusting journal entries and post to the ledger(s).
5. Take a trial balance after adjusting (adjusted trial balance).
6. Prepare the financial statements from the second trial balance.
7. Prepare closing journal entries and post to the ledger(s).
8. Take a trial balance after closing (post-closing trial balance).
9. Prepare reversing entries (optional) and post to the ledger(s).

This list of procedures constitutes a complete accounting cycle that is normally performed in every fiscal period.

USING A WORK SHEET

OBJECTIVE 8
Prepare a 10-column work sheet.

To facilitate the end-of-period (monthly, quarterly, or annually) accounting and reporting process, a work sheet is often used. A **work sheet** is a columnar sheet of paper used to adjust the account balances and prepare the financial statements. Use of a work sheet helps the accountant prepare the financial statements on a more timely basis. It is not necessary to delay preparation of the financial statements until the adjusting and closing entries are journalized and posted. The **10-column work sheet** illustrated in this chapter (Illustration 3-25 on page 93) provides columns for the first trial balance, adjustments, adjusted trial balance, income statement, and balance sheet.

The work sheet does not replace the financial statements. Instead, it is an informal device for accumulating and sorting information needed for the financial statements. Completing the work sheet provides considerable assurance that all of the details related to the end-of-period accounting and statement preparation have been properly brought together.

Adjustments Entered on the Work Sheet

Items (a) through (f) below serve as the basis for the adjusting entries made in the work sheet shown in Illustration 3-25.

(a) Furniture and equipment is depreciated at the rate of 10% per year based on original cost of $67,000.

(b) Estimated bad debts, one-quarter of 1% of sales ($400,000).

(c) Insurance expired during the year, $360.

(d) Interest accrued on notes receivable as of December 31, $800.

(e) The Rent Expense account contains $500 rent paid in advance, which is applicable to next year.

(f) Property taxes accrued December 31, $2,000.

The adjusting entries shown on the December 31, 2002, work sheet are as follows:

(a)		
Depreciation Expense—Furniture and Equipment	6,700	
Accumulated Depreciation—Furniture and Equipment		6,700
(b)		
Bad Debt Expense	1,000	
Allowance for Doubtful Accounts		1,000
(c)		
Insurance Expense	360	
Prepaid Insurance		360
(d)		
Interest Receivable	800	
Interest Revenue		800
(e)		
Prepaid Rent Expense	500	
Rent Expense		500
(f)		
Property Tax Expense	2,000	
Property Tax Payable		2,000

These adjusting entries are transferred to the Adjustments columns of the work sheet, and each may be designated by letter. The accounts that are set up as a result of the adjusting entries and that are not already in the trial balance are listed below the totals of the trial balance, as illustrated on the work sheet. The Adjustments columns are then totaled and balanced.

Work Sheet Columns

Trial Balance Columns

Data for the trial balance are obtained from the ledger balances of Uptown Cabinet Corp. at December 31. The amount for Merchandise Inventory, $40,000, is the year-end inventory amount, which results from the application of a perpetual inventory system.

Adjustments Columns

After all adjustment data are entered on the work sheet, the equality of the adjustment columns is established. The balances in all accounts are then extended to the adjusted trial balance columns.

Adjusted Trial Balance

The adjusted trial balance shows the balance of all accounts after adjustment at the end of the accounting period. For example, the $2,000 shown opposite the Allowance for Doubtful Accounts in the Trial Balance Cr. column is added to the $1,000 in the Adjustments Cr. column. The $3,000 total is then extended to the Adjusted Trial Balance Cr. column. Similarly, the $900 debit opposite Prepaid Insurance is reduced by the $360 credit in the Adjustments column. The result, $540, is shown in the Adjusted Trial Balance Dr. column.

Income Statement and Balance Sheet Columns

All the debit items in the Adjusted Trial Balance columns are extended into the Income Statement or Balance Sheet columns to the right. All the credit items are similarly extended. The next step is to total the Income Statement columns; the figure necessary to balance the debit and credit columns is the pretax income or loss for the period. The income before income taxes of $15,640 is shown in the Income Statement Dr. column because revenues exceeded expenses by that amount.

Income Taxes and Net Income

The federal and state income tax expense and related tax liability are computed next. The company applies an effective rate of 22% to arrive at $3,440. Because the Adjustments columns have been balanced, this adjustment is entered in the Income Statement Dr. column as Income Tax Expense and in the Balance Sheet Cr. column as Income Tax Payable. The following adjusting journal entry is recorded on December 31, 2002, and posted to the general ledger as well as entered on the work sheet.

A	=	L	+	SE
		+3,440		−3,440

(g)

Income Tax Expense	3,440	
Income Tax Payable		3,440

Next the Income Statement columns are balanced with the income taxes included. The $12,200 difference between the debit and credit columns in this illustration represents net income. The net income of $12,200 is entered in the Income Statement Dr. column to achieve equality and in the Balance Sheet Cr. column as the increase in retained earnings.

ILLUSTRATION 3-25 Use of a Work Sheet

UPTOWN CABINET CORP.
Ten-Column Work Sheet
For the Year Ended December 31, 2002

Accounts	Trial Balance Dr.	Trial Balance Cr.	Adjustments Dr.	Adjustments Cr.	Adjusted Trial Balance Dr.	Adjusted Trial Balance Cr.	Income Statement Dr.	Income Statement Cr.	Balance Sheet Dr.	Balance Sheet Cr.
Cash	1,200				1,200				1,200	
Notes receivable	16,000				16,000				16,000	
Accounts receivable	41,000				41,000				41,000	
Allowance for doubtful accounts		2,000		(b) 1,000		3,000				3,000
Merchandise inventory	40,000				40,000				40,000	
Prepaid insurance	900			(c) 360	540				540	
Furniture and equipment	67,000				67,000				67,000	
Accumulated depreciation—furniture and equipment		12,000		(a) 6,700		18,700				18,700
Notes payable		20,000				20,000				20,000
Accounts payable		13,500				13,500				13,500
Bonds payable		30,000				30,000				30,000
Common stock		50,000				50,000				50,000
Retained earnings, Jan. 1, 2002		14,200				14,200				14,200
Sales		400,000				400,000		400,000		
Cost of goods sold	316,000				316,000		316,000			
Sales salaries expense	20,000				20,000		20,000			
Advertising expense	2,200				2,200		2,200			
Traveling expense	8,000				8,000		8,000			
Salaries, office and general	19,000				19,000		19,000			
Telephone and Internet expense	600				600		600			
Rent expense	4,800			(e) 500	4,300		4,300			
Property tax expense	3,300		(f) 2,000		5,300		5,300			
Interest expense	1,700				1,700		1,700			
Totals	541,700	541,700								
Depreciation expense—furniture and equipment			(a) 6,700		6,700		6,700			
Bad debt expense			(b) 1,000		1,000		1,000			
Insurance expense			(c) 360		360		360			
Interest receivable			(d) 800		800				800	
Interest revenue				(d) 800		800		800		
Prepaid rent expense			(e) 500		500				500	
Property tax payable				(f) 2,000		2,000				2,000
Totals			11,360	11,360	552,200	552,200	385,160	400,800		
Income before income taxes							15,640			
Totals							400,800	400,800		
Income before income taxes								15,640		
Income tax expense			(g) 3,440				3,440			
Income tax payable				(g) 3,440						3,440
Net income							12,200			12,200
Totals							15,640	15,640	167,040	167,040

Preparing Financial Statements from a Work Sheet

The work sheet provides the information needed for preparation of the financial statements without reference to the ledger or other records. In addition, the data have been sorted into appropriate columns, which facilitates the preparation of the statements.

The financial statements prepared from the 10-column work sheet illustrated are: Income Statement for the Year Ended December 31, 2002 (Illustration 3-26), Statement of Retained Earnings for the Year Ended December 31, 2002 (Illustration 3-27), and Balance Sheet as of December 31, 2002 (Illustration 3-28), as shown below and on the next page.

ILLUSTRATION 3-26
An Income Statement

UPTOWN CABINET CORP. Income Statement For the Year Ended December 31, 2002			
Net sales			$400,000
Cost of goods sold			316,000
Gross profit on sales			84,000
Selling expenses			
Sales salaries expense		$20,000	
Advertising expense		2,200	
Traveling expense		8,000	
Total selling expenses		30,200	
Administrative expenses			
Salaries, office and general	$19,000		
Telephone and Internet expense	600		
Rent expense	4,300		
Property tax expense	5,300		
Depreciation expense—furniture and equipment	6,700		
Bad debt expense	1,000		
Insurance expense	360		
Total administrative expenses		37,260	
Total selling and administrative expenses			67,460
Income from operations			16,540
Other revenues and gains			
Interest revenue			800
Other expenses and losses			17,340
Interest expense			1,700
Income before income taxes			15,640
Income taxes			3,440
Net income			$ 12,200
Earnings per share			$1.22

ILLUSTRATION 3-27
A Statement of Retained Earnings

UPTOWN CABINET CORP. Statement of Retained Earnings For the Year Ended December 31, 2002	
Retained earnings, Jan. 1, 2002	$14,200
Add net income for 2002	12,200
Retained earnings, Dec. 31, 2002	$26,400

Income Statement

The income statement presented is that of a trading or merchandising concern; if a manufacturing concern were illustrated, three inventory accounts would be involved: raw materials, work in process, and finished goods. When these accounts are used, a supplementary statement entitled Cost of Goods Manufactured must be prepared.

ILLUSTRATION 3-28
A Balance Sheet

UPTOWN CABINET CORP. Balance Sheet As of December 31, 2002			
Assets			
Current assets			
Cash			$ 1,200
Notes receivable	$16,000		
Accounts receivable	41,000		
Interest receivable	800	$57,800	
Less: Allowance for doubtful accounts		3,000	54,800
Merchandise inventory			40,000
Prepaid insurance			540
Prepaid rent			500
Total current assets			97,040
Property, plant, and equipment			
Furniture and equipment		67,000	
Less: Accumulated depreciation		18,700	
Total property, plant, and equipment			48,300
Total assets			$145,340
Liabilities and Stockholders' Equity			
Current liabilities			
Notes payable			$ 20,000
Accounts payable			13,500
Property tax payable			2,000
Income tax payable			3,440
Total current liabilities			38,940
Long-term liabilities			
Bonds payable, due June 30, 2007			30,000
Total liabilities			68,940
Stockholders' equity			
Common stock, $5.00 par value, issued and outstanding, 10,000 shares		$50,000	
Retained earnings		26,400	
Total stockholders' equity			76,400
Total liabilities and stockholders' equity			$145,340

Statement of Retained Earnings

The net income earned by a corporation may be retained in the business or it may be distributed to stockholders by payment of dividends. In the illustration the net income earned during the year was added to the balance of retained earnings on January 1, thereby increasing the balance of retained earnings to $26,400 on December 31. No dividends were declared during the year.

Balance Sheet

The balance sheet prepared from the 10-column work sheet contains new items resulting from year-end adjusting entries. Interest receivable, unexpired insurance, and prepaid rent expense are included as current assets. These assets are considered current because they will be converted into cash or consumed in the ordinary routine of the business within a relatively short period of time. The amount of Allowance for Doubtful Accounts is deducted from the total of accounts, notes, and interest receivable because it is estimated that only $54,800 of $57,800 will be collected in cash.

In the property, plant, and equipment section the accumulated depreciation is deducted from the cost of the furniture and equipment; the difference represents the book or carrying value of the furniture and equipment.

Property tax payable is shown as a current liability because it is an obligation that is payable within a year. Other short-term accrued liabilities would also be shown as current liabilities.

The bonds payable, due in 2007, are long-term liabilities and are shown in a separate section. (Interest on the bonds was paid on December 31.)

Because Uptown Cabinet Corp. is a corporation, the capital section of the balance sheet, called the stockholders' equity section in the illustration, is somewhat different from the capital section for a proprietorship. Total stockholders' equity consists of the common stock, which is the original investment by stockholders, and the earnings retained in the business.

Closing Entries

The entries for the closing process are as follows:

General Journal
December 31, 2002

Interest Revenue	800	
Sales	400,000	
Cost of Goods Sold		316,000
Sales Salaries Expense		20,000
Advertising Expense		2,200
Traveling Expense		8,000
Salaries, Office and General		19,000
Telephone and Internet Expense		600
Rent Expense		4,300
Property Tax Expense		5,300
Depreciation Expense—Furniture and Equipment		6,700
Bad Debt Expense		1,000
Insurance Expense		360
Interest Expense		1,700
Income Tax Expense		3,440
Income Summary		12,200
(To close revenues and expenses to Income Summary)		
Income Summary	12,200	
Retained Earnings		12,200
(To close Income Summary to Retained Earnings)		

Monthly Statements, Yearly Closing

The use of a work sheet at the end of each month or quarter permits the preparation of interim financial statements even though the books are closed only at the end of each year. For example, assume that a business closes its books on December 31 but that monthly financial statements are desired. At the end of January a work sheet similar to the one illustrated in this chapter can be prepared to supply the information needed for statements for January. At the end of February a work sheet can be used again. Note that because the accounts were not closed at the end of January, the income statement taken from the work sheet on February 28 will present the net income for two months. If an income statement for only the month of February is wanted, it can be obtained by subtracting the items in the January income statement from the corresponding items in the income statement for the two months of January and February.

A statement of retained earnings for February only also may be obtained by subtracting the January items. The balance sheet prepared from the February work sheet, however, shows assets, liabilities, and stockholders' equity as of February 28, the specific date for which a balance sheet is desired.

The March work sheet would show the revenues and expenses for three months, and the subtraction of the revenues and expenses for the first two months could be made to supply the amounts needed for an income statement for the month of March only, and so on throughout the year.

SUMMARY OF LEARNING OBJECTIVES

1 **Understand basic accounting terminology.** It is important to understand the following eleven terms. (1) Event. (2) Transaction. (3) Account. (4) Real and nominal accounts. (5) Ledger. (6) Journal. (7) Posting. (8) Trial balance. (9) Adjusting entries. (10) Financial statements. (11) Closing entries.

2 **Explain double-entry rules.** The left side of any account is the debit side; the right side is the credit side. All asset and expense accounts are increased on the left or debit side and decreased on the right or credit side. Conversely, all liability and revenue accounts are increased on the right or credit side and decreased on the left or debit side. Stockholders' equity accounts, Common Stock and Retained Earnings, are increased on the credit side, whereas Dividends is increased on the debit side.

3 **Identify steps in the accounting cycle.** The basic steps in the accounting cycle are (1) identification and measurement of transactions and other events; (2) journalization; (3) posting; (4) unadjusted trial balance; (5) adjustments; (6) adjusted trial balance; (7) statement preparation; and (8) closing.

4 **Record transactions in journals, post to ledger accounts, and prepare a trial balance.** The simplest journal form is a chronological listing of transactions and events expressed in terms of debits and credits to particular accounts. The items entered in a general journal must be transferred (posted) to the general ledger. An unadjusted trial balance should be prepared at the end of a given period after the entries have been recorded in the journal and posted to the ledger.

5 **Explain the reasons for preparing adjusting entries.** Adjustments are necessary to achieve a proper matching of revenues and expenses so as to determine net income for the current period and to achieve an accurate statement of end-of-the-period balances in assets, liabilities, and owners' equity accounts.

6 **Prepare closing entries.** In the closing process all of the revenue and expense account balances (income statement items) are transferred to a clearing account called Income Summary, which is used only at the end of the fiscal year. Revenues and expenses are matched in the Income Summary account. The net result of this matching, which represents the net income or net loss for the period, is then transferred to an owners' equity account (retained earnings for a corporation and capital accounts for proprietorships and partnerships).

7 **Explain how inventory accounts are adjusted at year-end.** Under a perpetual inventory system the balance in the Inventory account should represent the ending inventory amount. When the inventory records are maintained in a periodic inventory system, a Purchases account is used; the Inventory account is unchanged during the period. The Inventory account represents the beginning inventory amount throughout the period. At the end of the accounting period the inventory account must be adjusted by closing out the beginning inventory amount and recording the ending inventory amount.

8 **Prepare a 10-column work sheet.** The 10-column work sheet provides columns for the first trial balance, adjustments, adjusted trial balance, income statement, and balance sheet. The work sheet does not replace the financial statements. Instead, it is the accountant's informal device for accumulating and sorting information needed for the financial statements.

KEY TERMS

account, *69*
accounting cycle, *73*
accounting information system, *68*
accrued expenses, *84*
accrued revenues, *83*
adjusted trial balance, *69*
adjusting entry, *78*
balance sheet, *69*
book value, *82*
closing entries, *69*
closing process, *88*
contra asset account, *82*
credit, *70*
debit, *70*
depreciation, *81*
double-entry accounting, *70*
event, *69*
financial statements, *69*
general journal, *75*
general ledger, *75*
income statement, *69*
journal, *69*
ledger, *69*
nominal accounts, *69*
periodic inventory system, *89*
perpetual inventory system, *89*
post-closing trial balance, *69*
posting, *76*
prepaid expense, *79*
real accounts, *69*
reversing entries, *90*
special journals, *75*
statement of cash flows, *69*
statement of retained earnings, *69*
T-account, *75*
transaction, *69*
trial balance, *76*
unearned revenues, *82*
useful life, *81*
work sheet, *91*

APPENDIX 3A

Cash Basis Accounting versus Accrual Basis Accounting

DIFFERENCES BETWEEN CASH AND ACCRUAL BASES

OBJECTIVE 9
After studying Appendix 3A, you should be able to: Differentiate the cash basis of accounting from the accrual basis of accounting.

Most companies use the **accrual basis of accounting**: they recognize revenue when it is earned and recognize expenses in the period incurred, without regard to the time of receipt or payment of cash. Some small enterprises and the average individual taxpayer, however, use a strict or modified cash basis approach. Under the **strict cash basis of accounting**, revenue is recorded only when the cash is received and expenses are recorded only when the cash is paid. The determination of income on the cash basis rests upon the collection of revenue and the payment of expenses, and the revenue recognition and the matching principles are ignored. Consequently, cash basis financial statements are not in conformity with generally accepted accounting principles.

To illustrate and contrast accrual basis accounting and cash basis accounting, assume that Quality Contractor signs an agreement to construct a garage for $22,000. In January, Quality Contractor begins construction, incurs costs of $18,000 on credit, and by the end of January delivers a finished garage to the buyer. In February, Quality Contractor collects $22,000 cash from the customer. In March, Quality pays the $18,000 due the creditors. The net incomes for each month under cash basis accounting and accrual basis accounting are as follows:

ILLUSTRATION 3A-1
Income Statement—Cash Basis

QUALITY CONTRACTOR
Income Statement—Cash Basis
For the Month of

	January	February	March	Total
Cash receipts	$ –0–	$22,000	$ –0–	$22,000
Cash payments	–0–	–0–	18,000	18,000
Net income (loss)	$ –0–	$22,000	$(18,000)	$ 4,000

ILLUSTRATION 3A-2
Income Statement—Accrual Basis

QUALITY CONTRACTOR
Income Statement—Accrual Basis
For the Month of

	January	February	March	Total
Revenues	$22,000	$ –0–	$ –0–	$22,000
Expenses	18,000	–0–	–0–	18,000
Net income (loss)	$ 4,000	$ –0–	$ –0–	$ 4,000

For the three months combined, total net income is the same under both cash basis accounting and accrual basis accounting; the difference is in the **timing** of net income.

The balance sheet is also affected by the basis of accounting. For instance, if cash basis accounting were used, Quality Contractor's balance sheets at each month-end would appear as follows:

ILLUSTRATION 3A-3
Balance Sheets—Cash Basis

QUALITY CONTRACTOR
Balance Sheets—Cash Basis
As of

	January 31	February 28	March 31
Assets			
Cash	$ –0–	$22,000	$4,000
Total assets	$ –0–	$22,000	$4,000
Liabilities and Owners' Equity			
Owners' equity	$ –0–	$22,000	$4,000
Total liabilities and owners' equity	$ –0–	$22,000	$4,000

If accrual basis accounting were used, Quality Contractor's balance sheets at each month-end would appear as follows:

ILLUSTRATION 3A-4
Balance Sheets—Accrual Basis

QUALITY CONTRACTOR
Balance Sheets—Accrual Basis
As of

	January 31	February 28	March 31
Assets			
Cash	$ –0–	$22,000	$4,000
Accounts receivable	22,000	–0–	–0–
Total assets	$22,000	$22,000	$4,000
Liabilities and Owners' Equity			
Accounts payable	$18,000	$18,000	$ –0–
Owners' equity	4,000	4,000	4,000
Total liabilities and owners' equity	$22,000	$22,000	$4,000

An analysis of the preceding income statements and balance sheets shows the ways in which cash basis accounting is inconsistent with basic accounting theory:

1. The cash basis understates revenues and assets from the construction and delivery of the garage in January. It ignores the $22,000 accounts receivable, representing a near-term future cash inflow.
2. The cash basis understates expenses incurred with the construction of the garage and the liability outstanding at the end of January. It ignores the $18,000 accounts payable, representing a near-term future cash outflow.
3. The cash basis understates owners' equity in January by not recognizing the revenues and the asset until February, and it overstates owners' equity in February by not recognizing the expenses and the liability until March.

In short, cash basis accounting violates the theory underlying the elements of financial statements.

The **modified cash basis**, a mixture of cash basis and accrual basis, is the method often followed by professional services firms (doctors, lawyers, accountants, consultants) and by retail, real estate, and agricultural operations. It is the pure cash basis of accounting with modifications that have substantial support, such as capitalizing and depreciating plant assets or recording inventory.[1]

CONVERSION FROM CASH BASIS TO ACCRUAL BASIS

Not infrequently a cash basis or a modified cash basis set of financial statements is converted to the accrual basis for presentation to investors and creditors. To illustrate this conversion, assume that Dr. Diane Windsor keeps her accounting records on a cash basis. In the year 2002, Dr. Windsor received $300,000 from her patients and paid $170,000 for operating expenses, resulting in an excess of cash receipts over disbursements of $130,000 ($300,000 − $170,000). At January 1 and December 31, 2002, she has accounts receivable, unearned service revenue, accrued liabilities, and prepaid expenses as follows:

ILLUSTRATION 3A-5
Financial Information Related to Dr. Diane Windsor

	January 1, 2002	December 31, 2002
Accounts receivable	$12,000	$9,000
Unearned service revenue	–0–	4,000
Accrued liabilities	2,000	5,500
Prepaid expenses	1,800	2,700

Service Revenue Computation

To convert the amount of cash received from patients to service revenue on an accrual basis, changes in accounts receivable and unearned service revenue during the year must be considered. Accounts receivable at the beginning of the year represents revenues earned last year that are collected this year. Ending accounts receivable indicates revenues earned this year that are not yet collected. Therefore, beginning accounts receivable is subtracted and ending accounts receivable is added to arrive at revenue on an accrual basis, as shown in Illustration 3A-6.

ILLUSTRATION 3A-6
Conversion of Cash Receipts to Revenue— Accounts Receivable

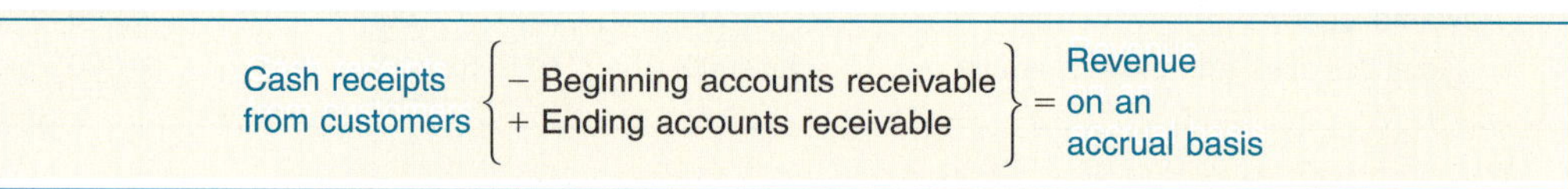

Using similar analysis, beginning unearned service revenue represents cash received last year for revenues earned this year. Ending unearned service revenue results from collections this year that will be recognized as revenue next year. Therefore, beginning unearned service revenue is added and ending unearned service revenue is subtracted to arrive at revenue on an accrual basis, as shown in Illustration 3A-7.

---

[1]A cash or modified cash basis might be used in the following situations:

(1) A company that is primarily interested in cash flows (for example, a group of physicians that distributes cash-basis earnings for salaries and bonuses).

(2) A company that has a limited number of financial statement users (small, closely held company with little or no debt).

(3) A company that has operations that are relatively straightforward (small amounts of inventory, long-term assets, or long-term debt).

Cash receipts from customers	+ Beginning unearned service revenue − Ending unearned service revenue	= Revenue on an accrual basis

ILLUSTRATION 3A-7
Conversion of Cash Receipts to Revenue—Unearned Service Revenue

Cash collected from customers, therefore, is converted to service revenue on an accrual basis as follows:

Cash receipts from customers		$300,000
− Beginning accounts receivable	$(12,000)	
+ Ending accounts receivable	9,000	
+ Beginning unearned service revenue	−0−	
− Ending unearned service revenue	(4,000)	(7,000)
Service revenue (accrual)		$293,000

ILLUSTRATION 3A-8
Conversion of Cash Receipts to Service Revenue

Operating Expense Computation

To convert cash paid for operating expenses during the year to operating expenses on an accrual basis, you must consider changes in prepaid expenses and accrued liabilities during the year. Beginning prepaid expenses should be recognized as expenses this year. (The cash payment occurred last year.) Therefore, the beginning prepaid expenses balance is added to cash paid for operating expenses to arrive at operating expense on an accrual basis.

Conversely, ending prepaid expenses result from cash payments made this year for expenses to be reported next year. (The expense recognition is deferred to a future period.) As a result, ending prepaid expenses are deducted from cash paid for expenses, as shown in Illustration 3A-9.

Cash paid for operating expenses	+ Beginning prepaid expenses − Ending prepaid expenses	= Expenses on an accrual basis

ILLUSTRATION 3A-9
Conversion of Cash Payments to Expenses—Prepaid Expenses

Using similar analysis, beginning accrued liabilities result from expenses recognized last year that require cash payments this year. Ending accrued liabilities relate to expenses recognized this year that have not been paid. Beginning accrued liabilities, therefore, are deducted and ending accrued liabilities added to cash paid for expenses to arrive at expense on an accrual basis, as shown in Illustration 3A-10.

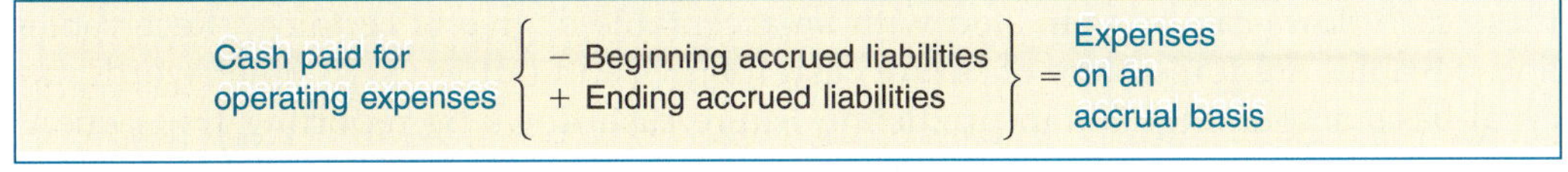

Cash paid for operating expenses	− Beginning accrued liabilities + Ending accrued liabilities	= Expenses on an accrual basis

ILLUSTRATION 3A-10
Conversion of Cash Payments to Expenses—Accrued Liabilities

Cash paid for operating expenses, therefore, is converted to operating expenses on an accrual basis for Dr. Diane Windsor as follows:

Cash paid for operating expenses		$170,000
+ Beginning prepaid expense	$1,800	
− Ending prepaid expense	(2,700)	
− Beginning accrued liabilities	(2,000)	
+ Ending accrued liabilities	5,500	2,600
Operating expenses (accrual)		$172,600

ILLUSTRATION 3A-11
Conversion of Cash Paid to Operating Expenses

This entire conversion can be shown in work sheet form as follows:

ILLUSTRATION 3A-12
Conversion of Statement of Cash Receipts and Disbursements to Income Statement

DIANE WINDSOR, D.D.S.
Conversion of Income Statement Data from Cash Basis to Accrual Basis
For the Year 2002

	Cash Basis	Adjustments Add	Adjustments Deduct	Accrual Basis
Collections from customers	$300,000			
− Accounts receivable, Jan. 1			$12,000	
+ Accounts receivable, Dec. 31		$9,000		
+ Unearned service revenue, Jan. 1		—	—	
− Unearned service revenue, Dec. 31			4,000	
Service revenue				$293,000
Disbursement for expenses	170,000			
+ Prepaid expenses, Jan. 1		1,800		
− Prepaid expenses, Dec. 31			2,700	
− Accrued liabilities, Jan. 1			2,000	
+ Accrued liabilities, Dec. 31		5,500		
Operating expenses				172,600
Excess of cash collections over disbursements—cash basis	$130,000			
Net income—accrual basis				$120,400

Using this approach, collections and disbursements on a cash basis are adjusted to revenue and expense on an accrual basis to arrive at accrual net income. In any conversion from the cash basis to the accrual basis, depreciation or amortization expense is an expense in arriving at net income on an accrual basis.

THEORETICAL WEAKNESSES OF THE CASH BASIS

The cash basis does report exactly when cash is received and when cash is disbursed. To many people that information represents something solid, something concrete. Isn't cash what it is all about? Does it make sense to invent something, design it, produce it, market and sell it, if you aren't going to get cash for it in the end? It is frequently said, "Cash is the real bottom line." It is also said, "Cash is the oil that lubricates the economy." If so, then what is the merit of accrual accounting?

Today's economy is considerably more lubricated by credit than by cash. And the accrual basis, not the cash basis, recognizes all aspects of the credit phenomenon. Investors, creditors, and other decision makers seek timely information about an enterprise's future cash flows. Accrual basis accounting provides this information by reporting the cash inflows and outflows associated with earnings activities as soon as these cash flows can be estimated with an acceptable degree of certainty. Receivables and payables are forecasters of future cash inflows and outflows. In other words, accrual basis accounting aids in predicting future cash flows by reporting transactions and other events with cash consequences at the time the transactions and events occur, rather than when the cash is received and paid.

KEY TERMS

accrual basis, *98*
modified cash basis, *100*
strict cash basis, *98*

SUMMARY OF LEARNING OBJECTIVE FOR APPENDIX 3A

9 **Differentiate the cash basis of accounting from the accrual basis of accounting.** Accrual basis accounting provides information about cash inflows and outflows associated with earnings activities as soon as these cash flows can be estimated with an acceptable degree of certainty. That is, accrual basis accounting aids in predicting future cash flows by reporting transactions and events with cash consequences at the time the transactions and events occur, rather than when the cash is received and paid.

APPENDIX 3B

Using Reversing Entries

The purpose of reversing entries is to simplify the recording of transactions in the next accounting period. The use of reversing entries does not change the amounts reported in the financial statements for the previous period.

OBJECTIVE 10
After studying Appendix 3B, you should be able to: Identify adjusting entries that may be reversed.

ILLUSTRATION OF REVERSING ENTRIES—ACCRUALS

Reversing entries are most often used to reverse two types of adjusting entries: accrued revenues and accrued expenses. To illustrate the optional use of reversing entries for accrued expenses, we will use the following transaction and adjustment data:

1. October 24 (initial salary entry): $4,000 of salaries incurred between October 1 and October 24 are paid.
2. October 31 (adjusting entry): Salaries incurred between October 25 and October 31 are $1,200. These will be paid in the November 8 payroll.
3. November 8 (subsequent salary entry): Salaries paid are $2,500. Of this amount, $1,200 applied to accrued wages payable at October 31 and $1,300 was incurred between November 1 and November 8.

The comparative entries are shown in Illustration 3B-1.

ILLUSTRATION 3B-1
Comparison of Entries for Accruals, with and without Reversing Entries

Reversing Entries Not Used				Reversing Entries Used			
Initial Salary Entry							
Oct. 24	Salaries Expense	4,000		Oct. 24	Salaries Expense	4,000	
	Cash		4,000		Cash		4,000
Adjusting Entry							
Oct. 31	Salaries Expense	1,200		Oct. 31	Salaries Expense	1,200	
	Salaries Payable		1,200		Salaries Payable		1,200
Closing Entry							
Oct. 31	Income Summary	5,200		Oct. 31	Income Summary	5,200	
	Salaries Expense		5,200		Salaries Expense		5,200
Reversing Entry							
Nov. 1	No entry is made.			Nov. 1	Salaries Payable	1,200	
					Salaries Expense		1,200
Subsequent Salary Entry							
Nov. 8	Salaries Payable	1,200		Nov. 8	Salaries Expense	2,500	
	Salaries Expense	1,300			Cash		2,500
	Cash		2,500				

The comparative entries show that the first three entries are the same whether or not reversing entries are used. The last two entries, however, are different. The November 1 reversing entry eliminates the $1,200 balance in Salaries Payable that was created by the October 31 adjusting entry. The reversing entry also creates a $1,200 credit balance in the Salaries Expense account. As you know, it is unusual for an expense account to have a credit balance; however, the balance is correct in this instance. It is correct because the entire amount of the first salary payment in the new accounting period will be debited to Salaries Expense. This debit will eliminate the credit balance, and the resulting debit balance in the expense account will equal the salaries expense incurred in the new accounting period ($1,300 in this example).

When reversing entries are made, all cash payments of expenses can be debited to the expense account. This means that on November 8 (and every payday) Salaries Expense can be debited for the amount paid without regard to the existence of any accrued salaries payable. Being able to make the same entry each time simplifies the recording process in an accounting system.

ILLUSTRATION OF REVERSING ENTRIES—PREPAYMENTS

Up to this point, we have assumed that all prepayments are recorded as prepaid expense or unearned revenue. In some cases, prepayments are recorded directly in expense or revenue accounts. When this occurs, prepayments may also be reversed. To illustrate the use of reversing entries for prepaid expenses, we will use the following transaction and adjustment data:

1. December 10 (initial entry): $20,000 of office supplies are purchased with cash.
2. December 31 (adjusting entry): $5,000 of office supplies on hand.

The comparative entries are shown in Illustration 3B-2.

Reversing Entries Not Used				Reversing Entries Used			
Initial Purchase of Supplies Entry							
Dec. 10	Office Supplies	20,000		Dec. 10	Office Supplies Expense	20,000	
	Cash		20,000		Cash		20,000
Adjusting Entry							
Dec. 31	Office Supplies Expense	15,000		Dec. 31	Office Supplies	5,000	
	Office Supplies		15,000		Office Supplies Expense		5,000
Closing Entry							
Dec. 31	Income Summary	15,000		Dec. 31	Income Summary	15,000	
	Office Supplies Expense		15,000		Office Supplies Expense		15,000
Reversing Entry							
Jan. 1	No entry			Jan. 1	Office Supplies Expense	5,000	
					Office Supplies		5,000

ILLUSTRATION 3B-2
Comparison of Entries for Prepayments, with and without Reversing Entries

After the adjusting entry on December 31 (regardless of whether reversing entries are used) the asset account Office Supplies shows a balance of $5,000 and Office Supplies Expense a balance of $15,000. If Office Supplies Expense initially was debited when the supplies were purchased, a reversing entry is made to return to the expense account the cost of unconsumed supplies. The company then continues to debit Office Supplies Expense for additional purchases of office supplies during the next period.

With respect to prepaid items, why are all such items not entered originally into real accounts (assets and liabilities), thus making reversing entries unnecessary? Sometimes this practice is followed. It is particularly advantageous for items that need to be apportioned over several periods (e.g., supplies and parts inventories). However, items that do not follow this regular pattern and that may or may not involve two or more periods are ordinarily entered initially in revenue or expense accounts. The revenue and expense accounts may not require adjusting and are systematically closed to Income Summary. Using the nominal accounts adds consistency to the accounting system and makes the recording more efficient, particularly when a large number of such transactions occur during the year. For example, the bookkeeper knows that when an invoice is received for other than a capital asset acquisition, the amount is expensed. The bookkeeper need not worry at the time the invoice is received whether or not the item will result in a prepaid expense at the end of the period, because adjustments will be made at the end of the period.

SUMMARY OF REVERSING ENTRIES

A summary of guidelines for reversing entries is as follows:

1. All accrued items should be reversed.
2. All prepaid items for which the original cash transaction was debited or credited to an expense or revenue account should be reversed.
3. Adjusting entries for depreciation and bad debts are not reversed.

Recognize that reversing entries do not have to be used; therefore, some accountants avoid them entirely.

SUMMARY OF LEARNING OBJECTIVE FOR APPENDIX 3B

10 **Identify adjusting entries that may be reversed.** Reversing entries are most often used to reverse two types of adjusting entries: accrued revenues and accrued expenses. Prepayments may also be reversed if the initial entry to record the transaction is made to an expense or revenue account.

Note: All **asterisked** Questions, Exercises, Problems, and Cases relate to material contained in an appendix to the chapter.

QUESTIONS

1 Give an example of a transaction that results in

(a) A decrease in an asset and a decrease in a liability.

(b) A decrease in one asset and an increase in another asset.

(c) A decrease in one liability and an increase in another liability.

2 Do the following events represent business transactions? Explain your answer in each case.

(a) A computer is purchased on account.

(b) A customer returns merchandise and is given credit on account.

(c) A prospective employee is interviewed.

(d) The owner of the business withdraws cash from the business for personal use.

(e) Merchandise is ordered for delivery next month.

3 Name the accounts debited and credited for each of the following transactions:

(a) Billing a customer for work done.

(b) Receipt of cash from customer on account.

(c) Purchase of office supplies on account.

(d) Purchase of 15 gallons of gasoline for the delivery truck.

4 Why are revenue and expense accounts called temporary or nominal accounts?

5 Omar Morena, a fellow student, contends that the double-entry system means that each transaction must be recorded twice. Is Omar correct? Explain.

6 Is it necessary that a trial balance be taken periodically? What purpose does it serve?

7 Indicate whether each of the items below is a real or nominal account and whether it appears in the balance sheet or the income statement.

(a) Prepaid Rent.

(b) Salaries and Wages Payable.

(c) Merchandise Inventory.

(d) Accumulated Depreciation.

(e) Office Equipment.

(f) Income from Services.

(g) Office Salaries Expense.

(h) Supplies on Hand.

8 Employees are paid every Saturday for the preceding work week. If a balance sheet is prepared on Wednesday, December 31, what does the amount of wages earned during the first three days of the week (12/29, 12/30, 12/31) represent? Explain.

9 (a) How do the components of revenues and expenses differ between a merchandising company and a service enterprise? (b) Explain the income measurement process of a merchandising company.

10 What is the purpose of the Cost of Goods Sold account (assume a periodic inventory system)?

11 Under a perpetual system, what is the purpose of the Cost of Goods Sold account?

12 If the cost of a new microcomputer and printer ($3,900) purchased for office use were recorded as a debit to Purchases, what would be the effect of the error on the balance sheet and income statement in the period in which the error was made?

13 What differences are there between the trial balance before closing and the trial balance after closing with respect to the following?

(a) Accounts Payable.
(b) Expense accounts.
(c) Revenue accounts.
(d) Retained Earnings account.
(e) Cash.

14 What are "adjusting entries" and why are they necessary?

15 What are "closing entries" and why are they necessary?

16 Paul Molitor, maintenance supervisor for Blue Jay Insurance Co., has purchased a riding lawnmower and accessories to be used in maintaining the grounds around corporate headquarters. He has sent the following information to the accounting department:

Cost of mower and accessories	$3,000	Date purchased	7/1/01
Estimated useful life	5 yrs	Monthly salary of groundskeeper	$1,100
		Estimated annual fuel cost	$150

Compute the amount of depreciation expense (related to the mower and accessories) that should be reported on Blue Jay's December 31, 2001, income statement. Assume straight-line depreciation.

17 Selanne Enterprises made the following entry on December 31, 2001.

Dec. 31, 2001	Interest Expense	10,000	
	Interest Payable		10,000
	(To record interest expense due on loan from Anaheim National Bank.)		

What entry would Anaheim National Bank make regarding its outstanding loan to Selanne Enterprises? Explain why this must be the case.

18 "A worksheet is a permanent accounting record, and its use is required in the accounting cycle." Do you agree? Explain.

***19** Distinguish between cash basis accounting and accrual basis accounting. Why for most business enterprises is accrual basis accounting acceptable and the cash basis unacceptable in the preparation of an income statement and a balance sheet?

***20** Why are beginning accrued wages subtracted from, and ending accrued wages added to, wages paid during the year when wages expense for the year is computed?

***21** List two types of transactions that would receive different accounting treatment using (a) strict cash basis accounting and (b) a modified cash basis.

***22** What are reversing entries, and why are they used?

BRIEF EXERCISES

BE3-1 Transactions for Argot Company for the month of May are presented below. Prepare journal entries for each of these transactions. (You may omit explanations.)

May	1	B.D. Argot invests $3,000 cash in exchange for common stock in a small welding corporation.
	3	Buys equipment on account for $1,100.
	13	Pays $400 to landlord for May rent.
	21	Bills Noble Corp. $500 for welding work done.

BE3-2 Brett Favre Repair Shop had the following transactions during the first month of business. Journalize the transactions.

August	2	Invested $12,000 cash and $2,500 of equipment in the business.
	7	Purchased supplies on account for $400. (Debit asset account.)
	12	Performed services for clients, for which $1,300 was collected in cash and $670 was billed to the clients.
	15	Paid August rent, $600.
	19	Counted supplies and determined that only $270 of the supplies purchased on August 7 are still on hand.

BE3-3 On July 1, 2002, Blair Co. pays $18,000 to Hindi Insurance Co. for a 3-year insurance contract. Both companies have fiscal years ending December 31. For Blair Co. journalize the entry on July 1 and the adjusting entry on December 31.

BE3-4 Using the data in BE3-3, journalize the entry on July 1 and the adjusting entry on December 31 for Hindi Insurance Co. Hindi uses the accounts Unearned Insurance Revenue and Insurance Revenue.

BE3-5 On August 1, George Bell Company paid $8,400 in advance for 2 years' insurance coverage. Prepare Bell's August 1 journal entry and the annual adjusting entry on December 31.

BE3-6 Mogilny Corporation owns a warehouse. On November 1, it rented storage space to a lessee (tenant) for 3 months for a total cash payment of $2,700 received in advance. Prepare Mogilny's November 1 journal entry and the December 31 annual adjusting entry.

BE3-7 Catherine Janeway Company's weekly payroll, paid on Fridays, totals $6,000. Employees work a 5-day week. Prepare Janeway's adjusting entry on Wednesday, December 31 and the journal entry to record the $6,000 cash payment on Friday, January 2.

BE3-8 Included in Martinez Company's December 31 trial balance is a note receivable of $10,000. The note is a 4-month, 12% note dated October 1. Prepare Martinez's December 31 adjusting entry to record $300 of accrued interest, and the February 1 journal entry to record receipt of $10,400 from the borrower.

BE3-9 Prepare the following adjusting entries at December 31 for DeGads Co.

1. Interest on notes payable of $400 is accrued.
2. Fees earned but unbilled total $1,400.
3. Salaries earned by employees of $700 have not been recorded.
4. Bad debt expense for year is $900.

Use the following account titles: Service Revenue, Accounts Receivable, Interest Expense, Interest Payable, Salaries Expense, Salaries Payable, Allowance for Doubtful Accounts, and Bad Debt Expense.

BE3-10 At the end of its first year of operations, the trial balance of Rafael Company shows Equipment $30,000 and zero balances in Accumulated Depreciation—Equipment and Depreciation Expense. Depreciation for the year is estimated to be $3,000. Prepare the adjusting entry for depreciation at December 31, and indicate the balance sheet presentation for the equipment at December 31.

BE3-11 Willis Corporation has beginning inventory $81,000; Purchases $540,000; Freight-in $16,200; Purchase Returns $5,800; Purchase Discounts $5,000; and ending inventory $70,200. Compute cost of goods sold.

BE3-12 Karen Sepaniak has year-end account balances of Sales $828,900; Interest Revenue $13,500; Cost of Goods Sold $556,200; Operating Expenses $189,000; Income Tax Expense $35,100; and Dividends $18,900. Prepare the year-end closing entries.

***BE3-13** Smith Company had cash receipts from customers in 2002 of $152,000. Cash payments for operating expenses were $97,000. Smith has determined that at January 1, accounts receivable was $13,000, and prepaid expenses were $17,500. At December 31, accounts receivable was $18,600, and prepaid expenses were $23,200. Compute (a) service revenue and (b) operating expenses.

***BE3-14** Pelican Company made a December 31 adjusting entry to debit Salaries Expense and credit Salaries Payable for $3,600. On January 2, Pelican paid the weekly payroll of $6,000. Prepare Pelican's (a) January 1 reversing entry, (b) January 2 entry (assuming the reversing entry was prepared), and (c) January 2 entry (assuming the reversing entry was not prepared).

EXERCISES

E3-1 (Transaction Analysis—Service Company) Beverly Crusher is a licensed CPA. During the first month of operations of her business (a sole proprietorship), the following events and transactions occurred.

April	2	Invested $32,000 cash and equipment valued at $14,000 in the business.
	2	Hired a secretary-receptionist at a salary of $290 per week payable monthly.
	3	Purchased supplies on account $700 (debit an asset account).
	7	Paid office rent of $600 for the month.
	11	Completed a tax assignment and billed client $1,100 for services rendered. (Use service revenue account.)
	12	Received $3,200 advance on a management consulting engagement.
	17	Received cash of $2,300 for services completed for Ferengi Co.
	21	Paid insurance expense $110.
	30	Paid secretary-receptionist $1,160 for the month.
	30	A count of supplies indicated that $120 of supplies had been used.
	30	Purchased a new computer for $6,100 with personal funds. (The computer will be used exclusively for business purposes.)

Instructions

Journalize the transactions in the general journal (omit explanations).

E3-2 (Corrected Trial Balance) The trial balance of Wanda Landowska Company shown below does not balance. Your review of the ledger reveals the following: (a) each account had a normal balance, (b) the debit footings in Prepaid Insurance, Accounts Payable, and Property Tax Expense were each understated $100, (c) transposition errors were made in Accounts Receivable and Service Revenue; the correct balances are $2,750 and $6,690, respectively, (d) a debit posting to Advertising Expense of $300 was omitted, and (e) a $1,500 cash drawing by the owner was debited to Wanda Landowska, Capital, and credited to Cash.

WANDA LANDOWSKA COMPANY
Trial Balance
April 30, 2001

	Debit	Credit
Cash	$ 4,800	
Accounts Receivable	2,570	
Prepaid Insurance	700	
Equipment		$ 8,000
Accounts Payable		4,500
Property Tax Payable	560	
Wanda Landowska, Capital		11,200
Service Revenue	6,960	
Salaries Expense	4,200	
Advertising Expense	1,100	
Property Tax Expense		800
	$20,890	$24,500

Instructions

Prepare a correct trial balance.

E3-3 (Corrected Trial Balance) The trial balance of Blues Traveler Corporation does not balance.

BLUES TRAVELER CORPORATION
Trial Balance
April 30

	Debit	Credit
Cash	$ 5,912	
Accounts Receivable	5,240	
Supplies on Hand	2,967	
Furniture and Equipment	6,100	
Accounts Payable		$ 7,044
Common Stock		8,000
Retained Earnings		2,000
Service Revenue		5,200
Office Expense	4,320	
	$24,539	$22,244

An examination of the ledger shows these errors.

1. Cash received from a customer on account was recorded (both debit and credit) as $1,380 instead of $1,830.
2. The purchase on account of a computer costing $3,200 was recorded as a debit to Office Expense and a credit to Accounts Payable.
3. Services were performed on account for a client, $2,250, for which Accounts Receivable was debited $2,250 and Service Revenue was credited $225.
4. A payment of $95 for telephone charges was entered as a debit to Office Expenses and a debit to Cash.
5. The Service Revenue account was totaled at $5,200 instead of $5,280.

Instructions

From this information prepare a corrected trial balance.

E3-4 (Corrected Trial Balance) The trial balance of Antoine Watteau Co. shown below does not balance.

ANTOINE WATTEAU CO.
Trial Balance
June 30, 2002

	Debit	Credit
Cash		$ 2,870
Accounts Receivable	$ 3,231	
Supplies	800	
Equipment	3,800	
Accounts Payable		2,666
Unearned Service Revenue	1,200	
Common Stock		6,000
Retained Earnings		3,000
Service Revenue		2,380
Wages Expense	3,400	
Office Expense	940	
	$13,371	$16,916

Each of the listed accounts has a normal balance per the general ledger. An examination of the ledger and journal reveals the following errors.

1. Cash received from a customer on account was debited for $570 and Accounts Receivable was credited for the same amount. The actual collection was for $750.
2. The purchase of a computer printer on account for $500 was recorded as a debit to Supplies for $500 and a credit to Accounts Payable for $500.
3. Services were performed on account for a client for $890. Accounts Receivable was debited for $890 and Service Revenue was credited for $89.
4. A payment of $65 for telephone charges was recorded as a debit to Office Expense for $65 and a debit to Cash for $65.
5. When the Unearned Service Revenue account was reviewed, it was found that $325 of the balance was earned prior to June 30.
6. A debit posting to Wages Expense of $670 was omitted.
7. A payment on account for $206 was credited to Cash for $206 and credited to Accounts Payable for $260.
8. A dividend of $575 was debited to Wages Expense for $575 and credited to Cash for $575.

Instructions

Prepare a correct trial balance. (Note: It may be necessary to add one or more accounts to the trial balance.)

E3-5 (Adjusting Entries) The ledger of Duggan Rental Agency on March 31 of the current year includes the following selected accounts before adjusting entries have been prepared.

	Debit	Credit
Prepaid Insurance	$ 3,600	
Supplies	2,800	
Equipment	25,000	
Accumulated Depreciation—Equipment		$ 8,400
Notes Payable		20,000
Unearned Rent Revenue		9,300
Rent Revenue		60,000
Interest Expense	–0–	
Wage Expense	14,000	

An analysis of the accounts shows the following:

1. The equipment depreciates $250 per month.
2. One-third of the unearned rent was earned during the quarter.
3. Interest of $500 is accrued on the notes payable.

4. Supplies on hand total $850.
5. Insurance expires at the rate of $300 per month.

Instructions

Prepare the adjusting entries at March 31, assuming that adjusting entries are made quarterly. Additional accounts are: Depreciation Expense, Insurance Expense, Interest Payable, and Supplies Expense.

E3-6 (Adjusting Entries) Karen Weller, D.D.S., opened a dental practice on January 1, 2002. During the first month of operations the following transactions occurred.

1. Performed services for patients who had dental plan insurance. At January 31, $750 of such services was earned but not yet billed to the insurance companies.
2. Utility expenses incurred but not paid prior to January 31 totaled $520.
3. Purchased dental equipment on January 1 for $80,000, paying $20,000 in cash and signing a $60,000, 3-year-note payable. The equipment depreciates $400 per month. Interest is $500 per month.
4. Purchased a one-year malpractice insurance policy on January 1 for $12,000.
5. Purchased $1,600 of dental supplies. On January 31, determined that $500 of supplies were on hand.

Instructions

Prepare the adjusting entries on January 31. Account titles are: Accumulated Depreciation—Dental Equipment, Depreciation Expense, Service Revenue, Accounts Receivable, Insurance Expense, Interest Expense, Interest Payable, Prepaid Insurance, Supplies, Supplies Expense, Utilities Expense, and Utilities Payable.

E3-7 (Analyze Adjusted Data) A partial adjusted trial balance of Piper Company at January 31, 2002, shows the following:

PIPER COMPANY
Adjusted Trial Balance
January 31, 2002

	Debit	Credit
Supplies	$ 700	
Prepaid Insurance	2,400	
Salaries Payable		$ 800
Unearned Revenue		750
Supplies Expense	950	
Insurance Expense	400	
Salaries Expense	1,800	
Service Revenue		2,000

Instructions

Answer the following questions, assuming the year begins January 1:

(a) If the amount in Supplies Expense is the January 31 adjusting entry, and $850 of supplies was purchased in January, what was the balance in Supplies on January 1?

(b) If the amount in Insurance Expense is the January 31 adjusting entry, and the original insurance premium was for one year, what was the total premium and when was the policy purchased?

(c) If $2,500 of salaries was paid in January, what was the balance in Salaries Payable at December 31, 2001?

(d) If $1,600 was received in January for services performed in January, what was the balance in Unearned Revenue at December 31, 2001?

E3-8 (Adjusting Entries) Bjorn Borg is the new owner of Ace Computer Services. At the end of August 2001, his first month of ownership, Bjorn is trying to prepare monthly financial statements. Below is some information related to unrecorded expenses that the business incurred during August.

1. At August 31, Mr. Borg owed his employees $1,900 in wages that would be paid on September 1.
2. At the end of the month he had not yet received the month's utility bill. Based on past experience, he estimated the bill would be approximately $600.
3. On August 1, Mr. Borg borrowed $30,000 from a local bank on a 15-year mortgage. The annual interest rate is 8%.
4. A telephone bill in the amount of $117 covering August charges is unpaid at August 31.

Instructions
Prepare the adjusting journal entries as of August 31, 2001, suggested by the information above.

E3-9 (Adjusting Entries) Selected accounts of Urdu Company are shown below.

Supplies

	Debit		Credit
Beg. Bal.	800	10/31	470

Accounts Receivable

	Debit		Credit
10/17	2,400		
10/31	1,650		

Salaries Expense

	Debit		Credit
10/15	800		
10/31	600		

Salaries Payable

	Debit		Credit
		10/31	600

Unearned Service Revenue

	Debit		Credit
10/31	400	10/20	650

Supplies Expense

	Debit		Credit
10/31	470		

Service Revenue

	Debit		Credit
		10/17	2,400
		10/31	1,650
		10/31	400

Instructions
From an analysis of the T-accounts, reconstruct (a) the October transaction entries, and (b) the adjusting journal entries that were made on October 31, 2001.

E3-10 (Adjusting Entries) Greco Resort opened for business on June 1 with eight air-conditioned units. Its trial balance on August 31 is as follows:

GRECO RESORT
Trial Balance
August 31, 2001

	Debit	Credit
Cash	$ 19,600	
Prepaid Insurance	4,500	
Supplies	2,600	
Land	20,000	
Cottages	120,000	
Furniture	16,000	
Accounts Payable		$ 4,500
Unearned Rent Revenue		4,600
Mortgage Payable		60,000
Common Stock		91,000
Retained Earnings		14,000
Dividends	5,000	
Rent Revenue		76,200
Salaries Expense	44,800	
Utilities Expense	9,200	
Repair Expense	3,600	
	$245,300	$245,300

Other data:

1. The balance in prepaid insurance is a one-year premium paid on June 1, 2001.
2. An inventory count on August 31 shows $450 of supplies on hand.
3. Annual depreciation rates are cottages (4%) and furniture (10%). Salvage value is estimated to be 10% of cost.
4. Unearned Rent Revenue of $3,800 was earned prior to August 31.
5. Salaries of $375 were unpaid at August 31.
6. Rentals of $800 were due from tenants at August 31.
7. The mortgage interest rate is 8% per year.

Instructions
(a) Journalize the adjusting entries on August 31 for the 3-month period June 1–August 31.
(b) Prepare an adjusted trial balance on August 31.

E3-11 (Closing Entries) The adjusted trial balance of Lopez Company shows the following data pertaining to sales at the end of its fiscal year October 31, 2001: Sales $800,000, Freight-out $12,000, Sales Returns and Allowances $24,000, and Sales Discounts $15,000.

Instructions

(a) Prepare the sales revenues section of the income statement.
(b) Prepare separate closing entries for (1) sales, and (2) the contra accounts to sales.

E3-12 (Closing Entries) Presented is information related to Gonzales Corporation for the month of January 2001.

Cost of goods sold	$208,000	Salary expense	$ 61,000
Freight-out	7,000	Sales discounts	8,000
Insurance expense	12,000	Sales returns and allowances	13,000
Rent expense	20,000	Sales	350,000

Instructions

Prepare the necessary closing entries.

E3-13 (Work Sheet) Presented below are selected accounts for Alvarez Company as reported in the work sheet at the end of May 2001.

Accounts	Adjusted Trial Balance		Income Statement		Balance Sheet	
	Dr.	Cr.	Dr.	Cr.	Dr.	Cr.
Cash	9,000					
Merchandise Inventory	80,000					
Sales		450,000				
Sales Returns and Allowances	10,000					
Sales Discounts	5,000					
Cost of Goods Sold	250,000					

Instructions

Complete the work sheet by extending amounts reported in the adjusted trial balance to the appropriate columns in the work sheet. Do not total individual columns.

E3-14 (Missing Amounts) Presented below is financial information for two different companies:

	Alatorre Company	Eduardo Company
Sales	$90,000	(d)
Sales returns	(a)	$ 5,000
Net sales	81,000	95,000
Cost of goods sold	56,000	(e)
Gross profit	(b)	38,000
Operating expenses	15,000	23,000
Net income	(c)	15,000

Instructions

Compute the missing amounts.

E3-15 (Find Missing Amounts—Periodic Inventory) Financial information is presented below for four different companies.

	Pamela's Cosmetics	Dean's Grocery	Anderson Wholesalers	Baywatch Supply Co.
Sales	$78,000	(c)	$144,000	$100,000
Sales returns	(a)	$ 5,000	12,000	9,000
Net sales	74,000	94,000	132,000	(g)
Beginning inventory	16,000	(d)	44,000	24,000
Purchases	88,000	100,000	(e)	85,000

Purchase returns	6,000	10,000	8,000	(h)
Ending inventory	(b)	48,000	30,000	28,000
Cost of goods sold	64,000	72,000	(f)	72,000
Gross profit	10,000	22,000	18,000	(i)

Instructions

Determine the missing amounts (a–i). Show all computations.

E3-16 (Cost of Goods Sold Section—Periodic Inventory) The trial balance of the Neville Mariner Company at the end of its fiscal year, August 31, 2002, includes the following accounts: Merchandise Inventory $17,500, Purchases $149,400, Sales $200,000, Freight-in $4,000, Sales Returns and Allowances $4,000, Freight-out $1,000, and Purchase Returns and Allowances $2,000. The ending merchandise inventory is $25,000.

Instructions

Prepare a cost of goods sold section for the year ending August 31.

E3-17 (Closing Entries for a Corporation) Presented below are selected account balances for Homer Winslow Co. as of December 31, 2002.

Merchandise Inventory 12/31/02	$ 60,000	Cost of Goods Sold	$225,700
Common Stock	75,000	Selling Expenses	16,000
Retained Earnings	45,000	Administrative Expenses	38,000
Dividends	18,000	Income Tax Expense	30,000
Sales Returns and Allowances	12,000		
Sales Discounts	15,000		
Sales	410,000		

Instructions

Prepare closing entries for Homer Winslow Co. on December 31, 2002.

E3-18 (Work Sheet Preparation) The trial balance of R.L. Stein Roofing at March 31, 2002 is as follows:

R.L. STEIN ROOFING
Trial Balance
March 31, 2002

	Debit	Credit
Cash	$ 2,300	
Accounts Receivable	2,600	
Roofing Supplies	1,100	
Equipment	6,000	
Accumulated Depreciation—Equipment		$ 1,200
Accounts Payable		1,100
Unearned Service Revenue		300
Common Stock		6,400
Retained Earnings		600
Service Revenue		3,000
Salaries Expense	500	
Miscellaneous Expense	100	
	$12,600	$12,600

Other data:

1. A physical count reveals only $520 of roofing supplies on hand.
2. Equipment is depreciated at a rate of $120 per month.
3. Unearned service revenue amounted to $100 on March 31.
4. Accrued salaries are $850.

Instructions

Enter the trial balance on a work sheet and complete the work sheet, assuming that the adjustments relate only to the month of March. (Ignore income taxes.)

E3-19 (Work Sheet and Balance Sheet Presentation) The adjusted trial balance of Ed Bradley Co. work sheet for the month ended April 30, 2001, contains the following:

ED BRADLEY CO.
Work Sheet (partial)
For the Month Ended April 30, 2001

Account Titles	Adjusted Trial Balance		Income Statement		Balance Sheet	
	Dr.	Cr.	Dr.	Cr.	Dr.	Cr.
Cash	$19,472					
Accounts Receivable	6,920					
Prepaid Rent	2,280					
Equipment	18,050					
Accumulated Depreciation		$ 4,895				
Notes Payable		5,700				
Accounts Payable		5,472				
Bradley, Capital		34,960				
Bradley, Drawing	6,650					
Service Revenue		11,590				
Salaries Expense	6,840					
Rent Expense	2,260					
Depreciation Expense	145					
Interest Expense	83					
Interest Payable		83				

Instructions

Complete the work sheet and prepare a balance sheet as illustrated in this chapter.

E3-20 (Partial Work Sheet Preparation) Jurassic Park Co. prepares monthly financial statements from a work sheet. Selected portions of the January work sheet showed the following data:

JURASSIC PARK CO.
Work Sheet (partial)
For Month Ended January 31, 2002

Account Title	Trial Balance		Adjustments		Adjusted Trial Balance	
	Dr.	Cr.	Dr.	Cr.	Dr.	Cr.
Supplies	3,256			(a) 1,500	1,756	
Accumulated Depreciation		6,682		(b) 257		6,939
Interest Payable		100		(c) 50		150
Supplies Expense			(a) 1,500		1,500	
Depreciation Expense			(b) 257		257	
Interest Expense			(c) 50		50	

During February no events occurred that affected these accounts, but at the end of February the following information was available:

(a) Supplies on hand	$715
(b) Monthly depreciation	$257
(c) Accrued interest	$ 50

Instructions

Reproduce the data that would appear in the February work sheet and indicate the amounts that would be shown in the February income statement.

E3-21 (Transactions of a Corporation, Including Investment and Dividend) Scratch Miniature Golf and Driving Range Inc. was opened on March 1 by Scott Verplank. The following selected events and transactions occurred during March:

Mar.	1	Invested $50,000 cash in the business in exchange for common stock.
	3	Purchased Lee Janzen's Golf Land for $38,000 cash. The price consists of land, $10,000; building, $22,000; and equipment, $6,000. (Make one compound entry.)
	5	Advertised the opening of the driving range and miniature golf course, paying advertising expenses of $1,600.
	6	Paid cash $1,480 for a one-year insurance policy.
	10	Purchased golf equipment for $2,500 from Sluman Company payable in 30 days.
	18	Received golf fees of $1,200 in cash.
	25	Declared and paid a $500 cash dividend.
	30	Paid wages of $900.
	30	Paid Sluman Company in full.
	31	Received $750 of fees in cash.

Scott Verplank uses the following accounts: Cash; Prepaid Insurance; Land; Buildings; Equipment; Accounts Payable; Common Stock; Dividends; Service Revenue; Advertising Expense; and Wages Expense.

Instructions

Journalize the March transactions.

***E3-22 (Cash and Accrual Basis)** Robin Williams Company maintains its books on the accrual basis. The company reported insurance expense of $19,450 in its 2001 income statement. Prepaid insurance at December 31, 2001, amounted to $5,740; cash paid for insurance during the year 2001 totaled $24,100. There was no accrued insurance expense either at the beginning or at the end of 2001.

Instructions

What was the amount, if any, of prepaid insurance at January 1, 2001? Show computations.

***E3-23 (Cash to Accrual Basis)** Jill Accardo, M.D., maintains the accounting records of Accardo Clinic on a cash basis. During 2001, Dr. Accardo collected $142,600 from her patients and paid $55,470 in expenses. At January 1, 2001, and December 31, 2001, she had accounts receivable, unearned service revenue, accrued expenses, and prepaid expenses as follows (all long-lived assets are rented):

	January 1, 2001	December 31, 2001
Accounts receivable	$9,250	$15,927
Unearned service revenue	2,840	4,111
Accrued expenses	3,435	2,108
Prepaid expenses	1,917	3,232

Instructions

Prepare a schedule that converts Dr. Accardo's "excess of cash collected over cash disbursed" for the year 2001 to net income on an accrual basis for the year 2001.

***E3-24 (Cash and Accrual Basis)** Wayne Rogers Corp. maintains its financial records on the cash basis of accounting. Interested in securing a long-term loan from its regular bank, Wayne Rogers Corp. requests you as its independent CPA to convert its cash basis income statement data to the accrual basis. You are provided with the following summarized data covering 1999, 2000, and 2001:

	1999	2000	2001
Cash receipts from sales:			
On 1999 sales	$295,000	$160,000	$ 30,000
On 2000 sales	–0–	355,000	90,000
On 2001 sales			408,000
Cash payments for expenses:			
On 1999 expenses	185,000	67,000	25,000
On 2000 expenses	40,000[a]	160,000	55,000
On 2001 expenses		45,000[b]	218,000

[a]Prepayments of 2000 expense.
[b]Prepayments of 2001 expense.

Instructions

(a) Using the data above, prepare abbreviated income statements for the years 1999 and 2000 on the cash basis.

(b) Using the data above, prepare abbreviated income statements for the years 1999 and 2000 on the accrual basis.

***E3-25 (Adjusting and Reversing Entries)** On December 31, adjusting information for James Lyman Corporation is as follows:

1. Estimated depreciation on equipment $1,100.

2. Personal property taxes amounting to $525 have accrued but are unrecorded and unpaid.
3. Employees' wages earned but unpaid and unrecorded $1,200.
4. Unearned Service Revenue balance includes $1,500 that has been earned.
5. Interest of $250 on a $25,000 note receivable has accrued.

Instructions

(a) Prepare adjusting journal entries.
(b) Prepare reversing journal entries.

***E3-26 (Closing and Reversing Entries)** On December 31, the adjusted trial balance of Cree Co. Inc. shows the following selected data:

Accounts Receivable	$4,300	Service Revenue	$96,000
Interest Expense	7,800	Interest Payable	2,400

Analysis shows that adjusting entries were made for (a) $4,300 of services performed but not billed, and (b) $2,400 of accrued but unpaid interest.

Instructions

(a) Prepare the closing entries for the temporary accounts at December 31.
(b) Prepare the reversing entries on January 1.
(c) Enter the adjusted trial balance data in the four accounts. Post the entries in (a) and (b) and rule and balance the accounts. (Use T-accounts.)
(d) Prepare the entries to record (1) the collection of the accrued commissions on January 10, and (2) the payment of all interest due ($3,000) on January 15.
(e) Post the entries in (d) to the temporary accounts.

***E3-27 (Adjusting and Reversing Entries)** When the accounts of Daniel Barenboim Inc. are examined, the adjusting data listed below are uncovered on December 31, the end of an annual fiscal period.

1. The prepaid insurance account shows a debit of $5,280, representing the cost of a 2-year fire insurance policy dated August 1 of the current year.
2. On November 1, Rental Revenue was credited for $1,800, representing revenue from a subrental for a 3-month period beginning on that date.
3. Purchase of advertising materials for $800 during the year was recorded in the Advertising Expense account. On December 31, advertising materials of $290 are on hand.
4. Interest of $770 has accrued on notes payable.

Instructions

Prepare in general journal form: (a) the adjusting entry for each item; (b) the reversing entry for each item where appropriate.

PROBLEMS

P3-1 (Transactions, Financial Statements—Service Company) Listed below are the transactions of Isao Aoki, D.D.S., for the month of September:

Sept.	1	Isao Aoki begins practice as a dentist and invests $20,000 cash.
	2	Purchases furniture and dental equipment on account from Green Jacket Co. for $17,280.
	4	Pays rent for office space, $680 for the month.
	4	Employs a receptionist, Michael Bradley.
	5	Purchases dental supplies for cash, $942.
	8	Receives cash of $1,690 from patients for services performed.
	10	Pays miscellaneous office expenses, $430.
	14	Bills patients $5,120 for services performed.
	18	Pays Green Jacket Co. on account, $3,600.
	19	Withdraws $3,000 cash from the business for personal use.
	20	Receives $980 from patients on account.
	25	Bills patients $2,110 for services performed.
	30	Pays the following expenses in cash: office salaries, $1,400; miscellaneous office expenses, $85.
	30	Dental supplies used during September, $330.

Instructions

(a) Enter the transactions shown above in appropriate general ledger accounts. Use the following ledger accounts: Cash; Accounts Receivable; Supplies on Hand; Furniture and Equipment; Accumulated Depreciation; Accounts Payable; Isao Aoki, Capital; Service Revenue; Rent Expense; Miscellaneous Office Expense; Office Salaries Expense; Supplies Expense; Depreciation Expense; and Income Summary. Allow 10 lines for the Cash and Income Summary accounts, and 5 lines for each of the other accounts needed. Record depreciation using a 5-year life on the furniture and equipment, the straight-line method, and no salvage value. Do not use a drawing account.

(b) Prepare a trial balance.

(c) Prepare an income statement, a balance sheet, and a statement of owner's equity.

(d) Close the ledger.

(e) Prepare a post-closing trial balance.

P3-2 (Adjusting Entries and Financial Statements) Yount Advertising Agency was founded by Thomas Grant in January of 1997. Presented below are both the adjusted and unadjusted trial balances as of December 31, 2001.

YOUNT ADVERTISING AGENCY
Trial Balance
December 31, 2001

	Unadjusted		Adjusted	
	Dr.	Cr.	Dr.	Cr.
Cash	$ 11,000		$ 11,000	
Accounts Receivable	20,000		21,500	
Art Supplies	8,400		5,000	
Prepaid Insurance	3,350		2,500	
Printing Equipment	60,000		60,000	
Accumulated Depreciation		$ 28,000		$ 35,000
Accounts Payable		5,000		5,000
Interest Payable		–0–		150
Notes Payable		5,000		5,000
Unearned Advertising Revenue		7,000		5,600
Salaries Payable		–0–		1,300
Common Stock		10,000		10,000
Retained Earnings		3,500		3,500
Advertising Revenue		58,600		61,500
Salaries Expense	10,000		11,300	
Insurance Expense			850	
Interest Expense	350		500	
Depreciation Expense			7,000	
Art Supplies Expense			3,400	
Rent Expense	4,000		4,000	
	$117,100	$117,100	$127,050	$127,050

Instructions

(a) Journalize the annual adjusting entries that were made.

(b) Prepare an income statement and a statement of owner's equity for the year ending December 31, 2001, and a balance sheet at December 31.

(c) Answer the following questions:

(1) If the note has been outstanding 3 months, what is the annual interest rate on that note?

(2) If the company paid $13,500 in salaries in 2001, what was the balance in Salaries Payable on December 31, 2000?

P3-3 (Adjusting Entries) A review of the ledger of Oklahoma Company at December 31, 2001, produces the following data pertaining to the preparation of annual adjusting entries.

1. Salaries Payable $0. There are eight salaried employees. Salaries are paid every Friday for the current week. Five employees receive a salary of $700 each per week, and three employees earn $500 each per week. December 31 is a Tuesday. Employees do not work weekends. All employees worked the last 2 days of December.
2. Unearned Rent Revenue $369,000. The company began subleasing office space in its new building on November 1. Each tenant is required to make a $5,000 security deposit that is not refundable

until occupancy is terminated. At December 31, the company had the following rental contracts that are paid in full for the entire term of the lease.

Date	Term (in months)	Monthly Rent	Number of Leases
Nov. 1	6	$4,000	5
Dec. 1	6	$8,500	4

3. Prepaid Advertising $13,200. This balance consists of payments on two advertising contracts. The contracts provide for monthly advertising in two trade magazines. The terms of the contracts are as follows:

Contract	Date	Amount	Number of Magazine Issues
A650	May 1	$6,000	12
B974	Oct. 1	7,200	24

The first advertisement runs in the month in which the contract is signed.

4. Notes Payable $80,000. This balance consists of a note for one year at an annual interest rate of 12%, dated June 1.

Instructions

Prepare the adjusting entries at December 31, 2001. (Show all computations).

P3-4 (Financial Statements and Closing Entries) The completed financial statement columns of the work sheet for Parsons Company are shown below.

PARSONS COMPANY
Work Sheet
For the Year Ended December 31, 2002

Account No.	Account Titles	Income Statement Dr.	Income Statement Cr.	Balance Sheet Dr.	Balance Sheet Cr.
101	Cash			8,200	
112	Accounts Receivable			7,500	
130	Prepaid Insurance			1,800	
157	Equipment			28,000	
167	Accumulated Depreciation				8,600
201	Accounts Payable				12,000
212	Salaries Payable				3,000
301	Common Stock				20,000
306	Retained Earnings				6,800
400	Service Revenue		42,000		
622	Repair Expense	3,200			
711	Depreciation Expense	2,800			
722	Insurance Expense	1,200			
726	Salaries Expense	36,000			
732	Utilities Expense	3,700			
	Totals	46,900	42,000	45,500	50,400
	Net Loss		4,900	4,900	
		46,900	46,900	50,400	50,400

Instructions

(a) Prepare an income statement, retained earnings statement, and a classified balance sheet. Parsons' stockholders made an additional investment in the business of $4,000 during 2002.

(b) Prepare the closing entries.

(c) Post the closing entries and rule and balance the accounts. Use T-accounts. Income Summary is No. 350.

(d) Prepare a post-closing trial balance.

P3-5 (Work Sheet, Balance Sheet, Adjusting and Closing Entries) Noah's Ark has a fiscal year ending on September 30. Selected data from the September 30 work sheet are presented below:

NOAH'S ARK
Work Sheet
For the Year Ended September 30, 2002

	Trial Balance		Adjusted Trial Balance	
	Dr.	Cr.	Dr.	Cr.
Cash	37,400		37,400	
Supplies	18,600		1,200	
Prepaid Insurance	31,900		3,900	
Land	80,000		80,000	
Equipment	120,000		120,000	
Accumulated Depreciation		36,200		43,000
Accounts Payable		14,600		14,600
Unearned Admissions Revenue		2,700		1,700
Mortgage Payable		50,000		50,000
N. Y. Berge, Capital		109,700		109,700
N. Y. Berge, Drawing	14,000		14,000	
Admissions Revenue		278,500		279,500
Salaries Expense	109,000		109,000	
Repair Expense	30,500		30,500	
Advertising Expense	9,400		9,400	
Utilities Expense	16,900		16,900	
Property Taxes Expense	18,000		21,000	
Interest Expense	6,000		12,000	
Totals	491,700	491,700		
Insurance Expense			28,000	
Supplies Expense			17,400	
Interest Payable				6,000
Depreciation Expense			6,800	
Property Taxes Payable				3,000
Totals			507,500	507,500

Instructions

(a) Prepare a complete work sheet.

(b) Prepare a classified balance sheet. (*Note:* $10,000 of the mortgage payable is due for payment in the next fiscal year.)

(c) Journalize the adjusting entries using the work sheet as a basis.

(d) Journalize the closing entries using the work sheet as a basis.

(e) Prepare a post-closing trial balance.

P3-6 (Financial Statements, Adjusting and Closing Entries) The trial balance of Bishop Fashion Center contained the following accounts at November 30, the end of the company's fiscal year.

BISHOP FASHION CENTER
Trial Balance
November 30, 2002

	Debit	Credit
Cash	$ 26,700	
Accounts Receivable	33,700	
Merchandise Inventory	45,000	
Store Supplies	5,500	
Store Equipment	85,000	
Accumulated Depreciation—Store Equipment		$ 18,000
Delivery Equipment	48,000	
Accumulated Depreciation—Delivery Equipment		6,000
Notes Payable		51,000
Accounts Payable		48,500
Common Stock		90,000
Retained Earnings		8,000

Sales		757,200
Sales Returns and Allowances	4,200	
Cost of Goods Sold	497,400	
Salaries Expense	140,000	
Advertising Expense	26,400	
Utilities Expense	14,000	
Repair Expense	12,100	
Delivery Expense	16,700	
Rent Expense	24,000	
	$978,700	$978,700

Adjustment data:

1. Store supplies on hand totaled $3,500.
2. Depreciation is $9,000 on the store equipment and $7,000 on the delivery equipment.
3. Interest of $11,000 is accrued on notes payable at November 30.

Other data:

1. Salaries expense is 70% selling and 30% administrative.
2. Rent expense and utilities expense are 80% selling and 20% administrative.
3. $30,000 of notes payable are due for payment next year.
4. Repair expense is 100% administrative.

Instructions

(a) Enter the trial balance on a work sheet and complete the work sheet.
(b) Prepare a multiple-step income statement and retained earnings statement for the year and a classified balance sheet as of November 30, 2002.
(c) Journalize the adjusting entries.
(d) Journalize the closing entries.
(e) Prepare a post-closing trial balance.

P3-7 (Financial Statements, Adjusting and Closing Entries) The Rusch Department Store is located near the Village shopping mall. At the end of the company's fiscal year on December 31, 2002, the following accounts appeared in two of its trial balances.

	Unadjusted	Adjusted
Accounts Payable	$ 79,300	$ 79,300
Accounts Receivable	50,300	50,300
Accumulated Depreciation—Building	42,100	52,500
Accumulated Depreciation—Equipment	29,600	42,900
Building	190,000	190,000
Cash	23,000	23,000
Common Stock	160,000	160,000
Retained Earnings	16,600	16,600
Cost of Goods Sold	412,700	412,700
Depreciation Expense—Building		10,400
Depreciation Expense—Equipment		13,300
Dividends	28,000	28,000
Equipment	110,000	110,000
Insurance Expense		7,200
Interest Expense	3,000	11,000
Interest Payable		8,000
Interest Revenue	4,000	4,000
Merchandise Inventory	75,000	75,000
Mortgage Payable	80,000	80,000
Office Salaries Expense	32,000	32,000
Prepaid Insurance	9,600	2,400
Property Taxes Expense		4,800
Property Taxes Payable		4,800
Sales Salaries Expense	76,000	76,000
Sales	628,000	628,000
Sales Commissions Expense	11,000	14,500
Sales Commissions Payable		3,500
Sales Returns and Allowances	8,000	8,000
Utilities Expense	11,000	11,000

Analysis reveals the following additional data:

1. Insurance expense and utilities expense are 60% selling and 40% administrative.
2. $20,000 of the mortgage payable is due for payment next year.
3. Depreciation on the building and property tax expense are administrative expenses; depreciation on the equipment is a selling expense.

Instructions

(a) Prepare a multiple-step income statement, a retained earnings statement, and a classified balance sheet.

(b) Journalize the adjusting entries that were made.

(c) Journalize the closing entries that are necessary.

P3-8 (Adjusting Entries) The accounts listed below appeared in the December 31 trial balance of the Jane Alexander Theater.

	Debit	Credit
Equipment	$192,000	
Accumulated Depreciation—Equipment		$ 60,000
Notes Payable		90,000
Admissions Revenue		380,000
Advertising Expense	13,680	
Salaries Expense	57,600	
Interest Expense	1,400	

Instructions

(a) From the account balances listed above and the information given below, prepare the annual adjusting entries necessary on December 31.

(1) The equipment has an estimated life of 16 years and a salvage value of $40,000 at the end of that time. (Use straight-line method.)

(2) The note payable is a 90-day note given to the bank October 20 and bearing interest at 10%. (Use 360 days for denominator.)

(3) In December 2,000 coupon admission books were sold at $25 each; they could be used for admission any time after January 1.

(4) Advertising expense paid in advance and included in Advertising Expense, $1,100.

(5) Salaries accrued but unpaid, $4,700.

(b) What amounts should be shown for each of the following on the income statement for the year?

(1) Interest expense.

(2) Admissions revenue.

(3) Advertising expense.

(4) Salaries expense.

P3-9 (Adjusting Entries and Financial Statements) Presented below are the trial balance and the other information related to Muhammad Ali, a consulting engineer.

MUHAMMAD ALI, CONSULTING ENGINEER
Trial Balance
December 31, 2001

	Debit	Credit
Cash	$ 31,500	
Accounts Receivable	49,600	
Allowance for Doubtful Accounts		$ 750
Engineering Supplies Inventory	1,960	
Unexpired Insurance	1,100	
Furniture and Equipment	25,000	
Accumulated Depreciation—Furniture and Equipment		6,250
Notes Payable		7,200
Muhammad Ali, Capital		35,010
Service Revenue		100,000
Rent Expense	9,750	
Office Salaries Expense	28,500	
Heat, Light, and Water Expense	1,080	
Miscellaneous Office Expense	720	
	$149,210	$149,210

1. Fees received in advance from clients, $6,900.
2. Services performed for clients that were not recorded by December 31, $4,900.
3. Bad debt expense for the year is $1,430.
4. Insurance expired during the year, $480.
5. Furniture and equipment is being depreciated at $12\frac{1}{2}$% per year.
6. Muhammad Ali gave the bank a 90-day, 10% note for $7,200 on December 1, 2001.
7. Rent of the building is $750 per month. The rent for 2001 has been paid, as has that for January 2002.
8. Office salaries earned but unpaid December 31, 2001, $2,510.

Instructions

(a) From the trial balance and other information given, prepare annual adjusting entries as of December 31, 2001.

(b) Prepare an income statement for 2001, a balance sheet, and a statement of owner's equity. Muhammad Ali withdrew $17,000 cash for personal use during the year.

P3-10 (Adjusting Entries and Financial Statements) Ana Alicia Advertising Corporation was founded by Ana Alicia in January of 1998. Presented below are both the adjusted and unadjusted trial balances as of December 31, 2002.

ANA ALICIA ADVERTISING CORPORATION
Trial Balance
December 31, 2002

	Unadjusted		Adjusted	
	Dr.	Cr.	Dr.	Cr.
Cash	$ 7,000		$ 7,000	
Accounts Receivable	19,000		22,000	
Art Supplies	8,500		5,500	
Prepaid Insurance	3,250		2,500	
Printing Equipment	60,000		60,000	
Accumulated Depreciation		$ 27,000		$33,750
Accounts Payable		5,000		5,000
Interest Payable				150
Notes Payable		5,000		5,000
Unearned Service Revenue		7,000		5,600
Salaries Payable				1,500
Common Stock		10,000		10,000
Retained Earnings		4,500		4,500
Service Revenue		58,600		63,000
Salaries Expense	10,000		11,500	
Insurance Expense			750	
Interest Expense	350		500	
Depreciation Expense			6,750	
Art Supplies Expense	5,000		8,000	
Rent Expense	4,000		4,000	
	$117,100	$117,100	$128,500	$128,500

Instructions

(a) Journalize the annual adjusting entries that were made.

(b) Prepare an income statement and a statement of retained earnings for the year ending December 31, 2002, and a balance sheet at December 31.

(c) Answer the following questions:

(1) If the useful life of equipment is 8 years, what is the expected salvage value?

(2) If the note has been outstanding 3 months, what is the annual interest rate on that note?

(3) If the company paid $12,500 in salaries in 2002, what was the balance in Salaries Payable on December 31, 2001?

P3-11 (Adjusting Entries) Presented below is information related to Jillian Anderson, Realtor, at the close of the fiscal year ending December 31.

1. Jillian had paid the local newspaper $335 for an advertisement to be run in January of the next year, charging it to Advertising Expense.

2. On November 1 Jillian borrowed $9,000 from Yorkville Bank issuing a 90-day, 10% note.
3. Salaries and wages due and unpaid December 31: sales, $1,420; office clerks, $1,060.
4. Interest accrued to date on Grant Muldaur's note, which Jillian holds, $500.
5. Estimated loss on bad debts, $1,210 for the period.
6. Stamps and stationery on hand, $110, charged to Stationery and Postage Expense account when purchased.
7. Jillian has not yet paid the December rent on the building her business occupies, $1,000.
8. Insurance paid November 1 for one year, $930, charged to Prepaid Insurance when paid.
9. Property taxes accrued, $1,670.
10. On December 1 Jillian gave Laura Palmer her (Jillian's) 60-day, 12% note for $6,000 on account.
11. On October 31 Jillian received $2,580 from Douglas Raines in payment of 6 months' rent for office space occupied by him in the building and credited Unearned Rent Revenue.
12. On September 1 she paid 6 months' rent in advance on a warehouse, $6,600, and debited the asset account Prepaid Rent Expense.
13. The bill from the Twin Peaks Light & Power Company for December has been received but not yet entered or paid, $510.
14. Estimated depreciation on furniture and equipment, $1,400.

Instructions

Prepare annual adjusting entries as of December 31.

P3-12 (Adjusting and Closing) Following is the trial balance of the Platteville Golf Club, Inc. as of December 31. The books are closed annually on December 31.

PLATTEVILLE GOLF CLUB, INC.
Trial Balance
December 31

	Debit	Credit
Cash	$ 15,000	
Accounts Receivable	13,000	
Allowance for Doubtful Accounts		$ 1,100
Land	350,000	
Buildings	120,000	
Accumulated Depreciation of Buildings		38,400
Equipment	150,000	
Accumulated Depreciation of Equipment		70,000
Unexpired Insurance	9,000	
Common Stock		400,000
Retained Earnings		82,000
Dues Revenue		200,000
Greens Fee Revenue		8,100
Rental Revenue		15,400
Utilities Expense	54,000	
Salaries Expense	80,000	
Maintenance Expense	24,000	
	$815,000	$815,000

Instructions

(a) Enter the balances in ledger accounts. Allow five lines for each account.

(b) From the trial balance and the information given, prepare annual adjusting entries and post to the ledger accounts.

(1) The buildings have an estimated life of 25 years with no salvage value (straight-line method).

(2) The equipment is depreciated at 10% per year.

(3) Insurance expired during the year, $3,500.

(4) The rental revenue represents the amount received for 11 months for dining facilities. The December rent has not yet been received.

(5) It is estimated that 15% of the accounts receivable will be uncollectible.

(6) Salaries earned but not paid by December 31, $3,600.

(7) Dues paid in advance by members, $8,900.

(c) Prepare an adjusted trial balance.

(d) Prepare closing entries and post.

P3-13 (Adjusting and Closing) Presented below is the December 31 trial balance of Nancy Drew Boutique.

NANCY DREW BOUTIQUE
Trial Balance
December 31

	Debit	Credit
Cash	$ 18,500	
Accounts Receivable	42,000	
Allowance for Doubtful Accounts		$ 700
Inventory, December 31	80,000	
Furniture and Equipment	84,000	
Accumulated Depreciation of Furniture and Equipment		35,000
Prepaid Insurance	5,100	
Notes Payable		28,000
Common Stock		80,600
Retained Earnings		10,000
Sales		600,000
Cost of Goods Sold	398,000	
Sales Salaries Expense	50,000	
Advertising Expense	6,700	
Administrative Salaries Expense	65,000	
Office Expense	5,000	
	$754,300	$754,300

Instructions

(a) Construct T-accounts and enter the balances shown.

(b) Prepare adjusting journal entries for the following and post to the T-accounts. Open additional T-accounts as necessary. (The books are closed yearly on December 31.)

- **(1)** Bad debts are estimated to be $1,400.
- **(2)** Furniture and equipment is depreciated based on a 6-year life (no salvage).
- **(3)** Insurance expired during the year, $2,550.
- **(4)** Interest accrued on notes payable, $3,360.
- **(5)** Sales salaries earned but not paid, $2,400.
- **(6)** Advertising paid in advance, $700.
- **(7)** Office supplies on hand, $1,500, charged to Office Expense when purchased.

(c) Prepare closing entries and post to the accounts.

***P3-14 (Cash and Accrual Basis)** On January 1, 2002, Jill Monroe and Jenni Meno formed a computer sales and service enterprise in Soapsville, Arkansas by investing $90,000 cash. The new company, Razorback Sales and Service, has the following transactions during January:

1. Pays $6,000 in advance for 3 months' rent of office, showroom, and repair space.
2. Purchases 40 personal computers at a cost of $1,500 each, 6 graphics computers at a cost of $3,000 each, and 25 printers at a cost of $450 each, paying cash upon delivery.
3. Sales, repair, and office employees earn $12,600 in salaries during January, of which $3,000 was still payable at the end of January.
4. Sells 30 personal computers at $2,550 each, 4 graphics computers for $4,500 each, and 15 printers for $750 each; $75,000 is received in cash in January and $30,750 is sold on a deferred payment basis.
5. Other operating expenses of $8,400 are incurred and paid for during January; $2,000 of incurred expenses are payable at January 31.

Instructions

(a) Using the transaction data above, prepare (1) a cash basis income statement and (2) an accrual basis income statement for the month of January.

(b) Using the transaction data above, prepare (1) a cash basis balance sheet and (2) an accrual basis balance sheet as of January 31, 2002.

(c) Identify the items in the cash basis financial statements that make cash basis accounting inconsistent with the theory underlying the elements of financial statements.

***P3-15 (Cash to Accrual)** Dr. John Gleason, M.D., maintains the accounting records of Bones Clinic on a cash basis. During 2001, Dr. Gleason collected $146,000 from his patients and paid $55,470 in expenses.

At January 1, 2001, and December 31, 2001, he had accounts receivable, unearned service revenue, accrued expenses, and prepaid expenses as follows (all long-lived assets are rented):

	January 1, 2001	December 31, 2001
Accounts receivable	$9,250	$16,100
Unearned service revenue	2,840	1,620
Accrued expenses	3,435	2,200
Prepaid expenses	2,000	1,775

Instructions

Last week Dr. Gleason asked you, his CPA, to help him determine his income on the accrual basis. Write a letter to him explaining what you did to calculate net income on the accrual basis. Be sure to state net income on the accrual basis and to include a schedule of your calculations.

USING YOUR JUDGMENT

FINANCIAL REPORTING PROBLEM: INTEL CORPORATION

The financial statements of Intel are presented in Appendix 5B. Refer to these financial statements and the accompanying notes to answer the following questions.

Instructions

(a) What were Intel's total assets at December 30, 1998? At December 31, 1997?

(b) How much cash (and cash equivalents) did Intel have on December 30, 1998?

(c) What were Intel's research and development costs in 1996? In 1998?

(d) What were Intel's net revenues in 1996? In 1998?

(e) Using Intel's financial statements and related notes, identify items that may result in adjusting entries for prepayments and accruals.

(f) What were the amounts of Intel's depreciation expense in 1996, 1997, and 1998?

FINANCIAL STATEMENT ANALYSIS CASE

Kellogg Company

Kellogg Company has its headquarters in Battle Creek, Michigan. The company manufactures and sells ready-to-eat breakfast cereals and convenience foods including toaster pastries and cereal bars.

Selected data from Kellogg Company's 1998 annual report follows: (dollar amounts and share data in millions)

	1998	1997	1996
Net sales	$6,762.1	$6,830.1	$6,676.6
Cost of goods sold	3,282.6	3,270.1	3,122.9
Selling and administrative expense	2,513.9	2,366.8	2,458.7
Net income	502.6	546.0	531.0

In its 1998 annual report, Kellogg Company outlined its plans for the future, which it described as its five point "strategy for growth." A brief description of these plans follows.

1. **Leading the food industry in innovation**—Kellogg Company is rolling out a broader grain-based product portfolio, including great-tasting new cereals, innovative convenience foods, and new grain-based products outside our traditional lines.
2. **Investing in our largest cereal markets**—During 1999, Kellogg will invest in growth in our seven largest cereal markets.
3. **Accelerating the global growth of our convenience foods business**—Kellogg is focusing both on an expanded geographic distribution and new distribution channels, particularly single-serve channels.
4. **Continuing to reduce cost**—From ongoing cost-reduction programs, we anticipate more than $50 million in incremental savings in 1999.
5. **Creating a more focused and accountable organization**—Kellogg's objective is to develop a talented, diverse global workforce with every person focused on the largest, most important activities.

Instructions

(a) For each of the strategies, describe how gross profit and net income are likely to be affected.

(b) Compute the percentage change in sales, gross profit, operating costs (cost of goods sold plus selling and administrative expenses), and net income from year to year for each of the three years shown.

Evaluate Kellogg Company's performance. Which trend seems to be least favorable? Do you think the global strategies described will improve that trend? Explain.

COMPARATIVE ANALYSIS CASE

The Coca-Cola Company versus PepsiCo, Inc.

Go to the Digital Tool and answer the following questions regarding **The Coca-Cola Company** and **PepsiCo, Inc.**

Instructions

(a) Which company had the greater percentage increase in total assets from 1997 to 1998?

(b) Using the Selected Financial Data section of these two companies, determine their 5-year compound growth rates related to net sales and income from continuing operations.

(c) What company had more depreciation and amortization expense for 1998? Provide a rationale as to why there is a difference in these amounts between the two companies.

RESEARCH CASES

Case 1

The Enterprise Standard Industrial Classification (SIC) coding scheme, a published classification of firms into separate industries, is commonly used in practice. SIC codes permit identification of company activities on three levels of detail. Two-digit codes designate a "major group," three-digit codes designate an "industry group," while four-digit codes identify a specific "industry."

Instructions

Use the *Standard Industrial Classification Manual* (published by the U.S. Government's Office of Management and Budget in 1987) to answer the following questions.

(a) On what basis are SIC codes assigned to companies?

(b) Identify the major group/industry group/industry represented by the following codes: 12, 271, 3571, 7033, 75, and 872.

(c) Identify the SIC code for the following industries:
(1) Golfing equipment—manufacturing
(2) Worm farms
(3) Felt tip markers—manufacturing
(4) Household appliance stores, electric or gas—retail
(5) Advertising agencies

(d) You are interested in examining several companies in the passenger airline industry. Determine the appropriate two-, three-, and four-digit SIC codes. Use *Wards Business Directory of U.S. Private and Public Companies (Vol. 5)* to compile a list of the five largest parent companies (by total sales) in the industry. *Note:* If Wards is not available, alternative sources include *Standard & Poor's Register of Corporations, Directors, and Executives, Standard & Poor's Industry Surveys,* and the Dun & Bradstreet *Million Dollar Directory.*

Case 2

The March 1995 issue of *Management Review* includes an article by Barbara Ettorre, entitled "How Motorola Closes Its Books in Two Days."

Instructions

Read the article and answer the following questions.

(a) How often does Motorola close its books? How long did the process used to take?

(b) What was the major change Motorola initiated to shorten the closing process?

(c) What incentive does Motorola offer to ensure accurate and timely information?

(d) In a given year, how many journal entry lines does Motorola process?

(e) Provide an example of an external force that prevents Motorola from closing faster than a day-and-a-half.

(f) According to Motorola's corporate vice president and controller, how do external financial statement users perceive companies that release information early?

ETHICS CASE

Ernest Banks is the manager and accountant for a small company privately owned by three individuals. Banks always has given the owners cash-based financial statements. The owners are not accountants and do not understand how financial statements are prepared. Recently, the business has experienced strong growth, and inventory, accounts receivable, and fixed assets have become more significant company assets. Banks understands generally accepted accounting principles and knows that net income would be lower if he prepared accrual-based financial statements. He is afraid that if he gave the owners financial statements prepared on an accrual basis, they would think he is not managing the business well; they might even decide to fire him.

Instructions

Answer the following questions.

(a) What are the ethical issues involved?

(b) What should Banks do?

CHAPTER 4

Income Statement and Related Information

What Is the Bottom Line?

Automaker DaimlerChrysler recently released its first financial results as a merged company. Its financial results were as follows:

DaimlerChrysler	Income Comparisons ($ billions)		
	1997	1998	% Change
Operating income	$4.51	$5.72	+29%
Net income	7.15	5.28	−26%

As shown, net income decreased $1.87 billion, or 26%, from 1997 to 1998. However, DaimlerChrysler stressed that one-time merger charges and other unusual items caused the decrease. Some analysts argue that a more relevant income measure in this case would be operating income, which excludes these special charges. For DaimlerChrysler, it makes a big difference which income measure is used, because its income from operations *increased* 29%.

What number, net income or income from operations, should an analyst use in evaluating companies that have unusual items? Some argue that operating income should be used because it is more representative of what will happen in the future. Others disagree, noting that special items are often no longer special. For example, one study noted that in 1997 companies in Standard & Poor's 500 index wrote off unusual items totaling on average $7.04 per share, topping the previous high of $6.61 in 1993. Why all these write-offs when the economy is booming? One reason is to front-load expenses. Charging three or four years' future expenses as unusual in the current year means that earnings will be better in the future. Call this write-off a restructuring charge, and the belief is that Wall Street will forgive you.

Another example is McDonald's Corporation. It wanted to write off $350 million as a restructuring charge, which included $190 million to install new, costly kitchen equipment. The SEC questioned the $190 million item, noting that upgrading kitchen equipment in the restaurant business is normal and should be a charge to operating expense. The SEC prevailed, and McDonald's had to show these costs as normal expenses, reducing its income from operations.

Some argue that companies have always taken write-offs as restructuring charges, so what's the big deal? The problem is that the increasing use of restructuring and other one-time charges to bury normal expenses distorts what is really happening. And if such distortion continues, annual performance numbers such as income from operations or net income become less useful. In that case, we all lose.

LEARNING OBJECTIVES

After studying this chapter, you should be able to:

1. **Identify the uses and limitations of an income statement.**
2. **Prepare a single-step income statement.**
3. **Prepare a multiple-step income statement.**
4. **Explain how irregular items are reported.**
5. **Explain intraperiod tax allocation.**
6. **Explain where earnings per share information is reported.**
7. **Prepare a retained earnings statement.**
8. **Explain how other comprehensive income is reported.**

PREVIEW OF CHAPTER 4

As shown in the opening story, DaimlerChrysler's net income and income from operations can be substantially different. As a result, the way items are reported within the income statement can affect its usefulness. The purpose of this chapter is to examine the many different types of revenues, expenses, gains, and losses that affect the income statement and related information. The content and organization of this chapter are as follows:

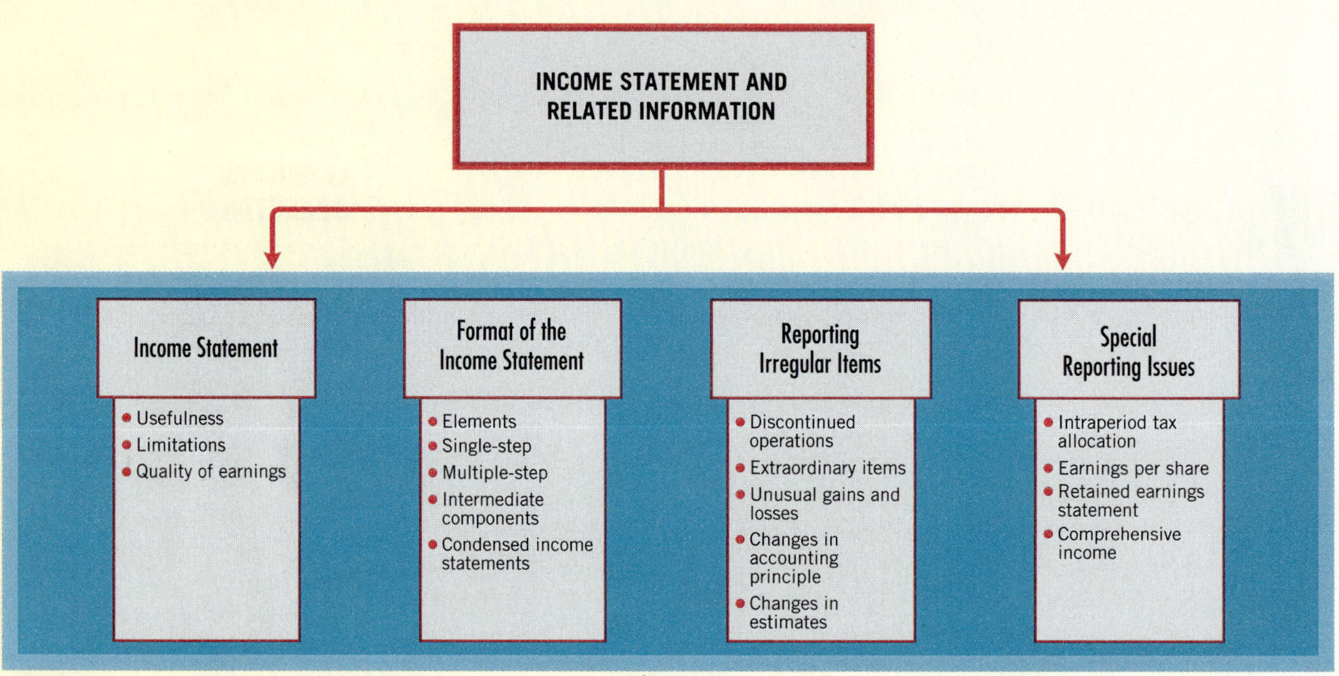

OBJECTIVE 1
Identify the uses and limitations of an income statement.

INCOME STATEMENT

The **income statement**, often called the statement of income or statement of earnings,[1] is the report that measures the success of enterprise operations for a given period of time. The business and investment community uses this report to determine profitability, investment value, and credit worthiness. It provides investors and creditors with information that helps them predict the **amounts, timing, and uncertainty of future cash flows**.

Usefulness of the Income Statement

The income statement helps users of financial statements predict future cash flows in a number of ways. For example, investors and creditors can use the information in the income statement to:

[1]*Accounting Trends and Techniques—1999* (New York: AICPA) indicates that for the 600 companies surveyed the term *income* was employed in the title of 298 income statements. The term *operations* was second in acceptance with 180, and the term *earnings* was used by 117 companies.

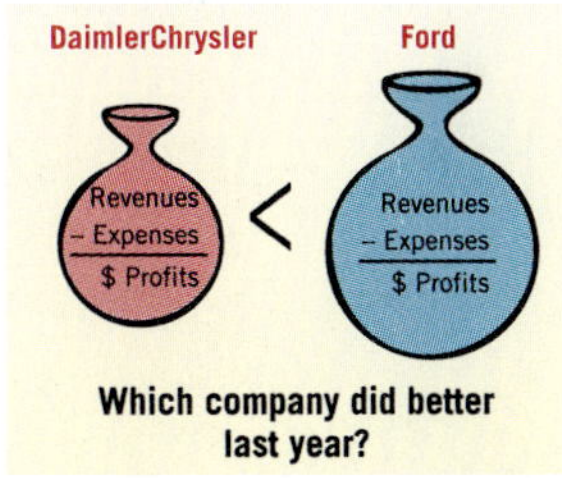

1. **Evaluate the past performance of the enterprise.** By examining revenues and expenses, you can tell how the company performed and compare its performance to its competitors. For example, the income data provided by **DaimlerChrysler** in the opening story can be used to compare its performance to that of **Ford**.

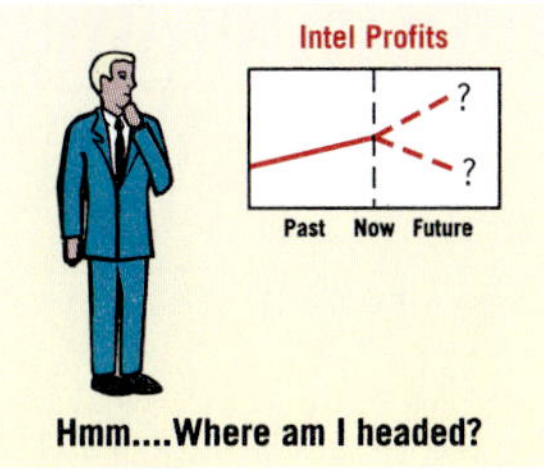

2. **Provide a basis for predicting future performance.** Information about past performance can be used to determine important trends that, if continued, provide information about future performance. For example, **Intel** has reported consistent increases in revenues in recent years. Although success in the past does not necessarily mean the company will be successful in the future, predictions of future revenues, and hence earnings and cash flows, can be made with some confidence, if a reasonable correlation exists between past and future performance.

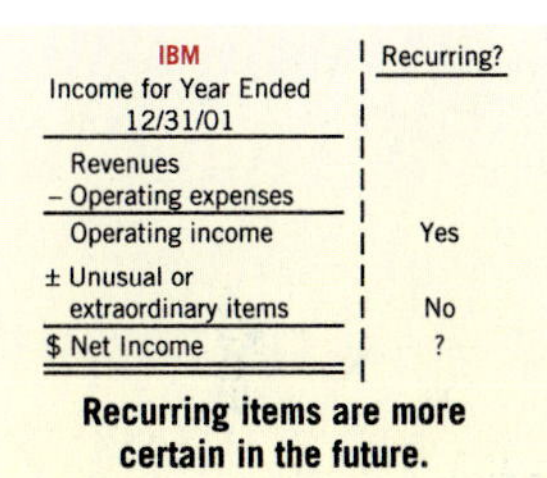

3. **Help assess the risk or uncertainty of achieving future cash flows.** Information on the various components of income—revenues, expenses, gains, and losses—highlights the relationships among them and can be used to assess the risk of not achieving a particular level of cash flows in the future. For example, segregating **IBM**'s operating performance from other nonrecurring sources of income is useful because operations are usually the primary means by which revenues and cash are generated. Thus, results from continuing operations usually have greater significance for predicting future performance than do results from nonrecurring activities and events.

In summary, information in the income statement—revenues, expenses, gains, and losses—helps users evaluate past performance and provides insights into achieving a particular level of cash flows in the future.

Limitations of the Income Statement

Because net income is an estimate and reflects a number of assumptions, income statement users need to be aware of certain limitations associated with the information contained in the income statement. Some of these limitations include:

1. **Items that cannot be measured reliably are not reported in the income statement.** Current practice prohibits recognition of certain items from the determination of income even though the effects of these items arguably affect the performance of an entity from one point in time to another. For example, unrealized gains and losses on certain investment securities may not be recorded in income when there is uncertainty that the changes in value will ever be realized. In addition, more and more companies, like **Cisco Systems** and **Microsoft**, have experienced increases in value due to brand recognition, customer service, and product quality. Presently, a common framework for identifying and reporting these types of values has not been developed.

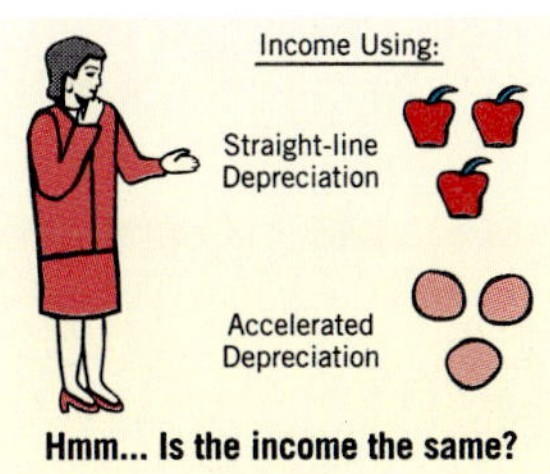

2. **Income numbers are affected by the accounting methods employed.** For example, one company may choose to depreciate its plant assets on an accelerated basis; another chooses straight-line depreciation. Assuming all other factors are equal, the income for the first company will be lower, even though the companies are essentially the same. In effect, we are comparing apples to oranges.

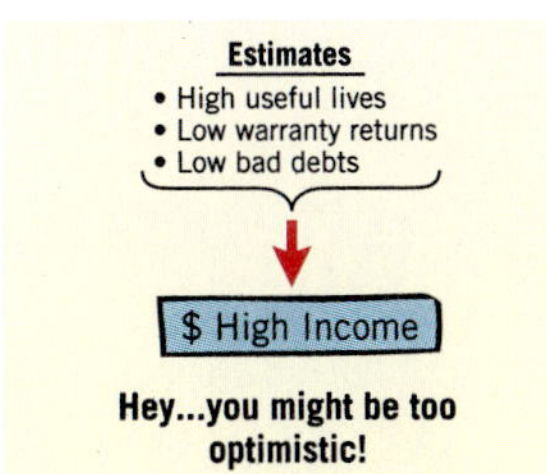

3. **Income measurement involves judgment.** For example, one company in good faith may estimate the useful life of an asset to be 20 years while another company uses a 15-year estimate for the same type of asset. Similarly, some companies may make overly optimistic estimates of future warranty returns and bad debt write-offs, which results in lower expense and higher income.

In summary, several limitations of the income statement reduce the usefulness of this statement for predicting the amounts, timing, and uncertainty of future cash flows.

Quality of Earnings

Our discussion to this point has highlighted the importance of information in the income statement for investment and credit decisions, including the evaluation of the company and its managers.[2] Companies try to meet or beat Wall Street expectations so that the market price of their stock and the value of management's stock options increase. As a result, companies have incentives to manage income to meet earnings targets or to make earnings look less risky.

Recently, the SEC has expressed concern that the motivations to meet earnings targets may be overriding good business practices. As a result, the quality of earnings and the quality of financial reporting are eroding. As indicated by the SEC chairman, "Managing may be giving way to manipulation; integrity may be losing out to illusion.[3] Therefore the SEC has started to take decisive action to prevent the practice of earnings management.

What is **earnings management**? It is often defined as the planned timing of revenues, expenses, gains, and losses to smooth out bumps in earnings. In most cases, earnings management is used to increase income in the current year at the expense of income in future years. For example, companies prematurely recognize sales before they are complete in order to boost earnings. As one commentator noted, ". . . it's like popping a cork in a bottle of wine before it is ready."

Earnings management can also be used to decrease current earnings in order to increase income in the future. The classic case is the use of "cookie jar" reserves, which are established by using unrealistic assumptions to estimate liabilities for such items as sales returns, loan losses, and warranty returns. These reserves can then be reduced in the future to increase income. For example, **W.R. Grace** has come under fire for allegedly stashing away $55 million of excess profits from 1991 to 1996. During the early 1990s, Grace was growing fast, with profits increasing 30% annually. Analysts' targets had Grace growing 24% each year. Worried that they could not continue to meet these growth expectations, management began stashing away excess profits in an all-purpose reserve. In 1995, when profits were not meeting expectations, Grace wanted to reduce this reserve and so increase income. The SEC objected, noting that generally accepted accounting principles would be violated if Grace were to do so.

Such earnings management has a negative effect on the **quality of earnings** if it distorts the information in a way that is less useful for predicting future earnings and cash flows. Markets are based on trust, and it is imperative that the bond between shareholders and the company be strong. If investors or others lose faith in the numbers reported in the financial statements, U.S. capital markets will be damaged. As mentioned in the opening story, heightened scrutiny of earnings management is warranted to ensure the quality of earnings and investors' confidence in the income statement.

FORMAT OF THE INCOME STATEMENT

Elements of the Income Statement

Net income results from revenue, expense, gain, and loss transactions. These transactions are summarized in the income statement. This method of income measurement is called the **transaction approach** because it focuses on the income-related activities

[2]In support of the usefulness of income information, accounting researchers have documented that the market prices of companies change when income is reported to the market. See W.H. Beaver, "The Information Content of Annual Earnings Announcements," *Empirical Research in Accounting: Selected Studies, Journal of Accounting Research* (Supplement 1968), pp. 67–92.

[3]A. Levitt, the "Numbers Game." Remarks to NYU Center for Law and Business, September 28, 1998 (Securities and Exchange Commission, 1998).

that have occurred during the period.[4] Income can be further classified by customer, product line, or function or by operating and nonoperating, continuing and discontinued, and regular and irregular categories.[5] More formal definitions of income-related items, referred to as the major elements of the income statement, are as follows:

ELEMENTS OF FINANCIAL STATEMENTS

REVENUES. Inflows or other enhancements of assets of an entity or settlements of its liabilities during a period from delivering or producing goods, rendering services, or other activities that constitute the entity's ongoing major or central operations.

EXPENSES. Outflows or other using-up of assets or incurrences of liabilities during a period from delivering or producing goods, rendering services, or carrying out other activities that constitute the entity's ongoing major or central operations.

GAINS. Increases in equity (net assets) from peripheral or incidental transactions of an entity except those that result from revenues or investments by owners.

LOSSES. Decreases in equity (net assets) from peripheral or incidental transactions of an entity except those that result from expenses or distributions to owners.[6]

Revenues take many forms, such as sales, fees, interest, dividends, and rents. Expenses also take many forms, such as cost of goods sold, depreciation, interest, rent, salaries and wages, and taxes. Gains and losses also are of many types, resulting from the sale of investments, sale of plant assets, settlement of liabilities, write-offs of assets due to obsolescence or casualty, and theft.

The distinction between revenues and gains and the distinction between expenses and losses depend to a great extent on the typical activities of the enterprise. For example, when **McDonald's** sells a hamburger, the selling price is recorded as revenue. However, when McDonald's sells a french-fryer, any excess of the selling price over the book value would be recorded as a gain. This difference in treatment results because the sale of the hamburger is part of McDonald's regular operations while the sale of the french-fryer is not. Similarly, when a manufacturer of french-fryers sells a fryer, the proceeds from the sale would be recorded as revenue.

INTERNATIONAL INSIGHT

In many nations, financial reporting is prepared on the same basis as tax returns. In such cases, companies have incentives to minimize reported income.

The importance of reporting these elements should not be underestimated. For most decision makers, the parts of a financial statement will often be more useful than the whole. As indicated earlier, investors and creditors are interested in predicting the amounts, timing, and uncertainty of future income and cash flows. Having income statement elements shown in some detail and in comparison form with prior years' data, decision makers are better able to assess future income and cash flows.

---

[4]The most common alternative to the transaction approach is the **capital maintenance approach** to income measurement. Under this approach, income for the period is determined based on the change in equity, after adjusting for capital contributions (e.g., investments by owners) or distributions (e.g., dividends). The main drawback associated with the capital maintenance approach is that the components of income are not evident in its measurement. The Internal Revenue Service uses the capital maintenance approach to identify unreported income and refers to this approach as the "net worth check."

[5]The term irregular encompasses transactions and other events that are derived from developments outside the normal operations of the business.

[6]"Elements of Financial Statements," *Statement of Financial Accounting Concepts No. 6* (Stamford, Conn.: FASB, 1985), pars. 78–89.

Single-Step Income Statements

OBJECTIVE 2
Prepare a single-step income statement.

In reporting revenues, gains, expenses, and losses, a format known as the **single-step income statement** is often used. In the single-step statement, just two groupings exist: revenues and expenses. Expenses are deducted from revenues to arrive at net income or loss. The expression "single-step" is derived from the single subtraction necessary to arrive at net income. Frequently income tax is reported separately as the last item before net income to indicate its relationship to income before income tax.

For example, Illustration 4-1 shows the single-step income statement of Dan Deines Company.

ILLUSTRATION 4-1
Single-step Income Statement

DAN DEINES COMPANY
Income Statement
For the Year Ended December 31, 2002

Revenues	
Net sales	$2,972,413
Dividend revenue	98,500
Rental revenue	72,910
Total revenues	3,143,823
Expenses	
Cost of goods sold	1,982,541
Selling expenses	453,028
Administrative expenses	350,771
Interest expense	126,060
Income tax expense	66,934
Total expenses	2,979,334
Net income	$ 164,489
Earnings per common share	$1.74

The single-step form of income statement is widely used in financial reporting, although in recent years, the multiple-step form described below has regained its former popularity.[7]

The primary advantage of the single-step format lies in the simplicity of presentation and the absence of any implication that one type of revenue or expense item has priority over another. Potential classification problems are thus eliminated.

Multiple-Step Income Statements

OBJECTIVE 3
Prepare a multiple-step income statement.

Some contend that including other important revenue and expense data makes the income statement more informative and more useful. These further classifications include:

1. A separation of operating and nonoperating activities of the company. For example, enterprises often present an income from operations figure and then sections entitled "other revenues and gains" and "other expenses and losses." These other categories include interest revenue and expense, gains or losses from sales of miscellaneous items, and dividends received.
2. A classification of expenses by functions, such as merchandising or manufacturing (cost of goods sold), selling, and administration. This permits immediate comparison with costs of previous years and with the cost of other departments during the same year.

A **multiple-step income statement** is used to recognize these additional relationships. This statement recognizes a separation of operating transactions from nonoperating

[7] *Accounting Trends and Techniques—1999.* Of the 600 companies surveyed by the AICPA, 443 employed the multiple-step form, and 157 employed the single-step income statement format. This is a reversal from 1983, when 314 used the single-step form and 286 used the multiple-step form.

transactions and matches costs and expenses with related revenues. It highlights certain intermediate components of income that are used for the computation of ratios used to assess the performance of the enterprise.

To illustrate, Dan Deines Company's multiple-step statement of income is presented in Illustration 4-2. Note, for example, that in arriving at net income, three subtotals are

ILLUSTRATION 4-2
Multiple-step Income Statement

DAN DEINES COMPANY Income Statement For the Year Ended December 31, 2002			
Sales Revenue			
Sales			$3,053,081
Less: Sales discounts		$ 24,241	
Sales returns and allowances		56,427	80,668
Net sales revenue			2,972,413
Cost of Goods Sold			
Merchandise inventory, Jan. 1, 2002		461,219	
Purchases	$1,989,693		
Less: Purchase discounts	19,270		
Net purchases	1,970,423		
Freight and transportation-in	40,612	2,011,035	
Total merchandise available for sale		2,472,254	
Less: Merchandise inventory, Dec. 31, 2002		489,713	
Cost of goods sold			1,982,541
Gross profit on sales			989,872
Operating Expenses			
Selling expenses			
Sales salaries and commissions	202,644		
Sales office salaries	59,200		
Travel and entertainment	48,940		
Advertising expense	38,315		
Freight and transportation-out	41,209		
Shipping supplies and expense	24,712		
Postage and stationery	16,788		
Depreciation of sales equipment	9,005		
Telephone and Internet expense	12,215	453,028	
Administrative expenses			
Officers' salaries	186,000		
Office salaries	61,200		
Legal and professional services	23,721		
Utilities expense	23,275		
Insurance expense	17,029		
Depreciation of building	18,059		
Depreciation of office equipment	16,000		
Stationery, supplies, and postage	2,875		
Miscellaneous office expenses	2,612	350,771	803,799
Income from operations			186,073
Other Revenues and Gains			
Dividend revenue		98,500	
Rental revenue		72,910	171,410
			357,483
Other Expenses and Losses			
Interest on bonds and notes			126,060
Income before income tax			231,423
Income tax			66,934
Net income for the year			$ 164,489
Earnings per common share			$1.74

presented: net sales revenue, gross profit, and income from operations. The disclosure of net sales revenue is useful because regular revenues are reported as a separate item. Irregular or incidental revenues are disclosed elsewhere in the income statement. As a result, trends in revenue from continuing operations should be easier to understand and analyze. Similarly, the reporting of gross profit provides a useful number for evaluating performance and assessing future earnings. A study of the trend in gross profits may show how successfully a company uses its resources; it may also be a basis for understanding how profit margins have changed as a result of competitive pressure.

Finally, disclosing income from operations highlights the difference between regular and irregular or incidental activities. This disclosure helps users recognize that incidental or irregular activities are unlikely to continue at the same level. Furthermore, disclosure of operating earnings may assist in comparing different companies and assessing operating efficiencies.

Intermediate Components of the Income Statement

When a multiple-step income statement is used, some or all of the following sections or subsections may be prepared:

INCOME STATEMENT SECTIONS

1. **Operating Section.** A report of the revenues and expenses of the company's principal operations.
   - (a) **Sales or Revenue Section.** A subsection presenting sales, discounts, allowances, returns, and other related information. Its purpose is to arrive at the net amount of sales revenue.
   - (b) **Cost of Goods Sold Section.** A subsection that shows the cost of goods that were sold to produce the sales.
   - (c) **Selling Expenses.** A subsection that lists expenses resulting from the company's efforts to make sales.
   - (d) **Administrative or General Expenses.** A subsection reporting expenses of general administration.
2. **Nonoperating Section.** A report of revenues and expenses resulting from secondary or auxiliary activities of the company. In addition, special gains and losses that are infrequent or unusual, but not both, are normally reported in this section. Generally these items break down into two main subsections:
   - (a) **Other Revenues and Gains.** A list of the revenues earned or gains incurred, generally net of related expenses, from nonoperating transactions.
   - (b) **Other Expenses and Losses.** A list of the expenses or losses incurred, generally net of any related incomes, from nonoperating transactions.
3. **Income Tax.** A short section reporting federal and state taxes levied on income from continuing operations.
4. **Discontinued Operations.** Material gains or losses resulting from the disposition of a segment of the business.
5. **Extraordinary Items.** Unusual and infrequent material gains and losses.
6. **Cumulative Effect of a Change in Accounting Principle.**
7. **Earnings Per Share.**[8]

[8]Earnings per share or net loss per share is required to be included on the face of the income statement.

Items 1, 2, 3, and 7 are shown in the Dan Deines Company income statement in Illustration 4-2.

Although the content of the operating section is always the same, the organization of the material need not be as described above. The breakdown above uses a **natural expense classification** and is commonly used for manufacturing concerns and for merchandising companies in the wholesale trade. Another classification of operating expenses recommended for retail stores uses a **functional expense classification** of administrative, occupancy, publicity, buying, and selling expenses.

Usually, financial statements that are provided to external users have less detail than internal management reports. The latter tend to have more expense categories—usually grouped along lines of responsibility. This detail allows top management to judge staff performance.

Whether a single-step or a multiple-step income statement is used, irregular transactions such as discontinued operations, extraordinary items, and cumulative effect of changes in accounting principles should be reported separately following income from continuing operations.

Condensed Income Statements

In some cases it is impossible to present in a single income statement of convenient size all the desired expense detail. This problem is solved by including only the totals of expense groups in the statement of income and preparing supplementary schedules of expenses to support the totals. With this format, the income statement itself may be reduced to a few lines on a single sheet. For this reason, readers who wish to study all the reported data on operations must give their attention to the supporting schedules. The income statement shown in Illustration 4-3 for Dan Deines Company is a condensed version of the more detailed multiple-step statement presented earlier and is more representative of the type found in practice.

ILLUSTRATION 4-3
Condensed Income Statement

DAN DEINES COMPANY
Income Statement
For the Year Ended December 31, 2002

Net sales		$2,972,413
Cost of goods sold		1,982,541
Gross profit		989,872
Selling expenses (see Note D)	$453,028	
Administrative expenses	350,771	803,799
Income from operations		186,073
Other revenues and gains		171,410
		357,483
Other expenses and losses		126,060
Income before income tax		231,423
Income tax		66,934
Net income for the year		$ 164,489
Earnings per share		$1.74

An example of a supporting schedule, cross-referenced as Note D and detailing the selling expenses, is shown on page 138 in Illustration 4-4.

How much detail to include in the income statement is always a problem. On the one hand, we want to present a simple, summarized statement so that a reader can readily discover important factors. On the other hand, we want to disclose the results of all activities and to provide more than just a skeleton report. Certain basic elements are always included, but as we'll see they can be presented in various formats.

ILLUSTRATION 4-4
Sample Supporting Schedule

Note D: Selling expenses	
Sales salaries and commissions	$202,644
Sales office salaries	59,200
Travel and entertainment	48,940
Advertising expense	38,315
Freight and transportation-out	41,209
Shipping supplies and expense	24,712
Postage and stationery	16,788
Depreciation of sales equipment	9,005
Telephone and Internet expense	12,215
Total selling expenses	$453,028

REPORTING IRREGULAR ITEMS

OBJECTIVE 4
Explain how irregular items are reported.

Either the single-step or the multiple-step income statement may be used for financial reporting purposes: Flexibility in the presentation of the components of income is thereby permitted. In two important areas, however, specific guidelines have been developed. These two areas relate to what is included in income and how certain unusual or irregular items are reported.

What should be included in net income has been a controversy for many years. For example, should irregular gains and losses and corrections of revenues and expenses of prior years be closed directly to Retained Earnings and therefore not be reported in the income statement? Or should they first be presented in the income statement and then carried to Retained Earnings along with the net income or loss for the period? In general, **income measurement follows an all-inclusive approach. This approach indicates that most items, even irregular ones, are recorded in income.**[9] One exception is errors in prior years' income measurement. Because these items have affected earnings already reported in a prior period, errors from prior periods are not included in current income. Rather, these items are recorded as adjustments to retained earnings.[10]

INTERNATIONAL INSIGHT

In many countries the "modified all-inclusive" income statement approach does not parallel that of the U.S. For example, some gains and losses are not reported on the income statement. Rather, they are taken directly to owners' equity accounts.

Currently there is growing debate concerning **how** irregular items that are part of current income should be reported within the income statement. This issue is extremely important, because the reporting of irregular items on the income statement is substantial. For example, Illustration 4-5 identifies the most common types and number of irregular items reported in a survey of 600 large companies. As indicated, restructuring charges, which many times contain write-offs and other one-time items, were reported by nearly one-third of the surveyed firms. About 20% of the surveyed firms re-

ILLUSTRATION 4-5
Number of Irregular Items Reported in a Recent Year by 600 Large Companies

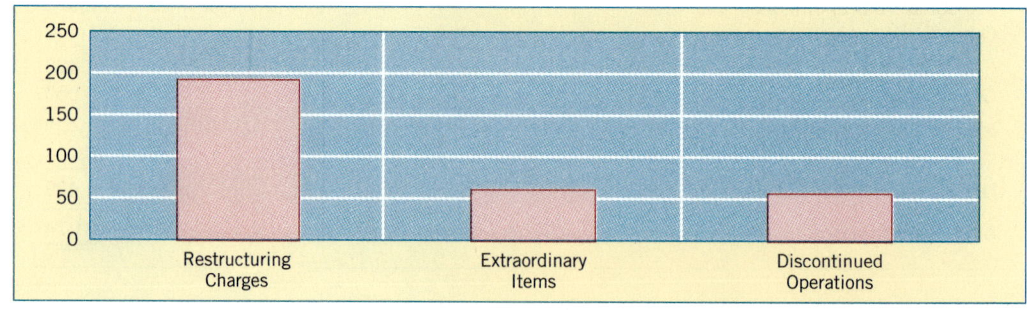

[9]As discussed later in this chapter, the FASB has issued a statement of concepts that offers some guidance on this topic—"Recognition and Measurement in Financial Statements of Business Enterprises," *Statement of Financial Accounting Concepts No. 5* (Stamford, Conn.: FASB, 1984).

[10]This is referred to as "prior period adjustments." Another example of items that bypass the income statement are the gains or losses arising from investment securities and pension adjustments—both cases where there is uncertainty about the realization of these gains or losses. These gains and losses are recorded in owners' equity until they are realized.

ported either an extraordinary item or a discontinued operation charge.[11] Thus, developing a framework for reporting irregular items is important to ensure that financial statement users have reliable income information.[12]

Many users advocate a **current operating performance approach** to income reporting. These analysts argue that the most useful income measure will reflect only regular and recurring revenue and expense elements. Irregular items do not reflect an enterprise's future earning power. As discussed in the opening story about **DaimlerChrysler**, operating-income supporters believe that inclusion of one-time items such as write-offs and restructuring charges reduces the predictive value of the income measure.

In contrast, others warn that a focus on operating income potentially misses important information about a firm's performance. Any gain or loss experienced by the firm, whether directly or indirectly related to operations, contributes to its long-run profitability. As one analyst notes, "write-offs matter. . . . They speak to the volatility of (past) earnings."[13] As a result, some nonoperating items can be used to assess the riskiness of future earnings. Furthermore, determining which items are operating and which items are irregular requires judgment and could lead to differences in the treatment of irregular items and to possible manipulation of income measures.

In this regard a recent study reported that users believe that management sometimes reports unusual losses as nonrecurring but reports unusual gains as part of regular income.[14] For example, when **Gabelli Asset Management** announced its first quarterly earnings, it failed to mention the bottom line income number. Instead Gabelli highlighted a "pro-forma" profit that was adjusted for the effects of a special compensation arrangement for management. Including the effects of these expenses resulted in a loss for the first quarter. Although users do not believe that management intentionally misrepresents accounting results, there is concern that much of the information that companies disseminate is too promotional and that troubled companies take great pains to present their results in the best light.

So, what to do? The accounting profession has **adopted a modified all-inclusive concept and requires application of this approach in practice**. A number of subsequent pronouncements require **irregular items** to be highlighted so that the reader of financial statements can better determine the long-run earning power of the enterprise. These items fall into five general categories:

1. Discontinued operations.
2. Extraordinary items.
3. Unusual gains and losses.
4. Changes in accounting principle.
5. Changes in estimates.

Discontinued Operations

As indicated in Illustration 4-5, one of the most common types of irregular items relates to discontinued operations. To qualify as a discontinued operation, the assets, results of operations, and activities of a segment of a business must be clearly distinguishable, physically and operationally, from the other assets, results of operations, and activities of the entity.

---

[11] *Accounting Trends and Techniques—1998* (New York: AICPA).

[12] The FASB and other international accounting standard setters continue to study the best way to report income. See *Reporting Financial Performance: A Proposed Approach* (Norwalk, Conn.: FASB, September 1999).

[13] D. McDermott, "Latest Profit Data Stir Old Debate Between Net and Operating Income," *The Wall Street Journal,* May 3, 1999.

[14] AICPA Special Committee on Financial Reporting, "The Information Needs of Investors and Creditors," November 1993, p. 13.

The reporting requirements for discontinued operations are complex. In general, a separate income statement category for the gain or loss from **disposal of a segment of a business** must be provided. In addition, the **results of operations of a segment that has been or will be disposed of** are reported in conjunction with the gain or loss on disposal—separately from continuing operations. The effects of discontinued operations are shown net of tax as a separate category, after continuing operations but before extraordinary items.[15]

To illustrate, Multiplex Products, Inc., a highly diversified company, decides to discontinue its electronics division. During the current year, the electronics division lost $300,000 (net of tax) and was sold at the end of the year at a loss of $500,000 (net of tax). The information is shown on the current year's income statement as follows:

ILLUSTRATION 4-6
Income Statement Presentation of Discontinued Operations

Income from continuing operations		$20,000,000
Discontinued operations		
Loss from operation of discontinued electronics division (net of tax)	$300,000	
Loss from disposal of electronics division (net of tax)	500,000	800,000
Net income		$19,200,000

Note that the phrase **"Income from continuing operations"** is used only when gains or losses on discontinued operations occur.

Disposal of assets incidental to the evolution of the entity's business is not considered to be disposal of a segment of the business. **Disposals of assets that do *not* qualify as disposals of a segment** of a business include the following:

1. Disposal of *part* of a line of business.
2. Shifting production or marketing activities for a particular line of business from one location to another.
3. Phasing out of a product line or class of service.
4. Other changes due to a technological improvement.

Examples that would qualify as a disposal of a segment of a business are: (1) sale by a meat-packing company of a 53% interest in a professional football team, or (2) sale by a communications company of all of its radio stations but none of its television stations or publishing houses.

Conversely, examples that would not qualify are (1) discontinuance by a children's wear manufacturer of its operations in Italy but not elsewhere, or (2) sale by a diversified company of one furniture-manufacturing subsidiary but not all furniture-manufacturing subsidiaries. Judgment must be exercised in defining a disposal of a segment of a business because the criteria are difficult to apply in some cases.

Extraordinary Items

Extraordinary items are defined as nonrecurring **material** items that differ significantly from the entity's typical business activities. The criteria for extraordinary items are as follows:

> Extraordinary items are events and transactions that are distinguished by their unusual nature **and** by the infrequency of their occurrence. **Both** of the following criteria must be met to classify an event or transaction as an extraordinary item:

[15]The reporting requirements for discontinued operations are complex. These complexities are discussed more fully in the appendix to this chapter. Our purpose here is to illustrate the basic presentation of this information on the income statement.

(a) **Unusual Nature.** The underlying event or transaction should possess a high degree of abnormality and be of a type clearly unrelated to, or only incidentally related to, the ordinary and typical activities of the entity, taking into account the environment in which the entity operates.

(b) **Infrequency of Occurrence.** The underlying event or transaction should be of a type that would not reasonably be expected to recur in the foreseeable future, taking into account the environment in which the entity operates.[16]

For further clarification, the APB specified that the following gains and losses are **not extraordinary items**:

(a) Write-down or write-off of receivables, inventories, equipment leased to others, deferred research and development costs, or other intangible assets.

(b) Gains or losses from exchange or translation of foreign currencies, including those relating to major devaluations and revaluations.

(c) Gains or losses on disposal of a segment of a business.

(d) Other gains or losses from sale or abandonment of property, plant, or equipment used in the business.

(e) Effects of a strike, including those against competitors and major suppliers.

(f) Adjustment of accruals on long-term contracts.[17]

The items listed above are not considered extraordinary "because they are usual in nature and may be expected to recur as a consequence of customary and continuing business activities."

Only rarely does an event or transaction clearly meet the criteria for an extraordinary item.[18] For example, gains or losses such as (a) and (d) above would be classified as extraordinary if they are a **direct result of a major casualty** (such as an earthquake), **an expropriation**, or **a prohibition under a newly enacted law or regulation**. Such circumstances would clearly meet the criteria of unusual and infrequent. A good example of an extraordinary item is the approximately $36 million loss incurred by **Weyerhaeuser Company** (forest and lumber) as a result of volcanic activity at Mount St. Helens. Standing timber, logs, buildings, equipment, and transportation systems covering 68,000 acres were destroyed by the volcanic eruption.

In determining whether an item is extraordinary, **the environment in which the entity operates is of primary importance**. The environment includes such factors as industry characteristics, geographic location, and the nature and extent of governmental regulations. Thus, extraordinary item treatment is accorded the loss from hail damages to a tobacco grower's crops because severe damage from hailstorms in its locality is rare. On the other hand, frost damage to a citrus grower's crop in Florida does not qualify as extraordinary because frost damage is normally experienced every three or four years. In this environment, the criterion of infrequency is not met.

Classification of items as extraordinary differs across nations. Even in countries in which the criteria for identifying extraordinary items are similar, they are not interpreted identically; thus, what is extraordinary in the U.S. is not necessarily extraordinary elsewhere.

Similarly, when a company sells the only significant security investment it has ever owned, the gain or loss meets the criteria of an extraordinary item. Another company, however, that has a portfolio of securities acquired for investment purposes would not have an extraordinary item. Sale of such securities would be considered part of its ordinary and typical activities.

There are **exceptions** to the general rules provided above. The disposal of a business segment at a gain or loss [item (c) above], which is not an extraordinary item, re-

[16]"Reporting the Results of Operations," *Opinions of the Accounting Principles Board No. 30* (New York: AICPA, 1973), par. 20.

[17]Ibid., par. 23.

[18]Some contend that the criteria for an extraordinary item are so restrictive that only such items as a single chemist who knew the secret formula for an enterprise's mixing solution but was eaten by a tiger on a big game hunt or a plant facility that was smashed by a meteor would qualify for extraordinary item treatment.

quires special accounting treatment. In addition, **material gains and losses from extinguishment of debt** should be reported as an extraordinary item even though these gains or losses do not meet the normal criteria mentioned above for extraordinary items.[19] The rationale for this position will be discussed in Chapter 14.

In addition, considerable judgment must be exercised in determining whether an item should be reported as extraordinary. For example, some paper companies have had their forest lands condemned by the government for state or national parks or forests. Is such an event extraordinary, or is it part of normal operations? Such determination is not easy; much depends on the frequency of previous condemnations, the expectation of future condemnations, materiality, and the like.[20]

Extraordinary items are to be shown net of taxes in a separate section in the income statement, usually just before net income. After listing the usual revenues, costs and expenses, and income taxes, the remainder of the statement shows:

ILLUSTRATION 4-7
Income Statement Placement of Extraordinary Items

Income before extraordinary items
Extraordinary items (less applicable income tax of $________)
Net income

For example, **Keystone Consolidated Industries, Inc.** presented its extraordinary loss in this manner:

ILLUSTRATION 4-8
Income Statement Presentation of Extraordinary Items

KEYSTONE CONSOLIDATED INDUSTRIES, INC.

Income before extraordinary item	$11,638,000
Extraordinary item—flood loss (Note E)	1,216,000
Net income	$10,422,000

Note E: Extraordinary Item. The Keystone Steel and Wire Division's Steel Works experienced a flash flood on June 22. The extraordinary item represents the estimated cost, net of related income taxes of $1,279,000, to restore the steel works to full operation.

Unusual Gains and Losses

Because of the restrictive criteria for extraordinary items, financial statement users must carefully examine the financial statements for items that are **unusual or infrequent but not both**. As indicated earlier, items such as write-downs of inventories and gains and losses from fluctuation of foreign exchange are not considered extraordinary items. Thus, these items are sometimes shown with the normal, recurring revenues, costs, and expenses. If they are not material in amount, they are combined with other items in the income statement. If they are material, they must be disclosed separately, but are shown **above** "income (loss) before extraordinary items."

For example, **Pepsico, Inc.** presented an unusual charge in the following manner in its income statement:

[19]"Reporting Gains and Losses from Extinguishment of Debt," *Statement of Financial Accounting Standards No. 4* (Stamford, Conn.: FASB, 1975), par. 8.

[20]It is often difficult to determine what is extraordinary, because assessing the materiality of individual items requires judgment. However, in making materiality judgments, extraordinary items should be considered individually, and not in the aggregate. "Reporting the Results of Operations," op. cit., par. 24.

ILLUSTRATION 4-9
Income Statement Presentation of Unusual Charges

PEPSICO, INC.
(in millions)

Net sales	$20,917
Costs and expenses, net	
Cost of sales	8,525
Selling, general, and administrative expenses	9,241
Amortization of intangible assets	199
Unusual items (Note 2)	290
Operating income	$2,662

Note 2 (Restructuring Charge)

Dispose and write down assets	$183
Improve productivity	94
Strengthen the international bottler structure	13
Net loss	$290

The net charge to strengthen the international bottler structure includes proceeds of $87 million associated with a settlement related to a previous Venezuelan bottler agreement, which were partially offset by related costs.

As indicated in Illustration 4-5, restructuring charges, like the one reported by Pepsico, have been common in recent years.[21] There has been a tendency to **report unusual items in a separate section just above income from operations before income taxes and extraordinary items**, especially when there are multiple unusual items. For example, when General Electric Company experienced multiple unusual items in one year, it reported them in a separate "Unusual items" section of the income statement below "Income before unusual items and income taxes." When a multiple-step income statement is being prepared for homework purposes, unusual gains and losses should be reported in the other revenues and gains or other expenses and losses section unless you are instructed to prepare a separate unusual items section.[22]

In dealing with events that are either unusual or nonrecurring but not both, the profession attempted to prevent a practice that many believed was misleading. Companies often reported such transactions on a net-of-tax basis and prominently displayed the earnings per share effect of these items. Although not captioned extraordinary items, they are presented in the same manner. Some had referred to these as "first cousins" to extraordinary items. As a consequence, the Board specifically **prohibited a net-of-tax treatment for such items** to ensure that users of financial statements can easily differentiate extraordinary items—which are reported net of tax—from material items that are unusual or infrequent, but not both.

[21]Hardly a day goes by that *The Wall Street Journal* does not announce that a well-known company has taken a restructuring charge. A restructuring charge relates to a major reorganization of company affairs, such as costs associated with employee layoffs, plant closing costs, write-offs of assets, and so on. A restructuring charge should not be reported as an extraordinary item, because these write-offs are considered part of a company's ordinary and typical activities.

Research in this area questions whether the "big bath" works. See, for example, Don Fried, Michael Schiff, and Ashwenpaul C. Sondhi, *Impairments and Writeoffs of Long-Lived Assets* (Montvale, NJ: NAA), and John A. Elliot and Wayne Shaw, "Write-offs as Accounting Procedures to Manage Perceptions," *Journal of Accounting Research* (Supplement, 1988).

[22]As indicated in the opening story, many companies are reporting "one-time items." However, some companies have taken restructuring charges practically every year. Citicorp (now Citigroup) took restructuring charges six years in a row, between 1988 and 1993, and Eastman Kodak Co. did so five out of six years in 1989–1994. Recent research on the market reaction to income containing "one-time" items indicates that the market discounts the earnings of companies that report a series of "nonrecurring" items. Such evidence supports the contention that these elements reduce the quality of earnings. J. Elliott and D. Hanna, "Repeated Accounting Write-offs and the Information Content of Earnings," *Journal of Accounting Research* (Supplement, 1996).

UNDERLYING CONCEPTS

Companies can change principles, but it must be demonstrated that the newly adopted principle is preferable to the old one. Such changes mean that consistency from period to period is lost.

Changes in Accounting Principle

Changes in accounting occur frequently in practice, because important events or conditions may be in dispute or uncertain at the statement date. One type of accounting change, therefore, comprises the normal recurring corrections and adjustments that are made by every business enterprise. Another accounting change results when an accounting principle is adopted that is different from the one previously used. Changes in accounting principle would include a change in the method of inventory pricing from FIFO to average cost or a change in depreciation from the double-declining to the straight-line method.[23]

Changes in accounting principle are recognized by including the cumulative effect as of the beginning of the year, net of tax in the current year's income statement. This amount is based on a retroactive computation of changing to a new accounting principle. **The effect on net income of adopting the new accounting principle should be disclosed as a separate item following extraordinary items in the income statement.**

To illustrate, Gaubert Inc. decided in March 2002 to change from the sum-of-the-years'-digits method of computing depreciation on its plant assets to the straight-line method. The assets originally cost $100,000 in 2000 and have a service life of four years. The data assumed for this illustration and the manner of reporting the change are as shown in Illustration 4-10.

ILLUSTRATION 4-10
Calculation of a Change in Accounting Principle

Year	Sum-of-the-Years'-Digits Depreciation	Straight-Line Depreciation	Excess of Sum-of-the-Years'-Digits over Straight-Line Method
2000	$40,000	$25,000	$15,000
2001	30,000	25,000	5,000
Total			$20,000

The information presented in the 2002 financial statements is shown in Illustration 4-11. (The tax rate was 30%.)

ILLUSTRATION 4-11
Income Statement Presentation of a Change in Accounting Principle

Income before extraordinary item and cumulative effect of a change in accounting principle	$120,000
Extraordinary item—casualty loss (net of $12,000 tax)	(28,000)
Cumulative effect on prior years of retroactive application of new depreciation method (net of $6,000 tax)	14,000
Net income	$106,000

Changes in Estimates

Estimates are inherent in the accounting process. Estimates are made, for example, of useful lives and salvage values of depreciable assets, of uncollectible receivables, of inventory obsolescence, and of the number of periods expected to benefit from a particular expenditure. Not infrequently, as time passes, as circumstances change, or as additional information is obtained, even estimates originally made in good faith must be changed. Such **changes in estimates** are accounted for in the period of change if they affect only that period, or in the period of change and future periods if the change affects both.

[23]"Accounting Changes," *Opinions of the Accounting Principles Board No. 20* (New York: AICPA, 1971), par. 18. Chapter 23 examines in greater detail the problems related to accounting changes; our purpose now is to provide general guidance for the major types of transactions affecting the income statement.

To illustrate a change in estimate that affects only the period of change, assume that DuPage Materials Corp. has consistently estimated its bad debt expense at 1% of credit sales. In 2001, however, DuPage's controller determines that the estimate of bad debts for the current year's credit sales must be revised upward to 2%, or double the prior years' percentage. Using 2% results in a bad debt charge of $240,000 or double the amount using the 1% estimate for prior years. The 2% rate is necessary to reduce accounts receivable to net realizable value. The provision is recorded at December 31, 2001, as follows:

Bad Debt Expense	240,000	
Allowance for Doubtful Accounts		240,000

The entire change in estimate is included in 2001 income because no future periods are affected by the change. **Changes in estimate are not handled retroactively**, that is, carried back to adjust prior years. Changes in estimate that affect both the current period and future periods are examined in greater detail in Chapter 23. **Changes in estimate are not considered errors (prior period adjustments) or extraordinary items.**

Summary of Irregular Items

The public accounting profession now tends to accept a modified all-inclusive income concept instead of the current operating performance concept. Except for a couple of items (discussed later in this chapter) that are charged or credited directly to retained earnings, all other irregular gains or losses or nonrecurring items are closed to Income Summary and are included in the income statement. Of these, **discontinued operations of a segment** of a business is classified as a separate item in the income statement after continuing operations. The **unusual, material, nonrecurring items** that are significantly different from the typical or customary business activities are shown in a separate section for **"extraordinary items"** below discontinued operations. Other items of a material amount that are of an **unusual or nonrecurring** nature and are **not considered extraordinary** are separately disclosed. In addition, the cumulative adjustment that occurs when a change in accounting principles develops is disclosed as a separate item just before net income.

UNDERLYING CONCEPTS

The AICPA Special Committee on Financial Reporting indicates a company's core activities—usual and recurring events—provide the best historical data from which users determine trends and relationships and make their predictions about the future. Therefore, the effects of core and non-core activities should be separately displayed.

Because of the numerous intermediate income figures that are created by the reporting of these irregular items, careful evaluation of information reported by the financial press is needed. Illustration 4-12 (page 146) summarizes the basic concepts previously discussed. Although the chart is simplified, it provides a useful framework for determining the proper treatment of special items affecting the income statement.

SPECIAL REPORTING ISSUES

Intraperiod Tax Allocation

OBJECTIVE 5
Explain intraperiod tax allocation.

We noted that certain irregular items are shown on the income statement net of tax. Many believe that the resulting income tax effect should be directly associated with that event or item. In other words, the tax expense for the year should be related, where possible, to **specific** items on the income statement to provide a more informative disclosure to statement users. This procedure is called **intraperiod tax allocation**, that is, allocation within a period. Its main purpose is to relate the income tax expense of the fiscal period to the items that affect the amount of the tax provisions. Intraperiod tax allocation is used for the following items: (1) income from continuing operations, (2) discontinued operations, (3) extraordinary items, and (4) changes in accounting principle. The general concept is **"let the tax follow the income."**

The income tax expense attributable to "income from continuing operations" is computed by finding the income tax expense related to revenue and to expense transactions used in determining this income. In this tax computation, no effect is given to the tax consequences of the items excluded from the determination of "income from continuing operations." A separate tax effect is then associated with each irregular item.

ILLUSTRATION 4-12 Summary of Irregular Items in the Income Statement

Type of Situation[a]	Criteria	Examples	Placement on Financial Statements
Discontinued operations	Disposal of a segment of a business constituting a separate line of business or class of customer.	Sale by diversified company of major division that represents only activities in electronics industry. Food distributor that sells wholesale to supermarket chains and through fast-food restaurants decides to discontinue the division that sells to one of two classes of customers.	Shown in separate section of the income statement after continuing operations but before extraordinary items. (Shown net of tax.)
Extraordinary items	Material, and both unusual and infrequent (nonrecurring).	Gains or losses resulting from casualties, an expropriation, or a prohibition under a new law.[b]	Separate section in the income statement entitled extraordinary items. (Shown net of tax.)
Unusual gains or losses, not considered extraordinary	Material; character typical of the customary business activities; unusual or infrequent but not both.	Write-downs of receivables, inventories; adjustments of accrued contract prices; gains or losses from fluctuations of foreign exchange; gains or losses from sales of assets used in business.	Separate section in income statement above income before extraordinary items. Often reported in other revenues and gains or other expenses and losses section. (Not shown net of tax.)
Changes in principle[c]	Change from one generally accepted principle to another.	Changing the basis of inventory pricing from FIFO to average cost; change in the method of depreciation from accelerated to straight-line.	Cumulative effect of the change is reflected in the income statement between the captions extraordinary items and net income. (Shown net of tax.)
Changes in estimates	Normal, recurring corrections and adjustments.	Changes in the realizability of receivables and inventories; changes in estimated lives of equipment, intangible assets; changes in estimated liability for warranty costs, income taxes, and salary payments.	Change in income statement only in the account affected. (Not shown net of tax.)

[a]This summary provides only the general rules to be followed in accounting for the various situations described above. Exceptions do exist in some of these situations.

[b]Material gains and losses from extinguishment of debt are considered extraordinary, even though criteria for extraordinary items may not be met.

[c]The general rule per *APB Opinion No. 20* is to use the cumulative effect approach. However, all the recent FASB pronouncements require or permit the retroactive method whenever a new standard is adopted for the first time.

Extraordinary Gains

In applying the concept of intraperiod tax allocation, assume that Schindler Co. has income before income tax and extraordinary item of $250,000 and an extraordinary gain from the sale of a single stock investment of $100,000. If the income tax rate is assumed to be 30%, the following information is presented on the income statement:

ILLUSTRATION 4-13
Intraperiod Tax Allocation, Extraordinary Gain

Income before income tax and extraordinary item		$250,000
Income tax		75,000
Income before extraordinary item		175,000
Extraordinary gain—sale of investment	$100,000	
Less: Applicable income tax	30,000	70,000
Net income		$245,000

The income tax of $75,000 ($250,000 × 30%) attributable to "income before income tax and extraordinary item" is determined from revenue and expense transactions related

to this income. In this income tax computation, the tax consequences of items excluded from the determination of "income before income tax and extraordinary item" are not considered. The "extraordinary gain—sale of investment" then shows a separate tax effect of $30,000.

Extraordinary Losses

To illustrate the reporting of an extraordinary loss, assume that Schindler Co. has income before income tax and extraordinary item of $250,000 and an extraordinary loss from a major casualty of $100,000. Assuming a 30% tax rate, the presentation of income tax on the income statement would be as follows:

ILLUSTRATION 4-14
Intraperiod Tax Allocation, Extraordinary Loss

Income before income tax and extraordinary item		$250,000
Income tax		75,000
Income before extraordinary item		175,000
Extraordinary item—loss from casualty	$100,000	
Less: Applicable income tax reduction	30,000	70,000
Net income		$105,000

In this case, the loss provides a positive tax benefit of $30,000 and, therefore, is subtracted from the $100,000 loss.

An extraordinary item may be reported "net of tax" with note disclosure as illustrated below:

ILLUSTRATION 4-15
Note Disclosure of Intraperiod Tax Allocation

Income before income tax and extraordinary item	$250,000
Income tax	75,000
Income before extraordinary item	175,000
Extraordinary item, less applicable income tax reduction (Note 1)	70,000
Net income	$105,000

Note 1: During the year the Company suffered a major casualty loss of $70,000, net of applicable income tax reduction of $30,000.

Earnings per Share

OBJECTIVE 6
Explain where earnings per share information is reported.

The results of a company's operations are customarily summed up in one important figure: net income. As if this condensation were not enough of a simplification, the financial world has widely accepted an even more distilled and compact figure as its most significant business indicator—**earnings per share.**

The computation of earnings per share is usually straightforward. **Net income minus preferred dividends (income available to common stockholders) is divided by the weighted average of common shares outstanding to arrive at earnings per share.**[24] To illustrate, assume that Lancer, Inc. reports net income of $350,000 and declares and pays preferred dividends of $50,000 for the year. The weighted average number of common shares outstanding during the year is 100,000 shares. Earnings per share is $3.00, as computed in Illustration 4-16.

ILLUSTRATION 4-16
Equation Illustrating Computation of Earnings per Share

$$\frac{\text{Net Income} - \text{Preferred Dividends}}{\text{Weighted Average of Common Shares Outstanding}} = \text{Earnings per Share}$$

$$\frac{\$350{,}000 - \$50{,}000}{100{,}000} = \$3.00$$

[24]In the calculation of earnings per share, preferred dividends are deducted from net income if declared or if cumulative though not declared.

Note that the EPS figure measures the number of dollars earned by each share of common stock—but not the dollar amount paid to stockholders in the form of dividends.

"Net income per share" or "earnings per share" is a ratio commonly used in prospectuses, proxy material, and annual reports to stockholders. It is also highlighted in the financial press, by statistical services like Standard & Poor's, and by Wall Street securities analysts. Because of its importance, **earnings per share is required to be disclosed on the face of the income statement**. A company that reports a discontinued operation, an extraordinary item, or the cumulative effect of a change in accounting principle, must report per share amounts for these line items either on the face of the income statement or in the notes to the financial statements.[25]

To illustrate both the income statement order of presentation and the earnings per share data, we present an income statement for Poquito Industries Inc. in Illustration 4-17. Notice the order in which data are shown. In addition, per share information is shown at the bottom. Assume that the company had 100,000 shares outstanding for the entire year. The Poquito Industries Inc. income statement, in Illustration 4-17, is highly condensed. Items such as the "Unusual charge," "Discontinued operations," "Extraordinary item," and the "Change in accounting principle" would have to be described fully and appropriately in the statement or related notes.

ILLUSTRATION 4-17
Income Statement

POQUITO INDUSTRIES INC.
Income Statement
For the Year Ended December 31, 2001

Sales revenue		$1,480,000
Cost of goods sold		600,000
Gross profit		880,000
Selling and administrative expenses		320,000
Income from operations		560,000
Other revenues and gains		
Interest revenue		10,000
Other expenses and losses		
Loss on disposal of part of Textile Division	$ (5,000)	
Unusual charge—loss on sale of investments	(45,000)	(50,000)
Income from continuing operations before income tax		520,000
Income tax		208,000
Income from continuing operations		312,000
Discontinued operations		
Income from operations of Pizza Division, less applicable income tax of $24,800	54,000	
Loss on disposal of Pizza Division, less applicable income tax of $41,000	(90,000)	(36,000)
Income before extraordinary item and cumulative effect of accounting change		276,000
Extraordinary item—loss from earthquake, less applicable income tax of $23,000		(45,000)
Cumulative effect on prior years of retroactive application of new depreciation method, less applicable income tax of $30,900		(60,000)
Net income		$ 171,000
Per share of common stock		
Income from continuing operations		$3.12
Income from operations of discontinued division, net of tax		.54
Loss on disposal of discontinued operation, net of tax		(.90)
Income before extraordinary item and cumulative effect		2.76
Extraordinary loss, net of tax		(.45)
Cumulative effect of change in accounting principle, net of tax		(.60)
Net income		$1.71

[25]"Earnings Per Share," *Statement of Financial Accounting Standards No. 128* (Norwalk, Conn.: FASB, 1996).

Many corporations have simple capital structures that include only common stock. For these companies, a presentation such as "earnings per common share" is appropriate on the income statement. In many instances, however, companies' earnings per share are subject to dilution (reduction) in the future because existing contingencies permit the issuance of additional common shares.[26]

In summary, the simplicity and availability of figures for per share earnings lead inevitably to their widespread use. Because of the undue importance that the public, even the well-informed public, attaches to earnings per share, the earnings per share figure must be made as meaningful as possible.

Retained Earnings Statement

OBJECTIVE 7
Prepare a retained earnings statement.

Net income increases retained earnings and a net loss decreases retained earnings. Both cash and stock dividends decrease retained earnings. Prior period adjustments may either increase or decrease retained earnings. A **prior period adjustment** is a correction of an error in the financial statements of a prior period. Prior period adjustments (net of tax) are charged or credited to the opening balance of retained earnings, and thus excluded from the determination of net income for the current period.

Information related to retained earnings may be shown in different ways. For example, some companies prepare a separate retained earnings statement, as shown in Illustration 4-18.

ILLUSTRATION 4-18
Retained Earnings Statement

TIGER WOODS INC.
Retained Earnings Statement
For the Year Ended December 31, 2002

Balance, January 1, as reported		$1,050,000
Correction for understatement of net income in prior period (inventory error)		50,000
Balance, January 1, as adjusted		1,100,000
Add: Net income		360,000
		1,460,000
Less: Cash dividends	$100,000	
Stock dividends	200,000	300,000
Balance, December 31		$1,160,000

The reconciliation of the beginning to the ending balance in retained earnings provides information about why net assets increased or decreased during the year. The association of dividend distributions with net income for the period indicates what management is doing with earnings: It may be "plowing back" into the business part or all of the earnings, distributing all current income, or distributing current income plus the accumulated earnings of prior years.

Appropriations of Retained Earnings

Retained earnings is often restricted—**appropriated**—in accordance with contractual requirements, board of directors' policy, or the apparent necessity of the moment. The amounts of retained earnings appropriated are transferred to **Appropriated Retained Earnings**. The retained earnings section may therefore report two separate amounts—(1) retained earnings free (unrestricted) and (2) retained earnings appropriated (restricted). The total of these two amounts equals the total retained earnings.[27]

---

[26]Ibid. The computational problems involved in accounting for these dilutive securities in earnings per share computations are discussed in Chapter 17.

[27]*Accounting Trends and Techniques—1999* (New York: AICPA) indicates that most companies (577 of 600 surveyed) present changes in retained earnings either within the statement of stockholders' equity (562 firms) or in a separate statement of retained earnings. Only 7 of the 600 companies prepare a combined statement of income and retained earnings.

Comprehensive Income

As indicated earlier, the all-inclusive income concept is used in determining financial performance for a period of time. Under this concept, all revenues, expenses, and gains and losses recognized during the period are included in income. However, over time, specific exceptions to this general concept have developed so that certain items now bypass income and are reported directly in equity. An example of one of these items is unrealized gains and losses on available-for-sale securities.[28]

Why are these gains and losses on available-for-sale securities excluded from net income? Because disclosing them separately (1) reduces the volatility of net income due to fluctuations in fair value, yet (2) informs the financial statement user of the gain or loss that would be incurred if the securities were sold at fair value.

Items that bypass the income statement are included under the concept of comprehensive income. **Comprehensive income** includes all changes in equity during a period except those resulting from investments by owners and distributions to owners. Comprehensive income, therefore, includes all revenues and gains, expenses and losses reported in net income, and, in addition it includes gains and losses that bypass net income but affect stockholders' equity. These items that bypass the income statement are referred to as **other comprehensive income**.

The users of financial statements have expressed concern over the increasing number of items that are being reported as other comprehensive income (adjustments to stockholders' equity). As one set of writers noted, equity is becoming a dumpster for an amorphous and growing mass of important information. As more and different types of items are reported as adjustments to stockholders' equity, many argue that a separate new statement is needed to report the information in an organized way.

OBJECTIVE 8
Explain how other comprehensive income is reported.

Recently, the FASB evaluated several approaches to providing more information about other comprehensive income items. It decided that the components of other comprehensive income must be displayed in one of three ways: **(1) a second separate income statement; (2) a combined income statement of comprehensive income; or (3) as a part of the statement of stockholders' equity.**[29]

Regardless of the format used, net income must be added to other comprehensive income to arrive at comprehensive income. Earnings per share information related to comprehensive income is not required. To illustrate these three presentation formats, assume that V. Gill Inc. reports the following information for 2002: sales revenue $800,000, cost of goods sold $600,000, operating expenses $90,000, and an unrealized holding gain on available-for-sale securities of $30,000, net of tax.[30]

Second Income Statement

The two-income statement format is shown in Illustration 4-19 on the next page. Reporting comprehensive income in a separate statement indicates that the gains and losses identified as other comprehensive income have the same status as traditional gains and losses. In addition, the relationship of the traditional income statement to the comprehensive income statement is apparent because net income is the starting point in the comprehensive income statement.

[28]Available-for-sale securities are further discussed in Chapter 18. Examples of other comprehensive items are translation gains and losses on foreign currency, excess of additional pension liability over unrecognized prior service cost, and unrealized gains and losses on certain hedging transactions.

[29]"Reporting Comprehensive Income," *Statement of Financial Accounting Standards No. 130* (Norwalk, Conn.: FASB, June 1997).

[30]A company is required to display the components of other comprehensive income either (1) net of related tax effects or (2) before related tax effects with one amount shown for the aggregate amount of tax related to the total amount of other comprehensive income. Under either alternative, each component of other comprehensive income must be shown, net of related taxes either in the face of the statement or in the notes.

ILLUSTRATION 4-19
Two-Statement Format: Comprehensive Income

V. GILL INC. Income Statement For the Year Ended December 31, 2002	
Sales revenue	$800,000
Cost of goods sold	600,000
Gross profit	200,000
Operating expenses	90,000
Net income	$110,000

V. GILL INC. Comprehensive Income Statement For the Year Ended December 31, 2002	
Net income	$110,000
Other comprehensive income	
Unrealized holding gain, net of tax	30,000
Comprehensive income	$140,000

Combined Income Statement

The second approach provides a combined statement in which the traditional net income would be a subtotal, with total comprehensive income shown as a final total. A combined statement of comprehensive income is shown in Illustration 4-20 below:

ILLUSTRATION 4-20
Combined Income Statement Format: Comprehensive Income

V. GILL INC. Combined Statement of Comprehensive Income For the Year Ended December 31, 2002	
Sales revenue	$800,000
Cost of goods sold	600,000
Gross profit	200,000
Operating expenses	90,000
Net income	110,000
Unrealized holding gain, net of tax	30,000
Comprehensive income	$140,000

As shown, comprehensive income is $140,000 and net income is $110,000; the difference is due to the unrealized holding gain of $30,000. The combined statement has the advantage of not requiring the creation of a new financial statement. However, burying net income in a subtotal on the statement is a disadvantage.

Statement of Stockholders' Equity

A third approach is to report other comprehensive income items in a **statement of stockholders' equity** (often referred to as statement of changes in stockholders' equity). This statement reports the changes in each stockholder's equity account and in total stockholders' equity during the year. The statement of stockholders' equity is often **prepared in columnar form** with columns for each account and for total stockholders' equity.

To illustrate its presentation, assume the same information above related to V. Gill Inc. and that the company had the following stockholder equity account balances at the beginning of 2002: Common Stock $300,000; Retained Earnings $50,000; and Accumulated Other Comprehensive Income $60,000. No changes in the Common Stock account occurred during the year. A statement of stockholders' equity for V. Gill Inc. is shown in Illustration 4-21 on the next page.

ILLUSTRATION 4-21
Presentation of Comprehensive Income Items in Stockholders' Equity Statement

Go to the Digital Tool for examples of comprehensive income reporting.

V. GILL INC.
Statement of Stockholders' Equity
For the Year Ended December 31, 2002

	Total	Comprehensive Income	Retained Earnings	Accumulated Other Comprehensive Income	Common Stock
Beginning balance	$410,000		$ 50,000	$60,000	$300,000
Comprehensive income					
Net income	110,000	$110,000	110,000		
Other comprehensive income					
Unrealized holding gain, net of tax	30,000	30,000		30,000	
Comprehensive income		$140,000			
Ending balance	$550,000		$160,000	$90,000	$300,000

Most companies use the statement of stockholders' equity approach to provide information related to the components of other comprehensive income. Many companies already provide a statement of stockholders' equity; adding additional columns to display information related to comprehensive income is not costly.

Balance Sheet Presentation

Regardless of the display format used, the **accumulated other comprehensive income** of $90,000 is reported in the stockholders' equity section of the balance sheet of V. Gill Inc. as follows:

ILLUSTRATION 4-22
Presentation of Accumulated Other Comprehensive Income in the Balance Sheet

V. GILL INC.
Balance Sheet
As of December 31, 2002
(Stockholders' Equity Section)

Stockholders' equity	
Common stock	$300,000
Retained earnings	160,000
Accumulated other comprehensive income	90,000
Total stockholders' equity	$550,000

By providing information on the components of comprehensive income as well as total accumulated other comprehensive income, the firm communicates information about all changes in net assets.[31] With this information, users will be better able to understand the quality of the company's earnings. This information should help users predict the amount, timing, and uncertainty of future cash flows.

Observations on Comprehensive Income

The FASB encourages, but does not require, that the term comprehensive income be used. The reason is that many oppose the use of the term comprehensive income because they believe this amount is neither "comprehensive" nor is it "income." Therefore, many companies will undoubtedly use terms such as "total nonowner changes in equity" instead of comprehensive income.

As indicated earlier, it is also likely that most companies will not report the components of comprehensive income using an income statement approach. Rather, the in-

[31]Note that prior period adjustments and the cumulative effect of changes in accounting principle are not considered other comprehensive income items.

formation related to comprehensive income will be reported in the statement of stockholders' equity. If companies choose to report the components of other comprehensive income in a statement of stockholders' equity, that statement must be displayed as a primary financial statement.[32]

SUMMARY OF LEARNING OBJECTIVES

1 Identify the uses and limitations of an income statement. The income statement provides investors and creditors with information that helps them predict the amounts, timing, and uncertainty of future cash flows. Also, the income statement helps users determine the risk (level of uncertainty) of not achieving particular cash flows. The limitations of an income statement are: (1) the statement does not include many items that contribute to general growth and well-being of an enterprise; (2) income numbers are often affected by the accounting methods used; and (3) income measures are subject to estimates.

The *transaction approach* focuses on the activities that have occurred during a given period; instead of presenting only a net change, it discloses the components of the change. The transaction approach to income measurement requires the use of revenue, expense, loss, and gain accounts.

2 Prepare a single-step income statement. In a single-step income statement, just two groupings exist: revenues and expenses. Expenses are deducted from revenues to arrive at net income or loss—a single subtraction. Frequently, income tax is reported separately as the last item before net income to indicate its relationship to income before income tax.

3 Prepare a multiple-step income statement. A multiple-step income statement shows two further classifications: (1) a separation of operating results from those obtained through the subordinate or nonoperating activities of the company; and (2) a classification of expenses by functions, such as merchandising or manufacturing, selling, and administration.

4 Explain how irregular items are reported. Irregular gains or losses or nonrecurring items are generally closed to Income Summary and are included in the income statement. These are treated in the income statement as follows: (1) Discontinued operation of a segment of a business is classified as a separate item, after continuing operations. (2) The unusual, material, nonrecurring items that are significantly different from the customary business activities are shown in a separate section for extraordinary items, below discontinued operations. (3) Other items of a material amount that are of an unusual or nonrecurring nature and are not considered extraordinary are separately disclosed. (4) The cumulative adjustment that occurs when a change in accounting principles develops is disclosed as a separate item, just before net income.

5 Explain intraperiod tax allocation. The tax expense for the year should be related, where possible, to specific items on the income statement, to provide a more informative disclosure to statement users. This procedure is called intraperiod tax allocation, that is, allocation within a period. Its main purpose is to relate the income tax expense for the fiscal period to the following items that affect the amount of the tax provisions: (1) income from continuing operations, (2) discontinued operations, (3) extraordinary items, and (4) changes in accounting principle.

KEY TERMS

- accumulated other comprehensive income, *152*
- all-inclusive approach, *138*
- appropriated retained earnings, *149*
- capital maintenance approach, *133n*
- changes in estimate, *144*
- comprehensive income, *150*
- current operating performance approach, *139*
- earnings management, *132*
- earnings per share, *147*
- income statement, *130*
- intraperiod tax allocation, *145*
- irregular items, *139*
- modified all-inclusive concept, *139*
- multiple-step income statement, *134*
- other comprehensive income, *150*
- prior period adjustments, *149*
- quality of earnings, *132*
- single-step income statement, *134*
- statement of stockholders' equity, *151*
- transaction approach, *132*

[32]Some companies such as **General Motors** have provided a statement of stockholders' equity only in the notes to the financial statements. If it chooses to report its comprehensive income information in the statement of stockholders' equity, it will now have to give it equal prominence with the balance sheet, income statement, and statement of cash flows.

6 **Explain where earnings per share information is reported.** Because of the inherent dangers of focusing attention solely on earnings per share, the profession concluded that earnings per share must be disclosed on the face of the income statement. A company that reports a discontinued operation, an extraordinary item, or the cumulative effect of a change in accounting principle must report per share amounts for these line items either on the face of the income statement or in the notes to the financial statements.

7 **Prepare a retained earnings statement.** The retained earnings statement should disclose net income (loss), dividends, prior period adjustments, and transfers to and from retained earnings (appropriations).

8 **Explain how other comprehensive income is reported.** The components of other comprehensive income are reported in a second statement, a combined income statement of comprehensive income, or in a statement of stockholders' equity.

APPENDIX 4A

Accounting for Discontinued Operations

OBJECTIVE 9
After studying Appendix 4A, you should be able to: Measure and report gains and losses from discontinued operations.

The chapter discussed how and where gains and losses related to discontinued operations are reported on the income statement. This appendix discusses the more technical aspects of how such a gain or loss is computed, along with related reporting issues.

Recall that the assets, results of operations, and activities of a **business segment** must be clearly distinguishable, physically and operationally, to qualify for discontinued operations treatment. Recall, too, that in the income statement, discontinued operations are classified as a separate item, net of tax, after continuing operations.

FIRST ILLUSTRATION—NO PHASE-OUT PERIOD

To illustrate the accounting for a discontinued operation, assume that the board of directors of Heartland Inc. decided on October 1, 2000, to sell a division of the company called Concept Cassettes. Concept Cassettes had provided cassette tapes for Heartland's 15 retail stores. Heartland's management could see that the compact disc was revolutionizing the recording industry and would soon render its cassette tape division unprofitable. Fortunately, a buyer was available immediately, and the division was sold on October 1, 2000.

Heartland Inc. had income of $2,000,000 for the year 2000, not including a $150,000 loss from operations of Concept Cassettes from January 1 to October 1, 2000. Heartland Inc. was able to sell the division at a gain of $400,000. Its tax rate on all items was 30%.

Heartland's accountants first must decide whether to treat the sale as a discontinued operation. The assets and operations of Concept Cassettes can be easily identified, and the cassette business is distinct from Heartland's other lines of business. Accordingly, **the disposal of Concept Cassettes does constitute the disposal of a segment of the business.**

For the period up to the time management commits itself to sell the division, the revenues and expenses of the discontinued operations are aggregated and reported as income or loss on discontinued operations, net of tax. The date at which time management formally commits itself to a formal plan to dispose of a segment of the business is referred to as the **measurement date**. In this case, it is October 1, 2000. The plan of disposal should include, as a minimum:

1. Identification of the major assets to be disposed of.
2. The expected method of disposal.
3. The period expected to be required for completion of the disposal.
4. An active program to find a buyer if disposal is to be by sale.
5. Estimated results of operations of the segment from the measurement date to the disposal date.
6. Estimated proceeds or salvage to be realized by disposal.

Because the segment has actually been sold on October 1, 2000, a gain or loss on disposal is computed. This date is referred to as the **disposal date**. Because the measurement date and the disposal date are the same, no unusual complications occur. The following diagram illustrates Heartland's situation:

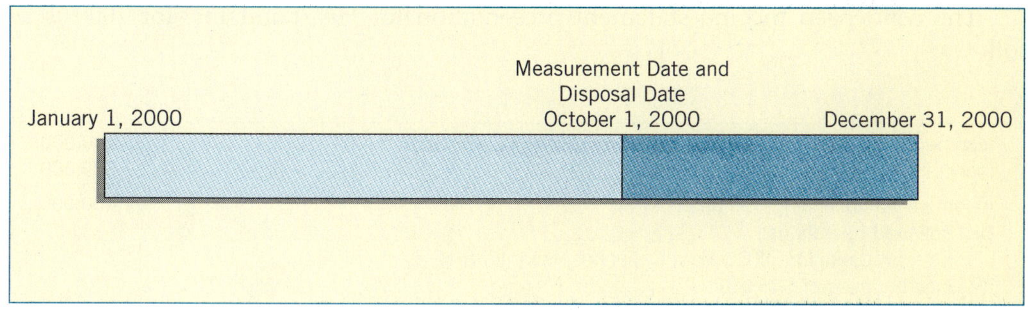

ILLUSTRATION 4A-1
Example of Discontinued Operations with No Phase-Out Period

The condensed income statement presentation for Heartland Inc. for 2000 is as follows:

ILLUSTRATION 4A-2
Presentation of Discontinued Operations, No Phase-Out Period

Income from continuing operations before income taxes		$2,000,000
Income taxes		600,000
Income from continuing operations		1,400,000
Discontinued operations:		
Loss from operation of Concept Cassettes, less applicable income taxes of $45,000	$(105,000)	
Gain on disposal of Concept Cassettes, less applicable income taxes of $120,000	280,000	175,000
Net income		$1,575,000

SECOND ILLUSTRATION—PHASE-OUT PERIOD

In practice the measurement date and the disposal date are rarely the same. Normally, the disposal date would be later than the measurement date. Thus, **the gain or loss on disposal would be the sum of**:

1. Income (loss) from the measurement date to the disposal date (called the **phase-out period**).
2. Gain (loss) on the disposal of the net assets.

The reason for aggregating the above two items to compute the gain (loss) on disposal is that the selling company needs a reasonable period to phase out its discontinued operations. The income (loss) from operations of the discontinued segment is part of the computation of the gain (loss) on disposal because the phase-out period often enables the seller to obtain a better selling price.

To illustrate the combination of these two components, assume that Heartland's sale of Concept Cassettes does not occur until December 1, 2000, at which time it is sold at a gain of $350,000. During the period October 1, 2000, to December 1, 2000, the Concept Cassettes division suffered a loss of $50,000 from operations. The following diagram illustrates Heartland's situation.

ILLUSTRATION 4A-3
Example of Discontinued Operations with Phase-Out Period

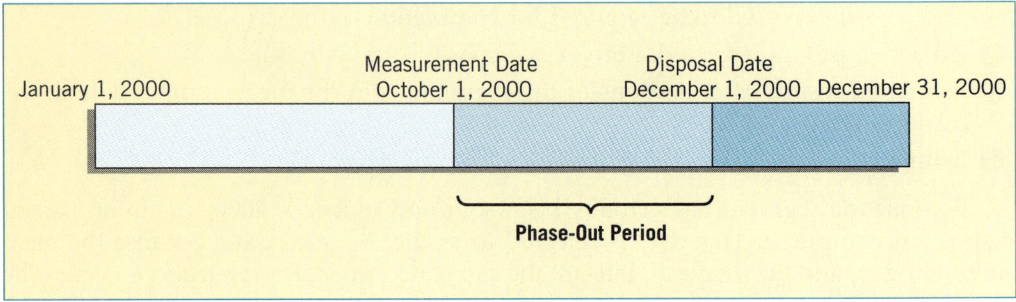

The condensed income statement presentation for Heartland Inc. for 2000 is as follows:

ILLUSTRATION 4A-4
Presentation of Discontinued Operations with Phase-Out Period

Income from continuing operations before income taxes		$2,000,000
Income taxes		600,000
Income from continuing operations		1,400,000
Discontinued operations:		
Loss from operation of Concept Cassettes, less applicable income taxes of $45,000	$(105,000)	
Gain on disposal of Concept Cassettes, including operating loss of $50,000 and gain on disposal of $350,000, less applicable income taxes of $90,000	210,000	105,000
Net income		$1,505,000

THIRD ILLUSTRATION—EXTENDED PHASE-OUT PERIOD

In the preceding illustration, the disposal of the discontinued operation occurred in the same accounting period as the measurement date. As a result, determining the proper gain or loss on the disposal of Concept Cassettes at the end of year was straightforward. However, the phase-out period often extends into another year. In this case, *APB Opinion No. 30* states that **if a loss is expected on disposal, the estimated loss should be reported at the measurement date. If a gain on disposal is expected, it should be recognized when realized, which is ordinarily the disposal date.** In other words, the profession has taken a conservative position by recognizing losses immediately but deferring gains until realized.

Implementing these general rules can be troublesome. In order to determine the gain or loss on disposal of the segment, the income (loss) from operations must be estimated and then combined with the estimated gain (loss) on sale. If a net loss results, then it is recognized at the measurement date. If a net gain arises, it generally is recognized at the date of disposal. **The major exception is when realized gains exceed estimated unrealized and realized net losses. In that special case, realized gains can be recognized in the period of the measurement date.**

Net Loss

To illustrate, assume that Heartland Inc. expects to sell its Concept Cassettes division on May 1, 2001, at a gain of $350,000. In addition, from October 1, 2000, to December 31, 2000, it realized a loss of $400,000 on operations for this segment and expects to lose an additional $200,000 on it from January 1, 2001, to May 1, 2001. The following diagram illustrates Heartland's situation.

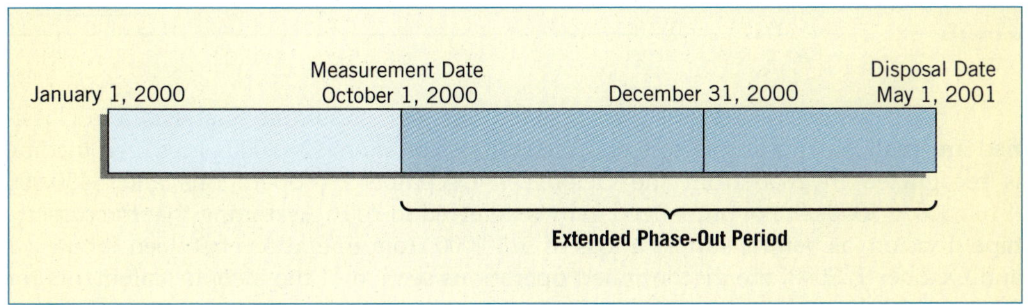

ILLUSTRATION 4A-5
Example of Discontinued Operations with Extended Phase-Out Period

The computation of the net gain or loss on disposal is shown in Illustration 4A-6.

ILLUSTRATION 4A-6
Computation of the Net Loss on Disposal

Realized loss on operations October 1–December 31, 2000	$(400,000)
Expected loss on operations January 1–May 1, 2001	(200,000)
Expected gain on sale of assets on May 1, 2001	350,000
Net loss on disposal	$(250,000)

Given that a net loss on disposal is expected, the loss on disposal is recognized in the period of the measurement date. The condensed income statement presentation for Heartland Inc. for 2000 is therefore reported as shown in Illustration 4A-7.

ILLUSTRATION 4A-7
Presentation of Expected Loss from Discontinued Operations

Income from continuing operations before income taxes		$2,000,000
Income taxes		600,000
Income from continuing operations		1,400,000
Discontinued operations:		
Loss from operation of Concept Cassettes, net of applicable income taxes of $45,000	$(105,000)	
Loss on disposal of Concept Cassettes, including provision for losses during phase-out period, $600,000, and estimated gain on sale of assets, $350,000, net of applicable income taxes of $75,000	(175,000)	(280,000)
Net income		$1,120,000

If the estimated amounts of any of the items later prove to be incorrect, the correction should be reported in the later period when the estimate is determined to be incorrect. Prior periods should not be restated.

Net Gain

To illustrate recognition of a realized gain and deferral of an unrealized gain in the same discontinued operation, assume that Heartland Inc. expects to sell its Concept Cassettes division on May 1, 2001, at a gain of $350,000. In addition, from October 1,

2000, to December 31, 2000, it realized income of $200,000 on operations for this segment and expects to earn an additional $100,000 of profit on it from January 1, 2001, to May 1, 2001. The computation of the net gain or loss on disposal is as follows:

ILLUSTRATION 4A-8
Computation of Net Gain on Disposal

Realized income on operations October 1–December 31, 2000	$200,000
Expected income on operations January 1–May 1, 2001	100,000
Expected gain on sale of assets on May 1, 2001	350,000
Net gain on disposal	$650,000

When a net gain on disposal is expected, the gain should be analyzed and classified into realized and unrealized amounts. In this situation, $200,000 of realized income is recognized in 2000 from the October 1–December 31 operations and $450,000 ($100,000 + $350,000) of unrealized gain is deferred to 2001. Assuming that the cassette tape division, as before, suffers a loss of $150,000 from operations between January 1 and October 1, 2000, the discontinued operations section of the income statements for 2000 and 2001 would appear as follows:

ILLUSTRATION 4A-9
Presentation of Gain from Discontinued Operations

2000		
Discontinued operations:		
Loss from operations of Concept Cassettes, less applicable income taxes of $45,000	$(105,000)	
Gain on disposal of Concept Cassettes, less applicable income taxes of $60,000	140,000	35,000
2001		
Discontinued operations:		
Gain on disposal of Concept Cassettes, less applicable income taxes of $135,000		$315,000

If a net unrealized loss of $150,000 had been expected during the 2001 portion of the extended phase-out period, instead of the $450,000 unrealized gain noted above, a net realized gain on disposal of $50,000 ($200,000 − $150,000) before income taxes would be recognized in 2000.

Summary

UNDERLYING CONCEPTS
This accounting treatment is the application of conservatism: recognize all losses, but only realized gains.

All realized and estimated unrealized gains and losses related to the extended phase-out period are netted as one "event" after the measurement date. To determine the amount to be reported on the "gain or loss from disposal of a segment" line (the second line of the discontinued operations section), the following simple algorithm may be used: If an overall loss is computed for the extended phase-out period, the amount reported is the overall loss; if an overall gain is computed, the amount reported is the lesser of the overall gain or the realized gain.

EXTENDED PHASE-OUT—ADDITIONAL EXAMPLES

Provided in Illustration 4A-10 are some additional cases to help you understand how the gain (loss) on disposal of a segment of a business is reported for an extended phase-out period. We will use the same measurement and disposal dates as in the previous situation. All situations are reported on a pretax basis.

In Case 2, all three components related to the gain (loss) on disposal were losses; therefore **a net loss of $1,400,000 is reported at the measurement date.**

Disposals of Segments Involving Extended Phase-Out of Discontinued Operations

	Realized Income (Loss) on Operations October 1, 2000–December 31, 2000	Expected Income (Loss) on Operations January 1, 2001–May 1, 2001	Expected Gain (Loss) on Sale of Assets	Gain (Loss) on Disposal of Segment	
Case 1	$(400,000)	$(200,000)	$350,000	2000	$ (250,000)
				2001	0
Case 2	(300,000)	(600,000)	(500,000)	2000	$(1,400,000)
				2001	0
Case 3	100,000	400,000	(600,000)	2000	$ (100,000)
				2001	0
Case 4	(500,000)	(300,000)	900,000	2000	0
				2001	$ 100,000
Case 5	400,000	300,000	250,000	2000	$ 400,000
				2001	$ 550,000
Case 6	600,000	(200,000)	(300,000)	2000	$ 100,000
				2001	0
Case 7	400,000	(300,000)	350,000	2000	$ 400,000
				2001	$ 50,000
Case 8	400,000	(350,000)	300,000	2000	$ 350,000
				2001	0

ILLUSTRATION 4A-10
Gains or Losses Involving Extended Phase-Out of Discontinued Operations

In Case 3, the loss of $600,000 on the sale of the segment assets is greater than the realized $100,000 and expected $400,000 income from operations; therefore **a net loss of $100,000 is reported at the measurement date.**

In Case 4, the gain of $900,000 on the sale of the segment assets is greater than the realized $500,000 and expected $300,000 losses from operations; therefore **a net gain of $100,000 is reported at the disposal date.**

In Case 5, both components of operations report income, and a gain is expected on the sale of the segment assets. As a result, the **realized income from operations of $400,000 can be reported at the date of measurement** because there are no realized or estimated losses. **The remaining estimated gain of $550,000 ($300,000 + $250,000) is deferred and recognized at the disposal date.**

In Case 6, the realized income from operations of $600,000 exceeds the estimated losses from operations $200,000 and sale $300,000. As a result, **a realized gain of $100,000 is reported at the end of 2000, because the net gain is realized.**

In Case 7, the net gain on disposal is expected to be $450,000, of which $400,000 is realized and $50,000 is unrealized. **The realized $400,000 is recognized in 2000 and the net unrealized gain of $50,000** (the net of a $300,000 expected loss from operations in 2001 and a $350,000 expected gain from disposal in 2001) is recognized in 2001.

In Case 8, the net gain on disposal is expected to be $350,000, all of which is realized and, therefore, recognized in 2000. **The $400,000 of realized income from operations is reduced by the net expected unrealized loss of $50,000** from 2001 (the expected loss from operations of $350,000 less the expected gain on sale of $300,000).

DISCLOSURE REQUIREMENTS

Amounts of income taxes applicable to the results of discontinued operations and the gain or loss from disposal of the segment should be disclosed on the face of the income statement or related notes. Revenues applicable to the discontinued operations should be separately disclosed in the related notes.

In addition to the amounts that should be reported in the financial statements, the notes to the financial statements for the period encompassing the measurement date should disclose:

1. The identity of the segment of the business that has been or will be discontinued.
2. The expected disposal date, if known.
3. The expected manner of disposition.
4. A description of the remaining assets and liabilities of the segment at the balance sheet date.
5. The income or loss from operations and any proceeds from disposal of the segment during the period from the measurement date to the date of the balance sheet.

An example of the income statement and the note disclosure taken from the annual report of **Fluor Corporation** is shown in Illustration 4A-11.

ILLUSTRATION 4A-11
Note Disclosure of Discontinued Operations

FLUOR CORPORATION

Income from continuing operations before income taxes		$171,800,000
Income taxes		91,100,000
Income from continuing operations		80,700,000
Discontinued operations—Note G:		
Loss from operation of Distribution Group (net of income tax benefit of $22,952,000)	$(27,000,000)	
Loss on disposal of Distribution Group, including provision for estimated operating losses during phase-out period (net of income tax benefit of $15,538,000)	(26,000,000)	(53,000,000)
Net income		$ 27,700,000

Note G: Discontinued Operations. During the fourth quarter of the current year, the company adopted a plan to dispose of the Distribution Group through sale or liquidation. Negotiations for the sale of two of the companies are currently being conducted with the respective management groups. At October 31, the net assets of discontinued operations, consisting primarily of inventories, trade receivables, and warehouse facilities have been reclassified as current assets at estimated net realizable value.

Revenues from discontinued operations, including the Goldston Transportation Group which was sold during the year, were $368,551,000. Included in the loss on disposal is a pretax provision of $2,115,000 for estimated operating losses during the phase-out period.

Go to the Digital Tool for additional disclosures of discontinued operations.

Companies frequently segregate the assets and liabilities of the segment on the balance sheet into net current and net noncurrent amounts, identifying these elements as related to discontinued operations.

As previously stated, if the estimates on income or losses from operations during the phase-out period and on gains or losses on the sale of assets prove to be incorrect, the correction should be reported in the period when the estimate is determined to be incorrect; prior periods are not restated. An example of such a correction is disclosed in a note to the financial statements of **BMC Industries Inc.**

ILLUSTRATION 4A-12
Example of Note Explaining Correction to Financial Statement

BMC INDUSTRIES INC.

Note 3: Discontinued Operations. In the prior year, the Company estimated a loss on the disposal of the discontinued operations of $60,000,000, which included a provision of approximately $8,000,000 for operating losses through the anticipated disposal periods. Actual operating losses exceeded the estimate by approximately $10,000,000, and the loss on the disposal of discontinued operations is expected to be approximately $5,000,000 less than the original estimate. Accordingly, the accompanying Consolidated Statement of Operations for the current year includes an additional provision for loss on disposal of $5,000,000.

Note that the amount of the correction—in the case of BMC Industries, $5,000,000—is reported net of tax in the discontinued operations section of the income statement.

SUMMARY OF LEARNING OBJECTIVE FOR APPENDIX 4A

9 **Measure and report gains and losses from discontinued operations.** The accountant may be required to report gains and losses from discontinued operations (sale of a segment of the business) under three different situations: (1) no phase-out period, (2) a phase-out period, and (3) an extended phase-out period. The gain or loss on disposal of a segment involves the sum of: (1) income or loss from operations to the measurement date, and (2) the gain or loss on the disposal of the business segment (operating incomes or losses during the phase-out period and the gain or loss on the sale of the net assets). These two items are reported separately net of tax among the irregular items in the income statement.

KEY TERMS

disposal date, 155
measurement date, 155
phase-out period, 155

Note: All **asterisked** Questions, Exercises, Problems, and Conceptual Cases relate to material contained in the appendix to the chapter.

QUESTIONS

1 What kinds of questions about future cash flows do investors and creditors attempt to answer with information in the income statement?

2 How can information based on past transactions be used to predict future cash flows?

3 Identify at least two situations in which important changes in value are not reported in the income statement.

4 Identify at least two situations in which application of different accounting methods or accounting estimates results in difficulties in comparing companies.

5 Explain the transaction approach to measuring income. Why is the transaction approach to income measurement preferable to other ways of measuring income?

6 What is earnings management?

7 How can earnings management affect the quality of earnings?

8 Why should caution be exercised in the use of the income figure derived in an income statement? What are the objectives of generally accepted accounting principles in their application to the income statement?

9 A *Wall Street Journal* article noted that if Canon Inc. had written off film costs in the first quarter as fast as some of its competitors, Canon would have had a loss instead of a profit. One analyst noted therefore that Canon's quality of earnings was low. What does the term "quality of earnings" mean?

10 What is the major distinction (a) between revenues and gains and (b) between expenses and losses?

11 What are the advantages and disadvantages of the "single-step" income statement?

12 What is the basis for distinguishing between operating and nonoperating items?

13 Distinguish between the "all-inclusive" income statement and the "current operating performance" income statement. According to present generally accepted accounting principles, which is recommended? Explain.

14 How should prior period adjustments be reported in the financial statements? Give an example of a prior period adjustment.

15 Discuss the appropriate treatment in the financial statements of each of the following:

(a) An amount of $113,000 realized in excess of the cash surrender value of an insurance policy on the life of one of the founders of the company who died during the year.

(b) A profit-sharing bonus to employees computed as a percentage of net income.

(c) Additional depreciation on factory machinery because of an error in computing depreciation for the previous year.

(d) Rent received from subletting a portion of the office space.

(e) A patent infringement suit, brought two years ago against the company by another company, was settled this year by a cash payment of $725,000.

(f) A reduction in the Allowance for Doubtful Accounts balance, because the account appears to be considerably in excess of the probable loss from uncollectible receivables.

16 Indicate where the following items would ordinarily appear on the financial statements of Allepo, Inc. for the year 2001.

(a) The service life of certain equipment was changed from 8 to 5 years. If a 5-year life had been used previously, additional depreciation of $425,000 would have been charged.

(b) In 2001 a flood destroyed a warehouse that had a book value of $1,600,000. Floods are rare in this locality.

(c) In 2001 the company wrote off $1,000,000 of inventory that was considered obsolete.

(d) An income tax refund related to the 1998 tax year was received.

(e) In 1998, a supply warehouse with an expected useful life of 7 years was erroneously expensed.

(f) Allepo, Inc. changed its depreciation from double-declining to straight-line on machinery in 2001. The cumulative effect of the change was $925,000 (net of tax).

17 Give the section of a multiple-step income statement in which each of the following is shown.

(a) Loss on inventory write-down.

(b) Loss from strike.

(c) Bad debt expense.

(d) Loss on disposal of a segment of the business.

(e) Gain on sale of machinery.

(f) Interest revenue.

(g) Depreciation expense.

(h) Material write-offs of notes receivable.

18 Barry Bonds Land Development, Inc. purchased land for $70,000 and spent $30,000 developing it. It then sold the land for $160,000. Tom Glavine Manufacturing purchased land for a future plant site for $100,000. Due to a change in plans, Glavine later sold the land for $160,000. Should these two companies report the land sales, both at gains of $60,000, in a similar manner?

19 You run into Bart Simpson at a party and begin discussing financial statements. Bart says "I prefer the single-step income statement because the multiple-step format generally overstates income." How should you respond to Bart?

20 Federov Corporation has eight expense accounts in its general ledger which could be classified as selling expenses. Should Federov report these eight expenses separately in its income statement or simply report one total amount for selling expenses?

21 Jose DeLeon Investments reported an unusual gain from the sale of certain assets in its 2001 income statement. How does intraperiod tax allocation affect the reporting of this unusual gain?

22 What effect does intraperiod tax allocation have on reported net income?

23 Jane Pauley Company computed earnings per share as follows:

$$\frac{\text{Net Income}}{\text{Common Shares Outstanding at Year End}}$$

Jane Pauley has a simple capital structure. What possible errors might the company have made in the computation? Explain.

24 Maria Shriver Corporation reported 2001 earnings per share of $7.21. In 2002, Maria Shriver reported earnings per share as follows:

On income before extraordinary item	$6.40
On extraordinary item	1.88
On net income	$8.28

Is the increase in earnings per share from $7.21 to $8.28 a favorable trend?

25 What is meant by "tax allocation within a period"? What is the justification for such practice?

26 When does tax allocation within a period become necessary? How should this allocation be handled?

27 During 2001, Natsume Sozeki Company earned income of $1,000,000 before federal income taxes and realized a gain of $450,000 on a government-forced condemnation sale of a division plant facility. The income is subject to federal income taxation at the rate of 34%; the gain on the sale of the plant is taxed at 30%. Proper accounting suggests that the unusual gain be reported as an extraordinary item. Illustrate an appropriate presentation of these items in the income statement.

28 On January 30, 2001, a suit was filed against Pierogi Corporation under the Environmental Protection Act. On August 6, 2002, Pierogi Corporation agreed to settle the action and pay $920,000 in damages to certain current and former employees. How should this settlement be reported in the 2002 financial statements? Discuss.

29 Tiger Paper Company decided to close two small pulp mills in Conway, New Hampshire, and Corvallis, Oregon. Would these closings be reported in a separate section entitled Discontinued Operations after Income from Continuing Operations? Discuss.

30 What major types of items are reported in the retained earnings statement?

31 Generally accepted accounting principles usually require the use of accrual accounting to "fairly present" income. If the cash receipts and disbursements method of accounting will "clearly reflect" taxable income, why does this method not usually also "fairly present" income?

32 State some of the more serious problems encountered in seeking to achieve the ideal measurement of periodic net income. Explain what accountants do as a practical alternative.

33 What is meant by the terms components, elements, and items as they relate to the income statement? Why might items have to be disclosed in the income statement?

34 What are the three ways that other comprehensive income may be displayed (reported)?

35 How are the measurement and disposal dates defined for a disposal of a segment of a business?

36 How are gains or losses on disposal of a segment of a business determined?

37 How should the disposal of a segment of a business be disclosed in the income statement?

BRIEF EXERCISES

BE4-1 Tim Allen Co. had sales revenue of $540,000 in 2001. Other items recorded during the year were:

Cost of goods sold	$320,000
Wage expense	120,000
Income tax expense	25,000
Increase in value of company reputation	15,000
Other operating expenses	10,000
Unrealized gain on value of patents	20,000

Prepare a single-step income statement for Allen for 2001. Allen has 100,000 shares of stock outstanding.

BE4-2 Kirstie Alley Corporation had net sales of $1,780,000 and investment revenue of $103,000 in 2002. Its 2002 expenses were: cost of goods sold, $1,190,000; selling expenses, $272,000; administrative expenses, $211,000; interest expense, $76,000; and income tax expense, $40,000. Prepare a single-step income statement for Kirstie Alley Corporation, which has 10,000 shares of stock outstanding.

BE4-3 Use the information provided in BE4-2 for Kirstie Alley Corporation to prepare a multiple-step income statement.

BE4-4 Green Day Corporation had income from continuing operations of $12,600,000 in 2002. During 2002, it disposed of its restaurant division at an after-tax loss of $189,000. Prior to disposal, the division operated at a loss of $315,000 (net of tax) in 2002. Green Day had 10,000,000 shares of common stock outstanding during 2002. Prepare a partial income statement for Green Day beginning with income from continuing operations.

BE4-5 Boyz II Men Corporation had income before income taxes for 2002 of $7,300,000. In addition, it suffered an unusual and infrequent pretax loss of $770,000 from a volcano eruption. The corporation's tax rate is 30%. Prepare a partial income statement for Boyz II Men beginning with income before income taxes. The corporation had 5,000,000 shares of common stock outstanding during 2002.

BE4-6 Shawn Bradley Company changed from straight-line depreciation to double-declining balance depreciation at the beginning of 2002. The plant assets originally cost $1,500,000 in 2000. Using straight-line depreciation, depreciation expense is $60,000 per year. Under the double-declining balance method, depreciation expense would be $120,000; $110,400; and $101,568 for 2000, 2001, and 2002. If Bradley's tax rate is 30%, by what amount would the cumulative effect of a change in accounting principle increase or decrease 2002 net income?

BE4-7 Jana Kingston Company has recorded bad debts expense in the past at a rate of 1½% of net sales. In 2002, Kingston decides to increase its estimate to 2%. If the new rate had been used in prior years, cumulative bad debt expense would have been $380,000 instead of $285,000. In 2002, bad debt expense will be $120,000 instead of $90,000. If Kingston's tax rate is 30%, what amount should it report as the cumulative effect of changing estimated bad debt rate?

BE4-8 In 2002, Kirby Puckett Corporation reported net income of $1,200,000. It declared and paid preferred stock dividends of $250,000. During 2002, Puckett had a weighted average of 190,000 common shares outstanding. Compute Puckett's 2002 earnings per share.

BE4-9 Turgeon Corporation had retained earnings of $529,000 at January 1, 2002. Net income in 2002 was $1,496,000 and cash dividends of $650,000 were declared and paid. Prepare a 2002 retained earnings statement for Turgeon Corporation.

BE4-10 Use the information provided in BE4-9 to prepare a retained earnings statement for Turgeon Corporation, assuming that in 2002 Turgeon discovered that it had overstated 2000 depreciation by $125,000 (net of tax).

BE4-11 On January 1, 2001, Creative Works Inc. had cash and common stock of $60,000. At that date the company had no other asset, liability or equity balances. On January 2, 2001, it purchased for cash $20,000 of equity securities that it classified as available-for-sale. It received cash dividends of $3,000 during the year on these securities. In addition, it has an unrealized holding gain on these securities of $5,000 net of tax. Determine the following amounts for 2001: (a) net income; (b) comprehensive income; (c) other comprehensive income; and (d) accumulated other comprehensive income (end of 2001).

***BE4-12** Garok Company decided on Sept. 1, 2002, to dispose of its Cardassian Division. The Cardassian Division operated at a loss of $190,000 during the first 8 months of 2002 and a loss of $114,000 during the last 4 months of the year. Garok estimates the division will incur a loss of $130,000 in 2003 before it is sold at a gain of $85,000. Garok's tax rate is 30%. Prepare the discontinued operations section of Garok's 2002 income statement.

EXERCISES

E4-1 (Computation of Net Income) Presented below are changes in all the account balances of Fritz Reiner Furniture Co. during the current year, except for retained earnings.

	Increase (Decrease)		Increase (Decrease)
Cash	$ 79,000	Accounts payable	$(51,000)
Accounts receivable (net)	45,000	Bonds payable	82,000
Inventory	127,000	Common stock	125,000
Investments	(47,000)	Additional paid-in capital	13,000

Instructions

Compute the net income for the current year, assuming that there were no entries in the Retained Earnings account except for net income and a dividend declaration of $19,000 which was paid in the current year.

E4-2 (Compute Net Income—Capital Maintenance Approach) Presented below is selected information pertaining to the Videohound Video Company during 2002:

Cash balance, January 1, 2002	$ 13,000
Accounts receivable, January 1, 2002	19,000
Collections from customers in 2002	210,000
Capital account balance, January 1, 2002	38,000
Total assets, January 1, 2002	75,000
Cash investment added, July 1, 2002	5,000
Total assets, December 31, 2002	101,000
Cash balance, December 31, 2002	20,000
Accounts receivable, December 31, 2002	36,000
Merchandise taken for personal use	11,000
Total liabilities, December 31, 2002	41,000

Instructions

Compute the net income for 2002.

E4-3 (Income Statement Items) Presented below are certain account balances of Paczki Products Co.

Rental revenue	$ 6,500	Sales discounts	7,800
Interest expense	12,700	Selling expenses	99,400
Beginning retained earnings	114,400	Sales	390,000
Ending retained earnings	134,000	Income tax	31,000
Dividends earned	71,000	Cost of goods sold	184,400
Sales returns	$ 12,400	Administrative expenses	82,500

Instructions

From the foregoing, compute the following: (a) total net revenue; (b) net income; (c) dividends declared during the current year.

E4-4 (Single-step Income Statement) The financial records of LeRoi Jones Inc. were destroyed by fire at the end of 2002. Fortunately the controller had kept certain statistical data related to the income statement as presented below.

1. The beginning merchandise inventory was $92,000 and decreased 20% during the current year.
2. Sales discounts amount to $17,000.
3. 20,000 shares of common stock were outstanding for the entire year.
4. Interest expense was $20,000.
5. The income tax rate is 30%.
6. Cost of goods sold amounts to $500,000.
7. Administrative expenses are 20% of cost of goods sold but only 8% of gross sales.
8. Four-fifths of the operating expenses relate to sales activities.

Instructions

From the foregoing information prepare an income statement for the year 2002 in single-step form.

E4-5 (Multiple-step and Single-step) Two accountants for the firm of Elwes and Wright are arguing about the merits of presenting an income statement in a multiple-step versus a single-step format. The discussion involves the following 2002 information related to P. Bride Company ($000 omitted).

Administrative expense	
Officers' salaries	$ 4,900
Depreciation of office furniture and equipment	3,960
Cost of goods sold	60,570
Rental revenue	17,230
Selling expense	
Transportation-out	2,690
Sales commissions	7,980
Depreciation of sales equipment	6,480
Sales	96,500
Income tax	9,070
Interest expense on bonds payable	1,860

Instructions

(a) Prepare an income statement for the year 2002 using the multiple-step form. Common shares outstanding for 2002 total 40,550 (000 omitted).
(b) Prepare an income statement for the year 2002 using the single-step form.
(c) Which one do you prefer? Discuss.

E4-6 (Multiple-step and Extraordinary Items) The following balances were taken from the books of Maria Conchita Alonzo Corp. on December 31, 2002.

Interest revenue	$ 86,000	Accumulated depreciation—equipment	$ 40,000
Cash	51,000	Accumulated depreciation—building	28,000
Sales	1,380,000	Notes receivable	155,000
Accounts receivable	150,000	Selling expenses	194,000
Prepaid insurance	20,000	Accounts payable	170,000
Sales returns and allowances	150,000	Bonds payable	100,000
Allowance for doubtful accounts	7,000	Administrative and general expenses	97,000
Sales discounts	45,000	Accrued liabilities	32,000
Land	100,000	Interest expense	60,000
Equipment	200,000	Notes payable	100,000
Building	140,000	Loss from earthquake damage (extraordinary item)	150,000
Cost of goods sold	621,000	Common stock	500,000
		Retained earnings	21,000

Assume the total effective tax rate on all items is 34%.

Instructions

Prepare a multiple-step income statement; 100,000 shares of common stock were outstanding during the year.

E4-7 (Multiple-step and Single-step) The accountant of Whitney Houston Shoe Co. has compiled the following information from the company's records as a basis for an income statement for the year ended December 31, 2002.

Rental revenue	$ 29,000
Interest on notes payable	18,000
Market appreciation on land above cost	31,000
Wages and salaries—sales	114,800
Materials and supplies—sales	17,600
Income tax	37,400
Wages and salaries—administrative	135,900
Other administrative expense	51,700
Cost of goods sold	496,000
Net sales	980,000
Depreciation on plant assets (70% selling, 30% administrative)	65,000
Dividends declared	16,000

There were 20,000 shares of common stock outstanding during the year.

Instructions

(a) Prepare a multiple-step income statement.
(b) Prepare a single-step income statement.
(c) Which format do you prefer? Discuss.

E4-8 (Multiple-step and Single-step—Periodic Inventory Method) Presented below is income statement information related to Klingon Corporation for the year 2002.

Administrative expenses:		Transportation-in	$ 14,000
Officers' salaries	$ 39,000	Purchase discounts	10,000
Depreciation expense—building	28,500	Inventory (beginning)	120,000
Office supplies expense	9,500	Sales returns and allowances	15,000
Inventory (ending)	137,000	Selling expenses:	
Flood damage (pretax extraordinary item)	50,000	Sales salaries	71,000
Purchases	600,000	Depreciation expense—store equipment	18,000
Sales	930,000	Store supplies expense	9,000

In addition, the corporation has other revenue from dividends received of $20,000 and other expense of interest on notes payable of $9,000. There are 20,000 shares of common stock outstanding for the year. The total effective tax rate on all income is 34%.

Instructions

(a) Prepare a multiple-step income statement for 2002.
(b) Prepare a single-step income statement for 2002.
(c) Discuss the relative merits of the two income statements.

E4-9 (Multiple-step Statement with Retained Earnings) Presented below is information related to Ivan Calderon Corp. for the year 2002.

Net sales	$1,300,000	Write-off of inventory due to obsolescence	$ 80,000
Cost of goods sold	780,000	Depreciation expense omitted by accident in 2001	55,000
Selling expenses	65,000	Casualty loss (extraordinary item) before taxes	50,000
Administrative expenses	48,000	Dividends declared	45,000
Dividend revenue	20,000	Retained earnings at December 31, 2001	980,000
Interest revenue	7,000	Effective tax rate of 34% on all items	

Instructions

(a) Prepare a multiple-step income statement for 2002. Assume that 60,000 shares of common stock are outstanding.
(b) Prepare a separate retained earnings statement for 2002.

E4-10 (Earnings Per Share) The stockholders' equity section of Tkachuk Corporation appears below as of December 31, 2002:

8% cumulative preferred stock, $50 par value, authorized 100,000 shares, outstanding 90,000 shares		$ 4,500,000
Common stock, $1.00 par, authorized and issued 10 million shares		10,000,000
Additional paid-in capital		20,500,000
Retained earnings	$134,000,000	
Net income	33,000,000	167,000,000
		$202,000,000

Net income for 2002 reflects a total effective tax rate of 34%. Included in the net income figure is a loss of $18,000,000 (before tax) as a result of a major casualty.

Instructions

Compute earnings per share data as it should appear on the financial statements of Tkachuk Corporation.

E4-11 (Condensed Income Statement—Periodic Inventory Method) Presented below are selected ledger accounts of Spock Corporation at December 31, 2002:

Cash	$ 185,000	Travel and entertainment	$ 69,000
Merchandise inventory	535,000	Accounting and legal services	33,000
Sales	4,275,000	Insurance expense	24,000
Advances from customers	117,000	Advertising	54,000
Purchases	2,786,000	Transportation-out	93,000
Sales discounts	34,000	Depreciation of office	48,000
Purchase discounts	27,000	Depreciation of sales equipment	36,000
Sales salaries	284,000	Telephone—sales	17,000
Office salaries	346,000	Utilities—office	32,000
Purchase returns	15,000	Miscellaneous office expenses	8,000
Sales returns	79,000	Rental revenue	240,000

Transportation-in	72,000	Extraordinary loss (before tax)	70,000
Accounts receivable	142,500	Interest expense	176,000
Sales commissions	83,000	Common stock ($10 par)	900,000

Spock's effective tax rate on all items is 34%. A physical inventory indicates that the ending inventory is $686,000.

Instructions

Prepare a condensed 2002 income statement for Spock Corporation.

E4-12 (Retained Earnings Statement) Eddie Zambrano Corporation began operations on January 1, 1999. During its first 3 years of operations, Zambrano reported net income and declared dividends as follows:

	Net income	Dividends declared
1999	$ 40,000	$–0–
2000	125,000	50,000
2001	160,000	50,000

The following information relates to 2002:

Income before income tax	$240,000
Prior period adjustment: understatement of 2000 depreciation expense (before taxes)	$ 25,000
Cumulative decrease in income from change in inventory methods (before taxes)	$ 35,000
Dividends declared (of this amount, $25,000 will be paid on Jan. 15, 2003)	$100,000
Effective tax rate	40%

Instructions

(a) Prepare a 2002 retained earnings statement for Eddie Zambrano Corporation.

(b) Assume Eddie Zambrano Corp. appropriated retained earnings in the amount of $70,000 on December 31, 2002. After this action, what would Zambrano report as total retained earnings in its December 31, 2002, balance sheet?

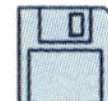

E4-13 (Earnings per Share) At December 31, 2001, Shiga Naoya Corporation had the following stock outstanding:

10% cumulative preferred stock, $100 par, 107,500 shares	$10,750,000
Common stock, $5 par, 4,000,000 shares	20,000,000

During 2002, Shiga Naoya's only stock transaction was the issuance of 400,000 shares of common on April 1. During 2002, the following also occurred:

Income from continuing operations before taxes	$23,650,000
Discontinued operations (loss before taxes)	$ 3,225,000
Preferred dividends declared	$ 1,075,000
Common dividends declared	$ 2,200,000
Effective tax rate	35%

Instructions

Compute earnings per share data as it should appear in the 2002 income statement of Shiga Naoya Corporation.

E4-14 (Comprehensive Income) C. Reither Co. reports the following information for 2002: sales revenue, $700,000; cost of goods sold, $500,000; operating expenses, $80,000; and an unrealized holding loss on available-for-sale securities for 2002 of $60,000. It declared and paid a cash dividend of $10,000 in 2002.

Instructions

(a) Show how comprehensive income is reported using the separate income statement format.

(b) Show how comprehensive income is reported using the combined income statement format.

E4-15 (Comprehensive Income) C. Reither Co. has January 1, 2002, balances in common stock, $350,000; accumulated other comprehensive income, $80,000; and retained earnings, $90,000. It issued no stock during 2002.

Instructions

Using the information from E4-14, prepare a statement of stockholders' equity.

E4-16 (Various Reporting Formats) The following information was taken from the records of Roland Carlson Inc. for the year 2002. Income tax applicable to income from continuing operations $187,000; income tax applicable to loss on discontinued operations $25,500; income tax applicable to extraordinary gain $32,300; income tax applicable to extraordinary loss $20,400; and unrealized holding gain on available-for-sale securities $15,000.

Extraordinary gain	$ 95,000	Cash dividends declared	$ 150,000
Loss on discontinued operations	75,000	Retained earnings January 1, 2002	600,000
Administrative expenses	240,000	Cost of goods sold	850,000
Rent revenue	40,000	Selling expenses	300,000
Extraordinary loss	60,000	Sales	1,900,000

Shares outstanding during 2002 were 100,000.

Instructions

(a) Prepare a single-step income statement for 2002.
(b) Prepare a retained earnings statement for 2002.
(c) Show how comprehensive income is reported using the combined income statement format.

***E4-17 (Discontinued Operations)** Assume that Lyle Alzado Inc. decides to sell WBTV, its television subsidiary, in 2001. This sale qualifies for discontinued operations treatment. Pertinent data regarding the operations of the TV subsidiary are as follows:

Loss from operations from beginning of year to measurement date, $1,000,000 (net of tax).

Realized loss from operations from measurement date to end of 2001, $700,000 (net of tax).

Estimated income from operations from end of year to disposal date of June 1, 2002, $400,000 (net of tax).

Estimated gain on sale of net assets on June 1, 2002, $150,000 (net of tax).

Instructions

(a) What is the gain (loss) on the disposal of the segment reported in 2001? In 2002?
(b) Prepare the discontinued operations section of the income statement for the year ended 2001.
(c) If the amount reported in 2001 as gain or loss from disposal of a segment by Lyle Alzado Inc. proves to be materially incorrect, when and how is the correction reported, if at all?
(d) If the TV subsidiary had a realized income of $100,000 (net of tax) instead of a realized loss from the measurement date to the end of 2001, what is the gain or loss on disposal of the segment reported in 2001? In 2002?

***E4-18 (Discontinued Operations)** On October 5, 2002, Blues Inc.'s board of directors decided to dispose of the Jake and Elwood Division. Blues is a real estate firm with approximately 25% of its income from management of apartment complexes. The Jake and Elwood Division contracts to clean apartments after tenants move out in the Blues complexes and several others. The board decided to dispose of the division because of unfavorable operating results.

Net income for Blues was $91,000 after tax (assume a 30% rate) for the fiscal year ended December 31, 2002. The Jake and Elwood Division accounted for only $4,200 (after tax) of this amount and only $1,050 (after tax) in the fourth quarter. Jake and Elwood accounted for $50,000 in revenues, of which $8,000 were earned in the last quarter. The average number of common shares outstanding was 20,000 for the year.

Because of the unfavorable results and the extreme competition, the board believes selling the business intact is impossible. Their final decision is to complete all current contracts, the last of which expires on May 3, 2004, and then auction off the cleaning equipment on May 10, 2004. This, the only asset of the division, will have a depreciated value of $25,000 at the disposal date. The board believes the sale proceeds will approximate $5,000 after the auction expenses and estimates Jake and Elwood earnings in fiscal year 2003 as $3,800 (before tax), with a loss of $3,000 (before tax) in fiscal year 2004.

Instructions

Prepare the income statement and the appropriate footnotes that relate to the Jake and Elwood Division for 2002. The income statement should begin with income from continuing operations before income taxes. Earnings per share computations are not required.

PROBLEMS

P4-1 (Multi-step Income, Retained Earnings) Presented below is information related to American Horse Company for 2002.

Retained earnings balance, January 1, 2002	$ 980,000
Sales for the year	25,000,000
Cost of goods sold	17,000,000

Interest revenue	70,000
Selling and administrative expenses	4,700,000
Write-off of goodwill (not tax deductible)	520,000
Federal income taxes for 2002	905,000
Assessment for additional 1999 income taxes (normal recurring)	300,000
Gain on the sale of investments (normal recurring)	110,000
Loss due to flood damage—extraordinary item (net of tax)	390,000
Loss on the disposition of the wholesale division (net of tax)	440,000
Loss on operations of the wholesale division (net of tax)	90,000
Dividends declared on common stock	250,000
Dividends declared on preferred stock	70,000

Instructions

Prepare a multi-step income statement and a retained earnings statement. American Horse Company decided to discontinue its entire wholesale operations and to retain its manufacturing operations. On September 15, American Horse sold the wholesale operations to Rogers Company. During 2002, there were 300,000 shares of common stock outstanding all year.

P4-2 (Single-step Income, Retained Earnings, Periodic Inventory) Presented below is the trial balance of Mary J. Blige Corporation at December 31, 2002.

MARY J. BLIGE CORPORATION
Trial Balance
Year Ended December 31, 2002

	Debits	Credits
Purchase discounts		$ 10,000
Cash	$ 205,100	
Accounts receivable	105,000	
Rent revenue		18,000
Retained earnings		260,000
Salaries payable		18,000
Sales		1,000,000
Notes receivable	110,000	
Accounts payable		49,000
Accumulated depreciation—equipment		28,000
Sales discounts	14,500	
Sales returns	17,500	
Notes payable		70,000
Selling expenses	232,000	
Administrative expenses	99,000	
Common stock		300,000
Income tax expense	38,500	
Cash dividends	45,000	
Allowance for doubtful accounts		5,000
Supplies	14,000	
Freight-in	20,000	
Land	70,000	
Equipment	140,000	
Bonds payable		100,000
Gain on sale of land		30,000
Accumulated depreciation—building		19,600
Merchandise inventory	89,000	
Building	98,000	
Purchases	610,000	
Totals	$1,907,600	$1,907,600

A physical count of inventory on December 31 resulted in an inventory amount of $124,000.

Instructions

Prepare a single-step income statement and a retained earnings statement. Assume that the only changes in the retained earnings during the current year were from net income and dividends. Thirty thousand shares of common stock were outstanding the entire year.

P4-3 (Irregular Items) Tony Rich Inc. reported income from continuing operations before taxes during 2002 of $790,000. Additional transactions occurring in 2002 but not considered in the $790,000 are as follows:

1. The corporation experienced an uninsured flood loss (extraordinary) in the amount of $80,000 during the year. The tax rate on this item is 46%.
2. At the beginning of 2000, the corporation purchased a machine for $54,000 (salvage value of $9,000) that had a useful life of 6 years. The bookkeeper used straight-line depreciation for 2000, 2001, and 2002 but failed to deduct the salvage value in computing the depreciation base.
3. Sale of securities held as a part of its portfolio resulted in a loss of $57,000 (pretax).
4. When its president died, the corporation realized $110,000 from an insurance policy. The cash surrender value of this policy had been carried on the books as an investment in the amount of $46,000 (the gain is nontaxable).
5. The corporation disposed of its recreational division at a loss of $115,000 before taxes. Assume that this transaction meets the criteria for discontinued operations.
6. The corporation decided to change its method of inventory pricing from average cost to the FIFO method. The effect of this change on prior years is to increase 2000 income by $60,000 and decrease 2001 income by $20,000 before taxes. The FIFO method has been used for 2002. The tax rate on these items is 40%.

Instructions

Prepare an income statement for the year 2002 starting with income from continuing operations before taxes. Compute earnings per share as it should be shown on the face of the income statement. Common shares outstanding for the year are 80,000 shares. (Assume a tax rate of 30% on all items, unless indicated otherwise.)

P4-4 (Multiple- and Single-step Income, Retained Earnings) The following account balances were included in the trial balance of J.R. Reid Corporation at June 30, 2002.

Sales	$1,678,500	Depreciation of office furniture and equipment	$ 7,250
Sales discounts	31,150	Real estate and other local taxes	7,320
Cost of goods sold	896,770	Bad debt expense—selling	4,850
Sales salaries	56,260	Building expense—prorated to administration	9,130
Sales commissions	97,600	Miscellaneous office expenses	6,000
Travel expense—salespersons	28,930	Sales returns	62,300
Freight-out	21,400	Dividends received	38,000
Entertainment expense	14,820	Bond interest expense	18,000
Telephone and Internet—sales	9,030	Income taxes	133,000
Depreciation of sales equipment	4,980	Depreciation understatement due to error—1999 (net of tax)	17,700
Building expense—prorated to sales	6,200	Dividends declared on preferred stock	9,000
Miscellaneous selling expenses	4,715	Dividends declared on common stock	32,000
Office supplies used	3,450		
Telephone and Internet—administration	2,820		

The Unappropriated Retained Earnings account had a balance of $287,000 at June 30, 2002, before closing; the only entry in that account during the year was a debit of $50,000 to establish an Appropriation for Bond Retirement. There are 80,000 shares of common stock outstanding.

Instructions

(a) Using the multiple-step form, prepare an income statement and an unappropriated retained earnings statement for the year ended June 30, 2002.

(b) Using the single-step form, prepare an income statement and an unappropriated retained earnings statement for the year ended June 30, 2002.

P4-5 (Irregular Items) Presented below is a combined single-step income and retained earnings statement for Sandy Freewalt Company for 2001.

	(000 omitted)
Net sales	$640,000
Cost and expenses:	
Cost of goods sold	500,000

Selling, general, and administrative expenses		66,000
Other, net		17,000
		583,000
Income before income tax		57,000
Income tax		19,400
Net income		37,600
Retained earnings at beginning of period, as previously reported	141,000	
Adjustment required for correction of error	(7,000)	
Retained earnings at beginning of period, as restated		134,000
Dividends on common stock		(12,200)
Retained earnings at end of period		$159,400

Additional facts are as follows:

1. "Selling, general, and administrative expenses" for 2001 included a usual but infrequently occurring charge of $10,500,000.
2. "Other, net" for 2001 included an extraordinary item (charge) of $9,000,000. If the extraordinary item (charge) had not occurred, income taxes for 2001 would have been $22,400,000 instead of $19,400,000.
3. "Adjustment required for correction of an error" was a result of a change in estimate (useful life of certain assets reduced to 8 years and a catch-up adjustment made).
4. Sandy Freewalt Company disclosed earnings per common share for net income in the notes to the financial statements.

Instructions

Determine from these additional facts whether the presentation of the facts in the Sandy Freewalt Company income and retained earnings statement is appropriate. If the presentation is not appropriate, describe the appropriate presentation and discuss its theoretical rationale. (Do not prepare a revised statement.)

P4-6 (Retained Earnings Statement, Prior Period Adjustment) Below is the retained earnings account for the year 2002 for LeClair Corp.

Retained earnings, January 1, 2002		$257,600
Add:		
Gain on sale of investments (net of tax)	$41,200	
Net income	84,500	
Refund on litigation with government, related to the year 1999 (net of tax)	21,600	
Recognition of income earned in 2001, but omitted from income statement in that year (net of tax)	25,400	172,700
		430,300
Deduct:		
Loss on discontinued operations (net of tax)	25,000	
Write-off of goodwill	60,000	
Cumulative effect on income in changing from straight-line depreciation to accelerated depreciation in 2002 (net of tax)	18,200	
Cash dividends declared	32,000	135,200
Retained earnings, December 31, 2002		$295,100

Instructions

(a) Prepare a corrected retained earnings statement. LeClair Corp. normally sells investments of the type mentioned above.

(b) State where the items that do not appear in the corrected retained earnings statement should be shown.

P4-7 (Income Statement and Irregular Items) The Rufino Tamayo Corporation commenced business on January 1, 1999. Recently the corporation has had several unusual accounting problems related to the presentation of its income statement for financial reporting purposes.

You have been the CPA for Rufino Tamayo Corporation for several years and have been asked to examine the following data.

RUFINO TAMAYO CORPORATION
Income Statement
For the Year Ended December 31, 2002

Sales	$9,500,000
Cost of goods sold	5,900,000
Gross profit	3,600,000
Selling and administrative expense	1,300,000
Income before income tax	2,300,000
Income tax (30%)	690,000
Net income	$1,610,000

In addition, this information was provided:

1. The controller mentioned that the corporation has had difficulty in collecting on several of their receivables. For this reason, the bad debt write-off was increased from 1% to 2% of sales. The controller estimates that if this rate had been used in past periods, an additional $83,000 worth of expense would have been charged. The bad debt expense for the current period was calculated using the new rate and is part of selling and administrative expense.
2. Common shares outstanding at the end of 2002 totaled 400,000. No additional shares were purchased or sold during 2002.
3. Rufino Tamayo noted also that the following items were not included in the income statement.
   (a) Inventory in the amount of $72,000 was obsolete.
   (b) The major casualty loss suffered by the corporation was partially uninsured and cost $127,000, net of tax (extraordinary item).
4. Retained earnings as of January 1, 2002, was $2,800,000. Cash dividends of $700,000 were paid in 2002.
5. In January 2002, Rufino Tamayo Corporation changed its method of accounting for plant assets from the straight-line method to the accelerated method (double-declining balance). The controller has prepared a schedule indicating what depreciation expense would have been in previous periods if the double-declining method had been used. (The effective tax rate for 1999, 2000, and 2001 was 30%.)

	Depreciation Expense under Straight-Line	Depreciation Expense under Double-Declining	Difference
1999	$ 75,000	$150,000	$ 75,000
2000	75,000	112,500	37,500
2001	75,000	84,375	9,375
	$225,000	$346,875	$121,875

6. In 2002, Rufino Tamayo discovered that two errors were made in previous years. First, when it took a physical inventory at the end of 1999, one of the count sheets was apparently lost. The ending inventory for 1999 was therefore understated by $95,000. The inventory was correctly taken in 2000, 2001, and 2002. Also, the corporation found that in 2001 it had failed to record $40,000 as an expense for sales commissions. The effective tax rate for 1999, 2000, and 2001 was 30%. The sales commissions for 2001 are included in 2002 expenses.

Instructions

Prepare the income statement for Rufino Tamayo Corporation in accordance with professional pronouncements. Do not prepare notes to the financial statements.

P4-8 (Income Statement, Irregular Items) Rap Corp. has 100,000 shares of common stock outstanding. In 2002, the company reports income from continuing operations before taxes of $1,210,000. Additional transactions not considered in the $1,210,000 are as follows:

1. In 2002, Rap Corp. sold equipment for $40,000. The machine had originally cost $80,000 and had accumulated depreciation of $36,000. The gain or loss is considered ordinary.
2. The company discontinued operations of one of its subsidiaries during the current year at a loss of $190,000 before taxes. Assume that this transaction meets the criteria for discontinued operations. The loss on operations of the discontinued subsidiary was $90,000 before taxes; the loss from disposal of the subsidiary was $100,000 before taxes.

3. The sum of $100,000, applicable to a breached 1998 contract, was received as a result of a lawsuit. Prior to the award, legal counsel was uncertain about the outcome of the suit and had not established a receivable.
4. In 2002, the company reviewed its accounts receivable and determined that $26,000 of accounts receivable that had been carried for years appeared unlikely to be collected.
5. An internal audit discovered that amortization of intangible assets was understated by $35,000 (net of tax) in a prior period. The amount was charged against retained earnings.
6. The company sold its only investment in common stock during the year at a gain of $145,000. The gain is taxed at a total effective rate of 40%. Assume that the transaction meets the requirements of an extraordinary item.

Instructions

Analyze the above information and prepare an income statement for the year 2002, starting with income from continuing operations before income taxes. Compute earnings per share as it should be shown on the face of the income statement. (Assume a total effective tax rate of 38% on all items, unless otherwise indicated.)

***P4-9 (Discontinued Operations)** Bill Campbell Corporation management formally decided to discontinue operation of its Rocketeer Division on November 1, 2000. Campbell is a successful corporation with earnings in excess of $38.5 million before taxes for each of the past 5 years. The Rocketeer Division is being discontinued because it has not contributed to this profitable performance.

The principal assets of this division are the land, plant, and equipment used to manufacture engine components. The land, plant, and equipment had a net book value of $56 million on November 1, 2000.

Campbell's management has entered into negotiations for a cash sale of the facility for $39 million. The expected date of the sale and final disposal of the segment is July 1, 2001.

Campbell Corporation has a fiscal year ending May 31. The results of operations for the Rocketeer Division for the 2000–2001 fiscal year and the estimated results for June 2001 are presented below. The before-tax losses after October 31, 2000, are computed without depreciation on the plant and equipment because the net book value as of November 1, 2000, is being used as a basis of negotiation for the sale.

Period	Before-tax Income (Loss)
June 1, 2000–October 31, 2000	$(4,100,000)
November 1, 2000–May 31, 2001	$(5,900,000)
June 1–30, 2001 (estimated)	$(750,000)

The Rocketeer Division will be accounted for as a discontinued operation on Campbell's 2000–2001 fiscal year financial statements. Campbell is subject to a 30% tax rate (federal and state income taxes) on operating income and all gains and losses.

Instructions

(a) Explain how the Rocketeer Division's assets would be reported on Bill Campbell Corporation's balance sheet as of May 31, 2001.

(b) Explain how the discontinued operations and pending sale of the Rocketeer Division would be reported on Bill Campbell Corporation's income statement for the year ended May 31, 2001.

(c) Explain what information ordinarily should be disclosed in the notes to the financial statements regarding discontinued operations.

(CMA adapted)

CONCEPTUAL CASES

C4-1 (Identification of Income Statement Deficiencies) John Amos Corporation was incorporated and began business on January 1, 2001. It has been successful and now requires a bank loan for additional working capital to finance expansion. The bank has requested an audited income statement for the year 2001. The accountant for John Amos Corporation provides you with the following income statement which John Amos plans to submit to the bank:

JOHN AMOS CORPORATION
Income Statement

Sales	$850,000
Dividends	32,300
Gain on recovery of insurance proceeds from earthquake loss (extraordinary)	38,500
	920,800

Less:		
Selling expenses	$100,100	
Cost of goods sold	510,000	
Advertising expense	13,700	
Loss on obsolescence of inventories	34,000	
Loss on discontinued operations	48,600	
Administrative expense	73,400	780,800
Income before income tax		140,000
Income tax		56,000
Net income		$ 84,000

Instructions

Indicate the deficiencies in the income statement presented above. Assume that the corporation desires a single-step income statement.

C4-2 (Income Reporting Deficiencies) The following represents a recent income statement for **Boeing Company**:

Sales	$21,924,000,000
Costs and expenses	20,773,000,000
Income from operations	1,151,000,000
Other income	122,000,000
Interest and debt expense	(130,000,000)
Earnings before income taxes	1,143,000,000
Income taxes	(287,000,000)
Net income	$ 856,000,000

It includes only *five* separate numbers (two of which are in billions of dollars), *two* subtotals, and the net earnings figure.

Instructions

(a) Indicate the deficiencies in the income statement.

(b) What recommendations would you make to Boeing to improve the usefulness of its income statement?

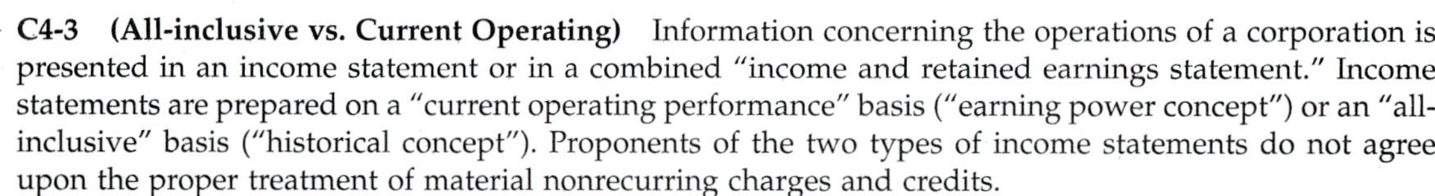

C4-3 (All-inclusive vs. Current Operating) Information concerning the operations of a corporation is presented in an income statement or in a combined "income and retained earnings statement." Income statements are prepared on a "current operating performance" basis ("earning power concept") or an "all-inclusive" basis ("historical concept"). Proponents of the two types of income statements do not agree upon the proper treatment of material nonrecurring charges and credits.

Instructions

(a) Define "current operating performance" and "all-inclusive" as used above.

(b) Explain the differences in content and organization of a "current operating performance" income statement and an "all-inclusive" income statement. Include a discussion of the proper treatment of material nonrecurring charges and credits.

(c) Give the principal arguments for the use of each of the three statements, "all-inclusive" income statement, "current operating performance" income statement, and a combined "income and retained earnings statement."

(AICPA adapted)

C4-4 (Extraordinary Items) Jeff Foxworthy, vice-president of finance for Red Neck Company, has recently been asked to discuss with the company's division controllers the proper accounting for extraordinary items. Jeff Foxworthy prepared the factual situations presented below as a basis for discussion.

1. An earthquake destroys one of the oil refineries owned by a large multinational oil company. Earthquakes are rare in this geographical location.
2. A publicly held company has incurred a substantial loss in the unsuccessful registration of a bond issue.
3. A large portion of a cigarette manufacturer's tobacco crops are destroyed by a hailstorm. Severe damage from hailstorms is rare in this locality.

4. A large diversified company sells a block of shares from its portfolio of securities acquired for investment purposes.
5. A company sells a block of common stock of a publicly traded company. The block of shares, which represents less than 10% of the publicly held company, is the only security investment the company has ever owned.
6. A company that operates a chain of warehouses sells the excess land surrounding one of its warehouses. When the company buys property to establish a new warehouse, it usually buys more land than it expects to use for the warehouse with the expectation that the land will appreciate in value. Twice during the past 5 years the company sold excess land.
7. A textile manufacturer with only one plant moves to another location and sustains relocation costs of $725,000.
8. A company experiences a material loss in the repurchase of a large bond issue that has been outstanding for 3 years. The company regularly repurchases bonds of this nature.
9. A railroad experiences an unusual flood loss to part of its track system. Flood losses normally occur every 3 or 4 years.
10. A machine tool company sells the only land it owns. The land was acquired 10 years ago for future expansion, but shortly thereafter the company abandoned all plans for expansion but decided to hold the land for appreciation.

Instructions

Determine whether the foregoing items should be classified as extraordinary items. Present a rationale for your position.

C4-5 (Earnings Management) Grace Inc. has recently reported steadily increasing income. The company reported income of $20,000 in 1998, $25,000 in 1999, and $30,000 in 2000. A number of market analysts have recommended that investors buy the stock because they expect the steady growth in income to continue. Grace is approaching the end of its fiscal year in 2001, and it again appears to be a good year. However, it has not yet recorded warranty expense.

Based on prior experience, this year's warranty expense should be around $5,000, but some top management has approached the controller to suggest a larger, more conservative warranty expense should be recorded this year. Income before warranty expense is $43,000. Specifically, by recording an $8,000 warranty accrual this year, Grace could report an increase in income for this year and still be in a position to cover its warranty costs in future years.

Instructions

(a) What is earnings management?
(b) What is the effect of the proposed accounting in 2001? In 2002?
(c) What is the appropriate accounting in this situation?

C4-6 (Income Reporting Items) Woody Allen Corp. is an entertainment firm that derives approximately 30% of its income from the Casino Royale Division, which manages gambling facilities. As auditor for Woody Allen Corp., you have recently overheard the following discussion between the controller and financial vice-president.

VICE-PRESIDENT: If we sell the Casino Royale Division, it seems ridiculous to segregate the results of the sale in the income statement. Separate categories tend to be absurd and confusing to the stockholders. I believe that we should simply report the gain on the sale as other income or expense without detail.

CONTROLLER: Professional pronouncements would require that we disclose this information separately in the income statement. If a sale of this type is considered unusual and infrequent, it must be reported as an extraordinary item.

VICE-PRESIDENT: What about the walkout we had last month when our employees were upset about their commission income? Would this situation not also be an extraordinary item?

CONTROLLER: I am not sure whether this item would be reported as extraordinary or not.

VICE-PRESIDENT: Oh well, it doesn't make any difference because the net effect of all these items is immaterial, so no disclosure is necessary.

Instructions

(a) On the basis of the foregoing discussion, answer the following questions: Who is correct about handling the sale? What would be the income statement presentation for the sale of the Casino Royale Division?

(b) How should the walkout by the employees be reported?
(c) What do you think about the vice-president's observation on materiality?
(d) What are the earnings per share implications of these topics?

C4-7 (Identification of Extraordinary Items) Loni Anderson Company is a major manufacturer of foodstuffs whose products are sold in grocery and convenience stores throughout the United States. The company's name is well known and respected because its products have been marketed nationally for over 50 years.

In April 2001 the company was forced to recall one of its major products. A total of 35 persons in Oshkosh were treated for severe intestinal pain, and eventually 3 people died from complications. All of the people had consumed Anderson's product.

The product causing the problem was traced to one specific lot. Anderson keeps samples from all lots of foodstuffs. After thorough testing, Anderson and the legal authorities confirmed that the product had been tampered with after it had left the company's plant and was no longer under the company's control.

All of the product was recalled from the market—the only time an Anderson product has been recalled nationally and the only time for tampering. Persons who still had the product in their homes, even though it was not from the affected lot, were encouraged to return the product for credit or refund. A media campaign was designed and implemented by the company to explain what had happened and what the company was doing to minimize any chance of recurrence. Anderson decided to continue the product with the same trade name and same wholesale price. However, the packaging was redesigned completely to be tamper resistant and safety sealed. This required the purchase and installation of new equipment.

The corporate accounting staff recommended that the costs associated with the tampered product be treated as an extraordinary charge on the 2001 financial statements. Corporate accounting was asked to identify the various costs that could be associated with the tampered product and related recall. These costs ($000 omitted) are as follows.

1. Credits and refunds to stores and consumers	$30,000
2. Insurance to cover lost sales and idle plant costs for possible future recalls	5,000
3. Transportation costs and off-site warehousing of returned product	2,000
4. Future security measures for other Anderson products	4,000
5. Testing of returned product and inventory	900
6. Destruction of returned product and inventory	2,400
7. Public relations program to reestablish brand credibility	4,200
8. Communication program to inform customers, answer inquiries, prepare press releases, etc.	1,600
9. Higher cost arising from new packaging	800
10. Investigation of possible involvement of employees, former employees, competitors, etc.	500
11. Packaging redesign and testing	2,000
12. Purchase and installation of new packaging equipment	6,000
13. Legal costs for defense against liability suits	750
14. Lost sales revenue due to recall	32,000

Anderson's estimated earnings before income taxes and before consideration of any of the above items for the year ending December 31, 2001, are $225 million.

Instructions

(a) Loni Anderson Company plans to recognize the costs associated with the product tampering and recall as an extraordinary charge.
  (1) Explain why Anderson could classify this occurrence as an extraordinary charge.
  (2) Describe the placement and terminology used to present the extraordinary charge in the 2001 income statement.

(b) Refer to the 14 cost items identified by the corporate accounting staff of Anderson Company.
  (1) Identify the cost items by number that should be included in the extraordinary charge for 2001.
  (2) For any item that is not included in the extraordinary charge, explain why it would not be included in the extraordinary charge.

(CMA adapted)

C4-8 (All-inclusive vs. Current Operating—Periodic Inventory) Aaron Neville, controller for Tatooed Heart Inc., has recently prepared an income statement for 2002. Mr. Neville admits that he has not examined any recent professional pronouncements, but believes that the following presentation presents fairly the financial progress of this company during the current period.

TATOOED HEART INC.
Income Statement
For the Year Ended December 31, 2002

Sales			$377,852
Less: Sales returns and allowances			16,320
Net sales			361,532
Cost of goods sold:			
Inventory, January 1, 2002		$ 50,235	
Purchases	$192,143		
Less: Purchase discounts	3,142	189,001	
Cost of goods available for sale		239,236	
Inventory, December 31, 2002		41,124	
Cost of goods sold			198,112
Gross profit			163,420
Selling expenses		41,850	
Administrative expenses		32,142	73,992
Income before income tax			89,428
Other revenues and gains			
Dividends received			40,000
			129,428
Income tax			43,900
Net income			$ 85,528

TATOOED HEART INC.
Retained Earnings Statement
For the Year Ended December 31, 2002

Retained earnings, January 1, 2002			$216,000
Add:			
Net income for 2002	$85,528		
Gain from casualty (net of tax)	10,000		
Gain on sale of plant assets	21,400	$116,928	
Deduct:			
Loss on expropriation (net of tax)	13,000		
Cash dividends declared on common stock	30,000		
Correction of mathematical error in depreciating plant assets in 2000 (net of tax)	17,186	(60,186)	56,742
Retained earnings, December 31, 2002			$272,742

Instructions

(a) Determine whether these statements are prepared under the "current operating" or "all-inclusive" concept of income. Cite specific details.

(b) Which method do you favor and why?

(c) Which method must be used, and how should the information be presented? Common shares outstanding for the year are 50,000 shares.

For questionable items, use the classification that ordinarily would be appropriate.

C4-9 (Identification of Income Statement Weaknesses) The following financial statement was prepared by employees of Cynthia Taylor Corporation.

CYNTHIA TAYLOR CORPORATION
Income Statement
Year Ended December 31, 2002

Revenues	
Gross sales, including sales taxes	$1,044,300
Less: Returns, allowances, and cash discounts	56,200

Net sales	988,100
Dividends, interest, and purchase discounts	30,250
Recoveries of accounts written off in prior years	13,850
Total revenues	1,032,200
Costs and expenses	
Cost of goods sold, including sales taxes	465,900
Salaries and related payroll expenses	60,500
Rent	19,100
Freight-in and freight-out	3,400
Bad debt expense	24,000
Addition to reserve for possible inventory losses	3,800
Total costs and expenses	576,700
Income before extraordinary items	455,500
Extraordinary items	
Loss on discontinued styles (Note 1)	37,000
Loss on sale of marketable securities (Note 2)	39,050
Loss on sale of warehouse (Note 3)	86,350
Retroactive settlement of federal income taxes for 2001 and 2000 (Note 4)	34,500
Total extraordinary items	196,900
Net income	$ 258,600
Net income per share of common stock	$2.30

Note 1: New styles and rapidly changing consumer preferences resulted in a $37,000 loss on the disposal of discontinued styles and related accessories.

Note 2: The corporation sold an investment in marketable securities at a loss of $39,050. The corporation normally sells securities of this nature.

Note 3: The corporation sold one of its warehouses at an $86,350 loss.

Note 4: The corporation was charged $34,500 retroactively for additional income taxes resulting from a settlement in 1999. Of this amount, $17,000 was applicable to 2001, and the balance was applicable to 2000. Litigation of this nature is recurring for this company.

Instructions

Identify and discuss the weaknesses in classification and disclosure in the single-step income statement above. You should explain why these treatments are weaknesses and what the proper presentation of the items would be in accordance with recent professional pronouncements.

C4-10 (Classification of Income Statement Items) As audit partner for Noriyuki and Morita, you are in charge of reviewing the classification of unusual items that have occurred during the current year. The following (material) items have come to your attention:

1. A merchandising company incorrectly overstated its ending inventory 2 years ago. Inventory for all other periods is correctly computed.
2. An automobile dealer sells for $137,000 an extremely rare 1930 S type Invicta which it purchased for $21,000 10 years ago. The Invicta is the only such display item the dealer owns.
3. A drilling company during the current year extended the estimated useful life of certain drilling equipment from 9 to 15 years. As a result, depreciation for the current year was lowered.
4. A retail outlet changed its computation for bad debt expense from 1% to 1/2 of 1% of sales because of changes in its customer clientele.
5. A mining concern sells a foreign subsidiary engaged in uranium mining, although it (the seller) continues to engage in uranium mining in other countries.
6. A steel company changes from straight-line depreciation to accelerated depreciation in accounting for its plant assets.
7. A construction company, at great expense, prepared a major proposal for a government loan. The loan is not approved.
8. A water pump manufacturer has had large losses resulting from a strike by its employees early in the year.
9. Depreciation for a prior period was incorrectly understated by $950,000. The error was discovered in the current year.
10. A large sheep rancher suffered a major loss because the state required that all sheep in the state be killed to halt the spread of a rare disease. Such a situation has not occurred in the state for 20 years.

11. A food distributor that sells wholesale to supermarket chains and to fast-food restaurants (two major classes of customers) decides to discontinue the division that sells to one of the two classes of customers.

Instructions

From the foregoing information, indicate in what section of the income statement or retained earnings statement these items should be classified. Provide a brief rationale for your position.

C4-11 (Comprehensive Income) Ferguson Arthur, Jr., controller for Jenkins Corporation, is preparing the company's financial statements at year-end. Currently, he is focusing on the income statement and determining the format for reporting comprehensive income. During the year, the company earned net income of $400,000 and had unrealized gains on available-for-sale securities of $20,000. In the previous year net income was $410,000, and the company had no unrealized gains or losses.

Instructions

(a) Show how income and comprehensive income will be reported on a comparative basis for the current and prior years, using the separate income statement format.

(b) Show how income and comprehensive income will be reported on a comparative basis for the current and prior years, using the combined income statement format.

(c) Which format should Arthur recommend?

***C4-12 (Discontinued Operations)** You are working on the audit team for a multi-divisional, calendar year-end client with annual sales of $90 million. The company primarily sells electronic transistors to small customers and has one division that deals in acoustic transmitters for Navy submarines. The Red October Division has approximately $18 million in sales.

It's an evening in February 2001, and the audit work is complete. You're working in the client's office on the report, when you overhear a conversation between the financial vice-president, the treasurer, and the controller. They're discussing the sale of the Red October Division, expected to take place in June of this year, and the related reporting problems.

The vice-president thinks no segregation of the sale is necessary in the income statement because separate categories tend to be abused and confuse the stockholders. The treasurer disagrees. He feels that if an item is unusual or infrequent, it should be classified as an extraordinary item, including the sale of the Red October Division. The controller says an item should be both infrequent and unusual to be extraordinary. He feels the sale of the Red October Division should be shown separately, but not as an extraordinary item.

The sale is not new to you because you read about it in the minutes of the December 16, 2000, board of directors meeting. The minutes indicated plans to sell the transmitter plant and equipment by June 30, 2001, to its major competitor, who seems interested. The board estimates that net income and sales will remain constant until the sale, on which the company expects a $700,000 profit.

You also hear the controller disagree with the vice-president that the results of the strike last year and the sale of the old transistor ovens, formerly used in manufacturing, would also be extraordinary items. In addition, the treasurer thinks the government regulation issued last month, which made much of their inventory of raw material useless, would be extraordinary. The regulations set beta emission standards at levels lower than those in the raw materials supply, and there's no alternative use for the materials. Finally, the controller claims the discussion is academic. Since the net effect of all three items is immaterial, no disclosure is required.

Instructions

(a) Does the Red October Division qualify as a segment of a business in more than one way? If so, why?

(b) Does the Red October Division qualify as a discontinued operation? Why?

(c) Do the minutes indicate that a formal plan has been established? If not, why?

(d) When should the gain be recognized? What if a loss were anticipated?

(e) Who is correct about reporting the sale? What would the income statement presentation be for the next fiscal year?

(f) Who is right about whether the strike, the sale of fixed assets and the imposition of a new government regulation constitute extraordinary items?

(g) What do you think about the controller's observation on materiality?

(h) What are the earnings per share ramifications of these topics?

USING YOUR JUDGMENT

FINANCIAL REPORTING PROBLEM: INTEL CORPORATION

The financial statements of Intel and accompanying notes, as presented in the Company's 1998 Annual Report, are in Appendix 5B.

Instructions

Refer to this information and answer the following questions:

(a) What type of income statement format does Intel use? Indicate why this format might be used to present income statement information.

(b) What are Intel's primary revenue sources?

(c) Compute Intel's gross profit for each of the years 1996–1998. Explain why cost of sales has increased over these years.

(d) Why does Intel make a distinction between operating and nonoperating revenue? Explain what happened to Intel's nonoperating revenue in 1998.

(e) What financial ratios did Intel choose to report in its "Facts and Figures" section covering the years 1989–1998?

FINANCIAL STATEMENT ANALYSIS CASES

Case 1: Comptronix Corporation

Comptronix Corporation manufactures circuit boards and other electronic parts used in computers, computer peripherals, medical devices, and testing equipment. During a recent year, the company ceased operations in two locations. A manufacturing facility in San Jose, California, was sold and one in Colorado Springs, Colorado, was closed. The products that had been manufactured in both locations were similar to those manufactured in the remaining plants.

The sale of the San Jose facility was completed in the same year. Suppose that the operating loss from this facility was $400,000, net of applicable tax benefit of $103,000, and that the sale of the assets resulted in a $4.7 million loss based on a book value of $7.2 million.

Instructions

(a) Should Comptronix account for this as a discontinued segment? Why or why not?

(b) Describe how the sale of the San Jose facility should be shown on the income statement of Comptronix if the company determined that it should be shown as a discontinued segment.

(c) Describe how the sale of the San Jose facility should be shown on the income statement of Comptronix if the company determined that it should *not* be shown as a discontinued segment.

Case 2: Dresser Industries

Dresser Industries provides products and services to oil and natural gas exploration, production, transmission and processing companies. A recent income statement is reproduced below. Dollar amounts are in millions.

Sales	$2,697.0
Service revenues	1,933.9
Share of earnings of unconsolidated affiliates	92.4
Total revenues	4,723.3
Cost of sales	1,722.7
Cost of services	1,799.9
Total costs of sales and services	3,522.6

Gross earnings	1,200.7
Selling, engineering, administrative and general expenses	(919.8)
Special charges	(70.0)
Other income (deductions)	
Interest expense	(47.4)
Interest earned	19.1
Other, net	4.8
Earnings before income taxes and other items below	187.4
Income taxes	(79.4)
Minority interest	(10.3)
Earnings from continuing operations	97.7
Discontinued operations	(35.3)
Earnings before extraordinary items and accounting changes	62.4
Extraordinary items	(6.3)
Cumulative effect of accounting changes	(393.8)
Net earnings (loss)	$(337.7)

Instructions

Assume that 177,636,000 shares of stock were issued and outstanding. Prepare the per-share portion of the income statement. Remember to begin with Income from Continuing Operations.

COMPARATIVE ANALYSIS CASE

The Coca-Cola Company versus PepsiCo Inc.

Instructions

Go to the Digital Tool and answer the following questions about the financial reporting by Coca-Cola and PepsiCo.

(a) What type of income format(s) is used by these two companies? Identify any differences in income statement format between these two companies.

(b) What are the gross profits, operating profit, and net income for these two companies over the 3-year period 1996–1998? Which company has had better financial results over this period of time?

(c) Identify the irregular items reported by these two companies in their income statements over the 3-year period 1996–1998. Do these irregular items appear to be significant?

(d) In PepsiCo's Management Analysis section under results of operation, examine the company's presentation of "Operating Profit" and "Income and Income Per Share Before Cumulative Effect of Accounting Changes." Why do you believe PepsiCo reports information on both a "reported" and "ongoing" basis?

RESEARCH CASES

Case 1

Most libraries maintain the annual reports of large companies on file or on microfiche.

Instructions

Obtain the 1998 annual reports for UAL Corp. and NIKE, Inc., and answer the following questions concerning their income statements. (*Note:* Larger libraries may have CD-ROM products such as *Laser Disclosure* or *Compact Disclosure.* UAL and NIKE are also on the Digital Tool or can be found online in the SEC EDGAR database.)

(a) Describe the major differences between the income statement formats.

(b) Identify any irregular items on either of the income statements.

(c) UAL includes a separate line for depreciation expense, while NIKE does not. Why is this the case? Does NIKE's depreciation expense appear on another financial statement?

(d) UAL's income statement includes significantly more detail than NIKE's. Which presentation do you prefer? Why?

Case 2

The April 1996 issue of the *Journal of Accountancy* includes an article by Dennis R. Beresford, L. Todd Johnson, and Cheri L. Reither, entitled "Is a Second Income Statement Needed?"

Instructions

Read the article and answer the following questions.

(a) One what basis would the "second income statement" be prepared? Briefly describe this basis.

(b) Why is there a perceived need for a second income statement?

(c) Identify three alternatives for reporting the proposed measure of income.

INTERNATIONAL REPORTING CASE

Presented below is the income statement for a British company, Avon Rubber PLC.

AVON RUBBER PLC

Consolidated Profit and Loss Account
for the year ended 3 October 1998

	Total £'000
Turnover	
Continuing activities	251,531
Acquisitions	15,554
Total turnover	**267,085**
Cost of sales	(216,174)
Gross profit	50,911
Net operating expenses	(28,586)
Share of operating profits of joint ventures and associated companies	26
Operating profit	
Continuing activities	19,361
Acquisitions	2,990
Total operating profit	**22,351**
Profit on sale of property	993
Loss on sale of fixed asset investment	(275)
Profit on ordinary activities before interest	**23,069**
Interest payable	(3,014)
Interest receivable	3,850
Profit on ordinary activities before taxation	**23,905**
Taxation	(7,003)
Profit on ordinary activities after taxation	**16,902**
Minority interests	254
Profit for the year	**17,156**
Basic earnings per ordinary share	**62.4p**

Instructions

(a) Review the Avon Rubber income statement and identify at least three differences between this British income statement and an income statement of a U.S. company as presented in the chapter.

(b) Identify any irregular items reported by Avon Rubber. Is the reporting of these irregular items in Avon's income statement similar to reporting of these items in U.S. companies' income statements? Explain.

ETHICS CASE

Arthur Miller, controller for the Salem Corporation, is preparing the company's income statement at year-end. He notes that the company lost a considerable sum on the sale of some equipment it had decided to replace. Since the company has sold equipment routinely in the past, Miller knows the losses cannot be reported as extraordinary. He also does not want to highlight it as a material loss since he feels that will reflect poorly on him and the company. He reasons that if the company had recorded more depreciation during the assets' lives, the losses would not be so great. Since depreciation is included among the company's operating expenses, he wants to report the losses along with the company's expenses, where he hopes it will not be noticed.

Instructions

(a) What are the ethical issues involved?

(b) What should Miller do?

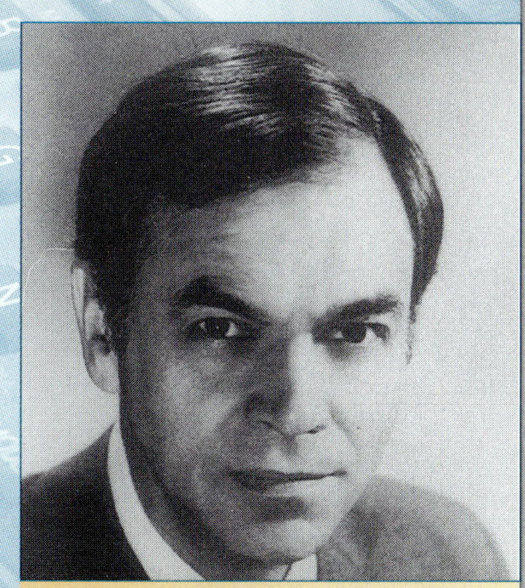

A visit with
Robert Sack

Robert Sack teaches accounting and ethics at the Darden Graduate School of Business at the University of Virginia. Prior to joining academia, Mr. Sack was chief accountant in the Enforcement Division of the Securities & Exchange Commission. He was also a partner at what is now Deloitte & Touche.

PERSPECTIVES ON
Accounting Ethics

The ethics rules for accountants seem complex. What part of the rule structure draws the most attention from people in practice? The rules are complex because maintaining independence in today's business world is complex. I think the one area that has created the most tension is the requirement that an auditor must not have a financial interest in his or her client. The rule seems obvious, but some people are so enthusiastic about their clients that they want to participate in the client's success. One of the Big Five firms was recently very embarrassed to find that several people in an office had purchased stock in a client of that office. It was a serious breach of ethics, and of the rules of the profession. When that situation was discovered, the firm undertook a more thorough examination across its offices and found even more violations. The individuals have been disciplined, the firm is embarrassed, and the credibility of the profession took it on the nose.

As with any set of "rules," we find that we are caught up in a web of interpretations. For example, it seems clear that, as the audit partner for a client, I ought not have any financial involvement with that client, whether in the form of a stock investment or a loan to or from the client. However, would it be all right if my wife invested in the stock of that client? How about her father? Or the estate of my aunt, for which I am executor? Those are all legitimate questions, and they must be answered. As we struggle to answer those questions, protecting the substance of the rules but treating the individuals fairly, we may lose sight of our overall goal—and that is to assure the independence of the audit function in our financial society.

You refer to the difficult problems that are sure to come our way. Can you give us some examples? Let's say you're a junior auditor on an engagement, and the senior on the job is under a lot of pressure to bring this job in on budget. He tells you to report ten hours of work per day even though you really worked twelve hours. As the junior, you probably feel a little uncertain about your abilities, and you are sure you have wasted time. Besides, you really don't want to make waves with this person who will be evaluating your performance at the end of this engagement. It will be very tempting to go along with the senior's request. But someone has to stand up and say,

"Sorry, that's not right." Asking for the falsification of a time report, and giving in to that request, poisons the environment on that engagement. If it's OK to fudge the time on the job, it will be tempting to fudge the completion of an audit test.

Can you give us some examples of higher-level ethical dilemmas that audit people confront? In the last several years, the SEC has brought enforcement actions against individual members of an audit team, acknowledging that the primary responsibility rests with the signing partner, but also arguing that the staff people have a professional responsibility to keep the firm from making a mistake. In one case, the manager on the job had been fighting with the client over some accounting adjustments. The manager was called out of town to wrap up another audit, and the partner agreed to bring the first audit to a close.

When the manager came back and found that the job was done and that the partner had accepted the client's position, he was confronted with a very difficult ethical choice. To whom did he owe loyalty? To the partner, his superior? To the firm? To the client? To the readers of the financial statements? In the end, the manager signed off on the papers and said nothing about the adjustments that he had fought for so vigorously. Someone else on the audit team alerted the national office of the firm, which, after a thorough review, recalled the audit report and admitted that the partner and manager had made a mistake. Both the partner and the manager were sanctioned by the SEC for their failure to adhere to professional standards. It is easy to say in hindsight, but how much better off everyone would have been if the manager had stood his ground when he saw that the partner had given in to the client.

Now that the Big Eight has merged down to the Big Five, do you think that independence has been compromised? No. It might actually enhance independence. Five firms—Arthur Andersen, Deloitte & Touche, Ernst & Young, KPMG Peat Marwick, and PricewaterhouseCoopers—audit most of the nation's public companies. Because of the size and power the firms have, the competitive pressures for individual clients ought to be reduced, and therefore there should be less pressure on in-the-field independence. The firms' larger reputations are likely to be more important than a relationship with any one client.

That's not to say that the consolidation is without problems. A blue ribbon panel commissioned by the Public Oversight Board urged the firms to be very careful as they expanded in scope and size, to preserve the unique atmosphere required for the audit function. Auditing is different from the other elements of a professional services firm in that the audit client is a vague, amorphous thing called the public interest. That obligation for the public interest is the basis of the profession's code of ethics and, more importantly, for the required independent attitude. Preserving that attitude, within the hurly-burly of a multi-disciplinary firm, is a challenge that will need consistent monitoring by the firms themselves and by the profession.

Is the issue of independence also relevant for management accountants? Yes, but in a different context than that of the independent auditor. Let's say you are a management accountant with XYZ Corp. The company has a hot lead for a major sale, and a team is created to make the final pitch to the potential customer. You are included on the team because you are going to explain to the customer why the financing package you are proposing will save a great deal of money. The team closes the sale and everybody celebrates. But the next morning, you have to change your hat and evaluate the transaction against the GAAP revenue recognition standards. If there are some serious contingencies in the customer's acceptance of the deal, then it might not qualify as revenue. As a professional accountant, you must exercise a judgment that is independent of the interests of your team. The dual role that we expect management accountants to play, working as part of management but also acting as the primary gatekeeper for financial reporting, requires a great deal of personal integrity and independence.

Do you see any ethical issues in financial reporting for Internet companies? Traditional accounting systems are oriented towards reporting net income. But now we have companies whose shares trade on other information, such as market share and eyeball count. If you're the CFO of such a company, and you know that the investment community is looking at these new measures of performance, you must make sure that your company's data are honest and accurate. As the independent CPA, it's particularly important that you can be satisfied that this non-traditional information is reliable, even if it is not covered by your standard opinion—you must not allow your client to distort operating data, for the long-term good of the client and your client relationship.

CHAPTER 5

Balance Sheet and Statement of Cash Flows

Warning Signs!

Commodore International reported earnings of $4.66 per share in one year, up approximately 63% over the prior year. Yet, its stock price dropped from a high of 60⅝ to less than 30 over this one-year period. Why? The balance sheet indicated that accounts receivable increased substantially and the composition of the inventory changed dramatically. The substantial receivables buildup indicated that the receivables collection was a problem. Furthermore, while inventory overall remained stable, finished goods inventory increased 50%. In other words, goods were piling up because sales were lagging. Savvy investors, who saw the trouble signs in the financial statements, began selling their stock. In the following year, Commodore reported a fourth quarter loss of $124 million caused by substantial inventory write-offs.

Another notable recent example is **Sunbeam**, which recorded stellar market performance following the hiring of "Chainsaw Al" Dunlap as CEO. Mr. Dunlap arrived at Sunbeam with a track record of turning around troubled companies, and Sunbeam shares soared nearly 300% in the wake of his hiring. However, some analysts were concerned that growing inventory and receivables balances at Sunbeam warned of hard times ahead. In fact, within a year the Sunbeam bubble burst and the stock price fell below pre-Chainsaw Al levels, once the market discovered that the growth in inventories and receivables would lead to lower sales and profits.

Earnings declines at Commodore and Sunbeam could have been predicted, given the deteriorating financial information provided in the balance sheet and statement of cash flows. And just as these deteriorating financial statements warned of trouble, improving balance sheet and related cash flow quality often foreshadows long-term improvements in earnings.

LEARNING OBJECTIVES

After studying this chapter, you should be able to:

1. **Identify the uses and limitations of a balance sheet.**
2. **Identify the major classifications of the balance sheet.**
3. **Prepare a classified balance sheet using the report and account formats.**
4. **Identify balance sheet information requiring supplemental disclosure.**
5. **Identify major disclosure techniques for the balance sheet.**
6. **Indicate the purpose of the statement of cash flows.**
7. **Identify the content of the statement of cash flows.**
8. **Prepare a statement of cash flows.**
9. **Understand the usefulness of the statement of cash flows.**

PREVIEW OF CHAPTER 5

Until recently, readers of financial statements merely skimmed the balance sheet and all but ignored the cash flow statement. However, these financial statements offer important information. For example, as shown in the opening story involving **Commodore International** and **Sunbeam Corporation**, surprises in earnings per share could have been anticipated if these financial statements had not been overlooked. The purpose of this chapter is to examine the many different types of assets, liabilities, and stockholders' equity items that affect the balance sheet and the statement of cash flows. The content and organization of this chapter are as follows:

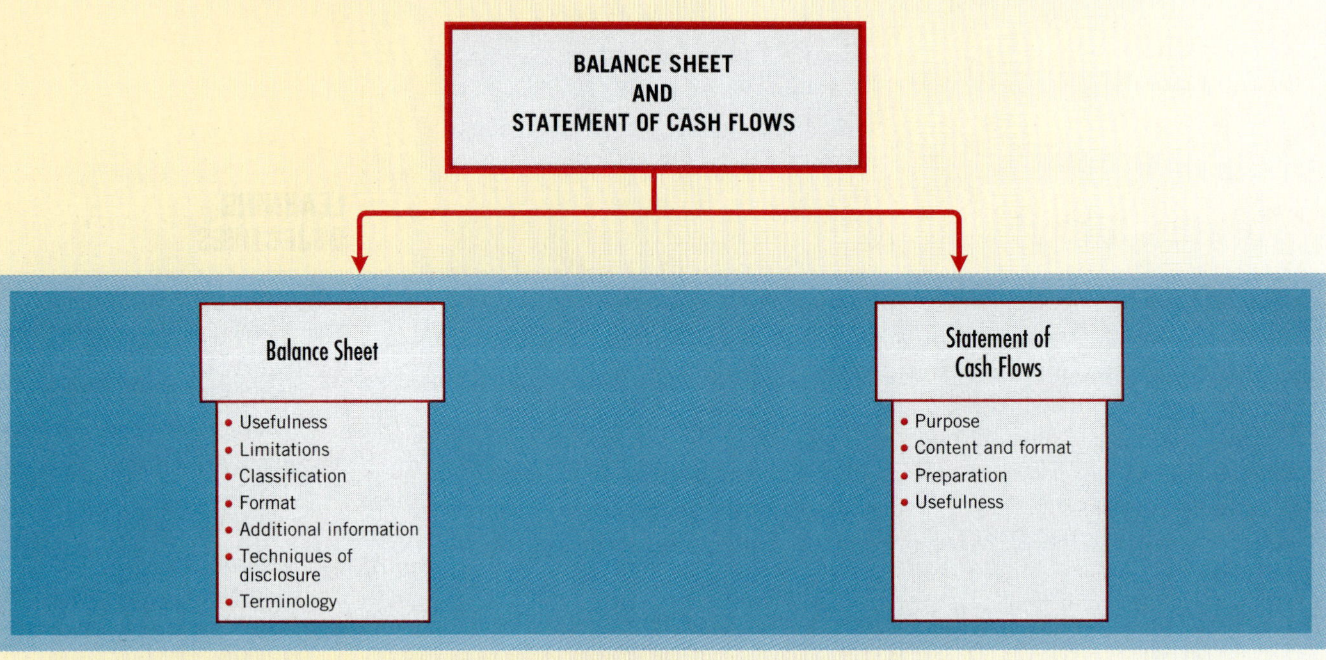

SECTION 1 BALANCE SHEET

The **balance sheet**, sometimes referred to as the statement of financial position, reports the assets, liabilities, and stockholders' equity of a business enterprise at a specific date. This financial statement provides information about the nature and amounts of investments in enterprise resources, obligations to creditors, and the owners' equity in net resources.[1] It therefore helps in predicting the amounts, timing, and uncertainty of future cash flows.

OBJECTIVE 1
Identify the uses and limitations of a balance sheet.

USEFULNESS OF THE BALANCE SHEET

By providing information on assets, liabilities, and stockholders' equity, the balance sheet provides a basis for computing rates of return and evaluating the capital structure of the enterprise. As illustrated in the opening story about Commodore and Sun-

[1]*Accounting Trends and Techniques—1999* indicates that approximately 95% of the companies surveyed used the term "balance sheet." The term "statement of financial position" is used infrequently, although it is conceptually appealing.

beam, information in the balance sheet is also used to assess enterprise risk[2] and future cash flows. In this regard, the balance sheet is useful for analyzing a company's liquidity, solvency, and financial flexibility, as described below.

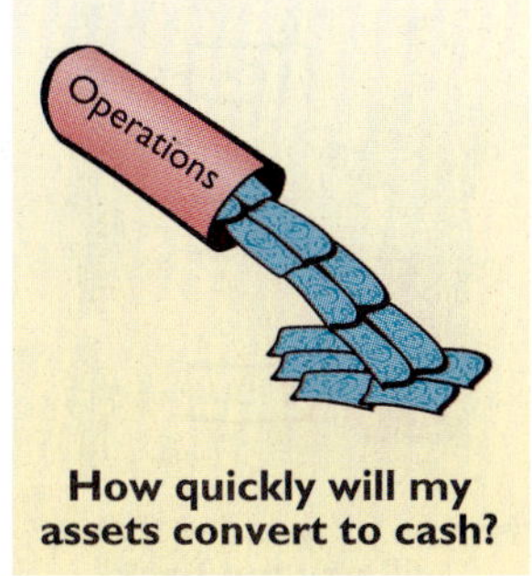

How quickly will my assets convert to cash?

Liquidity describes "the amount of time that is expected to elapse until an asset is realized or otherwise converted into cash or until a liability has to be paid."[3] Creditors are interested in short-term liquidity ratios, such as cash (or near cash) to short-term liabilities, because they indicate whether the enterprise will have the resources to pay its current and maturing obligations. Similarly, stockholders assess liquidity to evaluate the possibility of future cash dividends or the buyback of shares. In general, the greater the liquidity, the lower the risk of enterprise failure.[4]

Solvency refers to the ability of an enterprise to pay its debts as they mature. For example, when a company carries a high level of long-term debt relative to assets, it has lower solvency than a similar company with a low level of long-term debt. Companies with higher debt are relatively more risky because more of their assets will be required to meet these fixed obligations (such as interest and principal payments).

We are drowning in a sea of debt!

Liquidity and solvency affect an entity's **financial flexibility**, which measures the "ability of an enterprise to take effective actions to alter the amounts and timing of cash flows so it can respond to unexpected needs and opportunities."[5] For example, a company may become so loaded with debt—so financially inflexible—that its sources of cash to finance expansion or to pay off maturing debt are limited or nonexistent. An enterprise with a high degree of financial flexibility is better able to survive bad times, to recover from unexpected setbacks, and to take advantage of profitable and unexpected investment opportunities. Generally, the greater the financial flexibility, the lower the risk of enterprise failure.

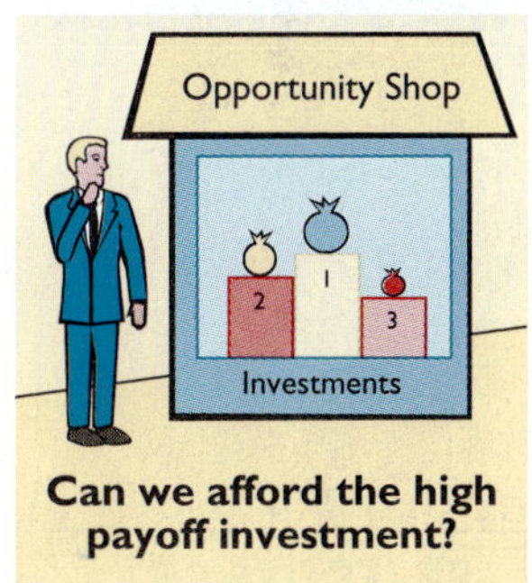

Can we afford the high payoff investment?

Lack of liquidity, solvency, and inadequate financial flexibility seriously affected the U.S. airline industry in the 1980s and again in the early 1990s. **American**, **Eastern**, **United**, and **TWA** all reported quarterly operating losses that stemmed primarily from high interest costs, increased fuel costs, and price cutting resulting from deregulation. Because of operating losses and lowered liquidity, some airlines asked their employees to sign labor contracts that provided no wage increases. Other airlines, already heavily in debt and lacking financial flexibility and liquidity, had to cancel orders for new, more efficient aircraft. TWA had to sell routes and planes to raise cash. Some of the major airlines (such as **Braniff**, **Continental**, **Eastern**, **Midway**, and **America West**) even declared bankruptcy. This financial distress was not an insiders' secret. The airlines' balance sheets clearly revealed their financial inflexibility and low liquidity.

LIMITATIONS OF THE BALANCE SHEET

Because the income statement and the balance sheet are interrelated, it is not surprising that the balance sheet has many of the same limitations as the income statement. Here are some of the major limitations of the balance sheet:

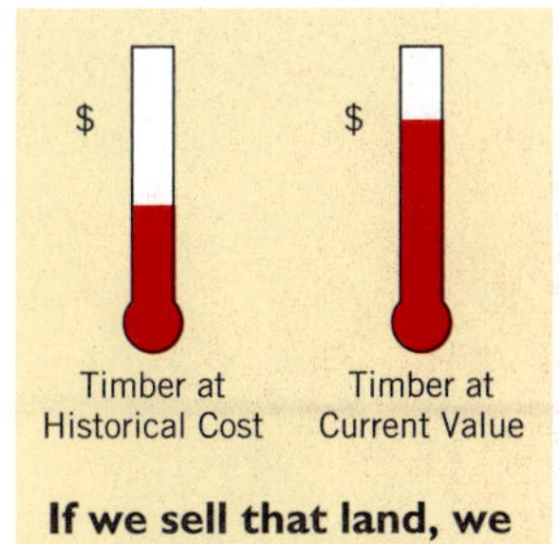

If we sell that land, we could get more than we paid.

1. Most assets and liabilities are stated at **historical cost**. As a result, the information reported in the balance sheet has higher reliability but is subject to the criticism that a more relevant current fair value is not reported. For example, **Georgia Pa-**

[2]Risk is an expression of the unpredictability of future events, transactions, circumstances, and results of the enterprise.

[3]"Reporting Income, Cash Flows, and Financial Position of Business Enterprises," *Proposed Statement of Financial Accounting Concepts* (Stamford, Conn.: FASB, 1981), par. 29.

[4]Liquidity measures are important inputs to bankruptcy prediction models, such as those developed by Altman and others. See G. White, A. Sondhi, and D. Fried, *The Analysis of Financial Statements* (New York: John Wiley & Sons, 1997), Chapter 18.

[5]"Reporting Income, Cash Flows, and Financial Position of Business Enterprises," *Proposed Statement of Financial Accounting Concepts* (Stamford, Conn.: FASB, 1981), par. 25.

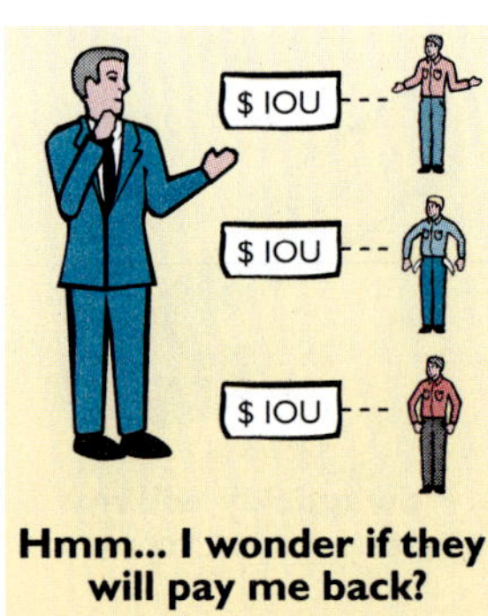

Hmm... I wonder if they will pay me back?

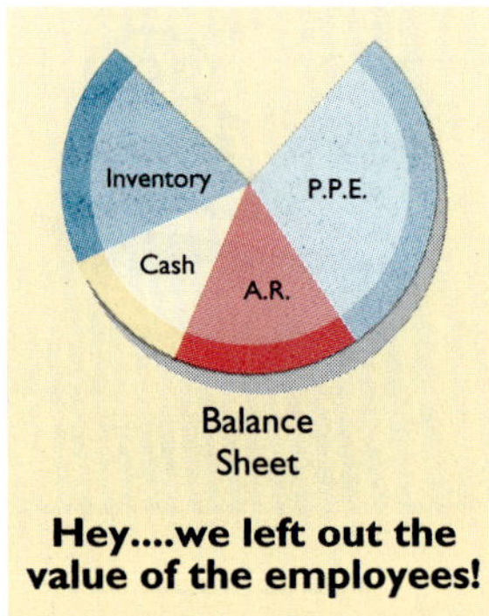

Hey....we left out the value of the employees!

cific owns timber and other assets that may appreciate in value after they are purchased; this increase is not reported unless the assets are sold.

2. **Judgments and estimates** are used in determining many of the items reported in the balance sheet. For example, **Gateway 2000** makes estimates of the amount of receivables that it will collect, the useful life of its warehouses, and the number of computers that will be returned under warranty in arriving at the amounts reported in its balance sheet.
3. The balance sheet necessarily **omits many items that are of financial value** to the business but cannot be recorded objectively. For example, the knowledge and skill of **Intel** employees in developing new computer chips are arguably the company's most significant asset. However, because it is difficult to reliably measure the value of employees and other intangible assets (such as customer base, research superiority, and reputation), these items are not recognized in the balance sheet. Similarly, many liabilities are also reported in an "off-balance sheet" manner, if reported at all.[6]

One of the most significant challenges facing the accounting profession is the limitations of financial statements. As indicated in Chapter 1, the AICPA has recently concluded a study examining the information needs of investors and creditors. Some major observations are related to the balance sheet: Users oppose replacing the current historical-cost-based accounting model with a fair value accounting model. However, they view fair value information as useful for particular types of assets and liabilities and in certain types of industries. Also, users want companies to disclose information about the estimates and assumptions used to determine material asset and liability amounts. Finally, they want more qualitative and quantitative information about the risks associated with financial instruments and off-balance-sheet financing arrangements.[7]

CLASSIFICATION IN THE BALANCE SHEET

OBJECTIVE 2
Identify the major classifications of the balance sheet.

Balance sheet accounts are **classified** so that similar items are grouped together to arrive at significant subtotals. Furthermore, the material is arranged so that important relationships are shown.

The FASB has often noted that the parts and subsections of financial statements can be more informative than the whole. Therefore, as one would expect, the reporting of summary accounts alone (total assets, net assets, total liabilities, etc.) is discouraged. Individual items should be separately reported and classified in sufficient detail to permit users to assess the amounts, timing, and uncertainty of future cash flows, as well as the evaluation of liquidity and financial flexibility, profitability, and risk.

Classification in financial statements helps analysts by grouping items with similar characteristics and separating items with different characteristics:[8]

1. Assets that differ in their **type or expected function** in the central operations or other activities of the enterprise should be reported as separate items. For example, merchandise inventories should be reported separately from property, plant, and equipment.

[6]Several of these omitted items (such as leases and through-put arrangements) are discussed in later chapters. See AICPA Special Committee on Financial Reporting, "Improving Business Reporting—A Customer Focus," *Journal of Accountancy,* Supplement, October 1994, for a discussion of issues surrounding off-balance sheet items.

[7]AICPA Special Committee on Financial Reporting, "Meeting the Information Needs of Investors and Creditors," *Journal of Accountancy,* Supplement, September 1994.

[8]"Reporting Income, Cash Flows, and Financial Positions of Business Enterprises," *Proposed Statement of Financial Accounting Concepts* (Stamford, Conn.: FASB, 1981), par. 51.

2. Assets and liabilities with **different implications for the financial flexibility** of the enterprise should be reported as separate items. For example, assets used in operations should be reported separately from assets held for investment and assets subject to restrictions such as leased equipment.
3. Assets and liabilities with **different general liquidity characteristics** should be reported as separate items. For example, cash should be reported separately from inventories.

The three general classes of items included in the balance sheet are assets, liabilities, and equity. Here is how we defined them in Chapter 2:

ELEMENTS OF THE BALANCE SHEET

1. ***Assets.*** Probable future economic benefits obtained or controlled by a particular entity as a result of past transactions or events.
2. ***Liabilities.*** Probable future sacrifices of economic benefits arising from present obligations of a particular entity to transfer assets or provide services to other entities in the future as a result of past transactions or events.
3. ***Equity.*** Residual interest in the assets of an entity that remains after deducting its liabilities. In a business enterprise, the equity is the ownership interest.[9]

These items are then divided into several subclassifications. Illustration 5-1 indicates the general format of balance sheet presentation.

Assets	Liabilities and Owners' Equity
Current assets	Current liabilities
Long-term investments	Long-term debt
Property, plant, and equipment	Owners' equity
Intangible assets	Capital stock
Other assets	Additional paid-in capital
	Retained earnings

ILLUSTRATION 5-1
Balance Sheet Classifications

The balance sheet may be classified in some other manner, but there is very little departure from these major subdivisions in practice. If a proprietorship or partnership is involved, the classifications within the owners' equity section are presented a little differently, as will be shown later in the chapter.

Current Assets

Current assets **are cash and other assets expected to be converted into cash, sold, or consumed either in one year or in the operating cycle, whichever is longer.** The operating cycle is the average time between the acquisition of materials and supplies and the realization of cash through sales of the product for which the materials and supplies were acquired. The cycle operates from cash through inventory, production, and receivables back to cash. When there are several operating cycles within one year, the one-year period is used. If the operating cycle is more than one year, the longer period is used.

Current assets are presented in the balance sheet in order of liquidity. The five major items found in the current assets section are cash, short-term investments, re-

[9]"Elements of Financial Statements of Business Enterprises," *Statement of Financial Accounting Concepts No. 6* (Stamford, Conn.: FASB, 1985), paras. 25, 35 and 49.

Basic balance sheet formats differ across nations. For example, in Great Britain and in nations influenced by British financial reporting, the balance sheet is presented with the least liquid asset accounts appearing first and cash appearing last.

ceivables, inventories, and prepayments. **Cash** is included at its stated value; **short-term investments** are generally valued at fair value; **accounts receivable** are stated at the estimated amount collectible; **inventories** generally are included at cost or the lower of cost or market; and **prepaid items** are valued at cost.

The above items are not considered current assets if they are not expected to be realized in one year or in the operating cycle, whichever is longer. For example, cash restricted for purposes other than payment of current obligations or for use in current operations is excluded from the current assets section. **Generally, the rule is that if an asset is to be turned into cash or is to be used to pay a current liability within a year or the operating cycle, whichever is longer, it is classified as current.** This requirement is subject to exceptions. An investment in common stock is classified as either a current asset or a noncurrent asset depending on management's intent. When a company has small holdings of common stocks or bonds that are going to be held long-term, they should not be classified as current.

Although a current asset is well defined, certain theoretical problems develop. One problem is justifying the inclusion of prepaid expense in the current assets section. The normal justification is that if these items had not been paid in advance, they would require the use of current assets during the operating cycle. If we follow this logic to its ultimate conclusion, however, any asset purchased previously saves the use of current assets during the operating cycle and would be considered current.

Another problem occurs in the current asset definition when fixed assets are consumed during the operating cycle. A literal interpretation of the accounting profession's position on this matter would indicate that an amount equal to the current depreciation and amortization charges on the noncurrent assets should be placed in the current assets section at the beginning of the year, because they will be consumed in the next operating cycle. This conceptual problem is ignored, which illustrates that the formal distinction made between current and noncurrent assets is somewhat arbitrary.[10]

Cash

Any restrictions on the general availability of cash or any commitments on its probable disposition must be disclosed. An example of such a presentation is excerpted from the Annual Report of **Owens-Corning Fiberglas Corp.** below:

ILLUSTRATION 5-2
Balance Sheet Presentation of Restricted Cash

OWENS-CORNING FIBERGLAS CORP.

Current assets	
Cash	$ 3,927,000
Restricted cash (Note 22)	85,043,000

Note 22: Restricted Funds. The Company has 222,885,000 Brazilian cruzados (approximately $15,000,000) of restricted funds deposited in a Brazilian bank account representing a recent dividend payment from a Brazilian subsidiary. Those funds are expected to be available to the Company in the next year.

The Company also has 116,707,000 Swiss Francs (approximately $70,000,000) in trust and restricted for payment of the Company's maturing bonds payable in Swiss Francs.

In the example above, cash was restricted to meet an obligation due currently and, therefore, was included under current assets. If cash is restricted for purposes other

[10]For an interesting discussion of the shortcomings of the current and noncurrent classification framework, see Loyd Heath, "Financial Reporting and the Evaluation of Solvency," *Accounting Research Monograph No. 3* (New York: AICPA, 1978), pp. 43–69. The principal recommendation is that the current and noncurrent classification be abolished, and that assets and liabilities simply be listed without classification in their present order. This approach is justified on the basis that any classification scheme is arbitrary and that users of the financial statements can assemble the data in the manner they believe most appropriate.

than current obligations, it is excluded from current assets. An example of a noncurrent presentation is excerpted from the Annual Report of **The Penn Traffic Company** below:

ILLUSTRATION 5-3
Balance Sheet Presentation of Noncurrent Restricted Cash

THE PENN TRAFFIC COMPANY

Current assets	
Cash and short-term investments	$9,123,000
Other assets	
Restricted funds (Note 1)	8,101,000

Note 1: Restricted Funds. During the current year, the Company entered into a long-term debt agreement for construction of a new perishables distribution center. The principal amount has been included in long-term debt, and the unexpended cash proceeds at year end have been reported as restricted funds.

Short-Term Investments

Investments in debt and equity securities are grouped into three separate portfolios for valuation and reporting purposes. These portfolios are categorized as follows:

> **Held-to-maturity:** Debt securities that the enterprise has the positive intent and ability to hold to maturity.
>
> **Trading:** Debt and equity securities bought and held primarily for sale in the near term to generate income on short-term price differences.
>
> **Available-for-sale:** Debt and equity securities not classified as held-to-maturity or trading securities.

Trading securities (whether debt or equity) should be reported as current assets. Individual held-to-maturity and available-for-sale securities are classified as current or noncurrent depending upon the circumstances. All trading and available-for-sale securities are to be reported at fair value.[11]

The example below is excerpted from the Annual Report of **Anchor BanCorp Wisconsin Inc.**

ILLUSTRATION 5-4
Balance Sheet Presentation of Investments in Securities

ANCHOR BANCORP WISCONSIN INC.
(in thousands)

Assets	
Cash and cash equivalents	$ 45,784
Securities available for sale	
Investment securities	10,284
Mortgage-related securities	51,814
Securities held to maturity	
Mortgage-related securities (fair value of $134.2 million)	135,896
Loans receivable, net	
Held for sale	16,542
Held for investment	1,066,945
Foreclosed properties and repossessed assets, net	5,294

[11] "Accounting for Certain Investments in Debt and Equity Securities," *Statement of Financial Accounting Standards No. 115* (Norwalk, Conn.: FASB, 1993).

Receivables

Any anticipated loss due to uncollectibles, the amount and nature of any nontrade receivables, and any receivables designated or pledged as collateral should be clearly identified. Mack Trucks, Inc. reported its receivables as follows:

ILLUSTRATION 5-5
Balance Sheet Presentation of Receivables

MACK TRUCKS, INC.

Current assets	
Trade receivables	
Accounts receivable	$102,212,000
Affiliated companies	1,157,000
Installment notes and contracts	625,000
Total	103,994,000
Less: Allowance for uncollectible accounts	8,194,000
Trade receivables—net	95,800,000
Receivables from unconsolidated financial subsidiaries	22,106,000

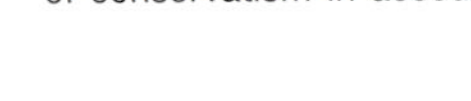

UNDERLYING CONCEPTS

The lower of cost or market valuation is an example of the use of conservatism in accounting.

Inventories

For a proper presentation of inventories, the basis of valuation (i.e., lower of cost or market) and the method of pricing (FIFO or LIFO) are disclosed. For a manufacturing concern (like General Signal Corporation, shown below), the stage of completion of the inventories is also indicated.

ILLUSTRATION 5-6
Balance Sheet Presentation of Inventories, Showing Stage of Completion

GENERAL SIGNAL CORPORATION

Current assets		
Inventories—at the lower of cost (determined by the first-in, first-out method) or market		
Finished goods	$103,405,000	
Work in process	126,667,000	
Raw materials and purchased parts	167,972,000	$398,044,000

Weyerhaeuser Company, a forestry company and lumber manufacturer with several finished goods product lines, reported its inventory as follows:

ILLUSTRATION 5-7
Balance Sheet Presentation of Inventories, Showing Product Lines

WEYERHAEUSER COMPANY

Current assets	
Inventories—at FIFO lower of cost or market	
Logs and chips	$ 68,471,000
Lumber, plywood and panels	86,741,000
Pulp, newsprint and paper	47,377,000
Containerboard, paperboard, containers and cartons	59,682,000
Other products	161,717,000
Total product inventories	423,988,000
Materials and supplies	175,540,000

Prepaid Expenses

Prepaid expenses included in current assets are expenditures already made for benefits (usually services) to be received within one year or the operating cycle, whichever is longer.[12] These items are current assets because if they had not already been paid, they would require the use of cash during the next year or the operating cycle. A common example is the payment in advance for an insurance policy. It is classified as a prepaid expense at the time of the expenditure because the payment precedes the receipt of the benefit of coverage. Prepaid expenses are reported at the amount of the unexpired or unconsumed cost. Other common prepaid expenses include prepaid rent, advertising, taxes, and office or operating supplies. **Munsingwear, Inc.**, for example, listed its prepaid expenses in current assets as follows:

MUNSINGWEAR, INC.

Current assets	
Inventories	$18,013,000
Prepaid expenses	1,492,000
Net assets related to discontinued operations	5,162,000

ILLUSTRATION 5-8
Balance Sheet Presentation of Prepaid Expenses

Companies often include insurance and other prepayments for two or three years in current assets even though part of the advance payment applies to periods beyond one year or the current operating cycle.

Long-Term Investments

Long-term investments, often referred to simply as investments, normally consist of one of four types:

1. Investments in securities, such as bonds, common stock, or long-term notes.
2. Investments in tangible fixed assets not currently used in operations, such as land held for speculation.
3. Investments set aside in special funds such as a sinking fund, pension fund, or plant expansion fund. The cash surrender value of life insurance is included here.
4. Investments in nonconsolidated subsidiaries or affiliated companies.

Long-term investments are to be held for many years. They are not acquired with the intention of disposing of them in the near future. They are usually presented on the balance sheet just below Current Assets in a separate section called Investments. Many securities that are properly shown among long-term investments are, in fact, readily marketable. But they are not included as current assets unless the intent is to convert them to cash in the short-term—within a year or in the operating cycle, whichever is longer. Securities classified as available-for-sale should be reported at fair value. Securities classified as held-to-maturity are reported at amortized cost.

Alco Standard Corporation reported its investments section between Current Assets and Property, Plant, and Equipment in the following manner:

ALCO STANDARD CORPORATION

Investments	
Investment in Alco Health Services Corporation	$ 62,255,000
Other investments	37,533,000
Long-term receivables	22,191,000
Total investments	121,979,000

ILLUSTRATION 5-9
Balance Sheet Presentation of Long-Term Investments

[12] *Accounting Trends and Techniques—1999* in its survey of 600 annual reports identified 336 companies that reported prepaid expenses.

Property, Plant, and Equipment

Property, plant, and equipment are properties of a durable nature used in the regular operations of the business. These assets consist of physical property such as land, buildings, machinery, furniture, tools, and wasting resources (timberland, minerals). With the exception of land, most assets are either depreciable (such as buildings) or depletable (such as timberlands or oil reserves).

Mattel, Inc., a manufacturer of toys and games, presented its property, plant, and equipment in its balance sheet as follows:

ILLUSTRATION 5-10
Balance Sheet Presentation of Property, Plant, and Equipment

MATTEL, INC.

Property, plant, and equipment	
Land	$ 5,812,000
Buildings	46,490,000
Machinery and equipment	72,513,000
Capitalized leases	39,425,000
Leasehold improvements	19,068,000
	183,308,000
Less: Accumulated depreciation	55,496,000
	127,812,000
Tools, dies and molds, less amortization	37,053,000
Property, plant, and equipment, net	164,865,000

The basis of valuing the property, plant, and equipment, any liens against the properties, and accumulated depreciation should be disclosed—usually in notes to the statements.

Intangible Assets

Intangible assets lack physical substance and usually have a high degree of uncertainty concerning their future benefits. They include patents, copyrights, franchises, goodwill, trademarks, trade names, and secret processes. Generally, all of these intangibles are written off (amortized) to expense over 5 to 40 years. Intangibles can represent significant economic resources, yet financial analysts often ignore them, and accountants write them down or off arbitrarily because valuation is difficult.

Unipack Corporation reported intangible assets in its balance sheet as follows:

ILLUSTRATION 5-11
Balance Sheet Presentation of Intangible Assets

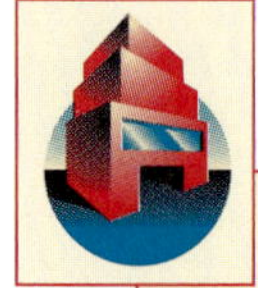

UNIPACK CORPORATION

Intangible assets	
Goodwill less $57,827 accumulated amortization	$145,617
Patents, licenses, and trademarks less $198,026 accumulated amortization	371,005
Software development costs less $46,280 accumulated amortization	120,214
Total intangibles	636,836

Other Assets

The items included in the section Other Assets vary widely in practice. Some of the items commonly included are deferred charges (long-term prepaid expenses), noncurrent receivables, intangible assets, assets in special funds, deferred income taxes, property held for sale, and advances to subsidiaries. Such a section unfortunately is too general a classification. Instead, it should be restricted to unusual items sufficiently different from assets included in specific categories.

Current Liabilities

Current liabilities are the obligations that are reasonably expected to be liquidated either through the use of current assets or the creation of other current liabilities.

This concept includes:

1. Payables resulting from the acquisition of goods and services: accounts payable, wages payable, taxes payable, and so on.
2. Collections received in advance for the delivery of goods or performance of services such as unearned rent revenue or unearned subscriptions revenue.
3. Other liabilities whose liquidation will take place within the operating cycle such as the portion of long-term bonds to be paid in the current period, or short-term obligations arising from purchase of equipment.

At times, a liability payable next year is not included in the current liabilities section. This occurs either when the debt is expected to be refinanced through another long-term issue,[13] or when the debt is retired out of noncurrent assets. This approach is used because liquidation does not result from the use of current assets or the creation of other current liabilities.

Current liabilities are not reported in any consistent order. The items most commonly listed first are notes payable, accounts payable, or short-term debt; income taxes payable, current maturities of long-term debt, or other current liabilities are commonly listed last. An example of **Dresser Industries**' current liabilities section is shown below.

ILLUSTRATION 5-12
Balance Sheet Presentation of Current Liabilities

DRESSER INDUSTRIES, INC.

Current liabilities	
Short-term debt	$ 22,500,000
Accounts payable—public	240,400,000
Accounts payable to unconsolidated affiliates	18,200,000
Advances from customers on contracts	161,100,000
Accrued compensation and benefits	169,400,000
Accrued warranty costs	34,100,000
Accrued taxes other than income taxes	21,900,000
Accrued interest	28,300,000
Other accrued liabilities	151,000,000
Income taxes payable	112,200,000
Current portion of long-term debt	12,400,000
Total current liabilities	971,500,000

Current liabilities include such items as trade and nontrade notes and accounts payable, advances received from customers, and current maturities of long-term debt. Income taxes and other accrued items are classified separately, if material. Any secured liability—for example, stock held as collateral on notes payable—is fully described in the notes so that the assets providing the security can be identified.

The excess of total current assets over total current liabilities is referred to as **working capital** (sometimes called **net working capital**). Working capital represents the net

[13]A detailed discussion of accounting for debt expected to be refinanced is found in Chapter 13 and in "Classification of Short-term Obligations Expected to Be Refinanced," *Statement of Financial Accounting Standards No. 6* (Stamford, Conn.: FASB, 1975).

amount of a company's relatively liquid resources. That is, it is the liquid buffer available to meet the financial demands of the operating cycle. Working capital as an amount is seldom disclosed on the balance sheet, but it is computed by bankers and other creditors as an indicator of the short-run liquidity of a company. In order to determine the actual liquidity and availability of working capital to meet current obligations, however, one must analyze the composition of the current assets and their nearness to cash.[14]

Long-Term Liabilities

Long-term liabilities are obligations that are not reasonably expected to be liquidated within the normal operating cycle but, instead, are payable at some date beyond that time. Bonds payable, notes payable, some deferred income tax amounts, lease obligations, and pension obligations are the most common examples. Generally, a great deal of supplementary disclosure is needed for this section, because most long-term debt is subject to various covenants and restrictions for the protection of lenders.[15] Long-term liabilities that mature within the current operating cycle are classified as current liabilities if their liquidation requires the use of current assets.

Generally, long-term liabilities are of three types:

1. Obligations arising from specific financing situations, such as the issuance of bonds, long-term lease obligations, and long-term notes payable.
2. Obligations arising from the ordinary operations of the enterprise, such as pension obligations and deferred income tax liabilities.
3. Obligations that are dependent upon the occurrence or nonoccurrence of one or more future events to confirm the amount payable, or the payee, or the date payable, such as service or product warranties and other contingencies.

It is desirable to report any premium or discount separately as an addition to or subtraction from the bonds payable. The terms of all long-term liability agreements (including maturity date or dates, rates of interest, nature of obligation, and any security pledged to support the debt) are frequently described in notes to the financial statements. An example of the financial statement and accompanying note presentation is shown in Illustration 5-13 on the next page in the excerpt from **The Great Atlantic & Pacific Tea Company**'s financials.

Financial Instruments

Financial instruments are defined as cash, an ownership interest, or a contractual right to receive or obligation to deliver cash or another financial instrument. Such contractual rights to receive cash or other financial instruments are assets, whereas contractual obligations to pay are liabilities. Cash, investments, accounts receivable, and payables are examples of financial instruments.

---

[14]The FASB in a discussion memorandum has suggested alternative classification of assets that might help financial statement users assess the nature, amounts, and liquidity of available resources. See "Reporting Funds Flows, Liquidity, and Financial Flexibility," *FASB Discussion Memorandum* (Stamford, Conn.: FASB, 1980), Chapters 8 and 9.

[15]The pertinent rights and privileges of the various securities (both debt and equity) outstanding are usually explained in the notes to the financial statements. Examples of information that should be disclosed are dividend and liquidation preferences, participation rights, call prices and dates, conversion or exercise prices or rates and pertinent dates, sinking fund requirements, unusual voting rights, and significant terms of contracts to issue additional shares. "Disclosure of Information about Capital Structure," *Statement of Financial Accounting Standards No. 129* (Norwalk: FASB, 1997), par. 4.

ILLUSTRATION 5-13
Balance Sheet Presentation of Long-Term Debt

THE GREAT ATLANTIC & PACIFIC TEA COMPANY, INC.

Total current liabilities	$978,109,000
Long-term debt (See note)	254,312,000
Obligations under capital leases	252,618,000
Deferred income taxes	57,167,000
Other non-current liabilities	127,321,000
Note: Indebtedness. Debt consists of:	
9.5% Senior notes, due in annual installments of $10,000,000	$ 40,000,000
Mortgages and other notes due through 2011 (average interest rate of 9.9%)	107,604,000
Bank borrowings at 9.7%	67,225,000
Commercial paper at 9.4%	100,102,000
	314,931,000
Less: Current portion	(60,619,000)
Total long-term debt	$254,312,000

Financial instruments are increasing both in use and variety. As a consequence of the increasing use of financial instruments, companies are required to disclose both the carrying value and the estimated fair values of their financial instruments. For example, Intel provides extensive disclosures of the fair value of its financial instrument assets and liabilities (see p. 229). More extensive discussion of financial instrument accounting and reporting is provided in Chapters 7, 13, 14, 17, and 18.

Owners' Equity

The **owners' equity** (stockholders' equity) section is one of the most difficult sections to prepare and understand. This is due to the complexity of capital stock agreements and the various restrictions on residual equity imposed by state corporation laws, liability agreements, and boards of directors. The section is usually divided into three parts:

STOCKHOLDERS' EQUITY SECTION

1. ***Capital Stock.*** The par or stated value of the shares issued.
2. ***Additional Paid-In Capital.*** The excess of amounts paid in over the par or stated value.
3. ***Retained Earnings.*** The corporation's undistributed earnings.

The major disclosure requirements for capital stock are the authorized, issued, and outstanding par value amounts. The additional paid-in capital is usually presented in one amount, although subtotals are informative if the sources of additional capital are varied and material. The retained earnings section may be divided between the unappropriated (the amount that is usually available for dividend distribution) and any amounts that are restricted (e.g., by bond indentures or other loan agreements). In addition, any capital stock reacquired (treasury stock) is shown as a reduction of stockholders' equity. As indicated in Chapter 4, accumulated other comprehensive income (loss) is shown as an addition (reduction) to stockholders' equity, if applicable.

The ownership or stockholders' equity accounts in a corporation are considerably different from those in a partnership or proprietorship. Partners' permanent capital accounts and the balance in their temporary accounts (drawing accounts) are shown separately. Proprietorships ordinarily use a single capital account that handles all of the owner's equity transactions.

Presented below is an example of the stockholders' equity section from Quanex Corporation.

ILLUSTRATION 5-14
Balance Sheet Presentation of Stockholders' Equity

QUANEX CORPORATION
(in thousands)

Stockholders' equity (Note 12):	
Preferred stock, no par value, 1,000,000 shares authorized; 345,000 issued and outstanding	$ 86,250
Common stock, $.50 par value, 25,000,000 shares authorized; 13,638,005 shares issued and outstanding	6,819
Additional paid-in capital	87,260
Retained earnings	57,263
	$237,592

BALANCE SHEET FORMAT

OBJECTIVE 3
Prepare a classified balance sheet using the report and account formats.

One common arrangement followed in the presentation of a classified balance sheet is called the **account form**. It lists assets by sections on the left side and liabilities and stockholders' equity by sections on the right side. The main disadvantage is the need for two facing pages. To avoid the use of facing pages, the **report form**, shown in Illustration 5-15 (page 201), lists liabilities and stockholders' equity directly below assets on the same page.[16] (Also see Intel's balance sheet on page 222 for the report form.)

Other balance sheet formats are used infrequently. For example, current liabilities are sometimes deducted from current assets to arrive at working capital, or all liabilities are deducted from all assets. Caterpillar, for instance, is one of the few large companies to prepare its balance sheet in this latter unorthodox format, referred to as the **financial position form**.

ADDITIONAL INFORMATION REPORTED

UNDERLYING CONCEPTS
The basis for inclusion of additional information should meet the full disclosure principle; that is, the information should be of sufficient importance to influence the judgment of an informed user.

The balance sheet is not complete simply because the assets, liabilities, and owners' equity accounts have been listed. Great importance is given to supplemental information. It may be information not presented elsewhere in the statement, or it may be an elaboration or qualification of items in the balance sheet. There are normally three types of information that are supplemental to account titles and amounts presented in the balance sheet:

OBJECTIVE 4
Identify balance sheet information requiring supplemental disclosure.

SUPPLEMENTAL BALANCE SHEET INFORMATION

1. ***Contingencies.*** Material events that have an uncertain outcome.
2. ***Accounting Policies.*** Explanations of the valuation methods used or the basic assumptions made concerning inventory valuations, depreciation methods, investments in subsidiaries, etc.
3. ***Contractual Situations.*** Explanations of certain restrictions or covenants attached to specific assets or, more likely, to liabilities.

[16] *Accounting Trends and Techniques—1999* indicates that all of the 600 companies surveyed use either the "report form" (465) or the "account form" (135), sometimes collectively referred to as the "customary form."

ILLUSTRATION 5-15
Classified Report Form Balance Sheet

SCIENTIFIC PRODUCTS, INC.
Balance Sheet
December 31, 2001

Assets			
Current assets			
Cash		$ 42,485	
Available-for-sale securities—at fair value		28,250	
Accounts receivable	$165,824		
Less: Allowance for doubtful accounts	1,850	163,974	
Notes receivable		23,000	
Inventories—at average cost		489,713	
Supplies on hand		9,780	
Prepaid expenses		16,252	
Total current assets			$ 773,454
Long-term investments			
Investments in Warren Co.			87,500
Property, plant, and equipment			
Land—at cost		125,000	
Buildings—at cost	975,800		
Less: Accumulated depreciation	341,200	634,600	
Total property, plant, and equipment			759,600
Intangible assets			
Goodwill			100,000
Total assets			$1,720,554
Liabilities and Stockholders' Equity			
Current liabilities			
Notes payable to banks		$ 50,000	
Accounts payable		197,532	
Accrued interest on notes payable		500	
Income taxes payable		62,520	
Accrued salaries, wages, and other liabilities		9,500	
Deposits received from customers		420	
Total current liabilities			$ 320,472
Long-term debt			
Twenty-year 12% debentures, due January 1, 2011			500,000
Total liabilities			820,472
Stockholders' equity			
Paid in on capital stock			
Preferred, 7%, cumulative			
Authorized, issued, and outstanding, 30,000 shares of $10 par value	$300,000		
Common—			
Authorized, 500,000 shares of $1.00 par value; issued and outstanding, 400,000 shares	400,000		
Additional paid-in capital	37,500	737,500	
Earnings retained in the business		162,582	
Total stockholders' equity			900,082
Total liabilities and stockholders' equity			$1,720,554

UNDERLYING CONCEPTS

The presentation of balance sheet information meets one of the objectives of financial reporting—to provide information about enterprise resources, claims to resources, and changes in them.

Contingencies

A **contingency** is defined as an existing situation involving uncertainty as to possible gain (gain contingency) or loss (loss contingency) that will ultimately be resolved when one or more future events occur or fail to occur. In short, they are material events that have an uncertain future. Examples of gain contingencies are tax operating loss carry-forwards or company litigation against another party. Typical loss contingencies relate to litigation, environmental issues, possible tax assessments, or government investigation. The accounting and reporting requirements involving contingencies are examined fully in Chapter 13, and, therefore, additional discussion is not provided here.

Accounting Policies

APB Opinion No. 22 recommends disclosure for all significant accounting principles and methods that involve selection from among alternatives or those that are peculiar to a given industry.[17] For instance, inventories can be computed under several cost flow assumptions (such as LIFO and FIFO); plant and equipment can be depreciated under several accepted methods of cost allocation (such as double-declining balance and straight-line); and investments can be carried at different valuations (such as cost, equity, and fair value). Sophisticated users of financial statements know of these possibilities and examine the statements closely to determine the methods used.

Companies are also required to disclose information about the nature of their operations, the use of estimates in preparing financial statements, certain significant estimates, and vulnerabilities due to certain concentrations.[18] An example of such a disclosure is provided below.

ILLUSTRATION 5-16
Balance Sheet Disclosure of Significant Risks and Uncertainties

CHESAPEAKE CORPORATION

Risks and Uncertainties: Chesapeake operates in three business segments which offer a diversity of products over a broad geographic base. The Company is not dependent on any single customer, group of customers, market, geographic area or supplier of materials, labor or services. Financial statements include, where necessary, amounts based on the judgments and estimates of management. These estimates include allowances for bad debts, accruals for landfill closing costs, environmental remediation costs, loss contingencies for litigation, self-insured medical and workers' compensation insurance and income taxes and determinations of discount and other rate assumptions for pensions and postretirement benefit expenses.

Disclosure of significant accounting principles and methods and of risks and uncertainties is particularly useful if given in a separate **Summary of Significant Accounting Policies** preceding the notes to the financial statements or as the initial note.

Contractual Situations

In addition to contingencies and different methods of valuation, contractual situations of significance should be disclosed in the notes to the financial statements. It is mandatory, for example, that the essential provisions of lease contracts, pension obligations, and stock option plans be clearly stated in the notes. The analyst who examines a set of financial statements wants to know not only the amount of the liabilities, but also how the different contractual provisions affect the company at present and in the future.

Commitments related to obligations to maintain working capital, to limit the payment of dividends, to restrict the use of assets, and to require the maintenance of certain financial ratios must all be disclosed if material. Considerable judgment is necessary to determine whether omission of such information is misleading. The axiom in this situation is, "When in doubt, disclose." It is better to disclose a little too much information than not enough.

---

[17]"Disclosure of Accounting Policies," *Opinions of the Accounting Principles Board No. 22* (New York: AICPA, 1972).

[18]"Disclosure of Certain Significant Risks and Uncertainties," *Statement of Position 94-6* (New York: AICPA, 1994).

The accountant's judgment should reflect ethical considerations, because the manner of disclosing the accounting principles, methods, and other items that have important effects on the enterprise may subtly represent the interests of a particular stakeholder (at the expense of others). A reader, for example, may benefit by the highlighting of information in comprehensive notes, whereas the company—not wishing to emphasize certain information— may choose to provide limited (rather than comprehensive) note information.

TECHNIQUES OF DISCLOSURE

The effect of various contingencies on financial condition, the methods of valuing assets, and the companies' contracts and agreements should be disclosed as completely and as intelligently as possible. These methods of disclosing pertinent information are available: parenthetical explanations, notes, cross reference and contra items, and supporting schedules.

OBJECTIVE 5
Identify major disclosure techniques for the balance sheet.

Parenthetical Explanations

Additional information is often provided by parenthetical explanations following the item. For example, investments in available-for-sale securities are shown on the balance sheet under Investments as follows:

Investments in available-for-sale securities (cost, $330,586)—at fair value	$401,500

UNDERLYING CONCEPTS

The user-specific quality of understandability requires accountants to be careful in describing transactions and events.

This device permits disclosure of additional pertinent balance sheet information that adds clarity and completeness. It has an advantage over a note because it brings the additional information into the body of the statement where it is less likely to be overlooked. Of course, lengthy parenthetical explanations that might distract the reader from the balance sheet information must be used with care.

Notes

Notes are used if additional explanations cannot be shown conveniently as parenthetical explanations. For example, inventory costing methods are reported in **The Quaker Oats Company**'s accompanying notes as follows:

ILLUSTRATION 5-17
Notes Disclosure

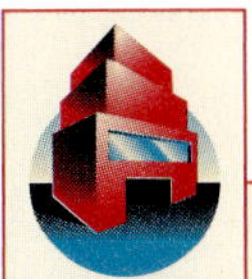

THE QUAKER OATS COMPANY

Inventories (Note 1)	
Finished goods	$326,000,000
Grain and raw materials	114,100,000
Packaging materials and supplies	39,000,000
Total inventories	479,100,000

Note 1: Inventories. Inventories are valued at the lower of cost or market, using various cost methods, and include the cost of raw materials, labor, and overhead. The percentage of year-end inventories valued using each of the methods is as follows:

Average quarterly cost	21%
Last-in, first-out (LIFO)	65%
First-in, first-out (FIFO)	14%

If the LIFO method of valuing certain inventories was not used, total inventories would have been $60,100,000 higher than reported.

Notes are commonly used to disclose the existence and amount of any preferred stock dividends in arrears, the terms of or obligations imposed by purchase commitments, special financial arrangements and instruments, depreciation policies, any changes in the application of accounting principles, and the existence of contingencies. The following notes illustrate a common method of presenting such information:

ILLUSTRATION 5-18
More Notes Disclosures

CONSOLIDATED PAPERS, INC.

Note 7: Commitments. The company had capital expenditure purchase commitments outstanding of approximately $17 million.

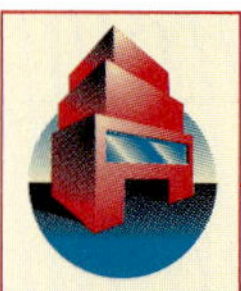

ALBERTO-CULVER COMPANY

Note 3: Long-Term Debt. Various borrowing arrangements impose restrictions on such items as total debt, working capital, dividend payments, treasury stock purchases and interest expense. The company was in compliance with these arrangements and $68 million of consolidated retained earnings was not restricted as to the payment of dividends and purchases of treasury stock.

AMPCO-PITTSBURGH CORPORATION

Note 11: Change in Accounting Estimate. The Corporation revised its estimate of the useful lives of certain machinery and equipment. Previously, all machinery and equipment, whether new when placed in use or not, were in one class and depreciated over 15 years. The change principally applies to assets purchased new when placed in use. Those lives are now extended to 20 years. These changes were made to better reflect the estimated periods during which such assets will remain in service. The change had the effect of reducing depreciation expense and increasing net income by approximately $991,000 ($.10 per share).

The notes must present all essential facts as completely and succinctly as possible. Careless wording may mislead rather than aid readers. Notes should add to the total information made available in the financial statements, not raise unanswered questions or contradict other portions of the statements.

Cross Reference and Contra Items

A direct relationship between an asset and a liability is "cross referenced" on the balance sheet. For example, on December 31, 2001, among the current assets this might be shown:

Cash on deposit with sinking fund trustee for redemption of bonds payable—see Current liabilities	$800,000

Included among the current liabilities is the amount of bonds payable to be redeemed within one year:

Bonds payable to be redeemed in 2002—see Current assets	$2,300,000

This cross reference points out that $2,300,000 of bonds payable are to be redeemed currently, for which only $800,000 in cash has been set aside. Therefore, the additional cash needed must come from unrestricted cash, from sales of investments, from profits, or from some other source. The same information can be shown parenthetically, if this technique is preferred.

Another common procedure is to establish contra or adjunct accounts. A **contra account** on a balance sheet is an item that reduces either an asset, liability, or owners' equity account. Examples include Accumulated Depreciation and Discount on Bonds Payable. Contra accounts provide some flexibility in presenting the financial information. With the use of the Accumulated Depreciation account, for example, a reader of the statement can see the original cost of the asset as well as the depreciation to date.

An **adjunct account**, on the other hand, increases either an asset, liability, or owners' equity account. An example is Premium on Bonds Payable, which, when added to the Bonds Payable account, describes the total bond liability of the enterprise.

Supporting Schedules

Often a separate schedule is needed to present more detailed information about certain assets or liabilities, because the balance sheet provides just a single summary item.

ILLUSTRATION 5-19
Disclosure through Use of Supporting Schedules

Property, plant, and equipment	
Land, buildings, equipment, and other fixed assets—net (see Schedule 3)	$643,300

A separate schedule then might be presented as follows:

Schedule 3
LAND, BUILDINGS, EQUIPMENT, AND OTHER FIXED ASSETS

	Total	Land	Buildings	Equip.	Other Fixed Assets
Balance January 1, 2002	$740,000	$46,000	$358,000	$260,000	$76,000
Additions in 2002	161,200		120,000	38,000	3,200
	901,200	46,000	478,000	298,000	79,200
Assets retired or sold in 2002	31,700			27,000	4,700
Balance December 31, 2002	869,500	46,000	478,000	271,000	74,500
Depreciation taken to January 1, 2002	196,000		102,000	78,000	16,000
Depreciation taken in 2002	56,000		28,000	24,000	4,000
	252,000		130,000	102,000	20,000
Depreciation on assets retired in 2002	25,800			22,000	3,800
Depreciation accumulated December 31, 2002	226,200		130,000	80,000	16,200
Book value of assets	$643,300	$46,000	$348,000	$191,000	$58,300

INTERNATIONAL INSIGHT

Internationally, accounting terminology is problematic. Confusing differences arise even between nations that share a language. For example, U.S. investors normally think of "stock" as "equity" or "ownership," but the British refer to inventory as "stocks." In the U.S. "fixed assets" generally refers to "property, plant, and equipment," while in Britain the category includes more items.

TERMINOLOGY

The account titles in the general ledger do not necessarily represent the best terminology for balance sheet purposes. Account titles are often brief and include technical terms that are understood only by accountants. But balance sheets are examined by many persons who are not acquainted with the technical vocabulary of accounting. Thus, they should contain descriptions that will be generally understood and not be subject to misinterpretation.

The profession has recommended that the word **reserve** be used only to describe an appropriation of retained earnings. This term had been used in several ways: to describe amounts deducted from assets (contra accounts such as accumulated depreciation and allowance for doubtful accounts), and as a part of the title of contingent or estimated liabilities. Because of the different meanings attached to this term, misinterpretation often resulted from its use. The use of "reserve" only to describe appropriated retained earnings has resulted in a better understanding of its significance when it appears in a balance sheet. However, the term "appropriated" appears more logical, and its use should be encouraged.

For years the profession has recommended that the use of the word **surplus** be discontinued in balance sheet presentations of owners' equity. The use of the terms capital surplus, paid-in surplus, and earned surplus is confusing. Although condemned by the profession, these terms appear all too frequently in current financial statements.

SECTION 2 STATEMENT OF CASH FLOWS

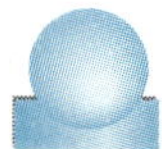

UNDERLYING CONCEPTS

The statement of cash flows meets one of the objectives of financial reporting—to help assess the amounts, timing, and uncertainty of future cash flows.

In Chapter 2, "assessing the amounts, timing, and uncertainty of cash flows" was presented as one of the three basic objectives of financial reporting. The balance sheet, the income statement, and the statement of stockholders' equity each present, to a limited extent and in a fragmented manner, information about the cash flows of an enterprise during a period. For instance, comparative balance sheets might show what new assets have been acquired or disposed of and what liabilities have been incurred or liquidated. The income statement provides information about resources, but not exactly cash, provided by operations. The statement of stockholders' equity shows the amount of cash used to pay dividends or purchase treasury stock. But none of these statements presents a detailed summary of all the cash inflows and outflows, or the sources and uses of cash during the period. To fill this need, the FASB requires the **statement of cash flows** (also called the **cash flow statement**).[19]

PURPOSE OF THE STATEMENT OF CASH FLOWS

OBJECTIVE 6
Indicate the purpose of the statement of cash flows.

The primary purpose of a statement of cash flows is to provide relevant information about the cash receipts and cash payments of an enterprise during a period. To achieve this purpose, the statement of cash flows reports (1) the cash effects of operations during a period, (2) investing transactions, (3) financing transactions, and (4) the net increase or decrease in cash during the period.[20]

Reporting the sources, uses, and net increase or decrease in cash helps investors, creditors, and others know what is happening to a company's most liquid resource. Because most individuals maintain their checkbook and prepare their tax return on a cash basis, they can relate to the statement of cash flows and comprehend the causes and effects of cash inflows and outflows and the net increase or decrease in cash. The statement of cash flows provides answers to the following simple but important questions:

1. Where did the cash come from during the period?
2. What was the cash used for during the period?
3. What was the change in the cash balance during the period?

[19]"Statement of Cash Flows," *Statement of Financial Accounting Standards No. 95* (Stamford, Conn.: FASB, 1987).

[20]The basis recommended by the FASB is actually "cash and cash equivalents." Cash equivalents are short-term, highly liquid investments such as Treasury bills, commercial paper, and money market funds purchased with cash that is in excess of immediate needs.

CONTENT AND FORMAT OF THE STATEMENT OF CASH FLOWS

OBJECTIVE 7
Identify the content of the statement of cash flows.

Cash receipts and cash payments during a period are classified in the statement of cash flows into three different activities—operating, investing, and financing activities. These classifications are defined as follows:

1. **Operating activities** involve the cash effects of transactions that enter into the determination of net income.
2. **Investing activities** include making and collecting loans and acquiring and disposing of investments (both debt and equity) and property, plant, and equipment.
3. **Financing activities** involve liability and owners' equity items. They include (a) obtaining resources from owners and providing them with a return on (and a return of) their investment and (b) borrowing money from creditors and repaying the amounts borrowed.

With cash flows classified into those three categories, the statement of cash flows has assumed the following basic format:

ILLUSTRATION 5-20
Basic Format of Cash Flow Statement

Statement of Cash Flows	
Cash flows from operating activities	$XXX
Cash flows from investing activities	XXX
Cash flows from financing activities	XXX
Net increase (decrease) in cash	XXX
Cash at beginning of year	XXX
Cash at end of year	$XXX

The inflows and outflows of cash classified by activity are shown in Illustration 5-21.

ILLUSTRATION 5-21
Cash Inflows and Outflows

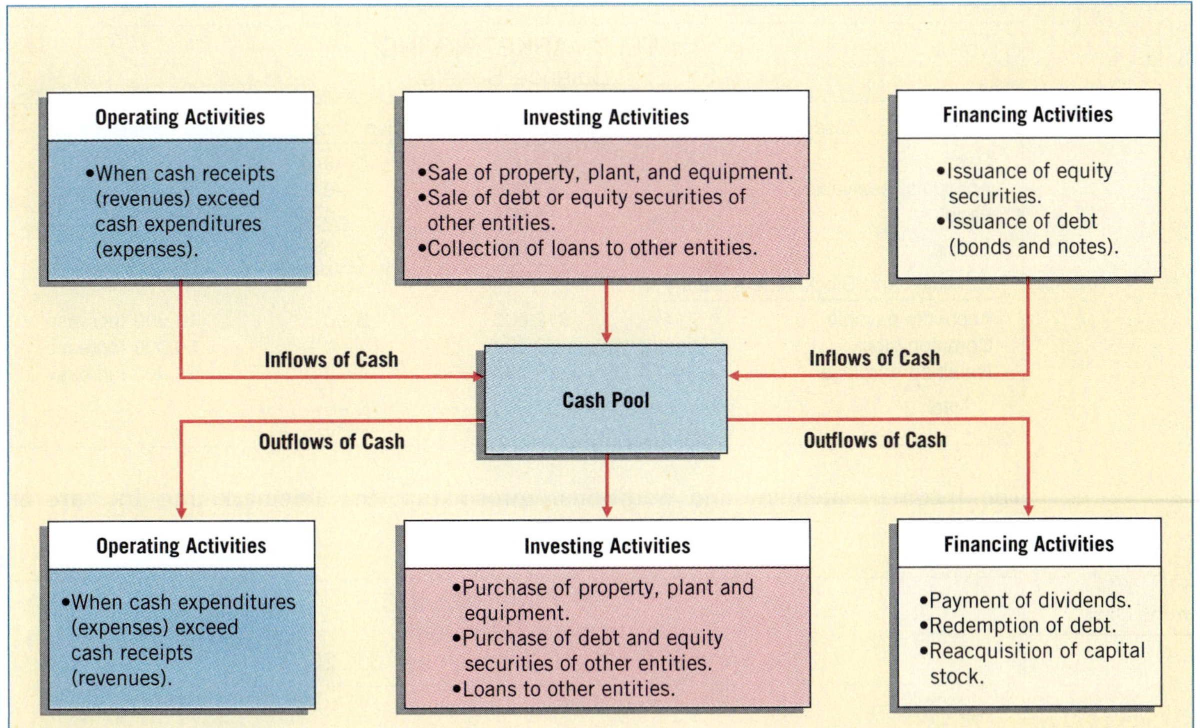

The statement's value is that it helps users evaluate liquidity, solvency, and financial flexibility. Liquidity refers to the "nearness to cash" of assets and liabilities. **Solvency** refers to the firms' ability to pay its debts as they mature. And **financial flexibility** refers to a firm's ability to respond and adapt to financial adversity and unexpected needs and opportunities.

We have devoted Chapter 24 entirely to the preparation and content of the statement of cash flows. Our comprehensive coverage of this topic has been deferred to that later chapter so that we can cover in the intervening chapters several elements and complex topics that make up the content of a typical statement of cash flows. The presentation in this chapter is introductory, a reminder of the existence of the statement of cash flows and its usefulness.

PREPARATION OF THE STATEMENT OF CASH FLOWS

OBJECTIVE 8
Prepare a statement of cash flows.

The information to prepare the statement of cash flows usually comes from (1) comparative balance sheets, (2) the current income statement, and (3) selected transaction data. Preparing the statement of cash flows from these sources involves the following steps:

1. Determine the cash provided by operations.
2. Determine the cash provided by or used in investing and financing activities.
3. Determine the change (increase or decrease) in cash during the period.
4. Reconcile the change in cash with the beginning and the ending cash balances.

INTERNATIONAL INSIGHT

Statements of cash flows are not required in all countries. Some nations require a statement reporting sources and applications of "funds" (often defined as working capital); others have no requirement for either cash or funds flow statements.

The following simple illustration demonstrates how these steps are applied in the preparation of a statement of cash flows.

Telemarketing Inc. in its first year of operations issued on January 1, 2002, 50,000 shares of $1.00 par value common stock for $50,000 cash. The company rented its office space, furniture, and telecommunications equipment and performed surveys and marketing services throughout the first year. In June 2002 the company purchased land for $15,000. The comparative balance sheets at the beginning and end of the year 2002 are shown in Illustration 5-22.

ILLUSTRATION 5-22
Comparative Balance Sheets

TELEMARKETING INC.
Balance Sheets

Assets	Dec. 31, 2002	Jan. 1, 2002	Increase/Decrease
Cash	$31,000	$ -0-	$31,000 Increase
Accounts receivable	41,000	-0-	41,000 Increase
Land	15,000	-0-	15,000 Increase
Total	$87,000	$ -0-	
Liabilities and Stockholders' Equity			
Accounts payable	$12,000	$ -0-	12,000 Increase
Common stock	50,000	-0-	50,000 Increase
Retained earnings	25,000	-0-	25,000 Increase
Total	$87,000	$ -0-	

The income statement and additional information for Telemarketing Inc. are as follows:

ILLUSTRATION 5-23
Income Statement Data

TELEMARKETING INC.
Income Statement
For the Year Ended December 31, 2002

Revenues	$172,000
Operating expenses	120,000
Income before income taxes	52,000
Income tax expense	13,000
Net income	$ 39,000

Additional information:
Dividends of $14,000 were paid during the year.

Cash provided by operations (the excess of cash receipts over cash payments) is determined by converting net income on an accrual basis to a cash basis. This is accomplished by adding to or deducting from net income those items in the income statement not affecting cash. This procedure requires an analysis not only of the current year's income statement but also of the comparative balance sheets and selected transaction data.

Analysis of Telemarketing's comparative balance sheets reveals two items that give rise to noncash credits or charges to the income statement: (1) the increase in accounts receivable reflects a noncash credit of $41,000 to revenues, and (2) the increase in accounts payable reflects a noncash charge of $12,000 to expenses. **To arrive at cash provided by operations, the increase in accounts receivable must be deducted from net income, and the increase in accounts payable must be added back to net income.**

As a result of the accounts receivable and accounts payable adjustments, cash provided by operations is determined to be $10,000, computed as follows:

ILLUSTRATION 5-24
Computation of Net Cash Provided by Operations

Net income		$39,000
Adjustments to reconcile net income to net cash provided by operating activities:		
Increase in accounts receivable	$(41,000)	
Increase in accounts payable	12,000	(29,000)
Net cash provided by operating activities		$10,000

The increase of $50,000 in common stock resulting from the issuance of 50,000 shares for cash, is classified as a financing activity. Likewise, the payment of $14,000 cash in dividends is a financing activity. Telemarketing Inc.'s only investing activity was the land purchase. The statement of cash flows for Telemarketing Inc. for 2002 is as follows:

ILLUSTRATION 5-25
Statement of Cash Flows

TELEMARKETING INC.
Statement of Cash Flows
For the Year Ended December 31, 2002

Cash flows from operating activities		
Net income		$39,000
Adjustments to reconcile net income to net cash provided by operating activities:		
Increase in accounts receivable	$(41,000)	
Increase in accounts payable	12,000	(29,000)
Net cash provided by operating activities		10,000
Cash flows from investing activities		
Purchase of land	(15,000)	
Net cash used by investing activities		(15,000)
Cash flows from financing activities		
Issuance of common stock	50,000	
Payment of cash dividends	(14,000)	
Net cash provided by financing activities		36,000
Net increase in cash		31,000
Cash at beginning of year		–0–
Cash at end of year		$31,000

International Accounting Standard 7 requires a statement of cash flows. Both international standards and U.S. GAAP specify that the cash flows must be classified as operating, investing, or financing.

The increase in cash of $31,000 reported in the statement of cash flows agrees with the increase of $31,000 in the Cash account calculated from the comparative balance sheets.

An illustration of a more comprehensive statement of cash flows is presented in Illustration 5-26 (page 210).

ILLUSTRATION 5-26
Comprehensive Statement of Cash Flows

NESTOR COMPANY Statement of Cash Flows For the Year Ended December 31, 2002		
Cash flows from operating activities		
Net income		$320,750
Adjustments to reconcile net income to net cash provided by operating activities:		
Depreciation expense	$88,400	
Amortization of intangibles	16,300	
Gain on sale of plant assets	(8,700)	
Increase in accounts receivable (net)	(11,000)	
Decrease in inventory	15,500	
Decrease in accounts payable	(9,500)	91,000
Net cash provided by operating activities		411,750
Cash flows from investing activities		
Sale of plant assets	90,500	
Purchase of equipment	(182,500)	
Purchase of land	(70,000)	
Net cash used by investing activities		(162,000)
Cash flows from financing activities		
Payment of cash dividend	(19,800)	
Issuance of common stock	100,000	
Redemption of bonds	(50,000)	
Net cash provided by financing activities		30,200
Net increase in cash		279,950
Cash at beginning of year		135,000
Cash at end of year		$414,950

USEFULNESS OF THE STATEMENT OF CASH FLOWS

OBJECTIVE 9
Understand the usefulness of the statement of cash flows.

"Happiness is a positive cash flow" is certainly true. Although net income provides a long-term measure of a company's success or failure, cash is the lifeblood of a company. Without cash, a company will not survive. For small and newly developing companies, cash flow is the single most important element of survival. In a recent survey of over 60,000 companies that failed, over 60 percent blamed their failure on factors linked to cash flows. Even medium and large companies indicate a major concern in controlling cash flow.

Creditors examine the cash flow statement carefully because they are concerned about being paid. A good starting point in their examination is to find net cash provided by operating activities. A high amount of net cash provided by operating activities indicates that a company is able to generate sufficient cash internally from operations to pay its bills without further borrowing. Conversely, a low or negative amount of net cash provided by operating activities indicates that a company cannot generate enough cash internally from its operations and, therefore, must borrow or issue equity securities to acquire additional cash. Consequently, creditors look for answers to the following questions in the company's cash flow statements:

1. How successful is the company in generating net cash provided by operating activities?
2. What are the trends in net cash flow provided by operating activities over time?
3. What are the major reasons for the positive or negative net cash provided by operating activities?

You should recognize that companies can fail even though they are profitable. The difference between net income and net cash provided by operating activities can be substantial. Companies such as **W.T. Grant Company** and **Prime Motor Inn**, for example, reported high net income numbers but negative net cash provided by operating activities. Eventually both these companies filed for bankruptcy.

As discussed in the opening story, the reasons for the difference between a positive net income and a negative net cash provided by operating activities are substantial increases in receivables and/or inventory. To illustrate, Ho Inc. in its first year of operations reported a net income of $80,000. Its net cash provided by operating activities, however, was a negative $95,000, as shown in Illustration 5-27.

ILLUSTRATION 5-27
Negative Net Cash Provided by Operating Activities

HO INC. Net Cash Flow from Operating Activities		
Cash flows from operating activities		
Net income		$ 80,000
Adjustments to reconcile net income to net cash provided by operating activities:		
Increase in receivables	$(75,000)	
Increase in inventories	(100,000)	(175,000)
Net cash provided by operating activities		$(95,000)

Note that the negative net cash provided by operating activities occurred for Ho even though it reported a positive net income. Ho could easily experience a "cash crunch" because it has tied up its cash in receivables and inventory. If problems in collecting receivables occur or inventory is slow moving or becomes obsolete, the creditors of Ho may have difficulty collecting on their loans.

Financial Liquidity

One relationship (ratio) that is often used to assess liquidity is the **current cash debt coverage ratio**. It indicates whether the company can pay off its current liabilities in a given year from its operations. The formula for this ratio is:

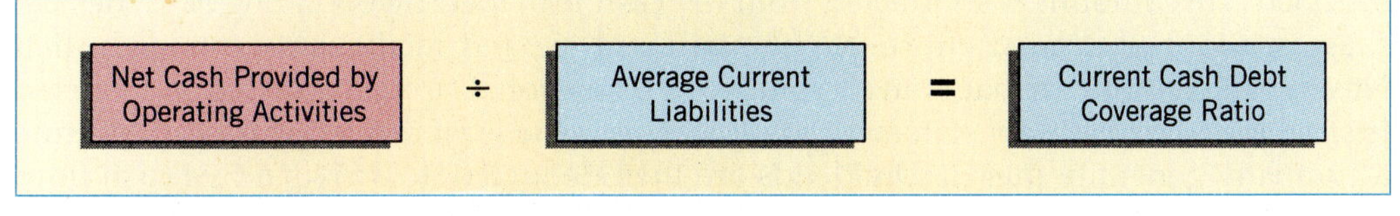

ILLUSTRATION 5-28
Formula for Current Cash Debt Coverage Ratio

The higher this ratio, the less likely a company will have liquidity problems. For example, a ratio near 1:1 is good because it indicates that the company can meet all of its current obligations from internally generated cash flow.

Financial Flexibility

A more long-run measure which provides information on financial flexibility is the **cash debt coverage ratio**. This ratio indicates a company's ability to repay its liabilities from net cash provided by operating activities, without having to liquidate the assets employed in its operations. The formula for this ratio is:

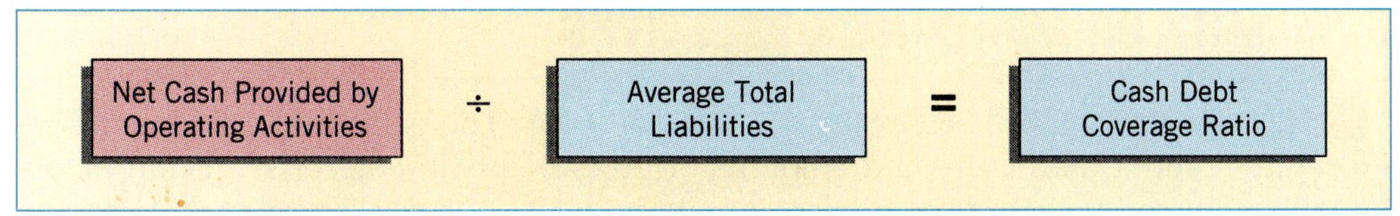

ILLUSTRATION 5-29
Formula for Cash Debt Coverage Ratio

The higher this ratio, the less likely the company will experience difficulty in meeting its obligations as they come due. As a result, it signals whether the company can pay its debts and survive if external sources of funds become limited or too expensive.

Free Cash Flow

A more sophisticated way to examine a company's financial flexibility is to develop a free cash flow analysis. This analysis starts with net cash provided by operating activities and ends with **free cash flow**, which is calculated as net cash provided by operating activities less capital expenditures and dividends.[21] Free cash flow is the amount of discretionary cash flow a company has for purchasing additional investments, retiring its debt, purchasing treasury stock, or simply adding to its liquidity. This measure indicates a company's level of financial flexibility. Questions that a free cash flow analysis answers are:

1. Is the company able to pay its dividends without resorting to external financing?
2. If business operations decline, will the company be able to maintain its needed capital investment?
3. What is the free cash flow that can be used for additional investment, retirement of debt, purchase of treasury stock, or addition to liquidity?

Presented below is a free cash flow analysis using the cash flow statement for Nestor Company shown in Illustration 5-26 (page 210):

ILLUSTRATION 5-30
Free Cash Flow Computation

NESTOR COMPANY
Free Cash Flow Analysis

Net cash provided by operating activities	$411,750
Less: Capital expenditures	(252,500)
Dividends	(19,800)
Free cash flow	$139,450

This analysis shows that Nestor has a positive, and substantial, net cash provided by operating activities of $411,750. Nestor reports on its statement of cash flows that it purchased equipment of $182,500 and land of $70,000 for total capital spending of $252,500. This amount is subtracted from net cash provided by operating activities because without continued efforts to maintain and expand facilities it is unlikely that Nestor can continue to maintain its competitive position. Capital spending is deducted first on the free cash flow statement to indicate it is the least discretionary expenditure a company generally makes. Dividends are then deducted, to arrive at free cash flow. Although a company can cut its dividend, it will usually do so only in a financial emergency. Nestor has more than sufficient cash flow to meet its dividend payment and therefore has satisfactory financial flexibility.

Nestor used its free cash flow to redeem bonds and add to its liquidity. If it finds additional investments that are profitable, it can increase its spending without putting its dividend or basic capital spending in jeopardy. Companies that have strong financial flexibility can take advantage of profitable investments even in tough times. In addition, strong financial flexibility frees companies from worry about survival in poor economic times. In fact, those with strong financial flexibility often fare better in poor economic times because they can take advantage of opportunities that other companies cannot.

SUMMARY OF LEARNING OBJECTIVES

1 **Identify the uses and limitations of a balance sheet.** The balance sheet provides information about the nature and amounts of investments in enterprise resources, obligations to creditors, and the owners' equity in net resources. The balance sheet contributes to financial reporting by providing a basis for (1) computing rates of return,

[21]In determining free cash flows, some companies do not subtract dividends because they believe these expenditures to be discretionary.

(2) evaluating the capital structure of the enterprise, and (3) assessing the liquidity, solvency, and financial flexibility of the enterprise. The limitations of a balance sheet are: (1) The balance sheet does not reflect current value because accountants have adopted a historical cost basis in valuing and reporting assets and liabilities. (2) Judgments and estimates must be used in preparing a balance sheet. The collectibility of receivables, the salability of inventory, and the useful life of long-term tangible and intangible assets are difficult to determine. (3) The balance sheet omits many items that are of financial value to the business but cannot be recorded objectively, such as human resources, customer base, and reputation.

2 Identify the major classifications of the balance sheet. The general elements of the balance sheet are assets, liabilities, and equity. The major classifications within the balance sheet on the asset side are current assets; long-term investments; property, plant, and equipment; intangible assets; and other assets. The major classifications of liabilities are current and long-term liabilities. In a corporation, owners' equity is generally classified as capital stock, additional paid-in capital, and retained earnings.

3 Prepare a classified balance sheet using the report and account formats. The report form lists liabilities and stockholders' equity directly below assets on the same page. The account form lists assets by sections on the left side and liabilities and stockholders' equity by sections on the right side.

4 Identify balance sheet information requiring supplemental disclosure. Three types of information normally are supplemental to account titles and amounts presented in the balance sheet: (1) *Contingencies:* Material events that have an uncertain outcome. (2) *Accounting policies:* Explanations of the valuation methods used or the basic assumptions made concerning inventory valuation, depreciation methods, investments in subsidiaries, etc. (3) *Contractual situations:* Explanations of certain restrictions or covenants attached to specific assets or, more likely, to liabilities.

5 Identify major disclosure techniques for the balance sheet. There are four methods of disclosing pertinent information in the balance sheet: (1) *Parenthetical explanations:* Additional information or description is often provided by parenthetical explanations following the item. (2) *Notes:* Notes are used if additional explanations or descriptions cannot be shown conveniently as parenthetical explanations. (3) *Cross reference and contra items:* A direct relationship between an asset and a liability is "cross referenced" on the balance sheet. (4) *Supporting schedules:* Often a separate schedule is needed to present more detailed information about certain assets or liabilities, because the balance sheet provides just a single summary item.

6 Indicate the purpose of the statement of cash flows. The primary purpose of a statement of cash flows is to provide relevant information about the cash receipts and cash payments of an enterprise during a period. Reporting the sources, uses, and net increase or decrease in cash enables investors, creditors, and others to know what is happening to a company's most liquid resource.

7 Identify the content of the statement of cash flows. Cash receipts and cash payments during a period are classified in the statement of cash flows into three different activities: (1) *Operating activities:* Involve the cash effects of transactions that enter into the determination of net income. (2) *Investing activities:* Include making and collecting loans and acquiring and disposing of investments (both debt and equity) and property, plant, and equipment. (3) *Financing activities:* Involve liability and owners' equity items and include (a) obtaining capital from owners and providing them with a return on their investment and (b) borrowing money from creditors and repaying the amounts borrowed.

8 Prepare a statement of cash flows. The information to prepare the statement of cash flows usually comes from (1) comparative balance sheets, (2) the current income statement, and (3) selected transaction data. Preparing the statement of cash flows from these sources involves the following steps: (1) determine the cash provided by

KEY TERMS

account form, *200*
adjunct account, *205*
available-for-sale securities, *193*
balance sheet, *188*
cash debt coverage ratio, *211*
contra account, *205*
current assets, *191*
current cash debt coverage ratio, *211*
current liabilities, *197*
financial flexibility, *189*
financial instruments, *198*
financial position form, *200*
financing activities, *207*
free cash flow, *212*
held-to-maturity securities, *193*
intangible assets, *196*
investing activities, *207*
liquidity, *189*
long-term investments, *195*
long-term liabilities, *198*
operating activities, *207*
owners' (stockholders') equity, *199*
property, plant, and equipment, *196*
report form, *200*
reserve, *205*
solvency, *189*
statement of cash flows, *206*
trading securities, *193*
working capital, *197*

operations; (2) determine the cash provided by or used in investing and financing activities; (3) determine the change (increase or decrease) in cash during the period; and (4) reconcile the change in cash with the beginning and the ending cash balances.

9 **Understand the usefulness of the statement of cash flows.** Creditors examine the cash flow statement carefully because they are concerned about being paid. The amount and trend of net cash flow provided by operating activities in relation to the company's liabilities is helpful in making this assessment. In addition, measures such as a free cash flow analysis provide creditors and stockholders with a better picture of the company's financial flexibility.

APPENDIX 5A Ratio Analysis—A Reference

USING RATIOS TO ANALYZE FINANCIAL PERFORMANCE

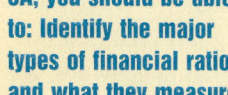

OBJECTIVE 10
After studying Appendix 5A, you should be able to: Identify the major types of financial ratios and what they measure.

Qualitative information from financial statements can be gathered by examining relationships between items on the statements and identifying trends in these relationships. A useful starting point in developing this information is the application of ratio analysis.

A **ratio** expresses the mathematical relationship between one quantity and another. **Ratio analysis** expresses the relationship among selected financial statement data. The relationship is expressed in terms of either a percentage, a rate, or a simple proportion. To illustrate, recently **IBM Corporation** had current assets of $41,338 million and current liabilities of $29,226 million. The relationship is determined by dividing current assets by current liabilities. The alternative means of expression are:

Percentage: Current assets are 141% of current liabilities.
Rate: Current assets are 1.41 times as great as current liabilities.
Proportion: The relationship of current assets to liabilities is 1.41:1.

For analysis of financial statements, ratios can be classified into four types, as follows:

MAJOR TYPES OF RATIOS

Liquidity Ratios. Measures of the enterprise's short-run ability to pay its maturing obligations.
Activity Ratios. Measures of how effectively the enterprise is using the assets employed.
Profitability Ratios. Measures of the degree of success or failure of a given enterprise or division for a given period of time.
Coverage Ratios. Measures of the degree of protection for long-term creditors and investors.

Go to the Digital Tool for an expanded discussion of financial statement analysis.

In Chapter 5 two ratios related to the statement of cash flows were discussed. Throughout the remainder of the textbook, ratios are provided to help you understand and interpret the information presented. In an Appendix to Chapter 25, a discussion of financial statement analysis, of which ratio analysis is one part, is presented. In Il-

ILLUSTRATION 5A-1 A Summary of Financial Ratios

Ratio	Formula	Purpose or Use
I. Liquidity		
1. Current ratio	Current assets / Current liabilities	Measures short-term debt-paying ability
2. Quick or acid-test ratio	Cash, marketable securities, and receivables (net) / Current liabilities	Measures immediate short-term liquidity
3. Current cash debt coverage ratio	Net cash provided by operating activities / Average current liabilities	Measures a company's ability to pay off its current liabilities in a given year from its operations
II. Activity		
4. Receivable turnover	Net sales / Average trade receivables (net)	Measures liquidity of receivables
5. Inventory turnover	Cost of goods sold / Average inventory	Measures liquidity of inventory
6. Asset turnover	Net sales / Average total assets	Measures how efficiently assets are used to generate sales
III. Profitability		
7. Profit margin on sales	Net income / Net sales	Measures net income generated by each dollar of sales
8. Rate of return on assets	Net income / Average total assets	Measures overall profitability of assets
9. Rate of return on common stock equity	Net income minus preferred dividends / Average common stockholders' equity	Measures profitability of owners' investment
10. Earnings per share	Net income minus preferred dividends / Weighted shares outstanding	Measures net income earned on each share of common stock
11. Price earnings ratio	Market price of stock / Earnings per share	Measures the ratio of the market price per share to earnings per share
12. Payout ratio	Cash dividends / Net income	Measures percentage of earnings distributed in the form of cash dividends
IV. Coverage		
13. Debt to total assets	Total debt / Total assets or equities	Measures the percentage of total assets provided by creditors
14. Times interest earned	Income before interest charges and taxes / Interest charges	Measures ability to meet interest payments as they come due
15. Cash debt coverage ratio	Net cash provided by operating activities / Average total liabilities	Measures a company's ability to repay its total liabilities in a given year from its operations
16. Book value per share	Common stockholders' equity / Outstanding shares	Measures the amount each share would receive if the company were liquidated at the amounts reported on the balance sheet

lustration 5A-1 are the ratios that will be used throughout the text. You should find this chart helpful as you examine these ratios in more detail in the following chapters.

SUMMARY OF LEARNING OBJECTIVE FOR APPENDIX 5A

⑩ **Identify the major types of financial ratios and what they measure.** Ratios express the mathematical relationship between one quantity and another, in terms of either a percentage, a rate, or a proportion. Liquidity ratios measure the short-run ability to pay maturing obligations. Activity ratios measure the effectiveness of asset usage. Profitability ratios measure the success or failure of an enterprise. Coverage ratios measure the degree of protection for long-term creditors and investors.

KEY TERMS

activity ratios, *214*
coverage ratios, *214*
liquidity ratios, *214*
profitability ratios, *214*
ratio analysis, *214*

APPENDIX 5B
Specimen Financial Statements

To the Student:

The following 26 pages contain the financial statements, accompanying notes and other information from the 1998 Annual Report of **Intel Corporation**, the world's leading manufacturer of microprocessors and semiconductors and one of the largest and most profitable U.S. companies in the fast-growing, ever-changing computer industry. Because of its size, worldwide scope, and diversity of operations, Intel's accounting and reporting practices are affected by most of the accounting topics covered in this textbook and by nearly every facet of generally accepted accounting principles. Of all U.S. industrial companies in 1998, Intel was 40th largest in sales ($26.3 billion), 11th most profitable in terms of return on assets (19.3%), 5th in terms of market value ($207.2 billion), and 6th in net profit margin (23.1%). Intel employs over 64,000 workers and in 1998 was named by *Fortune* magazine as the third most admired company in America.

We do not expect that you will comprehend Intel's financial statements and the accompanying notes in their entirety at your first reading. But we expect that by the time you complete the coverage of the material in this text, your level of understanding and interpretive ability will have grown enormously.

At this point we recommend that you take 20 to 30 minutes to scan the statements and notes, to familiarize yourself with the contents and accounting elements. Throughout the following 20 chapters, when you are asked to refer to specific parts of Intel's financials, do so! Then, when you have completed reading this book, we challenge you to reread Intel's financials to see how much greater and more sophisticated is your understanding of them.

Financial summary

intel®

Ten Years Ended December 26, 1998

(In millions—except employees)	Employees at year-end (in thousands)	Net investment in property, plant & equipment	Total assets	Long-term debt & put warrants	Stock-holders' equity	Additions to property, plant & equipment[†]
1998	64.5	$11,609	$31,471	$ 903	$23,377	$ 4,032
1997	63.7	$10,666	$28,880	$ 2,489	$19,295	$ 4,501
1996	48.5	$ 8,487	$23,735	$ 1,003	$16,872	$ 3,024
1995	41.6	$ 7,471	$17,504	$ 1,125	$12,140	$ 3,550
1994	32.6	$ 5,367	$13,816	$ 1,136	$ 9,267	$ 2,441
1993	29.5	$ 3,996	$11,344	$ 1,114	$ 7,500	$ 1,933
1992	25.8	$ 2,816	$ 8,089	$ 622	$ 5,445	$ 1,228
1991	24.6	$ 2,163	$ 6,292	$ 503	$ 4,418	$ 948
1990	23.9	$ 1,658	$ 5,376	$ 345	$ 3,592	$ 680
1989	21.7	$ 1,284	$ 3,994	$ 412	$ 2,549	$ 422

(In millions—except per share amounts)	Net revenues	Cost of sales	Research & development	Operating income	Net income	Basic earnings per share	Diluted earnings per share	Dividends declared per share	Dividends paid per share	Weighted average diluted shares outstanding
1998	$26,273	$12,144	$ 2,674	$ 8,379	$ 6,068	$ 1.82	$ 1.73	$ .050	$ .065	3,517
1997	$25,070	$ 9,945	$ 2,347	$ 9,887	$ 6,945	$ 2.12	$ 1.93	$ .058	$ .055	3,590
1996	$20,847	$ 9,164	$ 1,808	$ 7,553	$ 5,157	$ 1.57	$ 1.45	$ .048	$ .045	3,551
1995	$16,202	$ 7,811	$ 1,296	$ 5,252	$ 3,566	$ 1.08	$ 1.01	$ .038	$ .035	3,536
1994	$11,521	$ 5,576	$ 1,111	$ 3,387	$ 2,288	$ .69	$ .65	$ .029	$ .028	3,496
1993	$ 8,782	$ 3,252	$ 970	$ 3,392	$ 2,295	$ .69	$ .65	$ .025	$ .025	3,528
1992	$ 5,844	$ 2,557	$ 780	$ 1,490	$ 1,067	$ .32	$ .31	$ .013	$ .006	3,436
1991	$ 4,779	$ 2,316	$ 618	$ 1,080	$ 819	$ .25	$ .24	—	—	3,344
1990	$ 3,921	$ 1,930	$ 517	$ 858	$ 650	$ .21	$ .20	—	—	3,247
1989	$ 3,127	$ 1,721	$ 365	$ 557	$ 391	$ .13	$ .13	—	—	3,020

Share and per share amounts shown have been adjusted for stock splits through April 1999, including the stock split declared in January 1999.

[†]Additions to property, plant and equipment in 1998 included $475 million for capital assets acquired from Digital Equipment Corporation.

Facts and figures

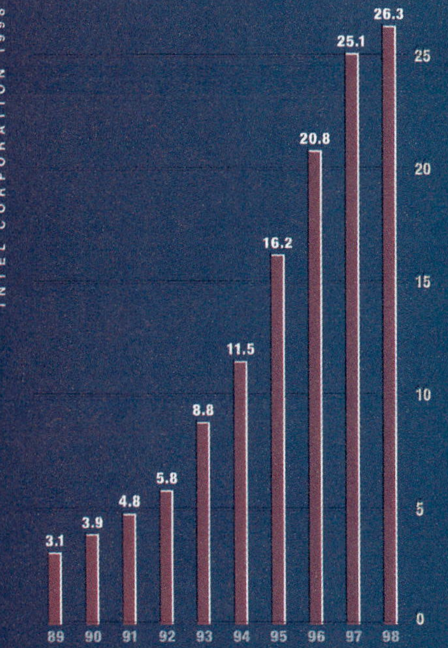

Net revenues
(Dollars in billions)

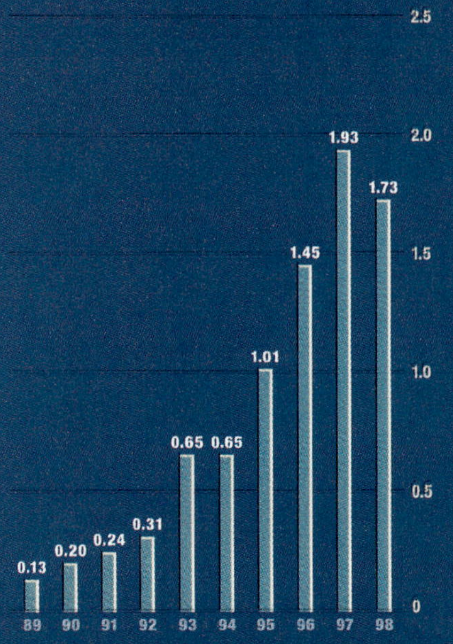

Diluted earnings per share
(Dollars, adjusted for stock splits)

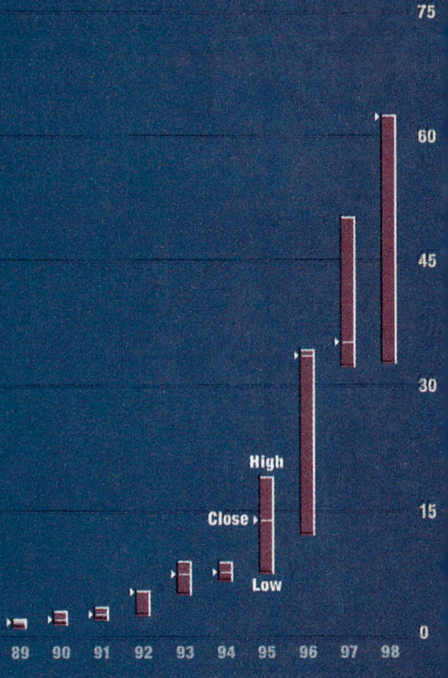

Stock price trading ranges by fiscal year
(Dollars, adjusted for stock splits)

1998: challenges an

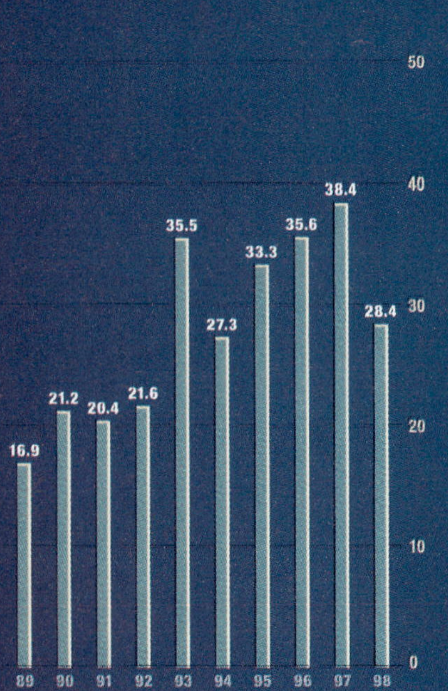

Return on average stockholders' equity
(Percent)

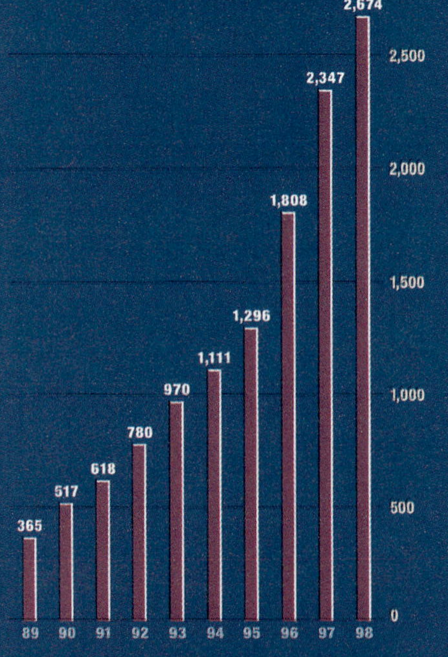

Research and development
(Dollars in millions)

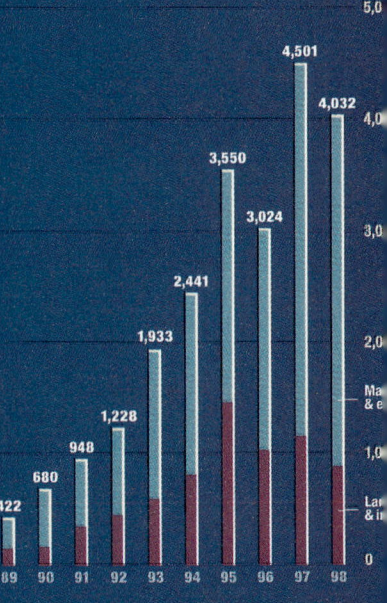

422
680
948
1,228
1,933
2,441
3,550
3,024
4,501
4,032
0
89 90 91 92 93 94 95 96 97 98

Capital additions to property, plant and equipment†
(Dollars in millions)

Past performance does not guarantee future results.
Share and per share amounts shown have been adjusted for stock splits through April 1999, including the stock split declared in January 1999.
†Capital additions for 1998 included assets acquired from Digital Equipment Corporation.

To our stockholders

We faced extraordinary business conditions in 1998. Competition in the value PC market segment, inventory corrections among some of our large customers in the first half of the year and an economic slowdown in some parts of the world all took their toll. As a consequence, our financial results in the first half of the year were not as strong as we would have liked. Revenues for the year were up 5%, with net income down 13% to $6.1 billion. At the same time, beneath these choppy waters, we were undergoing a fundamental sea change in how we see our business. The Internet is transforming the nature of the computing industry. As a leading provider of key computing and communications building blocks, we play a central role in this revolution. We are confident that our actions have helped us ride out the turbulence of 1998, and we are excited about our strategic plans to help drive the development of an increasingly connected computing world.

New products for all levels. With hindsight, it's clear that we were caught off guard by the increase in demand for low-cost PCs. We were late in recognizing the emergence of this value PC market segment—and the competition took advantage of our delay. While our global position remains strong, we lost market share in the U.S. retail segment of the market (which is about 10% of the worldwide PC market). We have redoubled our efforts to regain that share, with focused product development.

In response to the evolving computing marketplace, it was clear that we had to drive our business in a new way. We developed a broad game plan that would enable us to participate in every level of the newly segmented computing market. We revamped our microprocessor lineup with new products created specifically for each computing segment:

an exciting sea change

⇒ Our Intel® Celeron™ microprocessor, introduced in April and followed in August by an enhanced version, offers entry-level PC buyers good value and reliable Intel technology. By the end of 1998, it was the second-highest volume PC microprocessor in the world, second only to the Pentium® II microprocessor.

⇒ Our Pentium II microprocessor remains the heart of our business. Ideal for the performance desktop and entry-level servers and workstations, this powerful processor makes up the majority of units we sold worldwide in 1998.

⇒ The powerhouse Pentium® II Xeon™ microprocessor, introduced in August, is specifically designed for mid- and high-range servers and workstations. Manufacturers can benefit by designing systems to harness the power of multiple high-performance processors. Demand for servers and workstations is increasing, and within both of these segments, sales of systems based on Intel architecture are growing much faster than the overall segment.

Our segmentation strategy is designed to allow us to participate profitably in various segments of the computing market and to pursue new growth opportunities in the high-end server and workstation market segments. Supported by our strong branding program, which conveys the benefits of Intel technology and the attributes of the products at each level, our segmentation strategy is working as intended.

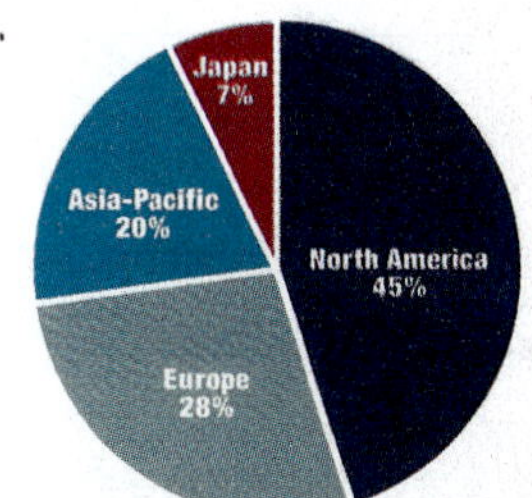

1998 Geographic breakdown of revenues
(Percent)

Adjusting to a cost-competitive environment. 1998 found us operating in a more cost competitive marketplace. We responded by setting aggressive new targets in cost management and manufacturing efficiency. With belt tightening in discretionary spending and some headcount reductions, we adjusted to an environment that demands leaner operations. We ended the year with headcount down 2% (excluding acquisitions) and our human resources employed in the areas of maximum return.

We also made great strides in manufacturing efficiency through a successful and rapid ramp to our new 0.25-micron process technology. With each new generation of our manufacturing process, the dimensions shrink on the finished chip, giving higher product yields as well as more powerful products.

In 1998, we also developed an innovative new packaging technology for our microprocessors, the Organic LAN Grid Array, that provides higher performance and versatility at lower cost for the final product. We are the only major chip maker using this packaging. We continue to invest in the state-of-the-art manufacturing facilities and R&D programs that make such innovations possible, spending $4 billion for capital additions and $2.7 billion for R&D in 1998.

The Internet drives an industry shift. Throughout the turbulence of the first half of the year, we were also adapting to a more fundamental shift in our business. Ten years ago, people bought PCs for personal productivity needs—spreadsheets, word processing and the like. Today, the number one reason people buy PCs is to get on the Internet. As the computing universe becomes connected, the demands on PCs and the entire computing infrastructure are expanding.

On a networked PC, every click of the mouse sets in motion a series of invisible and demanding tasks: compression and decompression of bulky downloads, encryption, virus scans and security checks, among others. These tasks have to be executed quickly and accurately behind the scenes, and they require powerful PCs. At the same time, behind the connected PCs is a large number of powerful servers, delivering data to the desktop and performing some of those compute-intensive functions. The number of servers is increasing as the Internet expands, providing a growing market segment for our products. We consider this opportunity so significant that more than half of Intel's microprocessor R&D investment is now committed to workstations and servers.

We also have a rapidly growing network products business, with software and hardware products designed to make it easier to connect and manage networked PCs for small businesses, large enterprises and home users. As part of our commitment to networking, we acquired Case Technology and Dayna Communications Inc. in 1997, and have entered into an agreement to acquire Shiva Corporation. These companies provide key technologies for improving Internet performance.

In addition to providing the powerful processors that are the key building blocks of the Internet and network products, we are engaging with other industry leaders in initiatives to expand Internet capabilities and product offerings. In 1998, our Corporate Business Development group made more than 100 new equity investments to help spur development of computer and Internet capabilities.

The Internet has stimulated the most intensely competitive cycle and development boom in the history of the computing industry. Being connected is now at the center of people's computing experience. The resulting opportunities have made our direction clear: to help drive the growth of the connected world. In 1999 and beyond, we will pursue our strategic intent to be a major force behind the Internet revolution.

Gordon E. Moore
Chairman Emeritus

Andrew S. Grove
Chairman

Craig R. Barrett
President and CEO

At the time of the Annual Meeting of Stockholders in May 1998, Craig Barrett was elected Chief Executive Officer of Intel Corporation, and Andy Grove was elected Chairman of the Board. Gordon Moore is now Chairman Emeritus. This is the latest phase of a management transition that has been under way for years and reflects our dedication to continuity in the executive office.

Report of Ernst & Young LLP, independent auditors

The Board of Directors and Stockholders, Intel Corporation

We have audited the accompanying consolidated balance sheets of Intel Corporation as of December 26, 1998 and December 27, 1997, and the related consolidated statements of income, stockholders' equity, and cash flows for each of the three years in the period ended December 26, 1998. These financial statements are the responsibility of the Company's management. Our responsibility is to express an opinion on these financial statements based on our audits.

We conducted our audits in accordance with generally accepted auditing standards. Those standards require that we plan and perform the audit to obtain reasonable assurance about whether the financial statements are free of material misstatement. An audit includes examining, on a test basis, evidence supporting the amounts and disclosures in the financial statements. An audit also includes assessing the accounting principles used and significant estimates made by management, as well as evaluating the overall financial statement presentation. We believe that our audits provide a reasonable basis for our opinion.

In our opinion, the consolidated financial statements referred to above present fairly, in all material respects, the consolidated financial position of Intel Corporation at December 26, 1998 and December 27, 1997, and the consolidated results of its operations and its cash flows for each of the three years in the period ended December 26, 1998, in conformity with generally accepted accounting principles.

Ernst & Young LLP

San Jose, California
January 11, 1999

Consolidated statements of income

Three years ended December 26, 1998
(In millions—except per share amounts)

	1998	1997	1996
Net revenues	**$26,273**	**$25,070**	**$20,847**
Cost of sales	12,144	9,945	9,164
Research and development	2,509	2,347	1,808
Marketing, general and administrative	3,076	2,891	2,322
Purchased in-process research and development	165	—	—
Operating costs and expenses	17,894	15,183	13,294
Operating income	**8,379**	**9,887**	**7,553**
Interest expense	(34)	(27)	(25)
Interest income and other, net	792	799	406
Income before taxes	**9,137**	**10,659**	**7,934**
Provision for taxes	3,069	3,714	2,777
Net income	**$ 6,068**	**$ 6,945**	**$ 5,157**
Basic earnings per common share	**$ 1.82**	**$ 2.12**	**$ 1.57**
Diluted earnings per common share	**$ 1.73**	**$ 1.93**	**$ 1.45**
Weighted average common shares outstanding	**3,336**	**3,271**	**3,290**
Dilutive effect of:			
Employee stock options	159	204	187
1998 Step-Up Warrants	22	115	74
Weighted average common shares outstanding, assuming dilution	**3,517**	**3,590**	**3,551**

See accompanying notes.

Consolidated balance sheets

December 26, 1998 and December 27, 1997 (In millions—except per share amounts)	1998	1997
Assets		
Current assets:		
Cash and cash equivalents	$ 2,038	$ 4,102
Short-term investments	5,272	5,630
Trading assets	316	195
Accounts receivable, net of allowance for doubtful accounts of $62 ($65 in 1997)	3,527	3,438
Inventories	1,582	1,697
Deferred tax assets	618	676
Other current assets	122	129
Total current assets	**13,475**	**15,867**
Property, plant and equipment:		
Land and buildings	6,297	5,113
Machinery and equipment	13,149	10,577
Construction in progress	1,622	2,437
	21,068	18,127
Less accumulated depreciation	9,459	7,461
Property, plant and equipment, net	**11,609**	**10,666**
Long-term investments	**5,365**	**1,839**
Other assets	**1,022**	**508**
Total assets	**$31,471**	**$28,880**
Liabilities and stockholders' equity		
Current liabilities:		
Short-term debt	$ 159	$ 212
Long-term debt redeemable within one year	—	110
Accounts payable	1,244	1,407
Accrued compensation and benefits	1,285	1,268
Deferred income on shipments to distributors	606	516
Accrued advertising	458	500
Other accrued liabilities	1,094	842
Income taxes payable	958	1,165
Total current liabilities	**5,804**	**6,020**
Long-term debt	**702**	**448**
Deferred tax liabilities	**1,387**	**1,076**
Put warrants	**201**	**2,041**
Commitments and contingencies		
Stockholders' equity:		
Preferred Stock, $.001 par value, 50 shares authorized; none issued	—	—
Common Stock, $.001 par value, 4,500 shares authorized; 3,315 issued and outstanding (3,256 in 1997) and capital in excess of par value	4,822	3,311
Retained earnings	17,952	15,926
Accumulated other comprehensive income	603	58
Total stockholders' equity	**23,377**	**19,295**
Total liabilities and stockholders' equity	**$31,471**	**$28,880**

See accompanying notes.

Consolidated statements of cash flows

intel

Three years ended December 26, 1998 (In millions)	1998	1997	1996
Cash and cash equivalents, beginning of year	**$ 4,102**	**$ 4,165**	**$ 1,463**
Cash flows provided by (used for) operating activities:			
Net income	6,068	6,945	5,157
Adjustments to reconcile net income to net cash provided by (used for) operating activities:			
Depreciation	2,807	2,192	1,888
Net loss on retirements of property, plant and equipment	282	130	120
Deferred taxes	77	6	179
Purchased in-process research and development	165	—	—
Changes in assets and liabilities:			
Accounts receivable	(38)	285	(607)
Inventories	167	(404)	711
Accounts payable	(180)	438	105
Accrued compensation and benefits	17	140	370
Income taxes payable	(211)	179	185
Tax benefit from employee stock plans	415	224	196
Other assets and liabilities	(378)	(127)	439
Total adjustments	3,123	3,063	3,586
Net cash provided by operating activities	**9,191**	**10,008**	**8,743**
Cash flows provided by (used for) investing activities:			
Additions to property, plant and equipment	(3,557)	(4,501)	(3,024)
Purchase of Chips and Technologies, Inc., net of cash acquired	(321)	—	—
Purchase of Digital Equipment Corporation semiconductor operations	(585)	—	—
Purchases of available-for-sale investments	(10,925)	(9,224)	(4,683)
Sales of available-for-sale investments	201	153	225
Maturities and other changes in available-for-sale investments	8,681	6,713	2,214
Net cash (used for) investing activities	**(6,506)**	**(6,859)**	**(5,268)**
Cash flows provided by (used for) financing activities:			
(Decrease) increase in short-term debt, net	(83)	(177)	43
Additions to long-term debt	169	172	317
Retirement of long-term debt	—	(300)	—
Proceeds from sales of shares through employee stock plans and other	507	317	257
Proceeds from exercise of 1998 Step-Up Warrants	1,620	40	4
Proceeds from sales of put warrants	40	288	56
Repurchase and retirement of Common Stock	(6,785)	(3,372)	(1,302)
Payment of dividends to stockholders	(217)	(180)	(148)
Net cash (used for) financing activities	**(4,749)**	**(3,212)**	**(773)**
Net (decrease) increase in cash and cash equivalents	**(2,064)**	**(63)**	**2,702**
Cash and cash equivalents, end of year	**$ 2,038**	**$ 4,102**	**$ 4,165**
Supplemental disclosures of cash flow information:			
Cash paid during the year for:			
Interest	$ 40	$ 37	$ 51
Income taxes	$ 2,784	$ 3,305	$ 2,217

See accompanying notes.

Consolidated statements of stockholders' equity

intel®

Three years ended December 26, 1998 (In millions—except per share amounts)	Common Stock and capital in excess of par value		Retained earnings	Accumulated other comprehensive income	Total
	Number of shares	Amount			
Balance at December 30, 1995	**3,286**	**$ 2,583**	**$ 9,505**	**$ 52**	**$12,140**
Components of comprehensive income:					
Net income	—	—	5,157	—	5,157
Change in unrealized gain on available-for-sale investments	—	—	—	70	70
Total comprehensive income					5,227
Proceeds from sales of shares through employee stock plans, tax benefit of $196 and other	65	457	—	—	457
Proceeds from sales of put warrants	—	56	—	—	56
Reclassification of put warrant obligation, net	—	70	272	—	342
Repurchase and retirement of Common Stock	(68)	(269)	(925)	—	(1,194)
Cash dividends declared ($.048 per share)	—	—	(156)	—	(156)
Balance at December 28, 1996	**3,283**	**2,897**	**13,853**	**122**	**16,872**
Components of comprehensive income:					
Net income	—	—	6,945	—	6,945
Change in unrealized gain on available-for-sale investments	—	—	—	(64)	(64)
Total comprehensive income					6,881
Proceeds from sales of shares through employee stock plans, tax benefit of $224 and other	61	581	(1)	—	580
Proceeds from sales of put warrants	—	288	—	—	288
Reclassification of put warrant obligation, net	—	(144)	(1,622)	—	(1,766)
Repurchase and retirement of Common Stock	(88)	(311)	(3,061)	—	(3,372)
Cash dividends declared ($.058 per share)	—	—	(188)	—	(188)
Balance at December 27, 1997	**3,256**	**3,311**	**15,926**	**58**	**19,295**
Components of comprehensive income:					
Net income	—	—	6,068	—	6,068
Change in unrealized gain on available-for-sale investments	—	—	—	545	545
Total comprehensive income					6,613
Proceeds from sales of shares through employee stock plans, tax benefit of $415 and other	66	922	—	—	922
Proceeds from exercise of 1998 Step-Up Warrants	155	1,620	—	—	1,620
Proceeds from sales of put warrants	—	40	—	—	40
Reclassification of put warrant obligation, net	—	53	588	—	641
Repurchase and retirement of Common Stock	(162)	(1,124)	(4,462)	—	(5,586)
Cash dividends declared ($.050 per share)	—	—	(168)	—	(168)
Balance at December 26, 1998	**3,315**	**$ 4,822**	**$17,952**	**$ 603**	**$23,377**

See accompanying notes.

Notes to consolidated financial statements

Accounting policies

Fiscal year. Intel Corporation ("Intel" or "the Company") has a fiscal year that ends the last Saturday in December. Fiscal years 1998, 1997 and 1996, each 52-week years, ended on December 26, 27 and 28, respectively. Periodically there will be a 53-week year. The next 53-week year will end on December 30, 2000.

Basis of presentation. The consolidated financial statements include the accounts of Intel and its wholly owned subsidiaries. Significant intercompany accounts and transactions have been eliminated. Accounts denominated in foreign currencies have been remeasured using the U.S. dollar as the functional currency.

The preparation of financial statements in conformity with generally accepted accounting principles requires management to make estimates and assumptions that affect the amounts reported in the financial statements and accompanying notes. Actual results could differ from those estimates.

Investments. Highly liquid investments with insignificant interest rate risk and with original maturities of three months or less are classified as cash and cash equivalents. Investments with maturities greater than three months and less than one year are classified as short-term investments. Investments with maturities greater than one year are classified as long-term investments.

The Company's policy is to protect the value of its investment portfolio and to minimize principal risk by earning returns based on current interest rates. The Company enters into certain equity investments for the promotion of business and strategic objectives, and typically does not attempt to reduce or eliminate the inherent market risks on these investments. A substantial majority of the Company's marketable investments are classified as available-for-sale as of the balance sheet date and are reported at fair value, with unrealized gains and losses, net of tax, recorded in stockholders' equity. The cost of securities sold is based on the specific identification method. Realized gains or losses and declines in value, if any, judged to be other than temporary on available-for-sale securities are reported in other income or expense. Investments in non-marketable instruments are recorded at the lower of cost or market and included in other assets.

Trading assets. The Company maintains its trading asset portfolio to generate returns that offset changes in certain liabilities related to deferred compensation arrangements. The trading assets consist of marketable equity securities and are stated at fair value. Both realized and unrealized gains and losses are included in other income or expense and generally offset the change in the deferred compensation liability, which is also included in other income or expense. Net gains on the trading asset portfolio were $66 million, $37 million and $12 million in 1998, 1997 and 1996, respectively.

Fair values of financial instruments. Fair values of cash and cash equivalents approximate cost due to the short period of time to maturity. Fair values of long-term investments, long-term debt, short-term investments, short-term debt, long-term debt redeemable within one year, trading assets, non-marketable instruments, swaps, currency forward contracts, currency options and options hedging marketable instruments are based on quoted market prices or pricing models using current market rates. No consideration is given to liquidity issues in valuing debt.

Derivative financial instruments. The Company utilizes derivative financial instruments to reduce financial market risks. These instruments are used to hedge foreign currency, equity and interest rate market exposures of underlying assets, liabilities and other obligations. The Company also uses derivatives to create synthetic instruments, for example, buying and selling put and call options on the same underlying security, to generate money market like returns with a similar level of risk. The Company does not use derivative financial instruments for speculative or trading purposes. The Company's accounting policies for these instruments are based on whether they meet the Company's criteria for designation as hedging transactions. The criteria the Company uses for designating an instrument as a hedge include the instrument's effectiveness in risk reduction and one-to-one matching of derivative instruments to underlying transactions. Gains and losses on currency forward contracts, and options that are designated and effective as hedges of anticipated transactions, for which a firm commitment has been attained, are deferred and recognized in income in the same period that the underlying transactions are settled. Gains and losses on currency forward contracts, options and swaps that are designated and effective as hedges of existing transactions are recognized in income in the same period as losses and gains on the underlying transactions are recognized and generally offset. Gains and losses on any instruments not meeting the above criteria are recognized in income in the current period. If an underlying hedged transaction is terminated earlier than initially anticipated, the offsetting gain or loss on the related derivative instrument would be recognized in income in the same period. Subsequent gains or losses on the related derivative instrument would be recognized in income in each period until the instrument matures, is terminated or is sold. Income or expense on swaps is accrued as an adjustment to the yield of the related investments or debt they hedge.

Notes to consolidated financial statements

Inventories. Inventories are stated at the lower of cost or market. Cost is computed on a currently adjusted standard basis (which approximates actual cost on a current average or first-in, first-out basis). Inventories at fiscal year-ends were as follows:

(In millions)	1998	1997
Raw materials	$ 206	$ 255
Work in process	795	928
Finished goods	581	514
Total	**$ 1,582**	**$ 1,697**

Property, plant and equipment. Property, plant and equipment are stated at cost. Depreciation is computed for financial reporting purposes principally using the straight-line method over the following estimated useful lives: machinery and equipment, 2–4 years; buildings, 4–40 years.

Deferred income on shipments to distributors. Certain of the Company's sales are made to distributors under agreements allowing price protection and/or right of return on merchandise unsold by the distributors. Because of frequent sales price reductions and rapid technological obsolescence in the industry, Intel defers recognition of such sales until the merchandise is sold by the distributors.

Advertising. Cooperative advertising obligations are accrued and the costs expensed at the same time the related revenues are recognized. All other advertising costs are expensed as incurred. Advertising expense was $1.3 billion, $1.2 billion and $974 million in 1998, 1997 and 1996, respectively.

Interest. Interest as well as gains and losses related to contractual agreements to hedge certain investment positions and debt (see "Derivative financial instruments") are recorded as net interest income or expense. Interest expense capitalized as a component of construction costs was $6 million, $9 million and $33 million for 1998, 1997 and 1996, respectively.

Earnings per share. Basic earnings per common share are computed using the weighted average number of common shares outstanding during the period. Diluted earnings per common share incorporate the incremental shares issuable upon the assumed exercise of stock options and warrants. For portions of 1998, certain of the Company's stock options were excluded from the calculation of diluted earnings per share because they were antidilutive, but these options could be dilutive in the future.

Stock distribution. On January 27, 1999, the Company announced a two-for-one stock split in the form of a special stock distribution payable April 11, 1999 to stockholders of record as of March 23, 1999. On July 13, 1997, the Company effected a two-for-one stock split in the form of a special stock distribution to stockholders of record as of June 10, 1997. All share, per share, Common Stock, stock option and warrant amounts herein have been restated to reflect the effects of these splits.

Reclassifications. Certain amounts reported in previous years have been reclassified to conform to the 1998 presentation.

Recent accounting pronouncements. The Company intends to adopt Statement of Financial Accounting Standards ("SFAS") No. 133, "Accounting for Derivative Instruments and Hedging Activities," as of the beginning of its fiscal year 2000. The Standard will require the Company to recognize all derivatives on the balance sheet at fair value. Derivatives that are not hedges must be adjusted to fair value through income. If the derivative is a hedge, depending on the nature of the hedge, changes in the fair value of derivatives will either be offset against the change in fair value of the hedged assets, liabilities or firm commitments through earnings, or recognized in other comprehensive income until the hedged item is recognized in earnings. The change in a derivative's fair value related to the ineffective portion of a hedge, if any, will be immediately recognized in earnings. The effect of adopting the Standard is currently being evaluated but is not expected to have a material effect on the Company's financial position or overall trends in results of operations.

Common Stock

1998 Step-Up Warrants. In 1993, the Company issued 160 million 1998 Step-Up Warrants to purchase 160 million shares of Common Stock. This transaction resulted in an increase of $287 million in Common Stock and capital in excess of par value, representing net proceeds from the offering. The Warrants became exercisable in May 1993 at an effective price of $8.9375 per share of Common Stock, subject to annual increases to a maximum price of $10.4375 per share effective in March 1997. Between December 27, 1997 and March 14, 1998, approximately 155 million Warrants were exercised, and shares of Common Stock were issued for proceeds of $1.6 billion. The expiration date of these Warrants was March 14, 1998.

Stock repurchase program. The Company has an ongoing authorization, as amended, from the Board of Directors to repurchase up to 760 million shares of Intel's Common Stock in open market or negotiated transactions. During 1998, the Company repurchased 161.7 million shares of Common Stock at a cost of $6.8 billion. As of December 26, 1998, the Company had repurchased and retired approximately 588.6 million shares at a cost of $13.6 billion since the program began in 1990. As of December 26, 1998, after allowing for 5 million shares to cover outstanding put warrants, 166.4 million shares remained available under the repurchase authorization.

Notes to consolidated financial statements

Put warrants

In a series of private placements from 1991 through 1998, the Company sold put warrants that entitle the holder of each warrant to sell to the Company, by physical delivery, one share of Common Stock at a specified price. Activity during the past three years is summarized as follows:

(In millions)	Cumulative net premium received	Put warrants outstanding: Number of warrants	Put warrants outstanding: Potential obligation
December 30, 1995	**$ 279**	**48.0**	**$ 725**
Sales	56	36.0	603
Exercises	—	(7.2)	(108)
Expirations	—	(58.8)	(945)
December 28, 1996	**335**	**18.0**	**275**
Sales	288	92.6	3,525
Expirations	—	(58.0)	(1,759)
December 27, 1997	**623**	**52.6**	**2,041**
Sales	40	15.0	588
Exercises	—	(30.0)	(1,199)
Expirations	—	(32.6)	(1,229)
December 26, 1998	**$ 663**	**5.0**	**$ 201**

The amount related to Intel's potential repurchase obligation has been reclassified from stockholders' equity to put warrants. The 5 million put warrants outstanding at December 26, 1998 expire on various dates in January and February 1999 and have exercise prices ranging from $40 to $41 per share, with an average exercise price of $40 per share. There is no significant effect on diluted earnings per share for the periods presented.

Borrowings

Short-term debt. Non-interest-bearing short-term debt at fiscal year-ends was as follows:

(In millions)	1998	1997
Borrowed under lines of credit	$ 10	$ 32
Drafts payable	149	180
Total	**$ 159**	**$ 212**

The Company also borrows under commercial paper programs. Maximum borrowings under commercial paper programs reached $325 million during 1998 and $175 million during 1997. This debt is rated A-1+ by Standard and Poor's and P-1 by Moody's. Proceeds are used to fund short-term working capital needs.

Long-term debt. Long-term debt at fiscal year-ends was as follows:

(In millions)	1998	1997
Payable in U.S. dollars:		
AFICA Bonds due 2013 at 3.9%–4.25%	$ 110	$ 110
Other U.S. dollar debt	5	6
Payable in other currencies:		
Irish punt due 2000–2027 at 5%–12%	541	396
Greek drachma due 2001	46	46
Subtotal	702	558
Less long-term debt redeemable within one year	—	(110)
Total	**$ 702**	**$ 448**

The Company has guaranteed repayment of principal and interest on the AFICA Bonds issued by the Puerto Rico Industrial, Tourist, Educational, Medical and Environmental Control Facilities Financing Authority ("AFICA"). During 1998, the bonds were repriced and a portion remarketed, with interest rates effective through 2003 of 4.25% on the $80 million of Series A bonds and 3.90% on the $30 million of Series B bonds. The bonds are adjustable and redeemable at the option of either the Company or the bondholder every five years through 2013 and are next adjustable and redeemable in 2003. The additional and the existing Irish punt borrowings were made in connection with the financing of manufacturing facilities in Ireland, and Intel has invested the proceeds in Irish punt denominated instruments of similar maturity to hedge foreign currency and interest rate exposures. The Greek drachma borrowings were made under a tax incentive program in Ireland, and the proceeds and cash flows have been swapped to U.S. dollars.

Under shelf registration statements filed with the Securities and Exchange Commission, Intel had the authority to issue up to $3.3 billion in the aggregate of Common Stock, Preferred Stock, depositary shares, debt securities and warrants to purchase the Company's or other issuers' Common Stock, Preferred Stock and debt securities, and, subject to certain limits, stock index warrants and foreign currency exchange units. In 1993, Intel completed an offering of Step-Up Warrants (see "1998 Step-Up Warrants") under these registration statements. The Company may issue up to $1.4 billion in additional securities under effective registration statements.

As of December 26, 1998, aggregate debt maturities were as follows: 2000–$9 million; 2001–$57 million; 2002–$22 million; 2003–$130 million; and thereafter–$484 million.

Investments

The returns on a majority of the Company's marketable investments in long-term fixed rate debt and certain equity securities are swapped to U.S. dollar LIBOR-based returns. The currency risks of investments denominated in foreign

Notes to consolidated financial statements

currencies are hedged with foreign currency borrowings, currency forward contracts or currency interest rate swaps (see "Derivative financial instruments" under "Accounting policies").

Investments with maturities of greater than six months consist primarily of A and A2 or better rated financial instruments and counterparties. Investments with maturities of up to six months consist primarily of A-1 and P-1 or better rated financial instruments and counterparties. Foreign government regulations imposed upon investment alternatives of foreign subsidiaries, or the absence of A and A2 rated counterparties in certain countries, result in some minor exceptions. Intel's practice is to obtain and secure available collateral from counterparties against obligations whenever Intel deems appropriate. At December 26, 1998, investments were placed with approximately 185 different counterparties.

Investments at December 26, 1998 were as follows:

(In millions)	Cost	Gross unrealized gains	Gross unrealized losses	Estimated fair value
U.S. government securities	$ 2,824	$ —	$ (11)	$ 2,813
Commercial paper	2,694	5	(2)	2,697
Floating rate notes	1,273	2	(2)	1,273
Corporate bonds	1,153	51	(17)	1,187
Bank time deposits	1,135	1	(1)	1,135
Loan participations	625	—	—	625
Repurchase agreements	124	—	—	124
Securities of foreign governments	36	1	(1)	36
Other debt securities	160	—	—	160
Total debt securities	10,024	60	(34)	10,050
Hedged equity	100	—	(2)	98
Marketable strategic equity securities	822	979	(44)	1,757
Preferred stock and other equity	140	1	—	141
Total equity securities	1,062	980	(46)	1,996
Options creating synthetic money market instruments	474	—	—	474
Swaps hedging investments in debt securities	—	19	(52)	(33)
Swaps hedging investments in equity securities	—	2	—	2
Currency forward contracts hedging investments in debt securities	—	2	(4)	(2)
Total available-for-sale securities	**11,560**	**1,063**	**(136)**	**12,487**
Less amounts classified as cash equivalents	(1,850)	—	—	(1,850)
Total investments	**$ 9,710**	**$ 1,063**	**$ (136)**	**$10,637**

Investments at December 27, 1997 were as follows:

(In millions)	Cost	Gross unrealized gains	Gross unrealized losses	Estimated fair value
Commercial paper	$ 3,572	$ 1	$ (9)	$ 3,564
Bank time deposits	2,369	—	(2)	2,367
Corporate bonds	1,788	12	(73)	1,727
Floating rate notes	843	1	(2)	842
Loan participations	743	—	—	743
Repurchase agreements	515	—	—	515
Securities of foreign governments	75	—	(6)	69
Fixed rate notes	32	—	—	32
Other debt securities	294	—	(1)	293
Total debt securities	10,231	14	(93)	10,152
Hedged equity	504	9	(17)	496
Marketable strategic equity securities	279	130	(34)	375
Preferred stock and other equity	341	1	(7)	335
Total equity securities	1,124	140	(58)	1,206
Swaps hedging investments in debt securities	—	76	(12)	64
Swaps hedging investments in equity securities	—	17	(9)	8
Currency forward contracts hedging investments in debt securities	—	16	(1)	15
Total available-for-sale securities	**11,355**	**263**	**(173)**	**11,445**
Less amounts classified as cash equivalents	(3,976)	—	—	(3,976)
Total investments	**$ 7,379**	**$ 263**	**$ (173)**	**$ 7,469**

Available-for-sale securities with a fair value at the date of sale of $227 million, $153 million and $225 million were sold in 1998, 1997 and 1996, respectively. The gross realized gains on these sales totaled $185 million, $106 million and $7 million, respectively.

The amortized cost and estimated fair value of investments in debt securities at December 26, 1998, by contractual maturity, were as follows:

(In millions)	Cost	Estimated fair value
Due in 1 year or less	$ 6,412	$ 6,436
Due in 1–2 years	3,097	3,099
Due in 2–5 years	65	65
Due after 5 years	450	450
Total investments in debt securities	**$10,024**	**$10,050**

Notes to consolidated financial statements

Derivative financial instruments

Outstanding notional amounts for derivative financial instruments at fiscal year-ends were as follows:

(In millions)	1998	1997
Swaps hedging investments in debt securities	$ 2,526	$ 2,017
Swaps hedging investments in equity securities	$ 100	$ 604
Swaps hedging debt	$ 156	$ 156
Currency forward contracts	$ 830	$ 1,724
Currency options	$ —	$ 55
Options creating synthetic money market instruments	$ 2,086	$ —

While the contract or notional amounts provide one measure of the volume of these transactions, they do not represent the amount of the Company's exposure to credit risk. The amounts potentially subject to credit risk (arising from the possible inability of counterparties to meet the terms of their contracts) are generally limited to the amounts, if any, by which the counterparties' obligations exceed the obligations of the Company. The Company controls credit risk through credit approvals, limits and monitoring procedures. Credit rating criteria for derivative financial instruments are similar to those for investments.

Swap agreements. The Company utilizes swap agreements to exchange the foreign currency, equity and interest rate returns of its investment and debt portfolios for floating U.S. dollar interest rate based returns. The floating rates on swaps are based primarily on U.S. dollar LIBOR and are reset on a monthly, quarterly or semiannual basis.

Pay rates on swaps hedging investments in debt securities match the yields on the underlying investments they hedge. Payments on swaps hedging investments in equity securities match the equity returns on the underlying investments they hedge. Receive rates on swaps hedging debt match the expense on the underlying debt they hedge. Maturity dates of swaps match those of the underlying investment or the debt they hedge. There is approximately a one-to-one matching of swaps to investments and debt. Swap agreements generally remain in effect until expiration.

Weighted average pay and receive rates, average maturities and range of maturities on swaps at December 26, 1998 were as follows:

	Weighted average pay rate	Weighted average receive rate	Weighted average maturity	Range of maturities
Swaps hedging investments in U.S. dollar debt securities	5.4%	5.1%	0.5 years	0–2 years
Swaps hedging investments in foreign currency debt securities	5.5%	5.5%	0.7 years	0–2 years
Swaps hedging investments in equity securities	N/A	5.8%	1.0 years	0–1 years
Swaps hedging debt	5.6%	5.7%	4.1 years	2–5 years

Note: Pay and receive rates are based on the reset rates that were in effect at December 26, 1998.

Other foreign currency instruments. Intel transacts business in various foreign currencies, primarily Japanese yen and certain other Asian and European currencies. The Company has established revenue and balance sheet hedging programs to protect against reductions in value and volatility of future cash flows caused by changes in foreign exchange rates. The Company utilizes currency forward contracts and currency options in these hedging programs. The maturities on these instruments are less than 12 months.

Fair values of financial instruments

The estimated fair values of financial instruments outstanding at fiscal year-ends were as follows:

	1998		1997	
(In millions)	Carrying amount	Estimated fair value	Carrying amount	Estimated fair value
Cash and cash equivalents	$ 2,038	$ 2,038	$ 4,102	$ 4,102
Short-term investments	$ 4,821	$ 4,821	$ 5,561	$ 5,561
Trading assets	$ 316	$ 316	$ 195	$ 195
Long-term investments	$ 5,375	$ 5,375	$ 1,821	$ 1,821
Non-marketable instruments	$ 571	$ 716	$ 387	$ 497
Options creating synthetic money market instruments	$ 474	$ 474	$ —	$ —
Swaps hedging investments in debt securities	$ (33)	$ (33)	$ 64	$ 64
Swaps hedging investments in equity securities	$ 2	$ 2	$ 8	$ 8
Short-term debt	$ (159)	$ (159)	$ (212)	$ (212)
Long-term debt redeemable within one year	$ —	$ —	$ (110)	$ (109)
Long-term debt	$ (702)	$ (696)	$ (448)	$ (448)
Swaps hedging debt	$ —	$ 1	$ —	$ (1)
Currency forward contracts	$ (1)	$ (1)	$ 26	$ 28
Currency options	$ —	$ —	$ 1	$ 1

Notes to consolidated financial statements

Concentrations of credit risk

Financial instruments that potentially subject the Company to concentrations of credit risk consist principally of investments and trade receivables. Intel places its investments with high-credit-quality counterparties and, by policy, limits the amount of credit exposure to any one counterparty based on Intel's analysis of that counterparty's relative credit standing. A majority of the Company's trade receivables are derived from sales to manufacturers of computer systems, with the remainder spread across various other industries. The Company's five largest customers accounted for approximately 42% of net revenues for 1998. At December 26, 1998, these customers accounted for approximately 39% of net accounts receivable.

The Company endeavors to keep pace with the evolving computing industry and has adopted credit policies and standards intended to accommodate industry growth and inherent risk. Management believes that credit risks are moderated by the diversity of the Company's end customers and geographic sales areas. Intel performs ongoing credit evaluations of its customers' financial condition and requires collateral as deemed necessary.

Interest income and other

(In millions)	1998	1997	1996
Interest income	$ 593	$ 562	$ 364
Foreign currency gains	11	63	26
Other income, net	188	174	16
Total	**$ 792**	**$ 799**	**$ 406**

Other income for 1998 and 1997 included approximately $185 and $106 million, respectively, from sales of a portion of the Company's investments in marketable strategic equity securities.

Comprehensive income

The Company adopted SFAS No. 130, "Reporting Comprehensive Income," at the beginning of fiscal 1998. The adoption had no impact on net income or total stockholders' equity. Comprehensive income consists of net income and other comprehensive income.

The components of other comprehensive income and related tax effects were as follows:

(In millions)	1998	1997	1996
Gains on investments during the year, net of tax of $(357), $(4) and $(37) in 1998, 1997 and 1996, respectively	$ 665	$ 5	$ 75
Less: adjustment for gains included in net income, net of tax of $65, $37 and $2 in 1998, 1997 and 1996, respectively	(120)	(69)	(5)
Other comprehensive income	**$ 545**	**$ (64)**	**$ 70**

Accumulated other comprehensive income presented in the accompanying consolidated balance sheets consists of the accumulated net unrealized gain on available-for-sale investments.

Provision for taxes

Income before taxes and the provision for taxes consisted of the following:

(In millions)	1998	1997	1996
Income before taxes:			
U.S.	$ 6,677	$ 8,033	$ 5,515
Foreign	2,460	2,626	2,419
Total income before taxes	**$ 9,137**	**$10,659**	**$ 7,934**
Provision for taxes:			
Federal:			
Current	$ 2,321	$ 2,930	$ 2,046
Deferred	145	30	8
	2,466	2,960	2,054
State:			
Current	320	384	286
Foreign:			
Current	351	394	266
Deferred	(68)	(24)	171
	283	370	437
Total provision for taxes	**$ 3,069**	**$ 3,714**	**$ 2,777**
Effective tax rate	**33.6%**	**34.8%**	**35.0%**

The tax benefit associated with dispositions from employee stock plans reduced taxes currently payable for 1998 by $415 million ($224 million and $196 million for 1997 and 1996, respectively).

Notes to consolidated financial statements

The provision for taxes reconciles to the amount computed by applying the statutory federal rate of 35% to income before taxes as follows:

(In millions)	1998	1997	1996
Computed expected tax	$ 3,198	$ 3,731	$ 2,777
State taxes, net of federal benefits	208	249	186
Foreign income taxed at different rates	(339)	(111)	(127)
Other	2	(155)	(59)
Provision for taxes	**$ 3,069**	**$ 3,714**	**$ 2,777**

Deferred income taxes reflect the net tax effects of temporary differences between the carrying amount of assets and liabilities for financial reporting purposes and the amounts used for income tax purposes.

Significant components of the Company's deferred tax assets and liabilities at fiscal year-ends were as follows:

(In millions)	1998	1997
Deferred tax assets		
Accrued compensation and benefits	$ 117	$ 76
Deferred income	181	200
Inventory valuation and related reserves	106	163
Interest and taxes	52	49
Other, net	162	188
	618	676
Deferred tax liabilities		
Depreciation	(911)	(882)
Unremitted earnings of certain subsidiaries	(152)	(162)
Unrealized gain on investments	(324)	(32)
	(1,387)	(1,076)
Net deferred tax (liability)	**$ (769)**	**$ (400)**

U.S. income taxes were not provided for on a cumulative total of approximately $2.2 billion of undistributed earnings for certain non-U.S. subsidiaries. The Company intends to reinvest these earnings indefinitely in operations outside the United States.

During 1998, the Company settled all tax and related interest for years 1991 through 1996 with the Internal Revenue Service ("IRS"). The settlement did not result in a material effect on the Company's 1998 financial statements. Years after 1996 are open to examination by the IRS. Management believes that adequate amounts of tax and related interest and penalties, if any, have been provided for any adjustments that may result for these years.

Employee benefit plans

Stock option plans. Intel has a stock option plan under which officers, key employees and non-employee directors may be granted options to purchase shares of the Company's authorized but unissued Common Stock. The Company also has a stock option plan under which stock options may be granted to employees other than officers and directors. The Company's Executive Long-Term Stock Option Plan, under which certain key employees, including officers, have been granted stock options, terminated in September 1998. Although this termination will not affect options granted prior to this date, no further grants may be made under this plan. Under all of the plans, the option exercise price is equal to the fair market value of Intel Common Stock at the date of grant.

Options currently expire no later than 10 years from the grant date, and generally vest within 5 years. Proceeds received by the Company from exercises are credited to Common Stock and capital in excess of par value. Additional information with respect to stock option plan activity is as follows:

		Outstanding options	
(In millions)	Shares available for options	Number of shares	Weighted average exercise price
December 30, 1995	**173.8**	**342.0**	**$ 5.30**
Grants	(53.4)	53.4	$ 17.28
Exercises	—	(47.4)	$ 2.47
Cancellations	10.2	(10.2)	$ 8.53
December 28, 1996	**130.6**	**337.8**	**$ 7.49**
Additional shares reserved	260.0	—	—
Grants	(63.0)	63.0	$ 36.23
Exercises	—	(47.2)	$ 3.06
Cancellations	8.8	(8.8)	$ 16.38
December 27, 1997	**336.4**	**344.8**	**$ 13.12**
Grants	(48.0)	48.0	$ 38.35
Exercises	—	(63.0)	$ 4.59
Cancellations	17.3	(17.3)	$ 23.64
Lapsed under terminated plans	(38.5)	—	—
December 26, 1998	**267.2**	**312.5**	**$ 18.13**
Options exercisable at:			
December 28, 1996		114.5	$ 2.86
December 27, 1997		115.2	$ 3.66
December 26, 1998		103.8	$ 6.11

The range of option exercise prices for options outstanding at December 26, 1998 was $1.46 to $60.80. The range of exercise prices for options is wide, primarily due to the increasing price of the Company's stock over the period in which the option grants were awarded.

Notes to consolidated financial statements

The following tables summarize information about options outstanding at December 26, 1998:

	Outstanding options		
Range of exercise prices	Number of shares (in millions)	Weighted average contract-ual life (in years)	Weighted average exercise price
$1.46–$5.55	55.8	2.2	$ 2.83
$5.62–$11.10	70.2	4.9	$ 7.18
$11.42–$34.75	89.2	6.9	$ 15.16
$34.85–$60.80	97.3	8.8	$ 37.51
Total	**312.5**	**6.2**	**$ 18.13**

	Exercisable options	
Range of exercise prices	Number of shares (in millions)	Weighted average exercise price
$1.46–$5.55	55.8	$ 2.83
$5.62–$11.10	37.6	$ 6.16
$11.42–$34.75	7.0	$ 16.82
$34.85–$60.80	3.4	$ 37.53
Total	**103.8**	**$ 6.11**

These options will expire if not exercised at specific dates ranging from January 1999 to December 2008. Option exercise prices for options exercised during the three-year period ended December 26, 1998 ranged from $0.78 to $48.97.

Stock Participation Plan. Under this plan, eligible employees may purchase shares of Intel's Common Stock at 85% of fair market value at specific, predetermined dates. Of the 472 million shares authorized to be issued under the plan, 79.7 million shares remained available for issuance at December 26, 1998. Employees purchased 6.3 million shares in 1998 (9 million in 1997 and 14 million in 1996) for $229 million ($191 million and $140 million in 1997 and 1996, respectively).

Pro forma information. The Company has elected to follow APB Opinion No. 25, "Accounting for Stock Issued to Employees," in accounting for its employee stock options because, as discussed below, the alternative fair value accounting provided for under SFAS No. 123, "Accounting for Stock-Based Compensation," requires the use of option valuation models that were not developed for use in valuing employee stock options. Under APB No. 25, because the exercise price of the Company's employee stock options equals the market price of the underlying stock on the date of grant, no compensation expense is recognized in the Company's financial statements.

Pro forma information regarding net income and earnings per share is required by SFAS No. 123. This information is required to be determined as if the Company had accounted for its employee stock options (including shares issued under the Stock Participation Plan, collectively called "options") granted subsequent to December 31, 1994 under the fair value method of that statement. The fair value of options granted in 1998, 1997 and 1996 reported below has been estimated at the date of grant using a Black-Scholes option pricing model with the following weighted average assumptions:

Employee stock options	1998	1997	1996
Expected life (in years)	6.5	6.5	6.5
Risk-free interest rate	5.3%	6.6%	6.5%
Volatility	.36	.36	.36
Dividend yield	.2%	.1%	.2%

Stock Participation Plan shares	1998	1997	1996
Expected life (in years)	.5	.5	.5
Risk-free interest rate	5.2%	5.3%	5.3%
Volatility	.42	.40	.36
Dividend yield	.2%	.1%	.2%

The Black-Scholes option valuation model was developed for use in estimating the fair value of traded options that have no vesting restrictions and are fully transferable. In addition, option valuation models require the input of highly subjective assumptions, including the expected stock price volatility. Because the Company's options have characteristics significantly different from those of traded options, and because changes in the subjective input assumptions can materially affect the fair value estimate, in the opinion of management, the existing models do not necessarily provide a reliable single measure of the fair value of its options. The weighted average estimated fair value of employee stock options granted during 1998, 1997 and 1996 was $17.91, $17.67 and $8.17 per share, respectively. The weighted average estimated fair value of shares granted under the Stock Participation Plan during 1998, 1997 and 1996 was $10.92, $11.04 and $4.05, respectively.

For purposes of pro forma disclosures, the estimated fair value of the options is amortized to expense over the options' vesting periods. The Company's pro forma information follows (in millions except for earnings per share information):

	1998	1997	1996
Pro forma net income	$ 5,755	$ 6,735	$ 5,046
Pro forma basic earnings per share	$ 1.73	$ 2.06	$ 1.53
Pro forma diluted earnings per share	$ 1.66	$ 1.88	$ 1.42

Notes to consolidated financial statements

The effects on pro forma disclosures of applying SFAS No. 123 are not likely to be representative of the effects on pro forma disclosures of future years. Because SFAS No. 123 is applicable only to options granted subsequent to December 31, 1994, the pro forma effect will not be fully reflected until 1999.

Retirement plans. The Company provides tax-qualified profit-sharing retirement plans (the "Qualified Plans") for the benefit of eligible employees in the U.S. and Puerto Rico and certain foreign countries. The plans are designed to provide employees with an accumulation of funds for retirement on a tax-deferred basis and provide for annual discretionary employer contributions to trust funds.

The Company also provides a non-qualified profit-sharing retirement plan (the "Non-Qualified Plan") for the benefit of eligible employees in the U.S. This plan is designed to permit certain discretionary employer contributions in excess of the tax limits applicable to the Qualified Plans and to permit employee deferrals in excess of certain tax limits. This plan is unfunded.

The Company accrued $291 million for the Qualified Plans and the Non-Qualified Plan in 1998 ($273 million in 1997 and $209 million in 1996). The Company expects to fund approximately $283 million for the 1998 contribution to the Qualified Plans and to allocate approximately $13 million for the Non-Qualified Plan, including the utilization of amounts accrued in prior years. A remaining accrual of approximately $205 million carried forward from prior years is expected to be contributed to these plans when allowable under IRS regulations and plan rules.

Contributions made by the Company vest based on the employee's years of service. Vesting begins after three years of service in 20% annual increments until the employee is 100% vested after seven years.

The Company provides tax-qualified defined-benefit pension plans for the benefit of eligible employees in the U.S. and Puerto Rico. Each plan provides for minimum pension benefits that are determined by a participant's years of service, final average compensation (taking into account the participant's social security wage base) and the value of the Company's contributions, plus earnings, in the Qualified Plan. If the participant's balance in the Qualified Plan exceeds the pension guarantee, the participant will receive benefits from the Qualified Plan only. Intel's funding policy is consistent with the funding requirements of federal laws and regulations. The Company also provides defined-benefit pension plans in certain foreign countries. The Company's funding policy for foreign defined-benefit pension plans is consistent with the local requirements in each country. These defined-benefit pension plans had no material impact on the Company's financial statements for the periods presented.

The Company provides postemployment benefits for retired employees in the U.S. Upon retirement, eligible employees are credited with a defined dollar amount based on years of service. These credits can be used to pay all or a portion of the cost to purchase coverage in an Intel-sponsored medical plan. These benefits had no material impact on the Company's financial statements for the periods presented.

Acquisitions

In May 1998, the Company purchased the semiconductor operations of Digital Equipment Corporation, including manufacturing facilities in Massachusetts as well as development operations in Israel and Texas. The original cash purchase price of $625 million was adjusted to $585 million as a result of revisions to the valuations of certain capital assets as contemplated in the original purchase agreement. The purchase price remains subject to adjustment for asset valuation in accordance with the agreement. Assets acquired consisted primarily of property, plant and equipment. Following the completion of the purchase, lawsuits between the companies that had been pending since 1997 were dismissed with prejudice.

In January 1998, the Company acquired the outstanding shares of Chips and Technologies, Inc., a supplier of graphics accelerator chips for mobile computing products. The purchase price was approximately $430 million ($321 million in net cash). The Company recorded a non-deductible charge of $165 million for purchased in-process research and development, representing the appraised value of products still in the development stage that were not considered to have reached technological feasibility.

Commitments

The Company leases a portion of its capital equipment and certain of its facilities under operating leases that expire at various dates through 2010. Rental expense was $64 million in 1998, $69 million in 1997 and $57 million in 1996. Minimum rental commitments under all non-cancelable leases with an initial term in excess of one year are payable as follows: 1999–$35 million; 2000–$28 million; 2001–$22 million; 2002–$20 million; 2003–$15 million; 2004 and beyond–$22 million. Commitments for construction or purchase of property, plant and equipment approximated $2.1 billion at December 26, 1998. In connection with certain manufacturing arrangements, Intel had minimum purchase commitments of approximately $83 million at December 26, 1998 for flash memory.

In October 1998, Intel announced that it had entered into a definitive agreement to acquire Shiva Corporation ("Shiva"), whose products include remote access and virtual private networking solutions for the small to medium enterprise market segment and the remote access needs of campuses and branch offices. Intel expects that the total cash required to complete the transaction will be approximately $185 million, before consideration of any cash to be acquired.

Notes to consolidated financial statements

Contingencies

In November 1997, Intergraph Corporation ("Intergraph") filed suit in Federal District Court in Alabama generally alleging that Intel attempted to coerce Intergraph into relinquishing certain patent rights. The suit initially alleged that Intel infringes three Intergraph microprocessor-related patents and has been amended to add two other patents. The suit also includes alleged violations of antitrust laws and various state law claims. The suit seeks injunctive relief and unspecified damages. Intel has counterclaimed that the Intergraph patents are invalid and alleges infringement of seven Intel patents, breach of contract and misappropriation of trade secrets. In April 1998, the Court ordered Intel to continue to deal with Intergraph on the same terms as it treats allegedly similarly situated customers with respect to confidential information and product supply. Intel's appeal of this order was heard in December 1998. In June 1998, Intel filed a motion for summary judgment on Intergraph's patent claims on the grounds that Intel is licensed to use those patents. In July 1998, the Company received a letter stating that Intergraph believes that the patent damages will be "several billion dollars by the time of trial." In addition, Intergraph alleges that Intel's infringement is willful and that any damages awarded should be trebled. The letter also stated that Intergraph believes that antitrust, unfair competition and tort and contract damages will be "hundreds of millions of dollars by the time of trial." The Company disputes Intergraph's claims and intends to defend the lawsuit vigorously.

The Company is currently party to various legal proceedings, including that noted above. While management, including internal counsel, currently believes that the ultimate outcome of these proceedings, individually and in the aggregate, will not have a material adverse effect on the Company's financial position or overall trends in results of operations, litigation is subject to inherent uncertainties. Were an unfavorable ruling to occur, there exists the possibility of a material adverse impact on the net income of the period in which the ruling occurs.

Intel has been named to the California and U.S. Superfund lists for three of its sites and has completed, along with two other companies, a Remedial Investigation/Feasibility study with the U.S. Environmental Protection Agency ("EPA") to evaluate the groundwater in areas adjacent to one of its former sites. The EPA has issued a Record of Decision with respect to a groundwater cleanup plan at that site, including expected costs to complete. Under the California and U.S. Superfund statutes, liability for cleanup of this site and the adjacent area is joint and several. The Company, however, has reached agreement with those same two companies which significantly limits the Company's liabilities under the proposed cleanup plan. Also, the Company has completed extensive studies at its other sites and is engaged in cleanup at several of these sites. In the opinion of management, including internal counsel, the potential losses to the Company in excess of amounts already accrued arising out of these matters would not have a material adverse effect on the Company's financial position or overall trends in results of operations, even if joint and several liability were to be assessed.

The estimate of the potential impact on the Company's financial position or overall results of operations for the above legal proceedings could change in the future.

Operating segment and geographic information

Intel adopted SFAS No. 131, "Disclosures about Segments of an Enterprise and Related Information," in 1998. SFAS No. 131 establishes standards for reporting information about operating segments and related disclosures about products, geographic information and major customers. Operating segment information for 1997 and 1996 is also presented in accordance with SFAS No. 131.

Intel designs, develops, manufactures and markets microcomputer components and related products at various levels of integration. The Company is organized into four product line operating segments: Intel Architecture Business Group, Computing Enhancement Group, Network Communications Group and New Business Group. Each of these groups has a vice president who reports directly to the Chief Executive Officer ("CEO"). The CEO allocates resources to each of these groups using information on their revenues and operating profits before interest and taxes. The CEO has been identified as the Chief Operating Decision Maker as defined by SFAS No. 131.

The Intel Architecture Business Group's products include the Pentium® family of microprocessors, and microprocessors and related board-level products based on the P6 microarchitecture (including the Pentium® II processor, the Intel® Celeron™ processor and the Pentium® II Xeon™ processor). Sales of microprocessors and related board-level products based on the P6 microarchitecture represented a majority of the Company's 1998 revenues and a substantial majority of its 1998 gross margin. The Computing Enhancement Group's

Notes to consolidated financial statements

products include chipsets, embedded processors (including embedded Pentium® processors), microcontrollers, flash memory products and graphics products. The Network Communications Group's products include fast Ethernet connections, hubs, switches and routers. The New Business Group's products include systems management software, digital imaging products, and video and data conferencing products. Intel's products in all operating groups are sold directly to original equipment manufacturers, retail and industrial distributors, and resellers throughout the world.

In addition to the aforementioned operating segments, the sales and marketing, manufacturing, finance and administration groups also report to the CEO. Expenses of these groups are allocated to the operating segments and are included in the operating results reported below. Certain corporate-level operating expenses (primarily profit-dependent bonus expenses) and reserves for deferred income on shipments to distributors are not allocated to operating segments and are included in "all other" in the reconciliation of operating profits reported below.

Although the Company has four operating segments, only the Intel Architecture Business Group and Computing Enhancement Group are reportable segments under the criteria of SFAS No. 131. Intel does not identify or allocate assets or depreciation by operating segment, nor does the CEO evaluate groups on these criteria. Operating segments do not sell products to each other, and accordingly, there are no intersegment revenues to be reported. Intel does not allocate interest and other income, interest expense or taxes to operating segments. The accounting policies for segment reporting are the same as for the Company as a whole (see "Accounting policies").

Information on reportable segments for the three years ended December 26, 1998 is as follows:

(In millions)	1998	1997	1996
Intel Architecture Business Group			
Revenues	$21,545	$20,782	$17,000
Operating profit	$ 9,077	$10,659	$ 7,666
Computing Enhancement Group			
Revenues	$ 4,047	$ 3,793	$ 3,622
Operating profit	$ 358	$ 529	$ 940
All other			
Revenues	$ 681	$ 495	$ 225
Operating (loss)	$ (1,056)	$ (1,301)	$ (1,053)
Total			
Revenues	$26,273	$25,070	$20,847
Operating profit	$ 8,379	$ 9,887	$ 7,553

In 1998, one customer accounted for 13% of the Company's revenues and another customer accounted for 11%. In 1997, one customer accounted for 12% of the Company's revenues. In 1996, no customer exceeded 10% of the Company's revenues. A substantial majority of the sales to these customers were Intel Architecture Business Group products, but these customers also purchased Computing Enhancement Group products.

Enterprise-wide information is provided in accordance with SFAS No. 131. Geographic revenue information for the three years ended December 26, 1998 is based on the location of the selling entity. Property, plant and equipment information is based on the physical location of the assets at the end of each of the fiscal years.

Revenues from unaffiliated customers by geographic region were as follows:

(In millions)	1998	1997	1996
United States	$11,663	$11,053	$ 8,668
Europe	7,452	6,774	5,876
Asia-Pacific	5,309	4,754	3,844
Japan	1,849	2,489	2,459
Total revenues	**$26,273**	**$25,070**	**$20,847**

Net property, plant and equipment by country was as follows:

(In millions)	1998	1997
United States	$ 8,076	$ 8,022
Ireland	1,287	919
Other foreign countries	2,246	1,725
Total property, plant and equipment, net	**$11,609**	**$10,666**

Management's discussion and analysis
of financial condition and results of operations

Results of operations

Intel posted record net revenues in 1998, for the 12th consecutive year, increasing by 5% from 1997, and by 20% from 1996 to 1997. The increases in both periods were primarily due to higher revenues from sales of microprocessors by the Intel Architecture Business Group and to a lesser extent due to increases in revenues of the Computing Enhancement Group.

Cost of sales increased by 22% from 1997 to 1998, primarily due to microprocessor unit volume growth and additional costs associated with purchased components for the Single Edge Contact ("SEC") cartridge housing the Pentium® II processor. From 1996 to 1997, cost of sales increased by 8.5% primarily due to microprocessor unit volume growth, costs related to the 0.25-micron microprocessor manufacturing process ramp and shifts in product mix, partially offset by factory efficiencies due to the increased volumes. The gross margin percentage was 54% in 1998, compared to 60% in 1997 and 56% in 1996. See "Outlook" for a discussion of gross margin expectations.

Research and development spending grew by 14% from 1997 to 1998, primarily due to increased spending on development of microprocessor products and the charge for in-process research and development related to the acquisition of Chips and Technologies, Inc. (See the discussion about purchased in-process research and development under "Computing Enhancement Group segment.") Research and development spending increased 30% from 1996 to 1997 due to substantially increased investment in both microprocessor product development and manufacturing technology development.

Marketing, general and administrative spending grew 6% in 1998, primarily due to the Intel Inside® cooperative advertising program and merchandising spending, partially offset by lower profit-dependent bonus expenses. From 1996 to 1997, marketing, general and administrative spending grew 25%, primarily due to merchandising spending, the Intel Inside program and higher profit-dependent expenses.

Interest expense increased $7 million from 1997 to 1998 due to higher average borrowing balances and lower interest capitalization. Interest and other income was essentially unchanged for the same period, with higher gains on sales of equity securities and higher interest income offset by lower foreign currency gains. For 1997 compared to 1996, interest expense was essentially unchanged, and interest and other income increased by $393 million, primarily due to higher average investment balances and higher gains on sales of equity investments.

The Company's effective income tax rate decreased to 33.6% in 1998 from 34.8% in 1997 and 35.0% in 1996. Foreign income taxed at rates different from U.S. rates contributed to the lower tax rate in 1998.

Intel Architecture Business Group segment. Revenues increased 4% from 1997 to 1998, primarily due to higher volumes of microprocessors sold, particularly processors based on the P6 microarchitecture (including the Intel® Celeron,™

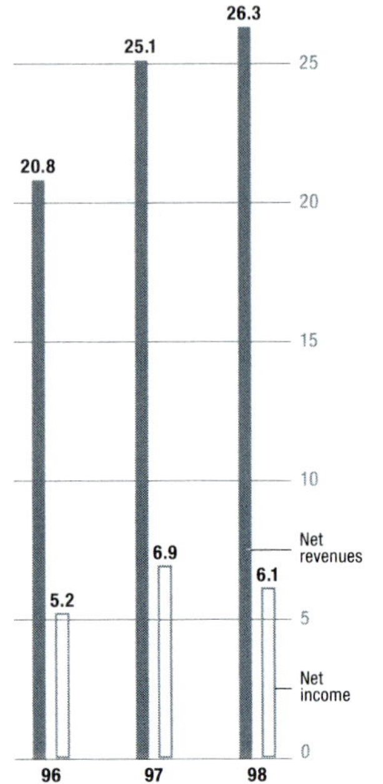

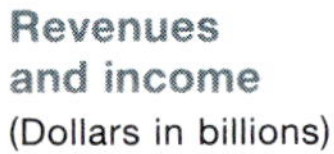
Revenues and income
(Dollars in billions)

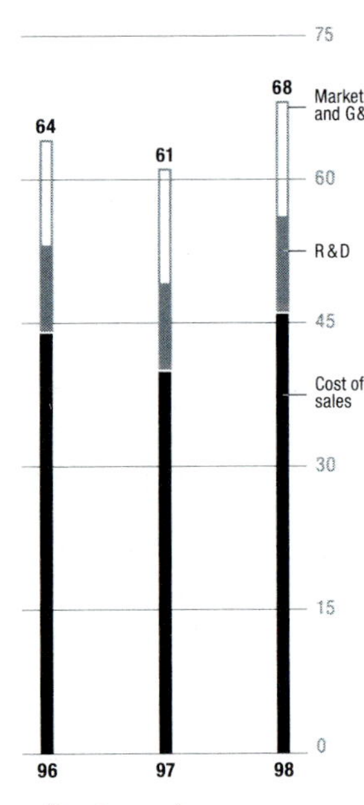

Costs and expenses
(Percent of revenues)

Pentium II, Pentium® Pro and Pentium® II Xeon™ processors). The higher volumes were partially offset by lower average selling prices. Revenues for this operating segment increased 22% from 1996 to 1997, primarily due to higher volumes of the Pentium® microprocessor family (including processors with Intel's MMX™ media enhancement technology) and Pentium Pro processor, and the introduction of the Pentium II processor, along with increased average selling prices in the first half of 1997 compared to the first half of 1996.

During 1998, sales of microprocessors and related board-level products based on the P6 microarchitecture comprised a majority of the Company's consolidated revenues and a substantial majority of its gross margin. Sales of these microprocessors first became a significant portion of the Company's revenues and gross margin in 1997. Also during 1998, sales of Pentium family processors, including Pentium processors with MMX technology, were a rapidly declining but still significant portion of the Company's revenues and gross margin. During 1997, sales of the Pentium family processors were a majority of the Company's revenues and gross margin, and in 1996 were a majority of its revenues and a substantial majority of its gross margin.

Operating profit for the Intel Architecture Business Group operating segment decreased 15% from 1997 to 1998, primarily due to the increased costs related to the SEC cartridge in the Pentium II processor and the lower average selling prices of processors in the first half of 1998 compared to the first half of 1997. In the second half of 1998, gross margin improved compared to the first half of the year as the transition to the P6 microarchitecture was largely complete and the SEC cartridge had no further incremental impact on the gross margin percentage. In addition, in the second half of 1998, this operating segment began to see the benefit of the Company's cost reduction efforts. Operating profit for the segment increased 39% from 1996 to 1997 due to the increase in processor unit volumes and higher average selling prices in the first half of 1997 arising from the ramp of the Pentium processor with MMX technology.

Computing Enhancement Group segment. Revenues increased 7% from 1997 to 1998 and 5% from 1996 to 1997. Revenues from sales of chipsets represented a majority of revenues for this operating segment only in 1998. Chipset revenues increased primarily due to higher average selling prices in 1998 compared to 1997, and primarily due to increased unit volumes from 1996 to 1997. These increases were partially offset in both periods by decreases in revenues from sales of flash memory and embedded processors.

Operating profits for the Computing Enhancement Group operating segment declined 32% from 1997 to 1998 and 44% from 1996 to 1997, primarily due to competitive pressures in flash memory products, partially offset by increased profitability of chipsets. In 1998, the results were also negatively affected by the purchase of Chips and Technologies, Inc. ("C&T"), including the related $165 million charge for purchased in-process research and development.

In the first quarter of 1998, the Company purchased C&T for a total price of approximately $430 million. C&T had a product line of mobile graphics controllers based on 2D and video graphics technologies, and their major development activities included new technologies for embedded memory and 3D graphics. Other development projects included improvements to the existing 2D and video technologies, and several other new business product lines, all of which were individually insignificant.

Intel obtained an outside valuation of C&T, and values were assigned to developed technology, in-process research and development, customer base and assembled workforce. The valuations of developed technology and in-process research and development were established using an income-based approach. Revenue estimates for each product line under development were based on discussions with management, existing product family revenues, anticipated product development schedules, product sales cycles and estimated life of each of the technologies. Revenue estimates were then compared for reasonableness to external industry sources on expected market growth. Percentages of product revenues for each project were designated as developed, in-process and future yet-to-be-defined. Revenues on the products under development were estimated to begin in 1998 and continue through 2006, with the majority of the revenues related to in-process technology occurring between 2001 and 2003. Operating expenses, including cost of goods sold, were estimated based primarily on C&T's historical experience. The resulting operating income was adjusted for a charge for the use of contributory assets and income tax expense using Intel's tax rate. The risk-adjusted discount rate applied to after-

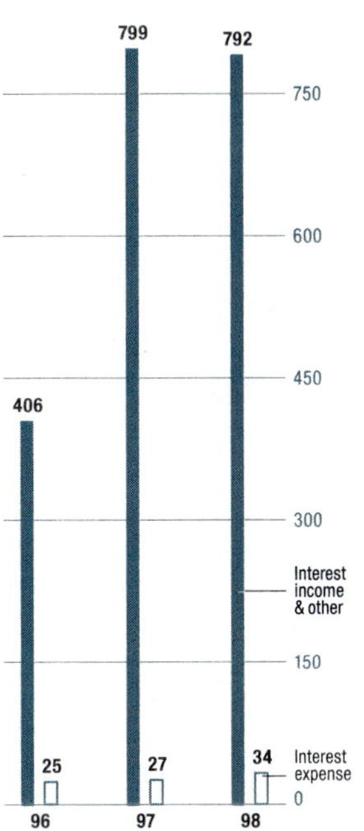

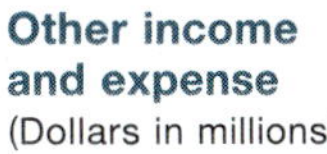
Other income and expense
(Dollars in millions)

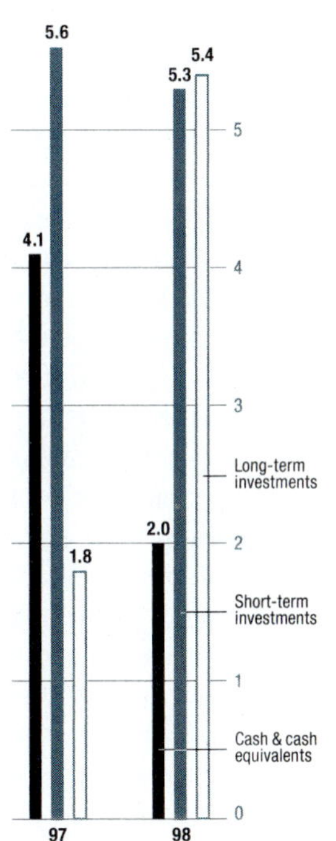

Cash and investments
(Dollars in billions)

tax cash flow was 15% for developed technology and 20% for in-process technology, compared to an estimated weighted-average cost of capital for C&T of approximately 10%.

The total value of in-process research and development was estimated to be approximately $165 million. Costs to complete all of the in-process projects were estimated to be $30 million. Approximately 70% of the estimated in-process research and development was attributable to the embedded memory technology and the 3D technology that were expected to be used together and separately in products under development. Development of the first in a series of mobile graphics products using the embedded memory technology was estimated to be approximately 80% complete and was completed in August 1998. The 3D technology was at an earlier stage of development with a minimal amount of work completed at the time of the acquisition. Close to the time of the acquisition, Intel also began working with another company to license their 3D technology for a line of desktop graphics controllers. Subsequent to the acquisition, a decision was made that the mobile and desktop product lines should have compatible 3D technology, and further development of the C&T 3D technology was stopped.

Financial condition

The Company's financial condition remains very strong. At December 26, 1998, total cash, trading assets, and short- and long-term investments totaled $13 billion, up from $11.8 billion at December 27, 1997. Cash provided by operating activities was $9.2 billion in 1998, compared to $10 billion and $8.7 billion in 1997 and 1996, respectively.

The Company used $6.5 billion in cash for investing activities during 1998, compared to $6.9 billion during 1997 and $5.3 billion during 1996. Capital expenditures totaled $3.6 billion in 1998, as the Company continued to invest in property, plant and equipment, primarily for additional microprocessor manufacturing capacity and the transition of manufacturing technology. The Company also purchased the semiconductor manufacturing operations of Digital Equipment Corporation for $585 million, including $475 million in capital assets. The Company had committed approximately $2.1 billion for the purchase or construction of property, plant and equipment as of December 26, 1998. See "Outlook" for a discussion of capital expenditure expectations in 1999. In addition, during 1998 the Company used $321 million in cash to purchase C&T and $500 million to acquire a non-voting equity interest in Micron Technology, Inc.

Inventory levels in total decreased in 1998, with a decrease in raw materials and work-in-process inventory, partially offset by an increase in finished goods inventory. The increase in accounts receivable in 1998 was mainly due to the higher level of revenues. The Company's five largest customers accounted for approximately 42% of net revenues for 1998. One customer accounted for 13% of revenues and another accounted for 11% in 1998. One customer accounted for 12% of revenues in 1997 and no customer accounted for more than 10% of revenues in 1996. At December 26, 1998, the five largest customers accounted for approximately 39% of net accounts receivable.

The Company used $4.7 billion for financing activities in 1998, compared to $3.2 billion and $773 million in 1997 and 1996, respectively. The major financing applications of cash in 1998 were for repurchase of 161.7 million shares of Common Stock, adjusted for the stock split declared in January 1999, for $6.8 billion (including $1.2 billion for exercised put warrants). The major financing applications of cash in 1997 and 1996 were for stock repurchases totaling $3.4 billion and $1.3 billion (including $108 million for exercised put warrants), respectively, as well as for a $300 million repayment in 1997 under a private reverse repurchase arrangement. Financing sources of cash during 1998 included $507 million in proceeds from the sale of shares, primarily pursuant to employee stock plans ($317 million in 1997 and $257 million in 1996) and $1.6 billion in proceeds from the exercise of 1998 Step-Up Warrants ($40 million in 1997 and $4 million in 1996). Financing sources in 1996 also included $300 million under the private reverse repurchase arrangement.

As part of its authorized stock repurchase program, the Company had outstanding put warrants at the end of 1998, with the potential obligation to buy back 5 million shares of its Common Stock at an aggregate price of $201 million. The exercise price of these warrants ranged from $40 to $41 per share, with an average exercise price of $40 per share as of December 26, 1998.

Other sources of liquidity include authorized commercial paper borrowings of $700 million. The Company also maintains the ability to issue an aggregate of approximately $1.4 billion in debt, equity and other securities under Securities and Exchange Commission shelf registration statements.

In October 1998, the Company announced that it had entered into a definitive agreement to acquire Shiva Corporation ("Shiva"). Intel expects that the total cash required to complete the transaction will be approximately $185 million, before consideration of any cash to be acquired.

The Company believes that it has the financial resources needed to meet business requirements in the foreseeable future, including the acquisition of Shiva, capital expenditures for the expansion or upgrading of worldwide manufacturing capacity, working capital requirements, the potential put warrant obligation and the dividend program.

Financial market risks

The Company is exposed to financial market risks, including changes in interest rates, foreign currency exchange rates and marketable equity security prices. To mitigate these risks, the Company utilizes derivative financial instruments. The Company does not use derivative financial instruments for speculative or trading purposes. All of the potential changes noted below are based on sensitivity analyses performed on the Company's financial positions at December 26, 1998 and December 27, 1997. Actual results may differ materially.

The primary objective of the Company's investment activities is to preserve principal while at the same time maximizing yields, without significantly increasing risk. To achieve this objective, the returns on a substantial majority of the Company's marketable investments in long-term fixed rate debt and certain equity securities, excluding equity investments entered into for strategic purposes, are swapped to U.S. dollar LIBOR-based returns. A hypothetical 60 basis point increase in interest rates would result in an approximate $30 million decrease (less than 0.3%) in the fair value of the Company's available-for-sale securities as of the end of 1998 ($18 million as of the end of 1997).

The Company hedges currency risks of investments denominated in foreign currencies with foreign currency borrowings, currency forward contracts and currency interest rate swaps. Gains and losses on these foreign currency investments would generally be offset by corresponding losses and gains on the related hedging instruments, resulting in negligible net exposure to the Company.

A substantial majority of the Company's revenue, expense and capital purchasing activities are transacted in U.S. dollars. However, the Company does enter into these transactions in other foreign currencies, primarily Japanese yen and certain other Asian and European currencies. To protect against reductions in value and the volatility of future cash flows caused by changes in foreign exchange rates, the Company has established revenue, expense and balance sheet hedging programs. Currency forward contracts and currency options are utilized in these hedging programs. The Company's hedging programs reduce, but do not always entirely eliminate, the impact of foreign currency exchange rate movements. For example, an adverse change in exchange rates (defined as 20% in certain Asian currencies and 10% in all other currencies) would result in an adverse impact on income before taxes of less than $20 million as of the end of each of 1998 and 1997.

The Company is exposed to equity price risks on the marketable portion of equity securities included in its portfolio of investments entered into for the promotion of business and strategic objectives. These investments are generally in companies in the high-technology industry sector, many of which are small capitalization stocks. The Company typically does not attempt to reduce or eliminate its market exposure on these securities. A 20% adverse change in equity prices would result in an approximate $350 million decrease in the fair value of the Company's available-for-sale securities as of the end of 1998 ($75 million as of the end of 1997). The increase compared to 1997 reflects the increase in the dollar value of the Company's marketable strategic equity securities, a significant portion of which represents unrealized market appreciation. Approximately $825 million of the value of these equity securities as of the end of 1998 consisted of the investment in Micron Technology, Inc., described above under "Financial condition."

Outlook

This outlook section contains a number of forward-looking statements, all of which are based on current expectations. Actual results may differ materially. These statements do not reflect the potential impact of any mergers or acquisitions that had not closed as of the end of 1998.

Intel expects that the total number of computers using Intel's Pentium family processors, P6 microarchitecture processors (including Intel Celeron, Pentium II, Pentium® III, Pentium II Xeon and Pentium® III Xeon™ processors) and other semiconductor components sold worldwide will continue to grow in 1999. The Company's financial results are substantially dependent on sales of these microprocessors by the Intel Architecture Business Group and other semiconductor components sold by the Computing Enhancement Group. Revenues are also a function of the mix of microprocessor types and speeds sold as well as the mix of related motherboards, purchased components and other semiconductor products, all of which are difficult to forecast. Because of the large price difference between types of microprocessors, this mix affects the average price Intel will realize and has a large impact on Intel's revenues. The Company's expectations regarding growth in the computing industry worldwide are dependent in part on the growth in usage of the Internet and the expansion of Internet product offerings. The expectations are also subject to the impact of economic conditions in various geographic regions, including the ongoing financial difficulties in the Asian markets and certain emerging markets in other regions.

Intel's strategy is to introduce ever higher performance microprocessors tailored for the different segments of the worldwide computing market, using a tiered branding approach. In line with this strategy, the Company is seeking to develop higher performance microprocessors specifically for each computing segment: the Intel Celeron processor for entry-level PC buyers interested in a value PC, the Pentium II and Pentium III processors for the performance desktop and entry-level servers and workstations, and the Pentium II Xeon and Pentium III Xeon processors for mid-range and high-end servers and workstations. The Company plans to cultivate new businesses and continue to work with the computing industry to expand Internet capabilities and product offerings and to develop compelling software applications that can take advantage of this higher performance, thus driving demand toward the newer products in each computing market segment. The Company may continue to take various steps, including reducing microprocessor prices at such times as it deems appropriate, in order to increase acceptance of its latest technology and to remain competitive within each relevant market segment.

The Company's gross margin varies depending on the mix of types and speeds of processors sold and the mix of microprocessors and related motherboards and purchased components within a product family. The Company's Pentium II processor is packaged with purchased components in the SEC cartridge, and the inclusion of purchased components has tended to increase absolute margin dollars but to lower the gross margin percentage. However, the Company has also been developing new packaging formats that use fewer purchased components. These new packaging formats are expected to reduce costs on certain microprocessor products. In addition, the Company expects to have reduced costs due to continued productivity improvements on its existing manufacturing processes during 1999. Various other factors—including unit volumes, yield issues associated with production at factories, ramp of new technologies, excess or obsolete inventory, variations in inventory valuation and mix of shipments of other semiconductors—will also continue to affect the amount of cost of sales and the variability of gross margin percentages in future quarters.

Intel's current gross margin expectation for 1999 is 57% plus or minus a few points compared to 54% for 1998. Intel's primary goal is to get its advanced technology to the marketplace, and the Company sometimes may implement strategies that increase margin dollars but lower margin percentages, for example, the Company's plans to grow in non-microprocessor areas that have the potential to expand computing and communications capabilities. In addition, from time to time the Company may forecast a range of gross margin percentages for the coming quarter. Actual results may differ from these estimates.

The Company has expanded semiconductor manufacturing and assembly and test capacity over the last few years, and continues to plan capacity based on the assumed continued success of its strategy and the acceptance of its products in specific market segments. The Company expects that capital spending will decrease to approximately $3 billion in 1999, primarily as a result of reduced investment for new facilities and improved utilization of equipment. If the market demand does not continue to grow and move rapidly toward higher performance products in the various market segments, revenues and gross margin may be affected, the capacity installed might be under-utilized and capital spending may be slowed. Revenues and gross margin may also be affected if the Company does not add capacity fast enough to meet market demand. This spending plan is dependent upon expectations regarding production efficiencies and delivery times of various machinery and equipment. Depreciation and amortization for 1999 is expected to be approximately $3.4 billion, an increase of approximately $600 million from 1998. Most of this increase would be included in cost of sales and research and development spending.

The industry in which Intel operates is characterized by very short product life cycles, and the Company's continued success is dependent on technological advances, including the development and implementation of new processes and new strategic products for specific market segments. Since Intel considers it imperative to maintain a strong research and development program, spending for research and development in 1999 is expected to increase to approximately $3 billion. The Company intends to continue spending to promote its products and to increase the value of its product brands. Based on current forecasts, spending for marketing, general and administrative expenses is also expected to increase in 1999.

The Company currently expects its tax rate to be 33.5% for 1999. This estimate is based on current tax law and the current estimate of earnings, and is subject to change.

Intel has established a team to address the issues raised by the introduction of the Single European Currency ("Euro") on January 1, 1999 and during the transition period through January 1, 2002. Intel's internal systems that are affected by the initial introduction of the Euro have been made Euro capable without material system modification costs. Further internal systems changes will be made during the three-year transition phase in preparation for the ultimate withdrawal of the legacy currencies in July 2002, and the costs of these changes are not expected to be material. The Company does not presently expect that introduction and use of the Euro will materially affect the Company's foreign exchange and hedging activities, or the Company's use of derivative instruments, or will result in any material increase in costs to the Company. While Intel will continue to evaluate the impact of the Euro introduction over time, based on currently available information, management does not believe that the introduction of the Euro will have a material adverse impact on the Company's financial condition or overall trends in results of operations.

Like many other companies, Intel is subject to risks from the year 2000 computer issue. If internal systems do not correctly recognize and process date information beyond the year 1999, there could be an adverse impact on the Company's operations. Two other related issues could also lead to incorrect calculations or failures: i) some systems' programming assigns special meaning to certain dates, such as 9/9/99 and ii) the fact that the year 2000 is a leap year.

The Company has established a comprehensive program with dedicated program management and executive-level sponsorship to deal with year 2000 issues. The Company is addressing its most critical internal systems first and has categorized as "critical" or "priority" those systems whose failure would cause an extended shutdown of all or part of a factory, could cause personal injury or would have a sustained and significant detrimental financial impact. The Company is also testing customer and supplier interfaces with its internal systems as appropriate. These activities are intended to encompass all major categories of systems in use by the Company, including network and communications infrastructure, manufacturing, facilities management, sales, finance and human resources. The Company's approach prioritizes functions and systems worldwide, and all divisions and facilities are working toward the same global milestones.

The Company's semiconductor manufacturing and assembly and test ("manufacturing") equipment and systems are highly automated, incorporating PCs, embedded processors and related software to control scheduling, inventory tracking, statistical analysis and automated manufacturing. A significant portion of the Company's year 2000 efforts on internal systems is intended to prevent disruption to manufacturing operations.

As of December 1998, approximately 99% of the Company's critical and priority manufacturing systems, and 85% of critical and priority non-manufacturing systems, were determined to be already year 2000 capable, or remediation needed (replacements, changes, upgrades or workarounds) has been determined and unit testing completed. Deployment of replacements, changes and upgrades has been completed for 93% of manufacturing systems and 84% of non-manufacturing systems. The Company has planned a comprehensive program of integration testing of internal systems. The integration testing began in the third quarter of 1998 and will continue into 1999 as necessary.

The following table indicates the phases of the year 2000 project related to the Company's critical and priority internal systems and the expected time frames.

Phases of the project	Start date	End date
High-level assessment of systems	1996	Q3 1998 (actual)
Detailed assessment, remediation and unit testing	1996	Q1 1999 (expected)
Deployment	1997	Mid-1999 (expected)
Integration testing	Q3 1998	Mid-1999 (expected)

Intel is also actively working with suppliers of products and services to determine the extent to which the suppliers' operations and the products and services they provide are year 2000 capable, and to monitor their progress toward year 2000 capability. Highest priority is being placed on working with critical suppliers, defined by Intel as those whose failure would shut down manufacturing or other critical operations within a short period of time. The Company has made inquiries of its major suppliers and has received responses to its initial inquiries from 100% of critical suppliers.

Follow-up activities seek to determine whether the supplier is taking all appropriate steps to fix year 2000 problems and to be prepared to continue functioning effectively as a supplier in accordance with Intel's standards and requirements. Contingency plans are being developed to address issues related to suppliers that are not considered to be making sufficient progress in becoming year 2000 capable.

The Company is also developing contingency plans to address possible changes in customer order patterns due to year 2000 issues. As with suppliers, the readiness of customers to deal with year 2000 issues may affect their operations and their ability to order and pay for products. Intel has surveyed its major direct customers about their year 2000 readiness in critical areas of their operations. The results identified certain key areas to be addressed by the customers. Intel is also communicating information about its own readiness to customers and is conducting seminars to help communicate the methodologies and processes used in Intel's year 2000 programs.

Intel believes that its most reasonably likely worst-case year 2000 scenarios would relate to problems with the systems of third parties rather than with the Company's internal systems or its products. Because the Company has less control over assessing and remediating the year 2000 problems of third parties, the Company believes the risks are greatest with infrastructure (e.g., electricity supply and water and sewer service), telecommunications, transportation supply chains and critical suppliers of materials.

The Company's microprocessor production is conducted in a network of domestic and foreign facilities. Each location relies on local private and governmental suppliers for electricity, water, sewer and other needed supplies. Failure of an electricity grid or an uneven supply of power, for example, would be a worst-case scenario that would completely shut down the affected facilities. Electrical failure could also shut down airports and other transportation facilities.

The Company does not generally maintain facilities that would allow it to generate its own electrical or water supply in lieu of that supplied by utilities. To the extent possible, the Company is working with the infrastructure suppliers for its manufacturing sites, major subcontractor sites and relevant transportation hubs to seek to better ensure continuity of infrastructure services. Contingency planning regarding major infrastructure failure generally emphasizes planned increases in inventory levels of specific products and the shift of production to unaffected sites. By the end of 1999, Intel expects to have in place a buffer supply of finished goods inventory and is evaluating where to locate inventory geographically in light of infrastructure concerns. In addition, multiple plants engage in similar tasks in the Intel system, and production can be expanded at some sites to partially make up for capacity unavailable elsewhere. Although overall capacity would be reduced, it is not expected that the entire production system would halt due to the unavailability of one or two facilities.

A worst-case scenario involving a critical supplier of materials would be the partial or complete shutdown of the supplier and its resulting inability to provide critical supplies to the Company on a timely basis. The Company does not maintain the capability to replace most third-party supplies with internal production. Where efforts to work with critical suppliers to ensure year 2000 capability have not been successful, contingency planning generally emphasizes the identification of substitute and second-source suppliers, and in certain situations includes a planned increase in the level of inventory carried. In an industry characterized by rapid technological change, higher levels of raw materials and finished goods inventories involve increased risk of inventory obsolescence and the potential for write-downs in the value of inventory.

The Company is not in a position to identify or to avoid all possible scenarios; however, the Company is currently assessing scenarios and taking steps to mitigate the impacts of various scenarios if they were to occur. This contingency planning will continue through 1999 as the Company learns more about the preparations and vulnerabilities of third parties regarding year 2000 issues. Due to the large number of variables involved, the Company cannot provide an estimate of the damage it might suffer if any of these scenarios were to occur.

The Company also has a program ... and other issues.

Intel believes that it has the product offerings, facilities, personnel, and competitive and financial resources for continued business success, but future revenues, costs, margins and profits are all influenced by a number of factors, including those discussed above, all of which are inherently difficult to forecast.

Financial information by quarter (unaudited)

intel®

(In millions—except per share amounts) 1998 for quarter ended		December 26	September 26	June 27	March 28
Net revenues		$ 7,614	$ 6,731	$ 5,927	$ 6,001
Cost of sales		$ 3,176	$ 3,192	$ 3,027	$ 2,749
Net income [(A)]		$ 2,064	$ 1,559	$ 1,172	$ 1,273
Basic earnings per share		$ .62	$ .46	$ .35	$ .39
Diluted earnings per share		$ .59	$ .44	$ .33	$ .36
Dividends per share [(B)]	Declared	$ —	$ .035	$ —	$ .015
	Paid	$ .020	$ .015	$ .015	$ .015
Market price range Common Stock [(C)]	High	$ 62.50	$ 45.72	$ 42.41	$ 47.09
	Low	$ 39.22	$ 35.59	$ 32.97	$ 35.13
Market price range Step-Up Warrants [(C)]	High	$ —	$ —	$ —	$ 36.56
	Low	$ —	$ —	$ —	$ 24.73

(In millions—except per share amounts) 1997 for quarter ended		December 27	September 27	June 28	March 29
Net revenues		$ 6,507	$ 6,155	$ 5,960	$ 6,448
Cost of sales		$ 2,691	$ 2,604	$ 2,343	$ 2,307
Net income		$ 1,743	$ 1,574	$ 1,645	$ 1,983
Basic earnings per share		$ 53	$ .48	$ .50	$ .61
Diluted earnings per share		$ .49	$ .44	$ .46	$ .55
Dividends per share [(B)]	Declared	$ .0150	$ .0150	$ .0150	$ .0125
	Paid	$ .0150	$ .0150	$ .0125	$ .0125
Market price range Common Stock [(C)]	High	$ 47.69	$ 50.25	$ 42.33	$ 41.19
	Low	$ 34.56	$ 34.77	$ 32.63	$ 32.59
Market price range Step-Up Warrants [(C)]	High	$ 37.34	$ 39.94	$ 32.08	$ 31.31
	Low	$ 24.19	$ 24.78	$ 22.66	$ 22.53

[(A)] *Net income for the first quarter of 1998 reflected a $165 million charge for purchased in-process research and development related to the acquisition of Chips and Technologies, Inc.*

[(B)] *As of the second quarter of 1998, the Company adopted a new dividend declaration schedule which results in the Board of Directors considering two dividend declarations in the first and third quarters of the year and no declarations in the second and fourth quarters. A dividend was paid in each quarter of 1998. Intel plans to continue its dividend program. However, dividends are dependent on future earnings, capital requirements and financial condition.*

[(C)] *Intel's Common Stock (symbol INTC) trades on The Nasdaq Stock Market* and is quoted in the* Wall Street Journal *and other newspapers. Intel's 1998 Step-Up Warrants traded on The Nasdaq Stock Market prior to their March 1998 expiration. Intel's Common Stock also trades on the The Swiss Exchange. At December 26, 1998, there were approximately 203,000 registered holders of Common Stock. All stock and warrant prices are closing prices per The Nasdaq Stock Market, as adjusted for stock splits.*

Note: All **asterisked** Questions, Exercises, Problems, and Conceptual Cases relate to material contained in the appendix to the chapter.

QUESTIONS

1 How does information from the balance sheet help users of the financial statements?

2 What is meant by solvency? What information in the balance sheet can be used to assess a company's solvency?

3 A recent financial magazine indicated that a drug company had good financial flexibility. What is meant by financial flexibility and why is it important?

4 Discuss at least two situations in which estimates could affect the usefulness of information in the balance sheet.

5 Jones Company reported an increase in inventories in the past year. Discuss the effect of this change on the current ratio. What does this tell a statement user about Jones Company's liquidity?

6 What is meant by liquidity? Rank the following assets from one to five in order of liquidity.

(a) Goodwill.
(b) Inventories.
(c) Buildings.
(d) Short-term investments.
(e) Accounts receivable.

7 What are the major limitations of the balance sheet as a source of information?

8 Discuss at least two items that are important to the value of companies like Intel or IBM but that are not recorded in their balance sheets. What are some reasons why these items are not recorded in the balance sheet?

9 How does separating current assets from property, plant, and equipment in the balance sheet help analysts?

10 In its December 31, 2002, balance sheet Oakley Corporation reported as an asset "Net notes and accounts receivable, $7,100,000." What other disclosures are necessary?

11 Should available-for-sale securities always be reported as a current asset? Explain.

12 What is the relationship between current assets and current liabilities?

13 The New York Knicks, Inc. sold 10,000 season tickets at $1,000 each. By December 31, 2002, 18 of the 40 home games had been played. What amount should be reported as a current liability at December 31, 2002?

14 What is working capital? How does working capital relate to the operating cycle?

15 In what section of the balance sheet should the following items appear, and what balance sheet terminology would you use?

(a) Treasury stock (recorded at cost, which is below par).
(b) Checking account at bank.
(c) Land (held as an investment).
(d) Reserve for sinking fund.
(e) Unamortized premium on bonds payable.
(f) Investment in copyrights.
(g) Employees' pension fund (consisting of cash and securities).
(h) Premium on capital stock.
(i) Long-term investments (pledged against bank loans payable).

16 Where should the following items be shown on the balance sheet, if shown at all?

(a) Allowance for doubtful accounts receivable.
(b) Merchandise held on consignment.
(c) Advances received on sales contract.
(d) Cash surrender value of life insurance.
(e) Land.
(f) Merchandise out on consignment.
(g) Pension fund on deposit with a trustee (under a trust revocable at depositor's option).
(h) Franchises.
(i) Accumulated depreciation of plant and equipment.
(j) Materials in transit—purchased f.o.b. destination.

17 State the generally accepted accounting principle (standard) applicable to the balance sheet valuation of each of the following assets.

(a) Trade accounts receivable.
(b) Land.
(c) Inventories.
(d) Trading securities (common stock of other companies).
(e) Prepaid expenses.

18 Refer to the definition of assets on page 191. Discuss how a leased building might qualify as an asset of the lessee under this definition.

19 Christine Agazzi says, "Retained earnings should be reported as an asset, since it is earnings which are reinvested in the business." How would you respond to Agazzi?

20 The creditors of Nick Anderson Company agree to accept promissory notes for the amount of its indebtedness with a proviso that two-thirds of the annual profits must be applied to their liquidation. How should these notes be reported on the balance sheet of the issuing company? Give a reason for your answer.

21 What are some of the techniques of disclosure for the balance sheet?

22 What is a "Summary of Significant Accounting Policies"?

23 What types of contractual obligations must be disclosed in great detail in the notes to the balance sheet? Why do you think these detailed provisions should be disclosed?

24 What is the profession's recommendation in regard to the use of the term "surplus"? Explain.

25 What is the purpose of a statement of cash flows? How does it differ from a balance sheet and an income statement?

26 The net income for the year for Won Long, Inc. is $750,000, but the statement of cash flows reports that the cash provided by operating activities is $640,000. What might account for the difference?

27 Net income for the year for Jenkins, Inc. was $750,000, but the statement of cash flows reports that cash provided by operating activities was $860,000. What might account for the difference?

28 Differentiate between operating activities, investing activities, and financing activities.

29 Each of the following items must be considered in preparing a statement of cash flows. Indicate where each item is to be reported in the statement, if at all. Assume that net income is reported as $90,000.

(a) Accounts receivable increased from $32,000 to $39,000 from the beginning to the end of the year.

(b) During the year, 10,000 shares of preferred stock with a par value of $100 a share were issued at $115 per share.

(c) Depreciation expense amounted to $14,000, and bond premium amortization amounted to $5,000.

(d) Land increased from $10,000 to $30,000.

30 Marker Co. has net cash provided by operating activities of $900,000. Its average current liabilities for the period are $1,000,000, and its average total liabilities are $1,500,000. Comment on the company's liquidity and financial flexibility, given this information.

31 Net income for the year for Hatfield, Inc. was $750,000, but the statement of cash flows reports that cash provided by operating activities was $860,000. Hatfield also reported capital expenditures of $75,000 and paid dividends in the amount of $20,000. Compute Hatfield's free cash flow.

32 What is the purpose of a free cash flow analysis?

BRIEF EXERCISES

BE5-1 La Bouche Corporation has the following accounts included in its 12/31/02 trial balance: Accounts Receivable $110,000; Inventories $290,000; Allowance for Doubtful Accounts $8,000; Patents $72,000; Prepaid Insurance $9,500; Accounts Payable $77,000; Cash $27,000. Prepare the current assets section of the balance sheet listing the accounts in proper sequence.

BE5-2 Included in Goo Goo Dolls Company's 12/31/02 trial balance are the following accounts: Prepaid Rent $5,200; Held-to-Maturity Securities $61,000; Unearned Fees $17,000; Land Held for Investment $39,000; Long-term Receivables $42,000. Prepare the long-term investments section of the balance sheet.

BE5-3 Adam Ant Company's 12/31/02 trial balance includes the following accounts: Inventories $120,000; Buildings $207,000; Accumulated Depreciation–Equipment $19,000; Equipment $190,000; Land Held for Investment $46,000; Accumulated Depreciation–Buildings $45,000; Land $61,000; Capital Leases $70,000. Prepare the property, plant, and equipment section of the balance sheet.

BE5-4 Mason Corporation has the following accounts included in its 12/31/02 trial balance: Trading Securities $21,000; Goodwill $150,000; Prepaid Insurance $12,000; Patents $220,000; Franchises $110,000. Prepare the intangible assets section of the balance sheet.

BE5-5 Included in Ewing Company's 12/31/02 trial balance are the following accounts: Accounts Payable $240,000; Obligations under Capital Leases $375,000; Discount on Bonds Payable $24,000; Advances from Customers $41,000; Bonds Payable $400,000; Wages Payable $27,000; Interest Payable $12,000; Income Taxes Payable $29,000. Prepare the current liabilities section of the balance sheet.

BE5-6 Use the information presented in BE5-5 for Ewing Company to prepare the long-term liabilities section of the balance sheet.

BE5-7 Young Company's 12/31/02 trial balance includes the following accounts: Investment in Common Stock $70,000; Retained Earnings $114,000; Trademarks $31,000; Preferred Stock $172,000; Common Stock $55,000; Deferred Income Taxes $88,000; Additional Paid-in Capital $174,000. Prepare the stockholders' equity section of the balance sheet.

BE5-8 Midwest Beverage Company reported the following items in the most recent year:

Net income	$40,000
Dividends paid	5,000
Increase in accounts receivable	10,000
Increase in accounts payable	5,000
Purchase of equipment (capital expenditure)	8,000
Depreciation expense	4,000
Issue of notes payable	20,000

Compute cash from operations, the net change in cash during the year, and free cash flow for Midwest.

BE5-9 Kes Company reported 2002 net income of $151,000. During 2002, accounts receivable increased by $13,000 and accounts payable increased by $9,500. Depreciation expense was $39,000. Prepare the cash flows from operating activities section of the statement of cash flows.

BE5-10 Yorkis Perez Corporation engaged in the following cash transactions during 2002:

Sale of land and building	$181,000
Purchase of treasury stock	40,000
Purchase of land	37,000
Payment of cash dividend	85,000
Purchase of equipment	53,000
Issuance of common stock	147,000
Retirement of bonds	100,000

Compute the net cash provided (used) by investing activities.

BE5-11 Use the information presented in BE5-10 for Yorkis Perez Corporation to compute the net cash used (provided) by financing activities.

BE5-12 Using the information in BE5-10, determine Yorkis Perez's free cash flow, assuming that it reported net cash provided by operating activities of $400,000.

EXERCISES

E5-1 (Balance Sheet Classifications) Presented below are a number of balance sheet accounts of Deep Blue Something, Inc.:

1. Investment in Preferred Stock
2. Treasury Stock
3. Common Stock Distributable
4. Cash Dividends Payable
5. Accumulated Depreciation
6. Warehouse in Process of Construction
7. Petty Cash
8. Accrued Interest on Notes Payable
9. Deficit
10. Trading Securities
11. Income Taxes Payable
12. Unearned Subscription Revenue
13. Work in Process
14. Accrued Vacation Pay

Instructions

For each of the accounts above, indicate the proper balance sheet classification. In the case of borderline items, indicate the additional information that would be required to determine the proper classification.

E5-2 (Classification of Balance Sheet Accounts) Presented below are the captions of Faulk Company's balance sheet:

A. Current Assets
B. Investments
C. Property, Plant, and Equipment
D. Intangible Assets
E. Other Assets
F. Current Liabilities
G. Noncurrent Liabilities
H. Capital Stock
I. Additional Paid-in Capital
J. Retained Earnings

Instructions

Indicate by letter where each of the following items would be classified:

1. Preferred stock
2. Goodwill
3. Wages payable
4. Trade accounts payable
5. Buildings
6. Trading securities
7. Current portion of long-term debt
8. Premium on bonds payable
9. Allowance for doubtful accounts
10. Accounts receivable
11. Cash surrender value of life insurance
12. Notes payable (due next year)
13. Office supplies
14. Common stock
15. Land
16. Bond sinking fund
17. Merchandise inventory
18. Prepaid insurance
19. Bonds payable
20. Taxes payable

E5-3 (Classification of Balance Sheet Accounts) Assume that Fielder Enterprises uses the following headings on its balance sheet:

A. Current Assets
B. Investments
C. Property, Plant, and Equipment
D. Intangible Assets
E. Other Assets
F. Current Liabilities
G. Long-term Liabilities
H. Capital Stock
I. Paid-in Capital in Excess of Par
J. Retained Earnings

Instructions

Indicate by letter how each of the following usually should be classified. If an item should appear in a note to the financial statements, use the letter "N" to indicate this fact. If an item need not be reported at all on the balance sheet, use the letter "X."

1. Unexpired insurance.
2. Stock owned in affiliated companies.
3. Unearned subscriptions.
4. Advances to suppliers.
5. Unearned rent.
6. Treasury stock.
7. Premium on preferred stock.
8. Copyrights.
9. Petty cash fund.
10. Sales tax payable.
11. Accrued interest on notes receivable.
12. Twenty-year issue of bonds payable which will mature within the next year. (No sinking fund exists, and refunding is not planned.)
13. Machinery retired from use and held for sale.
14. Fully depreciated machine still in use.
15. Organization costs.
16. Accrued interest on bonds payable.
17. Salaries that company budget shows will be paid to employees within the next year.
18. Discount on bonds payable. (Assume related to bonds payable in No. 12.)
19. Accumulated depreciation.

E5-4 (Preparation of a Classified Balance Sheet) Assume that Denis Savard Inc. has the following accounts at the end of the current year.

1. Common Stock
2. Discount on Bonds Payable
3. Treasury Stock (at cost)
4. Common Stock Subscribed
5. Raw Materials
6. Preferred Stock Investments—Long-term
7. Unearned Rent
8. Work in Process
9. Copyrights
10. Buildings
11. Notes Receivable (short-term)
12. Cash
13. Accrued Salaries Payable
14. Accumulated Depreciation—Buildings
15. Cash Restricted for Plant Expansion
16. Land Held for Future Plant Site
17. Allowance for Doubtful Accounts—Accounts Receivable
18. Retained Earnings—Unappropriated
19. Premium on Common Stock
20. Unearned Subscriptions
21. Receivables—Officers (due in one year)
22. Finished Goods
23. Accounts Receivable
24. Bonds Payable (due in 4 years)
25. Stock Subscriptions Receivable

Instructions

Prepare a classified balance sheet in good form (no monetary amounts are necessary).

E5-5 (Preparation of a Corrected Balance Sheet) Uhura Company has decided to expand its operations. The bookkeeper recently completed the balance sheet presented below in order to obtain additional funds for expansion.

UHURA COMPANY
Balance Sheet
For the Year Ended 2002

Current assets	
Cash (net of bank overdraft of $30,000)	$200,000
Accounts receivable (net)	340,000
Inventories at lower of average cost or market	401,000
Trading securities—at cost (fair value $120,000)	140,000
Property, plant, and equipment	
Building (net)	570,000
Office equipment (net)	160,000
Land held for future use	175,000
Intangible assets	
Goodwill	80,000
Cash surrender value of life insurance	90,000
Prepaid expenses	12,000

Current liabilities	
Accounts payable	105,000
Notes payable (due next year)	125,000
Pension obligation	82,000
Rent payable	49,000
Premium on bonds payable	53,000
Long-term liabilities	
Bonds payable	500,000
Stockholders' equity	
Common stock, $1.00 par, authorized 400,000 shares, issued 290,000	290,000
Additional paid-in capital	160,000
Retained earnings	?

Instructions

Prepare a revised balance sheet given the available information. Assume that the accumulated depreciation balance for the buildings is $160,000 and for the office equipment, $105,000. The allowance for doubtful accounts has a balance of $17,000. The pension obligation is considered a long-term liability.

E5-6 (Corrections of a Balance Sheet) The bookkeeper for Geronimo Company has prepared the following balance sheet as of July 31, 2002:

GERONIMO COMPANY
Balance Sheet
As of July 31, 2002

Cash	$ 69,000	Notes and accounts payable	$ 44,000
Accounts receivable (net)	40,500	Long-term liabilities	75,000
Inventories	60,000	Stockholders' equity	155,500
Equipment (net)	84,000		$274,500
Patents	21,000		
	$274,500		

The following additional information is provided:

1. Cash includes $1,200 in a petty cash fund and $15,000 in a bond sinking fund.
2. The net accounts receivable balance is comprised of the following three items: (a) accounts receivable—debit balances $52,000; (b) accounts receivable—credit balances $8,000; (c) allowance for doubtful accounts $3,500.
3. Merchandise inventory costing $5,300 was shipped out on consignment on July 31, 2002. The ending inventory balance does not include the consigned goods. Receivables in the amount of $5,300 were recognized on these consigned goods.
4. Equipment had a cost of $112,000 and an accumulated depreciation balance of $28,000.
5. Taxes payable of $6,000 were accrued on July 31. Geronimo Company, however, had set up a cash fund to meet this obligation. This cash fund was not included in the cash balance, but was offset against the taxes payable amount.

Instructions

Prepare a corrected classified balance sheet as of July 31, 2002, from the available information, adjusting the account balances using the additional information.

E5-7 (Current Assets Section of the Balance Sheet) Presented below are selected accounts of Yasunari Kawabata Company at December 31, 2002:

Finished goods	$ 52,000	Cost of goods sold	2,100,000
Revenue received in advance	90,000	Notes receivable	40,000
Bank overdraft	8,000	Accounts receivable	161,000
Equipment	253,000	Raw materials	207,000
Work-in-process	34,000	Supplies expense	60,000
Cash	37,000	Allowance for doubtful accounts	12,000
Short-term investments in stock	31,000	Licenses	18,000
Customer advances	36,000	Additional paid-in capital	88,000
Cash restricted for plant expansion	50,000	Treasury stock	22,000

The following additional information is available:

1. Inventories are valued at lower of cost or market using LIFO.
2. Equipment is recorded at cost. Accumulated depreciation, computed on a straight-line basis, is $50,600.
3. The short-term investments have a fair value of $29,000 (assume they are trading securities).
4. The notes receivable are due April 30, 2004, with interest receivable every April 30. The notes bear interest at 12%. (*Hint:* Accrue interest due on December 31, 2002).
5. The allowance for doubtful accounts applies to the accounts receivable. Accounts receivable of $50,000 are pledged as collateral on a bank loan.
6. Licenses are recorded net of accumulated amortization of $14,000.
7. Treasury stock is recorded at cost.

Instructions

Prepare the current assets section of Yasunari Kawabata Company's December 31, 2002, balance sheet, with appropriate disclosures.

E5-8 (Current vs. Long-term Liabilities) Frederic Chopin Corporation is preparing its December 31, 2002, balance sheet. The following items may be reported as either a current or long-term liability.

1. On December 15, 2002, Chopin declared a cash dividend of $2.50 per share to stockholders of record on December 31. The dividend is payable on January 15, 2003. Chopin has issued 1,000,000 shares of common stock, of which 50,000 shares are held in treasury.
2. Also on December 31, Chopin declared a 10% stock dividend to stockholders of record on January 15, 2003. The dividend will be distributed on January 31, 2003. Chopin's common stock has a par value of $10 per share and a market value of $38 per share.
3. At December 31, bonds payable of $100,000,000 are outstanding. The bonds pay 12% interest every September 30 and mature in installments of $25,000,000 every September 30, beginning September 30, 2003.
4. At December 31, 2001, customer advances were $12,000,000. During 2002, Chopin collected $30,000,000 of customer advances, and advances of $25,000,000 were earned.
5. At December 31, 2002, retained earnings appropriated for future inventory losses is $15,000,000.

Instructions

For each item above indicate the dollar amounts to be reported as a current liability and as a long-term liability, if any.

E5-9 (Current Assets and Current Liabilities) The current assets and liabilities sections of the balance sheet of Allessandro Scarlatti Company appear as follows:

ALLESSANDRO SCARLATTI COMPANY
Balance Sheet (partial)
December 31, 2002

Cash		$ 40,000	Accounts payable	$61,000
Accounts receivable	$89,000		Notes payable	67,000
Less: Allowance for doubtful accounts	7,000	82,000		$128,000
Inventories		171,000		
Prepaid expenses		9,000		
		$302,000		

The following errors in the corporation's accounting have been discovered:

1. January 2003 cash disbursements entered as of December 2002 included payments of accounts payable in the amount of $39,000, on which a cash discount of 2% was taken.
2. The inventory included $27,000 of merchandise that had been received at December 31 but for which no purchase invoices had been received or entered. Of this amount, $12,000 had been received on consignment; the remainder was purchased f.o.b. destination, terms 2/10, n/30.
3. Sales for the first four days in January 2003 in the amount of $30,000 were entered in the sales book as of December 31, 2002. Of these, $21,500 were sales on account and the remainder were cash sales.
4. Cash, not including cash sales, collected in January 2003 and entered as of December 31, 2002, totaled $35,324. Of this amount, $23,324 was received on account after cash discounts of 2% had been deducted; the remainder represented the proceeds of a bank loan.

Instructions

(a) Restate the current assets and liabilities sections of the balance sheet in accordance with good accounting practice. (Assume that both accounts receivable and accounts payable are recorded gross.)

(b) State the net effect of your adjustments on Allesandro Scarlatti Company's retained earnings balance.

E5-10 (Statement of Cash Flows—Classifications) The major classifications of activities reported in the statement of cash flows are operating, investing, and financing. Classify each of the transactions listed below as:

1. Operating activity—add to net income.
2. Operating activity—deduct from net income.
3. Investing activity.
4. Financing activity.
5. Not reported as a cash flow.

The transactions are as follows:

(a) Issuance of capital stock.
(b) Purchase of land and building.
(c) Redemption of bonds.
(d) Sale of equipment.
(e) Depreciation of machinery.
(f) Amortization of patent.
(g) Issuance of bonds for plant assets.
(h) Payment of cash dividends.
(i) Exchange of furniture for office equipment.
(j) Purchase of treasury stock.
(k) Loss on sale of equipment.
(l) Increase in accounts receivable during the year.
(m) Decrease in accounts payable during the year.

E5-11 (Preparation of a Statement of Cash Flows) The comparative balance sheets of Constantine Cavamanlis Inc. at the beginning and the end of the year 2002 appear below.

CONSTANTINE CAVAMANLIS INC.
Balance Sheets

Assets	Dec. 31, 2002	Jan. 1, 2002	Inc./Dec.
Cash	$ 45,000	$ 13,000	$32,000 Inc.
Accounts receivable	91,000	88,000	3,000 Inc.
Equipment	39,000	22,000	17,000 Inc.
Less: Accumulated depreciation	(17,000)	(11,000)	6,000 Inc.
Total	$158,000	$112,000	
Liabilities and Stockholders' Equity			
Accounts payable	$ 20,000	$ 15,000	5,000 Inc.
Common stock	100,000	80,000	20,000 Inc.
Retained earnings	38,000	17,000	21,000 Inc.
Total	$158,000	$112,000	

Net income of $44,000 was reported and dividends of $23,000 were paid in 2002. New equipment was purchased and none was sold.

Instructions

Prepare a statement of cash flows for the year 2002.

E5-12 (Preparation of a Statement of Cash Flows) Presented below is a condensed version of the comparative balance sheets for Zubin Metha Corporation for the last two years at December 31:

	2002	2001
Cash	$177,000	$ 78,000
Accounts receivable	180,000	185,000
Investments	52,000	74,000
Equipment	298,000	240,000
Less: Accumulated depreciation	(106,000)	(89,000)
Current liabilities	134,000	151,000
Capital stock	160,000	160,000
Retained earnings	307,000	177,000

Additional information:
Investments were sold at a loss (not extraordinary) of $10,000; no equipment was sold; cash dividends paid were $30,000; and net income was $160,000.

Instructions

(a) Prepare a statement of cash flows for 2002 for Zubin Metha Corporation.
(b) Determine Zubin Metha Corporation's free cash flow.

E5-13 (Preparation of a Statement of Cash Flows) A comparative balance sheet for Shabbona Corporation is presented below.

	December 31	
Assets	2002	2001
Cash	$ 73,000	$ 22,000
Accounts receivable	82,000	66,000
Inventories	180,000	189,000
Land	71,000	110,000
Equipment	260,000	200,000
Accumulated depreciation—equipment	(69,000)	(42,000)
Total	$597,000	$545,000
Liabilities and Stockholders' Equity		
Accounts payable	$ 34,000	$ 47,000
Bonds payable	150,000	200,000
Common stock ($1 par)	214,000	164,000
Retained earnings	199,000	134,000
Total	$597,000	$545,000

Additional information:

1. Net income for 2002 was $125,000.
2. Cash dividends of $60,000 were declared and paid.
3. Bonds payable amounting to $50,000 were retired through issuance of common stock.

Instructions

(a) Prepare a statement of cash flows for 2002 for Shabbona Corporation.
(b) Determine Shabbona Corporation's current cash debt ratio, cash debt coverage ratio, and free cash flow. Comment on its liquidity and financial flexibility.

E5-14 (Preparation of a Balance Sheet) Presented below is the trial balance of William Melvin Kelly Corporation at December 31, 2002.

	Debits	Credits
Cash	$ 197,000	
Sales		$ 8,100,000
Trading Securities (at cost, $145,000)	153,000	
Cost of Goods Sold	4,800,000	
Long-term Investments in Bonds	299,000	
Long-term Investments in Stocks	277,000	
Short-term Notes Payable		90,000
Accounts Payable		455,000
Selling Expenses	2,000,000	
Investment Revenue		63,000
Land	260,000	
Buildings	1,040,000	
Dividends Payable		136,000
Accrued Liabilities		96,000
Accounts Receivable	435,000	
Accumulated Depreciation—Buildings		152,000
Allowance for Doubtful Accounts		25,000
Administrative Expenses	900,000	
Interest Expense	211,000	
Inventories	597,000	
Extraordinary Gain		80,000
Prior Period Adjustment—Depr. Error	140,000	

Long-term Notes Payable		900,000
Equipment	600,000	
Bonds Payable		1,000,000
Accumulated Depreciation—Equipment		60,000
Franchise (net of $80,000 amort.)	160,000	
Common Stock ($5 par)		1,000,000
Treasury Stock	191,000	
Patent (net of $30,000 amort.)	195,000	
Retained Earnings		218,000
Additional Paid-in Capital		80,000
Totals	$12,455,000	$12,455,000

Instructions

Prepare a balance sheet at December 31, 2002, for William Melvin Kelly Corporation. Ignore income taxes.

E5-15 (Preparation of a Statement of Cash Flows and a Balance Sheet) Grant Wood Corporation's balance sheet at the end of 2001 included the following items:

Current assets	$235,000	Current liabilities	$150,000
Land	30,000	Bonds payable	100,000
Building	120,000	Common stock	180,000
Equipment	90,000	Retained earnings	44,000
Accum. depr.—build.	(30,000)	Total	$474,000
Accum. depr.—equip.	(11,000)		
Patents	40,000		
Total	$474,000		

The following information is available for 2002.

1. Net income was $55,000.
2. Equipment (cost $20,000 and accumulated depreciation, $8,000) was sold for $10,000.
3. Depreciation expense was $4,000 on the building and $9,000 on equipment.
4. Patent amortization was $2,500.
5. Current assets other than cash increased by $29,000. Current liabilities increased by $13,000.
6. An addition to the building was completed at a cost of $27,000.
7. A long-term investment in stock was purchased for $16,000.
8. Bonds payable of $50,000 were issued.
9. Cash dividends of $30,000 were declared and paid.
10. Treasury stock was purchased at a cost of $11,000.

Instructions

(a) Prepare a statement of cash flows for 2002.
(b) Prepare a balance sheet at December 31, 2002.

***E5-16 (Preparation of a Statement of Cash Flows, Analysis)** The comparative balance sheets of Madrasah Corporation at the beginning and end of the year 2002 appear below.

MADRASAH CORPORATION
Balance Sheets

Assets	Dec. 31, 2002	Jan. 1, 2002	Inc./Dec.
Cash	$ 20,000	$ 13,000	$ 7,000 Inc.
Accounts receivable	106,000	88,000	18,000 Inc.
Equipment	39,000	22,000	17,000 Inc.
Less: Accumulated depreciation	(17,000)	(11,000)	6,000 Inc.
Total	$148,000	$112,000	
Liabilities and Stockholders' Equity			
Accounts payable	$ 20,000	$ 15,000	5,000 Inc.
Common stock	100,000	80,000	20,000 Inc.
Retained earnings	28,000	17,000	11,000 Inc.
Total	$148,000	$112,000	

Net income of $44,000 was reported and dividends of $33,000 were paid in 2002. New equipment was purchased and none was sold.

Instructions

(a) Prepare a statement of cash flows for the year 2002.
(b) Compute the current ratio as of January 1, 2002, and December 31, 2002, and compute free cash flow for the year 2002.
(c) In light of the analysis in (b), comment on Madrasah's liquidity and financial flexibility.

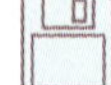

***E5-17 (Preparation of a Statement of Cash Flows, Analysis)** A comparative balance sheet for Nicholson Industries Inc. is presented below.

NICHOLSON INDUSTRIES INC.
Balance Sheets

	December 31	
Assets	2002	2001
Cash	$ 13,000	$ 22,000
Accounts receivable	112,000	66,000
Inventories	220,000	189,000
Land	71,000	110,000
Equipment	260,000	200,000
Accumulated depreciation—equipment	(69,000)	(42,000)
Total	$607,000	$545,000
Liabilities and Stockholders' Equity		
Accounts payable	$ 44,000	$ 47,000
Bonds payable	150,000	200,000
Common stock ($1 par)	214,000	164,000
Retained earnings	199,000	134,000
Total	$607,000	$545,000

Additional information:

1. Net income for 2002 was $125,000.
2. Cash dividends of $60,000 were declared and paid.
3. Bonds payable amounting to $50,000 were retired through issuance of common stock.

Instructions

(a) Prepare a statement of cash flows for the year 2002 for Nicholson.
(b) Compute the current and acid-test ratios for 2001 and 2002.
(c) Compute Nicholson's free cash flow and the current cash debt coverage ratio for 2002.
(d) Based on the analyses in (b) and (c), comment on Nicholson's liquidity and financial flexibility.

PROBLEMS

P5-1 (Preparation of a Classified Balance Sheet, Periodic Inventory) Presented below is a list of accounts in alphabetical order.

Accounts Receivable
Accrued Wages
Accumulated Depreciation—Buildings
Accumulated Depreciation—Equipment
Advances to Employees
Advertising Expense
Allowance for Doubtful Accounts
Bond Sinking Fund
Bonds Payable
Building
Cash in Bank
Cash on Hand
Cash Surrender Value of Life Insurance
Commission Expense
Common Stock
Copyright (net of amortization)
Dividends Payable
Equipment
FICA Taxes Payable
Gain on Sale of Equipment
Interest Receivable
Inventory—Beginning
Inventory—Ending
Land

Land for Future Plant Site	Purchases
Loss from Flood	Purchase Returns and Allowances
Notes Payable	Retained Earnings
Patent (net of amortization)	Sales
Pension Obligations	Sales Discounts
Petty Cash	Sales Salaries
Preferred Stock	Trading Securities
Premium on Bonds Payable	Transportation-in
Premium on Preferred Stock	Treasury Stock (at cost)
Prepaid Rent	Unearned Subscriptions

Instructions

Prepare a classified balance sheet in good form. (No monetary amounts are to be shown.)

P5-2 (Balance Sheet Preparation) Presented below are a number of balance sheet items for Jay Leno, Inc., for the current year, 2002.

Goodwill	$ 125,000	Accumulated depreciation—equipment	$ 292,000
Payroll taxes payable	177,591	Inventories	239,800
Bonds payable	300,000	Rent payable—short-term	45,000
Discount on bonds payable	15,000	Taxes payable	98,362
Cash	360,000	Long-term rental obligations	480,000
Land	480,000	Common stock, $1 par value	200,000
Notes receivable	545,700	Preferred stock, $10 par value	150,000
Notes payable to banks	265,000	Prepaid expenses	87,920
Accounts payable	590,000	Equipment	1,470,000
Retained earnings	?	Trading securities	121,000
Refundable federal and state income taxes	97,630	Accumulated depreciation—building	170,200
Unsecured notes payable (long-term)	1,600,000	Building	1,640,000

Instructions

Prepare a classified balance sheet in good form. Common stock authorized was 400,000 shares, and preferred stock authorized was 20,000 shares. Assume that notes receivable and notes payable are short-term, unless stated otherwise. Cost and fair value of marketable securities are the same.

P5-3 (Balance Sheet Adjustment and Preparation) The adjusted trial balance of Side Kicks Company and other related information for the year 2002 is presented below.

SIDE KICKS COMPANY
Adjusted Trial Balance
December 31, 2002

	Debits	Credits
Cash	$ 41,000	
Accounts Receivable	163,500	
Allowance for Doubtful Accounts		$ 8,700
Prepaid Insurance	5,900	
Inventory	308,500	
Long-term Investments	339,000	
Land	85,000	
Construction Work in Progress	124,000	
Patents	36,000	
Equipment	400,000	
Accumulated Depreciation of Equipment		140,000
Unamortized Discount on Bonds Payable	20,000	
Accounts Payable		148,000
Accrued Expenses		49,200
Notes Payable		94,000
Bonds Payable		400,000
Capital Stock		500,000
Premium on Capital Stock		45,000
Retained Earnings		138,000
	$1,522,900	$1,522,900

Additional information:

1. The inventory has a replacement market value of $353,000. The LIFO method of inventory value is used.
2. The cost and fair value of the long-term investments that consist of stocks and bonds is the same.
3. The amount of the Construction Work in Progress account represents the costs expended to date on a building in the process of construction. (The company rents factory space at the present time.) The land on which the building is being constructed cost $85,000, as shown in the trial balance.
4. The patents were purchased by the company at a cost of $36,000 and are being amortized on a straight-line basis.
5. Of the unamortized discount on bonds payable, $2,000 will be amortized in 2003.
6. The notes payable represent bank loans that are secured by long-term investments carried at $120,000. These bank loans are due in 2003.
7. The bonds payable bear interest at 11% payable every December 31, and are due January 1, 2013.
8. Six hundred thousand shares of common stock of a par value of $1 were authorized, of which 500,000 shares were issued are outstanding.

Instructions

Prepare a balance sheet as of December 31, 2002, so that all important information is fully disclosed.

P5-4 (Preparation of a Corrected Balance Sheet) Presented below is the balance sheet of Tom Cruise Corporation as of December 31, 2002.

TOM CRUISE CORPORATION
Balance Sheet
December 31, 2002

Assets	
Goodwill (Note 2)	$ 120,000
Building (Note 1)	1,640,000
Inventories	312,100
Land	750,000
Accounts receivable	170,000
Treasury stock (50,000 shares, no par)	87,000
Cash on hand	175,900
Assets allocated to trustee for plant expansion	
Cash in bank	70,000
U.S. Treasury notes, at cost and fair value	138,000
	$3,463,000
Equities	
Notes payable (Note 3)	$ 600,000
Common stock, authorized and issued, 1,000,000 shares, no par	1,150,000
Retained earnings	658,000
Appreciation capital (Note 1)	570,000
Federal income taxes payable	75,000
Reserve for depreciation of building	410,000
	$3,463,000

Note 1: Buildings are stated at cost, except for one building that was recorded at appraised value. The excess of appraisal value over cost was $570,000. Depreciation has been recorded based on cost.

Note 2: Goodwill in the amount of $120,000 was recognized because the company believed that book value was not an accurate representation of the fair market value of the company. The gain of $120,000 was credited to Retained Earnings.

Note 3: Notes payable are long-term except for the current installment due of $100,000.

Instructions

Prepare a corrected classified balance sheet in good form. The notes above are for information only.

P5-5 (Balance Sheet Adjustment and Preparation) Presented on the next page is the balance sheet of Stephen King Corporation for the current year, 2002.

STEPHEN KING CORPORATION
Balance Sheet
December 31, 2002

Current assets	$ 435,000	Current liabilities	$ 330,000
Investments	640,000	Long-term liabilities	1,000,000
Property, plant, and equipment	1,720,000	Stockholders' equity	1,770,000
Intangible assets	305,000		$3,100,000
	$3,100,000		

The following information is presented:

1. The current assets section includes: cash $100,000, accounts receivable $170,000 less $10,000 for allowance for doubtful accounts, inventories $180,000, and prepaid revenue $5,000. The cash balance is composed of $114,000, less a bank overdraft of $14,000. Inventories are stated on the lower of FIFO cost or market.
2. The investments section includes the cash surrender value of a life insurance contract $40,000; investments in common stock, short-term (trading) $80,000 and long-term (available-for-sale) $140,000; bond sinking fund $250,000; and organization costs $130,000. The cost and fair value of investments in common stock are the same.
3. Property, plant, and equipment includes buildings $1,040,000 less accumulated depreciation $360,000; equipment $450,000 less accumulated depreciation $180,000; land $500,000; and land held for future use $270,000.
4. Intangible assets include a franchise $165,000, goodwill $100,000, and discount on bonds payable $40,000.
5. Current liabilities include accounts payable $90,000, notes payable—short-term $80,000 and long-term $120,000, and taxes payable $40,000.
6. Long-term liabilities are composed solely of 10% bonds payable due 2010.
7. Stockholders' equity has preferred stock, no par value, authorized 200,000 shares, issued 70,000 shares for $450,000, and common stock, $1.00 par value, authorized 400,000 shares, issued 100,000 shares at an average price of $10. In addition, the corporation has retained earnings of $320,000.

Instructions

Prepare a balance sheet in good form, adjusting the amounts in each balance sheet classification as affected by the "information" given above.

P5-6 (Preparation of a Statement of Cash Flows and a Balance Sheet) Alistair Cooke Inc. had the following balance sheet at the end of operations for 2001:

ALISTAIR COOKE INC.
Balance Sheet
December 31, 2001

Cash	$ 20,000	Accounts payable	$ 30,000
Accounts receivable	21,200	Long-term notes payable	41,000
Investments	32,000	Capital stock	100,000
Plant assets (net)	81,000	Retained earnings	23,200
Land	40,000		$194,200
	$194,200		

During 2002 the following occurred:

1. Alistair Cooke Inc. sold part of its investment portfolio for $17,000. This transaction resulted in a gain of $3,400 for the firm. The company often sells and buys securities of this nature.
2. A tract of land was purchased for $18,000 cash.
3. Long-term notes payable in the amount of $16,000 were retired before maturity by paying $16,000 cash.
4. An additional $24,000 in capital stock was issued at par.
5. Dividends totalling $8,200 were declared and paid to stockholders.
6. Net income for 2002 was $32,000 after allowing for depreciation of $12,000.

7. Land was purchased through the issuance of $30,000 in bonds.
8. At December 31, 2002, Cash was $39,000, Accounts Receivable was $41,600, and Accounts Payable remained at $30,000.

Instructions

(a) Prepare a statement of cash flows for 2002.
(b) Prepare the balance sheet as it would appear at December 31, 2002.
(c) How might the statement of cash flows help the user of the financial statements? Compute two cash flow ratios.

P5-7 (Income Statement and Balance Sheet Preparation) Mary Anne Spier has prepared baked goods for resale since 1991. She started a baking business in her home and has been operating in a rented building with a storefront since 1996. Spier incorporated the business as MAS Inc. on January 1, 2002, with an initial stock issue of 1,000 shares of common stock at a par value of $2.50 per share. Mary Anne Spier is the principal stockholder of MAS Inc.

Sales have increased 30 percent annually since operations began at the present location, and additional equipment is needed to accommodate expected continued growth. Spier wishes to purchase some additional baking equipment and to finance the equipment through a long-term note from a commercial bank. Wisconsin State Bank & Trust has asked Spier to submit an income statement for MAS Inc. for the first 5 months of 2002 and a balance sheet as of May 31, 2002.

Spier assembled the following information from the cash basis records of the corporation for use in preparing the financial statements requested by the bank.

1. The check register showed the following 2002 deposits through May 31.

Sale of common stock	$ 2,500
Cash sales	22,770
Rebates from purchases	130
Collections on credit sales	5,320
Bank loan proceeds	2,880
	$33,600

2. The following amounts were disbursed through May 31, 2002.

Baking materials	$14,400
Rent	1,800
Salaries and wages	5,500
Maintenance	110
Utilities	4,000
Insurance premium	1,920
Equipment	3,000
Principal and interest payment on bank loan	312
Advertising	424
	$31,466

3. Unpaid invoices at May 31, 2002, were as follows.

Baking materials	$ 256
Utilities	270
	$ 526

4. Customer records showed uncollected sales of $4,226 at May 31, 2002.
5. Baking materials costing $1,840 were on hand at May 31, 2002. There were no materials in process or finished goods on hand at that date. No materials were on hand or in process and no finished goods were on hand at January 1, 2002.
6. The note evidencing the 3-year bank loan is dated January 1, 2002, and states a simple interest rate of 10%. The loan requires quarterly payments on April 1, July 1, October 1, and January 1 consisting of equal principal payments plus accrued interest since the last payment.
7. Mary Anne Spier receives a salary of $750 on the last day of each month. The other employees had been paid through Friday, May 25, 2002, and were due an additional $240 on May 31, 2002.
8. New display cases and equipment costing $3,000 were purchased on January 2, 2002, and have an estimated useful life of 5 years. These are the only fixed assets currently used in the business. Straight-line depreciation is to be used for book purposes.
9. Rent was paid for 6 months in advance on January 2, 2002.
10. A one-year insurance policy was purchased on January 2, 2002.
11. MAS Inc. is subject to an income tax rate of 20%.

12. Payments and collections pertaining to the unincorporated business through December 31, 2001, were not included in the records of the corporation, and no cash was transferred from the unincorporated business to the corporation.

Instructions

Using the accrual basis of accounting, prepare for MAS Inc.:

(a) An income statement for the 5 months ended May 31, 2002.
(b) A balance sheet as of May 31, 2002.

(CMA adapted)

P5-8 (Preparation of a Statement of Cash Flows and Balance Sheet) Roger Mudd Inc. had the following balance sheet at the end of operations for 2001:

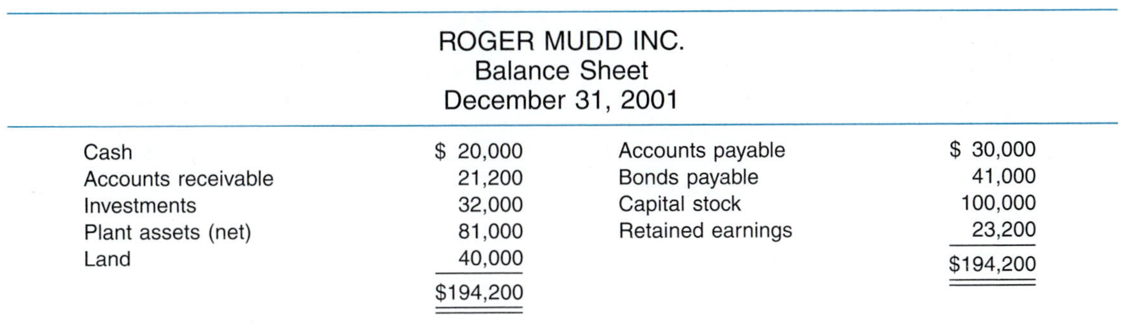

ROGER MUDD INC.
Balance Sheet
December 31, 2001

Cash	$ 20,000	Accounts payable	$ 30,000
Accounts receivable	21,200	Bonds payable	41,000
Investments	32,000	Capital stock	100,000
Plant assets (net)	81,000	Retained earnings	23,200
Land	40,000		$194,200
	$194,200		

During 2002 the following occurred:

1. Mudd liquidated its investment portfolio at a loss of $3,000.
2. A tract of land was purchased for $38,000.
3. An additional $26,000 in common stock was issued at par.
4. Dividends totaling $10,000 were declared and paid to stockholders.
5. Net income for 2002 was $35,000, including $12,000 in depreciation expense.
6. Land was purchased through the issuance of $30,000 in additional bonds.
7. At December 31, 2002, Cash was $66,200, Accounts Receivable was $42,000, and Accounts Payable was $40,000.

Instructions

(a) Prepare a statement of cash flows for the year 2002 for Mudd.
(b) Prepare the balance sheet as it would appear at December 31, 2002.
(c) Compute the current and acid-test ratios for 2001 and 2002.
(d) Compute Mudd's free cash flow and the current cash debt coverage ratio for 2002.
(e) Use the analysis of Mudd to illustrate how information in the balance sheet and statement of cash flows helps the user of the financial statements.

CONCEPTUAL CASES

C5-1 (Reporting the Financial Effects of Varied Transactions) In an examination of Juan Acevedo Corporation as of December 31, 2002, you have learned that the following situations exist. No entries have been made in the accounting records for these items.

1. The corporation erected its present factory building in 1987. Depreciation was calculated by the straight-line method, using an estimated life of 35 years. Early in 2002, the board of directors conducted a careful survey and estimated that the factory building had a remaining useful life of 25 years as of January 1, 2002.
2. An additional assessment of 2001 income taxes was levied and paid in 2002.
3. When calculating the accrual for officers' salaries at December 31, 2002, it was discovered that the accrual for officers' salaries for December 31, 2001, had been overstated.
4. On December 15, 2002, Acevedo Corporation declared a 1% common stock dividend on its common stock outstanding, payable February 1, 2003, to the common stockholders of record December 31, 2002.

5. Acevedo Corporation, which is on a calendar-year basis, changed its inventory method as of January 1, 2002. The inventory for December 31, 2001, was costed by the average method, and the inventory for December 31, 2002, was costed by the FIFO method.

Instructions

Describe fully how each of the items above should be reported in the financial statements of Acevedo Corporation for the year 2002.

C5-2 (Current Asset and Liability Classification) Below are the titles of a number of debit and credit accounts as they might appear on the balance sheet of Ethan Allen Corporation as of October 31, 2002.

Debits	Credits
Interest accrued on U.S. government securities	Capital stock—preferred
Notes receivable	11% first mortgage bonds due in 2009
Petty cash fund	Preferred cash dividend, payable Nov. 1, 2002
U.S. government securities	Allowance for doubtful accounts receivable
Treasury stock	Federal income taxes payable
Unamortized bond discount	Customers' advances (on contracts to be completed next year)
Cash in bank	Premium on bonds redeemable in 2002
Land	Officers' 2002 bonus accrued
Inventory of operating parts and supplies	Accrued payroll
Inventory of raw materials	Notes payable
Patents	Accrued interest on bonds
Cash and U.S. government bonds set aside for property additions	Accumulated depreciation
Investment in subsidiary	Accounts payable
Accounts receivable	Capital in excess of par
U.S. government contracts	Accrued interest on notes payable
Regular	8% first mortgage bonds to be redeemed in 2002 out of current assets
Installments—due next year	
Installments—due after next year	
Goodwill	
Inventory of finished goods	
Inventory of work in process	
Deficit	

Instructions

Select the current asset and current liability items from among these debits and credits. If there appear to be certain borderline cases that you are unable to classify without further information, mention them and explain your difficulty, or give your reasons for making questionable classifications, if any.

(AICPA adapted)

C5-3 (Identifying Balance Sheet Deficiencies) The assets of LaShon Johnson Corporation are presented below (000s omitted):

LASHON JOHNSON CORPORATION
Balance Sheet (partial)
December 31, 2002

Assets

Current assets		
Cash		$ 100,000
Unclaimed payroll checks		27,500
Marketable securities (cost $30,000) at fair value		37,000
Accounts receivable (less bad debt reserve)		75,000
Inventories—at lower of cost (determined by the next-in, first-out method) or market		240,000
Total current assets		479,500
Tangible assets		
Land (less accumulated depreciation)		80,000
Buildings and equipment	$800,000	
Less: Accumulated depreciation	250,000	550,000
Net tangible assets		630,000

Long-term investments	
Stocks and bonds	100,000
Treasury stock	70,000
Total long-term investments	170,000
Other assets	
Discount on bonds payable	19,400
Sinking fund	975,000
Total other assets	994,400
Total assets	$2,273,900

Instructions

Indicate the deficiencies, if any, in the foregoing presentation of LaShon Johnson Corporation's assets. Marketable securities are considered trading securities.

C5-4 (Critique of Balance Sheet Format and Content) Presented below is the balance sheet of Bellemy Brothers Corporation (000s omitted):

BELLEMY BROTHERS CORPORATION
Balance Sheet
December 31, 2002

Assets		
Current assets		
Cash	$26,000	
Marketable securities	18,000	
Accounts receivable	25,000	
Merchandise inventory	20,000	
Supplies inventory	4,000	
Stock investment in Subsidiary Company	20,000	$113,000
Investments		
Treasury stock		25,000
Property, plant, and equipment		
Buildings and land	91,000	
Less: Reserve for depreciation	31,000	60,000
Other assets		
Cash surrender value of life insurance		19,000
		$217,000
Liabilities and Capital		
Current liabilities		
Accounts payable	$22,000	
Reserve for income taxes	15,000	
Customers' accounts with credit balances	1	$ 37,001
Deferred credits		
Unamortized premium on bonds payable		2,000
Long-term liabilities		
Bonds payable		60,000
Total liabilities		99,001
Capital stock		
Capital stock, par $5	85,000	
Earned surplus	24,999	
Cash dividends declared	8,000	117,999
		$217,000

Instructions

Evaluate the balance sheet presented. State briefly the proper treatment of any item criticized.

C5-5 (Identifying Balance Sheet Deficiencies) The financial statement below was prepared by employees of your client, Walt Whitman Co. The statement is unaccompanied by notes.

WALT WHITMAN CO.
Balance Sheet
As of November 30, 2002

Current assets				
Cash			$ 100,000	
Accounts receivable (less allowance of $30,000 for doubtful accounts)			419,900	
Inventories			1,954,000	$2,473,900
Less: Current liabilities				
Accounts payable			306,400	
Accrued payroll			28,260	
Accrued interest on mortgage note			12,000	
Estimated taxes payable			66,000	412,660
Net working capital				2,061,240
Property, plant, and equipment (at cost)				
	Cost	Depreciation	Value	
Land and buildings	$ 983,300	$410,000	$ 573,300	
Machinery and equipment	1,135,700	568,699	567,001	
	$2,119,000	$978,699		1,140,301
Deferred charges				
Prepaid taxes and other expenses			23,700	
Unamortized discount on mortgage note			10,800	34,500
Total net working capital and noncurrent assets				3,236,041
Less: Deferred liabilities				
Mortgage note payable			300,000	
Unearned revenue			1,808,000	2,108,000
Total net assets				$1,128,041
Stockholders' equity				
10% Preferred stock at par value				$ 300,000
Common stock at par value				397,000
Paid-in surplus				210,000
Retained earnings				265,641
Treasury stock at cost (400 shares)				(44,600)
Total stockholders' equity				$1,128,041

Instructions

Indicate the deficiencies, if any, in the balance sheet above in regard to form, terminology, descriptions, content, and the like.

C5-6 (Cash Flow Analysis) The partner in charge of the James Spencer Corporation audit comes by your desk and leaves a letter he has started to the CEO and a copy of the cash flow statement for the year ended December 31, 2001. Because he must leave on an emergency, he asks you to finish the letter by explaining: (1) the disparity between net income and cash flow; (2) the importance of operating cash flow; (3) the renewable source(s) of cash flow; and (4) possible suggestions to improve the cash position.

JAMES SPENCER CORPORATION
Statement of Cash Flows
For the Year Ended December 31, 2001

Cash flows from operating activities		
Net income		$100,000
Adjustments to reconcile net income to net cash provided by operating activities:		
Depreciation expense	$ 10,000	
Amortization expense	1,000	
Loss on sale of fixed assets	5,000	
Increase in accounts receivable (net)	(40,000)	
Increase in inventory	(35,000)	

Decrease in accounts payable	(41,000)	(100,000)
Net cash provided by operating activities		–0–
Cash flows from investing activities		
Sale of plant assets	$ 25,000	
Purchase of equipment	(100,000)	
Purchase of land	(200,000)	
Net cash used by investing activities		(275,000)
Cash flows from financing activities		
Payment of dividends	$ (10,000)	
Redemption of bonds	(100,000)	
Net cash used by financing activities		(110,000)
Net decrease in cash		(385,000)
Cash balance, January 1, 2001		400,000
Cash balance, December 31, 2001		$ 15,000

Date

James Spencer, III, CEO
James Spencer Corporation
125 Wall Street
Middleton, Kansas 67458

Dear Mr. Spencer:

I have good news and bad news about the financial statements for the year ended December 31, 2001. The good news is that net income of $100,000 is close to what we predicted in the strategic plan last year, indicating strong performance this year. The bad news is that the cash balance is seriously low. Enclosed is the Statement of Cash Flows, which best illustrates how both of these situations occurred simultaneously . . .

Instructions
Complete the letter to the CEO, including the four components requested by your boss.

USING YOUR JUDGMENT

FINANCIAL REPORTING PROBLEM: INTEL CORPORATION

The financial statements of Intel Corporation appear in Appendix 5B.

Instructions

Refer to those financial statements and the accompanying notes to answer the following questions.

(a) What alternative formats could Intel have adopted for its balance sheet? Which format did it adopt?

(b) Identify the various techniques of disclosure Intel might have used to disclose additional pertinent financial information. Which technique does it use in its financials?

(c) Why are certain investments included in Intel's short-term investments? In long-term investments? What valuation basis does Intel use to report its investments? How much working capital did Intel have on December 26, 1998? December 27, 1997?

(d) What were Intel's cash flows from its operating, investing, and financing activities for 1998? What were its trends in net cash provided by operating activities over the period 1996–1998? Explain why a decrease in accounts payable is deducted from net income to arrive at net cash provided by operating activities.

(e) Compute Intel's (1) current cash debt coverage ratio, (2) cash debt coverage ratio, and (3) free cash flow for 1998. What do these ratios indicate about the financial condition of Intel?

FINANCIAL STATEMENT ANALYSIS CASES

Case 1 Uniroyal Technology Corporation

Uniroyal Technology Corporation (UTC), with corporate offices in Sarasota, Florida, is organized into three operating segments. The high-performance plastics segment is responsible for research, development, and manufacture of a wide variety of products, including orthopedic braces, graffiti-resistant seats for buses and airplanes, and a static-resistant plastic used in the central processing units of microcomputers. The coated fabrics segment manufactures products such as automobile seating, door and instrument panels, and specialty items such as waterproof seats for personal watercraft and stain-resistant, easy-cleaning upholstery fabrics. The foams and adhesives segment develops and manufactures products used in commercial roofing applications.

The following items relate to operations in a recent year:

1. Serious pressure was placed on profitability by sharply increasing raw material prices. Some raw materials increased in price 50% during the past year. Cost containment programs were instituted and product prices were increased whenever possible, which resulted in profit margins actually improving over the course of the year.
2. The company entered into a revolving credit agreement, under which UTC may borrow the lesser of $15,000,000 or 80% of eligible accounts receivable. At the end of the year, approximately $4,000,000 was outstanding under this agreement. The company plans to use this line of credit in the upcoming year to finance operations and expansion.

Instructions

(a) Should investors be informed of raw materials price increases, such as described in item **1**? Does the fact that the company successfully met the challenge of higher prices affect the answer? Explain.

(b) How should the information in item **2** be presented in the financial statements of UTC?

Case 2 Sherwin-Williams Company

Sherwin-Williams, based in Cleveland, Ohio, manufactures a wide variety of paint and other coatings, which are marketed through its specialty stores and in other retail outlets. The company also manufactures paint for automobiles. The Automotive Division has had financial difficulty. During a recent year, five branch locations of the Automotive Division were closed, and new management was put in place for the branches remaining.

The following titles were shown on Sherwin-Williams' balance sheet for that year:

Accounts payable
Accounts receivable, less allowance
Accrued taxes
Buildings
Cash and cash equivalents
Common stock
Construction in progress
Deferred pension assets
Employee compensation payable
Finished goods inventories
Intangibles and other assets
Land
Long-term debt
Machinery and equipment
Other accruals
Other capital
Other current assets
Other long-term liabilities
Postretirement benefits other than pensions
Retained earnings
Short-term investments
Taxes withheld
Work in process and raw materials inventories

Instructions

(a) Organize the accounts in the general order in which they would have been presented in a classified balance sheet.

(b) When several of the branch locations of the Automotive Division were closed, what balance sheet accounts were most likely affected? Did the balance in those accounts decrease or increase?

COMPARATIVE ANALYSIS CASE

The Coca-Cola Company versus PepsiCo Inc.

Instructions

Go to the Digital Tool and use information found there to answer the following questions about The Coca-Cola Company and PepsiCo.

(a) What format(s) did these companies use to present their balance sheets?

(b) How much working capital did each of these companies have at the end of 1998? Speculate as to their rationale for the amount of working capital they maintain.

(c) What is the most significant difference in the asset structure of the two companies? What causes this difference?

(d) What are the companies' annual and 5-year growth rates in total assets and total debt?

(e) What were these two companies' trends in net cash provided by operating activities over the period 1996–1998?

(f) Compute both companies' (1) current cash debt coverage ratio, (2) cash debt coverage ratio, and (3) free cash flow. What do these ratios indicate about the financial condition of these two companies?

(g) What ratios do each of these companies use in their management's discussion and analysis section to explain their financial condition related to debt financing?

RESEARCH CASES

Case 1

Publicity-owned companies registered with the Securities and Exchange Commission electronically file required reports via the EDGAR (Electronic Data Gathering, Analysis, and Retrieval) system.

EDGAR can easily be accessed via the Internet (http://www.sec.gov) using the following steps:

1. Select "EDGAR Database of Corporate Information" from the home page.
2. Select "Search the EDGAR Database."
3. Select "CIK (Central Index Key) and Ticker Symbol Lookup" and enter the name(s) of the company(ies) you are investigating. Write down the CIK number(s) and return to the previous page.
4. To examine filings, click on "Search the EDGAR Archives" and enter the appropriate CIK number (including all zeroes). When the list of filings appears, click on the desired filing under the "Company name" column.

Instructions

(a) Determine the CIK numbers for the following companies: **Ford Motor Company**, **Wisconsin Electric Power Company**, and **Orion Pictures**.

(b) Examine the balance sheet formats included in the following filings: (1) Ford Motor Co. Form 10-K filed 3/17/99, (2) Wisconsin Electric Power Co. annual report to shareholders (10-KIA) filed 4/15/99, and (3) Orion Pictures Form 10-K filed 4/14/95. Do you notice anything "unusual" about the balance sheet formats? Why do you think the balance sheets are presented in this manner?

Case 2

The January 1995 issue of *The CPA Journal* incudes an article by John D. Gould, entitled "A Second Opinion on International Accounting Standards."

Instructions

Read the article and answer the following questions.

(a) With regard to compliance with U.S. GAAP, what are the two alternatives for foreign issuers desiring to register securities with the U.S. Securities and Exchange Commission?

(b) In general, how do German accounting principles differ from U.S. GAAP?

(c) What does the author assert regarding the costs to German companies of complying with U.S. GAAP versus International Accounting Standards?

(d) According to the author, what are the advantages of the proposed SEC rule changes for filings by foreign companies?

(e) While the author predicts that international accounting standards are "unlikely to be accepted in practice," what useful purpose has the International Accounting Standards Committee served?

INTERNATIONAL REPORTING CASE

Presented below is the balance sheet for J. Sainsbury PLC, a British company.

Instructions

(a) Identify at least three differences in balance sheet reporting between British and U.S. firms, as shown in Sainsbury's balance sheet.

(b) Review Sainsbury's balance sheet and identify how the format of this financial statement provides useful information, as illustrated in the chapter.

J. SAINSBURY, PLC

Balance Sheets
3 April 1999

	1999 £m
Fixed assets	
Tangible assets	6,409
Investments	41
	6,450
Current assets	
Stocks	843
Debtors	249
Investments	17
Sainsbury's Bank	1,766
Cash at bank and in hand	725
	3,600
Creditors: due within one year	
Sainsbury's Bank	(1,669)
Other	(2,880)
	(4,549)

Net current liabilities	(949)
Total assets less current liabilities	5,501
Creditors: due after one year	(804)
Provisions for liabilities and charges	(8)
Total net assets	4,689
Capital and reserves	
Called up share capital	480
Share premium account	1,359
Revaluation reserve	38
Profit and loss account	2,767
Equity shareholders' funds	4,644
Minority equity interest	45
Total capital employed	4,689

ETHICS CASE

Andrea Pafko, corporate comptroller for Nicholson Industries, is trying to decide how to present "Property, plant, and equipment" in the balance sheet. She realizes that the statement of cash flows will show that the company made a significant investment in purchasing new equipment this year, but overall she knows the company's plant assets are rather old. She feels that she can disclose one figure titled "Property, plant, and equipment, net of depreciation," and the result will be a low figure. However, it will not disclose the age of the assets. If she chooses to show the cost less accumulated depreciation, the age of the assets will be apparent. She proposes the following:

Property, plant, and equipment, net of depreciation	$10,000,000
rather than	
Property, plant and equipment	$50,000,000
Less: Accumulated depreciation	(40,000,000)
Net book value	$10,000,000

Instructions

Answer the following questions:

(a) What are the ethical issues involved?

(b) What should Pafko do?

A visit with
Michael Lehman

Michael Lehman is chief financial officer for Sun Microsystems, Inc., a leading supplier of global network computing products and software. During his tenure with Sun, investors have enjoyed more than a 40-fold increase in Sun's stock market value. As CFO, he is responsible for Sun's finance, legal, human resources, real estate, and information resource functions. Prior to joining Sun in 1987, he was a senior manager in the San Francisco office of PricewaterhouseCoopers.

PERSPECTIVES ON

Quality Corporate Reporting

How would you describe your interaction with the Wall Street community? One place where I get involved—along with our CEO and chief operating officer—is the quarterly earnings conference call. This is a formal two-hour session in which we announce the results of the quarter and provide perspective and color to it. In addition, there is an annual industry meeting—a day and a half event in which we present our company in front of the financial community. Then I'll participate in a selected number of conferences hosted by the major brokerage firms such as Goldman Sachs, Morgan Stanley Dean Witter, and Merrill Lynch where I'll typically speak in front of several hundred people. I will also go on "buy side" tours once a quarter on their turf where we try to visit many of the top twenty financial institutions that are holding our stock—and some who we would like to hold our stock. Sun Microsystems also has an investor relations department that reports to me. The IR people conduct the routine day-to-day business with the investment community, whether it's the sell-side brokerage firms or the buy-side institutions.

In addition, there's a lot of information that we convey over the Internet. For instance, if you go to the Investor Relations area of our Web site at www.sun.com, you can view a Webcast of our 1999 stockholder's meeting, an online version of our most recent annual report, a list of Wall Street analysts who follow our stock, and much more.

What types of issues do you struggle with in terms of keeping Wall Street expectations where they ought to be? One of the biggest challenges that we all face is how to walk that fine line in terms of setting expectations and also keeping your company safe from what I'll call frivolous lawsuits. About half of the time that I spend with Wall Street is setting the right expectations for revenue and profit growth. And once we get comfortable with what we believe we're going to go after internally, then my job is—as subtly as possible, and as indirectly as possible—to try to get Wall Street into a reasonable range that's near that.

Especially given the phenomenal increase in your stock price, do you think that making sure that this is done right is even more critical? Well, the stakes are definitely higher, but I think the stock is where it is partly because we've been able to manage expectations—and deliver on our promises—for five years in a row. While Wall Street likes growth in revenues and earnings, they also like consistency and predictability. So the art of managing the Street is managing expectations as well as making sure that the company hits those numbers.

Your background is heavily financial, so how did you learn these other disciplines that you manage—human resources, legal, real estate, information technology, public policy in Washington, D.C.? It's a combination of always seeking more and broader experiences and responsibilities. I sought it out; it wasn't just handed to me. You have to go out and seek some experiences that will help put you in that position, and then you have to earn the confidence and trust of the people who are running those functions. Also, it comes from the trust that the CEO has in me as a business partner, not just a finance person.

What would you say is the most significant accounting issue facing your industry? Revenue recognition is still the biggest single challenge facing our industry. Sometimes the way a business transaction is structured can be affected by accounting rules. For example, we recently did a transaction with a company that's going to be laying the infrastructure to provide digital content to companies. They're a public company, but they don't have a lot of revenue. They wanted us to be their technology supplier, but they also wanted us to make an equity investment in them to help legitimize them in the market. They wanted pretty aggressive long-term lease financing from us. The challenge for us was to structure a deal including lease financing, warrants, and an equity investment that would allow us as a company to make sufficient money on the deal to compensate us for the risk, and to simultaneously allow us to recognize revenue appropriately over time.

What FASB activities would ultimately affect Sun Microsystems? The FASB continues to refine areas such as revenue recognition, stock option accounting, and business combinations. Often, the FASB struggles with an issue for years, and they often come up with a solution that nobody likes. As a result, you see the advent of a non-GAAP item like "cash earnings per share" being reported to shareholders. Companies are reporting net income before one-time items, before goodwill amortization and R&D expense, in order to arrive at a normalized operating income number, which of course is a non-GAAP concept. We really report two income statements—one that focuses on required GAAP accounting and the other one that we called "operating income." We're just saying that you need to take away the one-time items to have truly comparable financial statements, quarter-in and quarter-out.

Do the analysts say, "Gee, thanks for telling us that, because now we know what your real earning power is, as opposed to GAAP numbers"? I think it's very important to point out that when you write off $100 million one quarter for purchased R&D and you write off nothing a year later, and you try to compare those periods, it's apples and oranges. So it's very important to separate the impact of one-time items.

The argument from the FASB is that Wall Street will make that distinction anyway. But I think that we need to present the information in a way that they're used to seeing it, which is by excluding the one-time item. Frankly, the only income statement that I talk about when I do my Wall Street presentations is the income statement without one-time items. Of course, I will also show the GAAP reported numbers.

What advice do you give college students who want to follow in your footsteps? First of all, I encourage them to find a way to differentiate themselves as they're going forward in their college careers. Whether it's mastering a foreign language, or working outside the United States, or working outside of their chosen discipline, I'm constantly telling the people who work for me to get out of their comfort zones. Go work in sales for a while, go work in information technology for a while. You will be a much better finance person/business partner if you have done some of that.

Second, try to be very clear about where you want to go and what you're willing to do to go make it happen. My belief is that you can pretty much create the kind of career you want, if you're focused on it, and you go out and make it happen. It doesn't just happen to you. The other thing that I tell people is that you can't always predict the future. I had no idea that I was going to leave Price Waterhouse and go to work at Sun, and I had no idea that Sun was going to become the company that it became. But I was constantly positioning myself in terms of background and experience to have more choices.

CHAPTER 6

Accounting and the Time Value of Money

The Magic of Interest

Sidney Homer, author of *A History of Interest Rates,* wrote, "$1,000 invested at a mere 8% for 400 years would grow to $23 quadrillion—$5 million for every human on earth. But the first 100 years are the hardest."

This startling quote highlights the power of time and compounding interest on money. Equally significant, although not mentioned in the quote, is the fact that a small difference in the interest rate makes a big difference in the amount of monies accumulated over time. Taking a more realistic example, assume that you had $20,000 in a tax-free retirement account. Half the money is in stocks returning 12% and the other half in bonds earning 8%. Assuming reinvested profits and quarterly compounding, your bonds would be worth $22,080 after ten years, a doubling of their value. But your stocks, returning 4% more, would be worth $32,620, or triple your initial value. The following chart shows this impact.

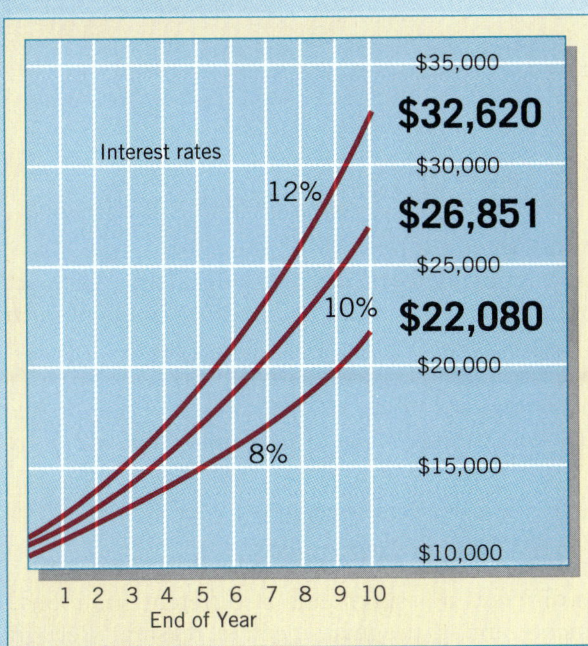

Money received tomorrow is not the same as money received today. Business people are acutely aware of this timing factor, and they invest and borrow only after carefully analyzing the relative present or future values of the cash flows.

LEARNING OBJECTIVES

After studying this chapter, you should be able to:

1. **Identify accounting topics where time value of money is relevant.**
2. **Distinguish between simple and compound interest.**
3. **Learn how to use appropriate compound interest tables.**
4. **Identify variables fundamental to solving interest problems.**
5. **Solve future and present value of 1 problems.**
6. **Solve future value of ordinary and annuity due problems.**
7. **Solve present value of ordinary and annuity due problems.**

PREVIEW OF CHAPTER 6

As indicated in the opening story, the timing of the returns on investments has an important effect on the worth of the investment (asset), and the timing of debt repayments has a similarly important effect on the value of the debt commitment (liability). As a financial expert, you will be expected to make present and future value measurements and to understand their implications. The purpose of this chapter is to present the tools and techniques that will help you measure the present value of future cash inflows and outflows. The content and organization of the chapter are as follows:

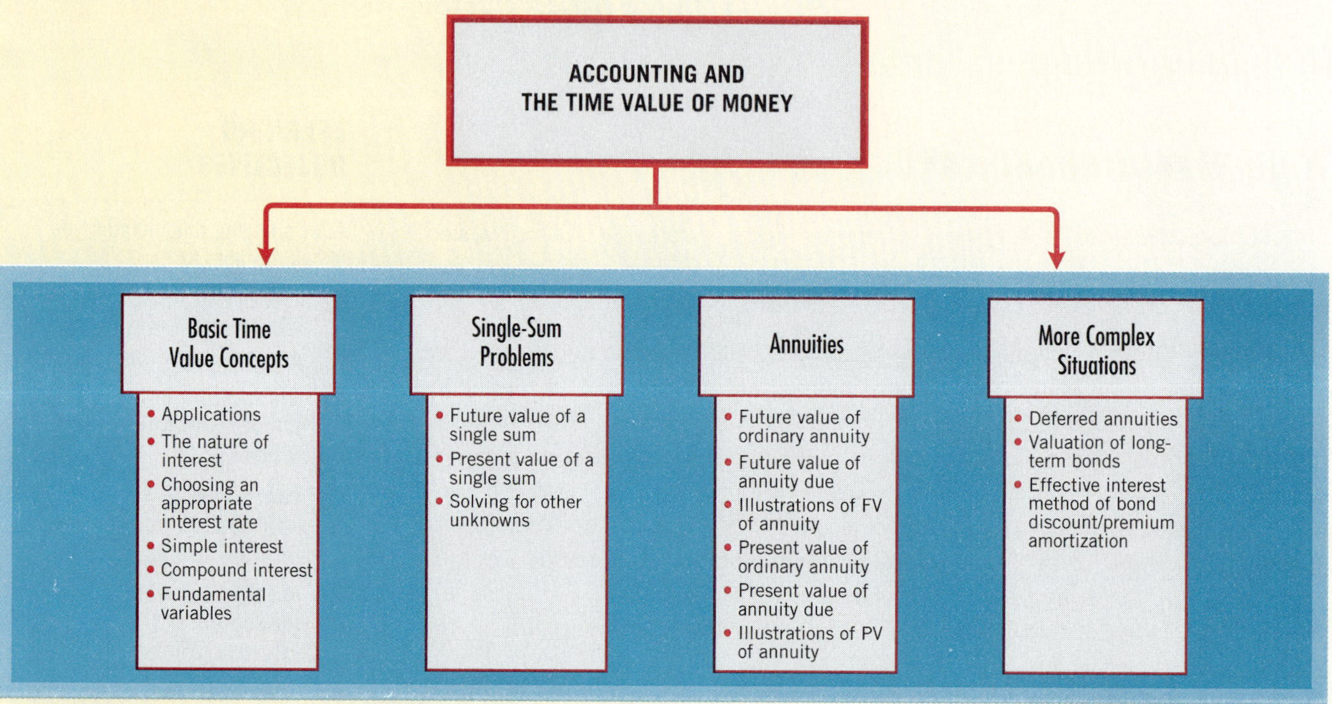

BASIC TIME VALUE CONCEPTS

In accounting (and finance), the term **time value of money** is used to indicate a relationship between time and money—that a dollar received today is worth more than a dollar promised at some time in the future. Why? Because of the opportunity to invest today's dollar and receive interest on the investment. Yet, when you have to decide among various investment or borrowing alternatives, it is essential to be able to compare today's dollar and tomorrow's dollar on the same footing—to "compare apples to apples." We do that by using the concept of **present value**, which has many applications in accounting.

Applications of Time Value Concepts

Financial reporting uses different measurements in different situations. Present value is one of these measurements, and its usage has been increasing.[1] Recognizing that fact, the FASB has issued a concepts statement that provides a framework for using expected

[1]Many of the recent standards, such as FASB Statements No. 106, 107, 109, 113, 114, 116, 118, 121, and 122, addressed the issue of present value somewhere in the pronouncement or related basis for conclusions.

future cash flows and present values as a basis for measurement.[2] Why is a new concepts statement in this area needed? In the past, most accounting calculations of present value have been based on the most likely cash flow amount and a single discount factor. The new statement introduces an expected cash flow approach that uses a **range of cash flows** and incorporates the probabilities of those cash flows to provide a more relevant measurement.

For example, if there is a 30% probability that the cash flow will be $100, a 50% probability that it will be $200, and a 20% probability that it will be $300, the expected cash flow is $190 [($100 × .3) + ($200 × .5) + ($300 × .2)]. Under traditional present value approaches, the most likely estimate ($200) would be used, but that estimate does not consider the different probabilities of the possible cash flows. As a result, the expected cash flow measure should provide more relevant present value measurements. Although the expected cash flow method is currently used in some accounting measurements, such as pensions and other post-retirement benefits, the concepts statement discusses how this approach can be extended to other present value–based accounting measurements.

Some of the applications of present value-based measurements to accounting topics are listed below, several of which are required in succeeding chapters of this textbook:

OBJECTIVE 1
Identify accounting topics where the time value of money is relevant.

PRESENT VALUE-BASED ACCOUNTING MEASUREMENTS

1. ***Notes.*** Valuing noncurrent receivables and payables that carry no stated interest rate or a lower than market interest rate.
2. ***Leases.*** Valuing assets and obligations to be capitalized under long-term leases and measuring the amount of the lease payments and annual leasehold amortization.
3. ***Amortization of Premiums and Discounts.*** Measuring amortization of premium or discount on both bond investments and bonds payable.
4. ***Pensions and Other Postretirement Benefits.*** Measuring service cost components of employers' postretirement benefits expense and postretirement benefits obligation.
5. ***Long-Term Assets.*** Evaluating alternative long-term investments by discounting future cash flows. Determining the value of assets acquired under deferred payment contracts. Measuring impairments of assets.
6. ***Sinking Funds.*** Determining the contributions necessary to accumulate a fund for debt retirements.
7. ***Business Combinations.*** Determining the value of receivables, payables, liabilities, accruals, and commitments acquired or assumed in a "purchase."
8. ***Disclosures.*** Measuring the value of future cash flows from oil and gas reserves for disclosure in supplementary information.
9. ***Installment Contracts.*** Measuring periodic payments on long-term purchase contracts.[3]

In addition to accounting and business applications, compound interest, annuity, and present value concepts apply to personal finance and investment decisions. In purchasing a home or car, planning for retirement, and evaluating alternative investments, you will need to understand time value of money concepts.

---

[2] "Using Cash Flow Information and Present Value in Accounting Measurements," *Statement of Financial Accounting Concepts No. 7* (Norwalk, Conn.: FASB, 2000).

[3] A complete list of where GAAP specifically forbids and requires discounting is presented in an article by Roman L. Weil, "Role of the Time Value of Money in Financial Reporting," *Accounting Horizons*, December 1990, pp. 47–67.

The Nature of Interest

Interest is payment for the use of money. It is the excess cash received or repaid over and above the amount lent or borrowed (**principal**). For example, if the Corner Bank lends you $1,000 with the understanding that you will repay $1,150, then the excess over $1,000, or $150, represents interest expense. Or if you lend your roommate $100 and then collect $110 in full payment, the $10 excess represents interest revenue.

The amount of interest to be paid is generally stated as a rate over a specific period of time. For example, if you used $1,000 for one year before repaying $1,150, the rate of interest is 15% per year ($150 ÷ $1,000). The custom of expressing interest as a percentage rate is an established business practice.[4] In fact, business managers make investing and borrowing decisions on the basis of the rate of interest involved rather than on the actual dollar amount of interest to be received or paid.

How is the interest rate determined? One of the most important factors is the level of credit risk (risk of nonpayment) involved. Other factors being equal, the higher the credit risk, the higher the interest rate. Low-risk borrowers like **Microsoft** or **Intel** can probably obtain a loan at or slightly below the going market rate of interest. You or the neighborhood delicatessen, on the other hand, would probably be charged several percentage points above the market rate, if you can get a loan at all!

The amount of interest involved in any financing transaction is a function of three variables:

VARIABLES IN INTEREST COMPUTATION

1. ***Principal.*** The amount borrowed or invested.
2. ***Interest Rate.*** A percentage of the outstanding principal.
3. ***Time.*** The number of years or fractional portion of a year that the principal is outstanding.

The larger the principal amount, or the higher the interest rate, or the longer the time period, the larger the dollar amount of interest.

Choosing an Appropriate Interest Rate

A perplexing problem is the selection of an appropriate interest rate to measure assets and liabilities. Consider the following debates that have taken place in practice.

1. In oil and gas accounting, the Securities and Exchange Commission (SEC) at one time recommended that the fair value of oil and gas reserves in the ground be computed at the present value of the future revenues discounted at a flat 10% rate. The SEC argued that the use of one rate leads to comparability and that a rate of this magnitude provides a reasonable representation of the present value of future oil and gas reserves. Others disagreed, noting that a 10% rate was unrealistic for two reasons. First, it ignores the current level of interest rate benchmarks such as the prime rate. Second, not all companies and situations deserve the same rate because of differences in risk.
2. In trying to resolve the problem of capitalizing interest cost incurred (recording as an asset) during construction, the profession encountered support for two different measurement bases. Some accountants favored capitalizing the interest cost associated with the specific borrowing. Others disagreed, arguing that a weighed av-

[4]Federal law requires the disclosure of interest rates on an **annual basis** in all contracts. That is, instead of stating the rate as "1% per month," it must be stated as "12% per year" if it is simple interest or "12.68% per year" if it is compounded monthly.

erage is preferable because the borrowing on any specific project affects the borrowing costs of the entire company as it relates to other projects.

How then should we select an interest rate for purposes of present value computations? In the past, interest rates have often been selected on the basis of expediency (availability), regulatory stipulations, and ease of auditability. No consistent approach has been adopted. This is not surprising, given the wide variety of rates from which to choose, such as the general borrowing rate (prime rate), a specific borrowing rate for a given company, opportunity cost rate, investment rate of return, cost-of-capital rate on a weighted-average basis, and so on.

An interest rate has three components:

THREE COMPONENTS OF INTEREST

1. *Pure Rate of Interest* (2%–4%). This would be the amount a lender would charge if there were no possibilities of default and no expectation of inflation.
2. *Credit Risk Rate of Interest* (0%–5%). The government has little or no credit risk (i.e., risk of nonpayment) when it issues bonds; a business enterprise, however, depending upon its financial stability, profitability, etc., can have a low or a high credit risk.
3. *Expected Inflation Rate of Interest* (0%–?). Lenders recognize that in an inflationary economy, they are being paid back with less valuable dollars. As a result, they increase their interest rate to compensate for this loss in purchasing power. When inflationary expectations are high, interest rates are high.

Identifying and mixing these three components in the appropriate ratio for any given company or investor at any given moment is not easy. Yet, the relevance and reliability of accounting information depend on the selection of appropriate interest rates.

Throughout the remainder of this chapter, we will focus on the mechanics of computing present values and future values. In most cases, interest rates will be provided. Occasionally, a problem will ask you to solve for the interest rate as the only unknown variable.

Simple Interest

OBJECTIVE 2
Distinguish between simple and compound interest.

Simple interest is computed on the amount of the principal only. It is the return on (or growth of) the principal for one time period. Simple interest is commonly expressed as follows.[5]

$$\text{Interest} = p \times i \times n$$

where

$$p = \text{principal}$$
$$i = \text{rate of interest for a single period}$$
$$n = \text{number of periods.}$$

To illustrate, if you borrow $1,000 for 3 years with a simple interest rate of 15% per year, the total interest you will pay is $450, computed as follows:

$$\begin{aligned}\text{Interest} &= (p)(i)(n)\\ &= (\$1{,}000)(.15)(3)\\ &= \$450\end{aligned}$$

[5]Simple interest is traditionally expressed in textbooks in business mathematics or business finance as: I(interest) = P(principal) × R(rate) × T(time).

If you borrow $1,000 for 3 months at 15%, the interest is $37.50, computed as follows:

$$\text{Interest} = (\$1{,}000)(.15)(.25)$$
$$= \$37.50$$

Compound Interest

John Maynard Keynes, the legendary English economist, supposedly called it magic. Mayer Rothschild, the founder of the famous European banking firm, is said to have proclaimed it the eighth wonder of the world. Today people continue to extol its wonder and its power. The object of their affection is compound interest.

Compound interest is computed on principal **and** on any interest earned that has not been paid or withdrawn. It is the return on (or growth of) the principal for two or more time periods. Compounding computes interest not only on the principal but also on the interest earned to date on that principal, assuming the interest is left on deposit.[6]

To illustrate the difference between simple and compound interest, assume that you deposit $1,000 in the Last National Bank, where it will earn simple interest of 9% per year, and you deposit another $1,000 in the First State Bank, where it will earn compound interest of 9% per year compounded annually. Also assume that in both cases you will not withdraw any interest until 3 years from the date of deposit. The computation of interest to be received and the accumulated year-end balance are indicated in Illustration 6-1.

ILLUSTRATION 6-1
Simple vs. Compound Interest

Last National Bank

Simple Interest Calculation	Simple Interest	Accumulated Year-end Balance
Year 1 $1,000.00 × 9%	$ 90.00	$1,090.00
Year 2 $1,000.00 × 9%	90.00	$1,180.00
Year 3 $1,000.00 × 9%	90.00	$1,270.00
	$270.00	

First State Bank

Compound Interest Calculation	Compound Interest	Accumulated Year-end Balance
Year 1 $1,000.00 × 9%	$ 90.00	$1,090.00
Year 2 $1,090.00 × 9%	98.10	$1,188.10
Year 3 $1,188.10 × 9%	106.93	$1,295.03
	$295.03	

$25.03 Difference

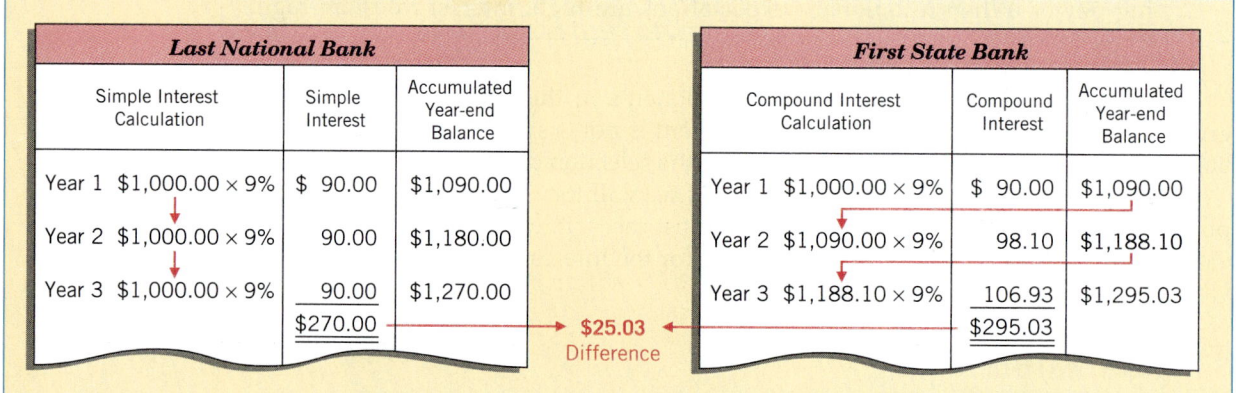

Note in the illustration above that simple interest uses the initial principal of $1,000 to compute the interest in all 3 years. Compound interest uses the accumulated balance (principal plus interest to date) at each year-end to compute interest in the succeeding year—which explains why your compound interest account is larger.

Obviously if you had a choice between investing your money at simple interest or at compound interest, you would choose compound interest, all other things—especially risk—being equal. In the example, compounding provides $25.03 of additional interest revenue. For practical purposes compounding assumes that unpaid interest earned becomes a part of the principal, and the accumulated balance at the end of each year becomes the new principal sum on which interest is earned during the next year.

[6]Here is an illustration of the power of *time* and *compounding* interest on money. In 1626, Peter Minuit bought Manhattan Island from the Manhattoe Indians for $24 worth of trinkets and beads. If the Indians had taken a boat to Holland, invested the $24 in Dutch securities returning just 6% per year, and kept the money and interest invested at 6%, by 1971 they would have had $13 billion, enough to buy back Manhattan and still have a couple of billion dollars left for doodads (*Forbes,* June 1, 1971). By 2000, 374 years after the trade, the $24 would have grown to approximately $69 billion—or to $72 trillion had the money compounded at 8%.

Compound interest is the typical interest computation applied in business situations, particularly in our economy where large amounts of long-lived assets are used productively and financed over long periods of time. Financial managers view and evaluate their investment opportunities in terms of a series of periodic returns, each of which can be reinvested to yield additional returns. Simple interest is usually applicable only to short-term investments and debts that involve a time span of one year or less.

Compound Interest Tables (see pages 324–333)

Five different types of compound interest tables are presented at the end of this chapter. These tables should help you study this chapter as well as solve later problems involving interest.[7] The titles of these five tables and their contents are:

OBJECTIVE 3
Learn how to use appropriate compound interest tables.

INTEREST TABLES AND CONTENTS

1. *Future Value of 1* table. Contains the amounts to which 1 will accumulate if deposited now at a specified rate and left for a specified number of periods. (Table 6-1)
2. *Present Value of 1* table. Contains the amounts that must be deposited now at a specified rate of interest to equal 1 at the end of a specified number of periods. (Table 6-2)
3. *Future Value of an Ordinary Annuity of 1* table. Contains the amounts to which periodic rents of 1 will accumulate if the payments (rents) are invested at the **end** of each period at a specified rate of interest for a specified number of periods. (Table 6-3)
4. *Present Value of an Ordinary Annuity of 1* table. Contains the amounts that must be deposited now at a specified rate of interest to permit withdrawals of 1 at the **end** of regular periodic intervals for the specified number of periods. (Table 6-4)
5. *Present Value of an Annuity Due of 1* table. Contains the amounts that must be deposited now at a specified rate of interest to permit withdrawals of 1 at the **beginning** of regular periodic intervals for the specified number of periods. (Table 6-5)

The excerpt below illustrates the general format and content of these tables. This excerpt from Table 6-1 indicates how much principal plus interest a dollar accumulates to at the end of each of five periods at three different rates of compound interest.

ILLUSTRATION 6-2
Excerpt from Table 6-1

FUTURE VALUE OF 1 AT COMPOUND INTEREST
(Excerpt from Table 6-1, page 325)

Period	9%	10%	11%
1	1.09000	1.10000	1.11000
2	1.18810	1.21000	1.23210
3	1.29503	1.33100	1.36763
4	1.41158	1.46410	1.51807
5	1.53862	1.61051	1.68506

The compound tables are computed using basic formulas. For example, the formula to determine the future value factor (*FVF*) for 1 is:

$$FVF_{n,i} = (1 + i)^n$$

[7]Compound interest tables make no allowance for inflation or deflation. If you need to consider the changes in the purchasing power of the dollar, you have to do so outside the framework of these tables or by adjusting the interest rate to reflect inflation.

where

$$FVF_{n,i} = \text{future value factor for } n \text{ periods at } i \text{ interest}$$
$$n = \text{number of periods}$$
$$i = \text{rate of interest for a single period}$$

The $FVF_{n,i}$ and other time value of money formulas are programmed into financial calculators and spreadsheet programs. The use of these tools to solve time value of money problems is illustrated in the appendix to this chapter.

To illustrate the use of interest tables to calculate compound amounts, assuming an interest rate of 9%, the future value to which 1 accumulates (the future value factor) is shown below.

ILLUSTRATION 6-3
Accumulation of Compound Amounts

Period	Beginning-of-Period Amount	×	Multiplier $(1 + i)$	=	End-of-Period Amount*	Formula $(1 + i)^n$
1	1.00000		1.09		1.09000	$(1.09)^1$
2	1.09000		1.09		1.18810	$(1.09)^2$
3	1.18810		1.09		1.29503	$(1.09)^3$

*Note that these amounts appear in Table 6-1 in the 9% column.

Throughout the discussion of compound interest tables the use of the term **periods** instead of **years** is intentional. Interest is generally expressed in terms of an annual rate, but in many business circumstances the compounding period is less than one year. In such circumstances the annual interest rate must be converted to correspond to the length of the period. The process is to convert the "annual interest rate" into the "compounding period interest rate" by **dividing the annual rate by the number of compounding periods per year**.

In addition, the number of periods is determined by **multiplying the number of years involved by the number of compounding periods per year**. To illustrate, assume that $1.00 is invested for 6 years at 8% annual interest compounded **quarterly**. Using Table 6-1, page 324, we can determine the amount to which this $1.00 will accumulate: read the factor that appears in the 2% column on the 24th row—6 years × 4 compounding periods per year, namely 1.60844, or approximately $1.61. Thus, the term **periods**, not **years**, is used in all compound interest tables to express the quantity of n.

The following schedule shows how to determine (1) the interest rate per compounding period and (2) the number of compounding periods in four situations of differing compounding frequency.[8]

ILLUSTRATION 6-4
Frequency of Compounding

12% Annual Interest Rate over 5 Years Compounded	Interest Rate per Compounding Period	Number of Compounding Periods
Annually (1)	.12 ÷ 1 = .12	5 years × 1 compounding per year = 5 periods
Semiannually (2)	.12 ÷ 2 = .06	5 years × 2 compoundings per year = 10 periods
Quarterly (4)	.12 ÷ 4 = .03	5 years × 4 compoundings per year = 20 periods
Monthly (12)	.12 ÷ 12 = .01	5 years × 12 compoundings per year = 60 periods

[8]Because interest is theoretically earned (accruing) every second of every day, it is possible to calculate interest that is **compounded continuously**. Computations involving continuous compounding are facilitated through the use of the natural, or Napierian, system of logarithms. As a practical matter, however, most business transactions assume interest to be compounded no more frequently than daily.

How often interest is compounded can make a substantial difference in the rate of return. For example, a 9% annual interest compounded **daily** provides a 9.42% yield, or a difference of .42%. The 9.42% is referred to as the **effective yield**.[9] The annual interest rate (9%) is called the **stated**, **nominal**, or **face rate**. When the compounding frequency is greater than once a year, the effective interest rate will always be greater than the stated rate.

The schedule below shows how compounding for five different time periods affects the effective yield and the amount earned by an investment of $10,000 for one year.

ILLUSTRATION 6-5
Comparison of Different Compounding Periods

Interest Rate	Compounding Periods: Annually	Semiannually	Quarterly	Monthly	Daily
8%	8.00% $800	8.16% $816	8.24% $824	8.30% $830	8.33% $833
9%	9.00% $900	9.20% $920	9.31% $931	9.38% $938	9.42% $942
10%	10.00% $1,000	10.25% $1,025	10.38% $1,038	10.47% $1,047	10.52% $1,052

Fundamental Variables

The following four variables are fundamental to all compound interest problems:

OBJECTIVE 4
Identify variables fundamental to solving interest problems.

FUNDAMENTAL VARIABLES

1. ***Rate of Interest.*** This rate, unless otherwise stated, is an annual rate that must be adjusted to reflect the length of the compounding period if less than a year.
2. ***Number of Time Periods.*** This is the number of compounding periods (a period may be equal to or less than a year).
3. ***Future Value.*** The value at a future date of a given sum or sums invested assuming compound interest.
4. ***Present Value.*** The value now (present time) of a future sum or sums discounted assuming compound interest.

[9]The formula for calculating the **effective rate** in situations where the compounding frequency (n) is greater than once a year is as follows:

$$\text{Effective rate} = (1 + i)^n - 1$$

To illustrate, if the stated annual rate is 8% compounded quarterly (or 2% per quarter), the effective annual rate is:

$$\begin{aligned}\text{Effective rate} &= (1 + .02)^4 - 1\\ &= (1.02)^4 - 1\\ &= 1.0824 - 1\\ &= .0824\\ &= 8.24\%\end{aligned}$$

The relationship of these four fundamental variables is depicted in the following **time diagram**:

ILLUSTRATION 6-6
Basic Time Diagram

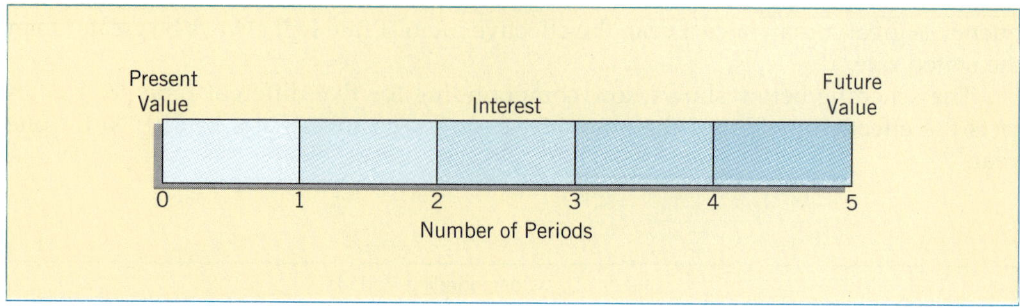

In some cases all four of these variables are known, but in many business situations at least one variable is unknown. As an aid to better understanding the problems and to finding solutions, we encourage you to sketch compound interest problems in the form of the preceding time diagram.

SINGLE-SUM PROBLEMS

Many business and investment decisions involve a single amount of money that either exists now or will in the future. Single-sum problems can generally be classified into one of the following two categories:

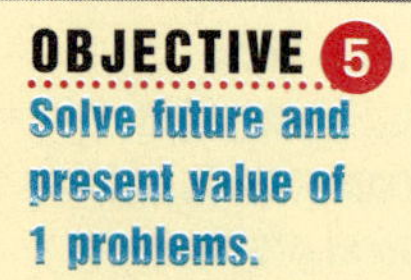

OBJECTIVE 5
Solve future and present value of 1 problems.

1. Computing the **unknown future value** of a known single sum of money that is invested now for a certain number of periods at a certain interest rate.
2. Computing the **unknown present value** of a known single sum of money in the future that is discounted for a certain number of periods at a certain interest rate.

When analyzing the information provided, you determine first whether it is a future value problem or a present value problem. **If you are solving for a future value,** all cash flows must be *accumulated* to a future point. In this instance, the effect of interest is to increase the amounts or values over time so that the future value is greater than the present value. However, **if you are solving for a present value,** all cash flows must be *discounted* from the future to the present. In this case, the **discounting** reduces the amounts or values so that the present value is less than the future amount.

Preparation of time diagrams aids in identifying the unknown as an item in the future or the present. Sometimes it is neither a future value nor a present value that is to be determined but, rather, the interest or discount rate or the number of compounding or discounting periods.

Future Value of a Single Sum

To determine the **future value** of a single sum, multiply the future value factor by its present value (principal), as follows:

$$FV = PV\ (FVF_{n,i})$$

where

FV = future value

PV = present value (principal or single sum)

$FVF_{n,i}$ = future value factor for n periods at i interest

To illustrate, what is the future value of $50,000 invested for 5 years compounded annually at an interest rate of 11%? In time-diagram form, this investment situation would appear as follows:

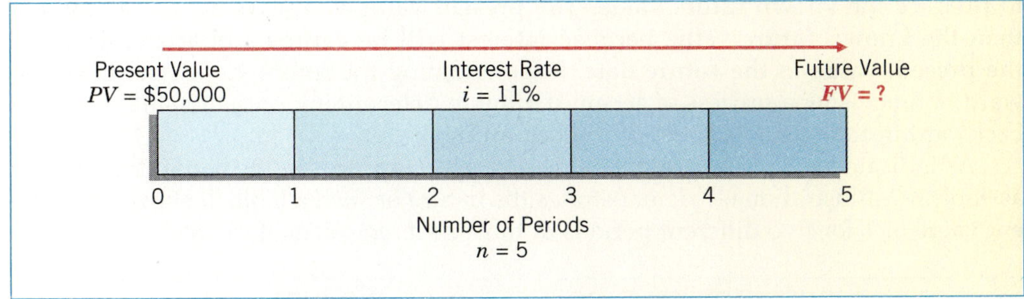

Using the formula, this investment problem is solved as follows:

$$\text{Future value} = PV\,(FVF_{n,i})$$
$$= \$50{,}000\,(FVF_{5,11\%})$$
$$= \$50{,}000\,(1 + .11)^5$$
$$= \$50{,}000\,(1.68506)$$
$$= \$84{,}253$$

To determine the future value factor of 1.68506 in the formula above, use a financial calculator or read the appropriate table, in this case Table 6-1 (11% column and the 5-period row).

This time diagram and formula approach can be applied to a routine business situation. To illustrate, Commonwealth Edison Company deposited $250 million in an escrow account with the Northern Trust Company at the beginning of 2000 as a commitment toward a power plant to be completed December 31, 2003. How much will be on deposit at the end of 4 years if interest is 10%, compounded semiannually?

With a known present value of $250 million, a total of 8 compounding periods (4 × 2), and an interest rate of 5% per compounding period (.10 ÷ 2), this problem can be time diagrammed and the future value determined as follows:

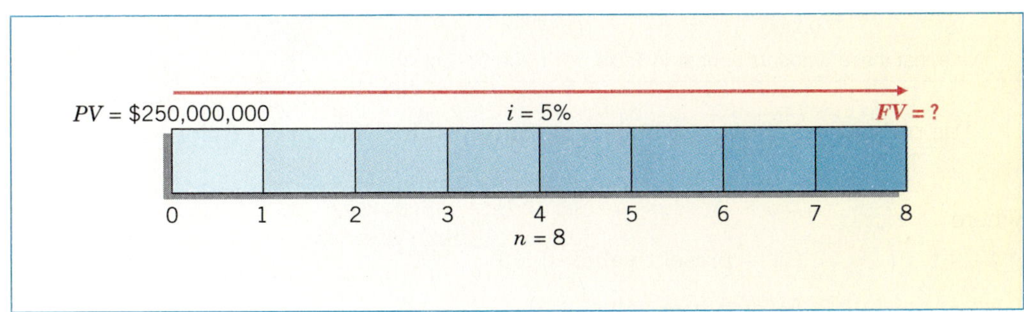

$$\text{Future value} = \$250{,}000{,}000\,(FVF_{8,5\%})$$
$$= \$250{,}000{,}000\,(1 + .05)^8$$
$$= \$250{,}000{,}000\,(1.47746)$$
$$= \$369{,}365{,}000$$

Using a future value factor found in Table 6-1 (5% column, 8-period row), we find that the deposit of $250 million will accumulate to $369,365,000 by December 31, 2003.

Present Value of a Single Sum

The example at the top of the page showed that $50,000 invested at an annually compounded interest rate of 11% will be worth $84,253 at the end of 5 years. It follows, then, that $84,253, 5 years in the future is worth $50,000 now; that is, $50,000 is the present value of $84,253. The **present value** is the amount that must be invested now to produce the known future value. **The present value is always a smaller amount than the known future value because interest will be earned and accumulated on the present value to the future date.** In determining the future value, we move forward in time using a process of **accumulation**; in determining present value, we move backward in time using a process of **discounting**.

As indicated earlier, a "present value of 1 table" appears at the end of this chapter as Table 6-2. Illustration 6-7 demonstrates the nature of such a table. It shows the present value of 1 for five different periods at three different rates of interest.

ILLUSTRATION 6-7
Excerpt from Table 6-2

PRESENT VALUE OF 1 AT COMPOUND INTEREST
(Excerpt from Table 6-2, page 327)

Period	9%	10%	11%
1	0.91743	0.90909	0.90090
2	0.84168	0.82645	0.81162
3	0.77218	0.75132	0.73119
4	0.70843	0.68301	0.65873
5	0.64993	0.62092	0.59345

The present value of 1 (present value factor) may be expressed as a formula:

$$PVF_{n,i} = \frac{1}{(1 + i)^n}$$

where

$PVF_{n,i}$ = present value factor for n periods at i interest

To illustrate, assuming an interest rate of 9%, the present value of 1 discounted for three different periods is as follows:

ILLUSTRATION 6-8
Present Value of $1 Discounted at 9% for Three Periods

Discount Periods	1	÷	$(1 + i)^n$	=	Present Value*	Formula $1/(1 + i)^n$
1	1.00000		1.09		.91743	$1/(1.09)^1$
2	1.00000		$(1.09)^2$		.84168	$1/(1.09)^2$
3	1.00000		$(1.09)^3$		.77218	$1/(1.09)^3$

*Note that these amounts appear in Table 6-2 in the 9% column.

The present value of any single sum (future value) then, is as follows:

$$PV = FV\ (PVF_{n,i})$$

where

PV = present value

FV = future value

$PVF_{n,i}$ = present value factor for n periods at i interest

To illustrate, what is the present value of $84,253 to be received or paid in 5 years discounted at 11% compounded annually? In time-diagram form, this problem is drawn as follows:

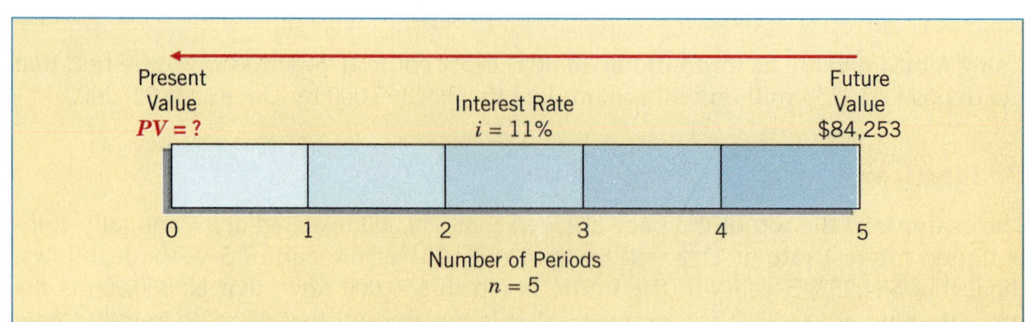

Using the formula, this problem is solved as follows:

$$\text{Present value} = FV\ (PVF_{n,i})$$
$$= \$84{,}253\ (PVF_{5,11\%})$$
$$= \$84{,}253\left(\frac{1}{(1 + .11)^5}\right)$$
$$= \$84{,}253\ (.59345)$$
$$= \$50{,}000$$

To determine the present value factor of .59345, use a financial calculator or read the present value of a single sum in Table 6-2 (11% column, 5-period row).

The time diagram and formula approach can be applied in a variety of situations. For example, assume that your rich uncle proposes to give you \$2,000 for a trip to Europe when you graduate from college 3 years from now. He proposes to finance the trip by investing a sum of money now at 8% compound interest that will provide you with \$2,000 upon your graduation. The only conditions are that you graduate and that you tell him how much to invest now.

To impress your uncle, you might set up the following time diagram and solve this problem as follows:

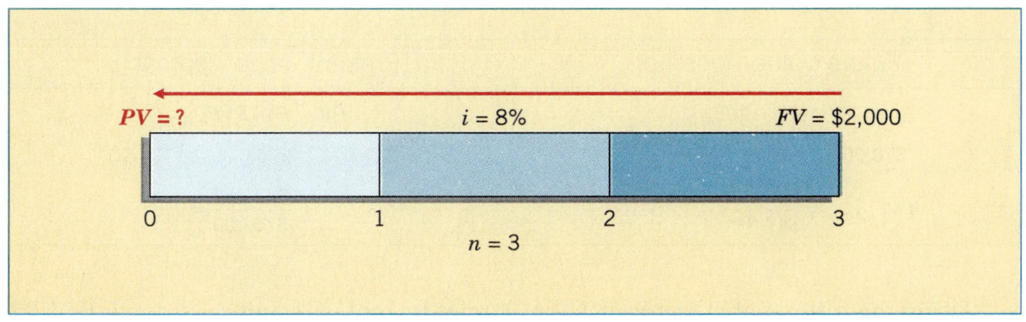

$$\text{Present value} = \$2{,}000\ (PVF_{3,8\%})$$
$$= \$2{,}000\left(\frac{1}{(1 + .08)^3}\right)$$
$$= \$2{,}000\ (.79383)$$
$$= \$1{,}587.66$$

Advise your uncle to invest \$1,587.66 now to provide you with \$2,000 upon graduation. To satisfy your uncle's other condition, you must pass this course and many more.

Solving for Other Unknowns in Single-Sum Problems

In computing either the future value or the present value in the previous single-sum illustrations, both the number of periods and the interest rate were known. In many business situations, both the future value and the present value are known, but the number of periods or the interest rate is unknown. The following two illustrations are single-sum problems (future value and present value) with either an unknown number of periods (n) or an unknown interest rate (i). These illustrations and the accompanying solutions demonstrate that if any three of the four values (future value, FV; present value, PV; number of periods, n; interest rate, i) are known, the remaining unknown variable can be derived.

Illustration—Computation of the Number of Periods

The Village of Somonauk wants to accumulate \$70,000 for the construction of a veterans monument in the town square. If at the beginning of the current year the Village deposited $47,811 in a memorial fund that earns 10% interest compounded annually, how many years will it take to accumulate $70,000 in the memorial fund?

In this illustration, both the present value ($47,811) and the future value ($70,000) are known along with the interest rate of 10%. A time diagram of this investment problem is as follows:

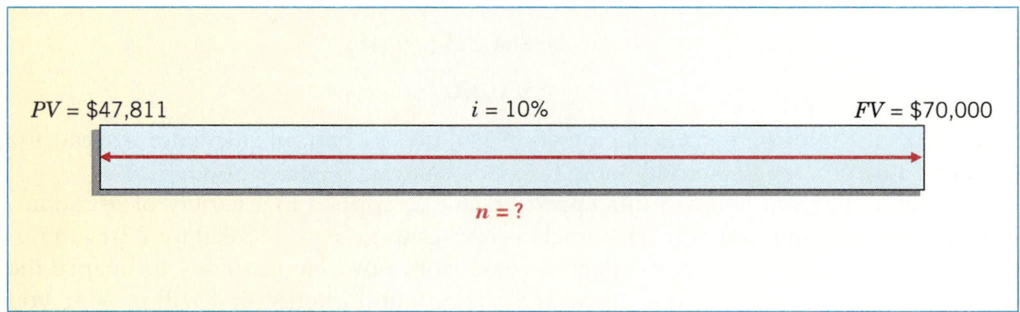

Because both the present value and the future value are known, we can solve for the unknown number of periods using either the future value or the present value formulas as shown below:

ILLUSTRATION 6-9
Solving for Unknown Number of Periods

Future Value Approach	Present Value Approach
$FV = PV\,(FVF_{n,10\%})$	$PV = FV\,(PVF_{n,10\%})$
$\$70{,}000 = \$47{,}811\,(FVF_{n,10\%})$	$\$47{,}811 = \$70{,}000\,(PVF_{n,10\%})$
$FVF_{n,10\%} = \dfrac{\$70{,}000}{\$47{,}811} = 1.46410$	$PVF_{n,10\%} = \dfrac{\$47{,}811}{\$70{,}000} = .68301$

Using the future value factor of 1.46410, refer to Table 6-1 and read down the 10% column to find that factor in the 4-period row. Thus, it will take 4 years for the $47,811 to accumulate to $70,000 if invested at 10% interest compounded annually. Using the present value factor of .68301, refer to Table 6-2 and read down the 10% column to find again that factor in the 4-period row.

Illustration—Computation of the Interest Rate

Advanced Design, Inc. wishes to have $1,409,870 for basic research 5 years from now. The firm currently has $800,000 to invest for that purpose. At what rate of interest must the $800,000 be invested to fund basic research projects of $1,409,870, 5 years from now?

A time diagram of this investment situation is as follows:

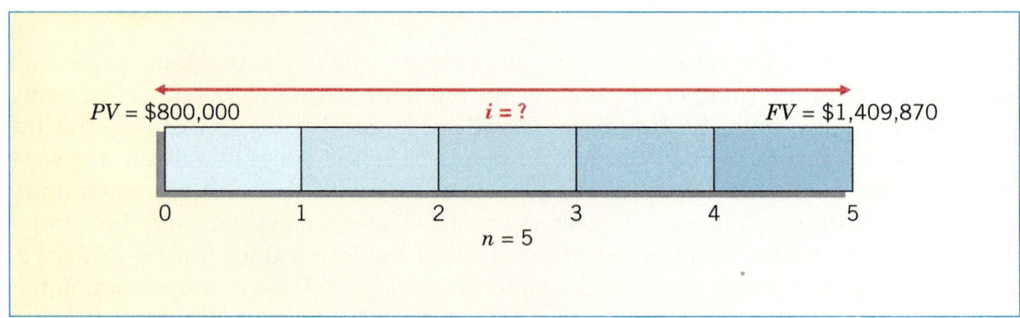

The unknown interest rate may be determined from either the future value approach or the present value approach as shown in Illustration 6-10 on the next page.

Future Value Approach	Present Value Approach
$FV = PV\,(FVF_{5,i})$	$PV = FV\,(PVF_{5,i})$
$\$1{,}409{,}870 = \$800{,}000\,(FVF_{5,i})$	$\$800{,}000 = \$1{,}409{,}870\,(PVF_{5,i})$
$FVF_{5,i} = \frac{\$1{,}409{,}870}{\$800{,}000} = 1.76234$	$PVF_{5,i} = \frac{\$800{,}000}{\$1{,}409{,}870} = .56743$

ILLUSTRATION 6-10
Solving for Unknown Interest Rate

Using the future value factor of 1.76234, refer to Table 6-1 and read across the 5-period row to find that factor in the 12% column. Thus, the $800,000 must be invested at 12% to accumulate to $1,409,870 in 5 years. And, using the present value factor of .56743 and Table 6-2, again find that factor at the juncture of the 5-period row and the 12% column.

ANNUITIES

The preceding discussion involved only the accumulation or discounting of a single principal sum. Individuals frequently encounter situations in which a series of dollar amounts are to be paid or received periodically, such as loans or sales to be repaid in installments, invested funds that will be partially recovered at regular intervals, or cost savings that are realized repeatedly. A life insurance contract is probably the most common and most familiar type of transaction involving a series of equal payments made at equal intervals of time. Such a process of periodic saving represents the accumulation of a sum of money through an annuity. An **annuity** by definition requires that (1) the periodic payments or receipts (called **rents**) always be the same amount, (2) the **interval** between such rents always be the same, and (3) the **interest be compounded** once each interval. The **future value of an annuity** is the sum of all the rents plus the accumulated compound interest on them.

It should be noted that the rents may occur at either the beginning or the end of the periods. To distinguish annuities under these two alternatives, an annuity is classified as an **ordinary annuity** if the rents occur at the end of each period, and as an **annuity due** if the rents occur at the beginning of each period.

Future Value of an Ordinary Annuity

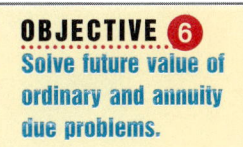

OBJECTIVE 6
Solve future value of ordinary and annuity due problems.

One approach to the problem of determining the future value to which an annuity will accumulate is to compute the value to which **each** of the rents in the series will accumulate and then total their individual future values. For example, assume that $1 is deposited at the **end** of each of 5 years (an ordinary annuity) and earns 12% interest compounded annually. The future value can be computed as follows using the "future value of 1" table (Table 6-1) for each of the five $1 rents:

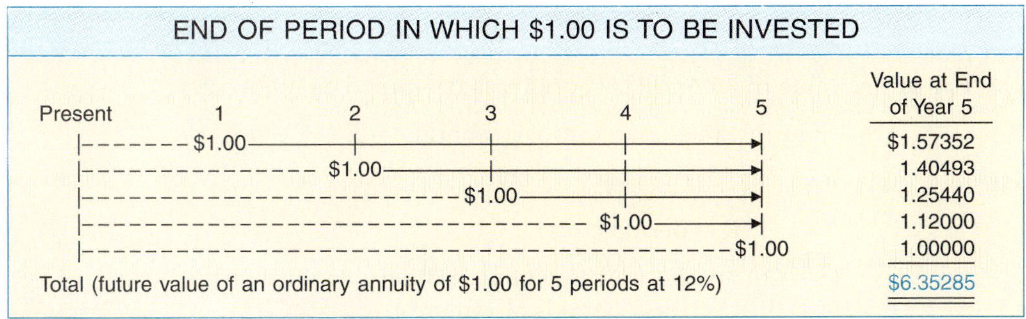
END OF PERIOD IN WHICH $1.00 IS TO BE INVESTED

Present	1	2	3	4	5	Value at End of Year 5
	$1.00				→	$1.57352
		$1.00			→	1.40493
			$1.00		→	1.25440
				$1.00	→	1.12000
					$1.00	1.00000
Total (future value of an ordinary annuity of $1.00 for 5 periods at 12%)						$6.35285

ILLUSTRATION 6-11
Solving for the Future Value of an Ordinary Annuity

Because the rents that compose an ordinary annuity are deposited at the end of the period, they can earn no interest during the period in which they are originally deposited. For example, the third rent earns interest for only two periods (periods four and five). Obviously the third rent earns no interest for the first two periods since it is not deposited until the third period; furthermore, it can earn no interest for the third period since it is not deposited until the end of the third period. Any time the future value of an ordinary annuity is computed, the number of compounding periods will always be **one less than the number of rents**.

Although the foregoing procedure for computing the future value of an ordinary annuity will always produce the correct answer, it can become cumbersome if the number of rents is large. A more efficient way of expressing the future value of an ordinary annuity of 1 is in a formula that is a summation of the individual rents plus the compound interest:

$$FVF\text{-}OA_{n,i} = \frac{(1+i)^n - 1}{i}$$

where

$$FVF\text{-}OA_{n,i} = \text{future value factor of an ordinary annuity}$$

$$i = \text{rate of interest per period}$$

$$n = \text{number of compounding periods}$$

For example, $FVF\text{-}OA_{5,12\%}$ refers to the value to which an ordinary annuity of 1 will accumulate in 5 periods at 12% interest.

Using the formula above, tables have been developed similar to those used for the "future value of 1" and the "present value of 1" for both an ordinary annuity and an annuity due. The table in Illustration 6-12 is an excerpt from the "future value of an ordinary annuity of 1" table.

ILLUSTRATION 6-12
Excerpt from Table 6-3

FUTURE VALUE OF AN ORDINARY ANNUITY OF 1
(Excerpt from Table 6-3, page 329)

Period	10%	11%	12%
1	1.00000	1.00000	1.00000
2	2.10000	2.11000	2.12000
3	3.31000	3.34210	3.37440
4	4.64100	4.70973	4.77933
5	6.10510	6.22780	6.35285*

*Note that this annuity table factor is the same as the sum of the future values of 1 factors shown in Illustration 6-11.

Interpreting the table, if $1.00 is invested at the end of each year for 4 years at 11% interest compounded annually, the value of the annuity at the end of the fourth year will be $4.71 (4.70973 × $1.00). Multiply the factor from the appropriate line and column of the table by the dollar amount of **one rent** involved in an ordinary annuity. The result: the accumulated sum of the rents and the compound interest to the date of the last rent.

The future value of an ordinary annuity is computed as follows:

$$\text{Future value of an ordinary annuity} = R\ (FVF\text{-}OA_{n,i})$$

where

$$R = \text{periodic rent}$$

$$FVF\text{-}OA_{n,i} = \text{future value of an ordinary annuity factor for } n \text{ periods at } i \text{ interest}$$

To illustrate, what is the future value of five $5,000 deposits made at the end of each of the next 5 years, earning interest of 12%? In time-diagram form, this problem is drawn as follows:

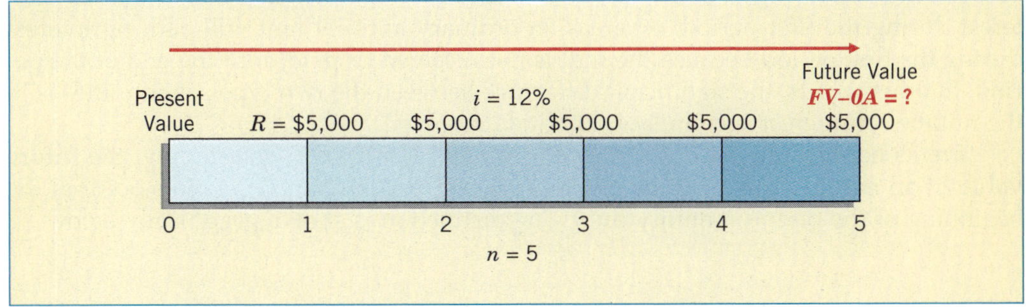

Using the formula, this investment problem is solved as follows:

$$\text{Future value of an ordinary annuity} = R\,(FVF\text{-}OA_{n,i})$$
$$= \$5{,}000\,(FVF\text{-}OA_{5,12\%})$$
$$= \$5{,}000\left(\frac{(1+.12)^5-1}{.12}\right)$$
$$= \$5{,}000\,(6.35285)$$
$$= \$31{,}764.25$$

We can determine the future value of an ordinary annuity factor of 6.35285 in the formula above using a financial calculator or by reading the appropriate table, in this case Table 6-3 (12% column and the 5-period row).

To illustrate these computations in a business situation, assume that Hightown Electronics decides to deposit $75,000 at the end of each 6-month period for the next 3 years for the purpose of accumulating enough money to meet debts that mature in 3 years. What is the future value that will be on deposit at the end of 3 years if the annual interest rate is 10%?

The time diagram and formula solution are as follows:

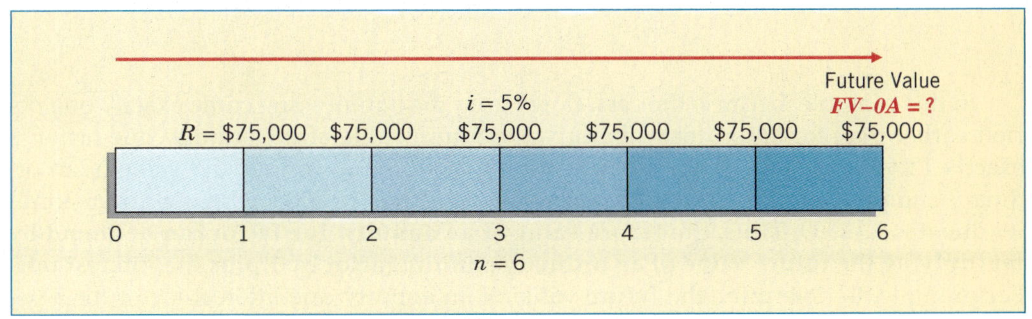

$$\text{Future value of an ordinary annuity} = R\,(FVF\text{-}OA_{n,i})$$
$$= \$75{,}000\,(FVF\text{-}OA_{6,5\%})$$
$$= \$75{,}000\left(\frac{(1+.05)^6-1}{.05}\right)$$
$$= \$75{,}000\,(6.80191)$$
$$= \$510{,}143.25$$

Thus, six 6-month deposits of $75,000 earning 5% per period will grow to $510,143.25.

Future Value of an Annuity Due

The preceding analysis of an ordinary annuity was based on the assumption that the periodic rents occur at the **end** of each period. An annuity due assumes periodic rents occur at the **beginning** of each period. This means an annuity due will accumulate interest during the first period, whereas an ordinary annuity rent will earn no interest during the first period because the rent is not received or paid until the end of the period. In other words, the significant difference between the two types of annuities is in the number of interest accumulation periods involved.

If rents occur at the end of a period (ordinary annuity), in determining the **future value of an annuity** there will be one less interest period than if the rents occur at the beginning of the period (annuity due). The distinction is shown graphically below.

ILLUSTRATION 6-13
Comparison of the Future Value of an Ordinary Annuity with an Annuity Due

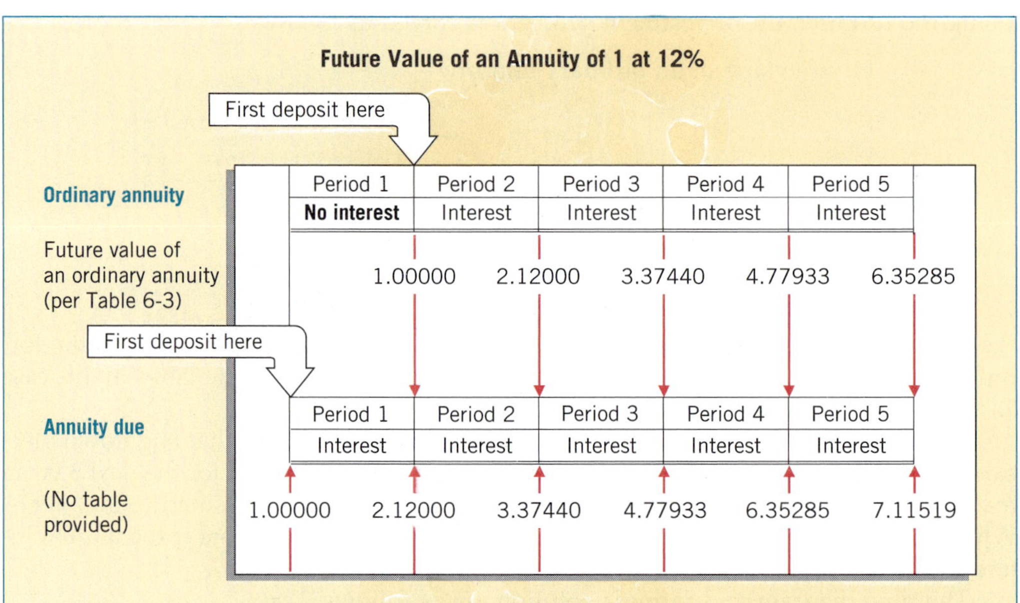

In this example, because the cash flows from the annuity due come exactly one period earlier than for an ordinary annuity, the future value of the annuity due factor is exactly 12% higher than the ordinary annuity factor. For example, the value of an ordinary annuity factor at the end of period one at 12% is 1.00000, whereas for an annuity due it is 1.12000. **Thus, the future value of an annuity due factor can be found by multiplying the future value of an ordinary annuity factor by 1 plus the interest rate.** For example, to determine the future value of an annuity due interest factor for 5 periods at 12% compound interest, simply multiply the future value of an ordinary annuity interest factor for 5 periods (6.35285) by one plus the interest rate (1 + .12), to arrive at 7.11519 (6.35285 × 1.12).

To illustrate the use of the ordinary annuity tables in converting to an annuity due, assume that Sue Lotadough plans to deposit $800 a year on each birthday of her son Howard, starting today, his tenth birthday, at 12% interest compounded annually. Sue wants to know the amount she will have accumulated for college expenses by her son's eighteenth birthday. If the first deposit is made on Howard's tenth birthday, Sue will make a total of 8 deposits over the life of the annuity (assume no deposit on the eighteenth birthday). Because all the deposits will be made at the beginning of the periods, they represent an annuity due.

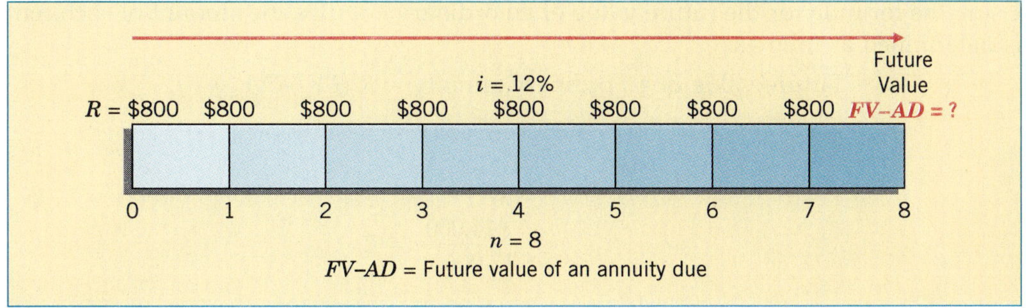

Referring to the "future value of an ordinary annuity of 1" table for 8 periods at 12%, we find a factor of 12.29969. This factor is then multiplied by (1 + .12) to arrive at the future value of an annuity due factor. As a result, the accumulated value on Howard's eighteenth birthday is computed as follows:

ILLUSTRATION 6-14
Computation of Accumulated Value of Annuity Due

1. Future value of an ordinary annuity of 1 for 8 periods at 12% (Table 6-3)	12.29969
2. Factor (1 + .12)	× 1.12
3. Future value of an annuity due of 1 for 8 periods at 12%	13.77565
4. Periodic deposit (rent)	× $800
5. Accumulated value on son's eighteenth birthday	$11,020.52

Depending on the college he chooses, Howard may have only enough to finance his first year of school.

Illustrations of Future Value of Annuity Problems

In the foregoing annuity examples three values were known—amount of each rent, interest rate, and number of periods. They were used to determine the fourth value, future value, which was unknown. The first two future value problems presented illustrate the computations of (1) the amount of the rents and (2) the number of rents. The third problem illustrates the computation of the future value of an annuity due.

Computation of Rent

Assume that you wish to accumulate $14,000 for a down payment on a condominium apartment 5 years from now; for the next 5 years you can earn an annual return of 8% compounded semiannually. How much should you deposit at the end of each 6-month period?

The $14,000 is the future value of 10 (5 × 2) semiannual end-of-period payments of an unknown amount, at an interest rate of 4% (8% ÷ 2). This problem appears in the form of a time diagram as follows:

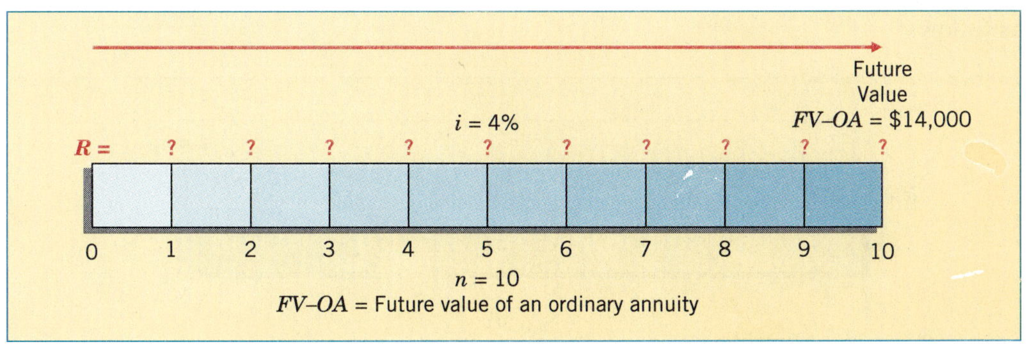

Using the formula for the future value of an ordinary annuity, the amount of each rent is determined as follows:

$$\text{Future value of an ordinary annuity} = R\ (FVF\text{-}OA_{n,i})$$

$$\$14{,}000 = R\ (FVF\text{-}OA_{10,4\%})$$

$$\$14{,}000 = R(12.00611)$$

$$\frac{\$14{,}000}{12.00611} = R$$

$$R = \$1{,}166.07$$

Thus, you must make 10 semiannual deposits of $1,166.07 each in order to accumulate $14,000 for your down payment.

Computation of the Number of Periodic Rents

Suppose that your company wishes to accumulate $117,332 by making periodic deposits of $20,000 at the end of each year that will earn 8% compounded annually while accumulating. How many deposits must be made?

The $117,332 represents the future value of n(?) $20,000 deposits, at an 8% annual rate of interest. This problem appears in the form of a time diagram as follows:

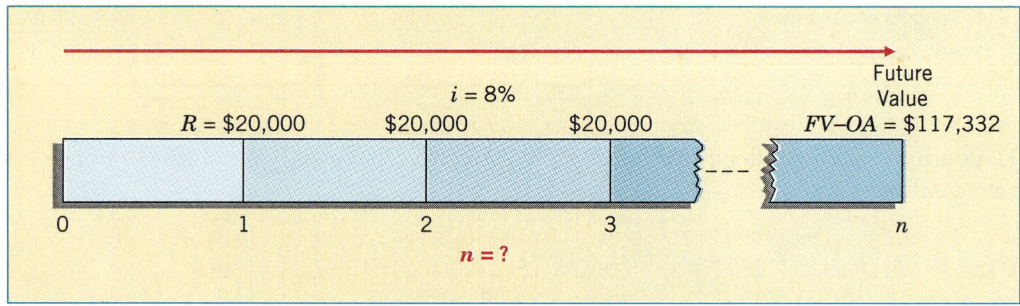

Using the future value of an ordinary annuity formula, we obtain the following factor:

$$\text{Future value of an ordinary annuity} = R\ (FVF\text{-}OA_{n,i})$$

$$\$117{,}332 = \$20{,}000\ (FVF\text{-}OA_{n,8\%})$$

$$FVF\text{-}OA_{n,8\%} = \frac{\$117{,}332}{\$20{,}000} = 5.86660$$

Using Table 6-3 and reading down the 8% column, we find 5.86660 in the 5-period row. Thus, five deposits of $20,000 each must be made.

Computation of the Future Value

Walter Goodwrench, a mechanic, has taken on weekend work in the hope of creating his own retirement fund. Mr. Goodwrench deposits $2,500 today in a savings account that earns 9% interest. He plans to deposit $2,500 every year for a total of 30 years. How much cash will have accumulated in Mr. Goodwrench's retirement savings account when he retires in 30 years? This problem appears in the form of a time diagram as follows:

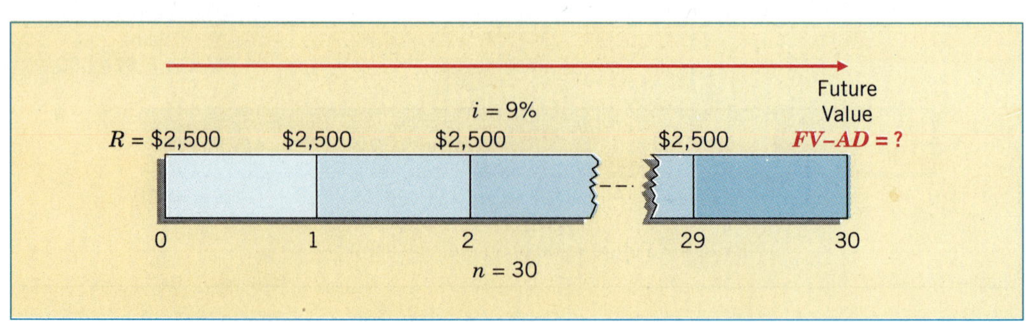

Using the "future value of an ordinary annuity of 1" table, the solution is computed as follows:

1. Future value of an ordinary annuity of 1 for 30 periods at 9%	136.30754
2. Factor (1 + .09)	× 1.09
3. Future value of an annuity due of 1 for 30 periods at 9%	148.57522
4. Periodic rent	× $2,500
5. Accumulated value at end of 30 years	$371,438

ILLUSTRATION 6-15
Computation of Accumulated Value of an Annuity Due

Present Value of an Ordinary Annuity

OBJECTIVE 7
Solve present value of ordinary and annuity due problems.

The present value of an annuity is **the single sum** that, if invested at compound interest now, would provide for an annuity (a series of withdrawals) for a certain number of future periods. In other words, the present value of an ordinary annuity is the present value of a series of equal rents to be withdrawn at equal intervals.

One approach to finding the present value of an annuity is to determine the present value of each of the rents in the series and then total their individual present values. For example, an annuity of $1.00 to be received at the **end** of each of 5 periods may be viewed as separate amounts; the present value of each is computed from the table of present values (see pages 326–327), assuming an interest rate of 12%.

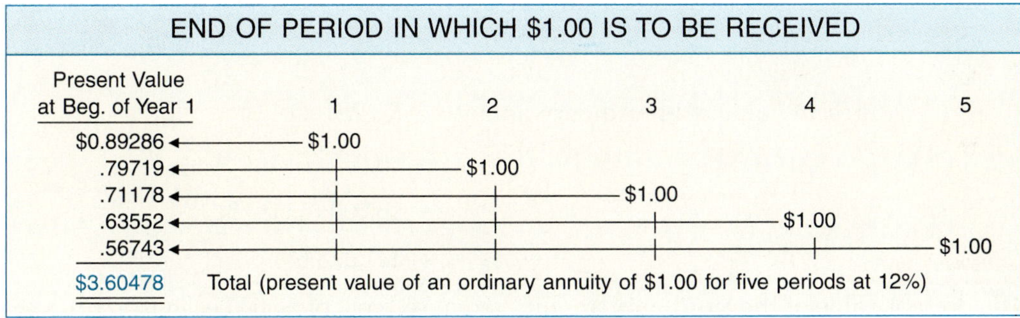

ILLUSTRATION 6-16
Solving for the Present Value of an Ordinary Annuity

This computation tells us that if we invest the single sum of $3.60 today at 12% interest for 5 periods, we will be able to withdraw $1.00 at the end of each period for 5 periods. This cumbersome procedure can be summarized by:

$$PVF\text{-}OA_{n,i} = \frac{1 - \dfrac{1}{(1+i)^n}}{i}$$

The expression $PVF\text{-}OA_{n,i}$ refers to the present value of an ordinary annuity of 1 factor for n periods at i interest. Using this formula, present value of ordinary annuity tables are prepared. An excerpt from such a table is shown below:

PRESENT VALUE OF AN ORDINARY ANNUITY OF 1
(Excerpt from Table 6-4, page 331)

Period	10%	11%	12%
1	0.90909	0.90090	0.89286
2	1.73554	1.71252	1.69005
3	2.48685	2.44371	2.40183
4	3.16986	3.10245	3.03735
5	3.79079	3.69590	3.60478*

*Note that this annuity table factor is equal to the sum of the present value of 1 factors shown in Illustration 6-16.

ILLUSTRATION 6-17
Excerpt from Table 6-4

The general formula for the present value of any ordinary annuity is as follows:

$$\text{Present value of an ordinary annuity} = R\ (PVF\text{-}OA_{n,i})$$

where

$$R = \text{periodic rent (ordinary annuity)}$$

$$PVF\text{-}OA_{n,i} = \text{present value of an ordinary annuity of 1 for } n \text{ periods at } i \text{ interest}$$

To illustrate, what is the present value of rental receipts of $6,000 each to be received at the end of each of the next 5 years when discounted at 12%? This problem may be time-diagrammed and solved as follows:

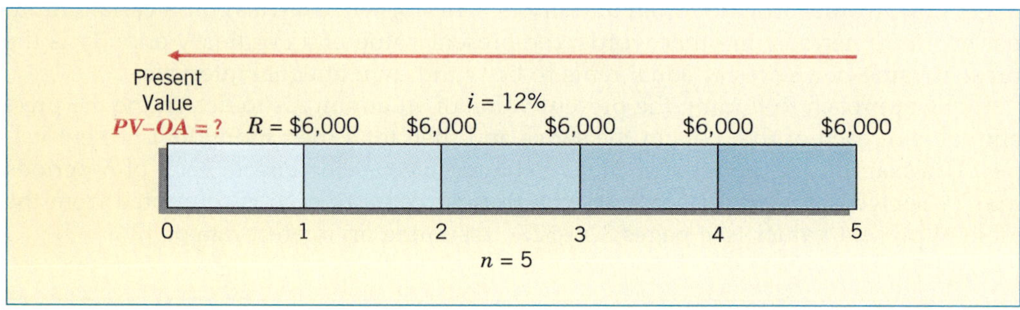

$$\begin{aligned}\text{Present value of an ordinary annuity} &= R\ (PVF\text{-}OA_{n,i})\\ &= \$6{,}000\ (PVF\text{-}OA_{5,12\%})\\ &= \$6{,}000\ (3.60478)\\ &= \$21{,}628.68\end{aligned}$$

The present value of the 5 ordinary annuity rental receipts of $6,000 each is $21,628.68. Determining the present value of the ordinary annuity factor 3.60478 can be accomplished using a financial calculator or by reading the appropriate table, in this case Table 6-4 (12% column and 5-period row).

Present Value of an Annuity Due

In the discussion of the present value of an ordinary annuity, the final rent was discounted back the same number of periods that there were rents. In determining the present value of an annuity due, there is always one fewer discount period. This distinction is shown graphically in Illustration 6-18 on the next page.

Because each cash flow comes exactly one period sooner in the present value of the annuity due, the present value of the cash flows is exactly 12% higher than the present value of an ordinary annuity. Thus, **the present value of an annuity due factor can be found by multiplying the present value of an ordinary annuity factor by 1 plus the interest rate.**

To determine the present value of an annuity due interest factor for 5 periods at 12% interest, take the present value of an ordinary annuity for 5 periods at 12% interest (3.60478) and multiply it by 1.12 to arrive at the present value of an annuity due, 4.03735 (3.60478 × 1.12). Because the payment and receipt of rentals at the beginning of periods (such as leases, insurance, and subscriptions) are as common as those at the end of the periods (referred to as "in arrears"), we have provided present value annuity due factors in the form of Table 6-5.

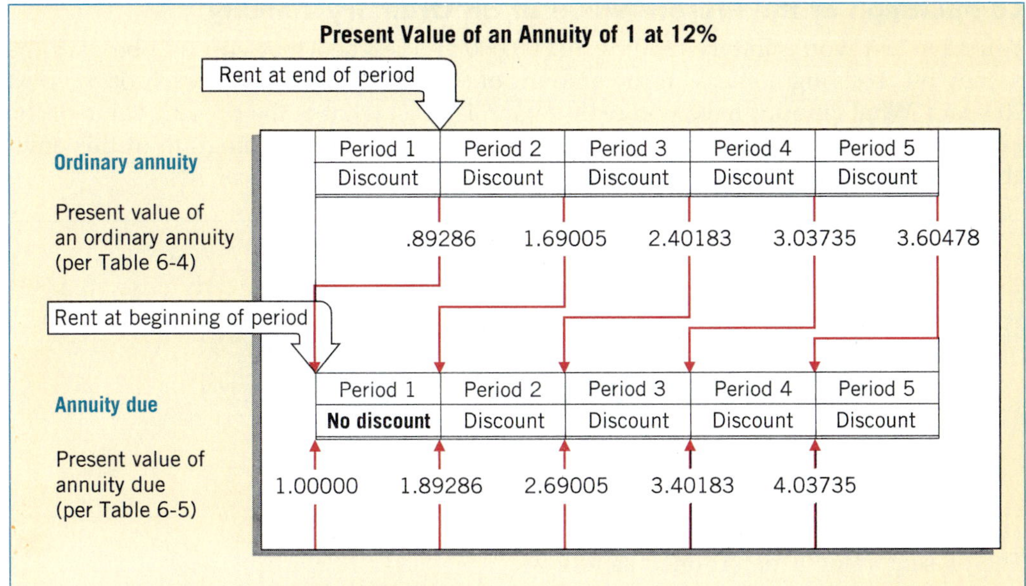

ILLUSTRATION 6-18
Comparison of Present Value of an Ordinary Annuity with an Annuity Due

Space Odyssey, Inc., rents a communications satellite for 4 years with annual rental payments of $4.8 million to be made at the beginning of each year. If the relevant annual interest rate is 11%, what is the present value of the rental obligations?

This problem is time-diagrammed as follows:

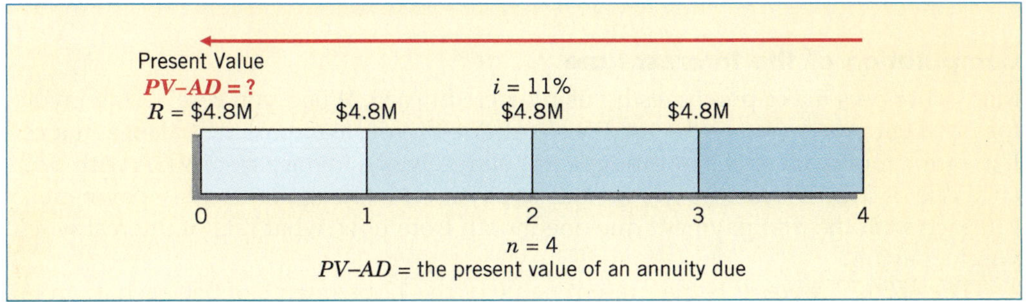

This problem is solved in the following manner.

1. Present value of an ordinary annuity of 1 for 4 periods at 11% (Table 6-4)	3.10245
2. Factor (1 + .11)	× 1.11
3. Present value of an annuity due of 1 for 4 periods at 11%	3.44372
4. Periodic deposit (rent)	× $4,800,000
5. Present value of payments	$16,529,856

ILLUSTRATION 6-19
Computation of Present Value of an Annuity Due

Since we have Table 6-5 for present value of an annuity due problems, we can also locate the desired factor 3.44372 and compute the present value of the lease payments to be $16,529,856.

Illustrations of Present Value of Annuity Problems

The following three illustrations demonstrate the computation of (1) the present value, (2) the interest rate, and (3) the amount of each rent.

Computation of the Present Value of an Ordinary Annuity

You have just won a lottery totaling $4,000,000 and learned that you will be paid the money by receiving a check in the amount of $200,000 at the end of each of the next 20 years. What amount have you really won? That is, what is the present value of the $200,000 checks you will receive over the next 20 years? A time diagram of this enviable situation is as follows (assuming an appropriate interest rate of 10%):

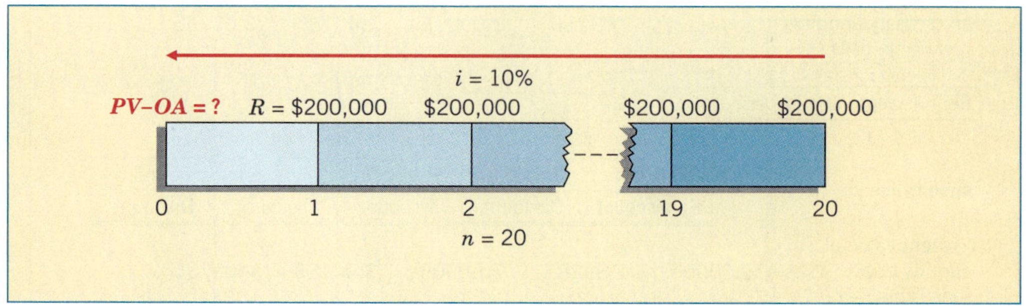

The present value is determined as follows:

$$\text{Present value of an ordinary annuity} = R\ (PVF\text{-}OA_{n,i})$$
$$= \$200{,}000\ (PVF\text{-}OA_{20,10\%})$$
$$= \$200{,}000\ (8.51356)$$
$$= \$1{,}702{,}712$$

As a result, if the state deposits $1,702,712 now and earns 10% interest, it can withdraw $200,000 a year for 20 years to pay you the $4,000,000.

Computation of the Interest Rate

Many shoppers make purchases by using a credit card. When you receive the invoice for payment you may pay the total amount due or you may pay the balance in a certain number of payments. For example, if you receive an invoice from VISA with a balance due of $528.77 and you are invited to pay it off in 12 equal monthly payments of $50 each with the first payment due one month from now, what rate of interest would you be paying?

The $528.77 represents the present value of the 12 payments of $50 each at an unknown rate of interest. This situation in the form of a time diagram appears as follows:

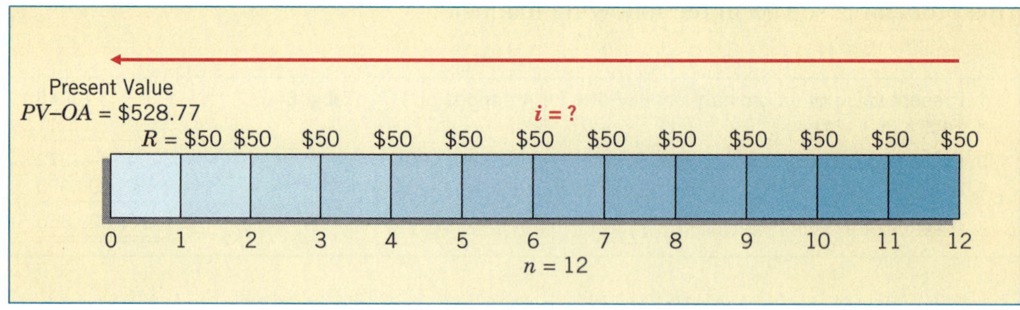

The rate is determined as follows:

$$\text{Present value of an ordinary annuity} = R\ (PVF\text{-}OA_{n,i})$$
$$\$528.77 = \$50\ (PVF\text{-}OA_{12,i})$$
$$(PVF\text{-}OA_{12,i}) = \frac{\$528.77}{\$50} = 10.57540$$

Referring to Table 6-4 and reading across the 12-period row, we find 10.57534 in the 2% column. Since 2% is a monthly rate, the nominal annual rate of interest is 24%

(12 × 2%), and the effective annual rate is 26.82413% $[(1 + .02)^{12} - 1]$. Obviously, you're better off paying the entire bill now if you possibly can.

Computation of a Periodic Rent

Norm and Jackie Remmers have saved $18,000 to finance their daughter Dawna's college education. The money has been deposited in the Bloomington Savings and Loan Association and is earning 10% interest compounded semiannually. What equal amounts can their daughter withdraw at the end of every 6 months during the next 4 years while she attends college, without exhausting the fund? This is time-diagrammed as follows:

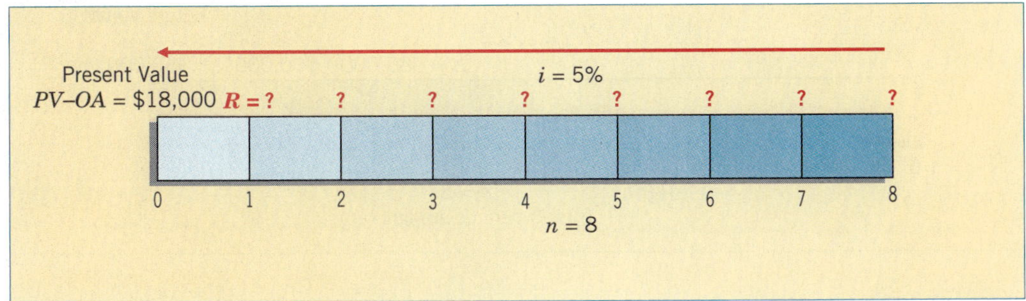

The answer is not determined simply by dividing $18,000 by 8 withdrawals because that would ignore the interest earned on the money remaining on deposit. Taking into consideration that interest is compounded semiannually at 5% (10% ÷ 2) for 8 periods (4 years × 2), and using the same present value of an ordinary annuity formula, we determine the amount of each withdrawal that she can make as follows:

$$\text{Present value of an ordinary annuity} = R\,(PVF\text{-}OA_{n,i})$$

$$\$18{,}000 = R\,(PVF\text{-}OA_{8,5\%})$$

$$\$18{,}000 = R\,(6.46321)$$

$$R = \$2{,}784.99$$

MORE COMPLEX SITUATIONS

Often it is necessary to use more than one table to solve time value problems. The business problem encountered may require that computations of both present value of a single sum and present value of an annuity be made. Two common situations are:

1. Deferred annuities.
2. Bond problems.

Deferred Annuities

A **deferred annuity** is an annuity in which the rents begin after a specified number of periods. A deferred annuity does not begin to produce rents until 2 or more periods have expired. For example, "an **ordinary annuity** of six annual rents deferred 4 years" means that no rents will occur during the first 4 years, and that the first of the six rents will occur at the end of the fifth year. "An **annuity due** of six annual rents deferred 4 years" means that no rents will occur during the first 4 years, and that the first of six rents will occur at the beginning of the fifth year.

Future Value of a Deferred Annuity

In the case of the future value of a deferred annuity the computations are relatively straightforward. Because there is no accumulation or investment on which interest may accrue, the future value of a deferred annuity is the same as the future value of an annuity not deferred. That is, the deferral period is ignored in computing the future value.

To illustrate, assume that Sutton Corporation plans to purchase a land site in 6 years for the construction of its new corporate headquarters. Because of cash flow problems, Sutton is able to budget deposits of $80,000 that are expected to earn 12% annually only at the end of the fourth, fifth, and sixth periods. What future value will Sutton have accumulated at the end of the sixth year?

A time diagram of this situation is as follows:

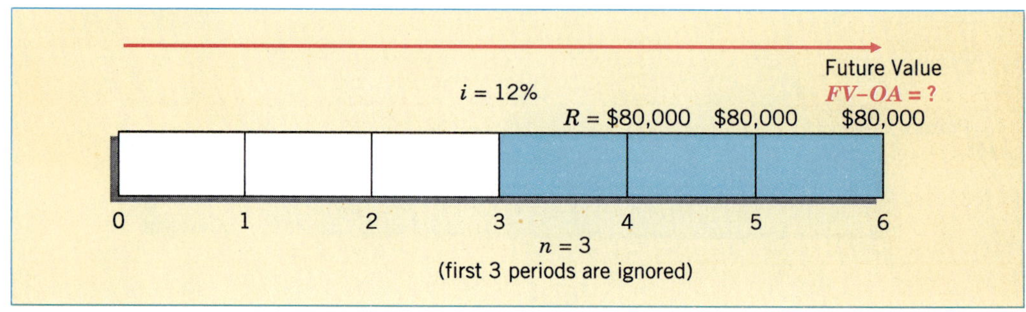

The value accumulated is determined by using the standard formula for the future value of an ordinary annuity:

$$\text{Future value of an ordinary annuity} = R\,(FVF\text{-}OA_{n,i})$$
$$= \$80{,}000\,(FVF\text{-}OA_{3,12\%})$$
$$= \$80{,}000\,(3.37440)$$
$$= \$269{,}952$$

Present Value of a Deferred Annuity

In computing the present value of a deferred annuity, the interest that accrues on the original investment during the deferral period must be recognized.

To compute the present value of a deferred annuity, we compute the present value of an ordinary annuity of 1 as if the rents had occurred for the entire period, and then subtract the present value of rents which were not received during the deferral period. We are left with the present value of the rents actually received subsequent to the deferral period.

To illustrate, Tom Bytehead has developed and copyrighted a software computer program that is a tutorial for students in advanced accounting. He agrees to sell the copyright to Campus Micro Systems for six annual payments of $5,000 each. The payments are to begin 5 years from today. Given an annual interest rate of 8%, what is the present value of the six payments?

This situation is an ordinary annuity of six payments deferred four periods. The following time diagram helps to visualize this sales agreement:

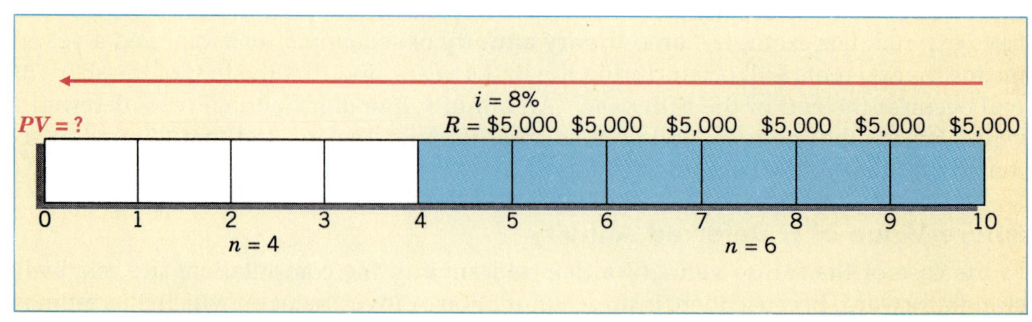

Two options are available to solve this problem. The first is to use only Table 6-4 as follows:

ILLUSTRATION 6-20
Computation of the Present Value of a Deferred Annuity

1. Each periodic rent		$5,000
2. Present value of an ordinary annuity of 1 for total periods (10) [number of rents (6) plus number of deferred periods (4)] at 8%	6.71008	
3. Less: Present value of an ordinary annuity of 1 for the number of deferred periods (4) at 8%	−3.31213	
4. Difference		× 3.39795
5. Present value of six rents of $5,000 deferred 4 periods		$16,989.75

The subtraction of the present value of an annuity of 1 for the deferred periods eliminates the nonexistent rents during the deferral period and converts the present value of an ordinary annuity of $1.00 for 10 periods to the present value of 6 rents of $1.00, deferred 4 periods.

Alternatively, the present value of the 6 rents could be computed using both Table 6-2 and Table 6-4. One can first discount the annuity 6 periods, but because the annuity is deferred 4 periods, the present value of the annuity must then be treated as a future amount to be discounted another 4 periods. A time diagram illustrates this two-step process as follows:

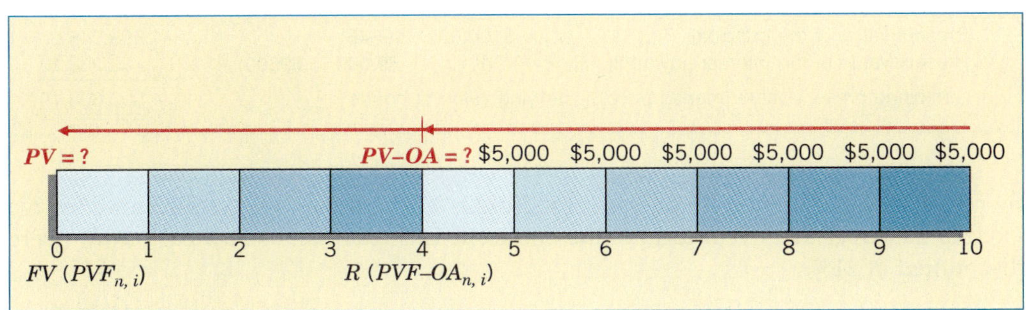

Step 1: Present value of an ordinary annuity $= R\ (PVF\text{-}OA_{n,i})$

$= \$5{,}000\ (PVF\text{-}OA_{6,8\%})$

$= \$5{,}000\ (4.62288)$
(Table 6-4 Present value of an ordinary annuity)

$= \$23{,}114.40$

Step 2: Present value $= FV\ (PVF_{n,i})$

$= \$23{,}114.40\ (PVF_{4,8\%})$

$= \$23{,}114.40\ (.73503)$
(Table 6-2 Present value of a single sum)

$= \$16{,}989.78$

The present value of $16,989.78 computed above is the same result although computed differently from the first illustration.

Valuation of Long-Term Bonds

A long-term bond produces two cash flows: (1) periodic interest payments during the life of the bond, and (2) the principal (face value) paid at maturity. At the date of issue, bond buyers determine the present value of these two cash flows using the market rate of interest.

The periodic interest payments represent an annuity, and the principal represents a single-sum problem. The current market value of the bonds is the combined present values of the interest annuity and the principal amount.

To illustrate, Alltech Corporation on January 1, 2001, issues $100,000 of 9% bonds due in 5 years with interest payable annually at year-end. The current market rate of interest for bonds of similar risk is 11%. What will the buyers pay for this bond issue?

The time diagram depicting both cash flows is shown below:

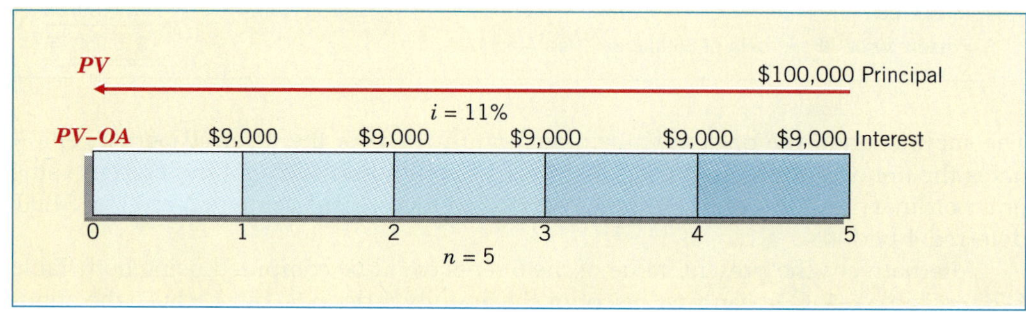

The present value of the two cash flows is computed by discounting at 11% as follows:

ILLUSTRATION 6-21
Computation of the Present Value of an Interest-Bearing Bond

1. Present value of the principal: $FV\ (PVF_{5,11\%})$ = $100,000 (.59345)	$59,345.00
2. Present value of the interest payments: $R\ (PVF\text{-}OA_{5,11\%})$ = $9,000 (3.69590)	33,263.10
3. Combined present value (market price)—carrying value of bonds	$92,608.10

By paying $92,608.10 at date of issue, the buyers of the bonds will realize an effective yield of 11% over the 5-year term of the bonds. This is true because the cash flows were discounted at 11%.

Effective Interest Method of Amortization of Bond Discount or Premium

In the Alltech Corporation bond issue, Illustration 6-21, the bonds were issued at a discount computed as follows:

ILLUSTRATION 6-22
Computation of Bond Discount

Maturity value (face amount) of bonds		$100,000.00
Present value of the principal	$59,345.00	
Present value of the interest	33,263.10	
Proceeds (present value and cash received)		92,608.10
Discount on bonds issued		$ 7,391.90

This discount of $7,391.90 under acceptable accrual accounting is amortized (written off) over the life of the bond issue to interest expense.

The profession's preferred procedure for amortization of a discount or premium is the **effective interest method** (also called **present value amortization**). Under the effective interest method:

1. Bond interest expense is computed first by multiplying the carrying value of the bonds at the beginning of the period by the effective interest rate.
2. The bond discount or premium amortization is then determined by comparing the bond interest expense with the interest to be paid.

The computation of the amortization is depicted graphically as follows:

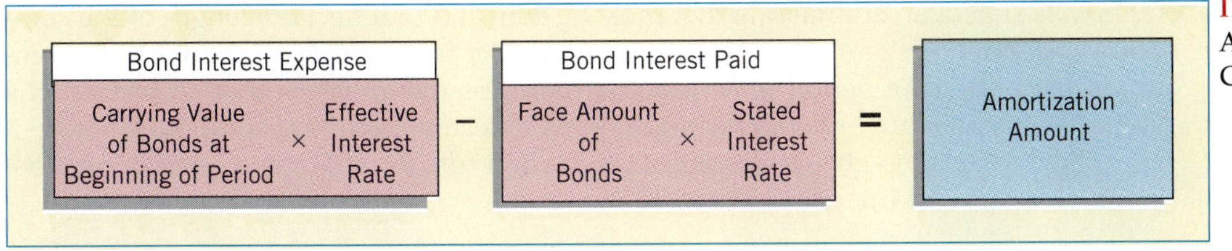

ILLUSTRATION 6-23
Amortization Computation

The effective interest method produces a periodic interest expense equal to **a constant percentage of the carrying value of the bonds.** Since the percentage used is the effective rate of interest incurred by the borrower at the time of issuance, the effective interest method results in matching expenses with revenues.

The effective interest method of amortization can be illustrated using the data from the Alltech Corporation example, where $100,000 face value of bonds were issued at a discount of $7,391.90, resulting in a carrying value of $92,608.10. The effective interest amortization schedule is shown in Illustration 6-24:

ILLUSTRATION 6-24
Effective Interest Amortization Schedule

SCHEDULE OF BOND DISCOUNT AMORTIZATION
5-Year, 9% Bonds Sold to Yield 11%

Date	Cash Interest Paid	Interest Expense	Bond Discount Amortization	Carrying Value of Bonds
1/1/01				$92,608.10
12/31/01	$9,000[a]	$10,186.89[b]	$1,186.89[c]	93,794.99[d]
12/31/02	9,000	10,317.45	1,317.45	95,112.44
12/31/03	9,000	10,462.37	1,462.37	96,574.81
12/31/04	9,000	10,623.23	1,623.23	98,198.04
12/31/05	9,000	10,801.96	1,801.96	100,000.00
	$45,000	$52,391.90	$7,391.90	

[a]$100,000 × .09 = $9,000
[b]$92,608.10 × .11 = $10,186.89
[c]$10,186.89 − $9,000 = $1,186.89
[d]$92,608.10 + $1,186.89 = $93,794.99

The amortization schedule illustrated above is used for note and bond transactions in Chapters 7 and 14.

SUMMARY OF LEARNING OBJECTIVES

1 Identify accounting topics where the time value of money is relevant. Some of the applications of present value–based measurements to accounting topics are: (1) notes, (2) leases, (3) amortization of premiums and discounts, (4) pensions and other postretirement benefits, (5) long-term assets, (6) sinking funds, (7) business combinations, (8) disclosures, and (9) installment contracts.

2 Distinguish between simple and compound interest. See Fundamental Concepts following this Summary.

3 Learn how to use appropriate compound interest tables. In order to identify the appropriate compound interest table to use of the five given, you must identify whether you are solving for (1) the future value of a single sum, (2) the present value of a single sum, (3) the future value of a series of sums (an annuity), or (4) the present value of a series of sums (an annuity). In addition, when a series of sums (an annuity) is involved, you must identify whether these sums are received or paid (1) at the beginning of each period (annuity due) or (2) at the end of each period (ordinary annuity).

4 Identify variables fundamental to solving interest problems. The following four variables are fundamental to all compound interest problems: (1) *Rate of interest:* unless

KEY TERMS

annuity, 283
annuity due, 283
compound interest, 274
deferred annuity, 293
discounting, 278
effective interest method, 296
effective yield, 277
face rate, 277
future value, 278
interest, 272
nominal rate, 277
ordinary annuity, 283
present value, 279
principal, 272
simple interest, 273
stated rate, 277
time value of money, 270

otherwise stated, an annual rate that must be adjusted to reflect the length of the compounding period if less than a year. (2) *Number of time periods:* the number of compounding periods (a period may be equal to or less than a year). (3) *Future value:* the value at a future date of a given sum or sums invested assuming compound interest. (4) *Present value:* the value now (present time) of a future sum or sums discounted assuming compound interest.

5 **Solve future and present value of 1 problems.** See Fundamental Concepts following this Summary, items 5(a) and 6(a).

6 **Solve future value of ordinary and annuity due problems.** See Fundamental Concepts following this Summary, item 5(b).

7 **Solve present value of ordinary and annuity due problems.** See Fundamental Concepts following this Summary, item 6(b).

FUNDAMENTAL CONCEPTS

1 ***Simple Interest.*** Interest on principal only, regardless of interest that may have accrued in the past.

2 ***Compound Interest.*** Interest accrues on the unpaid interest of past periods as well as on the principal.

3 ***Rate of Interest.*** Interest is usually expressed as an annual rate, but when the compounding period is shorter than one year, the interest rate for the shorter period must be determined.

4 ***Annuity.*** A series of payments or receipts (called rents) that occur at equal intervals of time.
Types of annuities:
   - **(a)** ***Ordinary Annuity.*** Each rent is payable (receivable) at the end of the period.
   - **(b)** ***Annuity Due.*** Each rent is payable (receivable) at the beginning of the period.

5 ***Future Value.*** Value at a later date of a single sum that is invested at compound interest.
   - **(a)** ***Future Value of 1*** (or value of a single sum). The future value of $1.00 (or a single given sum), *FV*, at the end of n periods at i compound interest rate (Table 6-1).
   - **(b)** ***Future Value of an Annuity.*** The future value of a series of rents invested at compound interest; in other words, the accumulated total that results from a series of equal deposits at regular intervals invested at compound interest. Both deposits and interest increase the accumulation.
      - **(1)** ***Future Value of an Ordinary Annuity.*** The future value on the date of the last rent.
      - **(2)** ***Future Value of an Annuity Due.*** The future value one period after the date of the last rent. When an annuity due table is not available, use Table 6-3 with the following formula:

$$\text{Value of annuity due of 1 for } n \text{ rents} = (\text{Value of ordinary annuity for } n \text{ rents}) \times (1 + \text{interest rate}).$$

6 ***Present Value.*** The value at an earlier date (usually now) of a given future sum discounted at compound interest.
   - **(a)** ***Present Value of 1*** (or present value of a single sum). The present value (worth) of $1.00 (or a given sum), due n periods hence, discounted at i compound interest (Table 6-2).

(b) ***Present Value of an Annuity.*** The present value (worth) of a series of rents discounted at compound interest; in other words, it is the sum when invested at compound interest that will permit a series of equal withdrawals at regular intervals.

(1) ***Present Value of an Ordinary Annuity.*** The value now of $1.00 to be received or paid at the end of each period (rents) for n periods, discounted at i compound interest (Table 6-4).

(2) ***Present Value of an Annuity Due.*** The value now of $1.00 to be received or paid at the beginning of each period (rents) for n periods, discounted at i compound interest (Table 6-5). To use Table 6-4 for an annuity due, apply this formula:

Present value of annuity due of 1 for n rents = (Present value of an ordinary annuity of n rents) × (1 + interest rate).

APPENDIX 6A

Technology Tools for Time Value Problems

OBJECTIVE 8
After studying Appendix 6A, you should be able to: Use a financial calculator or a spreadsheet to solve time value of money problems.

Business professionals, once they have mastered the underlying concepts shown in Chapter 6, will often use a financial (business) calculator or computerized spreadsheet to solve time value of money problems. In many cases, one of these tools must be used if interest rates or time periods do not correspond with the information provided in the compound interest tables.

FINANCIAL CALCULATORS — SECTION 1

Financial calculators allow you to solve present and future value problems by entering the time value of money variables into the calculator. The five most common keys used to solve time value of money problems are pictured below:[1]

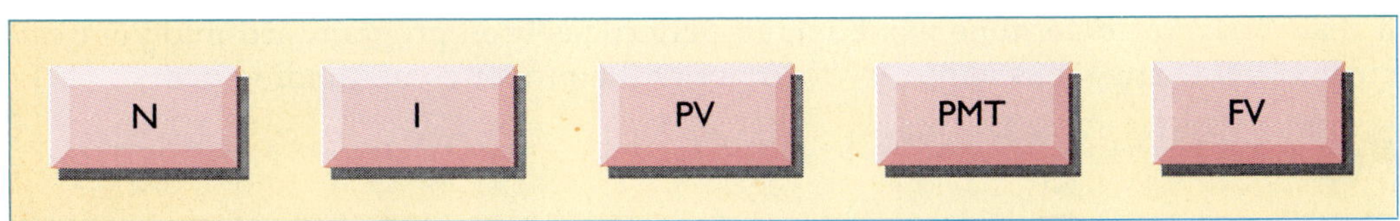

[1]On many calculators, these keys are actual buttons on the face of the calculator; on others, they are shown on the display after accessing a present value menu.

where:

N = number of periods

I = interest rate per period (some calculators use I/YR or i)

PV = present value (occurs at the beginning of the first period)

PMT = payment (all payments are equal, and none are skipped)

FV = future value (occurs at the end of the last period)

In solving time value of money problems in this appendix, you will generally be given three of four variables and will have to solve for the remaining variable. The fifth key (the key not used) is given a value of zero to ensure that this variable is not used in the computation.

FUTURE VALUE OF A SINGLE SUM

To illustrate the use of a financial calculator, let's assume that you want to know the future value of $50,000 invested to earn 11%, compounded annually for 5 years.

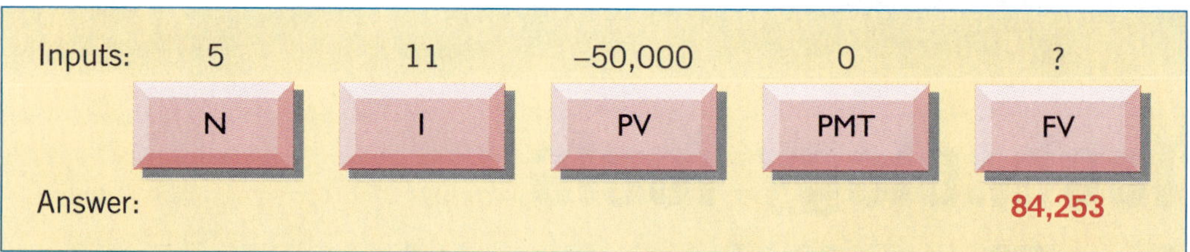

The diagram shows you the information to enter into the calculator (inputs): N = 5, I = 11, PV = −50,000, and PMT = 0. FV is then pressed to yield the answer: $84,253. This is the same answer as shown on p. 279, when compound interest tables were used to compute the future value of a single sum. As indicated, the PMT key was given a value of zero because a series of payments did not occur in this problem.

Plus and Minus

The use of plus and minus signs in time value of money problems using a financial calculator can be confusing. Most financial calculators are programmed so that the positive and negative cash flows in any problem offset each other. In the future value problem above, we identified the 50,000 initial investment as a negative (outflow); the answer 84,253 was shown as a positive, reflecting a cash inflow. If the 50,000 were entered as a positive, then the final answer would have been reported as a negative (−84,253). Hopefully, the sign convention will not cause confusion. If you understand what is required in a problem, you should be able to interpret a positive or negative amount in determining the solution to a problem.

Compounding Periods

In the problem above, we assumed that compounding occurs once a year. Some financial calculators have a default setting, which assumes compounding occurs 12 times a year. You must determine what default period has been programmed into your calculator and change it as necessary to arrive at the proper compounding period.

Rounding

Most financial calculators store and calculate using 12 decimal places. As a result, because compound interest tables generally have factors only up to 5 decimal places, a slight difference in the final answer can result. In most time value of money problems, the final answer will not include more than two decimal points.

PRESENT VALUE OF A SINGLE SUM

To illustrate how a present value problem is solved using a financial calculator, assume that you want to know the present value of $84,253 to be received in 5 years, discounted at 11% compounded annually.

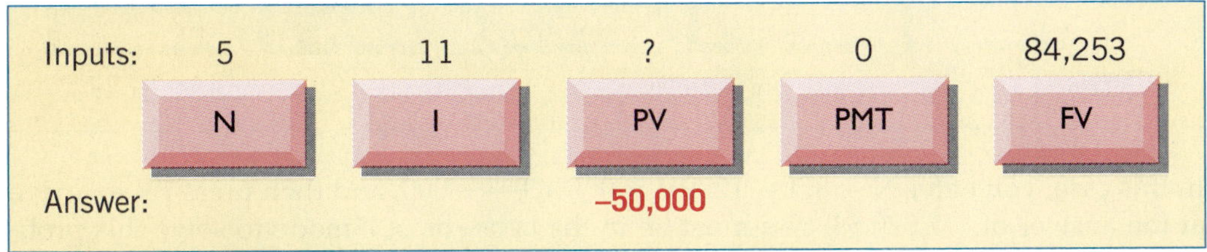

In this case, you enter N = 5, I = 11, PMT = 0, FV = 84,253, and then press the PV key to find the present value of $50,000.

FUTURE VALUE OF AN ORDINARY ANNUITY

To illustrate the future value of an ordinary annuity, assume that you are asked to determine the future value of five $5,000 deposits made at the end of each of the next 5 years, each of which earns interest at 12%, compounded annually.

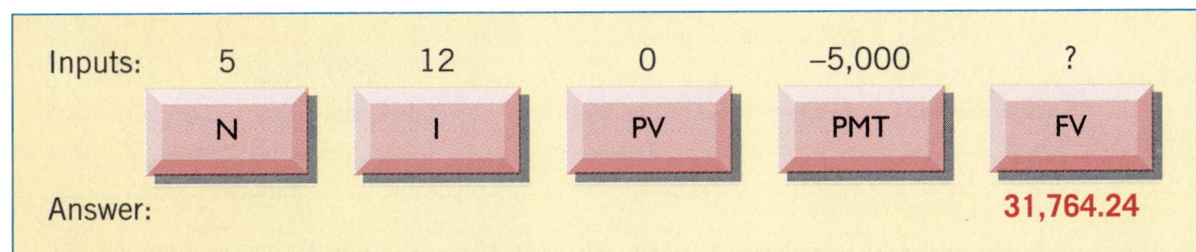

In this case, you enter N = 5, I = 12, PV = 0, PMT = −5,000, and then press FV to arrive at the answer of $31,764.24.[2] The $5,000 payments are shown as negatives because the deposits represent cash outflows that will accumulate with interest to the amount to be received (cash inflow) at the end of 5 years.

FUTURE VALUE OF AN ANNUITY DUE

Recall from the discussion in the chapter that in any annuity problem you must determine whether the periodic payments occur at the beginning or the end of the period. If the first payment occurs at the beginning of the period, most financial calculators have a key marked "Begin" (or "Due") that you press to switch from the end-of-period payment mode (for an ordinary annuity) to beginning-of-period payment mode (for an annuity due). For most calculators, the word BEGIN is displayed to indicate that the calculator is set for an annuity due problem. (Some calculators use DUE.)

To illustrate a future value of an annuity due problem, assume that Sue Lotadough plans to deposit $800 per year in a fund on each of her son's birthdays, starting today (his tenth birthday). All amounts on deposit in the fund will earn 12% compounded

[2]Note on page 285 that the answer using the compound interest tables is $31,764.25—a difference of 1 cent due to rounding.

annually. Sue wants to know the amount she will have accumulated for college expenses on her son's eighteenth birthday. She will make 8 deposits into the fund. (Assume no deposit will be made on the eighteenth birthday.)

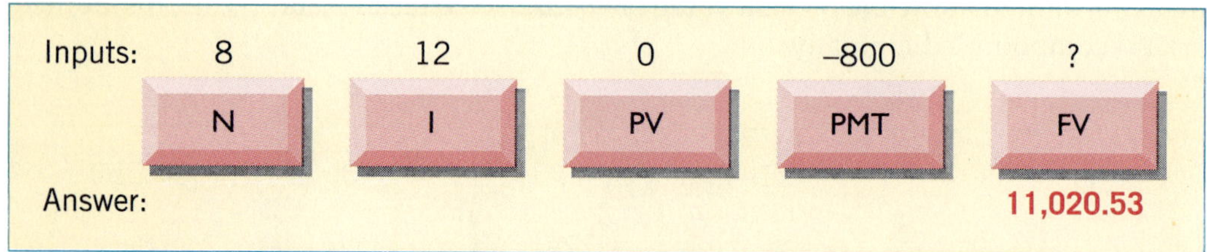

In this case, you enter N = 8, I = 12, PV = 0, PMT = −800, and then press FV to arrive at the answer of $11,020.53. You must be in the BEGIN or DUE mode to solve this problem correctly; before starting to solve any annuity problem, make sure that your calculator is switched to the proper mode.

PRESENT VALUE OF AN ORDINARY ANNUITY

To illustrate how to solve a present value of an ordinary annuity problem using a financial calculator, assume that you are asked to determine the present value of rental receipts of $6,000 each to be received at the end of each of the next 5 years, when discounted at 12%.

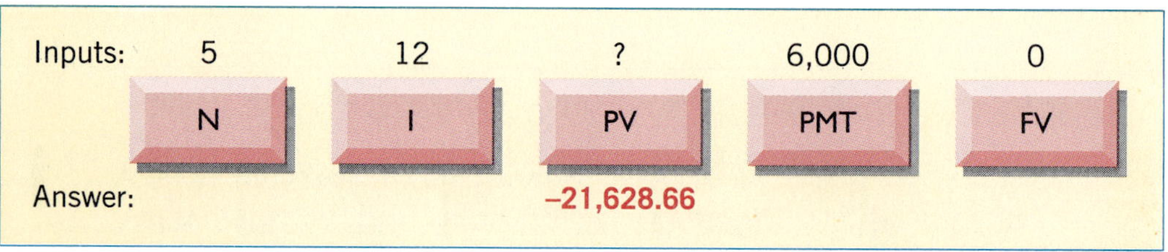

In this case, you enter N = 5, I = 12, PMT = 6,000, FV = 0, and then press PV to arrive at the answer of $21,628.66.[3]

USEFUL FEATURES OF THE FINANCIAL CALCULATOR

With a financial calculator you can solve for any interest rate or for any number of periods in a time value of money problem. Here are some illustrations of these features.

Auto Loan. Assume you are financing a new car with a 3-year loan. The loan has a 9.5% nominal annual interest rate, compounded monthly. The price of the car is $6,000, and you want to determine the monthly payments, assuming that the payments start one month after the purchase.

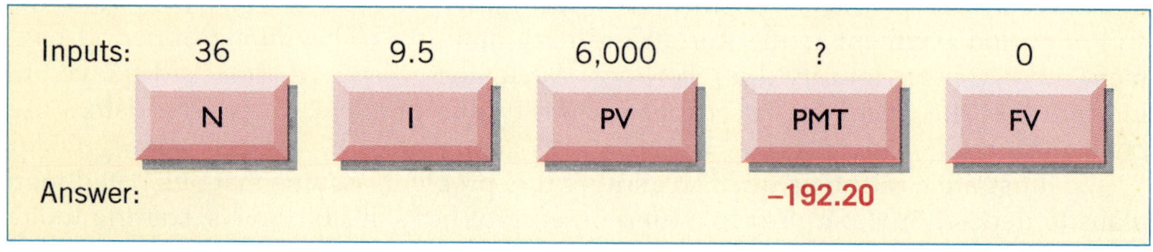

[3]If the rental payments were received at the beginning of the year, then it would be necessary to switch to the BEGIN or DUE mode. In this case, the present value of the payments would be $24,224.10.

Thus, by entering N = 36 (12 × 3), I = 9.5, PV = 6,000, FV = 0, and then pressing PMT, you can determine that the monthly payments will be $192.20. Note that the payment key is usually programmed for 12 payments per year. Thus, you must change the default (compounding period) if the payments are different than monthly.

Mortgage Loan Amount. Let's say you are evaluating financing options for a loan on your house. You decide that the maximum mortgage payment you can afford is $700 per month. The annual interest rate is 8.4%. If you get a mortgage that requires you to make monthly payments over a 15-year period, what is the maximum purchase price you can afford?

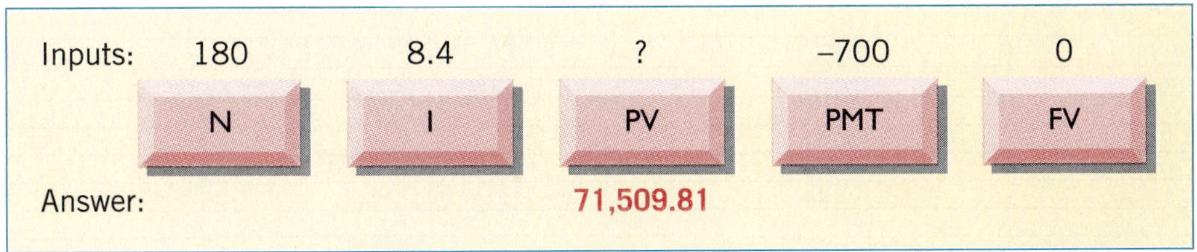

Entering N = 180 (12 × 15 years), I = 8.4, PMT = −700, FV = 0, and pressing PV, you find a present value of $71,509.81—the maximum house price you can afford, given that you want to keep your mortgage payments at $700. Note that by changing any of the variables, you can quickly conduct "what-if" analyses for different factual situations.

Individual Retirement Account (IRA). Assume you opened an IRA on April 15, 1990, with a deposit of $2,000. Since then you have deposited $100 in the account every two weeks (26 deposits per year, with the first $100 deposit made on April 29, 1990). The account pays 7.6% annual interest compounded semi-monthly (with each deposit). How much will be in the account on April 15, 2000?

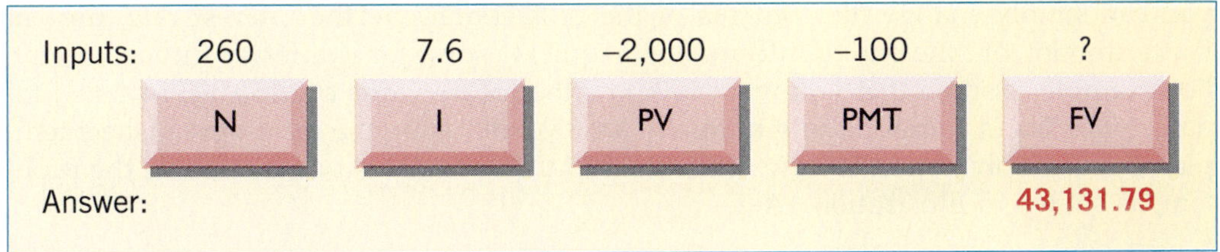

By entering N = 260 (26 × 10 years), I = 7.6, PV = −2,000, PMT = −100, and pressing FV, you determine the future value of $43,131.79. This is the amount that the IRA will grow to over the 10-year period. Note that in this problem we use four of the keys and solve for the fifth. Thus, we combine the future value of a single sum and of an annuity. Other problems similar to this will be illustrated in Chapters 7 and 14.

SPREADSHEET APPLICATIONS — SECTION 2

Instead of using a financial calculator, some professionals develop a computerized spreadsheet, such as Excel or Lotus, to solve time value of money problems. One way to use a spreadsheet is to program into the spreadsheet cells the future value and present value formulas discussed in the chapter. Once programmed, the spreadsheet "template" can then be used to solve time value of money problems.

FUTURE VALUE OF A SINGLE SUM

Assume that you want to know the future value of $50,000 invested to earn 11%, compounded annually for 5 years. To solve this problem using a spreadsheet, you enter the formula for the future value factors into a spreadsheet with references to cells containing the information needed. Illustration 6A-1 shows an excerpt from such a spreadsheet, in which the necessary elements for the future value factor have been entered.

ILLUSTRATION 6A-1
Spreadsheet Template for Future Value of a Single Sum—$50,000 at 11% for 5 Years

	A	B	C	D	E	F
1	Future Value of a Single Sum					
2						
3	Interest Rate per Period (i%)	11.00%				
4						
5	Number of Periods (n)	5				
6						
7	Present Value (PV)	$50,000.00	The following formula is inserted in this cell to yield this factor: =+(1+B3)^B5			
8						
9	Future Value Factor	1.68506				
10						
11	Future Value	$84,252.91	The following formula is inserted in this cell to yield this amount: =+(B7*B9)			
12						
13						

As indicated, the interest rate is entered into cell B3, and the number of periods is entered into cell B5. The future value factor in cell B9 is computed using the following cell reference formula: (1 + B3)^B5, corresponding to the future value formula—$(1 + i)^n$—developed in the chapter and used to generate the future value tables. This spreadsheet template provides the solution to the problem by multiplying cell B7 (containing the present value or the initial investment) times cell B9 (the future value factor) to yield $84,252.91—the same answer obtained by manually using the tables.

The power of the spreadsheet application is that once the formula is programmed, you can simply change the contents of the cells containing the interest rate, present value amount, or time period information to quickly solve for a different future amount. For example, assume that you want to know the future value of $150,000 invested today at 9.25% and compounding annually for 8 years. Using the same spreadsheet template, you simply enter the new amounts into the spreadsheet cells to solve the problem, as shown in Illustration 6A-2.

ILLUSTRATION 6A-2
Spreadsheet Template for Future Value of a Single Sum—$150,000 at 9.25% for 8 Years

	A	B	C	D	E	F
1	Future Value of a Single Sum					
2						
3	Interest Rate per Period (i%)	9.25%				
4						
5	Number of Periods (n)	8				
6						
7	Present Value (PV)	$150,000.00	The following formula is inserted in this cell to yield this factor: =+(1+B3)^B5			
8						
9	Future Value Factor	2.02942				
10						
11	Future Value	$304,412.74	The following formula is inserted in this cell to yield this amount: =+(B7*B9)			
12						
13						

Note that the formulas in cells B9 and B11 do not change—only the inputs (interest rate, present value, and/or periods) do. Furthermore, by using the general formula, we can solve a problem for which the tables do not contain the relevant factor. In this case, the 9.25% interest rate is not contained in the compound interest tables.

PRESENT VALUE OF A SINGLE SUM

To illustrate the use of the spreadsheet to solve a present value problem involving a single sum, assume you wish to determine the present value of a single payment of $2,000 to be received in 3 years. The relevant discount rate is 7%. The spreadsheet solution to this problem is shown in Illustration 6A-3.

ILLUSTRATION 6A-3
Spreadsheet Template for Present Value of a Single Sum

	A	B	C	D	E	F
14	Present Value of a Single Sum					
15						
16	Interest Rate per Period (i%)	7.00%				
17						
18	Number of Periods (n)	3				
19						
20	Future Value (FV)	$2,000.00	The following formula is inserted in this cell to yield this factor: =+1/((1+B16)^B18)			
21						
22	Present Value Factor	0.81630				
23						
24	**Present Value**	**$1,632.60**	The following formula is inserted in this cell to yield this amount: =+(B20*B22)			
25						
26						

FUTURE VALUE OF AN ANNUITY

Spreadsheet templates also can be developed for time value of money problems involving annuities. For example, assume you will receive three equal payments of $2,000 at the end of each of the next 3 years. You plan to deposit these payments in a money market fund that will earn 8% compounded annually. You want to determine how much the fund will be worth at the end of the third year. Again, a spreadsheet template can be developed to solve this problem, as shown in Illustration 6A-4.

ILLUSTRATION 6A-4
Spreadsheet Template for Future Value of an Annuity

	A	B	C	D	E	F
28	Future Value of an Annuity					
29						
30	Interest Rate per Period (i%)	8.00%				
31						
32	Number of Periods (n)	3				
33						
34	Payments	$2,000.00	The following formula is inserted in this cell to yield this factor: =+(((1+B30)^B32)−1)/B30			
35						
36	Future Value Factor-Ordinary Annuity	3.24640				
37						
38	**Future Value**	**$6,492.80**	The following formula is inserted in this cell to yield this amount: =+(B34*B36)			
39						
40						

As indicated, the future value of these payments will be $6,492.80. The template used to determine this amount is similar to our earlier single-sum example, except that the future value factor is based on the following future value of an annuity formula: $[(1 + i)^n - 1]/i$. This formula is built into the template with the following cell-referenced formula: (((1 + B30)^B32) − 1)/B30. This formula uses the cell contents from B30 (interest rate) and B32 (number of periods) to yield the correct factor. The factor is then multiplied by the payment amounts (B34) to arrive at the future value of the annuity. As with our earlier single-sum example, once this template is developed, similar ordinary annuity problems can be quickly solved by changing the interest rate, number of periods, or the amount of payments.

PRESENT VALUE OF ANNUITY

To illustrate a spreadsheet template for determining the present value of annuities, consider the following problem. You want to know the value today of five $6,000 rent payments to be received at the end of each of the next 5 years, assuming a discount rate of 10.5%. A spreadsheet template to solve problems such as this is shown in Illustration 6A-5.

ILLUSTRATION 6A-5
Spreadsheet Template for Present Value of an Annuity

	A	B	C	D	E	F
41	Present Value of an Annuity					
42						
43	Interest Rate per Period (i%)	10.50%				
44						
45	Number of Periods (n)	5				
46						
47	Payments (in the future)	$6,000.00				
48						
49	Present Value Factor-Ordinary Annuity	3.74286				
50						
51	Present Value Factor-Annuity Due	4.13586				
52						
53	Present Value-Ordinary Annuity	$22,457.15				
54						
55	Present Value-Annuity Due	$24,815.15				
56						
57						

The following formula is inserted in this cell to yield this factor: =+(1−(1/(1+B43)^B45))/B43

The following formula is inserted in this cell to yield this amount: =1+((1−(1/(1+B43)^(B45−1)))/B43)

The following formula is inserted in this cell to yield this amount: =+(B47*B49)

The following formula is inserted in this cell to yield this amount: =+(B47*B51)

Within this template, two present value of annuity factors are generated—one for ordinary annuities (in cell B53) and one for an annuity due (in cell B55). Thus, if the 6 payments will be made at the end of the period (ordinary annuity), the present value of the payments is $22,457.15. However, if the payments are made at the beginning of the period (annuity due), the present value of the payments is $24,815.15. Thus, once the template is developed, it provides an efficient way to examine the impact of alternative payment features on present values.

SUMMARY OF TEMPLATES

Go to the Digital Tool to access a spreadsheet file containing these templates.

In summary, as shown in our examples above, computer spreadsheet templates can be developed to solve common time value of money problems, including problems that are not easily solved using typical present value and future value tables. Illustration 6A-6 shows in one spreadsheet all of the templates illustrated above. Note that once these general templates are developed, they can be easily copied to other spreadsheets in order to solve other problems or do time value of money analyses.

DETERMINING PAYMENTS

The present value of annuity template just illustrated also can be adapted to solve other unknowns, such as interest rate, number of periods, or payments. Assume that you owe $10,000 on your student loan and you want to determine the monthly payments

ILLUSTRATION 6A-6 Time Value of Money Templates

	A	B	C	D	E	F
1	Future Value of a Single Sum					
2						
3	Interest Rate per Period (i%)	11.00%				
4						
5	Number of Periods (n)	5				
6						
7	Present Value (PV)	$50,000.00				
8						
9	Future Value Factor	1.68506	The following formula is inserted in this cell to yield this factor: =+(1+B3)^B5			
10						
11	**Future Value**	**$84,252.91**	The following formula is inserted in this cell to yield this amount: =+(B7*B9)			
12						
13						
14	Present Value of a Single Sum					
15						
16	Interest Rate per Period (i%)	7.00%				
17						
18	Number of Periods (n)	3				
19						
20	Future Value (FV)	$2,000.00				
21						
22	Present Value Factor	0.81630	The following formula is inserted in this cell to yield this factor: =+1/((1+B16)^B18)			
23						
24	**Present Value**	**$1,632.60**	The following formula is inserted in this cell to yield this amount: =+(B20*B22)			
25						
26						
27						
28	Future Value of an Annuity					
29						
30	Interest Rate per Period (i%)	8.00%				
31						
32	Number of Periods (n)	3				
33						
34	Payments	$2,000.00				
35						
36	Future Value Factor-Ordinary Annuity	3.24640	The following formula is inserted in this cell to yield this factor: =+(((1+B30)^B32)−1)/B30			
37						
38	**Future Value**	**$6,492.80**	The following formula is inserted in this cell to yield this amount: =+(B34*B36)			
39						
40						
41	Present Value of an Annuity					
42						
43	Interest Rate per Period (i%)	10.50%				
44						
45	Number of Periods (n)	5				
46						
47	Payments (in the future)	$6,000.00				
48						
49	Present Value Factor-Ordinary Annuity	3.74286	The following formula is inserted in this cell to yield this factor: =+(1−(1/(1+B43)^B45))/B43			
50						
51	Present Value Factor-Annuity Due	4.13586	The following formula is inserted in this cell to yield this factor: =1+((1−(1/(1+B43)^(B45−1)))/B43)			
52						
53	**Present Value-Ordinary Annuity**	**$22,457.15**	The following formula is inserted in this cell to yield this amount: =+(B47*B49)			
54						
55	**Present Value-Annuity Due**	**$24,815.15**	The following formula is inserted in this cell to yield this amount: =+(B47*B51)			
56						
57						
58						

that will be required to pay off the loan. The loan is structured to make equal monthly payments over 5 years, beginning at the end of your first month on the job, and at an annual interest rate of 9%, with interest compounding monthly. A spreadsheet solution to this problem is shown in Illustration 6A-7 (page 308).

The unknown quantity in this problem is the payments, which are determined by dividing the present value ($10,000 owed today) by the present value of an ordinary

	A	B	C	D	E	F
38	Determining Loan Payments					
39						
40	Annual Interest Rate	9.00%				
41	Term of Loan (Years)	5				
42	Payment per Year	12				
43	Interest Rate per Period (i%)	0.75%				
44						
45	Number of Periods (n)	60				
46						
47	Present Value (PV)	$10,000.00				
48						
49	Present Value Factor-Ordinary Annuity	48.17337				
50						
51	Payments	$207.58				
52						
53						

The following formula is inserted in this cell to get the effective rate: =+(B40/B42)

The following formula is inserted in this cell to get the number of periods: =+(B41*B42)

The following formula is inserted in this cell to yield this factor: =+(1−(1/(1+B43)^B45))/B43

The following formula is inserted in this cell to yield the payment: =+(B47/B49)

ILLUSTRATION 6A-7
Spreadsheet Template for Determining Loan Payments

annuity factor. Thus, 60 equal payments of $207.58 will pay off the principal and interest components of your student loan.[4]

Once spreadsheet templates have been developed, it is easy to experiment with different interest rates, number of periods, or payments (given other time value variables). This "what-if" type of analysis makes the use of spreadsheet templates or financial calculators a must for any professional solving complex time value of money problems.

SUMMARY OF LEARNING OBJECTIVE FOR APPENDIX 6A

8 **Use a financial calculator or a spreadsheet to solve time value of money problems.** A financial calculator or computerized spreadsheet can be used to solve time value of money problems. By entering into the calculator amounts for all but one of the unknown elements (periods, interest rate, payments, future or present value), a financial calculator can be used to solve the same and additional problems as those solved with the time value of money tables. Particularly useful situations involve interest rates and compounding periods not presented in the tables. Spreadsheets can be used in a similar fashion to solve time value of money problems and are particularly useful in conducting sensitivity analysis in time value of money problems.

[4]Spreadsheet programs also contain a number of time value of money functions that can be used to solve many time value of money problems. In essence these functions already have the present value and future value formulas built into them. In most spreadsheet programs, these functions are inserted into a cell by point-and-click capabilities from a function menu.

Note: All **asterisked** Exercises and Problems relate to material contained in the chapter appendix; a calculator is needed for these assignments.

QUESTIONS

1 What is the time value of money? Why should accountants have an understanding of compound interest, annuities, and present value concepts?

2 Identify three situations in which accounting measures are based on present values. Do these present value applications involve single sums or annuities, or both single sums and annuities? Explain.

3 What is the nature of interest? Distinguish between "simple interest" and "compound interest."

4 What are the components of an interest rate? Why is it important for accountants to understand these components?

5 Presented are a number of values taken from compound interest tables involving the same number of periods and the same rate of interest. Indicate what each of these four values represents.

(a) 6.71008 **(c)** .46319

(b) 2.15892 **(d)** 14.48656

6 Bill Jones is considering two investment options for a $1,000 gift he received for graduation. Both investments have 8% annual interest rates. One offers quarterly compounding, the other compounds on a semiannual basis. Which investment should he choose? Why?

7 Brenda Starr deposited $18,000 in a money market certificate that provides interest of 10% compounded quarterly if the amount is maintained for 3 years. How much will Brenda Starr have at the end of 3 years?

8 Charlie Brown will receive $50,000 on December 31, 2007 (5 years from now) from a trust fund established by his father. Assuming the appropriate interest rate for discounting is 12% (compounded semiannually), what is the present value of this amount today?

9 What are the primary characteristics of an annuity? Differentiate between an "ordinary annuity" and an "annuity due."

10 Linus, Inc. owes $30,000 to Peanuts Company. How much would Linus have to pay each year if the debt is retired through four equal payments (made at the end of the year), given an interest rate on the debt of 12%? (Round to two decimal places.)

11 The Lockhorns are planning for a retirement home. They estimate they will need $160,000, 4 years from now to purchase this home. Assuming an interest rate of 10%, what amount must be deposited at the end of each of the 4 years to fund the home price? (Round to two decimal places.)

12 Assume the same situation as in Question 11, except that the four equal amounts are deposited at the beginning of the period rather than at the end. In this case, what amount must be deposited at the beginning of each period? (Round to two decimals.)

13 Explain how the future value of an ordinary annuity interest table is converted to the future value of an annuity due interest table.

14 Explain how the present value of an ordinary annuity interest table is converted to the present value of an annuity due interest table.

15 In a book named *Treasure*, the reader has to figure out where a 2.2 pound, 24 kt gold horse has been buried. If the horse is found, a prize of $25,000 a year for 20 years is provided. The actual cost of the publisher to purchase an annuity to pay for the prize is $210,000. What interest rate (to the nearest percent) was used to determine the amount of the annuity? (Assume end-of-year payments.)

16 Greg Norman Enterprises leases property to Tiger Woods, Inc. Because Tiger Woods, Inc. is experiencing financial difficulty, Norman agrees to receive five rents of $10,000 at the end of each year, with the rents deferred 3 years. What is the present value of the five rents discounted at 12%?

17 Answer the following questions:

(a) On May 1, 2001, Liselotte Neumann Company sold some machinery to Tee-off Company on an installment contract basis. The contract required five equal annual payments, with the first payment due on May 1, 2001. What present value concept is appropriate for this situation?

(b) On June 1, 2001, Mike Brisky Inc. purchased a new machine that it does not have to pay for until May 1, 2003. The total payment on May 1, 2003, will include both principal and interest. Assuming interest at a 12% rate, the cost of the machine would be the total payment multiplied by what time value of money concept?

(c) Kelly Gibson Inc. wishes to know how much money it will have available in 5 years if five equal amounts of $35,000 are invested, with the first amount invested immediately. What interest table is appropriate for this situation?

(d) Patty Sheehan invests in a "jumbo" $200,000, 3-year certificate of deposit at First Wisconsin Bank. What table would be used to determine the amount accumulated at the end of 3 years?

18 Recently Vickie Maher was interested in purchasing a Honda Acura. The salesperson indicated that the price of the car was either $27,000 cash or $6,900 at the end of each of 5 years. Compute the effective interest rate to the nearest percent that Vickie would pay if she chooses to make the five annual payments.

19 Recently, property/casualty insurance companies have been criticized because they reserve for the total loss as much as 5 years before it may happen. Recently the IRS has joined the debate because they say the full reserve is unfair from a taxation viewpoint. What do you believe is the IRS position?

BRIEF EXERCISES

BE6-1 Steve Allen invested $10,000 today in a fund that earns 8% compounded annually. To what amount will the investment grow in 3 years? To what amount would the investment grow in 3 years if the fund earns 8% annual interest compounded semiannually?

BE6-2 Itzak Perlman needs $20,000 in 4 years. What amount must he invest today if his investment earns 12% compounded annually? What amount must he invest if his investment earns 12% annual interest compounded quarterly?

BE6-3 Janet Jackson will invest $30,000 today. She needs $222,000 in 21 years. What annual interest rate must she earn?

BE6-4 Dan Webster will invest $10,000 today in a fund that earns 5% annual interest. How many years will it take for the fund to grow to $13,400?

BE6-5 Anne Boleyn will invest $5,000 a year for 20 years in a fund that will earn 12% annual interest. If the first payment into the fund occurs today, what amount will be in the fund in 20 years? If the first payment occurs at year-end, what amount will be in the fund in 20 years?

BE6-6 William Cullen Bryant needs $200,000 in 10 years. How much must he invest at the end of each year, at 11% interest, to meet his needs?

BE6-7 Jack Thompson's lifelong dream is to own his own fishing boat to use in his retirement. Jack has recently come into an inheritance of $400,000. He estimates that the boat he wants will cost $350,000 when he retires in 5 years. How much of his inheritance must he invest at an annual rate of 12% (compounded annually) to buy the boat at retirement?

BE6-8 Refer to the data in BE6-7. Assuming quarterly compounding of amounts invested at 12%, how much of Jack Thompson's inheritance must be invested to have enough at retirement to buy the boat?

BE6-9 Luther Vandross is investing $12,961 at the end of each year in a fund that earns 10% interest. In how many years will the fund be at $100,000?

BE6-10 Grupo Rana wants to withdraw $20,000 each year for 10 years from a fund that earns 8% interest. How much must he invest today if the first withdrawal is at year-end? How much must he invest today if the first withdrawal takes place immediately?

BE6-11 Mark Twain's VISA balance is $1,124.40. He may pay it off in 18 equal end-of-month payments of $75 each. What interest rate is Mark paying?

BE6-12 Corinne Dunbar is investing $200,000 in a fund that earns 8% interest compounded annually. What equal amounts can Corinne withdraw at the end of each of the next 20 years?

BE6-13 Bayou Inc. will deposit $20,000 in a 12% fund at the end of each year for 8 years beginning December 31, 2002. What amount will be in the fund immediately after the last deposit?

BE6-14 Hollis Stacy wants to create a fund today that will enable her to withdraw $20,000 per year for 8 years, with the first withdrawal to take place 5 years from today. If the fund earns 8% interest, how much must Hollis invest today?

BE6-15 Acadian Inc. issues $1,000,000 of 7% bonds due in 10 years with interest payable at year-end. The current market rate of interest for bonds of similar risk is 8%. What amount will Acadian receive when it issues the bonds?

BE6-16 Walt Frazier is settling a $20,000 loan due today by making 6 equal annual payments of $4,864.51. Determine the interest rate on this loan, if the payments begin one year after the loan is signed.

BE6-17 Consider the loan in BE6-16. What payments must Walt Frazier make to settle the loan at the same interest rate but with the 6 payments beginning on the day the loan is signed?

EXERCISES

(Interest rates are per annum unless otherwise indicated.)

E6-1 (Using Interest Tables) For each of the following cases, indicate (a) to what rate columns and (b) to what number of periods you would refer in looking up the interest factor.

1. In a future value of 1 table

Annual Rate	Number of Years Invested	Compounded
a. 9%	9	Annually
b. 12%	5	Quarterly
c. 10%	15	Semiannually

2. In a present value of an annuity of 1 table

Annual Rate	Number of Years Involved	Number of Rents Involved	Frequency of Rents
a. 9%	25	25	Annually
b. 10%	15	30	Semiannually
c. 12%	7	28	Quarterly

E6-2 (Simple and Compound Interest Computations) Alan Jackson invests $20,000 at 8% annual interest, leaving the money invested without withdrawing any of the interest for 8 years. At the end of the 8 years, Alan withdrew the accumulated amount of money.

Instructions

(a) Compute the amount Alan would withdraw assuming the investment earns simple interest.
(b) Compute the amount Alan would withdraw assuming the investment earns interest compounded annually.
(c) Compute the amount Alan would withdraw assuming the investment earns interest compounded semiannually.

E6-3 (Computation of Future Values and Present Values) Using the appropriate interest table, answer each of the following questions (each case is independent of the others).

(a) What is the future value of $7,000 at the end of 5 periods at 8% compounded interest?
(b) What is the present value of $7,000 due 8 periods hence, discounted at 11%?
(c) What is the future value of 15 periodic payments of $7,000 each made at the end of each period and compounded at 10%?
(d) What is the present value of $7,000 to be received at the end of each of 20 periods, discounted at 5% compound interest?

E6-4 (Computation of Future Values and Present Values) Using the appropriate interest table, answer the following questions (each case is independent of the others).

(a) What is the future value of 20 periodic payments of $4,000 each made at the beginning of each period and compounded at 8%?
(b) What is the present value of $2,500 to be received at the beginning of each of 30 periods, discounted at 10% compound interest?
(c) What is the future value of 15 deposits of $2,000 each made at the beginning of each period and compounded at 10%? (Future value as of the end of the fifteenth period.)
(d) What is the present value of six receipts of $1,000 each received at the beginning of each period, discounted at 9% compounded interest?

E6-5 (Computation of Present Value) Using the appropriate interest table, compute the present values of the following periodic amounts due at the end of the designated periods.

(a) $30,000 receivable at the end of each period for 8 periods compounded at 12%.
(b) $30,000 payments to be made at the end of each period for 16 periods at 9%.
(c) $30,000 payable at the end of the seventh, eighth, ninth, and tenth periods at 12%.

E6-6 (Future Value and Present Value Problems) Presented below are three unrelated situations:

(a) Horace Grant Company recently signed a lease for a new office building, for a lease period of 10 years. Under the lease agreement, a security deposit of $12,000 is made, with the deposit to be returned at the expiration of the lease, with interest compounded at 10% per year. What amount will the company receive at the time the lease expires?
(b) Sharone Wright Corporation, having recently issued a $20 million, 15-year bond issue, is committed to make annual sinking fund deposits of $600,000. The deposits are made on the last day of each year, and yield a return of 10%. Will the fund at the end of 15 years be sufficient to retire the bonds? If not, what will the deficiency be?
(c) Under the terms of his salary agreement, president Rex Walters has an option of receiving either an immediate bonus of $40,000, or a deferred bonus of $70,000, payable in 10 years. Ignoring tax considerations, and assuming a relevant interest rate of 8%, which form of settlement should Walters accept?

E6-7 (Computation of Bond Prices) What would you pay for a $50,000 debenture bond that matures in 15 years and pays $5,000 a year in interest if you wanted to earn a yield of:

(a) 8%? **(b)** 10%? **(c)** 12%?

E6-8 (Computations for a Retirement Fund) Clarence Weatherspoon, a super salesman contemplating retirement on his fifty-fifth birthday, decides to create a fund on an 8% basis that will enable him to withdraw $20,000 per year on June 30, beginning in 2006, and continuing through 2009. To develop this fund, Clarence intends to make equal contributions on June 30 of each of the years 2002–2005.

Instructions

(a) How much must the balance of the fund equal on June 30, 2005, in order for Clarence Weatherspoon to satisfy his objective?

(b) What are each of Clarence's contributions to the fund?

E6-9 (Unknown Rate) LEW Company purchased a machine at a price of $100,000 by signing a note payable, which requires a single payment of $123,210 in 2 years. Assuming annual compounding of interest, what rate of interest is being paid on the loan?

E6-10 (Unknown Periods and Unknown Interest Rate) Consider the following independent situations:

(a) Jerry Stackhouse wishes to become a millionaire. His money market fund has a balance of $92,296 and has a guaranteed interest of 10%. How many years must Jerry leave that balance in the fund in order to get his desired $1,000,000?

(b) Assume that Russell Maryland desires to accumulate $1 million in 15 years using his money market fund balance of $182,696. At what interest rate must Russell's investment compound annually?

E6-11 (Evaluation of Purchase Options) Sosa Excavating Inc. is purchasing a bulldozer. The equipment has a price of $100,000. The manufacturer has offered a payment plan that would allow Sosa to make 10 equal annual payments of $16,274.53, with the first payment due one year after the purchase.

Instructions

(a) How much total interest will Sosa pay on this payment plan?

(b) Sosa could borrow $100,000 from its bank to finance the purchase at an annual rate of 9%. Should Sosa borrow from the bank or use the manufacturer's payment plan to pay for the equipment?

E6-12 (Analysis of Alternatives) The Black Knights Inc., a manufacturer of high-sugar, low-sodium, low-cholesterol TV dinners, would like to increase its market share in the Sunbelt. In order to do so, Black Knights has decided to locate a new factory in the Panama City area. Black Knights will either buy or lease a site depending upon which is more advantageous. The site location committee has narrowed down the available sites to the following three buildings.

Building A: Purchase for a cash price of $600,000, useful life 25 years.

Building B: Lease for 25 years with annual lease payments of $69,000 being made at the beginning of the year.

Building C: Purchase for $650,000 cash. This building is larger than needed; however, the excess space can be sublet for 25 years at a net annual rental of $7,000. Rental payments will be received at the end of each year. The Black Knights Inc. has no aversion to being a landlord.

Instructions

In which building would you recommend that The Black Knights Inc. locate, assuming a 12% cost of funds?

E6-13 (Amount in Trust) Tim Salmon intends to invest $10,000 in a trust on January 10 of every year, 1999 through 2013. He anticipates that interest rates will change during that period of time as follows:

1/10/99–1/10/02	10%
1/11/02–1/10/09	11%
1/11/09–1/10/13	12%

How much will Tim have in trust on January 10, 2013?

E6-14 (Amount Needed to Retire Stock) Alexandra Inc. is a computer software development company. In recent years, the company has experienced significant growth in sales. As a result, the board of directors has decided to raise funds by issuing redeemable preferred stock to meet the need for expansion. On January 1, 2000, the company issued 100,000 shares of 12% redeemable preferred stock with the intent to redeem this preferred stock on January 1, 2010. The redemption price per share of preferred stock will be $25.

As the controller of the company, Al Iskan is asked to set up a plan to accumulate the funds that will be needed to retire the redeemable preferred stock on January 1, 2010. He expects that the company will have a surplus of funds of $125,000 each year for the next 10 years and decides to set up a sinking fund for these funds. Beginning January 1, 2001, the company will deposit $125,000 into the sinking fund annually for 10 years. The sinking fund is expected to generate 10% interest and compound annually. However, the sinking fund will not be sufficient for the redemption of preferred stock. Therefore, Al plans to deposit on January 1, 2005, a single amount of money into a savings account which is expected to earn 9% interest.

Instructions

Help Al Iskan to determine the amount to be deposited on January 1, 2005.

E6-15 (Computation of Bond Liability) Katarina Witt Inc. manufactures skating equipment. Recently the vice president of operations of the company has requested construction of a new plant to meet the increasing needs for the company's skates. After a careful evaluation of the request, the board of directors has decided to raise funds for the new plant by issuing $2,000,000 of 11% term corporate bonds on March 1, 2001, due on March 1, 2016, with interest payable each March 1 and September 1. At the time of issuance, the market interest rate for similar financial instruments is 10%.

Instructions

As the controller of the company, determine the selling price of the bonds.

E6-16 (Computation of Pension Liability) Nerwin, Inc. is a furniture manufacturing company with 50 employees. Recently, after a long negotiation with the local labor union, the company decided to initiate a pension plan as a part of its compensation plan. The plan will start on January 1, 2001. Each employee covered by the plan is entitled to a pension payment each year after retirement. As required by accounting standards, the controller of the company needs to report the pension obligation (liability). On the basis of a discussion with the supervisor of the Personnel Department and an actuary from an insurance company, the controller develops the following information related to the pension plan:

Average length of time to retirement	15 years
Expected life duration after retirement	10 years
Total pension payment expected each year after retirement for all employees. Payment made at the end of the year.	$700,000 per year

The interest rate to be used is 8%.

Instructions

On the basis of the information above, determine the present value of the pension obligation (liability).

E6-17 (Investment Decision) Scottie Pippen just received a signing bonus of $1,000,000. His plan is to invest this payment in a fund that will earn 8%, compounded annually.

Instructions

(a) If Pippen plans to establish the Scottie Pippen Foundation once the fund grows to $1,999,000, how many years until he can establish the foundation?

(b) Instead of investing the entire $1,000,000, Pippen invests $300,000 today and plans to make 9 equal annual investments into the fund beginning one year from today. What amount should the payments be if Pippen plans to establish the $1,999,000 foundation at the end of 9 years?

E6-18 (Retirement of Debt) Jesper Parnevik borrowed $70,000 on March 1, 2000. This amount plus accrued interest at 12% compounded semiannually is to be repaid March 1, 2010. To retire this debt, Jesper plans to contribute to a debt retirement fund five equal amounts starting on March 1, 2005, and for the next 4 years. The fund is expected to earn 10% per annum.

Instructions

How much must be contributed each year by Jesper Parnevik to provide a fund sufficient to retire the debt on March 1, 2010?

E6-19 (Computation of Bond Liability) Your client, Faith Hill Inc., has acquired Tracy Lawrence Manufacturing Company in a business combination that is to be accounted for as a purchase transaction (at fair market value). Along with the assets and business of Tracy Lawrence, Faith Hill assumed an outstanding debenture bond issue having a principal amount of $8,000,000 with interest payable semiannually at a stated rate of 8%. Tracy Lawrence received $7,300,000 in proceeds from the issuance 5 years ago. The bonds are currently 20 years from maturity. Equivalent securities command a 12% rate of interest, interest paid semiannually.

Instructions

Your client requests your advice regarding the amount to record for the acquired bond issue.

E6-20 (Computation of Amount of Rentals) Your client, Vince Gill Leasing Company, is preparing a contract to lease a machine to Souvenirs Corporation for a period of 25 years. Gill has an investment cost of $365,755 in the machine, which has a useful life of 25 years and no salvage value at the end of that time. Your client is interested in earning an 11% return on its investment and has agreed to accept 25 equal rental payments at the end of each of the next 25 years.

Instructions

You are requested to provide Gill with the amount of each of the 25 rental payments that will yield an 11% return on investment.

E6-21 (Least Costly Payoff) Sonic Hedgehog Corporation has outstanding a contractual debt. The corporation has available two means of settlement: It can either make immediate payment of $2,600,000, or it can make annual payments of $300,000 for 15 years, each payment due on the last day of the year.

Instructions

Which method of payment do you recommend, assuming an expected effective interest rate of 8% during the future period?

E6-22 (Least Costly Payoff) Assuming the same facts as those in E6-21 except that the payments must begin now and be made on the first day of each of the 15 years, what payment method would you recommend?

***E6-23 (Determine Interest Rate)** Reba McEntire wishes to invest $19,000 on July 1, 2001, and have it accumulate to $49,000 by July 1, 2011.

Instructions

At what exact annual rate of interest must Reba invest the $19,000?

***E6-24 (Determine Interest Rate)** On July 17, 2000, Tim McGraw borrowed $42,000 from his grandfather to open a clothing store. Starting July 17, 2001, Tim has to make ten equal annual payments of $6,500 each to repay the loan.

Instructions

What interest rate is Tim paying?

***E6-25 (Determine Interest Rate)** As the purchaser of a new house, Patty Loveless has signed a mortgage note to pay the Memphis National Bank and Trust Co. $14,000 every 6 months for 20 years, at the end of which time she will own the house. At the date the mortgage is signed the purchase price was $198,000, and a down payment of $20,000 was made. The first payment will be made 6 months after the date the mortgage is signed.

Instructions

Compute the exact rate of interest earned on the mortgage by the bank.

PROBLEMS

(Interest rates are per annum unless otherwise indicated.)

P6-1 (Various Time Value Situations) Answer each of these unrelated questions.

(a) On January 1, 2001, Rather Corporation sold a building that cost $250,000 and that had accumulated depreciation of $100,000 on the date of sale. Rather received as consideration a $275,000 non-interest-bearing note due on January 1, 2004. There was no established exchange price for the building, and the note had no ready market. The prevailing rate of interest for a note of this type on January 1, 2001, was 9%. At what amount should the gain from the sale of the building be reported?

(b) On January 1, 2001, Rather Corporation purchased 200 of the $1,000 face value, 9%, 10-year bonds of Walters Inc. The bonds mature on January 1, 2011, and pay interest annually beginning January 1, 2002. Rather Corporation purchased the bonds to yield 11%. How much did Rather pay for the bonds?

(c) Rather Corporation bought a new machine and agreed to pay for it in equal annual installments of $4,000 at the end of each of the next 10 years. Assuming that a prevailing interest rate of 8% applies to this contract, how much should Rather record as the cost of the machine?

(d) Rather Corporation purchased a special tractor on December 31, 2001. The purchase agreement stipulated that Rather should pay $20,000 at the time of purchase and $5,000 at the end of each of the next 8 years. The tractor should be recorded on December 31, 2001, at what amount, assuming an appropriate interest rate of 12%?

(e) Rather Corporation wants to withdraw $100,000 (including principal) from an investment fund at the end of each year for 9 years. What should be the required initial investment at the beginning of the first year if the fund earns 11%?

P6-2 (Various Time Value Situations) Using the appropriate interest table, provide the solution to each of the following four questions by computing the unknowns.

(a) What is the amount of the payments that Tom Brokaw must make at the end of each of 8 years to accumulate a fund of $70,000 by the end of the eighth year, if the fund earns 8% interest, compounded annually?

(b) Peter Jennings is 40 years old today and he wishes to accumulate $500,000 by his sixty-fifth birthday so he can retire to his summer place on Lake Hopatcong. He wishes to accumulate this amount by making equal deposits on his fortieth through his sixty-fourth birthdays. What annual deposit must Peter make if the fund will earn 12% interest compounded annually?

(c) Jane Pauley has $20,000 to invest today at 9% to pay a debt of $56,253. How many years will it take her to accumulate enough to liquidate the debt?

(d) Maria Shriver has a $27,600 debt that she wishes to repay 4 years from today; she has $18,181 that she intends to invest for the 4 years. What rate of interest will she need to earn annually in order to accumulate enough to pay the debt?

P6-3 (Investment Problem) Mack Aroni, a bank robber, is worried about his retirement. He decides to start a savings account. Mack deposits annually his net share of the "loot," which consists of $75,000 per year, for 3 years beginning January 1, 2001. Mack is arrested on January 4, 2003 (after making the third deposit), and spends the rest of 2003 and most of 2004 in jail. He escapes in September of 2004. He resumes his savings plan with semiannual deposits of $30,000 each beginning January 1, 2005. Assume that the bank's interest rate was 9% compounded annually from January 1, 2001, through January 1, 2004, and 12% annual rate compounded semiannually thereafter.

Instructions

When Mack retires on January 1, 2008 (6 months after his last deposit), what is the balance in his savings account?

P6-4 (Analysis of Alternatives) Derrick Coleman Inc. has decided to surface and maintain for 10 years a vacant lot next to one of its discount-retail outlets to serve as a parking lot for customers. Management is considering the following bids involving two different qualities of surfacing for a parking area of 12,000 square yards:

Bid A: A surface that costs $5.25 per square yard to install. This surface will have to be replaced at the end of 5 years. The annual maintenance cost on this surface is estimated at 20 cents per square yard for each year except the last year of its service. The replacement surface will be similar to the initial surface.

Bid B: A surface that costs $9.50 per square yard to install. This surface has a probable useful life of 10 years and will require annual maintenance in each year except the last year, at an estimated cost of 9 cents per square yard.

Instructions

Prepare computations showing which bid should be accepted by Derrick Coleman Inc. You may assume that the cost of capital is 9%, that the annual maintenance expenditures are incurred at the end of each year, and that prices are not expected to change during the next 10 years.

P6-5 (Various Time Value Situations) Solve for the unknowns in each of the following three situations using the interest tables.

(a) Mr. and Mrs. Scott Williams have decided to provide for their handicapped son by investing $187,400 today in an annuity at 8% interest, compounded annually. They feel their son should receive approximately $20,000 per year beginning one year from today. The investment of the $187,400 will provide approximately $20,000 per year for how many years before being depleted?

(b) Chris Webber wishes to invest $150,000 today to ensure $18,610 payments to his son at the end of each year for the next 15 years. At what approximate interest rate must the $150,000 be invested?

(c) On June 1, 2001, Cheryl Miller purchases 20 acres of farmland from her neighbor, Juwann Howard, and agrees to pay the purchase price in five payments of $21,000 each, the first payment to be payable June 1, 2005. (Assume interest compounded annually at the rate of 9% is implicit in the payments.) What is the purchase price of the 20 acres?

P6-6 (Evaluating Payment Alternatives) Terry O'Malley has just learned he has won a $900,000 prize in the lottery. The lottery has given him two options for receiving the payments: (1) If Terry takes all the money today, the state and federal governments will deduct taxes at a rate of 46% immediately. (2) Alternatively, the lottery offers Terry a payout of 20 equal payments of $62,000 with the first payment occurring when Terry turns in the winning ticket. Terry will be taxed on each of these payments at a rate of 25%.

Instructions

Assuming Terry can earn an 8% rate of return (compounded annually) on any money invested during this period, which pay-out option should he choose?

P6-7 (Analysis of Alternatives) Sally Brown died, leaving to her husband Linus an insurance policy contract that provides that the beneficiary (Linus) can choose any one of the following four options.

(a) $55,000 immediate cash.
(b) $3,700 every 3 months payable at the end of each quarter for 5 years.
(c) $18,000 immediate cash and $1,600 every 3 months for 10 years, payable at the beginning of each 3-month period.
(d) $4,000 every 3 months for 3 years and $1,200 each quarter for the following 25 quarters, all payments payable at the end of each quarter.

Instructions

If money is worth 2½% per quarter, compounded quarterly, which option would you recommend that Linus exercise?

P6-8 (Various Time Value Situations) Provide a solution to each of the following situations by computing the unknowns (use the interest tables).

(a) Laura Davies invests in a $180,000 annuity insurance policy at 9% compounded annually on February 8, 2002. The first of 20 receipts from the annuity is payable to Laura 10 years after the annuity is purchased, or on February 8, 2012. What will be the amount of each of the 20 equal annual receipts?
(b) Jim Harbaugh owes a debt of $30,000 from the purchase of his new sports car. The debt bears interest of 8% payable annually. Jim wishes to pay the debt and interest in eight annual installments, beginning one year hence. What equal annual installments will pay the debt and interest?
(c) On January 1, 2002, Neil O'Donnel offers to buy Scott Mitchell's used combine for $45,000, payable in 10 equal installments, which are to include 9% interest on the unpaid balance and a portion of the principal with the first payment to be made on January 1, 2002. How much will each payment be?

P6-9 (Purchase Price of a Business) During the past year, Nicole Bobek planted a new vineyard on 150 acres of land that she leases for $27,000 a year. She has asked you as her accountant to assist her in determining the value of her vineyard operation.

The vineyard will bear no grapes for the first 5 years (1–5). In the next 5 years (6–10), Nicole estimates that the vines will bear grapes that can be sold for $60,000 each year. For the next 20 years (11–30) she expects the harvest will provide annual revenues of $100,000. But during the last 10 years (31–40) of the vineyard's life she estimates that revenues will decline to $80,000 per year.

During the first 5 years the annual cost of pruning, fertilizing, and caring for the vineyard is estimated at $9,000; during the years of production, 6–40, these costs will rise to $10,000 per year. The relevant market rate of interest for the entire period is 12%. Assume that all receipts and payments are made at the end of each year.

Instructions

Dick Button has offered to buy Nicole's vineyard business by assuming the 40-year lease. On the basis of the current value of the business what is the minimum price Nicole should accept?

P6-10 (Investment Decision) Mrs. Paul plans to establish an annuity arrangement whereby her four children would each receive $3,700 on December 25 of the years 2004 to 2018, inclusive. Variations in the interest rates during that period of time are estimated as follows:

12/26/03–12/25/08	12%
12/26/08–12/25/14	11%
12/26/14–12/25/18	9%

Instructions

Compute the amount that Mrs. Paul must invest on December 26, 2003, to assure these annual payments to her children.

P6-11 (Time Value Concepts Applied to Solve Business Problems) Answer the following questions related to Mark Grace Inc.

(a) Mark Grace Inc. has $572,000 to invest. The company is trying to decide between two alternative uses of the funds. One alternative provides $80,000 at the end of each year for 12 years, and the other is to receive a single lump sum payment of $1,900,000 at the end of the 12 years. Which alternative should Grace select? Assume the interest rate is constant over the entire investment.

(b) Mark Grace Inc. has completed the purchase of new IBM computers. The fair market value of the equipment is $824,150. The purchase agreement specifies an immediate down payment of $200,000 and semiannual payments of $76,952 beginning at the end of 6 months for 5 years. What is the interest rate, to the nearest percent, used in discounting this purchase transaction?

(c) Mark Grace Inc. loans money to John Kruk Corporation in the amount of $600,000. Grace accepts an 8% note due in 7 years with interest payable semiannually. After 2 years (and receipt of interest for 2 years), Grace needs money and therefore sells the note to Chicago National Bank, which demands interest on the note of 10% compounded semiannually. What is the amount Grace will receive on the sale of the note?

(d) Mark Grace Inc. wishes to accumulate $1,300,000 by December 31, 2011, to retire bonds outstanding. The company deposits $300,000 on December 31, 2001, which will earn interest at 10% compounded quarterly, to help in the retirement of this debt. In addition, the company wants to know how much should be deposited at the end of each quarter for 10 years to ensure that $1,300,000 is available at the end of 2011. (The quarterly deposits will also earn at a rate of 10%, compounded quarterly.) Round to even dollars.

P6-12 (Analysis of Alternatives) Homer Simpson Inc., a manufacturer of steel school lockers, plans to purchase a new punch press for use in its manufacturing process. After contacting the appropriate vendors, the purchasing department received differing terms and options from each vendor. The Engineering Department has determined that each vendor's punch press is substantially identical and each has a useful life of 20 years. In addition, Engineering has estimated that required year-end maintenance costs will be $1,000 per year for the first 5 years, $2,000 per year for the next 10 years, and $3,000 per year for the last 5 years. Following is each vendor's sale package.

Vendor A: $45,000 cash at time of delivery and 10 year-end payments of $15,000 each. Vendor A offers all its customers the right to purchase at the time of sale a separate 20-year maintenance service contract under which Vendor A will perform all year-end maintenance at a one-time initial cost of $10,000.

Vendor B: Forty seminannual payments of $8,000 each with the first installment due upon delivery. Vendor B will perform all year-end maintenance for the next 20 years at no extra charge.

Vendor C: Full cash price of $125,000 will be due upon delivery.

Instructions

Assuming that both Vendor A and B will be able to perform the required year-end maintenance, that Simpson's cost of funds is 10%, and the machine will be purchased on January 1, from which vendor should the press be purchased?

P6-13 (Analysis of Business Problems) Jean-Luc is a financial executive with Starship Enterprises. Although Jean-Luc has not had any formal training in finance or accounting, he has a "good sense" for numbers and has helped the company grow from a very small company ($500,000 sales) to a large operation ($45 million in sales). With the business growing steadily, however, the company needs to make a number of difficult financial decisions in which Jean-Luc feels a little "over his head." He therefore has decided to hire a new employee with "numbers" expertise to help him. As a basis for determining whom to employ, he has decided to ask each prospective employee to prepare answers to questions relating to the following situations he has encountered recently. Here are the questions.

(a) In 1999, Starship Enterprises negotiated and closed a long-term lease contract for newly constructed truck terminals and freight storage facilities. The buildings were constructed on land owned by the company. On January 1, 2000, Starship took possession of the leased property. The 20-year lease is effective for the period January 1, 2000, through December 31, 2019. Advance rental payments of $800,000 are payable to the lessor (owner of facilities) on January 1 of each of the first 10 years of the lease term. Advance payments of $300,000 are due on January 1 for each of the last 10 years of the lease term. Starship has an option to purchase all the leased facilities for $1.00 on December 31, 2019. At the time the lease was negotiated, the fair market value of the truck terminals and freight storage facilities was approximately $7,200,000. If the company had borrowed the money to purchase the facilities, it would have had to pay 10% interest. Should the company have purchased rather than leased the facilities?

(b) Last year the company exchanged a piece of land for a noninterest-bearing note. The note is to be paid at the rate of $12,000 per year for 9 years, beginning one year from the date of disposal of the land. An appropriate rate of interest for the note was 11%. At the time the land was originally purchased, it cost $90,000. What is the fair value of the note?

(c) The company has always followed the policy to take any cash discounts on goods purchased. Recently the company purchased a large amount of raw materials at a price of $800,000 with terms 2/10, n/30 on which it took the discount. Starship has recently estimated its cost of funds at 10%. Should Starship continue this policy of always taking the cash discount?

P6-14 (Analysis of Various Business Problems) Bela Koroly has had a difficult year as controller for Pommel Inc. The company lost a considerable amount of money this year, and now the board of directors has decided to hire a management consulting team to review the major financial decisions made over the last 3 years. As controller, Koroly has been asked by the board to highlight the three major financial decisions over the last 2 years, and indicate what decisions the company made.

(a) During this period, the company had to decide to replace its old equipment in the plant with automated equipment. A schedule relating to pertinent information about the old equipment and automated equipment is as follows:

	Old Equipment	Automated Equipment
Original cost (new)	$2,800,000	$2,000,000
Accumulated depreciation to date	100,000	—
Current salvage value	50,000	—
Estimated cost savings each year over old equipment (Assume that cost savings occur at the end of each year.)	—	500,000
Remaining useful life	6 years	6 years
Salvage value at end of 6 years	—	—

Pommel Inc. decided to continue using the old equipment. Its cost of funds was 10%.

(b) During this period, the company had $25,000,000 to invest. The company had two principal alternatives for the use of investment funds. These alternatives are provided below.

	Project I Investment	Project II Investment
Required investment	$25,000,000	$25,000,000
Annual cash inflows (Assume they will be received at the end of each year.)	9,000,000	
Cash inflows at the end of the 9th year		90,000,000
Life of the project	9 years	9 years

Pommel decided to invest its funds in Project I. The cost of funds is 10%.

(c) Pommel has 400 employees. At the end of each year, it has given a bonus to its employees based on their productivity. The total bonus in a year is approximately $1 million. A number of the employees indicated that they would prefer a pension plan rather than a bonus payment each year because they have a tendency to spend the bonus immediately. Pertinent data related to a bonus plan versus a pension plan are provided below:

	Bonus Plan	Pension Plan
Number of employees	400	400
Length of time to retirement	15 years	15 years
Expected life duration after retirement	—	12 years
Bonus payment expected until retirement (paid at end of year)	$1,000,000/year	—
Pension payment expected at retirement (to be paid at the beginning of each year, starting at the beginning of the 16th year)	—	$3,200,000/year

The cost of funds in this case is assumed to be 10%. The company decided to go with the pension plan.

Instructions

Assuming that you are one of the management consultants working for the board of directors, would you agree with these decisions?

P6-15 (Analysis of Lease vs. Purchase) Jose Rijo Inc. owns and operates a number of hardware stores in the New England region. Recently the company has decided to locate another store in a rapidly growing area of Maryland; the company is trying to decide whether to purchase or lease the building and related facilities.

Purchase: The company can purchase the site, construct the building, and purchase all store fixtures. The cost would be $1,650,000. An immediate down payment of $400,000 is required, and the remaining $1,250,000 would be paid off over 5 years at $300,000 per year (including interest). The property is expected to have a useful life of 12 years and then it will be sold for $500,000. As the owner of the property, the company will have the following out-of-pocket expenses each period:

Property taxes (to be paid at the end of each year)	$40,000
Insurance (to be paid at the beginning of each year)	27,000
Other (primarily maintenance which occurs at the end of each year)	16,000
	$83,000

Lease: First National Bank has agreed to purchase the site, construct the building, and install the appropriate fixtures for Rijo Inc. if Rijo will lease the completed facility for 12 years. The annual costs for the lease would be $240,000. Rijo would have no responsibility related to the facility over the 12 years. The terms of the lease are that Rijo would be required to make 12 annual payments (the first payment to be made at the time the store opens and then each following year). In addition, a deposit of $100,000 is required when the store is opened which will be returned at the end of the twelfth year, assuming no unusual damage to the building structure or fixtures.

Currently the cost of funds for Rijo Inc. is 10%.

Instructions

Which of the two approaches should Rijo Inc. follow?

P6-16 (Business Problems) Presented below are a series of time value of money problems. Solve each of them.

(a) Your client, Kate Janeway, wishes to provide for the payment of an obligation of $250,000 due on July 1, 2007. Kate plans to deposit $20,000 in a special fund each July 1 for 8 years, starting July 1, 2000. She will begin her savings plan by making a deposit on July 1, 1999, of an amount which, with its accumulated interest, will bring the fund up to $250,000 at the maturity of the obligation. She expects that the fund will earn interest at the rate of 4% compounded annually. Compute the amount to be deposited on July 1, 1999.

(b) Many employers establish pension plans for their employees. Accountants are often required to determine the present value of pension obligations for financial reporting. To illustrate, assume that on January 1, 1999, Tuvok Corporation initiated a pension plan under which each of its employees would receive a pension annuity of $10,000 per year beginning one year after retirement and continuing until death. Employee A will retire at the end of 2005 and, according to mortality tables, is expected to live long enough to receive eight pension payments. What is the present value of Tuvok Corporation's pension obligation for employee A at the beginning of 1999 if the interest rate is 10%?

(c) Neelix Company purchases bonds from Ocampa Corporation in the amount of $500,000. The bonds are 10-year, 12% bonds that pay interest semiannually. After 3 years (and receipt of interest for 3 years), Neelix needs money and, therefore, sells the bonds to Nystrum Company, which demands interest at 16% compounded semiannually. What is the amount that Neelix will receive on the sale of the bonds?

P6-17 (Analysis of Business Problems) Bill Jenkins owns a hardware store, and he is facing several business decisions that involve time value of money considerations. He has asked your advice on the following situations.

(a) Jenkins plans to purchase a delivery truck. The truck, which has a useful life of 6 years, could be leased by making 6 equal annual payments of $3,000, beginning on the day the lease is signed. Alternatively, Jenkins could borrow at the bank at an annual rate of 10%, in order to purchase the truck at a price of $13,900 plus a title fee of $400. Under both the lease and purchase options, Jenkins would be responsible for insurance and maintenance on the truck. Should Jenkins lease or buy?

(b) Jenkins is considering issuing bonds with a face value of $100,000 and a coupon rate of 11%. The bonds mature in 7 years and pay interest semiannually. The current market interest rate on similar securities is 12%. How much cash will Jenkins receive if he issues the bonds today?

(c) Jenkins has received information from his investment banker that market interest rates are likely to decline to 10% in the next week. How much cash will Jenkins receive on the bond issue if he waits and the market rate declines to 10%?

(d) If the bonds in (b) are issued, Jenkins plans to establish a fund to pay off the bondholders at maturity. The fund will be established from the cost savings from new equipment purchased with the proceeds. He plans to make a $20,000 deposit into the fund after 2 years, and then make 5 equal annual payments into the fund at the end of each year. The fund will earn interest at a rate of 8%, compounded annually. What must the amount of the payments be in order to have enough in the fund to pay off the bond principal at maturity?

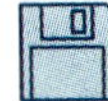

P6-18 (Pension Funding) You have been hired as a benefit consultant by Maugarite Alomar, the owner of Attic Angels. She wants to establish a retirement plan for herself and her three employees. Maugarite has provided the following information: The retirement plan is to be based upon annual salary for the last year before retirement and is to provide 50% of Maugarite's last-year annual salary and 40% of the last-year annual salary for each employee. The plan will make annual payments at the beginning of each year for 20 years from the date of retirement. Maugarite wishes to fund the plan by making 15 annual deposits beginning January 1, 2001. Invested funds will earn 12% compounded annually. Information about plan participants as of January 1, 2001, is as follows:

Maugarite Alomar, owner: Current annual salary of $40,000; estimated retirement date January 1, 2026.

Kenny Rogers, flower arranger: Current annual salary of $30,000; estimated retirement date January 1, 2031.

Anita Baker, sales clerk: Current annual salary of $15,000; estimated retirement date January 1, 2021.

Willie Nelson, part-time bookkeeper: Current annual salary of $15,000; estimated retirement date January 1, 2016.

In the past, Maugarite has given herself and each employee a year-end salary increase of 4%. Maugarite plans to continue this policy in the future.

Instructions

(a) Based upon the above information, what will be the annual retirement benefit for each plan participant? (Round to the nearest dollar.) (*Hint:* Maugarite will receive raises for 24 years.)

(b) What amount must be on deposit at the end of 15 years to ensure that all benefits will be paid? (Round to the nearest dollar.)

(c) What is the amount of each annual deposit Maugarite must make to the retirement plan?

***P6-19 (Various Time Value of Money Situations)** Using a financial calculator, provide a solution to each of the following questions.

(a) What is the amount of the payments that Karla Zehms must make at the end of each of 8 years to accumulate a fund of $70,000 by the end of the eighth year, if the fund earns 7.25% interest, compounded annually?

(b) Bill Yawn is 40 years old today, and he wishes to accumulate $500,000 by his sixty-fifth birthday so he can retire to his summer place on Lake Winnebago. He wishes to accumulate this amount by making equal deposits on his fortieth through sixty-fourth birthdays. What annual deposit must Bill make if the fund will earn 9.65% interest compounded annually?

(c) Jane Mayer has a $26,000 debt that she wishes to repay 4 years from today; she has $17,000 that she intends to invest for the 4 years. What rate of interest will she need to earn annually in order to accumulate enough to pay the debt?

***P6-20 (Various Time Value of Money Situations)** Using a financial calculator, solve for the unknowns in each of the following situations.

(a) Wayne Eski wishes to invest $150,000 today to ensure payments of $20,000 to his son at the end of each year for the next 15 years. At what interest rate must the $150,000 be invested? (Round the answer to two decimal points.)

(b) On June 1, 2001, Shelley Long purchases lakefront property from her neighbor, Joey Brenner, and agrees to pay the purchase price in seven payments of $16,000 each, the first payment to be payable June 1, 2002. (Assume that interest compounded at an annual rate of 7.35% is implicit in the payments.) What is the purchase price of the property?

(c) On January 1, 2001, Cooke Corporation purchased 200 of the $1,000 face value, 8% coupon, 10-year bonds of Howe Inc. The bonds mature on January 1, 2011, and pay interest annually beginning January 1, 2002. Cooke purchased the bonds to yield 10.65%. How much did Cooke pay for the bonds?

***P6-21 (Various Time Value of Money Situations)** Using a financial calculator, provide a solution to each of the following situations.

(a) On March 12, 2002, William Scott invests in a $180,000 insurance policy that earns 5.25% compounded annually. The annuity policy allows William to receive annual payments, the first of which is payable to William on March 12, 2003. What will be the amount of each of the 20 equal annual receipts?

(b) Bill Schroeder owes a debt of $35,000 from the purchase of his new sport utility vehicle. The debt bears annual interest of 9.1% compounded monthly. Bill wishes to pay the debt and interest in equal monthly payments over 8 years, beginning one month hence. What equal monthly payments will pay off the debt and interest?

(c) On January 1, 2002, Sammy Sosa offers to buy Mark Grace's used snowmobile for $8,000, payable in five equal installments, which are to include 8.25% interest on the unpaid balance and a portion of the principal. If the first payment is to be made on January 1, 2002, how much will each payment be?

(d) Repeat the requirements in part (c), assuming Sosa makes the first payment on December 31, 2002.

USING YOUR JUDGMENT

FINANCIAL REPORTING PROBLEM: INTEL CORPORATION

The financial statements and accompanying notes of Intel Corporation are presented in Appendix 5B.

Instructions

(a) Examining each item in Intel's balance sheet, identify those items that require present value, discounting, or interest computations in establishing the amount reported. (The accompanying notes are an additional source for this information.)

(b) (1) What interest rates are disclosed by Intel as being used to compute interest and present values? (2) Why are there so many different interest rates applied to Intel's financial statement elements (assets, liabilities, revenues, and expenses)?

FINANCIAL STATEMENT ANALYSIS CASE

Consolidated Natural Gas Company

Consolidated Natural Gas Company (CNG), with corporate headquarters in Pittsburgh, Pennsylvania, is one of the largest producers, transporters, distributors, and marketers of natural gas in North America.

During 1998, the company experienced a decrease in the value of its gas and oil producing properties, and a special charge to income was recorded in order to reduce the carrying value of those assets. The company also wrote down oil and gas properties in 1997 and 1996.

In addition, special charges were incurred for severance pay and early retirement incentives as CNG reduced its workforce in 1996.

Assume the following information: In 1997, CNG estimated the cash inflows from its oil and gas producing properties to be $350,000 per year. During 1998, the write-downs described above caused the estimate to be decreased to $275,000 per year. Production costs (cash outflows) associated with all these properties were estimated to be $125,000 per year in 1997, but this amount was revised to $175,000 per year in 1998.

Instructions

(Assume that all cash flows occur at the end of the year.)

(a) Calculate the present value of net cash flows for 1997–1999 (three years) using the 1997 estimates, and a 10% discount factor.

(b) Calculate the present value of net cash flows for 1998–2000 (three years) using the 1998 estimates, and a 10% discount factor.

(c) Compare the results using the two estimates. Is information on future cash flows from oil and gas producing properties useful, considering that the estimates must be revised each year? Explain.

RESEARCH CASES

Case 1

To access the Internet and EDGAR, follow the steps outlined in Research Case 1 on page 263.

Firms registered with the U.S. Securities and Exchange Commission (SEC) are required to file an annual report on Form 10-K within 90 days of their fiscal year end. The Form 10-K includes certain information not provided in a firm's annual report to shareholders.

Instructions

Examine the most recent Form 10-K of a company of your choice and answer the following questions.

(a) Each 10-K is required to include information regarding several aspects of a firm, referenced by item numbers. Identify the 14 items included in the 10-K.

(b) Each 10-K must include the firm's financial statements. Does the 10-K you examined include the firm's financial statements? If not, how did the firm comply with the financial statement requirement?

(c) What financial statement schedules are included with the 10-K you examined?

Case 2

The May 1996 issue of the *Journal of Accountancy* includes an article by Paul Miller and Paul Bahnson entitled "Four Steps to Useful Present Values."

Instructions

Read the article and answer the following questions.

(a) Present value techniques are designed to understand the relationship between what two observed facts?

(b) According to the authors, present value measurements for financial reporting are useful only if they follow four steps. Identify these four steps.

(c) What are the authors' recommendations regarding present value measurements?

ETHICS CASE

James Qualls, newly appointed controller of KBS, is considering ways to reduce his company's expenditures on annual pension costs. One way to do this is to switch KBS's pension fund assets from First Security to NET Life. KBS is a very well-respected computer manufacturer that recently has experienced a sharp decline in its financial performance for the first time in its 25-year history. Despite financial problems, KBS still is committed to providing its employees with good pension and postretirement health benefits.

Under its present plan with First Security, KBS is obligated to pay $43 million to meet the expected value of future pension benefits that are payable to employees as an annuity upon their retirement from the company. On the other hand, NET Life requires KBS to pay only $35 million for identical future pension benefits. First Security is one of the oldest and most reputable insurance companies in North America. NET Life has a much weaker reputation in the insurance industry. In pondering the significant difference in annual pension costs, Qualls asks himself, "Is this too good to be true?"

Instructions

Answer the following questions:

(a) Why might NET Life's pension cost requirement be $8 million less than First Security's requirement for the same future value?

(b) What ethical issues should James Qualls consider before switching KBS's pension fund assets?

(c) Who are the stakeholders that could be affected by Qualls's decision?

TABLE 6-1 FUTURE VALUE OF 1 (FUTURE VALUE OF A SINGLE SUM)

$$FVF_{n,i} = (1 + i)^n$$

(n) Periods	2%	2½%	3%	4%	5%	6%
1	1.02000	1.02500	1.03000	1.04000	1.05000	1.06000
2	1.04040	1.05063	1.06090	1.08160	1.10250	1.12360
3	1.06121	1.07689	1.09273	1.12486	1.15763	1.19102
4	1.08243	1.10381	1.12551	1.16986	1.21551	1.26248
5	1.10408	1.13141	1.15927	1.21665	1.27628	1.33823
6	1.12616	1.15969	1.19405	1.26532	1.34010	1.41852
7	1.14869	1.18869	1.22987	1.31593	1.40710	1.50363
8	1.17166	1.21840	1.26677	1.36857	1.47746	1.59385
9	1.19509	1.24886	1.30477	1.42331	1.55133	1.68948
10	1.21899	1.28008	1.34392	1.48024	1.62889	1.79085
11	1.24337	1.31209	1.38423	1.53945	1.71034	1.89830
12	1.26824	1.34489	1.42576	1.60103	1.79586	2.01220
13	1.29361	1.37851	1.46853	1.66507	1.88565	2.13293
14	1.31948	1.41297	1.51259	1.73168	1.97993	2.26090
15	1.34587	1.44830	1.55797	1.80094	2.07893	2.39656
16	1.37279	1.48451	1.60471	1.87298	2.18287	2.54035
17	1.40024	1.52162	1.65285	1.94790	2.29202	2.69277
18	1.42825	1.55966	1.70243	2.02582	2.40662	2.85434
19	1.45681	1.59865	1.75351	2.10685	2.52695	3.02560
20	1.48595	1.63862	1.80611	2.19112	2.65330	3.20714
21	1.51567	1.67958	1.86029	2.27877	2.78596	3.39956
22	1.54598	1.72157	1.91610	2.36992	2.92526	3.60354
23	1.57690	1.76461	1.97359	2.46472	3.07152	3.81975
24	1.60844	1.80873	2.03279	2.56330	3.22510	4.04893
25	1.64061	1.85394	2.09378	2.66584	3.38635	4.29187
26	1.67342	1.90029	2.15659	2.77247	3.55567	4.54938
27	1.70689	1.94780	2.22129	2.88337	3.73346	4.82235
28	1.74102	1.99650	2.28793	2.99870	3.92013	5.11169
29	1.77584	2.04641	2.35657	3.11865	4.11614	5.41839
30	1.81136	2.09757	2.42726	3.24340	4.32194	5.74349
31	1.84759	2.15001	2.50008	3.37313	4.53804	6.08810
32	1.88454	2.20376	2.57508	3.50806	4.76494	6.45339
33	1.92223	2.25885	2.65234	3.64838	5.00319	6.84059
34	1.96068	2.31532	2.73191	3.79432	5.25335	7.25103
35	1.99989	2.37321	2.81386	3.94609	5.51602	7.68609
36	2.03989	2.43254	2.89828	4.10393	5.79182	8.14725
37	2.08069	2.49335	2.98523	4.26809	6.08141	8.63609
38	2.12230	2.55568	3.07478	4.43881	6.38548	9.15425
39	2.16474	2.61957	3.16703	4.61637	6.70475	9.70351
40	2.20804	2.68506	3.26204	4.80102	7.03999	10.28572

TABLE 6-1 FUTURE VALUE OF 1

8%	9%	10%	11%	12%	15%	(n) Periods
1.08000	1.09000	1.10000	1.11000	1.12000	1.15000	1
1.16640	1.18810	1.21000	1.23210	1.25440	1.32250	2
1.25971	1.29503	1.33100	1.36763	1.40493	1.52088	3
1.36049	1.41158	1.46410	1.51807	1.57352	1.74901	4
1.46933	1.53862	1.61051	1.68506	1.76234	2.01136	5
1.58687	1.67710	1.77156	1.87041	1.97382	2.31306	6
1.71382	1.82804	1.94872	2.07616	2.21068	2.66002	7
1.85093	1.99256	2.14359	2.30454	2.47596	3.05902	8
1.99900	2.17189	2.35795	2.55803	2.77308	3.51788	9
2.15892	2.36736	2.59374	2.83942	3.10585	4.04556	10
2.33164	2.58043	2.85312	3.15176	3.47855	4.65239	11
2.51817	2.81267	3.13843	3.49845	3.89598	5.35025	12
2.71962	3.06581	3.45227	3.88328	4.36349	6.15279	13
2.93719	3.34173	3.79750	4.31044	4.88711	7.07571	14
3.17217	3.64248	4.17725	4.78459	5.47357	8.13706	15
3.42594	3.97031	4.59497	5.31089	6.13039	9.35762	16
3.70002	4.32763	5.05447	5.89509	6.86604	10.76126	17
3.99602	4.71712	5.55992	6.54355	7.68997	12.37545	18
4.31570	5.14166	6.11591	7.26334	8.61276	14.23177	19
4.66096	5.60441	6.72750	8.06231	9.64629	16.36654	20
5.03383	6.10881	7.40025	8.94917	10.80385	18.82152	21
5.43654	6.65860	8.14028	9.93357	12.10031	21.64475	22
5.87146	7.25787	8.95430	11.02627	13.55235	24.89146	23
6.34118	7.91108	9.84973	12.23916	15.17863	28.62518	24
6.84847	8.62308	10.83471	13.58546	17.00000	32.91895	25
7.39635	9.39916	11.91818	15.07986	19.04007	37.85680	26
7.98806	10.24508	13.10999	16.73865	21.32488	43.53532	27
8.62711	11.16714	14.42099	18.57990	23.88387	50.06561	28
9.31727	12.17218	15.86309	20.62369	26.74993	57.57545	29
10.06266	13.26768	17.44940	22.89230	29.95992	66.21177	30
10.86767	14.46177	19.19434	25.41045	33.55511	76.14354	31
11.73708	15.76333	21.11378	28.20560	37.58173	87.56507	32
12.67605	17.18203	23.22515	31.30821	42.09153	100.69983	33
13.69013	18.72841	25.54767	34.75212	47.14252	115.80480	34
14.78534	20.41397	28.10244	38.57485	52.79962	133.17552	35
15.96817	22.25123	30.91268	42.81808	59.13557	153.15185	36
17.24563	24.25384	34.00395	47.52807	66.23184	176.12463	37
18.62528	26.43668	37.40434	52.75616	74.17966	202.54332	38
20.11530	28.81598	41.14479	58.55934	83.08122	232.92482	39
21.72452	31.40942	45.25926	65.00087	93.05097	267.86355	40

TABLE 6-2 PRESENT VALUE OF 1 (PRESENT VALUE OF A SINGLE SUM)

$$PVF_{n,i} = \frac{1}{(1+i)^n} = (1+i)^{-n}$$

(n) Periods	2%	2½%	3%	4%	5%	6%
1	.98039	.97561	.97087	.96154	.95238	.94340
2	.96117	.95181	.94260	.92456	.90703	.89000
3	.94232	.92860	.91514	.88900	.86384	.83962
4	.92385	.90595	.88849	.85480	.82270	.79209
5	.90573	.88385	.86261	.82193	.78353	.74726
6	.88797	.86230	.83748	.79031	.74622	.70496
7	.87056	.84127	.81309	.75992	.71068	.66506
8	.85349	.82075	.78941	.73069	.67684	.62741
9	.83676	.80073	.76642	.70259	.64461	.59190
10	.82035	.78120	.74409	.67556	.61391	.55839
11	.80426	.76214	.72242	.64958	.58468	.52679
12	.78849	.74356	.70138	.62460	.55684	.49697
13	.77303	.72542	.68095	.60057	.53032	.46884
14	.75788	.70773	.66112	.57748	.50507	.44230
15	.74301	.69047	.64186	.55526	.48102	.41727
16	.72845	.67362	.62317	.53391	.45811	.39365
17	.71416	.65720	.60502	.51337	.43630	.37136
18	.70016	.64117	.58739	.49363	.41552	.35034
19	.68643	.62553	.57029	.47464	.39573	.33051
20	.67297	.61027	.55368	.45639	.37689	.31180
21	.65978	.59539	.53755	.43883	.35894	.29416
22	.64684	.58086	.52189	.42196	.34185	.22751
23	.63416	.56670	.50669	.40573	.32557	.26180
24	.62172	.55288	.49193	.39012	.31007	.24698
25	.60953	.53939	.47761	.37512	.29530	.23300
26	.59758	.52623	.46369	.36069	.28124	.21981
27	.58586	.51340	.45019	.34682	.26785	.20737
28	.57437	.50088	.43708	.33348	.25509	.19563
29	.56311	.48866	.42435	.32065	.24295	.18456
30	.55207	.47674	.41199	.30832	.23138	.17411
31	.54125	.46511	.39999	.29646	.22036	.16425
32	.53063	.45377	.38834	.28506	.20987	.15496
33	.52023	.44270	.37703	.27409	.19987	.14619
34	.51003	.43191	.36604	.26355	.19035	.13791
35	.50003	.42137	.35538	.25342	.18129	.13011
36	.49022	.41109	.34503	.24367	.17266	.12274
37	.48061	.40107	.33498	.23430	.16444	.11579
38	.47119	.39128	.32523	.22529	.15661	.10924
39	.46195	.38174	.31575	.21662	.14915	.10306
40	.45289	.37243	.30656	.20829	.14205	.09722

TABLE 6-2 PRESENT VALUE OF 1

8%	9%	10%	11%	12%	15%	(n) Periods
.92593	.91743	.90909	.90090	.89286	.86957	1
.85734	.84168	.82645	.81162	.79719	.75614	2
.79383	.77218	.75132	.73119	.71178	.65752	3
.73503	.70843	.68301	.65873	.63552	.57175	4
.68058	.64993	.62092	.59345	.56743	.49718	5
.63017	.59627	.56447	.53464	.50663	.43233	6
.58349	.54703	.51316	.48166	.45235	.37594	7
.54027	.50187	.46651	.43393	.40388	.32690	8
.50025	.46043	.42410	.39092	.36061	.28426	9
.46319	.42241	.38554	.35218	.32197	.24719	10
.42888	.38753	.35049	.31728	.28748	.21494	11
.39711	.35554	.31863	.28584	.25668	.18691	12
.36770	.32618	.28966	.25751	.22917	.16253	13
.34046	.29925	.26333	.23199	.20462	.14133	14
.31524	.27454	.23939	.20900	.18270	.12289	15
.29189	.25187	.21763	.18829	.16312	.10687	16
.27027	.23107	.19785	.16963	.14564	.09293	17
.25025	.21199	.17986	.15282	.13004	.08081	18
.23171	.19449	.16351	.13768	.11611	.07027	19
.21455	.17843	.14864	.12403	.10367	.06110	20
.19866	.16370	.13513	.11174	.09256	.05313	21
.18394	.15018	.12285	.10067	.08264	.04620	22
.17032	.13778	.11168	.09069	.07379	.04017	23
.15770	.12641	.10153	.08170	.06588	.03493	24
.14602	.11597	.09230	.07361	.05882	.03038	25
.13520	.10639	.08391	.06631	.05252	.02642	26
.12519	.09761	.07628	.05974	.04689	.02297	27
.11591	.08955	.06934	.05382	.04187	.01997	28
.10733	.08216	.06304	.04849	.03738	.01737	29
.09938	.07537	.05731	.04368	.03338	.01510	30
.09202	.06915	.05210	.03935	.02980	.01313	31
.08520	.06344	.04736	.03545	.02661	.01142	32
.07889	.05820	.04306	.03194	.02376	.00993	33
.07305	.05340	.03914	.02878	.02121	.00864	34
.06763	.04899	.03558	.02592	.01894	.00751	35
.06262	.04494	.03235	.02335	.01691	.00653	36
.05799	.04123	.02941	.02104	.01510	.00568	37
.05369	.03783	.02674	.01896	.01348	.00494	38
.04971	.03470	.02430	.01708	.01204	.00429	39
.04603	.03184	.02210	.01538	.01075	.00373	40

TABLE 6-3 FUTURE VALUE OF AN ORDINARY ANNUITY OF 1

$$FVF\text{-}OA_{n,i} = \frac{(1+i)^n - 1}{i}$$

(n) Periods	2%	2½%	3%	4%	5%	6%
1	1.00000	1.00000	1.00000	1.00000	1.00000	1.00000
2	2.02000	2.02500	2.03000	2.04000	2.05000	2.06000
3	3.06040	3.07563	3.09090	3.12160	3.15250	3.18360
4	4.12161	4.15252	4.18363	4.24646	4.31013	4.37462
5	5.20404	5.25633	5.30914	5.41632	5.52563	5.63709
6	6.30812	6.38774	6.46841	6.63298	6.80191	6.97532
7	7.43428	7.54743	7.66246	7.89829	8.14201	8.39384
8	8.58297	8.73612	8.89234	9.21423	9.54911	9.89747
9	9.75463	9.95452	10.15911	10.58280	11.02656	11.49132
10	10.94972	11.20338	11.46338	12.00611	12.57789	13.18079
11	12.16872	12.48347	12.80780	13.48635	14.20679	14.97164
12	13.41209	13.79555	14.19203	15.02581	15.91713	16.86994
13	14.68033	15.14044	15.61779	16.62684	17.71298	18.88214
14	15.97394	16.51895	17.08632	18.29191	19.59863	21.01507
15	17.29342	17.93193	18.59891	20.02359	21.57856	23.27597
16	18.63929	19.38022	20.15688	21.82453	23.65749	25.67253
17	20.01207	20.86473	21.76159	23.69751	25.84037	28.21288
18	21.41231	22.38635	23.41444	25.64541	28.13238	30.90565
19	22.84056	23.94601	25.11687	27.67123	30.53900	33.75999
20	24.29737	25.54466	26.87037	29.77808	33.06595	36.78559
21	25.78332	27.18327	28.67649	31.96920	35.71925	39.99273
22	27.29898	28.86286	30.53678	34.24797	38.50521	43.39229
23	28.84496	30.58443	32.45288	36.61789	41.43048	46.99583
24	30.42186	32.34904	34.42647	39.08260	44.50200	50.81558
25	32.03030	34.15776	36.45926	41.64591	47.72710	54.86451
26	33.67091	36.01171	38.55304	44.31174	51.11345	59.15638
27	35.34432	37.91200	40.70963	47.08421	54.66913	63.70577
28	37.05121	39.85980	42.93092	49.96758	58.40258	68.52811
29	38.79223	41.85630	45.21885	52.96629	62.32271	73.63980
30	40.56808	43.90270	47.57542	56.08494	66.43885	79.05819
31	42.37944	46.00027	50.00268	59.32834	70.76079	84.80168
32	44.22703	48.15028	52.50276	62.70147	75.29883	90.88978
33	46.11157	50.35403	55.07784	66.20953	80.06377	97.34316
34	48.03380	52.61289	57.73018	69.85791	85.06696	104.18376
35	49.99448	54.92821	60.46208	73.65222	90.32031	111.43478
36	51.99437	57.30141	63.27594	77.59831	95.83632	119.12087
37	54.03425	59.73395	66.17422	81.70225	101.62814	127.26812
38	56.11494	62.22730	69.15945	85.97034	107.70955	135.90421
39	58.23724	64.78298	72.23423	90.40915	114.09502	145.05846
40	60.40198	67.40255	75.40126	95.02552	120.79977	154.76197

TABLE 6-3 FUTURE VALUE OF AN ORDINARY ANNUITY OF 1

8%	9%	10%	11%	12%	15%	(n) Periods
1.00000	1.00000	1.00000	1.00000	1.00000	1.00000	1
2.08000	2.09000	2.10000	2.11000	2.12000	2.15000	2
3.24640	3.27810	3.31000	3.34210	3.37440	3.47250	3
4.50611	4.57313	4.64100	4.70973	4.77933	4.99338	4
5.86660	5.98471	6.10510	6.22780	6.35285	6.74238	5
7.33592	7.52334	7.71561	7.91286	8.11519	8.75374	6
8.92280	9.20044	9.48717	9.78327	10.08901	11.06680	7
10.63663	11.02847	11.43589	11.85943	12.29969	13.72682	8
12.48756	13.02104	13.57948	14.16397	14.77566	16.78584	9
14.48656	15.19293	15.93743	16.72201	17.54874	20.30372	10
16.64549	17.56029	18.53117	19.56143	20.65458	24.34928	11
18.97713	20.14072	21.38428	22.71319	24.13313	29.00167	12
21.49530	22.95339	24.52271	26.21164	28.02911	34.35192	13
24.21492	26.01919	27.97498	30.09492	32.39260	40.50471	14
27.15211	29.36092	31.77248	34.40536	37.27972	47.58041	15
30.32428	33.00340	35.94973	39.18995	42.75328	55.71747	16
33.75023	36.97371	40.54470	44.50084	48.88367	65.07509	17
37.45024	41.30134	45.59917	50.39593	55.74972	75.83636	18
41.44626	46.01846	51.15909	56.93949	63.43968	88.21181	19
45.76196	51.16012	57.27500	64.20283	72.05244	102.44358	20
50.42292	56.76453	64.00250	72.26514	81.69874	118.81012	21
55.45676	62.87334	71.40275	81.21431	92.50258	137.63164	22
60.89330	69.53194	79.54302	91.14788	104.60289	159.27638	23
66.76476	76.78981	88.49733	102.17415	118.15524	184.16784	24
73.10594	84.70090	98.34706	114.41331	133.33387	212.79302	25
79.95442	93.32398	109.18177	127.99877	150.33393	245.71197	26
87.35077	102.72314	121.09994	143.07864	169.37401	283.56877	27
95.33883	112.96822	134.20994	159.81729	190.69889	327.10408	28
103.96594	124.13536	148.63093	178.39719	214.58275	377.16969	29
113.28321	136.30754	164.49402	199.02088	241.33268	434.74515	30
123.34587	149.57522	181.94343	221.91317	271.29261	500.95692	31
134.21354	164.03699	201.13777	247.32362	304.84772	577.10046	32
145.95062	179.80032	222.25154	275.52922	342.42945	644.66553	33
158.62667	196.98234	245.47670	306.83744	384.52098	765.36535	34
172.31680	215.71076	271.02437	341.58955	431.66350	881.17016	35
187.10215	236.12472	299.12681	380.16441	484.46312	1014.34568	36
203.07032	258.37595	330.03949	422.98249	543.59869	1167.49753	37
220.31595	282.62978	364.04343	470.51056	609.83053	1343.62216	38
238.94122	309.06646	401.44778	523.26673	684.01020	1546.16549	39
259.05652	337.88245	442.59256	581.82607	767.09142	1779.09031	40

TABLE 6-4 PRESENT VALUE OF AN ORDINARY ANNUITY OF 1

$$\text{PVF-OA}_{n,i} = \frac{1 - \frac{1}{(1+i)^n}}{i}$$

(n) Periods	2%	2½%	3%	4%	5%	6%
1	.98039	.97561	.97087	.96154	.95238	.94340
2	1.94156	1.92742	1.91347	1.88609	1.85941	1.83339
3	2.88388	2.85602	2.82861	2.77509	2.72325	2.67301
4	3.80773	3.76197	3.71710	3.62990	3.54595	3.46511
5	4.71346	4.64583	4.57971	4.45182	4.32948	4.21236
6	5.60143	5.50813	5.41719	5.24214	5.07569	4.91732
7	6.47199	6.34939	6.23028	6.00205	5.78637	5.58238
8	7.32548	7.17014	7.01969	6.73274	6.46321	6.20979
9	8.16224	7.97087	7.78611	7.43533	7.10782	6.80169
10	8.98259	8.75206	8.53020	8.11090	7.72173	7.36009
11	9.78685	9.51421	9.25262	8.76048	8.30641	7.88687
12	10.57534	10.25776	9.95400	9.38507	8.86325	8.38384
13	11.34837	10.98319	10.63496	9.98565	9.39357	8.85268
14	12.10625	11.69091	11.29607	10.56312	9.89864	9.29498
15	12.84926	12.38138	11.93794	11.11839	10.37966	9.71225
16	13.57771	13.05500	12.56110	11.65230	10.83777	10.10590
17	14.29187	13.71220	13.16612	12.16567	11.27407	10.47726
18	14.99203	14.35336	13.75351	12.65930	11.68959	10.82760
19	15.67846	14.97889	14.32380	13.13394	12.08532	11.15812
20	16.35143	15.58916	14.87747	13.59033	12.46221	11.46992
21	17.01121	16.18455	15.41502	14.02916	12.82115	11.76408
22	17.65805	16.76541	15.93692	14.45112	13.16300	12.04158
23	18.29220	17.33211	16.44361	14.85684	13.48857	12.30338
24	18.91393	17.88499	16.93554	15.24696	13.79864	12.55036
25	19.52346	18.42438	17.41315	15.62208	14.09394	12.78336
26	20.12104	18.95061	17.87684	15.98277	14.37519	13.00317
27	20.70690	19.46401	18.32703	16.32959	14.64303	13.21053
28	21.28127	19.96489	18.76411	16.66306	14.89813	13.40616
29	21.84438	20.45355	19.18845	16.98371	15.14107	13.59072
30	22.39646	20.93029	19.60044	17.29203	15.37245	13.76483
31	22.93770	21.39541	20.00043	17.58849	15.59281	13.92909
32	23.46833	21.84918	20.38877	17.87355	15.80268	14.08404
33	23.98856	22.29188	20.76579	18.14765	16.00255	14.23023
34	24.49859	22.72379	21.13184	18.41120	16.19290	14.36814
35	24.99862	23.14516	21.48722	18.66461	16.37419	14.49825
36	25.48884	23.55625	21.83225	18.90828	16.54685	14.62099
37	25.96945	23.95732	22.16724	19.14258	16.71129	14.73678
38	26.44064	24.34860	22.49246	19.36786	16.86789	14.84602
39	26.90259	24.73034	22.80822	19.58448	17.01704	14.94907
40	27.35548	25.10278	23.11477	19.79277	17.15909	15.04630

TABLE 6-4 PRESENT VALUE OF AN ORDINARY ANNUITY OF 1

8%	9%	10%	11%	12%	15%	(n) Periods
.92593	.91743	.90909	.90090	.89286	.86957	1
1.78326	1.75911	1.73554	1.71252	1.69005	1.62571	2
2.57710	2.53130	2.48685	2.44371	2.40183	2.28323	3
3.31213	3.23972	3.16986	3.10245	3.03735	2.85498	4
3.99271	3.88965	3.79079	3.69590	3.60478	3.35216	5
4.62288	4.48592	4.35526	4.23054	4.11141	3.78448	6
5.20637	5.03295	4.86842	4.71220	4.56376	4.16042	7
5.74664	5.53482	5.33493	5.14612	4.96764	4.48732	8
6.24689	5.99525	5.75902	5.53705	5.32825	4.77158	9
6.71008	6.41766	6.14457	5.88923	5.65022	5.01877	10
7.13896	6.80519	6.49506	6.20652	5.93770	5.23371	11
7.53608	7.16073	6.81369	6.49236	6.19437	5.42062	12
7.90378	7.48690	7.10336	6.74987	6.42355	5.58315	13
8.24424	7.78615	7.36669	6.98187	6.62817	5.72448	14
8.55948	8.06069	7.60608	7.19087	6.81086	5.84737	15
8.85137	8.31256	7.82371	7.37916	6.97399	5.95424	16
9.12164	8.54363	8.02155	7.54879	7.11963	6.04716	17
9.37189	8.75563	8.20141	7.70162	7.24967	6.12797	18
9.60360	8.95012	8.36492	7.83929	7.36578	6.19823	19
9.81815	9.12855	8.51356	7.96333	7.46944	6.25933	20
10.01680	9.29224	8.64869	8.07507	7.56200	6.31246	21
10.20074	9.44243	8.77154	8.17574	7.64465	6.35866	22
10.37106	9.58021	8.88322	8.26643	7.71843	6.39884	23
10.52876	9.70661	8.98474	8.34814	7.78432	6.43377	24
10.67478	9.82258	9.07704	8.42174	7.84314	6.46415	25
10.80998	9.92897	9.16095	8.48806	7.89566	6.49056	26
10.93516	10.02658	9.23722	8.54780	7.94255	6.51353	27
11.05108	10.11613	9.30657	8.60162	7.98442	6.53351	28
11.15841	10.19828	9.36961	8.65011	8.02181	6.55088	29
11.25778	10.27365	9.42691	8.69379	8.05518	6.56598	30
11.34980	10.34280	9.47901	8.73315	8.08499	6.57911	31
11.43500	10.40624	9.52638	8.76860	8.11159	6.59053	32
11.51389	10.46444	9.56943	8.80054	8.13535	6.60046	33
11.58693	10.51784	9.60858	8.82932	8.15656	6.60910	34
11.65457	10.56682	9.64416	8.85524	8.17550	6.61661	35
11.71719	10.61176	9.67651	8.87859	8.19241	6.62314	36
11.77518	10.65299	9.70592	8.89963	8.20751	6.62882	37
11.82887	10.69082	9.73265	8.91859	8.22099	6.63375	38
11.87858	10.72552	9.75697	8.93567	8.23303	6.63805	39
11.92461	10.75736	9.77905	8.95105	8.24378	6.64178	40

TABLE 6-5 PRESENT VALUE OF AN ANNUITY DUE OF 1

$$\text{PVF-AD}_{n,i} = 1 + \frac{1 - \dfrac{1}{(1+i)^{n-1}}}{i}$$

(n) Periods	2%	2½%	3%	4%	5%	6%
1	1.00000	1.00000	1.00000	1.00000	1.00000	1.00000
2	1.98039	1.97561	1.97087	1.96154	1.95238	1.94340
3	2.94156	2.92742	2.91347	2.88609	2.85941	2.83339
4	3.88388	3.85602	3.82861	3.77509	3.72325	3.67301
5	4.80773	4.76197	4.71710	4.62990	4.54595	4.46511
6	5.71346	5.64583	5.57971	5.45182	5.32948	5.21236
7	6.60143	6.50813	6.41719	6.24214	6.07569	5.91732
8	7.47199	7.34939	7.23028	7.00205	6.78637	6.58238
9	8.32548	8.17014	8.01969	7.73274	7.46321	7.20979
10	9.16224	8.97087	8.78611	8.43533	8.10782	7.80169
11	9.98259	9.75206	9.53020	9.11090	8.72173	8.36009
12	10.78685	10.51421	10.25262	9.76048	9.30641	8.88687
13	11.57534	11.25776	10.95400	10.38507	9.86325	9.38384
14	12.34837	11.98319	11.63496	10.98565	10.39357	9.85268
15	13.10625	12.69091	12.29607	11.56312	10.89864	10.29498
16	13.84926	13.38138	12.93794	12.11839	11.37966	10.71225
17	14.57771	14.05500	13.56110	12.65230	11.83777	11.10590
18	15.29187	14.71220	14.16612	13.16567	12.27407	11.47726
19	15.99203	15.35336	14.75351	13.65930	12.68959	11.82760
20	16.67846	15.97889	15.32380	14.13394	13.08532	12.15812
21	17.35143	16.58916	15.87747	14.59033	13.46221	12.46992
22	18.01121	17.18455	16.41502	15.02916	13.82115	12.76408
23	18.65805	17.76541	16.93692	15.45112	14.16300	13.04158
24	19.29220	18.33211	17.44361	15.85684	14.48857	13.30338
25	19.91393	18.88499	17.93554	16.24696	14.79864	13.55036
26	20.52346	19.42438	18.41315	16.62208	15.09394	13.78336
27	21.12104	19.95061	18.87684	16.98277	15.37519	14.00317
28	21.70690	20.46401	19.32703	17.32959	15.64303	14.21053
29	22.28127	20.96489	19.76411	17.66306	15.89813	14.40616
30	22.84438	21.45355	20.18845	17.98371	16.14107	14.59072
31	23.39646	21.93029	20.60044	18.29203	16.37245	14.76483
32	23.93770	22.39541	21.00043	18.58849	16.59281	14.92909
33	24.46833	22.84918	21.38877	18.87355	16.80268	15.08404
34	24.98856	23.29188	21.76579	19.14765	17.00255	15.23023
35	25.49859	23.72379	22.13184	19.41120	17.19290	15.36814
36	25.99862	24.14516	22.48722	19.66461	17.37419	15.49825
37	26.48884	24.55625	22.83225	19.90828	17.54685	15.62099
38	26.96945	24.95732	23.16724	20.14258	17.71129	15.73678
39	27.44064	25.34860	23.49246	20.36786	17.86789	15.84602
40	27.90259	25.73034	23.80822	20.58448	18.01704	15.94907

TABLE 6-5 PRESENT VALUE OF AN ANNUITY DUE OF 1

8%	9%	10%	11%	12%	15%	(n) Periods
1.00000	1.00000	1.00000	1.00000	1.00000	1.00000	1
1.92593	1.91743	1.90909	1.90090	1.89286	1.86957	2
2.78326	2.75911	2.73554	2.71252	2.69005	2.62571	3
3.57710	3.53130	3.48685	3.44371	3.40183	3.28323	4
4.31213	4.23972	4.16986	4.10245	4.03735	3.85498	5
4.99271	4.88965	4.79079	4.69590	4.60478	4.35216	6
5.62288	5.48592	5.35526	5.23054	5.11141	4.78448	7
6.20637	6.03295	5.86842	5.71220	5.56376	5.16042	8
6.74664	6.53482	6.33493	6.14612	5.96764	5.48732	9
7.24689	6.99525	6.75902	6.53705	6.32825	5.77158	10
7.71008	7.41766	7.14457	6.88923	6.65022	6.01877	11
8.13896	7.80519	7.49506	7.20652	6.93770	6.23371	12
8.53608	8.16073	7.81369	7.49236	7.19437	6.42062	13
8.90378	8.48690	8.10336	7.74987	7.42355	6.58315	14
9.24424	8.78615	8.36669	7.98187	7.62817	6.72448	15
9.55948	9.06069	8.60608	8.19087	7.81086	6.84737	16
9.85137	9.31256	8.82371	8.37916	7.97399	6.95424	17
10.12164	9.54363	9.02155	8.54879	8.11963	7.04716	18
10.37189	9.75563	9.20141	8.70162	8.24967	7.12797	19
10.60360	9.95012	9.36492	8.83929	8.36578	7.19823	20
10.81815	10.12855	9.51356	8.96333	8.46944	7.25933	21
11.01680	10.29224	9.64869	9.07507	8.56200	7.31246	22
11.20074	10.44243	9.77154	9.17574	8.64465	7.35866	23
11.37106	10.58021	9.88322	9.26643	8.71843	7.39884	24
11.52876	10.70661	9.98474	9.34814	8.78432	7.43377	25
11.67478	10.82258	10.07704	9.42174	8.84314	7.46415	26
11.80998	10.92897	10.16095	9.48806	8.89566	7.49056	27
11.93518	11.02658	10.23722	9.54780	8.94255	7.51353	28
12.05108	11.11613	10.30657	9.60162	8.98442	7.53351	29
12.15841	11.19828	10.36961	9.65011	9.02181	7.55088	30
12.25778	11.27365	10.42691	9.69379	9.05518	7.56598	31
12.34980	11.34280	10.47901	9.73315	9.08499	7.57911	32
12.43500	11.40624	10.52638	9.76860	9.11159	7.59053	33
12.51389	11.46444	10.56943	9.80054	9.13535	7.60046	34
12.58693	11.51784	10.60858	9.82932	9.15656	7.60910	35
12.65457	11.56682	10.64416	9.85524	9.17550	7.61661	36
12.71719	11.61176	10.67651	9.87859	9.19241	7.62314	37
12.77518	11.65299	10.70592	9.89963	9.20751	7.62882	38
12.82887	11.69082	10.73265	9.91859	9.22099	7.63375	39
12.87858	11.72552	10.75697	9.93567	9.23303	7.63805	40

CHAPTER 7

Cash and Receivables

Ugly Duckling or Swan?

Ugly Duckling Corporation is a used car dealer that has carved out a niche by selling cars to customers with questionable credit histories. Ugly Duckling and other "sub-prime lenders" attempt to make a profit by loaning money to riskier borrowers so they can purchase automobiles or homes. To compensate for the higher probability of default of these customers, sub-prime lenders charge higher rates of interest on these high-risk loans.

In theory, this strategy should work. Although some borrowers will not be able to repay their loans, Ugly Duckling plans to make up these losses based on the higher interest payments received from borrowers who do not default and who continue to pay on their loans. Furthermore, in many instances these companies are able to package their sub-prime loans and sell them as securities (a process called securitization). If they receive more for the securities than the amount at which the loans are recorded on the books, they record a gain on the sale of the asset. Recognition of these gains at the time of sale is appropriate if Ugly Duckling can arrive at a reasonable estimate of the proportion of the loans that will not be repaid.

However, estimating the proportion of these high-risk loans that are likely to default is difficult. If rates are not set high enough to cover unexpected higher rates of default, Ugly Duckling and other sub-prime lenders will be in a severe cash squeeze. In addition, if too many of the loans that were sold default, Ugly Duckling will have to take them back, thereby eliminating any gain they recorded on the original sale. Indeed, early in 1998 Green Tree Financial Corporation, a leading lender in the sub-prime housing market, reported 1997 write-downs of $190 million and restated 1996 earnings downward by $200 million, in part due to optimistic assumptions on its high-risk loans.

Thus, the sub-prime lending business is a risky one, and depending on default and interest rate assumptions on these receivables, companies like Ugly Duckling may not survive to grow into a lending swan.

LEARNING OBJECTIVES

After studying this chapter, you should be able to:

1. **Identify items considered cash.**
2. **Indicate how cash and related items are reported.**
3. **Define receivables and identify the different types of receivables.**
4. **Explain accounting issues related to recognition of accounts receivable.**
5. **Explain accounting issues related to valuation of accounts receivable.**
6. **Explain accounting issues related to recognition of notes receivable.**
7. **Explain accounting issues related to valuation of notes receivable.**
8. **Explain accounting issues related to disposition of accounts and notes receivable.**
9. **Explain how receivables are reported and analyzed.**

PREVIEW OF CHAPTER 7

As the opening story indicates, difficulties associated with estimating the collectibility of accounts receivable resulted in significant write-downs and restatements of earnings for businesses that rely on credit sales. The purpose of this chapter is to discuss two assets of importance to companies such as **Ugly Duckling** and **Greentree Financial**—cash and receivables. The content and organization of the chapter are as follows:

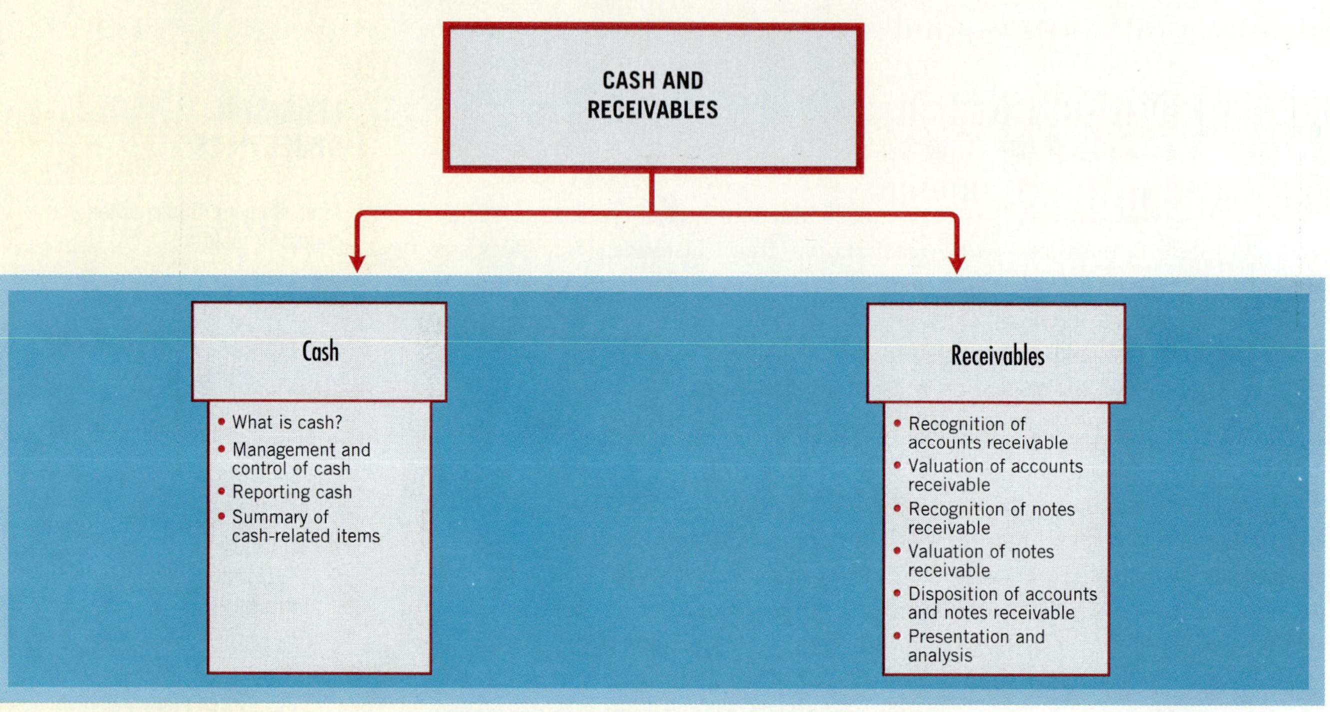

SECTION 1 CASH

WHAT IS CASH?

Cash, the most liquid of assets, is the standard medium of exchange and the basis for measuring and accounting for all other items. It is generally classified as a current asset. To be reported as **cash**, it must be readily available for the payment of current obligations, and it must be free from any contractual restriction that limits its use in satisfying debts.

Cash consists of coin, currency, and available funds on deposit at the bank. Negotiable instruments such as money orders, certified checks, cashier's checks, personal checks, and bank drafts are also viewed as cash. Savings accounts are usually classified as cash, although the bank has the legal right to demand notice before withdrawal. But, because prior notice is rarely demanded by banks, savings accounts are considered cash.

Money market funds, money market savings certificates, certificates of deposit (CDs), and similar types of deposits and "short-term paper"[1] that provide small investors with an opportunity to earn high rates of interest are more appropriately classified as temporary investments than as cash. The reason is that these securities usually contain restrictions or penalties on their conversion to cash. Money market funds that provide checking account privileges, however, are usually classified as cash.

Certain items present classification problems: **Postdated checks and I.O.U.s** are treated as receivables. **Travel advances** are properly treated as receivables if the advances are to be collected from the employees or deducted from their salaries. Otherwise, classification of the travel advance as a prepaid expense is more appropriate. **Postage stamps on hand** are classified as part of office supplies inventory or as a prepaid expense. **Petty cash funds and change funds** are included in current assets as cash because these funds are used to meet current operating expenses and to liquidate current liabilities.

MANAGEMENT AND CONTROL OF CASH

Cash is the asset most susceptible to improper diversion and use. Two problems of accounting for cash transactions face management: (1) Proper controls must be established to ensure that no unauthorized transactions are entered into by officers or employees; and (2) information necessary to the proper management of cash on hand and cash transactions must be provided. Yet even with sophisticated control devices errors can and do happen. *The Wall Street Journal* ran a story entitled "A $7.8 Million Error Has a Happy Ending for a Horrified Bank," which described how **Manufacturers Hanover Trust Co.** mailed about $7.8 million too much in cash dividends to its stockholders. As implied in the headline, most of the monies were subsequently returned.

To safeguard cash and to ensure the accuracy of the accounting records for cash, effective **internal control** over cash is imperative. There are new challenges to maintaining control over liquid assets as more and more transactions are conducted with the swipe of a debit or credit card. For example, over 25% of bill payments in the United States are now being made through the use of digital cash (credit cards, debit cards, and electronic transfers).[2] In addition, electronic commerce conducted over the Internet continues to grow. Estimated holiday sales over the Internet in 1999 were expected to triple the volume of the 1998 holiday season, which has been dubbed the first e-holiday. Each of these trends contributes to the shift from cold cash to digital cash and poses new challenges for the control of cash. The appendix to this chapter discusses some of the basic control procedures used to ensure that cash is reported correctly.

---

[1]A variety of "short-term paper" is available for investment. For example, **certificates of deposit** (CDs) represent formal evidence of indebtedness, issued by a bank, subject to withdrawal under the specific terms of the instrument. Issued in $10,000 and $100,000 denominations, they mature in 30 to 360 days and generally pay interest at the short-term interest rate in effect at the date of issuance. **Money market savings certificates** are issued by banks and savings and loan associations in denominations of $10,000 or more for 6-month periods (6 to 48 months). The interest rate is tied to the 26-week Treasury bill rate. In **money market funds,** a variation of the mutual fund, the yield is determined by the mix of Treasury bills and commercial paper making up the fund's portfolio. Most money market funds require an initial minimum investment of $5,000; many allow withdrawal by check or wire transfer. **Treasury bills** are U.S. government obligations generally having 91- and 182-day maturities; they are sold in $10,000 denominations at weekly government auctions. **Commercial paper** is a short-term note (30 to 270 days) issued by corporations with good credit ratings. Issued in $5,000 and $10,000 denominations, these notes generally yield a higher rate than Treasury bills.

[2]Non-U.S. consumers are even bigger users of digital cash than U.S. consumers. For example, non-check payments in Japan and Europe are over 70% of all payment transactions. U.S. consumers' continued use of checks and cash for payment raises other fraud concerns, though, as duplication technology makes it easier for crooks to forge checks and currency.

REPORTING CASH

OBJECTIVE 2
Indicate how cash and related items are reported.

Although the reporting of cash is relatively straightforward, there are a number of issues that merit special attention. These issues relate to the reporting of:

1. Restricted cash.
2. Bank overdrafts.
3. Cash equivalents.

Restricted Cash

Compensating Balances

Banks and other lending institutions often require customers to whom they lend money to maintain minimum cash balances in checking or savings accounts. These minimum balances, called **compensating balances**, are defined by the SEC as: "that portion of any demand deposit (or any time deposit or certificate of deposit) maintained by a corporation which constitutes support for existing borrowing arrangements of the corporation with a lending institution. Such arrangements would include both outstanding borrowings and the assurance of future credit availability."[3]

Compensating balances may be payment for bank services rendered to the company for which there is no direct fee, for example, check processing and lockbox management. By requiring a compensating balance, the bank achieves an effective interest rate on a loan that is higher than the stated rate because it has use of the restricted amount that must remain on deposit.

To illustrate, assume that on January 1, 2002, Biddle Co. borrowed $10,000,000 for one year from First Union Bank at an interest rate of 10%. In addition, Biddle is required to keep a compensatory balance of $2,000,000 on deposit at First Union, which will earn 6%. Normally, Biddle would deposit $1,000,000 at the bank for transaction purposes. The effective interest that Biddle pays on this loan is 10.4% computed as follows:

ILLUSTRATION 7-1
Computation of Interest Cost

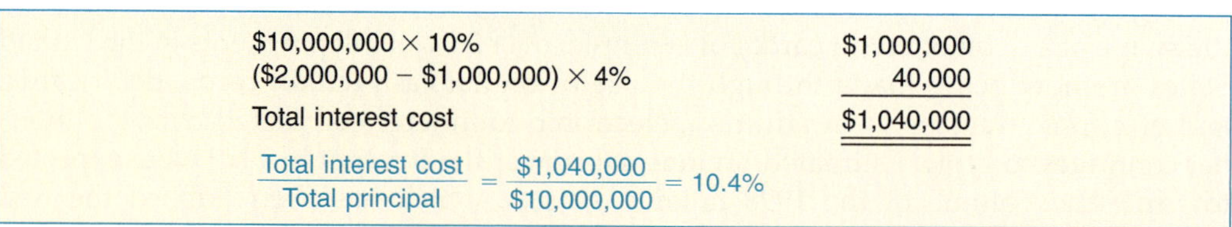

$10,000,000 × 10%	$1,000,000
($2,000,000 − $1,000,000) × 4%	40,000
Total interest cost	$1,040,000

$$\frac{\text{Total interest cost}}{\text{Total principal}} = \frac{\$1,040,000}{\$10,000,000} = 10.4\%$$

Biddle pays $1,000,000 interest on the original loan of $10,000,000, and it is required to maintain an additional $1,000,000 cash balance on which it can earn only 6%. If it has to borrow this additional $1,000,000, it will be losing 4% (10% − 6%) on every dollar borrowed.

The need for the disclosure of compensating balances was highlighted in the 1970s when a number of companies were involved in a liquidity crisis. Many investors believed that the cash reported on the balance sheet was fully available to meeting recurring obligations, but these funds were actually restricted because of the need for these companies to maintain compensating cash balances at various lending institutions.

The SEC recommends that **legally restricted deposits** held as compensating balances against **short-term** borrowing arrangements be stated separately among the "cash and cash equivalent items" in Current Assets. Restricted deposits held as compensating balances against **long-term** borrowing arrangements should be separately classified as noncurrent assets in either the Investments or Other Assets sections, using a caption such as "Cash on Deposit Maintained as Compensating Balance."

[3]*Accounting Series Release No. 148,* "Amendments to Regulations S-X and Related Interpretations and Guidelines Regarding the Disclosure of Compensating Balances and Short-Term Borrowing Arrangements," Securities and Exchange Commission (November 13, 1973). The SEC defines 15% of liquid assets (current cash balances, whether restricted or not, plus marketable securities) as being material.

In cases where compensating balance arrangements exist without agreements that restrict the use of cash amounts shown on the balance sheet, the arrangements and the amounts involved should be described in the notes. Compensating balances that are maintained under an agreement to assure future credit availability also must be disclosed separately in the notes, together with the amount and duration of such agreement.

Agribrands International reported the following information regarding compensating balances:

ILLUSTRATION 7-2
Disclosure of Compensating Balances

AGRIBRANDS INTERNATIONAL

Note: Compensating Balances. Notes payable of $46.9 million had a weighted average interest rate of 18.0% at the end of the year. At year-end, substantially all notes payable are denominated in local currencies and are due to banks. Compensating balance arrangements ensure future credit availability and do not restrict the withdrawal of funds. Under these arrangements, Agribrands maintained compensating bank balances of $21.6 million.

Other Types of Restrictions

Petty cash, payroll, and dividend funds are examples of cash set aside for a particular purpose. In most situations, these fund balances are not material and therefore are not segregated from cash when reported in the financial statements. When material in amount, restricted cash is segregated from "regular" cash for reporting purposes. The **restricted cash** is classified either in the Current Assets or in the Long-term Assets section, depending on the date of availability or disbursement. Classification in the current section is appropriate if the cash is to be used (within a year or the operating cycle, whichever is longer) for payment of existing or maturing obligations. On the other hand, if the cash is to be held for a longer period of time, the restricted cash is shown in the long-term section of the balance sheet.

Among other potential restrictions, companies need to determine whether any of the cash in accounts outside the U.S. is restricted by regulations against exportation of currency.

Cash classified in the long-term section is frequently set aside for plant expansion, retirement of long-term debt or, in the case of **International Thoroughbred Breeders**, for entry fee deposits.

ILLUSTRATION 7-3
Disclosure of Restricted Cash

INTERNATIONAL THOROUGHBRED BREEDERS

Restricted cash and investments (See Note)	$3,730,000

Note: Restricted Cash. At year-end, the Company had approximately $3,730,000, which was classified as restricted cash and investments. These funds are primarily cash received from horsemen for nomination and entry fees to be applied to upcoming racing meets, purse winnings held in trust for horsemen, and amounts held for unclaimed ticketholder winnings.

Bank Overdrafts

Bank overdrafts occur when a check is written for more than the amount in the cash account. They should be reported in the current liabilities section and are usually added to the amount reported as accounts payable. If material, these items should be separately disclosed either on the face of the balance sheet or in the related notes.[4]

Go to the Digital Tool for additional disclosures of restricted cash.

[4]Bank overdrafts usually occur because of a simple oversight by the company writing the check. Banks often expect companies to have overdrafts from time to time and therefore negotiate a fee as payment for this possible occurrence. However, in the early 1980s, **E. F. Hutton** (a large brokerage firm) intentionally began overdrawing its accounts by astronomical amounts—on some days exceeding $1 billion—thus obtaining interest-free loans which it could invest. Because the amounts were so large and fees were not negotiated in advance, E. F. Hutton came under criminal investigation for its actions.

Bank overdrafts are generally not offset against the cash account. A major exception is when available cash is present in another account in the same bank on which the overdraft occurred. Offsetting in this case is required.

Cash Equivalents

A current classification that has become popular is "cash and cash equivalents."[5] **Cash equivalents** are short-term, highly liquid investments that are both (a) readily convertible to known amounts of cash, and (b) so near their maturity that they present insignificant risk of changes in interest rates. Generally only investments with original maturities of 3 months or less qualify under these definitions. Examples of cash equivalents are Treasury bills, commercial paper, and money market funds. Some companies combine cash with temporary investments on the balance sheet. In these cases, the amount of the temporary investments is described either parenthetically or in the notes.

SUMMARY OF CASH-RELATED ITEMS

Cash and cash equivalents include the medium of exchange and most negotiable instruments. If the item cannot be converted to coin or currency on short notice, it is separately classified as an investment, as a receivable, or as a prepaid expense. Cash that is not available for payment of currently maturing liabilities is segregated and classified in the long-term assets section. Illustration 7-4 summarizes the classification of cash-related items.

ILLUSTRATION 7-4
Classification of Cash-Related Items

Classification of Cash, Cash Equivalents, and Noncash Items

Item	Classification	Comment
Cash	Cash	If unrestricted, report as cash. If restricted, identify and classify as current and noncurrent assets.
Petty cash and change funds	Cash	Report as cash.
Short-term paper	Cash equivalents	Investments with maturity of less than 3 months, often combined with cash.
Short-term paper	Temporary investments	Investments with maturity of 3 to 12 months.
Postdated checks and IOU's	Receivables	Assumed to be collectible.
Travel advances	Receivables	Assumed to be collected from employees or deducted from their salaries.
Postage on hand (as stamps or in postage meters)	Prepaid expenses	May also be classified as office supplies inventory.
Bank overdrafts	Current liability	If right of offset exists, reduce cash.
Compensating balances		
1. Legally restricted	Cash separately classified as a deposit maintained as compensating balance	Classify as current or noncurrent in the balance sheet.
2. Arrangement without legal restriction	Cash with note disclosure	Disclose separately in notes details of the arrangement.

[5]*Accounting Trends and Techniques—1999,* indicates that approximately 10% of the companies surveyed use the caption "cash," 84% use "cash and cash equivalents," and 6% use a caption such as "cash and marketable securities" or similar terminology.

RECEIVABLES

SECTION 2

OBJECTIVE 3
Define receivables and identify the different types of receivables.

Receivables are claims held against customers and others for money, goods, or services. For financial statement purposes, receivables are classified as either **current** (short-term) or **noncurrent** (long-term). **Current receivables** are expected to be collected within a year or during the current operating cycle, whichever is longer. All other receivables are classified as **noncurrent**. Receivables are further classified in the balance sheet as either trade or nontrade receivables.

Trade receivables are amounts owed by customers for goods sold and services rendered as part of normal business operations. Trade receivables, usually the most significant an enterprise possesses, may be subclassified into accounts receivable and notes receivable. **Accounts receivable** are oral promises of the purchaser to pay for goods and services sold. They are normally collectible within 30 to 60 days and represent "open accounts" resulting from short-term extensions of credit. **Notes receivable** are written promises to pay a certain sum of money on a specified future date. They may arise from sales, financing, or other transactions. Notes may be short-term or long-term.

Nontrade receivables arise from a variety of transactions and can be written promises either to pay or to deliver. Some examples of nontrade receivables are:

1. Advances to officers and employees.
2. Advances to subsidiaries.
3. Deposits to cover potential damages or losses.
4. Deposits as a guarantee of performance or payment.
5. Dividends and interest receivable.
6. Claims against:
   - **(a)** Insurance companies for casualties sustained.
   - **(b)** Defendants under suit.
   - **(c)** Governmental bodies for tax refunds.
   - **(d)** Common carriers for damaged or lost goods.
   - **(e)** Creditors for returned, damaged, or lost goods.
   - **(f)** Customers for returnable items (crates, containers, etc.).

Because of the peculiar nature of nontrade receivables, they are generally classified and reported as separate items in the balance sheet. Illustration 7-5 shows the reporting of

ILLUSTRATION 7-5
Receivables Balance Sheet Presentations

ADOLPH COORS COMPANY

(in thousands)	
Current assets	
Cash and cash equivalents	$160,038
Short-term investments	96,190
Accounts and notes receivable	
Trade, less allowance for doubtful accounts of $299	106,962
Subsidiaries	11,896
Other, less allowance for certain claims of $584	7,751
Inventories	102,660
Other supplies, less allowance for obsolete supplies of $3,968	27,729
Prepaid expenses and other assets	12,848
Deferred tax asset	22,917
Total current assets	$548,991

TEMTEX INDUSTRIES, INC.

(in thousands)	
Current assets	
Cash and cash equivalents	$ 407
Accounts receivable (less allowance for doubtful accounts: $292)	5,598
Inventories	9,077
Prepaid expenses and other assets	227
Income taxes receivable	35
Deferred tax asset	607
Total current assets	$15,951

trade and non-trade receivables in the balance sheets of Adolph Coors Company and Temtex Industries.

The basic issues in accounting for accounts and notes receivable are the same: **recognition**, **valuation**, and **disposition**. We will discuss these basic issues of accounts and notes receivable in the following sequence:

1. Recognition and valuation of accounts receivable.
2. Recognition and valuation of notes receivable.
3. Disposition of accounts and notes receivable.

RECOGNITION OF ACCOUNTS RECEIVABLE

OBJECTIVE 4
Explain accounting issues related to recognition of accounts receivable.

In most receivables transactions, the amount to be recognized is the exchange price between the two parties. **The exchange price is the amount due from the debtor** (a customer or a borrower) and is generally evidenced by some type of business document, often an invoice. Two factors that may complicate the measurement of the exchange price are (1) the availability of discounts (trade and cash discounts) and (2) the length of time between the sale and the due date of payments (the interest element).

Trade Discounts

Customers are often quoted prices on the basis of list or catalog prices that may be subject to a trade or quantity discount. Such **trade discounts** are used to avoid frequent changes in catalogs, to quote different prices for different quantities purchased, or to hide the true invoice price from competitors.

Trade discounts are commonly quoted in percentages. For example, if your textbook has a list price of $60.00 and the publisher sells it to college bookstores for list less a 30% trade discount, the receivable recorded by the publisher is $42.00 per textbook. The normal practice is simply to deduct the trade discount from the list price and bill the customer net.

As another example, Maxwell House at one time sold a 10 oz. jar of its instant coffee listing at $4.65 to supermarkets for $3.90, a trade discount of approximately 16%. The supermarkets in turn sold the instant coffee for $3.99 per jar. Maxwell House records the receivable and related sales revenue at $3.90 per jar, not $4.65.

Cash Discounts (Sales Discounts)

Cash discounts (**sales discounts**) are offered as an inducement for prompt payment. They are communicated in terms that read, for example, 2/10, n/30 (2% if paid within 10 days, gross amount due in 30 days), or 2/10, E.O.M. (2% if paid within 10 days of the end of the month).

Companies that fail to take sales discounts are usually not employing their money advantageously. An enterprise that receives a 1% reduction in the sales price for payment within 10 days, total payment due within 30 days, is effectively earning 18.25% (.01 ÷ [20/365]), or at least avoiding that rate of interest cost. For this reason, companies usually take the discount unless their cash is severely limited.

The easiest and most commonly used method of recording sales and related sales discount transactions is to enter the receivable and sale at the gross amount. Under this method, sales discounts are recognized in the accounts only when payment is received within the discount period. Sales discounts would then be shown in the income statement as a deduction from sales to arrive at net sales.

Some contend that sales discounts not taken reflect penalties added to an established price to encourage prompt payment. That is, the seller offers sales on account at a slightly higher price than if selling for cash, and the increase is offset by the cash discount offered. Thus, customers who pay within the discount period purchase at the cash price; those who pay after expiration of the discount period are penalized because they must pay an amount in excess of the cash price. If this reasoning is used, sales and receivables are recorded net, and any discounts not taken are subsequently debited to Accounts Receivable and credited to Sales Discounts Forfeited. The following entries illustrate the difference between the gross and net methods.

ILLUSTRATION 7-6
Entries under Gross and Net Methods of Recording Cash (Sales) Discounts

Gross Method			Net Method		
Sales of $10,000, terms 2/10, n/30:					
Accounts Receivable	10,000		Accounts Receivable	9,800	
Sales		10,000	Sales		9,800
Payment of $4,000 received within discount period:					
Cash	3,920		Cash	3,920	
Sales Discounts	80		Accounts Receivable		3,920
Accounts Receivable		4,000			
Payment of $6,000 received after discount period:					
Cash	6,000		Accounts Receivable	120	
Accounts Receivable		6,000	Sales Discounts Forfeited		120
			Cash	6,000	
			Accounts Receivable		6,000

If the gross method is employed, sales discounts are reported as a deduction from sales in the income statement. Proper matching would dictate that a reasonable estimate of material amounts of expected discounts to be taken also should be charged against sales. If the net method is used, Sales Discounts Forfeited are considered as an other revenue item.[6]

Theoretically, the recognition of Sales Discounts Forfeited is correct because the receivable is stated closer to its realizable value and the net sale figure measures the revenue earned from the sale. As a practical matter, however, the net method is seldom used because it requires additional analysis and bookkeeping. For one thing, the net method requires adjusting entries to record sales discounts forfeited on accounts receivable that have passed the discount period.

Nonrecognition of Interest Element

Ideally, receivables should be measured in terms of their present value, that is, the discounted value of the cash to be received in the future. When expected cash receipts require a waiting period, the receivable face amount is not worth the amount that is ultimately received.

To illustrate, assume that a company makes a sale on account for $1,000 with payment due in 4 months. The applicable annual rate of interest is 12%, and payment is made at the end of 4 months. The present value of that receivable is not $1,000 but $961.54 ($1,000 × .96154, Table 6-2; $n = 1, i = 4\%$). In other words, $1,000 to be received 4 months from now is not the same as $1,000 received today.

UNDERLYING CONCEPTS

Materiality means it must make a difference to a decision maker. The FASB believes that present value concepts can be ignored for short-term notes.

Theoretically, any revenue after the period of sale is interest revenue. In practice, interest revenue related to accounts receivable is ignored because the amount of the discount is not usually material in relation to the net income for the period. The pro-

[6]To the extent that discounts not taken reflect a short-term financing, some argue that an interest revenue account could be used to record these amounts.

fession specifically excludes from the present value considerations "receivables arising from transactions with customers in the normal course of business which are due in customary trade terms not exceeding approximately one year."[7]

VALUATION OF ACCOUNTS RECEIVABLE

OBJECTIVE 5
Explain accounting issues related to valuation of accounts receivable.

Having recorded receivables at their face value (the amount due), the problem of financial statement presentation then occurs. Reporting of receivables involves (1) classification and (2) valuation on the balance sheet.

Classification, as already discussed, involves a determination of the length of time each receivable will be outstanding. Receivables intended to be collected within a year or the operating cycle, whichever is longer, are classified as current; all other receivables are classified as long-term.

The valuation of receivables is slightly more complex. **Short-term receivables are valued and reported at net realizable value—the net amount expected to be received in cash**, which is not necessarily the amount legally receivable. Determining net realizable value requires an estimation of both uncollectible receivables and any returns or allowances to be granted.

Uncollectible Accounts Receivable

As one accountant so aptly noted, the credit manager's idea of heaven probably would be a place where everyone (eventually) paid his or her debts.[8] The recent experience of Sears, as shown in Illustration 7-7, indicates the importance of credit sales for many companies. Note that while credit cards represent the largest source of Sears' profits, its increased bad debt expense has led to a lower stock price.

ILLUSTRATION 7-7
Sears' Credit Card Growth and Stock Performance

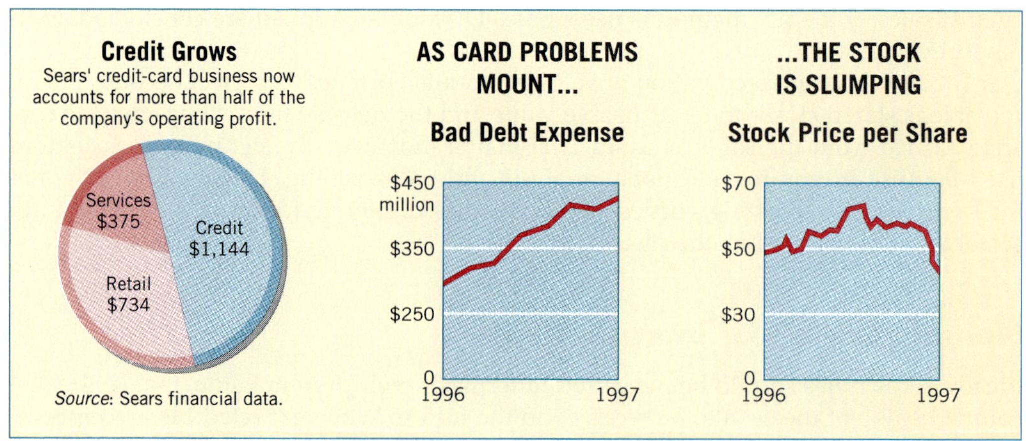

Sales on any basis other than for cash make possible the subsequent failure to collect the account. An uncollectible account receivable is a loss of revenue that requires, through proper entry in the accounts, a decrease in the asset accounts receivable and

[7]"Interest on Receivables and Payables," *Opinions of the Accounting Principles Board No. 21* (New York: AICPA, 1971), par. 3(a). According to *APB Opinion No. 21,* all receivables are subject to present value measurement techniques and interest imputation, if necessary, except for the following specifically excluded types:

1. Normal accounts receivable due within one year.
2. Security deposits, retainages, advances, or progress payments.
3. Transactions between parent and subsidiary.
4. Receivables due at some indeterminable future date.

[8]William J. Vatter, *Managerial Accounting* (Englewood Cliffs, N.J.: Prentice-Hall, 1950), p. 60.

a related decrease in income and stockholders' equity. The loss in revenue and the decrease in income are recognized by recording bad debt expense.

The chief problem in recording uncollectible accounts receivable is establishing the time at which to record the loss. Two general procedures are in use:

METHODS FOR RECORDING UNCOLLECTIBLES

1. ***Direct Write-Off Method.*** No entry is made until a specific account has definitely been established as uncollectible. Then the loss is recorded by crediting Accounts Receivable and debiting Bad Debt Expense.
2. ***Allowance Method.*** An estimate is made of the expected uncollectible accounts from all sales made on account or from the total of outstanding receivables. This estimate is entered as an expense and an indirect reduction in accounts receivable (via an increase in the allowance account) in the period in which the sale is recorded.

The direct write-off method records the bad debt in the year it is determined that a specific receivable cannot be collected. The allowance method enters the expense on an estimated basis in the accounting period in which the sales on account are made.

Supporters of the **direct write-off method** contend that facts, not estimates, are recorded. It assumes that a good account receivable resulted from each sale, and that later events proved certain accounts to be uncollectible and worthless. From a practical standpoint this method is simple and convenient to apply, although receivables do not generally become worthless at an identifiable moment of time. The direct write-off method is theoretically deficient because it usually does not match costs with revenues of the period, nor does it result in receivables being stated at estimated realizable value on the balance sheet. **As a result, its use is not considered appropriate, except when the amount uncollectible is immaterial.**

Advocates of the **allowance method** believe that bad debt expense should be recorded in the same period as the sale to obtain a proper matching of expenses and revenues and to achieve a proper carrying value for accounts receivable. They support the position that although estimates are involved, the percentage of receivables that will not be collected can be predicted from past experiences, present market conditions, and an analysis of the outstanding balances. Many companies set their credit policies to provide for a certain percentage of uncollectible accounts. (In fact, many feel that failure to reach that percentage means that sales are being lost by credit policies that are too restrictive.)

Because the collectibility of receivables is considered a loss contingency, the allowance method is appropriate in situations where it is probable that an asset has been impaired and that the amount of the loss can be reasonably estimated.[9] A receivable is a prospective cash inflow, and the probability of its collection must be considered in valuing this inflow. These estimates normally are made either on (1) the basis of percentage of sales or (2) the basis of outstanding receivables.

Percentage-of-Sales (Income Statement) Approach

If there is a fairly stable relationship between previous years' credit sales and bad debts, then that relationship can be turned into a percentage and used to determine this year's bad debt expense.

The **percentage-of-sales approach** matches costs with revenues because it relates the charge to the period in which the sale is recorded. To illustrate, assume that Chad Shumway Corp. estimates from past experience that about 2% of credit sales become

UNDERLYING CONCEPTS

The percentage-of-sales method is a good illustration of the use of the matching principle which relates expenses to revenues earned.

[9] "Accounting for Contingencies," *Statement of Financial Accounting Standards No. 5* (Stamford, Conn.: FASB, 1975), par. 8.

uncollectible. If Shumway Corp. has credit sales of $400,000 in 2001, the entry to record bad debt expense using the percentage-of-sales method is as follows:

Bad Debt Expense	8,000	
Allowance for Doubtful Accounts		8,000

The Allowance for Doubtful Accounts is a valuation account (i.e., a contra asset) and is subtracted from trade receivables on the balance sheet.[10] The amount of bad debt expense and the related credit to the allowance account are unaffected by any balance currently existing in the allowance account. Because the bad debt expense estimate is related to a nominal account (Sales), and any balance in the allowance is ignored, this method is frequently referred to as the **income statement approach**. A proper matching of cost and revenues is therefore achieved.

Percentage-of-Receivables (Balance Sheet) Approach

Using past experience, a company can estimate the percentage of its outstanding receivables that will become uncollectible, without identifying specific accounts. This procedure provides a reasonably accurate estimate of the receivables' realizable value, but does not fit the concept of matching cost and revenues. Rather, its objective is to report receivables in the balance sheet at net realizable values; hence it is referred to as the **percentage-of-receivables** (or **balance sheet**) **approach**.

In the People's Republic of China the rates for providing for bad debts are established by state regulation.

The percentage of receivables may be applied using one **composite rate** that reflects an estimate of the uncollectible receivables. Another approach that is more sensitive to the actual status of the accounts receivable sets up an **aging schedule** and applies a different percentage based on past experience to the various age categories. An aging schedule is frequently used in practice. It indicates which accounts require special attention by providing the age of such accounts receivable. The following schedule of Wilson & Co. is an example.

ILLUSTRATION 7-8
Accounts Receivable Aging Schedule

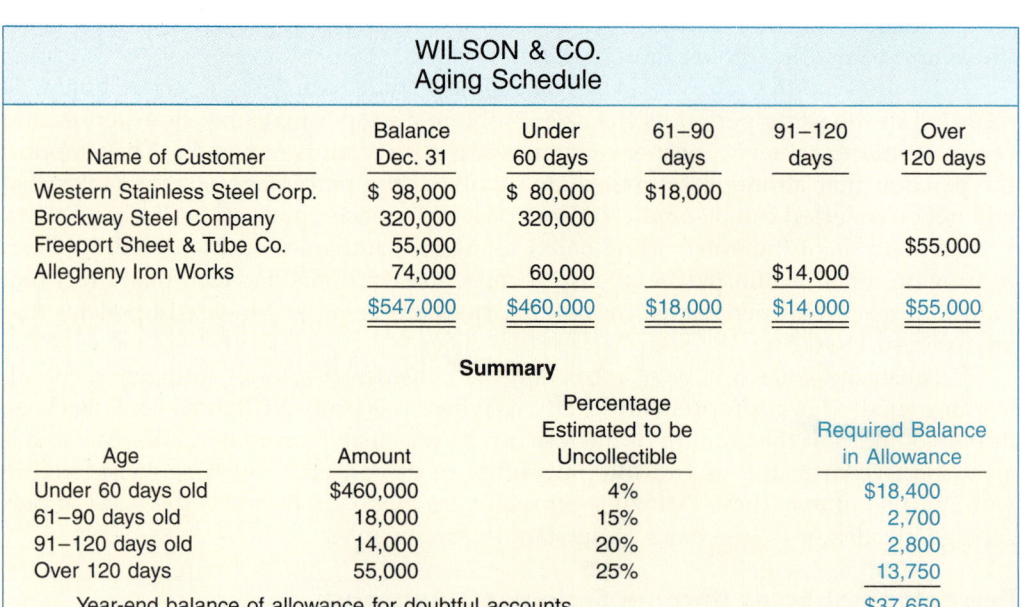

WILSON & CO.
Aging Schedule

Name of Customer	Balance Dec. 31	Under 60 days	61–90 days	91–120 days	Over 120 days
Western Stainless Steel Corp.	$ 98,000	$ 80,000	$18,000		
Brockway Steel Company	320,000	320,000			
Freeport Sheet & Tube Co.	55,000				$55,000
Allegheny Iron Works	74,000	60,000		$14,000	
	$547,000	$460,000	$18,000	$14,000	$55,000

Summary

Age	Amount	Percentage Estimated to be Uncollectible	Required Balance in Allowance
Under 60 days old	$460,000	4%	$18,400
61–90 days old	18,000	15%	2,700
91–120 days old	14,000	20%	2,800
Over 120 days	55,000	25%	13,750
Year-end balance of allowance for doubtful accounts			$37,650

The amount $37,650 would be the bad debt expense to be reported for this year, assuming that no balance existed in the allowance account.

[10]The account description employed for the allowance account is usually Allowance for Doubtful Accounts or simply Allowance. *Accounting Trends and Techniques—1999,* for example, indicates that approximately 81% of the companies surveyed used "allowance" in their description.

To change the illustration slightly, **assume that the allowance account had a credit balance of $800 before adjustment**. In this case, the amount to be added to the allowance account is $36,850 ($37,650 − $800), and the following entry is made.

Bad Debt Expense	36,850	
Allowance for Doubtful Accounts		36,850

The balance in the Allowance account is therefore stated at $37,650. **If the Allowance balance before adjustment had a debit balance of $200**, then the amount to be recorded for bad debt expense would be $37,850 ($37,650 desired balance + $200 debit balance). In the percentage-of-receivables method, the balance in the allowance account **cannot be ignored**, because the percentage is related to a real account (Accounts Receivable).

An aging schedule is usually not prepared to determine the bad debt expense. Rather, it is prepared as a control device to determine the composition of receivables and to identify delinquent accounts. The estimated loss percentage developed for each category is based on previous loss experience and the advice of credit department personnel. Regardless of whether a composite rate or an aging schedule is employed, the primary objective of the percentage of outstanding receivables method for financial statement purposes is to report receivables in the balance sheet at net realizable value. However, it is deficient in that it may not match the bad debt expense to the period in which the sale takes place.

The allowance for doubtful accounts as a percentage of receivables will vary, depending upon the industry and the economic climate. Companies such as Eastman Kodak, General Electric, and Monsanto have recorded allowances ranging from $3.00 to $6.00 per $100 of accounts receivable. Others such as CPC International ($1.48), Texaco ($1.23), and USX Corp. ($0.78) are examples of large enterprises that have had bad debt allowances of less than $1.50 per $100. At the other extreme are hospitals that allow for $15.00 to $20.00 per $100.00 of accounts receivable.[11]

In summary, the percentage-of-receivables method results in a more accurate valuation of receivables on the balance sheet. From a matching viewpoint, the percentage-of-sales approach provides the better results. The following diagram relates these methods to the basic theory:

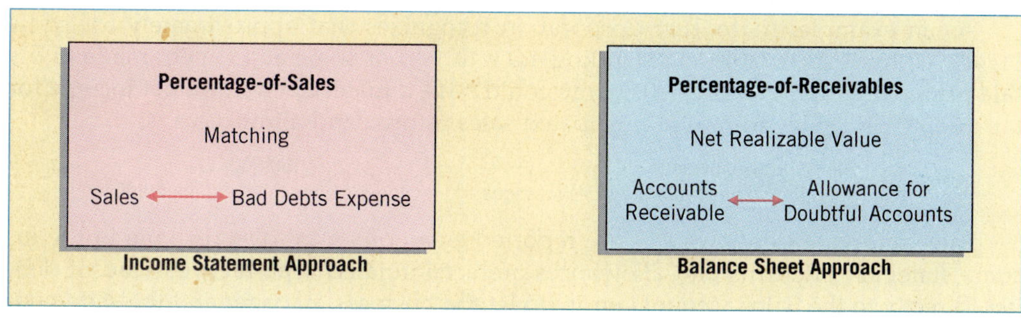

ILLUSTRATION 7-9
Comparison of Methods for Estimating Uncollectibles

The account title employed for the allowance account is usually Allowance for Doubtful Accounts or simply Allowance.

Regardless of the method chosen, determining the expense associated with uncollectible accounts is an area of accounting that is subject to a large degree of judgment. Recently there has been concern that some banks are using this judgment to manage

[11]A U.S. Department of Commerce study indicated, as a general rule, the following relationships between the age of accounts receivable and their uncollectibility:

30 days or less	4% uncollectible
31–60 days	10% uncollectible
61–90 days	17% uncollectible
91–120 days	26% uncollectible

After 120 days, an approximate 3–4% increase in uncollectibles for every 30 days outstanding occurs for the remainder of the first year.

The U.S. has been critical of some countries' use of excess reserves to manage income. These same countries would argue that Suntrust Banks' accounting for loan losses is a similar practice.

earnings. By overestimating the amounts of uncollectible loans in a good earnings year, the bank can "save for a rainy day" in a future period. In future (less profitable) periods, the overly conservative allowance for loan loss account can be reduced to increase earnings. In this regard, the SEC brought action against **Suntrust Banks**, requiring a reversal of $100 million of bad debt expense. This reversal increased aftertax profit by $61 million.[12]

Collection of Accounts Receivable Written Off

When a particular account receivable is determined to be uncollectible, the balance is removed from the books by debiting Allowance for Doubtful Accounts and crediting Accounts Receivable. If a collection is made on a receivable that was previously written off, the procedure is first to reestablish the receivable by debiting Accounts Receivable and crediting Allowance for Doubtful Accounts. An entry is then made to debit Cash and credit the customer's account for the amount received.

If the direct write-off approach is employed, the amount collected is debited to Cash and credited to a revenue account entitled Uncollectible Amounts Recovered, with proper notation in the customer's account.

Sales Returns and Allowances

To properly match expenses to sales revenues, it is sometimes necessary to establish additional allowance accounts. These allowance accounts are reported as contra accounts to accounts receivable, and they establish the receivables at net realizable value. The most common is allowance for sales returns and allowances.

Many question the soundness of recording returns and allowances in the current period when they are derived from sales made in the preceding period. Normally, however, the amount of mismatched returns and allowances is not material, if such items are handled consistently from year to year. Yet, if a company completes a few special orders involving large amounts near the end of the accounting period, **sales returns and allowances** should be anticipated in the period of the sale to avoid distorting the income statement of the current period. And, there are some companies that by their nature have significant returns and customarily establish an allowance for sales returns.

As an example, Astro Turf Corporation recognizes that approximately 5% of its $1,000,000 trade receivables outstanding are returned or some adjustment made to the sale price. Omission of a $50,000 charge could have a material effect on net income for the period. The entry to reflect anticipated sales returns and allowances is:

Sales Returns and Allowances	50,000	
Allowance for Sales Returns and Allowances		50,000

Sales returns and allowances are reported as an offset to sales revenue in the income statement. Returns and allowances are accumulated separately instead of debited directly to the Sales account simply to let the business manager and the statement reader know their magnitude. The allowance is an asset valuation account (contra asset) and is deducted from total accounts receivable.

In most cases, the inclusion in the income statement of all returns and allowances made during the period, whether or not they resulted from the current period's sales, is an acceptable accounting procedure justified by practicality and immateriality.[13]

---

[12]Recall from the earnings management discussion in Chapter 4 that increasing or decreasing income through management manipulation can reduce the quality of financial reports.

[13]An interesting sidelight to the entire problem of returns and allowances is determining when a sale is a sale. In certain circumstances the seller is exposed to such a high risk of ownership through possible return of the property that the entire transaction is nullified and the sale not recognized. Such situations have developed particularly in sales to related parties. This subject is discussed in more detail in Chapters 8 and 19.

RECOGNITION OF NOTES RECEIVABLE

A note receivable is supported by a formal **promissory note**, a written promise to pay a certain sum of money at a specific future date. Such a note is a negotiable instrument that is signed by a **maker** in favor of a designated **payee** who may legally and readily sell or otherwise transfer the note to others. Although notes contain an interest element because of the time value of money, notes are classified as interest-bearing or noninterest-bearing. **Interest-bearing notes** have a stated rate of interest, whereas **zero-interest-bearing notes** (noninterest-bearing) include interest as part of their face amount instead of stating it explicitly. Notes receivable are considered fairly liquid, even if long-term, because they may be easily converted to cash.

Notes receivable are frequently accepted from customers who need to extend the payment period of an outstanding receivable. Notes are also sometimes required of high-risk or new customers. In addition, notes are often used in loans to employees and subsidiaries and in the sales of property, plant, and equipment. In some industries (e.g., the pleasure and sport boat industry) all credit sales are supported by notes. The majority of notes, however, originate from lending transactions. The basic issues in accounting for notes receivable are the same as those for accounts receivable: recognition, valuation, and disposition.

OBJECTIVE 6
Explain accounting issues related to recognition of notes receivable.

Short-term notes are generally recorded at face value (less allowances) because the interest implicit in the maturity value is immaterial. A general rule is that notes treated as cash equivalents (maturities of 3 months or less) are not subject to premium or discount amortization. Long-term notes receivable, however, should be recorded and reported at the **present value of the cash expected to be collected**. When the interest stated on an interest-bearing note is equal to the effective (market) rate of interest, the note sells at face value.[14] When the stated rate is different from the market rate, the cash exchanged (present value) is different from the face value of the note. The difference between the face value and the cash exchanged, either a discount or a premium, is then recorded and amortized over the life of a note to approximate the effective (market) interest rate.

Note Issued at Face Value

To illustrate the discounting of a note issued at face value, assume that Bigelow Corp. lends Scandinavian Imports $10,000 in exchange for a $10,000, 3-year note bearing interest at 10% annually. The market rate of interest for a note of similar risk is also 10%. This time diagram depicting both cash flows is shown below:

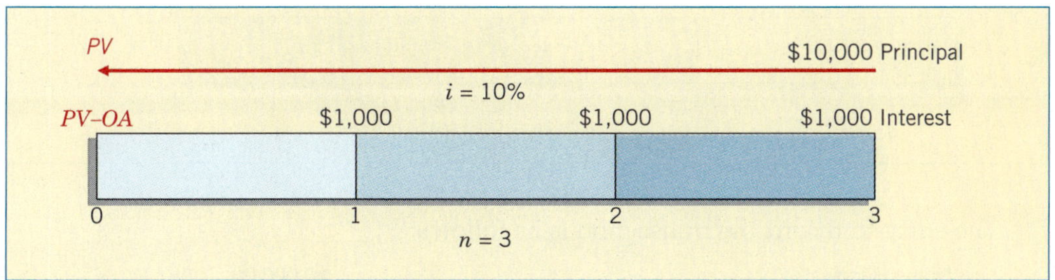

[14]The **stated interest rate**, also referred to as the face rate or the coupon rate, is the rate contracted as part of the note. The **effective interest rate**, also referred to as the market rate or the effective yield, is the rate used in the market to determine the value of the note—that is, the discount rate used to determine present value.

The present value or exchange price of the note is computed as follows:

ILLUSTRATION 7-10
Present Value of Note—Stated and Market Rates the Same

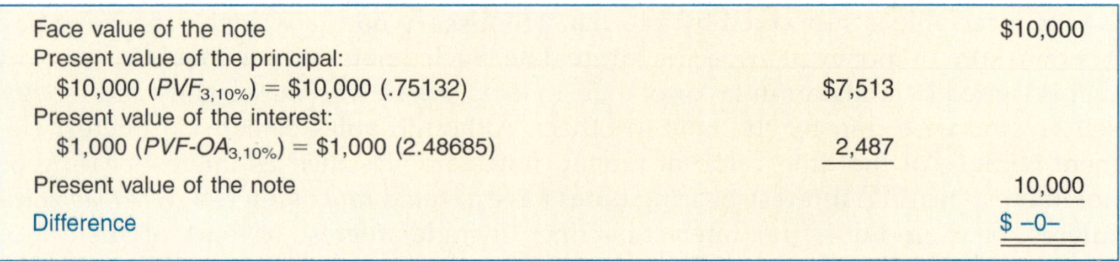

Face value of the note		$10,000
Present value of the principal:		
$10,000 ($PVF_{3,10\%}$) = $10,000 (.75132)	$7,513	
Present value of the interest:		
$1,000 ($PVF\text{-}OA_{3,10\%}$) = $1,000 (2.48685)	2,487	
Present value of the note		10,000
Difference		$ –0–

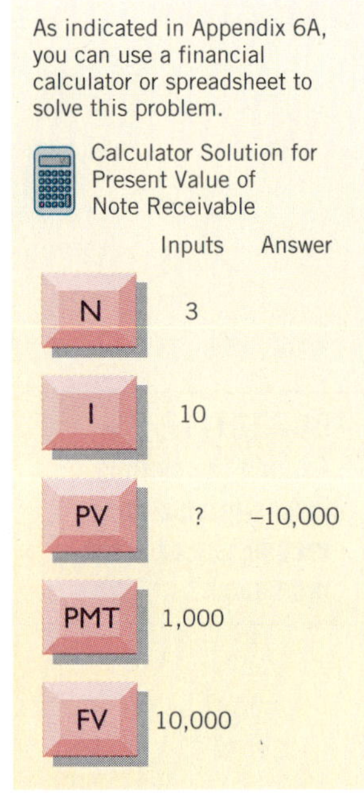

As indicated in Appendix 6A, you can use a financial calculator or spreadsheet to solve this problem.
Calculator Solution for Present Value of Note Receivable
Inputs
Answer
N
3
I
10
PV
?
–10,000
PMT
1,000
FV
10,000

In this case, the present value of the note and its face value are the same, that is, $10,000, because the effective and stated rates of interest are also the same. The receipt of the note is recorded by Bigelow Corp. as follows:

Notes Receivable	10,000	
Cash		10,000

Bigelow Corp. would recognize the interest earned each year as follows:

Cash	1,000	
Interest Revenue		1,000

Note Not Issued at Face Value

Zero-Interest-Bearing Notes

If a zero-interest-bearing note is received solely for cash, its present value is the cash paid to the issuer. Because both the future amount and the present value of the note are known, the interest rate can be computed, i.e., it is implied. The **implicit interest rate** is the rate that equates the cash paid with the amounts receivable in the future. The difference between the future (face) amount and the present value (cash paid) is recorded as a discount and amortized to interest revenue over the life of the note.

To illustrate, Jeremiah Company receives a 3-year, $10,000 zero-interest-bearing note, the present value of which is $7,721.80. The implicit rate that equates the total cash to be received ($10,000 at maturity) to the present value of the future cash flows ($7,721.80) is 9% (the present value of 1 for 3 periods at 9% is .77218). The time diagram depicting the one cash flow is shown below.

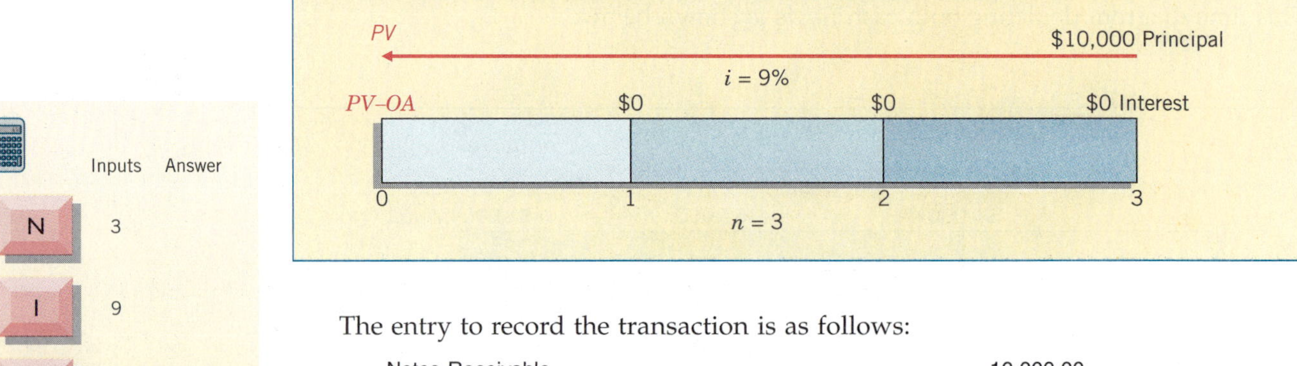

Inputs Answer

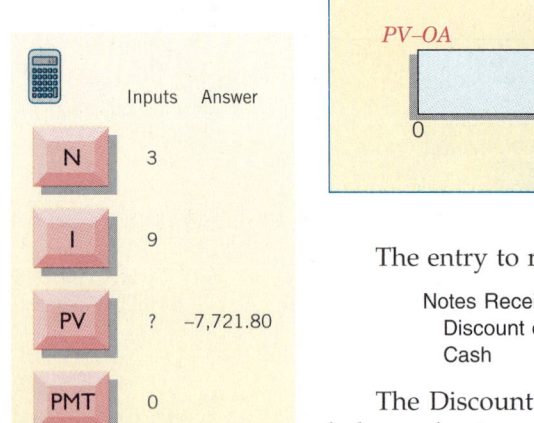

	Inputs	Answer
N	3	
I	9	
PV	?	–7,721.80
PMT	0	
FV	10,000	

The entry to record the transaction is as follows:

Notes Receivable	10,000.00	
Discount on Notes Receivable ($10,000 – $7,721.80)		2,278.20
Cash		7,721.80

The Discount on Notes Receivable is a valuation account and is reported on the balance sheet as a contra-asset account to notes receivable. The discount is then amortized, and interest revenue is recognized annually using the **effective interest method**. The 3-year discount amortization and interest revenue schedule is shown in Illustration 7-11 on the next page.

ILLUSTRATION 7-11
Discount Amortization Schedule—Effective Interest Method

Schedule of Note Discount Amortization
Effective Interest Method
0% Note Discounted at 9%

	Cash Received	Interest Revenue	Discount Amortized	Carrying Amount of Note
Date of issue				$ 7,721.80
End of year 1	$-0-	$ 694.96[a]	$ 694.96[b]	8,416.76[c]
End of year 2	-0-	757.51	757.51	9,174.27
End of year 3	-0-	825.73[d]	825.73	10,000.00
	$-0-	$2,278.20	$2,278.20	

[a]$7,721.80 × .09 = $694.96
[b]$694.96 − 0 = $694.96
[c]$7,721.80 + $694.96 = $8,416.76
[d]5¢ adjustment to compensate for rounding

Interest revenue at the end of the first year using the effective interest method is recorded as follows:

Discount on Notes Receivable	694.96	
Interest Revenue ($7,721.80 × 9%)		694.96

The amount of the discount, $2,278.20 in this case, represents the interest revenue to be received from the note over the three years.

Interest-Bearing Notes

Often the stated rate and the effective rate are different. The zero-interest-bearing case above is one example of such a situation.

To illustrate a more common situation, assume that Morgan Corp. made a loan to Marie Co. and received in exchange a 3-year, $10,000 note bearing interest at 10% annually. The market rate of interest for a note of similar risk is 12%. The time diagram depicting both cash flows is shown below:

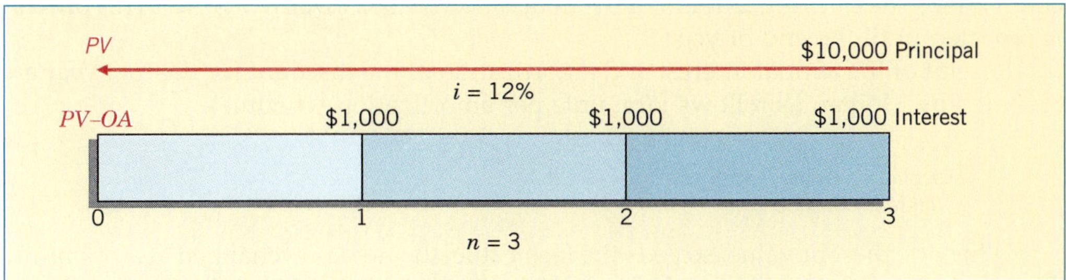

The present value of the two cash flows is computed as follows:

ILLUSTRATION 7-12
Computation of Present Value—Effective Rate Different from Stated Rate

Face value of the note		$10,000
Present value of the principal:		
$10,000 ($PVF_{3,12\%}$) = $10,000 (.71178)	$7,118	
Present value of the interest:		
$1,000 ($PVF\text{-}OA_{3,12\%}$) = $1,000 (2.40183)	2,402	
Present value of the note		9,520
Difference (Discount)		$ 480

In this case, because the effective rate of interest (12%) is greater than the stated rate (10%), the present value of the note is less than the face value; that is, the note was exchanged at a **discount**. The receipt of the note at a discount is recorded by Morgan as follows:

Notes Receivable	10,000	
Discount on Notes Receivable		480
Cash		9,520

The discount is then amortized and interest revenue is recognized annually using the **effective interest method**. The 3-year discount amortization and interest revenue schedule is shown below:

ILLUSTRATION 7-13
Discount Amortization Schedule—Effective Interest Method

Schedule of Note Discount Amortization
Effective Interest Method
10% Note Discounted at 12%

	Cash Received	Interest Revenue	Discount Amortized	Carrying Amount of Note
Date of issue				$ 9,520
End of year 1	$1,000[a]	$1,142[b]	$142[c]	9,662[d]
End of year 2	1,000	1,159	159	9,821
End of year 3	1,000	1,179	179	10,000
	$3,000	$3,480	$480	

[a]$10,000 × 10% = $1,000
[b]$9,520 × 12% = $1,142
[c]$1,142 − $1,000 = $142
[d]$9,520 + $142 = $9,662

On the date of issue, the note has a present value of $9,520. Its unamortized discount—additional interest revenue to be spread over the 3-year life of the note—is $480.

At the end of year 1, Morgan receives $1,000 in cash. But its interest revenue is $1,142 ($9,520 × 12%). The difference between $1,000 and $1,142 is the amortized discount, $142. The carrying amount of the note is now $9,662 ($9,520 + $142). This process is repeated until the end of year 3.

Receipt of the annual interest and amortization of the discount for the first year are recorded by Morgan as follows (amounts per amortization schedule):

Cash	1,000	
Discount on Notes Receivable	142	
Interest Revenue		1,142

When the present value exceeds the face value, the note is exchanged at a premium. The premium on a note receivable is recorded as a debit and amortized using the effective interest method over the life of the note as annual reductions in the amount of interest revenue recognized.

Special Situations

The note transactions just discussed are the common types of situations encountered in practice. Special situations are as follows:

1. Notes received for cash and other rights.
2. Notes received for property, goods, or services.
3. Imputed interest.

Notes Received for Cash and Other Rights

The lender may also accept a **note in exchange for cash and other rights and privileges**. For example, Ideal Equipment Co. accepts a 5-year, $100,000, zero-interest-bearing note from Outland Steel Corp. plus the right to purchase 10,000 tons of steel at a bargain price in exchange for $100,000 in cash. Assume that the current rate of interest that would be charged on another note without the right to purchase at a bargain is 10%. The acceptance of the note is recorded and the present value of the note is computed as follows:

Notes Receivable	100,000	
Prepaid Purchases	37,908	
Discount on Notes Receivable		37,908*
Cash		100,000

*Present value = $100,000 × ($PVF_{5,10\%}$) = $100,000 × .62092 = $62,092;
Discount = $100,000 − $62,092 = $37,908.

The difference between the $62,092 present value of the note and its maturity value of $100,000 represents implicit interest of $37,908. It is amortized to interest revenue over the 5-year life of the note using the effective interest method. The excess of the $100,000 over the $62,092 represents an asset, Prepaid Purchases. Prepaid Purchases is allocated to purchases or inventory in proportion to the number of tons of steel purchased each year relative to the total 10,000 tons for which a bargain price is available. For example, if 3,000 tons of steel were purchased during the first year of the 5-year bargain period, the following entry would be recorded by Ideal Equipment:

Purchases (Inventory)	11,372	
Prepaid Purchases		11,372
(3,000/10,000 × $37,908)		

Note that although prepaid purchases and the discount on notes receivable are both recorded initially at the same amount, $37,908, they are written off differently. Prepaid purchases are written off in the ratio of tons purchased, whereas the discount is amortized using the effective interest method. The value of the right or privilege, in this case the price reduction, aids in determining the interest implicit in the transaction.

Notes Received for Property, Goods, or Services

When a **note is received in exchange for property, goods, or services** in a bargained transaction entered into at arm's length, the stated interest rate is presumed to be fair unless:

1. No interest rate is stated, or
2. The stated interest rate is unreasonable, or
3. The face amount of the note is materially different from the current cash sales price for the same or similar items or from the current market value of the debt instrument.[15]

In these circumstances, the present value of the note is measured by the fair value of the property, goods, or services or by an amount that reasonably approximates the market value of the note.

To illustrate, Oasis Development Co. sold a corner lot to Rusty Pelican as a restaurant site and accepted in exchange a 5-year note having a maturity value of $35,247 and no stated interest rate. The land originally cost Oasis $14,000 and at the date of sale had an appraised fair value of $20,000. Given the criterion above, it is acceptable to use the fair market value of the land, $20,000, as the present value of the note. The entry to record the sale therefore is:

Notes Receivable	35,247	
Discount on Notes Receivable ($35,247 − $20,000)		15,247
Land		14,000
Gain on Sale of Land ($20,000 − $14,000)		6,000

The discount is amortized to interest revenue over the 5-year life of the note using the effective interest method.

[15]"Interest on Receivables and Payables," *Opinions of the Accounting Principles Board No. 21* (New York: AICPA, 1971), par. 12.

Imputed Interest

In note transactions, the effective or real interest rate is either evident or determinable by other factors involved in the exchange, such as the fair market value of what is given or received. But, if the fair value of the property, goods, services, or other rights is not determinable and if the note has no ready market, the problem of determining the present value of the note is more difficult. To estimate the present value of a note under such circumstances, an applicable interest rate that may differ from the stated interest rate must be approximated. This process of interest-rate approximation is called **imputation**, and the resulting interest rate is called an **imputed interest rate**. The imputed interest rate is used to establish the present value of the note by discounting, at that rate, all future receipts (interest and principal) on the note.

> The objective for computing the appropriate interest rate is to approximate the rate which would have resulted if an independent borrower and an independent lender had negotiated a similar transaction under comparable terms and conditions with the option to pay the cash price upon purchase or to give a note for the amount of the purchase which bears the prevailing rate of interest to maturity. The rate used for valuation purposes will normally be at least equal to the rate at which the debtor can obtain financing of a similar nature from other sources at the date of the transaction.[16]

The choice of a rate is affected by the prevailing rates for similar instruments of issuers with similar credit ratings. It is also affected specifically by restrictive covenants, collateral, payment schedule, the existing prime interest rate, etc. Determination of the imputed interest rate is made when the note is received; any subsequent changes in prevailing interest rates are ignored.

To illustrate, assume that on December 31, 2001, Brown Interiors Company rendered architectural services and accepted in exchange a long-term promissory note with a face value of $550,000, a due date of December 31, 2006, and a stated interest rate of 2%, interest receivable at the end of each year. The fair value of the services is not readily determinable, and the note is not readily marketable. Given the circumstances—the maker's credit rating, the absence of collateral, the prime rate, and the prevailing interest rate on the maker's outstanding debt—an 8% interest rate is determined to be appropriate. The time diagram depicting both cash flows is shown below:

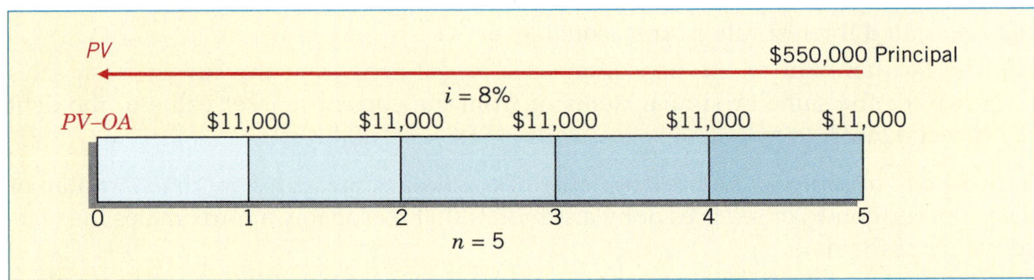

The present value of the note and the imputed fair value of the architectural services are computed as follows:

ILLUSTRATION 7-14
Computation of Present Value—Imputed Interest Rate

Face value of the note		$550,000
Present value of $550,000 due in 5 years at 8%—$550,000 ($PVF_{5,8\%}$) = $550,000 × .68058	$374,319	
Present value of $11,000 ($550,000 × .02) payable annually for 5 years at 8%—$11,000 ($PVF\text{-}OA_{5,8\%}$) = $11,000 × 3.99271	43,920	
Present value of the note		418,239
Discount		$131,761

[16]Ibid., par. 13.

The value of the services is thus determined to be $418,239, the current value of the note. The receipt of the note in exchange for the services is recorded as follows:

December 31, 2001		
Notes Receivable	550,000	
Discount on Notes Receivable		131,761
Revenue from Services		418,239

An amortization schedule similar to Illustration 7-13 is then prepared to help record transactions in future periods.

VALUATION OF NOTES RECEIVABLE

OBJECTIVE 7
Explain accounting issues related to valuation of notes receivable.

Like accounts receivable, short-term notes receivable are recorded and reported at their net realizable value; that is, at their face amount less all necessary allowances. The primary notes receivable allowance account is Allowance for Doubtful Accounts. The computations and estimations involved in valuing short-term notes receivable and in recording bad debt expense and the related allowance are **exactly the same as for trade accounts receivable**. Either a percentage of sales revenue or an analysis of the receivables can be used to estimate the amount of uncollectibles.

Long-term notes receivable, however, pose additional estimation problems. We need only look at the problems our financial institutions, most notably money-center banks, have had in collecting receivables from energy loans, real estate loans, and loans to less-developed countries.[17]

A note receivable is considered **impaired** when it is probable that the creditor will be unable to collect all amounts due (both principal and interest) according to the contractual terms of the loan. In that case, the present value of the expected future cash flows is determined by discounting those flows at the historical effective rate. This present value amount is deducted from the carrying amount of the receivable to measure the loss. Impairments, as well as restructurings, of receivables and debts are discussed and illustrated in considerable detail in Appendix 14A.

DISPOSITION OF ACCOUNTS AND NOTES RECEIVABLE

OBJECTIVE 8
Explain accounting issues related to disposition of accounts and notes receivable.

In the normal course of events, accounts and notes receivable are collected when due and removed from the books. However, as credit sales and receivables have grown in size and significance, this "normal course of events" has evolved. **In order to accelerate the receipt of cash from receivables, the owner may transfer accounts or notes receivables to anther company for cash.**

There are various reasons for this early transfer. First, for competitive reasons, providing sales financing for customers is virtually mandatory in many industries. In the sale of durable goods, such as automobiles, trucks, industrial and farm equipment, computers, and appliances, a large majority of sales are on an installment contract basis. Many major companies in these industries have created wholly-owned subsidiaries specializing in receivables financing. General Motors Corp. has General Motors Acceptance Corp. (GMAC), and Sears has Sears Roebuck Acceptance Corp. (SRAC).

Second, the **holder** may sell receivables because money is tight and access to normal credit is not available or is prohibitively expensive. Also, a firm may have to sell its receivables, instead of borrowing, to avoid violating existing lending agreements.

Finally, billing and collection of receivables are often time-consuming and costly. Credit card companies such as MasterCard, VISA, American Express, Diners Club, and others take over the collection process and provide merchants with immediate cash.

[17]A wise person once said that a bank lending money to a Third World country is like lending money to one's children: you should never expect to get the interest, let alone the principal.

Conversely, some **purchasers** of receivables buy them to obtain the legal protection of ownership rights afforded a purchaser of assets versus the lesser rights afforded a secured creditor. In addition, banks and other lending institutions may be forced to purchase receivables because of legal lending limits; that is, they cannot make any additional loans but they can buy receivables and charge a fee for this service.

The transfer of receivables to a third party for cash is accomplished in one of two ways:

1. Secured borrowing.
2. Sales of receivables.

Secured Borrowing

Receivables are often used as collateral in a borrowing transaction. A creditor often requires that the debtor designate (assign) or pledge[18] receivables as security for the loan. If the loan is not paid when due, the creditor has the right to convert the collateral to cash—that is, to collect the receivables.

To illustrate, on March 1, 2001, Howat Mills, Inc., provides (assigns) $700,000 of its accounts receivable to Citizens Bank as collateral for a $500,000 note. Howat Mills will continue to collect the accounts receivable; the account debtors are not notified of the arrangement. Citizens Bank assesses a finance charge of 1% of the accounts receivable and interest on the note of 12%. Settlement by Howat Mills to the bank is made monthly for all cash collected on the receivables.

ILLUSTRATION 7-15
Entries for Transfer of Receivables—Secured Borrowing

Howat Mills, Inc.			Citizens Bank		
Transfer of accounts receivable and issuance of note on March 1, 2001:					
Cash	493,000		Notes Receivable	500,000	
Finance Charge	7,000*		Finance Revenue		7,000*
Notes Payable		500,000	Cash		493,000
*(1% × $700,000)					
Collection in March of $440,000 of accounts less cash discounts of $6,000. In addition, sales returns of $14,000 were received:					
Cash	434,000				
Sales Discounts	6,000				
Sales Returns	14,000		(No entry)		
Accounts Receivable		454,000			
($440,000 + $14,000 = $454,000)					
Remitted March collections plus accrued interest to the bank on April 1:					
Interest Expense	5,000*		Cash	439,000	
Notes Payable	434,000		Interest Revenue		5,000*
Cash		439,000	Notes Receivable		434,000
*($500,000 × .12 × 1/12)					
Collection in April of the balance of accounts less $2,000 written off as uncollectible:					
Cash	244,000				
Allow. for Doubtful Accts.	2,000		(No entry)		
Accounts Receivable		246,000*			
*($700,000 – $454,000)					
Remitted the balance due of $66,000 ($500,000 – $434,000) on the note plus interest on May 1:					
Interest Expense	660*		Cash	66,660	
Notes Payable	66,000		Interest Revenue		660*
Cash		66,660	Notes Receivable		66,000
*($66,000 × .12 × 1/12)					

[18]If the receivables are transferred to the transferee for custodial purposes, the custodial arrangement is often referred to as a **pledge**.

In addition to recording the collection of receivables, all discounts, returns and allowances, and bad debts must be recognized. Each month the proceeds from the collection of the accounts receivable are used to retire the note obligation. In addition, interest on the note is paid.[19]

Sales of Receivables

Sales of receivables have increased substantially in recent years. A common type is a sale to a factor. **Factors** are finance companies or banks that buy receivables from businesses for a fee and then collect the remittances directly from the customers. **Factoring receivables** is traditionally associated with the textile, apparel, footwear, furniture, and home furnishing industries.[20] An illustration of a factoring arrangement is shown below.

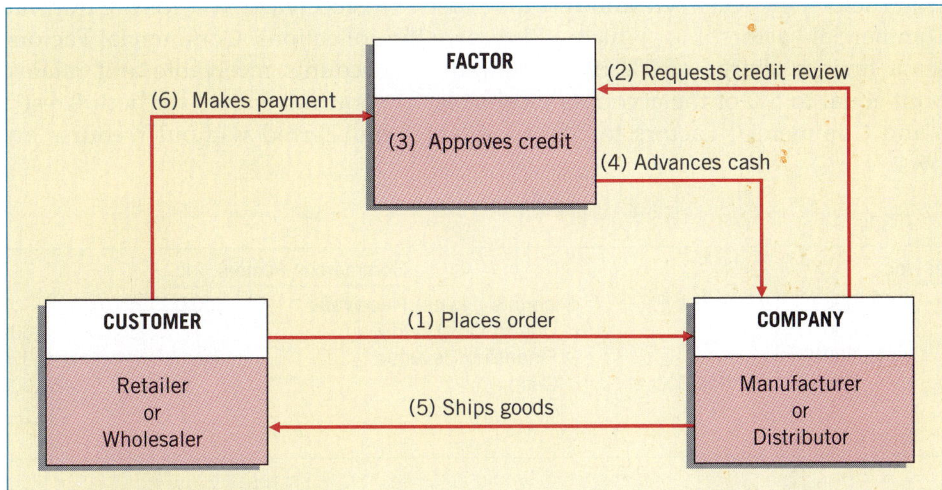

ILLUSTRATION 7-16
Basic Procedures in Factoring

As indicated in the opening story, a recent phenomenon in the sale (transfer) of receivables is securitization. **Securitization** takes a pool of assets such as credit card receivables, mortgage receivables, or car loan receivables and sells shares in these pools of interest and principal payments (in effect, creating securities backed by these pools of assets). Virtually every asset with a payment stream and a long-term payment history is a candidate for securitization.

The differences between factoring and securitization are that factoring usually involves sale to only one company, fees are high, the quality of the receivables is low, and the seller afterward does not service the receivables. In a securitization, many investors are involved, margins are tight, the receivables are of higher quality, and the seller usually continues to service the receivables.

---

[19]What happens if Citizens Bank collected the transferred accounts receivable rather than Howat Mills? In that case, Citizens Bank would simply remit the cash proceeds to Howat Mills, and Howat Mills would make the same entries shown in Illustration 7-15. As a result, the receivables used as collateral are reported as an asset on the transferors' balance sheet. In some cases, if the transferee can sell or pledge the receivables received from the transferor, the transferee may be required to report an additional asset and related liability.

[20]Credit cards like MasterCard and VISA are a type of factoring arrangement. Typically the purchaser of the receivable charges a 3/4 % to 1 1/2% commission of the receivables purchased (the commission is 4–5% for credit card factoring).

In either a factoring or a securitization transaction, receivables are sold on either a **without recourse** or a **with recourse** basis.[21]

Sale without Recourse

When receivables are sold **without recourse**, the purchaser assumes the risk of collectibility and absorbs any credit losses. The transfer of accounts receivable in a nonrecourse transaction is an outright sale of the receivables both in form (transfer of title) and substance (transfer of control). In nonrecourse transactions, as in any sale of assets, Cash is debited for the proceeds. Accounts Receivable is credited for the face value of the receivables. The difference, reduced by any provision for probable adjustments (discounts, returns, allowances, etc.), is recognized as a Loss on the Sale of Receivables. The seller uses a Due from Factor account (reported as a receivable) to account for the proceeds retained by the factor to cover probable sales discounts, sales returns, and sales allowances.

Go to the Digital Tool for a comprehensive illustration of sale without recourse.

To illustrate, Crest Textiles, Inc. factors $500,000 of accounts receivable with Commercial Factors, Inc., on a **without recourse** basis. The receivable records are transferred to Commercial Factors, Inc., which will receive the collections. Commercial Factors assesses a finance charge of 3% of the amount of accounts receivable and retains an amount equal to 5% of the accounts receivable. The journal entries for both Crest Textiles and Commercial Factors for the receivables transferred without recourse are as follows:

Crest Textiles, Inc.			Commercial Factors, Inc.		
Cash	460,000		Accounts (Notes) Receivable	500,000	
Due from Factor	25,000*		Due to Crest Textiles		25,000
Loss on Sale of Receivables	15,000**		Financing Revenue		15,000
Accounts (Notes) Receivable		500,000	Cash		460,000
*(5% × $500,000)					
**(3% × $500,000)					

ILLUSTRATION 7-17
Entries for Sale of Receivables Without Recourse

In recognition of the sale of receivables, Crest Textiles records a loss of $15,000. The factor's net income will be the difference between the financing revenue of $15,000 and the amount of any uncollectible receivables.

Sale with Recourse

If receivables are sold **with recourse**, the seller guarantees payment to the purchaser in the event the debtor fails to pay. To record this type of transaction, a **financial components approach** is used, because the seller has a continuing involvement with the receivable.[22] In this approach, each party to the sale recognizes the assets and liabilities that it controls after the sale and no longer recognizes the assets and liabilities that were sold or extinguished.

To illustrate, assume the same information as in Illustration 7-17 for Crest Textiles and for Commercial Factors except that the receivables are sold on a with recourse ba-

[21]**Recourse** is the right of a transferee of receivables to receive payment from the transferor of those receivables for (1) failure of the debtors to pay when due, (2) the effects of prepayments, or (3) adjustments resulting from defects in the eligibility of the transferred receivables. See "Accounting for Transfers and Servicing of Financial Assets and Extinguishments of Liabilities," *Statement of Financial Accounting Standards No. 125* (Stamford, Conn.: FASB, 1996), pp. 3–4.

[22]Previous accounting standards generally required that the transferor account for financial assets transferred as an inseparable unit that had been entirely sold or entirely retained. Those standards were difficult to apply and produced inconsistent and arbitrary results. Values are now assigned to such components as the recourse provision, servicing rights, and agreement to reacquire.

sis. It is determined that this recourse obligation has a fair value of $6,000. To determine the loss on the sale of the receivables by Crest Textiles, the net proceeds from the sale are computed:

ILLUSTRATION 7-18
Net Proceeds Computation

Cash received	$460,000	
Due from factor	25,000	$485,000
Less: Recourse obligation		6,000
Net proceeds		$479,000

Net proceeds are cash or other assets received in a sale less any liabilities incurred. The loss is then computed as follows:

ILLUSTRATION 7-19
Loss on Sale Computation

Carrying (book) value	$500,000
Net proceeds	479,000
Loss on sale of receivables	$ 21,000

The journal entries for both Crest Textiles and Commercial Factors for the receivables sold with recourse are as follows:

ILLUSTRATION 7-20
Entries for Sale of Receivables with Recourse

Crest Textiles, Inc.			Commercial Factors, Inc.		
Cash	460,000		Accounts Receivable	500,000	
Due from Factor	25,000		Due to Crest Textiles		25,000
Loss on Sale of Receivables	21,000		Financing Revenue		15,000
Accounts (Notes) Receivable		500,000	Cash		460,000
Recourse Liability		6,000			

In this case, Crest Textiles recognizes a loss of $21,000. In addition, a liability of $6,000 is recorded to indicate the probable payment to Commercial Factors for uncollectible receivables. If all the receivables are collected, Crest Textiles would eliminate its recourse liability and increase income. Commercial Factors' net income is the financing revenue of $15,000 because it will have no bad debts related to these receivables.

Secured Borrowing versus Sale

The FASB concluded that a sale occurs only if the seller surrenders control of the receivables to the buyer. The following three conditions must be met before a sale can be recorded:

The IASC has a similar conceptual approach to the sale of receivables, although it provides more flexibility in implementation.

1. The transferred asset has been isolated from the transferor (put beyond reach of the transferor and its creditors).
2. The transferees have obtained the right to pledge or exchange either the transferred assets or beneficial interests in the transferred assets.
3. The transferor does not maintain effective control over the transferred assets through an agreement to repurchase or redeem them before their maturity.

If the three conditions are met, a sale occurs. Otherwise, the transferor should record the transfer as a secured borrowing. If sale accounting is appropriate, it is still necessary to consider assets obtained and liabilities incurred in the transaction. The rules of accounting for transfers of receivables are shown in Illustration 7-21.

ILLUSTRATION 7-21
Accounting for Transfers of Receivables

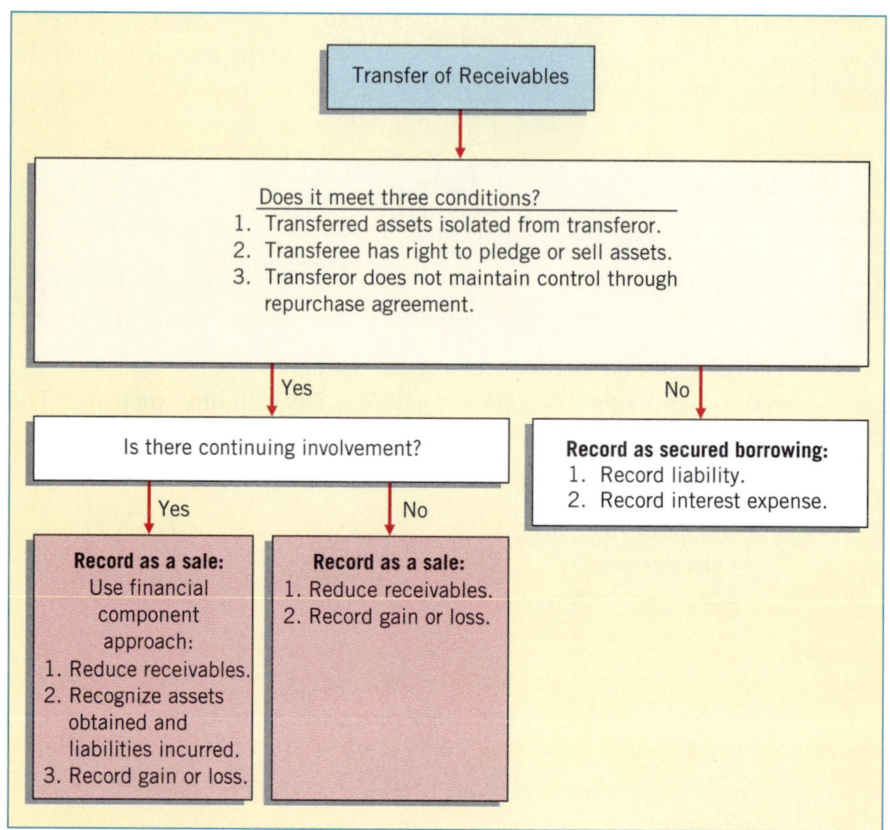

As shown in Illustration 7-21, if there is continuing involvement in a sale transaction, the assets obtained and liabilities incurred must be recorded at fair value.

PRESENTATION AND ANALYSIS

Presentation of Receivables

OBJECTIVE 9
Explain how receivables are reported and analyzed.

The general rules in classifying receivables are: (1) segregate the different types of receivables that an enterprise possesses, if material; (2) ensure that the valuation accounts are appropriately offset against the proper receivable accounts; (3) determine that receivables classified in the current assets section will be converted into cash within the year or the operating cycle, whichever is longer; (4) disclose any loss contingencies that exist on the receivables; (5) disclose any receivables designated or pledged as collateral; (6) disclose all significant concentrations of credit risk arising from receivables.[23]

---

[23]Concentrations of credit risk exist when receivables have common characteristics that may affect their collection. These common characteristics might be companies in the same industry or same region of the country. For example, financial statements users want to know if a substantial amount of receivables are with defense contractors or with companies in the Middle East. No numerical guidelines are provided as to what is meant by a "concentration of credit risk." When a concentration is identified, three items should be disclosed: (1) information on the characteristic that determines the concentration should be identified, (2) the amount of loss that could occur upon nonperformance, and (3) information on any collateral related to the receivable. "Disclosure of Information About Financial Instruments with Off-Balance-Sheet Risk and Financial Instruments with Concentrations of Credit Risk," *Statement of Financial Accounting Standards No. 105* (Norwalk, Conn.: FASB, 1990).

The asset sections of Colton Corporation's balance sheet shown below illustrate many of the disclosures required for receivables:

ILLUSTRATION 7-22
Disclosure of Receivables

COLTON CORPORATION
Balance Sheet (partial)
As of December 31, 2001

Current assets		
Cash and cash equivalents		$ 1,870,250
Accounts receivable (Note 2)	$8,977,673	
Less: Allowance for doubtful accounts	500,226	
	8,477,447	
Advances to subsidiaries due 9/30/02	2,090,000	
Notes receivable—trade (Note 2)	1,532,000	
Federal income taxes refundable	146,704	
Dividends and interest receivable	75,500	
Other receivables and claims (including debit balances in accounts payable)	174,620	12,496,271
Total current assets		14,366,521
Noncurrent receivables		
Notes receivable from officers and key employees		376,090
Claims receivable (litigation settlement to be collected over four years)		585,000

Note 2: Accounts and Notes Receivable
In November 2001, the Company arranged with a finance company to refinance a part of its indebtedness. The loan is evidenced by a 12% note payable. The note is payable on demand and is secured by substantially all the accounts receivable.

Go to the Digital Tool for additional disclosures of receivables.

Holding receivables that will be paid in a foreign currency represents risk that the exchange rate may move against the company, causing a decrease in the amount collected in terms of U.S. dollars. Companies engaged in cross-border transactions often "hedge" these receivables by buying contracts to exchange currencies at specified amounts at future dates.

Analysis of Receivables

Financial ratios are frequently computed to evaluate the liquidity of a company's accounts receivable. The ratio used to assess the liquidity of the receivables is the **receivables turnover ratio**. This ratio measures the number of times, on average, receivables are collected during the period. The ratio is computed by dividing net sales by average receivables (net) outstanding during the year. Theoretically, the numerator should include only net credit sales. This information is frequently not available, however, and if the relative amounts of credit and cash sales remain fairly constant, the trend indicated by the ratio will still be valid. Unless seasonal factors are significant, average receivables outstanding can be computed from the beginning and ending balances of net trade receivables.

To illustrate, **Gateway 2000** reported 1998 net sales of $7,468 million, its beginning and ending accounts receivable balances were $511 million and $559 million, respectively. Its accounts receivables turnover ratio is computed as follows:

ILLUSTRATION 7-23
Computation of Accounts Receivable Turnover

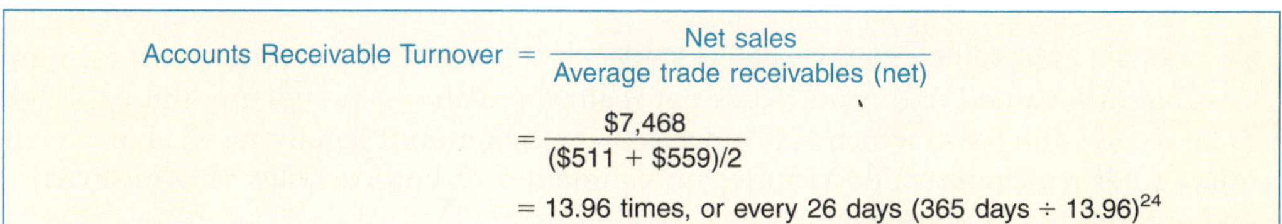

$$\text{Accounts Receivable Turnover} = \frac{\text{Net sales}}{\text{Average trade receivables (net)}}$$

$$= \frac{\$7,468}{(\$511 + \$559)/2}$$

$$= 13.96 \text{ times, or every 26 days (365 days} \div 13.96)^{24}$$

[24]Often the receivables turnover is transformed to **days to collect accounts receivable** or days outstanding—an average collection period. In this case, 13.96 is divided into 365 days to obtain 26 days. Several figures other than 365 could be used here; a most common alternative is 360 days because it is divisable by 30 (days) and 12 (months). Use 365 days in any homework computations.

UNDERLYING CONCEPTS

Providing information that will help users assess an enterprises's current liquidity and prospective cash flows is a primary objective of accounting.

This information provides some indication of the quality of the receivables, and also an idea of how successful the firm is in collecting its outstanding receivables. If possible, an aging schedule should also be prepared to determine how long receivables have been outstanding. It is possible that a satisfactory receivables turnover may have resulted because certain receivables were collected quickly though others have been outstanding for a relatively long period. An aging schedule would reveal such patterns.

SUMMARY OF LEARNING OBJECTIVES

1 Identify items considered cash. To be reported as "cash," an asset must be readily available for the payment of current obligations and free from contractual restrictions that limit its use in satisfying debts. Cash consists of coin, currency, and available funds on deposit at the bank. Negotiable instruments such as money orders, certified checks, cashier's checks, personal checks, and bank drafts are also viewed as cash. Savings accounts are usually classified as cash.

2 Indicate how cash and related items are reported. Cash is reported as a current asset in the balance sheet. The reporting of other related items are: (1) *Restricted cash:* The SEC recommends that legally restricted deposits held as compensating balances against short-term borrowing be stated separately among the "cash and cash equivalent items" in Current Assets. Restricted deposits held against long-term borrowing arrangements should be separately classified as noncurrent assets in either the Investments or Other Assets sections. (2) *Bank overdrafts:* They should be reported in the current liabilities section and are usually added to the amount reported as accounts payable. If material, these items should be separately disclosed either on the face of the balance sheet or in the related notes. (3) *Cash equivalents:* This item is often reported together with cash as "cash and cash equivalents."

3 Define receivables and identify the different types of receivables. Receivables are claims held against customers and others for money, goods, or services. The receivables are classified into three types: (1) current or noncurrent; (2) trade or nontrade; (3) accounts receivable or notes receivable.

4 Explain accounting issues related to recognition of accounts receivable. Two issues that may complicate the measurement of accounts receivable are: (1) The availability of discounts (trade and cash discounts) and (2) the length of time between the sale and the payment due dates (the interest element).

Ideally, receivables should be measured in terms of their present value—that is, the discounted value of the cash to be received in the future. The profession specifically excludes from the present value considerations receivables arising from normal business transactions that are due in customary trade terms within approximately one year.

5 Explain accounting issues related to valuation of accounts receivable. Short-term receivables are valued and reported at net realizable value—the net amount expected to be received in cash, which is not necessarily the amount legally receivable. Determining net realizable value requires an estimation of both uncollectible receivables and any returns or allowances.

6 Explain accounting issues related to recognition of notes receivable. Short-term notes are recorded at face value. Long-term notes receivable are recorded at the present value of the cash expected to be collected. When the interest stated on an interest-bearing note is equal to the effective (market) rate of interest, the note sells at face value. When the stated rate is different from the effective rate, either a discount or premium is recorded.

KEY TERMS

accounts receivable, *341*
aging schedule, *346*
allowance method, *345*
bank overdrafts, *339*
cash, *336*
cash discounts, *342*
cash equivalents, *340*
compensating balances, *338*
direct write-off method, *345*
factoring receivables, *357*
financial components approach, *358*
imputed interest rate, *354*
net realizable value, *344*
nontrade receivables, *341*
notes receivable, *341*
percentage-of-receivables approach, *346*
percentage-of-sales approach, *345*
promissory note, *349*
receivables, *341*
receivables turnover ratio, *361*
restricted cash, *339*
sales discounts, *342*
sales returns and allowances, *348*
securitization, *357*
trade discounts, *342*
trade receivables, *341*
with recourse, *358*
without recourse, *358*
zero-interest-bearing notes, *349*

7 **Explain accounting issues related to valuation of notes receivable.** Like accounts receivable, short-term notes receivable are recorded and reported at their net realizable value. The same is also true of long-term receivables. Special issues relate to impairments and notes receivable past due.

8 **Explain accounting issues related to disposition of accounts and notes receivable.** To accelerate the receipt of cash from receivables, the owner may transfer the receivables to another company for cash. The transfer of receivables to a third party for cash may be accomplished in one of two ways: (1) *Secured borrowing:* A creditor often requires that the debtor designate or pledge receivables as security for the loan. (2) *Sales (factoring) of receivables:* Factors are finance companies or banks that buy receivables from businesses and then collect the remittances directly from the customers. In many cases, transferors may have some continuing involvement with the receivable sold. A financial components approach is used to record this type of transaction.

9 **Explain how receivables are reported and analyzed.** Disclosure of receivables requires valuation accounts be appropriately offset against receivables, receivables be appropriately classified as current or noncurrent, pledged or designated receivables be identified, and concentrations of risks arising from receivables be identified. Receivables may be analyzed relative to turnover and the days outstanding.

Cash Controls

As indicated in Chapter 7, cash creates many management and control problems. The purpose of this appendix is to discuss some of the basic control issues related to cash.

OBJECTIVE 10
After studying Appendix 7A, you should be able to: Explain common techniques employed to control cash.

USING BANK ACCOUNTS

A company can vary the number and location of banks and the types of bank accounts to obtain desired control objectives. For large companies operating in multiple locations, the location of bank accounts can be important. Establishing collection accounts in strategic locations can accelerate the flow of cash into the company by shortening the time between a customer's mailing of a payment and the company's use of the cash. Multiple collection centers generally are used to reduce the size of a company's **collection float**, which is the difference between the amount on deposit according to the company's records and the amount of collected cash according to the bank record.

INTERNATIONAL INSIGHT

Multinational corporations often have cash accounts in more than one currency. For financial statement purposes these currencies are typically translated into U.S. dollars using the exchange rate in effect at the balance sheet date.

The **general checking account** is the principal bank account in most companies and frequently the only bank account in small businesses. Cash is deposited in and disbursed from this account as all transactions are cycled through it. Deposits from and disbursements to all other bank accounts are made through the general checking account.

Imprest bank accounts are used to make a specific amount of cash available for a limited purpose. The account acts as a clearing account for a large volume of checks or for a specific type of check. The specific and intended amount to be cleared through the imprest account is deposited by transferring that amount from the general checking account or other source. Impress bank accounts are often used for disbursing payroll checks, dividends, commissions, bonuses, confidential expenses (e.g., officers' salaries), and travel expenses.

Lockbox accounts are frequently used by large, multilocation companies to make collections in cities within areas of heaviest customer billing. The company rents a local post office box and authorizes a local bank to pick up the remittances mailed to that box number. The bank empties the box at least once a day and immediately credits the company's account for collections. The greatest advantage of a lockbox is that it accelerates the availability of collected cash. Generally, in a lockbox arrangement the bank microfilms the checks for record purposes and provides the company with a deposit slip, a list of collections, and any customer correspondence. If the control over cash is improved and if the income generated from accelerating the receipt of funds exceeds the cost of the lockbox system, then it is considered a worthwhile undertaking.

THE IMPREST PETTY CASH SYSTEM

Almost every company finds it necessary to pay small amounts for a great many things such as employee's lunches, taxi fares, minor office supplies, and other miscellaneous expenses. It is frequently impractical to require that such disbursements be made by check, yet some control over them is important. A simple method of obtaining reasonable control, while adhering to the rule of disbursement by check, is the **imprest system for petty cash** disbursements.

This is how the system works:

1. Someone is designated petty cash custodian and given a small amount of currency from which to make small payments. The transfer of funds to petty cash is recorded as:

Petty Cash	300	
Cash		300

2. As disbursements are made, the petty cash custodian obtains signed receipts from each individual to whom cash is paid. If possible, evidence of the disbursement should be attached to the petty cash receipt. Petty cash transactions are not recorded until the fund is reimbursed, and then such entries are recorded by someone other than the petty cash custodian.

3. When the supply of cash runs low, the custodian presents to the general cashier a request for reimbursement supported by the petty cash receipts and other disbursement evidence. The custodian receives a company check to replenish the fund. At this point, transactions are recorded based on petty cash receipts:

Office Supplies Expense	42	
Postage Expense	53	
Entertainment Expense	76	
Cash Over and Short	2	
Cash		173

4. If it is decided that the amount of cash in the petty cash fund is excessive, an adjustment may be made as follows (lowering the fund balance from \$300 to \$250):

Cash	50	
Petty Cash		50

Entries are made to the Petty Cash account only to increase or decrease the size of the fund.

A **Cash Over and Short** account is used when the petty cash fund fails to prove out. When this occurs, it is usually due to an error (failure to provide correct change, overpayment of expense, lost receipt, etc.). If cash proves out **short** (i.e., the sum of the receipts and cash in the fund is less than the imprest amount), the shortage is debited to the Cash Over and Short account. If it proves out **over,** the overage is credited to Cash Over and Short. This account is left open until the end of the year, when it is closed and generally shown on the income statement as an other expense or revenue.

There are usually expense items in the fund except immediately after reimbursement; therefore, if accurate financial statements are desired, the funds must be reimbursed at the end of each accounting period and also when nearly depleted.

Under the imprest system the petty cash custodian is responsible at all times for the amount of the fund on hand either as cash or in the form of signed receipts. These receipts provide the evidence required by the disbursing officer to issue a reimbursement check. Two additional procedures are followed to obtain more complete control over the petty cash fund:

1. Surprise counts of the fund are made from time to time by a superior of the petty cash custodian to determine that the fund is being accounted for satisfactorily.
2. Petty cash receipts are canceled or mutilated after they have been submitted for reimbursement, so that they cannot be used to secure a second reimbursement.

PHYSICAL PROTECTION OF CASH BALANCES

Not only must cash receipts and cash disbursements be safeguarded through internal control measures, but also the cash on hand and in banks must be protected. Because receipts become cash on hand and disbursements are made from cash in banks, adequate control of receipts and disbursements is a part of the protection of cash balances. Certain other procedures, however, should be given some consideration.

Physical protection of cash is so elementary a necessity that it requires little discussion. Every effort should be made to minimize the cash on hand in the office. A petty cash fund, the current day's receipts, and perhaps funds for making change should be all that is on hand at any one time. Insofar as possible, these funds should be kept in a vault, safe, or locked cash drawer. Each day's receipts should be transmitted intact to the bank as soon as practicable. Accurately stating the amount of available cash both in internal management reports and in external financial statements is also extremely important.

Every company has a record of cash received, disbursed, and the balance. Because of the many cash transactions, however, errors or omissions may be made in keeping this record. Therefore, it is necessary periodically to prove the balance shown in the general ledger. Cash actually present in the office—petty cash, change funds, and undeposited receipts—can be counted, for comparison with the company records. Cash on deposit is not available for count and is proved by preparing a bank reconciliation—a reconciliation of the company's record and the bank's record of the company's cash.

RECONCILIATION OF BANK BALANCES

At the end of each calendar month the bank supplies each customer with a **bank statement** (a copy of the bank's account with the customer) together with the customer's checks that have been paid by the bank during the month.[1] If no errors were made by the bank or the customer, if all deposits made and all checks drawn by the customer reached the bank within the same month, and if no unusual transactions occurred that affected either the company's or the bank's record of cash, the balance of cash reported

[1] As mentioned in Chapter 7, use of paper checks continues to be a popular means of payment. However, ready availability of desktop publishing software and hardware has created new opportunities for check fraud in the form of duplicate, altered, and forged checks. At the same time, new fraud-fighting technologies, such as ultraviolet imaging, high-capacity barcodes, and biometrics are being developed. These technologies convert paper documents into document files that are processed electronically, thereby reducing the risk of fraud.

by the bank to the customer would be the same as that shown in the customer's own records. This condition seldom occurs for one or more of the following reasons:

RECONCILING ITEMS

1. ***Deposits in Transit.*** End-of-month deposits of cash recorded on the depositor's books in one month are received and recorded by the bank in the following month.
2. ***Outstanding Checks.*** Checks written by the depositor are recorded when written but may not be recorded by—or "clear"—the bank until the next month.
3. ***Bank Charges.*** Charges recorded by the bank against the depositor's balance for such items as bank services, printing checks, **not-sufficient-funds (NSF) checks**, and safe-deposit box rentals. The depositor may not be aware of these charges until the receipt of the bank statement.
4. ***Bank Credits.*** Collections or deposits by the bank for the benefit of the depositor that may be unknown to the depositor until receipt of the bank statement. Examples are note collection for the depositor and interest earned on interest-bearing checking accounts.
5. ***Bank or Depositor Errors.*** Errors on either the part of the bank or the part of the depositor cause the bank balance to disagree with the depositor's book balance.

Hence, differences between the depositor's record of cash and the bank's record are usual and expected. Therefore, the two must be reconciled to determine the nature of the differences between the two amounts.

A **bank reconciliation** is a schedule explaining any differences between the bank's and the company's records of cash. If the difference results only from transactions not yet recorded by the bank, the company's record of cash is considered correct. But, if some part of the difference arises from other items, the bank's records or the company's records must be adjusted.

Two forms of bank reconciliation may be prepared. One form reconciles from the bank statement balance to the book balance or vice versa. The other form reconciles both the bank balance and the book balance to a correct cash balance. This latter form is more widely used. A sample of that form and its common reconciling items are shown in Illustration 7A-1.

ILLUSTRATION 7A-1
Bank Reconciliation Form and Content

Balance per bank statement (end of period)		$$$
Add: Deposits in transit	$$	
Undeposited receipts (cash on hand)	$$	
Bank errors that understate the bank statement balance	$$	$$
Deduct: Outstanding checks	$$	$$$
Bank errors that overstate the bank statement balance	$$	$$
Correct cash balance		$$$
Balance per depositor's books		$$$
Add: Bank credits and collections not yet recorded in the books	$$	
Book errors that understate the book balance	$$	$$
		$$$
Deduct: Bank charges not yet recorded in the books	$$	
Book errors that overstate the book balance	$$	$$
Correct cash balance		$$$

This form of reconciliation consists of two sections: (1) "Balance per bank statement" and (2) "Balance per depositor's books." Both sections end with the same "correct cash balance." The correct cash balance is the amount to which the books must be adjusted and is the amount reported on the balance sheet. **Adjusting journal entries are prepared for all the addition and deduction items appearing in the "Balance per depositor's books" section**. Any errors attributable to the bank should be called to the bank's attention immediately.

To illustrate, Nugget Mining Company's books show a cash balance at the Denver National Bank on November 30, 2001, of $20,502. The bank statement covering the month of November shows an ending balance of $22,190. An examination of Nugget's accounting records and November bank statement identified the following reconciling items:

1. A deposit of $3,680 was mailed November 30 but does not appear on the bank statement.
2. Checks written in November but not charged to the November bank statement are:

Check #7327	$ 150
#7348	4,820
#7349	31

3. Nugget has not yet recorded the $600 of interest collected by the bank November 20 on Sequoia Co. bonds held by the bank for Nugget.
4. Bank service charges of $18 are not yet recorded on Nugget's books.
5. One of Nugget's customer's checks for $220 was returned with the bank statement and marked "NSF." The bank treated this bad check as a disbursement.
6. Nugget discovered that check #7322, written in November for $131 in payment of an account payable, had been incorrectly recorded in their books as $311.
7. A check for Nugent Oil Co. in the amount of $175 that had been incorrectly charged to Nugget Mining accompanied the bank statement.

The reconciliation of bank and book balances to the correct cash balance of $21,044 would appear as follows:

ILLUSTRATION 7A-2
Sample Bank Reconciliation

NUGGET MINING COMPANY
Bank Reconciliation
Denver National Bank, November 30, 2001

Balance per bank statement (end of period)			$22,190
Add: Deposit in transit	(1)	$3,680	
Bank error—incorrect check charged to account by bank	(7)	175	3,855
			26,045
Deduct: Outstanding checks	(2)		5,001
Correct cash balance			$21,044
Balance per books			$20,502
Add: Interest collected by the bank	(3)	$ 600	
Error in recording check #7322	(6)	180	780
			21,282
Deduct: Bank service charges	(4)	18	
NSF check returned	(5)	220	238
Correct cash balance			$21,044

The journal entries required to adjust and correct Nugget Mining's books in early December 2001 are taken from the items in the "Balance per books" section and are as follows:

Cash	600	
Interest Revenue		600
(To record interest on Sequoia Co. bonds, collected by bank)		

Go to the Digital Tool for an expanded discussion of a four-column bank reconciliation.

Cash	180	
Accounts Payable		180
(To correct error in recording amount of check #7322)		
Office Expense—Bank Charges	18	
Cash		18
(To record bank service charges for November)		
Accounts Receivable	220	
Cash		220
(To record customer's check returned NSF)		

When the entries are posted, Nugget's cash account will have a balance of $21,044. Nugget should return the Nugent Oil Co. check to Denver National Bank, informing the bank of the error.

KEY TERMS

bank reconciliation, *366*
imprest system for petty cash, *364*
not-sufficient-funds (NSF) checks, *366*

SUMMARY OF LEARNING OBJECTIVE FOR APPENDIX 7A

10 Explain common techniques employed to control cash. The common techniques employed to control cash are: (1) *Using bank accounts:* a company can vary the number and location of banks and the types of accounts to obtain desired control objectives. (2) *The imprest petty cash system:* It may be impractical to require small amounts of various expenses be paid by check, yet some control over them is important. (3) *Physical protection of cash balances:* Adequate control of receipts and disbursements is a part of the protection of cash balances. Every effort should be made to minimize the cash on hand in the office. (4) *Reconciliation of bank balances:* Cash on deposit is not available for count and is proved by preparing a bank reconciliation.

Note: All **asterisked** Questions, Brief Exercises, Exercises, Problems, and Conceptual Cases relate to material covered in the appendix to the chapter.

QUESTIONS

1 What may be included under the heading of "cash"?

2 In what accounts should the following items be classified?
- (a) Coins and currency.
- (b) U.S. Treasury (government) bonds.
- (c) Certificate of deposit.
- (d) Cash in a bank that is in receivership.
- (e) NSF check (returned with bank statement).
- (f) Deposit in foreign bank (exchangeability limited).
- (g) Postdated checks.
- (h) Cash (to be used for retirement of long-term bonds).
- (i) Deposits in transit.
- (j) 100 shares of America Online stock (intention is to sell in one year or less).
- (k) Savings and checking accounts.
- (l) Petty cash.
- (m) Stamps.
- (n) Travel advances.

3 Define a "compensating balance." How should a compensating balance be reported?

4 Michael Tilsen Thomas Inc. reported in a recent annual report "Restricted cash for debt redemption." What section of the balance sheet would report this item?

5 What are the reasons that a company gives trade discounts? Why are trade discounts not recorded in the accounts like cash discounts?

6 What are two methods of recording accounts receivable transactions when a cash discount situation is involved? Which is more theoretically correct? Which is used in practice more of the time? Why?

7 What are the basic problems that occur in the valuation of accounts receivable?

8 Why is the account Allowance for Sales Returns and Allowances sometimes used?

9 What is the theoretical justification of the allowance method as contrasted with the direct write-off method of accounting for bad debts?

10 Indicate how well the percentage-of-sales method and the aging method accomplish the objectives of the allowance method of accounting for bad debts.

11 Of what merit is the contention that the allowance method lacks the objectivity of the direct write-off method? Discuss in terms of accounting's measurement function.

12 Explain how the accounting for bad debts can be used for earnings management.

13 Because of calamitous earthquake losses, Kishwaukee Company, one of your client's oldest and largest customers, suddenly and unexpectedly became bankrupt. Approximately 30% of your client's total sales have been made to Kishwaukee Company during each of the past several years. The amount due from Kishwaukee Company—none of which is collectible—equals 22% of total accounts receivable, an amount that is considerably in excess of what was determined to be an adequate provision for doubtful accounts at the close of the preceding year. How would your client record the write-off of the Kishwaukee Company receivable if it is using the allowance method of accounting for bad debts? Justify your suggested treatment.

14 What is the normal procedure for handling the collection of accounts receivable previously written off using the direct write-off method? The allowance method?

15 On January 1, 2001, John Singer Co. sells property for which it had paid $690,000 to Sargent Company, receiving in return Sargent's zero-interest-bearing note for $1,000,000 payable in 5 years. What entry would John Singer make to record the sale, assuming that John Singer frequently sells similar items of property for a cash sales price of $620,000?

16 What is "imputed interest"? In what situations is it necessary to impute an interest rate for notes receivable? What are the considerations in imputing an appropriate interest rate?

17 Indicate three reasons why a company might sell its receivables to another company.

18 When is the financial components approach to recording the transfers of receivables used? When should a transfer of receivables be recorded as a sale?

19 Hale Hardware is planning to factor some of its receivables. The cash received will be used to pay for inventory purchases. The factor has indicated that it will require "recourse" on the sold receivables. Explain to the controller of Hale Hardware what "recourse" is and how the recourse will be reflected in Hale's financial statements after the sale of the receivables.

20 The Morley Safer Company includes in its trial balance for December 31 an item for Accounts Receivable, $769,000. This balance consists of the following items:

Due from regular customers	$523,000
Refund receivable on prior year's income taxes (an established claim)	15,500
Loans to officers	22,000
Loan to wholly owned subsidiary	45,500
Advances to creditors for goods ordered	61,000
Accounts receivable assigned as security for loans payable	75,000
Notes receivable past due plus interest on these notes	27,000
Total	$769,000

Illustrate how these items should be shown in the balance sheet as of December 31.

21 What is the accounts receivable turnover ratio, and what type of information does it provide?

22 You are evaluating Hawthorn Downs Racetrack for a potential loan. An examination of the notes to the financial statements indicates restricted cash at year-end amounts to $100,000. Explain how you would use this information in evaluating Hawthorn's liquidity.

***23** Distinguish among the following: (1) a general checking account, (2) an imprest bank account, and (3) a lockbox account.

BRIEF EXERCISES

BE7-1 Stowe Enterprises owns the following assets at December 31, 2002:

Cash in bank—savings account	63,000	Checking account balance	17,000
Cash on hand	9,300	Postdated checks	750
Cash refund due from IRS	31,400	Certificates of deposit (180-day)	90,000

What amount should be reported as cash?

BE7-2 Hawthorne Corporation on July 1, 2001, obtained a $4,000,000, 6-month loan at an annual rate of 11% from Salem Bank. As part of the loan agreement, Hawthorne is required to maintain a $500,000 compensating balance in a checking account at Salem Bank. Normally Hawthorne would maintain only a balance of $200,000 in this checking account. The checking account pays 4% interest. Determine the effective interest rate paid by Hawthorne for this loan.

BE7-3 Saturn Company made sales of $25,000 with terms 1/10, n/30. Within the discount period it received payment from customers owing $15,000; after the discount period it received payment from customers owing $10,000. If Saturn uses the gross method of recording sales, prepare journal entries for the transactions described above.

BE7-4 Use the information presented for Saturn Company in BE7-3. If Saturn uses the net method of recording sales, prepare journal entries for the transactions described.

BE7-5 Battle Tank, Incorporated, had net sales in 2001 of $1,200,000. At December 31, 2001, before adjusting entries, the balances in selected accounts were: Accounts Receivable, $250,000 debit, and Allowance for Doubtful Accounts, $2,100 credit. If Battle Tank estimates that 2% of its net sales will prove to be uncollectible, prepare the December 31, 2001, journal entry to record bad debt expense.

BE7-6 Use the information presented for Battle Tank, Incorporated, in BE7-5.

(a) Instead of estimating the uncollectibles at 2% of net sales, assume that 10% of accounts receivable will prove to be uncollectible. Prepare the entry to record bad debts expense.

(b) Instead of estimating uncollectibles at 2% of net sales, assume Battle Tank prepares an aging schedule that estimates total uncollectible accounts at $24,600. Prepare the entry to record bad debts expense.

BE7-7 Addams Family Importers sold goods to Acme Decorators for $20,000 on November 1, 2001, accepting Acme's $20,000, 6-month, 12% note. Prepare Addams' November 1 entry, December 31 annual adjusting entry, and May 1 entry for the collection of the note and interest.

BE7-8 Aero Acrobats lent $15,944 to Afterburner, Inc., accepting Afterburner's 2-year, $20,000, zero-interest-bearing note. The implied interest is 12%. Prepare Aero's journal entries for the initial transaction, recognition of interest each year, and the collection of $20,000 at maturity.

BE7-9 On October 1, 2001, Akira, Inc., assigns $1,000,000 of its accounts receivable to Alisia National Bank as collateral for a $700,000 note. The bank assesses a finance charge of 2% of the receivables assigned and interest on the note of 13%. Prepare the October 1 journal entries for both Akira and Alisia.

BE7-10 Landstalker Enterprises sold $400,000 of accounts receivable to Leander Factors, Inc., on a without recourse basis. Leander Factors assesses a finance charge of 4% of the amount of accounts receivable and retains an amount equal to 5% of accounts receivable. Prepare journal entries for both Landstalker and Leander.

BE7-11 Use the information presented for Landstalker Enterprises in BE7-10. Assume the receivables are sold with recourse. Prepare the journal entry for Landstalker to record the sale, assuming the recourse obligation has a fair value of $6,000.

BE7-12 Keyser Woodcrafters sells $200,000 of receivables to Commercial Factors, Inc. on a recourse basis. Commercial assesses a finance charge of 5% and retains an amount equal to 4% of accounts receivable. Keyser estimates the fair value of the recourse obligation to be $8,000. Prepare the journal entry for Keyser to record the sale.

BE7-13 Use the information presented for Keyser Woodcrafters in BE7-12 but assume that the recourse obligation has a fair value of $4,000, instead of $8,000. Discuss the effects of this change in the value of the recourse obligation on Keyser's balance sheet and income statement.

BE7-14 The financial statements of **General Mills, Inc.** report net sales of $5,416,000,000. Accounts receivable are $277,300,000 at the beginning of the year and $337,800,000 at the end of the year. Compute General Mills' accounts receivable turnover ratio. Compute General Mills' average collection period for accounts receivable in days.

***BE7-15** Genesis Company designated Alex Kidd as petty cash custodian and established a petty cash fund of $200. The fund is reimbursed when the cash in the fund is at $17. Petty cash receipts indicate funds were disbursed for office supplies, $94, and miscellaneous expense, $87. Prepare journal entries for the establishment of the fund and the reimbursement.

***BE7-16** Jaguar Corporation is preparing a bank reconciliation and has identified the following potential reconciling items. For each item, indicate if it is (1) added to balance per bank statement, (2) deducted from balance per bank statement, (3) added to balance per books, or (4) deducted from balance per books.

(a) Deposit in transit, $5,500.
(b) Interest credited to Jaguar's account, $31.
(c) Bank service charges, $25.
(d) Outstanding checks, $7,422.
(e) NSF check returned, $377.

***BE7-17** Use the information presented for Jaguar Corporation in BE7-16. Prepare any entries necessary to make Jaguar's accounting records correct and complete.

EXERCISES

E7-1 (Determining Cash Balance) The controller for Clint Eastwood Co. is attempting to determine the amount of cash to be reported on its December 31, 2001, balance sheet. The following information is provided:

1. Commercial savings account of $600,000 and a commercial checking account balance of $900,000 are held at First National Bank of Yojimbo.
2. Money market fund account held at Volonte Co. (a mutual fund organization) that permits Eastwood to write checks on this balance, $5,000,000.
3. Travel advances of $180,000 for executive travel for the first quarter of next year (employee to reimburse through salary reduction).
4. A separate cash fund in the amount of $1,500,000 is restricted for the retirement of long-term debt.
5. Petty cash fund of $1,000.
6. An I.O.U. from Marianne Koch, a company officer, in the amount of $190,000.
7. A bank overdraft of $110,000 has occurred at one of the banks the company uses to deposit its cash receipts. At the present time, the company has no deposits at this bank.
8. The company has two certificates of deposit, each totaling $500,000. These certificates of deposit have a maturity of 120 days.
9. Eastwood has received a check that is dated January 12, 2002, in the amount of $125,000.
10. Eastwood has agreed to maintain a cash balance of $500,000 at all times at First National Bank of Yojimbo to ensure future credit availability.
11. Eastwood has purchased $2,100,000 of commercial paper of Sergio Leone Co. which is due in 60 days.
12. Currency and coin on hand amounted to $7,700.

Instructions

(a) Compute the amount of cash to be reported on Eastwood Co.'s balance sheet at December 31, 2001.

(b) Indicate the proper reporting for items that are not reported as cash on the December 31, 2001, balance sheet.

E7-2 (Determine Cash Balance) Presented below are a number of independent situations. For each individual situation, determine the amount that should be reported as cash. If the item(s) is not reported as cash, explain the rationale.

1. Checking account balance $925,000; certificate of deposit $1,400,000; cash advance to subsidiary of $980,000; utility deposit paid to gas company $180.
2. Checking account balance $600,000; an overdraft in special checking account at same bank as normal checking account of $17,000; cash held in a bond sinking fund $200,000; petty cash fund $300; coins and currency on hand $1,350.
3. Checking account balance $590,000; postdated check from customer $11,000; cash restricted due to maintaining compensating balance requirement of $100,000; certified check from customer $9,800; postage stamps on hand $620.
4. Checking account balance at bank $37,000; money market balance at mutual fund (has checking privileges) $48,000; NSF check received from customer $800.
5. Checking account balance $700,000; cash restricted for future plant expansion $500,000; short-term Treasury bills $180,000; cash advance received from customer $900 (not included in checking account balance); cash advance of $7,000 to company executive, payable on demand; refundable deposit of $26,000 paid to federal government to guarantee performance on construction contract.

E7-3 (Financial Statement Presentation of Receivables) Jack Gleason Company shows a balance of $181,140 in the Accounts Receivable account on December 31, 2001. The balance consists of the following:

Installment accounts due in 2002	$23,000
Installment accounts due after 2002	34,000
Overpayments to creditors	2,640
Due from regular customers, of which $40,000 represents accounts pledged as security for a bank loan	79,000
Advances to employees	1,500
Advance to subsidiary company (made in 1996)	81,000

Instructions

Illustrate how the information above should be shown on the balance sheet of Jack Gleason Company on December 31, 2001.

E7-4 (Determine Ending Accounts Receivable) Your accounts receivable clerk, Ms. Mitra Adams, to whom you pay a salary of $1,500 per month, has just purchased a new Cadillac. You decided to test the accuracy of the accounts receivable balance of $82,000 as shown in the ledger.

The following information is available for your *first year* in business:

(1) Collections from customers	$198,000
(2) Merchandise purchased	320,000
(3) Ending merchandise inventory	90,000
(4) Goods are marked to sell at 40% above cost	

Instructions

Compute an estimate of the ending balance of accounts receivable from customers that should appear in the ledger and any apparent shortages. Assume that all sales are made on account.

E7-5 (Record Sales Gross and Net) On June 3, Benedict Arnold Company sold to Chester Arthur merchandise having a sale price of $3,000 with terms of 2/10, n/60, f.o.b. shipping point. An invoice totaling $90, terms n/30, was received by Chester on June 8 from the John Booth Transport Service for the freight cost. On receipt of the goods, June 5, Chester notified the Benedict Arnold Company that merchandise costing $500 contained flaws that rendered it worthless; the same day Benedict Arnold Company issued a credit memo covering the worthless merchandise and asked that it be returned at company expense. The freight on the returned merchandise was $25, paid by Benedict Arnold Company on June 7. On June 12, the company received a check for the balance due from Chester Arthur.

Instructions

(a) Prepare journal entries on the Benedict Arnold Company books to record all the events noted above under each of the following bases:

(1) Sales and receivables are entered at gross selling price.

(2) Sales and receivables are entered at net of cash discounts.

(b) Prepare the journal entry under basis 2, assuming that Chester Arthur did not remit payment until July 29.

E7-6 (Computing Bad Debts) At January 1, 2002, the credit balance in the Allowance for Doubtful Accounts of the Van Amos Company was $400,000. For 2002, the provision for doubtful accounts is based on a percentage of net sales. Net sales for 2002 were $70,000,000. On the basis of the latest available facts, the 2002 provision for doubtful accounts is estimated to be 0.8% of net sales. During 2002, uncollectible receivables amounting to $500,000 were written off against the allowance for doubtful accounts.

Instructions

Prepare a schedule computing the balance in Van Amos' Allowance for Doubtful Accounts at December 31, 2002.

E7-7 (Computing Bad Debts and Preparing Journal Entries) The trial balance before adjustment of Patsy Cline Inc. shows the following balances:

	Dr.	Cr.
Accounts Receivable	$90,000	
Allowance for Doubtful Accounts	1,750	
Sales (all on credit)		$680,000
Sales Returns and Allowances	30,000	

Instructions

Give the entry for estimated bad debts assuming that the allowance is to provide for doubtful accounts on the basis of (a) 4% of gross accounts receivable and (b) 1% of net sales.

E7-8 (Bad Debt Reporting) The chief accountant for Emily Dickinson Corporation provides you with the following list of accounts receivable written off in the current year.

Date	Customer	Amount
March 31	E. L. Masters Company	$7,800
June 30	Stephen Crane Associates	6,700
September 30	Amy Lowell's Dress Shop	7,000
December 31	R. Frost, Inc.	9,830

Emily Dickinson Corporation follows the policy of debiting Bad Debt Expense as accounts are written off. The chief accountant maintains that this procedure is appropriate for financial statement purposes because the Internal Revenue Service will not accept other methods for recognizing bad debts.

All of Emily Dickinson Corporation's sales are on a 30-day credit basis. Sales for the current year total $2,200,000, and research has determined that bad debt losses approximate 2% of sales.

Instructions

(a) Do you agree or disagree with Emily Dickinson Corporation policy concerning recognition of bad debt expense? Why or why not?

(b) By what amount would net income differ if bad debt expense was computed using the percentage-of-sales approach?

E7-9 (Bad Debts—Aging) Gerard Manley, Inc. includes the following account among its trade receivables.

Hopkins Co.

1/1	Balance forward	700	1/28	Cash (#1710)	1,100
1/20	Invoice #1710	1,100	4/2	Cash (#2116)	1,350
3/14	Invoice #2116	1,350	4/10	Cash (1/1 Balance)	155
4/12	Invoice #2412	1,710	4/30	Cash (#2412)	1,000
9/5	Invoice #3614	490	9/20	Cash (#3614 and part of #2412)	790
10/17	Invoice #4912	860	10/31	Cash (#4912)	860
11/18	Invoice #5681	2,000	12/1	Cash (#5681)	1,250
12/20	Invoice #6347	800	12/29	Cash (#6347)	800

Instructions

Age the balance and specify any items that apparently require particular attention at year-end.

E7-10 (Journalizing Various Receivable Transactions) Presented below is information related to James Garfield Corp.

July 1 James Garfield Corp. sold to Warren Harding Co. merchandise having a sales price of $8,000 with terms 2/10, net/60. Garfield records its sales and receivables net.

3 Warren Harding Co. returned defective merchandise having a sales price of $700.

5 Accounts receivable of $9,000 (gross) are factored with Andrew Jackson Credit Corp. without recourse at a financing charge of 9%. Cash is received for the proceeds; collections are handled by the finance company. (These accounts were all past the discount period.)

9 Specific accounts receivable of $9,000 (gross) are pledged to Alf Landon Credit Corp. as security for a loan of $6,000 at a finance charge of 6% of the amount of the loan. The finance company will make the collections. (All the accounts receivable are past the discount period.)

Dec. 29 Warren Harding Co. notifies Garfield that it is bankrupt and will pay only 10% of its account. Give the entry to write off the uncollectible balance using the allowance method. (Note: First record the increase in the receivable on July 11 when the discount period passed.)

Instructions

Prepare all necessary entries in general journal form for Garfield Corp.

E7-11 (Assigned Accounts Receivable) Presented below is information related to A. E. Housman Co.

1. Customers' accounts in the amount of $40,000 are assigned (designated) to the W. B. Yeats Finance Company as security for a loan of $30,000. The finance charge is 4% of the amount borrowed.
2. Cash collections on assigned accounts amount to $18,000.
3. Collections on assigned accounts to date, plus a $300 check for interest on the loan, are forwarded to W. B. Yeats Finance Company.
4. Additional collections on assigned accounts amount to $16,200.
5. The loan is paid in full plus additional interest of $120.

Instructions

Prepare entries in journal form for A. E. Housman Co.

E7-12 (Journalizing Various Receivable Transactions) The trial balance before adjustment for Judy Collins Company shows the following balances:

	Dr.	Cr.
Accounts Receivable	$82,000	
Allowance for Doubtful Accounts	2,120	
Sales		$430,000
Sales Returns and Allowances	7,600	

Instructions

Using the data above, give the journal entries required to record each of the following cases (each situation is independent):

1. To obtain additional cash, Collins factors without recourse $25,000 of accounts receivable with Stills Finance. The finance charge is 10% of the amount factored.

2. To obtain a one-year loan of $55,000, Collins assigns $65,000 of specific receivable accounts to Crosby Financial. The finance charge is 8% of the loan; the cash is received and the accounts turned over to Crosby Financial.
3. The company wants to maintain the Allowance for Doubtful Accounts at 5% of gross accounts receivable.
4. The company wishes to increase the allowance by 1½% of net sales.

E7-13 (Transfer of Receivables with Recourse) Ames Quartet Inc. factors receivables with a carrying amount of $200,000 to Joffrey Company for $160,000 on a with recourse basis.

Instructions

The recourse provision has a fair value of $1,000. This transaction should be recorded as a sale. Prepare the appropriate journal entry to record this transaction on the books of Ames Quartet Inc.

E7-14 (Transfer of Receivables with Recourse) Whitney Houston Corporation factors $175,000 of accounts receivable with Kathleen Battle Financing, Inc. on a with recourse basis. Kathleen Battle Financing will collect the receivables. The receivable records are transferred to Kathleen Battle Financing on August 15, 2001. Kathleen Battle Financing assesses a finance charge of 2% of the amount of accounts receivable and also reserves an amount equal to 4% of accounts receivable to cover probable adjustments.

Instructions

(a) What conditions must be met for a transfer of receivables with recourse to be accounted for as a sale?

(b) Assume the conditions from part (a) are met. Prepare the journal entry on August 15, 2001, for Whitney Houston to record the sale of receivables, assuming the recourse obligation has a fair value of $2,000.

E7-15 (Transfer of Receivables Without Recourse) JFK Corp. factors $300,000 of accounts receivable with LBJ Finance Corporation on a without recourse basis on July 1, 2001. The receivable records are transferred to LBJ Finance, which will receive the collections. LBJ Finance assesses a finance charge of 1½% of the amount of accounts receivable and retains an amount equal to 4% of accounts receivable to cover sales discounts, returns, and allowances. The transaction is to be recorded as a sale.

Instructions

(a) Prepare the journal entry on July 1, 2001, for JFK Corp. to record the sale of receivables without recourse.

(b) Prepare the journal entry on July 1, 2001, for LBJ Finance Corporation to record the purchase of receivables without recourse.

E7-16 (Note Transactions at Unrealistic Interest Rates) On July 1, 2002, Agincourt Inc. made two sales:

1. It sold land having a fair market value of $700,000 in exchange for a 4-year noninterest-bearing promissory note in the face amount of $1,101,460. The land is carried on Agincourt's books at a cost of $590,000.
2. It rendered services in exchange for a 3%, 8-year promissory note having a face value of $400,000 (interest payable annually).

Agincourt Inc. recently had to pay 8% interest for money that it borrowed from British National Bank. The customers in these two transactions have credit ratings that require them to borrow money at 12% interest.

Instructions

Record the two journal entries that should be recorded by Agincourt Inc. for the sales transactions above that took place on July 1, 2002.

E7-17 (Note Receivable at Unrealistic Interest Rates) On December 31, 2002, James Fenimore Company sold some of its product to Cooper Company, accepting a $340,000 noninterest-bearing note, receivable in full on December 31, 2005. James Fenimore Company enjoys a high credit rating and, therefore, borrows funds from its several lines of credit at 9%. Cooper Company, however, pays 12% for its borrowed funds. The product sold is carried on the books of James Fenimore Company at a manufactured cost of $180,000. Assume that the effective interest method is used for discount amortization.

Instructions

(a) Prepare journal entries to record the sale on December 31, 2002, by James Fenimore Company. Assume that a perpetual inventory system is used.

(b) Prepare the journal entry on the books of James Fenimore Company for the year 2003 that are necessitated by the sales transaction of December 31, 2002. Preparation of an amortization schedule may be of assistance.

(c) Prepare the journal entry on the books of James Fenimore Company for the year 2004 that are necessitated by the sale on December 31, 2002.

E7-18 (Analysis of Receivables) Presented below is information for Jones Company.

1. Beginning of the year Accounts Receivable balance was $15,000.
2. Net sales for the year were $185,000. (Credit sales were $100,000 of the total sales.) Jones does not offer cash discounts.
3. Collections on accounts receivable during the year were $70,000.

Instructions

(a) Prepare (summary) journal entries to record the items noted above.

(b) Compute Jones' accounts receivable turnover ratio for the year.

(c) Use the turnover ratio computed in (b) to analyze Jones' liquidity. The turnover ratio last year was 13.65.

E7-19 (Transfer of Receivables) Use the information for Jones Company as presented in E7-18. Jones is planning to factor some accounts receivable at the end of the year. Accounts totaling $25,000 will be transferred to Credit Factors, Inc. with recourse. Credit Factors will retain 5% of the balances and assesses a finance charge of 4%. The fair value of the recourse obligation is $1,200.

Instructions

(a) Prepare the journal entry to record the sale of receivables.

(b) Compute Jones' accounts receivables turnover ratio for the year, assuming the receivables are sold, and discuss how factoring of receivables affects the turnover ratio.

***E7-20 (Petty Cash)** Carolyn Keene, Inc. decided to establish a petty cash fund to help ensure internal control over its small cash expenditures. The following information is available for the month of April.

1. On April 1, it established a petty cash fund in the amount of $200.
2. A summary of the petty cash expenditures made by the petty cash custodian as of April 10 is as follows:

Delivery charges paid on merchandise purchased	$60.00
Supplies purchased and used	25.00
Postage expense	33.00
I.O.U. from employees	17.00
Miscellaneous expense	36.00

The petty cash fund was replenished on April 10. The balance in the fund was $27.

3. The petty cash fund balance was increased $100 to $300 on April 20.

Instructions

Prepare the journal entries to record transactions related to petty cash for the month of April.

***E7-21 (Petty Cash)** The petty cash fund of Fonzarelli's Auto Repair Service, a sole proprietorship, contains the following:

1. Coins and currency		$15.20
2. Postage stamps		2.90
3. An I.O.U. from Richie Cunningham, an employee, for cash advance		40.00
4. Check payable to Fonzarelli's Auto Repair from Pottsie Weber, an employee, marked NSF		34.00
5. Vouchers for the following:		
Stamps	$ 20.00	
Two Rose Bowl tickets for Nick Fonzarelli	170.00	
Printer cartridge	14.35	204.35
		$296.45

The general ledger account Petty Cash has a balance of $300.00.

Instructions

Prepare the journal entry to record the reimbursement of the petty cash fund.

***E7-22 (Bank Reconciliation and Adjusting Entries)** Angela Lansbury Company deposits all receipts and makes all payments by check. The following information is available from the cash records.

June 30 Bank Reconciliation

Balance per bank	$7,000
Add: Deposits in transit	1,540
Deduct: Outstanding checks	(2,000)
Balance per books	$6,540

Month of July Results

	Per Bank	Per Books
Balance July 31	$8,650	$9,250
July deposits	5,000	5,810
July checks	4,000	3,100
July note collected (not included in July deposits)	1,000	—
July bank service charge	15	—
July NSF check from a customer, returned by the bank (recorded by bank as a charge)	335	—

Instructions

(a) Prepare a bank reconciliation going from balance per bank and balance per book to correct cash balance.

(b) Prepare the general journal entry or entries to correct the Cash account.

***E7-23 (Bank Reconciliation and Adjusting Entries)** Logan Bruno Company has just received the August 31, 2001, bank statement, which is summarized below:

County National Bank	Disbursements	Receipts	Balance
Balance, August 1			$ 9,369
Deposits during August		$32,200	41,569
Note collected for depositor, including $40 interest		1,040	42,609
Checks cleared during August	$34,500		8,109
Bank service charges	20		8,089
Balance, August 31			8,089

The general ledger Cash account contained the following entries for the month of August:

Cash			
Balance, August 1	10,050	Disbursements in August	34,903
Receipts during August	35,000		

Deposits in transit at August 31 are $3,800, and checks outstanding at August 31 are determined to total $1,050. Cash on hand at August 31 is $310. The bookkeeper improperly entered one check in the books at $146.50 which was written for $164.50 for supplies (expense); it cleared the bank during the month of August.

Instructions

(a) Prepare a bank reconciliation dated August 31, 2001, proceeding to a correct balance.

(b) Prepare any entries necessary to make the books correct and complete.

(c) What amount of cash should be reported in the August 31 balance sheet?

PROBLEMS

P7-1 (Determine Proper Cash Balance) Dumaine Equipment Co. closes its books regularly on December 31, but at the end of 2001 it held its cash book open so that a more favorable balance sheet could be prepared for credit purposes. Cash receipts and disbursements for the first 10 days of January were recorded as December transactions. The following information is given.

1. January cash receipts recorded in the December cash book totaled $39,640, of which $22,000 represents cash sales and $17,640 represents collections on account for which cash discounts of $360 were given.
2. January cash disbursements recorded in the December check register liquidated accounts payable of $26,450 on which discounts of $250 were taken.
3. The ledger has not been closed for 2001.
4. The amount shown as inventory was determined by physical count on December 31, 2001.

Instructions

(a) Prepare any entries you consider necessary to correct Dumaine's accounts at December 31.

(b) To what extent was Dumaine Equipment Co. able to show a more favorable balance sheet at December 31 by holding its cash book open? (Use ratio analysis.) Assume that the balance sheet that was prepared by the company showed the following amounts:

	Dr.	Cr.
Cash	$39,000	
Receivables	42,000	
Inventories	67,000	
Accounts payable		$45,000
Other current liabilities		14,200

P7-2 (Bad Debt Reporting) Presented below are a series of unrelated situations.

1. Spock Company's unadjusted trial balance at December 31, 2001, included the following accounts:

	Debit	Credit
Allowance for doubtful accounts	$ 4,000	
Sales		$1,500,000
Sales returns and allowances	70,000	

Spock Company estimates its bad debt expense to be 1½% of net sales. Determine its bad debt expense for 2001.

2. An analysis and aging of Scotty Corp. accounts receivable at December 31, 2001, disclosed the following:

Amounts estimated to be uncollectible	$ 180,000
Accounts receivable	1,750,000
Allowance for doubtful accounts (per books)	125,000

What is the net realizable value of Scotty's receivables at December 31, 2001?

3. Uhura Co. provides for doubtful accounts based on 3% of credit sales. The following data are available for 2001.

Credit sales during 2001	$2,100,000
Allowance for doubtful accounts 1/1/01	17,000
Collection of accounts written off in prior years (customer credit was reestablished)	8,000
Customer accounts written off as uncollectible during 2001	30,000

What is the balance in the Allowance for Doubtful Accounts at December 31, 2001?

4. At the end of its first year of operations, December 31, 2001, Chekov Inc. reported the following information:

Accounts receivable, net of allowance for doubtful accounts	$950,000
Customer accounts written off as uncollectible during 2001	24,000
Bad debt expense for 2001	84,000

What should be the balance in accounts receivable at December 31, 2001, before subtracting the allowance for doubtful accounts?

5. The following accounts were taken from Chappel Inc.'s balance sheet at December 31, 2001.

	Debit	Credit
Net credit sales		$750,000
Allowance for doubtful accounts	$ 14,000	
Accounts receivable	410,000	

If doubtful accounts are 3% of accounts receivable, determine the bad debt expense to be reported for 2001.

Instructions

Answer the questions relating to each of the five independent situations as requested.

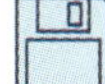

P7-3 (Bad Debt Reporting—Aging) Ignace Paderewski Corporation operates in an industry that has a high rate of bad debts. Before any year-end adjustments, the balance in Paderewski's Accounts Receivable account was $555,000 and the Allowance for Doubtful Accounts had a credit balance of $35,000. The year-end balance reported in the balance sheet for the Allowance for Doubtful Accounts will be based on the aging schedule shown below.

Days Account Outstanding	Amount	Probability of Collection
Less than 16 days	$300,000	.98
Between 16 and 30 days	100,000	.90
Between 31 and 45 days	80,000	.85
Between 46 and 60 days	40,000	.75
Between 61 and 75 days	20,000	.40
Over 75 days	15,000	.00

Instructions

(a) What is the appropriate balance for the Allowance for Doubtful Accounts at year-end?

(b) Show how accounts receivable would be presented on the balance sheet.

(c) What is the dollar effect of the year-end bad debt adjustment on the before-tax income?

(CMA adapted)

P7-4 (Bad Debt Reporting) From inception of operations to December 31, 2002, Blaise Pascal Corporation provided for uncollectible accounts receivable under the allowance method: provisions were made monthly at 2% of credit sales; bad debts written off were charged to the allowance account; recoveries of bad debts previously written off were credited to the allowance account; and no year-end adjustments to the allowance account were made. Pascal's usual credit terms are net 30 days.

The balance in the Allowance for Doubtful Accounts was $154,000 at January 1, 2002. During 2002 credit sales totaled $9,000,000, interim provisions for doubtful accounts were made at 2% of credit sales, $95,000 of bad debts were written off, and recoveries of accounts previously written off amounted to $15,000. Pascal installed a computer facility in November 2002 and an aging of accounts receivable was prepared for the first time as of December 31, 2002. A summary of the aging is as follows:

Classification by Month of Sale	Balance in Each Category	Estimated % Uncollectible
November–December 2002	$1,080,000	2%
July–October	650,000	10%
January–June	420,000	25%
Prior to 1/1/02	150,000	70%
	$2,300,000	

Based on the review of collectibility of the account balances in the "prior to 1/1/02" aging category, additional receivables totaling $60,000 were written off as of December 31, 2002. The 70% uncollectible estimate applies to the remaining $90,000 in the category. Effective with the year ended December 31, 2002, Pascal adopted a new accounting method for estimating the allowance for doubtful accounts at the amount indicated by the year-end aging analysis of accounts receivable.

Instructions

(a) Prepare a schedule analyzing the changes in the Allowance for Doubtful Accounts for the year ended December 31, 2002. Show supporting computations in good form. (*Hint:* In computing the 12/31/02 allowance, subtract the $60,000 write-off).

(b) Prepare the journal entry for the year-end adjustment to the Allowance for Doubtful Accounts balance as of December 31, 2002.

(AICPA adapted)

P7-5 (Bad Debt Reporting) Presented below is information related to the Accounts Receivable accounts of Gulistan Inc. during the current year 2002.

1. An aging schedule of the accounts receivable as of December 31, 2002, is as follows:

Age	Net Debit Balance	% to Be Applied after Correction Is Made
Under 60 days	$172,342	1%
61–90 days	136,490	3%
91–120 days	39,924*	6%
Over 120 days	23,644	$4,200 definitely uncollectible; estimated remainder uncollectible is 25%
	$372,400	

*The $2,740 write-off of receivables is related to the 91-to-120 day category.

2. The Accounts Receivable control account has a debit balance of $372,400 on December 31, 2002.

3. Two entries were made in the Bad Debt Expense account during the year: (1) a debit on December 31 for the amount credited to Allowance for Doubtful Accounts, and (2) a credit for $2,740 on November 3, 2002, and a debit to Allowance for Doubtful Accounts because of a bankruptcy.
4. The Allowance for Doubtful Accounts is as follows for 2002:

Allowance for Doubtful Accounts					
Nov. 3	Uncollectible accounts written off	2,740	Jan. 1	Beginning balance	8,750
			Dec. 31	5% of $372,400	18,620

5. A credit balance exists in the Accounts Receivable (61–90 days) of $4,840, which represents an advance on a sales contract.

Instructions

Assuming that the books have not been closed for 2002, make the necessary correcting entries.

P7-6 (Journalize Various Account and Notes Receivable Transactions) The balance sheet of Antonio Vivaldi Company at December 31, 2001, includes the following:

Notes receivable	$ 36,000	
Accounts receivable	182,100	
Less: Allowance for doubtful accounts	17,300	200,800

Transactions in 2002 include the following:

1. Accounts receivable of $138,000 were collected including accounts of $40,000 on which 2% sales discounts were allowed.
2. $6,300 was received in payment of an account which was written off the books as worthless in 2000. (*Hint:* Reestablish the receivable account.)
3. Customer accounts of $17,500 were written off during the year.
4. At year-end the Allowance for Doubtful Accounts was estimated to need a balance of $20,000. This estimate is based on an analysis of aged accounts receivable.

Instructions

Prepare all journal entries necessary to reflect the transactions above.

P7-7 (Assigned Accounts Receivable—Journal Entries) Nikos Company finances some of its current operations by assigning accounts receivable to a finance company. On July 1, 2002, it assigned, under guarantee, specific accounts amounting to $100,000; the finance company advanced to Nikos 80% of the accounts assigned (20% of the total to be withheld until the finance company has made its full recovery), less a finance charge of ½% of the total accounts assigned.

On July 31 Nikos Company received a statement that the finance company had collected $55,000 of these accounts and had made an additional charge of ½% of the total accounts outstanding as of July 31. This charge is to be deducted at the time of the first remittance due Nikos Company from the finance company. (*Hint:* Make entries at this time.) On August 31, 2002, Nikos Company received a second statement from the finance company, together with a check for the amount due. The statement indicated that the finance company had collected an additional $30,000 and had made a further charge of ½% of the balance outstanding as of August 31.

Instructions

Make all entries on the books of Nikos Company that are involved in the transactions above.

(AICPA adapted)

P7-8 (Notes Receivable Journal Entries) Heinrich Boll Sports Company produces soccer, football, and track shoes. The treasurer has recently completed negotiations in which Heinrich Boll Sports agrees to loan Max Frisch Company, a leather supplier, $500,000. Max Frisch Company will issue a noninterest-bearing note due in 5 years (a 12% interest rate is appropriate), and has agreed to furnish Heinrich Boll Sports with leather at prices that are 10% lower than those usually charged.

Instructions

(a) Prepare the accounting entry to record this transaction on Heinrich Boll Sports Company's books.
(b) Determine the balances at the end of each year the note is outstanding for the following accounts for Heinrich Boll Sports Company: Notes receivable, Unamortized discount, Interest revenue.

P7-9 (Notes Receivable Journal Entries) On December 31, 2002, Menachem Inc. rendered services to Begin Corporation at an agreed price of $91,844.10, accepting $36,000 down and agreeing to accept the balance in four equal installments of $18,000 receivable each December 31. An assumed interest rate of 11% is imputed.

Instructions

Prepare the entries that would be recorded by Menachem Inc. for the sale and for the receipts and interest on the following dates. (Assume that the effective interest method is used for amortization purposes).

(a) December 31, 2002. **(c)** December 31, 2004. **(e)** December 31, 2006.
(b) December 31, 2003. **(d)** December 31, 2005.

P7-10 (Comprehensive Accounts Receivable) Jair Lynch Supply produces paints and related products for sale to the construction industry throughout the southwest United States. While sales have remained relatively stable despite a decline in the amount of new construction, there has been a noticeable change in the timeliness with which Lynch's customers are paying their bills.

Lynch sells its products on payment terms of 2/10, n/30. In the past, over 75 percent of the credit customers have taken advantage of the discount by paying within 10 days of the invoice date. During the fiscal year ended November 30, 2001, the number of customers taking the full 30 days to pay has increased. Current indications are that less than 60% of the customers are now taking the discount. Uncollectible accounts as a percentage of total credit sales have risen from the 1.5% provided in past years to 4.0% in the current year.

In response to a request for more information on the deterioration of accounts receivable collections, Lynch's controller has prepared the following report.

JAIR LYNCH SUPPLY
Accounts Receivable Collections
November 30, 2001

The fact that some credit accounts will prove uncollectible is normal, and annual bad debt write-offs had been 1.5% of total credit sales for many years. However, during the 2000–01 fiscal year, this percentage increased to 4.0%. The current accounts receivable balance is $1,500,000, and the condition of this balance in terms of age and probability of collection is shown below.

Proportion of Total	Age Categories	Probability of Collection
64.0%	1 to 10 days	99.0%
18.0	11 to 30 days	97.5
8.0	Past due 31 to 60 days	95.0
5.0	Past due 61 to 120 days	80.0
3.0	Past due 121 to 180 days	65.0
2.0	Past due over 180 days	20.0

At the beginning of the fiscal year, December 1, 2000, the Allowance for Doubtful Accounts had a credit balance of $27,300. Lynch has provided for a monthly bad debt expense accrual during the fiscal year just ended based on the assumption that 4% of total credit sales will be uncollectible. Total credit sales for the 2000–01 fiscal year amounted to $8,000,000, and write-offs of uncollectible accounts during the year totaled $292,500.

Instructions

(a) Prepare an accounts receivable aging schedule at November 30, 2001, for Jair Lynch Supply using the age categories identified in the controller's report showing:
 (1) the amount of accounts receivable outstanding for each age category and in total.
 (2) the estimated amount that is uncollectible for each category and in total.

(b) Compute the amount of the year-end adjustment necessary to bring Jair Lynch Supply's Allowance for Doubtful Accounts to the balance indicated by the aging analysis.

(c) Calculate the net realizable value of Jair Lynch Supply's accounts receivable at November 30, 2001. Ignore any discounts that may be applicable to the accounts not yet due.

(d) Describe the accounting to be performed for subsequent collections of previously written-off accounts receivable.

(CMA adapted)

P7-11 (Comprehensive Receivables Problem) Connecticut Inc. had the following long-term receivable account balances at December 31, 2001:

Note receivable from sale of division	$1,800,000
Note receivable from officer	400,000

Transactions during 2002 and other information relating to Connecticut's long-term receivables were as follows:

1. The $1,800,000 note receivable is dated May 1, 2001, bears interest at 9%, and represents the balance of the consideration received from the sale of Connecticut's electronics division to New York

Company. Principal payments of $600,000 plus appropriate interest are due on May 1, 2002, 2003, and 2004. The first principal and interest payment was made on May 1, 2002. Collection of the note installments is reasonably assured.

2. The $400,000 note receivable is dated December 31, 2001, bears interest at 8%, and is due on December 31, 2004. The note is due from Marcus Camby, president of Connecticut Inc. and is collateralized by 10,000 shares of Connecticut's common stock. Interest is payable annually on December 31, and all interest payments were paid on their due dates through December 31, 2002. The quoted market price of Connecticut's common stock was $45 per share on December 31, 2002.
3. On April 1, 2002, Connecticut sold a patent to Pennsylvania Company in exchange for a $200,000 noninterest-bearing note due on April 1, 2004. There was no established exchange price for the patent, and the note had no ready market. The prevailing rate of interest for a note of this type at April 1, 2002, was 12%. The present value of $1 for two periods at 12% is 0.797 (use this factor). The patent had a carrying value of $40,000 at January 1, 2002, and the amortization for the year ended December 31, 2002, would have been $8,000. The collection of the note receivable from Pennsylvania is reasonably assured.
4. On July 1, 2002, Connecticut sold a parcel of land to Harrisburg Company for $200,000 under an installment sale contract. Harrisburg made a $60,000 cash down payment on July 1, 2002, and signed a 4-year 11% note for the $140,000 balance. The equal annual payments of principal and interest on the note will be $45,125 payable on July 1, 2003, through July 1, 2006. The land could have been sold at an established cash price of $200,000. The cost of the land to Connecticut was $150,000. Circumstances are such that the collection of the installments on the note is reasonably assured.

Instructions

(a) Prepare the long-term receivables section of Connecticut's balance sheet at December 31, 2002.

(b) Prepare a schedule showing the current portion of the long-term receivables and accrued interest receivable that would appear in Connecticut's balance sheet at December 31, 2002.

(c) Prepare a schedule showing interest revenue from the long-term receivables that would appear on Connecticut's income statement for the year ended December 31, 2002.

P7-12 (Various Receivables Transactions) Mike Horn Company manufactures sweatshirts for sale to athletic-wear retailers. The following summary information was available for Horn for the year ended December 31, 2001:

Cash	$20,000
Trade accounts receivable (net)	40,000
Inventories	85,000
Accounts payable	65,000
Other current liabilities	15,000

Part 1

During 2002, Horn had the following transactions:

1. Total sales were $450,000.
2. $200,000 of total sales were made on a credit basis (trade accounts receivable).
3. On June 30, sales of $50,000 to a major customer were settled with Horn accepting a 1-year $50,000 note, bearing 11% interest, payable at maturity.
4. Horn collected $160,000 on trade accounts receivable during the year.
5. At December 31, 2002, Cash has a balance of $15,000, Inventories had a balance of $80,000, Accounts Payable were $70,000, and other current liabilities were $16,000.

Instructions

(a) Prepare (summary) journal entries to record the items noted above.

(b) Compute the current ratio and the receivables turnover ratio for Horn at December 31, 2002. Use these measures to analyze Horn's liquidity. The receivables turnover ratio last year was 10.37.

Part 2

Now assume that at year-end 2002, Horn enters into the following transactions related to the company's receivables:

1. Horn transfers the note receivable to Plains Bank for $50,000 cash plus accrued interest. Given the creditworthiness of Horn's customer, the bank accepts the note without recourse and assesses a finance charge of 1.5%.
2. Horn factors some accounts receivable at the end of the year. Accounts totaling $40,000 are transferred to First Factors, Inc. with recourse. First Factors will receive the collections from Horn's customers and retains 6% of the balances. Horn is assessed a finance charge of 4% on this transfer. The fair value of the recourse obligation is $4,000.

Instructions

(c) Prepare the journal entry to record the transfer of the note receivable to Plains Bank.
(d) Prepare the journal entry to record the sale of receivables.
(e) Compute the current ratio and the receivables turnover ratio for Horn at December 31, 2002. Use these measures to analyze Horn's liquidity. The receivables turnover ratio last year was 10.37.
(f) Discuss how the ratio analysis in (e) would be affected if Horn had transferred the receivables in a secured borrowing transaction.

P7-13 (Income Effects of Receivables Transactions) Radisson Company requires additional cash for its business. Radisson has decided to use its accounts receivable to raise the additional cash and has asked you to determine the income statement effects of the following contemplated transactions.

1. On July 1, 2001, Radisson assigned $400,000 of accounts receivable to Stickum Finance Company. Radisson received an advance from Stickum of 85% of the assigned accounts receivable less a commission of 3% on the advance. Prior to December 31, 2001, Radisson collected $220,000 on the assigned accounts receivable, and remitted $232,720 to Stickum, $12,720 of which represented interest on the advance from Stickum.
2. On December 1, 2001, Radisson sold $300,000 of net accounts receivable to Wunsch Company for $250,000. The receivables were sold outright on a without recourse basis.
3. On December 31, 2001, an advance of $120,000 was received from First Bank by pledging $160,000 of Radisson's accounts receivable. Radisson's first payment to First Bank is due on January 30, 2002.

Instructions

Prepare a schedule showing the income statement effects for the year ended December 31, 2001, as a result of the above facts.

***P7-14 (Petty Cash, Bank Reconciliation)** Bill Howe is reviewing the cash accounting for Kappeler, Inc., a local mailing service. Howe's review will focus on the petty cash account and the bank reconciliation for the month ended May 31, 2001. He has collected the following information from Kappeler's bookkeeper for this task.

Petty Cash

1. The petty cash fund was established on May 10, 2001, in the amount of $250.00.
2. Expenditures from the fund by the custodian as of May 31, 2001, were evidenced by approved receipts for the following:

Postage expense	$33.00
Mailing labels and other supplies	75.00
I.O.U. from employees	30.00
Shipping charges	57.45
Newspaper advertising	22.80
Miscellaneous expense	15.35

On May 31, 2001, the petty cash fund was replenished and increased to $300.00; currency and coin in the fund at that time totaled $16.40.

Bank Reconciliation

THIRD NATIONAL BANK
Bank Statement

	Disbursements	Receipts	Balance
Balance, May 1, 2001			$8,769
Deposits		$28,000	
Note payment direct from customer (interest of $30)		930	
Checks cleared during May	$31,150		
Bank service charges	27		
Balance, May 31, 2001			6,522

Kappeler's Cash Account

Balance, May 1, 2001	$ 9,150
Deposits during May 2001	31,000
Checks written during May 2001	(31,835)

Deposits in transit are determined to be $3,000, and checks outstanding at May 31 total $550. Cash on hand (besides petty cash) at May 31, 2001, is $246.

Instructions

(a) Prepare the journal entries to record the transactions related to the petty cash fund for May.

(b) Prepare a bank reconciliation dated May 31, 2001, proceeding to a correct balance, and prepare the journal entries necessary to make the books correct and complete.

(c) What amount of cash should be reported in the May 31, 2001, balance sheet?

***P7-15 (Bank Reconciliation and Adjusting Entries)** The cash account of Jose Orozco Co. showed a ledger balance of $3,969.85 on June 30, 2001. The bank statement as of that date showed a balance of $4,150. Upon comparing the statement with the cash records, the following facts were determined:

1. There were bank service charges for June of $25.00.
2. A bank memo stated that Bao Dai's note for $900 and interest of $36 had been collected on June 29, and the bank had made a charge of $5.50 on the collection. (No entry had been made on Orozco's books when Bao Dai's note was sent to the bank for collection.)
3. Receipts for June 30 for $2,890 were not deposited until July 2.
4. Checks outstanding on June 30 totaled $2,136.05.
5. The bank had charged the Orozco Co.'s account for a customer's uncollectible check amounting to $453.20 on June 29.
6. A customer's check for $90 had been entered as $60 in the cash receipts journal by Orozco on June 15.
7. Check no. 742 in the amount of $491 had been entered in the cashbook as $419, and check no. 747 in the amount of $58.20 had been entered as $582. Both checks had been issued to pay for purchases of equipment.

Instructions

(a) Prepare a bank reconciliation dated June 30, 2001, proceeding to a correct cash balance.

(b) Prepare any entries necessary to make the books correct and complete.

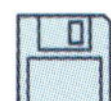
***P7-16 (Bank Reconciliation and Adjusting Entries)** Presented below is information related to Tanizaki Inc.

Balance per books at October 31, $41,847.85; receipts, $173,523.91; disbursements, $166,193.54. Balance per bank statement November 30, $56,274.20.

The following checks were outstanding at November 30:

1224	$1,635.29
1230	2,468.30
1232	3,625.15
1233	482.17

Included with the November bank statement and not recorded by the company were a bank debit memo for $27.40 covering bank charges for the month, a debit memo for $572.13 for a customer's check returned and marked NSF, and a credit memo for $1,400 representing bond interest collected by the bank in the name of Tanizaki Inc. Cash on hand at November 30 recorded and awaiting deposit amounted to $1,915.40.

Instructions

(a) Prepare a bank reconciliation (to the correct balance) at November 30, 2001, for Tanizaki Inc. from the information above.

(a) Prepare any journal entries required to adjust the cash account at November 30.

***P7-17 (Bank Reconciliation)** Presented below is information related to Junichiro Industries.

JUNICHIRO INDUSTRIES
Bank Reconciliation
May 31, 2001

Balance per bank statement		$30,928.46
Less: Outstanding checks		
No. 6124	$2,125.00	
No. 6138	932.65	
No. 6139	960.57	
No. 6140	1,420.00	5,438.22
		25,490.24
Add deposit in transit		4,710.56
Balance per books (correct balance)		$30,200.80

Check Register—June

Date	Payee	No.	Invoice Amount	Discount	Cash
June 1	Ren Mfg.	6141	$ 237.50		$ 237.50
1	Stimpy Mfg.	6142	915.00	$ 9.15	905.85
8	Rugrats Co., Inc.	6143	122.90	2.45	120.45
9	Ren Mfg.	6144	306.40		306.40
10	Petty Cash	6145	89.93		89.93
17	Muppet Babies Photo	6146	706.00	14.12	691.88
22	Hey Dude Publishing	6147	447.50		447.50
23	Payroll Account	6148	4,130.00		4,130.00
25	Dragnet Tools, Inc.	6149	390.75	3.91	386.84
28	Double Dare Insurance Agency	6150	1,050.00		1,050.00
28	Get Smart Construction	6151	2,250.00		2,250.00
29	MMT, Inc.	6152	750.00		750.00
30	Lassie Co.	6153	400.00	8.00	392.00
			$11,795.98	$37.63	$11,758.35

NICKELODEON STATE BANK
Bank Statement
General Checking Account of Junichiro Industries—June 2001

Debits			Date	Credits	Balance
					$30,928.46
$2,125.00	$ 237.50	$ 905.85	June 1	$4,710.56	32,370.67
932.65	120.45		12	1,507.06	32,824.63
1,420.00	447.50	306.40	23	1,458.55	32,109.28
4,130.00		11.05 (BC)	26		27,968.23
89.93	2,250.00	1,050.00	28	4,157.48	28,735.78

Cash received June 29 and 30 and deposited in the mail for the general checking account June 30 amounted to $4,607.96. Because the cash account balance at June 30 is not given, it must be calculated from other information in the problem.

Instructions
From the information above, prepare a bank reconciliation (to the correct balance) as of June 30, 2001, for Junichiro Industries.

CONCEPTUAL CASES

C7-1 (Bad Debt Accounting) Ariel Company has significant amounts of trade accounts receivable. Ariel uses the allowance method to estimate bad debts instead of the direct write-off method. During the year, some specific accounts were written off as uncollectible, and some that were previously written off as uncollectible were collected.

Instructions

(a) What are the deficiencies of the direct write-off method?

(b) What are the two basic allowance methods used to estimate bad debts, and what is the theoretical justification for each?

(c) How should Ariel account for the collection of the specific accounts previously written off as uncollectible?

C7-2 (Various Receivable Accounting Issues) Anne Archer Company uses the net method of accounting for sales discounts. Anne Archer also offers trade discounts to various groups of buyers.

On August 1, 2001, Archer sold some accounts receivable on a without recourse basis. Archer incurred a finance charge.

Archer also has some notes receivable bearing an appropriate rate of interest. The principal and total interest are due at maturity. The notes were received on October 1, 2001, and mature on September 30, 2003. Archer's operating cycle is less than one year.

Instructions

(a) (1) Using the net method, how should Archer account for the sales discounts at the date of sale? What is the rationale for the amount recorded as sales under the net method?

(2) Using the net method, what is the effect on Archer's sales revenues and net income when customers do not take the sales discounts?

(b) What is the effect of trade discounts on sales revenues and accounts receivable? Why?

(c) How should Archer account for the accounts receivable factored on August 1, 2001? Why?

(d) How should Archer account for the note receivable and the related interest on December 31, 2001? Why?

C7-3 (Bad Debt Reporting Issues) Ben Gazarra conducts a wholesale merchandising business that sells approximately 5,000 items per month with a total monthly average sales value of $250,000. Its annual bad debt ratio has been approximately 1½% of sales. In recent discussions with his bookkeeper, Mr. Gazarra has become confused by all the alternatives apparently available in handling the Allowance for Doubtful Accounts balance. The following information has been shown.

1. An allowance can be set up (a) on the basis of a percentage of sales or (b) on the basis of a valuation of all past due or otherwise questionable accounts receivable—those considered uncollectible being charged to such allowance at the close of the accounting period or specific items charged off directly against (1) Gross Sales, or to (2) Bad Debt Expense in the year in which they are determined to be uncollectible.
2. Collection agency and legal fees, and so on, incurred in connection with the attempted recovery of bad debts can be charged to (a) Bad Debt Expense, (b) Allowance for Doubtful Accounts, (c) Legal Expense, or (d) General Expense.
3. Debts previously written off in whole or in part but currently recovered can be credited to (a) Other Revenue, (b) Bad Debt Expense, or (c) Allowance for Doubtful Accounts.

Instructions

Which of the foregoing methods would you recommend to Mr. Gazarra in regard to (1) allowances and charge-offs, (2) collection expenses, and (3) recoveries? State briefly and clearly the reasons supporting your recommendations.

C7-4 (Basic Note and Accounts Receivable Transactions)

Part 1

On July 1, 2002, Eve Arden Company, a calendar-year company, sold special-order merchandise on credit and received in return an interest-bearing note receivable from the customer. Eve Arden Company will receive interest at the prevailing rate for a note of this type. Both the principal and interest are due in one lump sum on June 30, 2003.

Instructions

When should Eve Arden Company report interest income from the note receivable? Discuss the rationale for your answer.

Part 2

On December 31, 2002, Eve Arden Company had significant amounts of accounts receivable as a result of credit sales to its customers. Eve Arden Company uses the allowance method based on credit sales to estimate bad debts. Past experience indicates that 2% of credit sales normally will not be collected. This pattern is expected to continue.

Instructions

(a) Discuss the rationale for using the allowance method based on credit sales to estimate bad debts. Contrast this method with the allowance method based on the balance in the trade receivables accounts.

(b) How should Eve Arden Company report the allowance for bad debts account on its balance sheet at December 31, 2002? Also, describe the alternatives, if any, for presentation of bad debt expense in Eve Arden Company's 2002 income statement.

(AICPA adapted)

C7-5 (Bad Debt Reporting Issues) The Rosita Arenas Company sells office equipment and supplies to many organizations in the city and surrounding area on contract terms of 2/10, n/30. In the past, over

75% of the credit customers have taken advantage of the discount by paying within 10 days of the invoice date.

The number of customers taking the full 30 days to pay has increased within the last year. Current indications are that less than 60% of the customers are now taking the discount. Bad debts as a percentage of gross credit sales have risen from the 1.5% provided in past years to about 4% in the current year.

The controller has responded to a request for more information on the deterioration in collections of accounts receivable with the report reproduced below.

THE ROSITA ARENAS COMPANY
Finance Committee Report—Accounts Receivable Collections
May 31, 2002

The fact that some credit accounts will prove uncollectible is normal. Annual bad debt write-offs have been 1.5% of gross credit sales over the past five years. During the last fiscal year, this percentage increased to slightly less than 4%. The current Accounts Receivable balance is $1,600,000. The condition of this balance in terms of age and probability of collection is as follows:

Proportion of Total	Age Categories	Probability of Collection
68%	not yet due	99%
15%	less than 30 days past due	96½%
8%	30 to 60 days past due	95%
5%	61 to 120 days past due	91%
2½%	121 to 180 days past due	70%
1½%	over 180 days past due	20%

The Allowance for Doubtful Accounts had a credit balance of $43,300 on June 1, 2001. The Rosita Arenas Company has provided for a monthly bad debts expense accrual during the current fiscal year based on the assumption that 4% of gross credit sales will be uncollectible. Total gross credit sales for the 2001–02 fiscal year amounted to $4,000,000. Write-offs of bad accounts during the year totaled $145,000.

Instructions

(a) Prepare an accounts receivable aging schedule for The Rosita Arenas Company using the age categories identified in the controller's report to the Finance Committee showing:
  (1) The amount of accounts receivable outstanding for each age category and in total.
  (2) The estimated amount that is uncollectible for each category and in total.

(b) Compute the amount of the year-end adjustment necessary to bring Allowance for Doubtful Accounts to the balance indicated by the age analysis. Then prepare the necessary journal entry to adjust the accounting records.

(c) In a recessionary environment with tight credit and high interest rates:
  (1) Identify steps The Rosita Arenas Company might consider to improve the accounts receivable situation.
  (2) Then evaluate each step identified in terms of the risks and costs involved.

(CMA adapted)

C7-6 (Sale of Notes Receivable) Sergey Luzov Wholesalers Co. sells industrial equipment for a standard 3-year note receivable. Revenue is recognized at time of sale. Each note is secured by a lien on the equipment and has a face amount equal to the equipment's list price. Each note's stated interest rate is below the customer's market rate at date of sale. All notes are to be collected in three equal annual installments beginning one year after sale. Some of the notes are subsequently sold to a bank with recourse, some are subsequently sold without recourse, and some are retained by Luzov. At year end, Luzov evaluates all outstanding notes receivable and provides for estimated losses arising from defaults.

Instructions

(a) What is the appropriate valuation basis for Luzov's notes receivable at the date it sells equipment?

(b) How should Luzov account for the sale, without recourse, of a February 1, 2001, note receivable sold on May 1, 2001? Why is it appropriate to account for it in this way?

(c) At December 31, 2001, how should Luzov measure and account for the impact of estimated losses resulting from notes receivable that it
  (1) Retained and did **not** sell?
  (2) Sold to bank with recourse?

(AICPA adapted)

C7-7 (Noninterest-Bearing Note Receivable) On September 30, 2001, Tiger Machinery Co. sold a machine and accepted the customer's noninterest-bearing note. Tiger normally makes sales on a cash basis. Since the machine was unique, its sales price was not determinable using Tiger's normal pricing practices.

After receiving the first of two equal annual installments on September 30, 2002, Tiger immediately sold the note with recourse. On October 9, 2003, Tiger received notice that the note was dishonored, and it paid all amounts due. At all times prior to default, the note was reasonably expected to be paid in full.

Instructions

(a) **(1)** How should Tiger determine the sales price of the machine?
(2) How should Tiger report the effects of the noninterest-bearing note on its income statement for the year ended December 31, 2001? Why is this accounting presentation appropriate?

(b) What are the effects of the sale of the note receivable with recourse on Tiger's income statement for the year ended December 31, 2002, and its balance sheet at December 31, 2002?

(c) How should Tiger account for the effects of the note being dishonored?

C7-8 (Reporting of Notes Receivable, Interest, and Sale of Receivables) On July 1, 2002, Gale Sondergaard Company sold special-order merchandise on credit and received in return an interest-bearing note receivable from the customer. Sondergaard will receive interest at the prevailing rate for a note of this type. Both the principal and interest are due in one lump sum on June 30, 2003.

On September 1, 2002, Sondergaard sold special-order merchandise on credit and received in return a noninterest-bearing note receivable from the customer. The prevailing rate of interest for a note of this type is determinable. The note receivable is due in one lump sum on August 31, 2004.

Sondergaard also has significant amounts of trade accounts receivable as a result of credit sales to its customers. On October 1, 2002, some trade accounts receivable were assigned to Irene Dunne Finance Company on a non-notification (Sondergaard handles collections) basis for an advance of 75% of their amount at an interest charge of 12% on the balance outstanding.

On November 1, 2002, other trade accounts receivable were sold on a without recourse basis. The factor withheld 5% of the trade accounts receivable factored as protection against sales returns and allowances and charged a finance charge of 3%.

Instructions

(a) How should Sondergaard determine the interest income for 2002 on the:
(1) Interest-bearing note receivable? Why?
(2) Noninterest-bearing note receivable? Why?

(b) How should Sondergaard report the interest-bearing note receivable and the noninterest-bearing note receivable on its balance sheet at December 31, 2002?

(c) How should Sondergaard account for subsequent collections on the trade accounts receivable assigned on October 1, 2002, and the payments to Irene Dunne Finance? Why?

(d) How should Sondergaard account for the trade accounts receivable factored on November 1, 2002? Why?

(AICPA adapted)

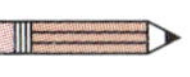

C7-9 (Accounting for Non-interest-Bearing Note) Soon after beginning the year-end audit work on March 10 at Alan Arkin Company, the auditor has the following conversation with the controller.

CONTROLLER: The year ended March 31st should be our most profitable in history and, as a consequence, the Board of Directors has just awarded the officers generous bonuses.

AUDITOR: I thought profits were down this year in the industry, according to your latest interim report.

CONTROLLER: Well, they were down, but 10 days ago we closed a deal that will give us a substantial increase for the year.

AUDITOR: Oh, what was it?

CONTROLLER: Well, you remember a few years ago our former president bought stock in Rocketeer Enterprises because he had those grandiose ideas about becoming a conglomerate. For 6 years we have not been able to sell this stock, which cost us $3,000,000 and has not paid a nickel in dividends. Thursday we sold this stock to Campbell Inc. for $4,000,000. So, we will have a gain of $700,000 ($1,000,000 pretax) which will increase our net income for the year to $4,000,000, compared with last year's $3,800,000. As far as I know, we'll be the only company in the industry to register an increase in net income this year. That should help the market value of the stock!

AUDITOR: Do you expect to receive the $4,000,000 in cash by March 31st, your fiscal year-end?

CONTROLLER: No. Although Campbell Inc. is an excellent company, they are a little tight for cash because of their rapid growth. Consequently, they are going to give us a $4,000,000 noninterest-bearing note due $400,000 per year for the next 10 years. The first payment is due on March 31 of next year.

AUDITOR: Why is the note noninterest-bearing?

CONTROLLER: Because that's what everybody agreed to. Since we don't have any interest-bearing debt, the funds invested in the note do not cost us anything and besides, we were not getting any dividends on the Rocketeer Enterprises stock.

Instructions

Do you agree with the way the controller has accounted for the transaction? If not, how should the transaction be accounted for?

C7-10 (Receivables Management) As the manager of the accounts receivable department for Vicki Maher Leather Goods, Ltd., you recently noticed that Percy Shelley, your accounts receivable clerk who is paid $1,200 per month, has been wearing unusually tasteful and expensive clothing. (This is Vicki Maher's first year in business.) This morning, Shelley drove up to work in a brand new Lexus.

Naturally suspicious by nature, you decide to test the accuracy of the accounts receivable balance of $132,000 as shown in the ledger. The following information is available for your first year (precisely 9 months ended September 30, 2001) in business:

(1) Collections from customers	$198,000
(2) Merchandise purchased	360,000
(3) Ending merchandise inventory	90,000
(4) Goods are marked to sell at 40% above cost.	

Instructions

Assuming all sales were made on account, compute the ending accounts receivable balance that should appear in the ledger, noting any apparent shortage. Then, draft a memo dated October 3, 2001, to John Castle, the branch manager, explaining the facts in this situation. Remember that this problem is serious, and you do not want to make hasty accusations.

USING YOUR JUDGMENT

FINANCIAL REPORTING PROBLEM: INTEL CORPORATION

The financial statements of Intel Corporation appear in Appendix 5B.

Instructions

Refer to these financial statements and the accompanying notes to answer the following questions.

(a) What criteria does Intel use to differentiate among (1) "cash and cash equivalents," (2) "short-term investments," and (3) "long-term investments" as reported in its balance sheet?

(b) As of December 26, 1998, what balances did Intel have in cash and cash equivalents and short-term investments? Why does Intel have such a large amount in highly liquid assets?

(c) In recent years the accounting profession has encouraged companies to disclose any concentration of risk not apparent in their financial statements. What risks relative to accounts receivable does Intel disclose in its Notes to Consolidated Financial Statements?

FINANCIAL STATEMENT ANALYSIS CASE

Occidental Petroleum Corporation

Occidental Petroleum Corporation reported the following information in its 1998 Annual Report:

OCCIDENTAL PETROLEUM CORPORATION

Consolidated Balance Sheets
(in millions)

Assets at December 31,	1998	1997
Current assets		
Cash and cash equivalents	$ 96	$ 113
Trade receivables, net of reserves of $23 in 1998 and $24 in 1997	340	603
Receivables from joint ventures, partnerships, and other	1,586	210
Inventories	500	604
Prepaid expenses and other	273	395
Total current assets	2,795	1,925
Long-term receivables, net	121	153

Notes to Consolidated Financial Statements

Cash and Cash Equivalents. Cash equivalents consist of highly liquid money-market mutual funds and bank deposits with initial maturities of three months or less. Cash equivalents totaled approximately $58 million and $50 million at December 31, 1998 and 1997, respectively.

Trade Receivables In 1992, Occidental entered into an agreement to sell, under a revolving sale program, an undivided percentage ownership interest in a designated pool of trade receivables, with limited recourse. Under this program, Occidental serves as the collection agent with respect to the receivables sold. An interest in new receivables is sold as collections are made from customers. As of December 31, 1998, Occidental had received net cash proceeds totaling $360 million. Fees and expenses under this program are included in selling, general and administrative and other operating expenses. During the years ended December 31, 1998, 1997, and 1996, the cost of this program amounted to approximately 5.9 percent, 5.9 percent and 5.8 percent, respectively, of the weighted average amount of proceeds received.

Instructions

(a) What items other than coin and currency may be included in "cash"?

(b) What items may be included in "cash equivalents"?

(c) What are compensating balance arrangements, and how should they be reported in financial statements?

(d) What are the possible differences between cash equivalents and short-term (temporary) investments?

(e) Why is petty cash not reported in the financial statements?

(f) What is the difference between a demand deposit and a time deposit?

(g) What types of arrangements, events, or situations result in restricted cash?

COMPARATIVE ANALYSIS CASE

The Coca-Cola Company versus PepsiCo Inc.

Instructions

Go to the Digital Tool and use the information about **The Coca-Cola Company** and **PepsiCo** to answer the following questions.

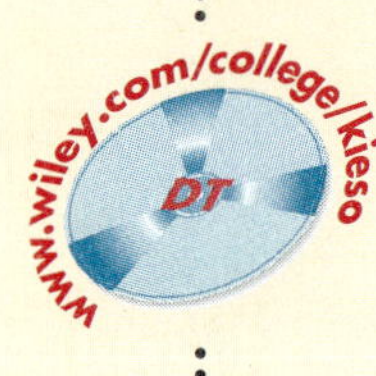

(a) What were the cash and cash equivalents reported by Coca-Cola and PepsiCo at the end of 1998? What does each company classify as cash equivalents?

(b) What were the accounts receivable (net) for Coca-Cola and PepsiCo at the end of 1998? Which company reports the greater allowance for doubtful accounts receivable (amount and percentage of gross receivable) at the end of 1998?

(c) Assuming that all "net operating revenues" (Coca-Cola) and all "net sales" (PepsiCo) were net *credit* sales, compute the receivables turnover ratio for 1998 for Coca-Cola and PepsiCo; also compute the days outstanding for receivables. What is your evaluation of the difference?

RESEARCH CASES

Case 1

Accounting Trends and Techniques, published annually by the American Institute of Certified Public Accountants, is a survey of 600 annual reports to stockholders. The survey covers selected industrial, merchandising, and service companies.

Instructions

Examine the section regarding the use of receivables for financing and answer the following questions.

(a) For the most recent year, how many of the companies surveyed disclosed (1) receivables sold, and (2) receivables used as collateral?

(b) Examine the disclosure provided by a company that sold receivables and a company that used its receivables as collateral. Summarize the major terms of the transactions.

Case 2

The May 6, 1996, issue of *Forbes* includes an article by Matthew Schifrin and Howard Rudnitsky entitled "Rx for Receivables."

Instructions

Read the article and answer the following questions.

(a) Why has the pharmacy business moved from a cash-based business to a receivables-based business?

(b) What is the economic motivation for pharmacists to sell their receivables?

(c) What is the economic motivation for the Pharmacy Fund to purchase the receivables?

ETHICS CASE

Rudolph Company is a subsidiary of Hundley Corp. The controller believes that the yearly allowance for doubtful accounts for Rudolph should be 2% of net credit sales. The president, nervous that the parent company might expect the subsidiary to sustain its 10% growth rate, suggests that the controller increase the allowance for doubtful accounts to 3% yearly. The supervisor thinks that the lower net income, which reflects a 6% growth rate, will be a more sustainable rate for Rudolph Company.

Instructions

Answer the following questions:

(a) Should the controller be concerned with Rudolph Company's growth rate in estimating the allowance? Explain your answer.

(b) Does the president's request pose an ethical dilemma for the controller? Give your reasons.

CHAPTER 8

Valuation of Inventories: A Cost Basis Approach

LEARNING OBJECTIVES

After studying this chapter, you should be able to:

1. **Identify major classifications of inventory.**
2. **Distinguish between perpetual and periodic inventory systems.**
3. **Identify the effects of inventory errors on the financial statements.**
4. **Identify the items that should be included as inventory cost.**
5. **Describe and compare the flow assumptions used in accounting for inventories.**
6. **Explain the significance and use of a LIFO reserve.**
7. **Explain the effect of LIFO liquidations.**
8. **Explain the dollar-value LIFO method.**
9. **Identify the major advantages and disadvantages of LIFO.**
10. **Identify the reasons why a given inventory method is selected.**

Where's My Inventory?

Recent cases of fraudulent financial reporting have emphasized the importance of inventory. According to *The Wall Street Journal,* "Creating phantom inventory instantly benefits a company's bottom line."[1] For example, it is alleged that **Phar-Mor Inc.**, a deep-discount store chain, overstated its profits by $50 million by keeping in its inventory records items that had already been sold, maintaining secret inventory records, and creating phantom inventory.

Similarly, **Crazy Eddie Inc.**'s new management alleged that previous management had created phantom inventory and profits. The company, known in the New York area for its wacky TV commercials, said its former management inflated the inventory count by $10 million by drafting phony count sheets and improperly including merchandise that was being returned to suppliers. The total shortfall for the consumer electronics retailer was later determined to be $65 million.[2] In short, Crazy Eddie went crazy.

At **Kurzweil Applied Intelligence Inc.** millions of dollars in phony inventory sales were booked during a two-year period that straddled two audits and an initial public stock offering. Employees dummied up phony shipping documents and logbooks to support bogus sales transactions. High-tech equipment was shipped all right, but not to customers. Instead, the goods were shipped to a public warehouse for "temporary" storage; Kurzweil still had ownership. Some "sold" equipment sat in storage for 17 months. To foil auditors' attempts to verify the existence of the "sold" inventory, Kurzweil employees moved the goods from warehouse to warehouse. To cover the fraudulently recorded sales transactions, as auditors closed in, the still-hidden goods were brought back, under the pretense that they were returned by customers. When the fraud was finally exposed in mid-1994, the bottom dropped out of Kurzweil's stock.[3]

---

[1] "Inventory Chicanery Tempts More Firms, Fools More Auditors," *The Wall Street Journal,* December 12, 1992, p. A1. Overstatement of ending inventory reduces cost of sales and thus increases profits.

[2] "Short Circuit: How Mounting Woes at Crazy Eddie Sank a Turnaround Effort," *The Wall Street Journal,* July 10, 1989, p. A1. "Peat Settles Crazy Eddie Case," *Accounting Today,* April 19, 1993, p. 37.

[3] "Anatomy of a Fraud," *Business Week,* September 16, 1996, pp. 90–94.

PREVIEW OF CHAPTER 8

As indicated in the opening story, inventories are often a significant portion of a company's total assets. As a result, improper accounting and reporting for this asset can materially affect the financial statements. The purpose of this chapter is to discuss the basic issues related to accounting and reporting for the costs of inventory. The content and organization of the chapter are as follows:

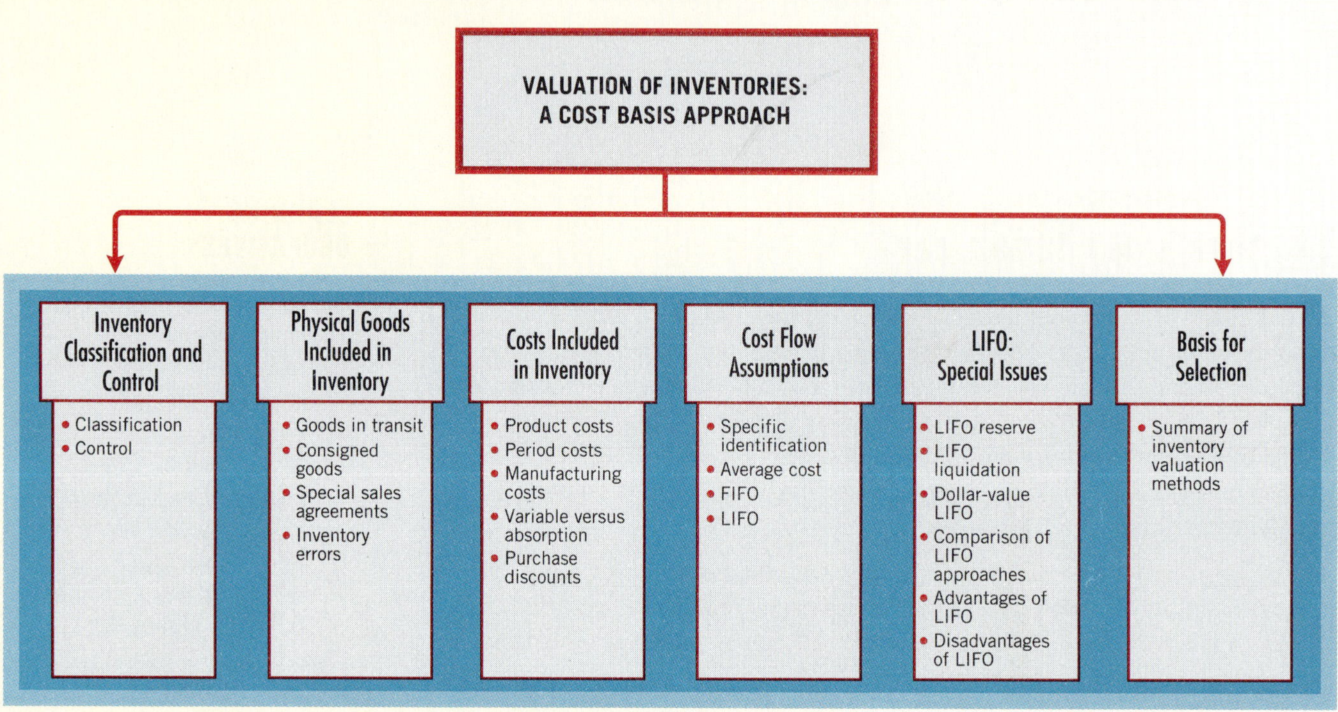

INVENTORY CLASSIFICATION AND CONTROL

Classification

OBJECTIVE 1
Identify major classifications of inventory.

Inventories are asset items held for sale in the ordinary course of business or goods that will be used or consumed in the production of goods to be sold. The description and measurement of inventory require careful attention because the investment in inventories is frequently the largest current asset of merchandising (retail) and manufacturing businesses.

A **merchandising concern,** such as **Wal-Mart**, ordinarily purchases its merchandise in a form ready for sale. It reports the cost assigned to unsold units left on hand as **merchandise inventory**. Only one inventory account, Merchandise Inventory, appears in the financial statements. **Manufacturing concerns**, on the other hand, produce goods to be sold to the merchandising firms. Many of the largest U.S. businesses are manufacturers—**Boeing**, **IBM**, **Exxon Mobil**, **Procter & Gamble**, **Ford**, **Motorola**, to name only a few. Although the products they produce may be quite different, manufacturers normally have three inventory accounts—Raw Materials, Work in Process, and Finished Goods.

Go to the Digital Tool for additional inventory disclosures.

The cost assigned to goods and materials on hand but not yet placed into production is reported as **raw materials inventory**. Raw materials include the wood to make a baseball bat or the steel to make a car. These materials ultimately can be traced directly to the end product.

At any point in a continuous production process some units are not completely processed. The cost of the raw material on which production has been started but not completed, plus the direct labor cost applied specifically to this material and a ratable share of manufacturing overhead costs, constitute the **work in process inventory**.

The costs identified with the completed but unsold units on hand at the end of the fiscal period are reported as **finished goods inventory**. The current assets sections presented in Illustration 8-1 contrast the financial statement presentation of inventories of a merchandising company and those of a manufacturing company. The remainder of the balance sheet is essentially similar for the two types of companies.

ILLUSTRATION 8-1
Comparison of Current Assets Presentation for Merchandising and Manufacturing Companies

Merchandising Company
WAL-MART
Balance Sheet
January 31, 1999

Current assets (in millions)	
Cash and cash equivalents	$ 1,879
Receivables	1,118
Inventories at LIFO cost	17,076
Prepaid expenses and other	1,059
Total current assets	$21,132

Manufacturing Company
ADOLPH COORS COMPANY
Balance Sheet
December 27, 1998

Current assets (in millions)		
Cash and cash equivalents		$160
Short-term investments		96
Accounts and notes receivable (net)		126
Inventories:		
Finished	$38	
In process	25	
Raw materials	34	
Packaging materials	6	
Total inventories		103
Prepaid expenses and other		64
Total current assets		$549

A manufacturing company also might include a **manufacturing** or **factory supplies inventory** account. In it would be items such as machine oils, nails, cleaning materials, and the like that are used in production but are not the primary materials being processed. The flow of costs through a merchandising company is different from that of a manufacturing company, as shown in Illustration 8-2 (page 396).

UNDERLYING CONCEPTS

Because inventory provides future economic benefits to the company (revenue from sales), it meets the definition of an asset. Inventory costs will be matched against revenue in the period that sales occur.

Control

For various reasons, management is vitally interested in inventory planning and control. An accurate accounting system with up-to-date records is essential. If unsalable items have accumulated in the inventory, a potential loss exists. Sales and customers may be lost if products ordered by customers are not available in the desired style, quality, and quantity. Also, businesses must monitor inventory levels carefully to limit the financing costs of carrying large inventories. In recent years, with the introduction and use of "just-in-time" (JIT) inventory order systems and better supplier relationships, inventory levels have become leaner for many enterprises.[4]

OBJECTIVE 2
Distinguish between perpetual and periodic inventory systems.

Perpetual System

As indicated in Chapter 3, inventory records may be maintained on a perpetual or periodic basis. Under a **perpetual inventory system**, a continuous record of changes in inventory is maintained in the Inventory account. That is, all purchases and sales (is-

[4]Wal-Mart provides a classic example of the use of tight inventory controls. Department managers use a scanner which when placed over the bar code corresponding to a particular item will tell you how many items were sold yesterday, last week, and over the same period last year. It will tell you how many of those items are in stock, how many are on the way, and how many the neighboring Wal-Marts are carrying, in case one store runs out.

ILLUSTRATION 8-2
Flow of Costs through Manufacturing and Merchandising Companies

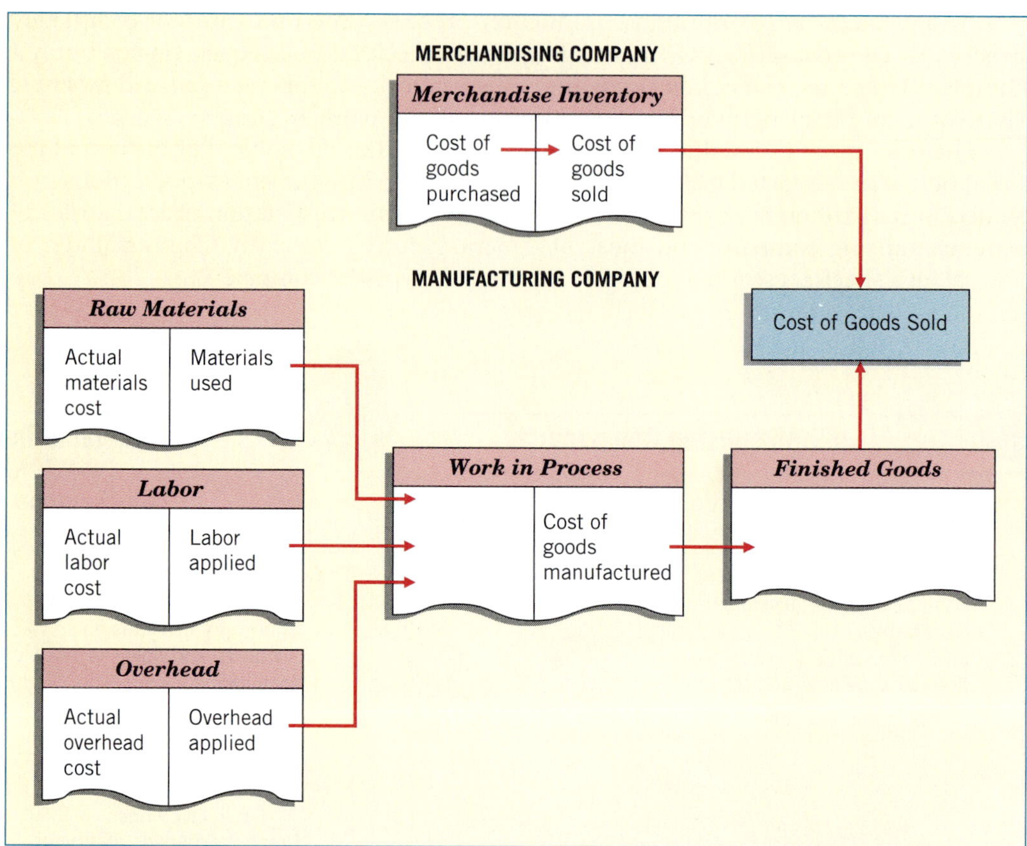

sues) of goods are recorded directly in the Inventory account **as they occur**. The accounting features of a perpetual inventory system are:

1. Purchases of merchandise for resale or raw materials for production are debited to Inventory rather than to Purchases.
2. Freight-in, purchase returns and allowances, and purchase discounts are recorded in Inventory rather than in separate accounts.
3. Cost of goods sold is recognized for each sale by debiting the account, Cost of Goods Sold, and crediting Inventory.
4. Inventory is a control account that is supported by a subsidiary ledger of individual inventory records. The subsidiary records show the quantity and cost of each type of inventory on hand.

The perpetual inventory system provides a continuous record of the balances in both the Inventory account and the Cost of Goods Sold account.

Under a computerized recordkeeping system, additions to and issuances from inventory can be recorded nearly instantaneously. The popularity and affordability of computerized accounting software have made the perpetual system cost-effective for many kinds of businesses. Recording sales with optical scanners at the cash register has been incorporated into perpetual inventory systems at many retail stores.

Periodic System

Under a **periodic inventory system**, the quantity of inventory on hand is determined, as its name implies, only periodically. All acquisitions of inventory during the accounting period are recorded by debits to a Purchases account. The total in the Purchases account at the end of the accounting period is added to the cost of the inventory on hand at the beginning of the period to determine the total cost of the goods available for sale during the period. Ending inventory is subtracted from the cost of goods available for sale to compute the cost of goods sold. Note that under a periodic inventory system, the cost of goods sold is a residual amount that is dependent upon a physically counted ending inventory.

The **physical inventory count** required by a periodic system is taken once a year at the end of the year.[5] However, most companies need more current information regarding their inventory levels to protect against stockouts or overpurchasing and to aid in the preparation of monthly or quarterly financial data. As a consequence, many companies use a **modified perpetual inventory system** in which increases and decreases in quantities only—not dollar amounts—are kept in a detailed inventory record. It is merely a memorandum device outside the double-entry system which helps in determining the level of inventory at any point in time.

Whether a company maintains a perpetual inventory in quantities and dollars, quantities only, or has no perpetual inventory record at all, it probably takes a physical inventory once a year. No matter what type of inventory records are in use or how well organized the procedures for recording purchases and requisitions, the danger of loss and error is always present. Waste, breakage, theft, improper entry, failure to prepare or record requisitions, and any number of similar possibilities may cause the inventory records to differ from the actual inventory on hand. This requires periodic verification of the inventory records by actual count, weight, or measurement. These counts are compared with the detailed inventory records. The records are corrected to agree with the quantities actually on hand.

Insofar as possible, the physical inventory should be taken near the end of a company's fiscal year so that correct inventory quantities are available for use in preparing annual accounting reports and statements. Because this is not always possible, however, physical inventories taken within two or three months of the year's end are satisfactory, if the detailed inventory records are maintained with a fair degree of accuracy.

To illustrate the difference between a perpetual and a periodic system, assume that Fesmire Company had the following transactions during the current year:

Beginning inventory	100 units at \$ 6 = \$ 600
Purchases	900 units at \$ 6 = \$5,400
Sales	600 units at \$12 = \$7,200
Ending inventory	400 units at \$ 6 = \$2,400

The entries to record these transactions during the current year are shown in Illustration 8-3.

ILLUSTRATION 8-3
Comparative Entries—Perpetual vs. Periodic

Perpetual Inventory System			Periodic Inventory System		
1. Beginning inventory, 100 units at \$6:					
The inventory account shows the inventory on hand at \$600.			The inventory account shows the inventory on hand at \$600.		
2. Purchase 900 units at \$6:					
Inventory	5,400		Purchases	5,400	
Accounts Payable		5,400	Accounts Payable		5,400
3. Sale of \$600 units at \$12:					
Accounts Receivable	7,200		Accounts Receivable	7,200	
Sales		7,200	Sales		7,200
Cost of Goods Sold (600 at \$6)	3,600		(No entry)		
Inventory		3,600			
4. End-of-period entries for inventory accounts, 400 units at \$6:					
No entry necessary.			Inventory (ending, by count)	2,400	
The account, Inventory, shows the ending balance of \$2,400			Cost of Goods Sold	3,600	
(\$600 + \$5,400 − \$3,600).			Purchases		5,400
			Inventory (beginning)		600

[5]In recent years, some companies have developed methods of determining inventories, including statistical sampling, that are sufficiently reliable to make unnecessary an annual physical count of each item of inventory.

When a perpetual inventory system is used and a difference exists between the perpetual inventory balance and the physical inventory count, a separate entry is needed to adjust the perpetual inventory account. To illustrate, assume that at the end of the reporting period, the perpetual inventory account reported an inventory balance of $4,000, but a physical count indicated $3,800 was actually on hand. The entry to record the necessary writedown is as follows:

Inventory Over and Short	200	
Inventory		200

Perpetual inventory overages and shortages generally represent a misstatement of cost of goods sold. The difference is a result of normal and expected shrinkage, breakage, shoplifting, incorrect record keeping, and the like. Inventory Over and Short would therefore be an adjustment of cost of goods sold. In practice, the account Inventory Over and Short is sometimes reported in the other revenues and gains or other expenses and losses section of the income statement, depending on its balance. Note that in a periodic inventory system the account Inventory Over and Short does not arise because there are no accounting records available against which to compare the physical count. Thus, inventory overages and shortages are buried in cost of goods sold.

BASIC ISSUES IN INVENTORY VALUATION

Because the goods sold or used during an accounting period seldom correspond exactly to the goods bought or produced during that period, the physical inventory either increases or decreases. The cost of all the goods available for sale or use should be allocated between the goods that were sold or used and those that are still on hand. The **cost of goods available for sale or use** is the sum of (1) the cost of the goods on hand at the beginning of the period and (2) the cost of the goods acquired or produced during the period. The **cost of goods sold** is the difference between the cost of goods available for sale during the period and the cost of goods on hand at the end of the period.

ILLUSTRATION 8-4
Computation of Cost of Goods Sold

Beginning inventory, Jan. 1	$100,000
Cost of goods acquired or produced during the year	800,000
Total cost of goods available for sale	900,000
Ending inventory, Dec. 31	200,000
Cost of goods sold during the year	$700,000

The valuation of inventories can be a complex process that requires determination of:

1. **The physical goods to be included in inventory** (who owns the goods?—goods in transit, consigned goods, special sales agreements).
2. **The costs to be included in inventory** (product vs. period costs, variable costing vs. absorption costing).
3. **The cost flow assumption to be adopted** (specific identification, average cost, FIFO, LIFO, retail, etc.).

We will explore these basic issues in the next three sections of the chapter.

PHYSICAL GOODS INCLUDED IN INVENTORY

Technically, purchases should be recorded when legal title to the goods passes to the buyer. General practice, however, is to record acquisitions when the goods are received, because it is difficult for the buyer to determine the exact time of legal passage of title for every purchase. In addition, no material error is likely to result from such a practice if it is consistently applied. Illustration 8-5 indicates the general guidelines used in evaluating whether the seller or the buyer reports an item as inventory.

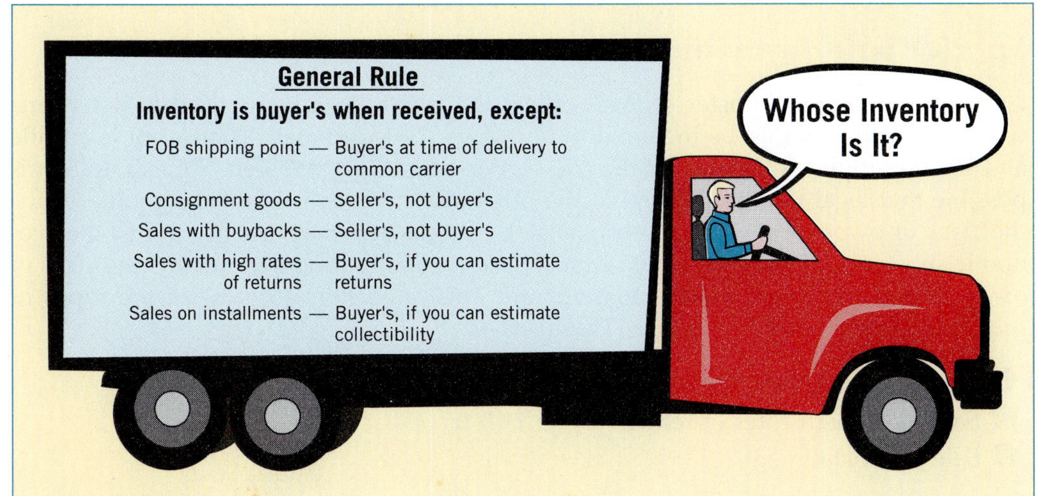

ILLUSTRATION 8-5
Guidelines for Determining Ownership

Goods in Transit

Sometimes purchased merchandise is in transit—not yet received—at the end of a fiscal period. The accounting for these shipped goods depends on who owns them. That can be determined by application of the "passage of title" rule. If the goods are shipped **f.o.b. shipping point**, title passes to the buyer when the seller delivers the goods to the common carrier, who acts as an agent for the buyer. (The abbreviation f.o.b. stands for free on board.) If the goods are shipped **f.o.b. destination**, title does not pass until the buyer receives the goods from the common carrier. "Shipping point" and "destination" are often designated by a particular location, for example, f.o.b. Denver.

The accounting rule is that goods to which legal title has passed should be recorded as purchases of the fiscal period. Goods shipped f.o.b. shipping point that are in transit at the end of the period belong to the buyer and should be shown in the buyer's records. Legal title to these goods passed to the buyer when the goods were shipped. To disregard such purchases would result in an understatement of inventories and accounts payable in the balance sheet and an understatement of purchases and ending inventories in the income statement.

Consigned Goods

A specialized method of marketing certain products uses a device known as a **consignment** shipment. Under this arrangement, one party (the consignor) ships merchandise to another (the consignee), who acts as the consignor's agent in selling the **consigned goods**. The consignee agrees to accept the goods without any liability, except to exercise due care and reasonable protection from loss or damage, until the goods are sold to a third party. When the consignee sells the goods, the revenue less a selling commission and expenses incurred in accomplishing the sale is remitted to the consignor.

Goods out on consignment remain the property of the consignor and are included in the consignor's inventory at purchase price or production cost. Occasionally, the inventory out on consignment is shown as a separate item, but unless the amount is large there is little need for this. Sometimes the inventory on consignment is reported in the notes to the financial statements. For example, **Eagle Clothes, Inc.** reported the following related to consigned goods: "Inventories consist of finished goods shipped on consignment to customers of the Company's subsidiary **April-Marcus, Inc.**"

The consignee makes no entry to the inventory account for goods received because they are the property of the consignor. The consignee should be extremely careful *not* to include any of the goods consigned as a part of inventory.

Special Sale Agreements

As indicated earlier, transfer of legal title is the general guideline used to determine whether an item should be included in inventory. Unfortunately, transfer of legal title and the underlying substance of the transaction often do not match. For example, it is possible that legal title has passed to the purchaser but the seller of the goods retains the risks of ownership. Conversely, transfer of legal title may not occur, but the economic substance of the transaction is such that the seller no longer retains the risks of ownership. Three special sale situations are illustrated here to indicate the types of problems encountered in practice. These are:

1. Sales with buyback agreement.
2. Sales with high rates of return.
3. Sales on installment.

Sales with Buyback Agreement

Sometimes an enterprise finances its inventory without reporting either the liability or the inventory on its balance sheet. Such an approach—often referred to as a **product financing arrangement**—usually involves a "sale" with either an implicit or explicit "buyback" agreement. To illustrate, Hill Enterprises transfers ("sells") inventory to Chase, Inc. and simultaneously agrees to repurchase this merchandise at a specified price over a specified period of time. Chase then uses the inventory as collateral and borrows against it. Chase uses the loan proceeds to pay Hill. Hill repurchases the inventory in the future, and Chase employs the proceeds from repayment to meet its loan obligation.

UNDERLYING CONCEPTS

Recognizing revenue at the time the inventory is "parked" violates the revenue recognition principle. This principle requires that the earning process be substantially completed; in this case, the economic benefits remain under the control of the seller.

The essence of this transaction is that Hill Enterprises is financing its inventory—and retaining risk of ownership—even though technical legal title to the merchandise was transferred to Chase. The advantage to Hill Enterprises in structuring a transaction in this manner is the avoidance of personal property taxes in certain states, the removal of the current liability from its balance sheet, and the ability to manipulate income. The advantages to Chase are that the purchase of the goods may solve a LIFO liquidation problem (discussed later), or that Chase may be interested in a reciprocal agreement at a later date.

These arrangements are often described in practice as "**parking transactions**," because the seller simply parks the inventory on another enterprise's balance sheet for a short period of time. When a repurchase agreement exists at a set price and this price covers all costs of the inventory plus related holding costs, the inventory and related liability should be reported on the seller's books.[6]

Sales with High Rates of Return

Formal or informal agreements often exist in industries such as publishing, music, and toys and sporting goods that permit inventory to be returned for a full or partial refund. To illustrate, Quality Publishing Company sells textbooks to Campus Bookstores with an agreement that any books not sold may be returned for full credit. In the past,

[6] "Accounting for Product Financing Arrangements," *Statement of Financial Accounting Standards No. 49* (Stamford, Conn.: FASB, 1981).

approximately 25% of the textbooks sold to Campus Bookstores were returned. How should Quality Publishing report its sales transactions? One alternative is to record the sale at the full amount and establish an estimated sales returns and allowances account. A second possibility is to not record any sale until circumstances indicate the amount of inventory the buyer will return. The key question is: Under what circumstances should the inventory be considered sold and removed from Quality's inventory? The answer is that when the amount of returns can be reasonably estimated, the goods should be considered sold. Conversely, if returns are unpredictable, removal of these goods from the inventory of the seller is inappropriate.[7]

Sales on Installment

"Goods sold on installment" describes any type of sale in which payment is required in periodic installments over an extended period of time. Because the risk of loss from uncollectibles is higher in installment sale situations than in other sales transactions, the seller often withholds legal title to the merchandise until all the payments have been made. The question is whether the inventory should be considered sold, even though legal title has not passed. The answer is that **the goods should be excluded from the seller's inventory if the percentage of bad debts can be reasonably estimated**. Installment sales are discussed here to show that in some cases, the goods should be removed from inventory, although legal title may not have passed.

UNDERLYING CONCEPTS

Revenues should be recognized because they have been substantially earned and are reasonably estimable. Collection is not the most critical event because bad debts can be reasonably estimated.

Effect of Inventory Errors

OBJECTIVE 3
Identify the effects of inventory errors on the financial statements.

As related in the opening stories about **Phar-Mor Inc.**, **Crazy Eddie Inc.**, and **Kurzweil Applied Intelligence Inc.**, items incorrectly included or excluded in determining cost of goods sold by inventory misstatements will result in errors in the financial statements. Let's look at two cases.

Ending Inventory Misstated

What would happen if the beginning inventory and purchases are recorded correctly, but some items are not included in ending inventory? In this situation, we would have the following effects on the financial statements at the end of the period:

ILLUSTRATION 8-6
Financial Statement Effects of Misstated Ending Inventory

Balance Sheet		Income Statement	
Inventory	Understated	Cost of goods sold	Overstated
Retained earnings	Understated		
Working capital (current assets less current liabilities)	Understated	Net income	Understated
Current ratio (current assets divided by current liabilities)	Understated		

Working capital and the current ratio are understated because ending inventory is understated; net income is understated because cost of goods sold is overstated.

To illustrate the effect on net income over a two-year period, assume that the ending inventory of Jay Weiseman Corp. is understated by $10,000 and that all other items are correctly stated. The effect of this error will be to decrease net income in the current year and to increase net income in the following year. The error will be counterbalanced (offset) in the next period because beginning inventory will be understated and net income will be overstated. Both net income figures are misstated, but the total for the two years is correct, as shown in Illustration 8-7.

UNDERLYING CONCEPTS

When inventory is misstated, its presentation lacks representational faithfulness.

[7]"Revenue Recognition When Right of Return Exists," *Statement of Financial Accounting Standards No. 48* (Stamford, Conn.: FASB, 1981).

ILLUSTRATION 8-7
Effect of Ending Inventory Error on Two Periods

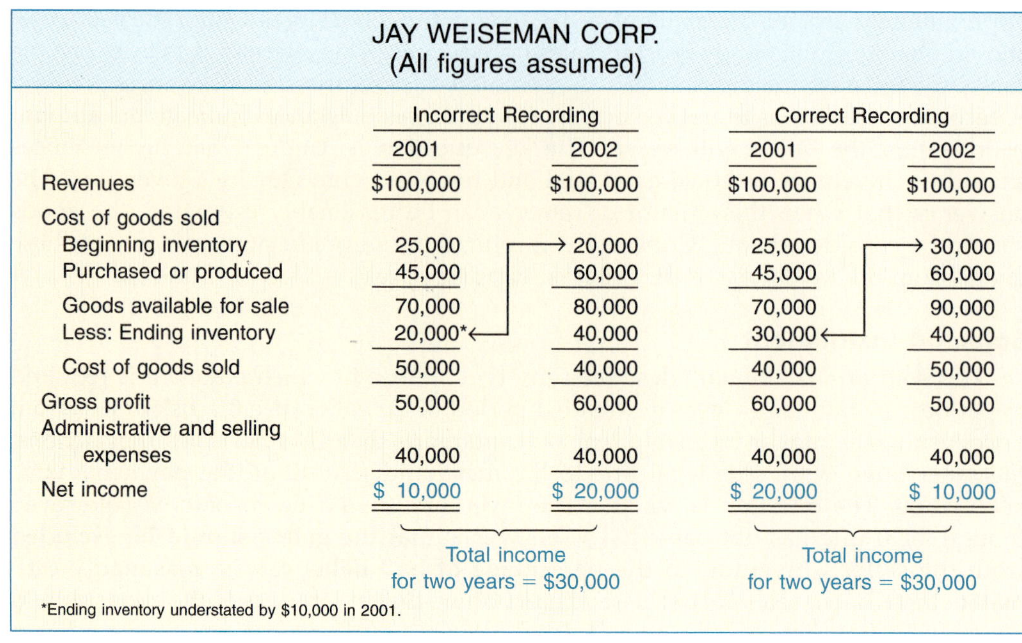

JAY WEISEMAN CORP.
(All figures assumed)

	Incorrect Recording		Correct Recording	
	2001	2002	2001	2002
Revenues	$100,000	$100,000	$100,000	$100,000
Cost of goods sold				
Beginning inventory	25,000	20,000	25,000	30,000
Purchased or produced	45,000	60,000	45,000	60,000
Goods available for sale	70,000	80,000	70,000	90,000
Less: Ending inventory	20,000*	40,000	30,000	40,000
Cost of goods sold	50,000	40,000	40,000	50,000
Gross profit	50,000	60,000	60,000	50,000
Administrative and selling expenses	40,000	40,000	40,000	40,000
Net income	$ 10,000	$ 20,000	$ 20,000	$ 10,000

Total income for two years = $30,000 (Incorrect Recording)
Total income for two years = $30,000 (Correct Recording)

*Ending inventory understated by $10,000 in 2001.

If ending inventory is *overstated*, the reverse effect occurs. Inventory, working capital, current ratio, and net income are overstated and cost of goods sold is understated. The effect of the error on net income will be counterbalanced in the next year, but both years' net income figures will be misstated.

Purchases and Inventory Misstated

Suppose that certain goods that the company owns are not recorded as a purchase and are not counted in ending inventory. The effect on the financial statements (assuming this is a purchase on account) is as follows:

ILLUSTRATION 8-8
Financial Statement Effects of Misstated Purchases and Inventory

Balance Sheet		Income Statement	
Inventory	Understated	Purchases	Understated
Retained earnings	No effect	Cost of goods sold	No effect
Accounts payable	Understated	Net income	No effect
Working capital	No effect	Inventory (ending)	Understated
Current ratio	Overstated		

To omit goods from purchases and inventory results in an understatement of inventory and accounts payable in the balance sheet and an understatement of purchases and ending inventory in the income statement. Net income for the period is not affected by the omission of such goods because purchases and ending inventory are both understated by the same amount—the error thereby offsetting itself in cost of goods sold. Total working capital is unchanged, but the **current ratio** is overstated because of the omission of equal amounts from inventory and accounts payable.

To illustrate the effect on the current ratio, assume that Larry Mall Company understated accounts payable and ending inventory by $40,000. The understated and correct data are shown below.

ILLUSTRATION 8-9
Effects of Purchases and Ending Inventory Errors

Purchases and Ending Inventory Understated		Purchases and Ending Inventory Correct	
Current assets	$120,000	Current assets	$160,000
Current liabilities	$ 40,000	Current liabilities	$ 80,000
Current ratio	3 to 1	Current ratio	2 to 1

The correct ratio is 2 to 1 rather than 3 to 1. Thus, understatement of accounts payable and ending inventory can lead to a "window dressing" of the current ratio—can make it appear better than it is.

If both purchases (on account) and ending inventory are overstated, then the effects on the balance sheet are exactly the reverse. Inventory and accounts payable are overstated and the current ratio is understated; working capital is not affected. Cost of goods sold and net income are not affected because the errors offset one another.

We cannot overemphasize the importance of a proper inventory computation in presenting accurate financial statements. For example, **Leslie Fay**, a women's apparel maker, had accounting irregularities that wiped out one year's net income and caused a restatement of the prior year's earnings. One reason: it inflated inventory and deflated cost of goods sold. Or remember **Phar-Mor Inc.**, mentioned earlier. Or, **Anixter Bros. Inc.** had to restate its income by $1.7 million because an accountant in the antenna manufacturing division overstated the ending inventory, thereby reducing its cost of sales. Similarly, **AM International** allegedly recorded as sold products that were only being rented. As a result, inaccurate inventory figures added $7.9 million to pretax income.

COSTS INCLUDED IN INVENTORY

OBJECTIVE 4
Identify the items that should be included as inventory cost.

One of the most important problems in dealing with inventories concerns the amount at which the inventory should be carried in the accounts. **The acquisition of inventories, like other assets, is generally accounted for on a basis of cost.** (Other bases are discussed in Chapter 9.)

Product Costs

Product costs are those costs that "attach" to the inventory and are recorded in the inventory account. These costs are directly connected with the bringing of goods to the place of business of the buyer and converting such goods to a salable condition. Such charges would include freight charges on goods purchased, other direct costs of acquisition, and labor and other production costs incurred in processing the goods up to the time of sale.

It would seem proper also to allocate to inventories a share of any buying costs or expenses of a purchasing department, storage costs, and other costs incurred in storing or handling the goods before they are sold. Because of the practical difficulties involved in allocating such costs and expenses, however, these items are not ordinarily included in valuing inventories.

Period Costs

Selling expenses and, under ordinary circumstances, **general and administrative expenses** are not considered to be directly related to the acquisition or production of goods and, therefore, are not considered to be a part of inventories. Such costs are **period costs**.

Conceptually, these expenses are as much a cost of the product as the initial purchase price and related freight charges attached to the product. Why then are these costs not considered inventoriable items? Selling expenses are generally considered as more directly related to the cost of goods sold than to the unsold inventory. In most cases, though, the costs, especially administrative expenses, are so unrelated or indirectly related to the immediate production process that any allocation is purely arbitrary.

Interest costs associated with getting inventories ready for sale usually are expensed as incurred. A major argument for this approach is that interest costs are really a cost of financing. Others have argued, however, that interest costs incurred to finance activities associated with bringing inventories to a condition and place ready for sale are as much a cost of the asset as materials, labor, and overhead and, therefore, should be capitalized.[8] **The FASB has ruled that interest costs related to assets constructed for internal use or assets produced as discrete projects (such as ships or real estate projects) for sale or lease should be capitalized.**[9] The FASB emphasized that these discrete projects should take considerable time, entail substantial expenditures, and be likely to involve significant amounts of interest cost. Interest costs should not be capitalized for inventories that are routinely manufactured or otherwise produced in large quantities on a repetitive basis, because the informational benefit does not justify the cost.

UNDERLYING CONCEPTS

In capitalizing interest, both constraints—materiality and cost/benefit—are applied.

Manufacturing Costs

As previously indicated, a business that manufactures goods utilizes three inventory accounts—Raw Materials, Work in Process, and Finished Goods. Work in process and finished goods include direct materials, direct labor, and manufacturing overhead costs. Manufacturing overhead costs include indirect material, indirect labor, and such items as depreciation, taxes, insurance, heat, and electricity incurred in the manufacturing process.

Variable Costing Versus Absorption Costing

INTERNATIONAL INSIGHT

Components of inventory differ internationally. In determining the cost of inventories, U.S. practice requires the inclusion not only of direct material and labor but also of variable and fixed manufacturing overhead. In other nations (India and Chile, for example) only direct materials and labor are included.

In a **variable costing system** (frequently called a direct costing system), all costs must be classified as variable or fixed. **Variable costs** are those that fluctuate in direct proportion to changes in output, and **fixed costs** are those that remain constant in spite of changes in output. Under variable costing only costs that vary directly with the production volume are charged to products as manufacturing takes place. Because variable costing is so useful to management in decision making, cost control, and budget preparation, it is widely used internally. However, it is not acceptable for tax purposes or for use in published financial reports (external reporting) because it understates the company's investment in inventories.

Under **absorption costing** (often referred to as full costing), all manufacturing costs, variable and fixed, direct and indirect, that are incurred in the factory or production process attach to the product and are included in the cost of inventory. Absorption costing (full costing) is required by GAAP as the basis of inventory valuation for financial statements. A modified version of absorption costing is required for tax purposes too.[10]

Treatment of Purchase Discounts

The use of a **Purchase Discounts** account indicates that the company is reporting its purchases and accounts payable at the gross amount. Another approach is to record the purchases and accounts payable at an amount **net** of the cash discounts. This treat-

---

[8]The reporting rules related to interest cost capitalization have their greatest impact in accounting for long-term assets and, therefore, are discussed in detail in Chapter 10.

[9]"Capitalization of Interest Cost," *Statement of Financial Accounting Standards No. 34* (Stamford, Conn.: FASB, 1979).

[10]The Tax Reform Act of 1986 required that all manufacturers and most wholesalers and retailers replace the previously existing full absorption costing provisions with the following new rules related to costs to be capitalized as inventory. **These tax rules require that in addition to direct material and direct labor, indirect costs that directly benefit or are incurred by reason of the performance of a production or resale activity must be capitalized.**

In December 1986, the FASB's Emerging Issues Task Force concluded that the fact that a cost (such as bidding, warehousing, purchasing, officer salaries, and administrative and selling expenses) is capitalizable for tax purposes does not, in itself, indicate that capitalizing the cost for financial reporting is preferable—or even appropriate. Task Force members, however, indicated that certain of the additional costs that now have to be capitalized for tax purposes **may be** capitalizable for financial reporting purposes, but only after the individual facts and circumstances have been analyzed.

ment is considered to be better because (1) it provides a correct reporting of the cost of the asset and related liability, and (2) it presents the opportunity to measure inefficiency of management if the discount is not taken. In the net approach, the failure to take a purchase discount within the discount period is recorded in a Purchase Discounts Lost account (for which management is responsible). To illustrate the difference between the gross and net methods, assume the following transactions:

ILLUSTRATION 8-10
Entries under Gross and Net Methods

Gross Method			Net Method		
Purchase cost $10,000, terms 2/10, net 30:					
Purchases	10,000		Purchases	9,800	
Accounts Payable		10,000	Accounts Payable		9,800
Invoices of $4,000 are paid within discount period:					
Accounts Payable	4,000		Accounts Payable	3,920	
Purchase Discounts		80	Cash		3,920
Cash		3,920			
Invoices of $6,000 are paid after discount period:					
Accounts Payable	6,000		Accounts Payable	5,880	
Cash		6,000	Purchase Discounts Lost	120	
			Cash		6,000

If the **gross method** is employed, purchase discounts should be reported as a deduction from purchases on the income statement. If the **net method** is used, purchase discounts lost should be considered a financial expense and reported in the other expenses and losses section of the income statement. Many believe that the difficulty involved in using the somewhat more complicated net method is not justified considering the resulting benefits. This could account for the widespread use of the less logical but simpler gross method. In addition, some contend that management is reluctant to report the amount of purchase discounts lost in the financial statements.

UNDERLYING CONCEPTS

Not using the net method because of resultant difficulties is an example of the application of the cost-benefit constraint.

WHAT COST FLOW ASSUMPTION SHOULD BE ADOPTED?

OBJECTIVE 5
Describe and compare the flow assumptions used in accounting for inventories.

During any given fiscal period it is very likely that merchandise will be purchased at several different prices. If inventories are to be priced at cost and numerous purchases have been made at different unit costs, which of the various cost prices should be used? Conceptually, a specific identification of the given items sold and unsold seems optimal, but this measure is often not only expensive but impossible to achieve. Consequently, one of several systematic inventory **cost flow assumptions** is used. Indeed, the actual physical flow of goods and the cost flow assumption are often quite different. **There is no requirement that the cost flow assumption adopted be consistent with the physical movement of goods.** The major objective in selecting a method should be to choose the one that, under the circumstances, most clearly reflects periodic income.[11]

To illustrate, assume that Call-Mart Inc. had the following transactions in its first month of operations.

Date	Purchases	Sold or Issued	Balance
March 2	2,000 @ $4.00		2,000 units
March 15	6,000 @ $4.40		8,000 units
March 19		4,000 units	4,000 units
March 30	2,000 @ $4.75		6,000 units

[11]"Restatement and Revision of Accounting Research Bulletins," *Accounting Research Bulletin No. 43* (New York: AICPA, 1953), Ch. 4, Statement 4.

From this information, we can compute the ending inventory of 6,000 units and the cost of goods available for sale (beginning inventory + purchases) of $43,900 [(2,000 @ $4.00) + (6,000 @ $4.40) + (2,000 @ $4.75)]. The question is, which price or prices should be assigned to the 6,000 units of ending inventory? The answer depends on which cost flow assumption is employed.

Specific Identification

Specific identification calls for identifying each item sold and each item in inventory. The costs of the specific items sold are included in the cost of goods sold, and the costs of the specific items on hand are included in the inventory. This method may be used only in instances where it is practical to separate physically the different purchases made. It can be successfully applied in situations where a relatively small number of costly, easily distinguishable items are handled. In the retail trade this includes some types of jewelry, fur coats, automobiles, and some furniture. In manufacturing it includes special orders and many products manufactured under a job cost system.

To illustrate the specific identification method, assume that Call-Mart Inc.'s 6,000 units of inventory is composed of 1,000 units from the March 2 purchase, 3,000 from the March 15 purchase, and 2,000 from the March 30 purchase. The ending inventory and cost of goods sold would be computed as shown in Illustration 8-11.

ILLUSTRATION 8-11
Specific Identification Method

Date	No. of Units	Unit Cost	Total Cost
March 2	1,000	$4.00	$ 4,000
March 15	3,000	4.40	13,200
March 30	2,000	4.75	9,500
Ending inventory	6,000		$26,700

Cost of goods available for sale (computed in previous section)	$43,900
Deduct: Ending inventory	26,700
Cost of goods sold	$17,200

Conceptually, this method appears ideal because actual costs are matched against actual revenue, and ending inventory is reported at actual cost. In other words, under specific identification the cost flow matches the physical flow of the goods. On closer observation, however, this method has certain deficiencies.

One argument against specific identification is that it makes it possible to manipulate net income. For example, assume that a wholesaler purchases otherwise identical plywood early in the year at three different prices. When the plywood is sold, the wholesaler can select either the lowest or the highest price to charge to expense simply by selecting the plywood from a specific lot for delivery to the customer. A business manager, therefore, can manipulate net income simply by delivering to the customer the higher- or lower-priced item, depending on whether higher or lower reported earnings is desired for the period.

Another problem relates to the arbitrary allocation of costs that sometimes occurs with specific inventory items. In certain circumstances, it is difficult to relate adequately, for example, shipping charges, storage costs, and discounts directly to a given inventory item. The alternative, then, is to allocate these costs somewhat arbitrarily, which leads to a "breakdown" in the precision of the specific identification method.[12]

[12] A good illustration of the cost allocation problem arises in the motion picture industry. Often actors and actresses receive a percentage of net income for a given movie or television program. Some actors who had these arrangements, have alleged that their programs have been extremely profitable to the motion picture studios but they have received little in the way of profit sharing. Actors contend that the studios allocate additional costs to successful projects to ensure that there will be no profits to share.

Average Cost

As the name implies, the **average cost method** prices items in the inventory on the basis of the average cost of all similar goods available during the period. To illustrate, assuming that Call-Mart Inc. used the periodic inventory method, the ending inventory and cost of goods sold would be computed as follows using a **weighted-average method**:

ILLUSTRATION 8-12
Weighted-Average Method—Periodic Inventory

Date of Invoice	No. Units	Unit Cost	Total Cost
March 2	2,000	$4.00	$ 8,000
March 15	6,000	4.40	26,400
March 30	2,000	4.75	9,500
Total goods available	10,000		$43,900

Weighted-average cost per unit $\frac{\$43,900}{10,000} = \$4.39$

Inventory in units 6,000 units
Ending inventory 6,000 × $4.39 = $26,340

Cost of goods available for sale	$43,900
Deduct: Ending inventory	26,340
Cost of goods sold	$17,560

If the company has a beginning inventory, it is included both in the total units available and in the total cost of goods available in computing the average cost per unit.

Another average cost method is the **moving-average method**, which is used with perpetual inventory records. The application of the average cost method for perpetual records is shown in Illustration 8-13.

ILLUSTRATION 8-13
Moving-Average Method—Perpetual Inventory

Date	Purchased		Sold or Issued	Balance	
March 2	(2,000 @ $4.00)	$ 8,000		(2,000 @ $4.00)	$ 8,000
March 15	(6,000 @ 4.40)	26,400		(8,000 @ 4.30)	34,400
March 19			(4,000 @ $4.30) $17,200	(4,000 @ 4.30)	17,200
March 30	(2,000 @ 4.75)	9,500		(6,000 @ 4.45)	26,700

In this method, a new average unit cost is computed each time a purchase is made. On March 15, after 6,000 units are purchased for $26,400, 8,000 units costing $34,400 ($8,000 plus $26,400) are on hand. The average unit cost is $34,400 divided by 8,000, or $4.30. This unit cost is used in costing withdrawals until another purchase is made, when a new average unit cost is computed. Accordingly, the cost of the 4,000 units withdrawn on March 19 is shown at $4.30, a total cost of goods sold of $17,200. On March 30, following the purchase of 2,000 units for $9,500, a new unit cost of $4.45 is determined for an ending inventory of $26,700.

The use of the average cost methods is usually justified on the basis of practical rather than conceptual reasons. These methods are simple to apply, objective, and not as subject to income manipulation as some of the other inventory pricing methods. In addition, proponents of the average cost methods argue that it is often impossible to measure a specific physical flow of inventory and therefore it is better to cost items on an average price basis. This argument is particularly persuasive when the inventory involved is relatively homogeneous in nature.

First-In, First-Out (FIFO)

The **FIFO method** assumes that goods are used in the order in which they are purchased. In other words, it assumes that **the first goods purchased are the first used** (in a manufacturing concern) **or sold** (in a merchandising concern). The inventory remaining must therefore represent the most recent purchases.

To illustrate, assume that Call-Mart Inc. uses the periodic inventory system (amount of inventory computed only at the end of the month). The cost of the ending inventory is computed by taking the cost of the most recent purchase and working back until all units in the inventory are accounted for. The ending inventory and cost of goods sold are determined as shown in Illustration 8-14.

ILLUSTRATION 8-14
FIFO Method—Periodic Inventory

Date	No. Units	Unit Cost	Total Cost
March 30	2,000	$4.75	$ 9,500
March 15	4,000	4.40	17,600
Ending inventory	6,000		$27,100

Cost of goods available for sale	$43,900
Deduct: Ending inventory	27,100
Cost of goods sold	$16,800

If a perpetual inventory system in quantities and dollars is used, a cost figure is attached to each withdrawal. Then the cost of the 4,000 units removed on March 19 would be made up of the items purchased on March 2 and March 15. The inventory on a FIFO basis perpetual system for Call-Mart Inc. is shown in Illustration 8-15.

ILLUSTRATION 8-15
FIFO Method—Perpetual Inventory

Date	Purchased		Sold or Issued	Balance	
March 2	(2,000 @ $4.00)	$ 8,000		2,000 @ $4.00	$ 8,000
March 15	(6,000 @ 4.40)	26,400		2,000 @ 4.00 6,000 @ 4.40	34,400
March 19			2,000 @ $4.00 2,000 @ 4.40 ($16,800)	4,000 @ 4.40	17,600
March 30	(2,000 @ 4.75)	9,500		4,000 @ 4.40 2,000 @ 4.75	27,100

The ending inventory in this situation is $27,100, and the cost of goods sold is $16,800 [(2,000 @ 4.00) + (2,000 @ $4.40)].

Notice that in these two FIFO examples, the cost of goods sold and ending inventory are the same. **In all cases where FIFO is used, the inventory and cost of goods sold would be the same at the end of the month whether a perpetual or periodic system is used.** This is true because the same costs will always be first in and, therefore, first out whether cost of goods sold is computed as goods are sold throughout the accounting period (the perpetual system) or as a residual at the end of the accounting period (the periodic system).

One objective of FIFO is to approximate the physical flow of goods. When the physical flow of goods is actually first-in, first-out, the FIFO method closely approximates specific identification. At the same time, it does not permit manipulation of income because the enterprise is not free to pick a certain cost item to be charged to expense.

Another advantage of the FIFO method is that the ending inventory is close to current cost. Because the first goods in are the first goods out, the ending inventory amount will be composed of the most recent purchases. This is particularly true where the inventory turnover is rapid. This approach generally provides a reasonable approximation of replacement cost on the balance sheet when price changes have not occurred since the most recent purchases.

The basic disadvantage of the FIFO method is that current costs are not matched against current revenues on the income statement. The oldest costs are charged against the more current revenue, which can lead to distortions in gross profit and net income.

INTERNATIONAL INSIGHT

Until recently, LIFO was typically used only in the United States. However, LIFO is acceptable under the Directives of the European Union, and its use has now spread in some degree to other countries. Nonetheless, LIFO is still used primarily in the United States and is still prohibited in several nations, including, for example, Australia, Hong Kong, and the United Kingdom.

Last-In, First-Out (LIFO)

The **LIFO method** first matches against revenue the cost of the last goods purchased. If a periodic inventory is used, then it would be assumed that **the cost of the total quantity sold or issued during the month would have come from the most recent**

purchases. The ending inventory would be priced by using the total units as a basis of computation and disregarding the exact dates involved. The example below assumes that the cost of the 4,000 units withdrawn absorbed the 2,000 units purchased on March 30 and 2,000 of the 6,000 units purchased on March 15. The inventory and related cost of goods sold would then be computed as shown in Illustration 8-16.

ILLUSTRATION 8-16
LIFO Method—Periodic Inventory

Date of Invoice	No. Units	Unit Cost	Total Cost
March 2	2,000	$4.00	$ 8,000
March 15	4,000	4.40	17,600
Ending inventory	6,000		$25,600

Goods available for sale	$43,900
Deduct: Ending inventory	25,600
Cost of goods sold	$18,300

If a perpetual inventory record is kept in quantities and dollars, application of the last-in, first-out method will result in **different ending inventory and cost of goods sold amounts**, as shown in Illustration 8-17.

ILLUSTRATION 8-17
LIFO Method—Perpetual Inventory

Date	Purchased		Sold or Issued	Balance	
March 2	(2,000 @ $4.00)	$ 8,000		2,000 @ $4.00	$ 8,000
March 15	(6,000 @ 4.40)	26,400		2,000 @ 4.00 6,000 @ 4.40	34,400
March 19			(4,000 @ $4.40) $17,600	2,000 @ 4.00 2,000 @ 4.40	16,800
March 30	(2,000 @ 4.75)	9,500		2,000 @ 4.00 2,000 @ 4.40 2,000 @ 4.75	26,300

The month-end periodic inventory computation presented in Illustration 8-16 (inventory $25,600 and cost of goods sold $18,300) shows a different amount from the perpetual inventory computation (inventory $26,300 and cost of goods sold $17,600). This is because the periodic system matches the total withdrawals for the month with the total purchases for the month in applying the last-in, first-out method, whereas the perpetual system matches each withdrawal with the immediately preceding purchases. In effect, the periodic computation assumed that the cost of the goods that were purchased on March 30 were included in the sale or issue on March 19.

SPECIAL ISSUES RELATED TO LIFO

LIFO Reserve

OBJECTIVE 6
Explain the significance and use of a LIFO reserve.

Many companies use LIFO for tax and external reporting purposes, but maintain a FIFO, average cost, or standard cost system for internal reporting purposes. There are several reasons to do so: (1) Companies often base their pricing decisions on a FIFO, average, or standard cost assumption, rather than on a LIFO basis. (2) Record keeping on some other basis is easier because the LIFO assumption usually does not approximate the physical flow of the product. (3) Profit-sharing and other bonus arrangements are often not based on a LIFO inventory assumption. Finally, (4) the use of a pure LIFO system is troublesome for interim periods, for which estimates must be made of year-end quantities and prices.

The difference between the inventory method used for internal reporting purposes and LIFO is referred to as the Allowance to Reduce Inventory to LIFO or the **LIFO reserve**. The change in the allowance balance from one period to the next is called the **LIFO effect**. The LIFO effect is the adjustment that must be made to the accounting records in a given year. To illustrate, assume that Acme Boot Company uses the FIFO method for internal reporting purposes and LIFO for external reporting purposes. At January 1, 2002, the Allowance to Reduce Inventory to LIFO balance was $20,000 and the ending balance should be $50,000. The LIFO effect is therefore $30,000, and the following entry is made at year-end:

Cost of Goods Sold	30,000	
Allowance to Reduce Inventory to LIFO		30,000

The Allowance to Reduce Inventory to LIFO would be deducted from inventory to ensure that the inventory is stated on a LIFO basis at year-end.

The AICPA Task Force on LIFO Inventory Problems concluded that either the LIFO reserve or the replacement cost of the inventory should be disclosed.[13] Two types of this kind of disclosure are shown below.

ILLUSTRATION 8-18
Note Disclosures of LIFO Reserve

AMERICAN MAIZE-PRODUCTS COMPANY

Inventories (Note 3)	$80,320,000

Note 3: Inventories. At December 31, $31,516,000 of inventories were valued using the LIFO method. This amount is less than the corresponding replacement value by $3,765,000.

BROWN GROUP, INC.

Inventories, net of adjustment to last-in, first-out cost of $68,736,000 (Note D)	$309,426,000

Note D: Inventories. Inventories are valued at the lower of cost or market determined principally by the last-in, first-out (LIFO) method. If the first-in, first-out (FIFO) cost method has been used, inventories would have been $68,736,000 higher.

Go to the Digital Tool for additional LIFO reserve disclosures.

LIFO Liquidation

OBJECTIVE 7
Explain the effect of LIFO liquidations.

Up to this point, we have emphasized a **specific goods approach** to costing LIFO inventories (also called traditional LIFO or unit LIFO). This approach is often unrealistic for two reasons:

1. When a company has many different inventory items, the accounting cost of keeping track of each inventory item is expensive.
2. Erosion of the LIFO inventory can easily occur (referred to as **LIFO liquidation**). This often leads to distortions of net income and substantial tax payments.

To understand the LIFO liquidation problem, assume that Basler Co. has 30,000 pounds of steel in its inventory on December 31, 2002, costed on a specific goods LIFO approach.

Ending Inventory (2002)

	Pounds	Unit Cost	LIFO Cost
1999	8,000	$ 4	$ 32,000
2000	10,000	6	60,000
2001	7,000	9	63,000
2002	5,000	10	50,000
	30,000		$205,000

[13]The AICPA Task Force on LIFO Inventory Problems defined **LIFO reserve** for its purposes as "the difference between (a) inventory at the lower of LIFO cost or market and (b) inventory at replacement cost or at the lower of cost determined by some acceptable inventory accounting method (such as FIFO or average cost) or market." *Issues Paper* (New York: AICPA, November 30, 1984), par. 2–24. The SEC has endorsed this issues paper, and therefore it has authoritative status for GAAP purposes.

As indicated, the ending 2002 inventory for Basler Co. comprises costs from past periods. These costs are called **layers** (increases from period to period), with the first layer identified as the base layer. The layers for Basler are shown in Illustration 8-19.

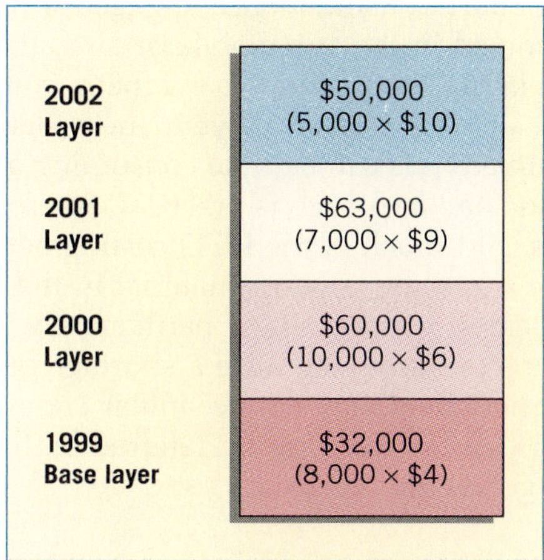

ILLUSTRATION 8-19
Layers of LIFO Inventory

The price of steel has increased over the 4-year period. In 2003, Basler Co. experienced metal shortages and had to liquidate much of its inventory (a LIFO liquidation). At the end of 2003, only 6,000 pounds of steel remained in inventory. Because the company is using LIFO, the most recent layer, 2002, is liquidated first, followed by the 2001 layer, and so on. The result: costs from preceding periods are matched against sales revenues reported in current dollars. This leads to a distortion in net income and a substantial tax bill in the current period. These effects are shown in Illustration 8-20. Unfortunately LIFO liquidations can occur frequently when a specific goods LIFO approach is employed.

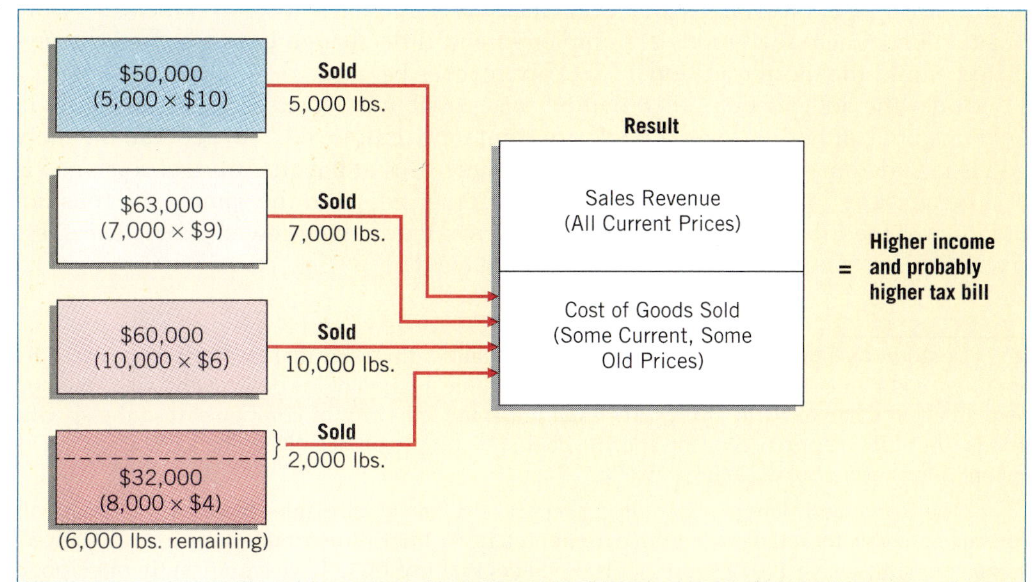

ILLUSTRATION 8-20
LIFO Liquidation

To alleviate the LIFO liquidation problems and to simplify the accounting, goods can be combined into pools. A **pool** is defined as a group of items of a similar nature. Thus, instead of only identical units, a number of similar units or products are combined and accounted for together. This method is referred to as the **specific goods pooled LIFO approach**. Using the specific goods pooled LIFO approach, LIFO liquidations are less likely to happen because the reduction of one quantity in the pool may be offset by an increase in another.

The specific goods pooled LIFO approach eliminates some of the disadvantages of the specific goods (traditional) accounting for LIFO inventories. This pooled approach, using quantities as its measurement basis, however, creates other problems.

First, most companies are continually changing the mix of their products, materials, and production methods. A business once engaged in manufacturing train locomotives may now be involved in the automobile or aircraft business. A business that had used cotton fabric in its clothing now uses synthetic fabric (dacron, nylon, etc.). If a pooled approach using quantities is employed, such changes mean that the pools must be continually redefined; this can be time consuming and costly.

Second, even when such an approach is practical, an erosion ("LIFO liquidation") of the layers often results, and much of the LIFO costing benefit is lost. An erosion of the layers results because a specific good or material in the pool may be replaced by another good or material either temporarily or permanently. This replacement may occur for competitive reasons or simply because a shortage of a certain material exists. Whatever the reason, the new item may not be similar enough to be treated as part of the old pool. Therefore any inflationary profit deferred on the old goods may have to be recognized as the old goods are replaced.

Dollar-Value LIFO

OBJECTIVE 8
Explain the dollar-value LIFO method.

To overcome the problems of redefining pools and eroding layers, the dollar-value LIFO method was developed. **An important feature of the dollar-value LIFO method is that increases and decreases in a pool are determined and measured in terms of total dollar value, not the physical quantity of the goods in the inventory pool.**

Such an approach has two important advantages over the specific goods pooled approach. First, a broader range of goods may be included in a dollar-value LIFO pool. Second, in a dollar-value LIFO pool, replacement is permitted if it is a similar material, or similar in use, or interchangeable. (In contrast, in a specific goods LIFO pool, an item may be replaced only with an item that is substantially identical.)

Thus, dollar-value LIFO techniques help protect LIFO layers from erosion. Because of this advantage, the dollar-value LIFO method is frequently used in practice.[14] Only in situations where few goods are employed and little change in product mix is predicted would the more traditional LIFO approaches be used.

Under the dollar-value LIFO method, it is possible to have the entire inventory in only one pool, although several pools are commonly employed.[15] In general, the more goods included in a pool, the more likely that decreases in the quantities of some goods will be offset by increases in the quantities of other goods in the same pool; thus liquidation of the LIFO layers is avoided. It follows that having fewer pools means less cost and less chance of a reduction of a LIFO layer.[16]

---

[14]A study by James M. Reeve and Keith G. Stanga disclosed that the vast majority of respondent companies applying LIFO use the dollar-value method or the dollar-value retail method (explained in Chapter 9) to apply LIFO. Only a small minority of companies use the specific goods (unit LIFO) approach or the specific goods pooling approach. See "The LIFO Pooling Decision," *Accounting Horizons,* June 1987, p. 27.

[15]The Reeve and Stanga study (ibid.) reports that most companies have only a few pools (the median is six for retailers and three for nonretailers), but the distributions are highly skewed; some companies have 100 or more pools. Retailers that use LIFO have significantly more pools than nonretailers. About a third of the nonretailers (mostly manufacturers) use a single pool for their entire LIFO inventory.

[16]In a later study, William R. Coon and Randall B. Hayes point out that when quantities are increasing, multiple pools over a period of time may produce (under rather general conditions) significantly higher cost of goods sold deductions than a single-pool approach. When a stock-out occurs, a single-pool approach may lessen the layer liquidation for that year, but it may not erase the cumulative cost of goods sold advantage accruing to the use of multiple pools built up over the preceding years. See "The Dollar Value LIFO Pooling Decision: The Conventional Wisdom Is Too General," *Accounting Horizons,* December 1989, pp. 57–70.

Dollar-Value LIFO Illustration

To illustrate how the dollar-value LIFO method works, assume that dollar-value LIFO was first adopted (base period) on December 31, 2001, that the inventory at current prices on that date was $20,000, and that the inventory on December 31, 2002, at current prices is $26,400. We should not conclude that the quantity has increased 32% during the year ($26,400 ÷ $20,000 = 132%). First, we need to ask: What is the value of the ending inventory in terms of beginning-of-the-year prices? Assuming that prices have increased 20% during the year, the ending inventory at beginning-of-the-year prices amounts to $22,000 ($26,400 ÷ 120%). Therefore, the inventory quantity has increased 10%, or from $20,000 to $22,000 in terms of beginning-of-the-year prices.

The next step is to price this real-dollar quantity increase. This real-dollar quantity increase of $2,000 valued at year-end prices is $2,400 (120% × $2,000). This increment (layer) of $2,400, when added to the beginning inventory of $20,000, gives a total of $22,400 for the December 31, 2002, inventory, as shown below:

First layer—(beginning inventory) in terms of 100	$20,000
Second layer—(2002 increase) in terms of 120	2,400
Dollar-value LIFO inventory, December 31, 2002	$22,400

It should be emphasized that **a layer is formed only when the ending inventory at base-year prices exceeds the beginning inventory at base-year prices**. And only when a new layer is formed must a new index be computed.

Comprehensive Dollar-Value LIFO Illustration

To illustrate the use of the dollar-value LIFO method in a more complex situation, assume that Bismark Company develops the following information:

December 31	Inventory at End-of-Year Prices	÷	Price Index (percentage)	=	End-of-Year Inventory at Base-Year Prices
(Base year) 1999	$200,000		100		$200,000
2000	299,000		115		260,000
2001	300,000		120		250,000
2002	351,000		130		270,000

At December 31, 1999, the ending inventory under dollar-value LIFO is simply the $200,000 computed as shown in Illustration 8-21.

Ending Inventory at Base-Year Prices	Layer at Base-Year Prices		Price Index (percentage)		Ending Inventory at LIFO Cost
$200,000	$200,000	×	100	=	$200,000

ILLUSTRATION 8-21
Computation of 1999 Inventory at LIFO Cost

At December 31, 2000, a comparison of the ending inventory at base-year prices ($260,000) with the beginning inventory at base-year prices ($200,000), indicates that the quantity of goods has increased $60,000 ($260,000 − $200,000). This increment (layer) is then priced at the 2000 index of 115% to arrive at a new layer of $69,000. Ending inventory for 2000 is $269,000, composed of the beginning inventory of $200,000 and the new layer of $69,000. These computations are shown in Illustration 8-22.

Ending Inventory at Base-Year Prices	Layers at Base-Year Prices		Price Index (percentage)		Ending Inventory at LIFO Cost
$260,000	→ 1999 $200,000	×	100	=	$200,000
	→ 2000 60,000	×	115	=	69,000
	$260,000				$269,000

ILLUSTRATION 8-22
Computation of 2000 Inventory at LIFO Cost

At December 31, 2001, a comparison of the ending inventory at base-year prices ($250,000) with the beginning inventory at base-year prices ($260,000) indicates that the quantity of goods has decreased $10,000 ($250,000 – $260,000). If the ending inventory at base-year prices is less than the beginning inventory at base-year prices, **the decrease must be subtracted from the most recently added layer. When a decrease occurs, previous layers must be "peeled off" at the prices in existence when the layers were added**. In Bismark Company's situation, this means that $10,000 in base-year prices must be removed from the 2000 layer of $60,000 at base-year prices. The balance of $50,000 ($60,000 – $10,000) at base-year prices must be valued at the 2000 price index of 115%, so this 2000 layer now is valued at $57,500 ($50,000 × 115%). The ending inventory is therefore computed at $257,500, consisting of the beginning inventory of $200,000 and the second layer, $57,500. The computations for 2001 are shown in Illustration 8-23.

ILLUSTRATION 8-23
Computation of 2001 Inventory at LIFO Cost

Ending Inventory at Base-Year Prices	Layers at Base-Year Prices			Price Index (percentage)		Ending Inventory at LIFO Cost
$250,000	→ 1999	$200,000	×	100	=	$200,000
	→ 2000	50,000	×	115	=	57,500
		$250,000				$257,500

Note that if a layer or base (or portion thereof) has been eliminated, it cannot be rebuilt in future periods. That is, it is gone forever.

At December 31, 2002, a comparison of the ending inventory at base-year prices ($270,000) with the beginning inventory at base-year prices ($250,000) indicates that the dollar quantity of goods has increased $20,000 ($270,000 – $250,000) in terms of base-year prices. After converting the $20,000 increase to the 2002 price index, the ending inventory is $283,500, composed of the beginning layer of $200,000, a 2000 layer of $57,500, and a 2002 layer of $26,000 ($20,000 × 130%). This computation is shown in Illustration 8-24.

ILLUSTRATION 8-24
Computation of 2002 Inventory at LIFO Cost

Ending Inventory at Base-Year Prices	Layers at Base-Year Prices			Price Index (percentage)		Ending Inventory at LIFO Cost
$270,000	→ 1999	$200,000	×	100	=	$200,000
	→ 2000	50,000	×	115	=	57,500
	→ 2002	20,000	×	130	=	26,000
		$270,000				$283,500

The ending inventory at base-year prices must always equal the total of the layers at base-year prices. Checking that this situation exists will help to ensure that the dollar-value computation is made correctly.

Selecting a Price Index

Obviously, price changes are critical in dollar-value LIFO. How are the price indexes determined? Many companies use the general price-level index prepared and published monthly by the federal government; the most popular general external price-level index is the Consumers Price Index for Urban Consumers (CPI-U).[17] Specific external price indexes are also widely used. For instance, specific indexes are computed and published daily for most commodities (gold, silver, other metals, corn, wheat, and other

[17]Indexes may be **general** (composed of several commodities, goods, or services) or **specific** (for one commodity, good, or service), and they may be **external** (computed by an outside party, such as the government, commodity exchange, or trade association) or **internal** (computed by the enterprise for its own product or service).

farm products). Many trade associations prepare indexes for specific product lines or industries. Any of these indexes may be used for dollar-value LIFO purposes.

When a specific external price index is not readily available or relevant, a company may compute its own specific internal price index. The desired approach is to price ending inventory at the most current cost. Current cost is ordinarily determined by referring to the actual cost of those goods most recently purchased. The price index provides a measure of the change in price or cost levels between the base year and the current year. An index is computed for each year after the base year. The general formula for computing the index is as follows:

$$\frac{\text{Ending Inventory for the Period at Current Cost}}{\text{Ending Inventory for the Period at Base-Year Cost}} = \text{Price Index for Current Year}$$

ILLUSTRATION 8-25
Formula for Computing a Price Index

This approach is generally referred to as the **double-extension method** because the value of the units in inventory is extended at both base-year prices and current-year prices. To illustrate this computation, assume that Toledo Company's base-year inventory (January 1, 2002) was composed of the following:

Items	Quantity	Cost per Unit	Total Cost
A	1,000	$ 6	$ 6,000
B	2,000	20	40,000
January 1, 2002, inventory at base-year costs			$46,000

Examination of the ending inventory indicates that 3,000 units of Item A and 6,000 units of Item B are held on December 31, 2002. The most recent actual purchases related to these items were as follows:

Items	Purchase Date	Quantity Purchased	Cost per Unit
A	December 1, 2002	4,000	$ 7
B	December 15, 2002	5,000	25
B	November 16, 2002	1,000	22

We double-extend the inventory as shown in Illustration 8-26.

ILLUSTRATION 8-26
Double-Extension Method of Determining a Price Index

	12/31/02 Inventory at Base-Year Costs			12/31/02 Inventory at Current-Year Costs		
Items	Units	Base-Year Cost per Unit	Total	Units	Current-Year Cost per Unit	Total
A	3,000	$ 6	$ 18,000	3,000	$ 7	$ 21,000
B	6,000	20	120,000	5,000	25	125,000
B				1,000	22	22,000
			$138,000			$168,000

After the inventories are double-extended, the formula above is used to develop the index for the current year (2002) as shown in Illustration 8-27.

$$\frac{\text{Ending Inventory for the Period at Current Cost}}{\text{Ending Inventory for the Period at Base-Year Cost}} = \frac{\$168{,}000}{\$138{,}000} = 121.74\%$$

ILLUSTRATION 8-27
Computation of 2002 Index

This index (121.74%) is then applied to the layer added in 2002. Note in this illustration that Toledo Company used the most recent actual purchases to determine current cost; other approaches such as FIFO and average cost may also be used. Whichever flow assumption is adopted, consistent use from one period to another is required.[18]

Use of the double-extension method is time consuming and difficult where substantial technological change has occurred or where a large number of items is involved. That is, as time passes, a new base-year cost must be determined for new products, and a base-year cost must be kept for each inventory item.[19]

Comparison of LIFO Approaches

Three different approaches to computing LIFO inventories are presented in this chapter—specific goods LIFO, specific goods pooled LIFO, and dollar-value LIFO. As indicated earlier, the use of the specific goods LIFO is unrealistic because most enterprises have numerous goods in inventory at the end of a period, and costing (pricing) them on a unit basis is extremely expensive and time consuming.

The specific goods pooled LIFO approach is better in that it reduces record keeping and clerical costs. In addition, it is more difficult to erode the layers because the reduction of one quantity in the pool may be offset by an increase in another. Nonetheless, the pooled approach using quantities as its measurement basis can lead to untimely LIFO liquidations.

As a result, **dollar-value LIFO is the method employed by most companies that currently use a LIFO system**. Although the approach appears complex, the logic and the computations are actually quite simple, once an appropriate index is determined.

This is not to suggest that problems do not exist with the dollar-value LIFO method. The selection of the items to be put in a pool can be subjective.[20] Such a determination, however, is extremely important because manipulation of the items in a pool without conceptual justification can affect reported net income. For example, the SEC noted that some companies have set up pools that are easy to liquidate. As a result, when the company wants to increase its income, it decreases inventory, thereby matching low-cost inventory items to current revenues.

To curb this practice, the SEC has taken a much harder line on the number of pools that companies may establish. In the well-publicized **Stauffer Chemical Company** case, Stauffer had increased the number of LIFO pools from 8 to 280, boosting its net income by \$16,515,000 or approximately 13%.[21] Stauffer justified the change in its Annual Report on the basis of "achieving a better matching of cost and revenue." The SEC required Stauffer to reduce the number of its inventory pools, contending that some pools were inappropriate and alleging income manipulation.

---

[18]Another approach to finding an index is the **link-chain method**. Under the link-chain method the base cost of ending inventory is determined by applying a cumulative index to the dollar value of the ending inventory. The cumulative index is the relationship of the current-year prices to those of the prior year (based on either double-extension or an index) multiplied by the prior year's cumulative index. Thus each year's index may be characterized as a link in a chain of indexes back to the base year. It is not illustrated here because its use is limited.

[19]Another approach, which was initially sanctioned by the Internal Revenue Service for tax purposes, may be used to simplify the analysis. Under this method, an index is obtained by reference to an outside source or by double-extending only a sample portion of the inventory. For example, all companies are allowed to use 80% of the inflation rate reported by the appropriate consumer or producer price indexes prepared by the Bureau of Labor Statistics (BLS) as their inflation rate for a LIFO pool. Small companies (less than \$5 million in sales) can use 100% of the inflation rate reported by such indexes as their inflation rate. Once the index is obtained, the ending inventory at current cost is divided by the index to find the base-year cost. Using generally available external indexes greatly simplifies LIFO computations, as internal indexes need not be computed. Although this approach was initially established for reporting taxable income, it is permissible to use this method for financial reporting as well.

[20]It is suggested that companies analyze how inventory purchases are affected by price changes, how goods are stocked, how goods are used, and if future liquidations are likely. See William R. Cron and Randall Hayes, "The Dollar Value LIFO Pooling Decision: The Conventional Wisdom Is Too General," *Accounting Horizons*, December 1989, p. 57.

[21]Commerce Clearing House, *SEC Accounting Rules* (Chicago: CCH, 1983), par. 4035.

Major Advantages of LIFO Approaches

OBJECTIVE 9
Identify the major advantages and disadvantages of LIFO.

One obvious advantage of LIFO approaches is that in certain situations the LIFO cost flow actually approximates the physical flow of the goods in and out of inventory. For instance, in the case of a coal pile, the last coal in is the first coal out because it is on the top of the pile. The coal remover is not going to take the coal from the bottom of the pile! The coal that is going to be taken first is the coal that was placed on the pile last.

However, the coal pile situation is one of only a few situations where the actual physical flow corresponds to LIFO. Therefore most adherents of LIFO use other arguments for its widespread employment, as follows:

Matching

In LIFO, the more recent costs are matched against current revenues to provide a better measure of current earnings. During periods of inflation, many challenge the quality of non-LIFO earnings, noting that by failing to match current costs against current revenues, **transitory or "paper" profits ("inventory profits") are created**. Inventory profits occur when the inventory costs matched against sales are less than the inventory replacement cost. The cost of goods sold therefore is understated and profit is overstated. Using LIFO (rather than a method such as FIFO), current costs are matched against revenues and inventory profits are thereby reduced.

Tax Benefits

Tax benefits are the major reason why LIFO has become popular. As long as the price level increases and inventory quantities do not decrease, a deferral of income tax occurs, because the items most recently purchased at the higher price level are matched against revenues. For example, when Fuqua Industries decided to switch to LIFO, it had a resultant tax savings of about $4 million. Even if the price level decreases later, the company has been given a temporary deferral of its income taxes.[22] The tax law requires that if a company uses LIFO for tax purposes, it must also use LIFO for financial accounting purposes[23] (although neither tax law nor GAAP requires a company to pool its inventories in the same manner for book and tax purposes). This requirement is often referred to as the **LIFO conformity rule**. Other inventory valuation methods do not have this requirement. Unfortunately, the general attitude too frequently is: "Whatever is good for tax is good for financial reporting."

LIFO tends to be found in financial statements in countries where it is allowed for tax purposes, such as Belgium, Germany, Japan, South Korea, and Taiwan.

Improved Cash Flow

Improved cash flow is related to the tax benefits, because taxes must be paid in cash. As a consequence, some companies not receiving LIFO tax benefits are forced to borrow to finance replacement of existing inventory levels, and interest costs can be staggering. Fuqua Industries expected to save approximately $400,000 in interest costs by switching to LIFO. Even if the company has plenty of cash to pay its taxes, LIFO permits management to invest these funds and earn a return unavailable to those using FIFO.[24]

---

[22]In periods of rising prices, the use of fewer pools will translate into greater income tax benefits through the use of LIFO. The use of fewer pools allows inventory reductions of some items to be offset by inventory increases in others. In contrast, the use of more pools increases the likelihood that old, low-cost inventory layers will be liquidated and tax consequences will be negative. See Reeve and Stanga, *Accounting Horizons*, pp. 28–29.

[23]Management often selects an accounting procedure because a lower tax results from its use, instead of an accounting method that is conceptually more appealing. Throughout this textbook, an effort has been made to identify accounting procedures that provide income tax benefits to the user.

[24]Note that, even though some would receive substantial tax benefits if they switched to LIFO, they have chosen not to. Some of the reasons for not changing to LIFO are presented in Gary C. Biddle, "Accounting Methods and Management Decisions: The Case of Inventory Costing and Inventory Policy," *The Journal of Accounting Research*, Supplement 1980.

Future Earnings Hedge

With LIFO, a company's future reported earnings will not be affected substantially by future price declines. LIFO eliminates or substantially minimizes write-downs to market as a result of price decreases. The reason: since the most recent inventory is sold first, there isn't much ending inventory sitting around at high prices vulnerable to a price decline. In contrast, inventory costed under FIFO is more vulnerable to price declines, which can reduce net income substantially.

Major Disadvantages of LIFO Approaches

Despite its advantages, LIFO has the following drawbacks:

Reduced Earnings

Many corporate managers view the lower profits reported under the LIFO method in inflationary times as a distinct disadvantage and would rather have higher reported profits than lower taxes. Some fear that an accounting change to LIFO may be misunderstood by investors and that, as a result of the lower profits, the price of the company's stock will fall. In fact, though, there is some evidence to refute this contention. Non-LIFO earnings are now highly suspect and may be severely penalized by Wall Street.

Inventory Understated

LIFO may have a distorting effect on a company's balance sheet. The inventory valuation is normally outdated because the oldest costs remain in inventory. This understatement makes the working capital position of the company appear worse than it really is.

The magnitude and direction of this variation between the carrying amount of inventory and its current price depend on the degree and direction of the price changes and the amount of inventory turnover.[25] The combined effect of rising product prices and avoidance of inventory liquidations increases the difference between the inventory carrying value at LIFO and current prices of that inventory, thereby magnifying the balance sheet distortion attributed to the use of LIFO.[26]

Physical Flow

LIFO does not approximate the physical flow of the items except in peculiar situations (such as the coal pile). Originally LIFO could be used only in certain circumstances. This situation has changed over the years to the point where physical flow characteristics no longer play an important role in determining whether LIFO may be employed.

Current Cost Income Not Measured

LIFO falls short of measuring current cost (replacement cost) income, though not as far short as FIFO. When measuring current cost income, the cost of goods sold should consist not of the most recently incurred costs but rather of the cost that will be incurred to replace the goods that have been sold. Using replacement cost is referred to as the

---

[25] In 1986, the Accounting Standards Executive Committee (AcSEC) of the AICPA considered but voted down (by 8 to 6) a draft issues paper that explored an intriguing alternative to the way some companies report inventories in their financial statements. Under the suggested method, dubbed LIFO/FIFO, a company would use LIFO to measure cost of goods sold in its income statement and FIFO to report inventories in its balance sheet. See M. P. Bohan and S. Rubin, "LIFO/FIFO: How Would It Work?" *Journal of Accountancy,* September 1986, p. 106.

[26] This position is supported by the findings of James M. Reeve and Keith G. Stanga, "Balance Sheet Impact of Using LIFO: An Empirical Study," *Accounting Horizons,* September 1987, pp. 9–15.

next-in, first-out method, which is not currently acceptable for purposes of inventory valuation.

Involuntary Liquidation

If the base or layers of old costs are eliminated, strange results can occur because old, irrelevant costs can be matched against current revenues. A distortion in reported income for a given period may result, as well as consequences that are detrimental from an income tax point of view.[27]

For example, **Allied Corporation** reported net earnings of $.09 per share in a year in which its inventory reductions resulted in liquidations of LIFO inventory quantities. The effect of the inventory reduction was to increase income by $13 million or $.17 per share. The income tax problem is particularly severe when the involuntary liquidation results from a strike or a shortage of materials. In these situations, companies may incur high tax bills when they can least afford to pay taxes.

Poor Buying Habits

Because of the liquidation problem, LIFO may cause poor buying habits. A company may simply purchase more goods and match these goods against revenue to ensure that the old costs are not charged to expense. Furthermore, the possibility always exists with LIFO that a company will attempt to manipulate its net income at the end of the year simply by altering its pattern of purchases.[28]

Because price rises have been the general way of life in the U.S. economy during the last four decades, LIFO has provided a tax advantage over FIFO. During periods of price decreases, this tax advantage could become a disadvantage. And during periods of stable prices, FIFO and LIFO methods of inventory costing would generally produce identical results.

One survey uncovered the following reasons why companies reject LIFO:[29]

ILLUSTRATION 8-28
Why Do Companies Reject LIFO? Summary of Responses

Reasons to Reject LIFO	Number	% of Total*
No expected tax benefits		
No required tax payment	34	16%
Declining prices	31	15
Rapid inventory turnover	30	14
Immaterial inventory	26	12
Miscellaneous tax related	38	17
	159	74%
Regulatory or other restrictions	26	12%
Excessive cost		
High administrative costs	29	14
LIFO liquidation–related costs	12	6
	41	20%
Other adverse consequences		
Lower reported earnings	18	8
Bad accounting	7	3
	25	11%

*Percentage totals more than 100% as some companies offered more than one explanation.

Despite an effort to eliminate it, LIFO remains acceptable under international accounting standards.

[27]The AICPA Task Force on LIFO Inventory Problems recommends that the effects on income of LIFO inventory liquidations be disclosed in the notes to the financial statements but that the effects not receive special treatment in the income statement. *Issues Paper* (New York: AICPA, 1984), pp. 36–37.

[28]For example, one reason why **General Tire and Rubber** at one time accelerated raw material purchases at the end of the year was to minimize the book profit from a liquidation of LIFO inventories and to minimize income taxes for the year.

[29]Michael H. Granof and Daniel Short, "Why Do Companies Reject LIFO?" *Journal of Accounting, Auditing, and Finance,* Summer 1984, pp. 323–333, Table 1, p. 327.

BASIS FOR SELECTION OF INVENTORY METHOD

OBJECTIVE 10
Identify the reasons why a given inventory method is selected.

How does one choose among the various inventory methods? Although no absolute rules can be stated, preferability for LIFO can ordinarily be established in either of the following circumstances: (1) if selling prices and revenues have been increasing faster than costs, thereby distorting income, and (2) in situations where LIFO has been traditional, such as department stores and industries where a fairly constant "base stock" is present such as refining, chemicals, and glass.[30]

Conversely, LIFO would probably not be appropriate: (1) where prices tend to lag behind costs; (2) in situations where specific identification is traditional, such as in the sale of automobiles, farm equipment, art, and antique jewelry; or (3) where unit costs tend to decrease as production increases, thereby nullifying the tax benefit that LIFO might provide.[31]

Tax consequences are another consideration. Switching from FIFO to LIFO usually results in an immediate tax benefit. However, switching from LIFO to FIFO can result in a substantial tax burden. For example, when **Chrysler** (now DaimlerChrysler) changed from LIFO to FIFO, it became responsible for an additional $53 million in taxes that had been deferred over 14 years of LIFO inventory valuation. Why, then, would Chrysler, and other companies, change to FIFO? The major reason was the profit crunch of that era. Although Chrysler showed a loss of $7.6 million after the switch, the loss would have been $20 million *more* if the company had not changed its inventory valuation back to FIFO from LIFO.

It is questionable whether companies should switch from LIFO to FIFO for the sole purpose of increasing reported earnings.[32] Intuitively one would assume that companies with higher reported earnings would have a higher share (common stock price) valuation. Some studies have indicated, however, that the users of financial data exhibit a much higher sophistication than might be expected. Share prices are the same and, in some cases, even higher under LIFO in spite of lower reported earnings.[33]

The concern about reduced income resulting from adoption of LIFO has even less substance now because the IRS has relaxed the LIFO conformity rule which required a company that employed LIFO for tax purposes to use it for book purposes as well. The IRS has relaxed restrictions against providing non-LIFO income numbers as supplementary information. As a result, the profession now permits supplemental non-LIFO disclosures but not on the face of the income statement. The supplemental disclosure, while not intended to override the basic LIFO method adopted for financial

[30]*Accounting Trends and Techniques—1999* reports that of 944 inventory method disclosures, 319 used LIFO, 409 used FIFO, 176 used average cost, and 40 used other methods.

[31]See Barry E. Cushing and Marc J. LeClere, "Evidence on the Determinants of Inventory Accounting Policy Choice," *The Accounting Review*, April 1992, pp. 355–366, Table 4, p. 363, for a list of factors hypothesized to affect FIFO–LIFO choices.

[32]Because of steady or falling raw materials costs and costs savings from electronic data interchange and just-in-time technologies in recent years, many businesses using LIFO are no longer experiencing substantial tax benefits from LIFO. Even some companies for which LIFO is creating a benefit are finding that the administrative costs associated with LIFO are higher than the LIFO benefit obtained. As a result, some companies are deciding to move to FIFO or average cost.

[33]See, for example, Shyam Sunder, "Relationship Between Accounting Changes and Stock Prices: Problems of Measurement and Some Empirical Evidence," *Empirical Research in Accounting: Selected Studies, 1973* (Chicago: University of Chicago), pp. 1–40. But see Robert Moren Brown, "Short-Range Market Reaction to Changes to LIFO Accounting Using Preliminary Earnings Announcement Dates," *The Journal of Accounting Research*, Spring 1980, which found that companies that do change to LIFO suffer a short-run decline in the price of their stock; see also William E. Ricks, "Market's Response to the 1974 LIFO Adoptions," *The Journal of Accounting Research*, Autumn 1982, pp. 367–387.

reporting, may be useful in comparing operating income and working capital with companies not on LIFO.

For example, **J. C. Penney, Inc.** (a LIFO user) in its Annual Report presented the following information.

ILLUSTRATION 8-29
Supplemental Non-LIFO Disclosure

J. C. PENNEY, INC.

Some companies in the retail industry use the FIFO method in valuing part or all of their inventories. Had J. C. Penney used the FIFO method and made no other assumptions with respect to changes in income resulting therefrom, income and income per share from continuing operations would have been:

Income from continuing operations (in millions)	$325
Income from continuing operations per share	$4.63

Another user of LIFO, **Weyerhaeuser Company**, made the following disclosure in its Annual Report relative to product inventories carried in its balance sheet at $423,988,000 (current period) and $379,399,000 (prior period):

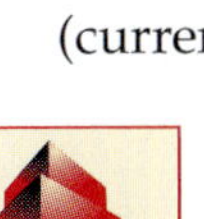

ILLUSTRATION 8-30
Supplemental Non-LIFO Disclosure

WEYERHAEUSER COMPANY

Had the FIFO method been used to cost all inventories, the amounts at which product inventories are stated would have been $178,122,000 and $183,001,000 greater during the current and prior period, respectively.

Relaxation of the LIFO conformity rule has led more companies to select LIFO as their inventory valuation method because they will be able to disclose FIFO income numbers in the financial reports if they so desire.[34]

Often the inventory methods are used in combination with other methods. For example, most companies never use LIFO totally, but rather use it in combination with other valuation approaches. One reason is that certain product lines can be highly susceptible to deflation instead of inflation. In addition, if the level of inventory is unstable, unwanted involuntary liquidations may result in certain product lines if LIFO is used. Finally, where inventory turnover in certain product lines is high, the additional recordkeeping and expense are not justified by LIFO. Average cost is often used in such cases because it is easy to compute.[35]

This variety of inventory methods has been devised to assist in accurate computation of net income rather than to permit manipulation of reported income. Hence, it is recommended that the pricing method most suitable to a company be selected and, once selected, be applied consistently thereafter. If conditions indicate that the inventory pricing method in use is unsuitable, serious consideration should be given to all other possibilities before selecting another method. Any change should be clearly explained and its effect disclosed in the financial statements.

[34]Note that a company can use one variation of LIFO for financial reporting purposes and another for tax without violating the LIFO conformity rule. Such a relaxation has caused many problems because the general approach to accounting for LIFO has been "whatever is good for tax is good for financial reporting." The AICPA published a useful paper on this subject entitled "Identification and Discussion of Certain Financial Accounting and Reporting Issues Concerning LIFO Inventories" (New York: AICPA, November 30, 1984).

[35]For an interesting discussion of the reasons for and against the use of FIFO and average cost, see Michael H. Granof and Daniel G. Short "For Some Companies, FIFO Accounting Makes Sense," *The Wall Street Journal*, August 30, 1982, and the subsequent rebuttal by Gary C. Biddle "Taking Stock of Inventory Accounting Choices," *The Wall Street Journal*, September 15, 1982.

Inventory Valuation Methods—Summary Analysis

A number of inventory valuation methods are described in the preceding sections of this chapter. A brief summary of the three major inventory methods, assuming periodic inventory procedures, is presented below to show the differing effects these valuation methods have on the financial statements. The first schedule provides selected data for the comparison as follows:

Selected Data

Given		
Beginning cash balance		$ 7,000
Beginning retained earnings		$10,000
Beginning inventory:	4,000 units @ $3	$12,000
Purchases:	6,000 units @ $4	$24,000
Sales:	5,000 units @ $12	$60,000
Operating expenses		$10,000
Income tax rate		40%

The comparative results of using average cost, FIFO, and LIFO on net income are computed as shown in Illustration 8-31.

ILLUSTRATION 8-31
Comparative Results of Average Cost, FIFO, and LIFO Methods

	Average Cost	FIFO	LIFO
Sales	$60,000	$60,000	$60,000
Cost of goods sold	18,000[a]	16,000[b]	20,000[c]
Gross profit	42,000	44,000	40,000
Operating expenses	10,000	10,000	10,000
Income before taxes	32,000	34,000	30,000
Income taxes (40%)	12,800	13,600	12,000
Net income	$19,200	$20,400	$18,000

[a]4,000 @ $3 = $12,000
6,000 @ $4 = 24,000
$36,000
$36,000 ÷ 10,000 = $3.60
$3.60 × 5,000 = $18,000

[b]4,000 @ $3 = $12,000
1,000 @ $4 = 4,000
$16,000

[c]5,000 @ $4 = $20,000

Notice that gross profit and net income are lowest under LIFO, highest under FIFO, and somewhere in the middle under average cost.

The table below then shows the final balances of selected items at the end of the period:

ILLUSTRATION 8-32
Balances of Selected Items Under Alternative Inventory Valuation Methods

	Inventory	Gross Profit	Taxes	Net Income	Retained Earnings	Cash
Average Cost	$18,000 (5,000 × $3.60)	$42,000	$12,800	$19,200	$29,200 ($10,000 + $19,200)	$20,200[a]
FIFO	$20,000 (5,000 × $4)	$44,000	$13,600	$20,400	$30,400 ($10,000 + $20,400)	$19,400[a]
LIFO	$16,000 (4,000 × $3) (1,000 × $4)	$40,000	$12,000	$18,000	$28,000 ($10,000 + $18,000)	$21,000[a]

[a]Cash at year-end	=	Beg. balance	+	sales	−	purchases	−	operating expenses	−	taxes
Average cost—$20,200	=	$7,000	+	$60,000	−	$24,000	−	$10,000	−	$12,800
FIFO—$19,400	=	$7,000	+	$60,000	−	$24,000	−	$10,000	−	$13,600
LIFO—$21,000	=	$7,000	+	$60,000	−	$24,000	−	$10,000	−	$12,000

LIFO results in the highest cash balance at year-end because taxes are lower. This example assumes prices are rising; the opposite result occurs if prices are declining.

SUMMARY OF LEARNING OBJECTIVES

1 Identify major classifications of inventory. Only one inventory account, Merchandise Inventory, appears in the financial statements of a merchandising concern. A manufacturer normally has three inventory accounts: Raw Materials, Work in Process, and Finished Goods. The cost assigned to goods and materials on hand but not yet placed into production is reported as raw materials inventory. The cost of the raw materials on which production has been started but not completed, plus the direct labor cost applied specifically to this material and a ratable share of manufacturing overhead costs, constitute the work in process inventory. The costs identified with the completed but unsold units on hand at the end of the fiscal period are reported as finished goods inventory.

2 Distinguish between perpetual and periodic inventory systems. Under a perpetual inventory system, a continuous record of changes in inventory is maintained in the Inventory account. That is, all purchases and sales (issues) of goods are recorded directly in the Inventory account as they occur. Under a periodic inventory system, the quantity of inventory on hand is determined only periodically. The Inventory account remains the same and a Purchases account is debited. Cost of goods sold is determined at the end of the period using a formula. Ending inventory is ascertained by physical count.

3 Identify the effects of inventory errors on the financial statements. *If the ending inventory is misstated,* (1) the inventory, retained earnings, working capital, and current ratio in the balance sheet will be misstated, and (2) the cost of goods sold and net income in the income statement will be misstated. *If purchases and inventory are misstated,* (1) the inventory, accounts payable, and current ratio will be misstated, and (2) purchases and ending inventory in the income statement will be misstated.

4 Identify the items that should be included as inventory cost. Product costs are directly connected with the bringing of goods to the place of business of the buyer and converting such goods to a salable condition. Such charges would include freight charges on goods purchased, other direct costs of acquisition, and labor and other production costs incurred in processing the goods up to the time of sale. Manufacturing overhead costs that include indirect material, indirect labor, and such items as depreciation, taxes, insurance, heat, and electricity incurred in the manufacturing process are also allocated to inventory.

5 Describe and compare the flow assumptions used in accounting for inventories. (1) *Average cost* prices items in the inventory on the basis of the average cost of all similar goods available during the period. (2) *First-in, first-out (FIFO)* assumes that goods are used in the order in which they are purchased. The inventory remaining must therefore represent the most recent purchases. (3) *Last-in, first-out (LIFO)* matches the cost of the last goods purchased against revenue.

6 Explain the significance and use of a LIFO reserve. The difference between the inventory method used for internal reporting purposes and LIFO is referred to as the Allowance to Reduce Inventory to LIFO. Either the LIFO reserve or the replacement cost of the inventory should be disclosed.

7 Explain the effect of LIFO liquidations. The effect of LIFO liquidations is that costs from preceding periods are matched against sales revenues reported in current dollars. This leads to a distortion in net income and a substantial tax bill in the current period. LIFO liquidations can occur frequently when a specific goods LIFO approach is employed.

8 Explain the dollar-value LIFO method. An important feature of the dollar-value LIFO method is that increases and decreases in a pool are determined and measured in terms of total dollar value, not the physical quantity of the goods in the inventory pool.

KEY TERMS

9 Identify the major advantages and disadvantages of LIFO. The major advantages of LIFO are: (1) recent costs are matched against current revenues to provide a better measure of current earnings; (2) as long as the price level increases and inventory quantities do not decrease, a deferral of income tax occurs in LIFO; (3) because of the deferral of income tax, there is improvement of cash flow; (4) a company's future reported earnings will not be affected substantially by future price declines (future earnings hedge). Major disadvantages are: (1) reduced earnings, (2) understated inventory, and (3) no approximated physical flow of the items except in peculiar situations.

10 Identify the reasons why a given inventory method is selected. Preferability of LIFO can ordinarily be established if: (1) selling prices and revenues have been increasing faster than costs, and (2) LIFO has been traditional, such as department stores and industries like refining, chemicals, and glass where a fairly constant "base stock" is present. Conversely, LIFO would probably not be appropriate: (1) where prices tend to lag behind costs; (2) in situations where specific identification is traditional, such as in the sales of automobiles, farm equipment, art, and antique jewelry; and (3) where unit costs tend to decrease as production increases, thereby nullifying the tax benefit that LIFO might provide.

QUESTIONS

1 In what ways are the inventory accounts of a retailing concern different from those of a manufacturing enterprise?

2 Why should inventories be included in (a) a statement of financial position and (b) the computation of net income?

3 What is the difference between a perpetual inventory and a physical inventory? If a company maintains a perpetual inventory, should its physical inventory at any date be equal to the amount indicated by the perpetual inventory records? Why?

4 Mariah Carey, Inc. indicated in a recent annual report that approximately $19 million of merchandise was received on consignment. Should Mariah Carey, Inc. report this amount on its balance sheet? Explain.

5 What is a product financing arrangement? How should product financing arrangements be reported in the financial statements?

6 Where, if at all, should the following items be classified on a balance sheet?

(a) Goods out on approval to customers.

(b) Goods in transit that were recently purchased f.o.b. destination.

(c) Land held by a realty firm for sale.

(d) Raw materials.

(e) Goods received on consignment.

(f) Manufacturing supplies.

7 At the balance sheet date Paula Abdul Company held title to goods in transit amounting to $214,000. This amount was omitted from the purchases figure for the year and also from the ending inventory. What is the effect of this omission on the net income for the year as calculated when the books are closed? On the company's financial position as shown in its balance sheet? Is materiality a factor in determining whether an adjustment for this item should be made?

8 Define "cost" as applied to the valuation of inventories.

9 What is the difference between variable costing and conventional absorption costing? Is variable costing acceptable for external financial reporting and for income tax purposes? Why?

10 Dana Barros Corp. is considering alternate methods of accounting for the cash discounts it takes when paying suppliers promptly. One method suggested was to report these discounts as financial income when payments are made. Comment on the propriety of this approach.

11 Harold Baines Inc. purchases 300 units of an item at an invoice cost of $30,000. What is the cost per unit? If the goods are shipped f.o.b. shipping point and the freight bill was $1,500, what is the cost per unit if Baines Inc. pays the freight charges? If these items were bought on 2/10, n/30 terms and the invoice and the freight bill were paid within the 10-day period, what would be the cost per unit?

12 Specific identification is sometimes said to be the ideal method of assigning cost to inventory and to cost of goods sold. Briefly indicate the arguments for and against this method of inventory valuation.

13 First-in, first-out; weighted average; and last-in, first-out methods are often used instead of specific identification for inventory valuation purposes. Compare these methods with the specific identification method, discussing the theoretical propriety of each method in the determination of income and asset valuation.

14 How might a company obtain a price index in order to apply dollar-value LIFO?

15 Describe the LIFO double-extension method. Using the following information, compute the index at December 31, 2002, applying the double-extension method to a LIFO pool consisting of 25,500 units of product A and 10,350 units of product B: the base-year cost of product A is $10.20 and of product B is $37.00; the price at December 31, 2002, for product A is $19.00 and for product B is $45.60.

16 As compared with the FIFO method of costing inventories, does the LIFO method result in a larger or smaller net income in a period of rising prices? What is the comparative effect on net income in a period of falling prices?

17 What is the dollar-value method of LIFO inventory valuation? What advantage does the dollar-value method have over the specific goods approach of LIFO inventory valuation? Why will the traditional LIFO inventory costing method and the dollar-value LIFO inventory costing method produce different inventory valuations if the composition of the inventory base changes?

18 Explain the following terms:

(a) LIFO layer. **(b)** LIFO reserve. **(c)** LIFO effect.

19 On December 31, 2001, the inventory of Mario Lemieux Company amounts to $800,000. During 2002, the company decides to use the dollar-value LIFO method of costing inventories. On December 31, 2002, the inventory is $1,026,000 at December 31, 2002, prices. Using the December 31, 2001, price level of 100 and the December 31, 2002, price level of 108, compute the inventory value at December 31, 2002, under the dollar-value LIFO method.

20 In an article that appeared in *The Wall Street Journal*, the phrases "phantom (paper) profits" and "high LIFO profits" through involuntary liquidation were used. Explain these phrases.

BRIEF EXERCISES

BE8-1 Included in the December 31 trial balance of Billie Joel Company are the following assets:

Cash	$ 190,000	Work in process	$200,000
Equipment (net)	1,100,000	Receivables (net)	400,000
Prepaid insurance	41,000	Patents	110,000
Raw materials	335,000	Finished goods	150,000

Prepare the current assets section of the December 31 balance sheet.

BE8-2 Alanis Morrissette Company uses a perpetual inventory system. Its beginning inventory consists of 50 units that cost $30 each. During June, the company purchased 150 units at $30 each, returned 6 units for credit, and sold 125 units at $50 each. Journalize the June transactions.

BE8-3 Mayberry Company took a physical inventory on December 31 and determined that goods costing $200,000 were on hand. Not included in the physical count were $15,000 of goods purchased from Taylor Corporation, f.o.b. shipping point; and $22,000 of goods sold to Mount Pilot Company for $30,000, f.o.b. destination. Both the Taylor purchase and the Mount Pilot sale were in transit at year-end. What amount should Mayberry report as its December 31 inventory?

BE8-4 Gavin Bryars Enterprises reported cost of goods sold for 2002 of $1,400,000 and retained earnings of $5,200,000 at December 31, 2002. Gavin Bryars later discovered that its ending inventories at December 31, 2001 and 2002, were overstated by $110,000 and $45,000, respectively. Determine the corrected amounts for 2002 cost of goods sold and December 31, 2002, retained earnings.

BE8-5 Jose Zorilla Company uses a periodic inventory system. For April, when the company sold 700 units, the following information is available:

	Units	Unit Cost	Total Cost
April 1 inventory	250	$10	$ 2,500
April 15 purchase	400	12	4,800
April 23 purchase	350	13	4,550
	1,000		$11,850

Compute the April 30 inventory and the April cost of goods sold using the average cost method.

BE8-6 Data for Jose Zorilla Company are presented in BE8-5. Compute the April 30 inventory and the April cost of goods sold using the FIFO method.

BE8-7 Data for Jose Zorilla Company are presented in BE8-5. Compute the April 30 inventory and the April cost of goods sold using the LIFO method.

BE8-8 Easy-E Company had ending inventory at end-of-year prices of $100,000 at 12/31/00; $123,200 at 12/31/01; and $134,560 at 12/31/02. The year-end price indexes were 100 at 12/31/00, 110 at 12/31/01, and 116 at 12/31/02. Compute the ending inventory for Easy-E Company for 2000 through 2002 using the dollar-value LIFO method.

BE8-9 Wingers uses the dollar-value LIFO method of computing its inventory. Data for the past 3 years follow:

Year Ended December 31	Inventory at Current-year Cost	Price Index
1999	$19,750	100
2000	21,708	108
2001	25,935	114

Instructions

Compute the value of the 2000 and 2001 inventories using the dollar-value LIFO method.

EXERCISES

E8-1 (Inventoriable Costs) Presented below is a list of items that may or may not be reported as inventory in a company's December 31 balance sheet.

1. Goods out on consignment at another company's store.
2. Goods sold on an installment basis (bad debts can be reasonably estimated).
3. Goods purchased f.o.b. shipping point that are in transit at December 31.
4. Goods purchased f.o.b. destination that are in transit at December 31.
5. Goods sold to another company, for which our company has signed an agreement to repurchase at a set price that covers all costs related to the inventory.
6. Goods sold where large returns are predictable.
7. Goods sold f.o.b. shipping point that are in transit at December 31.
8. Freight charges on goods purchased.
9. Factory labor costs incurred on goods still unsold.
10. Interest costs incurred for inventories that are routinely manufactured.
11. Costs incurred to advertise goods held for resale.
12. Materials on hand not yet placed into production by a manufacturing firm.
13. Office supplies.
14. Raw materials on which a manufacturing firm has started production, but which are not completely processed.
15. Factory supplies.
16. Goods held on consignment from another company.
17. Costs identified with units completed by a manufacturing firm, but not yet sold.
18. Goods sold f.o.b. destination that are in transit at December 31.
19. Temporary investments in stocks and bonds that will be resold in the near future.

Instructions

Indicate which of these items would typically be reported as inventory in the financial statements. If an item should **not** be reported as inventory, indicate how it should be reported in the financial statements.

E8-2 (Inventoriable Costs) In your audit of the Jose Oliva Company, you find that a physical inventory on December 31, 2000, showed merchandise with a cost of $441,000 was on hand at that date. You also discover the following items were all excluded from the $441,000.

1. Merchandise of $61,000 which is held by Oliva on consignment. The consignor is the Max Suzuki Company.
2. Merchandise costing $38,000 which was shipped by Oliva f.o.b. destination to a customer on December 31, 2000. The customer was expected to receive the merchandise on January 6, 2001.
3. Merchandise costing $46,000 which was shipped by Oliva f.o.b. shipping point to a customer on December 29, 2000. The customer was scheduled to receive the merchandise on January 2, 2001.
4. Merchandise costing $83,000 shipped by a vendor f.o.b. destination on December 30, 2000, and received by Oliva on January 4, 2001.
5. Merchandise costing $51,000 shipped by a vendor f.o.b. seller on December 31, 2000, and received by Oliva on January 5, 2001.

Instructions

Based on the above information, calculate the amount that should appear on Oliva's balance sheet at December 31, 2000, for inventory.

E8-3 (Inventoriable Costs) In an annual audit of Jan Matejko Company at December 31, 2002, you find the following transactions near the closing date.

1. A special machine, fabricated to order for a customer, was finished and specifically segregated in the back part of the shipping room on December 31, 2002. The customer was billed on that date and the machine excluded from inventory although it was shipped on January 4, 2003.
2. Merchandise costing $2,800 was received on January 3, 2003, and the related purchase invoice recorded January 5. The invoice showed the shipment was made on December 29, 2002, f.o.b. destination.
3. A packing case containing a product costing $3,400 was standing in the shipping room when the physical inventory was taken. It was not included in the inventory because it was marked "Hold for shipping instructions." Your investigation revealed that the customer's order was dated December 18, 2002, but that the case was shipped and the customer billed on January 10, 2003. The product was a stock item of your client.
4. Merchandise received on January 6, 2003, costing $680 was entered in the purchase journal on January 7, 2003. The invoice showed shipment was made f.o.b. supplier's warehouse on December 31, 2002. Because it was not on hand at December 31, it was not included in inventory.
5. Merchandise costing $720 was received on December 28, 2002, and the invoice was not recorded. You located it in the hands of the purchasing agent; it was marked "on consignment."

Instructions

Assuming that each of the amounts is material, state whether the merchandise should be included in the client's inventory and give your reason for your decision on each item.

E8-4 (Inventoriable Costs—Perpetual) Colin Davis Machine Company maintains a general ledger account for each class of inventory, debiting such accounts for increases during the period and crediting them for decreases. The transactions below relate to the Raw Materials inventory account, which is debited for materials purchased and credited for materials requisitioned for use.

1. An invoice for $8,100, terms f.o.b. destination, was received and entered January 2, 2002. The receiving report shows that the materials were received December 28, 2001.
2. Materials costing $28,000, shipped f.o.b. destination, were not entered by December 31, 2001, "because they were in a railroad car on the company's siding on that date and had not been unloaded."
3. Materials costing $7,300 were returned to the creditor on December 29, 2001, and were shipped f.o.b. shipping point. The return was entered on that date, even though the materials are not expected to reach the creditor's place of business until January 6, 2002.
4. An invoice for $7,500, terms f.o.b. shipping point, was received and entered December 30, 2001. The receiving report shows that the materials were received January 4, 2002, and the bill of lading shows that they were shipped January 2, 2002.
5. Materials costing $19,800 were received December 30, 2001, but no entry was made for them because "they were ordered with a specified delivery of no earlier than January 10, 2002."

Instructions

Prepare correcting general journal entries required at December 31, 2001, assuming that the books have not been closed.

E8-5 (Inventoriable Costs—Error Adjustments) Craig Company asks you to review its December 31, 2002, inventory values and prepare the necessary adjustments to the books. The following information is given to you.

1. Craig uses the periodic method of recording inventory. A physical count reveals $234,890 of inventory on hand at December 31, 2002.
2. Not included in the physical count of inventory is $13,420 of merchandise purchased on December 15 from Browser. This merchandise was shipped f.o.b. shipping point on December 29 and arrived in January. The invoice arrived and was recorded on December 31.
3. Included in inventory is merchandise sold to Champy on December 30, f.o.b. destination. This merchandise was shipped after it was counted. The invoice was prepared and recorded as a sale on account for $12,800 on December 31. The merchandise cost $7,350, and Champy received it on January 3.
4. Included in inventory was merchandise received from Dudley on December 31 with an invoice price of $15,630. The merchandise was shipped f.o.b. destination. The invoice, which has not yet arrived, has not been recorded.
5. Not included in inventory is $8,540 of merchandise purchased from Glowser Industries. This merchandise was received on December 31 after the inventory had been counted. The invoice was received and recorded on December 30.

6. Included in inventory was $10,438 of inventory held by Craig on consignment from Jackel Industries.
7. Included in inventory is merchandise sold to Kemp f.o.b. shipping point. This merchandise was shipped after it was counted. The invoice was prepared and recorded as a sale for $18,900 on December 31. The cost of this merchandise was $10,520, and Kemp received the merchandise on January 5.
8. Excluded from inventory was a carton labeled "Please accept for credit." This carton contains merchandise costing $1,500 which had been sold to a customer for $2,600. No entry had been made to the books to reflect the return, but none of the returned merchandise seemed damaged.

Instructions

(a) Determine the proper inventory balance for Craig Company at December 31, 2002.

(b) Prepare any correcting entries to adjust inventory to its proper amount at December 31, 2002. Assume the books have not been closed.

E8-6 (Determining Merchandise Amounts—Periodic) Two or more items are omitted in each of the following tabulations of income statement data. Fill in the amounts that are missing.

	2000	2001	2002
Sales	$290,000	$______	$410,000
Sales returns	11,000	13,000	______
Net sales	______	347,000	______
Beginning inventory	20,000	32,000	______
Ending inventory	______	______	______
Purchases	______	260,000	298,000
Purchase returns and allowances	5,000	8,000	10,000
Transportation-in	8,000	9,000	12,000
Cost of goods sold	233,000	______	293,000
Gross profit on sales	46,000	91,000	97,000

E8-7 (Financial Statement Presentation of Manufacturing Amounts—Periodic) Navajo Company is a manufacturing firm. Presented below is selected information from its 2001 accounting records.

Raw materials inventory, 1/1/01	$ 30,800	Transportation-out	$ 8,000
Raw materials inventory, 12/31/01	37,400	Selling expenses	300,000
Work in process inventory, 1/1/01	72,600	Administrative expenses	180,000
Work in process inventory, 12/31/01	61,600	Purchase discounts	10,640
Finished goods inventory, 1/1/01	35,200	Purchase returns and allowances	6,460
Finished goods inventory, 12/31/01	22,000	Interest expense	15,000
Purchases	278,600	Direct labor	440,000
Transportation-in	6,600	Manufacturing overhead	330,000

Instructions

(a) Compute raw materials used.

(b) Compute the cost of goods manufactured.

(c) Compute cost of goods sold.

(d) Indicate how inventories would be reported in the December 31, 2001, balance sheet.

E8-8 (Purchases Recorded Net) Presented below are transactions related to Tom Brokaw, Inc.

May 10	Purchased goods billed at $15,000 subject to cash discount terms of 2/10, n/60.
11	Purchased goods billed at $13,200 subject to terms of 1/15, n/30.
19	Paid invoice of May 10.
24	Purchased goods billed at $11,500 subject to cash discount terms of 2/10, n/30.

Instructions

(a) Prepare general journal entries for the transactions above under the assumption that purchases are to be recorded at net amounts after cash discounts and that discounts lost are to be treated as financial expense.

(b) Assuming no purchase or payment transactions other than those given above, prepare the adjusting entry required on May 31 if financial statements are to be prepared as of that date.

E8-9 (Purchases Recorded, Gross Method) Cruise Industries purchased $10,800 of merchandise on February 1, 2002, subject to a trade discount of 10% and with credit terms of 3/15, n/60. It returned $2,500 (gross price before trade or cash discount) on February 4. The invoice was paid on February 13.

Instructions

(a) Assuming that Cruise uses the perpetual method for recording merchandise transactions, record the purchase, return, and payment using the gross method.

(b) Assuming that Cruise uses the periodic method for recording merchandise transactions, record the purchase, return, and payment using the gross method.
(c) At what amount would the purchase on February 1 be recorded if the net method were used?

E8-10 (Periodic versus Perpetual Entries) The Fong Sai-Yuk Company sells one product. Presented below is information for January for the Fong Sai-Yuk Company.

Jan. 1	Inventory	100 units at $5 each
4	Sale	80 units at $8 each
11	Purchase	150 units at $6 each
13	Sale	120 units at $8.75 each
20	Purchase	160 units at $7 each
27	Sale	100 units at $9 each

Fong Sai-Yuk uses the FIFO cost flow assumption. All purchases and sales are on account.

Instructions
(a) Assume Fong Sai-Yuk uses a periodic system. Prepare all necessary journal entries, including the end-of-month closing entry to record cost of goods sold. A physical count indicates that the ending inventory for January is 110 units.
(b) Compute gross profit using the periodic system.
(c) Assume Fong Sai-Yuk uses a perpetual system. Prepare all necessary journal entries.
(d) Compute gross profit using the perpetual system.

E8-11 (Inventory Errors—Periodic) Ann M. Martin Company makes the following errors during the current year.

1. Ending inventory is overstated, but purchases are recorded correctly.
2. Both ending inventory and purchases on account are understated. (Assume this purchase was recorded in the following year.)
3. Ending inventory is correct, but a purchase on account was not recorded. (Assume this purchase was recorded in the following year.)

Instructions
Indicate the effect of each of these errors on working capital, current ratio (assume that the current ratio is greater than 1), retained earnings, and net income for the current year and the subsequent year.

E8-12 (Inventory Errors) Marcy Walker Company has a calendar-year accounting period. The following errors have been discovered in 2002.

1. The December 31, 2000, merchandise inventory had been understated by $21,000.
2. Merchandise purchased on account during 2001 was recorded on the books for the first time in February 2002, when the original invoice for the correct amount of $5,430 arrived. The merchandise had arrived December 28, 2001, and was included in the December 31, 2001, merchandise inventory. The invoice arrived late because of a mixup on the wholesaler's part.
3. Accrued interest of $1,300 at December 31, 2001, on notes receivable had not been recorded until the cash for the interest was received in March 2002.

Instructions
(a) Compute the effect each error had on the 2001 net income.
(b) Compute the effect, if any, each error had on the related December 31, 2001, balance sheet items.

E8-13 (Inventory Errors) At December 31, 2001, Stacy McGill Corporation reported current assets of $370,000 and current liabilities of $200,000. The following items may have been recorded incorrectly.

1. Goods purchased costing $22,000 were shipped f.o.b. shipping point by a supplier on December 28. McGill received and recorded the invoice on December 29, but the goods were not included in McGill's physical count of inventory because they were not received until January 4.
2. Goods purchased costing $15,000 were shipped f.o.b. destination by a supplier on December 26. McGill received and recorded the invoice on December 31, but the goods were not included in McGill's physical count of inventory because they were not received until January 2.
3. Goods held on consignment from Claudia Kishi Company were included in McGill's physical count of inventory at $13,000.
4. Freight-in of $3,000 was debited to advertising expense on December 28.

Instructions
(a) Compute the current ratio based on McGill's balance sheet.
(b) Recompute the current ratio after corrections are made.
(c) By what amount will income (before taxes) be adjusted up or down as a result of the corrections?

E8-14 (Inventory Errors) The net income per books of Linda Patrick Company was determined without knowledge of the errors indicated.

Year	Net Income per Books	Error in Ending Inventory	
1997	$50,000	Overstated	$ 3,000
1998	52,000	Overstated	9,000
1999	54,000	Understated	11,000
2000	56,000	No error	
2001	58,000	Understated	2,000
2002	60,000	Overstated	8,000

Instructions

Prepare a work sheet to show the adjusted net income figure for each of the 6 years after taking into account the inventory errors.

E8-15 (FIFO and LIFO—Periodic and Perpetual) Inventory information for Part 311 of Monique Aaron Corp. discloses the following information for the month of June:

June 1	Balance	300 units @ $10	June 10	Sold	200 units @ $24
11	Purchased	800 units @ $12	15	Sold	500 units @ $25
20	Purchased	500 units @ $13	27	Sold	300 units @ $27

Instructions

(a) Assuming that the periodic inventory method is used, compute the cost of goods sold and ending inventory under (1) LIFO and (2) FIFO.

(b) Assuming that the perpetual inventory method is used and costs are computed at the time of each withdrawal, what is the value of the ending inventory at LIFO?

(c) Assuming that the perpetual inventory method is used and costs are computed at the time of each withdrawal, what is the gross profit if the inventory is valued at FIFO?

(d) Why is it stated that LIFO usually produces a lower gross profit than FIFO?

E8-16 (FIFO, LIFO and Average Cost Determination) John Adams Company's record of transactions for the month of April was as follows:

Purchases			Sales	
April 1 (balance on hand)	600 @ $6.00		April 3	500 @ $10.00
4	1,500 @ 6.08		9	1,400 @ 10.00
8	800 @ 6.40		11	600 @ 11.00
13	1,200 @ 6.50		23	1,200 @ 11.00
21	700 @ 6.60		27	900 @ 12.00
29	500 @ 6.79			4,600
	5,300			

Instructions

(a) Assuming that perpetual inventory records are kept in units only, compute the inventory at April 30 using (1) LIFO and (2) average cost.

(b) Assuming that perpetual inventory records are kept in dollars, determine the inventory using (1) FIFO and (2) LIFO.

(c) Compute cost of goods sold assuming periodic inventory procedures and inventory priced at FIFO.

(d) In an inflationary period, which inventory method—FIFO, LIFO, average cost—will show the highest net income?

E8-17 (FIFO, LIFO, Average Cost Inventory) Shania Twain Company was formed on December 1, 2000. The following information is available from Twain's inventory records for Product BAP:

	Units	Unit Cost
January 1, 2001 (beginning inventory)	600	$ 8.00
Purchases:		
January 5, 2001	1,200	9.00
January 25, 2001	1,300	10.00
February 16, 2001	800	11.00
March 26, 2001	600	12.00

A physical inventory on March 31, 2001, shows 1,600 units on hand.

Instructions
Prepare schedules to compute the ending inventory at March 31, 2001, under each of the following inventory methods:

(a) FIFO. **(b)** LIFO. **(c)** Weighted average.

E8-18 (Compute FIFO, LIFO, Average Cost—Periodic) Presented below is information related to Blowfish radios for the Hootie Company for the month of July:

Date	Transaction	Units In	Unit Cost	Total	Units Sold	Selling Price	Total
July 1	Balance	100	$4.10	$ 410			
6	Purchase	800	4.20	3,360			
7	Sale				300	$7.00	$ 2,100
10	Sale				300	7.30	2,190
12	Purchase	400	4.50	1,800			
15	Sale				200	7.40	1,480
18	Purchase	300	4.60	1,380			
22	Sale				400	7.40	2,960
25	Purchase	500	4.58	2,290			
30	Sale				200	7.50	1,500
	Totals	2,100		$9,240	1,400		$10,230

Instructions

(a) Assuming that the periodic inventory method is used, compute the inventory cost at July 31 under each of the following cost flow assumptions:
  (1) FIFO.
  (2) LIFO.
  (3) Weighted-average. (Round the weighted-average unit cost to the nearest one-tenth of one cent.)

(b) Answer the following questions:
  (1) Which of the methods used above will yield the lowest figure for gross profit for the income statement? Explain why.
  (2) Which of the methods used above will yield the lowest figure for ending inventory for the balance sheet? Explain why.

E8-19 (FIFO and LIFO—Periodic and Perpetual) The following is a record of Pervis Ellison Company's transactions for Boston teapots for the month of May 2002:

May 1 Balance 400 units @ $20	May 10 Sale 300 units @ $38
12 Purchase 600 units @ $25	20 Sale 540 units @ $38
28 Purchase 400 units @ $30	

Instructions

(a) Assuming that perpetual inventories are **not** maintained and that a physical count at the end of the month shows 560 units on hand, what is the cost of the ending inventory using (1) FIFO and (2) LIFO?

(b) Assuming that perpetual records are maintained and they tie into the general ledger, calculate the ending inventory using (1) FIFO and (2) LIFO.

E8-20 (FIFO and LIFO; Income Statement Presentation) The board of directors of Deion Sanders Corporation is considering whether or not it should instruct the accounting department to shift from a first-in, first-out (FIFO) basis of pricing inventories to a last-in, first-out (LIFO) basis. The following information is available.

Sales	21,000 units @ $50
Inventory, January 1	6,000 units @ 20
Purchases	6,000 units @ 22
	10,000 units @ 25
	7,000 units @ 30
Inventory, December 31	8,000 units @ ?
Operating expenses	$200,000

Instructions
Prepare a condensed income statement for the year on both bases for comparative purposes.

E8-21 (FIFO and LIFO Effects) You are the vice-president of finance of Sandy Alomar Corporation, a retail company that prepared two different schedules of gross margin for the first quarter ended March 31, 2002. These schedules appear below.

	Sales ($5 per unit)	Cost of Goods Sold	Gross Margin
Schedule 1	$150,000	$124,900	$25,100
Schedule 2	150,000	129,400	20,600

The computation of cost of goods sold in each schedule is based on the following data:

	Units	Cost per Unit	Total Cost
Beginning inventory, January 1	10,000	$4.00	$40,000
Purchase, January 10	8,000	4.20	33,600
Purchase, January 30	6,000	4.25	25,500
Purchase, February 11	9,000	4.30	38,700
Purchase, March 17	11,000	4.40	48,400

Jane Torville, the president of the corporation, cannot understand how two different gross margins can be computed from the same set of data. As the vice-president of finance you have explained to Ms. Torville that the two schedules are based on different assumptions concerning the flow of inventory costs, i.e., first-in, first-out; and last-in, first-out. Schedules 1 and 2 were not necessarily prepared in this sequence of cost flow assumptions.

Instructions

Prepare two separate schedules computing cost of goods sold and supporting schedules showing the composition of the ending inventory under both cost flow assumptions.

E8-22 (FIFO and LIFO—Periodic) Howie Long Shop began operations on January 2, 2002. The following stock record card for footballs was taken from the records at the end of the year.

Date	Voucher	Terms	Units Received	Unit Invoice Cost	Gross Invoice Amount
1/15	10624	Net 30	50	$20.00	$1,000.00
3/15	11437	1/5, net 30	65	16.00	1,040.00
6/20	21332	1/10, net 30	90	15.00	1,350.00
9/12	27644	1/10, net 30	84	12.00	1,008.00
11/24	31269	1/10, net 30	76	11.00	836.00
	Totals		365		$5,234.00

A physical inventory on December 31, 2002, reveals that 100 footballs were in stock. The bookkeeper informs you that all the discounts were taken. Assume that Howie Long Shop uses the invoice price less discount for recording purchases.

Instructions

(a) Compute the December 31, 2002, inventory using the FIFO method.
(b) Compute the 2002 cost of goods sold using the LIFO method.
(c) What method would you recommend to the owner to minimize income taxes in 2002, using the inventory information for footballs as a guide?

E8-23 (LIFO Effect) The following example was provided to encourage the use of the LIFO method:

> In a nutshell, LIFO subtracts inflation from inventory costs, deducts it from taxable income, and records it in a LIFO reserve account on the books. The LIFO benefit grows as inflation widens the gap between current-year and past-year (minus inflation) inventory costs. This gap is:

	With LIFO	Without LIFO
Revenue	$3,200,000	$3,200,000
Cost of goods sold	2,800,000	2,800,000
Operating expenses	150,000	150,000
Operating income	250,000	250,000
LIFO adjustment	40,000	0
Taxable income	$210,000	$250,000
Income taxes @ 36%	$ 75,600	$ 90,000
Cash flow	$174,400	$160,000
Extra cash	$14,400	0
Increased cash flow	9%	0%

Instructions

(a) Explain what is meant by the LIFO reserve account.
(b) How does LIFO subtract inflation from inventory costs?
(c) Explain how the cash flow of $174,400 in this example was computed. Explain why this amount may not be correct.
(d) Why does a company that uses LIFO have extra cash? Explain whether this situation will always exist.

E8-24 (Alternative Inventory Methods—Comprehensive) Tori Amos Corporation began operations on December 1, 2001. The only inventory transaction in 2001 was the purchase of inventory on December 10, 2001, at a cost of $20 per unit. None of this inventory was sold in 2001. Relevant information is as follows:

Ending inventory units		
December 31, 2001		100
December 31, 2002, by purchase date		
December 2, 2002	100	
July 20, 2002	50	150

During the year the following purchases and sales were made:

Purchases		Sales	
March 15	300 units at $24	April 10	200
July 20	300 units at 25	August 20	300
September 4	200 units at 28	November 18	150
December 2	100 units at 30	December 12	200

The company uses the periodic inventory method.

Instructions

(a) Determine ending inventory under (1) specific identification, (2) FIFO, (3) LIFO periodic, and (4) average cost.
(b) Determine ending inventory using dollar-value LIFO. Assume that the December 2, 2002, purchase cost is the current cost of inventory (*Hint*: The beginning inventory is the base layer priced at $20 per unit).

E8-25 (Dollar-Value LIFO) Oasis Company has used the dollar-value LIFO method for inventory cost determination for many years. The following data were extracted from Oasis' records:

Date	Price Index	Ending Inventory at Base Prices	Ending Inventory at Dollar-Value LIFO
December 31, 2000	105	$92,000	$92,600
December 31, 2001	?	97,000	98,350

Instructions

Calculate the index used for 2001 that yielded the above results.

E8-26 (Dollar-Value LIFO) The dollar-value LIFO method was adopted by Enya Corp. on January 1, 2002. Its inventory on that date was $160,000. On December 31, 2002, the inventory at prices existing on that date amounted to $140,000. The price level at January 1, 2002, was 100, and the price level at December 31, 2002, was 112.

Instructions

(a) Compute the amount of the inventory at December 31, 2002, under the dollar-value LIFO method.
(b) On December 31, 2003, the inventory at prices existing on that date was $172,500, and the price level was 115. Compute the inventory on that date under the dollar-value LIFO method.

E8-27 (Dollar-Value LIFO) Presented below is information related to Dino Radja Company.

Date	Ending Inventory (End-of-Year Prices)	Price Index
December 31, 1999	$ 80,000	100
December 31, 2000	115,500	105
December 31, 2001	108,000	120
December 31, 2002	122,200	130
December 31, 2003	154,000	140
December 31, 2004	176,900	145

Instructions

Compute the ending inventory for Dino Radja Company for 1999 through 2004 using the dollar-value LIFO method.

E8-28 (Dollar-Value LIFO) The following information relates to the Jimmy Johnson Company.

Date	Ending Inventory (End-of-Year Prices)	Price Index
December 31, 1998	$ 70,000	100
December 31, 1999	90,300	105
December 31, 2000	95,120	116
December 31, 2001	105,600	120
December 31, 2002	100,000	125

Instructions

Use the dollar-value LIFO method to compute the ending inventory for Johnson Company for 1998 through 2002.

PROBLEMS

P8-1 (Various Inventory Issues) The following independent situations relate to inventory accounting.

1. Jag Co. purchased goods with a list price of $150,000, subject to trade discounts of 20% and 10%, with no cash discounts allowable. How much should Jag Co. record as the cost of these goods?
2. Francis Company's inventory of $1,100,000 at December 31, 2001, was based on a physical count of goods priced at cost and before any year-end adjustments relating to the following items:
   a. Goods shipped f.o.b. shipping point on December 24, 2001, from a vendor at an invoice cost of $69,000 to Francis Company were received on January 4, 2002.
   b. The physical count included $29,000 of goods billed to Sakic Corp. f.o.b. shipping point on December 31, 2001. The carrier picked up these goods on January 3, 2002.

   What amount should Francis report as inventory on its balance sheet?
3. Mark Messier Corp. had 1,500 units of part M.O. on hand May 1, 2001, costing $21 each. Purchases of part M.O. during May were as follows:

	Units	Unit Cost
May 9	2,000	$22.00
17	3,500	23.00
26	1,000	24.00

   A physical count on May 31, 2001, shows 2,100 units of part M.O. on hand. Using the FIFO method, what is the cost of part M.O. inventory at May 31, 2001? Using the LIFO method, what is the inventory cost? Using the average cost method, what is the inventory cost?
4. Forsberg Company adopted the dollar-value LIFO method on January 1, 2001 (using internal price indexes and multiple pools). The following data are available for inventory pool A for the 2 years following adoption of LIFO.

Inventory	At Base-Year Cost	At Current-Year Cost
1/1/01	$200,000	$200,000
12/31/01	240,000	252,000
12/31/02	256,000	286,720

   Computing an internal price index and using the dollar-value LIFO method, at what amount should the inventory be reported at December 31, 2002?
5. Eric Lindros Inc., a retail store chain, had the following information in its general ledger for the year 2002:

Merchandise purchased for resale	$909,400
Interest on notes payable to vendors	8,700
Purchase returns	16,500
Freight-in	22,000
Freight-out	17,100
Cash discounts on purchases	6,800

   What is Lindros' inventoriable cost for 2002?

Instructions

Answer each of the questions above about inventories and explain your answers.

P8-2 (Inventory Adjustments) James T. Kirk Company, a manufacturer of small tools, provided the following information from its accounting records for the year ended December 31, 2002:

Inventory at December 31, 2002 (based on physical count of goods in Kirk's plant, at cost, on December 31, 2002)	$1,520,000
Accounts payable at December 31, 2002	1,200,000
Net sales (sales less sales returns)	8,150,000

Additional information is as follows:

1. Included in the physical count were tools billed to a customer f.o.b. shipping point on December 31, 2002. These tools had a cost of $31,000 and were billed at $40,000. The shipment was on Kirk's loading dock waiting to be picked up by the common carrier.
2. Goods were in transit from a vendor to Kirk on December 31, 2002. The invoice cost was $71,000, and the goods were shipped f.o.b. shipping point on December 29, 2002.
3. Work in process inventory costing $30,000 was sent to an outside processor for plating on December 30, 2002.
4. Tools returned by customers and held pending inspection in the returned goods area on December 31, 2002, were not included in the physical count. On January 8, 2003, the tools costing $32,000 were inspected and returned to inventory. Credit memos totaling $47,000 were issued to the customers on the same date.
5. Tools shipped to a customer f.o.b. destination on December 26, 2002, were in transit at December 31, 2002, and had a cost of $21,000. Upon notification of receipt by the customer on January 2, 2003, Kirk issued a sales invoice for $42,000.
6. Goods, with an invoice cost of $27,000, received from a vendor at 5:00 p.m. on December 31, 2002, were recorded on a receiving report dated January 2, 2003. The goods were not included in the physical count, but the invoice was included in accounts payable at December 31, 2002.
7. Goods received from a vendor on December 26, 2002, were included in the physical count. However, the related $56,000 vendor invoice was not included in accounts payable at December 31, 2002, because the accounts payable copy of the receiving report was lost.
8. On January 3, 2003, a monthly freight bill in the amount of $6,000 was received. The bill specifically related to merchandise purchased in December 2002, one-half of which was still in the inventory at December 31, 2002. The freight charges were not included in either the inventory or in accounts payable at December 31, 2002.

Instructions

Using the format shown below, prepare a schedule of adjustments as of December 31, 2002, to the initial amounts per Kirk's accounting records. Show separately the effect, if any, of each of the eight transactions on the December 31, 2002, amounts. If the transactions would have no effect on the initial amount shown, enter NONE.

	Inventory	Accounts Payable	Net Sales
Initial amounts	$1,520,000	$1,200,000	$8,150,000
Adjustments—increase (decrease)			
1			
2			
3			
4			
5			
6			
7			
8			
Total adjustments			
Adjusted amounts	$	$	$

(AICPA adapted)

P8-3 (Purchases Recorded Gross and Net) Some of the transactions of William Dubois Company during August are listed below. Dubois uses the periodic inventory method.

August 10	Purchased merchandise on account, $9,000, terms 2/10, n/30.
13	Returned part of the purchase of August 10, $1,200, and received credit on account.

15 Purchased merchandise on account, $12,000, terms 1/10, n/60.
25 Purchased merchandise on account, $15,000, terms 2/10, n/30.
28 Paid invoice of August 15 in full.

Instructions

(a) Assuming that purchases are recorded at gross amounts and that discounts are to be recorded when taken:
(1) Prepare general journal entries to record the transactions.
(2) Describe how the various items would be shown in the financial statements.

(b) Assuming that purchases are recorded at net amounts and that discounts lost are treated as financial expenses:
(1) Prepare general journal entries to enter the transactions.
(2) Prepare the adjusting entry necessary on August 31 if financial statements are to be prepared at that time.
(3) Describe how the various items would be shown in the financial statements.

(c) Which of the two methods do you prefer and why?

P8-4 (Compute FIFO, LIFO, and Average Cost—Periodic and Perpetual) Taos Company's record of transactions concerning part X for the month of April was as follows:

Purchases		Sales	
April 1 (balance on hand)	100 @ $5.00	April 5	300
4	400 @ 5.10	12	200
11	300 @ 5.30	27	800
18	200 @ 5.35	28	100
26	500 @ 5.60		
30	200 @ 5.80		

Instructions

(a) Compute the inventory at April 30 on each of the following bases. Assume that perpetual inventory records are kept in units only. Carry unit costs to the nearest cent.
(1) First-in, first-out (FIFO).
(2) Last-in, first-out (LIFO).
(3) Average cost.

(b) If the perpetual inventory record is kept in dollars, and costs are computed at the time of each withdrawal, what amount would be shown as ending inventory in 1, 2, and 3 above? Carry average unit costs to four decimal places.

P8-5 (Compute FIFO, LIFO and Average Cost—Periodic and Perpetual) Some of the information found on a detail inventory card for David Letterman Inc. for the first month of operations is as follows:

	Received		Issued,	Balance,
Date	No. of Units	Unit Cost	No. of Units	No. of Units
January 2	1,200	$3.00		1,200
7			700	500
10	600	3.20		1,100
13			500	600
18	1,000	3.30	300	1,300
20			1,100	200
23	1,300	3.40		1,500
26			800	700
28	1,500	3.60		2,200
31			1,300	900

Instructions

(a) From these data compute the ending inventory on each of the following bases. Assume that perpetual inventory records are kept in units only. Carry unit costs to the nearest cent and ending inventory to the nearest dollar.
(1) First-in, first-out (FIFO).
(2) Last-in, first-out (LIFO).
(3) Average cost.

(b) If the perpetual inventory record is kept in dollars, and costs are computed at the time of each withdrawal, would the amounts shown as ending inventory in 1, 2, and 3 above be the same? Explain and compute.

P8-6 (Compute FIFO, LIFO, Average Cost—Periodic and Perpetual) Iowa Company is a multi-product firm. Presented below is information concerning one of its products, the Hawkeye:

Date	Transaction	Quantity	Price/Cost
1/1	Beginning inventory	1,000	$12
2/4	Purchase	2,000	18
2/20	Sale	2,500	30
4/2	Purchase	3,000	23
11/4	Sale	2,000	33

Instructions

Compute cost of goods sold, assuming Iowa uses:

(a) Periodic system, FIFO cost flow.
(b) Perpetual system, FIFO cost flow.
(c) Periodic system, LIFO cost flow.
(d) Perpetual system, LIFO cost flow.
(e) Periodic system, weighted-average cost flow.
(f) Perpetual system, moving-average cost flow.

P8-7 (Financial Statement Effects of FIFO and LIFO) The management of Maine Company has asked its accounting department to describe the effect upon the company's financial position and its income statements of accounting for inventories on the LIFO rather than the FIFO basis during 2002 and 2003. The accounting department is to assume that the change to LIFO would have been effective on January 1, 2002, and that the initial LIFO base would have been the inventory value on December 31, 2001. Presented below are the company's financial statements and other data for the years 2002 and 2003 when the FIFO method was employed.

	Financial Position as of		
	12/31/01	12/31/02	12/31/03
Cash	$ 90,000	$130,000	$ 141,600
Accounts receivable	80,000	100,000	120,000
Inventory	120,000	140,000	180,000
Other assets	160,000	170,000	200,000
Total assets	$450,000	$540,000	$ 641,600
Accounts payable	$ 40,000	$ 60,000	$ 80,000
Other liabilities	70,000	80,000	110,000
Common stock	200,000	200,000	200,000
Retained earnings	140,000	200,000	251,600
Total equities	$450,000	$540,000	$ 641,600

	Income for Years Ended	
	12/31/02	12/31/03
Sales	$900,000	$1,350,000
Less: Cost of goods sold	505,000	770,000
Other expenses	205,000	304,000
	710,000	1,074,000
Net income before income taxes	190,000	276,000
Income taxes (40%)	76,000	110,400
Net income	$114,000	$ 165,600

Other data:

1. Inventory on hand at 12/31/01 consisted of 40,000 units valued at $3.00 each.
2. Sales (all units sold at the same price in a given year):

   2002—150,000 units @ $6.00 each   2003—180,000 units @ $7.50 each

3. Purchases (all units purchased at the same price in given year):

   2002—150,000 units @ $3.50 each   2003—180,000 units @ $4.50 each

4. Income taxes at the effective rate of 40% are paid on December 31 each year.

Instructions

Name the account(s) presented in the financial statements that would have different amounts for 2003 if LIFO rather than FIFO had been used, and state the new amount for each account that is named. Show computations.

(CMA adapted)

P8-8 (Dollar-Value LIFO) Falcon's Televisions produces television sets in three categories: portable, midsize, and console. On January 1, 2001, Falcon adopted dollar-value LIFO and decided to use a single inventory pool. The company's January 1 inventory consists of:

Category	Quantity	Cost per Unit	Total Cost
Portable	6,000	$100	$ 600,000
Midsize	8,000	250	2,000,000
Console	3,000	400	1,200,000
	17,000		$3,800,000

During 2001, the company had the following purchases and sales:

Category	Quantity Purchased	Cost per Unit	Quantity Sold	Selling Price per Unit
Portable	15,000	$120	14,000	$150
Midsize	20,000	300	24,000	405
Console	10,000	460	6,000	600
	45,000		44,000	

Instructions

(Round to four decimals.)

(a) Compute ending inventory, cost of goods sold, and gross profit.

(b) Assume the company uses three inventory pools instead of one. Repeat instruction (a).

P8-9 (LIFO Effect on Income) Kristi Yamaguchi Inc. sells two products: figure skates and speed skates. At December 31, 2002, Yamaguchi used the first-in, first-out (FIFO) inventory method. Effective January 1, 2003, Yamaguchi changed to the last-in, first-out (LIFO) inventory method. The cumulative effect of this change is not determinable and, as a result, the ending inventory of 2002 for which the FIFO method was used is also the beginning inventory for 2003 for the LIFO method. Any layers added during 2003 should be costed by reference to the first acquisitions of 2003 and any layers liquidated during 2003 should be considered a permanent liquidation.

The following information was available from Yamaguchi's inventory records for the 2 most recent years:

	Figure Skates		Speed Skates	
	Units	Unit Cost	Units	Unit Cost
2002 purchases				
January 7	7,000	$40.00	22,000	$20.00
April 16	12,000	45.00		
November 8	17,000	54.00	18,500	34.00
December 13	9,000	62.00		
2003 purchases				
February 11	3,000	66.00	23,000	36.00
May 20	8,000	75.00		
October 15	20,000	81.00		
December 23			15,500	42.00
Units on hand				
December 31, 2002	15,100		15,000	
December 31, 2003	18,000		13,200	

Instructions

Compute the effect on income before income taxes for the year ended December 31, 2003, resulting from the change from the FIFO to the LIFO inventory method.

(AICPA adapted)

P8-10 (Internal Indexes—Dollar-Value LIFO) On January 1, 2001, Addis Abeba Wholesalers Inc. adopted the dollar-value LIFO inventory method for income tax and external financial reporting purposes. However, Abeba continued to use the FIFO inventory method for internal accounting and management purposes. In applying the LIFO method, Abeba uses internal conversion price indexes and the multiple pools approach under which substantially identical inventory items are grouped into LIFO inventory pools. The following data were available for inventory pool no. 1, which comprises products A and B, for the 2 years following the adoption of LIFO:

	FIFO Basis per Records		
	Units	Unit Cost	Total Cost
Inventory, 1/1/01			
Product A	10,000	$30	$300,000
Product B	9,000	25	225,000
			$525,000
Inventory, 12/31/01			
Product A	17,000	35	$595,000
Product B	9,000	26	234,000
			$829,000
Inventory, 12/31/02			
Product A	13,000	40	$520,000
Product B	10,000	32	320,000
			$840,000

Instructions

(a) Prepare a schedule to compute the internal conversion price indexes for 2001 and 2002. Round indexes to two decimal places.

(b) Prepare a schedule to compute the inventory amounts at December 31, 2001 and 2002, using the dollar-value LIFO inventory method.

(AICPA adapted)

P8-11 (Internal Indexes—Dollar-Value LIFO) Presented below is information related to Mellon Collie Corporation for the last 3 years:

Item	Quantities in Ending Inventories	Base-Year Cost Unit Cost	Base-Year Cost Amount	Current-Year Cost Unit Cost	Current-Year Cost Amount
December 31, 2000					
A	9,000	$2.00	$18,000	$2.40	$21,600
B	6,000	3.00	18,000	3.55	21,300
C	4,000	5.00	20,000	5.40	21,600
		Totals	$56,000		$64,500
December 31, 2001					
A	9,000	$2.00	$18,000	$2.60	$23,400
B	6,800	3.00	20,400	3.75	25,500
C	6,000	5.00	30,000	6.40	38,400
		Totals	$68,400		$87,300
December 31, 2002					
A	8,000	$2.00	$16,000	$2.70	$21,600
B	8,000	3.00	24,000	4.00	32,000
C	6,000	5.00	30,000	6.20	37,200
		Totals	$70,000		$90,800

Instructions

Compute the ending inventories under the dollar-value method for 2000, 2001, and 2002. The base period is January 1, 2000, and the beginning inventory cost at that date was $45,000. Compute indexes to two decimal places.

P8-12 (Dollar-Value LIFO) Warren Dunn Company cans a variety of vegetable-type soups. Recently, the company decided to value its inventories using dollar-value LIFO pools. The clerk who accounts for inventories does not understand how to value the inventory pools using this new method, so, as a private consultant, you have been asked to teach him how this new method works.

He has provided you with the following information about purchases made over a 6-year period:

Date	Ending Inventory (End-of-Year Prices)	Price Index
Dec. 31, 1996	$ 80,000	100
Dec. 31, 1997	115,500	105
Dec. 31, 1998	108,000	120
Dec. 31, 1999	131,300	130
Dec. 31, 2000	154,000	140
Dec. 31, 2001	174,000	145

You have already explained to him how this inventory method is maintained, but he would feel better about it if you were to leave him detailed instructions explaining how these calculations are done and why he needs to put all inventories at a base-year value.

Instructions

(a) Compute the ending inventory for Warren Dunn Company for 1996 through 2001 using dollar-value LIFO.

(b) Using your computation schedules as your illustration, write a step-by-step set of instructions explaining how the calculations are done. Begin your explanation by briefly explaining the theory behind this inventory method, including the purpose of putting all amounts into base-year price levels.

CONCEPTUAL CASES

C8-1 (Inventoriable Costs) You are asked to travel to Milwaukee to observe and verify the inventory of the Milwaukee branch of one of your clients. You arrive on Thursday, December 30, and find that the inventory procedures have just been started. You spot a railway car on the sidetrack at the unloading door and ask the warehouse superintendent Predrag Danilovic how he plans to inventory the contents of the car. He responds: "We are not going to include the contents in the inventory."

Later in the day, you ask the bookkeeper for the invoice on the carload and the related freight bill. The invoice lists the various items, prices, and extensions of the goods in the car. You note that the carload was shipped December 24 from Albuquerque, f.o.b. Albuquerque, and that the total invoice price of the goods in the car was $35,300. The freight bill called for a payment of $1,500. Terms were net 30 days. The bookkeeper affirms the fact that this invoice is to be held for recording in January.

Instructions

(a) Does your client have a liability that should be recorded at December 31? Discuss.

(b) Prepare a journal entry(ies), if required, to reflect any accounting adjustment required. Assume a perpetual inventory system is used by your client.

(c) For what possible reason(s) might your client wish to postpone recording the transaction?

C8-2 (Inventoriable Costs) Alonzo Spellman, an inventory control specialist, is interested in better understanding the accounting for inventories. Although Alonzo understands the more sophisticated computer inventory control systems, he has little knowledge of how inventory cost is determined. In studying the records of Ditka Enterprises, which sells normal brand-name goods from its own store and on consignment through Wannstedt Inc., he asks you to answer the following questions.

Instructions

(a) Should Ditka Enterprises include in its inventory normal brand-name goods purchased from its suppliers but not yet received if the terms of purchase are f.o.b. shipping point (manufacturer's plant)? Why?

(b) Should Ditka Enterprises include freight-in expenditures as an inventory cost? Why?

(c) If Ditka Enterprises purchases its goods on terms 2/10, net 30, should the purchases be recorded gross or net? Why?

(d) What are products on consignment? How should they be reported in the financial statements?

(AICPA adapted)

C8-3 (Inventoriable Costs) Jack McDowell, the controller for McDowell Lumber Company, has recently hired you as assistant controller. He wishes to determine your expertise in the area of inventory accounting and therefore asks you to answer the following unrelated questions:

(a) A company is involved in the wholesaling and retailing of automobile tires for foreign cars. Most of the inventory is imported, and it is valued on the company's records at the actual inventory cost plus freight-in. At year-end, the warehousing costs are prorated over cost of goods sold and ending inventory. Are warehousing costs considered a product cost or a period cost?

(b) A certain portion of a company's "inventory" is composed of obsolete items. Should obsolete items that are not currently consumed in the production of "goods or services to be available for sale" be classified as part of inventory?

(c) A company purchases airplanes for sale to others. However, until they are sold, the company charters and services the planes. What is the proper way to report these airplanes in the company's financial statements?

(d) A company wants to buy coal deposits but does not want the financing for the purchase to be reported on its financial statements. The company therefore establishes a trust to acquire the coal deposits. The company agrees to buy the coal over a certain period of time at specified prices. The trust is able to finance the coal purchase and pay off the loan as it is paid by the company for the minerals. How should this transaction be reported?

C8-4 (Accounting Treatment of Purchase Discounts) Wayne Gretzky Corp., a household appliances dealer, purchases its inventories from various suppliers. Gretzky has consistently stated its inventories at the lower of cost (FIFO) or market.

Instructions

Gretzky is considering alternate methods of accounting for the cash discounts it takes when paying its suppliers promptly. From a theoretical standpoint, discuss the acceptability of each of the following methods:

(a) Financial income when payments are made.

(b) Reduction of cost of goods sold for period when payments are made.

(c) Direct reduction of purchase cost.

(AICPA adapted)

C8-5 (General Inventory Issues) In January 2002, Wesley Crusher Inc. requested and secured permission from the commissioner of the Internal Revenue Service to compute inventories under the last-in, first-out (LIFO) method and elected to determine inventory cost under the dollar-value method. Crusher Inc. satisfied the commissioner that cost could be accurately determined by use of an index number computed from a representative sample selected from the company's single inventory pool.

Instructions

(a) Why should inventories be included in (1) a balance sheet and (2) the computation of net income?

(b) The Internal Revenue Code allows some accountable events to be considered differently for income tax reporting purposes and financial accounting purposes, while other accountable events must be reported the same for both purposes. Discuss why it might be desirable to report some accountable events differently for financial accounting purposes than for income tax reporting purposes.

(c) Discuss the ways and conditions under which the FIFO and LIFO inventory costing methods produce different inventory valuations. Do not discuss procedures for computing inventory cost.

(AICPA adapted)

C8-6 (Variable Costing and Financial Statement Presentation) Akihito Co. is a manufacturing business with relatively heavy fixed costs and large inventories of finished goods. These inventories constitute a very material item on the balance sheet. The company has a departmental cost accounting system that assigns all manufacturing costs to the product each period.

Edward Gierek, controller of the company, has informed you that the management is giving serious consideration to the adoption of variable (direct) costing as a method of accounting for plant operations and inventory valuation. The management wishes to have your opinion of the effect, if any, that such a change would have on: (1) the year-end financial position, and (2) the net income for the year.

Instructions

State your reply to the request and the reasons for your conclusions.

(AICPA adapted)

C8-7 (LIFO Inventory Advantages) Jean Honore, president of Fragonard Co., recently read an article that claimed that at least 100 of the country's largest 500 companies were either adopting or considering adopting the last-in, first-out (LIFO) method for valuing inventories. The article stated that the firms were switching to LIFO to (1) neutralize the effect of inflation in their financial statements, (2) eliminate inventory profits, and (3) reduce income taxes. Ms. Honore wonders if the switch would benefit her company.

Fragonard currently uses the first-in, first-out (FIFO) method of inventory valuation in its periodic inventory system. The company has a high inventory turnover rate, and inventories represent a significant proportion of the assets.

Ms. Honore has been told that the LIFO system is more costly to operate and will provide little benefit to companies with high turnover. She intends to use the inventory method that is best for the company in the long run rather than selecting a method just because it is the current fad.

Instructions

(a) Explain to Ms. Honore what "inventory profits" are and how the LIFO method of inventory valuation could reduce them.

(b) Explain to Ms. Honore the conditions that must exist for Fragonard Co. to receive tax benefits from a switch to the LIFO method.

C8-8 (Average Cost, FIFO, and LIFO) Prepare a memorandum containing responses to the following items.

(a) Describe the cost flow assumptions used in average cost, FIFO, and LIFO methods of inventory valuation.

(b) Distinguish between weighted average cost and moving average cost for inventory costing purposes.

(c) Identify the effects on both the balance sheet and the income statement of using the LIFO method instead of the FIFO method for inventory costing purposes over a substantial time period when purchase prices of inventoriable items are rising. State why these effects take place.

C8-9 (LIFO Application and Advantages) The Neshki Corporation is a medium-sized manufacturing company with two divisions and three subsidiaries, all located in the United States. The Metallic Division manufactures metal castings for the automotive industry, and the Plastic Division produces small plastic items for electrical products and other uses. The three subsidiaries manufacture various products for other industrial users.

Neshki Corporation plans to change from the lower of first-in, first-out (FIFO) cost or market method of inventory valuation to the last-in, first-out (LIFO) method of inventory valuation to obtain tax benefits. To make the method acceptable for tax purposes, the change also will be made for its annual financial statements.

Instructions

(a) Describe the establishment of and subsequent pricing procedures for each of the following LIFO inventory methods:

(1) LIFO applied to units of product when the periodic inventory system is used.

(2) Application of the dollar-value method to LIFO units of product.

(b) Discuss the specific advantages and disadvantages of using the dollar-value LIFO application as compared to specific goods LIFO (unit LIFO). Ignore income tax considerations.

(c) Discuss the general advantages and disadvantages claimed for LIFO methods.

C8-10 (Dollar-Value LIFO Issues) Maria Callas Co. is considering switching from the specific goods LIFO approach to the dollar-value LIFO approach. Because the financial personnel at Callas know very little about dollar-value LIFO, they ask you to answer the following questions.

(a) What is a LIFO pool?

(b) Is it possible to use a LIFO pool concept and not use dollar-value LIFO? Explain.

(c) What is a LIFO liquidation?

(d) How are price indexes used in the dollar-value LIFO method?

(e) What are the advantages of dollar-value LIFO over specific goods LIFO?

C8-11 (FIFO and LIFO) Günter Grass Company is considering changing its inventory valuation method from FIFO to LIFO because of the potential tax savings. However, the management wishes to consider all of the effects on the company, including its reported performance, before making the final decision.

The inventory account, currently valued on the FIFO basis, consists of 1,000,000 units at $7 per unit on January 1, 2002. There are 1,000,000 shares of common stock outstanding as of January 1, 2002, and the cash balance is $400,000.

The company has made the following forecasts for the period 2002–2004.

	2002	2003	2004
Unit sales (in millions of units)	1.1	1.0	1.3
Sales price per unit	$10	$10	$12
Unit purchases (in millions of units)	1.0	1.1	1.2
Purchase price per unit	$7	$8	$9
Annual depreciation (in thousands of dollars)	$300	$300	$300
Cash dividends per share	$.15	$.15	$.15
Cash payments for additions to and replacement of plant and equipment (in thousands of dollars)	$350	$350	$350

Income tax rate	40%	40%	40%
Operating expense (exclusive of depreciation) as a percent of sales	15%	15%	15%
Common shares outstanding (in millions)	1	1	1

Instructions

(a) Prepare a schedule that illustrates and compares the following data for Günter Grass Company under the FIFO and the LIFO inventory method for 2002–2004. Assume the company would begin LIFO at the beginning of 2002.

(1) Year-end inventory balances. **(3)** Earnings per share.
(2) Annual net income after taxes. **(4)** Cash balance.

Assume all sales are collected in the year of sale and all purchases, operating expenses, and taxes are paid during the year incurred.

(b) Using the data above, your answer to (a), and any additional issues you believe need to be considered, prepare a report that recommends whether or not Günter Grass Company should change to the LIFO inventory method. Support your conclusions with appropriate arguments.

(CMA adapted)

USING YOUR JUDGMENT

FINANCIAL STATEMENT ANALYSIS CASES

T J International

T J International was founded in 1969 as Trus Joist International. The firm, a manufacturer of specialty building products, has its headquarters in Boise, Idaho. The company, through its partnership in the Trus Joist MacMillan joint venture, develops and manufactures engineered lumber. This product is a high-quality substitute for structural lumber, and uses lower-grade wood and materials formerly considered waste. The company also is majority owner of the Outlook Window Partnership, which is a consortium of three wood and vinyl window manufacturers.

Following is T J International's adapted income statement and information concerning inventories from its annual report.

T J INTERNATIONAL

Sales	$618,876,000
Cost of goods sold	475,476,000
Gross profit	143,400,000
Selling and administrative expenses	102,112,000
Income from operations	41,288,000
Other expense	24,712,000
Income before income tax	16,576,000
Income taxes	7,728,000
Net income	$ 8,848,000

Inventories. Inventories are valued at the lower of cost or market and include material, labor, and production overhead costs. Inventories consisted of the following:

	Current Year	Prior Year
Finished goods	$27,512,000	$23,830,000
Raw materials and work-in-progress	34,363,000	33,244,000
	61,875,000	57,074,000
Reduction to LIFO cost	(5,263,000)	(3,993,000)
	$56,612,000	$53,081,000

The last-in, first-out (LIFO) method is used for determining the cost of lumber, veneer, Microllam lumber, TJI joists, and open web joists. Approximately 35 percent of total inventories at the end of the current year were valued using the LIFO method. The first-in, first-out (FIFO) method is used to determine the cost of all other inventories.

Instructions

(a) How much would income before taxes have been if FIFO costing had been used to value all inventories?

(b) If the income tax rate is 46.6%, what would income tax have been if FIFO costing had been used to value all inventories? In your opinion, is this difference in net income between the two methods material? Explain.

(c) Does the use of a different costing system for different types of inventory mean that there is a different physical flow of goods among the different types of inventory? Explain.

Noven Pharmaceuticals, Inc.

Noven Pharmaceuticals, Inc., headquartered in Miami, Florida, describes itself in a recent annual report as follows:

> Noven is a place of ideas—a company where scientific excellence and state-of-the-art manufacturing combine to create new answers to human needs. Our transdermal delivery systems speed drugs painlessly and effortlessly into the bloodstream by means of a simple skin patch. This technology has proven applications in estrogen replacement, but at Noven we are developing a variety of systems incorporating bestselling drugs that fight everything from asthma, anxiety and dental pain to cancer, heart disease and neurological illness. Our research portfolio also includes new technologies, such as iontophoresis, in which drugs are delivered through the skin by means of electrical currents, as well as products that could satisfy broad consumer needs, such as our anti-microbial mouthrinse.

Noven also reported in its annual report that its activities to date have consisted of product development efforts, some of which have been independent and some of which have been completed in conjunction with Rhone-Poulenc Rorer (RPR) and Ciba-Geigy. The revenues so far have consisted of money received from licensing fees, "milestone" payments (payments made under licensing agreements when certain stages of the development of a certain product have been completed), and interest on its investments. The company expects that it will have significant revenue in the upcoming fiscal year from the launch of its first product, a transdermal estrogen delivery system.

The current assets portion of Noven's balance sheet follows:

Cash and cash equivalents	$12,070,272
Securities held to maturity	23,445,070
Inventory of supplies	1,264,553
Prepaid and other current assets	825,159
Total current assets	$37,605,054

Inventory of supplies is recorded at the lower of cost (first-in, first-out) or net realizable value and consists mainly of supplies for research and development.

Instructions

(a) What would you expect the physical flow of goods for a pharmaceutical manufacturer to be most like: FIFO, LIFO, or random (flow of goods does not follow a set pattern)? Explain.

(b) What are some of the factors that Noven should consider as it selects an inventory measurement method?

(c) Suppose that Noven had $49,000 in an inventory of transdermal estrogen delivery patches. These patches are from an initial production run, and will be sold during the coming year. Why do you think that this amount is not shown in a separate inventory account? In which of the accounts shown is the inventory likely to be? At what point will the inventory be transferred to a separate inventory account?

RESEARCH CASES

Case 1

As indicated in the chapter, the FIFO and LIFO inventory methods can result in significantly different income statement and balance sheet figures. However, it is possible to convert income for a LIFO firm to its FIFO-based equivalent. To assist financial statement users in this task, firms using LIFO are required to disclose in their footnotes the "LIFO reserve" (LR)—i.e., the difference between the inventory balance shown on the balance sheet and the amount that would have been reported had the firm used current cost (or FIFO). The following equation can be used to convert LIFO cost of goods sold (COGS) to FIFO COGS:

$$COGS_{FIFO} = COGS_{LIFO} - \text{LIFO effect}$$

where

$$\text{LIFO effect} = [LR_{ending} - LR_{beginning}]$$

.com/college/kieso

Go to the Digital Tool for examples of LIFO reserves.

The following equation can be used to convert LIFO net income (NI) to FIFO net income.

$$NI_{FIFO} = NI_{LIFO} + (\text{LIFO effect})\ (1 - \text{tax rate})$$

Instructions

Obtain the annual report of a firm that reports a LIFO reserve in its footnotes.

(a) Identify the LIFO reserve at the two most recent balance sheet dates.

(b) Determine the LIFO effect during the most recent year.

(c) By how much would cost of goods sold during the most recent year change if the firm used FIFO?

(d) By how much would net income during the most recent year change if the firm used FIFO? (*Hint:* To estimate the tax rate, divide income tax expense by income before taxes.)

Case 2

The "Fortune 500" issue of *Fortune* magazine can serve as a useful reference. This annual issue, generally appearing in late April or early May, contains a great deal of information regarding the largest U.S. industrial and service companies.

Instructions

Examine the most recent edition and answer the following questions.

(a) Identify the three largest U.S. corporations in terms of revenue, profit, assets, market value, and employees.

(b) Identify the largest corporation in your state (by total revenue).

ETHICS CASE

Gamble Company uses the LIFO method for inventory costing. In an effort to lower net income, company president Oscar Gamble tells the plant accountant to take the unusual step of recommending to the purchasing department a large purchase of inventory at year-end. The price of the item to be purchased has nearly doubled during the year, and the item represents a major portion of inventory value.

Instructions

Answer the following questions:

(a) Identify the major stakeholders. If the plant accountant recommends the purchase, what are the consequences?

(b) If Gamble Company were using the FIFO method of inventory costing, would Oscar Gamble give the same order? Why or why not?

A visit with
Sue McGrath

Suzanne P. McGrath, CPA, owns Vision Capital Management, a money management firm in Portland, Oregon, that she founded in 1999. Prior to that, she was a managing director and stockbroker with Piper Jaffray, a regional investment firm. She holds a bachelor's degree in mathematics from Oregon State University.

PERSPECTIVES ON

Money Management

It looks like you've had several careers since college. That's true. After graduating from Oregon State, I became a high school math teacher, during which time I began taking correspondence courses to get 30 accounting hours that are required to take the CPA exam. I passed the exam and began working for what is now Grant Thornton. I then started my own CPA firm, which was called Lang McGrath and Co., P.C. Another regional firm approached me and offered to buy my interest. At the time, I was ready to leave public accounting for new challenges. I became a stockbroker in 1983, working for a local firm called Black & Co., where I stayed until 1990, and then moved to Piper Jaffray, which was acquired by U.S. Bancorp in 1998. In August of 1999, I started my own money management firm. I am a Registered Investment Advisor, which means I have full discretion over client funds. I manage their money, a minimum of $1 million, for a fee, rather than a commission.

Are you also a financial planner? Registered Investment Advisors are a type of financial planner, but my focus is more narrowly on the success of a client's investments. A financial planner coordinates investment advisors, insurance brokers, the CPA, the attorney, and any other advisors to come up with an overall financial plan. In reality, I act as my clients' financial planner because they typically don't have one. Often clients ask me to meet with their attorneys to draft their wills and trusts and to do estate planning. I may meet with their CPA to do tax planning. Right now, I'm analyzing my clients' unrealized gains and losses to see if it makes sense to sell stock to net gains against losses for tax purposes. So, all of these fields are interrelated.

Why did you leave public accounting? Because I had an attractive offer to buy my interest in the firm at a time when I was interested in planning for my clients' future rather than thinking in historical terms. And while CPAs help clients make financial plans for the future, the primary focus is still on reporting financial results, conducting audits, preparing tax returns, and installing computer systems—a historical view. Of course, my timing was great because the stock market was about to embark on the century's greatest bull market that began in 1982 when the Dow Jones Industrial Average was about 800. I could see that this baby boomer population that's talked about so much in the media—people my age—would need a lot more forward planning.

What skills were transferable from accounting to money management? Number one, the organizational skills that I learned as a CPA made me a standout in the brokerage industry, because most stockbrokers had virtually no records. They usually had two books on their desks—often with manual entries that might be out of date. One was a book that had each client's name and what had been purchased for them, when and how much. So it would say, "For Mr. Jones I bought 100 shares of IBM at 82 on X/X/XX." Another book listed all the holders of IBM, which might be 20 or 30 people. Brokerage statements back then didn't even list the price of the securities. People wanted to know how they were doing, but the brokerage industry wasn't very good at supplying that information. I could see that my accounting and organizing skills would be a big advantage in attracting clients.

Number two, my ability to analyze financial statements was very helpful. I could quickly glance at a financial statement and see trends in sales and earnings that the typical salesperson couldn't see. Brokers were trained in sales, not accounting, and they relied on the firm's analysts to make recommendations on individual stocks.

Third, I had a built-in client base. Most of my accounting clients became my investment clients. Instead of being a typical stockbroker who focused on transactions, I built an investments practice that was very similar to my practice in public accounting. The big difference, of course, is that as a CPA, I was usually a hero by saving my client money. A mistake could usually be fixed at a low cost, whether it was a financial statement or a tax return. In the investment business, you're a hero or a bum depending on how the stock turns out. So you have to retrain your clients to think about their investments over the long term. When I started out, I made some mistakes that had to do with not recognizing the risk associated with individual securities. It didn't take me long to see that creating a diversified portfolio was one of the keys to success.

How is your investment style different because of your accounting background? Undoubtedly, it has affected the way I look at investments, because I won't invest without studying a company's financial statements. In a go-go market where investors are ignoring red ink, it can hurt me because I might not invest in an Internet company with no earnings. Meanwhile, the stock soars—but I was trained to look for profits. My style is to look for sales—and earnings growth.

The first thing I do when considering a stock is to go into a database and compare that company to its industry peers and the overall market. Unlike many analysts who look only at the income statement and balance sheet, I give equal billing to the statement of cash flows, which can give early warning signs that a company is going to get into trouble. It can also signal that a company's true performance is better than its earnings per share would indicate. But I also consider factors that have nothing to do with accounting, such as the products and services the company has to offer.

Has the investment field become too crowded? No. I think it offers unlimited opportunities for people who want to dig in and work hard. While the industry has attracted a huge number of people because of its reputation for high compensation, there is a surprising number of mediocre people in the field. My advice to college students who are thinking about entering this business is to take a broad array of courses. Don't just study business. Take courses in history, art, and science, and be as well rounded academically as possible because investing money requires some knowledge about many topics. When you graduate from college, find a mentor and work under his or her guidance—whether it's at a large firm or a small boutique.

When you're analyzing financial statements, what accounting issues concern you? In general, I believe that Wall Street can adjust to changes in accounting methods, whether it is the elimination of pooling accounting or a more conservative method for valuing stock options. But there are certain issues that worry me, such as discrepancies on when certain companies recognize revenue. If it turns out that they're booking sales prematurely, as has been the case recently with certain technology companies, then you can't rely on the financial information. Accurate revenue recognition is particularly important in this era when so many high-flying companies are losing money. Accounting irregularities kill stock prices, and Wall Street can be very unforgiving. I have bought shares in companies whose stocks have been cut in half merely from the accusation of "cooking the books." Even though the company is exonerated from the accusation, the stock takes years to recover.

CHAPTER 9

Inventories: Additional Valuation Issues

What Do Inventory Changes Tell Us?

Department stores face an ongoing challenge to have enough inventory on hand to meet customer demand, but at the same time not to accumulate too much inventory if demand for the product is less than expected. If demand falls short of expectations, the department store may be forced to reduce the price. For example, the following chart shows recent quarterly sales and inventory trends for major retailers compared to the same quarter in the prior year:[1]

Company	Sales	Inventory
Sears, Roebuck and Co.	+9.4%	+14.0%
J.C. Penney Co.	+4.8	+12.9
Nordstrom Inc.	+5.3	+12.6
Kmart Corp.	+4.1	+8.9
Federated Department Stores	+3.3	+8.0
Dillard's Inc.	+4.3	+7.0
May Department Stores	+7.6	+7.0
Wal-Mart Stores	+11.6	−2.0

Note that for six of these eight retailers, inventories have grown faster than sales from one year to the next. This trend should raise warning flags for investors in retail company stocks, because rising levels of inventories indicate that fewer shoppers are turning out to buy merchandise compared to activity in the prior period. Note that such a scenario will be reflected in lower inventory turnover ratios. As one analyst remarked, ". . . when inventory grows faster than sales, profits drop." That is, when retailers face slower sales and growing inventory, then markdowns in prices are usually not far behind. These markdowns, in turn, lead to lower sales revenue and income as profit margins on sales are squeezed.

Research supporting these observations has found that increases in inventory for retailers translate into lower prices and therefore lower net income.[2] Interestingly, the same research found that, for manufacturers, only increases in finished goods inventory lead to future profit decline. Increases in raw materials and work-in-process inventories provide a signal that the company is building its inventory to meet increased demand, and therefore future sales and income will be higher. These research results reinforce the usefulness of the GAAP requirement that a manufacturer's inventory components should be disclosed on the balance sheet or in related notes.

[1]S. Pulliam, "Heard on the Street," *The Wall Street Journal,* May 21, 1997, p. C1.

[2]Victor Bernard and J. Noel, "Do Inventory Disclosures Predict Sales and Earnings?" *Journal of Accounting, Auditing, and Finance,* March 1991, pp. 145–182.

LEARNING OBJECTIVES

After studying this chapter, you should be able to:

1. **Explain and apply the lower of cost or market rule.**
2. **Identify when inventories are valued at net realizable value.**
3. **Explain when the relative sales value method is used to value inventories.**
4. **Explain accounting issues related to purchase commitments.**
5. **Determine ending inventory by applying the gross profit method.**
6. **Determine ending inventory by applying the retail inventory method.**
7. **Explain how inventory is reported and analyzed.**

PREVIEW OF CHAPTER 9

As indicated in the opening story, information on inventories and changes in inventory is relevant to predicting profits. The purpose of this chapter is to discuss and illustrate some of the valuation and estimation concepts that are used to develop relevant inventory information. The content and organization of the chapter are as follows:

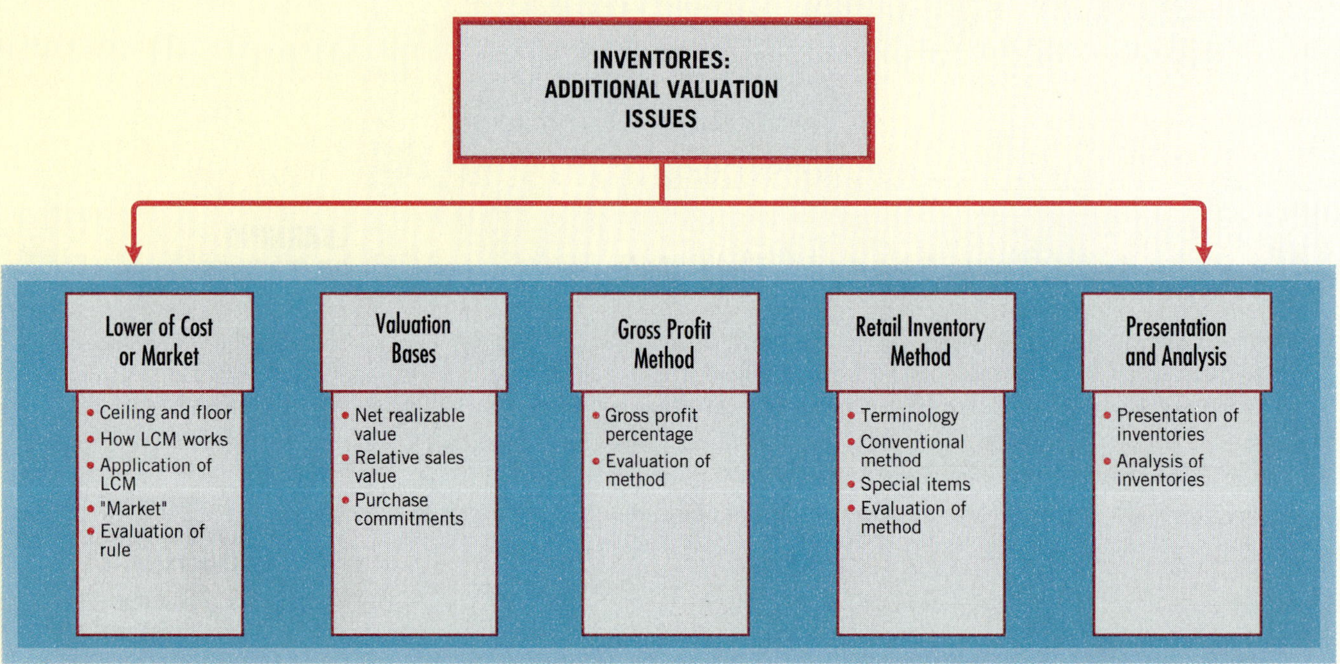

LOWER OF COST OR MARKET

OBJECTIVE 1
Explain and apply the lower of cost or market rule.

As noted in Chapter 8, inventories are recorded at their original cost. However, a major departure from the historical cost principle is made in the area of inventory valuation if inventory declines in value below its original cost. Whatever the reason for a decline—obsolescence, price-level changes, damaged goods, and so forth—the inventory should be written down to reflect this loss. **The general rule is that the historical cost principle is abandoned when the future utility (revenue-producing ability) of the asset is no longer as great as its original cost.**

Inventories that experience a decline in utility are valued therefore on the basis of the lower of cost or market, instead of on an original cost basis. **Cost** is the acquisition price of inventory computed using one of the historical cost-based methods—specific identification, average cost, FIFO, or LIFO. The term **market** in the phrase "the lower of cost or market" (LCM) generally means the cost to replace the item by purchase or reproduction. In a retailing business the term "market" refers to the market in which goods were purchased, not the market in which they are sold; in manufacturing, the term "market" refers to the cost to reproduce. Thus the rule really means that **goods are to be valued at cost or cost to replace, whichever is lower**. For example, a Casio calculator wristwatch that costs a retailer $30.00 when purchased, that can be sold for $48.95, and that can be replaced for $25.00 should be valued at $25.00 for inventory purposes under the lower of cost or market rule. The lower of cost or market rule of valuation can be used after any of the cost flow methods discussed in Chapter 8 have been applied to determine the inventory cost.

A departure from cost is justified because **a loss of utility should be charged against revenues in the period in which the loss occurs**, not in the period in which it is sold. In addition, the lower of cost or market method is **a conservative approach to inventory valuation**. That is, when doubt exists about the value of an asset, it is preferable to undervalue rather than to overvalue it.

UNDERLYING CONCEPTS

The use of the lower of cost or market method is an excellent example of the conservatism constraint.

Lower of Cost or Market—Ceiling and Floor

Why use replacement cost to represent market value? The reason is that a decline in the replacement cost of an item usually reflects or predicts a decline in selling price. Using replacement cost allows a company to maintain a consistent rate of gross profit on sales (normal profit margin). Sometimes, however, a reduction in the replacement cost of an item does not indicate a corresponding reduction in its utility. Then, two additional valuation limitations are used to value ending inventory—net realizable value and net realizable value less a normal profit margin.

Net realizable value (NRV) is defined as the estimated selling price in the ordinary course of business less reasonably predictable costs of completion and disposal. A normal profit margin is subtracted from that amount to arrive at **net realizable value less a normal profit margin**.

To illustrate, assuming that Jerry Mander Corp. has unfinished inventory with a sales value of $1,000, estimated cost of completion of $300, and a normal profit margin of 10% of sales, the following can be determined:

Inventory—sales value	$1,000
Less: Estimated cost of completion and disposal	300
Net realizable value	700
Less: Allowance for normal profit margin (10% of sales)	100
Net realizable value less a normal profit margin	$ 600

ILLUSTRATION 9-1
Computation of Net Realizable Value

The general rule of lower of cost or market is: inventory is valued at the lower of cost or market, with market limited to an amount that is not more than net realizable value or less than net realizable value less a normal profit margin.[3]

What is the rationale for these two limitations? The **upper (ceiling)** and **lower (floor) limits** for the value of the inventory are intended to prevent the inventory from being reported at an amount in excess of the net selling price or at an amount less than the net selling price less a normal profit margin. The maximum limitation, **not to exceed the net realizable value (ceiling)**, covers obsolete, damaged, or shopworn material and prevents overstatement of inventories and understatement of the loss in the current period. That is, if the replacement cost of an item is greater than its net realizable value, inventory should not be reported at replacement cost because the company can receive only the selling price less cost of disposal. To report the inventory at replacement cost would result in an overstatement of inventory and an understated loss in the current period. To illustrate, assume that Staples paid $1,000 for a laser printer that can now be replaced for $900 and whose net realizable value is $700. At what amount should the laser printer be reported in the financial statements? To report the replacement cost of $900 overstates the ending inventory and understates the loss for the period. The printer should, therefore, be reported at $700.

UNDERLYING CONCEPTS

Setting a floor and a ceiling increases the relevancy of the inventory presentation. The inventory figure provides a better understanding of how much revenue the inventory will generate.

The minimum limitation, **not to be less than net realizable value reduced by an allowance for an approximately normal profit margin (floor)**, deters understatement of inventory and overstatement of the loss in the current period. It establishes a floor below which the inventory should not be priced regardless of replacement cost. It makes no sense to price inventory below net realizable value less a normal margin because

[3]"Restatement and Revision of Accounting Research Bulletins," *Accounting Research Bulletin No. 43* (New York: AICPA, 1953), Ch. 4, par. 8.

this minimum amount (floor) measures what the company can receive for the inventory and still earn a normal profit. These guidelines are illustrated graphically in Illustration 9-2.

ILLUSTRATION 9-2
Inventory Valuation—Lower of Cost or Market

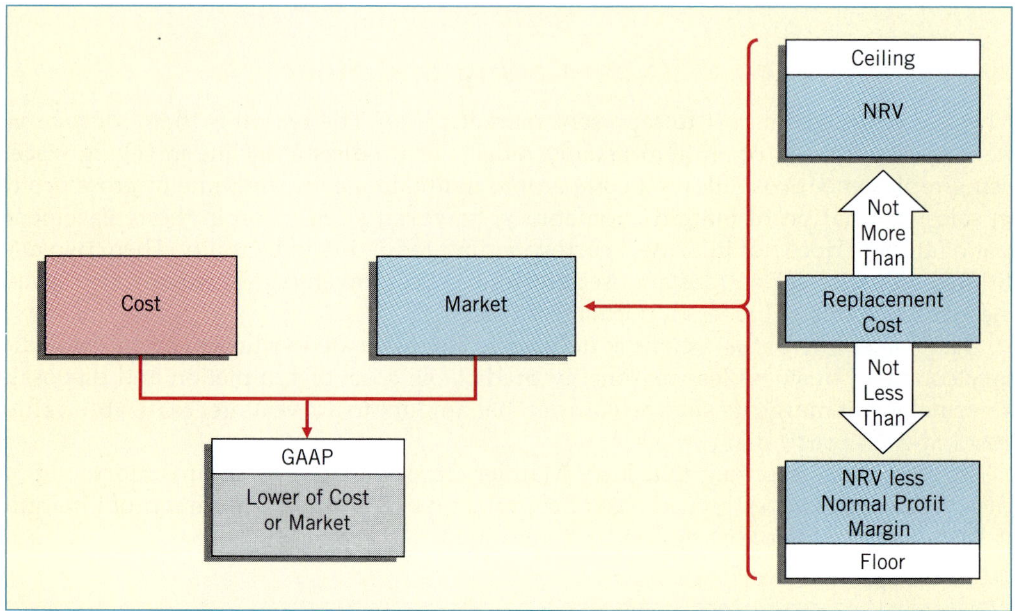

How Lower of Cost or Market Works

The amount that is compared to cost, often referred to as **designated market value**, is **always the middle value of three amounts**: replacement cost, net realizable value, and net realizable value less a normal profit margin. To illustrate how designated market value is computed, assume the following information relative to the inventory of Regner Foods, Inc.

ILLUSTRATION 9-3
Computation of Designated Market Value

Food	Replacement Cost	Net Realizable Value (Ceiling)	Net Realizable Value Less a Normal Profit Margin (Floor)	Designated Market Value
Spinach	$ 88,000	$120,000	$104,000	$104,000
Carrots	90,000	100,000	70,000	90,000
Cut beans	45,000	40,000	27,500	40,000
Peas	36,000	72,000	48,000	48,000
Mixed vegetables	105,000	92,000	80,000	92,000

Designated Market Value Decision:

Spinach	Net realizable value less a normal profit margin is selected because it is the middle value.
Carrots	Replacement cost is selected because it is the middle value.
Cut beans	Net realizable value is selected because it is the middle value.
Peas	Net realizable value less a normal profit margin is selected because it is the middle value.
Mixed vegetables	Net realizable value is selected because it is the middle value.

Designated market value is then compared to cost to determine the lower of cost or market. To illustrate, the final inventory value for Regner Foods is determined as follows:

ILLUSTRATION 9-4
Determining Final Inventory Value

Food	Cost	Replacement Cost	Net Realizable Value (Ceiling)	Net Realizable Value Less a Normal Profit Margin (Floor)	Designated Market Value	Final Inventory Value
Spinach	$ 80,000	$ 88,000	$120,000	$104,000	$104,000	$ 80,000
Carrots	100,000	90,000	100,000	70,000	90,000	90,000
Cut beans	50,000	45,000	40,000	27,500	40,000	40,000
Peas	90,000	36,000	72,000	48,000	48,000	48,000
Mixed vegetables	95,000	105,000	92,000	80,000	92,000	92,000
						$350,000

Final Inventory Value:

Spinach	Cost ($80,000) is selected because it is lower than designated market value (net realizable value less a normal profit margin).
Carrots	Designated market value (replacement cost, $90,000) is selected because it is lower than cost.
Cut beans	Designated market value (net realizable value, $40,000) is selected because it is lower than cost.
Peas	Designated market value (net realizable value less a normal profit margin, $48,000) is selected because it is lower than cost.
Mixed vegetables	Designated market value (net realizable value, $92,000) is selected because it is lower than cost.

The application of the lower of cost or market rule incorporates only losses in value that occur in the normal course of business from such causes as style changes, shift in demand, or regular shop wear. Damaged or deteriorated goods are reduced to net realizable value. When material, such goods may be carried in separate inventory accounts.

Methods of Applying Lower of Cost or Market

In the previous illustration for Regner Foods, we assumed that the lower of cost or market rule was applied to each individual type of food. However, the lower of cost or market rule may be "applied either directly to each item, to each category, or to the total of the inventory." Increases in market prices tend to offset decreases in market prices, if a major category or total inventory approach is followed in applying the lower of cost or market rule. To illustrate, assume that Regner Foods separates its food products into frozen and canned for purposes of designating major categories.

ILLUSTRATION 9-5
Alternative Applications of Lower of Cost or Market

			Lower of Cost or Market By:		
	Cost	Designated Market	Individual Items	Major Categories	Total Inventory
Frozen					
Spinach	$ 80,000	$104,000	$ 80,000		
Carrots	100,000	90,000	90,000		
Cut beans	50,000	40,000	40,000		
Total frozen	230,000	234,000		$230,000	
Canned					
Peas	90,000	48,000	48,000		
Mixed vegetables	95,000	92,000	92,000		
Total canned	185,000	140,000		140,000	
Total	$415,000	$374,000	$350,000	$370,000	$374,000

If the lower of cost or market rule is applied to individual items, the amount of inventory is $350,000; if applied to major categories, it is $370,000; if applied to the total inventory, it is $374,000. The reason for the difference is that market values higher than cost are offset against market values lower than cost when the major categories or total inventory approach is adopted. For Regner Foods, the high market value for spinach is partially offset when the major categories approach is adopted, and it is totally offset when the total inventory approach is used.

The most common practice is to price the inventory on an item-by-item basis. For one thing, tax rules require that an individual item basis be used unless it involves practical difficulties. In addition, the individual item approach gives the most conservative valuation for balance sheet purposes.[4] Inventory is often priced on a total inventory basis when there is only one end product (comprised of many different raw materials) because the main concern is the pricing of the final inventory. If several end products are produced, a category approach might be used. The method selected should be the one that most clearly reflects income. **Whichever method is selected, it should be applied consistently from one period to another.**[5]

Recording "Market" Instead of Cost

Two methods are used for recording inventory at market. One method, referred to as the **direct method**, substitutes the market value figure for cost when valuing the inventory. As a result, no loss is reported in the income statement because the loss is buried in cost of goods sold. The second method, referred to as the **indirect method** or **allowance method**, does not change the cost amount, but establishes a separate contra asset account and a loss account to record the writeoff.

The following illustrations of entries under both methods are based on the following inventory data:

Inventory	At Cost	At Market
Beginning of the period	$65,000	$65,000
End of the period	82,000	70,000

The following entries assume the use of a **periodic** inventory system.

[4]If a company uses dollar-value LIFO, determining the LIFO cost of an individual item may be more difficult. The company might decide that it is more appropriate to apply the lower of cost or market rule to the total amount of each pool. The AICPA Task Force on LIFO Inventory Problems concluded that the most reasonable approach to applying the lower of cost or market provisions to LIFO inventories is to base the determination on reasonable groupings of items and that a pool constitutes a reasonable grouping. Both the Task Force and AcSEC, however, support the use of the item-by-item approach for identifying product obsolescence and product discontinuance write-downs and write-offs.

[5]Inventory accounting for financial statement purposes can be different from income tax purposes. For example, the lower of cost or market rule cannot be used with LIFO for tax purposes. There is nothing, however, to prevent the use of the lower of cost or market and LIFO for financial accounting purposes. In addition, for financial accounting purposes, companies often write down slow-moving inventory because experience indicates that some of it will not be sold for many years, if at all. However, to be deductible for tax purposes a write-down in inventory value resulting from the application of the lower of cost or market rule can be taken only in the year in which the actual decline in the sale price of the item occurs, and the write-down must be computed on an individual item basis rather than on classes of inventory or on the inventory as a whole.

ILLUSTRATION 9-6
Accounting for the Reduction of Inventory to Market—Periodic Inventory System

Ending Inventory Recorded at Market (Direct Method)			Ending Inventory Recorded at Cost and Reduced to Market (Indirect or Allowance Method)		
To close beginning inventory:					
Cost of Goods Sold (or Income Summary)	65,000		Cost of Goods Sold (or Income Summary)	65,000	
Inventory		65,000	Inventory		65,000
To record ending inventory:					
Inventory	70,000		Inventory	82,000	
Cost of Goods Sold (or Income Summary)		70,000	Cost of Goods Sold (or Income Summary)		82,000
To write down inventory to market:					
No entry			Loss Due to Market Decline of Inventory	12,000	
			Allowance to Reduce Inventory to Market		12,000

If the company had used a **perpetual** inventory system, the entries would be as follows:

ILLUSTRATION 9-7
Accounting for the Reduction of Inventory to Market—Perpetual Inventory System

(No inventory closing entries are necessary under the perpetual method; only the reduction to market is recorded.)

Direct Method			Indirect or Allowance Method		
To reduce inventory from cost to market:					
Cost of Goods Sold	12,000		Loss Due to Market Decline of Inventory	12,000	
Inventory		12,000	Allowance to Reduce Inventory to Market		12,000

The advantage of identifying the loss due to market decline is that it is shown separately from cost of goods sold in the income statement (not as an extraordinary item); the cost of goods sold for the year is not distorted. The data from the preceding illustration are used to contrast the differing amounts reported in the income statements below.

ILLUSTRATION 9-8
Income Statement Presentation—Direct and Indirect Methods of Reducing Inventory to Market

Direct Method

Revenue from sales		$200,000
Cost of goods sold		
Inventory, Jan. 1	$ 65,000	
Purchases	125,000	
Goods available	190,000	
Inventory, Dec. 31 (at market which is lower than cost)	70,000	
Cost of goods sold		120,000
Gross profit on sales		$ 80,000

Indirect or Allowance Method

Revenue from sales		$200,000
Cost of goods sold		
Inventory, Jan. 1	$ 65,000	
Purchases	125,000	
Goods available	190,000	
Inventory, Dec. 31 (at cost)	82,000	
Cost of goods sold		108,000
Gross profit on sales		92,000
Loss due to market decline of inventory		12,000
		$ 80,000

The second presentation is preferable, because it clearly discloses the loss resulting from the market decline of inventory prices. The first presentation buries the loss in the cost of goods sold. The Allowance to Reduce Inventory to Market would be reported on the balance sheet as a $12,000 deduction from the inventory. This deduction permits both the income statement and the balance sheet to show the ending inventory of $82,000, although the balance sheet shows a net amount of $70,000. It also keeps subsidiary inventory ledgers and records in correspondence with the control account without changing unit prices.

UNDERLYING CONCEPTS

The income statement under the first presentation lacks *representational faithfulness.* The cost of goods sold does not represent what it purports to represent. However, allowing the first presentation illustrates the concept of materiality. The presentation does not affect net income and would not "change the judgment of a reasonable person."

Although use of an allowance account permits balance sheet disclosure of the inventory at cost and the lower of cost or market, it raises the problem of how to dispose of the balance of the new account in the following period. If the merchandise in question is still on hand, the allowance account should be retained. Otherwise, beginning inventory and cost of goods are overstated. But if the goods have been sold, then the account should be closed. A "new allowance account" is then established for any decline in inventory value that has taken place in the current year.[6]

Some accountants leave this account on the books and merely adjust the balance at the next year-end to agree with the discrepancy between cost and the lower of cost or market at that balance sheet date. Thus, if prices are falling, a loss is recorded. If prices are rising, a loss recorded in prior years is recovered and a "gain" (which is not really a gain, but a recovery of a previously recognized loss) is recorded, as illustrated in the example below.

ILLUSTRATION 9-9
Effect on Net Income of Reducing Inventory to Market

Date	Inventory at Cost	Inventory at Market	Amount Required in Valuation Account	Adjustment of Valuation Account Balance	Effect on Net Income
Dec. 31, 2000	$188,000	$176,000	$12,000	$12,000 inc.	Loss
Dec. 31, 2001	194,000	187,000	7,000	5,000 dec.	Gain
Dec. 31, 2002	173,000	174,000	0	7,000 dec.	Gain
Dec. 31, 2003	182,000	180,000	2,000	2,000 inc.	Loss

UNDERLYING CONCEPTS

The inconsistency in the presentation of inventory is an example of the trade-off between *relevancy and reliability.* Market is more relevant than cost, and cost is more reliable than market. Apparently, relevance takes precedence in a down market, and reliability is more important than relevancy in an up market.

This net "gain" can be thought of as the excess of the credit effect of closing the beginning allowance balance over the debit effect of setting up the current year-end allowance account. Recognition of gain or loss has the same effect on net income as closing the allowance balance to beginning inventory or to cost of goods sold. Recovery of the loss up to the original cost is permitted, **but it may not exceed original cost.**

Evaluation of the Lower of Cost or Market Rule

The lower of cost or market rule suffers some conceptual deficiencies:

1. Decreases in the value of the asset and the charge to expense are recognized in the period in which the loss in utility occurs—not in the period of sale. On the other hand, increases in the value of the asset are recognized only at the point of sale. This treatment is inconsistent and can lead to distortions in income data.
2. Application of the rule results in inconsistency because the inventory of a company may be valued at cost in one year and at market in the next year.
3. Lower of cost or market values the inventory in the balance sheet conservatively, but its effect on the income statement may or may not be conservative. Net income for the year in which the loss is taken is definitely lower; net income of the subsequent period may be higher than normal if the expected reductions in sales price do not materialize.

INTERNATIONAL INSIGHT

In Japan, companies typically value their inventories at cost, rather than at lower of cost or market.

[6]The AICPA Task Force on LIFO Inventory Problems concluded that for LIFO inventories the allowance from the prior year should be closed and that the allowance at the end of the year should be based on a new lower of cost or market computation. *Issues Paper* (New York: AICPA, November 30, 1984), pp. 50–55.

4 Application of the lower of cost or market rule uses a "normal profit" in determining inventory values. Since "normal profit" is an estimated figure based upon past experience (and might not be attained in the future), it is not objective in nature and presents an opportunity for income manipulation.

Many financial statement users appreciate the lower of cost or market rule because they at least know that the inventory is not overstated. In addition, recognizing all losses but anticipating no gains generally results in lower income.

VALUATION BASES

Valuation at Net Realizable Value

OBJECTIVE 2
Identify when inventories are valued at net realizable value.

For the most part, inventory is recorded at cost or the lower of cost or market.[7] However, many believe that market should always be defined as net realizable value (rather than replacement cost) for purposes of applying the lower of cost or market rule. This argument is based on the fact that net realizable value is the amount that will be collected from this inventory in the future.[8] Under limited circumstances, support exists for **recording inventory at net realizable value (selling price less estimated costs to complete and sell)** even if that amount is above cost. This exception to the normal recognition rule is permitted where (1) there is a controlled market with a quoted price applicable to all quantities and (2) no significant costs of disposal are involved. Inventories of certain minerals (rare metals especially) are ordinarily reported at selling prices because there is often a controlled market without significant costs of disposal. A similar treatment is given agricultural products that are immediately marketable at quoted prices.

In the Netherlands, Canada, and the United Kingdom, inventory is valued at "lower of cost or market," but in contrast to the U.S., *market* in these nations is defined as "net realizable value." The U.S. is the only country that defines *market* as something other than net realizable value.

Another reason for allowing this method of valuation is that sometimes the cost figures are too difficult to obtain. In a manufacturing plant, various raw materials and purchased parts are put together to create a finished product. The various items in inventory, whether completely or partially finished, can be accounted for on a basis of cost because the cost of each individual component part is known. In a meat-packing house, however, a different situation prevails. The "raw material" consists of cattle, hogs, or sheep, each unit of which is purchased as a whole and then divided into parts that are the products. Instead of one product out of many raw materials or parts, many products are made from one "unit" of raw material. To allocate the cost of the animal "on the hoof" into the cost of ribs, chucks, and shoulders, for instance, is a practical

[7]Manufacturing companies frequently employ a **standardized cost system** that predetermines the unit costs for material, labor, and manufacturing overhead and values raw materials, work in process, and finished goods inventories at their standard costs. For financial reporting purposes the pricing of inventories at standard costs is acceptable if there is no significant difference between the actual costs and standard costs. If there is a significant difference, the inventory amounts should be adjusted to actual cost. In *Accounting Research and Terminology Bulletin, Final Edition* the profession notes that **"standard costs are acceptable if adjusted at reasonable intervals to reflect current conditions."** Burlington Industries and Hewlett-Packard are examples of companies that use standard costs for valuing at least a portion of their inventory.

[8] "The Accounting Basis of Inventories," *Accounting Research Study No. 13* (New York: AICPA, 1973) recommends that net realizable value be adopted. It also should be noted that a literal interpretation of the rules of lower of cost or market is frequently not applied in practice. For example, the lower limit, net realizable value less a normal markup, is rarely computed and applied because it is a fairly subjective computation. In addition, inventory is often not reduced to market unless its disposition is expected to result in a loss. Furthermore, if the net realizable value of finished goods exceeds cost, it is usually assumed that both work in process and raw materials do also. In practice, therefore, *ARB No. 43* is considered a guide, and professional judgment is often exercised in lieu of following this pronouncement literally.

impossibility. It is much easier and more useful to determine the market price of the various products and value them in the inventory at selling price less the various costs, such as shipping and handling, necessary to get them to market. Hence, because of a peculiarity of the meat-packing industry, **inventories are sometimes carried at sales price less distribution costs.**

Valuation Using Relative Sales Value

OBJECTIVE 3
Explain when the relative sales value method is used to value inventories.

A special problem arises when a group of varying units is purchased at a single **lump sum price**, a so-called **basket purchase**. Assume that Woodland Developers purchases land for $1 million that can be subdivided in 400 lots. These lots are of different sizes and shapes but can be roughly sorted into three groups graded A, B, and C. As lots are sold, the purchase cost of $1 million is apportioned among the lots sold and the lots remaining on hand.

It is inappropriate to divide 400 lots into the total cost of $1 million to get a cost of $2,500 for each lot, because they vary in size, shape, and attractiveness. When such a situation is encountered—and it is not at all unusual—the common and most logical practice is to allocate the total cost among the various units on the basis of their relative sales value. For the example given, the allocation works out as follows:

ILLUSTRATION 9-10
Allocation of Costs, Using Relative Sales Value

Lots	Number of Lots	Sales Price Per Lot	Total Sales Price	Relative Sales Price	Total Cost	Cost Allocated to Lots	Cost Per Lot
A	100	$10,000	$1,000,000	100/250	$1,000,000	$ 400,000	$4,000
B	100	6,000	600,000	60/250	1,000,000	240,000	2,400
C	200	4,500	900,000	90/250	1,000,000	360,000	1,800
			$2,500,000			$1,000,000	

The cost of lots sold can be computed by using the amounts given in the column for "Cost Per Lot," and the gross profit is determined as follows:

ILLUSTRATION 9-11
Determination of Gross Profit, Using Relative Sales Value

Lots	Number of Lots Sold	Cost Per Lot	Cost of Lots Sold	Sales	Gross Profit
A	77	$4,000	$308,000	$ 770,000	$ 462,000
B	80	2,400	192,000	480,000	288,000
C	100	1,800	180,000	450,000	270,000
			$680,000	$1,700,000	$1,020,000

The ending inventory is therefore $320,000 ($1,000,000 − $680,000). This inventory amount can also be computed in another manner. The ratio of cost to selling price for all the lots is $1 million divided by $2,500,000, or 40%. Accordingly, if the total sales price of lots sold is, say $1,700,000, then the cost of these lots sold is 40% of $1,700,000, or $680,000. The inventory of lots on hand is then $1 million less $680,000, or $320,000.

The relative sales value method is used throughout the petroleum industry to value (at cost) the many products and by-products obtained from a barrel of crude oil.

Purchase Commitments—A Special Problem

OBJECTIVE 4
Explain accounting issues related to purchase commitments.

In many lines of business, the survival and continued profitability of a firm depends on it having a sufficient stock of merchandise to meet all customer demands. Consequently, it is quite common for a company to agree to buy inventory weeks, months, or even years in advance. Such arrangements may be made on the basis of estimated or firm sales commitments by the company's customers. Generally, title to the merchandise or materials described in these **purchase commitments** has not passed to the buyer. Indeed, the goods may exist only as natural resources or, in the case of commodities, as unplanted seed, or in the case of a product, as work in process.

Usually it is neither necessary nor proper for the buyer to make any entries to reflect commitments for purchases of goods that have not been shipped by the seller. Ordinary orders, for which the prices are determined at the time of shipment and **which are subject to cancellation** by the buyer or seller, do not represent either an asset or a liability to the buyer. Therefore they need not be recorded in the books or reported in the financial statements.

Even with formal, noncancelable purchase contracts, no asset or liability is recognized at the date of inception, **because the contract is "executory" in nature**: neither party has fulfilled its part of the contract. However, if material, such contract details should be disclosed in the buyer's balance sheet in a note.

ILLUSTRATION 9-12
Disclosure of Purchase Commitment

> **Note 1:** Contracts for the purchase of raw materials in 2002 have been executed in the amount of $600,000. The market price of such raw materials on December 31, 2001, is $640,000.

In the foregoing illustration the contracted price was less than the market price at the balance sheet date. **If the contracted price is in excess of market and it is expected that losses will occur when the purchase is effected, losses should be recognized in the period during which such declines in market prices take place.**[9]

In the early 1980s, many Northwest forest product companies such as **Boise Cascade**, **Georgia-Pacific**, **Weyerhaeuser**, and **St. Regis** signed long-term timber-cutting contracts with the United States Forest Service. These contracts required that the companies pay $310 per thousand board feet for timber-cutting rights. Unfortunately, the market price for timber-cutting rights in late 1984 dropped to $80 per thousand board feet. As a result, a number of these companies had long-term contracts that, if fulfilled, projected substantial future losses.

To illustrate the accounting problem, assume that St. Regis Paper Co. signed timber-cutting contracts to be executed in 2002 at a firm price of $10,000,000 and that the market price of the timber cutting rights on December 31, 2001, dropped to $7,000,000. The following entry is made on December 31, 2001:

Unrealized Holding Gain or Loss—Income (Purchase Commitments)	3,000,000	
Estimated Liability on Purchase Commitments		3,000,000

UNDERLYING CONCEPTS

Reporting the loss is *conservative.* However, reporting the decline in market price is debatable because no asset is recorded. This area demonstrates the need for good definitions of assets and liabilities.

This unrealized holding loss would be reported in the income statement under Other Expenses and Losses. The Estimated Liability on Purchase Commitments is reported in the current liabilities section of the balance sheet because the contract is to be executed within the next fiscal year. When St. Regis cuts the timber at a cost of $10 million, the following entry would be made:

Purchases (Inventory)	7,000,000	
Estimated Liability on Purchase Commitments	3,000,000	
Cash		10,000,000

The company paid $10 million for a contract worth only $7 million. The loss was recorded in the previous period—when the price actually declined.

If the price is partially or fully recovered before the timber is cut, the Estimated Liability on Purchase Commitments is reduced. A resulting gain is then reported in the period of the price increase for the amount of the partial or full recovery. For example, Congress permitted some of these companies to buy out of their contracts at reduced prices in order to avoid some potential bankruptcies. To illustrate, assume that St. Regis is permitted to reduce its contract price and therefore its commitment by $1,000,000. The entry to record this transaction is as follows:

Estimated Liability on Purchase Commitments	1,000,000	
Unrealized Holding Gain or Loss—Income (Purchase Commitments)		1,000,000

[9] *Accounting Research Bulletin No. 43,* op. cit., par. 16.

If the market price at the time the timber is cut is more than $2,000,000 below the contract price, St. Regis will have to recognize an additional loss in the period of cutting and record the purchase at the lower of cost or market.

The purchasers in purchase commitments can protect themselves against the possibility of market price declines of goods under contract by hedging. **Hedging** is accomplished through a futures contract in which the purchaser in the purchase commitment simultaneously contracts to a future sale of the same quantity of the same or similar goods at a fixed price. When a company holds a buy position in a purchase commitment and a sell position in a futures contract in the same commodity, it will be better off under one contract by approximately (maybe exactly) the same amount by which it is worse off under the other contract. That is, a loss on one will be offset by a gain on the other. For example, if St. Regis Paper Co. had hedged its purchase commitment contract by selling futures contracts for timber rights of the same amount, its loss of $3,000,000 on the purchase commitment would have been offset by a $3,000,000 gain on the futures contract.[10]

Accounting for purchase commitments (and, for that matter, all commitments) is unsettled and controversial. Some argue that these contracts should be reported as assets and liabilities at the time the contract is signed.[11] Others believe that the present recognition at the delivery date is more appropriate. *FASB Concepts Statement No. 6* states that "a purchase commitment involves both an item that might be recorded as an asset and an item that might be recorded as a liability. That is, it involves both a right to receive assets and an obligation to pay. . . . If both the right to receive assets and the obligation to pay were recorded at the time of the purchase commitment, the nature of the loss and the valuation account that records it when the price falls would be clearly seen." Although the discussion in *Concepts Statement No. 6* does not exclude the possibility of recording assets and liabilities for purchase commitments, it contains no conclusions or implications about whether they should be recorded.[12]

THE GROSS PROFIT METHOD OF ESTIMATING INVENTORY

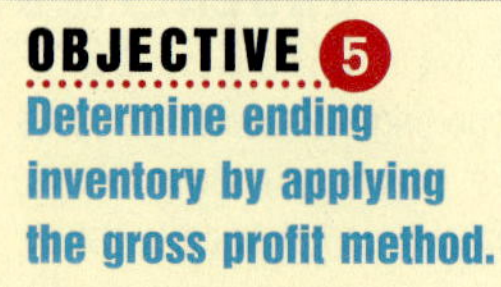

OBJECTIVE 5
Determine ending inventory by applying the gross profit method.

Recall that the basic purpose of taking a physical inventory is to verify the accuracy of the perpetual inventory records or, if no records exist, to arrive at an inventory amount. Sometimes, taking a physical inventory is impractical. Then, substitute measures are used to approximate inventory on hand. One substitute method of verifying or determining the inventory amount is called the gross profit method (often called the gross margin method). This method is widely used by auditors in situations (e.g., interim reports) where only an estimate of the company's inventory is needed. It is also used where either inventory or inventory records have been destroyed by fire or other catastrophe.

[10]A complete discussion regarding hedging and the use of derivatives such as futures is provided in Appendix 18A.

[11]See, for example, Yuji Ijiri, *Recognition of Contractual Rights and Obligations, Research Report* (Stamford, Conn.: FASB, 1980), who argues that firm purchase commitments should be capitalized. "Firm" means that it is unlikely that performance under the contract can be avoided without a severe penalty.

Also, see Mahendra R. Gujarathi and Stanley F. Biggs, "Accounting for Purchase Commitments: Some Issues and Recommendations," *Accounting Horizons,* September 1988, pages 75–78, who conclude, "Recording an asset and liability on the date of inception for the noncancelable purchase commitments is suggested as the first significant step towards alleviating the accounting problems associated with the issue. At year-end, the potential gains and losses should be treated as contingencies under FASB 5 which provides a coherent structure for the accounting and informative disclosure for such gains and losses."

[12]"Elements of Financial Statements," *Statement of Financial Accounting Concepts No. 6* (Stamford, Conn.: FASB, 1985), pars. 251–253.

The **gross profit method** is based on three assumptions: (1) the beginning inventory plus purchases equal total goods to be accounted for; (2) goods not sold must be on hand; and (3) if the sales, reduced to cost, are deducted from the sum of the opening inventory plus purchases, the result is the ending inventory.

To illustrate, assume that Cetus Corp. has a beginning inventory of $60,000 and purchases of $200,000, both at cost. Sales at selling price amount to $280,000. The gross profit on selling price is 30%. The gross margin method is applied as follows:

ILLUSTRATION 9-13
Application of Gross Profit Method

Beginning inventory (at cost)		$ 60,000
Purchases (at cost)		200,000
Goods available (at cost)		260,000
Sales (at selling price)	$280,000	
Less: Gross profit (30% of $280,000)	84,000	
Sales (at cost)		196,000
Approximate inventory (at cost)		$ 64,000

All the information needed to compute Cetus' inventory at cost, except for the gross profit percentage, is available in the current period's records. The gross profit percentage is determined by reviewing company policies or prior period records. In some cases, this percentage must be adjusted if prior periods are not considered representative of the current period.[13]

Computation of Gross Profit Percentage

In most situations, the **gross profit percentage** is given as a percentage of selling price. The previous illustration, for example, used a 30% gross profit on sales. Gross profit on selling price is the common method for quoting the profit for several reasons: (1) Most goods are stated on a retail basis, not a cost basis. (2) A profit quoted on selling price is lower than one based on cost, and this lower rate gives a favorable impression to the consumer. (3) The gross profit based on selling price can never exceed 100%.[14]

In the previous example, the gross profit was a given. But how was that figure derived? To see how a gross profit percentage is computed, assume that an article cost

[13]An alternative method of estimating inventory using the gross profit percentage, considered by some to be less complicated than the traditional method illustrated above, uses the standard income statement format as follows (assume the same data as in the Cetus Corp. illustration above):

Sales		$280,000			$280,000
Cost of sales					
Beginning inventory	$ 60,000			$ 60,000	
Purchases	200,000			200,000	
Goods available for sale	260,000			260,000	
Ending inventory	(3) ?			(3) 64,000 Est.	
Cost of goods sold		(2) ?			(2)196,000 Est.
Gross profit on sales (30%)		(1) ?			(1) 84,000 Est.

Compute the unknowns as follows: first the gross profit amount, then cost of goods sold, and then the ending inventory.

(1) $280,000 × 30% = $84,000 (gross profit on sales):
(2) $280,000 − $84,000 = $196,000 (cost of goods sold).
(3) $260,000 − $196,000 = $64,000 (ending inventory).

[14]The terms "gross margin percentage," "rate of gross profit," and "percentage markup" are synonymous, although "markup" is more commonly used in reference to cost and "gross profit" in reference to sales.

\$15.00 and sells for \$20.00, a gross profit of \$5.00. This markup is ¼ or 25% of retail and ⅓ or 33⅓% of cost:

ILLUSTRATION 9-14
Computation of Gross Profit Percentage

$$\frac{\text{Markup}}{\text{Retail}} = \frac{\$\ 5.00}{\$20.00} = 25\% \text{ at retail} \qquad \frac{\text{Markup}}{\text{Cost}} = \frac{\$\ 5.00}{\$15.00} = 33\tfrac{1}{3}\% \text{ on cost}$$

Although it is normal to compute the gross profit on the basis of selling price, you should understand the basic relationship between markup on cost and markup on selling price.

For example, assume that you were told that the markup on cost for a given item is 25%. What, then, is the **gross profit on selling price**? To find the answer, assume that the selling price of the item is \$1.00. In this case, the following formula applies:

$$\text{Cost} + \text{Gross profit} = \text{Selling price}$$

$$C + .25C = SP$$

$$(1 + .25)C = SP$$

$$1.25C = \$1.00$$

$$C = \$0.80$$

The gross profit equals \$0.20 (\$1.00 − \$0.80), and the rate of gross profit on selling price is therefore 20% (\$0.20/\$1.00).

Conversely, assume that you were told that the gross profit on selling price is 20%. What is the **markup on cost**? To find the answer, again assume that the selling price is \$1.00. Again, the same formula holds:

$$\text{Cost} + \text{Gross profit} = \text{Selling price}$$

$$C + .20SP = SP$$

$$C = (1 - .20)SP$$

$$C = .80SP$$

$$C = .80(\$1.00)$$

$$C = \$0.80$$

Here, as in the example above, the markup equals \$0.20 (\$1.00 − \$0.80), and the markup on cost is 25% (\$0.20/\$0.80).

Retailers use the following formulas to express these relationships:

ILLUSTRATION 9-15
Formulas Relating to Gross Profit

1. $\text{Gross profit on selling price} = \dfrac{\text{Percentage markup on cost}}{100\% + \text{Percentage markup on cost}}$

2. $\text{Percentage markup on cost} = \dfrac{\text{Gross profit on selling price}}{100\% - \text{Gross profit on selling price}}$

To understand how these formulas are employed, consider the following calculations:

ILLUSTRATION 9-16
Application of Gross Profit Formulas

Gross Profit on Selling Price		Percentage Markup on Cost
Given: 20%	→	$\frac{.20}{1.00 - .20} = 25\%$
Given: 25%	→	$\frac{.25}{1.00 - .25} = 33\tfrac{1}{3}\%$
$\frac{.25}{1.00 + .25} = 20\%$	←	Given: 25%
$\frac{.50}{1.00 + .50} = 33\tfrac{1}{3}\%$	←	Given: 50%

Because selling price is greater than cost, and with the gross profit amount the same for both, **gross profit on selling price will always be less than the related percentage based on cost**. It should be emphasized that sales may not be multiplied by a cost-based markup percentage; the gross profit percentage must be converted to a percentage based on selling price.

Gross profits are closely followed by managements and analysts. A small change in the gross profit rate can have a significant effect on the bottom line. In 1993, **Apple Computer** suffered a textbook case of shrinking gross profits. In response to pricing wars in the personal computer market, Apple was forced to quickly reduce the price of its signature Macintosh computers—reducing prices more quickly than it could reduce its costs. As a result its gross profit rate fell from 44% in 1992 to 40% in 1993. While the drop of 4% may appear small, its impact on the bottom line caused Apple's stock price to drop from $57 per share on June 1, 1993, to $27.50 by mid-July 1993. A similar effect (a 40% plummet in stock price) occurred when **Woolworth Corp.** disclosed a "correction of gross profits" due to a reporting of inaccurate gross profits in at least three of the company's quarterly reports during the fiscal year ended January 29, 1994.[15]

Evaluation of Gross Profit Method

What are the major disadvantages of the gross profit method? One major disadvantage is that **it provides an estimate**; as a result, a physical inventory must be taken once a year to verify that the inventory is actually on hand. Second, the gross profit method **uses past percentages** in determining the markup. Although the past can often provide answers to the future, a current rate is more appropriate. It is important to emphasize that whenever significant fluctuations occur, the percentage should be adjusted as appropriate. Third, **care must be taken in applying a blanket gross profit rate**. Frequently, a store or department handles merchandise with widely varying rates of gross profit. In these situations, the gross profit method may have to be applied by subsections, lines of merchandise, or a similar basis that classifies merchandise according to their respective rates of gross profit.

The gross profit method is not normally acceptable for financial reporting purposes because it provides only an estimate. A physical inventory is needed as additional verification that the inventory indicated in the records is actually on hand. Nevertheless, the gross profit method is permitted to determine ending inventory for interim (generally quarterly) reporting purposes provided the use of this method is disclosed. Note that the gross profit method will follow closely the inventory method used (FIFO, LIFO, average cost) because it is based on historical records.

RETAIL INVENTORY METHOD

> **OBJECTIVE 6**
> Determine ending inventory by applying the retail inventory method.

Accounting for inventory in a retail operation presents several challenges. Retailers with certain types of inventory may use the specific identification method to value their inventories. Such an approach makes sense when individual inventory units are significant, such as automobiles, pianos, or fur coats. However, imagine attempting to use such an approach at **Kmart**, **True-Value Hardware**, **Sears**, or **Bloomingdales**—high-volume retailers that have many different types of merchandise. It would be extremely difficult to determine the cost of each sale, to enter cost codes on the tickets, to change the codes to reflect declines in value of the merchandise, to allocate costs such as transportation, and so on.

An alternative is to compile the inventories at retail prices. In most retail concerns, an observable pattern between cost and price exists. Retail prices can therefore be converted to cost through formula. This method, called the **retail inventory method, re-**

---

[15]"Two Top Woolworth Officers Step Down Amid Probe of Accounting Irregularities," *The Wall Street Journal*, April 4, 1994, p. A3.

quires that a record be kept of (1) the total cost and retail value of goods purchased, (2) the total cost and retail value of the goods available for sale, and (3) the sales for the period.

Here is how it works: The sales for the period are deducted from the retail value of the goods available for sale, to produce an estimated inventory (goods on hand) at retail. The ratio of cost to retail for all goods passing through a department or firm is then determined by dividing the total goods available for sale at cost by the total goods available at retail. The inventory valued at retail is converted to ending inventory at cost by applying the cost-to-retail ratio. Use of the retail inventory method is very common. For example, **Safeway** supermarkets uses the retail inventory method as do the department stores of **Dayton Hudson Corp**. The retail inventory method is illustrated below for Jordan-Guess Inc.

ILLUSTRATION 9-17
Retail Inventory Method

JORDAN-GUESS INC.
(current period)

	Cost	Retail
Beginning inventory	$14,000	$ 20,000
Purchases	63,000	90,000
Goods available for sale	$77,000	110,000
Deduct: Sales		85,000
Ending inventory, at retail		$ 25,000
Ratio of cost to retail ($77,000 ÷ $110,000)		**70%**
Ending inventory at cost (70% of $25,000)		**$ 17,500**

To avoid a potential overstatement of the inventory, periodic inventory counts are made, especially in retail operations where loss due to shoplifting and breakage is common.

There are different versions of the retail inventory method—the conventional (lower of average cost or market) method, the cost method, the LIFO retail method, and the dollar-value LIFO retail method. Regardless of which version is used, the retail inventory method is sanctioned by the IRS, various retail associations, and the accounting profession. One of its advantages is that the inventory balance **can be approximated without a physical count**.

The retail inventory method is particularly useful for any type of interim report, because a fairly quick and reliable measure of the inventory value is usually needed. Insurance adjusters often use this approach to estimate losses from fire, flood, or other type of casualty. This method also acts as a **control device** because any deviations from a physical count at the end of the year have to be explained. In addition, the retail method **expedites the physical inventory count** at the end of the year. The crew taking the physical inventory need record only the retail price of each item; there is no need to look up each item's invoice cost, thereby saving time and expense.

Retail Method Terminology

The amounts shown in the Retail column of Illustration 9-17 represent the original retail prices, assuming no price changes. Sales prices are frequently marked up or down. For retailers, the term **markup** means an additional markup of the original retail price. (In another context, such as the gross profit discussion on page 462, we often think of markup on the basis of cost.) **Markup cancellations** are decreases in prices of merchandise that had been marked up above the original retail price.

Markdowns below the original sales prices may be necessary because of a decrease in the general level of prices, special sales, soiled or damaged goods, overstocking, and competition. Markdowns are common in retailing these days. **Markdown cancellations** occur when the markdowns are later offset by increases in the prices of goods that had been marked down—such as after a one-day sale, for example. Neither a markup cancellation nor a markdown cancellation can exceed the original markup or markdown.

To illustrate these different concepts, assume that the Designer Clothing Store recently purchased 100 dress shirts from Marroway, Inc. The cost for these shirts was $1,500, or $15.00 a shirt. Designer Clothing established the selling price on these shirts at $30.00 a shirt. The manager noted that the shirts were selling quickly, so he added a markup of $5.00 per shirt. This markup made the price too high for customers and sales lagged. The manager then reduced the price to $32.00. At this point we would say that Designer Clothing has had a markup of $5.00 and a markup cancellation of $3.00. As soon as the major marketing season passed, the manager marked the remaining shirts down to a sales price of $23.00. At this point, an additional markup cancellation of $2.00 has taken place and a $7.00 markdown has occurred. If the shirts are later written up to $24.00, a markdown cancellation of $1.00 would occur.

Retail Inventory Method with Markups and Markdowns—Conventional Method

Retailers use markup and markdown concepts in developing the proper inventory valuation at the end of the accounting period. To obtain the appropriate inventory figures, proper treatment must be given to markups, markup cancellations, markdowns, and markdown cancellations.

To illustrate the different possibilities, consider the data for In-Fashion Stores Inc., shown in Illustration 9-18. In-Fashion's ending inventory at cost can be calculated under two assumptions, A and B (the reasons for the two will be explained later):

Assumption A: Computes a cost ratio after markups (and markup cancellations) but before markdowns.

Assumption B: Computes a cost ratio after both markups and markdowns (and cancellations).

ILLUSTRATION 9-18
Retail Inventory Method with Markups and Markdowns

	Cost	Retail
Beginning inventory	$ 500	$ 1,000
Purchases (net)	20,000	35,000
Markups		3,000
Markup cancellations		1,000
Markdowns		2,500
Markdown cancellations		2,000
Sales (net)		25,000

IN-FASHION STORES INC.

	Cost		Retail	
Beginning inventory	$ 500		$ 1,000	
Purchases (net)	20,000		35,000	
Merchandise available for sale	20,500		36,000	
Add:				
Markups		$3,000		
Less: Markup cancellations		(1,000)		
Net markups			2,000	
	20,500		38,000	
Cost-to-retail ratio $\frac{\$20,500}{\$38,000} = 53.9\%$				(A)
Deduct:				
Markdowns		2,500		
Less: Markdown cancellations		(2,000)		
Net markdowns			500	
	$20,500		37,500	
Cost-to-retail ratio $\frac{\$20,500}{\$37,500} = 54.7\%$				(B)
Deduct: Sales (net)			25,000	
Ending inventory at retail			$12,500	

The computations for In-Fashion Stores are:

Ending inventory at retail × Cost ratio = Value of ending inventory		
Assumption A: $12,500 ×	53.9%	= $6,737.50
Assumption B: $12,500 ×	54.7%	= $6,837.50

The question becomes: Which assumption and which percentage should be employed to compute the ending inventory valuation?

The answer depends on the retail inventory method chosen. **The conventional retail inventory method uses assumption A only. It is designed to approximate the lower of average cost or market.** We will refer to this approach as the **lower of cost or market approach** or the **conventional retail inventory method**. To understand why the markups but not the markdowns are considered in the cost percentage, we must understand how a retail outlet operates. Markup normally indicates that the market value of the item has increased. On the other hand, a markdown means that a decline in the utility of that item has occurred. Therefore, if we attempt to approximate the lower of cost or market, markdowns are considered a current loss and are not involved in the calculation of the cost-to-retail ratio. Thus, the cost-to-retail ratio is lower, which leads to an approximate lower of cost or market.

An example will make this clear. Two items were purchased for $5.00 apiece, and the original sales price was established at $10.00 each. One item was subsequently written down to $2.00. Assuming no sales for the period, **if markdowns are considered** in the cost-to-retail ratio (assumption B, above), we compute the ending inventory in the following manner:

ILLUSTRATION 9-19
Retail Inventory Method Including Markdowns—Cost Method

Markdowns Included in Cost-to-Retail Ratio

	Cost	Retail
Purchases	$10.00	$20.00
Deduct: Markdowns		8.00
Ending inventory, at retail		$12.00

Cost-to-retail ratio $\frac{\$10.00}{\$12.00} = 83.3\%$

Ending inventory at cost ($12.00 × .833) = $10.00

This approach is the **cost method**. It reflects an average cost of the two items of the commodity without considering the loss on the one item.

If markdowns are not considered, the result is the lower of cost or market method (assumption A). The calculation is made as shown below.

ILLUSTRATION 9-20
Retail Inventory Method Excluding Markdowns—Conventional Method (LCM)

Markdowns Not Included in Cost-to-Retail Ratio

	Cost	Retail
Purchases	$10.00	$20.00
Cost-to-retail ratio $\frac{\$10.00}{\$20.00} = 50\%$		
Deduct: Markdowns		8.00
Ending inventory, at retail		$12.00

Ending inventory, at cost ($12 × .50) = $6.00

Under the conventional retail inventory method (when markdowns are **not** considered in computing the cost-to-retail ratio), the ratio would be 50% ($10.00/$20.00), and ending inventory would be $6.00 ($12.00 × .50).

The inventory valuation of $6.00 reflects two inventory items, one inventoried at $5.00, the other at $1.00. Basically, the sales price was reduced from $10.00 to $2.00 and the cost reduced from $5.00 to $1.00.[16] To approximate the lower of cost or market, therefore, the **cost-to-retail ratio** must be established by dividing the cost of goods available by the sum of the original retail price of these goods plus the net markups; the markdowns and markdown cancellations are excluded. The basic format for the retail inventory method using the lower of cost or market approach is shown in Illustration 9-21 using the In-Fashion Stores information.

ILLUSTRATION 9-21
Comprehensive Conventional Retail Inventory Method Format

IN-FASHION STORES INC.			
	Cost		Retail
Beginning inventory	$ 500.00		$ 1,000.00
Purchases (net)	20,000.00		35,000.00
Totals	20,500.00		36,000.00
Add: Net markups			
Markups		$3,000.00	
Markup cancellations		1,000.00	2,000.00
Totals	$20,500.00 ←	→	38,000.00
Deduct: Net markdowns			
Markdowns		2,500.00	
Markdown cancellations		2,000.00	500.00
Sales price of goods available			37,500.00
Deduct: Sales (net)			25,000.00
Ending inventory, at retail			$12,500.00

$$\text{Cost-to-retail ratio} = \frac{\text{Cost of goods available}}{\text{Original retail price of goods available, plus net markups}}$$

$$= \frac{\$20{,}500}{\$38{,}000} = 53.9\%$$

Ending inventory at lower of cost or market (53.9% × $12,500.00)	$ 6,737.50

Because an averaging effect occurs, an exact lower of cost or market inventory valuation is ordinarily not obtained, but an adequate approximation can be achieved. In contrast, adding net markups **and** deducting net markdowns yields **approximate cost.**

Special Items Relating to Retail Method

The retail inventory method becomes more complicated when such items as freight-in, purchase returns and allowances, and purchase discounts are involved. **Freight costs** are treated as a part of the purchase cost. **Purchase returns** are ordinarily considered as a reduction of the price at both cost and retail; and **purchase discounts and allowances** usually are considered as a reduction of the cost of purchases. When the purchase allowance is not reflected by a reduction in the selling price, no adjustment is made to the retail column. In short, the treatment for the items affecting the cost column of the retail inventory approach follows the computation for cost of goods available for sale.

Note also that **sales returns and allowances** are considered as proper adjustments to gross sales; **sales discounts**, however, are not recognized when sales are recorded gross. To adjust for the sales discount account in such a situation would provide an ending inventory figure at retail that would be overvalued.

In addition, a number of special items require careful analysis. **Transfers-in** from another department, for example, should be reported in the same way as purchases from an outside enterprise. **Normal shortages** (breakage, damage, theft, shrinkage) should reduce the retail column because these goods are no longer available for sale. Such costs are reflected in the selling price because a certain amount of shortage is con-

[16]This figure is really not market (replacement cost), but is net realizable value less the normal margin that is allowed. In other words, the sale price of the goods written down is $2.00, but subtracting a normal margin of 50% ($5.00 cost, $10.00 price), the figure becomes $1.00.

sidered normal in a retail enterprise. As a result, this amount is not considered in computing the cost to retail percentage. Rather, it is shown as a deduction similar to sales to arrive at ending inventory at retail. **Abnormal shortages** should be deducted from both the cost and retail columns and reported as a special inventory amount or as a loss. To do otherwise distorts the cost-to-retail ratio and overstates ending inventory. Finally, companies often provide their employees with special discounts to encourage loyalty, better performance, and so on. **Employee discounts** should be deducted from the retail column in the same way as sales. These discounts should not be considered in the cost-to-retail percentage because they do not reflect an overall change in the selling price.

Illustration 9-22 shows some of these concepts. The company, Feminine Executive Apparel, determines its inventory using the conventional retail inventory method.

ILLUSTRATION 9-22
Conventional Retail Inventory Method—Special Items Included

FEMININE EXECUTIVE APPAREL

	Cost		Retail
Beginning inventory	$ 1,000		$ 1,800
Purchases	30,000		60,000
Freight-in	600		—
Purchase returns	(1,500)		(3,000)
Totals	30,100		58,800
Net markups			9,000
Abnormal shortage	(1,200)		(2,000)
Totals	$28,900 ⟵	⟶	65,800
Deduct:			
Net markdowns			1,400
Sales		$36,000	
Sales returns		(900)	35,100
Employee discounts			800
Normal shortage			1,300
			$27,200

Cost-to-retail ratio $= \frac{\$28,900}{\$65,800} = 43.9\%$

Ending inventory at lower of cost or market (43.9% × $27,200) = $11,940.80

Evaluation of Retail Inventory Method

The retail inventory method of computing inventory is used widely (1) to permit the computation of net income without a physical count of inventory, (2) as a control measure in determining inventory shortages, (3) in regulating quantities of merchandise on hand, and (4) for insurance information.

One characteristic of the retail inventory method is that it **has an averaging effect on varying rates of gross profit**. When applied to an entire business where rates of gross profit vary among departments, no allowance is made for possible distortion of results because of such differences. Some companies refine the retail method under such conditions by computing inventory separately by departments or by classes of merchandise with similar gross profits. In addition, the reliability of this method assumes that the distribution of items in inventory is similar to the "mix" in the total goods available for sale.

PRESENTATION AND ANALYSIS

Presentation of Inventories

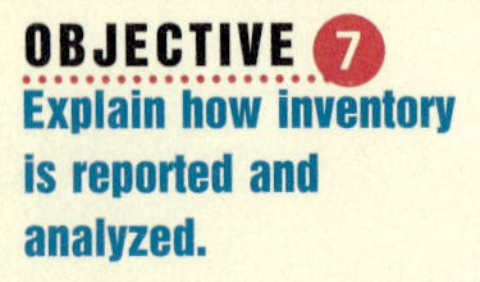

OBJECTIVE 7
Explain how inventory is reported and analyzed.

Accounting standards require financial statement disclosure of the composition of the inventory, inventory financing arrangements, and the inventory costing methods employed. The standards also require the consistent application of costing methods from one period to another.

Manufacturers should report the inventory composition either in the balance sheet or in a separate schedule in the notes. As indicated in the opening story, the relative mix of raw materials, work in process, and finished goods is important in assessing liquidity and in computing the stage of inventory completion.

Go to the Digital Tool for additional inventory disclosures.

Significant or unusual financing arrangements relating to inventories may require note disclosure. Examples are: transactions with related parties, product financing arrangements, firm purchase commitments, involuntary liquidation of LIFO inventories, and pledging of inventories as collateral. Inventories pledged as collateral for a loan should be presented in the current assets section rather than as an offset to the liability.

The basis upon which inventory amounts are stated (lower of cost or market) and the method used in determining cost (LIFO, FIFO, average cost, etc.) should also be reported. For example, the annual report of **Mumford of Wyoming** contains the following disclosures:

ILLUSTRATION 9-23
Disclosure of Inventory Methods

MUMFORD OF WYOMING

Note A: Significant Accounting Policies

Live feeder cattle and feed—last-in, first-out (LIFO) cost, which is below approximate market	$854,800
Live range cattle—lower of principally identified cost or market	$1,240,500
Live sheep and supplies—lower of first-in, first-out (FIFO) cost or market	$674,000
Dressed meat and by-products—principally at market less allowances for distribution and selling expenses	$362,630

The preceding illustration shows that a company can use different pricing methods for different elements of its inventory. If Mumford changes the method of pricing any of its inventory elements, a change in accounting principle must be reported. For example, if Mumford changes its method of accounting for live sheep from FIFO to average cost, this change, along with the effect on income, should be separately reported in the financial statements. Changes in accounting principle require an explanatory paragraph in the auditor's report describing the change in method.

In Switzerland, inventory may be reported on the balance sheet at amounts substantially (one-third or more) below cost or market due to provisions of the tax code. Further, Swiss accounting principles do not require any specific disclosures related to inventories.

American Brands, Inc. reported its inventories in its Annual Report as follows (note the "trade practice" followed in classifying inventories among the current assets):

ILLUSTRATION 9-24
Disclosure of Trade Practice in Valuing Inventories

AMERICAN BRANDS, INC.

Current assets

Inventories (Note 2)	
Leaf tobacco	$ 563,424,000
Bulk whiskey	232,759,000
Other raw materials, supplies and work in process	238,906,000
Finished products	658,326,000
	1,693,415,000

Note 2: Inventories

Inventories are priced at the lower of cost (average; first-in, first-out; and minor amounts at last-in, first-out) or market. In accordance with generally recognized trade practice, the leaf tobacco and bulk whiskey inventories are classified as current assets, although part of such inventories due to the duration of the aging process, ordinarily will not be sold within one year.

The following inventory disclosures by **Newmont Gold Company** reveal the application of different bases of valuation, including market value, for different classifications of inventory.

ILLUSTRATION 9-25
Disclosure of Different Bases of Valuation

NEWMONT GOLD COMPANY

Current assets		
Inventories (Note 2)		$44,303,000
Noncurrent assets		
Inventories—ore in stockpiles (Note 2)		$5,250,000

Note 2: Inventories

Inventories included in current assets at December 31 were:

Ore and in-process inventory	$11,303,000
Gold bullion and gold precipitates	24,209,000
Materials and supplies	8,791,000
	$44,303,000

Ore and in-process inventory and materials and supplies are stated at the lower of average cost or net realizable value. Gold bullion and gold precipitates are stated at market value, less a provision for estimated refining and delivery charges. Expenditures capitalized as ore and in-process inventory include labor, material and other production costs.

Noncurrent inventories are stated at the lower of average cost or net realizable value and represent ore in stockpiles anticipated to be processed in future years.

Analysis of Inventories

As illustrated in the opening story, the amount of inventory that a company carries can have significant economic consequences. As a result, inventories must be managed. But, inventory management is a double-edged sword that requires constant attention. On the one hand, management wants to have a great variety and quantity on hand so customers have the greatest selection and always find what they want in stock. However, such an inventory policy may incur excessive carrying costs (e.g., investment, storage, insurance, taxes, obsolescence, and damage). On the other hand, low inventory levels lead to stockouts, lost sales, and disgruntled customers. Financial ratios can be used to help chart a middle course between these two dangers. Common ratios used in the management and evaluation of inventory levels are inventory turnover and a related measure, average days to sell the inventory.

The **inventory turnover ratio** measures the number of times on average the inventory was sold during the period. Its purpose is to measure the liquidity of the inventory. A manager may extrapolate from past turnover experience how long the inventory now in stock will take to be sold. The inventory turnover is computed by dividing the cost of goods sold by the average inventory on hand during the period. Unless seasonal factors are significant, average inventory can be computed from the beginning and ending inventory balances. For example, in its 1998 annual report **Kellogg Company** reported a beginning inventory of $434.3 million, an ending inventory of $451.4 million, and cost of goods sold of $3,282.6 million for the year. The inventory turnover formula and Kellogg Company's 1998 ratio computation are shown below.

ILLUSTRATION 9-26
Inventory Turnover Ratio

$$\text{Inventory Turnover} = \frac{\text{Cost of Goods Sold}}{\text{Average Inventory}}$$

$$= \frac{\$3{,}282.6}{\frac{\$434.3 + \$451.4}{2}} = 7.4 \text{ times}$$

A variant of the inventory turnover ratio is the **average days to sell inventory**, which represents the average number of days' sales for which inventory is on hand. For example, the inventory turnover for Kellogg Company of 7.4 times divided into 365 is approximately 49 days.

There are typical levels of inventory in every industry. However, companies that are able to keep their inventory at lower levels with higher turnovers than those of their competitors, and still satisfy customer needs, are the most successful.

SUMMARY OF LEARNING OBJECTIVES

1 **Explain and apply the lower of cost or market rule.** If inventory declines in value below its original cost for whatever reason, the inventory should be written down to reflect this loss. The general rule is that the historical cost principle is abandoned when the future utility (revenue-producing ability) of the asset is no longer as great as its original cost.

2 **Identify when inventories are valued at net realizable value.** Inventories are valued at net realizable value when (1) there is a controlled market with a quoted price applicable to all quantities, (2) no significant costs of disposal are involved, and (3) the cost figures are too difficult to obtain.

3 **Explain when the relative sales value method is used to value inventories.** When a group of varying units is purchased at a single lump sum price, a so-called basket purchase, the total purchase price may be allocated to the individual items on the basis of relative sales value.

4 **Explain accounting issues related to purchase commitments.** Accounting for purchase commitments is controversial. Some argue that these contracts should be reported as assets and liabilities at the time the contract is signed; others believe that the present recognition at the delivery date is most appropriate. The FASB neither excludes nor recommends the recording of assets and liabilities for purchase commitments but notes that if they were recorded at the time of commitment, "the nature of the loss and the valuation account that records it when the price falls would be clearly seen."

5 **Determine ending inventory by applying the gross profit method.** The steps to determine ending inventory by applying the gross profit method are as follows: (1) Compute the gross profit percentage on selling price; (2) compute gross profit by multiplying net sales by the gross profit percentage; (3) compute cost of goods sold by subtracting gross profit from net sales; (4) compute ending inventory by subtracting cost of goods sold from total goods available for sale.

6 **Determine ending inventory by applying the retail inventory method.** The steps to determine ending inventory by applying the conventional retail method are: (1) the sales for the period are deducted from the retail value of the goods available for sale to produce an estimated inventory at retail; (2) the ratio of cost to retail for all goods passing through a department or firm is then determined by dividing the total goods available for sale at cost by the total goods available at retail; (3) the inventory valued at retail is converted to approximate cost by applying the cost-to-retail ratio.

7 **Explain how inventory is reported and analyzed.** Accounting standards require financial statement disclosure of: (1) the composition of the inventory (in the balance sheet or a separate schedule in the notes); (2) significant or unusual inventory financing arrangements; and (3) inventory costing methods employed (which may differ for different elements of inventory). Accounting standards also require the consistent application of costing methods from one period to another. Common ratios used in the management and evaluation of inventory levels are inventory turnover and a related measure, average days to sell the inventory.

KEY TERMS

average days to sell inventory, *471*
conventional retail inventory method, *466*
cost-to-retail ratio, *467*
designated market value, *452*
gross profit method, *461*
gross profit percentage, *461*
hedging, *460*
inventory turnover ratio, *470*
lower (floor) limit, *451*
lower of cost or market (LCM), *451*
lump sum (basket) purchase, *458*
markdown, *464*
markdown cancellations, *464*
market (for LCM), *450*
markup, *464*
markup cancellations, *464*
net realizable value (NRV), *451*
net realizable value less a normal profit margin, *451*
purchase commitments, *458*
retail inventory method, *463*
upper (ceiling) limit, *451*

LIFO Retail Methods

Many argue that the conventional retail method follows a flow assumption that does not match current cost against current revenues. They suggest that a LIFO assumption be adopted to obtain a better matching of costs and revenues.

LIFO RETAIL METHODS

OBJECTIVE 8
After studying Appendix 9A, you should be able to: Determine ending inventory by applying the LIFO retail methods.

Many retail establishments have changed from the more conventional treatment to a **LIFO retail method** for the tax advantages associated with valuing inventories on a LIFO basis.

The application of LIFO retail is made under two assumptions: (1) stable prices and (2) fluctuating prices.

Stable Prices—LIFO Retail Method

Computing the final inventory balance assuming a LIFO flow is much more complex than the calculation for the conventional retail method. Under the LIFO retail method, **both markups and markdowns are considered** in obtaining the proper cost-to-retail percentage. Furthermore, since the LIFO method is concerned only with the additional layer, or the amount that should be subtracted from the previous layer, the beginning inventory is excluded from the cost-to-retail percentage. **A major assumption of the LIFO retail method—one that is debatable—is that the markups and markdowns apply only to the goods purchased during the current period and not to the beginning inventory.** In addition, to simplify the accounting, we have assumed that the price level has remained unchanged. The concepts are presented in Illustration 9A-1.

ILLUSTRATION 9A-1
LIFO Retail Method—Stable Prices

	Cost		Retail
Beginning inventory—2001	$ 27,000		$ 45,000
Net purchases during the period	346,500		480,000
Net markups			20,000
Net markdowns			(5,000)
Total (excluding beginning inventory)	346,500	←→	495,000
Total (including beginning inventory)	$373,500		540,000
Net sales during the period			(484,000)
Ending inventory at retail			$ 56,000
Establishment of cost-to-retail percentage under assumptions of LIFO retail ($346,500 ÷ $495,000)		70%	

Illustration 9A-2 indicates that the inventory is composed of two layers: the beginning inventory and the additional increase that occurred in the inventory this period (2001). When we start the next period (2002), the beginning inventory will be composed of those two layers, and if an increase in inventory occurs again, an additional layer will be added.

ILLUSTRATION 9A-2
Ending Inventory at LIFO Cost, 2001—Stable Prices

Ending Inventory at Retail Prices—2001	Layers at Retail Prices			Cost-to-Retail (Percentage)		Ending Inventory at LIFO Cost
$56,000	2000	$45,000	×	60%[a]	=	$27,000
	2001	11,000	×	70	=	7,700
		$56,000				$34,700

[a] $\frac{\$27,000}{\$45,000}$ (prior year's cost-to-retail)

However, if the final inventory figure is below the beginning inventory, it is necessary to reduce the beginning inventory starting with the most recent layer. For example, assume that the ending inventory for 2002 at retail is $50,000. The computation of the ending inventory at cost is shown below.

ILLUSTRATION 9A-3
Ending Inventory at LIFO Cost, 2002—Stable Prices

Ending Inventory at Retail Prices—2002	Layers at Retail Prices			Cost-to-Retail (Percentage)		Ending Inventory at LIFO Cost
$50,000	2000	$45,000	×	60%	=	$27,000
	2001	5,000	×	70	=	3,500
		$50,000				$30,500

Notice that the 2001 layer is reduced from $11,000 to $5,000.

Fluctuating Prices—Dollar-Value LIFO Retail Method

The computation of the LIFO retail method was simplified in the previous illustration because changes in the selling price of the inventory were ignored. Let us now assume that a change in the price level of the inventories occurs (as is usual). If the price level does change, **the price change must be eliminated** because we are measuring the real increase in inventory, not the dollar increase.

To illustrate, assume that the beginning inventory had a retail market value of $10,000 and the ending inventory a retail market value of $15,000. If the price level has risen from 100 to 125, it is inappropriate to suggest that a real increase in inventory of $5,000 has occurred. Instead, the ending inventory at retail should be deflated as indicated by the computation shown below.

ILLUSTRATION 9A-4
Ending Inventory at Retail—Deflated and Restated

Ending inventory at retail (deflated) $15,000 ÷ 1.25*	$12,000	
Beginning inventory at retail	10,000	
Real increase in inventory at retail	$ 2,000	
Ending inventory at retail on LIFO basis:		
First layer	$10,000	
Second layer ($2,000 × 1.25)	2,500	$12,500

*1.25 = 125 ÷ 100

This approach is essentially the dollar-value LIFO method previously discussed in Chapter 8. In computing the LIFO inventory under a dollar-value LIFO approach, the dollar increase in inventory is found and deflated to beginning-of-the-year prices to determine whether actual increases or decreases in quantity have occurred. If an increase in quantities occurs, this increase is priced at the new index to compute the value of the new layer. If a decrease in quantities happens, it is subtracted from the most recent layers to the extent necessary.

The following computations, taken from Illustration 9A-1, illustrate the differences between the **dollar-value LIFO retail method** and the regular LIFO retail approach. Assume that the current 2001 price index is 112 (prior year = 100) and that the inventory ($56,000) has remained unchanged. In comparing these two illustrations, note that the computations involved in finding the cost-to-retail percentage are exactly the same. However, the dollar-value method determines the increase that has occurred in the inventory in terms of base-year prices.

ILLUSTRATION 9A-5
Dollar-Value LIFO Retail Method—Fluctuating Prices

	Cost		Retail
Beginning inventory—2001	$ 27,000		$ 45,000
Net purchases during the period	346,500		480,000
Net markups			20,000
Net markdowns			(5,000)
Total (excluding beginning inventory)	346,500 ←	→	495,000
Total (including beginning inventory)	$373,500		540,000
Net sales during the period at retail			(484,000)
Ending inventory at retail			$ 56,000
Establishment of cost-to-retail percentage under assumptions of LIFO retail ($346,500 ÷ $495,000)		70%	
A. Ending inventory at retail prices deflated to base year prices $56,000 ÷ 112 =		$50,000	
B. Beginning inventory (retail) at base-year prices		45,000	
C. Inventory increase (retail) from beginning of period		$ 5,000	

From this information, we compute the inventory amount at cost:

ILLUSTRATION 9A-6
Ending Inventory at LIFO Cost, 2001—Fluctuating Prices

Ending Inventory at Base-Year Retail Prices—2001	Layers at Base-Year Retail Prices			Price Index (percentage)		Cost-to-Retail (percentage)		Ending Inventory at LIFO Cost
$50,000 →	2000	$45,000	×	100%	×	60%	=	$27,000
→	2001	5,000	×	112	×	70	=	3,920
		$50,000						$30,920

As illustrated above, layers of a particular year must be restated to the prices in effect in the year when the layer was added before the conversion to cost takes place.

Note the difference between the LIFO approach (stable prices) and the dollar-value LIFO method as indicated below:

ILLUSTRATION 9A-7
Comparison of Effect of Price Assumptions

	LIFO (stable prices)	LIFO (fluctuating prices)
Beginning inventory	$27,000	$27,000
Increment	7,700	3,920
Ending inventory	$34,700	$30,920

The difference of $3,780 ($34,700 − $30,920) is a result of an increase in the price of goods, not of an increase in the quantity of goods.

Subsequent Adjustments under Dollar-Value LIFO Retail

The dollar-value LIFO retail method follows the same procedures in subsequent periods as the traditional dollar-value method discussed in Chapter 8. That is, when a real increase in inventory occurs, a new layer is added. Using the data from the previous illustration, assume that the retail value of the 2002 ending inventory at current prices is $64,800, the 2002 price index is 120% of base-year, and the cost-to-retail percentage is 75%. In base-year dollars, the ending inventory is therefore $54,000 ($64,800/120%). The computation of the ending inventory at LIFO cost is as follows:

ILLUSTRATION 9A-8
Ending Inventory at LIFO Cost, 2002—Fluctuating Prices

Ending Inventory at Base-Year Retail Prices—2002	Layers at Base-Year Retail Prices			Price Index (percentage)		Cost-to-Retail (percentage)		Ending Inventory at LIFO Cost
$54,000	→ 2000	$45,000	×	100%	×	60%	=	$27,000
	→ 2001	5,000	×	112	×	70	=	3,920
	→ 2002	4,000	×	120	×	75	=	3,600
		$54,000						$34,520

Conversely, when a real decrease in inventory develops, previous layers are "peeled off" at prices in existence when the layers were added. To illustrate, assume that in 2002 the ending inventory in base-year prices is $48,000. The computation of the LIFO inventory is as follows:

ILLUSTRATION 9A-9
Ending Inventory at LIFO Cost, 2002—Fluctuating Prices

Ending Inventory at Base-Year Retail Prices—2002	Layers at Base-Year Retail Prices			Price Index (percentage)		Cost-to-Retail (percentage)		Ending Inventory at LIFO Cost
$48,000	→ 2000	$45,000	×	100%	×	60%	=	$27,000
	→ 2001	3,000	×	112	×	70	=	2,352
		$48,000						$29,352

The advantages and disadvantages of the lower of cost or market method (conventional retail) versus LIFO retail are the same for retail as for nonretail operations. As a practical matter, the selection of the retail inventory method to be used often involves determining which method provides a lower taxable income. Although it might appear that retail LIFO will provide the lower taxable income in a period of rising prices, such is not always the case. LIFO will provide an approximate current cost matching, but the ending inventory is stated at cost. The conventional retail method may have a large write-off because of the use of the lower of cost or market approach which may offset the LIFO current cost matching.

CHANGING FROM CONVENTIONAL RETAIL TO LIFO

When changing from the conventional retail method to LIFO retail, neither a cumulative adjustment nor a retroactive adjustment can be made easily. Because conventional retail is a lower of cost or market approach, the beginning inventory must be restated to a cost basis. The usual approach is to compute the cost basis from the purchases of the prior year, adjusted for both markups and markdowns.[1] To illustrate, assume that Clark Clothing Store employs the conventional retail method but wishes to change to the LIFO retail method beginning in 2002. The amounts shown by the firm's books are as follows:

	At Cost	At Retail
Inventory, January 1, 2001	$ 5,210	$ 15,000
Net purchases in 2001	47,250	100,000
Net markups in 2001		7,000
Net markdowns in 2001		2,000
Sales in 2001		95,000

[1]A logical question to ask is, "Why are only the purchases from the prior period considered and not also the beginning inventory?" Apparently the IRS believes that "the purchases-only approach" provides a more reasonable cost basis. The IRS position is debatable. However, for our purposes, it seems appropriate to use the purchases-only approach.

Ending inventory under the **conventional retail method** for 2001 is computed as shown in Illustration 9A-10.

ILLUSTRATION 9A-10
Conventional Retail Inventory Method

	Cost	Retail
Inventory January 1, 2001	$ 5,210	$ 15,000
Net purchases	47,250	100,000
Net additional markups		7,000
	$52,460	122,000
Net markdowns		(2,000)
Sales		(95,000)
Ending inventory at retail		$ 25,000
Establishment of cost-to-retail percentage ($52,460 ÷ $122,000)	43%	
December 31, 2001, inventory at cost		
Inventory at retail		$ 25,000
Cost-to-retail ratio		43%
Inventory at cost under conventional retail		$ 10,750

The ending inventory for 2001 under the **LIFO retail method** can then be quickly approximated in the following way.

ILLUSTRATION 9A-11
Conversion to LIFO Retail Inventory Method

December 31, 2001, Inventory at LIFO cost

	Retail		Ratio		LIFO
Ending inventory	$25,000	×	45%[a]	=	$11,250

[a]The cost-to-retail ratio was computed as follows:

$$\frac{\text{Net purchases at cost}}{\text{Net purchases at retail plus markups less markdowns}} = \frac{\$47{,}250}{\$100{,}000 + \$7{,}000 - \$2{,}000} = 45\%$$

The difference of $500 ($11,250 – $10,750) between the LIFO retail method and the conventional retail method in the ending inventory for 2001 is the amount by which the beginning inventory for 2002 must be adjusted. The entry to adjust the inventory to a cost basis is as follows:

Inventory	500	
Adjustment to Record Inventory at Cost		500

KEY TERMS

dollar-value LIFO retail method, *473*
LIFO retail method, *472*

SUMMARY OF LEARNING OBJECTIVE FOR APPENDIX 9A

8 **Determine ending inventory by applying the LIFO retail methods.** The application of LIFO retail is made under two assumptions: stable prices and fluctuating prices. *Procedures under stable prices:* (a) Because the LIFO method is a cost method, both the markups and the markdowns must be considered in obtaining the proper cost-to-retail percentage. (b) Since the LIFO method is concerned only with the additional layer, or the amount that should be subtracted from the previous layer, the beginning inventory is excluded from the cost-to-retail percentage. (c) The markups and markdowns apply only to the goods purchased during the current period and not to the beginning inventory. *Procedures under fluctuating prices:* The steps are the same as for stable prices except that in computing the LIFO inventory under a dollar-value LIFO approach, the dollar increase in inventory is found and deflated to beginning-of-the-year prices to determine whether actual increases or decreases in quantity have occurred. If quantities increase, this increase is priced at the new index to compute the new layer. If quantities decrease, the decrease is subtracted from the most recent layers to the extent necessary.

FROM CLASSROOM TO CAREER

DAVID MINIKEN
is a senior auditor with Sweeney Conrad, a Seattle-based CPA firm. Prior to joining Sweeney Conrad, Mr. Miniken held several accounting positions with Boeing, the giant aircraft company. He holds a Bachelor of Arts in accounting from the University of Washington and an MBA from Seattle University.

How did you decide on accounting as a career?

I think it was my fourth major in college. I started out pre-med, then went to physical education, then forestry, and then business. Once I settled on business, then I chose what I thought would be the best route to employment.

What was the hardest part of your transition from college to the working world?

Going to work eight hours a day during the summer when the weather's nice outside. You have to get up early every day and go to work, and you have only a few weeks vacation each year. Another reality of working in public accounting is the pressure to get your work done on a time budget.

What non-accounting skills have been important to you as you've progressed in your career?

Communication and interpersonal skills are critical. As an auditor, I spend most of my time at a client's office. I'm interacting with a dozen people who may wish to help me, but for some I'm really more of a nuisance, because they've got their day-to-day work to do. You want to get along well with a client.

Are clients ever disrespectful to you?

Sometimes we have clients who may wish to communicate directly with the partner—not staff or seniors—on the engagement. And I can certainly understand that. I'm not the ultimate authority here at Sweeney Conrad. But the fact is that the staff is on the front lines of the engagement. If it's a low-risk area of the audit, then it often makes sense to have the person with the lower billing rate handle that type of question.

What kind of clients do you have?

All of our audit clients are privately held. I've probably audited companies in 20 different industries. Right now, I'm working with a trucking company in which each driver is actually an independent franchisee rather than an employee. So this week I've had to educate myself about how you treat a transaction in which the firm has to repossess some of those franchises that weren't working out so well. And I haven't had any franchising clients in the past. So there's always something new. You're always learning.

You started out in public accounting after several years at Boeing. How has that affected your career progression?

The only real impact is that a number of my peers are six or seven years younger without families. There's no doubt that being in public accounting with its emphasis on hourly billing takes up a lot of time. I've got small children, and I want to spend lots of time with my family, too. My friends who are lawyers are going through the same thing.

Since you're a campus recruiter for your firm, what are you looking for in a prospective employee?

I'm looking for someone with good communications skills who seems easy to get along with and has a good attitude. I don't expect much technically from somebody coming straight out of school. It's also a big positive if the candidate has done some research so that he or she knows a little bit about our firm.

Note: All **asterisked** Questions, Brief Exercises, Exercises, Problems, and Conceptual Cases relate to material contained in the appendix to the chapter.

QUESTIONS

1 Where there is evidence that the utility of inventory goods, as part of their disposal in the ordinary course of business, will be less than cost, what is the proper accounting treatment?

2 Explain the rationale for the ceiling and floor in the lower of cost or market method of valuing inventories.

3 Why are inventories valued at the lower of cost or market? What are the arguments against the use of the lower of cost or market method of valuing inventories?

4 What approaches may be employed in applying the lower of cost or market procedure? Which approach is normally used and why?

5 In some instances accounting principles require a departure from valuing inventories at cost alone. Determine the proper unit inventory price in the following cases:

	Cases				
	1	2	3	4	5
Cost	$15.90	$16.10	$15.90	$15.90	$15.90
Net realizable value	14.30	19.20	15.20	10.40	16.40
Net realizable value less normal profit	12.80	17.60	13.75	8.80	14.80
Market (replacement cost)	14.80	17.20	12.80	9.70	16.80

6 What method(s) might be used in the accounts to record a loss due to a price decline in the inventories? Discuss.

7 What factors might call for inventory valuation at sales prices (net realizable value or market price)?

8 Under what circumstances is relative sales value an appropriate basis for determining the price assigned to inventory?

9 At December 31, 2002, James Arness Co. has outstanding purchase commitments for purchase of 150,000 gallons, at $6.40 per gallon, of a raw material to be used in its manufacturing process. The company prices its raw material inventory at cost or market, whichever is lower. Assuming that the market price as of December 31, 2002, is $5.90, how would you treat this situation in the accounts?

10 What are the major uses of the gross profit method?

11 Distinguish between gross profit as a percentage of cost and gross profit as a percentage of sales price. Convert the following gross profit percentages based on cost to gross profit percentages based on sales price: 20% and 33⅓%. Convert the following gross profit percentages based on sales price to gross profit percentages based on cost: 33⅓% and 60%.

12 Carole Lombard Co. with annual net sales of $6 million maintains a markup of 25% based on cost. Lombard's expenses average 15% of net sales. What is Lombard's gross profit and net profit in dollars?

13 A fire destroys all of the merchandise of Rosanna Arquette Company on February 10, 2002. Presented below is information compiled up to the date of the fire.

Inventory, January 1, 2002	$ 400,000
Sales to February 10, 2002	1,750,000
Purchases to February 10, 2002	1,140,000
Freight-in to February 10, 2002	60,000
Rate of gross profit on selling price	40%

What is the approximate inventory on February 10, 2002?

14 What conditions must exist for the retail inventory method to provide valid results?

15 The conventional retail inventory method yields results that are essentially the same as those yielded by the lower of cost or market method. Explain. Prepare an illustration of how the retail inventory method reduces inventory to market.

16 (a) Determine the ending inventory under the conventional retail method for the furniture department of Gin Blossoms Department Stores from the following data.

	Cost	Retail
Inventory, Jan. 1	$ 149,000	$ 283,500
Purchases	1,400,000	2,160,000
Freight-in	70,000	
Markups, net		92,000
Markdowns, net		48,000
Sales		2,235,000

(b) If the results of a physical inventory indicated an inventory at retail of $240,000, what inferences would you draw?

17 Bodeans Company reported inventory in its balance sheet as follows:

Inventories $115,756,800

What additional disclosures might be necessary to present the inventory fairly?

18 Of what significance is inventory turnover to a retail store?

***19** What modifications to the conventional retail method are necessary to approximate a LIFO retail flow?

BRIEF EXERCISES

BE9-1 Presented below is information related to Alstott Inc.'s inventory

(per unit)	Skis	Boots	Parkas
Historical cost	$190.00	$106.00	$53.00
Selling price	217.00	145.00	73.75
Cost to distribute	19.00	8.00	2.50
Current replacement cost	203.00	105.00	51.00
Normal profit margin	32.00	29.00	21.25

Determine the following: (a) the two limits to market value (i.e., the ceiling and the floor) that should be used in the lower of cost or market computation for skis; (b) the cost amount that should be used in the lower of cost or market comparison of boots; and (c) the market amount that should be used to value parkas on the basis of the lower of cost or market.

BE9-2 Robin Corporation has the following four items in its ending inventory:

Item	Cost	Replacement Cost	Net Realizable Value (NRV)	NRV Less Normal Profit Margin
Jokers	$2,000	$1,900	$2,100	$1,600
Penguins	5,000	5,100	4,950	4,100
Riddlers	4,400	4,550	4,625	3,700
Scarecrows	3,200	2,990	3,830	3,070

Determine the final lower of cost of market inventory value for each item.

BE9-3 Battletoads Inc. uses a perpetual inventory system. At January 1, 2002, inventory was $214,000 at both cost and market value. At December 31, 2002, the inventory was $286,000 at cost and $269,000 at market value. Prepare the necessary December 31 entry under (a) the direct method and (b) the indirect method.

BE9-4 PC Plus buys 1,000 computer game CDs from a distributor who is discontinuing those games. The purchase price for the lot is $6,000. PC Plus will group the CDs into three price categories for resale, as indicated below:

Group	No. of CDs	Price per CD
1	100	$ 5.00
2	800	10.00
3	100	15.00

Determine the cost per CD for each group, using the relative sales value method.

BE9-5 Beavis Company signed a long-term noncancelable purchase commitment with a major supplier to purchase raw materials in 2002 at a cost of $1,000,000. At December 31, 2001, the raw materials to be purchased have a market value of $930,000. Prepare any necessary December 31 entry.

BE9-6 Use the information for Beavis Company from BE9-5. In 2002, Beavis paid $1,000,000 to obtain the raw materials which were worth $930,000. Prepare the entry to record the purchase.

BE9-7 Big Hurt Corporation's April 30 inventory was destroyed by fire. January 1 inventory was $150,000, and purchases for January through April totaled $500,000. Sales for the same period were $700,000. Big Hurt's normal gross profit percentage is 31%. Using the gross profit method, estimate Big Hurt's April 30 inventory that was destroyed by fire.

BE9-8 Bimini Inc. had beginning inventory of $12,000 at cost and $20,000 at retail. Net purchases were $120,000 at cost and $170,000 at retail. Net markups were $10,000; net markdowns were $7,000; and sales were $157,000. Compute ending inventory at cost using the conventional retail method.

BE9-9 In its 1998 Annual Report, Deere and Company reported inventory of $1,287 million on October 31, 1998, and $1,073 million on October 31, 1997, cost of goods sold of $9,234 million for fiscal year 1998, and net sales of $11,926 million. Compute Deere and Company's inventory turnover and the average days to sell inventory for the fiscal year 1998.

***BE9-10** Use the information for Bimini Inc. from BE9-8. Compute ending inventory at cost using the LIFO retail method.

***BE9-11** Use the information for Bimini Inc. from BE9-8, and assume the price level increased from 100 at the beginning of the year to 120 at year-end. Compute ending inventory at cost using the dollar-value LIFO retail method.

EXERCISES

E9-1 (Lower of Cost or Market) The inventory of 3T Company on December 31, 2002, consists of these items:

Part No.	Quantity	Cost per Unit	Cost to Replace per Unit
110	600	$90	$100
111	1,000	60	52
112	500	80	76
113	200	170	180
120	400	205	208
121[a]	1,600	16	14
122	300	240	235

[a]Part No. 121 is obsolete and has a realizable value of $0.20 each as scrap.

Instructions

(a) Determine the inventory as of December 31, 2002, by the lower of cost or market method, applying this method directly to each item.

(b) Determine the inventory by the lower of cost or market method, applying the method to the total of the inventory.

E9-2 (Lower of Cost or Market) Smashing Pumpkins Company uses the lower of cost or market method, on an individual-item basis, in pricing its inventory items. The inventory at December 31, 2002, consists of products D, E, F, G, H, and I. Relevant per-unit data for these products appear below:

	Item D	Item E	Item F	Item G	Item H	Item I
Estimated selling price	$120	$110	$95	$90	$110	$90
Cost	75	80	80	80	50	36
Replacement cost	120	72	70	30	70	30
Estimated selling expense	30	30	30	25	30	30
Normal profit	20	20	20	20	20	20

Instructions

Using the lower of cost or market rule, determine the proper unit value for balance sheet reporting purposes at December 31, 2002, for each of the inventory items above.

E9-3 (Lower of Cost or Market) Michael Bolton Company follows the practice of pricing its inventory at the lower of cost or market, on an individual-item basis.

Item No.	Quantity	Cost per Unit	Cost to Replace	Estimated Selling Price	Cost of Completion and Disposal	Normal Profit
1320	1,200	$3.20	$3.00	$4.50	$.35	$1.25
1333	900	2.70	2.30	3.50	.50	.50
1426	800	4.50	3.70	5.00	.40	1.00
1437	1,000	3.60	3.10	3.20	.25	.90
1510	700	2.25	2.00	3.25	.80	.60
1522	500	3.00	2.70	3.80	.40	.50
1573	3,000	1.80	1.60	2.50	.75	.50
1626	1,000	4.70	5.20	6.00	.50	1.00

Instructions

From the information above, determine the amount of Bolton Company inventory.

E9-4 (Lower of Cost or Market—Journal Entries) Corrs Company began operations in 2001 and determined its ending inventory at cost and at lower of cost or market at December 31, 2001, and December 31, 2002. This information is presented below:

	Cost	Lower of Cost or Market
12/31/01	$346,000	$327,000
12/31/02	410,000	395,000

Instructions

(a) Prepare the journal entries required at 12/31/01 and 12/31/02, assuming that the inventory is recorded at market, and a periodic inventory system (direct method) is used.

(b) Prepare journal entries required at 12/31/01 and 12/31/02, assuming that the inventory is recorded at cost and an allowance account is adjusted at each year-end under a periodic system.

(c) Which of the two methods above provides the higher net income in each year?

E9-5 (Lower of Cost or Market—Valuation Account) Presented below is information related to Candlebox Enterprises:

	Jan. 31	Feb. 28	Mar. 31	Apr. 30
Inventory at cost	$15,000	$15,100	$17,000	$13,000
Inventory at the lower of cost or market	14,500	12,600	15,600	12,300
Purchases for the month		20,000	24,000	26,500
Sales for the month		29,000	35,000	40,000

Instructions

(a) From the information, prepare (as far as the data permit) monthly income statements in columnar form for February, March, and April. The inventory is to be shown in the statement at cost, the gain or loss due to market fluctuations is to be shown separately, and a valuation account is to be set up for the difference between cost and the lower of cost or market.

(b) Prepare the journal entry required to establish the valuation account at January 31 and entries to adjust it monthly thereafter.

E9-6 (Lower of Cost or Market—Error Effect) Winans Company uses the lower of cost or market method, on an individual-item basis, in pricing its inventory items. The inventory at December 31, 2001, included product X. Relevant per-unit data for product X appear below:

Estimated selling price	$45
Cost	40
Replacement cost	35
Estimated selling expense	14
Normal profit	9

There were 1,000 units of product X on hand at December 31, 2001. Product X was incorrectly valued at $35 per unit for reporting purposes. All 1,000 units were sold in 2002.

Instructions

Compute the effect of this error on net income for 2001 and the effect on net income for 2002, and indicate the direction of the misstatement for each year.

E9-7 (Relative Sales Value Method) Phil Collins Realty Corporation purchased a tract of unimproved land for $55,000. This land was improved and subdivided into building lots at an additional cost of $34,460. These building lots were all of the same size but owing to differences in location were offered for sale at different prices as follows:

Group	No. of Lots	Price per Lot
1	9	$3,000
2	15	4,000
3	17	2,400

Operating expenses for the year allocated to this project total $18,200. Lots unsold at the year-end were as follows:

Group 1	5 lots
Group 2	7 lots
Group 3	2 lots

Instructions

At the end of the fiscal year Phil Collins Realty Corporation instructs you to arrive at the net income realized on this operation to date.

E9-8 (Relative Sales Value Method) During 2002, Pretenders Furniture Company purchases a carload of wicker chairs. The manufacturer sells the chairs to Pretenders for a lump sum of $59,850, because it is discontinuing manufacturing operations and wishes to dispose of its entire stock. Three types of chairs are included in the carload. The three types and the estimated selling price for each are listed below.

Type	No. of Chairs	Estimated Selling Price Each
Lounge chairs	400	$90
Armchairs	300	80
Straight chairs	700	50

During 2002, Pretenders sells 200 lounge chairs, 100 armchairs, and 120 straight chairs.

Instructions

What is the amount of gross profit realized during 2002? What is the amount of inventory of unsold wicker chairs on December 31, 2002?

E9-9 (Purchase Commitments) Marvin Gaye Company has been having difficulty obtaining key raw materials for its manufacturing process. The company therefore signed a long-term noncancelable purchase commitment with its largest supplier of this raw material on November 30, 2002, at an agreed price of $400,000. At December 31, 2002, the raw material had declined in price to $365,000.

Instructions

What entry would you make on December 31, 2002, to recognize these facts?

E9-10 (Purchase Commitments) At December 31, 2002, Indigo Girls Company has outstanding noncancelable purchase commitments for 36,000 gallons, at $3.00 per gallon, of raw material to be used in its manufacturing process. The company prices its raw material inventory at cost or market, whichever is lower.

Instructions

(a) Assuming that the market price as of December 31, 2002, is $3.30, how would this matter be treated in the accounts and statements? Explain.

(b) Assuming that the market price as of December 31, 2002, is $2.70, instead of $3.30, how would you treat this situation in the accounts and statements?

(c) Give the entry in January 2003, when the 36,000-gallon shipment is received, assuming that the situation given in (b) above existed at December 31, 2002, and that the market price in January 2003 was $2.70 per gallon. Give an explanation of your treatment.

E9-11 (Gross Profit Method) Each of the following gross profit percentages is expressed in terms of cost.

1. 20%.
2. 25%.
3. 33⅓%.
4. 50%.

Instructions

Indicate the gross profit percentage in terms of sales for each of the above.

E9-12 (Gross Profit Method) Mark Price Company uses the gross profit method to estimate inventory for monthly reporting purposes. Presented below is information for the month of May:

Inventory, May 1	$ 160,000
Purchases (gross)	640,000
Freight-in	30,000
Sales	1,000,000
Sales returns	70,000
Purchase discounts	12,000

Instructions

(a) Compute the estimated inventory at May 31, assuming that the gross profit is 30% of sales.

(b) Compute the estimated inventory at May 31, assuming that the gross profit is 30% of cost.

E9-13 (Gross Profit Method) Tim Legler requires an estimate of the cost of goods lost by fire on March 9. Merchandise on hand on January 1 was $38,000. Purchases since January 1 were $72,000; freight-in, $3,400; purchase returns and allowances, $2,400. Sales are made at 33⅓% above cost and totaled $100,000 to March 9. Goods costing $10,900 were left undamaged by the fire; remaining goods were destroyed.

Instructions

(a) Compute the cost of goods destroyed.

(b) Compute the cost of goods destroyed, assuming that the gross profit is 33⅓% of sales.

E9-14 (Gross Profit Method) Rasheed Wallace Company lost most of its inventory in a fire in December just before the year-end physical inventory was taken. The corporation's books disclosed the following:

Beginning inventory	$170,000	Sales	$650,000
Purchases for the year	390,000	Sales returns	24,000
Purchase returns	30,000	Rate of gross margin on sales	40%

Merchandise with a selling price of $21,000 remained undamaged after the fire. Damaged merchandise with an original selling price of $15,000 had a net realizable value of $5,300.

Instructions

Compute the amount of the loss as a result of the fire, assuming that the corporation had no insurance coverage.

E9-15 (Gross Profit Method) You are called by Calbert Cheany of Wizard Co. on July 16 and asked to prepare a claim for insurance as a result of a theft that took place the night before. You suggest that an inventory be taken immediately. The following data are available:

Inventory, July 1	$ 38,000
Purchases—goods placed in stock July 1–15	85,000
Sales—goods delivered to customers (gross)	116,000
Sales returns—goods returned to stock	4,000

Your client reports that the goods on hand on July 16 cost $30,500, but you determine that this figure includes goods of $6,000 received on a consignment basis. Your past records show that sales are made at approximately 40% over cost.

Instructions

Compute the claim against the insurance company.

E9-16 (Gross Profit Method) Gheorghe Moresan Lumber Company handles three principal lines of merchandise with these varying rates of gross profit on cost:

Lumber	25%
Millwork	30%
Hardware and fittings	40%

On August 18, a fire destroyed the office, lumber shed, and a considerable portion of the lumber stacked in the yard. To file a report of loss for insurance purposes, the company must know what the inventories were immediately preceding the fire. No detail or perpetual inventory records of any kind were maintained. The only pertinent information you are able to obtain are the following facts from the general ledger, which was kept in a fireproof vault and thus escaped destruction.

	Lumber	Millwork	Hardware
Inventory, Jan. 1, 2002	$ 250,000	$ 90,000	$ 45,000
Purchases to Aug. 18, 2002	1,500,000	375,000	160,000
Sales to Aug. 18, 2002	2,080,000	533,000	210,000

Instructions

Submit your estimate of the inventory amounts immediately preceding the fire.

E9-17 (Gross Profit Method) Presented below is information related to Warren Moon Corporation for the current year:

Beginning inventory	$ 600,000	
Purchases	1,500,000	
Total goods available for sale		$2,100,000
Sales		2,500,000

Instructions

Compute the ending inventory, assuming that **(a)** gross profit is 45% of sales; **(b)** gross profit is 60% of cost; **(c)** gross profit is 35% of sales; and **(d)** gross profit is 25% of cost.

E9-18 (Retail Inventory Method) Presented below is information related to Bobby Engram Company:

	Cost	Retail
Beginning inventory	$ 58,000	$100,000
Purchases (net)	122,000	200,000
Net markups		10,345
Net markdowns		26,135
Sales		186,000

Instructions

(a) Compute the ending inventory at retail.

(b) Compute a cost-to-retail percentage (round to two decimals):

(1) Excluding both markups and markdowns.

(2) Excluding markups but including markdowns.

(3) Excluding markdowns but including markups.

(4) Including both markdowns and markups.

(c) Which of the methods in (b) above (1, 2, 3, or 4)

(1) Provides the most conservative estimate of ending inventory?

(2) Provides an approximation of lower of cost or market?
(3) Is used in the conventional retail method?
(d) Compute ending inventory at lower of cost or market (round to nearest dollar).
(e) Compute cost of goods sold based on (d).
(f) Compute gross margin based on (d).

E9-19 (Retail Inventory Method) Presented below is information related to Ricky Henderson Company.

	Cost	Retail
Beginning inventory	$ 200,000	$ 280,000
Purchases	1,375,000	2,140,000
Markups		95,000
Markup cancellations		15,000
Markdowns		35,000
Markdown cancellations		5,000
Sales		2,200,000

Instructions

Compute the inventory by the conventional retail inventory method.

E9-20 (Retail Inventory Method) The records of Ellen's Boutique report the following data for the month of April.

Sales	$99,000	Purchases (at cost)	$48,000
Sales returns	2,000	Purchases (at sales price)	88,000
Additional markups	10,000	Purchase returns (at cost)	2,000
Markup cancellations	1,500	Purchase returns (at sales price)	3,000
Markdowns	9,300	Beginning inventory (at cost)	30,000
Markdown cancellations	2,800	Beginning inventory (at sales price)	46,500
Freight on purchases	2,400		

Instructions

Compute the ending inventory by the conventional retail inventory method.

E9-21 (Analysis of Inventories) The financial statements of General Mills, Inc's. 1999 Annual Report disclose the following information:

(in millions)	May 26, 1999	May 28, 1998	May 29, 1997
Inventories	$426.7	$389.7	$360.4

	Fiscal Year	
	1999	1998
Sales	$6,246.1	$6,033.0
Cost of goods sold	2,593.5	2,537.9
Net income	534.5	421.8

Instructions

Compute General Mills' **(a)** inventory turnover and **(b)** the average days to sell inventory for 1999 and 1998.

***E9-22 (Retail Inventory Method—Conventional and LIFO)** Helen Keller Company began operations on January 1, 2000, adopting the conventional retail inventory system. None of its merchandise was marked down in 2000 and, because there was no beginning inventory, its ending inventory for 2000 of $38,100 would have been the same under either the conventional retail system or the LIFO retail system. On December 31, 2001, the store management considers adopting the LIFO retail system, and desires to know how the December 31, 2001, inventory would appear under both systems. All pertinent data regarding purchases, sales, markups, and markdowns are shown below. There has been no change in the price level.

	Cost	Retail
Inventory, Jan. 1, 2001	$ 38,100	$ 60,000
Markdowns (net)		13,000
Markups (net)		22,000
Purchases (net)	130,900	178,000
Sales (net)		167,000

Instructions

Determine the cost of the 2001 ending inventory under both **(a)** the conventional retail method and **(b)** the LIFO retail method.

***E9-23 (Retail Inventory Method—Conventional and LIFO)** Leonard Bernstein Company began operations late in 2000 and adopted the conventional retail inventory method. Because there was no beginning inventory for 2000 and no markdowns during 2000, the ending inventory for 2000 was $14,000 under both the conventional retail method and the LIFO retail method. At the end of the 2001, management wants to compare the results of applying the conventional and LIFO retail methods. There was no change in the price level during 2001. The following data are available for computations:

	Cost	Retail
Inventory, January 1, 2001	$14,000	$20,000
Sales		80,000
Net markups		9,000
Net markdowns		1,600
Purchases	58,800	81,000
Freight-in	7,500	
Estimated theft		2,000

Instructions

Compute the cost of the 2001 ending inventory under both **(a)** the conventional retail method and **(b)** the LIFO retail method.

***E9-24 (Dollar-Value LIFO Retail)** You assemble the following information for Seneca Department Store, which computes its inventory under the dollar-value LIFO method.

	Cost	Retail
Inventory on January 1, 2001	$216,000	$300,000
Purchases	364,800	480,000
Increase in price level for year		9%

Instructions

Compute the cost of the inventory on December 31, 2002, assuming that the inventory at retail is **(a)** $294,300 and **(b)** $365,150.

***E9-25 (Dollar-Value LIFO Retail)** Presented below is information related to Langston Hughes Corporation:

	Price Index	LIFO Cost	Retail
Inventory on December 31, 2002, when dollar-value LIFO is adopted	100	$36,000	$ 74,500
Inventory, December 31, 2003	110	?	100,100

Instructions

Compute the ending inventory under the dollar-value LIFO method at December 31, 2003. The cost-to-retail ratio for 2003 was 60%.

***E9-26 (Conventional Retail and Dollar-Value LIFO Retail)** Black Feet Corporation began operations on January 1, 2001, with a beginning inventory of $30,100 at cost and $50,000 at retail. The following information relates to 2001:

	Retail
Net purchases ($108,500 at cost)	$150,000
Net markups	10,000
Net markdowns	5,000
Sales	126,900

Instructions

(a) Assume Black Feet decided to adopt the conventional retail method. Compute the ending inventory to be reported in the balance sheet.

(b) Assume instead that Black Feet decides to adopt the dollar-value LIFO retail method. The appropriate price indexes are 100 at January 1 and 110 at December 31. Compute the ending inventory to be reported in the balance sheet.

(c) On the basis of the information in part (b), compute cost of goods sold.

***E9-27 (Dollar-Value LIFO Retail)** The Connie Chung Corporation adopted the dollar-value LIFO retail inventory method on January 1, 2000. At that time the inventory had a cost of $54,000 and a retail price of $100,000. The following information is available:

	Year-End Inventory at Retail	Current Year Cost—Retail %	Year-End Price Index
2000	$118,720	57%	106
2001	138,750	60%	111
2002	125,350	61%	115
2003	162,500	58%	125

The price index at January 1, 2000, is 100.

Instructions

Compute the ending inventory at December 31 of the years 2000–2003. Round to the nearest dollar.

*E9-28 **(Change to LIFO Retail)** John Olerud Ltd., a local retailing concern in the Bronx, N.Y., has decided to change from the conventional retail inventory method to the LIFO retail method starting on January 1, 2002. The company recomputed its ending inventory for 2001 in accordance with the procedures necessary to switch to LIFO retail. The inventory computed was $212,600.

Instructions

Assuming that John Olerud Ltd.'s ending inventory for 2001 under the conventional retail inventory method was $205,000, prepare the appropriate journal entry on January 1, 2002.

PROBLEMS

P9-1 (Lower of Cost or Market) Grant Wood Company manufactures desks. Most of the company's desks are standard models and are sold on the basis of catalog prices. At December 31, 2002, the following finished desks appear in the company's inventory:

Finished Desks	A	B	C	D
2002 catalog selling price	$450	$480	$900	$1,050
FIFO cost per inventory list 12/31/02	470	450	830	960
Estimated current cost to manufacture (at December 31, 2002, and early 2003)	460	440	610	1,000
Sales commissions and estimated other costs of disposal	45	60	90	130
2003 catalog selling price	500	540	900	1,200

The 2002 catalog was in effect through November 2002, and the 2003 catalog is effective as of December 1, 2002. All catalog prices are net of the usual discounts. Generally, the company attempts to obtain a 20% gross margin on selling price and has usually been successful in doing so.

Instructions

At what amount should each of the four desks appear in the company's December 31, 2002, inventory, assuming that the company has adopted a lower of FIFO cost or market approach for valuation of inventories on an individual-item basis?

P9-2 (Lower of Cost or Market) T. Allen Home Improvement Company installs replacement siding, windows, and louvered glass doors for single family homes and condominium complexes in northern New Jersey and southern New York. The company is in the process of preparing its annual financial statements for the fiscal year ended May 31, 2001, and Tim Taylor, controller for T. Allen, has gathered the following data concerning inventory.

At May 31, 2001, the balance in T. Allen's Raw Material Inventory account was $408,000, and the Allowance to Reduce Inventory to Market had a credit balance of $29,500. Taylor summarized the relevant inventory cost and market data at May 31, 2001, in the schedule below.

Taylor assigned Patricia Richardson, an intern from a local college, the task of calculating the amount that should appear on T. Allen's May 31, 2001, financial statements for inventory under the lower of cost or market rule as applied to each item in inventory. Richardson expressed concern over departing from the cost principle.

	Cost	Replacement Cost	Sales Price	Net Realizable Value	Normal Profit
Aluminum siding	$ 70,000	$ 62,500	$ 64,000	$ 56,000	$ 5,100
Cedar shake siding	86,000	79,400	94,000	84,800	7,400
Louvered glass doors	112,000	124,000	186,400	168,300	18,500
Thermal windows	140,000	122,000	154,800	140,000	15,400
Total	$408,000	$387,900	$499,200	$449,100	$46,400

Instructions

(a) **(1)** Determine the proper balance in the Allowance to Reduce Inventory to Market at May 31, 2001.

(2) For the fiscal year ended May 31, 2001, determine the amount of the gain or loss that would be recorded due to the change in the Allowance to Reduce Inventory to Market.

(b) Explain the rationale for the use of the lower of cost or market rule as it applies to inventories.

(CMA adapted)

P9-3 (Lower of Cost or Market) Jonathan Brandis Company is a food wholesaler that supplies independent grocery stores in the immediate region. The company has a perpetual inventory system for all of its food products. The first-in, first-out (FIFO) method of inventory valuation is used to determine the cost of the inventory at the end of each month. Transactions and other related information regarding two of the items (instant coffee and sugar) carried by Brandis are given below for October 2001, the last month of Brandis' fiscal year.

	Instant Coffee	Sugar
Standard unit of packaging:	Case containing 24, one-pound jars	Baler containing 12, five-pound bags
Inventory, 10/1/01:	1,000 cases @ $60.20 per case	500 balers @ $6.50 per baler
Purchases:	**1.** 10/10/01—1,600 cases @ $62.10 per case plus freight of $480. **2.** 10/20/01—2,400 cases @ $64.00 per case plus freight of $480.	**1.** 10/5/01—850 balers @ $5.76 per baler plus freight of $320. **2.** 10/16/01—640 balers @ $6.00 per baler plus freight of $320. **3.** 10/24/01—600 balers @ $6.20 per baler plus freight of $360.
Purchase terms:	2/10, net/30, f.o.b. shipping point	Net 30 days, f.o.b. shipping point
October sales:	3,600 cases @ $76.00 per case	1,950 balers @ $8.00 per baler
Returns and allowances:	A customer returned 50 cases that had been shipped by error. The customer's account was credited for $3,800.	As the October 16 purchase was unloaded, 20 balers were discovered damaged. A representative of the trucking firm confirmed the damage and the balers were discarded. Credit of $120 for the merchandise and $10 for the freight was received by Brandis.
Inventory values 10/31/01:		
• Net realizable value	$66.00 per case	$6.60 per baler
• Net realizable value less a normal profit of 15%	$56.10 per case	$5.61 per baler

Brandis' sales terms are 1/10, net/30, f.o.b. shipping point. Brandis records all purchases net of purchase discounts and takes all purchase discounts. The most recent quoted price for coffee is $60 per case and for sugar $6.10 per baler before freight and purchase discounts.

Instructions

(a) Calculate the number of units in inventory and the FIFO unit cost for instant coffee and sugar as of October 31, 2001.

(b) Brandis Company applies the lower of cost or market rule in valuing its year-end inventory. Calculate the total dollar amount of the inventory for instant coffee and sugar applying the lower of cost or market rule on an individual-product basis.

(c) Could Brandis Company apply the lower of cost or market rule to groups of products or the inventory as a whole rather than on an individual product basis? Explain your answer.

(CMA adapted)

P9-4 (Entries for Lower of Cost or Market—Direct and Allowance) Mary Stuart Company determined its ending inventory at cost and at lower of cost or market at December 31, 2000, December 31, 2001, and December 31, 2002, as shown below:

	Cost	Lower of Cost or Market
12/31/00	$650,000	$650,000
12/31/01	780,000	722,000
12/31/02	900,000	830,000

Instructions

(a) Prepare the journal entries required at 12/31/01 and 12/31/02 assuming that a periodic inventory system and the direct method of adjusting to market is used.

(b) Prepare the journal entries required at 12/31/01 and 12/31/02 assuming that a periodic inventory is recorded at cost and reduced to market through the use of an allowance account (indirect method).

P9-5 (Gross Profit Method) David Hasselhoff Company lost most of its inventory in a fire in December just before the year-end physical inventory was taken. Corporate records disclose the following:

Inventory (beginning)	$ 80,000	Sales	$415,000
Purchases	280,000	Sales returns	21,000
Purchase returns	28,000	Gross profit % based on selling price	34%

Merchandise with a selling price of $30,000 remained undamaged after the fire, and damaged merchandise has a salvage value of $7,150. The company does not carry fire insurance on its inventory.

Instructions

Prepare a formal labeled schedule computing the fire loss incurred. (Do not use the retail inventory method.)

P9-6 (Gross Profit Method) On April 15, 2002, fire damaged the office and warehouse of John Kimmel Corporation. The only accounting record saved was the general ledger, from which the trial balance below was prepared.

JOHN KIMMEL CORPORATION
Trial Balance
March 31, 2002

Cash	$ 20,000	
Accounts receivable	40,000	
Inventory, December 31, 2001	75,000	
Land	35,000	
Building and equipment	110,000	
Accumulated depreciation		$ 41,300
Other assets	3,600	
Accounts payable		23,700
Other expense accruals		10,200
Capital stock		100,000
Retained earnings		52,000
Sales		135,000
Purchases	52,000	
Other expenses	26,600	
	$362,200	$362,200

The following data and information have been gathered:

1. The fiscal year of the corporation ends on December 31.
2. An examination of the April bank statement and canceled checks revealed that checks written during the period April 1–15 totaled $13,000: $5,700 paid to accounts payable as of March 31, $3,400 for April merchandise shipments, and $3,900 paid for other expenses. Deposits during the same period amounted to $12,950, which consisted of receipts on account from customers with the exception of a $950 refund from a vendor for merchandise returned in April.
3. Correspondence with suppliers revealed unrecorded obligations at April 15 of $10,600 for April merchandise shipments, including $2,300 for shipments in transit (f.o.b. shipping point) on that date.
4. Customers acknowledged indebtedness of $36,000 at April 15, 2002. It was also estimated that customers owed another $8,000 that will never be acknowledged or recovered. Of the acknowledged indebtedness, $600 will probably be uncollectible.
5. The companies insuring the inventory agreed that the corporation's fire-loss claim should be based on the assumption that the overall gross profit ratio for the past 2 years was in effect during the current year. The corporation's audited financial statements disclosed this information:

	Year Ended December 31	
	2001	2000
Net sales	$530,000	$390,000
Net purchases	280,000	235,000
Beginning inventory	50,000	75,200
Ending inventory	75,000	50,000

6. Inventory with a cost of $7,000 was salvaged and sold for $3,500. The balance of the inventory was a total loss.

Instructions

Prepare a schedule computing the amount of inventory fire loss. The supporting schedule of the computation of the gross profit should be in good form.

(AICPA adapted)

P9-7 (Retail Inventory Method) The records for the Clothing Department of Magdalena Aguilar's Discount Store are summarized below for the month of January.

Inventory; January 1: at retail, $25,000; at cost, $17,000
Purchases in January: at retail, $137,000; at cost, $86,500
Freight-in: $7,000
Purchase returns: at retail, $3,000; at cost, $2,300
Purchase allowances: $2,200
Transfers in from suburb branch: at retail, $13,000; at cost, $9,200
Net markups: $8,000
Net markdowns: $4,000
Inventory losses due to normal breakage, etc.: at retail, $400
Sales at retail: $85,000
Sales returns: $2,400

Instructions

Compute the inventory for this department as of January 31, at **(a)** retail and **(b)** lower of average cost or market.

P9-8 (Retail Inventory Method) Presented below is information related to Edward Braddock Inc.

	Cost	Retail
Inventory, 12/31/01	$250,000	$ 390,000
Purchases	914,500	1,460,000
Purchase returns	60,000	80,000
Purchase discounts	18,000	—
Gross sales (after employee discounts)	—	1,460,000
Sales returns	—	97,500
Markups	—	120,000
Markup cancellations	—	40,000
Markdowns	—	45,000
Markdown cancellations	—	20,000
Freight-in	79,000	—
Employee discounts granted	—	8,000
Loss from breakage (normal)	—	2,500

Instructions

Assuming that Edward Braddock Inc. uses the conventional retail inventory method, compute the cost of its ending inventory at December 31, 2002.

P9-9 (Retail Inventory Method) Jared Jones Inc. uses the retail inventory method to estimate ending inventory for its monthly financial statements. The following data pertain to a single department for the month of October 2002.

Inventory, October 1, 2002	
At cost	$ 52,000
At retail	78,000
Purchases (exclusive of freight and returns)	
At cost	262,000
At retail	423,000
Freight-in	16,600
Purchase returns	
At cost	5,600
At retail	8,000

Additional markups	9,000
Markup cancellations	2,000
Markdowns (net)	3,600
Normal spoilage and breakage	10,000
Sales	380,000

Instructions

(a) Using the conventional retail method, prepare a schedule computing estimated lower of cost or market inventory for October 31, 2002.

(b) A department store using the conventional retail inventory method estimates the cost of its ending inventory as $60,000. An accurate physical count reveals only $47,000 of inventory at lower of cost or market. List the factors that may have caused the difference between the computed inventory and the physical count.

P9-10 (Statement and Note Disclosure, LCM, and Purchase Commitment) Garth Brooks Specialty Company, a division of Fresh Horses Inc., manufactures three models of gear shift components for bicycles that are sold to bicycle manufacturers, retailers, and catalog outlets. Since beginning operations in 1969, Brooks has used normal absorption costing and has assumed a first-in, first-out cost flow in its perpetual inventory system. Except for overhead, manufacturing costs are accumulated using actual costs. Overhead is applied to production using predetermined overhead rates. The balances of the inventory accounts at the end of Brooks' fiscal year, November 30, 2001, are shown below. The inventories are stated at cost before any year-end adjustments.

Finished goods	$647,000
Work-in-process	112,500
Raw materials	240,000
Factory supplies	69,000

The following information relates to Brooks' inventory and operations.

1. The finished goods inventory consists of the items analyzed below.

	Cost	Market
Down tube shifter		
Standard model	$ 67,500	$ 67,000
Click adjustment model	94,500	87,000
Deluxe model	108,000	110,000
Total down tube shifters	270,000	264,000
Bar end shifter		
Standard model	83,000	90,050
Click adjustment model	99,000	97,550
Total bar end shifters	182,000	187,600
Head tube shifter		
Standard model	78,000	77,650
Click adjustment model	117,000	119,300
Total head tube shifters	195,000	196,950
Total finished goods	$647,000	$648,550

2. One-half of the head tube shifter finished goods inventory is held by catalog outlets on consignment.
3. Three-quarters of the bar end shifter finished goods inventory has been pledged as collateral for a bank loan.
4. One-half of the raw materials balance represents derailleurs acquired at a contracted price 20 percent above the current market price. The market value of the rest of the raw materials is $127,400.
5. The total market value of the work-in-process inventory is $108,700.
6. Included in the cost of factory supplies are obsolete items with an historical cost of $4,200. The market value of the remaining factory supplies is $65,900.
7. Brooks applies the lower of cost or market method to each of the three types of shifters in finished goods inventory. For each of the other three inventory accounts, Brooks applies the lower of cost or market method to the total of each inventory account.
8. Consider all amounts presented above to be material in relation to Brooks' financial statements taken as a whole.

Instructions

(a) Prepare the inventory section of Brooks' statement of financial position as of November 30, 2001, including any required note(s).

(b) Without prejudice to your answer to requirement (a), assume that the market value of Brooks' inventories is less than cost. Explain how this decline would be presented in Brooks' income statement for the fiscal year ended November 30, 2001.

(c) Assume that Brooks has a firm purchase commitment for the same type of derailleur included in the raw materials inventory as of November 30, 2001, and that the purchase commitment is at a contracted price 15 percent greater than the current market price. These derailleurs are to be delivered to Brooks after November 30, 2001. Discuss the impact, if any, that this purchase commitment would have on Brooks' financial statements prepared for the fiscal year ended November 30, 2001.

(CMA adapted)

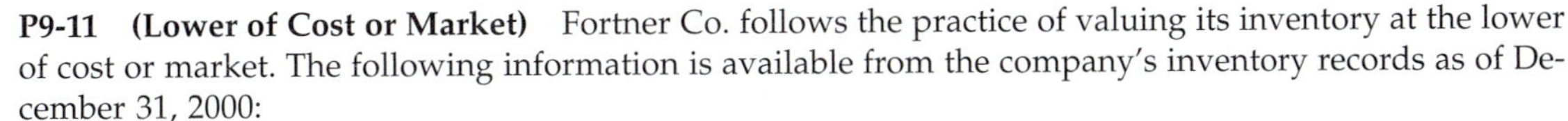

P9-11 (Lower of Cost or Market) Fortner Co. follows the practice of valuing its inventory at the lower of cost or market. The following information is available from the company's inventory records as of December 31, 2000:

Item	Quantity	Unit Cost	Replacement Cost/Unit	Estimated Selling Price/Unit	Completion & Disposal Cost/Unit	Normal Profit Margin/Unit
A	1,100	$7.50	$8.40	$10.50	$1.50	$1.80
B	800	8.20	8.00	9.40	.90	1.20
C	1,000	5.60	5.40	7.20	1.10	.60
D	1,000	3.80	4.20	6.30	.80	1.50
E	1,400	6.40	6.30	6.80	.70	1.00

Instructions

Finn Berge is an accounting clerk in the accounting department of Fortner Co., and he cannot understand why the market value keeps changing from replacement cost to net realizable value to something that he cannot even figure out. Finn is very confused, and he is the one who records inventory purchases and calculates ending inventory. You are the manager of the department and an accountant.

(a) Calculate the lower of cost or market using the "individual item" approach.

(b) Show the journal entry he will need to make in order to write down the ending inventory from cost to market.

(c) Then write a memo to Finn explaining what designated market value is as well as how it is computed. Use your calculations to aid in your explanation.

***P9-12 (Conventional and Dollar-Value LIFO Retail)** As of January 1, 2002, Carl Sandburg Inc. installed the retail method of accounting for its merchandise inventory.

To prepare the store's financial statements at June 30, 2002, you obtain these data.

	Cost	Selling Price
Inventory, January 1	$ 30,000	$ 43,000
Markdowns		10,500
Markups		9,200
Markdown cancellations		6,500
Markup cancellations		3,200
Purchases	108,800	155,000
Sales		159,000
Purchase returns and allowances	2,800	4,000
Sales returns and allowances		8,000

Instructions

(a) Prepare a schedule to compute Sandburg's June 30, 2002, inventory under the conventional retail method of accounting for inventories.

(b) Without prejudice to your solution to part (a), assume that you computed the June 30, 2002, inventory to be $54,000 at retail and the ratio of cost to retail to be 70%. The general price level has increased from 100 at January 1, 2002, to 108 at June 30, 2002. Prepare a schedule to compute the June 30, 2002, inventory at the June 30 price level under the dollar-value LIFO retail method.

(AICPA adapted)

***P9-13 (Retail, LIFO Retail, and Inventory Shortage)** Late in 1998, Sara Teasdale and four other investors took the chain of Sprint Department Stores private, and the company has just completed its third year of operations under the ownership of the investment group. Elinor Wylie, controller of Sprint Department Stores, is in the process of preparing the year-end financial statements. Based on the preliminary financial statements, Teasdale has expressed concern over inventory shortages, and she has asked Wylie to determine whether an abnormal amount of theft and breakage has occurred. The accounting records of Sprint Department Stores contain the following amounts on November 30, 2001, the end of the fiscal year.

	Cost	Retail
Beginning inventory	$ 68,000	$100,000
Purchases	248,200	400,000
Net markups		50,000
Net markdowns		110,000
Sales		330,000

According to the November 30, 2001, physical inventory, the actual inventory at retail is $107,000.

Instructions

(a) Describe the circumstances under which the retail inventory method would be applied, and the advantages of using the retail inventory method.

(b) Assuming that prices have been stable, calculate the value, at cost, of Sprint Department Stores' ending inventory using the last-in, first-out (LIFO) retail method. Be sure to furnish supporting calculations.

(c) Estimate the amount of shortage, at retail, that has occurred at Sprint Department Stores during the year ended November 30, 2001.

(d) Complications in the retail method can be caused by such items as (1) freight-in expense, (2) purchase returns and allowances, (3) sales returns and allowances, and (4) employee discounts. Explain how each of these four special items is handled in the retail inventory method.

(CMA adapted)

***P9-14 (Change to LIFO Retail)** Ulysses Grant Stores Inc., which uses the conventional retail inventory method, wishes to change to the LIFO retail method beginning with the accounting year ending December 31, 2001.

Amounts as shown below appear on the store's books before adjustment:

	At Cost	At Retail
Inventory, January 1, 2001	$ 13,600	$ 24,000
Purchases in 2001	116,200	184,000
Markups in 2001		12,000
Markdowns in 2001		5,500
Sales in 2001		170,000

You are to assume that all markups and markdowns apply to 2001 purchases, and that it is appropriate to treat the entire inventory as a single department.

Instructions

Compute the inventory at December 31, 2001, under:

(a) The conventional retail method.

(b) The last-in, first-out retail method, effecting the change in method as of January 1, 2001. Assume that the cost-to-retail percentage for 2000 was recomputed correctly in accordance with procedures necessary to change to LIFO. This ratio was 57%.

(AICPA adapted)

***P9-15 (Change to LIFO Retail; Dollar-Value LIFO Retail)** Rudyard Kipling Department Store converted from the conventional retail method to the LIFO retail method on January 1, 2000, and is now considering converting to the dollar-value LIFO inventory method. During your examination of the financial statements for the year ended December 31, 2001, management requested that you furnish a summary showing certain computations of inventory cost for the past 3 years.

Here is the available information.

1. The inventory at January 1, 1999, had a retail value of $56,000 and cost of $26,700 based on the conventional retail method.
2. Transactions during 1999 were as follows:

	Cost	Retail
Gross purchases	$311,000	$554,000
Purchase returns	5,200	10,000
Purchase discounts	6,000	
Gross sales (after employee discounts)		551,000
Sales returns		9,000

Employee discounts		3,000
Freight-in	17,600	
Net markups		20,000
Net markdowns		12,000

3. The retail value of the December 31, 2000, inventory was $73,500, the cost ratio for 2000 under the LIFO retail method was 61%, and the regional price index was 105% of the January 1, 2000, price level.
4. The retail value of the December 31, 2001, inventory was $65,880, the cost ratio for 2001 under the LIFO retail method was 60%, and the regional price index was 108% of the January 1, 2000, price level.

Instructions

(a) Prepare a schedule showing the computation of the cost of inventory on hand at December 31, 1999, based on the conventional retail method.

(b) Prepare a schedule showing the recomputation of the inventory to be reported on December 31, 1999, in accordance with procedures necessary to convert from the conventional retail method to the LIFO retail method beginning January 1, 2000. Assume that the retail value of the December 31, 1999, inventory was $63,000.

(c) Without prejudice to your solution to part (b), assume that you computed the December 31, 1999, inventory (retail value $63,000) under the LIFO retail method at a cost of $34,965. Prepare a schedule showing the computations of the cost of the store's 2000 and 2001 year-end inventories under the dollar-value LIFO method.

(AICPA adapted)

CONCEPTUAL CASES

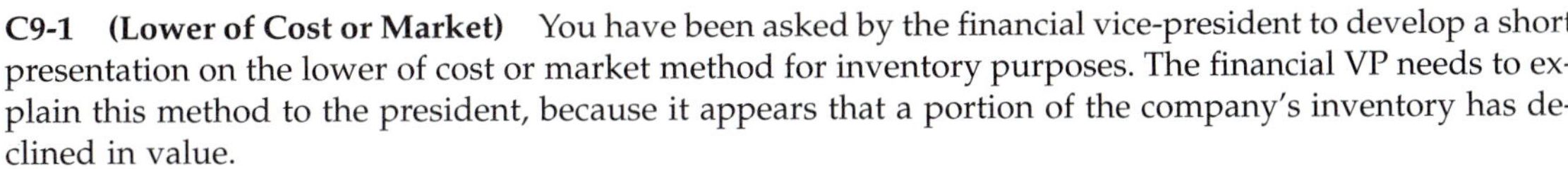

C9-1 (Lower of Cost or Market) You have been asked by the financial vice-president to develop a short presentation on the lower of cost or market method for inventory purposes. The financial VP needs to explain this method to the president, because it appears that a portion of the company's inventory has declined in value.

Instructions

The financial VP asks you to answer the following questions.

(a) What is the purpose of the lower of cost or market method?

(b) What is meant by market? (*Hint*: Discuss the ceiling and floor constraints.)

(c) Do you apply the lower of cost or market method to each individual item, to a category, or to the total of the inventory? Explain.

(d) What are the potential disadvantages of the lower of cost or market method?

C9-2 (Lower of Cost or Market) YoYoMa Inc. manufactures and sells four products, the inventories of which are priced at cost or market, whichever is lower. A normal profit margin rate of 30% is usually maintained on each of the four products.

The following information was compiled as of December 31, 2001.

Product	Original Cost	Cost to Replace	Estimated Cost to Dispose	Expected Selling Price[a]
A	$17.50	$14.00	$ 6.00	$ 30.00
B	48.00	78.00	26.00	100.00
C	35.00	42.00	15.00	80.00
D	47.50	45.00	20.50	95.00

[a]Normal margin is 30% of selling price.

Instructions

(a) Why are expected selling prices important in the application of the lower of cost or market rule?

(b) Prepare a schedule containing unit values (including "floor" and "ceiling") for determining the lower of cost or market on an individual-product basis. The last column of the schedule should contain for each product the unit value for the purpose of inventory valuation resulting from the application of the lower of cost or market rule.

C9-3 (Lower of Cost or Market) Lena Horne Corporation purchased a significant amount of raw materials inventory for a new product that it is manufacturing.

Horne uses the lower of cost or market rule for these raw materials. The replacement cost of the raw materials is above the net realizable value, and both are below the original cost.

Horne uses the average cost inventory method for these raw materials. In the last 2 years, each purchase has been at a lower price than the previous purchase, and the ending inventory quantity for each period has been higher than the beginning inventory quantity for that period.

Instructions

(a) **(1)** At which amount should Horne's raw materials inventory be reported on the balance sheet? Why?

(2) In general, why is the lower of cost or market rule used to report inventory?

(b) What would have been the effect on ending inventory and cost of goods sold had Horne used the LIFO inventory method instead of the average cost inventory method for the raw materials? Why?

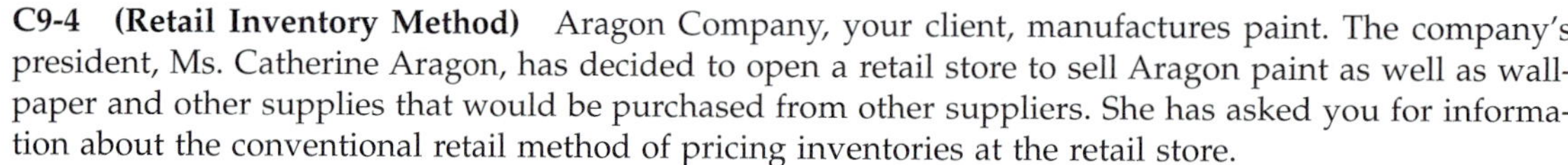

C9-4 (Retail Inventory Method) Aragon Company, your client, manufactures paint. The company's president, Ms. Catherine Aragon, has decided to open a retail store to sell Aragon paint as well as wallpaper and other supplies that would be purchased from other suppliers. She has asked you for information about the conventional retail method of pricing inventories at the retail store.

Instructions

Prepare a report to the president explaining the retail method of pricing inventories. Your report should include these points:

(a) Description and accounting features of the method.

(b) The conditions that may distort the results under the method.

(c) A comparison of the advantages of using the retail method with those of using cost methods of inventory pricing.

(d) The accounting theory underlying the treatment of net markdowns and net markups under the method.

(AICPA adapted)

C9-5 (Cost Determination, LCM, Retail Method) E. A. Poe Corporation, a retailer and wholesaler of national brand-name household lighting fixtures, purchases its inventories from various suppliers.

Instructions

(a) **(1)** What criteria should be used to determine which of Poe's costs are inventoriable?

(2) Are Poe's administrative costs inventoriable? Defend your answer.

(b) **(1)** Poe uses the lower of cost or market rule for its wholesale inventories. What are the theoretical arguments for that rule?

(2) The replacement cost of the inventories is below the net realizable value less a normal profit margin, which, in turn, is below the original cost. What amount should be used to value the inventories? Why?

(c) Poe calculates the estimated cost of its ending inventories held for sale at retail using the conventional retail inventory method. How would Poe treat the beginning inventories and net markdowns in calculating the cost ratio used to determine its ending inventories? Why?

(AICPA adapted)

***C9-6 (Retail Inventory Method and LIFO Retail)** Presented below are a number of items that may be encountered in computing the cost to retail percentage when using the conventional retail method or the LIFO retail method.

1. Markdowns.
2. Markdown cancellations.
3. Cost of items transferred in from other departments.
4. Retail value of items transferred in from other departments.
5. Sales discounts.
6. Purchases discounts (purchases recorded gross).
7. Estimated retail value of goods broken or stolen.
8. Cost of beginning inventory.
9. Retail value of beginning inventory.
10. Cost of purchases.
11. Retail value of purchases.
12. Markups.
13. Markup cancellations.
14. Employee discounts (sales recorded net).

Instructions

For each of the items listed above, indicate whether this item would be considered in the cost to retail percentage under **(a)** conventional retail and **(b)** LIFO retail.

USING YOUR JUDGMENT

FINANCIAL REPORTING PROBLEM: INTEL CORPORATION

The financial statements of Intel are presented in Appendix 5B.

Instructions

Refer to these financial statements and the accompanying notes to answer the following questions.

(a) How does Intel value its inventories? Which inventory costing method does Intel use as a basis for reporting its inventories?

(b) How does Intel report its inventories in the balance sheet? In the notes to its financial statements, what three descriptions are used to classify its inventories?

(c) What was the dollar amount and percentage change in Intel's inventories from December 27, 1997, to December 26, 1998?

(d) What was Intel's inventory turnover ratio in 1998? What is its gross profit percentage? Evaluate Intel's inventory turnover ratio and gross profit percentage.

(e) What are Intel's gross profit margin expectations for 1999? Explain.

FINANCIAL STATEMENT ANALYSIS CASES

Case 1 Sonic, Inc.

Sonic, Inc., reported the following information regarding 1999–2000 inventory:

SONIC, INC.

	2000	1999
Current assets		
Cash	$ 153,010	$ 538,489
Accounts receivable, net of allowance for doubtful accounts of $46,000 in 2000 and $160,000 in 1999	1,627,980	2,596,291
Inventories (Note 2)	1,340,494	1,734,873
Other current assets	123,388	90,592
Assets of discontinued operations	—	32,815
Total current assets	3,244,872	4,993,060

Notes to Consolidated Financial Statements

Note 1 (in part): Nature of Business and Significant Accounting Policies

Inventories—Inventories are stated at the lower of cost or market. Cost is determined by the last-in, first-out (LIFO) method by the parent company and by the first-in, first-out (FIFO) method by its subsidiaries.

Note 2: Inventories

Inventories consist of the following:

	2000	1999
Raw materials	$1,264,646	$2,321,178
Work in process	240,988	171,222
Finished goods and display units	129,406	711,252
Total inventories	1,635,040	3,203,652
Less: Amount classified as long-term	294,546	1,468,779
Current portion	$1,340,494	$1,734,873

Inventories are stated at the lower of cost determined by the LIFO method or market for Sonic, Inc. Inventories for the two wholly-owned subsidiaries, Sonic Command, Inc. (U.S.) and Sonic Limited (U.K.) are stated on the FIFO method which amounted to $566,000 at October 31, 1999. No inventory is stated on the FIFO method at October 31, 2000. Included in inventory stated at FIFO cost was $32,815 at October 31, 1999, of Sonic Command inventory classified as an asset from discontinued operations (see Note 14). If the FIFO method had been used for the entire consolidated group, inventories after an adjustment to the lower of cost or market, would have been approximately $2,000,000 and $3,800,000 at October 31, 2000 and 1999, respectively.

Inventory has been written down to estimated net realizable value, and results of operations for 2000, 1999, and 1998 include a corresponding charge of approximately $868,000, $960,000, and $273,000, respectively, which represents the excess of LIFO cost over market.

Inventory of $294,546 and $1,468,779 at October 31, 2000 and 1999, respectively, shown on the balance sheet as a noncurrent asset represents that portion of the inventory that is not expected to be sold currently.

Reduction in inventory quantities during the years ended October 31, 2000, 1999, and 1998 resulted in liquidation of LIFO inventory quantities carried at a lower cost prevailing in prior years as compared with the cost of fiscal 2000 purchases. The effect of these reductions was to decrease the net loss by approximately $24,000, $157,000 and $90,000 at October 31, 2000, 1999, and 1998, respectively.

Instructions

(a) Why might Sonic, Inc., use two different methods for valuing inventory?

(b) Comment on why Sonic, Inc., might disclose how its LIFO inventories would be valued under FIFO.

(c) Why does the LIFO liquidation reduce operating costs?

(d) Comment on whether Sonic would report more or less income if it had been on a FIFO basis for all its inventory.

Case 2 Barrick Gold Corporation

Barrick Gold Corporation, with headquarters in Toronto, Canada, is the world's most profitable and largest gold mining company outside South Africa. Part of the key to Barrick's success has been due to its ability to maintain cash flow while improving production and increasing its reserves of gold-containing property. During 1995, Barrick achieved record growth in cash flow, production, and reserves.

The company maintains an aggressive policy of developing previously identified target areas that have the possibility of a large amount of gold ore, and that have not been previously developed. Barrick limits the riskiness of this development by choosing only properties that are located in politically stable regions, and by the company's use of internally generated funds, rather than debt, to finance growth.

Barrick's inventories are as follows:

Inventories (in millions, US dollars)	1995
Current	
Gold in process	$54.8
Mine operating supplies	53.1
	$107.9
Non-current (included in property, plant, and equipment)	
Ore in stockpiles	$60.5

Instructions

(a) Why do you think that there are no finished goods inventories? Why do you think the raw material, ore in stockpiles, is considered to be a non-current asset?

(b) Consider that Barrick has no finished goods inventories. What journal entries are made to record a sale?

(c) Suppose that gold bullion that cost $1.8 million to produce was sold for $2.4 million. The journal entry was made to record the sale, but no entry was made to remove the gold from the gold in process inventory. How would this error affect the following?

Balance Sheet		Income Statement	
Inventory	?	Cost of goods sold	?
Retained earnings	?	Net income	?
Accounts payable	?		
Working capital	?		
Current ratio	?		

COMPARATIVE ANALYSIS CASE

The Coca-Cola Company versus PepsiCo, Inc.

Instructions

Go to the Digital Tool and, using **The Coca-Cola Company** and the **PepsiCo, Inc.** annual report information, answer the following questions.

(a) What is the amount of inventory reported by Coca-Cola at December 31, 1998, and by PepsiCo at December 26, 1998? What percent of total assets is invested in inventory by each company?

(b) What inventory costing methods are used by Coca-Cola and PepsiCo? How does each company value its inventories?

(c) In the notes, what classifications (descriptions) are used by Coca-Cola and PepsiCo to categorize their inventories?

(d) Compute and compare the inventory turnover ratios and days to sell inventory for 1998 for Coca-Cola and PepsiCo. Indicate why there might be a significant difference between the two companies.

RESEARCH CASES

Case 1

Numerous companies have established home pages on the Internet, for example, **Boston Beer Company** (http://www.samadams.com), **Ford Motor Company** (http://www.ford.com), and **Kodak** (http://www.kodak.com). You undoubtedly have noticed company Internet addresses in television commercials or magazine advertisements.

Instructions

Examine the home pages of any two companies and answer the following questions.

(a) What type of information is available?

(b) Is any accounting-related information presented?

(c) Would you describe the home page as informative, promotional, or both? Why?

Case 2

The September 23, 1994, edition of *The Wall Street Journal* includes an article entitled "**CompUSA** Auctions Notebook Computers Through Bulk Sale."

Instructions

Read the article and answer the following questions:

(a) At what amount did CompUSA estimate the retail value of the computers? What was the estimate made by one of the bidders?

(b) What was wrong with the computers?

(c) What were the rules of the auction as specified by CompUSA?

(d) CompUSA had just recorded a $3 million inventory write-down in the preceding quarter. Based on the information in the article, does it appear that additional write-downs were called for?

ETHICS CASES

Case 1

The market value of Lake Corporation's inventory has declined below its cost. Vickie Maher, the controller, wants to use the allowance method to write down inventory because it more clearly discloses the decline in market value, and it does not distort the cost of goods sold. Her supervisor, financial vice-president Doug Brucki, prefers the direct method to write down inventory because it does not call attention to the decline in market value.

Instructions

Answer the following questions:

(a) What, if any, is the ethical issue involved?

(b) Is any stakeholder harmed if Brucki's preference is used?

(c) What should Vickie Maher do?

Case 2

Vineland Company signed a long-term purchase contract to buy timber from the United States Forest Service at $300 per thousand board feet. Under these terms, Vineland must cut and pay $6,000,000 for this timber during the next year. Currently the market value is $250 per thousand board feet. At this rate, the market price is $5,000,000. Ruben Walker, the controller, wants to recognize the loss in value on the year-end financial statements; but the financial vice-president, Billie Hands, argues that the loss is temporary and should be ignored. Walker notes that market value has remained near $250 for many months, and he sees no sign of significant change.

Instructions

Answer the following questions:

(a) What are the ethical issues, if any?

(b) Is any particular stakeholder harmed by the financial vice-president's decision?

(c) What should the controller do?

CHAPTER 10

Acquisition and Disposition of Property, Plant, and Equipment

LEARNING OBJECTIVES

After studying this chapter, you should be able to:

1. **Describe the major characteristics of property, plant, and equipment.**
2. **Identify the costs included in the initial valuation of land, buildings, and equipment.**
3. **Describe the accounting problems associated with self-constructed assets.**
4. **Describe the accounting problems associated with interest capitalization.**
5. **Understand accounting issues related to acquiring and valuing plant assets.**
6. **Describe the accounting treatment for costs subsequent to acquisition.**
7. **Describe the accounting treatment for the disposal of property, plant, and equipment.**

Landfill Accounting That SMELLS

A classic case of deferring too many costs is **Chambers Development Co.**, a developer of landfills. In 1991, Chambers' earnings rose 45 percent. Net sales approached $322 million, a ten-fold increase in just five years. This amazing growth, not uncommon for waste management firms in the 1980s, was powered by the acquisition and rapid development of new landfills. During 1991, its stock price rose from $16.13 to $37. Unfortunately, on March 17, 1992, in a tersely worded statement, Chambers revealed that its profit growth had been greatly overstated. The highly profitable company was not so profitable after all. In October 1992, Chambers restated income for 1991 and several prior years, wiping out $362 million in earnings and retained earnings. Not surprisingly, the next day, Chambers' stock plunged 63%—from $30.50 to $11.13 in one day!

What happened? As Chambers' stockholders would learn, the company had been deferring recognition of certain "indirect" landfill development expenses by capitalizing these costs and writing them off over the life of the landfills (three to ten years). The deferred expenses included executives' salaries and travel, legal and public relations costs, and security guard contracts, along with costs of initiating new trash hauling routes. These capitalized costs were tucked near the bottom of the balance sheet under the heading "other assets" on a line described "deferred costs." As one Wall Street analyst remarked, "Whenever you see an asset called 'deferred anything' hold on to your pocketbook."

While Chambers says it is now recognizing rather than deferring indirect costs, it is continuing to defer substantial interest costs that most firms expense. This concerns investors and analysts because it is consistent with Chambers' penchant for showing generous earnings growth through liberal accounting practices. As one observer noted, "What got them in trouble is that they'd led the world to believe they were using conservative accounting methods when they weren't."[1] Once a company gets this kind of dubious reputation, the investment community loses faith in the quality of its reported earnings for years to come.

[1] "Audit Report Shows How Far Chambers Would Go for Profits," *The Wall Street Journal*, October 21, 1992, p. A1.

PREVIEW OF CHAPTER 10

As indicated in the opening story, Chambers Development Co. used questionable criteria to capitalize certain costs and report them as assets. The purpose of this chapter is to discuss (1) the proper accounting for costs related to property, plant, and equipment, and (2) the accounting methods used to record the retirement or disposal of these costs. Depreciation—allocating costs of property, plant, and equipment to accounting periods—is presented in Chapter 11. The content and organization of this chapter are as follows.

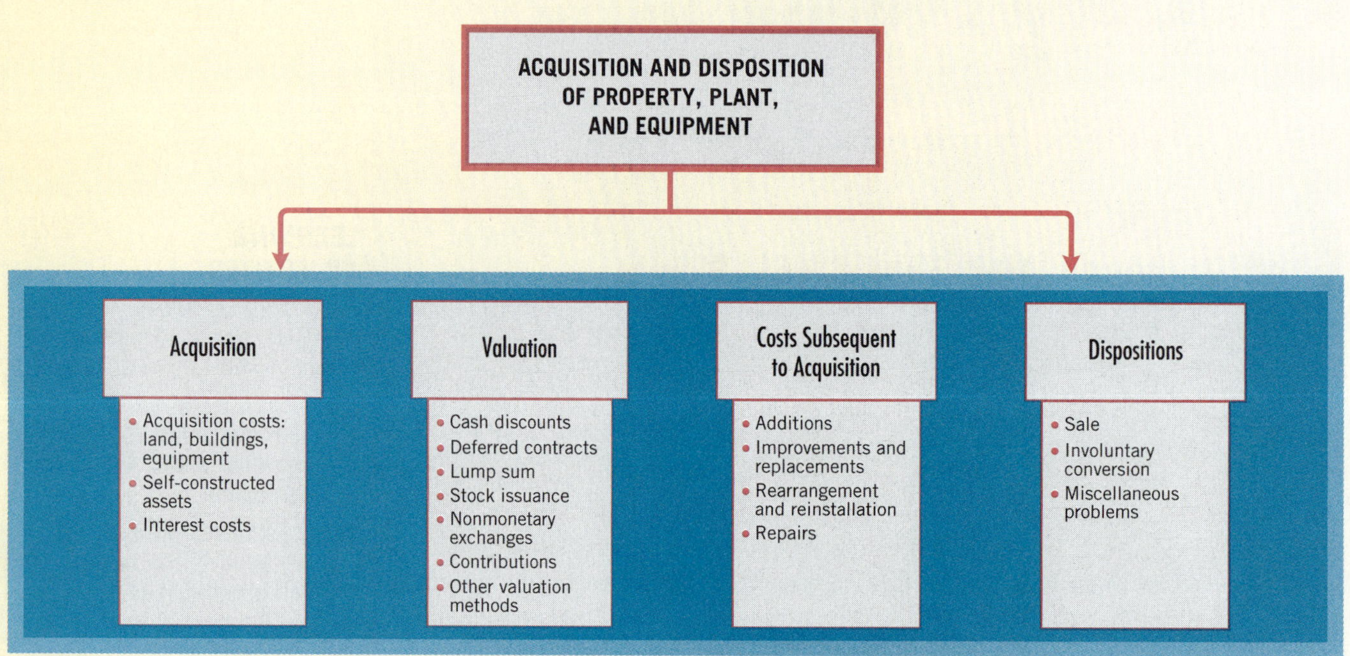

OBJECTIVE 1
Describe the major characteristics of property, plant, and equipment.

Almost every business enterprise of any size or activity uses assets of a durable nature. Such assets, commonly referred to as **property, plant, and equipment**; **plant assets**; or **fixed assets**, include land, building structures (offices, factories, warehouses), and equipment (machinery, furniture, tools). These terms are used interchangeably throughout this textbook. The major characteristics of property, plant, and equipment are:

1. ***They are acquired for use in operations and not for resale.*** Only assets used in normal business operations should be classified as property, plant, and equipment. An idle building is more appropriately classified separately as an investment; land held by land developers or subdividers is classified as inventory.
2. ***They are long-term in nature and usually subject to depreciation.*** Property, plant, and equipment yield services over a number of years. The investment in these assets is assigned to future periods through periodic depreciation charges. The exception is land, which is not depreciated unless a material decrease in value occurs, such as a loss in fertility of agricultural land because of poor crop rotation, drought, or soil erosion.
3. ***They possess physical substance.*** Property, plant, and equipment are characterized by physical existence or substance and thus are differentiated from intangible assets, such as patents or goodwill. Unlike raw material, however, property, plant, and equipment do not physically become part of a product held for resale.

ACQUISITION OF PROPERTY, PLANT, AND EQUIPMENT

Historical cost is the usual basis for valuing property, plant, and equipment. **Historical cost is measured by the cash or cash equivalent price of obtaining the asset and bringing it to the location and condition necessary for its intended use.** The purchase price, freight costs, sales taxes, and installation costs of a productive asset are considered part of the asset's cost. These costs are allocated to future periods through depreciation. Any related costs incurred **after the asset's acquisition**, such as additions, improvements, or replacements, are **added to the asset's cost if they provide future service potential**. Otherwise they are expensed immediately.

OBJECTIVE 2
Identify the costs included in the initial valuation of land, buildings, and equipment.

Cost should be the basis used at the acquisition date because the cash or cash equivalent price best measures the asset's value at that time. Disagreement does exist concerning differences between historical cost and other valuation methods (such as replacement cost or fair market value) arising after acquisition. *APB Opinion No. 6* states that "property, plant, and equipment should not be written up to reflect appraisal, market, or current values which are above cost." Although minor exceptions are noted, current standards indicate that departures from historical cost are rare.

UNDERLYING CONCEPTS

Market value is relevant to inventory but less so for property, plant, and equipment which, consistent with the going concern assumption, are held for use in the business, not for sale like inventory.

The main reasons for this position are (1) at the date of acquisition, cost reflects fair value; (2) historical cost involves actual, not hypothetical transactions, and as a result is the most reliable; and (3) gains and losses should not be anticipated but should be recognized when the asset is sold.

Several other valuation methods have been considered, such as (1) constant dollar accounting (adjustments for general price-level changes), (2) current cost accounting (adjustments for specific price-level changes), (3) net realizable value, or (4) a combination of constant dollar accounting and current cost or net realizable value.

Go to the Digital Tool for an expanded discussion of alternative valuation methods.

Cost of Land

All expenditures made to acquire land and to ready it for use are considered part of the land cost. Land costs typically include (1) the purchase price, (2) closing costs, such as title to the land, attorney's fees, and recording fees, (3) costs incurred in getting the land in condition for its intended use, such as grading, filling, draining, and clearing, (4) assumption of any liens, mortgages, or encumbrances on the property, and (5) any additional land improvements that have an indefinite life.

When land has been purchased for the purpose of constructing a building, all costs incurred up to the excavation for the new building are considered land costs. **Removal of old buildings—clearing, grading, and filling—are considered land costs because these costs are necessary to get the land in condition for its intended purpose.** Any proceeds obtained in the process of getting the land ready for its intended use, such as salvage receipts on the demolition of an old building or the sale of cleared timber, are treated as **reductions in the price of the land**.

INTERNATIONAL INSIGHT

In many nations, such as Great Britain and Brazil, companies are allowed to revalue their fixed assets at amounts above historical cost. These revaluations may be at appraisal values or at amounts linked to a specified index. Other nations, such as Japan and Germany, do not allow such revaluations.

In some cases, the purchaser of land has to assume certain obligations on the land such as back taxes or liens. In such situations, the cost of the land is the cash paid for it, plus the encumbrances. In other words, if the purchase price of the land is $50,000 cash, but accrued property taxes of $5,000 and liens of $10,000 are assumed, the cost of the land is $65,000.

Special assessments for local improvements, such as pavements, street lights, sewers, and drainage systems, are usually charged to the Land account because they are relatively permanent in nature and are maintained and replaced by the local government body. In addition, permanent improvements made by the owner, such as landscaping, are properly chargeable to the Land account. **Improvements with limited lives**, such as private driveways, walks, fences, and parking lots, are recorded separately as Land Improvements so they can be depreciated over their estimated lives.

Generally, land is part of property, plant, and equipment. If the major purpose of acquiring and holding land is speculative, however, it is more appropriately classified as an investment. If the land is held by a real estate concern for resale, it should be classified as inventory.

In cases where land is held as an investment, what accounting treatment should be given taxes, insurance, and other direct costs incurred while holding the land? Many believe these costs should be capitalized because the revenue from the investment still has not been received. This approach is reasonable and seems justified except in cases where the asset is currently producing revenue (such as rental property).

Cost of Buildings

INTERNATIONAL INSIGHT

Under international accounting standards historical cost is the benchmark (preferred) treatment for property, plant, and equipment. However, it is also allowable to use revalued amounts. If revaluation is used, companies are required to revalue the class of assets regularly.

The cost of buildings should include all expenditures related directly to their acquisition or construction. These costs include (1) materials, labor, and overhead costs incurred during construction and (2) professional fees and building permits. Generally, companies contract to have their buildings constructed. All costs incurred, from excavation to completion, are considered part of the building costs.

One accounting problem is deciding what to do about an old building that is on the site of a newly proposed building. Is the cost of removal of the old building a cost of the land or a cost of the new building? The answer is that if land is purchased with an old building on it, then the cost of demolition less its salvage value is a cost of getting the land ready for its intended use and relates to the land rather than to the new building. As indicated earlier, all costs of getting an asset ready for its intended use are costs of that asset.

Cost of Equipment

The term "equipment" in accounting includes delivery equipment, office equipment, machinery, furniture and fixtures, furnishings, factory equipment, and similar fixed assets. The cost of such assets includes the purchase price, freight and handling charges incurred, insurance on the equipment while in transit, cost of special foundations if required, assembling and installation costs, and costs of conducting trial runs. Costs thus include all expenditures incurred in acquiring the equipment and preparing it for use.

Self-Constructed Assets

OBJECTIVE 3
Describe the accounting problems associated with self-constructed assets.

Occasionally companies (particularly in the railroad and utility industries) construct their own assets. Determining the cost of such machinery and other fixed assets can be a problem. Without a purchase price or contract price, the company must allocate costs and expenses to arrive at the cost of the **self-constructed asset**. Materials and direct labor used in construction pose no problem; these costs can be traced directly to work and material orders related to the fixed assets constructed.

However, the assignment of indirect costs of manufacturing creates special problems. These indirect costs, called **overhead** or burden, include power, heat, light, insurance, property taxes on factory buildings and equipment, factory supervisory labor, depreciation of fixed assets, and supplies.

These costs might be handled in one of three ways:

1. ***Assign No Fixed Overhead to the Cost of the Constructed Asset.*** The major argument for this treatment is that indirect overhead is generally fixed in nature and does not increase as a result of constructing one's own plant or equipment. This approach assumes that the company will have the same costs regardless of whether the company constructs the asset or not, so to charge a portion of the overhead costs to the equipment will normally relieve current expenses and consequently overstate income of the current period. In contrast, variable overhead costs that increase as a result of the construction are assigned to the cost of the asset.
2. ***Assign a Portion of All Overhead to the Construction Process.*** This approach, a full costing concept, is appropriate if one believes that costs attach to all products and assets manufactured or constructed. This procedure assigns overhead costs to

construction as it would to normal production. Advocates say that failure to allocate overhead costs understates the initial cost of the asset and results in an inaccurate future allocation.

3. ***Allocate on the Basis of Lost Production.*** A third alternative is to allocate to the construction project the cost of any curtailed production that occurs because the asset is built instead of purchased. This method is conceptually appealing, but is based on "what might have occurred"—an opportunity cost concept—which is difficult to measure.

A pro rata portion of the fixed overhead should be assigned to the asset to obtain its cost. This treatment is employed extensively because many believe a better matching of costs with revenues is obtained. If the allocated overhead results in recording construction costs in excess of the costs that would be charged by an outside independent producer, the excess overhead should be recorded as a period loss rather than be capitalized, to avoid capitalizing the asset at more than its probable market value.

Interest Costs During Construction

OBJECTIVE 4
Describe the accounting problems associated with interest capitalization.

The proper accounting for interest costs has been a long-standing controversy. Three approaches have been suggested to account for the interest incurred in financing the construction or acquisition of property, plant, and equipment:

1. ***Capitalize No Interest Charges During Construction.*** Under this approach interest is considered a cost of financing and not a cost of construction. It is contended that if the company had used stock financing rather than debt financing, this expense would not have been incurred. The major argument against this approach is that an implicit interest cost is associated with the use of cash regardless of its source; if stock financing is employed, a real cost exists to the stockholders although a contractual claim does not take place.
2. ***Charge Construction with All Costs of Funds Employed, Whether Identifiable or Not.*** This method maintains that one part of the cost of construction is the cost of financing, whether by debt, cash, or stock financing. An asset should be charged with all costs necessary to get it ready for its intended use. Interest, whether actual or imputed, is a cost of building, just as labor, materials, and overhead are costs. A major criticism of this approach is that imputation of a cost of equity capital is subjective and outside the framework of an historical cost system.
3. ***Capitalize Only the Actual Interest Costs Incurred During Construction.*** This approach relies on the historical cost concept that only actual transactions are recorded. It is argued that interest incurred is as much a cost of acquiring the asset as the cost of the materials, labor, and other resources used. As a result, a company that uses debt financing will have an asset of higher cost than an enterprise that uses stock financing. The results achieved by this approach are considered unsatisfactory by some because the cost of an asset should be the same whether cash, debt financing, or stock financing is employed.

Illustration 10-1 on the next page shows the interest costs (if any) that would be added to the cost of an asset under the three capitalization approaches.

As indicated, in general, capitalizing actual interest (with modification) is the approach recommended under GAAP. This method is in accordance with the concept that the historical cost of acquiring an asset includes all costs (including interest) incurred to bring the asset to the condition and location necessary for its intended use. The rationale for this approach is that during construction the asset is not generating revenues, and therefore interest costs should be deferred (capitalized).[2] Once construction is completed, the asset is ready for its intended use and revenues can be earned. At this

[2]"Capitalization of Interest Cost," *Statement of Financial Accounting Standards No. 34* (Stamford, Conn.: FASB, 1979).

ILLUSTRATION 10-1
Capitalization of Interest Costs

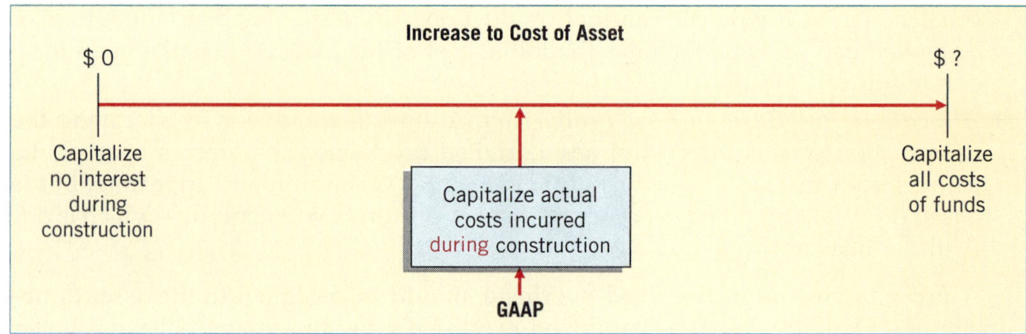

point interest should be reported as an expense and matched to these revenues. It follows that any interest cost incurred in purchasing an asset that is ready for its intended use should be expensed.

To implement this general approach, three items must be considered:

1. Qualifying assets.
2. Capitalization period.
3. Amount to capitalize.

Qualifying Assets

To qualify for interest capitalization, assets must require a period of time to get them ready for their intended use. Interest costs are capitalized starting with the first expenditure related to the asset, and capitalization continues until the asset is substantially completed and ready for its intended use.

Assets that qualify for interest cost capitalization include assets under construction for an enterprise's own use (including buildings, plants, and large machinery) and assets intended for sale or lease that are constructed or otherwise produced as discrete projects (e.g., ships or real estate developments).

Examples of assets that do not qualify for interest capitalization are (1) assets that are in use or ready for their intended use, and (2) assets that are not being used in the earnings activities of the enterprise and that are not undergoing the activities necessary to get them ready for use (such as land that is not being developed and assets not being used because of obsolescence, excess capacity, or need for repair).

Capitalization Period

INTERNATIONAL INSIGHT

Under international accounting standards, capitalization of interest is allowed, but it is not the preferred treatment. The benchmark treatment is to expense interest in the period incurred.

The **capitalization period** is the period of time during which interest must be capitalized. It begins when three conditions are present:

1. Expenditures for the asset have been made.
2. Activities that are necessary to get the asset ready for its intended use are in progress.
3. Interest cost is being incurred.

Interest capitalization **continues as long as these three conditions are present**. The capitalization period ends when the asset is substantially complete and ready for its intended use.

Amount to Capitalize

The amount of interest to be capitalized is limited to the lower of actual interest cost incurred during the period or avoidable interest. **Avoidable interest** is the amount of interest cost during the period that theoretically could have been avoided if expenditures for the asset had not been made. If the actual interest cost for the period is $90,000 and the avoidable interest is $80,000, only $80,000 is capitalized. Or, if the actual interest cost is $80,000 and the avoidable interest is $90,000, only $80,000 is capitalized. In no situation should interest cost include a cost of capital charge for stockholders' equity. And, interest capitalization is required for a qualifying asset only if its effect, compared with the effect of expensing interest, is material.[3]

To apply the avoidable interest concept, the potential amount of interest that may be capitalized during an accounting period is determined by multiplying the interest rate(s) by the **weighted-average accumulated expenditures** for qualifying assets during the period.

Weighted-Average Accumulated Expenditures. In computing the weighted-average accumulated expenditures, the construction expenditures are weighted by the amount of time (fraction of a year or accounting period) that interest cost could be incurred on the expenditure. To illustrate, assume a 17-month bridge construction project with current-year payments to the contractor of $240,000 on March 1, $480,000 on July 1, and $360,000 on November 1. The weighted-average accumulated expenditures for the year ended December 31 are computed as follows:

ILLUSTRATION 10-2
Computation of Weighted-Average Accumulated Expenditures

Expenditures					
Date	Amount	×	Capitalization Period*	=	Weighted-Average Accumulated Expenditures
March 1	$ 240,000		10/12		$200,000
July 1	480,000		6/12		240,000
November 1	360,000		2/12		60,000
	$1,080,000				$500,000

*Months between date of expenditure and date interest capitalization stops or end of year, whichever comes first (in this case December 31).

To compute the weighted-average accumulated expenditures, we weight the expenditures by the amount of time that interest cost could be incurred on each one. For the March 1 expenditure a 10 months' interest cost can be associated with the expenditure, whereas for the expenditure on July 1, only 6 months' interest costs can be incurred, and for the expenditure made on November 1, only 2 months of interest cost is incurred.

Interest Rates. The principles to be used in selecting the appropriate interest rates to be applied to the weighted-average accumulated expenditures are:

1. For the portion of weighted-average accumulated expenditures that is less than or equal to any amounts borrowed specifically to finance construction of the assets, **use the interest rate incurred on the specific borrowings.**
2. For the portion of weighted-average accumulated expenditures that is greater than any debt incurred specifically to finance construction of the assets, **use a weighted average of interest rates incurred on all other outstanding debt during the period.**[4]

An illustration of the computation of a weighted-average interest rate for debt greater than the amount incurred specifically to finance construction of the assets is shown in Illustration 10-3 on the next page.

Comprehensive Illustration of Interest Capitalization

To illustrate the issues related to interest capitalization, assume that on November 1, 2000, Shalla Company contracted with Pfeifer Construction Co. to have a building con-

[3]Ibid., summary paragraph.

[4]The interest rate to be used may be based exclusively on an average rate of all the borrowings, if desired. For our purposes, we will use the specific borrowing rate followed by the average interest rate because we believe it to be more conceptually consistent. Either method can be used; *FASB Statement No. 34* does not provide explicit guidance on this measurement. For a discussion of this issue and others related to interest capitalization, see Kathryn M. Means and Paul M. Kazenski, "SFAS 34: Recipe for Diversity," *Accounting Horizons,* September 1988; and Wendy A. Duffy, "A Graphical Analysis of Interest Capitalization," *Journal of Accounting Education,* Fall 1990.

ILLUSTRATION 10-3
Computation of Weighted-Average Interest Rate

	Principal	Interest
12%, 2-year note	$ 600,000	$ 72,000
9%, 10-year bonds	2,000,000	180,000
7.5%, 20-year bonds	5,000,000	375,000
	$7,600,000	$627,000

$$\text{Weighted-average interest rate} = \frac{\text{Total interest}}{\text{Total principal}} = \frac{\$627,000}{\$7,600,000} = 8.25\%$$

structed for $1,400,000 on land costing $100,000 (purchased from the contractor and included in the first payment). Shalla made the following payments to the construction company during 2001:

January 1	March 1	May 1	December 31	Total
$210,000	$300,000	$540,000	$450,000	$1,500,000

Construction was completed and the building was ready for occupancy on December 31, 2001. Shalla Company had the following debt outstanding at December 31, 2001:

Specific Construction Debt

1. 15%, 3-year note to finance purchase of land and construction of the building, dated December 31, 2000, with interest payable annually on December 31 — $750,000

Other Debt

2. 10%, 5-year note payable, dated December 31, 1997, with interest payable annually on December 31 — $550,000
3. 12%, 10-year bonds issued December 31, 1996, with interest payable annually on December 31 — $600,000

The weighted-average accumulated expenditures during 2001 are computed as follows:

ILLUSTRATION 10-4
Computation of Weighted-Average Accumulated Expenditures

Expenditures		×	Current Year Capitalization	=	Weighted-Average
Date	Amount		Period*		Accumulated Expenditures
January 1	$ 210,000		12/12		$210,000
March 1	300,000		10/12		250,000
May 1	540,000		8/12		360,000
December 31	450,000		0		0
	$1,500,000				$820,000

Note that the expenditure made on December 31, the last day of the year, does not have any interest cost.

The avoidable interest is computed as follows:

ILLUSTRATION 10-5
Computation of Avoidable Interest

Weighted-Average Accumulated Expenditures	×	Interest Rate	=	Avoidable Interest
$750,000		.15 (construction note)		$112,500
70,000[a]		.1104 (weighted average of other debt)[b]		7,728
$820,000				$120,228

[a]The amount by which the weighted-average accumulated expenditures exceeds the specific construction loan.

[b]Weighted-average interest rate computation:

	Principal	Interest
10%, 5-year note	$ 550,000	$ 55,000
12%, 10-year bonds	600,000	72,000
	$1,150,000	$127,000

$$\text{Weighted-average interest rate} = \frac{\text{Total interest}}{\text{Total principal}} = \frac{\$127,000}{\$1,150,000} = 11.04\%$$

The actual interest cost, which represents the maximum amount of interest that may be capitalized during 2001, is computed as shown below.

Construction note	$750,000 × .15	=	$112,500
5-year note	$550,000 × .10	=	55,000
10-year bonds	$600,000 × .12	=	72,000
Actual interest			$239,500

ILLUSTRATION 10-6
Computation of Actual Interest Cost

The interest cost to be capitalized is the lesser of $120,228 (avoidable interest) or $239,500 (actual interest), which is $120,228.

The journal entries made by Shalla Company during 2001 would be as follows:

	Debit	Credit
January 1		
Land	100,000	
Building (or Construction in Process)	110,000	
Cash		210,000
March 1		
Building	300,000	
Cash		300,000
May 1		
Building	540,000	
Cash		540,000
December 31		
Building	450,000	
Cash		450,000
Building (Capitalized Interest)	120,228	
Interest Expense ($239,500 − $120,228)	119,272	
Cash ($112,500 + $55,000 + $72,000)		239,500

Capitalized interest cost should be written off as part of depreciation over the useful life of the assets involved and not over the term of the debt. The total interest cost incurred during the period should be disclosed, with the portion charged to expense and the portion capitalized indicated.

At December 31, 2001, Shalla would disclose the amount of interest capitalized either as part of the nonoperating section of the income statement or in the notes accompanying the financial statements. Both forms of disclosure are illustrated below.

Income from operations		XXXX
Other expenses and losses:		
Interest expense	$239,500	
Less: Capitalized interest	120,228	119,272
Income before taxes on income		XXXX
Income taxes		XXX
Net income		XXXX

ILLUSTRATION 10-7
Capitalized Interest Reported in the Income Statement

Note 1: Accounting Policies. *Capitalized Interest.* During 2001 total interest cost was $239,500, of which $120,228 was capitalized and $119,272 was charged to expense.

ILLUSTRATION 10-8
Capitalized Interest Disclosed in a Note

Special Issues Related to Interest Capitalization

Three issues related to interest capitalization merit special attention:

1. Expenditures for land.
2. Interest revenue.
3. Significance of interest capitalization.

Expenditures for Land. When land is purchased with the intention of developing it for a particular use, interest costs associated with those expenditures qualify for interest capitalization. If land is purchased as a site for a structure (such as a plant site), interest costs capitalized during the period of construction are part of the cost of the plant, not the land. In the Shalla illustration where land was acquired for a structure, all interest costs capitalized (including those related to land expenditures) should be allocated to the cost of the building. Conversely, if land is being developed for lot sales, any capitalized interest cost should be part of the acquisition cost of the developed land. However, interest costs involved in purchasing land held **for speculation** should **not** be capitalized because the asset is ready for its intended use.

Interest Revenue. Companies frequently borrow money to finance construction of assets and temporarily invest the excess borrowed funds in interest-bearing securities until the funds are needed to pay for construction. During the early stages of construction, interest revenue earned may exceed the interest cost incurred on the borrowed funds.

The question is whether it is appropriate to offset interest revenue against interest cost when determining the amount of interest to be capitalized as a part of the construction cost of assets. According to *FASB Statement No. 62* on capitalization of interest cost, **interest revenue should not be netted or offset against interest cost**, except in cases involving externally restricted tax exempt borrowings. Temporary or short-term investment decisions are not related to the interest incurred as part of the acquisition cost of assets. Therefore, the interest incurred on qualifying assets should be capitalized whether or not excess funds are temporarily invested in short-term securities. Some are critical of this accounting because a company can defer the interest cost but report the interest revenue in the current period.

Significance of Interest Capitalization. The requirement of interest capitalization can have a substantive impact on the financial statements of business enterprises. When **Jim Walter Corporation**'s earnings dropped from $1.51 to $1.17 per share, the building manufacturer, looking for ways to regain its profitability, was able to pick up an additional 11 cents per share by capitalizing the interest on coal mining projects and several plants under construction.

Public utilities have been permitted to capitalize interest during construction (whether actual or imputed) for many years.[5] For example, at one time it was estimated that **Duke Power**'s net income of $58.5 million would be reduced by more than 85% if capitalized interest costs were shown as an expense. As shown in Illustration 10-9, **Anadarko Petroleum Corporation** capitalized nearly 30 percent of its total interest costs in a recent year.

ILLUSTRATION 10-9
Disclosure of Interest Costs

ANADARKO PETROLEUM CORPORATION

Financial Footnotes

Total interest costs incurred during the year were $82,415,000. Of this amount, the Company capitalized $24,716,000. Capitalized interest is included as part of the cost of oil and gas properties. The capitalization rates are based on the Company's weighted-average cost of borrowings used to finance the expenditures.

[5]Nonutility companies traditionally had not capitalized any interest cost during construction, whether actual or imputed. In the early 1970s, however, a number of companies decided to do so. The reason for this switch was to prevent the decline in earnings that resulted when an enterprise expensed these interest costs. In 1974, the SEC in *ASR No. 163* declared a temporary moratorium on the capitalization of interest costs for most nonutility companies, indicating that these practices were leading to noncomparability of financial data. In 1979, the FASB finally standardized accounting for interest costs during construction.

Public utility companies are allowed to include in the costs of additions to plant and equipment an "allowance for funds used during construction" (AFUDC) in conformity with Federal Energy Regulatory Commission pronouncements. AFUDC includes not only interest on borrowed funds but also an **imputed interest on equity funds** used during construction.

The interest capitalization requirement, while now universally adopted, is still debated. From a conceptual viewpoint, many believe that either no interest cost should be capitalized or all interest costs, actual or imputed, should be capitalized for the reasons mentioned earlier in this section.

VALUATION

We have seen that **an asset should be recorded at the fair market value of what is given up or the fair value of the asset received, whichever is more clearly evident.** Fair market value, however, is sometimes obscured by the process through which the asset is acquired. As an example, assume that land and buildings are bought together for one price. How are separate values for the land and building determined? A number of accounting problems of this nature are examined in the following sections.

OBJECTIVE 5
Understand accounting issues related to acquiring and valuing plant assets.

Cash Discounts

When plant assets are purchased subject to cash discounts for prompt payment, how should the discount be reported? If the discount is taken, it should be considered a reduction in the purchase price of the asset. What is not clear, however, is whether a reduction in the asset cost should occur even if the discount is not taken.

Two points of view exist on this matter. Under one approach, the discount, whether taken or not, is considered a reduction in the cost of the asset. The rationale for this approach is that the real cost of the asset is the cash or cash equivalent price of the asset. In addition, some argue that the terms of cash discounts are so attractive that failure to take them indicates management error or inefficiency. Proponents of the other approach argue that the discount should not always be considered a loss because the terms may be unfavorable or because it might not be prudent for the company to take the discount. At present, both methods are employed in practice. The former method is generally preferred.

Deferred Payment Contracts

Plant assets are purchased frequently on long-term credit contracts through the use of notes, mortgages, bonds, or equipment obligations. **To properly reflect cost, assets purchased on long-term credit contracts should be accounted for at the present value of the consideration exchanged between the contracting parties at the date of the transaction.** For example, an asset purchased today in exchange for a $10,000 zero-interest-bearing note payable 4 years from now should not be recorded at $10,000. The present value of the $10,000 note establishes the exchange price of the transaction (the purchase price of the asset). Assuming an appropriate interest rate of 12% at which to discount this single payment of $10,000 due 4 years from now, this asset should be recorded at $6,355.20 [$10,000 × .63552; see Table 6-2 for the present value of a single sum, $PV =$ $10,000 ($PVF_{4,12\%}$)].

When no interest rate is stated, or if the specified rate is unreasonable, an appropriate interest rate must be imputed. The objective is to approximate the interest rate that the buyer and seller would negotiate at arm's length in a similar borrowing transaction. Factors to be considered in imputing an interest rate are the borrower's credit rating, the amount and maturity date of the note, and prevailing interest rates. If determinable, the cash exchange price of the asset acquired should be used as the basis for recording the asset and measuring the interest element.

To illustrate, Sutter Company purchases a specially built robot spray painter for its production line. The company issues a $100,000, 5-year, zero-interest-bearing note to Wrigley Robotics, Inc. for the new equipment when the prevailing market rate of interest for obligations of this nature is 10%. Sutter is to pay off the note in five $20,000 installments made at the end of each year. The fair market value of this specially built robot is not readily determinable and must therefore be approximated by establishing the market value (present value) of the note. Computation of the present value of the note and the date of purchase and dates of payment entries are as follows:

Date of Purchase

Equipment	75,816*	
Discount on Notes Payable	24,184	
Notes Payable		100,000

*Present value of note = $20,000 ($PVF\text{-}OA_{5,10\%}$)
= $20,000 (3.79079) Table 6-4
= $75,816

End of First Year

Interest Expense	7,582	
Notes Payable	20,000	
Cash		20,000
Discount on Notes Payable		7,582

Interest expense in the first year under the effective interest approach is $7,582 [($100,000 − $24,184) × 10%]. The entry at the end of the second year to record interest and principal payment is as follows:

End of Second Year

Interest Expense	6,340	
Notes Payable	20,000	
Cash		20,000
Discount on Notes Payable		6,340

Interest expense in the second year under the effective interest approach is $6,340 [($100,000 − $24,184) − ($20,000 − $7,582)] × 10%.

If an interest rate were not imputed for such deferred payment contracts, the asset would be recorded at an amount greater than its fair value. In addition, interest expense reported in the income statement would be understated for all periods involved.

Lump Sum Purchase

A special problem of pricing fixed assets arises when a group of plant assets is purchased at a single **lump sum price**. When such a situation occurs, and it is not at all unusual, the practice is to allocate the total cost among the various assets on the basis of their relative fair market values. The assumption is that costs will vary in direct proportion to sales value. This is the same principle that is applied to allocate a lump sum cost among different inventory items.

To determine fair market value, any of the following might be used: an appraisal for insurance purposes, the assessed valuation for property taxes, or simply an independent appraisal by an engineer or other appraiser.

To illustrate, Norduct Homes, Inc. decides to purchase several assets of a small heating concern, Comfort Heating, for $80,000. Comfort Heating is in the process of liquidation, and its assets sold are:

	Book Value	Fair Market Value
Inventory	$30,000	$ 25,000
Land	20,000	25,000
Building	35,000	50,000
	$85,000	$100,000

The $80,000 purchase price would be allocated on the basis of the relative fair market values (assuming specific identification of costs is not practicable) in the following manner:

Inventory	$\frac{\$25{,}000}{\$100{,}000} \times \$80{,}000 = \$20{,}000$	
Land	$\frac{\$25{,}000}{\$100{,}000} \times \$80{,}000 = \$20{,}000$	
Building	$\frac{\$50{,}000}{\$100{,}000} \times \$80{,}000 = \$40{,}000$	

ILLUSTRATION 10-10
Allocation of Purchase Price—Relative Fair Market Value Basis

Issuance of Stock

When property is acquired by issuance of securities, such as common stock, the cost of the property is not properly measured by the par or stated value of such stock. If the stock is being actively traded, **the market value of the stock issued is a fair indication of the cost of the property acquired because the stock is a good measure of the current cash equivalent price.**

For example, Upgrade Living Co. decides to purchase some adjacent land for expansion of its carpeting and cabinet operation. In lieu of paying cash for the land, the company issues to Deedland Company 5,000 shares of common stock (par value $10) that have a fair market value of $12 per share. Upgrade Living Co. would make the following entry.

Land (5,000 × $12)	60,000	
Common Stock		50,000
Additional Paid-In Capital		10,000

If the market value of the common stock exchanged is not determinable, the market value of the property should be established and used as the basis for recording the asset and issuance of the common stock.[6]

Exchanges of Nonmonetary Assets

The proper accounting for exchanges of nonmonetary assets (such as inventories and property, plant, and equipment) is controversial.[7] Some argue that the accounting for these types of exchanges should be based on the fair value of the asset given up or the fair value of the asset received, with a gain or loss recognized. Others believe that the accounting should be based on the recorded amount (book value) of the asset given up, with no gain or loss recognized. Still others favor an approach that would recognize losses in all cases, but defer gains in special situations.

Ordinarily accounting for the exchange of **nonmonetary assets** should be based on **the fair value of the asset given up or the fair value of the asset received, whichever is clearly more evident.**[8] Thus, any gains or losses on the exchange **should be recognized immediately**. The rationale for such immediate recognition is that the earnings process related to these assets is completed and, therefore, a gain or loss should be recognized. This approach is always employed when the assets are **dissimilar** in nature, such as the exchange of computers for a truck, or the exchange of equipment for inventory. If the fair value of either asset is not reasonably determinable, the book value of the asset given up is usually used as the basis for recording the nonmonetary exchange.

[6]When the fair market value of the stock is used as the basis of valuation, careful consideration must be given to the effect that the issuance of additional shares will have on the existing market price. Where the effect on market price appears significant, an independent appraisal of the asset received should be made. This valuation should be employed as the basis for valuation of the asset as well as for the stock issued. In the unusual case where the fair market value of the stock or the fair market value of the asset cannot be determined objectively, the board of directors of the corporation may set the value.

[7]Nonmonetary assets are items whose price in terms of the monetary unit may change over time, whereas monetary assets—cash and short- or long-term accounts and notes receivable—are fixed in terms of units of currency by contract or otherwise.

[8]"Accounting for Nonmonetary Transactions," *Opinions of the Accounting Principles Board No. 29* (New York: AICPA, 1973), par 18.

The general rule of immediate recognition is modified when exchanges of **similar** nonmonetary assets occur for gain situations. For example, when a company exchanges its inventory items with inventory of another company because of color, size, etc. to facilitate sale to an outside customer, the earnings process is not considered completed and a **gain** should not be recognized. Likewise if a company trades **similar productive assets** such as land for land or equipment for equipment, the earnings process is not considered complete and, therefore, **a gain should not be recognized**. However, if the exchange transaction involving **similar assets** would result in a loss, **the loss is recognized immediately**.

In certain situations, gains on exchange of similar nonmonetary assets may be recognized where **monetary consideration (boot)** is received. When monetary consideration such as cash is received in addition to the nonmonetary asset, it is assumed that a portion of the earnings process is completed and, therefore, a partial gain is recognized (see footnote 9).[9] The alternative exchange situations are summarized in Illustration 10-11.

ILLUSTRATION 10-11
Accounting for Exchanges

Type of Exchange	Accounting Guidance	Rationale
Dissimilar assets	Recognize gains and losses immediately.	Earnings process is complete.
Similar assets — No cash received	Defer gains; recognize losses immediately.	Earnings process is not complete.
Similar assets — Cash received	Recognize partial gain; recognize losses immediately.* *If cash is 25% or more of the fair value of the exchange, recognize entire gain because earnings process is complete.	Earnings process is partially complete.*

To illustrate the accounting for these different types of transactions, we will look at the following three situations:

1. Accounting for dissimilar assets.
2. Accounting for similar assets—loss situation.
3. Accounting for similar assets—gain situation.

Dissimilar Assets

The cost of a nonmonetary asset acquired in exchange for a **dissimilar nonmonetary asset** is usually recorded at the **fair value of the asset given up**, and a gain or loss is recognized. The **fair value of the asset received** should be used only if it is more clearly evident than the fair value of the asset given up.

[9]When the monetary consideration is significant, i.e., **25% or more** of the fair value of the exchange, the transaction is considered a **monetary exchange** by both parties. In such "monetary" exchanges the fair values are used to measure the gains or losses that are recognized in their entirety. *EITF Issue No. 86-29,* "Nonmonetary Transactions: Magnitude of Boot and the Exception to the Use of Fair Value," *Emerging Issues Task Force Abstracts* (October 1, 1987).

To illustrate, Interstate Transportation Company exchanged a number of used trucks plus cash for vacant land that might be used for a future plant site. The trucks have a combined book value of $42,000 (cost $64,000 less $22,000 accumulated depreciation). Interstate's purchasing agent, who has had previous dealings in the second-hand market, indicates that the trucks have a fair market value of $49,000. In addition to the trucks, Interstate must pay $17,000 cash for the land. The cost of the land to Interstate is $66,000 computed as follows:

ILLUSTRATION 10-12
Computation of Land Cost

Fair value of trucks exchanged	$49,000
Cash paid	17,000
Cost of land	$66,000

The journal entry to record the exchange transaction is:

Land	66,000	
Accumulated Depreciation—Trucks	22,000	
Trucks		64,000
Gain on Disposal of Trucks		7,000
Cash		17,000

The gain is the difference between the fair value of the trucks and their book value. It is verified as follows:

ILLUSTRATION 10-13
Computation of Gain on Disposal of Used Trucks

Fair value of trucks		$49,000
Cost of trucks	$64,000	
Less: Accumulated depreciation	22,000	
Book value of trucks		42,000
Gain on disposal of used trucks		$ 7,000

It follows that if the fair value of the trucks was $39,000 instead of $49,000, a loss on the exchange of $3,000 ($42,000 − $39,000) would be reported. In either case, as a result of the exchange of dissimilar assets, the earnings process on the used trucks has been completed and **a gain or loss should be recognized**.

Similar Assets—Loss Situation

Similar nonmonetary assets are those that are of the same general type, or that perform the same function, or that are employed in the same line of business. When similar nonmonetary assets are exchanged and a loss results, the loss should be recognized immediately. For example, Information Processing, Inc. trades its used machine for a new model. The machine given up has a book value of $8,000 (original cost $12,000 less $4,000 accumulated depreciation) and a fair value of $6,000. It is traded for a new model that has a list price of $16,000. In negotiations with the seller, a trade-in allowance of $9,000 is finally agreed on for the used machine. The cash payment that must be made for the new asset and the cost of the new machine are computed as follows:

ILLUSTRATION 10-14
Computation of Cost of New Machine

List price of new machine	$16,000
Less: Trade-in allowance for used machine	9,000
Cash payment due	7,000
Fair value of used machine	6,000
Cost of new machine	$13,000

The journal entry to record this transaction is:

Equipment	13,000	
Accumulated Depreciation—Equipment	4,000	
Loss on Disposal of Equipment	2,000	
Equipment		12,000
Cash		7,000

The loss on the disposal of the used machine can be verified as follows:

ILLUSTRATION 10-15
Computation of Loss on Disposal of Used Machine

Fair value of used machine	$6,000
Book value of used machine	8,000
Loss on disposal of used machine	$2,000

Why was the trade-in allowance or the book value of the old asset not used as a basis for the new equipment? The trade-in allowance is not used because it included a price concession (similar to a price discount) to the purchaser. Few individuals pay list price for a new car. Trade-in allowances on the used car are often inflated so that actual selling prices are below list prices. To record the car at list price would state it at an amount in excess of its cash equivalent price because the new car's list price is usually inflated. Use of book value in this situation would overstate the value of the new machine by $2,000. Because assets should not be valued at more than their cash equivalent price, the loss should be recognized immediately rather than added to the cost of the newly acquired asset.

Similar Assets—Gain Situation, No Cash Received

The accounting treatment for exchanges of **similar** nonmonetary assets when a gain develops is more complex. If the exchange does not complete the earnings process, then any **gain should be deferred.**

The real estate industry provides a good example of why the accounting profession decided not to recognize gains on exchanges of similar nonmonetary assets. In this industry, it is common practice for companies to "swap" real estate holdings. Assume that Landmark Company and Hillfarm, Inc. each had undeveloped land on which they intended to build shopping centers. Appraisals indicated that the land of both companies had increased significantly in value. The companies decided to exchange (swap) their undeveloped land, record a gain, and report their new parcels of land at current fair values. But, should gains be recognized at this point? No: the earnings process is not completed because the companies remain in the same economic position after the swap as before. Therefore, the asset acquired should be recorded at book value with no gain recognized. In contrast, had book value exceeded fair value, a loss would be recognized immediately.

Davis Rent-A-Car has a rental fleet of automobiles consisting primarily of Ford Motor Company products. Davis' management is interested in increasing the variety of automobiles in its rental fleet by adding numerous General Motors models. Davis arranges with Nertz Rent-A-Car to exchange a group of Ford automobiles with a fair value of $160,000 and a book value of $135,000 (cost $150,000 less accumulated depreciation $15,000) for a number of Chevy and Pontiac models with a fair value of $170,000; Davis pays $10,000 in cash in addition to the Ford automobiles exchanged. The total gain to Davis Rent-A-Car is computed as shown in Illustration 10-16.

ILLUSTRATION 10-16
Computation of Gain (Unrecognized)

Fair value of Ford automobiles exchanged	$160,000
Book value of Ford automobiles exchanged	135,000
Total gain (unrecognized)	$ 25,000

But the earnings process is not considered completed in this transaction. The company still has a fleet of cars, although different models. Therefore, the total gain is deferred and the basis of the General Motors automobiles is reduced via two different but acceptable computations as shown below:

Fair value of GM automobiles	$170,000	OR	Book value of Ford automobiles	$135,000
Less: Gain deferred	(25,000)		Cash paid	10,000
Basis of GM automobiles	$145,000		Basis of GM automobiles	$145,000

ILLUSTRATION 10-17
Basis of New Automobiles—Fair Value vs. Book Value

The entry by Davis to record this transaction is as follows:

Automobiles (GM)	145,000	
Accumulated Depreciation—Automobiles	15,000	
Automobiles (Ford)		150,000
Cash		10,000

The gain that reduced the basis of the new automobiles will be recognized when those automobiles are sold to an outside party. While these automobiles are held, depreciation charges will be lower and net income will be higher in subsequent periods because of the reduced basis.

Similar Assets—Gain Situation, Some Cash Received

The accounting issue of gain recognition becomes more difficult if monetary consideration such as cash is **received** in an exchange of similar nonmonetary assets. When cash is received, part of the nonmonetary asset is considered sold and part exchanged; therefore, only a portion of the gain is deferred. The general formula for gain recognition when some cash is received is as follows:

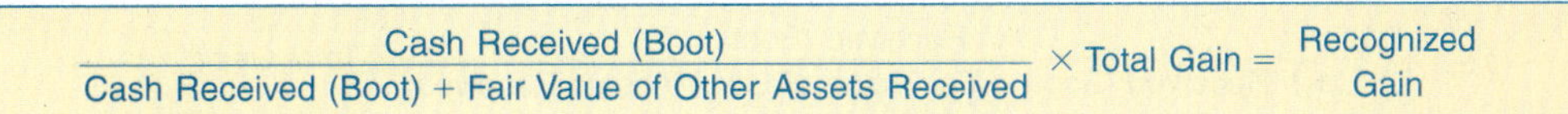

$$\frac{\text{Cash Received (Boot)}}{\text{Cash Received (Boot)} + \text{Fair Value of Other Assets Received}} \times \text{Total Gain} = \text{Recognized Gain}$$

ILLUSTRATION 10-18
Formula for Gain Recognition, Some Cash Received

If the book value of Nertz's Chevy and Pontiac automobiles exchanged in the foregoing example is $136,000 (cost $200,000 less accumulated depreciation $64,000), then the total gain on the exchange to Nertz would be computed as follows:

Fair value of GM automobiles exchanged	$170,000
Book value of GM automobiles exchanged	136,000
Total gain	$ 34,000

ILLUSTRATION 10-19
Computation of Total Gain

But, because Nertz received $10,000 in cash, the recognized gain on this transaction is computed as follows:

$$\frac{\$10{,}000}{\$10{,}000 + \$160{,}000} \times \$34{,}000 = \$2{,}000$$

ILLUSTRATION 10-20
Computation of Recognized Gain Based on Ratio of Cash Received

The ratio of monetary assets ($10,000) to the total consideration received ($10,000 + $160,000) is the portion of the total gain ($34,000) to be recognized—that is, $2,000. Because only a gain of $2,000 is recognized on this transaction, the remaining $32,000 ($34,000 − $2,000) is deferred and reduces the basis (recorded cost) of the new automobiles. The computation of the basis is as follows:

Fair value of Ford automobiles	$160,000	OR	Book value of GM automobiles	$136,000
Less: Gain deferred	(32,000)		Portion of book value presumed sold	(8,000)*
Basis of Ford automobiles	$128,000		Basis of Ford automobiles	$128,000

$^{*}\ \dfrac{\$10{,}000}{\$170{,}000} \times \$136{,}000 = \$8{,}000$

ILLUSTRATION 10-21
Basis of New Automobiles—Fair Value vs. Book Value

The entry by Nertz to record this transaction is as follows:

Cash	10,000	
Automobiles (Ford)	128,000	
Accumulated Depreciation—Automobiles (GM)	64,000	
Automobiles (GM)		200,000
Gain on Disposal of GM Automobiles		2,000

The rationale for this treatment is as follows: Before the exchange, Nertz Rent-A-Car had an unrecognized gain of $34,000, as evidenced by the difference between the book value ($136,000) and the fair value ($170,000) of its GM automobiles. When the exchange occurred, a portion ($10,000/$170,000 or 1/17) of the fair value was converted to a more liquid asset. The ratio of this liquid asset ($10,000) to the total consideration received ($160,000 + $10,000) is the portion of the gain ($34,000) realized. Thus, a gain of $2,000 (1/17 × $34,000) is recognized and recorded.

Presented below in summary form are the accounting requirements for recognizing gains and losses on exchanges of nonmonetary assets.[10]

ILLUSTRATION 10-22
Summary of Gain and Loss Recognition on Exchanges of Nonmonetary Assets

1. Compute the total gain or loss on the transaction, which is equal to the difference between the fair value of the asset given up and the book value of the asset given up.
2. If a loss is computed in 1, always recognize the entire loss.
3. If a gain is computed in 1,
   (a) and the earnings process is considered completed, the entire gain is recognized (dissimilar assets).
   (b) and the earnings process is not considered completed (similar assets),
      (1) and no cash is involved, no gain is recognized.
      (2) and some cash is given, no gain is recognized.
      (3) and some cash is received, the following portion of the gain is recognized:

$$\frac{\text{Cash Received (Boot)}}{\text{Cash Received (Boot)} + \text{Fair Value of Other Assets Received}} \times \text{Total Gain*}$$

*If the amount of cash exchanged is 25% or more, recognize entire gain.

An enterprise that engages in one or more nonmonetary exchanges during a period should disclose in financial statements for the period the nature of the transactions, the method of accounting for the assets transferred, and gains or losses recognized on transfers.[11]

Accounting for Contributions

Companies sometimes receive or make contributions (donations or gifts). Such contributions are referred to as **nonreciprocal transfers** because they are transfers of assets in one direction. A contribution is often some type of asset (such as cash, securities, land, buildings, or use of facilities), but it also could be the forgiveness of a debt.

When assets are acquired as a donation, a strict cost concept dictates that the valuation of the asset should be zero. A departure from the cost principle seems justified, however, because the only costs incurred (legal fees and other relatively minor expenditures) do not constitute a reasonable basis of accounting for the assets acquired. To record nothing is to ignore the economic realities of an increase in wealth and assets. Therefore, **the fair value of the asset should be used to establish its value on the books**.

Two general approaches have been used to record the credit for the asset received. Some believe the credit should be to Donated Capital (an additional paid-in capital account). The increase in assets is viewed more as contributed capital than as earned rev-

[10]Adapted from an article by Robert Capettini and Thomas E. King, "Exchanges of Nonmonetary Assets: Some Changes," *The Accounting Review,* January 1976.

[11]"Accounting for Nonmonetary Transactions," op. cit., par. 28.

enue. Others argue that capital is contributed only by the owners of the business and that donations are benefits to the enterprise that should be reported as revenues from contributions. At issue is whether the revenue should be reported immediately or over the period that the asset is employed. To attract new industry a city may offer land, but the receiving enterprise may incur additional costs in the future (transportation, higher state income taxes, etc.) because the location is not the most desirable. As a consequence, some argue that the revenue should be deferred and recognized as the costs are incurred.

In a recent standard, the FASB has taken the position that, **in general, contributions received should be recognized as revenues in the period received.**[12] Contributions would be measured at the fair value of the assets received.[13] To illustrate, Max Wayer Meat Packing, Inc. has recently accepted a donation of land with a fair value of $150,000 from the Memphis Industrial Development Corp. in return for a promise to build a packing plant in Memphis. Max Wayer's entry is:

Land	150,000	
Contribution Revenue		150,000

When a nonmonetary asset is contributed, the amount of the donation should be recorded as an expense at the fair value of the donated asset. If a difference exists between the fair value of the asset and its book value, a gain or loss should be recognized. To illustrate, Kline Industries donates land that cost $80,000 and has a fair market value of $110,000 to the city of Los Angeles for a city park. The entry to record this donation would be:

Contribution Expense	110,000	
Land		80,000
Gain on Disposal of Land		30,000

In some cases, companies will promise to give (pledge) some type of asset in the future. The question is whether this promise should be recorded immediately or at the time the assets are given. If the promise is **unconditional** (depends only on the passage of time or on demand by the recipient for performance), the contribution expense and related payable should be reported. If the promise is **conditional**, the expense is recognized in the period benefited by the contribution, which is generally when the asset is transferred.

Other Asset Valuation Methods

As indicated above, an exception to the historical cost principle arises in the acquisition of plant assets through donation, which is based on fair value. Another approach that is sometimes allowed and not considered a violation of historical cost is a concept often referred to as **prudent cost**. This concept states that if for some reason you were ignorant about a certain price and paid too much for the asset originally, it is theoretically preferable to charge a loss immediately.

As an example, assume that a company constructs an asset at a cost substantially in excess of its present economic usefulness. In this case, it would be appropriate to charge these excess costs as a loss to the current period, rather than capitalize them as part of the cost of the asset. This problem seldom develops because at the outset individuals either use good reasoning in paying a given price or fail to recognize any such errors.

[12]"Accounting for Contributions Received and Contributions Made," *Statement of Financial Accounting Standards No. 116* (Norwalk, Conn.: FASB, 1993). Transfers of assets from governmental units to business enterprises are excluded from the scope of this standard. However, we believe that the basic requirements should hold also for these types of contributions, and therefore all assets should be recorded at fair value and all credits should be recorded as revenue.

[13]"Accounting for Nonmonetary Transactions," op. cit., par. 18. Also, *FASB No. 116* indicates that expenses on contributions made should be recorded at the fair value of the assets given up.

On the other hand, a purchase that is obtained at a bargain, or a piece of equipment internally constructed at a cost savings, should not result in immediate recognition of a gain under any circumstances. Although immediate recognition of a gain is conceptually appealing, the implications of such a treatment would be to change completely the entire basis of accounting.

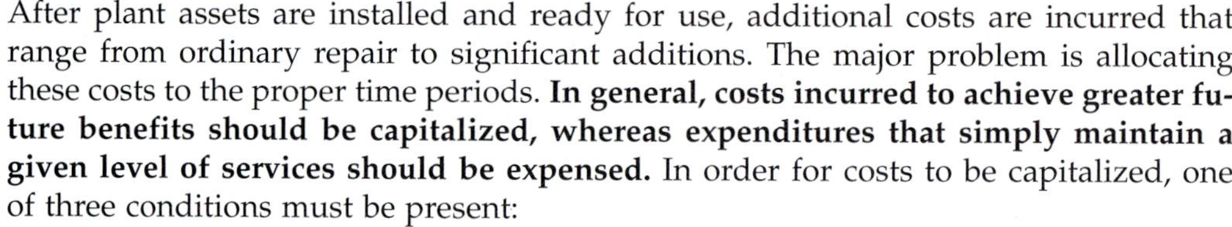

COSTS SUBSEQUENT TO ACQUISITION

OBJECTIVE 6
Describe the accounting treatment for costs subsequent to acquisition.

After plant assets are installed and ready for use, additional costs are incurred that range from ordinary repair to significant additions. The major problem is allocating these costs to the proper time periods. **In general, costs incurred to achieve greater future benefits should be capitalized, whereas expenditures that simply maintain a given level of services should be expensed.** In order for costs to be capitalized, one of three conditions must be present:

1. The useful life of the asset must be increased.
2. The quantity of units produced from the asset must be increased.
3. The quality of the units produced must be enhanced.

Expenditures that do not increase an asset's future benefits should be expensed. Ordinary repairs are expenditures that maintain the existing condition of the asset or restore it to normal operating efficiency and should be expensed immediately.

UNDERLYING CONCEPTS

Expensing long-lived ash trays and waste baskets is an application of the materiality constraint.

Most expenditures below an established arbitrary minimum amount are expensed rather than capitalized. Many enterprises have adopted the rule that expenditures below, say, $100 or $500, should always be expensed. Although conceptually this treatment may not be correct, expediency demands it. Otherwise, depreciation schedules would have to be set up for such items as wastepaper baskets and ash trays.

The distinction between a **capital (asset) expenditure** and a **revenue (expense) expenditure** is not always clear-cut. Determining the **property unit** with which costs should be associated is critical. If a fully equipped steamship is considered a property unit, then replacement of the engine might be considered an expense. On the other hand, if the ship's engine is considered a property unit, then its replacement would be capitalized. **AT&T** at one time argued that it should be permitted to expense its station connectors (wires that connect your telephone to the outside wall). Previously, these wires had been capitalized and depreciated over an 8-year period. AT&T argued that continual home occupancy changes resulted in so much rewiring that expensing these wires was more appropriate. The Federal Communications Commission approved this request, and the cost of wiring is now expensed. This decision is significant: it was at one time estimated that the cost of phone installation in Illinois would triple as a result of this accounting change. In most cases, **consistent application of a capital/expense policy** is more important than attempting to provide general theoretical guidelines for each transaction.

Generally, four major types of expenditures are incurred relative to existing assets.

MAJOR TYPES OF EXPENDITURES

ADDITIONS. Increase or extension of existing assets.

IMPROVEMENTS AND REPLACEMENTS. Substitution of an improved asset for an existing one.

REARRANGEMENT AND REINSTALLATION. Movement of assets from one location to another.

REPAIRS. Expenditures that maintain assets in condition for operation.

Additions

Additions should present no major accounting problems. By definition, **any addition to plant assets is capitalized** because a new asset has been created. The addition of a wing to a hospital or the addition of an air conditioning system to an office, for example, increases the service potential of that facility. Such expenditures should be capitalized and matched against the revenues that will result in future periods.

The most difficult problem that develops in this area is accounting for any changes related to the existing structure as a result of the addition. Is the cost that is incurred to tear down an old wall to make room for the addition a cost of the addition or an expense or loss of the period? The answer is that it depends on the original intent. If the company had anticipated that an addition was going to be added later, then this cost of removal is a proper cost of the addition. But if the company had not anticipated this development, it should properly be reported as a loss in the current period on the basis that the company was inefficient in its planning. Normally, the carrying amount of the old wall remains in the accounts, although theoretically it should be removed.

Improvements and Replacements

Improvements (often referred to as betterments) and replacements are substitutions of one asset for another. What is the difference between an improvement and a replacement? An improvement is the substitution of a **better asset** for the one currently used (say, a concrete floor for a wooden floor). A replacement, on the other hand, is the substitution of a **similar asset** (a wooden floor for a wooden floor).

Many times improvements and replacements result from a general policy to modernize or rehabilitate an older building or piece of equipment. The problem is differentiating these types of expenditure from normal repairs. Does the expenditure increase the **future service potential** of the asset, or does it merely **maintain the existing level** of service? Frequently, the answer is not clear-cut, and good judgment must be used in order to classify these expenditures.

If it is determined that the expenditure increases the future service potential of the asset and, therefore, should be capitalized, the accounting is handled in one of three ways, depending on the circumstances.

1. ***Substitution Approach.*** Conceptually, the substitution approach is the correct procedure if the carrying amount of the old asset is available. If the carrying amount of the old asset can be determined, it is a simple matter to remove the cost of the old asset and replace it with the cost of the new asset.

   To illustrate, Instinct Enterprises decides to replace the pipes in its plumbing system. A plumber suggests that in place of the cast iron pipes and copper tubing, a newly developed plastic tubing be used. The old pipe and tubing have a book value of $15,000 (cost of $150,000 less accumulated depreciation of $135,000), and a scrap value of $1,000. The plastic tubing system has a cost of $125,000. Assuming that Instinct has to pay $124,000 for the new tubing after exchanging the old tubing, the entry is:

Plumbing System	125,000	
Accumulated Depreciation	135,000	
Loss on Disposal of Plant Assets	14,000	
Plumbing System		150,000
Cash ($125,000 − $1,000)		124,000

   The problem is determining the book value of the old asset. Generally, the components of a given asset depreciate at different rates, but no separate accounting is made. As an example, the tires, motor, and body of a truck depreciate at different rates, but most companies use only one depreciation rate for the entire truck. Separate depreciation rates could be set for each component, but it would be impractical. If the carrying amount of the old asset cannot be determined, one of two other approaches is adopted.

2. ***Capitalizing the New Cost.*** The justification for capitalizing the cost of the improvement or replacement is that even though the carrying amount of the old asset is not removed from the accounts, sufficient depreciation was taken on the item to reduce the carrying amount almost to zero. Although this assumption may not be true in every case, the differences are not often significant. Improvements are usually handled in this manner.
3. ***Charging to Accumulated Depreciation.*** There are times when the quantity or quality of the asset itself has not been improved, but its useful life has been extended. Replacements, particularly, may extend the useful life of the asset, yet may not improve its quality or quantity. In these circumstances, the expenditure may be debited to Accumulated Depreciation rather than to an asset account. The theory behind this approach is that the replacement extends the useful life of the asset and thereby recaptures some or all of the past depreciation. The net carrying amount of the asset is the same whether the asset is debited or the accumulated depreciation is debited.

Rearrangement and Reinstallation

Rearrangement and reinstallation costs, which are expenditures intended to benefit future periods, are different from additions, replacements, and improvements. An example is the rearrangement and reinstallation of a group of machines to facilitate future production. If the original installation cost and the accumulated depreciation taken to date can be determined or estimated, the rearrangement and reinstallation cost is handled as a replacement. If not, which is generally the case, the new costs (if material in amount) should be capitalized as an asset to be amortized over those future periods expected to benefit. If these costs are not material, if they cannot be separated from other operating expenses, or if their future benefit is questionable, they should be immediately expensed.

Repairs

Ordinary repairs are expenditures made to maintain plant assets in operating condition; they are charged to an expense account in the period in which they are incurred on the basis that **it is the primary period benefited**. Replacing minor parts, lubricating and adjusting equipment, repainting, and cleaning are examples of maintenance charges that occur regularly and are treated as ordinary operating expenses.

It is often difficult to distinguish a repair from an improvement or replacement. The major consideration is whether the expenditure benefits more than one year or one operating cycle, whichever is longer. If a **major repair** (such as an overhaul) occurs, several periods will benefit and the cost should be handled as an addition, improvement, or replacement.

If income statements are prepared for short periods of time, say, monthly or quarterly, the same principles apply. Ordinary repairs and other regular maintenance charges for an annual period may benefit several quarters, and allocation of the cost among the periods concerned might be required. A company will often find it advantageous to concentrate its repair program at a certain time of the year, perhaps during the period of least activity or when the plant is shut down for vacation. Short-term comparative statements might be misleading if such expenditures were shown as expenses of the quarter in which they were incurred. To give comparability to monthly or quarterly income statements, an account such as Allowance for Repairs might be used so that repair costs could be better assigned to periods benefited.

To illustrate, Cricket Tractor Company estimated that its total repair expense for the year would be $720,000. It decided to charge each quarter for a portion of the repair cost even though the total cost for the year would occur in only two quarters.

End of First Quarter (zero repair costs incurred)

Repair Expense	180,000	
Allowance for Repairs (1/4 × $720,000)		180,000

End of Second Quarter ($344,000 repair costs incurred)

Allowance for Repairs	344,000	
Cash, Wages Payable, Inventory, etc.		344,000
Repair Expense	180,000	
Allowance for Repairs (1/4 × $720,000)		180,000

End of Third Quarter (zero repair costs incurred)

Repair Expense	180,000	
Allowance for Repairs (1/4 × $720,000)		180,000

End of Fourth Quarter ($380,800 repair costs incurred)

Allowance for Repairs	380,800	
Cash, Wages Payable, Inventory, etc.		380,800
Repair Expense	184,800	
Allowance for Repairs ($344,000 + $380,800 − $180,000 − $180,000 − $180,000)		184,800

Ordinarily, no balance in the Allowance for Repairs account should be carried over to the following year. The fourth quarter would normally absorb the variation from estimates. If balance sheets are prepared during the year, the Allowance account should be added to or subtracted from the property, plant, and equipment section to obtain a proper valuation.

Some advocate accruing estimated repair costs beyond one year on the assumption that depreciation does not take into consideration the incurrence of repair costs. For example, in aircraft overhaul and open hearth furnace rebuilding, an allowance for repairs is sometimes established because the amount of repairs can be estimated with a high degree of certainty. Although conceptually appealing, it is difficult to justify the Allowance for Repairs account as a liability because one might ask, To whom do you owe the liability? Placement in the stockholders' equity section is also illogical because no addition to the stockholders' investment has taken place. One possibility might be to treat allowance for repairs as an addition to or subtraction from the asset on the basis that the value has changed. In general, expenses should not be anticipated before they arise unless estimates of the future are reasonably predictable.

Summary of Costs Subsequent to Acquisition

The following schedule summarizes the accounting treatment for various costs incurred subsequent to the acquisition of capitalized assets.

ILLUSTRATION 10-23
Summary of Costs Subsequent to Acquisition of Property, Plant, and Equipment

Type of Expenditure	Normal Accounting Treatment
Additions	Capitalize cost of addition to asset account.
Improvements and replacements	(a) **Carrying value known:** Remove cost of and accumulated depreciation on old asset, recognizing any gain or loss. Capitalize cost of improvement/replacement. (b) **Carrying value unknown:** 1. If the asset's useful life is extended, debit accumulated depreciation for cost of improvement/replacement. 2. If the quantity or quality of the asset's productivity is increased, capitalize cost of improvement/replacement to asset account.
Rearrangement and reinstallation	(a) If original installation cost is **known**, account for cost of rearrangement/reinstallation as a replacement (carrying value known). (b) If original installation cost is **unknown** and rearrangement/reinstallation cost is **material** in amount and benefits future periods, capitalize as an asset. (c) If original installation cost is **unknown** and rearrangement/reinstallation cost is **not material or future benefit is questionable**, expense the cost when incurred.
Repairs	(a) **Ordinary:** Expense cost of repairs when incurred. (b) **Major:** As appropriate, treat as an addition, improvement, or replacement.

DISPOSITIONS OF PLANT ASSETS

OBJECTIVE 7
Describe the accounting treatment for the disposal of property, plant, and equipment.

Plant assets may be retired voluntarily or disposed of by sale, exchange, involuntary conversion, or abandonment. Regardless of the time of disposal, depreciation must be taken up to the date of disposition, and then all accounts related to the retired asset should be removed. Ideally, the book value of the specific plant asset would be equal to its disposal value. But this is generally not the case. As a result, a gain or loss develops. The reason: depreciation is an estimate of cost allocation and not a process of valuation. **The gain or loss is really a correction of net income** for the years during which the fixed asset was used. If it had been possible at the time of acquisition to forecast the exact date of disposal and the amount to be realized at disposition, then a more accurate estimate of depreciation could have been recorded and no gain or loss would be incurred.

Gains or losses on the retirement of plant assets should be shown in the income statement along with other items that arise from customary business activities. If, however, the "operations of a segment of a business" are sold, abandoned, spun off, or otherwise disposed of, then the results of "continuing operations" should be reported separately from "discontinued operations." Any gain or loss from disposal of a segment of a business should be reported with the related results of discontinued operations and not as an extraordinary item.

Sale of Plant Assets

Depreciation must be recorded for the period of time between the date of the last depreciation entry and the date of sale. To illustrate, assume that depreciation on a machine costing $18,000 has been recorded for 9 years at the rate of $1,200 per year. If the machine is sold in the middle of the tenth year for $7,000, the entry to record depreciation to the date of sale is:

Depreciation Expense	600	
Accumulated Depreciation—Machinery		600

This separate entry ordinarily is not made because most companies enter all depreciation, including this amount, in one entry at the end of the year. In either case the entry for the sale of the asset is:

Cash	7,000	
Accumulated Depreciation—Machinery [($1,200 × 9) + $600]	11,400	
Machinery		18,000
Gain on Disposal of Machinery		400

The book value of the machinery at the time of the sale is $6,600 ($18,000 − $11,400); because it is sold for $7,000, the amount of the gain on the sale is $400.

Involuntary Conversion

Sometimes, an asset's service is terminated through some type of **involuntary conversion** such as fire, flood, theft, or condemnation. The gains or losses are treated no differently from those in any other type of disposition except that **they are often reported in the extraordinary items section of the income statement**.

To illustrate, Camel Transport Corp. was forced to sell a plant located on company property that stood directly in the path of an interstate highway. For a number of years the state had sought to purchase the land on which the plant stood, but the company resisted. The state ultimately exercised its right of eminent domain and was upheld by the courts. In settlement, Camel received $500,000, which was substantially in excess of the $200,000 book value of the plant and land (cost of $400,000 less accumulated depreciation of $200,000). The following entry was made:

Cash	500,000	
Accumulated Depreciation—Plant Assets	200,000	
Plant Assets		400,000
Gain on Disposal of Plant Assets		300,000

However, some object to the recognition of a gain or loss in certain involuntary conversions. For example, the federal government often condemns forests for national parks; as a result, the paper companies that owned these forests are required to report a gain or loss on the condemnation. However, companies such as **Georgia-Pacific** contend that because they must replace this condemned forest land immediately, they are in the same economic position as they were before and no gain or loss should be reported. The issue is whether the condemnation and subsequent purchase should be viewed as one or two transactions. *FASB Interpretation No. 30* rules against the companies by requiring "that gain or loss be recognized when a nonmonetary asset is involuntarily converted to monetary assets even though an enterprise reinvests or is obligated to reinvest the monetary assets in replacement nonmonetary assets."[14]

The gain or loss that develops on these types of unusual, nonrecurring transactions should be shown as an extraordinary item. Similar treatment is given to other types of involuntary conversions such as those resulting from a major casualty (such as an earthquake) or an expropriation, assuming that it meets other conditions for extraordinary item treatment. The difference between the amount recovered (condemnation award or insurance recovery), if any, and the asset's book value is reported as a gain or loss.

Miscellaneous Problems

If an asset is scrapped or abandoned without any cash recovery, a loss should be recognized equal to the asset's book value. If scrap value exists, the gain or loss that occurs is the difference between the asset's scrap value and its book value. If an asset still can be used even though it is fully depreciated, it may be kept on the books at historical cost less depreciation, or the asset may be carried at scrap value.

Disclosure of the amount of fully depreciated assets in service should be made in notes to the financial statements. For example, **Petroleum Equipment Tools Inc.** in its Annual Report disclosed: "The amount of fully depreciated assets included in property, plant, and equipment at December 31 amounted to approximately $98,900,000."

SUMMARY OF LEARNING OBJECTIVES

1 Describe the major characteristics of property, plant, and equipment. The major characteristics of property, plant, and equipment are: (1) They are acquired for use in operations and not for resale; (2) they are long-term in nature and usually subject to depreciation; and (3) they possess physical substance.

2 Identify the costs included in the initial valuation of land, buildings, and equipment. *Cost of land:* Includes all expenditures made to acquire land and to ready it for use. Land costs typically include (1) the purchase price; (2) closing costs, such as title to the land, attorney's fees, and recording fees; (3) costs incurred in getting the land in condition for its intended use, such as grading, filling, draining, and clearing; (4) assumption of any liens, mortgages, or encumbrances on the property; and (5) any additional land improvements that have an indefinite life.

Cost of buildings: Includes all expenditures related directly to their acquisition or construction. These costs include (1) materials, labor, and overhead costs incurred during construction and (2) professional fees and building permits.

KEY TERMS

additions, *519*
avoidable interest, *504*
betterments, *519*
capital expenditure, *518*
capitalization period, *504*
dissimilar nonmonetary asset, *512*
fixed assets, *500*
historical cost, *501*
improvements (betterments), *519*
involuntary conversion, *522*
lump sum price, *510*
major repairs, *520*
nonmonetary assets, *511*
nonreciprocal transfers, *516*
ordinary repairs, *520*
plant assets, *500*
property, plant, and equipment, *500*
prudent cost, *517*
rearrangement and reinstallation costs, *520*
replacements, *519*
revenue expenditure, *518*
self-constructed asset, *502*
similar nonmonetary assets, *513*
weighted-average accumulated expenditures, *505*

[14]"Accounting for Involuntary Conversions of Nonmonetary Assets to Monetary Assets," *FASB Interpretation No. 30* (Stamford, Conn.: FASB, 1979), summary paragraph.

Cost of equipment: Includes the purchase price, freight and handling charges incurred, insurance on the equipment while in transit, cost of special foundations if required, assembling and installation costs, and costs of conducting trial runs.

3 Describe the accounting problems associated with self-constructed assets. The assignment of indirect costs of manufacturing creates special problems because these costs cannot be traced directly to work and material orders related to the fixed assets constructed. These costs might be handled in one of three ways: (1) Assign no fixed overhead to the cost of the constructed asset, (2) assign a portion of all overhead to the construction process, or (3) allocate on the basis of lost production. The second method is used extensively in practice.

4 Describe the accounting problems associated with interest capitalization. Only actual interest (with modifications) should be capitalized. The rationale for this approach is that during construction, the asset is not generating revenue and therefore interest cost should be deferred (capitalized); once construction is completed, the asset is ready for its intended use and revenues can be earned. Any interest cost incurred in purchasing an asset that is ready for its intended use should be expensed.

5 Understand accounting issues related to acquiring and valuing plant assets. The following issues relate to acquiring and valuing plant assets: (1) *Cash discounts:* Whether taken or not, they are generally considered a reduction in the cost of the asset; the real cost of the asset is the cash or cash equivalent price of the asset. (2) *Assets purchased on long-term credit contracts:* Are accounted for at the present value of the consideration exchanged between the contracting parties. (3) *Lump sum purchase:* Allocate the total cost among the various assets on the basis of their relative fair market values. (4) *Issuance of stock:* If the stock is actively traded, the market value of the stock issued is a fair indication of the cost of the property acquired. If the market value of the common stock exchanged is not determinable, the value of the property should be established and used as the basis for recording the asset and issuance of the common stock. (5) *Exchanges of property, plant, and equipment.* See Illustrations 10-11 and 10-22 for summaries of how to account for exchanges. (6) *Contributions:* Should be recorded at the fair value of the asset received and a related credit should be made to revenue for the same amount.

6 Describe the accounting treatment for costs subsequent to acquisition. See Illustration 10-23 for a summary of how to account for costs subsequent to acquisition.

7 Describe the accounting treatment for the disposal of property, plant, and equipment. Regardless of the time of disposal, depreciation must be taken up to the date of disposition, and then all accounts related to the retired asset should be removed. Gains or losses on the retirement of plant assets should be shown in the income statement along with other items that arise from customary business activities. Gains or losses on involuntary conversions should be reported as extraordinary items. If an asset is scrapped or abandoned without any cash recovery, a loss should be recognized equal to the asset's book value. If scrap value exists, the gain or loss that occurs is the difference between the asset's scrap value and its book value.

QUESTIONS

1 What are the major characteristics of plant assets?

2 Esplanade Inc. owns land that it purchased on January 1, 1994, for $420,000. At December 31, 2001, its current value is $770,000 as determined by appraisal. At what amount should Esplanade report this asset on its December 31, 2001, balance sheet? Explain.

3 Name the items, in addition to the amount paid to the former owner or contractor, that may properly be included as part of the acquisition cost of the following plant assets:

(a) Land.

(b) Machinery and equipment.

(c) Buildings.

4 Indicate where the following items would be shown on a balance sheet.

(a) A lien that was attached to the land when purchased.

(b) Landscaping costs.

(c) Attorney's fees and recording fees related to purchasing land.

(d) Variable overhead related to construction of machinery.

(e) A parking lot servicing employees in the building.

(f) Cost of temporary building for workers during construction of building.

(g) Interest expense on bonds payable incurred during construction of a building.

(h) Assessments for sidewalks that are maintained by the city.

(i) The cost of demolishing an old building that was on the land when purchased.

5 Three positions have normally been taken with respect to the recording of fixed manufacturing overhead as an element of the cost of plant assets constructed by a company for its own use:

(a) It should be excluded completely.

(b) It should be included at the same rate as is charged to normal operations.

(c) It should be allocated on the basis of the lost production that occurs from normal operations.

What are the circumstances or rationale that support or deny the application of these methods?

6 The Buildings account of Diego Rivera Inc. includes the following items that were used in determining the basis for depreciating the cost of a building:

(a) Organization and promotion expenses.

(b) Architect's fees.

(c) Interest and taxes during construction.

(d) Commission paid on the sale of capital stock.

(e) Bond discount.

Do you agree with these charges? If not, how would you deal with each of the items above in the corporation's books and in its annual financial statements?

7 Jones Company has purchased two tracts of land. One tract will be the site of its new manufacturing plant, while the other is being purchased with the hope that it will be sold in the next year at a profit. How should these two tracts of land be reported in the balance sheet?

8 One financial accounting issue encountered when a company constructs its own plant is whether the interest cost on funds borrowed to finance construction should be capitalized and then amortized over the life of the assets constructed. What is a common accounting justification for capitalizing such interest?

9 Provide examples of assets that do not qualify for interest capitalization.

10 What interest rates should be used in determining the amount of interest to be capitalized? How should the amount of interest to be capitalized be determined?

11 How should the amount of interest capitalized be disclosed in the footnotes to the financial statements? How should interest revenue from temporarily invested excess funds borrowed to finance the construction of assets be accounted for?

12 Discuss the basic accounting problem that arises in handling each of the following situations.

(a) Assets purchased by issuance of capital stock.

(b) Acquisition of plant assets by gift or donation.

(c) Purchase of a plant asset subject to a cash discount.

(d) Assets purchased on a long-term credit basis.

(e) A group of assets acquired for a lump sum.

(f) An asset traded in or exchanged for another asset.

13 Yukio Mishima Industries acquired equipment this year to be used in its operations. The equipment was delivered by the suppliers, installed by Mishima, and placed into operation. Some of it was purchased for cash with discounts available for prompt payment. Some of it was purchased under long-term payment plans for which the interest charges approximated prevailing rates. What costs should Mishima capitalize for the new equipment purchased this year? Explain.

14 Adam Mickiewicz Co. purchased for $2,200,000 property that included both land and a building to be used in operations. The seller's book value was $300,000 for the land and $900,000 for the building. By appraisal, the fair market value was estimated to be $500,000 for the land and $2,000,000 for the building. At what amount should Mickiewicz report the land and the building at the end of the year?

15 Richardson Co. acquires machinery by paying $10,000 cash and signing a $5,000, 2-year, zero-interest-bearing note payable. The note has a present value of $4,058, and Richardson purchased a similar machine last month for $13,500. At what cost should the new equipment be recorded?

16 Ron Dayne is evaluating two recent transactions involving exchanges of equipment. In one case, similar assets were exchanged; in the second situation, dissimilar assets were exchanged. Explain to Ron the differences in accounting for these two situations.

17 Saadi Company purchased a heavy-duty truck on July 1, 1998, for $30,000. It was estimated that it would have a useful life of 10 years and then would have a trade-in value of $6,000. It was traded on August 1, 2002, for a similar truck costing $39,000; $13,000 was allowed as trade-in value (also fair value) on the old truck and $26,000 was paid in cash. What is the entry to record the trade-in? The company uses the straight-line method.

18 Once equipment has been installed and placed in operation, subsequent expenditures relating to this equipment are frequently thought of as repairs or general maintenance and, hence, chargeable to operations in the period in which the expenditure is made. Actually, determination of whether such an expenditure should be charged to operations or capitalized involves a much more careful analysis of the character of the expenditure. What are the factors that should be considered in making such a decision? Discuss fully.

19 What accounting treatment is normally given to the following items in accounting for plant assets?

(a) Additions.

(b) Major repairs.

(c) Improvements and replacements.

20 New machinery, which replaced a number of employees, was installed and put in operation in the last month of the fiscal year. The employees had been dismissed after payment of an extra month's wages and this amount was added to the cost of the machinery. Discuss the propriety of the charge and, if it was improper, describe the proper treatment.

21 To what extent do you consider the following items to be proper costs of the fixed asset? Give reasons for your opinions.

(a) Overhead of a business that builds its own equipment.

(b) Cost of constructing new models of machinery.

(c) Cash discounts on purchases of equipment.

(d) Interest paid during construction of a building.

(e) Cost of a safety device installed on a machine.

(f) Freight on equipment returned before installation, for replacement by other equipment of greater capacity.

(g) Cost of moving machinery to a new location.

(h) Cost of plywood partitions erected as part of the remodeling of the office.

(i) Replastering of a section of the building.

(j) Cost of a new motor for one of the trucks.

22 Recently, Michelangelo Manufacturing Co. presented the account "Allowance for Repairs" in the long-term liability section. Evaluate this procedure.

23 Dimitri Enterprises has a number of fully depreciated assets that are still being used in the main operations of the business. Because the assets are fully depreciated, the president of the company decides not to show them on the balance sheet or disclose this information in the footnotes. Evaluate this procedure.

24 What are the general rules for how gains or losses on retirement of plant assets should be reported in income?

BRIEF EXERCISES

BE10-1 Bonanza Brothers Inc. purchased land at a price of $27,000. Closing costs were $1,400. An old building was removed at a cost of $12,200. What amount should be recorded as the cost of the land?

BE10-2 Brett Hull Company is constructing a building. Construction began on February 1 and was completed on December 31. Expenditures were $1,500,000 on March 1, $1,200,000 on June 1, and $3,000,000 on December 31. Compute Hull's weighted-average accumulated expenditures for interest capitalization purposes.

BE10-3 Brett Hull Company (see BE10-2) borrowed $1,000,000 on March 1 on a 5-year, 12% note to help finance construction of the building. In addition, the company had outstanding all year a 13%, 5-year, $2,000,000 note payable and a 15%, 4-year, $3,500,000 note payable. Compute the weighted-average interest rate used for interest capitalization purposes.

BE10-4 Use the information for Brett Hull Company from BE10-2 and BE10-3. Compute avoidable interest for Brett Hull Company.

BE10-5 Chavez Corporation purchased a truck by issuing an $80,000, 4-year, noninterest-bearing note to Equinox Inc. The market rate of interest for obligations of this nature is 12%. Prepare the journal entry to record the purchase of this truck.

BE10-6 Cool Spot Inc. purchased land, building and equipment from Pinball Wizard Corporation for a cash payment of $306,000. The estimated fair values of the assets are land $60,000; building $220,000; and equipment $80,000. At what amounts should each of the three assets be recorded?

BE10-7 Dark Wizard Company obtained land by issuing 2,000 shares of its $10 par value common stock. The land was recently appraised at $85,000. The common stock is actively traded at $41 per share. Prepare the journal entry to record the acquisition of the land.

BE10-8 Strider Corporation traded a used truck (cost $20,000, accumulated depreciation $18,000) for a small computer worth $3,700. Strider also paid $1,000 in the transaction. Prepare the journal entry to record the exchange.

BE10-9 Sloan Company traded a used welding machine (cost $9,000, accumulated depreciation $3,000) for office equipment with an estimated fair value of $5,000. Sloan also paid $2,000 cash in the transaction. Prepare the journal entry to record the exchange.

BE10-10 Bubey Company traded a used truck for a new truck. The used truck cost $30,000 and has accumulated depreciation of $27,000. The new truck is worth $35,000. Bubey also made a cash payment of $33,000. Prepare Bubey's entry to record the exchange.

BE10-11 Buck Rogers Corporation traded a used truck for a new truck. The used truck cost $20,000 and has accumulated depreciation of $17,000. The new truck is worth $35,000. Rogers also made a cash payment of $33,000. Prepare Rogers' entry to record the exchange.

BE10-12 Indicate which of the following costs should be expensed when incurred.

- **(a)** $13,000 paid to rearrange and reinstall machinery.
- **(b)** $200 paid for tune-up and oil change on delivery truck.
- **(c)** $200,000 paid for addition to building.
- **(d)** $7,000 paid to replace a wooden floor with a concrete floor.
- **(e)** $2,000 paid for a major overhaul on a truck, which extends useful life.
- **(f)** $700,000 paid for relocation of company headquarters.

BE10-13 Sim City Corporation owns machinery that cost $20,000 when purchased on January 1, 1998. Depreciation has been recorded at a rate of $3,000 per year, resulting in a balance in accumulated depreciation of $9,000 at December 31, 2000. The machinery is sold on September 1, 2001, for $10,500. Prepare journal entries to (a) update depreciation for 2001 and (b) record the sale.

BE10-14 Use the information presented for Sim City Corporation in BE10-13, but assume the machinery is sold for $5,200 instead of $10,500. Prepare journal entries to (a) update depreciation for 2001 and (b) record the sale.

EXERCISES

E10-1 (Acquisition Costs of Realty) The following expenditures and receipts are related to land, land improvements, and buildings acquired for use in a business enterprise. The receipts are enclosed in parentheses.

(a)	Money borrowed to pay building contractor (signed a note)	$(275,000)
(b)	Payment for construction from note proceeds	275,000
(c)	Cost of land fill and clearing	8,000
(d)	Delinquent real estate taxes on property assumed by purchaser	7,000
(e)	Premium on 6-month insurance policy during construction	6,000
(f)	Refund of 1-month insurance premium because construction completed early	(1,000)
(g)	Architect's fee on building	22,000
(h)	Cost of real estate purchased as a plant site (land $200,000 and building $50,000)	250,000
(i)	Commission fee paid to real estate agency	9,000
(j)	Installation of fences around property	4,000
(k)	Cost of razing and removing building	11,000
(l)	Proceeds from salvage of demolished building	(5,000)
(m)	Interest paid during construction on money borrowed for construction	13,000
(n)	Cost of parking lots and driveways	19,000
(o)	Cost of trees and shrubbery planted (permanent in nature)	14,000
(p)	Excavation costs for new building	3,000

Instructions

Identify each item by letter and list the items in columnar form, as shown below. All receipt amounts should be reported in parentheses. For any amounts entered in the Other Accounts column also indicate the account title.

Item	Land	Land Improvements	Building	Other Accounts

E10-2 (Acquisition Costs of Realty) Martin Buber Co. purchased land as a factory site for $400,000. The process of tearing down two old buildings on the site and constructing the factory required 6 months.

The company paid $42,000 to raze the old buildings and sold salvaged lumber and brick for $6,300. Legal fees of $1,850 were paid for title investigation and drawing the purchase contract. Payment to an engineering firm was made for a land survey, $2,200, and for drawing the factory plans, $68,000. The land survey had to be made before definitive plans could be drawn. Title insurance on the property cost $1,500, and a liability insurance premium paid during construction was $900. The contractor's charge for construction was $2,740,000. The company paid the contractor in two installments: $1,200,000 at the end of 3 months and $1,540,000 upon completion. Interest costs of $170,000 were incurred to finance the construction.

Instructions

Determine the cost of the land and the cost of the building as they should be recorded on the books of Martin Buber Co. Assume that the land survey was for the building.

E10-3 (Acquisition Costs of Trucks) Alexei Urmanov Corporation operates a retail computer store. To improve delivery services to customers, the company purchases four new trucks on April 1, 2001. The terms of acquisition for each truck are described below:

1. Truck #1 has a list price of $15,000 and is acquired for a cash payment of $13,900.
2. Truck #2 has a list price of $16,000 and is acquired for a down payment of $2,000 cash and a non-interest-bearing note with a face amount of $14,000. The note is due April 1, 2002. Urmanov would normally have to pay interest at a rate of 10% for such a borrowing, and the dealership has an incremental borrowing rate of 8%.
3. Truck #3 has a list price of $16,000. It is acquired in exchange for a computer system that Urmanov carries in inventory. The computer system cost $12,000 and is normally sold by Urmanov for $15,200. Urmanov uses a perpetual inventory system.
4. Truck #4 has a list price of $14,000. It is acquired in exchange for 1,000 shares of common stock in Urmanov Corporation. The stock has a par value per share of $10 and a market value of $13 per share.

Instructions

Prepare the appropriate journal entries for the foregoing transactions for Urmanov Corporation.

E10-4 (Purchase and Self-Constructed Cost of Assets) Worf Co. both purchases and constructs various equipment it uses in its operations. The following items for two different types of equipment were recorded in random order during the calendar year 2002.

Purchase	
Cash paid for equipment, including sales tax of $5,000	$105,000
Freight and insurance cost while in transit	2,000
Cost of moving equipment into place at factory	3,100
Wage cost for technicians to test equipment	4,000
Insurance premium paid during first year of operation on this equipment	1,500
Special plumbing fixtures required for new equipment	8,000
Repair cost incurred in first year of operations related to this equipment	1,300
Construction	
Material and purchased parts (gross cost $200,000; failed to take 2% cash discount)	$200,000
Imputed interest on funds used during construction (stock financing)	14,000
Labor costs	190,000
Allocated overhead costs (fixed—$20,000; variable—$30,000)	50,000
Profit on self-construction	30,000
Cost of installing equipment	4,400

Instructions

Compute the total cost for each of these two pieces of equipment. If an item is not capitalized as a cost of the equipment, indicate how it should be reported.

E10-5 (Treatment of Various Costs) Ben Sisko Supply Company, a newly formed corporation, incurred the following expenditures related to Land, to Buildings, and to Machinery and Equipment.

Abstract company's fee for title search		$ 520
Architect's fees		2,800
Cash paid for land and dilapidated building thereon		87,000
Removal of old building	$20,000	
Less: Salvage	5,500	14,500
Surveying before construction		370
Interest on short-term loans during construction		7,400
Excavation before construction for basement		19,000

Machinery purchased (subject to 2% cash discount, which was not taken)	55,000
Freight on machinery purchased	1,340
Storage charges on machinery, necessitated by noncompletion of building when machinery was delivered	2,180
New building constructed (building construction took 6 months from date of purchase of land and old building)	485,000
Assessment by city for drainage project	1,600
Hauling charges for delivery of machinery from storage to new building	620
Installation of machinery	2,000
Trees, shrubs, and other landscaping after completion of building (permanent in nature)	5,400

Instructions

Determine the amounts that should be debited to Land, to Buildings, and to Machinery and Equipment. Assume the benefits of capitalizing interest during construction exceed the cost of implementation. Indicate how any costs not debited to these accounts should be recorded.

E10-6 (Correction of Improper Cost Entries) Plant acquisitions for selected companies are as follows:

1. Belanna Industries Inc. acquired land, buildings, and equipment from a bankrupt company, Torres Co., for a lump sum price of $700,000. At the time of purchase, Torres assets had the following book and appraisal values:

	Book Values	Appraisal Values
Land	$200,000	$150,000
Buildings	250,000	350,000
Equipment	300,000	300,000

To be conservative, the company decided to take the lower of the two values for each asset acquired. The following entry was made:

Land	150,000	
Buildings	250,000	
Equipment	300,000	
Cash		700,000

2. Harry Enterprises purchased store equipment by making a $2,000 cash down payment and signing a 1-year, $23,000, 10% note payable. The purchase was recorded as follows:

Store Equipment	27,300	
Cash		2,000
Note Payable		23,000
Interest Payable		2,300

3. Kim Company purchased office equipment for $20,000, terms 2/10, n/30. Because the company intended to take the discount, it made no entry until it paid for the acquisition. The entry was:

Office Equipment	20,000	
Cash		19,600
Purchase Discounts		400

4. Kaisson Inc. recently received at zero cost land from the Village of Cardassia as an inducement to locate its business in the Village. The appraised value of the land is $27,000. The company made no entry to record the land because it had no cost basis.
5. Zimmerman Company built a warehouse for $600,000. It could have purchased the building for $740,000. The controller made the following entry:

Warehouse	740,000	
Cash		600,000
Profit on Construction		140,000

Instructions

Prepare the entry that should have been made at the date of each acquisition.

E10-7 (Capitalization of Interest) Harrisburg Furniture Company started construction of a combination office and warehouse building for its own use at an estimated cost of $5,000,000 on January 1, 2001. Harrisburg expected to complete the building by December 31, 2001. Harrisburg has the following debt obligations outstanding during the construction period.

Construction loan—12% interest, payable semiannually, issued December 31, 2000	$2,000,000

Short-term loan—10% interest, payable monthly, and principal payable at maturity on May 30, 2002	1,400,000
Long-term loan—11% interest, payable on January 1 of each year. Principal payable on January 1, 2005	1,000,000

Instructions (Carry all computations to two decimal places.)

(a) Assume that Harrisburg completed the office and warehouse building on December 31, 2001, as planned at a total cost of $5,200,000, and the weighted average of accumulated expenditures was $3,600,000. Compute the avoidable interest on this project.

(b) Compute the depreciation expense for the year ended December 31, 2002. Harrisburg elected to depreciate the building on a straight-line basis and determined that the asset has a useful life of 30 years and a salvage value of $300,000.

E10-8 (Capitalization of Interest) On December 31, 2000, Alma-Ata Inc. borrowed $3,000,000 at 12% payable annually to finance the construction of a new building. In 2001, the company made the following expenditures related to this building: March 1, $360,000; June 1, $600,000; July 1, $1,500,000; December 1, $1,500,000. Additional information is provided as follows:

1.	Other debt outstanding	
	10-year, 13% bond, December 31, 1994, interest payable annually	$4,000,000
	6-year, 10% note, dated December 31, 1998, interest payable annually	$1,600,000
2.	March 1, 2001, expenditure included land costs of $150,000	
3.	Interest revenue earned in 2001	$49,000

Instructions

(a) Determine the amount of interest to be capitalized in 2001 in relation to the construction of the building.

(b) Prepare the journal entry to record the capitalization of interest and the recognition of interest expense, if any, at December 31, 2001.

E10-9 (Capitalization of Interest) On July 31, 2001, Amsterdam Company engaged Minsk Tooling Company to construct a special-purpose piece of factory machinery. Construction was begun immediately and was completed on November 1, 2001. To help finance construction, on July 31 Amsterdam issued a $300,000, 3-year, 12% note payable at Netherlands National Bank, on which interest is payable each July 31. $200,000 of the proceeds of the note was paid to Minsk on July 31. The remainder of the proceeds was temporarily invested in short-term marketable securities at 10% until November 1. On November 1, Amsterdam made a final $100,000 payment to Minsk. Other than the note to Netherlands, Amsterdam's only outstanding liability at December 31, 2001, is a $30,000, 8%, 6-year note payable, dated January 1, 1998, on which interest is payable each December 31.

Instructions

(a) Calculate the interest revenue, weighted-average accumulated expenditures, avoidable interest, and total interest cost to be capitalized during 2001. Round all computations to the nearest dollar.

(b) Prepare the journal entries needed on the books of Amsterdam Company at each of the following dates:

(1) July 31, 2001.
(2) November 1, 2001.
(3) December 31, 2001.

E10-10 (Capitalization of Interest) The following three situations involve the capitalization of interest:

Situation I

On January 1, 2001, Oksana Baiul, Inc. signed a fixed-price contract to have Builder Associates construct a major plant facility at a cost of $4,000,000. It was estimated that it would take 3 years to complete the project. Also on January 1, 2001, to finance the construction cost, Oksana Baiul borrowed $4,000,000 payable in 10 annual installments of $400,000, plus interest at the rate of 10%. During 2001, Oksana Baiul made deposit and progress payments totaling $1,500,000 under the contract; the weighted-average amount of accumulated expenditures was $800,000 for the year. The excess borrowed funds were invested in short-term securities, from which Oksana Baiul realized investment income of $250,000.

Instructions

What amount should Oksana Baiul report as capitalized interest at December 31, 2001?

Situation II

During 2001, Midori Ito Corporation constructed and manufactured certain assets and incurred the following interest costs in connection with those activities:

	Interest Costs Incurred
Warehouse constructed for Ito's own use	$30,000
Special-order machine for sale to unrelated customer, produced according to customer's specifications	9,000
Inventories routinely manufactured, produced on a repetitive basis	8,000

All of these assets required an extended period of time for completion.

Instructions

Assuming the effect of interest capitalization is material, what is the total amount of interest costs to be capitalized?

Situation III

Peggy Fleming, Inc. has a fiscal year ending April 30. On May 1, 2001, Peggy Fleming borrowed $10,000,000 at 11% to finance construction of its own building. Repayments of the loan are to commence the month following completion of the building. During the year ended April 30, 2002, expenditures for the partially completed structure totaled $7,000,000. These expenditures were incurred evenly throughout the year. Interest earned on the unexpended portion of the loan amounted to $650,000 for the year.

Instructions

How much should be shown as capitalized interest on Peggy Fleming's financial statements at April 30, 2002?

(CPA adapted)

E10-11 (Entries for Equipment Acquisitions) Jane Geddes Engineering Corporation purchased conveyor equipment with a list price of $10,000. The vendor's credit terms were 2/10, n/30. Presented below are three independent cases related to the equipment. Assume that the purchases of equipment are recorded gross. (Round to nearest dollar.)

(a) Geddes paid cash for the equipment 8 days after the purchase.

(b) Geddes traded in equipment with a book value of $2,000 (initial cost $8,000), and paid $9,500 in cash one month after the purchase. The old equipment could have been sold for $400 at the date of trade (assume similar equipment).

(c) Geddes gave the vendor a $10,800 non-interest-bearing note for the equipment on the date of purchase. The note was due in one year and was paid on time. Assume that the effective interest rate in the market was 9%.

Instructions

Prepare the general journal entries required to record the acquisition and payment in each of the independent cases above. Round to the nearest dollar.

E10-12 (Entries for Asset Acquisition, Including Self-Construction) Below are transactions related to Fred Couples Company.

(a) The City of Pebble Beach gives the company 5 acres of land as a plant site. The market value of this land is determined to be $81,000.

(b) 13,000 shares of common stock with a par value of $50 per share are issued in exchange for land and buildings. The property has been appraised at a fair market value of $810,000, of which $180,000 has been allocated to land and $630,000 to buildings. The stock of Fred Couples Company is not listed on any exchange, but a block of 100 shares was sold by a stockholder 12 months ago at $65 per share, and a block of 200 shares was sold by another stockholder 18 months ago at $58 per share.

(c) No entry has been made to remove from the accounts for Materials, Direct Labor, and Overhead the amounts properly chargeable to plant asset accounts for machinery constructed during the year. The following information is given relative to costs of the machinery constructed.

Materials used	$12,500
Factory supplies used	900
Direct labor incurred	15,000
Additional overhead (over regular) caused by construction of machinery, excluding factory supplies used	2,700
Fixed overhead rate applied to regular manufacturing operations	60% of direct labor cost
Cost of similar machinery if it had been purchased from outside suppliers	44,000

Instructions

Prepare journal entries on the books of Fred Couples Company to record these transactions.

E10-13 (Entries for Acquisition of Assets) Presented below is information related to Zonker Company.

1. On July 6 Zonker Company acquired the plant assets of Doonesbury Company, which had discontinued operations. The appraised value of the property is:

Land	$ 400,000
Building	1,200,000
Machinery and equipment	800,000
Total	$2,400,000

Zonker Company gave 12,500 shares of its $100 par value common stock in exchange. The stock had a market value of $168 per share on the date of the purchase of the property.

2. Zonker Company expended the following amounts in cash between July 6 and December 15, the date when it first occupied the building:

Repairs to building	$105,000
Construction of bases for machinery to be installed later	135,000
Driveways and parking lots	122,000
Remodeling of office space in building, including new partitions and walls	161,000
Special assessment by city on land	18,000

3. On December 20, the company paid cash for machinery, $260,000, subject to a 2% cash discount, and freight on machinery of $10,500.

Instructions

Prepare entries on the books of Zonker Company for these transactions.

E10-14 (Purchase of Equipment with Non-Interest-Bearing Debt) Chippewas Inc. has decided to purchase equipment from Central Michigan Industries on January 2, 2001, to expand its production capacity to meet customers' demand for its product. Chippewas issues an $800,000, 5-year, non-interest-bearing note to Central Michigan for the new equipment when the prevailing market rate of interest for obligations of this nature is 12%. The company will pay off the note in five $160,000 installments due at the end of each year over the life of the note.

Instructions

(a) Prepare the journal entry(ies) at the date of purchase. (Round to nearest dollar in all computations.)
(b) Prepare the journal entry(ies) at the end of the first year to record the payment and interest, assuming that the company employs the effective interest method.
(c) Prepare the journal entry(ies) at the end of the second year to record the payment and interest.
(d) Assuming that the equipment had a 10-year life and no salvage value, prepare the journal entry necessary to record depreciation in the first year. (Straight-line depreciation is employed.)

E10-15 (Purchase of Computer with Non-Interest-Bearing Debt) Cardinals Corporation purchased a computer on December 31, 2000, for $105,000, paying $30,000 down and agreeing to pay the balance in five equal installments of $15,000 payable each December 31 beginning in 2001. An assumed interest rate of 10% is implicit in the purchase price.

Instructions

(a) Prepare the journal entry(ies) at the date of purchase. (Round to two decimal places.)
(b) Prepare the journal entry(ies) at December 31, 2001, to record the payment and interest (effective interest method employed).
(c) Prepare the journal entry(ies) at December 31, 2002, to record the payment and interest (effective interest method employed).

E10-16 (Asset Acquisition) Hayes Industries purchased the following assets and constructed a building as well. All this was done during the current year.

Assets 1 and 2

These assets were purchased as a lump sum for $100,000 cash. The following information was gathered.

Description	Initial Cost on Seller's Books	Depreciation to Date on Seller's Books	Book Value on Seller's Books	Appraised Value
Machinery	$100,000	$50,000	$50,000	$85,000
Office equipment	60,000	10,000	50,000	45,000

Asset 3
This machine was acquired by making a $10,000 down payment and issuing a $30,000, 2-year, zero-interest-bearing note. The note is to be paid off in two $15,000 installments made at the end of the first and second years. It was estimated that the asset could have been purchased outright for $35,900.

Asset 4
This machinery was acquired by trading in similar used machinery. Facts concerning the trade-in are as follows:

Cost of machinery traded	$100,000
Accumulated depreciation to date of sale	40,000
Fair market value of machinery traded	80,000
Cash received	10,000
Fair market value of machinery acquired	70,000

Asset 5
Office equipment was acquired by issuing 100 shares of $8 par value common stock. The stock had a market value of $11 per share.

Construction of Building
A building was constructed on land purchased last year at a cost of $150,000. Construction began on February 1 and was completed on November 1. The payments to the contractor were as follows:

Date	Payment
2/1	$120,000
6/1	360,000
9/1	480,000
11/1	100,000

To finance construction of the building, a $600,000, 12% construction loan was taken out on June 1. The loan was repaid on November 1. The firm had $200,000 of other outstanding debt during the year at a borrowing rate of 8%.

Instructions
Record the acquisition of each of these assets.

E10-17 (Nonmonetary Exchange with Boot) Busytown Corporation, which manufactures shoes, hired a recent college graduate to work in its accounting department. On the first day of work, the accountant was assigned to total a batch of invoices with the use of an adding machine. Before long, the accountant, who had never before seen such a machine, managed to break the machine. Busytown Corporation gave the machine plus $340 to Dick Tracy Business Machine Company (dealer) in exchange for a new machine. Assume the following information about the machines:

	Busytown Corp. (Old Machine)	Dick Tracy Co. (New Machine)
Machine cost	$290	$270
Accumulated depreciation	140	–0–
Fair value	85	425

Instructions
For each company, prepare the necessary journal entry to record the exchange.

E10-18 (Nonmonetary Exchange with Boot) Cannondale Company purchased an electric wax melter on April 30, 2002, by trading in its old gas model and paying the balance in cash. The following data relate to the purchase:

List price of new melter	$15,800
Cash paid	10,000
Cost of old melter (5-year life, $700 residual value)	11,200
Accumulated depreciation—old melter (straight-line)	6,300
Second-hand market value of old melter	5,200

Instructions
Prepare the journal entry(ies) necessary to record this exchange, assuming that the melters exchanged are (a) similar in nature, and (b) dissimilar in nature. Cannondale's fiscal year ends on December 31, and depreciation has been recorded through December 31, 2001.

E10-19 (Nonmonetary Exchange with Boot) Carlos Arruza Company exchanged equipment used in its manufacturing operations plus $3,000 in cash for similar equipment used in the operations of Tony LoBianco Company. The following information pertains to the exchange:

	Carlos Arruza Co.	Tony LoBianco Co.
Equipment (cost)	$28,000	$28,000
Accumulated depreciation	19,000	10,000
Fair value of equipment	12,500	15,500
Cash given up	3,000	

Instructions

Prepare the journal entries to record the exchange on the books of both companies.

E10-20 (Nonmonetary Exchange with Boot) Dana Ashbrook Inc. has negotiated the purchase of a new piece of automatic equipment at a price of $8,000 plus trade-in, f.o.b. factory. Dana Ashbrook Inc. paid $8,000 cash and traded in used equipment. The used equipment had originally cost $62,000; it had a book value of $42,000 and a secondhand market value of $47,800, as indicated by recent transactions involving similar equipment. Freight and installation charges for the new equipment required a cash payment of $1,100.

Instructions

(a) Prepare the general journal entry to record this transaction, assuming that the assets Dana Ashbrook Inc. exchanged are similar in nature.

(b) Assuming the same facts as in (a) except that the assets exchanged are dissimilar in nature, prepare the general journal entry to record this transaction.

E10-21 (Analysis of Subsequent Expenditures) King Donovan Resources Group has been in its plant facility for 15 years. Although the plant is quite functional, numerous repair costs are incurred to maintain it in sound working order. The company's plant asset book value is currently $800,000, as indicated below:

Original cost	$1,200,000
Accumulated depreciation	400,000
	$ 800,000

During the current year, the following expenditures were made to the plant facility:

(a) Because of increased demands for its product, the company increased its plant capacity by building a new addition at a cost of $270,000.

(b) The entire plant was repainted at a cost of $23,000.

(c) The roof was an asbestos cement slate; for safety purposes it was removed and replaced with a wood shingle roof at a cost of $61,000. Book value of the old roof was $41,000.

(d) The electrical system was completely updated at a cost of $22,000. The cost of the old electrical system was not known. It is estimated that the useful life of the building will not change as a result of this updating.

(e) A series of major repairs were made at a cost of $47,000, because parts of the wood structure were rotting. The cost of the old wood structure was not known. These extensive repairs are estimated to increase the useful life of the building.

Instructions

Indicate how each of these transactions would be recorded in the accounting records.

E10-22 (Analysis of Subsequent Expenditures) The following transactions occurred during 2002. Assume that depreciation of 10% per year is charged on all machinery and 5% per year on buildings, on a straight-line basis, with no estimated salvage value. Depreciation is charged for a full year on all fixed assets acquired during the year, and no depreciation is charged on fixed assets disposed of during the year.

Jan. 30 A building that cost $132,000 in 1985 is torn down to make room for a new building. The wrecking contractor was paid $5,100 and was permitted to keep all materials salvaged.

Mar. 10 Machinery that was purchased in 1995 for $16,000 is sold for $2,900 cash, f.o.b. purchaser's plant. Freight of $300 is paid on this machinery.

Mar. 20 A gear breaks on a machine that cost $9,000 in 1997, and is replaced at a cost of $385. The replacement does not extend the useful life of the machine.

May 18 A special base installed for a machine in 1996 when the machine was purchased has to be replaced at a cost of $5,500 because of defective workmanship on the original base. The cost of the machinery was $14,200 in 1996; the cost of the base was $3,500, and this amount was charged to the Machinery account in 1996.

June 23 One of the buildings is repainted at a cost of $6,900. It had not been painted since it was constructed in 1998.

Instructions

Prepare general journal entries for the transactions. (Round to nearest dollar.)

E10-23 (Analysis of Subsequent Expenditures) Plant assets often require expenditures subsequent to acquisition. It is important that they be accounted for properly. Any errors will affect both the balance sheets and income statements for a number of years.

Instructions

For each of the following items, indicate whether the expenditure should be capitalized (C) or expensed (E) in the period incurred.

(a) ________ Improvement.
(b) ________ Replacement of a minor broken part on a machine.
(c) ________ Expenditure that increases the useful life of an existing asset.
(d) ________ Expenditure that increases the efficiency and effectiveness of a productive asset but does not increase its salvage value.
(e) ________ Expenditure that increases the efficiency and effectiveness of a productive asset and increases the asset's salvage value.
(f) ________ Expenditure that increases the quality of the output of the productive asset.
(g) ________ Improvement to a machine that increased its fair market value and its production capacity by 30% without extending the machine's useful life.
(h) ________ Ordinary repairs.
(i) ________ Improvement.
(j) ________ Interest on borrowing necessary to finance a major overhaul of machinery. The overhaul extended the life of the machinery.

E10-24 (Entries for Disposition of Assets) On December 31, 2001, Travis Tritt Inc. has a machine with a book value of $940,000. The original cost and related accumulated depreciation at this date are as follows:

Machine	$1,300,000
Accumulated depreciation	360,000
	$ 940,000

Depreciation is computed at $60,000 per year on a straight-line basis.

Instructions

Presented below is a set of independent situations. For each independent situation, indicate the journal entry to be made to record the transaction. Make sure that depreciation entries are made to update the book value of the machine prior to its disposal.

(a) A fire completely destroys the machine on August 31, 2002. An insurance settlement of $430,000 was received for this casualty. Assume the settlement was received immediately.
(b) On April 1, 2002, Tritt sold the machine for $1,040,000 to Dwight Yoakam Company.
(c) On July 31, 2002, the company donated this machine to the Mountain King City Council. The fair market value of the machine at the time of the donation was estimated to be $1,100,000.

E10-25 (Disposition of Assets) On April 1, 2001, Gloria Estefan Company received a condemnation award of $430,000 cash as compensation for the forced sale of the company's land and building, which stood in the path of a new state highway. The land and building cost $60,000 and $280,000, respectively, when they were acquired. At April 1, 2001, the accumulated depreciation relating to the building amounted to $160,000. On August 1, 2001, Estafan purchased a piece of replacement property for cash. The new land cost $90,000, and the new building cost $400,000.

Instructions

Prepare the journal entries to record the transactions on April 1 and August 1, 2001.

PROBLEMS

P10-1 (Classification of Acquisition and Other Asset Costs) At December 31, 2000, certain accounts included in the property, plant, and equipment section of Craig Ehlo Company's balance sheet had the following balances:

Land	$230,000
Buildings	890,000
Leasehold improvements	660,000
Machinery and equipment	875,000

During 2001 the following transactions occurred:

Land site number 621 was acquired for $850,000. In addition, to acquire the land Ehlo paid a $51,000 commission to a real estate agent. Costs of $35,000 were incurred to clear the land. During the course of clearing the land, timber and gravel were recovered and sold for $13,000.

A second tract of land (site number 622) with a building was acquired for $420,000. The closing statement indicated that the land value was $300,000 and the building value was $120,000. Shortly after acquisition, the building was demolished at a cost of $41,000. A new building was constructed for $330,000 plus the following costs:

Excavation fees	$38,000
Architectural design fees	11,000
Building permit fee	2,500
Imputed interest on funds used during construction (stock financing)	8,500

The building was completed and occupied on September 30, 2001.

A third tract of land (site number 623) was acquired for $650,000 and was put on the market for resale.

During December 2001 costs of $89,000 were incurred to improve leased office space. The related lease will terminate on December 31, 2003, and is not expected to be renewed. (*Hint:* Leasehold improvements should be handled in the same manner as land improvements.)

A group of new machines was purchased under a royalty agreement that provides for payment of royalties based on units of production for the machines. The invoice price of the machines was $87,000, freight costs were $3,300, installation costs were $2,400, and royalty payments for 2001 were $17,500.

Instructions

(a) Prepare a detailed analysis of the changes in each of the following balance sheet accounts for 2001:

Land	Leasehold improvements
Buildings	Machinery and equipment

Disregard the related accumulated depreciation accounts.

(b) List the items in the situation that were not used to determine the answer to (a) above, and indicate where, or if, these items should be included in Ehlo's financial statements.

(AICPA adapted)

P10-2 (Classification of Acquisition Costs) Selected accounts included in the property, plant, and equipment section of Spud Webb Corporation's balance sheet at December 31, 2000, had the following balances:

Land	$ 300,000
Land improvements	140,000
Buildings	1,100,000
Machinery and equipment	960,000

During 2001 the following transactions occurred:

1. A tract of land was acquired for $150,000 as a potential future building site.
2. A plant facility consisting of land and building was acquired from Ken Norman Company in exchange for 20,000 shares of Webb's common stock. On the acquisition date, Webb's stock had a closing market price of $37 per share on a national stock exchange. The plant facility was carried on Norman's books at $110,000 for land and $320,000 for the building at the exchange date. Current appraised values for the land and building, respectively, are $230,000 and $690,000.
3. Items of machinery and equipment were purchased at a total cost of $400,000. Additional costs were incurred as follows:

Freight and unloading	$13,000
Sales taxes	20,000
Installation	26,000

4. Expenditures totaling $95,000 were made for new parking lots, streets, and sidewalks at the corporation's various plant locations. These expenditures had an estimated useful life of 15 years.
5. A machine costing $80,000 on January 1, 1993, was scrapped on June 30, 2001. Double-declining-balance depreciation has been recorded on the basis of a 10-year life.
6. A machine was sold for $20,000 on July 1, 2001. Original cost of the machine was $44,000 on January 1, 1998, and it was depreciated on the straight-line basis over an estimated useful life of 7 years and a salvage value of $2,000.

Instructions

(a) Prepare a detailed analysis of the changes in each of the following balance sheet accounts for 2001:

Land
Land improvements
Buildings
Machinery and equipment

(*Hint:* Disregard the related accumulated depreciation accounts.)

(b) List the items in the fact situation that were not used to determine the answer to (a), showing the pertinent amounts and supporting computations in good form for each item. In addition, indicate where, or if, these items should be included in Spud Webb's financial statements.

(AICPA adapted)

P10-3 (Classification of Land and Building Costs) Lenny Wilkins Company was incorporated on January 2, 2002, but was unable to begin manufacturing activities until July 1, 2002, because new factory facilities were not completed until that date.

The Land and Building account at December 31, 2002, was as follows:

January 31, 2002	Land and building	$160,000
February 28, 2002	Cost of removal of building	9,800
May 1, 2002	Partial payment of new construction	60,000
May 1, 2002	Legal fees paid	3,770
June 1, 2002	Second payment on new construction	40,000
June 1, 2002	Insurance premium	2,280
June 1, 2002	Special tax assessment	4,000
June 30, 2002	General expenses	36,300
July 1, 2002	Final payment on new construction	40,000
December 31, 2002	Asset write-up	43,800
		399,950
December 31, 2002	Depreciation—2002 at 1%	4,000
	Account balance	$395,950

The following additional information is to be considered:

1. To acquire land and building the company paid $80,000 cash and 800 shares of its 8% cumulative preferred stock, par value $100 per share. Fair market value of the stock is $107 per share.
2. Cost of removal of old buildings amounted to $9,800, and the demolition company retained all materials of the building.
3. Legal fees covered the following:

Cost of organization	$ 610
Examination of title covering purchase of land	1,300
Legal work in connection with construction contract	1,860
	$3,770

4. Insurance premium covered the building for a 2-year term beginning May 1, 2002.
5. The special tax assessment covered street improvements that are permanent in nature.
6. General expenses covered the following for the period from January 2, 2002, to June 30, 2002.

President's salary	$32,100
Plant superintendent covering supervision of new building	4,200
	$36,300

7. Because of a general increase in construction costs after entering into the building contract, the board of directors increased the value of the building $43,800, believing that such an increase was justified to reflect the current market at the time the building was completed. Retained earnings was credited for this amount.
8. Estimated life of building—50 years.
   Writeoff for 2002—1% of asset value (1% of $400,000, or $4,000).

Instructions

(a) Prepare entries to reflect correct land, building, and depreciation allowance accounts at December 31, 2002.

(b) Show the proper presentation of land, building, and depreciation on the balance sheet at December 31, 2002.

(AICPA adapted)

P10-4 (Dispositions, Including Condemnation, Demolition, and Trade-in) Presented below is a schedule of property dispositions for Frank Thomas Co.

Schedule of Property Dispositions

	Cost	Accumulated Depreciation	Cash Proceeds	Fair Market Value	Nature of Disposition
Land	$40,000	—	$31,000	$31,000	Condemnation
Building	15,000	—	3,600	—	Demolition
Warehouse	70,000	$11,000	74,000	74,000	Destruction by fire
Machine	8,000	3,200	900	7,200	Trade-in
Furniture	10,000	7,850	—	3,100	Contribution
Automobile	8,000	3,460	2,960	2,960	Sale

The following additional information is available:

Land
On February 15, a condemnation award was received as consideration for unimproved land held primarily as an investment, and on March 31, another parcel of unimproved land to be held as an investment was purchased at a cost of $35,000.

Building
On April 2, land and building were purchased at a total cost of $75,000, of which 20% was allocated to the building on the corporate books. The real estate was acquired with the intention of demolishing the building, and this was accomplished during the month of November. Cash proceeds received in November represent the net proceeds from demolition of the building.

Warehouse
On June 30, the warehouse was destroyed by fire. The warehouse was purchased January 2, 1988, and had depreciated $11,000. On December 27, the insurance proceeds and other funds were used to purchase a replacement warehouse at a cost of $90,000.

Machine
On December 26, the machine was exchanged for another machine having a fair market value of $6,300 and cash of $900 was received.

Furniture
On August 15, furniture was contributed to a qualified charitable organization. No other contributions were made or pledged during the year.

Automobile
On November 3, the automobile was sold to Ozzie Guillen, a stockholder.

Instructions
Indicate how these items would be reported on the income statement of Frank Thomas Co.

(AICPA adapted)

P10-5 (Classification of Costs and Interest Capitalization) On January 1, 2001, George Solti Corporation purchased for $600,000 a tract of land (site number 101) with a building. Solti paid a real estate broker's commission of $36,000, legal fees of $6,000, and title guarantee insurance of $18,000. The closing statement indicated that the land value was $500,000 and the building value was $100,000. Shortly after acquisition, the building was razed at a cost of $54,000.

Solti entered into a $3,000,000 fixed-price contract with Slatkin Builders, Inc. on March 1, 2001, for the construction of an office building on land site number 101. The building was completed and occupied on September 30, 2002. Additional construction costs were incurred as follows:

Plans, specifications, and blueprints	$21,000
Architects' fees for design and supervision	82,000

The building is estimated to have a 40-year life from date of completion and will be depreciated using the 150% declining balance method.

To finance construction costs, Solti borrowed $3,000,000 on March 1, 2001. The loan is payable in ten annual installments of $300,000 plus interest at the rate of 10%. Solti's weighted-average amounts of accumulated building construction expenditures were as follows:

For the period March 1 to December 31, 2001	$1,200,000
For the period January 1 to September 30, 2002	1,900,000

Instructions

(a) Prepare a schedule that discloses the individual costs making up the balance in the land account in respect of land site number 101 as of September 30, 2002.

(b) Prepare a schedule that discloses the individual costs that should be capitalized in the office building account as of September 30, 2002. Show supporting computations in good form.

(AICPA adapted)

P10-6 (Interest During Construction) Jerry Landscaping began construction of a new plant on December 1, 1999. On this date the company purchased a parcel of land for $142,000 in cash. In addition, it paid $2,000 in surveying costs and $4,000 for a title insurance policy. An old dwelling on the premises was demolished at a cost of $3,000, with $1,000 being received from the sale of materials.

Architectural plans were also formalized on December 1, 1999, when the architect was paid $30,000. The necessary building permits costing $3,000 were obtained from the city and paid for on December 1 as well. The excavation work began during the first week in December with payments made to the contractor as follows:

Date of Payment	Amount of Payment
March 1	$240,000
May 1	360,000
July 1	60,000

The building was completed on July 1, 2000.

To finance construction of this plant, Jerry borrowed $600,000 from the bank on December 1, 1999. Jerry had no other borrowings. The $600,000 was a 10-year loan bearing interest at 8%.

Instructions

Compute the balance in each of the following accounts at December 31, 1999, and December 31, 2000:

(a) Land.

(b) Buildings.

(c) Interest Expense.

P10-7 (Capitalization of Interest) Wordcrafters Inc. is a book distributor that had been operating in its original facility since 1976. The increase in certification programs and continuing education requirements in several professions has contributed to an annual growth rate of 15% for Wordcrafters since 1996. Wordcrafters' original facility became obsolete by early 2001 because of the increased sales volume and the fact that Wordcrafters now carries tapes and disks in addition to books.

On June 1, 2001, Wordcrafters contracted with Favre Construction to have a new building constructed for $5,000,000 on land owned by Wordcrafters. The payments made by Wordcrafters to Favre Construction are shown in the schedule below.

Date	Amount
July 30, 2001	$1,200,000
January 30, 2002	1,500,000
May 30, 2002	1,300,000
Total payments	$4,000,000

Construction was completed and the building was ready for occupancy on May 27, 2002. Wordcrafters had no new borrowings directly associated with the new building but had the following debt outstanding at May 31, 2002, the end of its fiscal year:

14½%, 5-year note payable of $2,000,000, dated April 1, 1998, with interest payable annually on April 1.

12%, 10-year bond issue of $3,000,000 sold at par on June 30, 1994, with interest payable annually on June 30.

The new building qualifies for interest capitalization. The effect of capitalizing the interest on the new building, compared with the effect of expensing the interest, is material.

Instructions

(a) Compute the weighted average accumulated expenditures on Wordcrafters' new building during the capitalization period.

(b) Compute the avoidable interest on Wordcrafters' new building.

(c) Some interest cost of Wordcrafters Inc. is capitalized for the year ended May 31, 2002.
  (1) Identify the items relating to interest costs that must be disclosed in Wordcrafters' financial statements.
  (2) Compute the amount of each of the items that must be disclosed.

(CMA adapted)

P10-8 (Nonmonetary Exchanges with Boot) Susquehanna Corporation wishes to exchange a machine used in its operations. Susquehanna has received the following offers from other companies in the industry:

1. Choctaw Company offered to exchange a similar machine plus $23,000.
2. Powhatan Company offered to exchange a similar machine.
3. Shawnee Company offered to exchange a similar machine, but wanted $8,000 in addition to Susquehanna's machine.

In addition, Susquehanna contacted Seminole Corporation, a dealer in machines. To obtain a new machine, Susquehanna must pay $93,000 in addition to trading in its old machine.

	Susquehanna	Choctaw	Powhatan	Shawnee	Seminole
Machine cost	$160,000	$120,000	$147,000	$160,000	$130,000
Accumulated depreciation	50,000	45,000	71,000	75,000	–0–
Fair value	92,000	69,000	92,000	100,000	185,000

Instructions
For each of the four independent situations, prepare the journal entries to record the exchange on the books of each company. (Round to nearest dollar.)

P10-9 (Nonmonetary Exchanges with Boot) On August 1, 2002, Arna, Inc. exchanged productive assets with Bontemps, Inc. Arna's asset is referred to below as "Asset A" and Bontemps' is referred to as "Asset B." The following facts pertain to these assets:

	Asset A	Asset B
Original cost	$96,000	$110,000
Accumulated depreciation (to date of exchange)	45,000	52,000
Fair market value at date of exchange	60,000	75,000
Cash paid by Arna, Inc.	15,000	
Cash received by Bontemps, Inc.		15,000

Instructions
(a) Assume that Assets A and B are dissimilar, and record the exchange for both Arna, Inc. and Bontemps, Inc. in accordance with generally accepted accounting principles.
(b) Assume that Assets A and B are similar, and record the exchange for both Arna, Inc. and Bontemps, Inc. in accordance with generally accepted accounting principles.

P10-10 (Nonmonetary Exchanges with Boot) During the current year, Garrison Construction trades an old crane that has a book value of $80,000 (original cost $140,000 less accumulated depreciation $60,000) for a new crane from Keillor Manufacturing Co. The new crane cost Keillor $165,000 to manufacture and is classified as inventory. The following information is also available.

	Garrison Const.	Keillor Mfg. Co.
Fair market value of old crane	$ 72,000	
Fair market value of new crane		$190,000
Cash paid	118,000	
Cash received		118,000

Instructions
(a) Assume that this exchange is considered to involve dissimilar assets and prepare the journal entries on the books of (1) Garrison Construction and (2) Keillor Manufacturing.
(b) Assume that this exchange is considered to involve similar assets and prepare the journal entries on the books of (1) Garrison Construction and (2) Keillor Manufacturing.
(c) Assuming the same facts as those in (a), except that the fair market value of the old crane is $98,000 and the cash paid is $92,000, prepare the journal entries on the books of (1) Garrison Construction and (2) Keillor Manufacturing.
(d) Assuming the same facts as those in (b), except that the fair market value of the old crane is $87,000 and the cash paid $103,000, prepare the journal entries on the books of (1) Garrison Construction and (2) Keillor Manufacturing.

P10-11 (Costs of Self-Constructed Assets) George Fayne Mining Co. received a $760,000 low bid from a reputable manufacturer for the construction of special production equipment needed by Fayne in an expansion program. Because the company's own plant was not operating at capacity, Fayne decided to construct the equipment there and recorded the following production costs related to the construction:

Services of consulting engineer	$ 40,000
Work subcontracted	31,000
Materials	300,000
Plant labor normally assigned to production	114,000
Plant labor normally assigned to maintenance	160,000
Total	$645,000

Management prefers to record the cost of the equipment under the incremental cost method. Approximately 40% of the company's production is devoted to government supply contracts which are all based in some way on cost. The contracts require that any self-constructed equipment be allocated its full share of all costs related to the construction.

The following information is also available:

1. The production labor was for partial fabrication of the equipment in the plant. Skilled personnel were required and were assigned from other projects. The maintenance labor would have been idle time of nonproduction plant employees who would have been retained on the payroll whether or not their services were utilized.
2. Payroll taxes and employee fringe benefits are approximately 35% of labor cost and are included in manufacturing overhead cost. Total manufacturing overhead for the year was $6,084,000, including the $160,000 maintenance labor used to construct the equipment.
3. Manufacturing overhead is approximately 60% variable and is applied on the basis of production labor cost. Production labor cost for the year for the corporation's normal products totaled $8,286,000.
4. General and administrative expenses include $27,000 of allocated executive salary cost and $13,750 of postage, telephone, supplies, and miscellaneous expenses identifiable with this equipment construction.

Instructions

(a) Prepare a schedule computing the amount that should be reported as the full cost of the constructed equipment to meet the requirements of the government contracts. Any supporting computations should be in good form.

(b) Prepare a schedule computing the incremental cost of the constructed equipment.

(c) What is the greatest amount that should be capitalized as the cost of the equipment? Why?

(AICPA adapted)

P10-12 (Purchases by Deferred Payment, Lump-sum, and Nonmonetary Exchanges) Kent Adamson Company is a manufacturer of ballet shoes and is experiencing a period of sustained growth. In an effort to expand its production capacity to meet the increased demand for its product, the company recently made several acquisitions of plant and equipment. Tod Mullinger, newly hired in the position of fixed-asset accountant, requested that Watt Kaster, Adamson's controller, review the following transactions.

Transaction 1

On June 1, 2001, Adamson Company purchased equipment from Venghaus Corporation. Adamson issued a $20,000, 4-year, non-interest-bearing note to Venghaus for the new equipment. Adamson will pay off the note in four equal installments due at the end of each of the next 4 years. At the date of the transaction, the prevailing market rate of interest for obligations of this nature was 10%. Freight costs of $425 and installation costs of $500 were incurred in completing this transaction. The appropriate factors for the time value of money at a 10% rate of interest are given below.

Future value of $1 for 4 periods	1.46
Future value of an ordinary annuity for 4 periods	4.64
Present value of $1 for 4 periods	0.68
Present value of an ordinary annuity for 4 periods	3.17

Transaction 2

On December 1, 2001, Adamson Company purchased several assets of Haukap Shoes Inc., a small shoe manufacturer whose owner was retiring. The purchase amounted to $210,000 and included the assets listed below. Adamson Company engaged the services of Tennyson Appraisal Inc., an independent appraiser, to determine the fair market values of the assets which are also presented below.

	Haukap Book Value	Fair Market Value
Inventory	$ 60,000	$ 50,000
Land	40,000	80,000
Building	70,000	120,000
	$170,000	$250,000

During its fiscal year ended May 31, 2002, Adamson incurred $8,000 for interest expense in connection with the financing of these assets.

Transaction 3

On March 1, 2002, Adamson Company exchanged a number of used trucks plus cash for vacant land adjacent to its plant site. Adamson intends to use the land for a parking lot. The trucks had a combined book value of $35,000, as Adamson had recorded $20,000 of accumulated depreciation against these assets. Adamson's purchasing agent, who has had previous dealings in the second-hand market, indicated that the trucks had a fair market value of $46,000 at the time of the transaction. In addition to the trucks, Adamson Company paid $19,000 cash for the land.

Instructions

(a) Plant assets such as land, buildings, and equipment receive special accounting treatment. Describe the major characteristics of these assets that differentiate them from other types of assets.

(b) For each of the three transactions described above, determine the value at which Adamson Company should record the acquired assets. Support your calculations with an explanation of the underlying rationale.

(c) The books of Adamson Company show the following additional transactions for the fiscal year ended May 31, 2002.

1. Acquisition of a building for speculative purposes.
2. Purchase of a 2-year insurance policy covering plant equipment.
3. Purchase of the rights for the exclusive use of a process used in the manufacture of ballet shoes.

For each of these transactions, indicate whether the asset should be classified as a plant asset. If it is a plant asset, explain why it is. If it is not a plant asset, explain why not, and identify the proper classification.

(CMA adapted)

CONCEPTUAL CASES

C10-1 (Options to Purchase Property) Your client, Salvador Plastics Co., found three suitable sites, each having certain unique advantages, for a new plant facility. In order to thoroughly investigate the advantages and disadvantages of each site, 1-year options were purchased for an amount equal to 6% of the contract price of each site. The costs of the options cannot be applied against the contracts. Before the options expired, one of the sites was purchased at the contract price of $400,000. The option on this site had cost $24,000. The two options not exercised had cost $16,000 each.

Instructions

Present arguments in support of recording the cost of the land at each of the following amounts.

(a) $400,000.
(b) $424,000.
(c) $456,000.

(AICPA adapted)

C10-2 (Acquisition, Improvements, and Sale of Realty) William Bradford Company purchased land for use as its corporate headquarters. A small factory that was on the land when it was purchased was torn down before construction of the office building began. Furthermore, a substantial amount of rock blasting and removal had to be done to the site before construction of the building foundation began. Because the office building was set back on the land far from the public road, Bradford Company had the contractor construct a paved road that led from the public road to the parking lot of the office building.

Three years after the office building was occupied, Bradford Company added four stories to the office building. The four stories had an estimated useful life of 5 years more than the remaining estimated useful life of the original office building.

Ten years later the land and building were sold at an amount more than their net book value, and Bradford Company had a new office building constructed in another state for use as its new corporate headquarters.

Instructions

(a) Which of the expenditures above should be capitalized? How should each be depreciated or amortized? Discuss the rationale for your answers.

(b) How would the sale of the land and building be accounted for? Include in your answer an explanation of how to determine the net book value at the date of sale. Discuss the rationale for your answer.

C10-3 (Accounting for Self-Constructed Assets) Shanette Medical Labs, Inc., began operations 5 years ago producing stetrics, a new type of instrument it hoped to sell to doctors, dentists, and hospitals. The demand for stetrics far exceeded initial expectations, and the company was unable to produce enough stetrics to meet demand.

The company was manufacturing its product on equipment that it built at the start of its operations. To meet demand, more efficient equipment was needed. The company decided to design and build the equipment, because the equipment currently available on the market was unsuitable for producing stetrics.

In 2001, a section of the plant was devoted to development of the new equipment and a special staff was hired. Within 6 months a machine developed at a cost of $714,000 increased production dramatically and reduced labor costs substantially. Elated by the success of the new machine, the company built three more machines of the same type at a cost of $441,000 each.

Instructions

(a) In general, what costs should be capitalized for self-constructed equipment?

(b) Discuss the propriety of including in the capitalized cost of self-constructed assets:

  (1) The increase in overhead caused by the self-construction of fixed assets.

  (2) A proportionate share of overhead on the same basis as that applied to goods manufactured for sale.

(c) Discuss the proper accounting treatment of the $273,000 ($714,000 − $441,000) by which the cost of the first machine exceeded the cost of the subsequent machines. This additional cost should not be considered research and development costs.

C10-4 (Capitalization of Interest) Zucker Airline is converting from piston-type planes to jets. Delivery time for the jets is 3 years, during which substantial progress payments must be made. The multimillion-dollar cost of the planes cannot be financed from working capital; Zucker must borrow funds for the payments.

Because of high interest rates and the large sum to be borrowed, management estimates that interest costs in the second year of the period will be equal to one-third of income before interest and taxes, and one-half of such income in the third year.

After conversion, Zucker's passenger-carrying capacity will be doubled with no increase in the number of planes, although the investment in planes would be substantially increased. The jet planes have a 7-year service life.

Instructions

Give your recommendation concerning the proper accounting for interest during the conversion period. Support your recommendation with reasons and suggested accounting treatment. (Disregard income tax implications.)

(AICPA adapted)

C10-5 (Capitalization of Interest) Petri Magazine Company started construction of a warehouse building for its own use at an estimated cost of $6,000,000 on January 1, 1999, and completed the building on December 31, 1999. During the construction period, Petri has the following debt obligations outstanding:

Construction loan—12% interest, payable semiannually, issued December 31, 1998	$2,000,000
Short-term loan—10% interest, payable monthly, and principal payable at maturity, on May 30, 2000	1,400,000
Long-term loan—11% interest, payable on January 1 of each year. Principal payable on January 1, 2002	2,000,000

Total cost amounted to $6,200,000, and the weighted average of accumulated expenditures was $4,000,000.

Dee Pettepiece, the president of the company, has been shown the costs associated with this construction project and capitalized on the balance sheet. She is bothered by the "avoidable interest" included in the cost. She argues that, first, all the interest is unavoidable—no one lends money without expecting to be compensated for it. Second, why can't the company use all the interest on all the loans when computing this avoidable interest? Finally, why can't her company capitalize all the annual interest that accrued over the period of construction?

Instructions

You are the manager of accounting for the company. In a memo, explain what avoidable interest is, how you computed it (being especially careful to explain why you used the interest rates that you did), and why the company cannot capitalize all its interest for the year. Attach a schedule supporting any computations that you use.

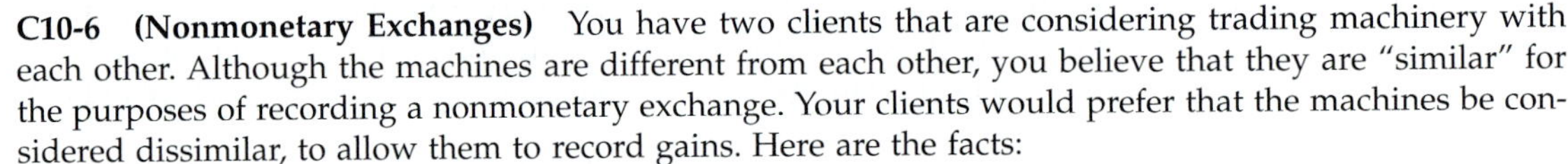

C10-6 (Nonmonetary Exchanges) You have two clients that are considering trading machinery with each other. Although the machines are different from each other, you believe that they are "similar" for the purposes of recording a nonmonetary exchange. Your clients would prefer that the machines be considered dissimilar, to allow them to record gains. Here are the facts:

	Client A	Client B
Original cost	$100,000	$150,000
Accumulated depreciation	40,000	80,000
Market value	90,000	120,000
Cash received (paid)	(30,000)	30,000

Instructions

(a) Record the trade-in on Client A's books assuming the assets are dissimilar.
(b) Record the trade-in on Client A's books assuming the assets are similar.
(c) Write a memo to the controller of Company A indicating and explaining the dollar impact on current and future statements of treating the assets as "similar" versus "dissimilar."
(d) Record the entry on Client B's books assuming the assets are dissimilar.
(e) Record the entry on Client B's books assuming the assets are similar.
(f) Write a memo to the controller of Company B indicating and explaining the dollar impact on current and future statements of treating the assets as "similar" versus "dissimilar."

C10-7 (Assets Acquired through Issuance of Stock) You have been engaged to examine the financial statements of Richard Corporation for the year ending December 31, 2001. Richard was organized in January 2001 by Messrs. Dean and Anderson, original owners of options to acquire oil leases on 5,000 acres of land for $1,200,000. They expected that (1) the oil leases would be acquired by the corporation and (2) subsequently 180,000 shares of the corporation's common stock would be sold to the public at $20 per share. In February 2002, they exchanged their options, $400,000 cash, and $200,000 of other assets for 75,000 shares of common stock of the corporation. The corporation's board of directors appraised the leases at $2,100,000, basing its appraisal on the price of other acreage recently leased in the same area. The options were, therefore, recorded at $900,000 ($2,100,000 − $1,200,000 option price).

The options were exercised by the corporation in March 2002, prior to the sale of common stock to the public in April 2002. Leases on approximately 500 acres of land were abandoned as worthless during the year.

Instructions

(a) Why is the valuation of assets acquired by a corporation in exchange for its own common stock sometimes difficult?
(b) **(1)** What reasoning might Richard Corporation use to support valuing the leases at $2,100,000, the amount of the appraisal by the board of directors?
(2) Assuming that the board's appraisal was sincere, what steps might Richard Corporation have taken to strengthen its position to use the $2,100,000 value and to provide additional information if questions were raised about possible overvaluation of the leases?
(c) Discuss the propriety of charging one-tenth of the recorded value of the leases to expense at December 31, 2002, because leases on 500 acres of land were abandoned during the year.

(AICPA adapted)

C10-8 (Costs of Acquisition) The invoice price of a machine is $40,000. Various other costs relating to the acquisition and installation of the machine including transportation, electrical wiring, special base, and so on amount to $7,500. The machine has an estimated life of 10 years, with no residual value at the end of that period.

The owner of the business suggests that the incidental costs of $7,500 be charged to expense immediately for the following reasons.

1. If the machine should be sold, these costs cannot be recovered in the sales price.
2. The inclusion of the $7,500 in the machinery account on the books will not necessarily result in a closer approximation of the market price of this asset over the years, because of the possibility of changing demand and supply levels.
3. Charging the $7,500 to expense immediately will reduce federal income taxes.

Instructions

Discuss each of the points raised by the owner of the business.

(AICPA adapted)

USING YOUR JUDGMENT

FINANCIAL STATEMENT ANALYSIS CASE

Johnson & Johnson

Johnson & Johnson, the world's leading and most diversified health care corporation, serves its customers through specialized worldwide franchises. Each of its franchises consists of a number of companies throughout the world that focus on a particular health care market, such as surgical sutures, consumer pharmaceuticals, or contact lenses. Information related to its property, plant, and equipment in its 1998 annual report is shown in the notes to the financial statements as follows.

Note 1: Depreciation of Property

The company utilizes the straight-line method of depreciation for financial statement purposes for all additions to property, plant, and equipment.

Note 3: Property, Plant, and Equipment

At the end of 1998 and 1997, property, plant, and equipment at cost and accumulated depreciation consisted of:

(dollars in millions)	1998	1997
Land and land improvements	$ 459	$ 407
Buildings and building equipment	2,922	2,895
Machinery and equipment	5,575	5,224
Construction in progress	1,068	918
	10,024	9,444
Less: Accumulated depreciation	3,784	3,634
	$ 6,240	$5,810

The Company capitalizes interest expense as part of the cost of construction of facilities and equipment. Interest expense capitalized in 1998, 1997, and 1996 was $71, $40, and $55 million, respectively.

Upon retirement or other disposal of fixed assets, the cost and related amount of accumulated depreciation or amortization are eliminated from the asset and reserve accounts, respectively. The difference, if any, between the net asset value and the proceeds is adjusted to income.

In Johnson & Johnson's cash flow statement, the following selected information is provided:

Net cash flows from operating activities	$ 4,886
Cash flows from investing activities	
Additions to property, plant, and equipment	(1,460)
Proceeds from the disposal of assets	71
Acquisition of businesses, net of cash acquired (Note 17)	(3,481)
Other, principally marketable securities	(769)
Net cash used by investing activities	(5,639)
Cash flows from financing activities	
Dividends to shareowners	(1,305)
Repurchase of common stock	(930)
Proceeds from short-term debt	2,424
Retirement of short-term debt	(226)
Proceeds from long-term debt	86
Retirement of long-term debt	(416)
Proceeds from the exercise of stock options	269
Net cash used by financing activities	(98)
Effect of exchange rate changes on cash and cash equivalents	25
(Decrease) increase in cash and cash equivalents	(826)
Cash and cash equivalents, beginning of year (Note 1)	2,753
Cash and cash equivalents, end of year (Note 1)	$ 1,927

Supplemental cash flow data
Cash paid during the year for:

Interest, net of portion capitalized	$ 89
Income taxes	1,310

Instructions

(a) What was the cost of buildings and building equipment at the end of 1998?

(b) Does Johnson & Johnson use a conservative or liberal method to depreciate its property, plant, and equipment?

(c) What was the actual interest expense incurred by the company in 1998?

(d) What is Johnson & Johnson's free cash flow? From the information provided, comment on Johnson & Johnson's financial flexibility.

RESEARCH CASE

The December 18, 1995, issue of *Forbes* includes an article by Rita Koselka entitled "Tall Story."

Instructions

Read the article and answer the following questions.

(a) What is the biggest expense in running a video rental store?

(b) Over how long a period does Hollywood Entertainment Corp. depreciate its videotapes? How did the author arrive at this figure?

(c) The author asserts that, once a store is fully stocked, depreciation expense should be approximately equal to the cost of new tapes. Calculate and compare the ratio of depreciation expense to new purchases for Hollywood and Blockbuster.

(d) If Hollywood can open a new store for $400,000 or buy an existing store for $1.2 million, why might investors value Hollywood at an average of $3 million per store?

ETHICS CASE

Field Company purchased a warehouse in a downtown district where land values are rapidly increasing. Adolph Phillips, controller, and Wilma Smith, financial vice-president, are trying to allocate the cost of the purchase between the land and the building. Phillips, noting that depreciation can be taken only on the building, favors placing a very high proportion of the cost on the warehouse itself, thus reducing taxable income and income taxes. Smith, his supervisor, argues that the allocation should recognize the increasing value of the land, regardless of the depreciation potential of the warehouse. Besides, she says, net income is negatively impacted by additional depreciation and will cause the company's stock price to go down.

Instructions

Answer the following questions:

(a) What stakeholder interests are in conflict?

(b) What ethical issues does Phillips face?

(c) How should these costs be allocated?

CHAPTER 11

Depreciation, Impairments, and Depletion

Impairment, Impairment Everywhere

As shown below, companies are reporting significant impairments on long-lived assets.

Company	Nature of Impairment	Amount
Hanneford Brothers Co.	Stores	$40 million in 4th quarter of 1997
Sodak Gaming Inc.	Riverboat	$6 million in 4th quarter of 1997
Au Bon Pain Co.	Fixed assets of business unit to be sold	$17.7 million in 3rd quarter of 1998
Ross Technologies	Subsidiary and other assets	11.2 million in 4th quarter of 1998
Damark International	Computer software and hardware, and furniture and fixtures	$10.2 million in 4th quarter of 1998

Each of these write-offs is recorded in accordance with *Statement of Financial Accounting Standards No. 121,* "Accounting for the Impairment of Long-lived Assets and for Long-lived Assets to Be Disposed of" (*SFAS No. 121*). For example, **Sodak Gaming Inc.** reported that its write-down on the Miss Marquette Riverboat was recorded after the company decided that this asset would not be as profitable as originally thought. Similarly, both **Au Bon Pain Co.** and **Ross Technologies** recorded impairments on assets in businesses that they were planning to sell. Before *SFAS No. 121,* companies generally waited to record impairments or write-downs until it was certain that the impairment was permanent. As a result, investors and creditors often learned too late that long-lived assets had declined in value.

International accounting standard-setters have also addressed this problem. For example, the United Kingdom's accounting standard-setting body recently issued a standard on impairment as well. According to its chairperson, Sir David Tweedy, companies ". . . will no longer be able to pretend that long-standing losses . . . (on long-lived assets) . . . are only temporary." Sir David noted that the new rule attacks "scoundrel accounting" in which companies charge low amounts of depreciation on long-lived assets, resulting in unrealistically high valuations of fixed assets in financial statements.

Thus, while impairments are on the rise in the United States and elsewhere, investors are now receiving better information about fixed asset values in financial statements.

LEARNING OBJECTIVES

After studying this chapter, you should be able to:

1. **Explain the concept of depreciation.**
2. **Identify the factors involved in the depreciation process.**
3. **Compare activity, straight-line, and decreasing charge methods of depreciation.**
4. **Explain special depreciation methods.**
5. **Identify reasons why depreciation methods are selected.**
6. **Explain the accounting issues related to asset impairment.**
7. **Explain the accounting procedures for depletion of natural resources.**
8. **Explain how property, plant, equipment, and natural resources are reported and analyzed.**

PREVIEW OF CHAPTER 11

As noted in the opening story, accounting standard-setters around the world have developed new rules on impairments. These rules recognize that when economic conditions change, some type of write-off of cost is needed to indicate that the usefulness of an asset has declined. The purpose of this chapter is to examine the depreciation process and the methods of writing off the cost of tangible assets and natural resources. The content and organization of the chapter are as follows:

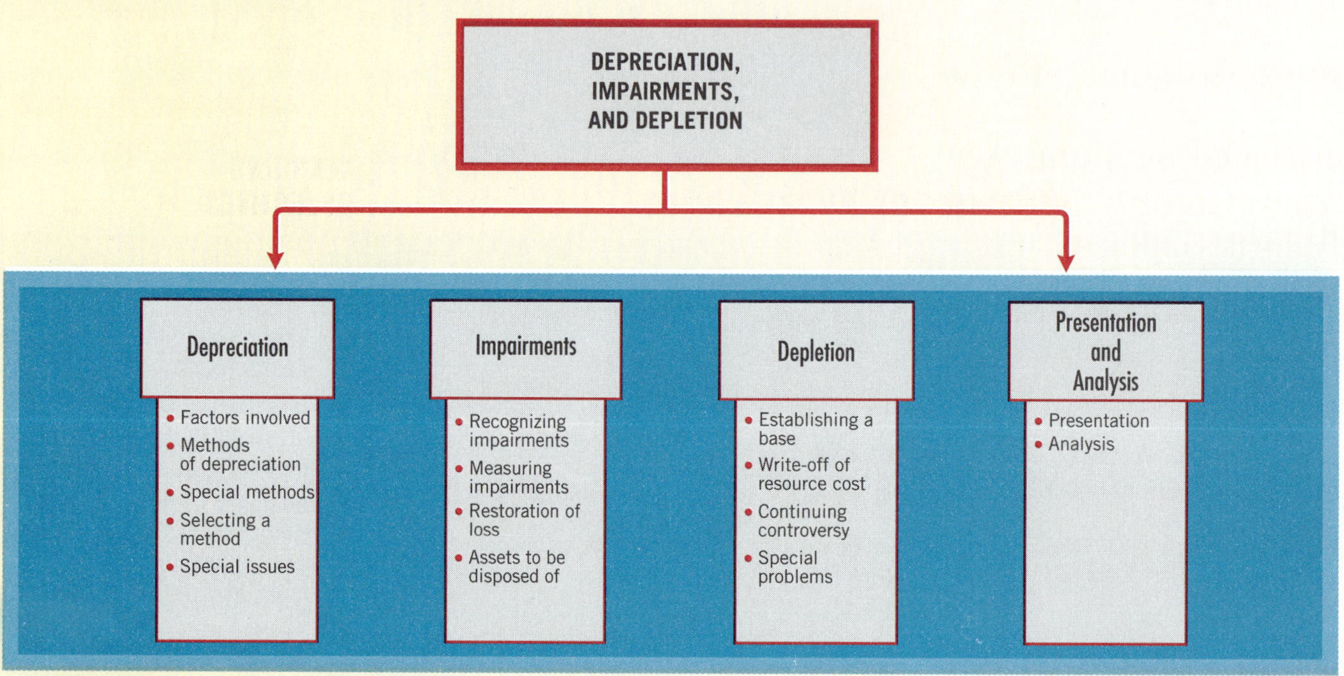

DEPRECIATION—A METHOD OF COST ALLOCATION

OBJECTIVE 1
Explain the concept of depreciation.

Most individuals at one time or another purchase and trade in an automobile. In discussions with the automobile dealer, depreciation is a consideration on two points. First, how much has the old car "depreciated"? That is, what is the trade-in value? Second, how fast will the new car depreciate? That is, what will its trade-in value be? In both cases depreciation is thought of as a loss in value.

To accountants, however, **depreciation is not a matter of valuation but a means of cost allocation**. Assets are not depreciated on the basis of a decline in their fair market value, but on the basis of systematic charges to expense. **Depreciation is defined as the accounting process of allocating the cost of tangible assets to expense in a systematic and rational manner to those periods expected to benefit from the use of the asset.**

This approach is employed because the value of the asset may fluctuate between the time the asset is purchased and the time it is sold or junked. Attempts to measure these interim value changes have not been well received by accountants because values are difficult to measure objectively. Therefore, the asset's cost is charged to depreciation expense over its estimated life, making no attempts to value the asset at fair market value between acquisition and disposition. The cost allocation approach is used because a matching of costs with revenues occurs and because fluctuations in market value are tenuous and difficult to measure.

When long-lived assets are written off, the term **depreciation** is most often used to indicate that tangible plant assets have declined in value. Where natural resources, such as timber, gravel, oil, and coal, are involved, the term **depletion** is employed. The expiration of intangible assets, such as patents or goodwill, is called **amortization**.

Factors Involved in the Depreciation Process

Before a pattern of charges to revenue can be established, three basic questions must be answered:

OBJECTIVE 2
Identify the factors involved in the depreciation process.

1. What depreciable base is to be used for the asset?
2. What is the asset's useful life?
3. What method of cost apportionment is best for this asset?

The answers to these questions involve the distillation of several estimates into one single figure. The calculations on which depreciation is based assume perfect knowledge of the future, which is never attainable.

Depreciable Base for the Asset

The base established for depreciation is a function of two factors: the original cost and salvage or disposal value. We discussed historical cost in Chapter 10. **Salvage value** is the estimated amount that will be received at the time the asset is sold or removed from service. It is the amount to which the asset must be written down or depreciated during its useful life. To illustrate, if an asset has a cost of $10,000 and a salvage value of $1,000, its depreciation base is $9,000.

Original cost	$10,000
Less: Salvage value	1,000
Depreciation base	$ 9,000

ILLUSTRATION 11-1
Computation of Depreciation Base

From a practical standpoint, salvage value is often considered to be zero because its valuation is small. Some long-lived assets, however, have substantial salvage values.

Companies also differ as to their estimate of salvage value. At one time **Leasco**, **Greyhound Corp.**, and **Boothe Computer** all depreciated the same IBM computer equipment on a straight-line basis, but Leasco and Greyhound assumed a 10% salvage value, whereas Boothe assumed zero.

Estimation of Service Lives

The service life of an asset and its physical life are often not the same. A piece of machinery may be physically capable of producing a given product for many years beyond its service life, but the equipment is not used for all of those years because the cost of producing the product in later years may be too high. For example, the old Slater cotton mill in Pawtucket, Rhode Island, is preserved in remarkable physical condition as an historic landmark in American industrial development, although its service life was terminated many years ago.[1]

Assets are retired for two reasons: **physical factors** (such as casualty or expiration of physical life) and **economic factors** (obsolescence). Physical factors are the wear and tear, decay, and casualties that make it difficult for the asset to perform indefinitely. These physical factors set the outside limit for the service life of an asset.

In the U.S., depreciation must take into account any expected obsolescence. In many nations this is not required.

The economic or functional factors can be classified into three categories: inadequacy, supersession, and obsolescence. **Inadequacy** results when an asset ceases to be useful to a given enterprise because the demands of the firm have increased. Example:

[1]Taken from J. D. Coughlan and W. K. Strand, *Depreciation Accounting, Taxes and Business Decisions* (New York: The Ronald Press, 1969), pp. 10–12.

the need for a larger building to handle increased production. Although the old building may still be sound, it may have become inadequate for that enterprise's purposes. **Supersession** is the replacement of one asset with another more efficient and economical asset. Example: the replacement of the mainframe computer with a PC network, or the replacement of the Boeing 767 with the Boeing 777. **Obsolescence** is the catchall for situations not involving inadequacy and supersession. Because the distinction between these categories appears artificial, it is probably best to consider economic factors totally instead of trying to make distinctions that are not clear-cut.

To illustrate the concepts of physical and economic factors, consider a new nuclear power plant. Which do you think would be more important in determining the useful life of a nuclear power plant—physical factors or economic factors? The limiting factors seem to be (1) ecological considerations, (2) competition from other power sources, and (3) safety concerns. Physical life does not appear to be the primary factor affecting useful life. Although the plant's physical life may be far from over, the plant may become obsolete in 10 years.

For a house, physical factors undoubtedly are more important than the economic or functional factors relative to useful life. Whenever the physical nature of the asset is the primary determinant of useful life, maintenance plays an extremely vital role. The better the maintenance, the longer the life of the asset.[2]

In some cases, arbitrary service lives are selected; in others, sophisticated statistical methods are employed to establish a useful life for accounting purposes. In many cases, the primary basis for estimating the useful life of an asset is the enterprise's past experience with the same or similar assets. In a highly industrial economy such as that of the United States, where research and innovation are so prominent, technological factors have as much effect, if not more, on service lives of tangible plant assets as physical factors do.

Methods of Depreciation

The third factor involved in the depreciation process is the **method** of cost apportionment. The profession requires that the depreciation method employed be "systematic and rational."

A number of depreciation methods are used. They may be classified as follows.

Depreciation is an attempt to match the cost of an asset to the periods that benefit from the use of that asset.

1. Activity method (units of use or production).
2. Straight-line method.
3. Decreasing charge methods (accelerated):
   (a) Sum-of-the-years'-digits.
   (b) Declining-balance method.
4. Special depreciation methods:
   (a) Group and composite methods.
   (b) Hybrid or combination methods.[3]

To illustrate some of these depreciation methods, assume that Stanley Coal Mines recently purchased an additional crane for digging purposes. Pertinent data concerning the purchase of the crane are:

---

[2]The airline industry also illustrates the type of problem involved in estimation. In the past, aircraft were assumed not to wear out—they just became obsolete. However, some jets have been in service as long as 20 years, and maintenance of these aircraft has become increasingly expensive. In addition, the public's concern about worn-out aircraft has been heightened by some recent air disasters. As a result, some airlines are finding it necessary to replace aircraft not because of obsolescence but because of physical deterioration.

[3]*Accounting Trends and Techniques—1999* reports that of its 600 surveyed companies various depreciation methods were used for financial reporting purposes: straight-line, 577; declining-balance 25; sum-of-the-years'-digits, 9; accelerated method (not specified), 43; units of production, 36. No utility or transportation companies (the ones that use the "special depreciation methods") are included in the AICPA's survey.

Cost of crane	$500,000
Estimated useful life	5 years
Estimated salvage value	$ 50,000
Productive life in hours	30,000 hours

ILLUSTRATION 11-2
Data Used to Illustrate Depreciation Methods

Activity Method

OBJECTIVE 3
Compare activity, straight-line, and decreasing charge methods of depreciation.

The **activity method** (also called the variable charge approach) assumes that depreciation is **a function of use or productivity instead of the passage of time.** The life of the asset is considered in terms of either the **output** it provides (units it produces), or an **input** measure such as the number of hours it works. Conceptually, the proper cost association is established in terms of output instead of hours used, but often the output is not easily measurable. In such cases, an input measure such as machine hours is a more appropriate method of measuring the dollar amount of depreciation charges for a given accounting period.

The crane poses no particular problem because the usage (hours) is relatively easy to measure. If the crane is used 4,000 hours the first year, the depreciation charge is:

$$\frac{\text{(Cost less salvage)} \times \text{Hours this year}}{\text{Total estimated hours}} = \text{Depreciation charge}$$

$$\frac{(\$500{,}000 - \$50{,}000) \times 4{,}000}{30{,}000} = \$60{,}000$$

ILLUSTRATION 11-3
Depreciation Calculation, Activity Method—Crane Example

The major limitation of this method is that it is not appropriate in situations in which depreciation is a function of time instead of activity. For example, a building is subject to a great deal of steady deterioration from the elements (time) regardless of its use. In addition, where an asset is subject to economic or functional factors, independent of its use, the activity method loses much of its significance. For example, if a company is expanding rapidly, a particular building may soon become obsolete for its intended purposes. In both cases, activity is irrelevant. Another problem in using an activity method is that an estimate of units of output or service hours received is often difficult to determine.

Where loss of services is a result of activity or productivity, the activity method will best match costs and revenues. Companies that desire low depreciation during periods of low productivity and high depreciation during high productivity either adopt or switch to an activity method. In this way, a plant running at 40% of capacity generates 60% lower depreciation charges. **Inland Steel**, for example, switched to units-of-production depreciation at one time and reduced its losses by $43 million, or $1.20 per share.[4]

Straight-Line Method

UNDERLYING CONCEPTS

If those benefits flow on a "straight-line" basis, then justification exists for matching the cost of the asset on a straight-line basis with these benefits.

The **straight-line method** considers depreciation a **function of time rather than a function of usage.** This method is widely employed in practice because of its simplicity. The straight-line procedure is often the most conceptually appropriate, too. When creeping obsolescence is the primary reason for a limited service life, the decline in usefulness may be constant from period to period. The depreciation charge for the crane is computed as follows.

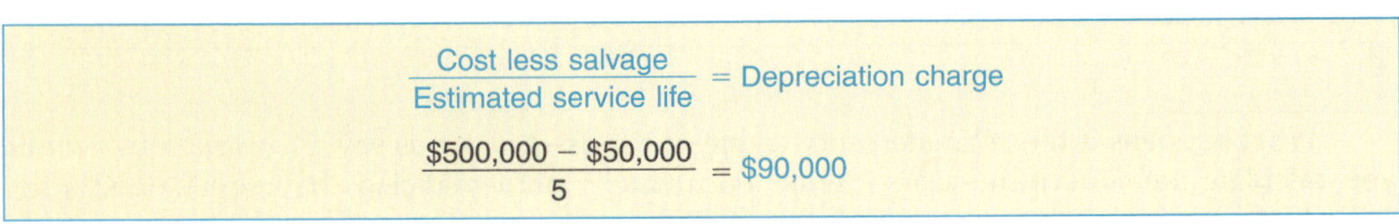

$$\frac{\text{Cost less salvage}}{\text{Estimated service life}} = \text{Depreciation charge}$$

$$\frac{\$500{,}000 - \$50{,}000}{5} = \$90{,}000$$

ILLUSTRATION 11-4
Depreciation Calculation, Straight-Line Method—Crane Example

[4]"Double Standard," *Forbes*, November 22, 1982, p. 178.

The major objection to the straight-line method is that it rests on two unrealistic assumptions: (1) the asset's economic usefulness is the same each year, and (2) the repair and maintenance expense is essentially the same each period.

One additional problem that occurs in using straight-line—as well as some others—is that distortions in the rate of return analysis (income/assets) develop. Illustration 11-5 indicates how the rate of return increases, given constant revenue flows, because the asset's book value decreases.

ILLUSTRATION 11-5
Depreciation and Rate of Return Analysis—Crane Example

Year	Depreciation Expense	Undepreciated Asset Balance (book value)	Income (after depreciation expense)	Rate of Return (income ÷ assets)
0		$500,000		
1	$90,000	410,000	$100,000	24.4%
2	90,000	320,000	100,000	31.2%
3	90,000	230,000	100,000	43.5%
4	90,000	140,000	100,000	71.4%
5	90,000	50,000	100,000	200.0%

Decreasing Charge Methods

The **decreasing charge methods**—often called **accelerated depreciation methods**—provide for a higher depreciation cost in the earlier years and lower charges in later periods. The main justification for this approach is that more depreciation should be charged in earlier years because the asset suffers its greatest loss of services in those years. Another argument presented is that the accelerated methods provide a constant cost because the depreciation charge is lower in the later periods, at the time when the repair and maintenance costs are often higher. Generally, one of two decreasing charge methods is employed: the sum-of-the-years'-digits method or the declining-balance method.

UNDERLYING CONCEPTS

The matching concept does not justify a constant charge to income. If the benefits from the asset decline as the asset gets older, then a decreasing charge to income would better match cost to benefits.

Sum-of-the-Years'-Digits. The **sum-of-the-years'-digits method** results in a decreasing depreciation charge based on a decreasing fraction of depreciable cost (original cost less salvage value). Each fraction uses the sum of the years as a denominator (5 + 4 + 3 + 2 + 1 = 15) and the number of years of estimated life remaining as of the beginning of the year as a numerator. In this method, the numerator decreases year by year and the denominator remains constant (5/15, 4/15, 3/15, 2/15, and 1/15). At the end of the asset's useful life, the balance remaining should be equal to the salvage value. This method of computation is shown in Illustration 11-6 below.[5]

ILLUSTRATION 11-6
Sum-of-the-Years'-Digits Depreciation Schedule—Crane Example

Year	Depreciation Base	Remaining Life in Years	Depreciation Fraction	Depreciation Expense	Book Value, End of Year
1	$450,000	5	5/15	$150,000	$350,000
2	450,000	4	4/15	120,000	230,000
3	450,000	3	3/15	90,000	140,000
4	450,000	2	2/15	60,000	80,000
5	450,000	1	1/15	30,000	50,000[a]
		15	15/15	$450,000	

[a]Salvage value.

[5]What happens if the estimated service life of the asset is, let us say, 51 years? How would you calculate the sum-of-the-years'-digits? Fortunately mathematicians have developed a formula that permits easy computation. It is as follows:

$$\frac{n(n+1)}{2} = \frac{51(51+1)}{2} = 1{,}326$$

Declining-Balance Method. Another decreasing charge method is the **declining-balance method**, which utilizes a depreciation rate (expressed as a percentage) that is some multiple of the straight-line method. For example, the double-declining rate for a 10-year asset would be 20% (double the straight-line rate, which is 1/10 or 10%). The declining-balance rate remains constant and is applied to the reducing book value each year. Unlike other methods, in the declining-balance method the salvage value is not deducted in computing the depreciation base. The declining-balance rate is multiplied by the book value of the asset at the beginning of each period. Since the book value of the asset is reduced each period by the depreciation charge, the constant-declining-balance rate is applied to a successively lower book value which results in lower depreciation charges each year. This process continues until the book value of the asset is reduced to its estimated salvage value, at which time depreciation is discontinued.

INTERNATIONAL INSIGHT

German companies depreciate their fixed assets at a much faster rate than U.S. companies because German tax laws permit accelerated depreciation of up to triple the straight-line rate.

As indicated above, various multiples are used in practice, such as twice (200%) the straight-line rate (**double-declining-balance method**) and 150% of the straight-line rate. Using the double-declining approach in the crane example, Stanley Coal Mines would have the depreciation charges shown in Illustration 11-7 below.

ILLUSTRATION 11-7
Double-Declining Depreciation Schedule—Crane Example

Year	Book Value of Asset First of Year	Rate on Declining Balance[a]	Debit Depreciation Expense	Balance Accumulated Depreciation	Book Value, End of Year
1	$500,000	40%	$200,000	$200,000	$300,000
2	300,000	40%	120,000	320,000	180,000
3	180,000	40%	72,000	392,000	108,000
4	108,000	40%	43,200	435,200	64,800
5	64,800	40%	14,800[b]	450,000	50,000

[a]Based on twice the straight-line rate of 20% ($90,000/$450,000 = 20%; 20% × 2 = 40%).
[b]Limited to $14,800 because book value should not be less than salvage value.

Enterprises often switch from the declining-balance method to the sum-of-the-years'-digits or straight-line method near the end of the asset's useful life to ensure that the asset is depreciated only to its salvage value.[6]

Special Depreciation Methods

Sometimes an enterprise does not select one of the more popular depreciation methods because the assets involved have unique characteristics, or the nature of the industry dictates that a special depreciation method be adopted. Two of these special methods are discussed below.

1. Group and composite methods.
2. Hybrid or combination methods.

Group and Composite Methods

Multiple-asset accounts are often depreciated using one rate. For example, an enterprise such as **American Telephone and Telegraph Co.** might depreciate telephone poles, microwave systems, or switchboards by groups.

[6]A pure form of the declining-balance method (sometimes appropriately called the "fixed percentage of book value method") has also been suggested as a possibility. This approach finds a rate that depreciates the asset exactly to salvage value at the end of its expected useful life. The formula for determination of this rate is as follows:

$$\text{Depreciation rate} = 1 - \sqrt[n]{\frac{\text{Salvage value}}{\text{Acquisition cost}}}$$

The life in years is n. Once the depreciation rate is computed, it is applied on the declining book value of the asset from period to period, which means that depreciation expense will be successively lower. This method is not used extensively in practice because the computations are cumbersome and it is not permitted for tax purposes.

Two methods of depreciating multiple-asset accounts are employed: the group method and the composite method. The term **"group" refers to a collection of assets that are similar in nature; "composite" refers to a collection of assets that are dissimilar in nature**. The **group method** is frequently used when the assets are fairly homogeneous and have approximately the same useful lives. The **composite approach** is used when the assets are heterogeneous and have different lives. The group method more closely approximates a single-unit cost procedure because the dispersion from the average is not as great. The method of computation for group or composite is essentially the same: find an average and depreciate on that basis.

To illustrate, Mooney Motors depreciates its fleet of cars, trucks, and campers on a composite basis. The depreciation rate is established in this manner:

ILLUSTRATION 11-8
Depreciation Calculation, Composite Basis

Asset	Original Cost	Residual Value	Depreciable Cost	Estimated Life (yrs.)	Depreciation per Year (straight-line)
Cars	$145,000	$25,000	$120,000	3	$40,000
Trucks	44,000	4,000	40,000	4	10,000
Campers	35,000	5,000	30,000	5	6,000
	$224,000	$34,000	$190,000		$56,000

$$\text{Composite depreciation rate} = \frac{\$56{,}000}{\$224{,}000} = 25\%$$

Composite life = 3.39 years ($190,000 ÷ $56,000)

The **composite depreciation rate** is determined by dividing the depreciation per year by the total cost of the assets. If there are no changes in the asset account, the group of assets will be depreciated to the residual or salvage value at the rate of $56,000 ($224,000 × 25%) a year. As a result, it will take Mooney 3.39 years (composite life as indicated above) to depreciate these assets.

The differences between the group or composite method and the single-unit depreciation method become accentuated when we look at asset retirements. If an asset is retired before, or after, the average service life of the group is reached, the resulting gain or loss is buried in the Accumulated Depreciation account. This practice is justified because some assets will be retired before the average service life and others after the average life. For this reason, the debit to Accumulated Depreciation is the difference between original cost and cash received. No gain or loss on disposition is recorded. To illustrate, suppose that one of the campers with a cost of $5,000 was sold for $2,600 at the end of the third year. The entry is:

Accumulated Depreciation	2,400	
Cash	2,600	
Cars, Trucks, and Campers		5,000

If a new type of asset is purchased (mopeds, for example), a new depreciation rate must be computed and applied in subsequent periods.

A typical financial statement disclosure of the group depreciation method is shown for **Ampco-Pittsburg Corporation** as follows:

ILLUSTRATION 11-9
Disclosure of Group Depreciation Method

AMPCO-PITTSBURG CORPORATION

Depreciation rates are based on estimated useful lives of the asset groups. Gains or losses on normal retirements or replacements of depreciable assets, subject to composite depreciation methods, are not recognized; the difference between the cost of the assets retired or replaced and the related salvage value is charged or credited to the accumulated depreciation.

The group or composite method simplifies the bookkeeping process and tends to average out errors caused by over- or underdepreciation. As a result, periodic income is not distorted by gains or losses on disposals of assets.

On the other hand, the unit method has several advantages over the group or composite methods: (1) it simplifies the computation mathematically; (2) it identifies gains and losses on disposal; (3) it isolates depreciation on idle equipment; and (4) it represents the best estimate of the depreciation of each asset, not the result of averaging the cost over a longer period of time. As a consequence, the unit method is generally used in practice and is generally assumed to be used in homework problems unless stated otherwise.

Hybrid or Combination Methods

In addition to the aforementioned depreciation methods, companies are free to develop their own special or tailor-made depreciation methods. GAAP requires only that the method result in the allocation of an asset's cost over the asset's life in a systematic and rational manner.

Go to the Digital Tool for discussion of other special depreciation methods.

A hybrid depreciation method widely used in the steel industry is a combination straight-line/activity approach referred to as the **production variable method**. The following note from **WHX Corporation**'s 1998 Annual Report explains one variation of this method.

ILLUSTRATION 11-10
Disclosure of Hybrid Depreciation Method

WHX CORPORATION

The Company utilizes the modified units of production method of depreciation which recognizes that the depreciation of steelmaking machinery is related to the physical wear of the equipment as well as a time factor. The modified units of production method provides for straight-line depreciation charges modified (adjusted) by the level of raw steel production. In 1997 depreciation under the modified units of production method was $21.6 million or 40% less than straight-line depreciation, and in 1998 it was $1.1 million or 2% more than straight-line depreciation.

Selecting a Depreciation Method

OBJECTIVE 5
Identify reasons why depreciation methods are selected.

Which depreciation method should be selected? Many believe that the **method which best matches revenues and expenses** should be used. For example, if revenues generated by the asset are constant over the asset's useful life, straight-line depreciation is employed. On the other hand, if revenues are higher (or lower) at the beginning, some form of decreasing (or increasing) charge method of depreciation appears justified. Others argue that it is difficult in most cases to project future revenues and therefore **simplicity** (the straight-line method) should govern. Similarly, others argue that whatever is used for tax purposes should be used for book purposes because it **eliminates some record-keeping costs**.

In most non-Anglo-Saxon nations, companies are not permitted to use one depreciation method for financial statements and a different method for tax returns. The financial statements must conform to the tax return.

Because it is difficult to defend one approach as more useful than another on a conceptual basis, the selection of the depreciation method is often made on more practical grounds. Many companies use the straight-line method for book purposes and adopt the accelerated depreciation method for tax purposes. This provides the best of both worlds—a **lower tax** and usually a **higher net income** for financial reporting purposes. At one time, **U.S. Steel** (now USX) changed its method of depreciation from an accelerated to a straight-line method for financial reporting purposes. Many observers note that the reason for the change was to report higher income so that it would be less susceptible to takeover by another enterprise. In effect, U.S. Steel wanted to report higher income so that the market value of its stock would rise.[7] In 1995 the giant chemical company **Du Pont** switched from accelerated depreciation to straight-line for a $250 million drop in depreciation expense and a warning that the eventual impact on net income would depend "on the level of future capital spending" (averaging $3.5 billion annually from 1993 to 1995).

INTERNATIONAL INSIGHT

Some have even used an economic consequences argument that Canadian real estate companies (which may use an increasing charge method) have a competitive edge over U.S. real estate companies.

The real estate industry is frustrated with depreciation accounting because it argues that real estate often does not decline in value. In addition, because real estate is highly debt financed, most real estate concerns report losses in earlier years when the sum of depreciation and interest charges exceeds the revenues from the real estate project. The industry argues for some form of increasing charge method of depreciation (lower depreciation at the beginning and higher depreciation at the end), so that higher total assets and net income are reported in the earlier years of the project.[8]

Tax policy also has an impact. In the 1980s railroads changed from a special-industry method of accounting for railroad tracks to a more traditional method of capitalizing these track costs and depreciating them. Although the railroads wished to use the traditional method for many years, they had been reluctant to switch because higher tax deductions were achieved through their special methods. The railroads feared that changing to a more traditional method of depreciating for financial reporting purposes might suggest to Congress that this method be used for tax purposes. Ultimately, Congress provided favorable tax legislation to the industry, and the concern was alleviated. As a result, companies have changed to traditional methods of depreciation.

To summarize, the selection of a depreciation method involves factors such as the nature and uncertainty of revenue flows, matching costs and revenues, effect on income and asset book values, tax considerations, and record-keeping costs.

Special Depreciation Issues

Several special issues related to depreciation remain to be discussed. The major issues are:

1. How should depreciation be computed for partial periods?
2. Does depreciation provide for the replacement of assets?
3. How are revisions in depreciation rates handled?

Depreciation and Partial Periods

Plant assets are seldom purchased on the first day of a fiscal period or disposed of on the last day of a fiscal period. A practical question is: How much depreciation should

[7]This assumption is highly tenuous. It is based on the belief that stock market analysts will not be able to recognize that the change in depreciation methods is purely cosmetic and therefore will give more value to the stock after the change. In fact, research in this area reports just the opposite. One study showed that companies that switched from accelerated to straight-line (which increased income) experienced declines in stock value after the change; see Robert J. Kaplan and Richard Roll, "Investor Evaluation of Accounting Information: Some Empirical Evidence," *The Journal of Business,* April 1972, pp. 225–257. Others have noted that switches to more liberal accounting policies (generating higher income numbers) have resulted in lower stock market performance. One rationale is that such changes signal that the company is in trouble and also leads to skepticism about management's attitudes and behavior.

[8]In this regard, real estate investment trusts (REITs) often report (in addition to net income) an earnings measure, funds from operations (FFO), that adjusts income for depreciation expense and other noncash expenses. This method is not GAAP, and there is mixed empirical evidence about whether FFO or GAAP income is more useful to real estate investment trust investors. See, for example, Richard Gore and David Stott, "Toward a More Informative Measure of Operating Performance in the REIT Industry: Net Income vs. FFO," *Accounting Horizons,* December 1998; and Linda Vincent, "The Information Content of FFO for REITs," *Journal of Accounting and Economics,* January 1999.

be charged for the partial periods involved? Assume, for example, that an automated drill machine with a 5-year life is purchased by Steeltex Company for $45,000 (no salvage value) on June 10, 2000. The company's fiscal year ends December 31, and depreciation is charged for 6⅔ months during that year. The total depreciation for a full year (assuming straight-line depreciation) is $9,000 ($45,000/5), and the depreciation for the first, partial year is:

$$\frac{6\tfrac{2}{3}}{12} \times \$9{,}000 = \$5{,}000$$

The partial-period calculation is relatively simple when straight-line depreciation is used. But how is partial period depreciation handled when an accelerated method such as sum-of-the-years'-digits or double-declining balance is used? As an illustration, assume that an asset was purchased for $10,000 on July 1, 2000, with an estimated useful life of 5 years; the depreciation figures for 2000, 2001, and 2002 are shown in Illustration 11-11.

ILLUSTRATION 11-11
Calculation of Partial-Period Depreciation, Two Methods

	Sum-of-the-Years'-Digits		Double-Declining Balance	
1st full year	(5/15 × $10,000) = $3,333.33		(40% × $10,000) = $4,000	
2nd full year	(4/15 × 10,000) = 2,666.67		(40% × 6,000) = 2,400	
3rd full year	(3/15 × 10,000) = 2,000.00		(40% × 3,600) = 1,440	
Depreciation from July 1, 2000, to December 31, 2000				
6/12 × $3,333.33 =		$1,666.67	6/12 x $4,000 =	$2,000
Depreciation for 2001				
6/12 × $3,333.33 =		$1,666.67	6/12 × $4,000 =	$2,000
6/12 × 2,666.67 =		1,333.33	6/12 × 2,400 =	1,200
		$3,000.00		$3,200
			or ($10,000 − $2,000) × 40% =	$3,200
Depreciation for 2002				
6/12 × $2,666.67 =		$1,333.33	6/12 × $2,400 =	$1,200
6/12 × 2,000.00 =		1,000.00	6/12 × 1,440 =	720
		$2,333.33		$1,920
			or ($10,000 − $5,200) × 40% =	$1,920

In computing depreciation expense for partial periods, it is necessary to determine the depreciation expense for the full year and then to prorate this depreciation expense between the two periods involved. This process should continue throughout the useful life of the asset.

Sometimes the process of allocating costs to a partial period is modified to handle acquisitions and disposals of plant assets more simply. Depreciation may be computed for the full period on the opening balance in the asset account and no depreciation is charged on acquisitions during the year. Other variations charge a full year's depreciation on assets used for a full year, or charge one-half year's depreciation in the year of acquisition and in the year of disposal (referred to as the "half-year" convention), or charge a full year in the year of acquisition and none in the year of disposal.

A company is at liberty to adopt any one of these several fractional-year policies in allocating cost to the first and last years of an asset's life so long as the method is applied consistently. However, **unless otherwise stipulated, depreciation is normally computed on the basis of the nearest full month.** Illustration 11-12 shows depreciation allocated under five different fractional-year policies using the straight-line method on the $45,000 automated drill machine purchased on June 10, 2000, by Steeltex Company discussed earlier.

ILLUSTRATION 11-12
Fractional-Year Depreciation Policies

Machine Cost = $45,000	Depreciation Allocated per Period Over 5-Year Life*					
Fractional-Year Policy	2000	2001	2002	2003	2004	2005
1. Nearest fraction of a year.	$5,000[a]	$9,000	$9,000	$9,000	$9,000	$4,000[b]
2. Nearest full month.	5,250[c]	9,000	9,000	9,000	9,000	3,750[d]
3. Half year in period of acquisition and disposal.	4,500	9,000	9,000	9,000	9,000	4,500
4. Full year in period of acquisition, none in period of disposal.	9,000	9,000	9,000	9,000	9,000	–0–
5. None in period of acquisition, full year in period of disposal.	–0–	9,000	9,000	9,000	9,000	9,000

[a]6.667/12 ($9,000) [b]5.333/12 ($9,000) [c]7/12 ($9,000) [d]5/12 ($9,000)
*Rounded to nearest dollar.

Depreciation and Replacement of Fixed Assets

A common misconception about depreciation is that it provides funds for the replacement of fixed assets. Depreciation is similar to any other expense in that it reduces net income, but it differs in that **it does not involve a current cash outflow.**

To illustrate why depreciation does not provide funds for replacement of plant assets, assume that a business starts operating with plant assets of $500,000, which have a useful life of 5 years. The company's balance sheet at the beginning of the period is:

Plant assets	$500,000	Owners' equity	$500,000

Now if we assume that the enterprise earned no revenue over the 5 years, the income statements are:

	Year 1	Year 2	Year 3	Year 4	Year 5
Revenue	$ –0–	$ –0–	$ –0–	$ –0–	$ –0–
Depreciation	(100,000)	(100,000)	(100,000)	(100,000)	(100,000)
Loss	$(100,000)	$(100,000)	$(100,000)	$(100,000)	$(100,000)

The balance sheet at the end of the 5 years is:

Plant assets	–0–	Owners' equity	–0–

This extreme example illustrates that depreciation in no way provides funds for the replacement of assets. **The funds for the replacement of the assets come from the revenues** (generated through use of the asset); without the revenues no income materializes and no cash inflow results. A separate decision must be made by management to set aside cash to accumulate asset replacement funds.

Revision of Depreciation Rates

When a plant asset is purchased, depreciation rates are carefully determined based on past experience with similar assets and other pertinent information. The provisions for depreciation are only estimates, however, and it may be necessary to revise them during the life of the asset. Unexpected physical deterioration or unforeseen obsolescence may make the useful life of the asset less than originally estimated. Improved maintenance procedures, revision of operating procedures, or similar developments may prolong the life of the asset beyond the expected period.[9]

For example, assume that machinery originally costing $90,000 is estimated to have a 20-year life with no salvage value. However, during year 11 it is estimated that the machine will be used an additional 20 years. Its total life, therefore, will be 30 years instead of 20. Depreciation has been recorded at the rate of 1/20 of $90,000, or $4,500 per year by the straight-line method. On the basis of a 30-year life, depreciation should have been 1/30 of $90,000, or $3,000 per year. Depreciation, therefore, has been overestimated, and net income has been understated by $1,500 for each of the past 10 years, or a total amount of $15,000. The amount of the difference can be computed as shown below.

ILLUSTRATION 11-13
Computation of Accumulated Difference Due to Revisions

	Per Year	For 10 Years
Depreciation charged per books (1/20 × $90,000)	$4,500	$45,000
Depreciation based on a 30-year life (1/30 × $90,000)	3,000	30,000
Excess depreciation charged	$1,500	$15,000

Changes in estimate should be handled in the current and prospective periods. No changes should be made in previously reported results. Opening balances are not adjusted, and no attempt is made to "catch up" for prior periods. The reason is that changes in estimates are a continual and inherent part of any estimation process, and continual restatement of prior periods would occur for revisions of estimates unless they are handled prospectively. Therefore, no entry is made at the time the change in estimate occurs, and charges for depreciation in subsequent periods (assuming use of the straight-line method) are based on **dividing the remaining book value less any salvage value by the remaining estimated life**:

ILLUSTRATION 11-14
Computing Depreciation after Revision of Estimated Life

Machinery	$90,000
Less: Accumulated depreciation	45,000
Book value of machinery at end of 10th year	$45,000

Depreciation (future periods) = $45,000 book value ÷ 20 years remaining life = $2,250

The entry to record depreciation for each of the remaining 20 years is:

Depreciation Expense	2,250	
Accumulated Depreciation—Machinery		2,250

IMPAIRMENTS

OBJECTIVE 6
Explain the accounting issues related to asset impairment.

The general accounting standard of **lower of cost or market for inventories does not apply to property, plant, and equipment**. Even when property, plant, and equipment has suffered partial obsolescence, accountants have been reluctant to reduce the carry-

[9]As an example of a change in operating procedures, **General Motors** (GM) used to write off its tools—such as dies and equipment used to manufacture car bodies—over the life of the body type. Through this procedure, it expensed tools twice as fast as **Ford** and three times as fast as **DaimlerChrysler**. However, it slowed the depreciation process on these tools and lengthened the lives on its plant and equipment. These revisions had the effect of reducing depreciation and amortization charges by approximately $1.23 billion, or $2.55 per share, in the year of the change.

ing amount of the asset. This reluctance occurs because, unlike inventories, it is difficult to arrive at a fair value for property, plant, and equipment that is not subjective and arbitrary. For example, Falconbridge Ltd. Nickel Mines had to decide whether all or a part of its property, plant, and equipment in a nickel-mining operation in the Dominican Republic should be written off. The project had been incurring losses because nickel prices were low and operating costs were high. Only if nickel prices increased by approximately 33% would the project be reasonably profitable. Whether a write-off was appropriate depended on the future price of nickel. Even if the decision were made to write off the asset, another important question would be: How much should be written off?[10]

UNDERLYING CONCEPTS

The *going concern* concept assumes that the firm can recover the cost of the investment in its assets. Under GAAP the fair value of long-lived assets is not reported because a *going* concern does not plan to sell such assets. However, if the assumption of being able to recover the cost of the investment is not valid, then a reduction in value should be reported.

Recognizing Impairments

As discussed in the opening story, a new standard on impairments of long-lived assets was recently issued.[11] In this standard, an impairment occurs when the carrying amount of an asset is not recoverable and, therefore, a write-off is needed. Various events and changes in circumstances might lead to an impairment. Examples are:

a. A significant decrease in the market value of an asset.

b. A significant change in the extent or manner in which an asset is used.

c. A significant adverse change in legal factors or in the business climate that affects the value of an asset.

d. An accumulation of costs significantly in excess of the amount originally expected to acquire or construct an asset.

e. A projection or forecast that demonstrates continuing losses associated with an asset.

If these events or changes in circumstances indicate that the carrying amount of the asset may not be recoverable, a recoverability test is used to determine whether an impairment has occurred. To apply the first step of the recoverability test, you estimate the future net cash flows expected from the **use of that asset and its eventual disposition**. If the sum of the expected future net cash flows (undiscounted) is **less than the carrying amount** of the asset, the asset is considered impaired. Conversely, if the sum of the expected future net cash flows (undiscounted) is **equal to or greater than the carrying amount** of the asset, no impairment has occurred.

The recoverability test is a screening device to determine whether an impairment has occurred. For example, if the expected future net cash flows from an asset are $400,000 and its carrying amount is $350,000, no impairment has occurred. However, if the expected future net cash flows are $300,000, an impairment has occurred. The rationale for the recoverability test is the basic presumption that a balance sheet should report long-lived assets at no more than the carrying amounts that are recoverable.

Measuring Impairments

If the recoverability test indicates that an impairment has occurred, a loss is computed. **The impairment loss is the amount by which the carrying amount of the asset exceeds its fair value.** The fair value of an asset is measured by its market value if an active market for it exists. If no active market exists, the **present value of expected future net cash flows** should be used. The company's market rate of interest should be

[10]Even given these difficult valuation problems, many companies during the earlier part of the 1990s, before issuance of the standard, took a number of large write-offs. One study, for example, noted that write-offs of long-lived assets during a recent 5-year period totaled over $50 billion. Also it has been estimated that over one-third of the largest companies in the United States in recent years have taken restructuring losses of some amount.

[11]"Accounting for the Impairment of Long-lived Assets and for Long-lived Assets to Be Disposed of," *Statement of Financial Accounting Standards No. 121* (Norwalk, Conn.: 1995).

used in discounting to present value. To summarize, the process of determining an impairment loss is as follows:

1. Review events or changes in circumstances for possible impairment.
2. If the review indicates impairment, apply the recoverability test. If the sum of the expected future net cash flows from the long-lived asset is less than the carrying amount of the asset, an impairment has occurred.
3. Assuming an impairment, the impairment loss is the amount by which the carrying amount of the asset is greater than the fair value of the asset. The fair value is the market value or the present value.

Illustration One

M. Alou Inc. has an asset that, due to changes in its use, is reviewed for possible impairment. The asset's carrying amount is $600,000 ($800,000 cost less $200,000 accumulated depreciation). The expected future net cash flows (undiscounted) from the use of the asset and its eventual disposition are determined to be $650,000.

The recoverability test indicates that the $650,000 of expected future net cash flows from the asset's use exceed its carrying amount of $600,000. As a result, no impairment is assumed to have occurred. The undiscounted future net cash flows must be less than the carrying amount for an asset to be deemed impaired and for the impairment loss to be measured. Therefore, M. Alou Inc. will not recognize an impairment loss in this case.

Illustration Two

Assume the same facts as Illustration One, except that the expected future net cash flows from Alou's equipment is $580,000 (instead of $650,000). The recoverability test indicates that the expected future net cash flows of $580,000 from the use of the asset are less than its carrying amount of $600,000. Therefore an impairment has occurred. The difference between the carrying amount of Alou's asset and its fair value is the impairment loss. This asset has a market value of $525,000. The computation of the loss is:

Carrying amount of the equipment	$600,000
Fair value of equipment (market value)	525,000
Loss on impairment	$ 75,000

ILLUSTRATION 11-15
Computation of Impairment Loss

The entry to record the impairment loss is as follows:

Loss on Impairment	75,000	
Accumulated Depreciation		75,000

The impairment loss is reported as part of income from continuing operations, generally in the other expenses and losses section. This loss should **not be reported as an extraordinary item**. Costs associated with an impairment loss are the same costs that would flow through operations and be reported as part of continuing operations. These assets will continue to be used in operations and, therefore, the loss should not be reported below income from continuing operations.

A company that recognizes an impairment loss should disclose the asset(s) impaired, the events leading to the impairment, the amount of the loss, and how fair value was determined (disclosing the interest rate used, if appropriate).

U.S. oil companies are particularly affected by this new standard because for the first time they have to assess each of their producing fields on a case-by-case basis. In the past, oil fields were evaluated on a total company basis. **Texaco**, for instance, took a $640 million fourth-quarter charge in 1995 that swung a quarterly profit into a loss. Other 1995 oil company impairment charges were reported by **Mobil**, now Exxon Mobil ($487 million), **Amoco**, now BP-Amoco ($380 million), **Ashland Inc.** ($90 million), and **Phillips Petroleum** ($49 million).

As shown in Illustration 11-16, Dreyer's Grand Ice Cream Inc. disclosed an impairment as follows:

ILLUSTRATION 11-16
Disclosure of Impairment

DREYER'S GRAND ICE CREAM INC.

Impairment of Long-Lived Assets
The Company reviews long-lived assets and certain identifiable intangibles, including goodwill and distribution rights, for impairment whenever events or changes in circumstances indicate that the carrying amount of an asset may not be recoverable. The assessment of impairment is based on the estimated undiscounted future cash flows from operating activities compared with the carrying value of the assets. If the undiscounted future cash flows of an asset are less than the carrying value, a write-down will be recorded, measured by the amount of the difference between the carrying value and the fair value of the asset. Assets to be disposed of are recorded at the lower of carrying amount or fair value less costs to sell. Such assets are not depreciated while held for sale.

The Company decided to exit the equipment manufacturing business associated with its Grand Soft ice cream unit and recorded $8.6 million in impairment charges.

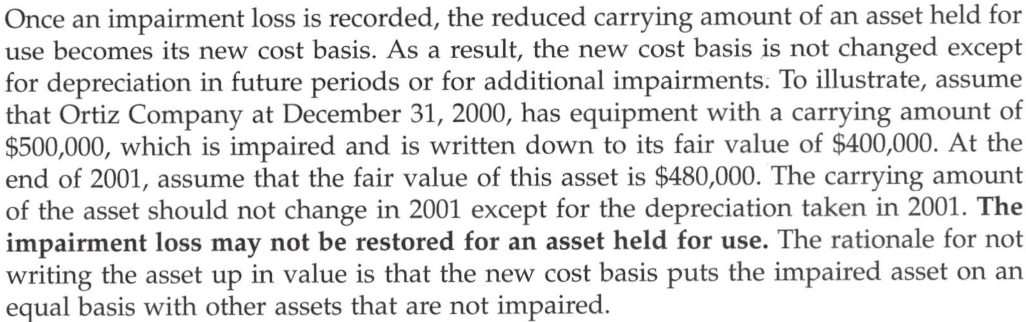

Restoration of Impairment Loss

INTERNATIONAL INSIGHT

International accounting standards permit write-ups for subsequent recoveries of impairment whereas U.S. GAAP prohibits those write-ups, except for assets to be disposed of.

Once an impairment loss is recorded, the reduced carrying amount of an asset held for use becomes its new cost basis. As a result, the new cost basis is not changed except for depreciation in future periods or for additional impairments. To illustrate, assume that Ortiz Company at December 31, 2000, has equipment with a carrying amount of $500,000, which is impaired and is written down to its fair value of $400,000. At the end of 2001, assume that the fair value of this asset is $480,000. The carrying amount of the asset should not change in 2001 except for the depreciation taken in 2001. **The impairment loss may not be restored for an asset held for use.** The rationale for not writing the asset up in value is that the new cost basis puts the impaired asset on an equal basis with other assets that are not impaired.

Assets to Be Disposed Of

What happens if the impaired asset is intended to be disposed of instead of held for use? In this case, the impaired asset is reported at the lower of cost or fair value less cost to sell (net realizable value). Because the asset is intended to be disposed of in a short period of time, net realizable value is used in order to provide a better measure of the net cash flows that will be received from this asset.

Assets that are being held for disposal are not depreciated during the period they are held. The rationale is that depreciation is inconsistent with the notion of assets to be disposed of and with the use of the lower of cost or net realizable value. In other words, **assets held for disposal are like inventory and should be reported at the lower of cost or net realizable value**.

Because assets held for disposal will be recovered through sale rather than through operations, they are continually revalued. Each period they are reported at the lower of cost or net realizable value. Thus **an asset held for disposal can be written up or down in future periods, as long as the write-up is never greater than the carrying amount of the asset before the impairment**. Losses or gains related to these impaired assets should be reported as part of **income from continuing operations**. The disclosure requirements for these assets are complex; we leave that issue for an advanced course. A summary of the key concepts in accounting for impairments is presented in Illustration 11-17 on the next page.

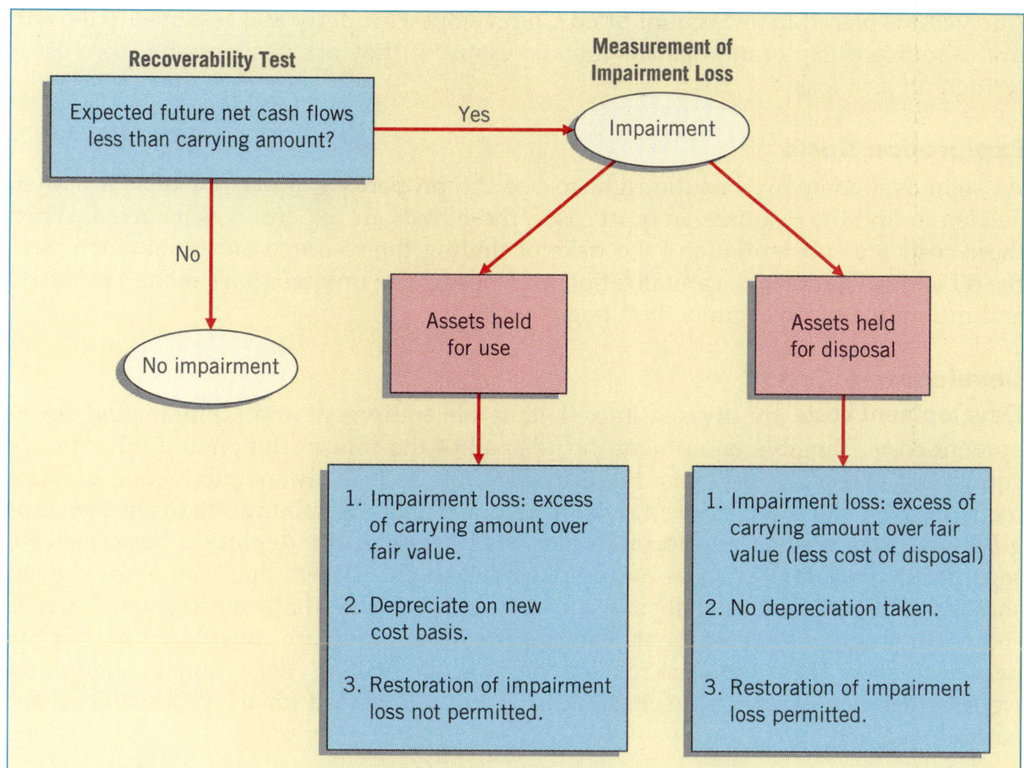

ILLUSTRATION 11-17
Graphic of Accounting for Impairments

DEPLETION

OBJECTIVE 7 Explain the accounting procedures for depletion of natural resources.

Natural resources, often called wasting assets, include petroleum, minerals, and timber. They are characterized by two main features: (1) the complete removal (consumption) of the asset, and (2) replacement of the asset only by an act of nature. Unlike plant and equipment, natural resources are consumed physically over the period of use and do not maintain their physical characteristics. Still, the accounting problems associated with natural resources are similar to those encountered with fixed assets. The questions to be answered are:

1. How is the cost basis for write-off (depletion) established?
2. What pattern of allocation should be employed?

Establishing a Depletion Base

How do we determine the depletion base for natural resources? Sizable expenditures are needed to find these natural resources, and for every successful discovery there are many "failures." Furthermore, long delays are encountered between the time the costs are incurred and the benefits are obtained from the extracted resources. As a result, a conservative policy frequently is adopted in accounting for the expenditures incurred in finding and extracting natural resources. The computation of the depletion base involves four factors: (1) acquisition cost of the deposit, (2) exploration costs, (3) development costs, and (4) restoration costs.

Acquisition Costs

Acquisition cost is the price paid to obtain the property right to search and find an undiscovered natural resource or the price paid for an already discovered resource. In some cases, property is leased and special royalty payments paid to the owner if a productive natural resource is found and is commercially profitable. Generally, the acquisition cost is placed in an account titled Undeveloped Property and assigned to the natural resource if exploration efforts are successful. If they are unsuccessful, the cost is written off as a loss.

Exploration Costs

As soon as a company has the right to use the property, **exploration costs** are often needed to find the resource. In most cases, these costs are expensed as incurred. When these costs are substantial and the risks of finding the resource uncertain (such as in the oil and gas industry), capitalization may occur. The unique issues related to the oil and gas industry are examined on page 567.

Development Costs

Development costs are divided into: (1) tangible equipment and (2) intangible development costs. Tangible equipment includes all of the transportation and other heavy equipment necessary to extract the resource and get it ready for production or shipment. Because the asset can be moved from one drilling or mining site to another, **tangible equipment costs are normally not considered in the depletion base**. Instead, separate depreciation charges are employed. Tangible assets that cannot be moved should be depreciated over their useful life or the life of the resource, whichever is shorter. **Intangible development costs, on the other hand, are considered part of the depletion base.** These costs are for such items as the drilling costs, tunnels, shafts, and wells, which have no tangible characteristics but are needed for the production of the natural resource.

Restoration Costs

Companies sometimes incur substantial costs to restore property to its natural state after extraction has occurred. These **restoration costs** should be added to the depletion base for purposes of computing the depletion cost per unit. It follows that any salvage value received on the property should be deducted from the depletion base.

Write-Off of Resource Cost

As soon as the depletion base is established, the next problem is determining how the cost of the natural resource should be allocated to accounting periods. Normally, depletion is computed on the units of production method (activity approach), which means that depletion is a function of the number of units withdrawn during the period. In adopting this approach, the total cost of the natural resource less salvage value is divided by the number of units estimated to be in the resource deposit, to obtain a cost per unit of product. This cost per unit is multiplied by the number of units extracted to compute depletion.

For example, MaClede Co. has acquired the right to use 1,000 acres of land in Alaska to mine for gold. The lease cost is \$50,000; the related exploration costs on the property are \$100,000; and intangible development costs incurred in opening the mine are \$850,000. Total costs related to the mine before the first ounce of gold is extracted are, therefore, \$1,000,000. MaClede estimates that the mine will provide approximately 100,000 ounces of gold. The depletion rate established is computed in the following manner:

ILLUSTRATION 11-18
Computation of Depletion Rate

$$\frac{\text{Total cost} - \text{Salvage value}}{\text{Total estimated units available}} = \text{Depletion cost per unit}$$

$$\frac{\$1{,}000{,}000}{100{,}000} = \$10.00 \text{ per ounce}$$

If 25,000 ounces are extracted in the first year, then the depletion for the year is \$250,000 (25,000 ounces at \$10.00). The entry to record the depletion is:

Inventory	250,000	
Accumulated Depletion		250,000

Inventory is first debited for the total depletion for the year, and then is credited for the cost of materials sold during the year. The amount not sold remains in inventory and is reported in the current assets section.

In some instances an Accumulated Depletion account is not used, and the credit goes directly to the natural resources asset account. The balance sheet presents the cost of the property and the amount of accumulated depletion entered to date as follows:

ILLUSTRATION 11-19
Balance Sheet Presentation of Natural Resource

Gold mine (at cost)	$1,000,000	
Less: Accumulated depletion	250,000	$750,000

In the income statement the depletion cost is part of the cost of goods sold.

The tangible equipment used in extracting the gold may also be depreciated on a units of production basis, especially if the estimated lives of the equipment can be directly assigned to one given resource deposit. If the equipment is used on more than one job, other cost allocation methods such as straight-line or accelerated depreciation methods would be more appropriate.

Continuing Controversy

A major controversy relates to the accounting for exploration costs in the oil and gas industry. Conceptually, the question is whether unsuccessful exploration costs are a cost of those that are successful. Some believe that unsuccessful ventures are a cost of those that are successful (**full cost concept**) because the cost of drilling a dry hole is a cost that is needed to find the commercially profitable wells. Those who believe that only the costs of successful projects should be capitalized (**successful efforts concept**) contend that an unsuccessful company will end up capitalizing many costs that will make it, over a short period of time, show no less income than does one that is successful.[12] In addition, the only relevant measure for a single property unit is the cost directly related to that unit. The remainder of the costs should be reported as period charges.

The FASB has attempted to narrow the available alternatives but has met with little success. Here is a brief history of the debate.

1. **1977—The FASB issued *Statement No. 19,* which required oil and gas companies to follow successful efforts accounting.** However, after small oil and gas producers, voicing strong opposition, lobbied extensively in Congress, governmental agencies assessed the implications of this standard from a public interest perspective and reacted contrary to the FASB's position.[13]
2. **1978—In response to criticisms of the FASB's actions, the SEC reexamined the issue and found both successful efforts and full cost accounting inadequate because neither reflects the economic substance of oil and gas exploration.** As a substitute, the SEC argued in favor of a yet-to-be developed method, **reserve recognition accounting (RRA)**, which it believed would provide more useful informa-

[12]Large international oil companies such as **Exxon Mobil** use the successful efforts approach. Full-cost accounting is used by most of the smaller, exploration-oriented companies. The differences in net income figures under the two methods can be staggering. It was estimated that **Texaco**'s full-cost accounting increased its reported profits by $500 million over a 10-year period.

[13]The Department of Energy indicated that companies using the full-cost method at that time would reduce their exploration activities because of the unfavorable earnings impact associated with successful efforts accounting. The Justice Department asked the SEC to postpone adoption of one uniform method of accounting in the oil and gas industry until the SEC could determine whether the information reported to investors would be enhanced and competition constrained by adoption of the successful efforts method.

tion. Under RRA, as soon as a company discovers oil, it reports the value of the oil on the balance sheet and in the income statement. Thus, RRA is a current value approach as opposed to full costing and successful efforts, which are historical cost approaches.[14]

3 **1979–1981—As a result of the SEC's actions, the FASB had no choice but to issue another standard that suspended the requirement that companies follow successful efforts accounting.** Therefore, full costing again became permissible. In attempting to implement RRA, however, the SEC encountered practical problems in estimating **(1) the amount of the reserves, (2) the future production costs, (3) the periods of expected disposal, (4) the discount rate, and (5) the selling price**. An estimate for each of these elements is necessary to arrive at an accurate valuation of the existing oil or gas reserve. If the oil or gas reserve is not to be extracted and sold for several years, estimating the future selling price, the appropriate discount rate, and the future costs of extraction and delivery can each be a formidable task.

4 **1981—The SEC announced that it had abandoned RRA as a potential accounting recognition method in the primary financial statements of oil and gas producers.** Because of the inherent uncertainty of determining recoverable quantities of proved oil and gas reserves, the SEC indicated that RRA does not currently possess the required degree of reliability for use as a primary method of financial reporting. However, the SEC continued to stress that some form of value-based disclosure was needed for oil and gas reserves. As a result, the FASB issued *Statement No. 69,* "Disclosure about Oil and Gas Producing Activities," which requires current value disclosures.

5 **1986—One requirement of full-cost accounting is that costs can only be capitalized up to a ceiling, the height of which is determined by the present value of company reserves.** Capitalized costs above that ceiling have to be expensed. In 1986 the price of oil plummeted and as a result a number of companies faced massive write-offs of their reserves because capitalized costs exceeded the present value of the companies' reserves. Companies lobbied for leniency, but the SEC decided that the write-offs had to be taken. As a result, **Mesa Limited Partnerships**' $31 million profit was restated to a $169 million loss and **Pacific Lighting**'s $44.5 million profit was changed to a $70.5 million loss.

Either the full-cost approach or the successful efforts approach is currently acceptable. It does seem ironic that Congress directed the FASB to develop one method of accounting for the oil and gas industry, and when the FASB did so, the government chose not to accept it. Subsequently, the government (SEC) attempted to develop a new approach, failed, and then urged the FASB to develop the disclosure requirements in this area. After all these changes, alternatives still exist in the oil and gas industry.

UNDERLYING CONCEPTS

Failure to consider the economic consequences of accounting principles is a frequent criticism of the profession. However, the neutrality concept requires that the statements be free from bias. Freedom from bias requires that the statements reflect economic reality, even if undesirable effects occur.

This controversy in the oil and gas industry provides a number of lessons to the student in accounting. First, it demonstrates the strong influence that the federal government has in financial reporting matters. Second, the concern for economic consequences places considerable pressure on the FASB to weigh the economic effects of any required standard. Third, the experience with RRA highlights the problems that are encountered when a change from an historical cost to a current value approach is proposed. Fourth, this controversy illustrates the difficulty of establishing standards when affected groups have differing viewpoints. And finally, it reinforces the need for a conceptual framework with carefully developed guidelines for recognition, measurement, and reporting, so that issues of this nature hopefully may be more easily resolved in the future.

---

[14]The use of RRA would make a substantial difference in the balance sheets and income statements of oil companies. For example, **Atlantic Richfield Co.** at one time reported net producing property of $2.6 billion. If RRA were adopted, the same properties would be valued at $11.8 billion. Similarly, **Standard Oil of Ohio**, which reported net producing properties of $1.7 billion, would have reported approximately $10.7 billion under RRA.

Special Problems in Depletion Accounting

Accounting for natural resources has some interesting problems that are uncommon to most other types of assets. These problems are divided into four categories:

1. Difficulty of estimating recoverable reserves.
2. Problems of discovery value.
3. Tax aspects of natural resources.
4. Accounting for liquidating dividends.

Estimating Recoverable Reserves

Not infrequently the estimate of recoverable reserves has to be changed either because new information has become available or because production processes have become more sophisticated. Natural resources such as oil and gas deposits and some rare metals have recently provided the greatest challenges. Estimates of these reserves are in large measure "knowledgeable guesses."

This problem is the **same as accounting for changes in estimates for the useful lives of plant and equipment**. The procedure is to revise the depletion rate on a prospective basis by dividing the remaining cost by the estimate of the new recoverable reserves. This approach has much merit because the required estimates are so tenuous.

Discovery Value

Discovery value accounting and reserve recognition accounting are similar. RRA is specifically related to the oil and gas industry, whereas discovery value is a broader term associated with the whole natural resources area. As indicated earlier, accountants do not recognize discovery values. However, if discovery value were to be recorded, an asset account would be debited and an Unrealized Appreciation account would be credited. Unrealized Appreciation is part of stockholders' equity. Unrealized Appreciation would then be transferred to revenue as the natural resources are sold.

A similar issue arises with resources such as growing timber, aging liquor, and maturing livestock that increase in value over time. One method is to record the increase in value as the accretion occurs. Debit the asset account and credit revenue or an unrealized revenue account. These increases can be substantial. Boise Cascade's timber resources were at one time valued at $1.7 billion, whereas its book value was approximately $289 million. Accountants have been hesitant to record these increases because of the uncertainty regarding the final sales price and the problem of estimating the costs involved in getting the resources ready for sale.

Tax Aspects of Natural Resources

The tax aspects of accounting for most natural resources have comprised some of the most controversial provisions of the Internal Revenue Code (IRC). The tax law has long provided a deduction for the greater of **cost** or percentage depletion against revenue from oil, gas, and most minerals. The percentage or statutory depletion allows a write-off ranging from 5% to 22% (depending on the natural resource) of gross revenue received. As a result, the amount of depletion may exceed the cost assigned to a given natural resource. An asset's carrying amount may be zero, but a depletion deduction may still be taken if the enterprise has gross revenue. The significance of the percentage depletion allowance is now greatly reduced because it has been repealed for most oil and gas companies and is of only limited use in most other situations.

Liquidating Dividends

A company often owns as its only major asset a certain property from which it intends to extract natural resources. If the company does not expect to purchase additional properties, it may distribute gradually to stockholders their capital investments by paying dividends greater than the amount of accumulated net income. The major accounting problem is to distinguish between dividends that are a return of capital and those that are not. The company issuing a **liquidating dividend** should debit Paid-in Capital in Excess of Par for that portion related to the original investment instead of Retained Earnings, because the dividend is a return of part of the investor's original contribution.

To illustrate, at year-end, Callahan Mining had a retained earnings balance of $1,650,000, accumulated depletion on mineral properties of $2,100,000, and paid-in capital in excess of par of $5,435,493. Callahan's board declared a dividend of $3.00 a share on the 1,000,000 shares outstanding. The entry to record the $3,000,000 cash dividend is as follows:

Retained Earnings	1,650,000	
Paid-in Capital in Excess of Par	1,350,000	
Cash		3,000,000

Stockholders must be informed that each $3.00 dividend per share represents a $1.65 ($1,650,000 ÷ 1,000,000 shares) per share return on investment and a $1.35 ($1,350,000 ÷ 1,000,000 shares) per share liquidating dividend.

PRESENTATION AND ANALYSIS

Presentation of Property, Plant, Equipment, and Natural Resources

OBJECTIVE 8
Explain how property, plant, equipment, and natural resources are reported and analyzed.

The basis of valuation—usually historical cost—for property, plant, equipment, and natural resources should be disclosed along with pledges, liens, and other commitments related to these assets. Any liability secured by property, plant, equipment, and natural resources should not be offset against these assets, but should be reported in the liability section. Property, plant, equipment, and natural resources not currently employed as producing assets in the business (such as idle facilities or land held as an investment) should be segregated from assets used in operations.

When assets are depreciated, a valuation account normally called Accumulated Depreciation is credited. The employment of an Accumulated Depreciation account permits the user of the financial statements to see the original cost of the asset and the amount of depreciation that has been charged to expense in past years. When assets are depleted, some companies use an Accumulated Depletion account. Many companies, however, simply credit the natural resource account directly. The rationale for this approach is that the natural resources are physically consumed and, therefore, direct reduction of the cost of the natural resources is appropriate.

Because of the significant impact on the financial statements of the depreciation method(s) used, the following disclosures should be made:

a. Depreciation expense for the period.

b. Balances of major classes of depreciable assets, by nature and function.

c. Accumulated depreciation, either by major classes of depreciable assets or in total.

d. A general description of the method or methods used in computing depreciation with respect to major classes of depreciable assets.[15]

For natural resources, special disclosure requirements relate to the oil and gas industry. Companies engaged in these activities must disclose in their financial statements (1) the basic method of accounting for those costs incurred in oil and gas producing activities (e.g., full cost versus successful efforts) and (2) the manner of disposing

[15]"Omnibus Opinion–1967," *Opinions of the Accounting Principles Board No. 12* (New York: AICPA, 1967), par. 5. Some believe that the average useful life of the assets or the range of years for asset life is significant information that should be disclosed.

of costs relating to oil and gas producing activities (e.g., expensing immediately versus depreciation and depletion).[16]

The 1998 Annual Report of **Boise Cascade Corporation** in Illustration 11-20 illustrates an acceptable disclosure using condensed balance sheet data supplemented with details and policies in notes to the financial statements.

ILLUSTRATION 11-20
Disclosures for Property, Plant, Equipment, and Natural Resources

BOISE CASCADE CORPORATION

	1998	1997
	(expressed in thousands)	
Property (Note 1)		
Property and equipment		
Land and land improvements	$ 63,307	$ 57,260
Buildings and improvements	575,509	554,712
Machinery and equipment	4,082,724	4,055,065
	4,721,540	4,667,037
Accumulated depreciation	(2,150,385)	(2,037,352)
	2,571,155	2,629,685
Timber, timberlands, and timber deposits	270,570	273,001
	$2,841,725	$2,902,686

Notes to Financial Statements

Note 1 (in part): Summary of Significant Accounting Policies

Property. Property and equipment are recorded at cost. Cost includes expenditures for major improvements and replacements and the net amount of interest cost associated with significant capital additions. Capitalized interest was $1,341,000 in 1998, $10,575,000 in 1997, and $17,778,000 in 1996. Substantially all of our paper and wood products manufacturing facilities determine depreciation by the units-of-production method, and other operations use the straight-line method. Gains and losses from sales and retirements are included in income as they occur except at certain pulp and paper mills that use composite depreciation methods. At those facilities, gains and losses are included in accumulated depreciation. Beginning in 1999, we will discontinue the use of composite depreciation. This change is not expected to have a material impact on our results of operations or financial position. Depreciation is computed over the following estimated useful lives:

Buildings and improvements	5 to 40 years
Furniture and fixtures	5 to 10 years
Machinery, equipment, and delivery trucks	3 to 20 years
Leasehold improvements	5 to 10 years

Cost of company timber harvested and amortization of logging roads are determined on the basis of the annual amount of timber cut in relation to the total amount of recoverable timber. Timber and timberlands are stated at cost, less the accumulated cost of timber previously harvested.

Go to the Digital Tool for additional property, plant, equipment, and natural resources disclosures.

Analysis of Property, Plant, Equipment, and Natural Resources

Assets may be analyzed relative to activity (turnover) and profitability. How efficiently a company uses its assets to generate sales is measured by the **asset turnover ratio**. This ratio is determined by dividing net sales by average total assets for the period.

[16]Public companies, in addition to these two required disclosures, must include as supplementary information numerous schedules reporting reserve quantities; capitalized costs; acquisition, exploration, and development activities; and a standardized measure of discounted future net cash flows related to proved oil and gas reserve quantities. See "Disclosures about Oil and Gas Producing Activities," *Statement of Financial Accounting Standards Board No. 69* (Stamford, Conn.: FASB, 1982).

The resulting number is the dollars of sales produced by each dollar invested in assets. To illustrate, we will use the following data from **Tootsie Roll Industries** 1998 annual report:

TOOTSIE ROLL INDUSTRIES

	(in millions)
Net sales	\$388.7
Total assets, 12/31/98	487.4
Total assets, 12/31/97	436.7
Net income	67.5

ILLUSTRATION 11-21
Asset Turnover Ratio

$$\text{Asset turnover} = \frac{\text{Net sales}}{\text{Average total assets}}$$

$$= \frac{\$388.7}{\frac{\$487.4 + \$436.7}{2}}$$

$$= .84$$

The asset turnover ratio shows that Tootsie Roll generated sales of \$0.84 per dollar of assets in the year ended December 31, 1998.

Asset turnover ratios vary considerably among industries. For example, a large utility company like **Union Electric Company** (now Ameren L/E) has a ratio of 0.36 times, and a large grocery chain like **Atlantic and Pacific Tea** (A&P) has a ratio of 3.6 times.

Employment of the **profit margin on sales ratio** (rate of return on sales) in conjunction with the asset turnover ratio offers an interplay that leads to a **rate of return on total assets**. By using the Tootsie Roll Industries data shown above, the profit margin on sales ratio and the rate of return on total assets are computed as follows:

ILLUSTRATION 11-22
Profit Margin on Sales

$$\text{Profit margin on sales} = \frac{\text{Net income}}{\text{Net sales}}$$

$$= \frac{\$67.5}{\$388.7}$$

$$= 17.4\%$$

$$\text{Rate of return on total assets} = \text{Profit margin on sales} \times \text{Asset turnover}$$

$$= 17.4\% \times .84$$

$$= 14.6\%$$

The profit margin on sales does not answer the question of how profitably a company uses its assets. But by relating the profit margin on sales to the asset turnover during a period of time, it is possible to ascertain how profitably the assets were used during that period of time.

The **rate of return on assets** (ROA) can be directly computed by dividing net income by average total assets. By using Tootsie Roll's data, the ratio is computed as follows:

ILLUSTRATION 11-23
Rate of Return on Assets

$$\text{Rate of return on assets} = \frac{\text{Net income}}{\text{Average total assets}}$$

$$= \frac{\$67.5}{\frac{\$487.4 + \$436.7}{2}}$$

$$= 14.6\%$$

The 14.6% rate of return computed in this manner is identical to the 14.6% rate computed by multiplying the profit margin on sales by the asset turnover. The rate of return on assets is a good measure of profitability because it combines the effects of profit margin and asset turnover.

SUMMARY OF LEARNING OBJECTIVES

1 **Explain the concept of depreciation.** Depreciation is the accounting process of allocating the cost of tangible assets to expense in a systematic and rational manner to those periods expected to benefit from the use of the asset.

2 **Identify the factors involved in the depreciation process.** Three factors involved in the depreciation process are: (1) determining the depreciation base for the asset, (2) estimating service lives, and (3) selecting a method of cost apportionment (depreciation).

3 **Compare activity, straight-line, and decreasing charge methods of depreciation.** (1) *Activity method:* Assumes that depreciation is a function of use or productivity instead of the passage of time. The life of the asset is considered in terms of either the output it provides, or an input measure such as the number of hours it works. (2) *Straight-line method:* Considers depreciation a function of time instead of a function of usage. This method is widely employed in practice because of its simplicity. The straight-line procedure is often the most conceptually appropriate when the decline in usefulness is constant from period to period. (3) *Decreasing charge methods:* Provide for a higher depreciation cost in the earlier years and lower charges in later periods. The main justification for this approach is that the asset suffers the greatest loss of services in those years.

4 **Explain special depreciation methods.** Two special depreciation methods are: (1) *Group and composite methods:* The term *group* refers to a collection of assets that are similar in nature; *composite* refers to a collection of assets that are dissimilar in nature. The group method is frequently used where the assets are fairly homogeneous and have approximately the same useful lives. The composite approach is used when the assets are heterogeneous and have different lives. (2) *Hybrid or combination methods:* A hybrid depreciation method widely used in the steel industry is a combination straight-line/activity approach referred to as the production variable method.

5 **Identify reasons why depreciation methods are selected.** The selection of a depreciation method involves factors such as the nature and uncertainty of revenue flows, matching costs and revenues, effect on income and asset book values, tax considerations, and record-keeping costs.

6 **Explain the accounting issues related to asset impairment.** The process to determine an impairment loss is as follows: (1) Review events and changes in circumstances for possible impairment. (2) If events or changes suggest impairment, determine if the sum of the expected future net cash flows from the long-lived asset is less than the carrying amount of the asset. If less, measure the impairment loss. (3) The impairment loss is the amount by which the carrying amount of the asset is greater than the fair value of the asset. After an impairment loss is recorded, the reduced carrying amount of the long-lived asset is now considered its new cost basis. Impairment losses may not be restored for assets held for use. If the asset is expected to be disposed of, the impaired asset should be reported at the lower of cost or net realizable value. It is not depreciated. It can be continuously revalued, as long as the write-up is never greater than the carrying amount before impairment.

7 **Explain the accounting procedures for depletion of natural resources.** The accounting procedures for depletion of natural resources are (1) establishment of depletion base, and (2) write-off of resource cost. Four factors are involved in establishing the depletion base: (a) *acquisition costs,* (b) *exploration costs,* (c) *development costs,* and (d)

KEY TERMS

accelerated depreciation methods, *554*
activity method, *553*
amortization, *551*
asset turnover ratio, *571*
composite approach, *556*
composite depreciation rate, *556*
declining-balance method, *555*
decreasing charge methods, *554*
depletion, *551*
depreciation, *550*
development costs, *566*
discovery value, *569*
double-declining-balance method, *555*
exploration costs, *566*
full cost concept, *567*
group and composite methods, *556*
impairment, *562*
inadequacy, *551*
liquidating dividends, *570*
natural resources, *565*
obsolescence, *552*
percentage depletion, *569*
profit margin on sales ratio, *572*
rate of return on assets (ROA), *572*
recoverability test, *562*
reserve recognition accounting (RRA), *567*
restoration costs, *566*
salvage value, *551*
straight-line method, *553*
successful efforts concept, *567*
sum-of-the-years'-digits method, *554*
supersession, *552*

restoration costs. To write off resource cost, normally, depletion is computed on the units of production method, which means that depletion is a function of the number of units withdrawn during the period. In adopting this approach, the total cost of the natural resource less salvage value is divided by the number of units estimated to be in the resource deposit, to obtain a cost per unit of product. This cost per unit is multiplied by the number of units withdrawn to compute depletion.

8 Explain how property, plant, equipment, and natural resources are reported and analyzed. The basis of valuation for property, plant, equipment, and natural resources should be disclosed along with pledges, liens, and other commitments related to these assets. Any liability secured by property, plant, equipment, and natural resources should not be offset against these assets, but should be reported in the liability section. When assets are depreciated, a valuation account normally called Accumulated Depreciation is credited. When assets are depleted, an accumulated depletion account may be used or the depletion may be credited directly to the natural resource account. Companies engaged in significant oil and gas producing activities must provide special additional disclosures about these activities. Analysis may be performed to evaluate the asset turnover rate, the profit margin on sales, and the rate of return on assets.

APPENDIX 11A

Income Tax Depreciation

MODIFIED ACCELERATED COST RECOVERY SYSTEM

OBJECTIVE 9
After studying Appendix 11A, you should be able to: Describe income tax methods of depreciation.

For the most part, issues related to the computation of income taxes are not discussed in a financial accounting course. However, because the concepts of tax depreciation are similar to those of book depreciation, and because tax depreciation methods are sometimes adopted for book purposes, an overview of this subject is presented.

Efforts to stimulate capital investment through faster write-offs and to bring more uniformity to the write-off period resulted in enactment of the Accelerated Cost Recovery System (ACRS) as part of the Economic Recovery Tax Act of 1981. For assets purchased in the years 1981 through 1986, ACRS and its preestablished "cost recovery periods" for various classes of assets are used.

A **Modified Accelerated Cost Recovery System**, known as **MACRS**, was enacted by Congress in the Tax Reform Act of 1986. It applies to depreciable assets placed in service in 1987 and later. The following discussion is based on these MACRS rules. Tax depreciation rules are subject to change annually.

The computation of depreciation under MACRS differs from the computation under GAAP in three respects: (1) a mandated tax life, which is generally shorter than the economic life; (2) cost recovery on an accelerated basis; and (3) an assigned salvage value of zero.

Tax Lives (Recovery Periods)

Each item of depreciable property is assigned to a property class. The recovery period (depreciable tax life) of an asset depends on the property class.[1] The MACRS property classes are presented below:

3-year property—includes small tools, horses, and assets used in research and development activities

5-year property—includes automobiles, trucks, computers and peripheral equipment, and office machines

7-year property—includes office furniture and fixtures, agriculture equipment, oil exploration and development equipment, railroad track, manufacturing equipment, and any property not designated by law as being in any other class

10-year property—includes railroad tank cars, mobile homes, boilers, and certain public utility property

15-year property—includes roads, shrubbery, and certain low-income housing

20-year property—includes waste-water treatment plants and sewer systems

27.5-year property—includes residential rental property

39-year property—includes nonresidential real property

ILLUSTRATION 11A-1
MACRS Property Classes

Tax Depreciation Methods

The depreciation expense is computed based on the tax basis, usually the cost, of the asset. The depreciation method depends on the life of the assets as mandated by the MACRS property class, as shown below:

MACRS Property Class	Depreciation Method
3-, 5-, 7-, and 10-year property	Double-declining-balance
15- and 20-year property	150% declining-balance
27.5- and 39-year property	Straight-line

ILLUSTRATION 11A-2
Depreciation Method for Various MACRS Property Classes

When one of the accelerated methods is used, a change is made to the straight-line method in the first year in which straight-line depreciation exceeds the accelerated depreciation. Depreciation computations for income tax purposes are based on the half-year convention; that is, a half year of depreciation is allowable in the year of acquisition and in the year of disposition.[2] An asset is depreciated to a zero value so that there is no salvage value at the end of its MACRS life.

The application of these depreciation methods is simplified by using IRS published tables as shown in Illustration 11A-3 (page 576).

Illustration—MACRS System

To illustrate depreciation computations under both the MACRS system and GAAP straight-line accounting, assume the following facts for a computer and peripheral equipment purchased by Denise Rode Company on January 1, 2000:

---

[1]Tax depreciation has changed numerous times during the 1980s and 1990s. For example, since 1980, six different depreciation requirements have been enacted. The tax life of certain real property has moved from 35 years in 1980 to 15 in 1981, 18 in 1982, 19 in 1984, 31.5 in 1986, and 39 in 1993. As one writer noted, "It appears that the useful life of a depreciation law is 2.2 years."

[2]Mid-quarter and mid-month conventions are required for MACRS purposes in certain circumstances.

Acquisition date	January 1, 2000
Cost	$100,000
Estimated useful life	7 years
Estimated salvage value	$16,000
MACRS class life	5 years
MACRS method	200% declining-balance
GAAP method	Straight-line
Disposal proceeds—January 2, 2007	$11,000

ILLUSTRATION 11A-3
IRS Table of MACRS Depreciation Rates, by Property Class

MACRS Depreciation Rates by Class of Property

Recovery Year	3-year (200% DB)	5-year (200% DB)	7-year (200% DB)	10-year (200% DB)	15-year (150% DB)	20-year (150% DB)
1	33.33	20.00	14.29	10.00	5.00	3.750
2	44.45	32.00	24.49	18.00	9.50	7.219
3	14.81*	19.20	17.49	14.40	8.55	6.677
4	7.41	11.52*	12.49	11.52	7.70	6.177
5		11.52	8.93*	9.22	6.93	5.713
6		5.76	8.92	7.37	6.23	5.285
7			8.93	6.55*	5.90*	4.888
8			4.46	6.55	5.90	4.522
9				6.56	5.91	4.462*
10				6.55	5.90	4.461
11				3.28	5.91	4.462
12					5.90	4.461
13					5.91	4.462
14					5.90	4.461
15					5.91	4.462
16					2.95	4.461
17						4.462
18						4.461
19						4.462
20						4.461
21						2.231

*Switchover to straight-line depreciation.

Using the rates from the MACRS depreciation rate schedule for a 5-year class of property, depreciation is computed as follows for tax purposes:

ILLUSTRATION 11A-4
Computation of MACRS Depreciation

MACRS Depreciation

2000	$100,000 × .20 =	$ 20,000
2001	$100,000 × .32 =	32,000
2002	$100,000 × .192 =	19,200
2003	$100,000 × .1152 =	11,520
2004	$100,000 × .1152 =	11,520
2005	$100,000 × .0576 =	5,760
	Total depreciation	$100,000

The depreciation under GAAP straight-line method with $16,000 of estimated salvage value and an estimated useful life of 7 years is computed as follows:

ILLUSTRATION 11A-5
Computation of GAAP Depreciation

GAAP Depreciation

($100,000 − $16,000) ÷ 7 =	$12,000 annual depreciation
	× 7 years
1/1/00–1/2/07	$84,000 total depreciation

The MACRS depreciation recovers the total cost of the asset on an accelerated basis. But, a taxable gain of $11,000 results from the sale of the asset at January 2, 2007. Therefore, the net effect on taxable income for the years 2000 through 2007 is $89,000 ($100,000 depreciation minus $11,000 gain).

Under GAAP, a loss on disposal of $5,000 ($16,000 book value − $11,000 disposal proceeds) is recognized. The net effect on income before income taxes for the years 2000 through 2007 is $89,000 ($84,000 depreciation plus $5,000 loss), the same as the net effect of MACRS on taxable income.

Even though the net effects are equal in amount, the deferral of income tax payments under MACRS from early in the life of the asset to later in life is desirable when considering present value concepts. The different amounts of depreciation for income tax reporting and financial GAAP reporting in each year are a matter of timing and result in temporary differences, which require interperiod tax allocation. (See Chapter 20 for an extended treatment of this topic.)

Optional Straight-line Method

An alternate MACRS method to determine depreciation deductions is based on the straight-line method. Often referred to as the optional (elective) straight-line method, it applies to the six classes of property described earlier. Under the alternate MACRS, the straight-line method is generally applied to the MACRS recovery periods. Salvage value is ignored. Under the optional straight-line method, in the first year the property is placed in service, half of the amount of depreciation that would be permitted for a full year is generally deducted (half-year convention). Use the half-year convention for homework problems.

Tax versus Book Depreciation

GAAP requires that the cost of depreciable assets be allocated to expense over the expected useful life of the asset in a systematic and rational manner. Some argue that from a cost-benefit perspective it would be better for companies to adopt the MACRS approach to eliminate the necessity of maintaining two different sets of records. However, because the objectives of the tax laws and financial reporting are different, the adoption of one method for both tax and book purposes in all cases would be unfortunate. The purpose of taxation is to raise revenue from constituents in an equitable manner; the purpose of financial reporting is to reflect the economic substance of a transaction as closely as possible and to help predict the amounts, timing, and uncertainty of future cash flows.

In Switzerland, depreciation in the financial statements conforms to that on the tax returns. As a consequence, companies may depreciate as much as 80% of the cost of assets in the first year.

SUMMARY OF LEARNING OBJECTIVE FOR APPENDIX 11A

9 **Describe income tax methods of depreciation.** A Modified Accelerated Cost Recovery System (MACRS) was enacted by Congress in the Tax Return Act of 1986. It applies to depreciable assets placed in service in 1987 and later. The computation of depreciation under MACRS differs from the computation under GAAP in three respects: (1) a mandated tax life, which is generally shorter than the economic life; (2) cost recovery on an accelerated basis; and (3) an assigned salvage value of zero.

KEY TERMS

Modified Accelerated Cost Recovery System (MACRS), 574

Note: All **asterisked** Questions, Brief Exercises, Exercises, Problems, and Conceptual Cases relate to material contained in the appendix to the chapter.

QUESTIONS

1 Distinguish between depreciation, depletion, and amortization.

2 Identify the factors that are relevant in determining the annual depreciation charge, and explain whether these factors are determined objectively or whether they are based on judgment.

3 Some believe that accounting depreciation measures the decline in the value of fixed assets. Do you agree? Explain.

4 Explain how estimation of service lives can result in unrealistically high valuations of fixed assets.

5 The plant manager of a manufacturing firm suggested in a conference of the company's executives that accountants should speed up depreciation on the machinery in the finishing department because improvements were rapidly making those machines obsolete and a depreciation fund big enough to cover their replacement is needed. Discuss the accounting concept of depreciation and the effect on a business concern of the depreciation recorded for plant assets, paying particular attention to the issues raised by the plant manager.

6 For what reasons are plant assets retired? Define inadequacy, supersession, and obsolescence.

7 What basic questions must be answered before the amount of the depreciation charge can be computed?

8 Elizabeth Ashley Company purchased a machine on January 2, 2000, for $600,000. The machine has an estimated useful life of 5 years and a salvage value of $100,000. Depreciation was computed by the 150% declining-balance method. What is the amount of accumulated depreciation at the end of December 31, 2001?

9 Linda Blair Company purchased machinery for $120,000 on January 1, 2001. It is estimated that the machinery will have a useful life of 20 years, scrap value of $15,000, production of 84,000 units, and working hours of 42,000. During 2001 the company uses the machinery for 14,300 hours, and the machinery produces 20,000 units. Compute depreciation under the straight-line, units-of-output, working-hours, sum-of-the-years'-digits, and declining-balance (use 10% as the annual rate) methods.

10 What are the major factors considered in determining what depreciation method to use?

11 Under what conditions is it appropriate for a business to use the composite method of depreciation for its plant assets? What are the advantages and disadvantages of this method?

12 If Ed Asner, Inc. uses the composite method and its composite rate is 7.5% per year, what entry should it make when plant assets that originally cost $50,000 and have been used for 10 years are sold for $16,000?

13 A building that was purchased December 31, 1976, for $2,400,000 was originally estimated to have a life of 50 years with no salvage value at the end of that time. Depreciation has been recorded through 2000. During 2001 an examination of the building by an engineering firm discloses that its estimated useful life is 15 years after 2000. What should be the amount of depreciation for 2001?

14 Armand Assante, president of Flatbush Company, has recently noted that depreciation increases cash provided by operations and, therefore, depreciation is a good source of funds. Do you agree? Discuss.

15 Melanie Mayron purchased a computer for $6,000 on July 1, 2001. She intends to depreciate it over 4 years using the double-declining balance method. Salvage value is $1,000. Compute depreciation for 2002.

16 Astaire Inc. is considering the write-down of its long-term plant because of a lack of profitability. Explain to the management of Astaire how to determine whether a write-off is permitted.

17 Last year Wilde Company recorded an impairment on an asset held for use. Recent appraisals indicate that the asset has increased in value. Should Wilde record this recovery in value?

18 Kuga Co. has equipment with a carrying amount of $700,000. The expected future net cash flows from the equipment is $705,000 and its fair value is $590,000. The equipment is expected to be used in operations in the future. What amount (if any) should Kuga report as an impairment to its equipment?

19 Explain how gains or losses on impaired assets should be reported in income.

20 It has been suggested that plant and equipment could be replaced more quickly if depreciation rates for income tax and accounting purposes were substantially increased. As a result, business operations would receive the benefit of more modern and more efficient plant facilities. Discuss the merits of this proposition.

21 Neither depreciation on replacement cost nor depreciation adjusted for changes in the purchasing power of the dollar has been recognized as generally accepted accounting practice for inclusion in the primary financial statements. Briefly present the accounting treatment that might be used to assist in the maintenance of the ability of a company to replace its productive capacity.

22 List (a) the similarities and (b) the differences in the accounting treatments of depreciation and cost depletion.

23 Describe cost depletion and percentage depletion. Why is the percentage depletion method permitted?

24 In what way may the use of percentage depletion violate sound accounting theory?

25 In the extractive industries, businesses may pay dividends in excess of net income. What is the maximum permissible? How can this practice be justified?

26 The following statement appeared in a financial magazine: "RRA— or Rah-Rah, as it's sometimes dubbed— has kicked up quite a storm. Oil companies, for example, are convinced that the approach is misleading. Major accounting firms agree." What is RRA? Why might oil companies believe that this approach is misleading?

27 Adriana Oil uses successful efforts accounting and also provides full-cost results as well. Under full-cost, Adriana Oil would have reported retained earnings of $42 million and net income of $4 million. Under successful efforts, retained earnings were $29 million and net income was $3 million. Explain the difference between full costing and successful efforts accounting.

28 Kellogg Company in 1998 reports net income of $502.6 million, net sales of $6.8 billion, and average total assets of $4.96 billion. What is Kellogg's asset turnover ratio? What is Kellogg's rate of return on assets?

***29** What is a modified accelerated cost recovery system (MACRS)? Speculate as to why this system is now required for tax purposes.

BRIEF EXERCISES

BE11-1 Castlevania Corporation purchased a truck at the beginning of 2001 for $42,000. The truck is estimated to have a salvage value of $2,000 and a useful life of 160,000 miles. It was driven 23,000 miles in 2001 and 31,000 miles in 2002. Compute depreciation expense for 2001 and 2002.

BE11-2 Cheetah Company purchased machinery on January 1, 2001, for $60,000. The machinery is estimated to have a salvage value of $6,000 after a useful life of 8 years. (a) Compute 2001 depreciation expense using the straight-line method. (b) Compute 2001 depreciation expense using the straight-line method assuming the machinery was purchased on September 1, 2001.

BE11-3 Use the information for Cheetah Company given in BE11-2. (a) Compute 2001 depreciation expense using the sum-of-the-years'-digits method. (b) Compute 2001 depreciation expense using the sum-of-the-years'-digits method assuming the machinery was purchased on April 1, 2001.

BE11-4 Use the information for Cheetah Company given in BE11-2. (a) Compute 2001 depreciation expense using the double-declining balance method. (b) Compute 2001 depreciation expense using the double-declining balance method assuming the machinery was purchased on October 1, 2001.

BE11-5 Garfield Company purchased a machine on July 1, 1999, for $25,000. Garfield paid $200 in title fees and county property tax of $125 on the machine. In addition, Garfield paid $500 shipping charges for delivery, and $475 was paid to a local contractor to build and wire a platform for the machine on the plant floor. The machine has an estimated useful life of 6 years with a scrap value of $3,000. Determine the depreciation base of Garfield's new machine. Garfield uses straight-line depreciation.

BE11-6 Battlesport Inc. owns the following assets:

Asset	Cost	Salvage	Estimated Useful Life
A	$70,000	$ 7,000	10 years
B	50,000	10,000	5 years
C	82,000	4,000	12 years

Compute the composite depreciation rate and the composite life of Battlesport's assets.

BE11-7 Myst Company purchased a computer for $7,000 on January 1, 2000. Straight-line depreciation is used, based on a 5-year life and a $1,000 salvage value. In 2002, the estimates are revised. Myst now feels the computer will be used until December 31, 2003, when it can be sold for $500. Compute the 2002 depreciation.

BE11-8 Dinoland Company owns machinery that cost $900,000 and has accumulated depreciation of $360,000. The expected future net cash flows from the use of the asset are expected to be $500,000. The fair value of the equipment is $400,000. Prepare the journal entry, if any, to record the impairment loss.

BE11-9 Genghis Khan Corporation acquires a coal mine at a cost of $400,000. Intangible development costs total $100,000. After extraction has occurred, $75,000 will be spent to restore the property, after which it can be sold for $160,000. Khan estimates that 4,000 tons of coal can be extracted. If 700 tons are extracted the first year, prepare the journal entry to record depletion.

BE11-10 In its 1998 Annual Report **Caterpillar Inc.** reports beginning of the year total assets of $20,756 million, end-of-the-year total assets of $25,128 million, total sales of $20,977 million, and net income of $1,513 million. (a) Compute Caterpillar's asset turnover ratio. (b) Compute Caterpillar's profit margin on sales. (c) Compute Caterpillar's rate of return on assets (1) using asset turnover and profit margin, and (2) using net income.

***BE11-11** Timecap Corporation purchased an asset at a cost of $40,000 on March 1, 2002. The asset has a useful life of 8 years and a salvage value of $4,000. For tax purposes, the MACRS class life is 5 years. Compute tax depreciation for each year 2002–2007.

EXERCISES

E11-1 (Depreciation Computations—SL, SYD, DDB) Deluxe Ezra Company purchases equipment on January 1, Year 1, at a cost of $469,000. The asset is expected to have a service life of 12 years and a salvage value of $40,000.

Instructions

(a) Compute the amount of depreciation for each of Years 1 through 3 using the straight-line depreciation method.

(b) Compute the amount of depreciation for each of Years 1 through 3 using the sum-of-the-years'-digits method.

(c) Compute the amount of depreciation for each of Years 1 through 3 using the double-declining balance method. (In performing your calculations, round constant percentage to the nearest one-hundredth of a point and round answers to the nearest dollar.)

E11-2 (Depreciation—Conceptual Understanding) Rembrandt Company acquired a plant asset at the beginning of Year 1. The asset has an estimated service life of 5 years. An employee has prepared depreciation schedules for this asset using three different methods to compare the results of using one method with the results of using other methods. You are to assume that the following schedules have been correctly prepared for this asset using (1) the straight-line method, (2) the sum-of-the-years'-digits method, and (3) the double-declining balance method.

Year	Straight-line	Sum-of-the-Years'-Digits	Double-declining Balance
1	$ 9,000	$15,000	$20,000
2	9,000	12,000	12,000
3	9,000	9,000	7,200
4	9,000	6,000	4,320
5	9,000	3,000	1,480
Total	$45,000	$45,000	$45,000

Instructions

Answer the following questions:

(a) What is the cost of the asset being depreciated?

(b) What amount, if any, was used in the depreciation calculations for the salvage value for this asset?

(c) Which method will produce the highest charge to income in Year 1?

(d) Which method will produce the highest charge to income in Year 4?

(e) Which method will produce the highest book value for the asset at the end of Year 3?

(f) If the asset is sold at the end of Year 3, which method would yield the highest gain (or lowest loss) on disposal of the asset?

E11-3 (Depreciation Computations—SYD, DDB—Partial Periods) Judds Company purchased a new plant asset on April 1, 2001, at a cost of $711,000. It was estimated to have a service life of 20 years and a salvage value of $60,000. Judds' accounting period is the calendar year.

Instructions

(a) Compute the depreciation for this asset for 2001 and 2002 using the sum-of-the-years'-digits method.

(b) Compute the depreciation for this asset for 2001 and 2002 using the double-declining balance method.

E11-4 (Depreciation Computations—Five Methods) Jon Seceda Furnace Corp. purchased machinery for $315,000 on May 1, 2001. It is estimated that it will have a useful life of 10 years, scrap value of $15,000, production of 240,000 units, and working hours of 25,000. During 2002 Seceda Corp. uses the machinery for 2,650 hours, and the machinery produces 25,500 units.

Instructions

From the information given, compute the depreciation charge for 2002 under each of the following methods (round to three decimal places):

(a) Straight-line
(b) Units-of-output.
(c) Working hours.
(d) Sum-of-the-years'-digits.
(e) Declining-balance (use 20% as the annual rate).

E11-5 (Depreciation Computations—Four Methods) Robert Parish Corporation purchased a new machine for its assembly process on August 1, 2001. The cost of this machine was $117,900. The company estimated that the machine would have a trade-in value of $12,900 at the end of its service life. Its life is estimated at 5 years and its working hours are estimated at 21,000 hours. Year-end is December 31.

Instructions

Compute the depreciation expense under the following methods: (1) straight-line depreciation for 2001, (2) activity method for 2001, assuming that machine usage was 800 hours, (3) sum-of-the-years'-digits for 2002, and (4) double-declining balance for 2002. Each of the foregoing should be considered unrelated.

E11-6 (Depreciation Computations—Five Methods, Partial Periods) Muggsy Bogues Company purchased equipment for $212,000 on October 1, 2000. It is estimated that the equipment will have a useful life of 8 years and a salvage value of $12,000. Estimated production is 40,000 units and estimated working hours 20,000. During 2000, Bogues uses the equipment for 525 hours and the equipment produces 1,000 units.

Instructions

Compute depreciation expense under each of the following methods. Bogues is on a calendar-year basis ending December 31.

(a) Straight-line method for 2000.
(b) Activity method (units of output) for 2000.
(c) Activity method (working hours) for 2000.
(d) Sum-of-the-years'-digits method for 2002.
(e) Double-declining balance method for 2001.

E11-7 (Different Methods of Depreciation) Jackel Industries presents you with the following information:

Description	Date Purchased	Cost	Salvage Value	Life in Years	Depreciation Method	Accumulated Depreciation to 12/31/01	Depreciation for 2002
Machine A	2/12/00	$142,500	$16,000	10	(a)	$33,350	(b)
Machine B	8/15/99	(c)	21,000	5	SL	29,000	(d)
Machine C	7/21/98	75,400	23,500	8	DDB	(e)	(f)
Machine D	10/12/(g)	219,000	69,000	5	SYD	70,000	(h)

Instructions

Complete the table for the year ended December 31, 2002. The company depreciates all assests using the half-year convention.

E11-8 (Depreciation Computation—Replacement, Nonmonetary Exchange) George Zidek Corporation bought a machine on June 1, 1999, for $31,000, f.o.b. the place of manufacture. Freight to the point where it was set up was $200, and $500 was expended to install it. The machine's useful life was estimated at 10 years, with a scrap value of $2,500. On June 1, 2000, an essential part of the machine is replaced, at a cost of $1,980, with one designed to reduce the cost of operating the machine. On June 1, 2003, the company buys a new machine of greater capacity for $35,000, delivered, trading in the old machine which has a fair market value and trade-in allowance of $20,000. To prepare the old machine for removal from the plant cost $75, and expenditures to install the new one were $1,500. It is estimated that the new machine has a useful life of 10 years, with a scrap value of $4,000 at the end of that time.

Instructions

Assuming that depreciation is to be computed on the straight-line basis, compute the annual depreciation on the new equipment that should be provided for the fiscal year beginning June 1, 2003. (Round to the nearest dollar.)

E11-9 (Composite Depreciation) Presented below is information related to Dell Curry Manufacturing Corporation:

Asset	Cost	Estimated Scrap	Estimated Life (in years)
A	$40,500	$5,500	10
B	33,600	4,800	9
C	36,000	3,600	9
D	19,000	1,500	7
E	23,500	2,500	6

Instructions

(a) Compute the rate of depreciation per year to be applied to the plant assets under the composite method.

(b) Prepare the adjusting entry necessary at the end of the year to record depreciation for the year.

(c) Prepare the entry to record the sale of fixed asset D for cash of $4,800. It was used for 6 years, and depreciation was entered under the composite method.

E11-10 (Depreciation Computations, SYD) The Five Satins Company purchased a piece of equipment at the beginning of 1998. The equipment cost $430,000. It has an estimated service life of 8 years and an expected salvage value of $70,000. The sum-of-the-years'-digits method of depreciation is being used. Someone has already correctly prepared a depreciation schedule for this asset. This schedule shows that $60,000 will be depreciated for a particular calendar year.

Instructions

Show calculations to determine for what particular year the depreciation amount for this asset will be $60,000.

E11-11 (Depreciation—Change in Estimate) Machinery purchased for $60,000 by Joe Montana Co. in 1997 was originally estimated to have a life of 8 years with a salvage value of $4,000 at the end of that time. Depreciation has been entered for 5 years on this basis. In 2002, it is determined that the total estimated life (including 2002) should be 10 years with a salvage value of $4,500 at the end of that time. Assume straight-line depreciation.

Instructions

(a) Prepare the entry to correct the prior years' depreciation, if necessary.

(b) Prepare the entry to record depreciation for 2002.

E11-12 (Depreciation Computation—Addition, Change in Estimate) In 1974, Herman Moore Company completed the construction of a building at a cost of $2,000,000 and first occupied it in January 1975. It was estimated that the building will have a useful life of 40 years, and a salvage value of $60,000 at the end of that time.

Early in 1985, an addition to the building was constructed at a cost of $500,000. At that time it was estimated that the remaining life of the building would be, as originally estimated, an additional 30 years, and that the addition would have a life of 30 years, and a salvage value of $20,000.

In 2003, it is determined that the probable life of the building and addition will extend to the end of 2034 or 20 years beyond the original estimate.

Instructions

(a) Using the straight-line method, compute the annual depreciation that would have been charged from 1975 through 1984.

(b) Compute the annual depreciation that would have been charged from 1985 through 2002.

(c) Prepare the entry, if necessary, to adjust the account balances because of the revision of the estimated life in 2003.

(d) Compute the annual depreciation to be charged beginning with 2003.

E11-13 (Depreciation—Replacement, Change in Estimate) Orel Hershiser Company constructed a building at a cost of $2,200,000 and occupied it beginning in January 1982. It was estimated at that time that its life would be 40 years, with no salvage value.

In January 2002, a new roof was installed at a cost of $300,000, and it was estimated then that the building would have a useful life of 25 years from that date. The cost of the old roof was $160,000.

Instructions

(a) What amount of depreciation should have been charged annually from the years 1982 to 2001? (Assume straight-line depreciation.)

(b) What entry should be made in 2002 to record the replacement of the roof?

(c) Prepare the entry in January 2002, to record the revision in the estimated life of the building, if necessary.

(d) What amount of depreciation should be charged for the year 2002?

E11-14 (Error Analysis and Depreciation, SL and SYD) Mike Devereaux Company shows the following entries in its Equipment account for 2002; all amounts are based on historical cost.

Equipment						
2002			2002			
Jan. 1	Balance	134,750	June 30	Cost of equipment sold (purchased prior to 1999)	23,000	
Aug. 10	Purchases	32,000				
12	Freight on equipment purchased	700				
25	Installation costs	2,700				
Nov. 10	Repairs	500				

Instructions

(a) Prepare any correcting entries necessary.

(b) Assuming that depreciation is to be charged for a full year on the ending balance in the asset account, compute the proper depreciation charge for 2002 under each of the methods listed below. Assume an estimated life of 10 years, with no salvage value. The machinery included in the January 1, 2002, balance was purchased in 2000.

1. Straight-line.

2. Sum-of-the-years'-digits.

E11-15 (Depreciation for Fractional Periods) On March 10, 2003, Lost World Company sells equipment that it purchased for $192,000 on August 20, 1996. It was originally estimated that the equipment would have a life of 12 years and a scrap value of $16,800 at the end of that time, and depreciation has been computed on that basis. The company uses the straight-line method of depreciation.

Instructions

(a) Compute the depreciation charge on this equipment for 1996, for 2003, and the total charge for the period from 1997 to 2002, inclusive, under each of the six following assumptions with respect to partial periods.

(1) Depreciation is computed for the exact period of time during which the asset is owned. (Use 365 days for base.)

(2) Depreciation is computed for the full year on the January 1 balance in the asset account.

(3) Depreciation is computed for the full year on the December 31 balance in the asset account.

(4) Depreciation for one-half year is charged on plant assets acquired or disposed of during the year.

(5) Depreciation is computed on additions from the beginning of the month following acquisition and on disposals to the beginning of the month following disposal.

(6) Depreciation is computed for a full period on all assets in use for over one-half year, and no depreciation is charged on assets in use for less than one-half year. (Use 365 days for base.)

(b) Briefly evaluate the methods above, considering them from the point of view of basic accounting theory as well as simplicity of application.

E11-16 (Impairment) Presented below is information related to equipment owned by Suarez Company at December 31, 2002.

Cost	$9,000,000
Accumulated depreciation to date	1,000,000
Expected future net cash flows	7,000,000
Fair value	4,800,000

Assume that Suarez will continue to use this asset in the future. As of December 31, 2002, the equipment has a remaining useful life of 4 years.

Instructions

(a) Prepare the journal entry (if any) to record the impairment of the asset at December 31, 2002.

(b) Prepare the journal entry to record depreciation expense for 2003.

(c) The fair value of the equipment at December 31, 2003, is $5,100,000. Prepare the journal entry (if any) necessary to record this increase in fair value.

E11-17 (Impairment) Assume the same information as E11-16, except that Suarez intends to dispose of the equipment in the coming year. It is expected that the cost of disposal will be $20,000.

Instructions

(a) Prepare the journal entry (if any) to record the impairment of the asset at December 31, 2002.

(b) Prepare the journal entry (if any) to record depreciation expense for 2003.

(c) The asset was not sold by December 31, 2003. The fair value of the equipment on that date is $5,300,000. Prepare the journal entry (if any) necessary to record this increase in fair value. It is expected that the cost of disposal is still $20,000.

E11-18 (Impairment) The management of Luis Andujar Inc. was discussing whether certain equipment should be written off as a charge to current operations because of obsolescence. This equipment has a cost of $900,000 with depreciation to date of $400,000 as of December 31, 2001. On December 31, 2001, management projected its future net cash flows from this equipment to be $300,000 and its fair value to be $230,000. The company intends to use this equipment in the future.

Instructions

(a) Prepare the journal entry (if any) to record the impairment at December 31, 2001.
(b) Where should the gain or loss (if any) on the write-down be reported in the income statement?
(c) At December 31, 2002, the equipment's fair value increased to $260,000. Prepare the journal entry (if any) to record this increase in fair value.
(d) What accounting issues did management face in accounting for this impairment?

E11-19 (Depletion Computations—Timber) Stanislaw Timber Company owns 9,000 acres of timberland purchased in 1990 at a cost of $1,400 per acre. At the time of purchase the land without the timber was valued at $400 per acre. In 1991, Stanislaw built fire lands and roads, with a life of 30 years, at a cost of $84,000. Every year Stanislaw sprays to prevent disease at a cost of $3,000 per year and spends $7,000 to maintain the fire lanes and roads. During 1992, Stanislaw selectively logged and sold 700,000 board feet of timber, of the estimated 3,500,000 board feet. In 1993, Stanislaw planted new seedlings to replace the trees cut at a cost of $100,000.

Instructions

(a) Determine the depreciation expense and the cost of timber sold related to depletion for 1992.
(b) Stanislaw has not logged since 1992. If Stanislaw logged and sold 900,000 board feet of timber in 2003, when the timber cruise (appraiser) estimated 5,000,000 board feet, determine the cost of timber sold related to depletion for 2003.

E11-20 (Depletion Computations—Oil) Diderot Drilling Company has leased property on which oil has been discovered. Wells on this property produced 18,000 barrels of oil during the past year that sold at an average sales price of $15 per barrel. Total oil resources of this property are estimated to be 250,000 barrels.

The lease provided for an outright payment of $500,000 to the lessor before drilling could be commenced and an annual rental of $31,500. A premium of 5% of the sales price of every barrel of oil removed is to be paid annually to the lessor. In addition, the lessee is to clean up all the waste and debris from drilling and to bear the costs of reconditioning the land for farming when the wells are abandoned. It is estimated that this clean-up and reconditioning will cost $30,000.

Instructions

From the provisions of the lease agreement, you are to compute the cost per barrel for the past year, exclusive of operating costs, to Diderot Drilling Company.

E11-21 (Depletion Computations—Timber) Forda Lumber Company owns a 7,000-acre tract of timber purchased in 1995 at a cost of $1,300 per acre. At the time of purchase the land was estimated to have a value of $300 per acre without the timber. Forda Lumber Company has not logged this tract since it was purchased. In 2002, Forda had the timber cruised. The cruise (appraiser) estimated that each acre contained 8,000 board feet of timber. In 2002, Forda built 10 miles of roads at a cost of $7,840 per mile. After the roads were completed, Forda logged and sold 3,500 trees containing 850,000 board feet.

Instructions

(a) Determine the cost of timber sold related to depletion for 2002.
(b) If Forda depreciates the logging roads on the basis of timber cut, determine the depreciation expense for 2002.
(c) If Forda plants five seedlings at a cost of $4 per seedling for each tree cut, how should Forda treat the reforestation?

E11-22 (Depletion Computations—Mining) Alcide Mining Company purchased land on February 1, 2001, at a cost of $1,190,000. It estimated that a total of 60,000 tons of mineral was available for mining. After it has removed all the natural resources, the company will be required to restore the property to its previous state because of strict environmental protection laws. It estimates the cost of this restoration at $90,000. It believes it will be able to sell the property afterwards for $100,000. It incurred developmental costs of $200,000 before it was able to do any mining. In 2001 resources removed totaled 30,000 tons. It sold 22,000 tons.

Instructions (Round to two decimals)
Compute the following information for 2001: (1) per unit material cost; (2) total material cost of 12/31/01 inventory; and (3) total material cost in cost of goods sold at 12/31/01.

E11-23 (Depletion Computations—Minerals) At the beginning of 2001, Aristotle Company acquired a mine for $970,000. Of this amount, $100,000 was ascribed to the land value and the remaining portion to the minerals in the mine. Surveys conducted by geologists have indicated that approximately 12,000,000 units of the ore appear to be in the mine. Aristotle incurred $170,000 of development costs associated with this mine prior to any extraction of minerals and estimates that it will require $40,000 to prepare the land for an alternative use when all of the mineral has been removed. During 2001, 2,500,000 units of ore were extracted and 2,100,000 of these units were sold.

Instructions
Compute (1) the total amount of depletion of 2001, and (2) the amount that is charged as an expense for 2001 for the cost of the minerals sold during 2001.

E11-24 (Ratio Analysis) The 1999 Annual Report of **Microsoft Corporation** contains the following information:

(in millions)	June 30, 1998	June 30, 1999
Total assets	$22,357	$37,156
Total liabilities	5,730	8,718
Net sales	15,262	19,747
Net income	4,490	7,785

Instructions
Compute the following ratios for Microsoft for 1999:

(a) Asset turnover ratio.
(b) Rate of return on assets.
(c) Profit margin on sales.
(d) How can the asset turnover ratio be used to compute the rate of return on assets?

***E11-25 (Book vs. Tax (MACRS) Depreciation)** Futabatei Enterprises purchased a delivery truck on January 1, 2002, at a cost of $27,000. The truck has a useful life of 7 years with an estimated salvage value of $6,000. The straight-line method is used for book purposes. For tax purposes the truck, having an MACRS class life of 7 years, is classified as 5-year property; the optional MACRS tax rate tables are used to compute depreciation. In addition, assume that for 2002 and 2003 the company has revenues of $200,000 and operating expenses (excluding depreciation) of $130,000.

Instructions
(a) Prepare income statements for 2002 and 2003. (The final amount reported on the income statement should be income before income taxes.)
(b) Compute taxable income for 2002 and 2003.
(c) Determine the total depreciation to be taken over the useful life of the delivery truck for both book and tax purposes.
(d) Explain why depreciation for book and tax purposes will generally be different over the useful life of a depreciable asset.

***E11-26 (Book vs. Tax (MACRS) Depreciation)** Shimei Inc. purchased computer equipment on March 1, 2001, for $31,000. The computer equipment has a useful life of 10 years and a salvage value of $1,000. For tax purposes, the MACRS class life is 5 years.

Instructions
(a) Assuming that the company uses the straight-line method for book and tax purposes, what is the depreciation expense reported in (1) the financial statements for 2001 and (2) the tax return for 2001?
(b) Assuming that the company uses the double-declining balance method for both book and tax purposes, what is the depreciation expense reported in (1) the financial statements for 2001 and (2) the tax return for 2001?
(c) Why is depreciation for tax purposes different from depreciation for book purposes even if the company uses the same depreciation method to compute them both?

PROBLEMS

P11-1 (Depreciation for Partial Period—SL, SYD, and DDB) Onassis Company purchased Machine #201 on May 1, 2001. The following information relating to Machine #201 was gathered at the end of May.

Price	$73,500
Credit terms	2/10, n/30
Freight-in costs	$ 970
Preparation and installation costs	$ 3,800
Labor costs during regular production operations	$10,500

It was expected that the machine could be used for 10 years, after which the salvage value would be zero. Onassis intends to use the machine for only 8 years, however, after which it expects to be able to sell it for $1,200. The invoice for Machine #201 was paid May 5, 2001. Onassis uses the calendar year as the basis for the preparation of financial statements.

Instructions

(a) Compute the depreciation expense for the years indicated using the following methods. (Round to the nearest dollar.)
- **(1)** Straight-line method for 2001.
- **(2)** Sum-of-the-years'-digits method for 2002.
- **(3)** Double-declining balance method for 2001.

(b) Suppose Jackie Ari, the president of Onassis, tells you that because the company is a new organization, she expects it will be several years before production and sales reach optimum levels. She asks you to recommend a depreciation method that will allocate less of the company's depreciation expense to the early years and more to later years of the assets' lives. What method would you recommend?

P11-2 (Depreciation for Partial Periods—SL, Act., SYD, and DDB) The cost of equipment purchased by Boris Becker, Inc., on June 1, 2001 is $67,000. It is estimated that the machine will have a $4,000 salvage value at the end of its service life. Its service life is estimated at 7 years; its total working hours are estimated at 42,000 and its total production is estimated at 525,000 units. During 2001 the machine was operated 6,000 hours and produced 55,000 units. During 2002 the machine was operated 5,500 hours and produced 48,000 units.

Instructions

Compute depreciation expense on the machine for the year ending December 31, 2001, and the year ending December 31, 2002, using the following methods:
- **(a)** Straight-line.
- **(b)** Units-of-output.
- **(c)** Working hours.
- **(d)** Sum-of-the-years'-digits.
- **(e)** Declining balance (twice the straight-line rate).

P11-3 (Depreciation—Partial Periods, Machinery) Goran Tool Company records depreciation annually at the end of the year. Its policy is to take a full year's depreciation on all assets used throughout the year and depreciation for one-half a year on all machines acquired or disposed of during the year. The depreciation rate for the machinery is 10% applied on a straight-line basis, with no estimated scrap value.

The balance of the Machinery account at the beginning of 2002 was $172,300; the Accumulated Depreciation on Machinery account had a balance of $72,900. The following transactions affecting the machinery accounts took place during the year.

Jan. 15 Machine No. 38, which cost $9,600 when acquired June 3, 1995, was retired and sold as scrap metal for $600.

Feb. 27 Machine No. 81 was purchased. The fair market value of this machine was $12,500. It replaces Machines No. 12 and No. 27, which were traded in on the new machine. Machine No. 12 was acquired Feb. 4, 1990, at a cost of $5,500 and is still carried in the accounts although fully depreciated and not in use; Machine No. 27 was acquired June 11, 1995, at a cost of $8,200. In addition to these two used machines, $9,000 was paid in cash. (Assume exchange of similar assets.)

Apr. 7 Machine No. 54 was equipped with electric control equipment at a cost of $940. This machine, originally equipped with simple hand controls, was purchased Dec. 11, 1998, for $1,800. The new electric controls can be attached to any one of several machines in the shop.

12 Machine No. 24 was repaired at a cost of $720 after a fire caused by a short circuit in the wiring burned out the motor and damaged certain essential parts.

July 22 Machines No. 25, 26, and 41 are sold for $3,100 cash. The purchase dates and cost of these machines are:

No. 25	$4,000	May 8, 1994
No. 26	3,200	May 8, 1994
No. 41	2,800	June 1, 1996

Instructions

(a) Record each transaction in general journal entry form.

(b) Compute and record depreciation for the year. No machines now included in the balance of the account were acquired before January 1, 1993.

P11-4 (Depreciation—SYD, Act., SL, and DDB) The following data relate to the Plant Assets account of Arthur Fiedler, Inc. at December 31, 2001:

Plant Assets

	A	B	C	D
Original cost	$35,000	$51,000	$80,000	$80,000
Year purchased	1996	1997	1998	2000
Useful life	10 years	15,000 hours	15 years	10 years
Salvage value	$ 3,100	$ 3,000	$ 5,000	$ 5,000
Depreciation method	Sum-of-the-years'-digits	Activity	Straight-line	Double-declining balance
Accum. Depr. through 2001[a]	$23,200	$35,200	$15,000	$16,000

[a]In the year an asset is purchased, Fiedler, Inc. does not record any depreciation expense on the asset. In the year an asset is retired or traded in, Fiedler, Inc. takes a full year's depreciation on the asset.

The following transactions occurred during 2002:

(a) On May 5, Asset A was sold for $13,000 cash. The company's bookkeeper recorded this retirement in the following manner in the cash receipts journal:

Cash	13,000	
Asset A		13,000

(b) On December 31, it was determined that Asset B had been used 2,100 hours during 2002.

(c) On December 31, before computing depreciation expense on Asset C, the management of Fiedler, Inc. decided the useful life remaining from 1/1/02 was 10 years.

(d) On December 31, it was discovered that a plant asset purchased in 2001 had been expensed completely in that year. This asset cost $22,000 and has a useful life of 10 years and no salvage value. Management has decided to use the double-declining balance method for this asset, which can be referred to as "Asset E."

Instructions

Prepare the necessary correcting entries for the year 2002. Record the appropriate depreciation expense on the above-mentioned assets.

P11-5 (Depreciation and Error Analysis) A depreciation schedule for semitrucks of Oglala Manufacturing Company was requested by your auditor soon after December 31, 2002, showing the additions, retirements, depreciation, and other data affecting the income of the company in the 4-year period 1999 to 2002, inclusive. The following data were ascertained:

Balance of Semitrucks account, Jan. 1, 1999:	
Truck No. 1 purchased Jan. 1 1996, cost	$18,000
Truck No. 2 purchased July 1, 1996, cost	22,000
Truck No. 3 purchased Jan. 1, 1998, cost	30,000
Truck No. 4 purchased July 1, 1998, cost	24,000
Balance, Jan. 1, 1999	$94,000

The Semitrucks—Accumulated Depreciation account previously adjusted to January 1, 1999, and duly entered in the ledger, had a balance on that date of $30,200 (depreciation on the four trucks from the respective dates of purchase, based on a 5-year life, no salvage value). No charges had been made against the account before January 1, 1999.

Transactions between January 1, 1999, and December 31, 2002, and their record in the ledger were as follows:

July 1, 1999 Truck No. 3 was traded for a larger one (No. 5), the agreed purchase price of which was $34,000. Oglala Mfg. Co. paid the automobile dealer $15,000 cash on the transaction. The entry was a debit to Semitrucks and a credit to Cash, $15,000.

Jan. 1, 2000	Truck No. 1 was sold for $3,500 cash; entry debited Cash and credited Semitrucks, $3,500.
July 1, 2001	A new truck (No. 6) was acquired for $36,000 cash and was charged at that amount to the Semitrucks account. (Assume truck No. 2 was not retired.)
July 1, 2001	Truck No. 4 was damaged in a wreck to such an extent that it was sold as junk for $700 cash. Oglala Mfg. Co. received $2,500 from the insurance company. The entry made by the bookkeeper was a debit to Cash, $3,200, and credits to Miscellaneous Income, $700, and Semitrucks, $2,500.

Entries for depreciation had been made at the close of each year as follows: 1999, $20,300; 2000, $21,100; 2001, $24,450; 2002, $27,800.

Instructions

(a) For each of the 4 years compute separately the increase or decrease in net income arising from the company's errors in determining or entering depreciation or in recording transactions affecting trucks, ignoring income tax considerations.

(b) Prepare one compound journal entry as of December 31, 2002, for adjustment of the Semitrucks account to reflect the correct balances as revealed by your schedule, assuming that the books have not been closed for 2002.

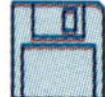

P11-6 (Depletion and Depreciation—Mining) Richard Wright Mining Company has purchased a tract of mineral land for $600,000. It is estimated that this tract will yield 120,000 tons of ore with sufficient mineral content to make mining and processing profitable. It is further estimated that 6,000 tons of ore will be mined the first and last year and 12,000 tons every year in between. The land will have a residual value of $30,000.

The company builds necessary structures and sheds on the site at a cost of $36,000. It is estimated that these structures can serve 15 years but, because they must be dismantled if they are to be moved, they have no scrap value. The company does not intend to use the buildings elsewhere. Mining machinery installed at the mine was purchased second-hand at a cost of $48,000. This machinery cost the former owner $100,000 and was 50% depreciated when purchased. Richard Wright Mining estimates that about half of this machinery will still be useful when the present mineral resources have been exhausted but that dismantling and removal costs will just about offset its value at that time. The company does not intend to use the machinery elsewhere. The remaining machinery will last until about one-half the present estimated mineral ore has been removed and will then be worthless. Cost is to be allocated equally between these two classes of machinery.

Instructions

(a) As chief accountant for the company, you are to prepare a schedule showing estimated depletion and depreciation costs for each year of the expected life of the mine.

(b) Also compute the depreciation and depletion for the first year assuming actual production of 7,000 tons. Nothing occurred during the year to cause the company engineers to change their estimates of either the mineral resources or the life of the structures and equipment.

P11-7 (Depletion, Timber, and Extraordinary Loss) Ted Koppel Logging and Lumber Company owns 3,000 acres of timberland on the north side of Mount St. Helens, which was purchased in 1968 at a cost of $550 per acre. In 1980, Kopple began selectively logging this timber tract. In May of 1980, Mount St. Helens erupted, burying the timberland of Koppel under a foot of ash. All of the timber on the Koppel tract was downed. In addition, the logging roads, built at a cost of $150,000, were destroyed, as well as the logging equipment, with a net book value of $300,000.

At the time of the eruption, Koppel had logged 20% of the estimated 500,000 board feet of timber. Prior to the eruption, Koppel estimated the land to have a value of $200 per acre after the timber was harvested. Koppel includes the logging roads in the depletion base.

Koppel estimates it will take 3 years to salvage the downed timber at a cost of $700,000. The timber can be sold for pulp wood at an estimated price of $3 per board foot. The value of the land is unknown, but must be considered nominal due to future uncertainties.

Instructions

(a) Determine the depletion cost per board foot for the timber harvested prior to the eruption of Mount St. Helens.

(b) Prepare the journal entry to record the depletion prior to the eruption.

(c) If this tract represents approximately half of the timber holdings of Koppel, determine the amount of the estimated loss and show how the losses of roads, machinery, and timber and the salvage of the timber should be reported in the financial statements of Koppel for the year ended December 31, 1980.

P11-8 (Natural Resources—Timber) Western Paper Products purchased 10,000 acres of forested timberland in March 2002. The company paid $1,700 per acre for this land, which was above the $800 per acre most farmers were paying for cleared land. During April, May, June, and July 2002, Western cut enough timber to build roads using moveable equipment purchased on April 1, 2002. The cost of the roads was $195,000, and the cost of the equipment was $189,000; this equipment was expected to have a $9,000 salvage value and would be used for the next 15 years. Western selected the straight-line method of depreciation for the moveable equipment. Western began actively harvesting timber in August and by December had harvested and sold 472,500 board feet of timber of the estimated 6,750,000 board feet available for cutting.

In March 2003, Western planted new seedlings in the area harvested during the winter. Cost of planting these seedlings was $120,000. In addition, Western spent $8,000 in road maintenance and $6,000 for pest spraying during calendar-year 2003. The road maintenance and spraying are annual costs. During 2003 Western harvested and sold 774,000 board feet of timber of the estimated 6,450,000 board feet available for cutting.

In March 2004, Western again planted new seedlings at a cost of $150,000, and also spent $15,000 on road maintenance and pest spraying. During 2004, the company harvested and sold 650,000 board feet of timber of the estimated 6,500,000 board feet available for cutting.

Instructions

Compute the amount of depreciation and depletion expense for each of the 3 years. Assume that the roads are usable only for logging and therefore are included in the depletion base.

P11-9 (Comprehensive Fixed Asset Problem) Selig Sporting Goods Inc. has been experiencing growth in the demand for its products over the last several years. The last two Olympic Games greatly increased the popularity of basketball around the world. As a result, a European sports retailing consortium entered into an agreement with Selig's Roundball Division to purchase basketballs and other accessories on an increasing basis over the next 5 years.

To be able to meet the quantity commitments of this agreement, Selig had to obtain additional manufacturing capacity. A real estate firm located an available factory in close proximity to Selig's Roundball manufacturing facility, and Selig agreed to purchase the factory and used machinery from Starks Athletic Equipment Company on October 1, 2000. Renovations were necessary to convert the factory for Selig's manufacturing use.

The terms of the agreement required Selig to pay Starks $50,000 when renovations started on January 1, 2001, with the balance to be paid as renovations were completed. The overall purchase price for the factory and machinery was $400,000. The building renovations were contracted to Malone Construction at $100,000. The payments made, as renovations progressed during 2001, are shown below. The factory was placed in service on January 1, 2002.

	1/1	4/1	10/1	12/31
Starks	$50,000	$100,000	$100,000	$150,000
Malone		30,000	30,000	40,000

On January 1, 2001, Selig secured a $500,000 line-of-credit with a 12% interest rate to finance the purchase cost of the factory and machinery, and the renovation costs. Selig drew down on the line-of-credit to meet the payment schedule shown above; this was Selig's only outstanding loan during 2001.

Rob Stewart, Selig's controller, will capitalize the maximum allowable interest costs for this project. Selig's policy regarding purchases of this nature is to use the appraisal value of the land for book purposes and prorate the balance of the purchase price over the remaining items. The building had originally cost Starks $300,000 and had a net book value of $50,000, while the machinery originally cost $125,000 and had a net book value of $40,000 on the date of sale. The land was recorded on Starks' books at $40,000. An appraisal, conducted by independent appraisers at the time of acquisition, valued the land at $280,000, the building at $105,000, and the machinery at $45,000.

Linda Safford, chief engineer, estimated that the renovated plant would be used for 15 years, with an estimated salvage value of $30,000. Safford estimated that the productive machinery would have a remaining useful life of 5 years and a salvage value of $3,000. Selig's depreciation policy specifies the 200% declining-balance method for machinery and the 150% declining-balance method for the plant. One-half year's depreciation is taken in the year the plant is placed in service and one-half year is allowed when the property is disposed of or retired. Selig uses a 360-day year for calculating interest costs.

Instructions

(a) Determine the amounts to be recorded on the books of Selig Sporting Goods Inc. as of December 31, 2001, for each of the following properties acquired from Starks Athletic Equipment Company.
(1) Land. **(2)** Building. **(3)** Machinery.

(b) Calculate Selig Sporting Goods Inc.'s 2002 depreciation expense, for book purposes, for each of the properties acquired from Starks Athletic Equipment Company.

(c) Discuss the arguments for and against the capitalization of interest costs.

(CMA adapted)

P11-10 (Impairment) Olsson Company uses special strapping equipment in its packaging business. The equipment was purchased in January 2001 for $8,000,000 and had an estimated useful life of 8 years with no salvage value. At December 31, 2002, new technology was introduced that would accelerate the obsolescence of Olsson's equipment. Olsson's controller estimates that expected future net cash flows on the equipment will be $5,300,000 and that the fair value of the equipment is $4,400,000. Olsson intends to continue using the equipment, but it is estimated that the remaining useful life is 4 years. Olsson uses straight-line depreciation.

Instructions

(a) Prepare the journal entry (if any) to record the impairment at December 31, 2002.

(b) Prepare any journal entries for the equipment at December 31, 2003. The fair value of the equipment at December 31, 2003, is estimated to be $4,600,000.

(c) Repeat the requirements for (a) and (b), assuming that Olsson intends to dispose of the equipment and that it has not been disposed of as of December 31, 2003.

P11-11 (Comprehensive Depreciation Computations) Anjelica Huston Corporation, a manufacturer of steel products, began operations on October 1, 2000. The accounting department of Huston has started the fixed-asset and depreciation schedule presented below. You have been asked to assist in completing this schedule. In addition to ascertaining that the data already on the schedule are correct, you have obtained the following information from the company's records and personnel:

1. Depreciation is computed from the first of the month of acquisition to the first of the month of disposition.
2. Land A and Building A were acquired from a predecessor corporation. Huston paid $820,000 for the land and building together. At the time of acquisition, the land had an appraised value of $90,000, and the building had an appraised value of $810,000.
3. Land B was acquired on October 2, 2000, in exchange for 2,500 newly issued shares of Huston's common stock. At the date of acquisition, the stock had a par value of $5 per share and a fair value of $30 per share. During October 2000, Huston paid $16,000 to demolish an existing building on this land so it could construct a new building.
4. Construction of Building B on the newly acquired land began on October 1, 2001. By September 30, 2002, Huston had paid $320,000 of the estimated total construction costs of $450,000. It is estimated that the building will be completed and occupied by July 2003.
5. Certain equipment was donated to the corporation by a local university. An independent appraisal of the equipment when donated placed the fair market value at $30,000 and the salvage value at $3,000.
6. Machinery A's total cost of $164,900 includes installation expense of $600 and normal repairs and maintenance of $14,900. Salvage value is estimated at $6,000. Machinery A was sold on February 1, 2002.
7. On October 1, 2001, Machinery B was acquired with a down payment of $5,740 and the remaining payments to be made in 11 annual installments of $6,000 each beginning October 1, 2001. The prevailing interest rate was 8%. The following data were abstracted from present-value tables (rounded):

Present value of $1.00 at 8%		Present value of an ordinary annuity of $1.00 at 8%	
10 years	.463	10 years	6.710
11 years	.429	11 years	7.139
15 years	.315	15 years	8.559

ANJELICA HUSTON CORPORATION
Fixed Asset and Depreciation Schedule
For Fiscal Years Ended September 30, 2001, and September 30, 2002

Assets	Acquisition Date	Cost	Salvage	Depreciation Method	Estimated Life in Years	Depreciation Expense Year Ended September 30 2001	2002
Land A	October 1, 2000	$ (1)	N/A	N/A	N/A	N/A	N/A
Building A	October 1, 2000	(2)	$40,000	Straight-line	(3)	$17,450	(4)
Land B	October 2, 2000	(5)	N/A	N/A	N/A	N/A	N/A
Building B	Under Construction	320,000 to date	—	Straight-line	30	—	(6)

Donated Equipment	October 2, 2000	(7)	3,000	150% declining balance	10	(8)	(9)
Machinery A	October 2, 2000	(10)	6,000	Sum-of-the-years'-digits	8	(11)	(12)
Machinery B	October 1, 2001	(13)	—	Straight-line	20	—	(14)

N/A—Not applicable

Instructions

For each numbered item on the foregoing schedule, supply the correct amount. Round each answer to the nearest dollar.

P11-12 (Depreciation for Partial Periods—SL, Act., SYD, and DDB) On January 1, 1999, a machine was purchased for $77,000. The machine has an estimated salvage value of $5,000 and an estimated useful life of 5 years. The machine can operate for 100,000 hours before it needs to be replaced. The company closed its books on December 31 and operates the machine as follows: 1999, 20,000 hrs; 2000, 25,000 hrs; 2001, 15,000 hrs; 2002, 30,000 hrs; 2003, 10,000 hrs.

Instructions

(a) Compute the annual depreciation charges over the machine's life assuming a December 31 year-end for each of the following depreciation methods:

(1) Straight-line method.
(2) Activity method.
(3) Sum-of-the-years'-digits method.
(4) Double-declining balance method.

(b) Assume a fiscal year-end of September 30. Compute the annual depreciation charges over the asset's life applying

(1) Straight-line method.
(2) Sum-of-the-years'-digits method.
(3) Double-declining balance method.

***P11-13 (Depreciation—SL, DDB, SYD, Act., and MACRS)** On January 1, 1999, Moshe Dayan Company, a small machine-tool manufacturer, acquired for $1,100,000 a piece of new industrial equipment. The new equipment had a useful life of 5 years, and the salvage value was estimated to be $50,000. Dayan estimates that the new equipment can produce 12,000 machine tools in its first year. It estimates that production will decline by 1,000 units per year over the remaining useful life of the equipment.

The following depreciation methods may be used: (1) straight-line; (2) double-declining balance; (3) sum-of-the-years'-digits; and (4) units-of-output. For tax purposes, the class life is 7 years. Use the MACRS tables for computing depreciation.

Instructions

(a) Which depreciation method would maximize net income for financial statement reporting for the 3-year period ending December 31, 2001? Prepare a schedule showing the amount of accumulated depreciation at December 31, 2001, under the method selected. Ignore present value, income tax, and deferred income tax considerations.

(b) Which depreciation method (MACRS or optional straight-line) would minimize net income for income tax reporting for the 3-year period ending December 31, 2001? Determine the amount of accumulated depreciation at December 31, 2001. Ignore present value considerations.

(AICPA adapted)

CONCEPTUAL CASES

C11-1 (Depreciation Basic Concepts) Prophet Manufacturing Company was organized January 1, 2002. During 2002, it has used in its reports to management the straight-line method of depreciating its plant assets.

On November 8 you are having a conference with Prophet's officers to discuss the depreciation method to be used for income tax and stockholder reporting. Frank Peretti, president of Prophet, has suggested the use of a new method, which he feels is more suitable than the straight-line method for the needs of the company during the period of rapid expansion of production and capacity that he foresees. Following is an example in which the proposed method is applied to a fixed asset with an original cost of $248,000, an estimated useful life of 5 years, and a scrap value of approximately $8,000.

Year	Years of Life Used	Fraction Rate	Depreciation Expense	Accumulated Depreciation at End of Year	Book Value at End of Year
1	1	1/15	$16,000	$ 16,000	$232,000
2	2	2/15	32,000	48,000	200,000
3	3	3/15	48,000	96,000	152,000
4	4	4/15	64,000	160,000	88,000
5	5	5/15	80,000	240,000	8,000

The president favors the new method because he has heard that:

1. It will increase the funds recovered during the years near the end of the assets' useful lives when maintenance and replacement disbursements are high.
2. It will result in increased write-offs in later years and thereby will reduce taxes.

Instructions

(a) What is the purpose of accounting for depreciation?

(b) Is the president's proposal within the scope of generally accepted accounting principles? In making your decision discuss the circumstances, if any, under which use of the method would be reasonable and those, if any, under which it would not be reasonable.

(c) The president wants your advice.

(1) Do depreciation charges recover or create funds? Explain.

(2) Assume that the Internal Revenue Service accepts the proposed depreciation method in this case. If the proposed method were used for stockholder and tax reporting purposes, how would it affect the availability of funds generated by operations?

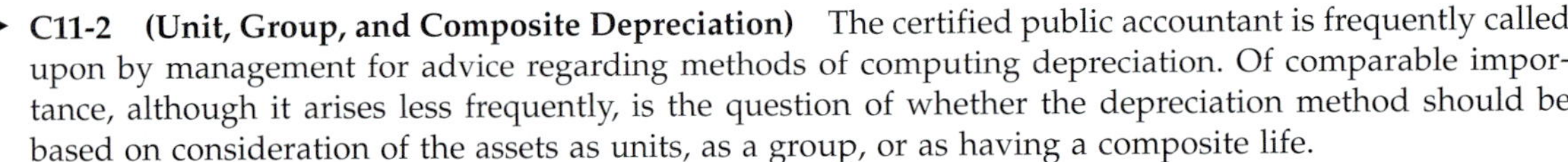

C11-2 (Unit, Group, and Composite Depreciation) The certified public accountant is frequently called upon by management for advice regarding methods of computing depreciation. Of comparable importance, although it arises less frequently, is the question of whether the depreciation method should be based on consideration of the assets as units, as a group, or as having a composite life.

Instructions

(a) Briefly describe the depreciation methods based on treating assets as (1) units and (2) a group or as having a composite life.

(b) Present the arguments for and against the use of each of the two methods.

(c) Describe how retirements are recorded under each of the two methods.

(AICPA adapted)

C11-3 (Depreciation—Strike, Units-of-Production, Obsolescence) Presented below are three different and unrelated situations involving depreciation accounting. Answer the question(s) at the end of each case situation.

Situation I

Recently, John Brown Company experienced a strike that affected a number of its operating plants. The controller of this company indicated that it was not appropriate to report depreciation expense during this period because the equipment did not depreciate and an improper matching of costs and revenues would result. She based her position on the following points:

1. It is inappropriate to charge the period with costs for which there are no related revenues arising from production.
2. The basic factor of depreciation in this instance is wear and tear, and because equipment was idle, no wear and tear occurred.

Instructions

Comment on the appropriateness of the controller's comments.

Situation II

Andrew Carnegie Company manufactures electrical appliances, most of which are used in homes. Company engineers have designed a new type of blender which, through the use of a few attachments, will perform more functions than any blender currently on the market. Demand for the new blender can be projected with reasonable probability. In order to make the blenders, Carnegie needs a specialized machine that is not available from outside sources. It has been decided to make such a machine in Carnegie's own plant.

Instructions

(a) Discuss the effect of projected demand in units for the new blenders (which may be steady, decreasing, or increasing) on the determination of a depreciation method for the machine.

(b) What other matters should be considered in determining the depreciation method? Ignore income tax considerations.

Situation III

Dorothea Dix Paper Company operates a 300-ton-per-day kraft pulp mill and four sawmills in Wisconsin. The company is in the process of expanding its pulp mill facilities to a capacity of 1,000 tons per day and plans to replace three of its older, less efficient sawmills with an expanded facility. One of the mills to be replaced did not operate for most of 2001 (current year), and there are no plans to reopen it before the new sawmill facility becomes operational.

In reviewing the depreciation rates and in discussing the residual values of the sawmills that were to be replaced, it was noted that if present depreciation rates were not adjusted, substantial amounts of plant costs on these three mills would not be depreciated by the time the new mill came on stream.

Instructions

What is the proper accounting for the four sawmills at the end of 2001?

C11-4 (Depreciation Concepts) As a cost accountant for San Francisco Cannery, you have been approached by Merton Miller, canning room supervisor, about the 2000 costs charged to his department. In particular, he is concerned about the line item "depreciation." Miller is very proud of the excellent condition of his canning room equipment. He has always been vigilant about keeping all equipment serviced and well oiled. He is sure that the huge charge to depreciation is a mistake; it does not at all reflect the cost of minimal wear and tear that the machines have experienced over the last year. He believes that the charge should be considerably lower.

The machines being depreciated are six automatic canning machines. All were put into use on January 1, 2000. Each cost $469,000, having a salvage value of $40,000 and a useful life of 12 years. San Francisco depreciates this and similar assets using double-declining balance. Miller has also pointed out that if you used straight-line depreciation the charge to his department would not be so great.

Instructions

Write a memo to Merton Miller to clear up his misunderstanding of the term "depreciation." Also, calculate year 1 depreciation on all machines using both methods. Explain the theoretical justification for double-declining balance and why, in the long run, the aggregate charge to depreciation will be the same under both methods.

USING YOUR JUDGMENT

FINANCIAL REPORTING PROBLEM: INTEL CORPORATION

The financial statements of Intel Corporation appear in Appendix 5B. Refer to these financial statements and the accompanying notes to answer the following questions.

Instructions

(a) What descriptions are used by Intel in its balance sheet to classify its property, plant, and equipment?

(b) What method or methods of depreciation does Intel Corporation use to depreciate its property, plant, and equipment?

(c) Over what estimated useful lives does Intel depreciate its property, plant, and equipment?

(d) What amounts for depreciation expense did Intel charge to its income statement in 1998, 1997, and 1996?

(e) What amounts of interest expense were capitalized by Intel as part of construction costs in 1998, 1997, and 1996?

(f) What were the additions to property, plant, and equipment made by Intel in 1998, 1997, and 1996?

FINANCIAL STATEMENT ANALYSIS CASES

Case 1 Boeing versus McDonnell Douglas

Boeing and McDonnell Douglas are two leaders in the manufacture of aircraft. In 1996 Boeing announced intentions to acquire McDonnell Douglas and create one huge corporation. Its competitors, primarily Airbus of Europe, are very concerned that they will not be able to compete with such a huge rival. In addition, customers are concerned that this will reduce the number of suppliers to a point where Boeing will be able to dictate prices. Provided below are figures taken from the 1995 financial statements of Boeing and McDonnell Douglas which allow a comparison of the operations of the two corporations prior to their merger.

(in millions of dollars)	Boeing	McDonnell Douglas
Total revenue	$19,515	$14,322
Net income (loss)	393	(416)
Total assets	22,098	10,466
Land	404	91
Buildings and fixtures	5,791	1,647
Machinery and equipment	7,251	2,161
Total property, plant, and equipment (at cost)	13,744	3,899
Accumulated depreciation	7,288	2,541
Depreciation expense	976	196

Instructions

(a) Based on the asset turnover ratio, which company used its assets more effectively to generate sales? Assume that total assets reported are a reasonable average of beginning and ending balances.

(b) Which company had a better profit margin on sales?

(c) Which company had the higher rate of return on total assets?

(d) Besides an increase in size, what other factors might have motivated this merger?

Case 2 McDonald's Corporation

McDonald's is the largest and best-known global food service retailer, with more than 24,000 restaurants in 114 countries. On any day, McDonald's serves approximately 1 percent of the world's population. Presented below is information related to property and equipment.

MCDONALD'S CORPORATION

Summary of Significant Accounting Policies Section

Property and Equipment. Property and equipment are stated at cost, with depreciation and amortization provided on the straight-line method over the following estimated useful lives: buildings—up to 40 years; leasehold improvements—lesser of useful lives of assets or lease terms including option periods; and equipment—3 to 12 years.

[In the notes to the financial statements:]

Other Operating (Income) Expense

(in millions)	1998	1997	1996
Net losses from property dispositions	$71.1	$29.1	$41.1
Other	18.1	(10.8)	3.1

Net losses from property dispositions in 1996 included $16.0 million for certain restaurant sites in Mexico, upon the adoption of *SFAS No. 121,* and in 1998 reflected an increased number of restaurant closings.

Property and Equipment

(in millions)	December 31, 1998	1997
Land	$ 3,812.1	$ 3,592.2
Buildings and improvements on owned land	7,665.8	7,289.7
Buildings and improvements on leased land	6,910.4	6,168.3
Equipment, signs and seating	2,728.8	2,345.1
Other	640.9	692.9
	21,758.0	20,088.2
Accumulated depreciation and amortization	(5,716.4)	(5,126.8)
Net property and equipment	$16,041.6	$14,961.4

Depreciation and amortization expense was (in millions): 1998—$808.0; 1997—$726.4; 1996—$673.4.

[In the management discussion and analysis section, the following schedule is provided:]

(in millions)	1998	1997	1996	1995	1994
Cash provided by operations	$2,766	$2,442	$2,461	$2,296	$1,926
Free cash flow	$ 887	$ 331	$ 86	$ 232	$ 387
Cash provided by operations as a percent of capital expenditures	147%	116%	104%	111%	125%
Cash provided by operations as a percent of average total debt	41%	41%	48%	49%	48%

Instructions

(a) What method of depreciation is used by McDonald's?

(b) Does depreciation and amortization expense cause cash flow from operations to increase? Explain.

(c) McDonald's indicates that it reported losses in accordance with *Financial Accounting Standard No. 121.* What criterion should McDonald's use to record an impairment loss?

(d) What does the schedule of cash flow measures indicate?

COMPARATIVE ANALYSIS CASE

The Coca-Cola Company versus PepsiCo. Inc.

Instructions

Go to the Digital Tool and use information about the Coca-Cola Company and PepsiCo found there to answer the following questions.

(a) What amount is reported in the balance sheets as property, plant, and equipment (net) of Coca-Cola at December 31, 1998, and of PepsiCo at December 30, 1998? What percentage of total assets is invested in property, plant, and equipment by each company?

(b) What depreciation methods are used by Coca-Cola and PepsiCo for property, plant, and equipment? How much depreciation was reported by Coca-Cola and PepsiCo in 1998, 1997, and 1996?

(c) Compute and compare the following ratios for Coca-Cola and PepsiCo for 1998:

(1) Asset turnover.

(2) Profit margin on sales.

(3) Ratio of return on assets.

(d) What amount was spent in 1998 for capital expenditures by Coca-Cola and PepsiCo? What amount of interest was capitalized in 1998?

(e) What references do Coca-Cola and PepsiCo make to any impairments of long-lived assets?

RESEARCH CASES

Case 1

A wealth of accounting-related information is available via the Internet. For example, the Rutgers Accounting Web (http://www.rutgers.edu/accounting/raw) offers access to a great variety of sources.

Instructions

Once in the Rutgers Accounting Web, click on "internet" to arrive at the "Accounting Resources on the Internet" page. (*Note:* Once on this page, you may have to click on the "text only" box to access the available information.)

(a) List the categories of information available through the "Accounting Resources on the Internet" page.

(b) Select any one of these categories and briefly describe the types of information available.

Case 2

The December 4, 1995, issue of *Forbes ASAP* includes an article by Umberto Tosi entitled "Digital Air."

Instructions

Read the article and answer the following questions.

(a) What does "AMIS" stand for?

(b) What are the primary features of AMIS?

(c) How did deregulation in the airline industry aid in the development of AMIS?

(d) How does AMIS help reduce maintenance costs?

INTERNATIONAL REPORTING CASE

Companies following international accounting standards are permitted to revalue fixed assets above the assets' historical costs. Such revaluations are allowed under various countries' standards and the standards issued by the International Accounting Standards Committee (IASC). Nestlé SA, headquartered in Switzerland, follows IASC standards; it disclosed the following information on revaluations of its tangible fixed assets. The revaluation reserve measures the amount by which tangible fixed assets are recorded above historical cost and is reported in Nestlé's stockholders' equity:

NESTLÉ SA

31 December 1997

Tangible fixed assets

The revaluation reserve included in the carrying value of net tangible fixed assets at net replacement value is as follows:

(in millions of Swiss francs)	Land and Buildings	Machinery and Equipment	Tools, Furniture, and Other Equipment	Vehicles	Total 1997
Net replacement value	9 492	10 727	1 571	378	22 168
Net book value	7 474	8 724	1 659	328	18 185
Revaluation reserve	2 018	2 003	−88	50	3 983

The following additional data were reported by Nestlé for 1997. Amounts for Tootsie Roll are provided for comparison:

	Nestlé (Swiss francs, in millions)	Tootsie Roll ($, in thousands)
Total revenues	69 998	375,594
Average total assets	52 857	413,924
Net income	4 005	60,682

Instructions

(a) Compute the following ratios for Nestlé and Tootsie Roll for 1997:
  (1) Return on assets.
  (2) Profit margin.
  (3) Asset turnover.
  How do these companies compare on these performance measures?

(b) Nestlé reports a revaluation reserve of 3,983 Swiss francs in 1997. Assume that 1,550 of this amount arose from an increase in the net replacement value of land and buildings during 1997. Prepare the journal entry to record this increase for 1997. (*Hint:* Credit the Revaluation Reserve account.)

(c) Under IASC standards, are Nestlé's assets and equity overstated? If so, why? When comparing Nestlé to U.S. companies, like Tootsie Roll, what adjustments would you need to make in order to have valid comparisons of ratios such as those computed in (a) above?

ETHICS CASE

Billy Williams, Sheffield Corporation's controller, is concerned that net income may be lower this year. He is afraid upper-level management might recommend cost reductions by laying off accounting staff, him included.

Williams knows that depreciation is a major expense for Sheffield. The company currently uses the double-declining balance method for both financial reporting and tax purposes, and he's thinking of a change to the straight-line method. That, of course, would require a cumulative-effect adjustment since it is a change in accounting principle and would be reported separately in the income statement. He doesn't want to highlight the method of increasing income in this manner. He thinks, "Why don't I increase the estimated useful lives and the salvage values? That will decrease depreciation expense and since the changes are accounted for prospectively, they will not be disclosed in the income statement. I may be able to save my job and those of my staff."

Instructions

Answer the following questions:

(a) Who are the stakeholders in this situation?

(b) What are the ethical issues involved?

(c) What should Williams do?

CHAPTER 12

Intangible Assets

Trying to Grasp the Intangible

In 1494, a mathematically minded Venetian monk named Luca Pacioli published his *Summa de Arithmetica, Geometrica,* the first accounting textbook. It illustrated double-entry accounting, a system that makes the modern corporation manageable, even possible. Today, half a millennium later, Pacioli's process, still pretty much intact, is being challenged like never before.

Pacioli's accounting system lets businesses keep track of changes in their assets. But this system deals primarily with *tangible assets* such as cash, inventory, investments, receivables, property, plant, and equipment. What go unrecorded are *intangible assets* such as quality of management, customer loyalty, information infrastructure, trade secrets, patents, goodwill, research, and, considered by some the ultimate intangible, *knowledge*—a company's intellectual capital. As present FASB chairman Edmund Jenkins attests, "The components of cost in a product today are largely R & D, intellectual assets, and services. The old accounting system, which tells us the cost of material and labor, isn't applicable." Argues Professor James Quinn of Dartmouth College, "Even in manufacturing, perhaps three-fourths of the value added derives from knowledge."[1]

This refrain is echoed by the managing editor of *Fortune* magazine, Walter Kiechel, who says, "To be sure, there are still industries in which the factory confers a competitive advantage. But this is changing fast, as more and more companies realize that their edge derives less from their machines, bricks, and mortar than from what we used to think of as the intangibles, like the brainpower resident in the corporation."[2]

In this emerging economy of knowledge, even some banks have concluded that "soft" assets (like computer programming know-how and information infrastructure) can be a better credit risk than "hard" assets (like buildings). But how should the "soft assets" be valued? Accountants get little solace from former FASB chairman Donald Kirk, who acknowledges, "There are arguments that balance sheets ignore certain intangibles, but the reporting issues of trying to recognize them are, in my mind, insurmountable."[3] It appears that the assets that really count are the ones accountants can't count—yet.

LEARNING OBJECTIVES

After studying this chapter, you should be able to:

1. **Describe the characteristics of intangible assets.**
2. **Explain the procedure for valuing and amortizing intangible assets.**
3. **Identify the types of specifically identifiable intangible assets.**
4. **Explain the conceptual issues related to goodwill.**
5. **Describe the accounting procedures for recording goodwill.**
6. **Identify the conceptual issues related to research and development costs.**
7. **Describe the accounting procedures for research and development costs and for other similar costs.**
8. **Indicate the presentation of intangibles and related items.**

---

[1]Thomas Stewart, "Your Company's Most Valuable Asset: Intellectual Capital," *Fortune,* October 3, 1994, p. 68.

[2]"Searching for Nonfiction in Financial Statements," *Fortune,* December 23, 1996, p. 38.

[3]Ibid.

PREVIEW OF CHAPTER 12

As the opening story indicates, the accounting and reporting of intangibles is taking on increasing importance in this information age. The purpose of this chapter is to explain the basic conceptual and reporting issues related to intangible assets. The content and organization of the chapter are as follows:

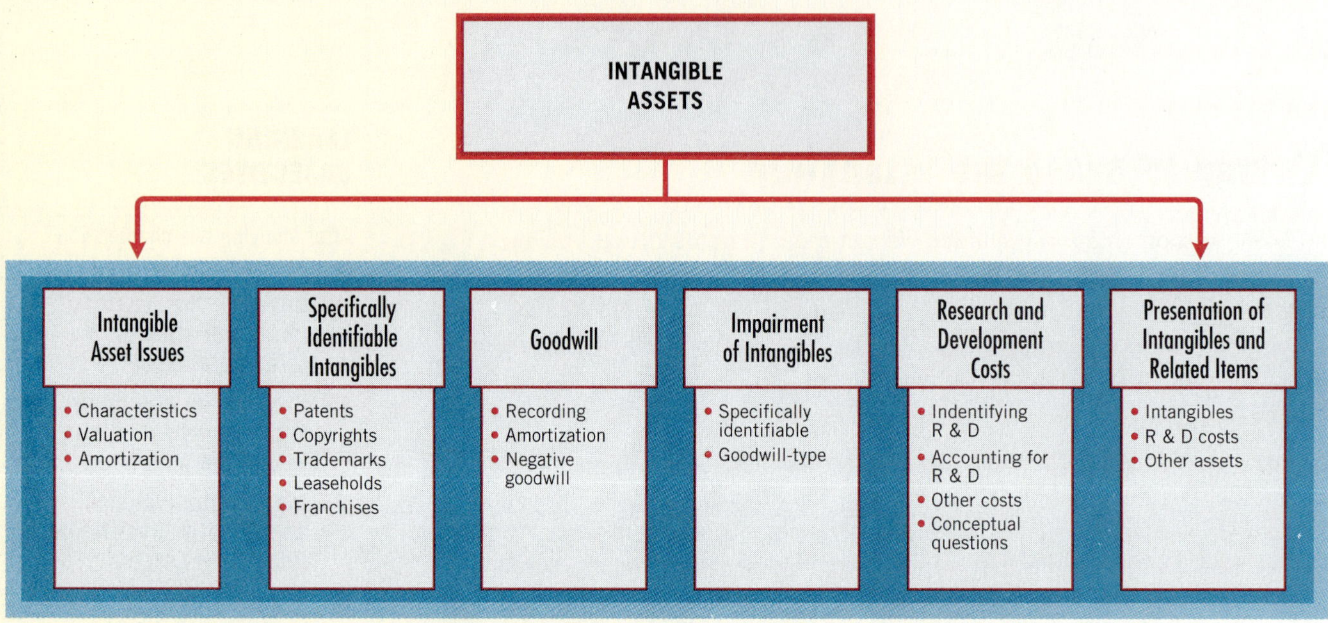

INTANGIBLE ASSET ISSUES

Characteristics

OBJECTIVE 1
Describe the characteristics of intangible assets.

Gap Inc.'s most important asset is not store fixtures—brand image is. The major asset of Coca-Cola is not its plant facilities—its secret formula for making Coke is. America Online's most important asset is not its Internet connection equipment—its subscriber base is. As these examples show, we have an economy dominated today by information and service providers, and their major assets are often intangible in nature. Accounting for these intangibles is difficult, and as a result many intangibles are presently not reported on a company's balance sheet. **Intangible assets** have three main characteristics.[4]

1. **They lack physical existence.** Unlike tangible assets such as property, plant, and equipment, intangible assets derive their value from the rights and privileges granted to the company using them.
2. **They are not financial instruments** Assets such as bank deposits, accounts receivable, and long-term investments in bonds and stocks lack physical substance, but are not classified as intangible assets. These assets are financial instruments and derive their value from the right (claim) to receive cash or cash equivalents in the future.

[4]"Business Combinations and Intangible Assets," *Proposed Statement of Financial Accounting Standards* (Norwalk, Conn.: FASB, 1999).

3. **They are long-term in nature and subject to amortization.** Intangible assets provide services over a period of years. Investments in these assets are normally assigned to future periods through periodic amortization charges.

The most common types of intangibles reported are patents, copyrights, franchises or licenses, trademarks or trade names, and goodwill. Intangible assets are often further subdivided on the basis of the following characteristics:

1. ***Identifiability.*** Separately identifiable or lacking specific identification.
2. ***Manner of Acquisition.*** Acquired singly, in groups, or in business combinations, or developed internally.
3. ***Expected Period of Benefit.*** Limited by law or contract, related to human or economic factors, or indefinite or indeterminate duration.
4. ***Separability from an Entire Enterprise.*** Rights transferable without title, salable, or inseparable from the enterprise or a substantial part of it.[5]

These subdivisions provide insight into how the reporting requirements for intangibles have developed.

Valuation

Purchased Intangibles

OBJECTIVE 2
Explain the procedure for valuing and amortizing intangible assets.

Intangibles purchased from another party are **recorded at cost**. Cost includes all costs of acquisition and expenditures necessary to make the intangible asset ready for its intended use—for example, purchase price, legal fees and other incidental expenses.

If intangibles are acquired for stock or in exchange for other assets, **the cost of the intangible is the fair market value of the consideration given or the fair market value of the intangible received, whichever is more clearly evident**. When several intangibles, or a combination of intangibles and tangibles, are bought in a "basket purchase," the cost should be allocated on the basis of fair market values or on the basis of relative sales values. Essentially the accounting treatment for purchased intangibles closely parallels that followed for purchased tangible assets. The profession has resisted employment of some other basis of valuation, such as current replacement costs or appraisal value for intangible assets.[6]

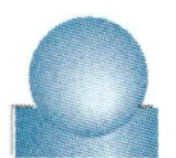

UNDERLYING CONCEPTS

The basic attributes of intangibles, their uncertainty as to future benefits, and their uniqueness, have discouraged valuation in excess of cost.

Internally-Created Intangibles

Costs incurred internally to create intangibles are generally expensed as incurred. Thus, even though a company may incur substantial research and development costs to create an intangible, these costs are expensed. Various reasons are given for this approach. Some argue that the costs incurred internally to create intangibles bear no relationship to their real value; therefore, expensing these costs is appropriate. Others note that with a purchased intangible, a reliable number for the cost of the intangible can be determined; with internally developed intangibles, it is difficult to associate costs with specific intangible assets. And others argue that due to the underlying subjectivity related to intangibles, a conservative approach should be followed—that is, expense as incurred. As a result, the **only internal costs capitalized are direct costs** incurred in obtaining the intangible, such as legal costs.

In Japan the cost of intangibles can be capitalized whether they are externally purchased or internally developed.

[5]"Intangible Assets," *Opinions of the Accounting Principles Board No. 17* (New York: AICPA, 1970), par. 10.

[6]Recognize that as intangible assets continue to grow in both size and scope, many people are demanding that these values be reported in a timely manner. How to make this happen is the subject of much debate because valuation problems are complex. See Steven M.H. Wallman, "The Future of Accounting and Disclosure in an Evolving World: The Need for Dramatic Change," *Accounting Horizons*, September 1995, pp. 81–91.

For subsequent discussion, we will classify intangibles into intangibles that are specifically identifiable, as contrasted to "goodwill-type" intangible assets (unidentifiable values). **Specifically identifiable** means that costs associated with obtaining a given intangible asset can be identified as a part of the cost of that intangible asset. In contrast, a **goodwill-type** intangible may create some right or privilege, but it is not specifically identifiable and it has an indeterminable life. The accounting treatments accorded these two types of intangibles are shown in Illustration 12-1.

ILLUSTRATION 12-1
Accounting for the Costs of Intangibles

	Manner Acquired	
Type of Intangible	Purchased	Internally Created
Specifically Identifiable Intangibles	Capitalize	Expense, except certain costs
Goodwill-type Intangibles	Capitalize	Expense

Amortization of Intangibles

As you learned in Chapter 11, the expiration of intangible assets is called **Amortization**. Intangible assets should be amortized by systematic charges to expense over their useful lives. Factors considered in determining useful life are:

1. Legal, regulatory, or contractual provisions.
2. Provisions for renewal or extension.
3. Effects of obsolescence, demand, competition, and other economic factors.
4. A useful life may parallel the service life expectancies of individuals or groups of employees.
5. Expected actions of competitors and others may restrict competitive advantages.
6. An apparently unlimited useful life may in fact be indefinite and benefits cannot be reasonably projected.
7. An intangible asset may be a composite of many individual factors with varying effective lives.[7]

Although in many nations it is standard practice to capitalize and amortize goodwill, practice varies widely. In a few countries goodwill is capitalized but not amortized, thus remaining as a permanent asset. In other nations goodwill is written off immediately.

One problem relating to the amortization of intangibles is that some intangibles have indeterminable useful lives. In this case, **intangible assets must be amortized over a period not exceeding 40 years.**[8] The 40-year requirement is based on the premise that only a few, if any, intangibles last forever. Sometimes, because useful life is difficult to determine, a 40-year period is employed because it is practical, although admittedly arbitrary. Another reason for this 40-year limitation is simply that it ensures that companies eventually write off their intangibles. Prior to the 40-year rule, there was evidence that some companies retained their intangibles (notably goodwill) indefinitely on their balance sheet for only one reason—to avoid the charge to expense that occurs when goodwill is written off.

Intangible assets acquired from other enterprises (notably goodwill) should not be written off at acquisition. Some contend that certain intangibles should not be carried as assets on the balance sheet under any circumstances but should be written off directly to retained earnings or additional paid-in capital. However, the immediate writeoff to retained earnings and additional paid-in capital is not acceptable because this approach denies the existence of an asset that has just been purchased.

[7]*APB Opinion No. 17*, op. cit., par. 27.

[8]Ibid., par. 10. We should note that the general rules for amortization would change if the proposed SFAS on business combinations and intangible assets is adopted. The proposed SFAS prescribes a 20-year useful life for all intangible assets. If certain conditions are met, the amortization period for intangible assets (other than goodwill) may exceed 20 years. In some situations, an intangible asset may not be amortized at all. Whether these recommendations will be adopted is difficult to determine at this point because many companies are upset with some of the key provisions of this proposed SFAS and are lobbying to have them changed.

Intangible assets are generally amortized on a straight-line basis (tax practice requires a straight-line approach), although there is no reason why another systematic approach might not be employed if the firm demonstrates that another method is more appropriate. In any case the method and period of amortization should be disclosed.

When intangible assets are amortized, the charges should be shown as expenses, and the credits should be made either to the appropriate asset accounts or to separate accumulated amortization accounts.

SPECIFICALLY IDENTIFIABLE INTANGIBLES

OBJECTIVE 3
Identify the types of specifically identifiable intangible assets.

Patents

Patents are granted by the U.S. Patent and Trademark Office. The two principal kinds of patents are **product patents**, which cover actual physical products, and **process patents**, which govern the process by which products are made. A patent gives the holder exclusive right to use, manufacture, and sell a product or process **for a period of 20 years** without interference or infringement by others. With this exclusive right, fortunes can be made. For example: companies such as Merck, Polaroid, and Xerox were founded on patents.[9] If a patent is purchased from an inventor (or other owner), the purchase price represents its cost. Other costs incurred in connection with securing a patent, as well as attorneys' fees and other unrecovered costs of a successful legal suit to protect the patent, can be capitalized as part of the patent cost. Research and development costs related to the **development** of the product, process, or idea that is subsequently patented **must be expensed as incurred**, however. See pages 614–616 for a more complete presentation of accounting for research and development costs.

The cost of a patent should be amortized over its legal life or its useful life (the period benefits are received), whichever is shorter. If a patent is owned from the date it is granted, and it is expected to be useful during its entire legal life, it should be amortized over 20 years. If it appears that the patent will be useful for a shorter period of time, say, for 5 years, its cost should be amortized to expense over 5 years. Changing demand, new inventions superseding old ones, inadequacy, and other factors often limit the useful life of a patent to less than the legal life. For example, the useful life of patents in the pharmaceutical and drug industry is frequently less than the legal life because of the testing and approval period that follows their issuance. A typical drug patent has 5 to 11 years knocked off its 20-year legal life because 1 to 4 years must be spent on tests on animals, 4 to 6 years on human tests, and 2 to 3 years for the Food and Drug Administration to review the tests—all after the patent is issued but before the product goes on a pharmacist's shelves.

From bioengineering to software design to the Internet,[10] battles over patents are heating up as global competition intensifies. For example, Priceline.com filed suit against Microsoft for launching Hotel Price Matcher, a service that operates pretty much like the name-your-own-price-system pioneered by Priceline. And Amazon.com filed a complaint against barnesandnoble.com, its bitter rival in the Web-retailing wars. The suit alleges that barnesandnoble.com is infringing on Amazon.com's patent for one-click shopping and asks the court to stop barnesandnoble.com from using its own quick-checkout system, called ExpressLane. **Legal fees and other costs incurred in successfully defending a patent suit are debited to Patents**, an asset account, because such a suit establishes the legal rights of the holder of the patent. Such costs should be amortized along with acquisition cost over the remaining useful life of the patent.

---

[9]Consider the opposite result: Sir Alexander Fleming, who discovered penicillin, decided not to use a patent to protect his discovery. He hoped that companies would produce it more quickly to help save sufferers. Companies, however, refused to develop it because they did not have the patent shield and, therefore, were afraid to make the investment.

[10]"Battle over Patents Threatens to Damp Web's Innovative Spirit," *The Wall Street Journal*, November 8, 1999.

Amortization of patents may be computed on a time basis or on a basis of units produced and may be credited directly to the Patents account. It is acceptable also, although less common, to credit an Accumulated Patent Amortization account. To illustrate, assume that Harcott Co. incurs $180,000 in legal costs on January 1, 2001, to successfully defend a patent. The patent has a useful life of 20 years, and is amortized on a straight-line basis. The entries to record the legal fees and the amortization at the end of each year are as follows:

January 1, 2001		
Patents	180,000	
Cash		180,000
(To record legal fees related to patent)		
December 31, 2001		
Patent Amortization Expense	9,000	
Patents (or Accumulated Patent Amortization)		9,000
(To record amortization of patent)		

Amortization on a units-of-production basis would be computed in a manner similar to that described for depreciation on property, plant, and equipment in Chapter 11, page 553.

Although a patent's useful life should not extend beyond its legal life of 20 years, small modifications or additions may lead to a new patent. The effect may be to extend the life of the old patent. In that case it is permissible to apply the unamortized costs of the old patent to the new patent if the new patent provides essentially the same benefits.[11] Alternatively, if a patent becomes worthless (impaired) because demand drops for the product produced, the asset should be written down or written off immediately to expense.

Copyrights

A **copyright** is a federally granted right that all authors, painters, musicians, sculptors, and other artists have in their creations and expressions. A copyright is granted for the **life of the creator plus 50 years**, and gives the owner, or heirs, the exclusive right to reproduce and sell an artistic or published work. Copyrights are not renewable. Like patents, they may be assigned or sold to other individuals. The costs of acquiring and defending a copyright may be capitalized, but the research and development costs involved must be expensed as incurred.

Generally, the useful life of the copyright is less than its legal life (life in being plus 50 years). The costs of the copyright should be allocated to the years in which the benefits are expected to be received, not to exceed 40 years. The difficulty of determining the number of years over which benefits will be received normally encourages the company to write these costs off over a fairly short period of time.

Copyrights can be valuable. **Really Useful Group** is a company that consists of copyrights on the musicals of Andrew Lloyd Webber—*Cats, Phantom of the Opera, Jesus Christ-Superstar,* and others. It has little in the way of hard assets, yet it has been valued at $300 million.[12]

Trademarks and Trade Names

A **trademark** or **trade name** is a word, phrase, or symbol that distinguishes or identifies a particular enterprise or product. The right to use a trademark or trade name under common law, whether it is registered or not, rests exclusively with the original user

[11]A good example is **Eli Lilly**'s drug Prozac (used to treat depression) which in 1998 accounted for 43% of its U.S. sales. The patent on Prozac is due to expire in 2001, but the company expects to get an additional 2 years of protection, to 2003, because the company has a second-use patent covering appetite disorders.

[12]Russell L. Parr, *Investing in Intangible Assets* (New York: John Wiley & Sons, Inc., 1991), p. 47.

as long as the original user continues to use it. Registration with the U.S. Patent and Trademark Office provides legal protection for an **indefinite number of renewals for periods of 20 years each**, so a business that uses an established trademark or trade name may properly consider it to have an unlimited life. Trade names like Kleenex, Pepsi-Cola, Oldsmobile, Excedrin, Wheaties, and Sunkist create immediate product identification in our minds, thereby enhancing marketability.

The value of a trademark or trade name can be substantial. Consider Internet domain names as an example. The name **Drugs.com** recently sold for $800,000, and the bidding for the name **Loans.com** approached $500,000.

INTERNATIONAL INSIGHT

Traditionally, when brand names are included in the acquisition of another company, the value of the brand name has been included in goodwill. In recent years, however, a number of firms in Great Britain and Australia have begun to value brand names separately in their balance sheets. This practice is highly controversial.

Company names themselves identify qualities and characteristics that the companies have worked hard and spent much to develop. In a recent year an estimated 1,230 companies took on new names in an attempt to forge new identities and paid over $250 million to corporate-identity consultants. Among these were **Primerica** (formerly American Can), **Navistar** (formerly International Harvester), **Nissan** (formerly Datsun), and **USX** (U.S. Steel).

If a trademark or trade name is acquired, its capitalizable cost is the purchase price. If a trademark or trade name is developed by the enterprise itself, the capitalizable cost includes attorney fees, registration fees, design costs, consulting fees, successful legal defense costs, and other expenditures directly related to securing it (excluding research and development costs). When the total cost of a trademark or trade name is insignificant, it can be expensed rather than capitalized.

Although the life of a trademark, trade name, or company name may be unlimited, for accounting purposes the cost must be amortized over the periods benefited, not to exceed 40 years. However, because of the uncertainty involved in estimating their useful life, the cost of trademarks and trade names is frequently amortized over a much shorter period of time.[13]

Leaseholds

A **leasehold** is a contractual understanding between a lessor (owner of property) and a lessee (renter of property) that grants the lessee **the right to use specific property, owned by the lessor, for a specific period of time in return for stipulated, and generally periodic, cash payments**. In most cases, the rent is included as an expense on the books of the lessee. Special problems, however, develop in the following situations.

Lease Prepayments

If the rent for the period of the lease is paid in advance, or if a lump sum payment is made in advance in addition to periodic rental payments, it is necessary to allocate this prepaid rent to the proper periods. The lessee has purchased the exclusive right to use the property for an extended period of time. These prepayments should be reported as a prepaid expense and not as an intangible asset.

UNDERLYING CONCEPTS

The treatment of leases is an example of the importance of the definition of an asset. The definition does not require ownership but it does require that the benefits of an asset flow to and be under the control of the entity.

Leasehold Improvements

Long-term leases ordinarily provide that any **leasehold improvements**, improvements made to the leased property, revert to the lessor at the end of the life of the lease. If the lessee constructs new buildings on leased land or reconstructs and improves existing buildings, **the lessee has the right to use such facilities during the life of the lease, but they become the property of the lessor when the lease expires**.

---

[13]To illustrate how various intangibles might arise from a given product, consider what the creators of the highly successful game, Trivial Pursuit, did to protect their creation. First, they copyrighted the 6,000 questions that are at the heart of the game. Then they shielded the Trivial Pursuit name by applying for a registered trademark. As a third mode of protection, the creators obtained a design patent on the playing board's design because it represents a unique graphic creation.

The lessee should charge the cost of the facilities to the Leasehold Improvements account and **depreciate the cost as operating expense over the remaining life of the lease, or the useful life of the improvements, whichever is shorter**. If a building with an estimated useful life of 25 years is constructed on land leased for 35 years, the cost of the building should be depreciated over 25 years. On the other hand, if the building has an estimated life of 50 years, it should be depreciated over 35 years, the life of the lease.

If the lease contains an option to renew for a period of additional years and the likelihood of renewal is too uncertain to warrant apportioning the cost over the longer period of time, the leasehold improvements are generally written off over the original term of the lease (assuming that the life of the lease is shorter than the useful life of the improvements). **Leasehold improvements are generally shown in the tangible property, plant, and equipment section**, although some accountants classify them as intangible assets. The rationale for intangible asset treatment is that the improvements revert to the lessor at the end of the lease and are therefore more of a right than a tangible asset.

Capital Leases

In some cases, the lease agreement transfers substantially all of the benefits and risks incident to ownership of the property so that the economic effect on the parties is similar to that of an installment purchase. As a result, the asset value recognized when a lease is capitalized is classified as a tangible rather than an intangible asset. Such a lease is referred to as a **capital lease**. We will cover the accounting for leases in more detail in Chapter 22.

Franchises and Licenses

When you drive down the street in an automobile purchased from a **Toyota** dealer, fill your tank at the corner **Texaco** station, eat lunch at **McDonald's**, cool off with one of **Baskin-Robbins**' 31 flavors, work at a **Coca-Cola** bottling plant, live in a home purchased through a **Century 21** real estate broker, or vacation at a **Holiday Inn** resort, you are dealing with franchises. A **franchise** is a contractual arrangement under which the franchisor grants the franchisee the right to sell certain products or services, to use certain trademarks or trade names, or to perform certain functions, usually within a designated geographical area.

The franchisor, having developed a unique concept or product, protects its concept or product through a patent, copyright, or trademark or trade name. The franchisee acquires the right to exploit the franchisor's idea or product by signing a franchise agreement.

Another type of franchise is the arrangement commonly entered into by a municipality (or other governmental body) and a business enterprise that uses public property. In such cases, a privately owned enterprise is permitted to use public property in performing its services. Examples are the use of public waterways for a ferry service, the use of public land for telephone or electric lines, the use of phone lines for cable TV, the use of city streets for a bus line, or the use of the airwaves for radio or TV broadcasting. Such operating rights, obtained through agreements with governmental units or agencies, are frequently referred to as **licenses** or **permits**.

Franchises and licenses may be for a definite period of time, for an indefinite period of time, or perpetual. The enterprise securing the franchise or license carries an intangible asset account entitled Franchise or License on its books only when there are costs (such as a lump sum payment in advance or legal fees and other expenditures) that are identified with the acquisition of the operating right. **The cost of a franchise (or license) with a limited life should be amortized as operating expense over the life of the franchise.** A franchise with an indefinite life, or a perpetual franchise, should be carried at cost and amortized over a reasonable period not to exceed 40 years.

If a franchise is deemed to be worthless, it should be written off immediately. For example, in 1980, Congress deregulated the trucking industry and opened to competition long-protected routes covered by franchises. Because these franchise rights were substantial, approximately 15% of the trucking industry's equity was eliminated; as a result, losses instead of profits were reported in the period of write-off.[14] For example, when **Roadway Express** wrote off all $26.8 million worth of these assets, it changed a $16.4 million profit for the quarter to a $10.4 million loss.

Annual payments made under a franchise agreement should be entered as operating expenses in the period in which they are incurred. They do not represent an asset to the concern since they do not relate to future rights to use public property.

GOODWILL

OBJECTIVE 4
Explain the conceptual issues related to goodwill.

Although companies are permitted to capitalize certain costs to develop specifically identifiable assets such as patents and copyrights, the amounts capitalized are generally not significant. Material amounts of intangible assets are recorded when companies purchase intangible assets, particularly in situations involving the purchase of another business (often referred to as a business combination).

In a business combination, the cost (purchase price) is assigned where possible to the identifiable tangible and intangible net assets, and the remainder is recorded in an intangible asset account called **Goodwill**. Goodwill is often referred to as the most intangible of the intangibles because it can only be identified with the business as a whole. The only way it can be sold is to sell the business.

The problem of determining the proper cost to allocate to intangible assets in a business combination is complex because of the many different types of intangibles that might be considered. Many of these types of intangibles are described below.[15]

1. **Intangible assets that relate to customers or market factors of the business:**

Lists (advertising, customers, mailing and so forth)	Production backlog
Customer routes	Retail shelfspace
Trademarks and brand names	Delivery system

2. **Intangible assets that have a fixed or definite life:**
   Agreements (consulting, income, royalty, manufacturing)
   Covenants not to compete
   Permits (construction, for example)
   Rights (broadcasting, gas allocation, landing, and so forth)

3. **Intangible assets that relate to innovation or technological advances within the business:**

Computer software	Technological know-how
Internet domain names and portals	Databases
Secret formulas and processes	

4. **Intangible assets with statutorily established useful lives:**

Patents	Franchises
Copyrights	Trademarks or trade names

5. **Intangible assets that relate to the value of the established employees or workforce of a business:**

Assembled workforce, trained staff	Technical expertise
Strong labor relations	Ongoing training program

6. **Intangible assets relating to the organizational structure of the company:**

Favorable financial arrangements	Favorable governmental relations
Easy access to capital markets	Outstanding credit rating

---

[14]Accounting for Intangible Assets of Motor Carriers," *Statement of Financial Accounting Standards No. 44* (Stamford, Conn.: FASB, 1980).

[15]Adapted from "Business Combinations and Intangible Assets," *Proposed Statement of Financial Accounting Standards* (Norwalk, Conn.: FASB, 1999).

It would be extremely difficult not only to identify certain types of intangibles but also to assign a value to them in a business combination. As a result, the approach followed is to record identifiable intangible assets that can be reliably measured. Other intangible assets that are difficult to identify or measure are recorded as goodwill.

Recording Goodwill

Internally Created Goodwill

OBJECTIVE 5
Describe the accounting procedures for recording goodwill.

Goodwill generated internally should not be capitalized in the accounts, because measuring the components of goodwill is simply too complex and associating any costs with future benefits too difficult. The future benefits of goodwill may have no relationship to the costs incurred in the development of that goodwill. To add to the mystery, goodwill may even exist in the absence of specific costs to develop it. In addition, because no objective transaction with outside parties has taken place, a great deal of subjectivity—even misrepresentation—might be involved.

Purchased Goodwill

UNDERLYING CONCEPTS

Capitalizing goodwill only when it is purchased in an arm's-length transaction and not capitalizing any goodwill generated internally is another example of reliability winning out over relevance.

Goodwill is recorded only when an entire business is purchased, because goodwill is a "going concern" valuation and cannot be separated from the business as a whole.[16] To record goodwill, the fair market value of the net tangible and identifiable intangible assets are compared with the purchase price of the acquired business. The difference is considered goodwill, which is why goodwill is sometimes referred to as a "plug" or "gap filler" or **"master valuation"** account. **Goodwill is the residual: the excess of cost over fair value of the identifiable net assets acquired.**

To illustrate, Multi-Diversified, Inc. decides that it needs a parts division to supplement its existing tractor distributorship. The president of Multi-Diversified is interested in buying a small concern in Chicago (Tractorling Company) that has an established reputation and is seeking a merger candidate. The balance sheet of Tractorling Company is presented in Illustration 12-2.

ILLUSTRATION 12-2
Tractorling Balance Sheet

TRACTORLING CO.
Balance Sheet
as of December 31, 2000

Assets		Equities	
Cash	$ 25,000	Current liabilities	$ 55,000
Receivables	35,000	Capital stock	100,000
Inventories	42,000	Retained earnings	100,000
Property, plant, and equipment, net	153,000		
Total assets	$255,000	Total equities	$255,000

After considerable negotiation, Tractorling Company decides to accept Multi-Diversified's offer of $400,000. What then is the value of the goodwill, if any?

The answer is not obvious. The fair market values of Tractorling's identifiable assets are not disclosed in its historical cost-based balance sheet. Suppose, though, that as the negotiations progressed, Multi-Diversified conducted an investigation of the underlying assets of Tractorling to determine the fair market value of the assets. Such an investigation may be accomplished either through a purchase audit undertaken

[16]See "Conceptual Framework for Financial Accounting and Reporting Elements of Financial Statements and Their Measurement," *FASB Discussion Memorandum* (Stamford, Conn.: FASB, 1976), p. 235.

by Multi-Diversified's auditors in order to estimate the values of the seller's assets, or an independent appraisal from some other source. The following valuations are determined.

ILLUSTRATION 12-3
Fair Market Value of Tractorling's Net Assets

Fair Market Values	
Cash	$ 25,000
Receivables	35,000
Inventories	122,000
Property, plant, and equipment, net	205,000
Patents	18,000
Liabilities	(55,000)
Fair market value of net assets	$350,000

Normally, differences between current fair market value and book value are more common among long-term assets, although significant differences can also develop in the current asset category. Cash obviously poses no problems, and receivables normally are fairly close to current valuation, although at times certain adjustments need to be made because of inadequate bad debt provisions. Liabilities usually are stated at book value, although if interest rates have changed since the liabilities were incurred, a different valuation (such as present value) might be appropriate. Careful analysis must be made to determine that no unrecorded liabilities are present.

The $80,000 difference in inventories ($122,000 − $42,000) could result from a number of factors, the most likely being that Tractorling Company uses LIFO. Recall that during periods of inflation, LIFO better matches expenses against revenues, but in doing so creates a balance sheet distortion. Ending inventory is comprised of older layers costed at lower valuations.

In many cases, the values of long-term assets such as property, plant, and equipment, and intangibles may have increased substantially over the years. This difference could be due to inaccurate estimates of useful lives, continual expensing of small expenditures (say, less than $300), inaccurate estimates of salvage values and the discovery of some unrecorded assets (as in Tractorling's case where Patents are discovered to have a fair value of $18,000). Or, replacement costs may have substantially increased.

Since the fair market value of net assets is now determined to be $350,000, why did Multi-Diversified pay $400,000? Undoubtedly, the seller pointed to an established reputation, good credit rating, top management team, well-trained employees, and so on, as factors that make the value of the business greater than $350,000. At the same time, Multi-Diversified placed a premium on the future earning power of these attributes as well as the basic asset structure of the enterprise today. At this point in the negotiations, price can be a function of many factors: the most important is probably sheer skill at the bargaining table.

The difference between the purchase price of $400,000 and the fair market value of $350,000 is labeled goodwill. Goodwill is viewed as one or a group of unidentifiable values (intangible assets) the cost of which "is measured by the difference between the cost of the group of assets or enterprise acquired and the sum of the assigned costs of individual tangible and identifiable intangible assets acquired less liabilities assumed."[17] This procedure for valuation is referred to as a **master valuation approach** because goodwill is assumed to cover all the values that cannot be specifically identified with any identifiable tangible or intangible asset; this approach is shown in Illustration 12-4.

[17] *APB Opinion No. 17*, op. cit., par. 26. The proposed SFAS, "Business Combinations and Intangible Assets," adopts this approach. The Board expressed concern about measuring goodwill as a residual but noted that there is no real measurement alternative, since goodwill is not separable from the enterprise as a whole.

ILLUSTRATION 12-4
Determination of Goodwill—Master Valuation Approach

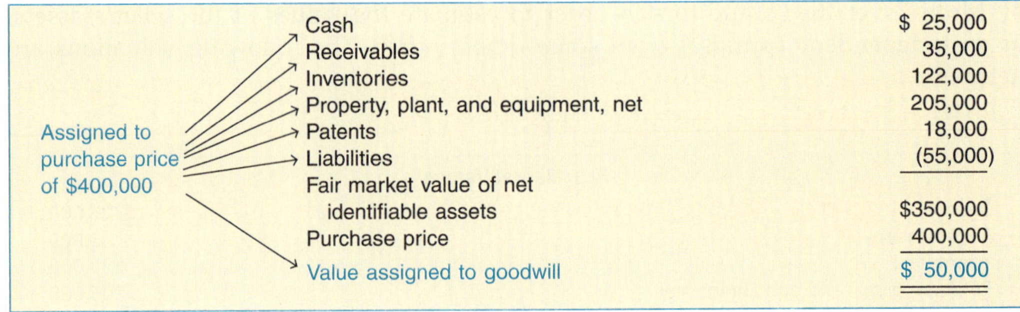

Assigned to purchase price of $400,000	Cash	$ 25,000
	Receivables	35,000
	Inventories	122,000
	Property, plant, and equipment, net	205,000
	Patents	18,000
	Liabilities	(55,000)
	Fair market value of net identifiable assets	$350,000
	Purchase price	400,000
	Value assigned to goodwill	$ 50,000

The entry to record this transaction would be as follows:

Cash	25,000	
Receivables	35,000	
Inventories	122,000	
Property, plant, and equipment	205,000	
Patents	18,000	
Goodwill	50,000	
Liabilities		55,000
Cash		400,000

Goodwill is often identified on the balance sheet as the **excess of cost over the fair value** of the net assets acquired.

Amortization of Goodwill

INTERNATIONAL INSIGHT

Until recently, companies in the United Kingdom were allowed to write off goodwill immediately against equity. In 1998, U.K. companies were required to capitalize and amortize goodwill. This change in goodwill accounting is an example of international accounting harmonization.

Once goodwill has been recognized in the accounts, the next question is how it should be amortized (if at all). Three basic approaches have been suggested.

1. **Charge goodwill off immediately to stockholders' equity.** *Accounting Research Study No. 10,* "Accounting for Goodwill," takes the position that goodwill differs from other types of assets and demands special attention.[18] Unlike other assets, it is not separable and distinct from the business as a whole and therefore is not an asset in the same sense as cash, receivables, or plant assets. In other words, goodwill cannot be sold without selling the business.

   Furthermore, say proponents of this approach, the accounting treatment for purchased goodwill and goodwill internally created should be consistent. Goodwill created internally is immediately expensed and does not appear as an asset: the same treatment should be accorded purchased goodwill. Amortization of purchased goodwill leads to double counting, because net income is reduced by amortization of the purchased goodwill as well as by the internal expenditure made to maintain or enhance the value of assets.

   Perhaps the best rationale for direct write-off is that determining the periods over which the future benefits are to be received is so difficult that immediate charging to stockholders' equity is justified.

2. **Retain goodwill indefinitely unless reduction in value occurs.** Many believe that goodwill can have an indefinite life and should be maintained as an asset until a decline in value occurs. They contend that some form of goodwill should always be an asset inasmuch as internal goodwill is being expensed to maintain or enhance the purchased goodwill. In addition, without sufficient evidence that a decline in value has occurred, a write-off of goodwill is both arbitrary and capricious and will lead to distortions in net income.

3. **Amortize goodwill over useful life.** Still others believe that goodwill's value eventually disappears and it is proper that the asset be charged to expense over the periods affected. This procedure provides a better matching of costs and revenues.

[18]George R. Catlett and Norman O. Olsen, "Accounting for Goodwill," *Accounting Research Study No. 10* (New York: AICPA, 1968), pp. 89–95.

APB Opinion No. 17 takes the position that goodwill should be written off over its useful life, which is dependent on a number of factors such as regulatory restrictions, demand, competition, and obsolescence. **The profession did note that goodwill should never be written off immediately or amortized over more than 40 years.**[19]

Immediate write-off was not considered proper, because it would lead to the untenable conclusion that goodwill has no future service potential. The profession merely prohibits the writing off of goodwill in the period of purchase and over a period exceeding 40 years; no other mention is made regarding another period. Some believe that a 5-year period for amortization would be appropriate unless a shorter period is obviously justified.[20] Such circumstances would include continuous losses or an exodus of managerial talent. A single loss year or a combination of loss years does not automatically necessitate a charge-off of the goodwill.

Goodwill amortization should be computed using the straight-line method unless another method is deemed more appropriate. It should be treated as a regular operating expense. Where the amortization is material, a disclosure of the charge is necessary, as well as the method and period of amortization. Goodwill amortization is now deductible for tax purposes.

The amortization practices associated with goodwill sometimes lead to major disagreements. When Ted Turner of **Turner Broadcasting** attempted to take over **CBS**, he was required to file income statements on what a combined Turner-CBS company would look like in subsequent years. Turner assigned the difference between what he proposed to pay and the book value of CBS entirely to goodwill and amortized this amount over 40 years. CBS disagreed, noting that some of CBS's assets should have been revalued and a smaller amount assigned to goodwill. These revalued assets have a shorter life than goodwill and would lower the net income of the combined Turner-CBS Company. Thus the merger would be supposedly less attractive to stockholders of CBS. Questions of valuation and amortization of goodwill were important considerations in this takeover battle which failed.

Negative Goodwill—Badwill

Negative goodwill, often appropriately dubbed badwill, or bargain purchase, arises when the fair market value of the assets acquired is higher than the purchase price of the assets. This situation is a result of market imperfection because the seller would be better off to sell the assets individually than in total. Situations do occur in which the purchase price is less than the value of the net identifiable assets and therefore a

---

[19]More companies than ever before have learned recently that by classifying some or all of an acquisition's cost as "purchased research and development," they can write off immediately a large chunk of what would otherwise have been capitalized as goodwill. In some cases, they have made the entire purchase price of companies vanish from the books on the day of acquisition. *The Wall Street Journal* (December 2, 1996, p. A2) reported the following acquisition R & D write-offs:

Acquiring Company	Acquired Company	Year	Total (000,000)	R & D Write-off	% of Price
Adobe Systems	Ares Software	1996	$ 15.6	$ 14.7	94%
3 Com	Axon Networks	1996	65.3	52.4	80
H&R Block	Epry	1995	106.4	83.5	78
IBM	Lotus	1995	3,236.0	1,840.0	57
Lotus	Edge Research	1994	5.4	5.4	100
Sphinx Pharm.	Genesis Pharm.	1993	3.8	3.8	100

[20]Recently the SEC has made it more difficult for companies to immediately expense these costs. For example, a recent study by Steven Henning and Wayne Shaw employed an approach based on stock valuation to determine the amount of goodwill that should not be amortized. See *Business Week,* August 30, 1999, p. 188. Also see J. Ron Colley and Ara G. Volkan, "Accounting for Goodwill," *Accounting Horizons,* March 1998, p. 40, where they argue that the current amortization period is too long.

credit develops; this credit is referred to as negative goodwill or **excess of fair value over the cost of assets acquired**. Companies that have negative goodwill are in a very interesting position because the amortization of this negative goodwill to revenue increases earnings.

APB Opinion No. 16 **takes the position that an excess of fair value over purchase price should be allocated to reduce proportionately the values assigned to noncurrent assets** of the acquired company (except long-term investments in marketable securities). If the allocation reduces the noncurrent assets to zero, the remainder of the excess over cost should be classified as a deferred credit and should be amortized systematically to revenue over the period estimated to be benefited but not in excess of 40 years. The method and period of amortization should be disclosed.[21]

IMPAIRMENT OF INTANGIBLE ASSETS

The general rules that apply to **impairments of long-lived assets also apply to intangibles**. As indicated in Chapter 11, long-lived assets to be held and used by a company are to be reviewed for impairment whenever events or changes in circumstances indicate that **the carrying amount of the assets may not be recoverable**. In performing the review for recoverability, the company would estimate the future cash flows expected to result from the use of the asset and its eventual disposition. If the sum of the expected future net cash flows (undiscounted) is less than the carrying amount of the asset, an impairment loss would be measured and recognized. Otherwise, an impairment loss would not be recognized.[22]

The impairment loss is the amount by which the carrying amount of the asset exceeds the fair value of the impaired asset. Illustrations of impairment for specifically identifiable and goodwill type intangibles are shown below.

Specifically Identifiable Intangibles

Assume that Lerch, Inc. has a patent on how to extract oil from shale rock. Unfortunately, reduced oil prices have made the shale oil technology somewhat unprofitable, and the patent has provided little income to date. As a result, a recoverability test is performed, and it is found that the expected net future cash flows from this patent are $35 million. Lerch's patent has a carrying amount of $60 million. Because the expected future net cash flows of $35 million are less than the carrying amount of $60 million, an impairment loss must be measured. Discounting the expected net future cash flows at its market rate of interest, Lerch determines the fair value of its patent to be $20 million. The impairment loss computation is shown in Illustration 12-5:

ILLUSTRATION 12-5
Computation of Loss on Impairment of Patent

Carrying amount of patent	$ 60,000,000
Fair value (based on present value computation)	20,000,000
Loss on impairment	$ 40,000,000

The journal entry to record this loss is:

Loss on Impairment	40,000,000	
Patents		40,000,000

[21]"Business Combinations," *Opinions of the Accounting Principles Board No. 16* (New York: AICPA, 1970), par. 91. Under the proposed SFAS, negative goodwill would be allocated pro rata first to intangible assets with no observable market value, and second to depreciable nonfinancial assets and any other acquired intangible assets. If the allocation results in these assets being written down to zero, the excess is recognized as an extraordinary gain.

[22]"Accounting for the Impairment of Long-Lived Assets," *Statement of Financial Accounting Standards No. 121* (Norwalk, Conn.: FASB, 1994).

After the impairment is recognized, the reduced carrying amount of the patents is its new cost basis. The patent's new cost should be amortized over its useful life or legal life, whichever is shorter. Even if oil prices increase in subsequent periods, and the value of the patent increases, **restoration of the previously recognized impairment loss is not permitted.**

Goodwill-Type Intangibles

Goodwill is a "going concern" valuation and cannot be separated from the other assets and liabilities which give it value. As a result, goodwill impairments involve a grouping of net assets.

To illustrate an impairment loss when goodwill is involved, assume that Kohlberg Corporation has three divisions in its company. One division, Pritt Products, was purchased four years ago for $2 million. Unfortunately, it has experienced operating losses over the last three quarters and management is reviewing the division for purposes of recognizing an impairment. The Pritt Division's net assets including the associated goodwill of $1,200,000 are listed in Illustration 12-6.

Cash	$ 200,000
Receivables	300,000
Inventory	400,000
Property, plant, and equipment (net)	800,000
Goodwill	1,200,000
Less: Accounts and notes payable	(500,000)
Net assets	$2,400,000

ILLUSTRATION 12-6
Pritt Division Net Assets

A recoverability test is performed and it is found that the expected net future cash flows from Pritt Division are $2,000,000. The fair value of the division is estimated to be $1,300,000, the present value of the expected future net cash flows. The impairment loss is computed as follows:

Carrying amount of Pritt Division	$2,400,000
Fair value	1,300,000
Loss on impairment	$1,100,000

ILLUSTRATION 12-7
Computation of Impairment Loss on Pritt Division

How should the impairment loss be allocated to the net assets of the Pritt Division? Various allocation approaches might be used. The FASB requires that where goodwill is associated with assets that are subject to the impairment loss, the carrying amount of the associated goodwill should be eliminated *before* the carrying amounts of impaired long-lived assets and identifiable intangibles are reduced to their fair values.

For Pritt Division, therefore, the total loss on impairment reduces only goodwill. The entry to record the impairment is:

Loss on Impairment	1,100,000	
Goodwill		1,100,000

If the impairment loss were greater than the carrying amount of goodwill, the additional loss would be used to reduce the remaining long-lived assets to fair value.[23]

[23]Once the goodwill is completely eliminated, the remaining loss would probably be allocated pro-rata, based on relative fair values, to those long-lived assets and identifiable intangible assets that had fair values less than their carrying amounts.

RESEARCH AND DEVELOPMENT COSTS

OBJECTIVE 6
Identify the conceptual issues related to research and development costs.

Research and development (R & D) costs are not in themselves intangible assets. The accounting for R & D costs is presented here, however, because research and development activities frequently result in the development of something that is patented or copyrighted (such as a new product, process, idea, formula, composition, or literary work).

Many businesses spend considerable sums of money on research and development to create new products or processes, to improve present products, and to discover new knowledge that may be valuable at some future date. The following schedule shows the outlays for R & D made by selected U.S. companies:

ILLUSTRATION 12-8
R & D Outlays, as Percentage of Sales and Profits

Company	R & D Dollars	% of Sales	% of Profits
Deere & Co.	$ 444,400,000	3.73%	43.51%
Dell	272,000,000	1.49%	18.63%
General Mills	70,000,000	1.12%	13.10%
Johnson & Johnson	2,269,000,000	9.59%	74.17%
Kellogg	121,900,000	1.80%	24.25%
Merck	1,821,100,000	6.77%	34.70%

INTERNATIONAL INSIGHT
Contrary to U.S. practice, in most other nations (the Netherlands, Canada, and Japan, for example) the capitalization of research and development costs is allowed under specified circumstances.

The difficulties in accounting for these research and development (R & D) expenditures are (1) identifying the costs associated with particular activities, projects, or achievements and (2) determining the magnitude of the future benefits and length of time over which such benefits may be realized. Because of these latter uncertainties, the accounting practice in this area has been simplified by requiring that **all research and development costs be charged to expense when incurred.**[24]

Identifying R & D Activities

To differentiate research and development costs from similar costs, the following definitions are used for **research activities** and **development activities.**[25]

ILLUSTRATION 12-9
R & D Activities

Research Activities	Development Activities
Planned search or critical investigation aimed at discovery of new knowledge.	Translation of research findings or other knowledge into a plan or design for a new product or process or for a significant improvement to an existing product or process whether intended for sale or use.
Examples Laboratory research aimed at discovery of new knowledge; searching for applications of new research findings.	**Examples** Conceptual formulation and design of possible product or process alternatives; construction of prototypes and operation of pilot plants.

[24]"Accounting for Research and Development Costs," *Statement of Financial Accounting Standards No. 2* (Stamford, Conn.: FASB, 1974), par. 12.

[25]Ibid., par. 8.

It should be emphasized that R & D activities do not include routine or periodic alternatives to existing products, production lines, manufacturing processes, and other ongoing operations even though these alterations may represent improvements. For example, routine ongoing efforts to refine, enrich, or improve the qualities of an existing product are not considered R & D activities.

Accounting for R & D Activities

The costs associated with R & D activities and the accounting treatment accorded them are as follows:

OBJECTIVE 7
Describe the accounting procedures for research and development costs and for other similar costs.

1. *Materials, Equipment, and Facilities.* Expense the entire costs, **unless the items have alternative future uses** (in other R & D projects or otherwise), then carry as inventory and allocate as consumed, or capitalize and depreciate as used.
2. *Personnel.* Salaries, wages, and other related costs of personnel engaged in R & D should be expensed as incurred.
3. *Purchased Intangibles.* Expense the entire cost, **unless the items have alternative future uses** (in other R & D projects or otherwise), then capitalize and amortize.
4. *Contract Services.* The costs of services performed by others in connection with the reporting company's R & D should be expensed as incurred.
5. *Indirect Costs.* A reasonable allocation of indirect costs shall be included in R & D costs, except for general and administrative cost, which must be clearly related in order to be included and expensed.[26]

International accounting standards require the capitalization of appropriate development expenditures. This conflicts with U.S. GAAP.

Consistent with item 1 above, if an enterprise owns a research facility consisting of buildings, laboratories, and equipment that conducts R & D activities and that has alternative future uses (in other R & D projects or otherwise), the facility should be accounted for as a capitalized operational asset. The depreciation and other costs related to such research facilities are accounted for as R & D expenses.[27]

To illustrate the identification of R & D activities and the accounting treatment of related costs, assume that Next Century Incorporated develops, produces, and markets laser machines for medical, industrial, and defense uses.[28] The types of expenditures related to its laser machine activities, along with the recommended accounting treatment, are listed in Illustration 12-10.

---

[26]Ibid., par. 11.

[27]Costs of research, exploration, and development activities that are unique to companies in the **extractive industries** (e.g., prospecting, acquisition of mineral rights, exploration, drilling, mining, and related mineral development) and those costs discussed which are similar to but not classified as R & D costs may be:

1. expensed as incurred,
2. capitalized and either depreciated or amortized over an appropriate period of time, or
3. accumulated as part of inventoriable costs.

Choice of the appropriate accounting treatment for such costs should be guided by the degree of certainty of future benefits and the principle of matching revenues and expenses.

[28]Sometimes enterprises conduct R & D activities for other entities under a **contractual arrangement**. In this case, the contract usually specifies that all direct costs, certain specific indirect costs, plus a profit element, should be reimbursed to the enterprise performing the R & D work. Because reimbursement is expected, such R & D costs should be recorded as a receivable. It is the company for whom the work has been performed that reports these costs as R & D and expenses them as incurred.

For a more complete discussion of how an enterprise should account for its obligation under an arrangement for the funding of its research and development by others, see "Research and Development Arrangements," *Statement of Financial Accounting Standards No. 68* (Stamford, Conn.: FASB, 1982).

ILLUSTRATION 12-10
Sample R & D Expenditures and Their Accounting Treatment

Next Century Incorporated

Type of Expenditure	Accounting Treatment
1. Construction of long-range research facility for use in current and future projects (three-story, 400,000-square-foot building).	Capitalize and depreciate as R & D expense.
2. Acquisition of R & D equipment for use on current project only.	Expense immediately as R & D.
3. Acquisition of machinery to be used on current and future R & D projects.	Capitalize and depreciate as R & D expense.
4. Purchase of materials to be used on current and future R & D projects.	Inventory and allocate to R & D projects; expense as consumed.
5. Salaries of research staff designing new laser bone scanner.	Expense immediately as R & D.
6. Research costs incurred under contract with New Horizon, Inc., and billable monthly.	Record as a receivable (reimbursable expenses).
7. Material, labor, and overhead costs of prototype laser scanner.	Expense immediately as R & D.
8. Costs of testing prototype and design modifications.	Expense immediately as R & D.
9. Legal fees to obtain patent on new laser scanner.	Capitalize as patent and amortize to overhead as part of cost of goods manufactured.
10. Executive salaries.	Expense as operating expense (general and administrative).
11. Cost of marketing research to promote new laser scanner.	Expense as operating expense (selling).
12. Engineering costs incurred to advance the laser scanner to full production stage.	Expense immediately as R & D.
13. Costs of successfully defending patent on laser scanner.	Capitalize as patent and amortize to overhead as part of cost of goods manufactured.
14. Commissions to sales staff marketing new laser scanner.	Expense as operating expense (selling).

Other Costs Similar to R & D Costs

Many costs have characteristics similar to research and development costs. Examples are:

1. Start-up costs for a new operation.
2. Initial operating losses.
3. Advertising costs.
4. Computer software costs.

For the most part, these costs are expensed as incurred, similar to the accounting for R & D costs. A brief explanation of these costs is provided below.

Start-up Costs

Start-up costs are costs incurred for one-time activities to start a new operation. Examples include opening a new plant, introducing a new product or service, or conducting business in a new territory or with a new class of customers. Start-up costs include organizational costs; these are costs incurred in the organizing of a new entity, such as legal and state fees of various types. The accounting for start-up costs is straightforward: **expense start-up costs as incurred**. The profession recognizes that these costs are incurred with the expectation that future revenues will occur or increased efficiencies will result. However, to determine the amount and timing of future benefits is so difficult that a conservative approach—expensing these costs as incurred—is required.[29]

[29]"Reporting on the Costs of Start-Up Activities," *Statement of Position 98-5* (New York: AICPA, 1998).

To illustrate the type of costs that should be expensed as start-up costs, assume that U.S.-based Hilo Beverage Company decides to construct a new plant in Brazil. This represents Hilo's first entry into the Brazilian market. As part of its overall strategy, Hilo plans to introduce the company's major U.S. brands into Brazil, on a locally produced basis. Following are some of the costs that might be involved with these start-up activities.

1. Travel-related costs, costs related to employee salaries, and costs related to feasibility studies, accounting, tax, and government affairs.
2. Training of local employees related to product, maintenance, computer systems, finance, and operations.
3. Recruiting, organizing, and training related to establishing a distribution network.

All of these costs are start-up costs and should be expensed as incurred.

It is not uncommon for start-up activities to occur at the same time as other activities, such as the acquisition or development of assets. For example, property, plant, and equipment or inventory used in Hilo's new plant should not be immediately expensed. These assets should be reported on the balance sheet and charged to operations using appropriate GAAP reporting guidelines.

Initial Operating Losses

Some contend that initial operating losses incurred in the start-up of a business should be capitalized, since they are unavoidable and are a cost of starting a business. For example, assume that Hilo lost money in its first year of operations and wished to capitalize this loss arguing that as the company becomes profitable, it will offset these losses in future periods. What do you think? We believe that this approach is unsound, since losses have no future service potential and therefore cannot be considered an asset.

Our position that operating losses should not be capitalized during the early years is supported by *Statement of Financial Accounting Standards No. 7,* which clarifies the accounting and reporting practices for **development stage enterprises**. **The FASB concludes that the accounting practices and reporting standards should be no different for an enterprise trying to establish a new business than they are for other enterprises.** The same "generally accepted accounting principles that apply to established operating enterprises shall govern the recognition of revenue by a development stage enterprise and shall determine whether a cost incurred by a development stage enterprise is to be charged to expense when incurred or is to be capitalized or deferred."[30]

Advertising Costs

Recently, **PepsiCo** hired supermodel Cindy Crawford to advertise its products. How should these advertising costs related to Cindy Crawford be reported? These costs could be expensed in a variety of ways:

1. When she has completed her acting assignment.
2. The first time the advertising takes place.
3. Over the estimated useful life of the advertising.

[30] "Accounting and Reporting by Development Stage Enterprises," *Statement of Financial Accounting Standards No. 7* (Stamford, Conn.: FASB, 1975), par. 10. A company is considered to be in the developing stages when its efforts are directed toward establishing a new business and either the principal operations have not started or no significant revenue has been earned. To evaluate the economic impact of applying the same accounting principles to development stage enterprises that apply to established operating enterprises, the FASB interviewed officers of fifteen venture capital companies. The consensus was that whether a development stage enterprise defers or expenses preoperating costs has little effect on the amount of, or the terms under which venture capital is provided. According to these officers, venture capital investors instead rely on an evaluation of potential cash flows resulting from an investigation of the technological, marketing, management, and financial aspects of the enterprise.

4. In an appropriate fashion to each of the three periods identified above.
5. Over the period revenues are expected to result.

After much discussion, the profession has concluded that future benefits from advertising generally are not sufficiently defined or measurable with a degree of reliability that is required to recognize these costs as an asset. **As a result, for the most part advertising costs must be expensed as incurred or the first time the advertising takes place.** These two alternatives are permitted because whichever approach is followed, the results are essentially the same. Tangible assets used in advertising, such as billboards or blimps, are recorded as assets because they do have alternative future use. Again the profession has taken a conservative approach to recording advertising costs because defining and measuring the future benefits are so difficult.[31]

Computer Software Costs

A special problem arises in distinguishing R & D costs from selling and administrative activities. The FASB's intent was that the acquisition, development, or improvement of a product or process by an enterprise **for use in its selling or administrative activities** be excluded from the definition of research and development activities. For example, the costs of software incurred by an airline in acquiring, developing, or improving its computerized reservation system, or the costs incurred during the development of a general management information system are not research and development costs. Accounting for computer software costs is a specialized and complicated accounting topic that is discussed and illustrated in an appendix to this chapter (Appendix 12A).

UNDERLYING CONCEPTS

The requirement that all R & D costs be expensed as incurred is an example of the conflict between relevance and reliability, with this requirement leaning strongly in support of reliability, as well as conservatism, consistency, and comparability. No attempt is made to match costs and revenues.

Conceptual Questions

The requirement that all R & D costs (and other costs mentioned in the previous section) incurred internally be expensed immediately is a conservative, practical solution that ensures consistency in practice and uniformity among companies. But the practice of immediately writing off expenditures made in the expectation of benefiting future periods cannot be justified on the grounds that it is good accounting theory.

Defendants of immediate expensing contend that from an income statement standpoint, long-run application of this standard frequently makes little difference. They contend that the amount of R & D cost charged to expense each accounting period would be about the same whether there is immediate expensing or capitalization and subsequent amortization because of the ongoing nature of most companies' R & D activities. Critics of this practice argue that the balance sheet should report an intangible asset related to expenditures that have future benefit. To preclude capitalization of all R & D expenditures removes from the balance sheet what may be a company's most valuable asset. This standard represents one of the many trade-offs made among relevance, reliability, and cost-benefit considerations.[32]

The International Accounting Standards Committee issued a standard that is in disagreement with the FASB's standard on accounting for R & D costs. The International Committee identified certain circumstances that justify the capitalization and deferral of development costs.

---

[31] "Reporting on Advertising Costs," *Statement of Position 93-7* (New York: AICPA, 1993). Note that there are some exceptions for immediate expensing of advertising costs when they relate to direct-response advertising, but this subject is beyond the scope of this book.

[32] Recent research suggests that capitalizing research and development costs may be helpful to investors. For example, one study showed that a significant relationship exists between R & D outlays and subsequent benefits in the form of increased productivity, earnings, and shareholder value for R & D–intensive companies. Baruch Lev and Theodore Sougiannis, "The Capitalization, Amortization, and Value-Relevance of R & D," *Journal of Accounting and Economics*, February 1996. In another study, it was found that there was a significant decline in earnings usefulness for companies that were forced to switch from capitalizing to expensing R & D costs and that the decline appears to persist over time. Martha L. Loudder and Bruce K. Behn, "Alternative Income Determination Rules and Earnings Usefulness: The Case of R & D Costs," *Contemporary Accounting Research*, Fall 1995.

PRESENTATION OF INTANGIBLES AND RELATED ITEMS

Intangibles

The reporting of intangibles differs from the reporting of property, plant, and equipment in that contra accounts are not normally shown. The amortization of intangibles is frequently credited directly to the intangible asset.[33]

The financial statements should disclose the method and period of amortization. Intangible assets shown net of amortization and related note information are shown for **PepsiCo** as follows:

OBJECTIVE 8
Indicate the presentation of intangibles and related items.

ILLUSTRATION 12-11
Balance Sheet Presentation and Related Note on Intangible Assets

PEPSICO, INC.
(in millions)

	1998	1997
Intangible assets, net (Note 8)	$8,996	$5,855

Note 8—Intangible Assets, net

	1998	1997
Goodwill	$5,131	$2,298
Reacquired franchise rights	3,118	2,860
Trademarks and other identifiable intangibles	747	697
	$8,996	$5,855

Identifiable intangible assets possess economic value but lack physical substance. These assets primarily arise from the allocation of purchase prices of businesses acquired. Amounts assigned to such identifiable intangibles are based on independent appraisals or internal estimates. Goodwill represents the residual purchase price after allocation to all identifiable net assets (see Note 2).

The above amounts are presented net of accumulated amortization of $1.9 billion at year-end 1998 and $1.7 billion at year-end 1997.

It should be noted that PepsiCo reports in a separate note that its intangible assets are amortized on a straight-line basis over appropriate periods, generally ranging from 20 to 40 years.[34]

Research and Development Costs

Acceptable accounting practice requires that disclosure be made in the financial statements (generally in the notes) of the total R & D costs charged to expense each period for which an income statement is presented. **Merck & Co., Inc.**, a global research pharmaceutical company, reported both internal and acquired research and development in its recent income statement.

[33]*Accounting Trends and Techniques—1999* reports that the most common type of intangible is goodwill followed by patents; trademarks, brand names, and copyrights; and then noncompete covenants, licenses, franchises, memberships, technology, and customer lists.

[34]The proposed SFAS on intangibles requires in most cases a maximum 20-year useful life. Under certain conditions, the proposal would permit the amortization period (other than for goodwill) to exceed 20 years. And in limited situations, an intangible asset may not need to be amortized.

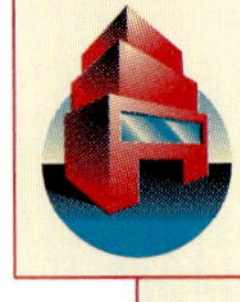

ILLUSTRATION 12-12
Income Statement Disclosure of R & D Costs

Go to the Digital Tool for additional disclosures of intangibles and R & D costs.

MERCK & CO., INC.

(in millions)

	Years Ended December 31		
	1998	1997	1996
Sales	$26,898.2	$23,636.9	$19,828.7
Costs, expenses, and other			
Materials and production	13,925.4	11,790.3	9,319.2
Marketing and administrative	4,511.4	4,299.2	3,841.3
Research and development	1,821.1	1,683.7	1,487.3
Acquired research	1,039.5	—	—
Equity income from affiliates	(884.3)	(727.9)	(600.7)
Gains on sales of businesses	(2,147.7)	(213.4)	—
Other (income) expense, net	499.7	342.7	240.8
	$18,765.1	$17,174.6	$14,287.9

In addition, Merck provides the following discussion in its annual report.

ILLUSTRATION 12-13
Merck's R & D Disclosure

MERCK & CO., INC.

Research and development in the pharmaceutical industry is inherently a long-term process. The following data show an unbroken trend of year-to-year increases in research and development spending. For the period 1989 to 1998, the compounded annual growth rate in research and development was 11%. Research and development expenses for 1999 are estimated to approximate $2.1 billion.

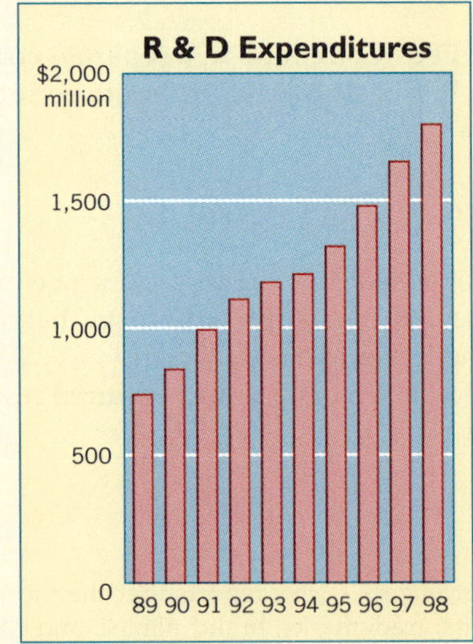

In 1998, in connection with the restructuring of AMI, the Company recorded a $1.04 billion charge for acquired research associated with 10 product candidates in Phase II or later stages of development and U.S. rights to future Astra products which have not yet entered Phase II, for which, at the acquisition date, commercial viability had not been established.

Other Assets

Other assets (sometimes referred to as **deferred charges**) is a classification often used to describe a number of different items that have debit balances, among them certain types of intangibles. How do these items happen to be classified in this section and not in a separate intangible section? In truth, the other asset section serves as a dumping ground for a number of small items. Some of these items are: property held for sale, prepaid pension costs, segregated cash or securities, cash surrender value of life insurance, and deferred income taxes. In many cases, deferred income taxes are separately identified.

SUMMARY OF LEARNING OBJECTIVES

1 Describe the characteristics of intangible assets. Intangible assets have three main characteristics: (1) They lack physical existence; (2) they are not financial instruments; and (3) they are long-term in nature and subject to amortization. Intangibles may be subdivided on the basis of the following characteristics: (1) *Identifiability:* separately identifiable or lacking specific identification. (2) *Manner of acquisition:* acquired singly, in groups, or in business combinations, or developed internally. (3) *Expected period of benefit:* limited by law or contract, related to human or economic factors, or indefinite or indeterminate duration. (4) *Separability from the enterprise:* rights transferable without title, salable, or inseparable from the enterprise or a substantial part of it.

2 Explain the procedure for valuing and amortizing intangible assets. Intangibles are recorded at cost. Cost includes all costs of acquisition and expenditures necessary to make the intangible asset ready for its intended use. If intangibles are acquired for stock or in exchange for other assets, the cost of the intangible is the fair market value of the consideration given or the fair market value of the intangible received, whichever is more clearly evident. When several intangibles, or a combination of intangibles and tangibles, are bought in a "basket purchase," the cost should be allocated on the basis of fair market values or on the basis of relative sales values. Intangible assets should be amortized by systematic charges to expense over their useful lives. Intangible assets must be amortized over a period not exceeding 40 years.

3 Identify the types of specifically identifiable intangible assets. The major identifiable assets are: (1) *Patents:* give the holder exclusive right to use, manufacture, and sell a product or process for a period of 20 years without interference or infringement by others. (2) *Copyrights:* a federally granted right that all authors, painters, musicians, sculptors, and other artists have in their creations and expressions. (3) *Trademarks and trade names:* a word, phrase, or symbol that distinguishes or identifies a particular enterprise or product. (4) *Leaseholds:* a contractual understanding between a lessor (owner of property) and a lessee (renter of property) that grants the lessee the right to use specific property, owned by the lessor, for a specific period of time in return for stipulated, and generally periodic, cash payments. (5) *Franchises and licenses:* a contractual arrangement under which the franchisor grants the franchisee the right to sell certain products or services, to use certain trademarks or trade names, or to perform certain functions, usually within a designated geographical area.

4 Explain the conceptual issues related to goodwill. Goodwill is unique because unlike receivables, inventories, and patents that can be sold or exchanged individually in the marketplace, goodwill can be identified only with the business as a whole. Goodwill is a "going concern" valuation and is recorded only when an entire business is purchased. Goodwill generated internally should not be capitalized in the accounts, because measuring the components of goodwill is simply too complex and associating any costs with future benefits too difficult. The future benefits of goodwill

KEY TERMS

amortization, *602*
capital lease, *606*
copyright, *604*
deferred charges, *621*
development activities, *614*
franchise, *606*
goodwill, *607*
intangible assets, *600*
leasehold, *605*
leasehold improvements, *605*
license, *606*
master valuation approach, *609*
negative goodwill (badwill), *611*
organizational costs, *616*
patent, *603*
research activities, *614*
research and development (R & D) costs, *614*
specifically identifiable intangible asset, *602*
start-up costs, *616*
trademark, trade name, *604*

may have no relationship to the costs incurred in the development of that goodwill. Goodwill may exist even in the absence of specific costs to develop it.

5 Describe the accounting procedures for recording goodwill. To record goodwill, the fair market value of the net tangible and identifiable intangible assets are compared with the purchase price of the acquired business. The difference is considered goodwill. Goodwill is the residual—the excess of cost over fair value of the identifiable net assets acquired. Goodwill is often identified on the balance sheet as the excess of cost over the fair value of the net assets acquired.

6 Identify the conceptual issues related to research and development costs. R & D costs are not in themselves intangible assets, but research and development activities frequently result in the development of something that is patented or copyrighted. The difficulties in accounting for R & D expenditures are (1) identifying the costs associated with particular activities, projects, or achievements and (2) determining the magnitude of the future benefits and length of time over which such benefits may be realized. Because of these latter uncertainties, the FASB has standardized and simplified accounting practice by requiring that all research and development costs be charged to expense when incurred.

7 Describe the accounting procedures for research and development costs and for other similar costs. The costs associated with R & D activities and the accounting treatment accorded them are as follows: (1) *Materials, equipment, and facilities:* Expense the entire costs, unless the items have alternative future uses, then carry as inventory and allocate as consumed, or capitalize and depreciate as used. (2) *Personnel:* Salaries, wages, and other related costs of personnel engaged in R & D should be expensed as incurred. (3) *Purchased intangibles:* Expense the entire cost, unless the items have alternative future uses, then capitalize and amortize. (4) *Contract services:* The costs of services performed by others in connection with the reporting company's R & D should be expensed as incurred. (5) *Indirect costs:* A reasonable allocation of indirect costs shall be included in R & D costs, except for general and administrative costs, which must be related to be included and expensed. Many costs have characteristics similar to R & D costs. Examples are start-up costs, initial operating losses, advertising costs, and computer software costs. For the most part, these costs are expensed as incurred, similar to the accounting for R & D costs.

8 Indicate the presentation of intangible and related items. The reporting of intangibles differs from the reporting of property, plant and equipment in that contra accounts are not normally shown. Disclosure must be made in the financial statements for the total R & D costs charged to expense each period for which an income statement is presented.

APPENDIX 12A

Accounting for Computer Software Costs

The development of computer software products takes on increasing importance as our economy continues to change from a manufacturing process orientation (tangible outputs) to an information flow society (intangible outputs).[1] This appendix discusses the basic issues involved in accounting for computer software.

OBJECTIVE 9
After studying Appendix 12A, you should be able to: Identify the accounting treatment for computer software costs.

DIVERSITY IN PRACTICE

Computer software may be either **purchased** or **created** by a company. It may be purchased or created for **external use** (such as spreadsheet applications like Excel or Lotus 1-2-3) or for **internal use** (e.g., to establish a better internal accounting system). Should costs incurred in developing the software be expensed immediately or capitalized and amortized in the future? Prior to 1985, some companies expensed all software costs, and others capitalized such costs. Still others differentiated such costs on the basis of whether the software was purchased or created, or whether it was used for external or internal purposes.

THE PROFESSION'S POSITION

A major question is whether the costs involved in developing software are research and development costs. If they are actually R & D, then the profession requires that they be expensed as incurred. If they are not research and development costs, then a strong case can be made for capitalization. As one financial executive of a software company who argues for capitalization noted: "The key distinction between our spending and R & D is recoverability. We know we are developing something we can sell."

In an attempt to resolve this issue (at least for companies that sell computer software), the FASB issued *Statement of Financial Accounting Standards No. 86,* "Accounting for the Costs of Computer Software to Be Sold, Leased, or Otherwise Marketed."[2] The major recommendations of this pronouncement are:

1. Costs incurred in creating a computer software product should be charged to research and development expense when incurred until **technological feasibility** has been established for the product.

[1]A major contributing factor was IBM's decision in 1969 to "unbundle" its hardware and software, that is, to state the cost of the hardware and software separately. Prior to the unbundling, most applications software was provided free with the hardware. This unbundling led to the creation of a whole new industry, the software industry, whose members began selling software to hardware users.

[2]"Accounting for the Cost of Computer Software to Be Sold, Leased, or Otherwise Marketed," *Statement of Financial Accounting Standards No. 86* (Stamford, Conn.: FASB, 1985). Also see, Robert W. McGee, *Accounting for Software* (Homewood, Ill.: Dow Jones–Irwin, 1985).

2. Technological feasibility is established upon completion of a detailed program design or working model.

In short, the FASB has taken a conservative position in regard to computer software costs. All costs must be expensed until the company has completed planning, designing, coding, and testing activities necessary to establish that the product can be produced to meet its design specifications. Subsequent costs incurred should be capitalized and amortized to current and future periods.

Two additional points should be emphasized. First, **if the software is purchased and it has alternative future uses, then it may be capitalized**. Second, **this standard applies only to the development of software that is to be sold, leased, or otherwise marketed to third parties** (i.e., for external use).

Recently the profession also indicated how to account for computer software to be used internally. It noted that activities performed during the preliminary project stage of development (conceptual formulation and evaluation of alternatives, for example) are similar to R & D costs and should be expensed immediately. However, once the software is at the application development stage (at the coding or installation into hardware stages, for example), its future economic benefits become probable and capitalization of costs is required. Costs subsequent to the application development stage related to training and application maintenance should be expensed as incurred.[3]

ACCOUNTING FOR CAPITALIZED SOFTWARE COSTS

If software costs are capitalized, then a proper amortization pattern for these costs must be established. **Companies are required to use the greater of (1) the ratio of current revenues to current and anticipated revenues (percent of revenue approach) or (2) the straight-line method over the remaining useful life of the asset (straight-line approach) as a basis for amortization.** These rules can result in the use of the ratio method one year and the straight-line method in another.

To illustrate, assume that AT&T has capitalized software costs of $10 million and its current (first-year) revenues from sales of this product are $4 million. AT&T anticipates earning $16 million in additional future revenues from this product, which is estimated to have an economic life of 4 years. Using the percent of revenue approach, the current (first) year's amortization would be $2 million ($10,000,000 × $4,000,000/$20,000,000). Using the straight-line approach, the amortization would be $2.5 million ($10,000,000/4 years). Thus the straight-line approach would be employed because it results in the greater amortization charge.

REPORTING SOFTWARE COSTS

Because much concern exists about the reliability of an asset such as software, the Board indicated that capitalized software costs should be valued at the **lower of unamortized cost or net realizable value**. If net realizable value is lower, then the capitalized software costs should be written down to this value. Once written down, it **may not be written back up**. In addition to the regular disclosures for R & D costs, the following should be reported in the financial statements:

1. Unamortized software costs.
2. The total amount charged to expense and amounts, if any, written down to net realizable value.

Once again these accounting and reporting requirements apply only to software **developed for external purposes**.

[3]"Accounting for the Costs of Computer Software Developed or Obtained for Internal Use," *Statement of Position 98-1* (New York: AICPA, 1998).

An example of software development cost disclosure, taken from the annual report of **Micrografx Inc.**, is shown below.

MICROGRAFX INC.

Capitalized software development costs and acquired product rights consist of the following (in thousands):

	June 30,	
	1998	1997
Capitalized software development costs	$9,077	$5,270
Less: Accumulated amortization	(5,886)	(1,986)
Capitalized software development costs, net	$3,191	$3,284
Acquired product rights	$6,477	$5,940
Less: Accumulated amortization	(3,784)	(2,359)
Acquired product rights, net	$2,693	$3,581

Significant Accounting Policies:

In accordance with Statement of Financial Accounting Standards ("SFAS") No. 86, "Accounting for the Costs of Computer Software to be Sold, Leased, or Otherwise Marketed," the Company capitalizes certain software development costs incurred after technological feasibility is achieved and also capitalizes costs of acquiring certain product rights in connection with the development of its computer software products. Capitalized costs are reported at the lower of unamortized cost or net realizable value. Capitalized software development costs and acquired product rights are amortized straight-line over the estimated economic life of the products, generally 12 to 18 months, which approximates amortization based on the ratio of current net sales over future estimated net sales. The Company begins amortization when the products are available for general release to customers. All other research and development expenditures are charged to research and development expense in the period incurred.

ILLUSTRATION 12A-1
Disclosure of Software Development Costs

SETTING STANDARDS FOR SOFTWARE ACCOUNTING

"It's unreasonable to expense all software costs, and it's unreasonable to capitalize all software costs," said **IBM**'s director of financial reporting. "If you subscribe to those two statements, then it follows that there is somewhere in between where development ends and capitalization begins. Now you have to define that point."[4] The FASB defined that point as "technological feasibility," which is established upon completion of a detailed program design or working model. The difficulty of applying this criterion to software is that, "there is no such thing as a real, specific, baseline design. But you could make it look like you have one as early or as late as you like," says Osman Erlop of **Hambrecht & Quist**.[5] That is, if you wish to capitalize, draw up a detailed program design quickly. If you want to expense lots of development costs, simply hold off writing a detailed program design. And, once capitalized, the costs are amortized over the useful life specified by the developer, which because of either constant redesign or supersession is generally quite short (2 to 4 years).

As another example, some companies "manage by the numbers"; that is, they are very careful to identify projects that are worthwhile and capitalize the computer software costs associated with them. They believe that good projects must be capitalized and amortized in the future; otherwise, the concept of properly matching expense and revenues is abused.

Other companies choose not to manage by the numbers and simply expense all these costs. Companies that expense all these costs have no use for a standard that

[4]"When Does Life Begin?" *Forbes,* June 16, 1986, pp. 72–74.

[5]Ibid.

requires capitalization. In their view, it would mean only that a more complex, more expensive cost accounting system would be required, one that would provide little if any benefit.

Financial analysts have reacted almost uniformly against any capitalization. They believe software costs should be expensed because of the rapid obsolescence of software and the potential for abuse that may result from capitalizing costs inappropriately. As Donald Kirk, a former chairman of the FASB, stated: "The Board is now faced with the problem of balancing what it thought was good theory with the costs for some companies of implementing a new accounting system with the concerns of users about the potential for abuse of the standard."[6]

Resolving the software accounting problem again demonstrates the difficulty of establishing reporting standards.

SUMMARY OF LEARNING OBJECTIVE FOR APPENDIX 12A

9 **Identify the accounting treatment for computer software costs.** Costs incurred in creating a software product should be charged to R & D expense when incurred until technological feasibility has been established for the product. Subsequent costs should be capitalized and amortized to current and future periods. Software that is purchased for sale or lease to third parties and has alternative future uses may be capitalized and amortized using the greater of the percent of revenue approach or the straight-line approach.

APPENDIX 12B

Valuing Goodwill

OBJECTIVE 10
After studying Appendix 12B, you should be able to: Explain various approaches to valuing goodwill.

In this chapter we discussed the generally accepted method of measuring and recording goodwill as the excess of cost over fair value of the identifiable net assets acquired in a business acquisition. Accountants are frequently asked to participate in the valuation of businesses as part of a planned business acquisition.

To determine the purchase price for a business and the resulting goodwill is a difficult and inexact process. As indicated, it is often possible to determine the fair value of identifiable assets. But how does a buyer value intangible factors like good management, good credit rating, and so on?

EXCESS EARNINGS APPROACH

One method is called the **excess earnings approach**. Using this approach, the total earning power that the company commands is computed. The next step is to calculate "normal earnings" by determining the normal rate of return on assets in that industry. **The**

[6]Donald J. Kirk, "Growing Temptation & Rising Expectation = Accelerating Regulation," *FASB Viewpoints*, June 12, 1985, p. 7.

difference between what the firm earns and what is normal in the industry is referred to as the excess earning power. This extra earning power indicates that there are unidentifiable values (intangible assets) that provide this increased earning power. Finding the value of goodwill then is a matter of discounting these excess future earnings to the present.

This approach appears to be a systematic and logical way of determining goodwill. However, each factor necessary to compute a value under this approach is subject to question. Generally, the problems relate to getting answers to the following questions:

1. What is a normal rate of return?
2. How does one determine the future earnings?
3. What discount rate should be applied to the excess earnings?
4. Over what period should the excess earnings be discounted?

Finding a Normal Rate of Return

Determining the normal rate of return for tangible and identifiable intangible assets requires analysis of companies similar to the enterprise in question. An industry average may be determined by examining annual reports or data from statistical services. Suppose that a rate of 15% is decided as normal for a concern such as Tractorling (see pages 608–610). In this case, the normal earnings are calculated in the following manner.[1]

ILLUSTRATION 12B-1
Calculation of Normal Earnings

Fair market value of Tractorling's net identifiable assets	$350,000
Normal rate of return	15%
Normal earnings	$ 52,500

Determining Future Earnings

The starting point for determining future earnings is normally the past earnings of the enterprise. Although estimates of future earnings are needed, the past often provides useful information concerning the enterprise's future earnings potential. Past earnings—generally 3 to 6 years—are also useful because estimates of the future are usually overly optimistic; the hard facts of previous periods bring a sobering reality to the negotiations.

Tractorling's net earnings for the last 5 years are as follows:

ILLUSTRATION 12B-2
Calculation of Average Earnings

Earnings History—Tractorling

		Average Earnings
1997	$ 60,000	$\frac{\$375,000}{5} = \$75,000$
1998	55,000	
1999	110,000[a]	
2000	70,000	
2001	80,000	
	$375,000	

[a]Includes extraordinary gain of $25,000.

The average net earnings for the last 5 years is $75,000 or a rate of return of approximately 21.4% on the current value of the assets excluding goodwill ($75,000 ÷ $350,000). Before we go further, however, we need to know whether $75,000 is representative of the future earnings of this enterprise.

[1]The fair value of Tractorling's assets (rather than historical cost) is used to compute the normal profit, because fair value is closer to the true value of the company's assets exclusive of goodwill.

Often past earnings of a company to be acquired need to be evaluated on the basis of the acquirer's own accounting procedures. Suppose, that in determining earnings power, Multi-Diversified measures earnings in relation to a FIFO inventory valuation figure rather than LIFO, which Tractorling employs, and that the use of LIFO reduced Tractorling's net income by $2,000 per year. In addition, Tractorling uses accelerated depreciation while Multi-Diversified uses straight-line. As a result, Tractorling's earnings were lower by $3,000.

Also, assets discovered on examination that might affect the earnings flow should be considered. Patent costs not previously recorded should be amortized, say, at the rate of $1,000 per period. Finally because the estimate of the future earnings is what we are attempting to determine, some items, like the extraordinary gain of $25,000, probably should not be considered. An analysis can now be made as follows:

ILLUSTRATION 12B-3
Calculation of Adjusted Net Earnings

Average net earnings per Tractorling computation		$75,000
Add		
Adjustment for switch from LIFO to FIFO	$2,000	
Adjustment for change from accelerated to straight-line approach	3,000	5,000
		80,000
Deduct		
Extraordinary gain ($25,000 ÷ 5)	5,000	
Patent amortization on straight-line basis	1,000	6,000
Adjusted average net earnings of Tractorling		$74,000

The excess earnings would be determined to be $21,500 ($74,000 – $52,500).

Choosing a Discount Rate to Apply to Excess Earnings

Determining the discount rate is a fairly subjective estimate.[2] **The lower the discount rate, the higher the value of the goodwill and vice versa.** To illustrate, assume that the excess earnings are $21,500 and that these earnings will continue indefinitely. If the excess earnings are capitalized at, say, a rate of 25% in perpetuity,[3] the results are:

---

[2]The following illustration shows how the capitalization rate might be computed for a small business:

A Method of Selecting a Capitalization Rate	
Long-term U.S. government bond rate	10%
Plus: Average premium return on small stocks over U.S. government bonds	10
Expected total rate of return on small publicly held stocks	20
Plus: Premium for greater risk and illiquidity	6
Total required expected rate of return, including inflation component	26
Less: Consensus long-term inflation expectation	6
Capitalization rate to apply to current earnings	20%

From Warren Kissin and Ronald Zulli, "Valuation of a Closely Held Business," *The Journal of Accountancy,* June 1988, p. 42.

[3]Why do we divide by the capitalization rate to arrive at the goodwill amount? Recall that the present value of an ordinary annuity is equal to:

$$PV\text{-}OA_{n,i} = \frac{1 - \dfrac{1}{(1+i)^n}}{i}$$

When a number is capitalized into perpetuity, $(1 + i)^n$ becomes so large that $1/(1 + i)^n$ essentially equals zero, which leaves $1/i$ or, as in the case above, $21,500/.25.

Capitalization at 25%		
Excess earnings / Capitalization rate	$21,500 / .25	= $86,000

ILLUSTRATION 12B-4
Capitalization of Excess Earnings at 25% in Perpetuity

If the excess earnings are capitalized in perpetuity at a somewhat lower rate, say 15%, a much higher goodwill figure results.

Capitalization at 15%		
Excess earnings / Capitalization rate	$21,500 / .15	= $143,333

ILLUSTRATION 12B-5
Capitalization of Excess Earnings at 15% in Perpetuity

Because the continuance of excess profits is uncertain, a conservative rate (higher than the normal rate) is usually employed. Factors that are considered in determining the rate are the stability of past earnings, the speculative nature of the business, and general economic conditions.

Choosing a Discounting Period for Excess Earnings

Determining the period over which excess earnings will exist is perhaps the most difficult problem associated with computing goodwill. If it is assumed that the excess earnings will last indefinitely, then goodwill is $143,333 as computed in the previous section (assuming a rate of 15%).

Another method of computing goodwill that gives the same answer, using the normal return of 15%, is to discount the total average earnings of the company and subtract the fair market value of the net identifiable assets as shown in Illustration 12B-6.

Average earnings capitalized at 15% in perpetuity ($74,000 ÷ 15%)	$493,333
Less: Fair market value of net identifiable assets	350,000
Present value of estimated earnings (goodwill)	$143,333

ILLUSTRATION 12B-6
Capitalization of Average Earnings Less Fair Value of Net Assets

Frequently, however, the excess earnings are assumed to last a limited number of years, say 10, and then it is necessary to discount these earnings only over that time. Assume that Multi-Diversified believes that the excess earnings of Tractorling will last 10 years and, because of the uncertainty surrounding this earning power, uses 25% as an appropriate rate of return. The present value of an annuity of $21,500 ($74,000 − $52,500) discounted at 25% for 10 years is $76,766.[4] That is the amount that Multi-Diversified should be willing to pay above the fair value of net identifiable assets.

OTHER METHODS OF VALUATION

A number of other methods of valuing goodwill exist.[5] Some accountants fail to discount but simply multiply the excess earnings by the number of years they believe the

[4]The present value of an annuity of one dollar received in a steady stream for 10 years in the future discounted at 25% is 3.57050 (3.57050 × $21,500 = $76,766).

[5]One article lists three "asset-based approaches" (tangible net worth, adjusted book value, and price-book value ratio methods) and three "earnings-based approaches" (capitalization of earnings, capitalization of excess earnings, and discounted cash flow methods) as the popular methods for valuing closely held businesses. See Warren Rissin and Ronald Zulli, "Valuation of a Closely Held Business," *The Journal of Accountancy,* June 1988, pp. 38–44.

excess earnings will continue. This approach, often referred to as the **number of years method**, is used to provide a rough measure for the goodwill factor. The approach has only the advantage of simplicity; it is sounder to recognize the discount factor.

An even simpler method is one that relies on multiples of average yearly earnings that are paid for other companies in the same industry. If Skyward Airlines was recently acquired for five times its average yearly earnings of $50 million, or $250 million, then Worldwide Airways, a close competitor, with $80 million in average yearly earnings would be worth $400 million.

Another method (similar to discounting excess earnings) is the **discounted free cash flow method**, which involves a projection of the acquired company's free cash flow over a long period, typically 10 or 20 years. The method first projects into the future a dozen or so important financial variables, including production, prices, noncash expenses (such as depreciation and amortization), taxes, and capital outlays, all adjusted for inflation. The objective is to determine the amount of cash that will accumulate over a specified number of years. The present value of the free cash flows is then computed. This amount represents the price to be paid for the business.[6]

For example, if Magnaputer Company is expected to generate $1 million a year for 20 years, and the buyer's rate-of-return objective is 15%, the buyer would be willing to pay about $6.26 million for Magnaputer Company. (The present value of $1 million to be received for 20 years discounted at 15% is $6,259,330.)

In practice, prospective buyers use a variety of methods to produce a "valuation curve" or range of prices. But the actual price paid may be more a factor of the buyer's or seller's ego and horse-trading acumen.

Valuation of goodwill is at best a highly uncertain process. The estimated value of goodwill depends on a number of factors, all of which are extremely tenuous and subject to bargaining.

KEY TERMS

discounted free cash flow method, 630
excess earnings approach, 626
number of years method, 630

SUMMARY OF LEARNING OBJECTIVE FOR APPENDIX 12B

10 Explain various approaches to valuing goodwill. One method of valuing goodwill is the excess earnings approach. Using this approach, the total earning power that the company commands is computed. The next step is to calculate "normal earnings" by determining the normal rate of return on assets in that industry. The difference between what the firm earns and what is normal in the industry is referred to as the excess earning power. This excess earning power indicates that there are unidentifiable values that provide the increased earning power. Finding the value of goodwill then is a matter of discounting these excess future earnings to the present. The number of years method of valuing goodwill, which simply multiplies the excess earnings by the number of years of expected excess earnings, is used to provide a rough measure for the goodwill factor. A third method of valuing goodwill is the discounted free cash flow method, which projects the amount of cash that will accumulate over a specified number of years and then finds the present value of that amount as today's value of the firm.

Note: All **asterisked** Questions, Brief Exercises, Problems, and Conceptual Cases relate to material contained in the appendixes to the chapter.

QUESTIONS

1 What are the major characteristics of intangible assets?

2 What problems of accounting for goodwill and similar intangibles are comparable to those of accounting for plant assets? What problems are different?

3 Many advocate the abandonment of historical cost for plant assets but argue that historical cost should be used in accounting for intangible assets. Are the two viewpoints inconsistent?

[6]Tim Metz, "Deciding How Much a Company Is Worth Often Depends on Whose Side You're On," *The Wall Street Journal,* March 18, 1981.

4 Intangible assets may be classified on a number of different bases. Explain the following bases: identifiability, manner of acquisition, expected period of benefit, and separability from an entire enterprise.

5 What are some examples of internally created intangibles? Why does the accounting profession make a distinction between internally created "goodwill-type" intangibles and other intangibles?

6 In 2001, Sheila Wright Corp. spent $420,000 for "goodwill" visits by sales personnel to key customers. The purpose of these visits was to build a solid, friendly relationship for the future and to gain insight into the problems and needs of the companies served. How should this expenditure be reported?

7 State the generally accepted accounting procedures for the amortization and write-down or write-off of capitalized intangible assets.

8 It has been argued, on the grounds of conservatism, that all intangible assets should be written off immediately after acquisition. Give the accounting arguments against this treatment.

9 Alonzo Mourning Company spent $190,000 developing a new process, $45,000 in legal fees to obtain a patent, and $91,000 to market the process that was patented, all in the year 2001. How should these costs be accounted for in 2001?

10 Indicate the period of time over which each of the following should be amortized.

(a) Research and development costs.

(b) Trademarks.

(c) Goodwill.

(d) Franchises.

(e) Patents.

(f) Leasehold improvements.

(g) Copyrights.

11 What is a lease prepayment? What are property rights capitalized by the lessee? What are leasehold improvements? Should any of these items be classified as an intangible asset?

12 On January 1, 1997, an intangible asset with a 35-year estimated useful life was acquired. On January 1, 2002, a review was made of the estimated useful life, and it was determined that the intangible asset had an estimated useful life of 45 more years. Assuming that the company wants to amortize this intangible over the maximum period possible, how many more years may this intangible be amortized?

13 Recently Penquin Corporation entered into a lease agreement with Eagle Developers, Inc. to lease some land for 25 years in southwest New Mexico. Penquin Corporation as lessee then built on this site a number of apartment buildings having a useful life of 35 years. The lease agreement states that the lessee has the option to renew the lease for another 20 years. Over what period should the apartments be depreciated?

14 Recently, a group of university students decided to incorporate for the purposes of selling a process to recycle the waste product from manufacturing cheese. Some of the initial costs involved were legal fees and office expenses incurred in starting the business, state incorporation fees, and stamp taxes. One student wishes to charge these costs against revenue in the current period; another wishes to defer these costs and amortize them in the future. Which student is correct?

15 What is goodwill? What is negative goodwill?

16 Under what circumstances is it appropriate to record goodwill in the accounts? How should goodwill, properly recorded on the books, be amortized in order to conform with generally accepted accounting principles?

17 In examining financial statements, financial analysts often write off goodwill immediately. Evaluate this procedure.

18 What is the nature of research and development costs? What other costs have similar characteristics?

19 Research and development activities may include (a) personnel costs, (b) materials and equipment costs, and (c) indirect costs. What is the recommended accounting treatment for these three types of R & D costs?

20 Which of the following activities should be expensed currently as R & D costs:

(a) Testing in search for or evaluation of product or process alternatives.

(b) Engineering follow-through in an early phase of commercial production.

(c) Legal work in connection with patent applications or litigation, and the sale or licensing of patents.

21 Indicate the proper accounting for the following items:

(a) Organization costs.

(b) Advertising costs.

(c) Operating losses.

22 In 2000, Cassie Logan Corporation developed a new product that will be marketed in 2001. In connection with the development of this product, the following costs were incurred in 2000: research and development costs, $420,000; materials and supplies consumed, $60,000; compensation paid to research consultants, $125,000. It is anticipated that these costs will be recovered in 2003. What is the amount of research and development costs that Cassie Logan should record in 2000 as a charge to expense?

23 An intangible asset with an estimated useful life of 30 years was acquired on January 1, 1991, for $450,000. On January 1, 2001, a review was made of intangible assets and their expected service lives and it was determined that this asset had an estimated useful life of 35 more years from the date of the review. What is the amount of amortization for this intangible asset for 2001?

***24** An article in the financial press stated "More than half of software maker Comserve's net worth is in a pile of tapes and ring-bound books. That raises some accountants' eyebrows." What is the profession's position regarding the incurrence of costs for computer software that will be sold?

***25** Matt Antonio, Inc. has incurred $6 million in developing a computer software product for sale to third parties. Of the $6 million costs incurred, $4 million is capitalized. The product produced from this development work has generated $2 million in 2001 and is anticipated to generate another $8 million in future years. The estimated useful life of the project is 4 years. How much of the capitalized costs should be amortized in 2001?

***26** In 2001, U-Learn Software developed a software package for assisting calculus instruction in business colleges, at a cost of $2,000,000. Although there are tens of thousands of calculus students in the market, college instructors seem to change their minds frequently on the use of teaching aids. And, not one package has yet been ordered or delivered. Prepare an argument to advocate expensing the development cost in the current year. Offer an argument for capitalizing the development cost over its estimated useful life. Which stakeholders are harmed or benefited by either approach?

***27** Explain how "average excess earnings" are determined. What is the justification for the use of this method of estimating goodwill?

***28** Discuss two methods for estimating the value of goodwill in determining the amount that should properly be paid for it.

BRIEF EXERCISES

BE12-1 Doom Troopers Corporation purchases a patent from Judge Dredd Company on January 1, 2002, for $64,000. The patent has a remaining legal life of 16 years. Doom Troopers feels the patent will be useful for 10 years. Prepare Doom Troopers' journal entries to record the purchase of the patent and 2002 amortization.

BE12-2 Use the information provided in BE12-1. Assume that at January 1, 2004, the carrying amount of the patent on Doom Troopers' books is $51,200. In January, Doom Troopers spends $24,000 successfully defending a patent suit. Doom Troopers still feels the patent will be useful until the end of 2011. Prepare the journal entries to record the $24,000 expenditure and 2004 amortization.

BE12-3 Dr. Robotnik's, Inc., spent $60,000 in attorney fees while developing the trade name of its new product, the Mean Bean Machine. Prepare the journal entries to record the $60,000 expenditure and the first year's amortization, using an 8-year life.

BE12-4 Incredible Hulk Corporation commenced operations in early 2002. The corporation incurred $70,000 of costs such as fees to underwriters, legal fees, state fees, and promotional expenditures during its formation. Prepare journal entries to record the $70,000 expenditure and 2002 amortization, if any. Assume a full year's amortization based on a 5-year life.

BE12-5 Cyborg Company leased a building on July 1, 2002, for 8 years ending June 30, 2010. The building has an estimated remaining useful life of 20 years. Cyborg immediately made improvements to the building. The improvements, which cost $89,120, have a useful life of 10 years. Prepare journal entries to record the $89,120 expenditure and 2002 amortization.

BE12-6 Knuckles Corporation obtained a franchise from Sonic Hedgehog Inc. for a cash payment of $100,000 on April 1, 2002. The franchise grants Knuckles the right to sell certain products and services for a period of 8 years. Prepare Knuckles' April 1 journal entry and December 31 adjusting entry.

BE12-7 On September 1, 2002, Dungeon Corporation acquired Dragon Enterprises for a cash payment of $750,000. At the time of purchase, Dragon's balance sheet showed assets of $620,000, liabilities of $200,000, and owners' equity of $420,000. The fair value of Dragon's assets is estimated to be $800,000. (a) Compute the amount of goodwill acquired by Dungeon. (b) Prepare the December 31 entry to record amortization, based on a 10-year life.

BE12-8 Nobunaga Corporation owns a patent that has a carrying amount of $330,000. Nobunaga expects future net cash flows from this patent to total $190,000. The fair value of the patent is $110,000. Prepare Nobunaga's journal entry, if necessary, to record the loss on impairment.

BE12-9 Evander Corporation purchased Holyfield Company 3 years ago and at that time recorded goodwill of $400,000. The carrying amount of the goodwill today is $340,000. The Holyfield Division's net assets, including the goodwill, have a carrying amount of $800,000. Evander expects net future cash flows of $700,000 from the Holyfield Division. The fair value of the division is estimated to be $525,000. Prepare Evander's journal entry, if necessary, to record impairment of the goodwill.

BE12-10 Dorsett Corporation incurred the following costs in 2002:

Cost of laboratory research aimed at discovery of new knowledge	$140,000
Cost of testing in search for product alternatives	100,000
Cost of engineering activity required to advance the design of a product to the manufacturing stage	210,000
	$450,000

Prepare the necessary 2002 journal entry or entries for Dorsett.

BE2-11 Indicate whether the following items are capitalized or expensed in the current year:

(a) purchase cost of a patent from a competitor;
(b) research and development costs;
(c) organizational costs; and
(d) costs incurred internally to create goodwill.

BE12-12 Langer Industries had one patent recorded on its books as of January 1, 2002. This patent had a book value of $240,000 and a remaining useful life of 8 years. During 2002, Langer incurred research and development costs of $96,000 and brought a patent infringement suit against a competitor. On December 1, 2002, Langer received the good news that its patent was valid and that its competitor could not use the process Langer had patented. The company incurred $85,000 to defend this patent. At what amount should patent(s) be reported on the December 31, 2002, balance sheet assuming monthly amortization of patents?

BE12-13 Wiggens Industries acquired two copyrights during 2002. One copyright related to a textbook that was developed internally at a cost of $9,900. This textbook is estimated to have a useful life of 3 years from September 1, 2002, the date it was published. The second copyright (a history research textbook) was purchased from University Press on December 1, 2002, for $19,200. This textbook has an indefinite useful life. How should these two copyrights be reported on Wiggens' balance sheet as of December 31, 2002? Assume that Wiggens will use the maximum period of amortization for intangibles, whenever possible.

***BE12-14** Earthworm Jim Corporation has capitalized software costs of $700,000, and sales of this product the first year totaled $420,000. Earthworm Jim anticipates earning $980,000 in additional future revenues from this product, which is estimated to have an economic life of 4 years. Compute the amount of software cost amortization for the first year.

***BE12-15** Nigel Mansel Corporation is interested in purchasing Indy Car Company. Indy's total net income during the last 5 years is $600,000. During one of those years, Indy reported an extraordinary gain of $80,000. The fair value of Indy's identifiable net assets is $560,000. A normal rate of return is 15%, and Mansel wishes to capitalize excess earnings at 20%. Compute the estimated value of Indy's goodwill.

EXERCISES

E12-1 (Classification Issues—Intangibles) Presented below is a list of items that could be included in the intangible assets section of the balance sheet.

1. Investment in a subsidiary company.
2. Timberland.
3. Cost of engineering activity required to advance the design of a product to the manufacturing stage.
4. Lease prepayment (6 months' rent paid in advance).
5. Cost of equipment obtained under a capital lease.
6. Cost of searching for applications of new research findings.
7. Costs incurred in the formation of a corporation.
8. Operating losses incurred in the start-up of a business.
9. Training costs incurred in start-up of new operation.
10. Purchase cost of a franchise.
11. Goodwill generated internally.
12. Cost of testing in search for product alternatives.

13. Goodwill acquired in the purchase of a business.
14. Cost of developing a patent.
15. Cost of purchasing a patent from an inventor.
16. Legal costs incurred in securing a patent.
17. Unrecovered costs of a successful legal suit to protect the patent.
18. Cost of conceptual formulation of possible product alternatives.
19. Cost of purchasing a copyright.
20. Research and development costs.
21. Long-term receivables.
22. Cost of developing a trademark.
23. Cost of purchasing a trademark.

Instructions

(a) Indicate which items on the list above would generally be reported as intangible assets in the balance sheet.

(b) Indicate how, if at all, the items not reportable as intangible assets would be reported in the financial statements.

E12-2 (Classification Issues—Intangibles) Presented below is selected account information related to Martin Burke Inc. as of December 21, 2001. All these accounts have debit balances.

Cable television franchises	Film contract rights
Music copyrights	Customer lists
Research and development costs	Prepaid expenses
Goodwill	Covenants not to compete
Cash	Brand names
Discount on notes payable	Notes receivable
Accounts receivable	Investments in affiliated companies
Property, plant, and equipment	Organization cost
Leasehold improvements	Land

Instructions

Identify which items should be classified as an intangible asset. For those items not classified as an intangible asset, indicate where they would be reported in the financial statements.

E12-3 (Classification Issues—Intangible Asset) Joni Hyde Inc. has the following amounts included in its general ledger at December 31, 2001:

Organization costs	$24,000
Trademarks	15,000
Discount on bonds payable	35,000
Deposits with advertising agency for ads to promote goodwill of company	10,000
Excess of cost over fair value of net identifiable assets of acquired subsidiary	75,000
Cost of equipment acquired for research and development projects; the equipment has an alternative future use	90,000
Costs of developing a secret formula for a product that is expected to be marketed for at least 20 years	80,000

Instructions

(a) On the basis of the information above, compute the total amount to be reported by Hyde for intangible assets on its balance sheet at December 31, 2001. Equipment has alternative future use.

(b) If an item is not to be included in intangible assets, explain its proper treatment for reporting purposes.

E12-4 (Intangible Amortization) Presented below is selected information for Alatorre Company. Answer each of the factual situations.

1. Alatorre purchased a patent from Vania Co. for $1,000,000 on January 1, 1998. The patent is being amortized over its remaining legal life of 10 years, expiring on January 1, 2008. During 2000, Alatorre determined that the economic benefits of the patent would not last longer than 6 years from the date of acquisition. What amount should be reported in the balance sheet for the patent, net of accumulated amortization, at December 31, 2000?
2. Alatorre bought a franchise from Alexander Co. on January 1, 1999, for $400,000. It is estimated that the franchise has a useful life of 60 years. Its carrying amount on Alexander's books at January 1, 1999, was $500,000. Alatorre has decided to amortize the franchise over the maximum period permitted. What amount should be amortized for the year ended December 31, 2000?

3. On January 1, 1996, Alatorre incurred organization costs of $275,000. Alatorre is amortizing these costs over 5 years. What amount, if any, should be reported as unamortized organization costs as of December 31, 2000?

E12-5 (Correct Intangible Asset Account) As the recently appointed auditor for William J. Bryan Corporation, you have been asked to examine selected accounts before the 6-month financial statements of June 30, 2001, are prepared. The controller for William J. Bryan Corporation mentions that only one account (shown below) is kept for Intangible Assets.

Intangible Assets

		Debit	Credit	Balance
January 4	Research and development costs	940,000		940,000
January 5	Legal costs to obtain patent	75,000		1,015,000
January 31	Payment of 7 months' rent on property leased by Bryan	91,000		1,106,000
February 11	Premium on common stock		250,000	856,000
March 31	Unamortized bond discount on bonds due March 31, 2021	84,000		940,000
April 30	Promotional expenses related to start-up of business	207,000		1,147,000
June 30	Operating losses for first 6 months	241,000		1,388,000

Instructions

Prepare the entry or entries necessary to correct this account. Assume that the patent has a useful life of 10 years.

E12-6 (Recording and Amortization of Intangibles) Rolanda Marshall Company, organized in 2001, has set up a single account for all intangible assets. The following summary discloses the debit entries that have been recorded during 2002:

1/2/02	Purchased patent (8-year life)	$ 350,000
4/1/02	Purchased goodwill (indefinite life)	360,000
7/1/02	Purchased franchise with 10-year life; expiration date 7/1/12	450,000
8/1/02	Payment of copyright (5-year life)	156,000
9/1/02	Research and development costs	215,000
		$1,531,000

Instructions

Prepare the necessary entries to clear the Intangible Assets account and to set up separate accounts for distinct types of intangibles. Make the entries as of December 31, 2002, recording any necessary amortization and reflecting all balances accurately as of that date (straight-line amortization).

E12-7 (Accounting for Trade Name) In early January of 2001, Gayle Crystal Corporation applied for a trade name, incurring legal costs of $16,000. In January of 2002, Gayle Crystal incurred $7,800 of legal fees in a successful defense of its trade name.

Instructions

(a) Compute 2001 amortization, 12/31/01 book value, 2002 amortization, and 12/31/02 book value if the company amortizes the trade name over the maximum allowable life.

(b) Repeat part (a), assuming a useful life of 5 years.

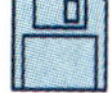

E12-8 (Accounting for Lease Transaction) William Rose Benet Inc. leases an old building which it intends to improve and use as a warehouse. To obtain the lease, the company pays a bonus of $72,000. Annual rental for the 6-year lease period is $120,000. No option to renew the lease or right to purchase the property is given.

After the lease is obtained, improvements costing $144,000 are made. The building has an estimated remaining useful life of 17 years.

Instructions

(a) What is the annual cost (excluding depreciation) of this lease to William Rose Benet Inc.?

(b) What amount of annual depreciation, if any, on a straight-line basis should William Rose Benet record?

E12-9 (Accounting for Organization Costs) Horace Greeley Corporation was organized in 2000 and began operations at the beginning of 2001. The company is involved in interior design consulting services. The following costs were incurred prior to the start of operations:

Attorney's fees in connection with organization of the company	$15,000
Improvements to leased offices prior to occupancy	25,000
Costs of meetings of incorporators to discuss organizational activities	7,000
State filing fees to incorporate	1,000
	$48,000

Instructions

(a) Compute the total amount of organization costs incurred by Greeley.
(b) Prepare the journal entry to record organization costs for 2001.

E12-10 (Accounting for Patents, Franchises, and R & D) Jimmy Carter Company has provided information on intangible assets as follows:

A patent was purchased from Gerald Ford Company for $2,000,000 on January 1, 2001. Carter estimated the remaining useful life of the patent to be 10 years. The patent was carried in Ford's accounting records at a net book value of $2,000,000 when Ford sold it to Carter.

During 2002, a franchise was purchased from the Ronald Reagan Company for $480,000. In addition, 5% of revenue from the franchise must be paid to Reagan. Revenue from the franchise for 2002 was $2,500,000. Carter estimates the useful life of the franchise to be 10 years and takes a full year's amortization in the year of purchase.

Carter incurred research and development costs in 2002 as follows:

Materials and equipment	$142,000
Personnel	189,000
Indirect costs	102,000
	$433,000

Carter estimates that these costs will be recouped by December 31, 2005.

On January 1, 2002, Carter, because of recent events in the field, estimates that the remaining life of the patent purchased on January 1, 2001, is only 5 years from January 1, 2002.

Instructions

(a) Prepare a schedule showing the intangibles section of Carter's balance sheet at December 31, 2002. Show supporting computations in good form.
(b) Prepare a schedule showing the income statement effect for the year ended December 31, 2002, as a result of the facts above. Show supporting computations in good form.

(AICPA adapted)

E12-11 (Accounting for Patents) During 1998, George Winston Corporation spent $170,000 in research and development costs. As a result, a new product called the New Age Piano was patented at additional legal and other costs of $18,000. The patent was obtained on October 1, 1998, and had a legal life of 20 years and a useful life of 10 years.

Instructions

(a) Prepare all journal entries required in 1998 and 1999 as a result of the transactions above.
(b) On June 1, 2000, Winston spent $9,480 to successfully prosecute a patent infringement. As a result, the estimate of useful life was extended to 12 years from June 1, 2000. Prepare all journal entries required in 2000 and 2001.
(c) In 2002, Winston determined that a competitor's product would make the New Age Piano obsolete and the patent worthless by December 31, 2003. Prepare all journal entries required in 2002 and 2003.

E12-12 (Accounting for Patents) Tones Industries has the following patents on its December 31, 2003, balance sheet:

Patent Item	Initial Cost	Date Acquired	Useful Life at Date Acquired
Patent A	$30,600	3/1/00	17 years
Patent B	$15,000	7/1/01	10 years
Patent C	$14,400	9/1/02	4 years

The following events occurred during the year ended December 31, 2004:

1. Research and development costs of $245,700 were incurred during the year.
2. Patent D was purchased on July 1 for $36,480. This patent has a useful life of $9\frac{1}{2}$ years.

3. As a result of reduced demands for certain products protected by Patent B, a possible impairment of Patent B's value may have occurred at December 31, 2004. The controller for Tones estimates the future cash flows from Patent B will be as follows:

For the Year Ended	Future Cash Flows
December 31, 2005	$2,000
December 31, 2006	2,000
December 31, 2007	2,000

The proper discount rate to be used for these flows is 8%. (Assume that the cash flows occur at the end of the year.)

Instructions

(a) Compute the total carrying amount of Tones' patents on its December 31, 2003, balance sheet.
(b) Compute the total carrying amount of Tones' patents on its December 31, 2004, balance sheet.

E12-13 (Accounting for Goodwill) Fred Moss, owner of Moss Interiors, is negotiating for the purchase of Zweifel Galleries. The condensed balance sheet of Zweifel is given in an abbreviated form below:

ZWEIFEL GALLERIES
Balance Sheet
As of December 31, 2002

Assets		**Liabilities and Stockholders' Equity**		
Cash	$100,000	Accounts payable		$ 50,000
Land	70,000	Long-term notes payable		300,000
Building (net)	200,000	Total liabilities		350,000
Equipment (net)	175,000	Common stock	$200,000	
Copyright (net)	30,000	Retained earnings	25,000	225,000
Total assets	$575,000	Total liabilities and stockholders' equity		$575,000

Moss and Zweifel agree that:

1. Land is undervalued by $30,000.
2. Equipment is overvalued by $5,000.

Zweifel agrees to sell the gallery to Moss for $350,000.

Instructions

Prepare the entry to record the purchase of Zweifel gallery on Moss' books.

E12-14 (Accounting for Goodwill) On July 1, 2001, Brigham Corporation purchased Young Company by paying $250,000 cash and issuing a $100,000 note payable to Steve Young. At July 1, 2001, the balance sheet of Young Company was as follows:

Cash	$ 50,000	Accounts payable	$200,000
Receivables	90,000	Young, capital	235,000
Inventory	100,000		$435,000
Land	40,000		
Buildings (net)	75,000		
Equipment (net)	70,000		
Trademarks	10,000		
	$435,000		

The recorded amounts all approximate current values except for land (worth $60,000), inventory (worth $125,000), and trademarks (worthless).

Instructions

(a) Prepare the July 1 entry for Brigham Corporation to record the purchase.
(b) Prepare the December 31 entry for Brigham Corporation to record amortization of goodwill. The goodwill is estimated to have a useful life of 50 years.

E12-15 (Intangible Impairment) Presented below is information related to copyrights owned by Walter de la Mare Company at December 31, 2002.

Cost	$8,600,000
Carrying amount	4,300,000
Expected future net cash flows	4,000,000
Fair value	3,200,000

Assume that Walter de la Mare Company will continue to use this copyright in the future. As of December 31, 2002, the copyright is estimated to have a remaining useful life of 10 years.

Instructions

(a) Prepare the journal entry (if any) to record the impairment of the asset at December 31, 2002. The company does not use accumulated amortization accounts.

(b) Prepare the journal entry to record amortization expense for 2003 related to the copyrights.

(c) The fair value of the copyright at December 31, 2003, is $3,400,000. Prepare the journal entry (if any) necessary to record the increase in fair value.

E12-16 (Goodwill Impairment) Presented below is net asset information (including associated goodwill of $200 million) related to the Carlos Division of Santana, Inc.

CARLOS DIVISION
Net Assets
as of December 31, 2002
(in millions)

Cash	$ 50
Receivables	200
Property, plant, and equipment (net)	2,600
Goodwill	200
Less: Notes payable	(2,700)
Net assets	$ 350

The purpose of this division is to develop a nuclear-powered aircraft. If successful, traveling delays associated with refueling could be substantially reduced. Many other benefits would also occur. To date, management has not had much success and is deciding whether a writedown at this time is appropriate. Management estimated its future net cash flows from the project to be $300 million. Management has also received an offer to purchase the division for $220 million.

Instructions

(a) Prepare the journal entry (if any) to record the impairment at December 31, 2002.

(b) At December 31, 2003, it is estimated that the division's fair value increased to $240 million. Prepare the journal entry (if any) to record this increase in fair value.

E12-17 (Accounting for R & D Costs) Leontyne Price Company from time to time embarks on a research program when a special project seems to offer possibilities. In 2001 the company expends $325,000 on a research project, but by the end of 2001 it is impossible to determine whether any benefit will be derived from it.

Instructions

(a) What account should be charged for the $325,000, and how should it be shown in the financial statements?

(b) The project is completed in 2002, and a successful patent is obtained. The R & D costs to complete the project are $110,000. The administrative and legal expenses incurred in obtaining patent number 472-1001-84 in 2002 total $16,000. The patent has an expected useful life of 5 years. Record these costs in journal entry form. Also, record patent amortization (full year) in 2002.

(c) In 2003, the company successfully defends the patent in extended litigation at a cost of $47,200, thereby extending the patent life to 12/31/10. What is the proper way to account for this cost? Also, record patent amortization (full year) in 2003.

(d) Additional engineering and consulting costs incurred in 2003 required to advance the design of a product to the manufacturing stage total $60,000. These costs enhance the design of the product considerably. Discuss the proper accounting treatment for this cost.

E12-18 (Accounting for R & D Costs) Josha Heifitz Company incurred the following costs during 2001:

Quality control during commercial production, including routine testing of products	$58,000
Laboratory research aimed at discovery of new knowledge	68,000
Engineering follow-through in an early phase of commercial production	15,000
Adaptation of an existing capability to a particular requirement or customer's need as a part of continuing commercial activity	13,000
Trouble-shooting in connection with breakdowns during commercial production	29,000
Searching for applications of new research findings	19,000

Instructions

Compute the total amount Josha Heifitz should classify and expense as research and development costs for 2001.

E12-19 (Accounting for R & D Costs) Thomas More Company incurred the following costs during 2001 in connection with its research and development activities:

Cost of equipment acquired that will have alternative uses in future research and development projects over the next 5 years (uses straight-line depreciation)	$280,000
Materials consumed in research and development projects	59,000
Consulting fees paid to outsiders for research and development projects	100,000
Personnel costs of persons involved in research and development projects	128,000
Indirect costs reasonably allocable to research and development projects	50,000
Materials purchased for future research and development projects	34,000

Instructions

Compute the amount to be reported as research and development expense by More on its income statement for 2001. Assume equipment is purchased at beginning of year.

E12-20 (Accounting for R & D Costs) Listed below are four independent situations involving research and development costs:

1. During 2002, Jake Sisco Co. incurred the following costs:

Research and development services performed by Miles Company for Sisco	$350,000
Testing for evaluation of new products	300,000
Laboratory research aimed at discovery of new knowledge	425,000

For the year ended December 31, 2002, Jake Sisco Co. should report research and development expense of how much?

2. Odo Corp. incurred the following costs during the year ended December 31, 2002:

Design, construction, and testing of preproduction prototypes and models	$290,000
Routine, on-going efforts to refine, enrich, or otherwise improve upon the qualities of an existing product	250,000
Quality control during commercial production including routine testing of products	300,000
Laboratory research aimed at discovery of new knowledge	420,000

What is the total amount to be classified and expensed as research and development for 2002?

3. Quark Company incurred costs in 2002 as follows:

Equipment acquired for use in various research and development projects	$900,000
Depreciation on the equipment above	210,000
Materials used in R & D	300,000
Compensation costs of personnel in R & D	400,000
Outside consulting fees for R & D work	220,000
Indirect costs appropriately allocated to R & D	260,000

What is the total amount of research and development that should be reported in Quark's 2002 income statement?

4. Julian Inc. incurred the following costs during the year ended December 31, 2002:

Laboratory research aimed at discovery of new knowledge	$200,000
Radical modification to the formulation of a chemical product	145,000
Research and development costs reimbursable under a contract to perform research and development for Bashir Inc.	350,000
Testing for evaluation of new products	225,000

What is the total amount to be classified and expensed as research and development for 2002?

Instructions
Provide the correct answer to each of the four situations.

***E12-21 (Accounting for Computer Software Costs)** New Jersey Inc. has capitalized computer software costs of $3,600,000 on its new "Trenton" software package. Revenues from 2001 (first year) sales are $2,000,000; additional future revenues from "Trenton" for the remainder of its economic life, through 2005, are estimated to be $10,000,000.

Instructions
(a) What method or methods of amortization are to be applied in the write-off of capitalized computer software costs?
(b) Compute the amount of amortization for 2001 for "Trenton."

***E12-22 (Accounting for Computer Software Costs)** During 2001, Delaware Enterprises spent $5,000,000 developing its new Dover software package. Of this amount, $2,200,000 was spent before technological feasibility was established for the product, which is to be marketed to third parties. The package was completed at December 31, 2001. Delaware expects a useful life of 8 years for this product with total revenues of $16,000,000. During the first year (2002), Delaware realizes revenues of $3,200,000.

Instructions
(a) Prepare journal entries required in 2001 for the foregoing facts.
(b) Prepare the entry to record amortization at December 31, 2002.
(c) At what amount should the computer software costs be reported in the December 31, 2002, balance sheet? Could the net realizable value of this asset affect your answer?
(d) What disclosures are required in the December 31, 2002, financial statements for the computer software costs?
(e) How would your answers for (a), (b), and (c) be different if the computer software was developed for internal use?

***E12-23 (Compute Goodwill)** The net assets of Frankie Beverly Company excluding goodwill totals $800,000 and earnings for the last 5 years total $890,000. Included in the latter figure are extraordinary gains of $75,000, nonrecurring losses of $40,000, and sales commissions of $15,000. In developing a sales price for the business a 14% return on net worth is considered normal for the industry, and annual excess earnings are to be capitalized at 20% in arriving at goodwill.

Instructions
Compute estimated goodwill.

***E12-24 (Compute Normal Earnings)** Cliff Barnes Petroleum Corporation's pretax accounting income for the year 2001 was $850,000 and included the following items:

Amortization of goodwill	$ 60,000
Amortization of identifiable intangibles	57,000
Depreciation on building	80,000
Extraordinary losses	44,000
Extraordinary gains	150,000
Profit-sharing payments to employees	65,000

Ewing Oil Industries is seeking to purchase Cliff Barnes Petroleum Corporation. In attempting to measure Barnes' normal earnings for 2001, Ewing determines that the fair value of the building is triple the book value and that the remaining economic life is double that used by Barnes. Ewing would continue the profit-sharing payments to employees; such payments are based on income before depreciation and amortization.

Instructions
Compute the normal earnings (for purposes of computing goodwill) of Barnes Petroleum Corporation for the year 2001.

***E12-25 (Compute Goodwill)** Texas News Inc. is considering acquiring Austin Company in total as a going concern. Texas makes the following computations and conclusions:

1. The fair value of the identifiable assets of Austin Company is $720,000.
2. The liabilities of Austin Company are $380,000.
3. A fair estimate of annual earnings for the indefinite future is $120,000 per year.
4. Considering the risk and potential of Austin Company, Texas feels that it must earn a 25% return on its investment.

Instructions

(a) How much should Texas be willing to pay for Austin Company?
(b) How much of the purchase price would be goodwill?

***E12-26 (Compute Goodwill)** As the president of Tennessee Recording Corp., you are considering purchasing Nashville CD Corp., whose balance sheet is summarized as follows:

Current assets	$ 300,000	Current liabilities	$ 300,000
Fixed assets (net of depreciation)	700,000	Long-term liabilities	500,000
Other assets	300,000	Common stock	400,000
		Retained earnings	100,000
Total	$1,300,000	Total	$1,300,000

The fair market value of current assets is $550,000 because of the undervaluation of inventory. The normal rate of return on net assets for the industry is 15%. The average expected annual earnings projected for Nashville CD Corp. is $140,000.

Instructions

Assuming that the excess earnings continue for 5 years, how much would you be willing to pay for goodwill? (Estimate goodwill by the present-value method.)

***E12-27 (Compute Goodwill)** Net income figures for Maryland Company are as follows:

1997—$64,000	2000—$80,000
1998—$50,000	2001—$75,000
1999—$81,000	

Tangible net assets of this company are appraised at $400,000 on December 31, 2001. This business is to be acquired by Annapolis Co. early in 2002.

Instructions

What amount should be paid for goodwill if:

(a) 14% is assumed to be a normal rate of return on net tangible assets, and average excess earnings for the last 5 years are to be capitalized at 25%?
(b) 12% is assumed to be a normal rate of return on net tangible assets, and payment is to be made for excess earnings for the last 4 years?

***E12-28 (Compute Goodwill)** Virginia Corporation is interested in acquiring Richmond Plastics Company. It has determined that Richmond Company's excess earnings have averaged approximately $150,000 annually over the last 6 years. Richmond Company agrees with the computation of $150,000 as the approximate excess earnings and feels that such amount should be capitalized over an unlimited period at a 20% rate. Virginia Corporation feels that because of increased competition the excess earnings of Richmond Company will continue for 7 years at best and that a 15% discount rate is appropriate.

Instructions

(a) How far apart are the positions of these two parties?
(b) Is there really any difference in the two approaches used by the two parties in evaluating Richmond Company's goodwill? Explain.

***E12-29 (Compute Goodwill)** West Virginia Corporation is contemplating the purchase of Charleston Industries and evaluating the amount of goodwill to be recognized in the purchase.

Charleston reported the following net incomes:

1996	$170,000
1997	200,000
1998	240,000
1999	250,000
2000	380,000

Charleston has indicated that 2000 net income included the sale of one of its warehouses at a gain of $115,000 (net of tax). Net identifiable assets of Charleston have a total fair market value of $900,000.

Instructions

Calculate goodwill in the following cases, assuming that expected income is to be a simple average of **normal income** for the past 5 years.

(a) Goodwill is determined by capitalizing average net earnings at 16%.
(b) Goodwill is determined by presuming a 16% return on identifiable net assets and capitalizing excess earnings at 25%.

***E12-30 (Compute Fair Value of Identifiable Assets)** Bret Harte Company bought a business that would yield exactly a 20% annual rate of return on its investment. Of the total amount paid for the business, $80,000 was deemed to be goodwill, and the remaining was attributable to the identifiable net assets.

Bret Harte Company projected that the estimated annual future earnings of the new business would be equal to its average annual ordinary earnings over the past 4 years. The total net income over the past 4 years was $380,000, which included an extraordinary loss of $35,000 in one year and an extraordinary gain of $115,000 in one of the other 3 years.

Instructions

Compute the fair market value of the identifiable net assets that Bret Harte Company purchased in this transaction.

PROBLEMS

P12-1 (Correct Intangible Asset Account) Esplanade Co., organized in 2000, has set up a single account for all intangible assets. The following summary discloses the debit entries that have been recorded during 2000 and 2001:

Intangible Assets

7/1/00	8-year franchise; expiration date 6/30/08	$ 42,000
10/1/00	Advance payment on leasehold (2-year lease)	28,000
12/31/00	Net loss for 2000 including state incorporation fee, $1,000, and related legal fees of organizing, $5,000 (all fees incurred in 2000)	16,000
1/2/01	Patent purchased (10-year life)	74,000
3/1/01	Cost of developing a secret formula (indefinite life)	75,000
4/1/01	Goodwill purchased (indefinite life)	278,400
6/1/01	Legal fee for successful defense of patent purchased above	12,650
9/1/01	Research and development costs	160,000

Instructions

Prepare the necessary entries to clear the Intangible Assets account and to set up separate accounts for distinct types of intangibles. Make the entries as of December 31, 2001, recording any necessary amortization and reflecting all balances accurately as of that date. (Assume a 40-year amortization for intangibles unless specified. Ignore income tax effects.)

P12-2 (Accounting for Patents) Ankara Laboratories holds a valuable patent (No. 758-6002-1A) on a precipitator that prevents certain types of air pollution. Ankara does not manufacture or sell the products and processes it develops; it conducts research and develops products and processes which it patents, and then assigns the patents to manufacturers on a royalty basis. Occasionally it sells a patent. The history of Ankara patent number 758-6002-1A is as follows:

Date	Activity	Cost
1991–1992	Research conducted to develop precipitator	$384,000
Jan. 1993	Design and construction of a prototype	87,600
March 1993	Testing of models	42,000
Jan. 1994	Fees paid engineers and lawyers to prepare patent application; patent granted July 1, 1994	62,050
Nov. 1995	Engineering activity necessary to advance the design of the precipitator to the manufacturing stage	81,500
Dec. 1996	Legal fees paid to successfully defend precipitator patent	35,700
April 1997	Research aimed at modifying the design of the patented precipitator	43,000
July 2001	Legal fees paid in unsuccessful patent infringement suit against a competitor	34,000

Ankara assumed a useful life of 17 years when it received the initial precipitator patent. On January 1, 1999, it revised its useful life estimate downward to 5 remaining years. Amortization is computed for a

full year if the cost is incurred prior to July 1, and no amortization for the year if the cost is incurred after June 30. The company's year ends December 31.

Instructions

Compute the carrying value of patent No. 758-6002-1A on each of the following dates:

(a) December 31, 1994.
(b) December 31, 1998.
(c) December 31, 2001.

P12-3 (Accounting for Franchise, Patents, and Trade Name) Information concerning Haerhpin Corporation's intangible assets is as follows:

1. On January 1, 2002, Haerhpin signed an agreement to operate as a franchisee of Hsian Copy Service, Inc. for an initial franchise fee of $75,000. Of this amount, $15,000 was paid when the agreement was signed and the balance is payable in 4 annual payments of $15,000 each, beginning January 1, 2003. The agreement provides that the down payment is not refundable and no future services are required of the franchisor. The present value at January 1, 2002, of the 4 annual payments discounted at 14% (the implicit rate for a loan of this type) is $43,700. The agreement also provides that 5% of the revenue from the franchise must be paid to the franchisor annually. Haerhpin's revenue from the franchise for 2002 was $950,000. Haerhpin estimates the useful life of the franchise to be 10 years. (*Hint:* You may refer to Appendix 19A to determine the proper accounting treatment for the franchise fee and payments.)
2. Haerhpin incurred $65,000 of experimental and development costs in its laboratory to develop a patent which was granted on January 2, 2002. Legal fees and other costs associated with registration of the patent totaled $13,600. Haerhpin estimates that the useful life of the patent will be 8 years.
3. A trademark was purchased from Shanghai Company for $32,000 on July 1, 1999. Expenditures for successful litigation in defense of the trademark totaling $8,160 were paid on July 1, 2002. Haerhpin estimates that the useful life of the trademark will be 20 years from the date of acquisition.

Instructions

(a) Prepare a schedule showing the intangible section of Haerhpin's balance sheet at December 31, 2002. Show supporting computations in good form.
(b) Prepare a schedule showing all expenses resulting from the transactions that would appear on Haerhpin's income statement for the year ended December 31, 2002. Show supporting computations in good form.

(AICPA adapted)

P12-4 (Amortization of Various Intangibles) The following information relates to the intangible assets of Rube Goldberg Product Company:

	Goodwill	Purchased Patent Costs
Original cost at 1/1/2001	$280,000	$48,000
Useful life at 1/1/2001 (estimated)	50 years	6 years

Instructions

(a) Assuming straight-line amortization, compute the amount of the amortization of **each** item for 2001 in accordance with generally accepted accounting principles.
(b) Prepare the journal entry for the amortization of goodwill for 2001.
(c) Assume that at January 1, 2002, Rube Goldberg Product Company incurred $6,000 of legal fees in successfully defending the rights to the patents. Prepare the entry for the year 2002 to amortize the patents.
(d) Assume that at the beginning of year 2003 the company decided that the patent costs would be applicable only for the years 2003 and 2004. (A competitor has developed a product that will eventually make Rube Goldberg Product's obsolete.) Record the amortization of the patent costs at the end of 2003.

P12-5 (Accounting for R & D Costs) During 1999, Florence Nightingale Tool Company purchased a building site for its proposed research and development laboratory at a cost of $60,000. Construction of the building was started in 1999. The building was completed on December 31, 2000, at a cost of $280,000 and was placed in service on January 2, 2001. The estimated useful life of the building for depreciation purposes was 20 years; the straight-line method of depreciation was to be employed and there was no estimated net salvage value.

Management estimates that about 50% of the projects of the research and development group will result in long-term benefits (i.e., at least 10 years) to the corporation. The remaining projects either benefit the current period or are abandoned before completion. A summary of the number of projects and the direct costs incurred in conjunction with the research and development activities for 2001 appears below.

Upon recommendation of the research and development group Florence Nightingale Tool Company acquired a patent for manufacturing rights at a cost of $80,000. The patent was acquired on April 1, 2000, and has an economic life of 10 years.

	Number of Projects	Salaries and Employee Benefits	Other Expenses (excluding Building Depreciation Charges)
Completed projects with long-term benefits	15	$ 90,000	$50,000
Abandoned projects or projects that benefit the current period	10	65,000	15,000
Projects in process—results indeterminate	5	40,000	12,000
Total	30	$195,000	$77,000

Instructions

If generally accepted accounting principles were followed, how would the items above relating to research and development activities be reported on the company's

(a) Income statement for 2001?
(b) Balance sheet as of December 31, 2001?

Be sure to give account titles and amounts, and briefly justify your presentation.

(CMA adapted)

***P12-6 (Accounting for Purchase of a Business)** Anshan Inc. has recently become interested in acquiring a South American plant to handle many of its production functions in that market. One possible candidate is La Paz Inc., a closely held corporation, whose owners have decided to sell their business if a proper settlement can be obtained. La Paz's balance sheet appears as follows:

Current assets	$150,000
Investments	50,000
Plant assets (net)	400,000
Total assets	$600,000
Current liabilities	$ 80,000
Long-term debt	100,000
Capital stock	50,000
Additional paid-in capital	170,000
Retained earnings	200,000
Total equities	$600,000

Anshan has hired Palermo Appraisal Corporation to determine the proper price to pay for La Paz Inc. The appraisal firm finds that the investments have a fair market value of $150,000 and that inventory is understated by $80,000. All other assets and equities are properly stated. An examination of the company's income for the last 4 years indicates that the net income has steadily increased. In 2001, the company had a net operating income of $100,000, and this income should increase 20% each year over the next 4 years. Anshan believes that a normal return in this type of business is 18% on net assets. The asset investment in the South American plant is expected to stay the same for the next 4 years.

Instructions

(a) Palermo Appraisal Corporation has indicated that the fair value of the company can be estimated in a number of ways. Prepare an estimate of the value of La Paz Inc., assuming that any goodwill will be computed as:
 (1) The capitalization of the average excess earnings of La Paz Inc. at 18%.
 (2) The purchase of average excess earnings over the next 4 years.
 (3) The capitalization of average excess earnings of La Paz Inc. at 24%.
 (4) The present value of the average excess earnings over the next four years discounted at 15%.

(b) La Paz Inc. is willing to sell the business for $1,000,000. How do you believe Palermo Appraisal should advise Anshan?

(c) If Anshan were to pay $770,000 to purchase the assets and assume the liabilities of La Paz Inc., how would this transaction be reflected on Anshan's books?

P12-7 (Comprehensive Problem on Intangibles) Yuka Sato Corporation was incorporated on January 3, 2000. The corporation's financial statements for its first year's operations were not examined by a CPA. You have been engaged to audit the financial statements for the year ended December 31, 2001, and your audit is substantially completed. The corporation's trial balance appears below.

YUKA SATO CORPORATION
Trial Balance
December 31, 2001

	Debit	Credit
Cash	$ 47,000	
Accounts Receivable	73,000	
Allowance for Doubtful Accounts		$ 1,460
Inventories	50,200	
Machinery	82,000	
Equipment	37,000	
Accumulated Depreciation		26,200
Patents	128,200	
Leasehold Improvements	36,100	
Prepaid Expenses	13,000	
Goodwill	30,000	
Licensing Agreement No. 1	60,000	
Licensing Agreement No. 2	56,000	
Accounts Payable		73,000
Unearned Revenue		17,280
Capital Stock		300,000
Retained Earnings, January 1, 2001		159,060
Sales		720,000
Cost of Goods Sold	475,000	
Selling and General Expenses	180,000	
Interest Expense	9,500	
Extraordinary Losses	20,000	
Totals	$1,297,000	$1,297,000

The following information relates to accounts that may yet require adjustment.

1. Patents for Sato's manufacturing process were acquired January 2, 2001, at a cost of $93,500. An additional $34,700 was spent in December 2001 to improve machinery covered by the patents and charged to the Patents account. Depreciation on fixed assets has been properly recorded for 2001 in accordance with Sato's practice, which provides a full year's depreciation for property on hand June 30 and no depreciation otherwise. Sato uses the straight-line method for all depreciation and amortization and the legal life on its patents.
2. On January 3, 2000, Sato purchased licensing agreement No. 1, which was believed to have an unlimited useful life. The balance in the Licensing Agreement No. 1 account includes its purchase price of $57,000 and expenses of $3,000 related to the acquisition. On January 1, 2001, Sato purchases licensing agreement No. 2, which has a life expectancy of 10 years. The balance in the Licensing Agreement No. 2 account includes its $54,000 purchase price and $6,000 in acquisition expenses, but it has been reduced by a credit of $4,000 for the advance collection of 2002 revenue from the agreement.

   In late December 2000, an explosion caused a permanent 70% reduction in the expected revenue-producing value of licensing agreement No. 1, and in January 2002, a flood caused additional damage that rendered the agreement worthless.
3. The balance in the Goodwill account results from legal expenses of $30,000 incurred for Sato's incorporation on January 3, 2000.
4. The Leasehold Improvements account includes (a) the $15,000 cost of improvements with a total estimated useful life of 12 years, which Sato, as tenant, made to leased premises in January 2000, (b) movable assembly line equipment costing $15,000 that was installed in the leased premises in December 2001, and (c) real estate taxes of $6,100 paid by Sato in 2001, which under the terms of the lease should have been paid by the landlord. Sato paid its rent in full during 2001. A 10-year nonrenewable lease was signed January 3, 2000, for the leased building that Sato used in manufacturing operations.

Instructions

Prepare an 8-column worksheet to adjust accounts that require adjustment and include columns for an income statement and a balance sheet.

A separate account should be used for the accumulation of each type of amortization and for each prior period adjustment. Formal adjusting journal entries and financial statements are **not** required. (*Hint:* Make sure that Licensing Agreement No. 1 is amortized over the maximum life required in *APB Opinion No. 17* before the explosion damage loss is determined.)

(AICPA adapted)

***P12-8 (Compute Goodwill)** Presented below are financial forecasts related to Barbara Bush Company for the next 10 years.

Forecasted average earnings (per year)	$ 70,000
Forecasted market value of net assets, exclusive of goodwill (average over 10 years)	340,000

Instructions

You have been asked to compute goodwill under the following methods. The normal rate of return on net assets for the industry is 15%.

(a) Goodwill is equal to 5 years' excess earnings.
(b) Goodwill is equal to the present value of 5 years' excess earnings discounted at 12%.
(c) Goodwill is equal to the average excess earnings capitalized at 16%.
(d) Goodwill is equal to average excess earnings capitalized at the normal rate of return for the industry of 15%.

***P12-9 (Compute Goodwill)** Batman Corp., a high-flying conglomerate, has recently been involved in discussions with Robin Inc. As its CPA, you have been instructed by Batman to conduct a purchase audit of Robin's books to determine a possible purchase price for Robin's net assets. The following information is found.

Total identifiable assets of Robin's (fair market value)	$250,000
Liabilities	60,000
Average rate of return on net assets for Robin's industry	15%
Forecasted earnings per year based on past earnings figures	35,000

Instructions

(a) Batman asked you to determine the purchase price on the basis of the following assumptions:
(1) Goodwill is equal to 3 years' excess earnings.
(2) Goodwill is equal to the present value of excess earnings discounted at 15% for 3 years.
(3) Goodwill is equal to the capitalization of excess earnings at 15%.
(4) Goodwill is equal to the capitalization of excess earnings at 25%.
(b) Batman asks you which of the methods above is the most theoretically sound. Justify your answer. Any assumptions made should be clearly indicated.

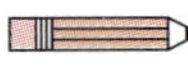

***P12-10 (Computation of Goodwill—Various Methods)** The president of Dane Co., Mrs. Joyce Pollachek, is considering purchasing Balloon Bunch Company. She thinks that the offer sounds pretty good, but she wants to consult a certified public accountant to be sure. Balloon Bunch Company is asking $78,000 over the fair market value of the net identifiable assets. Balloon Bunch's net income figures for the last 5 years are as follows:

1997—$64,000	2000—$80,000
1998—$50,000	2001—$70,000
1999—$81,000	

The tangible net assets of this company were appraised at $400,000 on December 31, 2001.

You have done some initial research on the balloon industry and discovered that the normal rate of return on net tangible assets is 13%. After analyzing variables such as stability of past earnings, the nature of the business, and general economic conditions, you have decided that the average excess earnings for the last 5 years should be capitalized at 25% and that the excess earnings will continue for about 5 more years. Further research led you to discover that the Happy Balloon Company, a competitor of similar size and profitability, was recently sold for six times its average yearly earnings ($90,000) for $540,000.

Instructions

(a) Prepare a schedule that includes the computation of Balloon Bunch Company's goodwill and purchase price under at least three methods.
(b) Write a letter to Mrs. Pollachek that includes:
(1) An explanation of the nature of goodwill.

(2) An explanation of the different acceptable methods of determining its fair value. (Include with your explanation of the different methods the rationale of how each method arrives at a goodwill value.)

(3) Advice for Mrs. Pollachek on how to determine her purchase price.

CONCEPTUAL CASES

C12-1 (Patent Cost) In examining the books of Annita Sorenstam Mfg. Company, you find on the December 31, 2001, balance sheet the item "Costs of patents, $922,000."

Referring to the ledger accounts, you note the following items regarding one patent acquired in 1998:

1998	Legal costs incurred in defending the validity of the patent	$ 55,000
2000	Legal costs in prosecuting an infringement suit	94,000
2001	Legal costs (additional expenses) in the infringement suit	44,500
2001	Cost of improvements (unpatented) on the patented device	151,200

There are no credits in the account, and no allowance for amortization has been set up on the books for any of the patents. Three other patents issued in 1995, 1997, and 1998 were developed by the staff of the client. The patented articles are currently very marketable, but it is estimated that they will be in demand only for the next few years.

Instructions

Discuss the items included in the Patent account from an accounting standpoint.

(AICPA adapted)

C12-2 (Accounting for Intangible-Type Expenditures) Missie McGeorge, Inc., is a large, publicly held corporation. Listed below are six selected expenditures made by the company during the current fiscal year ended April 30, 2001. The proper accounting treatment of these transactions must be determined in order that McGeorge's annual financial statements will be prepared in accordance with generally accepted accounting principles.

1. McGeorge, Inc. spent $3,000,000 on a program designed to improve relations with its dealers. This project was favorably received by the dealers and McGeorge's management believes that significant future benefits should be received from this program. The program was conducted during the fourth quarter of the current fiscal year.
2. A pilot plant was constructed during 2000–01 at a cost of $5,500,000 to test a new production process. The plant will be operated for approximately 5 years. At that time, the company will make a decision regarding the economic value of the process. The pilot plant is too small for commercial production, so it will be dismantled when the test is over.
3. McGeorge, Inc. purchased Eagle Company for $6,000,000 in cash in early August 2000. The fair market value of the identifiable assets of Eagle was $5,200,000.
4. During the first six months of the 2000–01 fiscal year, $400,000 was expended for legal work in connection with a successful patent application. The patent became effective November 1, 2000. The legal life of the patent is 20 years and the economic life of the patent is expected to be approximately 10 years.

Instructions

For each of the four expenditures presented, determine and justify:

(a) The amount, if any, that should be capitalized and be included on McGeorge's statement of financial position prepared as of April 30, 2001.

(b) The amount that should be included in McGeorge's statement of income for the year ended April 30, 2001.

(CMA adapted)

C12-3 (Accounting for Pollution Expenditure) Phil Mickelson Company operates several plants at which limestone is processed into quicklime and hydrated lime. The Eagle Ridge plant, where most of the equipment was installed many years ago, continually deposits a dusty white substance over the surrounding countryside. Citing the unsanitary condition of the neighboring community of Scales Mound, the pollution of the Galena River, and the high incidence of lung disease among workers at Eagle Ridge, the state's Pollution Control Agency has ordered the installation of air pollution control equipment. Also, the Agency has assessed a substantial penalty, which will be used to clean up Scales Mound. After considering the costs involved (which could not have been reasonably estimated prior to the Agency's action), Phil Mickelson Company decides to comply with the Agency's orders, the alternative being to cease operations at Eagle Ridge at the end of the current fiscal year. The officers of Mickelson agree that the air pollution control equipment should be capitalized and depreciated over its useful life, but they disagree over the period(s) to which the penalty should be charged.

Instructions

Discuss the conceptual merits and reporting requirements of accounting for the penalty as a:

(a) Charge to the current period.
(b) Correction of prior periods.
(c) Capitalizable item to be amortized over future periods.

(AICPA adapted)

C12-4 (Accounting for Pre-Opening Costs) After securing lease commitments from several major stores, Lobo Shopping Center, Inc. was organized and built a shopping center in a growing suburb.

The shopping center would have opened on schedule on January 1, 2001, if it had not been struck by a severe tornado in December; it opened for business on October 1, 2001. All of the additional construction costs that were incurred as a result of the tornado were covered by insurance.

In July 2000, in anticipation of the scheduled January opening, a permanent staff had been hired to promote the shopping center, obtain tenants for the uncommitted space, and manage the property.

A summary of some of the costs incurred in 2000 and the first nine months of 2001 follows.

	2000	January 1, 2001 through September 30, 2001
Interest on mortgage bonds	$720,000	$540,000
Cost of obtaining tenants	300,000	360,000
Promotional advertising	540,000	557,000

The promotional advertising campaign was designed to familiarize shoppers with the center. Had it been known in time that the center would not open until October 2001, the 2000 expenditure for promotional advertising would not have been made. The advertising had to be repeated in 2001.

All of the tenants who had leased space in the shipping center at the time of the tornado accepted the October occupancy date on condition that the monthly rental charges for the first 9 months of 2001 be canceled.

Instructions

Explain how each of the costs for 2000 and the first 9 months of 2001 should be treated in the accounts of the shopping center corporation. Give the reasons for each treatment.

(AICPA adapted)

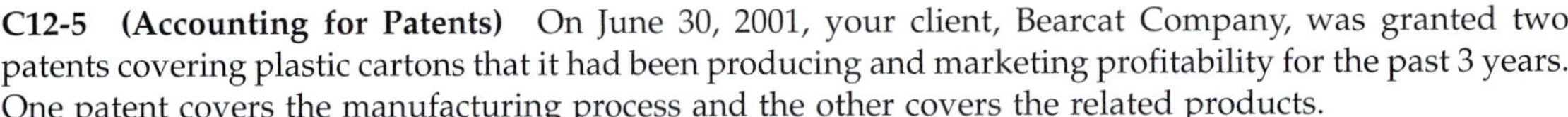

C12-5 (Accounting for Patents) On June 30, 2001, your client, Bearcat Company, was granted two patents covering plastic cartons that it had been producing and marketing profitability for the past 3 years. One patent covers the manufacturing process and the other covers the related products.

Bearcat executives tell you that these patents represent the most significant breakthrough in the industry in the past 30 years. The products have been marketed under the registered trademarks Evertight, Duratainer, and Sealrite. Licenses under the patents have already been granted by your client to other manufacturers in the United States and abroad and are producing substantial royalties.

On July 1, Bearcat commenced patent infringement actions against several companies whose names you recognize as those of substantial and prominent competitors. Bearcat's management is optimistic that these suits will result in a permanent injunction against the manufacture and sale of the infringing products and collection of damages for loss of profits caused by the alleged infringement.

The financial vice-president has suggested that the patents be recorded at the discounted value of expected net royalty receipts.

Instructions

(a) What is the meaning of "discounted value of expected net receipts"? Explain.
(b) How would such a value be calculated for net royalty receipts?
(c) What basis of valuation for Bearcat's patents would be generally accepted in accounting? Give supporting reasons for this basis.
(d) Assuming no practical problems of implementation and ignoring generally accepted accounting principles, what is the preferable basis of valuation for patents? Explain.
(e) What would be the preferable theoretical basis of amortization? Explain.
(f) What recognition, if any, should be made of the infringement litigation in the financial statements for the year ending September 30, 2001? Discuss.

(AICPA adapted)

C12-6 (Accounting for Goodwill) Ecco Co., a retail propane gas distributor, has increased its annual sales volume to a level three times greater than the annual sales of a dealer it purchased in 1998 in order to begin operations.

The board of directors of Ecco Co. recently received an offer to negotiate the sale of Ecco to a large competitor. As a result, the majority of the board wants to increase the stated value of goodwill on the balance sheet to reflect the larger sales volume developed through intensive promotion and the current market price of sales gallonage. A few of the board members, however, would prefer to eliminate goodwill altogether from the balance sheet in order to prevent "possible misinterpretations." Goodwill was recorded properly in 1998.

Instructions

(a) Discuss the meaning of the term "goodwill."

***(b)** List the techniques used to calculate the tentative value of goodwill in negotiations to purchase a going concern.

(c) Why are the book and market values of the goodwill of Ecco Co. different?

(d) Discuss the propriety of

- **(1)** Increasing the stated value of goodwill prior to the negotiations.
- **(2)** Eliminating goodwill completely from the balance sheet prior to negotiations.

(AICPA adapted)

C12-7 (Accounting for Research and Development Costs) Indiana Jones Co. is in the process of developing a revolutionary new product. A new division of the company was formed to develop, manufacture, and market this new product. As of year-end (December 31, 2001) the new product has not been manufactured for resale; however, a prototype unit was built and is in operation.

Throughout 2001 the new division incurred certain costs. These costs include design and engineering studies, prototype manufacturing costs, administrative expenses (including salaries of administrative personnel), and market research costs. In addition, approximately $900,000 in equipment (estimated useful life—10 years) was purchased for use in developing and manufacturing the new product. Approximately $315,000 of this equipment was built specifically for the design development of the new product; the remaining $585,000 of equipment was used to manufacture the pre-production prototype and will be used to manufacture the new product once it is in commercial production.

Instructions

(a) How are "research" and "development" defined in *Statement of Financial Accounting Standards No. 2?*

(b) Briefly indicate the practical and conceptual reasons for the conclusion reached by the Financial Accounting Standards Board on accounting and reporting practices for research and development costs.

(c) In accordance with *Statement of Financial Accounting Standards No. 2,* how should the various costs of Indiana Jones described above be recorded on the financial statements for the year ended December 31, 2001?

(AICPA adapted)

USING YOUR JUDGMENT

FINANCIAL REPORTING PROBLEM: INTEL CORPORATION

Refer to the financial statements and accompanying notes and discussion of Intel Corporation presented in Appendix 5B and answer the following questions:

Instructions

(a) Does Intel report any intangible assets, especially goodwill, in its 1998 financial statements and accompanying notes?

(b) How much research and development (R&D) cost was expensed by Intel in 1998 and 1997? What percentage of sales revenue and net income did Intel spend on R&D in 1998 and 1997? How much does Intel expect to spend on R&D in 1999?

FINANCIAL STATEMENT ANALYSIS CASE

Merck and Johnson & Johnson

Merck & Co., Inc. and Johnson & Johnson are two leading producers of health care products. Each has considerable assets, and each expends considerable funds each year toward the development of new products. The development of a new health care product is often very expensive, and risky. New products frequently must undergo considerable testing before approval for distribution to the public. For example, it took Johnson & Johnson 4 years and $200 million to develop its 1-DAY ACUVUE contact lenses. Below are some basic data compiled from the financial statements of these two companies.

(all dollars in millions)	Johnson & Johnson	Merck
Total assets	$15,668	$21,857
Total revenue	15,734	14,970
Net income	2,006	2,997
Research and development expense	1,278	1,230
Intangible assets	2,403	7,212

Instructions

(a) What kinds of intangible assets might a health care products company have? Does the composition of these intangibles matter to investors—that is, would it be perceived differently if all of Merck's intangibles were goodwill, than if all of its intangibles were patents?

(b) Suppose the president of Merck has come to you for advice. He has noted that by eliminating research and development expenditures the company could have reported $1.3 billion more in net income. He is frustrated because much of the research never results in a product, or the products take years to develop. He says shareholders are eager for higher returns, so he is considering eliminating research and development expenditures for at least a couple of years. What would you advise?

(c) The notes to Merck's financial statements note that Merck has goodwill of $4.1 billion. Where does recorded goodwill come from? Is it necessarily a good thing to have a lot of goodwill on your books?

COMPARATIVE ANALYSIS CASE

The Coca-Cola Company versus PepsiCo, Inc.

Instructions

Go to the Digital Tool and, using The Coca-Cola Company and PepsiCo, Inc. annual report information, answer the following questions.

(a) (1) What amounts for intangible assets were reported in their respective balance sheets by Coca-Cola and PepsiCo?
(2) What percentage of total assets is each of these reported amounts?
(3) What was the change in the amount of intangibles from 1997 to 1998 for Coca-Cola and PepsiCo?

(b) (1) On what basis and over what periods of time did Coca-Cola and PepsiCo amortize their intangible assets?
(2) What were the amounts of accumulated amortization reported by Coca-Cola and PepsiCo at the end of 1998 and 1997?
(3) What was the composition of identifiable and unidentifiable intangible assets reported by Coca-Cola and PepsiCo at the end of 1998?

(c) What caused the significant increase in PepsiCo's intangible assets in 1998?

RESEARCH CASES

Case 1

Instructions

Examine the financial statements and related footnotes for three companies of your choice, and answer the following questions with respect to each company.

(a) Identify any intangible assets included on the balance sheet.

(b) What is the useful life over which the intangibles are being amortized?

(c) Does the company utilize an Accumulated Amortization account?

(d) What were the company's research and development expenses in the most recent two years?

Case 2

The February 19, 1996, issue of *Fortune* includes an article by Thomas A. Stewart entitled "The Coins in the Knowledge Bank."

Instructions

Read the article and answer the following questions.

(a) What is the rationale for estimating the "knowledge bank" and reporting it on the balance sheet?

(b) What is the purpose of income measurement under the proposed approach?

(c) Why should capital spending be treated as an expense?

(d) What items treated as expenses under GAAP should be capitalized on the balance sheet?

(e) While the article admits that the method is subjective, why might it still be appropriate for financial reporting?

INTERNATIONAL REPORTING CASE

Presented below are data and accounting policy notes for the goodwill of three international drug companies. **Bayer**, a German company, prepares its statements in accordance with International Accounting Standards (IAS); **Smithkline Beecham** follows United Kingdom (U.K.) rules; and **Merck**, a U.S. company, prepares its financial statements in accordance with U.S. GAAP.

Related Information for 1998	Bayer (DM millions)	Smithkline Beecham (£ millions)	Merck ($ millions)
Amortization expense	136	69	264
Net income	3,157	606	5,248
Accumulated goodwill amortization	306	313	1,124
Stockholders' equity	24,991	1,747	31,853

The following accounting policy notes related to goodwill appeared with the companies' financial statements.

Bayer

Intangible assets that have been acquired are recognized at cost and amortized over their estimated useful lives. Goodwill, including that resulting from capital consolidation, is capitalized in accordance with *IAS 22* (Business Combinations) and normally is amortized over a period of 5 or at most 20 years.

Smithkline Beecham

Goodwill, representing the excess of the purchase consideration over the fair value of the net separable assets acquired, is capitalised and amortised over an appropriate period not exceeding 20 years. Prior to 1998, all goodwill, except for diversified goodwill, was eliminated in the Group balance sheet against reserves in the year of acquisition.

Merck

Goodwill represents the excess of acquisition costs over the fair value of net assets of businesses purchased and is amortized on a straight-line basis over periods up to 40 years.

Instructions

(a) Compute the return on equity for each of these companies, and use this analysis to briefly discuss the relative profitability of the three companies.

(b) Assume that each of the companies uses the maximum allowable amortization period for goodwill. Discuss how these companies' goodwill amortization policies affect your ability to compare their amortization expense and income.

(c) Some analysts believe that the only valid way to compare companies that follow different goodwill accounting practices is to treat all goodwill as an asset and record expense only if the goodwill is impaired.[1] Using the data above, make these adjustments, and compare the profitability of the three drug companies, comparing this information to your analysis in (a).

ETHICS CASE

Waveland Corporation's research and development department has an idea for a project it believes will culminate in a new product that would be very profitable for the company. Because the project will be very expensive, the department requests approval from Waveland Corporation's controller, Ron Santo.

Santo recognizes that corporate profits have been down lately and is hesitant to approve a project that will incur significant expenses that cannot be capitalized due to the requirement of *FASB Statement No. 2, Accounting for Research and Development Costs.* He knows that if they hire an outside firm that does the work and obtains a patent for the process, Waveland Corporation can purchase the patent from the outside firm and record the expenditure as an asset. Santo knows that the company's own R&D department is first-rate, and he is confident they can do the work well.

Instructions

Answer the following questions:

(a) Who are the stakeholders in this situation?

(b) What are the ethical issues involved?

(c) What should Santo do?

---

[1]Trevor Harris, *Apples to Apples: Accounting for Value in World Markets* (New York: Morgan Stanley Dean Witter, February 1998).

A visit with
Gary Valenzuela

Gary Valenzuela has served as the chief financial officer for Yahoo!, a global Internet media company that offers programming as well as guides to online content. Mr. Valenzuela is a CPA and holds a bachelor's degree in accounting from San Jose State University.

PERSPECTIVES ON

High-Tech Accounting

Since taking the company public in 1996, what has been your role with the company? Managing the tremendous growth, both internal and through acquisitions, has consumed most of my time. That includes growing Yahoo! on a global basis in some two dozen countries. My key roles include negotiating the transaction, setting a price, and looking at the impact on service as well as the bottom line. It has been a great challenge to make an acquisition, project the earnings impact of that acquisition to the financial community, and then actually meet or exceed those expectations. To give you an idea of our growth, in late 1997 we bought a company for $85 million that ultimately became Yahoo! Mail, which is now used by millions of people around the world. By early 1999, we were making billion-dollar acquisitions of companies such as GeoCities and broadcast.com. We own 34% of Yahoo! Japan, which was one of the first international Yahoo!s that we launched. Yahoo! Japan went public in November of 1997 and currently has a market capitalization of more than $22 billion.

Are you a typical Internet company that's growing revenues but bleeding red ink? No. Throughout this growth period, we've generally been profitable. Unlike some Internet companies, there has been a very strong, consistent record of profitability that has been built into the culture of our company. Many Internet companies have never been measured on the basis of being profitable as an enterprise. Shifting that mentality could be a big challenge for them.

As a company that uses stock to make acquisitions, how will the phase-out of pooling accounting affect you? Our view is that there is no sense fighting the SEC and international accounting standards organizations on this because it is going to go away. But we'll still do acquisitions. What we've been doing is focusing our investors on understanding cash flow and how purchase accounting generates non-cash amortization. If you look at our quarterly results, you'll see a P&L that includes all of the amortization according to GAAP. You'll also see a P&L that does not include non-cash charges. It's good to understand the impact of amortization, but it's also good to understand the impact of true cash earnings. Educating Wall Street and looking at the P&L from that point of view means you can do purchase transactions and incur amortization, but it's not cash and it's truly not thought of as having a real operating effect. There may actually be a positive that comes out of this accounting rule change because it frees companies to be more creative in the way they structure acquisitions. With purchase accounting, you can be very flexible. You can include performance payouts, which means the buyer pays more money later on if the company outperforms expectations. You can't do that with pooling accounting.

What's it like to work in Silicon Valley these days? It's exhilarating, exciting, and exhausting. It's beyond what you could have thought possible. And it's a powerful feeling, this notion that we are leaders in a new industry. We've tried to make Yahoo! very easy to use in order to reach the broadest possible audience without bogging it down with a lot of advertising.

How did you get started in accounting and finance? During my sophomore year in college, I had a part-time professor at San Jose State who was a controller at a local technology company. He mentioned that he might be hiring somebody. For about six months, I just hounded him for the position. Finally, he hired me, and I spent two years working in all types of accounting jobs. In the job market immediately after college, I had an advantage because I had real-world accounting experience.

After graduating from college in 1980, I spent two years with KPMG Peat Marwick, becoming a computer auditing specialist and receiving my CPA certificate. In 1982 I joined the internal audit staff at Syntex, a large pharmaceutical company. The job was appealing to me because of the computer audit emphasis and because it involved doing operational audits throughout the Syntex worldwide network, which required quite a bit of international travel. Then I was recruited—and this is a milestone event in my career—by Wyse Technology in 1984, joining them six months before they went public. That was an absolute rocketship. When I joined the company, its sales were about $17 million per year. Within three years, revenues reached $250 million.

At what point did you begin to move from accounting to finance? When I joined minicomputer-maker Pyramid Technology as corporate controller in the mid-1980s, my supervisor gave me a lot of flexibility to do a lot of different things. As a result, I became involved in tax, the treasury function, some business development activities, international operations, and a major systems project. I was able to work directly with the CEO and the entire management team, where I established a reputation as a person who would get something done. After being with the company about two and a half years, I became CFO after my mentor, the former CFO, left the company. A few years later, I joined a start-up Internet software company that was poised to go public. Nine months later, I negotiated the sale of that company to Cisco Systems. I started working at Yahoo! on February 1, 1996, where I immediately began preparations to take the company public.

What was your role in Yahoo!'s initial public offering? The role of a CFO in a well-executed IPO is to be the quarterback of the IPO process. The first step is forming your IPO team. Selecting investment bankers is a very key step. You go public only once, and those bankers will forever be associated with your name. We selected Goldman Sachs, Montgomery Securities, and Donaldson, Lufkin & Jenrette. Forming the IPO team also includes lawyers and accountants. Next, you put together a prospectus for potential investors, which is filed with the SEC. Then there's a waiting period, during which time you work on your "road show." We traveled to 15 cities in 11 days and made presentations to more than 400 investors.

We went public on April 12, 1996. The initial filing range was $10 to $12 per share. The stock opened at $24 and went to $43 on the first day, closing at $33. For the first six months of 1996, we reported revenues of about $5 million, but a net loss, which was expected. In comparison, we reported $16 million in net income on revenues of $388 million for the first nine months of 1999. In late 1999, the stock reached $400 per share—after splitting three times.

What advice do you have for college students? I would advise students to seize opportunities and not be scared off by risk. There have been some major challenges in my career. When I stepped into the role of CFO of Pyramid Technology, the company had just had one restructuring, was still losing money, and six months later I had to go back to the CEO and tell him that the restructuring was inadequate and that we had to take another $30 million restructuring charge. That was a definite career risk.

As this book went to press, Yahoo! announced Mr. Valenzuela's decision to retire from the company in July 2000, praising his "excellent job of developing and maintaining strong, credible relationships with Wall Street, financial analysts and Yahoo! shareholders alike. [He] provided the financial leadership that contributed to the company's strong record of operating performance. . . ."

CHAPTER 13

Current Liabilities and Contingencies

Microsoft's Liabilities—Good or Bad?

Users of financial statements generally examine current liabilities to assess a company's liquidity and overall financial flexibility. This is because many current liabilities such as accounts payable, wages payable, and taxes payable must be paid sooner rather than later. Thus, when these liabilities increase substantially, it raises a red flag about a company's financial position.

This is not always the case for all current liabilities. For example, Microsoft has a current liability entitled "Unearned Revenue" that has increased substantially year after year. Unearned revenue is a liability that arises from sales of Microsoft products such as *Windows* and *Office.* At the time of a sale, customers pay not only for the current version of the software but also for future improvements to the software. In this case, Microsoft recognizes sales revenue from the current version of the software and records as a liability (unearned revenue) the value of future upgrades to the software that are "owed" to customers.

Market analysts indicate that such an increase in unearned revenue, rather than raising a red flag, often provides a positive signal about sales and profitability. How can information from a liability account provide information about profitability? It works this way: When Microsoft sales are growing, its unearned revenue account increases. Thus, an *increase* in a liability is good news about Microsoft sales.

What happens if the unearned revenue liability declines? After steady increases in recent years, Microsoft's unearned revenue declined from the second to the third quarter of 1999. In response to this decline in unearned revenue, a number of mutual funds sold part of their Microsoft holdings. Many believed that a decline in Microsoft's unearned revenue is bad news for investors. As one analyst noted, when the growth in unearned revenues slows or reverses, as it did for Microsoft, it indicates that sales are slowing. Thus, increases in current liabilities can sometimes be viewed as good signs instead of bad.[1]

LEARNING OBJECTIVES

After studying this chapter, you should be able to:

1. **Define current liabilities and describe how they are valued.**
2. **Identify the nature and types of current liabilities.**
3. **Explain the classification issues of short-term debt expected to be refinanced.**
4. **Identify types of employee-related liabilities.**
5. **Identify the criteria used to account for and disclose gain and loss contingencies.**
6. **Explain the accounting for different types of loss contingencies.**
7. **Indicate how current liabilities and contingencies are presented and analyzed.**

[1]Based on David Bank, "Some Fans Cool to Microsoft, Citing Drop in Old Indicator," *The Wall Street Journal,* October 28, 1999.

PREVIEW OF CHAPTER 13

As the opening story indicates, careful analysis of current liabilities can provide insights about a company's liquidity and profitability. The purpose of this chapter is to explain the basic principles regarding accounting and reporting for current and contingent liabilities. Chapter 14 addresses issues related to long-term liabilities. The content and organization of this chapter are as follows:

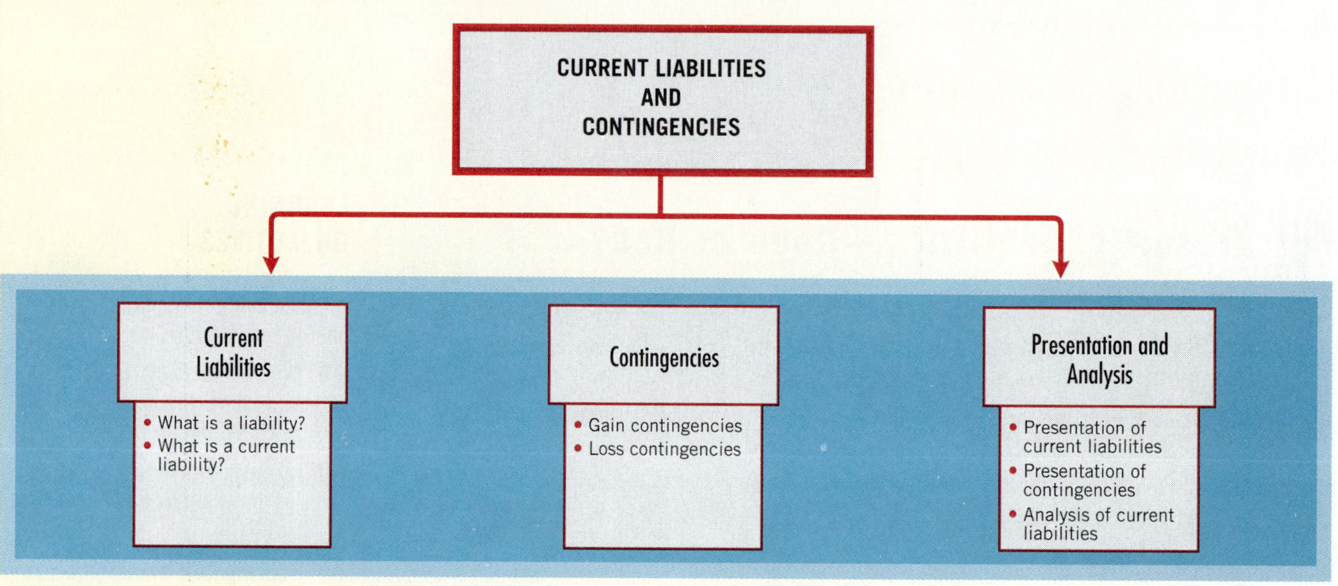

SECTION 1 CURRENT LIABILITIES

WHAT IS A LIABILITY?

The question, "What is a liability?" is not easy to answer. For example, one might ask whether preferred stock is a liability or an ownership claim. The first reaction is to say that preferred stock is in fact an ownership claim and should be reported as part of stockholders' equity. In fact, preferred stock has many elements of debt as well.[2] The issuer (and in some cases the holder) often has the right to call the stock within a specific period of time—making it similar to a repayment of principal. The dividend is in many cases almost guaranteed (cumulative provision)—making it look like interest. And preferred stock is but one of many financial instruments that are difficult to classify.[3]

[2]This illustration is not just a theoretical exercise. In practice, there are a number of preferred stock issues that have all the characteristics of a debt instrument, except that they are called and legally classified preferred stock. In some cases, the IRS has even permitted the dividend payments to be treated as interest expense for tax purposes. This issue is discussed further in Chapter 15.

[3]The FASB has issued a discussion memorandum addressing these issues: "Distinguishing between Liability and Equity Instruments and Accounting for Instruments with Characteristics of Both," Discussion Memorandum (Norwalk, Conn.: FASB, 1990). It is expected to issue an exposure draft during 2000 for a new standard on distinguishing between debt and equity.

To help resolve some of these controversies, the FASB, as part of its conceptual framework study, defined liabilities as **"probable future sacrifices of economic benefits arising from present obligations of a particular entity to transfer assets or provide services to other entities in the future as a result of past transactions or events."**[4] In other words, a liability has three essential characteristics:

1. It is a present obligation that entails settlement by probable future transfer or use of cash, goods, or services.
2. It is an unavoidable obligation.
3. The transaction or other event creating the obligation has already occurred.

Because liabilities involve future disbursements of assets or services, one of their most important features is the date on which they are payable. Currently maturing obligations must be satisfied promptly and in the ordinary course of business if operations are to be continued. Liabilities with a more distant due date do not, as a rule, represent a claim on the enterprise's current resources and are therefore in a slightly different category. This feature gives rise to the basic division of liabilities into (1) current liabilities and (2) long-term debt.

UNDERLYING CONCEPTS

To determine the appropriate classification of specific financial instruments, proper definitions of assets, liabilities, and equities are needed. The conceptual framework definitions are often used as the basis for resolving controversial classification issues.

WHAT IS A CURRENT LIABILITY?

OBJECTIVE 1
Define current liabilities and describe how they are valued.

Current assets are cash or other assets that can reasonably be expected to be converted into cash, sold, or consumed in operations within a single operating cycle or within a year if more than one cycle is completed each year. Current liabilities are **"obligations whose liquidation is reasonably expected to require use of existing resources properly classified as current assets, or the creation of other current liabilities."**[5] This definition has gained wide acceptance because it recognizes operating cycles of varying lengths in different industries and takes into consideration the important relationship between current assets and current liabilities.[6]

In France, the balance sheet does not show current liabilities in a separate category. Rather, debts are disclosed separately by maturity in the notes.

The operating cycle is the period of time elapsing between the acquisition of goods and services involved in the manufacturing process and the final cash realization resulting from sales and subsequent collections. Industries that manufacture products requiring an aging process and certain capital-intensive industries have an operating cycle of considerably more than one year. On the other hand, most retail and service establishments have several operating cycles within a year.

There are many different types of current liabilities. The following ones are covered in this chapter in this order.

OBJECTIVE 2
Identify the nature and types of current liabilities.

1. Accounts payable.
2. Notes payable.
3. Current maturities of long-term debt.
4. Short-term obligations expected to be refinanced.
5. Dividends payable.
6. Returnable deposits.
7. Unearned revenues.
8. Sales taxes payable.
9. Property taxes payable.
10. Income taxes payable.
11. Employee-related liabilities.

---

[4]"Elements of Financial Statements of Business Enterprises," *Statement of Financial Accounting Concepts No. 6* (Stamford, Conn.: FASB, 1980).

[5]Committee on Accounting Procedure, American Institute of Certified Public Accountants, "Accounting Research and Terminology Bulletins," Final Edition (New York: AICPA, 1961), p. 21.

[6]The FASB affirmed this concept of "maturity within one year or the operating cycle whichever is longer" in its definition of short-term obligations in *Statement No. 6*. "Classification of Short-term Obligations Expected to Be Refinanced," *Statement of Financial Accounting Standards No. 6* (Stamford, Conn.: FASB, 1975), par. 2.

Accounts Payable

Accounts payable, or **trade accounts payable**, are balances owed to others for goods, supplies, or services purchased on open account. Accounts payable arise because of the time lag between the receipt of services or acquisition of title to assets and the payment for them. This period of extended credit is usually found in the terms of the sale (e.g., 2/10, n/30 or 1/10, E.O.M.) and is commonly 30 to 60 days.

Most accounting systems are designed to record liabilities for purchases of goods when the goods are received or, practically, when the invoices are received. Frequently there is some delay in recording the goods and the related liability on the books. If title has passed to the purchaser before the goods are received, the transaction should be recorded at the time of title passage. Attention must be paid to transactions occurring near the end of one accounting period and at the beginning of the next to ascertain that the record of goods received (the inventory) is in agreement with the liability (accounts payable) and that both are recorded in the proper period.

Measuring the amount of an account payable poses no particular difficulty because the invoice received from the creditor specifies the due date and the exact outlay in money that is necessary to settle the account. The only calculation that may be necessary concerns the amount of cash discount. See Chapter 8 for illustrations of entries related to accounts payable and purchase discounts.

Notes Payable

Notes payable are written promises to pay a certain sum of money on a specified future date and may arise from purchases, financing, or other transactions. In some industries, notes (often referred to as **trade notes payable**) are required as part of the sales/purchases transaction in lieu of the normal extension of open account credit. Notes payable to banks or loan companies generally arise from cash loans. Notes may be classified as short-term or long-term, depending upon the payment due date. Notes may also be interest-bearing or zero-interest-bearing.

Interest-Bearing Note Issued

Assume that the Castle National Bank agrees to lend $100,000 on March 1, 2001, to Landscape Co. if Landscape Co. signs a $100,000, 12%, 4-month note. The entry to record the cash received by Landscape Co. on March 1 is:

March 1		
Cash	100,000	
Notes Payable		100,000
(To record issuance of 12%, 4-month note to Castle National Bank)		

If Landscape Co. prepares financial statements semiannually, an adjusting entry is required to recognize interest expense and interest payable of $4,000 ($100,000 × 12% × 4/12) at June 30. The adjusting entry is:

June 30		
Interest Expense	4,000	
Interest Payable		4,000
(To accrue interest for 4 months on Castle National Bank note)		

If Landscape prepared financial statements monthly, the adjusting entry at the end of each month would have been $1,000 ($100,000 × 12% × 1/12).

At maturity (July 1), Landscape Co. must pay the face value of the note ($100,000) plus $4,000 interest ($100,000 × 12% × 4/12).

The entry to record payment of the note and accrued interest is as follows:

July 1		
Notes Payable	100,000	
Interest Payable	4,000	
Cash		104,000
(To record payment of Castle National Bank interest-bearing note and accrued interest at maturity)		

Zero-Interest-Bearing Note Issued

A zero-interest-bearing note may be issued instead of an interest-bearing note. A zero-interest-bearing note does not explicitly state an interest rate on the face of the note. Interest is still charged, however, because the borrower is required at maturity to pay back an amount greater than the cash received at the issuance date. In other words, the borrower receives in cash the present value of the note. The present value equals the face value of the note at maturity minus the interest or discount charged by the lender for the term of the note. In essence, the bank takes its fee "up front" rather than on the date the note matures.

To illustrate, we will assume that Landscape Co. issues a $104,000, 4-month, zero-interest-bearing note to the Castle National Bank. The present value of the note is $100,000.[7] The entry to record this transaction for Landscape Co. is as follows:

March 1		
Cash	100,000	
Discount on Notes Payable	4,000	
Notes Payable		104,000
(To record issuance of 4-month, zero-interest-bearing note to Castle National Bank)		

The Notes Payable account is credited for the face value of the note, which is $4,000 more than the actual cash received. The difference between the cash received and the face value of the note is debited to Discount on Notes Payable. **Discount on Notes Payable is a contra account to Notes Payable and therefore is subtracted from Notes Payable on the balance sheet.** The balance sheet presentation on March 1 is as follows:

Current liabilities		
Notes payable	104,000	
Less: Discount on notes payable	4,000	100,000

ILLUSTRATION 13-1
Balance Sheet Presentation of Discount

The amount of the discount, $4,000 in this case, represents the cost of borrowing $100,000 for 4 months. Accordingly, the discount is charged to interest expense over the life of the note. That is, the Discount on Notes Payable balance **represents interest expense chargeable to future periods**. Thus, it would be incorrect to debit Interest Expense for $4,000 at the time the loan is obtained. Additional accounting issues related to notes payable are discussed in Chapter 14.

Current Maturities of Long-Term Debt

The portion of bonds, mortgage notes, and other long-term indebtedness that matures within the next fiscal year—**current maturities of long-term debt**—is reported as a current liability. When only a part of a long-term debt is to be paid within the next 12 months, as in the case of serial bonds that are to be retired through a series of annual installments, **the maturing portion of long-term debt is reported as a current liability**, the balance as a long-term debt.

[7]The bank discount rate used in this example to find the present value is 11.538%.

Long-term debts maturing currently should not be included as current liabilities if they are to be:

1. retired by assets accumulated for this purpose that properly have not been shown as current assets,
2. refinanced, or retired from the proceeds of a new debt issue (see next topic), or
3. converted into capital stock.

In these situations, the use of current assets or the creation of other current liabilities does not occur. Therefore, classification as a current liability is inappropriate. The plan for liquidation of such a debt should be disclosed either parenthetically or by a note to the financial statements.

However, a liability that is **due on demand** (callable by the creditor) or will be due on demand within a year (or operating cycle, if longer) should be classified as a current liability. Liabilities often become callable by the creditor when there is a violation of the debt agreement. For example, most debt agreements specify a given level of equity to debt be maintained, or specify that working capital be of a minimum amount. If an agreement is violated, classification of the debt as current is required because it is a reasonable expectation that existing working capital will be used to satisfy the debt. Only if it can be shown that it is **probable** that the violation will be cured (satisfied) within the grace period usually given in these agreements can the debt be classified as noncurrent.[8]

Short-Term Obligations Expected to Be Refinanced

OBJECTIVE 3
Explain the classification issues of short-term debt expected to be refinanced.

Short-term obligations are those debts that are scheduled to mature within one year after the date of an enterprise's balance sheet or within an enterprise's operating cycle, whichever is longer. Some **short-term obligations** are **expected to be refinanced** on a long-term basis and, therefore, are not expected to require the use of working capital during the next year (or operating cycle).[9]

At one time, the accounting profession generally supported the exclusion of short-term obligations from current liabilities if they were "expected to be refinanced." Because the profession provided no specific guidelines, however, determining whether a short-term obligation was "expected to be refinanced" was usually based solely on management's **intent** to refinance on a long-term basis. A company may obtain a 5-year bank loan but, because the bank prefers it, handle the actual financing with 90-day notes, which it must keep turning over (renewing). So what is the loan—a long-term debt or a current liability? Another example of this problem of classification was the **Penn Central Railroad** before it went bankrupt. The railroad was deep into short-term debt and commercial paper but classified it as long-term debt. Why? Because the railroad believed it had commitments from lenders to keep refinancing the short-term debt. When those commitments suddenly disappeared, it was good-bye Pennsy. As the Greek philosopher Epictetus once said, "Some things in this world are not and yet appear to be."

Refinancing Criteria

As a result of these classification problems, the profession set forth authoritative criteria for determining the circumstances under which short-term obligations may properly be excluded from current liabilities. An enterprise is required to exclude a short-term obligation from current liabilities only if **both** of the following conditions are met:

---

[8]"Classification of Obligations That Are Callable by the Creditor," *Statement of Financial Accounting Standards No. 78* (Stamford, Conn.: FASB, 1983).

[9]*Refinancing a short-term obligation on a long-term basis* means either replacing it with a long-term obligation or with equity securities, or renewing, extending, or replacing it with short-term obligations for an uninterrupted period extending beyond one year (or the operating cycle, if longer) from the date of the enterprise's balance sheet.

1. It must **intend to refinance** the obligation on a long-term basis, and
2. It must **demonstrate an ability** to consummate the refinancing.[10]

Intention to refinance on a long-term basis means the enterprise intends to refinance the short-term obligation so that the use of working capital will not be required during the ensuing fiscal year or operating cycle, if longer. The **ability** to consummate the refinancing may be demonstrated by:

(a) **Actually refinancing** the short-term obligation by issuing a long-term obligation or equity securities after the date of the balance sheet but before it is issued; or

(b) Entering into a **financing agreement** that clearly permits the enterprise to refinance the debt on a long-term basis on terms that are readily determinable.

If an actual refinancing occurs, the portion of the short-term obligation to be excluded from current liabilities may not exceed the proceeds from the new obligation or equity securities that are applied to retire the short-term obligation. For example, **Montavon Winery** with $3,000,000 of short-term debt issued 100,000 shares of common stock subsequent to the balance sheet date but before the balance sheet was issued, intending to use the proceeds to liquidate the short-term debt at its maturity. If the net proceeds from the sale of the 100,000 shares totaled $2,000,000, only that amount of the short-term debt could be excluded from current liabilities.

An additional question relates to whether a short-term obligation should be excluded from current liabilities if it is paid off after the balance sheet date and subsequently replaced by long-term debt before the balance sheet is issued. To illustrate, Marquardt Company pays off short-term debt of $40,000 on January 17, 2002 and issues long-term debt of $100,000 on February 3, 2002. Marquardt's financial statements dated December 31, 2001, are to be issued March 1, 2002. Because repayment of the short-term obligation **before** funds were obtained through long-term financing required the use of **existing** current assets, the profession requires that the short-term obligation be included in current liabilities at the balance sheet date (see graphical presentation below).

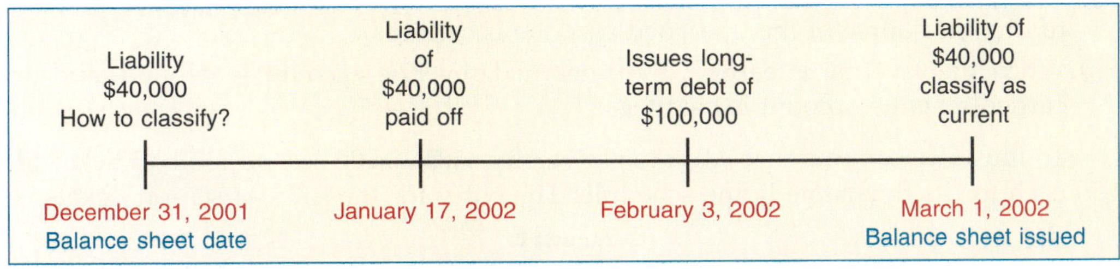

ILLUSTRATION 13-2
Short-Term Debt Paid Off after Balance Sheet Date and Later Replaced by Long-Term Debt

Dividends Payable

A **cash dividend payable** is an amount owed by a corporation to its stockholders as a result of board of directors' authorization. At the date of declaration the corporation assumes a liability that places the stockholders in the position of creditors in the amount of dividends declared. Because cash dividends are always paid within one year of declaration (generally within 3 months), they are classified as current liabilities.

Accumulated but undeclared dividends on cumulative preferred stock are not a recognized liability because **preferred dividends in arrears** are not an obligation until formal action is taken by the board of directors authorizing the distribution of earnings. Nevertheless, the amount of cumulative dividends unpaid should be disclosed in a note or it may be shown parenthetically in the capital stock section.

UNDERLYING CONCEPTS

Preferred dividends in arrears do represent a probable future economic sacrifice, but the expected sacrifice does not result from a past transaction or past event. The sacrifice will result from a future event (declaration by the board of directors). Note disclosure improves the predictive value of the financial statements.

[10] "Classification of Short-term Obligations Expected to Be Refinanced," *Statement of Financial Accounting Standards No. 6* (Stamford, Conn.: FASB, 1975), pars. 10 and 11.

Dividends payable in the form of additional shares of stock are not recognized as a liability. Such **stock dividends** (as discussed in Chapter 16) do not require future outlays of assets or services and are revocable by the board of directors at any time prior to issuance. Even so, such undistributed stock dividends are generally reported in the stockholders' equity section because they represent retained earnings in the process of transfer to paid-in capital.

Returnable Deposits

Current liabilities of a company may include **returnable cash deposits** received from customers and employees. Deposits may be received from customers to guarantee performance of a contract or service or as guarantees to cover payment of expected future obligations. For example, telephone companies often require a deposit upon installation of a phone. Deposits may also be received from customers as guarantees for possible damage to property left with the customer. Some companies require their employees to make deposits for the return of keys or other company property. The classification of these items as current or noncurrent liabilities is dependent on the time between the date of the deposit and the termination of the relationship that required the deposit.

Unearned Revenues

A magazine publisher such as **Golf Digest** may receive a customer's check when magazines are ordered, and an airline company, such as **American Airlines,** often sells tickets for future flights. Restaurants may issue meal tickets that can be exchanged or used for future meals. Who hasn't received or given a **McDonald's** gift certificate? And as discussed in the opening story, a company like **Microsoft** issues coupons that allow customers to upgrade to the next version of its software. How do these companies account for **unearned revenues** that are received before goods are delivered or services are rendered?

1. When the advance is received, Cash is debited, and a current liability account identifying the source of the unearned revenue is credited.
2. When the revenue is earned, the unearned revenue account is debited, and an earned revenue account is credited.

To illustrate, assume that Allstate University sells 10,000 season football tickets at $50 each for its five-game home schedule. The entry for the sales of season tickets is:

August 6		
Cash	500,000	
Unearned Football Ticket Revenue		500,000
(To record sale of 10,000 season tickets)		

As each game is completed, the following entry is made:

September 7		
Unearned Football Ticket Revenue	100,000	
Football Ticket Revenue		100,000
(To record football ticket revenues earned)		

Unearned Football Ticket Revenue is, therefore, unearned revenue and is reported as a current liability in the balance sheet. As revenue is earned, a transfer from unearned revenue to earned revenue occurs. Unearned revenue is material for some companies: In the airline industry, tickets sold for future flights represent almost 50% of total current liabilities. At **United Air Lines**, unearned ticket revenue is the largest current liability, recently amounting to over $1,429 million.

Illustration 13-3 shows specific unearned and earned revenue accounts used in selected types of businesses.

ILLUSTRATION 13-3
Unearned and Earned Revenue Accounts

Type of Business	Account Title	
	Unearned Revenue	Earned Revenue
Airline	Unearned Passenger Ticket Revenue	Passenger Revenue
Magazine publisher	Unearned Subscription Revenue	Subscription Revenue
Hotel	Unearned Rental Revenue	Rental Revenue
Auto dealer	Unearned Warranty Revenue	Warranty Revenue

The balance sheet should report obligations for any commitments that are redeemable in goods and services; the income statement should report revenues earned during the period.

Sales Taxes Payable

Sales taxes on transfers of tangible personal property and on certain services must be collected from customers and remitted to the proper governmental authority. A liability is set up to provide for taxes collected from customers but not yet remitted to the tax authority. The Sales Taxes Payable account should reflect the liability for sales taxes due various governments. The entry below is the proper one for a sale of $3,000 when a 4% sales tax is in effect.

Cash or Accounts Receivable	3,120	
Sales		3,000
Sales Taxes Payable		120

When the sales tax collections credited to the liability account are not equal to the liability as computed by the governmental formula, an adjustment of the liability account may be made by recognizing a gain or a loss on sales tax collections.

In many companies, however, the sales tax and the amount of the sale are not segregated at the time of sale; both are credited in total in the Sales account. In that case, to reflect correctly the actual amount of sales and the liability for sales taxes, the Sales account must be debited for the amount of the sales taxes due the government on these sales and the Sales Taxes Payable account credited for the same amount. As an illustration, assume that the Sales account balance of $150,000 includes sales taxes of 4%. Because the amount recorded in the Sales account is equal to sales plus 4% of sales, or 1.04 times the sales total, sales are $150,000 ÷ 1.04, or $144,230.77. The sales tax liability is $5,769.23 ($144,230.77 × 0.04; or $150,000 − $144,230.77), and the following entry would be made to record the amount due the taxing unit:

Sales	5,769.23	
Sales Taxes Payable		5,769.23

Property Taxes Payable

Local governmental units generally depend on property taxes as their primary source of revenue. Such taxes are based on the assessed value of both real and personal property and become a lien against the property at a date determined by law. This lien is a liability of the property owner and is a cost of the services of such property. The accounting questions that arise from property taxes are:

1. When should property owners record the liability?
2. To which accounting period should the cost be charged?

The accounting profession, in considering the various periods to which property taxes might be charged and how the liability should be reported, contends that generally, the most acceptable basis of providing for property taxes is monthly accrual on the taxpayer's books during the fiscal period of the taxing authority for which the taxes are paid. This method charges the taxes to the period subsequent to the lien date and **relates the expense to the period in which the taxes are used by the governmental unit to provide benefits to the property owner.**[11]

Assume that Seaboard Company, which closes its books each year on December 31, receives its property tax bill in May each year. The fiscal year for the city and county in which Seaboard Company is located begins on May 1 and ends on the following April 30. Property taxes of $36,000 are assessed against Seaboard Company property on January 1, 2001, and become a lien on May 1, 2001. Tax bills are sent out in May and are payable in equal installments on July 1 and September 1.

Entries to record the liability, monthly tax charges, and the tax payments for taxes becoming a lien on May 1, 2001 are shown below.

1. Entry, if any, on May 1, 2001 (lien date):

No entry

2. Monthly expense accrual for May 31 and June 30, 2001:

Property Tax Expense	3,000	
Property Taxes Payable		3,000

3. First tax payment on July 1, 2001:

Property Taxes Payable	6,000	
Prepaid Property Taxes	12,000	
Cash		18,000

4. Monthly expense accrual for July 31 and August 31, 2001:

Property Tax Expense	3,000	
Prepaid Property Taxes		3,000

5. Second tax payment on September 1, 2001:

Prepaid Property Taxes	18,000	
Cash		18,000

6. Monthly expense accrual for Sept. 30, 2001, through April 30, 2002:

Property Tax Expense	3,000	
Prepaid Property Taxes		3,000

Prepaid Property Taxes of $12,000 on July 1 represents a 4-month prepayment and $18,000 on September 1 represents a 6-month prepayment. At December 31, the account has 4 months of unexpired tax.[12]

Some advocate accruing property taxes by charges to expense during the fiscal year **ending on the lien date**, rather than during the fiscal year beginning on the lien date (the fiscal year of the tax authority). In such instances the property tax for the coming fiscal year must be estimated and charged monthly to Property Tax Expense and must be credited to Property Tax Payable. Under this method the entire amount of the tax

---

[11]Possible alternatives are: (a) year in which paid, (b) year ending on assessment (or lien) date, (c) year beginning on assessment (or lien) date, (d) calendar or fiscal year of taxpayer prior to assessment (or lien) date, (e) calendar or fiscal year of taxpayer including assessment (or lien) date, (f) calendar or fiscal year of taxpayer prior to payment date, (g) fiscal year of governing body levying the tax, and (h) year appearing on tax bill. Committee on Accounting Procedure, American Institute of Certified Public Accountants, *Accounting Research and Terminology Bulletin, Final Edition* (New York: AICPA, 1961), ch. 10, sec. A, par. 10.

[12]Some argue that the entire liability of $36,000 should be recorded on the lien date with a related debit to a Deferred Charge account. These individuals contend that the company has a legal liability at that date and therefore the full amount of the liability should be reported. We disagree. To report the full liability at the lien date necessitates the recording of a Deferred Property Tax Asset for unpaid property taxes—a dubious asset. In addition, the liability accrues as the property is used. If the property is sold, the buyer has the responsibility for the property taxes subsequent to purchase—not the seller.

is accrued by the lien date and the expense is therefore charged to the fiscal period preceding payment of the tax. Justification for this method exists when the assessment date precedes the lien date by a year or more, as is the case in some taxing units. In such instances, the amount is estimated and accrued by the property owner before receipt of the tax bill.

Recognizing that special circumstances can suggest the use of alternative accrual periods, the profession supports the view that **"consistency of application from year to year is the important consideration and selection of any of the periods mentioned is a matter for individual judgment."**[13]

Income Taxes Payable

Any federal or state income tax varies in proportion to the amount of annual income. Some consider the amount of income tax on annual income as an estimate because the computation of income (and the tax thereon) is subject to IRS review and approval. The meaning and application of numerous tax rules, especially new ones, are debatable and often dependent on a court's interpretation. Using the best information and advice available, a business must prepare an income tax return and compute the income tax payable resulting from the operations of the current period. The taxes payable on the income of a corporation, as computed per the tax return, should be classified as a current liability.[14]

Unlike the corporation, the proprietorship and the partnership are not taxable entities. Because the individual proprietor and the members of a partnership are subject to personal income taxes on their share of the business's taxable income, income tax liabilities do not appear on the financial statements of proprietorships and partnerships.

Most corporations must make periodic tax payments in an authorized bank depository or a Federal Reserve bank throughout the year. These payments are based upon estimates of the total annual tax liability. As the estimated total tax liability changes, the periodic contributions also change. If in a later year an additional tax is assessed on the income of an earlier year, Income Taxes Payable should be credited. The related debit should be charged to current operations.

Differences between taxable income under the tax laws and accounting income under generally accepted accounting principles sometimes occur. Because of these differences, the amount of income tax payable to the government in any given year may differ substantially from income tax expense, as reported on the financial statements. Chapter 20 is devoted solely to income tax matters and presents an extensive discussion of this complex and controversial problem.

Employee-Related Liabilities

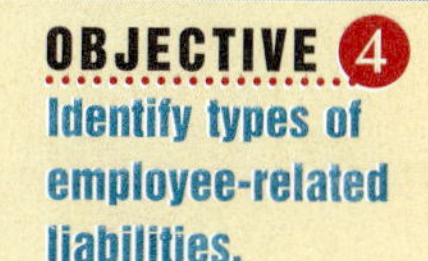
OBJECTIVE 4
Identify types of employee-related liabilities.

Amounts owed to employees for salaries or wages at the end of an accounting period are reported as a current liability. In addition, the following items related to employee compensation are often reported as current liabilities:

1. Payroll deductions.
2. Compensated absences.
3. Bonuses. (Accounting for bonuses is covered in Appendix 13A.)

Payroll Deductions

The most common types of payroll deductions are taxes and miscellaneous items such as insurance premiums, employee savings, and union dues. **To the extent the amounts**

[13] *Accounting Research and Terminology Bulletin,* Final Edition, par. 3.

[14] Corporate taxes are based on a progressive tax rate structure. Companies with taxable income of $50,000 or less are taxed at a 15% rate, while higher levels of income are taxed at rates ranging up to 39%.

deducted have not been remitted to the proper authority at the end of the accounting period, they should be recognized as current liabilities.

Social Security Taxes. Since January 1, 1937, Social Security legislation has provided federal old-age, survivor, and disability insurance (O.A.S.D.I.) benefits for certain individuals and their families through taxes levied on both the employer and the employee. All employers covered are required to collect the employee's share of this tax, by deducting it from the employee's gross pay, and to remit it to the government along with the employer's share. Both the employer and the employee are taxed at the same rate, currently 6.2% based on the employee's gross pay up to a $76,200 annual limit.

In 1965 Congress passed the first federal health insurance program for the aged—popularly known as Medicare. It is a two-part program designed to alleviate the high cost of medical care for those over age 65. The Basic Plan, which provides hospital and other institutional services, is financed by a separate Hospital Insurance tax paid by both the employee and the employer at the rate of 1.45% on the employee's total compensation. The Voluntary Plan takes care of the major part of doctors' bills and other medical and health services and is financed by monthly payments from all who enroll plus matching funds from the federal government.

The combination of the O.A.S.D.I. tax, often called Federal Insurance Contribution Act (F.I.C.A.) tax, and the federal Hospital Insurance Tax is commonly referred to as the **Social Security tax**. The combined rate for these taxes, 7.65% on an employee's wages to $76,200 and 1.45% in excess of $76,200, is changed intermittently by acts of Congress. **The amount of unremitted employee and employer Social Security tax on gross wages paid should be reported by the employer as a current liability.**

Unemployment Taxes. Another payroll tax levied by the federal government in cooperation with state governments provides a system of unemployment insurance. All employers who (1) paid wages of $1,500 or more during any calendar quarter in the year or preceding year or (2) employed at least one individual on at least one day in each of 20 weeks during the current or preceding calendar year are subject to the Federal Unemployment Tax Act (F.U.T.A.). This tax is levied only on the employer at a rate of 6.2% on the first $7,000 of compensation paid to each employee during the calendar year. The employer is allowed a tax credit not to exceed 5.4% for contributions paid to a state plan for unemployment compensation. Thus, if an employer is subject to a state unemployment tax of 5.4% or more, only 0.8% tax is due the federal government.

State unemployment compensation laws differ from the federal law and differ among various states. Therefore, employers must be familiar with the unemployment tax laws in each state in which they pay wages and salaries. Although the normal state tax may range from 3% to 7% or higher, all states provide for some form of merit rating under which a reduction in the state contribution rate is allowed. Employers who display by their benefit and contribution experience that they have provided steady employment may be entitled to this reduction—if the size of the state fund is adequate to provide the reduction. In order not to penalize an employer who has earned a reduction in the state contribution rate, the federal law allows a credit of 5.4% even though the effective state contribution rate is less than 5.4%.

To illustrate, Appliance Repair Co., which has a taxable payroll of $100,000, is subject to a federal rate of 6.2% and a state contribution rate of 5.7%. But because of stable employment experience, the company's state rate has been reduced to 1%. The computation of the federal and state unemployment taxes for Appliance Repair Co. is:

ILLUSTRATION 13-4
Computation of Unemployment Taxes

State unemployment tax payment (1%)($100,000)	$1,000
Federal unemployment tax (6.2% – 5.4%)($100,000)	800
Total federal and state unemployment tax	$1,800

The federal unemployment tax is paid quarterly with a tax form filed annually. State contributions generally are required to be paid quarterly. Because both the federal and the state unemployment taxes accrue on earned compensation, the amount of accrued but unpaid employer contributions **should be recorded as an operating expense and as a current liability when financial statements are prepared at year-end**.

Income Tax Withholding. Federal and some state income tax laws require employers to withhold from the pay of each employee the applicable income tax due on those wages. The amount of income tax withheld is computed by the employer according to a government-prescribed formula or withholding tax table. That amount depends on the length of the pay period and each employee's taxable wages, marital status, and claimed dependents. If the income tax withheld plus the employee and the employer Social Security taxes exceeds specified amounts per month, the employer is required to make remittances to the government during the month. Illustration 13-5 summarizes various payroll deductions and liabilities.

ILLUSTRATION 13-5
Summary of Payroll Liabilities

Item	Who Pays	
Income tax withholding FICA taxes—employee share Union dues	Employee	Employer reports these amounts as liabilities until remitted.
FICA taxes—employer share Federal unemployment State unemployment	Employer	

Illustration. Assume a weekly payroll of $10,000 entirely subject to F.I.C.A. and Medicare (7.65%), federal (0.8%) and state (4%) unemployment taxes with income tax withholding of $1,320 and union dues of $88 deducted.

The entry to record the wages and salaries paid and the **employee payroll deductions** would be:

Wages and Salaries Expense	10,000	
Withholding Taxes Payable		1,320
F.I.C.A. Taxes Payable		765
Union Dues Payable to Local No. 257		88
Cash		7,827

The entry to record the **employer payroll taxes** would be:

Payroll Tax Expense	1,245	
F.I.C.A. Taxes Payable		765
Federal Unemployment Tax Payable		80
State Unemployment Tax Payable		400

The employer is required to remit to the government its share of F.I.C.A. tax along with the amount of F.I.C.A. tax deducted from each employee's gross compensation. All unremitted employer F.I.C.A. taxes should be recorded as payroll tax expense and payroll tax payable.[15]

Compensated Absences

Compensated absences are absences from employment—such as vacation, illness, and holidays—for which employees are paid anyway. A liability should be accrued for the cost of compensation for future absences if **all** of the following conditions are met:[16]

[15] In a manufacturing enterprise, all of the payroll costs (wages, payroll taxes, and fringe benefits) are allocated to appropriate cost accounts such as Direct Labor, Indirect Labor, Sales Salaries, Administrative Salaries, and the like. This abbreviated and somewhat simplified discussion of payroll costs and deductions is not indicative of the volume of records and clerical work that may be involved in maintaining a sound and accurate payroll system.

[16] "Accounting for Compensated Absences," *Statement of Financial Accounting Standards No. 43* (Stamford, Conn.: FASB, 1980), par. 6.

UNDERLYING CONCEPTS

When these four conditions exist, all elements in the definition of a liability exist. In addition, the matching concept requires that the period receiving the services also should report the related expense.

(a) The employer's obligation relating to employees' rights to receive compensation for future absences is attributable to employees' services **already rendered,**

(b) The obligation relates to the rights that **vest or accumulate,**

(c) Payment of the compensation is **probable,** and

(d) The amount can be **reasonably estimated.**[17]

An example of an accrual for compensated absences is shown below in an excerpt from the balance sheet of **Clarcor Inc.** presented in its annual report.

ILLUSTRATION 13-6
Balance Sheet Presentation of Accrual for Compensated Absences

CLARCOR INC.

Current liabilities	
Accounts payable	$ 6,308
Accrued salaries, wages and commissions	2,278
Compensated absences	2,271
Accrued pension liabilities	1,023
Other accrued liabilities	4,572
	$16,452

If an employer meets conditions (a), (b), and (c) but does not accrue a liability because of a failure to meet condition (d), that fact should be disclosed. An example of such a disclosure is the following note from the financial statements of **Gotham Utility Company**:

ILLUSTRATION 13-7
Disclosure of Policy for Compensated Absences

GOTHAM UTILITY COMPANY

Employees of the Company are entitled to paid vacation, personal, and sick days off, depending on job status, length of service, and other factors. Due to numerous differing union contracts and other agreements with nonunion employees, it is impractical to estimate the amount of compensation for future absences, and, accordingly, no liability has been reported in the accompanying financial statements. The Company's policy is to recognize the cost of compensated absences when actually paid to employees; compensated absence payments to employees totaled $2,786,000.

Vested rights exist when an employer has an obligation to make payment to an employee even if his or her employment is terminated; thus, vested rights are not contingent on an employee's future service. **Accumulated rights** are those that can be carried forward to future periods if not used in the period in which earned. For example, assume that you have earned 4 days of vacation pay as of December 31, the end of

[17]These same four conditions are to be applied to accounting for **postemployment benefits. Postemployment benefits** are benefits provided by an enterprise to past or inactive employees **after employment but prior to retirement**. Examples include salary continuation, supplemental unemployment benefits, severance pay, job training, and continuation of health and life insurance coverage. The FASB recently issued *Statement No. 112,* "Employers' Accounting for Postemployment Benefits" which requires that the accounting treatment for compensated absences described in *FASB Statement No. 43* should be applied to postemployment benefits. "Employers' Accounting for Postemployment Benefits," *Statement of Financial Accounting Standards No. 112* (Norwalk, Conn.: FASB, November 1992), par. 18.

your employer's fiscal year, and that you will be paid for this vacation time even if you terminate employment. In this situation, your 4 days of vacation pay are considered vested and must be accrued. Now assume that your vacation days are not vested, but that you can carry the 4 days over into later periods. Although the rights are not vested, they are accumulated rights for which the employer must provide an accrual, allowing for estimated forfeitures due to turnover.

A modification of the general rules relates to the issue of **sick pay**. If sick pay benefits vest, accrual is required. If sick pay benefits accumulate but do not vest, accrual is permitted but not required. The reason for this distinction is that compensation that is designated as sick pay may be administered in one of two ways. In some companies, employees receive sick pay only if they are absent because of illness. Accrual of a liability is permitted but not required because its payment is contingent upon future employee illness. In other companies, employees are allowed to accumulate unused sick pay and take compensated time off from work even though they are not ill. For this type of sick pay, a liability must be accrued because it will be paid whether or not employees ever become ill.

The expense and related liability for compensated absences should be recognized in the year earned by employees. For example, if new employees receive rights to two weeks' paid vacation at the beginning of their second year of employment, the vacation pay is considered to be earned during the first year of employment.

What rate should be used to accrue the compensated absence cost—the current rate or an estimated future rate? *FASB Statement No. 43* is silent on this subject; therefore, it is likely that companies will use the current rather than future rate. The future rate is less certain and raises issues concerning the time value of money. To illustrate, assume that Amutron Inc. began operations on January 1, 2000. The company employs ten individuals who are paid $480 per week. Vacation weeks earned by all employees in 2000 were 20 weeks, but none were used during this period. In 2001, the vacation weeks were used when the current rate of pay was $540 per week for each employee. The entry at December 31, 2000 to accrue the accumulated vacation pay is as follows:

Wages Expense	9,600	
Vacation Wages Payable ($480 × 20)		9,600

At December 31, 2000 the company would report on its balance sheet a liability of $9,600. In 2001, the vacation pay related to 2000 would be recorded as follows:

Vacation Wages Payable	9,600	
Wages Expense	1,200	
Cash ($540 × 20)		10,800

In 2001 the vacation weeks were used; therefore, the liability is extinguished. Note that the difference between the amount of cash paid and the reduction in the liability account is recorded as an adjustment to Wages Expense in the period when paid. This difference arises because the liability account was accrued at the rates of pay in effect during the period when compensated time was earned. The cash paid, however, is based on the rates in effect during the period when compensated time is used. If the future rates of pay had been used to compute the accrual in 2000, then the cash paid in 2001 would have been equal to the liability.[18]

In Japan, bonuses to members of the Board of Directors and to the Commercial Code auditors are not treated as expenses. They are considered to be a distribution of profits and charged against retained earnings.

Bonus Agreements

For various reasons, many companies give a **bonus** to certain or all officers and employees in addition to their regular salary or wage. Frequently the bonus amount is dependent on the company's yearly profit. For example, **Ford Motor Company** has a plan whereby employees share in the success of the company's operations on the basis of a

[18]Some companies have obligations for benefits paid to employees after they retire. The accounting and reporting standards for postretirement benefit payments are complex. These standards relate to two different types of **postretirement benefits**: (1) pensions and (2) postretirement health care and life insurance benefits. These issues are discussed extensively in Chapter 21.

complicated formula using net income as its primary basis for computation. From the standpoint of the enterprise, **bonus payments to employees** may be considered additional wages and should be included as a deduction in determining the net income for the year.

To illustrate the entries for an employee bonus, assume a company whose income for the year 2001 is $100,000 will pay out bonuses of $10,714.29 in January 2002. (Computations of this and other bonuses are illustrated in Appendix 13A.) An adjusting entry dated December 31, 2001, is made to record the bonus as follows:

Employees' Bonus Expense	10,714.29	
Profit-Sharing Bonus Payable		10,714.29

In January 2002, when the bonus is paid, the journal entry would be:

Profit-Sharing Bonus Payable	10,714.29	
Cash		10,714.29

The expense account should appear in the income statement as an operating expense. **The liability, profit-sharing bonus payable, is usually payable within a short period of time and should be included as a current liability in the balance sheet.**

Similar to bonus arrangements are contractual agreements covering rents or royalty payments conditional on the amount of revenues earned or the quantity of product produced or extracted. Conditional expenses based on revenues or units produced are usually less difficult to compute than bonus arrangements. For example, if a lease calls for a fixed rent payment of $500 per month and 1% of all sales over $300,000 per year, the annual rent obligation would amount to $6,000 plus $.01 of each dollar of revenue over $300,000. Or, a royalty agreement may accrue to the patent owner $1.00 for every ton of product resulting from the patented process, or accrue to the mineral rights owner $.50 on every barrel of oil extracted. As each additional unit of product is produced or extracted, an additional obligation, usually a current liability, is created.

SECTION 2 CONTINGENCIES

A **contingency** is defined in *FASB Statement No. 5* "as an existing condition, situation, or set of circumstances involving uncertainty as to possible gain **(gain contingency)** or loss **(loss contingency)** to an enterprise that will ultimately be resolved when one or more future events occur or fail to occur."[19]

GAIN CONTINGENCIES

OBJECTIVE 5
Identify the criteria used to account for and disclose gain and loss contingencies.

Gain contingencies are claims or rights to receive assets (or have a liability reduced) whose existence is uncertain but which may become valid eventually.

The typical gain contingencies are:

1. Possible receipts of monies from gifts, donations, bonuses, and so on.
2. Possible refunds from the government in tax disputes.
3. Pending court cases where the probable outcome is favorable.
4. Tax loss carryforwards (discussed in Chapter 20).

Accountants have adopted a conservative policy in this area. Gain contingencies are not recorded. They are disclosed in the notes only when the probabilities are high that

[19]"Accounting for Contingencies," *Statement of Financial Accounting Standards No. 5* (Stamford, Conn.: FASB, 1975), par. 1.

a gain contingency will become a reality. As a result, it is unusual to find information about contingent gains in the financial statements and the accompanying notes. An example of a disclosure of a gain contingency is as follows:

BMC INDUSTRIES, INC.

Note 13: Legal Matters. In the first quarter, a U.S. District Court in Miami, Florida, awarded the Company a $5.1 million judgment against Barth Industries (Barth) of Cleveland, Ohio and its parent, Nesco Holdings, Inc. (Nesco). The judgment relates to an agreement under which Barth and Nesco were to help automate the plastic lens production plant in Fort Lauderdale, Florida. The Company has not recorded any income relating to this judgment because Barth and Nesco have filed an appeal.

ILLUSTRATION 13-8
Disclosure of Gain Contingency

LOSS CONTINGENCIES

Loss contingencies are situations involving uncertainty as to possible loss. A liability incurred as a result of a loss contingency is by definition a **contingent liability**. **Contingent liabilities** are obligations that are dependent upon the occurrence or nonoccurrence of one or more future events to confirm either the amount payable, the payee, the date payable, or its existence. That is, one or more of these factors depend upon a contingency.

When a loss contingency exists, the likelihood that the future event or events will confirm the incurrence of a liability can range from probable to remote. The FASB uses the terms **probable**, **reasonably possible**, and **remote** to identify three areas within that range and assigns the following meanings:

> **Probable.** The future event or events are likely to occur.
>
> **Reasonably possible.** The chance of the future event or events occurring is more than remote but less than likely.
>
> **Remote.** The chance of the future event or events occurring is slight.

An estimated loss from a loss contingency should be accrued by a charge to expense and a liability recorded only if **both** of the following conditions are met.[20]

1. Information available prior to the issuance of the financial statements indicates that it is **probable that a liability has been incurred** at the date of the financial statements.
2. The amount of the loss can be **reasonably estimated**.

Neither the exact payee nor the exact date payable need be known to record a liability. **What must be known is whether it is probable that a liability has been incurred.**

The second criterion indicates that an amount for the liability can be reasonably determined; otherwise, it should not be accrued as a liability. Evidence to determine a reasonable estimate of the liability may be based on the company's own experience, experience of other companies in the industry, engineering or research studies, legal advice, or educated guesses by personnel in the best position to know. The following excerpt from the annual report of Quaker State Oil Refining Corp. is an example of an accrual recorded for a loss contingency.

[20]Those loss contingencies that result in the incurrence of a liability are most relevant to the discussion in this chapter. Loss contingencies that result in the impairment of an asset (e.g., collectibility of receivables or threat of expropriation of assets) are discussed more fully in other sections of this textbook.

ILLUSTRATION 13-9
Disclosure of Accrual for Loss Contingency

QUAKER STATE OIL REFINING CORP.

Note 5: Contingencies. During the period from November 13 to December 23, a change in an additive component purchased from one of its suppliers caused certain oil refined and shipped to fail to meet the Company's low-temperature performance requirements. The Company has recalled this product and has arranged for reimbursement to its customers and the ultimate consumers of all costs associated with the product. Estimated cost of the recall program, net of estimated third party reimbursement, in the amount of $3,500,000 has been charged to current operations.

Use of the terms probable, reasonably possible, and remote as guidelines for classifying contingencies involves judgment and subjectivity. The items in Illustration 13-10 are examples of loss contingencies and the general accounting treatment accorded them.

ILLUSTRATION 13-10
Accounting Treatment of Loss Contingencies

Loss Related to	Usually Accrued	Not Accrued	May be Accrued*
1. Collectibility of receivables	X		
2. Obligations related to product warranties and product defects	X		
3. Premiums offered to customers	X		
4. Risk of loss or damage of enterprise property by fire, explosion, or other hazards		X	
5. General or unspecified business risks		X	
6. Risk of loss from catastrophes assumed by property and casualty insurance companies including reinsurance companies		X	
7. Threat of expropriation of assets			X
8. Pending or threatened litigation			X
9. Actual or possible claims and assessments**			X
10. Guarantees of indebtedness of others			X
11. Obligations of commercial banks under "standby letters of credit"			X
12. Agreements to repurchase receivables (or the related property) that have been sold			X

* Should be accrued when both criteria are met (probable and reasonably estimable).
**Estimated amounts of losses incurred prior to the balance sheet date but settled subsequently should be accrued as of the balance sheet date.

INTERNATIONAL INSIGHT

In Germany, company law allows firms to accrue losses for contingencies as long as they are possible and reasonable. Such provisions are one means of smoothing income.

Practicing accountants express concern over the diversity that now exists in the interpretation of "probable," "reasonably possible," and "remote." Current practice relies heavily on the exact language used in responses received from lawyers (such language is necessarily biased and protective rather than predictive). As a result, accruals and disclosures of contingencies vary considerably in practice. Some of the more common loss contingencies discussed in this chapter are:[21]

1. Litigation, claims, and assessments.
2. Guarantee and warranty costs.

[21] *Accounting Trends and Techniques—1999* reports that of the 600 companies surveyed, loss contingencies of the following nature and number were reported: litigation, 452; environmental, 266; insurance, 56; possible tax assessments, 54; governmental investigation, 31; and others, 56.

3. Premiums and coupons.
4. Environmental liabilities.
5. Self-insurance risks.

Note that general risk contingencies that are inherent in business operations, such as the possibility of war, strike, uninsurable catastrophes, or a business recession, are not reported in the notes to the financial statements.

Litigation, Claims, and Assessments

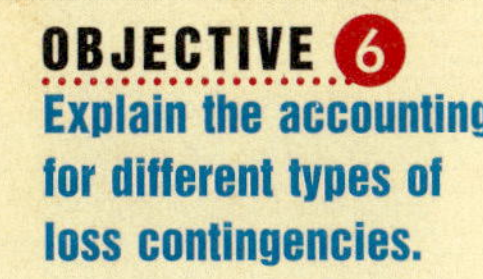

OBJECTIVE 6
Explain the accounting for different types of loss contingencies.

The following factors, among others, must be considered in determining whether a liability should be recorded with respect to **pending or threatened** litigation and actual or possible claims and assessments:

1. The **time period** in which the underlying cause of action occurred.
2. The **probability** of an unfavorable outcome.
3. The ability to make a **reasonable estimate** of the amount of loss.

To report a loss and a liability in the financial statements, the cause for litigation must have occurred on or before the date of the financial statements. It does not matter that the company did not become aware of the existence or possibility of the lawsuit or claims until after the date of the financial statements but before they are issued. To evaluate the probability of an unfavorable outcome, consider: the nature of the litigation; the progress of the case; the opinion of legal counsel; the experience of your company and others in similar cases; and any management response to the lawsuit.

The outcome of pending litigation, however, can seldom be predicted with any assurance. And, even if the evidence available at the balance sheet date does not favor the defendant, it is hardly reasonable to expect the company to publish in its financial statements a dollar estimate of the probable negative outcome. Such specific disclosures could weaken the company's position in the dispute and encourage the plaintiff to intensify its efforts. A typical example of the wording of such a disclosure is the note to the financial statements of **Apple Computer, Inc.**, relating to its litigation concerning repetitive stress injuries as shown in Illustration 13-11.

ILLUSTRATION 13-11
Disclosure of Litigation

APPLE COMPUTER, INC.

"Repetitive Stress Injury" Litigation. The Company is named in numerous lawsuits (fewer than 100) alleging that the plaintiff incurred so-called "repetitive stress injury" to the upper extremities as a result of using keyboards and/or mouse input devices sold by the Company. On October 4, in a trial of one of these cases (*Dorsey v. Apple*) in the United States District Court for the Eastern District of New York, the jury rendered a verdict in favor of the Company, and final judgment in favor of the Company has been entered. The other cases are in various stages of pretrial activity. These suits are similar to those filed against other major suppliers of personal computers. Ultimate resolution of the litigation against the Company may depend on progress in resolving this type of litigation in the industry overall.

With respect to **unfiled suits** and **unasserted claims and assessments**, a company must determine (1) the degree of **probability** that a suit may be filed or a claim or assessment may be asserted and (2) the **probability** of an unfavorable outcome. For example, assume that Nawtee Company is being investigated by the Federal Trade Commission for restraint of trade, and enforcement proceedings have been instituted. Such proceedings are often followed by private claims of triple damages for redress. In this case, Nawtee Company must determine the probability of the claims being asserted **and** the probability of triple damages being awarded. If both are probable, if the loss is reasonably estimable, and if the cause for action is dated on or before the date of the financial statements, then the liability should be accrued.[22]

Guarantee and Warranty Costs

A warranty **(product guarantee)** is a promise made by a seller to a buyer to make good on a deficiency of quantity, quality, or performance in a product. It is commonly used by manufacturers as a sales promotion technique. Automakers, for instance, "hyped" their sales by extending their new-car warranty to 7 years or 70,000 miles. For a specified period of time following the date of sale to the consumer, the manufacturer may promise to bear all or part of the cost of replacing defective parts, to perform any necessary repairs or servicing without charge, to refund the purchase price, or even to "double your money back."

Warranties and guarantees entail future costs, frequently significant additional costs, which are sometimes called "after costs" or "post-sale costs." Although the future cost is indefinite as to amount, due date, and even customer, a liability is probable in most cases and should be recognized in the accounts if it can be reasonably estimated. The amount of the liability is an estimate of all the costs that will be incurred after sale and delivery and that are incident to the correction of defects or deficiencies required under the warranty provisions. Warranty costs are a classic example of a loss contingency. There are two basic methods of accounting for warranty costs: (1) the cash basis method and (2) the accrual method.

Cash Basis

Under the **cash basis method**, warranty costs are charged to expense as they are incurred. In other words, **warranty costs are charged to the period in which the seller or manufacturer complies with the warranty**. No liability is recorded for future costs arising from warranties, nor is the period in which the sale is recorded necessarily charged with the costs of making good on outstanding warranties. Use of this method, the only one recognized for income tax purposes, is frequently justified for accounting on the basis of expediency when warranty costs are immaterial or when the warranty period is relatively short. The cash basis method is required when a warranty liability is not accrued in the year of sale either because

1. It is not probable that a liability has been incurred; or
2. The amount of the liability cannot be reasonably estimated.

Accrual Basis

If it is probable that customers will make claims under warranties relating to goods or services that have been sold and a reasonable estimate of the costs involved can be made, the accrual method must be used. Under the **accrual method**, warranty costs are charged to operating expense **in the year of sale**. It is the generally accepted method and should be used whenever the warranty is an integral and inseparable part of the sale and is viewed as a loss contingency. We refer to this approach as the **expense warranty approach**.

Illustration of Expense Warranty Approach. To illustrate the expense warranty method, assume that the Denson Machinery Company begins production on a new machine in July 2001, and sells 100 units at $5,000 each by its year-end, December 31, 2001. Each machine is under warranty for one year and the company has estimated, from past experience with a similar machine, that the warranty cost will probably average $200 per unit. Further, as a result of parts replacements and services rendered in com-

[22]Contingencies involving an unasserted claim or assessment need not be disclosed when no claimant has come forward unless (1) it is considered probable that a claim will be asserted and (2) there is a reasonable possibility that the outcome will be unfavorable.

pliance with machinery warranties, the company incurs $4,000 in warranty costs in 2001 and $16,000 in 2002.

1 Sale of 100 machines at $5,000 each, July through December 2001:

Cash or Accounts Receivable	500,000	
Sales		500,000

2 Recognition of warranty expense, July through December 2001:

Warranty Expense	4,000	
Cash, Inventory, Accrued Payroll		4,000
(Warranty costs incurred)		
Warranty Expense	16,000	
Estimated Liability under Warranties		16,000
(To accrue estimated warranty costs)		

The December 31, 2001, balance sheet would report Estimated Liability Under Warranties as a current liability of $16,000, and the income statement for 2001 would report Warranty Expense of $20,000.

3 Recognition of warranty costs incurred in 2002 (on 2001 machinery sales):

Estimated Liability under Warranties	16,000	
Cash, Inventory, or Accrued Payroll		16,000
(Warranty costs incurred)		

If the cash basis method were applied to the facts in the Denson Machinery Company example, $4,000 would be recorded as warranty expense in 2001 and $16,000 as warranty expense in 2002 with all of the sale price being recorded as revenue in 2001. In many instances, application of the cash basis method does not match the warranty costs relating to the products sold during a given period with the revenues derived from such products, and therefore it violates the matching principle. Where ongoing warranty policies exist year after year, the differences between the cash and the expense warranty basis probably would not be so great.

Sales Warranty Approach. A warranty is sometimes **sold separately from the product**. For example, when you purchase a television set or VCR, you will be entitled to the manufacturer's warranty. You also will undoubtedly be offered an extended warranty on the product at an additional cost.[23]

In this case, the seller should recognize separately the sale of the television or VCR with the manufacturer's warranty and the sale of the extended warranty.[24] This approach is referred to as the **sales warranty approach**. **Revenue on the sale of the extended warranty is deferred** and is generally recognized on a straight-line basis over the life of the contract. Revenue is deferred because the seller of the warranty has an obligation to perform services over the life of the contract. Only costs that vary with and are directly related to the sale of the contracts (mainly commissions) should be deferred and amortized. Costs such as employees' salaries, advertising, and general and administrative expenses that would have been incurred even if no contract were sold should be expensed as incurred.

To illustrate, assume you have just purchased a new automobile from Hanlin Auto for $20,000. In addition to the regular warranty on the auto (all repairs will be paid by the manufacturer for the first 36,000 miles or 3 years, whichever comes first), you purchase at a cost of $600 an extended warranty that protects you for an additional 3 years or 36,000 miles. The entry to record the sale of the automobile (with the regular

[23]A contract is separately priced **if the customer has the option to purchase** the services provided under the contract for an expressly stated amount separate from the price of the product. An extended warranty or product maintenance contract usually meets these conditions.

[24]"Accounting for Separately Extended Warranty and Product Maintenance Contracts," *FASB Technical Bulletin No. 90–1* (Stamford, Conn.: FASB, 1990).

warranty) and the sale of the extended warranty on January 2, 2001, on Hanlin Auto's books is:

Cash	20,600	
Sales		20,000
Unearned Warranty Revenue		600

The entry to recognize revenue at the end of the fourth year (using straight-line amortization) would be as follows:

Unearned Warranty Revenue	200	
Warranty Revenue		200

Because the extended warranty contract does not start until after the regular warranty expires, revenue is not recognized until the fourth year. If the costs of performing services under the extended warranty contract are incurred on other than a straight-line basis (as historical evidence might indicate), revenue should be recognized over the contract period in proportion to the costs expected to be incurred in performing services under the contract.[25]

Premiums and Coupons

UNDERLYING CONCEPTS

Warranties and coupons are loss contingencies that satisfy the conditions necessary for a liability. Regarding the income statement, the *matching principle* requires that the related expense be reported in the period in which the sale occurs.

Numerous companies offer (either on a limited or continuing basis) premiums to customers in return for boxtops, certificates, coupons, labels, or wrappers. The **premium** may be silverware, dishes, a small appliance, a toy, other goods, or free transportation.[26] Also, **printed coupons** that can be redeemed for a cash discount on items purchased are extremely popular.[27] A more recent marketing innovation is the **cash rebate**, which the buyer can obtain by returning the store receipt, a rebate coupon, and Universal Product Code (UPC label) or "bar code" to the manufacturer. These premiums, coupon offers, and rebates are made to stimulate sales, and their **costs should be charged to expense in the period of the sale** that benefits from the premium plan. At the end of the accounting period many of these premium offers may be outstanding and, when presented in subsequent periods, must be redeemed. **The number of outstanding premium offers that will be presented for redemption must be estimated in order to reflect the existing current liability and to match costs with revenues.** The

[25]Ibid, par. 3.

[26]Premium plans that have widespread adoption are the **frequent-flier programs** used by all major airlines. On the basis of mileage accumulated, frequent-flier members are awarded discounted or free airline tickets. Airline customers can earn miles toward free travel by making long-distance phone calls, staying in hotels, and charging gasoline and groceries on a credit card. Those free tickets represent an enormous potential liability because people using them may displace paying passengers.

When airlines first started offering frequent-flier bonuses, everyone assumed that they could accommodate the free-ticket holders with otherwise-empty seats. That made the additional cost of the program so minimal that airlines didn't accrue it or report the small liability. But, as more and more paying passengers have been crowded off of flights by frequent-flier awardees, the loss of revenues has grown enormously. For example, **United Airlines** recently reported a liability of $1.4 billion for advance ticket sales, some of which pertains to free frequent-flyer tickets.

Although the accounting for this transaction has been studied by the profession, no authoritative guidelines have been issued.

[27]Approximately 4% of coupons are redeemed. Redeemed coupons eventually make their way to the corporate headquarters of the stores that accept them. From there they are shipped in 50-pound boxes to Mexico's border towns (Juárez, Tijuana, Nuevo Laredo), where clearinghouses operated by **A. C. Nielsen Company** (of TV rating fame) count them and report back to the manufacturers who, in turn, reimburse the stores.

cost of premium offers should be charged to Premium Expense, and the outstanding obligations should be credited to an account titled Estimated Liability for Premiums.

Although the FASB did not include premium offers in its list of loss contingencies, the authors believe that **premium offers result in the probable existence of a liability at the date of the financial statements, can be reasonably estimated in amount, are contingent upon the occurrence of a future event (redemption), and, therefore, are a loss contingency** within the guidelines of *FASB Statement No. 5.*

The following example illustrates the accounting treatment accorded a premium offer. Fluffy Cakemix Company offered its customers a large nonbreakable mixing bowl in exchange for 25 cents and 10 boxtops. The mixing bowl costs Fluffy Cakemix Company 75 cents, and the company estimates that 60% of the boxtops will be redeemed. The premium offer began in June 2001 and resulted in the following transactions and entries during 2001.

1. To record purchase of 20,000 mixing bowls at 75 cents each:

Inventory of Premium Mixing Bowls	15,000	
Cash		15,000

2. To record sales of 300,000 boxes of cake mix at 80 cents:

Cash	240,000	
Sales		240,000

3. To record the actual redemption of 60,000 boxtops, the receipt of 25 cents per 10 boxtops, and the delivery of the mixing bowls:

Cash [(60,000 ÷ 10) × \$0.25]	1,500	
Premium Expense	3,000	
Inventory of Premium Mixing Bowls		4,500
[Computation: (60,000 ÷ 10) × \$0.75 = \$4,500]		

4. To record end-of-period adjusting entry for estimated liability for outstanding premium offers (boxtops):

Premium Expense	6,000		
Estimated Liability for Premiums			6,000
Computation:			
Total boxtops sold in 2001		300,000	
Total estimated redemptions (60%)		180,000	
Boxtops redeemed in 2001		60,000	
Estimated future redemptions		120,000	
Cost of estimated claims outstanding (120,000 ÷ 10) × (\$0.75 − \$0.25) = \$6,000			

The December 31, 2001, balance sheet of Fluffy Cakemix Company will report an Inventory of Premium Mixing Bowls of \$10,500 as a current asset and Estimated Liability for Premiums of \$6,000 as a current liability. The 2001 income statement will report a \$9,000 Premium Expense among the selling expenses.

Environmental Liabilities

Estimates to clean up existing toxic waste sites run to upward of \$752 billion over a 30-year period. In addition, the cost of cleaning up our air and preventing future deterioration of the environment is estimated to cost even more. The average environmental cost per firm in various industries at one time was: high-tech firms, \$2 million (6.1% of revenues); utilities, \$340 million (6.1% of revenues); steel and metals, \$50 million (2.9% of revenues), and oil companies, \$430 million (1.9% of revenues). Given that the average pretax profit of the 500 largest U.S. manufacturing companies recently was 7.7 percent of sales, these figures are staggering!

These costs will only grow when one considers "Superfund legislation": it provides not only a government-supported fund to clean up pollution, but a mandate to clean up existing waste sites. Further it provided the Environmental Protection Agency (EPA) with the power to clean up waste sites and charge the clean-up costs to parties the EPA deems responsible for contaminating the site. These potentially responsible parties have an onerous liability. The EPA estimates that it will likely cost an average of $25 million to clean up each polluted site. For the most troublesome sites, the cost could easily reach $100 million or more.

Presently **companies infrequently record any liability for these potential costs.** They note that the liability is a contingent liability that is not estimable. As a result, generally only a description regarding the possible liability is disclosed in the financial statements. An example of one company that did report a liability is provided in Illustration 13-12.

ILLUSTRATION 13-12
Disclosure of a Recorded Liability for Environmental Costs

CROWN CENTRAL PETROLEUM CORPORATION

Note G (in part): Contingencies—Environmental. Like other petroleum refiners and marketers, the Company's operations are subject to extensive and rapidly changing federal and state environmental regulations governing air emissions, waste water discharges, and solid and hazardous waste management activities. The Company's policy is to accrue environmental and clean-up related costs of a noncapital nature when it is both probable that a liability has been incurred and the amount can be reasonably estimated. While it is often extremely difficult to reasonably quantify future environmental related expenditures, the Company anticipates a substantial capital investment will be required over the next several years to comply with existing regulations. The Company had recorded a liability of approximately $10,485,000 to cover the estimated costs of compliance with environmental regulations which are not anticipated to be of a capital nature.

More extensive disclosure is needed regarding environmental liabilities. In addition, more of these liabilities should be recorded. The SEC believes that managements should not delay recognition of a liability due to significant uncertainty. The SEC argues that if the liability is within a range and no amount within the range is the best estimate, then management should recognize the minimum amount of the range; that is in accordance with *FASB Interpretation No. 14,* "Reasonable Estimation of the Amount of a Loss." The SEC also believes that environmental liabilities should be reported in the balance sheet independent of recoveries from third parties. Thus, possible insurance recoveries are not permitted to be netted against liabilities but must be shown separately. Because there is much litigation regarding recovery of insurance proceeds, these "assets" appear to be gain contingencies and, therefore, companies will not be reporting these on the balance sheet.[28]

UNDERLYING CONCEPTS

Even if the amount of losses is estimable with a high degree of certainty, the losses are not liabilities because they result from a future event and not from a past event.

Self-Insurance

A company may insure against many contingencies such as fire, flood, storm, and accident by taking out insurance policies and paying premiums to insurance companies.

[28]As indicated earlier, the FASB pronouncements on this topic require that, when some amount within the range appears at the time to be a better estimate than any other amount within the range, that amount is accrued. When no amount within the range is a better estimate than any other amount, the dollar amount at the low end of the range is **accrued** and the dollar amount at the high end of the range is **disclosed**. See *FASB Interpretation No. 14,* "Reasonable Estimation of the Amount of a Loss" (Stamford, Conn.: FASB, 1976), par. 3, and *FASB Statement No. 5,* "Accounting for Contingencies" (Stamford, Conn.: FASB, 1975).

Some contingencies are, however, not insurable, or the insurance rates are prohibitive (e.g., earthquakes and riots). For such contingencies, even though insurance may be available, some businesses adopt a policy of self-insurance.

Despite its name, **self-insurance** is **not insurance, but risk assumption**, and any company that assumes its own risks puts itself in the position of incurring expenses or losses as they occur. There is little theoretical justification for the establishment of a liability based on a hypothetical charge to insurance expense. This is "as if" accounting. The conditions for accrual stated in *FASB Statement No. 5* are not satisfied prior to the occurrence of the event; until that time there is no diminution in the value of the property. And unlike an insurance company, which has contractual obligations to reimburse policyholders for losses, a company can have no such obligation to itself and, hence, no liability either before or after the occurrence of damage.[29]

In Switzerland, companies may make provisions for general (non-specified) contingencies to the extent allowed by tax regulations.

The following note from the annual report of **Adolph Coors Company** is typical of the self-insurance disclosure.

ILLUSTRATION 13-13
Disclosure of Self-Insurance

ADOLPH COORS COMPANY

Notes to Financial Statements

Note 4: Commitments and Contingencies. It is generally the policy of the Company to act as a self-insurer for certain insurable risks consisting primarily of physical loss to corporate property, business interruption resulting from such loss, employee health insurance programs, and workers' compensation. Losses and claims are accrued as incurred.

Exposure to **risks of loss resulting from uninsured past injury to others**, however, is an existing condition involving uncertainty about the amount and timing of losses that may develop, in which case a contingency exists. A company with a fleet of vehicles would have to accrue uninsured losses resulting from injury to others or damage to the property of others that took place prior to the date of the financial statements (if the experience of the company or other information enables it to make a reasonable estimate of the liability). However, it should not establish a liability for **expected future injury** to others or damage to the property of others even if the amount of losses is reasonably estimable.

PRESENTATION AND ANALYSIS

Presentation of Current Liabilities

OBJECTIVE 7
Indicate how current liabilities and contingencies are presented and analyzed.

In practice, current liabilities are usually recorded in accounting records and reported in financial statements at their full maturity value. Because of the short time periods involved, frequently less than one year, the difference between the present value of a current liability and the maturity value is not usually large. The slight overstatement

[29]"Accounting for Contingencies," *FASB Statement No. 5,* op. cit., par. 28. A commentary in *Forbes* (June 15, 1974, p. 42) stated its position on this matter quite succinctly: "The simple and unquestionable fact of life is this: Business is cyclical and full of unexpected surprises. Is it the role of accounting to disguise this unpleasant fact and create a fairyland of smoothly rising earnings? Or, should accounting reflect reality, warts and all—floods, expropriations and all manner of rude shocks?"

of liabilities that results from carrying current liabilities at maturity value is accepted as immaterial. *APB Opinion No. 21,* "Interest on Receivables and Payables," specifically exempts from present value measurements those payables arising from transactions with suppliers in the normal course of business that do not exceed approximately one year.[30]

The current liability accounts are commonly presented as the first classification in the liabilities and stockholders' equity section of the balance sheet. Within the current liabilities section the accounts may be listed in order of maturity, in descending order of amount, or in order of liquidation preference. Presented in Illustration 13-14 is an excerpt of the **Sun Microsystems** published financial statements, which is a representative presentation of the current liabilities as found in the reports of large corporations:

ILLUSTRATION 13-14
Balance Sheet Presentation of Current Liabilities

SUN MICROSYSTEMS
(in thousands)

	1999	1998
Current liabilities		
Short-term borrowings	$ 1,646	$ 7,169
Accounts payable	753,838	495,603
Accrued payroll–related liabilities	520,068	315,929
Accrued liabilities and other	1,126,497	810,562
Deferred service revenues	422,115	264,967
Income taxes payable	402,813	188,641
Note payable	—	40,000
Total current liabilities	$3,226,977	$2,122,871

Go to the Digital Tool for additional disclosures of current liability sections.

Detail and supplemental information concerning current liabilities should be sufficient to meet the requirement of full disclosure. Secured liabilities should be identified clearly, and the related assets pledged as collateral indicated. If the due date of any liability can be extended, the details should be disclosed. Current liabilities should not be offset against assets that are to be applied to their liquidation. Current maturities of long-term debt should be classified as current liabilities.

A major exception exists when a currently maturing obligation is to be paid from assets classified as long-term. For example, if payments to retire a bond payable are made from a bond sinking fund classified as a long-term asset, the bonds payable should be reported in the long-term liabilities section. Presentation of this debt in the current liabilities section would distort the working capital position of the enterprise.

If a short-term obligation is excluded from current liabilities because of refinancing, the note to the financial statements should include:

1. A general description of the financing agreement.
2. The terms of any new obligation incurred or to be incurred.
3. The terms of any equity security issued or to be issued.

When refinancing on a long-term basis is expected to be accomplished through the issuance of equity securities, it is not appropriate to include the short-term obligation in owners' equity. At the date of the balance sheet, the obligation is a liability and not owners' equity. The disclosure requirements are shown in Illustration 13-15 for an actual refinancing situation.

[30]"Interest on Receivables and Payables," *Opinions of the Accounting Principles Board No. 21* (New York: AICPA, 1971), par. 3.

ILLUSTRATION 13-15
Actual Refinancing of Short-Term Debt

	December 31, 2000
Current liabilities	
Accounts payable	$ 3,600,000
Accrued payables	2,500,000
Income taxes payable	1,100,000
Current portion of long-term debt	1,000,000
Total current liabilities	$ 8,200,000
Long-term debt	
Notes payable refinanced in January 2001 (Note 1)	$ 2,000,000
11% bonds due serially through 2011	15,000,000
Total long-term debt	$17,000,000

Note 1: On January 19, 2001, the Company issued 50,000 shares of Common Stock and received proceeds totaling $2,385,000 of which $2,000,000 was used to liquidate notes payable that matured on February 1, 2001. Accordingly, such notes payable have been classified as long-term debt at December 31, 2000.

Go to the Digital Tool for additional disclosures of contingencies.

Presentation of Contingencies

A loss contingency and a liability is recorded if the loss is both probable and estimable. But, if the loss is **either probable or estimable but not both**, and if there is at least a **reasonable possibility** that a liability may have been incurred, the following disclosure in the notes is required:

1. The nature of the contingency.
2. An estimate of the possible loss or range of loss or a statement that an estimate cannot be made.

Presented in Illustration 13-16 is an extensive litigation disclosure note (taken from the financial statements of **Raymark Corporation**), which shows that although actual losses have been charged to operations and further liability possibly exists, no estimate of this liability is possible.

ILLUSTRATION 13-16
Disclosure of Loss Contingency through Litigation

RAYMARK CORPORATION

Note I: Litigation. Raymark is a defendant or co-defendant in a substantial number of lawsuits alleging wrongful injury and/or death from exposure to asbestos fibers in the air. The following table summarizes the activity in these lawsuits:

Claims	
Pending at beginning of year	8,719
Received during year	4,494
Settled or otherwise disposed of	(1,445)
Pending at end of year	11,768
Average indemnification cost	$3,364
Average cost per case, including defense costs	$6,499
Trial activity	
Verdicts for the Company	23
Total trials	36

The following table presents the cost of defending asbestos litigation, together with related insurance and workers' compensation expenses.

Included in operating profit	$ 1,872,000
Nonoperating expense	9,077,000
Total	$10,949,000

The Company is seeking to reasonably determine its liability. However, it is not possible to predict which theory of insurance will apply, the number of lawsuits still to be filed, the cost of settling and defending the existing and unfiled cases, or the ultimate impact of these lawsuits on the Company's consolidated financial statements.

U.S. GAAP provides more guidance on the content of disclosures about contingencies than do IASC standards.

Certain other contingent liabilities that should be disclosed even though the possibility of loss may be remote are the following:

1. Guarantees of indebtedness of others.
2. Obligations of commercial banks under "stand-by letters of credit."
3. Guarantees to repurchase receivables (or any related property) that have been sold or assigned.

Disclosure should include the nature and amount of the guarantee and, if estimable, the amount that could be recovered from outside parties. **Cities Service Company** disclosed its guarantees of indebtedness of others in the following note:

ILLUSTRATION 13-17
Disclosure of Guarantees of Indebtedness

CITIES SERVICE COMPANY

Note 10: Contingent Liabilities. The Company and certain subsidiaries have guaranteed debt obligations of approximately $62 million of companies in which substantial stock investments are held. Also, under long-term agreements with certain pipeline companies in which stock interests are held, the Company and its subsidiaries have agreed to provide minimum revenue for product shipments. The Company has guaranteed mortgage debt ($80 million) incurred by a 50 percent owned tanker affiliate for construction of tankers which are under long-term charter contracts to the Company and others. It is not anticipated that any loss will result from any of the above described agreements.

Analysis of Current Liabilities

The distinction between current liabilities and long-term debt is important because it provides information about the liquidity of the company. Liquidity regarding a liability is the time that is expected to elapse until a liability has to be paid. In other words, a liability soon to be paid is a current liability. A liquid company is better able to withstand a financial downturn. Also, it has a better chance of taking advantage of investment opportunities that develop.

As indicated, certain basic ratios such as net cash flow provided by operating activities to current liabilities, and the turnover ratios for receivables and inventory, are used to assess liquidity. Two other ratios used to examine liquidity are the current ratio and the acid-test ratio.

The **current ratio** is the ratio of total current assets to total current liabilities. The formula is shown below.

ILLUSTRATION 13-18
Formula for Current Ratio

$$\text{Current ratio} = \frac{\text{Current assets}}{\text{Current liabilities}}$$

It is frequently expressed as a coverage of so many times. Sometimes it is called the working capital ratio because working capital is the excess of current assets over current liabilities.

A satisfactory current ratio does not disclose that a portion of the current assets may be tied up in slow-moving inventories. With inventories, especially raw materials and work in process, there is a question of how long it will take to transform them into the finished product and what ultimately will be realized in the sale of the merchandise. Elimination of the inventories, along with any prepaid expenses from the current assets, might provide better information for the short-term creditors. Many analysts favor an **acid-test** or **quick ratio** that relates total current liabilities to cash, marketable securities, and receivables. The formula for this ratio is shown on page 683.

$$\text{Acid-test ratio} = \frac{\text{Cash} + \text{Marketable securities} + \text{Net receivables}}{\text{Current liabilities}}$$

ILLUSTRATION 13-19
Formula for Acid-test Ratio

To illustrate the computation of these two ratios, the following information for **Sun Microsystems** is provided:

ILLUSTRATION 13-20
Current Assets of Sun Microsystems

SUN MICROSYSTEMS
(in thousands)

	1999
Current assets	
Cash and cash equivalents	$1,088,972
Short-term investments	1,576,079
Accounts receivable, net of allowances	2,286,911
Inventories	307,873
Other current assets	856,515
Total current assets	$6,116,350

The total current liabilities for Sun Microsystems were $3,227 million (see Illustration 13-14). The computation of the current and acid-test ratios for Sun Microsystems are as follows:

ILLUSTRATION 13-21
Computation of Current and Acid-test Ratios

$$\text{Current ratio} = \frac{\text{Current assets}}{\text{Current liabilities}} = \frac{\$6{,}116.3}{\$3{,}227} = 1.9 \text{ times}$$

$$\text{Acid-test ratio} = \frac{\text{Cash and cash equivalents} + \text{Net receivables}}{\text{Current liabilities}} = \frac{\$4{,}952}{\$3{,}227} = 1.53 \text{ times}$$

From this information, it appears that Sun Microsystems' liquidity is adequate.

SUMMARY OF LEARNING OBJECTIVES

1 **Define current liabilities and describe how they are valued.** Current liabilities are obligations whose liquidation is reasonably expected to require the use of current assets or the creation of other current liabilities. Theoretically, liabilities should be measured by the present value of the future outlay of cash required to liquidate them. In practice, current liabilities are usually recorded in accounting records and reported in financial statements at their full maturity value.

2 **Identify the nature and types of current liabilities.** There are several types of liabilities: (1) accounts payable, (2) notes payable, (3) current maturities of long-term debt, (4) dividends payable, (5) returnable deposits, (6) unearned revenues, (7) taxes payable, and (8) employee-related liabilities.

3 **Explain the classification issues of short-term debt expected to be refinanced.** An enterprise is required to exclude a short-term obligation from current liabilities if both of the following conditions are met: (1) It must intend to refinance the obligation on

KEY TERMS

accumulated rights, *668*
acid-test (quick) ratio, *682*
assessments, *673*
bonus, *669*
cash dividend payable, *661*
claims, *673*
compensated absences, *667*
contingency, *670*
contingent liabilities, *671*
current liabilities, *657*
current maturities of long-term debt, *659*
current ratio, *682*
expense warranty approach, *674*
gain contingencies, *670*
liabilities, *657*
litigation, claims, and assessments, *673*
loss contingencies, *671*
notes payable (trade notes payable), *658*
operating cycle, *657*
preferred dividends in arrears, *661*
premiums, *676*
probable (contingency), *671*
reasonably possible (contingency), *671*
remote (contingency), *671*
returnable cash deposits, *662*
sales warranty approach, *675*
self-insurance, *679*
short-term obligations expected to be refinanced, *660*
Social Security tax, *666*
trade accounts payable, *658*
trade notes payable, *658*
unearned revenues, *662*
vested rights, *668*
warranty, *674*

a long-term basis, *and* (2) it must demonstrate an ability to consummate the refinancing.

4 Identify types of employee-related liabilities. The employee-related liabilities are: (1) payroll deductions; (2) compensated absences; and (3) bonus agreements.

5 Identify the criteria used to account for and disclose gain and loss contingencies. Gain contingencies are not recorded. They are disclosed in the notes only when the probabilities are high that a gain contingency will become a reality. An estimated loss from a loss contingency should be accrued by a charge to expense and a liability recorded only if both of the following conditions are met: (1) Information available prior to the issuance of the financial statements indicates that it is probable that a liability has been incurred at the date of the financial statements, and (2) the amount of the loss can be reasonably estimated.

6 Explain the accounting for different types of loss contingencies. (1) The following factors must be considered in determining whether a liability should be recorded with respect to pending or threatened litigation and actual or possible claims and assessments: (a) the time period in which the underlying cause for action occurred; (b) the probability of an unfavorable outcome; and (c) the ability to make a reasonable estimate of the amount of loss.

(2) If it is probable that customers will make claims under warranties relating to goods or services that have been sold and a reasonable estimate of the costs involved can be made, the accrual method must be used. Warranty costs under the accrual basis are charged to operating expense in the year of sale.

(3) Premiums, coupon offers, and rebates are made to stimulate sales, and their costs should be charged to expense in the period of the sale that benefits from the premium plan.

7 Indicate how current liabilities and contingencies are presented and analyzed. The current liability accounts are commonly presented as the first classification in the liabilities and stockholders' equity section of the balance sheet. Within the current liability section the accounts may be listed in order of maturity, in descending order of amount, or in order of liquidation preference. Detail and supplemental information concerning current liabilities should be sufficient to meet the requirement of full disclosure. If the loss is either probable or estimable but not both, and if there is at least a reasonable possibility that a liability may have been incurred, disclosure should be made in the notes of the nature of the contingency and an estimate given of the possible loss. Two ratios used to analyze liquidity are the current and acid-test ratios.

FROM CLASSROOM TO CAREER

DARIAN GRIFFIN

is a financial manager with S.C. Johnson & Son Wax in Racine, Wisconsin. S.C. Johnson is a leading maker of chemical specialty products for home, personal care, and insect control. Mr. Griffin is a 1991 graduate of the University of Wisconsin at Madison and is in the executive MBA program at Marquette University.

How did you decide on accounting as a career?

Well, I liked numbers and I liked business. Originally, I was majoring in actuarial science, but I found it to be too focused on math theory.

What's the toughest part of the transition from college to the working world?

In school, you can be anonymous and still do well, but in business you have to be sharp every day. At work, what you do has a cumulative effect on your career. If you miss an assignment or do poorly on a project, then it can hurt your long-term prospects with the company. In school, at the beginning of a semester you start with a clean slate.

Why did you choose industry instead of public accounting?

I wanted to get exposure to all areas of business, including manufacturing, research and development, and sales. During the summer before graduation, I interned at Johnson Wax and really liked the people with whom I was working. My first assignment was in the home care division, which includes products like Pledge and Glade air fresheners. My job was to prepare the financial schedules for the division. Early on, I had to refer back to my intermediate accounting course to set up accruals for our coupon programs. In my next job, I went into consolidation accounting, where I was responsible for making sure that the trial balances from overseas subsidiaries fit together.

How do you use intermediate accounting in your current position?

I do a lot of pro-forma income statements and balance sheets—accounting simulations—to determine whether a new product is going to generate an adequate return. I work with cost analysts in our division to figure out what it is going to cost us to make the product. In one way or another, I have used my accounting background in every job that I've had at this company.

What non-accounting skills are important to develop?

Leadership ability. As you advance, you end up having to lead and motivate other people. A good place to develop that skill is in school. Take advantage of every opportunity to hold leadership roles in extracurricular activities, whether it is a fraternity or sorority, the campus newspaper, student government, or athletics. Another good skill is oral and written communications. As accountants, we know the numbers and we understand them, but we can't operate in a vacuum. We have to explain the numbers and other assumptions to management.

How do you find time to pursue an MBA?

The program at Marquette fits in with my work schedule. I go to class every other Friday and Saturday, and it requires about 20 hours a week outside of class for homework and meetings.

You're doing this in addition to a full-time job. Do you have a family?

Yes, a wife and two kids. We made a family decision that the next 18 months would be a challenge, but that it would be worth it. I've become an early riser, so typically I do a lot of my studying in the morning before work. I'll wake up at 4 a.m., do some homework, go to work, and get home in time for dinner; then I'll spend a little time with my family, go to sleep, and then it starts all over again.

APPENDIX 13A

Computation of Employees' Bonuses

OBJECTIVE 8
After studying Appendix 13A, you should be able to: Compute employee bonuses under differing arrangements.

Because the amount of a bonus is an expense of the business, the problem of computing the amount of bonus based on income becomes more difficult. Say a company has income of $100,000 determined before considering the bonus expense. According to the terms of the bonus agreement, 20% of the income is to be set aside for distribution among the employees. If the bonus were not itself an expense to be deducted in determining net income, the amount of the bonus could be computed very simply as 20% of the income before bonus of $100,000. However, the bonus itself is an expense that must be deducted in arriving at the amount of income on which the bonus is to be based. Hence, $100,000 reduced by the bonus is the figure on which the bonus is to be computed. That is, the bonus is equal to 20% of $100,000 less the bonus. Stated algebraically:

$$\begin{aligned} B &= 0.20\ (\$100{,}000 - B) \\ B &= \$20{,}000 - 0.2B \\ 1.2B &= \$20{,}000 \\ B &= \$16{,}666.67 \end{aligned}$$

A similar problem results from the relationship of bonus payments to federal income taxes. Assume income of $100,000 computed without subtracting either the employees' bonus or taxes on income. The bonus is to be based on income **after deducting income taxes but before deducting the bonus**. The rate of income tax is 40% and the bonus of 20% is a deductible expense for tax purposes. The bonus is, therefore, equal to 20% of $100,000 minus the tax, and the tax is equal to 40% of $100,000 minus the bonus. Thus we have two simultaneous equations that, using B as the symbol for the bonus and T for the tax, may be stated algebraically as follows:

$$\begin{aligned} B &= 0.20\ (\$100{,}000 - T) \\ T &= 0.40\ (\$100{,}000 - B) \end{aligned}$$

These may be solved by substituting the value of T as indicated in the second equation for T in the first equation.

$$\begin{aligned} B &= 0.20\ [\$100{,}000 - 0.40\ (\$100{,}000 - B)] \\ B &= 0.20\ (\$100{,}000 - \$40{,}000 + 0.4B) \\ B &= 0.20\ (\$60{,}000 + 0.4B) \\ B &= \$12{,}000 + 0.08B \\ 0.92B &= \$12{,}000 \\ B &= \$13{,}043.48 \end{aligned}$$

Substituting this value for B into the second equation allows us to solve for T:

$$
\begin{aligned}
T &= 0.40\ (\$100{,}000 - \$13{,}043.48) \\
T &= 0.40\ (\$86{,}956.52) \\
T &= \$34{,}782.61
\end{aligned}
$$

To prove these amounts, both should be worked back into the original equation.

$$
\begin{aligned}
B &= 0.20\ (\$100{,}000 - T) \\
\$13{,}043.48 &= 0.20\ (\$100{,}000 - \$34{,}782.61) \\
\$13{,}043.48 &= 0.20\ (\$65{,}217.39) \\
\$13{,}043.48 &= \$13{,}043.48
\end{aligned}
$$

If the terms of the agreement provide for deducting both the tax and the bonus to arrive at the income figure on which the bonus is computed, the equations would be:

$$
\begin{aligned}
B &= 0.20\ (\$100{,}000 - B - T) \\
T &= 0.40\ (\$100{,}000 - B)
\end{aligned}
$$

Substituting the value of T from the second equation into the first equation enables us to solve for B:

$$
\begin{aligned}
B &= 0.20\ [\$100{,}000 - B - 0.40\ (\$100{,}000 - B)] \\
B &= 0.20\ (\$100{,}000 - B - \$40{,}000 + 0.4B) \\
B &= 0.20\ (\$60{,}000 - 0.6B) \\
B &= \$12{,}000 - 0.12B \\
1.12B &= \$12{,}000 \\
B &= \$10{,}714.29
\end{aligned}
$$

The value for B may then be substituted in the second equation above, and that equation solved for T:

$$
\begin{aligned}
T &= 0.40\ (\$100{,}000 - \$10{,}714.29) \\
T &= 0.40\ (\$89{,}285.71) \\
T &= \$35{,}714.28
\end{aligned}
$$

If these values are then substituted in the original bonus equation, they prove themselves as follows:

$$
\begin{aligned}
B &= 0.20\ (\$100{,}000 - B - T) \\
\$10{,}714.29 &= 0.20\ (\$100{,}000 - \$10{,}714.29 - \$35{,}714.28) \\
\$10{,}714.29 &= 0.20\ (\$53{,}571.43) \\
\$10{,}714.29 &= \$10{,}714.29
\end{aligned}
$$

Drawing up a legal document such as a bonus agreement is a task for a lawyer, not an accountant, although accountants are frequently called on to express an opinion on the agreement's feasibility. In this respect, one should always insist that the agreement state specifically whether income taxes and the bonus itself are expenses deductible in determining income for purposes of the bonus computation.

SUMMARY OF LEARNING OBJECTIVE FOR APPENDIX 13A

8 **Compute employee bonuses under differing arrangements.** Because the bonus is based on net income and is deductible in determining net income, the bonus may have to be determined algebraically. Its computation is made more difficult by the bonus being deductible for tax purposes and the taxes being deductible from the income on which the bonus is based.

Note: All **asterisked** Questions, Brief Exercises, Exercises, Problems, and Conceptual Cases relate to material contained in the appendix to the chapter.

QUESTIONS

1 Distinguish between a current liability and a long-term debt.

2 Assume that your friend Greg Jonas, who is a music major, asks you to define and discuss the nature of a liability. Assist him by preparing a definition of a liability and by explaining to him what you believe are the elements or factors inherent in the concept of a liability.

3 Why is the liability section of the balance sheet of primary significance to bankers?

4 How are current liabilities related by definition to current assets? How are current liabilities related to a company's operating cycle?

5 Jon Bryant, a newly hired loan analyst, is examining the current liabilities of a corporate loan applicant. He observes that unearned revenues have declined in the current year compared to the prior year. Is this a positive indicator about the client's liquidity? Explain.

6 How is present value related to the concept of a liability?

7 What is the nature of a "discount" on notes payable?

8 How should a debt callable by the creditor be reported in the debtor's financial statements?

9 Under what conditions should a short-term obligation be excluded from current liabilities?

10 What evidence is necessary to demonstrate the ability to consummate the refinancing of short-term debt?

11 Discuss the accounting treatment or disclosure that should be accorded a declared but unpaid cash dividend; an accumulated but undeclared dividend on cumulative preferred stock; a stock dividend distributable.

12 How does deferred or unearned revenue arise? Why can it be classified properly as a current liability? Give several examples of business activities that result in unearned revenues.

13 What are compensated absences?

14 Under what conditions must an employer accrue a liability for the cost of compensated absences?

15 Under what conditions is an employer required to accrue a liability for sick pay? Under what conditions is an employer permitted but not required to accrue a liability for sick pay?

16 Caitlin Carter operates a health food store, and she has been the only employee. Her business is growing, and she is considering hiring some additional staff to help her in the store. Explain to her the various payroll deductions that she will have to account for, including their potential impact on her financial statements, if she hires additional staff.

17 Over which two periods of time is the property tax most commonly allocated? Under what circumstances might each of these periods be justified as the period of expense?

18 Define (a) a contingency and (b) a contingent liability.

19 Under what conditions should a contingent liability be recorded?

20 Distinguish between a "current liability" and a "contingent liability." Give two examples of each type.

21 How are the terms "probable," "reasonably possible," and "remote" related to contingent liabilities?

22 Contrast the cash basis method and the accrual method of accounting for warranty costs.

23 Kren Company has had a record-breaking year in terms of growth in sales and profitability. However, market research indicates that it will experience operating losses in two of its major businesses next year. The controller has proposed that the company record a provision for these future losses this year, since it can afford to take the charge and still show good results. Advise the controller on the appropriateness of this charge.

24 How does the expense warranty approach differ from the sales warranty approach?

25 Zucker-Abrahams Airlines Inc. awards members of its Flightline program a second ticket at half price, valid for 2 years anywhere on its flight system, when a full-price ticket is purchased. How would you account for the full-fare and half-fare tickets?

26 Northeast Airlines Co. awards members of its Frequent Fliers Club one free round-trip ticket, anywhere on its flight system, for every 50,000 miles flown on its planes. How would you account for the free ticket award?

27 Should a liability be recorded for risk of loss due to lack of insurance coverage? Discuss.

28 What factors must be considered in determining whether or not to record a liability for pending litigation? For threatened litigation?

29 Within the current liability section, how do you believe the accounts should be listed? Defend your position.

30 How does the acid-test ratio differ from the current ratio? How are they similar?

31 When should liabilities for each of the following items be recorded on the books of an ordinary business corporation?

(a) Acquisition of goods by purchase on credit.

(b) Officers' salaries.

(c) Special bonus to employees.

(d) Dividends.

(e) Purchase commitments.

BRIEF EXERCISES

BE13-1 Congo Corporation uses a periodic inventory system and the gross method of accounting for purchase discounts. On July 1, Congo purchased $40,000 of inventory, terms 2/10, n/30, FOB shipping point. Congo paid freight costs of $1,200. On July 3, Congo returned damaged goods and received credit of $6,000. On July 10, Congo paid for the goods. Prepare all necessary journal entries for Congo.

BE13-2 Desert Storm Company borrowed $50,000 on November 1, 2001, by signing a $50,000, 9%, 3-month note. Prepare Desert Storm's November 1, 2001, entry; the December 31, 2001, annual adjusting entry; and the February 1, 2002, entry.

BE13-3 Kawasaki Corporation borrowed $50,000 on November 1, 2001, by signing a $51,125, 3-month, zero-interest-bearing note. Prepare Kawasaki's November 1, 2001, entry; the December 31, 2001, annual adjusting entry; and the February 1, 2002, entry.

BE13-4 At December 31, 2001, Fifa Corporation owes $500,000 on a note payable due February 15, 2002. (a) If Fifa refinances the obligation by issuing a long-term note on February 14 and using the proceeds to pay off the note due February 15, how much of the $500,000 should be reported as a current liability at December 31, 2001? (b) If Fifa pays off the note on February 15, 2002, and then borrows $1,000,000 on a long-term basis on March 1, how much of the $500,000 should be reported as a current liability at December 31, 2001?

BE13-5 Game Pro Magazine sold 10,000 annual subscriptions on August 1, 2001, for $18 each. Prepare Game Pro's August 1, 2001, journal entry and the December 31, 2001, annual adjusting entry.

BE13-6 Flintstones Corporation made credit sales of $30,000 which are subject to 6% sales tax. The corporation also made cash sales which totaled $19,610 including the 6% sales tax. (a) Prepare the entry to record Flintstones' credit sales. (b) Prepare the entry to record Flintstones' cash sales.

BE13-7 Final Fantasy Inc. receives its property tax bill from Jidoor County in December each year. The county uses the tax receipts to provide services from January through the following December. Tax payments are due February 1 and August 1. In December 2000, Final Fantasy received a tax bill of $14,760 for 2001. At January 31, the company recorded property tax expense and property taxes payable of $1,230 (1/12 of $14,760). Prepare Final Fantasy's February 1 entry (when half of the taxes are due), and the February 28 adjusting entry.

BE13-8 Future Zone Corporation's weekly payroll of $23,000 included FICA taxes withheld of $1,426, federal taxes withheld of $2,990, state taxes withheld of $920, and insurance premiums withheld of $250. Prepare the journal entry to record Future Zone's payroll.

BE13-9 Tale Spin Inc. provides paid vacations to its employees. At December 31, 2001, 30 employees have each earned 2 weeks of vacation time. The employees' average salary is $600 per week. Prepare Tale Spin's December 31, 2001, adjusting entry.

BE13-10 Gargoyle Corporation provides its officers with bonuses based on income. For 2001, the bonuses total $450,000 and are paid on February 15, 2002. Prepare Gargoyle's December 31, 2001, adjusting entry and the February 15, 2002, entry.

BE13-11 Justice League Inc. is involved in a lawsuit at December 31, 2001. (a) Prepare the December 31 entry assuming it is probable that Justice League will be liable for $700,000 as a result of this suit.

(b) Prepare the December 31 entry, if any, assuming it is *not* probable that Justice League will be liable for any payment as a result of this suit.

BE13-12 Kohlbeck Company recently was sued by a competitor for patent infringement. Attorneys have determined that it is probable that Kohlbeck will lose the case and that a reasonable estimate of damages to be paid by Kohlbeck is $200,000. In light of this case, Kohlbeck is considering establishing a $100,000 self-insurance allowance. What entry(ies), if any, should Kohlbeck record to recognize this loss contingency?

BE13-13 Frantic Factory provides a 2-year warranty with one of its products which was first sold in 2001. In that year, Frantic spent $70,000 servicing warranty claims. At year-end, Frantic estimates that an additional $500,000 will be spent in the future to service warranty claims related to 2001 sales. Prepare Frantic's journal entry to record the $70,000 expenditure, and the December 31 adjusting entry.

BE13-14 Herzog Zwei Corporation sells VCRs. The corporation also offers its customers a 2-year warranty contract. During 2001, Herzog Zwei sold 15,000 warranty contracts at $99 each. The corporation spent $180,000 servicing warranties during 2001, and it estimates that an additional $900,000 will be spent in the future to service the warranties. Prepare Herzog Zwei's journal entries for (a) the sale of contracts, (b) the cost of servicing the warranties, and (c) the recognition of warranty revenue.

BE13-15 Klax Company offers a set of building blocks to customers who send in 3 UPC codes from Klax cereal, along with 50¢. The blocks sets cost Klax $1.10 each to purchase and 60¢ each to mail to customers. During 2001, Klax sold 1,000,000 boxes of cereal. The company expects 30% of the UPC codes to be sent in. During 2001, 120,000 UPC codes were redeemed. Prepare Klax's December 31, 2001, adjusting entry.

***BE13-16** Locke Company provides its president, Cyan Garamonde, with a bonus equal to 10% of income after deducting income tax and bonus. Income *before* deducting income tax and bonus is $265,000, and the tax rate is 40%. Compute the amount of Cyan Garamonde's bonus.

EXERCISES

E13-1 (Balance Sheet Classification of Various Liabilities) How would each of the following items be reported on the balance sheet?

(a) Accrued vacation pay.
(b) Estimated taxes payable.
(c) Service warranties on appliance sales.
(d) Bank overdraft.
(e) Employee payroll deductions unremitted.
(f) Unpaid bonus to officers.
(g) Deposit received from customer to guarantee performance of a contract.
(h) Sales taxes payable.
(i) Gift certificates sold to customers but not yet redeemed.
(j) Premium offers outstanding.
(k) Discount on notes payable.
(l) Personal injury claim pending.
(m) Current maturities of long-term debts to be paid from current assets.
(n) Cash dividends declared but unpaid.
(o) Dividends in arrears on preferred stock.
(p) Loans from officers.

E13-2 (Accounts and Notes Payable) The following are selected 2001 transactions of Sean Astin Corporation:

Sept. 1 Purchased inventory from Encino Company on account for $50,000. Astin records purchases gross and uses a periodic inventory system.
Oct. 1 Issued a $50,000, 12-month, 12% note to Encino in payment of account.
Oct. 1 Borrowed $50,000 from the Shore Bank by signing a 12-month, noninterest-bearing $56,000 note.

Instructions

(a) Prepare journal entries for the selected transactions above.
(b) Prepare adjusting entries at December 31.
(c) Compute the total net liability to be reported on the December 31 balance sheet for:
  (1) the interest-bearing note.
  (2) the noninterest-bearing note.

E13-3 (Refinancing of Short-Term Debt) On December 31, 2001, Hattie McDaniel Company had $1,200,000 of short-term debt in the form of notes payable due February 2, 2002. On January 21, 2002, the company issued 25,000 shares of its common stock for $38 per share, receiving $950,000 proceeds after brokerage fees and other costs of issuance. On February 2, 2002, the proceeds from the stock sale, supplemented by an additional $250,000 cash, are used to liquidate the $1,200,000 debt. The December 31, 2001, balance sheet is issued on February 23, 2002.

Instructions

Show how the $1,200,000 of short-term debt should be presented on the December 31, 2001, balance sheet, including note disclosure.

E13-4 (Refinancing of Short-Term Debt) On December 31, 2001, Chris Atkins Company has $7,000,000 of short-term debt in the form of notes payable to Blue Lagoon State Bank due periodically in 2002. On January 28, 2002, Atkins enters into a refinancing agreement with Blue Lagoon that will permit it to borrow up to 60% of the gross amount of its accounts receivable. Receivables are expected to range between a low of $6,000,000 in May to a high of $8,000,000 in October during the year 2002. The interest cost of the maturing short-term debt is 15%, and the new agreement calls for a fluctuating interest at 1% above the prime rate on notes due in 2006. Atkin's December 31, 2001, balance sheet is issued on February 15, 2002.

Instructions

Prepare a partial balance sheet for Atkins at December 31, 2001, showing how its $7,000,000 of short-term debt should be presented, including footnote disclosures.

E13-5 (Compensated Absences) Zero Mostel Company began operations on January 2, 2000. It employs 9 individuals who work 8-hour days and are paid hourly. Each employee earns 10 paid vacation days and 6 paid sick days annually. Vacation days may be taken after January 15 of the year following the year in which they are earned. Sick days may be taken as soon as they are earned; unused sick days accumulate. Additional information is as follows:

Actual Hourly Wage Rate		Vacation Days Used by Each Employee		Sick Days Used by Each Employee	
2000	2001	2000	2001	2000	2001
$10	$11	0	9	4	5

Zero Mostel Company has chosen to accrue the cost of compensated absences at rates of pay in effect during the period when earned and to accrue sick pay when earned.

Instructions

(a) Prepare journal entries to record transactions related to compensated absences during 2000 and 2001.

(b) Compute the amounts of any liability for compensated absences that should be reported on the balance sheet at December 31, 2000 and 2001.

E13-6 (Compensated Absences) Assume the facts in the preceding exercise, except that Zero Mostel Company has chosen not to accrue paid sick leave until used, and has chosen to accrue vacation time at expected future rates of pay without discounting. The company used the following projected rates to accrue vacation time:

Year in Which Vacation Time Was Earned	Projected Future Pay Rates Used to Accrue Vacation Pay
2000	$10.75
2001	11.60

Instructions

(a) Prepare journal entries to record transactions related to compensated absences during 2000 and 2001.

(b) Compute the amounts of any liability for compensated absences that should be reported on the balance sheet at December 31, 2000, and 2001.

E13-7 (Adjusting Entry for Sales Tax) During the month of June, R. Attenborough Boutique had cash sales of $233,200 and credit sales of $153,700, both of which include the 6% sales tax that must be remitted to the state by July 15.

Instructions

Prepare the adjusting entry that should be recorded to fairly present the June 30 financial statements.

E13-8 (Payroll Tax Entries) The payroll of Rene Auber Company for September 2000 is as follows:

Total payroll was $480,000, of which $110,000 is exempt from Social Security tax because it represented amounts paid in excess of $76,200 to certain employees. The amount paid to employees in excess of $7,000 was $400,000. Income taxes in the amount of $90,000 were withheld, as was $9,000 in union dues. The state unemployment tax is 3.5%, but Auber Company is allowed a credit of 2.3% by the state for its unemployment experience. Also, assume that the current F.I.C.A. tax is 7.65% on an employee's wages to $76,200 and 1.45% in excess of $76,200. No employee for Auber makes more than $125,000. The federal unemployment tax rate is .8% after state credit.

Instructions

Prepare the necessary journal entries if the wages and salaries paid and the employer payroll taxes are recorded separately.

E13-9 (Payroll Tax Entries) Green Day Hardware Company's payroll for November 2001 is summarized below.

		Amount Subject to Payroll Taxes		
			Unemployment Tax	
Payroll	Wages Due	F.I.C.A.	Federal	State
Factory	$120,000	$120,000	$40,000	$40,000
Sales	44,000	32,000	4,000	4,000
Administrative	36,000	36,000	—	—
Total	$200,000	$188,000	$44,000	$44,000

At this point in the year some employees have already received wages in excess of those to which payroll taxes apply. Assume that the state unemployment tax is 2.5%. The F.I.C.A. rate is 7.65% on an employee's wages to $76,200 and 1.45% in excess of $76,200. Of the $188,000 wages subject to F.I.C.A. tax, $20,000 is in excess of $76,200 related to the sales wages. Federal unemployment tax rate is .8% after credits. Income tax withheld amounts to $16,000 for factory, $7,000 for sales, and $6,000 for administrative.

Instructions

(a) Prepare a schedule showing the employer's total cost of wages for November by function. (Round all computations to nearest dollar.)

(b) Prepare the journal entries to record the factory, sales, and administrative payrolls including the employer's payroll taxes.

E13-10 (Warranties) Soundgarden Company sold 200 copymaking machines in 2001 for $4,000 apiece, together with a one-year warranty. Maintenance on each machine during the warranty period averages $330.

Instructions

(a) Prepare entries to record the sale of the machines and the related warranty costs, assuming that the accrual method is used. Actual warranty costs incurred in 2001 were $17,000.

(b) On the basis of the data above, prepare the appropriate entries, assuming that the cash basis method is used.

E13-11 (Warranties) Sheryl Crow Equipment Company sold 500 Rollomatics during 2001 at $6,000 each. During 2001, Crow spent $20,000 servicing the 2-year warranties that accompany the Rollomatic. All applicable transactions are on a cash basis.

Instructions

(a) Prepare 2001 entries for Crow using the expense warranty approach. Assume that Crow estimates the total cost of servicing the warranties will be $120,000 for 2 years.

(b) Prepare 2001 entries for Crow assuming that the warranties are not an integral part of the sale. Assume that of the sales total, $150,000 relates to sales of warranty contracts. Crow estimates the total cost of servicing the warranties will be $120,000 for 2 years. Estimate revenues earned on the basis of costs incurred and estimated costs.

E13-12 (Liability for Returnable Containers) Candlebox Company sells its products in expensive, reusable containers. The customer is charged a deposit for each container delivered and receives a refund for each container returned within two years after the year of delivery. Candlebox accounts for the containers not returned within the time limit as being sold at the deposit amount. Information for 2001 is as follows:

Containers held by customers at December 31, 2000, from deliveries in:	1999	$170,000	
	2000	480,000	$650,000
Containers delivered in 2001			860,000
Containers returned in 2001 from deliveries in:	1999	$115,000	
	2000	280,000	
	2001	314,000	709,000

Instructions

(a) Prepare all journal entries required for Candlebox Company during 2001 for the returnable containers.

(b) Compute the total amount Candlebox should report as a liability for returnable containers at December 31, 2001.

(c) Should the liability computed in (b) above be reported as current or long-term?

(AICPA adapted)

E13-13 (Premium Entries) Yanni Company includes 1 coupon in each box of soap powder that it packs, and 10 coupons are redeemable for a premium (a kitchen utensil). In 2001, Yanni Company purchased 8,800 premiums at 80 cents each and sold 110,000 boxes of soap powder @ $3.30 per box; 44,000 coupons were presented for redemption in 2001. It is estimated that 60% of the coupons will eventually be presented for redemption.

Instructions

Prepare all the entries that would be made relative to sales of soap powder and to the premium plan in 2001.

E13-14 (Contingencies) Presented below are three independent situations. Answer the question at the end of each situation.

1. During 2001, Salt-n-Pepa Inc. became involved in a tax dispute with the IRS. Salt-n-Pepa's attorneys have indicated that they believe it is probable that Salt-n-Pepa will lose this dispute. They also believe that Salt-n-Pepa will have to pay the IRS between $900,000 and $1,400,000. After the 2001 financial statements were issued, the case was settled with the IRS for $1,200,000. What amount, if any, should be reported as a liability for this contingency as of December 31, 2001?
2. On October 1, 2001, Alan Jackson Chemical was identified as a potentially responsible party by the Environmental Protection Agency. Jackson's management along with its counsel have concluded that it is probable that Jackson will be responsible for damages, and a reasonable estimate of these damages is $5,000,000. Jackson's insurance policy of $9,000,000 has a deductible clause of $500,000. How should Alan Jackson Chemical report this information in its financial statements at December 31, 2001?
3. Melissa Etheridge Inc. had a manufacturing plant in Bosnia, which was destroyed in the civil war. It is not certain who will compensate Etheridge for this destruction, but Etheridge has been assured by governmental officials that it will receive a definite amount for this plant. The amount of the compensation will be less than the fair value of the plant, but more than its book value. How should the contingency be reported in the financial statements of Etheridge Inc.?

E13-15 (Premiums) Presented below are three independent situations.

1. Mark Grace Stamp Company records stamp service revenue and provides for the cost of redemptions in the year stamps are sold to licensees. Grace's past experience indicates that only 80% of the stamps sold to licensees will be redeemed. Grace's liability for stamp redemptions was $13,000,000 at December 31, 2000. Additional information for 2001 is as follows:

Stamp service revenue from stamps sold to licensees	$9,500,000
Cost of redemptions (stamps sold prior to 1/1/01)	6,000,000

If all the stamps sold in 2001 were presented for redemption in 2002, the redemption cost would be $5,200,000. What amount should Grace report as a liability for stamp redemptions at December 31, 2001?

2. In packages of its products, Sam Sosa Inc. includes coupons that may be presented at retail stores to obtain discounts on other Sosa products. Retailers are reimbursed for the face amount of coupons redeemed plus 10% of that amount for handling costs. Sosa honors requests for coupon redemption by retailers up to 3 months after the consumer expiration date. Sosa estimates that 60% of all coupons issued will ultimately be redeemed. Information relating to coupons issued by Sosa during 2001 is as follows:

Consumer expiration date	12/31/01
Total face amount of coupons issued	$800,000
Total payments to retailers as of 12/31/01	330,000

What amount should Sam Sosa report as a liability for unredeemed coupons at December 31, 2001?

3. Don Baylor Company sold 700,000 boxes of pie mix under a new sales promotional program. Each box contains one coupon, which submitted with $4.00, entitles the customer to a baking pan. Baylor pays $6.00 per pan and $0.50 for handling and shipping. Baylor estimates that 70% of the coupons will be redeemed, even though only 250,000 coupons had been processed during 2001. What amount should Baylor report as a liability for unredeemed coupons at December 31, 2001?

(AICPA adapted)

E13-16 (Financial Statement Impact of Liability Transactions) Presented below is a list of possible transactions.

1. Purchased inventory for $80,000 on account (assume perpetual system is used).
2. Issued an $80,000 note payable in payment on account (see item 1 above).
3. Recorded accrued interest on the note from item 2 above.
4. Borrowed $100,000 from the bank by signing a 6-month, $112,000, noninterest-bearing note.
5. Recognized 4 months' interest expense on the note from item 4 above.
6. Recorded cash sales of $75,260, which includes 6% sales tax.
7. Recorded wage expense of $35,000. The cash paid was $25,000; the difference was due to various amounts withheld.
8. Recorded employer's payroll taxes.
9. Accrued accumulated vacation pay.
10. Recorded accrued property taxes payable.
11. Recorded bonuses due to employees.
12. Recorded a contingent loss on a lawsuit that the company will probably lose.
13. Accrued warranty expense (assume expense warranty approach).
14. Paid warranty costs that were accrued in item 13 above.
15. Recorded sales of product and related warranties (assume sales warranty approach).
16. Paid warranty costs under contracts from item 15 above.
17. Recognized warranty revenue (see item 15 above).
18. Recorded estimated liability for premium claims outstanding.

Instructions

Set up a table using the format shown below and analyze the effect of the 18 transactions on the financial statement categories indicated.

#	Assets	Liabilities	Owners' Equity	Net Income
1				

Use the following code:

I: Increase D: Decrease NE: No net effect

E13-17 (Ratio Computations and Discussion) Sprague Company has been operating for several years, and on December 31, 2001, presented the following balance sheet:

SPRAGUE COMPANY
Balance Sheet
December 31, 2001

Cash	$ 40,000	Accounts payable	$ 80,000
Receivables	75,000	Mortgage payable	140,000
Inventories	95,000	Common stock ($1.00 par)	150,000
Plant assets (net)	220,000	Retained earnings	60,000
	$430,000		$430,000

The net income for 2001 was $25,000. Assume that total assets are the same in 2000 and 2001.

Instructions

Compute each of the following ratios. For each of the four indicate the manner in which it is computed and its significance as a tool in the analysis of the financial soundness of the company.

(a) Current ratio.
(b) Acid-test ratio.
(c) Debt to total assets.
(d) Rate of return on assets.

E13-18 (Ratio Computations and Analysis) Hood Company's condensed financial statements provide the following information:

HOOD COMPANY
Balance Sheet

	Dec. 31, 2001	Dec. 31, 2000
Cash	$ 52,000	$ 60,000
Accounts receivable (net)	198,000	80,000
Marketable securities (short-term)	80,000	40,000
Inventories	440,000	360,000
Prepaid expenses	3,000	7,000
Total current assets	$ 773,000	$ 547,000
Property, plant, and equipment (net)	857,000	853,000
Total assets	$1,630,000	$1,400,000
Current liabilities	240,000	160,000
Bonds payable	400,000	400,000
Common stockholders' equity	990,000	840,000
Total liabilities and stockholders' equity	$1,630,000	$1,400,000

Income Statement
For the Year Ended 2001

Sales	$1,640,000
Cost of goods sold	(800,000)
Gross profit	840,000
Selling and administrative expense	(440,000)
Interest expense	(40,000)
Net income	$ 360,000

Instructions

(a) Determine the following:

(1) Current ratio at December 31, 2001.

(2) Acid-test ratio at December 31, 2001.

(3) Accounts receivable turnover for 2001.

(4) Inventory turnover for 2001.

(5) Rate of return on assets for 2001.

(6) Profit margin on sales.

(b) Prepare a brief evaluation of the financial condition of Hood Company and of the adequacy of its profits.

E13-19 (Ratio Computations and Effect of Transactions) Presented below is information related to Carver Inc.:

CARVER INC.
Balance Sheet
December 31, 2001

Cash		$ 45,000	Notes payable (short-term)	$ 50,000
Receivables	$110,000		Accounts payable	32,000
Less: Allowance	15,000	95,000	Accrued liabilities	5,000
Inventories		170,000	Capital stock (par $5)	260,000
Prepaid insurance		8,000	Retained earnings	141,000
Land		20,000		
Equipment (net)		150,000		
		$488,000		$488,000

Income Statement For the Year Ended December 31, 2001		
Sales		$1,400,000
Cost of goods sold		
Inventory, Jan. 1, 2001	$200,000	
Purchases	790,000	
Cost of goods available for sale	990,000	
Inventory, Dec. 31, 2001	170,000	
Cost of goods sold		820,000
Gross profit on sales		580,000
Operating expenses		170,000
Net income		$ 410,000

Instructions

(a) Compute the following ratios or relationships of Carver Inc. Assume that the ending account balances are representative unless the information provided indicates differently.

(1) Current ratio.
(2) Inventory turnover.
(3) Receivables turnover.
(4) Earnings per share.
(5) Profit margin on sales.
(6) Rate of return on assets on December 31, 2001.

(b) Indicate for each of the following transactions whether the transaction would improve, weaken, or have no effect on the current ratio of Carver Inc. at December 31, 2001.

(1) Write off an uncollectible account receivable, $2,200.
(2) Purchase additional capital stock for cash.
(3) Pay $40,000 on notes payable (short-term).
(4) Collect $23,000 on accounts receivable.
(5) Buy equipment on account.
(6) Give an existing creditor a short-term note in settlement of account.

***E13-20 (Bonus Computation)** Jud Buechler, president of the Supporting Cast Company, has a bonus arrangement with the company under which he receives 15% of the net income (after deducting taxes and bonuses) each year. For the current year, the net income before deducting either the provision for income taxes or the bonus is $299,750. The bonus is deductible for tax purposes, and the effective tax rate may be assumed to be 40%.

Instructions

(a) Compute the amount of Jud Buechler's bonus.
(b) Compute the appropriate provision for federal income taxes for the year.
(c) Prepare the December 31 journal entry to record the bonus (which will not be paid until next year).

***E13-21 (Bonus Computation and Income Statement Preparation)** The incomplete income statement of Scottie Pippen Company appears below:

SCOTTIE PIPPEN COMPANY Income Statement For the Year 2001		
Revenue		$10,000,000
Cost of goods sold		7,000,000
Gross profit		3,000,000
Administrative and selling expenses	$1,000,000	
Profit-sharing bonus to employees	?	?
Income before income taxes		?
Income taxes		?
Net income		$?

The employee profit-sharing plan requires that 20% of all profits remaining after the deduction of the bonus and income taxes be distributed to the employees by the first day of the fourth month following each year-end. The federal income tax is 45%, and the bonus is tax-deductible.

Instructions

Complete the condensed income statement of Scottie Pippen Company for the year 2001.

***E13-22 (Bonus Compensation)** Alan Iverson Company has a profit-sharing agreement with its employees that provides for deposit in a pension trust for the benefit of the employees of 25% of the net income after deducting (1) federal taxes on income, (2) the amount of the annual pension contribution, and (3) a return of 10% on the stockholders' equity as of the end of the year 2001.

Instructions

Compute the amount of the pension contribution under the assumption that the stockholders' equity at the end of the year before adding the net income for the year is $700,000; that net income for the year before either the pension contribution or tax is $300,000; and that the pension contribution is deductible for tax purposes. Use 40% as the applicable rate of tax.

PROBLEMS

P13-1 (Current Liability Entries and Adjustments) Described below are certain transactions of James Edwards Corporation.

1. On February 2, the corporation purchased goods from Jack Haley Company for $50,000 subject to cash discount terms of 2/10, n/30. Purchases and accounts payable are recorded by the corporation at net amounts after cash discounts. The invoice was paid on February 26.
2. On April 1, the corporation bought a truck for $40,000 from General Motors Company, paying $4,000 in cash and signing a one-year, 12% note for the balance of the purchase price.
3. On May 1, the corporation borrowed $80,000 from Chicago National Bank by signing a $92,000 non-interest-bearing note due one year from May 1.
4. On August 1, the board of directors declared a $300,000 cash dividend that was payable on September 10 to stockholders of record on August 31.

Instructions

(a) Make all the journal entries necessary to record the transactions above using appropriate dates.

(b) James Edwards Corporation's year-end is December 31. Assuming that no adjusting entries relative to the transactions above have been recorded, prepare any adjusting journal entries concerning interest that are necessary to present fair financial statements at December 31. Assume straight-line amortization of discounts.

P13-2 (Current Liability Entries and Adjustments) Listed below are selected transactions of Kobe Bryant Department Store for the current year ending December 31.

1. On December 5, the store received $500 from the Phil Jackson Players as a deposit to be returned after certain furniture to be used in stage production was returned on January 15.
2. During December, cash sales totaled $834,750, which includes the 5% sales tax that must be remitted to the state by the fifteenth day of the following month.
3. On December 10, the store purchased for cash three delivery trucks for $99,000. The trucks were purchased in a state that applies a 5% sales tax.
4. The store follows the practice of accruing its property tax liability from the lien date. Property taxes of $66,000 became a lien on May 1 and were paid in two equal installments on July 1 and October 1.

Instructions

Prepare all the journal entries necessary to record the transactions noted above as they occurred and any adjusting journal entries relative to the transactions that would be required to present fair financial statements at December 31. Date each entry. For simplicity, assume that adjusting entries are recorded only once a year on December 31.

P13-3 (Payroll Tax Entries) Star Wars Company pays its office employee payroll weekly. Below is a partial list of employees and their payroll data for August. Because August is their vacation period, vacation pay is also listed.

Employee	Earnings to July 31	Weekly Pay	Vacation Pay to Be Received in August
Mark Hamill	$4,200	$180	—
Carrie Fisher	3,500	150	$300
Harrison Ford	2,700	110	220
Alec Guinness	7,400	250	—
Peter Cushing	8,000	290	580

Assume that the federal income tax withheld is 10% of wages. Union dues withheld are 2% of wages. Vacations are taken the second and third weeks of August by Fisher, Ford, and Cushing. The state unemployment tax rate is 2.5% and the federal is .8%, both on a $7,000 maximum. The F.I.C.A. rate is 7.65% on employee and employer on a maximum of $76,200 per employee. In addition, a 1.45% rate is charged both employer and employee for an employee's wage in excess of $76,200.

Instructions

Make the journal entries necessary for each of the four August payrolls. The entries for the payroll and for the company's liability are made separately. Also make the entry to record the monthly payment of accrued payroll liabilities.

P13-4 (Payroll Tax Entries) Below is a payroll sheet for Empire Import Company for the month of September 2001. The company is allowed a 1% unemployment compensation rate by the state; the federal unemployment tax rate is .8% and the maximum for both is $7,000. Assume a 10% federal income tax rate for all employees and a 7.65% F.I.C.A. tax on employee and employer on a maximum of $76,200. In addition, 1.45% is charged both employer and employee for an employee's wage in excess of $76,200 per employee.

Name	Earnings to Aug. 31	September Earnings	Income Tax Withholding	F.I.C.A.	State U.C.	Federal U.C.
B.D. Williams	$ 6,800	$ 800				
D. Prowse	6,300	700				
K. Baker	7,600	1,100				
F. Oz	13,600	1,900				
A. Daniels	105,000	15,000				
P. Mayhew	112,000	16,000				

Instructions

(a) Complete the payroll sheet and make the necessary entry to record the payment of the payroll.
(b) Make the entry to record the payroll tax expenses of Empire Import Company.
(c) Make the entry to record the payment of the payroll liabilities created. Assume that the company pays all payroll liabilities at the end of each month.

P13-5 (Warranties, Accrual, and Cash Basis) Davey Lopes Corporation sells portable computers under a 2-year warranty contract that requires the corporation to replace defective parts and to provide the necessary repair labor. During 2001 the corporation sells for cash 300 computers at a unit price of $3,500. On the basis of past experience, the 2-year warranty costs are estimated to be $155 for parts and $185 for labor per unit. (For simplicity, assume that all sales occurred on December 31, 2001.) The warranty is not sold separately from the computer.

Instructions

(a) Record any necessary journal entries in 2001, applying the cash basis method.
(b) Record any necessary journal entries in 2001, applying the expense warranty accrual method.
(c) What liability relative to these transactions would appear on the December 31, 2001, balance sheet and how would it be classified if the cash basis method is applied?
(d) What liability relative to these transactions would appear on the December 31, 2001, balance sheet and how would it be classified if the expense warranty accrual method is applied?

In 2002 the actual warranty costs to Davey Lopes Corporation were $21,400 for parts and $24,900 for labor.

(e) Record any necessary journal entries in 2002, applying the cash basis method.
(f) Record any necessary journal entries in 2002, applying the expense warranty accrual method.

P13-6 (Extended Warranties) Brett Perriman Company sells televisions at an average price of $750 and also offers to each customer a separate 3-year warranty contract for $75 that requires the company to perform periodic services and to replace defective parts. During 2001, the company sold 300 televisions and 270 warranty contracts for cash. It estimates the 3-year warranty costs as $20 for parts and $40 for labor and accounts for warranties separately. Assume sales occurred on December 31, 2001, income is recognized on the warranties, and straight-line recognition of warranty revenues occurs.

Instructions

(a) Record any necessary journal entries in 2001.

(b) What liability relative to these transactions would appear on the December 31, 2001, balance sheet and how would it be classified?

In 2002, Brett Perriman Company incurred actual costs relative to 2001 television warranty sales of $2,000 for parts and $3,000 for labor.

(c) Record any necessary journal entries in 2002 relative to 2001 television warranties.

(d) What amounts relative to the 2001 television warranties would appear on the December 31, 2002, balance sheet and how would they be classified?

P13-7 (Warranties, Accrual, and Cash Basis) Albert Belle Company sells a machine for $7,400 under a 12-month warranty agreement that requires the company to replace all defective parts and to provide the repair labor at no cost to the customers. With sales being made evenly throughout the year, the company sells 650 machines in 2002 (warranty expense is incurred half in 2002 and half in 2003). As a result of product testing, the company estimates that the warranty cost is $370 per machine ($170 parts and $200 labor).

Instructions

Assuming that actual warranty costs are incurred exactly as estimated, what journal entries would be made relative to these facts:

(a) Under application of the expense warranty accrual method for:
- **(1)** Sale of machinery in 2002?
- **(2)** Warranty costs incurred in 2002?
- **(3)** Warranty expense charged against 2002 revenues?
- **(4)** Warranty costs incurred in 2003?

(b) Under application of the cash basis method for:
- **(1)** Sale of machinery in 2002?
- **(2)** Warranty costs incurred in 2002?
- **(3)** Warranty expense charged against 2002 revenues?
- **(4)** Warranty costs incurred in 2003?

(c) What amount, if any, is disclosed in the balance sheet as a liability for future warranty costs as of December 31, 2002, under each method?

(d) Which method best reflects the income in 2002 and 2003 of Albert Belle Company? Why?

P13-8 (Premium Entries) To stimulate the sales of its Alladin breakfast cereal, the Khamsah Company places 1 coupon in each box. Five coupons are redeemable for a premium consisting of a children's hand puppet. In 2002, the company purchases 40,000 puppets at $1.50 each and sells 440,000 boxes of Alladin at $3.75 a box. From its experience with other similar premium offers, the company estimates that 40% of the coupons issued will be mailed back for redemption. During 2002, 105,000 coupons are presented for redemption.

Instructions

Prepare the journal entries that should be recorded in 2002 relative to the premium plan.

P13-9 (Premium Entries and Financial Statement Presentation) Roberto Hernandez Candy Company offers a CD single as a premium for every five candy bar wrappers presented by customers together with $2.00. The candy bars are sold by the company to distributors for 30 cents each. The purchase price of each CD to the company is $1.80; in addition it costs 30 cents to mail each CD. The results of the premium plan for the years 2001 and 2002 are as follows (all purchases and sales are for cash):

	2001	2002
CDs purchased	250,000	330,000
Candy bars sold	2,895,400	2,743,600
Wrappers redeemed	1,200,000	1,500,000
2001 wrappers expected to be redeemed in 2002	290,000	
2002 wrappers expected to be redeemed in 2003		350,000

Instructions

(a) Prepare the journal entries that should be made in 2001 and 2002 to record the transactions related to the premium plan of the Roberto Hernandez Candy Company.

(b) Indicate the account names, amounts, and classifications of the items related to the premium plan that would appear on the balance sheet and the income statement at the end of 2001 and 2002.

 **P13-10 (Loss Contingencies: Entries and Essay)** On November 24, 2001, 26 passengers on Tom Paris Airlines Flight No. 901 were injured upon landing when the plane skidded off the runway. Personal injury suits for damages totaling $5,000,000 were filed on January 11, 2002, against the airline by 18 injured passengers. The airline carries no insurance. Legal counsel has studied each suit and advised Paris that it can reasonably expect to pay 60% of the damages claimed. The financial statements for the year ended December 31, 2001, were issued February 27, 2002.

Instructions

(a) Prepare any disclosures and journal entries required by the airline in preparation of the December 31, 2001, financial statements.

(b) Ignoring the Nov. 24, 2001, accident, what liability due to the risk of loss from lack of insurance coverage should Tom Paris Airlines record or disclose? During the past decade the company has experienced at least one accident per year and incurred average damages of $3,200,000. Discuss fully.

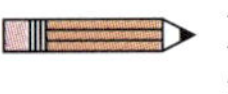 **P13-11 (Loss Contingencies: Entries and Essays)** Shoyo Corporation, in preparation of its December 31, 2001, financial statements, is attempting to determine the proper accounting treatment for each of the following situations:

1. As a result of uninsured accidents during the year, personal injury suits for $350,000 and $60,000 have been filed against the company. It is the judgment of Shoyo's legal counsel that an unfavorable outcome is unlikely in the $60,000 case but that an unfavorable verdict approximating $225,000 will probably result in the $350,000 case.
2. Shoyo Corporation owns a subsidiary in a foreign country that has a book value of $5,725,000 and an estimated fair value of $8,700,000. The foreign government has communicated to Shoyo its intention to expropriate the assets and business of all foreign investors. On the basis of settlements other firms have received from this same country, Shoyo expects to receive 40% of the fair value of its properties as final settlement.
3. Shoyo's chemical product division consisting of five plants is uninsurable because of the special risk of injury to employees and losses due to fire and explosion. The year 2001 is considered one of the safest (luckiest) in the division's history because no loss due to injury or casualty was suffered. Having suffered an average of three casualties a year during the rest of the past decade (ranging from $60,000 to $700,000), management is certain that next year the company will probably not be so fortunate.

Instructions

(a) Prepare the journal entries that should be recorded as of December 31, 2001, to recognize each of the situations above.

(b) Indicate what should be reported relative to each situation in the financial statements and accompanying notes. Explain why.

 **P13-12 (Warranties and Premiums)** Gloria Estefan's Music Emporium carries a wide variety of musical instruments, sound reproduction equipment, recorded music, and sheet music. Estefan's uses two sales promotion techniques—warranties and premiums—to attract customers.

Musical instruments and sound equipment are sold with a one-year warranty for replacement of parts and labor. The estimated warranty cost, based on past experience, is 2% of sales.

The premium is offered on the recorded and sheet music. Customers receive a coupon for each dollar spent on recorded music or sheet music. Customers may exchange 200 coupons and $20 for a CD player. Estefan's pays $34 for each CD player and estimates that 60% of the coupons given to customers will be redeemed.

Estefan's total sales for 2001 were $7,200,000—$5,400,000 from musical instruments and sound reproduction equipment and $1,800,000 from recorded music and sheet music. Replacement parts and labor for warranty work totaled $164,000 during 2001. A total of 6,500 CD players used in the premium program were purchased during the year and there were 1,200,000 coupons redeemed in 2001.

The accrual method is used by Estefan's to account for the warranty and premium costs for financial reporting purposes. The balances in the accounts related to warranties and premiums on January 1, 2001, were as shown below.

Inventory of Premium CD Players	$39,950
Estimated Premium Claims Outstanding	44,800
Estimated Liability from Warranties	136,000

Instructions

Gloria Estefan's Music Emporium is preparing its financial statements for the year ended December 31, 2001. Determine the amounts that will be shown on the 2001 financial statements for the following:

(1) Warranty Expense.
(2) Estimated Liability from Warranties.
(3) Premium Expense.
(4) Inventory of Premium CD Players.
(5) Estimated Premium Claims Outstanding.

(CMA adapted)

P13-13 (Liability Errors) You are the independent auditor engaged to audit Christine Agazzi Corporation's December 31, 2000, financial statements. Christine Agazzi manufactures household appliances. During the course of your audit, you discovered the following contingent liabilities:

1. Christine Agazzi began production on a new dishwasher in June 2000 and, by December 31, 2000, sold 100,000 to various retailers for $500 each. Each dishwasher is under a one-year warranty. The company estimates that its warranty expense per dishwasher will amount to $25. At year-end, the company had already paid out $1,000,000 in warranty expenses. Christine Agazzi's income statement shows warranty expenses of $1,000,000 for 2000. Agazzi accounts for warranty costs on the accrual basis.
2. In response to your attorney's letter, Robert Sklodowski, Esq., has informed you that Agazzi has been cited for dumping toxic waste into the Kishwaukee River. Clean-up costs and fines amount to $3,330,000. Although the case is still being contested, Sklodowski is certain that Agazzi will most probably have to pay the fine and clean-up costs. No disclosure of this situation was found in the financial statements.
3. Christine Agazzi is the defendant in a patent infringement lawsuit by Heidi Goldman over Agazzi's use of a hydraulic compressor in several of its products. Sklodowski claims that, if the suit goes against Agazzi, the loss may be as much as $5,000,000; however, Sklodowski believes the loss of this suit to be only reasonably possible. Again, no mention of this suit occurs in the financial statements.

As presented, these contingencies are not reported in accordance with GAAP which may create problems in issuing a clean audit report. You feel the need to note these problems in the work papers.

Instructions

Heading each page with the name of the company, balance sheet date, and a brief description of the problem, write a brief narrative for each of the above issues in the form of **a memorandum** to be incorporated in the audit work papers. Explain what led to the discovery of each problem, what the problem really is, and what you advised your client to do (along with any appropriate journal entries) in order to bring these contingencies in accordance with GAAP.

P13-14 (Various Current Liabilities) Alex Rodriguez Inc., a publishing company, is preparing its December 31, 2000, financial statements and must determine the proper accounting treatment for the following situations; they have retained your group to assist them in this task.

(a) Rodriguez sells subscriptions to several magazines for a 1-year, 2-year, or 3-year period. Cash receipts from subscribers are credited to magazine subscriptions collected in advance, and this account had a balance of $2,300,000 at December 31, 2000. Outstanding subscriptions at December 31, 2000, expire as follows:

During 2001—$600,000
During 2002— 500,000
During 2003— 800,000

(b) On January 2, 2000, Rodriguez discontinued collision, fire, and theft coverage on its delivery vehicles and became self-insured for these risks. Actual losses of $50,000 during 2000 were charged to delivery expense. The 1999 premium for the discontinued coverage amounted to $80,000 and the controller wants to set up a reserve for self-insurance by a debit to delivery expense of $30,000 and a credit to the reserve for self-insurance of $30,000.

(c) A suit for breach of contract seeking damages of $1,000,000 was filed by an author against Rodriguez on July 1, 2000. The company's legal counsel believes that an unfavorable outcome is probable. A reasonable estimate of the court's award to the plaintiff is in the range between $300,000 and $700,000. No amount within this range is a better estimate of potential damages than any other amount.

(d) During December 2000, a competitor company filed suit against Rodriguez for industrial espionage claiming $1,500,000 in damages. In the opinion of management and company counsel, it is reasonably possible that damages will be awarded to the plaintiff. However, the amount of potential damages awarded to the plaintiff cannot be reasonably estimated.

Instructions

For each of the above situations, provide the journal entry that should be recorded as of December 31, 2000, or explain why an entry should not be recorded.

(AICPA adapted)

***P13-15 (Bonus Computation)** Henryk Inc. has a contract with its president, Nathalie Sarraute, to pay her a bonus during each of the years 2000, 2001, 2002, and 2003. The federal income tax rate is 40% during the 4 years. The profit before deductions for bonus and federal income taxes was $250,000 in 2000, $308,000 in 2001, $350,000 in 2002, and $380,000 in 2003. The president's bonus of 12% is deductible for tax purposes in each year and is to be computed as follows:

(a) In 2000 the bonus is to be based on profit before deductions for bonus and income tax.
(b) In 2001 the bonus is to be based on profit after deduction of bonus but before deduction of income tax.
(c) In 2002 the bonus is to be based on profit before deduction of bonus but after deduction of income tax.
(d) In 2003 the bonus is to be based on profit after deductions for bonus and income tax.

Instructions
Compute the amounts of the bonus and the income tax for each of the 4 years.

P13-16 (Warranty, Bonus, and Coupon Computation) Victor Hugo Company must make computations and adjusting entries for the following independent situations at December 31, 2001:

1. Its line of amplifiers carries a 3-year warranty against defects. On the basis of past experience the estimated warranty costs related to dollar sales are: first year after sale—2% of sales; second year after sale—3% of sales; and third year after sale—4% of sales. Sales and actual warranty expenditures for the first 3 years of business were:

	Sales	Warranty Expenditures
1999	$ 800,000	$ 6,500
2000	1,100,000	17,200
2001	1,200,000	62,000

Instructions
Compute the amount that Hugo Company should report as a liability in its December 31, 2001, balance sheet. Assume that all sales are made evenly throughout each year with warranty expenses also evenly spaced relative to the rates above.

*2. Hugo Company's profit-sharing plan provides that the company will contribute to a fund an amount equal to one-fourth of its net income each year. Income before deducting the profit-sharing contribution and taxes for 2001 is $1,035,000. The applicable income tax rate is 40%, and the profit-sharing contribution is deductible for tax purposes.

Instructions
Compute the amount to be contributed to the profit-sharing fund for 2001.

3. With some of its products, Hugo Company includes coupons that are redeemable in merchandise. The coupons have no expiration date and, in the company's experience, 40% of them are redeemed. The liability for unredeemed coupons at December 31, 2000, was $9,000. During 2001, coupons worth $25,000 were issued, and merchandise worth $8,000 was distributed in exchange for coupons redeemed.

Instructions
Compute the amount of the liability that should appear on the December 31, 2001, balance sheet.

(AICPA adapted)

CONCEPTUAL CASES

C13-1 (Nature of Liabilities) Presented below is the current liabilities section of Nizami Corporation.

	($000) 2000	1999
Current Liabilities		
Notes payable	$ 68,713	$ 7,700
Accounts payable	179,496	101,379
Compensation to employees	60,312	31,649
Accrued liabilities	158,198	77,621
Income taxes payable	10,486	26,491
Current maturities of long-term debt	16,592	6,649
Total current liabilities	$493,797	$251,489

Instructions

Answer the following questions.

(a) What are the essential characteristics that make an item a liability?
(b) How does one distinguish between a current liability and a long-term liability?
(c) What are accrued liabilities? Give three examples of accrued liabilities that Nizami might have.
(d) What is the theoretically correct way to value liabilities? How are current liabilities usually valued?
(e) Why are notes payable reported first in the current liability section?
(f) What might be the items that comprise Nizami's liability for "Compensation to employees"?

C13-2 (Current versus Noncurrent Classification) D'Annunzio Corporation includes the following items in its liabilities at December 31, 2001:

1. Notes payable, $25,000,000, due June 30, 2002.
2. Deposits from customers on equipment ordered by them from D'Annunzio, $6,250,000.
3. Salaries payable, $3,750,000, due January 14, 2002.

Instructions

Indicate in what circumstances, if any, each of the three liabilities above would be excluded from current liabilities.

C13-3 (Current versus Noncurrent Classification) The following items are listed as liabilities on the balance sheet of Eleutherios Company on December 31, 2001:

Accounts payable	$ 420,000
Notes payable	750,000
Bonds payable	2,250,000

The accounts payable represent obligations to suppliers that were due in January 2002. The notes payable mature on various dates during 2002. The bonds payable mature on July 1, 2002.

These liabilities must be reported on the balance sheet in accordance with generally accepted accounting principles governing the classification of liabilities as current and noncurrent.

Instructions

(a) What is the general rule for determining whether a liability is classified as current or noncurrent?
(b) Under what conditions may any of Eleutherios Company's liabilities be classified as noncurrent? Explain your answer.

(CMA adapted)

C13-4 (Refinancing of Short-Term Debt) Levi Eshkol Corporation reports in the current liability section of its balance sheet at December 31, 2001 (its year-end), short-term obligations of $15,000,000, which includes the current portion of 12% long-term debt in the amount of $11,000,000 (matures in March 2002). Management has stated its intention to refinance the 12% debt whereby no portion of it will mature during 2002. The date of issuance of the financial statements is March 25, 2002.

Instructions

(a) Is management's intent enough to support long-term classification of the obligation in this situation?
(b) Assume that Eshkol Corporation issues $13,000,000 of 10-year debentures to the public in January 2002 and that management intends to use the proceeds to liquidate the $11,000,000 debt maturing in March 2002. Furthermore, assume that the debt maturing in March 2002 is paid from these proceeds prior to the issuance of the financial statements. Will this have any impact on the balance sheet classification at December 31, 2001? Explain your answer.
(c) Assume that Eshkol Corporation issues common stock to the public in January and that management intends to entirely liquidate the $11,000,000 debt maturing in March 2002 with the proceeds of this equity securities issue. In light of these events, should the $11,000,000 debt maturing in March 2002 be included in current liabilities at December 31, 2001?
(d) Assume that Eshkol Corporation, on February 15, 2002, entered into a financing agreement with a commercial bank that permits Eshkol Corporation to borrow at any time through 2003 up to $15,000,000 at the bank's prime rate of interest. Borrowings under the financing agreement mature three years after the date of the loan. The agreement is not cancelable except for violation of a provision with which compliance is objectively determinable. No violation of any provision exists at the date of issuance of the financial statements. Assume further that the current portion of long-term debt does not mature until August 2002. In addition, management intends to refinance the $11,000,000 obligation under the terms of the financial agreement with the bank, which is expected to be financially capable of honoring the agreement.

(1) Given these facts, should the $11,000,000 be classified as current on the balance sheet at December 31, 2001?

(2) Is disclosure of the refinancing method required?

C13-5 (Refinancing of Short-Term Debt) Medvedev Inc. issued $10,000,000 of short-term commercial paper during the year 2000 to finance construction of a plant. At December 31, 2000, the corporation's year-end, Medvedev intends to refinance the commercial paper by issuing long-term debt. However, because the corporation temporarily has excess cash, in January 2001 it liquidates $4,000,000 of the commercial paper as the paper matures. In February 2001, Medvedev completes an $18,000,000 long-term debt offering. Later during the month of February, it issues its December 31, 2000, financial statements. The proceeds of the long-term debt offering are to be used to replenish $4,000,000 in working capital, to pay $6,000,000 of commercial paper as it matures in March 2001, and to pay $8,000,000 of construction costs expected to be incurred later that year to complete the plant.

Instructions

(a) How should the $10,000,000 of commercial paper be classified on the December 31, 2000, January 31, 2001, and February 28, 2001, balance sheets? Give support for your answer and also consider the cash element.

(b) What would your answer be if, instead of a refinancing at the date of issuance of the financial statements, a financing agreement existed at that date?

C13-6 (Loss Contingencies) Animaniacs Company is a manufacturer of toys. During the year, the following situations arose:

1. A safety hazard related to one of its toy products was discovered. It is considered probable that liabilities have been incurred. On the basis of past experience, a reasonable estimate of the amount of loss can be made.
2. One of its small warehouses is located on the bank of a river and could no longer be insured against flood losses. No flood losses have occurred after the date that the insurance became unavailable.
3. This year, Animaniacs began promoting a new toy by including a coupon, redeemable for a movie ticket, in each toy's carton. The movie ticket, which cost Animaniacs $3, is purchased in advance and then mailed to the customer when the coupon is received by Animaniacs. Animaniacs estimated, based on past experience, that 60% of the coupons would be redeemed. Forty-five percent of the coupons were actually redeemed this year, and the remaining 15% of the coupons are expected to be redeemed next year.

Instructions

(a) How should Animaniacs report the safety hazard? Why? Do not discuss deferred income tax implications.

(b) How should Animaniacs report the noninsurable flood risk? Why?

(c) How should Animaniacs account for the toy promotion campaign in this year?

C13-7 (Loss Contingencies) On February 1, 2001, one of the huge storage tanks of Paunee Manufacturing Company exploded. Windows in houses and other buildings within a one-mile radius of the explosion were severely damaged, and a number of people were injured. As of February 15, 2001 (when the December 31, 2000, financial statements were completed and sent to the publisher for printing and public distribution), no suits had been filed or claims asserted against the company as a consequence of the explosion. The company fully anticipates that suits will be filed and claims asserted for injuries and damages. Because the casualty was uninsured and the company considered at fault, Paunee Manufacturing will have to cover the damages from its own resources.

Instructions

Discuss fully the accounting treatment and disclosures that should be accorded the casualty and related contingent losses in the financial statements dated December 31, 2000.

C13-8 (Loss Contingency) Presented below is a note disclosure for Ralph Ellison Corporation:

> **Litigation and Environmental:** The Company has been notified, or is a named or a potentially responsible party in a number of governmental (federal, state and local) and private actions associated with environmental matters, such as those relating to hazardous wastes, including certain sites which are on the United States EPA National Priorities List ("Superfund"). These actions seek cleanup costs, penalties and/or damages for personal injury or to property or natural resources.
>
> In 1999, the Company recorded a pre-tax charge of $56,229,000, included in the "Other Expense (Income)—Net" caption of the Company's Consolidated Statements of Income, as an additional provision for environmental matters. These expenditures are expected to take place over the next several years and are indicative of the Company's commitment to improve and maintain the environment

in which it operates. At December 31, 1999, environmental accruals amounted to $69,931,000, of which $61,535,000 are considered noncurrent and are included in the "Deferred Credits and Other Liabilities" caption of the Company's Consolidated Balance Sheets.

While it is impossible at this time to determine with certainty the ultimate outcome of environmental matters, it is management's opinion, based in part on the advice of independent counsel (after taking into account accruals and insurance coverage applicable to such actions) that when the costs are finally determined they will not have a material adverse effect on the financial position of the Company.

Instructions

Answer the following questions.

(a) What conditions must exist before a loss contingency can be recorded in the accounts?

(b) Suppose that Ralph Ellison Corporation could not reasonably estimate the amount of the loss, although it could establish with a high degree of probability the minimum and maximum loss possible. How should this information be reported in the financial statements?

(c) If the amount of the loss is uncertain, how would the loss contingency be reported in the financial statements?

C13-9 (Loss Contingencies) The following three independent sets of facts relate to (1) the possible accrual or (2) the possible disclosure of a loss contingency.

Situation I

Subsequent to the date of a set of financial statements, but prior to the issuance of the financial statements, a company enters into a contract that will probably result in a significant loss to the company. The amount of the loss can be reasonably estimated.

Situation II

A company offers a one-year warranty for the product that it manufactures. A history of warranty claims has been compiled and the probable amount of claims related to sales for a given period can be determined.

Situation III

A company has adopted a policy of recording self-insurance for any possible losses resulting from injury to others by the company's vehicles. The premium for an insurance policy for the same risk from an independent insurance company would have an annual cost of $4,000. During the period covered by the financial statements, there were no accidents involving the company's vehicles that resulted in injury to others.

Instructions

Discuss the accrual or type of disclosure necessary (if any) and the reason(s) why such disclosure is appropriate for each of the three independent sets of facts above.

(AICPA adapted)

C13-10 (Warranties and Loss Contingencies) The following two independent situations involve loss contingencies:

Part 1

Clarke Company sells two products, John and Henrick. Each carries a one-year warranty.

1. Product John—Product warranty costs, based on past experience, will normally be 1% of sales.
2. Product Henrick—Product warranty costs cannot be reasonably estimated because this is a new product line. However, the chief engineer believes that product warranty costs are likely to be incurred.

Instructions

How should Clarke report the estimated product warranty costs for each of the two types of merchandise above? Discuss the rationale for your answer. Do not discuss deferred income tax implications, or disclosures that should be made in Clarke's financial statements or notes.

Part 2

Toni Morrison Company is being sued for $4,000,000 for an injury caused to a child as a result of alleged negligence while the child was visiting the Toni Morrison Company plant in March 2001. The suit was filed in July 2001. Toni Morrison's lawyer states that it is probable that Toni Morrison will lose the suit and be found liable for a judgment costing anywhere from $400,000 to $2,000,000. However, the lawyer states that the most probable judgment is $800,000.

Instructions

How should Toni Morrison report the suit in its 2001 financial statements? Discuss the rationale for your answer. Include in your answer disclosures, if any, that should be made in Toni Morrison's financial statements or notes.

(AICPA adapted)

USING YOUR JUDGMENT

FINANCIAL REPORTING PROBLEM: INTEL CORPORATION

Instructions

Refer to the financial statements and other documents of Intel Corporation presented in Appendix 5A and answer the following questions:

(a) What was Intel Corporation's short-term debt and related weighted average interest rate in this debt?

(b) What was Intel's working capital, acid-test ratio, and current ratio? Comment on Intel's liquidity.

(c) What types of commitments and contingencies has Intel reported in its financial statements? What is management's reaction to these contingencies?

(d) Explain the nature of the current liability identified as "Deferred Income on Shipments to Distributors."

FINANCIAL STATEMENT ANALYSIS CASES

Case 1 Northland Cranberries

Despite being a publicly traded company only since 1987, Northland Cranberries of Wisconsin Rapids, Wisconsin, is one of the world's largest cranberry growers. Despite its short life as a publicly traded corporation, it has engaged in an aggressive growth strategy. As a consequence, the company has taken on significant amounts of both short-term and long-term debt. The following information is taken from recent annual reports of the company.

	Current Year	Prior Year
Current assets	$ 6,745,759	$ 5,598,054
Total assets	107,744,751	83,074,339
Current liabilities	10,168,685	4,484,687
Total liabilities	73,118,204	49,948,787
Stockholders' equity	34,626,547	33,125,552
Net sales	21,783,966	18,051,355
Cost of goods sold	13,057,275	8,751,220
Interest expense	3,654,006	2,393,792
Income tax expense	1,051,000	1,917,000
Net income	1,581,707	2,942,954

Instructions

(a) Evaluate the company's liquidity by calculating and analyzing working capital and the current ratio.

(b) The following discussion of the company's liquidity was provided by the company in the Management Discussion and Analysis section of the company's annual report. Comment on whether you agree with management's statements, and what might be done to remedy the situation.

The lower comparative current ratio in the current year was due to $3 million of short-term borrowing then outstanding which was incurred to fund the Yellow River Marsh acquisitions last year. As a result of the extreme seasonality of its business, the company does not believe that its current ratio or its underlying stated working capital at the current, fiscal year-end is a meaningful indication of the Company's liquidity. As of March 31 of each fiscal year, the Company has historically carried no significant amounts of inventories and by such date all of the Company's accounts receivable from its crop sold for processing under the supply agreements have been paid in cash, with the resulting cash received from such payments used to reduce indebtedness. The Company utilizes its revolving bank credit facility, together with cash generated from operations, to fund its working capital requirements throughout its growing season.

Case 2 Mohican Company

Presented below is the current liabilities section and related note of **Mohican Company**.

	Current Year	Prior Year
	(dollars in thousands)	
Current liabilities		
Current portion of long-term debt	$ 15,000	$ 10,000
Short-term debt	2,668	405
Accounts payable	29,495	42,427
Accrued warranty	16,843	16,741
Accrued marketing programs	17,512	16,585
Other accrued liabilities	35,653	33,290
Accrued and deferred income taxes	16,206	17,348
Total current liabilities	$133,377	$136,796

Notes to Consolidated Financial Statements

1 (in part): Summary of Significant Accounting Policies and Related Data

Accrued Warranty—The company provides an accrual for future warranty costs based upon the relationship of prior years' sales to actual warranty costs.

Instructions

Answer the following questions.

(a) What is the difference between the cash basis and the accrual basis of accounting for warranty costs?

(b) Under what circumstance, if any, would it be appropriate for Mohican Company to recognize deferred revenue on warranty contracts?

(c) If Mohican Company recognized deferred revenue on warranty contracts, how would it recognize this revenue in subsequent periods?

COMPARATIVE ANALYSIS CASE

The Coca-Cola Company versus PepsiCo Inc.

Instructions

Go to the Digital Tool, and using **The Coca-Cola Company** and **PepsiCo** annual report information, answer the following questions:

(a) How much working capital do each of these companies have at the end of 1998? Comment on the appropriateness of the working capital they maintain.

(b) Compute both company's (a) current cash debt coverage ratio, (b) cash debt coverage ratio, (c) current ratio, (d) acid-test ratio, (e) receivable turnover ratio and (f) inventory turnover ratio for 1998. Comment on each company's overall liquidity.

(c) In PepsiCo's financial statements, it reports in the long-term debt section "short-term borrowings, reclassified." How can short-term borrowings be classified as long-term debt? How much of PepsiCo's debt is categorized as variable rate?

(d) What types of loss or gain contingencies do these two companies have at December 31, 1998?

RESEARCH CASES

Case 1

Instructions

Obtain the most recent edition of *Accounting Trends and Techniques.* Examine the disclosures included under the section regarding gain contingencies, and answer the following questions.

(a) Determine the nature of each of the disclosed gain contingencies. Are there any common themes?

(b) How many of the footnotes include dollar amounts?

(c) What are the smallest and largest amounts disclosed?

Case 2

The December 1995 issue of *Management Accounting* includes a reprint of an article by Glenn Cheney entitled "It's Not Easy Being Green But Top Companies Are Trying."

Instructions

Read the article and answer the following questions.

(a) What portion of the Fortune 500 companies disclose their position on the environment? What type of information is included in these disclosures?

(b) How can companies save money by "being green"?

(c) What is the "take-back principle"?

(d) What is the role of public accountants in this area?

INTERNATIONAL REPORTING CASE

An important difference between U.S. and international accounting standards is the accounting for liabilities related to provisions. Due in part to differences in tax laws, accounting standards in some countries and the standards issued by the International Accounting Standards Committee (IASC) allow recognition of liabilities for items that would not meet the definition of a liability under U.S. GAAP. The following note disclosure for liabilities related to provisions was provided by **Hoechst A.G.**, a leading German drug company, in its 1998 annual report. Hoechst prepares its statements in accordance with IASC standards.

Other provisions	Dec. 31, 1998	Dec. 31, 1997
	(in DM millions)	
Taxes	2,350	2,349
Restructuring	709	1,109
Damage and product liability claims	795	553
Environmental protection	869	814
Self insurance loss provisions	631	870
Employee-related commitments	1,123	1,243
Other	2,274	2,538
Total	8,751	9,476
Current portion thereof	(5,013)	(5,679)

Hoechst reported the following additional items in its 1998 annual report. Data for **Merck & Co.**, a U.S. drug company, are provided for comparison.

	Hoechst (DM millions)	Merck ($ millions)
Current assets	20,528	10,229
Average current liabilities	5,346	5,819
Liquid assets	391	3,356
Receivables (net)	14,362	3,374
Cash flow from operations	4,628	5,328

Instructions

(a) Compute the following ratios for Hoechst and Merck: current ratio, acid-test ratio, and the current cash debt coverage ratio. Compare the liquidity of these two drug companies based on these ratios.

(b) Identify items in Hoechst's provision disclosure that likely would not be recognized as liabilities under U.S. GAAP. (*Hint:* Refer to Illustration 13-10 in the chapter.)

(c) Discuss how the items identified in (b) would affect the comparative analysis in part (a). What adjustments would you make in your analysis? Assume that 75% of the provisions for restructuring and self-insurance are current liabilities.

ETHICS CASE

The Ray Company, owner of Bleacher Mall, charges Creighton Clothing Store a rental fee of $600 per month plus 5% of yearly profits over $500,000. Harry Creighton, the owner of the store, directs his accountant, Burt Wilson, to increase the estimate of bad debt expense and warranty costs in order to keep profits at $475,000.

Instructions

Answer the following questions:

(a) Should Wilson follow his boss's directive?

(b) Who is harmed if the estimates are increased?

(c) Is Creighton's directive ethical?

CHAPTER 14

Long-Term Liabilities

How's the Weather?

What is the latest news in the bond world—changes in interest rates, default provisions, or bond ratings? Well, how about bond interest payments tied to changes in the weather, sometimes referred to as *weather bonds?*[1] To understand how weather bonds work, let's take a look at a recent issue of weather bonds by **Koch Industries**. Koch provides energy to utilities, distributors, and others around the country. It feels the heat financially when weather is colder than expected and the company has to buy energy in the open market to serve its clients. It also can experience losses if the weather is warmer than usual.

Koch structured a bond offering designed to deal with this problem. It offered two types of bonds to investors: high-yield senior bonds that are rated below investment grade (junk bonds), and another unrated and even riskier class of bonds. The senior bonds pay 10.5%. With these bonds, if the weather is colder than normal, the interest rate drops 1/2% for each one-quarter degree decline in average temperature. Conversely, the rate goes up by 1/2% if the weather is warmer by one-quarter of a degree. Investors even lose some of their original investment (principal) if weather deviates significantly from the average.

On the even-riskier unrated bonds, investors can expect a return of 30% if temperatures remain at the average. But there is a 50% chance that temperatures will shift, and then the investor may lose principal. It should be noted that certain investors like these types of bonds because they provide diversification in their portfolio. Mother Nature, rather than economic factors, affects the bond value so diversification is provided.

All this may sound strange, but recognize that more and more companies are issuing catastrophe-type bonds. For example, insurance companies are now issuing bonds to protect themselves from catastrophes such as earthquakes and storms. "Besides financial conditions, investors must now be concerned with meteorological matters as well."

[1]Adapted from Gregory Zuckerman and Deborah Lohse, "Weather Bonds Hedge Against Mother Nature's Profit Effects," *The Wall Street Journal,* October 26, 1999, p. C1.

LEARNING OBJECTIVES

After studying this chapter, you should be able to:

1. **Describe the formal procedures associated with issuing long-term debt.**
2. **Identify various types of bond issues.**
3. **Describe the accounting valuation for bonds at date of issuance.**
4. **Apply the methods of bond discount and premium amortization.**
5. **Describe the accounting procedures for the extinguishment of debt.**
6. **Explain the accounting procedures for long-term notes payable.**
7. **Explain the reporting of off-balance-sheet financing arrangements.**
8. **Indicate how long-term debt is presented and analyzed.**

PREVIEW OF CHAPTER 14

As indicated in the opening story, companies are devising innovative types of long-term debt issues. Long-term debt continues to play an important role today in our capital markets because companies—and governments—need large amounts of capital to finance their growth. In many cases, the most effective way to obtain the capital is through the issuance of long-term debt. The purpose of this chapter is to explain the accounting issues related to long-term debt. The content and organization of the chapter are as follows:

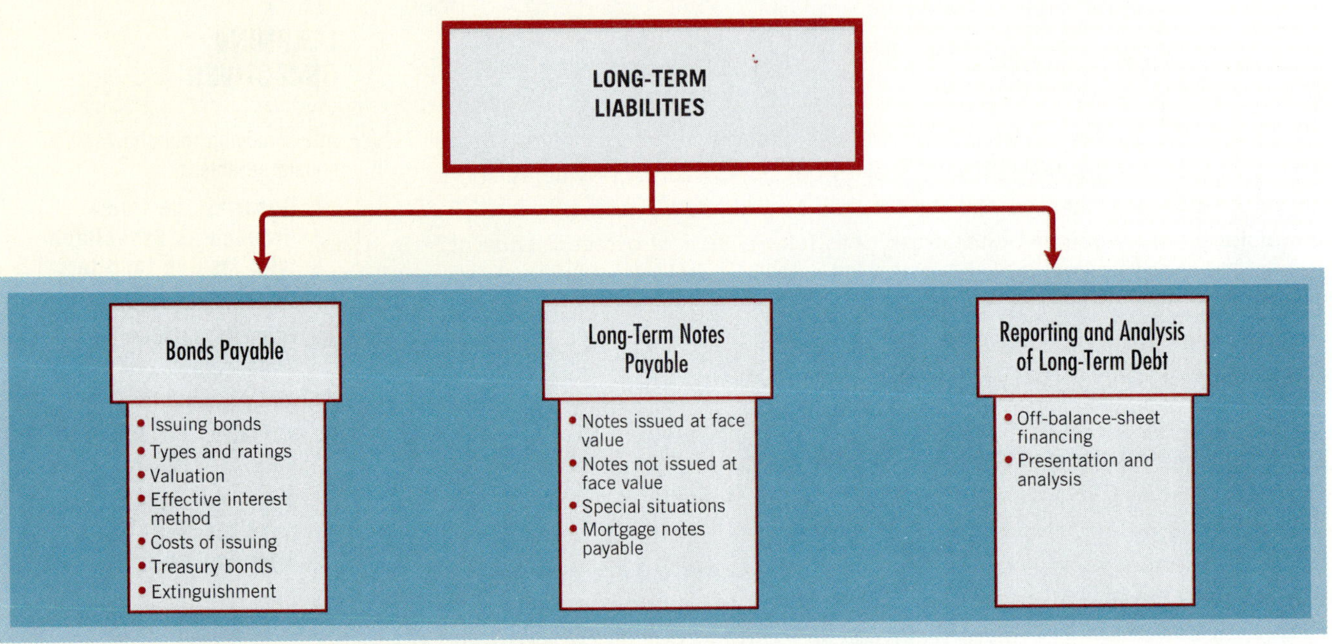

SECTION 1 BONDS PAYABLE

OBJECTIVE 1 Describe the formal procedures associated with issuing long-term debt.

Long-term debt consists of probable future sacrifices of economic benefits arising from present obligations that are not payable within a year or the operating cycle of the business, whichever is longer. Bonds payable, long-term notes payable, mortgages payable, pension liabilities, and lease liabilities are examples of long-term liabilities.

Incurring long-term debt is often accompanied by considerable formality. For example, the bylaws of corporations usually require approval by the board of directors and the stockholders before bonds can be issued or other long-term debt arrangements can be contracted.

Generally, long-term debt has various **covenants or restrictions** for the protection of both lenders and borrowers. The covenants and other terms of the agreement between the borrower and the lender are stated in the bond indenture or note agreement. Items often mentioned in the indenture or agreement include the amounts authorized to be issued, interest rate, due date or dates, call provisions, property pledged as security, sinking fund requirements, working capital and dividend restrictions, and limitations concerning the assumption of additional debt. Whenever these stipulations are important for a complete understanding of the financial position and the results of operations, they should be described in the body of the financial statements or the notes thereto.

Although it would seem that these covenants provide adequate protection to the long-term debt holder, many bondholders suffer considerable losses when additional debt is added to the capital structure. Consider what happened to bondholders in the leveraged buyout of **RJR Nabisco**. Solidly rated 9 3/8% bonds due in 2016 plunged 20% in value when management announced the leveraged buyout. Such a loss in value occurs because the additional debt added to the capital structure increases the likelihood of default. Although bondholders have covenants to protect them, they often are written in a manner that can be interpreted in a number of different ways.

ISSUING BONDS

Bonds are the most common type of long-term debt reported on a company's balance sheet. The main purpose of bonds is to borrow for the long term when the amount of capital needed is too large for one lender to supply. By issuing bonds in $100, $1,000, or $10,000 denominations, a large amount of long-term indebtedness can be divided into many small investing units, thus enabling more than one lender to participate in the loan.

A bond arises from a contract known as a **bond indenture** and represents a promise to pay: (1) a sum of money at a designated maturity rate, plus (2) periodic interest at a specified rate on the maturity amount (face value). Individual bonds are evidenced by a paper certificate and typically have a $1,000 face value. Bond interest payments usually are made semiannually, although the interest rate is generally expressed as an annual rate.

An entire bond issue may be sold to an investment banker who acts as a selling agent in the process of marketing the bonds. In such arrangements, investment bankers may either underwrite the entire issue by guaranteeing a certain sum to the corporation, thus taking the risk of selling the bonds for whatever price they can get (firm underwriting), or they may sell the bond issue for a commission to be deducted from the proceeds of the sale (best efforts underwriting). Alternatively, the issuing company may choose to place privately a bond issue by selling the bonds directly to a large institution, financial or otherwise, without the aid of an underwriter (private placement).

TYPES AND RATINGS OF BONDS

Some of the more common types of bonds found in practice are:

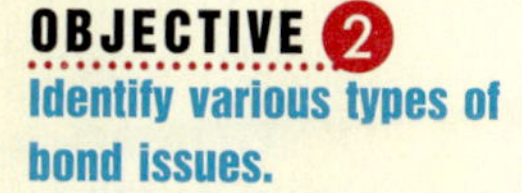
OBJECTIVE 2
Identify various types of bond issues.

TYPES OF BONDS

Secured and Unsecured Bonds. **Secured bonds** are backed by a pledge of some sort of collateral. Mortgage bonds are secured by a claim on real estate. Collateral trust bonds are secured by stocks and bonds of other corporations. Bonds not backed by collateral are **unsecured**. A **debenture bond** is unsecured. A "junk bond" is unsecured and also very risky, and therefore pays a high interest rate. These bonds are often used to finance leveraged buyouts.

Term, Serial Bonds, and Callable Bonds. Bond issues that mature on a single date are called **term bonds**, and issues that mature in installments are called **serial bonds**. Serially maturing bonds are frequently used by school or sanitary districts, municipalities, or other local taxing bodies that receive money through a special levy. **Callable bonds** give the issuer the right to call and retire the bonds prior to maturity.

Convertible, Commodity-Backed, and Deep Discount Bonds. If bonds are convertible into other securities of the corporation for a specified time after issuance, they are called **convertible bonds**. Accounting for bond conversions is discussed in Chapter 17. Two new types of bonds have been developed in an attempt to attract capital in a tight money market—commodity-backed bonds and deep discount bonds.

Commodity-backed bonds (also called **asset-linked bonds**) are redeemable in measures of a commodity, such as barrels of oil, tons of coal, or ounces of rare metal. To illustrate, **Sunshine Mining**, a silver mining producer, sold two issues of bonds redeemable with either $1,000 in cash or 50 ounces of silver, whichever is greater at maturity, and that have a stated interest rate of 8½%. The accounting problem is one of projecting the maturity value, especially since silver has fluctuated between $4 and $40 an ounce since issuance.

J. C. Penney Company sold the first publicly marketed long-term debt securities in the United States that do not bear interest. These **deep discount bonds**, also referred to as **zero-interest debenture bonds**, are sold at a discount that provides the buyer's total interest payoff at maturity. **Caesar's World Inc.**, a Las Vegas/Lake Tahoe gambling casino operator, proposed a unique version of the zero-interest bond.[2] Caesar's World proposed to issue 5,000 of $15,000 face amount bonds that would entitle each bondholder to spend two weeks a year at its Lake Tahoe resort in lieu of interest.

Registered and Bearer (Coupon) Bonds. Bonds issued in the name of the owner are **registered bonds** and require surrender of the certificate and issuance of a new certificate to complete a sale. A **bearer** or **coupon bond**, however, is not recorded in the name of the owner and may be transferred from one owner to another by mere delivery.

Income and Revenue Bonds. **Income bonds** pay no interest unless the issuing company is profitable. **Revenue bonds**, so called because the interest on them is paid from specified revenue sources, are most frequently issued by airports, school districts, counties, toll-road authorities, and governmental bodies.

Two major investment publication companies, Moody's Investors Service and Standard & Poor's Corporation, issue quality ratings on every public bond issue. The bond quality designations and rating symbols of these two firms are as follows:

ILLUSTRATION 14-1
Bond Quality Ratings

	Symbols	
Quality	Moody's	Standard & Poor's
Prime	Aaa	AAA
Excellent	Aa	AA
Upper medium	A	A
Lower medium	Baa	BBB
Marginally speculative	Ba	BB
Very speculative	B, Caa	B
Default	Ca, C	D

[2]"Caesar's World May Try Bond Issue Paying in Vacations," *The Wall Street Journal*, January 22, 1982, p. 32.

A quality rating is assigned to each new public bond issue and is a current assessment of the company's ability to pay with respect to a specific borrowing. The rating may be changed up or down during the issue's outstanding life because the quality is constantly monitored. The debt rating is not a recommendation to purchase, sell, or hold a security, because it does not comment on market prices or suitability for particular investors.

VALUATION OF BONDS PAYABLE—DISCOUNT AND PREMIUM

OBJECTIVE 3
Describe the accounting valuation for bonds at date of issuance.

The issuance and marketing of bonds to the public does not happen overnight. It usually takes weeks or even months. Underwriters must be arranged, Securities and Exchange Commission approval must be obtained, audits and issuance of a prospectus may be required, and certificates must be printed. Frequently, the terms in a bond indenture are established well in advance of the sale of the bonds. Between the time the terms are set and the bonds are issued, the market conditions and the financial position of the issuing corporation may change significantly. Such changes affect the marketability of the bonds and thus their selling price.

The selling price of a bond issue is set by such familiar phenomena as supply and demand of buyers and sellers, relative risk, market conditions, and the state of the economy. The investment community values a bond at the present value of its future cash flows, which consist of (1) interest and (2) principal. The rate used to compute the present value of these cash flows is the interest rate that provides an acceptable return on an investment commensurate with the issuer's risk characteristics.

Valuation of long-term debt varies internationally. In the U.S., discount and premium are booked and amortized over the life of the debt. In some countries (e.g., Sweden, Japan, Belgium), it is permissible to write off the discount and premium immediately.

The interest rate written in the terms of the bond indenture (and ordinarily printed on the bond certificate) is known as the **stated**, **coupon**, or **nominal rate**. This rate, which is set by the issuer of the bonds, is expressed as a percentage of the **face value**, also called the **par value**, **principal amount**, or **maturity value**, of the bonds. If the rate employed by the investment community (buyers) differs from the stated rate, the present value of the bonds computed by the buyers (and the current purchase price) will differ from the face value of the bonds. The difference between the face value and the present value of the bonds is either a discount or premium.[3] If the bonds sell for less than face value, they are sold at a **discount**. If the bonds sell for more than face value, they are sold at a **premium**.

The rate of interest actually earned by the bondholders is called the **effective yield**, or **market rate**. If bonds sell at a discount, the effective yield is higher than the stated rate. Conversely, if bonds sell at a premium, the effective yield is lower than the stated rate. While the bond is outstanding, its price is affected by several variables, most notably the market rate of interest. There is an inverse relationship between the market interest rate and the price of the bond. The proof of this is graphically portrayed in Illustration 14-2. These huge bond principal losses were due primarily to the Federal Reserve's 1.5% increase in the short-term interest rate in the mid-1990s.

[3]Until the 1950s it was common for corporations to issue bonds with low, even-percentage coupons (such as 4%) to demonstrate their financial solidity. Frequently, the result was large discounts. More recently, it has become acceptable to set the stated rate of interest on bonds in rather precise fractions (such as 10⅞%). Companies usually attempt to align the stated rate as closely as possible with the market or effective rate at the time of issue. While discounts and premiums continue to occur, their absolute magnitude tends to be much smaller; many times it is immaterial. Professor Bill N. Schwartz (Virginia Commonwealth University) studied the 685 new debt offerings in 1985. Of these, none were issued at a premium. Approximately 95% were issued either with no discount or at a price above 98. Now, however, zero-interest (deep discount) bonds are more popular which cause substantial discounts.

ILLUSTRATION 14-2
Effects of Interest Rate Change on Various Types of Outstanding Bonds

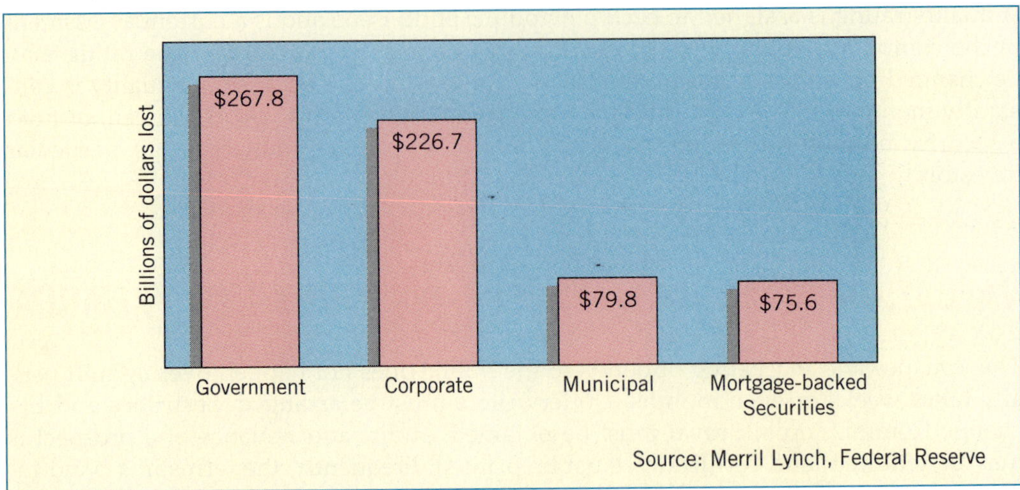

To illustrate the computation of the **present value of a bond issue**, consider ServiceMaster which issues $100,000 in bonds, due in 5 years with 9% interest payable annually at year-end. At the time of issue, the market rate for such bonds is 11%. The following time diagram depicts both the interest and the principal cash flows:

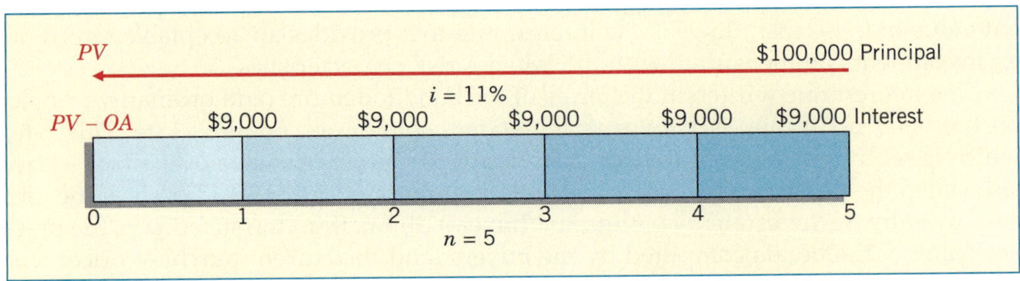

The actual principal and interest cash flows are discounted at an 11% rate for 5 periods as follows:

ILLUSTRATION 14-3
Present Value Computation of Bond Selling at a Discount

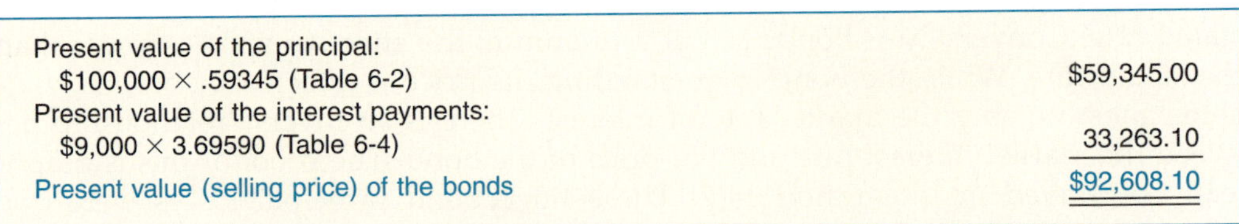

Present value of the principal:	
$100,000 × .59345 (Table 6-2)	$59,345.00
Present value of the interest payments:	
$9,000 × 3.69590 (Table 6-4)	33,263.10
Present value (selling price) of the bonds	$92,608.10

By paying $92,608.10 at the date of issue, the investors will realize an effective rate or yield of 11% over the 5-year term of the bonds. These bonds would sell at a discount of $7,391.90 ($100,000 − $92,608.10). The price at which the bonds sell is typically stated as a percentage of the face or par value of the bonds. For example, the ServiceMaster bonds sold for 92.6 (92.6% of par). If ServiceMaster had received $102,000, we would say the bonds sold for 102 (102% of par).

When bonds sell below face value, it means that investors demand a rate of interest higher than the stated rate. The investors are not satisfied with the stated rate because they can earn a greater rate on alternative investments of equal risk. They cannot change the stated rate, so they refuse to pay face value for the bonds. Thus, by changing the amount invested they alter the effective rate of interest. The investors receive interest at the stated rate computed on the face value, but they are earning at **an effective rate that is higher than the stated rate because they paid less than face**

value for the bonds. (An illustration of a bond that sells at a premium is shown in Illustrations 14-7 and 14-8.)

Bonds Issued at Par on Interest Date

When bonds are issued on an interest payment date at par (face value), no interest has accrued and no premium or discount exists. The accounting entry is made simply for the cash proceeds and the face value of the bonds. To illustrate, if 10-year term bonds with a par value of $800,000, dated January 1, 2001, and bearing interest at an annual rate of 10% payable semiannually on January 1 and July 1, are issued on January 1 at par, the entry on the books of the issuing corporation would be:

Cash	800,000	
Bonds Payable		800,000

The entry to record the first semiannual interest payment of $40,000 ($800,000 × .10 × 1/2) on July 1, 2001, would be as follows:

Bond Interest Expense	40,000	
Cash		40,000

The entry to record accrued interest expense at December 31, 2001 (year-end) would be as follows:

Bond Interest Expense	40,000	
Bond Interest Payable		40,000

Bonds Issued at Discount or Premium on Interest Date

OBJECTIVE 4
Apply the methods of bond discount and premium amortization.

If the $800,000 of bonds illustrated above were issued on January 1, 2001, at 97 (meaning 97% of par), the issuance would be recorded as follows:

Cash ($800,000 × .97)	776,000	
Discount on Bonds Payable	24,000	
Bonds Payable		800,000

Because of its relation to interest, as previously discussed, **the discount is amortized and charged to interest expense over the period of time that the bonds are outstanding.** Under the **straight-line method**,[4] the amount amortized each year is a constant amount. For example, using the bond discount above of $24,000, the amount amortized to interest expense each year for 10 years is $2,400 ($24,000 ÷ 10 years) and, if amortization is recorded annually, it is recorded as follows:

Bond Interest Expense	2,400	
Discount on Bonds Payable		2,400

At the end of the first year, 2001, as a result of the amortization entry above, the unamortized balance in Discount on Bonds Payable is $21,600, ($24,000 − $2,400).

If the bonds were dated and sold on October 1, 2001, and if the fiscal year of the corporation ended on December 31, the discount amortized during 2001 would be only 3/12 of 1/10 of $24,000, or $600. Three months of accrued interest must also be recorded on December 31.

Premium on Bonds Payable is accounted for in a manner similar to that for Discount on Bonds Payable. If the 10-year bonds of a par value of $800,000 are dated and sold on January 1, 2001, at 103, the following entry is made to record the issuance:

Cash ($800,000 × 1.03)	824,000	
Premium on Bonds Payable		24,000
Bonds Payable		800,000

[4]Although the effective interest method is preferred for amortization of discount or premium, to keep these initial illustrations simple, we have chosen to use the straight-line method (which is acceptable if the results obtained are not materially different from those produced by the effective interest method).

At the end of 2001 and for each year the bonds are outstanding, the entry to amortize the premium on a straight-line basis is:

Premium on Bonds Payable	2,400	
Bond Interest Expense		2,400

Bond interest expense is increased by amortization of a discount and decreased by amortization of a premium. Amortization of a discount or premium under the effective interest method is discussed later.

Some bonds are callable by the issuer after a certain date at a stated price so that the issuing corporation may have the opportunity to reduce its bonded indebtedness or take advantage of lower interest rates. **Whether callable or not, any premium or discount must be amortized over the life to maturity date because early redemption (call of the bond) is not a certainty.**

Bonds Issued between Interest Dates

Bond interest payments are usually made semiannually on dates specified in the bond indenture. When bonds are issued on other than the interest payment dates, **buyers of the bonds will pay the seller the interest accrued from the last interest payment date to the date of issue**. The purchasers of the bonds, in effect, pay the bond issuer in advance for that portion of the full 6-months' interest payment to which they are not entitled, not having held the bonds during that period. **The purchasers will receive the full 6-months' interest payment on the next semiannual interest payment date.**

To illustrate, if 10-year bonds of a par value of $800,000, dated January 1, 2001, and bearing interest at an annual rate of 10% payable semiannually on January 1 and July 1, are issued on March 1, 2001, at **par plus accrued interest**, the entry on the books of the issuing corporation is:

Cash	813,333	
Bonds Payable		800,000
Bond Interest Expense ($800,000 × .10 × 2/12)		13,333
(Interest Payable might be credited instead)		

The purchaser advances 2 months' interest, because on July 1, 2001, 4 months after the date of purchase, 6 months' interest will be received from the issuing company. The company makes the following entry on July 1, 2001:

Bond Interest Expense	40,000	
Cash		40,000

The expense account now contains a debit balance of $26,667, which represents the proper amount of interest expense, 4 months at 10% on $800,000.

The illustration above was simplified by having the January 1, 2001, bonds issued on March 1, 2001, **at par**. If, however, the 10% bonds were issued at 102, the entry on March 1 on the books of the issuing corporation would be:

Cash [($800,000 × 1.02) + ($800,000 × .10 × 2/12)]	829,333	
Bonds Payable		800,000
Premium on Bonds Payable ($800,000 × .02)		16,000
Bond Interest Expense		13,333

The premium would be amortized **from the date of sale**, March 1, 2001, not from the date of the bonds, January 1, 2001.

EFFECTIVE INTEREST METHOD

The profession's preferred procedure for amortization of a discount or premium is the **effective interest method** (also called **present value amortization**). Under the effective interest method:

1. Bond interest expense is computed first by multiplying the carrying value[5] of the bonds at the beginning of the period by the effective interest rate.
2. The bond discount or premium amortization is then determined by comparing the bond interest expense with the interest to be paid.

The computation of the amortization is depicted graphically as follows:

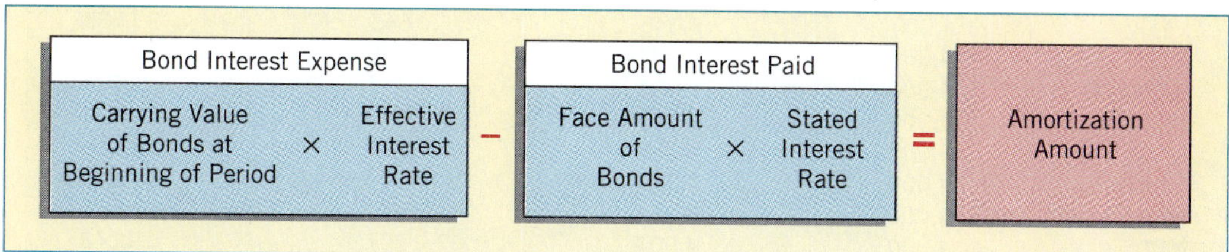

ILLUSTRATION 14-4
Bond Discount and Premium Amortization Computation

The effective interest method produces a periodic interest expense equal to **a constant percentage of the carrying value of the bonds.** Since the percentage is the effective rate of interest incurred by the borrower at the time of issuance, the effective interest method results in a better matching of expenses with revenues than the straight-line method.

Both the effective interest and straight-line methods result in the **same total amount of interest expense over the term of the bonds,** and the annual amounts of interest expense are generally quite similar. However, **when the annual amounts are materially different, the effective interest method is required under generally accepted accounting principles.**

Bonds Issued at a Discount

To illustrate amortization of a discount, Evermaster Corporation issued $100,000 of 8% term bonds on January 1, 2001, due on January 1, 2006, with interest payable each July 1 and January 1. Because the investors required an effective interest rate of 10%, they paid $92,278 for the $100,000 of bonds, creating a $7,722 discount. The $7,722 discount is computed as follows:[6]

ILLUSTRATION 14-5
Computation of Discount on Bonds Payable

Maturity value of bonds payable		$100,000
Present value of $100,000 due in 5 years at 10%, interest payable semiannually (Table 6-2); $FV(PVF_{10,5\%})$; ($100,000 × .61391)	$61,391	
Present value of $4,000 interest payable semiannually for 5 years at 10% annually (Table 6-4); $R(PVF\text{-}OA_{10,5\%})$; ($4,000 × 7.72173)	30,887	
Proceeds from sale of bonds		92,278
Discount on bonds payable		$ 7,722

The 5-year amortization schedule appears on page 720.

[5]The **book value,** also called the **carrying value,** equals the face amount minus any unamortized discount or plus any unamortized premium.

[6]Because interest is paid semiannually, the interest rate used is 5% (10% × 6/12). The number of periods is 10 (5 years × 2).

ILLUSTRATION 14-6
Bond Discount Amortization Schedule

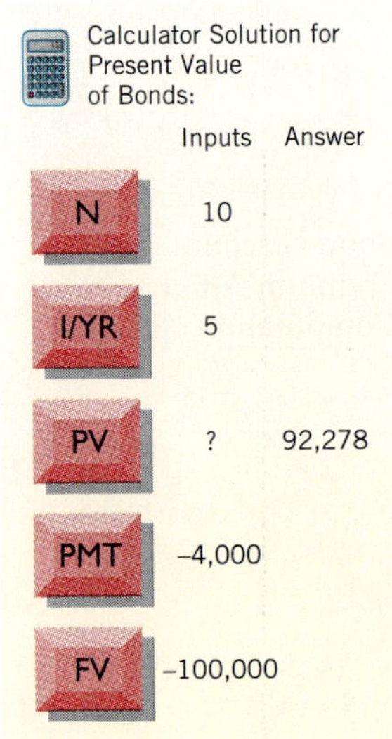

Schedule of Bond Discount Amortization
Effective Interest Method—Semiannual Interest Payments
5-Year, 8% Bonds Sold to Yield 10%

Date	Cash Paid	Interest Expense	Discount Amortized	Carrying Amount of Bonds
1/1/01				$ 92,278
7/1/01	$ 4,000[a]	$ 4,614[b]	$ 614[c]	92,892[d]
1/1/02	4,000	4,645	645	93,537
7/1/02	4,000	4,677	677	94,214
1/1/03	4,000	4,711	711	94,925
7/1/03	4,000	4,746	746	95,671
1/1/04	4,000	4,783	783	96,454
7/1/04	4,000	4,823	823	97,277
1/1/05	4,000	4,864	864	98,141
7/1/05	4,000	4,907	907	99,048
1/1/06	4,000	4,952	952	100,000
	$40,000	$47,722	$7,722	

[a]$4,000 = $100,000 × .08 × 6/12
[b]$4,614 = $92,278 × .10 × 6/12
[c]$614 = $4,614 − $4,000
[d]$92,892 = $92,278 + $614

The entry to record the issuance of Evermaster Corporation's bonds at a discount on January 1, 2001, is:

Cash	92,278	
Discount on Bonds Payable	7,722	
Bonds Payable		100,000

The journal entry to record the first interest payment on July 1, 2001, and amortization of the discount is:

Bond Interest Expense	4,614	
Discount on Bonds Payable		614
Cash		4,000

The journal entry to record the interest expense accrued at December 31, 2001 (year-end) and amortization of the discount is:

Bond Interest Expense	4,645	
Bond Interest Payable		4,000
Discount on Bonds Payable		645

Bonds Issued at Premium

If the market had been such that the investors were willing to accept an effective interest rate of 6% on the bond issue described above, they would have paid $108,530 or a premium of $8,530, computed as follows:

ILLUSTRATION 14-7
Computation of Premium on Bonds Payable

Maturity value of bonds payable		$100,000
Present value of $100,000 due in 5 years at 6%, interest payable semiannually (Table 6-2); $FV(PVF_{10,3\%})$; ($100,000 × .74409)	$74,409	
Present value of $4,000 interest payable semiannually for 5 years at 6% annually (Table 6-4); $R(PVF\text{-}OA_{10,3\%})$; ($4,000 × 8.53020)	34,121	
Proceeds from sale of bonds		108,530
Premium on bonds payable		$ 8,530

The 5-year amortization schedule appears on page 721.

ILLUSTRATION 14-8
Bond Premium Amortization Schedule

Schedule of Bond Premium Amortization Effective Interest Method—Semiannual Interest Payments 5-Year, 8% Bonds Sold to Yield 6%				
Date	Cash Paid	Interest Expense	Premium Amortized	Carrying Amount of Bonds
1/1/01				$108,530
7/1/01	$ 4,000[a]	$ 3,256[b]	$ 744[c]	107,786[d]
1/1/02	4,000	3,234	766	107,020
7/1/02	4,000	3,211	789	106,231
1/1/03	4,000	3,187	813	105,418
7/1/03	4,000	3,162	838	104,580
1/1/04	4,000	3,137	863	103,717
7/1/04	4,000	3,112	888	102,829
1/1/05	4,000	3,085	915	101,914
7/1/05	4,000	3,057	943	100,971
1/1/06	4,000	3,029	971	100,000
	$40,000	$31,470	$8,530	

[a]$4,000 = $100,000 × .08 × 6/12
[b]$3,256 = $108,530 × .06 × 6/12
[c]$744 = $4,000 − $3,256
[d]$107,786 = $108,530 − $744

Calculator Solution for Present Value of Bonds:

	Inputs	Answer
N	10	
I/YR	3	
PV	?	108,530
PMT	−4,000	
FV	−100,000	

The entry to record the issuance of Evermaster bonds at a premium on January 1, 2001, is:

Cash	108,530	
Premium on Bonds Payable		8,530
Bonds Payable		100,000

The journal entry to record the first interest payment on July 1, 2001, and amortization of the premium is:

Bond Interest Expense	3,256	
Premium on Bonds Payable	744	
Cash		4,000

The discount or premium should be amortized as an adjustment to interest expense over the life of the bond in such a way as to result in a **constant rate of interest** when applied to the carrying amount of debt outstanding at the beginning of any given period.[7] Although the effective interest method is recommended, the straight-line method is permitted if the results obtained are not materially different from those produced by the effective interest method.

Accruing Interest

In our previous examples, the interest payment dates and the date the financial statements were issued were the same. For example, when Evermaster sold bonds at a premium (page 720), the two interest payment dates coincided with the financial reporting dates. However, what happens if Evermaster wishes to report financial statements at the end of February 2001? In this case, the premium is prorated by the appropriate number of months to arrive at the proper interest expense as follows:

ILLUSTRATION 14-9
Computation of Interest Expense

Interest accrual ($4,000 × 2/6)	$1,333.33
Premium amortized ($744 × 2/6)	(248.00)
Interest expense (Jan.–Feb.)	$1,085.33

[7]"Interest on Receivables and Payables," *Opinions of the Accounting Principles Board No. 21* (New York: AICPA, 1971), par. 16.

The journal entry to record this accrual is as follows:

Bond Interest Expense	1,085.33	
Premium on Bonds Payable	248.00	
Bond Interest Payable		1,333.33

If the company prepares financial statements 6 months later, the same procedure is followed; that is, the premium amortized would be as follows:

ILLUSTRATION 14-10
Computation of Premium Amortization

Premium amortized (March–June) ($744 × 4/6)	$496.00
Premium amortized (July–August) ($766 × 2/6)	255.33
Premium amortized (March–August, 2001)	$751.33

The computation is much simpler if the straight-line method is employed. For example, in the Evermaster situation, the total premium is $8,530, which is allocated evenly over the 5-year period. Thus, premium amortization per month is $142.17 ($8,530 ÷ 60 months).

Classification of Discount and Premium

Discount on bonds payable is **not an asset** because it does not provide any future economic benefit. The enterprise has the use of the borrowed funds, but for that use it must pay interest. A bond discount means that the company borrowed less than the face or maturity value of the bond and therefore is faced with an actual (effective) interest rate higher than the stated (nominal) rate. Conceptually, discount on bonds payable is a liability valuation account; that is, it is a reduction of the face or maturity amount of the related liability.[8] This account is referred to as a **contra** account.

Premium on bonds payable has no existence apart from the related debt. The lower interest cost results because the proceeds of borrowing exceed the face or maturity amount of the debt. Conceptually, premium on bonds payable is a liability valuation account; that is, it is an addition to the face or maturity amount of the related liability.[9] This account is referred to as an **adjunct** account. As a result, the profession requires that **bond discount and bond premium be reported as a direct deduction from or addition to the face amount of the bond**.

COSTS OF ISSUING BONDS

The issuance of bonds involves engraving and printing costs, legal and accounting fees, commissions, promotion costs, and other similar charges. According to *APB Opinion No. 21*, these items should be debited to a **deferred charge** account (asset) for Unamortized Bond Issue Costs and amortized over the life of the debt, in a manner similar to that used for discount on bonds.[10]

The FASB, however, in *Concepts Statement No. 3* takes the position that debt issue cost can be treated as either an expense or a reduction of the related debt liability. Debt issue cost is not considered an asset because it provides no future economic benefit. The cost of issuing bonds in effect reduces the proceeds of the bonds issued and increases the effective interest rate and thus may be accounted for the same as the unamortized discount.

---

[8] "Elements of Financial Statements of Business Enterprises," *Statement of Financial Accounting Concepts No. 3* (Stamford, Conn.: FASB, 1980), par. 160.

[9] Ibid., par. 162.

[10] "Interest on Receivables and Payables," op. cit., par. 15.

There is an obvious difference between GAAP and *Concepts Statement No. 3*'s view of debt issue costs. Until a standard is issued to supersede *Opinion No. 21*, however, **acceptable GAAP for debt issue costs is to treat them as a deferred charge and amortize them over the life of the debt.**

To illustrate the accounting for costs of issuing bonds, assume that Microchip Corporation sold $20,000,000 of 10-year debenture bonds for $20,795,000 on January 1, 2002 (also the date of the bonds). Costs of issuing the bonds were $245,000. The entries at January 1, 2002, and December 31, 2002, for issuance of the bonds and amortization of the bond issue costs would be as follows:

January 1, 2002		
Cash	20,550,000	
Unamortized Bond Issue Costs	245,000	
Premium on Bonds Payable		795,000
Bonds Payable		20,000,000
(To record issuance of bonds)		
December 31, 2002		
Bond Issue Expense	24,500	
Unamortized Bond Issue Costs		24,500
(To amortize one year of bond issue costs—straight-line method)		

While the bond issue costs should be amortized using the effective interest method, the straight-line method is generally used in practice because it is easier and the results are not materially different.

TREASURY BONDS

Bonds payable that have been reacquired by the issuing corporation or its agent or trustee and have not been canceled are known as **treasury bonds**. They should be shown on the balance sheet at par value—as a deduction from the bonds payable issued to arrive at a net figure representing bonds payable outstanding. When they are sold or canceled, the Treasury Bonds account should be credited.

EXTINGUISHMENT OF DEBT

OBJECTIVE 5
Describe the accounting procedures for the extinguishment of debt.

How is the payment of debt—often referred to as **extinguishment of debt**—recorded? If the bonds (or any other form of debt security) are held to maturity, the answer is straightforward—no gain or loss is computed. Any premium or discount and any issue costs will be fully amortized at the date the bonds mature. As a result, the carrying amount will be equal to the maturity (face) value of the bond. As the maturity or face value is also equal to the bond's market value at that time, no gain or loss exists.

In some cases, debt is extinguished before its maturity date.[11] The amount paid on extinguishment or redemption before maturity, including any call premium and expense of reacquisition, is called the **reacquisition price**. On any specified date, the **net carrying amount** of the bonds is the amount payable at maturity, adjusted for unamortized premium or discount, and cost of issuance. Any excess of the net carrying

[11]Some companies have attempted to extinguish debt through an in-substance defeasance. **In-substance defeasance** is an arrangement whereby a company provides for the future repayment of one or more of its long-term debt issues by placing purchased securities in an irrevocable trust, the principal and interest of which are pledged to pay off the principal and interest of its own debt securities as they mature. The company, however, is not legally released from being the primary obligor under the debt that is still outstanding. In some cases, debt holders are not even aware of the transaction and continue to look to the company for repayment. This practice is not considered an extinguishment of debt and, therefore, no gain or loss is recorded.

amount over the reacquisition price is a **gain from extinguishment**, whereas the excess of the reacquisition price over the net carrying amount is a **loss from extinguishment**. At the time of reacquisition, **the unamortized premium or discount, and any costs of issue applicable to the bonds, must be amortized up to the reacquisition date**.

To illustrate, assume that on January 1, 1991, General Bell Corp. issued bonds with a par value of $800,000 at 97, due in 20 years. Bond issue costs totaling $16,000 were incurred. Eight years after the issue date, the entire issue is called at 101 and canceled.[12] The loss on redemption (extinguishment) is computed as follows (straight-line amortization is used for simplicity):

ILLUSTRATION 14-11
Computation of Loss on Redemption of Bonds

Reacquisition price ($800,000 × 1.01)		$808,000
Net carrying amount of bonds redeemed:		
Face value	$800,000	
Unamortized discount ($24,000* × 12/20)	(14,400)	
Unamortized issue costs ($16,000 × 12/20) (both amortized using straight-line basis)	(9,600)	776,000
Loss on redemption		$ 32,000

*[$800,000 × (1 − .97)]

The entry to record the reacquisition and cancellation of the bonds is:

Bonds Payable	800,000	
Loss on Redemption of Bonds (Extraordinary)	32,000	
Discount on Bonds Payable		14,400
Unamortized Bond Issue Costs		9,600
Cash		808,000

Note that it is often advantageous for the issuing corporation to acquire the entire outstanding bond issue and replace it with a new bond issue bearing a lower rate of interest. The replacement of an existing issuance with a new one is called **refunding**. Whether the early redemption or other extinguishment of outstanding bonds is a nonrefunding or a refunding situation, the difference (gain or loss) between the reacquisition price and the net carrying amount of the redeemed bonds should be recognized currently in income of the period of redemption, and **classified as an extraordinary item**.

Extraordinary item treatment applies whether an extinguishment is early, at a scheduled maturity date, or later, without regard to the criteria of "unusual in nature" and "infrequency of occurrence." These gains and losses are reported as extraordinary items so that readers of the financial statements can evaluate their significance.[13] The following disclosures are required:

1. A description of the extinguishment transactions, including the sources of any funds used to extinguish debt if it is practicable to identify the sources.

---

[12]The issuer of callable bonds is generally required to exercise the call on an interest date. Therefore, the amortization of any discount or premium will be up to date and there will be no accrued interest. However, early extinguishments through purchases of bonds in the open market are more likely to be on other than an interest date. If the purchase is not made on an interest date, the discount or premium must be amortized and the interest payable must be accrued from the last interest date to the date of purchase.

[13]Two types of extinguishment that are not reported as extraordinary items are (1) gains and losses that result from a conversion agreement that is part of the original debt covenant and (2) gains and losses from cash purchases of debt made to satisfy current or future sinking fund requirements.

2. The income tax effect in the period of extinguishment.
3. The per share amount of the aggregate gain or loss, net of related tax effect.

The following illustration presents disclosure on the face of the income statement and in a note to the financial statements for **Rohm and Haas Company**.

ILLUSTRATION 14-12
Disclosure of Debt Extinguishment

ROHM AND HAAS COMPANY
(in millions)

	1998	1997	1996
Earnings before extraordinary item	$453	$410	$363
Extraordinary loss on early extinguishment of debt (net of income tax benefit of $6)—Note 15	13	—	—
Net earnings	$440	$410	$363
Earnings per share before extraordinary item	$2.55		
Extraordinary loss, net of tax	.08		
Earnings per share	$2.47		

Note 15 (in part): Long-Term Debt
In 1998 the company retired $130 million of high interest long-term debt through a tender offer. These debt retirements resulted in an after-tax extraordinary loss of $13 million, or $.08 per share.

LONG-TERM NOTES PAYABLE

SECTION 2

OBJECTIVE 6
Explain the accounting procedures for long-term notes payable.

The difference between current notes payable and **long-term notes payable** is the maturity date. As discussed in Chapter 13, short-term notes payable are expected to be paid within a year or the operating cycle—whichever is longer. Long-term notes are similar in substance to bonds in that both have fixed maturity dates and carry either a stated or implicit interest rate. However, notes do not trade as readily as bonds in the organized public securities markets. Noncorporate and small corporate enterprises issue notes as their long-term instruments, whereas larger corporations issue both long-term notes and bonds.

Accounting for notes and bonds is quite similar. **Like a bond, a note is valued at the present value of its future interest and principal cash flows, with any discount or premium being similarly amortized over the life of the note.**[14] The computation of the present value of an **interest-bearing note**, the recording of its issuance, and the amortization of any discount or premium and accrual of interest are as shown for bonds on pages 715–722 of this chapter.

As you might expect, accounting for long-term notes payable parallels accounting for long-term notes receivable as was presented in Chapter 7.

[14]According to *APB Opinion No. 21,* all payables that represent commitments to pay money at a determinable future date are subject to present value measurement techniques, except for the following specifically excluded types:
1. Normal accounts payable due within one year.
2. Security deposits, retainages, advances, or progress payments.
3. Transactions between parent and subsidiary.
4. Convertible debt securities.
5. Obligations payable at some indeterminable future date.

NOTES ISSUED AT FACE VALUE

In Chapter 7, we discussed the recognition of a $10,000, 3-year note issued at face value by Scandinavian Imports to Bigelow Corp. In this transaction, the stated rate and the effective rate were both 10%. The time diagram and present value computation on page 350 of Chapter 7 (see Illustration 7-10) for Bigelow Corp. would be the same for the issuer of the note, Scandinavian Imports, in recognizing a note payable. Because the present value of the note and its face value are the same, $10,000, no premium or discount is recognized. The issuance of the note is recorded by Scandinavian Imports as follows:

Cash	10,000	
Notes Payable		10,000

Scandinavian Imports would recognize the interest incurred each year as follows:

Interest Expense	1,000	
Cash		1,000

NOTES NOT ISSUED AT FACE VALUE

Zero-Interest-Bearing Notes

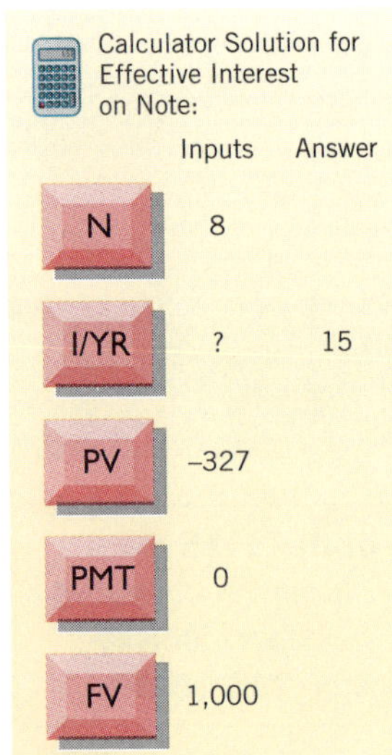

Calculator Solution for Effective Interest on Note:
Inputs Answer
N 8
I/YR ? 15
PV −327
PMT 0
FV 1,000

If a zero-interest-bearing (noninterest-bearing) note[15] is issued solely for cash, its present value is measured by the cash received by the issuer of the note. The implicit interest rate is the **rate that equates the cash received with the amounts received in the future.** The difference between the face amount and the present value (cash received) is recorded as **a discount and amortized to interest expense over the life of the note.**

An example of such a transaction is Beneficial Corporation's offering of $150 million of zero-coupon notes (deep discount bonds) having an 8-year life. With a face value of $1,000 each, these notes sold for $327—a deep discount of $673 each. The present value of each note is the cash proceeds of $327. The interest rate can be calculated by determining the interest rate that equates the amount currently paid by the investor with those amounts to be received in the future. Thus, Beneficial amortized the discount over the 8-year life of the notes using an effective interest rate of 15%.[16]

To illustrate the entries and the amortization schedule, assume that your company is the one that issued the 3-year, $10,000, zero-interest-bearing note to Jeremiah Company as illustrated on page 350 of Chapter 7 (notes receivable). The implicit rate that equated the total cash to be paid ($10,000 at maturity) to the present value of the future cash flows ($7,721.80 cash proceeds at date of issuance) was 9%. (The present value of $1 for 3 periods at 9% is $.77218.) The time diagram depicting the one cash flow is shown below:

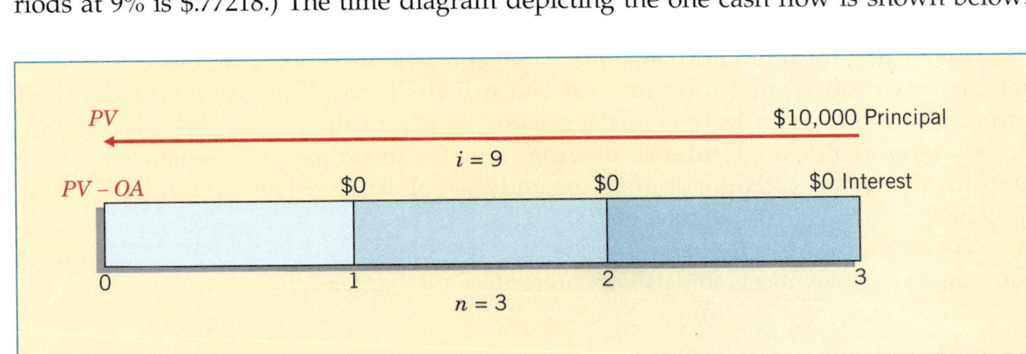

[15]Although the term "note" is used throughout this discussion, the basic principles and methodology are equally applicable to other long-term debt instruments, such as bonds.

[16] $\$327 = \$1{,}000\ (PVF_{8,i})$

$$PVF_{8,i} = \frac{\$327}{\$1{,}000} = .327$$

.327 = 15% (in Table 6-2 locate .32690).

Your entry to record issuance of the note is as follows:

Cash	7,721.80	
Discount on Notes Payable	2,278.20	
Notes Payable		10,000.00

The discount is amortized and interest expense is recognized annually using the **effective interest method**. The 3-year discount amortization and interest expense schedule is shown in Illustration 14-13. (This schedule is similar to the note receivable schedule of Jeremiah Company in Illustration 7-11.)

ILLUSTRATION 14-13
Schedule of Note Discount Amortization

Schedule of Note Discount Amortization
Effective Interest Method
0% Note Discounted at 9%

	Cash Paid	Interest Expense	Discount Amortized	Carrying Amount of Note
Date of issue				$ 7,721.80
End of year 1	$-0-	$ 694.96[a]	$ 694.96[b]	8,416.76[c]
End of year 2	-0-	757.51	757.51	9,174.27
End of year 3	-0-	825.73[d]	825.73	10,000.00
	$-0-	$2,278.20	$2,278.20	

[a]$7,721.80 × .09 = $694.96
[b]$694.96 − 0 = $694.96
[c]$7,721.80 + $694.96 = $8,416.76
[d]5¢ adjustment to compensate for rounding

Interest expense at the end of the first year using the effective interest method is recorded as follows:

Interest Expense ($7,721.80 × 9%)	694.96	
Discount on Notes Payable		694.96

The total amount of the discount, $2,278.20 in this case, represents the expense to be incurred on the note over the 3 years.

Interest-Bearing Notes

The zero-interest-bearing note above is an example of the extreme difference between the stated rate and the effective rate. In many cases, the difference between these rates is not so great. Take, for example, the illustration from Chapter 7 where Marie Co. issued a $10,000, 3-year note bearing interest at 10% to Morgan Corp. for cash. The market rate of interest for a note of similar risk is 12%. The time diagram depicting the cash flows and the computation of the present value of this note are shown on page 351 (Illustration 7-12). In this case, because the effective rate of interest (12%) is greater than the stated rate (10%), the present value of the note is less than the face value; that is, the note is exchanged at a **discount**. The issuance of the note is recorded by Marie Co. as follows:

Cash	9,520	
Discount on Notes Payable	480	
Notes Payable		10,000

The discount is then amortized and interest expense is recognized annually using the **effective interest method**. The 3-year discount amortization and interest expense schedule is shown in Illustration 14-14.

ILLUSTRATION 14-14
Schedule of Note Discount Amortization

Schedule of Note Discount Amortization
Effective Interest Method
10% Note Discounted at 12%

	Cash Paid	Interest Expense	Discount Amortized	Carrying Amount of Note
Date of issue				$ 9,520
End of year 1	$1,000[a]	$1,142[b]	$142[c]	9,662[d]
End of year 2	1,000	1,159	159	9,821
End of year 3	1,000	1,179	179	10,000
	$3,000	$3,480	$480	

[a]$10,000 × 10% = $1,000
[b]$9,520 × 12% = $1,142
[c]$1,142 − $1,000 = $142
[d]$9,520 + $142 = $9,662

Payment of the annual interest and amortization of the discount for the first year are recorded by Marie Co. as follows (amounts per amortization schedule):

Interest Expense	1,142	
Discount on Bonds Payable		142
Cash		1,000

When the present value exceeds the face value, the note is exchanged at a premium. The premium on a note payable is recorded as a credit and amortized using the effective interest method over the life of the note as annual reductions in the amount of interest expense recognized.

SPECIAL NOTE PAYABLE SITUATIONS

The note payable transactions just discussed are the common types of transactions encountered in practice. Three special situations are as follows:

1. Notes issued for cash and other rights.
2. Notes issued for property, goods, and services.
3. Imputed interest.

Notes Issued for Cash and Other Rights

Sometimes when a note is issued, additional rights or privileges are given to the recipient of the note. For example, a corporation issues at face value a zero-interest-bearing note payable that is to be repaid over 5 years with no stated interest. In exchange it agrees to sell merchandise to the lender at less than prevailing prices. In this circumstance, the difference between the present value of the payable and the amount of **cash received should be recorded by the issuer of the note (borrower/supplier) simultaneously as a discount (debit) on the note and an unearned revenue (credit) on the future sales.** The discount should be amortized as a charge to interest expense over the life of the note. The unearned revenue, equal in amount to the discount, reflects a partial prepayment for sales transactions that will occur over the next 5 years. This unearned revenue should be recognized as revenue when sales are made to the lender over the next 5 years.

UNDERLYING CONCEPTS
Nonrecognition of the discount and the unearned revenue would understate specific liabilities and future interest (both expense and revenue), thus lacking representational faithfulness.

To illustrate, assume that the face or maturity value of a 5-year, zero-interest-bearing note is $100,000, that it is issued at face value, and that the appropriate rate of interest is 10%. The conditions of the note provide that the recipient of the note (lender/customer) can purchase $500,000 of merchandise from the issuer of the note (borrower/supplier) at something less than regular selling price over the next 5 years. To record the loan, the issuer of the note records a discount of $37,908, the difference between the $100,000 face amount of the loan and its present value of $62,092 ($100,000

$\times PVF_{5,10\%} = \$100,000 \times .62092$); as the supplier of the merchandise, the issuer also records a credit to unearned revenue of $37,908. The issuer's journal entry is:

Cash	100,000	
Discount on Notes Payable	37,908	
Notes Payable		100,000
Unearned Revenue		37,908

The Discount on Notes Payable is subsequently amortized to interest expense using the effective interest method. The Unearned Revenue is recognized as revenue from the sale of merchandise and is prorated on the same basis that each period's sales to the lender-customer bear to the total sales to that customer for the term of the note. In this situation the write-off of the discount and the recognition of the unearned revenue are at different rates.

Notes Issued for Property, Goods, and Services

The second type of situation involves the issuance of a note for some noncash consideration such a property, goods, or services. When the debt instrument is exchanged for property, goods, or services in a bargained transaction entered into at arm's length, the stated interest rate is presumed to be fair unless:

1. No interest rate is stated, or
2. The stated interest rate is unreasonable, or
3. The stated face amount of the debt instrument is materially different from the current cash sales price for the same or similar items or from current market value of the debt instrument.

In these circumstances the present value of the debt instrument is measured by the fair value of the property, goods, or services or by an amount that reasonably approximates the market value of the note.[17] **The interest element other than that evidenced by any stated rate of interest is the difference between the face amount of the note and the fair value of the property.**

For example, assume that Scenic Development Company sold land having a cash sale price of $200,000 to Health Spa, Inc. in exchange for Health Spa's 5-year, $293,860 zero-interest-bearing note. The $200,000 cash sale price represents the present value of the $293,860 note discounted at 8% for 5 years. If the transaction is recorded on the sale date at the face amount of the note, $293,860, by both parties, Health Spa's Land account and Scenic's sales would be overstated by $93,860, because the $93,860 represents the interest for 5 years at an effective rate of 8%. Interest revenue to Scenic and interest expense to Health Spa for the 5-year period correspondingly would be understated by $93,860.

Because the difference between the cash sale price of $200,000 and the face amount of the note, $293,860, represents interest at an effective rate of 8%, the transaction is recorded at the exchange date as follows:

ILLUSTRATION 14-15
Entries for Noncash Note Transactions

Health Spa, Inc. Books			Scenic Development Company Books		
Land	200,000		Notes Receivable	293,860	
Discount on Notes Payable	93,860		Discount on Notes Rec.		93,860
Notes Payable		293,860	Sales		200,000

During the 5-year life of the note, Health Spa amortizes annually a portion of the discount of $93,860 as a charge to interest expense. Scenic Development records interest revenue totaling $93,860 over the 5-year period by also amortizing the discount.

[17]"Interest on Receivables and Payables," op. cit., par. 12.

The effective interest method is required, although other approaches to amortization may be used if the results obtained are not materially different from those that result from the effective interest method.

Imputed Interest

In instances when the stated rate is known to be unreasonable, the effective rate must be imputed (as explained in Chapter 7). Whenever the **imputed interest rate** is different from the stated rate at the date the note is issued, a discount or premium must be recognized and amortized in subsequent periods. Using the illustration from Chapter 7, assume that on December 31, 2001, Wunderlich Company issued a promissory note to Brown Interiors Company for architectural services. The note has a face value of $550,000, a due date of December 31, 2006, and bears a stated interest rate of 2%, payable at the end of each year. The fair value of the architectural services is not readily determinable, nor is the note readily marketable. On the basis of the credit rating of Wunderlich Company, the absence of collateral, the prime interest rate at that date, and the prevailing interest on Wunderlich's other outstanding debt, an 8% interest rate is imputed as appropriate in this circumstance. The time diagram depicting both cash flows is shown as follows.

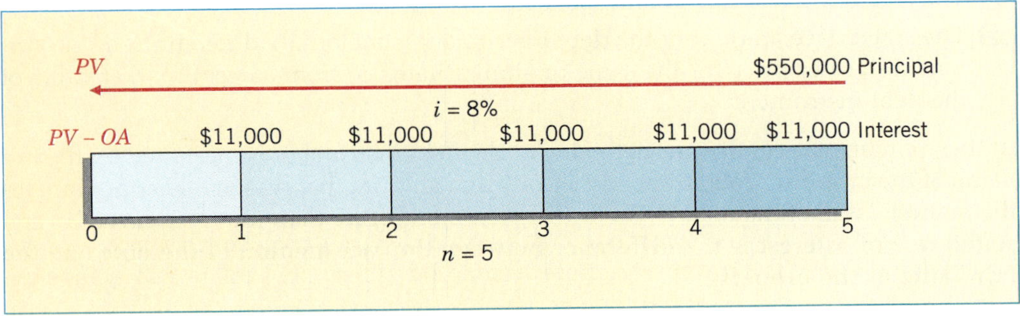

The present value of the note and the imputed fair value of the architectural services are determined as follows:

ILLUSTRATION 14-16
Computation of Imputed Fair Value and Note Discount

Face value of the note		$550,000
Present value of $550,000 due in 5 years at 8% interest payable annually (Table 6-2); $FV(PVF_{5,8\%})$; ($550,000 × .68058)	$374,319	
Present value of $11,000 interest payable annually for 5 years at 8%; $R(PVF\text{-}OA_{5,8\%})$; ($11,000 × 3.99271)	43,920	
Present value of the note		418,239
Discount on notes payable		$131,761

The issuance of the note and receipt of the architectural services are recorded as follows:

December 31, 2001

Building (or Construction in Process)	418,239	
Discount on Notes Payable	131,761	
Notes Payable		550,000

The 5-year amortization schedule appears on page 731.

ILLUSTRATION 14-17
Schedule of Discount Amortization Using Imputed Interest Rate

Schedule of Note Discount Amortization Effective Interest Method 2% Note Discounted at 8% (Imputed)				
Date	Cash Paid (2%)	Interest Expense (8%)	Discount Amortized	Carrying Amount of Note
12/31/01				$418,239
12/31/02	$11,000[a]	$ 33,459[b]	$ 22,459[c]	440,698[d]
12/31/03	11,000	35,256	24,256	464,954
12/31/04	11,000	37,196	26,196	491,150
12/31/05	11,000	39,292	28,292	519,442
12/31/06	11,000	41,558[e]	30,558	550,000
	$55,000	$186,761	$131,761	

[a]$550,000 × 2% = $11,000
[b]$418,239 × 8% = $33,459
[c]$33,459 − $11,000 = $22,459
[d]$418,239 + $22,459 = $440,698
[e]$3 adjustment to compensate for rounding.

Payment of the first year's interest and amortization of the discount is recorded as follows:

December 31, 2002

Interest Expense	33,459	
Discount on Notes Payable		22,459
Cash		11,000

MORTGAGE NOTES PAYABLE

The most common form of long-term notes payable is a mortgage note payable. A **mortgage note payable** is a promissory note secured by a document called a mortgage that pledges title to property as security for the loan. Mortgage notes payable are used more frequently by proprietorships and partnerships than by corporations, as corporations usually find that bond issues offer advantages in obtaining large loans. On the balance sheet, the liability should be reported using a title such as "Mortgage Notes Payable" or "Notes Payable—Secured," with a brief disclosure of the property pledged in notes to the financial statements.

The borrower usually receives cash in the face amount of the mortgage note. In that case, the face amount of the note is the true liability and no discount or premium is involved. When "points" are assessed by the lender, however, the total amount paid by the borrower exceeds the face amount of the note.[18] Points raise the effective interest rate above the rate specified in the note. A point is 1% of the face of the note. For example, assume that a 20-year mortgage note in the amount of $100,000 with a stated interest rate of 10.75% is given by you to Local Savings and Loan Association as part of the financing of your new house. If Local Savings demands 4 points to close the financing, you will receive 4% less than $100,000—or $96,000—but you will be obligated to repay the entire $100,000 at the rate of $1,015 per month. Because you received only $96,000, and must repay 100,000, your effective interest rate is increased to approximately 11.3% on the money you actually borrowed.

Mortgages may be payable in full at maturity or in installments over the life of the loan. If payable at maturity, the mortgage payable is shown as a long-term liability on the balance sheet until such time as the approaching maturity date warrants showing it as a current liability. If it is payable in installments, the current installments due are shown as current liabilities, with the remainder shown as a long-term liability.

[18]Points, in mortgage financing, are analogous to the original issue discount of bonds.

Because of unusually high, unstable interest rates and a tight money supply, the traditional **fixed-rate mortgage** recently has been partially supplanted with new and unique mortgage arrangements. Most lenders offer **variable-rate mortgages** (also called floating-rate or adjustable rate mortgages) featuring interest rates tied to changes in the fluctuating market rate. Generally the variable-rate lenders adjust the interest rate at either 1- or 3-year intervals, pegging the adjustments to changes in the prime rate or the U.S. Treasury bond rate.

SECTION 3 REPORTING AND ANALYSIS OF LONG-TERM DEBT

Reporting of long-term debt is one of the most controversial areas in financial reporting. Because long-term debt has a significant impact on the cash flows of the company, reporting requirements must be substantive and informative. One problem is that the definition of a liability established in *Concepts Statement No. 6* and the recognition criteria established in *Concepts Statement No. 5* are sufficiently imprecise that arguments can still be made that certain obligations need not be reported as debt.

OFF-BALANCE-SHEET FINANCING

OBJECTIVE 7
Explain the reporting of off-balance-sheet financing arrangements.

Off-balance-sheet financing is an attempt to borrow monies in such a way that the obligations are not recorded. It is an issue of extreme importance to accountants (as well as general management). As one writer noted, "The basic drives of humans are few: to get enough food, to find shelter, and to keep debt off the balance sheet."

Illustration

One form of off-balance-sheet financing occurs with **project financing arrangements**. These arrangements arise when (1) two or more entities form a new entity to construct an operating plant that will be used by both parties; (2) the new entity borrows funds to construct the project and repays the debt from the proceeds received from the project; (3) payment of the debt is guaranteed by the companies that formed the new entity. The advantage of such an arrangement is that **the companies that formed the new entity do not have to report the liability on their books**. To illustrate, assume that **Dow Chemical** and **Exxon Mobil** each put up $1 million and form a separate company to build a chemical plant to be used by both companies. The newly formed company borrows $48 million to construct the plant. The arrangement is illustrated below:

ILLUSTRATION 14-18
Project Financing Arrangement

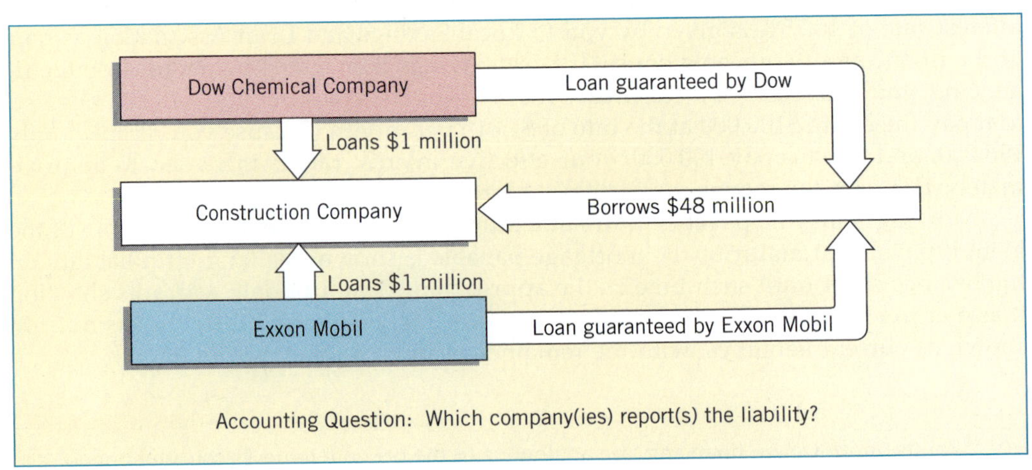

The answer is that each needs to disclose only that they guarantee debt repayment if the project's proceeds are inadequate to pay off the loan.[19]

In some cases, project financing arrangements become more formalized through the use of a variety of contracts. In a simple **take-or-pay contract**, a purchaser of goods signs an agreement with a seller to pay specified amounts periodically in return for an option to receive products. The purchaser must make specified minimum payments even if delivery of the contracted products is not taken. Often these take-or-pay contracts are associated with project financing arrangements. For example, in Illustration 14-18, Dow Chemical and Exxon Mobil sign an agreement that they will purchase products from this new plant and that they will make certain minimum payments **even if they do not take delivery of the goods**.

Through-put agreements are similar in concept to take-or-pay contracts, except that a service instead of a product is provided by the asset under construction. Assume that Dow and Exxon Mobil become involved in a project financing arrangement to build a pipeline to transport their various products. They sign an agreement that requires them to pay specified amounts in return for the transportation of the product. In addition, these companies are required to make cash payments **even if they do not provide the minimum quantities to be transported**.

Inconsistent methods have been used in practice to account for and disclose the unconditional obligation in a take-or-pay or through-put contract involved in a project financing arrangement. In general, most companies have attempted to develop these types of contracts to "get the debt off the balance sheet."

Rationale

Companies attempt to arrange off-balance-sheet financing for several reasons. First, many believe that **removing debt enhances the quality of the balance sheet** and permits credit to be obtained more readily and at less cost.

Second, loan covenants often impose a limitation on the amount of debt a company may have. As a result, off-balance-sheet financing is used because **these types of commitments might not be considered in computing the debt limitation**.

Third, it is argued by some that the asset side of the balance sheet is severely understated. For example, companies that use LIFO costing for inventories and depreciate assets on an accelerated basis will often have carrying amounts for inventories and property, plant, and equipment that are much lower than their current values. As an offset to these lower values, some managements believe that part of the debt does not have to be reported. In other words, **if assets were reported at current values**, less pressure would undoubtedly exist for off-balance-sheet financing arrangements.

Whether the arguments above have merit is debatable. The general idea "out of sight, out of mind" may not be true in accounting. Many users of financial statements indicate that they factor these off-balance-sheet financing arrangements into their computations when assessing debt to equity relationships. Similarly, many loan covenants also attempt to take these complex arrangements into account. Nevertheless, many companies still believe that benefits will accrue if certain obligations are not reported on the balance sheet.

The FASB response to these off-balance-sheet financing arrangements has been increased disclosure (note) requirements. This response is consistent with an "efficient markets" philosophy: the important question is not whether the presentation is off-balance sheet or not, but whether the items are disclosed at all.[20] The authors believe

[19]"Accounting for Contingencies," *Statement of Financial Accounting Standards No. 5* (Stamford, Conn.: FASB, 1975), par. 12.

[20]It is unlikely that the FASB will be able to stop all types of off-balance-sheet transactions. Financial information is the Holy Grail of Wall Street. Developing new financial instruments and arrangements to sell and market to customers is not only profitable, but also adds to the prestige of the investment firms that create them. Thus, new financial products will continue to appear that will test the ability of the FASB to develop appropriate accounting standards for them.

that financial reporting would be enhanced if more obligations were recorded on the balance sheet instead of merely described in the notes to the financial statements.[21]

PRESENTATION AND ANALYSIS OF LONG-TERM DEBT

Presentation of Long-Term Debt

OBJECTIVE 8
Indicate how long-term debt is presented and analyzed.

Companies that have large amounts and numerous issues of long-term debt frequently report only one amount in the balance sheet and support this with comments and schedules in the accompanying notes. Long-term debt that **matures within one year** should be reported as a current liability, unless retirement is to be accomplished with other than current assets. If the debt is to be refinanced, converted into stock, or is to be retired from a bond retirement fund, it should continue to be reported as noncurrent and accompanied with a note explaining the method to be used in its liquidation.[22]

Note disclosures generally indicate the nature of the liabilities, maturity dates, interest rates, call provisions, conversion privileges, restrictions imposed by the creditors, and assets designated or pledged as security. Any assets pledged as security for the debt should be shown in the assets section of the balance sheet. The fair value of the long-term debt should also be disclosed if it is practical to estimate fair value. Finally, disclosure is required of future payments for sinking fund requirements and maturity amounts of long-term debt during each of the next 5 years.[23] The purpose of these disclosures is to aid financial statement users in evaluating the amounts and timing of future cash flows. An example of the type of information provided is shown on page 735 for **Met-Pro Corporation**.

Note that if the company has any unconditional long-term obligations (such as project financing arrangements) that are not reported in the balance sheet, extensive note disclosure must be provided.[24]

Analysis of Long-Term Debt

Long-term creditors and stockholders are interested in a company's long-run solvency, particularly its ability to pay interest as it comes due and to repay the face value of the debt at maturity. Debt to total assets and times interest earned are two ratios that provide information about debt-paying ability and long-run solvency.

The **debt to total assets ratio** measures the percentage of the total assets provided by creditors. It is computed as shown in the following formula by dividing total debt (both current and long-term liabilities) by total assets:

ILLUSTRATION 14-19
Computation of Debt to Total Assets Ratio

$$\text{Debt to total assets} = \frac{\text{Total debt}}{\text{Total assets}}$$

The higher the percentage of debt to total assets, the greater the risk that the company may be unable to meet its maturing obligations.

[21]The FASB's recent efforts to report financial instrument derivatives on the balance sheet is a major breakthrough in this area. See Appendix 18B for discussion of the reporting issues related to these complex transactions.

[22]"Balance Sheet Classification of Short-Term Obligations Expected to Be Refinanced," *FASB Statement of Financial Accounting Standards No. 6* (Stamford, Conn.: FASB, 1975), par. 15. See also "Disclosure of Information about Capital Structure," *FASB Statement of Financial Accounting Standards No. 129* (Norwalk, Conn.: FASB, 1997), par. 4.

[23]"Disclosure of Long-Term Obligations," *Statement of Financial Accounting Standards No. 47* (Stamford, Conn.: FASB, 1981), par. 10.

[24]Ibid., par. 7.

ILLUSTRATION 14-20
Long-Term Debt Disclosure

MET-PRO CORPORATION

	1999	1998
Total current liabilities	$14,387,868	$11,267,545
Long-term debt (Notes 3, 7)	11,941,954	2,242,047
Other non-current liabilities	328,838	249,037
Deferred income taxes	304,874	384,782
Total liabilities	$26,963,534	$14,143,411

Note 3 (in part): Fair Value of Financial Instruments

Debt. The fair value and carrying amount of long-term debt (plus current portion) was as follows:

	January 31	
	1999	1998
Fair value	$13,891,334	$3,714,500
Carrying amount	14,067,047	3,684,011

Valuations for long-term debt are determined based on borrowing rates currently available to the Company for loans with similar terms and maturities.

Note 7 (in part): Debt

Long-Term Debt. Long-term debt consisted of the following:

	January 31	
	1999	1998
Note payable, bank, payable in quarterly installments of $300,000, plus interest at a fixed rate swap of 5.98%, maturing October 2008	$11,700,000	$ —
Notes payable, bank, payable in quarterly installments of $87,500, plus interest at a fixed rate of 7.51%, maturing September 2001	962,500	1,512,500
Notes payable, bank, payable in quarterly installments of $87,500, plus interest at a variable rate ranging from 6.25% to 6.59%, maturing September 2001	962,500	1,512,500
Notes payable, acquisition escrow accounts, balloon payments of $50,000 and $75,000 due on April 8, 1999 and June 11, 1999, plus interest at a fixed rate of 5.90%	125,000	250,000
Mortgage note payable, collateralized by property, payable in $10,267 monthly installments (including principal and interest), at a fixed interest rate of 8.50%, maturing January 2002	317,047	409,011
	14,067,047	3,684,011
Less: Current portion	2,125,093	1,441,964
	$11,941,954	$2,242,047

The above notes are subject to certain covenants, including maintenance of prescribed amounts of leverage and fixed charge coverage ratios.

Maturities of long-term debt were as follows:

Year Ending January 31	
2000	$ 2,125,093
2001	2,008,940
2002	1,833,014
2003	1,200,000
2004	1,200,000
Thereafter	5,700,000
	$14,067,047

Interest expense was $398,051, $325,718, and $300,170 for the years ended in 1999, 1998, and 1997, respectively.

The **times interest earned ratio** indicates the company's ability to meet interest payments as they come due. It is computed by dividing income before interest expense and income taxes by interest expense:

ILLUSTRATION 14-21
Computation of Times Interest Earned Ratio

$$\text{Times interest earned} = \frac{\text{Income before income taxes and interest expense}}{\text{Interest expense}}$$

To illustrate these ratios, we will use data from Hershey Foods Corporation's 1998 Annual Report, which disclosed total liabilities of $2,361 million, total assets of $3,404 million, interest expense of $86 million, income taxes of $216 million, and net income of $341 million. Hershey Foods' debt to total assets ratio is computed as follows:

$$\text{Debt to total assets} = \frac{\$2{,}361}{\$3{,}404} = 69.4\%$$

Hershey Foods' times interest earned ratio is computed as follows:

$$\text{Times interest earned} = \frac{(\$341 + \$86 + \$216)}{\$86} = 7.5 \text{ times}$$

Even though Hershey Foods has a relatively high debt to total assets percentage of 69.4%, its interest coverage of 7.5 times appears very safe.

SUMMARY OF LEARNING OBJECTIVES

1 Describe the formal procedures associated with issuing long-term debt. Incurring long-term debt is often a formal procedure. The bylaws of corporations usually require approval by the board of directors and the stockholders before bonds can be issued or other long-term debt arrangements can be contracted. Generally, long-term debt has various covenants or restrictions. The covenants and other terms of the agreement between the borrower and the lender are stated in the bond indenture or note agreement.

2 Identify various types of bond issues. (1) *Secured and unsecured bonds.* (2) *Term, serial bonds, and callable bonds.* (3) *Convertible, commodity-backed, and deep discount bonds.* (4) *Registered and bearer (coupon) bonds.* (5) *Income and revenue bonds.* The variety in the types of bonds is a result of attempts to attract capital from different investors and risk takers and to satisfy the cash flow needs of the issuers.

3 Describe the accounting valuation for bonds at date of issuance. The investment community values a bond at the present value of its future cash flows, which consist of interest and principal. The rate used to compute the present value of these cash flows is the interest rate that provides an acceptable return on an investment commensurate with the issuer's risk characteristics. The interest rate written in the terms of the bond indenture and ordinarily appearing on the bond certificate is the stated, coupon, or nominal rate. This rate, which is set by the issuer of the bonds, is expressed as a percentage of the face value, also called the par value, principal amount, or maturity value, of the bonds. If the rate employed by the buyers differs from the stated rate, the present value of the bonds computed by the buyers will differ from the face value of the bonds. The difference between the face value and the present value of the bonds is either a discount or premium.

4 Apply the methods of bond discount and premium amortization. The discount (premium) is amortized and charged (credited) to interest expense over the period of time that the bonds are outstanding. Bond interest expense is increased by amortization of a discount and decreased by amortization of a premium. The profession's preferred procedure for amortization of a discount or premium is the effective interest method.

KEY TERMS

bearer (coupon) bonds, *714*
bond discount, *715*
bond indenture, *713*
bond premium, *715*
callable bonds, *714*
carrying value, *719*
commodity-backed bonds, *714*
convertible bonds, *714*
debenture bonds, *713*
debt to total assets ratio, *734*
deep discount (zero-interest) debenture bonds, *714*
effective interest method, *718*
effective yield, or market rate, *715*
extinguishment of debt, *723*
face, par, principal or maturity value, *715*
imputed interest rate, *730*
income bonds, *714*
long-term debt, *712*
long-term notes payable, *725*

Under the effective interest method, (1) bond interest expense is computed by multiplying the carrying value of the bonds at the beginning of the period by the effective interest rate, and (2) the bond discount or premium amortization is then determined by comparing the bond interest expense with the interest to be paid.

5 Describe the accounting procedures for the extinguishment of debt. At the time of reacquisition, the unamortized premium or discount and any costs of issue applicable to the debt must be amortized up to the reacquisition date. The amount paid on extinguishment or redemption before maturity, including any call premium and expense of reacquisition, is the reacquisition price. On any specified date, the net carrying amount of the debt is the amount payable at maturity, adjusted for unamortized premium or discount, and cost of issuance. Any excess of the net carrying amount over the reacquisition price is a gain from extinguishment, whereas the excess of the reacquisition price over the net carrying amount is a loss from extinguishment. Gains and losses on extinguishments are recognized currently in income and classified as an extraordinary item.

6 Explain the accounting procedures for long-term notes payable. Accounting procedures for notes and bonds are quite similar. Like a bond, a note is valued at the present value of its future interest and principal cash flows, with any discount or premium being similarly amortized over the life of the note. Whenever the face amount of the note does not reasonably represent the present value of the consideration given or received in the exchange, the entire arrangement must be evaluated to properly record the exchange and the subsequent interest.

7 Explain the reporting of off-balance-sheet financing arrangements. Off-balance-sheet financing is an attempt to borrow funds in such a way that the obligations are not recorded. One type of off-balance-sheet financing occurs with project financing arrangements that may take the form of take-or-pay contracts or through-put agreements.

8 Indicate how long-term debt is presented and analyzed. Companies that have large amounts and numerous issues of long-term debt frequently report only one amount in the balance sheet and support this with comments and schedules in the accompanying notes. Any assets pledged as security for the debt should be shown in the assets section of the balance sheet. Long-term debt that matures within one year should be reported as a current liability, unless retirement is to be accomplished with other than current assets. If the debt is to be refinanced, converted into stock, or is to be retired from a bond retirement fund, it should continue to be reported as noncurrent and accompanied with a note explaining the method to be used in its liquidation. Disclosure is required of future payments for sinking fund requirements and maturity amounts of long-term debt during each of the next 5 years. Debt to total assets and times interest earned are two ratios that provide information about debt-paying ability and long-run solvency.

KEY TERMS (cont'd.)

- mortgage notes payable, *731*
- off-balance-sheet financing, *732*
- present value of a bond issue, *716*
- project financing arrangement, *732*
- refunding, *724*
- registered bonds, *714*
- revenue bonds, *714*
- secured bonds, *713*
- serial bonds, *713*
- stated, coupon, or nominal rate, *715*
- straight-line method, *717*
- take-or-pay contract, *733*
- term bonds, *713*
- through-put agreements, *733*
- times interest earned ratio, *736*
- treasury bonds, *723*
- zero-interest debenture bonds, *714*

APPENDIX 14A

Accounting for Troubled Debt

During periods of depressed economic conditions or other financial hardship, some debtors have difficulty meeting their financial obligations. For example, owing to rising interest rates and corporate mismanagement, the savings and loan industry

OBJECTIVE 9
After studying Appendix 14A, you should be able to: Distinguish between and account for (1) a loss on loan impairment, (2) a troubled debt restructuring that results in the settlement of a debt, and (3) a troubled debt restructuring that results in a continuation of debt with modification of terms.

experienced a decade of financial crises. The banking industry also faced credit concerns: During the late 1980s bad energy loans and the rescheduling of loans between "less developed countries," such as Argentina, Brazil, and Mexico, and major U.S. banks created considerable uncertainty about the soundness of our banking system. Electric utilities with large nuclear plant construction programs suffered from the financial strains of illiquidity. Companies such as **Public Service of New Hampshire**, **Continental Illinois Bank**, **Lions Capital**, and **Braniff Airlines** had to restructure their debts or in some other way be bailed out of negative cash flow situations.

ACCOUNTING ISSUES

The major accounting issues related to troubled debt situations involve recognition and measurement. In other words, when should a loss be recognized and at what amount?

To illustrate the major issue related to recognition, assume that Citybank has a $10,000,000, 5-year, 10% loan to Brazil with interest receivable annually. At the end of the third year, Citybank has determined that it probably will be able to collect $7,000,000 of this loan at maturity. Should it wait until the loan becomes uncollectible, or should it record a loss immediately? The general recognition principle is: **Losses should be recorded immediately if it is probable that the loss will occur.**

Assuming that Citybank decides to record a loss, at what amount should the loss be recorded? Three alternatives are:

1. *Aggregate Cash Flows.* Some argue that a loss should not be recorded unless the aggregate cash flows from the loan are less than its carrying amount. In the Citybank example, the aggregate cash flows expected are $7,000,000 of principal and $2,000,000 of interest ($10,000,000 × 10% × 2), for a total of $9,000,000. Thus, a loss of only $1,000,000 ($10,000,000 − $9,000,000) would be reported.

   Advocates of this position argue that Citybank will recover $9,000,000 of the $10,000,000 and, therefore, its loss is only $1,000,000. Others disagree, noting that this approach ignores present values. That is, the present value of the future cash flows is much less than $9,000,000 and, therefore, the loss is much greater than $1,000,000.

2. *Present Value—Historical Effective Rate.* Those who argue for the use of present value, however, disagree about the interest rate to use to discount the expected future cash flows. The two rates discussed are the **historical (original) effective rate** and the **market rate** at the time the loan is recognized as troubled. Those who favor the historical effective rate believe that losses should reflect only a deterioration in credit quality. When the historical effective loan rate is used, the value of the investment will change only if some of the legally contracted cash flows are reduced. A loss in this case is recognized because the expected future cash flows have changed. Interest rate changes caused by current economic events that affect the fair value of the loan are ignored.

3. *Present Value—Market Rate.* Others believe that expected future cash flows of a troubled loan should be discounted at market interest rates, which reflect current economic events and conditions that are commensurate with the risks involved. The historical effective interest rate reflects the risk characteristics of the loan at the time it was originated or acquired, but not at the time it is troubled. In short, proponents of the market rate believe that a fair value measure should be used.

This appendix addresses issues concerning the accounting by debtors and creditors for troubled debt. Two different types of situations result with troubled debt:

1. Impairments.
2. Restructurings:
   - **a.** Settlements.
   - **b.** Modification of terms.

In a troubled debt situation, the creditor usually first recognizes a loss on impairment. Subsequently either the terms of the loan are modified or the loan is settled on terms unfavorable to the creditor. In unusual cases, the creditor forces the debtor into bankruptcy in order to ensure the highest possible collection on the loan. Illustration 14A-1 shows this continuum:

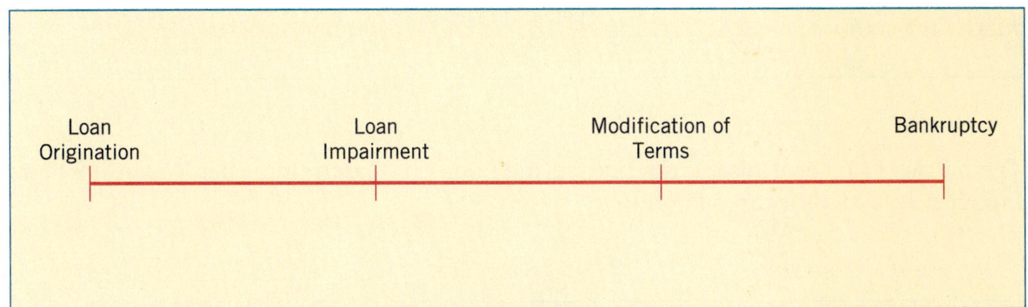

ILLUSTRATION 14A-1
Usual Progression in Troubled Debt Situations

IMPAIRMENTS

A loan[1] is considered **impaired** when it is **probable**,[2] based on current information and events, that the creditor will be unable to collect all amounts due (both principal and interest) according to the contractual terms of the loan. Creditors should apply their normal review procedures in making the judgment as to the probability of collection.[3] If a loan is considered impaired, the loss due to the **impairment** should be measured as the difference between the investment in the loan (generally the principal plus accrued interest) and the expected future cash flows discounted at the loan's historical effective interest rate.[4] In estimating future cash flows the creditor should employ all reasonable and supportable assumptions and projections.[5]

Illustration of Loss on Impairment

On December 31, 2001, Prospect Inc. issued a $500,000, 5-year, zero-interest-bearing note to Community Bank. The note was issued to yield 10% annual interest. As a result, Prospect received and Community Bank paid $310,460 ($500,000 × .62092) on December 31, 2001.[6] A time diagram illustrates the factors involved:

[1]*FASB Statement No. 114,* "Accounting by Creditors for Impairment of a Loan," (Norwalk, Conn.: FASB, May 1993), defines a loan as "a contractual right to receive money on demand or on fixed and determinable dates that is recognized as an asset in the creditor's statement of financial position." For example, accounts receivable with terms exceeding one year are considered loans.

[2]Recall the definitions of probable, reasonably possible, and remote with respect to contingencies, as defined in *FASB Statement No. 5.*

[3]Normal review procedures include examination of "watch lists," review of regulatory reports of examination, and examination of management reports of total loan amounts by borrower.

[4]The creditor may also, for the sake of expediency, use the market price of the loan (if such a price is available) or the fair value of collateral if it is a collateralized loan. *FASB Statement No. 114,* par. 13.

[5]*FASB Statement No. 114,* par. 15.

[6]Present value of $500,000 due in 5 years at 10%, annual compounding (Table 6-2) equals $500,000 x .62092.

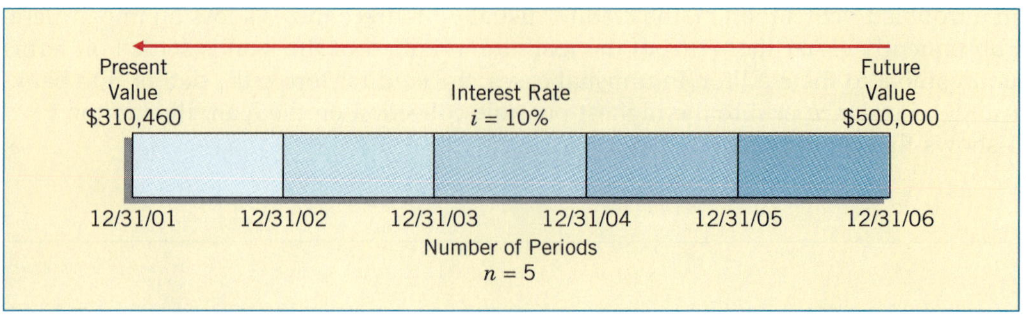

The entries to record this transaction on the books of Community Bank (creditor) and Prospect Inc. (debtor) are as follows:

ILLUSTRATION 14A-2
Creditor and Debtor Entries to Record Note

December 31, 2001					
Community Bank (Creditor)			**Prospect Inc. (Debtor)**		
Notes Receivable	500,000		Cash	310,460	
Discount on Notes Receivable		189,540	Discount on Notes Payable	189,540	
Cash		310,460	Notes Payable		500,000

Assuming that Community Bank and Prospect Inc. use the effective interest method to amortize discounts, Illustration 14A-3 shows the amortization of the discount and the increase in the carrying amount of the note over the life of the note.

ILLUSTRATION 14A-3
Schedule of Interest and Discount Amortization (Before Impairment)

Community Bank

Date	Cash Received (0%)	Interest Revenue (10%)	Discount Amortized	Carrying Amount of Note
12/31/01				$310,460
12/31/02	$0	$ 31,046[a]	$31,046	341,506[b]
12/31/03	0	34,151	34,151	375,657
12/31/04	0	37,566	37,566	413,223
12/31/05	0	41,322	41,322	454,545
12/31/06	0	45,455	45,455	500,000
Total	$0	$189,540	$189,540	

[a]$31,046 = $310,460 × .10
[b]$341,506 = $310,460 + $31,046

Unfortunately, during 2003 Prospect's business deteriorated due to increased competition and a faltering regional economy. After reviewing all available evidence at December 31, 2003, Community Bank determined that it was probable that Prospect would pay back only $300,000 of the principal at maturity. As a result, Community Bank decided that the loan was impaired, and that a loss should be recorded immediately.

To determine the loss, the first step is to compute the present value of the expected cash flows discounted at the historical effective rate of interest. This amount is $225,396. The time diagram on the next page highlights the factors involved in this computation.

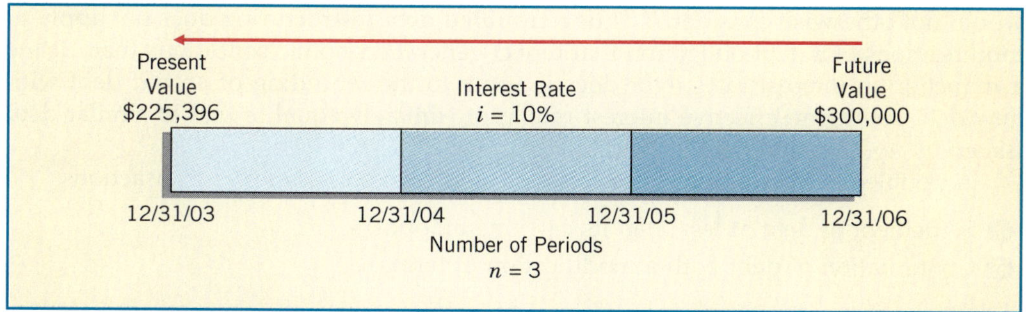

The loss due to impairment is equal to the difference between the present value of the expected future cash flows and the recorded carrying amount of the investment in the loan. The calculation of the loss is shown in Illustration 14A-4.

ILLUSTRATION 14A-4
Computation of Loss Due to Impairment

Carrying amount of investment (12/31/03)—Illustration 14A-3	$375,657
Less: Present value of $300,000 due in 3 years at 10% interest compounded annually (Table 6-2); $FV(PVF_{3,10\%})$; ($300,000 × .75132)	225,396
Loss due to impairment	$150,261

The loss due to the impairment is $150,261 not $200,000 ($500,000 − $300,000). The reason is that the loss is measured at a present value amount, not an undiscounted amount, at the time the loss is recorded.

The entry to record the loss is as follows:

ILLUSTRATION 14A-5
Creditor and Debtor Entries to Record Loss on Note

December 31, 2003			
Community Bank (Creditor)			**Prospect Inc. (Debtor)**
Bad Debt Expense	150,261		No entry
Allowance for Doubtful Accounts		150,261	

Community Bank (creditor) debits Bad Debt Expense for the expected loss. At the same time, it reduces the overall value of its loan receivable by crediting Allowance for Doubtful Accounts.[7] On the other hand, Prospect Inc. (debtor) makes no entry because it still legally owes $500,000.[8]

TROUBLED DEBT RESTRUCTURINGS

A **troubled debt restructuring** occurs when a creditor "for economic or legal reasons related to the debtor's financial difficulties grants a concession to the debtor that it

[7]In the event that the loan is written off, the loss is charged against the allowance. In subsequent periods, if the estimated expected cash flows are revised based on new information, the allowance account and bad debt account are adjusted (either increased or decreased depending whether conditions improved or worsened) in the same fashion as the original impairment. The terms "loss" and "bad debt expense" are used interchangeably throughout this discussion. Losses related to receivables transactions should be charged to Bad Debt Expense or the related Allowance for Doubtful Accounts because these are the accounts used to recognize changes in values affecting receivables.

[8]Many alternatives are permitted to recognize income in subsequent periods. See *FASB Statement No. 118,* "Accounting by Creditors for Impairment of a Loan—Income Recognition and Disclosures" (Norwalk, Conn.: FASB, October 1994) for appropriate methods.

would not otherwise consider."[9] Thus a **troubled** debt restructuring does not apply to modifications of a debt obligation that reflect general economic conditions that dictate a reduction in interest rates. Nor does it apply to the refunding of an old debt with new debt having an effective interest rate approximately equal to that of similar debt issued by nontroubled debtors.

A troubled debt restructuring involves one of two basic types of transactions:

1. Settlement of debt at less than its carrying amount.
2. Continuation of debt with a modification of terms.

Settlement of Debt

A transfer of noncash assets (real estate, receivables, or other assets) or the issuance of the debtor's stock can be used to settle a debt obligation in a troubled debt restructuring. In these situations, **the noncash assets or equity interest given should be accounted for at their fair market value.** The debtor is required to determine the excess of the carrying amount of the payable over the fair value of the assets or equity transferred (gain). Likewise, the creditor is required to determine the excess of the receivable over the fair value of those same assets or equity interests transferred (loss). The debtor recognizes an extraordinary gain equal to the amount of the excess, and the creditor normally would charge the excess (loss) against Allowance for Doubtful Accounts. In addition, the debtor recognizes a gain or loss on disposition of assets to the extent that the fair value of those assets differs from their carrying amount (book value).

To illustrate a transfer of assets, assume that American City Bank has loaned $20,000,000 to Union Mortgage Company. Union Mortgage in turn has invested these monies in residential apartment buildings, but because of low occupancy rates it cannot meet its loan obligations. American City Bank agrees to accept from Union Mortgage real estate with a fair market value of $16,000,000 in full settlement of the $20,000,000 loan obligation. The real estate has a recorded value of $21,000,000 on the books of Union Mortgage Company. The entry to record this transaction on the books of American City Bank (creditor) is as follows:

Real Estate	16,000,000	
Allowance for Doubtful Accounts	4,000,000	
Note Receivable from Union Mortgage Company		20,000,000

The real estate is recorded at fair market value, and a charge is made to the Allowance for Doubtful Accounts to reflect the bad debt write-off.

The entry to record this transaction on the books of Union Mortgage Company (debtor) is as follows:

Note Payable to American City Bank	20,000,000	
Loss on Disposition of Real Estate	5,000,000	
Real Estate		21,000,000
Gain on Restructuring of Debt (Extraordinary)		4,000,000

Union Mortgage Company has a loss on the disposition of real estate in the amount of $5,000,000 (the difference between the $21,000,000 book value and the $16,000,000 fair market value), which should be shown as an ordinary loss on the income statement. In addition, it has a gain on restructuring of debt of $4,000,000 (the difference between the $20,000,000 carrying amount of the note payable and the $16,000,000 fair market value of the real estate). **The gain on restructuring should be shown as an extraordinary item.**

To illustrate the granting of an equity interest, assume that American City Bank had agreed to accept from Union Mortgage Company 320,000 shares of Union's common stock ($10 par) that has a fair market value of $16,000,000 in full settlement of the

[9]"Accounting by Debtors and Creditors for Troubled Debt Restructurings," *FASB Statement No. 15* (Norwalk, Conn.: FASB, June, 1977), par. 1.

$20,000,000 loan obligation. The entry to record this transaction on the books of American City Bank (creditor) is as follows:

Investment	16,000,000	
Allowance for Doubtful Accounts	4,000,000	
Note Receivable from Union Mortgage Company		20,000,000

The stock received by American City Bank is recorded as an investment at the fair market value at the date of restructure.

The entry to record this transaction on the books of Union Mortgage Company (debtor) is as follows:

Note Payable to American City Bank	20,000,000	
Common Stock		3,200,000
Additional Paid-in Capital		12,800,000
Gain on Restructuring of Debt (Extraordinary)		4,000,000

The stock issued by Union Mortgage Company is recorded in the normal manner with the difference between the par value and the fair value of the stock recorded as additional paid-in capital.

Modification of Terms

In some cases, a debtor will have serious short-run cash flow problems that lead it to request one or a combination of the following modifications:

1. Reduction of the stated interest rate.
2. Extension of the maturity date of the face amount of the debt.
3. Reduction of the face amount of the debt.
4. Reduction or deferral of any accrued interest.

Prior to *FASB Statement No. 114,* debtors and creditors computed the gain or loss on restructuring based upon the undiscounted restructured cash flows. Under *FASB Statement No. 114,* the creditor's loss is based upon cash flows discounted at the historical effective rate of the loan. The FASB concluded that, "because loans are recorded originally at discounted amounts, the ongoing assessment for impairment should be made in a similar manner."[10] The debtor's gain will continue to be calculated based upon **undiscounted amounts,** as described in *FASB Statement No. 15.* As a consequence, **the gain recorded by the debtor will not equal the loss recorded by the creditor under many circumstances.**[11]

Two illustrations demonstrate the accounting for a troubled debt restructuring by debtors and creditors:

1. The debtor does not record a gain.
2. The debtor does record a gain.

In both instances the creditor has a loss.

Illustration 1—No Gain for Debtor

This illustration demonstrates a restructuring in which no gain is recorded by the debtor.[12] On December 31, 2001, Morgan National Bank enters into a debt restructur-

[10] *FASB Statement No. 114,* par. 42.

[11] In response to concerns expressed about this nonsymmetric treatment, the FASB stated that *Statement No. 114* does not address debtor accounting because the FASB was concerned that expansion of the scope of the statement would delay its issuance.

[12] Note that the examples given for restructuring assume no previous entries were made by the creditor for impairment. In actuality it is likely that, in accordance with *Statement No. 114,* the creditor would have already made an entry when the loan initially became impaired, and restructuring would simply require an adjustment of the initial estimated bad debt by the creditor. Recall, however, that the debtor makes no entry upon impairment.

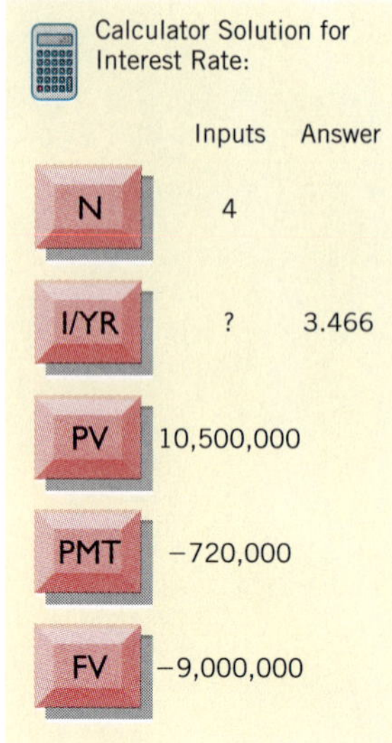

ing agreement with Resorts Development Company, which is experiencing financial difficulties. The bank restructures a $10,500,000 loan receivable issued at par (interest paid to date) by:

1. Reducing the principal obligation from $10,500,000 to $9,000,000,
2. Extending the maturity date from December 31, 2001, to December 31, 2005, and
3. Reducing the interest rate from 12% to 8%.

Debtor Calculations. The total future cash flow after restructuring of $11,880,000 ($9,000,000 of principal plus $2,880,000 of interest payments[13]) exceeds the total pre-restructuring carrying amount of the debt of $10,500,000. Consequently, **no gain is recorded and no adjustment is made by the debtor** to the carrying amount of the payable. As a result, no entry is made by Resorts Development Co. (debtor) at the date of restructuring.

A new effective interest rate must be computed by the debtor in order to record interest expense in future periods. The new effective interest rate equates the present value of the future cash flows specified by the new terms with the pre-restructuring carrying amount of the debt. In this case, the new rate is computed by relating the pre-restructure carrying amount ($10,500,000) to the total future cash flow ($11,880,000). The rate necessary to discount the total future cash flow ($11,880,000) to a present value equal to the remaining balance ($10,500,000) is 3.46613%.[14]

On the basis of the effective rate of 3.46613%, the schedule shown in Illustration 14A-6 is prepared.

ILLUSTRATION 14A-6
Schedule Showing Reduction of Carrying Amount of Note

RESORTS DEVELOPMENT CO. (DEBTOR)

Date	Interest Paid (8%)	Interest Expense (3.46613%)	Reduction of Carrying Amount	Carrying Amount of Note
12/31/01				$10,500,000
12/31/02	$ 720,000[a]	$ 363,944[b]	$ 356,056[c]	10,143,944
12/31/03	720,000	351,602	368,398	9,775,546
12/31/04	720,000	338,833	381,167	9,394,379
12/31/05	720,000	325,621	394,379	9,000,000
	$2,880,000	$1,380,000	$1,500,000	

[a]$720,000 = $9,000,000 × .08
[b]$363,944 = $10,500,000 × 3.46613%
[c]$356,056 = $720,000 − $363,944

Thus, on December 31, 2002 (date of first interest payment after restructure), the debtor makes the following entry:

December 31, 2002

Notes Payable	356,056	
Interest Expense	363,944	
Cash		720,000

[13]Total interest payments are: $9,000,000 × .08 × 4 years = $2,880,000.

[14]An accurate interest rate i can be found by using the formulas given at the tops of Tables 6-2 and 6-4 to set up the following equation:

$$\$10{,}500{,}000 = \underset{\text{(from Table 6-2)}}{\frac{1}{(1+i)^4}} \times \$9{,}000{,}000 + \underset{\text{(from Table 6-4)}}{\frac{1 - \frac{1}{(1+i)^4}}{i}} \times \$720{,}000$$

Solving algebraically for i, we find that $i = 3.46613\%$.

A similar entry (except for different amounts for debits to Notes Payable and Interest Expense) is made each year until maturity. At maturity, the following entry is made:

	December 31, 2005	
Notes Payable	9,000,000	
Cash		9,000,000

Creditor Calculations. Morgan National Bank (creditor) is required to calculate its loss based upon the expected future cash flows discounted at the historical effective rate of the loan. This loss is calculated as follows:

ILLUSTRATION 14A-7
Computation of Loss to Creditor on Restructuring

Pre-restructure carrying amount		$10,500,000
Present value of restructured cash flows:		
Present value of \$9,000,000 due in 4 years at 12%, interest payable annually (Table 6-2); $FV(PVF_{4,12\%})$; (\$9,000,000 × .63552)	$5,719,680	
Present value of \$720,000 interest payable annually for 4 years at 12% (Table 6-4); $R(PVF\text{-}OA_{4,12\%})$; (\$720,000 × 3.03735)	2,186,892	
Present value of restructured cash flows		7,906,572
Loss on restructuring		$ 2,593,428

As a result, Morgan National Bank records a bad debt expense account as follows (assuming no allowance balance has been established from recognition of an impairment):

Bad Debt Expense	2,593,428	
Allowance for Doubtful Accounts		2,593,428

In subsequent periods, interest revenue is reported based on the historical effective rate. Illustration 14A-8 provides the following interest and amortization information:

ILLUSTRATION 14A-8
Schedule of Interest and Amortization after Debt Restructuring

MORGAN NATIONAL BANK (CREDITOR)

Date	Interest Received (8%)	Interest Revenue (12%)	Increase of Carrying Amount	Carrying Amount of Note
12/31/01				$7,906,572
12/31/02	$ 720,000[a]	$ 948,789[b]	$ 228,789[c]	8,135,361
12/31/03	720,000	976,243	256,243	8,391,604
12/31/04	720,000	1,006,992	286,992	8,678,596
12/31/05	720,000	1,041,404[d]	321,404[d]	9,000,000
Total	$2,880,000	$3,973,428	$1,093,428	

[a]\$720,000 = \$9,000,000 × .08
[b]\$948,789 = \$7,906,572 × .12
[c]\$228,789 = \$948,789 − \$720,000
[d]\$28 adjustment to compensate for rounding.

On December 31, 2002, Morgan National Bank would make the following entry:

	December 31, 2002	
Cash	720,000	
Allowance for Doubtful Accounts	228,789	
Interest Revenue		948,789

A similar entry (except for different amounts debited to Allowance for Doubtful Accounts and credited to Interest Revenue) is made each year until maturity. At maturity, the following entry is made:

December 31, 2005		
Cash	9,000,000	
Allowance for doubtful accounts	1,500,000	
Notes Receivable		10,500,000

Illustration 2—Gain for Debtor

If the pre-restructure carrying amount exceeds the total future cash flows as a result of a modification of the terms, the debtor records a gain. To illustrate, assume the facts in the previous example except that Morgan National Bank reduced the principal to $7,000,000 (and extended the maturity date to December 31, 2005, and reduced the interest from 12% to 8%). The total future cash flow is now $9,240,000 ($7,000,000 of principal plus $2,240,000 of interest[15]), which is $1,260,000 less than the pre-restructure carrying amount of $10,500,000. Under these circumstances, Resorts Development Company (debtor) would reduce the carrying amount of its payable $1,260,000 and record an extraordinary gain of $1,260,000. On the other hand, Morgan National Bank (creditor) would debit its Bad Debt Expense for $4,350,444. This computation is shown in Illustration 14A-9.

ILLUSTRATION 14A-9
Computation of Loss to Creditor on Restructuring

Pre-restructure carrying amount		$10,500,000
Present value of restructured cash flows:		
Present value of $7,000,000 due in 4 years at 12%, interest payable annually (Table 6-2); $FV(PVF_{4,12\%})$; ($7,000,000 × .63552)	$4,448,640	
Present value of $560,000 interest payable annually for 4 years at 12% (Table 6-4); $R(PVF\text{-}OA_{4,12\%})$; ($560,000 × 3.03735)	1,700,916	6,149,556
Creditor's loss on restructuring		$ 4,350,444

Entries to record the gain and loss on the debtor's and creditor's books at the date of restructure, December 31, 2001, are as follows:

ILLUSTRATION 14A-10
Debtor and Creditor Entries to Record Gain and Loss on Note

December 31, 2001 (date of restructure)					
Resorts Development Co. (Debtor)			**Morgan National Bank (Creditor)**		
Notes Payable	1,260,000		Bad Debt Expense	4,350,444	
Gain on Restructuring of Debt (Extraordinary)		1,260,000	Allowance for Doubtful Accounts		4,350,444

For Resorts Development (debtor), because the new carrying value of the note ($10,500,000 − $1,260,000 = $9,240,000) equals the sum of the undiscounted cash flows ($9,240,000), the imputed interest rate is 0%. Consequently, all of the future cash flows reduce the principal balance, and no interest expense is recognized. For Morgan National the interest revenue would be reported in the same fashion as the previous example, that is, using the historical effective interest rate applied toward the newly discounted value of the note. Interest computations are shown in Illustration 14A-11.

[15]Total interest payments are: $7,000,000 × .08 × 4 years = $2,240,000.

ILLUSTRATION 14A-11
Schedule of Interest and Amortization after Debt Restructuring

Morgan National Bank (Creditor)				
Date	Cash Received (8%)	Interest Revenue (12%)	Increase in Carrying Amount	Carrying Amount of Note
12/31/01				$6,149,556
12/31/02	$ 560,000[a]	$ 737,947[b]	$177,947[c]	6,327,503
12/31/03	560,000	759,300	199,300	6,526,803
12/31/04	560,000	783,216	223,216	6,750,019
12/31/05	560,000	809,981[d]	249,981[d]	7,000,000
Total	$2,240,000	$3,090,444	$850,444	

[a]$560,000 = $7,000,000 × .08
[b]$737,947 = $6,149,556 × .12
[c]$177,947 = $737,947 − $560,000
[d]$21 adjustment to compensate for rounding.

ILLUSTRATION 14A-12
Debtor and Creditor Entries to Record Periodic Interest and Final Principal Payments

The following journal entries illustrate the accounting by debtor and creditor for periodic interest payments and final principal payment:

Resorts Development Co. (Debtor)			Morgan National Bank (Creditor)		
December 31, 2002 (date of first interest payment following restructure)					
Notes Payable	560,000		Cash	560,000	
Cash		560,000	Allowance for Doubtful Accounts	177,947	
			Interest Revenue		737,947
December 31, 2003, 2004, and 2005 (dates of 2nd, 3rd, and last interest payments)					
(Debit and credit same accounts as 12/31/02 using applicable amounts from appropriate amortization schedules.)					
December 31, 2005 (date of principal payment)					
Notes Payable	7,000,000		Cash	7,000,000	
Cash		7,000,000	Allowance for doubtful accounts	3,500,000	
			Notes Receivable		10,500,000

Evaluation

Under *Statement No. 15,* the FASB justified accounting for troubled debt restructurings at undiscounted values by saying that a restructuring involving a modification of terms is a continuation of an existing debt and is not a business transaction involving transfers of resources and obligations. Many challenged this approach. If a company has a $1,000,000 loan receivable earning interest at 10% and the interest rate is lowered to 5% because the debtor has financial problems, they believed that a loss should be recognized immediately to reflect the change in the economic relationship between the debtor and the creditor. The FASB contended that the creditor's primary objective is to recover its investment—as long as this is accomplished a loss should not be recognized.

The position taken by the FASB under *Statement No. 15* was the position lobbied for by financial institutions. They argued that the economic consequences of loss recognition would be devastating to their industry. During the troubled economic times of the early and mid-1970s and the late 1980s, many financial institutions would have had to take substantial losses if the usual present value techniques had been employed. They argued that the recognition of these losses might cause individuals to lose confidence in the financial system, which would make it more difficult for financial institutions to raise capital and to grant credit to marginal or small borrowers. They argued that some bankruptcies, perhaps even a recession, would result.

With the gift of hindsight, in light of the savings-and-loan crisis, it appears that the nonrecognition of losses under *Statement No. 15* hid the extent to which financial institutions had many bad loans on their books. In the aftermath of the savings-and-loan clean-up, bank regulators and accounting regulators have taken considerable steps toward improving the accounting and disclosure for loans.

SUMMARY OF ACCOUNTING FOR IMPAIRMENT AND TROUBLED DEBT RESTRUCTURINGS

ILLUSTRATION 14A-13
Procedures for Impairments and Troubled Debt Restructurings

Event	Accounting Procedure
1. Impairment	**Creditor:** Loss based upon difference between present value of future cash flows discounted at historical effective interest rate and carrying amount of note. Recognize interest revenue based upon new carrying amount and original effective rate. **Debtor:** No recognition
2. Restructurings—Settlement of Debt	
a. Transfer of noncash assets.	**Creditor:** Recognize loss on restructure. **Debtor:** Recognize gain on restructure and recognize gain or loss on asset transfer.
b. Granting of equity interest.	**Creditor:** Recognize loss on restructure. **Debtor:** Recognize gain on restructure.
3. Restructurings—Continuation of Debt with Modified Terms	
a. Carrying amount of debt is less than future cash flows (no gain for debtor).	**Creditor:** Recognize loss based upon present value of restructured cash flows. Recognize interest revenue based upon new recorded value and original effective rate. **Debtor:** Recognize no gain on restructure. Determine new effective interest rate to be used in recording interest expense.
b. Carrying amount of debt is greater than total future cash flows (gain for debtor).	**Creditor:** Recognize loss based upon present value of restructured cash flows. Recognize interest revenue based upon new recorded value and original effective rate. **Debtor:** Recognize gain on restructure and reduce carrying amount to the sum of the undiscounted cash flows. Recognize no interest expense over the remaining life of the debt.

The following disclosures for loan impairment and restructurings are required of creditors:[16]

ILLUSTRATION 14A-14
Disclosures of Creditors for Loan Impairment and Restructurings

DISCLOSURES OF CREDITORS

1. As of the date of each balance sheet presented, the total recorded investment in the impaired loans at the end of each period and (1) the amount of that recorded investment for which there is a related allowance for doubtful accounts determined in accordance with this statement and the amount of that allowance and (2) the amount of that recorded investment for which there is no related allowance for doubtful accounts determined in accordance with this statement
2. The creditor's policy for recognizing interest revenue on impaired loans, including how cash receipts are recorded
3. For each period for which results of operations are presented, the average recorded investment in the impaired loans during each period, the related amount of interest revenue recognized during the time within that period that the loans were impaired, and, unless not practicable, the amount of interest revenue recognized using a cash-basis method of accounting during the time within that period that the loans were impaired.
4. Activity in allowance for doubtful accounts, including beginning and ending balances.

[16] *FASB Statement No. 118,* par. 6.*i.*

The following disclosures for troubled debt restructures as of the date of each balance sheet presented are required of debtors:

DISCLOSURES OF DEBTORS
1. A description of the changes in terms or major features of settlement.
2. The aggregate gain on restructuring and the related tax effect.
3. The per-share amount of the aggregate gain on restructuring.
4. The aggregate gain or loss on transfers of assets.
5. Information on any contingent payments.

ILLUSTRATION 14A-15
Disclosures of Debtors for Restructurings

SUMMARY OF LEARNING OBJECTIVE FOR APPENDIX 14A

9 Distinguish between and account for (1) a loss on loan impairment, (2) a troubled debt restructuring that results in the settlement of a debt, and (3) a troubled debt restructuring that results in a continuation of debt with modification of terms. An impairment loan loss is based on the difference between the present value of the future cash flows and the carrying amount of the note. There are two types of settlement of debt restructurings: (1) transfer of noncash assets and (2) granting of equity interest. For accounting purposes there are also two types of restructurings with continuation of debt with modified terms: (1) the carrying amount of debt is less than the future cash flows, and (2) the carrying amount of debt is greater than the total future cash flows.

KEY TERMS

impairments, *739*
troubled debt restructuring, *741*

Note: All **asterisked** Questions, Brief Exercises, Exercises, Problems, and Conceptual Cases relate to material contained in the appendix to the chapter.

QUESTIONS

1 (a) From what sources might a corporation obtain funds through long-term debt? (b) What is a bond indenture? What does it contain? (c) What is a mortgage?

2 Differentiate between term bonds, mortgage bonds, collateral trust bonds, debenture bonds, income bonds, callable bonds, registered bonds, bearer or coupon bonds, convertible bonds, commodity-backed bonds, and deep discount bonds.

3 Distinguish between the following interest rates for bonds payable:

(a) yield rate
(b) nominal rate
(c) stated rate
(d) market rate
(e) effective rate

4 Distinguish between the following values relative to bonds payable:

(a) maturity value
(b) face value
(c) market value
(d) par value

5 Under what conditions of bond issuance does a discount on bonds payable arise? Under what conditions of bond issuance does a premium on bonds payable arise?

6 How should discount on bonds payable be reported on the financial statements? Premium on bonds payable?

7 What are the two methods of amortizing discount and premium on bonds payable? Explain each.

8 Zeno Company sells its bonds at a premium and applies the effective interest method in amortizing the premium. Will the annual interest expense increase or decrease over the life of the bonds? Explain.

9 How should the costs of issuing bonds be accounted for and classified in the financial statements?

10 Where should treasury bonds be shown on the balance sheet? Should treasury bonds be carried at par or at reacquisition cost?

11 What is the "call" feature of a bond issue? How does the call feature affect the amortization of bond premium or discount?

12 Why would a company wish to reduce its bond indebtedness before its bonds reach maturity? Indicate how this can be done and the correct accounting treatment for such a transaction.

13 How are gains and losses from extinguishment of a debt classified in the income statement? What disclosures are required of such transactions?

14 What is done to record properly a transaction involving the issuance of a non-interest-bearing long-term note in exchange for property?

15 How is the present value of a non-interest-bearing note computed?

16 When is the stated interest rate of a debt instrument presumed to be fair?

17 What are the considerations in imputing an appropriate interest rate?

18 Differentiate between a fixed-rate mortgage and a variable-rate mortgage.

19 What disclosures are required relative to long-term debt and sinking fund requirements?

20 What is off-balance-sheet financing? Why might a company be interested in using off-balance-sheet financing?

21 What are project financing arrangements?

22 What are take-or-pay contracts and through-put contracts?

***23** What are three measurement bases that might be used to value troubled debt? What are the advantages of each method?

***24** What are the general rules for measuring and recognizing gain or loss by both the debtor and the creditor in an impairment?

***25** What are the general rules for measuring gain or loss by both creditor and debtor in a troubled debt restructuring involving a settlement?

***26** **(a)** In a troubled debt situation, why might the creditor grant concessions to the debtor?

(b) What type of concessions might a creditor grant the debtor in a troubled debt situation?

(c) What is meant by "impairment" of a loan? Under what circumstances should a creditor or debtor recognize an impaired loan?

***27** What are the general rules for measuring and recognizing gain or loss by both the debtor and the creditor in a troubled debt restructuring involving a modification of terms?

***28** What is meant by "accounting symmetry" between the entries recorded by the debtor and creditor in a troubled debt restructuring involving a modification of terms? In what ways is the accounting for troubled debt restructurings and impairments non-symmetrical?

***29** Under what circumstances would a transaction be recorded as a troubled debt restructuring by only one of the two parties to the transaction?

***30** DC Bank agrees to restructure Talk Company's troubled debt situation by reducing the interest rate from 14% to 8% and extending the maturity date of the debt 5 additional years. Explain how Talk Company should account for this modification of terms in the restructuring of its debt to DC Bank.

***31** Assume that on January 1, 2000, the First Bank of Blackhawk enters into a debt restructuring agreement with Arista Sports Co., which is experiencing financial difficulties. The bank agrees to reduce both the principal obligation and interest rate. In this situation, what are the general rules for both debtor and creditor to measure and recognize gain or loss resulting from the debt restructuring?

***32** Assume that Toni Braxton Company has recently fallen into financial difficulties. By reviewing all available evidence on December 31, 2000, one creditor of Toni Braxton, the National American Bank, determined that Toni Braxton would pay back only 65% of the principal at maturity. As a result, the bank decided that the loan was impaired. If the loss is estimated to be $225,000, what entries should both Toni Braxton and National American Bank make to record this loss?

BRIEF EXERCISES

BE14-1 Ghostbusters Corporation issues $300,000 of 9% bonds, due in 10 years, with interest payable semiannually. At the time of issue, the market rate for such bonds is 10%. Compute the issue price of the bonds.

BE14-2 The Goofy Company issued $200,000 of 10% bonds on January 1, 2002. The bonds are due January 1, 2007, with interest payable each July 1 and January 1. The bonds are issued at face value. Prepare Goofy's journal entries for (a) the January issuance, (b) the July 1 interest payment, and (c) the December 31 adjusting entry.

BE14-3 Assume the bonds in BE14-2 were issued at 98. Prepare the journal entries for (a) January 1, (b) July 1, and (c) December 31. Assume The Goofy Company records straight-line amortization annually on December 31.

BE14-4 Assume the bonds in BE14-2 were issued at 103. Prepare the journal entries for (a) January 1, (b) July 1, and (c) December 31. Assume The Goofy Company records straight-line amortization annually on December 31.

BE14-5 Toy Story Corporation issued $500,000 of 12% bonds on May 1, 2002. The bonds were dated January 1, 2002, and mature January 1, 2007, with interest payable July 1 and January 1. The bonds were issued at face value plus accrued interest. Prepare Toy Story's journal entries for (a) the May 1 issuance, (b) the July 1 interest payment, and (c) the December 31 adjusting entry.

BE14-6 On January 1, 2002, Qix Corporation issued $400,000 of 7% bonds, due in 10 years. The bonds were issued for $372,816, and pay interest each July 1 and January 1. Qix uses the effective interest method. Prepare the company's journal entries for (a) the January 1 issuance, (b) the July 1 interest payment, and (c) the December 31 adjusting entry. Assume an effective interest rate of 8%.

BE14-7 Assume the bonds in BE14-6 were issued for $429,757 and the effective interest rate is 6%. Prepare the company's journal entries for (a) the January 1 issuance, (b) the July 1 interest payment, and (c) the December 31 adjusting entry.

BE14-8 Izzy Corporation issued $400,000 of 7% bonds on November 1, 2002, for $429,757. The bonds were dated November 1, 2002, and mature in 10 years, with interest payable each May 1 and November 1. Izzy uses the effective interest method with an effective rate of 6%. Prepare Izzy's December 31, 2002, adjusting entry.

BE14-9 At December 31, 2002, Treasure Land Corporation has the following account balances:

Bonds payable, due January 1, 2010	$2,000,000
Discount on bonds payable	98,000
Bond interest payable	80,000

Show how the above accounts should be presented on the December 31, 2002, balance sheet, including the proper classifications.

BE14-10 James Bond 007 Corporation issued 10-year bonds on January 1, 2002. Costs associated with the bond issuance were $180,000. Bond uses the straight-line method to amortize bond issue costs. Prepare the December 31, 2002, entry to record 1999 bond issue cost amortization.

BE14-11 On January 1, 2002, Uncharted Waters Corporation retired $600,000 of bonds at 99. At the time of retirement, the unamortized premium was $15,000 and unamortized bond issue costs were $5,250. Prepare the corporation's journal entry to record the reacquisition of the bonds.

BE14-12 Jennifer Capriati, Inc. issued a $100,000, 4-year, 11% note at face value to Forest Hills Bank on January 1, 2002, and received $100,000 cash. The note requires annual interest payments each December 31. Prepare Capriati's journal entries to record (a) the issuance of the note and (b) the December 31 interest payment.

BE14-13 Joe Montana Corporation issued a 4-year, $50,000, zero-interest-bearing note to John Madden Company on January 1, 2002, and received cash of $31,776. The implicit interest rate is 12%. Prepare Montana's journal entries for (a) the January 1 issuance and (b) the December 31 recognition of interest.

BE14-14 Larry Byrd Corporation issued a 4-year, $50,000, 5% note to Magic Johnson Company on January 1, 2002, and received a computer that normally sells for $39,369. The note requires annual interest payments each December 31. The market rate of interest for a note of similar risk is 12%. Prepare Larry Byrd's journal entries for (a) the January 1 issuance and (b) the December 31 interest.

BE14-15 King Corporation issued a 4-year, $50,000, zero-interest-bearing note to Salmon Company on January 1, 2002, and received cash of $50,000. In addition, King agreed to sell merchandise to Salmon at an amount less than regular selling price over the 4-year period. The market rate of interest for similar notes is 12%. Prepare King Corporation's January 1 journal entry.

EXERCISES

E14-1 (Classification of Liabilities) Presented below are various account balances of K.D. Lang Inc.:

(a) Unamortized premium on bonds payable, of which $3,000 will be amortized during the next year.
(b) Bank loans payable of a winery, due March 10, 2005. (The product requires aging for 5 years before sale.)
(c) Serial bonds payable, $1,000,000, of which $200,000 are due each July 31.
(d) Amounts withheld from employees' wages for income taxes.
(e) Notes payable due January 15, 2004.
(f) Credit balances in customers' accounts arising from returns and allowances after collection in full of account.
(g) Bonds payable of $2,000,000 maturing June 30, 2003.
(h) Overdraft of $1,000 in a bank account. (No other balances are carried at this bank.)
(i) Deposits made by customers who have ordered goods.

Instructions

Indicate whether each of the items above should be classified on December 31, 2002, as a current liability, a long-term liability, or under some other classification. Consider each one independently from all others; that is, do not assume that all of them relate to one particular business. If the classification of some of the items is doubtful, explain why in each case.

E14-2 (Classification) The following items are found in the financial statements:

(a) Discount on bonds payable
(b) Interest expense (credit balance)
(c) Unamortized bond issue costs
(d) Gain on repurchase of debt
(e) Mortgage payable (payable in equal amounts over next 3 years)
(f) Debenture bonds payable (maturing in 5 years)
(g) Notes payable (due in 4 years)
(h) Premium on bonds payable
(i) Treasury bonds
(j) Income bonds payable (due in 3 years)

Instructions

Indicate how each of these items should be classified in the financial statements.

E14-3 (Entries for Bond Transactions) Presented below are two independent situations:

1. On January 1, 2001, Paul Simon Company issued $200,000 of 9%, 10-year bonds at par. Interest is payable quarterly on April 1, July 1, October 1, and January 1.
2. On June 1, 2001, Graceland Company issued $100,000 of 12%, 10-year bonds dated January 1 at par plus accrued interest. Interest is payable semiannually on July 1 and January 1.

Instructions

For each of these two independent situations, prepare journal entries to record:

(a) The issuance of the bonds.
(b) The payment of interest on July 1.
(c) The accrual of interest on December 31.

E14-4 (Entries for Bond Transactions—Straight-Line) Celine Dion Company issued $600,000 of 10%, 20-year bonds on January 1, 2002, at 102. Interest is payable semiannually on July 1 and January 1. Dion Company uses the straight-line method of amortization for bond premium or discount.

Instructions

Prepare the journal entries to record:

(a) The issuance of the bonds.
(b) The payment of interest and the related amortization on July 1, 2002.
(c) The accrual of interest and the related amortization on December 31, 2002.

E14-5 (Entries for Bond Transactions—Effective Interest) Assume the same information as in E14-4, except that Celine Dion Company uses the effective interest method of amortization for bond premium or discount. Assume an effective yield of 9.75%.

Instructions

Prepare the journal entries to record the following. (Round to the nearest dollar.)

(a) The issuance of the bonds.
(b) The payment of interest and related amortization on July 1, 2002.
(c) The accrual of interest and the related amortization on December 31, 2002.

E14-6 (Amortization Schedules—Straight-line) Dan Majerle Company sells 10% bonds having a maturity value of $2,000,000 for $1,855,816. The bonds are dated January 1, 2001, and mature January 1, 2006. Interest is payable annually on January 1.

Instructions

Set up a schedule of interest expense and discount amortization under the straight-line method.

E14-7 (Amortization Schedule—Effective Interest) Assume the same information as E14-6.

Instructions

Set up a schedule of interest expense and discount amortization under the effective interest method. (*Hint:* The effective interest rate must be computed.)

E14-8 (Determine Proper Amounts in Account Balances) Presented below are three independent situations:

(a) CeCe Winans Corporation incurred the following costs in connection with the issuance of bonds: (1) printing and engraving costs, $12,000; (2) legal fees, $49,000, and (3) commissions paid to underwriter, $60,000. What amount should be reported as Unamortized Bond Issue Costs, and where should this amount be reported on the balance sheet?

(b) George Gershwin Co. sold $2,000,000 of 10%, 10-year bonds at 104 on January 1, 2001. The bonds were dated January 1, 2001, and pay interest on July 1 and January 1. If Gershwin uses the straight-line method to amortize bond premium or discount, determine the amount of interest expense to be reported on July 1, 2001, and December 31, 2001.

(c) Ron Kenoly Inc. issued $600,000 of 9%, 10-year bonds on June 30, 2001, for $562,500. This price provided a yield of 10% on the bonds. Interest is payable semiannually on December 31 and June 30. If Kenoly uses the effective interest method, determine the amount of interest expense to record if financial statements are issued on October 31, 2001.

E14-9 (Entries and Questions for Bond Transactions) On June 30, 2002, Mischa Auer Company issued $4,000,000 face value of 13%, 20-year bonds at $4,300,920, a yield of 12%. Auer uses the effective interest method to amortize bond premium or discount. The bonds pay semiannual interest on June 30 and December 31.

Instructions

(a) Prepare the journal entries to record the following transactions.
  (1) The issuance of the bonds on June 30, 2002.
  (2) The payment of interest and the amortization of the premium on December 31, 2002.
  (3) The payment of interest and the amortization of the premium on June 30, 2003.
  (4) The payment of interest and the amortization of the premium on December 31, 2003.

(b) Show the proper balance sheet presentation for the liability for bonds payable on the December 31, 2003, balance sheet.

(c) Provide the answers to the following questions.
  (1) What amount of interest expense is reported for 2003?
  (2) Will the bond interest expense reported in 2003 be the same as, greater than, or less than the amount that would be reported if the straight-line method of amortization were used?
  (3) Determine the total cost of borrowing over the life of the bond.
  (4) Will the total bond interest expense for the life of the bond be greater than, the same as, or less than the total interest expense if the straight-line method of amortization were used?

E14-10 (Entries for Bond Transactions) On January 1, 2001, Aumont Company sold 12% bonds having a maturity value of $500,000 for $537,907.37, which provides the bondholders with a 10% yield. The bonds are dated January 1, 2001, and mature January 1, 2006, with interest payable December 31 of each year. Aumont Company allocates interest and unamortized discount or premium on the effective interest basis.

Instructions

(a) Prepare the journal entry at the date of the bond issuance.
(b) Prepare a schedule of interest expense and bond amortization for 2001–2003.
(c) Prepare the journal entry to record the interest payment and the amortization for 2001.
(d) Prepare the journal entry to record the interest payment and the amortization for 2003.

E14-11 (Information Related to Various Bond Issues) Karen Austin Inc. has issued three types of debt on January 1, 2001, the start of the company's fiscal year.

(a) $10 million, 10-year, 15% unsecured bonds, interest payable quarterly. Bonds were priced to yield 12%.
(b) $25 million par of 10-year, zero-coupon bonds at a price to yield 12% per year.
(c) $20 million, 10-year, 10% mortgage bonds, interest payable annually to yield 12%.

Instructions

Prepare a schedule that identifies the following items for each bond: (1) maturity value, (2) number of interest periods over life of bond, (3) stated rate per each interest period, (4) effective interest rate per each interest period, (5) payment amount per period, and (6) present value of bonds at date of issue.

E14-12 (Entry for Retirement of Bond; Bond Issue Costs) On January 2, 1996, Banno Corporation issued $1,500,000 of 10% bonds at 97 due December 31, 2005. Legal and other costs of $24,000 were incurred in connection with the issue. Interest on the bonds is payable annually each December 31. The $24,000 issue costs are being deferred and amortized on a straight-line basis over the 10-year term of the bonds.

The discount on the bonds is also being amortized on a straight-line basis over the 10 years. (Straight-line is not materially different in effect from the preferable "interest method".)

The bonds are callable at 101 (i.e., at 101% of face amount), and on January 2, 2001, Banno called $900,000 face amount of the bonds and retired them.

Instructions

Ignoring income taxes, compute the amount of loss, if any, to be recognized by Banno as a result of retiring the $900,000 of bonds in 2001 and prepare the journal entry to record the retirement.

(AICPA adapted)

E14-13 (Entries for Retirement and Issuance of Bonds) Larry Hagman, Inc. had outstanding $6,000,000 of 11% bonds (interest payable July 31 and January 31) due in 10 years. On July 1, it issued $9,000,000 of 10%, 15-year bonds (interest payable July 1 and January 1) at 98. A portion of the proceeds was used to call the 11% bonds at 102 on August 1. Unamortized bond discount and issue cost applicable to the 11% bonds were $120,000 and $30,000, respectively.

Instructions

Prepare the journal entries necessary to record issue of the new bonds and the refunding of the bonds.

E14-14 (Entries for Retirement and Issuance of Bonds) On June 30, 1993, Gene Autry Company issued 12% bonds with a par value of $800,000 due in 20 years. They were issued at 98 and were callable at 104 at any date after June 30, 2001. Because of lower interest rates and a significant change in the company's credit rating, it was decided to call the entire issue on June 30, 2002, and to issue new bonds. New 10% bonds were sold in the amount of $1,000,000 at 102; they mature in 20 years. Autry Company uses straight-line amortization. Interest payment dates are December 31 and June 30.

Instructions

(a) Prepare journal entries to record the retirement of the old issue and the sale of the new issue on June 30, 2002.

(b) Prepare the entry required on December 31, 2002, to record the payment of the first 6 months' interest and the amortization of premium on the bonds.

E14-15 (Entries for Retirement and Issuance of Bonds) Linda Day George Company had bonds outstanding with a maturity value of $300,000. On April 30, 2002, when these bonds had an unamortized discount of $10,000, they were called in at 104. To pay for these bonds, George had issued other bonds a month earlier bearing a lower interest rate. The newly issued bonds had a life of 10 years. The new bonds were issued at 103 (face value $300,000). Issue costs related to the new bonds were $3,000.

Instructions

Ignoring interest, compute the gain or loss and record this refunding transaction.

(AICPA adapted)

E14-16 (Entries for Non-Interest-Bearing Debt) On January 1, 2002, Ellen Greene Company makes the two following acquisitions:

1. Purchases land having a fair market value of $200,000 by issuing a 5-year, non-interest-bearing promissory note in the face amount of $337,012.
2. Purchases equipment by issuing a 6%, 8-year promissory note having a maturity value of $250,000 (interest payable annually).

The company has to pay 11% interest for funds from its bank.

Instructions

(a) Record the two journal entries that should be recorded by Ellen Greene Company for the two purchases on January 1, 2002.

(b) Record the interest at the end of the first year on both notes using the effective interest method.

E14-17 (Imputation of Interest) Presented below are two independent situations:

(a) On January 1, 2002, Robin Wright Inc. purchased land that had an assessed value of $350,000 at the time of purchase. A $550,000, non-interest-bearing note due January 1, 2005, was given in exchange. There was no established exchange price for the land, nor a ready market value for the note. The interest rate charged on a note of this type is 12%. Determine at what amount the land should be recorded at January 1, 2002, and the interest expense to be reported in 2002 related to this transaction.

(b) On January 1, 2002, Sally Field Furniture Co. borrowed $5,000,000 (face value) from Gary Sinise Co., a major customer, through a non-interest-bearing note due in 4 years. Because the note was non-interest-bearing, Sally Field Furniture agreed to sell furniture to this customer at lower than market price. A 10% rate of interest is normally charged on this type of loan. Prepare the journal entry to record this transaction and determine the amount of interest expense to report for 2002.

E14-18 (Imputation of Interest with Right) On January 1, 2000, Margaret Avery Co. borrowed and received $400,000 from a major customer evidenced by a non-interest-bearing note due in 3 years. As consideration for the non-interest-bearing feature, Avery agrees to supply the customer's inventory needs for the loan period at lower than the market price. The appropriate rate at which to impute interest is 12%.

Instructions

(a) Prepare the journal entry to record the initial transaction on January 1, 2000. (Round all computations to the nearest dollar.)

(b) Prepare the journal entry to record any adjusting entries needed at December 31, 2000. Assume that the sales of Avery's product to this customer occur evenly over the 3-year period.

E14-19 (Long-Term Debt Disclosure) At December 31, 2000, Helen Reddy Company has outstanding three long-term debt issues. The first is a $2,000,000 note payable which matures June 30, 2003. The second is a $6,000,000 bond issue which matures September 30, 2004. The third is a $17,500,000 sinking fund debenture with annual sinking fund payments of $3,500,000 in each of the years 2002 through 2006.

Instructions

Prepare the note disclosure required by *FASB Statement No. 47,* "Disclosure of Long-term Obligations," for the long-term debt at December 31, 2000.

***E14-20 (Settlement of Debt)** Larisa Nieland Company owes $200,000 plus $18,000 of accrued interest to First State Bank. The debt is a 10-year, 10% note. During 2001, Larisa Nieland's business deteriorated due to a faltering regional economy. On December 31, 2001, First State Bank agrees to accept an old machine and cancel the entire debt. The machine has a cost of $390,000, accumulated depreciation of $221,000, and a fair market value of $190,000.

Instructions

(a) Prepare journal entries for Larisa Nieland Company and First State Bank to record this debt settlement.

(b) How should Larisa Nieland report the gain or loss on the disposition of machine and on restructuring of debt in its 2001 income statement?

(c) Assume that, instead of transferring the machine, Larisa Nieland decides to grant 15,000 shares of its common stock ($10 par) which has a fair market value of $190,000 in full settlement of the loan obligation. If First State Bank treats Larisa Nieland's stock as a trading investment, prepare the entries to record the transaction for both parties.

***E14-21 (Term Modification without Gain—Debtor's Entries)** On December 31, 2001, the Firstar Bank enters into a debt restructuring agreement with Nicole Bradtke Company, which is now experiencing financial trouble. The bank agrees to restructure a 12%, issued at par, $2,000,000 note receivable by the following modifications:

1. Reducing the principal obligation from $2,000,000 to $1,600,000.
2. Extending the maturity date from December 31, 2001, to December 31, 2004.
3. Reducing the interest rate from 12% to 10%.

Bradtke pays interest at the end of each year. On January 1, 2005, Bradtke Company pays $1,600,000 in cash to Firstar Bank.

Instructions

(a) Based on *FASB Statement No. 114,* will the gain recorded by Bradtke be equal to the loss recorded by Firstar Bank under the debt restructuring?

(b) Can Bradtke Company record a gain under the term modification mentioned above? Explain.

(c) Assuming that the interest rate Bradtke should use to compute interest expense in future periods is 1.4276%, prepare the interest payment schedule of the note for Bradtke Company after the debt restructuring.

(d) Prepare the interest payment entry for Bradtke Company on December 31, 2003.

(e) What entry should Bradtke make on January 1, 2005?

***E14-22 (Term Modification without Gain—Creditor's Entries)** Using the same information as in E14-21 above, answer the following questions related to Firstar Bank (creditor).

Instructions

(a) What interest rate should Firstar Bank use to calculate the loss on the debt restructuring?
(b) Compute the loss that Firstar Bank will suffer from the debt restructuring. Prepare the journal entry to record the loss.
(c) Prepare the interest receipt schedule for Firstar Bank after the debt restructuring.
(d) Prepare the interest receipt entry for Firstar Bank on December 31, 2003.
(e) What entry should Firstar Bank make on January 1, 2005?

***E14-23 (Term Modification with Gain—Debtor's Entries)** Use the same information as in E14-21 above except that Firstar Bank reduced the principal to $1,300,000 rather than $1,600,000. On January 1, 2005, Bradtke pays $1,300,000 in cash to Firstar Bank for the principal.

Instructions

(a) Can Bradtke Company record a gain under this term modification? If yes, compute the gain for Bradtke Company.
(b) Prepare the journal entries to record the gain on Bradtke's books.
(c) What interest rate should Bradtke use to compute its interest expense in future periods? Will your answer be the same as in E14-21 above? Why or why not?
(d) Prepare the interest payment schedule of the note for Bradtke Company after the debt restructuring.
(e) Prepare the interest payment entries for Bradtke Company on December 31, of 2002, 2003, and 2004.
(f) What entry should Bradtke make on January 1, 2005?

***E14-24 (Term Modification with Gain—Creditor's Entries)** Using the same information as in E14-21 and E14-23 above, answer the following questions related to Firstar Bank (creditor).

Instructions

(a) Compute the loss Firstar Bank will suffer under this new term modification. Prepare the journal entry to record the loss on Firstar's books.
(b) Prepare the interest receipt schedule for Firstar Bank after the debt restructuring.
(c) Prepare the interest receipt entry for Firstar Bank on December 31, 2002, 2003, and 2004.
(d) What entry should Firstar Bank make on January 1, 2005?

***E14-25 (Debtor/Creditor Entries for Settlement of Troubled Debt)** Petra Langrova Co. owes $199,800 to Mary Joe Fernandez Inc. The debt is a 10-year, 11% note. Because Petra Langrova Co. is in financial trouble, Mary Joe Fernandez Inc. agrees to accept some property and cancel the entire debt. The property has a book value of $80,000 and a fair market value of $120,000.

Instructions

(a) Prepare the journal entry on Langrova's books for debt restructure.
(b) Prepare the journal entry on Fernandez's books for debt restructure.

***E14-26 (Debtor/Creditor Entries for Modification of Troubled Debt)** Steffi Graf Corp. owes $225,000 to First Trust. The debt is a 10-year, 12% note due December 31, 2001. Because Graf Corp. is in financial trouble, First Trust agrees to extend the maturity date to December 31, 2003, reduce the principal to $200,000, and reduce the interest rate to 5%, payable annually on December 31.

Instructions

(a) Prepare the journal entries on Graf's books on December 31, 2001, 2002, 2003.
(b) Prepare the journal entries on First Trust's books on December 31, 2001, 2002, 2003.

***E14-27 (Impairments)** On December 31, 2000, Iva Majoli Company borrowed $62,092 from Paris Bank, signing a 5-year, $100,000 non-interest-bearing note. The note was issued to yield 10% interest. Unfortunately, during 2002, Majoli began to experience financial difficulty. As a result, at December 31, 2002, Paris Bank determined that it was probable that it would receive back only $75,000 at maturity. The market rate of interest on loans of this nature is now 11%.

Instructions

(a) Prepare the entry to record the issuance of the loan by Paris Bank on December 31, 2000.
(b) Prepare the entry (if any) to record the impairment of the loan on December 31, 2002, by Paris Bank.
(c) Prepare the entry (if any) to record the impairment of the loan on December 31, 2002, by Majoli Company.

***E14-28 (Impairments)** On December 31, 1999, Conchita Martinez Company signed a $1,000,000 note to Sauk City Bank. The market interest rate at that time was 12%. The stated interest rate on the note was

10%, payable annually. The note matures in 5 years. Unfortunately, because of lower sales, Conchita Martinez's financial situation worsened. On December 31, 2001, Sauk City Bank determined that it was probable that the company would pay back only $600,000 of the principal at maturity. However, it was considered likely that interest would continue to be paid, based on the $1,000,000 loan.

Instructions

(a) Determine the amount of cash Conchita Martinez received from the loan on December 31, 1999.
(b) Prepare a note amortization schedule for Sauk City Bank up to December 31, 2001.
(c) Determine the loss on impairment that Sauk City Bank should recognize on December 31, 2001.

PROBLEMS

P14-1 (Analysis of Amortization Schedule and Interest Entries) The following amortization and interest schedule reflects the issuance of 10-year bonds by Terrel Brandon Corporation on January 1, 1994, and the subsequent interest payments and charges. The company's year-end is December 31, and financial statements are prepared once yearly.

Amortization Schedule

Year	Cash	Interest	Amount Unamortized	Book Value
1/1/94			$5,651	$ 94,349
1994	$11,000	$11,322	5,329	94,671
1995	11,000	11,361	4,968	95,032
1996	11,000	11,404	4,564	95,436
1997	11,000	11,452	4,112	95,888
1998	11,000	11,507	3,605	96,395
1999	11,000	11,567	3,038	96,962
2000	11,000	11,635	2,403	97,597
2001	11,000	11,712	1,691	98,309
2002	11,000	11,797	894	99,106
2003	11,000	11,894		100,000

Instructions

(a) Indicate whether the bonds were issued at a premium or a discount and how you can determine this fact from the schedule.
(b) Indicate whether the amortization schedule is based on the straight-line method or the effective interest method and how you can determine which method is used.
(c) Determine the stated interest rate and the effective interest rate.
(d) On the basis of the schedule above, prepare the journal entry to record the issuance of the bonds on January 1, 1994.
(e) On the basis of the schedule above, prepare the journal entry or entries to reflect the bond transactions and accruals for 1994. (Interest is paid January 1.)
(f) On the basis of the schedule above, prepare the journal entry or entries to reflect the bond transactions and accruals for 2001. Brandon Corporation does not use reversing entries.

P14-2 (Issuance and Retirement of Bonds) Sam Sluggers Co. is building a new hockey arena at a cost of $2,000,000. It received a downpayment of $500,000 from local businesses to support the project, and now needs to borrow $1,500,000 to complete the project. It therefore decides to issue $1,500,000 of 10.5%, 10-year bonds. These bonds were issued on January 1, 1999, and pay interest annually on each January 1. The bonds yield 10%. Sluggers paid $50,000 in bond issue costs related to the bond sale.

Instructions

(a) Prepare the journal entry to record the issuance of the bonds and the related bond issue costs incurred on January 1, 1999.
(b) Prepare a bond amortization schedule up to and including January 1, 2003, using the effective interest method.
(c) Assume that on July 1, 2002, Sam Sluggers Co. retires half of the bonds at a cost of $800,000 plus accrued interest. Prepare the journal entry to record this retirement.

P14-3 (Negative Amortization) Slippery Sales Inc. developed a new sales gimmick to help sell its inventory of new automobiles. Because many new car buyers need financing, Slippery offered a low downpayment and low car payments for the first year after purchase. It believes that this promotion will bring in some new buyers.

On January 1, 2001, a customer purchased a new $25,000 automobile, making a downpayment of $1,000. The customer signed a note indicating that the annual rate of interest would be 8% and that quarterly payments would be made over 3 years. For the first year, Slippery required a $300 quarterly payment to be made on April 1, July 1, October 1, and January 1, 2002. After this one-year period, the customer was required to make regular quarterly payments that would pay off the loan as of January 1, 2004.

Instructions

(a) Prepare a note amortization schedule for the first year.
(b) Indicate the amount the customer owes on the contract at the end of the first year.
(c) Compute the amount of the new quarterly payments.
(d) Prepare a note amortization schedule for these new payments for the next 2 years.
(e) What do you think of the new sales promotion used by Slippery?

P14-4 (Issuance and Retirement of Bonds; Income Statement Presentation) Chris Mills Company issued its 9%, 25-year mortgage bonds in the principal amount of $5,000,000 on January 2, 1987, at a discount of $250,000, which it proceeded to amortize by charges to expense over the life of the issue on a straight-line basis. The indenture securing the issue provided that the bonds could be called for redemption in total but not in part at any time before maturity at 104% of the principal amount, but it did not provide for any sinking fund.

On December 18, 2001, the company issued its 11%, 20-year debenture bonds in the principal amount of $6,000,000 at 102, and the proceeds were used to redeem the 9%, 25-year mortgage bonds on January 2, 2002. The indenture securing the new issue did not provide for any sinking fund or for retirement before maturity.

Instructions

(a) Prepare journal entries to record the issuance of the 11% bonds and the retirement of the 9% bonds.
(b) Indicate the income statement treatment of the gain or loss from retirement and the note disclosure required. Assume 2002 income before extraordinary items of $3,200,000, a weighted number of shares outstanding of 1,500,000, and an income tax rate of 40%.

P14-5 (Comprehensive Bond Problem) In each of the following independent cases the company closes its books on December 31.

1. Danny Ferry Co. sells $250,000 of 10% bonds on March 1, 2001. The bonds pay interest on September 1 and March 1. The due date of the bonds is September 1, 2004. The bonds yield 12%. Give entries through December 31, 2002.
2. Brad Dougherty Co. sells $600,000 of 12% bonds on June 1, 2001. The bonds pay interest on December 1 and June 1. The due date of the bonds is June 1, 2005. The bonds yield 10%. On October 1, 2002, Dougherty buys back $120,000 worth of bonds for $126,000 (includes accrued interest). Give entries through December 1, 2003.

Instructions

(Round to the nearest dollar.)

For the two cases above prepare all of the relevant journal entries from the time of sale until the date indicated. Use the effective interest method for discount and premium amortization (construct amortization tables where applicable). Amortize premium or discount on interest dates and at year-end. (Assume that no reversing entries were made.)

P14-6 (Issuance of Bonds between Interest Dates, Straight-line, Retirement) Presented below are selected transactions on the books of Michael Cage Powerglide Corporation.

May 1, 2001	Bonds payable with a par value of $700,000, which are dated January 1, 2001, are sold at 106 plus accrued interest. They are coupon bonds, bear interest at 12% (payable annually at January 1), and mature January 1, 2011. (Use interest expense account for accrued interest.)
Dec. 31	Adjusting entries are made to record the accrued interest on the bonds, and the amortization of the proper amount of premium. (Use straight-line amortization.)
Jan. 1, 2002	Interest on the bonds is paid.
April 1	Bonds of par value of $420,000 are purchased at 102 plus accrued interest, and retired. (Bond premium is to be amortized only at the end of each year.)
Dec. 31	Adjusting entries are made to record the accrued interest on the bonds, and the proper amount of premium amortized.

Instructions

Prepare journal entries for the transactions above.

P14-7 (Entries for Life Cycle of Bonds) On April 1, 2001, Jerry Fontenot Company sold 12,000 of its 11%, 15-year, $1,000 face value bonds at 97. Interest payment dates are April 1 and October 1, and the company uses the straight-line method of bond discount amortization. On March 1, 2002, Fontenot took advantage of favorable prices of its stock to extinguish 3,000 of the bonds by issuing 100,000 shares of its $10 par value common stock. At this time, the accrued interest was paid in cash. The company's stock was selling for $31 per share on March 1, 2002.

Instructions

Prepare the journal entries needed on the books of Fontenot Company to record the following:

(a) April 1, 2001: issuance of the bonds.
(b) October 1, 2001: payment of semiannual interest.
(c) December 31, 2001: accrual of interest expense.
(d) March 1, 2002: extinguishment of 3,000 bonds. (No reversing entries made.)

P14-8 (Entries for Non-Interest-Bearing Debt) On December 31, 2001, Jose Luis Company acquired a computer from Cuevas Corporation by issuing a $400,000 non-interest-bearing note, payable in full on December 31, 2005. Jose Luis Company's credit rating permits it to borrow funds from its several lines of credit at 10%. The computer is expected to have a 5-year life and a $50,000 salvage value.

Instructions

(a) Prepare the journal entry for the purchase on December 31, 2001.
(b) Prepare any necessary adjusting entries relative to depreciation (use straight-line) and amortization (use effective interest method) on December 31, 2002.
(c) Prepare any necessary adjusting entries relative to depreciation and amortization on December 31, 2003.

P14-9 (Entries for Non-Interest-Bearing Debt; Payable in Installments) Sun Yat-sen Cosmetics Co. purchased machinery on December 31, 2000, paying $40,000 down and agreeing to pay the balance in four equal installments of $30,000 payable each December 31. An assumed interest of 12% is implicit in the purchase price.

Instructions

Prepare the journal entries that would be recorded for the purchase and for the payments and interest on the following dates:

(a) December 31, 2000.
(b) December 31, 2001.
(c) December 31, 2002.
(d) December 31, 2003.
(e) December 31, 2004.

P14-10 (Comprehensive Problem; Issuance, Classification, Reporting) Presented below are four independent situations:

(a) On March 1, 2002, Heide Co. issued at 103 plus accrued interest $3,000,000, 9% bonds. The bonds are dated January 1, 2002, and pay interest semiannually on July 1 and January 1. In addition, Heide Co. incurred $27,000 of bond issuance costs. Compute the net amount of cash received by Heide Co. as a result of the issuance of these bonds.

(b) On January 1, 2001, Reymont Co. issued 9% bonds with a face value of $500,000 for $469,280 to yield 10%. The bonds are dated January 1, 2001, and pay interest annually. What amount is reported for interest expense in 2001 related to these bonds, assuming that Reymont used the effective interest method for amortizing bond premium and discount?

(c) Czeslaw Building Co. has a number of long-term bonds outstanding at December 31, 2002. These long-term bonds have the following sinking fund requirements and maturities for the next 6 years.

	Sinking Fund	Maturities
2003	$300,000	$100,000
2004	100,000	250,000
2005	100,000	100,000
2006	200,000	—
2007	200,000	150,000
2008	200,000	100,000

Indicate how this information should be reported in the financial statements at December 31, 2002.

(d) In the long-term debt structure of Marie Curie Inc., the following three bonds were reported: mortgage bonds payable $10,000,000; collateral trust bonds $5,000,000; bonds maturing in installments, secured by plant equipment $4,000,000. Determine the total amount, if any, of debenture bonds outstanding.

P14-11 (Comprehensive Liability Problem; Balance Sheet Presentation) Honoré de Balzac Inc. has been producing quality children's apparel for more than 25 years. The company's fiscal year runs from April 1 to March 31. The following information relates to the obligations of Balzac as of March 31, 2002.

Bonds Payable

Balzac issued $5,000,000 of 11% bonds on July 1, 1996, at 96 which yielded proceeds of $4,800,000. The bonds will mature on July 1, 2006. Interest is paid semiannually on July 1 and January 1. Balzac uses the straight-line method to amortize the bond discount.

Notes Payable

Balzac has signed several long-term notes with financial institutions and insurance companies. The maturities of these notes are given in the schedule below. The total unpaid interest for all of these notes amounts to $210,000 on March 31, 2002.

Due Date	Amount Due
April 1, 2002	$ 200,000
July 1, 2002	300,000
October 1, 2002	150,000
January 1, 2003	150,000
April 1, 2003–March 31, 2004	600,000
April 1, 2004–March 31, 2005	500,000
April 1, 2005–March 31, 2006	700,000
April 1, 2006–March 31, 2007	400,000
April 1, 2007–March 31, 2008	500,000
	$3,500,000

Estimated Warranties

Balzac has a one-year product warranty on some selected items in its product line. The estimated warranty liability on sales made during the 2000–01 fiscal year and still outstanding as of March 31, 2001, amounted to $84,000. The warranty costs on sales made from April 1, 2001, through March 31, 2002, are estimated at $210,000. The actual warranty costs incurred during the current 2001–02 fiscal year are as follows:

Warranty claims honored on 2000–01 sales	$ 84,000
Warranty claims honored on 2001–02 sales	95,000
Total warranty claims honored	$179,000

Other Information

1. *Trade payables.* Accounts payable for supplies, goods and services purchased on open account amount to $370,000 as of March 31, 2002.
2. *Payroll related items.* Outstanding obligations related to Balzac's payroll as of March 31, 2002, are:

Accrued salaries and wages	$150,000
FICA taxes	22,000
State and federal income taxes withheld from employees	25,000
Other payroll deductions	5,000

3. *Taxes.* The following taxes incurred but not due until the next fiscal year are:

State and federal income taxes	$310,000
Property taxes	125,000
Sales and use taxes	182,000

4. *Miscellaneous accruals.* Other accruals not separately classified amount to $75,000 as of March 31, 2002.
5. *Dividends.* On March 15, 2002, Balzac's board of directors declared a cash dividend of $.40 per common share and a 10% common stock dividend. Both dividends were to be distributed on April 12, 2002, to the common stockholders of record at the close of business on March 31, 2002. Data regarding Balzac common stock are as follows:

Par value	$5 per share
Number of shares issued and outstanding	3,000,000 shares
Market values of common stock:	
March 15, 2002	$22.00 per share
March 31, 2002	21.50 per share
April 12, 2002	22.50 per share

Instructions

Prepare the liabilities section of the balance sheet and appropriate notes to the statement for Balzac Inc. as of March 31, 2002, as they should appear in its annual report to the stockholders.

(CMA adapted)

P14-12 (Effective Interest Method) Mathilda B. Reichenbacher, an intermediate accounting student, is having difficulty amortizing bond premiums and discounts using the effective interest method. Furthermore, she cannot understand why GAAP requires that this method be used instead of the straight-line method. She has come to you with the following problem, looking for help.

On June 30, 2000, Joan Elbert Company issued $3,000,000 face value of 13%, 20-year bonds at $3,225,690, a yield of 12%. Elbert Company uses the effective interest method to amortize bond premiums or discounts. The bonds pay semiannual interest on June 30 and December 31. Compute the amortization schedule for four periods.

Instructions

Using the data above for illustrative purposes, write a short memo (1–1.5 pages double-spaced) to Mathilda, explaining what the effective interest method is, why it is preferable, and how it is computed. (Do not forget to include an amortization schedule, referring to it whenever necessary.)

***P14-13 (Loan Impairment Entries)** On January 1, 2001, Bostan Company issued a $1,200,000, 5-year, zero-interest-bearing note to National Organization Bank. The note was issued to yield 8% annual interest. Unfortunately, during 2002, Bostan fell into financial trouble due to increased competition. After reviewing all available evidence on December 31, 2002, National Organization Bank decided that the loan was impaired. Bostan will probably pay back only $800,000 of the principal at maturity.

Instructions

(a) Prepare journal entries for both Bostan Company and National Organization Bank to record the issuance of the note on January 1, 2001. (Round to the nearest $10.)

(b) Assuming that both Bostan Company and National Organization Bank use the effective interest method to amortize the discount, prepare the amortization schedule for the note.

(c) Under what circumstances can National Organization Bank consider Bostan's note to be "impaired"?

(d) Compute the loss National Organization Bank will suffer from Bostan's financial distress on December 31, 2002. What journal entries should be made to record this loss?

***P14-14 (Debtor/Creditor Entries for Continuation of Troubled Debt)** Jeremy Hillary is the sole shareholder of Hillary Inc., which is currently under protection of the U.S. bankruptcy court. As a "debtor in possession," he has negotiated the following revised loan agreement with Valley Bank. Hillary Inc.'s $400,000, 12%, 10-year note was refinanced with a $400,000, 5%, 10-year note.

Instructions

(a) What is the accounting nature of this transaction?

(b) Prepare the journal entry to record this refinancing:

(1) On the books of Hillary Inc.

(2) On the books of Valley Bank.

(c) Discuss whether generally accepted accounting principles provide the proper information useful to managers and investors in this situation.

***P14-15 (Restructure of Note under Different Circumstances)** Sandro Corporation is having financial difficulty and therefore has asked Botticelli National Bank to restructure its $3 million note outstanding. The present note has 3 years remaining and pays a current rate of interest of 10%. The present market rate for a loan of this nature is 12%. The note was issued at its face value.

Instructions

Presented below are four independent situations. Prepare the journal entry that Sandro and Botticelli National Bank would make for each of these restructurings.

(a) Botticelli National Bank agrees to take an equity interest in Sandro by accepting common stock valued at $2,200,000 in exchange for relinquishing its claim on this note. The common stock has a par value of $1,000,000.

(b) Botticelli National Bank agrees to accept land in exchange for relinquishing its claim on this note. The land has a book value of $1,950,000 and a fair value of $2,400,000.

(c) Botticelli National Bank agrees to modify the terms of the note, indicating that Sandro does not have to pay any interest on the note over the 3-year period.

(d) Botticelli National Bank agrees to reduce the principal balance due to $2,500,000 and require interest only in the second and third year at a rate of 10%.

***P14-16 (Debtor/Creditor Entries for Continuation of Troubled Debt)** Dionysus Inc. owes Solomos Bank a 10-year, 15% note in the amount of $250,000. The note is due today, 12/31/01. Because Dionysus Inc. is in financial trouble, Solomos agrees to accept 60,000 shares of Dionysus's $1.00 par value common stock, which is selling for $1.40, reduce the face amount of the note to $150,000, extend the maturity date to 12/31/05, and reduce the interest rate to 6%. Interest will continue to be due on December 31 each year.

Instructions

(a) Prepare all the necessary journal entries on the books of Dionysus Inc. from restructure through maturity.

(b) Prepare all the necessary journal entries on the books of Solomos Bank from restructure through maturity.

***P14-17 (Entries for Troubled Debt Restructurings)** At December 31, 2000, Sioux Manufacturing Company had outstanding a $300,000, 12% note payable to Teton National Bank. Dated January 1, 1998, the note was due December 31, 2001, with interest payable each December 31. During 2001, Sioux notified Teton that it might be unable to meet the scheduled December 31, 2001, payment of principal and interest because of financial difficulties. On September 30, 2001, Teton sold the note, including interest accrued since December 31, 2000, for $280,000 to Osage Foundry, one of Sioux's oldest and largest customers. On December 31, 2000, Osage agreed to accept inventory costing $240,000 and worth $315,000 from Sioux in full settlement of the note.

Instructions

(a) Prepare the journal entry to record the September 30, 2001, transaction on the books of Teton, Sioux, and Osage. For each, indicate whether the transaction is a troubled debt restructuring.

(b) Prepare the journal entries to record the December 31, 2001, transaction on the books of Sioux and Osage. For each, indicate whether the transaction is a troubled debt restructuring.

***P14-18 (Debtor/Creditor Entries for Continuation of Troubled Debt with New Effective Interest)** Mildred Corp. owes D. Taylor Corp. a 10-year, 10% note in the amount of $110,000 plus $11,000 of accrued interest. The note is due today, December 31, 2001. Because Mildred Corp. is in financial trouble, D. Taylor Corp. agrees to forgive the accrued interest, $10,000 of the principal, and to extend the maturity date to December 31, 2004. Interest at 10% of revised principal will continue to be due on 12/31 each year.

Assume the following present value factors for 3 periods:

	2¼%	2⅜%	2½%	2⅝%	2¾%	3%
Single sum	.93543	.93201	.92859	.92521	.92184	.91514
Ordinary annuity of 1	2.86989	2.86295	2.85602	2.84913	2.84226	2.82861

Instructions

(a) Compute the new effective interest rate for Mildred Corp. following restructure. (*Hint:* Find the interest rate that establishes approximately $121,000 as the present value of the total future cash flows.)

(b) Prepare a schedule of debt reduction and interest expense for the years 2001 through 2004.

(c) Compute the gain or loss for D. Taylor Corp. and prepare a schedule of receivable reduction and interest revenue for the years 2001 through 2004.

(d) Prepare all the necessary journal entries on the books of Mildred Corp. for the years 2001, 2002, and 2003.

(e) Prepare all the necessary journal entries on the books of D. Taylor Corp. for the years 2001, 2002, and 2003.

CONCEPTUAL CASES

C14-1 (Bond Theory: Balance Sheet Presentations, Interest Rate, Premium) On January 1, 2002, Branagh Company issued for $1,075,230 its 20-year, 13% bonds that have a maturity value of $1,000,000 and pay interest semiannually on January 1 and July 1. Bond issue costs were not material in amount. Below are three presentations of the long-term liability section of the balance sheet that might be used for these bonds at the issue date:

1. Bonds payable (maturing January 1, 2022)	$1,000,000
Unamortized premium on bonds payable	75,230
Total bond liability	$1,075,230

2. Bonds payable—principal (face value $1,000,000 maturing January 1, 2022)	$ 97,220[a]
Bonds payable—interest (semiannual payment $65,000)	978,010[b]
Total bond liability	$1,075,230

3. Bonds payable—principal (maturing January 1, 2022)	$1,000,000
Bonds payable—interest ($65,000 per period for 40 periods)	2,600,000
Total bond liability	$3,600,000

[a]The present value of $1,000,000 due at the end of 40 (6-month) periods at the yield rate of 6% per period.
[b]The present value of $65,000 per period for 40 (6-month) periods at the yield rate of 6% per period.

Instructions

(a) Discuss the conceptual merit(s) of each of the date-of-issue balance sheet presentations shown above for these bonds.

(b) Explain why investors would pay $1,075,230 for bonds that have a maturity value of only $1,000,000.

(c) Assuming that a discount rate is needed to compute the carrying value of the obligations arising from a bond issue at any date during the life of the bonds, discuss the conceptual merit(s) of using for this purpose:
  (1) The coupon or nominal rate.
  (2) The effective or yield rate at date of issue.

(d) If the obligations arising from these bonds are to be carried at their present value computed by means of the current market rate of interest, how would the bond valuation at dates subsequent to the date of issue be affected by an increase or a decrease in the market rate of interest?

(AICPA adapted)

C14-2 (Various Long-Term Liability Conceptual Issues) Emma Thompson Company has completed a number of transactions during 2001. In January the company purchased under contract a machine at a total price of $1,200,000, payable over 5 years with installments of $240,000 per year. The seller has considered the transaction as an installment sale with the title transferring to Thompson at the time of the final payment.

On March 1, 2001, Thompson issued $10 million of general revenue bonds priced at 99 with a coupon of 10% payable July 1 and January 1 of each of the next 10 years. The July 1 interest was paid and on December 30 the company transferred $1,000,000 to the trustee, Hollywood Trust Company, for payment of the January 1, 1999, interest.

Due to the depressed market for the company's stock, Thompson purchased $500,000 par value of their 6% convertible bonds for a price of $455,000. It expects to resell the bonds when the price of its stock has recovered.

As the accountant for Emma Thompson Company, you have prepared the balance sheet as of December 31, 2001, and have presented it to the president of the company. You are asked the following questions about it:

1. Why has depreciation been charged on equipment being purchased under contract? Title has not passed to the company as yet and, therefore, they are not our assets. Why should the company not show on the left side of the balance sheet only the amount paid to date instead of showing the full contract price on the left side and the unpaid portion on the right side? After all, the seller considers the transaction an installment sale.
2. What is bond discount? As a debit balance, why is it not classified among the assets?
3. Bond interest is shown as a current liability. Did we not pay our trustee, Hollywood Trust Company, the full amount of interest due this period?
4. Treasury bonds are shown as a deduction from bonds payable issued. Why should they not be shown as an asset, since they can be sold again? Are they the same as bonds of other companies that we hold as investments?

Instructions

Outline your answers to these questions by writing a brief paragraph that will justify your treatment.

C14-3 (Bond Theory: Price, Presentation, and Retirement) On March 1, 2002, Chuck Norris Company sold its 5-year, $1,000 face value, 9% bonds dated March 1, 2002, at an effective annual interest rate (yield) of 11%. Interest is payable semiannually, and the first interest payment date is September 1, 2002. Norris uses the interest method of amortization. Bond issue costs were incurred in preparing and selling the bond issue. The bonds can be called by Norris at 101 at any time on or after March 1, 2003.

Instructions

(a) **(1)** How would the selling price of the bond be determined?

(2) Specify how all items related to the bonds would be presented in a balance sheet prepared immediately after the bond issue was sold.

(b) What items related to the bond issue would be included in Norris' 2002 income statement, and how would each be determined?

(c) Would the amount of bond discount amortization using the effective interest method of amortization be lower in the second or third year of the life of the bond issue? Why?

(d) Assuming that the bonds were called in and retired on March 1, 2003, how should Norris report the retirement of the bonds on the 2003 income statement?

(AICPA adapted)

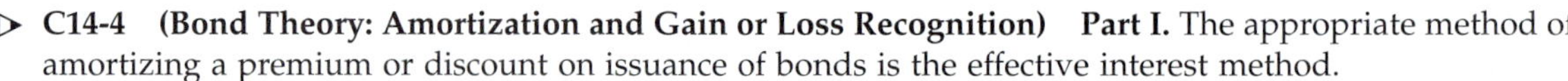

C14-4 (Bond Theory: Amortization and Gain or Loss Recognition) **Part I.** The appropriate method of amortizing a premium or discount on issuance of bonds is the effective interest method.

Instructions

(a) What is the effective interest method of amortization and how is it different from and similar to the straight-line method of amortization?

(b) How is amortization computed using the effective interest method, and why and how do amounts obtained using the effective interest method differ from amounts computed under the straight-line method?

Part II. Gains or losses from the early extinguishment of debt that is refunded can theoretically be accounted for in three ways:

1. Amortized over remaining life of old debt.
2. Amortized over the life of the new debt issue.
3. Recognized in the period of extinguishment.

Instructions

(a) Develop supporting arguments for each of the three theoretical methods of accounting for gains and losses from the early extinguishment of debt.

(b) Which of the methods above is generally accepted and how should the appropriate amount of gain or loss be shown in a company's financial statements?

(AICPA adapted)

C14-5 (Off-Balance-Sheet Financing) Brad Pitt Corporation is interested in building its own soda can manufacturing plant adjacent to its existing plant in Partyville, Kansas. The objective would be to ensure a steady supply of cans at a stable price and to minimize transportation costs. However, the company has been experiencing some financial problems and has been reluctant to borrow any additional cash to fund the project. The company is not concerned with the cash flow problems of making payments, but rather with the impact of adding additional long-term debt to their balance sheet.

The president of Pitt, Aidan Quinn, approached the president of the Aluminum Can Company (ACC), their major supplier, to see if some agreement could be reached. ACC was anxious to work out an arrangement, since it seemed inevitable that Pitt would begin their own can production. The Aluminum Can Company could not afford to lose the account.

After some discussion a two part plan was worked out. First ACC was to construct the plant on Pitt's land adjacent to the existing plant. Second, Pitt would sign a 20-year purchase agreement. Under the purchase agreement, Pitt would express its intention to buy all of its cans from ACC, paying a unit price which at normal capacity would cover labor and material, an operating management fee, and the debt service requirements on the plant. The expected unit price, if transportation costs are taken into consideration, is lower than current market. If Pitt did not take enough production in any one year and if the excess cans could not be sold at a high enough price on the open market, Pitt agrees to make up any cash shortfall so that ACC could make the payments on its debt. The bank will be willing to make a 20-year loan for the plant, taking the plant and the purchase agreement as collateral. At the end of 20 years the plant is to become the property of Pitt.

Instructions

(a) What are project financing arrangements?

(b) What are take-or-pay contracts?

(c) Should Pitt record the plant as an asset together with the related obligation?

(d) If not, should Pitt record an asset relating to the future commitment?

(e) What is meant by off-balance-sheet financing?

USING YOUR JUDGMENT

FINANCIAL REPORTING PROBLEM: INTEL CORPORATION

Refer to the financial statements and other documents of Intel Corporation presented in Appendix 5B and answer the following questions.

Instructions

(a) What are put warrants and why have they been reclassified from stockholders' equity to put warrants?

(b) What cash outflow obligations related to the repayment of long-term debt does Intel Corporation have over the next 5 years?

(c) Intel indicates that it believes that it has the ability to meet business requirements in the foreseeable future. Prepare an assessment of its solvency and financial flexibility using ratio analysis.

FINANCIAL STATEMENT ANALYSIS CASES

Case 1 Commonwealth Edison Co.

The following article appeared in *The Wall Street Journal:*

> **Bond Markets**
>
> *Giant Commonwealth Edison Issue Hits Resale Market With $70 Million Left Over*
>
> NEW YORK—Commonwealth Edison Co.'s slow-selling new 9¼% bonds were tossed onto the resale market at a reduced price with about $70 million still available from the $200 million offered Thursday, dealers said.
>
> The Chicago utility's bonds, rated double-A by Moody's and double-A-minus by Standard & Poor's, originally had been priced at 99.803, to yield 9.3% in 5 years. They were marked down yesterday the equivalent of about $5.50 for each $1,000 face amount, to about 99.25, where their yield jumped to 9.45%.

Instructions

(a) How will the development above affect the accounting for Commonwealth Edison's bond issue?

(b) Provide several possible explanations for the markdown and the slow sale of Commonwealth Edison's bonds.

Case 2 PepsiCo, Inc.

PepsiCo, Inc. based in Purchase, New York, is a leading company in the beverage industry.

Assume that the following events occurred relating to PepsiCo's long-term debt during 1999.

1. The company decided on February 1 to refinance $500 million in short-term 7.4% debt to make it long-term 6%.
2. $780 million of long-term zero-coupon bonds with an effective interest rate of 10.1% matured July 1 and were paid.
3. On October 1, the company issued $200 million in Australian dollar 6.3% bonds at 102 and $95 million in Italian lira 11.4% bonds at 99.
4. The company holds $100 million in perpetual foreign interest payment bonds that were issued in 1989, and presently have a rate of interest of 5.3%. These bonds are called perpetual because they have no stated due date. Instead, at the end of every 10-year period after the bond's issuance, the bondholders and PepsiCo have the option of redeeming the bonds. If either party desires to redeem the bonds, the bonds must be redeemed. If the bonds are not redeemed, a new interest rate is set, based on the then-prevailing interest rate for 10-year bonds. The company does not intend to cause

redemption of the bonds, but will reclassify this debt to current in 2000, since the bondholders could decide to redeem the bonds.

Instructions

(a) Consider event 1. What are some of the reasons the company may have decided to refinance this short-term debt, besides lowering the interest rate?

(b) What do you think are the benefits to the investor in purchasing zero-coupon bonds, such as those described in event 2? What journal entry would be required to record the payment of these bonds? If financial statements are prepared each December 31, in which year would the bonds have been included in short-term liabilities?

(c) Make the journal entry to record the bond issue described in event 3. Note that the bonds were issued on the same day, yet one was issued at a premium and the other at a discount. What are some of the reasons that this may have happened?

(d) What are the benefits to PepsiCo in having perpetual bonds as described in event 4? Suppose that in 1999 the bonds are not redeemed and the interest rate is adjusted to 6% from 7.5%. Make all necessary journal entries to record the renewal of the bonds and the change in rate.

COMPARATIVE ANALYSIS CASE

The Coca-Cola Company versus PepsiCo, Inc.

Instructions

Go to the Digital Tool and using the financial information for The Coca-Cola Company and PepsiCo, answer the following questions.

(a) Compute the debt to total assets ratio and the times interest earned ratio for these two companies. Comment on the quality of these two ratios for both Coca-Cola and PepsiCo.

(b) What financial measurements does the Coca-Cola Company use to manage its debt levels?

(c) What is the difference between the fair value and the historical cost (carrying amount) of each company's debt at year-end 1998? Why might a difference exist in these two amounts?

(d) Both companies have debt issued in foreign countries. Speculate as to why these companies may use foreign debt to finance their operations. What risks are involved in this strategy, and how might they adjust for this risk?

RESEARCH CASES

Case 1

Instructions

Use an appropriate source (such as those identified in the Chapter 2 Research Case) to identify a firm that recently had its bond rating changed. Answer the following questions.

(a) Which rating agency(ies) changed the rating?

(b) What was the bond rating before and after the change?

(c) What reasons did the rating agency give in support of its action? What accounting data was used as support?

(d) Are additional changes possible?

Case 2

The November 6, 1995, edition of *The Wall Street Journal* includes an article by Linda Sandler entitled "Kmart Is Pressured Over Obscure Bond 'Puts', Which Stir Worries Amid Tough Retail Times."

Instructions

Read the article and answer the following questions.

(a) What is the total dollar amount of the bond issue in question? Who purchased these bonds?

(b) What right does the "put option" give to bondholders?

(c) What amount is available under Kmart's bank lines? Why can't Kmart borrow under these lines to purchase the bonds? What is the most likely solution to the problem?

(d) Were the terms of the put bonds adequately disclosed?

ETHICS CASE

Roland Carlson is the president, founder, and majority owner of Thebeau Medical Corporation, an emerging medical technology products company. Thebeau is in dire need of additional capital to keep operating and to bring several promising products to final development, testing, and production. Roland, as owner of 51% of the outstanding stock, manages the company's operations. He places heavy emphasis on research and development and long-term growth. The other principal stockholder is Jana Kingston who, as a nonemployee investor, owns 40% of the stock. Jana would like to deemphasize the R & D functions and emphasize the marketing function to maximize short-run sales and profits from existing products. She believes this strategy would raise the market price of Thebeau's stock.

All of Roland's personal capital and borrowing power is tied up in his 51% stock ownership. He knows that any offering of additional shares of stock will dilute his controlling interest because he won't be able to participate in such an issuance. But, Jana has money and would likely buy enough shares to gain control of Thebeau. She then would dictate the company's future direction, even if it meant replacing Roland as president and CEO.

The company already has considerable debt. Raising additional debt will be costly, will adversely affect Thebeau's credit rating, and will increase the company's reported losses due to the growth in interest expense. Jana and the other minority stockholders express opposition to the assumption of additional debt, fearing the company will be pushed to the brink of bankruptcy. Wanting to maintain his control and to preserve the direction of "his" company, Roland is doing everything to avoid a stock issuance and is contemplating a large issuance of bonds, even if it means the bonds are issued with a high effective-interest rate.

Instructions

(a) Who are the stakeholders in this situation?

(b) What are the ethical issues in this case?

(c) What would you do if you were Roland?

CHAPTER 15

Stockholders' Equity: Contributed Capital

LEARNING OBJECTIVES

After studying this chapter, you should be able to:

1. **Discuss the characteristics of the corporate form of organization.**
2. **Identify the rights of stockholders.**
3. **Explain the key components of stockholders' equity.**
4. **Explain the accounting procedures for issuing shares of stock.**
5. **Identify the major reasons for purchasing treasury stock.**
6. **Explain the accounting for treasury stock.**
7. **Describe the major features of preferred stock.**
8. **Distinguish between debt and preferred stock.**
9. **Identify items reported as additional paid-in capital.**

Stocking Up

Quick, how did the market do yesterday? If asked this question, you probably responded that the market increased or decreased, based on the change in the Dow Jones Industrial Average. And just what is the Dow Jones Industrial Average (DJIA)? It is the average of 30 U.S. "blue-chip" (high-quality) stocks which represent the various sectors of the U.S. economy and have broad public ownership. **AT&T**, **American Express**, **Coca-Cola**, **Exxon Mobil**, **General Electric**, **Merck**, and **McDonald's** are examples of the type of companies found in this index.

The DJIA and other stock market indexes are becoming of increasing importance to most Americans. The reason: More and more of the country's wealth is tied up in the stock market. For example, the following chart shows the increase of stock as a percentage of U.S. household net worth over time.

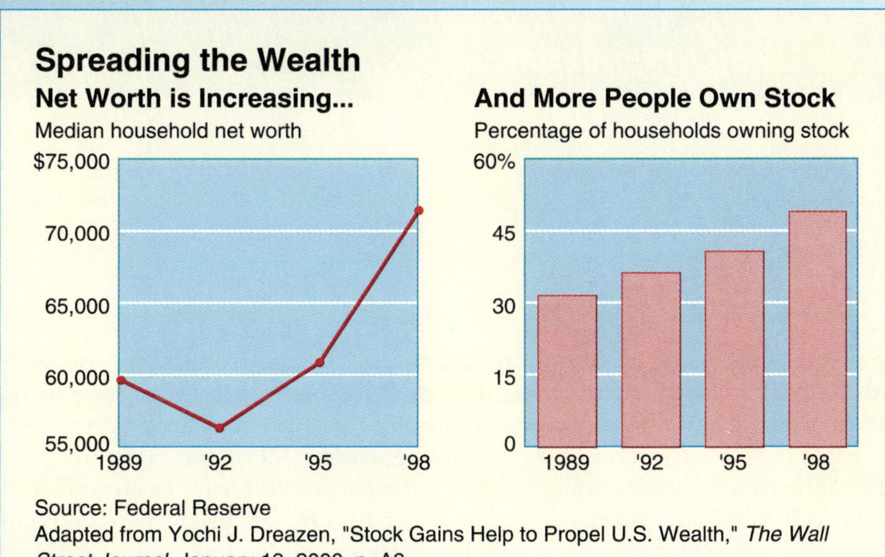

Source: Federal Reserve
Adapted from Yochi J. Dreazen, "Stock Gains Help to Propel U.S. Wealth," *The Wall Street Journal*, January 19, 2000, p. A2.

Fueled by stock-market gains, America's wealth grew at a strong pace in the latter half of the 1990s. At the same time, a record number of Americans at all income levels now own stock, intertwining their financial well-being with the stock market like never before. The percentage of Americans owning stock surged to 48.8% in 1998, up sharply from 40.4% in 1995. And for the first time in the history of the Federal Reserve Report, stock holdings now account for more than half of Americans' financial assets, up from 40% in 1995.

PREVIEW OF CHAPTER 15

As indicated from the opening story, more and more people are investing in the stock market. A public debate even has begun about whether some portion of Social Security funds should be invested in stocks. The stock market is of substantial importance in any economy that functions on private ownership. It provides a market where prices are established to serve as signals and incentives to guide the allocation of the economy's financial resources. The purpose of this chapter is to explain the various accounting issues related to the different types of stock that corporations issue. The content and organization of this chapter are as follows:

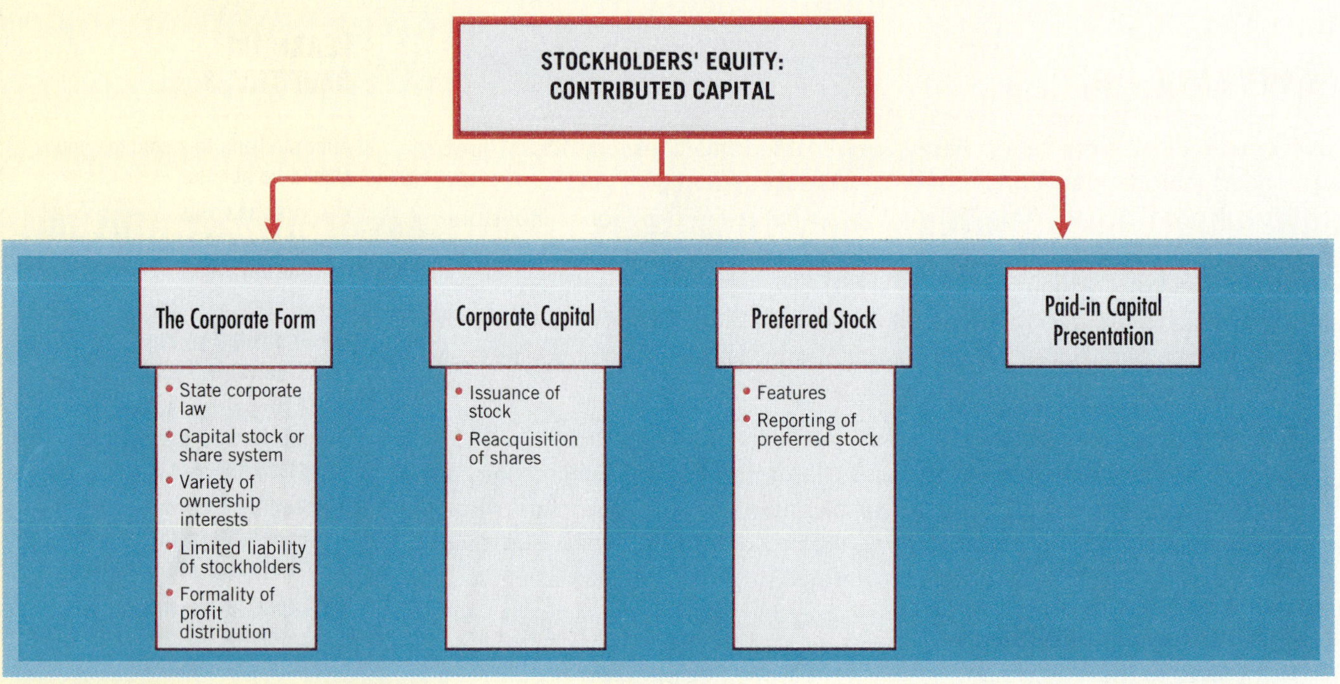

THE CORPORATE FORM

OBJECTIVE 1
Discuss the characteristics of the corporate form of organization.

Of the three **primary forms of business organization—the proprietorship, the partnership, and the corporation**—the dominant form of business is the corporate form. In terms of the aggregate amount of resources controlled, goods and services produced, and people employed, the corporation is by far the leader. All of the "Fortune 500" largest industrial firms are corporations. Although the corporate form has a number of advantages (as well as disadvantages) over the other two forms, its principal advantage is its facility for attracting and accumulating large amounts of capital.

Corporations may be classified by the nature of ownership as follows:

1. **Public sector corporations:** governmental units or business operations owned by governmental units (such as the Federal Deposit Insurance Corporation).
2. **Private sector corporations:**
   a. **Nonstock:** nonprofit in nature and no stock issued (such as churches, charities, and colleges).
   b. **Stock:** companies that operate for profit and issue stock.
      (i) **Closed corporations (nonpublic or private enterprises):** stock held by a few stockholders (perhaps a family) and not available for public purchase.

(ii) **Open corporations (public companies):** stock widely held and available for purchase by the public.
(a) **Listed corporation:** stock traded on an organized stock exchange.
(b) **Unlisted or over-the-counter corporation:** stock traded in a market in which securities dealers buy from and sell to the public.

INTERNATIONAL INSIGHT

In the United States, stockholders are treated equally as far as access to financial information. That is not always the case in other countries. For example, in Mexico foreign investors as well as minority investors often have difficulty obtaining financial data. These restrictions are rooted in the habits of companies that for many years have been tightly controlled by a few stockholders and managers.

Among the special characteristics of the corporate form that affect accounting are:

1. Influence of state corporate law.
2. Use of the capital stock or share system.
3. Development of a variety of ownership interests.
4. Limited liability of stockholders.
5. Formality of profit distribution.

State Corporate Law

Anyone who wishes to establish a corporation must submit **articles of incorporation** to the state in which incorporation is desired. Assuming the requirements are properly fulfilled, the corporation charter is issued, and the corporation is recognized as a legal entity subject to state law. Regardless of the number of states in which a corporation has operating divisions, it is incorporated in only one state.

It is to the company's advantage to incorporate in a state whose laws are favorable to the corporate form of business organization. **General Motors**, for example, is incorporated in Delaware; **USX Corp.** is a New Jersey corporation. Some corporations have increasingly been incorporating in states with laws favorable to existing management. For example, to thwart possible unfriendly takeovers, **Gulf Oil** changed its state of incorporation to Delaware. There, certain tactics against takeovers can be approved by the board of directors alone, without a vote of the shareholders.

Each state has its own business incorporation act, and the accounting for stockholders' equity follows the provisions of this act. In many cases states have adopted the principles contained in the Model Business Corporate Act prepared by the American Bar Association. State laws are complex and vary both in their provisions and in their definitions of certain terms. Some laws fail to define technical terms, and so terms often mean one thing in one state and another thing in a different state. These problems may be further compounded because legal authorities often interpret the effects and restrictions of the laws differently.[1]

Capital Stock or Share System

OBJECTIVE 2
Identify the rights of stockholders.

Stockholders' equity in a corporation is generally made up of a large number of units or shares. Within a given class of stock each share is exactly equal to every other share. Each owners's interest is determined by the number of shares possessed. If a company has but one class of stock divided into 1,000 shares, a person owning 500 shares controls one-half of the ownership interest of the corporation; one holding 10 shares has a one-hundredth interest.

Each share of stock has certain rights and privileges that can be restricted only by special contract at the time the shares are issued. One must examine the articles of incorporation, stock certificates, and the provisions of the state law to ascertain such restrictions on or variations from the standard rights and privileges. In the absence of restrictive provisions, each share carries the following rights:

1. To share proportionately in profits and losses.
2. To share proportionately in management (the right to vote for directors).
3. To share proportionately in corporate assets upon liquidation.

---

[1]Beatrice Melcher, "Stockholders' Equity," *Accounting Research Study No. 15* (New York: AICPA, 1973), p. 8.

4. To share proportionately in any new issues of stock of the same class—called the **preemptive right**.

The first three rights are to be expected in the ownership of any business; the last may be used in a corporation to protect each stockholder's proportional interest in the enterprise. **The preemptive right protects an existing stockholder from involuntary dilution of ownership interest.** Without this right, stockholders with a given percentage interest might find their interest reduced by the issuance of additional stock without their knowledge and at prices that were not favorable to them. Because the preemptive right that attaches to existing shares makes it inconvenient for corporations to make large issuances of additional stock, as they frequently do in acquiring other companies, it has been eliminated by many corporations.

The great advantage of the share system is the ease with which an interest in the business may be transferred from one individual to another. **Individuals owning shares in a corporation may sell them to others at any time and at any price without obtaining the consent of the company or other stockholders.** Each share is personal property of the owner and may be disposed of at will. All that is required of the corporation is that it maintain a list or subsidiary ledger of stockholders as a guide to dividend payments, issuance of stock rights, voting proxies, and the like. Because shares are freely and frequently transferred, it is necessary for the corporation to revise the subsidiary ledger of stockholders periodically, generally in advance of every dividend payment or stockholders' meeting. Also, the major stock exchanges require controls that the typical corporation finds uneconomic to provide. Thus **registrars and transfer agents** who specialize in providing services for recording and transferring stock are usually used. The negotiability of stock certificates is governed by the Uniform Stock Transfer Act and the Uniform Commercial Code.

The American and British systems of corporate governance and finance depend to a large extent on equity financing and the widely dispersed ownership of shares traded in highly liquid markets. The German and Japanese systems have relied more on debt financing, interlocking stock ownership, banker/directors, and worker/shareholder rights.

Variety of Ownership Interests

In every corporation one class of stock must represent the basic ownership interest. That class is called common stock. **Common stock** is the residual corporate interest that bears the ultimate risks of loss and receives the benefits of success. It is guaranteed neither dividends nor assets upon dissolution. But common stockholders generally control the management of the corporation and tend to profit most if the company is successful. In the event that a corporation has only one authorized issue of capital stock, that issue is by definition common stock, whether so designated in the charter or not.

In an effort to appeal to all types of investors, corporations may offer two or more classes of stock each with different rights or privileges. In the preceding section it was pointed out that each share of stock of a given issue has the same rights as other shares of the same issue and that there are four rights inherent in every share. By special stock contracts between the corporation and its stockholders, certain of these rights may be sacrificed by the stockholder in return for other special rights or privileges. Thus special classes of stock are created. Because they have certain preferential rights, they are usually called **preferred stock**. In return for any special preference, the preferred stockholder is always called on to sacrifice some of the inherent rights of capital stock interests.

A common type of preference is to give the preferred stockholders a prior claim on earnings. They are assured a dividend, usually at a stated rate, before any amount may be distributed to the common stockholders. In return for this preference the preferred stock may sacrifice its right to a voice in management or its right to share in profits beyond the stated rate.

A company may accomplish much the same thing by issuing two classes of common stock, Class A stock and Class B stock. In this case one of the issues is the common stock and the other issue has some preference or restriction of basic rights. For example, at one time **DeKalb Genetics Corporation** was organized with two classes of common stock, Class A and Class B. Both Class A and Class B participate equally (per share) in all dividend payments and have the same claim on assets in dissolution. The differences are that Class A is voting and Class B is not; Class B is traded publicly over the counter while Class A, which is "family owned," must be sold privately (Class A shares are convertible, one for one, into Class B shares but not vice versa). By issuing two classes of common stock, the Class A owners of DeKalb Genetics have obtained a ready market for the company's stock and yet provided an effective shield against outside takeover.[2]

Limited Liability of Stockholders

Those who "own" a corporation, the stockholders, contribute either property or services to the enterprise in return for ownership shares. **The property or service invested in the enterprise is the extent of a stockholder's possible loss.** That is, if the corporation sustains losses to such an extent that remaining assets are insufficient to pay creditors, no recourse can be had by the creditors against personal assets of the individual stockholders. In a partnership or proprietorship, personal assets of the owners can be attached to satisfy unpaid claims against the enterprise. Ownership interests in a corporation are legally protected against such a contingency. **The stockholders have limited liability—they may lose their investment but they cannot lose more than their investment.**

Stock that has a fixed per-share amount printed on each stock certificate is called **par value stock**. Par value has but one real significance: it establishes the maximum responsibility of a stockholder in the event of insolvency or other involuntary dissolution. Par value is thus not "value" in the ordinary sense of the word. It is merely an amount per share determined by the incorporators of the company and stated in the corporation charter or certificate of incorporation. Par value establishes the nominal value per share and is the minimum amount that must be paid in by each stockholder if the stock is to be fully paid when issued. A corporation may, however, issue its capital stock either above or below par, in which case the stock is said to be issued at a **premium or a discount**, respectively.[3]

If par value stock is issued at par or at a price above par and the corporation subsequently suffers losses so that assets to repay stockholders upon dissolution are insufficient, stockholders may lose their entire investment. If, however, the stock is issued at a price below par and the losses prove to be of such magnitude as to consume not only the stockholders' investments but also a portion of the assets required to repay creditors, the creditors can force the stockholders to pay in to the corporation the amount of the discount on their capital shares. Thus the original purchasers of stock issued at a price below par are **contingently liable** to creditors of the corporation. In other words, stockholders may lose their entire investment in a corporation if the investments are equal to or in excess of the par value of the shares they own, or, if the investments are less than their par value, they may lose the amount of their investment plus an additional amount equal to the discount at which they purchased the stock. The limited liability feature of corporate capital stock prevents them from losing any more than the par value of their stock plus any premium paid upon purchase.

It should be emphasized that **the contingent liability of a stockholder for stock purchased at a price below par**:

1. Is an obligation to the corporation's creditors, not to the corporation itself.
2. Becomes a real liability only if the amount below par must be collected in order to pay the creditors upon dissolution of the company.
3. Is the responsibility of the original certificate holder at the time of dissolution unless by contract such responsibility is transferred to a subsequent holder.

[2]Ironically, the voting class (which would necessarily be concerned about an unfriendly takeover) often gains the most if an acquisition does take place. That is, the acquirer is willing to pay a substantial premium for the voting shares, but not for the nonvoting ones.

[3]In most states capital stock may not be issued below par.

While the corporate form of organization grants the protective feature of limited liability to the stockholders, the corporation must guarantee not to distribute the amount of stockholders' investment unless all prior claims on corporate assets have been paid. **The corporation must maintain the corporate legal capital (generally par value of all capital stock issued) until dissolution**, and upon dissolution it must satisfy all prior claims before distributing any amounts to the stockholders.

In a proprietorship or partnership the owners can withdraw amounts at will because all their personal assets may be called on to protect creditors from loss. In a corporation, however, the owners cannot withdraw any amounts paid in because the only protection creditors have against loss is the amount paid in plus any discount below par.

Formality of Profit Distribution

The owners of an enterprise determine what is to be done with profits realized through operations. Profits may be left in the business to permit expansion or merely to provide a margin of safety, or they may be withdrawn and divided among the owners. In a proprietorship or partnership this decision is made by the owner or owners informally and requires no specific action. In a corporation, however, profit distribution is controlled by certain legal restrictions.

First, **distributions to owners must be in compliance with the state laws governing corporations**. Currently, the 50 states may be classified into one of three groups for purposes of comparing restrictions on distributions to owners.[4] Generally, in the largest group, distribution of dividends has to come from retained earnings or from current earnings. Chapter 16 covers this topic in more detail.

Second, **distributions to stockholders must be formally approved by the board of directors** and recorded in the minutes of their meetings. As the top executive body in the corporation, the board of directors must make certain that no distributions are made to stockholders that are not justified by profits, and directors are generally held personally liable to creditors if liabilities cannot be paid because company assets have been illegally paid out to stockholders.

Third, **dividends must be in full agreement with the capital stock contracts as to preferences, participation, and the like**. Once the corporation has entered into contracts with various classes of stockholders, the stipulations of such contracts must be observed.

CORPORATE CAPITAL

Owner's equity in a corporation is defined as stockholders' equity, shareholders' equity, or corporate capital. The following three categories normally appear as part of stockholders' equity:

1. Capital stock
2. Additional paid-in capital
3. Retained earnings

OBJECTIVE 3
Explain the key components of stockholders' equity.

The first two categories, capital stock and additional paid-in capital, constitute contributed (paid-in) capital; **retained earnings** represents the earned capital of the enterprise. **Contributed capital (paid-in capital)** is the total amount paid in on capital stock—the amount provided by stockholders to the corporation for use in the business. Contributed capital includes items such as the par value of all outstanding stock and premiums less discounts on issuance. **Earned capital** is the capital that develops if the

[4]See Michael L. Roberts, William D. Samson, and Michael T. Dugan, "The Stockholders' Equity Section: Form Without Substance," *Accounting Horizons*, December 1990, pp. 35–46.

business operates profitably; it consists of all undistributed income that remains invested in the enterprise.

The distinction between paid-in capital and retained earnings is important from both legal and economic points of view. Legally, dividends can be declared out of retained earnings in all states, but in many states dividends cannot be declared out of paid-in capital. Economically, management, shareholders, and others look to earnings for the continued existence and growth of the corporation.

Stockholders' equity is the difference between the assets and the liabilities of the enterprise. **Therefore, the owners' or stockholders' interest in a business enterprise is a residual interest.**[5] **Stockholders' (owners') equity** represents the cumulative net contributions by stockholders plus earnings that have been retained. As a residual interest, stockholders' equity has no existence apart from the assets and liabilities of the enterprise—stockholders' equity equals net assets. Stockholders' equity is not a claim to specific assets but a claim against a portion of the total assets. Its amount is not specified or fixed; it depends on the enterprise's profitability. Stockholders' equity grows if the enterprise is profitable, and it shrinks or may disappear entirely if the enterprise is unprofitable.

A final comment: Many different meanings are attached to the word **capital**, because the word often is construed differently by various user groups. **In corporation finance**, for example, capital commonly represents the total assets of the enterprise. **In law**, capital is considered that portion of stockholders' equity that is required by statute to be retained in the business for the protection of creditors. Generally, **legal capital (stated capital)** is the par value of all capital stock issued, but when shares without par value are issued, it may be:

1. Total consideration paid in for the shares.
2. A minimum amount stated in the applicable state incorporation law.
3. An arbitrary amount established by the board of directors at its discretion.

Accountants for the most part define capital more narrowly than total assets but more broadly than legal capital. **When accountants refer to capital they mean stockholders' equity or owners' equity.**

Issuance of Stock

OBJECTIVE 4
Explain the accounting procedures for issuing shares of stock.

In issuing stock, the following procedures are followed: First, the stock must be authorized by the state, generally in a certificate of incorporation or charter; next, shares are offered for sale and contracts to sell stock are entered into; then, amounts to be received for the stock are collected and the shares issued.

The accounting problems involved in the issuance of stock are discussed under the following topics:

1. Accounting for par value stock.
2. Accounting for no-par stock.
3. Accounting for stock sold on a subscription basis.
4. Accounting for stock issued in combination with other securities (lump sum sales).
5. Accounting for stock issued in noncash transactions.
6. Accounting for assessments on stock.
7. Accounting for costs of issuing stock.

Par Value Stock

As indicated earlier, the par value of a stock has no relationship to its fair market value. At present, the par value associated with most capital stock issuances is very low ($1,

[5] "Elements of Financial Statements," *Statement of Financial Accounting Concepts No. 6* (Stamford, Conn.: FASB, 1985), par. 60.

$5, $10), which contrasts dramatically with the situation in the early 1900s when practically all stock issued had a par value of $100. The reason for this change is to permit the original sale of stock at low amounts per share and to avoid the contingent liability associated with stock sold below par. Stock with a low par value is rarely, if ever, sold below par value. In addition, in states that charge a transfer tax based on the par value of the stock, a low par value may result in lower taxes.

To show the required information for issuance of par value stock, accounts must be kept for each class of stock as follows:

1. ***Preferred Stock or Common Stock.*** Reflects the par value of the corporation's issued shares. These accounts are credited when the shares are originally issued. No additional entries are made in these accounts unless additional shares are issued or shares are retired.
2. ***Paid-in Capital in Excess of Par or Additional Paid-in Capital.*** Indicates any excess over par value paid in by stockholders in return for the shares issued to them. Once paid in, the excess over par becomes a part of the corporation's additional paid-in capital, and the individual stockholder has no greater claim on the excess paid in than all other holders of the same class of shares.
3. ***Discount on Stock.*** Indicates that the stock has been issued at less than par. The original purchaser or the current holder of shares issued below par may be called on to pay in the amount of the discount if necessary to prevent creditors from sustaining loss upon liquidation of the corporation.

To illustrate how these accounts are used, assume that Colonial Corporation sold, for $1,100, one hundred shares of stock with a par value of $5 per share. The entry to record the issuance is:

Cash	1,100	
Common Stock		500
Paid-in Capital in Excess of Par (Premium on Common Stock)		600

If the stock had been issued in return for $300, the entry would have been recorded as follows:

Cash	300	
Paid-in Capital in Excess of Par (Discount on Common Stock)	200	
Common Stock		500

No entry is generally made in the general ledger accounts at the time the corporation receives its stock authorization from the state of incorporation.

No-Par Stock

Many states permit the issuance of capital stock without par value. **No-par stock** is shares issued with no per-share amount printed on the stock certificate. The reasons for issuance of no-par stock are twofold. First, issuance of no-par stock **avoids the contingent liability** that might occur if par value stock were issued at a discount. Second, some confusion exists over the relationship (or rather the absence of a relationship) between the par value and fair market value. If shares have no par value, **the questionable treatment of using par value as a basis for fair value never arises**. This circumstance is particularly advantageous whenever stock is issued for property items such as tangible or intangible fixed assets. The major disadvantages of no-par stock are that some states levy a high tax on these issues, and the total may be considered legal capital.

No-par shares, like par value shares, are sold for what they will bring, but unlike par value shares, they are issued without a premium or a discount. Therefore, no contingent liability accrues to the stockholders. The exact amount received represents the credit to common or preferred stock. For example, Video Electronics Corporation is organized with authorized common stock of 10,000 shares without par value. No entry, other than a memorandum entry, need be made for the authorization inasmuch as no amount is involved. If 500 shares are then issued for cash at $10 per share, the entry should be:

Cash	5,000	
Common Stock—No-Par Value		5,000

If another 500 shares are issued for $11 per share, the entry should be:

Cash	5,500	
Common Stock—No-Par Value		5,500

True no-par stock should be carried in the accounts at issue price without any complications due to additional paid-in capital or discount. But some states permit the issuance of no-par stock and then proceed either to require or, in some cases, to permit such stock to have a **stated value**; that is, a minimum value below which it cannot be issued. Thus, instead of becoming no-par stock it becomes, in effect, stock with a very low par value, open to all the criticism and abuses that first encouraged the development of no-par stock.[6]

If no-par stock is required to have a minimum issue price of $5 per share and no provision is made as to how amounts in excess of $5 per share are to be handled, the board of directors usually declares all such amounts to be additional paid-in capital, which in many states is fully or partially available for dividends. Thus, no-par value stock with either a minimum stated value or a stated value assigned by the board of directors permits a new corporation to commence its operations with additional paid-in capital that may be in excess of its stated capital. For example, if 1,000 of the shares with a $5 stated value were issued at $15 per share for cash, the entry could be either

Cash	15,000	
Common Stock		15,000

or

Cash	15,000	
Common Stock		5,000
Paid-in Capital in Excess of Stated Value		10,000

In most instances the obvious advantages to the corporation of setting up an initial Additional Paid-in Capital account will influence the board of directors to require the latter entry. Whether for this or for other reasons, the prevailing tendency is to account for no-par stock with stated value as if it were par value stock with par equal to the stated value.

Stock Sold on a Subscription Basis

The preceding discussion assumed that the stock was sold for cash, but stock may also be sold on a subscription basis. Sale of **subscribed stock** generally occurs when new, small companies "go public" or when corporations offer stock to employees to obtain employee participation in the ownership of the business. When stock is sold on a subscription basis, the full price of the stock is not received initially. Normally only a partial payment is made, and the stock is not issued until the full subscription price is received.

Accounting for Subscribed Stock. Two new accounts are used when stock is sold on a subscription basis. The first, **Common or Preferred Stock Subscribed**, indicates the corporation's obligation to issue shares of its stock upon payment of final subscription balances by those who have subscribed for stock. This account thus signifies a commitment against the unissued capital stock. Once the subscription price is fully paid, the Common or Preferred Stock Subscribed account is debited and the Common or Preferred Stock account is credited. Common or Preferred Stock Subscribed should be presented in the stockholders' equity section below Common or Preferred Stock.

---

[6] *Accounting Trends and Techniques—1999* indicates that its 600 surveyed companies reported 654 issues of outstanding common stock, 571 par value issues, and 59 no-par issues; 13 of the no-par issues were shown at their stated (assigned) values.

UNDERLYING CONCEPTS

Subscriptions Receivable would appear to fulfill all the requirements for an *asset.* As a result of a past transaction the company expects to receive a future economic benefit. An Allowance for Doubtful Accounts would disclose the collection risk in the same manner as for Accounts Receivable.

The second account, **Subscriptions Receivable**, indicates the amount yet to be collected before subscribed stock will be issued. Controversy exists concerning the presentation of Subscriptions Receivable on the balance sheet. Some argue that Subscriptions Receivable should be reported in the current assets section (assuming, of course, that payment on the receivable will be received within the operating cycle or one year, whichever is longer). They note that it is similar to trade accounts receivable. Trade accounts receivable grow out of sales transactions in the ordinary course of business; subscriptions receivable relate to the issuance of a concern's own stock and in a sense represent funds (capital contributions) not yet paid the corporation.

Others argue that Subscriptions Receivable should be reported as **a deduction from stockholders' equity** (similar to treasury stock recorded at cost). Their reasoning is that in most states no deficiency judgment can be sought for failure of a subscriber to pay the unpaid balance of a subscription receivable. Given the risk of collectibility, the SEC requires companies to use the **contra equity approach**.[7] For example, in the prospectus of **Morlan International, Inc.**, its subscriptions receivable was reported as a contra equity in the following manner (common stock subscribed is included in Common Stock rather than shown separately):

ILLUSTRATION 15-1
Treatment of Subscriptions Receivable

MORLAN INTERNATIONAL, INC.

Stockholders' equity	
Common stock, par value $.01 a share:	
Authorized 9,000,000 shares	
Issued 3,547,638 shares	$ 35,500
Additional capital	2,146,700
Retained earnings	3,878,600
Less: Subscriptions receivable	(148,500)
Total stockholders' equity	$5,912,300

Practice now generally follows the contra equity approach. Therefore, unless stated otherwise, this practice should be followed in working homework problems.

Most states consider common or preferred stock subscribed to be similar to outstanding common or preferred stock, which means that **individuals who have signed a valid subscription contract normally have the same rights and privileges as a stockholder who holds outstanding shares of stock.**

The journal entries for handling stock sold on a subscription basis are illustrated by the following example. Lubradite Corp. offers stock on a subscription basis to selected individuals, giving them the right to purchase 10 shares of stock (par value $5) at a price of $20 per share. Fifty individuals accept the company's offer and agree to pay 50% down and to pay the remaining 50% at the end of 6 months.

At date of issuance

Subscriptions Receivable (10 × $20 × 50)	10,000	
Common Stock Subscribed (10 × $5 × 50)		2,500
Paid-in Capital in Excess of Par		7,500
(To record receipt of subscriptions for 500 shares)		
Cash	5,000	
Subscriptions Receivable		5,000
(To record receipt of first installment representing 50% of total due on subscribed stock)		

[7]The SEC has specified that subscriptions receivable may be shown as an asset only if collected prior to the publication of the financial statements.

When the final payment is received and the stock is issued, the entries are:

Six months later

Cash	5,000	
Subscriptions Receivable		5,000
(To record receipt of final installment on subscribed stock)		
Common Stock Subscribed	2,500	
Common Stock		2,500
(To record issuance of 500 shares upon receipt of final installment from subscribers)		

Defaulted Subscription Accounts. Sometimes a subscriber is unable to pay all installments and defaults on the agreement. The question is what to do with the balance of the subscription account as well as the amount already paid in. The answer is a function of applicable state law. Some states permit the corporation to retain any amounts paid in on defaulted subscription accounts; other states require that any amount realized on the resale in excess of the amount due from the original subscriber be returned.

Stock Issued with Other Securities (Lump Sum Sales)

Generally, corporations sell classes of stock separately from one another so that the proceeds relative to each class, and ordinarily even relative to each lot, are known. Occasionally, two or more classes of securities are issued for a single payment or lump sum. It is not uncommon, for example, for more than one type or class of security to be issued in the acquisition of another company. The accounting problem in such **lump sum sales** is the allocation of the proceeds among the several classes of securities. The two methods of allocation available are (1) the proportional method and (2) the incremental method.

Proportional Method. If the fair market value or other sound basis for determining relative value is available for each class of security, **the lump sum received is allocated among the classes of securities on a proportional basis**, that is, the ratio that each is to the total. For instance, if 1,000 shares of $10 stated value common stock having a market value of $20 a share and 1,000 shares of $10 par value preferred stock having a market value of $12 a share are issued for a lump sum of $30,000, the allocation of the $30,000 to the two classes would be as shown below.

Fair market value of common (1,000 × $20) =	$20,000
Fair market value of preferred (1,000 × $12) =	12,000
Aggregate fair market value	$32,000
Allocated to common: $\frac{\$20,000}{\$32,000} \times \$30,000$ =	$18,750
Allocated to preferred: $\frac{\$12,000}{\$32,000} \times \$30,000$ =	11,250
Total allocation	$30,000

ILLUSTRATION 15-2
Allocation in Lump Sum Securities Issuance—Proportional Method

Incremental Method. In instances where the fair market value of all classes of securities is not determinable, the incremental method may be used. The market value of the securities is used as a basis for those classes that are known and the remainder of the lump sum is allocated to the class for which the market value is not known. For instance, if 1,000 shares of $10 stated value common stock having a market value of $20 and 1,000 shares of $10 par value preferred stock having no established market value are issued for a lump sum of $30,000, the allocation of the $30,000 to the two classes would be as follows:

ILLUSTRATION 15-3
Allocation in Lump Sum Securities Issuance—Incremental Method

Lump sum receipt	$30,000
Allocated to common (1,000 × $20)	20,000
Balance allocated to preferred	$10,000

If no fair market value is determinable for any of the classes of stock involved in a lump sum exchange, the allocation may have to be arbitrary. An expert's appraisal may be used. Or, if it is known that one or more of the classes of securities issued will have a determinable market value in the near future, the arbitrary basis may be used with the intent to make an adjustment when the future market value is established.

Stock Issued in Noncash Transactions

Accounting for the issuance of shares of stock for property or services involves an issue of valuation. **The general rule is: Stock issued for services or property other than cash should be recorded at either the fair market value of the stock issued or the fair market value of the noncash consideration received, whichever is more clearly determinable.**

If both are readily determinable and the transaction is the result of an arm's-length exchange, there will probably be little difference in their fair market values. In such cases it should not matter which value is regarded as the basis for valuing the exchange.

If the fair market value of the stock being issued and the property or services being received are not readily determinable, the value to be assigned is generally established by the board of directors or management at an amount that they consider fair and that is not controverted by available evidence. Independent appraisals usually serve as dependable bases. The use of the book, par, or stated values as a basis of valuation for these transactions should be avoided.

Unissued stock or treasury stock (issued shares that have been reacquired but not retired) may be exchanged for the property or services. If treasury shares are used, their cost should not be regarded as the decisive factor in establishing the fair market value of the property or services. Instead, the fair market value of the treasury stock, if known, should be used to value the property or services. If the fair market value of the treasury stock is not known, the fair market value of the property or services should be used, if determinable.

The following series of transactions illustrates the procedure for recording the issuance of 10,000 shares of $10 par value common stock for a patent, in various circumstances:

1. The fair market value of the patent is not readily determinable but the fair market value of the stock is known to be $140,000.

Patent	140,000	
Common Stock (10,000 shares × $10 per share)		100,000
Paid-in Capital in Excess of Par		40,000

2. The fair market value of the stock is not readily determinable, but the fair market value of the patent is determined to be $150,000.

Patent	150,000	
Common Stock (10,000 shares × $10 per share)		100,000
Paid-in Capital in Excess of Par		50,000

3. Neither the fair market value of the stock nor the fair market value of the patent is readily determinable. An independent consultant values the patent at $125,000, and the board of directors agrees with that valuation.

Patent	125,000	
Common Stock (10,000 shares × $10 share)		100,000
Paid-in Capital in Excess of Par		25,000

In corporate law, the board of directors is granted the power to set the value of noncash transactions. This power has been abused. The issuance of stock for property or services has resulted in cases of overstated corporate capital through intentional overvaluation of the property or services received. The overvaluation of the stockholders' equity resulting from inflated asset values creates what is referred to as **watered stock**. The "water" can be eliminated from the corporate structure by simply writing down the overvalued assets.

If as a result of the issuance of stock for property or services the recorded assets are undervalued, **secret reserves** are created. An understated corporate structure or secret reserve may also be achieved by other methods: excessive depreciation or amortization charges, expensing capital expenditures, excessive write-downs of inventories or receivables, or any other understatement of assets or overstatement of liabilities. An example of a liability overstatement is an excessive provision for estimated product warranties that ultimately results in an understatement of owners' equity, thereby creating a secret reserve.

Assessments on Stock

The laws of some states provide that a corporation may assess stockholders an additional amount above their original contribution. Although this situation occurs infrequently, when stockholders are assessed, they must either pay or possibly forfeit their existing shares. Upon receiving the assessments from the stockholders, the corporation should determine whether the original stock was sold at a discount or a premium. If the stock was originally sold at a discount, the additional proceeds are credited to the discount account. If the stock was originally issued at a premium, the account Additional Paid-in Capital Arising from Assessments is credited.

Costs of Issuing Stock

Direct costs incurred to sell stock, such as underwriting costs, accounting and legal fees, printing costs, and taxes, should be reported as a reduction of the amounts paid in. Issue costs are therefore debited to Additional Paid-in Capital because they are unrelated to corporate operations. In effect, **issue costs are a cost of financing** and should reduce the proceeds received from the sale of the stock.

Management salaries and other indirect costs related to the stock issue should be expensed as incurred because it is difficult to establish a relationship between these costs and the proceeds received upon sale. In addition, corporations annually incur costs for maintaining the stockholders' records and handling ownership transfers. These recurring costs, primarily registrar and transfer agents' fees, are normally charged to expense in the period in which incurred.

Reacquisition of Shares

It is not unusual for companies to buy back their own shares. In fact, share buybacks now exceed dividends as a form of distribution to stockholders.[8] **Merrill Lynch & Co.** estimated that in a recent year more than 1,400 corporations announced buyback programs totaling over $80 billion and 2.4 billion shares. Two of the biggest stock buyback programs were **General Motors**' purchase of 20% (64 million shares) of its stock for $4.8 billion and **Santa Fe Southern Pacific**'s buyback of 38% (60 million shares) of its stock for $3.4 billion in the mid-1990s. Data on recent corporate buybacks indicate that companies are continuing to spend millions of dollars to repurchase shares, as shown in the following table:

[8] At the beginning of the 1990s the situation was just the opposite; that is, share buybacks were less than half the level of dividends. Companies are extremely reluctant to reduce or eliminate their dividends, because they believe that this action would be viewed negatively by the market. On the other hand, many companies are no longer raising their dividends per share at the same percentage rate as increases in earnings per share, thus effectively reducing the dividend payout over time.

ILLUSTRATION 15-4
Recent Corporate Buybacks

Company	Year	Amount of Buyback (millions)	Percent of Shares
BankAmerica	1997	$2,025	4.6%
Coca-Cola	1998	445	3.5%
Eli Lilly & Co.	1998	2,000	2.6%
Gillette	1998	1,119	1.9%
Hewlett-Packard	1998	1,292	2.0%
Torchmark	1998	126	2.6%
XL Capital LTD	1998	255	2.5%

The reasons corporations purchase their outstanding stock are varied. Some major reasons are:

OBJECTIVE 5
Identify the major reasons for purchasing treasury stock.

1. ***To provide tax efficient distributions of excess cash to shareholders.*** Capital gain rates on sales of stock to the company by the stockholders are approximately half of what ordinary tax rates are. As a result, most stockholders will pay less tax if they receive cash in a buyback versus receiving a cash dividend.
2. ***To increase earnings per share and return on equity.*** By reducing shares outstanding and by reducing stockholders' equity, certain performance ratios often are enhanced.
3. ***To provide stock for employee stock compensation contracts or to meet potential merger needs.*** **Honeywell Inc.** reported that part of its purchase of one million common shares was to be used for employee stock option contracts. Other companies acquire shares to have them available for business acquisitions.
4. ***To thwart takeover attempts or to reduce the number of stockholders.*** By reducing the number of shares held by the public, existing owners and managements can keep "outsiders" from gaining control or significant influence. When Ted Turner attempted to acquire **CBS**, CBS started a substantial buyback of its stock. Stock purchases may also be used to eliminate dissident stockholders.
5. ***To make a market in the stock.*** As one company executive noted, "Our company is trying to establish a floor for the stock." By purchasing stock in the marketplace, a demand is created which may stabilize the stock price or, in fact, increase it.

Some publicly held corporations have chosen to "go private," that is, to eliminate public (outside) ownership entirely by purchasing all of their outstanding stock. Such a procedure is often accomplished through a **leveraged buyout (LBO)**, in which management or another employee group purchases the stock of the company and finances the purchase by using the assets of the company as collateral.

Once shares are reacquired, they may either be retired or held in the treasury for reissue. If not retired, such shares are referred to as **treasury shares** or **treasury stock**. Technically treasury stock is a corporation's own stock that has been reacquired after having been issued and fully paid.

UNDERLYING CONCEPTS

As indicated in Chapter 2, an asset should have probable future economic benefits. Treasury stock simply reduces common stock outstanding.

Treasury stock is not an asset. When treasury stock is purchased, a reduction occurs in both assets and stockholders' equity. It is inappropriate to imply that a corporation can own a part of itself. Treasury stock may be sold to obtain funds, but that possibility does not make treasury stock a balance sheet asset. When a corporation buys back some of its own outstanding stock, it has reduced its capitalization but has not acquired an asset. The possession of treasury stock does not give the corporation the right to vote, to exercise preemptive rights as a stockholder, to receive cash dividends, or to receive assets upon corporate liquidation. **Treasury stock is essentially the same as unissued capital stock,** and no one advocates classifying unissued capital stock as an asset in the balance sheet.[9]

Purchase of Treasury Stock

Two general methods of handling treasury stock in the accounts are the cost method and the par value method. Both methods are generally acceptable. The **cost method** enjoys more widespread use[10] and results in debiting the Treasury Stock account for the reacquisition cost and in reporting this account as a deduction from the total paid-in capital **and** retained earnings on the balance sheet. The **par** or **stated value method** records all transactions in treasury shares at their par value and reports the treasury stock as a deduction from capital stock only. No matter which method is used, the cost of the treasury shares acquired is considered a restriction on retained earnings in most states. Because the par or stated value method is little used, the accounting for this approach is discussed in the appendix to this chapter.

The cost method is generally used in accounting for treasury stock. This method derives its name from the fact that the Treasury Stock account is maintained at the cost of the shares purchased.[11] Under the cost method, the Treasury Stock account is debited for the cost of the shares acquired and upon reissuance of the shares is credited for this same cost. The price received for the stock when it was originally issued does not affect the entries to record the acquisition and reissuance of the treasury stock.

To illustrate, assume that Ho Company has issued 100,000 shares of $1 par value common stock at a price of $10 per share. In addition, it has retained earnings of $300,000. The stockholders' equity section on December 31, 2001, before purchase of treasury stock is as follows:

ILLUSTRATION 15-5
Stockholders' Equity with No Treasury Stock

Stockholders' equity	
Paid-in capital	
Common stock, $1 par value, 100,000 shares issued and outstanding	$ 100,000
Additional paid-in capital	900,000
Total paid-in capital	1,000,000
Retained earnings	300,000
Total stockholders' equity	$1,300,000

On January 20, 2002, Ho Company acquires 10,000 shares of its stock at $11 per share. The entry to record the reacquisition is:

January 20, 2002		
Treasury Stock	110,000	
Cash		110,000

[9]When treasury stock is held to meet a specific short-term obligation, such as treasury shares held for issuance under a deferred compensation plan, treasury stock can be reported as an asset in the balance sheet. For example, **General Motors Corporation** at one time reported treasury stock as a separate asset item entitled "Common Stocks Held for the Incentive Program." The justification for classifying these shares as assets is that they will be used to liquidate a specific liability that appears on the balance sheet. *Accounting Trends and Techniques—1999* reported that out of 600 companies surveyed, 392 disclosed treasury stock but none classified it as an asset.

[10]*Accounting Trends and Techniques—1999* indicates that of its selected list of 600 companies, 367 carried common stock in treasury at cost and only 23 at par or stated value; 2 companies carried preferred stock in treasury at cost and 1 at par or stated value.

[11]If numerous acquisitions of blocks of treasury shares are made at different prices, inventory costing methods—such as specific identification, average, or FIFO—may be used to identify the cost at date of reissuance.

Note that Treasury Stock is debited for the cost of the shares purchased. The original paid-in capital account, Common Stock, is not affected because the number of issued shares does not change. The same is true for the additional paid-in capital account. Treasury stock is deducted from total paid-in capital and retained earnings in the stockholders' equity section.

The stockholders' equity section for Ho Company after purchase of the treasury stock is as follows:

ILLUSTRATION 15-6
Stockholders' Equity with Treasury Stock

Stockholders' equity	
Paid-in capital	
Common stock, $1 par value, 100,000 shares issued and 90,000 outstanding	$ 100,000
Additional paid-in capital	900,000
Total paid-in capital	1,000,000
Retained earnings (see note)	300,000
Total paid-in capital and retained earnings	1,300,000
Less: Cost of treasury stock (10,000 shares)	110,000
Total stockholders' equity	$1,190,000

The cost of the treasury stock is subtracted from the total of common stock, additional paid-in capital, and retained earnings and therefore reduces stockholders' equity. Many states require a corporation to restrict retained earnings for the cost of treasury stock purchased. The restriction serves to keep intact the corporation's legal capital that is temporarily being held as treasury stock. When treasury stock is sold, the restriction is lifted.

Both the number of shares issued (100,000) and the number in the treasury (10,000) are disclosed. The difference is the number of shares of stock outstanding (90,000). The term **outstanding stock** means the number of shares of issued stock that are being held by stockholders.

Sale of Treasury Stock

Treasury stock is usually sold or retired. When treasury shares are sold, the accounting for the sale depends on the price. If the selling price of the treasury stock is equal to cost, the sale of the shares is recorded by a debit to Cash and a credit to Treasury Stock. In cases where the selling price of the treasury stock is not equal to cost, then accounting for treasury stock sold **above cost** differs from the accounting for treasury stock sold **below cost**. However, the sale of treasury stock either above or below cost increases both total assets and stockholders' equity.

Sale of Treasury Stock above Cost. When the selling price of shares of treasury stock is greater than cost, the difference is credited to Paid-in Capital from Treasury Stock. To illustrate, assume that 1,000 shares of treasury stock of Ho Company previously acquired at $11 per share are sold at $15 per share on March 10. The entry is as follows:

March 10, 2002		
Cash	15,000	
Treasury Stock		11,000
Paid-in Capital from Treasury Stock		4,000

There are two reasons why the $4,000 credit in the entry would not be made to Gain on Sale of Treasury Stock: (1) Gains on sales occur when **assets** are sold, and treasury stock is not an asset. (2) A corporation does not realize a gain or suffer a loss from stock transactions with its own stockholders. Thus, paid-in capital arising from the sale of treasury stock should not be included in the measurement of net income. Paid-in capital from treasury stock is listed separately on the balance sheet as a part of paid-in capital.

Sale of Treasury Stock below Cost. When treasury stock is sold below its cost, the excess of the cost over selling price is usually debited to Paid-in Capital from Treasury Stock. Thus, if Ho Company sells an additional 1,000 shares of treasury stock on March 21 at $8 per share, the entry is as follows:

March 21, 2002

Cash	8,000	
Paid-in Capital from Treasury Stock	3,000	
Treasury Stock		11,000

Observe from the two sale entries (sale above cost and sale below cost) that (1) Treasury Stock is credited at cost in each entry, (2) Paid-in Capital from Treasury Stock is used for the difference between the cost and the resale price of the shares, and (3) the original paid-in capital account, Common Stock, is not affected.

When the credit balance in Paid-in Capital from Treasury Stock is eliminated, any additional excess of cost over selling price is debited to Retained Earnings. To illustrate, assume that Ho Company sells an additional 1,000 shares at $8 per share on April 10. The balance in the Paid-in Capital from Treasury Stock account is:

ILLUSTRATION 15-7
Treasury Stock Transactions in Paid-in Capital Account

Paid-in Capital from Treasury Stock

Mar. 21	3,000	Mar. 10	4,000
		Balance	1,000

In this case, $1,000 of the excess is debited to Paid-in Capital from Treasury Stock, and the remainder is debited to Retained Earnings. The entry is:

April 10, 2002

Cash	8,000	
Paid-in Capital from Treasury Stock	1,000	
Retained Earnings	2,000	
Treasury Stock		11,000

Retiring Treasury Stock

The board of directors may approve the retirement of treasury shares. This decision results in cancellation of the treasury stock and a reduction in the number of shares of issued stock. Retired treasury shares have the status of authorized and unissued shares. The accounting effects are similar to the sale of treasury stock except that debits are made to the **paid-in capital accounts applicable to the retired shares** instead of to cash. For example, if the shares are originally sold at par, Common Stock is debited for the par value per share. If the shares are originally sold at $3 above par value, a debit to Paid-in Capital in Excess of Par Value for $3 per share is also required. To illustrate, assume that Ho Company retires 5,000 shares of its treasury stock. The entry to record this retirement is as follows:

Common Stock	5,000	
Paid-in Capital in Excess of Par	45,000	
Retained Earnings	5,000	
Treasury Stock		55,000

If the cost of treasury stock is less than the original issuance price, the difference should be credited to Paid-in Capital from Retirement of Treasury Stock. To illustrate, assume that Ho Company purchased treasury stock at $6 per share instead of $11 per share. Assuming that Ho Company retires 5,000 shares of its treasury stock, the entry to record the retirement is as follows:

Common Stock	5,000	
Paid-in Capital in Excess of Par	45,000	
Treasury Stock		30,000
Paid-in Capital from Retirement of Treasury Stock		20,000

There are two types of treasury stock retirements—actual and constructive. Cancellation of treasury shares through formal application to the secretary of state's office is an **actual retirement**. **Constructive retirement** effects the retirement on the financial statements by board authorization without formal cancellation through the secretary of state. The accounting is the same for actual and constructive retirements.

Other Methods of Accounting for Treasury Stock

Some countries which allow treasury stock purchases show such stock as an asset.

In some states treasury stock must be reported differently. For example, the applicable state law may require a permanent reduction of retained earnings, in which case the cost of the shares purchased in excess of the stated or par value would be charged to retained earnings. Many companies use the balance in Additional Paid-in Capital, regardless of its source, to absorb all charges resulting from treasury stock transactions or use a pro-rata allocation based on original issue price.[12]

Care should always be exercised in recording treasury stock transactions because of the considerable variety of possible requirements. The advice of an attorney is frequently desirable in this connection.

PREFERRED STOCK

OBJECTIVE 7
Describe the major features of preferred stock.

Preferred stock is a special class of shares that is designated "preferred" because it possesses certain preferences or features not possessed by the common stock.[13] The following features are those most often associated with preferred stock issues:

1. Preference as to dividends.
2. Preference as to assets in the event of liquidation.
3. Convertible into common stock.
4. Callable at the option of the corporation.
5. Nonvoting.

The features that distinguish preferred from common stock may be of a more restrictive and negative nature than preferences; for example, the preferred stock may be nonvoting, noncumulative, and nonparticipating.

Preferred stock is usually issued with a par value, and the dividend preference is expressed as a **percentage of the par value**. Thus, holders of 8% preferred stock with a $100 par value are entitled to an annual dividend of $8 per share. This stock is commonly referred to as 8% preferred stock. In the case of no-par preferred stock, a dividend preference is expressed as a **specific dollar amount** per share, for example, $7 per share. This stock is commonly referred to as $7 preferred stock. A preference as to dividends is not assurance that dividends will be paid; it is merely assurance that the stated dividend rate or amount applicable to the preferred stock must be paid before any dividends can be paid on the common stock.

Features of Preferred Stock

A corporation may attach whatever preferences or restrictions in whatever combination it desires to a preferred stock issue so long as it does not specifically violate its state incorporation law, and it may issue more than one class of preferred stock. The most common features attributed to preferred stock are discussed below.

---

[12]For example, the excess of cost over the reissuance price might be charged to Paid-in Capital in Excess of Par for a pro rata amount per share of any premium on the original sale of the stock, and any remaining excess is charged to Paid-in Capital from Treasury Stock and then to Retained Earnings.

[13]*Accounting Trends and Techniques—1999* reports that of its 600 surveyed companies, 99 had preferred stock outstanding; 84 had one class of preferred, and 15 had two classes.

1. ***Cumulative Preferred Stock.*** Dividends not paid in any year must be made up in a later year before any profits can be distributed to common stockholders. If the directors fail to declare a dividend at the normal date for dividend action, the dividend is said to have been "passed." Any passed dividend on cumulative preferred stock constitutes a **dividend in arrears**. Because no liability exists until the board of directors declares a dividend, a dividend in arrears is not recorded as a liability but is disclosed in a note to the financial statements. (At common law, if the corporate charter is silent about the cumulative feature, the preferred stock is considered to be cumulative.) Noncumulative preferred stock is seldom issued because a passed dividend is lost forever to the preferred stockholder and so this stock issue would be less marketable.

2. ***Participating Preferred Stock.*** Holders of participating preferred stock share ratably with the common stockholders in any profit distributions beyond the prescribed rate. That is 5% preferred stock, if fully participating, will receive not only its 5% return, but also dividends at the same rates as those paid to common stockholders if amounts in excess of 5% of par or stated value are paid to common stockholders. Also, participating preferred stock may not always be fully participating as described, but partially participating. For example, provision may be made that 5% preferred stock will be participating up to a maximum total rate of 10%, after which it ceases to participate in additional profit distributions; or 5% preferred stock may participate only in additional profit distributions that are in excess of a 9% dividend rate on the common stock. Although participating preferreds are not used extensively (unlike the cumulative provision), examples of companies that have used participating preferreds are **LTV Corporation**, **Southern California Edison**, and **Allied Products Corporation**.

3. ***Convertible Preferred Stock.*** The stockholders may at their option exchange preferred shares for common stock at a predetermined ratio. The convertible preferred stockholder not only enjoys a preferred claim on dividends but also has the option of converting into a common stockholder with unlimited participation in earnings.

4. ***Callable Preferred Stock.*** The issuing corporation can call or redeem at its option the outstanding preferred shares at specified future dates and at stipulated prices. Many preferred issues are callable. The call or redemption price is ordinarily set slightly above the original issuance price and is commonly stated in terms related to the par value. The callable feature permits the corporation to use the capital obtained through the issuance of such stock until the need has passed or it is no longer advantageous. The existence of a call price or prices tends to set a ceiling on the market value of the preferred shares unless they are convertible into common stock. When a preferred stock is called for redemption, any dividends in arrears must be paid.

Preferred stock is often issued instead of debt because a company's debt-to-equity ratio has become too high. In other instances, issuances are made through private placements with other corporations at a lower than market dividend rate because the acquiring corporation receives dividends that are largely tax free (owing to the IRS's 70% or 80% dividends received deduction).

Reporting of Preferred Stock

Preferred stock is generally reported at par value as the first item in the stockholders' equity section of a company's balance sheet. Any excess over par value is reported as part of additional paid-in capital. Dividends on preferred stock are considered a distribution of income and not an expense of the corporation. Companies must disclose the pertinent rights of the preferred stock outstanding.[14] For example, dividend and liquidation preferences, participation rights, call prices and dates, conversion or exercise prices and pertinent dates, sinking fund requirements, unusual voting rights, and significant terms of contracts to issue additional shares must be disclosed. The disclosure related to liquidation preferences should be made in the equity section of the balance sheet rather than in the notes to the financial statements to emphasize the possible effect of this restriction on future cash flows. Presented below is the stockholders' equity section of **Sequa Corporation** and related disclosures:

ILLUSTRATION 15-8
Stockholders' Equity Section

SEQUA CORPORATION

Stockholders' equity	
Preferred stock—$1 par value, 1,825,000 shares authorized; 797,000 shares of $5 cumulative convertible stock issued at December 31, 1998 (involuntary liquidation value—$17,181 at December 31, 1998)	$ 797,000
Class A common stock—no par value, 25,000,000 shares authorized; 7,273,000 shares issued at December 31, 1998	7,273,000
Class B common stock—no par value, 5,000,000 shares authorized; 3,727,000 shares issued at December 31, 1998	3,727,000
Capital in excess of par value	288,379,000
Accumulated other comprehensive loss	(1,016,000)
Retained earnings	444,669,000
	743,829,000
Less: Cost of treasury stock	78,377,000
Total shareholders' equity	$665,452,000

Note: Each share of $5.00 cumulative convertible preferred stock is convertible into 1.322 shares of Class A common stock. The preferred stock is redeemable, at the option of Sequa, at $100 per share.

OBJECTIVE 8
Distinguish between debt and preferred stock.

Preferred stock generally has no maturity date, and therefore no legal obligation exists to pay the preferred stockholder. As a result, preferred stock is classified as part of stockholders' equity. Recently more and more issuances of preferred stock have features that make the security more like debt (legal obligation to pay) than an equity instrument. For example, **redeemable preferred stock** is preferred stock that has a mandatory redemption period or a redemption feature that is outside the control of the issuer.[15]

[14] "Disclosure of Information about Capital Structure," *Statement of Financial Accounting Standards No. 129* (Norwalk, Conn.: FASB, 1997).

[15] It includes preferred stock that (1) has a fixed or determinable redemption date; (2) is redeemable at the option of the holder; or (3) has conditions for redemption that are not solely within the control of the issuer. Nonredeemable preferred stock is not redeemable or is redeemable solely at the option of the issuer. *Securities and Exchange Commission Release 33-6097* (Washington, D.C.: July 27, 1979). Note that the FASB has issued a discussion memorandum "Distinguishing between Liability and Equity Instruments and Accounting for Instruments with Characteristics of Both" that examines the conditions under which preferred stock would be reported as debt rather than as equity.

In these cases, the company has given to the holder a right to receive future cash flows of the company, and many believe this obligation should be reported as debt rather than equity. The FASB response to date has been to require disclosure in the notes of any redemption features of a preferred stock issued and a schedule of redemptions required within the next five years.

INTERNATIONAL INSIGHT

In Switzerland, there are no specific disclosure requirements for shareholders' equity. However, companies typically disclose separate categories of capital on the balance sheet.

Because of the increasing use of these types of securities, the SEC prohibits companies from combining preferred stock with common stock in financial statements. Amounts must be presented separately for redeemable preferred stock,[16] nonredeemable preferred stock, and common stock. The amounts applicable to these three categories cannot be totaled or combined for SEC reporting purposes. The general heading, **stockholders' equity, should not include redeemable preferred stock.**

To illustrate, assume that Perez Inc. has redeemable preferred stock in addition to common stock, additional paid-in capital, and retained earnings.[17] Perez Inc. presents this information as follows (all amounts assumed):

ILLUSTRATION 15-9
Balance Sheet Presentation of Redeemable Preferred Stock

PEREZ INC.	
Redeemable preferred stock	$ 63,000,000
Stockholders' equity	
Common stock @ $5 par value	
Authorized 100,000,000 shares, issued 40,000,000 shares	200,000,000
Additional paid-in capital	310,000,000
Total paid-in capital	510,000,000
Retained earnings	400,000,000
Total stockholders' equity	$910,000,000

Recent studies have noted that the attributes of preferred stock issuances have changed, with new issues more likely to be redeemable, callable, and exchangeable for debt, but less likely to be convertible into common stock. These changes appear to be in direct response to financial reporting standards, tax laws, and other regulations. Redeemable securities (often called trust preferred securities because of the legal form that is used) have been referred to as the Holy Grail of financial instruments. The reason: Trust preferred securities are treated as debt for tax purposes (dividends are therefore deductible for tax purposes) but not for financial reporting or debt-rating purposes. It is no wonder that the use of these types of securities is increasing dramatically.[18]

UNDERLYING CONCEPTS

Even though present GAAP does not dictate (or prohibit) separate classification, application of the FASB's qualitative characteristic of representational faithfulness would require that economic substance rather than the legal form or description of such securities dictate their financial statement classification.

[16]*SEC Release No. 33-6097,* op. cit.

[17]The initial carrying amount of redeemable preferred stock should be its fair market value at the date of issuance. If the fair value is less than the mandatory redemption amount, **periodic amortizations** using the interest method should be recorded so that the carrying value will equal the redemption amount on the mandatory redemption date. The initial carrying value should also be **periodically increased by dividends** that are not currently declared or paid but that will be due under the redemption agreement. In practice, the corresponding debit has been made to retained earnings (or to additional paid-in capital in the absence of retained earnings). This accounting treatment also applies when the redeemable preferred stock may be voluntarily redeemed by the issuer before the mandatory redemption date and when such preferred stock may be converted into another class of securities by the holder.

[18]See Ellen Engel, Merle Erickson, and Ed Maydew, "Debt-Equity Hybrid Securities," *Journal of Accounting Research,* Autumn, 1999; and Peter J. Frischmann, Paul D. Kimmel, and Terry D. Warfield, "Innovation in Preferred Stock: Current Developments and Implications for Financial Reporting," *Accounting Horizons,* September 1999.

OBJECTIVE 9
Identify items reported as additional paid-in capital.

PRESENTATION OF PAID-IN CAPITAL

As indicated throughout this chapter, additional paid-in capital arises from the issuance of capital stock. In addition, a number of other types of transactions affect additional paid-in capital. The basic transactions affecting additional paid-in capital are expressed in account form in Illustration 15-10.

ILLUSTRATION 15-10
Transactions that Affect Paid-in Capital

Additional Paid-in Capital	
1. Discounts on capital stock issued. 2. Sale of treasury stock below cost. 3. Absorption of a deficit in a recapitalization (quasi-reorganization).* 4. Declaration of a liquidating dividend.*	1. Premiums on capital stock issued. 2. Sale of treasury stock above cost. 3. Additional capital arising in recapitalizations or revisions in the capital structure (quasi-reorganizations).* 4. Additional assessments on stockholders. 5. Conversion of convertible bonds or preferred stock. 6. Declaration of a "small" (ordinary) stock dividend.*

*Discussed in Chapter 16.

In balance sheet presentation, **only one amount need appear**, Additional Paid-in Capital, to summarize all of these possible transactions.[19] A subsidiary ledger or separate general ledger accounts may be kept of the different sources of additional paid-in capital because certain state laws permit dividend distributions out of designated additional paid-in capital.

No operating gains or losses or extraordinary gains and losses may be debited or credited to Additional Paid-in Capital. The profession has long discouraged bypassing net income and retained earnings through the direct write-off of losses (e.g., write-offs of bond discount, goodwill, or obsolete plant and equipment) to additional paid-in capital accounts or other capital accounts.

KEY TERMS

additional paid-in capital, *776*
callable preferred stock, *787*
common stock, *772*
contra equity approach, *778*
contributed (paid-in) capital, *774*
convertible preferred stock, *787*
cost method, *783*
cumulative preferred stock, *787*
earned capital, *774*
legal capital, *775*
leveraged buyout, *782*
limited liability, *773*
lump sum sales, *779*
no-par stock, *776*
par (stated) value method, *783*
par value stock, *773*
participating preferred stock, *787*
preemptive right, *772*
preferred stock, *772*
redeemable preferred stock, *788*
residual interest, *775*
retained earnings, *774*
stated value, *777*
stockholders' (owners') equity, *775*
subscribed stock, *777*
treasury stock, *782*

SUMMARY OF LEARNING OBJECTIVES

1 Discuss the characteristics of the corporate form of organization. Among the specific characteristics of the corporate form that affect accounting are: (1) influence of state corporate law; (2) use of the capital stock or share system; (3) development of a variety of ownership interests; (4) limited liability of stockholders; (5) formality of profit distribution.

2 Identify the rights of stockholders. In the absence of restrictive provisions, each share of stock carries the following rights: (1) to share proportionately in profits and losses; (2) to share proportionately in management (the right to vote for directors); (3) to share proportionately in corporate assets upon liquidation; (4) to share proportionately in any new issues of stock of the same class (called the preemptive right).

3 Explain the key components of stockholders' equity. Stockholders' or owners' equity is classified into two categories: contributed capital and earned capital. Contributed capital (paid-in capital) is the term used to describe the total amount paid in on capital stock; put another way, it is the amount advanced by stockholders to the

[19] *Accounting Trends and Techniques—1999* reports that of its 600 surveyed companies, 527 had additional paid-in capital; 264 used the caption "Additional paid-in capital"; 139 used "Capital in excess of par or stated value" as the caption; 78 used "Paid-in capital" or "Additional capital"; and 46 used other captions.

corporation for use in the business. Contributed capital includes items such as the par value of all outstanding capital stock and premiums less any discounts on issuance. Earned capital is the capital that develops if the business operates profitably; it consists of all undistributed income that remains invested in the enterprise.

4 **Explain the accounting procedures for issuing shares of stock.** Accounts required to be kept for different types of stock are: (1) *Par value stock:* (a) preferred stock or common stock; (b) paid-in capital in excess of par or additional paid-in capital; and (c) discount on stock. (2) *No-par stock:* common stock or common stock and additional paid-in capital, if stated value used. (3) *Stock sold on a subscription basis:* (a) common or preferred stock subscribed; and (b) subscriptions receivable. *Stock issued in combination with other securities (lump sum sales).* The two methods of allocation available are (a) the proportional method; and (b) the incremental method. *Stock issued in noncash transactions:* When stock is issued for services or property other than cash, the property or services should be recorded at either the fair market value of the stock issued or the fair market value of the noncash consideration received, whichever is more clearly determinable.

5 **Identify the major reasons for purchasing treasury stock.** The reasons corporations purchase their outstanding stock are varied. Some major reasons are: (1) to provide tax-efficient distributions of excess cash to shareholders; (2) to increase earnings per share and return on equity; (3) to provide stock for employee stock compensation contracts or to meet potential merger needs; (4) to thwart takeover attempts or to reduce the number of stockholders; (5) to make a market in the stock.

6 **Explain the accounting for treasury stock.** The cost method is generally used in accounting for treasury stock. This method derives its name from the fact that the Treasury Stock account is maintained at the cost of the shares purchased. Under the cost method, the Treasury Stock account is debited for the cost of the shares acquired and is credited for this same cost upon reissuance. The price received for the stock when originally issued does not affect the entries to record the acquisition and reissuance of the treasury stock.

7 **Describe the major features of preferred stock.** Preferred stock is a special class of shares that possesses certain preferences or features not possessed by the common stock. The features that are most often associated with preferred stock issues are: (1) preference as to dividends; (2) preference as to assets in the event of liquidation; (3) convertible into common stock; (4) callable at the option of the corporation; (5) nonvoting.

8 **Distinguish between debt and preferred stock.** With the right combination of features (i.e., fixed return, no vote, redeemable), a preferred stockholder may possess more of the characteristics of a creditor than those of an owner. Preferred shares generally have no maturity date, but the preferred stockholder's relationship with the company may be terminated if the corporation exercises its call privilege. Many issuances of preferred stock have features that make the security more like debt than equity. As a result, companies must report separately redeemable preferred stock, nonredeemable preferred stock, and common stock. The amounts applicable to these three categories cannot be totaled or combined for financial reporting purposes.

9 **Identify items reported as additional paid-in capital.** Items reported as additional paid-in capital are: (1) discounts (premiums) on capital stock issued; (2) sale of treasury stock below (above) cost; (3) absorption of a deficit in a recapitalization or additional capital arising in recapitalizations or revisions in the capital structure (quasi-reorganization); (4) declaration of a liquidating dividend; (5) additional assessments on stockholders; (6) conversion of convertible bonds or preferred stock; (7) declaration of a "small" (ordinary) stock dividend.

APPENDIX 15A

Par Value Method

OBJECTIVE 10
After studying Appendix 15A, you should be able to: Explain the par value method of accounting for treasury stock.

Those who advocate accounting for treasury shares at par (or stated) value adhere to the theory that **the purchase or other acquisition of treasury shares is, in effect, a constructive retirement of those shares**. Inasmuch as the shares cannot be an asset, they must represent a retirement or at least a reduction of outstanding stock. Because outstanding shares are shown at par, they reason, **the reacquired shares must be carried at par** to indicate the proper reduction in stock outstanding.

PURCHASE OF TREASURY STOCK

To illustrate the accounting for treasury stock using the par value method, assume that Ho Company has issued 100,000 shares of $1 par value common stock at a price of $10 per share. In addition, it has retained earnings of $300,000. The stockholders' equity section on December 31, 2001, before purchase of treasury stock is as follows:

ILLUSTRATION 15A-1
Stockholders' Equity with No Treasury Stock

Stockholders' equity	
Paid-in capital	
Common stock, $1 par value 100,000 shares issued and outstanding	$ 100,000
Additional paid-in capital	900,000
Total paid-in capital	1,000,000
Retained earnings	300,000
Total stockholders' equity	$1,300,000

On January 20, 2002, Ho Company acquires 10,000 shares of its stock at $11 per share. The entry to record the reacquisition is:

January 20, 2002

Treasury Stock	10,000	
Paid-in Capital in Excess of Par	90,000[1]	
Retained Earnings	10,000	
Cash		110,000

Under the par value method, **the acquisition cost of treasury shares is compared with the amount received at the time of their original issue**. The Treasury Stock account is debited for the par value (or stated value) of the shares, and a pro rata amount of any excess over par (or stated value) on original issuance is charged to the related Paid-in Capital account. **Any excess of the acquisition cost over the original issue price is charged to Retained Earnings** and may be viewed as a dividend to the retiring stockholder. **If, however, the original issue price exceeds the acquisition price of the treasury stock, this difference is credited to Paid-in Capital from Treasury Stock** and may be viewed as a **capital contribution** from the retiring stockholders.

[1]This amount could be charged to Paid-in Capital from Treasury Stock if a balance existed in that account from previous transactions.

In the Ho Company example, because there was only one previous issuance of common stock (at $10 per share), the average price received is the same as the original issue price. Therefore, the $9 original excess over par per share is used to determine the total reduction in Paid-in Capital in Excess of Par. More typically, the average excess over par originally received per share is computed by dividing the total paid-in capital in excess of par from all original issuances of common stock by the number of common shares issued.

The stockholders' equity section for Ho Company after purchase of the treasury stock is as follows:

ILLUSTRATION 15A-2
Stockholders' Equity with Treasury Stock

Stockholders' equity	
Paid-in capital	
Common stock, $1 par value, 100,000 shares issued	$ 100,000
Less: Treasury stock (10,000 shares at par)	10,000
Common stock outstanding	90,000
Additional paid-in capital	810,000
Total paid-in capital	900,000
Retained earnings	290,000
Total stockholders' equity	$1,190,000

Under the par value method, treasury stock is reported in the balance sheet as a **deduction**—at par value of $10,000—from issued shares of the same class. Note also that additional paid-in capital is $90,000 less and retained earnings is $10,000 less than before the treasury stock transaction.

SALE OR RETIREMENT OF TREASURY STOCK

Treasury stock is usually sold or retired. If the treasury shares are sold or retired, the accounting treatment is similar to that accorded any original issuance of stock.

When the selling price of the shares is greater than par, the difference is credited to Paid-in Capital in Excess of Par. To illustrate, assume that 1,000 shares of treasury stock of Ho Company previously acquired at $11 per share are sold at $15 per share on March 10. The entry is as follows:

March 10, 2002		
Cash	15,000	
Treasury Stock		1,000
Paid-in Capital in Excess of Par		14,000

If the treasury stock is sold at less than par, Paid-in Capital from Treasury Stock is debited. A Discount on Capital Stock is not debited because no contingent liability exists on the part of the stockholders of the reissued shares.

If stock is retired, the par value of the treasury stock and related common stock is reduced. To illustrate, assume that Ho Company retires 5,000 shares of its treasury stock. The entry to record this retirement is as follows:

Common Stock	5,000	
Treasury Stock		5,000

The par value method maintains the integrity of the various sources of capital. The cost method avoids identifying and accounting for the premiums, discounts, and other amounts related to the original issue of the specific shares acquired. For that reason, it is the simpler and more popular method.

SUMMARY OF LEARNING OBJECTIVE FOR APPENDIX 15A

10 Explain the par value method of accounting for treasury stock. Under the par value method, the purchase of treasury shares is viewed as a constructive retirement of those shares. Inasmuch as the shares cannot be an asset, they must represent a retirement or at least a reduction of the outstanding stock. Because shares outstanding are shown at par, the reacquired shares must be carried at par to indicate the proper reduction in stock outstanding.

Note: All **asterisked** Questions, Brief Exercises, Exercises, Problems, and Conceptual Cases relate to material contained in the appendix to the chapter.

QUESTIONS

1 Distinguish between the following types of corporations:

(a) Public sector vs. private sector.

(b) Nonstock vs. stock.

(c) Closed vs. open.

(d) Listed vs. unlisted.

2 Differentiate between capital in a legal sense, capital in a corporate finance sense, and capital in an accounting sense.

3 Discuss the special characteristics of the corporate form of business that have a direct effect on owners' equity accounting.

4 In the absence of restrictive provisions, what are the basic rights of stockholders of a corporation?

5 Distinguish between common and preferred stock.

6 Why is the distinction between paid-in capital and retained earnings important?

7 Explain each of the following terms: authorized capital stock, unissued capital stock, issued capital stock, outstanding capital stock, subscribed stock, and treasury stock.

8 Distinguish between paid-in capital and stated capital.

9 What is meant by par value, and what is its significance to stockholders?

10 Describe the accounting for the issuance for cash of no-par value common stock at a price in excess of the stated value of the common stock.

11 When might the Stock Subscription Receivable account be classified as a current asset? As a deduction in the stockholders' equity section?

12 Describe the accounting for the subscription of common stock at a price in excess of the par value of the common stock.

13 Explain the difference between the proportional method and the incremental method of allocating the proceeds of lump sum sales of capital stock.

14 What are the different bases for stock valuation when assets other than cash are received for issued shares of stock?

15 Explain how underwriting costs and accounting and legal fees associated with the issuance of stock should be recorded.

16 For what reasons might a corporation purchase its own stock?

***17** Distinguish between the cost method and the par value method of accounting for treasury stock.

18 Discuss the propriety of showing:

(a) Treasury stock as an asset.

(b) "Gain" or "loss" on sale of treasury stock as additions to or deductions from income.

(c) Dividends received on treasury stock as income.

19 What features or rights may alter the character of preferred stock?

20 Little Texas Inc. recently noted that its 4% preferred stock and 4% participating second preferred stock, which are both cumulative, have priority as to dividends up to 4% of their par value; its participating preferred stock participates equally with the common stock in any dividends in excess of 4%. What is meant by the term participating? Cumulative?

21 Where in the financial statements is preferred stock normally reported?

22 How should preferred stock redeemable by the holder be classified in the financial statements?

23 List possible sources of additional paid-in capital.

24 Goo Goo Dolls Inc. purchases 10,000 shares of its own previously issued $10 par common stock for $290,000. Assuming the shares are held in the treasury with intent to reissue, what effect does this transaction have on (a) net income, (b) total assets, (c) total paid-in capital, and (d) total stockholders' equity?

25 Indicate how each of the following accounts should be classified in the stockholders' equity section.

(a) Common Stock
(b) Retained Earnings
(c) Paid-in Capital in Excess of Par Value
(d) Treasury Stock
(e) Paid-in Capital from Treasury Stock
(f) Paid-in Capital in Excess of Stated Value
(g) Preferred Stock

***26** How is stockholders' equity affected differently by using the par value method instead of the cost method for treasury stock purchases?

BRIEF EXERCISES

BE15-1 Lost Vikings Corporation issued 300 shares of $10 par value common stock for $4,100. Prepare Lost Vikings' journal entry.

BE15-2 Lotus Turbo Inc. issued 200 shares of $5 par value common stock for $850. Prepare Lotus Turbo's journal entry.

BE15-3 Shinobi Corporation issued 600 shares of no-par common stock for $10,200. Prepare Shinobi's journal entry if (a) the stock has no stated value, and (b) the stock has a stated value of $2 per share.

BE15-4 Rambo Inc. sells 300 shares of its $10 par value common stock on a subscription basis at $45 per share. On June 1, Rambo accepts a 40% down payment. On December 1, Rambo collects the remaining 60% and issues the shares. Prepare Rambo's journal entries.

BE15-5 Lufia Corporation has the following account balances at December 31, 2001:

Common stock, $5 par value	$ 210,000
Subscriptions receivable	90,000
Retained earnings	2,340,000
Paid-in capital in excess of par	1,320,000

Prepare Lufia's December 31, 2001, stockholders' equity section.

BE15-6 Primal Rage Corporation issued 300 shares of $10 par value common stock and 100 shares of $50 par value preferred stock for a lump sum of $14,200. The common stock has a market value of $20 per share, and the preferred stock has a market value of $90 per share. Prepare the journal entry to record the issuance.

BE15-7 On February 1, 2001, Mario Andretti Corporation issued 2,000 shares of its $5 par value common stock for land worth $31,000. Prepare the February 1, 2001, journal entry.

BE15-8 Powerdrive Corporation issued 2,000 shares of its $10 par value common stock for $70,000. Powerdrive also incurred $1,500 of costs associated with issuing the stock. Prepare Powerdrive's journal entry to record the issuance of the company's stock.

BE15-9 Maverick Inc. has outstanding 10,000 shares of $10 par value common stock. On July 1, 2001, Maverick reacquired 100 shares at $85 per share. On September 1, Maverick reissued 60 shares at $90 per share. On November 1, Maverick reissued 40 shares at $83 per share. Prepare Maverick's journal entries to record these transactions using the cost method.

BE15-10 Power Rangers Corporation has outstanding 20,000 shares of $5 par value common stock. On August 1, 2001, Power Rangers reacquired 200 shares at $75 per share. On November 1, Power Rangers reissued the 200 shares at $70 per share. Power Rangers had no previous treasury stock transactions. Prepare Power Rangers' journal entries to record these transactions using the cost method.

BE15-11 Mickey Mouse Inc. is holding 500 shares of its own $5 par value common stock as treasury stock. The stock was originally issued at $13 per share and was reacquired at $14 per share. Mickey Mouse uses the cost method of accounting for treasury stock. Prepare the necessary journal entry if Mickey Mouse formally retires the treasury stock.

BE15-12 Popeye Corporation issued 450 shares of $100 par value preferred stock for $61,500. Prepare Popeye's journal entry.

***BE15-13** Mega Man Corporation has outstanding 100,000 shares of $10 par value common stock which was originally issued at an average price of $24 per share. Mega Man reacquires 300 shares at $33 per share and later reissues the shares at $37 per share. Mega Man uses the par value method of accounting for treasury stock. Prepare the journal entries to record the two transactions.

***BE15-14** Use the information from BE15-13, except assume the treasury stock was reacquired at $21 per share and later reissued at $23 per share. Prepare Mega Man's journal entries to record the two transactions.

***BE15-15** Use the information from BE15-11, except assume that Mickey Mouse uses the par value method of accounting for treasury stock. Prepare the necessary journal entry if Mickey Mouse formally retires the treasury stock.

EXERCISES

E15-1 (Recording the Issuances of Common Stock) During its first year of operations, Collin Raye Corporation had the following transactions pertaining to its common stock.

Jan. 10	Issued 80,000 shares for cash at $6 per share.
Mar. 1	Issued 5,000 shares to attorneys in payment of a bill for $35,000 for services rendered in helping the company to incorporate.
July 1	Issued 30,000 shares for cash at $8 per share.
Sept. 1	Issued 60,000 shares for cash at $10 per share.

Instructions

(a) Prepare the journal entries for these transactions, assuming that the common stock has a par value of $5 per share.

(b) Prepare the journal entries for these transactions, assuming that the common stock is no par with a stated value of $3 per share.

E15-2 (Recording the Issuance of Common and Preferred Stock) Kathleen Battle Corporation was organized on January 1, 2001. It is authorized to issue 10,000 shares of 8%, $100 par value preferred stock, and 500,000 shares of no par common stock with a stated value of $1 per share. The following stock transactions were completed during the first year.

Jan. 10	Issued 80,000 shares of common stock for cash at $5 per share.
Mar. 1	Issued 5,000 shares of preferred stock for cash at $108 per share.
Apr. 1	Issued 24,000 shares of common stock for land. The asking price of the land was $90,000; the fair market value of the land was $80,000.
May 1	Issued 80,000 shares of common stock for cash at $7 per share.
Aug. 1	Issued 10,000 shares of common stock to attorneys in payment of their bill of $50,000 for services rendered in helping the company organize.
Sept. 1	Issued 10,000 shares of common stock for cash at $9 per share.
Nov. 1	Issued 1,000 shares of preferred stock for cash at $112 per share.

Instructions

Prepare the journal entries to record the above transactions.

E15-3 (Subscribed Stock) James Galway Inc. intends to sell capital stock to raise additional capital to allow for expansion in the rapidly growing service industry. The corporation decides to sell this stock through a subscription basis and publicly notifies the investment world. The stock is a $5 par value issue and 30,000 shares are offered at $25 a share. The terms of the subscription are 40% down and the balance at the end of six months. All shares are subscribed for during the offering period.

Instructions

Give the journal entry for the original subscription, the collection of the down payments, the collection of the balance of the subscription price, and the issuance of the common stock.

E15-4 (Stock Issued for Nonmonetary Assets) Faith Hill Products, Inc., was formed to operate a manufacturing plant in Warnersville. The events for the formation of the corporation include the following:

1. 5,000 shares of no-par common stock were issued to investors at $22 per share.
2. 8,000 shares were issued to acquire used equipment that has a depreciated book value to the seller of $140,000.

Instructions

Prepare journal entries for the transactions above.

E15-5 (Stock Issued for Land) Twenty-five thousand shares reacquired by Elixir Corporation for $53 per share were exchanged for undeveloped land that has an appraised value of $1,700,000. At the time of the exchange the common stock was trading at $62 per share on an organized exchange.

Instructions

(a) Prepare the journal entry to record the acquisition of land assuming the stock was originally recorded on the cost method.

(b) Briefly identify the possible alternatives (including those that are totally unacceptable) for quantifying the cost of the land and briefly support your choice.

E15-6 (Lump Sum Sale of Stock with Bonds) Faith Evans Corporation is a regional company which is an SEC registrant. The corporation's securities are thinly traded through the NASDAQ (National Association of Securities Dealers Quotes). Faith Evans Corp. has issued 10,000 units. Each unit consists of a $500 par, 12% subordinated debenture and 10 shares of $5 par common stock. The investment banker has retained 400 units as the underwriting fee. The other 9,600 units were sold to outside investors for cash at $880 per unit. Prior to this sale the two-week ask price of common stock was $40 per share. Twelve percent is a reasonable market yield for the debentures.

Instructions

(a) Prepare the journal entry to record the transaction above:

(1) Employing the incremental method assuming the interest rate on the debentures is the best market measure.

(2) Employing the proportional method using the recent price quotes on the common stock.

(b) Briefly explain which method is, in your opinion, the better method.

E15-7 (Lump Sum Sales of Stock with Preferred Stock) Dave Matthew Inc. issues 500 shares of $10 par value common stock and 100 shares of $100 par value preferred stock for a lump sum of $100,000.

Instructions

(a) Prepare the journal entry for the issuance when the market value of the common shares is $165 each and market value of the preferred is $230 each.

(b) Prepare the journal entry for the issuance when only the market value of the common stock is known and it is $170 per share.

E15-8 (Lump Sum Sale of Stock with Preferred) Cyndi Lauper Company was organized with 50,000 shares of $100 par value, 9% preferred stock and 100,000 shares of common stock without par value. During the first year, 1,000 shares of preferred and 1,000 shares of common were issued for a lump sum price of $180,000.

Instructions

What entry should be made to record this transaction under each of the following independent conditions:

(a) Shortly after the transaction described above, 500 shares of preferred stock were sold at $116.

(b) The directors have established a stated value of $75 a share for the common stock.

(c) At the date of issuance, the preferred stock had a market price of $140 per share and the common stock had a market price of $40 per share.

E15-9 (Stock Issuances and Repurchase) Lindsey Hunter Corporation is authorized to issue 50,000 shares of $5 par value common stock. During 2001, Lindsey Hunter took part in the following selected transactions:

1. Issued 5,000 shares of stock at $45 per share, less costs related to the issuance of the stock totaling $7,000.
2. Issued 1,000 shares of stock for land appraised at $50,000. The stock was actively traded on a national stock exchange at approximately $46 per share on the date of issuance.
3. Purchased 500 shares of treasury stock at $43 per share. The treasury shares purchased were issued in 2000 at $40 per share.

Instructions

(a) Prepare a journal entry to record item 1.

(b) Prepare a journal entry to record item 2.

(c) Prepare a journal entry to record item 3 using the cost method.

E15-10 (Effect of Treasury Stock Transactions on Financials) Joe Dumars Company has outstanding 40,000 shares of $5 par common stock which had been issued at $30 per share. Joe Dumars then entered into the following transactions:

1. Purchased 5,000 treasury shares at $45 per share.
2. Resold 2,000 of the treasury shares at $49 per share.
3. Resold 500 of the treasury shares at $40 per share.
4. Retired the remaining treasury shares.

Instructions

Use the following code to indicate the effect each of the four transactions has on the financial statement categories listed in the table below, assuming Joe Dumars Company uses the cost method: (I = Increase; D = Decrease; NE = No effect).

#	Assets	Liabilities	Stockholders' Equity	Paid-in Capital	Retained Earnings	Net Income
1						
2						
3						
4						

E15-11 (Preferred Stock Entries and Dividends) Otis Thorpe Corporation has 10,000 shares of $100 par value, 8%, preferred stock and 50,000 shares of $10 par value common stock outstanding at December 31, 2001.

Instructions

Answer the questions in each of the following independent situations:

(a) If the preferred stock is cumulative and dividends were last paid on the preferred stock on December 31, 1998, what are the dividends in arrears that should be reported on the December 31, 2001, balance sheet? How should these dividends be reported?

(b) If the preferred stock is convertible into seven shares of $10 par value common stock and 4,000 shares are converted, what entry is required for the conversion assuming the preferred stock was issued at par value?

(c) If the preferred stock was issued at $107 per share, how should the preferred stock be reported in the stockholders' equity section?

E15-12 (Stockholders' Equity Section) Doug Collins Corporation's charter authorized 100,000 shares of $10 par value common stock, and 30,000 shares of 6% cumulative and nonparticipating preferred stock, par value $100 per share. The corporation engaged in the following stock transactions through December 31, 2001: 30,000 shares of common stock were issued for $350,000 and 12,000 shares of preferred stock for machinery valued at $1,475,000. Subscriptions for 4,500 shares of common have been taken, and 40% of the subscription price of $16 per share has been collected. The stock will be issued upon collection of the subscription price in full. Treasury stock of 1,000 shares of common has been purchased for $15 and accounted for under the cost method. The Retained Earnings balance is $180,000.

Instructions

Prepare the stockholders' equity section of the balance sheet in good form. Assume that state law requires that the amount of retained earnings available for dividends be restricted by an amount equal to the cost of treasury shares acquired.

E15-13 (Correcting Entries for Equity Transactions) Pistons Inc. recently hired a new accountant with extensive experience in accounting for partnerships. Because of the pressure of the new job, the accountant was unable to review what he had learned earlier about corporation accounting. During the first month, he made the following entries for the corporation's capital stock.

May 2	Cash	192,000	
	Capital Stock		192,000
	(Issued 12,000 shares of $5 par value common stock at $16 per share)		
10	Cash	600,000	
	Capital Stock		600,000
	(Issued 10,000 shares of $30 par value preferred stock at $60 per share)		
15	Capital Stock	15,000	
	Cash		15,000
	(Purchased 1,000 shares of common stock for the treasury at $15 per share)		
31	Cash	8,500	
	Capital Stock		5,000
	Gain on Sale of Stock		3,500
	(Sold 500 shares of treasury stock at $17 per share)		

Instructions

On the basis of the explanation for each entry, prepare the entries that should have been made for the capital stock transactions.

E15-14 (Analysis of Equity Data and Equity Section Preparation) For a recent 2-year period, the balance sheet of Santana Dotson Company showed the following stockholders' equity data in millions.

	2002	2001
Additional paid-in capital	$ 931	$ 817
Common stock—par	545	540
Retained earnings	7,167	5,226
Treasury stock	1,564	918
Total stockholders' equity	$7,079	$5,665
Common stock shares issued	218	216
Common stock shares authorized	500	500
Treasury stock shares	34	27

Instructions

(a) Answer the following questions.
  (1) What is the par value of the common stock?
  (2) Was the cost per share of acquiring treasury stock higher in 2002 or in 2001?
(b) Prepare the stockholders' equity section for 2002.

***E15-15 (Treasury Stock—Par Value and Cost Methods)** Carver Smith Corporation reacquired 40,000 of its common shares in the market at $53 per share. The per share par value is $1; the average issue price was $30 per share.

Instructions

(a) Record the purchase assuming:
  (1) The par value method.
  (2) The cost method.
(b) Which of the methods will provide the financial statement reader with more useful information? Briefly explain.

***E15-16 (Treasury Stock—Par Value and Cost Methods)** Grant Hill Inc. has outstanding 35,000 shares of $10 par common stock which has been issued at $25 per share. On July 5, 2001, Grant Hill repurchased 1,000 of these shares at $41 per share. The company then retired the treasury shares.

Instructions

Give the appropriate journal entries for the acquisition and retirement of the treasury stock under:
(a) The cost method.
(b) The par value method.

***E15-17 (Effect of Treasury Stock Transactions on Financials—Par Value Method)** Joe Dumars Company has outstanding 40,000 shares of $5 par common stock which had been issued at $30 per share. Joe Dumars then entered into the following transactions:

1. Purchased 5,000 treasury shares at $45 per share.
2. Resold 2,000 of the treasury shares at $49 per share.
3. Resold 500 of the treasury shares at $40 per share.
4. Retired the remaining treasury shares.

Instructions

Use the following code to indicate the effect each of the four transactions has on the financial statement categories listed in the table below, assuming Joe Dumars Company uses the par value method: (I = Increase; D = Decrease; NE = No effect).

#	Assets	Liabilities	Stockholders' Equity	Paid-in Capital	Retained Earnings	Net Income
1						
2						
3						
4						

PROBLEMS

P15-1 (Subscriptions, Treasury Stock, and Lump Sum Issuances) The Nells Company had the following stockholders' equity on January 1, 2002.

Preferred stock, $100 par value, 8% cumulative, 10,000 shares authorized, no shares issued	$ —
Common stock, 200,000 shares authorized, 100,000 shares issued and outstanding, $2 par	200,000
Paid-in capital in excess of par (original issue)	2,300,000
Retained earnings, unappropriated	1,800,000
Total stockholders' equity	$4,300,000

The following transactions occurred, in the order given, during 2002:

1. Subscriptions were sold for 10,000 shares of common stock at $28 per share. The first payment was for $13 per share.
2. The second payment was for $15 per share. All payments were received on the second payment except for 1,000 shares.
3. Per the subscription contract, which requires that defaulting subscribers have all their payments refunded, Nells sends a refund check to the defaulting subscribers. At this point, common stock is issued to subscribers that have fully paid on the contract.
4. 10,000 shares of treasury stock were purchased at $20 per share. Nells uses the cost method of accounting for treasury shares.
5. All 10,000 shares of treasury stock were sold for $24 per share.
6. 2,000 shares of preferred stock and 3,000 shares of common stock were sold together for $290,000. The common stock had a market value of $27 per share.

Instructions

Prepare the journal entries to record the transactions for Nells Company for 2002.

P15-2 (Treasury Stock Transactions and Presentation) Jodz Company had the following stockholders' equity as of January 1, 2002.

Common stock, $5 par value, 20,000 shares issued	$100,000
Paid-in capital in excess of par	300,000
Retained earnings	320,000
Total stockholders' equity	$720,000

During 2002, the following transactions occurred:

Feb. 1	Jodz repurchased 2,000 shares of treasury stock at a price of $18 per share.
Mar. 1	800 shares of treasury stock repurchased above were reissued at $17 per share.
Mar. 18	500 shares of treasury stock repurchased above were reissued at $14 per share.
Apr. 22	600 shares of treasury stock repurchased above were reissued at $20 per share.

Instructions

(a) Prepare the journal entries to record the treasury stock transactions in 2002, assuming Jodz uses the cost method.

(b) Prepare the stockholders' equity section as of April 30, 2002. Net income for the first 4 months of 2002 was $110,000.

P15-3 (Equity Transactions and Statement Preparation) On January 5, 2001, Drabek Corporation received a charter granting the right to issue 5,000 shares of $100 par value, 8% cumulative and nonparticipating preferred stock and 50,000 shares of $5 par value common stock. It then completed these transactions:

Jan. 11	Accepted subscriptions to 20,000 shares of common stock at $16 per share; 40% down payments accompanied the subscription.
Feb. 1	Issued Robb Nen Corp. 4,000 shares of preferred stock for the following assets: machinery with a fair market value of $50,000; a factory building with a fair market value of $110,000; and land with an appraised value of $270,000.
Apr. 15	Collected the balance of the subscription price on the common shares and issued the stock.
July 29	Purchased 1,800 shares of common stock at $19 per share (use cost method).
Aug. 10	Sold the 1,800 treasury shares at $14 per share.
Dec. 31	Declared a $0.25 per share cash dividend on the common stock and declared the preferred dividend.
Dec. 31	Closed the Income Summary account. There was a $175,700 net income.

Instructions

(a) Record the journal entries for the transactions listed above.

(b) Prepare the stockholders' equity section of Drabek Corporation's balance sheet as of December 31, 2001.

P15-4 (Equity Transactions and Statement Preparation) Amado Company has two classes of capital stock outstanding: 8%, $20 par preferred and $5 par common. At December 31, 2000, the following accounts were included in stockholders' equity:

Preferred Stock, 150,000 shares	$ 3,000,000
Common Stock, 2,000,000 shares	10,000,000
Paid-in Capital in Excess of Par—Preferred	200,000
Paid-in Capital in Excess of Par—Common	27,000,000
Retained Earnings	4,500,000

The following transactions affected stockholders' equity during 2001:

Jan. 1	25,000 shares of preferred stock issued at $22 per share.
Feb. 1	40,000 shares of common stock issued at $20 per share.
June 1	2-for-1 stock split (par value reduced to $2.50).
July 1	30,000 shares of common treasury stock purchased at $9 per share. Amado uses the cost method.
Sept. 15	10,000 shares of treasury stock reissued at $11 per share.
Dec. 31	Net income is $2,100,000.
Dec. 31	The preferred dividend is declared, and a common dividend of 50¢ per share is declared.

Instructions

Prepare the stockholders' equity section for Amado Company at December 31, 2001. Show all supporting computations.

P15-5 (Stock Transactions—Assessment and Lump Sum) Shikai Corporation's charter authorized issuance of 100,000 shares of $10 par value common stock and 50,000 shares of $50 preferred stock. The following transactions involving the issuance of shares of stock were completed. Each transaction is independent of the others.

1. Issued a $10,000, 9% bond payable at par and gave as a bonus one share of preferred stock, which at that time was selling for $106 a share.
2. Issued 500 shares of common stock for machinery. The machinery had been appraised at $7,100; the seller's book value was $6,200. The most recent market price of the common stock is $15 a share.
3. Voted a 10% assessment on both the 10,000 shares of outstanding common and the 1,000 shares of outstanding preferred. The assessment was paid in full.
4. Issued 375 shares of common and 100 shares of preferred for a lump sum amounting to $11,300. The common had been selling at $14 and the preferred at $65.
5. Issued 200 shares of common and 50 shares of preferred for furniture and fixtures. The common had a fair market value of $16 per share and the furniture and fixtures were appraised at $6,200.

Instructions

Record the transactions listed above in journal entry form.

P15-6 (Treasury Stock—Cost Method) Before Polska Corporation engages in the treasury stock transactions listed below, its general ledger reflects, among others, the following account balances (par value of its stock is $30 per share).

Paid-in Capital in Excess of Par	Common Stock	Retained Earnings
Balance $99,000	Balance $270,000	Balance $80,000

Instructions

Record the treasury stock transactions (given below) under the cost method of handling treasury stock; use the FIFO method for purchase-sale purposes.

(a) Bought 380 shares of treasury stock at $39 per share.

(b) Bought 300 shares of treasury stock at $43 per share.

(c) Sold 350 shares of treasury stock at $42 per share.

(d) Sold 120 shares of treasury stock at $38 per share.

(e) Retired the remaining shares in the treasury.

P15-7 (Reacquisition of Stock—FIFO and Weighted Average) Indiana Inc. is a closely held toy manufacturer in the Midwest. You have been engaged as the independent public accountant to perform the first audit of Indiana. It is agreed that only current-year (2002) financial statements will be audited.

The following stockholder's equity information has been developed from Indiana records on December 31, 2001:

Common stock, no par value; no stated value; authorized 30,000 shares; issued 9,000 shares	$405,000
Retained earnings	180,000

The following stock transactions took place during 2002:

1. On March 15, Indiana issued 7,000 shares of common stock to Derrick McKey for $63 per share.
2. On March 31, Indiana reacquired 4,000 shares of common stock from Reggie Miller (Indiana's founder) for $74 per share. These shares were canceled and retired upon receipt.

For the year 2002, Indiana reported net income of $125,000.

Instructions

(a) How should the stockholders' equity information be reported in the Indiana financial statements for the year ended December 31, 2002 (1) assuming specific identification of the shares is impossible and (2) assuming application of the FIFO method? The company uses the cost method of accounting for treasury stock transactions.

(b) How would your answer in part (a) have been altered if Indiana had treated the reacquired shares as treasury stock carried at cost rather than retired?

(c) On December 30, 2003, Indiana's board of directors changed the common stock from no par, no stated value to no par with a $10 stated value per share. How will the stockholders' equity section be affected if comparative financial statements are prepared at December 31, 2003? (Apply the method used in (a)(1).)

P15-8 (Prepare Stockholders' Equity Section) Heinrich Corporation had the following stockholders' equity at January 1, 2002:

Preferred stock, 8%, $100 par value, 10,000 shares authorized, 4,000 shares issued	$ 400,000
Common stock, $2 par value, 200,000 shares authorized, 80,000 shares issued	160,000
Common stock subscribed, 10,000 shares	20,000
Additional paid-in capital—preferred	20,000
Additional paid-in capital—common	940,000
Retained earnings	780,000
	2,320,000
Less: Common stock subscriptions receivable	40,000
Total stockholders' equity	$2,280,000

During 2002 the following transactions occurred:

1. 100 shares of common stock were exchanged for equipment. The market value of the stock on the exchange date was $12 per share.
2. 1,000 shares of common stock and 100 shares of preferred stock were sold for the lump sum price of $24,500. The common stock had a market price of $14 at the time of the sale.
3. 2,000 shares of preferred stock were sold for cash at $102 per share.
4. All of the subscribers paid their subscription prices into the firm.
5. The shares of common stock were issued.
6. 1,000 shares of common stock were repurchased by the corporation at $15 per share.
7. 800 of these shares were resold at $18 per share by year-end. Heinrich uses the cost method of accounting for treasury stock.
8. Income for 2002 was $246,000.

Instructions

Prepare the stockholder's equity section of Heinrich Corporation as of December 31, 2002. (The use of T-accounts may help you organize the material.)

P15-9 (Treasury Stock—Cost Method—Equity Section Preparation) Constantine Company has the following owners' equity accounts at December 31, 2000:

Common Stock—$100 par value, authorized 8,000 shares	$480,000
Retained Earnings	294,000

Instructions

(a) Prepare entries in journal form to record the following transactions, which took place during 2001. (*Hint:* Debit retained earnings in transaction 6.)

(1) 240 shares of outstanding stock were purchased at 97. (These are to be accounted for using the cost method.)
(2) A $20 per share cash dividend was declared.
(3) The dividend declared in No. 2 above was paid.
(4) The treasury shares purchased in No. 1 above were resold at 102.
(5) 500 shares of outstanding stock were purchased at 103.
(6) 120 shares of outstanding stock were purchased at 106 and retired.
(7) 330 of the shares purchased in No. 5 above were resold at 96.

(b) Prepare the stockholders' equity section of Constantine Company's balance sheet after giving effect to these transactions, assuming that the net income for 2001 was $94,000.

P15-10 (Redeemable Preferred Stock) The following information relates to Altoona Industries, Inc.:

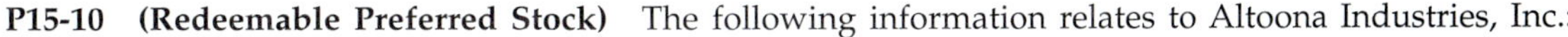

Altoona Industries, Inc.

	2002	2001
($000)		
Series A first preferred stock—subject to mandatory redemption ($4,062,000 liquidation value in 2002 and 2001); $1.00 par value; authorized 100,000 shares; issued 40,625 shares in 2002 and 2001 (note 6)	$ 4,062	$ 4,062
Common stockholders' equity:		
Common stock, $.10 par value; authorized 20,000,000 shares; issued 5,522,602 shares in 2002 and 5,280,602 in 2001	552	528
Additional paid-in capital	10,463	6,014
Retained earnings	25,286	17,110
Common stockholders' equity	36,301	23,652

Notes to Consolidated Financial Statements Note 6: Redeemable Preferred Stock. The Company's preferred stock consists of 250,000 authorized shares of $1.00 par value First Preferred Stock of which 40,620 shares of Series A First Preferred Stock were outstanding at December 31, 2002. The Series A First Preferred Stock, which is not convertible, has a carrying value of $80.00 per share representing fair value at date of issuance based upon an independent appraisal and sales to third parties, plus accumulated accretion. The shares are entitled to cumulative dividends of $12.70 annually ($3.175 per quarter) per share and must be redeemed at 10% per year commencing on December 31, 2005, at $100.00 per share plus accrued and unpaid dividends. The Company, at its option, may redeem at that price in each year in which mandatory redemption is required an additional number of shares not exceeding the mandatory redemption and may redeem all or any part of the shares at that price plus a premium amounting to $3.55 in 2003 and declining proportionately thereafter through 2011 after which there will be no premium.

Altoona had total debt of $85,979 in 2002. A restrictive covenant on some of the debt prohibits Altoona from additional borrowing if the debt/equity ratio exceeds 2.5 or if retained earnings falls below $17,000.

Instructions

Prepare responses to the following questions based on the above information.

(a) Does the Series A preferred stock have characteristics more like common stock or like debt? Explain.
(b) What are the present GAAP requirements for redeemable preferred stock?
(c) Is Altoona in violation of its debt covenants in 2002, based upon the reported numbers above? Would your answer change if Altoona classifies the redeemable stock as debt?
(d) How should redeemable preferred stock be reported?

***P15-11 (Treasury Stock Analysis)** The stockholders' equity section of Georges Bizet Company's balance sheet at December 31, 2002, was as follows:

Common stock—$100 par (authorized 50,000 shares, issued and outstanding 15,000 shares)	$1,500,000
Paid-in capital in excess of par	150,000
Retained earnings	210,000
Total stockholders' equity	$1,860,000

On January 2, 2003, having idle cash, the company repurchased 800 shares of its stock for $91,200. During the year it sold 150 of the reacquired shares at $117 per share, another 150 at $110 per share, and legally retired the remaining 500 shares.

Instructions

(a) Discuss the possible alternatives in handling these transactions.

(b) Prepare journal entries for each transaction in accordance with the method that you believe should be applied.

***P15-12 (Stock Transaction and Equity Section Preparation)** Transactions of Kalila Company are as follows:

1. The company is granted a charter that authorizes issuance of 15,000 shares of $100 par value preferred stock and 15,000 shares of common stock without par value.
2. 8,000 shares of common stock are issued to founders of the corporation for land valued by the Board of Directors at $210,000. The Board establishes a par value of $5 a share for the common stock.
3. 4,200 shares of preferred stock are sold for cash at 110.
4. 600 shares of common stock are sold to an officer of the corporation for $42 a share.
5. 300 shares of outstanding preferred stock are purchased for cash at par.
6. 400 shares of outstanding preferred stock are purchased for cash at 98.
7. 500 shares of the outstanding common stock issued in No. 2 above are purchased at $49 a share.
8. 200 shares of repurchased preferred stock are reissued at 102.
9. 2,100 shares of preferred stock are issued at 99.
10. 400 shares of reacquired common stock are reissued for $39 a share.
11. 200 shares of the common stock sold in No. 10 above are repurchased for $30 a share.

Instructions

(a) Prepare entries in journal form to record the transactions listed above. No other transactions affecting the capital stock accounts have occurred. Treasury stock is to be entered in the Treasury Stock accounts at par.

(b) Assuming that the company has retained earnings from operations of $132,000, prepare the stockholders' equity section of its balance sheet after considering all the transactions given.

***P15-13 (Treasury Stock—Par Value Method)** Before Polska Corporation engages in the treasury stock transactions listed below, its general ledger reflects, among others, the following account balances (par value of its stock is $30 per share).

Paid-in Capital in Excess of Par	Common Stock	Retained Earnings
Balance $99,000	Balance $270,000	Balance $80,000

Instructions

Record the treasury stock transactions (given below) under the par value method of handling treasury stock.

(a) Bought 380 shares of treasury stock at $39 per share.
(b) Bought 300 shares of treasury stock at $43 per share.
(c) Sold 350 shares of treasury stock at $42 per share.
(d) Sold 120 shares of treasury stock at $38 per share.
(e) Retired the remaining shares in the treasury.

***P15-14 (Cost and Par Value Methods)** John Uteg International, a relatively new corporation, has just become liquid enough to reacquire some of its own $1 par common stock in the market for $45 per share. It decided to repurchase 40,000 shares. The company has 200,000 shares of common stock authorized and 100,000 outstanding. All shares were originally issued at $30 per share. Retained Earnings amounts to $2,420,000. Since John Uteg is only beginning to reacquire its own stock, it has not yet decided how to account for this treasury stock.

As the company's independent auditor, you have been asked by the president, Larry Falcetto, to compare the cost and par value methods, indicating which would provide more valuable, theoretically sound financial information to financial statement users.

Instructions

Using the foregoing data, draft a memo to the president comparing the two methods. Include separate appendixes illustrating the journal entries under each method and the stockholders' equity portion of the balance sheet, referring to these in your memo whenever necessary. Include the balance sheet effect of each method in your discussion. Which would you recommend as the more useful method? Might other considerations enter into your choice?

CONCEPTUAL CASES

C15-1 (Preemptive Rights and Dilution of Ownership) Alvarado Computer Company is a small, closely held corporation. Eighty percent of the stock is held by Eduardo Alvarado, President; of the remainder, 10% is held by members of his family and 10% by Shaunda Jones, a former officer who is now retired. The balance sheet of the company at June 30, 2001, was substantially as shown below:

Assets		Liabilities and Stockholders' Equity	
Cash	$ 22,000	Current liabilities	$ 50,000
Other	450,000	Capital stock	250,000
	$472,000	Retained earnings	172,000
			$472,000

Additional authorized capital stock of $300,000 par value had never been issued. To strengthen the cash position of the company, Eduardo Alvarado issued capital stock with a par value of $100,000 to himself at par for cash. At the next stockholders' meeting, Jones objected and claimed that her interests had been injured.

Instructions

(a) Which stockholder's right was ignored in the issue of shares to Eduardo Alvarado?

(b) How may the damage to Jones' interests be repaired most simply?

(c) If Eduardo Alvarado offered Jones a personal cash settlement and they agreed to employ you as an impartial arbitrator to determine the amount, what settlement would you propose? Present your calculations with sufficient explanation to satisfy both parties.

C15-2 (Subscribed Stock and Subscription Receivable) Apache Corporation sold 50,000 shares of its $10 par value common stock on a subscription basis for $40 per share. By December 31, 2001, collections on these subscriptions totaled $1,300,000. No subscriptions have yet been paid in full.

Instructions

(a) Discuss the meaning of the account Common Stock Subscribed and indicate how it is reported in the financial statements.

(b) Discuss the arguments in favor of reporting Subscriptions Receivable as a current asset.

(c) Discuss the arguments in favor of reporting Subscriptions Receivable as a contra equity account.

(d) Indicate how these 50,000 shares would be presented on Apache's December 31, 2001, balance sheet under the method discussed in (c) above.

C15-3 (Issuance of Stock for Land) Hopee Corporation is planning to issue 3,000 shares of its own $10 par value common stock for 2 acres of land to be used as a building site.

Instructions

(a) What general rule should be applied to determine the amount at which the land should be recorded?

(b) Under what circumstances should this transaction be recorded at the fair market value of the land?

(c) Under what circumstances should this transaction be recorded at the fair market value of the stock issued?

(d) Assume Hopee intentionally records this transaction at an amount greater than the fair market value of the land and the stock. Discuss this situation.

C15-4 (Equipment Purchase with Treasury Stock) Iroquois Corporation purchased $175,000 worth of equipment in 2002 for $100,000 cash and a promise to deliver an indeterminate number of treasury shares of its $5 par common stock, with a market value of $25,000 on January 1 of each year for the next 4 years. Hence $100,000 in "market value" of treasury shares will be required to discharge the $75,000 balance due on the equipment.

The corporation then acquired 5,000 shares of its own stock in the expectation that the market value of the stock would increase substantially before the delivery dates.

Instructions

(a) Discuss the propriety of recording the equipment at

(1) $100,000 (the cash payment).

(2) $175,000 (the cash price of the equipment).

(3) $200,000 (the $100,000 cash payment plus the $100,000 market value of treasury stock that must be transferred to the vendor in order to settle the obligation according to the terms of the agreement).

(b) Discuss the arguments for treating the balance due as
   (1) A liability.
   (2) Treasury stock subscribed.

(c) Assuming that legal requirements do not affect the decision, discuss the arguments for treating the corporation's treasury shares as
   (1) An asset awaiting ultimate disposition.
   (2) A capital element awaiting ultimate disposition.

(AICPA adapted)

C15-5 (Secret Reserves and Watered Stock) It has been said that (1) the use of the LIFO inventory method during an extended period of rising prices and (2) the expensing of all human-resource costs are among the accepted accounting practices that help create "secret reserves."

Instructions

(a) What is a "secret reserve"? How can "secret reserves" be created or enlarged?

(b) What is the basis for saying that the two specific practices cited above tend to create "secret reserves"?

(c) Is it possible to create a "secret reserve" in connection with accounting for a liability? If so, explain or give an example.

(d) What are the objections to the creation of "secret reserves"?

(e) It has also been said that "watered stock" is the opposite of a "secret reserve." What is "watered stock"?

(f) Describe the general circumstances in which "watered stock" can arise.

(g) What steps can be taken to eliminate "water" from a capital structure?

(AICPA adapted)

USING YOUR JUDGMENT

FINANCIAL REPORTING PROBLEM: INTEL CORPORATION

Instructions

Refer to the financial statements and accompanying notes and discussion of Intel Corporation presented in Appendix 5B and answer the following questions.

(a) What is the par or stated value of Intel's preferred stock?

(b) What percentage of Intel's authorized preferred stock was issued at December 26, 1998?

(c) What is the par or stated value of Intel's common stock? Why is the par value so small?

(d) What percentage of Intel's authorized common stock was issued at December 26, 1998?

(e) How many shares of common stock were outstanding at December 26, 1998, and December 27, 1997?

(f) What is the nature and the extent of Intel's common stock repurchase plan? How many shares did Intel repurchase and retire in 1998? What was the effect on stockholders' equity of these stock repurchase and retirements in 1998?

(g) How many shares of common stock were issued in 1998 and for what purposes?

FINANCIAL STATEMENT ANALYSIS CASE

Kellogg Corporation

Kellogg Corporation is the world's leading producer of ready-to-eat cereal products. In recent years the company has taken numerous steps aimed at improving its profitability and earnings per share. Presented below are some basic facts for the Kellogg Corporation.

(all dollars in millions)	1998	1997
Net sales	$6,762	$6,830
Net income	503	546
Total assets	5,052	4,877
Total liabilities	4,162	3,880
Common stock, $.25 par value	104	104
Capital in excess of par value	105	93
Retained earnings	1,368	1,241
Treasury stock, at cost	394	157
Preferred stock	0	0
Number of shares outstanding (in millions)	408	414

Instructions

(a) What are some of the reasons that management purchases its own stock?

(b) Explain how earnings per share might be affected by treasury stock transactions.

(c) Calculate the ratio of debt to total assets for 1997 and 1998 and discuss the implications of the change.

COMPARATIVE ANALYSIS CASE

The Coca-Cola Company versus PepsiCo, Inc.

Instructions

Go to the Digital Tool and, using The Coca-Cola Company and PepsiCo, Inc. Annual Report information, answer the following questions.

(a) What is the par or stated value of Coca-Cola's and PepsiCo's common or capital stock?

(b) What percentage of authorized shares was issued by Coca-Cola at December 31, 1998, and by PepsiCo at December 26, 1998?

(c) How many shares are held as treasury stock by Coca-Cola at December 31, 1998, and by PepsiCo at December 26, 1998?

(d) How many Coca-Cola common shares are outstanding at December 31, 1998? How many PepsiCo shares of capital stock are outstanding at December 26, 1998?

(e) How do Coca-Cola and PepsiCo describe in their balance sheet the amount paid for shares of their common or capital stock in excess of the par value and what are these amounts as of December 31, 1998, and December 26, 1998, for Coca-Cola and PepsiCo respectively?

RESEARCH CASES

Case 1

Instructions

Use EDGAR or some other source to obtain the most recent proxy statement for the company of your choice. Be aware that EDGAR denotes final proxy materials by "DEF 14A," except for election contests ("DEFC14A") and mergers/acquisitions ("DEFM14A"). Examine the proxy statement and answer the following questions. (See bottom of page 263, Research Case 1, for access of EDGAR.)

(a) On what matters are the shareholders being asked to vote?

(b) Where is the annual meeting being held? Must a shareholder attend the annual meeting in order to vote?

(c) For each of the matters up for vote, what information is included in the proxy statement to aid shareholders in making their decisions?

(d) The proxy statement is generally the best source for identifying how company management is compensated. Examine the executive compensation section of the proxy statement and list the types of compensation received.

Case 2

The September 4, 1995, issue of *Fortune* includes an article by Richard D. Hylton entitled "Stock Buybacks Are Hot—Here's How You Can Cash In."

Instructions

Read the article and answer the following questions.

(a) What was the total amount of announced intentions to repurchase shares of stock in 1994? What was this figure during the first six months of 1995?

(b) The goal of many of these repurchase programs was to increase the price of the remaining outstanding shares. Identify the three factors that will determine the impact of repurchases on share price.

(c) What did Microsoft do with the shares it repurchased? Why might they use repurchased shares for this purpose rather than issuing new shares?

ETHICS CASES

Case 1

Morris Lester is the accounting manager of LBC, which is a closely held and rapidly growing retail sporting equipment concern with 60 stores located throughout New York and New England. Morris has been asked by the CFO, Kathy Morgan, to review two agreed-upon alternatives for the purchase of a newly constructed warehouse facility located in Pittsfield, Massachusetts (defined as follows):

Option 1

New Building	$1,500,000	
LBC Common Stock ($100 Par Value)		$1,000,000
Paid-in Capital in Excess of Par		500,000

Option 2

New Building	$1,350,000	
Notes Payable (with Contractor)		$1,200,000
Cash		150,000

In addition to the above facts and figures, Morris knows that LBC would probably prefer the first option because Kathy Morgan told him earlier that, ". . . the company is experiencing tough working capital problems due to its rapid expansion in recent years."

Instructions

(a) Assuming that the value of the new warehouse was independently appraised by a real estate consulting firm at $1.5 million, what are the ethical implications that should be considered by Morris when considering both options?

(b) Assuming that the value of the new warehouse was independently appraised by a real estate consulting firm at $1.35 million, what are the ethical implications that should be considered by Morris when considering both options?

(c) Who could be harmed if LBC chose to inflate its asset values in a "watered stock" transaction?

(d) Explain how your answers to the above questions would change if LBC were a publicly traded corporation.

Case 2

Jean Loptien, president of Sycamore Corporation, is concerned about several large stockholders who have been very vocal lately in their criticisms of her leadership. She thinks they might mount a campaign to have her removed as the corporation's CEO. She decides that buying them out by purchasing their shares could eliminate them as opponents, and she is confident they would accept a "good" offer. Loptien knows the corporation's cash position is decent, so it has the cash to complete the transaction. She also knows the purchase of these shares will increase earnings per share, which should make other investors quite happy.*

Instructions

Answer the following questions:

(a) Who are the stakeholders in this situation?

(b) What are the ethical issues involved?

(c) Should Loptien authorize the transaction?

---

*Earnings per share is calculated by dividing net income available for the common shareholders by the weighted average number of shares outstanding. Therefore, if the number of shares outstanding is decreased by purchasing treasury shares, earnings per share increases.

CHAPTER 16

Stockholders' Equity: Retained Earnings

Splitsville, Where More May Be More

A recent survey of New York Stock Exchange companies shows the increase in the use of stock splits by major companies:[1]

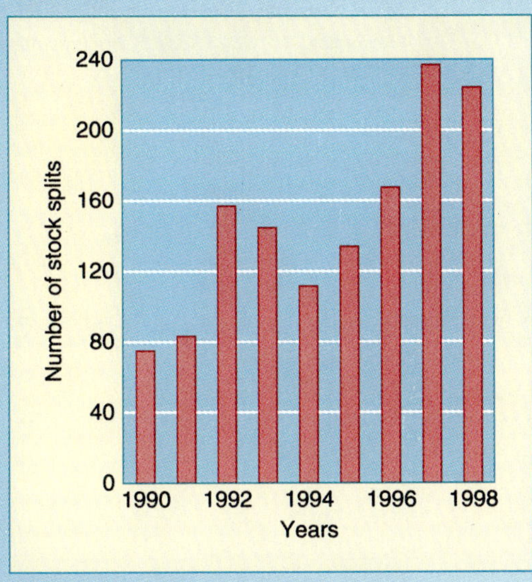

Companies recognize that stock splits may be cosmetic, but investors like them. Although a potential stock division is not sufficient reason to buy a stock, studies have shown that shares that split usually outperform those that don't, as well as the market as a whole, for several years after the split.

A stock split does not boost one's proportionate ownership of a company, yet many investors get a psychological lift from owning more shares. Nor does a stock dividend bolster a corporation's earning prospects, but a dividend boost typically accompanies a split, and this possibility attracts more investors. Also, the lower share price after the stock has split (typically down to the $60–$80 range) invites further buying by small investors. In all, as a Standard & Poor's investment newsletter states, "Companies that declare splits usually are doing well, and management is confident that earnings will continue to trend higher." Investors have seen the results of stock splits and have read them as positive signals.[2]

[1]Data from the New York Stock Exchange.

[2]Adapted from Shirley A. Lazo, "Splitsville, Where More May Be More," *Barron's*, June 3, 1996, p. 60.

LEARNING OBJECTIVES

After studying this chapter, you should be able to:

1. **Describe the policies used in distributing dividends.**
2. **Identify the various forms of dividend distributions.**
3. **Explain the accounting for small and large stock dividends.**
4. **Distinguish between stock dividends and stock splits.**
5. **Explain the effect of different types of preferred stock dividends.**
6. **Identify the reasons for appropriating retained earnings.**
7. **Explain accounting and reporting for appropriated retained earnings.**
8. **Indicate how stockholders' equity is presented and analyzed.**

PREVIEW OF CHAPTER 16

As indicated in the opening story, companies use stock splits and stock dividends to send positive signals to their shareholders. In addition, many companies provide other types of dividend distributions. The purpose of this chapter is to discuss these and other transactions that affect retained earnings. The content and organization of the chapter are as follows:

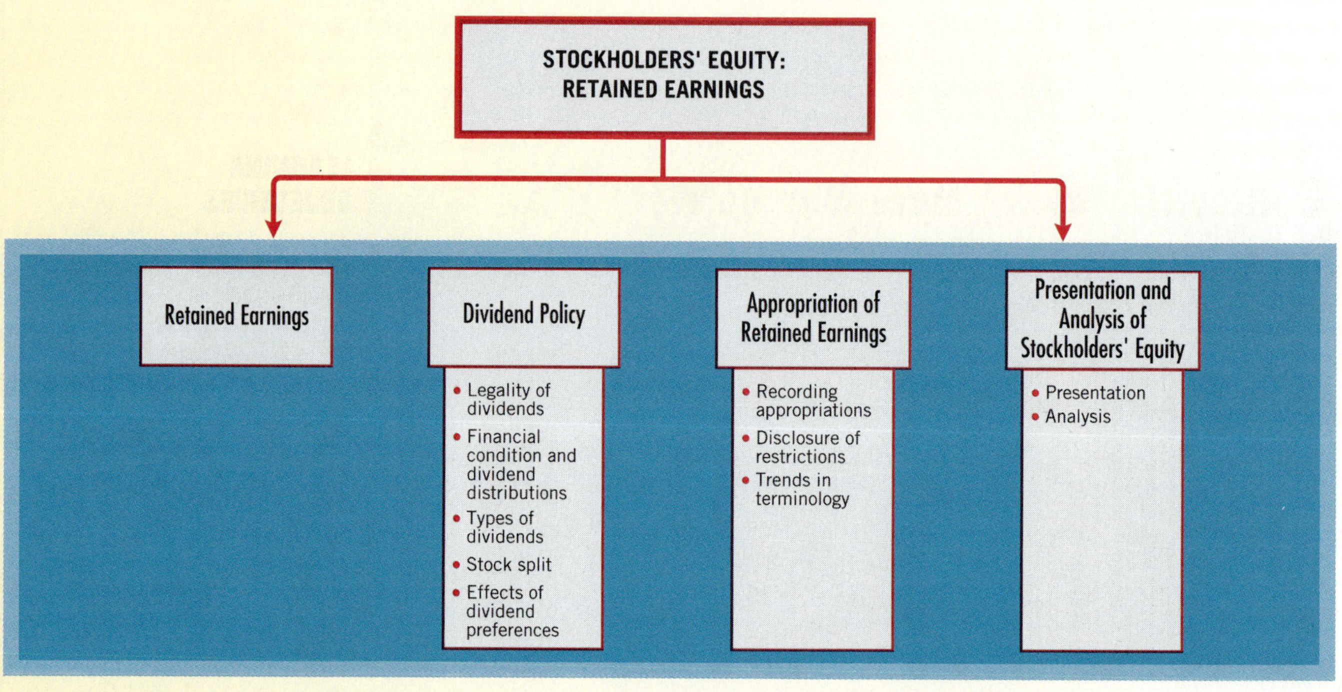

RETAINED EARNINGS

The basic source of **retained earnings**—earnings retained for use in the business—is income from operations. Stockholders assume the greatest risk in enterprise operations and stand any losses or share in any profits resulting from enterprise activities. Any income not distributed among the stockholders thus becomes additional stockholders' equity. Net income includes a considerable variety of income sources. These include the main operation of the enterprise (such as manufacturing and selling a given product), plus any ancillary activities (such as disposing of scrap or renting out unused space), plus the results of extraordinary and unusual items. All give rise to net income that increases retained earnings. The more common items that either increase or decrease retained earnings are expressed in account form below.

ILLUSTRATION 16-1
Transactions that Affect Retained Earnings

Retained Earnings	
1. Net loss	1. Net income
2. Prior period adjustments (error corrections) and certain changes in accounting principle	2. Prior period adjustments (error corrections) and certain changes in accounting principle
3. Cash or scrip dividends	3. Adjustments due to quasi-reorganization
4. Stock dividends	
5. Property dividends	
6. Some treasury stock transactions	

Chapter 4 pointed out that the results of irregular transactions should be reported in the income statement, not the retained earnings statement. However, prior period adjustments (error corrections) should be reported as adjustments to beginning retained earnings, bypassing completely the current income statement.

DIVIDEND POLICY

OBJECTIVE 1
Describe the policies used in distributing dividends.

Determining the proper amount of dividends to pay is a difficult financial management decision. Companies that are paying dividends are extremely reluctant to reduce or eliminate their dividend, because they believe that this action could be viewed negatively by the securities market. As a consequence, companies that have been paying cash dividends will make every effort to continue to do so. In addition, the type of shareholder the company has (taxable or nontaxable, retail investor or institutional investor) plays a large role in determining dividend policy. For example, a nontaxable entity will probably prefer cash dividends rather than a share buyback because tax considerations are not as important. As indicated in Chapter 15, more companies are becoming involved in share buyback programs and are either not starting or not increasing their present dividend program significantly.

Very few companies pay dividends in amounts equal to their legally available retained earnings. The major reasons are as follows:

1. Agreements (bond covenants) with specific creditors to retain all or a portion of the earnings, in the form of assets, to build up additional protection against possible loss.
2. Some state corporation laws require that earnings equivalent to the cost of treasury shares purchased be restricted against dividend declarations.
3. Desire to retain assets that would otherwise be paid out as dividends, to finance growth or expansion. This is sometimes called internal financing, reinvesting earnings, or "plowing" the profits back into the business.
4. Desire to smooth out dividend payments from year to year by accumulating earnings in good years and using such accumulated earnings as a basis for dividends in bad years.
5. Desire to build up a cushion or buffer against possible losses or errors in the calculation of profits.

The reasons above are probably self-explanatory except for the second. The laws of some states require that the corporation's legal capital be restricted from distribution to stockholders so that it may serve as a protection against loss for creditors.[3]

If a company is considering declaring a dividend, two preliminary questions must be asked:

1. Is the condition of the corporation such that a dividend is **legally permissible**?
2. Is the condition of the corporation such that a dividend is **economically sound**?

Legality of Dividends

The legality of a dividend can be determined only by reviewing the applicable state law. Currently, the 50 states may be classified into one of three groups for purposes of comparing restrictions on dividends and other distributions to owners.[4] The largest

---

[3]If the corporation buys its own outstanding stock, it has reduced its legal capital and distributed assets to stockholders. If this were permitted, the corporation could, by purchasing treasury stock at any price desired, return to the stockholders their investments and leave creditors with little or no protection against loss.

[4]Michael L. Roberts, William D. Samson, and Michael T. Dugan, "The Stockholders' Equity Section: Form Without Substance," *Accounting Horizons,* December 1990, pp. 35–46.

group permits distributions to stockholders as long as the corporation is not insolvent. Insolvency is defined as the inability to pay debts as they come due in the normal course of business. Generally, in these states distribution in the form of dividends has to come from retained earnings or from current earnings.

A second group either follows the 1984 Revised Model Business Corporation Act or has distribution restrictions similar to it. That is, (1) the corporation must be solvent, and (2) distributions must not exceed the fair value of net assets. Under the latter criterion, distributions are not limited to retained earnings or GAAP determined current earnings. Instead of being tied to the book value of the assets, distributions are linked to the fair (appraised) value of the assets—a notable new criterion.

The remaining states use a variety of hybrid restrictions that consist of solvency and balance sheet tests of liquidity and risk. To avoid illegal distribution of corporate assets to stockholders, the relevant state corporation act should be examined and legal advice obtained.

Unfortunately, current financial statement disclosures do not include basic information such as: whether a corporation is in compliance with state legal requirements; the corporation's capacity to make distributions; or, occasionally, what legal restrictions exist regarding distributions to stockholders.

An example of the inadequacies of such disclosures is the 1987–88 stockholders' equity balance sheet sections of **Holiday Corporation** (former owner of Holiday Inns of America). Its 1987 balance sheet reported total stockholders' equity of $639 million. The 1988 balance sheet, however, revealed a **$770 million deficit** in Holiday's total stockholders' equity. How did this deficit develop? During the year, Holiday distributed a $65 per share dividend to prevent a hostile takeover. This $1.55 billion dividend to stockholders, financed with borrowed money, not only exceeded Holiday's retained earnings (then about $400 million), but exceeded total stockholders' equity as well by $770 million.

UNDERLYING CONCEPTS

Here is where substance over form is demonstrated. The limitations of the historical cost principle are highlighted by an inability to address the situation.

Holiday was allowed to distribute the $1.55 billion dividend (legally, under Delaware law) because the fair value of its assets exceeded its liabilities after the distribution; that is, on a fair value basis it had positive equity. Yet, the traditional balance sheet disclosures in the equity section or the accompanying notes do not contain any information (either before or after the dividend distribution), enabling financial statement readers to assess Holiday's capacity for making such distributions.

Because the traditional equivalency of minimum legal capital and par value no longer holds in many states, the stockholders' equity accounting presentation of par value, additional paid-in capital, and retained earnings is being eroded. It implies that some amount, represented by a portion of stockholders' equity, exists to protect creditors, when in many instances, it may not.

Financial Condition and Dividend Distributions

Good management of a business requires attention to more than the legality of dividend distributions. Consideration must be given to economic conditions, most importantly, liquidity. Assume an extreme situation as follows:

ILLUSTRATION 16-2
Balance Sheet, Showing a Lack of Liquidity

Balance Sheet			
Plant assets	$500,000	Capital stock	$400,000
		Retained earnings	100,000
	$500,000		$500,000

The depicted company has a retained earnings credit balance and generally, unless it is restricted, can declare a dividend of $100,000. But because all its assets are plant assets and used in operations, payment of a cash dividend of $100,000 would require the sale of plant assets or borrowing.

Even if we assume a balance sheet showing current assets, the question remains as to whether those cash assets are needed for other purposes.

ILLUSTRATION 16-3
Balance Sheet, Showing Cash but Minimal Working Capital

Balance Sheet				
Cash	$100,000	Current liabilities		$ 60,000
Plant assets	460,000	Capital stock	$400,000	
	$560,000	Retained earnings	100,000	500,000
				$560,000

The existence of current liabilities implies very strongly that some of the cash is needed to meet current debts as they mature. In addition, day-by-day cash requirements for payrolls and other expenditures not included in current liabilities also require cash.

Thus, before a dividend is declared, management must consider **availability of funds to pay the dividend**. Other demands for cash should perhaps be investigated by preparing a cash forecast. A dividend should not be paid unless both the present and future financial position appear to warrant the distribution.

Directors must also consider the effect of inflation and replacement costs before making a dividend commitment. During a period of significant inflation, some costs charged to expense under historical cost accounting are understated in terms of comparative purchasing power. Income is thereby overstated because certain costs have not been adjusted for inflation. For example, **St. Regis Paper Company** reported historical cost net income of $179 million, but when it was adjusted for general inflation, net income was only $68 million. Yet St. Regis paid cash dividends of $72 million. Were cash dividends excessive?

The SEC encourages companies to disclose their dividend policy in their annual report. Those that (1) have earnings but fail to pay dividends or (2) do not expect to pay dividends in the forseeable future are encouraged to report this information. In addition, companies that have had a consistent pattern of paying dividends are encouraged to indicate whether they intend to continue this practice in the future.

Two disclosures relative to the policy of payment or nonpayment of dividends are those of **Kellogg Company** and **Atmel Corporation** presented below.

ILLUSTRATION 16-4
Disclosures about Dividend Payment Policy

KELLOGG COMPANY

Dividend News. We are pleased to report that the Kellogg Company dividend rose in 1998 for the 42nd consecutive year, with an increase of 5 cents per share to $.92.

ATMEL CORPORATION

Dividend Policy. The Company has not paid any dividends on its capital stock. The Company presently intends to retain any earnings for use in business and therefore does not anticipate paying cash dividends on its outstanding shares in the foreseeable future. In addition, the Company's bank credit agreement restricts the Company's ability to pay cash dividends without the bank's consent.

Types of Dividends

OBJECTIVE 2
Identify the various forms of dividend distributions.

Dividend distributions generally are based either on accumulated profits, that is, retained earnings, or on some other capital item such as additional paid-in capital. The natural expectation of any stockholder who receives a dividend is that the corporation has operated successfully and that he or she is receiving a share of its profits. A **liquidating dividend**—that is, a dividend not based on retained earnings—should be adequately described in the accompanying message to the stockholders so that there will be no misunderstanding about its source. Dividends are of the following types:

1. Cash dividends.
2. Property dividends.
3. Scrip dividends.
4. Liquidating dividends.
5. Stock dividends.

Dividends are commonly paid in cash but occasionally are paid in stock, scrip, or some other asset.[5] **All dividends, except for stock dividends, reduce the total stockholders' equity in the corporation,** because the equity is reduced either through an immediate or promised future distribution of assets. When a stock dividend is declared, the corporation does not pay out assets or incur a liability. It issues additional shares of stock to each stockholder and nothing more.

Cash Dividends

The board of directors votes on the declaration of **cash dividends**, and if the resolution is properly approved, the dividend is declared. Before it is paid, a current list of stockholders must be prepared. For this reason there is usually a time lag between declaration and payment. A resolution approved at the January 10 (**date of declaration**) meeting of the board of directors might be declared payable February 5 (**date of payment**) to all stockholders of record January 25 (**date of record**).[6]

The period from January 10 to January 25 gives time for any transfers in process to be completed and registered with the transfer agent. The time from January 25 to February 5 provides an opportunity for the transfer agent or accounting department, depending on who does this work, to prepare a list of stockholders as of January 25 and to prepare and mail dividend checks.

A declared cash dividend is a liability and, because payment is generally required very soon, is usually a current liability. The following entries are required to record the declaration and payment of an ordinary dividend payable in cash. For example, Roadway Freight Corp. on June 10 declared a cash dividend of 50 cents a share on 1.8 million shares payable July 16 to all stockholders of record June 24.

At date of declaration (June 10)		
Retained Earnings (Cash Dividends Declared)	900,000	
Dividends Payable		900,000
At date of record (June 24)		
No entry		
At date of payment (July 16)		
Dividends Payable	900,000	
Cash		900,000

To set up a ledger account that shows the amount of dividends declared during the year, Cash Dividends Declared might be debited instead of Retained Earnings at the time of declaration. This account is then closed to Retained Earnings at year-end.

[5] *Accounting Trends and Techniques—1999* reported that of its 600 surveyed companies, 435 paid a cash dividend on common stock, 83 paid a cash dividend on preferred stock, 9 issued stock dividends, and 10 issued or paid dividends in kind. Some companies declare more than one type of dividend in a given year.

[6] Theoretically, the ex-dividend date is the day after the date of record. However, to allow time for transfer of the shares, the stock exchanges generally advance the ex-dividend date 2 to 4 days. Therefore, the party who owns the stock on the day prior to the expressed ex-dividend date receives the dividends, and the party who buys the stock on and after the ex-dividend date does not receive the dividend. Between the declaration date and the ex-dividend date, the market price of the stock includes the dividend.

Dividends may be declared either as a certain percent of par, such as a 6% dividend on preferred stock, or as an amount per share, such as 60 cents per share on no-par common stock. In the first case, the rate is multiplied by the par value of outstanding shares to get the total dividend; in the second, the amount per share is multiplied by the number of shares outstanding. **Cash dividends are not declared and paid on treasury stock.**

As a less preferred but still allowable treatment, international accounting standards permit firms to reduce equity by the amount of proposed dividends prior to their legal declaration.

Dividend policies vary among corporations. Some older, well-established firms take pride in a long, unbroken string of quarterly dividend payments. They would lower or pass the dividend only if forced to do so by a sustained decline in earnings or a critical shortage of cash.

"Growth" companies, on the other hand, pay little or no cash dividends because their policy is to expand as rapidly as internal and external financing permit. Neither **Quest Medical, Inc.**, a small growth company, nor **Federal Express Corporation,** a large growth company, has ever paid cash dividends to their common stockholders. These investors hope that the price of their shares will appreciate in value and that they will realize a profit when they sell their shares. As indicated earlier, many companies are less concerned with dividend payout, and more focused on increasing share price, stock repurchase programs, and corporate earnings.

Property Dividends

Dividends payable in assets of the corporation other than cash are called **property dividends** or **dividends in kind**. Property dividends may be merchandise, real estate, or investments, or whatever form the board of directors designates. **Ranchers Exploration and Development Corp.** reported one year that it would pay a fourth-quarter dividend in gold bars instead of cash. Because of the obvious difficulties of divisibility of units and delivery to stockholders, the usual property dividend is in the form of securities of other companies that the distributing corporation holds as an investment.

For example, when **DuPont**'s 23% stock interest in **General Motors** was held by the Supreme Court to be in violation of antitrust laws, DuPont was ordered to divest itself of the GM stock within 10 years. The stock represented 63 million shares of GM's 281 million shares then outstanding. DuPont couldn't sell the shares in one block of 63 million, nor could it sell 6 million shares annually for the next 10 years without severely depressing the value of the GM stock. At that time the entire yearly trading volume in GM stock did not exceed 6 million shares. DuPont solved its problem by declaring a property dividend and distributing the GM shares as a dividend to its own stockholders.

Dresser Industries, Inc. distributed a dividend in kind and reported its accounting for the distribution as follows:

DRESSER INDUSTRIES, INC.

Notes to Consolidated Financial Statements

Note B: Dividend in Kind. The Company divested its industrial products and equipment businesses. The divestiture/spin-off was accomplished by a distribution of one INDRESCO share for every five shares of the Company's common stock. The distribution is included as charges totaling $413.9 million to retained earnings and accumulated translation adjustment in the statement of shareholders' investment.

ILLUSTRATION 16-5
Disclosure of a Dividend in Kind

A property dividend is a nonreciprocal transfer[7] of nonmonetary assets between an enterprise and its owners. Prior to the issuance of *APB Opinion No. 29,* the accounting for such transfers was based on the carrying amount (book value) of the non-

[7] A nonreciprocal transfer of assets or services is in one direction, either from or to an enterprise.

monetary assets transferred. This practice was based on the rationale that there is no sale or arm's-length transaction on which to base a gain or loss and that only this method is consistent with the historical cost basis of accounting. However, the profession's current position is quite clear on this matter:

> A transfer of a nonmonetary asset to a stockholder or to another entity in a nonreciprocal transfer should be recorded at the fair value of the asset transferred, and a gain or loss should be recognized on the disposition of the asset.[8]

The **fair value** of the nonmonetary asset distributed is measured by the amount that would be realizable in an outright sale at or near the time of the distribution. Such an amount should be determined by referring to estimated realizable values in cash transactions of the same or similar assets, quoted market prices, independent appraisals, and other available evidence.[9]

The failure to recognize the fair value of nonmonetary assets transferred may both misstate the dividend and fail to recognize gains and losses on nonmonetary assets that have already been earned or incurred by the enterprise. Recording the dividend at fair value permits future comparisons of dividend rates. If cash must be distributed to stockholders in place of the nonmonetary asset, determination of the amount to be distributed is simplified.

When the property dividend is declared, the corporation should **restate at fair value the property to be distributed, recognizing any gain or loss** as the difference between the property's fair value and carrying value at date of declaration. The declared dividend may then be recorded as a debit to Retained Earnings (or Property Dividends Declared) and a credit to Property Dividends Payable at an amount equal to the fair value of the property to be distributed. Upon distribution of the dividend, Property Dividends Payable is debited, and the account containing the distributed asset (restated at fair value) is credited.

For example, Trendler, Inc., transferred to stockholders some of its investments in marketable securities costing $1,250,000 by declaring a property dividend on December 28, 2000, to be distributed on January 30, 2001, to stockholders of record on January 15, 2001. At the date of declaration the securities have a market value of $2,000,000. The entries are as follows:

At date of declaration (December 28, 2000)		
Investments in Securities	750,000	
Gain on Appreciation of Securities		750,000
Retained Earnings (Property Dividends Declared)	2,000,000	
Property Dividends Payable		2,000,000
At date of distribution (January 30, 2001)		
Property Dividends Payable	2,000,000	
Investments in Securities		2,000,000

Scrip Dividends

A **scrip dividend**—dividend payable in scrip—means that instead of paying the dividend now, the corporation has elected to pay it at some later date. **The scrip issued to stockholders as a dividend is merely a special form of note payable.** For example, at one time the Bank of Puerto Rico issued a $9 million note as a dividend that matured ten years later, at which time each holder of the corporation's 3 million common shares

[8]"Accounting for Nonmonetary Transactions," *Opinions of the Accounting Principles Board No. 29* (New York: AICPA, 1973), par. 18.

[9]According to *APB Opinion No. 29*, accounting for the distribution of nonmonetary assets to owners of an enterprise in a spin-off or other form of reorganization or liquidation should be based on the **book value** (after reduction, if appropriate, for an indicated impairment of value) of the nonmonetary assets distributed. This is an exception to the fair value treatment prescribed for nonmonetary distributions.

received $3 a share. Scrip dividends may be declared when the corporation has a sufficient retained earnings balance but is short of cash. The recipient of the scrip dividend may hold it until the due date, if one is specified, and collect the dividend or may sell it to obtain immediate cash.

When a scrip dividend is declared, the corporation debits Retained Earnings (or Scrip Dividend Declared) and credits Scrip Dividend Payable or Notes Payable to Stockholders, **reporting the payable as a liability** on the balance sheet. Upon payment, Scrip Dividend Payable is debited and Cash credited. If the scrip bears interest, the interest portion of the cash payment should be debited to Interest Expense and not treated as part of the dividend. For example, Berg Canning Company avoided missing its 84th consecutive quarterly dividend by declaring on May 27 a scrip dividend in the form of two-month promissory notes amounting to 80 cents a share on 2,545,000 shares outstanding and payable at the date of record, June 5. The notes paid interest of 10% per annum and matured on July 27. The entries are as follows:

At date of declaration (May 27)		
Retained Earnings (Scrip Dividend Declared)	2,036,000	
Notes Payable to Stockholders ($.80 × 2,545,000)		2,036,000
At date of payment (July 27)		
Notes Payable to Stockholders	2,036,000	
Interest Expense ($2,036,000 × 2/12 × .10)[a]	33,933	
Cash		2,069,933

[a]The interest runs from the date of declaration to the date of payment.

Liquidating Dividends

Some corporations use paid-in capital as a basis for dividends. Without proper disclosure of this fact, stockholders may erroneously believe the corporation has been operating at a profit. A further result could be subsequent sale of additional shares at a higher price than is warranted. This type of deception, intentional or unintentional, can be avoided by requiring that a clear statement of the source of every dividend accompany the dividend check.

Dividends based on other than retained earnings are sometimes described as **liquidating dividends**, thus implying that they are a return of the stockholder's investment rather than of profits. In other words, **any dividend not based on earnings is a reduction of corporate paid-in capital and, to that extent, it is a liquidating dividend**. We noted in Chapter 11 that companies in the extractive industries may pay dividends equal to the total of accumulated income and depletion. The portion of these dividends in excess of accumulated income represents a return of part of the stockholder's investment.

For example, McChesney Mines Inc. issued a "dividend" to its common stockholders of $1,200,000. The cash dividend announcement noted that $900,000 should be considered income and the remainder a return of capital. The entries are:

At date of declaration		
Retained Earnings	900,000	
Additional Paid-in Capital	300,000	
Dividends Payable		1,200,000
At date of payment		
Dividends Payable	1,200,000	
Cash		1,200,000

In some cases, management may simply decide to cease business and declare a liquidating dividend. In these cases, liquidation may take place over a number of years to ensure an orderly and fair sale of assets. For example, when **Overseas National Airways** was dissolved, it agreed to pay a liquidating dividend to its stockholders over a period of years equivalent to $8.60 per share. Each liquidating dividend payment in such cases reduces paid-in capital.

Stock Dividends

If the management wishes to "capitalize" part of the earnings (i.e., reclassify amounts from earned to contributed capital), and thus retain earnings in the business on a permanent basis, it may issue a stock dividend. In this case, **no assets are distributed**, and each stockholder has exactly the same proportionate interest in the corporation and the same total book value after the stock dividend was issued as before it was declared. Of course, the book value per share is lower because an increased number of shares is held.

While accountants agree that a **stock dividend** is the nonreciprocal issuance by a corporation of its own stock to its stockholders on a pro rata basis, they do not agree on the proper entries to be made at the time of a stock dividend. Some believe that the **par value** of the stock issued as a dividend should be transferred from retained earnings to capital stock. Others believe that the **fair value** of the stock issued—its market value at the declaration date—should be transferred from retained earnings to capital stock and additional paid-in capital.

UNDERLYING CONCEPTS

If the intent of the CAP was to punish companies that used stock dividends by requiring fair value, it violated the neutrality concept; that is, that standard-setting should be even-handed.

The fair value position was originally adopted in this country, at least in part, in order to influence the stock dividend policies of corporations. Evidently in 1941 both the New York Stock Exchange and a majority of the Committee on Accounting Procedure (CAP) regarded periodic stock dividends as objectionable. The CAP therefore acted to make it more difficult for corporations to sustain a series of such stock dividends out of their accumulated earnings by requiring the use of fair market value when it was substantially in excess of book value.[10]

OBJECTIVE 3
Explain the accounting for small and large stock dividends.

When the stock dividend is less than 20–25% of the common shares outstanding at the time of the dividend declaration, the accounting profession requires that the **fair market value** of the stock issued be transferred from retained earnings.[11] Stock dividends of less than 20–25% are often referred to as **small (ordinary) stock dividends**. This method of handling stock dividends is justified on the grounds that "many recipients of stock dividends look upon them as distributions of corporate earnings and usually in an amount equivalent to the fair value of the additional shares received."[12] We do not consider this a convincing argument. It is generally agreed that stock dividends are not income to the recipients, and, therefore, sound accounting should not recommend procedures simply because some recipients think they are income.[13]

To illustrate a small stock dividend, assume that a corporation has outstanding 1,000 shares of $100 par value capital stock and retained earnings of $50,000. If the cor-

---

[10]This represented perhaps the earliest instance of an accounting pronouncement being affected by "economic consequences," because the Committee on Accounting Procedure described its action as being required by "proper accounting and corporate policy." See Stephen A. Zeff, "The Rise of 'Economic Consequences,'" *The Journal of Accountancy*, December 1978, pp. 53–66.

[11]American Institute of Certified Public Accountants, *Accounting Research and Terminology Bulletins*, No. 43 (New York: AICPA, 1961), Ch. 7, par. 10. A minor exception is that if the stock dividend is used to increase the marketability of the shares, par value may be used.

[12]Ibid., par. 10. One study concluded that *small* stock dividends do not always produce significant amounts of extra value on the date after issuance (ex date) and that *large* stock dividends almost always fail to generate extra value on the ex-dividend date. Taylor W. Foster III and Don Vickrey, "The Information Content of Stock Dividend Announcements," *The Accounting Review*, Vol. LIII, No. 2, April 1978, pp. 360–370.

[13]The case against treating an ordinary stock dividend as income is supported under either an **entity** or **proprietary assumption** regarding the business enterprise. If the corporation is considered an entity separate from the stockholders, the income of the corporation is corporate income and not income to the stockholders, although the equity of the stockholders in the corporation increases. This position argues that a dividend is not income to the recipients until it is realized by them as a result of a division or severance of corporate assets. The stock dividend merely distributes the "recipients'" equity over a larger number of shares. Under this interpretation, selling the stock received as a dividend has the effect of reducing the recipients' proportionate share of the corporation's equity. Under the proprietary assumption, income of the corporation is considered income to the owners, and, hence, a stock dividend represents only a reclassification of equity, inasmuch as there is no change in total proprietorship.

poration declares a 10% stock dividend, it issues 100 additional shares to current stockholders. If it is assumed that the fair value of the stock at the time of the stock dividend is $130 per share, the entry is:

At date of declaration

Retained Earnings (Stock Dividend Declared)	13,000	
Common Stock Dividend Distributable		10,000
Paid-in Capital in Excess of Par		3,000

INTERNATIONAL INSIGHT

Revaluation of assets is likely to result in revaluation capital. Such capital is available as the basis for stock dividends in some countries and for cash dividends in others. Some countries require the accumulation of such capital but do not permit it to be used as the basis for either form of dividend.

Note that no asset or liability has been affected. The entry merely reflects a reclassification of stockholders' equity. If a balance sheet is prepared between the dates of declaration and distribution, the common stock dividend distributable should be shown in the stockholders' equity section as an addition to capital stock (whereas cash or property dividends payable are shown as current liabilities).

When the stock is issued, the entry is

At date of distribution

Common Stock Dividend Distributable	10,000	
Common Stock		10,000

No matter what the fair value is at the time of the stock dividend, each stockholder retains the same proportionate interest in the corporation.

Some state statutes specifically prohibit the issuance of stock dividends on treasury stock. In those states that permit treasury shares to participate in the distribution accompanying a stock dividend or stock split, practice is influenced by the planned use of the treasury shares. For example, if the treasury shares are intended for issuance in connection with employee stock options, the treasury shares may participate in the distribution because the number of shares under option is usually adjusted for any stock dividends or splits. But unless there are specific uses for the treasury stock, no useful purpose is served by issuing additional shares to the treasury stock since they are essentially equivalent to authorized but unissued shares.

ILLUSTRATION 16-6
Effects of a Small (10%) Stock Dividend

Before dividend:	
Capital stock, 1,000 shares of $100 par	$100,000
Retained earnings	50,000
Total stockholders' equity	$150,000
Stockholders' interests:	
A. 400 shares, 40% interest, book value	$ 60,000
B. 500 shares, 50% interest, book value	75,000
C. 100 shares, 10% interest, book value	15,000
	$150,000
After declaration but before distribution of 10% stock dividend:	
If fair value ($130) is used as basis for entry	
Capital stock, 1,000 shares at $100 par	$100,000
Common stock distributable, 100 shares at $100 par	10,000
Paid-in capital in excess of par	3,000
Retained earnings ($50,000 − $13,000)	37,000
Total stockholders' equity	$150,000
After declaration and distribution of 10% stock dividend:	
If fair value ($130) is used as basis for entry	
Capital stock, 1,100 shares at $100 par	$110,000
Paid-in capital in excess of par	3,000
Retained earnings ($50,000 − $13,000)	37,000
Total stockholders' equity	$150,000
Stockholders' interest:	
A. 440 shares, 40% interest, book value	$ 60,000
B. 550 shares, 50% interest, book value	75,000
C. 110 shares, 10% interest, book value	15,000
	$150,000

To continue with our example of the effect of the small stock dividend, note in Illustration 16-6 on page 821 that the total stockholders' equity has not changed as a result of the stock dividend. Also note that the proportion of the total shares outstanding held by each stockholder is unchanged.

Stock Split

If a company has undistributed earnings over several years and a sizable balance in retained earnings has accumulated, the market value of its outstanding shares is likely to increase. Stock that was issued at prices less than $50 a share can easily attain a market value in excess of $200 a share. The higher the market price of a stock, the less readily it can be purchased by some investors. The managements of many corporations believe that for better public relations, wider ownership of the corporation stock is desirable. They wish, therefore, to have a market price sufficiently low to be within range of the majority of potential investors. To reduce the market value of shares, the common device of a **stock split** is employed.[14] For example, after its stock price increased by 25-fold during 1999, **Qualcomm Inc.** split its stock 4-for-1. Qualcomm's stock had risen above $500 per share, raising concerns that Qualcomm could not meet an analyst target of $1,000 per share. The split reduced the analysts' target to $250, which could better be met with wider distribution of shares at lower trading prices.[15]

From an accounting standpoint, **no entry is recorded for a stock split**; a memorandum note, however, is made to indicate that the par value of the shares has changed, and that the number of shares has increased. The lack of change in stockholders' equity is portrayed in Illustration 16-7 of a 2-for-1 stock split on 1,000 shares of $100 par value stock with the par being halved upon issuance of the additional shares:

ILLUSTRATION 16-7
Effects of a Stock Split

Stockholders' Equity before 2-for-1 Split		Stockholders' Equity after 2-for-1 Split	
Common stock, 1,000 shares at $100 par	$100,000	Common stock, 2,000 shares at $50 par	$100,000
Retained earnings	50,000	Retained earnings	50,000
	$150,000		$150,000

Stock Split and Stock Dividend Differentiated

OBJECTIVE 4
Distinguish between stock dividends and stock splits.

From a legal standpoint a stock split is distinguished from a stock dividend, because a stock split results in an increase in the number of shares outstanding and a corresponding decrease in the par or stated value per share. **A stock dividend, although it results in an increase in the number of shares outstanding, does not decrease the par value; thus it increases the total par value of outstanding shares.**

The reasons for issuing a stock dividend are numerous and varied. Stock dividends can be more of a publicity gesture, because they are considered by many as dividends

[14]The *DH&S Review,* May 12, 1986, page 7, listed the following as reasons behind a stock split:

1. To adjust the market price of the company's shares to a level where more individuals can afford to invest in the stock.
2. To spread the stockholder base by increasing the number of shares outstanding and making them more marketable.
3. To benefit existing stockholders by allowing them to take advantage of an imperfect market adjustment following the split.

[15]Some companies use reverse stock splits. A **reverse stock split** reduces the number of shares outstanding and increases the per share price. This technique is used when the stock price is unusually low or when management wishes to take control of the company. For example, two officers of **Metropolitan Maintenance Co.** took their company private by forcing a 1-for-3,000 reverse stock split on their stockholders. For every 3,000 old shares, one new share was issued. But anyone who had fewer than 3,000 shares received only cash for his or her stock. Only the two officers owned more than 3,000 shares, so they now own all the stock. A nice squeeze play! *Forbes,* November 19, 1984, p. 54.

and, consequently, the corporation is not criticized for retention of profits. Some corporations even lead their stockholders to believe that a stock dividend is equivalent to a cash dividend. For instance, the Board of Directors of **Wickes Companies Inc.** declared a 2½% stock dividend "in lieu of the quarterly cash dividend, which had been 26¢ per share." E. L. McNeely, chairman of Wickes, said, "This dividend continues Wickes' 88-year record of uninterrupted dividend payments." More defensible perhaps, the corporation may simply wish to retain profits in the business by capitalizing a part of retained earnings. In such a situation, a transfer is made on declaration of a stock dividend from earned capital to contributed or permanent capital.

A stock dividend, like a stock split, also may be used to increase the marketability of the stock, although marketability is often a secondary consideration. If the stock dividend is large, it has the same effect on market price as a stock split. The profession has taken the position that **whenever additional shares are issued for the purpose of reducing the unit market price, then the distribution more closely resembles a stock split than a stock dividend. This effect usually results only if the number of shares issued is more than 20–25% of the number of shares previously outstanding.**[16] A stock dividend of more than 20–25% of the number of shares previously outstanding is called a **large stock dividend**.[17] The profession also recommends that such a distribution not be called a stock dividend, but it might properly be called "a split-up effected in the form of a dividend" or "stock split." Also, since the par value of the outstanding shares is not altered, the transfer from retained earnings is only in the amount required by statute. Ordinarily this means a transfer from retained earnings to capital stock **for the par value of the stock issued** as opposed to a transfer of the market value of the shares issued as in the case of a small stock dividend.[18] For example, **Brown Group, Inc.** at one time authorized a 2-for-1 split, effected in the form of a stock dividend. As a result of this authorization, approximately 10.5 million shares were distributed and more than $39 million representing the par value of the shares issued was transferred from Retained Earnings to the Common Stock account.

To illustrate a large stock dividend (stock split-up effected in the form of a dividend), Rockland Steel, Inc. declared a 30% stock dividend on November 20, payable December 29 to stockholders of record December 12. At the date of declaration, 1,000,000 shares, par value $10, are outstanding and with a fair market value of $200 per share. The entries are:

At date of declaration (November 20)

Retained Earnings		3,000,000	
Common Stock Dividend Distributable			3,000,000
Computation: 1,000,000 shares	300,000 Additional shares		
× 30%	× $10 Par value		
300,000	$3,000,000		

At date of distribution (December 29)

Common Stock Dividend Distributable	3,000,000	
Common Stock		3,000,000

Illustration 16-8 summarizes and compares the effects of various types of dividends and stock splits on various elements of the financial statements:

---

[16] *Accounting Research and Terminology Bulletin No. 43*, par. 13.

[17] The SEC has added more precision to the 20–25% rule. Specifically, the SEC indicates that distributions of 25% or more should be considered a "split-up effected in the form of a dividend." Distributions of less than 25% should be accounted for as a stock dividend. The SEC more precisely defined GAAP here, and as a result the SEC rule is followed by public companies.

[18] Often, a split-up effected in the form of a dividend is debited to paid-in capital instead of retained earnings to indicate that this transaction should affect only paid-in capital accounts. No reduction of retained earnings is required except as indicated by legal requirements. For homework purposes, assume that the debit is to Retained Earnings. See, for example, Taylor W. Foster III and Edmund Scribner, "Accounting for Stock Dividends and Stock Splits: Corrections to Textbook Coverage," *Issues in Accounting Education*, February 1998.

ILLUSTRATION 16-8
Effects of Dividends and Stock Splits on Financial Statement Elements

Effect on:	Declaration of Cash Dividend	Payment of Cash Dividend	Declaration and Distribution of Small Stock Dividend	Declaration and Distribution of Large Stock Dividend	Stock Split
Retained earnings	Decrease	–0–	Decrease[a]	Decrease[b]	–0–
Capital stock	–0–	–0–	Increase[b]	Increase[b]	–0–
Additional paid-in capital	–0–	–0–	Increase[c]	–0–	–0–
Total stockholders' equity	Decrease	–0–	–0–	–0–	–0–
Working capital	Decrease	–0–	–0–	–0–	–0–
Total assets	–0–	Decrease	–0–	–0–	–0–
Number of shares outstanding	–0–	–0–	Increase	Increase	Increase

[a]Market value of shares. [b]Par or stated value of shares. [c]Excess of market value over par.

OBJECTIVE 5
Explain the effect of different types of preferred stock dividends.

Effects of Dividend Preferences

The examples given below illustrate the **effects of** various **dividend preferences** on dividend distributions to common and preferred stockholders. Assume that in a given year, $50,000 is to be distributed as cash dividends, outstanding common stock has a par value of $400,000, and 6% preferred stock has a par value of $100,000. Dividends would be distributed to each class as shown below, employing the assumptions given.

1. If the preferred stock is noncumulative and nonparticipating:

ILLUSTRATION 16-9
Dividend Distribution, Noncumulative and Nonparticipating Preferred

	Preferred	Common	Total
6% of $100,000	$6,000		$ 6,000
The remainder to common		$44,000	44,000
Totals	$6,000	$44,000	$50,000

2. If the preferred stock is cumulative and nonparticipating, and dividends were not paid on the preferred stock in the preceding 2 years:

ILLUSTRATION 16-10
Dividend Distribution, Cumulative and Nonparticipating Preferred, with Dividends in Arrears

	Preferred	Common	Total
Dividends in arrears, 6% of $100,000 for 2 years	$12,000		$12,000
Current year's dividend, 6% of $100,000	6,000		6,000
The remainder to common		$32,000	32,000
Totals	$18,000	$32,000	$50,000

3. If the preferred stock is noncumulative and is fully participating:[19]

[19]When preferred stock is participating, there may be different agreements as to how the participation feature is to be executed. However, in the absence of any specific agreement the following procedure is recommended:

a. After the preferred stock is assigned its current year's dividend, the common stock will receive a "like" percentage of par value outstanding. In example (3), this amounts to 6% of $400,000.
b. If there is a remainder of declared dividends for participation by the preferred and common stock, this remainder will be shared in proportion to the par value dollars outstanding in each class of stock. In example (3) this proportion is:

$$\text{Preferred } \frac{\$100{,}000}{\$500{,}000} \times \$20{,}000 = \$4{,}000$$

$$\text{Common } \frac{\$400{,}000}{\$500{,}000} \times \$20{,}000 = \$16{,}000$$

	Preferred	Common	Total
Current year's dividend, 6%	$ 6,000	$24,000	$30,000
Participating dividend of 4%	4,000	16,000	20,000
Totals	$10,000	$40,000	$50,000

The participating dividend was determined as follows:		
Current year's dividend:		
Preferred, 6% of $100,000 =	$ 6,000	
Common, 6% of $400,000 =	24,000	$ 30,000
Amount available for participation ($50,000 − $30,000)		$ 20,000
Par value of stock that is to participate ($100,000 + $400,000)		$500,000
Rate of participation ($20,000 ÷ $500,000)		4%
Participating dividend:		
Preferred, 4% of $100,000		$ 4,000
Common, 4% of $400,000		16,000
		$ 20,000

ILLUSTRATION 16-11
Dividend Distribution, Noncumulative and Fully Participating Preferred

4 If the preferred stock is cumulative and is fully participating, and if dividends were not paid on the preferred stock in the preceding 2 years (the same procedure as described in example (3) is used in this example to effect the participation feature):

	Preferred	Common	Total
Dividends in arrears, 6% of $100,000 for 2 years	$12,000		$12,000
Current year's dividend, 6%	6,000	$24,000	30,000
Participating dividend, 1.6% ($8,000 ÷ $500,000)	1,600	6,400	8,000
Totals	$19,600	$30,400	$50,000

ILLUSTRATION 16-12
Dividend Distribution, Cumulative and Fully Participating Preferred, with Dividends in Arrears

APPROPRIATION OF RETAINED EARNINGS

OBJECTIVE 6
Identify the reasons for appropriating retained earnings.

The act of appropriating retained earnings is a policy matter requiring approval by the board of directors. According to *FASB Statement No. 5,* the appropriation of retained earnings is acceptable practice, "provided that it is shown within the stockholders' equity section of the balance sheet and is clearly identified as an appropriation of retained earnings."[20]

Appropriation of retained earnings is **nothing more than reclassification of retained earnings for a specific purpose**. An appropriation does not set aside cash: It discloses that management does not intend to distribute assets as a dividend up to the amount of the appropriation because these assets are needed by the corporation for a specified purpose. The unappropriated retained earnings is debited (reduced) by the amount of the appropriation, and a new account for the specific purpose is established and credited for the transferred amount. When the appropriation is no longer necessary, either because the specific purpose has been accomplished or the loss has occurred or because it no longer appears as a possibility, the appropriation should be returned to unappropriated retained earnings. In accordance with *FASB Statement No. 5,* **"costs or losses shall not be charged to an appropriation of retained earnings, and no part of the appropriation shall be transferred to income."**[21]

[20]"Accounting for Contingencies," *Statement of Financial Accounting Standards No. 5* (Stamford, Conn.: FASB, March 1975), par. 15.

[21]Ibid., par. 15.

INTERNATIONAL INSIGHT

In some nations, companies are legally required to create reserves (appropriations) for creditor protection. They must allocate profits to reserves at a specified annual rate until the amount of the required reserve is accumulated.

Various reasons are advanced for appropriations of retained earnings. These include:

1. **Legal restrictions.** As indicated earlier, some state laws prohibit the purchase of treasury stock by the corporation unless earnings available for dividends are present. Retained earnings in an amount equal to the cost of any treasury stock acquired are restricted. Earnings must be retained to substitute for capital stock temporarily acquired as treasury stock.
2. **Contractual restrictions.** Bond indentures frequently contain a requirement that retained earnings in specified amounts be appropriated each year during the life of the bonds. The appropriation created under such a provision is commonly called Appropriation for Sinking Fund or Appropriation for Bonded Indebtedness.
3. **Existence of possible or expected loss.** Appropriations might be established for estimated losses due to lawsuits, unfavorable contractual obligations, and other contingencies.
4. **Protection of working capital position.** The board of directors may authorize the creation of an "Appropriation for Working Capital" out of retained earnings in order to indicate that the amount specified is not available for dividends because it is desirable to maintain a strong current position. Another example involves a decision made to finance a building program by internal financing. An "Appropriation for Plant Expansion" is created to indicate that retained earnings in the amount appropriated will not be considered by the directors as available for dividends.

Some corporations establish appropriations for general contingencies, or appropriate retained earnings for unspecified purposes. In some cases this is justified by statutory or contractual restrictions. In other cases no adequate explanation for such actions is available. The FASB does not encourage the establishment of general or unspecified appropriations.

Recording Appropriation of Retained Earnings

OBJECTIVE 7
Explain accounting and reporting for appropriated retained earnings.

When a company records an appropriation in the accounts, the unappropriated retained earnings must be reduced by the amount of the appropriation and a new account must be established to receive the amount transferred. The new account Appropriated Retained Earnings is simply a subclassification of total retained earnings. If the appropriation merely augments a previously established amount, the account already in use should receive the credit. The appropriation is recorded as a debit to Retained Earnings and a credit to an appropriately named account that itself is just a subdivision of retained earnings. For example:

(a) An Appropriation for Plant Expansion is to be created by transfer from Retained Earnings of $400,000 a year for 5 years. The entry for each year would be:

Retained Earnings	400,000	
Retained Earnings Appropriated for Plant Expansion		400,000

(b) At the end of 5 years the appropriation would have a balance of $2,000,000. If we assume that the expansion plan has been completed, the appropriation is no longer required and can be returned to retained earnings.

Retained Earnings Appropriated for Plant Expansion	2,000,000	
Retained Earnings		2,000,000

Return of such an appropriation to retained earnings has the effect of increasing unappropriated retained earnings considerably without affecting the assets or current position. In effect, over the 5 years the company has expanded by reinvesting assets acquired through the earnings process.

Disclosure of Restrictions on Retained Earnings

In many corporations restrictions on retained earnings or dividends exist, but no formal journal entries are made. Such restrictions are **best disclosed by note**. Parenthetical notations are sometimes used, but restrictions imposed by bond indentures and loan agreements commonly require an extended explanation; notes provide a medium for more complete explanations and free the financial statements from abbreviated notations. The note disclosure should reveal the source of the restriction, pertinent provisions, and the amount of retained earnings subject to restriction, or the amount not restricted.

Restrictions may be based on the retention of a certain retained earnings balance, the corporation's ability to observe certain working capital requirements, additional borrowing, and on other considerations. The following example from the annual report of **Alberto-Culver Company** illustrates a note disclosing potential restrictions on retained earnings and dividends.

INTERNATIONAL INSIGHT

In Switzerland, companies are allowed to create income reserves. That is, they reduce income in years with good profits by allocating it to reserves on the balance sheet. In less profitable years, they are able to reallocate from the reserves to improve income. This "smoothes" income across years.

ALBERTO-CULVER COMPANY

Note 3 (in part): The $200 million revolving credit facility, the term note due September 2000, and the receivables agreement impose restrictions on such items as total debt, working capital, dividend payments, treasury stock purchases, and interest expense. At September 30, 1998, the company was in compliance with these arrangements, and $220 million of consolidated retained earnings was not restricted as to the payment of dividends.

ILLUSTRATION 16-13
Disclosure of Restrictions on Retained Earnings and Dividends

Trends in Terminology

As discussed in Chapter 5, the profession's recommendations relating to changes in terminology have been directed primarily to the balance sheet presentation of stockholders' equity so that words or phrases used will more accurately describe the nature of the amounts shown.

The accounting profession has suggested the term "surplus" not be used in financial statements. Substitute terminology is recommended because the term "surplus" connotes a residual or "something not needed." The use of the term is gradually decreasing. **"Retained earnings"** or some similar phrase has generally replaced "earned surplus." Apparently, consensus regarding the terminology to replace "capital surplus" and "paid-in surplus" has not yet been reached, inasmuch as these two terms still appear in some financial statements. **"Capital in excess of par (or stated value)"** or **"additional paid-in capital"** are gaining favor over the term "paid-in surplus."[22] The persistent use of "surplus" terms by some leading corporations can perhaps be attributed to the numerous state incorporation acts that still contain antiquated terminology in their provisions regulating the issuance of stock and other equity transactions.

Formerly, the term "reserve" was used in accounting to describe such diverse items as accumulated depreciation, allowances for doubtful accounts, current liabilities, and segregations of retained earnings. **The profession recommends that use of the word "reserve" be confined to appropriations of retained earnings if it is to be used at all.** The general adoption of this recommendation could help to clear up one of the most troublesome terminology areas in accounting.[23]

---

[22] *Accounting Trends and Techniques—1999* reports that the use of the term "surplus" is gradually declining. In its survey of 600 companies, 30 out of 527 companies reporting additional paid-in capital used either "capital surplus" or "paid-in surplus" for the caption. Only 1 company used the term "earned surplus."

[23] *Accounting Trends and Techniques—1999* reports that of its list of 600 selected companies, 147 continued incorrectly to use the term "reserve" in the assets or liabilities section of the balance sheet.

PRESENTATION AND ANALYSIS OF STOCKHOLDERS' EQUITY

Presentation

OBJECTIVE 8
Indicate how stockholders' equity is presented and analyzed.

The following three categories normally appear as part of stockholders' equity:

1. Capital stock (legal capital).
2. Additional paid-in capital (capital in excess of par or stated value).
3. Retained earnings or deficit.

The first two categories, capital stock and additional paid-in capital, constitute contributed (or paid-in) capital; retained earnings represents the earned capital of the enterprise. These three categories are reported in summarized form in all enterprises' balance sheets. More detail of additions and deductions to specific stockholders' equity accounts are frequently reported in a separate statement of stockholders' equity.

Balance Sheet

The presentation below is an example of a comprehensive stockholders' equity section taken from a balance sheet that includes most of the equity items discussed in Chapters 15 and 16.

ILLUSTRATION 16-14
Comprehensive Stockholders' Equity Presentation

FROST CORPORATION
Stockholders' Equity
December 31, 2000

Capital stock		
Preferred stock, $100 par value, 7% cumulative, 100,000 shares authorized, 30,000 shares issued and outstanding		$ 3,000,000
Common stock, no par, stated value $10 per share, 500,000 shares authorized, 400,000 shares issued		4,000,000
Common stock dividend distributable, 20,000 shares		200,000
Total capital stock		7,200,000
Additional paid-in capital		
Excess over par—preferred	$ 150,000	
Excess over stated value—common	840,000	990,000
Total paid-in capital		8,190,000
Retained earnings		
Appropriated for plant expansion	2,200,000	
Unappropriated	2,160,000	4,360,000
Total paid-in capital and retained earnings		12,550,000
Less: Cost of treasury stock (2,000 shares, common)		(190,000)
Accumulated other comprehensive loss[24]		(360,000)
Total stockholders' equity		$12,000,000

[24]A number of items may be included in the accumulated other comprehensive loss. Among these items are "foreign currency translation adjustments" (covered in advanced accounting), "unrealized holding gains and losses for available-for-sale securities" (covered in Chapter 18), "excess of additional pension liability over unrecognized prior service cost" (covered in Chapter 21), "guarantees of employee stock option plan (ESOP) debt," "unearned or deferred compensation related to employee stock award plans," and others. *Accounting Trends and Techniques—1999* reports that of its 600 surveyed companies reporting other items in the equity section, 442 reported cumulative translation adjustments, 186 reported minimum pension liability adjustments, 148 reported unrealized losses/gains on certain investments, 119 reported unearned compensation, and 46 reported guarantees of ESOP debt. A number of companies had more than one item.

A company should disclose the pertinent rights and privileges of the various securities outstanding.[25]

Statement of Stockholders' Equity

Statements of stockholders' equity are frequently presented in the following basic format:

1. Balance at the beginning of the period.
2. Additions.
3. Deductions.
4. Balance at the end of the period.

The disclosure of changes in the separate accounts comprising stockholders' equity is required to make the financial statements sufficiently informative.[26] Disclosure of such changes may take the form of separate statements or may be made in the basic financial statements or notes thereto.[27]

A **columnar format** for the presentation of changes in stockholders' equity items in published annual reports is gaining in popularity; an example is **Goodyear Tire Company**'s statement of stockholders' equity shown in Illustration 16-15.

ILLUSTRATION 16-15
Columnar Format for Statement of Stockholders' Equity

GOODYEAR TIRE COMPANY

Statement of Stockholders' Equity

(Dollars in millions, except per share)	Common Stock Shares	Common Stock Amount	Additional Paid-in Capital	Retained Earnings	Accumulated Other Comprehensive Income: Foreign Currency Translation	Accumulated Other Comprehensive Income: Minimum Pension Liability	Total Shareholders' Equity
Balance at December 31, 1997 (after deducting 39,089,885 treasury shares)	156,588,783	$156.6	$1,061.6	$2,983.4	$(778.0)	$(28.1)	$3,395.5
Comprehensive income							
Net income				682.3			
Foreign currency translation					(99.6)		
Minimum pension liability (net of tax of $.2)						1.9	
Total comprehensive income							584.6
Cash dividends—$1.20 per share				(187.9)			(187.9)
Common stock acquired	(1,500,000)	(1.5)	(83.7)				(85.2)
Common stock issued from treasury:							
Stock compensation plans	854,752	.8	38.0				38.8
Balance at December 31, 1998 (after deducting 39,735,133 treasury shares)	155,943,535	$155.9	$1,015.9	$3,477.8	$(877.6)	$(26.2)	$3,745.8

[25]"Disclosure of Information about Capital Structure," *Statement of Financial Accounting Standards No. 129* (Norwalk, Conn.: FASB, February 1997), par. 4.

[26]If a company has other comprehensive income, and total comprehensive income is computed only in the statement of stockholders' equity, the statement of stockholders' equity must be displayed with the same prominence as other financial statements. "Reporting Comprehensive Income," *Statement of Financial Accounting Standards No. 130* (Norwalk, Conn.: FASB, June 1997).

[27]*Accounting Trends and Techniques—1999* reports that of the 600 companies surveyed, 562 presented statements of stockholders' equity, 15 presented separate statements of retained earnings only, 7 presented combined statements of income and retained earnings, and 16 presented changes in equity items in the notes only.

The annual report of Intel in the Appendix to Chapter 5, page 224, includes a 3-year comprehensive illustration of the various items that commonly appear as either additions or deductions in a "Statement of Shareholders' Equity."

Analysis

Several ratios use stockholders' equity related amounts to evaluate a company's profitability and long-term solvency. The following four ratios are discussed and illustrated below: (1) rate of return on common stock equity, (2) payout ratio, (3) price earnings ratio, and (4) book value per share.

Rate of Return on Common Stock Equity

A widely used ratio that measures profitability from the common stockholders' viewpoint is **rate of return on common stock equity**. This ratio shows how many dollars of net income were earned for each dollar invested by the owners. It is computed by dividing net income less preferred dividends by average common stockholders' equity. For example, assume that Gerber's Inc. had net income of $360,000, declared and paid preferred dividends of $54,000, and average common stockholders' equity of $2,550,000. Gerber's ratio is computed in this manner:

ILLUSTRATION 16-16
Computation of Rate of Return on Common Stock Equity

$$\text{Rate of Return on Common Stock Equity} = \frac{\text{Net income} - \text{Preferred dividends}}{\text{Average common stockholders' equity}}$$

$$= \frac{\$360{,}000 - \$54{,}000}{\$2{,}550{,}000}$$

$$= 12\%$$

As evidenced above, because preferred stock is present, preferred dividends are deducted from net income to compute income available to common stockholders. Similarly the par value of preferred stock is deducted from total stockholders' equity to arrive at the amount of common stock equity used in this ratio.

When the rate of return on total assets is lower than the rate of return on the common stockholders investment, the company is said to be trading on the equity at a gain. **Trading on the equity** describes the practice of using borrowed money at fixed interest rates or issuing preferred stock with constant dividend rates in hopes of obtaining a higher rate of return on the money used. These issues must be given a prior claim on some or all of the corporate assets. Thus, the advantage to common stockholders of trading on the equity must come from borrowing at a lower rate of interest than the rate of return obtained on the assets borrowed. If this can be done, the capital obtained from bondholders or preferred stockholders earns enough to pay the interest or preferred dividends and to leave a margin for the common stockholders. When this condition exists, trading on the equity is profitable.

Payout Ratio

Another measure of profitability is the **payout ratio**, which is the ratio of cash dividends to net income. If preferred stock is outstanding, this ratio is computed for common stockholders by dividing cash dividends paid to common stockholders by net income available to common stockholders. Assuming that Troy Co. has cash dividends of $100,000 and net income of $500,000, and no preferred stock outstanding, the payout ratio is computed in the following manner:

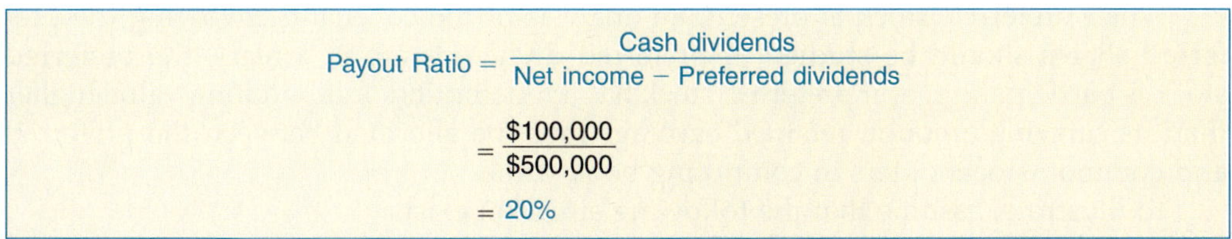

$$\text{Payout Ratio} = \frac{\text{Cash dividends}}{\text{Net income} - \text{Preferred dividends}}$$

$$= \frac{\$100{,}000}{\$500{,}000}$$

$$= 20\%$$

ILLUSTRATION 16-17
Computation of Payout Ratio

It is important to some investors that the payout be sufficiently high to provide a good yield on the stock.[28] However, payout ratios have declined for many companies because many investors view appreciation in the value of the stock as more important than the amount of the dividend.

Price Earnings Ratio

The **price earnings (P/E) ratio** is an oft-quoted statistic used by analysts in discussing the investment possibility of a given enterprise. It is computed by dividing the market price of the stock by its earnings per share. For example, Soreson Co. has a market price of $50 and earnings per share of $4. Its price earnings ratio is computed as follows:

$$\text{Price Earnings Ratio} = \frac{\text{Market price of stock}}{\text{Earnings per share}}$$

$$= \frac{\$50}{\$4}$$

$$= 12.5$$

ILLUSTRATION 16-18
Computation of Price Earnings Ratio

The average price earnings ratio for the 30 stocks that constitute the Dow Jones Industrial Average in January 2000 was 31.7. A steady drop in a company's price earnings ratio indicates that investors are wary of the firm's growth potential. Some companies have high P/E ratios (also called "multiples"), while others have low multiples. For instance, **Home Depot** in 2000 enjoyed a P/E ratio of 53, while **Ford Motor** had a low P/E ratio of 7.3. The reason for this difference is linked to several factors: relative risk, stability of earnings, trends in earnings, and the market's perception of the company's growth potential.

Book Value Per Share

A much-used basis for evaluating net worth is found in the **book value** or **equity value per share** of stock. Book value per share of stock is the amount each share would receive if the company were liquidated **on the basis of amounts reported on the balance sheet**. However, the figure loses much of its relevance if the valuations on the balance sheet do not approximate fair market value of the assets. **Book value per share** is computed by dividing common stockholders' equity by outstanding common shares. Assuming that Chen Corporation's common stockholders' equity is $1,000,000 and it has 100,000 shares of common stock outstanding, its book value per share is computed as follows:

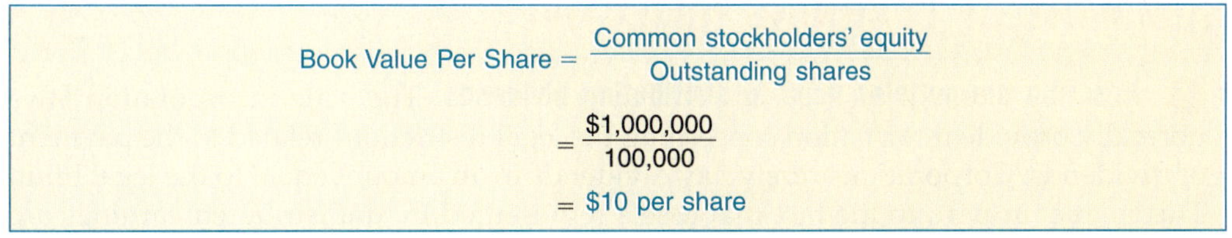

$$\text{Book Value Per Share} = \frac{\text{Common stockholders' equity}}{\text{Outstanding shares}}$$

$$= \frac{\$1{,}000{,}000}{100{,}000}$$

$$= \$10 \text{ per share}$$

ILLUSTRATION 16-19
Computation of Book Value Per Share

[28]Another closely watched ratio is the dividend yield—the cash dividend per share divided by the market price of the stock. This ratio affords investors some idea of the rate of return that will be received in cash dividends from their investment.

When preferred stock is present, an analysis of the covenants involving the preferred shares should be studied. If preferred dividends are in arrears, the preferred stock is participating, or if preferred stock has a redemption or liquidating value higher than its carrying amount, retained earnings must be allocated between the preferred and common stockholders in computing book value.

To illustrate, assume that the following situation exists:

ILLUSTRATION 16-20
Computation of Book Value Per Share—No Dividends in Arrears

Stockholders' equity	Preferred	Common
Preferred stock, 5%	$300,000	
Common stock		$400,000
Excess of issue price over par of common stock		37,500
Retained earnings		162,582
Totals	$300,000	$600,082
Shares outstanding		4,000
Book value per share		$150.02

In the preceding computation it is assumed that no preferred dividends are in arrears and that the preferred is not participating. Now assume that the same facts exist except that the 5% preferred is cumulative, participating up to 8%, and that dividends for three years before the current year are in arrears. The book value of the common stock is then computed as follows, assuming that no action has yet been taken concerning dividends for the current year.

ILLUSTRATION 16-21
Computation of Book Value Per Share—With Dividends in Arrears

Stockholders' equity	Preferred	Common
Preferred stock, 5%	$300,000	
Common stock		$400,000
Excess of issue price over par of common stock		37,500
Retained earnings:		
Dividends in arrears (3 years at 5% a year)	45,000	
Current year requirement at 5%	15,000	20,000
Participating—additional 3%	9,000	12,000
Remainder to common		61,582
Totals	$369,000	$531,082
Shares outstanding		4,000
Book value per share		$132.77

In connection with the book value computation, the analyst must know how to handle the following items: the number of authorized and unissued shares; the number of treasury shares on hand; any commitments with respect to the issuance of unissued shares or the reissuance of treasury shares; and the relative rights and privileges of the various types of stock authorized.

SUMMARY OF LEARNING OBJECTIVES

1 **Describe the policies used in distributing dividends.** The state incorporation laws normally provide information concerning the legal restrictions related to the payment of dividends. Corporations rarely pay dividends in an amount equal to the legal limit. This is due, in part, to the fact that assets represented by undistributed earnings are used to finance future operations of the business. If a company is considering declaring a dividend, two preliminary questions must be asked: (1) Is the condition of the corporation such that the dividend is **legally permissible**? (2) Is the condition of the corporation such that a dividend is **economically sound**?

2 Identify the various forms of dividend distributions. Dividends are of the following types: (1) cash dividends, (2) property dividends, (3) scrip dividends (instead of paying a dividend now, the corporation has elected to pay it at some later date; the scrip issued to stockholders as a dividend is merely a special form of note payable), (4) liquidating dividends (dividends based on other than retained earnings are sometimes described as liquidating dividends), (5) stock dividends (the nonreciprocal issuance by a corporation of its own stock to its stockholders on a pro rata basis).

3 Explain the accounting for small and large stock dividends. Generally accepted accounting principles require that the accounting for small stock dividends (less than 20 or 25%) be based on the fair market value of the stock issued. When a stock dividend is declared, Retained Earnings is debited at the fair market value of the stock to be distributed. The entry includes a credit to Common Stock Dividend Distributable at par value times the number of shares, with any excess credited to Paid-in Capital in Excess of Par. Common stock dividend distributable is reported in the stockholders' equity section between the declaration date and the date of issuance. If the number of shares issued exceeds 20 or 25% of the shares outstanding (large stock dividend), Retained Earnings is debited at par value, and there is no additional paid-in capital.

4 Distinguish between stock dividends and stock splits. A stock dividend is a capitalization of retained earnings that results in a reduction in retained earnings and a corresponding increase in certain contributed capital accounts. The par value and total stockholders' equity remain unchanged with a stock dividend. Also, all stockholders retain their same proportionate share of ownership in the corporation. A stock split results in an increase or decrease in the number of shares outstanding, with a corresponding decrease or increase in the par or stated value per share. No accounting entry is required for a stock split. Similar to a stock dividend, the total dollar amount of all stockholders' equity accounts remains unchanged. A stock split is usually intended to improve the marketability of the shares by reducing the market price of the stock being split.

5 Explain the effect of different types of preferred stock dividends. Dividends paid to shareholders are affected by the dividend preferences of the preferred stock. Preferred stock can be: (1) cumulative or noncumulative, and (2) fully participating, partially participating, or nonparticipating.

6 Identify the reasons for appropriating retained earnings. An appropriation of retained earnings serves to restrict for a specific purpose the payout of retained earnings. In general, the reason for retained earnings appropriations is the corporation's desire to reduce the basis upon which dividends are declared (unappropriated credit balance in retained earnings).

7 Explain accounting and reporting for appropriated retained earnings. To establish an appropriation of retained earnings, a corporation prepares a journal entry, debiting unappropriated retained earnings and crediting a specific appropriations account (for example, Retained Earnings Appropriated for Sinking Fund). The entry is confined to stockholders' equity accounts and does not directly affect corporate assets or liabilities. The only way to dispose of an appropriation of retained earnings is to reverse the entry that created the appropriation. Appropriations of retained earnings are frequently disclosed in the notes to the financial statements as an alternative to making a formal entry against retained earnings.

8 Indicate how stockholders' equity is presented and analyzed. The stockholders equity section of a balance sheet includes capital stock, additional paid-in capital, and retained earnings. Additional items that might also be presented are treasury stock and accumulated other comprehensive income. A statement of stockholders' equity is often provided. Common ratios used in this area are: rate of return on common stock equity, payout ratio, price earnings ratio, and book value per share.

KEY TERMS

- appropriation of retained earnings, *825*
- book value per share, *831*
- cash dividends, *816*
- large stock dividend, *823*
- liquidating dividends, *819*
- payout ratio, *830*
- price earnings ratio, *831*
- property dividends, *817*
- rate of return on common stock equity, *830*
- retained earnings, *812*
- scrip dividends, *818*
- small (ordinary) stock dividends, *820*
- statement of stockholders' equity, *829*
- stock dividends, *820*
- stock split, *822*
- trading on the equity, *830*

APPENDIX 16A

Quasi-Reorganization

OBJECTIVE 9
After studying Appendix 16A, you should be able to: Describe the accounting for a quasi-reorganization.

A corporation that consistently suffers net losses accumulates negative retained earnings, or a deficit. The laws of many states provide that no dividends may be declared and paid so long as a corporation's paid-in capital has been reduced by a deficit. In these states, a corporation with a debit balance of retained earnings must accumulate sufficient profits to offset the deficit before dividends may be paid.

This situation may be a real hardship on a corporation and its stockholders. A company that has operated unsuccessfully for several years and accumulated a deficit may have finally "turned the corner." Development of new products and new markets, a new management group, or improved economic conditions may point to much improved operating results. But, if the state law prohibits dividends until the deficit has been replaced by earnings, the stockholders must wait until such profits have been earned, which may take a considerable period of time. Furthermore, future success may depend on obtaining additional funds through the sale of stock. If no dividends can be paid for some time, the market price of any new stock issue is likely to be low, if such stock can be marketed at all.

Thus, a company with excellent prospects may be prevented from accomplishing its plans because of a deficit, although present management may have had nothing whatever to do with the years over which the deficit was accumulated. To permit the corporation to proceed with its plans might well be to the advantage of all interests in the enterprise; to require it to eliminate the deficit through profits might actually force it to liquidate.

A procedure provided for in some state laws eliminates an accumulated deficit and permits the company to proceed on much the same basis as if it had been legally reorganized, without the difficulty and expenses generally connected with a legal reorganization. This procedure, known as a **quasi-reorganization**, is justified under the concept of an accounting "fresh start."

ACCOUNTING APPROACHES

A quasi-reorganization may be accomplished under two accounting procedures. The simpler procedure, referred to as a **deficit reclassification**, results solely in eliminating a deficit in retained earnings without restating assets or liabilities. The accounting procedure is limited to a reclassification of a deficit in reported retained earnings as a reduction of paid-in capital.

No net asset writeup is permitted in a quasi-reorganization. The reason: Conservatism, as indicated in Chapter 2.

The more complex accounting procedure, referred to as an **accounting reorganization** type of quasi-reorganization, involves restating the assets of the enterprise to their fair values and the liabilities to their present values with the net amount of these adjustments added to or deducted from the deficit.[1] The balance in the retained earnings ac-

[1]The SEC states in *SAB 78, Quasi-Reorganization* (Topic 5.S), dated August 25, 1988, that write-ups of assets or reductions of liabilities to fair and present values in a quasi-reorganization are limited to an amount sufficient to offset decreases in other assets or increases in other liabilities in their fair and present values. Therefore, there should be **no net asset writeup** in a quasi-reorganization.

Also, the SEC does not allow the "deficit reclassification" type quasi-reorganization (the simpler form) to be used by publicly held companies; thus, it may be used only by privately held companies. Both public and private companies may use the accounting reorganization type (i.e., restating assets and liabilities and eliminating the deficit).

count (debit or credit) is then closed to other capital accounts, usually Additional Paid-in Capital, so that the company has a "fresh start" with a zero balance in retained earnings.

Entries Illustrated

The series of entries shown below illustrates the accounting procedures applied in an "accounting reorganization" type of quasi-reorganization. Assume New Horizons Inc. shows a deficit of $1,000,000 before a quasi-reorganization is effected on June 30, 2001.

1 Restatement of assets and liabilities to recognize unrecorded gains and losses

Plant Assets (gain on writeup)	400,000	
Long-term Liabilities (gain on writedown)	150,000	
Retained Earnings (net adjustment)	200,000	
Intangible Assets (loss on writedown)		525,000
Inventories (loss on writedown)		225,000

2 Reduction in par value of 60,000 shares of common stock outstanding from $100 per share to $75 per share (This procedure creates sufficient additional paid-in capital to absorb the deficit)

Common Stock	1,500,000	
Additional Paid-in Capital		1,500,000

3 Elimination of deficit against additional paid-in capital

Additional Paid-in Capital	1,200,000	
Retained Earnings ($1,000,000 + $200,000)		1,200,000

Disclosure

In connection with the foregoing accounting procedures, the following requirements must be fulfilled:

1. The proposed quasi-reorganization procedure should be submitted to and receive the approval of the corporation's stockholders before it is put into effect.
2. The new asset and liability valuations should be fair and not deliberately understate or overstate assets, liabilities, and earnings.
3. After the quasi-reorganization the corporation must have a zero balance of retained earnings, although it may have additional paid-in capital arising from the quasi-reorganization.
4. In subsequent reports the retained earnings must be "dated" (1) for a period of approximately 10 years to show the fact and the date of the quasi-reorganization, and (2) for a period of at least 3 years from the quasi-reorganization date, the amount of accumulated deficit eliminated should be disclosed as illustrated in the following excerpt from the 2003 balance sheet of New Horizons, Inc.[2]

ILLUSTRATION 16A-1
Disclosure of Quasi-Reorganization in the Balance Sheet

New Horizons, Inc.	
Stockholders' equity	
Common stock, $75 par value, 60,000 shares authorized and issued	$4,500,000
Additional paid-in capital arising from reduction in par value of common stock	300,000
Retained earnings since June 30, 2001, when a deficit of $1,000,000 was eliminated through a quasi-reorganization	593,640
	$5,393,640

In times of general economic or specific industry recession or depression, the use of the quasi-reorganization procedure becomes more common as companies attempt to turn around and get a fresh start. For example, **First Wisconsin Mortgage Trust**,

[2] *Regulation S-X*, Securities and Exchange Commission, Rule 5-02(31)6.

because of severe real estate losses, effected a quasi-reorganization. Similarly, **Lockheed Corporation**, given its large losses on the L-1011 Tri Star program, decided to use the quasi-reorganization approach to offset a large deficit balance in retained earnings. And **Astrotech International Corporation** eliminated a $28 million deficit in Retained Earnings as it changed from an investment company to an operating company through the quasi-reorganization approach.

An example of a quasi-reorganization disclosure, shown in Illustration 16A-2, is excerpted from the Annual Report of **Midway Airlines Corporation**.

ILLUSTRATION 16A-2
Disclosure of Quasi-Reorganization in the Notes

MIDWAY AIRLINES CORPORATION

Statement of Stockholders' Equity

(000 omitted)	Preferred Stock Amount	Common Stock Amount	Additional Paid-in Capital	Retained Earnings (Accumulated Deficit)	Total
Balance at December 31, 1996	$ 11	$100	$30,989	$(70,342)	$(39,242)
Cancellation of prior stock in connection with recapitalization	(11)	(100)	111	—	—
Issuance of preferred stock	37	—	14,963	—	15,000
Issuance of common stock	—	21	8,551	—	8,572
Issuance of common stock warrants in connection with debt restructuring	—	—	1,571	—	1,571
Contributed capital	—	—	1,314	—	1,314
Reclassification of accumulated deficit pursuant to quasi-reorganization	—	—	(49,812)	49,812	—
Conversion of preferred stock	(37)	37	—	—	—
Issuance of common stock in connection with initial public offering	—	27	37,677	—	37,704
Net income	—	—	—	24,894	24,894
Balance at December 31, 1997	$—	$ 85	$45,364	$ 4,364	$ 49,813

Quasi-Reorganization. As a result of the February 11, 1997 recapitalization, debt restructurings and retention of a new chief executive officer, the Company's Board of Directors approved a corporate readjustment of the Company's accounts in the form of a quasi-reorganization which was effected on June 30, 1997.

A quasi-reorganization is an accounting procedure which results in eliminating the accumulated deficit in retained earnings. This accounting procedure is limited to a reclassification of accumulated deficit as a reduction of paid-in capital. The Company believes the quasi-reorganization was appropriate because on completion of the recapitalization, the debt restructurings, and the installation of a new chief executive officer, the Company had substantially reduced its outstanding indebtedness, had formulated revised operating plans and as a result thereof would be able to devote its resources to its continuing operations. Because assets had been stated at approximate fair values, the quasi-reorganization had no effect on recorded assets.

The authoritative literature and accounting standards on quasi-reorganizations are generally antiquated and are permissive rather than mandatory. Moreover, "there are financial accounting and reporting issues concerning quasi-reorganizations for which the authoritative accounting literature provides no guidance or for which the guidance provided is unclear or conflicting."[3] As a result, accounting for quasi-reorganizations is in need of study and clarification.

[3]"Quasi-Reorganization," *Issues Paper 88-1* (New York: AICPA, September 22, 1988), 75 pp. This issues paper prepared by an AICPA Accounting Standards Division task force identified 46 issues that need to be resolved relative to accounting and reporting for quasi-reorganizations.

SUMMARY OF LEARNING OBJECTIVE FOR APPENDIX 16A

9 Describe the accounting for a quasi-reorganization. A corporation that has accumulated a large debit balance (deficit) in retained earnings may, under the laws of certain states, enter into a process known as a quasi-reorganization. This procedure consists of the following steps: (1) All assets are revalued at appropriate current values so the company will not be burdened with excessive inventory or fixed asset valuations in following years. Any loss on revaluation increases the deficit. (2) Paid-in or other types of capital must be available or must be created, at least equal in amount to the deficit. If no such capital exists, it is created through donation of outstanding stock, or by some similar means. (3) The deficit is then eliminated by a charge against paid-in capital. In addition to the steps above, a quasi-reorganization requires: (1) approval by stockholders, (2) fair and unbiased valuation of assets, (3) a zero balance in retained earnings at the conclusion of the reorganization, (4) the date of the quasi-reorganization shown with retained earnings for the succeeding 10 years, and (5) balance sheet disclosure of the amount of the deficit eliminated, for 3 years.

KEY TERMS

accounting reorganization, *834*
deficit reclassification, *834*
quasi-reorganization, *834*

Note: All **asterisked** Questions, Brief Exercises, Exercises, Problems, and Conceptual Cases relate to material contained in the appendix to the chapter.

QUESTIONS

1 Distinguish among the following: contributed capital, earned capital, and equity capital.

2 What are some of the common items that increase or decrease retained earnings?

3 What factors influence the dividend policy of a company?

4 What are the characteristics of state incorporation laws relative to the legality of dividend payments?

5 Very few companies pay dividends in amounts equal to their retained earnings legally available for dividends. Why?

6 What are the principal considerations of a board of directors in making decisions involving dividend declarations? Discuss briefly.

7 In a report from the FASB, it was noted that on a price-level basis (adjusted for specific prices), dividends exceeded profits. As a result, some industries, such as primary and fabricated metals, are in effect undergoing gradual liquidation. Explain what this statement means.

8 Dividends are sometimes said to have been paid "out of retained earnings." What is the error in that statement?

9 Distinguish among: cash dividends, property dividends, scrip dividends, liquidating dividends, and stock dividends.

10 Describe the accounting entry for a stock dividend. Describe the accounting entry for a stock split.

11 Stock splits and stock dividends may be used by a corporation to change the number of shares of its stock outstanding.

(a) What is meant by a stock split effected in the form of a dividend?

(b) From an accounting viewpoint, explain how the stock split effected in the form of a dividend differs from an ordinary stock dividend.

(c) How should a stock dividend that has been declared but not yet issued be classified in a statement of financial position? Why?

12 The following comment appeared in the notes of Belinda Alvarado Corporation's annual report: "Such distributions, representing proceeds from the sale of James Buchanan, Inc. were paid in the form of partial liquidating dividends and were in lieu of a portion of the Company's ordinary cash dividends." How would a partial liquidating dividend be accounted for in the financial records?

13 This comment appeared in the annual report of Rodriguez Lopez Inc.: "The Company could pay cash or property dividends on the Class A common stock without paying cash or property dividends on the Class B common stock, but if the Company pays any cash or property dividends on the Class B common stock, it would be required to pay at least the same dividend on the Class A common stock." How is a property dividend accounted for in the financial records?

14 Thomas Dewey Corporation has consistently reported a significant amount of income and has accumulated a large balance of retained earnings. At a recent stockholders' meeting, the company's policy of declaring little or no dividends caused some controversy.

(a) Why might Thomas Dewey Corporation establish such a conservative dividend policy?

(b) What steps might Thomas Dewey take to reduce the amount of retained earnings available for dividends?

15 Aaron Burr Corp. had $100,000 of 10%, $20 par value preferred stock and 12,000 shares of $25 par value common stock outstanding throughout 2001.

(a) Assuming that total dividends declared in 2001 were $88,000, and that the preferred stock is not cumulative but is fully participating, each common share should receive 2001 dividends of what amount?

(b) Assuming that total dividends declared in 2001 were $88,000, and that the preferred stock is fully participating and cumulative with preferred dividends in arrears for 2000, preferred stockholders should receive 2001 dividends totaling what amount?

(c) Assuming that total dividends declared in 2001 were $30,000, that cumulative nonparticipating preferred stock was issued on January 1, 2000, and that $5,000 of preferred dividends were declared and paid in 2000, the common stockholders should receive 2001 dividends totaling what amount?

16 For what reasons might a company appropriate a portion of its retained earnings?

17 How should appropriations of retained earnings be created and written off?

18 Comment on the propriety of William Byrd Company reporting "paid-in surplus" and "earned surplus" in the equity section of its balance sheet.

19 Indicate the misuse and the proper use of the term "reserve."

20 What are some of the ways in which retained earnings may be restricted?

21 Is there a duplication of charges to current year's costs or expenses where a sinking fund appropriation is created for the retirement of bonds, as well as accumulated depreciation with respect to the capital assets by which such bonds are secured? Discuss briefly the point raised by this question.

***22** Outline the accounting steps involved in accomplishing a quasi-reorganization.

***23** Under what circumstances would a corporation consider submitting itself to a quasi-reorganization?

***24** What disclosures are required in the balance sheet for years subsequent to a quasi-reorganization?

BRIEF EXERCISES

BE16-1 Micro Machines Inc. declared a cash dividend of $1.50 per share on its 2 million outstanding shares. The dividend was declared on August 1, payable on September 9 to all stockholders of record on August 15. Prepare all journal entries necessary on those three dates.

BE16-2 Ren Inc. owns shares of Stimpy Corporation stock classified as available-for-sale securities. At December 31, 2001, the available-for-sale securities were carried in Ren's accounting records at their cost of $875,000 which equals their market value. On September 21, 2002, when the market value of the securities was $1,400,000, Ren declared a property dividend whereby the Stimpy securities are to be distributed on October 23, 2002, to stockholders of record on October 8, 2002. Prepare all journal entries necessary on those three dates.

BE16-3 Might and Magic Inc. declared a scrip dividend of $3.00 per share on its 100,000 outstanding shares. The dividend was declared on January 30, and is payable with interest, at a 12% annual rate, on October 31. Prepare all journal entries necessary on those two dates.

BE16-4 Radical Rex Mining Company declared, on April 20, a dividend of $700,000 payable on June 1. Of this amount, $125,000 is a return of capital. Prepare the April 20 and June 1 entries for Radical Rex.

BE16-5 Mike Holmgren Football Corporation has outstanding 200,000 shares of $10 par value common stock. The corporation declares a 5% stock dividend when the fair value of the stock is $65 per share. Prepare the journal entries for Mike Holmgren Football Corporation for both the date of declaration and the date of distribution.

BE16-6 Use the information from BE16-5, but assume Mike Holmgren Football Corporation declared a 100% stock dividend rather than a 5% stock dividend. Prepare the journal entries for both the date of declaration and the date of distribution.

BE16-7 Power Piggs Corporation has outstanding 300,000 shares of $15 par value common stock. Power Piggs declares a 3-for-1 stock split. (a) How many shares are outstanding after the split? (b) What is the par value per share after the split? (c) What is the total par value after the split? (d) What journal entry is necessary to record the split?

BE16-8 Minnesota Fats Corporation has outstanding 10,000 shares of $100 par value, 8% preferred stock and 60,000 shares of $10 par value common stock. The preferred stock was issued in January 1999, and no dividends were declared in 1999 or 2000. In 2001, Minnesota Fats declares a cash dividend of $300,000. How will the dividend be shared by common and preferred if the preferred is (a) noncumulative and (b) cumulative?

BE16-9 Pocahontas Inc. has retained earnings of $2,100,000 at December 31, 2001. On that date the board of directors decides to appropriate $800,000 of retained earnings for a legal contingency. (a) Prepare the entry to record the appropriation. (b) Indicate the amount reported as total retained earnings after the appropriation.

***BE16-10** Monster Truck Corporation went through a quasi-reorganization by writing down plant assets by $125,000, reducing par value on its 40,000 outstanding shares from $15 to $5, and eliminating its deficit, which was $250,000 prior to the quasi-reorganization. Prepare Monster Truck's entries to record the quasi-reorganization.

EXERCISES

E16-1 (Equity Items on the Balance Sheet) The following are selected transactions that may affect stockholders' equity.

1. Recorded accrued interest earned on a note receivable.
2. Declared a cash dividend.
3. Declared and distributed a stock split.
4. Recorded a retained earnings appropriation.
5. Recorded the expiration of insurance coverage that was previously recorded as prepaid insurance.
6. Paid the cash dividend declared in item 2 above.
7. Recorded accrued interest expense on a note payable.
8. Recorded an increase in value of an investment that will be distributed as a property dividend.
9. Declared a property dividend (see item 8 above).
10. Distributed the investment to stockholders (see items 8 and 9 above).
11. Declared a stock dividend.
12. Distributed the stock dividend declared in item 11.

Instructions

In the table below, indicate the effect each of the twelve transactions has on the financial statement elements listed. Use the following code:

I = Increase D = Decrease NE = No effect

Item	Assets	Liabilities	Stockholders' Equity	Paid-in Capital	Retained Earnings	Net Income

E16-2 (Classification of Equity Items) Stockholders' equity on the balance sheet of Cherese Thomas Corp. is composed of three major sections. They are: A. Capital stock; B. Additional paid-in capital; and C. Retained earnings.

Instructions

Classify each of the following items as affecting one of the three sections above or as D, an item not to be included in stockholders' equity.

(a) Net income
(b) Dividends Payable
(c) Stock split
(d) Property dividends declared
(e) Preferred stock
(f) Common stock subscribed
(g) Retained earnings appropriated
(h) Sinking fund
(i) Paid-in capital in excess of par—common

E16-3 (Cash Dividend and Liquidating Dividend) Lotoya Davis Corporation has ten million shares of common stock issued and outstanding. On June 1 the board of directors voted an 80 cents per share cash dividend to stockholders of record as of June 14, payable June 30.

Instructions

(a) Prepare the journal entry for each of the dates above assuming the dividend represents a distribution of earnings.
(b) How would the entry differ if the dividend were a liquidating dividend?
(c) Assume Lotoya Davis Corporation holds 300,000 common shares in the treasury and as a matter of administrative convenience dividends are paid on treasury shares. How should this cash receipt be recorded?

E16-4 (Preferred Dividends) The outstanding capital stock of Edna Millay Corporation consists of 2,000 shares of $100 par value, 8% preferred, and 5,000 shares of $50 par value common.

Instructions

Assuming that the company has retained earnings of $90,000, all of which is to be paid out in dividends, and that preferred dividends were not paid during the two years preceding the current year, state how much each class of stock should receive under each of the following conditions:

(a) The preferred stock is noncumulative and nonparticipating.
(b) The preferred stock is cumulative and nonparticipating.
(c) The preferred stock is cumulative and participating.

E16-5 (Preferred Dividends) Archibald MacLeish Company's ledger shows the following balances on December 31, 2002:

7% Preferred stock — $10 par value, outstanding 20,000 shares	$ 200,000
Common stock—$100 par value, outstanding 30,000 shares	3,000,000
Retained earnings	630,000

Instructions

Assuming that the directors decide to declare total dividends in the amount of $366,000, determine how much each class of stock should receive under each of the conditions stated below. One year's dividends are in arrears on the preferred stock.

(a) The preferred stock is cumulative and fully participating.
(b) The preferred stock is noncumulative and nonparticipating.
(c) The preferred stock is noncumulative and is participating in distributions in excess of a 10% dividend rate on the common stock.

E16-6 (Stock Split and Stock Dividend) The common stock of Alexander Hamilton Inc. is currently selling at $120 per share. The directors wish to reduce the share price and increase share volume prior to a new issue. The per share par value is $10; book value is $70 per share. Nine million shares are issued and outstanding.

Instructions

Prepare the necessary journal entries assuming:

(a) The board votes a 2-for-1 stock split.
(b) The board votes a 100% stock dividend.
(c) Briefly discuss the accounting and securities market differences between these two methods of increasing the number of shares outstanding.

E16-7 (Stock Dividends) Henry Hudson Inc. has 5 million shares issued and outstanding. The per share par value is $1, book value is $32 per share, and market value is $40 per share.

Instructions

Prepare the necessary journal entry for the date of declaration and date of issue assuming:

(a) A 10% stock dividend is declared.

(b) A 50% stock dividend is declared.

(c) If Hudson has 500,000 shares of treasury stock, should the stock dividend be applied to the treasury shares? Explain.

(d) What is the amount of the corporation's liability for the period from the declaration date to the distribution date?

E16-8 (Entries for Stock Dividends and Stock Splits) The stockholders' equity accounts of G.K. Chesterton Company have the following balances on December 31, 2002:

Common stock, $10 par, 300,000 shares issued and outstanding	$3,000,000
Paid-in capital in excess of par	1,200,000
Retained earnings	5,600,000

Shares of G.K. Chesterton Company stock are currently selling on the Midwest Stock Exchange at $37.

Instructions

Prepare the appropriate journal entries for each of the following cases:

(a) A stock dividend of 5% is declared and issued.

(b) A stock dividend of 100% is declared and issued.

(c) A 2-for-1 stock split is declared and issued.

E16-9 (Dividend Entries) The following data were taken from the balance sheet accounts of John Masefield Corporation on December 31, 2001:

Current assets	$540,000
Investments	624,000
Common stock (par value $10)	500,000
Paid-in capital in excess of par	150,000
Retained earnings	840,000

Instructions

Prepare the required journal entries for the following unrelated items:

(a) A 5% stock dividend is declared and distributed at a time when the market value of the shares is $39 per share.

(b) A scrip dividend of $80,000 is declared.

(c) The par value of the capital stock is reduced to $2 with a 5-for-1 stock split.

(d) A dividend is declared January 5, 2002, and paid January 25, 2002, in bonds held as an investment; the bonds have a book value of $100,000 and a fair market value of $135,000.

E16-10 (Computation of Retained Earnings) The following information has been taken from the ledger accounts of Isaac Stern Corporation:

Total income since incorporation	$317,000
Total cash dividends paid	60,000
Proceeds from sale of donated stock	40,000
Total value of stock dividends distributed	30,000
Gains on treasury stock transactions	18,000
Unamortized discount on bonds payable	32,000
Appropriated for plant expansion	70,000

Instructions

Determine the current balance of unappropriated retained earnings.

E16-11 (Retained Earnings Appropriations and Disclosures) At December 31, 2000, the retained earnings account of Duke Ellington Inc. had a balance of $320,000. There was no appropriation at this time. During 2001, net income was $235,000. Cash dividends declared during the year were $50,000 on preferred stock and $70,000 on common stock. A stock dividend on common stock resulted in an $88,000 charge to retained earnings. At December 31, 2001, the board of directors decided to create an appropriation for contingencies of $125,000 because of an outstanding lawsuit that does not meet the criteria for accrual.

Instructions

(a) Prepare the journal entry to record the appropriation at December 31, 2001.

(b) Prepare a statement of unappropriated retained earnings for 2001.

(c) Prepare the retained earnings section of the December 31, 2001, balance sheet.

(d) Assume that in May 2002, the lawsuit is settled and Duke Ellington agrees to pay $113,000. At this time, the board of directors also decides to eliminate the appropriation. Prepare all necessary entries.

(e) Return to part (a), but assume that Duke Ellington decided to disclose the appropriation through a footnote at December 31, 2001, instead of preparing a formal journal entry. Prepare the necessary footnote.

E16-12 (Stockholders' Equity Section) Bruno Corporation's post-closing trial balance at December 31, 2001, was as follows:

BRUNO CORPORATION
Post-Closing Trial Balance
December 31, 2001

	Dr.	Cr.
Accounts payable		$ 310,000
Accounts receivable	$ 480,000	
Accumulated depreciation—building and equipment		185,000
Additional paid-in capital—common		
In excess of par value		1,300,000
From sale of treasury stock		160,000
Allowance for doubtful accounts		30,000
Bonds payable		300,000
Building and equipment	1,450,000	
Cash	190,000	
Common stock ($1 par value)		200,000
Dividends payable on preferred stock—cash		4,000
Inventories	560,000	
Land	400,000	
Preferred stock ($50 par value)		500,000
Prepaid expenses	40,000	
Retained earnings		301,000
Treasury stock—common at cost	170,000	
Totals	$3,290,000	$3,290,000

At December 31, 2001, Bruno had the following number of common and preferred shares:

	Common	Preferred
Authorized	600,000	60,000
Issued	200,000	10,000
Outstanding	190,000	10,000

The dividends on preferred stock are $4 cumulative. In addition, the preferred stock has a preference in liquidation of $50 per share.

Instructions

Prepare the stockholders' equity section of Bruno's balance sheet at December 31, 2001.

(AICPA adapted)

E16-13 (Participating Preferred, Stock Dividend, and Treasury Stock Retirement) The following is the stockholders' equity section of Jane Seymour Corp. at December 31, 2001:

Common stock, $20 par; authorized 200,000 shares; issued 90,000 shares	$ 1,800,000
Preferred stock,* $50 par; authorized 100,000 shares; issued 15,000 shares	750,000
Additional paid-in capital	3,150,000
Total paid-in capital	5,700,000
Retained earnings	5,213,000
Total paid-in capital and retained earnings	10,913,000
Less: Cost of treasury stock (7,500 common shares)	(742,500)
Total stockholders' equity	$10,170,500

*The preferred stock has a 12% dividend rate, is cumulative, and is participating in distributions in excess of a 15% dividend rate on the common stock.

Instructions

(a) No dividends have been paid in 1999 or 2000. On December 31, 2001, Seymour wants to pay a cash dividend of $4.00 a share to common stockholders. How much cash would be needed for the **total amount paid** to preferred and common stockholders?

(b) Instead, Jane Seymour will declare a 15% stock dividend on the outstanding common stock. The market value of the stock is $103 per share. Prepare the entry on the date of declaration.

(c) Instead, Jane Seymour will retire the treasury stock. It was originally issued at $55 a share. The current market value is $103 per share. Prepare the entry to record the retirement.

E16-14 (Dividends and Stockholders' Equity Section) Anne Cleves Company reported the following amounts in the stockholders' equity section of its December 31, 2000, balance sheet:

Preferred stock, 10%, $100 par (10,000 shares authorized, 2,000 shares issued)	$200,000
Common stock, $5 par (100,000 shares authorized, 20,000 shares issued)	100,000
Additional paid-in capital	125,000
Retained earnings	450,000
Total	$875,000

During 2001, Cleves took part in the following transactions concerning stockholders' equity.

1. Paid the annual 2000 $10 per share dividend on preferred stock and a $2 per share dividend on common stock. These dividends had been declared on December 31, 2000.
2. Purchased 1,700 shares of its own outstanding common stock for $40 per share. Cleves uses the cost method.
3. Reissued 700 treasury shares for land valued at $30,000.
4. Issued 500 shares of preferred stock at $105 per share.
5. Declared a 10% stock dividend on the outstanding common stock when the stock is selling for $45 per share.
6. Issued the stock dividend.
7. Declared the annual 2001 $10 per share dividend on preferred stock and the $2 par share dividend on common stock. These dividends are payable in 2002.
8. Appropriated retained earnings for plant expansion, $200,000.

Instructions

(a) Prepare journal entries to record the transactions described above.

(b) Prepare the December 31, 2001, stockholders' equity section. Assume 2001 net income was $330,000.

E16-15 (Comparison of Alternative Forms of Financing) Shown below is the liabilities and stockholders' equity section of the balance sheet for Jana Kingston Company and Mary Ann Benson Company. Each has assets totaling $4,200,000.

Jana Kingston Co.		Mary Ann Benson Co.	
Current liabilities	$ 300,000	Current liabilities	$ 600,000
Long-term debt, 10%	1,200,000	Common stock ($20 par)	2,900,000
Common stock ($20 par)	2,000,000	Retained earnings (Cash dividends, $328,000)	700,000
Retained earnings (Cash dividends, $220,000)	700,000		
	$4,200,000		$4,200,000

For the year each company has earned the same income before interest and taxes.

	Jana Kingston Co.	Mary Ann Benson Co.
Income before interest and taxes	$1,200,000	$1,200,000
Interest expense	120,000	–0–
	1,080,000	1,200,000
Income taxes (45%)	486,000	540,000
Net income	$ 594,000	$ 660,000

At year end, the market price of Kingston's stock was $101 per share and Benson's was $63.50.

Instructions

(a) Which company is more profitable in terms of return on total assets?

(b) Which company is more profitable in terms of return on stockholders' equity?

(c) Which company has the greater net income per share of stock? Neither company issued or reacquired shares during the year.

(d) From the point of view of income, is it advantageous to the stockholders of Jana Kingston Co. to have the long-term debt outstanding? Why?

(e) What is each company's price earnings ratio?

(f) What is the book value per share for each company?

E16-16 (Trading on the Equity Analysis) Presented below is information from the annual report of Emporia Plastics, Inc.

Operating income	$ 532,150
Bond interest expense	135,000
	397,150
Income taxes	183,432
Net income	$ 213,718
Bonds payable	$1,000,000
Common stock	875,000
Appropriation for contingencies	75,000
Retained earnings, unappropriated	300,000

Instructions

Is Emporia Plastics Inc. trading on the equity successfully? Explain.

E16-17 (Computation of Book Value per Share) Morgan Sondgeroth Inc. began operations in January 1999 and reported the following results for each of its 3 years of operations:

1999 $260,000 net loss 2000 $40,000 net loss 2001 $800,000 net income

At December 31, 2001, Morgan Sondgeroth Inc. capital accounts were as follows:

8% cumulative preferred stock, par value $100; authorized, issued, and outstanding 5,000 shares	$500,000
Common stock, par value $1.00; authorized 1,000,000 shares; issued and outstanding 750,000 shares	$750,000

Morgan Sondgeroth Inc. has never paid a cash or stock dividend. There has been no change in the capital accounts since Sondgeroth began operations. The state law permits dividends only from retained earnings.

Instructions

(a) Compute the book value of the common stock at December 31, 2001.

(b) Compute the book value of the common stock at December 31, 2001, assuming that the preferred stock has a liquidating value of $106 per share.

***E16-18 (Quasi-Reorganization)** The following account balances are available from the ledger of Glamorgan Corporation on December 31, 2000:

Common Stock—$50 par value, 20,000 shares authorized and outstanding	$1,000,000
Retained Earnings (deficit)	(190,000)

As of January 2, 2001, the corporation gave effect to a stockholder-approved quasi-reorganization by reducing the par value of the stock to $35 a share, writing down plant assets by $85,600, and eliminating the deficit.

Instructions

Prepare the required journal entries for the quasi-reorganization of Glamorgan Corporation.

***E16-19 (Quasi-Reorganization)** The condensed balance sheets of John Ross Company immediately before and one year after it had completed a quasi-reorganization appear below:

	Before Quasi	One Year After		Before Quasi	One Year After
Current assets	$ 300,000	$ 420,000	Common stock	$2,400,000	$1,550,000
Plant assets (net)	1,700,000	1,290,000	Premium on common	220,000	
			Retained earnings	(620,000)	160,000
	$2,000,000	$1,710,000		$2,000,000	$1,710,000

For the year following the quasi-reorganization, John Ross Company reported net income of $190,000, depreciation expense of $80,000, and paid a cash dividend of $30,000. As part of the quasi-reorganization, the company wrote down inventories by $120,000. No purchases or sales of plant assets and no stock transactions occurred in the year following the quasi-reorganization.

Instructions

Prepare all the journal entries made at the time of the quasi-reorganization.

***E16-20 (Quasi-Reorganization)** Trudy Borke Corporation is under protection of the bankruptcy court and has the following account balances at June 30, 2000.

Cash	$ (5,000)	Accounts payable	$ 450,000
Accounts receivable	320,000	Notes payable	605,000
Inventory	450,000	Taxes and wages	60,000
Equipment	860,000	Mortgage payable	150,000
Accumulated depreciation	(525,000)	Common stock	50,000
Intangibles	80,000	Retained earnings	(135,000)
Total	$1,180,000	Total	$1,180,000

The court has accepted the following proposed settlement of the company's affairs. Write down the assets by the following amounts:

Accounts receivable	$ 40,000
Inventory	$160,000
Intangibles	$ 80,000

The trade creditors (accounts payable) will reduce their claim by 30%, will accept one-year notes for 50% of their claim, and retain their current claim for the remaining 20%. The tax, wage, and mortgage claims will remain unchanged. The current common stock will be surrendered to the corporation and cancelled. In consideration thereof, the current stockholders shall be held harmless from any possible personal liability. The current holder of the note payable shall receive 1,000 shares of no par common stock in full satisfaction of the note payable. After these adjustments have been made the retained earnings shall be raised to zero by a charge against invested capital.

Instructions

(a) Prepare a balance sheet at June 30, 2000, that reflects the events listed above.
(b) Briefly discuss the nature of a quasi-reorganization.

PROBLEMS

P16-1 (Correction of Equity Items) As the newly appointed controller for Aretha Franklin Company, you are interested in analyzing the "Additional Capital" account of the company in order to present an accurate balance sheet. Your assistant, Diana Ross, who has analyzed the account from the inception of the company, submits the following summary:

	Debits	Credits
Cash dividends—preferred	$ 114,000	
Cash dividends—common	340,000	
Excess of amount paid in over par value of common stock		430,000
Discount on preferred stock	60,000	
Net income		780,000
Contra to appraisal increase of land		400,000
Additional assessments of prior years' income taxes	91,000	
Extraordinary gain		22,500
Treasury stock, preferred; issued and reacquired, at par	250,000	
Extraordinary loss	118,500	
Correction of a prior period error	55,000	
	1,028,500	1,632,500
Credit balance of additional capital account	604,000	
	$1,632,500	$1,632,500

Instructions

(a) Prepare a journal entry to close the single "Additional Capital" account now used and to establish appropriately classified accounts. Indicate how you derive the balance of each new account.

(b) If generally accepted accounting principles had been followed, what amount should have been shown as total net income?

P16-2 (Equity Shortage and Treasury Stock Settlement) The balance sheet of Bajor Inc. shows $400,000 capital stock consisting of 4,000 shares of $100 par, and retained earnings of $144,000. As controller of the company, you find that Ro Laren, the assistant treasurer, is $83,000 short in her accounts and had concealed this shortage by adding the amount to the inventory. She owns 750 shares of the company's stock and, in settlement of the shortage, offers this stock at its book value. The offer is accepted; the company pays her the excess value and distributes the 750 shares thus acquired to the other stockholders.

Instructions

(a) What amount should Bajor Inc. pay the assistant treasurer?
(b) By what journal entries should the foregoing transactions be recorded? (Treasury stock is recorded using the cost method.)
(c) What is the total stockholders' equity after the distribution noted above?
(d) What would have been done if Bajor Inc. had had a deficit of $85,000 and the 750 shares had been accepted at par?

P16-3 (Preferred Stock Dividends) Monie Love Inc. began operations in January 1998 and had the following reported net income or loss for each of its 5 years of operations:

1998	$ 225,000 loss
1999	140,000 loss
2000	180,000 loss
2001	422,500 income
2002	1,535,000 income

At December 31, 2002, Monie Love capital accounts were as follows:

Common stock, par value $15 per share; authorized 200,000 shares; issued and outstanding 50,000 shares	$ 750,000
8% nonparticipating noncumulative preferred stock, par value $100 per share; authorized, issued and outstanding 5,000 shares	500,000
5% fully participating cumulative preferred stock, par value $150 per share; authorized, issued and outstanding 10,000 shares	1,500,000

Monie Love has never paid a cash or stock dividend. There has been no change in the capital accounts since Monie Love began operations. The appropriate state law permits dividends only from retained earnings.

Instructions

Prepare a work sheet showing the maximum amount available for cash dividends on December 31, 2002, and how it would be distributable to the holders of the common shares and each of the preferred shares. Show supporting computations in good form.

(AICPA adapted)

P16-4 (Stock Dividend Involving Exchangeable Shares and Cash in Lieu of Fractional Shares) The board of directors of Edna Ferber Corporation on December 1, 2002, declared a 4% stock dividend on the common stock of the corporation, payable on December 28, 2002, only to the holders of record at the close of business December 15, 2002. They stipulated that cash dividends were to be paid in lieu of issuing any fractional shares. They also directed that the amount to be charged against retained earnings should be an amount equal to the market value of the stock on the record date multiplied by the total of (a) the number of shares issued as a stock dividend, and (b) the number of shares on which cash is paid in place of the issuance of fractional shares. The following facts are given:

1. At the dividend record date:

(a) Shares of Ferber common issued	3,048,750
(b) Shares of Ferber common held in treasury	1,100
(c) Shares of Ferber common included in (a) above held by persons who will receive cash in lieu of fractional shares	222,750

2. Values of Ferber common were:

Par value	$ 5
Market value at December 1st and 15th	$21
Book value at December 1st and 15th	$14

Instructions

Prepare entries and explanations to record the payment of the dividend.

(AICPA adapted)

P16-5 (Cash Dividend Entries) The books of John Dos Passos Corporation carried the following account balances as of December 31, 2001:

Cash	$ 195,000
Preferred stock, 6% cumulative, nonparticipating, $50 par	750,000
Common stock, no par value, 300,000 shares issued	1,500,000
Paid-in capital in excess of par (preferred)	150,000
Treasury stock (common 4,200 shares at cost)	33,600
Retained earnings	105,000

The preferred stock has dividends in arrears for the past year (2001)—to be settled by issuance of preferred stock.

The board of directors, at their annual meeting on December 21, 2002, declared the following: "The current year dividends shall be 6% on the preferred and $.30 per share on the common; the dividends in arrears shall be paid by issuing one share of treasury stock for each ten shares of preferred held."

The preferred is currently selling at $80 per share and the common at $8 per share. Net income for 2002 is estimated at $77,000.

Instructions

(a) Prepare the journal entries required for the dividend declaration and payment, assuming that they occur simultaneously.

(b) Could John Dos Passos Corporation give the preferred stockholders 2 years' dividends and common stockholders a 30 cents per share dividend, all in cash?

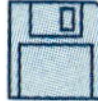

P16-6 (Preferred Stock Dividends) Cajun Company has outstanding 2,500 shares of $100 par, 6% preferred stock and 15,000 shares of $10 par value common. The schedule below shows the amount of dividends paid out over the last 4 years.

Instructions

Allocate the dividends to each type of stock under assumptions (a) and (b). Express your answers in per-share amounts using the following format.

		Assumptions			
		(a) Preferred, noncumulative, and nonparticipating		(b) Preferred, cumulative, and fully participating	
Year	Paid-out	Preferred	Common	Preferred	Common
1999	$13,000				
2000	$26,000				
2001	$57,000				
2002	$76,000				

P16-7 (Dividends and splits) Gutsy Company provides you with the following condensed balance sheet information.

Assets		Liabilities and Stockholders' Equity		
Current assets	$ 40,000	Current and long-term liabilities		$100,000
Investments in ABC stock		Stockholders' equity		
(10,000 shares at cost)	60,000	Common stock ($2 par)	$ 20,000	
Equipment (net)	250,000	Paid-in capital in excess of par	110,000	
Intangibles	60,000	Retained earnings	180,000	310,000
Total assets	$410,000	Total liabilities and stockholders' equity		$410,000

Instructions

For each transaction below, indicate the dollar impact (if any) on the following five items: (1) total assets, (2) common stock, (3) paid-in capital in excess of par, (4) retained earnings, and (5) stockholders' equity. (Each situation is independent.)

(a) Gutsy declares and pays a $.50 per share dividend.

(b) Gutsy declares and issues a 10% stock dividend when the market price of the stock is $14 per share.

(c) Gutsy declares and issues a 40% stock dividend when the market price of the stock is $15 per share.

(d) Gutsy declares and distributes a property dividend. Gutsy gives one share of ABC stock for every two shares of Gutsy Company stock held. ABC is selling for $10 per share on the date the property dividend is declared.

(e) Gutsy declares a 2-for-1 stock split and issues new shares.

P16-8 (Entries for Stockholders' Equity Transactions) Some of the account balances of Mali Vai Company at December 31, 2001, are shown below.

6% Preferred Stock ($100 par, 2,000 shares authorized)	$ 20,000
Paid-in Capital in Excess of Par—Preferred Stock	3,000
Common Stock ($10 par, 100,000 shares authorized)	500,000
Paid-in Capital in Excess of Par—Common Stock	100,000
Unappropriated Retained Earnings	304,000
Treasury Stock—Preferred (50 shares at cost)	5,500
Treasury Stock—Common (1,000 shares at cost)	16,000
Retained Earnings Appropriated for Contingencies	75,000
Retained Earnings Appropriated for Fire Insurance	95,000

The price of the company's common stock has been increasing steadily on the market; it was $21 on January 1, 2002, advanced to $24 by July 1, and to $27 at the end of the year 2002. The preferred stock is not openly traded but was appraised at $120 per share during 2002.

Instructions

Give the proper journal entries for each of the following:

(a) The company incurred a fire loss of $71,000 to its warehouse.

(b) The company declared a property dividend on April 1. Each common stockholder was to receive one share of Washington for every 10 shares outstanding. Mali Vai had 8,000 shares of Washington (2% of total outstanding stock) which was purchased in 1999 for $68,400. The market value of Washington stock was $16 per share on April 1. Record appreciation only on the shares distributed.

(c) The company resold the 50 shares of preferred stock held in the treasury for $116 per share.

(d) On July 1, the company declared a 5% stock dividend to the common (outstanding) stockholders.

(e) The city of Wimble, in an effort to persuade the company to expand into that city, donated to Mali Vai Company a plot of land with an appraised value of $42,000 (credit to Revenue from Contribution).

(f) At the annual board of directors meeting, the board decided to "Set up an appropriation in retained earnings for the future construction of a new plant. Such appropriation to be for $125,000 per year. Also, to increase the appropriation for contingencies by $25,000 and to eliminate the appropriation for fire insurance and begin purchasing such insurance from London Insurance Company."

P16-9 (Equity Entries and Retained Earnings Statement) The stockholders' equity section of Girod Company balance sheet on January 1 of the current year is as follows:

Paid-in capital		
Common stock, par $100, 20,000 shares authorized, 10,000 shares issued	$1,000,000	
Paid-in capital in excess of par	400,000	
Total paid-in capital		$1,400,000
Retained earnings		
Unappropriated	328,800	
Appropriated for plant expansion	120,000	
Appropriated for treasury stock	61,200	
Total retained earnings		510,000
		1,910,000
Less: Cost of treasury stock (600 shares)		61,200
Total stockholders' equity		$1,848,800

The following selected transactions occurred during the year:

1. Paid cash dividends of $1.25 per share on the common stock. The dividend had been properly recorded when declared last year. (State law prohibits cash or stock dividends on treasury shares.)

2. Declared a 10% stock dividend on the common stock when the shares were selling at $113 each in the market.
3. Made a prior period adjustment to correct an error of $70,000 which overstated net income in the previous year. The error was the result of an overstatement of ending inventory.
4. Sold all of the treasury shares for $70,200.
5. Issued the certificates for the stock dividend.
6. The board appropriated $40,000 of retained earnings for plant expansion, eliminated the appropriation for treasury stock, and declared a cash dividend of $1.65 per share on the common stock.
7. The company reported net income of $235,000 for the year.

Instructions

(a) Prepare journal entries for the selected transactions above (ignore income taxes).
(b) Compute the unappropriated retained earnings balance at December 31.

P16-10 (Equity Entries and Balance Sheet Presentation) On December 15, 2001, the directors of Geordi Laforge Corporation voted to appropriate $90,000 of retained earnings and to retain in the business assets equal to the appropriation for use in expanding the corporation's factory building. This was the fourth of such appropriations; after it was recorded, the stockholders' equity section of Laforge's balance sheet appeared as follows:

Stockholders' equity		
Common stock, $10 par value, 300,000 shares authorized, 200,000 shares issued and outstanding		$2,000,000
Paid-in capital in excess of par		3,600,000
Total paid-in capital		5,600,000
Retained earnings		
Unappropriated	$1,800,000	
Appropriated for plant expansion	360,000	
Total retained earnings		2,160,000
Total stockholders' equity		$7,760,000

On January 9, 2002, the corporation entered into a contract for the construction of the factory addition for which the retained earnings were appropriated. On November 1, 2002, the addition was completed and the contractor was paid the contract price of $330,000.

On December 14, 2002, the board of directors voted to return the balance of the Retained Earnings Appropriated for Plant Expansion account to Unappropriated Retained Earnings. They also voted a 25,000 share stock dividend distributable on January 23, 2003, to the January 15, 2003, stockholders of record. The stock dividend was paid per the board's resolution. The corporation's stock was selling at $47 in the market on December 14, 2002. Laforge reported net income of $530,000 for 2001 and $600,000 for 2002.

Instructions

(a) Prepare the appropriate journal entries for Laforge Corporation for the information above (December 15, 2001, to January 23, 2003, inclusive).
(b) Prepare the stockholders' equity section of the balance sheet for Laforge at December 31, 2002, in proper accounting form.

P16-11 (Stockholders' Equity Section of Balance Sheet) The following is a summary of all relevant transactions of Jadzia Dax Corporation since it was organized in 1999:

> In 1999, 15,000 shares were authorized and 7,000 shares of common stock ($50 par value) were issued at a price of $57. In 2000, 1,000 shares were issued as a stock dividend when the stock was selling for $62. Three hundred shares of common stock were bought in 2001 at a cost of $66 per share. These 300 shares are still in the company treasury. (State law requires an appropriation of retained earnings equal to cost of treasury stock.)
>
> In 2000, 10,000 preferred shares were authorized and the company issued 4,000 of them ($100 par value) at $113. Some of the preferred stock was reacquired by the company and later reissued for $4,700 more than it cost the company.
>
> The corporation has earned a total of $610,000 in net income after income taxes and paid out a total of $312,600 in cash dividends since incorporation. An appropriation was made in 2001 by the board of directors from retained earnings in the amount of $75,000 for Fixed Asset Replacements.

Instructions

Prepare the stockholders' equity section of the balance sheet in proper form for Jadzia Dax Corporation as of December 31, 2001. Account for treasury stock using the cost method.

P16-12 (Stock and Cash Dividends) Gul Ducat Corporation has outstanding 2,000,000 shares of common stock of a par value of $10 each. The balance in its retained earnings account at January 1, 2001, was $24,000,000, and it then had Additional Paid-in Capital of $5,000,000. During 2001, the company's net income was $5,700,000. A cash dividend of 60¢ a share was paid June 30, 2001, and a 6% stock dividend was distributed to stockholders of record at the close of business on December 31, 2001. You have been asked to advise on the proper accounting treatment of the stock dividend.

The existing stock of the company is quoted on a national stock exchange. The market price of the stock has been as follows:

October 31, 2001	$31
November 30, 2001	33
December 31, 2001	38
Average price over the two-month period	35

Instructions

(a) Prepare a journal entry to record the cash dividend.

(b) Prepare a journal entry to record the stock dividend.

(c) Prepare the stockholders' equity section (including schedules of retained earnings and additional paid-in capital) of the balance sheet of Gul Ducat Corporation for the year 2001 on the basis of the foregoing information. Draft a note to the financial statements setting forth the basis of the accounting for the stock dividend and add separately appropriate comments or explanations regarding the basis chosen.

P16-13 (Analysis and Classification of Equity Transactions) Ohio Company was formed on July 1, 1998. It was authorized to issue 300,000 shares of $10 par value common stock and 100,000 shares of 8% $25 par value, cumulative and nonparticipating preferred stock. Ohio Company has a July 1–June 30 fiscal year.

The following information relates to the stockholders' equity accounts of Ohio Company:

Common Stock

Prior to the 2000–01 fiscal year, Ohio Company had 110,000 shares of outstanding common stock issued as follows:

1. 95,000 shares were issued for cash on July 1, 1998, at $31 per share.
2. On July 24, 1998, 5,000 shares were exchanged for a plot of land which cost the seller $70,000 in 1992 and had an estimated market value of $220,000 on July 24, 1998.
3. 10,000 shares were issued on March 1, 2000; the shares had been subscribed for $42 per share on October 31, 1999.

During the 2000–01 fiscal year, the following transactions regarding common stock took place:

October 1, 2000	Subscriptions were received for 10,000 shares at $46 per share. Cash of $92,000 was received in full payment for 2,000 shares and stock certificates were issued. The remaining subscription for 8,000 shares were to be paid in full by September 30, 2001, at which time the certificates were to be issued.
November 30, 2000	Ohio purchased 2,000 shares of its own stock on the open market at $39 per share. Ohio uses the cost method for treasury stock.
December 15, 2000	Ohio declared a 5% stock dividend for stockholders of record on January 15, 2001, to be issued on January 31, 2001. Ohio was having a liquidity problem and could not afford a cash dividend at the time. Ohio's common stock was selling at $52 per share on December 15, 2000.
June 20, 2001	Ohio sold 500 shares of its own common stock that it had purchased on November 30, 2000, for $21,000.

Preferred Stock

Ohio issued 50,000 shares of preferred stock at $44 per share on July 1, 1999.

Cash Dividends

Ohio has followed a schedule of declaring cash dividends in December and June with payment being made to stockholders of record in the following month. The cash dividends which have been declared since inception of the company through June 30, 2001, are shown below:

Declaration Date	Common Stock	Preferred Stock
12/15/99	$.30 per share	$1.00 per share
6/15/00	$.30 per share	$1.00 per share
12/15/00	—	$1.00 per share

No cash dividends were declared during June 2001 due to the company's liquidity problems.

Retained Earnings

As of June 30, 2000, Ohio's retained earnings account had a balance of $690,000. For the fiscal year ending June 30, 2001, Ohio reported net income of $40,000.

In March of 2000, Ohio received a term loan from Columbus National Bank. The bank requires Ohio to establish a sinking fund and restrict retained earnings for an amount equal to the sinking fund deposit. The annual sinking fund payment of $50,000 is due on April 30 each year; the first payment was made on schedule on April 30, 2001.

Instructions

Prepare the stockholders' equity section of the Balance Sheet, including appropriate notes, for Ohio Company as of June 30, 2001, as it should appear in its annual report to the shareholders.

(CMA adapted)

P16-14 (Stock Dividends and Stock Split) Jenny Durdil Inc. is selling its $10 par common stock for $120 per share. Five million shares are currently issued and outstanding. The board of directors wishes to stimulate interest in Jenny Durdil common stock before a forthcoming stock issue but does not wish to distribute capital at this time. The board also believes that too many adjustments to the Stockholders' Equity section, especially Retained Earnings, might discourage potential investors.

The board has considered three options for stimulating interest in the stock:

1. A 20% stock dividend
2. A 100% stock dividend
3. A 2-for-1 stock split.

Acting as financial advisor to the board, you have been asked to report briefly on each option and, considering the board's wishes, make a recommendation. Discuss the effects of each of the foregoing options.

CONCEPTUAL CASES

C16-1 (Conceptual Issues—Equity) Statements of Financial Accounting Concepts set forth financial accounting and reporting objectives and fundamentals that will be used by the Financial Accounting Standards Board in developing standards. *Concepts Statement No. 6* was issued to replace *Concepts Statement No. 3,* and it defines various elements of financial statements.

Instructions

Answer the following questions based on *SFAC No. 6.*

(a) Define and discuss the term "equity."
(b) What transactions or events change owners' equity?
(c) Define "investments by owners" and provide examples of this type of transaction. What financial statement element other than equity is typically affected by owner investments?
(d) Define "distributions to owners" and provide examples of this type of transaction. What financial statement element other than equity is typically affected by distributions?
(e) What are examples of changes within owners' equity that do not change the total amount of owners' equity?

C16-2 (Stock Dividends and Splits) The directors of Amman Corporation are considering the issuance of a stock dividend. They have asked you to discuss the proposed action by answering the following questions.

Instructions

(a) What is a stock dividend? How is a stock dividend distinguished from a stock split (1) From a legal standpoint? (2) From an accounting standpoint?
(b) For what reasons does a corporation usually declare a stock dividend? A stock split?
(c) Discuss the amount, if any, of retained earnings to be capitalized in connection with a stock dividend.

(AICPA adapted)

C16-3 (Stock Dividends) Kitakyushu Inc., a client, is considering the authorization of a 10% common stock dividend to common stockholders. The financial vice president of Kitakyushu wishes to discuss the accounting implications of such an authorization with you before the next meeting of the board of directors.

Instructions

(a) The first topic the vice president wishes to discuss is the nature of the stock dividend to the recipient. Discuss the case against considering the stock dividend as income to the recipient.

(b) The other topic for discussion is the propriety of issuing the stock dividend to all "stockholders of record" or to "stockholders of record exclusive of shares held in the name of the corporation as treasury stock." Discuss the case against issuing stock dividends on treasury shares.

(AICPA adapted)

C16-4 (Stock Dividend, Cash Dividend, and Treasury Stock) Hsuchou Company has 30,000 shares of $10 par value common stock authorized and 20,000 shares issued and outstanding. On August 15, 2001, Hsuchou purchased 1,000 shares of treasury stock for $16 per share. Hsuchou uses the cost method to account for treasury stock. On September 14, 2001, Hsuchou sold 500 shares of the treasury stock for $20 per share.

In October 2001, Hsuchou declared and distributed 1,950 shares as a stock dividend from unissued shares when the market value of the common stock was $21 per share.

On December 20, 2001, Hsuchou declared a $1 per share cash dividend, payable on January 10, 2002, to shareholders of record on December 31, 2001.

Instructions

(a) How should Hsuchou account for the purchase and sale of the treasury stock, and how should the treasury stock be presented in the balance sheet at December 31, 2001?

(b) How should Hsuchou account for the stock dividend, and how would it affect the stockholders' equity at December 31, 2001? Why?

(c) How should Hsuchou account for the cash dividend, and how would it affect the balance sheet at December 31, 2001? Why?

(AICPA adapted)

***C16-5 (Quasi-Reorganization)** Jackie Henning Company, a medium-sized manufacturer, has been experiencing losses for the 5 years that it has been doing business. Although the operations for the year just ended resulted in a loss, several important changes resulted in a profitable fourth quarter, and the future operations of the company are expected to be profitable. The treasurer, Peter Henning, suggests that there be a quasi-reorganization to eliminate the accumulated deficit of $650,000.

Instructions

(a) What are the characteristics of a quasi-reorganization? In other words, of what does it consist?

(b) List the conditions under which a quasi-reorganization generally is justified.

(c) Discuss the propriety of the treasurer's proposals to eliminate the deficit of $650,000.

(AICPA adapted)

***C16-6 (Quasi-Reorganization)** After operating several years, Char Lewis Corporation showed a net worth of $1,500,000, of which $300,000 was represented by 3,000 shares of $100 each, and $1,200,000 was retained earnings. Subsequently, three additional shares were issued for each share held, which made the capital stock $1,200,000 and retained earnings $300,000. The operations of later years showed an aggregate loss of $840,000, leaving a deficit of $540,000.

The corporation then reduced the par value of each share of stock to 25% of its former value, thus restoring the capital to the original amount of $300,000. The deficit was absorbed and the retained earnings shown as $360,000. It is argued that this amount represents the net operating results since organization and is, therefore, retained earnings.

Instructions

Write a memorandum, giving your opinion of these transactions; disregard their legal aspects.

USING YOUR JUDGMENT

FINANCIAL REPORTING PROBLEM: INTEL CORPORATION

Instructions

Refer to the financial statements and accompanying notes and discussion of Intel Corporation presented in Appendix 5B and answer the following questions.

(a) What amount of cash dividends per share was declared by Intel in 1998? What was the dollar amount effect of the cash dividends on Intel's stockholders' equity?

(b) What is Intel's rate of return on common stock equity for 1998 and 1997?

(c) What is Intel's payout ratio for 1998 and 1997?

(d) What is Intel's book value per share at December 26, 1998, and December 27, 1997?

(e) What was the market price range (high/low) of Intel's common stock during the quarter ended December 26, 1998?

(f) Using the high price per share in the fourth quarter of 1998, what was the price earnings ratio for Intel?

FINANCIAL STATEMENT ANALYSIS CASES

Case 1: Wiebold, Incorporated

The following note related to stockholders' equity was reported in Wiebold's annual report:

> On February 1, 1998, the Board of Directors declared a 3-for-2 stock split, distributed on February 22, 1998, to shareholders of record on February 10, 1998. Accordingly, all numbers of common shares, except unissued shares and treasury shares, and all per share data have been restated to reflect this stock split in addition to the 3-for-2 stock split declared on January 27, 1997, distributed on February 26, 1997, to shareholders of record on February 10, 1997.
>
> On the basis of amounts declared and paid, the annualized quarterly dividends per share were $0.80 in 1997, $0.75 in 1996, and $0.71 in 1995.

Instructions

(a) What is the significance of the date of record and the date of distribution?

(b) Why might Weibold have declared a 3-for-2 for stock split?

(c) What impact does Wiebold's stock split have on (1) total stockholders' equity; (2) total par value; (3) outstanding shares, and (4) book value per share?

Case 2: Garrister Information Systems Corp.

Garrister Information Systems has two classes of preferred stock—A and C—in addition to its common stock. The 1,300 shares of Series A preferred stock are nonvoting, have a 12% cumulative dividend, have liquidation preference rights over the Series C preferred stock and the common stock, and are callable by the company at any time for $1,000 per share plus cumulative unpaid dividends. Each share of Series A preferred stock is convertible into 500 shares of common stock. As of March 31, 1998, the cumulative unpaid dividends on the Series A preferred stock totaled $254,000.

Instructions

(a) Should the $254,000 in dividends not paid be reported as a liability on the balance sheet?

(b) If the par value of the Class A preferred stock is $100 per share, what dollar amount in dividends can the shareholders expect annually on the Class A preferred stock?

COMPARATIVE ANALYSIS CASE

The Coca-Cola Company versus PepsiCo, Inc.

Instructions

Go to the Digital Tool and, using The Coca-Cola Company and PepsiCo, Inc. Annual Report information, answer the following questions.

(a) What amounts of cash dividends per share were declared by Coca-Cola and PepsiCo in 1998? What were the dollar amount effects of the cash dividends on each company's stockholders' equity?

(b) What are Coca-Cola's and PepsiCo's rate of return on common/capital stock equity for 1998 and 1997? Which company gets the higher return on the equity of its shareholders?

(c) What are Coca-Cola's and PepsiCo's payout ratios for 1998?

(d) What was the market price range (high/low) for Coca-Cola's common stock and PepsiCo's capital stock during the fourth quarter of 1998? Which company's (Coca-Cola's or PepsiCo's) stock price increased more (%) during 1998?

(e) What was Coca-Cola's price-earnings ratio at December 31, 1998? What was PepsiCo's price-earnings ratio at December 26, 1998?

RESEARCH CASES

Case 1

As indicated in the chapter, companies are required to disclose changes in the separate accounts comprising stockholders' equity.

Instructions

Examine the financial statements of two companies of your choice and answer the following questions with regard to each company.

(a) Are the changes in the stockholders' equity accounts presented in a separate statement or in the notes to the financial statements?

(b) Is a separate statement of retained earnings presented?

(c) Which of the stockholders' equity account balances changed during the period covered? Identify the reason(s) for these changes.

Case 2

The October 3, 1994, issue of *Barron's* includes an article by Shirley A. Lazo entitled "Split Decision: One Way To Lift Shares."

Instructions

Read the article and answer the following questions.

(a) Why might a stock dividend/split have a positive effect on shareholder wealth?

(b) Why might a stock dividend/split have a negative effect on shareholder wealth?

(c) According to the study described in the article, what happens to the stock prices of banks during the month following a stock dividend/split?

(d) What conclusion was drawn from the study?

ETHICS CASES

*Case 1

"You can't writeup assets," said Nick Toby, internal audit director of Paula Nofftz International Inc., to his boss, Jim Coffin, vice president and chief financial officer. "Nonsense," said Jim, "I can do this as part of a quasi-reorganization of our company." For the last 3 years, Paula Nofftz International, a farm equipment manufacturing firm, has experienced a downturn in its profits resulting from stiff competition with overseas firms and increasing direct labor costs. Though the prospects are still gloomy, the company is hoping to turn a profit by modernizing its property, plant, and equipment (PP&E). This will require Paula Nofftz International to raise a lot of money.

Over the past few months, Jim tried to raise funds from various financial institutions. They are unwilling to consider lending capital, however, because the company's net book value of fixed assets on the balance sheet, based on historic cost, was not ample to sustain major funding. Jim attempted to explain to bankers and investors that these assets were more valuable than their recorded amounts, given that the company used accelerated depreciation methods and tended to underestimate the useful lives of assets. Jim also believes that the company's land and buildings are substantially undervalued because of rising real estate prices over the past several years.

Jim's idea is a simple one: First, declare a large dividend to shareholders of the company, such that Retained Earnings would have a large debit balance. Then, writeup the fixed assets of Paula Nofftz International to an amount equal to the deficit in the Retained Earnings account.

Instructions

(a) What are the ethical implications of Jim Coffin's creative accounting scheme?

(b) Who could be harmed if the accounting reorganization were implemented and Paula Nofftz International Inc. received additional funding?

(c) Why can't a company writeup assets when the fair value of these assets exceed their original cost?

Case 2

Donald Young, comptroller for Center Company, wants to discuss with the company president, Rhonda Santo, the possibility of paying a stock dividend. Young knows the company does not have an abundance of cash, yet he is certain Santo would like to give the stockholders something of value this year since it has been a few years since the company has paid any dividends. Young also is concerned that their cash position will not improve significantly in the near future. He feels that stockholders look to retained earnings and, if they see a large balance, believe (erroneously, of course) that the company can pay a cash dividend.

Young wants to propose that the company pay a 100% stock dividend as opposed to a cash dividend or a 2-for-1 stock split. He reasons (1) that the stockholders will receive something of value, other than cash, and (2) that retained earnings will be reduced by the stock dividend (as opposed to a split which does not affect retained earnings) so stockholders will be less likely to expect cash dividends in the near future.

Instructions

Answer the following questions:

(a) What are the ethical issues involved?

(b) Do you agree with Young's reasoning?

CHAPTER 17

Dilutive Securities and Earnings per Share

LEARNING OBJECTIVES

After studying this chapter, you should be able to:

1. **Describe the accounting for the issuance, conversion, and retirement of convertible securities.**
2. **Explain the accounting for convertible preferred stock.**
3. **Contrast the accounting for stock warrants and stock warrants issued with other securities.**
4. **Describe the accounting for stock compensation plans under generally accepted accounting principles.**
5. **Explain the controversy involving stock compensation plans.**
6. **Compute earnings per share in a simple capital structure.**
7. **Compute earnings per share in a complex capital structure.**

Mergers Dilute Earnings per Share

The "urge to merge" that dominated the business scene in the 1960s developed into merger mania in the 1980s. The 1990s saw fewer mergers than the 1980s, but those that did take place were some of the largest ever. Typical mergers in the 1990s were combinations of information, entertainment, or financial (banking) companies. For example, **Bell Atlantic Corp.** and **Nynex Corp.** combined in a $22.7 billion deal, **Time** acquired **Warner Communications** for $10.1 billion, **Walt Disney Co.** purchased **Capital Cities/ABC, Inc.**, **Chemical Bank** joined with **Chase Manhattan Corp.**, and **Boeing** bought **McDonnell Douglas Corp.** Even larger were the mergers of **Nations Bank** and **BankAmerica** ($62 billion), and **Bell Atlantic** and **GTE** ($71 billion) in 1998. Sweeping deregulation triggered many of the deals in telecommunications, banking, and utilities; cuts in military spending changed the landscape for aerospace firms.[1]

One consequence of heavy merger activity is an increase in the use of securities such as convertible bonds, convertible preferred stocks, stock warrants, and contingent shares to structure these deals. Although not common stock in form, these securities enable their holders to obtain common stock upon exercise or conversion. They are called **dilutive securities** or **potential common stock** because a reduction—dilution—in earnings per share often results when these securities become common stock.

During the 1960s, corporate officers recognized that the issuance of dilutive securities in a merger did not have the same immediate adverse effect on earnings per share as the issuance of common stock. In addition, many companies found that issuance of convertible securities did not seem to upset common stockholders, even though the common stockholders' interests were substantially diluted when these securities were later converted or exercised.

As a consequence of the massive mergers in the 1990s, the presence of dilutive securities on corporate balance sheets is now very prevalent. The usage of stock option plans, which also are dilutive in nature, is increasing. These option plans are used mainly to attract and retain executive talent and to provide tax relief for executives in high tax brackets.

[1] Farrell Kramer, "Mergers Have Been in Fashion in 1996, With Seven Big Ones," *St. Louis Post-Dispatch,* December 16, 1996, p. A7; and Geoffrey Colvin, "The Year of the Mega Merger," *Fortune,* January 11, 1999, p. 62.

PREVIEW OF CHAPTER 17

The widespread use of dilutive securities has led the accounting profession to examine the area closely. Specifically, the profession has directed its attention to accounting for these securities at date of issuance and to the presentation of earnings per share figures that recognize their effect. The first section of this chapter discusses convertible securities, warrants, stock options, and contingent shares. The second section indicates how these securities are used in earnings per share computations. The content and organization of the chapter are as follows:

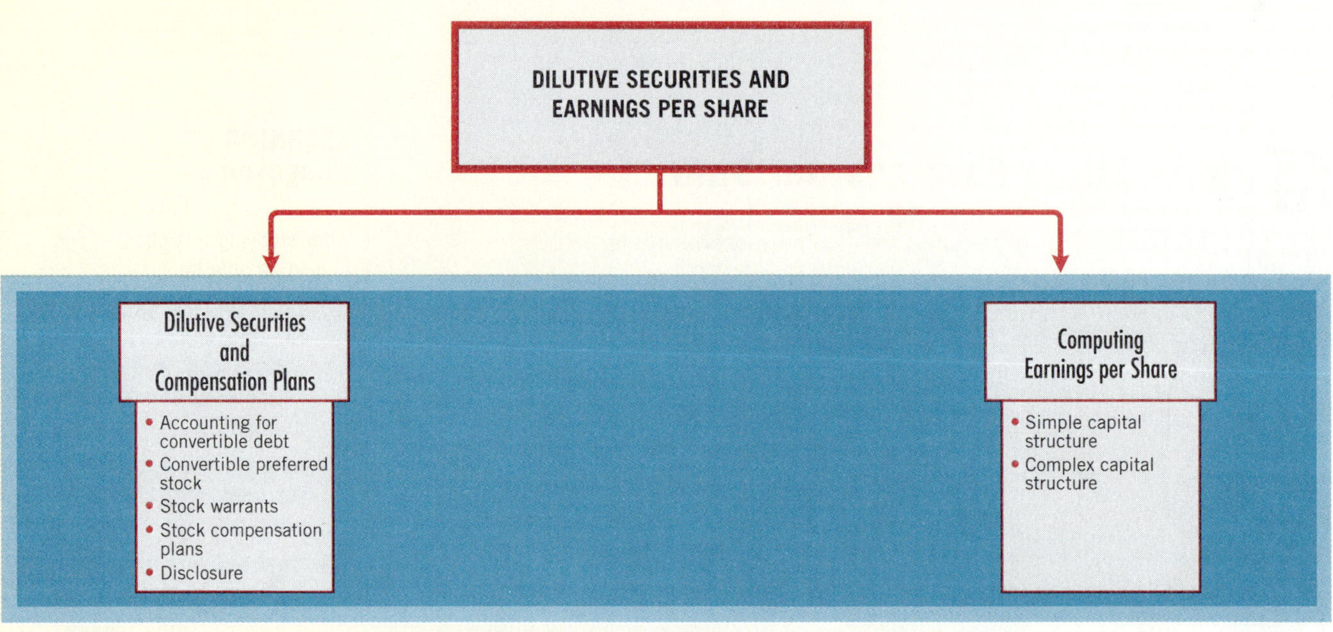

SECTION 1 DILUTIVE SECURITIES AND COMPENSATION PLANS

ACCOUNTING FOR CONVERTIBLE DEBT

OBJECTIVE 1
Describe the accounting for the issuance, conversion, and retirement of convertible securities.

If bonds can be converted into other corporate securities during some specified period of time after issuance, they are called **convertible bonds**. **A convertible bond combines the benefits of a bond with the privilege of exchanging it for stock at the holder's option.** It is purchased by investors who desire the security of a bond holding—guaranteed interest—plus the added option of conversion if the value of the stock appreciates significantly.

Corporations issue convertibles for two main reasons. One is the desire to raise equity capital without giving up more ownership control than necessary. To illustrate, assume that a company wants to raise $1,000,000 at a time when its common stock is selling at $45 per share. Such an issue would require sale of 22,222 shares (ignoring issue costs). By selling 1,000 bonds at $1,000 par, each convertible into 20 shares of common stock, the enterprise may raise $1,000,000 by committing only 20,000 shares of its common stock.

A second reason why companies issue convertible securities is to obtain common stock financing at cheaper rates. Many enterprises could issue debt only at high interest rates unless a convertible covenant were attached. The conversion privilege entices the investor to accept a lower interest rate than would normally be the case on a straight debt issue. For example, **Amazon.com** recently issued convertible bonds that pay interest at an effective yield of 4.75%, which is much lower than Amazon.com would have to pay if it issued straight debt. For this lower interest rate, the investor receives the right to buy Amazon.com's common stock at a fixed price until maturity.[2]

Accounting for convertible debt involves reporting issues at the time of (1) issuance, (2) conversion, and (3) retirement.

At Time of Issuance

The method for recording convertible bonds **at the date of issue follows the method used to record straight debt issues** (with none of the proceeds recorded as equity). Any discount or premium that results from the issuance of convertible bonds is amortized to its maturity date because it is difficult to predict when, if at all, conversion will occur. However, the accounting for convertible debt as a straight debt issue is controversial; we discuss it more fully later in this chapter.

At Time of Conversion

If bonds are converted into other securities, the principal accounting problem is to determine the amount at which to record the securities exchanged for the bond. Assume Hilton, Inc. issued at a premium of $60 a $1,000 bond convertible into 10 shares of common stock (par value $10). At the time of conversion the unamortized premium is $50, the market value of the bond is $1,200, and the stock is quoted on the market at $120. **The book value method of recording the conversion of the bonds is the method most commonly used in practice and is considered GAAP.** To illustrate the specifics of this approach, the entry for the conversion of the Hilton, Inc. bonds would be:

Bonds Payable	1,000	
Premium on Bonds Payable	50	
Common Stock		100
Paid-in Capital in Excess of Par		950

Support for the book value approach is based on the argument that an agreement was established at the date of the issuance either to pay a stated amount of cash at maturity or to issue a stated number of shares of equity securities. Therefore, when the debt is converted to equity in accordance with the preexisting contract terms, no gain or loss should be recognized upon conversion.[3]

---

[2]As with any investment, a buyer has to be careful. For example, **Wherehouse Entertainment Inc.**, which had 6 1/4% convertibles outstanding, was taken private in a leveraged buyout. As a result, the convertible was suddenly as risky as a junk bond of a highly leveraged company with a coupon of only 6 1/4%. As one holder of the convertibles noted, "What's even worse is that the company will be so loaded down with debt that it probably won't have enough cash flow to make its interest payments. And the convertible debt we hold is subordinated to the rest of Wherehouse's debt." These types of situations have made convertibles less attractive and have led to the introduction of takeover protection covenants in some convertible bond offerings. Or, sometimes convertibles are permitted to be called at par and therefore the conversion premium may be lost.

[3]An alternative approach that has some conceptual merit uses the market value to record the conversion. The entry under the **market value approach** (market price = $1,200) would be:

Bonds Payable	1,000	
Premium on Bonds Payable	50	
Loss on Redemption of Bonds Payable	150	
Common Stock		100
Paid-in Capital in Excess of Par		1,100

Because the conversion described above is initiated by the holder of the debt instrument (rather than the issuer), it is not an "early extinguishment of debt." As a result, the gain or loss would not be classified as an extraordinary item.

Induced Conversions

Sometimes the issuer wishes to induce prompt conversion of its convertible debt to equity securities in order to reduce interest costs or to improve its debt to equity ratio. As a result, the issuer may offer some form of additional consideration (such as cash or common stock), called a "sweetener," to **induce conversion**. The sweetener should be reported as an expense of the current period at an amount equal to the fair value of the additional securities or other consideration given.

Assume that Helloid, Inc. has outstanding $1,000,000 par value convertible debentures convertible into 100,000 shares of $1 par value common stock. Helloid wishes to reduce its annual interest cost. To do so, Helloid agrees to pay the holders of its convertible debentures an additional $80,000 if they will convert. Assuming conversion occurs, the following entry is made:

Debt Conversion Expense	80,000	
Bonds Payable	1,000,000	
Common Stock		100,000
Additional Paid-in Capital		900,000
Cash		80,000

The additional $80,000 is recorded as **an expense of the current period** and not as a reduction of equity. Some argue that the cost of a conversion inducement is a cost of obtaining equity capital. As a result, they contend, it should be recognized as a cost of—a reduction of—the equity capital acquired and not as an expense. However, the FASB indicated that when an additional payment is needed to make bondholders convert, the payment is for a service (bondholders converting at a given time) and should be reported as an expense. This expense is not reported as an extraordinary item.[4]

Retirement of Convertible Debt

Should the retirement of convertible debt be considered a debt transaction or an equity transaction? In theory, it could be either. If it is treated as a debt transaction, the difference between the carrying amount of the retired convertible debt and the cash paid should result in a charge or credit to income. If it is an equity transaction, the difference should go to additional paid-in capital.

To answer the question, we need to remember that the method for recording the **issuance** of convertible bonds follows that used in recording straight debt issues. Specifically this means that no portion of the proceeds should be attributable to the conversion feature and credited to Additional Paid-in Capital. Although theoretical objections to this approach can be raised, to be consistent, a gain or loss on **retiring convertible debt needs to be recognized in the same way as a gain or loss on retiring debt** that is not convertible. For this reason, differences between the cash acquisition price of debt and its carrying amount should be reported **currently in income as a gain or loss.**[5] As indicated in Chapter 14, material gains or losses on extingishment of debt are considered extraordinary items.

Nevertheless, failure to recognize the equity feature of convertible debt when issued creates problems upon early extinguishment. Assume that the **Amazon.com** convertible debt discussed earlier was issued at a time when the investment community attaches value to the conversion feature. Subsequently the price of Amazon.com stock decreases so sharply that the conversion feature has little or no value. If Amazon.com extinguishes its convertible debt early, a large gain develops because the book value of the debt will exceed the retirement price. Many consider this treatment incorrect, because the reduction in value of the convertible debt relates to its equity features, not

---

[4]"Induced Conversions of Convertible Debt," *Statement of Financial Accounting Standards No. 84* (Stamford, Conn.: FASB, 1985).

[5]"Early Extinguishment of Debt," *Opinions of the Accounting Principles Board No. 26* (New York: AICPA, 1972).

its debt features. Therefore, they argue, an adjustment to Additional Paid-in Capital should be made. However, present practice requires that an extraordinary gain or loss be recognized at the time of early extinguishment.

CONVERTIBLE PREFERRED STOCK

OBJECTIVE 2
Explain the accounting for convertible preferred stock.

The major difference in accounting for a convertible bond and a **convertible preferred stock** at the date of issue is that convertible bonds are considered liabilities, whereas convertible preferreds (unless mandatory redemption exists) are considered a part of stockholders' equity.

In addition, when convertible preferred stocks are exercised, there is no theoretical justification for recognition of a gain or loss. No gain or loss is recognized when the entity deals with stockholders in their capacity as business owners. The **book value method is employed**: Preferred Stock, along with any related Additional Paid-in Capital, is debited; Common Stock and Additional Paid-in Capital (if an excess exists) are credited.

A different treatment develops when the par value of the common stock issued exceeds the book value of the preferred stock. In that case, Retained Earnings is usually debited for the difference.

Assume Host Enterprises issued 1,000 shares of common stock (par value $2) upon conversion of 1,000 shares of preferred stock (par value $1) that was originally issued for a $200 premium. The entry would be:

Convertible Preferred Stock	1,000	
Paid-in Capital in Excess of Par (Premium on Preferred Stock)	200	
Retained Earnings	800	
Common Stock		2,000

The rationale for the debit to Retained Earnings is that the preferred stockholders are offered an additional return to facilitate their conversion to common stock. In this example, the additional return is charged to retained earnings. Many states, however, require that this charge simply reduce additional paid-in capital from other sources.

STOCK WARRANTS

OBJECTIVE 3
Contrast the accounting for stock warrants and stock warrants issued with other securities.

Warrants are certificates entitling the holder to acquire shares of stock at a certain price within a stated period. This option is similar to the conversion privilege because warrants, if exercised, become common stock and usually have a dilutive effect (reduce earnings per share) similar to that of the conversion of convertible securities. However, a substantial difference between convertible securities and stock warrants is that upon exercise of the warrants, the holder has to pay a certain amount of money to obtain the shares.

The issuance of warrants or options to buy additional shares normally arises under three situations:

1. When issuing different types of securities, such as bonds or preferred stock, warrants are often included to make the **security more attractive**—to provide an "equity kicker."
2. Upon the issuance of additional common stock, existing stockholders have a **preemptive right to purchase common stock** first. Warrants may be issued to evidence that right.
3. Warrants, often referred to as stock options, are given as **compensation to executives and employees**.

The problems in accounting for stock warrants are complex and present many difficulties—some of which remain unresolved.

Stock Warrants Issued with Other Securities

Warrants issued with other securities are basically long-term options to buy common stock at a fixed price. Although some perpetual warrants are traded, generally their life is 5 years, occasionally 10.

A warrant works like this: **Tenneco, Inc.** offered a unit comprising one share of stock and one detachable warrant exercisable at $24.25 per share and good for 5 years. The unit sold for 22¾ ($22.75) and since the price of the common the day before the sale was 19⅞ ($19.88), the difference suggests a price of 2⅞ ($2.87) for the warrants.

In this situation, the warrants had an apparent value of 2⅞ ($2.87), even though it would not be profitable at present for the purchaser to exercise the warrant and buy the stock, because the price of the stock is much below the exercise price of $24.25.[6] The investor pays for the warrant to receive a possible future call on the stock at a fixed price when the price has risen significantly. For example, if the price of the stock rises to $30, the investor has gained $2.88 ($30 minus $24.25 minus $2.87) on an investment of $2.87, a 100% increase! But, if the price never rises, the investor loses the full $2.87.[7]

The proceeds from the sale of debt with **detachable stock warrants** should be allocated between the two securities.[8] The profession takes the position that two separable instruments are involved, that is, (1) a bond and (2) a warrant giving the holder the right to purchase common stock at a certain price. Warrants that are detachable can be traded separately from the debt and, therefore, a market value can be determined. The two methods of allocation available are:

1. The proportional method.
2. The incremental method.

Proportional Method

AT&T's offering of detachable 5-year warrants to buy one share of common stock (par value $5) at $25 (at a time when a share was selling for approximately $50) enabled it to price its offering of bonds at par with a moderate 8¾% yield. To place a value on the two securities one would determine (1) the value of the bonds without the warrants and (2) the value of the warrants. For example, assume that AT&T's bonds (par $1,000) sold for 99 without the warrants soon after they were issued. The market value of the warrants at that time was $30. Prior to sale the warrants will not have a market value. The allocation is based on an estimate of market value, generally as established by an investment banker, or on the relative market value of the bonds and the warrants soon after they are issued and traded. The price paid for 10,000, $1,000 bonds with the warrants attached was par, or $10,000,000. The allocation between the bonds and warrants would be made in this manner:

ILLUSTRATION 17-1
Proportional Allocation of Proceeds between Bonds and Warrants

Fair market value of bonds (without warrants) ($10,000,000 × .99)	=	$ 9,900,000
Fair market value of warrants (10,000 × $30)	=	300,000
Aggregate fair market value		$10,200,000
Allocated to bonds:	$\frac{\$9,900,000}{\$10,200,000} \times \$10,000,000 =$	$ 9,705,882
Allocated to warrants:	$\frac{\$300,000}{\$10,200,000} \times \$10,000,000 =$	294,118
Total allocation		$10,000,000

[6]Later in this discussion it will be shown that the value of the warrant is normally determined on the basis of a relative market value approach because of the difficulty of imputing a warrant value in any other manner.

[7]From the illustration, it is apparent that buying warrants can be an "all or nothing" proposition.

[8]A detachable warrant means that the warrant can sell separately from the bond. *APB Opinion No. 14* makes a distinction between detachable and nondetachable warrants because nondetachable warrants must be sold with the security as a complete package; thus, no allocation is permitted.

In this situation the bonds sell at a discount and are recorded as follows:

Cash	9,705,882	
Discount on Bonds Payable	294,118	
Bonds Payable		10,000,000

In addition, the company sells warrants that are credited to paid-in capital. The entry is as follows:

Cash	294,118	
Paid-in Capital—Stock Warrants		294,118

The entries may be combined if desired; they are shown separately here to indicate that the purchaser of the bond is buying not only a bond, but also a possible future claim on common stock.

Assuming that all 10,000 warrants are exercised (one warrant per one share of stock), the following entry would be made:

Cash (10,000 × $25)	250,000	
Paid-in Capital—Stock Warrants	294,118	
Common Stock (10,000 × $5)		50,000
Paid-in Capital in Excess of Par		494,118

What if the warrants are not exercised? In that case, Paid-in Capital—Stock Warrants is debited for $294,118 and Paid-in Capital from Expired Warrants is credited for a like amount. The additional paid-in capital reverts to the former stockholders.

Incremental Method

In instances where the fair value of either the warrants or the bonds is not determinable, the incremental method used in lump sum security purchases (explained in Chapter 15, page 779) may be used. That is, the security for which the market value is determinable is used and the remainder of the purchase price is allocated to the security for which the market value is not known. Assume that the market price of the AT&T warrants was known to be $300,000, but the market price of the bonds without the warrants could not be determined. In this case, the amount allocated to the warrants and the stock would be as follows:

ILLUSTRATION 17-2
Incremental Allocation of Proceeds between Bonds and Warrants

Lump sum receipt	$10,000,000
Allocated to the warrants	300,000
Balance allocated to bonds	$ 9,700,000

Conceptual Questions

The question arises whether the allocation of value to the warrants is consistent with the handling accorded convertible debt, in which no value is allocated to the conversion privilege. The Board stated that the features of a convertible security are **inseparable** in the sense that choices are mutually exclusive: the holder either converts or redeems the bonds for cash, but cannot do both. No basis, therefore, exists for recognizing the conversion value in the accounts. The Board, however, indicated that the issuance of bonds with **detachable warrants** involves two securities, one a debt security, which will remain outstanding until maturity, and the other a warrant to purchase common stock. At the time of issuance, separable instruments exist, and therefore separate treatment is justified. **Nondetachable warrants,** however, **do not require an allocation of the proceeds between the bonds and the warrants**. The entire proceeds are recorded as debt.

UNDERLYING CONCEPTS

Reporting a convertible bond solely as debt is not representationally faithful. However, the cost-benefit constraint is used to justify the failure to allocate between debt and equity.

Many argue that the conversion feature is not significantly different in nature from the call represented by a warrant. The question is whether, although the legal forms are different, sufficient similarities of substance exist to support the same accounting treatment. Some contend that inseparability per se is not a sufficient basis for restricting allocation between identifiable components of a transaction. Examples of allocation between assets of value in a single transaction are not uncommon, such as allocation of values in basket purchases and separation of principal and interest in capitalizing long-term leases. Critics of the current accounting for convertibles say that to deny recognition of value to the conversion feature merely looks to the form of the instrument and does not deal with the substance of the transaction.

The authors disagree with the FASB as well. In both situations (convertible debt and debt issued with warrants), the investor has made a payment to the firm for an equity feature—the right to acquire an equity instrument in the future. The only real distinction between them is that the additional payment made when the equity instrument is formally acquired takes different forms. The warrant holder pays additional cash to the issuing firm; the convertible debt holder pays for stock by forgoing the receipt of interest from conversion date until maturity date and by forgoing the receipt of the maturity value itself. Thus, it is argued that the difference is one of method or form of payment only, rather than one of substance. **Until the profession officially reverses its stand in regard to accounting for convertible debt, however, only bonds issued with detachable stock warrants will result in accounting recognition of the equity feature.**[9]

INTERNATIONAL INSIGHT

International accounting standards require that the issuer of convertible debt record the liability and equity components separately.

Rights to Subscribe to Additional Shares

If the directors of a corporation decide to issue new shares of stock, the old stockholders generally have the right (preemptive privilege) to purchase newly issued shares in proportion to their holdings. The privilege, referred to as a **stock right**, saves existing stockholders from suffering a dilution of voting rights without their consent, and it may allow them to purchase stock somewhat below its market value. The warrants issued in these situations are of short duration, unlike the warrants issued with other securities.

The certificate representing the stock right states the number of shares the holder of the right may purchase, as well as the price at which the new shares may be purchased. Each share owned ordinarily gives the owner one stock right. The price is normally less than the current market value of such shares, which gives the rights a value in themselves. From the time they are issued until they expire, they may be purchased and sold like any other security.

No entry is required when rights are issued to existing stockholders. Only a memorandum entry is needed to indicate the number of rights issued to existing stockholders and to ensure that the company has additional unissued stock registered for issuance in case the rights are exercised. No formal entry is made at this time because no stock has been issued and no cash has been received.

If the rights are exercised, usually a cash payment of some type is involved. If the cash received is equal to the par value, an entry crediting Common Stock at par value is made. If it is in excess of par value, a credit to Paid-in Capital in Excess of Par develops; if it is less than par value, a charge to Paid-in Capital is appropriate.

STOCK COMPENSATION PLANS

Another form of warrant arises in stock compensation plans used to pay and motivate employees. This warrant is a **stock option**, which gives selected employees the option to purchase common stock at a given price over an extended period of time. Stock op-

[9]Recent research indicates that estimates of the debt and equity components of convertible bonds are subject to considerable measurement error. (Mary Barth, Wayne Landsman, and Richard Rendleman, Jr. "Option Pricing–Based Bond Value Estimates and a Fundamental Components Approach to Account for Corporate Debt," *The Accounting Review,* January 1998.) The FASB is currently working on a project that will address the accounting for securities with both debt and equity features, such as convertible bonds. A proposed standard is expected to be issued for comment in 2000.

tions are very popular because they meet the objectives of an effective compensation program.

Effective compensation has been a subject of considerable interest lately. A consensus of opinion is that effective compensation programs are ones that (1) motivate employees to high levels of performance, (2) help retain executives and allow for recruitment of new talent, (3) base compensation on employee and company performance, (4) maximize the employee's after-tax benefit and minimize the employee's after-tax cost, and (5) use performance criteria over which the employee has control. Although straight cash compensation plans (salary and, perhaps, bonus) are an important part of any compensation program, they are oriented to the short run. Many companies recognize that a more long-run compensation plan is often needed in addition to a cash component.

Long-term compensation plans attempt to develop in the executive a strong loyalty toward the company. An effective way to accomplish this goal is to give the employees "a piece of the action"—that is, an equity interest based on changes in long-term measures such as increases in earnings per share, revenues, stock price, or market share. These plans, generally referred to as **stock option plans**, come in many different forms. Essentially, they provide the executive with the opportunity to receive stock or cash in the future if the performance of the company (however measured) is satisfactory.

Stock options are the fastest-growing segment of executive pay. Executives want stock option contracts because options can make them instant millionaires if the company is successful. For example, for 365 of the largest U.S. companies, long-term compensation was mostly from exercised stock options. Here is an example of some of the higher awards and average compensation for all companies surveyed in 1998.

ILLUSTRATION 17-3
Executive Option Compensation

Top-Paid CEOs

($000)	1998 Salary and Bonus	Long-Term Compensation (Options)	Total Pay
1. Michael Eisner, Walt Disney	$5,764	$569,828	$575,592
2. Mel Karmazin, CBS	4,000	197,934	201,934
3. Sanford Weill, Citigroup	7,430	159,663	167,093
4. Stephen Case, America Online	1,177	158,057	159,233
5. Craig Barrett, Intel	2,280	114,232	116,511
6. John Welch, General Electric	10,105	73,559	83,664
7. Henry Schacht, Lucent Technologies	2,020	65,016	67,037
8. L. Dennis Kozlowski, Tyco International	3,750	61,514	65,264
9. Henry Silverman, Cendant	2,818	61,063	63,882
10. M. Douglas Ivester, Coca-Cola	2,750	54,572	57,322

Source: Based on Jennifer Rheingold and Ronald Grover, "Special Report: Executive Pay," *Business Week*, April 19, 1999.

Averages for All 365 Companies Surveyed

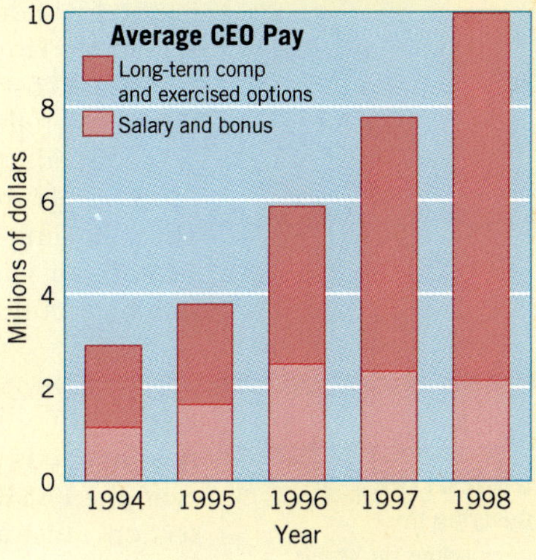

Data: *Business Week* Annual Executive Pay Survey

The Major Accounting Issue

To illustrate the most contentious accounting issue related to stock option plans, suppose that you are an employee for Hurdle Inc. and you are granted options to purchase 10,000 shares of the firm's common stock as part of your compensation. The date you receive the options is referred to as the **grant date**. The options are good for 10 years;

the market price and the exercise price for the stock are both $20 at the grant date. What is the value of the compensation you just received?

Some believe you have not received anything; that is, the difference between the market price and the exercise price is zero and therefore no compensation results. Others argue these options have value: if the stock price goes above $20 any time over the next 10 years and you exercise these options, substantial compensation results. For example, if at the end of the fourth year, the market price of the stock is $30 and you exercise your options, you will have earned $100,000 [10,000 options × ($30 − $20)], ignoring income taxes.

How should the granting of these options be reported by Hurdle Inc.? In the past, GAAP required that compensation cost be measured by the excess of the market price of the stock over its exercise price at the grant date. This approach is referred to as the **intrinsic value method** because the computation is not dependent on external circumstances: **it is the difference between the market price of the stock and the exercise price of the options at the grant date.** Hurdle would therefore not recognize any compensation expense related to your options because at the grant date the market price and exercise price were the same.

Recently the FASB issued *Statement of Financial Accounting Standards No. 123* "Accounting for Stock-Based Compensation" which **encourages but does not require recognition of compensation cost for the fair value of stock-based compensation paid to employees for their services.**[10] The FASB position is that the accounting for the cost of employee services should be based on the value of compensation paid, which is presumed to be a measure of the value of the services received. Accordingly, the compensation cost arising from employee stock options should be measured based on the fair value of the stock options granted.[11] To determine this value, acceptable option pricing models are used to value options at the date of grant. This approach is referred to as the **fair value method** because the option value is estimated based on the many factors which determine its underlying value.[12]

The FASB met considerable resistance when it proposed requiring the fair value method for recognizing the costs of stock options in the financial statements. As a result, under the final standard, a company **can choose** to use either the intrinsic value method or fair value method when accounting for compensation cost on the income statement. However, if a company uses the intrinsic value method to recognize compensation costs for employee stock options, it must provide expanded disclosures in the notes on these costs. Specifically, companies that choose the intrinsic value method are required to disclose in a note to the financial statements pro-forma net income and earnings per share (if presented by the company), as if it had used the fair value method. The following sections discuss the accounting for stock options under both the intrinsic and fair value methods as well as the political debate surrounding stock compensation accounting.

Accounting for Stock Compensation

OBJECTIVE 4
Describe the accounting for stock compensation plans under generally accepted accounting principles.

A company is given a choice in the recognition method for stock compensation; however, **the FASB encourages adoption of the fair value method.** Our discussion in this section illustrates both methods. Stock option plans involve two main accounting issues:

1. How should compensation expense be determined?
2. Over what periods should compensation expense be allocated?

[10]"Accounting for Stock-Based Compensation," *Statement of Financial Accounting Standards No. 123* (Norwalk, Conn.: FASB, 1995).

[11]Stock options issued to non-employees in exchange for other goods or services must be recognized according to the fair value method in *SFAS 123.*

[12]These factors include the volatility of the underlying stock, the expected life of the options, the risk-free rate during the option life, and expected dividends during the option life.

Determining Expense

Using the fair value method, total compensation expense is computed based on the fair value of the options expected to vest[13] on the date the options are granted to the employee(s) (i.e., the **grant date**). Fair value for public companies is to be estimated using an option pricing model, with some adjustments for the unique factors of employee stock options. No adjustments are made after the grant date, in response to subsequent changes in the stock price—either up or down.[14]

Under the intrinsic value method (*APB Opinion No. 25*), total compensation cost is computed as the excess of the market price of the stock over the option price on the date when both the number of shares to which employees are entitled and the option or purchase price for those shares are known (the **measurement date**). For many plans, this measurement date is the **grant date**. However, the measurement date may be later for plans with variable terms (either number of shares and/or option price are not known) that depend on events after the date of grant. For such variable plans, compensation expense may have to be estimated on the basis of assumptions as to the final number of shares and the option price (usually at the exercise date).

Allocating Compensation Expense

In general, under both the fair and intrinsic value methods, compensation expense is recognized in the periods in which the employee performs the service—the **service period**. Unless otherwise specified, the service period is the vesting period—the time between the grant date and the vesting date. Thus, total compensation cost is determined at the grant date and allocated to the periods benefited by the employees' services.

Illustration

To illustrate the accounting for a stock option plan, assume that on November 1, 2000, the stockholders of Chen Company approve a plan that grants the company's five executives options to purchase 2,000 shares each of the company's $1 par value common stock. The options are granted on January 1, 2001, and may be exercised at any time within the next ten years. The option price per share is $60, and the market price of the stock at the date of grant is $70 per share. Using the intrinsic value method, the total compensation expense is computed below.

Market value of 10,000 shares at date of grant ($70 per share)	$700,000
Option price of 10,000 shares at date of grant ($60 per share)	600,000
Total compensation expense (intrinsic value)	$100,000

Using the fair value method, total compensation expense is computed by applying an acceptable fair value option pricing model (such as the Black-Scholes option pricing model). To keep this illustration simple, we will assume that the fair value option pricing model determines total compensation expense to be $220,000.

Basic Entries. The value of the options under either method is recognized as an expense in the periods in which the employee performs services. In the case of Chen Company, assume that the documents associated with issuance of the options indicate that the expected period of benefit is 2 years, starting with the grant date. The journal entries to record the transactions related to this option contract using both the intrinsic value and fair value method are shown on the following page:

[13]Vested means "to earn the rights to." An employee's award becomes vested at the date that the employee's right to receive or retain shares of stock or cash under the award is no longer contingent on remaining in the service of the employer.

[14]Nonpublic companies are permitted to use a minimum value method to estimate the value of the options. The minimum value method does not consider the volatility of the stock price when estimating option value. Nonpublic companies frequently do not have data with which to estimate this element of option value.

ILLUSTRATION 17-4
Comparison of Entries for Option Contract—Intrinsic Value and Fair Value Methods

Intrinsic Value			Fair Value		
At date of grant (January 1, 2001):					
No entry			No entry		
To record compensation expense for 2001 (December 31, 2001):					
Compensation Expense	50,000		Compensation Expense	110,000	
Paid-in Capital—Stock Options		50,000	Paid-in Capital—Stock Options		110,000
($100,000 ÷ 2)			($220,000 ÷ 2)		
To record compensation expense for 2002 (December 31, 2002):					
Compensation Expense	50,000		Compensation Expense	110,000	
Paid-in Capital—Stock Options		50,000	Paid-in Capital—Stock Options		110,000

Under both methods, compensation expense is allocated evenly over the 2-year service period. The only difference between the two methods is the amount of compensation recognized.

Exercise. If 20% or 2,000 of the 10,000 options were exercised on June 1, 2004 (3 years and 5 months after date of grant), the following journal entry would be recorded using the **intrinsic value method**.

June 1, 2004		
Cash (2,000 × $60)	120,000	
Paid-in Capital—Stock Options (20% × $100,000)	20,000	
Common Stock (2,000 × $1.00)		2,000
Paid-in Capital in Excess of Par		138,000

Using the **fair value approach**, the entry would be:

June 1, 2004		
Cash (2,000 × $60)	120,000	
Paid-in Capital—Stock Options (20% × $220,000)	44,000	
Common Stock (2,000 × $1.00)		2,000
Paid-in Capital in Excess of Par		162,000

Expiration. If the remaining stock options are not exercised before their expiration date, the balance in the Paid-in Capital—Stock Options account should be transferred to a more properly titled paid-in capital account, such as Paid-in Capital from Expired Stock Options. The entry to record this transaction at the date of expiration would be as follows:

ILLUSTRATION 17-5
Comparison of Entries for Stock Option Expiration—Intrinsic Value and Fair Value Methods

Intrinsic Value			Fair Value		
January 1, 2011 (Expiration date):					
Paid-in Capital—Stock Options	80,000		Paid-in Capital—Stock Options	176,000	
Paid-in Capital from Expired Stock Options (80% × $100,000)		80,000	Paid-in Capital from Expired Stock Options (80% × $220,000)		176,000

Adjustment. The fact that a stock option is not exercised does not nullify the propriety of recording the costs of services received from executives and attributable to the stock option plan. Under GAAP, compensation expense is, therefore, not adjusted upon expiration of the options. However, if a stock option is forfeited because **an employee fails to satisfy a service requirement** (e.g., leaves employment), the estimate of compensation expense recorded in the current period should be adjusted (as a change in estimate). This change in estimate would be recorded by debiting Paid-in Capital—Stock Options and crediting Compensation Expense, thereby decreasing compensation expense in the period of forfeiture.

Types of Plans

Many different types of plans are used to compensate key executives. In all these plans the amount of the reward depends upon future events. Consequently, continued employment is a necessary element in almost all types of plans. The popularity of a given plan usually depends on prospects in the stock market and tax considerations. For example, if it appears that appreciation will occur in a company's stock, a plan that offers the option to purchase stock is attractive to an executive. Conversely, if it appears that price appreciation is unlikely, then compensation might be tied to some performance measure such as an increase in book value or earnings per share.

Three common compensation plans that illustrate different objectives are:

1. Stock option plans (incentive or nonqualified).
2. Stock appreciation rights plans.
3. Performance-type plans.

Most plans follow the general guideline for reporting established in the previous sections. A more detailed discussion of these plans is presented in Appendix 17A.

Noncompensatory Plans

In some companies, stock purchase plans permit all employees to purchase stock at a discounted price for a short period of time. These plans are usually classified as noncompensatory. Noncompensatory means that the primary purpose of the plan is not to compensate the employees but, rather, to enable the employer to secure equity capital or to induce widespread ownership of an enterprise's common stock among employees. Thus, compensation expense is not reported for these plans. **Noncompensatory plans** have three characteristics:

1. Substantially all full-time employees may participate on an equitable basis.
2. The discount from market price is small; that is, it does not exceed the greater of a per share discount reasonably offered to stockholders or the per share amount of costs avoided by not having to raise cash in a public offering.
3. The plan offers no substantive option feature.

For example, Masthead Company had a stock purchase plan under which employees who meet minimal employment qualifications are entitled to purchase Masthead stock at a 5% reduction from market price for a short period of time. The reduction from market price is not considered compensatory because the per share amount of the costs avoided by not having to raise the cash in a public offering is equal to 5%. **Plans that do not possess all of the above mentioned three characteristics are classified as compensatory.**

DISCLOSURE OF COMPENSATION PLANS

To comply with *SFAS No. 123*, companies offering stock-based compensation plans must determine the fair value of the options. Companies must then decide whether to use the fair value method and recognize expense in the income statement, or to use the intrinsic value approach and disclose in the notes the pro forma impact on net income and earnings per share (if presented), as if the fair value method had been used.

Regardless of whether the intrinsic value or fair value method is used, full disclosure should be made about the status of these plans at the end of the periods presented, including the number of shares under option, options exercised and forfeited, the weighted average option prices for these categories, the weighted average fair value of options granted during the year, and the average remaining contractual life of the options outstanding.[15] In addition to information about the status of the stock option plans, companies must also disclose the method and significant assumptions used to estimate the fair values of the stock options.

[15]These data should be reported separately for each different type of plan offered to employees.

Illustration 17-6 provides the disclosure by **Gateway 2000, Inc.** which accounts for its stock options using the intrinsic value method:

ILLUSTRATION 17-6
Disclosure of Stock Option Plans by Gateway 2000, Inc.

GATEWAY 2000, INC.

Note 6: Stock Option Plans. The Company maintains various stock option plans for its employees. Employee options are generally granted at the fair market value of the related common stock at the date of grant. These options generally vest over a four-year period from the date of grant or the employee's initial date of employment. In addition, these options expire, if not exercised, ten years from the date of grant. The Company also maintains option plans for non-employee directors. Option grants to non-employee directors generally have an exercise price equal to the fair market value of the related common stock on the date of grant. These options generally vest over one to three-year periods and expire, if not exercised, ten years from the date of grant.

For all of the Company's stock option plans, options for 1,283,000, 2,582,000 and 2,728,000 shares of common stock were exercisable at December 31, 1996, 1997 and 1998 with a weighted average exercise price of $4.28, $9.86 and $17.42, respectively. In addition, options for 672,000, 556,000 and 280,000 shares of Class A common stock were exercisable at December 31, 1996, 1997 and 1998 with a weighted average exercise price of $2.06, $2.01 and $1.93, respectively. Class A common stock may be converted into an equal number of shares of common stock at any time. There were 12,309,000, 8,328,000 and 11,265,000 shares of common stock available for grant under the plans at December 31, 1996, 1997 and 1998, respectively.

Go to the Digital Tool for additional examples of stock option disclosures.

The following table summarizes activity under the stock option plans for 1996, 1997 and 1998 (in thousands, except per share amounts):

	Common Stock	Weighted-Average Price	Class A Common Stock	Weighted-Average Price
Outstanding, December 31, 1995	8,739	$ 3.16	962	$2.14
Granted	3,260	15.75	—	—
Exercised	(6,305)	1.43	(241)	2.13
Forfeited	(254)	14.15	(8)	3.25
Outstanding, December 31, 1996	5,440	12.20	713	2.12
Granted	5,253	36.08	—	—
Exercised	(463)	11.56	(153)	2.50
Forfeited	(775)	23.69	—	—
Outstanding, December 31, 1997	9,455	22.98	560	2.02
Granted	6,118	45.17	—	—
Exercised	(2,143)	16.59	(280)	2.10
Forfeited	(1,103)	32.76	—	—
Outstanding, December 31, 1998	12,327	$34.19	280	$1.93

The following table summarizes information about the Company's Common Stock options outstanding at December 31, 1998 (in thousands, except per share amounts):

	Options Outstanding			Options Exercisable	
Range of Exercise Prices	Number Outstanding at 12/31/98	Weighted-Average Remaining Contractual Life	Weighted-Average Price	Number Exercisable at 12/31/98	Weighted-Average Price
$ 1.19–13.38	1,928	5.57	$ 9.01	1,259	$ 6.76
13.44–29.07	2,287	7.65	22.93	939	20.01
29.31–33.75	2,405	8.87	33.06	267	32.35
34.00–44.75	2,811	8.94	39.55	262	43.88
45.06–62.50	2,896	9.68	55.56	1	61.75

The weighted average fair value per share of options granted during 1996, 1997 and 1998 was $9.65, $21.61 and $27.33, respectively. The fair value of these options was estimated on the date of grant using the Black-Scholes option pricing model with the following weighted-average assumptions used for all grants in 1996, 1997 and 1998: dividend yield of zero percent; expected volatility of 60 percent; risk-free interest rates ranging from 4.7 to 7.2 percent; and expected lives of the options of three and one-half years from the date of vesting.

If *APB Opinion No. 25* is used in the financial statements, companies must still disclose the pro-forma net income and pro-forma earnings per share (if presented), as if the fair value method had been used to account for the stock-based compensation cost. Illustration 17-7 illustrates this disclosure, as provided by **Gateway 2000, Inc.**

GATEWAY 2000, INC.

ILLUSTRATION 17-7
Disclosure of Pro-Forma Effect of Stock Option Plans

Since all stock options have been granted with exercise prices equal to the fair market value of the related common stock at the date of grant, no compensation expense has been recognized under the Company's stock option plans. Had compensation cost under the plans been determined based on the estimated fair value of the stock options granted in 1996, 1997 and 1998, net income and net income per share would have been reduced to the pro forma amounts indicated below:

	1996	1997	1998
	(in thousands, except per share amounts)		
Net income—as reported	$250,679	$109,797	$346,399
Net income—pro forma	$241,729	$ 85,804	$297,470
Net income per share—as reported			
Basic	$ 1.64	$ .71	$ 2.23
Diluted	$ 1.60	$ .70	$ 2.18
Net income per share—pro forma			
Basic	$ 1.58	$ .56	$ 1.91
Diluted	$ 1.55	$ .55	$ 1.87

The pro forma effect on net income for 1996, 1997 and 1998 is not fully representative of the pro forma effect on net income in future years because it does not take into consideration pro forma compensation expense related to the vesting of grants made prior to 1995.

Debate over Stock Option Accounting

OBJECTIVE 5
Explain the controversy involving stock compensation plans.

In general, use of the fair value approach results in greater compensation costs relative to the intrinsic value model reflected in *APB Opinion No. 25.* For example, a recent study of the companies in the Standard & Poor's 500 stock index documented that on average earnings in 1998 were overstated by 5% through the use of the intrinsic value method. And some companies, such as **Guidant**, **3Com**, and **Cendant**, reported earnings under the intrinsic value model that were up to three times higher than earnings using the fair value method.

It is an understatement to say that corporate America was unhappy with the initial requirement to record compensation expense for these plans. Many small high-technology companies were particularly vocal in their opposition, arguing that only through offering stock options can they attract top professional management. They contend that if they are forced to recognize large amounts of compensation expense under these plans, they will be at a competitive disadvantage with larger companies that can withstand higher compensation charges. As one high-tech executive stated: "If your goal is to attack fat-cat executive compensation in multi-billion dollar firms, then please do so! But not at the expense of the people who are 'running lean and mean,' trying to build businesses and creating jobs in the process."

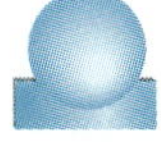

UNDERLYING CONCEPTS

The stock option controversy involves economic consequence issues. The FASB believes the neutrality concept should be followed; others disagree, noting that factors other than accounting theory should be considered.

A chronology of events related to this standard demonstrates the difficulty in standard-setting when various stakeholders believe they are adversely affected.

1. ***In June 1993 the FASB issued an exposure draft on stock options.*** The recommendations were that the value of stock options issued to employees is compensation which should be recognized in the financial statements. Nonrecognition of these costs results in financial statements that are neither credible nor representationally faithful. The draft recommended that option pricing models be used to estimate the value of stock options. In addition, disclosures related to these plans would be enhanced.

2 ***The exposure draft met a blizzard of opposition from the business community.*** Some argued stock option plans were not compensation expense; some contended that it was impossible to develop appropriate option pricing models; others said that these standards would be disastrous to American business. The economic consequences argument was used extensively. In mid-1993 Congresswoman Anna Eshoo (California) submitted a congressional resolution calling for the FASB *not* to change its current accounting rules. Eshoo stated that the FASB proposal "poses a threat to economic recovery and entrepreneurship in the United States. . . . (it) hurts low- and mid-level employees and stunts the growth of new-growth sectors, such as high technology which relies heavily on entrepreneurship."

3 ***On June 30, 1993, the Equity Expansion Act of 1993 was introduced by Senator Joseph Lieberman (Connecticut).*** The bill mandates that the SEC require that no compensation expense be reported on the income statement for stock option plans. Senator Lieberman's bill could have forced the FASB to bend to political pressure and thereby set a precedent for interfering in the operations of the Board.

4 ***During the latter part of 1993, the FASB looked for political support but found few supporters.*** The SEC commissioners all expressed reservations about the FASB's proposed ruling. However, the chief accountant of the SEC spoke in opposition to much of the lobbying effort directed against the FASB.

5 ***In early 1994 a group of senators wrote to the SEC.*** They expressed concern "that the credibility of the financial reporting process may be harmed significantly if Congress, in order to further economic or political goals, either discourages the FASB from revising what the FASB believes to be a deficient standard or overrules the FASB by writing an accounting standard directly into the Federal securities laws."

6 ***In late 1994, the FASB decided to encourage, rather than require, recognition of compensation cost based on the fair value method and require expanded disclosures.*** The FASB adopted the disclosure approach because they were concerned that the "divisiveness of the debate" could threaten the future of accounting standard-setting in the private sector. The final standard was issued in October 1995.

The stock option saga is a classic example of the difficulty the FASB faces in issuing an accounting standard. Many powerful interests aligned against the Board; even some who initially appeared to support the Board's actions later reversed themselves. The whole incident is troubling because the debate for the most part is not about the **proper accounting** but more about the **economic consequences** of the standards. If we continue to write standards so that some social, economic, or public policy goal is achieved, it will not be too long before financial reporting will lose its credibility.

SECTION 2 COMPUTING EARNINGS PER SHARE

In many nations (e.g., Switzerland, Sweden, Spain, and Mexico) there is no legal requirement to disclose earnings per share.

Earnings per share data are frequently reported in the financial press and are widely used by stockholders and potential investors in evaluating the profitability of a company. **Earnings per share** indicates the income earned by each share of common stock. Thus, **earnings per share is reported only for common stock**. For example, if Oscar Co. has net income of $300,000 and a weighted average of 100,000 shares of common stock outstanding for the year, earnings per share is $3 ($300,000 ÷ 100,000).

Because of the importance of earnings per share information, most companies are required to report this information on the face of the income statement.[16] The excep-

[16]"Earnings per Share," *Statement of Financial Accounting Standards No. 128* (Norwalk, Conn.: FASB, 1997). For an article on the usefulness of EPS reported data and the application of the qualitative characteristics of accounting information to EPS data, see Lola W. Dudley, "A Critical Look at EPS," *Journal of Accountancy*, August 1985, pp. 102–11.

tion is nonpublic companies; because of cost-benefit considerations they do not have to report this information.[17] Generally, earnings per share information is reported below net income in the income statement. For Oscar Co. the presentation would be as follows:

Net income	$300,000
Earnings per share	$3.00

ILLUSTRATION 17-8
Income Statement Presentation of EPS

When the income statement contains intermediate components of income, earnings per share should be disclosed for each component. The following is representative:

Earnings per share:	
Income from continuing operations	$4.00
Loss from discontinued operations, net of tax	.60
Income before extraordinary item and cumulative effect of change in accounting principle	3.40
Extraordinary gain, net of tax	1.00
Cumulative effect of change in accounting principle, net of tax	.50
Net income	$4.90

ILLUSTRATION 17-9
Income Statement Presentation of EPS Components

These disclosures enable the user of the financial statements to recognize the effects of income from continuing operations on EPS, as distinguished from income or loss from irregular items.[18]

EARNINGS PER SHARE—SIMPLE CAPITAL STRUCTURE

OBJECTIVE 6
Compute earnings per share in a simple capital structure.

A corporation's capital structure is **simple** if it consists only of common stock or includes no **potential common stock** that upon conversion or exercise could dilute earnings per common share. (A capital structure is **complex** if it includes securities that could have a dilutive effect on earnings per common share.) The computation of earnings per share for a simple capital structure involves two items (other than net income)—preferred stock dividends and weighted average number of shares outstanding.

Preferred Stock Dividends

As indicated earlier, earnings per share relates to earnings per common share. When a company has both common and preferred stock outstanding, **the current year preferred stock dividend is subtracted from net income to arrive at income available to common stockholders**. The formula for computing earnings per share is then as follows:

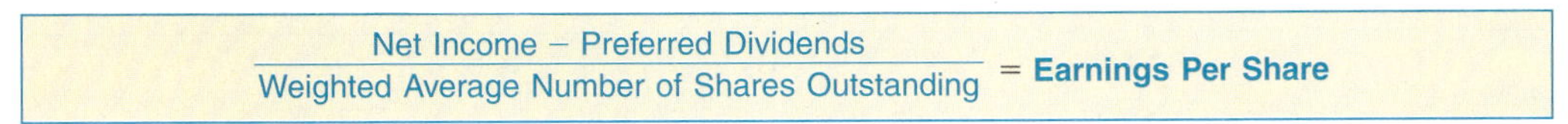

$$\frac{\text{Net Income} - \text{Preferred Dividends}}{\text{Weighted Average Number of Shares Outstanding}} = \textbf{Earnings Per Share}$$

ILLUSTRATION 17-10
Formula for Computing Earnings per Share

[17]A nonpublic enterprise is an enterprise other than (1) whose debt or equity securities are traded in a public market on a foreign or domestic stock exchange or in the over-the-counter market (including securities quoted locally or regionally) or (2) that is required to file financial statements with the SEC. An enterprise is no longer considered a nonpublic enterprise when its financial statements are issued in preparation for the sale of any class of securities in a public market.

[18]Per share amounts for discontinued operations, an extraordinary item, or the cumulative effect of an accounting change in a period should be presented either on the face of the income statement or in the notes to the financial statements.

In reporting earnings per share information, dividends on preferred stock should be subtracted from each of the intermediate components of income (income from continuing operations and income before extraordinary items) and finally from net income to arrive at income available to common stockholders. If dividends on preferred stock are declared and a net loss occurs, **the preferred dividend is added to the loss** for purposes of computing the loss per share. If the preferred stock is cumulative and the dividend is not declared in the current year, **an amount equal to the dividend that should have been declared for the current year only** should be subtracted from net income or added to the net loss. Dividends in arrears for previous years should have been included in the previous years' computations.

INTERNATIONAL INSIGHT

Where EPS disclosure is prevalent, it is usually based on the weighted average of shares outstanding. Some countries such as Australia, France, Japan, and Mexico use the number of shares outstanding at year-end.

Weighted Average Number of Shares Outstanding

In all computations of earnings per share, the **weighted average number of shares outstanding** during the period constitutes the basis for the per share amounts reported. Shares issued or purchased during the period affect the amount outstanding and must be **weighted by the fraction of the period they are outstanding**. The rationale for this approach is to find the equivalent number of whole shares outstanding for the year. To illustrate, assume that Stallone Inc. has the following changes in its common stock shares outstanding for the period.

ILLUSTRATION 17-11
Shares Outstanding, Ending Balance—Stallone Inc.

Date	Share Changes	Shares Outstanding
January 1	Beginning balance	90,000
April 1	Issued 30,000 shares for cash	30,000
		120,000
July 1	Purchased 39,000 shares	39,000
		81,000
November 1	Issued 60,000 shares for cash	60,000
December 31	Ending balance	141,000

To compute the weighted average number of shares outstanding, the following computation is made.

ILLUSTRATION 17-12
Weighted Average Number of Shares Outstanding

Dates Outstanding	(A) Shares Outstanding	(B) Fraction of Year	(C) Weighted Shares (A × B)
Jan. 1—Apr. 1	90,000	3/12	22,500
Apr. 1—July 1	120,000	3/12	30,000
July 1—Nov. 1	81,000	4/12	27,000
Nov. 1—Dec. 31	141,000	2/12	23,500
Weighted average number of shares outstanding			103,000

As illustrated, 90,000 shares were outstanding for 3 months, which translates to 22,500 whole shares for the entire year. Because additional shares were issued on April 1, the shares outstanding change and these shares must be weighted for the time outstanding. When 39,000 shares were purchased on July 1, the shares outstanding were reduced and again a new computation must be made to determine the proper weighted shares outstanding.

Stock Dividends and Stock Splits

When **stock dividends** or **stock splits** occur, computation of the weighted average number of shares requires restatement of the shares outstanding before the stock dividend or split. For example, assume that a corporation had 100,000 shares outstanding on January 1 and issued a 25% stock dividend on June 30. For purposes of computing a weighted average for the current year, the additional 25,000 shares outstanding as a result of the stock dividend are assumed to have been **outstanding since the beginning of the year**. Thus the weighted average for the year would be 125,000 shares.

The issuance of a stock dividend or stock split is restated, but the issuance or repurchase of stock for cash is not. Why? The reason is that stock splits and stock dividends do not increase or decrease the net assets of the enterprise; only additional shares of stock are issued and, therefore, the weighted average shares must be restated. By restating, valid comparisons of earnings per share can be made between periods before and after the stock split or stock dividend. Conversely, the issuance or purchase of stock for cash changes the amount of net assets. As a result, the company either earns more or less in the future as a result of this change in net assets. Stated another way, **a stock dividend or split does not change the shareholders' total investment**—it only increases (unless it is a reverse stock split) the number of common shares representing this investment.

To illustrate how a stock dividend affects the computation of the weighted average number of shares outstanding, assume that Rambo Company has the following changes in its common stock shares during the year.

ILLUSTRATION 17-13
Shares Outstanding, Ending Balance—Rambo Company

Date	Share Changes	Shares Outstanding
January 1	Beginning balance	100,000
March 1	Issued 20,000 shares for cash	20,000
		120,000
June 1	60,000 additional shares (50% stock dividend)	60,000
		180,000
November 1	Issued 30,000 shares for cash	30,000
December 31	Ending balance	210,000

The computation of the weighted average number of shares outstanding would be as follows:

ILLUSTRATION 17-14
Weighted Average Number of Shares Outstanding—Stock Issue and Stock Dividend

Dates Outstanding	(A) Shares Outstanding	(B) Restatement	(C) Fraction of Year	(D) Weighted Shares (A × B × C)
Jan. 1—Mar. 1	100,000	1.50	2/12	25,000
Mar. 1—June 1	120,000	1.50	3/12	45,000
June 1—Nov. 1	180,000		5/12	75,000
Nov. 1—Dec. 31	210,000		2/12	35,000
Weighted average number of shares outstanding				180,000

The shares outstanding prior to the stock dividend must be restated. The shares outstanding from January 1 to June 1 are adjusted for the stock dividend, so that these shares are stated on the same basis as shares issued subsequent to the stock dividend. Shares issued after the stock dividend do not have to be restated because they are on the new basis. The stock dividend simply restates existing shares. The same type of treatment occurs for a stock split.

If a stock dividend or stock split occurs after the end of the year, but before the financial statements are issued, the weighted average number of shares outstanding for the year (and any other years presented in comparative form) must be restated. For example, assume that Hendricks Company computes its weighted average number of shares to be 100,000 for the year ended December 31, 2001. On January 15, 2002, before the financial statements are issued, the company splits its stock 3 for 1. In this case, the weighted average number of shares used in computing earnings per share for 2001 would be 300,000 shares. If earnings per share information for 2000 is provided as comparative information, it also must be adjusted for the stock split.

Comprehensive Illustration

Sylvester Corporation has income before extraordinary item of $580,000 and an extraordinary gain, net of tax of $240,000. In addition, it has declared preferred dividends of $1 per share on 100,000 shares of preferred stock outstanding. Sylvester Corporation also has the following changes in its common stock shares outstanding during 2001.

ILLUSTRATION 17-15
Shares Outstanding, Ending Balance—Sylvester Corp.

Dates	Share Changes	Shares Outstanding
January 1	Beginning balance	180,000
May 1	Purchased 30,000 treasury shares	30,000
		150,000
July 1	300,000 additional shares (3 for 1 stock split)	300,000
		450,000
December 31	Issued 50,000 shares for cash	50,000
December 31	Ending balance	500,000

To compute the earnings per share information, the weighted average number of shares outstanding is determined as follows:

ILLUSTRATION 17-16
Weighted Average Number of Shares Outstanding

Dates Outstanding	(A) Shares Outstanding	(B) Restatement	(C) Fraction of Year	(D) Weighted Shares (A × B × C)
Jan. 1—May 1	180,000	3	4/12	180,000
May 1—Dec. 31	150,000	3	8/12	300,000
Weighted average number of shares outstanding				480,000

In computing the weighted average number of shares, the shares sold on December 31, 2001, are ignored because they have not been outstanding during the year. The weighted average number of shares is then divided into income before extraordinary item and net income to determine earnings per share. Sylvester Corporation's preferred dividends of $100,000 are subtracted from income before extraordinary item ($580,000) to arrive at income before extraordinary item available to common stockholders of $480,000 ($580,000 − $100,000). Deducting the preferred dividends from the income before extraordinary item has the effect of also reducing net income without affecting the amount of the extraordinary item. The final amount is referred to as **income available to common stockholders**.

ILLUSTRATION 17-17
Computation of Income Available to Common Stockholders

	(a) Income Information	(b) Weighted Shares	(c) Earnings per Share (A ÷ B)
Income before extraordinary item available to common stockholders	$480,000*	480,000	$1.00
Extraordinary gain (net of tax)	240,000	480,000	.50
Income available to common stockholders	$720,000	480,000	$1.50

*$580,000 − $100,000

Disclosure of the per share amount for the extraordinary item (net of tax) must be reported either on the face of the income statement or in the notes to the financial statements. Income and per share information reported on the face of the income statement would be as follows:

Income before extraordinary item	$580,000
Extraordinary gain, net of tax	240,000
Net income	$820,000
Earnings per share:	
Income before extraordinary item	$1.00
Extraordinary item, net of tax	.50
Net income	$1.50

ILLUSTRATION 17-18
Earnings per Share, with Extraordinary Item

EARNINGS PER SHARE—COMPLEX CAPITAL STRUCTURE

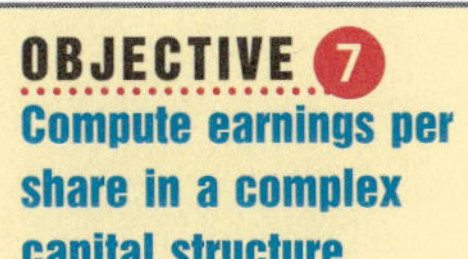

OBJECTIVE 7
Compute earnings per share in a complex capital structure.

One problem with a **basic EPS** computation is that it fails to recognize the potentially dilutive impact on outstanding stock when a corporation has dilutive securities in its capital structure. Dilutive securities present a serious problem because conversion or exercise often has an adverse effect on earnings per share. This adverse effect can be significant and, more important, unexpected unless financial statements call attention to the potential dilutive effect in some manner.[19]

A complex capital structure exists when a corporation has convertible securities, options, warrants or other rights that upon conversion or exercise could dilute earnings per share. Therefore when a company has a complex capital structure, both a basic and diluted earnings per share are generally reported.

The computation of **diluted EPS** is similar to the computation of basic EPS. The difference is that diluted EPS includes the effect of all dilutive potential common shares that were outstanding during the period. The formula in Illustration 17-19 shows the relationship between basic EPS and diluted EPS.

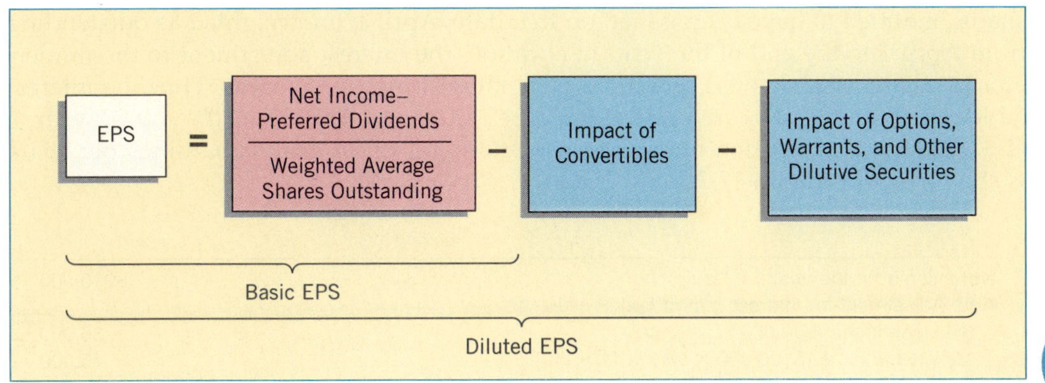

ILLUSTRATION 17-19
Relation between Basic and Diluted EPS

The provisions in U.S. GAAP are substantially the same as those in International Accounting Standard No. 33, *Earnings per Share,* recently issued by the IASC. The FASB and IASC worked together on this standard to achieve international comparability related to EPS presentations.

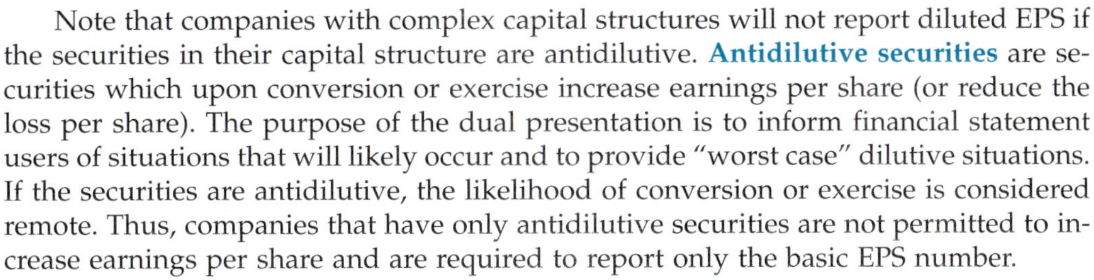

Note that companies with complex capital structures will not report diluted EPS if the securities in their capital structure are antidilutive. **Antidilutive securities** are securities which upon conversion or exercise increase earnings per share (or reduce the loss per share). The purpose of the dual presentation is to inform financial statement users of situations that will likely occur and to provide "worst case" dilutive situations. If the securities are antidilutive, the likelihood of conversion or exercise is considered remote. Thus, companies that have only antidilutive securities are not permitted to increase earnings per share and are required to report only the basic EPS number.

[19]As noted in the opening story, issuance of these types of securities in mergers and compensation plans is more and more prevalent.

The computation of basic EPS was illustrated in the prior section. The discussion in the following sections addresses the effects of convertible and other dilutive securities on EPS calculations.

Diluted EPS—Convertible Securities

At conversion, convertible securities are exchanged for common stock. The method used to measure the dilutive effects of potential conversion on EPS is called the **if-converted method**. The if-converted method for a convertible bond assumes (1) the conversion of the convertible securities at the beginning of the period (or at the time of issuance of the security, if issued during the period), and (2) the elimination of related interest, net of tax. Thus the **denominator**—the weighted average number of shares outstanding—is increased by the additional shares assumed issued. The **numerator**—net income—is increased by the amount of interest expense, net of tax associated with those potential common shares.

Comprehensive Illustration—If-Converted Method

As an example, Marshy Field Corporation has net income for the year of $210,000 and a weighted average number of common shares outstanding during the period of 100,000 shares. The basic earnings per share is, therefore, $2.10 ($210,000 ÷ 100,000). The company has two convertible debenture bond issues outstanding. One is a 6% issue sold at 100 (total $1,000,000) in a prior year and convertible into 20,000 common shares. The other is a 10% issue sold at 100 (total $1,000,000) on April 1 of the current year and convertible into 32,000 common shares. The tax rate is 40%.

As shown in Illustration 17-20, to determine the numerator, we add back the interest on the if-converted securities less the related tax effect. Because the if-converted method assumes conversion as of the beginning of the year, no interest on the convertibles is assumed to be paid during the year. The interest on the 6% convertibles is $60,000 for the year ($1,000,000 × 6%). The increased tax expense is $24,000 ($60,000 × .40), and the interest added back net of taxes is $36,000 [$60,000 − $24,000 or simply $60,000 × (1 − .40)].

Because 10% convertibles are issued subsequent to the beginning of the year, the shares assumed to have been issued on that date, April 1, are weighted as outstanding from April 1 to the end of the year. In addition, the interest adjustment to the numerator for these bonds would only reflect the interest for nine months. Thus the interest added back on the 10% convertible would be $45,000 [$1,000,000 × 10% × 9/12 year × (1 − .4)]. The computation of earnings (the numerator) for diluted earnings per share is shown in Illustration 17-20.

ILLUSTRATION 17-20
Computation of Adjusted Net Income

Net income for the year	$210,000
Add: Adjustment for interest (net of tax)	
6% debentures ($60,000 × [1 − .40])	36,000
10% debentures ($100,000 × 9/12 × [1 − .40])	45,000
Adjusted net income	$291,000

The computation for shares adjusted for dilutive securities (the denominator) for diluted earnings per share is shown in Illustration 17-21:

ILLUSTRATION 17-21
Computation of Weighted Average Number of Shares

Weighted average number of shares outstanding	100,000
Add: Shares assumed to be issued:	
6% debentures (as of beginning of year)	20,000
10% debentures (as of date of issue, April 1; 9/12 × 32,000)	24,000
Weighted average number of shares adjusted for dilutive securities	144,000

Marshy Field would then report earnings per share based on a dual presentation on the face of the income statement; basic and diluted earnings per share are reported.[20] The presentation is shown in Illustration 17-22.

Net income for the year	$210,000
Earnings per Share (Note X)	
Basic earnings per share ($210,000 ÷ 100,000)	$2.10
Diluted earnings per share ($291,000 ÷ 144,000)	$2.02

ILLUSTRATION 17-22
Earnings per Share Disclosure

Other Factors

The example above assumed that Marshy Field's bonds were sold at the face amount. If the bonds are sold at a premium or discount, interest expense must be adjusted each period to account for this occurrence. Therefore, the amount of interest expense added back, net of tax, to net income is the interest expense reported on the income statement, not the interest paid in cash during the period.

In addition, the conversion rate on a dilutive security may change over the period the dilutive security is outstanding. In this situation, for the diluted EPS computation, the **most advantageous conversion rate available to the holder is used**. For example, assume that a convertible bond was issued January 1, 2000, with a conversion rate of 10 common shares for each bond starting January 1, 2002; beginning January 1, 2005, the conversion rate is 12 common shares for each bond; and beginning January 1, 2009, it is 15 common shares for each bond. In computing diluted EPS in 2000, the conversion rate of 15 shares to one bond is used.

Finally, if the 6% convertible debentures were instead 6% convertible preferred stock, the convertible preferred would be considered potential common shares and included in shares outstanding in diluted EPS calculations. Preferred dividends are not subtracted from net income in computing the numerator because it is assumed that the convertible preferreds are converted and are outstanding as common stock for purposes of computing EPS. Net income is used as the numerator—**no tax effect** is computed because preferred dividends generally are not deductible for tax purposes.

Diluted EPS—Options and Warrants

Stock options and warrants outstanding (whether or not presently exercisable) are included in diluted earnings per share unless they are antidilutive. Options and warrants and their equivalents are included in earnings per share computations through the **treasury stock method**.

The treasury stock method assumes that the options or warrants are exercised at the beginning of the year (or date of issue if later) and the proceeds from the exercise of options and warrants are used to purchase common stock for the treasury. If the exercise price is lower than the market price of the stock, then the proceeds from exercise are not sufficient to buy back all the shares. The incremental shares remaining are added to the weighted average number of shares outstanding for purposes of computing diluted earnings per share.

For example, if the exercise price of a warrant is $5 and the fair market value of the stock is $15, the treasury stock method would increase the shares outstanding. Exercise of the warrant would result in one additional share outstanding, but the $5 received for the one share issued is not sufficient to purchase one share in the market at $15. Three warrants would have to be exercised (and three additional shares issued) to produce enough money ($15) to acquire one share in the market. Thus, a net increase of two shares outstanding would result.

[20] Conversion of bonds is dilutive because EPS with conversion ($2.02) is less than basic EPS ($2.10).

In terms of larger numbers, assume 1,500 options outstanding at an exercise price of $30 for a common share and a common stock market price per share of $50. Through application of the treasury stock method there would be 600 **incremental shares** outstanding, computed as follows:[21]

ILLUSTRATION 17-23
Computation of Incremental Shares

Proceeds from exercise of 1,500 options (1,500 × $30)	$45,000
Shares issued upon exercise of options	1,500
Treasury shares purchasable with proceeds ($45,000 ÷ $50)	900
Incremental shares outstanding (potential common shares)	600

Thus, if the exercise price of the option or warrant is **lower** than the market price of the stock, dilution occurs. If the exercise price of the option or warrant is **higher** than the market price of the stock, common shares are reduced. In this case, the options or warrants are **antidilutive** because their assumed exercise leads to an increase in earnings per share.

For both options and warrants, exercise is not assumed unless the average market price of the stock is above the exercise price during the period being reported.[22] As a practical matter, a simple average of the weekly or monthly prices is adequate, so long as the prices do not fluctuate significantly.

Comprehensive Illustration—Treasury Stock Method

To illustrate application of the treasury stock method, assume that Kubitz Industries, Inc. has net income for the period of $220,000. The average number of shares outstanding for the period was 100,000 shares. Hence, basic EPS—ignoring all dilutive securities—is $2.20. The average number of shares under outstanding options (although not exercisable at this time), at an option price of $20 per share, is 5,000 shares. The average market price of the common stock during the year was $28. The computation is shown below.

ILLUSTRATION 17-24
Computation of Earnings per Share–Treasury Stock Method

	Basic Earnings per Share	Diluted Earnings per Share
Average number of shares under option outstanding:		5000
Option price per share		× $20
Proceeds upon exercise of options		$100,000
Average market price of common stock		$28
Treasury shares that could be repurchased with proceeds ($100,000 ÷ $28)		3,571
Excess of shares under option over the treasury shares that could be repurchased (5,000 − 3,571)—Potential common incremental shares		1,429
Average number of common shares outstanding	100,000	100,000
Total average number of common shares outstanding and potential common shares	100,000 (A)	101,429 (C)
Net income for the year	$220,000 (B)	$220,000 (D)
Earnings per share	$2.20 (B ÷ A)	$2.17 (D ÷ C)

[21]The incremental number of shares may be more simply computed:

$$\frac{\text{Market Price} - \text{Option Price}}{\text{Market Price}} \times \text{Number of Options} = \text{Number of Shares}$$

$$\frac{\$50 - \$30}{\$50} \times 1{,}500 \text{ options} = 600 \text{ shares}$$

[22]It might be noted that options and warrants have essentially the same assumptions and computational problems, although the warrants may allow or require the tendering of some other security such as debt in lieu of cash upon exercise. In such situations, the accounting becomes quite complex, and the reader should refer to the standard for its proper disposition.

Contingent Issue Agreement

In business combinations, the acquirer may promise to issue additional shares—referred to as contingent shares—if certain conditions are met. If these shares are issuable upon the **mere passage of time or upon the attainment of a certain earnings or market price level, and this level is met at the end of the year,** they should be considered as outstanding for the computation of diluted earnings per share.[23]

For example, assume that Walz Corporation purchased Cardella Company and agreed to give the stockholders of Cardella Company 20,000 additional shares in 2004 if Cardella's net income in 2003 is $90,000; in 2002 Cardella Company's net income is $100,000. Because the 2003 stipulated earnings of $90,000 are already being attained, diluted earnings per share of Walz for 2002 would include the 20,000 contingent shares in the shares outstanding computation.

Antidilution Revisited

In computing diluted EPS, the aggregate of all dilutive securities must be considered. But first we must determine which potentially dilutive securities are in fact individually dilutive and which are antidilutive. Any security that is antidilutive should be excluded and cannot be used to offset dilutive securities.

Recall that antidilutive securities are securities whose inclusion in earnings per share computations would increase earnings per share (or reduce net loss per share). Convertible debt is antidilutive if the addition to income of the interest (net of tax) causes a greater percentage increase in income (numerator) than conversion of the bonds causes a percentage increase in common and potentially dilutive shares (denominator). In other words, convertible debt is antidilutive if conversion of the security causes common stock earnings to increase by a greater amount per additional common share than earnings per share was before the conversion.

To illustrate, assume that Kohl Corporation has a 6%, $1,000,000 debt issue that is convertible into 10,000 common shares. Net income for the year is $210,000, the weighted average number of common shares outstanding is 100,000 shares, and the tax rate is 40%. In this case assumed conversion of the debt into common stock at the beginning of the year requires the following adjustments of net income and the weighted average number of shares outstanding:

ILLUSTRATION 17-25
Test for Antidilution

Net income for the year	$210,000	Average number of shares outstanding	100,000
Add: Adjustment for interest (net of tax) on 6% debentures $60,000 × (1 − .40)	36,000	Add: Shares issued upon assumed conversion of debt	10,000
Adjusted net income	$246,000	Average number of common and potential common shares	110,000

Basic EPS = $210,000 ÷ 100,000 = $2.10
Diluted EPS = $246,000 ÷ 110,000 = $2.24 = **Antidilutive**

As a shortcut, the convertible debt also can be identified as antidilutive by comparing the EPS resulting from conversion, $3.60 ($36,000 additional earnings ÷ 10,000 additional shares), with EPS before inclusion of the convertible debt, $2.10.

With options or warrants, whenever the exercise price is higher than the market price, the security is antidilutive. **Antidilutive securities should be ignored in all calculations and should not be considered in computing diluted earnings per share.** This approach is reasonable because the profession's intent was to inform the investor of the **possible dilution** that might occur in reported earnings per share and not to be

[23]In addition to contingent issuances of stock, other types of situations that might lead to dilution are the issuance of participating securities and two-class common shares. The reporting of these types of securities in EPS computations is beyond the scope of this textbook.

concerned with securities that, if converted or exercised, would result in an increase in earnings per share. Appendix 17B to this chapter provides an extended example of how antidilution is considered in a complex situation with multiple securities.

EPS Presentation and Disclosure

If a corporation's capital structure is complex, the earnings per share presentation would be as follows:

ILLUSTRATION 17-26
EPS Presentation—Complex Capital Structure

Earnings per common share	
Basic earnings per share	$3.30
Diluted earnings per share	$2.70

When the earnings of a period include irregular items, per share amounts (where applicable) should be shown for income from continuing operations, income before extraordinary items, income before accounting change, and net income. Companies that report a discontinued operation, an extraordinary item, or the cumulative effect of an accounting change should present per share amounts for those line items either on the face of the income statement or in the notes to the financial statements. A presentation reporting extraordinary items only is presented in Illustration 17-27.

ILLUSTRATION 17-27
EPS Presentation, with Extraordinary Item

Basic earnings per share	
Income before extraordinary item	$3.80
Extraordinary item	.80
Net income	$3.00
Diluted earnings per share	
Income before extraordinary item	$3.35
Extraordinary item	.65
Net income	$2.70

Earnings per share amounts must be shown for all periods presented and all prior period earnings per share amounts presented should be restated for stock dividends and stock splits. If diluted EPS data are reported for at least one period, it should be reported for all periods presented, even if it is the same as basic EPS. When results of operations of a prior period have been restated as a result of a prior period adjustment, the earnings per share data shown for the prior periods should also be restated. The effect of the restatement should be disclosed in the year of the restatement.

Complex capital structures and dual presentation of earnings require the following additional disclosures in note form:

1. Description of pertinent rights and privileges of the various securities outstanding.
2. A reconciliation of the numerators and denominators of the basic and diluted per share computations, including individual income and share amount effects of all securities that affect EPS.
3. The effect given preferred dividends in determining income available to common stockholders in computing basic EPS.
4. Securities that could potentially dilute basic EPS in the future that were not included in the computation because they would be antidilutive.
5. Effect of conversions subsequent to year-end, but before statements have been issued.

Illustration 17-28 presents the reconciliation and the related disclosure that is needed to meet disclosure requirements of this standard.

ILLUSTRATION 17-28
Reconciliation for Basic and Diluted EPS

	For the Year Ended 2002		
	Income (Numerator)	Shares (Denominator)	Per-Share Amount
Income before extraordinary item and accounting change	$7,500,000		
Less: Preferred stock dividends	(45,000)		
Basic EPS			
Income available to common stockholders	7,455,000	3,991,666	$1.87
Warrants		30,768	
Convertible preferred stock	45,000	308,333	
4% convertible bonds (net of tax)	60,000	50,000	
Diluted EPS			
Income available to common stockholders + assumed conversions	$7,560,000	4,380,767	$1.73

Stock options to purchase 1,000,000 shares of common stock at $85 per share were outstanding during the second half of 2002 but were not included in the computation of diluted EPS because the options' exercise price was greater than the average market price of the common shares. The options were still outstanding at the end of year 2002 and expire on June 30, 2012.[24]

Summary

As you can see, computation of earnings per share is a complex issue. It is a controversial area because many securities, although technically not common stock, have many of its basic characteristics. Some companies have issued these types of securities rather than common stock in order to avoid an adverse dilutive effect on earnings per share.

Illustration 17-29 displays graphically the elementary points of calculating earnings per share in a simple capital structure.

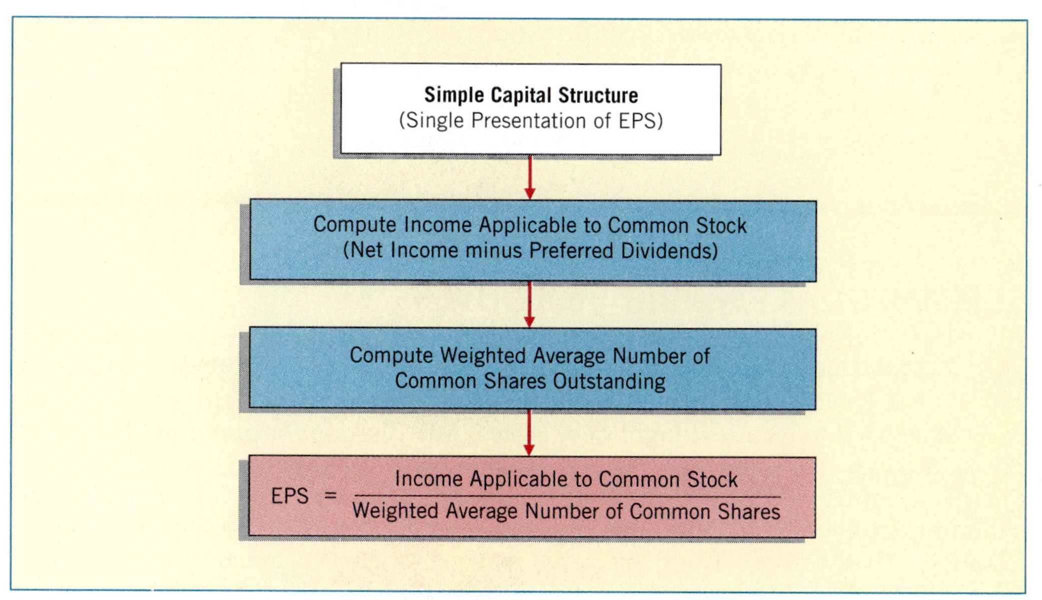

ILLUSTRATION 17-29
Calculating EPS, Simple Capital Structure

[24]Note that *Statement No. 123* has specific disclosure requirements as well regarding stock option plans and earnings per share disclosures.

Illustration 17-30 shows the calculation of earnings per share for a complex capital structure.

ILLUSTRATION 17-30
Calculating EPS, Complex Capital Structure

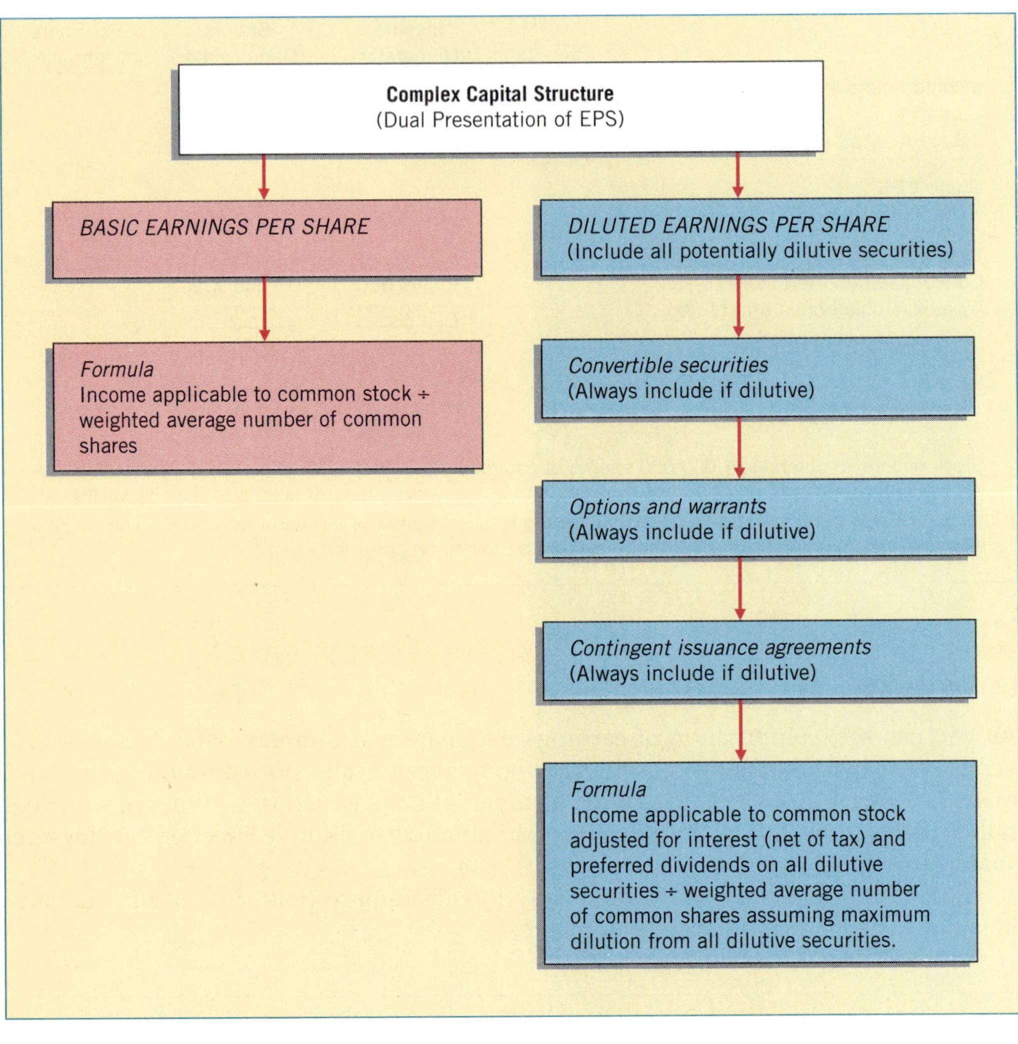

KEY TERMS

- antidilutive securities, *877*
- basic EPS, *877*
- complex capital structure, *873*
- convertible bonds, *858*
- convertible preferred stock, *861*
- detachable stock warrants, *862*
- diluted EPS, *877*
- dilutive securities, *857*
- earnings per share, *872*
- fair value method, *866*
- grant date, *865*
- if-converted method, *878*
- income available to common stockholders, *873*
- induced conversion, *860*
- intrinsic value method, *866*
- measurement date, *867*
- noncompensatory plans, *869*
- potential common stock, *857*
- service period, *867*
- simple capital structure, *873*
- stock option, *864*
- stock option plans, *865*
- stock right, *864*
- treasury stock method, *879*
- warrants, *861*
- weighted average number of shares outstanding, *874*

SUMMARY OF LEARNING OBJECTIVES

1 Describe the accounting for the issuance, conversion, and retirement of convertible securities. The method for recording convertible bonds at the date of issuance follows that used to record straight debt issues. Any discount or premium that results from the issuance of convertible bonds is amortized assuming the bonds will be held to maturity. If bonds are converted into other securities, the principal accounting problem is to determine the amount at which to record the securities exchanged for the bond. The book value method is used in practice and is considered GAAP. The retirement of convertible debt is considered a debt retirement, and the difference between the carrying amount of the retired convertible debt and the cash paid should result in an extraordinary charge or credit to income.

2 Explain the accounting for convertible preferred stock. When convertible preferred stock is converted, the book value method is employed; Preferred Stock, along with any related Additional Paid-in Capital, is debited, and Common Stock and Additional Paid-in Capital (if an excess exists) are credited.

3 Contrast the accounting for stock warrants and stock warrants issued with other securities. *Stock rights:* No entry is required when rights are issued to existing stockholders. Only a memorandum entry is needed to indicate the number of rights issued to existing stockholders and to ensure that the company has additional unissued stock registered for issuance in case the rights are exercised. *Stock warrants:* The proceeds from the sale of debt with detachable stock warrants should be allocated between the two securities. Warrants that are detachable can be traded separately from the debt, and therefore, a market value can be determined. The two methods of allocation available are the proportional method and the incremental method. Nondetachable warrants do not require an allocation of the proceeds between the bonds and the warrants. The entire proceeds are recorded as debt.

4 Describe the accounting for stock compensation plans under GAAP. Companies are given a choice in the recognition approach to stock compensation; however, the FASB encourages adoption of the fair value method. Using the fair value approach, total compensation expense is computed based on the fair value of the options that are expected to vest on the grant date. Under the intrinsic value approach, total compensation cost is computed as the excess of the market price of the stock over the option price on the date when both the number of shares to which employees are entitled and the option or purchase price for those shares are known. Under both the fair and intrinsic value methods, compensation expense is recognized in the periods in which the employee performs the services.

5 Explain the controversy involving stock compensation plans. When first proposed, there was considerable opposition to the recognition provisions contained in the fair value approach, because that approach could result in substantial compensation expense that was not previously recognized. Corporate America, particularly the small, high technology sector, was quite vocal in its opposition to the proposed standard. They believed that they would be placed at a competitive disadvantage with larger companies that can withstand higher compensation charges. In response to this opposition, which was based primarily on economic consequences arguments, the FASB decided to encourage, rather than require, recognition of compensation cost based on the fair value method and require expanded disclosures.

6 Compute earnings per share in a simple capital structure. When a company has both common and preferred stock outstanding, the current year preferred stock dividend is subtracted from net income to arrive at income available to common stockholders. The formula for computing earnings per share is net income less preferred stock dividends divided by the weighted average of shares outstanding.

7 Compute earnings per share in a complex capital structure. A complex capital structure requires a dual presentation of earnings per share, each with equal prominence on the face of the income statement. These two presentations are referred to as basic earnings per share and diluted earnings per share. Basic earnings per share is based on the number of weighted average common shares outstanding (i.e., equivalent to EPS for a simple capital structure). Diluted earnings per share indicates the dilution of earnings per share that would have occurred if all potential issuances of common stock that would have reduced earnings per share had taken place.

APPENDIX 17A

Stock Options— Additional Complications

OBJECTIVE 8
After studying Appendix 17A, you should be able to: Explain the accounting for various stock option plans under APB Opinion No. 25.

Before 1995, accounting for stock options was governed by the provisions in *APB Opinion No. 25.* This appendix discusses the provisions of *APB Opinion No. 25* because many companies do not adopt the recognition guidelines provided in *SFAS No. 123.* In addition, an expanded discussion of the types of plans used to compensate key executives is provided.

DETERMINING COMPENSATION EXPENSE

UNDERLYING CONCEPTS

GAAP is often characterized as misleading when compensation is measured at the grant date, using the excess of the market price of the stock over the exercise price. GAAP in this case is reliable, but many question the relevance of the compensation reported.

Under *APB Opinion No. 25,* total compensation expense is computed as the excess of the market price of the stock **over the option price on the measurement date.**[1] The measurement date is the first date on which are known both (1) the number of shares that an individual employee is entitled to receive and (2) the option or purchase price. The measurement date for many plans is the date an **option is granted to an employee** (i.e., the grant date). The measurement date may be later than the grant date in plans with variable terms (either number of shares or option price or both not known) that depend on events after date of grant. Usually the measurement date for plans with variable terms is the **date of exercise**.

If the number of shares or the option price, or both, are unknown, compensation expense may have to be estimated on the basis of assumptions about the final number of shares and the option price.

Three common plans that illustrate different accounting issues are:

1. Stock option plans (incentive or nonqualified).
2. Stock appreciation rights plans.
3. Performance-type plans.

Stock Option Plans

A stock option plan can be either an incentive stock option plan or a nonqualified (or nonstatutory) stock option plan. The distinction between an incentive and a nonqualified stock option plan is based on the IRS Code and relates to the tax treatment afforded the plan.

From the perspective of the executive, the **incentive stock option** provides a greater tax advantage. In these plans, an executive pays no tax on the difference between the market price of the stock and the option price when the stock is purchased. Subsequently, when the shares are sold, the executive pays tax on that difference at either capital gains rates (20%) or ordinary income tax rates (usually higher than capital gains

[1]"Accounting for Stock Issued to Employees," *Opinions of the Accounting Principles Board No. 25* (New York: AICPA, 1972).

rates), depending upon the executive's holding period.[2] Conversely, an executive who receives a nonqualified stock option must pay taxes, at ordinary income tax rates, on the difference between the market price of the stock and the option price at the time the stock is purchased. Thus, under an incentive stock option, the payment of the tax is deferred and may be less.

From the perspective of the company, the **nonqualified option plan** provides greater tax advantages. No tax deduction is received in an incentive stock option plan, whereas in a nonqualified stock option plan the company receives a tax deduction equal to the difference between the market price and option price at the date the employee purchases the stock. To illustrate, assume that Hubbard, Inc. grants options to purchase 10,000 shares at an option price of $10 when the current market price of the stock is $10; the shares are purchased at a time when the market price is $20; and the executive sells the shares one year later at $20. A comparison of the effect of both plans on the executive and on the company is shown in Illustration 17A-1.

ILLUSTRATION 17A-1
Comparison of Incentive and Nonqualified Stock Option Plans

	Incentive Stock Option[3]	Nonqualified Stock Option
Effect on Executive:		
(assuming 36% tax bracket)		
Profit on exercise [10,000 × ($20 − $10)]	$100,000	$100,000
Tax on exercise ($100,000 × 36%)	–0–	$ 36,000
Tax on sale ($100,000 × 20%)	$ 20,000	–0–
After-tax benefit	$ 80,000	$ 64,000
Effect on Company:		
(assuming 34% corporate rate)	Zero tax deduction resulting in no tax benefit.	$100,000 tax deduction resulting in a $34,000 tax benefit.

In effect, the executive in Hubbard, Inc.'s case would incur an $80,000 benefit under the incentive stock option plan and a $64,000 benefit under the nonqualified stock option plan. The tax is also deferred until the stock is sold under the incentive stock option plan. The company receives no benefit from an incentive stock option but a $100,000 tax deduction (which becomes a $34,000 tax benefit) for the nonqualified stock option.

Incentive Stock Option Plan

Why would companies want to issue incentive stock options? The major reason is to attract high-quality personnel, and many companies believe that incentive stock options are a greater attraction than nonqualified plans. Incentive stock options are particularly helpful to smaller higher-technology enterprises that have little cash and perhaps so little taxable income that the tax deduction is not important. Granting such options helps them attract and retain key personnel for whom they must compete against larger, established companies.

In an incentive stock option plan the tax laws require that the market price of the stock and the option price at the date of grant be equal. The tax laws do not require this equality in nonqualified plans. **No compensation expense is, therefore, recorded**

[2]After the year 2000, capital gains will be taxed at rates not to exceed 18%, as long as the stock is held for more than 5 years.

[3]For an ISO, the executive has an alternative minimum tax (AMT) preference upon exercise, which may lead to tax payments under AMT rules. The illustration also assumes that the executive receiving an ISO receives favorable capital gains treatment.

for an incentive stock option because no excess of market price over the option price exists at the date of grant (the measurement date in this case).[4]

Nonqualified Stock Option Plans

Nonqualified stock option plans usually involve compensation expense because the market price exceeds the option price **at the date of grant** (the measurement date). Total compensation cost is measured by this difference and then allocated to the periods benefited. The option price is set by the terms of the grant and generally remains the same throughout the option period. The market price of the shares under option, however, may vary materially in the extended period during which the option is outstanding.

The options in the Chen Company illustration on pages 867–868 were nonqualified stock options. Recall that under the fair value approach (*SFAS No. 123*), the total compensation expense is measured at the grant date based on the fair value of the options that are expected to vest. Under the intrinsic value approach, compensation expense is recorded for the excess of the market price over the exercise price at the grant date.

Stock Appreciation Rights

One of the main advantages of a **nonqualified stock option** plan is that an executive may acquire shares of stock having a market price substantially above the option price. A major disadvantage is that an executive must pay income tax on the difference between the market price of the stock and the option price at the **date of exercise**. This can be a financial hardship for an executive who wishes to keep the stock (rather than sell it immediately) because he or she would have to pay not only income tax but the option price as well. Note that for **incentive stock options**, much the same problem exists; that is, the executive may have to borrow to finance the exercise price, which leads to related interest costs.

One solution to this problem was the creation of **stock appreciation rights (SARs)**. In this type of plan, the executive is given the right to receive compensation equal to the **share appreciation**, which is defined as the excess of the market price of the stock at the date of exercise over a pre-established price. This share appreciation may be paid in cash, shares, or a combination of both. The major advantage of SARs is that the executive often does not have to make a cash outlay at the date of exercise, but receives a payment for the share appreciation. Unlike shares acquired under a stock option plan, the shares that constitute the basis for computing the appreciation in a SARs plan are not issued. The executive is awarded only cash or stock having a market value equivalent to the appreciation.

As indicated earlier, the usual date for measuring compensation related to stock compensation plans is the date of grant. However, with SARs, the final amount of cash or shares (or a combination of the two) to be distributed is not known until the date of exercise—the measurement date. Therefore total compensation cannot be measured until this date.

How then should compensation expense be recorded during the interim periods from the date of grant to the date of exercise? Such a determination is not easy because it is impossible to know what total compensation cost will be until the date of exercise,

---

[4]Recently, the FASB has proposed rules under which expense may be recorded on incentive stock options that are re-priced after the original grant (FASB, "Proposed Interpretation: Accounting for Certain Transactions Involving Stock Compensation," March 31, 1999). Repricing occurs when, following a decline in the stock price, a company resets the option price to a lower level, thereby making it more likely that the option will be "in the money" and valuable to the executive. Many companies are upset with this proposed accounting because they argue that re-pricing is appropriate to protect executives from market downturns outside of their control. See John Byrne, "How to Reward Failure: Reprice Stock Options," *Business Week*, October 12, 1998.

and the service period will probably not coincide with the exercise date. The best estimate of total compensation cost for the plan at any interim period is the difference between the **current market price** of the stock and the **option price** multiplied by the number of stock appreciation rights outstanding. This total estimated compensation cost is then allocated over the service period, to record an expense (or a decrease in expense if market price falls) in each period.[5] At the end of each interim period, total compensation expense reported to date should equal the percentage of the total service period that has elapsed multiplied by the estimated compensation cost.

For example, if at the end of an interim period the service period is 40% complete and total estimated compensation is $100,000, then cumulative compensation expense reported to date should equal $40,000 ($100,000 x .40). As another illustration, in the first year of a 4-year plan, the company charges one-fourth of the appreciation to date. In the second year, it charges off two-fourths or 50% of the appreciation to date less the amount already recognized in the first year. In the third year, it charges off three-fourths of the appreciation to date less the amount recognized previously, and in the fourth year it charges off the remaining compensation expense. We will refer to this method as the **percentage approach** for allocating compensation expense.

A special problem arises when the exercise date is later than the service period. In the previous example, if the SARs were not exercised at the end of 4 years it would be necessary to account for the difference in the market price and the option price in the fifth year. In this case, compensation expense is adjusted whenever a change in the market price of the stock **occurs in subsequent reporting periods until the rights expire or are exercised, whichever comes first.**

Increases or decreases in the market value of those shares between the date of grant and the exercise date, therefore, result in a change in the measure of compensation. Some periods will have credits to compensation expense if the quoted market price of the stock falls from one period to the next; the credit to compensation expense, however, cannot exceed previously recognized compensation expense. In other words, **cumulative compensation expense cannot be negative.**

To illustrate, assume that American Hotels, Inc. establishes a SARs program on January 1, 2001, which entitles executives to receive cash at the date of exercise (anytime in the next 5 years) for the difference between the market price of the stock and the preestablished price of $10 on 10,000 SARs; the market price of the stock on December 31, 2001, is $13, and the service period runs for 2 years (2001–2002). Illustration 17A-2 indicates the amount of compensation expense to be recorded each period, assuming that the executives hold the SARs for 3 years, at which time the rights are exercised.

ILLUSTRATION 17A-2
Compensation Expense, Stock Appreciation Rights

Stock Appreciation Rights
Schedule of Compensation Expense

(1) Date	(2) Market Price	(3) Pre-established Price (10,000 SARs)	(4) Cumulative Compensation Recognizable[a]	(5) Percentage Accrued[b]	(6) Cumulative Compensation Accrued to Date	Expense 2001	Expense 2002	Expense 2003
12/31/01	$13	$10	$30,000	50%	$ 15,000	$15,000		
					55,000		$55,000	
12/31/02	17	10	70,000	100%	70,000			
					(20,000)			$(20,000)
12/31/03	15	10	50,000	100%	$ 50,000			

[a]Cumulative compensation for unexercised SARs to be allocated to periods of service.
[b]The percentage accrued is based upon a 2-year service period (2001–2002).

[5]"Accounting for Stock Appreciation Rights and Other Variable Stock Option or Award Plans," *FASB Interpretation No. 28* (Stamford, Conn.: FASB, 1978), par. 2.

In 2001 American Hotels would record compensation expense of $15,000 because 50% of the $30,000 total of compensation cost estimated at December 31, 2001, is allocable to 2001.

In 2002 the market price increased to $17 per share; therefore, the additional compensation expense of $55,000 ($70,000 minus $15,000) was recorded. The SARs were held through 2003, during which time the stock decreased to $15. The decrease is recognized by recording a $20,000 credit to compensation expense and a debit to Liability under Stock Appreciation Plan. Note that after the service period ends, since the rights are still outstanding, the rights are adjusted to market at December 31, 2003. Any such credit to compensation expense cannot exceed previous charges to expense attributable to that plan.

As the compensation expense is recorded each period, the corresponding credit should be to a liability account if the stock appreciation is to be paid in cash. If stock is to be issued, then a more appropriate credit would be to Paid-in Capital. The entry to record compensation expense in the first year, assuming that the SARs ultimately will be paid in cash, is as follows:

Compensation Expense	15,000	
Liability under Stock Appreciation Plan		15,000

The liability account would be credited again in 2002 for $55,000 and debited for $20,000 in 2003 when the negative compensation expense is recorded. The entry to record the negative compensation expense is as follows:

Liability under Stock Appreciation Plan	20,000	
Compensation Expense		20,000

At December 31, 2003, the executives receive $50,000; the entry removing the liability is as follows:

Liability under Stock Appreciation Plan	50,000	
Cash		50,000

Because compensation expense is measured by the difference between market prices of the stock from period to period, multiplied by the number of SARs, compensation expense can increase or decrease substantially from one period to the next.

For this reason, companies with substantial stock appreciation rights plans may choose to use *SFAS No. 123* guidelines because the total compensation expense is determined at the date of grant. Subsequent changes in market price are therefore ignored; total compensation expense may be lower under *SFAS No. 123.*

SARs are often issued in combination with compensatory stock options (referred to as **tandem** or **combination plans**) and the executive must then select which of the two sets of terms to exercise, thereby canceling the other. The existence of alternative plans running concurrently poses additional problems. You must determine, on the basis of the facts available each period, which of the two plans has the higher probability of exercise and then account for this plan and ignore the other.

Performance-Type Plans

Some executives have become disenchanted with stock compensation plans whose ultimate payment depends on an increase in the market price of the common stock. They do not like having their compensation and judgment of performance at the mercy of the stock market's erratic behavior. As a result, there has been a substantial increase in the use of plans whereby executives receive common stock (or cash) if specified performance criteria are attained during the performance period (generally 3 to 5 years). Most of the 200 largest companies now have some type of plan that does not rely on stock price appreciation.

The **performance criteria** employed usually are increases in return on assets or equity, growth in sales, growth in earnings per share (EPS), or a combination of these factors. A good illustration of this type of plan is that of **Atlantic Richfield**, which at one time offered performance units valued in excess of $700,000 to the chairman of the board. These performance units are payable in 5 years, contingent upon the company's meeting certain levels of return on stockholders' equity and cash dividends.

As another example, **Honeywell** uses growth in EPS as its performance criterion. When certain levels of EPS are achieved, executives receive shares of stock. If the company achieves an average annual EPS growth of 13%, the executive will earn 100% of the shares. The maximum allowable is 130%, which would require a 17% growth rate; below 9% the executives receive nothing.

A performance-type plan's measurement date is the date of exercise because the number of shares that will be issued or the cash that will be paid out when performance is achieved are not known at the date of grant. The compensation cost is allocated to the periods involved in the same manner as with stock appreciation rights; that is, the percentage approach is used.

Tandem or combination awards are popular with these plans. The executive has the choice of selecting between a performance or stock option award. Companies such as **General Electric** and **Xerox** have adopted plans of this nature. In these cases the executive has the best of both worlds: if either the stock price increases or the performance goal is achieved, the executive gains. Sometimes, the executive receives both types of plans, so that the monies received from the performance plan can finance the exercise price on the stock option plan.

Summary of Compensation Plans

A summary of compensation plans and their major characteristics is provided in Illustration 17A-3.

ILLUSTRATION 17A-3
Summary of Compensation Plans

Type of Plan	Measurement Date	Measurement of Compensation	Allocation Period	Allocation Method
Incentive stock option				
APB Opinion No. 25	Grant	Market price less exercise price	N/A (no compensation expense)	N/A (no compensation expense)
SFAS No. 123	Grant	Option pricing model	Service	Straight-line
Nonqualified stock option				
APB Opinion No. 25	Grant	Market price less exercise price	Service	Straight-line
SFAS No. 123	Grant	Option pricing model	Service	Straight-line
Stock appreciation rights				
APB Opinion No. 25	Exercise	Market price less exercise price	Service	Percentage approach for service period, then mark to market
SFAS No. 123	Grant	Option pricing model	Service	Straight-line
Performance-type plan				
APB Opinion No. 25	Exercise	Market value of shares issued	Service	Percentage approach for service period, then mark to market
SFAS No. 123	Exercise	Market value of shares issued	Service	Percentage approach for service period, then mark to market

KEY TERMS

date of exercise, *886*
incentive stock option plan, *886*
nonqualified stock option plan, *887*
percentage approach, *889*
share appreciation, *888*
stock appreciation rights (SARs), *888*
tandem (combination) plans, *890*

SUMMARY OF LEARNING OBJECTIVE FOR APPENDIX 17A

8 Explain the accounting for various stock option plans under APB Opinion No. 25. (1) *Incentive stock option plans:* The market price and exercise price on the grant date must be equal. Because there is no compensation expense, there is no allocation problem. (2) *Nonqualified stock option plans:* Compensation is the difference between the market price and exercise price on the grant date. Compensation expense is allocated by the straight-line method during the service period. (3) *Stock appreciation rights:* The compensation is measured by the difference between market price and exercise price on the exercise date. The compensation expense is allocated by the percentage approach over the service period, then marked to market. (4) *Performance-type plan:* Compensation is measured by the market value of shares issued on the exercise date. Compensation expense is allocated by the percentage approach over the service period, then marked to market. See also Illustration 17A-3.

APPENDIX 17B

Comprehensive Earnings per Share Illustration

The purpose of this appendix is to illustrate the method of computing dilution when many securities are involved. The following section of the balance sheet of Webster Corporation is presented for analysis; assumptions related to the capital structure follow:

ILLUSTRATION 17B-1
Balance Sheet for Comprehensive Illustration

WEBSTER CORPORATION Selected Balance Sheet Information At December 31, 2001	
Long-term debt:	
Notes payable, 14%	$ 1,000,000
8% convertible bonds payable	2,500,000
10% convertible bonds payable	2,500,000
Total long-term debt	$ 6,000,000
Stockholders' equity:	
10% cumulative, convertible preferred stock, par value $100; 100,000 shares authorized, 25,000 shares issued and outstanding	$ 2,500,000
Common stock, par value $1, 5,000,000 shares authorized, 500,000 shares issued and outstanding	500,000
Additional paid-in capital	2,000,000
Retained earnings	9,000,000
Total stockholders' equity	$14,000,000

OBJECTIVE 9
After studying Appendix 17B, you should be able to: Compute earnings per share in a complex situation.

Notes and Assumptions
December 31, 2001

1. Options were granted in July 1999 to purchase 50,000 shares of common stock at \$20 per share. The average market price of Webster's common stock during 2001 was \$30 per share. No options were exercised during 2001.
2. Both the 8% and 10% convertible bonds were issued in 2000 at face value. Each convertible bond is convertible into 40 shares of common stock (each bond has a face value of \$1,000).
3. The 10% cumulative, convertible preferred stock was issued at the beginning of 2001 at par. Each share of preferred is convertible into four shares of common stock.
4. The average income tax rate is 40%.
5. The 500,000 shares of common stock were outstanding during the entire year.
6. Preferred dividends were not declared in 2001.
7. Net income was \$1,750,000 in 2001.
8. No bonds or preferred stock were converted during 2001.

The computation of basic earnings per share for 2001 starts with the amount based upon the weighted average of common shares outstanding, as shown in Illustration 17B-2.

ILLUSTRATION 17B-2
Computation of Earnings per Share—Simple Capital Structure

Net income	\$1,750,000
Less: 10% cumulative, convertible preferred stock dividend requirements	250,000
Income applicable to common stockholders	\$1,500,000
Weighted average number of common shares outstanding	500,000
Earnings per common share	\$3.00

Note the following points concerning the calculation above.

1. When preferred stock is cumulative, the preferred dividend is subtracted to arrive at income applicable to common stock whether the dividend is declared or not.
2. The earnings per share of \$3 must be computed as a starting point, because it is the per share amount that is subject to reduction due to the existence of convertible securities and options.

DILUTED EARNINGS PER SHARE

The steps for computing diluted earnings per share are:

1. Determine, for each dilutive security, the per share effect assuming exercise/conversion.
2. Rank the results from step 1 from smallest to largest earnings effect per share; that is, rank the results from most dilutive to least dilutive.
3. Beginning with the earnings per share based upon the weighted average of common shares outstanding (\$3), recalculate earnings per share by adding the smallest per share effects from step 2. If the results from this recalculation are less than \$3, proceed to the next smallest per share effect and recalculate earnings per share. This process is continued so long as each recalculated earnings per share is smaller than the previous amount. The process will end either because there are no more securities to test or a particular security maintains or increases earnings per share (is antidilutive).

We'll now apply the three steps to Webster Corporation. (Note that net income and income available to common stockholders are not the same if preferred dividends are declared or cumulative.) Webster Corporation has four securities (options, 8% and 10% convertible bonds, and the convertible preferred stock) that could reduce EPS.

The first step in the computation of diluted earnings per share is to determine a per share effect for each potentially dilutive security. Illustrations 17B-3 through 17B-6 illustrate these computations.

ILLUSTRATION 17B-3
Per Share Effect of Options (Treasury Stock Method), Diluted Earnings per Share

Number of shares under option	50,000
Option price per share	× $20
Proceeds upon assumed exercise of options	$1,000,000
Average 2001 market price of common	$30
Treasury shares that could be acquired with proceeds ($1,000,000 ÷ $30)	33,333
Excess of shares under option over treasury shares that could be repurchased (50,000 − 33,333)	16,667
Per share effect:	
Incremental Numerator Effect: None / Incremental Denominator Effect: 16,667 shares =	$0

ILLUSTRATION 17B-4
Per Share Effect of 8% Bonds (If-Converted Method), Diluted Earnings per Share

Interest expense for year (8% × $2,500,000)	$200,000
Income tax reduction due to interest (40% × $200,000)	80,000
Interest expense avoided (net of tax)	$120,000
Number of common shares issued assuming conversion of bonds (2,500 bonds × 40 shares)	100,000
Per share effect:	
Incremental Numerator Effect: $120,000 / Incremental Denominator Effect: 100,000 shares =	$1.20

ILLUSTRATION 17B-5
Per Share Effect of 10% Bonds (If-Converted Method), Diluted Earnings per Share

Interest expense for year (10% × $2,500,000)	$250,000
Income tax reduction due to interest (40% × $250,000)	100,000
Interest expense avoided (net of tax)	$150,000
Number of common shares issued assuming conversion of bonds (2,500 bonds × 40 shares)	100,000
Per share effect:	
Incremental Numerator Effect: $150,000 / Incremental Denominator Effect: 100,000 shares =	$1.50

ILLUSTRATION 17B-6
Per Share Effect of 10% Convertible Preferred (If-Converted Method), Diluted Earnings per Share

Dividend requirement on cumulative preferred (25,000 shares × $10)	$250,000
Income tax effect (dividends not a tax deduction)	none
Dividend requirement avoided	$250,000
Number of common shares issued assuming conversion of preferred (4 × 25,000 shares)	100,000
Per share effect:	
Incremental Numerator Effect: $250,000 / Incremental Denominator Effect: 100,000 shares =	$2.50

Illustration 17B-7 shows the ranking of all four potentially dilutive securities.

	Effect per Share
1. Options	$ 0
2. 8% convertible bonds	1.20
3. 10% convertible bonds	1.50
4. 10% convertible preferred	2.50

ILLUSTRATION 17B-7
Ranking of per Share Effects (Smallest to Largest), Diluted Earnings per Share

The next step is to determine earnings per share giving effect to the ranking in Illustration 17B-7. Starting with the earnings per share of $3 computed previously, add the incremental effects of the options to the original calculation, as follows:

Options	
Income applicable to common stockholders	$1,500,000
Add: Incremental numerator effect of options	none
Total	$1,500,000
Weighted average number of common shares outstanding	500,000
Add: Incremental denominator effect of options (Illustration 17B-3)	16,667
Total	516,667
Recomputed earnings per share ($1,500,000 ÷ 516,667 shares)	$2.90

ILLUSTRATION 17B-8
Recomputation of EPS Using Incremental Effect of Options

Since the recomputed earnings per share is reduced (from $3 to $2.90), the effect of the options is dilutive. Again, this effect could have been anticipated because the average market price ($30) exceeded the option price ($20).

Recomputed earnings per share, assuming the 8% bonds are converted, is as follows:

8% Convertible Bonds	
Numerator from previous calculation	$1,500,000
Add: Interest expense avoided (net of tax)	120,000
Total	$1,620,000
Denominator from previous calculation (shares)	516,667
Add: Number of common shares assumed issued upon conversion of bonds	100,000
Total	616,667
Recomputed earnings per share ($1,620,000 ÷ 616,667 shares)	$2.63

ILLUSTRATION 17B-9
Recomputation of EPS Using Incremental Effect of 8% Convertible Bonds

Since the recomputed earnings per share is reduced (from $2.90 to $2.63), the effect of the 8% bonds is dilutive.

Next, earnings per share is recomputed assuming the conversion of the 10% bonds. This is shown below:

10% Convertible Bonds	
Numerator from previous calculation	$1,620,000
Add: Interest expense avoided (net of tax)	150,000
Total	$1,770,000
Denominator from previous calculation (shares)	616,667
Add: Number of common shares assumed issued upon conversion of bonds	100,000
Total	716,667
Recomputed earnings per share ($1,770,000 ÷ 716,667 shares)	$2.47

ILLUSTRATION 17B-10
Recomputation of EPS Using Incremental Effect of 10% Convertible Bonds

Since the recomputed earnings per share is reduced (from $2.63 to $2.47), the effect of the 10% convertible bonds is dilutive.

The final step is the recomputation that includes the 10% preferred stock. This is shown below.

ILLUSTRATION 17B-11
Recomputation of EPS Using Incremental Effect of 10% Convertible Preferred

10% Convertible Preferred	
Numerator from previous calculation	$1,770,000
Add: Dividend requirement avoided	250,000
Total	$2,020,000
Denominator from previous calculation (shares)	716,667
Add: Number of common shares assumed issued upon conversion of preferred	100,000
Total	816,667
Recomputed earnings per share ($2,020,000 ÷ 816,667 shares)	$2.47

Since the recomputed earnings per share is not reduced, the effect of the 10% convertible preferred is not dilutive. Diluted earnings per share is $2.47, and the per share effects of the preferred are not used in the computation.

Finally, the disclosure of earnings per share on the income statement for Webster Corporation is shown below.

ILLUSTRATION 17B-12
Income Statement Presentation, EPS

Net income	$1,750,000
Basic earnings per common share (Note X)	$3.00
Diluted earnings per common share	$2.47

A company uses **income from continuing operations (adjusted for preferred dividends) to determine whether potential common stock is dilutive or antidilutive.** (Some refer to this measure as the **control number**.) To illustrate, assume that Barton Company provides the following information:

ILLUSTRATION 17B-13
Barton Company Data

Income from continuing operations	$2,400,000
Loss from discontinued operations	3,600,000
Net loss	$1,200,000
Weighted average shares of common stock outstanding	1,000,000
Potential common stock	200,000

The computation of basic and dilutive earnings per share is as follows:

ILLUSTRATION 17B-14
Basic and Diluted EPS

Basic earnings per share	
Income from continuing operations	$2.40
Loss from discontinued operations	3.60
Net loss	$1.20
Diluted earnings per share	
Income from continuing operations	$2.00
Loss from discontinued operations	3.00
Net loss	$1.00

As shown in Illustration 17B-14, basic earnings per share from continuing operations is higher than the diluted earnings per share from continuing operations. The reason:

The diluted earnings per share from continuing operations includes an additional 200,000 shares of potential common stock in its denominator.[1]

Income from continuing operations is used as the control number because many companies will show income from continuing operations (or a similar line item above net income if it appears on the income statement), but report a final net loss due to a loss on discontinued operations. If the final net loss is used as the control number, basic and diluted earnings per share would be the same because the potential common shares are antidilutive.[2]

Go to the Digital Tool for another EPS illustration with multiple dilutive securities.

SUMMARY OF LEARNING OBJECTIVE FOR APPENDIX 17B

9 **Compute earnings per share in a complex situation.** For diluted EPS, (1) determine, for each potentially dilutive security, the per share effect assuming exercise/conversion; (2) rank from most dilutive to least dilutive; (3) recalculate EPS starting with the most dilutive, and continue adding securities until EPS increases (is antidilutive).

KEY TERMS

control number, *896*

Note: All **asterisked** Questions, Brief Exercises, Exercises Problems, and Conceptual Cases relate to material contained in the appendix to the chapter.

QUESTIONS

1 Why might increased merger activity lead to the issuance of dilutive securities?

2 Briefly explain why corporations issue convertible securities.

3 Discuss the similarities and the differences between convertible debt and debt issued with stock warrants.

4 Plantagenet Corp. offered holders of its 1,000 convertible bonds a premium of $160 per bond to induce conversion into shares of its common stock. Upon conversion of all the bonds, Plantagenet Corp. recorded the $160,000 premium as a reduction of paid-in capital. Comment on Plantagenet's treatment of the $160,000 "sweetener."

5 Explain how the conversion feature of convertible debt has a value (a) to the issuer and (b) to the purchaser.

6 What are the arguments for giving separate accounting recognition to the conversion feature of debentures?

7 Four years after issue, debentures with a face value of $1,000,000 and book value of $960,000 are tendered for conversion into 80,000 shares of common stock immediately after an interest payment date when the market price of the debentures is 104 and the common stock is selling at $14 per share (par value $10). The company records the conversion as follows:

Bonds Payable	1,000,000	
Discount on Bonds Payable		40,000
Common Stock		800,000
Paid-in Capital in Excess of Par		160,000

Discuss the propriety of this accounting treatment.

8 On July 1, 2001, Roberts Corporation issued $3,000,000 of 9% bonds payable in 20 years. The bonds include detachable warrants giving the bondholder the right to purchase for $30 one share of $1 par value common stock at any time during the next 10 years. The bonds were sold for $3,000,000. The value of the warrants at the time of issuance was $200,000. Prepare the journal entry to record this transaction.

9 What are stock rights? How does the issuing company account for them?

10 Briefly explain the accounting requirements for stock compensation plans under *Statement of Financial Accounting Standards No. 123.*

11 Weiland Corporation has an employee stock purchase plan which permits all full-time employees to purchase

[1]A company that does not report a discontinued operation but reports an extraordinary item or the cumulative effect of a change in accounting principle should use that line item (for example, income before extraordinary items) as the control number.

[2]If a loss from continuing operations is reported, basic and diluted earnings per share will be the same because potential common stock will be antidilutive, even if the company reports final net income. The Board believes that comparability of EPS information will be improved by using income from continuing operations as the control number.

10 shares of common stock on the third anniversary of their employment and an additional 15 shares on each subsequent anniversary date. The purchase price is set at the market price on the date purchased and no commission is charged. Discuss whether this plan would be considered compensatory.

12 What date or event does the profession believe should be used in determining the value of a stock option? What arguments support this position?

13 Over what period of time should compensation cost be allocated?

14 How is compensation expense computed using the fair value approach?

15 At December 31, 2001, Amad Company had 600,000 shares of common stock issued and outstanding, 400,000 of which had been issued and outstanding throughout the year, and 200,000 of which were issued on October 1, 2001. Net income for 2001 was $3,000,000 and dividends declared on preferred stock were $400,000. Compute Amad's earnings per common share (round to the nearest penny).

16 What effect do stock dividends or stock splits have on the computation of the weighted average number of shares outstanding?

17 Define the following terms.

(a) Basic earnings per share.

(b) Potentially dilutive security.

(c) Diluted earnings per share.

(d) Complex capital structure.

(e) Potential common stock.

18 What are the computational guidelines for determining whether a convertible security is to be reported as part of diluted earnings per share?

19 Discuss why options and warrants may be considered potentially dilutive common shares for the computation of diluted earnings per share.

20 Explain how convertible securities are determined to be potentially dilutive common shares and how those convertible senior securities that are not considered to be potentially dilutive common shares enter into the determination of earnings per share data.

21 Explain the treasury stock method as it applies to options and warrants in computing dilutive earnings per share data.

22 Earnings per share can affect market prices of common stock. Can market prices affect earnings per share? Explain.

23 What is meant by the term antidilution? Give an example.

24 What type of earnings per share presentation is required in a complex capital structure?

***25** How is antidilution determined when multiple securities are involved?

BRIEF EXERCISES

BE17-1 Sasha Verbitsky Corporation has outstanding 1,000 $1,000 bonds, each convertible into 50 shares of $10 par value common stock. The bonds are converted on December 31, 2002, when the unamortized discount is $30,000, and the market price of the stock is $21 per share. Record the conversion using the market value approach.

BE17-2 Use the information for Sasha Verbitsky Corporation given in BE17-1. Record the conversion using the book value approach.

BE17-3 Malik Sealy Corporation issued 2,000 shares of $10 par value common stock upon conversion of 1,000 shares of $50 par value preferred stock. The preferred stock was originally issued at $55 per share. The common stock is trading at $26 per share at the time of conversion. Record the conversion of the preferred stock.

BE17-4 Divac Corporation issued 1,000 $1,000 bonds at 101. Each bond was issued with one detachable stock warrant. After issuance, the bonds were selling in the market at 98, and the warrants had a market value of $40. Use the proportional method to record the issuance of the bonds and warrants.

BE17-5 Ceballos Corporation issued 1,000 $1,000 bonds at 101. Each bond was issued with one detachable stock warrant. After issuance, the bonds were selling separately at 98. The market price of the warrants without the bonds cannot be determined. Use the incremental method to record the issuance of the bonds and warrants.

BE17-6 On January 1, 2002, Johnson Corporation granted 5,000 options to executives. Each option entitles the holder to purchase one share of Johnson's $5 par value common stock at $50 per share at any time during the next 5 years. The market price of the stock is $65 per share on the date of grant. The period of benefit is two years. Prepare Johnson's journal entries for January 1, 2002, and December 31, 2002 and 2003, using the intrinsic value method.

BE17-7 Use the information given for Johnson Corporation in BE17-6. Assume the fair value option pricing model determines that total compensation expense is $140,000. Prepare Johnson's journal entries for January 1, 2002, and December 31, 2002 and 2003, using the fair value method.

BE17-8 Haley Corporation had 2002 net income of $1,200,000. During 2002, Haley paid a dividend of $2 per share on 100,000 shares of preferred stock. During 2002, Haley had outstanding 250,000 shares of common stock. Compute Haley's 2002 earnings per share.

BE17-9 Barkley Corporation had 120,000 shares of stock outstanding on January 1, 2002. On May 1, 2002, Barkley issued 45,000 shares. On July 1, Barkley purchased 10,000 treasury shares, which were reissued on October 1. Compute Barkley's weighted average number of shares outstanding for 2002.

BE17-10 Green Corporation had 200,000 shares of common stock outstanding on January 1, 2002. On May 1, Green issued 30,000 shares. **(a)** Compute the weighted average number of shares outstanding if the 30,000 shares were issued for cash. **(b)** Compute the weighted average number of shares outstanding if the 30,000 shares were issued in a stock dividend.

BE17-11 Strickland Corporation earned net income of $300,000 in 2002 and had 100,000 shares of common stock outstanding throughout the year. Also outstanding all year was $400,000 of 10% bonds, which are convertible into 16,000 shares of common. Strickland's tax rate is 40%. Compute Strickland's 2002 diluted earnings per share.

BE17-12 Sabonis Corporation reported net income of $400,000 in 2002 and had 50,000 shares of common stock outstanding throughout the year. Also outstanding all year were 5,000 shares of cumulative preferred stock, each convertible into 2 shares of common. The preferred stock pays an annual dividend of $5 per share. Sabonis' tax rate is 40%. Compute Sabonis' 2002 diluted earnings per share.

BE17-13 Sarunas Corporation reported net income of $300,000 in 2002 and had 200,000 shares of common stock outstanding throughout the year. Also outstanding all year were 30,000 options to purchase common stock at $10 per share. The average market price of the stock during the year was $15. Compute diluted earnings per share.

BE17-14 The 2002 income statement of Schrempf Corporation showed net income of $480,000 and an extraordinary loss of $120,000. Schrempf had 50,000 shares of common stock outstanding all year. Prepare Schrempf's income statement presentation of earnings per share.

***BE17-15** Sam Perkins, Inc. established a stock appreciation rights (SAR) program on January 1, 2001, which entitles executives to receive cash at the date of exercise for the difference between the market price of the stock and the preestablished price of $20 on 5,000 SARs. The required service period is two years. The market price of the stock is $22 on December 31, 2001, and $29 on December 31, 2002. The SARs are exercised on January 1, 2003. Compute Perkins' compensation expense for 2001 and 2002.

EXERCISES

E17-1 (Issuance and Conversion of Bonds) For each of the unrelated transactions described below, present the entry(ies) required to record each transaction.

1. Grand Corp. issued $20,000,000 par value 10% convertible bonds at 99. If the bonds had not been convertible, the company's investment banker estimates they would have been sold at 95. Expenses of issuing the bonds were $70,000.
2. Hoosier Company issued $20,000,000 par value 10% bonds at 98. One detachable stock purchase warrant was issued with each $100 par value bond. At the time of issuance, the warrants were selling for $4.
3. On July 1, 2001, Trady Company called its 11% convertible debentures for conversion. The $10,000,000 par value bonds were converted into 1,000,000 shares of $1 par value common stock. On July 1, there was $55,000 of unamortized discount applicable to the bonds, and the company paid an additional $75,000 to the bondholders to induce conversion of all the bonds. The company records the conversion using the book value method.

E17-2 (Conversion of Bonds) Aubrey Inc. issued $4,000,000 of 10%, 10-year convertible bonds on June 1, 2001, at 98 plus accrued interest. The bonds were dated April 1, 2001, with interest payable April 1 and October 1. Bond discount is amortized semiannually on a straight-line basis.

On April 1, 2002, $1,500,000 of these bonds were converted into 30,000 shares of $20 par value common stock. Accrued interest was paid in cash at the time of conversion.

Instructions

(a) Prepare the entry to record the interest expense at October 1, 2001. Assume that accrued interest payable was credited when the bonds were issued. (Round to nearest dollar.)

(b) Prepare the entry(ies) to record the conversion on April 1, 2002. (Book value method is used.) Assume that the entry to record amortization of the bond discount and interest payment has been made.

E17-3 (Conversion of Bonds) Vargo Company has bonds payable outstanding in the amount of $500,000 and the Premium on Bonds Payable account has a balance of $7,500. Each $1,000 bond is convertible into 20 shares of preferred stock of par value of $50 per share. All bonds are converted into preferred stock.

Instructions

(a) Assuming that the book value method was used, what entry would be made?

(b) Assuming that the bonds are quoted on the market at 102 and that the preferred stock may be sold on the market at $50 7/8, make the entry to record the conversion of the bonds to preferred stock. (Use the market value approach.)

E17-4 (Conversion of Bonds) On January 1, 2000, when its $30 par value common stock was selling for $80 per share, Plato Corp. issued $10,000,000 of 8% convertible debentures due in 20 years. The conversion option allowed the holder of each $1,000 bond to convert the bond into five shares of the corporation's common stock. The debentures were issued for $10,800,000. The present value of the bond payments at the time of issuance was $8,500,000 and the corporation believes the difference between the present value and the amount paid is attributable to the conversion feature. On January 1, 2001, the corporation's $30 par value common stock was split 2 for 1, and the conversion rate for the bonds was adjusted accordingly. On January 1, 2002, when the corporation's $15 par value common stock was selling for $135 per share, holders of 30% of the convertible debentures exercised their conversion options. The corporation uses the straight-line method for amortizing any bond discounts or premiums.

Instructions

(a) Prepare in general journal form the entry to record the original issuance of the convertible debentures.

(b) Prepare in general journal form the entry to record the exercise of the conversion option, using the book value method. Show supporting computations in good form.

E17-5 (Conversion of Bonds) The December 31, 2001, balance sheet of Kepler Corp. is as follows:

10% Callable, Convertible Bonds Payable (semiannual interest dates April 30 and October 31; convertible into 6 shares of $25 par value common stock per $1,000 of bond principal; maturity date April 30, 2007)	$500,000	
Discount on Bonds Payable	10,240	$489,760

On March 5, 2002, Kepler Corp. called all of the bonds as of April 30 for the principal plus interest through April 30. By April 30 all bondholders had exercised their conversion to common stock as of the interest payment date. Consequently, on April 30, Kepler Corp. paid the semiannual interest and issued shares of common stock for the bonds. The discount is amortized on a straight-line basis. Kepler uses the book value method.

Instructions

Prepare the entry(ies) to record the interest expense and conversion on April 30, 2002. Reversing entries were made on January 1, 2002. (Round to the nearest dollar.)

E17-6 (Conversion of Bonds) On January 1, 2001, Gottlieb Corporation issued $4,000,000 of 10-year, 8% convertible debentures at 102. Interest is to be paid semiannually on June 30 and December 31. Each $1,000 debenture can be converted into eight shares of Gottlieb Corporation $100 par value common stock after December 31, 2002.

On January 1, 2003, $400,000 of debentures are converted into common stock, which is then selling at $110. An additional $400,000 of debentures are converted on March 31, 2003. The market price of the common stock is then $115. Accrued interest at March 31 will be paid on the next interest date.

Bond premium is amortized on a straight-line basis.

Instructions

Make the necessary journal entries for:

(a) December 31, 2002.

(b) January 1, 2003.

(c) March 31, 2003.

(d) June 30, 2003.

Record the conversions using the book value method.

E17-7 (Issuance of Bonds with Warrants) Illiad Inc. has decided to raise additional capital by issuing \$170,000 face value of bonds with a coupon rate of 10%. In discussions with their investment bankers, it was determined that to help the sale of the bonds, detachable stock warrants should be issued at the rate of one warrant for each \$100 bond sold. The value of the bonds without the warrants is considered to be \$136,000, and the value of the warrants in the market is \$24,000. The bonds sold in the market at issuance for \$152,000.

Instructions

(a) What entry should be made at the time of the issuance of the bonds and warrants?

(b) If the warrants were nondetachable, would the entries be different? Discuss.

E17-8 (Issuance of Bonds with Detachable Warrants) On September 1, 2001, Sands Company sold at 104 (plus accrued interest) 4,000 of its 9%, 10-year, \$1,000 face value, nonconvertible bonds with detachable stock warrants. Each bond carried two detachable warrants; each warrant was for one share of common stock at a specified option price of \$15 per share. Shortly after issuance, the warrants were quoted on the market for \$3 each. No market value can be determined for the bonds above. Interest is payable on December 1 and June 1. Bond issue costs of \$30,000 were incurred.

Instructions

Prepare in general journal format the entry to record the issuance of the bonds.

(AICPA adapted)

E17-9 (Issuance of Bonds with Stock Warrants) On May 1, 2001, Friendly Company issued 2,000 \$1,000 bonds at 102. Each bond was issued with one detachable stock warrant. Shortly after issuance, the bonds were selling at 98, but the market value of the warrants cannot be determined.

Instructions

(a) Prepare the entry to record the issuance of the bonds and warrants.

(b) Assume the same facts as part (a), except that the warrants had a fair value of \$30. Prepare the entry to record the issuance of the bonds and warrants.

E17-10 (Issuance and Exercise of Stock Options) On November 1, 2001, Columbo Company adopted a stock option plan that granted options to key executives to purchase 30,000 shares of the company's \$10 par value common stock. The options were granted on January 2, 2002, and were exercisable 2 years after the date of grant if the grantee was still an employee of the company; the options expired 6 years from date of grant. The option price was set at \$40 and the fair value option pricing model determines the total compensation expense to be \$450,000.

All of the options were exercised during the year 2004; 20,000 on January 3 when the market price was \$67, and 10,000 on May 1 when the market price was \$77 a share.

Instructions

Prepare journal entries relating to the stock option plan for the years 2002, 2003, and 2004 under the fair value method. Assume that the employee performs services equally in 2002 and 2003.

E17-11 (Issuance, Exercise, and Termination of Stock Options) On January 1, 2002, Titania Inc. granted stock options to officers and key employees for the purchase of 20,000 shares of the company's \$10 par common stock at \$25 per share. The options were exercisable within a 5-year period beginning January 1, 2004, by grantees still in the employ of the company, and expiring December 31, 2008. The service period for this award is 2 years. Assume that the fair value option pricing model determines total compensation expense to be \$350,000.

On April 1, 2003, 2,000 option shares were terminated when the employees resigned from the company. The market value of the common stock was \$35 per share on this date.

On March 31, 2004, 12,000 option shares were exercised when the market value of the common stock was \$40 per share.

Instructions

Prepare journal entries using the fair value method to record issuance of the stock options, termination of the stock options, exercise of the stock options, and charges to compensation expense, for the years ended December 31, 2002, 2003, and 2004.

E17-12 (Issuance, Exercise, and Termination of Stock Options) On January 1, 2000, Nichols Corporation granted 10,000 options to key executives. Each option allows the executive to purchase one share of Nichols' \$5 par value common stock at a price of \$20 per share. The options were exercisable within a 2-year period beginning January 1, 2002, if the grantee is still employed by the company at the time of the exercise. On the grant date, Nichols' stock was trading at \$25 per share, and a fair value option-pricing model determines total compensation to be \$400,000.

On May 1, 2002, 8,000 options were exercised when the market price of Nichols' stock was $30 per share. The remaining options lapsed in 2004 because executives decided not to exercise their options.

Instructions

Prepare the necessary journal entries related to the stock option plan for the years 2000 through 2004. Nichols uses the fair value approach to account for stock options.

***E17-13 (Stock Appreciation Rights)** On December 31, 1997, Beckford Company issues 150,000 stock appreciation rights to its officers entitling them to receive cash for the difference between the market price of its stock and a preestablished price of $10. The market price fluctuates as follows: 12/31/98—$14; 12/31/99—$8; 12/31/00—$20; 12/31/01—$19. The service period is 4 years and the exercise period is 7 years. The company elects to use *APB Opinion No. 25* accounting for this transaction.

Instructions

(a) Prepare a schedule that shows the amount of compensation expense allocable to each year affected by the stock appreciation rights plan.

(b) Prepare the entry at December 31, 2001, to record compensation expense, if any, in 2001.

(c) Prepare the entry on December 31, 2001, assuming that all 150,000 SARs are exercised.

***E17-14 (Stock Appreciation Rights)** Capulet Company establishes a stock appreciation rights program that entitles its new president Ben Davis to receive cash for the difference between the market price of the stock and a preestablished price of $30 (also market price) on December 31, 1998, on 30,000 SARs. The date of grant is December 31, 1998 and the required employment (service) period is 4 years. President Davis exercises all of the SARs in 2004. The market value of the stock fluctuates as follows: 12/31/99—$36; 12/31/00—$39; 12/31/01—$45; 12/31/02—$36; 12/31/03—$48. The company elects to use *APB Opinion No. 25* accounting for this transaction.

Instructions

(a) Prepare a 5-year (1999–2003) schedule of compensation expense pertaining to the 30,000 SARs granted President Davis.

(b) Prepare the journal entry for compensation expense in 1999, 2002, and 2003 relative to the 30,000 SARs.

E17-15 (Weighted Average Number of Shares) Newton Inc. uses a calendar year for financial reporting. The company is authorized to issue 9,000,000 shares of $10 par common stock. At no time has Newton issued any potentially dilutive securities. Listed below is a summary of Newton's common stock activities.

1. Number of common shares issued and outstanding at December 31, 1999	2,000,000
2. Shares issued as a result of a 10% stock dividend on September 30, 2000	200,000
3. Shares issued for cash on March 31, 2001	2,000,000
Number of common shares issued and outstanding at December 31, 2001	4,200,000
4. A 2-for-1 stock split of Newton's common stock took place on March 31, 2002.	

Instructions

(a) Compute the weighted average number of common shares used in computing earnings per common share for 2000 on the 2001 comparative income statement.

(b) Compute the weighted average number of common shares used in computing earnings per common share for 2001 on the 2001 comparative income statement.

(c) Compute the weighted average number of common shares to be used in computing earnings per common share for 2001 on the 2002 comparative income statement.

(d) Compute the weighted average number of common shares to be used in computing earnings per common share for 2002 on the 2002 comparative income statement.

(CMA adapted)

E17-16 (EPS: Simple Capital Structure) On January 1, 2002, Wilke Corp. had 480,000 shares of common stock outstanding. During 2002, it had the following transactions that affected the common stock account.

February 1	Issued 120,000 shares
March 1	Issued a 10% stock dividend
May 1	Acquired 100,000 shares of treasury stock
June 1	Issued a 3-for-1 stock split
October 1	Reissued 60,000 shares of treasury stock

Instructions

(a) Determine the weighted average number of shares outstanding as of December 31, 2002.

(b) Assume that Wilke Corp. earned net income of $3,456,000 during 2002. In addition, it had 100,000 shares of 9%, $100 par nonconvertible, noncumulative preferred stock outstanding for the entire year. Because of liquidity considerations, however, the company did not declare and pay a preferred dividend in 2002. Compute earnings per share for 2002, using the weighted average number of shares determined in part (a).

(c) Assume the same facts as in part (b), except that the preferred stock was cumulative. Compute earnings per share for 2002.

(d) Assume the same facts as in part (b), except that net income included an extraordinary gain of $864,000 and a loss from discontinued operations of $432,000. Both items are net of applicable income taxes. Compute earnings per share for 2002.

E17-17 (EPS: Simple Capital Structure) Ace Company had 200,000 shares of common stock outstanding on December 31, 2002. During the year 2003 the company issued 8,000 shares on May 1 and retired 14,000 shares on October 31. For the year 2003 Ace Company reported net income of $249,690 after a casualty loss of $40,600 (net of tax).

Instructions

What earnings per share data should be reported at the bottom of its income statement, assuming that the casualty loss is extraordinary?

E17-18 (EPS: Simple Capital Structure) Flagstad Inc. presented the following data:

Net income	$2,500,000
Preferred stock: 50,000 shares outstanding, $100 par, 8% cumulative, not convertible	5,000,000
Common stock: Shares outstanding 1/1	750,000
Issued for cash, 5/1	300,000
Acquired treasury stock for cash, 8/1	150,000
2-for-1 stock split, 10/1	

Instructions

Compute earnings per share.

E17-19 (EPS: Simple Capital Structure) A portion of the combined statement of income and retained earnings of Seminole Inc. for the current year follows:

Income before extraordinary item		$15,000,000
Extraordinary loss, net of applicable income tax (Note 1)		1,340,000
Net income		13,660,000
Retained earnings at the beginning of the year		83,250,000
		96,910,000
Dividends declared:		
On preferred stock—$6.00 per share	$ 300,000	
On common stock—$1.75 per share	14,875,000	15,175,000
Retained earnings at the end of the year		$81,735,000

Note 1. During the year, Seminole Inc. suffered a major casualty loss of $1,340,000 after applicable income tax reduction of $1,200,000.

At the end of the current year, Seminole Inc. has outstanding 8,500,000 shares of $10 par common stock and 50,000 shares of 6% preferred.

On April 1 of the current year, Seminole Inc. issued 1,000,000 shares of common stock for $32 per share to help finance the casualty.

Instructions

Compute the earnings per share on common stock for the current year as it should be reported to stockholders.

E17-20 (EPS: Simple Capital Structure) On January 1, 2002, Lennon Industries had stock outstanding as follows:

6% Cumulative preferred stock, $100 par value, issued and outstanding 10,000 shares	$1,000,000
Common stock, $10 par value, issued and outstanding 200,000 shares	2,000,000

To acquire the net assets of three smaller companies, Lennon authorized the issuance of an additional 160,000 common shares. The acquisitions took place as follows:

	Date of Acquisition	Shares Issued
Company A	April 1, 2002	50,000
Company B	July 1, 2002	80,000
Company C	October 1, 2002	30,000

On May 14, 2002, Lennon realized a $90,000 (before taxes) insurance gain on the expropriation of investments originally purchased in 1991.

On December 31, 2002, Lennon recorded net income of $300,000 before tax and exclusive of the gain.

Instructions

Assuming a 50% tax rate, compute the earnings per share data that should appear on the financial statements of Lennon Industries as of December 31, 2002. Assume that the expropriation is extraordinary.

E17-21 (EPS: Simple Capital Structure) At January 1, 2002, Langley Company's outstanding shares included:

280,000 shares of $50 par value, 7% cumulative preferred stock
900,000 shares of $1 par value common stock

Net income for 2002 was $2,530,000. No cash dividends were declared or paid during 2002. On February 15, 2003, however, all preferred dividends in arrears were paid, together with a 5% stock dividend on common shares. There were no dividends in arrears prior to 2002.

On April 1, 2002, 450,000 shares of common stock were sold for $10 per share and on October 1, 2002, 110,000 shares of common stock were purchased for $20 per share and held as treasury stock.

Instructions

Compute earnings per share for 2002. Assume that financial statements for 2002 were issued in March 2003.

E17-22 (EPS with Convertible Bonds, Various Situations) In 2000 Bonaparte Enterprises issued, at par, 60 $1,000, 8% bonds, each convertible into 100 shares of common stock. Bonaparte had revenues of $17,500 and expenses other than interest and taxes of $8,400 for 2001 (assume that the tax rate is 40%). Throughout 2001, 2,000 shares of common stock were outstanding; none of the bonds was converted or redeemed.

Instructions

(a) Compute diluted earnings per share for 2001.

(b) Assume the same facts as those assumed for part (a), except that the 60 bonds were issued on September 1, 2001 (rather than in 2000), and none have been converted or redeemed.

(c) Assume the same facts as assumed for part (a), except that 20 of the 60 bonds were actually converted on July 1, 2001.

E17-23 (EPS with Convertible Bonds) On June 1, 1999, Mowbray Company and Surrey Company merged to form Lancaster Inc. A total of 800,000 shares were issued to complete the merger. The new corporation reports on a calendar-year basis.

On April 1, 2001, the company issued an additional 400,000 shares of stock for cash. All 1,200,000 shares were outstanding on December 31, 2001.

Lancaster Inc. also issued $600,000 of 20-year, 8% convertible bonds at par on July 1, 2001. Each $1,000 bond converts to 40 shares of common at any interest date. None of the bonds have been converted to date.

Lancaster Inc. is preparing its annual report for the fiscal year ending December 31, 2001. The annual report will show earnings per share figures based upon a reported after-tax net income of $1,540,000 (the tax rate is 40%).

Instructions

Determine for 2001:

(a) The number of shares to be used for calculating:
  (1) Basic earnings per share.
  (2) Diluted earnings per share.

(b) The earnings figures to be used for calculating:
  (1) Basic earnings per share.
  (2) Diluted earnings per share.

(CMA adapted)

E17-24 (EPS with Convertible Bonds and Preferred Stock) The Simon Corporation issued 10-year, $5,000,000 par, 7% callable convertible subordinated debentures on January 2, 2001. The bonds have a par value of $1,000, with interest payable annually. The current conversion ratio is 14:1, and in 2 years it will increase to 18:1. At the date of issue, the bonds were sold at 98. Bond discount is amortized on a straight-line basis. Simon's effective tax was 35%. Net income in 2001 was $9,500,000, and the company had 2,000,000 shares outstanding during the entire year.

Instructions

(a) Prepare a schedule to compute both basic and diluted earnings per share.
(b) Discuss how the schedule would differ if the security was convertible preferred stock.

E17-25 (EPS with Convertible Bonds and Preferred Stock) On January 1, 2001, Crocker Company issued 10-year, $2,000,000 face value, 6% bonds, at par. Each $1,000 bond is convertible into 15 shares of Crocker common stock. Crocker's net income in 2001 was $300,000, and its tax rate was 40%. The company had 100,000 common stock outstanding throughout 2001. None of the bonds were exercised in 2001.

Instructions

(a) Compute diluted earnings per share for 2001.
(b) Compute diluted earnings per share for 2001, assuming the same facts as above, except that $1,000,000 of 6% convertible preferred stock was issued instead of the bonds. Each $100 preferred share is convertible into 5 shares of Crocker common stock.

E17-26 (EPS with Options, Various Situations) Venzuela Company's net income for 2001 is $50,000. The only potentially dilutive securities outstanding were 1,000 options issued during 2000, each exercisable for one share at $6. None has been exercised, and 10,000 shares of common were outstanding during 2001. The average market price of Venzuela's stock during 2001 was $20.

Instructions

(a) Compute diluted earnings per share (round to nearest cent).
(b) Assume the same facts as those assumed for part (a), except that the 1,000 options were issued on October 1, 2001 (rather than in 2000). The average market price during the last 3 months of 2001 was $20.

E17-27 (EPS with Contingent Issuance Agreement) Winsor Inc. recently purchased Holiday Corp., a large midwestern home painting corporation. One of the terms of the merger was that if Holiday's income for 2001 was $110,000 or more, 10,000 additional shares would be issued to Holiday's stockholders in 2002. Holiday's income for 2000 was $120,000.

Instructions

(a) Would the contingent shares have to be considered in Winsor's 2000 earnings per share computations?
(b) Assume the same facts, except that the 10,000 shares are contingent on Holiday's achieving a net income of $130,000 in 2001. Would the contingent shares have to be considered in Winsor's earnings per share computations for 2000?

E17-28 (EPS with Warrants) Howat Corporation earned $360,000 during a period when it had an average of 100,000 shares of common stock outstanding. The common stock sold at an average market price of $15 per share during the period. Also outstanding were 15,000 warrants that could be exercised to purchase one share of common stock for $10 for each warrant exercised.

Instructions

(a) Are the warrants dilutive?
(b) Compute basic earnings per share.
(c) Compute diluted earnings per share.

PROBLEMS

P17-1 (Entries for Various Dilutive Securities) The stockholders' equity section of McLean Inc. at the beginning of the current year appears below:

Common stock, $10 par value, authorized 1,000,000 shares, 300,000 shares issued and outstanding	$3,000,000
Paid-in capital in excess of par	600,000
Retained earnings	570,000

During the current year the following transactions occurred:

1. The company issued to the stockholders 100,000 rights. Ten rights are needed to buy one share of stock at $32. The rights were void after 30 days. The market price of the stock at this time was $34 per share.
2. The company sold to the public a $200,000, 10% bond issue at par. The company also issued with each $100 bond one detachable stock purchase warrant, which provided for the purchase of common stock at $30 per share. Shortly after issuance, similar bonds without warrants were selling at 96 and the warrants at $8.
3. All but 10,000 of the rights issued in (1) were exercised in 30 days.
4. At the end of the year, 80% of the warrants in (2) had been exercised, and the remaining were outstanding and in good standing.
5. During the current year, the company granted stock options for 5,000 shares of common stock to company executives. The company using a fair value option pricing model determines that each option is worth $10. The option price is $30. The options were to expire at year-end and were considered compensation for the current year.
6. All but 1,000 shares related to the stock option plan were exercised by year-end. The expiration resulted because one of the executives failed to fulfill an obligation related to the employment contract.

Instructions

(a) Prepare general journal entries for the current year to record the transactions listed above.

(b) Prepare the stockholders' equity section of the balance sheet at the end of the current year. Assume that retained earnings at the end of the current year is $750,000.

P17-2 (Entries for Conversion, Amortization, and Interest of Bonds) Counter Inc. issued $1,500,000 of convertible 10-year bonds on July 1, 2001. The bonds provide for 12% interest payable semiannually on January 1 and July 1. The discount in connection with the issue was $34,000, which is being amortized monthly on a straight-line basis.

The bonds are convertible after one year into 8 shares of Counter Inc.'s $100 par value common stock for each $1,000 of bonds.

On August 1, 2002, $150,000 of bonds were turned in for conversion into common. Interest has been accrued monthly and paid as due. At the time of conversion any accrued interest on bonds being converted is paid in cash.

Instructions (Round to nearest dollar)

Prepare the journal entries to record the conversion, amortization, and interest in connection with the bonds as of:

(a) August 1, 2002 (assume the book value method is used).

(b) August 31, 2002.

(c) December 31, 2002, including closing entries for end-of-year.

(AICPA adapted)

P17-3 (Stock Option Plan) ISU Company adopted a stock option plan on November 30, 1999, that provided that 70,000 shares of $5 par value stock be designated as available for the granting of options to officers of the corporation at a price of $8 a share. The market value was $12 a share on November 30, 1999.

On January 2, 2000, options to purchase 28,000 shares were granted to president Don Pedro—15,000 for services to be rendered in 2000 and 13,000 for services to be rendered in 2001. Also on that date, options to purchase 14,000 shares were granted to vice president Beatrice Leonato—7,000 for services to be rendered in 2000 and 7,000 for services to be rendered in 2001. The market value of the stock was $14 a share on January 2, 2000. The options were exercisable for a period of one year following the year in which the services were rendered.

In 2001 neither the president nor the vice president exercised their options because the market price of the stock was below the exercise price. The market value of the stock was $7 a share on December 31, 2001, when the options for 2000 services lapsed.

On December 31, 2002, both president Pedro and vice president Leonato exercised their options for 13,000 and 7,000 shares, respectively, when the market price was $16 a share.

Instructions

Prepare the necessary journal entries in 1999 when the stock option plan was adopted, in 2000 when options were granted, in 2001 when options lapsed and in 2002 when options were exercised. The company elects to use the intrinsic value method following *APB Opinion No. 25.*

P17-4 (EPS with Complex Capital Structure) Diane Leto, controller at Dewey Yaeger Pharmaceutical Industries, a public company, is currently preparing the calculation for basic and diluted earnings per share and the related disclosure for Yaeger's external financial statements. Below is selected financial information for the fiscal year ended June 30, 2002.

DEWEY YAEGER PHARMACEUTICAL INDUSTRIES
Selected Statement of
Financial Position Information
June 30, 2002

Long-term debt	
Notes payable, 10%	$ 1,000,000
7% convertible bonds payable	5,000,000
10% bonds payable	6,000,000
Total long-term debt	$12,000,000
Shareholders' equity	
Preferred stock, 8.5% cumulative, $50 par value, 100,000 shares authorized, 25,000 shares issued and outstanding	$ 1,250,000
Common stock, $1 par, 10,000,000 shares authorized, 1,000,000 shares issued and outstanding	1,000,000
Additional paid-in capital	4,000,000
Retained earnings	6,000,000
Total shareholders' equity	$12,250,000

The following transactions have also occurred at Yaeger.

1. Options were granted in 2000 to purchase 100,000 shares at $15 per share. Although no options were exercised during 2002, the average price per common share during fiscal year 2002 was $20 per share.
2. Each bond was issued at face value. The 7% convertible debenture will convert into common stock at 50 shares per $1,000 bond. It is exercisable after 5 years and was issued in 2001.
3. The 8.5% preferred stock was issued in 2000.
4. There are no preferred dividends in arrears; however, preferred dividends were not declared in fiscal year 2002.
5. The 1,000,000 shares of common stock were outstanding for the entire 2002 fiscal year.
6. Net income for fiscal year 2002 was $1,500,000, and the average income tax rate is 40%.

Instructions

For the fiscal year ended June 30, 2002, calculate Dewey Yaeger Pharmaceutical Industries':

(a) Basic earnings per share.
(b) Diluted earnings per share.

P17-5 (Simple EPS and EPS with Stock Options) As auditor for Banquo & Associates, you have been assigned to check Duncan Corporation's computation of earnings per share for the current year. The controller, Mac Beth, has supplied you with the following computations:

Net income	$3,374,960
Common shares issued and outstanding:	
Beginning of year	1,285,000
End of year	1,200,000
Average	1,242,500
Earnings per share	

$$\frac{\$3,374,960}{1,242,500} = \$2.72 \text{ per share}$$

You have developed the following additional information:

1. There are no other equity securities in addition to the common shares.
2. There are no options or warrants outstanding to purchase common shares.
3. There are no convertible debt securities.
4. Activity in common shares during the year was as follows:

Outstanding, Jan. 1	1,285,000
Treasury shares acquired, Oct. 1	(250,000)
	1,035,000
Shares reissued, Dec. 1	165,000
Outstanding, Dec. 31	1,200,000

Instructions

(a) On the basis of the information above, do you agree with the controller's computation of earnings per share for the year? If you disagree, prepare a revised computation of earnings per share.

(b) Assume the same facts as those in (a), except that options had been issued to purchase 140,000 shares of common stock at $10 per share. These options were outstanding at the beginning of the year and none had been exercised or canceled during the year. The average market price of the common shares during the year was $25 and the ending market price was $35. Prepare a computation of earnings per share.

P17-6 (Basic EPS: Two-Year Presentation) Hillel Corporation is preparing the comparative financial statements for the annual report to its shareholders for fiscal years ended May 31, 2000, and May 31, 2001. The income from operations for each year was $1,800,000 and $2,500,000, respectively. In both years, the company incurred a 10% interest expense on $2,400,000 of debt, an obligation that requires interest-only payments for 5 years. The company experienced a loss of $500,000 from a fire in its Scotsland facility in February 2001, which was determined to be an extraordinary loss. The company uses a 40% effective tax rate for income taxes.

The capital structure of Hillel Corporation on June 1, 1999, consisted of 2 million shares of common stock outstanding and 20,000 shares of $50 par value, 8%, cumulative preferred stock. There were no preferred dividends in arrears, and the company had not issued any convertible securities, options, or warrants.

On October 1, 1999, Hillel sold an additional 500,000 shares of the common stock at $20 per share. Hillel distributed a 20% stock dividend on the common shares outstanding on January 1, 2000. On December 1, 2000, Hillel was able to sell an additional 800,000 shares of the common stock at $22 per share. These were the only common stock transactions that occurred during the two fiscal years.

Instructions

(a) Identify whether the capital structure at Hillel Corporation is a simple or complex capital structure, and explain why.

(b) Determine the weighted average number of shares that Hillel Corporation would use in calculating earnings per share for the fiscal year ended

(1) May 31, 2000.

(2) May 31, 2001.

(c) Prepare, in good form, a comparative income statement, beginning with income from operations, for Hillel Corporation for the fiscal years ended May 31, 2000, and May 31, 2001. This statement will be included in Hillel's annual report and should display the appropriate earnings per share presentations.

(CMA adapted)

P17-7 (EPS Computation of Basic and Diluted EPS) Edmund Halvor of the controller's office of East Aurora Corporation was given the assignment of determining the basic and diluted earnings per share values for the year ending December 31, 2001. Halvor has compiled the information listed below.

1. The company is authorized to issue 8,000,000 shares of $10 par value common stock. As of December 31, 2000, 3,000,000 shares had been issued and were outstanding.
2. The per share market prices of the common stock on selected dates were as follows:

	Price per Share
July 1, 2000	$20.00
January 1, 2001	21.00
April 1, 2001	25.00
July 1, 2001	11.00
August 1, 2001	10.50
November 1, 2001	9.00
December 31, 2001	10.00

3. A total of 700,000 shares of an authorized 1,200,000 shares of convertible preferred stock had been issued on July 1, 2000. The stock was issued at its par value of $25, and it has a cumulative dividend of $3 per share. The stock is convertible into common stock at the rate of one share of convertible preferred for one share of common. The rate of conversion is to be automatically adjusted

for stock splits and stock dividends. Dividends are paid quarterly on September 30, December 31, March 31, and June 30.

4. East Aurora Corporation is subject to a 40% income tax rate.
5. The after-tax net income for the year ended December 31, 2001 was $13,550,000.

The following specific activities took place during 2001.

1. January 1—A 5% common stock dividend was issued. The dividend had been declared on December 1, 2000, to all stockholders of record on December 29, 2000.
2. April 1—A total of 200,000 shares of the $3 convertible preferred stock was converted into common stock. The company issued new common stock and retired the preferred stock. This was the only conversion of the preferred stock during 2001.
3. July 1—A 2-for-1 split of the common stock became effective on this date. The Board of Directors had authorized the split on June 1.
4. August 1—A total of 300,000 shares of common stock were issued to acquire a factory building.
5. November 1—A total of 24,000 shares of common stock were purchased on the open market at $9 per share. These shares were to be held as treasury stock and were still in the treasury as of December 31, 2001.
6. Common stock cash dividends—Cash dividends to common stockholders were declared and paid as follows:
   April 15—$.30 per share
   October 15—$.20 per share
7. Preferred stock cash dividends—Cash dividends to preferred stockholders were declared and paid as scheduled.

Instructions

(a) Determine the number of shares used to compute basic earnings per share for the year ended December 31, 2001.

(b) Determine the number of shares used to compute diluted earnings per share for the year ended December 31, 2001.

(c) Compute the adjusted net income to be used as the numerator in the basic earnings per share calculation for the year ended December 31, 2001.

P17-8 (Computation of Basic and Diluted EPS) The following information pertains to Prancer Company for 2001:

Net income for the year	$1,200,000
8% convertible bonds issued at par ($1,000 per bond). Each bond is convertible into 40 shares of common stock.	2,000,000
6% convertible, cumulative preferred stock, $100 par value. Each share is convertible into 3 shares of common stock.	3,000,000
Common stock, $10 par value	6,000,000
Common stock options (granted in a prior year) to purchase 50,000 of common stock at $20 per share	500,000
Tax rate for 2001	40%
Average market price of common stock	$25 per share

There were no changes during 2001 in the number of common shares, preferred shares, or convertible bonds outstanding. There is no treasury stock.

Instructions

(a) Compute basic earnings per share for 2001.

(b) Compute diluted earnings per share for 2001.

P17-9 (EPS with Stock Dividend and Extraordinary Items) Cordelia Corporation is preparing the comparative financial statements to be included in the annual report to stockholders. Cordelia employs a fiscal year ending May 31.

Income from operations before income taxes for Cordelia was $1,400,000 and $660,000, respectively, for fiscal years ended May 31, 2001 and 2000. Cordelia experienced an extraordinary loss of $500,000 because of an earthquake on March 3, 2001. A 40% combined income tax rate pertains to any and all of Cordelia Corporation's profits, gains, and losses.

Cordelia's capital structure consists of preferred stock and common stock. The company has not issued any convertible securities or warrants and there are no outstanding stock options.

Cordelia issued 50,000 shares of $100 par value, 6% cumulative preferred stock in 1997. All of this stock is outstanding, and no preferred dividends are in arrears.

There were 1,500,000 shares of $1 par common stock outstanding on June 1, 1999. On September 1, 1999, Cordelia sold an additional 400,000 shares of the common stock at $17 per share. Cordelia distributed a 20% stock dividend on the common shares outstanding on December 1, 2000. These were the only common stock transactions during the past 2 fiscal years.

Instructions

(a) Determine the weighted average number of common shares that would be used in computing earnings per share on the current comparative income statement for:

(1) The year ended May 31, 2000.

(2) The year ended May 31, 2001.

(b) Starting with income from operations before income taxes, prepare a comparative income statement for the years ended May 31, 2001 and 2000. The statement will be part of Cordelia Corporation's annual report to stockholders and should include appropriate earnings per share presentation.

(c) The capital structure of a corporation is the result of its past financing decisions. Furthermore, the earnings per share data presented on a corporation's financial statements is dependent upon the capital structure.

(1) Explain why Cordelia Corporation is considered to have a simple capital structure.

(2) Describe how earnings per share data would be presented for a corporation that has a complex capital structure.

(CMA adapted)

CONCEPTUAL CASES

C17-1 (Warrants Issued with Bonds and Convertible Bonds) Incurring long-term debt with an arrangement whereby lenders receive an option to buy common stock during all or a portion of the time the debt is outstanding is a frequent corporate financing practice. In some situations the result is achieved through the issuance of convertible bonds; in others the debt instruments and the warrants to buy stock are separate.

Instructions

(a) **(1)** Describe the differences that exist in current accounting for original proceeds of the issuance of convertible bonds and of debt instruments with separate warrants to purchase common stock.

(2) Discuss the underlying rationale for the differences described in (a)1 above.

(3) Summarize the arguments that have been presented in favor of accounting for convertible bonds in the same manner as accounting for debt with separate warrants.

(b) At the start of the year Biron Company issued $18,000,000 of 12% notes along with warrants to buy 1,200,000 shares of its $10 par value common stock at $18 per share. The notes mature over the next 10 years starting one year from date of issuance with annual maturities of $1,800,000. At the time, Biron had 9,600,000 shares of common stock outstanding and the market price was $23 per share. The company received $20,040,000 for the notes and the warrants. For Biron Company, 12% was a relatively low borrowing rate. If offered alone, at this time, the notes would have been issued at a 22% discount. Prepare the journal entry (or entries) for the issuance of the notes and warrants for the cash consideration received.

(AICPA adapted)

C17-2 (Convertible Bonds) On February 1, 1998, Parsons Company sold its 5-year, $1,000 par value, 8% bonds, which were convertible at the option of the investor into Parsons Company common stock at a ratio of 10 shares of common stock for each bond. The convertible bonds were sold by Parsons Company at a discount. Interest is payable annually each February 1. On February 1, 2001, Wong Company, an investor in the Parsons Company convertible bonds, tendered 1,000 bonds for conversion into 10,000 shares of Parsons Company common stock that had a market value of $120 per share at the date of the conversion.

Instructions

How should Parsons Company account for the conversion of the convertible bonds into common stock under both the book value and market value methods? Discuss the rationale for each method.

(AICPA adapted)

C17-3 (Stock Warrants—Various Types) For various reasons a corporation may issue warrants to purchase shares of its common stock at specified prices that, depending on the circumstances, may be less than, equal to, or greater than the current market price. For example, warrants may be issued:

1. To existing stockholders on a pro rata basis.
2. To certain key employees under an incentive stock option plan.
3. To purchasers of the corporation's bonds.

Instructions

For each of the three examples of how stock warrants are used:

(a) Explain why they are used.
(b) Discuss the significance of the price (or prices) at which the warrants are issued (or granted) in relation to (1) the current market price of the company's stock, and (2) the length of time over which they can be exercised.
(c) Describe the information that should be disclosed in financial statements, or notes thereto, that are prepared when stock warrants are outstanding in the hands of the three groups listed above.

(AICPA adapted)

***C17-4 (Stock Options and Stock Appreciation Rights—Intrinsic Value Model)** In 1999 Sanford Co. adopted a plan to give additional incentive compensation to its dealers to sell its principal product, fire extinguishers. Under the plan Sanford transferred 9,000 shares of its $1 par value stock to a trust with the provision that Sanford would have to forfeit interest in the trust and no part of the trust fund could ever revert to Sanford. Shares were to be distributed to dealers on the basis of their shares of fire extinguisher purchases from Sanford (above certain minimum levels) over the 3-year period ending June 30, 2002.

In 1999 the stock was closely held. The book value of the stock was $7.90 per share as of June 30, 1999, and in 1999 additional shares were sold to existing stockholders for $8 per share. On the basis of this information, market value of the stock was determined to be $8 per share.

In 1999 when the shares were transferred to the trust, Sanford charged prepaid expenses for $72,000 ($8 per share market value) and credited capital stock for $9,000 and additional paid-in capital for $63,000. The prepaid expense was charged to operations over a 3-year period ended June 30, 2002.

Sanford sold a substantial number of shares of its stock to the public in 2001 at $60 per share.

In July 2002 all shares of the stock in the trust were distributed to the dealers. The market value of the shares at date of distribution of the stock from the trust had risen to $110 per share. Sanford obtained a tax deduction equal to that market value for the tax year ended June 30, 2003.

Instructions

(Note: Use *APB Opinion No. 25* to solve this problem.)

(a) How much should be reported as selling expense in each of the years noted above assuming that the company uses the intrinsic value model?
(b) Sanford is also considering other types of option plans. One such plan is a stock appreciation right (SAR) plan. What is a stock appreciation right plan? What is a potential disadvantage of a SAR plan from the viewpoint of the company?

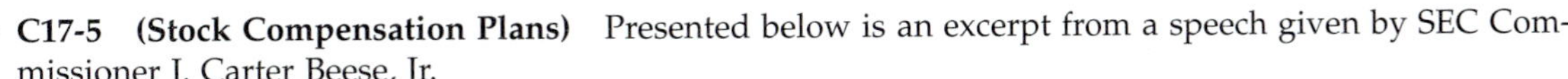

C17-5 (Stock Compensation Plans) Presented below is an excerpt from a speech given by SEC Commissioner J. Carter Beese, Jr.

> . . . I believe investors will be far better off if the value of stock options is reported in a footnote rather than on the face of the income statement. By allowing footnote disclosures, we will protect shareholders' current and future investments by not raising the cost of capital for the innovative, growth companies that depend on stock options to attract and retain key employees. I've said it before and I'll say it again: the stock option accounting debate essentially boils down to one thing—the cost of capital. And as long as we can adequately protect investors without raising the cost of capital to such a vital segment of our economy, why would we want to do it any other way?
>
> The FASB has made the assertion that when it comes to public policy, they lack the competence to weigh various national goals. I also agree with the sentiment that, as a general matter, Congress should not be in the business of writing accounting standards.
>
> But the SEC has the experience and the capability to determine exactly where to draw the regulatory lines to best serve investors and our capital markets. That is our mandate, and that is what we do, day in and day out.
>
> But we may have to act sooner rather than later. As we speak, the FASB's proposals are raising the cost of venture capital. That's because venture capitalists are pricing deals based on their exit strategies, which usually include cashing out in public offerings. The FASB's proposals, however, provide incentives for companies to stay private longer—they are able to use options more freely to attract and retain key employees, and they avoid the earnings hit that going public would entail. Even worse, as venture capital deals become less profitable because of the FASB's proposed actions, venture capitalists are starting to look overseas for alternative investment opportunities that lack the investment drag now associated with certain American ventures.

I acknowledge that the FASB deserves some degree of freedom to determine what they believe is the best accounting approach. At the same time, however, I cannot stand by idly for long and watch venture capital increase in price or even flee this country because of a myopic search for an accounting holy grail. At some point, I believe that the SEC must inject itself into this debate, and help the FASB determine what accounting approach is ultimately in the best interests of investors as a whole.

We owe it to shareholders, issuers and all market participants, and indeed our country, to make the best decision in accordance with the public good, not just technical accounting theory.

Instructions

(a) What are the major recommendations of *SFAS No. 123* on "Accounting for Stock-Based Compensation Plans"?

(b) Write a response to Commissioner Beese, defending the use of the concept of neutrality in financial accounting and reporting.

C17-6 (EPS: Preferred Dividends, Options, and Convertible Debt) "Earnings per share" (EPS) is the most featured single financial statistic about modern corporations. Daily published quotations of stock prices have recently been expanded to include for many securities a "times earnings" figure that is based on EPS. Stock analysts often focus their discussions on the EPS of the corporations they study.

Instructions

(a) Explain how dividends or dividend requirements on any class of preferred stock that may be outstanding affect the computation of EPS.

(b) One of the technical procedures applicable in EPS computations is the "treasury stock method." Briefly describe the circumstances under which it might be appropriate to apply the treasury stock method.

(c) Convertible debentures are considered potentially dilutive common shares. Explain how convertible debentures are handled for purposes of EPS computations.

(AICPA adapted)

C17-7 (EPS Concepts and Effect of Transactions on EPS) Fernandez Corporation, a new audit client of yours, has not reported earnings per share data in its annual reports to stockholders in the past. The treasurer, Angelo Balthazar, requested that you furnish information about the reporting of earnings per share data in the current year's annual report in accordance with generally accepted accounting principles.

Instructions

(a) Define the term "earnings per share" as it applies to a corporation with a capitalization structure composed of only one class of common stock and explain how earnings per share should be computed and how the information should be disclosed in the corporation's financial statements.

(b) Discuss the treatment, if any, that should be given to each of the following items in computing earnings per share of common stock for financial statement reporting.

(1) Outstanding preferred stock issued at a premium with a par value liquidation right.

(2) The exercise at a price below market value but above book value of a common stock option issued during the current fiscal year to officers of the corporation.

(3) The replacement of a machine immediately prior to the close of the current fiscal year at a cost 20% above the original cost of the replaced machine. The new machine will perform the same function as the old machine that was sold for its book value.

(4) The declaration of current dividends on cumulative preferred stock.

(5) The acquisition of some of the corporation's outstanding common stock during the current fiscal year. The stock was classified as treasury stock.

(6) A 2-for-1 stock split of common stock during the current fiscal year.

(7) A provision created out of retained earnings for a contingent liability from a possible lawsuit.

C17-8 (EPS, Anti-dilution) Matt Kacskos, a stockholder of Howat Corporation, has asked you, the firm's accountant, to explain why his stock warrants were not included in diluted EPS. In order to explain this situation, you must briefly explain what dilutive securities are, why they are included in the EPS calculation, and why some securities are antidilutive and thus not included in this calculation.

Instructions

Write Mr. Kacskos a 1–1.5 page letter explaining why the warrants are not included in the calculation. Use the following data to help you explain this situation.

Howat Corporation earned $228,000 during the period, when it had an average of 100,000 shares of common stock outstanding. The common stock sold at an average market price of $25 per share during the period. Also outstanding were 15,000 warrants that could be exercised to purchase one share of common stock at $30 per warrant.

USING YOUR JUDGMENT

FINANCIAL REPORTING PROBLEM: INTEL CORPORATION

Instructions

Refer to the financial statements and accompanying notes and discussion of Intel Corporation presented in Appendix 5B and answer the following questions.

(a) Under Intel's stock participation plan, eligible employees may purchase shares of Intel's common stock at 85% of fair market value. (1) How many shares are authorized to be issued under the plan? (2) How many were available for issuance at December 26, 1998? (3) How many shares were purchased by employees in 1998 under the plan and how much was paid for those shares?

(b) Intel has a stock option plan (referred to as the EOP plan) under which officers, key employees, and directors may be granted options to purchase Intel common stock. (1) What is the range of exercise prices for options outstanding under the EOP plan at December 26, 1998? (2) How many years from the grant date do these EOP plan options expire? (3) To what accounts are the proceeds from these option exercises credited? (4) What is the number of shares of outstanding options at December 26, 1998 under the EOP plan and at what weighted average exercise price? (5) How many options are exercisable under the EOP plan at December 26, 1998, and at what price?

(c) What number of weighted average common shares outstanding was used by Intel in computing earnings per share for 1998, 1997, and 1996? What was Intel's diluted earnings per share in 1998, 1997, and 1996?

FINANCIAL STATEMENT ANALYSIS CASE

Kellogg Company

Kellogg Company in its 1998 Annual Report in Note 1—Accounting Policies made the following comment about its accounting for employee stock options and other stock-based compensation:

> **Stock compensation.** The Company follows Accounting Principles Board Opinion (APB) #25, "Accounting for Stock Issued to Employees," in accounting for its employee stock options and other stock-based compensation. Under APB #25, because the exercise price of the Company's employee stock options equals the market price of the underlying stock on the date of the grant, no compensation expense is recognized. As permitted, the Company has elected to adopt only the disclosure provisions of Statement of Financial Accounting Standards (SFAS) #123, "Accounting for Stock-Based Compensation."

Instructions

In electing to adopt only the disclosure provisions of *FASB Statement No. 123*, what minimum disclosures was Kellogg Company required to make in its notes to the financial statement about its employee stock options and other stock-based compensation?

COMPARATIVE ANALYSIS CASE

The Coca-Cola Company versus PepsiCo, Inc.

Instructions

Go to the Digital Tool and using The Coca-Cola Company and PepsiCo, Inc. Annual Report information, answer the following questions.

(a) What employee stock option compensation plans are offered by Coca-Cola and PepsiCo?

(b) How many options are outstanding at year-end 1998 for both Coca-Cola and PepsiCo?

(c) How many options were granted by Coca-Cola and PepsiCo to officers and employees during 1998?

(d) How many options were exercised during 1998?

(e) What was the range of option prices exercised by Coca-Cola and PepsiCo employees during 1998?

(f) What are the weighted average number of shares used by Coca-Cola and PepsiCo in 1998, 1997, and 1996 to compute diluted earnings per share?

(g) What was the diluted net income per share for Coca-Cola and PepsiCo for 1998, 1997, and 1996?

RESEARCH CASES

Case 1

Instructions

Examine a copy of *Statement of Financial Accounting Standards No. 123,* "Accounting for Stock-Based Compensation," and answer the following questions.

(a) As indicated in Chapter 1, the passage of a new Financial Accounting Standards Board statement requires the support of five of the seven members of the Board. What was the vote with regard to SFAS 123? Which members of the Board dissented?

(b) What was the major objection cited by the dissenters? What reasoning was used to support this objection?

(c) The dissenters expressed a preference for measuring the fair value of stock options at the vesting date instead of the grant date. Under what circumstances would they have accepted the modified grant method? Why?

Case 2

The November 1995 issue the *The CPA Journal* includes an article by Anthony Cocco and Daniel Ivancevich entitled "Recognition of Footnote Disclosure of Compensatory Fixed Stock Options?"

Instructions

Read the article and answer the following questions.

(a) Identify two financial statement ratios that will be affected by recognition of fixed stock options. How will they be affected?

(b) Under what condition does the impact of expensing stock compensation take on less importance?

(c) What "signal" might be sent to investors if a company chooses to recognize stock compensation expense despite the negative impact on the financial statements?

(d) Do you feel that the example provided by the authors makes a strong case for recognition over disclosure?

INTERNATIONAL REPORTING CASE

Clearly Canadian Beverage is a Canadian company engaged in the manufacturing and distribution of its Clearly Canadian line of carbonated mineral water and natural fruit-flavored sparkling beverages, noncarbonated beverages, and bottled water. Its shares are traded on the NASDAQ exchange. Because its shares trade on a U.S. exchange, Clearly Canadian Beverage must either prepare its financial statements in accordance with U.S. GAAP or prepare a reconciliation of its financial statements (based on Canadian standards) to how they would be reported under U.S. GAAP. As a result of this requirement, Clearly Canadian presented the following information in its financial statements to meet the U.S. GAAP reconciliation requirement.

CLEARLY CANADIAN BEVERAGE

Reconciliation to Accounting Principles Generally Accepted in the United States of America
Differences in generally accepted accounting principles (GAAP) between Canada and the United States as they pertain to these consolidated financial statements are as follows:

	1998 $	1997 $
Net earnings (loss) under Canadian GAAP	310	(12,266)
Foreign currency adjustments—see note A	—	(408)
Earnings (loss) under U.S. GAAP	310	(12,674)
Unrealized holding gains (losses)—see note B	(1,044)	1,742
Foreign currency translation adjustments	(1,983)	—
Comprehensive loss—see note C	(2,717)	(10,932)
Basic earnings (loss) per post-consolidated share before comprehensive income (loss) adjustments (expressed in dollars)	0.05	(2.26)

Note A: Change in reporting currency. Under U.S. GAAP, a change in reporting currency would require a restatement of prior years' financial statements using a weighted average exchange rate for each year in the statement of operations, and current and historical rates for monetary and non-monetary assets and liabilities on the balance sheet.

Note B: Unrealized holding gains (losses). Under U.S. GAAP, the long-term investments in publicly traded companies would be shown at fair market value.

Note C: Comprehensive income (loss). U.S. GAAP requires disclosure of comprehensive income (loss), which is intended to reflect all changes in equity except those resulting from contributions to owners.

In addition, Clearly Canadian provided the following disclosure related to its stock compensation plans: Under a stock option plan, as amended and restated June 27, 1997, the Company may grant options to eligible employees of the Company, provided that the number of shares issuable does not exceed 941,176 post-consolidated common shares of the Company. Options may be issued under the stock option plan as determined at the sole discretion of the Company's board of directors. Options may be issued for a term of up to 10 years at an exercise price to be determined by the Company's board of directors, provided that the exercise price is not less than the average closing price of the Company's shares traded through the facilities of The Toronto Stock Exchange for the 10 trading days preceding the date on which the options are granted.

The Company applies APB Opinion 25, "Accounting for Stock Issued to Employees", and related Interpretations in accounting for the plan. Under APB Opinion 25, because the exercise price of the Company's employee stock options equals the market price of the underlying stock on the date of grant, no compensation cost is recognized.

Statement of Financial Accounting Standards No. 123, "Accounting for Stock-Based Compensation" (SFAS 123), requires the Company to provide pro forma information regarding net income and earnings per share as if compensation cost for the Company's stock option plans had been determined in accordance with the fair value based method prescribed in SFAS 123. The Company estimates the fair value of each stock option at the grant date by using the Black-Scholes option-pricing model with the following weighted-average assumptions used for grants in 1998: dividend yield of $nil (1997—$nil); expected volatility of 70% (1997—70%); risk-free interest rate of 4.7% (1997—4.54%); and expected life to nine years (1997—nine years).

Under the accounting provisions of SFAS 123, the Company's U.S. GAAP profit of $310,000 would have been decreased to a loss of $288,000.

Instructions

Use the information in the Clearly Canadian disclosure to respond to the following questions.

(a) What are the major differences between earnings reported by Clearly Canadian Beverage and earnings under U.S. GAAP?

(b) What are the major differences between earnings reported by Clearly Canadian Beverage and comprehensive income under U.S. GAAP?

(c) What do you think are some reasons why Clearly Canadian Beverage might not want to prepare its financial statements in accordance with U.S. GAAP?

(d) What is the impact of *SFAS 123* accounting on Clearly Canadian's profit? Why isn't this adjustment reflected in the reconciliation schedule?

ETHICS CASE

The executive officers of Coach Corporation have a performance-based compensation plan. The performance criteria of this plan is linked to growth in earnings per share. When annual EPS growth is 12%, the Coach executives earn 100% of the shares; if growth is 16%, they earn 125%. If EPS growth is lower than 8%, the executives receive no additional compensation.

In 2000, Joanna Becker, the controller of Coach, reviews year-end estimates of bad debt expense and warranty expense. She calculates the EPS growth at 15%. Peter Reiser, a member of the executive group, remarks over lunch one day that the estimate of bad debt expense might be decreased, increasing EPS growth to 16.1%. Becker is not sure she should do this because she believes that the current estimate of bad debts is sound. On the other hand, she recognizes that a great deal of subjectivity is involved in the computation.

Instructions

Answer the following questions:

(a) What, if any, is the ethical dilemma for Becker?

(b) Should Becker's knowledge of the compensation plan be a factor that influences her estimate?

(c) How should Becker respond to Reiser's request?

CHAPTER 18

Investments

Is Coke in Control Here?

The Coca-Cola Company (Coke) owns 42% of the shares of Coca-Cola Enterprises (a U.S. bottling business) and 43% of Coca-Cola Amatil (a European and Asian bottling business). These bottling businesses are very important to The Coca-Cola Company, because they are the primary distributors of Coca-Cola products. Furthermore, these companies are very dependent on Coca-Cola, which provides significant marketing and distribution development support. Indeed, an argument can be made that the bottling companies are controlled by Coca-Cola, because they would not exist without its support.

However, because The Coca-Cola Company does not own more than 50% of the shares in these companies, it does not prepare consolidated financial statements. Instead, Coca-Cola accounts for these investments using the equity method. Under the equity method, Coca-Cola reports a single income item for its profits from the bottlers, and only the net amount of its investment is reported in the balance sheet.

Equity method accounting gives Coca-Cola a pristine balance sheet and income statement, by keeping the assets and liabilities and the profit margins of these bottlers separate from its beverage-making business. What's more, as summarized in the following table, many countries allow proportional consolidation, an accounting method that includes part of the assets, liabilities, and income of investees in the financial statements of the investor company.

International Reporting of Less than 50% Equity Investments

Countries/Standards	Method(s) Allowed
U.S. GAAP: United Kingdom, Brazil, Mexico	Equity
IASC: France, Germany, Netherlands, Italy, Japan	Proportional consolidation or equity

This variation in practice makes it difficult to compare Coca-Cola to other international beverage companies and is part of the reason why U.S. and international accounting standards-setters are studying the accounting rules for equity investments like Coca-Cola's.[1]

[1]Based on Morgan Stanley Dean Witter, "Apples to Apples, Global Beverage: Thirst for Knowledge," May 25, 1999.

LEARNING OBJECTIVES

After studying this chapter, you should be able to:

1. **Identify the three categories of debt securities and describe the accounting and reporting treatment for each category.**
2. **Identify the categories of equity securities and describe the accounting and reporting treatment for each category.**
3. **Explain the equity method of accounting and compare it to the fair value method for equity securities.**
4. **Describe the disclosure requirements for investments in debt and equity securities.**
5. **Discuss the accounting for impairments of debt and equity investments.**
6. **Describe the accounting for transfer of investment securities between categories.**

PREVIEW OF CHAPTER 18

As indicated in the opening story, the measurement, recognition, and disclosure for certain investments are under study by U.S. and international standards-setters. This chapter addresses the accounting for debt and equity investments. Appendices to this chapter cover special issues related to investments and accounting for derivative instruments. The content and organization of this chapter are as follows:

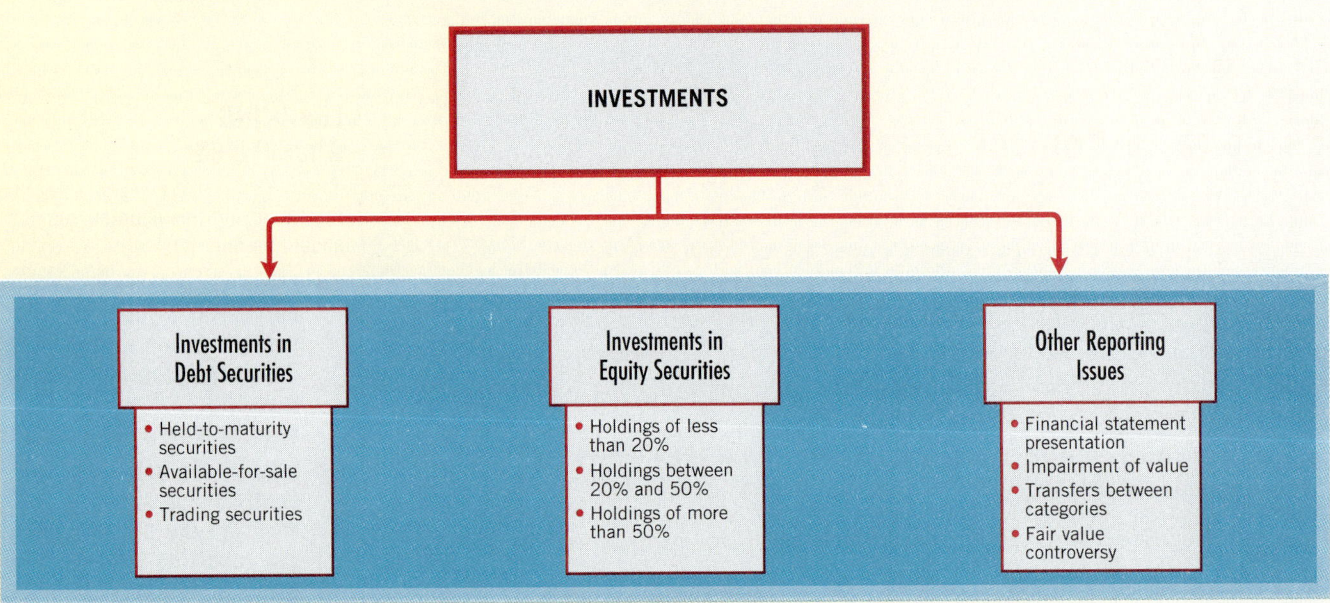

Companies have different motivations for investing in securities issued by other companies.[2] One motivation is to earn a high rate of return. A company can receive interest revenue from a debt investment or dividend revenue from an equity investment. In addition, capital gains on both types of securities can be realized. Another motivation for investing (in equity securities) is to secure certain operating or financing arrangements with another company. As in the opening story, **Coca-Cola** is able to exercise some control over bottler companies based on its significant (but not controlling) equity investment.

To provide useful information, the accounting for investments is based on the type of security (debt or equity) and management's intent with respect to the investment. As indicated in Illustration 18-1, our study of investments is organized by type of security. Within each section, we explain how the accounting for investments in debt and equity securities varies according to management intent.

[2]A **security** is a share, participation, or other interest in property or in an enterprise of the issuer or an obligation of the issuer that: (a) either is represented by an instrument issued in bearer or registered form or, if not represented by an instrument, is registered in books maintained to record transfers by or on behalf of the issuer; (b) is of a type commonly dealt in on securities exchanges or markets or, when represented by an instrument, is commonly recognized in any area in which it is issued or dealt in as a medium for investment; and (c) either is one of a class or series or by its terms is divisible into a class or series of shares, participations, interests, or obligations. From "Accounting for Certain Investments in Debt and Equity Securities," *Statement of Financial Accounting Standards No. 115* (Norwalk, Conn.: FASB, 1993), p. 48, par. 137.

Types of Security	Management Intent	Valuation Approach	Authoritative Literature
Debt (Section 1)	No plans to sell	Amortized cost	"Accounting for Certain Investments in Debt and Equity Securities," *SFAS No. 115*
	Plan to sell	Fair value	
Equity (Section 2)	Plan to sell	Fair value	
	Exercise some control	Equity method	"The Equity Method of Accounting for Investments in Common Stock," *APB Opinion No. 18*

ILLUSTRATION 18-1
Summary of Investment Accounting Approaches

INVESTMENTS IN DEBT SECURITIES

SECTION 1

Debt securities are instruments representing a creditor relationship with an enterprise. Debt securities include U.S. government securities, municipal securities, corporate bonds, convertible debt, commercial paper, and all securitized debt instruments. Trade accounts receivable and loans receivable are not debt securities because they do not meet the definition of a security.

Investments in debt securities are grouped into three separate categories for accounting and reporting purposes. These categories are as follows:

OBJECTIVE 1
Identify the three categories of debt securities and describe the accounting and reporting treatment for each category.

Held-to-maturity: Debt securities that the enterprise has the positive intent and ability to hold to maturity.

Trading: Debt securities bought and held primarily for sale in the near term to generate income on short-term price differences.

Available-for-sale: Debt securities not classified as held-to-maturity or trading securities.

Illustration 18-2 identifies these categories, along with the accounting and reporting treatments required for each.

Category	Valuation	Unrealized Holding Gains or Losses	Other Income Effects
Held-to-maturity	Amortized cost	Not recognized	Interest when earned; gains and losses from sale.
Trading securities	Fair value	Recognized in net income	Interest when earned; gains and losses from sale.
Available-for-sale	Fair value	Recognized as other comprehensive income and as separate component of stockholders' equity	Interest when earned; gains and losses from sale.

ILLUSTRATION 18-2
Accounting for Debt Securities by Category

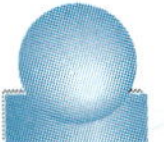

UNDERLYING CONCEPTS
Debt securities are reported at fair value not only because the information is relevant but also because it is reliable.

Amortized cost is the acquisition cost adjusted for the amortization of discount or premium, if appropriate. **Fair value** is the amount at which a financial instrument could be exchanged in a current transaction between willing parties, other than in a forced or liquidation sale.[3]

HELD-TO-MATURITY SECURITIES

Only debt securities can be classified as held-to-maturity because, by definition, equity securities have no maturity date. A debt security should be classified as **held-to-maturity** only if the reporting entity has **both (1) the positive intent** and **(2) the ability to hold those securities to maturity**. A company should not classify a debt security as held-to-maturity if the company intends to hold the security for an indefinite period of time. Likewise, if the enterprise anticipates that a sale may be necessary due to changes in interest rates, foreign currency risk, liquidity needs, or other asset-liability management reasons, the security should not be classified as held-to-maturity.[4]

Held-to-maturity securities are accounted for at amortized cost, not fair value. If management intends to hold certain investment securities to maturity and has no plans to sell them, fair values (selling prices) are not relevant for measuring and evaluating the cash flows associated with these securities. Finally, because held-to-maturity securities are not adjusted to fair value, they do not increase the volatility of either reported earnings or reported capital as do trading securities and available-for-sale securities.

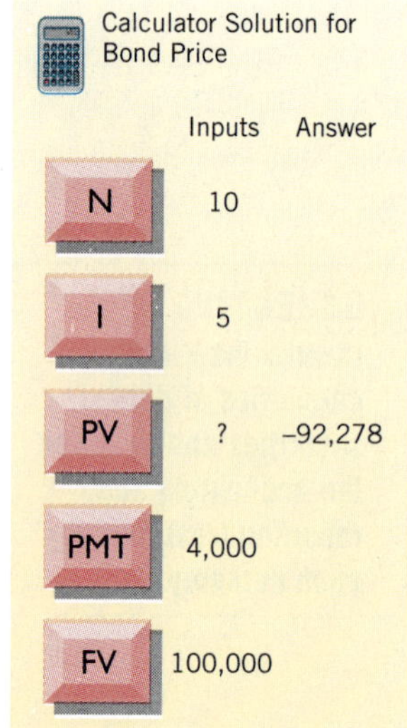

Calculator Solution for Bond Price
Inputs
Answer
N
10
I
5
PV
?
-92,278
PMT
4,000
FV
100,000

To illustrate the accounting for held-to-maturity debt securities, assume that Robinson Company purchased $100,000 of 8% bonds of Evermaster Corporation on January 1, 2001, paying $92,278. The bonds mature January 1, 2006; interest is payable each July 1 and January 1. The discount of $7,722 ($100,000 − $92,278) provided an effective interest yield of 10%. The entry to record the investment is:[5]

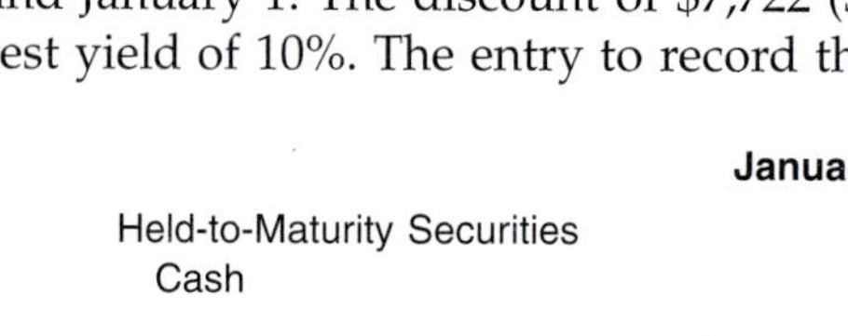

January 1, 2001		
Held-to-Maturity Securities	92,278	
Cash		92,278

A Held-to-Maturity Securities account is used to indicate the type of debt security purchased. Discounts and premiums on long-term investments in bonds are amortized in a manner similar to discounts and premiums on bonds payable, discussed in Chapter 14. Illustration 18-3 shows the effect of the discount amortization on the interest revenue recorded each period for the investment in Evermaster Corporation bonds.

[3]Ibid., pp. 47–48. The fair value is **readily determinable** if its sale price or other quotations are available on SEC registered exchanges, or, for over-the-counter securities, are published by recognized national publication systems. Foreign shares have readily determinable fair values if they trade in markets comparable in breadth and scope to the described U.S. markets.

[4]The FASB defines situations where, even though a security is sold before maturity, it has constructively been held to maturity, and thus does not represent a violation of the held-to-maturity requirement. These include selling a security close enough to maturity (such as three months) so that interest rate risk is no longer an important pricing factor. Additionally, if the enterprise has already collected a substantial portion of the principal of the security (at least 85%) it is considered to have been held to its maturity date.

[5]Investments acquired at par, at a discount, or at a premium are generally recorded in the accounts at cost, including brokerage and other fees but excluding the accrued interest; generally they are not recorded at maturity value. The use of a separate discount or premium account as a valuation account is acceptable procedure for investments, but in practice it has not been widely used. This traditional exclusion of a separate discount or premium account has not yet changed even though *APB Opinion No. 21* recommends the disclosure of unamortized discount or premium on notes and bonds receivable.

ILLUSTRATION 18-3
Schedule of Interest Revenue and Bond Discount Amortization—Effective Interest Method

8% Bonds Purchased to Yield 10%				
Date	Cash Received	Interest Revenue	Bond Discount Amortization	Carrying Amount of Bonds
1/1/01				$ 92,278
7/1/01	$ 4,000[a]	$ 4,614[b]	$ 614[c]	92,892[d]
1/1/02	4,000	4,645	645	93,537
7/1/02	4,000	4,677	677	94,214
1/1/03	4,000	4,711	711	94,925
7/1/03	4,000	4,746	746	95,671
1/1/04	4,000	4,783	783	96,454
7/1/04	4,000	4,823	823	97,277
1/1/05	4,000	4,864	864	98,141
7/1/05	4,000	4,907	907	99,048
1/1/06	4,000	4,952	952	100,000
	$40,000	$47,722	$7,722	

[a]$4,000 = $100,000 × .08 × 6/12
[b]$4,614 = $92,278 × .10 × 6/12
[c]$614 = $4,614 − $4,000
[d]$92,892 = $92,278 + $614

As indicated in Chapter 14, the **effective interest method** is required unless some other method—such as the straight-line method—yields a similar result. The effective interest method is applied to bond investments in a fashion similar to that described for bonds payable. The effective interest rate or yield is computed at the time of investment and is applied to its beginning carrying amount (book value) for each interest period to compute interest revenue. The investment carrying amount is increased by the amortized discount or decreased by the amortized premium in each period.

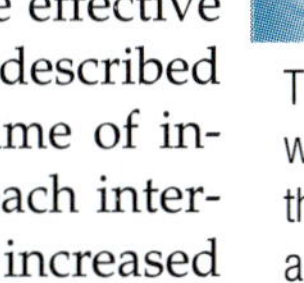

UNDERLYING CONCEPTS

The use of some simpler method which yields results similar to the effective interest method is an application of the materiality concept.

The journal entry to record the receipt of the first semiannual interest payment on July 1, 2001 (using the data in Illustration 18-3), is:

July 1, 2001

Cash	4,000	
Held-to-Maturity Securities	614	
Interest Revenue		4,614

Because Robinson Company is on a calendar-year basis, it accrues interest and amortizes the discount at December 31, 2001, as follows:

December 31, 2001

Interest Receivable	4,000	
Held-to-Maturity Securities	645	
Interest Revenue		4,645

Again, the interest and amortization amounts are provided in Illustration 18-3.

Robinson Company would report the following items related to its investment in Evermaster bonds in its December 31, 2001, financial statements:

ILLUSTRATION 18-4
Reporting of Held-to-Maturity Securities

Balance Sheet	
Current assets	
Interest receivable	$ 4,000
Long-term investments	
Held-to-maturity securities, at amortized cost	$93,537
Income Statement	
Other revenues and gains	
Interest revenue	$ 9,259

The sale of a held-to-maturity debt security close enough to its maturity date that a change in the market interest rates would not significantly affect the security's fair value may be considered a sale at maturity. If Robinson Company sells its investment in Evermaster bonds on November 1, 2005, for example, at 99¾ plus accrued interest, the following computations and entries would be made. The discount amortization from July 1, 2005, to November 1, 2005, is $635 (4/6 × $952). The entry to record this discount amortization is as follows:

November 1, 2005

Held-to-Maturity Securities	635	
Interest Revenue		635

The computation of the realized gain on the sale is shown in Illustration 18-5.

ILLUSTRATION 18-5
Computation of Gain on Sale of Bonds

Selling price of bonds (exclusive of accrued interest)		$99,750
Less: Book value of bonds on November 1, 2005:		
Amortized cost, July 1, 2005	$99,048	
Add: Discount amortized for the period July 1, 2005, to November 1, 2005	635	
		99,683
Gain on sale of bonds		$ 67

The entry to record the sale of the bonds is:

November 1, 2005

Cash	102,417	
Interest Revenue (4/6 × $4,000)		2,667
Held-to-Maturity Securities		99,683
Gain on Sale of Securities		67

The credit to Interest Revenue represents accrued interest for 4 months, for which the purchaser pays cash. The debit to Cash represents the selling price of the bonds, $99,750, plus accrued interest of $2,667. The credit to the Held-to-Maturity Securities account represents the book value of the bonds on the date of sale, and the credit to Gain on Sale of Securities represents the excess of the selling price over the book value of the bonds.

AVAILABLE-FOR-SALE SECURITIES

UNDERLYING CONCEPTS
Recognizing unrealized gains and losses is an application of the concept of comprehensive income.

Investments in debt securities that are in the **available-for-sale** category are reported at fair value. The unrealized gains and losses related to changes in the fair value of available-for-sale debt securities are recorded in an unrealized holding gain or loss account. This account is reported as other comprehensive income and as a separate component of stockholders' equity until realized. Thus, **changes in fair value are not reported as part of net income until the security is sold**. This approach reduces the volatility of net income.

Illustration: Single Security

To illustrate the accounting for available-for-sale securities, assume that Graff Corporation purchases $100,000, 10%, 5-year bonds on January 1, 2001, with interest payable on July 1 and January 1. The bonds sell for $108,111 which results in a bond premium of $8,111 and an effective interest rate of 8%.

The entry to record the purchase of the bonds is as follows:

January 1, 2001

Available-for-Sale Securities	108,111	
Cash		108,111

Illustration 18-6 discloses the effect of the premium amortization on the interest revenue recorded each period using the effective interest method.

ILLUSTRATION 18-6
Schedule of Interest Revenue and Bond Premium Amortization—Effective Interest Method

10% Bonds Purchased to Yield 8%

Date	Cash Received	Interest Revenue	Bond Premium Amortization	Carrying Amount of Bonds
1/1/01				$108,111
7/1/01	$ 5,000[a]	$ 4,324[b]	$ 676[c]	107,435[d]
1/1/02	5,000	4,297	703	106,732
7/1/02	5,000	4,269	731	106,001
1/1/03	5,000	4,240	760	105,241
7/1/03	5,000	4,210	790	104,451
1/1/04	5,000	4,178	822	103,629
7/1/04	5,000	4,145	855	102,774
1/1/05	5,000	4,111	889	101,885
7/1/05	5,000	4,075	925	100,960
1/1/06	5,000	4,040	960	100,000
	$50,000	$41,889	$8,111	

[a]$5,000 = $100,000 × .10 × 6/12
[b]$4,324 = $108,111 × .08 × 6/12
[c]$676 = $5,000 − $4,324
[d]$107,435 = $108,111 − $676

Calculator Solution for Bond Price

	Inputs	Answer
N	10	
I	4	
PV	?	−108,111
PMT	5,000	
FV	100,000	

The entry to record interest revenue on July 1, 2001, would be as follows:

July 1, 2001

Cash	5,000	
Available-for-Sale Securities		676
Interest Revenue		4,324

At December 31, 2001, Graff would make the following entry to recognize interest revenue:

December 31, 2001

Interest Receivable	5,000	
Available-for-Sale Securities		703
Interest Revenue		4,297

As a result, Graff would report interest revenue for 2001 of $8,621 ($4,324 + $4,297).

To apply the fair value method to these debt securities, assume that at year-end the fair value of the bonds is $105,000. Comparing this fair value with the carrying amount (amortized cost) of the bonds at December 31, 2001, as shown in Illustration 18-6, Graff recognizes an unrealized holding loss of $1,732 ($106,732 − $105,000). This loss is reported as other comprehensive income and as a separate component of stockholders' equity. The entry is as follows:

December 31, 2001

Unrealized Holding Gain or Loss—Equity	1,732	
Securities Fair Value Adjustment (Available-for-Sale)		1,732

A valuation account is used instead of crediting the Available-for-Sale Securities account. The use of the **Securities Fair Value Adjustment (Available-for-Sale) account** enables the company to maintain a record of its amortized cost. Because the adjustment account has a credit balance in this case, it is subtracted from the balance of the Available-for-Sale Securities account to arrive at fair value. The fair value is the amount reported on the balance sheet. At each reporting date, the bonds would be reported at fair value with an adjustment to the Unrealized Holding Gain or Loss—Equity account.

Illustration: Portfolio of Securities

To illustrate the accounting for a portfolio of securities, assume that Webb Corporation has two debt securities that are classified as available-for-sale. Illustration 18-7 provides information on amortized cost, fair value, and the amount of the unrealized gain or loss.

ILLUSTRATION 18-7
Computation of Securities Fair Value Adjustment—Available-for-Sale Securities (2002)

Available-for-Sale Debt Security Portfolio December 31, 2002			
Investments	Amortized Cost	Fair Value	Unrealized Gain (Loss)
Watson Corporation 8% bonds	$ 93,537	$103,600	$ 10,063
Anacomp Corporation 10% bonds	200,000	180,400	(19,600)
Total of portfolio	$293,537	$284,000	(9,537)
Previous securities fair value adjustment balance			0
Securities fair value adjustment—Cr.			$ (9,537)

The total fair value of Webb's available-for-sale portfolio is $284,000. The gross unrealized gains are $10,063 and the gross unrealized losses are $19,600 resulting in a net unrealized loss of $9,537. That is, the fair value of available-for-sale securities is $9,537 lower than its amortized cost. An adjusting entry is made to a valuation allowance to record the decrease in value and to record the loss as follows:

December 31, 2002		
Unrealized Holding Gain or Loss—Equity	9,537	
Securities Fair Value Adjustment (Available-for-Sale)		9,537

The unrealized holding loss of $9,537 is reported as other comprehensive income and a reduction of stockholders' equity. As indicated earlier, unrealized holding gains and losses related to investments that are classified in the available-for-sale category are not included in net income.

Sale of Available-for-Sale Securities

If bonds carried as investments in available-for-sale securities are sold before the maturity date, entries must be made to amortize the discount or premium to the date of sale and to remove from the Available-for-Sale Securities account the amortized cost of bonds sold. To illustrate, assume that the Webb Corporation sold the Watson bonds (from Illustration 18-7) on July 1, 2003, for $90,000. Assume that the entry to recognize the discount amortization and the receipt of interest through July 1, 2003, has been recorded and the amortized cost is $94,214. The computation of the realized loss is as follows:

ILLUSTRATION 18-8
Computation of Loss on Sale of Bonds

Amortized cost (Watson bonds)	$94,214
Less: Selling price of bonds	90,000
Loss on sale of bonds	$ 4,214

The entry to record the sale of the Watson bonds is as follows:

July 1, 2003		
Cash	90,000	
Loss on Sale of Securities	4,214	
Available-for-Sale Securities		94,214

This realized loss is reported in the Other Expenses and Losses section of the income statement. Assuming no other purchases and sales of bonds in 2003, Webb Corporation prepares the following information on December 31, 2003:

Available-for-Sale Debt Security Portfolio December 31, 2003			
Investments	Amortized Cost	Fair Value	Unrealized Gain (Loss)
Anacomp Corporation 10% bonds (total portfolio)	$200,000	$195,000	$(5,000)
Previous securities fair value adjustment balance—Cr.			(9,537)
Securities fair value adjustment—Dr.			$ 4,537

ILLUSTRATION 18-9
Computation of Securities Fair Value Adjustment—Available-for-Sale (2003)

As shown in Illustration 18-9, Webb Corporation has an unrealized holding loss of $5,000. However, the Securities Fair Value Adjustment account already has a credit balance of $9,537. To reduce the adjustment account balance to $5,000, it is debited for $4,537, as follows:

December 31, 2003		
Securities Fair Value Adjustment (Available-for-Sale)	4,537	
Unrealized Holding Gain or Loss—Equity		4,537

Financial Statement Presentation

Webb Corporation's December 31, 2003, balance sheet and the 2003 income statement would contain the following items and amounts (the Anacomp bonds are long-term investments but are not intended to be held to maturity):

Balance Sheet	
Current assets	
Interest receivable	$ xxx
Investments	
Available-for-sale securities, at fair value	$195,000
Stockholders' equity	
Accumulated other comprehensive loss	$ 5,000
Income Statement	
Other revenues and gains	
Interest revenue	$ xxx
Other expenses and losses	
Loss on sale of securities	$ 4,214

ILLUSTRATION 18-10
Reporting of Available-for-Sale Securities

Some favor including the unrealized holding gain or loss in net income rather than showing it as other comprehensive income.[6] However, some companies, particularly financial institutions, noted that recognizing gains and losses on assets, but not liabilities, would introduce substantial volatility in net income. They argued that often hedges exist between assets and liabilities so that gains in assets are offset by losses in liabilities, and vice versa. In short, to recognize gains and losses only on the asset side is unfair and not representative of the economic activities of the company.

This argument was convincing to the FASB. As a result, these unrealized gains and losses are **not included in net income**. However, even this approach does not solve some of the problems, because volatility of capital still results. This is of concern to financial institutions because regulators restrict financial institutions' operations based

[6]In Chapter 4, we discussed the reporting of other comprehensive income and the concept of comprehensive income. "Reporting Comprehensive Income," *Statement of Financial Accounting Standards No. 130* (Norwalk, Conn.: FASB, 1997).

upon their level of capital. In addition, companies can still manage their net income by engaging in gains trading (i.e., selling the winners and holding the losers).

TRADING SECURITIES

Trading securities are held with the intention of selling them in a short period of time. Trading in this context means frequent buying and selling, and trading securities are used to generate profits from short-term differences in price. The holding period for these securities is generally less than 3 months and more probably is measured in days or hours. **These securities are reported at fair value, with unrealized holding gains and losses reported as part of net income. Any discount or premium is not amortized.** A holding gain or loss is the net change in the fair value of a security from one period to another, exclusive of dividend or interest revenue recognized but not received. In short, the FASB says to adjust the trading securities to fair value, at each reporting date. In addition, the change in value is reported as part of net income, not other comprehensive income.

To illustrate, assume that on December 31, 2002, Western Publishing Corporation determined its trading securities portfolio to be as shown in Illustration 18-11 (assume that 2002 is the first year that Western Publishing held trading securities). At the date of acquisition, these trading securities were recorded at cost, including brokerage commissions and taxes, in the account entitled Trading Securities. This is the first valuation of this recently purchased portfolio.

ILLUSTRATION 18-11
Computation of Securities Fair Value Adjustment—Trading Securities Portfolio (2002)

Trading Debt Security Portfolio
December 31, 2002

Investments	Cost	Fair Value	Unrealized Gain (Loss)
Burlington Northern 10% bonds	$ 43,860	$ 51,500	$7,640
Chrysler Corporation 11% bonds	184,230	175,200	(9,030)
Time Warner 8% bonds	86,360	91,500	5,140
Total of portfolio	$314,450	$318,200	3,750
Previous securities fair value adjustment balance			0
Securities fair value adjustment—Dr.			$3,750

The total cost of Western's trading portfolio is $314,450. The gross unrealized gains are $12,780 ($7,640 + $5,140) and the gross unrealized losses are $9,030, resulting in a net unrealized gain of $3,750. The fair value of trading securities is $3,750 greater than its cost.

At December 31, an adjusting entry is made to a valuation allowance, referred to as Securities Fair Value Adjustment (Trading), to record the increase in value and to record the unrealized holding gain:

December 31, 2002

Securities Fair Value Adjustment (Trading)	3,750	
Unrealized Holding Gain or Loss—Income		3,750

Because the Securities Fair Value Adjustment account balance is a debit, it is added to the cost of the Trading Securities account to arrive at a fair value for the trading securities. The fair value of the securities is the amount reported on the balance sheet.

When securities are actively traded, the FASB believes that financial reporting is improved when the economic events affecting the company (changes in fair value) and related unrealized gains and losses are reported in the same period. Including changes in fair value in income provides more relevant information to current stockholders whose composition may be different next period.

INVESTMENTS IN EQUITY SECURITIES — SECTION 2

OBJECTIVE 2
Identify the categories of equity securities and describe the accounting and reporting treatment for each category.

Equity securities are described as securities representing ownership interests such as common, preferred, or other capital stock. They also include rights to acquire or dispose of ownership interests at an agreed-upon or determinable price such as warrants, rights, and call options or put options. Convertible debt securities and redeemable preferred stocks are not treated as equity securities. When equity securities are purchased, their cost includes the purchase price of the security plus broker's commissions and other fees incidental to the purchase.

The degree to which one corporation **(investor)** acquires an interest in the common stock of another corporation **(investee)** generally determines the accounting treatment for the investment subsequent to acquisition. Investments by one corporation in the common stock of another can be classified according to the percentage of the voting stock of the investee held by the investor:

1. Holdings of less than 20% (fair value method)—investor has passive interest.
2. Holdings between 20% and 50% (equity method)—investor has significant influence.
3. Holdings of more than 50% (consolidated statements)—investor has controlling interest.

Historically, consolidation practices in Europe differ in terms of how the group of companies is determined. The U.K. approach focuses on ownership and the legal right to control; in contrast, the German approach focuses on management control.

These levels of interest or influence and the corresponding valuation and reporting method that must be applied to the investment are graphically displayed in Illustration 18-12.

ILLUSTRATION 18-12
Levels of Influence Determine Accounting Methods

	0% ←→ 20%	20% ←→ 50%	50% ←→ 100%
Percentage of Ownership	0% ←→ 20%	20% ←→ 50%	50% ←→ 100%
Level of Influence	Little or None	Significant	Control
Valuation Method	Fair Value Method	Equity Method	Consolidation

The accounting and reporting for equity securities therefore depends upon the level of influence and the type of security involved, as shown in Illustration 18-13.

ILLUSTRATION 18-13
Accounting and Reporting for Equity Securities by Category

Category	Valuation	Unrealized Holding Gains or Losses	Other Income Effects
Holdings less than 20%			
1. Available-for-sale	Fair value	Recognized in other comprehensive income and as separate component of stockholders' equity	Dividends declared; gains and losses from sale.
2. Trading	Fair value	Recognized in net income	Dividends declared; gains and losses from sale.
Holdings between 20% and 50%	Equity	Not recognized	Proportionate shares of investee's net income (adjusted for appropriate amortization).
Holdings more than 50%	Consolidation	Not recognized	Not applicable

HOLDINGS OF LESS THAN 20%

As mentioned earlier, equity securities are recorded at cost. In some cases, cost is difficult to determine. For example, equity securities acquired in **exchange for noncash consideration** (property or services) should be recorded at (1) the fair value of the consideration given or (2) the fair value of the security received, whichever is more clearly determinable. The absence of clearly determinable values for the property or services or a market price for the security acquired may require the use of appraisals or estimates to arrive at a cost.

The purchase of two or more classes of securities for a lump sum price calls for the allocation of the cost to the different classes in some equitable manner. If fair values (market prices) are available for each class of security, the lump sum cost may be apportioned on the basis of the **relative fair values**. If the market price is available for one security but not for the other, the **incremental method** may be used and the market price assigned to the one and the cost excess to the other. If market prices are not available at the date of acquisition of several securities, it may be necessary to defer cost apportionment until evidence of at least one value becomes available. In some instances cost apportionment may have to wait until one of the securities is sold. In such cases, the proceeds from the sale of the one security may be subtracted from the lump sum cost, leaving the residual cost to be assigned as the cost of the other.[7]

When an investor has an interest of less than 20%, it is presumed that the investor has little or no influence over the investee. In such cases, if market prices are available, the investment is valued and reported subsequent to acquisition using the **fair value method**.[8] The fair value method requires that companies classify equity securities at acquisition as **available-for-sale securities** or **trading securities**. Because equity securities have no maturity date, they cannot be classified as held-to-maturity.

Available-for-Sale Securities

Available-for-sale securities when acquired are recorded at cost. To illustrate, assume that on November 3, 2002, Republic Corporation purchased common stock of three companies, each investment representing less than a 20% interest:

INTERNATIONAL INSIGHT

In Germany marketable securities (both trading and available-for-sale) are presented at lower of cost or market value.

	Cost
Northwest Industries, Inc.	$259,700
Campbell Soup Co.	317,500
St. Regis Pulp Co.	141,350
Total cost	$718,550

These investments would be recorded as follows:

November 3, 2002		
Available-for-Sale Securities	718,550	
Cash		718,550

[7]Accounting for numerous purchases of securities requires that information regarding the cost of individual purchases be preserved, as well as the dates of purchases and sales. If **specific identification** is not possible, the use of an **average cost** may be used for multiple purchases of the same class of security. The **first-in, first-out method** of assigning costs to investments at the time of sale is also acceptable and is normally employed.

[8]When market prices are not available, the investment is valued and reported at cost in periods subsequent to acquisition. This approach is often referred to as the **cost method**. Dividends are recognized as dividend revenue when received, and the portfolio is valued and reported at acquisition cost. No gains or losses are recognized until the securities are sold.

On December 6, 2002, Republic receives a cash dividend of $4,200 on its investment in the common stock of Campbell Soup Co. The cash dividend is recorded as follows:

December 6, 2002		
Cash	4,200	
Dividend Revenue		4,200

All three of the investee companies reported net income for the year but only Campbell Soup declared and paid a dividend to Republic. But, as indicated before, when an investor owns less than 20% of the common stock of another corporation, it is presumed that the investor has relatively little influence on the investee. As a result, **net income earned by the investee is not considered a proper basis for recognizing income from the investment by the investor**. The reason is that the investee may choose to retain for use in the business increased net assets resulting from profitable operations. Therefore, **net income is not considered earned by the investor until cash dividends are declared by the investee**.

At December 31, 2002, Republic's available-for-sale equity security portfolio has the following cost and fair value:

ILLUSTRATION 18-14
Computation of Securities Fair Value Adjustment—Available-for-Sale Equity Security Portfolio (2002)

Available-for-Sale Equity Security Portfolio
December 31, 2002

Investments	Cost	Fair Value	Unrealized Gain (Loss)
Northwest Industries, Inc.	$259,700	$275,000	$ 15,300
Campbell Soup Co.	317,500	304,000	(13,500)
St. Regis Pulp Co.	141,350	104,000	(37,350)
Total of portfolio	$718,550	$683,000	(35,550)
Previous securities fair value adjustment balance			0
Securities fair value adjustment—Cr.			$(35,550)

For Republic's available-for-sale equity securities portfolio the gross unrealized gains are $15,300 and the gross unrealized losses are $50,850 ($13,500 + $37,350), resulting in a net unrealized loss of $35,550. The fair value of the available-for-sale securities portfolio is $35,550 less than its cost. As with available-for-sale **debt** securities, the net unrealized gains and losses related to changes in the fair value of available-for-sale **equity** securities are recorded in an Unrealized Holding Gain or Loss—Equity account that is reported as a **part of other comprehensive income and as a component of stockholders' equity until realized.** In this case, Republic prepares an adjusting entry debiting the Unrealized Holding Gain or Loss—Equity account and crediting the Securities Fair Value Adjustment account to record the decrease in fair value and to record the loss as follows:

December 31, 2002		
Unrealized Holding Gain or Loss—Equity	35,550	
Securities Fair Value Adjustment (Available-for-Sale)		35,550

On January 23, 2003, Republic sold all of its Northwest Industries, Inc. common stock receiving net proceeds of $287,220. The realized gain on the sale is computed as follows:

ILLUSTRATION 18-15
Computation of Gain on Sale of Stock

Net proceeds from sale	$287,220
Cost of Northwest shares	259,700
Gain on sale of stock	$ 27,520

The sale is recorded as follows:

January 23, 2003		
Cash	287,220	
Available-for-Sale Securities		259,700
Gain on Sale of Stock		27,520

In addition, assume that on February 10, 2003, Republic purchased 20,000 shares of Continental Trucking at a market price of $12.75 per share plus brokerage commissions of $1,850 (total cost, $256,850).

On December 31, 2003, Republic's portfolio of available-for-sale securities is as follows:

ILLUSTRATION 18-16
Computation of Securities Fair Value Adjustment—Available-for-Sale Equity Security Portfolio (2003)

Available-for-Sale Equity Security Portfolio
December 31, 2003

Investments	Cost	Fair Value	Unrealized Gain (Loss)
Continental Trucking	$256,850	$278,350	$21,500
Campbell Soup Co.	317,500	362,550	45,050
St. Regis Pulp Co.	141,350	139,050	(2,300)
Total of portfolio	$715,700	$779,950	64,250
Previous securities fair value adjustment balance—Cr.			(35,550)
Securities fair value adjustment—Dr.			$99,800

At December 31, 2003, the fair value of Republic's available-for-sale equity securities portfolio exceeds cost by $64,250 (unrealized gain). The Securities Fair Value Adjustment account had a credit balance of $35,550 at December 31, 2002. To adjust Republic's December 31, 2003, available-for-sale portfolio to fair value requires that the Securities Fair Value Adjustment account be debited for $99,800 ($35,550 + $64,250). The entry to record this adjustment is as follows:

December 31, 2003		
Securities Fair Value Adjustment (Available-for-Sale)	99,800	
Unrealized Holding Gain or Loss—Equity		99,800

Trading Securities

The accounting entries to record trading equity securities are the same as for available-for-sale equity securities except for recording the unrealized holding gain or loss. For trading equity securities, the unrealized holding gain or loss is **reported as part of net income**. Thus, the account title Unrealized Holding Gain or Loss—Income is used. When a sale is made, the remainder of the gain or loss is recognized in income.

HOLDINGS BETWEEN 20% AND 50%

An investor corporation may hold an interest of less than 50% in an investee corporation and thus not possess legal control. However, as shown in the opening story about Coca-Cola, an investment in voting stock of less than 50% can still give Coke (the investor) the ability to exercise significant influence over the operating and financial policies of its bottlers.[9] To provide a guide for accounting for investors when 50% or less of the common voting stock is held and to develop an operational definition of "sig-

[9]"The Equity Method of Accounting for Investments in Common Stock," *Opinions of the Accounting Principles Board No. 18* (New York: AICPA, 1971), par. 17.

nificant influence," the APB in *Opinion No. 18* noted that ability to exercise influence may be indicated in several ways. Examples would be: representation on the board of directors, participation in policy-making processes, material intercompany transactions, interchange of managerial personnel, or technological dependency. Another important consideration is the extent of ownership by an investor in relation to the concentration of other shareholdings. However, substantial or majority ownership of the voting stock of an investee by another investor does not necessarily preclude the ability to exercise significant influence by the investor.[10]

Judgment is frequently required in determining whether an investment of 20% or more results in "significant influence" over the policies of an investee. In the late 1970s and early 1980s an increased number of "hostile" merger and takeover attempts created situations where "significant influence" over investees was difficult to determine. The FASB therefore provided examples of cases in which an investment of 20% or more might not enable an investor to exercise **significant influence**:

(a) The investee opposes the investor's acquisition of its stock. For example, the investee files suit against the investor, or files a complaint with a governmental regulatory agency.

(b) The investor and investee sign an agreement under which the investor surrenders significant shareholder rights. This commonly occurs when an investee is resisting a takeover attempt by the investor, and the investor agrees to limit its shareholding in the investee.

(c) The investor's ownership share does not result in "significant influence" because majority ownership of the investee is concentrated among a small group of shareholders who operate the investee without regard to the views of the investor.

(d) The investor needs or wants more financial information than that which is publicly issued by the investee, tries to obtain it from the investee, and fails.

(e) The investor tries and fails to obtain representation on the investee's board of directors.[11]

The FASB says this list of examples is not all-inclusive. It is meant to provide examples of the types of evidence requiring further analysis when determining whether or not an investor is able to exert "significant influence" over an investee.

To achieve a reasonable degree of uniformity in application of the "significant influence" criterion, the profession concluded that an investment (direct or indirect) of 20% or more of the voting stock of an investee should lead to a presumption that in the absence of evidence to the contrary, an investor has the ability to exercise significant influence over an investee.

In instances of "significant influence" (generally an investment of 20% or more), the investor is required to account for the investment using the **equity method**.

Equity Method

Under the **equity method** a substantive economic relationship is acknowledged between the investor and the investee. The investment is originally recorded at the cost of the shares acquired but is subsequently adjusted each period for changes in the net assets of the investee. That is, the **investment's carrying amount is periodically increased (decreased) by the investor's proportionate share of the earnings (losses) of the investee and decreased by all dividends received by the investor from the investee**. The equity method recognizes that investee's earnings increase investee's net assets, and that investee's losses and dividends decrease these net assets.

OBJECTIVE 3
Explain the equity method of accounting and compare it to the fair value method for equity securities.

[10]Ibid.

[11]"Criteria for Applying the Equity Method of Accounting for Investments in Common Stock," *Interpretations of the Financial Accounting Standards Board No. 35* (Stamford, Conn.: FASB, 1981).

To illustrate the equity method and compare it with the fair value method, assume that Maxi Company purchases a 20% interest in Mini Company. To apply the fair value method in this example, assume that Maxi does not have the ability to exercise significant influence and the securities are classified as available-for-sale. Where the equity method is applied in this example, assume that the 20% interest permits Maxi to exercise significant influence. The entries are shown in Illustration 18-17.

ILLUSTRATION 18-17
Comparison of Fair Value Method and Equity Method

Entries by Maxi Company

Fair Value Method			Equity Method		
On January 2, 2002, Maxi Company acquired 48,000 shares (20% of Mini Company common stock) at a cost of $10 a share.					
Available-for-Sale Securities	480,000		Investment in Mini Stock	480,000	
Cash		480,000	Cash		480,000
For the year 2002, Mini Company reported net income of $200,000; Maxi Company's share is 20% or $40,000.					
No entry			Investment in Mini Stock	40,000	
			Revenue from Investment		40,000
At December 31, 2002, the 48,000 shares of Mini Company have a fair value (market price) of $12 a share, or $576,000.					
Securities Fair Value Adjustment (Available-for-Sale)	96,000		No entry		
Unrealized Holding Gain or Loss—Equity		96,000			
On January 28, 2003, Mini Company announced and paid a cash dividend of $100,000; Maxi Company received 20% or $20,000.					
Cash	20,000		Cash	20,000	
Dividend Revenue		20,000	Investment in Mini Stock		20,000
For the year 2003, Mini reported a net loss of $50,000; Maxi Company's share is 20% or $10,000.					
No entry			Loss on Investment	10,000	
			Investment in Mini Stock		10,000
At December 31, 2003, the Mini Company 48,000 shares have a fair value (market price) of $11 a share, or $528,000.					
Unrealized Holding Gain or Loss—Equity	48,000		No entry		
Securities Fair Value Adjustment (Available-for-Sale)		48,000			

In the European Community, the Seventh Directive requires the use of the equity method of accounting for investments in affiliates. However, there is still strong disagreement internationally concerning accounting for such investments. Currently, some nations (U.S., U.K., Japan) require the use of the equity method; others (Sweden, Switzerland) do not.

UNDERLYING CONCEPTS

Revenue to be recognized should be earned and realized or realizable. A low level of ownership indicates that the income from an investee should be deferred until cash is received.

Note that under the fair value method only the cash dividends received from Mini Company are reported as revenue by Maxi Company. **The earning of net income by the investee is not considered a proper basis for recognition of income from the investment by the investor.** The reason is that increased net assets resulting from the investee's profitable operation may be permanently retained in the business by the investee. Therefore, revenue is not considered earned by the investor until dividends are received from the investee.

Under the equity method, Maxi Company reports as revenue its share of the net income reported by Mini Company; the cash dividends received from Mini Company are recorded as a decrease in the investment carrying value. As a result, the investor records its share of the net income of the investee in the year when it is earned. In this case, the investor can ensure that any net asset increases of the investee resulting from net income will be paid in dividends if desired. To wait until a dividend is received ignores the fact that the investor is better off if the investee has earned income.

Using dividends as a basis for recognizing income poses an additional problem. For example, assume that the investee reports a net loss, but the investor exerts influence to force a dividend payment from the investee. In this case, the investor reports income, even though the investee is experiencing a loss. **In other words, if dividends are used as a basis for recognizing income, the economics of the situation are not properly reported.**

Expanded Illustration of the Equity Method

Under the equity method, periodic investor revenue consists of the investor's proportionate share of investee earnings (adjusted to eliminate intercompany gains and losses) and **amortization of the difference between the investor's initial cost and the investor's proportionate share of the underlying book value of the investee at date of acquisition**. And, if the investee's net income includes extraordinary items, the investor treats a proportionate share of the extraordinary items as an extraordinary item, rather than as ordinary investment revenue before extraordinary items.

Assume that on January 1, 2002, Investor Company purchased 250,000 shares of Investee Company's 1,000,000 shares of outstanding common stock for $8,500,000. Investee Company's total net worth or book value was $30,000,000 at the date of Investor Company's 25% investment. Investor Company thereby paid $1,000,000 [$8,500,000 − .25($30,000,000)] in excess of book value. It was determined that $600,000 of this is attributable to its share of **undervalued depreciable assets** of Investee Company and $400,000 to **unrecorded goodwill**. Investor Company estimated the average remaining life of the undervalued assets to be 10 years and decided upon a 40-year amortization period for goodwill (the maximum length of time allowed). For the year 2002, Investee Company reported net income of $2,800,000 including an extraordinary loss of $400,000, and paid dividends at June 30, 2002 of $500,000 and at December 31, 2002 of $900,000. The following entries would be recorded on the books of Investor Company to report its long-term investment using the equity method.

January 1, 2002

Investment in Investee Stock	8,500,000	
Cash		8,500,000
(To record the acquisition of 250,000 shares of Investee Company common stock)		

June 30, 2002

Cash	125,000	
Investment in Investee Stock		125,000
[To record dividend received ($500,000 × .25) from Investee Company]		

The entries on December 31, however, are more complex. In addition to the dividend received, Investor Company must recognize its share of Investee Company's income. **Both an ordinary and extraordinary component must be recorded** by Investor Company, because Investee Company's income includes both. Furthermore, Investor Company paid more than the book value for an interest in Investee Company's net assets. As a result, this additional cost must be allocated to the proper accounting periods.

December 31, 2002

Investment in Investee Stock	700,000	
Loss from Investment (extraordinary)	100,000	
Revenue from Investment (ordinary)		800,000
[To record share of Investee Company ordinary income ($3,200,000 × .25) and extraordinary loss ($400,000 × .25)]		

December 31, 2002

Cash	225,000	
Investment in Investee Stock		225,000
[To record dividend received ($900,000 × .25) from Investee Company]		

December 31, 2002

Revenue from Investment (ordinary)		70,000	
Investment in Investee Stock			70,000
(To record amortization of investment cost in excess of book value represented by:			
Undervalued depreciable assets—$600,000 ÷ 10 =	$60,000		
Unrecorded goodwill—$400,000 ÷ 40 =	10,000		
Total	$70,000)		

The investment in Investee Company is presented in the balance sheet of Investor Company at a carrying amount of $8,780,000 computed as shown below.

ILLUSTRATION 18-18
Computation of Investment Carrying Amount

Investment in Investee Company		
Acquisition cost, 1/1/02	$8,500,000	
Plus: Share of 2002 income before extraordinary item	800,000	$9,300,000
Less: Share of extraordinary loss	100,000	
Dividends received 6/30 and 12/31	350,000	
Amortization of undervalued depreciable assets	60,000	
Amortization of unrecorded goodwill	10,000	520,000
Carrying amount, 12/31/02		$8,780,000

In the preceding illustration the investment cost exceeded the underlying book value. In some cases, an investor may acquire an investment at a **cost less than the underlying book value**. In such cases specific assets are assumed to be **overvalued** and, if depreciable, the excess of the investee's book value over the investor's acquisition cost is amortized into investment revenue over the remaining lives of the assets. Investment revenue is increased under the presumption that the investee's net income as reported is actually understated because the investee is charging depreciation on overstated asset values.

Investee Losses Exceed Carrying Amount

If an investor's share of the investee's losses exceeds the carrying amount of the investment, should the investor recognize additional losses? Ordinarily the investor should discontinue applying the equity method and not recognize additional losses.

If the investor's potential loss is not limited to the amount of its original investment (by guarantee of the investee's obligations or other commitment to provide further financial support), however, or if imminent return to profitable operations by the investee appears to be assured, it is appropriate for the investor to recognize additional losses.[12]

Changing from and to the Equity Method

If the investor level of influence of ownership falls below that necessary for continued use of the equity method, a change must be made to the fair value method. And an investment in common stock of an investee that has been accounted for by other than the equity method may become qualified for use of the equity method by an increase in the level of ownership. Both of these situations are discussed and illustrated in Chapter 23.

Go to the Digital Tool for disclosures related to equity investments.

Disclosures Required Under the Equity Method

The significance of an investment to the investor's financial position and operating results should determine the extent of disclosures. The following disclosures in the investor's financial statements generally apply to the equity method:

[12]"The Equity Method of Accounting for Investments in Common Stock," op. cit., par. 19(i).

1. The name of each investee and the percentage of ownership of common stock.
2. The accounting policies of the investor with respect to investments in common stock.
3. The difference, if any, between the amount in the investment account and the amount of underlying equity in the net assets of the investee.
4. The aggregate value of each identified investment based on quoted market price (if available).
5. When investments of 20% or more interest are in the aggregate material in relation to the financial position and operating results of an investor, it may be necessary to present summarized information concerning assets, liabilities, and results of operations of the investees, either individually or in groups, as appropriate.

In addition, the investor is expected to disclose the reasons for **not** using the equity method in cases of 20% or more ownership interest and ***for*** using the equity method in cases of less than 20% ownership interest.

UNDERLYING CONCEPTS

The consolidation of financial results of different companies follows the economic entity assumption and disregards legal entities. The key objective is to provide useful information to financial statement users.

HOLDINGS OF MORE THAN 50%

When one corporation acquires a voting interest of more than 50%—**controlling interest**—in another corporation, the investor corporation is referred to as the **parent** and the investee corporation as the **subsidiary**. The investment in the common stock of the subsidiary is presented as a long-term investment on the separate financial statements of the parent.

When the parent treats the subsidiary as an investment, **consolidated financial statements** are generally prepared instead of separate financial statements for the parent and the subsidiary. Consolidated financial statements disregard the distinction between separate legal entities and treat the parent and subsidiary corporations as a single economic entity. The subject of when and how to prepare consolidated financial statements is discussed extensively in advanced accounting. Whether or not consolidated financial statements are prepared, the investment in the subsidiary is generally accounted for on the parent's books **using the equity method** as explained in this chapter.

In contrast to U.S. firms, financial statements of non-U.S. companies often include both consolidated (group) statements and parent company financial statements.

OTHER REPORTING ISSUES — SECTION 3

We have identified the basic issues involved in accounting for investments in debt and equity securities. In addition, the following issues relate to both of these types of securities.

1. Financial statement presentation
2. Impairment of value
3. Transfers between categories
4. Fair value controversy

FINANCIAL STATEMENT PRESENTATION OF INVESTMENTS

Reclassification Adjustments

As indicated in Chapter 4, changes in unrealized holding gains and losses related to available-for-sale securities are reported as part of other comprehensive income. Companies have the option to display the components of other comprehensive income (1) in a combined statement of income and comprehensive income, (2) in a separate statement of comprehensive income that begins with net income, or (3) in a statement of stockholders' equity.

The reporting of changes in unrealized gains or losses in comprehensive income is straightforward unless securities are sold during the year. In this situation, double counting results when realized gains or losses are reported as part of net income but also are shown as part of other comprehensive income in the current period or in previous periods.

To ensure that gains and losses are not counted twice when a sale occurs, a **reclassification adjustment** is necessary. To illustrate, assume that Open Company has the following two available-for-sale securities in its portfolio at the end of 2001 (its first year of operations):

ILLUSTRATION 18-19
Available-for-Sale Security Portfolio (2001)

Investments	Cost	Fair Value	Unrealized Holding Gain (Loss)
Lehman Inc. common stocks	$ 80,000	$105,000	$25,000
Woods Co. common stocks	120,000	135,000	15,000
Total of portfolio	$200,000	$240,000	40,000
Previous securities fair value adjustment balance			-0-
Securities fair value adjustment—Dr.			$40,000

If Open Company reports net income in 2001 of $350,000, a statement of comprehensive income would be reported as follows:

ILLUSTRATION 18-20
Statement of Comprehensive Income (2001)

OPEN CO.
Statement of Comprehensive Income
For the Year Ended 12/31/01

Net income	$350,000
Other comprehensive income	
Holding gains arising during period	40,000
Comprehensive income	$390,000

During 2002, Open Company sold the Lehman Inc. common stock for $105,000 and realized a gain on the sale of $25,000 ($105,000 – $80,000). At the end of 2002, the fair value of the Woods Co. common stock increased an additional $20,000 to $155,000. The computation of the change in the securities fair value adjustment account is computed as follows:

ILLUSTRATION 18-21
Available-for-Sale Security Portfolio (2002)

Investments	Cost	Fair Value	Unrealized Holding Gain (Loss)
Woods Co. common stocks	$120,000	$155,000	$35,000
Previous securities fair value adjustment balance—Dr.			(40,000)
Securities fair value adjustment—Cr.			$ (5,000)

Illustration 18-21 indicates that an unrealized holding loss of $5,000 should be reported in comprehensive income in 2002. In addition, Open Company realized a gain of $25,000 on the sale of the Lehman common stock. Comprehensive income includes both realized and unrealized components, and therefore the total holding gain (loss) recognized in 2002 is $20,000, computed as follows:

ILLUSTRATION 18-22
Computation of Total Holding Gain (Loss)

Unrealized holding gain (loss)	$ (5,000)
Realized holding gain	25,000
Total holding gain recognized	**$ 20,000**

Open Company reports net income of $720,000 in 2002, which includes the realized gain on sale of the Lehman securities. A statement of comprehensive income for 2002 is shown in Illustration 18-23, indicating how the components of holding gains (losses) are reported.

ILLUSTRATION 18-23
Statement of Comprehensive Income (2002)

OPEN COMPANY Statement of Comprehensive Income For the Year Ended 12/31/02		
Net income (includes $25,000 realized gain on Lehman shares)		$720,000
Other comprehensive income		
Holding gains arising during period ($155,000 − $135,000)	$20,000	
Less: Reclassification adjustment for gains included in net income	(25,000)	(5,000)
Comprehensive income		$715,000

In 2001, the unrealized gain on the Lehman Co. common stock was included in comprehensive income. In 2002, it was sold and the realized gain reported in net income which increases comprehensive income again. To avoid double counting this gain, a reclassification adjustment is made to eliminate the realized gain from the computation of comprehensive income.

A company has the option to display reclassification adjustments on the face of the financial statement in which comprehensive income is reported or it may disclose these reclassification adjustments in the notes to the financial statements.

Comprehensive Illustration

To illustrate the reporting of investment securities and related gain or loss on available-for-sale securities, assume that on January 1, 2001, Hinges Co. had cash and common stock of $50,000.[13] At that date the company had no other asset, liability, or equity balance. On January 2, Hinges Co. purchased for cash $50,000 of equity securities that are classified as available-for-sale. On June 30, Hinges Co. sold part of the available-for-sale security portfolio, realizing a gain as follows:

ILLUSTRATION 18-24
Computation of Realized Gain

Fair value of securities sold	$22,000
Less: Cost of securities sold	20,000
Realized gain	$ 2,000

Hinges Co. did not purchase or sell any other securities during 2001. It received $3,000 in dividends during the year. At December 31, 2001, the remaining portfolio is:

ILLUSTRATION 18-25
Computation of Unrealized Gain

Fair value of portfolio	$34,000
Less: Cost of portfolio	30,000
Unrealized gain	$ 4,000

The company's income statement for 2001 is shown in Illustration 18-26.

[13]This example adapted from Dennis R. Beresford, L. Todd Johnson and Cheri L. Reither "Is a Second Income Statement Needed?" *Journal of Accountancy,* April 1996, p. 71.

ILLUSTRATION 18-26
Income Statement

HINGES CO. Income Statement For the Year Ended December 31, 2001	
Dividend revenue	$3,000
Realized gains on investment in securities	2,000
Net income	$5,000

The company decides to report its change in the unrealized holding gain in a statement of comprehensive income as follows:

ILLUSTRATION 18-27
Statement of Comprehensive Income

HINGES CO. Statement of Comprehensive Income For the Year Ended December 31, 2001		
Net income		$5,000
Other comprehensive income:		
Holding gains arising during the period	$6,000	
Less: Reclassification adjustment for gains included in net income	2,000	4,000
Comprehensive income		$9,000

Its statement of stockholders' equity would show the following:

ILLUSTRATION 18-28
Statement of Stockholders' Equity

HINGES CO.
Statement of Stockholders' Equity
For the Year Ended December 31, 2001

	Common Stock	Retained Earnings	Accumulated Other Comprehensive Income	Total
Beginning balance	$50,000	$-0-	$-0-	$50,000
Add: Net income		5,000		5,000
Other comprehensive income			4,000	4,000
Ending balance	$50,000	$5,000	$4,000	$59,000

A comparative balance sheet is shown below:

ILLUSTRATION 18-29
Comparative Balance Sheet

HINGES CO.
Comparative Balance Sheet

	1/1/01	12/31/01
Assets		
Cash	$50,000	$25,000
Available-for-sale securities		34,000
Total assets	$50,000	$59,000
Stockholders' equity		
Common stock	$50,000	$50,000
Retained earnings		5,000
Accumulated other comprehensive income		4,000
Total stockholders' equity	$50,000	$59,000

This example indicates how an unrealized gain or loss on available-for-sale securities affects all the financial statements. It should be noted that the components that comprise accumulated comprehensive income must be disclosed.

Companies are required to present individual amounts for the three categories of investments either on the balance sheet or in the related notes. Trading securities should be reported at aggregate fair value as current assets. Individual held-to-maturity and available-for-sale securities are classified as current or noncurrent depending upon the circumstances.

OBJECTIVE 4
Describe the disclosure requirements for investments in debt and equity securities.

Held-to-maturity securities should be classified as current or noncurrent, based on the maturity date of the individual securities. Debt securities identified as available-for-sale should be classified as current or noncurrent, based on maturities and expectations as to sales and redemptions in the following year. Equity securities identified as available-for-sale should be classified as current if these securities are available for use in current operations. Thus, if the invested cash used to purchase the equity securities is considered a contingency fund to be used whenever a need arises, then the securities should be classified as current.

For securities classified as available-for-sale and separately for securities classified as held-to-maturity, a company should describe:

(a) Aggregate fair value, gross unrealized holding gains, gross unrealized losses, and amortized cost basis by major security type (debt and equity).

(b) Information about the contractual maturities of debt securities. Maturity information may be combined in appropriate groupings such as (1) within 1 year, (2) after 1 year through 5 years, (3) after 5 years through 10 years, and (4) after 10 years.

Go to the Digital Tool for actual company disclosures related to investments and comprehensive income.

In classifying investments, management's expressed intent should be supported by evidence, such as the history of the company's investment activities, events subsequent to the balance sheet date, and the nature and purpose of the investment.

Companies have to be extremely careful with debt securities held to maturity. If a debt security in this category is sold prematurely, the sale may "taint" the entire held-to-maturity portfolio. That is, a management's statement regarding "intent" is no longer as credible and, therefore, the securities might have to be reclassified; this could lead to unfortunate consequences. An interesting by-product of this situation is that companies that wish to retire their debt securities early are finding it difficult to do so; the holder will not sell because the securities are classified as held-to-maturity.

IMPAIRMENT OF VALUE

OBJECTIVE 5
Discuss the accounting for impairments of debt and equity investments.

Every investment should be evaluated at each reporting date to determine if it has suffered a loss in value that is other than temporary (**impairment**). A bankruptcy or a significant liquidity crisis being experienced by an investee are examples of situations in which a loss in value to the investor may be permanent. **If the decline is judged to be other than temporary, the cost basis of the individual security is written down to a new cost basis.** The amount of the write-down is accounted for as a realized loss and, therefore, included in net income.

For debt securities, the impairment test is to determine whether "it is probable that the investor will be unable to collect all amounts due according to the contractual terms." **For equity securities**, the guideline is less precise. Any time realizable value is lower than the carrying amount of the investment, an impairment must be considered. Factors involved are the length of time and the extent to which the fair value has been less than cost, the financial condition and near-term prospects of the issuer, and the intent and ability of the investor company to retain its investment to allow for any anticipated recovery in fair value.

To illustrate an impairment, assume that Strickler Company holds available-for-sale bond securities with a par value and amortized cost of $1 million. The fair value of these securities is $800,000. Strickler has previously reported an unrealized loss on these securities of $200,000 as part of other comprehensive income. In evaluating the securities, Strickler now determines it probable that it will not be able to collect all amounts due. In this case, the unrealized loss of $200,000 will be reported as a loss on impairment of $200,000 and included in income, with the bonds stated at their new cost basis. The journal entry to record this impairment would be as follows:

Loss on Impairment	200,000	
Securities Fair Value Adjustment (Available-for-Sale)	200,000	
Unrealized Holding Gain or Loss—Equity		200,000
Available-for-Sale Securities		200,000

The new cost basis of the investment in debt securities is $800,000. Subsequent increases and decreases in the fair value of impaired available-for-sale securities are included as other comprehensive income.[14]

The impairment test used for debt and equity securities is based on a fair value test. This test is slightly different from the impairment test for loans discussed in Appendix 14A, which was based on discounted cash flows using the historical effective interest rate. The FASB rejected the discounted cash flow alternative for securities because of the availability of market price information.

TRANSFERS BETWEEN CATEGORIES

OBJECTIVE 6
Describe the accounting for transfer of investment securities between categories.

Transfers between any of the categories are accounted for at fair value. Thus, if available-for-sale securities are transferred to held-to-maturity investments, the new investment (held-to-maturity) is recorded at the date of transfer at **fair value** in the new category. Similarly, if held-to-maturity investments are transferred to available-for-sale investments, the new investments (available-for-sale) are recorded at **fair value**. This **fair value** rule assures that a company cannot escape recognition of fair value simply by transferring securities to the held-to-maturity category. Illustration 18-30 summarizes the accounting treatment for transfers. **This illustration assumes that adjusting entries to report changes in fair value for the current period are not yet recorded.**

FAIR VALUE CONTROVERSY

FASB Statement No. 115 leaves many issues unresolved. Many parties are dissatisfied with its results: some think it goes too far, others think it does not go far enough. In this section we look at some of the major unresolved issues.

Measurement Based on Intent

Debt securities can be classified as held-to-maturity, available-for-sale, or trading. As a result, three identical debt securities could be reported in three different ways in the financial statements. Some argue such treatment is confusing. Furthermore, the held-to-maturity category is based solely on intent, which is a subjective evaluation. What is not subjective is the market price of the debt instrument, which is observable in the marketplace. In other words, the three classifications are subjective, and therefore arbitrary classifications will result.

Gains Trading

Certain debt securities can be classified as held-to-maturity and therefore reported at amortized cost; other debt and equity securities can be classified as available-for-sale and reported at fair value with the unrealized gain or loss reported as other comprehensive income. In either case, a company can become involved in "gains trading" (also referred to as "cherry picking"). In **gains trading**, companies sell their "winners," reporting the gains in income, and hold on to the losers.

[14]Amortization of any discount related to the debt securities is not permitted after recording the impairment. The new cost basis of impaired held-to-maturity securities would not change unless additional impairment occurred.

ILLUSTRATION 18-30
Accounting for Transfers

Type of Transfer	Measurement Basis	Impact of Transfer on Stockholders' Equity	Impact of Transfer on Net Income
Transfer from Trading to Available-for-Sale	Security transferred at fair value at the date of transfer, which is the new cost basis of the security.	The unrealized gain or loss at the date of transfer increases or decreases stockholders' equity.	The unrealized gain or loss at the date of transfer is recognized in income.
Transfer from Available-for-Sale to Trading	Security transferred at fair value at the date of transfer, which is the new cost basis of the security.	The unrealized gain or loss at the date of transfer increases or decreases stockholders' equity.	The unrealized gain or loss at the date of transfer is recognized in income.
Transfer from Held-to-Maturity to Available-for-Sale*	Security transferred at fair value at the date of transfer.	The separate component of stockholders' equity is increased or decreased by the unrealized gain or loss at the date of transfer.	None
Transfer from Available-for-Sale to Held-to-Maturity	Security transferred at fair value at the date of transfer.	The unrealized gain or loss at the date of transfer carried as a separate component of stockholders' equity is amortized over the remaining life of the security.	None

**Statement No. 115* states that these types of transfers should be rare.

Go to the Digital Tool for examples of the entries for recording transfers between categories.

Liabilities Not Fairly Valued

Many argue that if investment securities are going to be reported at fair value, so also should liabilities. They note that by recognizing changes in value on only one side (the asset side), a high degree of volatility can occur in the income and stockholders' equity amounts. It is further argued that financial institutions are involved in asset and liability management (not just asset management) and that viewing only one side may lead managers to make uneconomic decisions as a result of the accounting. Although the Board was sympathetic with this view, it noted that certain debt securities were still reported at amortized cost and that other types of securities were excluded from the scope of this standard. In addition, serious valuation issues arose in relation to some types of liabilities. As a result, liabilities were excluded from consideration.[15]

Subjectivity of Fair Values

Some people question the relevance of fair value measures for investments in securities, arguing in favor of reporting based on amortized cost. They believe that amortized cost provides relevant information because it focuses on the decision to acquire the asset, the earning effects of that decision that will be realized over time, and the ultimate recoverable value of the asset. They argue that fair value ignores those concepts and focuses instead on the effects of transactions and events that do not involve the

---

[15]In a recent preliminary report concerning valuation of financial instruments, the FASB indicated its support for valuing liabilities at fair value. "Reporting Financial Instruments and Certain Related Assets and Liabilities at Fair Value," *FASB Preliminary Views* (Norwalk, Conn.: FASB, 1999).

enterprise, reflecting opportunity gains and losses whose recognition in the financial statement is, in their view, not appropriate until they are realized.

SUMMARY

The major debt and equity securities and their reporting treatment are summarized below.

ILLUSTRATION 18-31
Summary of Treatment of Major Debt and Equity Securities

Category	Balance Sheet	Income Statement
Trading (debt and equity securities)	Investments shown at fair value. Current assets.	Interest and dividends are recognized as revenue. Unrealized holding gains and losses are included in net income.
Available-for-sale (debt and equity securities)	Investments shown at fair value. Current or long-term assets. Unrealized holding gains and losses are a separate component of stockholders' equity.	Interest and dividends are recognized as revenue. Unrealized holding gains and losses are **not** included in net income but in other comprehensive income.
Held-to-maturity (debt securities)	Investments shown at amortized cost. Current or long-term assets.	Interest is recognized as revenue.
Equity method and/or consolidation (equity securities)	Investments originally are carried at cost, are periodically adjusted by the investor's share of the investee's earnings or losses, and are decreased by all dividends received from the investee. Classified long term.	Revenue is recognized to the extent of the investee's earnings or losses reported subsequent to the date of investment (adjusted by amortization of the difference between cost and underlying book value).

KEY TERMS

amortized cost, *919*
available-for-sale securities, *922*
consolidated financial statements, *935*
controlling interest, *935*
debt securities, *919*
effective interest method, *921*
equity method, *931*
equity securities, *927*
exchange for noncash consideration, *928*
fair value, *919*
fair value method, *928*
gains trading, *941*
held-to-maturity securities, *920*
holding gain or loss, *926*
impairment, *939*
incremental method, *928*
investee, *927*
investor, *927*
parent, *935*
reclassification adjustments, *936*
relative fair values, *928*
Securities Fair Value Adjustment account, *923*
security, *918*
significant influence, *931*
subsidiary, *935*
trading securities, *926*

SUMMARY OF LEARNING OBJECTIVES

1 Identify the three categories of debt securities and describe the accounting and reporting treatment for each category. (1) *Held-to-maturity debt securities* are carried and reported at amortized cost. (2) *Trading debt securities* are valued for reporting purposes at fair value, with unrealized holding gains or losses included in net income. (3) *Available-for-sale debt securities* are valued for reporting purposes at fair value, with unrealized holding gains or losses reported as other comprehensive income and as a separate component of stockholders' equity.

2 Identify the categories of equity securities and describe the accounting and reporting treatment for each category. The degree to which one corporation (investor) acquires an interest in the common stock of another corporation (investee) generally determines the accounting treatment for the investment. Long-term investments by one corporation in the common stock of another can be classified according to the percentage of the voting stock of the investee held by the investor.

3 Explain the equity method of accounting and compare it to the fair value method for equity securities. Under the equity method a substantive economic relationship is acknowledged between the investor and the investee. The investment is originally recorded at cost but is subsequently adjusted each period for changes in the net assets of the investee. That is, the investment's carrying amount is periodically increased (decreased) by the investor's proportionate share of the earnings (losses) of the investee and decreased by all dividends received by the investor from the investee. Under the fair value method the equity investment is reported by the investor at fair value each reporting period irrespective of the investee's earnings or dividends paid to the investor. The equity method is applied to investment holdings between 20% and 50% of ownership, whereas the fair value method is applied to holdings below 20%.

4 **Describe the disclosure requirements for investments in debt and equity securities.** A reclassification adjustment is necessary when realized gains or losses are reported as part of net income but also are shown as part of other comprehensive income in the current or in previous periods. Unrealized holding gains or losses related to available-for-sale securities should be reported in other comprehensive income and the aggregate balance as accumulated comprehensive income on the balance sheet. Trading securities should be reported at aggregate fair value as current assets. Individual held-to-maturity and available-for-sale securities are classified as current or noncurrent depending upon the circumstances. For available-for-sale and held-to-maturity securities, a company should describe: aggregate fair value, gross unrealized holding gains, gross unrealized losses, amortized cost basis by type (debt and equity), and information about the contractual maturity of debt securities.

5 **Discuss the accounting for impairments of debt and equity investments.** Impairments of debt and equity securities are losses in value that are determined to be other than temporary, are based on a fair value test, and are charged to income.

6 **Describe the accounting for transfer of investment securities between categories.** Transfers of securities between categories of investments are accounted for at fair value, with unrealized holding gains or losses treated in accordance with the nature of the transfer.

APPENDIX 18A

Special Issues Related to Investments

Special issues relate to accounting for investments: (1) revenue from investments in equity securities; (2) dividends received in stock; (3) stock rights; (4) cash surrender value of life insurance; and (5) accounting for funds.

OBJECTIVE 7
After studying Appendix 18A, you should be able to: Discuss the special issues that relate to accounting for investments.

REVENUE FROM INVESTMENTS IN EQUITY SECURITIES

Revenue recognized from investments—whether under the equity or the fair value method—should be included in the income statement of the investor. Under the fair value method, the dividends received (or receivable if declared but unpaid) are reported as dividend revenue.

The gains or losses on sales of investments also are factors in determining the net income for the period. The gain or loss resulting from the sale of long-term investments, unless it is the result of a major casualty, an expropriation, or the introduction of a new law prohibiting its ownership (which may be viewed as unusual and nonrecurring), is reported as **part of current income from operations** and is not an extraordinary item.

Dividends that are paid in some form of assets other than cash are called **property dividends**. In such instances, the fair market value of the property received becomes the basis for debiting an appropriate asset account and crediting Dividend Revenue.

Occasionally an investor receives a dividend that is in part, or entirely, a **liquidating dividend.**[1] The investor should reduce the investment account for the amount of the liquidating portion of the dividend and credit Dividend Revenue for the balance. To illustrate, assume that Donley Inc. purchases a 1% investment in Rodriguez Co. for $60,000 on December 31, 2001. In 2002, Rodriguez has no income but declares and pays a dividend of $3,000 to Donley. The entry by Donley to record this transaction is as follows:

Cash	3,000	
Available-for-Sale Securities		3,000

DIVIDENDS RECEIVED IN STOCK

If the investee corporation declares a dividend distributable in its own stock of the same class, instead of in cash, each stockholder owns a larger number of shares but retains the same proportionate interest in the firm as before. The issuing corporation has distributed no assets; it has merely transferred a specified amount of retained earnings to paid-in capital, thus indicating that this amount will not provide a basis in the future for cash dividends.

Therefore, shares received as a result of a stock dividend or stock split do not constitute revenue to the recipients. The reason they do not is that the recipients' interest in the issuing corporation is unchanged and the issuing corporation has not distributed any of its assets. The **recipient of such additional shares would make no formal entry**, but should make a memorandum entry and record a notation in the investments account to show that additional shares have been received.

Although no dollar amount is entered at the time of the receipt of stock dividends, the fact that additional shares have been received must be considered in computing the carrying amount of any shares sold. The cost of the original shares purchased (plus the effect of any adjustments under the equity method) now constitutes the total carrying amount of both those shares plus the additional shares received, because no price was paid for the additional shares. The carrying amount per share is computed by dividing the total shares into the carrying amount of the original shares purchased.

To illustrate, assume that 100 shares of Flemal Company common stock are purchased for $9,600, and that 2 years later the company issues to stockholders one additional share for every two shares held; 150 shares of stock that cost a total of $9,600 are then held. Therefore, if 60 shares are sold for $4,300, the carrying amount of the 60 shares would be computed as shown below, assuming that the investment has been accounted for under the fair value method.

ILLUSTRATION 18A-1
Computation of the Carrying Amount of Shares Received in a Stock Dividend

Cost of 100 shares originally purchased	$9,600
Cost of 50 shares received as stock dividend	0
Carrying amount of 150 shares held	$9,600

Carrying amount per share is $9,600/150, or $64.
Carrying amount of 60 shares sold is 60 × $64, or $3,840.

[1]A company can receive a dividend from preacquisition retained earnings of the investee, which the investor should treat as a liquidating dividend. From the investee's point of view, however, it is not a liquidating dividend.

The entry to record the sale is:

Cash	4,300	
Available-for-Sale Securities		3,840
Gain on Sale of Stock		460

A total of 90 shares is still retained, and they are carried in the Available-for-Sale Securities account at $9,600 − $3,840, or $5,760. Thus the carrying amount for those shares remaining is also $64 per share, or a total of $5,760 for the 90 shares.

STOCK RIGHTS

When a corporation is about to offer for sale additional shares of an issue already outstanding, it may forward to present holders of that issue certificates permitting them to purchase **additional shares in proportion to their present holdings**. These certificates represent rights to purchase additional shares and are called **stock rights**. In rights offerings, rights generally are issued on the basis of one right per share, but it may take many rights to purchase one new share.

The certificate representing the stock rights, called a **warrant**, states the number of shares that the holder of the right may purchase and also the price at which they may be purchased. If this price is less than the current market value of such shares, the rights have an intrinsic value, and from the time they are issued until they expire they may be purchased and sold like any other security.

Stock rights have three important dates:

1. The date the rights offering is announced.
2. The date as of which the certificates or rights are issued.
3. The date the rights expire.

From the date the right is announced until it is issued, the share of stock and the right are not separable, and the share is described as **rights-on**. After the certificate or right is received and up to the time it expires, the share and right can be sold separately. A share sold separately from an effective stock right is sold **ex-rights**.

When a right is received, the stockholders have actually received nothing that they did not have before, because the shares already owned brought them the right; they have received no distribution of the corporation assets. The carrying amount of the original shares held is now the carrying amount of those shares plus the rights, and it should be allocated between the two on the basis of their total market values at the time the rights are received. If the value allocated to the rights is maintained in a separate account, an entry would be made debiting Available-for-Sale Securities (Stock Rights) and crediting Available-for-Sale Securities.

Disposition of Rights

The investor who receives rights to purchase additional shares has three alternatives:

1. To exercise the rights by purchasing additional stock.
2. To sell the rights.
3. To permit them to expire without selling or using them.

If the investor buys additional stock, the carrying amount of the original shares allocated to the rights becomes a part of the carrying amount of the new shares purchased. If the investor sells the rights, the allocated carrying amount compared with the selling price determines the gain or loss on sale. If the investor permits the rights to expire, a loss is suffered, and the investment should be reduced accordingly. The following example illustrates the problem involved.

ILLUSTRATION 18A-2
Cost Allocations to Stock and to Rights

Shares owned before issuance of rights—100.
Cost of shares owned—$50 a share for a total cost of $5,000.
Rights received—one right for every share owned, or 100 rights; two rights are required to purchase one new share at $50.
Market value at date rights issued: Shares $60 a share
Rights $3 a right

Total market value of shares (100 × $60)	$6,000
Total market value of rights (100 × $3)	300
Combined market value	$6,300

Cost allocated to stock: $\frac{\$6{,}000}{\$6{,}300} \times \$5{,}000 = \$4{,}761.90$

Cost allocated to rights: $\frac{\$300}{\$6{,}300} \times \$5{,}000 = \quad 238.10$

$\$5{,}000.00$

Cost allocated to each share of stock: $\frac{\$4{,}761.90}{100} = \$47.619$

Cost allocated to each right: $\frac{\$238.10}{100} = \$2.381$

The reduction in the carrying amount of the stock from $5,000 to $4,761.90 and the acquisition of the rights with an allocated cost of $238.10 would be recorded as follows:

Available-for-Sale Securities (Stock Rights)	238.10	
Available-for-Sale Securities		238.10

If some of the original shares are later sold, their cost for purposes of determining gain or loss on sale is $47.619 per share, as computed above. If 10 of the original shares are sold at $58 per share, the entry would be:

Cash	580.00	
Available-for-Sale Securities		476.19
Gain on Sale of Stock		103.81

Entries for Stock Rights

Rights may be sold or used to purchase additional stock or permitted to expire. If 40 rights to purchase 20 shares of stock are sold at $3.00 each, the entry is:

Cash	120.00	
Available-for-Sale Securities (Stock Rights)		95.24
Gain on Sale of Stock Rights		24.76

The amount removed from the stock rights account is the amount allocated to 40 rights, 40 × $2.381.

If rights to purchase 20 shares of stock are exercised and 20 additional shares are purchased at the offer price of $50, the entry is:

Available-for-Sale Securities	1,095.24	
Cash		1,000.00
Available-for-Sale Securities (Stock Rights)		95.24

If these shares are sold in the future, their cost should be considered to be $1,095.24, or $54.762 per share—the price paid of $50 per share plus the amount allocated to two rights of $4.762.

If the remaining 20 rights are permitted to expire, the amount allocated to these rights should be removed from the general ledger account by this entry:

Loss on Expiration of Stock Rights	47.62	
Available-for-Sale Securities (Stock Rights)		47.62

The balances of the general ledger investment accounts are shown in Illustration 18A-3.

ILLUSTRATION 18A-3
Balances of General Ledger Investment Accounts

Available-for-Sale Securities (Stock)

Purchase of original 100 shares @ $50 per share	5,000.00	Cost allocated to 100 rights received	238.10
Purchase of 20 shares by exercise of rights	1,095.24	Sale of 10 shares of original purchase	476.19
		Balance	5,380.95
	6,095.24		6,095.24
Balance	5,380.95*		

*Analysis of Balance:

90 shares of original purchase, at allocated cost of $47.619 per share	$4,285.71
20 shares purchased through exercise of rights, carried at $54.762 per share (cash paid of $50.00, plus $4.762 for allocated cost of two rights)	1,095.24
Balance of account, as above	$5,380.95

Available-for-Sale Securities (Stock Rights)

Cost allocated to 100 rights received	283.10	Sale of 40 rights	95.24
		Exercise of 40 rights	95.24
		Expiration of 20 rights	47.62
	238.10		238.10
Balance	–0–		

CASH SURRENDER VALUE OF LIFE INSURANCE

There are many different kinds of insurance. The kinds usually carried by businesses include (1) casualty insurance, (2) liability insurance, and (3) life insurance. Certain types of **life insurance** constitute an investment, whereas casualty insurance and liability insurance do not. The three common types of life insurance policies that companies often carry on the lives of their principal officers are (a) **ordinary life**, (b) **limited payment**, and (c) **term insurance**. During the period that ordinary life and limited payment policies are in force, there is a cash surrender value and a loan value. Term insurance ordinarily has no cash surrender value or loan value.

If the insured officers or their heirs are the beneficiaries of the policy, the premiums paid by the company represent expense to the company and, for income tax purposes, income (excluding the first $50,000 of coverage) to the officer insured. In this case the cash surrender value of the policy does not represent an asset to the company.

If the company, however, is the beneficiary and has the right to cancel the policy at its own option, the cash surrender value of the policy or policies is an asset of the company. Accordingly, part of the premiums paid is not an expense, because the cash surrender value increases each year. Only the difference between the premium paid and the increase in cash surrender value represents expense to the company.

For example, if Zima Corporation pays an insurance premium of $2,300 on a $100,000 policy covering its president and, as a result, the cash surrender value of the policy increases from $15,000 to $16,400 during the period, the entry to record the premium payment is:

Life Insurance Expense	900	
Cash Surrender Value of Life Insurance	1,400	
Cash		2,300

If the insured officer were to die halfway through the most recent period of coverage for which the $2,300 premium payment was made, the following entry would be made (assuming cash surrender value of $15,700 and refund of a pro rata share of the premium paid):

Cash [$100,000 + (1/2 of $2,300)]	101,150	
Cash Surrender Value of Life Insurance		16,400
Life Insurance Expense (1/2 × $900)		450
Gain on Life Insurance Coverage ($100,000 − $15,700)		84,300

The gain on life insurance coverage is not generally reported as an extraordinary item because it is considered to be a "normal" business transaction.

The cash surrender value of such life insurance policies should be reported in the balance sheet as a **long-term investment**, inasmuch as it is unlikely that the policies will be surrendered and canceled in the immediate future. The premium is not deductible for tax purposes, however, and the proceeds of such policies are not taxable as income.

To illustrate such a disclosure, Alico Inc. reported information related to its cash surrender value as follows:

ILLUSTRATION 18A-4
Disclosure of Cash Surrender Value

ALICO INC.

Other investments (Note 4)

Cash surrender value of life insurance	$448,000

Note 4. The company purchased as owner and beneficiary, individual life insurance policies on the lives of certain officers and employees as a means of funding substantially all of such additional benefits. The company's accounting policy with respect to such insurance coverage is to charge operations with the annual premium cost, net of increase in cash surrender value.

FUNDS

Assets may be set aside in special funds for specific purposes and, therefore, become unavailable for ordinary operations of the business. Assets segregated in the special funds are then available when needed for the intended purposes.

There are two general types of funds: (1) those in which cash is set aside to meet specific current obligations, and (2) those that are not directly related to current operations and are therefore in the nature of long-term investments.

Several funds of the first type, discussed in preceding chapters, include the following:

Fund	Purpose
Petty Cash Fund	Payment of small expenditures, in currency
Payroll Cash Account	Payment of salaries and wages
Dividend Cash Account	Payment of dividends
Interest Fund	Payment of interest on long-term debt

In general, these funds are used to handle more expeditiously the payments of certain current obligations, to maintain better control over such expenditures, and to divide adequately the responsibility for cash disbursements. They are ordinarily shown as current assets (as part of Cash if immaterial), because the obligations to which they relate are ordinarily current liabilities.

Funds of the second type are similar to long-term investments, as they do not relate directly to current operations. They are ordinarily shown in the long-term investments section of the balance sheet or in a separate section if relatively large in amount. The more common funds of this type and the purpose of each are listed below:

Fund	Purpose
Sinking Fund	Payment of long-term debt
Plant Expansion Fund	Purchase or construction of additional plant
Stock Redemption Fund	Retirement of capital stock (usually preferred stock)
Contingency Fund	Payment of unforeseen obligations

Because the cash set aside will not be needed until some time in the future, it is usually invested in securities so that revenue may be earned on the fund assets. The assets of a fund may or may not be placed in the hands of a trustee. If appointed, the trustee becomes the custodian of the assets, accounts to the company for them, and reports fund revenues and expenses.

Entries for Funds

To keep track of the assets, revenues, and expenses of funds, it is desirable to maintain separate accounts. For example, if a fund is kept for the redemption of a preferred stock issue that was issued with a redemption provision at par after a certain date, the following accounts relating to that fund might be kept:

Stock Redemption Fund Cash
Stock Redemption Fund Investments
Stock Redemption Fund Revenue
Stock Redemption Fund Expenses
Gain on Sale of Stock Redemption Fund Investments
Loss on Sale of Stock Redemption Fund Investments

When cash is transferred from the regular cash account, perhaps periodically, the entry is:

Stock Redemption Fund Cash	30,000	
Cash		30,000

Securities purchased by the fund are recorded at cost:

Stock Redemption Fund Investments	27,000	
Stock Redemption Fund Cash		27,000

If securities purchased for the fund are to be held temporarily, they would be treated in the accounts in the same manner as short-term investments, described earlier in this chapter. If they are to be held for a long period of time, they are treated in accordance with the entries described for long-term investments. In both cases the securities purchased are recorded at cost when acquired, but if bonds are purchased as long-term investments for the fund, premium or discount should be amortized.

If we assume that the entry above records the purchase at a premium of 10-year bonds of a par value of $25,000 on April 1, the issue date, and that the bonds bear interest at 8%, the entry for the receipt of semiannual interest on October 1 is:

Stock Redemption Fund Cash	1,000	
Stock Redemption Fund Revenue		1,000

At December 31, entries are made to record amortization of premium for 9 months and to accrue interest on the bonds for 3 months:

Stock Redemption Fund Revenue	150	
Stock Redemption Fund Investments		150
(To record amortization of premium for 9 months, 9/12 of 1/10 of $2,000)		
Interest Receivable on Stock Redemption Fund Investments	500	
Stock Redemption Fund Revenue		500
(To record accrued interest for 3 months, 3/12 of 8% of $25,000)		

Expenses of the fund paid are recorded by debiting Stock Redemption Fund Expenses and crediting Stock Redemption Fund Cash.

When the investments held by the fund are disposed of, the entries to record the sale are similar to regular stock sales. Any revenue and expense accounts set up to record fund transactions should be closed to Income Summary at the end of the accounting period and reflected in earnings of the current period.

The entry for retirement of the preferred stock is:

Preferred Stock	500,000	
Stock Redemption Fund Cash		500,000

Any balance remaining in the Stock Redemption Fund Cash account is transferred back to a general cash account.

In some cases, a company purchases its own stock or bonds when it is using a stock redemption fund or sinking fund. In these situations, the treasury stock should be deducted from common stock (or the Stockholders' Equity section), and treasury bonds should be deducted from bonds payable. Dividend revenue or interest revenue should not be recorded for these securities.

Distinction between Funds and Reserves

Although funds and reserves (appropriations) are not similar, they are sometimes confused because they may be related and often have similar titles. A simple distinction may be drawn: **A fund is always an asset and always has a debit balance; a reserve (if used only in the limited sense recommended) is an appropriation of retained earnings, always has a credit balance, and is never an asset.**

This distinction is illustrated by reconsidering the entries made in connection with a stock redemption fund discussed earlier. The fund was originally established by the entry:

Stock Redemption Fund Cash	30,000	
Cash		30,000

Some of this cash was used to purchase investments; the assets of the fund were then cash and investments. Ultimately the investments were sold, and the stock redemption fund cash was used to retire the preferred stock.

If the company chose to do so, it could establish an appropriation for stock redemption at the same time to reduce the retained earnings apparently available for dividends. Appropriated retained earnings is established by periodic transfers from retained earnings, as follows:

Retained Earnings	30,000	
Appropriation for Stock Redemption		30,000

It will have a credit balance and will be shown in the stockholders' equity section of the balance sheet. When the stock is retired by payment of cash from the stock redemption fund, the appropriation is transferred back to retained earnings:

Appropriation for Stock Redemption	500,000	
Retained Earnings		500,000

The fund was an asset accumulated to retire stock and had a debit balance; the appropriation was a subdivision of retained earnings and had a credit balance. The fund was used to redeem the stock; the appropriation was transferred back to retained earnings.

SUMMARY OF LEARNING OBJECTIVE FOR APPENDIX 18A

7 **Discuss the special issues that relate to accounting for investments.** The special issues that relate to investments are: recognizing revenue from investments in equity securities; recognizing dividends received in shares of stock (stock dividends and stock splits); allocating cost between stocks and stock rights; accounting for changes in the cash surrender value of life insurance; and accounting for assets set aside in special funds.

APPENDIX 18B

Accounting for Derivative Instruments

It has been said that until the early 1970s most financial managers worked in a cozy, if unthrilling world. Since then, however, constant change caused by volatile markets, new technology, and deregulation has increased the risks to businesses. For example, in 1971 currencies were allowed to float freely. After that came oil price shocks, high inflation, and wide swings in interest rates. The response from the financial community was to develop products to manage the risks due to changes in market prices.

These products—often referred to as derivatives—are useful for risk management because the fair values or cash flows of these instruments can be used to offset the changes in fair values or cash flows of the assets that are at risk. The growth in use of derivatives has been aided by the development of powerful computing and communication technology, which provides new ways to analyze information about markets as well as the power to process high volumes of payments.

UNDERSTANDING DERIVATIVES

In order to understand derivatives, consider the following examples.

Illustration—Forward Contract

Let's assume that you believe that the price of Microsoft's stock will increase substantially in the next three months. Unfortunately, you do not have the cash resources to purchase the stock today. You therefore enter into a contract with your broker for delivery of 100 shares of Microsoft stock in three months at the price of $110 per share. As a result of the contract, you **have received the right** to receive 100 shares of Microsoft stock in three months and you **have an obligation** to pay $110 per share at that time. In this situation you have entered into a **forward contract**, a type of derivative. The benefit of this derivative contract to you is that you are able to buy Microsoft stock today and take delivery in three months. If the price goes up, as you expect, you win. If the price goes down, you lose.

Illustration—Option Contract

Let's suppose that instead of entering into the forward contract for delivery of the stock in three months, you tell your broker that you are undecided about whether to purchase Microsoft stock and need two weeks to decide. You enter into a different type of contract with your broker, one that gives you the right to purchase Microsoft stock at its current price any time within the next two weeks. As part of the contract the broker charges you $300 for holding the contract open for two weeks at a set price. In this situation, you have entered into an **option contract**, another type of derivative. As a result of this contract, **you have received the right, but not the obligation** to purchase this stock. The benefit of this contract to you is that if the price of the Microsoft stock increases in the next two weeks, you exercise your option. In this case, the cost of the stock to you is the price of the stock stated in the contract plus the cost of the option contract. If the price does not increase, you do not exercise the contract but you incur a cost for the option.

For both the forward contract and the option contract, the delivery of the stock was for a future date and the value of the contract was based on the underlying asset—the Microsoft stock. These financial instruments are referred to as **derivatives** because their value is *derived from* values of other assets (for example, stocks, bonds, or commodities) or is related to a market-determined indicator (for example, interest rates or the Standard and Poor's 500 stock composite index).

In this chapter, we will discuss the accounting for three different types of derivatives:

1. Financial forwards or financial futures.
2. Options.
3. Swaps.

WHO USES DERIVATIVES?

OBJECTIVE 8
After studying Appendix 18B, you should be able to: Explain who uses derivatives and why they are used.

Whether it is protection for changes in interest rates, the weather, stock prices, oil prices, or foreign currencies, derivative contracts can be used to smooth the fluctuations caused by various types of risks. In other words, any individual or company that wants to ensure against different types of business risks often can use derivative contracts to achieve this objective.

Producers and Consumers

To illustrate who might use derivatives, assume that Heartland Ag is a large producer of potatoes for the consumer market. Heartland believes the present price for potatoes is excellent, but unfortunately it will take two months to harvest its potatoes and deliver them to the market. Because Heartland Ag is concerned that the price of potatoes will drop, it signs a contract in which it agrees to sell its potatoes today at the current market price for delivery in two months.

Who would buy this contract? Suppose on the other side of the contract is McDonald's Corporation who wants to have potatoes (for French fries) in two months and is worried that prices will increase. McDonald's is therefore agreeable to delivery in two months at current prices because it knows that it will need potatoes in two months and that it can make an acceptable profit at this price level.

In this situation, if the price of potatoes increases before delivery, you might conclude that Heartland loses and McDonald's wins. Conversely, if prices decrease, Heartland wins and McDonald's loses. However the objective is not to gamble on the outcome. In other words, regardless of which way the price moves, both Heartland and McDonald's should be pleased because both have received a price at which an acceptable profit is obtained. In this case, Heartland is a **producer** and McDonald's is a **consumer**. Both companies are often referred to as **hedgers** because they are hedging their positions to ensure an acceptable financial result.

Commodity prices are volatile and depend on weather, crop disasters, and general economic conditions. For the producer and the consumer to plan effectively, it makes good sense to lock in specific future revenues or costs in order to run their businesses successfully.

Speculators and Arbitrageurs

In some cases, instead of McDonald's taking a position in the forward contract, a speculator may purchase the contract from Heartland. The **speculator** is betting that the price of potatoes will increase and therefore the value of the forward contract will increase. The speculator, who may be in the market for only a few hours, will then sell the forward contract to another speculator or to a company like McDonald's.

Another user of derivatives is **arbitrageurs**. These market players attempt to exploit inefficiencies in various derivative markets. They seek to lock in profits by simultaneously entering into transactions in two or more markets. For example, an arbitrageur might trade in a futures contract and at the same time in the commodity underlying the futures contract, hoping to achieve small price gains on the difference between the two. Speculators and arbitrageurs are very important to markets because they keep the market liquid on a daily basis.

WHY USE DERIVATIVES?

In the previous illustrations, we explained why Heartland Ag (the producer) and McDonald's (the consumer) would become involved in a derivative contract. Consider other types of situations that companies face.

1. Airlines, like **Delta**, **Southwest**, and **United**, are affected by changes in the price of jet fuel.
2. Financial institutions, such as **Citigroup**, **Bankers Trust**, and **M&I Bank**, are involved in borrowing and lending funds which are affected by changes in interest rates.
3. Multinational corporations, like **Cisco Systems**, **Coca-Cola**, and **General Electric**, are subject to changes in foreign exchange rates.

It is not surprising therefore that you find most corporations involved in some form of derivatives transactions. Here are some reasons given by companies in their annual reports as to why they use derivatives:

1. **Exxon Mobil** uses derivative instruments primarily for purposes of hedging its exposure to fluctuations in interest rates, foreign currency exchange rates, and hydrocarbon prices.
2. **Caterpillar**'s risk management policy includes the use of derivative financial instruments to manage foreign currency exchange rates, interest rates, and commodity price exposure.
3. **Johnson & Johnson** uses derivative financial instruments to manage the impact of interest rate and foreign exchange rate changes on earnings and cash flows.

Many corporations therefore use derivatives extensively and successfully. However, derivatives can be dangerous, and it is critical that all parties involved understand the risks and rewards associated with these contracts.[1]

BASIC PRINCIPLES IN ACCOUNTING FOR DERIVATIVES

OBJECTIVE 9
Understand the basic guidelines for accounting for derivatives.

In *SFAS No. 133*, the FASB concluded that derivatives such as forwards and options are assets and liabilities and should be reported in the balance sheet at **fair value**.[2] The Board believes that fair value will provide statement users the best information

[1]There are some well-publicized examples of companies that have suffered considerable losses using derivatives. For example, companies such as **Showa Shell Sekiyu** (Japan), **Metallgesellschaft** (Germany), **Procter & Gamble** (U.S.), and **Air Products & Chemicals** (U.S.) have incurred significant losses from investments in derivative instruments.

[2]Accounting for Derivative Instruments and Hedging Activities," *Statement of Financial Accounting Standards No. 133* (Stamford, Conn.: FASB, 1998). All derivative instruments, whether financial or not, are covered under this standard. Our discussion in this chapter focuses on derivative financial instruments because of their widespread use in practice.

about derivative financial instruments.[3] Relying on some other basis of valuation for derivatives, such as historical cost, does not make sense because many derivatives have a historical cost of zero. Furthermore, given the well-developed markets for derivatives and for the assets from which derivatives derive their value, the Board believed that reliable fair value amounts could be determined for derivative instruments.

On the income statement, any unrealized gain or loss should be recognized in income if the derivative is used for speculation purposes. If the derivative is used for hedging purposes, the accounting for any gain or loss depends on the type of hedge used. The accounting for hedged transactions is discussed later in the appendix.

In summary, the following guidelines are used in accounting for derivatives.

1. Derivatives should be recognized in the financial statements as assets and liabilities.
2. Derivatives should be reported at fair value.
3. Gains and losses resulting from speculation in derivatives should be recognized immediately in income.
4. Gains and losses resulting from hedge transactions are reported in different ways, depending upon the type of hedge.

ILLUSTRATION OF DERIVATIVE FINANCIAL INSTRUMENT—SPECULATION

OBJECTIVE 10
Describe the accounting for derivative financial instruments.

To illustrate the measurement and reporting of a derivative financial instrument for speculative purposes, we examine a derivative whose value is related to the market price of Laredo Inc. common stock. As in the previous Microsoft example, you could realize a gain from the increase in the value of the Laredo shares with the use of a derivative financial instrument, such as a call option.[4] A **call option** gives the holder the right, but not the obligation to buy shares at a preset price (often referred to as the **strike price** or the **exercise price**).

For example, assume you enter into a call option contract with Baird Investment Co., which gives you the option to purchase Laredo stock at $100 per share.[5] If the price of Laredo stock increases above $100, you can exercise this option and purchase the shares for $100 per share. If Laredo's stock never increases above $100 per share, the call option is worthless and you recognize a loss.

Accounting Entries

To illustrate the accounting for a call option, assume that you purchased a call option contract on January 2, 2000, when Laredo shares are trading at $100 per share. The terms of the contract give you the option to purchase 1,000 shares (referred to as the

---

[3]*Fair value* is defined as the amount at which an asset (or liability) could be bought (incurred) or sold (settled) between two willing parties (i.e., not forced or in liquidation). Quoted market prices in active markets are the best evidence of fair value and should be used if available. In the absence of market prices, the prices of similar assets or liabilities or accepted present value techniques can be used. "Disclosures About Fair Value of Financial Instruments," *Statement of Financial Accounting Standards No. 107* (Stamford, Conn.: FASB, 1991) paras. 5–6, 11. The Board's long-term objective is to require fair value measurement and recognition for all financial instruments (*SFAS No. 133,* para. 216).

[4]You could use a different type of option contract—a **put option**—to realize a gain if you speculate that the Laredo stock will decline in value. A put option gives the holder the option to sell shares at a preset price. Thus, a put option **increases** in value when the underlying asset **decreases** in value.

[5]Baird Investment Company is referred to as the **counterparty**. Counterparties frequently are investment bankers or other entities that hold inventories of financial instruments.

notional amount) of Laredo stock at an option price of $100 per share; the option expires on April 30, 2000. You purchase the call option for $400 and make the following entry:

January 2, 2000

Call Option	400	
Cash		400

This payment (referred to as the **option premium**) is generally much less than the cost of purchasing the shares directly. The option premium is comprised of two amounts: (1) intrinsic value and (2) time value. The formula to compute the option premium is as follows:

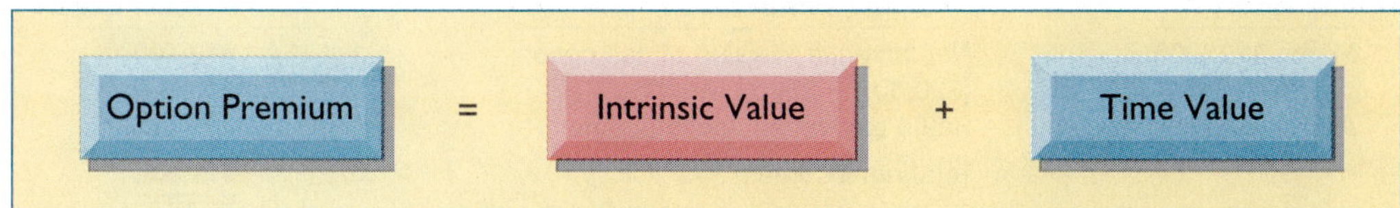

ILLUSTRATION 18B-1
Option Price Formula

Intrinsic value is the difference between the market price and the preset strike price at any point in time. It represents the amount realized by the option holder if the option were exercised immediately. On January 2, 2000, the intrinsic value is zero because the market price is equal to the preset strike price.

Time value refers to the option's value over and above its intrinsic value. Time value reflects the possibility that the option has a fair value greater than zero because there is some expectation that the price of Laredo shares will increase above the strike price during the option term. As indicated, the time value for the option is $400.[6]

On March 31, 2000, the price of Laredo shares has increased to $120 per share and the intrinsic value of the call option contract is now $20,000. That is, you could exercise the call option and purchase 1,000 shares from Baird Co. for $100 per share and then sell the shares in the market for $120 per share. This gives you a gain of $20,000 ($120,000 − $100,000) on the option contract.[7] The entry to record the increase in the intrinsic value of the option is as follows:

March 31, 2000

Call Option	20,000	
Unrealized Holding Gain or Loss—Income		20,000

A market appraisal indicates that the time value of the option at March 31, 2000, is $100.[8] The entry to record this change in value of the option is as follows:

March 31, 2000

Unrealized Holding Gain or Loss—Income	300	
Call Option ($400 − $100)		300

At March 31, 2000, the call option is reported in your balance sheet at fair value of $20,100.[9] The unrealized holding gain increases net income for the period, while the loss on the time value of the option decreases net income.

[6]This cost is estimated using option-pricing models, such as the Black-Scholes model. The fair value estimate is affected by the volatility of the underlying stock, the expected life of the option, the risk-free rate of interest, and expected dividends on the underlying stock during the option term.

[7]In practice, you generally do not have to actually buy and sell the Laredo shares to settle the option and realize the gain. This is referred to as the **net settlement** feature of option contracts.

[8]The decline in value reflects both the decreased likelihood that the Laredo shares will continue to increase in value over the option period and the shorter time to maturity of the option contract.

[9]As indicated earlier, the total value of the option at any point in time is equal to the intrinsic value plus the time value.

On April 1, 2000, the entry to record the settlement of the call option contract with Baird Investment Co. is as follows:

April 1, 2000		
Cash	20,000	
Loss on Settlement of Call Option	100	
Call Option		20,100

Illustration 18B-2 summarizes the effects of the call option contract on your net income.

ILLUSTRATION 18B-2
Effect on Income—Derivative Financial Instrument

Date	Transaction	Income (Loss) Effect
March 31, 2000	Net increase in value of call option ($20,000 – $300)	$19,700
April 1, 2000	Settle call option	(100)
	Total net income	$19,600

The accounting summarized in Illustration 18B-2 is in accord with *SFAS No. 133.* That is, because the call option meets the definition of an asset, it is recorded in the balance sheet on March 31, 2000. Furthermore, the call option is reported at fair value with any gains or losses reported in income.

Differences between Traditional and Derivative Financial Instruments

What is the difference between a traditional and derivative financial instrument? A derivative financial instrument has three basic characteristics:[10]

1. **The instrument has (1) one or more underlyings and (2) an identified payment provision.** An **underlying** is a specified interest rate, security price, commodity price, index of prices or rates, or other market-related variable. Payment is determined by the interaction of the underlying with the face amount or the number of shares, or other units specified in the derivative contract (referred to as notional amounts). For example, the value of the call option increased in value when the value of the Laredo stock increased. In this case, the underlying was the stock price. The change in the stock price is multiplied by the number of shares (notional amount) to arrive at the payment provision.
2. **The instrument requires little or no investment at the inception of the contract.** To illustrate, you paid a small premium to purchase the call option—an amount much less than if the Laredo shares were purchased as a direct investment.
3. **The instrument requires or permits net settlement.** As indicated in the call option example, you could realize a profit on the call option without taking possession of the shares. This **net settlement** feature serves to reduce the transaction costs associated with derivatives.

Illustration 18B-3 summarizes the differences between traditional and derivative financial instruments. We use a trading security for the traditional financial instrument and a call option as an example of a derivative financial instrument.

[10]In *SFAS No. 133,* the FASB identifies these same features as the key characteristics of derivatives. The FASB used these broad characteristics so that the definitions and hence the standard could be applied to yet-to-be-developed derivatives (para 249).

Feature	Traditional Financial Instrument (Trading Security)	Derivative Financial Instrument (Call Option)
Payment provision	Stock price times the number of shares.	Change in stock price (underlying) times number of shares (notional amount).
Initial investment	Investor pays full cost.	Initial investment is much less than full cost.
Settlement	Deliver stock to receive cash.	Receive cash equivalent, based on changes in stock price times the number of shares.

ILLUSTRATION 18B-3
Features of Traditional and Derivative Financial Instruments

As indicated, to make the initial investment in Laredo stock (traditional financial instrument), you would have to pay the full cost of this stock. If you purchase the Laredo stock and the price increases, you could profit. But you also are at risk for a loss if the Laredo shares decline in value. In contrast, derivatives require little initial investment and most derivatives are not exposed to all risks associated with ownership in the underlying. For example, the call option contract can only increase in value. That is, if the price of Laredo stock falls below $100 per share, you will not exercise the option, because the call option is worthless.

Finally, unlike the situation with a traditional financial instrument, you could realize a profit on the call option (related to the price of the Laredo stock) without ever having to take possession of the shares. These distinctions between traditional and derivative financial instruments explain in part the popularity of derivatives but also suggest that the accounting might be different.

DERIVATIVES USED FOR HEDGING

Flexibility in use and the low-cost features of derivatives relative to traditional financial instruments explain why derivatives have become so popular in recent years. An additional use for derivatives is in risk management. For example, companies such as **Coca-Cola**, **Exxon**, and **General Electric**, which borrow and lend substantial amounts in credit markets are exposed to significant **interest rate risk**. That is, they face substantial risk that the fair values or cash flows of interest-sensitive assets or liabilities will change if interest rates increase or decrease. These same companies also have significant international operations and are exposed to **exchange rate risk**—the risk that changes in foreign currency exchange rates will negatively impact the profitability of their international businesses.

Because the value and/or cash flows of derivative financial instruments can vary according to changes in interest rates or foreign currency exchange rates, derivatives can be used to offset the risks that a firm's fair values or cash flows will be negatively impacted by these market forces. This use of derivatives is referred to as **hedging**.

SFAS No. 133 established accounting and reporting standards for derivative financial instruments used in hedging activities.[11] Special accounting is allowed for two types of hedges—fair value and cash flow hedges.[12]

[11]The hedge accounting provisions of *SFAS No. 133* are the major new elements in the standard and contain some of the more difficult accounting issues. The provisions were needed because of growth in the quantity and variety of derivative financial instruments used for hedging and due to the lack of, and inconsistency in, existing accounting standards for derivatives used in hedging transactions.

[12]*SFAS No. 133* also addresses the accounting for certain foreign currency hedging transactions. In general, these transactions are special cases of the two hedges discussed here. Understanding of foreign currency hedging transactions requires knowledge of consolidation of multinational entities, which is beyond the scope of this textbook.

OBJECTIVE 11
Explain how to account for a fair value hedge.

Fair Value Hedge

In a **fair value hedge**, a derivative is used to hedge or offset the exposure to changes in the fair value of a recognized asset or liability or of an unrecognized firm commitment. In a perfectly hedged position, the gain or loss on the fair value of the derivative and that of the hedged asset or liability should be equal and offsetting. A common type of fair value hedge is the use of interest rate swaps (discussed below) to hedge the risk that changes in interest rates will impact the fair value of debt obligations. Another typical fair value hedge is the use of put options to hedge the risk that an equity investment will decline in value.

Interest Rate Swap—A Fair Value Hedge

Options and futures have certain disadvantages. First because they are traded on organized securities exchanges, options and futures have standardized terms and lack the flexibility needed to tailor contracts to specific circumstances. In addition, most types of derivatives have relatively short time horizons and therefore cannot be used to reduce any type of long-term risk exposure.

As a result, a very popular type of derivative used by many corporations is a swap. A **swap** is a transaction between two parties in which the first party promises to make a payment to the second party. Similarly the second party promises to make a simultaneous payment to the first party. The most common type of swap is the **interest rate swap**, in which one party makes payments based on a fixed or floating rate and the second party does just the opposite. In most cases, large money-center banks find the two parties and handle the flow of payments between the two parties, as shown below:

ILLUSTRATION 18B-4
Swap Transaction

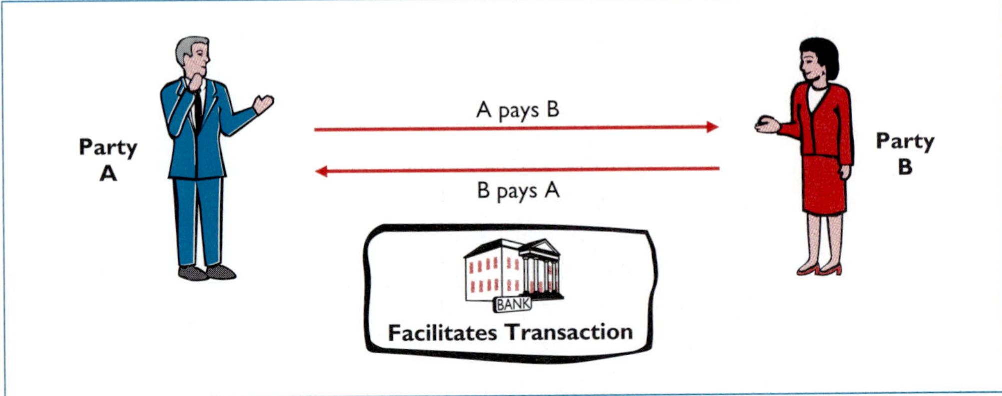

Accounting Entries

To illustrate the accounting for a fair value hedge, assume that Jones Company issues \$1,000,000 of 5-year, 8% fixed-rate bonds on January 2, 2001. The entry to record this transaction is as follows:

January 2, 2001		
Cash	1,000,000	
Bonds Payable		1,000,000

A fixed interest rate was offered to appeal to investors, but Jones is concerned that if market interest rates decline, the fair value of the liability will increase and the company will suffer an economic loss.[13] To protect against the risk of loss, Jones decides to hedge the risk of a decline in interest rates by entering into a 5-year **interest rate swap** contract. The terms of the swap contract to Jones are:

[13]This economic loss arises because Jones is locked into the 8% interest payments even if rates decline.

1. Jones will receive fixed payments at 8% (based on the $1,000,000 amount).
2. Jones will pay variable rates, based on the market rate in effect throughout the life of the swap contract. The variable rate at the inception of the contract is 6.8%.

As depicted in Illustration 18B-5, by using this swap Jones can change the interest on the bonds payable from a fixed rate to a variable rate.

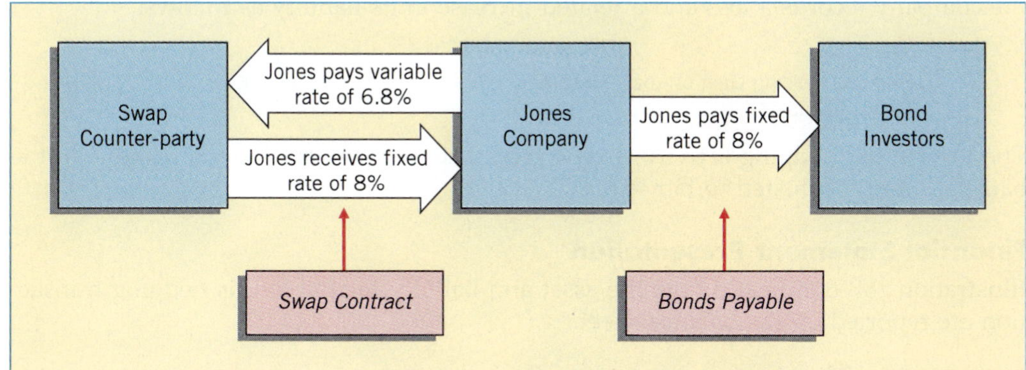

ILLUSTRATION 18B-5
Interest Rate Swap

The settlement dates for the swap correspond to the interest payment dates on the debt (December 31). On each interest payment (settlement date), Jones and the counterparty will compute the difference between current market interest rates and the fixed rate of 8% and determine the value of the swap.[14] As a result, if interest rates decline, the value of the swap contract to Jones increases (Jones has a gain), while at the same time Jones's fixed-rate debt obligation increases (Jones has an economic loss). The swap is an effective risk-management tool in this setting because its value is related to the same underlying (interest rates) that will affect the value of the fixed-rate bond payable. Thus, if the value of the swap goes up, it offsets the loss related to the debt obligation.

Assuming that the swap was entered into on January 2, 2001 (the same date as the issuance of the debt), the swap at this time has no value; therefore no entry is necessary:

January 2, 2001

No entry required. Memorandum to indicate that the swap contract is signed.

At the end of 2001, the interest payment on the bonds is made. The journal entry to record this transaction is as follows:

December 31, 2001

Interest Expense	80,000	
Cash (8% × $1,000,000)		80,000

At the end of 2001, market interest rates have declined substantially and therefore the value of the swap contract has increased. Recall (see Illustration 18B-5) that in the swap, Jones is to receive a fixed rate of 8%, or $80,000 ($1,000,000 × 8%), and pay a variable rate (which in this case is 6.8%), or $68,000. Jones therefore receives $12,000 ($80,000 − $68,000) as a settlement payment on the swap contract on the first interest payment date. The entry to record this transaction is as follows:

December 31, 2001

Cash	12,000	
Interest Expense		12,000

[14]The underlying for an interest rate swap is some index of market interest rates. The most commonly used index is the London Interbank Offer Rate, or LIBOR. In this example, we assumed the LIBOR is 6.8%.

In addition, a market appraisal indicates that the value of the interest rate swap has increased $40,000. This increase in value is recorded as follows:[15]

December 31, 2001		
Swap Contract	40,000	
Unrealized Holding Gain or Loss—Income		40,000

This swap contract is reported in the balance sheet, and the gain on the hedging transaction is reported in the income statement. Because interest rates have declined, the company records a loss and a related increase in its liability as follows:

December 31, 2001		
Unrealized Holding Gain or Loss—Income	40,000	
Bonds Payable		40,000

The loss on the hedging activity is reported in net income, and bonds payable in the balance sheet is adjusted to fair value.

Financial Statement Presentation

Illustration 18B-6 indicates how the asset and liability related to this hedging transaction are reported on the balance sheet.

ILLUSTRATION 18B-6
Balance Sheet Presentation of Fair Value Hedge

JONES COMPANY Balance Sheet (partial) December 31, 2001	
Current assets	
Swap contract	$40,000
Long-term liabilities	
Bonds payable	$1,040,000

The effect on the Jones Company balance sheet is the addition of the swap asset and an increase in the carrying value of the bonds payable. Illustration 18B-7 indicates how the effects of this swap transaction are reported in the income statement.

ILLUSTRATION 18B-7
Income Statement Presentation of Fair Value Hedge

JONES COMPANY Income Statement (partial) For the Year Ended December 31, 2001		
Interest expense ($80,000 – $12,000)		$68,000
Other income		
Unrealized holding gain—swap contract	$40,000	
Unrealized holding loss—bonds payable	(40,000)	
Net gain (loss)		$0

On the income statement, interest expense of $68,000 is reported. Jones has effectively changed the debt's interest rate from fixed to variable. That is, by receiving a fixed rate and paying a variable rate on the swap, the fixed rate on the bond payable is converted to variable, which results in an effective interest rate of 6.8% in 2001.[16] Also, the gain on the swap offsets the loss related to the debt obligation, and therefore the net gain or loss on the hedging activity is zero.

---

[15]Theoretically, this fair value change reflects the present value of expected future differences in variable and fixed interest rates.

[16]Similar accounting and measurement will be applied at future interest payment dates. Thus, if interest rates increase, Jones will continue to receive 8% on the swap (records a loss) but will also be locked into the fixed payments to the bondholders at an 8% rate (records a gain).

The overall impact of the swap transaction on the financial statements is shown in Illustration 18B-8.

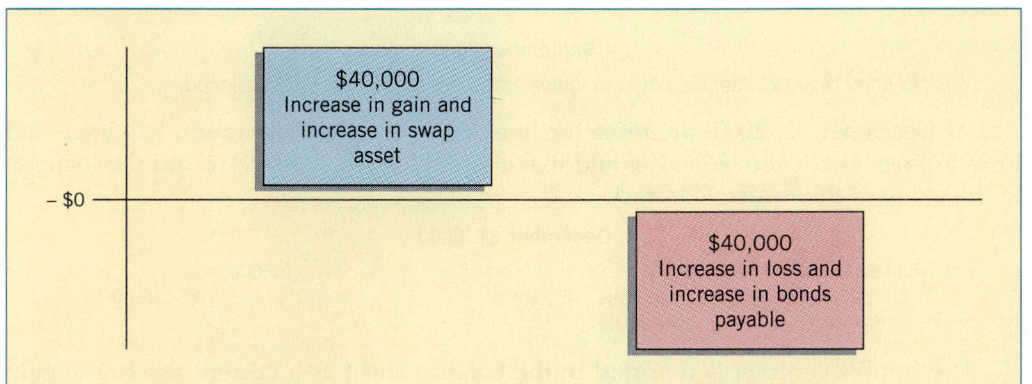

ILLUSTRATION 18B-8
Impact on Financial Statements of Fair Value Hedge

In summary, the accounting for fair value hedges (as illustrated in the Jones example) **records the derivative at its fair value in the balance sheet with any gains and losses recorded in income**. Thus, the gain on the swap offsets or hedges the loss on the bond payable due to the decline in interest rates. By adjusting the hedged item (the bond payable in the Jones case) to fair value, with the gain or loss recorded in earnings, the accounting for the Jones bond payable deviates from amortized cost. This special accounting is justified in order to report accurately the nature of the hedging relationship between the swap and the bond payable in the balance sheet (both the swap and the debt obligation are recorded at fair value) and in the income statement (offsetting gains and losses are reported in the same period).

Cash Flow Hedge

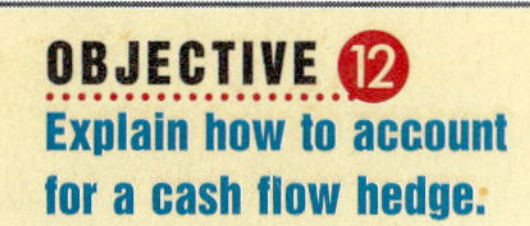

Cash flow hedges are used to hedge exposures to **cash flow risk**, which is exposure to the variability in cash flows. Special accounting is allowed for cash flow hedges. Generally, derivatives are measured and reported at fair value on the balance sheet, and gains and losses are reported directly in net income. However, derivatives used in cash flow hedges are accounted for at fair value on the balance sheet, but **gains or losses are recorded in equity as part of other comprehensive income**.

To illustrate the accounting for cash flow hedges, assume that in September 2000 Allied Can Co. anticipates purchasing 1,000 metric tons of aluminum in January 2001. Allied is concerned that prices for aluminum will increase in the next few months. To control its costs in producing cans, Allied wants to protect against possible price increases for aluminum inventory. To hedge the risk that it might have to pay higher prices for inventory in January 2001, Allied enters into an aluminum futures contract.

Under IASC rules, unrealized holding gains or losses on cash flow hedges are recorded as adjustments to the value of the hedged item, not in other comprehensive income.

A **futures contract** gives the holder the right and the obligation to purchase an asset at a preset price for a specified period of time.[17] In this case, the aluminum futures contract gives Allied the right and the obligation to purchase 1,000 metric tons of aluminum for $1,550 per ton. This contract price is good until the contract expires in January 2001. The underlying for this derivative is the price of aluminum. If the price of aluminum rises above $1,550, the value of the futures contract to Allied increases, because Allied will be able to purchase the aluminum at the lower price of $1,550 per ton.[18]

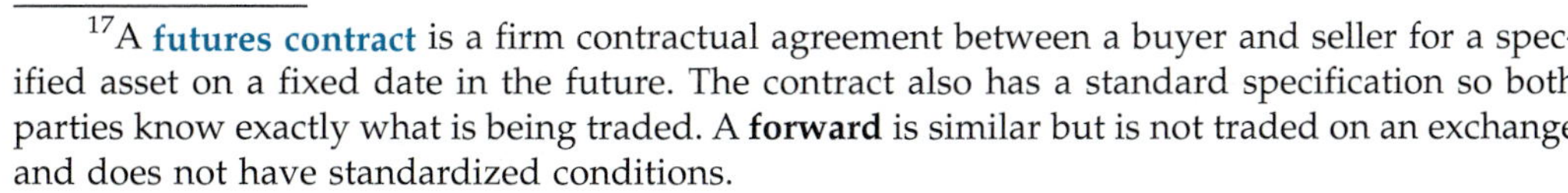

[17]A **futures contract** is a firm contractual agreement between a buyer and seller for a specified asset on a fixed date in the future. The contract also has a standard specification so both parties know exactly what is being traded. A **forward** is similar but is not traded on an exchange and does not have standardized conditions.

[18]As with the earlier call option example, the actual aluminum does not have to be exchanged. Rather, the parties to the futures contract settle by paying the cash difference between the futures price and the price of aluminum on each settlement date.

Assuming that the futures contract was entered into on September 1, 2000, and that the price to be paid today for inventory to be delivered in January—the **spot price**—was equal to the contract price, the futures contract has no value. Therefore no entry is necessary:

September 2000

No entry required. Memorandum to indicate that the futures contract is signed.

At December 31, 2000, the price for January delivery of aluminum has increased to $1,575 per metric ton. Allied would make the following entry to record the increase in the value of the futures contract:

December 31, 2000

Futures Contract	25,000	
Unrealized Holding Gain or Loss—Equity		25,000
([$1,575 − $1,550] × 1,000 tons)		

The futures contract is reported in the balance sheet as a current asset. The gain on the futures contract is reported as part of other comprehensive income. Since Allied has not yet purchased and sold the inventory, this is an **anticipated transaction**. In this type of transaction, gains or losses on the futures contract are accumulated in equity as part of other comprehensive income until the period in which the inventory is sold and earnings is affected.

In January 2001, Allied purchases 1,000 metric tons of aluminum for $1,575 and makes the following entry.[19]

January 2001

Aluminum Inventory	1,575,000	
Cash ($1,575 × 1,000 tons)		1,575,000

At the same time, Allied makes final settlement on the futures contract and makes the following entry:

January 2001

Cash	25,000	
Futures Contract ($1,575,000 − $1,550,000)		25,000

Through use of the futures contract derivative, Allied has been able to fix the cost of its inventory. The $25,000 futures contract settlement offsets the amount paid to purchase the inventory at the prevailing market price of $1,575,000, so that the net cash outflow is at $1,550 per metric ton, as desired. In this way, Allied has hedged the cash flow for the purchase of inventory, as depicted in Illustration 18B-9.

ILLUSTRATION 18B-9
Effect of Hedge on Cash Flows

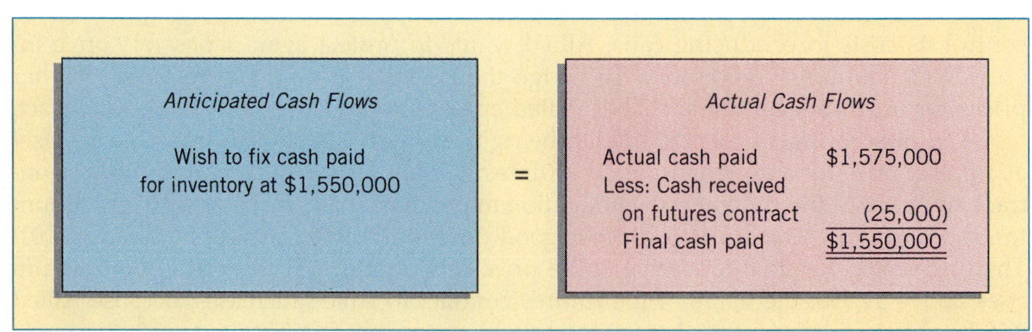

There are no income effects at this point. The gain on the futures contract is accumulated in equity as part of other comprehensive income until the period when the inventory is sold and earnings is affected through cost of goods sold.

[19]In practice, futures contracts are settled on a daily basis; for our purposes we show only one settlement for the entire amount.

For example, assume that the aluminum is processed into finished goods (cans). The total cost of the cans (including the aluminum purchases in January 2001) is $1,700,000. Allied sells the cans in July 2001 for $2,000,000. The entry to record this sale is as follows:

July 2001		
Cash	2,000,000	
Sales Revenue		2,000,000
Cost of Goods Sold	1,700,000	
Inventory (Cans)		1,700,000

Since the effect of the anticipated transaction has now affected earnings, Allied makes the following entry related to the hedging transaction:

July 2001		
Unrealized Holding Gain or Loss—Equity	25,000	
Cost of Goods Sold		25,000

The gain on the futures contract, which was reported as part of other comprehensive income, now reduces cost of goods sold. As a result, the cost of aluminum included in the overall cost of goods sold is $1,550,000. The futures contract has worked as planned to manage the cash paid for aluminum inventory and the amount of cost of goods sold.

OTHER REPORTING ISSUES

OBJECTIVE 13
Identify special reporting issues related to derivative financial instruments that cause unique accounting problems.

The examples above illustrate the basic reporting issues related to the accounting for derivatives. Additional issues of importance are as follows:

1. The accounting for embedded derivatives.
2. Qualifying hedge criteria.
3. Disclosures about financial instruments and derivatives.

Embedded Derivatives

As indicated at the beginning of this appendix, a major impetus for unifying and improving the accounting standards for derivatives was the rapid innovation in the development of complex financial instruments. In recent years, this innovation has led to the development of **hybrid securities**, which have characteristics of both debt and equity and often are a combination of traditional and derivative financial instruments. For example, a convertible bond (as discussed in Chapter 17) is a hybrid instrument because it is comprised of a debt security, referred to as the **host security**, combined with an option to convert the bond to shares of common stock, the **embedded derivative**.

To provide consistency in accounting for similar derivative instruments, embedded derivatives are required to be accounted for similarly to other derivative instruments. Therefore, a derivative that is embedded in a hybrid security should be separated from the host security and accounted for using the accounting for derivatives. This separation process is referred to as **bifurcation**.[20] Thus, an investor in a convertible bond is required to separate the stock option component of the instrument and account for the derivative (the stock option) at fair value and the host instrument (the debt) according to GAAP, as if there were no embedded derivative.[21]

[20]Such a derivative can also be designated as a hedging instrument, and the hedge accounting provisions outlined earlier in the chapter would be applied.

[21]The **issuer** of the convertible bonds would not bifurcate the option component of the convertible bonds payable. *SFAS No. 133* explicitly precludes embedded derivative accounting for an embedded derivative that is indexed to an entity's own common stock. If the conversion feature was tied to **another company's** stock, this derivative would be bifurcated.

Qualifying Hedge Criteria

INTERNATIONAL INSIGHT

IASC qualifying hedge criteria are similar to those used in *SFAS No. 133.*

The FASB identified certain criteria that hedging transactions must meet before the special accounting for hedges is required; these criteria are designed to ensure that hedge accounting is used in a consistent manner across different hedge transactions. The general criteria relate to the following areas:

1. **Designation, documentation, and risk management.** At inception of the hedge, there must be formal **documentation** of the hedging relationship, the entity's **risk management** objective, and the **strategy** for undertaking the hedge. **Designation** refers to identifying the hedging instrument, the hedged item or transaction, the nature of the risk being hedged, and how the hedging instrument will offset changes in the fair value or cash flows attributable to the hedged risk. The FASB decided that designation and documentation is critical to the implementation of the special hedge accounting model. Without these requirements, there was concern that companies would try to apply the hedge accounting provisions retroactively only in response to negative changes in market conditions, in order to offset the negative impact of a transaction on the financial statements. Allowing special hedge accounting in such a setting could mask the speculative nature of the original transaction.

2. **Effectiveness of the hedging relationship.** At inception and on an ongoing basis, the hedging relationship is expected to be **highly effective** in achieving offsetting changes in fair value or cash flows. Assessment of effectiveness is required whenever financial statements are prepared. The general guideline for effectiveness is that the fair values or cash flows of the hedging instrument (the derivative) and the hedged item exhibit a high degree of correlation. In practice, high effectiveness is assumed when the correlation is close to one (for example, within plus or minus .10). In our earlier hedging examples (interest rate swap and the futures contract on aluminum inventory), the fair values and cash flows were exactly correlated. That is, when the cash payment for the inventory purchase increased, it was offset dollar for dollar by the cash received on the futures contract. If the effectiveness criterion is not met, either at inception or because of changes following inception of the hedging relationship, special hedge accounting is no longer allowed, and the derivative should be accounted for as a freestanding derivative.[22]

3. **Effect on reported earnings of changes in fair values or cash flows.** A change in the fair value of a hedged item or variation in the cash flow of a hedged forecasted transaction must have the potential to change the amount recognized in reported earnings. There is no need for special hedge accounting, if both the hedging instrument and the hedged item are accounted for at fair value under existing GAAP. In this case, the offsetting gains and losses will be properly reflected in earnings. For example, special accounting is not needed for a fair value hedge of a trading security, because both the investment and the derivative are accounted for at fair value on the balance sheet with gains or losses reported in earnings. Thus, "special" hedge accounting is necessary only when there is a mismatch of the accounting effects for the hedging instrument and the hedged item under GAAP.[23]

[22]The accounting for the part of a derivative that is not effective in a hedge is at fair value with gains and losses recorded in income.

[23]An important criterion specific to cash flow hedges is that the forecasted transaction in a cash flow hedge "is likely to occur." This probability (defined as significantly greater than the term "more likely than not") should be supported by observable facts such as frequency of similar past transactions and the firm's financial and operational ability to carry out the transaction.

Disclosure Provisions

OBJECTIVE 14
Describe the disclosure requirements for traditional and derivative financial instruments.

Because *SFAS No. 133* provides comprehensive accounting guidance for derivatives, this standard replaces the disclosure provisions in *SFAS No. 105* and *SFAS No. 119* and amends the disclosure rules in *SFAS No. 107.*[24] Thus, *SFAS No. 107* provides general guidance for traditional financial instrument disclosures, and *SFAS No. 133* addresses the disclosures for derivative financial instruments.

As a consequence of these two pronouncements, the primary requirements for disclosures related to financial instruments are as follows:

1. A company should disclose the fair value and related carrying value of its financial instruments in the body of the financial statements, in a note, or in a summary table form that makes it clear whether the amounts represent assets or liabilities.
2. The fair value disclosures should distinguish between financial instruments held or issued for purposes other than trading. For derivative financial instruments, the firm should disclose its objectives for holding or issuing those instruments (speculation or hedging), the hedging context (fair value or cash flow), and its strategies for achieving risk management objectives.
3. In disclosing fair values of financial instruments, a company should not combine, aggregate, or net the fair value of separate financial instruments, even if those instruments are considered to be related.
4. A company should display as a separate classification of other comprehensive income the net gain or loss on derivative instruments designated in cash flow hedges.
5. Companies are encouraged, but not required, to provide quantitative information about market risks of derivative financial instruments, and also of its other assets and liabilities, that is consistent with the way the company manages and adjusts risks and that is useful for comparing the results of its use of derivative financial instruments.

While these additional disclosures of fair value provide useful information to financial statement users, they are generally provided as supplemental information only. The balance sheet continues to rely primarily on historical cost. Exceptions to this general rule are the fair value requirements for certain investment securities and derivative financial instruments, as illustrated earlier. Illustration 18B-10 on page 966 provides a fair value disclosure for **Intel Corporation**.

UNDERLYING CONCEPTS

Providing supplemental information on the fair values of financial instruments illustrates application of the full disclosure principle.

The fair values of cash and cash equivalents, short-term investments, and short-term debt approximate cost because of the immediate and short-term maturities of these financial instruments. The fair value of marketable securities (and some derivatives) is based on quoted market prices at the reporting date. The fair value of long-term debt and some derivatives is based on market prices for similar instruments or by discounting expected cash flows at rates currently available to the company for instruments with similar risks and maturities.

If a company is unable to arrive at an estimate of fair value, it must disclose information relevant to the estimate of fair value (such as the terms of the instrument) and the reason why it is unable to arrive at an estimate of fair value.[25]

[24]*SFAS No. 105* refers to "Disclosure of Information about Financial Instruments with Off-Balance Sheet Risk and Financial Instruments with Concentrations of Credit Risk," *Statement of Financial Accounting Standards No. 105* (Stamford, Conn.: FASB, 1990). *SFAS No. 119* refers to "Disclosure about Derivative Financial Instruments and Fair Value of Financial Instruments," *Statement of Financial Accounting Standards No. 119* (Stamford, Conn.: FASB, 1994).

[25]*SFAS No. 107* lists a number of exceptions to this requirement; most of these exceptions are covered in other standards. The exception list includes such items as: pension and post-retirement benefits; employee stock options; insurance contracts; lease contracts; warranties, rights, and obligations; purchase obligations; equity method investments; minority interests; and instruments classified as stockholders' equity in the entity's balance sheet.

ILLUSTRATION 18B-10
Intel Corporation Fair Value Disclosure

INTEL CORPORATION

Fair values of financial instruments
The estimated fair values of financial instruments outstanding at fiscal year-ends were as follows:

	1998		1997	
(in millions)	Carrying Amount	Estimated Fair Value	Carrying Amount	Estimated Fair Value
Cash and cash equivalents	$2,038	$2,038	$4,102	$4,102
Short-term investments	4,821	4,821	5,561	5,561
Trading assets	316	316	195	195
Long-term investments	5,375	5,375	1,821	1,821
Non-marketable instruments	571	716	387	497
Options creating synthetic money market instruments	474	474	—	—
Swaps hedging investments in debt securities	(33)	(33)	64	64
Swaps hedging investments in equity securities	2	2	8	8
Short-term debt	(159)	(159)	(212)	(212)
Long-term debt redeemable within one year	—	—	(110)	(109)
Long-term debt	(702)	(696)	(448)	(448)
Swaps hedging debt	—	1	—	(1)
Currency forward contracts	(1)	(1)	26	28
Currency options	—	—	1	1

Summary of *SFAS No. 133*

Illustration 18B-11 provides a summary of the accounting provisions for derivatives and hedging transactions.

ILLUSTRATION 18B-11
Summary of Derivative Accounting Under *SFAS 133*

Derivative Use	Accounting for Derivative	Accounting for Hedged Item	Common Example
Speculation	At fair value with unrealized holding gains and losses recorded in income.	Not applicable	Call or put option on an equity security.
Hedging			
Fair value	At fair value with holding gains and losses recorded in income.	At fair value with gains and losses recorded in income.	Interest rate swap hedge of a fixed-rate debt obligation.
Cash flow	At fair value with unrealized holding gains and losses from the hedge recorded in other comprehensive income and reclassified in income when the hedged transaction's cash flows affect earnings.	Use other generally accepted accounting principles for the hedged item.	Use of a futures contract to hedge a forecasted purchase of inventory.

As indicated in Illustration 18B-11, the general accounting for derivatives is based on fair values. *SFAS No. 133* also establishes **special accounting guidance** when derivatives are used **for hedging purposes**. For example, when an interest rate swap was used to hedge the bonds payable in a fair value hedge (see Jones Co. earlier), unrealized losses on the bonds payable were recorded in earnings, which is not GAAP for bonds issued without such a hedge. This special accounting is justified in order to accurately report the nature of the hedging relationship in the balance sheet (both the swap and the liability are recorded at fair value) and in the income statement (offsetting gains and losses are reported in the same period).

Special accounting also is used for cash flow hedges. Derivatives used in qualifying cash flow hedges are accounted for at fair value on the balance sheet, but unrealized holding gains or losses are recorded in other comprehensive income until the hedged item is sold or settled. In a cash flow hedge, the hedged item continues to be recorded at its historical cost.

COMPREHENSIVE HEDGE ACCOUNTING EXAMPLE

To demonstrate a comprehensive example of the hedge accounting provisions, using a fair value hedge, let's assume that on April 1, 2000, Hayward Co. purchased 100 shares of Sonoma stock at a market price of $100 per share. Hayward does not intend to actively trade this investment and consequently classifies the Sonoma investment as "available-for-sale." Hayward makes the following entry to record this available-for-sale investment:

April 1, 2000

Available-for-Sale Securities	10,000	
Cash		10,000

Available-for-sale securities are recorded at fair value on the balance sheet, and unrealized gains and losses are reported in equity as part of other comprehensive income.[26] Fortunately for Hayward, the value of the Sonoma shares increases to $125 per share during 2000. Hayward makes the following entry to record the gain on this investment:

December 31, 2000

Security Fair Value Adjustment (Available-for-Sale)	2,500	
Unrealized Holding Gain or Loss—Equity		2,500

Illustration 18B-12 indicates how the Sonoma investment is reported in Hayward's balance sheet:

ILLUSTRATION 18B-12
Balance Sheet Presentation of Available-for-Sale Securities

HAYWARD CO. Balance Sheet (partial) December 31, 2000	
Assets	
Available-for-sale securities (at fair value)	$12,500
Stockholders' Equity	
Accumulated other comprehensive income	
Unrealized holding gain	$2,500

While Hayward has benefited from an increase in the price of Sonoma shares, it is exposed to the risk that the price of the Sonoma stock will decline. To hedge this risk, Hayward locks in its gain on the Sonoma investment by purchasing a put option on 100 shares of Sonoma stock.

Hayward enters into the put option contract on January 2, 2001, and designates the option as a fair value hedge of the Sonoma investment. This put option (which expires in two years) gives Hayward the option to sell Sonoma shares at a price of $125. Since the exercise price is equal to the current market price, no entry is necessary at inception of the put option:[27]

[26]The distinction between trading and available-for-sale investments is discussed in Chapter 18.

[27]To simplify the example, we assume no premium is paid for the option.

January 2, 2001

No entry required. Memorandum to indicate that put option contract is signed and is designated as a fair value hedge for the Sonoma investment.

At December 31, 2001, the price of the Sonoma shares has declined to $120 per share. Hayward records the following entry for the Sonoma investment:

December 31, 2001

Unrealized Holding Gain or Loss—Income	500	
Security Fair Value Adjustment (Available-for-Sale)		500

Note that upon designation of the hedge, the accounting for the available-for-sale security changes from regular GAAP in that the unrealized holding loss is recorded in income, not in equity. If Hayward had not followed this accounting, a mismatch of gains and losses in the income statement would result. Thus, special accounting for the available-for-sale security is necessary in a fair value hedge.

The following journal entry records the increase in value of the put option on Sonoma shares:

December 31, 2001

Put Option	500	
Unrealized Holding Gain or Loss—Income		500

The decline in the price of Sonoma shares results in an increase in the fair value of the put option. That is, Hayward could realize a gain on the put option by purchasing 100 shares in the open market for $120 and then exercise the put option, selling the shares for $125. This results in a gain to Hayward of $500 (100 shares × [$125 − $120]).[28]

Illustration 18B-13 indicates how the amounts related to the Sonoma investment and the put option are reported.

ILLUSTRATION 18B-13
Balance Sheet Presentation of Fair Value Hedge

HAYWARD CO.
Balance Sheet (partial)
December 31, 2001

Assets	
Available-for-sale securities (at fair value)	$12,000
Put option	$500

The increase in fair value on the option offsets or hedges the decline in value on Hayward's available-for-sale security. By using fair value accounting for both financial instruments, the financial statements reflect the underlying substance of Hayward's net exposure to the risks of holding Sonoma stock. By using fair value accounting for both these financial instruments, the balance sheet reports the amount that Hayward would receive on the investment and the put option contract if they were sold and settled respectively.

Illustration 18B-14 illustrates the reporting of the effects of the hedging transaction on income for the year ended December 31, 2001.

ILLUSTRATION 18B-14
Income Statement Presentation of Fair Value Hedge

HAYWARD CO.
Income Statement (partial)
For the Year Ended December 31, 2001

Other Income	
Unrealized holding gain—put option	$500
Unrealized holding loss—available-for-sale securities	(500)

[28]In practice, Hayward generally does not have to actually buy and sell the Sonoma shares to realize this gain. Rather, unless the counterparty wants to hold Hayward shares, the contract can be "closed out" by having the counterparty pay Hayward $500 in cash. This is an example of the net settlement feature of derivatives.

The income statement indicates that the gain on the put option offsets the loss on the available-for-sale securities.[29] The reporting for these financial instruments, even when they reflect a hedging relationship, illustrates why the FASB argued that fair value accounting provides the most relevant information about financial instruments, including derivatives.

CONTROVERSY AND CONCLUDING REMARKS

SFAS No. 133 represents FASB's effort to develop accounting guidance for derivatives. Many believe that these new rules are needed to properly measure and report derivatives in financial statements. Others argue that reporting derivatives at fair value results in unrealized gains and losses that are difficult to interpret. Concerns also were raised concerning the complexity and cost of implementing the standard, since prior to *SFAS No. 133,* many derivatives were not recognized in financial statements.

The FASB, as part of its due process, worked to respond to these concerns. For example, from the beginning of the project in 1992, the FASB held over 100 meetings and received comments from over 400 constitutents or constituent groups. In response to these comments, the FASB revised the original proposal to make the provisions easier to apply. And recently, the FASB delayed the effective date for *SFAS No. 133* to give preparers more time to understand the standard and to develop the information systems necessary to implement the standard. More than 120 companies requested the delay, arguing that the rule could complicate companies' efforts to deal with the year 2000 (Y2K) problem. These Y2K problems arise when computers confuse the years 1900 and 2000 when making calculations.[30]

The authors believe that the long-term benefits of this standard will far outweigh any short-term implementation costs. As the volume and complexity of derivatives and hedging transactions continues to grow, the risk that investors and creditors will be exposed to unexpected losses arising from derivative transactions also increases. Without this standard, statement readers do not have comprehensive information in financial statements concerning many derivative financial instruments and the effects of hedging transactions using derivatives.

KEY TERMS

anticipated transaction, *962*
bifurcation, *963*
call option, *954*
cash flow hedge, *961*
derivative financial instrument, derivative, *952*
designation, *964*
documentation, *964*
embedded derivative, *963*
fair value, *953*
fair value hedge, *958*
futures contract, *961*
hedging, *957*
highly effective, *964*
host security, *963*
hybrid security, *963*
interest rate swap, *958*
intrinsic value, *955*
net settlement, *955*
notional amount, *955*
option premium, *955*
put option, *954*
risk management, *964*
spot price, *962*
strike (exercise) price, *954*
swap, *958*
time value, *955*
underlying, *956*

SUMMARY OF LEARNING OBJECTIVES FOR APPENDIX 18B

8 Explain who uses derivatives and why they are used. Any company or individual that wants to ensure against different types of business risks often uses derivative contracts to achieve this objective. In general, these transactions involve some type of hedge. Speculators also are in the market, attempting to find an enhanced return. Speculators are very important to the market because they keep the market liquid on a daily basis. Arbitrageurs also are in the market and attempt to exploit inefficiencies in various derivative contracts. Derivatives are used primarily for purposes of hedging a company's exposure to fluctuations in interest rates, foreign currency exchange rates, and commodity prices.

---

[29]Note that the fair value changes in the option contract will not offset **increases** in the value of the Hayward investment. Should the price of Sonoma stock increase above $125 per share, Hayward would have no incentive to exercise the put option.

[30]The original implementation date was set for June 15, 1999; the proposal will delay this until June 15, 2000. Interestingly, some companies have adopted the standard early because the rules provide better accounting for some derivatives relative to the rules in place before *SFAS No. 133.* "U.S. Companies Find New Accounting Rule Costly, Inefficient," by Paula Froelich, Dow Jones News Service (March 2, 1999). It is likely that this standard will be amended to address various implementation issues in the near future.

9 **Understand the basic guidelines for accounting for derivatives.** Derivatives should be recognized in the financial statements as assets and liabilities and reported at fair value. Gains and losses resulting from speculation should be recognized immediately in income. Gains and losses resulting from hedge transactions are reported in different ways, depending upon the type of hedge.

10 **Describe the accounting for derivative financial instruments.** Derivative financial instruments are reported in the balance sheet and recorded at fair value. Except for derivatives used in hedging, realized and unrealized gains and losses on derivative financial instruments are recorded in income.

11 **Explain how to account for a fair value hedge.** The derivative used in a qualifying fair value hedge is recorded at its fair value in the balance sheet with any gains and losses recorded in income. In addition, the item being hedged with the derivative is also accounted for at fair value. By adjusting the hedged item to fair value, with the gain or loss recorded in earnings, the accounting for the hedged item may deviate from GAAP in the absence of a hedge relationship. This special accounting is justified in order to report accurately the nature of the hedging relationship between the derivative hedging instruments and the hedged item (both are reported in the balance sheet, with offsetting gains and losses reported in income in the same period).

12 **Explain how to account for a cash flow hedge.** Derivatives used in qualifying cash flow hedges are accounted for at fair value on the balance sheet, but gains or losses are recorded in equity as part of other comprehensive income. These gains or losses are accumulated and reclassified in income when the hedged transaction's cash flows affect earnings. Accounting is according to GAAP for the hedged item.

13 **Identify special reporting issues related to derivative financial instruments that cause unique accounting problems.** A derivative that is embedded in a hybrid security should be separated from the host security and accounted for using the accounting for derivatives. This separation process is referred to as bifurcation. Special hedge accounting is allowed only for hedging relationships that meet certain criteria. The main criteria are that (1) there is formal documentation of the hedging relationship, the entity's risk management objective, and the strategy for undertaking the hedge, and that the derivative is designated as either a cash flow or fair value hedge; (2) the hedging relationship is expected to be highly effective in achieving offsetting changes in fair value or cash flows; and (3) "special" hedge accounting is necessary only when there is a mismatch of the accounting effects for the hedging instrument and the hedged item under GAAP.

14 **Describe the disclosure requirements for traditional and derivative financial instruments.** Companies must disclose the fair value and related carrying value of its financial instruments, and these disclosures should distinguish between amounts that represent assets or liabilities. The disclosures should distinguish between financial instruments held or issued for purposes other than trading. For derivative financial instruments, the firm should disclose whether the instruments are used for speculation or hedging. In disclosing fair values of financial instruments, a company should not combine, aggregate, or net the fair value of separate financial instruments, even if those instruments are considered to be related. A company should display as a separate classification of other comprehensive income the net gain or loss on derivative instruments designated in cash flow hedges. Companies are encouraged, but not required, to provide quantitative information about market risks of derivative financial instruments.

A visit with
Penelope Flugger

PENELOPE FLUGGER is a Managing Director of J.P. Morgan & Co. She joined the company in 1975 as an assistant comptroller, assuming responsibility for the audit department in 1982. In 1994, she assumed responsibility for control and quality initiatives in Morgan's technology and operations group. Before joining Morgan, she was an audit manager with Price Waterhouse. She holds a bachelor's degree in accounting from the University of Illinois and an MBA from Baruch College, CUNY.

PERSPECTIVES ON

Investment Banking Accounting

There weren't very many women in the accounting profession when you started, were there? When I was a student at the University of Illinois in the early 1960s, there were very few women students. But I had some great professors who were very encouraging and gave me the confidence to go into public accounting. When I graduated, there were only two "Big Eight" firms in Chicago who would hire women. I went to work for Price Waterhouse in New York in 1964 on the audit staff. That summer, 225 people started at Price Waterhouse in New York. There was only one other woman.

Why did you leave public accounting? I had some very good clients, some of the top clients of the firm, so I was lucky in that respect. After a few years, I started to specialize in the brokerage industry, which I found very interesting. I was PW's banking industry specialist and was involved in the AICPA banking committee. But I decided that I wasn't cut out for public accounting, particularly the salesmanship aspect, and decided that I wanted to work for one of the three big banks in New York City—Citicorp, Morgan, or Chase. Luckily, I got job offers from all three, and took the one from Morgan.

Describe some highlights of your career at J.P. Morgan. Initially, I was in charge of the bank's accounting policy and procedures department as well as being in charge of SEC reporting. After a few years, I moved into areas such as international banking and consolidations. From there, I got involved in systems development, because I was very interested in how to make financial reporting easier. After about seven years, the firm asked if I would take over the internal audit department, where I spent about ten years, changing the approach to internal auditing and developing a training program so that we could use it as an entry-level recruiting tool.

What suggestions have you had in the teaching of accounting and auditing? I met the authors of your book when I was a member of the Accounting Education Change Commission. Part of my interest was that changes in accounting education weren't keeping up with what we needed. When I was in auditing, I was complaining that I was hiring from colleges but had to completely retrain these new graduates because they just didn't understand the business. Because internal auditing was so hard to recruit for, I spent time with professors at the schools where we were recruiting. The students were taught discrete things about accounting, marketing, etc. without any idea about how to put it together. They couldn't figure out how things would flow through an organization. I would see people who would pass the CPA exam but couldn't relate it to business.

What has been your role as chairman of the Financial Executives Institute? The FEI is an organization of 14,000 financial executives of major corporations. We represent our members with regulatory bodies such as the FASB, AICPA, etc. In financial accounting, the major issue is how to make sure that accounting reflects business reality. For instance, we'll mark an asset to market, but in a hedge transaction we don't mark the liability to market, so there often seems to be a disconnect between accounting principles and the business reality. You try to keep a balance so that you don't fix one side and create a bigger problem. We also have committees dealing with taxation, pension fund investment, employee benefits, etc. We try to get our voice heard on issues such as the balanced budget, tax reduction, and other initiatives that we think are important.

What are some major issues currently facing you at J.P. Morgan? With the current focus on business process re-engineering and quality, we're spending a lot of time trying to identify our fixed and variable costs. In an investment banking firm you've got to adjust your costs quickly as the markets go up and down. If you don't have a handle on what's fixed and what's variable, your profits get adversely affected, and the market doesn't wait to give you time to fix that. If you build a fixed-cost system that accommodates 20,000 trades a day, and all of a sudden you're trading only 5,000 transactions in that particular instrument, then you have quadrupled the cost to process those transactions.

What are some advantages of industry vs. public accounting for new graduates? If you know what industry you want to go into, then I think you have a leg up in industry. Industry has changed the way it treats entry-level people. Training is much better now than it used to be. And there are more options. If you like consulting work like you would get in public accounting, then we also have a track that allows you to do consulting work. My advice to students is that when they take a job, they should be having fun. If you don't enjoy the job but you have to do it for 40 more years, then that can be a horrible life sentence. Most students take their first job based on who they interview with and where they think the glamour is. That's unfortunate, because the person they interview with is probably not who they're going to work with.

Note: All **asterisked** Questions, Exercises, Problems, and Conceptual Cases relate to material contained in the appendixes to the chapter.

QUESTIONS

1 Distinguish between a debt security and an equity security.

2 What purpose does the variety in bond features (types and characteristics) serve?

3 What is the cost of a long-term investment in bonds?

4 What are the problems of accounting for bond investments between interest dates?

5 Identify and explain the three types of classifications for investments in debt securities.

6 When should a debt security be classified as held-to-maturity?

7 Explain how trading securities are accounted for and reported.

8 At what amount should trading, available-for-sale, and held-to-maturity securities be reported on the balance sheet?

9 Indicate how unrealized holding gains and losses should be reported for investment securities classified as trading, available-for-sale, and held-to-maturity.

10 (a) Assuming no Securities Fair Value Adjustment (Available-for-Sale) account balance at the beginning of the year, prepare the adjusting entry at the end of the year if Laura Company has an unrealized holding loss of $70,000 on its available-for-sale securities. (b) Assume the same information as part (a), except that Laura Company has a debit balance in its Securities Fair Value Adjustment (Available-for-Sale) account of $10,000 at the beginning of the year. Prepare the adjusting entry at year-end.

11 On July 1, 2002, Ingalls Company purchased $2,000,000 of Wilder Company's 8% bonds, due on July 1, 2009. The bonds, which pay interest semiannually on January 1 and July 1, were purchased for $1,750,000 to yield 10%. Determine the amount of interest revenue Ingalls should report on its income statement for year ended December 31, 2002.

12 If the bonds in question 11 are classified as available-for-sale and they have a fair value at December 31, 2002, of $1,802,000, prepare the journal entry (if any) at December 31, 2002, to record this transaction.

13 How is the premium or discount handled relative to a trading debt security?

14 On what basis should stock acquired or exchanged for noncash consideration be recorded?

15 Identify and explain the different types of classifications for investment in equity securities.

16 Why are held-to-maturity investments applicable only to debt securities?

17 Emily Company sold 10,000 shares of Dickinson Co. common stock for $27.50 per share, incurring $1,770 in brokerage commissions. These securities were classified as trading and originally cost $250,000. Prepare the entry to record the sale of these securities.

18 Distinguish between the accounting treatment for available-for-sale equity securities and trading equity securities.

19 What constitutes "significant influence" when an investor's financial interest is below the 50% level?

20 Explain how the investment account is affected by investee activities under the equity method.

21 When the equity method is applied, what disclosures should be made in the investor's financial statements?

22 Molly Pitcher Co. uses the equity method to account for investments in common stock. What accounting should be made for dividends received in excess of Pitcher's share of investee's earnings subsequent to the date of investment?

23 Louisa Inc. uses the equity method to account for investments in Alcott common stock. The purchase price paid by Louisa implies a fair value of Alcott's depreciable assets in excess of Alcott's net asset carrying values. How should Louisa account for this excess?

24 In applying the equity method, what recognition, if any, does the investor give to the excess of its investment cost over its proportionate share of the investee book value at the date of acquisition? What recognition, if any, is given if the investment cost is less than the underlying book value?

25 Elizabeth Corp. has an investment carrying value (equity method) on its books of $170,000 representing a 40% interest in Dole Company, which suffered a $620,000 loss this year. How should Elizabeth Corp. handle its proportionate share of Dole's loss?

26 Where on the asset side of the balance sheet are trading securities, available-for-sale securities, and held-to-maturity securities reported? Explain.

27 Explain why reclassification adjustments are necessary.

28 Briefly discuss how a transfer of securities from the available-for-sale category to the trading category affects stockholders' equity and income.

29 When is a debt security considered impaired? Explain how to account for the impairment of an available-for-sale debt security.

***30** How is a stock dividend accounted for by the recipient? How is a stock split accounted for by the recipient?

***31** What three dates are significant in relation to stock rights? What are the alternatives available to the recipient of stock rights?

***32** Rosie Jones Co. owns 300 shares of Barb Mucha Corporation common stock acquired on June 10, 2002, at a total cost of $12,000. On December 2, 2003, Rosie Jones received 300 stock rights from Barb Mucha. Each right entitles the holder to acquire one share of stock for $45. The market price of Barb Mucha's stock on this date, ex-rights, was $50, and the market price of each right was $5. Rosie Jones sold its rights the same date for $5 a right less a $90 commission. Determine the gain on sale of the rights by Rosie Jones.

***33** Distinguish between a fund and a reserve.

***34** What are the two general types of funds? Give three examples of each type of fund.

***35** What is meant by the term underlying as it relates to derivative financial instruments?

***36** What are the main distinctions between a traditional financial instrument and a derivative financial instrument?

***37** What is the purpose of a fair value hedge?

***38** In what situation will bonds payable carrying amounts not be reported at cost or amortized cost?

***39** Why might a company become involved in an interest rate swap contract to receive fixed interest payments and pay variable?

***40** What is the purpose of a cash flow hedge?

***41** Where are gains and losses related to cash flow hedges involving anticipated transactions reported?

***42** What are hybrid securities? Give an example of a hybrid security.

BRIEF EXERCISES

BE18-1 Moonwalker Company purchased, as a held-to-maturity investment, $50,000 of the 9%, 5-year bonds of Prime Time Corporation for $46,304, which provides an 11% return. Prepare Moonwalker's journal entries for (a) the purchase of the investment, and (b) the receipt of annual interest and discount amortization. Assume effective interest amortization is used.

BE18-2 Mask Corporation purchased, as a held-to-maturity investment, $40,000 of the 8%, 5-year bonds of Phantasy Star, Inc. for $43,412, which provides a 6% return. The bonds pay interest semiannually. Prepare Masks' journal entries for (a) the purchase of the investment, and (b) the receipt of semiannual interest and premium amortization. Assume effective interest amortization is used.

BE18-3 Use the information from BE18-1, but assume the bonds are purchased as an available-for-sale security. Prepare Moonwalker's journal entries for (a) the purchase of the investment, (b) the receipt of annual interest and discount amortization, and (c) the year-end fair value adjustment. The bonds have a year-end fair value of $47,200.

BE18-4 Use the information from BE18-2, but assume the bonds are purchased as an available-for-sale security. Prepare Mask's journal entries for (a) the purchase of the investment, (b) the receipt of semiannual interest and premium amortization, and (c) the year-end fair value adjustment. Assume the first interest payment is received on December 31, when the fair value of the bonds is $42,900.

BE18-5 Pete Sampras Corporation purchased for $22,500 as a trading investment bonds with a face value of $20,000. At December 31, Sampras received annual interest of $2,000, and the fair value of the bonds was $20,900. Prepare Sampras' journal entries for (a) the purchase of the investment, (b) the interest received, and (c) the fair value adjustment.

BE18-6 Pacman Corporation purchased 300 shares of Galaga Inc. common stock as an available-for-sale investment for $9,900. During the year, Galaga paid a cash dividend of $3.25 per share. At year-end, Galaga stock was selling for $34.50 per share. Prepare Pacman's journal entries to record (a) the purchase of the investment, (b) the dividends received, and (c) the fair value adjustment.

BE18-7 Use the information from BE18-6, but assume the stock was purchased as a trading security. Prepare Pacman's journal entries to record (a) the purchase of the investment, (b) the dividends received, and (c) the fair value adjustment.

BE18-8 Penn Corporation purchased for $300,000 a 25% interest in Teller, Inc. This investment enables Penn to exert significant influence over Teller. During the year Teller earned net income of $180,000 and paid dividends of $60,000. Prepare Penn's journal entries related to this investment.

BE18-9 Muhammad Corporation purchased for $630,000 a 30% interest in Ali Corporation on January 2, 2002. At that time, the book value of Ali's net assets was $1,900,000. Any excess of cost over book value

2. The fair market value of the assets subject to depreciation is $680,000.
3. The company depreciates its assets on a straight-line basis; intangible assets are amortized over 10 years.
4. Amy Chow Company reports net income of $160,000 and declares and pays dividends of $125,000 in 2002.

Instructions

(a) Prepare the journal entry to record Strug's purchase of Chow Company.
(b) Prepare the journal entries to record Strug's equity in the net income and dividends of Chow Company for 2002.
(c) Assume the same facts as above, except that Chow's net income included an extraordinary loss (net of tax) of $30,000. Prepare the journal entries to record Strug's equity in the net income of Chow Company for 2002.

E18-16 (Equity Method with Revalued Assets) On January 1, 2001, Warner Corporation purchased 30% of the common shares of Vermeil Company for $180,000. The book value of Vermeil's net assets was $500,000 on that date. During the year, Vermeil earned net income of $80,000 and paid dividends of $20,000. Any excess of cost over book value is attributable to unrecorded goodwill and is amortized over 20 years.

Instructions

(a) Prepare the entries for Warner to record the purchase and any additional entries related to this investment in Vermeil Company in 2001.
(b) Repeat the requirements in part (a), assuming the same facts as above, except that Vermeil's net income included an extraordinary loss (net of tax) of $10,000.

E18-17 (Impairment of Debt Securities) Dominique Moceanu Corporation has municipal bonds classified as available-for-sale at December 31, 2001. These bonds have a par value of $800,000, an amortized cost of $800,000, and a fair value of $720,000. The unrealized loss of $80,000 previously recognized as other comprehensive income and as a separate component of stockholders' equity is now determined to be other than temporary; that is, the company believes that impairment accounting is now appropriate for these bonds.

Instructions

(a) Prepare the journal entry to recognize the impairment.
(b) What is the new cost basis of the municipal bonds? Given that the maturity value of the bonds is $800,000, should Moceanu Corporation accrete the difference between the carrying amount and the maturity value over the life of the bonds?
(c) At December 31, 2002, the fair value of the municipal bonds is $760,000. Prepare the entry (if any) to record this information.

***E18-18 (Determine Proper Income Reporting)** Presented below are three independent situations that you are to solve:

1. Lauren Bacall Inc. received dividends from its common stock investments during the year ended December 31, 2002, as follows:

   (a) A cash dividend of $12,000 is received from Big Sleep Corporation. (Bacall owns a 2% interest in Big Sleep.)
   (b) A cash dividend of $60,000 is received from Key Largo Corporation. (Bacall owns a 30% interest in Key Largo.) A majority of Bacall's directors are also directors of Key Largo Corporation.
   (c) A stock dividend of 300 shares from Orient Express Inc. was received on December 10, 2002, on which date the quoted market value of Orient's shares was $10 per share. Becall owns less than 1% of Orient's common stock.

   Determine how much dividend income Bacall should report in its 2002 income statement.
2. On January 3, 2002, Barbara Bach Co. purchased as a long-term investment 5,000 shares of Ringo Starr Co. common stock for $79 per share, which represents a 2% interest. On December 31, 2002, the market price of the stock was $83 per share. On March 3, 2003, it sold all 5,000 shares of Starr stock for $102 per share. The company regularly sells securities of this type. The income tax rate is 35%. Determine the amount of gain or loss on disposal that should be reported on the income statement in 2003.
3. Nastassia Kinski Co. owns a 5% interest in Magdalene Corporation, which declared a cash dividend of $620,000 on November 27, 2002, to shareholders of record on December 16, 2002, payable on January 6, 2003. In addition, on October 15, 2002, Kinski received a liquidating dividend of $10,200 from Terminal Velocity Company. Kinski owns 6% of Terminal Velocity Co. Determine the amount of dividend income Kinski should report in its financial statements for 2002.

***E18-19 (Entries for Stock Rights)** On January 10, 2001, Kevin Bacon Company purchased 240 shares, $50 par value (a 3% interest), of common stock of Diner Corporation for $24,000 as a long-term investment. On July 12, 2001, Diner Corporation announced that one right would be issued for every two shares of stock held.

July 30, 2001	Rights to purchase 120 shares of stock at $100 per share are received. The market value of the stock is $120 per share and the market value of the rights is $30 per right.
Aug. 10	The rights to purchase 50 shares of stock are sold at $29 per right.
Aug. 11	The additional 70 rights are exercised, and 70 shares of stock are purchased at $100 per share.
Nov. 15	50 shares of those purchased on January 10, 2001, are sold at $128 per share.

Instructions

Prepare general journal entries on the books of Bacon Company for each of the foregoing transactions.

***E18-20 (Entries for Stock Rights)** Pearl Bailey Company purchases 240 shares of common stock of Carmen Jones Inc. on February 17. The $100 par stock, costing $27,300, is to be a long-term investment for Bailey Company.

1. On June 30, Jones Inc. announces that rights are to be issued. One right will be received for every two shares owned.
2. The rights mentioned in (1) are received on July 15; 120 shares of $100 par stock may be purchased with these rights at par. The stock is currently selling for $120 per share. Market value of the stock rights is $20 per right.
3. On August 5, 70 rights are exercised, and 70 shares of stock are purchased at par.
4. On August 12, the remaining stock rights are sold at $23 per right.
5. On September 28, Bailey Company sells 50 shares of those purchased February 17, at $124 a share.

Instructions

Prepare necessary journal entries for the five numbered items above.

***E18-21 (Investment in Life Insurance Policy)** Bain Company pays the premiums on two insurance policies on the life of its president, Barbara Bain. Information concerning premiums paid in 2002 is given below.

					Cash Surrender Value	
Beneficiary	Face	Prem.	Dividends Cr. to Prem.	Net Prem.	1/1/02	12/31/02
1. Bain Co.	$250,000	$8,500	$2,940	$5,560	$35,000	$37,900
2. President's spouse	75,000	3,000		3,000	9,000	9,750

Instructions

(a) Prepare entries in journal form to record the payment of premiums in 2002.

(b) If the president died in January 2003, and the beneficiaries are paid the face amounts of the policies, what entry would the Bain Company make?

***E18-22 (Entries and Disclosure for Bond Sinking Fund)** The general ledger of Joe Don Baker Company shows an account for Bonds Payable with a balance of $2,000,000. Interest is payable on these bonds semiannually. Of the $2,000,000, bonds in the amount of $400,000 were recently purchased at par by the sinking fund trustee and are held in the sinking fund as an investment of the fund. The annual rate of interest is 10%.

Instructions

(a) What entry or entries should be made by Baker Company to record payment of the semiannual interest? (The company makes interest payments directly to bondholders.)

(b) Illustrate how the bonds payable and the sinking fund accounts should be shown in the balance sheet. Assume that the sinking fund investments other than Baker Company's bonds amount to $511,000, and that the sinking fund cash amounts to $16,000.

***E18-23 (Entries for Plant Expansion Fund, Numbers Omitted)** The transactions given below relate to a fund being accumulated by Mel Brooks Electrical Company over a period of 20 years for the construction of additional buildings.

1. Cash is transferred from the general cash account to the fund.
2. Preferred stock of Rick Moranis Company is purchased as an investment of the fund.
3. Bonds of John Candy Corporation are purchased between interest dates at a discount as an investment of the fund.
4. Expenses of the fund are paid from the fund cash.
5. Interest is collected on John Candy Corporation bonds.

6. Bonds held in the fund are sold at a gain between interest dates.
7. Dividends are received on Rick Moranis Company preferred stock.
8. Common stocks held in the fund are sold at a loss.
9. Cash is paid from the fund for building construction.
10. The cash balance remaining in the fund is transferred to general cash.

Instructions

Prepare journal entries to record the miscellaneous transactions listed above with amounts omitted.

***E18-24 (Derivative Transaction)** On January 2, 2000, Jones Company purchases a call option for $300 on Merchant common stock. The call option gives Jones the option to buy 1,000 shares of Merchant at a strike price of $50 per share. The market price of a Merchant share is $50 on January 2, 2000 (the intrinsic value is therefore $0). On March 31, 2000, the market price for Merchant stock is $53 per share, and the time value of the option is $200.

Instructions

(a) Prepare the journal entry to record the purchase of the call option on January 2, 2000.

(b) Prepare the journal entry(ies) to recognize the change in the fair value of the call option as of March 31, 2000.

(c) What was the effect on net income of entering into the derivative transaction for the period January 2 to March 31, 2000?

***E18-25 (Fair Value Hedge)** On January 2, 2001, MacCloud Co. issued a 4-year, $100,000 note at 6% fixed interest, interest payable semiannually. MacCloud now wants to change the note to a variable rate note.

As a result, on January 2, 2001, MacCloud Co. enters into an interest rate swap where it agrees to receive 6% fixed and pay LIBOR of 5.7% for the first 6 months on $100,000. At each 6-month period, the variable rate will be reset. The variable rate is reset to 6.7% on June 30, 2001.

Instructions

(a) Compute the net interest expense to be reported for this note and related swap transaction as of June 30, 2001.

(b) Compute the net interest expense to be reported for this note and related swap transaction as of December 31, 2001.

***E18-26 (Cash Flow Hedge)** On January 2, 2000, Parton Company issues a 5-year, $10,000,000 note at LIBOR, with interest paid annually. The variable rate is reset at the end of each year. The LIBOR rate for the first year is 5.8%.

Parton Company decides it prefers fixed-rate financing and wants to lock in a rate of 6%. As a result, Parton enters into an interest rate swap to pay 6% fixed and receive LIBOR based on $10 million. The variable rate is reset to 6.6% on January 2, 2001.

Instructions

(a) Compute the net interest expense to be reported for this note and related swap transactions as of December 31, 2000.

(b) Compute the net interest expense to be reported for this note and related swap transactions as of December 31, 2001.

***E18-27 (Fair Value Hedge)** Sarazan Company issues a 4-year, 7.5% fixed-rate interest only, nonprepayable $1,000,000 note payable on December 31, 2000. It decides to change the interest rate from a fixed rate to variable rate and enters into a swap agreement with M&S Corp. The swap agreement specifies that Sarazan will receive a fixed rate at 7.5% and pay variable with settlement dates that match the interest payments on the debt. Assume that interest rates have declined during 2001 and that Sarazan received $13,000 as an adjustment to interest expense for the settlement at December 31, 2001. The loss related to the debt (due to interest rate changes) was $48,000. The value of the swap contract increased $48,000.

Instructions

(a) Prepare the journal entry to record the payment of interest expense on December 31, 2001.

(b) Prepare the journal entry to record the receipt of the swap settlement on December 31, 2001.

(c) Prepare the journal entry to record the change in the fair value of the swap contract on December 31, 2001.

(d) Prepare the journal entry to record the change in the fair value of the debt on December 31, 2001.

***E18-28 (Fair Value Hedge)** Using the same information from E18-27, consider the effects of the swap on M&S Corp. The $1,000,000 nonprepayable note is classified as an available-for-sale security by M&S Corp.

Instructions

(a) Prepare the journal entry to record the receipt of interest revenue on December 31, 2001.

(b) Prepare the journal entry to record the payment of the swap settlement on December 31, 2001.

(c) Prepare the journal entry to record the change in the fair value of the swap contract on December 31, 2001.

(d) Prepare the journal entry to record the change in the fair value of the available-for-sale debt security on December 31, 2001.

PROBLEMS

P18-1 (Debt Securities) Presented below is an amortization schedule related to Kathy Baker Company's 5-year, $100,000 bond with a 7% interest rate and a 5% yield, purchased on December 31, 1999, for $108,660.

Date	Cash Received	Interest Revenue	Bond Premium Amortization	Carry Amount of Bonds
12/31/99				$108,660
12/31/00	$7,000	$5,433	$1,567	107,093
12/31/01	7,000	5,354	1,646	105,447
12/31/02	7,000	5,272	1,728	103,719
12/31/03	7,000	5,186	1,814	101,905
12/31/04	7,000	5,095	1,905	100,000

The following schedule presents a comparison of the amortized cost and fair value of the bonds at year-end:

	12/31/00	12/31/01	12/31/02	12/31/03	12/31/04
Amortized cost	$107,093	$105,447	$103,719	$101,905	$100,000
Fair value	$106,500	$107,500	$105,650	$103,000	$100,000

Instructions

(a) Prepare the journal entry to record the purchase of these bonds on December 31, 1999, assuming the bonds are classified as held-to-maturity securities.

(b) Prepare the journal entry(ies) related to the held-to-maturity bonds for 2000.

(c) Prepare the journal entry(ies) related to the held-to-maturity bonds for 2002.

(d) Prepare the journal entry(ies) to record the purchase of these bonds, assuming they are classified as available-for-sale.

(e) Prepare the journal entry(ies) related to the available-for-sale bonds for 2000.

(f) Prepare the journal entry(ies) related to the available-for-sale bonds for 2002.

P18-2 (Debt Securities Available-for-Sale) On January 1, 2002, Bon Jovi Company purchased $200,000, 8% bonds of Mercury Co. for $184,557. The bonds were purchased to yield 10% interest. Interest is payable semiannually on July 1 and January 1. The bonds mature on January 1, 2007. Bon Jovi Company uses the effective interest method to amortize discount or premium. On January 1, 2004, Bon Jovi Company sold the bonds for $185,363 after receiving interest to meet its liquidity needs.

Instructions

(a) Prepare the journal entry to record the purchase of bonds on January 1. Assume that the bonds are classified as available-for-sale.

(b) Prepare the amortization schedule for the bonds.

(c) Prepare the journal entries to record the semiannual interest on July 1, 2002, and December 31, 2002.

(d) If the fair value of Mercury bonds is $186,363 on December 31, 2003, prepare the necessary adjusting entry. (Assume the securities fair value adjustment balance on January 1, 2003, is a debit of $3,375.)

(e) Prepare the journal entry to record the sale of the bonds on January 1, 2004.

P18-3 (Available-for-Sale Debt Securities) Presented below is information taken from a bond investment amortization schedule with related fair values provided. These bonds are classified as available-for-sale.

	12/31/01	12/31/02	12/31/03
Amortized cost	$491,150	$519,442	$550,000
Fair value	$499,000	$506,000	$550,000

Instructions

(a) Indicate whether the bonds were purchased at a discount or at a premium.
(b) Indicate whether the amortization schedule is based on the effective interest method and how you can determine which method is used.
(c) Prepare the adjusting entry to record the bonds at fair value at December 31, 2001. The Securities Fair Value Adjustment account has a debit balance of $1,000 prior to adjustment.
(d) Prepare the adjusting entry to record the bonds at fair value at December 31, 2002.

P18-4 (Equity Securities Entries and Disclosures) Incognito Company has the following securities in its investment portfolio on December 31, 2001 (all securities were purchased in 2001): (1) 3,000 shares of Bush Co. common stock which cost $58,500, (2) 10,000 shares of David Sanborn Ltd. common stock which cost $580,000, and (3) 6,000 shares of Abba Company preferred stock which cost $255,000. The Securities Fair Value Adjustment account shows a credit of $10,100 at the end of 2001.

In 2002, Incognito completed the following securities transactions:

1. On January 15, sold 3,000 shares of Bush's common stock at $23 per share less fees of $2,150.
2. On April 17, purchased 1,000 shares of Tractors' common stock at $31.50 per share plus fees of $1,980.

On December 31, 2002, the market values per share of these securities were: Bush $20, Sanborn $62, Abba $40, and Tractors $29. In addition, the accounting supervisor of Incognito told you that, even though all these securities have readily determinable fair values, Incognito will not actively trade these securities because the top management intends to hold them for more than one year.

Instructions

(a) Prepare the entry for the security sale on January 15, 2002.
(b) Prepare the journal entry to record the security purchase on April 17, 2002.
(c) Compute the unrealized gains or losses and prepare the adjusting entry for Incognito on December 31, 2002.
(d) How should the unrealized gains or losses be reported on Incognito's balance sheet?

P18-5 (Trading and Available-for-Sale Securities Entries) Gypsy Kings Company has the following portfolio of investment securities at September 30, 2001, its last reporting date.

Trading Securities	Cost	Fair Value
Dan Fogelberg, Inc. common (5,000 shares)	$225,000	$200,000
Petra, Inc. preferred (3,500 shares)	133,000	140,000
Tim Weisberg Corp. common (1,000 shares)	180,000	179,000

On October 10, 2001, the Fogelberg shares were sold at a price of $54 per share. In addition, 3,000 shares of Los Tigres common stock were acquired at $59.50 per share on November 2, 2001. The December 31, 2001 fair values were: Petra $96,000, Los Tigres $132,000, and the Weisberg common $193,000. All the securities are classified as trading.

Instructions

(a) Prepare the journal entries to record the sale, purchase, and adjusting entries related to the trading securities in the last quarter of 2001.
(b) How would the entries in part (a) change if the securities were classified as available-for-sale?

P18-6 (Available-for-Sale and Held-to-Maturity Debt Securities Entries) The following information relates to the debt securities investments of the Yellowjackets Company.

1. On February 1, the company purchased 12% bonds of Vanessa Williams Co. having a par value of $500,000 at 100 plus accrued interest. Interest is payable April 1 and October 1.
2. On April 1, semiannual interest is received.
3. On July 1, 9% bonds of Chieftains, Inc. were purchased. These bonds with a par value of $200,000 were purchased at 100 plus accrued interest. Interest dates are June 1 and December 1.
4. On September 1, bonds of a par value of $100,000, purchased on February 1, are sold at 99 plus accrued interest.
5. On October 1, semiannual interest is received.
6. On December 1, semiannual interest is received.
7. On December 31, the fair value of the bonds purchased February 1 and July 1 are 95 and 93, respectively.

Instructions

(a) Prepare any journal entries you consider necessary, including year-end entries (December 31), assuming these are available-for-sale securities.

(b) If Yellowjackets classified these as held-to-maturity securities, explain how the journal entries would differ from those in part (a).

P18-7 (Applying Fair Value Method) Pacers Corp. is a medium-sized corporation specializing in quarrying stone for building construction. The company has long dominated the market, at one time achieving a 70% market penetration. During prosperous years, the company's profits, coupled with a conservative dividend policy, resulted in funds available for outside investment. Over the years, Pacers has had a policy of investing idle cash in equity securities. In particular, Pacers has made periodic investments in the company's principal supplier, Ricky Pierce Industries. Although the firm currently owns 12 percent of the outstanding common stock of Pierce Industries, Pacers does not have significant influence over the operations of Pierce Industries.

Cheryl Miller has recently joined Pacers as Assistant Controller, and her first assignment is to prepare the 2000 year-end adjusting entries for the accounts that are valued by the "fair value" rule for financial reporting purposes. Miller has gathered the following information about Pacers' pertinent accounts.

1. Pacers has trading securities related to Dale Davis Motors and Rik Smits Electric. During this fiscal year, Pacers purchased 100,000 shares of Davis Motors for $1,400,000; these shares currently have a market value of $1,600,000. Pacers' investment in Smits Electric has not been a profitable; the company acquired 50,000 shares of Smits in April 2000 at $20 per share, a purchase that currently has a value of $620,000.
2. Prior to 2000, Pacers invested $22,500,000 in Ricky Pierce Industries and has not changed its holdings this year. This investment in Ricky Pierce Industries was valued at $21,500,000 on December 31, 1999. Pacers' 12% ownership of Ricky Pierce Industries has a current market value of $22,275,000.

Instructions

(a) Prepare the appropriate adjusting entries for Pacers as of December 31, 2000, to reflect the application of the "fair value" rule for both classes of securities described above.

(b) For both classes of securities presented above, describe how the results of the valuation adjustments made in Instruction (a) would be reflected in the body of and/or notes to Pacers' 2000 financial statements.

P18-8 (Financial Statement Presentation of Available-for-Sale Investments) Woolford Company has the following portfolio of available-for-sale securities at December 31, 2001.

			Per Share	
Security	Quantity	Percent Interest	Cost	Market
Favre, Inc.	2,000 shares	8%	$11	$16
Walsh Corp.	5,000 shares	14%	23	17
Dilfer Company	4,000 shares	2%	31	24

Instructions

(a) What should be reported on Woolford's December 31, 2001, balance sheet relative to these long-term available-for-sale securities?

On December 31, 2002, Woolford's portfolio of available-for-sale securities consisted of the following common stocks.

			Per Share	
Security	Quantity	Percent Interest	Cost	Market
Walsh Corp.	5,000 shares	14%	$23	$30
Dilfer Company	4,000 shares	2%	31	23
Dilfer Company	2,000 shares	1%	25	23

At the end of year 2002, Woolford Company changed its intent relative to its investment in Favre, Inc. and reclassified the shares to trading securities status when the shares were selling for $9 per share.

(b) What should be reported on the face of Woolford's December 31, 2002, balance sheet relative to available-for-sale securities investments? What should be reported to reflect the transactions above in Woolford's 2002 income statement?

(c) Assuming that comparative financial statements for 2001 and 2002 are presented, draft the footnote necessary for full disclosure of Woolford's transactions and position in equity securities.

P18-9 (Gain on Sale of Securities and Comprehensive Income) On January 1, 2001, Enid Inc. had the following balance sheet:

ENID INC.
Balance Sheet
as of January 1, 2001

Assets		Equity	
Cash	$ 50,000	Common stock	$250,000
Available-for-sale securities	240,000	Accumulated other comprehensive income	40,000
Total	$290,000	Total	$290,000

The accumulated other comprehensive income related to unrealized holding gains on available-for-sale securities. The fair value of Enid Inc.'s available-for-sale securities at December 31, 2001, was $190,000; its cost was $120,000. No securities were purchased during the year. Enid Inc.'s income statement for 2001 was as follows (Ignore income taxes):

ENID INC.
Income Statement
For the Year Ended December 31, 2001

Dividend revenue	$15,000
Gain on sale of available-for-sale securities	20,000
Net income	$35,000

Instructions

(Assume all transactions during the year were for cash.)

(a) Prepare the journal entry to record the sale of the available-for-sale securities in 2001.
(b) Prepare a statement of comprehensive income for 2001.
(c) Prepare a balance sheet as of December 31, 2001.

P18-10 (Entries for Long-Term Investments) Octavio Paz Corp. carries an account in its general ledger called "Investments," which contained the following debits for investment purchases, and no credits.

Feb. 1, 2001	Chiang Kai-Shek Company common stock, $100 par, 200 shares	$ 37,400
April 1	U.S. Government bonds, 11%, due April 1, 2011, interest payable April 1 and October 1, 100 bonds of $1,000 par each	100,000
July 1	Claude Monet Company 12% bonds, par $50,000, dated March 1, 2001 purchased at 104 plus accrued interest, interest payable annually on March 1, due March 1, 2021	54,000

Instructions

(a) Prepare entries necessary to classify the amounts into proper accounts, assuming that all the securities are classified as available-for-sale.
(b) Prepare the entry to record the accrued interest and amortization of premium on December 31, 2001, using the straight-line method.
(c) The fair values of the securities on December 31, 2001, were:

Chiang Kai-shek Company common stock	$ 33,800 (1% interest)
U.S. Government bonds	124,700
Claude Monet Company bonds	58,600

What entry or entries, if any, would you recommend be made?
(d) The U.S. Government bonds were sold on July 1, 2002, for $119,200 plus accrued interest. Give the proper entry.

P18-11 (Available-for-Sale and Equity Method) Carlos Fuentes Incorporated is a publicly traded company that manufactures products to clean and demagnetize video and audio tape recorders and players. The company grew rapidly during its first 10 years and made three public offerings during this period. During its rapid growth period, Carlos Fuentes acquired common stock in Yukasato Inc. and Dimna Importers. In 1991 Fuentes acquired 25% of Yukasato's common stock for $588,000 and properly accounts for this investment using the equity method. For its fiscal year ended November 30, 1999, Yukasato Inc. reported net income of $250,000 and paid dividends of $100,000. In 1993 Fuentes acquired 10% of Dimna Importers' common stock for $204,000, and properly accounts for this investment using the fair value

method. Fuentes has a policy of investing idle cash in equity securities. The following data pertain to the securities in Fuentes' investment portfolio.

Available-for-Sale Securities at November 30, 2001

Security	Cost	Fair Value
Bettino Craxi Electric	$326,000	$314,000
Pierre Renoir Inc.	184,000	181,000
George Seferis Company	95,000	98,500
	$605,000	593,500
Dimna Importers	204,000	198,000
	$809,000	$791,500

Available-for-Sale Securities at November 30, 2002

Security	Cost	Fair Value
Bettino Craxi Electric	$326,000	$323,000
Pierre Renoir Inc.	184,000	180,000
Golda Meir Limited	105,000	108,000
	$615,000	611,000
Dimna Importers	204,000	205,000
	$819,000	$816,000

On November 14, 2002, Tasha Yar was hired by Funetes as assistant controller. Her first assignment was to propose the entries to record the November activity and the November 30, 2002, year-end adjusting entries for the investments in available-for-sale securities and the long-term investment in common stock. Using Fuentes' ledger of investment transactions and the data given above, Yar proposed the following entries and submitted them to Miles O'Brien, controller, for review.

Entry 1 (November 8, 2002)

Cash	99,500	
Available-for-Sale Securities		98,500
Gain on Sale of Securities		1,000
To record the sale of George Seferis Company stock for $99,500.		

Entry 2 (November 26, 2002)

Available-for-Sale Securities	105,000	
Cash		105,000
To record the purchase of Golda Meir common stock for $102,200 plus brokerage fees of $2,800.		

Entry 3 (November 30, 2002)

Unrealized Holding Gain or Loss—Equity	3,000	
Securities Fair Value Adjustment (Available-for-Sale)		3,000
To recognize a loss equal to the excess of cost over market value of equity securities.		

Entry 4 (November 30, 2002)

Cash	38,500	
Dividend Revenue		38,500
To record dividends received from securities.		
Yukasato Inc. $25,000		
Dimna Importers 9,000		
Bettino Craxi Electric 4,500		

Entry 5 (November 30, 2002)

Investment in Yukasato Inc.	62,500	
Revenue from Investment		62,500
To record share of Yukasato Inc. income under the equity method, $250,000 × .25		

Instructions

(a) Distinguish between the characteristics of available-for-sale investments and held-to-maturity investments.

(b) The journal entries proposed by Tasha Yar will establish the value of Fuentes Incorporated's equity investments to be reported on the company's external financial statements. Review each of the journal entries proposed by Yar and indicate whether or not it is in accordance with the applicable reporting standards. If an entry is incorrect, prepare the correct entry or entries that should have been made.

(c) Because Fuentes Incorporated owns more than 20% of Yukasato Inc., Miles O'Brien has adopted the equity method to account for the investment in Yukasato Inc. Under what circumstances would

it be inappropriate to use the equity method to account for a 25% interest in the common stock of Yukasato Inc.?

P18-12 (Fair Value and Equity Methods) On January 1, 2001, Howard Corporation acquired 10,000 of the 50,000 outstanding shares of common stock of Kline Company for $25 per share. The balance sheet of Kline Company reported the following information at the date of the acquisition:

Assets not subject to depreciation	$290,000
Assets subject to depreciation	860,000
Liabilities	150,000

Additional information:

1. Kline reported net income of $100,000 and paid dividends of $30,000 in 2001.
2. On the date of the acquisition, the fair value is the same as the book value for both the assets not subject to depreciation and the liabilities.
3. On the date of the acquisition, the fair value of the assets subject to depreciation is $960,000.
4. Kline's stock had a fair value of $24 per share on December 31, 2001.
5. Intangibles are amortized over 20 years and assets subject to depreciation have a remaining useful life of 8 years.

Instructions

(a) Prepare the journal entries for Howard Corporation for 2001, assuming that Howard *cannot* exercise significant influence over Kline Company.

(b) Prepare the journal entries for Howard Corporation for 2001, assuming that Howard can exercise significant influence over Kline Company.

P18-13 (Available-for-Sale Securities—Statement Presentation) Maryam Alvarez Corp. invested its excess cash in available-for-sale securities during 2000. As of December 31, 2000, the portfolio of available-for-sale securities consisted of the following common stocks:

Security	Quantity	Cost	Fair Value
Keesha Jones, Inc.	1,000 shares	$15,000	$21,000
Eola Corp.	2,000 shares	50,000	42,000
Yevette Aircraft	2,000 shares	72,000	60,000
	Totals	$137,000	$123,000

Instructions

(a) What should be reported on Alvarez' December 31, 2000, balance sheet relative to these securities? What should be reported on Alvarez' 2000 income statement?

On December 31, 2001, Alvarez' portfolio of available-for-sale securities consisted of the following common stocks:

Security	Quantity	Cost	Fair Value
Keesha Jones, Inc.	1,000 shares	$15,000	$20,000
Keesha Jones, Inc.	2,000 shares	38,000	40,000
King Company	1,000 shares	16,000	12,000
Yevette Aircraft	2,000 shares	72,000	22,000
	Totals	$141,000	$94,000

During the year 2001, Alvarez Corp. sold 2,000 shares of Eola Corp. for $38,200 and purchased 2,000 more shares of Keesha Jones, Inc. and 1,000 shares of King Company.

(b) What should be reported on Alvarez' December 31, 2001, balance sheet? What should be reported on Alvarez' 2001 income statement?

On December 31, 2002, Alvarez' portfolio of available-for-sale securities consisted of the following common stocks:

Security	Quantity	Cost	Fair Value
Yevette Aircraft	2,000 shares	$72,000	$82,000
King Company	500 shares	8,000	6,000
	Totals	$80,000	$88,000

During the year 2002, Alvarez Corp. sold 3,000 shares of Keesha Jones, Inc. for $39,900 and 500 shares of King Company at a loss of $2,700.

(c) What should be reported on the face of Alvarez' December 31, 2002, balance sheet? What should be reported on Alvarez' 2002 income statement?

(d) What would be reported in a statement of comprehensive income at (1) December 31, 2000; and (2) December 31, 2001?

***P18-14 (Stock Rights—Comprehensive)** Millard Company holds 300 shares of common stock of Fillmore's Decorating Inc. that it purchased for $31,629 as a long-term investment. On January 15, 2002, it is announced that one right will be issued for every 4 shares of Fillmore's Decorating Inc. stock held.

Instructions

(a) Prepare entries on Millard Company's books for the transactions below that occurred after the date of this announcement. Show all computations in good form.

(1) 100 shares of stock are sold rights-on for $11,500.

(2) Rights to purchase 50 additional shares of stock at par value of $100 per share are received. The market value of the stock on this date is $105 per share and the market value of the rights is $6 per right.

(3) The rights are exercised, and 50 additional shares are purchased at $100 per share.

(4) 100 shares of the stock originally held are sold at $106 per share.

(b) If the rights had not been exercised but instead had been sold at $6 per right, what would have been the amount of the gain or loss on the sale of the rights?

(c) If the stock purchased through the exercise of the rights is later sold at $107 per share, what is the amount of the gain or loss on the sale?

(d) If the rights had not been exercised, but had been allowed to expire, what would be the proper entry?

***P18-15 (Entries for Sinking Fund)** The transactions given below relate to a sinking fund for retirement of long-term bonds of John Fremont Roofing:

1. In accordance with the terms of the bond indenture, cash in the amount of $150,000 is transferred at the end of the first year, from the regular cash account to the sinking fund.
2. Cordell Hull Siding Company 10% bonds of a par value of $50,000, maturing in 5 years, are purchased for $47,000.
3. 500 shares of Robert Lee Company 8% preferred stock ($50 par value) are purchased at $54 per share.
4. Annual interest of $5,000 is received on Cordell Hull Siding Company bonds. (Amortize a full year of discount using straight-line amortization.)
5. Sinking fund expenses of $480 are paid from sinking fund cash.
6. Anne Hutchinson Glass Company 9% bonds with interest payable February 1 and August 1 are purchased on April 15 at par value of $60,000 plus accrued interest.
7. Dividends of $2,000 are received on Robert Lee Company preferred stock.
8. All the Hutchinson Glass Company bonds are sold on September 1 at 101 plus accrued interest. Assume interest collected August 1 was properly recorded.
9. Investments carried in the fund at $1,583,000 are sold for $1,538,000.
10. The fund contains cash of $1,627,000 after disposing of all investments and paying all expenses. $1,600,000 of this amount is used to retire the bonds payable at maturity date.
11. The remaining cash balance is returned to the general account.

Instructions

Prepare the journal entries required by John Fremont Roofing for the transactions above.

***P18-16 (Derivative Financial Instrument)** The treasurer of Miller Co. has read on the Internet that the stock price of Ewing Inc. is about to take off. In order to profit from this potential development, Miller Co. purchased a call option on Ewing common shares on July 7, 2000, for $240. The call option is for 200 shares (notional value), and the strike price is $70. The option expires on January 31, 2001. The following data are available with respect to the call option:

Date	Market Price of Ewing Shares	Time Value of Call Option
September 30, 2000	$77 per share	$180
December 31, 2000	$75 per share	65
January 4, 2001	$76 per share	30

Instructions

Prepare the journal entries for Miller Co. for the following dates:

(a) July 7, 2000—Investment in call option on Ewing shares.

(b) September 30, 2000—Miller prepared financial statements.

(c) December 31, 2000—Miller prepares financial statements.

(d) January 4, 2001—Miller settles the call option on the Ewing shares.

***P18-17 (Derivative Financial Instrument)** Johnstone Co. purchased a put option on Ewing common shares on July 7, 2000, for $240. The put option is for 200 shares, and the strike price

is $70. The option expires on January 31, 2001. The following data are available with respect to the put option:

Date	Market Price of Ewing Shares	Time Value of Put Option
September 30, 2000	$77 per share	$125
December 31, 2000	$75 per share	50
January 31, 2001	$78 per share	0

Instructions

Prepare the journal entries for Johnstone Co. for the following dates:

(a) January 7, 2000—Investment in put option on Ewing shares.
(b) September 30, 2000—Johnstone prepares financial statements.
(c) December 31, 2000—Johnstone prepares financial statements.
(d) January 31, 2001—Put option expires.

P18-18 (Free-standing Derivative) Warren Co. purchased a put option on Echo common shares on January 7, 2001, for $360. The put option is for 400 shares, and the strike price is $85. The option expires on July 31, 2001. The following data are available with respect to the put option:

Date	Market Price of Echo Shares	Time Value of Put Option
March 31, 2001	$80 per share	$200
June 30, 2001	$82 per share	90
July 6, 2001	$77 per share	25

Instructions

Prepare the journal entries for Warren Co. for the following dates:

(a) January 7, 2001—Investment in put option on Echo shares.
(b) March 31, 2001—Warren prepares financial statements.
(c) June 30, 2001—Warren prepares financial statements.
(d) July 6, 2001—Warren settles the call option on the Echo shares.

***P18-19 (Fair Value Hedge Interest Rate Swap)** On December 31, 2000, Mercantile Corp. had a $10,000,000 8% fixed rate note outstanding, payable in 2 years. It decides to enter into a 2-year swap with Chicago First Bank to convert the fixed-rate debt to variable-rate debt. The terms of the swap indicate that Mercantile will receive interest at a fixed rate of 8.0% and will pay a variable rate equal to the 6-month LIBOR rate, based on the $10,000,000 amount. The LIBOR rate on December 31, 2000, is 7%. The LIBOR rate will be reset every 6 months and will be used to determine the variable rate to be paid for the following 6-month period.

Mercantile Corp. designates the swap as a fair value hedge. Assume that the hedging relationship meets all the conditions necessary for hedge accounting. The 6-month LIBOR rate and the swap and debt fair values are as follows:

Date	6-Month LIBOR Rate	Swap Fair Value	Debt Fair Value
December 31, 2000	7.0%	—	$10,000,000
June 30, 2001	7.5%	(200,000)	9,800,000
December 31, 2001	6.0%	60,000	10,060,000

Instructions

(a) Present the journal entries to record the following transactions:
  (1) The entry, if any, to record the swap on December 31, 2000.
  (2) The entry to record the semiannual debt interest payment on June 30, 2001.
  (3) The entry to record the settlement of the semiannual swap amount receivables at 8%, less amount payable at LIBOR, 7%.
  (4) The entry to record the change in the fair value of the debt on June 30, 2001.
  (5) The entry to record the change in the fair value of the swap at June 30, 2001.
(b) Indicate the amount(s) reported on the balance sheet and income statement related to the debt and swap on December 31, 2000.
(c) Indicate the amount(s) reported on the balance sheet and income statement related to the debt and swap on June 30, 2001.
(d) Indicate the amount(s) reported on the balance sheet and income statement related to the debt and swap on December 31, 2001.

***P18-20 (Cash Flow Hedge)** LEW Jewelry Co. uses gold in the manufacture of its products. LEW anticipates that it will need to purchase 500 ounces of gold in October 2000, for jewelry that will be shipped for the holiday shopping season. However, if the price of gold increases, LEW's cost to produce its jewelry will increase, which could reduce its profit margins.

To hedge the risk of increased gold prices, on April 1, 2000, LEW enters into a gold futures contract and designates this futures contract as a cash flow hedge of the anticipated gold purchase. The notional amount of the contract is 500 ounces, and the terms of the contract give LEW the option to purchase gold at a price of $300 per ounce. The price will be good until the contract expires on October 31, 2000.

Assume the following data with respect to the price of the call options and the gold inventory purchase:

Date	Spot Price for October Delivery
April 1, 2000	$300 per ounce
June 30, 2000	$310 per ounce
September 30, 2000	$315 per ounce

Instructions

Prepare the journal entries for the following transactions:

(a) April 1, 2000—Inception of the futures contract, no premium paid.
(b) June 30, 2000—LEW Co. prepares financial statements.
(c) September 30, 2000—LEW Co. prepares financial statements.
(d) October 10, 2000—LEW Co. purchases 500 ounces of gold at $315 per ounce and settles the futures contract.
(e) December 20, 2000—LEW sells jewelry containing gold purchased in October 2000 for $350,000. The cost of the finished goods inventory is $200,000.
(f) Indicate the amount(s) reported on the balance sheet and income statement related to the futures contract on June 30, 2000.
(g) Indicate the amount(s) reported in the income statement related to the futures contract and the inventory transactions on December 31, 2000.

***P18-21 (Fair Value Hedge)** On November 3, 2001, Sprinkle Co. invested $200,000 in 4,000 shares of the common stock of Johnstone Co. Sprinkle classified this investment as available-for-sale. Sprinkle Co. is considering making a more significant investment in Johnstone Co. at some point in the future but has decided to wait and see how the stock does over the next several quarters.

To hedge against potential declines in the value of Johnstone stock during this period, Sprinkle also purchased a put option on the Johnstone stock. Sprinkle paid an option premium of $600 for the put option, which gives Sprinkle the option to sell 4,000 Johnstone shares at a strike price of $50 per share; the option expires on July 31, 2002. The following data are available with respect to the values of the Johnstone stock and the put option:

Date	Market Price of Johnstone Shares	Time Value of Put Option
December 31, 2001	$50 per share	$375
March 31, 2002	$45 per share	175
June 30, 2002	$43 per share	40

Instructions

(a) Prepare the journal entries for Sprinkle Co. for the following dates:
  (1) November 3, 2001—Investment in Johnstone stock and the put option on Johnstone shares.
  (2) December 31, 2001—Sprinkle Co. prepares financial statements.
  (3) March 31, 2002—Sprinkle prepares financial statements.
  (4) June 30, 2002—Sprinkle prepares financial statements.
  (5) July 1, 2002—Sprinkle settles the put option and sells the Johnstone shares for $43 per share.

(b) Indicate the amount(s) reported on the balance sheet and income statement related to the Johnstone investment and the put option on December 31, 2001.
(c) Indicate the amount(s) reported on the balance sheet and income statement related to the Johnstone investment and the put option on June 30, 2002.

CONCEPTUAL CASES

C18-1 (Issues Raised about Investment Securities) You have just started work for Andre Love Co. as part of the controller's group involved in current financial reporting problems. Jackie Franklin, controller for Love, is interested in your accounting background because the company has experienced a series of financial reporting surprises over the last few years. Recently, the controller has learned from the company's auditors that an FASB *Statement* may apply to its investment in securities. She assumes that you are familiar with this pronouncement and asks how the following situations should be reported in the financial statements.

Situation 1
Trading securities in the current asset section have a fair value of $4,200 lower than cost.

Situation 2
A trading security whose fair value is currently less than cost is transferred to the available-for-sale category.

Situation 3
An available-for-sale security, whose fair value is currently less than cost, is classified as noncurrent but is to be reclassified as current.

Situation 4
A company's portfolio of available-for-sale securities consists of the common stock of one company. At the end of the prior year the fair value of the security was 50% of original cost, and this reduction in market value was reported as an other than temporary impairment. However, at the end of the current year the fair value of the security had appreciated to twice the original cost.

Situation 5
The company has purchased some convertible debentures that it plans to hold for less than a year. The fair value of the convertible debenture is $7,700 below its cost.

Instructions

What is the effect upon carrying value and earnings for each of the situations above? Assume that these situations are unrelated.

C18-2 (Equity Securities) James Joyce Co. has the following available-for-sale securities outstanding on December 31, 2000 (its first year of operations):

	Cost	Fair Value
Anna Wickham Corp. Stock	$20,000	$19,000
D H Lawrence Company Stock	10,000	8,800
Edith Sitwell Company Stock	20,000	20,600
	$50,000	$48,400

During 2001 D H Lawrence Company stock was sold for $9,200, the difference between the $9,200 and the "fair value" of $8,800 being recorded as a "Gain on Sale of Securities." The market price of the stock on December 31, 2001, was: Anna Wickham Corp. stock—$19,900; Edith Sitwell Company stock—$20,500.

Instructions

(a) What justification is there for valuing available-for-sale securities at fair value and reporting the unrealized gain or loss as part of stockholders' equity?

(b) How should James Joyce Company apply this rule on December 31, 2000? Explain.

(c) Did James Joyce Company properly account for the sale of the D H Lawrence Company stock? Explain.

(d) Are there any additional entries necessary for James Joyce Company at December 31, 2001, to reflect the facts on the financial statements in accordance with generally accepted accounting principles? Explain.

(AICPA adapted)

C18-3 (Financial Statement Effect of Equity Securities) Presented below are three unrelated situations involving equity securities:

Situation 1
An equity security, whose market value is currently less than cost, is classified as available-for-sale but is to be reclassified as trading.

Situation 2
A noncurrent portfolio with an aggregate market value in excess of cost includes one particular security whose market value has declined to less than one-half of the original cost. The decline in value is considered to be other than temporary.

Situation 3
The portfolio of trading securities has a cost in excess of fair value of $13,500. The available-for-sale portfolio has a fair value in excess of cost of $28,600.

Instructions

What is the effect upon carrying value and earnings for each of the situations above? Complete your response to each situation before proceeding to the next situation.

C18-4 (Equity Securities, Current and Noncurrent) The Financial Accounting Standards Board issued its *Statement No. 115* to clarify accounting methods and procedures with respect to certain debt and all equity securities. An important part of the statement concerns the distinction between held-to-maturity, available-for-sale, and trading securities.

Instructions

(a) Why does a company maintain an investment portfolio of held-to-maturity, available-for-sale, and trading securities?

(b) What factors should be considered in determining whether investments in securities should be classified as held-to-maturity, available-for-sale, and trading, and how do these factors affect the accounting treatment for unrealized losses?

C18-5 (Investment Accounted for under the Equity Method) On July 1, 2002, Sylvia Warner Company purchased for cash 40% of the outstanding capital stock of Robert Graves Company. Both Sylvia Warner Company and Robert Graves Company have a December 31 year-end. Graves Company, whose common stock is actively traded in the over-the-counter market, reported its total net income for the year to Warner Company and also paid cash dividends on November 15, 2002, to Warner Company and its other stockholders.

Instructions

How should Warner Company report the above facts in its December 31, 2002, balance sheet and its income statement for the year then ended? Discuss the rationale for your answer.

(AICPA adapted)

C18-6 (Equity Investment) On July 1, 2001, Cheryl Munns Company purchased for cash 40% of the outstanding capital stock of Huber Corporation. Both Munns and Huber have a December 31 year-end. Huber Corporation, whose common stock is actively traded on the American Stock Exchange, paid a cash dividend on November 15, 2001, to Munns Company and its other stockholders. It also reported its total net income for the year of $920,000 to Munns Company.

Instructions

Prepare a one-page memorandum of instructions on how Cheryl Munns Company should report the above facts in its December 31, 2001, balance sheet and its 2001 income statement. In your memo, identify and describe the method of valuation you recommend. Provide rationale where you can. Address your memo to the chief accountant at Cheryl Munns Company.

***C18-7 (Investment in Life Insurance Policy)** In the course of your examination of the financial statements of Emanual Ax Corporation as of December 31, 2002, the following entry came to your attention.

January 4, 2002		
Receivable from Insurance Company	1,000,000	
Cash Surrender Value of Life Insurance Policies		132,000
Retained Earnings		163,000
Donated Capital from Life Insurance Proceeds		705,000
(Disposition of the proceeds of the life insurance policy on Mr. Cliburn's life. Mr. Cliburn died on January 1, 2002.)		

You are aware that Mr. Van Cliburn, an officer-stockholder in the small manufacturing firm, insisted that the corporation's board of directors authorize the purchase of an insurance policy to compensate for any loss of earning potential upon his death. The corporation paid $295,000 in premiums prior to Mr. Cliburn's death, and was the sole beneficiary of the policy. At the date of death there had been no premium prepayment and no rebate was due. In prior years cash surrender value in the amount of $132,000 had been recorded in the accounts.

Instructions

(a) What is the cash surrender value of a life insurance policy?

(b) How should the cash surrender value of a life insurance policy be classified in the financial statements while the policy is in force? Why?

(c) Comment on the propriety of the entry recording the insurance receivable.

***C18-8 (Basic Investment Concepts and Classification of Sinking Fund)**

Part A

To manufacture and sell its products, a company must invest in inventories, plant and equipment, and other operating assets. In addition, a manufacturing company often finds it desirable or necessary to invest a portion of its available resources, either directly or through the operation of special funds, in stocks, bonds, and other securities.

Instructions

(a) List the reasons why a manufacturing company might invest funds in stocks, bonds, and other securities.

(b) What are the criteria for classifying investments as current or noncurrent assets?

Part B

Because of favorable market prices, the trustee of George Washington Company's bond sinking fund invested the current year's contribution to the fund in the company's own bonds. The bonds are being held in the fund without cancellation. The fund also includes cash and securities of other companies.

Instructions

Describe three methods of classifying the bond sinking fund on the balance sheet of George Washington Company. Include a discussion of the propriety of using each method.

***C18-9 (Classification of Sinking Fund)** Clara Barton Inc. administers the sinking fund applicable to its own outstanding long-term bonds. The following four proposals relate to the accounting treatment of sinking fund cash and securities.

1. To mingle sinking fund cash with general cash and sinking fund securities with other securities, and to show both as current assets on the balance sheet.
2. To keep sinking fund cash in a separate bank account and sinking fund securities separate from other securities, but on the balance sheet to treat cash as a part of the general cash and the securities as part of general investments, both being shown as current assets.
3. To keep sinking fund cash in a separate bank account and sinking fund securities separate from other securities, but to combine the two accounts on the balance sheet under one caption, such as "Sinking Fund Cash and Investments," to be listed as a noncurrent asset.
4. To keep sinking fund cash in a separate bank account and sinking fund securities separate from other securities, and to identify each separately on the balance sheet among the current assets.

Instructions

Identify the proposal that is most appropriate. Give the reasons for your selection.

USING YOUR JUDGMENT

FINANCIAL REPORTING PROBLEM: INTEL CORPORATION

Instructions

Refer to the financial statements and accompanying notes and discussion of Intel Corporation presented in Appendix 5B and answer the following questions:

(a) What investments are reported by Intel in its balance sheet (description, classification, and amount) of December 26, 1998?

(b) What does Intel disclose in notes to the financial statements as its policy relative to its investments? How does Intel classify its marketable investments? What method of assigning cost to securities sold does Intel apply? How are Intel's investments in non-marketable instruments recorded and where are they reported in the balance sheet?

(c) Intel states in its notes that **all** of its marketable investments are reported at **fair value**. How is fair value determined by Intel?

(d) How does Intel use derivative financial instruments? What are Intel's accounting policies for its derivative instruments?

FINANCIAL STATEMENT ANALYSIS CASE

Union Planters

Union Planters is a Tennessee bank holding company (that is, it is a corporation that owns banks). It manages $32 billion in assets, the largest of which is its loan portfolio of $19 billion. In addition to its loan portfolio, however, like other banks it has significant debt and stock investments. The nature of these investments varies from short-term in nature to long-term in nature, and as a consequence, consistent with the requirements of accounting rules, Union Planters reports its investments in two different categories—trading and available-for-sale. The following facts were found in Union Planters' 1998 Annual Report:

(all dollars in millions)	Amortized Cost	Gross Unrealized Gains	Gross Unrealized Losses	Fair Value
Trading account assets	$ 275	—	—	$ 275
Securities available for sale	8,209	$108	$15	8,302
Net income				224
Net securities gains (losses)				(9)

Instructions

(a) Why do you suppose Union Planters purchases investments, rather than simply making loans? Why does it purchase investments that vary in nature both in terms of their maturities and in type (debt versus stock)?

(b) How must Union Planters account for its investments in each of the two categories?

(c) In what ways does classifying investments into two different categories assist investors in evaluating the profitability of a company like Union Planters?

(d) Suppose that the management of Union Planters was not happy with its 1998 net income. What step could it have taken with its investment portfolio that would have definitely increased 1998 reported profit? How much could it have increased reported profit? Why do you suppose it chose not to do this?

COMPARATIVE ANALYSIS CASE

The Coca-Cola Company versus PepsiCo, Inc.

Instructions

Go to the Digital Tool and, using The Coca-Cola Company and PepsiCo, Inc. Annual Report information, answer the following questions.

(a) Based on the information contained in these financial statements, determine each of the following for each company:

(1) Cash used in (for) investing activities during 1998 (from the Statement of Cash Flows).

(2) Cash used for acquisitions and investments in unconsolidated affiliates (or principally bottling companies) during 1998.

(3) Total investment in unconsolidated affiliates (or investments and other assets) at December 31, 1998.

(4) What conclusions concerning the management of investments can be drawn from these data?

(b) (1) Briefly identify from Coca-Cola's December 31, 1998, balance sheet the investments it reported as being accounted for under the equity method. (2) What is the amount of investments Coca-Cola reported in its 1998 balance sheet as "cost method investments," and what is the nature of these investments?

(c) In its note number 8 on Financial Instruments, what total amounts did Coca-Cola report at December 31, 1998, as: (1) trading securities; (2) available-for-sale securities; and (3) held-to-maturity securities?

(d) **(1)** Briefly, according to its note, what is PepsiCo's policy relative to the use of derivative instruments? **(2)** Briefly, what is Coca-Cola's policy relative to the use of derivative instruments?

RESEARCH CASES

Case 1

You have heard that G. D. Searle & Co. is developing a drug that will cure the common cold. Given the potentially enormous impact on the company's earnings and cash flow, you are interested in investing in Searle and want to do a background investigation.

Instructions

Use *Moody's Industrial Manual* to answer the following questions.

(a) What is the parent company of Searle? What portion of Searle does the parent own?

(b) When did the parent acquire Searle? What was the acquisition price?

(c) How would the financial results of Searle be reflected in the parent company's financial statements?

Case 2

The July 6, 1995, edition of *The Wall Street Journal* includes an article by Jim Carlton and David P. Hamilton entitled "Packard Bell Sells 20% Stake to NEC for $170 Million; Deal Gives Japanese Firm Unprecedented Access to the U.S. PC Market."

Instructions

Read the article and answer the following questions.

(a) Why did Packard Bell sell shares to NEC?

(b) Identify a similar transaction between two other computer companies.

(c) Under U.S. GAAP, how would NEC account for its investment in Packard Bell?

(d) Packard Bell was considering a sale of common shares to the general public. Why didn't it select this option?

ETHICS CASE

Addison Manufacturing holds a large portfolio of debt and equity securities as an investment. The fair value of the portfolio is greater than its original cost, even though some securities have decreased in value.

Ted Abernathy, the financial vice president, and Donna Nottebart, the controller, are near year-end in the process of classifying for the first time this securities portfolio in accordance with *FASB Statement No. 115.* Abernathy wants to classify those securities that have increased in value during the period as trading securities in order to increase net income this year. He wants to classify all the securities that have decreased in value as available-for-sale (the equity securities) and as held-to-maturity (the debt securities).

Nottebart disagrees and wants to classify those securities that have decreased in value as trading securities and those that have increased in value as available-for-sale (equity) and held-to-maturity (debt). She contends that the company is having a good earnings year and that recognizing the losses will help to smooth the income this year. As a result, the company will have built-in gains for future periods when the company may not be as profitable.

Instructions

Answer the following questions:

(a) Will classifying the portfolio as each proposes actually have the effect on earnings that each says it will?

(b) Is there anything unethical in what each of them proposes? Who are the stakeholders affected by their proposals?

(c) Assume that Abernathy and Nottebart properly classify the entire portfolio into trading, available-for-sale, and held-to-maturity categories, but then each proposes to sell just before year-end the securities with gains or with losses, as the case may be, to accomplish their effect on earnings. Is this unethical?

A visit with
Ed Jenkins

Edmund L. Jenkins, who holds an M.B.A. from the University of Michigan and a B.A from Albion College, is chairman of the Financial Accounting Standards Board in Norwalk, Connecticut. Prior to assuming this five-year term in 1997, Mr. Jenkins was a partner with Arthur Andersen & Co. Over a 38-year career at this Big Five accounting firm, Mr. Jenkins was directly involved in setting professional standards for Arthur Andersen's worldwide audit staff and partners. He was a founding member of the FASB's Emerging Issues Task Force and was Chairman of the AICPA Special Committee on Financial Reporting, which issued a path-breaking report in 1994. The report called for disclosure of a broader array of information such as business strategy, which was resisted by some business executives who were reluctant to disclose confidential information that would help competitors.

PERSPECTIVES ON

Standard Setting

How has the accounting profession changed over the past 30 years? The accounting profession has certainly expanded its scope of practice. When I entered the profession, services included traditional accounting and auditing, tax, and a narrow approach to consulting, usually related to the development and installation of information systems. But the demands of clients and the ability of CPAs to understand a company's business through their role as auditors created a demand for broader consulting services such as strategic planning and financing techniques. Today, we have a very broad, exciting scope of practice. Some might even say it's too exciting, that it has gone beyond where it should in terms of protecting the auditor's ability to be independent and objective.

What are your responsibilities as chairman of the FASB? I'm responsible for carrying out our mission, which is to see that financial reporting does the best possible job of meeting the information needs of investors as they go about carrying out their decision-making activities with respect to the allocation of capital. That means that we need to keep abreast of new types of transactions where standards may need to be developed, or to revamp standards that may need to be improved based on our research, which includes observing what goes on in the marketplace and listening to our constituents in the business community.

Accounting for stock options is particularly timely with so many Internet companies going public. But this has been a contentious issue for the Board. Why? The Board tried to change the standard about four or five years ago, but was unable to do so because of pressure from Congress. So, we're faced with having a standard in place, *APB Opinion 25,* which is more than 25 years old and was appropriate only when options were granted to half a dozen executives in the company. In recent years, the use of options has exploded in popularity, particularly in high technology, where it may represent the majority of the total compensation package for all employees. As a result, the impact on a company is much greater than was contemplated by the framers of *APB Opinion 25.* Today, we have ways of valuing options that weren't available 25 years ago. But current accounting says that you don't attribute any value to the option if it meets certain tests. Or, if you do value the option, you base it on the change in the underlying stock value, which may overstate the value of the option itself. So current accounting is an all-or-nothing approach to stock options, which creates an unrealistic recognition or lack of recognition of the cost involved in issuing options.

The FASB was originally established as an independent private-sector standards-setter not subject to the political process. Our goal has always been to develop information for investors and other users that is objective, that's neutral from a public policy standpoint, and that reflects the economics of the transaction. But on this issue, the FASB found itself in a position where going forward would have jeopardized its ability to remain in existence. The Board backed away, which in retrospect was unfortunate because it has served to encourage people to put pressure on us when they don't like the direction that a particular standard is going. For instance, our project on derivatives generated a lot of pressure from industry and in Congress, but we resisted it, and we were able to issue a new standard. Prior to our action, derivatives weren't accounted for at all, and the risk associated with their usage wasn't being communicated. Yet the implications of derivatives became very apparent when Orange County faced bankruptcy after its investment officers pursued there risky hedging strategies without adequate disclosure.

Are you receiving similar pressure with the new rules on business combinations? Yes. There are many companies that object to eliminating pooling-of-interest accounting, although we also have some companies that support its elimination. Today, companies have explicit strategies to grow through acquisition, often using highly valued stock as opposed to internal growth. The impact of the decision to use purchase versus pooling-of-interest accounting is much greater, especially with the very high stock multiples that we have today. That's because purchase accounting results in an annual goodwill charge-off that reflects the excess purchase price over the fair market value of assets. There has been a very significant trend outside of the U.S. to either eliminate or reduce the use of pooling. So all of those reasons entered into the Board's decision to move forward on this project.

How would you write off goodwill? There have been a number of suggestions on the topic. One is that you would write it off immediately upon acquisition, perhaps because you don't believe it meets the test of being an asset. Another approach is to recognize it, but not write it off at all, because unless a company is getting into trouble, goodwill doesn't have a finite life. It exists forever and might even grow if the company is successful enough. However, the approach that we've adopted is that goodwill should be amortized like any other asset, that sustaining goodwill arises from subsequent investment activity through advertising, high-quality products, good customer relations, and so on. Since it arises from efforts that take place subsequent to the business combination, it has a finite life, because without maintenance it would go away very fast.

What new issues are you tackling? There's a big question about whether the so-called "new economy," of technology and Internet companies requires an entirely different kind of financial reporting. In these companies, the intangible assets, e.g. software engineering talent or research and development, are often much more valuable than traditional fixed assets such as plant and equipment. At present, we do not have a good way to account for the cost or the benefit of these intangibles, whether purchased or generated internally. We're doing some basic research into that area now, and certainly it will be on our agenda as we look forward a few years.

Can new college graduates go to work for the FASB? Yes, we have a program which we call a Postgraduate Internship, where we take individuals, usually with bachelor's degrees, right off the campus, bring them to the FASB for a year in a paid position, and they work directly on projects. Frankly, it's amazing what they can do and the contributions they make. Every intern gets an opportunity to do research, develop positions, and make presentations to the Board on specific technical issues. The research might involve examining the accounting of various business transactions or looking at issues that have been raised in practice by accounting firms or the Securities and Exchange Commission. The accounting departments or business schools nominate candidates, and we accept about six or seven every year, although there are many more applicants. So it's quite competitive.

Can mid-career professionals go to work for you? Yes. We have a program which we call a Fellow Program, which takes experienced individuals, mostly from accounting firms but sometimes from industry or academia, who have been with their companies or firms for quite a long time, maybe ten years or so. They come in for two-year periods and then go back to their organizations, usually with a promotion, we hope.

CHAPTER 19

Revenue Recognition

Cyberspace Trading for Revenues

Since the time when early man traded tools for animal skins and frontier farmers traded cows for horses, barter has been an accepted form of commerce. Today, the practice of trading for goods and services appears to be catching on in a big way on the Internet. Consider **Sportsline, USA**. Its sports-related Internet advertising address is constantly being promoted on **CBS** telecasts of sporting events. This is not surprising, since CBS is part owner of this dot-com venture. How does Sportsline make money? Looking at the cash flow, it is not clear. For example, in the first half of 1999, none of Sportsline's revenue of $24 million was received in cash. Instead Sportsline sells advertising on its site in exchange for advertising and other services on its customers' Internet sites.

A lot of commerce is being transacted on such virtual trading posts, and much of the reported revenue comes from barter. For example, in a recent quarter, barter revenue comprised greater than 10 percent of the revenues at Internet companies such as **Ivillage**, **Salon.com**, **Earthweb**, **Verticalnet**, and **Edgar Online**. However, the growth in these types of exchanges is raising concerns that the financial picture for the Internet industry is being distorted. Because these companies rarely report positive net incomes, reported revenues (without deducting expenses) have become a key valuation indicator, with strong revenue growth leading to higher stock prices. As one expert noted, "Valuations for these companies are being driven by revenues, and barter creates the potential for distortion in a company's revenues."

This potential distortion has caught the attention of accounting regulators. Lynn Turner, the Securities and Exchange Commission's Chief Accountant, says he too is concerned about the proportion of dot-com revenues coming from barter and that his staff is monitoring these practices. According to Mr. Turner, "We want to make sure that the information being reported gives investors a true notion of what is really going on with revenues and that they are reliable numbers. . . . We're always concerned that someone will push the envelope too far." Some bartering dot-coms may be pushing the financial reporting envelope too far by trading relevant and reliable numbers for higher reported revenues.[1]

[1]Based on Edward Wyatt, "A Whole Other Type of E-Trade," *The New York Times*, October 20, 1999.

LEARNING OBJECTIVES

After studying this chapter, you should be able to:

1. **Apply the revenue recognition principle.**
2. **Describe accounting issues involved with revenue recognition at point of sale.**
3. **Apply the percentage-of-completion method for long-term contracts.**
4. **Apply the completed-contract method for long-term contracts.**
5. **Identify the proper accounting for losses on long-term contracts.**
6. **Describe the installment sales method of accounting.**
7. **Explain the cost recovery method of accounting.**

PREVIEW OF CHAPTER 19

As indicated in the opening story about barter transactions on the Internet, "When should revenue be recognized?" is a complex question. In some cases, the many methods of marketing products and services make it difficult to develop guidelines that will apply to all situations. The purpose of this chapter is to provide you with general guidelines used in most business transactions. The content and organization of the chapter are as follows:

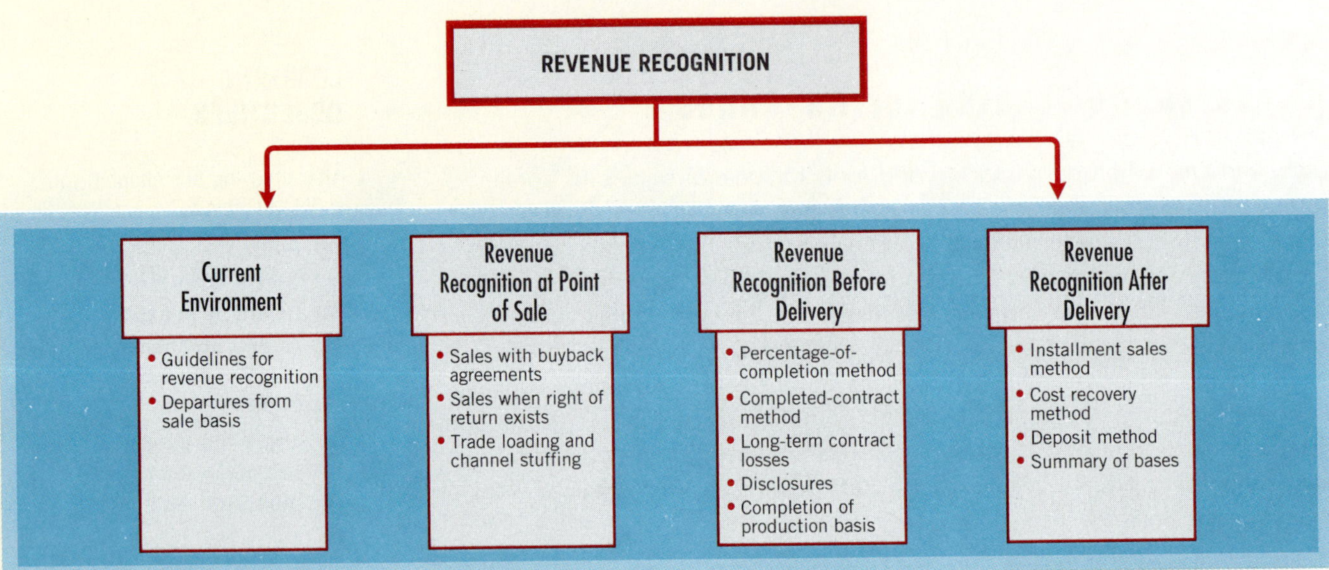

THE CURRENT ENVIRONMENT

The issue of the proper time to recognize revenue has received considerable attention over the last few years. A series of highly publicized cases of companies recognizing revenue prematurely has caused the SEC to increase its enforcement actions in this area. In some of these cases significant adjustments to previously issued financial statements were made. As indicated by Lynn Turner, chief accountant of the SEC, "When people cross over the boundaries of legitimate reporting, the Commission will take appropriate action to ensure the fairness and integrity that investors need and depend on every day."[2]

Inappropriate recognition of revenue can occur in any industry. Products that are sold to distributors for resale pose different risks than products or services that are sold directly to customers. Sales in high-technology industries where rapid product obsolescence is a significant issue pose different risks than sale of inventory with a longer life, such as farm or construction equipment, automobiles, trucks, and appliances.[3]

The opening story indicates the difficulties often associated with revenue recognition in new industries. As indicated, a number of dot-com companies have turned themselves into virtual trading posts, swapping ad space with one another. In these situa-

[2]The SEC has made it clear that it will not tolerate abuses of the financial reporting process and that those who fail to adhere to "certain standards" will be prosecuted.

[3]Adapted from American Institute of Certified Public Accountants, Inc., *Audit Issues in Revenue Recognition* (New York: AICPA, 1999).

tions, an equal amount of revenue and expense is reported, so there is no effect on cash flows and net income. But, Internet stocks often trade on revenue multiples, not earnings multiples, and therefore reporting of higher revenue amounts may affect stock valuations. In addition, the SEC has expressed concern that dot-com companies are increasing their revenue by including product sales in their revenue even though they are acting only as the distributor (middle-person) on behalf of other companies. In other words, dot-com companies should be reporting only a distribution (brokerage) fee for selling another company's products.[4]

Guidelines for Revenue Recognition

OBJECTIVE 1
Apply the revenue recognition principle.

In general, the guidelines for revenue recognition are quite broad. In addition, certain industries have very specific guidelines that provide additional insight into when revenue should be recognized. The **revenue recognition principle** provides that revenue is recognized[5] when (1) it is realized or realizable and (2) it is earned.[6] Revenues are **realized** when goods and services are exchanged for cash or claims to cash (receivables). Revenues are **realizable** when assets received in exchange are readily convertible to known amounts of cash or claims to cash. Revenues are **earned** when the entity has substantially accomplished what it must do to be entitled to the benefits represented by the revenues, that is, when the earnings process is complete or virtually complete.[7]

Four revenue transactions are recognized in accordance with this principle.

UNDERLYING CONCEPTS

Revenues are inflows of assets and/or settlements of liabilities from delivering or producing goods, rendering services, or other earning activities that constitute an enterprise's ongoing major or central operations during a period.

1. Revenue from selling products is recognized at the date of sale, usually interpreted to mean the date of delivery to customers.
2. Revenue from services rendered is recognized when services have been performed and are billable.
3. Revenue from permitting others to use enterprise assets, such as interest, rent, and royalties, is recognized as time passes or as the assets are used.
4. Revenue from disposing of assets other than products is recognized at the date of sale.

These revenue transactions are diagrammed in Illustration 19-1.

---

[4]Recently the SEC noted that if a company performs as an agent or broker without assuming the risks and rewards of ownership of the goods, sales should be reported on a net (fee) basis ("Revenue Recognition in Financial Statements," *SEC Staff Accounting Bulletin No. 101,* December 3, 1999).

[5]Recognition is "the process of formally recording or incorporating an item in the accounts and financial statements of an entity" (*SFAC No. 3,* par. 83). "Recognition includes depiction of an item in both words and numbers, with the amount included in the totals of the financial statements" (*SFAC No. 5,* par. 6). For an asset or liability, recognition involves recording not only acquisition or incurrence of the item but also later changes in it, including removal from the financial statements previously recognized.

Recognition is not the same as realization, although the two are sometimes used interchangeably in accounting literature and practice. *Realization* is "the process of converting noncash resources and rights into money and is most precisely used in accounting and financial reporting to refer to sales of assets for cash or claims to cash" (*SFAC No. 3,* par. 83).

[6]"Recognition and Measurement in Financial Statements of Business Enterprises," *Statement of Financial Accounting Concepts No. 5* (Stamford, Conn.: FASB, 1984), par. 83.

[7]Gains (as contrasted to revenues) commonly result from transactions and other events that do not involve an "earning process." For gain recognition, being earned is generally less significant than being realized or realizable. Gains are commonly recognized at the time of sale of an asset, disposition of a liability, or when prices of certain assets change.

Type of transaction	Sale of product from inventory	Rendering a service	Permitting use of an asset	Sale of asset other than inventory
Description of revenue	Revenue from sales	Revenue from fees or services	Revenue from interest, rents, and royalties	Gain or loss on disposition
Timing of revenue recognition	Date of sale (date of delivery)	Services performed and billable	As time passes or assets are used	Date of sale or trade-in

ILLUSTRATION 19-1
Revenue Recognition Classified by Nature of Transaction

The preceding statements describe the conceptual nature of revenue and are the basis of accounting for revenue transactions. Yet, in practice, there are departures from the revenue recognition principle (the full accrual method). Revenue is sometimes recognized at other points in the earning process, owing in great measure to the considerable variety of revenue transactions.

Departures from the Sale Basis

An FASB study found some common **reasons for departures from the sale basis**.[8] One reason is a desire to **recognize earlier** in the earning process than the time of sale the effect of earning activities (revenue) if there is a high degree of certainty about the amount of revenue earned. A second reason is a desire to **delay recognition** of revenue beyond the time of sale if the degree of uncertainty concerning the amount of either revenue or costs is sufficiently high or if the sale does not represent substantial completion of the earnings process.

This chapter is devoted exclusively to the discussion and illustration of two of the four general types of revenue transactions described earlier, namely, (1) selling products and (2) rendering services—both of which are **sales transactions**. The other two types of revenue transactions—(3) revenue from permitting others to use enterprise assets and (4) revenue from disposing of assets other than products—are discussed in several other sections of the textbook. Our discussion of product sales transactions is organized around the following topics:

Go to the Digital Tool for examples of revenue recognition policies.

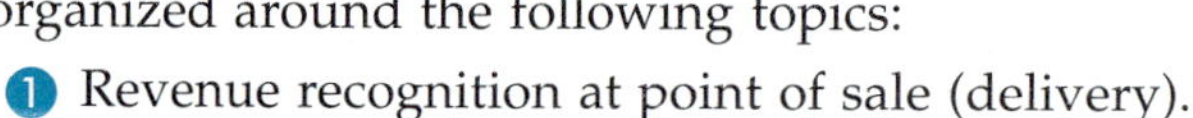

1. Revenue recognition at point of sale (delivery).
2. Revenue recognition before delivery.
3. Revenue recognition after delivery.
4. Revenue recognition for special sales transactions—franchises and consignments.

This organization of revenue recognition topics is depicted graphically below.

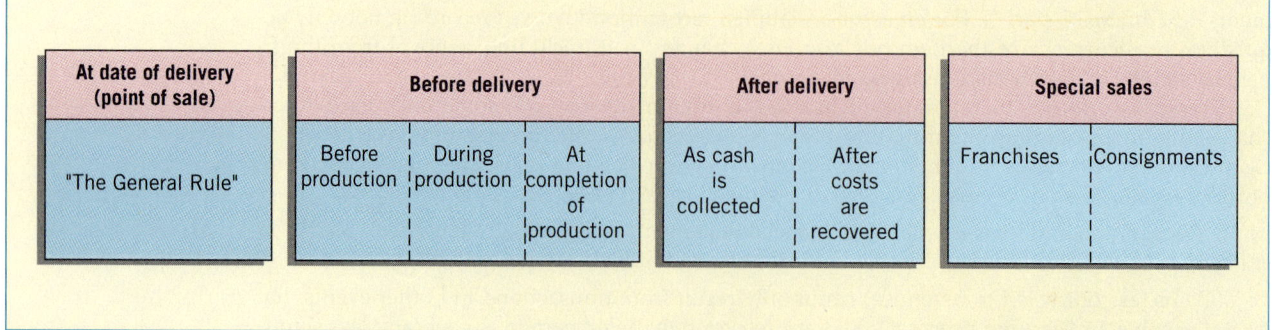

ILLUSTRATION 19-2
Revenue Recognition Alternatives

[8] Henry R. Jaenicke, *Survey of Present Practices in Recognizing Revenues, Expenses, Gains, and Losses,* A Research Report (Stamford, Conn.: FASB, 1981), p. 11.

REVENUE RECOGNITION AT POINT OF SALE (DELIVERY)

According to the FASB in *Concepts Statement No. 5,* the two conditions for recognizing revenue (being realized or realizable and being earned) are usually met by the time product or merchandise is delivered or services are rendered to customers.[9] Revenues from manufacturing and selling activities are commonly recognized at **point of sale** (usually meaning delivery).[10] Problems of implementation, however, can arise; three such situations are discussed below: (1) sales with buyback agreements, (2) sales when right of return exists, and (3) trade loading and channel stuffing.

OBJECTIVE 2
Describe accounting issues involved with revenue recognition at point of sale.

Sales with Buyback Agreements

If a company sells a product in one period and agrees to buy it back in the next accounting period, has the company sold the product? As indicated in Chapter 8, legal title has transferred in this situation, but the economic substance of the transaction is that retention of risks of ownership are retained by the seller. The profession has taken steps to curtail the recognition of revenue from this practice. When a repurchase agreement exists at a set price and this price covers all costs of the inventory plus related holding costs, the inventory and related liability remain on the seller's books.[11] In other words, no sale.

Sales When Right of Return Exists

Whether cash or credit sales are involved, a special problem arises with claims for returns and allowances. In Chapter 7, the accounting treatment for normal returns and allowances was presented. However, certain companies experience such a **high rate of returns**—a high ratio of returned merchandise to sales—that they find it necessary to postpone reporting sales until the return privilege has substantially expired. For example, in the publishing industry the rate of return approaches 25% for hardcover books and 65% for some magazines. Other types of companies that experience high return rates are perishable food dealers, rack jobbers or distributors who sell to retail outlets, record and tape companies, and some toy and sporting goods manufacturers. Returns in these industries are frequently made either through a right of contract or as a matter of practice involving "guaranteed sales" agreements or consignments.

UNDERLYING CONCEPTS

This is an example of *realized* but *unearned revenue.* When high rates of return exist and cannot be reasonably estimated, a question arises as to whether the earnings process has been substantially completed.

Three alternative revenue recognition methods are available when the seller is exposed to continued risks of ownership through return of the product. These are: (1) not recording a sale until all return privileges have expired; (2) recording the sale, but reducing sales by an estimate of future returns; and (3) recording the sale and accounting for the returns as they occur. The FASB concluded that if a company sells its product but gives the buyer the right to return it, then revenue from the sales transaction shall be recognized at the time of sale only if **all** of the following six conditions have been met.[12]

---

[9]It should be noted that the SEC believes that revenue is realized or realizable and earned when all of the following criteria are met: (1) Persuasive evidence of an arrangement exists; (2) delivery has occurred or services have been rendered; (3) the seller's price to the buyer is fixed or determinable; and (4) collectability is reasonably assured. See "Revenue Recognition in Financial Statements," *SEC Staff Accounting Bulletin No. 101,* December 3, 1999. The SEC provided more specific guidance because the general criteria were sometimes difficult to interpret.

[10]*Statement of Financial Accounting Concepts No. 5,* op. cit., par. 84.

[11]"Accounting for Product Financing Arrangements," *Statement of Financial Accounting Standards No. 49* (Stamford, Conn.: FASB, 1981).

[12]"Revenue Recognition When Right of Return Exists," *Statement of Financial Accounting Standards No. 48* (Stamford, Conn.: FASB, 1981), par. 6.

1. The seller's price to the buyer is substantially fixed or determinable at the date of sale.
2. The buyer has paid the seller, or the buyer is obligated to pay the seller and the obligation is not contingent on resale of the product.
3. The buyer's obligation to the seller would not be changed in the event of theft or physical destruction or damage of the product.
4. The buyer acquiring the product for resale has economic substance apart from that provided by the seller.
5. The seller does not have significant obligations for future performance to directly bring about resale of the product by the buyer.
6. The amount of future returns can be reasonably estimated.

What if revenue cannot be recognized at the time of sale because the six conditions are not met? In that case sales revenue and cost of sales that are not recognized at the time of sale because the six conditions above are not met should be recognized either when the return privilege has substantially expired or when those six conditions subsequently are met (whichever occurs first). Sales revenue and cost of sales reported in the income statement should be reduced to report estimated returns.

Trade Loading and Channel Stuffing

Some companies record revenues at date of delivery with neither buyback nor unlimited return provisions. Although they appear to be following acceptable point of sale revenue recognition practices, they are recognizing revenues and earnings prematurely. The domestic cigarette industry at one time engaged in a distribution practice known as **trade loading**. "Trade loading is a crazy, uneconomic, insidious practice through which manufacturers—trying to show sales, profits, and market share they don't actually have—induce their wholesale customers, known as the trade, to buy more product than they can promptly resell."[13] In total, the cigarette industry appears to have exaggerated a couple years' operating profits by as much as $600 million by taking the profits from future years.

In the computer software industry this same practice is referred to as **channel stuffing**. When a software maker needed to make its financial results look good, it offered deep discounts to its distributors to overbuy and recorded revenue when the software left the loading dock.[14] Of course, the distributors' inventories become bloated and the marketing channel gets stuffed but the software maker's financials are improved—but only to the detriment of future periods' results, unless the process is repeated.

Trade loading and channel stuffing hype sales, distort operating results, and window dress financial statements. If used without an appropriate allowance for sales returns, channel stuffing is a classic example of booking tomorrow's revenue today. **The practices of trade loading and channel stuffing need to be discouraged.** Business managers need to be aware of the ethical dangers of misleading the financial community by engaging in such practices to improve their financial statements.

REVENUE RECOGNITION BEFORE DELIVERY

For the most part, recognition at the point of sale (delivery) is used because most of the uncertainties concerning the earning process are removed and the exchange price is known. Under certain circumstances, however, revenue is recognized prior to completion and delivery. The most notable example is long-term construction contract accounting where the percentage-of-completion method is applicable.

[13] "The $600 Million Cigarette Scam," *Fortune,* December 4, 1989, p. 89.

[14] "Software's Dirty Little Secret," *Forbes,* May 15, 1989, p. 128.

Long-term contracts such as construction-type contracts, development of military and commercial aircraft, weapons delivery systems, and space exploration hardware frequently provide that the seller (builder) may bill the purchaser at intervals, as various points in the project are reached. When the project consists of separable units such as a group of buildings or miles of roadway, passage of title and billing may take place at stated stages of completion, such as the completion of each building unit or every 10 miles of road. Such contract provisions provide for delivery in installments, and the accounting records should report this by recording sales when installments are "delivered."[15]

Two distinctly different methods of accounting for long-term construction contracts are recognized.[16] They are:

INTERNATIONAL INSIGHT

International accounting standards are congruent with U.S. GAAP on long-term contract requirements.

1. **Percentage-of-Completion Method.** Revenues and gross profit are recognized each period based upon the progress of the construction, that is, the percentage of completion. Construction costs **plus gross profit earned to date** are accumulated in an inventory account (Construction in Process), and progress billings are accumulated in a contra inventory account (Billings on Construction in Process).
2. **Completed-Contract Method.** Revenues and gross profit are recognized only when the contract is completed. Construction costs are accumulated in an inventory account (Construction in Process), and progress billings are accumulated in a contra inventory account (Billings on Construction in Process).

The rationale for using percentage-of-completion accounting is that under most of these contracts the buyer and seller have obtained enforceable rights. The buyer has the legal right to require specific performance on the contract; the seller has the right to require progress payments that provide evidence of the buyer's ownership interest. As a result, a continuous sale occurs as the work progresses, and revenue should be recognized accordingly.

The profession requires that the percentage-of-completion method be used when estimates of progress toward completion, revenues, and costs are reasonably dependable and **all** the following conditions exist:[17]

UNDERLYING CONCEPTS

The percentage-of-completion method recognizes revenue from long-term contracts in the periods that the revenue is earned. The firm contract fixes the selling price. And, if costs are estimable and collection reasonably assured, the revenue recognition concept is not violated.

1. The contract clearly specifies the enforceable rights regarding goods or services to be provided and received by the parties, the consideration to be exchanged, and the manner and terms of settlement.
2. The buyer can be expected to satisfy all obligations under the contract.
3. The contractor can be expected to perform the contractual obligations.

The completed-contract method should be used only (1) when an entity has primarily short-term contracts, or (2) when the conditions for using the percentage-of-completion method cannot be met, or (3) when there are inherent hazards in the contract beyond the normal, recurring business risks. The presumption is that **percentage-of-completion is the better method and that the completed-contract method should be used only when the percentage-of-completion method is inappropriate**.

Percentage-of-Completion Method

OBJECTIVE 3
Apply the percentage-of-completion method for long-term contracts.

The **percentage-of-completion method** recognizes revenues, costs, and gross profit as progress is made toward completion on a long-term contract. To defer recognition of these items until completion of the entire contract is to misrepresent the efforts (costs)

[15]*Statement of Financial Accounting Concepts No. 5,* par. 84, item c.

[16]*Accounting Trends and Techniques—1999* reports that, of the 91 of its 600 sample companies that referred to long-term construction contracts, 88 used the percentage-of-completion method and 1 used the completed-contract method (2 were not determinable).

[17]"Accounting for Performance of Construction-Type and Certain Production-Type Contracts," *Statement of Position 81-1* (New York: AICPA, 1981), par. 23.

and accomplishments (revenues) of the interim accounting periods. In order to apply the percentage-of-completion method, one must have some basis or standard for measuring the progress toward completion at particular interim dates.

Measuring the Progress toward Completion

As one practicing accountant wrote, "The big problem in applying the percentage-of-completion method that cannot be demonstrated in an example has to do with the ability to make reasonably accurate estimates of completion and the final gross profit."[18] Various methods are used in practice to determine the **extent of progress toward completion**; the most common are "cost-to-cost method," "efforts expended methods," and "units of work performed method."

The objective of all the methods is to measure the extent of progress in terms of costs, units, or value added. The various measures (costs incurred, labor hours worked, tons produced, stories completed, etc.) are identified and classified as input and output measures. **Input measures** (costs incurred, labor hours worked) are made in terms of efforts devoted to a contract. **Output measures** (tons produced, stories of a building completed, miles of a highway completed) are made in terms of results. Neither are universally applicable to all long-term projects; their use requires careful tailoring to the circumstances and the exercise of judgment.

Both input and output measures have certain disadvantages. The input measure is based on an established relationship between a unit of input and productivity. If inefficiencies cause the productivity relationship to change, inaccurate measurements result. Another potential problem, called "front-end loading," produces higher estimates of completion by virtue of incurring significant costs up front. Some early-stage construction costs should be disregarded if they do not relate to contract performance, for example, costs of uninstalled materials or costs of subcontracts not yet performed.

Output measures can result in inaccurate measures if the units used are not comparable in time, effort, or cost to complete. For example, using stories completed can be deceiving; completing the first story of an eight-story building may require more than one-eighth the total cost because of the substructure and foundation construction.

One of the more popular input measures used to determine the progress toward completion is the **cost-to-cost basis**. Under the cost-to-cost basis, the percentage of completion is measured by comparing costs incurred to date with the most recent estimate of the total costs to complete the contract, as shown in the following formula:

ILLUSTRATION 19-3
Formula for Percentage of Completion, Cost-to-Cost Basis

$$\frac{\text{Costs incurred to date}}{\text{Most recent estimate of total costs}} = \text{Percent complete}$$

The percentage that costs incurred bear to total estimated costs is applied to the total revenue or the estimated total gross profit on the contract in arriving at the revenue or the gross profit amounts to be recognized to date.

ILLUSTRATION 19-4
Formula for Total Revenue to Be Recognized to Date

$$\text{Percent complete} \times \text{Estimated total revenue (or gross profit)} = \text{Revenue (or gross profit) to be recognized to date}$$

To find the amounts of revenue and gross profit recognized each period, we would need to subtract total revenue or gross profit recognized in prior periods, as shown in the following formula:

[18] Richard S. Hickok, "New Guidance for Construction Contractors: 'A Credit Plus,'" *The Journal of Accountancy*, March 1982, p. 46.

Revenue (or gross profit) to be recognized to date	−	Revenue (or gross profit) recognized in prior periods	=	Current period revenue (or gross profit)

ILLUSTRATION 19-5
Formula for Amount of Current Period Revenue, Cost-to-Cost Basis

Because **the profession specifically recommends the cost-to-cost method** (without excluding other bases for measuring progress toward completion), we have adopted it for use in our illustrations.[19]

Illustration of Percentage-of-Completion Method—Cost-to-Cost Basis

To illustrate the percentage-of-completion method, assume that the Hardhat Construction Company has a contract starting July 2001, to construct a $4,500,000 bridge that is expected to be completed in October 2003, at an estimated cost of $4,000,000. The following data pertain to the construction period (note that by the end of 2002 the estimated total cost has increased from $4,000,000 to $4,050,000):

	2001	2002	2003
Costs to date	$1,000,000	$2,916,000	$4,050,000
Estimated costs to complete	3,000,000	1,134,000	—
Progress billings during the year	900,000	2,400,000	1,200,000
Cash collected during the year	750,000	1,750,000	2,000,000

The percent complete would be computed as follows:

ILLUSTRATION 19-6
Application of Percentage-of-Completion Method, Cost-to-Cost Basis

	2001	2002	2003
Contract price	$4,500,000	$4,500,000	$4,500,000
Less estimated cost:			
Costs to date	1,000,000	2,916,000	4,050,000
Estimated costs to complete	3,000,000	1,134,000	—
Estimated total costs	4,000,000	4,050,000	4,050,000
Estimated total gross profit	$ 500,000	$ 450,000	$ 450,000
Percent complete:	25%	72%	100%
	($1,000,000 / $4,000,000)	($2,916,000 / $4,050,000)	($4,050,000 / $4,050,000)

On the basis of the data above, the following entries would be prepared to record (1) the costs of construction, (2) progress billings, and (3) collections. These entries appear as summaries of the many transactions that would be entered individually as they occur during the year:

ILLUSTRATION 19-7
Journal Entries—Percentage-of-Completion Method, Cost-to-Cost Basis

	2001		2002		2003	
To record cost of construction:						
Construction in Process	1,000,000		1,916,000		1,134,000	
Materials, Cash, Payables, etc.		1,000,000		1,916,000		1,134,000
To record progress billings:						
Accounts Receivable	900,000		2,400,000		1,200,000	
Billings on Construction in Process		900,000		2,400,000		1,200,000
To record collections:						
Cash	750,000		1,750,000		2,000,000	
Accounts Receivable		750,000		1,750,000		2,000,000

[19]Committee on Accounting Procedure, "Long-Term Construction-Type Contracts," *Accounting Research Bulletin No. 45* (New York: AICPA, 1955), p. 7.

In this illustration, the costs incurred to date as a proportion of the estimated total costs to be incurred on the project are a measure of the extent of progress toward completion. The estimated revenue and gross profit to be recognized for each year are calculated as follows:

ILLUSTRATION 19-8
Percentage-of-Completion, Revenue and Gross Profit, by Year

		2001	2002	2003
Revenue recognized in:				
2001	$4,500,000 × 25%	$1,125,000		
2002	$4,500,000 × 72%		$3,240,000	
	Less: Revenue recognized in 2001		1,125,000	
	Revenue in 2002		$2,115,000	
2003	$4,500,000 × 100%			$4,500,000
	Less: Revenue recognized in 2001 and 2002			3,240,000
	Revenue in 2003			$1,260,000
Gross profit recognized in:				
2001	$500,000 × 25%	$ 125,000		
2002	$450,000 × 72%		$ 324,000	
	Less: Gross profit recognized in 2001		125,000	
	Gross profit in 2002		$ 199,000	
2003	$450,000 × 100%			$ 450,000
	Less: Gross profit recognized in 2001 and 2002			324,000
	Gross profit in 2003			$ 126,000

The entries to recognize revenue and gross profit each year and to record completion and final approval of the contract are shown below.

ILLUSTRATION 19-9
Journal Entries to Recognize Revenue and Gross Profit and to Record Contract Completion—Percentage-of-Completion Method, Cost-to-Cost Basis

	2001		2002		2003	
To recognize revenue and gross profit:						
Construction in Process (gross profit)	125,000		199,000		126,000	
Construction Expenses	1,000,000		1,916,000		1,134,000	
Revenue from Long-Term Contract		1,125,000		2,115,000		1,260,000
To record completion of the contract:						
Billings on Construction in Process					4,500,000	
Construction in Process						4,500,000

Note that gross profit as computed above is debited to Construction in Process, while Revenue from Long-Term Contract is credited for the amounts as computed above. The difference between the amounts recognized each year for revenue and gross profit is debited to a nominal account, Construction Expenses (similar to cost of goods sold in a manufacturing enterprise), which is reported in the income statement. That amount is the actual cost of construction incurred in that period. For example, in the Hardhat Construction Company cost-to-cost illustration the actual costs of $1,000,000 in 2001 are used to compute both the gross profit of $125,000 and the percent complete (25%).

Costs must continue to be accumulated in the Construction in Process account to maintain a record of total costs incurred (plus recognized profit) to date. Although theoretically a series of "sales" takes place using the percentage-of-completion method, the inventory cost cannot be removed until the construction is completed and trans-

ferred to the new owner. The Construction in Process account would include the following summarized entries over the term of the construction project.

ILLUSTRATION 19-10
Content of Construction in Process Account—Percentage-of-Completion Method

Construction in Process				
2001 construction costs	$1,000,000	12/31/03	to close completed project	$4,500,000
2001 recognized gross profit	125,000			
2002 construction costs	1,916,000			
2002 recognized gross profit	199,000			
2003 construction costs	1,134,000			
2003 recognized gross profit	126,000			
Total	$4,500,000	Total		$4,500,000

The Hardhat Construction Company illustration contained a **change in estimate** in the second year, 2002, when the estimated total costs increased from $4,000,000 to $4,050,000. By adjusting the percent completed to the new estimate of total costs and then deducting the amount of revenues and gross profit recognized in prior periods from revenues and gross profit computed for progress to date, the change in estimate is accounted for in a **cumulative catch-up manner**. That is, the change in estimate is accounted for **in the period of change** so that the balance sheet at the end of the period of change and the accounting in subsequent periods are as they would have been if the revised estimate had been the original estimate.

Financial Statement Presentation—Percentage of Completion

Generally when a receivable from a sale is recorded, the Inventory account is reduced. In this case, however, both the receivable and the inventory continue to be carried. Subtracting the balance in the **Billings** account from Construction in Process avoids double-counting the inventory. During the life of the contract, the difference between the Construction in Process and the Billings on Construction in Process accounts is reported in the balance sheet **as a current asset if a debit, and as a current liability if a credit**.

When the costs incurred plus the gross profit recognized to date (the balance in Construction in Process) exceed the billings, this excess is reported as a current asset entitled "Cost and Recognized Profit in Excess of Billings." The unbilled portion of revenue recognized to date can be calculated at any time by subtracting the billings to date from the revenue recognized to date as illustrated below for 2001 for Hardhat Construction:

ILLUSTRATION 19-11
Computation of Unbilled Contract Price at 12/31/01

Contract revenue recognized to date: $\$4,500,000 \times \frac{\$1,000,000}{\$4,000,000} =$	$1,125,000
Billings to date	900,000
Unbilled revenue	$ 225,000

When the billings exceed costs incurred and gross profit to date, this excess is reported as a current liability entitled "Billings in Excess of Costs and Recognized Profit."

When a company has a number of projects, and costs exceed billings on some contracts and billings exceed costs on others, the contracts should be segregated. The asset side should include only those contracts on which costs and recognized profit exceed billings, and the liability side includes only those on which billings exceed costs and recognized profit. Separate disclosures of the dollar volume of billings and costs are preferable to a summary presentation of the net difference.

Using data from the previous illustration, the Hardhat Construction Company would report the status and results of its long-term construction activities under the percentage-of-completion method as follows:

ILLUSTRATION 19-12
Financial Statement Presentation—Percentage-of-Completion Method

HARDHAT CONSTRUCTION COMPANY				
		2001	2002	2003
Income Statement				
Revenue from long-term contracts		$1,125,000	$2,115,000	$1,260,000
Costs of construction		1,000,000	1,916,000	1,134,000
Gross profit		$ 125,000	$ 199,000	$ 126,000
Balance Sheet (12/31)				
Current assets				
Accounts receivable		$ 150,000	$ 800,000	
Inventories				
Construction in process	$1,125,000			
Less: Billings	900,000			
Costs and recognized profit in excess of billings		$ 225,000		
Current liabilities				
Billings ($3,300,000) in excess of costs and recognized profit ($3,240,000)			$ 60,000	

Note 1. Summary of significant accounting policies.
Long-Term Construction Contracts. The company recognizes revenues and reports profits from long-term construction contracts, its principal business, under the percentage-of-completion method of accounting. These contracts generally extend for periods in excess of one year. The amounts of revenues and profits recognized each year are based on the ratio of costs incurred to the total estimated costs. Costs included in construction in process include direct materials, direct labor, and project-related overhead. Corporate general and administrative expenses are charged to the periods as incurred and are not allocated to construction contracts.

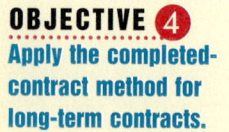

OBJECTIVE 4
Apply the completed-contract method for long-term contracts.

Completed-Contract Method

Under the **completed-contract method**, revenue and gross profit are recognized only at point of sale, that is, when the contract is completed. Costs of long-term contracts in process and current billings are accumulated, but there are **no interim charges or credits to income statement accounts for revenues, costs, and gross profit**.

UNDERLYING CONCEPTS

The completed-contract method does not violate the *matching concept* because the costs are also deferred until the completion of the contract.

The principal advantage of the completed-contract method is that reported revenue is based on final results rather than on estimates of unperformed work. Its major disadvantage is that it does not reflect current performance when the period of a contract extends into more than one accounting period. Although operations may be fairly uniform during the period of the contract, revenue is not reported until the year of completion, creating a distortion of earnings.

The **annual entries** to record costs of construction, progress billings, and collections from customers would be identical to those illustrated under the percentage-of-completion method with the significant exclusion of the recognition of revenue and gross profit. For the bridge project of Hardhat Construction Company illustrated on the preceding pages, the following entries are made in 2003 under the completed-contract method to recognize revenue and costs and to close out the inventory and billing accounts:

Billings on Construction in Process	4,500,000	
Revenue from Long-Term Contracts		4,500,000
Costs of Construction	4,050,000	
Construction in Process		4,050,000

Comparing the two methods in relation to the same bridge project, the Hardhat Construction Company would have recognized gross profit as follows:

ILLUSTRATION 19-13
Comparison of Gross Profit Recognized under Different Methods

	Percentage-of-Completion	Completed-Contract
2001	$125,000	$ 0
2002	199,000	0
2003	126,000	450,000

Hardhat Construction would report its long-term construction activities as follows:

ILLUSTRATION 19-14
Financial Statement Presentation—Completed-Contract Method

HARDHAT CONSTRUCTION COMPANY		2001	2002	2003
Income Statement				
Revenue from long-term contracts		—	—	$4,500,000
Costs of construction		—	—	4,050,000
Gross profit		—	—	$ 450,000
Balance Sheet (12/31)				
Current assets				
Accounts receivable		$150,000	$800,000	
Inventories				
Construction in process	$1,000,000			
Less: Billings	900,000			
Unbilled contract costs		$100,000		
Current liabilities				
Billings ($3,300,000) in excess of contract costs ($2,916,000)			$384,000	

Note 1. Summary of significant accounting policies.
Long-Term Construction Contracts. The company recognizes revenues and reports profits from long-term construction contracts, its principal business, under the completed-contract method. These contracts generally extend for periods in excess of one year. Contract costs and billings are accumulated during the periods of construction, but no revenues or profits are recognized until completion of the contract. Costs included in construction in process include direct material, direct labor, and project-related overhead. Corporate general and administrative expenses are charged to the periods as incurred.

Long-Term Contract Losses

OBJECTIVE 5
Identify the proper accounting for losses on long-term contracts.

Two types of losses can become evident under long-term contracts:[20]

1. ***Loss in Current Period on a Profitable Contract.*** This condition arises when, during construction, there is a significant increase in the estimated total contract costs but the increase does not eliminate all profit on the contract. Under the percentage-of-completion method only, the estimated cost increase requires a current period adjustment of excess gross profit recognized on the project in prior periods. This adjustment is recorded as a loss in the current period because it is a **change in accounting estimate** (discussed in Chapter 23).
2. ***Loss on an Unprofitable Contract.*** Cost estimates at the end of the current period may indicate that a loss will result on completion of the entire contract. Under both the percentage-of-completion and the completed-contract methods, the entire expected contract loss must be recognized in the current period.

The treatment described for unprofitable contracts is consistent with the accounting custom of anticipating foreseeable losses to avoid overstatement of current and future income (conservatism).

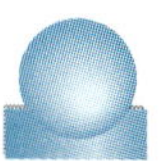

UNDERLYING CONCEPTS

Conservatism justifies recognizing the losses immediately. Loss recognition does not require *realization;* it only requires evidence that an impairment of asset value has occurred.

Loss in Current Period

To illustrate a loss in the current period on a contract expected to be profitable upon completion, assume that on December 31, 2002, Hardhat Construction Company estimates the costs to complete the bridge contract at $1,468,962 instead of $1,134,000 (refer to page 1007). Assuming all other data are the same as before, Hardhat would compute the percent complete and recognize the loss as shown in Illustration 19-15.

[20]Sak Bhamornsiri, "Losses from Construction Contracts," *The Journal of Accountancy*, April 1982, p. 26.

Compare these computations with those for 2002 in Illustration 19-6. The "percent complete" has dropped from 72% to 66½% due to the increase in estimated future costs to complete the contract.

The 2002 loss of $48,500 is a cumulative adjustment of the "excessive" gross profit recognized on the contract in 2001. **Instead of restating the prior period, the prior period misstatement is absorbed entirely in the current period.** In this illustration, the adjustment was large enough to result in recognition of a loss.

ILLUSTRATION 19-15
Computation of Recognizable Loss, 2002—Loss in Current Period

Cost to date (12/31/02)	$2,916,000
Estimated costs to complete (revised)	1,468,962
Estimated total costs	$4,384,962
Percent complete ($2,916,000 ÷ $4,384,962)	66½%
Revenue recognized in 2002 ($4,500,000 × 66½%) − $1,125,000	$1,867,500
Costs incurred in 2002	1,916,000
Loss recognized in 2002	$ 48,500

Hardhat Construction would record the loss in 2002 as follows:

Construction Expenses	1,916,000	
Construction in Process (loss)		48,500
Revenue from Long-Term Contract		1,867,500

The loss of $48,500 will be reported on the 2002 income statement as the difference between the reported revenues of $1,867,500 and the costs of $1,916,000.[21] **Under the completed-contract method, no loss is recognized in 2002 because the contract is still expected to result in a profit** to be recognized in the year of completion.

Loss on an Unprofitable Contract

To illustrate the accounting for an overall loss on a long-term contract, assume that at December 31, 2002, Hardhat Construction Company estimates the costs to complete the bridge contract at $1,640,250 instead of $1,134,000. Revised estimates relative to the bridge contract appear as follows:

	2001 Original Estimates	2002 Revised Estimates
Contract price	$4,500,000	$4,500,000
Estimated total cost	4,000,000	4,556,250*
Estimated gross profit	$ 500,000	
Estimated loss		$ (56,250)

*($2,916,000 + $1,640,250)

Under the percentage-of-completion method, $125,000 of gross profit was recognized in 2001 (see Illustration 19-8). This $125,000 must be offset in 2002 because it is no longer expected to be realized. In addition, the total estimated loss of $56,250 must be recognized in 2002 since losses must be recognized as soon as estimable. Therefore, a total loss of $181,250 ($125,000 + $56,250) must be recognized in 2002.

[21]In 2003 Hardhat Construction will recognize the remaining 33½% of the revenue, $1,507,500, with costs of $1,468,962 as expected, and report a gross profit of $38,538. The total gross profit over the 3 years of the contract would be $115,038 [$125,000 (2001) − $48,500 (2002) + $38,538 (2003)], which is the difference between the total contract revenue of $4,500,000 and the total contract costs of $4,384,962.

The revenue recognized in 2002 is computed as follows:

Revenue recognized in 2002:		
Contract price		$4,500,000
Percent complete		× 64%*
Revenue recognizable to date		2,880,000
Less: Revenue recognized prior to 2002		1,125,000
Revenue recognized in 2002		$1,755,000
*Cost to date (12/31/02)	$2,916,000	
Estimated cost to complete	1,640,250	
Estimated total costs	$4,556,250	
Percent complete: $2,916,000 ÷ $4,556,250 = 64%		

ILLUSTRATION 19-16
Computation of Revenue Recognizable, 2002—Unprofitable Contract

To compute the construction costs to be expensed in 2002 we add the total loss to be recognized in 2002 ($125,000 + $56,250) to the revenue to be recognized in 2002. This computation is shown below:

Revenue recognized in 2002 (computed above)		$1,755,000
Total loss recognized in 2002:		
Reversal of 2001 gross profit	$125,000	
Total estimated loss on the contract	56,250	181,250
Construction cost expensed in 2002		$1,936,250

ILLUSTRATION 19-17
Computation of Construction Expense, 2002—Unprofitable Contract

Hardhat Construction would record the long-term contract revenues, expenses, and loss in 2002 as follows:

Construction Expenses	1,936,250	
Construction in Process (Loss)		181,250
Revenue from Long-Term Contracts		1,755,000

At the end of 2002, Construction in Process has a balance of $2,859,750 as shown below:[22]

Construction in Process			
2001 Construction costs	1,000,000		
2001 Recognized gross profit	125,000		
2002 Construction costs	1,916,000	2002 Recognized loss	181,250
Balance 2,859,750			

ILLUSTRATION 19-18
Content of Construction in Process Account at End of 2002—Unprofitable Contract

Under the completed-contract method, the contract loss of $56,250 is also recognized in the year in which it first became evident through the following entry in 2002:

Loss from Long-Term Contracts	56,250	
Construction in Process (Loss)		56,250

[22]If the costs in 2003 are $1,640,250 as projected, at the end of 2003 the Construction in Process account will have a balance of $1,640,250 + $2,859,790, or $4,500,000, equal to the contract price. When the revenue remaining to be recognized in 2003 of $1,620,000 [$4,500,000 (total contract price) − $1,125,000 (2001) − $1,755,000 (2002)] is matched with the construction expense to be recognized in 2003 of $1,620,000 [total costs of $4,556,250 less the total costs recognized in prior years of $2,936,250 (2001, $1,000,000; 2002, $1,936,250)], a zero profit results. Thus the total loss has been recognized in 2002, the year in which it first became evident.

Just as the Billings account balance cannot exceed the contract price, neither can the balance in Construction in Process exceed the contract price. In circumstances where the Construction in Process balance exceeds the billings, the recognized loss may be deducted on the balance sheet from such accumulated costs. That is, under both the percentage-of-completion and the completed-contract methods, the provision for the loss (the credit) may be combined with Construction in Process, thereby reducing the inventory balance. In those circumstances, however (as in the 2002 illustration above), where the billings exceed the accumulated costs, the amount of the estimated loss must be reported separately on the balance sheet as a current liability. That is, under both the percentage-of-completion and the completed-contract methods, the amount of the loss of $56,250, as estimated in 2002, would be taken from the Construction in Process account and reported separately as a current liability entitled Estimated Liability from Long-Term Contracts.[23]

Disclosures in Financial Statements

In addition to making the financial statement disclosures required of all businesses, construction contractors usually make some unique disclosures. Generally these additional disclosures are made in the notes to the financial statements. For example, a construction contractor should disclose the method of recognizing revenue,[24] the basis used to classify assets and liabilities as current (the nature and length of the operating cycle), the basis for recording inventory, the effects of any revision of estimates, the amount of backlog on uncompleted contracts, and the details about receivables (billed and unbilled, maturity, interest rates, retainage provisions, and significant individual or group concentrations of credit risk).

Completion of Production Basis

This is not an exception to the revenue recognition principle. At the completion of production, realization is virtually assured and the earning process is substantially completed.

In certain cases revenue is recognized at the completion of production even though no sale has been made. Examples of such situations involve precious metals or agricultural products with assured prices. Under the **completion of production basis**, revenue is recognized when these metals are mined or agricultural crops harvested because the sales price is reasonably assured, the units are interchangeable, and no significant costs are involved in distributing the product (see discussion in Chapter 9, page 457, "Valuation at Net Realizable Value").[25] When sale or cash receipt precedes production and delivery, as in the case of magazine subscriptions, revenues may be recognized as earned by production and delivery.[26]

REVENUE RECOGNITION AFTER DELIVERY

In some cases, the collection of the sales price is not reasonably assured and revenue recognition is deferred. One of two methods is generally employed to defer revenue recognition until the cash is received, that is, **the installment sales method** or **the cost recovery method**. In some situations cash is received prior to delivery or transfer of the property and is recorded as a deposit because the sale transaction is incomplete. This is referred to as the **deposit method**.

---

[23]*Construction Contractors,* Audit and Accounting Guide (New York: AICPA, 1981), pp. 148–149.

[24]Ibid., p. 30.

[25]Such revenue satisfies the criteria of *Concepts Statement No. 5* since the assets are readily realizable and the earning process is virtually complete (see par. 84, item c).

[26]*Statement of Financial Accounting Concepts No. 5,* par. 84, item b.

Installment Sales Accounting Method

OBJECTIVE 6
Describe the installment sales method of accounting.

The installment sales method emphasizes collection rather than sale. It recognizes income in the periods of collection rather than in the period of sale. This method is justified on the basis that when there is no reasonable approach for estimating the degree of collectibility, revenue should not be recognized until cash is collected.

The expression "installment sales" is generally used to describe any type of sale for which payment is required in periodic installments over an extended period of time. It is used in retailing where all types of farm and home equipment and furnishings are sold on an installment basis. It is also sometimes used in the heavy equipment industry in which machine installations are paid for over a long period. A more recent application of the method is in land development sales.

Because payment for the product or property sold is spread over a relatively long period, the risk of loss resulting from uncollectible accounts is greater in installment sales transactions than in ordinary sales. Consequently, various devices are used to protect the seller. In merchandising, the two most common are (1) the use of a conditional sales contract that provides that title to the item sold does not pass to the purchaser until all payments have been made, and (2) use of notes secured by a chattel (personal property) mortgage on the article sold. Either of these permits the seller to "repossess" the goods sold if the purchaser defaults on one or more payments. The repossessed merchandise is then resold at whatever price it will bring to compensate the seller for the uncollected installments and the expense of repossession.

UNDERLYING CONCEPTS

Realization is a critical part of revenue recognition. Thus, if a high degree of uncertainty exists about collectibility, revenue recognition must be deferred.

Under the installment sales method of accounting, income recognition is deferred until the period of cash collection. Both revenues and costs of sales are recognized in the period of sale but the related gross profit is deferred to those periods in which cash is collected. Thus, **instead of the sale being deferred to the future periods of anticipated collection and then related costs and expenses being deferred, only the proportional gross profit is deferred,** which is equivalent to deferring both sales and cost of sales. Other expenses, that is, selling expense, administrative expense, and so on, are not deferred.

INTERNATIONAL INSIGHT

In Japan installment method accounting is frequently used whenever the collection period exceeds two years whether or not there is any uncertainty with regard to the collectibility of cash.

Thus, the theory that cost and expenses should be matched against sales is applied in installment sales transactions through the gross profit figure but no further. Companies using the installment sales method of accounting generally record operating expenses without regard to the fact that some portion of the year's gross profit is to be deferred. This practice is often justified on the basis that (1) these expenses do not follow sales as closely as does the cost of goods sold, and (2) accurate apportionment among periods would be so difficult that it could not be justified by the benefits gained.[27]

Acceptability of the Installment Sales Method

The use of the installment sales method for revenue recognition has fluctuated widely. Until the early 1960s it was widely used and accepted for installment sales transactions. As installment sales transactions increased during the sixties, somewhat paradoxically, acceptance and application of the installment sales method for financial accounting purposes decreased. In 1966 the APB concluded that except in special circumstances, "the installment method of recognizing revenue is not acceptable."[28]

The rationale for this position is that because the installment sales method of accounting recognizes no income until cash is collected, it is not in accordance with the accrual accounting concept. On the other hand, the installment sales method is

[27]In addition, other theoretical deficiencies of the installment sales method could be cited. For example, see Richard A. Scott and Rita K. Scott, "Installment Accounting: Is It Inconsistent?" *The Journal of Accountancy,* November 1979.

[28]"Omnibus Opinion," *Opinions of the Accounting Principles Board No. 10* (New York: AICPA, 1966), par. 12.

frequently justified on the grounds that the risk of not collecting an account receivable may be so great that the sale itself is not sufficient evidence that recognition should occur. In some cases, this reasoning may be valid but not in a majority of cases. The general approach is that if a sale has been completed, it should be recognized; if bad debts are expected, they should be recorded as separate estimates of uncollectibles. Although collection expenses, repossession expenses, and bad debts are an unavoidable part of installment sales activities, the incurrence of these costs and the collectibility of the receivables are reasonably predictable.

We study this topic in financial accounting because the method is acceptable in cases where a reasonable basis of estimating the degree of collectibility is deemed not to exist. In addition, weaknesses in the sales method of revenue recognition became very apparent when the franchise and land development booms of the 1960s and 1970s produced many failures and disillusioned investors. Application of the installment sales method to **franchise and license operations** resulted in the abuse described earlier as "front-end loading" (recognizing revenue prematurely, such as when the franchise is granted or the license issued rather than as it is earned or as the cash is received). Many **land development** ventures were susceptible to the same abuses. As a result, the FASB prescribes application of the installment sales method of accounting for sales of real estate under certain circumstances.[29]

Procedure for Deferring Revenue and Cost of Sales of Merchandise

One could easily work out a procedure that deferred both the uncollected portion of the sales price and the proportionate part of the cost of the goods sold. Instead of apportioning both sales price and cost over the period of collection, however, **only the gross profit is deferred**. This procedure has exactly the same effect as deferring both sales and cost of sales but requires only one deferred account rather than two.

The steps to be used are as follows:

For the sales in any one year:

1. During the year, record both sales and cost of sales in the regular way, using the special accounts described later, and compute the rate of gross profit on installment sales transactions.
2. At the end of the year, apply the rate of gross profit to the cash collections of the current year's installment sales to arrive at the realized gross profit.
3. The gross profit not realized should be deferred to future years.

For sales made in prior years:

1. The gross profit rate of each year's sales must be applied against cash collections of accounts receivable resulting from that year's sales to arrive at the realized gross profit.

From the preceding discussion of the general practice followed in taking up income from installment sales, it is apparent that special accounts must be used. These accounts provide certain special information required to determine the realized and unrealized gross profit in each year of operations. The requirements for special accounts are as follows:

---

[29]"Accounting for Sales of Real Estate," *Statement of Financial Accounting Standards No. 66* (Norwalk, Conn.: FASB, 1982), pars. 45–47. The installment sales method of accounting must be applied to a retail land sale that meets **all** of the following criteria: (1) the period of cancellation of the sale with refund of the down payment and any subsequent payments has expired; (2) cumulative cash payments equal or exceed 10% of the sales value; and (3) the seller is financially capable of providing all promised contract representations (e.g., land improvements, off-site facilities).

1. Installment sales transactions must be kept separate in the accounts from all other sales.
2. Gross profit on sales sold on installment must be determinable.
3. The amount of cash collected on installment sales accounts receivable must be known, and, further, the total collected on the current year's and on each preceding year's sales must be determinable.
4. Provision must be made for carrying forward each year's deferred gross profit.

In each year, ordinary operating expenses are charged to expense accounts and are closed to the Income Summary account as under customary accounting procedure. Thus, the only peculiarity in computing net income under the installment sales method as generally applied is **the deferral of gross profit until realized by accounts receivable collection**.

To illustrate the installment sales method in accounting for the sales of merchandise, assume the following data:

	2001	2002	2003
Installment sales	$200,000	$250,000	$240,000
Cost of installment sales	150,000	190,000	168,000
Gross profit	$ 50,000	$ 60,000	$ 72,000
Rate of gross profit on sales	25%[a]	24%[b]	30%[c]
Cash receipts			
2001 sales	$ 60,000	$100,000	$ 40,000
2002 sales		100,000	125,000
2003 sales			80,000

[a] $\frac{\$50,000}{\$200,000}$ [b] $\frac{\$60,000}{\$250,000}$ [c] $\frac{\$72,000}{\$240,000}$

To simplify the illustration, interest charges have been excluded. Summary entries in general journal form for year 2001 are shown below.

2001

Installment Accounts Receivable, 2001	200,000	
Installment Sales		200,000
(To record sales made on installment in 2001)		
Cash	60,000	
Installment Accounts Receivable, 2001		60,000
(To record cash collected on installment receivables)		
Cost of Installment Sales	150,000	
Inventory (or Purchases)		150,000
(To record cost of goods sold on installment in 2001 on either a perpetual or a periodic inventory basis)		
Installment Sales	200,000	
Cost of Installment Sales		150,000
Deferred Gross Profit, 2001		50,000
(To close installment sales and cost of installment sales for the year)		
Deferred Gross Profit, 2001	15,000	
Realized Gross Profit on Installment Sales		15,000
(To remove from deferred gross profit the profit realized through cash collections; $60,000 × 25%)		
Realized Gross Profit on Installment Sales	15,000	
Income Summary		15,000
(To close profits realized by collections)		

The realized and deferred gross profit is computed for the year 2001 as follows:

ILLUSTRATION 19-19
Computation of Realized and Deferred Gross Profit, Year 1

2001	
Rate of gross profit current year	25%
Cash collected on current year's sales	$60,000
Realized gross profit (25% of $60,000)	15,000
Gross profit to be deferred ($50,000 − $15,000)	35,000

Summary entries in journal form for year 2 (2002) are shown below.

2002		
Installment Accounts Receivable, 2002	250,000	
Installment Sales		250,000
(To record sales made on installment in 2002)		
Cash	200,000	
Installment Accounts Receivable, 2001		100,000
Installment Accounts Receivable, 2002		100,000
(To record cash collected on installment receivables)		
Cost of Installment Sales	190,000	
Inventory (or Purchases)		190,000
(To record cost of goods sold on installment in 2002)		
Installment Sales	250,000	
Cost of Installment Sales		190,000
Deferred Gross Profit, 2002		60,000
(To close installment sales and cost of installment sales for the year)		
Deferred Gross Profit, 2001 ($100,000 × 25%)	25,000	
Deferred Gross Profit, 2002 ($100,000 × 24%)	24,000	
Realized Gross Profit on Installment Sales		49,000
(To remove from deferred gross profit the profit realized through collections)		
Realized Gross Profit on Installment Sales	49,000	
Income Summary		49,000
(To close profits realized by collections)		

The realized and deferred gross profit is computed for the year 2002 as follows:

ILLUSTRATION 19-20
Computation of Realized and Deferred Gross Profit, Year 2

2002	
Current year's sales	
Rate of gross profit	24%
Cash collected on current year's sales	$100,000
Realized gross profit (24% of $100,000)	24,000
Gross profit to be deferred ($60,000 − $24,000)	36,000
Prior year's sales	
Rate of gross profit—2001	25%
Cash collected on 2001 sales	$100,000
Gross profit realized in 2002 on 2001 sales (25% of $100,000)	25,000
Total gross profit realized in 2002	
Realized on collections of 2001 sales	$ 25,000
Realized on collections of 2002 sales	24,000
Total	$ 49,000

The entries in 2003 would be similar to those of 2002, and the total gross profit taken up or realized would be $64,000, as shown by the following computations:

2003	
Current year's sales	
Rate of gross profit	30%
Cash collected on current year's sales	$ 80,000
Gross profit realized on 2003 sales (30% of $80,000)	24,000
Gross profit to be deferred ($72,000 − $24,000)	48,000
Prior years' sales	
2001 sales	
Rate of gross profit	25%
Cash collected	$ 40,000
Gross profit realized in 2003 on 2001 sales (25% of $40,000)	10,000
2002 sales	
Rate of gross profit	24%
Cash collected	$125,000
Gross profit realized in 2003 on 2002 sales (24% of $125,000)	30,000
Total gross profit realized in 2003	
Realized on collections of 2001 sales	$ 10,000
Realized on collections of 2002 sales	30,000
Realized on collections of 2003 sales	24,000
Total	$ 64,000

ILLUSTRATION 19-21
Computation of Realized and Deferred Gross Profit, Year 3

Additional Problems of Installment Sales Accounting

In addition to computing realized and deferred gross profit currently, other problems are involved in accounting for installment sales transactions. These problems are related to:

1. Interest on installment contracts.
2. Uncollectible accounts.
3. Defaults and repossessions.

Interest on Installment Contracts. Because the collection of installment receivables is spread over a long period, it is customary to charge the buyer interest on the unpaid balance. A schedule of equal payments consisting of interest and principal is set up. Each successive payment is attributable to a smaller amount of interest and a correspondingly larger amount attributable to principal, as shown in Illustration 19-22. This illustration assumes that an asset costing $2,400 is sold for $3,000 with interest of 8% included in the three installments of $1,164.10.

Date	Cash (Debit)	Interest Earned (Credit)	Installment Receivables (Credit)	Installment Unpaid Balance	Realized Gross Profit (20%)
1/2/01	—	—	—	$3,000.00	—
1/2/02	$1,164.10[a]	$240.00[b]	$ 924.10[c]	2,075.90[d]	$184.82[e]
1/2/03	1,164.10	166.07	998.03	1,077.87	199.61
1/2/04	1,164.10	86.23	1,077.87	−0−	215.57
					$600.00

[a]Periodic payment = Original unpaid balance ÷ PV of an annuity of $1.00 for three periods at 8%; $1,164.10 = $3,000 ÷ 2.57710.
[b]$3,000.00 × .08 = $240.
[c]$1,164.10 − $240.00 = $924.10.
[d]$3,000.00 − $924.10 = $2,075.90.
[e]$924.10 × .20 = $184.82.

ILLUSTRATION 19-22
Installment Payment Schedule

Interest should be accounted for separately from the gross profit recognized on the installment sales collections during the period. It is recognized as interest revenue at the time of the cash receipt.

Uncollectible Accounts. The problem of bad debts or uncollectible accounts receivable is somewhat different for concerns selling on an installment basis because of a repossession feature commonly incorporated in the sales agreement. This feature gives the selling company an opportunity to recoup any uncollectible accounts through repossession and resale of repossessed merchandise. If the experience of the company indicates that repossessions do not, as a rule, compensate for uncollectible balances, it may be advisable to provide for such losses through charges to a special bad debt expense account just as is done for other credit sales.

Defaults and Repossessions. Depending on the terms of the sales contract and the policy of the credit department, the seller can repossess merchandise sold under an installment arrangement if the purchaser fails to meet payment requirements. Repossessed merchandise may be reconditioned before being offered for sale. It may be resold for cash or installment payments.

The accounting for **repossessions** recognizes that the related installment receivable account is not collectible and that it should be written off. Along with the account receivable, the applicable deferred gross profit must be removed from the ledger using the following entry:

Repossessed Merchandise (an inventory account)	xx	
Deferred Gross Profit	xx	
Installment Accounts Receivable		xx

The entry above assumes that the repossessed merchandise is to be recorded on the books at exactly the amount of the uncollected account less the deferred gross profit applicable. This assumption may or may not be proper. The condition of the merchandise repossessed, the cost of reconditioning, and the market for second-hand merchandise of that particular type must all be considered. **The objective should be to put any asset acquired on the books at its fair value or, when fair value is not ascertainable, at the best possible approximation of fair value.** If the fair value of the merchandise repossessed is less than the uncollected balance less the deferred gross profit, a "loss on repossession" should be recorded at the date of repossession.

Some contend that repossessed merchandise should be entered at a valuation that will permit the company to make its regular rate of gross profit on resale. If it is entered at its approximated cost to purchase, the regular rate of gross profit could be provided for upon its ultimate sale, but that is completely a secondary consideration. It is more important that the asset acquired by repossession be recorded at fair value in accordance with the general practice of carrying assets at acquisition price as represented by the fair market value at the date of acquisition.

To illustrate the required entry, assume that a refrigerator was sold to Marilyn Hunt for $500 on September 1, 2001. Terms require a down payment of $200 and $20 on the first of every month for 15 months, starting October 1, 2001. It is further assumed that the refrigerator cost $300 and that it is sold to provide a 40% rate of gross profit on selling price. At the year-end, December 31, 2001, a total of $60 should have been collected in addition to the original down payment.

If Hunt makes her January and February payments in 2002 and then defaults, the account balances applicable to Hunt at time of default would be:

Installment Account Receivable ($500 − $200 − $20 − $20 − $20 − $20 − $20)	200 (dr.)
Deferred Gross Profit [40% × ($500 − $200 − $20 − $20 − $20)]	96 (cr.)

The deferred gross profit applicable to the Hunt account still has the December 31, 2001, balance because no entry has yet been made to take up gross profit realized by 2002 cash collections. The regular entry at the end of 2002, however, will take up the gross profit realized by all cash collections including amounts received from Hunt. Hence, the balance of deferred gross profit applicable to Hunt's account may be computed by applying the gross profit rate for the year of sale to the 2002 balance of Hunt's account receivable, 40% of \$200, or \$80. The account balances should therefore be considered as:

Installment Account Receivable (Hunt)	200 (dr.)
Deferred Gross Profit (applicable to Hunt after recognition of \$8 of profit in both January and February)	80 (cr.)

If the estimated fair value of the article repossessed is set at \$70, the following entry would be required to record the repossession:

Deferred Gross Profit	80	
Repossessed Merchandise	70	
Loss on Repossession	50	
Installment Account Receivable (Hunt)		200

The amount of the loss is determined by (1) subtracting the deferred gross profit from the amount of the account receivable, to determine the unrecovered cost (or book value) of the merchandise repossessed, and (2) subtracting the estimated fair value of the merchandise repossessed from the unrecovered cost to get the amount of the loss on repossession. The loss on the refrigerator in our example is computed as shown in Illustration 19-23.

ILLUSTRATION 19-23
Computation of Loss on Repossession

Balance of account receivable (representing uncollected selling price)	\$200
Less: Deferred gross profit	80
Unrecovered cost	120
Less: Estimated fair value of merchandise repossessed	70
Loss (Gain) on repossession	\$ 50

As pointed out earlier, the loss on repossession may be charged to Allowance for Doubtful Accounts if such an account is carried.

Financial Statement Presentation of Installment Sales Transactions

If installment sales transactions represent a significant part of total sales, full disclosure of installment sales, the cost of installment sales, and any expenses allocable to installment sales is desirable. If, however, installment sales transactions constitute an insignificant part of total sales, it may be satisfactory to include only the realized gross profit in the income statement as a special item following the gross profit on sales, as shown below.

ILLUSTRATION 19-24
Disclosure of Installment Sales Transactions—Insignificant Amount

HEALTH MACHINE COMPANY Statement of Income For the Year Ended December 31, 2002	
Sales	\$620,000
Cost of goods sold	490,000
Gross profit on sales	130,000
Gross profit realized on installment sales	51,000
Total gross profit on sales	\$181,000

If more complete disclosure of installment sales transactions is desired, a presentation similar to the following may be used:

ILLUSTRATION 19-25
Disclosure of Installment Sales Transactions—Significant Amount

HEALTH MACHINE COMPANY
Statement of Income
For the Year Ended December 31, 2002

	Installment Sales	Other Sales	Total
Sales	$248,000	$620,000	$868,000
Cost of goods sold	182,000	490,000	672,000
Gross profit on sales	66,000	130,000	196,000
Less: Deferred gross profit on installment sales of this year	47,000		47,000
Realized gross profit on this year's sales	19,000	130,000	149,000
Add: Gross profit realized on installment sales of prior years	32,000		32,000
Gross profit realized this year	$ 51,000	$130,000	$181,000

The apparent awkwardness of this method of presentation is difficult to avoid if full disclosure of installment sales transactions is to be provided in the income statement. One solution, of course, is to prepare a separate schedule showing installment sales transactions with only the final figure carried into the income statement.

In the balance sheet it is generally considered desirable to classify installment accounts receivable by year of collectibility. There is some question as to whether installment accounts that are not collectible for two or more years should be included in current assets. If installment sales are part of normal operations, they may be considered as current assets because they are collectible within the operating cycle of the business. Little confusion should result from this practice if maturity dates are fully disclosed, as illustrated in the following example:

ILLUSTRATION 19-26
Disclosure of Installment Accounts Receivable, by Year

Current assets		
Notes and accounts receivable		
Trade Customers	$78,800	
Less: Allowance for doubtful accounts	3,700	
	75,100	
Installment accounts collectible in 2002	22,600	
Installment accounts collectible in 2003	47,200	$144,900

On the other hand, receivables from an installment contract, or contracts, resulting from a transaction **not** related to normal operations should be reported in the Other Assets section if due beyond one year.

Repossessed merchandise is a part of inventory and should be included as such in the Current Asset section of the balance sheet. Any gain or loss on repossessions should be included in the income statement in the Other Revenues and Gains or Other Expenses and Losses section.

Deferred gross profit on installment sales is generally treated as unearned revenue and is classified as a current liability. Theoretically, deferred gross profit consists of three elements: (1) income tax liability to be paid when the sales are reported as realized revenue (current liability); (2) allowance for collection expense, bad debts, and repossession losses (deduction from installment accounts receivable); and (3) net income (retained earnings, restricted as to dividend availability). Because of the difficulty in allocating deferred gross profit among these three elements, however, the whole amount is frequently reported as unearned revenue.

In contrast, the FASB in *SFAC No. 3* states that "no matter how it is displayed in financial statements, deferred gross profit on installment sales is conceptually an asset valuation—that is, a reduction of an asset."[30] We support the FASB position but we

[30]See *Statement of Financial Accounting Concepts No. 3,* pars. 156–158.

recognize that until an official standard on this topic is issued, financial statements will probably continue to report such deferred gross profit as a current liability.

Cost Recovery Method

OBJECTIVE 7
Explain the cost recovery method of accounting.

Under the cost recovery method, no profit is recognized until cash payments by the buyer exceed the seller's cost of the merchandise sold. After all costs have been recovered, any additional cash collections are included in income. The income statement for the period of sale reports sales revenue, the cost of goods sold, and the gross profit—both the amount (if any) that is recognized during the period and the amount that is deferred. The deferred gross profit is offset against the related receivable—reduced by collections—on the balance sheet. Subsequent income statements report the gross profit as a separate item of revenue when it is recognized as earned.

APB Opinion No. 10 allows a seller to use the cost recovery method to account for sales in which "there is no reasonable basis for estimating collectibility." This method is required under *FASB Statements No. 45* (franchises) and *No. 66* (real estate) where a high degree of uncertainty exists related to the collection of receivables.[31]

To illustrate the cost recovery method, assume that early in 2001, Fesmire Manufacturing sells inventory with a cost of $25,000 to Higley Company for $36,000 with payments receivable of $18,000 in 2001, $12,000 in 2002, and $6,000 in 2003. If the cost recovery method applies to this sale transaction and the cash is collected on schedule, cash collections, revenue, cost, and gross profit are recognized as follows:[32]

ILLUSTRATION 19-27
Computation of Gross Profit—Cost Recovery Method

	2001	2002	2003
Cash collected	$18,000	$12,000	$6,000
Revenue	$36,000	–0–	–0–
Cost of goods sold	25,000	–0–	–0–
Deferred gross profit	11,000	$11,000	$6,000
Recognized gross profit	–0–	5,000*	6,000
Deferred gross profit balance (end of period)	$11,000	$ 6,000	$ –0–

*$25,000 – $18,000 = $7,000 of unrecovered cost at the end of 2001; $12,000 – $7,000 = $5,000, the excess of cash received in 2002 over unrecovered cost.

Under the cost recovery method, total revenue and cost of goods sold are reported in the period of sale similar to the installment sales method. However, unlike the installment sales method, which recognizes income as cash is collected, the cost recovery method recognizes profit only when cash collections exceed the total cost of the goods sold.

The journal entry to record the deferred gross profit on this transaction (after the sale and the cost of sale were recorded in the normal manner) at the end of 2001 is as follows:

[31]"Omnibus Opinion—1966," *Opinions of the Accounting Principles Board No. 10* (New York: AICPA, 1969), footnote 8, page 149; "Accounting for Franchise Fee Revenue," *Statement of Financial Accounting Standards No. 45* (Stamford, Conn.: FASB, 1981), par. 6; "Accounting for Sales of Real Estate," *Statement of Financial Accounting Standards No. 66,* pars. 62 and 63.

[32]An alternative format for computing the amount of gross profit recognized annually is shown below:

Year	Cash Received	Original Cost Recovered	Balance of Unrecovered Cost	Gross Profit Realized
Beginning balance	—	—	$25,000	—
12/31/01	$18,000	$18,000	7,000	$ –0–
12/31/02	12,000	7,000	–0–	5,000
12/31/03	6,000	–0–	–0–	6,000

2001		
Sales	36,000	
Cost of Sales		25,000
Deferred Gross Profit		11,000
(To close sales and cost of sales and to record deferred gross profit on sales accounted for under the cost recovery method)		

In 2002 and 2003, the deferred gross profit becomes realized gross profit as the cumulative cash collections exceed the total costs by recording the following entries:

2002		
Deferred Gross Profit	5,000	
Realized Gross Profit		5,000
(To recognize gross profit to the extent that cash collections in 2002 exceed costs)		

2003		
Deferred Gross Profit	6,000	
Realized Gross Profit		6,000
(To recognize gross profit to the extent that cash collections in 2003 exceed costs)		

Deposit Method

In some cases, cash is received from the buyer before transfer of the goods or property. There is not sufficient transfer of the risks and rewards of ownership for a sale to be recorded. In such cases the seller has not performed under the contract and has no claim against the purchaser. The method of accounting for these incomplete transactions is the **deposit method**. Under the deposit method the seller reports the cash received from the buyer as a deposit on the contract and classifies it as a liability (refundable deposit or customer advance) on the balance sheet. The seller continues to report the property as an asset on its balance sheet, along with any related existing debt. Also, the seller continues to charge depreciation expense as a period cost for the property. **No revenue or income should be recognized until the sale is complete.**[33] At that time, the deposit account is closed and one of the revenue recognition methods discussed in this chapter is applied to the sale.

The **major difference between the installment and cost recovery methods and the deposit method** is that in the installment and cost recovery methods it is assumed that the seller has performed on the contract, but cash collection is highly uncertain. In the deposit method, the seller has not performed and no legitimate claim exists. The **deposit method** postpones recognizing a sale until a determination can be made as to whether a sale has occurred for accounting purposes. Revenue recognition is delayed until a future event occurs. If there has not been sufficient transfer of risks and rewards of ownership, even if a deposit has been received, recognition of the sale should be postponed until sufficient transfer has occurred. In that sense, the deposit method is not a revenue recognition method as are the installment and cost recovery methods.

Summary of Product Revenue Recognition Bases

The revenue recognition bases or methods, the criteria for their use, and the reasons for departing from the sale basis are summarized in Illustration 19-28.

[33]*Statement of Financial Accounting Standards No. 66,* par. 65.

Recognition Basis (or Method of Applying a Basis)	Criteria for Use	Reason(s) for Departing from Sale Basis
Percentage-of-completion method	Long-term construction of property; dependable estimates of extent of progress and cost to complete; reasonable assurance of collectibility of contract price; expectation that both contractor and buyer can meet obligations; and absence of inherent hazards that make estimates doubtful.	Availability of evidence of ultimate proceeds; better measure of periodic income; avoidance of fluctuations in revenues, expenses, and income; performance is a "continuous sale" and therefore not a departure from the sale basis.
Completed-contract method	Use on short-term contracts, and whenever percentage-of-completion cannot be used on long-term contracts.	Existence of inherent hazards in the contract beyond the normal, recurring business risks; conditions for using the percentage-of-completion method are absent.
Completion-of-production basis	Immediate marketability at quoted prices; unit interchangeability; difficulty of determining costs; and no significant distribution costs.	Known or determinable revenues; inability to determine costs and thereby defer expense recognition until sale.
Installment sales method and cost recovery method	Absence of reasonable basis for estimating degree of collectibility and costs of collection.	Collectibility of the receivable is so uncertain that gross profit (or income) is not recognized until cash is actually received.
Deposit method	Cash received before the sales transaction is completed.	No recognition of revenue and income because there is not sufficient transfer of the risks and rewards of ownership.

ILLUSTRATION 19-28
Revenue Recognition Bases Other Than the Sale Basis for Products[34]

CONCLUDING REMARKS

As indicated, revenue recognition principles are sometimes difficult to apply and often vary by industry. Recently the SEC has attempted to provide more guidance in this area because of the concern that the revenue recognition principle is sometimes being incorrectly applied. In some cases there has even been intentional misstatement of revenue to achieve better financial results. The latter practice is fraudulent financial reporting, and the SEC is vigorously prosecuting these situations.

For our capital markets to be efficient, investors must have confidence that the financial information provided is both relevant and reliable. As a result, it is imperative that aggressive revenue recognition practices be eliminated. It is our hope that recent efforts by the SEC and the accounting profession will lead to higher quality reporting in this area.

SUMMARY OF LEARNING OBJECTIVES

1 **Apply the revenue recognition principle.** The revenue recognition principle provides that revenue is recognized (1) when it is realized or realizable and (2) when it is earned. Revenues are realized when goods and services are exchanged for cash or claims to cash. Revenues are realizable when assets received in exchanges are readily convertible to known amounts of cash or claims to cash. Revenues are earned when the

[34]Adapted from *Survey of Present Practices in Recognizing Revenues, Expenses, Gains, and Losses,* op. cit., pp. 12 and 13.

KEY TERMS

billings, *1009*
completed-contract method, *1010*
completion of production basis, *1014*
cost recovery method, *1023*
cost-to-cost basis, *1006*
deposit method, *1024*
earned revenues, *1001*
high rate of returns, *1003*
input measures, *1006*
installment sales method, *1015*
output measures, *1006*
percentage-of-completion method, *1005*
point of sale (delivery), *1003*
realizable revenues, *1001*
realized revenues, *1001*
repossessions, *1020*
revenue recognition principle, *1001*

entity has substantially accomplished what it must do to be entitled to the benefits represented by the revenues, that is, when the earnings process is complete or virtually complete.

2 Describe accounting issues involved with revenue recognition at point of sale. The two conditions for recognizing revenue are usually met by the time product or merchandise is delivered or services are rendered to customers. Revenues from manufacturing and selling activities are commonly recognized at time of sale. Problems of implementation can arise because of (1) sales with buyback agreements, (2) revenue recognition when right of return exists, and (3) trade loading and channel stuffing.

3 Apply the percentage-of-completion method for long-term contracts. To apply the percentage-of-completion method to long-term contracts, one must have some basis for measuring the progress toward completion at particular interim dates. One of the most popular input measures used to determine the progress toward completion is the cost-to-cost basis. Using this basis, the percentage of completion is measured by comparing costs incurred to date with the most recent estimate of the total costs to complete the contract. The percentage that costs incurred bear to total estimated costs is applied to the total revenue or the estimated total gross profit on the contract in arriving at the revenue or the gross profit amounts to be recognized to date.

4 Apply the completed-contract method for long-term contracts. Under this method, revenue and gross profit are recognized only at point of sale, that is, when the contract is completed. Costs of long-term contracts in process and current billings are accumulated, but there are no interim charges or credits to income statement accounts for revenues, costs, and gross profit. The annual entries to record costs of construction, progress billings, and collections from customers would be identical to those for the percentage-of-completion method with the significant exclusion of the recognition of revenue and gross profit.

5 Identify the proper accounting for losses on long-term contracts. Two types of losses can become evident under long-term contracts: (1) *Loss in current period on a profitable contract:* Under the percentage-of-completion method only, the estimated cost increase requires a current period adjustment of excess gross profit recognized on the project in prior periods. This adjustment is recorded as a loss in the current period because it is a change in accounting estimate. (2) *Loss on an unprofitable contract:* Under both the percentage-of-completion and the completed-contract methods, the entire expected contract loss must be recognized in the current period.

6 Describe the installment sales method of accounting. The installment sales method recognizes income in the periods of collection rather than in the period of sale. The installment method of accounting is justified on the basis that when there is no reasonable approach for estimating the degree of collectibility, revenue should not be recognized until cash is collected.

7 Explain the cost recovery method of accounting. Under the cost recovery method, no profit is recognized until cash payments by the buyer exceed the seller's cost of the merchandise sold. After all costs have been recovered, any additional cash collections are included in income. The income statement for the period of sale reports sales revenue, the cost of goods sold, and the gross profit—both the amount that is recognized during the period and the amount that is deferred. The deferred gross profit is offset against the related receivable on the balance sheet. Subsequent income statements report the gross profit as a separate item of revenue when it is recognized as earned.

APPENDIX **19A**

Revenue Recognition for Special Sales Transactions

To supplement our presentation of revenue recognition, we have chosen to cover two common yet unique types of business transactions—**franchises** and **consignments**.

FRANCHISES

OBJECTIVE 8
After studying Appendix 19A, you should be able to: Explain revenue recognition for franchises and consignment sales.

Accounting for franchise sales was chosen because of its popularity, complexity, and applicability to many of the previously discussed revenue recognition bases. In accounting for franchise sales, the accountant must analyze the transaction and, considering all the circumstances, must use judgment in selecting and applying one or more of the revenue recognition bases and then, possibly, monitor the situation over a long period of time.

As indicated throughout this chapter, revenue is recognized on the basis of two criteria: (1) when it is realized or realizable (occurrence of an exchange for cash or claims to cash), and (2) when it is earned (completion or virtual completion of the earnings process). These criteria are appropriate for most business activities, but for some sales transactions they simply do not adequately define when revenue should be recognized. The fast-growing franchise industry has given accountants special concern and challenge.

Four types of franchising arrangements have evolved: (1) manufacturer-retailer, (2) manufacturer-wholesaler, (3) service sponsor-retailer, and (4) wholesaler-retailer. The fastest growing category of franchising, and the one that caused a reexamination of appropriate accounting, has been the third category, **service sponsor-retailer**. Included in this category are such industries and businesses as:

Soft ice cream/frozen yogurt stores (Tastee Freeze, TCBY, Dairy Queen)
Food drive-ins (McDonald's, KFC, Burger King)
Restaurants (TGI Friday's, Pizza Hut, Denny's)
Motels (Holiday Inn, Marriott, Best Western)
Auto rentals (Avis, Hertz, National)
Part-time help (Manpower, Kelly Girl)
Others (H & R Block, Meineke Mufflers, 7-Eleven Stores)

Franchise companies derive their revenue from one or both of two sources: (1) from the sale of initial franchises and related assets or services, and (2) from continuing fees based on the operations of franchises. The **franchisor** (the party who grants business rights under the franchise) normally provides the **franchisee** (the party who operates the franchised business) with the following services:

1. Assistance in site selection.
   (a) Analyzing location.
   (b) Negotiating lease.

2. Evaluation of potential income.
3. Supervision of construction activity.
   (a) Obtaining financing.
   (b) Designing building.
   (c) Supervising contractor while building.
4. Assistance in the acquisition of signs, fixtures, and equipment.
5. Bookkeeping and advisory services.
   (a) Setting up franchisee's records.
   (b) Advising on income, real estate, and other taxes.
   (c) Advising on local regulations of the franchisee's business.
6. Employee and management training.
7. Quality control.
8. Advertising and promotion.[1]

During the 1960s and early 1970s it was standard practice for franchisors to recognize the entire franchise fee at the date of sale whether the fee was received then or was collectible over a long period of time. Frequently, franchisors recorded the entire amount as revenue in the year of sale even though many of the services were yet to be performed and uncertainty existed regarding the collection of the entire fee.[2] In effect the franchisors were counting their fried chickens before they were hatched.

However, a **franchise agreement** may provide for refunds to the franchisee if certain conditions are not met, and franchise fee profit can be reduced sharply by future costs of obligations and services to be rendered by the franchisor. To curb the abuses in revenue recognition that existed and to standardize the accounting and reporting practices in the franchise industry, the FASB issued *Statement No. 45.*

Initial Franchise Fees

The **initial franchise fee** is consideration for establishing the franchise relationship and providing some initial services. Initial franchise fees are to be recorded as revenue only when and as the franchisor makes "substantial performance" of the services it is obligated to perform and collection of the fee is reasonably assured. **Substantial performance** occurs when the franchisor has no remaining obligation to refund any cash received or excuse any nonpayment of a note and has performed all the initial services required under the contract. According to *FASB No. 45* "commencement of operations by the franchisee shall be presumed to be the earliest point at which substantial performance has occurred, unless it can be demonstrated that substantial performance of all obligations, including services rendered voluntarily, has occurred before that time."[3]

Illustration of Entries for Initial Franchise Fee

To illustrate, assume that Tum's Pizza Inc. charges an initial franchise fee of $50,000 for the right to operate as a franchisee of Tum's Pizza. Of this amount, $10,000 is payable when the agreement is signed and the balance is payable in five annual payments of $8,000 each. In return for the initial franchise fee, the franchisor will help locate the site, negotiate the lease or purchase of the site, supervise the construction activity, and provide the bookkeeping services. The credit rating of the franchisee indicates that money

[1]Archibald E. MacKay, "Accounting for Initial Franchise Fee Revenue," *The Journal of Accountancy,* January 1970, pp. 66–67.

[2]In 1987 and 1988 the SEC ordered a half-dozen fast-growing startup franchisors, including Jiffy Lube International, Moto Photo, Inc., Swensen's, Inc., and LePeep Restaurants, Inc., to defer their initial franchise fee recognition until earned. See "Claiming Tomorrow's Profits Today," *Forbes,* October 17, 1988, p. 78.

[3]"Accounting for Franchise Fee Revenue," *Statement of Financial Accounting Standards No. 45* (Stamford, Conn.: FASB, 1981), par. 5.

can be borrowed at 8%. The present value of an ordinary annuity of five annual receipts of $8,000 each discounted at 8% is $31,941.68. The discount of $8,058.32 represents the interest revenue to be accrued by the franchisor over the payment period.

1. If there is reasonable expectation that the down payment may be refunded and if substantial future services remain to be performed by Tum's Pizza Inc., the entry should be:

Cash	10,000.00	
Notes Receivable	40,000.00	
Discount on Notes Receivable		8,058.32
Unearned Franchise Fees		41,941.68

2. If the probability of refunding the initial franchise fee is extremely low, the amount of future services to be provided to the franchisee is minimal, collectibility of the note is reasonably assured, and substantial performance has occurred, the entry should be:

Cash	10,000.00	
Notes Receivable	40,000.00	
Discount on Notes Receivable		8,058.32
Revenue from Franchise Fees		41,941.68

3. If the initial down payment is not refundable, represents a fair measure of the services already provided, with a significant amount of services still to be performed by the franchisor in future periods, and collectibility of the note is reasonably assured, the entry should be:

Cash	10,000.00	
Notes Receivable	40,000.00	
Discount on Notes Receivable		8,058.32
Revenue from Franchise Fees		10,000.00
Unearned Franchise Fees		31,941.68

4. If the initial down payment is not refundable and no future services are required by the franchisor, but collection of the note is so uncertain that recognition of the note as an asset is unwarranted, the entry should be:

Cash	10,000	
Revenue from Franchise Fees		10,000

5. Under the same conditions as those listed under 4 except that the down payment is refundable or substantial services are yet to be performed, the entry should be:

Cash	10,000	
Unearned Franchise Fees		10,000

In cases 4 and 5—where collection of the note is extremely uncertain—cash collections may be recognized using the installment method or the cost recovery method.[4]

Continuing Franchise Fees

Continuing franchise fees are received in return for the continuing rights granted by the franchise agreement and for providing such services as management training, advertising and promotion, legal assistance, and other support. Continuing fees should be reported as revenue when they are earned and receivable from the franchisee, unless a portion of them has been designated for a particular purpose, such as providing a specified amount for building maintenance or local advertising. In that case, the

[4]A study that compared four revenue recognition procedures—installment sales basis, spreading recognition over the contract life, percentage-of-completion basis, and substantial performance—for franchise sales concluded that the percentage-of-completion method is the most acceptable revenue recognition method; the substantial performance method was found sometimes to yield ultra-conservative results. See Charles H. Calhoun III, "Accounting for Initial Franchise Fees: Is It a Dead Issue?" *The Journal of Accountancy*, February 1975, pp. 60–67.

portion deferred shall be an amount sufficient to cover the estimated cost in excess of continuing franchise fees and provide a reasonable profit on the continuing services.

Bargain Purchases

In addition to paying continuing franchise fees, franchisees frequently purchase some or all of their equipment and supplies from the franchisor. The franchisor would account for these sales as it would for any other product sales. Sometimes, however, the franchise agreement grants the franchisee the right to make **bargain purchases** of equipment or supplies after the initial franchise fee is paid. If the bargain price is lower than the normal selling price of the same product, or if it does not provide the franchisor a reasonable profit, then a portion of the initial franchise fee should be deferred. The deferred portion would be accounted for as an adjustment of the selling price when the franchisee subsequently purchases the equipment or supplies.

Options to Purchase

A franchise agreement may give the franchisor an **option to purchase** the franchisee's business. As a matter of management policy, the franchisor may reserve the right to purchase a profitable franchised outlet, or to purchase one that is in financial difficulty. If it is probable at the time the option is given that the franchisor will ultimately purchase the outlet, then the initial franchise fee should not be recognized as revenue but should be recorded as a liability. When the option is exercised, the liability would reduce the franchisor's investment in the outlet.

Franchisor's Cost

Franchise accounting also involves proper accounting for the **franchisor's cost**. The objective is to match related costs and revenues by reporting them as components of income in the same accounting period. Franchisors should ordinarily defer **direct costs** (usually incremental costs) relating to specific franchise sales for which revenue has not yet been recognized. Costs should not be deferred, however, without reference to anticipated revenue and its realizability.[5] **Indirect costs** of a regular and recurring nature such as selling and administrative expenses that are incurred irrespective of the level of franchise sales should be expensed as incurred.

Disclosures of Franchisors

Disclosure of all significant commitments and obligations resulting from franchise agreements, including a description of services that have not yet been substantially performed, is required. Any resolution of uncertainties regarding the collectibility of franchise fees should be disclosed. Initial franchise fees should be segregated from other franchise fee revenue if they are significant. Where possible, revenues and costs related to franchisor-owned outlets should be distinguished from those related to franchised outlets.

CONSIGNMENTS

In some arrangements the delivery of the goods by the manufacturer (or wholesaler) to the dealer (or retailer) is not considered to be full performance and a sale because the manufacturer retains title to the goods. This specialized method of marketing certain types of products makes use of a device known as a **consignment**. Under this arrangement, the **consignor** (manufacturer) ships merchandise to the **consignee**

[5]"Accounting for Franchise Fee Revenue," p. 17.

(dealer), who is to act as an agent for the consignor in selling the merchandise. Both consignor and consignee are interested in selling—the former to make a profit or develop a market, the latter to make a commission on the sales.

The consignee accepts the merchandise and agrees to exercise due diligence in caring for and selling it. Cash received from customers is remitted to the consignor by the consignee, after deducting a sales commission and any chargeable expenses.

A modified version of the sale basis of revenue recognition is used by the consignor. That is, revenue is recognized only after the consignor receives notification of sale and the cash remittance from the consignee. The merchandise is carried throughout the consignment as the inventory of the consignor, separately classified as Merchandise on Consignment. It is not recorded as an asset on the consignee's books. Upon sale of the merchandise, the consignee has a liability for the net amount due the consignor. The consignor periodically receives from the consignee a report called **account sales** that shows the merchandise received, merchandise sold, expenses chargeable to the consignment, and the cash remitted. Revenue is then recognized by the consignor.

To illustrate consignment accounting entries, assume that Nelba Manufacturing Co. ships merchandise costing $36,000 on consignment to Best Value Stores. Nelba pays $3,750 of freight costs and Best Value pays $2,250 for local advertising costs that are reimbursable from Nelba. By the end of the period, two-thirds of the consigned merchandise has been sold for $40,000 cash. Best Value notifies Nelba of the sales, retains a 10% commission, and remits the cash due Nelba. The following journal entries would be made by the consignor (Nelba) and the consignee (Best Value):

ILLUSTRATION 19A-1
Entries for Consignment Sales

NELBA MFG. CO. (Consignor)			BEST VALUE STORES (Consignee)		
Shipment of consigned merchandise					
Inventory on Consignment	36,000		No entry (record memo of merchandise		
Finished Goods Inventory		36,000	received).		
Payment of freight costs by consignor					
Inventory on Consignment	3,750		No entry.		
Cash		3,750			
Payment of advertising by consignee					
No entry until notified.			Receivable from Consignor	2,250	
			Cash		2,250
Sales of consigned merchandise					
No entry until notified.			Cash	40,000	
			Payable to Consignor		40,000
Notification of sales and expenses and remittance of amount due					
Cash	33,750		Payable to Consignor	40,000	
Advertising Expense	2,250		Receivable from Consignor		2,250
Commission Expense	4,000		Commission Revenue		4,000
Revenue from Consignment Sales		40,000	Cash		33,750
Adjustment of inventory on consignment for cost of sales					
Cost of Goods Sold	26,500		No entry.		
Inventory on Consignment		26,500			
[2/3 ($36,000 + $3,750) = $26,500]					

Under the consignment arrangement, the manufacturer (consignor) accepts the risk that the merchandise might not sell and relieves the dealer (consignee) of the need to commit part of its working capital to inventory. A variety of different systems and account titles are used to record consignments, but they all share the common goal of postponing the recognition of revenue until it is known that a sale to a third party has occurred.

KEY TERMS

account sales, *1031*
consignee, *1030*
consignment, *1030*
consignor, *1030*
continuing franchise fees, *1029*
franchisee, *1027*
franchisor, *1027*
initial franchise fee, *1028*
substantial performance, *1028*

SUMMARY OF LEARNING OBJECTIVE FOR APPENDIX 19A

8 **Explain revenue recognition for franchises and consignment sales.** In a franchise arrangement, the initial franchise fee is recorded as revenue only when and as the franchisor makes substantial performance of the services it is obligated to perform and collection of the fee is reasonably assured. Continuing franchise fees are recognized as revenue when they are earned and receivable from the franchisee. Revenue is recognized by the consignor when an account sales and the cash are received from the consignee.

FROM CLASSROOM TO CAREER

CLAIRE SCHULTE

is an audit manager with Deloitte & Touche (D&T), currently on a two-year assignment in London. She has been with the firm since 1994, when she graduated from the University of Portland as valedictorian with a double major in accounting and finance.

How did you move from the Portland, Oregon, office to the London office of D&T?

By sheer determination. My largest client in Portland was a life insurance company that recently "demutualized," which means they went from being owned by policyholders to public ownership on the New York Stock Exchange. I let a D&T partner in Portland know that I would like an assignment overseas, and at an international conference, he came across a partner in the United Kingdom who was looking for someone with life insurance experience. My purpose here is to work with another insurance company that is undergoing the demutualization process. The office in London is D&T's largest office in the world, and I'm working with clients operating in many different countries.

In what way are U.K. accounting rules different from U.S. GAAP?

Actually, this insurance client has operations in the U.S, the U.K, and Canada, so there are three sets of financial statements, all with different rules. For example, in the U.K., investments are carried at market value, and the income statement reflects gains or losses as these values change. In the U.S., the rules are more complicated, as Intermediate Accounting students who have studied *FASB Statement 115* can attest. Deloitte provides training to European professionals on U.S. accounting developments, so we don't fall behind on new FASB pronouncements while we're away from the U.S.

What advice would you give to college students who want to work overseas?

The first step might be to study abroad during college. In my sophomore year, I studied art, music, philosophy, political science, and theology in Salzburg, Austria. That gives you more credibility when you apply for an international assignment. Beyond that, I would say be persistent. If you really want to do something, it usually happens. One advantage of working for an international firm such as D&T is the opportunity for international assignments. Working abroad has allowed me to travel throughout Europe on business and on my personal time. The one potential drawback is that you become more and more specialized, and it might be difficult, although not impossible, to return to your home office back in the U.S.

How did you decide on accounting as a major?

I've always been business minded. As a nine-year-old kid, when Mt. St. Helens erupted, I went around and washed everybody's cars. In addition, I have role models in my family. My father was a professor of accounting at the University of Portland and eventually became vice president of finance for the university.

Note: All **asterisked** Questions, Exercises, Problems, and Conceptual Cases relate to material contained in the appendix to the chapter.

QUESTIONS

1 Explain the current environment regarding revenue recognition.

2 When is revenue conventionally recognized? What conditions should exist for the recognition at date of sale of all or part of the revenue and income of any sale transaction?

3 When is revenue recognized in the following situations: (a) Revenue from selling products? (b) Revenue from services rendered? (c) Revenue from permitting others to use enterprise assets? (d) Revenue from disposing of assets other than products?

4 Identify several types of sales transactions and indicate the types of business for which that type of transaction is common.

5 What are the three alternative accounting methods available to a seller that is exposed to continued risks of ownership through return of the product?

6 Under what conditions may a seller who is exposed to continued risks of a high rate of return of the product sold recognize sales transactions as current revenue?

7 What are the two basic methods of accounting for long-term construction contracts? Indicate the circumstances that determine when one or the other of these methods should be used.

8 F. Scott Fitzgerald Construction Co. has a $60 million contract to construct a highway overpass and cloverleaf. The total estimated cost for the project is $50 million. Costs incurred in the first year of the project are $9 million. F. Scott Fitzgerald Construction Co. appropriately uses the percentage-of-completion method. How much revenue and gross profit should F. Scott Fitzgerald recognize in the first year of the project?

9 For what reasons should the percentage-of-completion method be used over the completed-contract method whenever possible?

10 What methods are used in practice to determine the extent of progress toward completion? Identify some "input measures" and some "output measures" that might be used to determine the extent of progress.

11 What are the two types of losses that can become evident in accounting for long-term contracts? What is the nature of each type of loss? How is each type accounted for?

12 Under the percentage-of-completion method, how are the Construction in Process and the Billings on Construction in Process accounts reported in the balance sheet?

13 Explain the differences between the installment sales method and the cost recovery method.

14 Identify and briefly describe the two methods generally employed to account for the cash received in situations where the collection of the sales price is not reasonably assured.

15 What is the deposit method and when might it be applied?

16 What is the nature of an installment sale? How do installment sales differ from ordinary credit sales?

17 Describe the installment sales method of accounting.

18 How are operating expenses (not included in cost of goods sold) handled under the installment method of accounting? What is the justification for such treatment?

19 Jack London sold his condominium for $500,000 on September 14, 2000; he had paid $310,000 for it in 1992. London collected the selling price as follows: 2000, $80,000; 2001, $320,000; and 2002, $100,000. London appropriately uses the installment method. Prepare a schedule to determine the gross profit for 2000, 2001, and 2002 from the installment sale.

20 When interest is involved in installment sales transactions, how should it be treated for accounting purposes?

21 How should the results of installment sales be reported on the income statement?

22 At what time is it proper to recognize income in the following cases: (a) installment sales with no reasonable basis for estimating the degree of collectibility; (b) sales for future delivery; (c) merchandise shipped on consignment; (d) profit on incomplete construction contracts; and (e) subscriptions to publications?

23 When is revenue recognized under the cost recovery method?

24 When is revenue recognized under the deposit method? How does the deposit method differ from the installment sales and cost recovery methods?

***25** Why in franchise arrangements may it not be proper to recognize the entire franchise fee as revenue at the date of sale?

***26** How does the concept of "substantial performance" apply to accounting for franchise sales?

***27** How should a franchisor account for continuing franchise fees and routine sales of equipment and supplies to franchisees?

***28** What changes are made in the franchisor's recording of the initial franchise fee when the franchise agreement:

(a) Contains an option allowing the franchisor to purchase the franchised outlet, and it is likely that the option will be exercised?

(b) Allows the franchisee to purchase equipment and supplies from the franchisor at bargain prices?

***29** What is the nature of a sale on consignment? When is revenue recognized from a consignment sale?

BRIEF EXERCISES

BE19-1 Scooby Doo Music sold CDs to retailers and recorded sales revenue of $800,000. During 2002, retailers returned CDs to Scooby Doo and were granted credit of $78,000. Past experience indicates that the normal return rate is 15%. Prepare Scooby Doo's entries to record (a) the $78,000 of returns and (b) estimated returns at December 31, 2002.

BE19-2 Shock Wave, Inc. began work on a $7,000,000 contract in 2002 to construct an office building. During 2002, Shock Wave, Inc. incurred costs of $1,715,000, billed their customers for $1,200,000, and collected $960,000. At December 31, 2002, the estimated future costs to complete the project total $3,185,000. Prepare Shock Wave's 2002 journal entries using the percentage-of-completion method.

BE19-3 Shadow Blasters, Inc. began work on a $7,000,000 contract in 2002 to construct an office building. Shadow Blasters uses the percentage-of-completion method. At December 31, 2002, the balances in certain accounts were: construction in process, $2,450,000; accounts receivable, $240,000; and billings on construction in process, $1,200,000. Indicate how these accounts would be reported in Shadow Blasters' December 31, 2002, balance sheet.

BE19-4 Use the information from BE19-2, but assume Shock Wave uses the completed-contract method. Prepare the company's 2002 journal entries.

BE19-5 Cordero, Inc. began work on a $7,000,000 contract in 2002 to construct an office building. Cordero uses the completed-contract method. At December 31, 2002, the balances in certain accounts were construction in process, $1,715,000; accounts receivable, $240,000; and billings on construction in process, $1,200,000. Indicate how these accounts would be reported in Cordero's December 31, 2002, balance sheet.

BE19-6 Shaq Fu Construction Company began work on a $420,000 construction contract in 2002. During 2002, Shaq Fu incurred costs of $288,000, billed their customer for $215,000, and collected $175,000. At December 31, 2002, the estimated future costs to complete the project total $162,000. Prepare Shaq Fu's journal entry to record profit or loss using (a) the percentage-of-completion method and (b) the completed contract method, if any.

BE19-7 Thunder Paradise Corporation began selling goods on an installment basis on January 1, 2002. During 2002, Thunder Paradise had installment sales of $150,000; cash collections of $54,000; cost of installment sales of $105,000. Prepare the company's entries to record installment sales, cash collected, cost of installment sales, deferral of gross profit, and gross profit recognized, using the installment sales method.

BE19-8 Shinobi, Inc. sells goods on the installment basis and uses the installment sales method. Due to a customer default, Shinobi repossessed merchandise which was originally sold for $800, resulting in a gross profit rate of 40%. At the time of repossession, the uncollected balance is $560, and the fair value of the repossessed merchandise is $275. Prepare Shinobi's entry to record the repossession.

BE19-9 At December 31, 2002, Soul Star Corporation had the following account balances:

Installment Accounts Receivable, 2001	$ 65,000
Installment Accounts Receivable, 2002	110,000
Deferred Gross Profit, 2001	23,400
Deferred Gross Profit, 2002	40,700

Most of Soul Star's sales are made on a 2-year installment basis. Indicate how these accounts would be reported in Soul Star's December 31, 2002, balance sheet. The 2001 accounts are collectible in 2003, and the 2002 accounts are collectible in 2004.

BE19-10 Yogi Bear Corporation sold equipment to Magilla Company for $20,000. The equipment is on Yogi's books at a net amount of $14,000. Yogi collected $10,000 in 2001, $5,000 in 2002, and $5,000 in 2003. If Yogi uses the cost recovery method, what amount of gross profit will be recognized in each year?

***BE19-11** Speed Racer, Inc. charges an initial franchise fee of $75,000 for the right to operate as a franchisee of Speed Racer. Of this amount, $25,000 is collected immediately. The remainder is collected in 4 equal annual installments of $12,500 each. These installments have a present value of $39,623. There is reasonable expectation that the down payment may be refunded and substantial future services be performed by Speed Racer, Inc. Prepare the journal entry required by Speed Racer to record the franchise fee.

***BE19-12** Tom and Jerry Corporation shipped $20,000 of merchandise on consignment to Toons Company. Tom and Jerry paid freight costs of $2,000. Toons Company paid $500 for local advertising which is reimbursable from Tom and Jerry. By year-end, 60% of the merchandise had been sold for $22,300. Toons notified Tom and Jerry, retained a 10% commission, and remitted the cash due to Tom and Jerry. Prepare Tom and Jerry's entry when the cash is received.

EXERCISES

E19-1 (Revenue Recognition on Book Sales with High Returns) Justin Huish Publishing Co. publishes college textbooks that are sold to bookstores on the following terms. Each title has a fixed wholesale price, terms f.o.b. shipping point, and payment is due 60 days after shipment. The retailer may return a maximum of 30% of an order at the retailer's expense. Sales are made only to retailers who have good credit ratings. Past experience indicates that the normal return rate is 12% and the average collection period is 72 days.

Instructions

(a) Identify alternative revenue recognition tests that Huish could employ concerning textbook sales.
(b) Briefly discuss the reasoning for your answers in (a) above.
(c) In late July, Huish shipped books invoiced at $16,000,000. Prepare the journal entry to record this event that best conforms to generally accepted accounting principles and your answer to part (b).
(d) In October, $2 million of the invoiced July sales were returned according to the return policy, and the remaining $14 million was paid; prepare the entry recording the return and payment.

E19-2 (Sales Recorded Both Gross and Net) On June 3, David Reid Company sold to Kim Rhode merchandise having a sale price of $5,000 with terms of 2/10, n/60, f.o.b. shipping point. An invoice totaling $120, terms n/30, was received by Rhode on June 8 from the Olympic Transport Service for the freight cost. Upon receipt of the goods, June 5, Rhode notified Reid Company that merchandise costing $400 contained flaws that rendered it worthless; the same day Reid Company issued a credit memo covering the worthless merchandise and asked that it be returned at company expense. The freight on the returned merchandise was $24, paid by Reid Company on June 7. On June 12, the company received a check for the balance due from Rhode.

Instructions

(a) Prepare journal entries on Reid Company books to record all the events noted above under each of the following bases:
  (1) Sales and receivables are entered at gross selling price.
  (2) Sales and receivables are entered net of cash discounts.
(b) Prepare the journal entry under basis 2, assuming that Kim Rhode did not remit payment until August 5.

E19-3 (Revenue Recognition on Marina Sales with Discounts) Brooke Bennett Marina has 300 available slips that rent for $900 per season. Payments must be made in full at the start of the boating season, April 1. Slips for the next season may be reserved if paid for by December 31. Under a new policy, if payment is made by December 31, a 5% discount is allowed. The boating season ends October 31, and the marina has a December 31 year-end. To provide cash flow for major dock repairs, the marina operator is also offering a 25% discount to slip renters who pay for the second season following the current December 31.

For the fiscal year ended December 31, 2001, all 300 slips were rented at full price. Two hundred slips were reserved and paid for for the 2002 boating season, and 60 slips were reserved and paid for for the 2003 boating season.

Instructions

(a) Prepare the appropriate journal entries for fiscal 2001.
(b) Assume the marina operator is unsophisticated in business. Explain the managerial significance of the accounting above to this person.

E19-4 (Recognition of Profit on Long-Term Contracts) During 2001 Pierson Company started a construction job with a contract price of $1,500,000. The job was completed in 2003. The following information is available:

	2001	2002	2003
Costs incurred to date	$400,000	$935,000	$1,070,000
Estimated costs to complete	600,000	165,000	–0–
Billings to date	300,000	900,000	1,500,000
Collections to date	270,000	810,000	1,425,000

Instructions

(a) Compute the amount of gross profit to be recognized each year assuming the percentage-of-completion method is used.

(b) Prepare all necessary journal entries for 2002.

(c) Compute the amount of gross profit to be recognized each year assuming the completed-contract method is used.

E19-5 (Analysis of Percentage-of-Completion Financial Statements) In 2001, Beth Botsford Construction Corp. began construction work under a 3-year contract. The contract price was $1,000,000. Beth Botsford uses the percentage-of-completion method for financial accounting purposes. The income to be recognized each year is based on the proportion of cost incurred to total estimated costs for completing the contract. The financial statement presentations relating to this contract at December 31, 2001, follow:

Balance Sheet

Accounts receivable—construction contract billings		$21,500
Construction in progress	$65,000	
Less contract billings	61,500	
Cost of uncompleted contract in excess of billings		3,500

Income Statement

Income (before tax) on the contract recognized in 2001	$18,200

Instructions

(a) How much cash was collected in 2001 on this contract?

(b) What was the initial estimated total income before tax on this contract?

(AICPA adapted)

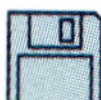

E19-6 (Gross Profit on Uncompleted Contract) On April 1, 2001, Brad Bridgewater Inc. entered into a cost-plus-fixed-fee contract to construct an electric generator for Tom Dolan Corporation. At the contract date, Bridgewater estimated that it would take 2 years to compete the project at a cost of $2,000,000. The fixed fee stipulated in the contract is $450,000. Bridgewater appropriately accounts for this contract under the percentage-of-completion method. During 2001 Bridgewater incurred costs of $700,000 related to the project. The estimated cost at December 31, 2001, to complete the contract is $1,300,000. Dolan was billed $600,000 under the contract.

Instructions

Prepare a schedule to compute the amount of gross profit to be recognized by Bridgewater under the contract for the year ended December 31, 2001. Show supporting computations in good form.

(AICPA adapted)

E19-7 (Recognition of Profit, Percentage-of-Completion) In 2001 Jeff Rouse Construction Company agreed to construct an apartment building at a price of $1,000,000. The information relating to the costs and billings for this contract is as follows:

	2001	2002	2003
Costs incurred to date	$280,000	$600,000	$ 785,000
Estimated costs yet to be incurred	520,000	200,000	–0–
Customer billings to date	150,000	400,000	1,000,000
Collection of billings to date	120,000	320,000	940,000

Instructions

(a) Assuming that the percentage-of-completion method is used: (1) compute the amount of gross profit to be recognized in 2001, and 2002, and (2) prepare journal entries for 2002.

(b) For 2002, show how the details related to this construction contract would be disclosed on the balance sheet and on the income statement.

E19-8 (Recognition of Revenue on Long-Term Contract and Entries) Amy Van Dyken Construction Company uses the percentage-of-completion method of accounting. In 2001, Van Dyken began work under contract #E2-D2, which provided for a contract price of $2,200,000. Other details follow:

	2001	2002
Costs incurred during the year	$ 480,000	$1,425,000
Estimated costs to complete, as of December 31	1,120,000	–0–
Billings during the year	420,000	1,680,000
Collections during the year	350,000	1,500,000

Instructions

(a) What portion of the total contract price would be recognized as revenue in 2001? In 2002?

(b) Assuming the same facts as those above except that Van Dyken uses the completed-contract method of accounting, what portion of the total contract price would be recognized as revenue in 2002?

(c) Prepare a complete set of journal entries for 2001 (using percentage-of-completion).

E19-9 (Recognition of Profit and Balance Sheet Amounts for Long-Term Contracts) Andre Agassi Construction Company began operations January 1, 2001. During the year, Andre Agassi Construction entered into a contract with Lindsey Davenport Corp. to construct a manufacturing facility. At that time, Agassi estimated that it would take 5 years to complete the facility at a total cost of $4,500,000. The total contract price for construction of the facility is $6,300,000. During the year, Agassi incurred $1,185,800 in construction costs related to the construction project. The estimated cost to complete the contract is $4,204,200. Lindsey Davenport Corp. was billed and paid 30% of the contract price.

Instructions

Prepare schedules to compute the amount of gross profit to be recognized for the year ended December 31, 2001, and the amount to be shown as "cost of uncompleted contract in excess of related billings" or "billings on uncompleted contract in excess of related costs" at December 31, 2001, under each of the following methods:

(a) Completed-contract method.

(b) Percentage-of-completion method.

Show supporting computations in good form.

(AICPA adapted)

E19-10 (Long-Term Contract Reporting) Derrick Adkins Construction Company began operations in 2001. Construction activity for the first year is shown below. All contracts are with different customers, and any work remaining at December 31, 2001, is expected to be completed in 2002.

Project	Total Contract Price	Billings through 12/31/01	Cash Collections through 12/31/01	Contract Costs Incurred through 12/31/01	Estimated Additional Costs to Complete
1	$ 560,000	$ 360,000	$340,000	$450,000	$140,000
2	670,000	220,000	210,000	126,000	504,000
3	500,000	500,000	440,000	330,000	–0–
	$1,730,000	$1,080,000	$990,000	$906,000	$644,000

Instructions

Prepare a partial income statement and balance sheet to indicate how the above information would be reported for financial statement purposes. Derrick Adkins Construction Company uses the completed-contract method.

E19-11 (Installment Sales Method Calculations, Entries) Austin Corporation appropriately uses the installment sales method of accounting to recognize income in its financial statements. The following information is available for 2001 and 2002:

	2001	2002
Installment sales	$900,000	$1,000,000
Cost of installment sales	630,000	680,000
Cash collections on 2001 sales	370,000	350,000
Cash collections on 2002 sales	–0–	475,000

Instructions

(a) Compute the amount of realized gross profit recognized in each year.

(b) Prepare all journal entries required in 2002.

E19-12 (Analysis of Installment Sales Accounts) Charles Austin Co. appropriately uses the installment sales method of accounting. On December 31, 2003, the books show balances as follows:

Installment Receivables	
2001	$11,000
2002	40,000
2003	80,000

Deferred Gross Profit	
2001	$ 7,000
2002	26,000
2003	95,000

Gross Profit on Sales	
2001	35%
2002	34%
2003	32%

Instructions

(a) Prepare the adjusting entry or entries required on December 31, 2003 to recognize 2003 realized gross profit. (Installment receivables have already been credited for cash receipts during 2003.)

(b) Compute the amount of cash collected in 2003 on accounts receivable each year.

E19-13 (Gross Profit Calculations and Repossessed Merchandise) Randy Barnes Corporation, which began business on January 1, 2001, appropriately uses the installment sales method of accounting. The following data were obtained for the years 2001 and 2002:

	2001	2002
Installment sales	$750,000	$840,000
Cost of installment sales	525,000	604,800
General & administrative expenses	70,000	84,000
Cash collections on sales of 2001	310,000	300,000
Cash collections on sales of 2002	–0–	400,000

Instructions

(a) Compute the balance in the deferred gross profit accounts on December 31, 2001, and on December 31, 2002.

(b) A 2001 sale resulted in default in 2003. At the date of default, the balance on the installment receivable was $12,000, and the repossessed merchandise had a fair value of $8,000. Prepare the entry to record the repossession.

(AICPA adapted)

E19-14 (Interest Revenue from Installment Sale) Gail Devers Corporation sells farm machinery on the installment plan. On July 1, 2001, Devers entered into an installment sale contract with Gwen Torrence Inc. for a 10-year period. Equal annual payments under the installment sale are $100,000 and are due on July 1. The first payment was made on July 1, 2001.

Additional information

1. The amount that would be realized on an outright sale of similar farm machinery is $676,000.
2. The cost of the farm machinery sold to Gwen Torrence Inc. is $500,000.
3. The finance charges relating to the installment period are $324,000 based on a stated interest rate of 10%, which is appropriate.
4. Circumstances are such that the collection of the installments due under the contract is reasonably assured.

Instructions

What income or loss before income taxes should Devers record for the year ended December 31, 2001, as a result of the transactive above?

(AICPA adapted)

E19-15 (Installment Method and Cost Recovery) Kenny Harrison Corp., a capital goods manufacturing business that started on January 4, 2001, and operates on a calendar-year basis, uses the installment method of profit recognition in accounting for all its sales. The following data were taken from the 2001 and 2002 records:

	2001	2002
Installment sales	$480,000	$620,000
Gross profit as a percent of costs	25%	28%
Cash collections on sales of 2001	$140,000	$240,000
Cash collections on sales of 2002	–0–	$180,000

The amounts given for cash collections exclude amounts collected for interest charges.

Instructions

(a) Compute the amount of realized gross profit to be recognized on the 2002 income statement, prepared using the installment method.

(b) State where the balance of Deferred Gross Profit would be reported on the financial statements for 2002.

(c) Compute the amount of realized gross profit to be recognized on the income statement, prepared using the cost recovery method.

(CIA adapted)

E19-16 (Installment Sales Method and Cost Recovery Method) On January 1, 2001, Barkly Company sold property for $200,000. The note will be collected as follows: $100,000 in 2001, $60,000 in 2002, and $40,000 in 2003. The property had cost Barkly $150,000 when it was purchased in 1999.

Instructions

(a) Compute the amount of gross profit realized each year assuming Barkly uses the cost recovery method.

(b) Compute the amount of gross profit realized each year assuming Barkly uses the installment sales method.

E19-17 (Cost Recovery Method) On January 1, 2002, Allen Johnson Company sold real estate that cost $110,000 to Carl Lewis for $120,000. Lewis agreed to pay for the purchase over 3 years by making three end-of-year equal payments of $52,557 that included 15% interest. Shortly after the sale, Allen Johnson Company learns distressing news about Lewis's financial circumstances and because collection is so uncertain decides to account for the sale using the cost recovery method.

Instructions

Applying the cost recovery method, prepare a schedule showing the amounts of cash collected, the increase (decrease) in deferred interest revenue, the balance of the receivable, the balance of the unrecovered cost, the gross profit realized, and the interest revenue realized for each of the 3 years assuming the payments are made as agreed.

E19-18 (Installment Sales—Default and Repossession) Michael Johnson Imports Inc. was involved in two default and repossession cases during the year:

1. A refrigerator was sold to Merlene Ottey for $1,800, including a 35% markup on selling price. Ottey made a down payment of 20%, four of the remaining 16 equal payments, and then defaulted on further payments. The refrigerator was repossessed, at which time the fair value was determined to be $800.
2. An oven that cost $1,200 was sold to Donovan Bailey for $1,600 on the installment basis. Bailey made a down payment of $240 and paid $80 a month for six months, after which he defaulted. The oven was repossessed and the estimated value at time of repossession was determined to be $750.

Instructions

Prepare journal entries to record each of these repossessions. (Ignore interest charges.)

E19-19 (Installment Sales—Default and Repossession) Kurt Angle Company uses the installment sales method in accounting for its installment sales. On January 1, 2002, Angle Company had an installment account receivable from Kay Bluhm with a balance of $1,800. During 2002, $400 was collected from Bluhm. When no further collection could be made, the merchandise sold to Bluhm was repossessed. The merchandise had a fair market value of $650 after the company spent $60 for reconditioning of the merchandise. The merchandise was originally sold with a gross profit rate of 40%.

Instructions

Prepare the entries on the books of Angle Company to record all transactions related to Bluhm during 2002. (Ignore interest charges.)

E19-20 (Cost Recovery Method) On January 1, 2002, Tom Brands sells 200 acres of farmland for $600,000, taking in exchange a 10% interest-bearing note. Tom Brands purchased the farmland in 1987 at a cost of $500,000. The note will be paid in three installments of $241,269 each on December 31, 2002, 2003, and 2004. Collectibility of the note is uncertain; Tom, therefore, uses the cost recovery method.

Instructions

Prepare for Tom a 3-year installment payment schedule (under the cost recovery method) that shows cash collections, deferred interest revenue, installment receivable balances, unrecovered cost, realized gross profit, and realized interest revenue by year.

***E19-21 (Franchise Entries)** Kendall Crossburgers Inc. charges an initial franchise fee of $70,000. Upon the signing of the agreement, a payment of $40,000 is due; thereafter, three annual payments of $10,000 are required. The credit rating of the franchisee is such that it would have to pay interest at 10% to borrow money.

Instructions

Prepare the entries to record the initial franchise fee on the books of the franchisor under the following assumptions:

(a) The down payment is not refundable, no future services are required by the franchisor, and collection of the note is reasonably assured.

(b) The franchisor has substantial services to perform, the down payment is refundable, and the collection of the note is very uncertain.

(c) The down payment is not refundable, collection of the note is reasonably certain, the franchisor has yet to perform a substantial amount of services, and the down payment represents a fair measure of the services already performed.

***E19-22 (Franchise Fee, Initial Down Payment)** On January 1, 2001, Svetlana Masterkova signed an agreement to operate as a franchisee of Short-Track Inc. for an initial franchise fee of $50,000. The amount of $20,000 was paid when the agreement was signed, and the balance is payable in five annual payments of $6,000 each, beginning January 1, 2002. The agreement provides that the down payment is not refundable and that no future services are required of the franchisor. Svetlana Masterkova's credit rating indicates that she can borrow money at 11% for a loan of this type.

Instructions

(a) How much should Short-Track record as revenue from franchise fees on January 1, 2001? At what amount should Svetlana record the acquisition cost of the franchise on January 1, 2001?

(b) What entry would be made by Short-Track on January 1, 2001, if the down payment is refundable and substantial future services remain to be performed by Short-Track?

(c) How much revenue from franchise fees would be recorded by Short-Track on January 1, 2001, if:

(1) The initial down payment is not refundable, it represents a fair measure of the services already provided, a significant amount of services is still to be performed by Short-Track in future periods, and collectibility of the note is reasonably assured?

(2) The initial down payment is not refundable and no future services are required by the franchisor, but collection of the note is so uncertain that recognition of the note as an asset is unwarranted?

(3) The initial down payment has not been earned and collection of the note is so uncertain that recognition of the note as an asset is unwarranted?

***E19-23 (Consignment Computations)** On May 3, 2001, Michelle Smith Company consigned 70 freezers, costing $500 each, to Angel Martino Company. The cost of shipping the freezers amounted to $840 and was paid by Smith Company. On December 30, 2001, an account sales was received from the consignee, reporting that 40 freezers had been sold for $700 each. Remittance was made by the consignee for the amount due, after deducting a commission of 6%, advertising of $200, and total installation costs of $320 on the freezers sold.

Instructions

(a) Compute the inventory value of the units unsold in the hands of the consignee.

(b) Compute the profit for the consignor for the units sold.

(c) Compute the amount of cash that will be remitted by the consignee.

PROBLEMS

P19-1 (Comprehensive Three-Part Revenue Recognition) Simona Amanar Industries has three operating divisions—Gina Construction Division, Gogean Publishing Division, and Chorkina Securities Division. Each division maintains its own accounting system and method of revenue recognition.

Gina Construction Division

During the fiscal year ended November 30, 2001, Gina Construction Division had one construction project in process. A $30,000,000 contract for construction of a civic center was granted on June 19, 2001, and construction began on August 1, 2001. Estimated costs of completion at the contract date were $25,000,000 over a 2-year time period from the date of the contract. On November 30, 2001, construction costs of $7,800,000 had been incurred and progress billings of $9,500,000 had been made. The construction costs to complete the remainder of the project were reviewed on November 30, 2001, and were estimated to amount to only $16,200,000 because of an expected decline in raw materials costs. Revenue recognition is based upon a percentage-of-completion method.

Gogean Publishing Division

The Gogean Publishing Division sells large volumes of novels to a few book distributors, which in turn sell to several national chains of bookstores. Gegean allows distributors to return up to 30% of sales, and distributors give the same terms to bookstores. While returns from individual titles fluctuate greatly, the returns from distributors have averaged 20% in each of the past 5 years. A total of $8,000,000 of paperback novel sales were made to distributors during fiscal 2001. On November 30, 2001, $2,500,000 of fiscal 2001 sales were still subject to return privileges over the next 6 months. The remaining $5,500,000 of fiscal 2001 sales had actual returns of 21%. Sales from fiscal 2000 totaling $2,000,000 were collected in fiscal 2001 less 18% returns. This division records revenue according to the method referred to as revenue recognition when the right of return exists.

Chorkina Securities Division
Chorkina Securities Division works through manufacturers' agents in various cities. Orders for alarm systems and down payments are forwarded from agents, and the Division ships the goods f.o.b. factory directly to customers (usually police departments and security guard companies). Customers are billed directly for the balance due plus actual shipping costs. The company received orders for $6,000,000 of goods during the fiscal year ended November 30, 2001. Down payments of $600,000 were received and $5,200,000 of goods were billed and shipped. Actual freight costs of $100,000 were also billed. Commissions of 10% on product price are paid to manufacturing agents after goods are shipped to customers. Such goods are warranted for 90 days after shipment, and warranty returns have been about 1% of sales. Revenue is recognized at the point of sale by this division.

Instructions

(a) There are a variety of methods of revenue recognition. Define and describe each of the following methods of revenue recognition and indicate whether each is in accordance with generally accepted accounting principles.
  (1) Point of sale.
  (2) Completion of production.
  (3) Percentage of completion.
  (4) Installment contract.

(b) Compute the revenue to be recognized in fiscal year 2001 for each of the three operating divisions of Simona Amanar Industries in accordance with generally accepted accounting principles.

P19-2 (Recognition of Profit on Long-Term Contract) Jenny Thompson Construction Company has entered into a contract beginning January 1, 2001, to build a parking complex. It has been estimated that the complex will cost $600,000 and will take three years to construct. The complex will be billed to the purchasing company at $900,000. The following data pertain to the construction period.

	2001	2002	2003
Costs to date	$270,000	$420,000	$600,000
Estimated costs to complete	330,000	180,000	–0–
Progress billings to date	270,000	550,000	900,000
Cash collected to date	240,000	500,000	900,000

Instructions

(a) Using the percentage-of-completion method, compute the estimated gross profit that would be recognized during each year of the construction period.

(b) Using the completed-contract method, compute the estimated gross profit that would be recognized during each year of the construction period.

P19-3 (Recognition of Profit and Entries on Long-Term Contract) On March 1, 2001, Winter Company entered into a contract to build an apartment building. It is estimated that the building will cost $2,000,000 and will take 3 years to complete. The contract price was $3,000,000. The following information pertains to the construction period:

	2001	2002	2003
Costs to date	$ 600,000	$1,560,000	$2,100,000
Estimated costs to complete	1,400,000	390,000	–0–
Progress billings to date	1,050,000	2,100,000	3,000,000
Cash collected to date	950,000	1,950,000	2,750,000

Instructions

(a) Compute the amount of gross profit to be recognized each year assuming the percentage-of-completion method is used.

(b) Prepare all necessary journal entries for 2003.

(c) Prepare a partial balance sheet for December 31, 2002, showing the balances in the receivables and inventory accounts.

P19-4 (Recognition of Profit and Balance Sheet Presentation, Percentage-of-Completion) On February 1, 2001, Amanda Beard Construction Company obtained a contract to build an athletic stadium. The stadium was to be built at a total cost of $5,400,000 and was scheduled for completion by September 1, 2003. One clause of the contract stated that Beard was to deduct $15,000 from the $6,600,000 billing price for each week that completion was delayed. Completion was delayed 6 weeks, which resulted in a $90,000 penalty. Below are the data pertaining to the construction period.

	2001	2002	2003
Costs to date	$1,782,000	$3,850,000	$5,500,000
Estimated costs to complete	3,618,000	1,650,000	–0–
Progress billings to date	1,200,000	3,100,000	6,510,000
Cash collected to date	1,000,000	2,800,000	6,510,000

Instructions

(a) Using the percentage-of-completion method, compute the estimated gross profit recognized in the years 2001–2003.

(b) Prepare a partial balance sheet for December 31, 2002, showing the balances in the receivable and inventory accounts.

P19-5 (Completed Contract and Percentage of Completion with Interim Loss) Gold Medal Custom Builders (GMCB) was established in 1972 by Whitney Hedgepeth and initially built high quality customized homes under contract with specific buyers. In the 1980s, Hedgepeth's two sons joined the firm and expanded GMCB's activities into the high-rise apartment and industrial plant markets. Upon the retirement of GMCB's long-time financial manager, Hedgepeth's sons recently hired Le Jingyi as controller for GMCB. Jingyi, a former college friend of Hedgepeth's sons, has been associated with a public accounting firm for the last 6 years.

Upon reviewing GMCB's accounting practices, Jingyi observed that GMCB followed the completed-contract method of revenue recognition, a carryover from the years when individual home building was the majority of GMCB's operations. Several years ago, the predominant portion of GMCB's activities shifted to the high-rise and industrial building areas. From land acquisition to the completion of construction, most building contracts cover several years. Under the circumstances, Jingyi believes that GMCB should follow the percentage-of-completion method of accounting. From a typical building contract, Jingyi developed the following data.

DAGMAR HAZE TRACTOR PLANT

Contract price: $8,000,000

	2000	2001	2002
Estimated costs	$2,010,000	$3,015,000	$1,675,000
Progress billings	1,000,000	2,500,000	4,500,000
Cash collections	800,000	2,300,000	4,900,000

Instructions

(a) Explain the difference between completed-contract revenue recognition and percentage-of-completion revenue recognition.

(b) Using the data provided for the Dagmar Haze Tractor Plant and assuming the percentage-of-completion method of revenue recognition is used, calculate GMCB's revenue and gross profit for 2000, 2001, and 2002, under **each** of the following circumstances.

(1) Assume that all costs are incurred, all billings to customers are made, and all collections from customers are received within 30 days of billing, as planned.

(2) Further assume that, as a result of unforeseen local ordinances and the fact that the building site was in a wetlands area, GMCB experienced cost overruns of $800,000 in 2000 to bring the site into compliance with the ordinances and to overcome wetlands barriers to construction.

(3) Further assume that, in addition to the cost overruns of $800,000 for this contract incurred under Instruction (b)2., inflationary factors over and above those anticipated in the development of the original contract cost have caused an additional cost overrun of $540,000 in 2001. It is not anticipated that any cost overruns will occur in 2002.

(CMA adapted)

P19-6 (Long-Term Contract with Interim Loss) On March 1, 2001, Franziska van Almsick Construction Company contracted to construct a factory building for Sandra Volker Manufacturing Inc. for a total contract price of $8,400,000. The building was completed by October 31, 2003. The annual contract costs incurred, estimated costs to complete the contract, and accumulated billings to Volker for 2001, 2002, and 2003 are given below:

	2001	2002	2003
Contract costs incurred during the year	$3,200,000	$2,600,000	$1,450,000
Estimated costs to complete the contract at 12/31	3,200,000	1,450,000	–0–
Billings to Volker during the year	3,200,000	3,500,000	1,700,000

Instructions

(a) Using the percentage-of-completion method, prepare schedules to compute the profit or loss to be recognized as a result of this contract for the years ended December 31, 2001, 2002, and 2003. (Ignore income taxes.)

(b) Using the completed-contract method, prepare schedules to compute the profit or loss to be recognized as a result of this contract for the years ended December 2001, 2002, and 2003. (Ignore incomes taxes.)

P19-7 (Long-Term Contract with an Overall Loss) On July 1, 2001, Kim Kyung-wook Construction Company Inc. contracted to build an office building for Fu Mingxia Corp. for a total contract price of $1,950,000. On July 1, Kyung-wook estimated that it would take between 2 and 3 years to complete the building. On December 31, 2003, the building was deemed substantially completed. Following are accumulated contract costs incurred, estimated costs to compete the contract, and accumulated billings to Mingxia for 2001, 2002, and 2003.

	At 12/31/01	At 12/31/02	At 12/31/03
Contract costs incurred to date	$ 150,000	$1,200,000	$2,100,000
Estimated costs to complete the contract	1,350,000	800,000	–0–
Billings to Mingxia	300,000	1,100,000	1,850,000

Instructions

(a) Using the percentage-of-completion method, prepare schedules to compute the profit or loss to be recognized as a result of this contract for the years ended December 31, 2001, 2002, and 2003. (Ignore income taxes.)

(b) Using the completed-contract method, prepare schedules to compute the profit or loss to be recognized as a result of this contract for the years ended December 2001, 2002, and 2003. (Ignore income taxes.)

P19-8 (Installment Sales Computations and Entries) Presented below is summarized information for Deng Yaping Co., which sells merchandise on the installment basis:

	2001	2002	2003
Sales (on installment plan)	$250,000	$260,000	$280,000
Cost of sales	150,000	163,800	182,000
Gross profit	$100,000	$ 96,200	$ 98,000
Collections from customers on:			
2001 installment sales	$ 75,000	$100,000	$ 50,000
2002 installment sales		100,000	120,000
2003 installment sales			110,000

Instructions

(a) Compute the realized gross profit for each of the years 2001, 2002, and 2003.

(b) Prepare in journal form all entries required in 2003, applying the installment sales method of accounting. (Ignore interest charges.)

P19-9 (Installment Sales Income Statements) Laura Flessel Stores sells merchandise on open account as well as on installment terms.

	2001	2002	2003
Sales on account	$385,000	$426,000	$525,000
Installment sales	320,000	275,000	380,000
Collections on installment sales			
Made in 2001	110,000	90,000	40,000
Made in 2002		110,000	140,000
Made in 2003			125,000
Cost of sales			
Sold on account	270,000	277,000	341,000
Sold on installment	214,400	167,750	224,200
Selling expenses	77,000	87,000	92,000
Administrative expenses	50,000	51,000	52,000

Instructions

From the data above, which cover the 3 years since Laura Flessel Stores commenced operations, determine the net income for each year, applying the installment sales method of accounting. (Ignore interest charges.)

P19-10 (Installment Sales Computations and Entries) Isabell Werth Stores sell appliances for cash and also on the installment plan. Entries to record cost of sales are made monthly.

ISABELL WERTH STORES
Trial Balance
December 31, 2003

	Dr.	Cr.
Cash	$153,000	
Installment Accounts Receivable, 2002	48,000	
Installment Accounts Receivable, 2003	91,000	
Inventory—New Merchandise	123,200	
Inventory—Repossessed Merchandise	24,000	
Accounts Payable		$98,500
Deferred Gross Profit, 2002		45,600
Capital Stock		170,000
Retained Earnings		93,900
Sales		343,000
Installment Sales		200,000
Cost of Sales	255,000	
Cost of Installment Sales	128,000	
Gain or Loss on Repossessions	800	
Selling and Administrative Expenses	128,000	
	$951,000	$951,000

The accounting department has prepared the following analysis of cash receipts for the year:

Cash sales (including repossessed merchandise)	$424,000
Installment accounts receivable, 2002	104,000
Installment accounts receivable, 2003	109,000
Other	36,000
Total	$673,000

Repossessions recorded during the year are summarized as follows:

	2002
Uncollected balance	$8,000
Loss on repossession	800
Repossessed merchandise	4,800

Instructions

From the trial balance and accompanying information:

(a) Compute the rate of gross profit for 2002 and 2003.

(b) Prepare closing entries as of December 31, 2003, under the installment sales method of accounting.

(c) Prepare a statement of income for the year ended December 31, 2003. Include only the realized gross profit in the income statement.

P19-11 (Installment Sales Entries) The following summarized information relates to the installment sales activity of Lisa Jacob Stores Inc. for the year 2001:

Installment sales during 2001	$500,000
Costs of goods sold on installment basis	330,000
Collections from customers	200,000
Unpaid balances on merchandise repossessed	24,000
Estimated value of merchandise repossessed	9,200

Instructions

(a) Prepare journal entries at the end of 2001 to record on the books of Lisa Jacob Stores, Inc. the summarized data above.

(b) Prepare the entry to record the gross profit realized during 2001.

P19-12 (Installment Sales Computation and Entries—Periodic Inventory) Catherine Fox Inc. sells merchandise for cash and also on the installment plan. Entries to record cost of goods sold are made at the end of each year.

Repossessions of merchandise (sold in 2002) were made in 2003 and were recorded correctly as follows:

Deferred Gross Profit, 2002	7,200	
Repossessed Merchandise	8,000	
Loss on Repossessions	2,800	
Installment Accounts Receivable, 2002		18,000

Part of this repossessed merchandise was sold for cash during 2003, and the sale was recorded by a debit to Cash and a credit to Sales.

The inventory of repossessed merchandise on hand December 31, 2003, is $4,000; of new merchandise, $127,400. There was no repossessed merchandise on hand January 1, 2003.

Collections on accounts receivable during 2000 were:

Installment Accounts Receivable, 2002	$80,000
Installment Accounts Receivable, 2003	50,000

The cost of the merchandise sold under the installment plan during 2003 was $117,000.

The rate of gross profit on 2002 and on 2003 installment sales can be computed from the information given above.

CATHERINE FOX INC.
Trial Balance
December 31, 2003

	Dr.	Cr.
Cash	$ 98,400	
Installment Accounts Receivable, 2002	80,000	
Installment Accounts Receivable, 2003	130,000	
Inventory, Jan. 1, 2003	120,000	
Repossessed Merchandise	8,000	
Accounts Payable		$ 47,200
Deferred Gross Profit, 2002		64,000
Capital Stock, Common		200,000
Retained Earnings		40,000
Sales		400,000
Installment Sales		180,000
Purchases	380,000	
Loss on Repossessions	2,800	
Operating Expenses	112,000	
	$931,200	$931,200

Instructions

(a) From the trial balance and other information given above, prepare adjusting and closing entries as of December 31, 2003.

(b) Prepare an income statement for the year ended December 31, 2003. Include only the realized gross profit in the income statement.

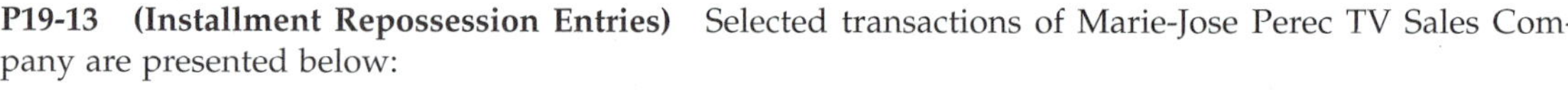

P19-13 (Installment Repossession Entries) Selected transactions of Marie-Jose Perec TV Sales Company are presented below:

1. A television set costing $560 is sold to Wang Junxia on November 1, 2002, for $800. Junxia makes a down payment of $200 and agrees to pay $30 on the first of each month for 20 months thereafter.
2. Junxia pays the $30 installment due December 1, 2002.
3. On December 31, 2002, the appropriate entries are made to record profit realized on the installment sales.
4. The first seven 2003 installments of $30 each are paid by Junxia. (Make one entry.)
5. In August 2003 the set is repossessed, after Junxia fails to pay the August 1 installment and indicates that he will be unable to continue the payments. The estimated fair value of the repossessed set is $100.

Instructions

Prepare journal entries to record on the books of Marie-Jose Perec TV Sales Company the transactions above. Closing entries should not be made.

P19-14 (Installment Sales Computations and Schedules) Valentina Vezzali Company, on January 2, 2001, entered into a contract with a manufacturing company to purchase room-size air conditioners and to sell the units on an installment plan with collections over approximately 30 months with no carrying charge.

For income tax purposes Vezzali Company elected to report income from its sales of air conditioners according to the installment sales method.

Purchases and sales of new units were as follows:

	Units Purchased		Units Sold	
Year	Quantity	Price Each	Quantity	Price Each
2001	1,400	$130	1,100	$200
2002	1,200	112	1,500	170
2003	900	136	800	182

Collections on installment sales were as follows:

	Collections Received		
	2001	2002	2003
2001 sales	$42,000	$88,000	$ 80,000
2002 sales		51,000	100,000
2003 sales			34,600

In 2003, 50 units from the 2002 sales were repossessed and sold for $80 each on the installment plan. At the time of repossession, $1,440 had been collected from the original purchasers and the units had a fair value of $3,000.

General and administrative expenses for 2003 were $60,000. No charge has been made against current income for the applicable insurance expense from a 3-year policy expiring June 30, 2004, costing $7,200, and for an advance payment of $12,000 on a new contract to purchase air conditioners beginning January 2, 2004.

Instructions

Assuming that the weighted-average method is used for determining the inventory cost, including repossessed merchandise, prepare schedules computing for 2001, 2002, and 2003:

(a) **(1)** The cost of goods sold on installments.
(2) The average unit cost of goods sold on installments for each year.
(b) The gross profit percentages for 2001, 2002, and 2003.
(c) The gain or loss on repossessions in 2003.
(d) The net income from installment sales for 2003 (ignore income taxes).

(AICPA adapted)

P19-15 (Completed-Contract Method) Renata Mauer Construction Company, Inc., entered into a firm fixed-price contract with Giovanna Trillini Clinic on July 1, 1999, to construct a four-story office building. At that time, Mauer estimated that it would take between 2 and 3 years to complete the project. The total contract price for construction of the building is $4,500,000. Mauer appropriately accounts for this contract under the completed-contract method in its financial statements and for income tax reporting. The building was deemed substantially completed on December 31, 2001. Estimated percentage of completion, accumulated contract costs incurred, estimated costs to complete the contract, and accumulated billings to the Trillini Clinic under the contract were as follows:

	At December 31, 1999	At December 31, 2000	At December 31, 2001
Percentage of completion	30%	65%	100%
Contract costs incurred	$1,140,000	$3,055,000	$4,800,000
Estimated costs to complete the contract	$2,660,000	$1,645,000	–0–
Billings to Trillini Clinic	$1,500,000	$2,500,000	$4,300,000

Instructions

(a) Prepare schedules to compute the amount to be shown as "cost of uncompleted contract in excess of related billings" or "billings on uncompleted contract in excess of related costs" at December 31, 1999, 2000, and 2001. Ignore income taxes. Show supporting computations in good form.

(b) Prepare schedules to compute the profit or loss to be recognized as a result of this contract for the years ended December 31, 1999, 2000, and 2001. Ignore income taxes. Show supporting computations in good form.

(AICPA adapted)

P19-16 (Revenue Recognition Methods—Comparison) Joy's Construction is in its fourth year of business. Joy performs long-term construction projects and accounts for them using the completed contract method. Joy built an apartment building at a price of $1,000,000. The costs and billings for this contract for the first three years are as follows:

	2000	2001	2002
Costs incurred to date	$320,000	$600,000	$ 790,000
Estimated costs yet to be incurred	480,000	200,000	–0–
Customer billings to date	150,000	410,000	1,000,000
Collection of billings to date	120,000	340,000	950,000

Joy has contacted you, a certified public accountant, about the following concern. She would like to attract some investors, but she believes that in order to recognize revenue she must first "deliver" the product. Therefore, on her balance sheet, she did not recognize any gross profits from the above contract until 2002, when she recognized the entire $210,000. That looked good for 2002, but the preceding years looked grim by comparison. She wants to know about an alternative to this completed-contract revenue recognition.

Instructions

Draft a letter to Joy, telling her about the percentage-of-completion method of recognizing revenue. Compare it to the completed-contract method. Explain the idea behind the percentage-of-completion method. In addition, illustrate how much revenue she could have recognized in 2000, 2001, and 2002 if she had used this method.

P19-17 (Comprehensive Problem—Long-Term Contracts) You have been engaged by Rich Mathre Construction Company to advise it concerning the proper accounting for a series of long-term contracts. Rich Mathre Construction Company commenced doing business on January 1, 2001. Construction activities for the first year of operations are shown below. All contract costs are with different customers, and any work remaining at December 31, 2001, is expected to be completed in 2002.

Project	Total Contract Price	Billings Through 12/31/01	Cash Collections Through 12/31/01	Contract Costs Incurred Through 12/31/01	Estimated Additional Costs to Complete
A	$ 300,000	$200,000	$180,000	$248,000	$ 67,000
B	350,000	110,000	105,000	67,800	271,200
C	280,000	280,000	255,000	186,000	–0–
D	200,000	35,000	25,000	123,000	87,000
E	240,000	205,000	200,000	185,000	15,000
	$1,370,000	$830,000	$765,000	$809,800	$440,200

Instructions

(a) Prepare a schedule to compute gross profit (loss) to be reported, unbilled contract costs and recognized profit, and billings in excess of costs and recognized profit using the percentage-of-completion method.

(b) Prepare a partial income statement and balance sheet to indicate how the information would be reported for financial statement purposes.

(c) Repeat the requirements for part (1) assuming Rich Mathre uses the completed-contract method.

(d) Using the responses above for illustrative purposes, prepare a brief report comparing the conceptual merits (both positive and negative) of the two revenue recognition approaches.

CONCEPTUAL CASES

C19-1 (Revenue Recognition—Alternative Methods) Alexsandra Isosev Industries has three operating divisions—Falilat Mining, Mourning Paperbacks, and Osygus Protection Devices. Each division maintains its own accounting system and method of revenue recognition.

Falilat Mining

Falilat Mining specializes in the extraction of precious metals such as silver, gold, and platinum. During the fiscal year ended November 30, 2001, Falilat entered into contracts worth $2,250,000 and shipped metals worth $2,000,000. A quarter of the shipments were made from inventories on hand at the beginning of the fiscal year while the remainder were made from metals that were mined during the year. Mining totals for the year, valued at market prices, were: silver at $750,000, gold at $1,300,000, and platinum at $490,000. Falilat uses the completion-of-production method to recognize revenue, because its operations meet the specified criteria, i.e., reasonably assured sales prices, interchangeable units, and insignificant distribution costs.

Mourning Paperbacks
Mourning Paperbacks sells large quantities of novels to a few book distributors that in turn sell to several national chains of bookstores. Mourning allows distributors to return up to 30 percent of sales, and distributors give the same terms to bookstores. While returns from individual titles fluctuate greatly, the returns from distributors have averaged 20 percent in each of the past 5 years. A total of $8,000,000 of paperback novel sales were made to distributors during the fiscal year. On November 30, 2001, $3,200,000 of fiscal 2001 sales were still subject to return privileges over the next 6 months. The remaining $4,800,000 of fiscal 2001 sales had actual returns of 21 percent. Sales from fiscal 2001 totaling $2,500,000 were collected in fiscal 2001, with less than 18 percent of sales returned. Mourning records revenue according to the method referred to as revenue recognition when the right of return exits, because all applicable criteria for use of this method are met by Mourning's operations.

Osygus Protection Devices
Osygus Protection Devices works through manufacturers' agents in various cities. Orders for alarm systems and down payments are forwarded from agents, and Osygus ships the goods f.o.b. shipping point. Customers are billed for the balance due plus actual shipping costs. The firm received orders for $6,000,000 of goods during the fiscal year ended November 30, 2001. Down payments of $600,000 were received, and $5,000,000 of goods were billed and shipped. Actual freight costs of $100,000 were also billed. Commissions of 10 percent on product price were paid to manufacturers' agents after the goods were shipped to customers. Such goods are warranted for 90 days after shipment, and warranty returns have been about 1 percent of sales. Revenue is recognized at the point of sale by Osygus.

Instructions

(a) There are a variety of methods for revenue recognition. Define and describe each of the following methods of revenue recognition and indicate whether each is in accordance with generally accepted accounting principles.
  (1) Completion-of-production method.
  (2) Percentage-of-completion method.
  (3) Installment sales method.

(b) Compute the revenue to be recognized in the fiscal year ended November 30, 2001, for
  (1) Falilat Mining.
  (2) Mourning Paperbacks.
  (3) Osygus Protection Devices.

(CMA adapted)

C19-2 (Recognition of Revenue—Theory) Revenue is usually recognized at the point of sale. Under special circumstances, however, bases other than the point of sale are used for the timing of revenue recognition.

Instructions

(a) Why is the point of sale usually used as the basis for the timing of revenue recognition?

(b) Disregarding the special circumstances when bases other than the point of sale are used, discuss the merits of each of the following objections to the sales basis of revenue recognition:
  (1) It is too conservative because revenue is earned throughout the entire process of production.
  (2) It is not conservative enough because accounts receivable do not represent disposable funds, sales returns and allowances may be made, and collection and bad debt expenses may be incurred in a later period.

(c) Revenue may also be recognized (1) during production and (2) when cash is received. For each of these two bases of timing revenue recognition, give an example of the circumstances in which it is properly used and discuss the accounting merits of its use in lieu of the sales basis.

(AICPA adapted)

C19-3 (Recognition of Revenue—Theory) The earning of revenue by a business enterprise is recognized for accounting purposes when the transaction is recorded. In some situations, revenue is recognized approximately as it is earned in the economic sense. In other situations, however, accountants have developed guidelines for recognizing revenue by other criteria, such as at the point of sale.

Instructions (Ignore income taxes.)

(a) Explain and justify why revenue is often recognized as earned at time of sale.

(b) Explain in what situations it would be appropriate to recognize revenue as the productive activity takes place.

(c) At what times, other than those included in (a) and (b) above, may it be appropriate to recognize revenue? Explain.

C19-4 (Recognition of Revenue—Trading Stamps) Alexei & Nemov Stamps, Inc., was formed early this year to sell trading stamps throughout the Southwest to retailers who distribute the stamps free to their customers. Books for accumulating the stamps and catalogs illustrating the merchandise for which the stamps may be exchanged are given free to retailers for distribution to stamp recipients. Centers with inventories of merchandise premiums have been established for redemption of the stamps. Retailers may not return unused stamps to Alexei & Nemov.

The following schedule expresses Alexei & Nemov's expectations as to percentages of a normal month's activity that will be attained. For this purpose, a "normal month's activity" is defined as the level of operations expected when expansion of activities ceases or tapers off to a stable rate. The company expects that this level will be attained in the third year and that sales of stamps will average $6,000,000 per month throughout the third year.

Month	Actual Stamp Sales Percent	Merchandise Premium Purchases Percent	Stamp Redemptions Percent
6th	30%	40%	10%
12th	60	60	45
18th	80	80	70
24th	90	90	80
30th	100	100	95

Alexei & Nemov plans to adopt an annual closing date at the end of each 12 months of operation.

Instructions

(a) Discuss the factors to be considered in determining when revenue should be recognized in measuring the income of a business enterprise.

(b) Discuss the accounting alternatives that should be considered by Alexei & Nemov Stamps, Inc., for the recognition of its revenues and related expenses.

(c) For each accounting alternative discussed in (b), give balance sheet accounts that should be used and indicate how each should be classified.

(AICPA adapted)

C19-5 (Recognition of Revenue from Subscriptions) *Cutting Edge* is a monthly magazine that has been on the market for 18 months. It currently has a circulation of 1.4 million copies. Currently negotiations are underway to obtain a bank loan in order to update their facilities. They are producing close to capacity and expect to grow at an average of 20% per year over the next 3 years.

After reviewing the financial statements of *Cutting Edge,* Gary Hall, the bank loan officer, had indicated that a loan could be offered to *Cutting Edge* only if they could increase their current ratio and decrease their debt to equity ratio to a specified level.

Alexander Popov, the marketing manager of *Cutting Edge,* has devised a plan to meet these requirements. Popov indicates that an advertising campaign can be initiated to immediately increase their circulation. The potential customers would be contacted after the purchase of another magazine's mailing list. The campaign would include:

1. An offer to subscribe to *Cutting Edge* at 3/4 the normal price.
2. A special offer to all new subscribers to receive the most current world atlas whenever requested at a guaranteed price of $2.00.
3. An unconditional guarantee that any subscriber will receive a full refund if dissatisfied with the magazine.

Although the offer of a full refund is risky, Popov claims that few people will ask for a refund after receiving half of their subscription issues. Popov notes that other magazine companies have tried this sales promotion technique and experienced great success. Their average cancellation rate was 25%. On the average, each company increased their initial circulation threefold and in the long run had increased circulation to twice that which existed before the promotion. In addition, 60% of the new subscribers are expected to take advantage of the atlas premium. Popov feels confident that the increased subscriptions from the advertising campaign will increase the current ratio and decrease the debt to equity ratio.

You are the controller of *Cutting Edge* and must give your opinion of the proposed plan.

Instructions

(a) When should revenue from the new subscriptions be recognized?

(b) How would you classify the estimated sales returns stemming from the unconditional guarantee?

(c) How should the atlas premium be recorded? Is the estimated premium claims a liability? Explain.
(d) Does the proposed plan achieve the goals of increasing the current ratio and decreasing the debt to equity ratio?

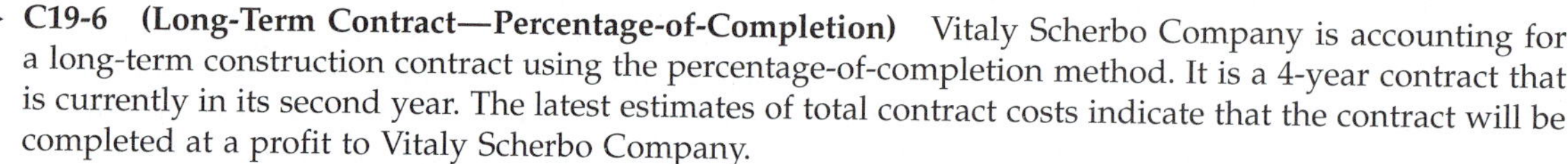

C19-6 (Long-Term Contract—Percentage-of-Completion) Vitaly Scherbo Company is accounting for a long-term construction contract using the percentage-of-completion method. It is a 4-year contract that is currently in its second year. The latest estimates of total contract costs indicate that the contract will be completed at a profit to Vitaly Scherbo Company.

Instructions

(a) What theoretical justification is there for Vitaly Scherbo Company's use of the percentage-of-completion method?
(b) How would progress billings be accounted for? Include in your discussion the classification of progress billings in Vitaly Scherbo Company financial statements.
(c) How would the income recognized in the second year of the 4-year contract be determined using the cost-to-cost method of determining percentage of completion?
(d) What would be the effect on earnings per share in the second year of the 4-year contract of using the percentage-of-completion method instead of the completed-contract method? Discuss.

(AICPA adapted)

C19-7 (Revenue Recognition—Real Estate Development) Pankratov Lakes is a new recreational real estate development which consists of 500 lake-front and lake-view lots. As a special incentive to the first 100 buyers of lake-view lots, the developer is offering 3 years of free financing on 10-year, 12% notes, no down payment, and one week at a nearby established resort—"a $1,200 value." The normal price per lot is $12,000. The cost per lake-view lot to the developer is an estimated average of $2,000. The development costs continue to be incurred; the actual average cost per lot is not known at this time. The resort promotion cost is $700 per lot. The notes are held by Davis Corp., a wholly owned subsidiary.

Instructions

(a) Discuss the revenue recognition and gross profit measurement issues raised by this situation.
(b) How would the developer's past financial and business experience influence your decision concerning the recording of these transactions?
(c) Assume 50 persons have accepted the offer, signed 10-year notes, and have stayed at the local resort. Prepare the journal entries that you believe are proper.
(d) What should be disclosed in the notes to the financial statements?

***C19-8 (Franchise Revenue)** Chou Foods Inc. sells franchises to independent operators throughout the northwestern part of the United States. The contract with the franchisee includes the following provisions:

1. The franchisee is charged an initial fee of $80,000. Of this amount, $30,000 is payable when the agreement is signed, and a $10,000 non-interest-bearing note is payable at the end of each of the 5 subsequent years.
2. All of the initial franchise fee collected by Chou Foods Inc. is to be refunded and the remaining obligation canceled if, for any reason, the franchisee fails to open his or her franchise.
3. In return for the initial franchise fee, Chou Foods Inc. agrees to (a) assist the franchisee in selecting the location for the business, (b) negotiate the lease for the land, (c) obtain financing and assist with building design, (d) supervise construction, (e) establish accounting and tax records, and (f) provide expert advice over a 5-year period relating to such matters as employee and management training, quality control, and promotion.
4. In addition to the initial franchise fee, the franchisee is required to pay to Chou Foods Inc. a monthly fee of 2% of sales for menu planning, receipt innovations, and the privilege of purchasing ingredients from Chou Foods Inc. at or below prevailing market prices.

Management of Chou Foods Inc. estimates that the value of the services rendered to the franchisee at the time the contract is signed amounts to at least $30,000. All franchisees to date have opened their locations at the scheduled time and none have defaulted on any of the notes receivable.

The credit ratings of all franchisees would entitle them to borrow at the current interest rate of 10%. The present value of an ordinary annuity of five annual receipts of $10,000 each discounted at 10% is $37,908.

Instructions

(a) Discuss the alternatives that Chou Foods Inc. might use to account for the initial franchise fees, evaluate each by applying generally accepted accounting principles, and give illustrative entries for each alternative.

(b) Given the nature of Chou Foods Inc.'s agreement with its franchisees, when should revenue be recognized? Discuss the question of revenue recognition for both the initial franchise fee and the additional monthly fee of 2% of sales and give illustrative entries for both types of revenue.

(c) Assuming that Chow Foods Inc. sells some franchises for $100,000, which includes a charge of $20,000 for the rental of equipment for its useful life of 10 years, that $50,000 of the fee is payable immediately and the balance on non-interest-bearing notes at $10,000 per year, that no portion of the $20,000 rental payment is refundable in case the franchisee goes out of business, and that title to the equipment remains with the franchisor, what would be the preferable method of accounting for the rental portion of the initial franchise fee? Explain.

(AICPA adapted)

USING YOUR JUDGMENT

FINANCIAL REPORTING PROBLEM: INTEL CORPORATION

Instructions

Refer to the financial statements and accompanying notes and discussion of Intel Corporation presented in Appendix 5B and answer the following questions.

(a) What were Intel's net revenues for 1998? Where did those revenues rank among Fortune's 500 largest industrial companies in 1998?

(b) What was the percentage of increase in Intel's revenues from 1997 to 1998? From 1996 to 1998? From 1993 to 1998?

(c) In its notes Intel states that it defers recognition of sales and income on shipments to distributors until the merchandise is sold by the distributors. What is the justification for deferring this recognition?

(d) In which foreign countries (geographic areas) did Intel experience significant revenues in 1998?

FINANCIAL STATEMENT ANALYSIS CASE

Westinghouse Electric Corporation

The following note appears in the "Summary of Significant Accounting Policies" section of the Annual Report of Westinghouse Electric Corporation.

> **Note 1 (in Part): Revenue Recognition.** Sales are primarily recorded as products are shipped and services are rendered. The percentage-of-completion method of accounting is used for nuclear steam supply system orders with delivery schedules generally in excess of five years and for certain construction projects where this method of accounting is consistent with industry practice.
>
> WFSI revenues are generally recognized on the accrual method. When accounts become delinquent for more than two payment periods, usually 60 days, income is recognized only as payments are received. Such delinquent accounts for which no payments are received in the current month, and other accounts on which income is not being recognized because the receipt of either principal or interest is questionable, are classified as nonearning receivables.

Instructions

(a) Identify the revenue recognition methods used by Westinghouse Electric as discussed in its note on significant accounting policies.

(b) Under what conditions are the revenue recognition methods identified in the first paragraph of Westinghouse's note above acceptable?

(c) From the information provided in the second paragraph of Westinghouse's note, identify the type of operation being described and defend the acceptability of the revenue recognition method.

COMPARATIVE ANALYSIS CASE

The Coca-Cola Company versus PepsiCo, Inc.

Instructions

Go to the Digital Tool site and, using The Coca-Cola Company and PepsiCo, Inc. Annual Report information, answer the following questions.

(a) What were Coca-Cola's and PepsiCo's net revenues (sales) for the year 1998? Which company increased its revenues the most (dollars and percentage) from 1997 to 1998?

(b) In which foreign countries (geographic areas) did Coca-Cola and PepsiCo experience significant revenues in 1998? Compare the amounts of foreign revenues to U.S. revenues for both Coca-Cola and PepsiCo.

RESEARCH CASES

Case 1

Companies registered with the Securities and Exchange Commission are required to file a current report on Form 8-K upon the occurrence of certain events.

Instructions

Use EDGAR or some other source to identify 8-Ks recently filed by two companies of your choice. Examine the 8-Ks and answer the following questions with regard to each.

(a) What corporate event or transaction triggered the filing of the Form 8-K?

(b) Identify any financial statements or exhibits included in the filing. How might these items help investors in evaluating the event/transaction?

Case 2

The December 19, 1994, issue of *Business Week* includes an article by Mark Maremont entitled "Numbers Game at **Bausch & Lomb**."

Instructions

Read the article and answer the following questions.

(a) What effect did the change in the contact lens division's sales strategy have on its 1993 sales and net income?

(b) According to the accounting experts referenced in the article, why was Bausch & Lomb not correct in recognizing revenue?

(c) How did Bausch & Lomb defend its accounting treatment?

(d) How was the problem resolved in October 1994?

ETHICS CASES

Case 1

Nimble Health and Racquet Club (NHRC), which operates eight clubs in the Chicago metropolitan area, offers one-year memberships. The members may use any of the eight facilities but must reserve racquetball court time and pay a separate fee before using the court. As an incentive to new customers, NHRC advertised that any customers not satisfied for any reason could receive a refund of the remaining portion of unused membership fees. Membership fees are due at the beginning of the individual membership period; however, customers are given the option of financing the membership fee over the membership period at a 15 percent interest rate.

Some customers have expressed a desire to take only the regularly scheduled aerobic classes without paying for a full membership. During the current fiscal year, NHRC began selling coupon books for aerobic classes only to accommodate these customers. Each book is dated and contains 50 coupons that may be redeemed for any regularly scheduled aerobic class over a one-year period. After the one-year period, unused coupons are no longer valid.

During 1995, NHRC expanded into the health equipment market by purchasing a local company that manufactures rowing machines and cross-country ski machines. These machines are used in NHRC's facilities and are sold through the clubs and mail order catalogs. Customers must make a 20 percent down payment when placing an equipment order; delivery is 60–90 days after order placement. The machines are sold with a 2-year unconditional guarantee. Based on past experience, NHRC expects the costs to repair machines under guarantee to be 4 percent of sales.

NHRC is in the process of preparing financial statements as of May 31, 2001, the end of its fiscal year. James Hogan, corporate controller, expressed concern over the company's performance for the year and decided to review the preliminary financial statements prepared by Barbara Hardy, NHRC's assistant controller. After reviewing the statements, Hogan proposed that the following changes be reflected in the May 31, 2001, published financial statements.

1. Membership revenue should be recognized when the membership fee is collected.
2. Revenue from the coupon books should be recognized when the books are sold.
3. Down payments on equipment purchases and expenses associated with the guarantee on the rowing and cross-country machines should be recognized when paid.

Hardy indicated to Hogan that the proposed changes are not in accordance with generally accepted accounting principles, but Hogan insisted that the changes be made. Hardy believes that Hogan wants to manipulate income to forestall any potential financial problems and increase his year-end bonus. At this point, Hardy is unsure what action to take.

Instructions

(a) **(1)** Describe when Nimble Health and Racquet Club (NHRC) should recognize revenue from membership fees, court rentals, and coupon book sales.

(2) Describe how NHRC should account for the down payments on equipment sales, explaining when this revenue should be recognized.

(3) Indicate when NHRC should recognize the expense associated with the guarantee of the rowing and cross-country machines.

(b) Discuss why James Hogan's proposed changes and his insistence that the financial statement changes be made is unethical. Structure your answer around or to include the following aspects of ethical conduct: competence, confidentiality, integrity, and/or objectivity.

(c) Identify some specific actions Barbara Hardy could take to resolve this situation.

(CMA adapted)

Case 2

Midwest Health Club offers one-year memberships. Membership fees are due in full at the beginning of the individual membership period. As an incentive to new customers, MHC advertised that any customers not satisfied for any reason could receive a refund of the remaining portion of unused membership fees. As a result of this policy, Stanley Hack, corporate controller, recognized revenue ratably over the life of the membership.

MHC is in the process of preparing its year-end financial statements. Phyllis Cavaretta, MHC's treasurer, is concerned about the company's lackluster performance this year. She reviews the financial statements Hack prepared and tells Hack to recognize membership revenue when the fees are received.

Instructions

Answer the following questions:

(a) What are the ethical issues involved?

(b) What should Hack do?

CHAPTER 20

Accounting for Income Taxes

Use It, but Don't Abuse It

As part of prudent management, companies are expected to manage all costs in order to maximize shareholder value. For example, good managers look for the best prices for raw materials and supplies that go into making their products, and are expected to be savvy bargainers in negotiating labor and other service contracts to minimize the overall cost of doing business.

Another set of costs that companies manage are those related to taxes. For example, by using accelerated depreciation methods for fixed assets, companies reduce their tax bills. With faster tax write-offs on fixed assets, companies report lower taxable income and pay lower taxes in the early years of the assets' lives, thereby managing tax costs.

What happens when companies cross the line from prudent tax management to abusive tax avoidance? Recently more companies appear to be crossing that line. As indicated in the following chart, corporate taxes as a share of profits have dropped from 26.6% in 1994 to just 21.8% in 1999.

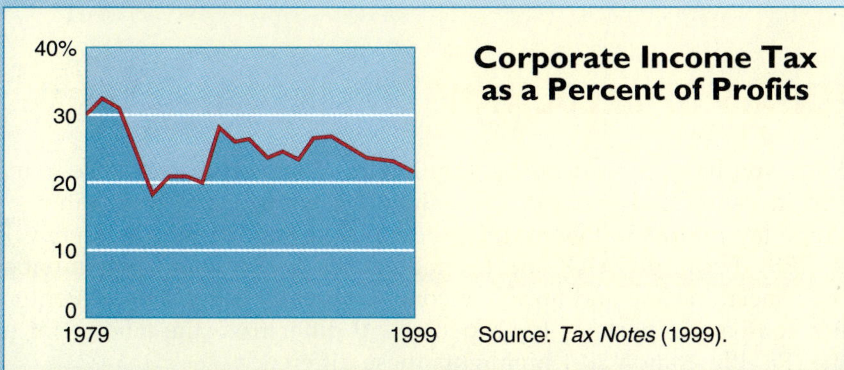

However, the IRS has been increasing its scrutiny of transactions that are done only to avoid taxes and that do not serve any legitimate business purpose. For example, in one recent case a company purchased and sold the same securities within an hour's time, simply to benefit from a multi-million dollar foreign tax credit. The tax judge in this case not only denied the credit but also imposed a 20% penalty. Thus, companies can manage their tax costs as long as they do not abuse the tax code.[1]

[1]Based on Howard Gleckman and Lorraine Woellert, "Kiss the Tax Shelter Good-bye? The Courts Crack Down on Egregious Corporate Tax Avoidance," *Business Week*, November 15, 1999, p. 50.

LEARNING OBJECTIVES

After studying this chapter, you should be able to:

1. **Identify differences between pretax financial income and taxable income.**
2. **Describe a temporary difference that results in future taxable amounts.**
3. **Describe a temporary difference that results in future deductible amounts.**
4. **Explain the purpose of a deferred tax asset valuation allowance.**
5. **Describe the presentation of income tax expense in the income statement.**
6. **Describe various temporary and permanent differences.**
7. **Explain the effect of various tax rates and tax rate changes on deferred income taxes.**
8. **Apply accounting procedures for a loss carryback and a loss carryforward.**
9. **Describe the presentation of deferred income taxes in financial statements.**
10. **Identify special issues related to deferred income taxes.**
11. **Indicate the basic principles of the asset-liability method.**

PREVIEW OF CHAPTER 20

As the opening story indicates, income taxes are a major cost of business to most corporations. As a result, companies spend a considerable amount of time and effort to minimize their tax payments. The purpose of this chapter is to discuss the basic guidelines that companies must follow in reporting income taxes. The content and organization of the chapter are as follows:

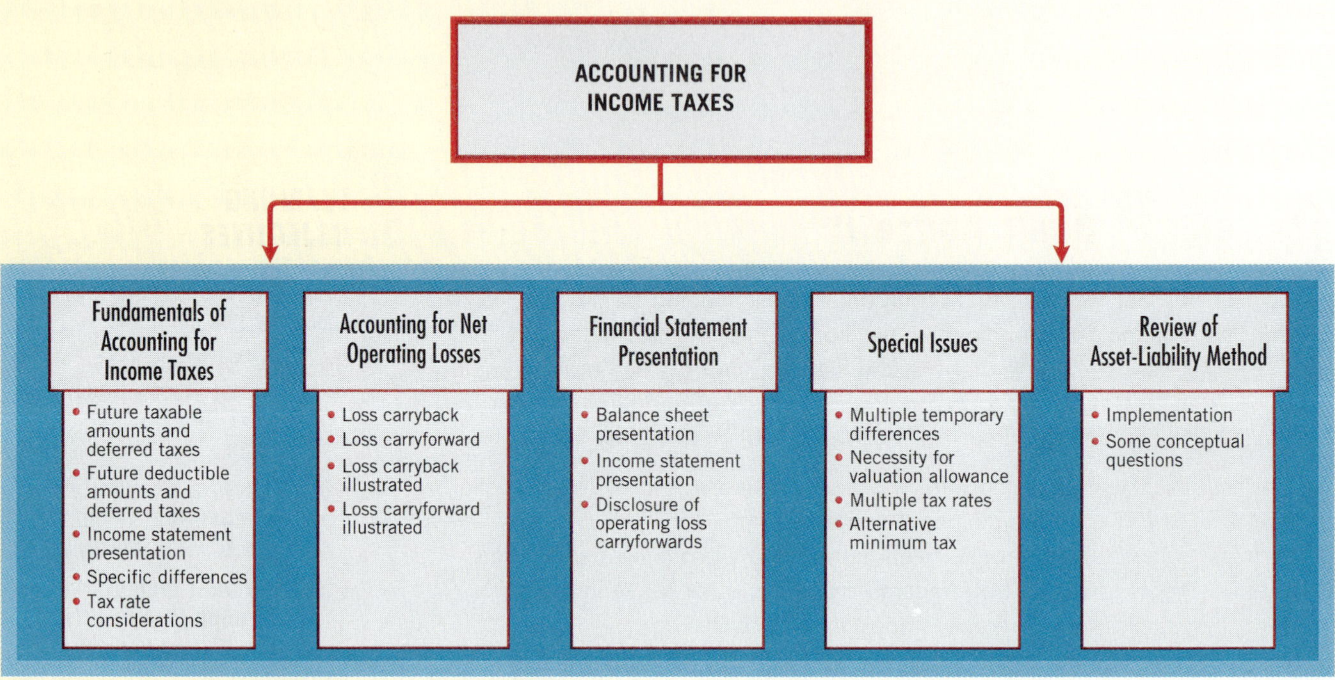

FUNDAMENTALS OF ACCOUNTING FOR INCOME TAXES

OBJECTIVE 1
Identify differences between pretax financial income and taxable income.

Up to this point, you have learned the basic guidelines that corporations use to report information to investors and creditors. You should recognize that corporations also must file income tax returns following the guidelines developed by the Internal Revenue Service (IRS). Because GAAP and tax regulations are different in a number of ways, pretax financial income and taxable income frequently differ. Consequently, the amount that a company reports as tax expense will differ from the amount of taxes payable to the IRS. Illustration 20-1 highlights these differences.

In some countries, taxable income and pretax financial income are the same. As a consequence, accounting for differences between tax and book income is not significant.

Pretax financial income is a financial reporting term often referred to as income before taxes, income for financial reporting purposes, or income for book purposes. Pretax financial income is determined according to GAAP and is measured with the objective of providing useful information to investors and creditors. **Taxable income** (income for tax purposes) is a tax accounting term used to indicate the amount upon which income tax payable is computed. Taxable income is determined according to the Internal Revenue Code (the tax code), which is designed to raise money to support government operations.

To illustrate how differences in GAAP and IRS rules affect financial reporting and taxable income, assume that Chelsea Inc. reported revenues of $130,000 and expenses of $60,000 in each of its first three years of operations. Illustration 20-2 shows the (partial) income statement over these three years.

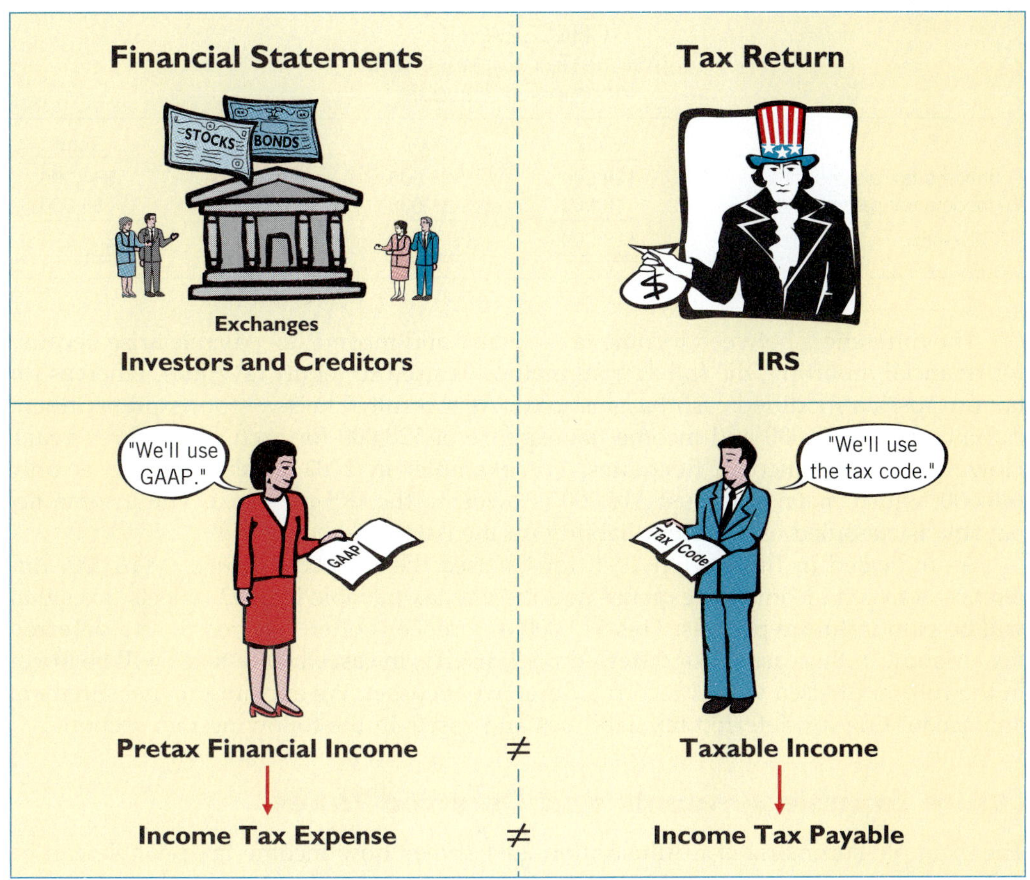

ILLUSTRATION 20-1
Fundamental Differences between Financial and Tax Reporting

ILLUSTRATION 20-2
Financial Reporting Income

CHELSEA INC. GAAP Reporting				
	2002	2003	2004	Total
Revenues	$130,000	$130,000	$130,000	
Expenses	60,000	60,000	60,000	
Pretax financial income	**$ 70,000**	**$ 70,000**	**$ 70,000**	**$210,000**
Income tax expense (40%)	$ 28,000	$ 28,000	$ 28,000	$ 84,000

For tax purposes (following the tax code), Chelsea reported the same expenses to the IRS in each of the years, but taxable revenues were $100,000 in 2002, $150,000 in 2003, and $140,000 in 2004 as shown in Illustration 20-3.

ILLUSTRATION 20-3
Tax Reporting Income

CHELSEA INC. Tax Reporting				
	2002	2003	2004	Total
Revenues	$100,000	$150,000	$140,000	
Expenses	60,000	60,000	60,000	
Taxable income	**$ 40,000**	**$ 90,000**	**$ 80,000**	**$210,000**
Income tax payable (40%)	$ 16,000	$ 36,000	$ 32,000	$ 84,000

Income tax expense and income tax payable differ over the three years but in total are the same, as shown in Illustration 20-4.

ILLUSTRATION 20-4
Comparison of Income Tax Expense to Income Tax Payable

CHELSEA INC.
Income Tax Expense and
Income Tax Payable

	2002	2003	2004	Total
Income tax expense	$28,000	$28,000	$28,000	$84,000
Income tax payable	16,000	36,000	32,000	84,000
Difference	$12,000	($ 8,000)	($ 4,000)	$ 0

The differences between income tax expense and income tax payable arise because for financial reporting, the full accrual method is used to report revenues, whereas for tax purposes a modified cash basis is used. As a result, Chelsea reports pretax financial income of $70,000 and income tax expense of $28,000 for each of the three years. However, taxable income fluctuates. For example, in 2002 taxable income is only $40,000, which means that just $16,000 is owed to the IRS that year. The income tax payable is classified as a current liability on the balance sheet.

As indicated in Illustration 20-4, for Chelsea the $12,000 ($28,000 − $16,000) difference between income tax expense and income tax payable in 2002 reflects taxes that will be paid in future periods. This $12,000 difference is often referred to as a **deferred tax amount**. In this case it is a **deferred tax liability**; in cases where taxes will be lower in the future, Chelsea would record a **deferred tax asset**. We explain the measurement and accounting for deferred tax liabilities and assets in the following two sections.

Future Taxable Amounts and Deferred Taxes

OBJECTIVE 2
Describe a temporary difference that results in future taxable amounts.

The example summarized in Illustration 20-4 shows how income tax payable can be different from income tax expense. One way that this can happen is when there are temporary differences between the amounts reported for tax purposes and those reported for book purposes. A **temporary difference** is the difference between the tax basis of an asset or liability and its reported (carrying or book) amount in the financial statements that will result in taxable amounts or deductible amounts in future years. **Taxable amounts** increase taxable income in future years, and **deductible amounts** decrease taxable income in future years.

In Chelsea Inc.'s situation, the only difference between the book basis and tax basis of the assets and liabilities relates to accounts receivable that arose from revenue recognized for book purposes. Illustration 20-5 indicates that accounts receivable are reported at $30,000 in the December 31, 2002, GAAP-basis balance sheet, but the receivables have a zero tax basis.

ILLUSTRATION 20-5
Temporary Difference, Sales Revenue

Per Books	12/31/02	Per Tax Return	12/31/02
Accounts receivable	$30,000	Accounts receivable	$-0-

What will happen to this $30,000 temporary difference that originated in 2002 for Chelsea Inc.? Assuming that Chelsea expects to collect $20,000 of the receivables in 2003 and $10,000 in 2004, this collection will result in future taxable amounts of $20,000 in 2003 and $10,000 in 2004. These future taxable amounts will cause taxable income to exceed pretax financial income in both 2003 and 2004.

In the FASB's view, an assumption inherent in a company's GAAP balance sheet is that the assets and liabilities will be recovered and settled at their reported amounts (carrying amounts). The FASB believes that this assumption creates a requirement under accrual accounting to recognize currently the deferred tax consequences of temporary differences, that is, the amount of income taxes that would be payable (or refundable) when the reported amounts of the assets are recovered and the liabilities are settled, respectively. The following diagram illustrates the reversal or turn around of the temporary difference described in Illustration 20-5 and the resulting taxable amounts in future periods.

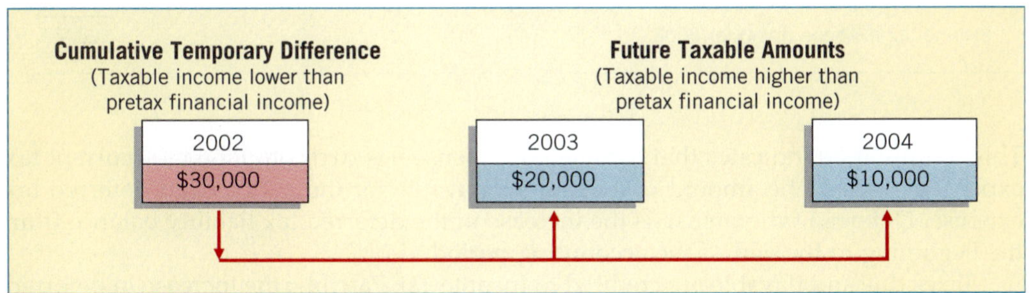

ILLUSTRATION 20-6
Reversal of Temporary Difference, Chelsea Inc.

We have assumed that Chelsea will collect the accounts receivable and report the $30,000 collection as taxable revenues in future tax returns. A payment of income tax in both 2003 and 2004 will therefore occur. We therefore should record in Chelsea's books in 2002 the deferred tax consequences of the revenue and related receivables reflected in the 2002 financial statements. This necessitates the recording of a deferred tax liability.

Deferred Tax Liability

A **deferred tax liability** is the deferred tax consequences attributable to taxable temporary differences. In other words, **a deferred tax liability represents the increase in taxes payable in future years as a result of taxable temporary differences existing at the end of the current year**. Recall from the Chelsea example that income tax payable is $16,000 ($40,000 × 40%) in 2002 (Illustration 20-4). In addition, a temporary difference exists at year-end because the revenue and related accounts receivable are reported differently for book and tax purposes. The book basis of accounts receivable is $30,000 and the tax basis is zero. Thus, the total deferred tax liability at the end of 2002 is $12,000, computed as follows:

ILLUSTRATION 20-7
Computation of Deferred Tax Liability, End of 2002

Book basis of accounts receivable	$30,000
Tax basis of accounts receivable	–0–
Cumulative temporary difference at the end of 2002	30,000
Tax rate	40%
Deferred tax liability at the end of 2002	$12,000

Another way to compute the deferred tax liability is to prepare a schedule that indicates the taxable amounts scheduled for the future as a result of existing temporary differences. Such a schedule is particularly useful when the computations become more complex.

ILLUSTRATION 20-8
Schedule of Future Taxable Amounts

	Future Years		
	2003	2004	Total
Future taxable amounts	$20,000	$10,000	$30,000
Tax rate	40%	40%	
Deferred tax liability at the end of 2002	$ 8,000	$ 4,000	$12,000

Because it is the first year of operations for Chelsea, there is no deferred tax liability at the beginning of the year. The income tax expense for 2002 is computed as follows:

ILLUSTRATION 20-9
Computation of Income Tax Expense, 2002

Deferred tax liability at end of 2002	$12,000
Deferred tax liability at beginning of 2002	–0–
Deferred tax expense for 2002	12,000
Current tax expense for 2002 (Income tax payable)	16,000
Income tax expense (total) for 2002	$28,000

This computation indicates that income tax expense has two components—current tax expense (which is the amount of income tax payable for the period) and deferred tax expense. **Deferred tax expense** is the increase in the deferred tax liability balance from the beginning to the end of the accounting period.

Taxes due and payable are credited to Income Tax Payable; the increase in deferred taxes is credited to Deferred Tax Liability; and the sum of those two items is debited to Income Tax Expense. For Chelsea Inc. the following entry is made at the end of 2002:

Income Tax Expense	28,000	
Income Tax Payable		16,000
Deferred Tax Liability		12,000

At the end of 2003 (the second year) the difference between the book basis and the tax basis of the accounts receivable is $10,000. This difference is multiplied by the applicable tax rate to arrive at the deferred tax liability of $4,000 ($10,000 × 40%) to be reported at the end of 2003. Income tax payable for 2003 is $36,000 (Illustration 20-3), the income tax expense for 2003 is as follows:

ILLUSTRATION 20-10
Computation of Income Tax Expense, 2003

Deferred tax liability at end of 2003	$ 4,000
Deferred tax liability at beginning of 2003	12,000
Deferred tax expense (benefit) for 2003	(8,000)
Current tax expense for 2003 (Income tax payable)	36,000
Income tax expense (total) for 2003	$28,000

The journal entry to record income tax expense, the change in the deferred tax liability, and income tax payable for 2003 is as follows:

Income Tax Expense	28,000	
Deferred Tax Liability	8,000	
Income Tax Payable		36,000

In the entry to record income taxes at the end of 2004, the Deferred Tax Liability is reduced by $4,000. The Deferred Tax Liability account appears as follows at the end of 2004:

ILLUSTRATION 20-11
Deferred Tax Liability Account after Reversals

Deferred Tax Liability			
2003	8,000	2002	12,000
2004	4,000		

The Deferred Tax Liability account has a zero balance at the end of 2004.

Some analysts dismiss deferred tax liabilities when assessing the financial strength of a company.[2] But the FASB indicates that the deferred tax liability meets the definition of a liability established in *Statement of Financial Accounting Concepts No. 6,* "Elements of Financial Statements" because:

1. ***It results from a past transaction.*** In the Chelsea example, services were performed for customers and revenue was recognized in 2002 for financial reporting purposes but was deferred for tax purposes.
2. ***It is a present obligation.*** Taxable income in future periods will be higher than pretax financial income as a result of this temporary difference. Thus, a present obligation exists.
3. ***It represents a future sacrifice.*** Taxable income and taxes due in future periods will result from events that have already occurred. The payment of these taxes when they come due is the future sacrifice.

Summary of Income Tax Accounting Objectives

One objective of accounting for income taxes is to recognize the amount of taxes payable or refundable for the current year. In Chelsea's case, income tax payable is $16,000 for 2002.

A **second objective** is to recognize deferred tax liabilities and assets for the future tax consequences of events that have already been recognized in the financial statements or tax returns. Chelsea sold services to customers that resulted in accounts receivable of $30,000 in 2002; the $30,000 was reported on the 2002 income statement—it was not reported on the tax return as income. It will appear on future tax returns as income when it is collected. As a result, a $30,000 temporary difference exists at the end of 2002 which will cause future taxable amounts. A deferred tax liability of $12,000 is reported on the balance sheet at the end of 2002, which represents the increase in taxes payable in future years ($8,000 in 2003 and $4,000 in 2004) as a result of a temporary difference existing at the end of the current year. The related deferred tax liability is reduced by $8,000 at the end of 2003 and by another $4,000 at the end of 2004.

In Japan and Korea, deferred taxes are not recognized; in Sweden, they are generally recognized only through consolidation.

In addition to affecting the balance sheet, deferred taxes have an impact on income tax expense in each of the three years affected. In 2002, taxable income ($40,000) is less than pretax financial income ($70,000). Income tax payable for 2002 is therefore $16,000 (based on taxable income). Deferred tax expense of $12,000 is caused by the increase in the Deferred Tax Liability account on the balance sheet. Income tax expense is then $28,000 for 2002.

In 2003 and 2004, however, taxable income will be more than pretax financial income due to the reversal of the temporary difference ($20,000 in 2003 and $10,000 in 2004). Income tax payable will therefore be higher than income tax expense in 2003 and 2004. The Deferred Tax Liability account will be debited for $8,000 in 2003 and $4,000 in 2004. Credits for these amounts are recorded in Income Tax Expense (often referred to as a **deferred tax benefit**).

Future Deductible Amounts and Deferred Taxes

OBJECTIVE 3
Describe a temporary difference that results in future deductible amounts.

Assume that during 2002, Cunningham Inc. estimated its warranty costs related to the sale of microwave ovens to be $500,000 paid evenly over the next 2 years. For book purposes, in 2002 Cunningham reported warranty expense and a related estimated liability for warranties of $500,000 in its financial statements. For tax purposes, **the war-**

[2]A study by D. Givoly and C. Hayn, "The Valuation of the Deferred Tax Liability: Evidence from the Stock Market," *The Accounting Review,* April 1992, provides evidence that the stock market views deferred tax liabilities arising from temporary differences as similar to other liabilities. More recently, a study by B. Ayers, "Deferred Tax Accounting Under *SFAS No. 109:* An Empirical Investigation of Its Incremental Value-Relevance Relative to *APB No. 11," The Accounting Review,* April 1998, indicates that *SFAS No. 109* increased the usefulness of deferred tax amounts in financial statements.

ranty tax deduction is not allowed until paid; therefore, no warranty liability is recognized on a tax basis balance sheet. Thus, the balance sheet difference at the end of 2002 is as follows:

ILLUSTRATION 20-12
Temporary Difference, Warranty Liability

Per Books	12/31/02	Per Tax Return	12/31/02
Estimated liability for warranties	$500,000	Estimated liability for warranties	$-0-

When the warranty liability is paid, an expense (deductible amount) will be reported for tax purposes. Because of this temporary difference, Cunningham Inc. should recognize in 2002 the tax benefits (positive tax consequences) for the tax deductions that will result from the future settlement of the liability. This future tax benefit is reported in the December 31, 2002, balance sheet as a **deferred tax asset**.

Another way to think about this situation is as follows: Deductible amounts will occur in future tax returns. These **future deductible amounts** will cause taxable income to be less than pretax financial income in the future as a result of an existing temporary difference. Cunningham's temporary difference originates (arises) in one period (2002) and reverses over two periods (2003 and 2004). This situation is diagramed as follows:

ILLUSTRATION 20-13
Reversal of Temporary Difference, Cunningham Inc.

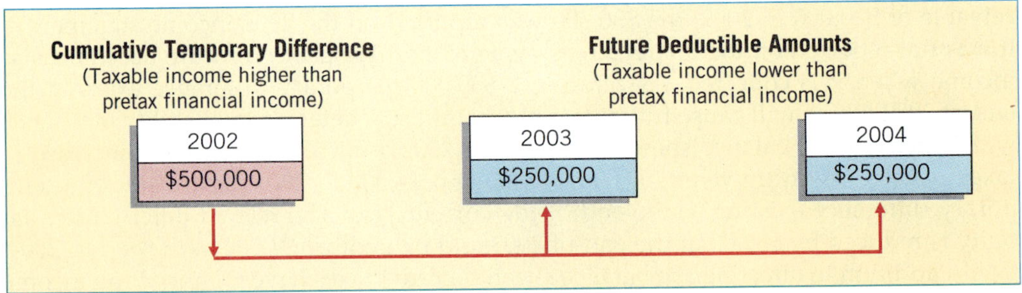

Deferred Tax Asset

A **deferred tax asset** is the deferred tax consequence attributable to deductible temporary differences. In other words, a **deferred tax asset represents the increase in taxes refundable (or saved) in future years as a result of deductible temporary differences existing at the end of the current year.**

To illustrate, assume that Hunt Co. accrues a loss and a related liability of $50,000 in 2002 for financial reporting purposes because of pending litigation. This amount is not deductible for tax purposes until the period the liability is paid, which is expected to be 2003. As a result, a deductible amount will occur in 2003 when the liability (Estimated Litigation Liability) is settled, causing taxable income to be lower than pretax financial income. The computation of the deferred tax asset at the end of 2002 (assuming a 40% tax rate) is as follows:

ILLUSTRATION 20-14
Computation of Deferred Tax Asset, End of 2002

Book basis of litigation liability	$50,000
Tax basis of litigation liability	–0–
Cumulative temporary difference at the end of 2002	50,000
Tax rate	40%
Deferred tax asset at the end of 2002	$20,000

Another way to compute the deferred tax asset is to prepare a schedule that indicates the deductible amounts scheduled for the future as a result of deductible temporary differences. This schedule is shown in Illustration 20-15.

ILLUSTRATION 20-15
Schedule of Future Deductible Amounts

	Future Years
Future deductible amounts	$50,000
Tax rate	40%
Deferred tax asset at the end of 2002	$20,000

Assuming that 2002 is Hunt's first year of operations, and income tax payable is $100,000, the income tax expense is computed as follows:

ILLUSTRATION 20-16
Computation of Income Tax Expense, 2002

Deferred tax asset at end of 2002	$ 20,000
Deferred tax asset at beginning of 2002	–0–
Deferred tax expense (benefit) for 2002	(20,000)
Current tax expense for 2002 (Income tax payable)	100,000
Income tax expense (total) for 2002	$ 80,000

The **deferred tax benefit** results from the increase in the deferred tax asset from the beginning to the end of the accounting period. The deferred tax benefit is a negative component of income tax expense. The total income tax expense of $80,000 on the income statement for 2002 is then comprised of two elements—current tax expense of $100,000 and deferred tax benefit of $20,000. For Hunt Co. the following journal entry is made at the end of 2002 to record income tax expense, deferred income taxes, and income tax payable.

Income Tax Expense	80,000	
Deferred Tax Asset	20,000	
Income Tax Payable		100,000

At the end of 2003 (the second year) the difference between the book value and the tax basis of the litigation liability is zero. Therefore, there is no deferred tax asset at this date. Assuming that income tax payable for 2003 is $140,000, the computation of income tax expense for 2003 is as follows:

ILLUSTRATION 20-17
Computation of Income Tax Expense, 2003

Deferred tax asset at the end of 2003	$ –0–
Deferred tax asset at the beginning of 2003	20,000
Deferred tax expense (benefit) for 2003	20,000
Current tax expense for 2003 (Income tax payable)	140,000
Income tax expense (total) for 2003	$160,000

The journal entry to record income taxes for 2003 is as follows:

Income Tax Expense	160,000	
Deferred Tax Asset		20,000
Income Tax Payable		140,000

The total income tax expense of $160,000 on the income statement for 2003 is then comprised of two elements—current tax expense of $140,000 and deferred tax expense of $20,000.

The Deferred Tax Asset account would appear as follows at the end of 2003:

ILLUSTRATION 20-18
Deferred Tax Asset Account after Reversals

Deferred Tax Asset			
2002	20,000	2003	20,000

A key issue in accounting for income taxes is whether a deferred tax asset should be recognized in the financial records. We believe that a deferred tax asset meets the three main conditions for an item to be recognized as an asset:

1. ***It results from a past transaction.*** In the Hunt Co. example, the accrual of the loss contingency is the past event that gives rise to a future deductible temporary difference.
2. ***It gives rise to a probable benefit in the future.*** Taxable income is higher than pretax financial income in the current year (2002). However, in the next year the exact opposite occurs; that is, taxable income is lower than pretax financial income. Because this deductible temporary difference reduces taxes payable in the future, a probable future benefit exists at the end of the current period.
3. ***The entity controls access to the benefits.*** Hunt Co. has the ability to obtain the benefit of existing deductible temporary differences by reducing its taxes payable in the future. Hunt Co. has the exclusive right to that benefit and can control others' access to it.

Deferred Tax Asset—Valuation Allowance

OBJECTIVE 4
Explain the purpose of a deferred tax asset valuation allowance.

A deferred tax asset is recognized for all deductible temporary differences. However, a deferred tax asset should be reduced by a valuation allowance if, based on all available evidence, **it is more likely than not** that some portion or all of the deferred tax asset **will not be realized**. More likely than not means a level of likelihood that is at least slightly more than 50%.

Assume that Jensen Co. has a deductible temporary difference of $1,000,000 at the end of its first year of operations. Its tax rate is 40%, which means a deferred tax asset of $400,000 ($1,000,000 × 40%) is recorded. Assuming that income taxes payable are $900,000, the journal entry to record income tax expense, the deferred tax asset, and income tax payable is as follows:

Income Tax Expense	500,000	
Deferred Tax Asset	400,000	
Income Tax Payable		900,000

After careful review of all available evidence, it is determined that it is more likely than not that $100,000 of this deferred tax asset will not be realized. The journal entry to record this reduction in asset value is as follows:

Income Tax Expense	100,000	
Allowance to Reduce Deferred Tax Asset to Expected Realizable Value		100,000

In this journal entry, income tax expense is increased in the current period because a favorable tax benefit is not expected to be realized for a portion of the deductible temporary difference. **A valuation allowance is simultaneously established to recognize the reduction in the carrying amount of the deferred tax asset.** This valuation account is a contra account and may be reported on the financial statements in the following manner:

ILLUSTRATION 20-19
Balance Sheet Presentation of Valuation Allowance Account

Deferred tax asset	$400,000
Less: Allowance to reduce deferred tax asset to expected realizable value	100,000
Deferred tax asset (net)	$300,000

This allowance account is evaluated at the end of each accounting period. If, at the end of the next period, the deferred tax asset is still $400,000, but now $350,000 of this asset is expected to be realized, then the following entry is made to adjust the valuation account:

Allowance to Reduce Deferred Tax Asset to Expected Realizable Value	50,000	
Income Tax Expense		50,000

All available evidence, both positive and negative, should be carefully considered to determine whether, based on the weight of available evidence, a valuation allowance is needed. For example, if the company has been experiencing a series of loss years, a reasonable assumption is that these losses will continue and the benefit of the future deductible amounts will be lost. The use of a valuation account under other conditions will be discussed later in the chapter.

Income Statement Presentation

OBJECTIVE 5
Describe the presentation of income tax expense in the income statement.

Whether the change in deferred income taxes should be added to or subtracted from income tax payable in computing income tax expense depends on the circumstances. For example, an increase in a deferred tax liability would be added to income tax payable. On the other hand, an increase in a deferred tax asset would be subtracted from income tax payable. The formula to compute income tax expense (benefit) is as follows:

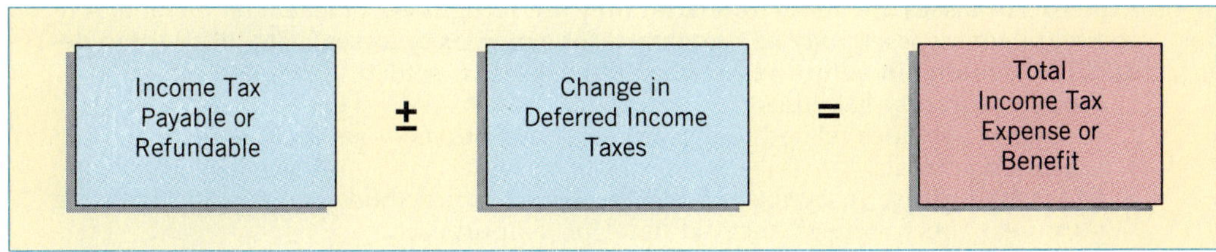

ILLUSTRATION 20-20
Formula to Compute Income Tax Expense

In the income statement or in the notes to the financial statements, the significant components of income tax expense attributable to continuing operations should be disclosed. Given the information related to Chelsea Inc. on page 1062, Chelsea's income statement might be reported as follows:

ILLUSTRATION 20-21
Income Statement Presentation of Income Tax Expense

CHELSEA INC.
Income Statement
For the Year Ending December 31, 2002

Revenues		$130,000
Expenses		60,000
Income before income taxes		70,000
Income tax expense		
Current	$16,000	
Deferred	12,000	28,000
Net income		$ 42,000

As illustrated, both the current portion (amount of income tax payable for the period) and the deferred portion of income tax expense are reported. Another option is to simply report the total income tax expense on the income statement, and then in the notes to the financial statements indicate the current and deferred portions. Income tax expense is often referred to as "Provision for Income Taxes." Using this terminology, the current provision is $16,000 and the provision for deferred taxes is $12,000.

Specific Differences

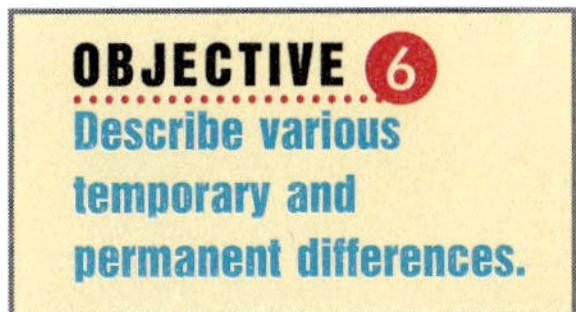

Numerous items create differences between pretax financial income and taxable income. For purposes of accounting recognition, these differences are of two types: (1) temporary differences, and (2) permanent differences.

Temporary Differences

Temporary differences that will result in taxable amounts in future years when the related assets are recovered are often called **taxable temporary differences**; temporary differences that will result in deductible amounts in future years when the related book liabilities are settled are often called **deductible temporary differences**. Taxable temporary differences give rise to recording deferred tax liabilities; deductible temporary differences give rise to recording deferred tax assets. Examples of temporary differences are provided in Illustration 20-22.[3]

ILLUSTRATION 20-22
Examples of Temporary Differences

A. **Revenues or gains are taxable after they are recognized in financial income.** An asset (e.g., accounts receivable or investment) may be recognized for revenues or gains that will result in **taxable amounts in future years** when the asset is recovered. Examples:
   1. Installment sale accounted for on the accrual basis for financial reporting purposes and on the installment (cash) basis for tax purposes.
   2. Contracts accounted for under the percentage-of-completion method for financial reporting purposes and a portion of related gross profit deferred for tax purposes.
   3. Investments accounted for under the equity method for financial reporting purposes and under the cost method for tax purposes.
   4. Gain on involuntary conversion of nonmonetary asset which is recognized for financial reporting purposes but deferred for tax purposes.

B. **Expenses or losses are deductible after they are recognized in financial income.** A liability (or contra asset) may be recognized for expenses or losses that will result in **deductible amounts in future years** when the liability is settled. Examples:
   1. Product warranty liabilities.
   2. Estimated liabilities related to discontinued operations or restructurings.
   3. Litigation accruals.
   4. Bad debt expense recognized using the allowance method for financial reporting purposes; direct write-off method used for tax purposes.

C. **Revenues or gains are taxable before they are recognized in financial income.** A liability may be recognized for an advance payment for goods or services to be provided in future years. For tax purposes, the advance payment is included in taxable income upon the receipt of cash. Future sacrifices to provide goods or services (or future refunds to those who cancel their orders) that settle the liability will result in **deductible amounts in future years**. Examples:
   1. Subscriptions received in advance.
   2. Advance rental receipts.
   3. Sales and leasebacks for financial reporting purposes (income deferral) and reported as sales for tax purposes.
   4. Prepaid contracts and royalties received in advance.

D. **Expenses or losses are deductible before they are recognized in financial income.** The cost of an asset may have been deducted for tax purposes faster than it was expensed for financial reporting purposes. Amounts received upon future recovery of the amount of the asset for financial reporting (through use or sale) will exceed the remaining tax basis of the asset and thereby result in **taxable amounts in future years**. Examples:
   1. Depreciable property, depletable resources, and intangibles.
   2. Deductible pension funding exceeding expense.
   3. Prepaid expenses that are deducted on the tax return in the period paid.

Determining a company's temporary differences may prove difficult. A company should prepare a balance sheet for tax purposes that can be compared with its GAAP balance sheet; many of the differences between the two balance sheets would be temporary differences.

Originating and Reversing Aspects of Temporary Differences. An **originating temporary difference** is the initial difference between the book basis and the tax basis of an asset or liability, regardless of whether the tax basis of the asset or liability exceeds or is exceeded by the book basis of the asset or liability. A **reversing difference**, on the

[3] *SFAS No. 109* gives more examples of temporary differences. We have presented the most common types.

other hand, occurs when a temporary difference that originated in prior periods is eliminated and the related tax effect is removed from the deferred tax account.

For example, assume that Sharp Co. has tax depreciation in excess of book depreciation of $2,000 in 1998, 1999, and 2000, and that it has an excess of book depreciation over tax depreciation of $3,000 in 2001 and 2002 for the same asset. Assuming a tax rate of 30% for all years involved, the Deferred Tax Liability account would reflect the following:

ILLUSTRATION 20-23
Tax Effects of Originating and Reversing Differences

	Deferred Tax Liability				
Tax Effects of Reversing Differences	2001	900	1998	600	Tax Effects of Originating Differences
	2002	900	1999	600	
			2000	600	

The originating differences for Sharp in each of the first three years would be $2,000, and the related tax effect of each originating difference would be $600. The reversing differences in 2001 and 2002 would each be $3,000, and the related tax effect of each would be $900.

Permanent Differences

Some differences between taxable income and pretax financial income are permanent. **Permanent differences** are caused by items that (1) enter into pretax financial income but **never** into taxable income or (2) enter into taxable income but **never** into pretax financial income.

Congress has enacted a variety of tax law provisions in an effort to attain certain political, economic, and social objectives. Some of these provisions exclude certain revenues from taxation, limit the deductibility of certain expenses, and permit the deduction of certain other expenses in excess of costs incurred. A corporation that has tax-free income, nondeductible expenses, or allowable deductions in excess of cost has an effective tax rate that is different from the statutory (regular) tax rate.

Since permanent differences affect only the period in which they occur, they do not give rise to future taxable or deductible amounts. As a result, **there are no deferred tax consequences to be recognized**. Examples of permanent differences are shown in Illustration 20-24.

ILLUSTRATION 20-24
Examples of Permanent Differences

A. **Items are recognized for financial reporting purposes but not for tax purposes.**
Examples:
1. Interest received on state and municipal obligations.
2. Expenses incurred in obtaining tax-exempt income.
3. Proceeds from life insurance carried by the company on key officers or employees.
4. Premiums paid for life insurance carried by the company on key officers or employees (company is beneficiary).
5. Fines and expenses resulting from a violation of law.
6. Compensation expense associated with certain employee stock options.

B. **Items are recognized for tax purposes but not for financial reporting purposes.**
Examples:
1. "Percentage depletion" of natural resources in excess of their cost.
2. The deduction for dividends received from U.S. corporations, generally 70% or 80%.

Temporary and Permanent Differences Illustrated

To illustrate the computations used when both temporary and permanent differences exist, assume that the Bio-Tech Company reports pretax financial income of $200,000 in each of the years 2000, 2001, and 2002. The company is subject to a 30% tax rate, and has the following differences between pretax financial income and taxable income:

1. An installment sale of $18,000 in 2000 is reported for tax purposes over an 18-month period at a constant amount per month beginning January 1, 2001. The entire sale is recognized for book purposes in 2000.
2. Premium paid for life insurance carried by the company on key officers is $5,000 in 2001 and 2002. This is not deductible for tax purposes, but is expensed for book purposes.

The first item is a temporary difference and the second is a permanent difference. The reconciliation of Bio-Tech Company's pretax financial income to taxable income and the computation of income tax payable is shown in Illustration 20-25.

ILLUSTRATION 20-25
Reconciliation and Computation of Income Taxes Payable

	2000	2001	2002
Pretax financial income	$200,000	$200,000	$200,000
Permanent difference			
Nondeductible expense		5,000	5,000
Temporary difference			
Installment sale	(18,000)	12,000	6,000
Taxable income	182,000	217,000	211,000
Tax rate	30%	30%	30%
Income tax payable	$ 54,600	$ 65,100	$ 63,300

Note that differences causing pretax financial income to exceed taxable income are deducted from pretax financial income when determining taxable income. Conversely, differences causing pretax financial income to be less than taxable income are added to pretax financial income in determining taxable income.

Both permanent and temporary differences are considered in reconciling pretax financial income to taxable income. Since the permanent difference (nondeductible expense) does not result in future taxable or deductible amounts, deferred income taxes are not recorded for this difference.

The journal entries to record income taxes for Bio-Tech for 2000, 2001, and 2002 are as follows:

December 31, 2000		
Income Tax Expense ($54,600 + $5,400)	60,000	
Deferred Tax Liability ($18,000 × 30%)		5,400
Income Tax Payable ($182,000 × 30%)		54,600

December 31, 2001		
Income Tax Expense ($65,100 − $3,600)	61,500	
Deferred Tax Liability ($12,000 × 30%)	3,600	
Income Tax Payable ($217,000 × 30%)		65,100

December 31, 2002		
Income Tax Expense ($63,300 − $1,800)	61,500	
Deferred Tax Liability ($6,000 × 30%)	1,800	
Income Tax Payable ($211,000 × 30%)		63,300

Bio-Tech has one temporary difference which originates in 2000 and reverses in 2001 and 2002. A deferred tax liability is recognized at the end of 2000 because the temporary difference causes future taxable amounts. As the temporary difference reverses, the deferred tax liability is reduced. There is no deferred tax amount associated with the difference caused by the nondeductible insurance expense because it is a permanent difference.

Although a statutory (enacted) tax rate of 30% applies for all three years, the effective rate is different. The **effective tax rate** is computed by dividing total income tax expense for the period by pretax financial income. The effective rate is 30% for 2000 ($60,000 ÷ $200,000 = 30%) and 30.75% for 2001 and 2002 ($61,500 ÷ $200,000 = 30.75%).

Tax Rate Considerations

OBJECTIVE 7
Explain the effect of various tax rates and tax rate changes on deferred income taxes.

In our previous illustrations, the enacted tax rate did not change from one year to the next. Thus, to compute the deferred income tax amount to be reported on the balance sheet, the cumulative temporary difference is simply multiplied by the current tax rate. Using Bio-Tech as an example, the cumulative temporary difference of $18,000 is multiplied by the enacted tax rate, 30% in this case, to arrive at a deferred tax liability of $5,400 ($18,000 × 30%) at the end of 2000.

Future Tax Rates

What happens if tax rates are different for future years? In this case, the **enacted tax rate** expected to apply should be used. Therefore, presently enacted changes in the tax rate that become effective for a particular future year(s) must be considered when determining the tax rate to apply to existing temporary differences. For example, assume that Warlen Co. at the end of 1999 has the following cumulative temporary difference of $300,000 computed as follows:

ILLUSTRATION 20-26
Computation of Cumulative Temporary Difference

Book basis of depreciable assets	$1,000,000
Tax basis of depreciable assets	700,000
Cumulative temporary difference	$ 300,000

Furthermore, assume that the $300,000 will reverse and result in taxable amounts in the following years when the enacted tax rates are as follows:

ILLUSTRATION 20-27
Deferred Tax Liability Based on Future Rates

	2000	2001	2002	2003	2004	Total
Future taxable amounts	$80,000	$70,000	$60,000	$50,000	$40,000	$300,000
Tax rate	40%	40%	35%	30%	30%	
Deferred tax liability	$32,000	$28,000	$21,000	$15,000	$12,000	$108,000

The total deferred tax liability at the end of 1999 is $108,000. Tax rates other than the current rate may be used only when the future tax rates have been enacted into law, as is apparently the case in this example. **If new rates are not yet enacted into law for future years, the current rate should be used.**

In determining the appropriate enacted tax rate for a given year, companies are required to use the **average tax rate**. The Internal Revenue Service and other taxing jurisdictions tax income on a graduated tax basis. For a U.S. corporation, the first $50,000 of taxable income is taxed at 15%, the next $25,000 at 25%, with higher incremental levels of income being taxed at rates as high as 39%. In computing deferred income taxes, companies for which graduated tax rates are a significant factor are therefore required to **determine the average tax rate and use that rate.**

Revision of Future Tax Rates

When a change in the tax rate is enacted into law, its effect on the existing deferred income tax accounts should be recorded immediately. **The effect is reported as an adjustment to income tax expense in the period of the change.**

Assume that on December 10, 1999, a new income tax act is signed into law that lowers the corporate tax rate from 40% to 35%, effective January 1, 2001. If Hostel Co. has one temporary difference at the beginning of 1999 related to $3 million of excess tax depreciation, then it has a Deferred Tax Liability account with a balance of $1,200,000 ($3,000,000 × 40%) at January 1, 1999. If taxable amounts related to this difference are scheduled to occur equally in 2000, 2001, and 2002, the deferred tax liability at the end of 1999 should be $1,100,000 computed as follows:

ILLUSTRATION 20-28
Schedule of Future Taxable Amounts and Related Tax Rates

	2000	2001	2002	Total
Future taxable amounts	$1,000,000	$1,000,000	$1,000,000	$3,000,000
Tax rate	40%	35%	35%	
Deferred tax liability	$ 400,000	$ 350,000	$ 350,000	$1,100,000

An entry, therefore, would be made at the end of 1999 to recognize the decrease of $100,000 ($1,200,000 − $1,100,000) in the deferred tax liability as follows:

Deferred Tax Liability	100,000	
Income Tax Expense		100,000

Corporate tax rates do not change often and, therefore, the current rate will usually be employed. However, state and foreign tax rates change more frequently and they require adjustments in deferred income taxes accordingly.[4]

ACCOUNTING FOR NET OPERATING LOSSES

OBJECTIVE 8
Apply accounting procedures for a loss carryback and a loss carryforward.

A **net operating loss (NOL)** occurs for tax purposes in a year when tax-deductible expenses exceed taxable revenues. An inequitable tax burden would result if companies were taxed during profitable periods without receiving any tax relief during periods of net operating losses. Under certain circumstances, therefore, the federal tax laws permit taxpayers to use the losses of one year to offset the profits of other years. This income-averaging provision is accomplished through the **carryback and carryforward of net operating losses**. Under this provision, a company pays no income taxes for a year in which it incurs a net operating loss. In addition, it may select one of the two options discussed below.

Loss Carryback

Through use of a **loss carryback**, a company may carry the net operating loss back 2 years and receive refunds for income taxes paid in those years. The loss must be applied to the earlier year first and then to the second year. Any loss remaining after the 2-year carryback may be **carried forward** up to 20 years to offset future taxable income. The following diagram illustrates the loss carryback procedure, assuming a loss in 2002.

ILLUSTRATION 20-29
Loss Carryback Procedure

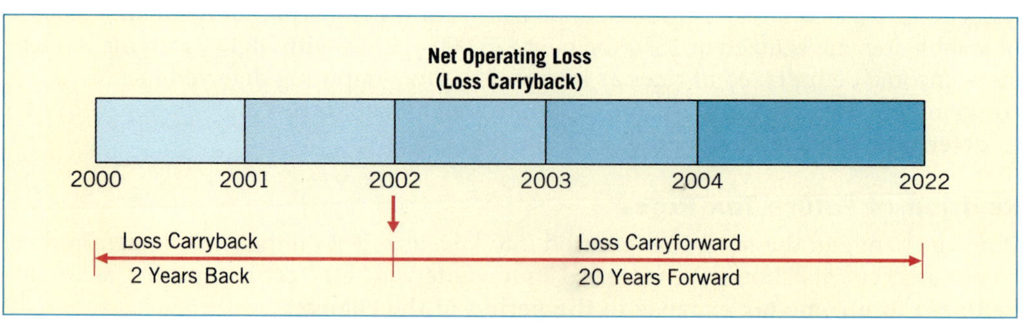

[4]Tax rate changes nearly always will have a substantial impact on income numbers and the reporting of deferred income taxes on the balance sheet. As a result, you can expect to hear an economic consequences argument every time that Congress decides to change the tax rates. For example, when Congress raised the corporate rate from 34% to 35% in 1993, companies took an additional "hit" to earnings if they were in a deferred tax liability position.

Loss Carryforward

A company may elect to forgo the loss carryback and use only the **loss carryforward** option, offsetting future taxable income for up to 20 years.[5] Illustration 20-30 shows this approach.

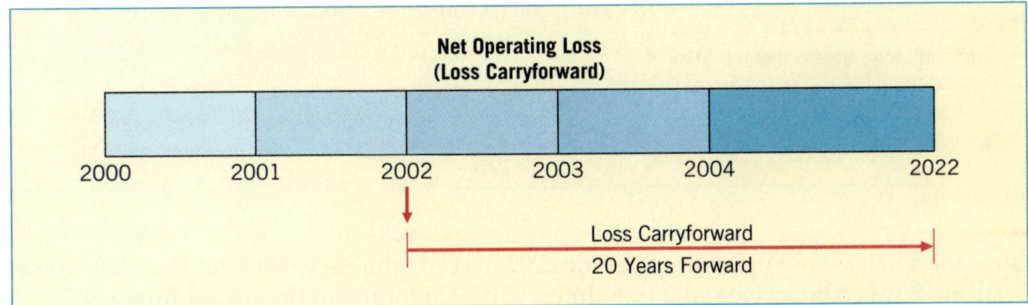

ILLUSTRATION 20-30
Loss Carryforward Procedure

Operating losses can be substantial. **IBM Corporation**'s total losses exceeded $15 billion dollars for the years 1992 and 1993, representing billions of dollars in potential tax savings. Companies that have suffered substantial losses are often attractive merger candidates because in certain cases the acquirer may use these losses to reduce its own income taxes.

Loss Carryback Illustrated

To illustrate the accounting procedures for a net operating loss carryback, assume that Groh Inc. has no temporary or permanent differences. Groh experiences the following:

Year	Taxable Income or Loss	Tax Rate	Tax Paid
1998	$ 50,000	35%	$17,500
1999	100,000	30%	30,000
2000	200,000	40%	80,000
2001	(500,000)	—	-0-

In 2001, Groh Inc. incurs a net operating loss that it decides to carry back. Under the law, the carryback must be applied first to the **second year preceding the loss year**. Therefore, the loss would be carried back first to 1999. Any unused loss would then be carried back to 2000. Accordingly, Groh would file amended tax returns for 1999 and 2000, receiving refunds for the $110,000 ($30,000 + $80,000) of taxes paid in those years.

For accounting as well as tax purposes, the $110,000 represents the **tax effect (tax benefit) of the loss carryback**. This tax effect should be recognized in 2001, the loss year. Since the tax loss gives rise to a refund that is both measurable and currently realizable, the associated tax benefit should be recognized in this loss period.

The following journal entry is appropriate for 2001:

Income Tax Refund Receivable	110,000	
Benefit Due to Loss Carryback (Income Tax Expense)		110,000

[5]The election to forgo the 2-year carryback period might be advantageous when a taxpayer had tax credit carryovers that might be wiped out and lost because of the carryback of the net operating loss. However, use of the carryback option provides an immediate inflow of cash at a time when alternate sources of cash may not be available. For this reason many companies with net operating losses, including companies that do not expect to return to profitable operations for a period of time, choose to carry their losses back.

The account debited, **Income Tax Refund Receivable**, is reported on the balance sheet as a current asset at December 31, 2001. The account credited is reported on the income statement for 2001 as follows:

ILLUSTRATION 20-31
Recognition of Benefit of the Loss Carryback in the Loss Year

GROH INC. Income Statement (partial) for 2001	
Operating loss before income taxes	$(500,000)
Income tax benefit	
Benefit due to loss carryback	110,000
Net loss	$(390,000)

Since the $500,000 net operating loss for 2001 exceeds the $300,000 total taxable income from the 2 preceding years, the remaining $200,000 loss is to be carried forward.

Loss Carryforward Illustrated

If a net operating loss is not fully absorbed through a carryback or if the company decides not to carry the loss back, then it can be carried forward for up to 20 years.[6] Because carryforwards are used to offset future taxable income, the **tax effect of a loss carryforward** represents **future tax savings**. Realization of the future tax benefit is dependent upon future earnings, the prospect of which may be highly uncertain.

The key accounting issue is whether there should be different requirements for recognition of a deferred tax asset for (a) deductible temporary differences and (b) operating loss carryforwards. The FASB's position is that in substance these items are the same—both are amounts that are deductible on tax returns in future years. As a result, the Board concluded that there should not be different requirements for recognition of a deferred tax asset from deductible temporary differences and operating loss carryforwards.[7]

Carryforward without Valuation Allowance

To illustrate the accounting for an operating loss carryforward, return to the Groh Inc. example from the preceding section. In 2001 the company would record the tax effect of the $200,000 loss carryforward as a deferred tax asset of $80,000 ($200,000 × 40%) assuming that the enacted future tax rate is 40%. The journal entries to record the benefits of the carryback and the carryforward in 2001 would be as follows:

To recognize benefit of loss carryback		
Income Tax Refund Receivable	110,000	
Benefit Due to Loss Carryback (Income Tax Expense)		110,000
To recognize benefit of loss carryforward		
Deferred Tax Asset	80,000	
Benefit Due to Loss Carryforward (Income Tax Expense)		80,000

The income tax refund receivable of $110,000 will be realized immediately as a refund of taxes paid in the past. A Deferred Tax Asset is established for the benefits of future tax savings. The two accounts credited are contra income tax expense items, which would be presented on the 2001 income statement as follows:

[6]The length of the carryforward period has varied. It has increased from 7 years to 20 years over a period of time.

[7]This requirement is controversial because many do not believe it is appropriate to recognize deferred tax assets except when they are assured beyond a reasonable doubt. Others argue that deferred tax assets for loss carryforwards should never be recognized until income is realized in the future.

ILLUSTRATION 20-32
Recognition of the Benefit of the Loss Carryback and Carryforward in the Loss Year

GROH INC. Income Statement (partial) for 2001		
Operating loss before income taxes		$(500,000)
Income tax benefit		
Benefit due to loss carryback	$110,000	
Benefit due to loss carryforward	80,000	190,000
Net loss		$(310,000)

The $110,000 **current tax benefit** is the income tax refundable for the year, which is determined by applying the carryback provisions of the tax law to the taxable loss for 2001. The $80,000 is the **deferred tax benefit** for the year, which results from an increase in the deferred tax asset.

For 2002, assume that Groh Inc. returns to profitable operations and has taxable income of $250,000 (prior to adjustment for the NOL carryforward) subject to a 40% tax rate. Groh Inc. would then realize the benefits of the carryforward for tax purposes in 2002 which were recognized for accounting purposes in 2001. The income tax payable for 2002 is computed as follows:

ILLUSTRATION 20-33
Computation of Income Tax Payable with Realized Loss Carryforward

Taxable income prior to loss carryforward	$250,000
Loss carryforward deduction	(200,000)
Taxable income for 2002	50,000
Tax rate	40%
Income tax payable for 2002	$ 20,000

The journal entry to record income taxes in 2002 would be as follows:

Income Tax Expense	100,000	
Deferred Tax Asset		80,000
Income Tax Payable		20,000

The Deferred Tax Asset account is reduced because the benefits of the NOL carryforward are realized in 2002.

The 2002 income statement that appears below would **not report** the tax effects of either the loss carryback or the loss carryforward, because both had been reported previously.

ILLUSTRATION 20-34
Presentation of the Benefit of Loss Carryforward Realized in 2002, Recognized in 2001

GROH INC. Income Statement (partial) for 2002		
Income before income taxes		$250,000
Income tax expense		
Current	$20,000	
Deferred	80,000	100,000
Net income		$150,000

Carryforward with Valuation Allowance

Return to the Groh Inc. example. Assume that it is more likely than not that the entire NOL carryforward will not be realized in future years. In this situation, Groh Inc. records the tax benefits of $110,000 associated with the $300,000 NOL carryback, as previously described. In addition, it records a Deferred Tax Asset of $80,000 ($200,000 ×

40%) for the potential benefits related to the loss carryforward and an allowance to reduce the deferred tax asset by the same amount. The journal entries in 2001 are as follows:

To recognize benefit of loss carryback		
Income Tax Refund Receivable	110,000	
Benefit Due to Loss Carryback (Income Tax Expense)		110,000
To recognize benefit of loss carryforward		
Deferred Tax Asset	80,000	
Benefit Due to Loss Carryforward (Income Tax Expense)		80,000
To record allowance amount		
Benefit Due to Loss Carryforward (Income Tax Expense)	80,000	
Allowance to Reduce Deferred Tax Asset to Expected Realizable Value		80,000

The latter entry indicates that because positive evidence of sufficient quality and quantity is not available to counteract the negative evidence, a valuation allowance is needed.

The presentation in the 2001 income statement would be as follows:

ILLUSTRATION 20-35
Recognition of Benefit of Loss Carryback Only

GROH INC. Income Statement (partial) for 2001	
Operating loss before income taxes	$(500,000)
Income tax benefit	
Benefit due to loss carryback	110,000
Net loss	$(390,000)

In 2002, assuming that the company has taxable income of $250,000 (before considering the carryforward) subject to a tax rate of 40%, the deferred tax asset is realized and the allowance is no longer needed. The following entries would be made:

To record current and deferred income taxes		
Income Tax Expense	100,000	
Deferred Tax Asset		80,000
Income Tax Payable		20,000
To eliminate allowance and recognize loss carryforward		
Allowance to Reduce Deferred Tax Asset to Expected Realizable Value	80,000	
Benefit Due to Loss Carryforward (Income Tax Expense)		80,000

The $80,000 Benefit Due to the Loss Carryforward is computed by multiplying the $200,000 loss carryforward by the 40% tax rate. This amount is reported on the 2002 income statement because it was not recognized in 2001. Assuming that the income for 2002 is derived from continuing operations, the income statement would be presented as follows:

ILLUSTRATION 20-36
Recognition of Benefit of Loss Carryforward When Realized

GROH INC. Income Statement (partial) for 2002		
Income before income taxes		$250,000
Income tax expense		
Current	$20,000	
Deferred	80,000	
Benefit due to loss carryforward	(80,000)	20,000
Net income		$230,000

Another method is to report only one line for total income tax expense of $20,000 on the face of the income statement and disclose the components of income tax expense in the notes to the financial statements.

FINANCIAL STATEMENT PRESENTATION

The proper presentation of income taxes in the financial statements is illustrated below.

Balance Sheet Presentation

OBJECTIVE 9
Describe the presentation of deferred income taxes in financial statements.

Deferred tax accounts are reported on the balance sheet as assets and liabilities. They should be classified as a net current amount and a net noncurrent amount. **An individual deferred tax liability or asset is classified as current or noncurrent based on the classification of the related asset or liability for financial reporting purposes.** A deferred tax asset or liability is considered to be related to an asset or liability if reduction of the asset or liability will cause the temporary difference to reverse or turn around. A deferred tax liability or asset that is not related to an asset or liability for financial reporting, including a deferred tax asset related to a loss carryforward, shall be classified according to the expected reversal date of the temporary difference.

To illustrate, assume that Morgan Inc. records bad debt expense using the allowance method for accounting purposes and the direct write-off method for tax purposes. The company currently has Accounts Receivable and Allowance for Doubtful Accounts balances of $2 million and $100,000, respectively. In addition, given a 40% tax rate, it has a debit balance in the Deferred Tax Asset account of $40,000 (40% × $100,000). The $40,000 debit balance in the Deferred Tax Asset account is considered to be related to the Accounts Receivable and the Allowance for Doubtful Accounts balances because collection or write-off of the receivables will cause the temporary difference to reverse. Therefore, the Deferred Tax Asset account is classified as current, the same as the Accounts Receivable and Allowance for Doubtful Accounts balances.

In practice, most companies engage in a large number of transactions that give rise to deferred taxes. The balances in the deferred tax accounts should be analyzed and classified on the balance sheet in two categories: one for the **net current amount** and one for the **net noncurrent amount**. This procedure is summarized as indicated below.

1. *Classify the amounts as current or noncurrent.* If they are related to a specific asset or liability, they should be classified in the same manner as the related asset or liability. If not so related, they should be classified on the basis of the expected reversal date of the temporary difference.

2. *Determine the net current amount* by summing the various deferred tax assets and liabilities classified as current. If the net result is an asset, report on the balance sheet as a current asset; if a liability, report as a current liability.

3. *Determine the net noncurrent amount* by summing the various deferred tax assets and liabilities classified as noncurrent. If the net result is an asset, report on the balance sheet as a noncurrent asset; if a liability, report as a long-term liability.

To illustrate, assume that K. Scott Company has four deferred tax items at December 31, 2002. An analysis reveals the following:

ILLUSTRATION 20-37
Classification of Temporary Differences as Current or Noncurrent

Temporary Difference	Resulting Deferred Tax (Asset)	Resulting Deferred Tax Liability	Related Balance Sheet Account	Classification
1. Rent collected in advance: recognized when earned for accounting purposes and when received for tax purposes.	$(42,000)		Unearned Rent	Current
2. Use of straight-line depreciation for accounting purposes and accelerated depreciation for tax purposes.		$214,000	Equipment	Noncurrent
3. Recognition of profits on installment sales during period of sale for accounting purposes and during period of collection for tax purposes.		45,000	Installment Accounts Receivable	Current
4. Warranty liabilities: recognized for accounting purposes at time of sale; for tax purposes at time paid.	(12,000)		Estimated Liability under Warranties	Current
Totals	$(54,000)	$259,000		

The deferred taxes to be classified as current net to a $9,000 asset ($42,000 + $12,000 − $45,000), and the deferred taxes to be classified as noncurrent net to a $214,000 liability. Consequently, deferred income taxes would appear as follows on K. Scott's December 31, 2002, balance sheet:

ILLUSTRATION 20-38
Balance Sheet Presentation of Deferred Income Taxes

Current assets	
Deferred tax asset	$ 9,000
Long-term liabilities	
Deferred tax liability	$214,000

As indicated earlier, a deferred tax asset or liability **may not be related** to an asset or liability for financial reporting purposes. One example is an operating loss carryforward. In this case, a deferred tax asset is recorded, but there is no related, identifiable asset or liability for financial reporting purposes. In these limited situations, deferred income taxes should be classified according to the **expected reversal date** of the temporary difference. That is, the tax effect of any temporary difference reversing next year should be reported as current and the remainder should be reported as noncurrent. If a deferred tax asset is noncurrent, it should be classified in the "Other assets" section.

The total of all deferred tax liabilities, the total of all deferred tax assets, and the total valuation allowance should be disclosed. In addition, (1) any net change during the year in the total valuation allowance and (2) the types of temporary differences, carryforwards, or carrybacks that give rise to significant portions of deferred tax liabilities and assets should be disclosed.

Income tax payable is shown as a current liability on the balance sheet. Corporations are required to make estimated tax payments to the Internal Revenue Service quarterly. These estimated payments are recorded by a debit to Prepaid Income Taxes. As a result, the balance of the Income Tax Payable is offset by the balance of the Prepaid Income Taxes account when reporting income taxes on the balance sheet.

Income Statement Presentation

Income tax expense (or benefit) should be allocated to continuing operations, discontinued operations, extraordinary items, the cumulative effect of accounting changes, and prior period adjustments. This approach is referred to as intraperiod tax allocation and is illustrated later in the chapter.

In addition, the significant components of income tax expense attributable to continuing operations should be disclosed:

1. Current tax expense or benefit.
2. Deferred tax expense or benefit, exclusive of other components listed below.
3. Investment tax credits.
4. Government grants (to the extent they are recognized as a reduction of income tax expense).
5. The benefits of operating loss carryforwards (resulting in a reduction of income tax expense).
6. Tax expense that results from allocating certain tax benefits either directly to paid-in capital or to reduce goodwill or other noncurrent intangible assets of an acquired entity.
7. Adjustments of a deferred tax liability or asset for enacted changes in tax laws or rates or a change in the tax status of an enterprise.
8. Adjustments of the beginning-of-the-year balance of a valuation allowance because of a change in circumstances that causes a change in judgment about the realizability of the related deferred tax asset in future years.

In the notes, companies are also required to reconcile (using percentages or dollar amounts) income tax expense attributable to continuing operations with the amount that results from applying domestic federal statutory tax rates to pretax income from continuing operations. The estimated amount and the nature of each significant reconciling item should be disclosed. An example from the 1998 Annual Report of **PepsiCo, Inc.** is presented in Illustration 20-39. For another example, refer to **Intel Corporation**'s Annual Report at the end of Chapter 5. (See Note on page 231).

Go to the Digital Tool for additional examples of deferred tax disclosures.

These income tax disclosures are required for several reasons. Some of the reasons are:

1. ***Assessment of Quality of Earnings.*** Many investors seeking to assess the quality of a company's earnings are interested in the reconciliation of pretax financial income to taxable income. Earnings that are enhanced by a favorable tax effect should be examined carefully, particularly if the tax effect is nonrecurring. For example, one year **Wang Laboratories** reported net income of $3.3 million, or 82 cents a share, versus $3.1 million, or 77 cents a share, in the preceding period. The entire increase in net income and then some resulted form a lower effective tax rate.
2. ***Better Predictions of Future Cash Flows.*** Examination of the deferred portion of income tax expense provides information as to whether taxes payable are likely to be higher or lower in the future. A close examination may disclose the company's policy regarding capitalization of costs, recognition of revenue, and other policies giving rise to a difference between pretax financial income and taxable income. As a result, it may be possible to predict future reductions in deferred tax liabilities leading to a loss of liquidity because actual tax payments will be higher than the tax expense reported on the income statement.[8]
3. ***Helpful in Setting Governmental Policy.*** Understanding the amount companies currently pay and the effective tax rate is helpful to government policymakers. In the early 1970s, when the oil companies were believed to have earned excess profits, many politicians and other interested parties attempted to determine their effective tax rates. Unfortunately, at that time such information was not available in published annual reports.

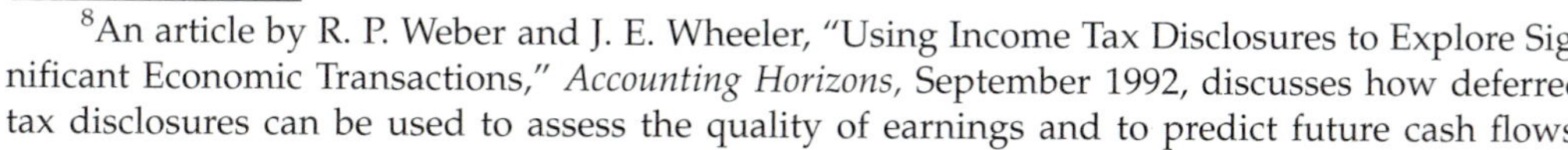

[8]An article by R. P. Weber and J. E. Wheeler, "Using Income Tax Disclosures to Explore Significant Economic Transactions," *Accounting Horizons,* September 1992, discusses how deferred tax disclosures can be used to assess the quality of earnings and to predict future cash flows.

ILLUSTRATION 20-39
Disclosure of Income Taxes—PepsiCo, Inc.

PEPSICO, INC.

Note 12: Income Taxes

U.S. and foreign income from continuing operations before income taxes:

	1998	1997	1996
U.S.	$1,629	$1,731	$1,630
Foreign	634	578	(64)
	$2,263	$2,309	$1,566

Provision for income taxes on income from continuing operations:

	1998	1997	1996
Current: Federal	$ (193)	$ 598	$ 254
Foreign	267	110	138
State	46	59	72
	120	767	464
Deferred: Federal	136	23	204
Foreign	4	15	(41)
State	10	13	(3)
	150	51	160
	$ 270	$ 818	$ 624

Reconciliation of the U.S. Federal statutory tax rate to our effective tax rate on continuing operations:

	1998	1997	1996
U.S. Federal statutory tax rate	35.0%	35.0%	35.0%
State income tax, net of Federal tax benefit	1.6	2.0	2.9
Effect of lower taxes on foreign results	(3.0)	(5.5)	(4.4)
Settlement of prior years' audit issues	(5.7)	(1.7)	(2.9)
Puerto Rico settlement	(21.8)	—	—
Effect of unusual impairment and other items	3.4	2.2	9.7
Other, net	2.4	3.4	(0.5)
Effective tax rate on continuing operations	11.9%	35.4%	39.8%

Deferred taxes are recorded to give recognition to temporary differences between the tax bases of assets or liabilities and their reported amounts in the financial statements. We record the tax effect of the temporary differences as deferred tax assets or deferred tax liabilities. Deferred tax assets generally represent items that can be used as a tax deduction or credit in future years. Deferred tax liabilities generally represent items that we have taken a tax deduction for, but have not yet recorded in the income statement.

Deferred tax liabilities (assets):

	1998	1997
Intangible assets other than nondeductible goodwill	$1,444	$1,363
Property, plant and equipment	665	500
Safe harbor leases	109	115
Zero coupon notes	79	84
Other	473	335
Gross deferred tax liabilities	2,770	2,397
Net operating loss carryforwards	(562)	(520)
Postretirement benefits	(246)	(247)
Various current liabilities and other	(702)	(510)
Gross deferred tax assets	(1,510)	(1,277)
Deferred tax assets valuation allowance	571	458
Net deferred tax assets	(939)	(819)
Net deferred tax liabilities	$1,831	$1,578
Included in:		
Prepaid expenses, deferred income taxes and other current assets	$ (172)	$ (119)
Deferred income taxes	2,003	1,697
	$1,831	$1,578

Deferred tax liabilities are not recognized for temporary differences related to investments in foreign subsidiaries and in unconsolidated foreign affiliates that are essentially permanent in duration. It would not be practicable to determine the amount of any such deferred tax liabilities.

Net operating losses of $2.7 billion at year-end 1998 were carried forward and are available to reduce future taxable income of certain subsidiaries in a number of foreign and state jurisdictions. These net operating losses will expire as follows: $96 million in 1999, $2.4 billion between 2000 and 2012, while $201 million may be carried forward indefinitely.

Disclosure of Operating Loss Carryforwards

The amounts and expiration dates of any operating loss carryforwards for tax purposes should be disclosed. From this disclosure, the reader can determine the amount of income that may be recognized in the future on which no income tax will be paid. For example, the PepsiCo disclosure in Illustration 20-39 indicates that PepsiCo has $2.7 billion in net operating loss carryforwards that can be used to reduce future taxes up to the year 2012.

Loss carryforwards can be extremely valuable to a potential acquirer. At one time, **Dalfort Company** received nearly $360 million in operating loss carryforwards and other credits as a result of its ownership of **Braniff Airlines**. Many speculate that Dalfort bought **Levitz Furniture Corp.** (a large discounter of quality furniture) so that it could offset its carryforward losses from Braniff against Levitz's earnings. Companies that have suffered substantial losses may find themselves worth more "dead" than alive because their tax losses have little value to themselves but great value to other enterprises. In short, substantial tax carryforwards can have real economic value.[9]

SPECIAL ISSUES

OBJECTIVE 10
Identify special issues related to deferred income taxes.

A number of issues merit special attention when accounting for deferred income taxes. These are as follows:

1. Multiple temporary differences.
2. Necessity for a valuation allowance.
3. Multiple tax rates.
4. Alternative minimum tax.

Multiple Temporary Differences

To simplify the accounting when multiple temporary differences are involved, the following schedules should prove useful. Assume that Griggs Co. has two temporary differences in its first year of operations, one involving an installment sale and the other involving warranty costs. Other assumptions made should be apparent from the presentation of the scheduled material.

ILLUSTRATION 20-40
Schedule of Future Taxable and Deductible Amounts

	Future Years		
	2003	2004	Total
Future taxable (deductible) amounts:			
Installment sale	$100,000	$100,000	$200,000
Warranty costs	(40,000)	(50,000)	(90,000)

The deferred income taxes to be reported at the end of 2002 are computed as follows:

ILLUSTRATION 20-41
Computation of Deferred Income Taxes

Temporary Differences	Future Taxable (Deductible) Amounts	Tax Rate	Deferred Tax (Asset)	Deferred Tax Liability
Installment sale	$200,000	40%		$80,000
Warranty costs	(90,000)	40%	$(36,000)	
	$110,000		$(36,000)	$80,000

Because of a flat rate, these totals can be reconciled: $110,000 × 40% = ($36,000) + $80,000

[9]The IRS frowns on acquisitions done solely to obtain operating loss carryforwards. If the merger is determined to be solely tax motivated, then the deductions will be disallowed. But because it is very difficult to determine whether a merger is or is not tax motivated, the "purchase of operating loss carryforwards" continues.

The journal entry to record income tax expense for 2002, assuming income tax payable is $500,000 is as follows:

Income Tax Expense	544,000	
Deferred Tax Asset	36,000	
Income Tax Payable		500,000
Deferred Tax Liability		80,000

Necessity for Valuation Allowance

All positive and negative information should be considered in determining whether a valuation allowance is needed. Whether a deferred tax asset will be realized depends on whether sufficient taxable income exists or will exist within the carryback or carryforward period available under tax law. The following possible sources of taxable income may be available under the tax law to realize a tax benefit for deductible temporary differences and carryforwards:

ILLUSTRATION 20-42
Possible Sources of Taxable Income

Taxable Income Sources

a. Future reversals of existing taxable temporary differences
b. Future taxable income exclusive of reversing temporary differences and carryforwards
c. Taxable income in prior carryback year(s) if carryback is permitted under the tax law
d. **Tax-planning strategies** that would, if necessary, be implemented to:
(1) Accelerate taxable amounts to utilize expiring carryforwards
(2) Change the character of taxable or deductible amounts from ordinary income or loss to capital gain or loss
(3) Switch from tax-exempt to taxable investments.[10]

If any one of these sources is sufficient to support a conclusion that a valuation allowance is not necessary, other sources need not be considered.

Forming a conclusion that a valuation allowance is not needed is difficult when there is negative evidence such as cumulative losses in recent years. Other examples of negative evidence include (but are not limited to) the following:

ILLUSTRATION 20-43
Negative Evidence to Support Need for Valuation Account

Negative Evidence

a. A history of operating loss or tax credit carryforwards expiring unused
b. Losses expected in early future years (by a presently profitable entity)
c. Unsettled circumstances that, if unfavorably resolved, would adversely affect future operations and profit levels on a continuing basis in future years
d. A carryback, carryforward period that is so brief that it would limit realization of tax benefits if (1) a significant deductible temporary difference is expected to reverse in a single year or (2) the enterprise operates in a traditionally cyclical business.

Examples (not prerequisites) of positive evidence that might support a conclusion that a valuation allowance is not needed when there is negative evidence include the following:

[10]"Accounting for Income Taxes," *Statement of Financial Accounting Standards No. 109* (Norwalk, Conn.: FASB, 1992). A tax planning strategy is an action that would be implemented to realize a tax benefit for an operating loss or tax credit carryforward before it expires. Tax planning strategies are considered when assessing the need for and amount of a valuation allowance for deferred tax assets.

ILLUSTRATION 20-44
Positive Evidence against Need for Valuation Account

Positive Evidence

a. Existing contracts or firm sales backlog that will produce more than enough taxable income to realize the deferred tax asset based on existing sale prices and cost structures
b. An excess of appreciated asset value over the tax basis of the entity's net assets in an amount sufficient to realize the deferred tax asset
c. A strong earnings history exclusive of the loss that created the future deductible amount (tax loss carryforward or deductible temporary difference) coupled with evidence indicating that the loss (for example, an unusual, infrequent, or extraordinary item) is an aberration rather than a continuing condition.[11]

The use of this valuation account provides management with an opportunity to manage its earnings. As one accounting expert notes: "The 'more likely than not' provision is perhaps the most judgmental clause in accounting." What some companies might do is set up valuation accounts and then use the valuation account to increase income as needed. Others could take the income immediately to increase capital or to offset large negative charges to income.[12]

Multiple Tax Rates

As indicated previously, the enacted future tax rate should be used to measure deferred taxes. This rate is applied to future taxable and deductible amounts arising from temporary differences. If there is a phased-in change in tax rates, selection of the future tax rate used to apply to a particular temporary difference requires some knowledge of when related taxable or deductible amounts will occur.

Deferred Tax Liability

Assume that Crandall Inc. at the end of 2002 (its third year of operations) has $2,400,000 of taxable temporary differences that are expected to result in taxable amounts of $800,000 in each of the following 3 years, 2003–2005. Enacted tax rates are 35% for 2001–2002, 40% for 2003–2005, and 45% for 2006 and thereafter. Assuming that taxable income is expected in 2003–2005, the deferred tax liability at December 31, 2002, is $960,000, which is computed as follows:

ILLUSTRATION 20-45
Computation of Deferred Tax Liability

	Future Years			
	2003	2004	2005	Total
Future taxable amounts	$800,000	$800,000	$800,000	$2,400,000
Enacted future tax rate	40%	40%	40%	
Deferred tax liability at 12/31/02	$320,000	$320,000	$320,000	$ 960,000

Now assume that Crandall Inc. is expected to incur **losses** for tax purposes in 2003–2005. The tax rate to use to compute the deferred tax liability is 35% if realization of the tax benefit for those losses in years 2003–2005 will be by loss carryback to 2001–2002. The deferred tax liability at December 31, 2002, under this assumption is $840,000 ($2,400,000 × 35%).

If, on the other hand, realization of the tax benefit for those tax losses in 2003–2005 will be by loss carryforward to 2006 and thereafter, the tax rate to be used is 45%. In

[11]Ibid., par. 23 and 24.

[12]A recent study of the valuation allowances recorded by companies since *SFAS No. 109* was issued indicates that valuation allowance balances are related to the factors identified as positive and negative evidence. There is little evidence that the valuation is used for earnings management. See G. S. Miller and D. J. Skinner, "Determinants of the Valuation Allowance for Deferred Tax Assets under *SFAS No. 109*," *The Accounting Review*, April 1998.

this situation, the deferred tax liability is $1,080,000 ($2,400,000 × 45%) at December 31, 2002.

Deferred Tax Asset

To illustrate the measurement of a deferred tax asset, assume that Miller Co. has a $9,000,000 deductible temporary difference at the end of 2002 (its second year of operations). The $9,000,000 is expected to result in tax deductions of $3,000,000 in each of the next three years (2003–2005). Enacted tax rates are 30% for 2001 and 2002 and 40% for 2003 and thereafter. The tax rate to be used to measure the deferred tax asset is 40% if Miller expects to realize a tax benefit for the deductible temporary differences by offsetting taxable income earned in future years. Under this assumption, the amount of the deferred tax asset at December 31, 2002, is $3,600,000 ($9,000,000 × 40%).

Alternatively, the tax rate to be used is 30% if Miller expects to realize a tax benefit for the deductible temporary differences by loss carryback refund (that is, if Miller expects tax losses rather than taxable income in the future). In this case, the deferred tax asset at December 31, 2002, is $2,700,000 ($9,000,000 x 30%).

Valuation Allowance

Assume that Miller reports a $3,600,000 ($9,000,000 × 40%) deferred tax asset at December 31, 2002, which is expected to be realized by offsetting taxable income in future years. Also assume that taxable income and taxes payable in both 2001 and 2002 were $4,500,000 and $1,350,000, respectively. Realization of a tax benefit of, at least, $2,700,000 is assured because carryback refunds totalling $2,700,000 ($9,000,000 × 30%) can be used even if no taxable income is earned in future years. Recognition of a valuation allowance for the other $900,000 ($3,600,000 − $2,700,000) of the deferred tax asset depends on management's assessment of whether, based on the weight of available evidence, a portion or all of the tax benefit of the deductible temporary differences will be realized in future years.

Alternative Minimum Tax

The current tax law requires a corporation to compute its potential tax liability using the regular tax system and an alternative minimum tax (AMT) system.[13] The **alternative minimum tax system** is used to ensure that corporations do not avoid paying a fair share of income taxes through various tax avoidance approaches.[14]

For any given year, a corporation's annual income tax liability is the greater of the regular tax or the alternative minimum tax. Any deferred income taxes are computed using the regular tax rate(s), without regard to whether the company is subject to the alternative minimum tax now or is expected to be affected by it in the future. A company that pays the alternative minimum tax is entitled to a credit against its regular tax liability in subsequent years. Thus, paying the AMT gives the entity a tax credit carryforward.

A **tax credit carryforward** is similar to a future deductible amount with one major difference. A future deductible amount will offset **future taxable income** and a tax credit carryforward will offset **income taxes payable** in the future. If a tax rate of 40% applies, a tax credit of $1,000 is more valuable than a deduction of $1,000. The former will save $1,000 in tax and the latter will save only $400 in tax.

---

[13]Companies most likely to be affected by the AMT are capital-intensive companies subject to significant depreciation deductions. Also companies that significantly reduce regular tax liabilities by using the completed-contract method, or by using the installment method for reporting sales of certain real property often pay taxes at AMT rates.

[14]The reason for the alternative minimum tax is quite simple: During the 1981–1984 period many of the nation's largest corporations paid little if any income tax, and few paid at the full statutory rate. The alternative minimum tax now ensures that most corporations will pay a certain minimum amount of tax.

A deferred tax asset is recognized for an AMT credit carryforward. The need for a related valuation allowance must then be assessed. The AMT computations and considerations are extremely complex and require a background in income tax accounting. We will generalize here to say that unless there is a significant amount of tax preference items (determined by a set of complex income tax rules), total taxes paid over the entire life of a company will be based on the regular tax system, not the AMT system; **thus, an AMT credit carryforward will usually be judged to be realized in the future and a related valuation account will not be necessary.**

REVIEW OF THE ASSET-LIABILITY METHOD

OBJECTIVE 11
Indicate the basic principles of the asset-liability method.

The FASB believes that the **asset-liability method** (sometime referred to as the liability approach) is the most consistent method for accounting for income taxes. One objective of this approach is to recognize the amount of taxes payable or refundable for the current year. A second objective is to recognize **deferred tax liabilities and assets** for the **future tax consequences** of events that have been recognized in the financial statements or tax returns.

To implement the objectives, the following basic principles are applied in accounting for income taxes at the date of the financial statements:

a. A current tax liability or asset is recognized for the estimated taxes payable or refundable on the tax return for the current year.

b. A deferred tax liability or asset is recognized for the estimated future tax effects attributable to temporary differences and carryforwards.

c. The measurement of current and deferred tax liabilities and assets is based on provisions of the enacted tax law; the effects of future changes in tax laws or rates are not anticipated.

d. The measurement of deferred tax assets is reduced, if necessary, by the amount of any tax benefits that, based on available evidence, are not expected to be realized.[15]

Nations that recognize deferred taxes using the liability method include, among others, Australia, Germany, the United Kingdom, and Spain. IASC standards for taxes also use the liability method. The European Directives do not specify the accounting for deferred taxes.

Implementation of the Asset-Liability Method

The procedures for the computation of deferred income taxes are as follows:

Annual Procedures

a. Identify (1) the types and amounts of existing temporary differences and (2) the nature and amount of each type of operating loss and tax credit carryforward and the remaining length of the carryforward period.

b. Measure the total deferred tax liability for taxable temporary differences using the applicable tax rate.

c. Measure the total deferred tax asset for deductible temporary differences and operating loss carryforwards using the applicable tax rate.

d. Measure deferred tax assets for each type of tax credit carryforward.

e. Reduce deferred tax assets by a **valuation allowance** if, based on the weight of available evidence, it is *more likely than not* that some portion or all of the deferred tax assets will not be realized. The valuation allowance should be sufficient to reduce the deferred tax assets to the amount that is more likely than not to be realized.[16]

ILLUSTRATION 20-46
Procedures for Computation of Deferred Income Taxes

These procedures are illustrated graphically in Illustration 20-47.

[15] "Accounting for Income Taxes," par. 6 and 8, 1992.

[16] "Accounting for Income Taxes," par. 17.

ILLUSTRATION 20-47
Procedures for Computing and Reporting Deferred Income Taxes

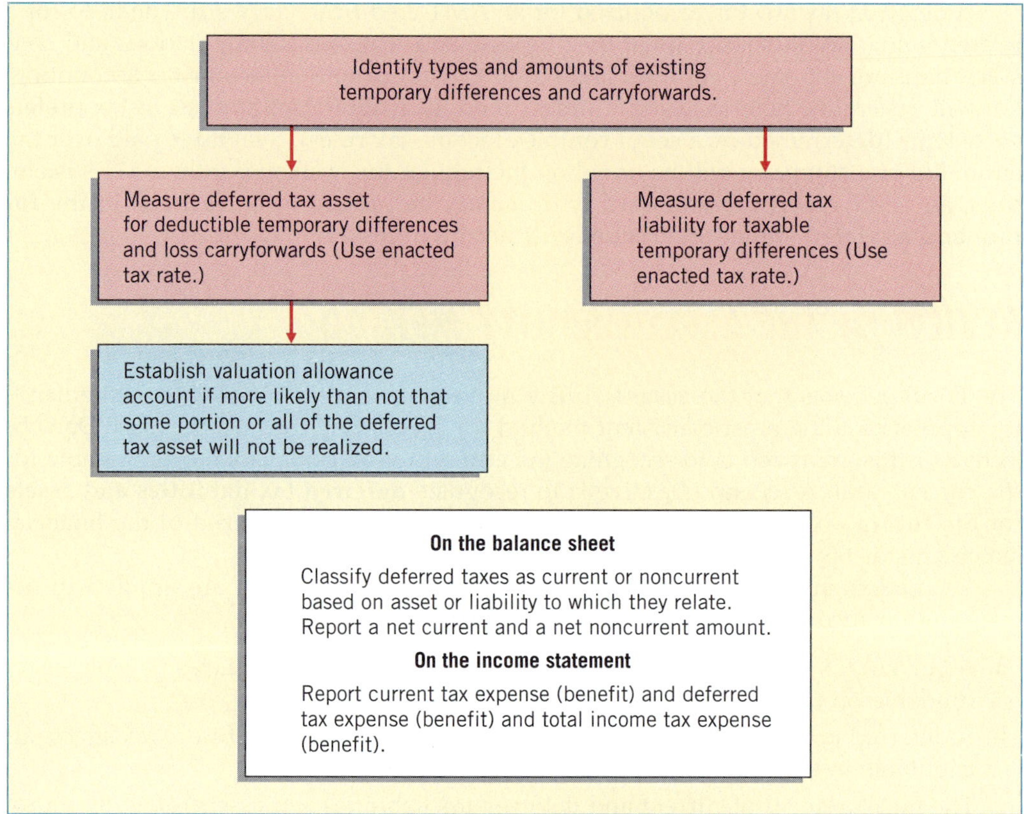

Some Conceptual Questions

The asset-liability method is the approach that the Board deemed most appropriate to record deferred income taxes. However, some conceptual questions remain. Presented below are three important issues.

1. ***Failure to Discount.*** Without discounting the asset or liability (that is, failing to consider its present value), financial statements do not indicate the appropriate benefit of tax deferral or the burden of tax prepayment. Thus, comparability of the financial statements is impaired because a dollar related to short-term deferral appears to be of the same value as a dollar of longer-term deferral.
2. ***Classification Issue.*** Consistent with the asset-liability approach, deferred tax assets and liabilities should be classified on the balance sheet based on when they will be realized or settled. Previously, the Board took the position that deferred taxes related to temporary differences reversing next period should be reported as current. Many believe this approach is correct and therefore disagree with the present requirements.
3. ***Dual Criteria for Recognition of Deferred Tax Asset.*** Many believe that future deductible amounts arising from net operating loss carryforwards are different from future deductible amounts arising from normal operations. One rationale provided is that a deferred tax asset arising from normal operations results in a tax prepayment—a prepaid tax asset. In the case of loss carryforwards, no tax prepayment has been made.

   Others argue that realization of a loss carryforward is less likely—and thus should require a more severe test—than for a net deductible amount arising from normal operations. Some have suggested that the test be changed from "more likely than not" to "probable" realization. Still others have indicated that because of the nature of net operating losses, deferred tax assets should never be established for these items.

The above controversies assume that the asset-liability approach is used. Others argue that completely different types of approaches should be used to report deferred income taxes.

As an aid to understanding deferred income taxes, the following glossary[17] is provided:

www.wiley.com/college/kieso

Go to the Digital Tool for a discussion of conceptual approaches to interperiod tax allocation.

KEY DEFERRED INCOME TAX TERMS

CARRYBACKS. Deductions or credits that cannot be utilized on the tax return during a year and that may be carried back to reduce taxable income or taxes paid in a prior year. An **operating loss carryback** is an excess of tax deductions over gross income in a year; a **tax credit carryback** is the amount by which tax credits available for utilization exceed statutory limitations.

CARRYFORWARDS. Deductions or credits that cannot be utilized on the tax return during a year and that may be carried forward to reduce taxable income or taxes payable in a future year. An **operating loss carryforward** is an excess of tax deductions over gross income in a year; a **tax credit carryforward** is the amount by which tax credits available for utilization exceed statutory limitations.

CURRENT TAX EXPENSE (BENEFIT). The amount of income taxes paid or payable (or refundable) for a year as determined by applying the provisions of the enacted tax law to the taxable income or excess of deductions over revenues for that year.

DEDUCTIBLE TEMPORARY DIFFERENCE. Temporary differences that result in deductible amounts in future years when the related asset or liability is recovered or settled, respectively.

DEFERRED TAX ASSET. The deferred tax consequences attributable to deductible temporary differences and carryforwards.

DEFERRED TAX CONSEQUENCES. The future effects on income taxes as measured by the enacted tax rate and provisions of the enacted tax law resulting from temporary differences and carryforwards at the end of the current year.

DEFERRED TAX EXPENSE (BENEFIT). The change during the year in an enterprise's deferred tax liabilities and assets.

DEFERRED TAX LIABILITY. The deferred tax consequences attributable to taxable temporary differences.

INCOME TAXES. Domestic and foreign federal (national), state, and local (including franchise) taxes based on income.

INCOME TAXES CURRENTLY PAYABLE (REFUNDABLE). Refer to current tax expense (benefit).

INCOME TAX EXPENSE (BENEFIT). The sum of current tax expense (benefit) and deferred tax expense (benefit).

TAXABLE INCOME. The excess of taxable revenues over tax deductible expenses and exemptions for the year as defined by the governmental taxing authority.

TAXABLE TEMPORARY DIFFERENCE. Temporary differences that result in taxable amounts in future years when the related asset or liability is recovered or settled, respectively.

TAX-PLANNING STRATEGY. An action that meets certain criteria and that would be implemented to realize a tax benefit for an operating loss or tax credit carryforward before it expires. Tax-planning strategies are considered when

[17]Ibid., Appendix E.

assessing the need for and amount of a valuation allowance for deferred tax assets.

TEMPORARY DIFFERENCE. A difference between the tax basis of an asset or liability and its reported amount in the financial statements that will result in taxable or deductible amounts in future years when the reported amount of the asset or liability is recovered or settled, respectively.

VALUATION ALLOWANCE. The portion of a deferred tax asset for which it is more likely than not that a tax benefit will not be realized.

KEY TERMS

alternative minimum tax system, *1084*
asset-liability method, *1085*
average tax rate, *1071*
current tax benefit or expense, *1075*
deductible amounts, *1060*
deductible temporary difference, *1068*
deferred tax asset, *1064*
deferred tax expense (benefit), *1062, 1063*
deferred tax liability, *1061*
effective tax rate, *1070*
enacted future tax rate, *1083*
enacted tax rate, *1071*
Income Tax Refund Receivable, *1074*
loss carryback, *1072*
loss carryforward, *1073*
more likely than not, *1066*
net current amount, *1077*
net noncurrent amount, *1077*
net operating loss (NOL), *1072*
originating temporary difference, *1068*
permanent difference, *1069*
pretax financial income, *1058*
reversing difference, *1068*
taxable amounts, *1060*
taxable income, *1058*
taxable temporary difference, *1068*
tax credit carryforward, *1084*
tax effect (tax benefit), *1073*
temporary difference, *1060*
valuation allowance, *1088*

SUMMARY OF LEARNING OBJECTIVES

1 **Identify differences between pretax financial income and taxable income.** Pretax financial income (or income for book purposes) is computed in accordance with generally accepted accounting principles. Taxable income (or income for tax purposes) is computed in accordance with prescribed tax regulations. Because tax regulations and GAAP are different in many ways, pretax financial income and taxable income frequently differ. Differences may exist, for example, in the timing of revenue recognition and the timing of expense recognition.

2 **Describe a temporary difference that results in future taxable amounts.** A credit sale that is recognized as revenue for book purposes in the period it is earned but is deferred and reported as revenue for tax purposes in the period it is collected will result in future taxable amounts. The future taxable amounts will occur in the periods the receivable is recovered and the collections are reported as revenue for tax purposes. This results in a deferred tax liability.

3 **Describe a temporary difference that results in future deductible amounts.** An accrued warranty expense that is paid for and is deductible for tax purposes in a period later than the period in which it is incurred and recognized for book purposes will result in future deductible amounts. The future deductible amounts will occur in the periods during which the related liability for book purposes is settled. This results in a deferred tax asset.

4 **Explain the purpose of a deferred tax asset valuation allowance.** A deferred tax asset should be reduced by a valuation allowance if, based on all available evidence, it is more likely than not (a level of likelihood that is at least slightly more than 50%) that some portion or all of the deferred tax asset will not be realized. All available evidence, both positive and negative, should be carefully considered to determine whether, based on the weight of available evidence, a valuation allowance is needed.

5 **Describe the presentation of income tax expense in the income statement.** The significant components of income tax expense should be disclosed in the income statement or in the notes to the financial statements. The most commonly encountered components are the current expense (or benefit) and the deferred expense (or benefit).

6 **Describe various temporary and permanent differences.** Examples of temporary differences are: (1) revenue or gains that are taxable after they are recognized in financial income; (2) expenses or losses that are deductible after they are recognized in financial income; (3) revenues or gains that are taxable before they are recognized in financial income; (4) expenses or losses that are deductible before they are recognized in financial income. Examples of permanent differences are: (1) items recognized for financial reporting purposes but not for tax purposes; and (2) items recognized for tax purposes but not for financial reporting purposes.

7 **Explain the effect of various tax rates and tax rate changes on deferred income taxes.** Tax rates other than the current rate may be used only when the future tax rates have been enacted into law. When a change in the tax rate is enacted into law, its effect on the deferred income tax accounts should be recognized immediately. The effects are reported as an adjustment to income tax expense in the period of the change.

8 **Apply accounting procedures for a loss carryback and a loss carryforward.** A company may carry a net operating loss back 2 years and receive refunds for income taxes paid in those years. The loss must be applied to the earlier year first and then to the second year. Any loss remaining after the 2-year carryback may be carried forward up to 20 years to offset future taxable income. A company may forgo the loss carryback and use the loss carryforward, offsetting future taxable income for up to 20 years.

9 **Describe the presentation of deferred income taxes in financial statements.** Deferred tax accounts are reported on the balance sheet as assets and liabilities. They should be classified as a net current and a net noncurrent amount. An individual deferred tax liability or asset is classified as current or noncurrent based on the classification of the related asset or liability for financial reporting. A deferred tax liability or asset that is not related to an asset or liability for financial reporting, including a deferred tax asset related to a loss carryforward, shall be classified according to the expected reversal date of the temporary difference.

10 **Identify special issues related to deferred income taxes.** A number of issues related to deferred income taxes are special: (1) multiple temporary differences; (2) necessity for a valuation allowance; (3) multiple tax rates; (4) alternative minimum tax.

11 **Indicate the basic principles of the asset-liability method.** The following basic principles are applied in accounting for income taxes at the date of the financial statements: (1) a current tax liability or asset is recognized for the estimated taxes payable or refundable on the tax return for the current year; (2) a deferred tax liability or asset is recognized for the estimated future tax effects attributable to temporary differences and carryforwards using the enacted tax rate; (3) the measurement of current and deferred tax liabilities and assets is based on provisions of the enacted tax law; (4) the measurement of deferred tax assets is reduced, if necessary, by the amount of any tax benefits that, based on available evidence, are not expected to be realized.

APPENDIX 20A

Comprehensive Illustration of Interperiod Tax Allocation

OBJECTIVE 12
After studying Appendix 20A, you should be able to: Understand and apply the concepts and procedures of interperiod tax allocation.

This appendix presents a comprehensive illustration of a deferred income tax problem with several temporary and permanent differences. The illustration follows one company through two complete years (2001 and 2002). **Study it carefully.** It should help you understand the concepts and procedures presented in the chapter.

FIRST YEAR—2001

Allman Company, which began operations at the beginning of 2001, produces various products on a contract basis. Each contract generates a gross profit of $80,000. Some of Allman's contracts provide for the customer to pay on an installment basis whereby one-fifth of the contract revenue is collected in each of the following four years. Gross profit is recognized in the year of completion for financial reporting purposes (accrual basis) and in the year cash is collected for tax purposes (installment basis).

Presented below is information related to Allman's operations for 2001:

1. In 2001, the company completed seven contracts that allow for the customer to pay on an installment basis. The related gross profit amount of $560,000 was recognized for financial reporting purposes, whereas only $112,000 of gross profit on installment sales was reported on the 2001 tax return.The future collections on the related installment receivables are expected to result in taxable amounts of $112,000 in each of the next four years.
2. At the beginning of 2001, Allman Company purchased depreciable assets with a cost of $540,000. For financial reporting purposes, Allman depreciates these assets using the straight-line method over a 6-year service life. For tax purposes, the assets fall in the 5-year recovery class and Allman uses the MACRS system. The depreciation schedules for both financial reporting and tax purposes follow:

Year	Depreciation for Financial Reporting Purposes	Depreciation for Tax Purposes	Difference
2001	$ 90,000	$108,000	$(18,000)
2002	90,000	172,800	(82,800)
2003	90,000	103,680	(13,680)
2004	90,000	62,208	27,792
2005	90,000	62,208	27,792
2006	90,000	31,104	58,896
	$540,000	$540,000	$ -0-

3. The company warrants their product for 2 years from the date of completion of a contract. During 2001 product warranty liability accrued for financial reporting purposes was $200,000, and the amount paid for the satisfaction of warranty liability was $44,000. The remaining $156,000 is expected to be settled by expenditures of $56,000 in 2002 and $100,000 in 2003.
4. In 2001 nontaxable municipal bond interest revenue was $28,000.
5. During 2001 nondeductible fines and penalties of $26,000 were paid.
6. Pretax financial income for 2001 amounts to $412,000.
7. Tax rates enacted before the end of 2001:

2001	50%
2002 and later years	40%

8. The accounting period is the calendar year.
9. The company is expected to have taxable income in all future years.

Taxable Income and Income Tax Payable—2001

The first step is to determine Allman Company's income tax payable for 2001 by calculating its taxable income. This computation is as follows:

ILLUSTRATION 20A-1
Computation of Taxable Income, 2001

Pretax financial income for 2001	$412,000
Permanent differences:	
Nontaxable revenue—municipal bond interest	(28,000)
Nondeductible expenses—fines and penalties	26,000
Temporary differences:	
Excess gross profit per books ($560,000 − $112,000)	(448,000)
Excess depreciation per tax ($108,000 − $90,000)	(18,000)
Excess warranty expense per books ($200,000 − $44,000)	156,000
Taxable income for 2001	$100,000

Income tax payable is computed on taxable income for $100,000 as follows:

ILLUSTRATION 20A-2
Computation of Income Tax Payable, End of 2001

Taxable income for 2001	$100,000
Tax rate	50%
Income tax payable (current tax expense) for 2001	$ 50,000

Computing Deferred Income Taxes—End of 2001

The following schedule is helpful in summarizing the temporary differences and the resulting future taxable and deductible amounts:

ILLUSTRATION 20A-3
Schedule of Future Taxable and Deductible Amounts, End of 2001

	Future Years					
	2002	2003	2004	2005	2006	Total
Future taxable (deductible) amounts:						
Installment sales	$112,000	$112,000	$112,000	$112,000		$448,000
Depreciation	(82,800)	(13,680)	27,792	27,792	$58,896	18,000
Warranty costs	(56,000)	(100,000)				(156,000)

The amounts of deferred income taxes to be reported at the end of 2001 are computed as follows:

ILLUSTRATION 20A-4
Computation of Deferred Income Taxes, End of 2001

Temporary Difference	Future Taxable (Deductible) Amounts	Tax Rate	Deferred Tax (Asset)	Deferred Tax Liability
Installment sales	$448,000	40%		$179,200
Depreciation	18,000	40%		7,200
Warranty costs	(156,000)	40%	$(62,400)	
Totals	$310,000		$(62,400)	$186,400*

*Because only a single tax rate is involved in all relevant years, these totals can be reconciled: $310,000 × 40% = ($62,400) + $186,400.

The temporary difference caused by the use of the accrual basis for financial reporting purposes and the installment method for tax purposes will result in future taxable amounts; hence, a deferred tax liability will arise. Because of the installment contracts completed in 2001, a temporary difference of $448,000 originates that will reverse in equal amounts over the next 4 years. The company is expected to have taxable income in all future years, and there is only one enacted tax rate applicable to all future years. Therefore, that rate (40%) is used to compute the entire deferred tax liability resulting from this temporary difference.

The temporary difference caused by different depreciation policies for books and for tax purposes originates over 3 years and then reverses over 3 years. This difference will cause deductible amounts in 2002 and 2003 and taxable amounts in 2004, 2005, and 2006, which sum to a net future taxable amount of $18,000 (which is the cumulative temporary difference at the end of 2001). Because the company is expected to have taxable income in all future years and because there is only one tax rate enacted for all of the relevant future years, that rate is applied to the net future taxable amount to determine the related net deferred tax liability.

The third temporary difference, caused by different methods of accounting for warranties, will result in deductible amounts in each of the 2 future years it takes to reverse. Because the company expects to report a positive income on all future tax returns and because there is only one tax rate enacted for each of the relevant future years, that 40% rate is used to calculate the resulting deferred tax asset.

Deferred Tax Expense (Benefit) and the Journal Entry to Record Income Taxes—2001

To determine the deferred tax expense (benefit), the beginning and ending balances of the deferred income tax accounts must be compared.

ILLUSTRATION 20A-5
Computation of Deferred Tax Expense (Benefit), 2001

Deferred tax asset at the end of 2001	$ 62,400
Deferred tax asset at the beginning of 2001	–0–
Deferred tax expense (benefit)	$ (62,400)
Deferred tax liability at the end of 2001	$186,400
Deferred tax liability at the beginning of 2001	–0–
Deferred tax expense (benefit)	$186,400

The $62,400 increase in the deferred tax asset causes a deferred tax benefit to be reflected in the income statement. The $186,400 increase in the deferred tax liability during 2001 results in a deferred tax expense. These two amounts **net** to a deferred tax expense of $124,000 for 2001.

ILLUSTRATION 20A-6
Computation of Net Deferred Tax Expense, 2001

Deferred tax expense (benefit)	$ (62,400)
Deferred tax expense (benefit)	186,400
Net deferred tax expense for 2001	$124,000

The total income tax expense is then computed as follows:

ILLUSTRATION 20A-7
Computation of Total Income Tax Expense, 2001

Current tax expense for 2001	$ 50,000
Deferred tax expense for 2001	124,000
Income tax expense (total) for 2001	$174,000

The journal entry to record income tax payable, deferred income taxes, and income tax expense is as follows:

Income Tax Expense	174,000	
Deferred Tax Asset	62,400	
Income Tax Payable		50,000
Deferred Tax Liability		186,400

Financial Statement Presentation—2001

Deferred tax assets and liabilities are to be classified as current and noncurrent on the balance sheet based on the classifications of related assets and liabilities. When there is more than one category of deferred taxes, they are classified into a net current amount and a net noncurrent amount. The classification of Allman's deferred tax accounts at the end of 2001 is as follows:

ILLUSTRATION 20A-8
Classification of Deferred Tax Accounts, End of 2001

Temporary Difference	Resulting Deferred Tax (Asset)	Resulting Deferred Tax Liability	Related Balance Sheet Account	Classification
Installment sales		$179,200	Installment Receivable	Current
Depreciation		7,200	Plant Assets	Noncurrent
Warranty costs	$(62,400)		Warranty Obligation	Current
Totals	$(62,400)	$186,400		

For the first temporary difference, there is a related asset on the balance sheet, installment accounts receivable. That asset is classified as a current asset because the company has a trade practice of selling to customers on an installment basis; hence, the resulting deferred tax liability is classified as a current liability. There are assets on the balance sheet that are related to the depreciation difference—the property, plant, and equipment being depreciated. The plant assets are classified as noncurrent; therefore, the resulting deferred tax liability is to be classified as noncurrent. Since Allman's operating cycle is at least 4 years in length, the entire $156,000 warranty obligation is classified as a current liability. Thus, the related deferred tax asset of $62,400 is classified as current.[1]

The balance sheet at the end of 2001 reports the following amounts:

ILLUSTRATION 20A-9
Balance Sheet Presentation of Deferred Taxes, 2001

Current liabilities	
Income tax payable	$ 50,000
Deferred tax liability ($179,200 − $62,400)	116,800
Long-term liabilities	
Deferred tax liability	$ 7,200

The income statement for 2001 reports the following:

ILLUSTRATION 20A-10
Income Statement Presentation of Income Tax Expense, 2001

Income before income taxes		$412,000
Income tax expense		
Current	$ 50,000	
Deferred	124,000	174,000
Net income		$238,000

[1]If Allman's operating cycle was less than one year in length, $56,000 of the warranty obligation would be expected to be settled within one year of the December 31, 2001, balance sheet and would require the use of current assets to settle it; thus $56,000 of the warranty obligation would be a current liability and the remaining $100,000 warranty obligation would be classified as a long-term (noncurrent) liability. This would mean $22,400 ($56,000 × 40%) of the related deferred tax asset would be classified as a current asset and $40,000 ($100,000 × 40%) of the deferred tax asset would be classified as a noncurrent asset. In doing homework problems, unless it is evident otherwise, assume a company's operating cycle is not longer than a year.

SECOND YEAR—2002

1. During 2002 the company collected $112,000 from customers for the receivables arising from contracts completed in 2001. Recovery of the remaining receivables is expected to result in taxable amounts of $112,000 in each of the following 3 years.
2. In 2002 the company completed four new contracts that allow for the customer to pay on an installment basis. These installment sales created new installment receivables. Future collections of these receivables will result in reporting gross profit of $64,000 for tax purposes in each of the next four years.
3. During 2002 Allman continued to depreciate the assets acquired in 2001 according to the depreciation schedules appearing on page 1090. Thus, depreciation amounted to $90,000 for financial reporting purposes and $172,800 for tax purposes.
4. An analysis at the end of 2002 of the product warranty liability account showed the following details:

Balance of liability at beginning of 2002	$156,000
Expense for 2002 income statement purposes	180,000
Amount paid for contracts completed in 2001	(56,000)
Amount paid for contracts completed in 2002	(50,000)
Balance of liability at end of 2002	$230,000

The balance of the liability is expected to require expenditures in the future as follows:

$100,000	in 2003 due to 2001 contracts
$ 50,000	in 2003 due to 2002 contracts
$ 80,000	in 2004 due to 2002 contracts
$230,000	

5. During 2002 nontaxable municipal bond interest revenue was $24,000.
6. A loss of $172,000 was accrued for financial reporting purposes because of pending litigation. This amount is not tax deductible until the period the loss is realized, which is estimated to be 2010.
7. Pretax financial income for 2002 amounts to $504,800.
8. The enacted tax rates still in effect are:

2001	50%
2002 and later years	40%

Taxable Income and Income Tax Payable—2002

The computation of taxable income for 2002 is as follows:

ILLUSTRATION 20A-11
Computation of Taxable Income, 2002

Pretax financial income for 2002	$504,800
Permanent difference:	
Nontaxable revenue—municipal bond interest	(24,000)
Reversing temporary differences:	
Collection on 2001 installment sales	112,000
Payments on warranties from 2001 contracts	(56,000)
Originating temporary differences:	
Excess gross profit per books—2002 contracts	(256,000)
Excess depreciation per tax	(82,800)
Excess warranty expense per books—2002 contracts	130,000
Loss accrual per books	172,000
Taxable income for 2002	$500,000

Income tax payable for 2002 is computed as follows:

ILLUSTRATION 20A-12
Computation of Income Tax Payable, End of 2002

Taxable income for 2002	$500,000
Tax rate	40%
Income tax payable (current tax expense) for 2002	$200,000

Computing Deferred Income Taxes—End of 2002

The following schedule is helpful in summarizing the temporary differences existing at the end of 2002 and the resulting future taxable and deductible amounts.

ILLUSTRATION 20A-13
Schedule of Future Taxable and Deductible Amounts, End of 2002

	Future Years					
	2003	2004	2005	2006	2010	Total
Future taxable (deductible) amounts:						
Installment sales—2001	$112,000	$112,000	$112,000			$336,000
Installment sales—2002	64,000	64,000	64,000	$64,000		256,000
Depreciation	(13,680)	27,792	27,792	58,896		100,800
Warranty costs	(150,000)	(80,000)				(230,000)
Loss accrual					$(172,000)	(172,000)

The amounts of deferred income taxes to be reported at the end of 2002 are computed as follows:

ILLUSTRATION 20A-14
Computation of Deferred Income Taxes, End of 2002

Temporary Difference	Future Taxable (Deductible) Amounts	Tax Rate	Deferred Tax (Asset)	Deferred Tax Liability
Installment sales	$592,000*	40%		$236,800
Depreciation	100,800	40%		40,320
Warranty costs	(230,000)	40%	$ (92,000)	
Loss accrual	(172,000)	40%	(68,800)	
Totals	$290,800		$(160,800)	$277,120**

*Cumulative temporary difference = $336,000 + $256,000
**Because of a flat tax rate, these totals can be reconciled: $290,800 × 40% = $(160,800) + $277,120

Deferred Tax Expense (Benefit) and the Journal Entry to Record Income Taxes—2002

To determine the deferred tax expense (benefit), the beginning and ending balances of the deferred income tax accounts must be compared.

ILLUSTRATION 20A-15
Computation of Deferred Tax Expense (Benefit), 2002

Deferred tax asset at the end of 2002	$160,800
Deferred tax asset at the beginning of 2002	62,400
Deferred tax expense (benefit)	$ (98,400)
Deferred tax liability at the end of 2002	$277,120
Deferred tax liability at the beginning of 2002	186,400
Deferred tax expense (benefit)	$ 90,720

The deferred tax expense (benefit) and the total income tax expense for 2002 are, therefore, as follows:

ILLUSTRATION 20A-16
Computation of Total Income Tax Expense, 2002

Deferred tax expense (benefit)	$ (98,400)
Deferred tax expense (benefit)	90,720
Deferred tax benefit for 2002	(7,680)
Current tax expense for 2002	200,000
Income tax expense (total) for 2002	$192,320

The deferred tax expense of $90,720 and the deferred tax benefit of $98,400 net to a deferred tax benefit of $7,680 for 2002.

The journal entry to record income taxes for 2002 is as follows:

Income Tax Expense	192,320	
Deferred Tax Asset	98,400	
Income Tax Payable		200,000
Deferred Tax Liability		90,720

Financial Statement Presentation — 2002

The classification of Allman's deferred tax accounts at the end of 2002 is as follows:

ILLUSTRATION 20A-17
Classification of Deferred Tax Accounts, End of 2002

Temporary Difference	Resulting Deferred Tax (Asset)	Resulting Deferred Tax Liability	Related Balance Sheet Account	Classification
Installment sales		$236,800	Installment Receivables	Current
Depreciation		40,320	Plant Assets	Noncurrent
Warranty costs	$ (92,000)		Warranty Obligation	Current
Loss accrual	(68,800)		Litigation Obligation	Noncurrent
Totals	$(160,800)	$277,120		

The new temporary difference introduced in 2002 (due to the litigation loss accrual) results in a litigation obligation that is classified as a long-term liability. Thus, the related deferred tax asset is noncurrent.

The balance sheet at the end of 2002 reports the following amounts:

ILLUSTRATION 20A-18
Balance Sheet Presentation of Deferred Taxes, End of 2002

Other assets (noncurrent)	
Deferred tax asset ($68,800 – $40,320)	$ 28,480
Current liabilities	
Income tax payable	$200,000
Deferred tax liability ($236,800 – $92,000)	144,800

The income statement for 2002 reports the following:

ILLUSTRATION 20A-19
Income Statement Presentation of Income Tax Expense, 2002

Income before income taxes		$504,800
Income tax expense		
Current	$200,000	
Deferred	(7,680)	192,320
Net income		$312,480

SUMMARY OF LEARNING OBJECTIVE FOR APPENDIX 20A

12 Understand and apply the concepts and procedures of interperiod tax allocation. Accounting for deferred taxes includes calculating taxable income and income tax payable for the year, computing deferred income taxes at the end of the year, determining deferred tax expense (benefit) and making the journal entry to record income taxes, and classifying deferred tax assets and liabilities as current and noncurrent in the financial statements.

QUESTIONS

1 Explain the difference between pretax financial income and taxable income.

2 What are the two objectives of accounting for income taxes?

3 Interest on municipal bonds is referred to as a permanent difference when determining the proper amount to report for deferred taxes. Explain the meaning of permanent differences and give two other examples.

4 Explain the meaning of a temporary difference as it relates to deferred tax computations and give three examples.

5 Differentiate between an originating temporary difference and a reversing difference.

6 The book basis of depreciable assets for Guinan Co. is $900,000, and the tax basis is $700,000 at the end of 2002. The enacted tax rate is 34% for all periods. Determine the amount of deferred taxes to be reported on the balance sheet at the end of 2002.

7 Borg Inc. has a deferred tax liability of $68,000 at the beginning of 2002. At the end of 2002, it reports accounts receivable on the books at $80,000 and the tax basis at zero (its only temporary difference). If the enacted tax rate is 34% for all periods, and income tax payable for the period is $230,000, determine the amount of total income tax expense to report for 2002.

8 What is the difference between a future taxable amount and a future deductible amount? When is it appropriate to record a valuation account for a deferred tax asset?

9 Pretax financial income for Mott Inc. is $300,000, and its taxable income is $100,000 for 2002. Its only temporary difference at the end of the period relates to a $90,000 difference due to excess depreciation for tax purposes. If the tax rate is 40% for all periods, compute the amount of income tax expense to report in 2002. No deferred income taxes existed at the beginning of the year.

10 How are deferred tax assets and deferred tax liabilities reported on the balance sheet?

11 Describe the procedures involved in segregating various deferred tax amounts into current and noncurrent categories.

12 How is it determined whether deferred tax amounts are considered to be "related" to specific assets or liability amounts?

13 At the end of the year, North Carolina Co. has pretax financial income of $550,000. Included in the $550,000 is $70,000 interest income on municipal bonds, $30,000 fine for dumping hazardous waste, and depreciation of $60,000. Depreciation for tax purposes is $45,000. Compute income taxes payable, assuming the tax rate is 30% for all periods.

14 Raleigh Co. has one temporary difference at the beginning of 2002 of $500,000. The deferred tax liability established for this amount is $150,000, based on a tax rate of 30%. The temporary difference will provide the following taxable amounts: $100,000 in 2003; $200,000 in 2004, and $200,000 in 2005. If a new tax rate for 2005 of 25% is enacted into law at the end of 2002, what is the journal entry necessary in 2002 (if any) to adjust deferred taxes?

15 What are some of the reasons that the components of income tax expense should be disclosed and a reconciliation between the effective tax rate and the statutory tax rate be provided?

16 Differentiate between "carryback" and "carryforward." Which can be accounted for with the greater certainty when it arises? Why?

17 What are the possible treatments for tax purposes of a net operating loss? What are the circumstances that determine the option to be applied? What is the proper treatment of a net operating loss for financial reporting purposes?

18 What is the alternative minimum tax and how does it affect the computation of deferred income taxes?

19 What controversy relates to the accounting for net operating loss carryforwards?

BRIEF EXERCISES

BE20-1 In 2002, Speedy Gonzalez Corporation had pretax financial income of $168,000 and taxable income of $110,000. The difference is due to the use of different depreciation methods for tax and accounting purposes. The effective tax rate is 40%. Compute the amount to be reported as income taxes payable at December 31, 2002.

BE20-2 At December 31, 2002, Thunderforce Inc. owned equipment that had a book value of $80,000 and a tax basis of $48,000 due to the use of different depreciation methods for accounting and tax purposes. The effective tax rate is 35%. Compute the amount Thunderforce should report as a deferred tax liability at December 31, 2002.

BE20-3 At December 31, 2001, Yserbius Corporation had a deferred tax liability of $25,000. At December 31, 2002, the deferred tax liability is $42,000. The corporation's 2002 current tax expense is $43,000. What amount should Yserbius report as total 2002 tax expense?

BE20-4 At December 31, 2002, Deep Space Nine Corporation had an estimated warranty liability of $125,000 for accounting purposes and $0 for tax purposes. (The warranty costs are not deductible until paid.) The effective tax rate is 40%. Compute the amount Deep Space Nine should report as a deferred tax asset at December 31, 2002.

BE20-5 At December 31, 2001, Next Generation Inc. had a deferred tax asset of $35,000. At December 31, 2002, the deferred tax asset is $59,000. The corporation's 2002 current tax expense is $61,000. What amount should Next Generation report as total 2002 tax expense?

BE20-6 At December 31, 2002, Stargate Corporation has a deferred tax asset of $200,000. After a careful review of all available evidence, it is determined that it is more likely than not that $80,000 of this deferred tax asset will not be realized. Prepare the necessary journal entry.

BE20-7 Steven Seagal Corporation had income before income taxes of $175,000 in 2002. Seagal's current income tax expense is $40,000, and deferred income tax expense is $30,000. Prepare Seagal's 2002 income statement, beginning with income before income taxes.

BE20-8 Tazmania Inc. had pretax financial income of $154,000 in 2002. Included in the computation of that amount is insurance expense of $4,000 which is not deductible for tax purposes. In addition, depreciation for tax purposes exceeds accounting depreciation by $14,000. Prepare Tazmania's journal entry to record 2002 taxes, assuming a tax rate of 45%.

BE20-9 Terminator Corporation has a cumulative temporary difference related to depreciation of $630,000 at December 31, 2002. This difference will reverse as follows: 2003, $42,000; 2004, $294,000; and 2005, $294,000. Enacted tax rates are 34% for 2003 and 2004, and 40% for 2005. Compute the amount Terminator should report as a deferred tax liability at December 31, 2002.

BE20-10 At December 31, 2001, Tick Corporation had a deferred tax liability of $680,000, resulting from future taxable amounts of $2,000,000 and an enacted tax rate of 34%. In May 2002, a new income tax act is signed into law that raises the tax rate to 38% for 2002 and future years. Prepare the journal entry for Tick to adjust the deferred tax liability.

BE20-11 Valis Corporation had the following tax information:

Year	Taxable Income	Tax Rate	Taxes Paid
1999	$300,000	35%	$105,000
2000	$325,000	30%	$ 97,500
2001	$400,000	30%	$120,000

In 2002 Valis suffered a net operating loss of $450,000, which it elected to carry back. The 2002 enacted tax rate is 29%. Prepare Valis's entry to record the effect of the loss carryback.

BE20-12 Zoop Inc. incurred a net operating loss of $500,000 in 2002. Combined income for 2000 and 2001 was $400,000. The tax rate for all years is 40%. Prepare the journal entries to record the benefits of the carryback and the carryforward.

BE20-13 Use the information for Zoop Inc. given in BE20-12. Assume that it is more likely than not that the entire net operating loss carryforward will not be realized in future years. Prepare all the journal entries necessary at the end of 2002.

BE20-14 Vectorman Corporation has temporary differences at 12/31/02 that result in the following deferred taxes:

Deferred tax liability—current	$38,000
Deferred tax asset—current	($52,000)
Deferred tax liability—noncurrent	$96,000
Deferred tax asset—noncurrent	($27,000)

Indicate how these balances would be presented in Vectorman's 12/31/02 balance sheet.

EXERCISES

E20-1 (One Temporary Difference, Future Taxable Amounts, One Rate, No Beginning Deferred Taxes) South Carolina Corporation has one temporary difference at the end of 2002 that will reverse and cause taxable amounts of $55,000 in 2003, $60,000 in 2004, and $65,000 in 2005. South Carolina's pretax financial income for 2002 is $300,000 and the tax rate is 30% for all years. There are no deferred taxes at the beginning of 2002.

Instructions

(a) Compute taxable income and income taxes payable for 2002.
(b) Prepare the journal entry to record income tax expense, deferred income taxes, and income taxes payable for 2002.
(c) Prepare the income tax expense section of the income statement for 2002, beginning with the line "Income before income taxes."

E20-2 (Two Differences, No Beginning Deferred Taxes, Tracked through 2 Years) The following information is available for Wenger Corporation for 2001:

1. Excess of tax depreciation over book depreciation, $40,000. This $40,000 difference will reverse equally over the years 2002–2005.
2. Deferral, for book purposes, of $20,000 of rent received in advance. The rent will be earned in 2002.
3. Pretax financial income, $300,000.
4. Tax rate for all years, 40%.

Instructions

(a) Compute taxable income for 2001.
(b) Prepare the journal entry to record income tax expense, deferred income taxes, and income taxes payable for 2001.
(c) Prepare the journal entry to record income tax expense, deferred income taxes, and income taxes payable for 2002, assuming taxable income of $325,000.

E20-3 (One Temporary Difference, Future Taxable Amounts, One Rate, Beginning Deferred Taxes) Bandung Corporation began 2002 with a $92,000 balance in the Deferred Tax Liability account. At the end of 2002, the related cumulative temporary difference amounts to $350,000, and it will reverse evenly over the next 2 years. Pretax accounting income for 2002 is $525,000, the tax rate for all years is 40%, and taxable income for 2002 is $405,000.

Instructions

(a) Compute income taxes payable for 2002.
(b) Prepare the journal entry to record income tax expense, deferred income taxes, and income taxes payable for 2002.
(c) Prepare the income tax expense section of the income statement for 2002 beginning with the line "Income before income taxes."

E20-4 (Three Differences, Compute Taxable Income, Entry for Taxes) Zurich Company reports pretax financial income of $70,000 for 2002. The following items cause taxable income to be different than pretax financial income:

1. Depreciation on the tax return is greater than depreciation on the income statement by $16,000.
2. Rent collected on the tax return is greater than rent earned on the income statement by $22,000.
3. Fines for pollution appear as an expense of $11,000 on the income statement.

Zurich's tax rate is 30% for all years and the company expects to report taxable income in all future years. There are no deferred taxes at the beginning of 2002.

Instructions

(a) Compute taxable income and income taxes payable for 2002.
(b) Prepare the journal entry to record income tax expense, deferred income taxes, and income taxes payable for 2002.

(c) Prepare the income tax expense section of the income statement for 2002, beginning with the line "Income before income taxes."
(d) Compute the effective income tax rate for 2002.

E20-5 (Two Temporary Differences, One Rate, Beginning Deferred Taxes) The following facts relate to Krung Thep Corporation:

1. Deferred tax liability, January 1, 2002, $40,000.
2. Deferred tax asset, January 1, 2002, $0.
3. Taxable income for 2002, $95,000.
4. Pretax financial income for 2002, $200,000.
5. Cumulative temporary difference at December 31, 2002, giving rise to future taxable amounts, $240,000.
6. Cumulative temporary difference at December 31, 2002, giving rise to future deductible amounts, $35,000.
7. Tax rate for all years, 40%.
8. The company is expected to operate profitably in the future.

Instructions

(a) Compute income taxes payable for 2002.
(b) Prepare the journal entry to record income tax expense, deferred income taxes, and income taxes payable for 2002.
(c) Prepare the income tax expense section of the income statement for 2002, beginning with the line "Income before income taxes."

E20-6 (Identify Temporary or Permanent Differences) Listed below are items that are commonly accounted for differently for financial reporting purposes than they are for tax purposes.

Instructions

For each item below, indicate whether it involves:

(a) A temporary difference that will result in future deductible amounts and, therefore, will usually give rise to a deferred income tax asset.
(b) A temporary difference that will result in future taxable amounts and, therefore, will usually give rise to a deferred income tax liability.
(c) A permanent difference.

Use the appropriate letter to indicate your answer for each.

_____ 1. The MACRS depreciation system is used for tax purposes, and the straight-line depreciation method is used for financial reporting purposes for some plant assets.
_____ 2. A landlord collects some rents in advance. Rents received are taxable in the period when they are received.
_____ 3. Expenses are incurred in obtaining tax-exempt income.
_____ 4. Costs of guarantees and warranties are estimated and accrued for financial reporting purposes.
_____ 5. Installment sales of investments are accounted for by the accrual method for financial reporting purposes and the installment method for tax purposes.
_____ 6. For some assets, straight-line depreciation is used for both financial reporting purposes and tax purposes but the assets' lives are shorter for tax purposes.
_____ 7. Interest is received on an investment in tax-exempt municipal obligations.
_____ 8. Proceeds are received from a life insurance company because of the death of a key officer (the company carries a policy on key officers).
_____ 9. The tax return reports a deduction for 80% of the dividends received from U.S. corporations. The cost method is used in accounting for the related investments for financial reporting purposes.
_____ 10. Estimated losses on pending lawsuits and claims are accrued for books. These losses are tax deductible in the period(s) when the related liabilities are settled.

E20-7 (Terminology, Relationships, Computations, Entries)

Instructions

Complete the following statements by filling in the blanks:

(a) In a period in which a taxable temporary difference reverses, the reversal will cause taxable income to be __________ (less than, greater than) pretax financial income.

(b) If a $76,000 balance in Deferred Tax Asset was computed by use of a 40% rate, the underlying cumulative temporary difference amounts to $________.

(c) Deferred taxes ________ (are, are not) recorded to account for permanent differences.

(d) If a taxable temporary difference originates in 2002, it will cause taxable income of 2002 to be ________ (less than, greater than) pretax financial income for 2002.

(e) If total tax expense is $50,000 and deferred tax expense is $65,000, then the current portion of the expense computation is referred to as current tax ________ (expense, benefit) of $________.

(f) If a corporation's tax return shows taxable income of $100,000 for Year 2 and a tax rate of 40%, how much will appear on the December 31, Year 2 balance sheet for "Income tax payable" if the company has made estimated tax payments of $36,500 for Year 2? $________

(g) An increase in the Deferred Tax Liability account on the balance sheet is recorded by a ________ (debit, credit) to the Income Tax Expense account.

(h) An income statement that reports current tax expense of $82,000 and deferred tax benefit of $23,000 will report total income tax expense of $________.

(i) A valuation account is needed whenever it is judged to be ________ that a portion of a deferred tax asset ________ (will be, will not be) realized.

(j) If the tax return shows total taxes due for the period of $75,000 but the income statement shows total income tax expense of $55,000, the difference of $20,000 is referred to as deferred tax ________ (expense, benefit).

E20-8 (One Temporary Difference through Three Years, One Rate) Odessa Company reports the following amounts in its first three years of operations:

	2002	2003	2004
Taxable income	160,000	139,000	140,000
Pretax financial income	200,000	120,000	125,000

The difference between taxable income and pretax financial income is due to one temporary difference. The tax rate is 40% for all years and the company expects to continue with profitable operations in the future.

Instructions

(a) For each year, (1) identify the amount of the temporary difference originating or reversing during that year, and (2) indicate the amount of the cumulative temporary difference at the end of the year.

(b) Indicate the balance in the related deferred tax account at the end of each year and identify it as either a deferred tax asset or liability.

E20-9 (Carryback and Carryforward of NOL, No Valuation Account, No Temporary Differences) The pretax financial income (or loss) figures for Jenny Spangler Company are as follows:

1997	$160,000
1998	250,000
1999	80,000
2000	(160,000)
2001	(380,000)
2002	120,000
2003	100,000

Pretax financial income (or loss) and taxable income (loss) were the same for all years involved. Assume a 45% tax rate for 1997 and 1998 and a 40% tax rate for the remaining years.

Instructions

Prepare the journal entries for the years 1999 to 2003 to record income tax expense and the effects of the net operating loss carrybacks and carryforwards assuming Jenny Spangler Company uses the carryback provision. All income and losses relate to normal operations. (In recording the benefits of a loss carryforward, assume that no valuation account is deemed necessary.)

E20-10 (2 NOLs, No Temporary Differences, No Valuation Account, Entries and Income Statement) Felicia Rashad Corporation has pretax financial income (or loss) equal to taxable income (or loss) form 1994 through 2002 as follows:

	Income (Loss)	Tax Rate
1994	$29,000	30%
1995	40,000	30%
1996	17,000	35%
1997	48,000	50%
1998	(150,000)	40%
1999	90,000	40%
2000	30,000	40%
2001	105,000	40%
2002	(60,000)	45%

Pretax financial income (loss) and taxable income (loss) were the same for all years since Rashad has been in business. Assume the carryback provision is employed for net operating losses. In recording the benefits of a loss carryforward, assume that it is more likely than not that the related benefits will be realized.

Instructions

(a) What entry(ies) for income taxes should be recorded for 1998?
(b) Indicate what the income tax expense portion of the income statement for 1998 should look like. Assume all income (loss) relates to continuing operations.
(c) What entry for income taxes should be recorded in 1999?
(d) How should the income tax expense section of the income statement for 1999 appear?
(e) What entry for income taxes should be recorded in 2002?
(f) How should the income tax expense section of the income statement for 2002 appear?

E20-11 (Three Differences, Classify Deferred Taxes) At December 31, 2001, Surya Bonilay Company had a net deferred tax liability of $375,000. An explanation of the items that compose this balance is as follows:

Temporary Differences	Resulting Balances in Deferred Taxes
1. Excess of tax depreciation over book depreciation	$200,000
2. Accrual, for book purposes, of estimated loss contingency from pending lawsuit that is expected to be settled in 2002. The loss will be deducted on the tax return when paid.	(50,000)
3. Accrual method used for book purposes and installment method used for tax purposes for an isolated installment sale of an investment.	225,000
	$375,000

In analyzing the temporary differences, you find that $30,000 of the depreciation temporary difference will reverse in 2002 and $120,000 of the temporary difference due to the installment sale will reverse in 2002. The tax rate for all years is 40%.

Instructions

Indicate the manner in which deferred taxes should be presented on Surya Bonilay Company's December 31, 2001, balance sheet.

E20-12 (Two Temporary Differences, One Rate, Beginning Deferred Taxes, Compute Pretax Financial Income) The following facts relate to Sabrina Duncan Corporation:

1. Deferred tax liability, January 1, 2002, $60,000.
2. Deferred tax asset, January 1, 2002, $20,000.
3. Taxable income for 2002, $105,000.
4. Cumulative temporary difference at December 31, 2002, giving rise to future taxable amounts, $230,000.
5. Cumulative temporary difference at December 31, 2002, giving rise to future deductible amounts, $95,000.
6. Tax rate for all years, 40%. No permanent differences exist.
7. The company is expected to operate profitably in the future.

Instructions

(a) Compute the amount of pretax financial income for 2002.
(b) Prepare the journal entry to record income tax expense, deferred income taxes, and income taxes payable for 2002.
(c) Prepare the income tax expense section of the income statement for 2002, beginning with the line "Income before income taxes."
(d) Compute the effective tax rate for 2002.

E20-13 (One Difference, Multiple Rates, Effect of Beginning Balance versus No Beginning Deferred Taxes) At the end of 2001, Lucretia McEvil Company has $180,000 of cumulative temporary differences that will result in reporting future taxable amounts as follows:

2002	$ 60,000
2003	50,000
2004	40,000
2005	30,000
	$180,000

Tax rates enacted as of the beginning of 2000 are:

2000 and 2001	40%
2002 and 2003	30%
2004 and later	25%

McEvil's taxable income for 2001 is $320,000. Taxable income is expected in all future years.

Instructions

(a) Prepare the journal entry for McEvil to record income taxes payable, deferred income taxes, and income tax expense for 2001, assuming that there were no deferred taxes at the end of 2000.

(b) Prepare the journal entry for McEvil to record income taxes payable, deferred income taxes, and income tax expense for 2001, assuming that there was a balance of $22,000 in a Deferred Tax Liability account at the end of 2000.

E20-14 (Deferred Tax Asset with and without Valuation Account) Jennifer Capriati Corp. has a deferred tax asset account with a balance of $150,000 at the end of 2001 due to a single cumulative temporary difference of $375,000. At the end of 2002 this same temporary difference has increased to a cumulative amount of $450,000. Taxable income for 2002 is $820,000. The tax rate is 40% for all years. No valuation account related to the deferred tax asset is in existence at the end of 2001.

Instructions

(a) Record income tax expense, deferred income taxes, and income taxes payable for 2002, assuming that it is more likely than not that the deferred tax asset will be realized.

(b) Assuming that it is more likely than not that $30,000 of the deferred tax asset will not be realized, prepare the journal entry at the end of 2002 to record the valuation account.

E20-15 (Deferred Tax Asset with Previous Valuation Account) Assume the same information as E20-14, except that at the end of 2001, Jennifer Capriati Corp. had a valuation account related to its deferred tax asset of $45,000.

Instructions

(a) Record income tax expense, deferred income taxes, and income taxes payable for 2002, assuming that it is more likely than not that the deferred tax asset will be realized in full.

(b) Record income tax expense, deferred income taxes, and income taxes payable for 2002, assuming that it is more likely than not that none of the deferred tax asset will be realized.

E20-16 (Deferred Tax Liability, Change in Tax Rate, Prepare Section of Income Statement) Jana Novotna Inc.'s only temporary difference at the beginning and end of 2001 is caused by a $3 million deferred gain for tax purposes for an installment sale of a plant asset, and the related receivable (only one-half of which is classified as a current asset) is due in equal installments in 2002 and 2003. The related deferred tax liability at the beginning of the year is $1,200,000. In the third quarter of 2001, a new tax rate of 34% is enacted into law and is scheduled to become effective for 2003. Taxable income for 2001 is $5,000,000 and taxable income is expected in all future years.

Instructions

(a) Determine the amount reported as a deferred tax liability at the end of 2001. Indicate proper classification(s).

(b) Prepare the journal entry (if any) necessary to adjust the deferred tax liability when the new tax rate is enacted into law.

(c) Draft the income tax expense portion of the income statement for 2001. Begin with the line "Income before income taxes." Assume no permanent differences exist.

E20-17 (Two Temporary Differences, Tracked through 3 Years, Multiple Rates) Taxable income and pretax financial income would be identical for Anke Huber Co. except for its treatments of gross profit on installment sales and estimated costs of warranties. The following income computations have been prepared:

Taxable income	2001	2002	2003
Excess of revenues over expenses (excluding two temporary differences)	$160,000	$210,000	$90,000
Installment gross profit collected	8,000	8,000	8,000
Expenditures for warranties	(5,000)	(5,000)	(5,000)
Taxable income	$163,000	$213,000	$93,000

Pretax financial income	2001	2002	2003
Excess of revenues over expenses (excluding two temporary differences)	$160,000	$210,000	$90,000
Installment gross profit earned	24,000	–0–	–0–
Estimated cost of warranties	(15,000)	–0–	–0–
Income before taxes	$169,000	$210,000	$90,000

The tax rates in effect are: 2001, 40%; 2002 and 2003, 45%. All tax rates were enacted into law on January 1, 2001. No deferred income taxes existed at the beginning of 2001. Taxable income is expected in all future years.

Instructions

Prepare the journal entry to record income tax expense, deferred income taxes, and income tax payable for 2001, 2002, and 2003.

E20-18 (Two Differences, Multiple Rates, No Beginning Deferred Taxes) In 2001, Wolf Company reported depreciation of $200,000 in its income statement. On its 2001 income tax return, Wolf reported depreciation of $320,000. Wolf's income statement also included $80,000 accrued warranty expense that will be deducted when paid for tax purposes. Wolf reported pretax financial income of $300,000 in 2001. The enacted tax rates are 35% for 2001 and 2002, and 40% for 2003 and subsequent years. The depreciation difference and warranty expense will reverse over the next four years as follows:

	Depreciation Difference	Warranty Expense
2002	$ 40,000	$10,000
2003	35,000	15,000
2004	25,000	25,000
2005	20,000	30,000
	$120,000	$80,000

Instructions

(a) Compute income taxes payable for 2001.

(b) Prepare the journal entry to record income tax expense, deferred income taxes, and income taxes payable for 2001.

(c) Prepare the income tax expense section of the income statement for 2001, beginning with the line "Income before taxes."

E20-19 (Two Differences, One Rate, Pretax Financial Loss) Jenny McCarthy Inc., in its first year of operations, has a pretax financial loss even though it has taxable income. A reconciliation between these two amounts for the calendar year 2002 is as follows:

Pretax financial loss	$ (50,000)
Estimated expenses that will be deductible for tax purposes when paid	2,000,000
Additional depreciation taken for tax purposes	(1,200,000)
Taxable income	$ 750,000

At the end of 2002, the reported amount of McCarthy's depreciable assets in the financial statements is $3 million, and the tax basis of these assets is $1.8 million. Future recovery of the depreciable assets will result in $1,200,000 of taxable amounts ($300,000 per year in years 2003–2006) over the 4-year remaining life of the assets. Also, a $2,000,000 estimated liability for litigation expenses has been recognized in the financial statements in 2002, but the related expenses will be deductible on the tax return in 2005 when the liability is expected to be settled. McCarthy expects to report taxable income in the next few years.

Instructions

Prepare the journal entry (if any) to record income tax expense, income tax payable, and deferred income taxes for 2002, assuming a tax rate of 40% for all periods.

E20-20 (Three Differences, Multiple Rates, Future Taxable Income) During 2002, Anna Nicole Smith Co.'s first year of operations, the company reports pretax financial income at $250,000. Smith's enacted tax rate is 45% for 2002 and 40% for all later years. Smith expects to have taxable income in each of the next 5 years. The effects on future tax returns of temporary differences existing at December 31, 2002, are summarized below:

	Future Years					
	2003	2004	2005	2006	2007	Total
Future taxable (deductible) amounts:						
Installment sales	$32,000	$32,000	$32,000			$ 96,000
Depreciation	6,000	6,000	6,000	$6,000	$6,000	30,000
Unearned rent	(50,000)	(50,000)				(100,000)

Instructions

(a) Complete the schedule below to compute deferred taxes at December 31, 2002.
(b) Compute taxable income for 2002.
(c) Prepare the journal entry to record income tax payable, deferred taxes, and income tax expense for 2002.

Temporary Difference	Future Taxable (Deductible) Amounts	Tax Rate	December 31, 2002 Deferred Tax (Asset)	Liability
Installment sales	$ 96,000			
Depreciation	30,000			
Unearned rent	(100,000)			
Totals	$			

E20-21 (Two Differences, One Rate, Beginning Deferred Balance, Compute Pretax Financial Income) Sharon Stone Co. establishes a $100 million liability at the end of 2002 for the estimated costs of closing two of its manufacturing facilities. All related closing costs will be paid and deducted on the tax return in 2003. Also, at the end of 2002, the company has $50 million of temporary differences due to excess depreciation for tax purposes, $7 million of which will reverse in 2003.

The enacted tax rate for all years is 40%, and the company pays taxes of $64 million on $160 million of taxable income in 2002. Stone expects to have taxable income in 2003.

Instructions

(a) Determine the deferred taxes to be reported at the end of 2002.
(b) Indicate how the deferred taxes computed in (a) are to be reported on the balance sheet.
(c) Assuming that the only deferred tax account at the beginning of 2002 was a deferred tax liability of $10,000,000, draft the income tax expense portion of the income statement for 2002 beginning with the line "Income before income taxes." (*Hint:* You must first compute (1) the amount of temporary difference underlying the beginning $10,000,000 deferred tax liability, then (2) the amount of temporary differences originating or reversing during the year, then (3) the amount of pretax financial income.)

E20-22 (Two Differences, No Beginning Deferred Taxes, Multiple Rates) Teri Hatcher Inc., in its first year of operations, has the following differences between the book basis and tax basis of its assets and liabilities at the end of 2001.

	Book Basis	Tax Basis
Equipment (net)	$400,000	$340,000
Estimated warranty liability	$200,000	$ –0–

It is estimated that the warranty liability will be settled in 2002. The difference in equipment (net) will result in taxable amounts of $20,000 in 2002, $30,000 in 2003, and $10,000 in 2004. The company has taxable income of $520,000 in 2001. As of the beginning of 2001, the enacted tax rate is 34% for 2001–2003, and 30% for 2004. Hatcher expects to report taxable income through 2004.

Instructions

(a) Prepare the journal entry to record income tax expense, deferred income taxes, and income tax payable for 2001.
(b) Indicate how deferred income taxes will be reported on the balance sheet at the end of 2001.

E20-23 (Depreciation, Temporary Difference Tracked over 5 Years) Patricia Ford Co. purchased depreciable assets costing $600,000 on January 2, 2000. For tax purposes, the company uses the elective straight-line depreciation method over the recovery period of 3 years. (*Hint:* The half-year convention must be used on these assets.) For financial reporting purposes, the company uses straight-line depreciation over 5 years. The enacted tax rate is 34% for all years. This depreciation difference is the only temporary difference the company has. Assume that Ford has taxable income of $240,000 in each of the years 2000–2004.

Instructions

Determine the amount of deferred income taxes and indicate where it should be reported in the balance sheet for each year from 2000 to 2004.

E20-24 (Two Temporary Differences, Multiple Rates, Future Taxable Income) Svetlana Boginskaya Inc. has two temporary differences at the end of 2001. The first difference stems from installment sales and the second one results from the accrual of a loss contingency. Boginskaya's accounting department has developed a schedule of future taxable and deductible amounts related to these temporary differences as follows:

	2002	2003	2004	2005
Taxable amounts	$40,000	$50,000	$60,000	$80,000
Deductible amounts		(15,000)	(19,000)	
	$40,000	$35,000	$41,000	$80,000

As of the beginning of 2001, the enacted tax rate is 34% for 2001 and 2002 and 38% for 2003–2006. At the beginning of 2001, the company had no deferred income taxes on its balance sheet. Taxable income for 2001 is $500,000. Taxable income is expected in all future years.

Instructions

(a) Prepare the journal entry to record income tax expense, deferred income taxes, and income taxes payable for 2001.

(b) Indicate how deferred income taxes would be classified on the balance sheet at the end of 2001.

E20-25 (Two Differences, One Rate, First Year) The differences between the book basis and tax basis of the assets and liabilities of JoAnn Castle Corporation at the end of 2001 are presented below:

	Book Basis	Tax Basis
Accounts receivable	$50,000	$–0–
Litigation liability	30,000	–0–

It is estimated that the litigation liability will be settled in 2002. The difference in accounts receivable will result in taxable amounts of $30,000 in 2002 and $20,000 in 2003. The company has taxable income of $350,000 in 2001 and is expected to have taxable income in each of the following 2 years. Its enacted tax rate is 34% for all years. This is the company's first year of operations. The operating cycle of the business is 2 years.

Instructions

(a) Prepare the journal entry to record income tax expense, deferred income taxes, and income tax payable for 2001.

(b) Indicate how deferred income taxes will be reported on the balance sheet at the end of 2001.

E20-26 (NOL Carryback and Carryforward, Valuation Account versus No Valuation Account) Spamela Hamderson Inc. reports the following pretax income (loss) for both financial reporting purposes and tax purposes (assume the carryback provision is used for a net operating loss):

Year	Pretax Income (Loss)	Tax Rate
2000	$120,000	34%
2001	90,000	34%
2002	(280,000)	38%
2003	220,000	38%

The tax rates listed were all enacted by the beginning of 2000.

Instructions

(a) Prepare the journal entries for the years 2000–2003 to record income tax expense (benefit) and income tax payable (refundable) and the tax effects of the loss carryback and carryforward, assuming that at the end of 2002 the benefits of the loss carryforward are judged more likely than not to be realized in the future.

(b) Using the assumption in (a), prepare the income tax section of the 2002 income statement beginning with the line "Operating loss before income taxes."

(c) Prepare the journal entries for 2002 and 2003, assuming that based on the weight of available evidence, it is more likely than not that one-fourth of the benefits of the carryforward will not be realized.

(d) Using the assumption in (c), prepare the income tax section of the 2002 income statement beginning with the line "Operating loss before income taxes."

E20-27 (NOL Carryback and Carryforward, Valuation Account Needed) Denise Beilman Inc. reports the following pretax income (loss) for both book and tax purposes (assume the carryback provision is used where possible for a net operating loss):

Year	Pretax Income (Loss)	Tax Rate
2000	$120,000	40%
2001	90,000	40%
2002	(280,000)	45%
2003	120,000	45%

The tax rates listed were all enacted by the beginning of 2000.

Instructions

(a) Prepare the journal entries for years 2000–2003 to record income tax expense (benefit) and income tax payable (refundable) and the tax effects of the loss carryback and carryforward, assuming that based on the weight of available evidence, it is more likely than not that one-half of the benefits of the carryforward will not be realized.

(b) Prepare the income tax section of the 2002 income statement beginning with the line "Operating loss before income taxes."

(c) Prepare the income tax section of the 2003 income statement beginning with the line "Income before income taxes."

E20-28 (NOL Carryback and Carryforward, Valuation Account Needed) Meyer reported the following pretax financial income (loss) for the years 2000–2004:

2000	$240,000
2001	350,000
2002	120,000
2003	(570,000)
2004	180,000

Pretax financial income (loss) and taxable income (loss) were the same for all years involved. The enacted tax rate was 34% for 2000 and 2001, and 40% for 2002–2004. Assume the carryback provision is used first for net operating losses.

Instructions

(a) Prepare the journal entries for the years 2002–2004 to record income tax expense, income tax payable (refundable), and the tax effects of the loss carryback and carryforward, assuming that based on the weight of available evidence, it is more likely than not that one-fifth of the benefits of the carryforward will not be realized.

(b) Prepare the income tax section of the 2003 income statement beginning with the line "Income (loss) before income taxes."

PROBLEMS

P20-1 (Three Differences, No Beginning Deferred Taxes, Multiple Rates) The following information is available for Swanson Corporation for 2001:

1. Depreciation reported on the tax return exceeded depreciation reported on the income statement by $100,000. This difference will reverse in equal amounts of $25,000 over the years 2002–2005.
2. Interest received on municipal bonds was $10,000.
3. Rent collected in advance on January 1, 2001, totaled $60,000 for a 3-year period. Of this amount, $40,000 was reported as unearned at December 31, for book purposes.
4. The tax rates are 40% for 2001 and 35% for 2002 and subsequent years.
5. Income taxes of $360,000 are due per the tax return for 2001.
6. No deferred taxes existed at the beginning of 2001.

Instructions

(a) Compute taxable income for 2001.
(b) Compute pretax financial income for 2001.
(c) Prepare the journal entries to record income tax expense, deferred income taxes, and income taxes payable for 2001 and 2002. Assume taxable income was $980,000 in 2002.
(d) Prepare the income tax expense section of the income statement for 2001, beginning with "Income before income taxes."

P20-2 (One Temporary Difference, Tracked for 4 Years, One Permanent Difference, Change in Rate) The pretax financial income of Kristal Parker-Gregory Company differs from its taxable income throughout each of 4 years as follows:

Year	Pretax Financial Income	Taxable Income	Tax Rate
2002	$280,000	$180,000	35%
2003	320,000	225,000	40%
2004	350,000	270,000	40%
2005	420,000	580,000	40%

Pretax financial income for each year includes a nondeductible expense of $30,000 (never deductible for tax purposes). The remainder of the difference between pretax financial income and taxable income in each period is due to one depreciation temporary difference. No deferred income taxes existed at the beginning of 2002.

Instructions

(a) Prepare journal entries to record income taxes in all 4 years. Assume that the change in the tax rate to 40% was not enacted until the beginning of 2003.
(b) Draft the income tax section of the income statement for 2003.

P20-3 (Second Year of Depreciation Difference, Two Differences, Single Rate, Extraordinary Item) The following information has been obtained for the Tracy Kerdyk Corporation.

1. Prior to 2001, taxable income and pretax financial income were identical.
2. Pretax financial income is $1,700,000 in 2001 and $1,400,000 in 2002.
3. On January 1, 2001, equipment costing $1,000,000 is purchased. It is to be depreciated on a straight-line basis over 5 years for tax purposes and over 8 years for financial reporting purposes. (*Hint:* Use the half-year convention for tax purposes.)
4. Interest of $60,000 was earned on tax-exempt municipal obligations in 2002.
5. Included in 2002 pretax financial income is an extraordinary gain of $200,000, which is fully taxable.
6. The tax rate is 35% for all periods.
7. Taxable income is expected in all future years.

Instructions

(a) Compute taxable income and income tax payable for 2002.
(b) Prepare the journal entry to record 2002 income tax expense, income tax payable, and deferred taxes.
(c) Prepare the bottom portion of Kerdyk's 2002 income statement, beginning with "Income before income taxes and extraordinary item."
(d) Indicate how deferred income taxes should be presented on the December 31, 2002, balance sheet.

P20-4 (Multiple Rates, Future Losses versus Future Income) Vijay Singh Co. started operations in 2001. A reconciliation of its pretax financial income to its taxable income for 2001 is as follows:

Pretax financial income	$24,000,000
Litigation accrual for book purposes	8,000,000
Excess depreciation for tax purposes	(3,000,000)
Taxable income	$29,000,000

As of the beginning of 2001, enacted tax rates are 35% for 2001 and 2002, and 40% for all subsequent years. It is estimated that the litigation accrual will be settled in 2006 and that the temporary difference due to the excess depreciation of tax purposes will reverse equally over the 3-year period from 2002 to 2004.

Instructions

(a) Determine the income tax payable, deferred income taxes, and income tax expense to be reported for 2001 assuming that taxable income is expected in all future years.

(b) Classify the deferred income taxes computed in (a) into current and noncurrent components. Explain where the deferred taxes should appear on the balance sheet.
(c) Determine the income tax payable, deferred income taxes, and income tax expense for 2001 assuming that net operating losses are expected to appear on tax returns for 2002 through 2006 and taxable income is very likely for 2007 and later years.
(d) Classify the deferred income taxes computed in (c) into current and noncurrent components. Explain where the deferred taxes should appear on the balance sheet.

P20-5 (Actual NOL without Valuation Account) Mark O'Meara Inc. reported the following pretax income (loss) and related tax rates during the years 1997–2003:

	Pretax Income (loss)	Tax Rate
1997	$ 40,000	30%
1998	25,000	30%
1999	60,000	30%
2000	80,000	40%
2001	(200,000)	45%
2002	70,000	40%
2003	90,000	35%

Pretax financial income (loss) and taxable income (loss) were the same for all years since O'Meara began business. The tax rates from 2000 to 2003 were enacted in 2000.

Instructions

(a) Prepare the journal entries for the years 2001–2003 to record income tax payable (refundable), income tax expense (benefit), and the tax effects of the loss carryback and carryforward. Assume that O'Meara elects the carryback provision where possible and expects to realize the benefits of any loss carryforward in the year that immediately follows the loss year.
(b) Indicate the effect the 2001 entry(ies) has on the December 31, 2001, balance sheet.
(c) Indicate how the bottom portion of the income statement, starting with "Operating loss before income taxes," would be reported in 2001.
(d) Indicate how the bottom portion of the income statement, starting with "Income before income taxes," would be reported in 2002.

P20-6 (Two Differences, Two Rates, Future Income Expected) Presented below are two independent situations related to future taxable and deductible amounts resulting from temporary differences existing at December 31, 2001.

1. Pirates Co. has developed the following schedule of future taxable and deductible amounts:

	2002	2003	2004	2005	2006
Taxable amounts	$300	$300	$300	$ 300	$300
Deductible amount	—	—	—	(1,400)	—

2. Eagles Co. has the following schedule of future taxable and deductible amounts:

	2002	2003	2004	2005
Taxable amounts	$300	$300	$ 300	$300
Deductible amount	—	—	(2,000)	—

Both Pirates Co. and Eagles Co. have taxable income of $3,000 in 2001 and expect to have taxable income in all future years. The tax rates enacted as of the beginning of 2001 are 30% for 2001–2004 and 35% for years thereafter. All of the underlying temporary differences relate to noncurrent assets and liabilities.

Instructions

For each of these two situations, compute the net amount of deferred income taxes to be reported at the end of 2001 and indicate how it should be classified on the balance sheet.

P20-7 (One Temporary Difference, Tracked 3 Years, Change in Rates, Income Statement Presentation) Gators Corp. sold an investment on an installment basis. The total gain of $60,000 was reported for financial reporting purposes in the period of sale. The company qualifies to use installment method for tax purposes. The installment period is 3 years; one-third of the sale price is collected in the period of sale. The tax rate was 35% in 2001 and 30% in 2002 and 2003. The 30% tax rate was not enacted in law until 2002. The accounting and tax data for the 3 years is shown below.

	Financial Accounting	Tax Return
2001 (35% tax rate)		
Income before temporary difference	$ 70,000	$70,000
Temporary difference	60,000	20,000
Income	$130,000	$90,000
2002 (30% tax rate)		
Income before temporary difference	$ 70,000	$70,000
Temporary difference	–0–	20,000
Income	$ 70,000	$90,000
2003 (30% tax rate)		
Income before temporary difference	$70,000	$70,000
Temporary difference	–0–	20,000
Income	$70,000	$90,000

Instructions

(a) Prepare the journal entries to record the income tax expense, deferred income taxes, and the income tax payable at the end of each year. No deferred income taxes existed at the beginning of 2001.

(b) Explain how the deferred taxes will appear on the balance sheet at the end of each year. (Assume the Installment Accounts Receivable is classified as a current asset.)

(c) Draft the income tax expense section of the income statement for each year, beginning with "Income before income taxes."

P20-8 (Two Differences, 2 Years, Compute Taxable Income and Pretax Financial Income) The following information was disclosed during the audit of Thomas Muster Inc.

1.

Year	Amount Due per Tax Return
2001	$140,000
2002	112,000

2. On January 1, 2001, equipment costing $400,000 is purchased. For financial reporting purposes, the company uses straight-line depreciation over a 5-year life. For tax purposes, the company uses the elective straight-line method over a 5-year life. (*Hint:* For tax purposes, the half-year convention must be used.)

3. In January 2002, $225,000 is collected in advance rental of a building for a 3-year period. The entire $225,000 is reported as taxable income in 2002, but $150,000 of the $225,000 is reported as unearned revenue in 2002 for financial reporting purposes. The remaining amount of unearned revenue is to be earned equally in 2003 and 2004.

4. The tax rate is 40% in 2001 and all subsequent periods. (*Hint:* To find taxable income in 2001 and 2002 the related income tax payable amounts will have to be grossed up.)

5. No temporary differences existed at the end of 2000. Muster expects to report taxable income in each of the next 5 years.

Instructions

(a) Determine the amount to report for deferred income taxes at the end of 2001 and indicate how it should be classified on the balance sheet.

(b) Prepare the journal entry to record income taxes for 2001.

(c) Draft the income tax section of the income statement for 2001 beginning with "Income before income taxes." (*Hint:* You must compute taxable income and then combine that with changes in cumulative temporary differences to arrive at pretax financial income.)

(d) Determine the deferred income taxes at the end of 2002 and indicate how they should be classified on the balance sheet.

(e) Prepare the journal entry to record income taxes for 2002.

(f) Draft the income tax section of the income statement for 2002 beginning with "Income before income taxes."

P20-9 (Five Differences, Compute Taxable Income and Deferred Taxes, Draft Income Statement) Martha King Company began operations at the beginning of 2000. The following information pertains to this company.

1. Pretax financial income for 2000 is $100,000.
2. The tax rate enacted for 2000 and future years is 40%
3. Differences between the 2000 income statement and tax return are listed below:
   (a) Warranty expense accrued for financial reporting purposes amounts to $5,000. Warranty deductions per the tax return amount to $2,000.
   (b) Gross profit on construction contracts using the percentage-of-completion method for books amounts to $92,000. Gross profit on construction contracts for tax purposes amounts to $62,000.
   (c) Depreciation of property, plant, and equipment for financial reporting purposes amounts to $60,000. Depreciation of these assets amounts to $80,000 for the tax return.
   (d) A $3,500 fine paid for violation of pollution laws was deducted in computing pretax financial income.
   (e) Interest revenue earned on an investment in tax-exempt municipal bonds amounts to $1,400. (Assume (a) is short-term in nature; assume (b) and(c) are long-term in nature.)
4. Taxable income is expected for the next few years.

Instructions

(a) Compute taxable income for 2000.
(b) Compute the deferred taxes at December 31, 2000, that relate to the temporary differences described above. Clearly label them as deferred tax asset or liability.
(c) Prepare the journal entry to record income tax expense, deferred taxes, and income taxes payable for 2000.
(d) Draft the income tax expense section of the income statement begining with "Income before income taxes."

CONCEPTUAL CASES

C20-1 (Objectives and Principles for Accounting for Income Taxes) The amount of income taxes due to the government for a period of time is rarely the amount reported on the income statement for that period as income tax expense.

Instructions

(a) Explain the objectives of accounting for income taxes in general purpose financial statements.
(b) Explain the basic principles that are applied in accounting for income taxes at the date of the financial statements to meet the objectives discussed in (a).
(c) List the steps in the annual computation of deferred tax liabilities and assets.

C20-2 (Basic Accounting for Temporary Differences) The Iva Majoli Company appropriately uses the asset-liability method to record deferred income taxes. Iva Majoli reports depreciation expense for certain machinery purchased this year using the modified accelerated cost recovery system (MACRS) for income tax purposes and the straight-line basis for financial reporting purposes. The tax deduction is the larger amount this year.

Iva Majoli received rent revenues in advance this year. These revenues are included in this year's taxable income. However, for financial reporting purposes, these revenues are reported as unearned revenues, a current liability.

Instructions

(a) What are the principles of the asset-liability approach?
(b) How would Majoli account for the temporary differences?
(c) How should Majoli classify the deferred tax consequences of the temporary differences on its balance sheet?

C20-3 (Identify Temporary Differences and Classification Criteria) The asset-liability approach for recording deferred income taxes is an integral part of generally accepted accounting principles.

Instructions

(a) Indicate whether each of the following independent situations should be treated as a temporary difference or a permanent difference and explain why.
   (1) Estimated warranty costs (covering a 3-year warranty) are expensed for financial reporting purposes at the time of sale but deducted for income tax purposes when paid.
   (2) Depreciation for book and income tax purposes differs because of different bases of carrying the related property, which was acquired in a trade-in. The different bases are a result of different rules used for book and tax purposes to compute the basis of property acquired in a trade-in.

(3) A company properly uses the equity method to account for its 30% investment in another company. The investee pays dividends that are about 10% of its annual earnings.
(4) A company reports a gain on an involuntary conversion of a nonmonetary asset to a monetary asset. The company elects to replace the property within the statutory period using the total proceeds so the gain is not reported on the current year's tax return.

(b) Discuss the nature of the deferred income tax accounts and possible classifications in a company's balance sheet. Indicate the manner in which these accounts are to be reported.

C20-4 (Identify Permanent or Temporary Differences, Future Taxable or Deductible Amounts, Deferred Tax Asset or Liability) Listed below are 16 of the more common items that are treated differently for financial reporting purposes than they are for tax purposes.

1. Excess of charge to accounting records (allowance method) over charge to tax return (direct write-off method) for uncollectible receivables.
2. Excess of accrued pension expense over amount paid.
3. The 80% deduction for dividends received from U.S. corporations.
4. Installment sales of investments are accounted for on the accrual basis for financial reporting purposes and on the installment (cash) basis for tax purposes.
5. Expenses incurred in obtaining tax-exempt income.
6. A trademark acquired directly from the government is capitalized and amortized over subsequent periods for accounting purposes and expensed for tax purposes.
7. Prepaid advertising expense deferred for accounting purposes and deducted as an expense for tax purposes.
8. Premiums paid on life insurance of officers (corporation is the beneficiary).
9. Penalty for filing a late tax return.
10. Proceeds of life insurance policies on lives of officers.
11. Estimated future warranty costs.
12. Fine for polluting.
13. Excess of tax depreciation over accounting depreciation.
14. Tax-exempt interest revenue.
15. Excess of percentage depletion for tax purposes over cost depletion.
16. Estimated gross profit on long-term construction contract is reported in the income statement; some of this gross profit is deferred for tax purposes.

Instructions

For each item above:

(a) Indicate if it is:
(1) A permanent difference, or
(2) A temporary difference.

(b) Indicate if it will:
(1) Create future taxable amounts, or
(2) Create future deductible amounts, or
(3) Not affect any future tax returns.

(c) Indicate if it usually will:
(1) Result in reporting a deferred tax liability, or
(2) Result in reporting a deferred tax asset, or
(3) Not result in reporting any deferred taxes.

C20-5 (Accounting and Classification of Deferred Income Taxes)

Part A

This year Lindsay Davenport Company has each of the following items in its income statement:

1. Gross profits on installment sales.
2. Revenues on long-term construction contracts.
3. Estimated costs of product warranty contracts.
4. Premiums on officers' life insurance with Davenport as beneficiary.

Instructions

(a) Under what conditions would deferred income taxes need to be reported in the financial statements?

(b) Specify when deferred income taxes would need to be recognized for each of the items above, and indicate the rationale for such recognition.

Part B

Davenport Company's president has heard that deferred income taxes can be classified in different ways in the balance sheet.

Instructions

Identify the conditions under which deferred income taxes would be classified as a noncurrent item in the balance sheet. What justification exists for such classification?

(AICPA adapted)

C20-6 (Explain Computation of Deferred Tax Liability for Multiple Tax Rates) At December 31, 2002, Martina Hingis Corporation has one temporary difference which will reverse and cause taxable amounts in 2003. In 2002 a new tax act set taxes equal to 45% for 2002, 40% for 2003, and 34% for 2004 and years thereafter.

Instructions

Explain what circumstances would call for Martina Hingis to compute its deferred tax liability at the end of 2002 by multiplying the cumulative temporary difference by:

(a) 45%.
(b) 40%.
(c) 34%.

C20-7 (Explain Future Taxable and Deductible Amounts, How Carryback and Carryforward Affects Deferred Taxes) Mary Joe Fernandez and Meredith McGrath are discussing accounting for income taxes. They are currently studying a schedule of taxable and deductible amounts that will arise in the future as a result of existing temporary differences. The schedule is as follows:

	Current Year	Future Years			
	2002	2003	2004	2005	2006
Taxable income	$850,000				
Taxable amounts		$375,000	$375,000	$ 375,000	$375,000
Deductible amounts				(2,400,000)	
Enacted tax rate	50%	45%	40%	35%	30%

Instructions

(a) Explain the concept of future taxable amounts and future deductible amounts as illustrated in the schedule.
(b) How do the carryback and carryforward provisions affect the reporting of deferred tax assets and deferred tax liabilities?

USING YOUR JUDGMENT

FINANCIAL REPORTING PROBLEM: INTEL CORPORATION

Instructions

Refer to the financial statements and accompanying notes and discussion of Intel Corporation presented in Appendix 5B and answer the following questions.

(a) What amounts relative to income taxes does Intel report in its:

(1) 1998 income statement?

(2) December 26, 1998 balance sheet?

(3) 1998 statement of cash flows?

(b) Intel's provision for income taxes in 1996, 1997, and 1998 was computed at what effective tax rates (see notes to the financial statements)?

(c) How much of Intel's 1998 total provision for income taxes was current tax expense and how much was deferred tax expense?

(d) What did Intel report as the significant components (the details) of its December 26, 1998 deferred tax assets and liabilities?

(e) Briefly, what does Intel disclose about the Internal Revenue Services's (IRS) examinations of its U.S. income tax returns?

FINANCIAL STATEMENT ANALYSIS CASE

Homestake Mining Company

Homestake Mining Company is a 120-year-old international gold mining company with substantial gold mining operations and exploration in the United States, Canada, and Australia. At December 31, 1998, Homestake reported the following items related to income taxes (thousands of dollars):

Total current taxes	$ 26,349
Total deferred taxes	(39,436)
Total income and mining taxes (the provision for taxes per its income statement)	(13,087)
Deferred tax liabilities	$303,050
Deferred tax assets, net of valuation allowance of $207,175	95,275
Net deferred tax liability	$207,775

Note 6: The classification of deferred tax assets and liabilities is based on the related asset or liability creating the deferred tax. Deferred taxes not related to a specific asset or liability are classified based on the estimated period of reversal.

Tax loss carryforwards (U.S., Canada, Australia, and Chile)	$71,151
Tax credit carryforwards	$12,007

Instructions

(a) What is the significance of Homestake's 1998 disclosure of "Current taxes" of $26,349 and "Deferred taxes" of $(39,436)?

(b) Explain the concept behind Homestake's disclosure of gross deferred tax liabilities (future taxable amounts) and gross deferred tax assets (future deductible amounts).

(c) Homestake reported tax loss carryforwards of $71,151 and tax credit carryforwards of $12,007. How do the carryback and carryforward provisions affect the reporting of deferred tax assets and deferred tax liabilities?

COMPARATIVE ANALYSIS CASE

The Coca-Cola Company versus PepsiCo, Inc.

Instruction

Go to the Digital Tool and, using The Coca-Cola Company and PepsiCo, Inc. Annual Report information, answer the following questions.

(a) What are the amounts of Coca-Cola's and PepsiCo's provision for income taxes for the year 1998? Of each company's 1998 provision for income taxes, what portion is current expense and what portion is deferred expense?

(b) What amount of cash was paid in 1998 for income taxes by Coca-Cola and by PepsiCo?

(c) What was the U.S. federal statutory tax rate in 1998? What was the effective tax rate in 1998 for Coca-Cola and PepsiCo? Why might their effective tax rates differ?

(d) For the year-end 1998 what amounts were reported by Coca-Cola and PepsiCo as (a) gross deferred tax assets and (b) gross deferred tax liabilities?

(e) Do either Coca-Cola or PepsiCo disclose any net operating loss carrybacks and/or carryforwards at year-end 1998? What are the amounts and when do the carryforwards expire?

RESEARCH CASES

Case 1

As discussed in the chapter, companies must consider all positive and negative information in determining whether a deferred tax asset valuation allowance is needed.

Instructions

Examine the balance sheets and income tax footnotes for two companies that have recorded deferred tax assets, and answer the following questions with regard to each company.

(a) What is the gross amount of the deferred tax asset recorded by the company? Express this amount as a percentage of total assets.

(b) Did the company record a valuation allowance? How large was the allowance?

(c) What evidence, if any, did the company cite with regard to the need for a valuation allowance? Do you consider the company's disclosure to be adequate?

Case 2

The deferred tax liability requires special considerations for financial statement readers.

Instructions

Obtain a recent edition of a financial statement analysis textbook, read the section related to the deferred tax liability, and answer the following questions.

(a) What are the major analytical issues associated with deferred tax liabilities?

(b) What type of adjustments to deferred tax liabilities do analysts make when examining financial statements?

INTERNATIONAL REPORTING CASE

Tomkins PLC is a British company that operates in four business sectors: industrial and automotive engineering; construction components; food manufacturing; and professional, garden, and leisure products. Tomkins prepares its accounts in accordance with United Kingdom (U.K.) accounting standards. Like U.S. reporting, U.K. financial reporting is investor-oriented. As a result, British companies report different income amounts for tax and financial reporting purposes. British companies receive different tax treatment for such items as depreciation (capital allowances), and they receive tax credits for operating losses. Tomkins reported income of £305 million in 1999 and reported total shareholders' funds of £2,221 million at May 31, 1999. Tomkins provided the following disclosures related to taxes in its May 31, 1999, annual report.

Principal Accounting Policies—Tax
The tax charge is based on the profit for the year and takes into account tax deferred due to timing differences between the treatment of certain items for tax and accounting purposes. Deferred tax is calculated under the liability method and it is considered probable that all liabilities will crystallise. Deferred tax assets are not recognised in respect of provisions for post-retirement benefits.

Note 5: Tax on Profit on Ordinary Activities

	1999 £ million	1998 £ million
Corporation tax at 31%	56.6	69.6
Overseas tax	85.5	95.8
Deferred tax–UK (see note 16)	5.1	(7.1)
–Overseas (see note 16)	7.3	9.2
Associated undertakings' tax	0.7	3.0
	155.2	170.5

The tax charge on exceptional items in 1999 and 1998 is £nil.

Note 16: Provisions for Liabilities and Charges

	1999 £ million	1998 £ million
The deferred tax provision comprises:		
Excess of capital allowances over depreciation charged	98.5	102.9
Other timing differences	40.8	25.5
Advance corporation tax recoverable	—	(30.3)
	139.3	98.1

Results under U.S. Accounting Principles
The consolidated financial statements are prepared in conformity with accounting principles generally accepted in the UK (UK GAAP) which differ in certain respects from those generally accepted in the United States (US GAAP). The significant areas of difference affecting the Tomkins consolidated financial statements are described below:

Deferred Income Tax. In Tomkins consolidated financial statements, deferred tax is calculated under the liability method and it is considered probable that all liabilities will crystallise. Deferred tax assets are not recognised in respect of provision for post-retirement benefits. Under US GAAP, deferred taxes are provided for all temporary differences on a full liability basis. Deferred tax assets are also recognized to the extent that their realisation is more likely than not.

If Tomkins had used U.S. GAAP for deferred taxes, its income would have been lower by £8.2 million in 1999. Stockholders' equity at May 31, 1999, would have been £87.5 million higher if Tompkins had applied U.S. GAAP.

Instructions

Use the information in the Tomkins disclosure to answer the following.

(a) Prepare the journal entry that would be required to reconcile Tomkins' income to U.S. GAAP for the differences in deferred taxes under U.S. and U.K. accounting standards.

(b) Prepare the journal entry that would be required to reconcile Tomkins' shareholders' equity to U.S. GAAP for the differences in deferred taxes under U.S. and U.K. accounting standards at the end of 1999.

(c) In light of the information disclosed under "Principal Accounting Policies—Tax," explain why you think Tomkins' equity under U.S. GAAP would be higher at May 31, 1999.

(d) Tomkins indicates that "Deferred tax is calculated under the liability method and it is considered probable that all (deferred tax) liabilities will crystallise [be realized]." Does this approach cause any problems in comparing the financial statements of U.S. and U.K. companies? Explain.

ETHICS CASE

Henrietta Aguirre, CPA, is the newly hired director of corporate taxation for Mesa Incorporated, which is a publicly traded corporation. Ms. Aguirre's first job with Mesa was the review of the company's accounting practices on deferred income taxes. In doing her review, she noted differences between tax and book depreciation methods that permitted Mesa to realize a sizable deferred tax liability on its balance sheet. As a result, Mesa did not have to report current income tax expenses. Aguirre also discovered that Mesa has an explicit policy of selling off fixed assets before they reversed in the deferred tax liability account. This policy, coupled with the rapid expansion of its fixed asset base, allowed Mesa to "defer" all income taxes payable for several years, even though it always has reported positive earnings and an increasing EPS. Aguirre checked with the legal department and found the policy to be legal, but she's uncomfortable with the ethics of it.

Instructions

Answer the following questions.

(a) Why would Mesa have an explicit policy of selling assets before they reversed in the deferred tax liability account?

(b) What are the ethical implications of Mesa's "deferral" of income taxes?

(c) Who could be harmed by Mesa's ability to "defer" income taxes payable for several years, despite positive earnings?

(d) In a situation such as this, what are Ms. Aguirre's professional responsibilities as a CPA?

CHAPTER 21

Accounting for Pensions and Postretirement Benefits

Who Wants to Be a Millionaire?

Many people dream of becoming millionaires. Increasingly, however, more and more of these people are finding that you do not have to win on a game show to have this dream come true. In the past decade, tax-favored retirement plans, in which employees receive tax incentives to save for retirement, have produced a growing number of "401K millionaires."

401K is the section number of the tax code that allows employees to contribute a part of their earnings to an investment fund that grows on a tax-deferred basis until the funds are withdrawn at retirement. In many cases, employers also contribute to the employee's retirement fund as part of the benefit package. In some cases these contributions are made in addition to the company-sponsored retirement plans, as a way to attract and retain good workers. Many employees like 401Ks because the employee can control the investment fund. In many company-sponsored plans, employees may not retain their retirement benefits if they do not stay at the company a long time.

Tax incentives combined with employee concerns that Social Security will not provide an adequate retirement income safety net have provided the impetus for employees to set up 401K-type plans. For example, the amounts contributed to these accounts more than tripled in the 1990s, with more than 44 million people owning accounts and a total of more than $1.5 trillion invested. Of these retirement investors, an increasing number are becoming millionaires by virtue of their contributions to these accounts and the strong stock market performance, since many of these funds are invested in common stocks. In 1995 there were 120 millionaires out of 700,000 401K accounts at T. Rowe Price. Within two years, T. Rowe Price reported 308 millionaires out of 870,000 401Ks.

The popularity of these plans, including their flexibility and the incentives they provide for individual savings, has even caught the eye of Congress as it debates ways to shore up the Social Security system. Recent estimates indicate that Social Security will be bankrupt by the year 2032. One proposal for dealing with the retirement shortfall is to allow workers to allocate part of their Social Security taxes to private investment funds, similar to a 401K.[1] So "who wants to be a millionaire?" More and more people are saying "I do," and many will be able to realize that dream by taking advantage of tax incentives and by taking control of their own retirement income planning.

[1]E. Schuerenberg, "Will Privatizing Fix Social Security?" *Fortune,* May 1, 1999, p. 129.

LEARNING OBJECTIVES

After studying this chapter, you should be able to:

1. **Distinguish between accounting for the employer's pension plan and accounting for the pension fund.**
2. **Identify types of pension plans and their characteristics.**
3. **Explain alternative measures for valuing the pension obligation.**
4. **Identify the components of pension expense.**
5. **Utilize a work sheet for employer's pension plan entries.**
6. **Describe the amortization of unrecognized prior service costs.**
7. **Explain the accounting procedure for recognizing unexpected gains and losses.**
8. **Explain the corridor approach to amortizing unrecognized gains and losses.**
9. **Explain the recognition of a minimum liability.**
10. **Describe the reporting requirements for pension plans in financial statements.**

PREVIEW OF CHAPTER 21

As the opening story indicates, many employees are increasingly concerned about retirement planning. To attract and reward high-quality employees, most companies have established pension plans to help employees meet their retirement savings goals. These companies offer investment programs for employee contributions, and some also contribute to employees' retirement funds as part of the overall compensation package. The substantial growth of these plans, both in number of employees covered and the dollar amounts of retirement benefits, has increased the significance of pension costs in relation to a company's financial position.[2] The purpose of this chapter is to discuss the accounting issues related to pension plans. The content and organization of the chapter are as follows:

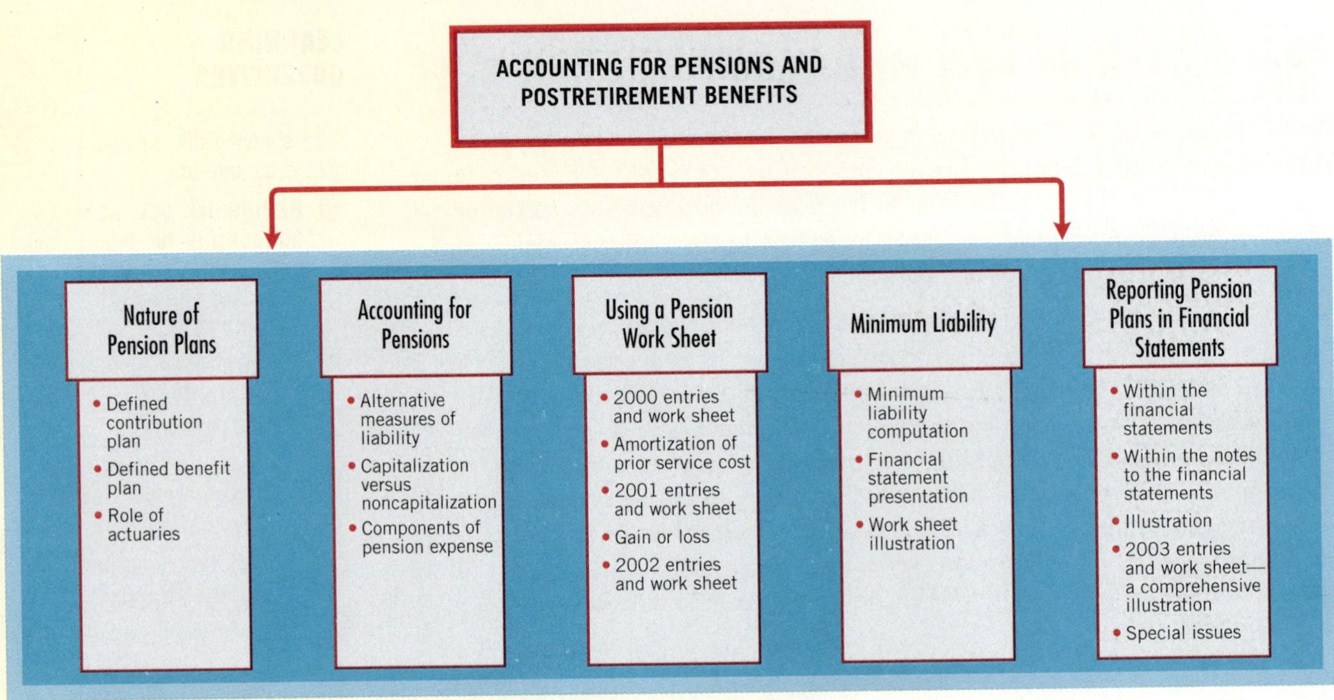

NATURE OF PENSION PLANS

OBJECTIVE 1
Distinguish between accounting for the employer's pension plan and accounting for the pension fund.

A **pension plan** is an arrangement whereby an employer provides benefits (payments) to employees after they retire for services they provided while they were working. Pension accounting may be divided and separately treated as **accounting for the employer** and **accounting for the pension fund**. The company or employer is the organization sponsoring the pension plan. It incurs the cost and makes contributions to the pension fund. The fund or plan is the entity that receives the contributions from the employer, administers the pension assets, and makes the benefit payments to the pension recipients (retired employees). Illustration 21-1 shows the three entities involved in a pension plan and indicates the flow of cash between them.

[2]For example, in 1980, private pension plans had assets of $671.3 billion. By 1997, pension plan assets totaled nearly $5 trillion.

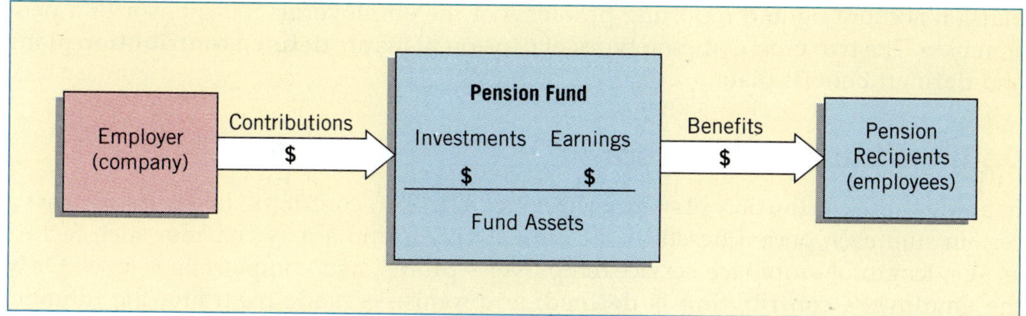

ILLUSTRATION 21-1
Flow of Cash among Pension Plan Participants

The pension plan above is being **funded**:[3] that is, the employer (company) sets funds aside for future pension benefits by making payments to a funding agency that is responsible for accumulating the assets of the pension fund and for making payments to the recipients as the benefits become due. In an insured plan, the funding agency is an insurance company; in a trust fund plan, the funding agency is a trustee.

Some plans are **contributory**; in these, the employees bear part of the cost of the stated benefits or voluntarily make payments to increase their benefits. Other plans are **noncontributory**, in which the employer bears the entire cost. Companies generally design **qualified pension plans** in accord with federal income tax requirements that permit **deductibility of the employer's contributions to the pension fund and tax-free status of earnings from pension fund assets.**

The need for proper administration of and sound accounting for pension funds becomes apparent when one appreciates the size of these funds. Listed below are the pension fund assets and pension expenses of seven major companies as of December 31, 1998.

ILLUSTRATION 21-2
Pension Fund Assets and Expense

Company ($ in millions)	Size of Pension Fund	1998 Pension Expense	Pension Expense as % of Operating Profit
Ford	$52,377	$1,071	16.0%
General Motors	80,983	1,642	35.6
Kellogg's	1,318	46	5.1
John Deere	5,661	100	6.4
Caterpillar	8,756	4	0.2
Coca-Cola	1,516	68	1.4
Pepsi	2,045	83	3.2

As indicated, pension expense is a substantial percentage of total profit for many companies.[4]

The fund should be a separate legal and accounting entity for which a set of books is maintained and financial statements are prepared. Maintaining books and records and preparing financial statements for the fund, known as "accounting for employee benefit plans," is not the subject of this chapter.[5] Instead this chapter is devoted to the

[3]When used as a verb, **fund** means to pay to a funding agency (as to fund future pension benefits or to fund pension cost). Used as a noun, it refers to assets accumulated in the hands of a funding agency (trustee) for the purpose of meeting pension benefits when they become due.

[4]Some have suggested that pension funds are the new owners of America's giant corporations. A recent study indicates that during the 1990s, pension funds (private and public) held or owned approximately 25% of the market value of corporate stock outstanding and accounted for 32% of the daily trading volume on the New York Stock Exchange. The enormous size (and the social significance) of these funds is staggering.

[5]The FASB issued a separate standard covering the accounting and reporting for employee benefit plans. "Accounting and Reporting by Defined Benefit Pension Plans," *Statement of Financial Accounting Standards No. 35* (Stamford, Conn.: FASB, 1979).

pension accounting and reporting problems of the employer as the sponsor of a pension plan. The two most common types of pension plans are **defined contribution plans** and **defined benefit plans**.

Defined Contribution Plan

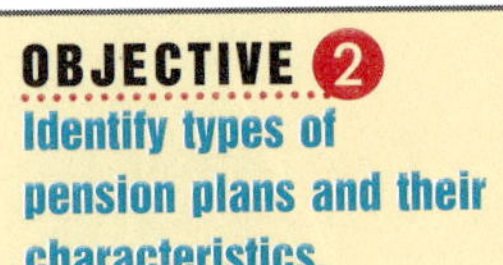

OBJECTIVE 2
Identify types of pension plans and their characteristics.

In a **defined contribution plan**, the employer agrees to contribute to a pension trust a certain sum each period based on a formula. This formula may consider such factors as age, length of employee service, employer's profits, and compensation level. **Only the employer's contribution is defined**; no promise is made regarding the ultimate benefits paid out to the employees.

The size of the pension benefits that the employee finally collects under the plan depends on the amounts originally contributed to the pension trust, the income accumulated in the trust, and the treatment of forfeitures of funds caused by early terminations of other employees. The amounts originally contributed are usually turned over to an **independent third-party trustee** who acts on behalf of the beneficiaries—the participating employees. The trustee assumes ownership of the pension assets and is accountable for their investment and distribution. The trust is separate and distinct from the employer.

The accounting for a defined contribution plan is straightforward. The employee gets the benefit of gain or the risk of loss from the assets contributed to the pension plan. The employer's responsibility is simply to make a contribution each year based on the formula established in the plan. As a result, the employer's annual cost (pension expense) is just the amount that it is obligated to contribute to the pension trust. A liability is reported on the employer's balance sheet only if the contribution has not been made in full, and an asset is reported only if more than the required amount has been contributed.

Go to the Digital Tool to examine disclosures for defined contribution plans.

In addition to pension expense, the only disclosures required by the employer under a defined contribution plan are a plan description, including employee groups covered, the basis for determining contributions, and the nature and effect of significant matters affecting comparability from period to period.[6]

Defined Benefit Plan

A **defined benefit plan** defines the benefits that the employee will receive at the time of retirement. The formula that is typically used provides for the benefits to be a function of the employee's years of service and the employee's compensation level when he or she nears retirement. It is necessary to determine what the contribution should be today to meet the pension benefit commitments that will arise at retirement. Many different contribution approaches could be used. Whatever funding method is employed, it should provide enough money at retirement to meet the benefits defined by the plan.

The employees are the beneficiaries of a defined contribution trust, but the employer is the beneficiary of a defined benefit trust. The trust's primary purpose under a defined benefit plan is to safeguard assets and to invest them so that there will be enough to pay the employer's obligation to the employees when they retire. **In form**, the trust is a separate entity; **in substance**, the trust assets and liabilities belong to the employer. That is, **as long as the plan continues, the employer is responsible for the payment of the defined benefits (without regard to what happens in the trust)**. Any shortfall in the accumulated assets held by the trust must be made up by the employer. Any excess accumulated in the trust can be recaptured by the employer, either through reduced future funding or through a reversion of funds.

Outside the U.S., private pension plans are less common because many other nations tend to rely on government-sponsored pension plans. Consequently, accounting for defined benefit pension plans is typically a less important issue elsewhere.

The accounting for a defined benefit plan is complex. Because the benefits are defined in terms of uncertain future variables, an appropriate funding pattern must be

[6]"Employers' Accounting for Pension Plans," *Statement of Financial Accounting Standards No. 87* (Stamford, Conn.: FASB, 1985), pars. 63–66.

established to assure that enough funds will be available at retirement to provide the benefits promised. This funding level depends on a number of factors such as turnover, mortality, length of employee service, compensation levels, and interest earnings.

Employers are at risk with defined benefit plans because they must be sure to make enough contributions to meet the cost of benefits that are defined in the plan. The expense recognized each period is not necessarily equal to the cash contribution. Similarly, the liability is controversial because its measurement and recognition relate to unknown future variables. Unfortunately, the accounting issues related to this type of plan are complex. **Our discussion in the following sections primarily deals with defined benefit plans.**[7]

The Role of Actuaries in Pension Accounting

Because the problems associated with pension plans involve complicated actuarial considerations, **actuaries** are engaged to ensure that the plan is appropriate for the employee group covered.[8] Actuaries are individuals who are trained through a long and rigorous certification program to assign probabilities to future events and their financial effects. The insurance industry employs actuaries to assess risks and to advise on the setting of premiums and other aspects of insurance policies. Employers rely heavily on actuaries for assistance in developing, implementing, and funding pension plans.

It is actuaries who make predictions (called actuarial assumptions) of mortality rates, employee turnover, interest and earnings rates, early retirement frequency, future salaries, and any other factors necessary to operate a pension plan. They assist by computing the various pension measures that affect the financial statements, such as the pension obligation, the annual cost of servicing the plan, and the cost of amendments to the plan. In summary, accounting for defined benefit pension plans is highly reliant upon information and measurements provided by actuaries.

ACCOUNTING FOR PENSIONS

In accounting for pension plans, two questions arise: (1) What amounts of employer's liability and of pension obligation should be reported in the financial statements? (2) What is the pension expense for the period? Attempting to answer the first question has produced much controversy.

[7]As discussed in the opening story, although defined benefit plans continue to be used, recent trends indicate growing participation in defined contribution plans. For example, a recent survey of over 45 million employees indicates that defined benefit plan participation was at 50% of full-time employees in 1997 (down from 59% in 1991). Participation in defined contribution plans grew from 48% of full-time employees in 1991 to 57% of full-time employees in 1997 (U.S. Department of Labor, Bureau of Labor Statistics, News Release, "Employee Benefits in Medium and Large Private Establishments, 1997," January 7, 1999). The recordkeeping requirements for the defined benefit plans are onerous and, therefore, companies have become more reluctant to use these plans. Also, the benefits in a defined contribution plan are easier for the employee to understand; they tend to prefer them over the defined benefit plan. In terms of total assets, recent Federal Reserve statistics indicate that assets in private defined benefit and contribution plans were about equal in 1998 (more than $2 trillion in each). In some cases, a defined contribution plan is offered in combination with a defined benefit plan.

[8]An actuary's primary purpose is to ensure that the company has established an appropriate funding pattern to meet its pension obligations. This computation entails the development of a set of assumptions and continued monitoring of these assumptions to assure their realism. That the general public has little understanding of what an actuary does is illustrated by the following excerpt from *The Wall Street Journal:* "A polling organization once asked the general public what an actuary was and received among its more coherent responses the opinion that it was a place where you put dead actors."

Alternative Measures of the Liability

OBJECTIVE 3
Explain alternative measures for valuing the pension obligation.

Most agree that an employer's **pension obligation** is the deferred compensation obligation it has to its employees for their service under the terms of the pension plan, but there are alternative ways of measuring it.[9] One measure of the obligation is to base it only on the benefits vested to the employees. **Vested benefits** are those that the employee is entitled to receive even if the employee renders no additional services under the plan. Under most pension plans, a certain minimum number of years of service to the employer is required before an employee achieves vested benefits status. The **vested benefit obligation** is computed using current salary levels and includes only vested benefits.

Another measure of the obligation is to base the computation of the deferred compensation amount on all years of service performed by employees under the plan—both vested and nonvested—using **current salary levels**. This measurement of the pension obligation is called the **accumulated benefit obligation**.

A third measure bases the computation of the deferred compensation amount on both vested and nonvested service **using future salaries.** This measurement of the pension obligation is called the **projected benefit obligation**. Because future salaries are expected to be higher than current salaries, this approach results in the largest measurement of the pension obligation.

The choice between these measures is critical because it affects the amount of the pension liability and the annual pension expense reported. The diagram in Illustration 21-3 presents the differences in these three measurements. Regardless of the approach used, the estimated future benefits to be paid are discounted to present value.

ILLUSTRATION 21-3
Different Measures of the Pension Obligation

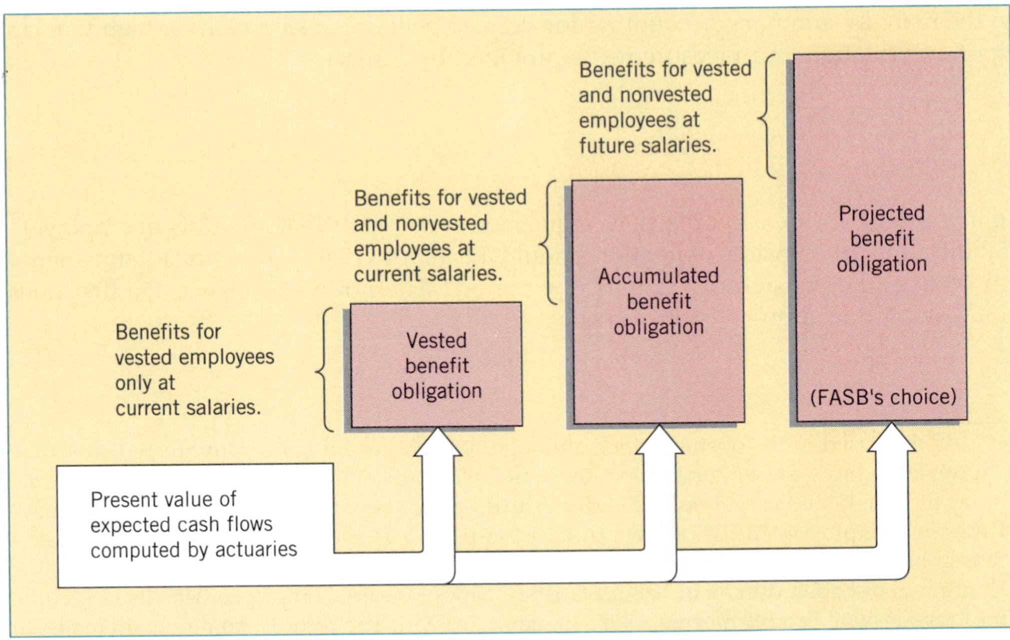

INTERNATIONAL INSIGHT

Japan is the most rapidly aging nation in the developed world, with 24% of the population expected to be over 65 by the year 2015, compared with 17% in Europe and 15% in the U.S.

Minor changes in the interest rate used to discount pension benefits can dramatically affect the measurement of the employer's obligation. For example, a 1% decrease in the discount rate can increase pension liabilities 15%. Discount rates used to measure the pension liability are required to be changed at each measurement date to reflect current interest rates.

---

[9]One measure of the pension obligation is to determine the amount that the Pension Benefit Guaranty Corporation would require the employer to pay if it defaulted (this amount is limited to 30% of the employer's net worth). The accounting profession rejected this approach for financial reporting because it is too hypothetical and ignores the going concern concept.

Which of these approaches did the profession adopt? **In general, the profession adopted the projected benefit obligation, which is the present value of vested and nonvested benefits accrued to date based on employees' future salary levels.**[10] As you will learn later, however, the profession uses the accumulated benefit obligation in certain situations.

INTERNATIONAL INSIGHT

Whereas the U.S. requires companies to base pension expense on estimated future compensation levels, Germany and Japan do not.

Those critical of the projected benefit obligation argue that using future salary levels is tantamount to adding future obligations to existing ones. Those in favor of the projected benefit obligation contend that a promise by an employer to pay benefits based on a percentage of the employees' future salary is far different from a promise to pay a percentage of their current salary, and such a difference should be reflected in the pension liability and pension expense.

Capitalization versus Noncapitalization

Prior to issuance of *FASB Statement No. 87,* accounting for pension plans followed a **noncapitalization approach**. Noncapitalization, often referred to as **off-balance-sheet financing**, was achieved because the balance sheet reported an asset or liability for the pension plan arrangement only if the amount actually funded during the year by the employer was different from the amount reported by the employer as pension expense for the year. As the employees worked during each year, the employer incurred pension cost and became obligated to fund that amount by making cash payments to the pension fund (viewed as a third-party trust). When the trust paid benefits to retirees, the employer recorded no entries because its own assets or liabilities were not reduced.

The accounting profession has been tending toward a **capitalization approach**, supporting the **economic substance** of the pension plan arrangement over its legal form. Under this view, the employer has a liability for pension benefits that it has promised to pay for employee services already performed. As pension expense is incurred—as the employees work—the employer's liability increases. Funding the plan has no effect on the amount of the liability; only the employer's promises and the employee's services affect the liability. The pension liability is reduced through the payment of benefits to retired employees.

Under a defined benefit plan, if additional funds are necessary to meet the pension obligation, the source is the employer. From the capitalization point of view, underfunding does not increase the liability, and funding more than the amount expensed does not create a prepaid expense. Capitalization means measuring and reporting in the financial statements a fair representation of the employers' pension assets and liabilities.

The FASB in *Statement No. 87* adopted an approach that leans toward capitalization. But, proposals to adopt a full capitalization (total accrual) approach, requiring the recognition of balance sheet items where none existed before, were strongly opposed. *FASB Statement No. 87* **represents a compromise that combines some of the features of capitalization with some of the features of noncapitalization**. As we will learn in more detail later in this chapter, some elements of the pension plan are not recognized in the accounts and the financial statements (that is, not capitalized).

Because of this, the accounting for pensions, outlined in *Statement No. 87* and demonstrated in the balance of this chapter, is not perfectly logical, totally complete, or conceptually sound. The FASB is not entirely at fault. Because of the financial complexity of defined benefit pensions, many well-intentioned, competent people could not agree on the economic substance of such plans. As a result, they did not agree on how to account for them. Because of the difficulties in gaining a consensus among

---

[10]When the term "present value of benefits" is used throughout this chapter, it really means the actuarial present value of benefits. Actuarial present value is the amount payable adjusted to reflect the time value of money **and** the probability of payment (by means of decrements for events such as death, disability, withdrawals, or retirement) between the present date and the expected date of payment. For simplicity, we will use the term "present value" instead of "actuarial present value" in our discussion.

the Board members and support from preparers as well as users of financial statements, *Statement No. 87* involves several compromises that make it less than an ideal application of the capitalization method. In its defense, however, *Statement No. 87* is a great improvement over previous accounting pronouncements and represents a first step toward a conceptually sound approach to employers' accounting for pension plans.

Components of Pension Expense

OBJECTIVE 4
Identify the components of pension expense.

There is broad agreement that pension cost should be accounted for on the **accrual basis.**[11] The profession recognizes that **accounting for pension plans requires measurement of the cost and its identification with the appropriate time periods**. The determination of pension cost, however, is extremely complicated because it is a function of the following components:

1. **Service Cost.** Service cost is the expense caused by the increase in pension benefits payable (the projected benefit obligation) to employees because of their services rendered during the current year. Actuaries compute **service cost** as the present value of the new benefits earned by employees during the year.

UNDERLYING CONCEPTS

The matching concept and the definition of a liability justify accounting for pension cost on the accrual basis. This requires recording an expense when the future benefits are earned by the employees and recognizing an existing obligation to pay pensions later based on current services received.

2. **Interest on the Liability.** Because a pension is a deferred compensation arrangement, there is a time value of money factor. As a result, it is recorded on a discounted basis. **Interest expense accrues each year on the projected benefit obligation just as it does on any discounted debt.** The accountant receives help from the actuary in selecting the interest rate, referred to as the **settlement rate**.
3. **Actual Return on Plan Assets.** The return earned by the accumulated pension fund assets in a particular year is relevant in measuring the net cost to the employer of sponsoring an employee pension plan. Therefore, **annual pension expense should be adjusted for interest and dividends that accumulate within the fund as well as increases and decreases in the market value of the fund assets**.
4. **Amortization of Unrecognized Prior Service Cost.** Pension plan amendments (including initiation of a pension plan) often include provisions to increase benefits (in rare situations to decrease benefits) for employee service provided in prior years. Because plan amendments are granted with the expectation that the employer will realize economic benefits in future periods, **the cost (prior service cost) of providing these retroactive benefits is allocated to pension expense in the future, specifically to the remaining service-years of the affected employees**.
5. **Gain or Loss.** Volatility in pension expense can be caused by sudden and large changes in the market value of plan assets and by changes in the projected benefit obligation (which changes when actuarial assumptions are modified or when actual experience differs from expected experience). Two items comprise this gain or loss: (1) the difference between the actual return and the expected return on plan assets and (2) amortization of the unrecognized net gain or loss from previous periods. This computation is complex and will be discussed later in the chapter.

The **components of pension expense** and their effect on total pension expense (increase or decrease) are shown in Illustration 21-4.

[11]Until the mid-1960s, with few exceptions, companies applied the **cash basis** of accounting to pension plans by recognizing the amount paid in a particular accounting period as the pension expense for the period. The problem was that the amount paid or funded in a fiscal period depended on financial management and was too often discretionary. For example, funding could be based on the availability of cash, the level of earnings, or other factors unrelated to the requirements of the plan. Application of the cash basis made it possible to manipulate the amount of pension expense appearing in the income statement simply by varying the cash paid to the pension fund.

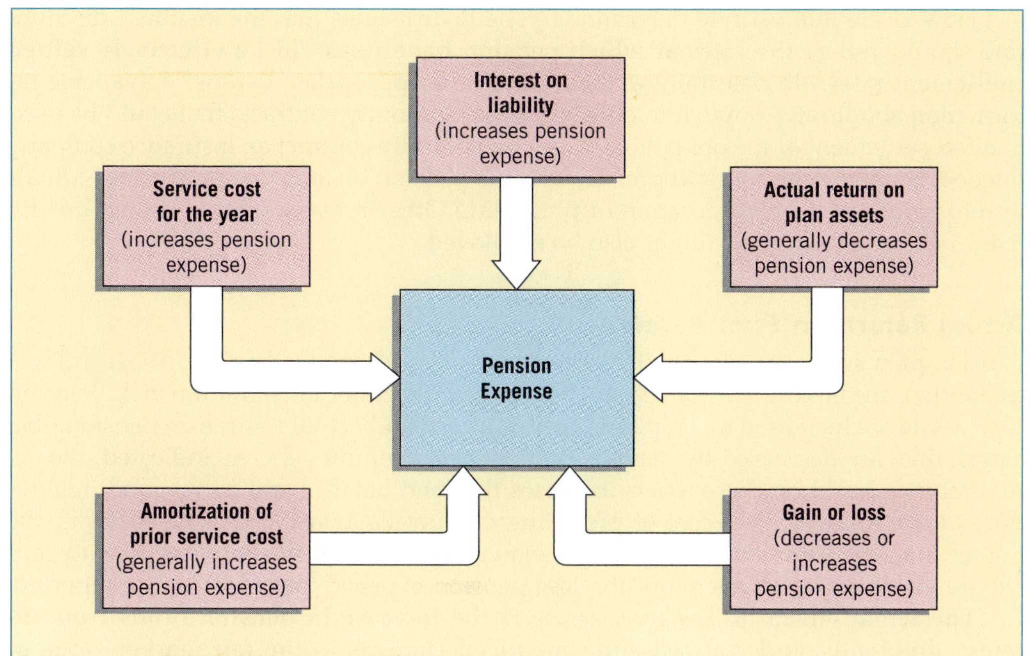

ILLUSTRATION 21-4
Components of Annual Pension Expense

Service Cost

In *FASB Statement No. 87,* the Board states that the service cost component recognized in a period **should be determined as the actuarial present value of benefits attributed by the pension benefit formula to employee service during the period**. That is, the actuary predicts the additional benefits that must be paid under the plan's benefit formula as a result of the employees' current year's service and then discounts the cost of those future benefits back to their present value.

The Board concluded that **future compensation levels had to be considered in measuring the present obligation and periodic pension expense if the plan benefit formula incorporated them**. In other words, the present obligation resulting from a promise to pay a benefit of 1% of an employee's **final pay** is different from an employer's promise to pay 1% of **current pay**. To ignore this fact would be to ignore an important aspect of pension expense. Thus, the **benefits/years-of-service actuarial method** is the approach adopted by the FASB.

Some object to this determination, arguing that a company should have more freedom to select an expense recognition pattern. Others believe that incorporating future salary increases into current pension expense is accounting for events that have not happened yet. They argue that if the plan were terminated today, only liabilities for accumulated benefits would have to be paid. **Nevertheless the Board indicates that the projected benefit obligation provides a more realistic measure on a going concern basis of the employer's obligation under the plan and, therefore, should be used as the basis for determining service cost.**

Interest on the Liability

The second component of pension expense is interest on the liability, or interest expense. As indicated earlier, a pension is a deferred compensation arrangement under which this element of wages is deferred and a liability is created. Because the liability is not paid until maturity, it is recorded on a discounted basis and accrues interest over the life of the employee. **The interest component is the interest for the period on the projected benefit obligation outstanding during the period.** The FASB did not address the question of how often to compound the interest cost. To simplify our illustrations and problem materials, we use a simple interest computation, applying it to the beginning-of-the-year balance of the projected benefit liability.

How is the interest rate determined? The Board states that the assumed discount rate should **reflect the rates at which pension benefits could be effectively settled (settlement rates)**. In determining these rates, it is appropriate to look to available information about rates implicit in current prices of annuity contracts that could be used to effect settlement of the obligation. (Under an annuity contract an insurance company unconditionally guarantees to provide specific pension benefits to specific individuals in return for a fixed consideration or premium.) Other rates of return on high-quality fixed-income investments might also be employed.

Actual Return on Plan Assets

Pension plan assets are usually investments in stocks, bonds, other securities, and real estate that are held to earn a reasonable return, generally at minimum risk. Pension plan assets are increased by employer contributions and actual returns on pension plan assets; they are decreased by benefits paid to retired employees. As indicated, the actual return earned on these assets increases the fund balance and correspondingly reduces the employer's net cost of providing employees' pension benefits. That is, the higher the actual return on the pension plan assets, the less the employer has to contribute eventually and, therefore the less pension expense that needs to be reported.

The actual return on the plan assets is the increase in pension funds from interest, dividends, and realized and unrealized changes in the fair market value of the plan assets. The actual return is computed by adjusting the change in the plan assets for the effects of contributions during the year and benefits paid out during the year. The following equation, or a variation thereof, can be used to compute the actual return:

ILLUSTRATION 21-5
Equation for Computing Actual Return

$$\text{Actual Return} = \left(\begin{array}{l}\text{Plan Assets} \\ \text{Ending Balance}\end{array} - \begin{array}{l}\text{Plan Assets} \\ \text{Beginning Balance}\end{array}\right) - \text{Contributions} - \text{Benefits Paid}$$

Stated another way, the actual return on plan assets is the difference between the **fair value of the plan assets** at the beginning of the period and the end of the period, adjusted for contributions and benefit payments. Computation of the actual return on the basis of the equation above is illustrated below using some assumed amounts:

ILLUSTRATION 21-6
Computation of Actual Return on Plan Assets

Fair value of plan assets at end of period		$5,000,000
Deduct: Fair value of plan assets at beginning of period		4,200,000
Increase in fair value of plan assets		800,000
Deduct: Contributions to plan during period	$500,000	
Less benefits paid during period	300,000	200,000
Actual return on plan assets		$ 600,000

If the actual return on the plan assets is positive (gain) during the period, it is subtracted in the computation of pension expense. If the actual return is negative (loss) during the period, it is added in the computation of pension expense.[12]

[12]At this point, we are using the actual rate of return. As shown later, for purposes of computing pension expense, the expected rate of return is used.

USING A PENSION WORK SHEET

Before covering in detail the other pension expense components (amortization of unrecognized prior service cost and gains and losses) which seem to get progressively more complex, we will illustrate the basic accounting entries for the first three components: (1) service cost, (2) interest on the liability, and (3) actual return on plan assets.

Important to accounting for pensions under *Statement No. 87* is the fact that **several significant items of the pension plan are unrecognized in the accounts and in the financial statements**. Among the compromises the FASB made in issuing *Statement No. 87* was the nonrecognition (noncapitalization) of the following pension items:

1. Projected benefit obligation.
2. Pension plan assets.
3. Unrecognized prior service costs.
4. Unrecognized net gain or loss.

As discussed later, the employer is required to **disclose in notes** to the financial statements all of these four noncapitalized items, but they are not recognized in the body of the financial statements. In addition, the exact amount of these items must be known at all times because they are used in the computation of annual pension expense. Therefore, **in order to track these off-balance-sheet pension items, memo entries and accounts have to be maintained outside the formal general ledger accounting system**. A work sheet unique to pension accounting will be utilized to record both the formal entries and the memo entries to keep track of all the employer's relevant pension plan items and components.[13]

OBJECTIVE 5
Utilize a work sheet for employer's pension plan entries.

The format of the **pension work sheet** is shown below:

ILLUSTRATION 21-7
Basic Format of Pension Work Sheet

Pension Work Sheet

	General Journal Entries			Memo Record	
Items	Annual Pension Expense	Cash	Prepaid/ Accrued Cost	Projected Benefit Obligation	Plan Assets

The left-hand "General Journal Entries" columns of the work sheet record entries in the formal general ledger accounts. The right-hand "Memo Record" columns maintain balances on the unrecognized (noncapitalized) pension items. On the first line of the work sheet, the beginning balances (if any) are recorded. Subsequently, transactions and events related to the pension plan are recorded, using debits and credits and using both sets of records as if they were one for recording the entries. For each transaction or event, the debits must equal the credits. The balance in the Prepaid/Accrued Cost column should equal the net balance in the memo record.

2000 Entries and Work Sheet

To illustrate the use of a work sheet and how it helps in accounting for a pension plan, assume that on January 1, 2000, Zarle Company adopts *FASB Statement No. 87* to account for its defined benefit pension plan. The following facts apply to the pension plan for the year 2000:

[13]The use of this pension entry work sheet is recommended and illustrated by Paul B. W. Miller, "The New Pension Accounting (Part 2)," *Journal of Accountancy,* February 1987, pp. 86–94.

Plan assets, January 1, 2000, are $100,000.

Projected benefit obligation, January 1, 2000, is $100,000.

Annual service cost is $9,000.

Settlement rate is 10%.

Actual return on plan assets is $10,000.

Contributions (funding) are $8,000.

Benefits paid to retirees during the year are $7,000.

Using the data presented above, the work sheet in Illustration 21-8 presents the beginning balances and all of the pension entries recorded by Zarle Company in 2000. The beginning balances for the projected benefit obligation and the pension plan assets are recorded on the first line of the work sheet in the memo record. They are not recorded in the formal general journal and, therefore, are not reported as a liability and an asset in the financial statements of Zarle Company. These two significant pension items are off-balance-sheet amounts that affect pension expense but are not recorded as assets and liabilities in the employer's books.

ILLUSTRATION 21-8
Pension Work Sheet—2000

	General Journal Entries			Memo Record	
Items	Annual Pension Expense	Cash	Prepaid/ Accrued Cost	Projected Benefit Obligation	Plan Assets
Balance, Jan. 1, 2000			—	100,000 Cr.	100,000 Dr.
(a) Service cost	9,000 Dr.			9,000 Cr.	
(b) Interest cost	10,000 Dr.			10,000 Cr.	
(c) Actual return	10,000 Cr.				10,000 Dr.
(d) Contributions		8,000 Cr.			8,000 Dr.
(e) Benefits				7,000 Dr.	7,000 Cr.
Journal entry for 2000	9,000 Dr.	8,000 Cr.	1,000 Cr.*		
Balance, Dec. 31, 2000			1,000 Cr.**	112,000 Cr.	111,000 Dr.

*$9,000 – $8,000 = $1,000.
**$112,000 – $111,000 = $1,000.

Entry (a) records the service cost component, which increases pension expense $9,000 and increases the liability (projected benefit obligation) $9,000. Entry (b) accrues the interest expense component, which increases both the liability and the pension expense by $10,000 (the beginning projected benefit obligation multiplied by the settlement rate of 10%). Entry (c) records the actual return on the plan assets, which increases the plan assets and decreases the pension expense. Entry (d) records Zarle Company's contribution (funding) of assets to the pension fund; cash is decreased $8,000 and plan assets are increased $8,000. Entry (e) records the benefit payments made to retirees, which results in equal $7,000 decreases to the plan assets and the projected benefit obligation.

The "formal journal entry" on December 31, which is the entry made to formally record the pension expense in 2000, is as follows:

2000		
Pension Expense	9,000	
Cash		8,000
Prepaid/Accrued Pension Cost		1,000

The credit to Prepaid/Accrued Pension Cost for $1,000 represents the difference between the 2000 pension expense of $9,000 and the amount funded of $8,000. Prepaid/Accrued Pension Cost (credit) is a liability because the plan is underfunded by $1,000. The Prepaid/Accrued Pension Cost account balance of $1,000 also equals the net of the balances in the memo accounts. This reconciliation of the off-balance-sheet items with the prepaid/accrued pension cost reported in the balance sheet is shown in Illustration 21-9.

Projected benefit obligation (Credit)	$(112,000)
Plan assets at fair value (Debit)	111,000
Prepaid/accrued pension cost (Credit)	(1,000)

ILLUSTRATION 21-9
Pension Reconciliation Schedule—December 31, 2000

If the net of the memo record balances is a credit, the reconciling amount in the prepaid/accrued cost column will be a credit equal in amount. If the net of the memo record balances is a debit, the prepaid/accrued cost amount will be a debit equal in amount. The work sheet is designed to produce this reconciling feature which will be useful later in the preparation of the required notes related to pension disclosures.

In this illustration, the debit to Pension Expense exceeds the credit to Cash, resulting in a credit to Prepaid/Accrued Pension Cost—the recognition of a liability. If the credit to Cash exceeded the debit to Pension Expense, Prepaid/Accrued Pension Cost would be debited—the recognition of an asset.

Amortization of Unrecognized Prior Service Cost (PSC)

OBJECTIVE 6
Describe the amortization of unrecognized prior service costs.

When a defined benefit plan is either initiated (adopted) or amended, credit is often given to employees for years of service provided before the date of initiation or amendment. As a result of prior service credits, the projected benefit obligation is usually greater than it was before. In many cases, the increase in the projected benefit obligation is substantial. One question that arises is whether an expense and related liability for these **prior service costs (PSC)** should be fully reported at the time a plan is initiated or amended. The FASB has taken the position that no expense for these costs and in some cases no liability should be recognized at the time of the plan's adoption or amendment. The Board's rationale is that the employer would not provide credit for past years of service unless it expected to receive benefits in the future. As a result, **the retroactive benefits should not be recognized as pension expense entirely in the year of amendment but should be recognized during the service periods of those employees who are expected to receive benefits under the plan (the remaining service life of the covered active employees).**

The cost of the retroactive benefits (including benefits that are granted to existing retirees) is the increase in the projected benefit obligation at the date of the amendment. The amount of the prior service cost is computed by an actuary. Amortization of the unrecognized prior service cost is an accounting function performed with the assistance of an actuary.

INTERNATIONAL INSIGHT

In the U.S., prior service cost is generally amortized over the average remaining service life of employees. In Germany, prior service cost is recognized immediately. In the Netherlands, prior service cost may either be recognized immediately or directly charged to shareholders' equity.

The Board prefers a **years-of-service** amortization method that is similar to a units-of-production computation. First, the total number of service-years to be worked by all of the participating employees is computed. Second, the unrecognized prior service cost is divided by the total number of service-years, to obtain a cost per service-year (the unit cost). Third, the number of service-years consumed each year is multiplied by the cost per service-year, to obtain the annual amortization charge.

To illustrate the amortization of the unrecognized prior service cost under the years-of-service method, assume that Zarle Company's defined benefit pension plan covers 170 employees. In its negotiations with its employees, Zarle Company amends its pension plan on January 1, 2001, and grants $80,000 of prior service costs to its employees. The employees are grouped as follows according to expected years of retirement:

Group	Number of Employees	Expected Retirement on Dec. 31
A	40	2001
B	20	2002
C	40	2003
D	50	2004
E	20	2005
	170	

The computation of the service-years per year and the total service-years is shown in Illustration 21-10.

ILLUSTRATION 21-10
Computation of Service-Years

Year	Service-Years A	B	C	D	E	Total
2001	40	20	40	50	20	170
2002		20	40	50	20	130
2003			40	50	20	110
2004				50	20	70
2005					20	20
	40	40	120	200	100	500

Computed on the basis of a prior service cost of $80,000 and a total of 500 service-years for all years, the cost per service-year is $160 ($80,000 ÷ 500). The annual amount of amortization based on a $160 cost per service-year is computed as follows:

ILLUSTRATION 21-11
Computation of Annual Prior Service Cost Amortization

Year	Total Service-Years	×	Cost per Service-Year	=	Annual Amortization
2001	170		$160		$27,200
2002	130		160		20,800
2003	110		160		17,600
2004	70		160		11,200
2005	20		160		3,200
	500				$80,000

FASB Statement No. 87 allows an alternative method of computing amortization of unrecognized prior service cost; **employers may use straight-line amortization over the average remaining service life of the employees**. In this case, with 500 service years and 170 employees, the average would be 2.94 years (500 ÷ 170). Using this method, the $80,000 cost would be charged to expense at $27,211 ($80,000 ÷ 2.94) in 2001, $27,211 in 2002, and $25,578 ($27,211 × .94) in 2003.

If the Board had adopted full capitalization of all elements of the pension plan, the prior service cost would have been capitalized as an intangible asset—pension goodwill—and amortized over its useful life. The intangible asset (goodwill) comes from the assumption that the cost of additional pension benefits increases loyalty and productivity (and reduces turnover) among the affected employees. However, prior service cost is accounted for off-balance-sheet and is called **unrecognized prior service cost**. Although not recognized on the balance sheet, prior service cost is a factor in computing pension expense.

2001 Entries and Work Sheet

Continuing the Zarle Company illustration into 2001, we note that a January 1, 2001, amendment to the pension plan grants to employees prior service benefits having a present value of $80,000. The annual amortization amounts, as computed in the previous section using the years-of-service approach ($27,200 for 2001), are employed in this illustration. The following facts apply to the pension plan for the year 2001.

On January 1, 2001, Zarle Company grants prior service benefits having a present value of $80,000.

Annual service cost is $9,500.

Settlement rate is 10%.

Actual return on plan assets is $11,100.

Annual contributions (funding) are $20,000.

Benefits paid to retirees during the year are $8,000.

Amortization of prior service cost (PSC) using the years-of-service method is $27,200.

The following work sheet presents all of the pension entries and information recorded by Zarle Company in 2001:

ILLUSTRATION 21-12
Pension Work Sheet—2001

	General Journal Entries			Memo Record		
Items	Annual Pension Expense	Cash	Prepaid/Accrued Cost	Projected Benefit Obligation	Plan Assets	Unrecognized Prior Service Cost
Balance, Dec. 31, 2000			1,000 Cr.	112,000 Cr.	111,000 Dr.	
(f) Prior service cost				80,000 Cr.		80,000 Dr.
Balance, Jan. 1, 2001			1,000 Cr.	192,000 Cr.	111,000 Dr.	80,000 Dr.
(g) Service cost	9,500 Dr.			9,500 Cr.		
(h) Interest cost	19,200 Dr.[a]			19,200 Cr.		
(i) Actual return	11,100 Cr.				11,100 Dr.	
(j) Amortization of PSC	27,200 Dr.					27,200 Cr.
(k) Contributions		20,000 Cr.			20,000 Dr.	
(l) Benefits				8,000 Dr.	8,000 Cr.	
Journal entry for 2001	44,800 Dr.	20,000 Cr.	24,800 Cr.			
Balance, Dec. 31, 2001			25,800 Cr.	212,700 Cr.	134,100 Dr.	52,800 Dr.

[a]$19,200 = $192,000 × 10%.

The first line of the work sheet shows the beginning balances of the Prepaid/Accrued Pension Cost account and the memo accounts. Entry (f) records Zarle Company's granting of prior service cost by adding $80,000 to the projected benefit obligation and to the unrecognized (noncapitalized) prior service cost. Entries (g), (h), (i), (k), and (l) are similar to the corresponding entries in 2000. Entry (j) records the 2001 amortization of unrecognized prior service cost by debiting Pension Expense by $27,200 and crediting the new Unrecognized Prior Service Cost account by the same amount.

The journal entry on December 31 to formally record the pension expense—the sum of the annual pension expense column—for 2001 is as follows:

2001		
Pension Expense	44,800	
Cash		20,000
Prepaid/Accrued Pension Cost		24,800

Because the expense exceeds the funding, the Prepaid/Accrued Pension Cost account is credited for the $24,800 difference and is a liability. In 2001, as in 2000, the balance of the Prepaid/Accrued Pension Cost account ($25,800) is equal to the net of the balances in the memo accounts as shown in Illustration 21-13.

ILLUSTRATION 21-13
Pension Reconciliation Schedule—December 31, 2001

Projected benefit obligation (Credit)	$(212,700)
Plan assets at fair value (Debit)	134,100
Funded status	(78,600)
Unrecognized prior service cost (Debit)	52,800
Prepaid/accrued pension cost (Credit)	$ (25,800)

The reconciliation is the formula that makes the work sheet work. It relates the components of pension accounting, recorded and unrecorded, to one another.

Gain or Loss

OBJECTIVE 7
Explain the accounting procedure for recognizing unexpected gains and losses.

Of great concern to companies that have pension plans are the uncontrollable and unexpected swings in pension expense that could be caused by (1) sudden and large changes in the market value of plan assets and (2) changes in actuarial assumptions that affect the amount of the projected benefit obligation. If these gains or losses were to impact fully the financial statements in the period of realization or incurrence, substantial fluctuations in pension expense would result. Therefore, the profession decided to reduce the volatility associated with pension expense by using **smoothing techniques** that dampen and in some cases fully eliminate the fluctuations.

Smoothing Unexpected Gains and Losses on Plan Assets

One component of pension expense, actual return on plan assets, reduces pension expense (assuming the actual return is positive). A large change in the actual return can substantially affect pension expense for a year. Assume a company has a 40% return in the stock market for the year. Should this substantial, and perhaps one-time, event affect current pension expense?

Actuaries ignore current fluctuations when they develop a funding pattern to pay expected benefits in the future. They develop an **expected rate of return** and multiply it by an asset value weighted over a reasonable period of time to arrive at an **expected return on plan assets**. This return is then used to determine its funding pattern.

The Board adopted the actuary's approach to dampen wide swings that might occur in the actual return. That is, the expected return on the plan assets is to be included as a component of pension expense, not the actual return in a given year. To achieve this goal, the expected rate of return (the actuary's rate) is multiplied by the fair value of the plan assets or a market-related asset value of the plan assets (throughout our Zarle Company illustrations, market-related value and fair value of plan assets are assumed equal). The **market-related asset value is a calculated value that recognizes changes in fair value in a systematic and rational manner over not more than 5 years.**[14]

What happens to the difference between the expected return and the actual return, often referred to as the **unexpected gain or loss**—also called **asset gains and losses** by the FASB? Asset gains (occurring when actual return is greater than expected return) and asset losses (occurring when actual return is less than expected return) are recorded in an Unrecognized Net Gain or Loss account and combined with unrecognized gains and losses accumulated in prior years.

To illustrate the computation of an unexpected asset gain or loss and its related accounting, assume that Shierer Company in 2002 has an actual return on plan assets of \$16,000 when the expected return is \$13,410 (the expected rate of return of 10% times the beginning-of-the-year plan assets). The unexpected asset gain of \$2,590 (\$16,000 − \$13,410) is credited to Unrecognized Net Gain or Loss and debited to Pension Expense.

Smoothing Unexpected Gains and Losses on the Pension Liability

In estimating, the projected benefit obligation (the liability), actuaries make assumptions about such items as mortality rate, retirement rate, turnover rate, disability rate, and salary amounts. Any change in these actuarial assumptions changes the amount of the projected benefit obligation. Seldom does actual experience coincide exactly with the actuarial predictions. These unexpected gains or losses from changes in the projected benefit obligation are called **liability gains and losses**.

Liability gains (resulting from unexpected decreases in the liability balance) and liability losses (resulting from unexpected increases) are deferred (unrecognized). The liability gains and losses are combined in the same Unrecognized Net Gain or Loss

[14]Different ways of calculating market-related value may be used for different classes of assets (for example, an employer might use fair value for bonds and a 5-year-moving-average for equities), but the manner of determining market-related value should be applied consistently from year to year for each asset class.

account used for asset gains and losses. They are accumulated from year to year, off-balance-sheet, in a memo record account.

Corridor Amortization

OBJECTIVE 8
Explain the corridor approach to amortizing unrecognized gains and losses.

Because the asset gains and losses and the liability gains and losses can be offsetting, the accumulated total unrecognized net gain or loss may not grow very large. But, it is possible that no offsetting will occur and that the balance in the Unrecognized Net Gain or Loss account will continue to grow. To limit its growth, the FASB invented the **corridor approach** for amortizing the accumulated balance in the Unrecognized Gain or Loss account when it gets too large. **The unrecognized net gain or loss balance is considered too large and must be amortized when it exceeds the arbitrarily selected FASB criterion of 10% of the larger of the beginning balances of the projected benefit obligation or the market-related value of the plan assets.**

To illustrate the corridor approach, assume data on the projected benefit obligation and the plan assets over a period of 6 years as shown in Illustration 21-14.

ILLUSTRATION 21-14
Computation of the Corridor

Beginning-of-the-Year Balances	Projected Benefit Obligation	Market-Related Asset Value	Corridor* +/− 10%
1999	**$1,000,000**	$ 900,000	$100,000
2000	**1,200,000**	1,100,000	120,000
2001	1,300,000	**1,700,000**	170,000
2002	1,500,000	**2,250,000**	225,000
2003	1,700,000	**1,750,000**	175,000
2004	**1,800,000**	1,700,000	180,000

*The corridor becomes 10% of the larger (in boldface) of the projected benefit obligation or the market-related plan asset value.

How the corridor works becomes apparent when the data above are portrayed graphically as in the diagram in Illustration 21-15.

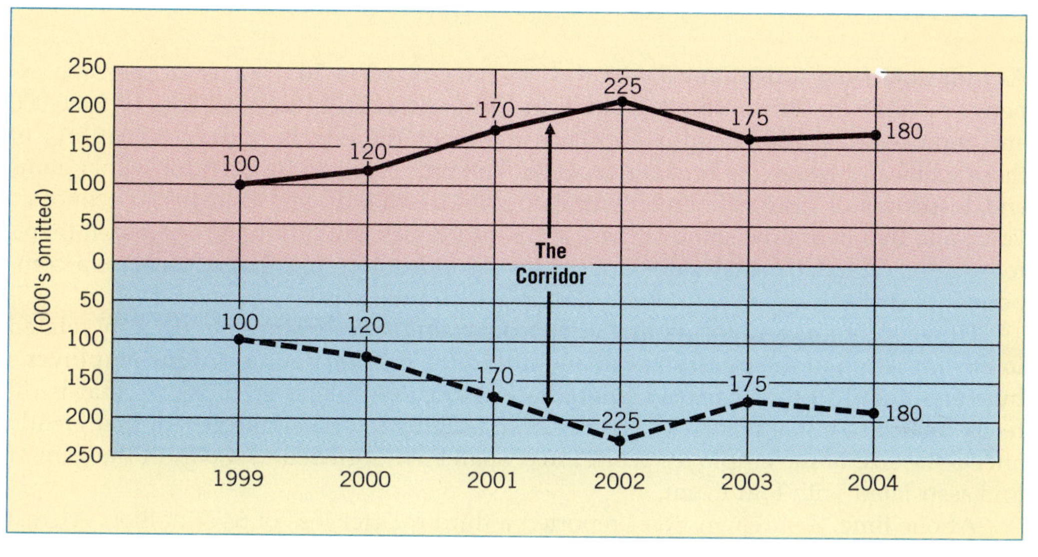

ILLUSTRATION 21-15
Graphic Illustration of the Corridor

If the balance of the Unrecognized Net Gain or Loss account stays within the upper and lower limits of the corridor, no amortization is required—the unrecognized net gain or loss balance is carried forward unchanged.

If amortization is required, the minimum amortization shall be the excess divided by the average remaining service period of active employees expected to receive benefits under the plan. Any systematic method of amortization of unrecognized gains and losses may be used in lieu of the minimum, provided it is greater than the minimum, is used consistently for both gains and losses, and is disclosed.

Illustration of Unrecognized Gains/Losses

In applying the corridor, the Board decided that amortization of the excess unrecognized net gain or loss should be included as a component of pension expense only if, at the **beginning of the year**, the unrecognized net gain or loss exceeded the corridor. That is, if no unrecognized net gain or loss exists at the beginning of the period, no recognition of gains or losses can result in that period.

To illustrate the amortization of unrecognized net gains and losses, assume the following information for Soft-White, Inc.:

	2000	2001	2002
		(beginning of the year)	
Projected benefit obligation	$2,100,000	$2,600,000	$2,900,000
Market-related asset value	2,600,000	2,800,000	2,700,000
Unrecognized net loss	–0–	400,000	300,000

If the average remaining service life of all active employees is 5.5 years, the schedule to amortize the unrecognized net loss is as follows:

ILLUSTRATION 21-16
Corridor Test and Gain/Loss Amortization Schedule

Year	Projected Benefit Obligation[a]	Plan Assets[a]	Corridor[b]	Cumulative Unrecognized Net Loss[a]	Minimum Amortization of Loss (For Current Year)
2000	$2,100,000	$2,600,000	$260,000	$ –0–	$ –0–
2001	2,600,000	2,800,000	280,000	400,000	21,818[c]
2002	2,900,000	2,700,000	290,000	678,182[d]	70,579[d]

[a]All as of the beginning of the period.
[b]10% of the greater of projected benefit obligation or plan assets market-related value.
[c]$400,000 − $280,000 = $120,000; $120,000 ÷ 5.5 = $21,818
[d]$400,000 − $21,818 + $300,000 = $678,182; $678,182 − $290,000 = $388,182; $388,182 ÷ 5.5 = $70,579.

As indicated from Illustration 21-16, the loss recognized in 2001 increased pension expense by $21,818. This amount is small in comparison with the total loss of $400,000 and indicates that the corridor approach dampens the effects (reduces volatility) of these gains and losses on pension expense. The rationale for the corridor is that gains and losses result from refinements in estimates as well as real changes in economic value and that over time some of these gains and losses will offset one another. It therefore seems reasonable that gains and losses should not be recognized fully as a component of pension expense in the period in which they arise.

However, gains and losses that arise from a single occurrence not directly related to the operation of the pension plan and not in the ordinary course of the employer's business should be recognized immediately. For example, a gain or loss that is directly related to a plant closing, a disposal of a segment, or a similar event that greatly affects the size of the employee work force, shall be recognized as a part of the gain or loss associated with that event.

At one time, **Bethlehem Steel** reported a third-quarter loss of $477 million. A great deal of this loss was attributable to future estimated benefits payable to workers who were permanently laid off. In this situation, the loss should be treated as an adjustment to the gain or loss on the plant closing and should not affect pension cost for the current or future periods.

Summary of Calculations for Asset Gain or Loss

The difference between the actual return on plan assets and the expected return on plan assets is the unexpected (deferred) asset gain or loss component. This component defers the difference between the actual return and expected return on plan assets in computing current year pension expense. Thus, after considering this component, **it is really the expected return on plan assets (not the actual return) that determines current pension expense.**

The amortized net gain or loss is determined by amortizing the unrecognized gain or loss at the beginning of the year subject to the corridor limitation. In other words, **if the unrecognized gain or loss is greater than the corridor, these net gains and losses are subject to amortization.** This minimum amortization is computed by dividing the net gains or losses subject to amortization by the average remaining service period. When the unexpected gain or loss is combined with the amortization of prior years' actuarial gains and losses, the net amortized and unexpected gains and losses is determined (often referred to simply as gain or loss). This summary is illustrated graphically below:

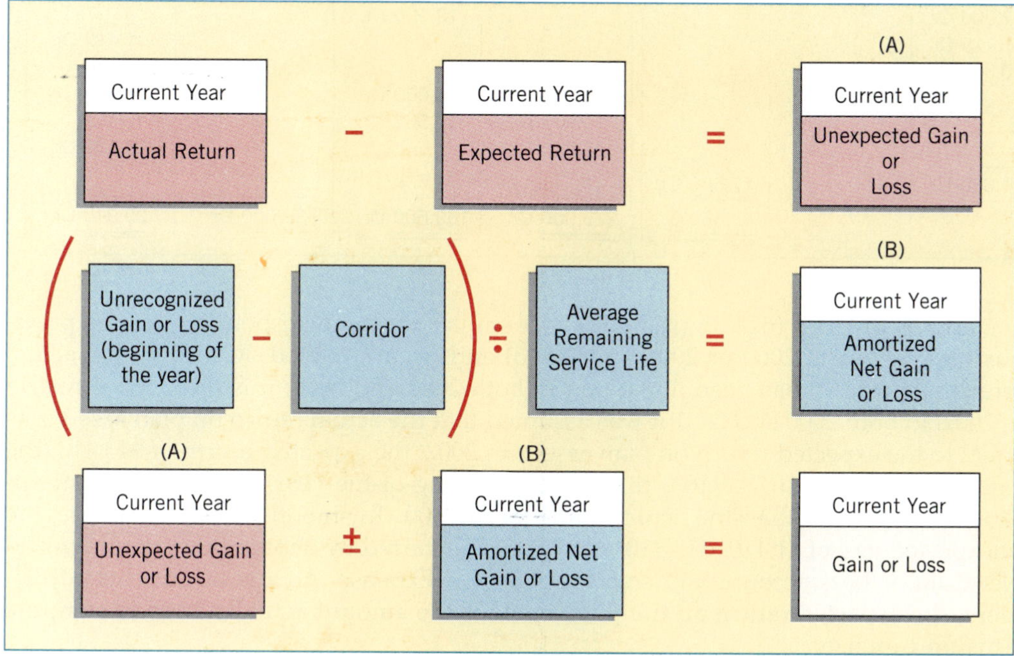

ILLUSTRATION 21-17
Graphic Summary of Gain or Loss Computation

In essence, these gains and losses are subject to triple smoothing. That is, the asset gain or loss is smoothed by using the expected return. Then the unrecognized gain or loss at the beginning of the year is not amortized unless it is greater than the corridor. Finally, the excess is spread over the remaining service life of existing employees.

2002 Entries and Work Sheet

Continuing the Zarle Company illustration, the following facts apply to the pension plan for 2002:

Annual service cost is $13,000.

Settlement rate is 10%; expected earnings rate is 10%.

Actual return on plan assets is $12,000.

Amortization of prior service cost (PSC) is $20,800.

Annual contributions (funding) are $24,000.

Benefits paid to retirees during the year are $10,500.

Changes in actuarial assumptions establish the end-of-year projected benefit obligation at $265,000.

The work sheet shown in Illustration 21-18 presents all of the pension entries and information recorded by Zarle Company in 2002. On the first line of the work sheet are recorded the beginning balances that relate to the pension plan. In this case, the beginning balances for Zarle Company are the ending balances from the 2001 Zarle Company pension work sheet in Illustration 21-12.

ILLUSTRATION 21-18
Pension Work Sheet—2002

	General Journal Entries			Memo Record			
Items	Annual Pension Expense	Cash	Prepaid/ Accrued Cost	Projected Benefit Obligation	Plan Assets	Unrecognized Prior Service Cost	Unrecognized Net Gain or Loss
Bal., December 31, 2001			25,800 Cr.	212,700 Cr.	134,100 Dr.	52,800 Dr.	
(m) Service cost	13,000 Dr.			13,000 Cr.			
(n) Interest cost	21,270 Dr.			21,270 Cr.			
(o) Actual return	12,000 Cr.				12,000 Dr.		
(p) Unexpected loss	1,410 Cr.						1,410 Dr.
(q) Amortization of PSC	20,800 Dr.					20,800 Cr.	
(r) Contributions		24,000 Cr.			24,000 Dr.		
(s) Benefits				10,500 Dr.	10,500 Cr.		
(t) Liability increase				28,530 Cr.			28,530 Dr.
Journal entry for 2002	41,660 Dr.	24,000 Cr.	17,660 Cr.				
Bal., December 31, 2002			43,460 Cr.	265,000 Cr.	159,600 Dr.	32,000 Dr.	29,940 Dr.

Entries (m), (n), (o), (q), (r), and (s) are similar to the corresponding entries previously explained in 2000 or 2001. Entries (o) and (p) are related. Recording the actual return in entry (o) has been illustrated in both 2000 and 2001; it is recorded similarly in 2002. In both 2000 and 2001 it was assumed that the actual return on plan assets was equal to the expected return on plan assets. In 2002, the expected return of $13,410 (the expected rate of return of 10% times the beginning-of-the-year plan assets balance of $134,100) is higher than the actual return of $12,000. To smooth pension expense, the unexpected loss of $1,410 ($13,410 − $12,000) is deferred by debiting the Unrecognized Net Gain or Loss account and crediting Pension Expense. **As a result of this adjustment, the expected return on the plan assets is the amount actually used to compute pension expense.**

Entry (t) records the change in the projected benefit obligation resulting from a change in actuarial assumptions. As indicated, the actuary has now computed the ending balance to be $265,000. Given that the memo record balance at December 31 is $236,470 ($212,700 + $13,000 + $21,270 − $10,500), a difference of $28,530 ($265,000 − $236,470) is indicated. This $28,530 increase in the employer's liability is an unexpected loss that is deferred by debiting it to the Unrecognized Net Gain or Loss account.

The journal entry on December 31 to formally record pension expense for 2002 is as follows:

2002		
Pension Expense	41,660	
Cash		24,000
Prepaid/Accrued Pension Cost		17,660

As illustrated in the work sheets of 2000 and 2001, the balance of the Prepaid/Accrued Pension Cost account at December 31, 2002, of $43,460 is equal to the net of the balances in the memo accounts as shown below:

ILLUSTRATION 21-19
Pension Reconciliation Schedule—December 31, 2002

Projected benefit obligation (Credit)	$(265,000)
Plan assets at fair value (Debit)	159,600
Funded status	(105,400)
Unrecognized prior service cost (Debit)	32,000
Unrecognized net loss (Debit)	29,940
Prepaid/accrued pension cost (Credit)	$ (43,460)

MINIMUM LIABILITY

If the FASB had decided to capitalize pension plan assets and liabilities, Zarle Company in our previous illustration would have reported on December 31, 2002, a liability of $265,000, plan assets of $159,600, and unrecognized prior service cost (goodwill) of $32,000 plus an unrecognized net loss of $29,940. Instead it reports only accrued pension cost of $43,460 as a liability. The Board was well aware of this discrepancy. It believed that an employer with a projected benefit obligation in excess of the fair value of pension plan assets has a liability and that an employer with a fair value of plan assets in excess of projected benefit obligation has an asset. Nevertheless, when the Board was faced with the final decision on this matter, it decided that to require the reporting of these amounts in the financial statements would be too great a change in practice at that time, because up to then none of these amounts had been reported in the balance sheet.

OBJECTIVE 9
Explain the recognition of a minimum liability.

The Board, therefore, developed a compromise approach that requires immediate recognition of a liability (referred to as the minimum liability) when the accumulated benefit obligation exceeds the fair value of plan assets. The purpose of this minimum liability requirement is to assure that if a significant plan amendment or actuarial loss occurs, a liability will be recognized at least to the extent of the unfunded portion of the accumulated benefit obligation.

Note that the plan assets are compared to the smaller **accumulated** benefit obligation instead of the larger projected benefit obligation. The rationale for using the accumulated benefit obligation is that if the liability were settled today, it would be settled on the basis of current salary rates, not future salary rates. Therefore, it is argued that the accumulated benefit obligation should be used, not the projected benefit obligation. Although the compromise approach frequently ignores a portion of the liability, it does help to report some balance sheet effects when a plan amendment or a large loss occurs. **The Board does not permit the recording of an additional asset if the fair value of the pension plan exceeds the accumulated benefit obligation.**

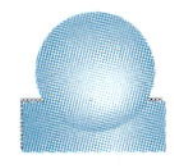

UNDERLYING CONCEPTS

Recognizing the smaller benefit obligation ignores the going concern concept. A going concern would not expect to settle the obligation today at current salaries and wages. A going concern would expect to settle the obligation based upon future salary levels.

Minimum Liability Computation

If a liability for accrued pension cost is already reported, only an additional liability to equal the required minimum liability (unfunded accumulated benefit) is recorded. To illustrate, assume that Largent Inc. amends its pension plan on December 31, 2000, giving retroactive benefits to its employees, as follows:

Projected benefit obligation	$8,000,000
Accumulated benefit obligation	7,000,000
Plan assets (at fair value)	5,000,000
Market-related asset value	4,900,000
Unrecognized prior service cost	2,500,000
Accrued pension cost	500,000

INTERNATIONAL INSIGHT

Only the U.S. requires companies to revalue their pension plan obligations each year. Other nations tend to require revaluation at approximately 3-year intervals.

The unfunded accumulated benefit is computed as follows:

ILLUSTRATION 21-20
Computation of Unfunded Accumulated Benefit (Minimum Liability)

Accumulated benefit obligation	$7,000,000
Plan assets (at fair value)	5,000,000
Unfunded accumulated benefit obligation (minimum liability)	$2,000,000

Note that the fair value of the plan assets is used, not the market-related asset value, to compute the unfunded accumulated benefit obligation. In this case, an additional $1,500,000 is required to be recorded as a liability and reported on the financial statements. The computation of the additional liability is as follows:

ILLUSTRATION 21-21
Computation of Additional Liability Required—Accrued Pension Cost Balance

Unfunded accumulated benefit obligation (minimum liability)	$2,000,000
Accrued pension cost (balance at December 31, 2000)	500,000
Additional liability required	$1,500,000

Largent Inc. would combine the **accrued pension cost** and the additional liability into one amount and report it in the balance sheet as accrued pension cost or pension liability in the amount of $2,000,000.

If Largent Inc. had a **prepaid pension cost** of $300,000 instead of an accrued pension cost of $500,000, an additional liability of $2,300,000 would be recorded as follows:

ILLUSTRATION 21-22
Computation of Additional Liability Required—Prepaid Pension Cost Balance

Unfunded accumulated benefit obligation (minimum liability)	$2,000,000
Prepaid pension cost	300,000
Additional liability required	$2,300,000

The existing balance in the prepaid pension cost (debit) is **combined** with the additional liability (credit) into one amount and reported as accrued pension cost or pension liability in the net amount of $2,000,000.

Financial Statement Presentation

IASC standards do not account for a minimum liability.

When it is necessary to adjust the accounts to recognize a minimum liability, the debit should be to an intangible asset that is called Intangible Asset—Deferred Pension Cost. The entry to record the liability and related intangible asset for Largent Inc. (first case) is:

Intangible Asset—Deferred Pension Cost	1,500,000	
Additional Pension Liability		1,500,000

One exception to the general rule of reporting an intangible asset is when the **additional liability exceeds the amount of unrecognized prior service cost.** In this case, the excess is debited to Excess of Additional Pension Liability Over Unrecognized Prior Service Cost. When the additional liability exceeds the unrecognized prior service cost, the excess must have resulted from an actuarial loss, such as an increase in the benefit obligation due to an increase in retiree longevity. The justification for recognizing an intangible asset up to the amount of the unrecognized prior service cost is that an amendment to an existing plan increases goodwill with employees and therefore benefits the company in the future. Such is not the case when the additional liability exceeds the unrecognized prior service cost.

When this excess develops, it should be reported as a reduction of other comprehensive income. In addition, its cumulative balance is reported as a component of accumulated other comprehensive income on the balance sheet. Because the excess of additional pension liability over unrecognized prior service cost reduces stockholders' equity, it is often referred to as a contra equity account. To illustrate, assume that Largent Inc. has common stock, with a total par value of $1,000,000, additional paid-in capital of $400,000, and retained earnings of $700,000. In addition, it has an additional liability that exceeds the unrecognized prior service cost by $200,000. A condensed version of Largent's stockholders' equity section is provided in Illustration 21-23.[15]

[15]This treatment is similar to the reporting of the unrealized holding loss on available-for-sale securities discussed in earlier chapters. Note that the components of accumulated other comprehensive income must be shown in the stockholders' equity section of the balance sheet, or the notes, or the statement of stockholders' equity.

ILLUSTRATION 21-23
Balance Sheet Presentation of Excess of Additional Pension Liability

Stockholders' Equity Section	
Common stock	$1,000,000
Additional paid-in capital	400,000
Total paid-in capital	1,400,000
Retained earnings	700,000
Accumulated other comprehensive income	(200,000)
Total stockholders' equity	$1,900,000

The amount of the additional liability required should be evaluated each reporting period along with the related intangible asset or contra equity account. At each reporting date, these items may be increased, decreased, or totally eliminated. Neither the intangible asset nor the contra equity account is amortized from period to period; the balances are merely adjusted up or down.

The minimum liability approach for the Zarle Company pension plan for all three years 2000, 2001, and 2002 is illustrated in the following schedule (values are assumed for the accumulated benefit obligation):

ILLUSTRATION 21-24
Minimum Liability Computations

	December 31		
	2000	2001	2002
Accumulated benefit obligation	$(80,000)	$(164,000)	$(240,600)
Plan assets at fair value	111,000	134,100	159,600
Unfunded accumulated benefit obligation (minimum liability)	$ -0-	(29,900)	(81,000)
Accrued pension cost	1,000	25,800	43,460
Additional liability	$ -0-	(4,100)	(37,540)
Unrecognized prior service cost*		52,800	32,000
Contra equity charge**		$ -0-	$ (5,540)

*Maximum intangible asset recognizable.
**Difference charged to Excess of Additional Pension Liability Over Unrecognized Prior Service Cost.

In 2000, the fair value of the plan assets exceeds the accumulated benefit obligation; therefore, no additional liability need be reported. **The Board does not permit the recognition of a net investment in the pension plan when the plan assets exceed the pension obligation.**

In 2001, the minimum liability amount ($29,900) exceeds the accrued pension cost liability already recorded ($25,800), so an additional liability of $4,100 ($29,900 − $25,800) is recorded as follows:

December 31, 2001		
Intangible Asset—Deferred Pension Cost	4,100	
Additional Pension Liability		4,100

In 2002, the minimum liability ($81,000) exceeds the accrued pension cost liability ($43,460), so an additional liability of $37,540 must be reported at the end of 2002. Since a balance of $4,100 already exists in the Additional Pension Liability account, it is credited for $33,440 ($37,540 − $4,100). Also, since the additional liability exceeds the unrecognized prior service cost by $5,540, the excess is debited to the contra equity account, Excess of Additional Pension Liability over Unrecognized Prior Service Cost. The remaining $27,900 ($33,440 − $5,540) is debited to the Intangible Asset—Deferred Pension Cost. The entry on December 31, 2002, to adjust the minimum liability is as follows:

December 31, 2002		
Intangible Asset—Deferred Pension Cost	27,900	
Excess of Additional Pension Liability over Unrecognized Prior Service Cost	5,540	
Additional Pension Liability		33,440

As the additional liability changes, the combined debit balance of the intangible asset and contra equity accounts fluctuates by the same amount.

Work Sheet Illustration

To illustrate how the pension work sheet is affected by the minimum liability computation, a revised version of the 2002 work sheet of Zarle Company is shown in Illustration 21-25. The boldface items [entry (u)] relate to adjustments caused by recognition of the minimum liability at the end of 2001 and 2002.

	General Journal Entries					
Items	Annual Pension Expense	Cash	Prepaid/ Accrued Cost	Additional Liability	Pension Intangible	Contra Equity
Balance, Dec. 31, 2001			25,800 Cr.	4,100 Cr.	4,100 Dr.	
(m) Service cost	13,000 Dr.					
(n) Interest cost	21,270 Dr.					
(o) Actual return	12,000 Cr.					
(p) Unexpected loss	1,410 Cr.					
(q) Amortization of PSC	20,800 Dr.					
(r) Contributions		24,000 Cr.				
(s) Benefits						
(t) Liability change (Incr.)						
(u) Minimum liab. adj.				**33,440 Cr.**	**27,900 Dr.**	**5,540 Dr.**
Journal entry for 2002	41,660 Dr.	24,000 Cr.	17,660 Cr.			
Balance, Dec. 31, 2002			43,460 Cr.	37,540 Cr.	32,000 Dr.	5,540 Dr.

	Memo Entries			
Items	Projected Benefit Obligation	Plan Assets	Unrecognized Prior Service Cost	Unrecognized Net Gain or Loss
Balance, Dec. 31, 2001	212,700 Cr.	134,100 Dr.	52,800 Dr.	
(m) Service cost	13,000 Cr.			
(n) Interest cost	21,270 Cr.			
(o) Actual return		12,000 Dr.		
(p) Unexpected loss				1,410 Dr.
(q) Amortization of PSC			20,800 Cr.	
(r) Contributions		24,000 Dr.		
(s) Benefits	10,500 Dr.	10,500 Cr.		
(t) Liability increase	28,530 Cr.			28,530 Dr.
(u) Minimum liab. adj.				
Journal entry for 2002				
Balance, Dec. 31, 2002	265,000 Cr.	159,600 Dr.	32,000 Dr.	29,940 Dr.

ILLUSTRATION 21-25
Revised Pension Work Sheet—2002, Revised to Include Minimum Liability Computation

As illustrated in prior work sheets, the balance in the Prepaid/Accrued Pension Cost account ($43,460) equals the net of the balances in the memo accounts ($265,000 − [$159,600 + $32,000 + $29,940]). In this case, the Additional Liability is combined with the Prepaid/Accrued Pension Cost to determine the minimum pension liability in the balance sheet. This computation is shown in Illustration 21-26.

Projected benefit obligation (Credit)	$(265,000)
Plan assets at fair value (Debit)	159,600
Funded status	(105,400)
Unrecognized prior service cost (Debit)	32,000
Unrecognized net loss (Debit)	29,940
Prepaid/accrued pension cost (Credit)	(43,460)
Additional liability (Credit)	(37,540)
Accrued pension cost liability recognized in the balance sheet (minimum liability)	$ (81,000)

ILLUSTRATION 21-26
Reconciliation Schedule—2002, Revised to Show Additional Pension Liability

REPORTING PENSION PLANS IN FINANCIAL STATEMENTS

OBJECTIVE 10
Describe the reporting requirements for pension plans in financial statements.

One might suspect that a phenomenon as significant and complex as pensions would involve extensive reporting and disclosure requirements. We will cover these requirements in two categories: (1) those within the financial statements, and (2) those within the notes to the financial statements.

Within the Financial Statements

If the amount funded (credit to Cash) by the employer to the pension trust is **less than the annual expense** (debit to Pension Expense), a credit balance accrual of the difference arises in the long-term liability section. It might be described as Accrued Pension Cost, Liability for Pension Expense Not Funded, or Due to Pension Fund. A liability is classified as current when it requires the disbursement of cash within the next year.

If the amount funded to the pension trust during the period is **greater than the amount charged to expense**, an asset equal to the difference arises. This asset is reported as Prepaid Pension Cost, Deferred Pension Expense, or Prepaid Pension Expense in the current assets section if it is current in nature, and in the other assets section if it is long-term in nature.

If the **accumulated benefit obligation exceeds the fair value of pension plan assets**, an additional liability is recorded. The debit is either to an Intangible Asset—Deferred Pension Cost or to a contra account to stockholders' equity entitled Excess of Additional Pension Liability Over Unrecognized Prior Service Cost. If the debit is less than unrecognized prior service cost, it is reported as an intangible asset. If the debit is greater than unrecognized prior service cost, the excess debit is reported as part of other comprehensive income and the accumulated balance as a component of accumulated other comprehensive income.

Within the Notes to the Financial Statements

Pension plans are frequently important to an understanding of financial position, results of operations, and cash flows of a company. Therefore, the following information, if not disclosed in the body of the financial statements, should be disclosed in the notes.[16]

1. A schedule showing all the major components of pension expense should be reported.
   Rationale: Information provided about the components of pension expense helps users better understand how pension expense is determined and is useful in forecasting a company's net income.

[16]"Employers' Disclosure about Pensions and Other Postretirement Benefits," *Statement of Financial Accounting Standards No. 132* (Stamford, Conn.: FASB, 1998). This statement modifies the disclosure requirements of *SFAS No. 87.* In our view, these new disclosure requirements are easier to understand and more streamlined than the disclosure requirements mandated prior to *SFAS No. 132.*

2. A **reconciliation** showing how the projected benefit obligation and the fair value of the plan assets changed from the beginning to the end of the period is required.
Rationale: Disclosing the projected benefit obligation, the fair value of the plan assets, and changes in them should help users understand the economics underlying the obligations and resources of these plans. The Board believes that explaining the changes in the projected benefit obligation and fair value of plan assets in the form of a reconciliation provides a more complete disclosure and makes the financial statements more understandable.

3. The **funded status** of the plan (difference between the projected benefit obligation and fair value of the plan assets) and the amounts recognized and not recognized in the financial statements must be disclosed.
Rationale: Providing a reconciliation of the plan's funded status to the amount reported in the balance sheet highlights the difference between the funded status and the balance sheet presentation.[17]

4. A disclosure of the rates used in measuring the benefit amounts (discount rate, expected return on plan assets, rate of compensation) should be disclosed.
Rationale: Disclosure of these rates permits the reader to determine the reasonableness of the assumptions applied in measuring the pension liability and pension expense.

In summary, the disclosure requirements are extensive, and purposely so. One factor that has been a challenge for useful pension reporting in the past has been the lack of consistency in terminology. Furthermore, a substantial amount of offsetting is inherent in the measurement of pension expense and the pension liability. These disclosures are designed to address these concerns and take some of the mystery out of pension reporting.

Illustration of Pension Note Disclosure

In the following sections we provide illustrations and explain the key pension disclosure elements.

Components of Pension Expense

The Board requires disclosure of the individual pension expense components—(1) service cost, (2) interest cost, (3) expected return on assets, (4) other deferrals and amortization—so that more sophisticated readers can understand how pension expense is determined. Providing information on the components should also be useful in predicting future pension expense. Using the information from the Zarle Company illustration—specifically, the expense component information taken from the left hand column of the work sheet in Illustration 21-25—an example of this part of the disclosure in presented in the following schedule:

ILLUSTRATION 21-27
Summary of Expense Components—2000, 2001, 2002

ZARLE COMPANY

Components of Net Periodic Pension Expense	2000	2001	2002
Service cost	$ 9,000	$ 9,500	$13,000
Interest cost	10,000	19,200	$21,270
Expected return on plan assets	(10,000)	(11,100)	(13,410)*
Amortization of prior service cost	–0–	27,200	20,800
Net periodic pension expense	$ 9,000	$44,800	$41,660

*Note that the expected return must be disclosed, not the actual. In 2002, the expected return is $13,410, which is the actual gain ($12,000) adjusted by the unrecognized loss ($1,410).

[17]The vested benefit obligation does not need to be disclosed, since it is not used in the accounting for the fund. If the accumulated benefit obligation is greater than the fair value of the plan assets, it must be disclosed to inform readers how the minimum liability was computed.

Reconciliation and Funded Status of Plan

By providing a reconciliation of the changes in the assets and liabilities from the beginning of the year to the end of the year, statement readers can better understand the underlying economics of the plan. In essence, this disclosure (reconciliation) contains the information in the pension work sheet for the projected benefit obligation and plan asset columns.

In addition, the Board also requires a disclosure of the funded status of the plan. That is, the off-balance-sheet assets, liabilities, and unrecognized gains and losses must be reconciled with the on-balance-sheet liability or asset. Many believe this is the key to understanding the accounting for pensions. Why is such a disclosure important? The FASB acknowledged that the delayed recognition of some pension elements may exclude the most current and the most relevant information about the pension plan from the financial statements. This important information, however, is provided within this disclosure.

UNDERLYING CONCEPTS

This represents another compromise between relevance and reliability. The disclosure of the unrecognized items attempts to balance these objectives.

Using the information for Zarle Company, the following schedule provides an example of the reconciliation.

ILLUSTRATION 21-28
Pension Disclosure for Zarle Company—2000, 2001, 2002

ZARLE COMPANY
Pension Disclosure

	2000	2001	2002
Change in benefit obligation			
Benefit obligation at beginning of year	$100,000	$112,000	$212,700
Service cost	9,000	9,500	13,000
Interest cost	10,000	19,200	21,270
Amendments (Prior service cost)	–0–	80,000	–0–
Actuarial loss	–0–	–0–	28,530
Benefits paid	(7,000)	(8,000)	(10,500)
Benefit obligation at end of year	112,000	212,700	265,000
Change in plan assets			
Fair value of plan assets at beginning of year	100,000	111,000	134,100
Actual return on plan assets	10,000	11,100	12,000
Contributions	8,000	20,000	24,000
Benefits paid	(7,000)	(8,000)	(10,500)
Fair value of plan assets at end of year	111,000	134,100	159,600
Funded status	(1,000)	(78,600)	(105,400)
Unrecognized net actuarial loss	–0–	–0–	29,940
Unrecognized prior service cost	–0–	52,800	32,000
Prepaid (accrued) benefit cost	**(1,000)**	**(25,800)**	**(43,460)**
Minimum liability adjustment included in:			
Intangible assets	–0–	(4,100)	(32,000)
Stockholders' equity	–0–	–0–	(5,540)
Accrued pension cost liability in the balance sheet	$ (1,000)	$ (29,900)	$ (81,000)

The 2000 column reveals that the projected benefit obligation is underfunded by $1,000. The 2001 column reveals that the underfunded liability of $78,600 is reported in the balance sheet at $29,900, due to the unrecognized prior service cost of $52,800 and the $4,100 additional liability. Finally, the 2002 column indicates that underfunded liability of $105,400 is recognized in the balance sheet at only $81,000 because of $32,000 in unrecognized prior service costs, $29,940 of unrecognized net loss, and $37,540 additional liability (with $5,540 of the minimum liability recorded in stockholders' equity).

UNDERLYING CONCEPTS

Does it make a difference to users of financial statements whether pension information is recognized in the financial statements or disclosed only in the notes? The FASB was not sure, so in accord with the full disclosure principle, it decided to provide extensive pension plan disclosures.

Illustration 21-29 provides the complete postretirement benefit disclosure for Gillette Company.[18] This disclosure shows how companies are providing information on the rates used in measuring the benefit amounts.

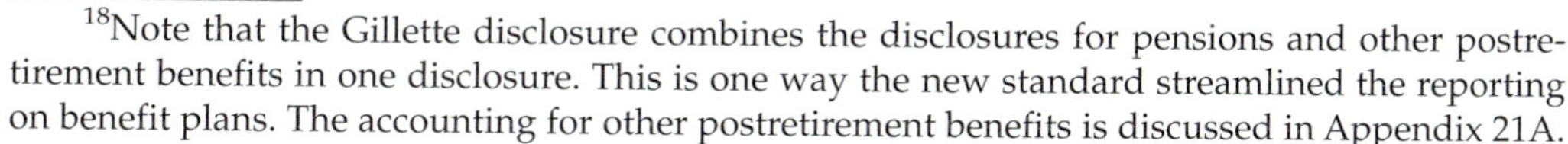

[18]Note that the Gillette disclosure combines the disclosures for pensions and other postretirement benefits in one disclosure. This is one way the new standard streamlined the reporting on benefit plans. The accounting for other postretirement benefits is discussed in Appendix 21A.

ILLUSTRATION 21-29
Gillette Company
Pension Disclosure

GILLETTE COMPANY

Pension Plans and Other Retiree Benefits. The company has various retirement programs, including defined benefit, defined contribution and other plans, that cover most employees worldwide. In 1998, the Company began funding its pension plans in Germany by contributing $252 million to a newly established pension trust. Other retiree benefits are health care and life insurance benefits provided to eligible retired employees, principally in the United States. The components of benefit expense follow.

	Pension Benefits			Other Retiree Benefits		
(Millions of dollars)	1998	1997	1996	1998	1997	1996
Components of new benefit expense						
Service cost-benefits earned	$ 67	$ 64	$ 61	$ 6	$ 5	$ 2
Interest cost on benefit obligation	123	115	109	17	17	19
Estimated return on assets	(157)	(118)	(103)	(3)	(2)	(2)
Net amortization	5	6	12	(7)	(8)	(3)
	38	67	79	13	12	16
Defined contribution plans	2	4	4	—	—	—
Foreign plans not on SFAS 87	10	8	7	—	—	—
Total benefit expense	$ 50	$ 79	$ 90	$13	$12	$16

The funded status of the Company's principal defined benefit and other retiree benefit plans and the amounts recognized in the balance sheet at December 31 follow.

	Pension Benefits		Other Retiree Benefits	
(Millions of dollars)	1998	1997	1998	1997
Change in benefit obligation:				
Balance at beginning of year	$1,790	$1,689	$ 248	$ 266
Benefit payments	(105)	(83)	(14)	(13)
Service and interest costs	190	179	23	22
Amendments	45	4	1	1
Actuarial (gains) losses	88	52	(16)	(28)
Currency translation adjustment	10	(51)	(2)	—
Balance at end of year	2,018	1,790	240	248
Change in fair value of plan assets:				
Balance at beginning of year	1,540	1,278	33	24
Actual return on plan assets	203	272	6	6
Employer contribution	299	57	(3)	3
Benefit payments	(86)	(69)	—	—
Currency translation adjustment	—	2	—	—
Balance at end of year	1,956	1,540	36	33
Plan assets less than benefit obligation	(62)	(250)	(204)	(215)
Unrecognized prior service cost and transition obligation	53	36	(1)	—
Unrecognized net loss (gain)	54	17	(100)	(87)
Minimum liability adjustment included in:				
Intangible assets	(17)	(15)	—	—
Stockholders' equity	(47)	(20)	—	—
Net accrued benefit cost included in consolidated balance sheet	$ (19)	$ (232)	$(305)	$(302)

The values at December 31 for pension plans with accumulated benefit obligations in excess of plan assets follow.

(Millions of dollars)	1998	1997
Projected benefit obligation	$570	$506
Accumulated benefit obligation	506	429
Fair value of plan assets	304	30

The weighted average assumptions used in determining related obligations of pension benefit plans are shown below.

(Percent)	1998	1997	1996
Discount rate	6.3	7.1	7.1
Long-term rate of return on assets	8.6	9.3	9.4
Rate of compensation increase	3.9	4.9	4.8

The weighted average assumptions used in determining related obligations of other retiree benefit plans are shown below.

(Percent)	1998	1997	1996
Discount rate	6.5	7.0	7.0
Long-term rate of return on assets	9.0	9.0	9.0

The assumed health care cost trend rate for 1999 is 6.5%, decreasing to 4.5% by 2001. A one percentage point increase in the trend rate would have increased the accumulated postretirement benefit obligation by 12%, and interest and service cost by 13%. A one percentage point decrease in the trend rate would have decreased the accumulated postretirement benefit obligation by 10%, and interest and service cost by 11%.

Go to the Digital Tool for additional postretirement benefit disclosures.

2003 Entries and Work Sheet—A Comprehensive Illustration

Incorporating the corridor computation, the minimum liability recognition, and the required disclosures, the Zarle Company pension plan accounting is continued based on the following facts for 2003:

> Service cost is $16,000.
>
> Settlement rate is 10%; expected rate of return 10%.
>
> Actual return on plan assets is $22,000.
>
> Amortization of unrecognized prior service cost is $17,600.
>
> Annual contributions (funding) are $27,000.
>
> Benefits paid to retirees during the year are $18,000.
>
> Accumulated benefit obligation is $263,000 at the end of 2003.
>
> Average service life of all covered employees is 20 years.

To facilitate accumulation and recording of the components of pension expense and maintenance of the unrecognized amounts related to the pension plan, the following work sheet is prepared from the basic data presented above. Beginning-of-the-year 2003 account balances are the December 31, 2002, balances from the revised 2002 pension work sheet of Zarle Company in Illustration 21-25.

ILLUSTRATION 21-30
Comprehensive Pension Work Sheet—2003

	General Journal Entries					
Items	Annual Pension Expense	Cash	Prepaid/ Accrued Cost	Additional Liability	Pension Intangible	Contra Equity Charge
Balance, Dec. 31, 2002			43,460 Cr.	37,540 Cr.	32,000 Dr.	5,540 Dr.
(aa) Service cost	16,000 Dr.					
(bb) Interest cost	26,500 Dr.					
(cc) Actual return	22,000 Cr.					
(dd) Unexpected gain	6,040 Dr.					
(ee) Amortization of PSC	17,600 Dr.					
(ff) Contributions		27,000 Cr.				
(gg) Benefits						
(hh) Unrecog. loss amort.	172 Dr.					
(ii) Minimum liab. adj.				25,912 Dr.	20,372 Cr.	5,540 Cr.
Journal entry for 2003	44,312 Dr.	27,000 Cr.	17,312 Cr.			
Balance Dec. 31, 2003			60,772 Cr.	11,628 Cr.	11,628 Dr.	-0-

	Memo Entries			
Items	Projected Benefit Obligation	Plan Assets	Unrecognized Prior Service Cost	Unrecognized Net Gain or Loss
Balance, Dec. 31, 2002	265,000 Cr.	159,600 Dr.	32,000 Dr.	29,940 Dr.
(aa) Service cost	16,000 Cr.			
(bb) Interest cost	26,500 Cr.			
(cc) Actual return		22,000 Dr.		
(dd) Unexpected gain				6,040 Cr.
(ee) Amortization of PSC			17,600 Cr.	
(ff) Contributions		27,000 Dr.		
(gg) Benefits	18,000 Dr.	18,000 Cr.		
(hh) Unrecog. loss amort.				172 Cr.
(ii) Minimum liab. adj.				
Journal entry for 2003				
Balance Dec. 31, 2003	289,500 Cr.	190,600 Dr.	14,400 Dr.	23,728 Dr.

Work Sheet Explanations and Entries

Entries (aa) through (gg) are similar to the corresponding entries previously explained in the prior years' work sheets with the exception of entry (dd). In 2002 the expected return on plan assets exceeded the actual return producing an unexpected loss. In 2003 the actual return of $22,000 exceeds the expected return of $15,960 ($159,600 × 10%), resulting in an unexpected gain of $6,040, entry (dd). By netting the gain of $6,040 against the actual return of $22,000, pension expense is affected only by the expected return of $15,960.

A new entry (hh) in Zarle Company's work sheet results from application of the corridor test on the accumulated balance of unrecognized net gain or loss. Zarle Company begins 2003 with a balance in the unrecognized net loss account of $29,940. The corridor criterion must be applied in 2003 to determine whether the balance is excessive and should be amortized. In 2003 the corridor is 10% of the larger of the beginning-of-the-year projected benefit obligation of $265,000 or the plan asset's market-related asset value (assumed to be fair market value) of $159,600. The corridor for 2003, thus, is $26,500 ($265,000 × 10%). Because the balance in the Unrecognized Net Loss account is $29,940, the excess (outside the corridor) is $3,440 ($29,940 − $26,500). The $3,440 excess is amortized over the average remaining service life of all employees. Using an average remaining service life of 20 years, the amortization in 2003 is $172 ($3,440 ÷ 20). In the 2003 pension work sheet, the $172 is recorded as a debit to Pension Expense and a credit to the Unrecognized Net Loss account. A schedule showing the computation of the $172 amortization charge is presented below:

ILLUSTRATION 21-31
Computation of 2003 Amortization Charge (Corridor Test)

2003 Corridor Test	
Unrecognized net (gain) or loss at beginning of year	$29,940
10% of larger of PBO or market-related asset value of plan assets	26,500
Amortizable amount	$ 3,440
Average service life of all employees	20 years
2003 amortization ($3,440 ÷ 20 years)	$172

The journal entry to formally record pension expense for 2003 is as follows:

2003		
Pension Expense	44,312	
Cash		27,000
Prepaid/Accrued Pension Cost		17,312

The minimum liability, additional liability, and the amount reported as a contra equity charge at the end of 2003 are computed as follows:

ILLUSTRATION 21-32
Minimum Liability Computation—2003

	December 31, 2003
Accumulated benefit obligation (ABO)	$(263,000)
Plan assets at fair value	190,600
Unfunded accumulated benefit obligation (minimum liability)	(72,400)
Accrued pension cost	60,772
Additional liability	(11,628)
Unrecognized prior service cost	14,400
Contra equity charge	$ –0–

As indicated in the above computation, the additional liability balance on December 31, 2003, is $11,628. The balance of $37,540 of additional liability carried over from 2002 requires a downward adjustment of $25,912 ($37,540 − $11,628). The balance in the pension intangible account should also be $11,628; it is, therefore, credited for $20,372 to reduce the balance of $32,000 to the desired amount of $11,628. Because the unrecognized prior service cost balance exceeds the additional liability, no contra equity charge is required. The entry to adjust the minimum liability (the three accounts related thereto) at December 31, 2003, is as follows:

2003		
Additional Pension Liability	25,912	
Intangible Asset—Deferred Pension Cost		20,372
Excess of Additional Pension Liability over Unrecognized Prior Service Cost		5,540

Financial Statement Presentation

The financial statements of Zarle Company at December 31, 2003, present the following items relative to its pension plan:

ILLUSTRATION 21-33
Balance Sheet Presentation of Pension Costs—2003

ZARLE COMPANY Balance Sheet As of December 31, 2003			
Assets		Liabilities	
Intangible assets		Long-term liabilities	
Deferred pension cost	$11,628	Accrued pension cost	$72,400

The prepaid/accrued pension cost balance of $60,772 and the additional liability balance of $11,628 on the work sheet are combined and reported as one pension liability of $72,400 in the balance sheet.

ILLUSTRATION 21-34
Income Statement Presentation of Pension Expense—2003

ZARLE COMPANY Income Statement For the Year Ended December 31, 2003	
Operating expenses	
Pension expense*	$44,312

*Pension expense is frequently reported as "Employee benefits."

ILLUSTRATION 21-35
Statement of Cash Flows Presentation of Pension Liability

ZARLE COMPANY Statement of Cash Flows For the Year Ended December 31, 2003		
Cash flow from operating activities		
Net income (assumed)		$905,000
Adjustments to reconcile net income to net cash provided by operating activities:		
Increase in accrued pension liability	$17,312	

Note: Significant noncash investing and financing activities
Decrease of $20,372 in intangible asset and decrease of $5,540 in contra equity due to decrease of $25,912 in minimum liability.

Note Disclosure

The minimum note disclosure by Zarle Company of the pension plan for 2003 is shown in Illustration 21-36. Note that in the reconciliation schedule in Illustration 21-36, the adjustment required to recognize the minimum liability of $11,628 is included in order to reconcile to the $72,400 accrued pension cost reported in the balance sheet.

ILLUSTRATION 21-36
Minimum Note Disclosure of Pension Plan, Zarle Company, 2003

ZARLE COMPANY
Notes to the Financial Statements

Note D. The company has a pension plan covering substantially all of its employees. The plan is noncontributory and provides pension benefits that are based on the employee's compensation during the three years immediately preceding retirement. The pension plan's assets consist of cash, stocks, and bonds. The company's funding policy is consistent with the relevant government (ERISA) and tax regulations.

Net pension expense for 2003 is comprised of the following components of pension cost:

Service cost	$16,000
Interest on projected benefit obligation	26,500
Expected return on plan assets	(15,960)
Net other components of pension expense[19]	17,772
Net pension expense	$44,312

The following schedule reports changes in the benefit obligation and plan assets during the year and reconciles the funded status of the plan with amounts reported in the company's balance sheet at December 31, 2003:

Change in benefit obligation	
Benefit obligation at beginning of year	$265,000
Service cost	16,000
Interest cost	26,500
Amendments (Prior service cost)	–0–
Actuarial gain	–0–
Benefits paid	(18,000)
Benefit obligation at end of year	289,500
Change in plan assets	
Fair value of plan assets at beginning of year	159,600
Actual return on plan assets	22,000
Contributions	27,000
Benefits paid	(18,000)
Fair value of plan assets at end of year	190,600
Funded status	(98,900)
Unrecognized net actuarial loss	23,728
Unrecognized prior service cost	14,400
Prepaid (accrued) benefit cost	**(60,772)**
Minimum liability adjustment included in:	
Intangible assets	(11,628)
Stockholders' equity	–0–
Accrued pension cost liability in the balance sheet	$ (72,400)

The weighted-average discount rate used in determining the 2003 projected benefit obligation was 10%. The rate of increase in future compensation levels used in computing the 2003 projected benefit obligation was 4.5%. The weighted-average expected long-term rate of return on the plan's assets was 10%.

Special Issues

The Pension Reform Act of 1974

The Employee Retirement Income Security Act of 1974 **(ERISA)** affects virtually every private retirement plan in the United States. It attempts to safeguard employees' pension rights by mandating many pension plan requirements, including minimum funding, participation, and vesting.

[19]"Net other components of pension expense" in this example is comprised of amortization of prior service cost ($17,600) plus amortization of the unrecognized loss ($172). Amortization of prior service cost and amortization of the unrecognized net gain or loss are combined when reporting the components of pension expense.

These requirements can influence the employers' costs significantly. Under this legislation, annual funding is no longer discretionary; an employer must fund the plan in accordance with an actuarial funding method that over time will be sufficient to pay for all pension obligations. If funding is not carried out in a reasonable manner, fines may be imposed and tax deductions denied.

UNDERLYING CONCEPTS

Many plans are underfunded but still quite viable. For example Loews Corp. has a $159 million shortfall. But Loew's had earnings of $594 million and a good net worth. Thus, the going concern assumption permits us to ignore these pension underfundings in many cases because in the long run they are not significant.

Plan administrators are required to publish a comprehensive description and summary of their plans and detailed annual reports accompanied by many supplementary schedules and statements. ERISA further mandates that the required reports, statements, and supplementary schedules be subjected to audit by qualified independent public accountants.

Another important provision of the Act is the creation of the Pension Benefit Guaranty Corporation (PBGC). **The PBGC's purpose is to administer terminated plans** and to impose liens on the employer's assets for certain unfunded pension liabilities. If a plan is terminated, the PBGC can effectively impose a lien against the employer's assets for the excess of the present value of guaranteed vested benefits over the pension fund assets. This lien generally has had the status of a tax lien and, therefore, takes priority over most other creditorship claims. This section of the Act gives the PBGC the power to force an involuntary termination of a pension plan whenever the risks related to nonpayment of the pension obligation seem too great. Because ERISA restricts the lien that the PBGC can impose to 30% of net worth, the PBGC must monitor all plans to ensure that net worth is sufficient to meet the pension benefit obligations.[20]

A large number of terminated plans have caused the PBGC to pay out substantial benefits. Currently the PBGC receives its funding from employers, who contribute a certain dollar amount for each employee covered under the plan.

An interesting accounting problem relates to the manner of disclosing the possible termination of a plan. When, for example, should a contingent liability be disclosed, if a company is experiencing financial difficulty and may not be able to meet its pension obligations if its plan is terminated? At present this issue is unresolved, and considerable judgment would be needed to analyze a company with these contingent liabilities.[21]

Pension Terminations

A congressman at one time noted that "employers are simply treating their employee pension plans like company piggy banks, to be raided at will." What this congressman was referring to is the practice by some companies that have pension plan assets in excess of projected benefit obligations of paying off the obligation and pocketing the difference. ERISA prevents companies from recapturing excess assets unless they pay participants what is owed to them and then terminate the plan. As a result, companies are buying annuities to pay off the pension claimants and using the excess funds for other corporate purposes.[22]

For example, pension plan terminations netted $363 million for Occidental Petroleum Corp., $95 million for Stroh's Brewery Co., $58 million for Kellogg Co., and $29 million for Western Airlines. Since 1980, many large companies have terminated their

[20]The major problems in underfunding are occurring in four labor-intensive industries—steel, autos, rubber, and airlines. General Motors' plan at one time was 92% funded but still had a deficit of over $6 billion.

[21]Pan American is a good illustration of how difficult it is to assess when to terminate. When Pan Am filed for bankruptcy in 1991, it had a pension liability of $900 million. From 1983 to 1991, the IRS gave it six waivers so it did not have to make contributions. When the plan was terminated, there was little net worth upon which a lien could be imposed.

[22]A real question exists as to whose money it is. Some argue that the excess funds belong to the employees, not the employer. In addition, given that the funds have been reverting to the employer, critics charge that cost-of-living increases and the possibility of other increased benefits are reduced, because companies will be reluctant to use those excess funds to pay for such increases.

pension plans and captured billions in surplus assets. All of this is quite legal, but is it ethical? It should be noted that federal legislation recently enacted requires the company to pay an excise tax of anywhere from 20% to 50% on the gains.

The accounting issue that arises from these terminations is whether a gain should be recognized by the corporation when these assets revert back to the company (often called **asset reversion** transactions). The issue is complex because, in some cases, a new defined benefit plan is started after the old one has been eliminated. Therefore some contend that there has been no change in substance, but merely one in form.

Up to this point the profession has required that these gains be reported if the companies switched from a defined benefit plan to a defined contribution plan. Otherwise, the gain is deferred and amortized over at least 10 years in the future. Many questioned this reporting treatment. As a result the FASB issued *FASB Statement No. 88* that requires recognition in earnings of a new gain or loss when the employer settles a pension obligation either by lump-sum cash payments to participants or by purchasing nonparticipating annuity contracts.[23]

Cash-Balance Pension Plans

Recently, some companies have adopted hybrid pension plans, which combine features of defined benefit and defined contribution plans. These **cash-balance plans** allow employees to transfer their pension benefits when they change employers. This portability-of-benefit feature is popular with younger workers who, unlike earlier generations of workers, expect to change employers several times during their working lives. Such plans are controversial because the change to a cash-balance plan often reduces benefits to older workers. Consequently, the introduction of these plans has drawn the attention of Congress and the IRS to ensure their fairness to all workers.[24]

From an accounting standpoint, cash-balance plans are accounted for similar to a defined benefit plan. This is because employers bear the investment risk in cash-balance plans. Interestingly, when an employer adopts a cash-balance plan, the measurement of the future benefit obligation to employees generally is lower, compared to a traditional defined benefit plan. As a result, when a defined benefit plan is converted to a cash-balance plan, the employer many times will record a negative prior service cost adjustment. The amortization of this prior service cost results in a reduction in pension expense.[25]

Concluding Observation

Hardly a day goes by without the financial press analyzing in depth some issues related to pension plans in the United States. This is hardly surprising, since U.S. pension funds now hold over $5 trillion in assets. As should be obvious by now, the accounting issues related to pension plans are complex. *FASB Statement No. 87* clarifies many of these issues and should help users understand the financial implications of a company's pension plans on its financial position, results of operations, and cash flows.

Critics still argue, however, that much remains to be done. One issue in particular relates to the delayed recognition of certain events. Changes in pension plan obliga-

[23]"Employers' Accounting for Settlements and Curtailments of Defined Benefit Pension Plans and for Termination Benefits," *Statement of Financial Accounting Standards No. 88* (Stamford, Conn.: FASB, 1985). Some companies have established pension poison pills as an antitakeover measure. These plans require asset reversions from termination of a plan to benefit employees and retirees rather than the acquiring company. For a discussion of pension poison pills, see Eugene E. Comiskey and Charles W. Mulford, "Interpreting Pension Disclosures: A Guide for Lending Officers," *Commercial Lending Review,* Winter 1993–94, Vol. 9, No. 1.

[24]E. Schultz, "IRS Set to Continue to Give Green Light on Pension Plan," *The Wall Street Journal*, September 2, 1999, p. A2.

[25]See A. T. Arcady and F. Mellors, "Cash-Balance Conversions," *Journal of Accountancy,* February 2000, pp. 22–28.

tions and changes in the value of plan assets are not recognized immediately but are systematically incorporated over subsequent periods.

SUMMARY OF LEARNING OBJECTIVES

1 Distinguish between accounting for the employer's pension plan and accounting for the pension fund. The company or employer is the organization sponsoring the pension plan. It incurs the cost and makes contributions to the pension fund. The fund or plan is the entity that receives the contributions from the employer, administers the pension assets, and makes the benefit payments to the pension recipients (retired employees). The fund should be a separate legal and accounting entity for which a set of books is maintained and financial statements are prepared.

2 Identify types of pension plans and their characteristics. The two most common types of pension arrangements are: (1) *Defined contribution plans:* the employer agrees to contribute to a pension trust a certain sum each period based on a formula. This formula may consider such factors as age, length of employee service, employer's profits, and compensation level. Only the employer's contribution is defined; no promise is made regarding the ultimate benefits paid out to the employees. (2) *Defined benefit plans:* define the benefits that the employee will receive at the time of retirement. The formula typically used provides for the benefits to be a function of the employee's years of service and the employer's compensation level when he or she nears retirement.

3 Explain alternative measures for valuing the pension obligation. One measure of the pension obligation bases it only on the benefits vested to the employees. Vested benefits are those that the employee is entitled to receive even if the employee renders no additional services under the plan. The *vested benefits pension obligation* is computed using current salary levels and includes only vested benefits. Another measure of the obligation, called the *accumulated benefit obligation,* bases the computation of the deferred compensation amount on all years of service performed by employees under the plan—both vested and nonvested—using current salary levels. A third measure, called the *projected benefit obligation,* bases the computation of the deferred compensation amount on both vested and nonvested service using future salaries.

4 Identify the components of pension expense. Pension expense is a function of the following components: (1) service cost; (2) interest on the liability; (3) actual return on plan assets; (4) amortization of unrecognized prior service cost; and (5) gain or loss.

5 Utilize a work sheet for pension plan entries. A work sheet unique to pension accounting may be utilized to record both the formal entries and the memo entries to keep track of all the employer's relevant pension plan items and components.

6 Describe the amortization of unrecognized prior service costs. The amount of the prior service cost is computed by an actuary. Amortization of the unrecognized prior service cost is an accounting function performed with the assistance of an actuary. The Board prefers a "years-of-service" amortization method that is similar to a units-of-production computation. First, the total estimated number of service-years to be worked by all of the participating employees is computed. Second, the unrecognized prior service cost is divided by the total number of service-years to obtain a cost per service-year (the unit cost). And third, the number of service-years consumed each year is multiplied by the cost per service-year to obtain the annual amortization charge.

KEY TERMS

accrued pension cost, *1140*
accumulated benefit obligation, *1124*
actual return on plan assets, *1128*
actuarial present value, *1127*
actuaries, *1123*
additional liability, *1139*
asset gains and losses, *1134*
cash-balance plans, *1152*
components of pension expense, *1126*
contributory pension plan, *1121*
corridor approach, *1135*
defined benefit plan, *1122*
defined contribution plan, *1122*
ERISA, *1150*
expected rate of return, *1134*
expected return on plan assets, *1134*
fair value of plan assets, *1128*
funded pension plan, *1121*
funded status, *1144*
interest on the liability (interest expense), *1127*
liability gains and losses, *1134*
market-related asset value, *1139*
minimum liability, *1139*
noncontributory pension plan, *1121*
pension plan, *1120*
pension work sheet, *1129*
prepaid pension cost, *1140*
prior service cost (PSC), *1131*
projected benefit obligation, *1124*
qualified pension plan, *1121*
reconciliation, *1144*
retroactive benefits, *1131*
service cost, *1127*

settlement rate, *1128*
unexpected gain or loss, *1134*
unrecognized net gain or loss, *1135*
unrecognized prior service cost, *1132*
vested benefit obligation, *1124*
vested benefits, *1124*
years-of-service method, *1131*

7 **Explain the accounting procedure for recognizing unexpected gains and losses.** In estimating the projected benefit obligation (the liability), actuaries make assumptions about such items as mortality rate, retirement rate, turnover rate, disability rate, and salary amounts. Any change in these actuarial assumptions changes the amount of the projected benefit obligation. These unexpected gains or losses from changes in the projected benefit obligation are liability gains and losses. Liability gains (resulting from unexpected decreases in the liability balance) and liability losses (resulting from unexpected increases) are deferred (unrecognized). The liability gains and losses are combined in the same Unrecognized Net Gain or Loss account used for asset gains and losses and are accumulated from year to year, off-balance-sheet, in a memo record account.

8 **Explain the corridor approach to amortizing unrecognized gains and losses.** The unrecognized net gain or loss balance is considered too large and must be amortized when it exceeds the arbitrarily selected FASB criterion of 10% of the larger of the beginning balances of the projected benefit obligation or the market-related value of the plan assets. If the balance of the unrecognized net gain or loss account stays within the upper and lower limits of the corridor, no amortization is required.

9 **Explain the recognition of a minimum liability.** Immediate recognition of a liability (referred to as the minimum liability) is required when the accumulated benefit obligation exceeds the fair value of plan assets. The purpose of this minimum liability requirement is to assure that if a significant plan amendment or actuarial loss occurs, a liability will be recognized at least to the extent of the unfunded portion of the accumulated benefit obligation.

10 **Describe the reporting requirements for pension plans in financial statements.** The current financial statement disclosure requirements for pension plans are as follows: (1) The components of net periodic pension expense for the period. (2) A schedule showing changes in the benefit obligation and plan assets during the year. (3) A schedule reconciling the funded status of the plan with amounts reported in the employer's statement of financial position. (4) The weighted-average assumed discount rate, the rate of compensation increase used to measure the projected benefit obligation, and the weighted-average expected long-term rate of return on plan assets.

FROM CLASSROOM TO CAREER

MICHELE LIPPERT
is the controller for evoke.com, an Internet communications company founded in 1997. Prior to her current position, she was an assistant controller for a cycling apparel company and, before that, a tax accountant with a mid-size CPA firm and an auditor with another firm. Lippert, who holds a bachelor's degree in accounting from Truman State University in Missouri, passed the CPA examination in one sitting.

What does evoke.com do?

We offer a comprehensive suite of Web-based voice, video, and data collaboration services that allow users to get business done better and faster. As an example, we allow clients to view a business presentation over the Internet while they are participating in a conference call. Perhaps 30 people throughout the country could view the same slide presentation, while interacting over the phone. Others who do not have access to telephone and computer simultaneously could still listen to the call through their computers, and push questions or comments on the presentation via the Internet. In addition, we can take video content, such as a video from a company's annual meeting, encode it, and present it over the Internet. We do a lot of work for the sports and entertainment industries, such as using cameras in racecars or presenting music videos for distribution over the Internet. Some presentations require a password, such as an annual meeting, which a company might want to restrict to shareholders. Other events could be open to anyone.

Why did you leave public accounting?

The hours were very long, sometimes for months at a time. Even though I still work long hours occasionally, I have found the money and benefits to be better in industry. And, of course, there's the lure of stock options. High-tech companies tend to start you at a lower salary, but offer options that could be very lucrative. It's risky, because a lot of venture-capital backed companies go out of business. Still, I don't have dependents, and I'm young enough to be able to take a risk like this.

What advice would you give students who would like to follow in your footsteps?

I don't think I could have done this straight out of college. Having a public accounting background helped me a lot. It gave me a basis for everything I'm doing right now. As we speak, we have auditors here, and my CPA background makes this go a lot smoother, because I know what they're looking for.

You've worked in auditing and tax. What's the difference?

Auditing requires you to go into a company, go through their accounts, and substantiate certain numbers to make sure everything is correctly stated. Once the audit is done, the tax people come in. They'll determine what is deductible for tax purposes and advise clients on actions they could take to lower taxes in the future. In addition, the tax people have to distinguish expenses allowable for financial statement purposes from those allowed for tax purposes. For instance, depreciation is calculated differently for tax and for book purposes. There's also a calculation that deals with capitalizing certain inventory costs for tax purposes that were expenses for financial statement purposes. Other items to be reconciled include disallowed tax expenses such as penalties and the 50% limitation on meals and entertainment.

Any tips on passing the CPA exam?

Learn the material the first time around, instead of trying to cram before the test.

APPENDIX 21A

Accounting for Postretirement Benefits

IBM Corporation's adoption of a new accounting standard on postretirement benefits in March 1991 resulted in a $2.3 billion charge and a historical curiosity—IBM's first-ever quarterly loss. General Electric Co. disclosed that its charge for adoption of the same new FASB standard would be $2.7 billion, and in the fourth quarter of 1993, AT&T Co. absorbed a $2.1 billion pretax hit for postretirement benefits. What is this standard, and how could its adoption have so grave an impact on companies' earnings?

ACCOUNTING GUIDANCE

After a decade of study, the FASB in December 1990 issued *Statement No. 106,* "Employers' Accounting for Postretirement Benefits Other Than Pensions." It alone is the cause for those large charges to income. This standard accounts for health care and other welfare benefits provided to retirees, their spouses, dependents, and beneficiaries.[1] These other welfare benefits include life insurance offered outside a pension plan, dental care as well as medical care, eye care, legal and tax services, tuition assistance, day care, and housing assistance.[2] Because health-care benefits are the largest of the other postretirement benefits, this item is used to illustrate accounting for postretirement benefits.

For many employers (about 95%) this standard required a change from the predominant practice of accounting for postretirement benefits on a pay-as-you-go (cash) basis to an accrual basis. Similar to pension accounting, the accrual basis necessitates measurement of the employer's obligation to provide future benefits and accrual of the cost during the years that the employee provides service.

One of the reasons companies have not prefunded these benefit plans is that payments to prefund health-care costs, unlike excess contributions to a pension trust, are not tax deductible. Another reason is that postretirement health-care benefits were once perceived to be a low-cost employee benefit that could be changed or eliminated at will and, therefore, not a legal liability. Now, the accounting definition of a liability goes beyond the notion of a legally enforceable claim to encompass equitable or

[1]*Accounting Trends and Techniques—1999* reports that of its 600 surveyed companies, 373 report benefit plans that provide postretirement health-care benefits. Surprisingly, such coverage translates into a total health-care liability estimated at more than $400 billion and perhaps as much as $2 trillion, which is largely unfunded.

[2]"OPEB" is the acronym frequently used to describe postretirement benefits covered by *FASB Statement No. 106.* This term came into being before the scope of the statement was narrowed from "other postemployment benefits" to "other postretirement benefits," thereby excluding postemployment benefits related to severance pay or wage continuation to disabled, terminated, or laid-off employees.

constructive obligations as well, making it clear that the postretirement benefit promise is a liability.[3]

DIFFERENCES BETWEEN PENSION BENEFITS AND HEALTH-CARE BENEFITS

OBJECTIVE 11
After studying Appendix 21A, you should be able to: Identify the differences between pensions and postretirement health-care benefits.

The FASB used *Statement No. 87* on pensions as a reference for the accounting prescribed in *Statement No. 106* on health-care and other nonpension postretirement benefits.[4] Why didn't the FASB cover both types of postretirement benefits in the earlier pension accounting statement? The apparent similarities between the two benefits mask some significant differences. These differences are shown in Illustration 21A-1.[5]

ILLUSTRATION 21A-1
Differences between Pensions and Postretirement Health-Care Benefits

Item	Pensions	Health-Care Benefits
Funding	Generally funded.	Generally *NOT* funded.
Benefit	Well-defined and level dollar amount.	Generally uncapped and great variability.
Beneficiary	Retiree (maybe some benefit to surviving spouse).	Retiree, spouse, and other dependents.
Benefit Payable	Monthly.	As needed and used.
Predictability	Variables are reasonably predictable.	Utilization difficult to predict. Level of cost varies geographically and fluctuates over time.

Two of the differences presented in Illustration 21A-1 highlight why measuring the future payments for health-care benefit plans is so much more difficult than for pension plans:

1. Many postretirement plans do not set a limit on health-care benefits. No matter how serious the illness or how long it lasts, the benefits continue to flow. (Even if the employer uses an insurance company plan, the premiums will escalate according to the increased benefits provided.)
2. The level of health-care benefit utilization and health-care costs is difficult to predict. The increased longevity and unexpected illnesses (e.g., AIDS) along with new medical technologies (e.g., MRI scans) and cures (e.g., radiation) cause changes in health-care utilization.

Additionally, although health-care benefits are generally covered by the fiduciary and reporting standards for employee benefit funds under ERISA, the stringent minimum vesting, participation, and funding standards that apply to pensions do not apply to health-care benefits. Nevertheless, as you will learn, many of the basic concepts and much of the accounting terminology and measurement methodology applicable to

---

[3]"Elements of Financial Statements," *Statement of Financial Accounting Concepts No. 6* (Stamford, Conn.: 1985), page 13, footnote 21.

[4]In November 1992 the FASB issued *Statement of Financial Accounting Standards No. 112*, "Employers' Accounting for Postemployment Benefits," which covers postemployment benefits that are not accounted for under *SFAS No. 87* (pensions), *SFAS No. 88* (settlements, curtailments, and termination benefits), or *SFAS No. 106* (postretirement benefits other than pensions). *SFAS No. 112* requires an employer to recognize the obligation to provide postemployment benefits in accordance with *SFAS No. 43*, similar to accounting for compensated absences (see Chapter 13). These *SFAS No. 112* benefits include, but are not limited to, salary continuation, disability-related benefits, severance benefits, and continuance of health-care benefits and life insurance for inactive or former (e.g., terminated, disabled, or deceased) employees or their beneficiaries.

[5]D. Gerald Searfoss and Naomi Erickson, "The Big Unfunded Liability: Postretirement Health-Care Benefits," *Journal of Accountancy*, November 1988, pp. 28–39.

pensions are applicable to other postretirement benefits accounting. Therefore, throughout the following discussion and illustrations, we point out the similarities and differences in the accounting and reporting for these two types of postretirement benefits.

POSTRETIREMENT BENEFITS ACCOUNTING PROVISIONS

Health-care and other postretirement benefits for current and future retirees and their dependents are forms of deferred compensation earned through employee service and subject to acrrual during the years an employee is working. The period of time over which the postretirement benefit cost is accrued, called the **attribution period**, is the period of service during which the employee earns the benefits under the terms of the plan. This attribution period (shown in Illustration 21A-2) generally begins when an employee is hired and ends on the date the employee is eligible to receive the benefits and ceases to earn additional benefits by performing service, the vesting date.[6]

ILLUSTRATION 21A-2
Range of Possible Attribution Periods

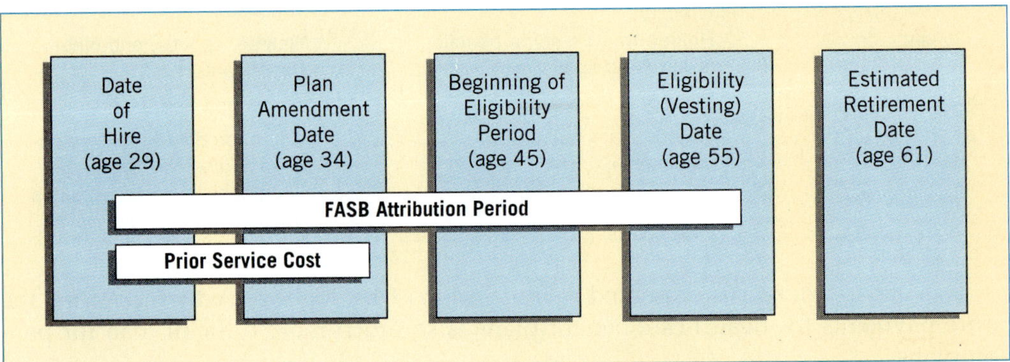

Obligations under Postretirement Benefits

In defining the obligation for postretirement benefits, many concepts similar to pension accounting are maintained, but some new and modified terms are designed specifically for postretirement benefits. Two of the most important are (a) expected postretirement benefit obligation and (b) accumulated postretirement benefit obligation.

Expected Postretirement Benefit Obligation (EPBO). The EPBO is the actuarial present value as of a particular date of **all benefits expected to be paid after retirement to employees and their dependents**. The EPBO is not recorded in the financial statements, but it is used in measuring periodic expense.

Accumulated Postretirement Benefit Obligation (APBO). The APBO is the actuarial present value of **future benefits attributed to employees' services rendered to a particular date**. The APBO is equal to the EPBO for retirees and active employees fully eligible for benefits. Before the date an employee achieves full eligibility, the APBO is only a portion of the EPBO. Or stated another way, the difference between the APBO and the EPBO is the future service costs of active employees who are not yet fully eligible.

Illustration 21A-3 contrasts the EPBO and the APBO.

[6]This is a benefit-years-of-service approach (the projected unit credit actuarial cost method). The FASB found no compelling reason to switch from the traditional pension accounting approach. It rejected the employee's full service period (i.e., to the estimated retirement date) because it was unable to identify any approach that would appropriately attribute benefits beyond the date full eligibility for those benefits is attained. Full eligibility is attained by meeting specified age, service, or age and service requirements of the plan.

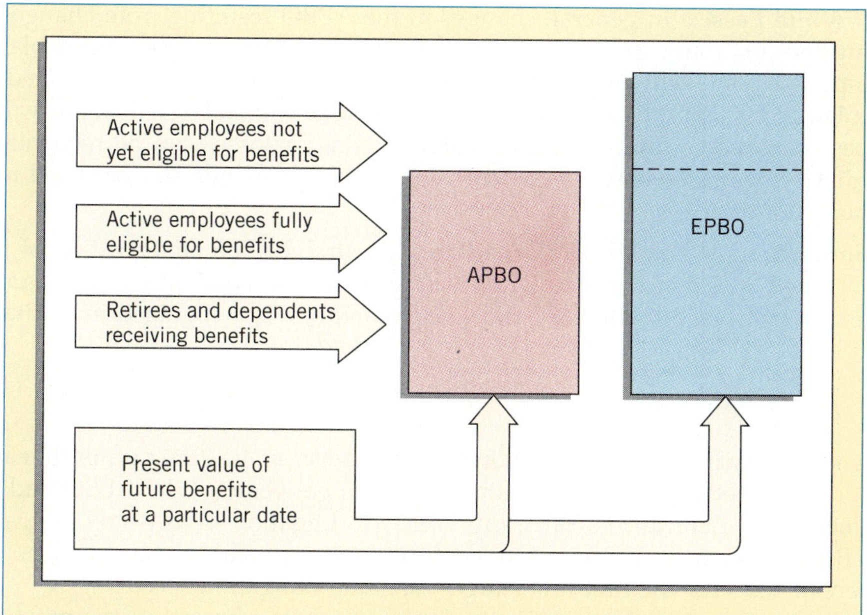

ILLUSTRATION 21A-3
APBO and EPBO Contrasted

At the date an employee is fully eligible (the end of the attribution period), the APBO and the EPBO relative to that employee are equal.

Postretirement Expense

Postretirement expense, also referred to as **net periodic postretirement benefit cost**, is the employer's annual postretirement benefit expense, which consists of many of the familiar components used to compute annual pension expense. The components of net periodic postretirement benefit cost are:[7]

1. ***Service Cost.*** The portion of the EPBO attributed to employee service during the period.
2. ***Interest Cost.*** The increase in the APBO attributable to the passage of time. It is computed by applying the beginning-of-the-year discount rate to the beginning-of-the-year APBO, adjusted for benefit payments to be made during the period. The discount rate is based on the rates of return on high-quality, fixed-income investments that are currently available.[8]
3. ***Actual Return on Plan Assets.*** The change in the fair value of the plan's assets adjusted for contributions and benefit payments made during the period. Because the postretirement expense is charged or credited for the gain or loss on plan assets (the difference between the actual and the expected return), this component is really expected return.
4. ***Amortization of Prior Service Cost.*** The amortization of the cost of retroactive benefits resulting from plan amendments or a plan initiation that takes place after *Statement No. 106* takes effect. The typical amortization period, beginning at the date of the plan amendment, is the remaining service periods through the full eligibility date.

---

[7] "Employers' Accounting for Postretirement Benefits Other Than Pensions," *Statement of Financial Accounting Standards No. 106* (Norwalk, Conn.: FASB, 1990), paras. 46–66. And see, James R. Wilbert and Kenneth E. Dakdduk, "The New FASB 106: How to Account for Postretirement Benefits," *Journal of Accountancy*, August 1991, pp. 36–41.

[8] The FASB concluded that the discount rate for measuring the present value of the postretirement benefit obligation and the service cost component should be the same as that applied to pension measurements. It chose not to label it the settlement rate in order to clarify that the objective of the discount rate is to measure the time value of money.

5 ***Gains and Losses.*** In general, changes in the APBO resulting from changes in assumptions or from experience different from that assumed. For funded plans, this component also includes the difference between actual return and expected return on plan assets (computed the same as for pensions—actual based on fair value and expected based on market-related value). Gains or losses can be recognized immediately or can be based on a "corridor approach" similar to that used for pension accounting.

6 ***Amortization of Transition Obligation.*** The straight-line amortization of the unrecognized APBO at the time *FASB Statement No. 106* is adopted. This component of expense is not present if the transition obligation is recognized immediately.

The Transition Amount

At the beginning of the year of adoption of *FASB Statement No. 106,* a **transition amount** (obligation or asset) is computed as the difference between (1) the APBO and (2) the fair value of the plan assets, plus any accrued obligation or less any prepaid cost (asset). Because most plans are unfunded and most employers are accruing postretirement benefit costs for the first time, large transition obligations occur.

The accounting treatment of this transition amount was one of the most controversial issues in postretirement benefit standard setting. The primary concern of many was that an immediate charge to expense for unrecognized past costs, accompanied by recognition of the total unrecognized liability, would have a large negative impact on reported earnings in the year of the change. Of equal concern to others was that the alternative, deferral and amortization of the expense, accompanied by a rapidly increasing liability, would be a drain on reported earnings for many years. And providing the option of immediate write-off or deferral and amortization was also problematic because of the lack of comparability that would result. Nevertheless, the FASB decided to permit employers to choose between the immediate recognition (e.g., the $2.3 billion charge taken by **IBM** in the first quarter of 1991) and deferral and amortization:

> **Immediate recognition**. As an immediate write-off, the transition amount is recognized in the income statement as the "effect of a change in accounting principle" (net of tax)[9] and in the balance sheet as a long-term liability entitled Postretirement Benefit Obligation. Restatement of previously issued annual financial statements is not permitted.
>
> **Deferred recognition**. Employers choosing deferred recognition must amortize the transition amount on a straight-line basis over the average remaining service period to expected retirement of the employees in place at the time of transition and expected to receive benefits.[10] If the remaining service period is less than 20 years, the employer may elect a 20-year amortization period. But, the transition amount may not be amortized more slowly than it is paid off (referred to as the "pay-as-you-go constraint").[11]

Once chosen, the method cannot be changed. That is, after once electing to amortize the transition amount, the employer cannot record the remainder of its unamor-

[9]The FASB uses the term "effect" rather than "cumulative effect," and because of the unique transition provision and calculations involved, the retroactive effects on prior periods are generally not determinable and therefore pro forma disclosures are not required. The per share effects of the accounting change are required to be shown on the face of the income statement.

[10]For amortization of the transition amount (and for gains and losses as well), the Board chose the longer "retirement date" as opposed to the "full eligibility date" for pragmatic reasons—the magnitude of the transition amount argued for a longer amortization period to minimize the effect on current financial statements.

[11]In pension accounting, the transition amount must be amortized over the average remaining service life of existing employees or optionally over a 15-year period if the remaining service life is less than 15 years.

tized transition obligation in a subsequent year under the immediate recognition method.

ILLUSTRATIVE ACCOUNTING ENTRIES

OBJECTIVE 12
Contrast accounting for pensions to accounting for other postretirement benefits.

Like pension accounting, several significant items of the postretirement plan are unrecognized in the accounts and in the financial statements. These off-balance-sheet items are:

1. Expected postretirement benefit obligation (EPBO)
2. Accumulated postretirement benefit obligation (APBO)
3. Postretirement benefit plan assets
4. Unrecognized transition amount
5. Unrecognized prior service cost
6. Unrecognized net gain or loss

The EPBO is not recognized in the financial statements or disclosed in the notes. It is recomputed each year and used by the actuary in measuring the annual service cost. Because of the numerous assumptions and actuarial complexity involved in measuring annual service cost, we have omitted these computations of the EPBO.

All five of the other off-balance-sheet items listed above must be disclosed by the employer in notes to the financial statements. In addition, as in pension accounting, the exact amount of these items must be known because they are used in the computation of postretirement expense. Therefore, in order to track these off-balance-sheet postretirement benefit items, the work sheet illustrated in pension accounting will be utilized to record both the formal general journal entries and the memo entries.

2000 Entries and Work Sheet

To illustrate the use of a work sheet in accounting for a postretirement benefits plan, assume that on January 1, 2000, Quest Company adopts *Statement No. 106* to account for its health-care benefit plan. The following facts apply to the postretirement benefits plan for the year 2000.

Plan assets at fair value on January 1, 2000, are zero.

Actual and expected returns on plan assets are zero.

APBO, January 1, 2000, is $400,000.

Service cost is $22,000.

No prior service cost exists.

Discount rate is 8%.

Contributions (funding) to plan during the year are $38,000.

Benefit payments to employees from plan are $28,000.

Average remaining service to full eligibility: 21 years.

Average remaining service to expected retirement: 25 years.

Transition amount to be amortized.

Using the preceding data, the following work sheet presents the beginning balances and all of the postretirement benefit entries recorded by Quest Company in 2000.

Items	Annual Postretirement Expense	Cash	Prepaid/ Accrued Cost	APBO	Plan Assets	Unrecognized Transition Amount
	General Journal Entries			Memo Record		
Balance, Jan. 1, 2000				400,000 Cr.		400,000 Dr.
(a) Service cost	22,000 Dr.			22,000 Cr.		
(b) Interest cost	32,000 Dr.			32,000 Cr.		
(c) Contributions		38,000 Cr.			38,000 Dr.	
(d) Benefits				28,000 Dr.	28,000 Cr.	
(e) Amortization: Transition	16,000 Dr.***					16,000 Cr.
Journal entry for 2000	70,000 Dr.	38,000 Cr.	32,000 Cr.*			
Balance, Dec. 31, 2000			32,000 Cr.**	426,000 Cr.	10,000 Dr.	384,000 Dr.

*$70,000 − $38,000 = $32,000.
**$426,000 − ($10,000 + $384,000) = $32,000
***$400,000 ÷ 25 = $16,000

ILLUSTRATION 21A-4
Postretirement Benefits Work Sheet—2000

On the first line of the work sheet, the beginning balances of the APBO and the unrecognized transition amount are recorded in the memo record columns. The transition amount is the difference between the APBO and the fair value of plan assets, in this case $400,000 ($400,000 − $0).

Entry (a) records the service cost component, which increases postretirement expense $22,000 and increases the liability (APBO) $22,000. Entry (b) accrues the interest expense component, which increases both the liability (APBO) and the expense by $32,000 (the beginning APBO multiplied by the discount rate of 8%). Entry (c) records Quest Company's contribution (funding) of assets to the postretirement benefit fund; cash is decreased $38,000 and plan assets are increased $38,000. Entry (d) records the benefit payments made to retirees, which results in equal $28,000 decreases to the plan assets and the liability (APBO). Entry (e) records the amortization of the unrecognized transition amount. It is amortized over the average remaining service to expected retirement, 25 years. The amortized amount of $16,000 ($400,000 ÷ 25) increases post retirement expense and decreases the unrecognized transition amount.

The entry on December 31, which is the adjusting entry made to formally record the postretirement expense in 2000, is as follows:

December 31, 2000		
Postretirement Expense	70,000	
Cash		38,000
Prepaid/Accrued Cost		32,000

The credit to Prepaid/Accrued Cost for $32,000 represents the difference between the 2000 postretirement expense of $70,000 and the amount funded of $38,000. The $32,000 credit balance is a liability because the plan is underfunded. The Prepaid/Accrued Cost account balance of $32,000 also equals the net of the balances in the memo accounts. This reconciliation of the off-balance-sheet items with the prepaid/accrued cost reported in the balance sheet is shown below (similar to the pension reconciliation schedule).

ILLUSTRATION 21A-5
Postretirement Benefits Reconciliation Schedule—December 31, 2000

Accumulated postretirement benefit obligation (Credit)	$(426,000)
Plan assets at fair value (Debit)	10,000
Funded status (Credit)	(416,000)
Unrecognized transition amount (Debit)	384,000
Prepaid/accrued cost (Credit)	$ (32,000)

Preparation of this reconciliation schedule is necessary as part of the required note disclosures.

Recognition of Gains and Losses

Gains and losses represent changes in the APBO or the value of plan assets resulting either from actual experience different from that expected or from changes in actuarial assumptions. The FASB noted that "recognizing the effects of revisions in estimates in full in the period in which they occur may produce financial statements that portray more volatility than is inherent in the employer's obligation."[12] Therefore, as in pension accounting, gains and losses are not required to be recognized immediately[13] but may be deferred in the period when they occur and amortized in future years.

The Corridor Approach

Consistent with pension accounting, deferred gains and losses are amortized as a component of net periodic expense if, as of the beginning of the period, they exceed a "corridor." The corridor is defined as the greater of 10% of the APBO or 10% of the market-related value of plan assets. The **corridor approach** is intended to reduce postretirement expense volatility by providing a reasonable opportunity for gains and losses to offset over time without affecting net periodic expense.

Amortization Methods

If amortization is required, the **minimum amortization amount** is the excess (beyond the corridor) gain or loss divided by the average remaining service life to expected retirement of all active employees. Any systematic method of amortization may be used provided that (1) the amount amortized in any period is equal to or greater than the minimum amount; (2) the method is applied consistently; and (3) the method is applied similarly for both gains and losses.

The amount of unrecognized gain or loss is recomputed each year and amortized over the average remaining service life if the net amount exceeds the "corridor."

2001 Entries and Work Sheet

Continuing the Quest Company illustration into 2001 the following facts apply to the postretirement benefits plan for the year 2001:

Actual return on plan assets is $600.

Expected return on plan assets is $800.

Discount rate is 8%.

Increase in APBO due to change in actuarial assumptions is $60,000.

Service cost is $26,000.

Contributions (funding) to plan during the year are $50,000.

Benefit payments to employees during the year are $35,000.

Average remaining service to full eligibility: 21 years.

Average remaining service to expected retirement: 25 years.

The work sheet in Illustration 21A-6 presents all of the postretirement benefit entries and information recorded by Quest Company in 2001. The beginning balances entered on the first line of the Quest Company work sheet are the ending balances from the 2000 Quest Company postretirement benefits work sheet in Illustration 21A-4.

---

[12] *FASB Statement No. 106,* par. 293.

[13] If an employer adopts a consistent policy of immediately recognizing gains and losses: (1) the amount of any **net gain** in excess of net losses previously recognized in income would first offset any unamortized **transition obligation**; and (2) the amount of any **net loss** in excess of net gains previously recognized in net income would first offset any unamortized **transition asset** (existence of a transition asset, however, is unlikely).

Items	Annual Postretirement Expense	Cash	Prepaid/ Accrued Cost	APBO	Plan Assets	Unrecognized Transition Amount	Unrecognized Net Gain or Loss
	General Journal Entries			Memo Record			
Balances, Jan. 1, 2001			32,000 Cr.	426,000 Cr.	10,000 Dr.	384,000 Dr.	
(f) Service cost	26,000 Dr.			26,000 Cr.			
(g) Interest cost	34,080 Dr.			34,080 Cr.			
(h) Actual return	600 Cr.				600 Dr.		
(i) Unexpected loss	200 Cr.						200 Dr.
(j) Contributions		50,000 Cr.			50,000 Dr.		
(k) Benefits				35,000 Dr.	35,000 Cr.		
(l) Amortization: Transition	16,000 Dr.					16,000 Cr.	
(m) Inc. in APBO—Loss				60,000 Cr.			60,000 Dr.
Journal entry for 2001	75,280 Dr.	50,000 Cr.	25,280 Cr.*				
Balance, Dec. 31, 2001			57,280 Cr.**	511,080 Cr.	25,600 Dr.	368,000 Dr.	60,200 Dr.

*$75,280 − $50,000 = $25,280
**$511,080 − ($25,600 + $368,000 + $60,200) = $57,280

ILLUSTRATION 21A-6
Postretirement Benefits Work Sheet—2001

Entries (f), (g), (j), (k), and (l) are similar to the corresponding entries previously explained in 2000. Entries (h) and (i) are related. The expected return of $800 is higher than the actual return of $600. To smooth postretirement expense, the unexpected loss of $200 ($800 − $600) is deferred by debiting Unrecognized Net Gain or Loss and crediting Postretirement Expense. As a result of this adjustment, the expected return on the plan assets is the amount actually used to compute postretirement expense.

Entry (m) records the change in the APBO resulting from a change in actuarial assumptions. This $60,000 increase in the employer's accumulated liability is an unexpected loss that is deferred by debiting it to Unrecognized Net Gain or Loss.

The journal entry on December 31 to formally record net periodic expense for 2001 is as follows:

December 31, 2001		
Postretirement Expense	75,280	
Cash		50,000
Prepaid/Accrued Cost		25,280

The balance of the Prepaid/Accrued Cost account as December 31, 2001, of $57,280 is equal to the net of the balances in the memo accounts as shown in the following reconciliation schedule.

ILLUSTRATION 21A-7
Postretirement Benefits Reconciliation Schedule—December 31, 2001

Accumulated postretirement benefit obligation (Credit)	$(511,080)
Plan assets at fair value (Debit)	25,600
Funded status (Credit)	(485,480)
Unrecognized transition amount (Debit)	368,000
Unrecognized net gain or loss (Debit)	60,200
Prepaid/accrued cost (Credit)	$ (57,280)

Amortization of Unrecognized Net Gain or Loss in 2002

Because of the beginning-of-the-year balance in unrecognized net gain or loss, the corridor test for amortization of the balance must be applied at the end of 2002. Illustration 21A-8 shows the computation of the amortization charge for unrecognized net gain or loss.

ILLUSTRATION 21A-8
Computation of Amortization Charge (Corridor Test)—2002

2002 Corridor Test	
Unrecognized net gain or loss at beginning of year	$60,200
10% of greater of APBO or market-related value of plan assets ($511,080 × .10)	51,108
Amortizable amount	$ 9,092
Average remaining service to expected retirement	25 years
2002 amortization of loss ($9,092 ÷ 25)	$364

DISCLOSURES IN NOTES TO THE FINANCIAL STATEMENTS

The disclosures required for other postretirement benefit plans are similar to and just as detailed and extensive as those required for pensions. By recognizing these similarities, under the provisions of *FASB Statement No. 132,* pension and other postretirement benefit disclosures can be combined. This disclosure for **Gillette Company** was provided in Illustration 21-29. As noted there, the following disclosures are required:

1. Postretirement expense for the period, separately identifying all components of that cost.
2. A schedule showing changes in postretirement benefit obligations and plan assets during the year.
3. A schedule reconciling the funded status of the plan with amounts reported in the employer's balance sheet, separately identifying the reconciling items.
4. The assumptions and rates used in computing the EPBO and APBO, including assumed health care cost trend rates; assumed discount rates; and the effect of a one-percentage-point increase in the assumed health care cost trend rate on the measurement of the APBO, the service cost, and the interest cost.

ACTUARIAL ASSUMPTIONS AND CONCEPTUAL ISSUES

The measurement of the EPBO and the APBO and the net periodic postretirement benefit cost is involved and complex. Due to the uncertainties in forecasting health care costs, rates of utilization, changes in government health programs, and the differences employed in nonmedical assumptions (discount rate, employee turnover, rate of pre-65 retirement, spouse-age difference, etc.), estimates of postretirement benefit costs may have a large margin of error. Is the information, therefore, relevant, reliable, or verifiable? The FASB concluded "that the obligation to provide postretirement benefits meets the definition of a liability, is representationally faithful, is relevant to financial statement users, and can be measured with sufficient reliability at a justifiable cost."[14] Failure to accrue an obligation and an expense prior to payment of benefits is considered to be an unfaithful representation of what financial statements purport to represent.[15]

The FASB took a momentous step by requiring the accrual of postretirement benefits as a liability. Many opposed the requirement warning that the standard would devastate earnings. Others argued that putting "soft" numbers on the balance sheet was inappropriate and, finally, others noted that it would force companies to curtail these benefits to employees.

[14]*FABS Statement No. 106,* par. 163.

[15]The FASB does not require recognition of a "minimum liability" for postretirement benefit plans. The Board concluded that the postretirement transition provisions that provide for delayed recognition should not be overridden by a requirement to recognize a liability that would accelerate recognition of that obligation in the balance sheet.

The authors believe that the FASB deserves special praise for this standard. Because the Board addressed this issue, companies now recognize the magnitude of these costs. This recognition has led to efforts to control escalating health-care costs. As John Ruffle, former president of the Financial Accounting Foundation noted, "The Board has done American industry a gigantic favor. Over the long term, industry will look back and say thanks."

KEY TERMS

accumulated postretirement benefit obligation (APBO), *1158*
attribution period, *1158*
corridor approach, *1163*
deferred recognition method, *1160*
expected postretirement benefit obligation (EPBO), *1158*
immediate recognition method, *1160*
minimum amortization amount, *1163*
transition amount, *1160*

SUMMARY OF LEARNING OBJECTIVES FOR APPENDIX 21A

11 Identify the differences between pensions and postretirement health-care benefits. Pension plans are generally funded, but health-care benefit plans are not. Pension benefits are generally well-defined and level in amount, but health-care benefits are generally uncapped and variable. Pension benefits are payable monthly, but health-care benefits are paid as needed and used. Pension plan variables are reasonably predictable, whereas health-care plan variables are difficult to predict.

12 Contrast accounting for pensions to accounting for other postretirement benefits. Many of the basic concepts and much of the accounting terminology and measurement methodology applicable to pensions also apply to other postretirement benefit accounting. Because other postretirement benefit plans are unfunded, large transition obligations occur; these may be immediately written off or amortized over 20 years. Two significant concepts peculiar to accounting for other postretirement benefits are (a) expected postretirement benefit obligation (EPBO) and (b) accumulated postretirement benefit obligation (APBO).

Note: All **asterisked** Questions, Brief Exercises, Exercises, Problems, and Conceptual Cases relate to material covered in the appendix to the chapter.

QUESTIONS

1 What is a private pension plan? How does a contributory pension plan differ from a noncontributory plan?

2 Differentiate between a defined contribution pension plan and a defined benefit pension plan. Explain how the employer's obligation differs between the two types of plans.

3 Differentiate between "accounting for the employer" and "accounting for the pension fund."

4 The meaning of the term "fund" depends on the context in which it is used. Explain its meaning when used as a noun. Explain its meaning when it is used as a verb.

5 What is the role of an actuary relative to pension plans? What are actuarial assumptions?

6 What factors must be considered by the actuary in measuring the amount of pension benefits under a defined benefit plan?

7 Name three approaches to measuring benefits from a pension plan and explain how they differ.

8 Distinguish between the noncapitalization approach and the capitalization approach with regard to accounting for pension plans. Which approach does *FASB Statement No. 87* adopt?

9 Explain how cash basis accounting for pension plans differs from accrual basis accounting for pension plans. Why is cash basis accounting generally considered unacceptable for pension plan accounting?

10 Identify the five components that comprise pension expense. Briefly explain the nature of each component.

11 What is service cost and what is the basis of its measurement?

12 In computing the interest component of pension expense, what interest rates may be used?

13 Explain the difference between service cost and prior service cost.

14 What is meant by "prior service cost"? When is prior service cost recognized as pension expense?

15 What are "liability gains and losses," and how are they accounted for?

16 If pension expense recognized in a period exceeds the current amount funded by the employer, what kind of account arises and how should it be reported in the financial statements? If the reverse occurs—that is, current funding by the employer exceeds the amount recognized as pension expense—what kind of account arises and how should it be reported?

17 Given the following items and amounts, compute the actual return on plan assets: fair value of plan assets at the beginning of the period, $9,200,000; benefits paid during the period, $1,400,000; contributions made during the period, $1,000,000; and fair value of the plan assets at the end of the period, $10,150,000.

18 How does an "asset gain or loss" develop in pension accounting? How does a "liability gain or loss" develop in pension accounting?

19 What is the meaning of "corridor amortization"?

20 Explain when a minimum liability is recognized and how it is reported in the financial statements.

21 Explain the nature of a debit to an intangible asset account when an additional pension liability must be recorded. How does the amount of unrecognized prior service cost influence the amount recognized as an intangible asset?

22 At the end of the current period, Jacob Inc. had an accumulated benefit obligation of $400,000, pension plan assets (at fair value) of $300,000, and a balance in prepaid pension cost of $41,000. Assuming that Jacob Inc. follows *FASB Statement No. 87,* what are the accounts and amounts that will be reported on the company's balance sheet as pension assets or pension liabilities?

23 At the end of the current year, Joshua Co. has unrecognized prior service cost of $9,150,000. In addition, it recognized a minimum liability of $10,500,000 for the year. Where should the unrecognized prior service cost be reported on the balance sheet? Where should the debit related to the establishment of the minimum liability be reported?

24 Determine the meaning of the following terms:

(a) Contributory plan.

(b) Vested benefits.

(c) Retroactive benefits.

(d) Years-of-service method.

25 Of what value to the financial statement reader is the schedule reconciling the funded status of the plan with amounts reported in the employer's balance sheet?

26 A headline in *The Wall Street Journal* stated "Firms Increasingly Tap Their Pension Funds to Use Excess Assets." What is the accounting issue related to the use of these "excess assets" by companies?

***27** What are postretirement benefits other than pensions?

***28** Why didn't the FASB cover both types of postretirement benefits—pensions and health-care—in the earlier pension accounting statement?

***29** What is the transition amount in pension accounting and the transition amount in postretirement benefit accounting? And, how does the accounting treatment for these transition amounts differ under *Statement Nos. 87* and *106*? Why is the accounting for the transition amount so controversial?

***30** What are the major differences between postretirement health-care benefits and pension benefits?

***31** What is the difference between the APBO and the EPBO? What are the components of postretirement expense?

BRIEF EXERCISES

BE21-1 The following information is available for Jack Borke Corporation for 2002:

Service	$29,000
Interest on P.B.O.	22,000
Return on plan assets	20,000
Amortization of unrecognized prior service cost	15,200
Amortization of unrecognized net loss	500

Compute Borke's 2002 pension expense.

BE21-2 For Becker Corporation, year-end plan assets were $2,000,000. At the beginning of the year, plan assets were $1,680,000. During the year, contributions to the pension fund were $120,000 while benefits paid were $200,000. Compute Becker's actual return on plan assets.

BE21-3 At January 1, 2002, Uddin Company had plan assets of $250,000 and a projected benefit obligation of the same amount. During 2002, service cost was $27,500, the settlement rate was 10%, actual and expected return on plan assets were $25,000, contributions were $20,000, and benefits paid were $17,500. Prepare a pension work sheet for Uddin Company for 2002.

BE21-4 For 2002, Potts Company had pension expense of $32,000 and contributed $25,000 to the pension fund. Prepare Potts Company's journal entry to record pension expense and funding.

BE21-5 Duesbury Corporation amended its pension plan on January 1, 2002, and granted $120,000 of unrecognized prior service costs to its employees. The employees are expected to provide 2,000 service years in the future, with 350 service years in 2002. Compute unrecognized prior service cost amortization for 2002.

BE21-6 At December 31, 2002, Conway Corporation had a projected benefit obligation of $510,000, plan assets of $322,000, unrecognized prior service cost of $127,000, and accrued pension cost of $61,000. Prepare a pension reconciliation schedule for Conway.

BE21-7 Hunt Corporation had a projected benefit obligation of $3,100,000 and plan assets of $3,300,000 at January 1, 2002. Hunt's unrecognized net pension loss was $475,000 at that time. The average remaining service period of Hunt's employees is 7.5 years. Compute Hunt's minimum amortization of pension loss.

BE21-8 Judy O'Neill Corporation provides the following information at December 31, 2001:

Accumulated benefit obligation	$2,800,000
Plan assets at fair value	2,000,000
Accrued pension cost	200,000
Unrecognized prior service cost	1,100,000

Compute the additional liability that O'Neill must record at December 31, 2001.

BE21-9 At December 31, 2002, Judy O'Neill Corporation (see BE21-8) has the following balances:

Accumulated benefit obligation	$3,400,000
Plan assets at fair value	2,420,000
Accrued pension cost	235,000
Unrecognized prior service cost	990,000

O'Neill's Additional Pension Liability was $600,000 at December 31, 2001. Prepare O'Neill's December 31, 1999, entry to adjust Additional Pension Liability.

BE21-10 At December 31, 2001, Jeremiah Corporation was not required to report any additional pension liability. At December 31, 2002, the additional liability required is $600,000, and unrecognized prior service cost was $425,000. Prepare Jeremiah's December 31, 2002, entry to adjust Additional Pension Liability.

***BE21-11** Caleb Corporation has the following information available concerning its postretirement benefit plan for 2002:

Service cost	$40,000
Interest cost	52,400
Actual return on plan assets	26,900
Amortization of unrecognized transition amount	24,600

Compute Caleb's 2002 postretirement expense.

***BE21-12** For 2002, Benjamin Inc. computed its annual postretirement expense as $240,900. Benjamin's contribution to the plan during 2002 was $160,000. Prepare Benjamin's 2002 entry to record postretirement expense.

EXERCISES

E21-1 (Pension Expense, Journal Entries) The following information is available for the pension plan of Kiley Company for the year 2001:

Actual and expected return on plan assets	$ 12,000
Benefits paid to retirees	40,000
Contributions (funding)	95,000
Interest/discount rate	10%
Prior service cost amortization	8,000
Projected benefit obligation, January 1, 2001	500,000
Service cost	60,000

Instructions

(a) Compute pension expense for the year 2001.

(b) Prepare the journal entry to record pension expense and the employer's contribution to the pension plan in 2001.

E21-2 (Computation of Pension Expense) Rebekah Company provides the following information about its defined benefit pension plan for the year 2002:

Service cost	$ 90,000
Contribution to the plan	105,000
Prior service cost amortization	10,000
Actual and expected return on plan assets	64,000
Benefits paid	40,000
Accrued pension cost liability at January 1, 2002	10,000
Plan assets at January 1, 2002	640,000
Projected benefit obligation at January 1, 2002	800,000
Unrecognized prior service cost balance at January 1, 2002	150,000
Interest/discount (settlement) rate	10%

Instructions
Compute the pension expense for the year 2002.

E21-3 (Preparation of Pension Work Sheet with Reconciliation) Using the information in E21-2 prepare a pension work sheet inserting January 1, 2002, balances, showing December 31, 2002, balances and the journal entry recording pension expense.

E21-4 (Basic Pension Work Sheet) The following facts apply to the pension plan of Trudy Borke Inc. for the year 2002:

Plan assets, January 1, 2002	$490,000
Projected benefit obligation, January 1, 2002	490,000
Settlement rate	8.5%
Annual pension service cost	40,000
Contributions (funding)	30,000
Actual return on plan assets	49,700
Benefits paid to retirees	33,400

Instructions
Using the preceding data, compute pension expense for the year 2002. As part of your solution, prepare a pension work sheet that shows the journal entry for pension expense for 2002 and the year-end balances in the related pension accounts.

E21-5 (Application of Years-of-Service Method) Janet Valente Company has five employees participating in its defined benefit pension plan. Expected years of future service for these employees at the beginning of 2002 are as follows:

Employee	Future Years of Service
Ed	3
Paul	4
Mary	6
Dave	6
Caroline	6

On January 1, 2002, the company amended its pension plan increasing its projected benefit obligation by $60,000.

Instructions
Compute the amount of prior service cost amortization for the years 2002 through 2007 using the years-of-service method setting up appropriate schedules.

E21-6 (Computation of Actual Return) James Paul Importers provides the following pension plan information:

Fair value of pension plan assets, January 1, 2002	$2,300,000
Fair value of pension plan assets, December 31, 2002	2,725,000
Contributions to the plan in 2002	250,000
Benefits paid retirees in 2002	350,000

Instructions
From the data above, compute the actual return on the plan assets for 2002.

E21-7 (Basic Pension Work Sheet) The following defined pension data of Doreen Corp. apply to the year 2002:

Projected benefit obligation, 1/1/02 (before amendment)	$560,000
Plan assets, 1/1/02	546,200
Prepaid/accrued pension cost (credit)	13,800
On January 1, 2002, Doreen Corp., through plan amendment, grants prior service benefits having a present value of	100,000
Settlement rate	9%
Annual pension service cost	58,000
Contributions (funding)	55,000
Actual return on plan assets	52,280
Benefits paid to retirees	40,000
Prior service cost amortization for 2002	17,000

Instructions

For 2002, prepare a pension work sheet for Doreen Corp. that shows the journal entry for pension expense and the year-end balances in the related pension accounts.

E21-8 (Application of the Corridor Approach) Dougherty Corp. has beginning-of-the-year present values for its projected benefit obligation and market-related values for its pension plan assets:

	Projected Benefit Obligation	Plan Assets Value
2000	$2,000,000	$1,900,000
2001	2,400,000	2,500,000
2002	2,900,000	2,600,000
2003	3,600,000	3,000,000

The average remaining service life per employee in 2000 and 2001 is 10 years and in 2002 and 2003 is 12 years. The unrecognized net gain or loss that occurred during each year is as follows: 2000, $280,000 loss; 2001, $90,000 loss; 2002, $10,000 loss; and 2003, $25,000 gain (in working the solution the unrecognized gains and losses must be aggregated to arrive at year-end balances).

Instructions

Using the corridor approach, compute the amount of unrecognized net gain or loss amortized and charged to pension expense in each of the four years, setting up an appropriate schedule.

E21-9 (Disclosures: Pension Expense and Reconciliation Schedule) Mildred Enterprises provides the following information relative to its defined benefit pension plan:

Balances or Values at December 31, 2002	
Projected benefit obligation	$2,737,000
Accumulated benefit obligation	1,980,000
Vested benefit obligation	1,645,852
Fair value of plan assets	2,278,329
Unrecognized prior service cost	205,000
Unrecognized net loss (1/1/02 balance, –0–)	45,680
Accrued pension cost liability	207,991
Other pension plan data:	
Service cost for 2002	$ 94,000
Unrecognized prior service cost amortization for 2002	45,000
Actual return on plan assets in 2002	130,000
Expected return on plan assets in 2002	175,680
Interest on January 1, 2002, projected benefit obligation	253,000
Contributions to plan in 2002	92,329
Benefits paid	140,000

Instructions

(a) Prepare the note disclosing the components of pension expense for the year 2002.

(b) Reconcile the funded status of the plan with the amount reported in the December 31, 2002, balance sheet.

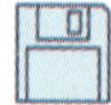

E21-10 (Pension Work Sheet with Reconciliation Schedule) Melanie Vail Corp. sponsors a defined benefit pension plan for its employees. On January 1, 2002, the following balances relate to this plan:

Plan assets	$480,000
Projected benefit obligation	625,000
Prepaid/accrued pension cost (credit)	45,000
Unrecognized prior service cost	100,000

As a result of the operation of the plan during 2002, the following additional data are provided by the actuary:

Service cost for 2002	$90,000
Settlement rate, 9%	
Actual return on plan assets in 2002	57,000
Amortization of prior service cost	19,000
Expected return on plan assets	52,000
Unexpected loss from change in projected benefit obligation, due to change in actuarial predictions	76,000
Contributions in 2002	99,000
Benefits paid retirees in 2002	85,000

Instructions

(a) Using the data above, compute pension expense for Melanie Vail Corp. for the year 2002 by preparing a pension work sheet that shows the journal entry for pension expense and the year-end balances in the related pension accounts.

(b) At December 31, 2002, prepare a schedule reconciling the funded status of the plan with the pension amount reported on the balance sheet.

E21-11 (Minimum Liability Computation, Entry) The following information is available for McGwire Corporation's defined benefit pension plan for the years 2001 and 2002.

	December 31,	
	2001	2002
Accrued pension cost balance	$ -0-	$ 45,000
Accumulated benefit obligation	260,000	370,000
Fair value of plan assets	255,000	300,000
Prepaid pension cost balance	30,000	-0-
Projected benefit obligation	350,000	455,000
Unrecognized prior service cost	125,000	110,000

Instructions

(a) Compute the amount of additional liability, if any, that McGwire must record at the end of each year.

(b) Prepare the journal entries, if any; necessary to record a minimum liability for 2001 and 2002.

E21-12 (Pension Expense, Journal Entries, Statement Presentation, Minimum Liability) Desiree Griseta Company sponsors a defined benefit pension plan for its employees. The following data relate to the operation of the plan for the year 2001 in which no benefits were paid:

1. The actuarial present value of future benefits earned by employees for services rendered in 2001 amounted to $56,000.
2. The company's funding policy requires a contribution to the pension trustee amounting to $145,000 for 2001.
3. As of January 1, 2001, the company had a projected benefit obligation of $1,000,000, an accumulated benefit obligation of $800,000, and an unrecognized prior service cost of $400,000. The fair value of pension plan assets amounted to $600,000 at the beginning of the year. The market-related asset value was equal to $600,000. The actual and expected return on plan assets was $54,000. The settlement rate was 9%. No gains or losses occurred in 2001 and no benefits were paid.
4. Amortization of unrecognized prior service cost was $40,000 in 2001 amortization of unrecognized net gain or loss was not required in 2001.

Instructions

(a) Determine the amounts of the components of pension expense that should be recognized by the company in 2001.

(b) Prepare the journal entry or entries to record pension expense and the employer's contribution to the pension trustee in 2001.

(c) Indicate the amounts that would be reported on the income statement and the balance sheet for the year 2001. The accumulated benefit obligation on December 31, 2001, was $830,000.

E21-13 (Pension Expense, Journal Entries, Minimum Liability, Statement Presentation) Nellie Altom Company received the following selected information from its pension plan trustee concerning the operation of the company's defined benefit pension plan for the year ended December 31, 2001.

	January 1, 2001	December 31, 2001
Projected benefit obligation	$2,000,000	$2,077,000
Market-related and fair value of plan assets	800,000	1,130,000
Accumulated benefit obligation	1,600,000	1,720,000
Actuarial (gains) losses (Unrecognized net (gain) or loss)	–0–	(200,000)

The service cost component of pension expense for employee services rendered in the current year amounted to $77,000 and the amortization of unrecognized prior service cost was $115,000. The company's actual funding (contributions) of the plan in 2001 amounted to $250,000. The expected return on plan assets and the actual rate were both 10%; the interest/discount (settlement) rate was 10%. No prepaid/accrued pension cost existed on January 1, 2001. Assume no benefits paid in 2001.

Instructions

(a) Determine the amounts of the components of pension expense that should be recognized by the company in 2001.

(b) Prepare the journal entries to record pension expense and the employer's contribution to the pension plan in 2001.

(c) Indicate the pension-related amounts that would be reported on the income statement and the balance sheet for Nellie Altom Company for the year 2001. (Compute the minimum liability.)

E21-14 (Computation of Actual Return, Gains and Losses, Corridor Test, Prior Service Cost, Minimum Liability, Pension Expense, and Reconciliation) Linda Berstler Company sponsors a defined benefit pension plan. The corporation's actuary provides the following information about the plan:

	January 1, 2002	December 31, 2002
Vested benefit obligation	$1,500	$1,900
Accumulated benefit obligation	1,900	2,730
Projected benefit obligation	2,800	3,645
Plan assets (fair value)	1,700	2,620
Settlement rate and expected rate of return		10%
Prepaid/(accrued) pension cost	–0–	?
Unrecognized prior service cost	1,100	?
Service cost for the year 2002		400
Contributions (funding in 2002)		800
Benefits paid in 2002		200

The average remaining service life per employee is 20 years.

Instructions

(a) Compute the actual return on the plan assets in 2002.

(b) Compute the amount of the unrecognized net gain or loss as of December 31, 2002 (assume the January 1, 2002, balance was zero).

(c) Compute the amount of unrecognized net gain or loss amortization for 2002 (corridor approach).

(d) Compute the amount of prior service cost amortization for 2002.

(e) Compute the minimum liability to be reported at December 31, 2002.

(f) Compute pension expense for 2002.

(g) Prepare a schedule reconciling the plan's funded status with the amounts reported in the December 31, 2002, balance sheet.

E21-15 (Work Sheet for E21-14) Using the information in E21-14 about Linda Berstler Company's defined benefit pension plan, prepare a 2002 pension work sheet with supplementary schedules of computations. Prepare the journal entries at December 31, 2002, to record pension expense and any "additional liability." Also, prepare a schedule reconciling the plan's funded status with the pension amounts reported in the balance sheet.

E21-16 (Pension Expense, Minimum Liability, Journal Entries) Walker Company provides the following information related to its defined benefit pension plan for 2001:

Accrued pension cost balance (January 1)	$ 25,000
Accumulated benefit obligation (December 31)	400,000
Actual and expected return on plan assets	15,000
Additional pension liability balance (January 1)	10,000
Contributions (funding) in 2001	150,000
Fair value of plan assets (December 31)	350,000
Interest/discount rate	10%
Projected benefit obligation (January 1)	700,000
Service cost	90,000

Instructions

(a) Compute pension expense and prepare the journal entry to record pension expense and the employer's contribution to the pension plan in 2001.

(b) Prepare the journal entry to record the minimum liability for 2001.

E21-17 (Pension Expense, Minimum Liability, Statement Presentation) Blum Foods Company obtained the following information from the insurance company that administers the company's employee-defined benefit pension plan:

	For Year Ended December 31		
	2001	2002	2003
Plan assets (at fair value)	$280,000	$398,000	$586,000
Accumulated benefit obligation	378,000	512,000	576,000
Pension expense	95,000	128,000	130,000
Employer's funding contribution	110,000	150,000	125,000
Prior service cost not yet recognized in earnings	494,230	451,365	400,438

Prior to 2001 cumulative pension expense was equal to cumulative contributions. The company has adopted the requirements of the FASB standard on "Employers' Accounting for Pensions." Assume that the market-related asset value is equal to the fair value of plan assets for all three years.

Instructions

(a) Prepare the journal entries to record pension expense, employer's funding contribution, and the adjustment to a minimum pension liability for the years 2001, 2002, and 2003. (Preparation of a pension work sheet is not a requirement of this exercise; insufficient information is given to prepare one.)

(b) Indicate the pension related amounts that would be reported on the company's income statement and balance sheet for 2001, 2002, and 2003.

E21-18 (Minimum Liability, Journal Entries, Balance Sheet Items) Presented below is partial information related to the pension fund of Rose Bryhan Inc.

Funded Status (end of year)	2001	2002	2003
Assets and obligations			
Market-related asset value	$1,300,000	$1,650,000	$1,900,000
Plan assets (at fair value)	1,300,000	1,670,000	1,950,000
Accumulated benefit obligation	1,150,000	1,480,000	2,060,000
Projected benefit obligation	1,600,000	1,910,000	2,500,000
Unfunded accumulated benefits			110,000
Overfunded accumulated benefits	150,000	190,000	
Amounts to be recognized			
(Accrued)/prepaid pension cost at beginning of year	$ –0–	$ 19,000	$ 16,000
Pension expense	(250,000)	(268,000)	(300,000)
Contribution	269,000	265,000	277,000
(Accrued)/prepaid pension cost at end of year	$ 19,000	$ 16,000	$ (7,000)

The company's unrecognized prior service cost is $637,000 at the end of 2003.

Instructions

(a) What pension-related amounts are reported on the balance sheet of Rose Bryhan Inc. for 2001, 2002, and 2003?

(b) What are the journal entries made to record pension expense in 2001, 2002, and 2003?

(c) What journal entries (if any) are necessary to record a minimum liability for 2001, 2002, and 2003?

E21-19 (Reconciliation Schedule, Minimum Liability, and Unrecognized Loss) Presented below is partial information related to Jean Burr Company at December 31, 2001:

Market-related asset value	$700,000
Projected benefit obligation	930,000
Accumulated benefit obligation	865,000
Plan assets (at fair value)	700,000
Vested benefits	200,000
Prior service cost not yet recognized in pension expense	120,000
Gains and losses	–0–

Instructions

(a) Present the schedule reconciling the funded status with the asset/liability reported on the balance sheet. Assume no asset or liability existed at the beginning of period for pensions on Jean Burr Company's balance sheet.

(b) Assume the same facts as in (a) except that Jean Burr Company has an unrecognized loss of $16,000 during 2001.

(c) Explain the rationale for the treatment of the unrecognized loss and the prior service cost not yet recognized in pension expense.

E21-20 (Amortization of Unrecognized Net Gain or Loss [Corridor Approach], Pension Expense Computation) The actuary for the pension plan of Joyce Bush Inc. calculated the following net gains and losses:

Unrecognized Net Gain or Loss	
Incurred during the Year	(Gain) or Loss
2001	$300,000
2002	480,000
2003	(210,000)
2004	(290,000)

Other information about the company's pension obligation and plan assets is as follows:

As of January 1,	Projected Benefit Obligation	Plan Assets (market-related asset value)
2001	$4,000,000	$2,400,000
2002	4,520,000	2,200,000
2003	4,980,000	2,600,000
2004	4,250,000	3,040,000

Joyce Bush Inc. has a stable labor force of 400 employees who are expected to receive benefits under the plan. The total service-years for all participating employees is 5,600. The beginning balance of unrecognized net gain or loss is zero on January 1, 2001. The market-related value and the fair value of plan assets are the same for the four-year period. Use the average remaining service life per employee as the basis for amortization.

Instructions

(Round to the nearest dollar)

Prepare a schedule which reflects the minimum amount of unrecognized net gain or loss amortized as a component of net periodic pension expense for each of the years 2001, 2002, 2003, and 2004. Apply the "corridor" approach in determining the amount to be amortized each year.

E21-21 (Amortization of Unrecognized Net Gain or Loss [Corridor Approach]) Lowell Company sponsors a defined benefit pension plan for its 600 employees. The company's actuary provided the following information about the plan:

	January 1,	December 31,	
	2001	2001	2002
Projected benefit obligation	$2,800,000	$3,650,000	$4,400,000
Accumulated benefit obligation	1,900,000	2,430,000	2,900,000
Plan assets (fair value and market related asset value)	1,700,000	2,900,000	2,100,000
Unrecognized net (gain) or loss (for purposes of the corridor calculation)	–0–	101,000	(24,000)
Discount rate (current settlement rate)	11%	8%	
Actual and expected asset return rate	10%	10%	

The average remaining service life per employee is 10.5 years. The service cost component of net periodic pension expense for employee services rendered amounted to $400,000 in 2001 and $475,000 in 2002. The unrecognized prior service cost on January 1, 2001, was $1,155,000. No benefits have been paid.

Instructions

(Round to the nearest dollar)

(a) Compute the amount of unrecognized prior service cost to be amortized as a component of net periodic pension expense for each of the years 2001 and 2002.

(b) Prepare a schedule which reflects the amount of unrecognized gain or loss to be amortized as a component of net periodic pension expense for 2001 and 2002.

(c) Determine the total amount of net periodic pension expense to be recognized by Lowell Company in 2001 and 2002.

***E21-22 (Postretirement Benefit Expense Computation)** Rose Chance Inc. provides the following information related to its postretirement benefits for the year 2003:

Accumulated postretirement benefit obligation at January 1, 2003	$810,000
Actual and expected return on plan assets	34,000
Unrecognized prior service cost amortization	21,000
Amortization of transition amount (loss)	5,000
Discount rate	10%
Service cost	88,000

Instructions

Compute postretirement benefit expense for 2003.

***E21-23 (Postretirement Benefit Expense Computation)** Marvelous Marvin Co. provides the following information about its postretirement benefit plan for the year 2002:

Service cost	$ 90,000
Prior service cost amortization	3,000
Contribution to the plan	16,000
Actual and expected return on plan assets	62,000
Benefits paid	40,000
Plan assets at January 1, 2002	710,000
Accumulated postretirement benefit obligation at January 1, 2002	810,000
Unrecognized prior service cost balance at January 1, 2002	20,000
Amortization of transition amount (Loss)	5,000
Unrecognized transition amount at January 1, 2002	80,000
Discount rate	9%

Instructions

Compute the postretirement benefit expense for 2002.

***E21-24 (Postretirement Benefit Work Sheet)** Using the information in *E21-23 prepare a work sheet inserting January 1, 2002, balances, showing December 31, 2002, balances, and the journal entry recording postretirement benefit expense.

***E21-25 (Postretirement Benefit Reconciliation Schedule)** Presented below is partial information related to Sandra Conley Co. at December 31, 2003:

Accumulated postretirement benefit obligation	$ 950,000
Expected postretirement benefit obligation	1,000,000
Plan assets (at fair value)	650,000
Prior service cost not yet recognized in postretirement expense	60,000
Gain and losses	–0–
Unrecognized transition amount (Loss)	100,000

Instructions

(a) Present the schedule reconciling the funded status with the asset/liability reported on the balance sheet. Assume no asset or liability existed at the beginning of the period for postretirement benefits on Sandra Conley Co.'s balance sheet.

(b) Assume the same facts as in (a) except that Sandra Conley Co. has an unrecognized loss of $20,000 during 2003.

PROBLEMS

P21-1 (Two-Year Work Sheet and Reconciliation Schedule) On January 1, 2002, Diana Peter Company has the following defined benefit pension plan balances:

Projected benefit obligation	$4,200,000
Fair value of plan assets	4,200,000

The interest (settlement) rate applicable to the plan is 10%. On January 1, 2003, the company amends its pension agreement so that prior service costs of $500,000 are created. Other data related to the pension plan are:

	2002	2003
Service costs	$150,000	$180,000
Unrecognized prior service costs amortization	–0–	90,000
Contributions (funding) to the plan	140,000	185,000
Benefits paid	200,000	280,000
Actual return on plan assets	252,000	260,000
Expected rate of return on assets	6%	8%

Instructions

(a) Prepare a pension work sheet for the pension plan for 2002 and 2003.

(b) As of December 31, 2003, prepare a schedule reconciling the funded status with the reported liability (accrued pension cost).

P21-2 (Three-Year Work Sheet, Journal Entries, and Reconciliation Schedules) Katie Day Company adopts acceptable accounting for its defined benefit pension plan on January 1, 2002, with the following beginning balances: Plan assets, $200,000; projected benefit obligation, $200,000. Other data relating to 3 years' operation of the plan are as follows:

	2002	2003	2004
Annual service cost	$16,000	$ 19,000	$ 26,000
Settlement rate and expected rate of return	10%	10%	10%
Actual return on plan assets	17,000	21,900	24,000
Annual funding (contributions)	16,000	40,000	48,000
Benefits paid	14,000	16,400	21,000
Unrecognized prior service cost (plan amended, 1/1/03)		160,000	
Amortization of unrecognized prior service cost		54,400	41,600
Change in actuarial assumptions establishes a December 31, 2004, projected benefit obligation of:			520,000

Instructions

(a) Prepare a pension work sheet presenting all 3 years' pension balances and activities.

(b) Prepare the journal entries (from the work sheet) to reflect all pension plan transactions and events at December 31 of each year.

(c) At December 31 of each year prepare a schedule reconciling the funded status of the plan with the pension amounts reported in the financial statements.

P21-3 (Pension Expense, Journal Entries, Minimum Pension Liability, Amortization of Unrecognized Loss, Reconciliation Schedule) Paul Dobson Company sponsors a defined benefit plan for its 100 employees. On January 1, 2001 (date company starts following *FASB Statement No. 87*), the company's actuary provided the following information:

Unrecognized prior service cost	$150,000
Pension plan assets (fair value and market-related asset value)	200,000
Accumulated benefit obligation	260,000
Projected benefit obligation	350,000

The average remaining service period for the participating employees is 10.5 years. All employees are expected to receive benefits under the plan. On December 31, 2001, the actuary calculated that the present value of future benefits earned for employee services rendered in the current year amounted to $52,000; the projected benefit obligation was $452,000; fair value of pension assets was $276,000; the accumulated benefit obligation amounted to $365,000; and the market-related asset value is $276,000. The expected return on plan assets and the discount rate on the projected benefit obligation were both 10%. The actual return on plan assets is $11,000. The company's current year's contribution to the pension plan amounted to $65,000. No benefits were paid during the year.

Instructions

(Round to the nearest dollar)

(a) Determine the components of pension expense that the company would recognize in 2001. (With only one year involved, you need not prepare a work sheet.)

(b) Prepare the journal entries to record the pension expense and the company's funding of the pension plan in 2001.

(c) Assume Paul Dobson Company elects to recognize the minimum pension liability in its balance sheet for the year ended December 31, 2001. Prepare the journal entry to record the minimum liability.

(d) Compute the amount of the 2001 increase/decrease in unrecognized gains or losses and the amount to be amortized in 2001 and 2002.

(e) Prepare a schedule reconciling the funded status of the plan with the pension amounts reported in the financial statement as of December 31, 2001.

P21-4 (Pension Expense, Minimum Liability, Journal Entries for Two Years) Mantle Company sponsors a defined benefit pension plan. The following information related to the pension plan is available for 2001 and 2002:

	2001	2002
Plan assets (fair value), December 31	$380,000	$465,000
Projected benefit obligation, January 1	600,000	700,000
Prepaid/(accrued) pension cost balance, January 1	(40,000)	?
Unrecognized prior service cost, January 1	250,000	240,000
Service cost	60,000	90,000
Actual and expected return on plan assets	24,000	30,000
Amortization of prior service cost	10,000	12,000
Contributions (funding)	110,000	120,000
Accumulated benefit obligation, December 31	500,000	550,000
Additional pension liability balance, January 1	50,000	?
Interest/settlement rate	9%	9%

Instructions

(a) Compute pension expense for 2001 and 2002.

(b) Prepare the journal entries to record the pension expense and the company's funding of the pension plan for both years.

(c) Compute the minimum liability for 2001 and 2002.

(d) Prepare the journal entries to record the minimum liability for both years.

P21-5 (Computation of Pension Expense, Amortization of Unrecognized Net Gain or Loss (Corridor Approach), Journal Entries for Three Years, and Minimum Pension Liability Computation) Dubel Toothpaste Company initiates a defined benefit pension plan for its 50 employees on January 1, 2001. The insurance company which administers the pension plan provided the following information for the years 2001, 2002, and 2003:

	For Year Ended December 31,		
	2001	2002	2003
Plan assets (fair value)	$50,000	$ 85,000	$170,000
Accumulated benefit obligation	45,000	165,000	292,000
Projected benefit obligation	55,000	200,000	324,000
Unrecognized net (gain) loss (for purposes of corridor calculation)	–0–	(24,500)	84,500
Employer's funding contribution (made at end of year)	50,000	60,000	95,000

There were no balances as of January 1, 2001, when the plan was initiated. The actual and expected return on plan assets was 10% over the 3-year period but the settlement rate used to discount the company's pension obligation was 13% in 2001, 11% in 2002, and 8% in 2003. The service cost component of net periodic pension expense amounted to the following: 2001, $55,000; 2002, $85,000; and 2003, $119,000. The average remaining service life per employee is 12 years. No benefits were paid in 2001, $30,000 of benefits were paid in 2002, and $18,500 of benefits were paid in 2003 (all benefits paid at end of year).

Instructions

(Round to the nearest dollar)

(a) Calculate the amount of net periodic pension expense that the company would recognize in 2001, 2002, and 2003.

(b) Prepare the journal entries to record net periodic pension expense, employer's funding contribution, and the adjustment to reflect a minimum pension liability for the years 2001, 2002, and 2003.

P21-6 (Computation of Unrecognized Prior Service Cost Amortization, Pension Expense, Journal Entries, Net Gain or Loss, and Reconciliation Schedule) Ekedahl Inc. has sponsored a noncontributory-defined benefit pension plan for its employees since 1984. Prior to 2001, cumulative net pension expense recognized equaled cumulative contributions to the plan. Management has elected to recognize the minimum pension liability requirement in the balance sheet for the year ending December 31, 2001. Other relevant information about the pension plan on January 1, 2001, is as follows:

1. The company has 200 employees who are expected to receive benefits under the plan. All these employees are expected to receive benefits under the plan. The average remaining service life per employee is 13 years.

2. The projected benefit obligation amounted to $5,000,000 and the fair value of pension plan assets was $3,000,000. The market-related asset value was also $3,000,000. Unrecognized prior service cost was $2,000,000.

On December 31, 2001, the projected benefit obligation and the accumulated benefit obligation were $4,750,000 and $4,025,000, respectively. The fair value of the pension plan assets amounted to $3,900,000 at the end of the year. The market-related asset value was $3,790,000. A 10% settlement rate and a 10% expected asset return rate was used in the actuarial present value computations in the pension plan. The present value of benefits attributed by the pension benefit formula to employee service in 2001 amounted to $200,000. The employer's contribution to the plan assets amounted to $575,000 in 2001. This problem assumes no payment of pension benefits.

Instructions

(Round all amounts to the nearest dollar)

(a) Prepare a schedule, based on the average remaining life per employee, showing the unrecognized prior service cost that would be amortized as a component of pension expense for 2001, 2002, and 2003.

(b) Compute pension expense for the year 2001.

(c) Prepare the journal entries required to report the accounting for the company's pension plan for 2001.

(d) Compute the amount of the 2001 increase/decrease in unrecognized net gains or losses and the amount to be amortized in 2001 and 2002.

(e) Prepare a schedule reconciling the funded status of the plan with the pension amounts reported in the financial statements as of December 31, 2001.

P21-7 (Pension Work Sheet, Minimum Liability) Farrey Corp. sponsors a defined benefit pension plan for its employees. On January 1, 2003, the following balances related to this plan:

Plan assets (fair value)	$520,000
Projected benefit obligation	725,000
Prepaid/accrued pension cost (credit)	33,000
Unrecognized prior service cost	81,000
Unrecognized net gain or loss (debit)	91,000

As a result of the operation of the plan during 2003, the actuary provided the following additional data at December 31, 2003:

Service cost for 2003	$108,000
Settlement rate, 9%; expected return rate, 10%.	
Actual return on assets in 2003	48,000
Amortization of prior service cost	25,000
Market-related asset value at 1/1/03	550,000
Contributions in 2003	138,000
Benefits paid retirees in 2003	85,000
Average remaining service life of active employees	10 years
Accumulated benefit obligation at 12/31/03	671,000

Instructions

Using the preceding data, compute pension expense for Farrey Corp. for the year 2003 by preparing a pension work sheet that shows the journal entry for pension expense and any additional pension liability. (The minimum pension liability must be computed and the corridor approach must be applied to the unrecognized gain or loss.) Use the market related asset value to compute the expected return.

P21-8 (Comprehensive 2-Year Work Sheet) Glesen Company sponsors a defined benefit pension plan for its employees. The following data relate to the operation of the plan for the years 2002 and 2003:

	2002	2003
Projected benefit obligation, January 1	$650,000	
Plan assets (fair value and market related value), January 1	410,000	
Prepaid/accrued pension cost (credit), January 1	80,000	
Additional pension liability, January 1	12,300	
Intangible asset-deferred pension cost, January 1	12,300	
Unrecognized prior service cost, January 1	160,000	
Service cost	40,000	$ 59,000
Settlement rate	10%	10%
Expected rate of return	10%	10%
Actual return on plan assets	36,000	61,000
Amortization of prior service cost	70,000	55,000

Annual contributions	72,000	81,000
Benefits paid retirees	31,500	54,000
Increase in projected benefit obligation due to changes in actuarial assumptions	87,000	–0–
Accumulated benefit obligation at December 31	721,800	789,000
Average service life of all employees		20 years
Vested benefit obligation at December 31		464,000

Instructions

(a) Prepare a pension work sheet presenting both years 2002 and 2003 and accompanying computations including the computation of the minimum liability (2002 and 2003) and amortization of the unrecognized loss (2003) using the corridor approach.

(b) Prepare the journal entries (from the work sheet) to reflect all pension plan transactions and events at December 31 of each year.

(c) At December 31, 2003, prepare a schedule reconciling the funded status of the pension plan with the pension amounts reported in the financial statements.

P21-9 (Comprehensive Pension Work Sheet) Connie Harpin was recently promoted to assistant controller of Glomski Corporation, having previously served Glomski as a staff accountant. One of the responsibilities of her new position is to prepare the annual pension accrual. Judy Gralapp, the corporate controller, provided Harpin with last year's workpapers and information from the actuary's annual report. The pension work sheet for the prior year is presented below.

	Journal Entry			Memo Records		
	Pension Expense	Cash	Prepaid (Accrued) Cost	Projected Benefit Obligation	Plan Assets	Unrecognized Prior Service Cost
June 1, 2001[1]				$(20,000)	$20,000	
Service cost[1]	$1,800			(1,800)		
Interest[2]	1,200			(1,200)		
Actual return[3]	(1,600)				1,600	
Contribution[1]		$(1,000)			1,000	
Benefits paid[1]				900	(900)	
Prior service cost[4]				(2,000)		$2,000
Journal entry	$1,400	$(1,000)	$(400)			
May 31, 2002, balance			$(400)	$(24,100)	$21,700	$2,000

[1]Per actuary's report.
[2]Beginning projected benefit obligation × settlement rate of 6%.
[3]Expected return was $1,600 (beginning plan assets × expected return of 8%).
[4]A plan amendment that granted employees retroactive benefits for work performed in earlier periods took effect on May 31, 2002. The amendment increased the May 31, 2002, projected benefit obligation by $2,000. No amortization was recorded in the fiscal year ended May 31, 2002.

Pertinent information from the actuary's report for the year ended May 31, 2003, is presented below. The report indicated no actuarial gains or losses in the fiscal year ended May 31, 2003.

Contribution	$ 425	Actual return on plan assets	$ 1,736
Service cost	$ 3,000	Benefits paid	$ 500
Settlement rate	6%	Average remaining service life	10 years
Expected return	8%	Fair value plan assets 5-31-02	$21,700
Accumulated benefit obligation 5-31-02	$21,000	Fair value plan assets 5-31-03	$23,361
Accumulated benefit obligation 5-31-03	$27,000		

When briefing Harpin, Gralapp indicated that the prior service cost is to be amortized over the average remaining service life. Gralapp also informed her that, in the current year, there will be an initial adoption of minimum pension liability reporting.

Instructions

(a) Prepare the pension worksheet for Glomski Corporation for the year ended May 31, 2003.

(b) Prepare the journal entries required to reflect the accounting for Glomski Corporation's pension plan for the year ended May 31, 2003.

(c) If the additional pension liability and the unrecognized prior service cost were $3,700 and $1,800, respectively, at May 31, 2003, explain how Glomski Corporation would report the $3,700 in its financial statements.

P21-10 (Comprehensive 2-Year Work Sheet) Ingrid Mount Co. has the following defined benefit pension plan balances on January 1, 2000:

Projected benefit obligation	$4,500,000
Fair value of plan assets	4,500,000

The interest (settlement) rate applicable to the plan is 10%. On January 1, 2001, the company amends its pension agreement so that prior service costs of $600,000 are created. Other data related to the pension plan are:

	2000	2001
Service costs	$150,000	$170,000
Unrecognized prior service costs amortization	–0–	90,000
Contributions (funding) to the plan	150,000	184,658
Benefits paid	220,000	280,000
Actual return on plan assets	252,000	250,000
Expected rate of return on assets	6%	8%

Instructions

(a) Prepare a pension work sheet for the pension plan in 2000.

(b) Prepare any journal entries related to the pension plan that would be needed at December 31, 2000.

(c) Prepare a pension work sheet for 2001 and any journal entries related to the pension plan as of December 31, 2001.

(d) As of December 31, 2001, prepare a schedule reconciling the funded status with the reported liability (accrued pension cost).

***P21-11 (Postretirement Benefit Work Sheet with Reconciliation)** Dusty Hass Foods Inc. sponsors a postretirement medical and dental benefit plan for its employees. The company adopts the provisions of *Statement No. 106* beginning January 1, 2002. The following balances relate to this plan on January 1, 2002.

Plan assets	$ 200,000
Expected postretirement benefit obligation	1,420,000
Accumulated postretirement benefit obligation	882,000
No prior service costs exist.	

As a result of the plan's operation during 2002, the following additional data are provided by the actuary:

Service cost for 2002 is $70,000
Discount rate is 9%
Contributions to plan in 2002 are $60,000
Expected return on plan assets is $9,000
Actual return on plan assets is $15,000
Benefits paid to employees from plan are $44,000
Average remaining service to full eligibility: 20 years
Average remaining service to expected retirement: 22 years
Transition amount to be amortized: ?

Instructions

(a) Using the preceding data, compute the net periodic postretirement benefit cost for 2002 by preparing a work sheet that shows the journal entry for postretirement expense and the year-end balances in the related postretirement benefit memo accounts. (Assume that contributions and benefits are paid at the end of the year.)

(b) At December 31, 2002, prepare a schedule reconciling the funded status of the plan with the postretirement amount reported on the balance sheet.

CONCEPTUAL CASES

C21-1 (Pension Terminology and Theory) Many business organizations have been concerned with providing for the retirement of employees since the late 1800s. During recent decades a marked increase in this concern has resulted in the establishment of private pension plans in most large companies and in many medium- and small-sized ones.

The substantial growth of these plans, both in numbers of employees covered and in amounts of retirement benefits, has increased the significance of pension cost in relation to the financial position, results of operations, and cash flows of many companies. In examining the costs of pension plans, a CPA encounters certain terms. The components of pension costs that the terms represent must be dealt with appropriately if generally accepted accounting principles are to be reflected in the financial statements of entities with pension plans.

Instructions

(a) Define a private pension plan. How does a contributory pension plan differ from a noncontributory plan?

(b) Differentiate between "accounting for the employer" and "accounting for the pension fund."

(c) Explain the terms "funded" and "pension liability" as they relate to:
  (1) The pension fund.
  (2) The employer.

(d) **(1)** Discuss the theoretical justification for accrual recognition of pension costs.
  (2) Discuss the relative objectivity of the measurement process of accrual versus cash (pay-as-you-go) accounting for annual pension costs.

(e) Distinguish among the following as they relate to pension plans:
  (1) Service cost.
  (2) Prior service costs.
  (3) Actuarial funding methods.
  (4) Vested benefits.

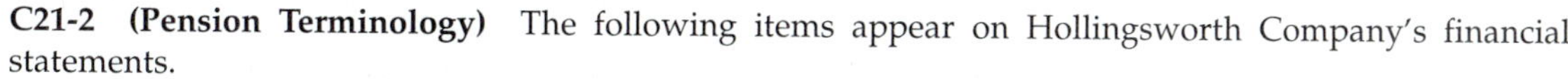

C21-2 (Pension Terminology) The following items appear on Hollingsworth Company's financial statements.

1. Under the caption Assets:
   Prepaid pension cost.
   Intangible asset—Deferred pension cost.
2. Under the caption Liabilities:
   Accrued pension cost.
3. Under the caption Stockholders' Equity:
   Excess of additional pension liability over unrecognized prior service cost as a component of Accumulated Other Comprehensive Income.
4. On the income statement:
   Pension expense.

Instructions

Explain the significance of each of the items above on corporate financial statements. (*Note:* All items set forth above are not necessarily to be found on the statements of a single company.)

C21-3 (Basic Terminology) In examining the costs of pension plans, Leah Hutcherson, CPA, encounters certain terms. The components of pension costs that the terms represent must be dealt with appropriately if generally accepted accounting principles are to be reflected in the financial statements of entities with pension plans.

Instructions

(a) **(1)** Discuss the theoretical justification for accrual recognition of pension costs.
  (2) Discuss the relative objectivity of the measurement process of accrual versus cash (pay-as-you-go) accounting for annual pension costs.

(b) Explain the following terms as they apply to accounting for pension plans:
  (1) Market-related asset value.
  (2) Actuarial funding methods.
  (3) Projected benefit obligation.
  (4) Corridor approach.

(c) What information should be disclosed about a company's pension plans in its financial statements and its notes?

(AICPA adapted)

C21-4 (Basic Concepts of Pension Reporting) Helen Kaufman, president of Express Mail Inc., is discussing the possibility of developing a pension plan for its employees with Esther Knox, controller, and Jason Nihles, assistant controller. Their conversation is as follows:

HELEN KAUFMAN: If we are going to compete with our competitors, we must have a pension plan to attract good talent.

ESTHER KNOX: I must warn you, Helen, that a pension plan will take a large bit out of our income. The only reason why we have been so profitable is the lack of a pension cost in our income statement. In some of our competitors' cases, pension expense is 30% of pretax income.

JASON NIHLES: Why do we have to worry about a pension cost now anyway? Benefits do not vest until after 10 years of service. If they do not vest, then we are not liable. We should not have to report an expense until we are legally liable to provide benefits.

HELEN KAUFMAN: But, Jason, the employees would want credit for prior service with full vesting 10 years after starting service, not 10 years after starting the plan. How would we allocate the large prior service cost?

JASON NIHLES: Well, I believe that the prior service cost is a cost of providing a pension plan for employees forever. It is an intangible asset that will not diminish in value because it will increase the morale of our present and future employees and provide us with a competitive edge in acquiring future employees.

HELEN KAUFMAN: I hate to disagree, but I believe the prior service cost is a benefit only to the present employees. This prior service is directly related to the composition of the employee group at the time the plan is initiated and is in no way related to any intangible benefit received by the company because of the plan's existence. Therefore, I propose that the prior service cost be amortized over the remaining lives of the existing employees.

ESTHER KNOX (somewhat perturbed): But what about the income statement? You two are arguing theory without consideration of our income figure.

HELEN KAUFMAN: Settle down, Esther.

ESTHER KNOX: Sorry, perhaps Jason's approach to resolving this approach is the best one. I am just not sure.

Instructions

(a) Assuming that Express Mail Inc. establishes a pension plan, how should their liability for pensions be computed in the first year?

(b) How should their liability be computed in subsequent years?

(c) How should pension expense be computed each year?

(d) Assuming that the pension fund is set up in a trusteed relationship, should the assets of the fund be reported on the books of Express Mail Inc.?

(e) What interest rate factor should be used in the present value computations?

(f) How should gains and losses be reported?

C21-5 (Major Pension Concepts) Lyons Corporation is a medium-sized manufacturer of paperboard containers and boxes. The corporation sponsors a noncontributory, defined benefit pension plan that covers its 250 employees. Spring Meissner has recently been hired as president of Lyons Corporation. While reviewing last year's financial statements with Sara Montgomery, controller, Meissner expressed confusion about several of the items in the footnote to the financial statements relating to the pension plan. In part, the footnote reads as follows.

> **Note J.** The company has a defined benefit pension plan covering substantially all of its employees. The benefits are based on years of service and the employee's compensation during the last four years of employment. The company's funding policy is to contribute annually the maximum amount allowed under the federal tax code. Contributions are intended to provide for benefits expected to be earned in the future as well as those earned to date.

Effective for the year ending December 31, 2001, Lyons Corporation adopted the provisions of *Statement of Financial Accounting Standard No. 87*—Employer's Accounting for Pensions. The net periodic pension expense on Lyons Corporation's comparative Income Statement was $72,000 in 2002 and $57,680 in 2001.

The following are selected figures from the plan's funded status and amount recognized in the Lyons Corporation's Statement of Financial Position at December 31, 2002 ($000 omitted):

Actuarial present value of benefit obligations:	
Accumulated benefit obligation (including vested benefits of $636)	$ (870)
Projected benefit obligation	$(1,200)
Plan assets at fair value	1,050
Projected benefit obligation in excess of plan assets	$ (150)

Given that Lyons Corporation's work force has been stable for the last 6 years, Meissner could not understand the increase in the net periodic pension expense. Montgomery explained that the net periodic pension expense consists of several elements, some of which may decrease of the net expense.

Instructions

(a) The determination of the net periodic pension expense is a function of five elements. List and briefly describe each of the elements.

(b) Describe the major difference and the major similarity between the accumulated benefit obligation and the projected benefit obligation.

(c) (1) Explain why pension gains and losses are not recognized on the income statement in the period in which they arise.

(2) Briefly describe how pension gains and losses are recognized.

(d) Under what conditions must Lyons recognize an additional minimum liability?

(CMA adapted)

C21-6 (Implications of *FASB Statement No. 87*) Ruth Moore and Carl Nies have to do a class presentation on the pension pronouncement "Employers' Accounting for Pension Plans." In developing the class presentation, they decided to provide the class with a series of questions related to pensions and then discuss the answers in class. Given that the class has all read *FASB Statement No. 87*, they felt this approach would provide a lively discussion. Here are the situations:

1. In an article in *Business Week* prior to *FASB No. 87*, it was reported that the discount rates used by the largest 200 companies for pension reporting ranged from 5 to 11%. How can such a situation exist, and does the new pension pronouncement alleviate this problem?
2. An article indicated that when *FASB Statement No. 87* was issued, it caused an increase in the liability for pensions for approximately 20% of companies. Why might this situation occur?
3. A recent article noted that while "smoothing" is not necessarily an accounting virtue, pension accounting has long been recognized as an exception—an area of accounting in which at least some dampening of market swings is appropriate. This is because pension funds are managed so that their performance is insulated from the extremes of short-term market swings. A pension expense that reflects the volatility of market swings might, for that reason, convey information of little relevance. Are these statements true?
4. Companies as diverse as **American Hospital Supply**, **Ashland Oil**, **Digital Equipment**, **GTE**, **Ralston Purina**, and **Signal Cos.** held assets twice as large as they needed to fund their pension plans at one time. Are these assets reported on the balance sheet of these companies per the pension pronouncement? If not, where are they reported?
5. Understanding the impact of the changes required in pension reporting requires detailed information about its pension plan(s) and an analysis of the relationship of many factors, particularly:
   (a) the type of plan(s) and any significant amendments.
   (b) the plan participants.
   (c) the funding status.
   (d) the actuarial funding method and assumptions currently used.
   What impact does each of these items have on financial statement presentation?
6. An article noted "You also need to decide whether to amortize gains and losses using the corridor method, or to use some other systematic method. Under the corridor approach, only gains and losses in excess of 10% of the greater of the projected benefit obligation or the plan assets would have to be amortized." What is the corridor method and what is its purpose?
7. Some companies may have to establish an intangible asset-deferred pension cost if the plan assets at fair value are less than the accumulated benefit obligation. What is the nature of this intangible asset and how is it amortized each period?
8. In its exposure draft on pensions, the Board required a note that discussed the sensitivity of pension expense to changes in the interest rate and the salary progression assumption. This note might read as follows:

At December 31, 2001, the weighted-average discount rate and rate of increase in future compensation levels used in determining the actuarial present value of the projected benefit obligation were 9% and 6%, respectively. Those assumptions can have a significant effect on the amounts reported. To illustrate, increasing the discount rate assumption to 10% would have decreased the projected benefit obligation and net periodic pension expense by $340,000 and $50,000, respectively, for the year ended December 31, 2001. Increasing the rate of change of future compensation levels to 7% would have increased the projected benefit obligation and net periodic pension cost by $180,000 and $30,000, respectively, for the year ended December 31, 2001.

Why do you believe this disclosure was eliminated from the final pronouncement?

Instructions

What answers do you believe Ruth and Carl gave to each of these questions?

C21-7 (Unrecognized Gains and Losses, Corridor Amortization) Rachel Avery, accounting clerk in the personnel office of Clarence G. Avery Corp., has begun to compute pension expense for 2001 but is not sure whether or not she should include the amortization of unrecognized gains/losses. She is currently working with the following beginning-of-the-year present values for the projected benefit obligation and market-related values for the pension plan:

	Projected Benefit Obligation	Plan Assets Value
1998	$2,200,000	$1,900,000
1999	2,400,000	2,600,000
2000	2,900,000	2,600,000
2001	3,900,000	3,000,000

The average remaining service life per employee in 1998 and 1999 is 10 years and in 2000 and 2001 is 12 years. The unrecognized net gain or loss that occurred during each year is as follows:

1998	$280,000 loss
1999	90,000 loss
2000	12,000 loss
2001	25,000 gain

(In working the solution, you must aggregate the unrecognized gains and losses to arrive at year-end balances.)

Instructions

You are the manager in charge of accounting. Write a memo to Rachel Avery, explaining why in some years she must amortize some of the unrecognized net gains and losses and in other years she does not need to. In order to explain this situation fully, you must compute the amount of unrecognized net gain or loss that is amortized and charged to pension expense in each of the 4 years listed above. Include an appropriate amortization schedule, referring to it whenever necessary.

USING YOUR JUDGMENT

FINANCIAL REPORTING PROBLEM: INTEL CORPORATION

Instructions

Refer to the financial statements and accompanying notes and discussion of Intel Corporation presented in Appendix 5B and answer the following questions.

(a) What kind of pension plan does Intel provide its employees in the United States (and Puerto Rico)? What does the plan provide employees?

(b) What was Intel's pension expense for 1998, 1997, and 1996 for the U.S. and Puerto Rico plans?

(c) What is the impact of Intel's pension plans on its financial statements?

(d) If you were an employee at Intel, would you be happy with the benefit package? Explain.

FINANCIAL STATEMENT ANALYSIS CASE

*General Electric

A *Wall Street Journal* article discussed a $1.8 billion charge to income made by General Electric for postretirement benefit costs. It was attributed to previously unrecognized health-care and life insurance cost. As financial vice president and controller for Peake, Inc., you found this article interesting because the president recently expressed concern about the company's rising health costs. The president, Martha Beyerlein, was particularly concerned with health care cost premiums being paid for retired employees. She wondered what charge Peake, Inc. will have to take for its postretirement benefit program.

Instructions

As financial vice president and controller of Peake, Inc., explain what the charge was that General Electric made against income and what the options are for Peake, Inc. in accounting for and reporting any transition amount when it adopts *FASB Statement No. 106.*

COMPARATIVE ANALYSIS CASE

The Coca-Cola Company versus PepsiCo, Inc.

Instructions

Go to the Digital Tool and, using The Coca-Cola Company and PepsiCo, Inc. Annual Report information, answer the following questions:

(a) What kind of pension plans do Coca-Cola and PepsiCo provide their employees?

(b) What are the pension plan funding policies of Coca-Cola and PepsiCo?

(c) What net periodic pension expense (cost) did Coca-Cola and PepsiCo report in 1998?

(d) What is the year-end 1998 funded status of Coca-Cola's and PepsiCo's U.S. plans?

(e) What relevant rates were used by Coca-Cola and PepsiCo in computing their pension amounts?

RESEARCH CASES

Case 1

Instructions

Examine the pension footnotes of three companies of your choice and answer the following questions.

(a) For each company, identify the following three assumptions: (1) the weighted-average discount rate, (2) the rate of compensation increase used to measure the projected benefit obligation, and (3) the weighted-average expected long-run rate of return on plan assets.

(b) Comment on any significant differences between the assumptions used by each firm.

(c) Did any of the companies change their assumptions during the period covered by the footnote? If so, what was the effect on the financial statements?

Case 2

The December 1995 issue of *Accounting Horizons* includes an article by Alan I. Blankley and Edward P. Swanson entitled "A Longitudinal Study of *SFAS 87* Pension Rate Assumptions." The article represents an excellent example of how academic research can address controversial accounting issues.

Instructions

Read the "introduction" section of the article and answer the following questions.

(a) According to the business press, firms are manipulating estimates of expected rates of return on plan assets and discount rates. What are the effects of these alleged manipulations?

(b) What was the reaction of the Securities and Exchange Commission?

(c) What is the purpose of the article? How did the authors obtain the data used in their study?

(d) What are the authors' major conclusions?

INTERNATIONAL REPORTING CASE

Volvo, a Swedish company that operates in the automotive and transport equipment industry, prepares its financial statements in accordance with Swedish accounting standards. In 1998, Volvo had income of 8,638 million SEK (Swedish Kronor) with assets of 204,426 million SEK at December 31, 1998. Volvo sponsors a pension plan for its employees in Sweden and the U.S. and provided the following disclosure related to its pension provisions in the notes to its financial statements:

VOLVO

Note 22: Provisions for postemployment benefits

	1996	1997	1998
Provisions for pensions	1,937	1,905	1,451
Provisions for other postemployment benefits	1,213	1,391	1,485
Total	3,150	3,296	2,936

The amounts shown for Provisions for postemployment benefits correspond to the actuarially calculated value of obligations not insured with a third party or secured through transfers of funds to pension foundations. The amount of pensions falling due within one year is included. The Swedish Group companies have insured their pension obligations with third parties. Group pension costs in 1998 amounted to 3,567. The greater part of pension costs consist of continuing payments to independent organizations that administer pension plans. Assets in pension foundations at market value exceeded the corresponding pension obligations by 425.

Volvo's shares trade on the NASDAQ in the United States (and on several European stock exchanges as well). As a consequence of listing its shares in the U.S., Volvo provides additional disclosure in its notes on the differences in accounting for its pension plans under U.S. and Swedish accounting standards. If Volvo had applied U.S. GAAP to its pensions, income would have been 313 million SEK higher in 1998, and stockholders' equity would have been 1,548 higher at December 31, 1998. The following excerpt about pension accounting differences between the U.S. and Sweden was taken from Volvo's notes.

Significant differences between Swedish and U.S. accounting principles

Note J: *Provision for pensions and other postemployment benefits.* The greater part of the Volvo Group's pension commitments are defined contribution plans; that is, they are met through regular payments to independent authorities or organs that administer pension plans. There is no difference between U.S. and Swedish accounting principles in accounting for these pension plans.

Other pension commitments are defined benefit plans; that is, the employee is entitled to receive a certain level of pension, usually related to the employee's final salary. In these cases the annual pension cost is calculated based on the current value of future pension payments. In Volvo's consolidated accounts, provisions for pensions and pension costs for the year in the individual companies are calculated based on local rules and directives. In accordance with U.S. GAAP provisions for pensions and pension costs for the year should always be calculated as specified in SFAS 87, "Employers Accounting for Pensions". The difference lies primarily in the choice of discount rates and the circumstance that U.S. calculations of capital-valuation, in contrast to the Swedish, are based on salaries calculated at time of retirement.

Instructions

Use the information on Volvo to respond to the following requirements.

(a) What are the key differences in accounting for pensions under U.S. and Swedish standards?

(b) Briefly explain how differences in U.S. and Swedish standards for pensions would affect the amounts reported in the financial statements.

(c) In light of the differences identified above, what are the likely reason(s) that Volvo's income and equity would be higher under U.S. GAAP than under Swedish accounting standards?

ETHICS CASES

Case 1

Cardinal Technology recently merged with College Electronix, a computer graphics manufacturing firm. In performing a comprehensive audit of CE's accounting system, Richard Nye, internal audit manager for Cardinal Technology, discovered that the new subsidiary did not capitalize pension assets and liabilities, subject to the requirements of *FASB Statement No. 87.*

The net present value of CE's pension assets was \$15.5 million, the vested benefit obligation was \$12.9 million, and the projected benefit obligation was \$17.4 million. Nye reported this audit finding to Renée Selma, the newly appointed controller of CE. A few days later Selma called Nye for his advice on what to do. Selma started her conversation by asking, "Can't we eliminate the negative income effect of our pension dilemma simply by terminating the employment of nonvested employees before the end of our fiscal year?"

Instructions

Answer the following question:

How should Nye respond to Selma's remark about firing nonvested employees?

Case 2

Philip Regan, Chief Executive Officer of Relief Dynamics Inc., a large defense contracting firm, is considering ways to improve the company's financial position after several years of sharply declining profitability. One way to do this is to reduce or completely eliminate Relief's commitment to present and future retirees who have full medical and dental benefits coverage. Despite financial problems, Relief still is committed to providing excellent pension benefits.

Instructions

Answer the following questions:

(a) What factors should Regan consider before making his decision to cut postretirement health benefits?

(b) Does your answer to the above question change if Relief Dynamics was paying Phil Regan, CEO, a salary of \$30 million per year?

(c) In your opinion, how did FASB's *Statement No. 106* influence the commitment of many organizations to its employees?

CHAPTER 22

Accounting for Leases

More Companies Ask "Why Buy?"

Leasing has grown tremendously in popularity and today is the fastest growing form of capital investment. Instead of borrowing money to buy an airplane, a computer, a nuclear core, or a satellite, a company leases it. Even the gambling casinos lease their slot machines. Airlines and railroads lease huge amounts of equipment; many hotel and motel chains lease their facilities; and most retail chains lease the bulk of their retail premises and warehouses. The popularity of leasing is evidenced in the fact that 541 of 600 companies surveyed by the AICPA in 1999 disclosed lease data.[1]

A classic example is the airline industry. Many travelers on airlines such as **United**, **Delta**, and **Southwest** believe the planes they are flying are owned by these airlines. But in many cases nothing could be further from the truth. Here are the lease percentages for the major U.S. airlines.

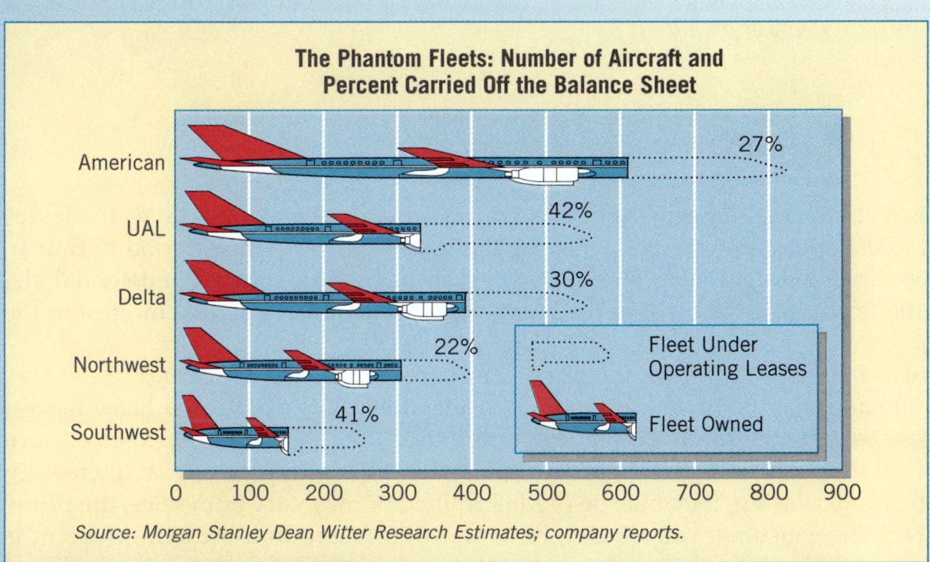

Source: Morgan Stanley Dean Witter Research Estimates; company reports.

Why do airline companies lease many of their airplanes? One reason is the favorable accounting treatment that airlines receive if they lease rather than purchase. By not reporting the airplane and related borrowing on their balance sheets, companies lower their debt to equity ratios. In addition, companies that lease often report higher net income in the earlier years of the life of the airplane.

LEARNING OBJECTIVES

After studying this chapter, you should be able to:

1. **Explain the nature, economic substance, and advantages of lease transactions.**
2. **Describe the accounting criteria and procedures for capitalizing leases by the lessee.**
3. **Contrast the operating and capitalization methods of recording leases.**
4. **Identify the classifications of leases for the lessor.**
5. **Describe the lessor's accounting for direct financing leases.**
6. **Identify special features of lease arrangements that cause unique accounting problems.**
7. **Describe the effect of residual values, guaranteed and unguaranteed, on lease accounting.**
8. **Describe the lessor's accounting for sales-type leases.**
9. **Describe the disclosure requirements for leases.**

[1]AICPA, *Accounting Trends and Techniques—1999.*

PREVIEW OF CHAPTER 22

Because of the increased significance and prevalence of lease arrangements indicated in the opening story, the need for uniform accounting and complete informative reporting of these transactions has intensified. In this chapter, we will look at the accounting issues related to leasing. The content and organization of this chapter are as follows:

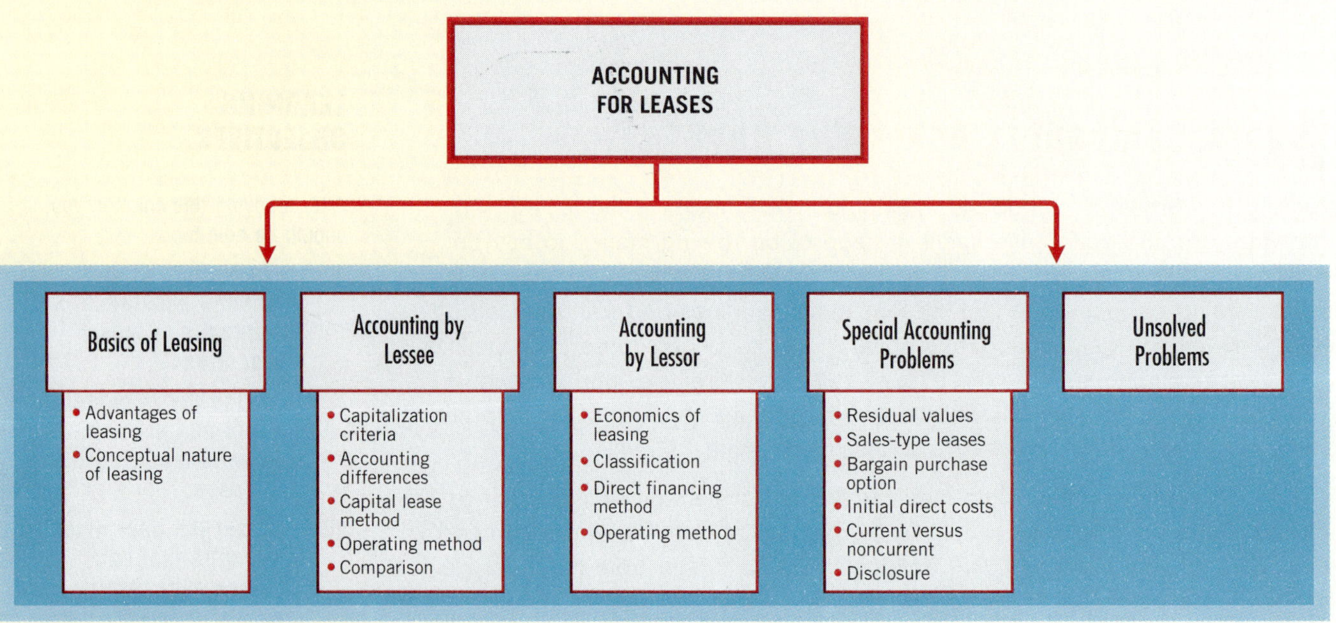

BASICS OF LEASING

OBJECTIVE 1
Explain the nature, economic substance, and advantages of lease transactions.

A **lease** is a contractual agreement between a **lessor** and a **lessee** that gives the lessee the right to use specific property, owned by the lessor, for a specified period of time in return for stipulated, and generally periodic, cash payments (rents). An essential element of the lease agreement is that the lessor conveys less than the total interest in the property.

Because a lease is a contract, the provisions agreed to by the lessor and lessee may vary widely and may be limited only by their ingenuity. The **duration—lease term—** of the lease may be anything from a short period of time to the entire expected economic life of the asset. The **rental payments** may be level from year to year, increasing in amount, or decreasing; they may be predetermined or may vary with sales, the prime interest rate, the consumer price index, or some other factor. In most cases the rent is set to enable the lessor to recover the cost of the asset plus a fair return over the life of the lease.

The **obligations for taxes, insurance, and maintenance** (executory costs) may be assumed by either the lessor or the lessee, or they may be divided. **Restrictions** comparable to bond indentures may limit the lessee's activities regarding dividend payments or the incurrence of further debt and lease obligations in order to protect the lessor from default on the rents. The lease contract may be **noncancelable** or may grant the right to **early termination** on payment of a set scale of prices plus a penalty. In case of **default**, the lessee may be liable for all future payments at once, receiving title to the property in exchange; or the lessor may have the right to sell to a third party and collect from the lessee all or a portion of the difference between the sale price and the lessor's unrecovered cost.

Alternatives for the lessee at termination of the lease may range from none to the right to purchase the leased asset at the fair market value or the right to renew or buy at a nominal price.

Advantages of Leasing

Although leasing is not without its disadvantages, the growth in its use suggests that it often has a genuine advantage over owning property. Some of the commonly discussed advantages to the lessee of leasing are:

1. ***100% Financing at Fixed Rates.*** Leases are often signed without requiring any money down from the lessee, which helps to conserve scarce cash—an especially desirable feature for new and developing companies. In addition, lease payments often remain fixed, which protects the lessee against inflation and increases in the cost of money. The following comment regarding a conventional loan is typical: "Our local bank finally came up to 80% of the purchase price but wouldn't go any higher, and they wanted a floating interest rate. We just couldn't afford the down payment and we needed to lock in a final payment rate we knew we could live with."
2. ***Protection against Obsolescence.*** Leasing equipment reduces risk of obsolescence to the lessee, and in many cases passes the risk of residual value to the lessor. For example, Syntex Corp. (a pharmaceutical maker) leases computers. Syntex is permitted under the lease agreement to turn in an old computer for a new model at any time, canceling the old lease and writing a new one. The cost of the new lease is added to the balance due on the old lease, less the old computer's trade-in value. As the treasurer of Syntex remarked, "Our instinct is to purchase." But if a new computer comes along in a short time "then leasing is just a heck of a lot more convenient than purchasing."
3. ***Flexibility.*** Lease agreements may contain less restrictive provisions than other debt agreements. Innovative lessors can tailor a lease agreement to the lessee's special needs. For instance, rental payments can be structured to meet the timing of cash revenues generated by the equipment so that payments are made when the equipment is productive.
4. ***Less Costly Financing.*** Some companies find leasing cheaper than other forms of financing. For example, start-up companies in depressed industries, or companies in low tax brackets may lease as a way of claiming tax benefits that might otherwise be lost. Depreciation deductions offer no benefit to companies that have little if any taxable income. Through leasing, these tax benefits are used by the leasing companies or financial institutions, which can pass some of these tax benefits back to the user of the asset in the form of lower rental payments.
5. ***Alternative Minimum Tax Problems.*** As indicated in Chapter 20, all companies are subject to an alternative minimum tax (AMT). Under the AMT rules, a portion of accelerated depreciation deductions are considered tax preference items that are added to a company's regular taxable income to arrive at the alternative minimum taxable income (AMTI). The company must pay whichever is higher—the regular tax or the AMT. Since ownership of equipment can contribute to an increase in AMTI and, ultimately, to an alternative minimum tax liability in excess of the regular tax liability, companies often find leasing a way to avoid the onerous alternative tax provisions.
6. ***Off-Balance-Sheet Financing.*** Certain leases do not add debt on a balance sheet or affect financial ratios, and they may add to borrowing capacity.[2] Such **off-balance-**

Some companies double dip. That is, the leasing rules of the lessor's and lessee's countries may be different, permitting both parties to be an owner of the asset. Thus, both lessor and lessee receive the tax benefits related to depreciation. By structuring the lease to take advantage of these international differences, both the lessee and lessor benefit.

[2]As demonstrated later in this chapter, certain types of lease arrangements are not capitalized on the balance sheet. The liability section is thereby relieved of large future lease commitments that, if recorded, would adversely affect the debt-to-equity ratio. The reluctance to record lease obligations as liabilities is one of the primary reasons capitalized lease accounting is resisted. For an excellent discussion on the effects of the failure to capitalize long-term lease commitments, see Eugene A. Imhoff, Jr., Robert C. Lipe, and David W. Wright, "Operating Leases: Impact of Constructive Capitalization," *Accounting Horizons,* March 1991.

sheet financing is critical to some companies. For example, as shown in our opening story, the airlines use lease arrangements extensively, which results in a great deal of off-balance-sheet financing. Illustration 22-1 indicates that debt levels are understated by a substantial amount for many airlines that lease aircraft.

ILLUSTRATION 22-1
Net Reported Debt and Debt Adjustment of Leases, 1997

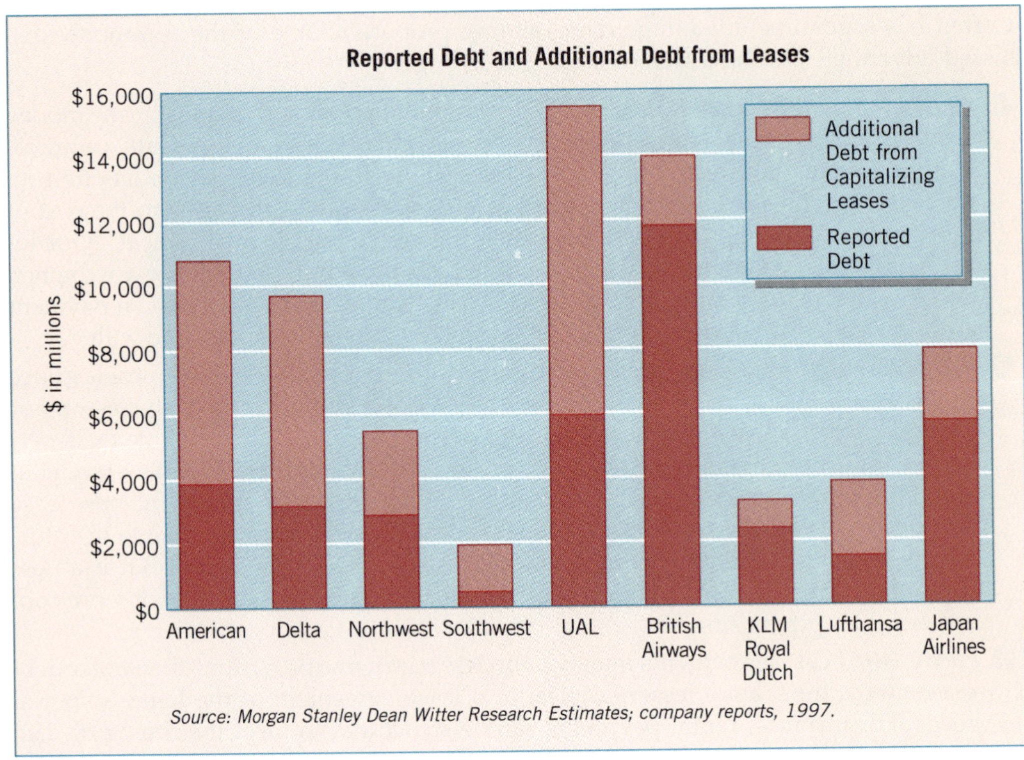

Source: Morgan Stanley Dean Witter Research Estimates; company reports, 1997.

Conceptual Nature of a Lease

If United Airlines borrows $47 million on a 10-year note from National City Bank to purchase a Boeing 757 jet plane, it is clear that an asset and related liability should be reported on United's balance sheet at that amount. If United purchases the 757 for $47,000,000 directly from Boeing through an installment purchase over 10 years, it is equally clear that an asset and related liability should be reported (i.e., the installment transaction should be "capitalized"). However, if United **leases** the Boeing 757 for 10 years through a noncancelable lease transaction with payments of the same amount as the installment purchase transaction, differences of opinion start to develop over how this transaction should be reported. The various views on capitalization of leases are as follows:

1. ***Do Not Capitalize Any Leased Assets.*** Because the lessee does not have ownership of the property, capitalization is considered inappropriate. Furthermore, a lease is an "executory" contract requiring continuing performance by both parties. Because other executory contracts (such as purchase commitments and employment contracts) are not capitalized at present, leases should not be capitalized, either.
2. ***Capitalize Leases That Are Similar to Installment Purchases.*** Accountants should report transactions in accordance with their economic substance; therefore, if installment purchases are capitalized, so also should leases that have similar characteristics. For example, United Airlines is committed to the same payments over a 10-year period for either a lease or an installment purchase; lessees make rental payments, whereas owners make mortgage payments. Why shouldn't the financial statements report these transactions in the same manner?

③ ***Capitalize All Long-Term Leases.*** Under this approach, the only requirement for capitalization is the long-term right to use the property. This property-rights approach capitalizes all long-term leases.[3]

④ ***Capitalize Firm Leases Where the Penalty for Nonperformance Is Substantial.*** A final approach is to capitalize only "firm" (noncancelable) contractual rights and obligations. "Firm" means that it is unlikely that performance under the lease can be avoided without a severe penalty.[4]

UNDERLYING CONCEPTS

The issue of how to report leases is the classic case of substance versus form. Although technically legal title does not pass in lease transactions, the benefits from the use of the property do transfer.

In short, the various viewpoints range from no capitalization to capitalization of all leases. The FASB apparently agrees with the capitalization approach when the lease is similar to an installment purchase, noting that **a lease that transfers substantially all of the benefits and risks of property ownership should be capitalized**. Transfer of ownership can be assumed only if there is a high degree of performance to the transfer, that is, the lease is noncancelable. **Noncancelable** means that the lease contract is cancelable only upon the outcome of some remote contingency or that the cancellation provisions and penalties of the contract are so costly to the lessee that cancellation probably will not occur. Only noncancelable leases may be capitalized.

This viewpoint leads to three basic conclusions: (1) The characteristics that indicate that substantially all of the benefits and risks of ownership have been transferred must be identified. (2) The same characteristics should apply consistently to the lessee and the lessor. (3) Those leases that do **not** transfer substantially all the benefits and risks of ownership are operating leases. They should not be capitalized but rather accounted for as rental payments and receipts.

ACCOUNTING BY LESSEE

OBJECTIVE 2
Describe the accounting criteria and procedures for capitalizing leases by the lessee.

If a lessee **capitalizes** a lease, the **lessee** records an asset and a liability generally equal to the present value of the rental payments. **The lessor**, having transferred substantially all the benefits and risks of ownership, recognizes a sale by removing the asset from the balance sheet and replacing it with a receivable. The typical journal entries for the lessee and the lessor, assuming equipment is leased and is capitalized, appear as follows:

ILLUSTRATION 22-2
Journal Entries for Capitalized Lease

Lessee			Lessor		
Leased Equipment	XXX		Lease Receivable (net)	XXX	
Lease Obligation		XXX	Equipment		XXX

Having capitalized the asset, the lessee records the depreciation. The lessor and lessee treat the lease rental payments as consisting of interest and principal.

If the lease is not capitalized, no asset is recorded by the lessee and no asset is removed from the lessor's books. When a lease payment is made, the lessee records rental expense and the lessor recognizes rental revenue.

For a lease to be recorded as a **capital lease**, the lease must be noncancelable, and meet one or more of the following four criteria:

---

[3]The property rights approach was originally recommended in a research study by the AICPA: John H. Myers, "Reporting of Leases in Financial Statements," *Accounting Research Study No. 4* (New York: AICPA, 1964), pp. 10–11. Recently, this view has received additional support. See Peter H. Knutson, "Financial Reporting in the 1990s and Beyond," Position Paper (Charlottesville, Va.: AIMR, 1993), and Warren McGregor, "Accounting for Leases: A New Approach," Special Report (Norwalk, Conn.: FASB, 1996).

[4]Yuji Ijiri, *Recognition of Contractual Rights and Obligations,* Research Report (Stamford, Conn.: FASB, 1980).

ILLUSTRATION 22-3
Capitalization Criteria for Lessee

Capitalization Criteria (Lessee)

- The lease transfers ownership of the property to the lessee.
- The lease contains a bargain purchase option.[5]
- The lease term is equal to 75% or more of the estimated economic life of the leased property.
- The present value of the minimum lease payments (excluding executory costs) equals or exceeds 90% of the fair value of the leased property.[6]

Leases that **do not meet any of the four criteria** are classified and accounted for by the lessee as **operating leases**. Illustration 22-4 shows that a lease meeting any one of the four criteria results in the lessee having a capital lease.

ILLUSTRATION 22-4
Diagram of Lessee's Criteria for Lease Classification

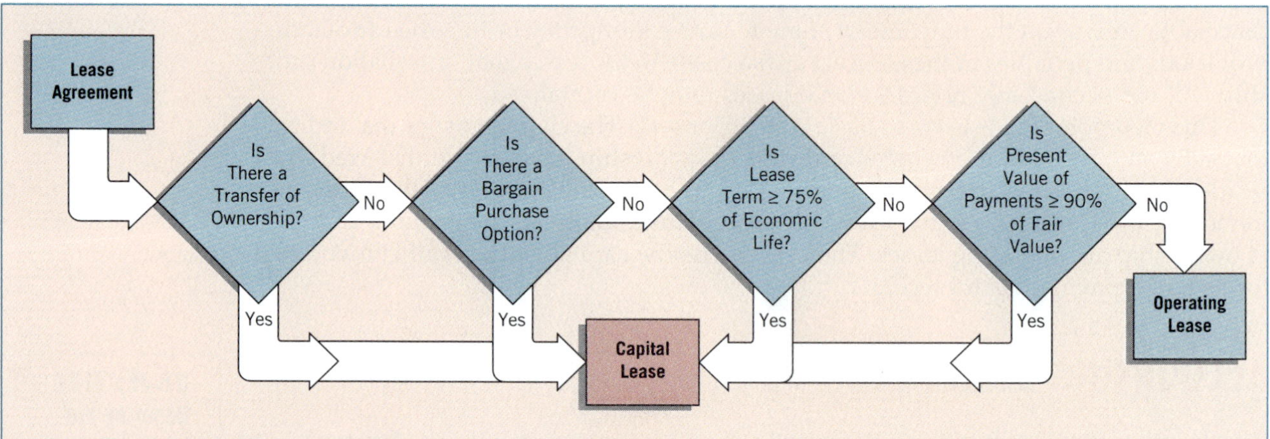

In keeping with the FASB's reasoning that a significant portion of the value of the asset is consumed in the first 75% of its life, neither the third nor the fourth criterion is to be applied when the inception of the lease occurs during the last 25% of the life of the asset.

Capitalization Criteria

The four **capitalization criteria** that apply to lessees are controversial and can be difficult to apply in practice. They are discussed in detail in the following pages.

Transfer of Ownership Test

If the lease transfers ownership of the asset to the lessee, it is a capital lease. This criterion is not controversial and is easily implemented in practice.

Bargain Purchase Option Test

UNDERLYING CONCEPTS

Capitalization of leases illustrates the necessity for good definitions. The lease fits the definition of an asset, as it gives the lessee the economic benefits that flow from the possession or the use of the asset.

A **bargain purchase option** is a provision allowing the lessee to purchase the leased property for a price that is **significantly lower** than the property's expected fair value at the date the option becomes exercisable. At the inception of the lease, the difference between the option price and the expected fair market value must be large enough to make exercise of the option reasonably assured.

For example, assume that you were to lease a Honda Accord for $599 per month for 40 months with an option to purchase for $100 at the end of the 40-month period. If the estimated fair value of the Honda Accord is $3,000 at the end of the 40 months,

[5] A bargain purchase option is defined in the next section.

[6] "Accounting for Leases," *FASB Statement No. 13* as amended and interpreted through May 1980 (Stamford, Conn.: FASB, 1980), par. 7.

the $100 option to purchase is clearly a bargain, and therefore capitalization is required. In other cases, the criterion may not be as easy to apply, and determining now that a certain future price is a bargain can be difficult.

Economic Life Test (75% Test)

If the lease period equals or exceeds 75% of the asset's economic life, most of the risks and rewards of ownership are transferred to the lessee, and capitalization is therefore appropriate. However, determining the lease term and the economic life of the asset can be troublesome.

The lease term is generally considered to be the fixed, noncancelable term of the lease. However, this period can be extended if a bargain renewal option is provided in the lease agreement. A **bargain renewal option** is a provision allowing the lessee to renew the lease for a rental that is lower than the expected fair rental at the date the option becomes exercisable. At the inception of the lease, the difference between the renewal rental and the expected fair rental must be great enough to make exercise of the option to renew reasonably assured.

For example, if a Dell PC is leased for 2 years at a rental of $100 per month and subsequently can be leased for $10 per month for another 2 years, it clearly is a bargain renewal option, and the lease term is considered to be 4 years. However, with bargain renewal options, as with bargain purchase options, it is sometimes difficult to determine what is a bargain.[7]

INTERNATIONAL INSIGHT

In some nations (e.g., Italy, Japan) accounting principles do not specify criteria for capitalization of leases. In others (e.g., Sweden, Switzerland) such criteria exist, but capitalization of the leases is optional.

Determining estimated economic life can also pose problems, especially if the leased item is a specialized item or has been used for a significant period of time. For example, determining the economic life of a nuclear core is extremely difficult because it is subject to much more than normal "wear and tear." The FASB takes the position that if the lease starts during the last 25% of the life of the asset, the economic life test cannot be used as a basis to classify a lease as a capital lease.

Recovery of Investment Test (90% Test)

If the present value of the minimum lease payments equals or exceeds 90% of the fair market value of the asset, then the leased asset should be capitalized. The rationale for this test is that if the present value of the minimum lease payments is reasonably close to the market price of the asset, the asset is effectively being purchased.

In determining the present value of the minimum lease payments, three important concepts are involved: (1) minimum lease payments, (2) executory costs, and (3) discount rate.

Minimum Lease Payments. These are payments the lessee is obligated to make or can be expected to make in connection with the leased property. **Minimum lease payments** include the following:

1. *Minimum Rental Payments*—Minimum payments the lessee is obligated to make to the lessor under the lease agreement. In some cases, the minimum rental payments may be equal to the minimum lease payments. However, the minimum lease payments also may include a guaranteed residual value (if any), penalty for failure to renew, or a bargain purchase option (if any), as noted on the next page.

[7]The original lease term is also extended for leases having the following: substantial penalties for nonrenewal; periods for which the lessor has the option to renew or extend the lease; renewal periods preceding the date a bargain purchase option becomes exercisable; and renewal periods in which any lessee guarantees of the lessor's debt are expected to be in effect or in which there will be a loan outstanding from the lessee to the lessor. The lease term, however, can never extend beyond the time a bargain purchase option becomes exercisable. "Accounting for Leases: Sale-Leaseback Transactions Involving Real Estate; Sales-Type Leases of Real Estate; Definition of the Lease Term; Initial Direct Costs of Direct Financing Leases," *Statement of Financial Accounting Standards No. 98* (Stamford, Conn.: FASB, 1988).

2. *Guaranteed Residual Value*—The residual value is the estimated fair (market) value of the leased property at the end of the lease term. The lessor often transfers the risk of loss to the lessee or to a third party through a guarantee of the estimated residual value. The **guaranteed residual value** is (1) the certain or determinable amount at which the lessor has the right to require the lessee to purchase the asset or (2) the amount the lessee or the third-party guarantor guarantees the lessor will realize. If it is not guaranteed in full, the **unguaranteed residual value** is the estimated residual value exclusive of any portion guaranteed.[8]
3. *Penalty for Failure to Renew or Extend the Lease*—The amount payable that is required of the lessee if the agreement specifies that the lease must be extended or renewed and the lessee fails to do so.
4. *Bargain Purchase Option*—As indicated earlier, an option given to the lessee to purchase the equipment at the end of the lease term at a price that is fixed sufficiently below the expected fair value, so that, at the inception of the lease, purchase appears to be reasonably assured.

Executory costs (defined below) are not included in the lessee's computation of the present value of the minimum lease payments.

Executory Costs. Like most assets, leased tangible assets require the incurrence of insurance, maintenance, and tax expenses—called **executory costs**—during their economic life. If the lessor retains responsibility for the payment of these "ownership-type costs," a portion of each lease payment that represents executory costs **should be excluded** in computing the present value of the minimum lease payments because it does not represent payment on or reduction of the obligation. If the portion of the minimum lease payments that represents executory costs is not determinable from the provisions of the lease, an estimate of such amount must be made. Many lease agreements, however, specify that executory costs be paid to the appropriate third parties directly by the lessee; in these cases, the rental payment can be used **without adjustment** in the present value computation.

Discount Rate. The lessee computes the present value of the minimum lease payments using the **lessee's incremental borrowing rate**, which is defined as: "The rate that, at the inception of the lease, the lessee would have incurred to borrow the funds necessary to buy the leased asset on a secured loan with repayment terms similar to the payment schedule called for in the lease."[9] Assume, for example, that Mortenson Inc. decides to lease computer equipment for a 5-year period at a cost of $10,000 a year. To determine whether the present value of these payments is less than 90% of the fair market value of the property, the lessee discounts the payments using its incremental borrowing rate. Determining that rate will often require judgment because it is based on a hypothetical purchase of the property.

However, there is one exception to this rule: If (1) the lessee knows the **implicit interest rate computed by the lessor** and (2) it is less than the lessee's incremental borrowing rate, then the **lessee must use the lessor's implicit rate**. The **interest rate implicit in the lease** is the discount rate that, when applied to the minimum lease payments and any unguaranteed residual value accruing to the lessor, causes the aggregate present value to be equal to the fair value of the leased property to the lessor.[10]

---

[8]A lease provision requiring the lessee to make up a residual value deficiency that is attributable to damage, extraordinary wear and tear, or excessive usage is not included in the minimum lease payments. Such costs are recognized as period costs when incurred. "Lessee Guarantee of the Residual Value of Leased Property," *FASB Interpretation No. 19* (Stamford, Conn.: FASB, 1977), par. 3.

[9]*FASB Statement No. 13*, op. cit., par. 5 (l).

[10]Ibid., par. 5 (k).

The purpose of this exception is twofold: First, the implicit rate of the lessor is generally a **more realistic rate** to use in determining the amount (if any) to report as the asset and related liability for the lessee. Second, the guideline is provided to ensure that the lessee **does not use an artificially high incremental borrowing rate** that would cause the present value of the minimum lease payments to be less than 90% of the fair market value of the property and thus make it possible to avoid capitalization of the asset and related liability. The lessee may argue that it cannot determine the implicit rate of the lessor and therefore the higher rate should be used. However, in many cases, the implicit rate used by the lessor can be approximated. The determination of whether or not a reasonable estimate could be made will require judgment, particularly where the result from using the incremental borrowing rate comes close to meeting the 90% test. Because **the lessee may not capitalize the leased property at more than its fair value** (as discussed later), the lessee is prevented from using an excessively low discount rate.

Asset and Liability Accounted for Differently

In a capital lease transaction, the lessee is using the lease as a source of financing. The lessor finances the transaction (provides the investment capital) through the leased asset, and the lessee makes rent payments, which actually are installment payments. Therefore, over the life of the property rented, **the rental payments to the lessor constitute a payment of principal plus interest**.

Asset and Liability Recorded

Under the capital lease method, the lessee treats the lease transaction as if an asset were being purchased in a financing transaction in which an asset is acquired and an obligation created. Therefore, the lessee records a capital lease as an asset and a liability at the lower of (1) the present value of the minimum lease payments (excluding executory costs) or (2) the fair market value of the leased asset at the inception of the lease. The rationale for this approach is that the leased asset should not be recorded for more than its fair market value.

Depreciation Period

One troublesome aspect of accounting for the depreciation of the capitalized leased asset relates to the period of depreciation. If the lease agreement transfers ownership of the asset to the lessee (criterion 1) or contains a bargain purchase option (criterion 2)—the leased asset is depreciated in a manner consistent with the lessee's normal depreciation policy for owned assets, **using the economic life of the asset**. On the other hand, if the lease does not transfer ownership or does not contain a bargain purchase option, then it is depreciated over the **term of the lease**. In this case, the leased asset reverts to the lessor after a certain period of time.

Effective Interest Method

Throughout the term of the lease, the **effective interest method** is used to allocate each lease payment between principal and interest. This method produces a periodic interest expense equal to a constant percentage of the carrying value of the lease obligation.

The discount rate used by the lessee to determine the present value of the minimum lease payments must be used by the lessee when applying the effective interest method to capital leases.

Depreciation Concept

Although the amounts initially capitalized as an asset and recorded as an obligation are computed at the same present value, the **depreciation of the asset and the discharge of the obligation are independent accounting processes** during the term of the lease. The lessee should depreciate the leased asset by applying conventional depreciation methods: straight-line, sum-of-the-years'-digits, declining-balance, units of production, etc.

The FASB uses the term "amortization" more frequently than "depreciation" to recognize intangible leased property rights. The authors prefer "depreciation" to describe the write-off of a tangible asset's expired services.

Capital Lease Method (Lessee)

Lessor Company and Lessee Company sign a lease agreement dated January 1, 2002, that calls for Lessor Company to lease equipment to Lessee Company beginning January 1, 2002. The terms and provisions of the lease agreement and other pertinent data are as follows:

1. The term of the lease is 5 years, and the lease agreement is noncancelable, requiring equal rental payments of $25,981.62 at the beginning of each year (annuity due basis).
2. The equipment has a fair value at the inception of the lease of $100,000, an estimated economic life of 5 years, and no residual value.
3. Lessee Company pays all of the executory costs directly to third parties except for the property taxes of $2,000 per year, which are included in the annual payments to the lessor.
4. The lease contains no renewal options, and the equipment reverts to Lessor Company at the termination of the lease.
5. Lessee Company's incremental borrowing rate is 11% per year.
6. Lessee Company depreciates on a straight-line basis similar equipment that it owns.
7. Lessor Company set the annual rental to earn a rate of return on its investment of 10% per year; this fact is known to Lessee Company.[11]

The lease meets the criteria for classification as a capital lease for the following reasons: (1) The lease term of 5 years, being equal to the equipment's estimated economic life of 5 years, satisfies the 75% test. (2) The present value of the minimum lease payments ($100,000 as computed below) exceeds 90% of the fair value of the property ($100,000).

The minimum lease payments are $119,908.10 ($23,981.62 × 5), and the amount capitalized as leased assets is computed as the present value of the minimum lease payments (excluding executory costs—property taxes of $2,000) as follows:

ILLUSTRATION 22-5
Computation of Capitalized Lease Payments

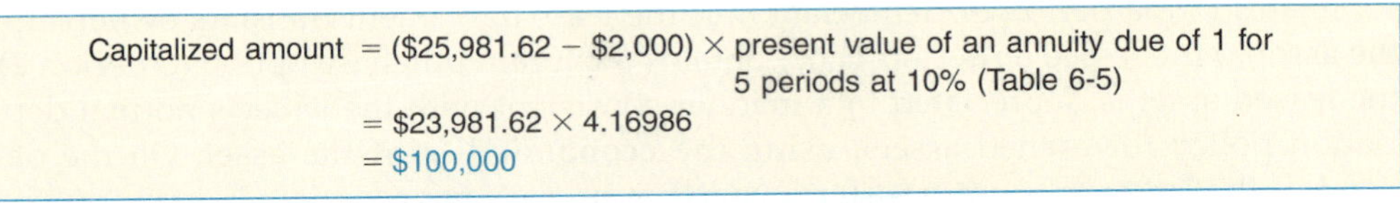
Capitalized amount = ($25,981.62 − $2,000) × present value of an annuity due of 1 for 5 periods at 10% (Table 6-5)
= $23,981.62 × 4.16986
= $100,000

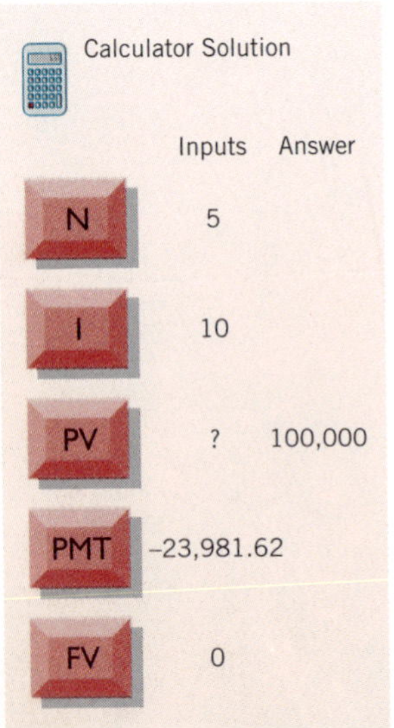

Calculator Solution
Inputs
Answer
N
5
I
10
PV
?
100,000
PMT
-23,981.62
FV
0

The lessor's implicit interest rate of 10% is used instead of the lessee's incremental borrowing rate of 11% because (1) it is lower and (2) the lessee has knowledge of it.

The entry to record the capital lease on Lessee Company's books on January 1, 2002, is:

Leased Equipment under Capital Leases	100,000	
Obligations under Capital Leases		100,000

Note that the preceding entry records the obligation at the net amount of $100,000 (the present value of the future rental payments) rather than at the gross amount of $119,908.10 ($23,981.62 × 5).

[11]If Lessee Company had an incremental borrowing rate of, say, 9% (lower than the 10% rate used by Lessor Company) and it did not know the rate used by Lessor Company, the present value computation would have yielded a capitalized amount of $101,675.35 ($23,981.62 × 4.23972). And, because this amount exceeds the $100,000 fair value of the equipment, Lessee Company would have had to capitalize the $100,000 and use 10% as its effective rate for amortization of the lease obligation.

The journal entry to record the **first lease payment on January 1, 2002**, is:

Property Tax Expense	2,000.00	
Obligations under Capital Leases	23,981.62	
Cash		25,981.62

Each lease payment of $25,981.62 consists of three elements: (1) a reduction in the lease obligation, (2) a financing cost (interest expense), and (3) executory costs (property taxes). The total financing cost (interest expense) over the term of the lease is $19,908.10, the difference between the present value of the lease payments ($100,000) and the actual cash disbursed, net of executory costs ($119,908.10). Therefore, the annual interest expense, applying the effective interest method, is a function of the outstanding obligation, as shown in Illustration 22-6:

ILLUSTRATION 22-6
Lease Amortization Schedule for Lessee—Annuity Due Basis

LESSEE COMPANY
Lease Amortization Schedule
(Annuity due basis)

Date	Annual Lease Payment	Executory Costs	Interest (10%) on Unpaid Obligation	Reduction of Lease Obligation	Lease Obligation
	(a)	(b)	(c)	(d)	(e)
1/1/02					$100,000.00
1/1/02	$ 25,981.62	$ 2,000	$ -0-	$ 23,981.62	76,018.38
1/1/03	25,981.62	2,000	7,601.84	16,379.78	59,638.60
1/1/04	25,981.62	2,000	5,963.86	18,017.76	41,620.84
1/1/05	25,981.62	2,000	4,162.08	19,819.54	21,801.30
1/1/06	25,981.62	2,000	2,180.32*	21,801.30	-0-
	$129,908.10	$10,000	$19,908.10	$100,000.00	

(a) Lease payment as required by lease.
(b) Executory costs included in rental payment.
(c) Ten percent of the preceding balance of (e) except for 1/1/02; since this is an annuity due, no time has elapsed at the date of the first payment and no interest has accrued.
(d) (a) minus (b) and (c).
(e) Preceding balance minus (d).
*Rounded by 19 cents.

At the end of Lessee Company's fiscal year, December 31, 2002, **accrued interest** is recorded as follows:

Interest Expense	7,601.84	
Interest Payable		7,601.84

Depreciation of the leased equipment over its lease term of 5 years, applying Lessee Company's normal depreciation policy (straight-line method), results in the following entry on December 31, 2002:

Depreciation Expense—Capital Leases	20,000	
Accumulated Depreciation—Capital Leases ($100,000 ÷ 5 years)		20,000

At December 31, 2002, the assets recorded under capital leases are separately identified on the lessee's balance sheet. Similarly, the related obligations are separately identified. The portion due within one year or the operating cycle, whichever is longer, is classified with current liabilities and the rest with noncurrent liabilities. For example, the current portion of the 12/31/02 total obligation of $76,018.38 in the lessee's amortization schedule is the amount of the reduction in the obligation in 2003, or $16,379.78. The liability section as it relates to lease transactions at 12/31/02 would appear as follows:

ILLUSTRATION 22-7
Reporting Current and Noncurrent Lease Liabilities

Current liabilities	
Interest payable	$ 7,601.84
Obligations under capital leases	16,379.78
Noncurrent liabilities	
Obligations under capital leases	$59,638.60

The journal entry to record the lease payment of January 1, 2003, is as follows:

Property Tax Expense	2,000.00	
Interest Expense (or Interest Payable)	7,601.84	
Obligations under Capital Leases	16,379.78	
Cash		25,981.62

Entries through 2006 would follow the pattern above. Other executory costs (insurance and maintenance) assumed by Lessee Company would be recorded in a manner similar to that used to record any other operating costs incurred on assets owned by Lessee Company.

Upon expiration of the lease, the amount capitalized as leased equipment is fully amortized and the lease obligation is fully discharged. If not purchased, the equipment would be returned to the lessor, and the leased equipment and related accumulated depreciation accounts would be removed from the books.[12] If the equipment is purchased at termination of the lease at a price of $5,000 and the estimated life of the equipment is changed from 5 to 7 years, the following entry might be made:

Equipment ($100,000 + $5,000)	105,000	
Accumulated Depreciation—Capital Leases	100,000	
Leased Equipment under Capital Leases		100,000
Accumulated Depreciation—Equipment		100,000
Cash		5,000

Operating Method (Lessee)

Under the **operating method**, rent expense (and the associated liability) accrues day by day to the lessee as the property is used. **The lessee assigns rent to the periods benefiting from the use of the asset and ignores, in the accounting, any commitments to make future payments.** Appropriate accruals or deferrals are made if the accounting period ends between cash payment dates. For example, assume that the capital lease illustrated in the previous section did not qualify as a capital lease and was therefore to be accounted for as an operating lease. The first-year charge to operations would have been $25,981.62, the amount of the rental payment. The journal entry to record this payment on January 1, 2002, would be as follows:

Rent Expense	25,981.62	
Cash		25,981.62

The rented asset, as well as any long-term liability for future rental payments, is not reported on the balance sheet. Rent expense would be reported on the income statement. In addition, **note disclosure is required for all operating leases that have noncancelable lease terms in excess of one year**. An illustration of the type of note disclosure required for an operating lease (as well as other types of leases) is provided in Illustrations 22-32 to 22-35 later in this chapter.

[12] If the lessee purchases a leased asset **during the term of a "capital lease,"** it is accounted for like a renewal or extension of a capital lease. "Any difference between the purchase price and the carrying amount of the lease obligation shall be recorded as an adjustment of the carrying amount of the asset." See "Accounting for Purchase of a Leased Asset by the Lessee During the Term of the Lease," *FASB Interpretation No. 26* (Stamford, Conn.: FASB, 1978), par. 5.

Comparison of Capital Lease with Operating Lease

As indicated on the previous page, if the lease had been accounted for as an operating lease, the first-year charge to operations would have been $25,981.62, the amount of the rental payment. Treating the transaction as a capital lease, however, resulted in a first-year charge of $29,601.84: depreciation of $20,000 (assuming straight-line), interest expense of $7,601.84 (per Illustration 22-8), and executory costs of $2,000. Illustration 22-8 shows that **while the total charges to operations are the same over the lease term whether the lease is accounted for as a capital lease or as an operating lease, under the capital lease treatment the charges are higher in the earlier years and lower in the later years.**[13]

OBJECTIVE 3
Contrast the operating and capitalization methods of recording leases.

ILLUSTRATION 22-8
Comparison of Charges to Operations—Capital vs. Operating Leases

LESSEE COMPANY
Schedule of Charges to Operations
Capital Lease versus Operating Lease

	Capital Lease					
Year	Depreciation	Executory Costs	Interest	Total Charge	Operating Lease Charge	Difference
2002	$ 20,000	$ 2,000	$ 7,601.84	$ 29,601.84	$ 25,981.62	$ 3,620.22
2003	20,000	2,000	5,963.86	27,963.86	25,981.62	1,982.24
2004	20,000	2,000	4,162.08	26,162.08	25,981.62	180.46
2005	20,000	2,000	2,180.32	24,180.32	25,981.62	(1,801.30)
2006	20,000	2,000	—	22,000.00	25,981.62	(3,981.62)
	$100,000	$10,000	$19,908.10	$129,908.10	$129,908.10	$ -0-

If an accelerated method of depreciation is used, the differences between the amounts charged to operations under the two methods would be even larger in the earlier and later years.

In addition, using the capital lease approach would have resulted in an asset and related liability of $100,000 initially reported on the balance sheet; no such asset or liability would be reported under the operating method. Therefore, the following differences occur if a capital lease instead of an operating lease is employed:

1. an increase in the amount of reported debt (both short-term and long-term),
2. an increase in the amount of total assets (specifically long-lived assets), and
3. a lower income early in the life of the lease and, therefore, lower retained earnings.

Thus, many companies believe that capital leases have a detrimental impact on their financial position as their debt to total equity ratio increases and their rate of return on total assets decreases. As a result, the business community resists capitalizing leases.

Whether their resistance is well founded is a matter of conjecture. From a cash flow point of view, the company is in the same position whether the lease is accounted for as an operating or a capital lease. The reason why managers often argue against capitalization is that it can more easily lead to **violation of loan covenants**; it can affect the **amount of compensation received** by owners (for example, a stock compensation plan tied to earnings); and finally, it can **lower rates of return** and **increase debt**

[13]The higher charges in the early years is one reason lessees are reluctant to adopt the capital lease accounting method. Lessees (especially those of real estate) claim that it is really no more costly to operate the leased asset in the early years than in the later years; thus, they advocate an even charge similar to that provided by the operating method.

to equity relationships, thus making the company less attractive to present and potential investors.[14]

ACCOUNTING BY LESSOR

INTERNATIONAL INSIGHT

In some countries, such as Germany, all leases can be off-balance sheet.

Earlier in this chapter we discussed leasing's advantages to the lessee. Three important benefits are available to the lessor:

1. ***Interest Revenue.*** Leasing is a form of financing; therefore, financial institutions and leasing companies find leasing attractive because it provides competitive interest margins.
2. ***Tax Incentives.*** In many cases, companies that lease cannot use the tax benefit, but leasing provides them with an opportunity to transfer such tax benefits to another party (the lessor) in return for a lower rental rate on the leased asset. To illustrate, **Boeing Aircraft** at one time sold one of its 767 jet planes to a wealthy investor who didn't need the plane but could use the tax benefit. The investor then leased the plane to a foreign airline, for whom the tax benefit was of no use. Everyone gained. Boeing was able to sell its 767, the investor received the tax benefits, and the foreign airline found a cheaper way to acquire a 767.[15]
3. ***High Residual Value.*** Another advantage to the lessor is the return of the property at the end of the lease term. Residual values can produce very large profits. **Citicorp** at one time assumed that the commercial aircraft it was leasing to the airline industry would have a residual value of 5% of their purchase price. It turned out that they were worth 150% of their cost—a handsome profit. However, 3 years later these same planes slumped to 80% of their cost, but still far more than 5%.

Economics of Leasing

The lessor determines the amount of the rental, basing it on the rate of return—the implicit rate—needed to justify leasing the asset. The key factors considered in establishing the rate of return are the credit standing of the lessee, the length of the lease, and the status of the residual value (guaranteed versus unguaranteed). In the Lessor Company/Lessee Company example on pages 1198–1200, the implicit rate of the lessor was 10%, the cost of the equipment to the lessor was $100,000 (also fair market value), and the estimated residual value was zero. Lessor Company determined the amount of the lease payment in the following manner:

ILLUSTRATION 22-9
Computation of Lease Payments

Fair market value of leased equipment	$100,000.00
Less: Present value of the residual value	–0–
Amount to be recovered by lessor through lease payments	$100,000.00
Five beginning-of-the-year lease payments to yield a 10% return ($100,000 ÷ 4.16986[a])	$ 23,981.62

[a]PV of an annuity due of 1 for 5 years at 10% (Table 6-5)

[14]One study indicates that management's behavior did change as a result of *FASB No. 13.* For example, many companies restructure their leases to avoid capitalization; others increase their purchases of assets instead of leasing; and others, faced with capitalization, postpone their debt offerings or issue stock instead. However, it is interesting to note that the study found no significant effect on stock or bond prices as a result of capitalization of leases. A. Rashad Abdel-khalik, "The Economic Effects on Lessees of *FASB Statement No. 13,* Accounting for Leases," Research Report (Stamford, Conn.: FASB, 1981).

[15]Some would argue that there is a loser—the U.S. government. The tax benefits enable the profitable investor to reduce or eliminate taxable income.

If a residual value were involved (whether guaranteed or not), the lessor would not have to recover as much from the lease payments. Therefore, the lease payments would be less (this situation is shown in Illustration 22-17).

Classification of Leases by the Lessor

OBJECTIVE 4
Identify the classifications of leases for the lessor.

From the standpoint of the **lessor**, all leases may be classified for accounting purposes as one of the following:

(a) Operating leases.
(b) Direct financing leases.
(c) Sales-type leases.

If at the date of the lease agreement (inception) the lessor is party to a lease that meets **one or more** of the following Group I criteria (1, 2, 3, and 4) and **both** of the following Group II criteria (1 and 2), the lessor shall classify and account for the arrangement as a direct financing lease or as a sales-type lease.[16] (Note that the Group I criteria are identical to the criteria that must be met in order for a lease to be classified as a capital lease by a lessee, as shown in Illustration 22-3.)

Capitalization Criteria (Lessor)

Group I

- The lease transfers ownership of the property to the lessee.
- The lease contains a bargain purchase option.
- The lease term is equal to 75% or more of the estimated economic life of the leased property.
- The present value of the minimum lease payments (excluding executory costs) equals or exceeds 90% of the fair value of the leased property.

Group II

- Collectibility of the payments required from the lessee is reasonably predictable.
- No important uncertainties surround the amount of unreimbursable costs yet to be incurred by the lessor under the lease (lessor's performance is substantially complete or future costs are reasonably predictable).

ILLUSTRATION 22-10
Capitalization Criteria for Lessor

U.S. GAAP is consistent with International Standard No. 17 (Accounting for Leases). However, the international standard is a relatively simple statement of basic principles, whereas the U.S. rules on leases are more prescriptive and detailed.

Why the Group II requirements? The answer is that the profession wants to make sure that the lessor has really transferred the risks and benefits of ownership. If collectibility of payments is not predictable or if performance by the lessor is incomplete, then the criteria for revenue recognition have not been met and it should be accounted for as an operating lease.

For example, computer leasing companies at one time used to buy IBM equipment, lease it, and remove the leased assets from their balance sheets. In leasing the asset, the computer lessors stated that they would be willing to substitute new IBM equipment if obsolescence occurred. However, when IBM introduced a new computer line, IBM refused to sell it to the computer leasing companies. As a result, a number of the lessors could not meet their contracts with their customers and were forced to take back the old equipment. What the computer leasing companies had taken off the books now had to be reinstated. Such a case demonstrates one reason for the Group II requirements.

The distinction for the lessor between a direct financing lease and a sales-type lease is the presence or absence of a manufacturer's or dealer's profit (or loss): A

[16] *FASB Statement No. 13,* op. cit., pars. 6, 7, and 8.

sales-type lease involves a manufacturer's or dealer's profit, and a direct financing lease does not. The profit (or loss) to the lessor is evidenced by the difference between the fair value of the leased property at the inception of the lease and the lessor's cost or carrying amount (book value). Normally, sales-type leases arise when manufacturers or dealers use leasing as a means of marketing their products. For example, a computer manufacturer will lease its computer equipment to businesses and institutions. Direct financing leases generally result from arrangements with lessors that are primarily engaged in financing operations, such as lease-finance companies, banks, insurance companies, and pension trusts. However, a lessor need not be a manufacturer or dealer to recognize a profit (or loss) at the inception of a lease that requires application of sales-type lease accounting.

All leases that do not qualify as direct financing or sales-type leases are classified and accounted for by the lessors as operating leases. Illustration 22-11 shows the circumstances under which a lease is classified as operating, direct financing, or sales-type for the lessor.

ILLUSTRATION 22-11
Diagram of Lessor's Criteria for Lease Classification

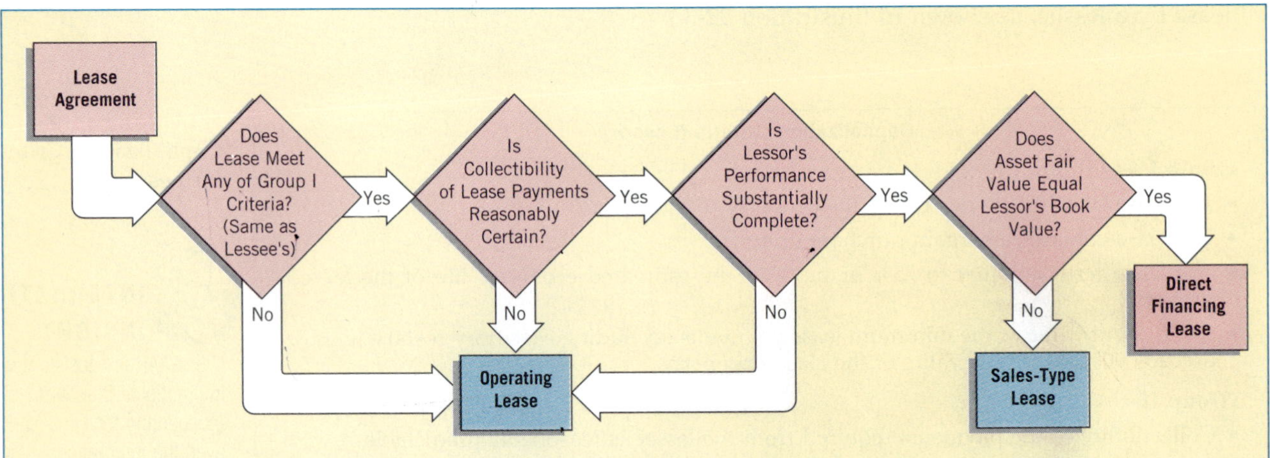

As a consequence of the additional Group II criteria for lessors, it is possible that a lessor having not met both criteria will classify a lease as an **operating** lease but the lessee will classify the same lease as a **capital** lease. In such an event, both the lessor and lessee will carry the asset on their books, and both will depreciate the capitalized asset.

For purposes of comparison with the lessee's accounting, only the operating and direct financing leases will be illustrated in the following section. The more complex sales-type lease will be discussed later in the chapter.

Direct Financing Method (Lessor)

OBJECTIVE 5
Describe the lessor's accounting for direct financing leases.

Leases that are in substance the financing of an asset purchase by a lessee require the lessor to substitute a "lease payments receivable" for the leased asset. The information necessary to record a **direct financing lease** is as shown on the next page.

The computation of the gross investment (lease payments receivable) is often confusing because of the uncertainty as to how to account for the residual values. Remember that "minimum lease payments" includes:

1. Rental payments (excluding executory costs).
2. Bargain purchase option (if any).
3. Guaranteed residual value (if any).
4. Penalty for failure to renew (if any).

DIRECT FINANCING TERMS

1. *Gross Investment ("Lease Payments Receivable").* The minimum lease payments plus the unguaranteed residual value accruing to the lessor at the end of the lease term.[17]
2. *Unearned Interest Revenue.* The difference between the gross investment (the receivable) and the fair market value of the property.[18]
3. *Net Investment.* The gross investment (the receivable) less the unearned interest revenue included therein.

When "lease payments receivable" is defined as minimum lease payments plus unguaranteed residual value, it means that residual value, both guaranteed (because it is included as part of "minimum lease payments") and unguaranteed (because it is added back in to compute the gross investment), is included as part of lease payments receivable if it is relevant to the lessor (that is, if the lessor expects to get the asset back).

In addition, if the lessor pays any executory costs, then the rental payment should be reduced by that amount for purposes of computing minimum lease payments. In other words, lease payments receivable includes:

1. Rental payments (less executory costs paid by the lessor).
2. Bargain purchase option (if any).
3. Guaranteed or unguaranteed residual value (if any).
4. Penalty for failure to renew (if any).

The **unearned interest revenue is amortized to revenue** over the lease term by applying the effective interest method. Thus, a constant rate of return is produced on the net investment in the lease.

The following presentation, utilizing the data from the preceding Lessor Company/Lessee Company illustration on pages 1198–1200, illustrates the accounting treatment accorded a direct financing lease. The information relevant to Lessor Company in accounting for this lease transaction is repeated as follows:

1. The term of the lease is 5 years beginning January 1, 2002, noncancelable, and requires equal rental payments of $25,981.62 at the beginning of each year; payments include $2,000 of executory costs (property taxes).
2. The equipment has a cost of $100,000 to Lessor Company, a fair value at the inception of the lease of $100,000, an estimated economic life of 5 years, and no residual value.
3. No initial direct costs were incurred in negotiating and closing the lease transaction.
4. The lease contains no renewable options and the equipment reverts to Lessor Company at the termination of the lease.

[17]Ibid., par. 17. If the lessee agrees to make up any deficiency below a stated amount that the lessor realizes in residual value at the end of the lease term, that stated amount is the guaranteed residual value.

Initially the unguaranteed residual value could be classified in a separate account. If the unguaranteed residual value is included in the Lease Payments Receivable account, it would be reclassified by the lessor at the end of the lease term if not purchased by the lessee.

[18]In a direct financing lease, the cost or carrying amount of the asset should be used instead of fair market value. In most cases, however, cost or carrying amount is equal to fair market value, so fair market value is used here. The use of fair market value will simplify subsequent discussion in this area. Significant differences between cost or carrying amount and fair market value exist for sales-type leases.

5. Collectibility is reasonably assured and no additional costs (with the exception of the property taxes being collected from the lessee) are to be incurred by Lessor Company.
6. Lessor Company set the annual lease payments to ensure a rate of return of 10% (implicit rate) on its investment as follows (as shown in Illustration 22-9):

ILLUSTRATION 22-12
Computation of Lease Payments

Fair market value of leased equipment	$100,000.00
Less: Present value of residual value	–0–
Amount to be recovered by lessor through lease payments	$100,000.00
Five beginning-of-the-year lease payments to yield a 10% return ($100,000 ÷ 4.16986[a])	$ 23,981.62

[a]PV of an annuity due of 1 for 5 years at 10% (Table 6-5).

The lease meets the criteria for classification as a direct financing lease because (1) the lease term exceeds 75% of the equipment's estimated economic life, (2) the present value of the minimum lease payments exceeds 90% of the equipment's fair value, (3) collectibility of the payments is reasonably assured, and (4) there are no further costs to be incurred by Lessor Company. It is not a sales-type lease because there is no difference between the fair value ($100,000) of the equipment and the lessor's cost ($100,000).

The lease payments receivable (gross investment) is calculated as follows:

ILLUSTRATION 22-13
Computation of Lease Payments Receivable

Lease payments receivable = Minimum lease payments minus executory costs paid by lessor plus unguaranteed residual value
= [($25,981.62 − $2,000) × 5] + $0
= $119,908.10

The unearned interest revenue is computed as the difference between the lease payments receivable and the lessor's fair market value of the leased asset:

ILLUSTRATION 22-14
Computation of Unearned Interest Revenue

Unearned interest revenue = Lease payments receivable minus asset's fair market value
= $119,908.10 − $100,000
= $19,908.10

The net investment in direct financing leases is $100,000; that is, the gross investment of $119,908.10 minus the unearned interest revenue of $19,908.10.

The lease of the asset, the resulting receivable, and the unearned interest revenue are recorded January 1, 2002 (the inception of the lease) as follows:

Lease Payments Receivable	119,908.10	
Equipment		100,000.00
Unearned Interest Revenue—Leases		19,908.10

The unearned interest revenue is classified on the balance sheet as a deduction from the lease payments receivable if the receivable is reported gross. Generally, the lease payments receivable, although **recorded** at the gross investment amount, is **reported** in the balance sheet at the "net investment" amount (gross investment less unearned interest revenue) and entitled "Net investment in capital leases." It is classified either as current or noncurrent, depending upon when the net investment is to be recovered.

The leased equipment with a cost of $100,000, which represents Lessor Company's investment, is replaced with a net lease receivable. In a manner similar to the lessee's treatment of interest, Lessor Company applies the effective interest method and recognizes interest revenue as a function of the unrecovered net investment, as shown in Illustration 22-15.

ILLUSTRATION 22-15
Lease Amortization Schedule for Lessor—Annuity Due Basis

LESSOR COMPANY
Lease Amortization Schedule
(Annuity due basis)

Date	Annual Lease Payment	Executory Costs	Interest (10%) on Net Investment	Net Investment Recovery	Net Investment
	(a)	(b)	(c)	(d)	(e)
1/1/02					$100,000.00
1/1/02	$ 25,981.62	$ 2,000.00	$ -0-	$ 23,981.62	76,018.38
1/1/03	25,981.62	2,000.00	7,601.84	16,379.78	59,638.60
1/1/04	25,981.62	2,000.00	5,963.86	18,017.76	41,620.84
1/1/05	25,981.62	2,000.00	4,162.08	19,819.54	21,801.30
1/1/06	25,981.62	2,000.00	2,180.32*	21,801.30	-0-
	$129,908.10	$10,000.00	$19,908.10	$100,000.00	

(a) Annual rental that provides a 10% return on net investment.
(b) Executory costs included in rental payment.
(c) Ten percent of the preceding balance of (e) except for 1/1/02.
(d) (a) minus (b) and (c).
(e) Preceding balance minus (d).
*Rounded by 19 cents.

On January 1, 2002, the journal entry to record receipt of the first year's lease payment is as follows:

Cash	25,981.62	
Lease Payments Receivable		23,981.62
Property Tax Expense/Property Taxes Payable		2,000.00

On 12/31/02 the interest revenue earned during the first year is recognized through the following entry:

Unearned Interest Revenue—Leases	7,601.84	
Interest Revenue—Leases		7,601.84

At December 31, 2002, the net investment under capital leases is reported in the lessor's balance sheet among current assets or noncurrent assets, or both. The portion due within one year or the operating cycle, whichever is longer, is classified as a current asset and the rest with noncurrent assets.

The total net investment at 12/31/02 is equal to $83,620.22 (the balance at 1/1/02, $76,018.38 plus interest receivable for 2002 of $7,601.84). The current portion is the net investment to be received in 2003, $16,379.78, plus the interest of $7,601.84. The remainder, $59,638.60 (Lease Payments Receivable of $71,944.86 [$23,981.62 × 3] minus Unearned Interest Revenue of $12,306.26 [$5,963.86 + $4,162.08 + $2,180.32]) should be reported in the noncurrent assets section.

The asset sections as it relates to lease transactions at 12/31/02 would appear as follows:

ILLUSTRATION 22-16
Reporting Lease Transactions by Lessor

Current assets	
Net investment in capital leases	$23,981.62
Noncurrent assets (investments)	
Net investment in capital leases	$59,638.60

The following entries record receipt of the second year's lease payment and recognition of the interest earned:

January 1, 2003

Cash	25,981.62	
Lease Payments Receivable		23,981.62
Property Tax Expense/Property Taxes Payable		2,000.00

December 31, 2003

Unearned Interest Revenue—Leases	5,963.86	
Interest Revenue—Leases		5,963.86

Journal entries through 2006 would follow the same pattern except that no entry would be recorded in 2006 (the last year) for earned interest. Because the receivable is fully collected by 1/1/06, no balance (investment) is outstanding during 2006 to which Lessor Company could attribute any interest. Upon expiration of the lease (whether an ordinary annuity or an annuity due), the gross receivable and the unearned interest revenue would be fully written off. **Lessor Company recorded no depreciation.** If the equipment is sold to Lessee Company for $5,000 upon expiration of the lease, Lessor Company would recognize disposition of the equipment as follows:

Cash	5,000	
Gain on Sale of Leased Equipment		5,000

Operating Method (Lessor)

Under the **operating method** each rental receipt by the lessor is recorded as rental revenue. The **leased asset is depreciated in the normal manner**, with the depreciation expense of the period matched against the rental revenue. The amount of revenue recognized in each accounting period is a level amount (straight-line basis) regardless of the lease provisions, unless another systematic and rational basis is more representative of the time pattern in which the benefit is derived from the leased asset. In addition to the depreciation charge, maintenance costs and the cost of any other services rendered under the provisions of the lease that pertain to the current accounting period are charged to expense. Costs paid to independent third parties such as appraisal fees, finder's fees, and costs of credit checks are amortized over the life of the lease.

To illustrate the operating method, assume that the direct financing lease illustrated above did not qualify as a capital lease and was therefore to be accounted for as an operating lease. The entry to record the cash rental receipt, assuming the $2,000 was for property tax expense, would be as follows:

Cash	25,981.62	
Rental Revenue		25,981.62

Depreciation is recorded by the lessor as follows (assuming a straight-line method, a cost basis of $100,000, and a 5-year life):

Depreciation Expense—Leased Equipment	20,000	
Accumulated Depreciation—Leased Equipment		20,000

If property taxes, insurance, maintenance, and other operating costs during the year are the obligation of the lessor, they are recorded as expenses chargeable against the gross rental revenues.

If the lessor owned plant assets that it used in addition to those leased to others, **the leased equipment and accompanying accumulated depreciation would be separately classified** in an account such as Equipment Leased to Others or Investment in Leased Property. If significant in amount or in terms of activity, the rental revenues and accompanying expenses are separated in the income statement from sales revenue and cost of goods sold.

SPECIAL ACCOUNTING PROBLEMS

OBJECTIVE 6
Identify special features of lease arrangements that cause unique accounting problems.

The features of lease arrangements that cause unique accounting problems are:

1. Residual values.
2. Sales-type leases (lessor).
3. Bargain purchase options.
4. Initial direct costs.

5 Current versus noncurrent.

6 Disclosure.

Residual Values

Up to this point, we have generally ignored discussion of residual values in order that the basic accounting issues related to lessee and lessor accounting could be developed. Accounting for residual values is complex and will probably provide you with the greatest challenge in understanding lease accounting.

Meaning of Residual Value

The residual value is the **estimated fair value** of the leased asset at the end of the lease term. Frequently, a significant residual value exists at the end of the lease term, especially when the economic life of the leased asset exceeds the lease term. If title does not pass automatically to the lessee (criterion 1) and a bargain purchase option does not exist (criterion 2), the lessee returns physical custody of the asset to the lessor at the end of the lease term.[19]

Guaranteed versus Unguaranteed

The residual value may be unguaranteed or guaranteed by the lessee. If the lessee agrees to make up any deficiency below a stated amount that the lessor realizes in residual value at the end of the lease term, that stated amount is the **guaranteed residual value**.

The guaranteed residual value is employed in lease arrangements for two reasons. The first is a business reason: It protects the lessor against any loss in estimated residual value, thereby ensuring the lessor of the desired rate of return on investment. The second is an accounting benefit that you will learn from the discussion at the end of this chapter.

Lease Payments

A guaranteed residual value—by definition—has more assurance of realization than does an unguaranteed residual value. As a result, the lessor may adjust lease payments because the certainty of recovery has been increased. After this rate is established, however, it makes no difference from an accounting point of view whether the residual value is guaranteed or unguaranteed. The net investment to be recorded by the lessor (once the rate is set) will be the same.

Assume the same data as in the Lessee Company/Lessor Company illustrations except that a residual value of $5,000 is estimated at the end of the 5-year lease term. In addition, a 10% return on investment (ROI) is assumed,[20] whether the residual value is guaranteed or unguaranteed. Lessor Company would compute the amount of the lease payments as follows:

ILLUSTRATION 22-17
Lessor's Computation of Lease Payments

Lessor's Computation of Lease Payments (10% ROI)
Guaranteed or Unguaranteed Residual Value
(Annuity due basis, including residual value)

Fair market value of leased asset to lessor	$100,000.00
Less: Present value of residual value ($5,000 × .62092, Table 6-2)	3,104.60
Amount to be recovered by lessor through lease payments	$ 96,895.40
Five periodic lease payments ($96,895.40 ÷ 4.16986, Table 6-5)	$ 23,237.09

[19]When the lease term and the economic life are not the same, the residual value and the salvage value of the asset will probably differ. For simplicity, we will assume that residual value and salvage value are the same, even when the economic life and lease term vary.

[20]Technically the rate of return demanded by the lessor would be different depending upon whether the residual value was guaranteed or unguaranteed. We are ignoring this difference in subsequent sections to simplify the illustrations.

Contrast the foregoing lease payment amount to the lease payments of $23,981.62 as computed in Illustration 22-9, where no residual value existed. The payments are less because the lessor's total recoverable amount of $100,000 is reduced by the present value of the residual value.

Lessee Accounting for Residual Value

Whether the estimated residual value is guaranteed or unguaranteed has both economic and accounting consequence to the lessee. The accounting difference is that the **minimum lease payments**, the basis for capitalization, includes the guaranteed residual value but excludes the unguaranteed residual value.

OBJECTIVE 7
Describe the effect of residual values, guaranteed and unguaranteed, on lease accounting.

Guaranteed Residual Value (Lessee Accounting). A guaranteed residual value affects the lessee's computation of minimum lease payments and, therefore, the amounts capitalized as a leased asset and a lease obligation. In effect, **it is an additional lease payment that will be paid in property or cash, or both, at the end of the lease term.** Using the rental payments as computed by the lessor in Illustration 22-17, the minimum lease payments are $121,185.45 ([$23,237.09 × 5] + $5,000). The capitalized present value of the minimum lease payments (excluding executory costs) is computed as follows:

ILLUSTRATION 22-18
Computation of Lessee's Capitalized Amount—Guaranteed Residual Value

Lessee's Capitalized Amount (10% Rate) (Annuity due basis; including **guaranteed** residual value)	
Present value of five annual rental payments ($23,237.09 × 4.16986, Table 6-5)	$ 96,895.40
Present value of guaranteed residual value of $5,000 due five years after date of inception: ($5,000 × .62092, Table 6-2)	3,104.60
Lessee's capitalized amount	$100,000.00

Lessee Company's schedule of interest expense and amortization of the $100,000 lease obligation that produces a $5,000 final guaranteed residual value payment at the end of five years is shown in Illustration 22-19.

ILLUSTRATION 22-19
Lease Amortization Schedule for Lessee—Guaranteed Residual Value

LESSEE COMPANY
Lease Amortization Schedule
(Annuity due basis, **guaranteed** residual value—GRV)

Date	Lease Payment Plus GRV	Executory Costs	Interest (10%) on Unpaid Obligation	Reduction of Lease Obligation	Lease Obligation
	(a)	(b)	(c)	(d)	(e)
1/1/02					$100,000.00
1/1/02	$ 25,237.09	$ 2,000	-0-	$ 23,237.09	76,762.91
1/1/03	25,237.09	2,000	$ 7,676.29	15,560.80	61,202.11
1/1/04	25,237.09	2,000	6,120.21	17,116.88	44,085.23
1/1/05	25,237.09	2,000	4,408.52	18,828.57	25,256.66
1/1/06	25,237.09	2,000	2,525.67	20,711.42	4,545.24
12/31/06	5,000.00*		454.76**	4,545.24	-0-
	$131,185.45	$10,000	$21,185.45	$100,000.00	

(a) Annual lease payment as required by lease.
(b) Executory costs included in rental payment.
(c) Preceding balance of (e) × 10%, except 1/1/02.
(d) (a) minus (b) and (c).
(e) Preceding balance minus (d).

*Represents the guaranteed residual value.
**Rounded by 24 cents.

The journal entries (Illustration 22-24 on page 1213) to record the leased asset and obligation, depreciation, interest, property tax, and lease payments are then made on the basis that the residual value is guaranteed. The format of these entries is the same as illustrated earlier, although the amounts are different because of the guaranteed residual value. The leased asset is recorded at $100,000 and is depreciated over 5 years. To compute depreciation, the guaranteed residual value is subtracted from the cost of the leased asset. Assuming that the straight-line method is used, the depreciation expense each year is $19,000 ([$100,000 − $5,000] ÷ 5 years).

At the end of the lease term, before the lessee transfers the asset to the lessor, the lease asset and obligation accounts have the following balances:

Leased equipment under capital leases	$100,000.00	Interest payable	$ 454.76
Less: Accumulated depreciation—capital leases	95,000.00	Obligations under capital leases	4,545.24
	$ 5,000.00		$5,000.00

ILLUSTRATION 22-20
Account Balances on Lessee's Books at End of Lease Term—Guaranteed Residual Value

If, at the end of the lease, the fair market value of the residual value is less than $5,000, Lessee Company will have to record a loss. Assume that Lessee Company depreciated the leased asset down to its residual value of $5,000 but that the fair market value of the residual value at 12/31/06 was $3,000. In this case, the Lessee Company would have to report a loss of $2,000. The following journal entry would be made, assuming cash was paid to make up the residual value deficiency:

Loss on Capital Lease	2,000.00	
Interest Expense (or Interest Payable)	454.76	
Obligations under Capital Leases	4,545.24	
Accumulated Depreciation—Capital Leases	95,000.00	
Leased Equipment under Capital Leases		100,000.00
Cash		2,000.00

If the fair market value exceeds $5,000, a gain may be recognized. Gains on guaranteed residual values may be apportioned to the lessor and lessee in whatever ratio the parties initially agree.

If the lessee depreciated the total cost of the asset ($100,000), a misstatement would occur; that is, the carrying amount of the asset at the end of the lease term would be zero, but the obligation under the capital lease would be stated at $5,000. Thus, if the asset was worth $5,000, the lessee would end up reporting a gain of $5,000 when it transferred the asset to the lessor. As a result, depreciation would be overstated and net income understated in 2002–2005, but in the last year (2006) net income would be overstated.

Unguaranteed Residual Value (Lessee Accounting). An **unguaranteed residual value** from the lessee's viewpoint is the same as no residual value in terms of its effect upon the lessee's method of computing the minimum lease payments and the capitalization of the leased asset and the lease obligation. Assume the same facts as those above except that the $5,000 residual value is **unguaranteed instead of guaranteed**. The amount of the annual lease payments would be the same, $23,237.09. Whether the residual value is guaranteed or unguaranteed, Lessor Company's amount to be recovered through lease rentals is the same, that is, $96,895.40. The minimum lease payments are $116,185.45 ($23,237.09 × 5). Lessee Company would capitalize the following amount:

Lessee's Capitalized Amount (10% Rate) (Annuity due basis, including **unguaranteed** residual value)	
Present value of 5 annual rental payments of $23,237.09 × 4.16986 (Table 6-5)	$96,895.40
Unguaranteed residual value of $5,000 (not capitalized by lessee)	–0–
Lessee's capitalized amount	$96,895.40

ILLUSTRATION 22-21
Computation of Lessee's Capitalized Amount—Unguaranteed Residual Value

The Lessee Company's schedule of interest expense and amortization of the lease obligation of $96,895.40, assuming an unguaranteed residual value of $5,000 at the end of 5 years, is shown in Illustration 22-22.

ILLUSTRATION 22-22
Lease Amortization Schedule for Lessee—Unguaranteed Residual Value

LESSEE COMPANY
Lease Amortization Schedule (10%)
(Annuity due basis, **unguaranteed** residual value)

Date	Annual Lease Payments	Executory Costs	Interest (10%) on Unpaid Obligation	Reduction of Lease Obligation	Lease Obligation
	(a)	(b)	(c)	(d)	(e)
1/1/02					$96,895.40
1/1/02	$ 25,237.09	$ 2,000	-0-	$23,237.09	73,658.31
1/1/03	25,237.09	2,000	$ 7,365.83	15,871.26	57,787.05
1/1/04	25,237.09	2,000	5,778.71	17,458.38	40,328.67
1/1/05	25,237.09	2,000	4,032.87	19,204.22	21,124.45
1/1/06	25,237.09	2,000	2,112.64*	21,124.45	-0-
	$126,185.45	$10,000	$19,290.05	$96,895.40	

(a) Annual lease payment as required by lease.
(b) Executory costs included in rental payment.
(c) Preceding balance of (e) × 10%.
(d) (a) minus (b) and (c).
(e) Preceding balance minus (d).
*Rounded by 19 cents.

The journal entries (Illustration 22-24 on page 1213) to record the leased asset and obligation, depreciation, interest, property tax, and payments on the lease obligation are then made on the basis that the residual value is unguaranteed. The format of these entries is the same as illustrated earlier. Note that the leased asset is recorded at $96,895.40 and is depreciated over 5 years. Assuming that the straight-line method is used, the depreciation expense each year is $19,379.08 ($96,895.40 ÷ 5 years). At the end of the lease term, before the lessee transfers the asset to the lessor, the following balances in the accounts result, as illustrated below.

ILLUSTRATION 22-23
Account Balances on Lessee's Books at End of Lease Term—Unguaranteed Residual Value

Leased equipment under capital leases	$96,895	Obligations under capital leases	$-0-
Less: Accumulated depreciation—capital leases	96,895		
	$ -0-		

Assuming that the asset had a fair market value of $3,000, no loss would be reported by the lessee. Assuming that the leased asset has been fully depreciated and that the lease obligation has been fully amortized, no entry is required at the end of the lease term, except to remove the asset from the books.

If the lessee depreciated the asset down to its unguaranteed residual value, a misstatement would occur. That is, the carrying amount of the leased asset would be $5,000 at the end of the lease, but the obligation under the capital lease would be stated at zero before the transfer of the asset. Thus, the lessee would end up reporting a loss of $5,000 when it transferred the asset to the lessor. Depreciation would be understated and net income is overstated in 2002–2005, but in the last year (2006) net income would be understated because of the recorded loss.

Lessee Entries Involving Residual Values. The entries by Lessee Company for both a guaranteed and an unguaranteed residual value are shown in Illustration 22-24 in comparative form.

ILLUSTRATION 22-24
Comparative Entries for Guaranteed and Unguaranteed Residual Values, Lessee Company

Guaranteed Residual Value			Unguaranteed Residual Value		
Capitalization of Lease 1/1/02:					
Leased Equipment under Capital Leases	100,000.00		Leased Equipment under Capital Leases	96,895.40	
Obligations under Capital Leases		100,000.00	Obligations under Capital Leases		96,895.40
First Payment 1/1/02:					
Property Tax Expense	2,000.00		Property Tax Expense	2,000.00	
Obligations under Capital Leases	23,237.09		Obligations under Capital Leases	23,237.09	
Cash		25,237.09	Cash		25,237.09
Adjusting Entry for Accrued Interest 12/31/02:					
Interest Expense	7,676.29		Interest Expense	7,365.83	
Interest Payable		7,676.29	Interest Payable		7,365.83
Entry to Record Depreciation 12/31/02:					
Depreciation Expense—Capital Leases	19,000.00		Depreciation Expense—Capital Leases	19,379.08	
Accumulated Depreciation—Capital Leases ([$100,000 − $5,000] ÷5 years)		19,000.00	Accumulated Depreciation—Capital Leases ($96,895.40 ÷ 5 years)		19,379.08
Second Payment 1/1/03:					
Property Tax Expense	2,000.00		Property Tax Expense	2,000.00	
Obligations under Capital Leases	15,560.80		Obligations under Capital Leases	15,871.26	
Interest Expense (or Interest Payable)	7,676.29		Interest Expense (or Interest Payable)	7,365.83	
Cash		25,237.09	Cash		25,237.09

Lessor Accounting for Residual Value

As indicated earlier, the net investment to be recovered by the lessor is the same whether the residual value is guaranteed or unguaranteed. The lessor works on the assumption that **the residual value will be realized at the end of the lease term whether guaranteed or unguaranteed**. The lease payments required by the lessor to earn a certain return on investment are the same ($23,237.09) whether the residual value is guaranteed or unguaranteed.

Using the Lessee Company/Lessor Company data and assuming a residual value (either guaranteed or unguaranteed) of $5,000 and classification of the lease as a direct financing lease, the following necessary amounts are computed:

ILLUSTRATION 22-25
Computation of Direct Financing Lease Amounts by Lessor

Gross investment = ($23,237.09 × 5) + $5,000 = $121,185.45
Unearned interest revenue = $121,185.45 − $100,000 = $21,185.45
Net investment = $121,185.45 − $21,185.45 = $100,000

The schedule for amortization with guaranteed or unguaranteed residual value is the same:

ILLUSTRATION 22-26
Lease Amortization Schedule, for Lessor—Guaranteed or Unguaranteed Residual Value

LESSOR COMPANY
Lease Amortization Schedule
(Annuity due basis, **guaranteed** or **unguaranteed** residual value)

Date	Annual Lease Payment Plus Residual Value	Executory Costs	Interest (10%) on Net Investment	Net Investment Recovery	Net Investment
	(a)	(b)	(c)	(d)	(e)
1/1/02					$100,000.00
1/1/02	$ 25,237.09	$ 2,000.00	$ -0-	$ 23,237.09	76,762.91
1/1/03	25,237.09	2,000.00	7,676.29	15,560.80	61,202.11
1/1/04	25,237.09	2,000.00	6,120.21	17,116.88	44,085.23
1/1/05	25,237.09	2,000.00	4,408.52	18,828.57	25,256.66
1/1/06	25,237.09	2,000.00	2,525.67	20,711.42	4,545.24
12/31/06	5,000.00	-0-	454.76*	4,545.24	-0-
	$131,185.45	$10,000.00	$21,185.45	$100,000.00	

(a) Annual lease payment as required by lease.
(b) Executory costs included in rental payment.
(c) Preceding balance of (e) × 10%, except 1/1/02.
(d) (a) minus (b) and (c).
(e) Preceding balance minus (d).
*Rounded by 24 cents.

Using the amounts computed above, the following entries would be made by Lessor Company during the first year for this direct financing lease. Note the similarity to the lessee's entries in Illustration 22-24:

ILLUSTRATION 22-27
Entries for Either Guaranteed or Unguaranteed Residual Value, Lessor Company

Inception of Lease 1/1/02:		
Lease Payments Receivable	121,185.45	
Equipment		100,000.00
Unearned Interest Revenue—Leases		21,185.45
First Payment Received 1/1/02:		
Cash	25,237.09	
Lease Payments Receivable		23,237.09
Property Tax Expense/Property Taxes Payable		2,000.00
Adjusting Entry for Accrued Interest 12/31/02:		
Unearned Interest Revenue—Leases	7,676.29	
Interest Revenue—Leases		7,676.29

Sales-Type Leases (Lessor)

As already indicated, the primary difference between a direct financing lease and a **sales-type lease** is the manufacturer's or dealer's gross profit (or loss). A diagram illustrating these relationships is shown in Illustration 22-28 below and on the next page:

ILLUSTRATION 22-28
Direct Financing versus Sales-Type Leases

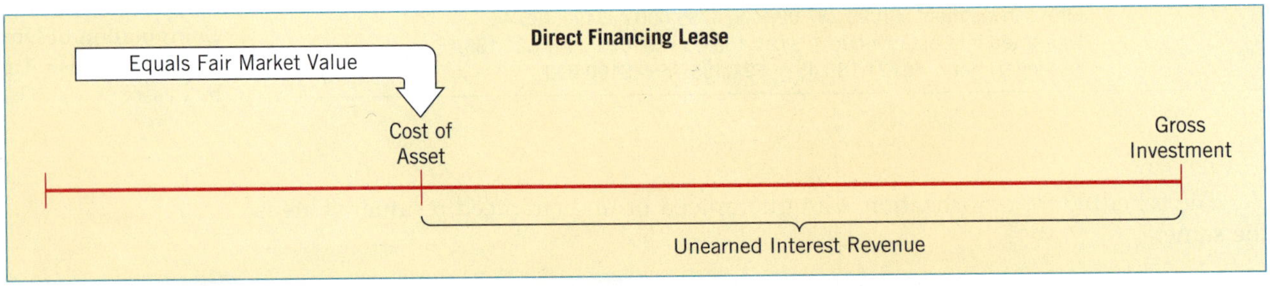

Sales-Type Lease

	Does Not Equal Fair Market Value → Cost of Asset	Sale Price of Asset	Gross Investment
	Gross Profit	Unearned Interest Revenue	

ILLUSTRATION 22-28
Continued

The information necessary to record the sales-type lease is as follows:

SALES-TYPE LEASE TERMS

1. *Gross Investment* (also "*Lease Payments Receivable*"). The minimum lease payments plus the unguaranteed residual value accruing to the lessor at the end of the lease term.
2. *Unearned Interest Revenue*. The gross investment less the fair market value of the asset.
3. *Sales Price of the Asset*. The present value of the minimum lease payments.
4. *Cost of Goods Sold*. The cost of the asset to the lessor, less the present value of any unguaranteed residual value.

The gross investment and the unearned interest revenue are the same whether a guaranteed or an unguaranteed residual value is involved.

OBJECTIVE 8
Describe the lessor's accounting for sales-type leases.

When recording sales revenue and cost of goods sold, there is a difference in the accounting for guaranteed and unguaranteed residual values. The guaranteed residual value can be considered part of sales revenue because the lessor knows that the entire asset has been sold. There is less certainty that the unguaranteed residual portion of the asset has been "sold" (i.e., will be realized); therefore, sales and cost of goods sold are recognized only for the portion of the asset for which realization is assured. However, **the gross profit amount on the sale of the asset is the same whether a guaranteed or unguaranteed residual value is involved**.

To illustrate a sales-type lease with a guaranteed residual value and a sales-type lease with an unguaranteed residual value, assume the same facts as in the preceding direct financing lease situation (pages 1205–1208). The estimated residual value is $5,000 (the present value of which is $3,104.60), and the leased equipment has an $85,000 cost to the dealer, Lessor Company. Assume that the fair market value of the residual value is $3,000 at the end of the lease term.

The amounts relevant to a sales-type lease are computed as follows:

ILLUSTRATION 22-29
Computation of Lease Amounts by Lessor Company—Sales-Type Lease

	Sales-Type Lease	
	Guaranteed Residual Value	Unguaranteed Residual Value
Gross investment	$121,185.45 ([$23,237.09 × 5] + $5,000)	Same
Unearned interest revenue	$21,185.45 ($121,185.45 – $100,000)	Same
Sales price of the asset	$100,000 ($96,895.40 + $3,104.60)	$96,895.40
Cost of goods sold	$85,000	$81,895.40 ($85,000 – $3,104.60)
Gross profit	$15,000 ($100,000 – $85,000)	$15,000 ($96,895.40 – $81,895.40)

The profit recorded by Lessor Company at the point of sale is the same, $15,000, whether the residual value is guaranteed or unguaranteed, **but the sales revenue and cost of goods sold amounts are different**. The present value of the unguaranteed residual value is deducted from sales revenue and cost of goods sold for two reasons: (1) the criteria for revenue recognition have not been met, and (2) matching expense against revenue not yet recognized is improper. The revenue recognition criteria have not been met **because of the uncertainty surrounding the realization of the unguaranteed residual value**.

The entries to record this transaction on January 1, 2002, and the receipt of the residual value at the end of the lease term are presented below.

ILLUSTRATION 22-30
Entries for Guaranteed and Unguaranteed Residual Values, Lessor Company—Sales-Type Lease

Guaranteed Residual Value			Unguaranteed Residual Value		
To record sales-type lease at inception (January 1, 2002):					
Cost of Goods Sold	85,000.00		Cost of Goods Sold	81,895.40	
Lease Payments Receivable	121,185.45		Lease Payments Receivable	121,185.45	
Sales Revenue		100,000.00	Sales Revenue		96,895.40
Unearned Interest Revenue		21,185.45	Unearned Interest Revenue		21,185.45
Inventory		85,000.00	Inventory		85,000.00
To record receipt of the first lease payment (January 1, 2002):					
Cash	25,237.09		Cash	25,237.09	
Lease Payments Receivable		23,237.09	Lease Payments Receivable		23,237.09
Prop. Tax Exp./Prop. Tax. Pay.		2,000.00	Prop. Tax Exp./Prop. Tax Pay.		2,000.00
To recognize interest revenue earned during the first year (December 31, 2002):					
Unearned Interest Revenue	7,676.29		Unearned Interest Revenue	7,676.29	
Interest Revenue		7,676.29	Interest Revenue		7,676.29
(See lease amortization schedule, Illustration 22-26 on page 1214.)					
To record receipt of the second lease payment (January 1, 2003):					
Cash	25,237.09		Cash	25,237.09	
Lease Payments Receivable		23,237.09	Lease Payments Receivable		23,237.09
Prop. Tax Exp./Prop. Tax Pay.		2,000.00	Prop. Tax Exp./Prop. Tax Pay.		2,000.00
To recognize interest revenue earned during the second year (December 31, 2003):					
Unearned Interest Revenue	6,120.21		Unearned Interest Revenue	6,120.21	
Interest Revenue		6,120.21	Interest Revenue		6,120.21
To record receipt of residual value at end of lease term (December 31, 2006):					
Inventory	3,000		Inventory	3,000	
Cash	2,000		Loss on Capital Lease	2,000	
Lease Payments Receivable		5,000	Lease Payments Receivable		5,000

The **estimated unguaranteed residual value in a sales-type lease** (and a direct financing-type lease) **must be reviewed periodically.** If the estimate of the unguaranteed residual value declines, the accounting for the transaction must be revised using the changed estimate. The decline represents a reduction in the lessor's net investment and is recognized as a loss in the period in which the residual estimate is reduced. Upward adjustments in estimated residual value are not recognized.

Bargain Purchase Option (Lessee)

A bargain purchase option allows the lessee to purchase the leased property for a future price that is substantially lower than the property's expected future fair value. The price is so favorable at the lease's inception that the future exercise of the option appears to be reasonably assured. If a bargain purchase option exists, **the lessee must increase the present value of the minimum lease payments by the present value of the option price.**

For example, assume that Lessee Company in the illustration on page 1210 had an option to buy the leased equipment for $5,000 at the end of the 5-year lease term when the fair value is expected to be $18,000. The significant difference between the option price and the fair value creates a bargain purchase option, the exercise of which is reasonably assured. Four computations are affected by a bargain purchase option in the same manner that they are by a guaranteed residual value: (1) the amount of the five lease payments necessary for the lessor to earn a 10% return on net investment, (2) the amount of the minimum lease payments, (3) the amount capitalized as leased assets and lease obligation, and (4) the amortization of the lease obligation. Therefore, the computations, amortization schedule, and entries that would be prepared for this $5,000 bargain purchase option are identical to those shown for the $5,000 guaranteed residual value.

The only difference between the accounting treatment for a bargain purchase option and a guaranteed residual value of identical amounts and circumstances is in the **computation of the annual depreciation**. In the case of a guaranteed residual value, the lessee depreciates the asset over the lease term, whereas in the case of a bargain purchase option, the lessee uses the **economic life** of the asset.

Initial Direct Costs (Lessor)

Initial direct costs are of two types.[21] The first, **incremental direct costs**, are costs paid to independent third parties, incurred in originating a lease arrangement. Examples would include cost of independent appraisal of collateral used to secure a lease, or the cost of an outside credit check of the lessee or a broker's fee for finding the lessee.

The second type, **internal direct costs**, are the costs directly related to specified activities performed **by the lessor** on a given lease. Examples are evaluating the prospective lessee's financial condition; evaluating and recording guarantees, collateral, and other security arrangements; negotiating lease terms and preparing and processing lease documents; and closing the transaction. The costs directly related to an employee's time spent on a specific lease transaction are also considered initial direct costs.

On the other hand, initial direct costs should **not** include **internal indirect costs** related to activities performed by the lessor for advertising, servicing existing leases, and establishing and monitoring credit policies; nor should they include costs for supervision and administration. In addition, expenses such as rent and depreciation are not considered initial direct costs.

For **operating leases**, the lessor should defer initial direct costs and **allocate them over the lease term** in proportion to the recognition of rental income. In a **sales-type lease** transaction, the lessor expenses the initial direct costs in the year of incurrence; that is, they are **expensed in the period** in which the profit on the sale is recognized.

In a **direct financing lease**, however, initial direct costs are added to the net investment in the lease and **amortized over the life of the lease as a yield adjustment**. In addition, the unamortized deferred initial direct costs that are part of the lessor's investment in the direct financing lease must be disclosed. If the carrying value of the asset in the lease is $4,000,000 and the lessor incurs initial direct costs of $35,000, then the net investment in the lease would be $4,035,000. The yield would be adjusted to ensure proper amortization of this amount over the life of the lease and would be lower than the initial rate of return.

Current versus Noncurrent

The classification of the lease obligation/net investment was presented earlier in an annuity due situation. As indicated in Illustration 22-7, the lessee's current liability is the payment ($23,981.62) to be made on January 1 of the next year. Similarly, as shown in

[21] "Accounting for Nonrefundable Fees and Costs Associated with Originating or Acquiring Loans and Initial Direct Costs of Leases," *Statement of Financial Accounting Standards No. 91* (Stamford: Conn.: FASB, 1987).

Illustration 22-16, the lessor's current asset is the amount to be collected ($23,981.62) on January 1 of the next year. In both of these annuity due instances, the balance sheet date is December 31 and the due date of the lease payment is January 1 (less than one year), so the present value ($23,981.62) of the payment due the following January 1 is the same as the rental payment ($23,981.62).

What happens if the situation is an ordinary annuity rather than an annuity due situation? For example, assume that the rent is to be paid at the end of the year (December 31) rather than at the beginning (January 1). *FASB Statement No. 13* does not indicate how to measure the current and noncurrent amounts; it requires that for the lessee the "obligations shall be separately identified on the balance sheet as obligations under capital leases and shall be subject to the same considerations as other obligations in classifying them with current and noncurrent liabilities in classified balance sheets."[22] **The most common method of measuring the current liability portion in ordinary annuity leases is the change in the present value method.**[23]

To illustrate the change in the present value method, assume an ordinary annuity situation with the same facts as the Lessee Company/Lessor Company case, excluding the $2,000 of executory costs. Because the rents are paid at the end of the period instead of at the beginning, the five rents are set at $26,379.73 to have an effective interest rate of 10%. The ordinary annuity amortization schedule appears as follows:

ILLUSTRATION 22-31
Lease Amortization Schedule—Ordinary Annuity Basis

LESSEE COMPANY/LESSOR COMPANY
Lease Amortization Schedule
(Ordinary annuity basis)

Date	Annual Lease Payment	Interest 10%	Reduction of Principal	Balance of Lease Obligation/ Net Investment
1/1/02				$100,000.00
12/31/02	$ 26,379.73	$10,000.00	$ 16,379.73	83,620.27
12/31/03	26,379.73	8,362.03	18,017.70	65,602.57
12/31/04	26,379.73	6,560.26	19,819.47	45,783.10
12/31/05	26,379.73	4,578.31	21,801.42	23,981.68
12/31/06	26,379.73	2,398.05*	23,981.68	-0-
	$131,898.65	$31,898.65	$100,000.00	

*Rounded by 12 cents.

The current portion of the lease obligation/net investment under the **change in the present value method** as of December 31, 2002, would be $18,017.70 ($83,620.27 − $65,602.57); and as of December 31, 2003, it would be $19,819.47 ($65,602.57 − $45,783.10). The portion of the lease obligation/net investment that is not current is classified as such; that is, $65,602.57 is the noncurrent portion at December 31, 2002.

Thus, both the annuity due and the ordinary annuity situations report the reduction of principal for the next period as a current liability/current asset. In the annuity due situation, interest is accrued during the year but is not paid until the next period. As a result, **a current liability/current asset arises for both the principal reduction and the interest** that was incurred/earned in the preceding period.

In the ordinary annuity situation, the interest accrued during the period is also paid in the same period; consequently, only the principal reduction is shown as a current liability/current asset.

[22]"Accounting for Leases," op. cit., par. 16.

[23]For additional discussion on this approach and possible alternatives, see R. J. Swieringa, "When Current Is Noncurrent and Vice Versa!" *The Accounting Review,* January 1984, pp. 123–30, and A. W. Richardson, "The Measurement of the Current Portion of the Long-Term Lease Obligations—Some Evidence from Practice," *The Accounting Review,* October 1985, pages 744–52.

Disclosing Lease Data

OBJECTIVE 9
Describe the disclosure requirements for leases.

Disclosures Required of the Lessee

The FASB requires that the following information with respect to leases be disclosed in the **lessee's** financial statements or in the notes.[24]

(a) For capital leases:
   i. The gross amount of assets at each balance sheet date categorized by nature or function. This information may be combined with comparable information for owned assets.
   ii. Future *minimum lease payments* as of the latest balance sheet date, in the aggregate and for each of five succeeding fiscal years. Separate deductions for *executory costs* included in the *minimum lease payments* and for the amount of imputed interest necessary to reduce net *minimum lease payments* to present value.
   iii. Total noncancelable minimum sublease rentals to be received in the future, as of the latest balance sheet date.
   iv. Total *contingent rentals.*
   v. Assets recorded under capital leases and the accumulated amortization thereon shall be separately identified in the lessee's balance sheet or notes. Likewise, related obligations shall be separately identified as obligations under capital leases. Depreciation on capitalized leased assets should be separately disclosed.

(b) For operating leases having initial or remaining noncancelable *lease terms* in excess of one year:
   i. Future minimum rental payments required as of the latest balance sheet date, in the aggregate and for each of the five succeeding fiscal years.
   ii. Total minimum rentals to be received in the future under noncancelable subleases as of the latest balance sheet date.

(c) For all operating leases, rental expense for each period with separate amounts for minimum rentals, *contingent rentals,* and sublease rentals. Rental payments under leases with *terms* of a month or less that were not renewed need not be included.

(d) A general description of the lessee's arrangements including, but not limited to:
   i. The basis on which *contingent rental* payments are determined.
   ii. The existence and terms of renewal or purchase options and escalation clauses.
   iii. Restrictions imposed by lease agreements, such as those concerning dividends, additional debt, and further leasing.

ILLUSTRATION 22-32
Lessee's Disclosures

Disclosures Required of the Lessor

The FASB requires that **lessors** disclose in the financial statements or in the notes the following information when leasing "is a significant part of the lessor's business activities in terms of revenue, net income, or assets."[25]

(a) For sales-type and direct financing leases:
   i. The components of the net investment in sales-type and direct financing leases as of each balance sheet date:
      a. Future *minimum lease payments* to be received, with separate deductions for (i) *executory costs* and (ii) the accumulated allowance for uncollectible *minimum lease payments* receivable.
      b. The *unguaranteed residual values* accruing to the lessor.
      c. Unearned revenue.
   ii. Future *minimum lease payments* to be received for each of the five succeeding fiscal years.
   iii. The amount of unearned revenue included in income to offset *initial direct costs* charged against income for each period for which an income statement is presented. (For direct financing leases only.)
   iv. Total *contingent rentals* included in income for each period for which an income statement is presented.

(b) For operating leases:
   i. The cost and carrying amount, if different, of leased property according to nature or function, and total amount of accumulated depreciation.
   ii. Minimum future rentals on noncancelable leases as of the latest balance sheet date, in aggregate and for each of five succeeding fiscal years.
   iii. Total *contingent rentals* included in income for each period for which an income statement is presented.

(c) A general description of the lessor's leasing arrangements.

ILLUSTRATION 22-33
Lessor's Disclosures

Disclosures Illustrated

The financial statement excerpts from the 1999 Annual Report of **The Penn Traffic Company** in Illustration 22-34 present the statement and note disclosures typical of a **lessee** having both capital leases and operating leases.

[24]"Accounting for Leases," *FASB Statement No. 13,* as amended and interpreted through May 1980 (Stamford, Conn.: FASB, 1980), par. 16.

[25]Ibid., par. 23.

ILLUSTRATION 22-34
Disclosure of Leases by Lessee

Go to the Digital Tool for additional lease disclosures.

PENN TRAFFIC COMPANY

(Dollar amounts in thousands)

Assets—Capital Leases (Note 6)	1999	1998
Capital leases	$157,667	$190,638
Less: Accumulated amortization	(66,735)	(75,057)
	90,932	115,581
Current Liabilities		
Current portion of obligations under capital leases (Note 6)	$ 11,516	$ 13,518
Noncurrent Liabilities		
Obligations under capital leases (Note 6)	98,029	121,436

Note 6: Leases

The Company principally operates in leased store facilities with terms of up to 20 years with renewable options for additional periods. The Company follows the provisions of Statement of Financial Accounting Standards No. 13, "Accounting for Leases" ("SFAS 13"), in determining the criteria for capital leases. Leases that do not meet such criteria are classified as operating leases and related rentals are charged to expense in the year incurred.

For Fiscal 1999, 1998 and 1997, capital lease amortization expense was $11.8 million, $13.8 million and $14.5 million, respectively.

The following is a summary by year of future minimum rental payments for capitalized leases and for operating leases that have initial or remaining noncancelable terms in excess of one year as of January 30, 1999:

Fiscal Years Ending:	Total	Operating	Capital
	(in thousands of dollars)		
2000	$ 60,728	$ 37,715	$ 23,013
2001	58,308	36,908	21,400
2002	53,080	34,172	18,908
2003	47,183	30,204	16,979
2004	42,037	27,557	14,480
Later years	295,008	198,633	96,375
Total minimum lease payments	$556,344	$365,189	191,155
Less: Executory costs			(477)
Net minimum capital lease payments			190,678
Less: Estimated amount representing interest			(81,133)
Present value of net minimum capital lease payments			109,545
Less: Current portion			(11,516)
Long-term obligations under capital lease at January 30, 1999			$ 98,029

Minimum rental payments and related executory costs for operating leases were as follows:

	Fiscal Year Ended		
	January 30, 1999	January 31, 1998	February 1, 1997
	(in thousands of dollars)		
Minimum rentals and executory costs	$ 46,250	$ 44,560	$ 45,067
Contingent rentals	3,082	2,691	2,760
Less: Sublease payments	(10,865)	(9,577)	(10,086)
Net rental payments	$ 38,467	$ 37,674	$ 37,741

The following note from the 1998 Annual Report of **Dana Corporation** illustrates the disclosures of a **lessor**.

ILLUSTRATION 22-35
Disclosure of Leases by Lessor

DANA CORPORATION

Notes to Financial Statements
(in millions)
Note 1 (In Part): Summary of Significant Accounting Policies
Lease Financing
Lease financing consists of direct financing leases, leveraged leases and equipment on operating leases. Income on direct financing leases is recognized by a method which produces a constant periodic rate of return on the outstanding investment in the lease. Income on leveraged leases is recognized by a method which produces a constant rate of return on the outstanding net investment in the lease, net of the related deferred tax liability, in the years in which the net investment is positive. Initial direct costs are deferred and amortized using the interest method over the lease period. Equipment under operating leases is recorded at cost, net of accumulated depreciation. Income from operating leases is recognized ratably over the term of the leases.

The components of the net investment in direct financing leases are as follows:

	December 31,	
	1997	1998
Total minimum lease payments	$743.7	$137.7
Residual values	89.5	34.8
Deferred initial direct costs	15.5	2.3
	848.7	174.8
Less: Unearned income	182.9	57.3
	$665.8	$117.5

The following is a schedule, by year, of total minimum lease payments receivable on direct financing leases as of December 31, 1998:

Year Ending December 31:	
1999	$ 23.9
2000	21.8
2001	18.5
2002	14.6
2003	11.5
Later years	47.4
Total minimum lease payments receivable	$137.7

LEASE ACCOUNTING—UNSOLVED PROBLEMS

As indicated at the beginning of this chapter, lease accounting is a much abused area in which strenuous efforts are being made to circumvent *Statement No. 13*. In practice, the accounting rules for capitalizing leases have been rendered partially ineffective by the strong desires of lessees to resist capitalization. Leasing generally involves large dollar amounts that when capitalized materially increase reported liabilities and adversely affect the debt-to-equity ratio. Lease capitalization is also resisted because charges to expense made in the early years of the lease term are higher under the capital lease method than under the operating method, frequently without tax benefit. As a consequence, "let's beat *Statement No. 13*" is one of the most popular games in town.[26]

[26]Richard Dieter, "Is Lessee Accounting Working?" *The CPA Journal*, August 1979, pp. 13–19. This article provides interesting examples of abuses of *Statement No. 13*, discusses the circumstances that led to the current situation, and proposes a solution.

To avoid leased asset capitalization, lease agreements are designed, written, and interpreted so that none of the four capitalized lease criteria are satisfied from the lessee's viewpoint. Devising lease agreements in such a way has not been too difficult when the following specifications have been met.

1. Make certain that the lease does not specify the transfer of title of the property to the lessee.
2. Do not write in a bargain purchase option.
3. Set the lease term at something less than 75% of the estimated economic life of the leased property.
4. Arrange for the present value of the minimum lease payments to be less than 90% of the fair value of the leased property.

The real challenge lies in disqualifying the lease as a capital lease to the lessee while having the same lease qualify as a capital (sales or financing) lease to the lessor. Unlike lessees, lessors try to avoid having lease arrangements classified as operating leases.[27]

Avoiding the first three criteria is relatively simple, but it takes a little ingenuity to avoid the "90% recovery test" for the lessee while satisfying it for the lessor. Two of the factors involved in this effort are (1) the use of the incremental borrowing rate by the lessee when it is higher than the implicit interest rate of the lessor, by making information about the implicit rate unavailable to the lessee; and (2) residual value guarantees.

The lessee's use of the higher interest rate is probably the more popular subterfuge. While lessees are knowledgeable about the fair value of the leased property and, of course, the rental payments, they generally are not aware of the estimated residual value used by the lessor. Therefore the lessee who does not know exactly the lessor's implicit interest rate might use a different incremental borrowing rate.

The residual value guarantee is the other unique, yet popular, device used by lessees and lessors. In fact, a whole new industry has emerged to circumvent symmetry between the lessee and the lessor in accounting for leases. The residual value guarantee has spawned numerous companies whose principal, or even sole, function is to guarantee the residual value of leased assets. These **third-party guarantors** (insurers), for a fee, assume the risk of deficiencies in leased asset residual value.

Because the guaranteed residual value is included in the minimum lease payments for the lessor, the 90% recovery of fair market value test is satisfied. The lease is a nonoperating lease to the lessor. But because the residual value is guaranteed by a third party, the minimum lease payments of the lessee do not include the guarantee. Thus, by merely transferring some of the risk to a third party, lessees can alter substantially the accounting treatment by converting what would otherwise be capital leases to operating leases.[28]

Much of this circumvention is encouraged by the nature of the criteria, which stem from weaknesses in the basic objective of *Statement No. 13.* Accounting standard-setting bodies continue to have poor experience with arbitrary break points or other size and percentage criteria—that is, rules like "90% of," "75% of," etc. Some believe that a more workable solution would be to require capitalization of all leases that ex-

[27]The reason is that most lessors are financial institutions and do not want these types of assets on their balance sheets. In fact, banks and savings and loans are not permitted to report these assets on their balance sheets except for relatively short periods of time. Furthermore, the capital lease transaction from the lessor's standpoint provides higher income flows in the earlier periods of the lease.

[28]As an aside, third-party guarantors have experienced some difficulty. **Lloyd's of London**, at one time, insured the fast growing U.S. computer-leasing industry in the amount of $2 billion against revenue losses and losses in residual value if leases were canceled. Because of "overnight" technological improvements and the successive introductions of more efficient and less expensive computers by computer manufacturers, lessees in abundance canceled their leases. As the market for second-hand computers became flooded and residual values plummeted, third-party guarantor Lloyd's of London projected a loss of $400 million. Much of the third-party guarantee business was stimulated by the lessees' and lessors' desire to circumvent *FASB Statement No. 13.*

tend for some defined period (such as one year) on the basis that the lessee has acquired an asset (a property right) and a corresponding liability rather than on the basis that the lease transfers substantially all the risks and rewards of ownership.

Three years after it issued *Statement No. 13,* a majority of the FASB expressed "the tentative view that, if *Statement 13* were to be reconsidered, they would support a property right approach in which all leases are included as 'rights to use property' and as 'lease obligations' in the lessee's balance sheet."[29] Recently, the FASB and other international standard setters have issued a report on lease accounting that proposes the capitalization of more leases.[30]

ILLUSTRATIONS OF DIFFERENT LEASE ARRANGEMENTS

To illustrate concepts discussed in this chapter, assume that Morgan Bakeries is involved in four different lease situations. Each of these leases is noncancelable and in no case does Morgan receive title to the properties leased during or at the end of the lease term. All leases start on January 1, 2002, with the first rental due at the beginning of the year. The additional information is shown in Illustration 22-36.

ILLUSTRATION 22-36
Illustrative Lease Situations, Lessors

	Harmon, Inc.	Arden's Oven Co.	Mendota Truck Co.	Appleland Computer
Type of property	Cabinets	Oven	Truck	Computer
Yearly rental	$6,000	$15,000	$5,582.62	$3,557.25
Lease term	20 years	10 years	3 years	3 years
Estimated economic life	30 years	25 years	7 years	5 years
Purchase option	None	$75,000 at end of 10 years $4,000 at end of 15 years	None	$3,000 at end of 3 years, which approximates fair market value
Renewal option	None	5-year renewal option at $15,000 per year	None	1 year at $1,500; no penalty for non-renewal; standard renewal clause
Fair market value at inception of lease	$60,000	$120,000	$20,000	$10,000
Cost of asset to lessor	$60,000	$120,000	$15,000	$10,000
Residual value				
Guaranteed	–0–	–0–	$7,000	–0–
Unguaranteed	$5,000	–0–	–0–	$3,000
Incremental borrowing rate of lessee	12%	12%	12%	12%
Executory costs paid by	*Lessee* $300 per year	*Lessee* $1,000 per year	*Lessee* $500 per year	*Lessor* Estimated to be $500 per year
Present value of minimum lease payments				
Using incremental borrowing rate of lessee	$50,194.68	$115,153.35	$20,000	$8,224.16
Using implicit rate of lessor	Not known	Not known	Not known	Known by lessee, $8,027.48
Estimated fair market value at end of lease	$5,000	$80,000 at end of 10 years $60,000 at end of 15 years	Not available	$3,000

[29]"Is Lessee Accounting Working?" op. cit., p. 19.

[30]H. Nailor and A. Lennard, "Capital Leases: Implementation of a New Approach," *Financial Accounting Series No. 206A* (Norwalk, Conn.: FASB, 2000).

Harmon, Inc.

The following is an analysis of the Harmon, Inc. lease:

1. **Transfer of title?** No.
2. **Bargain purchase option?** No.
3. **Economic life test (75% test).** The lease term is 20 years and the estimated economic life is 30 years. Thus it does **not** meet the 75% test.
4. **Recovery of investment test (90% test):**

Fair market value	$60,000	Rental payments	$ 6,000
Rate	90%	PV of annuity due for 20 years at 12%	× 8.36578
90% of fair market value	$54,000	PV of rental payments	$50,194.68

Because the present value of the minimum lease payments is less than 90% of the fair market value, the 90% test is not met. Both Morgan and Harmon should account for this lease as an operating lease, as indicated by the January 1, 2002, entries shown below.

ILLUSTRATION 22-37
Comparative Entries for Operating Lease

Morgan Bakeries (Lessee)			Harmon, Inc. (Lessor)		
Rent Expense	6,000		Cash	6,000	
Cash		6,000	Rental Revenue		6,000

Arden's Oven Co.

The following is an analysis of the Arden's Oven Co. lease.

1. **Transfer of title?** No.
2. **Bargain purchase option?** The $75,000 option at the end of 10 years does not appear to be sufficiently lower than the expected fair value of $80,000 to make it reasonably assured that it will be exercised. However, the $4,000 at the end of 15 years when the fair value is $60,000 does appear to be a bargain. From the information given, criterion 2 is therefore met. Note that both the guaranteed and the unguaranteed residual values are assigned zero values because the lessor does not expect to repossess the leased asset.
3. **Economic life test (75% test):** Given that a bargain purchase option exists, the lease term is the initial lease period of 10 years plus the 5-year renewal option since it precedes a bargain purchase option. Even though the lease term is now considered to be 15 years, this test is still not met because 75% of the economic life of 25 years is 18.75 years.
4. **Recovery of investment test (90% test):**

Fair market value	$120,000	Rental payments	$ 15,000.00
Rate	90%	PV of annuity due for 15 years at 12%	× 7.62817
90% of fair market value	$108,000	PV of rental payments	$114,422.55

PV of bargain purchase option: $= \$4,000(PVF_{15,12\%}) = \$4,000(.18270) = \$730.80$

PV of rental payments	$114,422.55
PV of bargain purchase option	730.80
PV of minimum lease payments	$115,153.35

The present value of the minimum lease payments if greater than 90% of the fair market value; therefore, the 90% test is met. Morgan Bakeries should account for this as a capital lease because both criterion 2 and criterion 4 are met. Assuming that Arden's implicit rate is the same as Morgan's incremental borrowing rate, the following entries are made on January 1, 2002.

ILLUSTRATION 22-38
Comparative Entries for Capital Lease—Bargain Purchase Option

Morgan Bakeries (Lessee)			Arden's Oven Co. (Lessor)		
Leased Asset—Oven	115,153.35		Lease Payments Receivable	229,000*	
Obligation under Capital Lease		115,153.35	Unearned Interest Revenue		109,000
			Asset—Oven		120,000
			*([$15,000 × 15] + $4,000)		

Morgan Bakeries would depreciate the leased asset over its economic life of 25 years, given the bargain purchase option. Arden's does not use sales-type accounting because the fair market value and the cost of the asset are the same at the inception of the lease.

Mendota Truck Co.

The following is an analysis of the Mendota Truck Co. lease.

1. **Transfer of title?** No.
2. **Bargain purchase option?** No.
3. **Economic life test (75% test):** The lease term is three years and the estimated economic life is seven years. Thus it does **not** meet the 75% test.
4. **Recovery of investment test (90% test):**

Fair market value	$20,000	Rental payments	$ 5,582.62
Rate	90%	PV of annuity due for 3 years at 12%	× 2.69005
90% of fair market value	$18,000	PV of rental payments	$15,017.54
		(Note: adjusted for $.01 due to rounding)	

PV of guaranteed residual value: = $7,000(PVF$_{3,12\%}$) = $7,000(.71178) = $4,982.46

PV of rental payments	$15,017.54
PV of guaranteed residual value	4,982.46
PV of minimum lease payments	$20,000.00

The present value of the minimum lease payments is greater than 90% of the fair market value; therefore, the 90% test is met. Assuming that Mendota's implicit rate is the same as Morgan's incremental borrowing rate, the following entries are made on January 1, 2002.

ILLUSTRATION 22-39
Comparative Entries for Capital Lease

Morgan Bakeries (Lessee)			Mendota Truck Co. (Lessor)		
Leased Asset—Truck	20,000.00		Lease Payments Receivable	23,747.86*	
Obligation under Capital Lease		20,000.00	Cost of Goods Sold	15,000.00	
			Inventory—Truck		15,000.00
			Sales		20,000.00
			Unearned Interest Revenue		3,747.86
			*[($5,582.62 × 3) + $7,000]		

The leased asset is depreciated by Morgan over three years to its guaranteed residual value.

Appleland Computer

The following is an analysis of the Appleland Computer lease.

1. **Transfer of title?** No.
2. **Bargain purchase option?** No. The option to purchase at the end of 3 years at approximate fair market value is clearly not a bargain.
3. **Economic life test (75% test):** The lease term is 3 years and no bargain renewal period exists. Therefore the 75% test is **not** met.
4. **Recovery of investment test (90% test):**

Fair market value	$10,000	Rental payments	$3,557.25
Rate	90%	Less executory costs	500.00
90% of fair market value	$ 9,000		3,057.25
		PV of annuity due factor for 3 years at 12%	× 2.69005
		PV of minimum lease payments using incremental borrowing rate	$8,224.16

The present value of the minimum lease payments using the incremental borrowing rate is $8,224.16; using the implicit rate, it is $8,027.48 (see Illustration 22-36). The implicit rate of the lessor is, therefore, higher than the incremental borrowing rate. Given this situation, the lessee uses the $8,224.16 (lower interest rate when discounting) when comparing with the 90% of fair market value. Because the present value of the minimum lease payments is lower than 90% of the fair market value, the recovery of investment test is **not** met.

The following entries are made on January 1, 2002, indicating an operating lease.

ILLUSTRATION 22-40
Comparative Entries for Operating Lease

Morgan Bakeries (Lessee)			Appleland Computer (Lessor)		
Rent Expense	3,557.25		Cash	3,557.25	
Cash		3,557.25	Rental Revenue		3,557.25

If the lease payments had been $3,557.25 with no executory costs involved, this lease arrangement would have qualified for capital lease accounting treatment.

SUMMARY OF LEARNING OBJECTIVES

1 **Explain the nature, economic substance, and advantages of lease transactions.** A lease is a contractual agreement between a lessor and a lessee that conveys to the lessee the right to use specific property (real or personal), owned by the lessor, for a specified period of time. In return for this right, the lessee agrees to make periodic cash payments (rents) to the lessor. The advantages of lease transactions are: (1) 100% financing; (2) protection against obsolescence, (3) flexibility, (4) less costly financing, (5) possible tax advantages, and (6) off-balance-sheet financing.

2 **Describe the accounting criteria and procedures for capitalizing leases by the lessee.** A lease is a capital lease if one or more of the following criteria are met: (1) the lease transfers ownership of the property to the lessee; (2) the lease contains a bargain purchase option; (3) the lease term is equal to 75% or more of the estimated economic life of the leased property; (4) the present value of the minimum lease payments (excluding executory costs) equals or exceeds 90% of the fair value of the leased property. For a capital lease, the lessee records an asset and a liability at the lower of (1) the present value of the minimum lease payments or (2) the fair market value of the leased asset at the inception of the lease.

3 Contrast the operating and capitalization methods of recording leases. The total charges to operations are the same over the lease term whether the lease is accounted for as a capital lease or as an operating lease; under the capital lease treatment, the charges are higher in the earlier years and lower in the later years. If an accelerated method of depreciation is used, the differences between the amounts charged to operations under the two methods would be even larger in the earlier and later years. The following occurs if a capital lease instead of an operating lease is employed: (1) an increase in the amount of reported debt (both short-term and long-term), (2) an increase in the amount of total assets (specifically long-lived assets), and (3) a lower income early in the life of the lease and, therefore, lower retained earnings.

4 Identify the classifications of leases for the lessor. From the standpoint of the lessor, all leases may be classified for accounting purpose as follows: (1) operating leases, (2) direct financing leases, (3) sales-type leases. The lessor should classify and account for an arrangement as a direct financing lease or a sales-type lease if, at the date of the lease agreement, one or more of the Group I criteria (as shown in learning objective 2 for lessees) are met and both of the following Group II criteria are met. *Group II:* (1) Collectibility of the payments required from the lessee is reasonably predictable; and (2) no important uncertainties surround the amount of unreimbursable costs yet to be incurred by the lessor under the lease. All leases that fail to meet the criteria are classified and accounted for by the lessor as operating leases.

5 Describe the lessor's accounting for direct financing leases. Leases that are in substance the financing of an asset purchase by a lessee require the lessor to substitute a "lease payments receivable" for the leased asset. The information necessary to record a direct financing lease is: (1) gross investment ("lease payments receivable"), (2) unearned interest revenue, and (3) net investment. There often is uncertainty as to how to account for the residual values when computing gross investment. When "lease payments receivable" is defined as minimum lease payments plus unguaranteed residual value, it means that the residual value, whether guaranteed or unguaranteed, is included as part of lease payments receivable if it is relevant to the lessor (i.e., if the lessor expects to get the asset back).

6 Identify special features of lease arrangements that cause unique accounting problems. The features of lease arrangements that cause unique accounting problems are: (1) residual values; (2) sales-type leases (lessor); (3) bargain purchase options; (4) initial direct costs; (5) current versus noncurrent; and (6) disclosures.

7 Describe the effect of residual values, guaranteed and unguaranteed, on lease accounting. Whether the estimated residual value is guaranteed or unguaranteed is of both economic and accounting consequence to the lessee. The accounting difference is that the minimum lease payments, the basis for capitalization, includes the guaranteed residual value but excludes the unguaranteed residual value. A guaranteed residual value affects the lessee's computation of minimum lease payments and, therefore, the amounts capitalized as a leased asset and a lease obligation. In effect, it is an additional lease payment that will be paid in property or cash, or both, at the end of the lease term. An unguaranteed residual value from the lessee's viewpoint is the same as no residual value in terms of its effect upon the lessee's method of computing the minimum lease payments and the capitalization of the leased asset and the lease obligation.

8 Describe the lessor's accounting for sales-type leases. The information needed to record the sales-type lease is as follows: (1) gross investment (also "lease payments receivable"); (2) unearned interest revenue; (3) sales price of the asset; and (4) cost of goods sold. The gross investment and the unearned interest revenue are the same whether a guaranteed or an unguaranteed residual value is involved. When recording sales revenue and cost of goods sold, there is a difference in the accounting for guaranteed and unguaranteed residual values. The guaranteed residual value can be

KEY TERMS

bargain purchase option, *1194*
bargain renewal option, *1195*
capital lease, *1193*
capitalization criteria, *1194*
capitalization of leases, *1192*
cost of goods sold (sales-type lease), *1215*
direct financing lease, *1204*
effective interest method, *1197*
executory costs, *1196*
gross investment, *1205, 1215*
guaranteed residual value, *1196*
implicit interest rate, *1196*
incremental borrowing rate, *1196*
initial direct costs, *1217*
lease, *1190*
lease payments receivable, *1205, 1215*
lease term, *1190*
lessee, *1190*
lessor, *1190*
manufacturer's or dealer's profit, *1203*
minimum lease payments, *1195*
net investment, *1205*
noncancelable, *1193*
off-balance-sheet financing, *1191*
operating lease, *1194*
sales price (sales-type lease), *1215*
sales-type lease, *1214*
third-party guarantors, *1222*
unearned interest revenue, *1205, 1215*
unguaranteed residual value, *1211*

considered part of sales revenue because the lessor knows that the entire asset has been sold. There is less certainty that the unguaranteed residual portion of the asset has been "sold"; therefore, sales and cost of goods sold are recognized only for the portion of the asset for which realization is assured. However, the gross profit amount on the sale of the asset is the same whether a guaranteed or unguaranteed residual value is involved.

Go to the Digital Tool for an expanded discussion of real estate leases and leveraged leases.

9 Describe the disclosure requirements for leases. The disclosure requirements for the **lessee** are classified as follows: (1) capital leases; (2) operating leases having initial or remaining noncancelable lease terms in excess of one year; (3) all operating leases; and (4) a general description of the lessee's arrangements. The disclosure requirements for the **lessor** are classified as follows: (1) sales-type and direct financing leases; (2) operating leases; and (3) a general description of the lessor's leasing arrangements.

APPENDIX 22A

Sale-Leasebacks

OBJECTIVE 10
After studying Appendix 22A, you should be able to: Describe the lessee's accounting for sale-leaseback transactions.

The term **sale-leaseback** describes a transaction in which the owner of the property (seller-lessee) sells the property to another and simultaneously leases it back from the new owner. The use of the property is generally continued without interruption.

Sale-leasebacks are common. Financial institutions (**Bank of America** and **First Chicago**) have used this technique for their administrative offices, public utilities (**Ohio Edison** and **Pinnacle West Corporation**) for their generating plants, and airlines (**Continental** and **Alaska Airlines**) for their aircraft. The advantages of a sale-leaseback from the seller's viewpoint usually involve two primary considerations.

1. *Financing*—If the purchase of equipment has already been financed, a sale-leaseback can allow the seller to refinance at lower rates, assuming rates have dropped. In addition, a sale-leaseback can provide another source of working capital, particularly when liquidity is tight.
2. *Taxes*—At the time a company purchased equipment, it may not have known that it would be subject to a minimum tax and that ownership might increase its minimum tax liability. By selling the property, the seller-lessee may deduct the entire lease payment, which is not subject to minimum tax considerations.

UNDERLYING CONCEPTS

A sale-leaseback is similar in substance to the parking of inventories discussed in Chapter 8. The ultimate economic benefits remain under the control of the "seller," thus the definition of an asset is satisfied.

DETERMINING ASSET USE

To the extent the **seller-lessee's use** of the asset sold continues after the sale, the sale-leaseback is really a form of financing, and therefore **no gain or loss should be recognized** on the transaction. In short, the seller-lessee is simply borrowing funds. On the other hand, if the **seller-lessee gives up the right to the use** of the asset sold, the transaction is in substance a sale, and **gain or loss recognition** is appropriate. Trying to ascertain when the lessee has given up the use of the asset is difficult, however, and complex rules have been formulated to identify this situation.[1] To understand the profession's position in this area, the basic accounting for the lessee and lessor are discussed below.

Lessee

If the lease meets one of the four criteria for treatment as a capital lease (see Illustration 22-4), the **seller-lessee accounts for the transaction as a sale and the lease as a capital lease**. Any profit or loss experienced by the seller-lessee from the sale of the assets that are leased back under a capital lease should be **deferred and amortized over the lease term** (or the economic life if either criterion 1 or 2 is satisfied) in proportion to the amortization of the leased assets. If Lessee, Inc. sells equipment having a book value of $580,000 and a fair value of $623,110 to Lessor, Inc. for $623,110 and leases the equipment back for $50,000 a year for 20 years, the profit of $43,110 should be amortized over the 20-year period at the same rate that the $623,110 is depreciated.[2] The $43,110 is credited to **"Unearned Profit on Sale-Leaseback."**

If none of the capital lease criteria are satisfied, **the seller-lessee accounts for the transaction as a sale and the lease as an operating lease**. Under an operating lease, such profit or loss should be deferred and amortized in proportion to the rental payments over the period of time the assets are expected to be used by the lessee.

There are exceptions to these two general rules. They are:

1. ***Losses Recognized***—The profession requires that, when the fair value of the asset is **less than the book value** (carrying amount), a loss must be recognized immediately up to the amount of the difference between the book value and fair value. For example, if Lessee, Inc. sells equipment having a book value of $650,000 and a fair value of $623,110, the difference of $26,890 should be charged to a loss account.[3]
2. ***Minor Leaseback***—Leasebacks in which the present value of the rental payments are 10% or less of the fair value of the asset are defined as **minor leasebacks**. In this case, the seller-lessee gives up most of the rights to the use of the asset sold. Therefore, the transaction is a sale, and full gain or loss recognition is appropriate. It is not a financing transaction because the risks of ownership have been transferred.[4]

Lessor

If the lease meets one of the criteria in Group I and both of the criteria in Group II (see Illustration 22-11), the **purchaser-lessor** records the transaction as a purchase and a direct financing lease. If the lease does not meet the criteria, the purchaser-lessor records the transaction as a purchase and an operating lease.

---

[1]Sales and leasebacks of real estate are often accounted for differently. A discussion of the issues related to these transactions is beyond the scope of this textbook. See *Statement of Financial Accounting Standards No. 98,* op. cit.

[2]*Statement of Financial Accounting Standards No. 28,* "Accounting for Sales with Leasebacks" (Stamford, Conn.: FASB, 1979).

[3]There can be two types of losses in sale-leaseback arrangements. One is a **real economic loss** that results when the carrying amount of the asset is higher than the fair market value of the asset. In this case, the loss should be recognized. An **artificial loss** results when the sale price is below the carrying amount of the asset but the fair market value is above the carrying amount. In this case the loss is more in the form of prepaid rent and should be deferred and amortized in the future.

[4]In some cases the seller-lessee retains more than a minor part but less than substantially all; the computations to arrive at these values are complex and beyond the scope of this textbook.

SALE-LEASEBACK ILLUSTRATION

To illustrate the accounting treatment accorded a sale-leaseback transaction, assume that Lessee Corp. on January 1, 2002, sells a used Boeing 747 having a carrying amount on its books of $75,500,000, to Lessor Corp. for $80,000,000 and immediately leases the aircraft back under the following conditions:

1. The term of the lease is 15 years, noncancelable, and requires equal rental payments of $10,487,443 at the beginning of each year.
2. The aircraft has a fair value of $80,000,000 on January 1, 2002, and an estimated economic life of 15 years.
3. Lessee Corp. pays all executory costs.
4. Lessee Corp. depreciates similar aircraft that it owns on a straight-line basis over 15 years.
5. The annual payments assure the lessor a 12% return.
6. The incremental borrowing rate of Lessee Corp. is 12%.

This lease is a capital lease to Lessee Corp. because the lease term exceeds 75% of the estimated life of the aircraft and because the present value of the lease payments exceeds 90% of the fair value of the aircraft to the lessor. Assuming that collectibility of the lease payments is reasonably predictable and that no important uncertainties exist in relation to unreimbursable costs yet to be incurred by the lessor, Lessor Corp. should classify this lease as a direct financing lease.

The typical journal entries to record the transactions relating to this lease for both Lessee Corp. and Lessor Corp. for the first year are presented below.

ILLUSTRATION 22A-1
Comparative Entries for Sale-Leaseback for Lessee and Lessor

Lessee Corp.			Lessor Corp.		
Sale of Aircraft by Lessee to Lessor Corp., January 1, 2002:					
Cash	80,000,000		Aircraft	80,000,000	
Aircraft		75,500,000	Cash		80,000,000
Unearned Profit on Sale-Leaseback		4,500,000	Lease Payments Receivable	157,311,645	
Leased Aircraft under Capital Leases	80,000,000		Aircraft		80,000,000
Obligations under Capital Leases		80,000,000	Unearned Interest Revenue		77,311,645
			($10,487,443 × 15 = $157,311,645)		
First Lease Payment, January 1, 2002:					
Obligations under Capital Leases	10,487,443		Cash	10,487,443	
Cash		10,487,443	Lease Payments Receivable		10,487,443
Incurrence and Payment of Executory Costs by Lessee Corp. throughout 2002:					
Insurance, Maintenance, Taxes, etc.	XXX		(No entry)		
Cash or Accounts Payable		XXX			
Depreciation Expense on the Aircraft, December 31, 2002:					
Depreciation Expense	5,333,333		(No entry)		
Accumulated Depr.—Capital Leases ($80,000,000 ÷ 15)		5,333,333			
Amortization of Profit on Sale-Leaseback by Lessee Corp., December 31, 2002:					
Unearned Profit on Sale-Leaseback	300,000		(No entry)		
Depreciation Expense ($4,500,000 ÷ 15)		300,000			

Note: A case might be made for crediting Revenue instead of Depreciation Expense.

	Lessee Corp.			Lessor Corp.		
Interest for 2002, December 31, 2002:						
Interest Expense	8,341,507[a]		Unearned Interest Revenue	8,341,507		
Interest Payable		8,341,507	Interest Revenue		8,341,507[a]	

[a]Partial Lease Amortization Schedule:

Date	Annual Rental Payment	Interest 12%	Reduction of Balance	Balance
1/1/02				$80,000,000
1/1/02	$10,487,443	$ –0–	$10,487,443	69,512,557
1/1/03	10,487,443	8,341,507	2,145,936	67,366,621

SUMMARY OF LEARNING OBJECTIVE FOR APPENDIX 22A

10 Describe the lessee's accounting for sale-leaseback transactions. If the lease meets one of the four criteria for treatment as a capital lease, the seller-lessee accounts for the transaction as a sale and the lease as a capital lease. Any profit experienced by the seller-lessee from the sale of the assets that are leased back under a capital lease should be deferred and amortized over the lease term (or the economic life if either criterion 1 or 2 is satisfied) in proportion to the amortization of the leased assets. If none of the capital lease criteria are satisfied, the seller-lessee accounts for the transaction as a sale and the lease as an operating lease. Under an operating lease, such profit should be deferred and amortized in proportion to the rental payments over the period of time the assets are expected to be used by the lessee.

KEY TERMS

minor leaseback, 1229
sale-leaseback, 1228

Note: All **asterisked** Questions, Exercises, Problems, and Conceptual Cases relate to material contained in the appendix to the chapter.

QUESTIONS

1 Jackie Remmers Co. is expanding its operations and is in the process of selecting the method of financing this program. After some investigation, the company determines that it may (1) issue bonds and with the proceeds purchase the needed assets, or (2) lease the assets on a long-term basis. Without knowing the comparative costs involved, answer these questions:

(a) What might be the advantages of leasing the assets instead of owning them?

(b) What might be the disadvantages of leasing the assets instead of owning them?

(c) In what way will the balance sheet be differently affected by leasing the assets as opposed to issuing bonds and purchasing the assets?

2 Mildred Natalie Corp. is considering leasing a significant amount of assets. The president, Joan Elaine Robinson, is attending an informal meeting in the afternoon with a potential lessor. Because her legal advisor cannot be reached, she has called on you, the controller, to brief her on the general provisions of lease agreements to which she should give consideration in such preliminary discussions with a possible lessor. Identify the general provisions of the lease agreement that the president should be told to include in her discussion with the potential lessor.

3 Identify the two recognized lease accounting methods for lessees and distinguish between them.

4 Wayne Higley Company rents a warehouse on a month-to-month basis for the storage of its excess inventory. The company periodically must rent space whenever its production greatly exceeds actual sales. For several years the company officials have discussed building their own storage facility, but this enthusiasm wavers when sales increase sufficiently to absorb the excess inventory. What is the nature of this type of lease arrangement, and what accounting treatment should be accorded it?

5 Distinguish between minimum rental payments and minimum lease payments, and indicate what is included in minimum lease payments.

6 Explain the distinction between a direct financing lease and a sales-type lease for a lessor.

7 Outline the accounting procedures involved in applying the operating method by a lessee.

8 Outline the accounting procedures involved in applying the capital lease method by a lessee.

9 Identify the lease classifications for lessors and the criteria that must be met for each classification.

10 Outline the accounting procedures involved in applying the direct financing method.

11 Outline the accounting procedures involved in applying the operating method by a lessor.

12 Joan Elbert Company is a manufacturer and lessor of computer equipment. What should be the nature of its lease arrangements with lessees if the company wishes to account for its lease transactions as sales-type leases?

13 Gordon Graham Corporation's lease arrangements qualify as sales-type leases at the time of entering into the transactions. How should the corporation recognize revenues and costs in these situations?

14 Joann Skabo, M.D. (lessee) has a noncancelable 20-year lease with Cheryl Countryman Realty, Inc. (lessor) for the use of a medical building. Taxes, insurance, and maintenance are paid by the lessee in addition to the fixed annual payments, of which the present value is equal to the fair market value of the leased property. At the end of the lease period, title becomes the lessee's at a nominal price. Considering the terms of the lease described above, comment on the nature of the lease transaction and the accounting treatment that should be accorded it by the lessee.

15 The residual value is the estimated fair value of the leased property at the end of the lease term.

(a) Of what significance is (1) an unguaranteed and (2) a guaranteed residual value in the lessee's accounting for a capitalized lease transaction?

(b) Of what significance is (1) an unguaranteed and (2) a guaranteed residual value in the lessor's accounting for a direct financing lease transaction?

16 How should changes in the estimated residual value be handled by the lessor?

17 Describe the effect of a "bargain purchase option" on accounting for a capital lease transaction by a lessee.

18 What are "initial direct costs" and how are they accounted for?

19 What disclosures should be made by a lessee if the leased assets and the related obligation are not capitalized?

***20** What is the nature of a "sale-leaseback" transaction?

BRIEF EXERCISES

BE22-1 WarpSpeed Corporation leased equipment from Photon Company. The lease term is 5 years and requires equal rental payments of $30,000 at the beginning of each year. The equipment has a fair value at the inception of the lease of $138,000, an estimated useful life of 8 years, and no residual value. WarpSpeed pays all executory costs directly to third parties. Photon set the annual rental to earn a rate of return of 10%, and this fact is known to WarpSpeed. The lease does not transfer title or contain a bargain purchase option. How should WarpSpeed classify this lease?

BE22-2 Waterworld Company leased equipment from Costner Company. The lease term is 4 years and requires equal rental payments of $37,283 at the beginning of each year. The equipment has a fair value at the inception of the lease of $130,000, an estimated useful life of 4 years, and no salvage value. Waterworld pays all executory costs directly to third parties. The appropriate interest rate is 10%. Prepare Waterworld's January 1, 2002, journal entries at the inception of the lease.

BE22-3 Rick Kleckner Corporation recorded a capital lease at $200,000 on January 1, 2002. The interest rate is 12%. Kleckner Corporation made the first lease payment of $35,947 on January 1, 2002. The lease requires eight annual payments. The equipment has a useful life of 8 years with no salvage value. Prepare Kleckner Corporation's December 31, 2002, adjusting entries.

BE22-4 Use the information for Rick Kleckner Corporation from BE22-3. Assume that at December 31, 2002, Kleckner made an adjusting entry to accrue interest expense of $19,686 on the lease. Prepare Kleckner's January 1, 2003, journal entry to record the second lease payment of $35,947.

BE22-5 Jana Kingston Corporation enters into a lease on January 1, 2002, that does not transfer ownership or contain a bargain purchase option. It covers 3 years of the equipment's 8-year useful life, and the present value of the minimum lease payments is less than 90% of the fair market value of the asset leased. Prepare Jana Kingston's journal entry to record its January 1, 2002, annual lease payment of $37,500.

BE22-6 Karen A. Henkel Corporation leased equipment that was carried at a cost of $150,000 to Sharon Swander Company. The term of the lease is 6 years beginning January 1, 2002, with equal rental payments of $30,677 at the beginning of each year. All executory costs are paid by Swander directly to third parties. The fair value of the equipment at the inception of the lease is $150,000. The equipment has a useful life of 6 years with no salvage value. The lease has an implicit interest rate of 9%, no bargain purchase option, and no transfer of title. Collectibility is reasonably assured with no additional cost to be incurred by Henkel. Prepare Karen A. Henkel Corporation's January 1, 2002, journal entries at the inception of the lease.

BE22-7 Use the information for Karen A. Henkel Corporation from BE22-6. Assume the direct financing lease was recorded at a present value of $150,000. Prepare Karen A. Henkel's December 31, 2002, entry to record interest.

BE22-8 Jennifer Brent Corporation owns equipment that cost $72,000 and has a useful life of 8 years with no salvage value. On January 1, 2002, Jennifer Brent leases the equipment to Donna Havaci Inc. for one year with one rental payment of $15,000 on January 1. Prepare Jennifer Brent Corporation's 2002 journal entries.

BE22-9 Indiana Jones Corporation enters into a 6-year lease of machinery on January 1, 2002, which requires 6 annual payments of $30,000 each, beginning January 1, 2002. In addition, Indiana Jones guarantees the lessor a residual value of $20,000 at lease-end. The machinery has a useful life of 6 years. Prepare Indiana Jones' January 1, 2002, journal entries assuming an interest rate of 10%.

BE22-10 Use the information for Indiana Jones Corporation from BE22-9. Assume that for Lost Ark Company, the lessor, collectibility is reasonably predictable, there are no important uncertainties concerning costs, and the carrying amount of the machinery is $155,013. Prepare Lost Ark's January 1, 2002, journal entries.

BE22-11 Starfleet Corporation manufactures replicators. On January 1, 2002, it leased to Ferengi Company a replicator that had cost $110,000 to manufacture. The lease agreement covers the 5-year useful life of the replicator and requires 5 equal annual rentals of $45,400 each. An interest rate of 12% is implicit in the lease agreement. Collectibility of the rentals is reasonably assured, and there are no important uncertainties concerning costs. Prepare Starfleet's January 1, 2002, journal entries.

***BE22-12** On January 1, 2002, Acme Animation sold a truck to Coyote Finance for $35,000 and immediately leased it back. The truck was carried on Acme's books at $28,000. The term of the lease is 5 years, and title transfers to Acme at lease-end. The lease requires five equal rental payments of $9,233 at the end of each year. The appropriate rate of interest is 10%, and the truck has a useful life of 5 years with no salvage value. Prepare Acme's 2002 journal entries.

EXERCISES

E22-1 (Lessee Entries; Capital Lease with Unguaranteed Residual Value) On January 1, 2001, Burke Corporation signed a 5-year noncancelable lease for a machine. The terms of the lease called for Burke to make annual payments of $8,668 at the beginning of each year, starting January 1, 2001. The machine has an estimated useful life of 6 years and a $5,000 unguaranteed residual value. The machine reverts back to the lessor at the end of the lease term. Burke uses the straight-line method of depreciation for all of its plant assets. Burke's incremental borrowing rate is 10%, and the Lessor's implicit rate is unknown.

Instructions

(a) What type of lease is this? Explain.
(b) Compute the present value of the minimum lease payments.
(c) Prepare all necessary journal entries for Burke for this lease through January 1, 2002.

E22-2 (Lessee Computations and Entries; Capital Lease with Guaranteed Residual Value) Pat Delaney Company leases an automobile with a fair value of $8,725 from John Simon Motors, Inc., on the following terms:

1. Noncancelable term of 50 months.
2. Rental of $200 per month (at end of each month; present value at 1% per month is $7,840).
3. Estimated residual value after 50 months is $1,180 (the present value at 1% per month is $715). Delaney Company guarantees the residual value of $1,180.
4. Estimated economic life of the automobile is 60 months.
5. Delaney Company's incremental borrowing rate is 12% a year (1% a month). Simon's implicit rate is unknown.

Instructions

(a) What is the nature of this lease to Delaney Company?
(b) What is the present value of the minimum lease payments?
(c) Record the lease on Delaney Company's books at the date of inception.

(d) Record the first month's depreciation on Delaney Company's books (assume straight-line).
(e) Record the first month's lease payment.

E22-3 (Lessee Entries; Capital Lease with Executory Costs and Unguaranteed Residual Value) On January 1, 2002, Lahey Paper co. signs a 10-year noncancelable lease agreement to lease a storage building from Sheffield Storage Company. The following information pertains to this lease agreement:

1. The agreement requires equal rental payments of $72,000 beginning on January 1, 2002.
2. The fair value of the building on January 1, 2002 is $440,000.
3. The building has an estimated economic life of 12 years, with an unguaranteed residual value of $10,000. Lahey Paper Co. depreciates similar buildings on the straight-line method.
4. The lease is nonrenewable. At the termination of the lease, the building reverts to the lessor.
5. Lahey Paper's incremental borrowing rate is 12% per year. The lessor's implicit rate is not known by Lahey Paper Co.
6. The yearly rental payment includes $2,470.51 of executory costs related to taxes on the property.

Instructions

Prepare the journal entries on the lessee's books to reflect the signing of the lease agreement and to record the payments and expenses related to this lease for the years 2002 and 2003. Lahey Paper's corporate year end is December 31.

E22-4 (Lessor Entries; Direct Financing Lease with Option to Purchase) Castle Leasing Company signs a lease agreement on January 1, 2002, to lease electronic equipment to Jan Way Company. The term of the noncancelable lease is 2 years and payments are required at the end of each year. The following information relates to this agreement:

1. Jan Way Company has the option to purchase the equipment for $16,000 upon the termination of the lease.
2. The equipment has a cost and fair value of $160,000 to Castle Leasing Company; the useful economic life is 2 years, with a salvage value of $16,000.
3. Jan Way Company is required to pay $5,000 each year to the lessor for executory costs.
4. Castle Leasing Company desires to earn a return of 10% on its investment.
5. Collectibility of the payments is reasonably predictable, and there are no important uncertainties surrounding the costs yet to be incurred by the lessor.

Instructions

(a) Prepare the journal entries on the books of Castle Leasing to reflect the payments received under the lease and to recognize income for the years 2002 and 2003.
(b) Assuming that Jan Way Company exercises its option to purchase the equipment on December 31, 2003, prepare the journal entry to reflect the sale on Castle's books.

E22-5 (Type of Lease; Amortization Schedule) Mike Maroscia Leasing Company leases a new machine that has a cost and fair value of $95,000 to Maggie Sharrer Corporation on a 3-year noncancelable contract. Maggie Sharrer Corporation agrees to assume all risks of normal ownership including such costs as insurance, taxes, and maintenance. The machine has a 3-year useful life and no residual value. The lease was signed on January 1, 2002; Mike Maroscia Leasing Company expects to earn a 9% return on its investment. The annual rentals are payable on each December 31.

Instructions

(a) Discuss the nature of the lease arrangement and the accounting method that each party to the lease should apply.
(b) Prepare an amortization schedule that would be suitable for both the lessor and the lessee and that covers all the years involved.

E22-6 (Lessor Entries; Sales-Type Lease) Crosley Company, a machinery dealer, leased a machine to Dexter Corporation on January 1, 2001. The lease is for an 8-year period and requires equal annual payments of $35,013 at the beginning of each year. The first payment is received on January 1, 2001. Crosley had purchased the machine during 2000 for $160,000. Collectibility of lease payments is reasonably predictable, and no important uncertainties surround the amount of costs yet to be incurred by Crosley. Crosley set the annual rental to ensure an 11% rate of return. The machine has an economic life of 10 years with no residual value and reverts to Crosley at the termination of the lease.

Instructions

(a) Compute the amount of each of the following:
    (1) Gross investment.
    (2) Unearned interest revenue.
(b) Prepare all necessary journal entries for Crosley for 2001.

E22-7 (Lessee-Lessor Entries; Sales-Type Lease) On January 1, 2001, Bensen Company leased equipment to Flynn Corporation. The following information pertains to this lease:

1. The term of the noncancelable lease is 6 years, with no renewal option. The equipment reverts to the lessor at the termination of the lease.
2. Equal rental payments are due on January 1 of each year, beginning in 2001.
3. The fair value of the equipment on January 1, 2001, is $150,000, and its cost is $120,000.
4. The equipment has an economic life of 8 years, with an unguaranteed residual value of $10,000. Flynn depreciates all of its equipment on a straight-line basis.
5. Bensen set the annual rental to ensure an 11% rate of return. Flynn's incremental borrowing rate is 12%, and the implicit rate of the lessor is unknown.
6. Collectibility of lease payments is reasonably predictable, and no important uncertainties surround the amount of costs yet to be incurred by the lessor.

Instructions

(a) Discuss the nature of this lease to Bensen and Flynn.
(b) Calculate the amount of the annual rental payment.
(c) Prepare all the necessary journal entries for Flynn for 2001.
(d) Prepare all the necessary journal entries for Bensen for 2001.

E22-8 (Lessee Entries with Bargain Purchase Option) The following facts pertain to a noncancelable lease agreement between Mike Mooney Leasing Company and Denise Rode Company, a lessee.

Inception date:	May 1, 2001
Annual lease payment due at the beginning of each year, beginning with May 1, 2001	$21,227.65
Bargain purchase option price at end of lease term	$ 4,000.00
Lease term	5 years
Economic life of leased equipment	10 years
Lessor's cost	$65,000.00
Fair value of asset at May 1, 2001	$91,000.00
Lessor's implicit rate	10%
Lessee's incremental borrowing rate	10%

The collectibility of the lease payments is reasonably predictable, and there are no important uncertainties surrounding the costs yet to be incurred by the lessor. The lessee assumes responsibility for all executory costs.

Instructions

(Round all numbers to the nearest cent.)

(a) Discuss the nature of this lease to Rode Company.
(b) Discuss the nature of this lease to Mooney Company.
(c) Prepare a lease amortization schedule for Rode Company for the 5-year lease term.
(d) Prepare the journal entries on the lessee's books to reflect the signing of the lease agreement and to record the payments and expenses related to this lease for the years 2001 and 2002. Rode's annual accounting period ends on December 31. Reversing entries are used by Rode.

E22-9 (Lessor Entries with Bargain Purchase Option) A lease agreement between Mooney Leasing Company and Rode Company is described in E22-8.

Instructions

(Round all numbers to the nearest cent.)

Refer to the data in E22-8 and do the following for the lessor:

(a) Compute the amount of gross investment at the inception of the lease.
(b) Compute the amount of net investment at the inception of the lease.
(c) Prepare a lease amortization schedule for Mooney Leasing Company for the 5-year lease term.
(d) Prepare the journal entries to reflect the signing of the lease agreement and to record the receipts and income related to this lease for the years 2001, 2002, and 2003. The lessor's accounting period ends on December 31. Reversing entries are not used by Mooney.

E22-10 (Computation of Rental; Journal Entries for Lessor) Morgan Marie Leasing Company signs an agreement on January 1, 2001, to lease equipment to Cole William Company. The following information relates to this agreement.

1. The term of the noncancelable lease is 6 years with no renewal option. The equipment has an estimated economic life of 6 years.

2. The cost of the asset to the lessor is $245,000. The fair value of the asset at January 1, 2001, is $245,000.
3. The asset will revert to the lessor at the end of the lease term at which time the asset is expected to have a residual value of $43,622, none of which is guaranteed.
4. Cole William Company assumes direct responsibility for all executory costs.
5. The agreement requires equal annual rental payments, beginning on January 1, 2001.
6. Collectibility of the lease payments is reasonably predictable. There are no important uncertainties surrounding the amount of costs yet to be incurred by the lessor.

Instructions

(Round all numbers to the nearest cent.)

(a) Assuming the lessor desires a 10% rate of return on its investment, calculate the amount of the annual rental payment required. Round to the nearest dollar.

(b) Prepare an amortization schedule that would be suitable for the lessor for the lease term.

(c) Prepare all of the journal entries for the lessor for 2001 and 2002 to record the lease agreement, the receipt of lease payments, and the recognition of income. Assume the lessor's annual accounting period ends on December 31.

E22-11 (Amortization Schedule and Journal Entries for Lessee) Laura Potts Leasing Company signs an agreement on January 1, 2001, to lease equipment to Janet Plote Company. The following information relates to this agreement.

1. The term of the noncancelable lease is 5 years with no renewal option. The equipment has an estimated economic life of 5 years.
2. The fair value of the asset at January 1, 2001, is $80,000.
3. The asset will revert to the lessor at the end of the lease term, at which time the asset is expected to have a residual value of $7,000, none of which is guaranteed.
4. Plote Company assumes direct responsibility for all executory costs, which include the following annual amounts: (1) $900 to Rocky Mountain Insurance Company for insurance; (2) $1,600 to Laclede County for property taxes.
5. The agreement requires equal annual rental payments of $18,142.95 to the lessor, beginning on January 1, 2001.
6. The lessee's incremental borrowing rate is 12%. The lessor's implicit rate is 10% and is known to the lessee.
7. Plote Company uses the straight-line depreciation method for all equipment.
8. Plote uses reversing entries when appropriate.

Instructions

(Round all numbers to the nearest cent.)

(a) Prepare an amortization schedule that would be suitable for the lessee for the lease term.

(b) Prepare all of the journal entries for the lessee for 2001 and 2002 to record the lease agreement, the lease payments, and all expenses related to this lease. Assume the lessee's annual accounting period ends on December 31.

E22-12 (Accounting for an Operating Lease) On January 1, 2001, Doug Nelson Co. leased a building to Patrick Wise Inc. The relevant information related to the lease is as follows:

1. The lease arrangement is for 10 years.
2. The leased building cost $4,500,000 and was purchased for cash on January 1, 2001.
3. The building is depreciated on a straight-line basis. Its estimated economic life is 50 years.
4. Lease payments are $275,000 per year and are made at the end of the year.
5. Property tax expense of $85,000 and insurance expense of $10,000 on the building were incurred by Nelson in the first year. Payment on these two items was made at the end of the year.
6. Both the lessor and the lessee are on a calendar-year basis.

Instructions

(a) Prepare the journal entries that Nelson Co. should make in 2001.

(b) Prepare the journal entries that Wise Inc. should make in 2001.

(c) If Nelson paid $30,000 to a real estate broker on January 1, 2001, as a fee for finding the lessee, how much should be reported as an expense for this item in 2001 by Nelson Co.?

E22-13 (Accounting for an Operating Lease) On January 1, 2002, a machine was purchased for $900,000 by Tom Young Co. The machine is expected to have an 8-year life with no salvage value. It is to be depreciated on a straight-line basis. The machine was leased to St. Leger Inc. on January 1, 2002, at an annual rental of $210,000. Other relevant information is as follows:

1. The lease term is for 3 years.
2. Tom Young Co. incurred maintenance and other executory costs of $25,000 in 2002 related to this lease.
3. The machine could have been sold by Tom Young Co. for $940,000 instead of leasing it.
4. St. Leger is required to pay a rent security deposit of $35,000 and to prepay the last month's rent of $17,500.

Instructions

(a) How much should Tom Young Co. report as income before income tax on this lease for 2002?
(b) What amount should St. Leger Inc. report for rent expense for 2002 on this lease?

E22-14 (Operating Lease for Lessee and Lessor) On February 20, 2001, Barbara Brent Inc., purchased a machine for $1,500,000 for the purpose of leasing it. The machine is expected to have a 10-year life, no residual value, and will be depreciated on the straight-line basis. The machine was leased to Chuck Rudy Company on March 1, 2001, for a 4-year period at a monthly rental of $19,500. There is no provision for the renewal of the lease or purchase of the machine by the lessee at the expiration of the lease term. Brent paid $30,000 of commissions associated with negotiating the lease in February 2001:

Instructions

(a) What expense should Chuck Rudy Company record as a result of the facts above for the year ended December 31, 2001? Show supporting computations in good form.
(b) What income or loss before income taxes should Brent record as a result of the facts above for the year ended December 31, 2001? (*Hint:* Amortize commissions over the life of the lease.)

(AICPA adapted)

***E22-15 (Sale and Leaseback)** On January 1, 2001, Hein Do Corporation sells a computer to Liquidity Finance Co. for $680,000 and immediately leases the computer back. The relevant information is as follows:

1. The computer was carried on Hein Do's books at a value of $600,000.
2. The term of the noncancelable lease is 10 years; title will transfer to Hein Do.
3. The lease agreement requires equal rental payments of $110,666.81 at the end of each year.
4. The incremental borrowing rate of Hein Do Corporation is 12%. Hein Do is aware that Liquidity Finance Co. set the annual rental to insure a rate of return of 10%.
5. The computer has a fair value of $680,000 on January 1, 2001, and an estimated economic life of 10 years.
6. Hein Do pays executory costs of $9,000 per year.

Instructions

Prepare the journal entries for both the lessee and the lessor for 2001 to reflect the sale and leaseback agreement. No uncertainties exist, and collectibility is reasonably certain.

***E22-16 (Lessee-Lessor, Sale-Leaseback)** Presented below are four independent situations:

(a) On December 31, 2002, Nancy Zarle Inc. sold computer equipment to Erin Daniell Co. and immediately leased it back for 10 years. The sales price of the equipment was $520,000, its carrying amount $400,000, and its estimated remaining economic life 12 years. Determine the amount of deferred revenue to be reported from the sale of the computer equipment on December 31, 2002.
(b) On December 31, 2002, Linda Wasicsko Co. sold a machine to Cross Co. and simultaneously leased it back for one year. The sale price of the machine was $480,000, the carrying amount $420,000, and it had an estimated remaining useful life of 14 years. The present value of the rental payments for the one year is $35,000. At December 31, 2002, how much should Linda Wasicsko report as deferred revenue from the sale of the machine?
(c) On January 1, 2002, Joe McKane Corp. sold an airplane with an estimated useful life of 10 years. At the same time, Joe McKane leased back the plane for 10 years. The sales price of the airplane was $500,000, the carrying amount $379,000, and the annual rental $73,975.22. Joe McKane Corp. intends to depreciate the leased asset using the sum-of-the-years'-digits depreciation method. Discuss how the gain on the sale should be reported at the end of 2002 in the financial statements.
(d) On January 1, 2002, Dick Sondgeroth Co. sold equipment with an estimated useful life of 5 years. At the same time, Dick Sondgeroth leased back the equipment for 2 years under a lease classified as an operating lease. The sales price (fair market value) of the equipment was $212,700, the carrying amount was $300,000, the monthly rental under the lease $6,000, and the present value of the rental payments $115,753. For the year ended December 31, 2002, determine which items would be reported on its income statement for the sale-leaseback transaction.

PROBLEMS

P22-1 (Lessee-Lessor Entries; Sales-Type Lease) Stine Leasing Company agrees to lease machinery to Potter Corporation on January 1, 2001. The following information relates to the lease agreement:

1. The term of the lease is 7 years with no renewal option, and the machinery has an estimated economic life of 9 years.
2. The cost of the machinery is $420,000, and the fair value of the asset on 1/1/01 is $560,000.
3. At the end of the lease term the asset reverts to the lessor. At the end of the lease term the asset is expected to have a guaranteed residual value of $80,000. Potter depreciates all of its equipment on a straight-line basis.
4. The lease agreement requires equal annual rental payments, beginning on January 1, 2001.
5. The collectibility of the lease payments is reasonably predictable and there are no important uncertainties surrounding the amount of costs yet to be incurred by the lessor.
6. Stine desires a 10% rate of return on its investments. Potter's incremental borrowing rate is 11%, and the lessor's implicit rate is unknown.

Instructions

(a) Discuss the nature of this lease for both the lessee and the lessor.
(b) Calculate the amount of the annual rental payment required.
(c) Compute the present value of the minimum lease payments.
(d) Prepare the journal entries Potter would make in 2001 and 2002 related to the lease arrangement.
(e) Prepare the journal entries Stine would make in 2001 and 2002.

P22-2 (Lessee-Lessor Entries; Operating Lease) Synergetics Inc. leased a new crane to M. K. Gumowski Construction under a 5-year noncancelable contract starting January 1, 2002. Terms of the lease require payments of $22,000 each January 1, starting January 1, 2002. Synergetics will pay insurance, taxes, and maintenance charges on the crane, which has an estimated life of 12 years, a fair value of $160,000, and a cost to Synergetics of $160,000. The estimated fair value of the crane is expected to be $45,000 at the end of the lease term. No bargain purchase or renewal options are included in the contract. Both Synergetics and Gumowski adjust and close books annually at December 31. Collectibility of the lease payments is reasonably certain and no uncertainties exist relative to unreimbursable lessor costs. Gumowski's incremental borrowing rate is 10% and Synergetics' implicit interest rate of 9% is known to Gumowski.

Instructions

(a) Identify the type of lease involved and give reasons for your classification. Discuss the accounting treatment that should be applied by both the lessee and the lessor.
(b) Prepare all the entries related to the lease contract and leased asset for the year 2002 for the lessee and lessor, assuming:
  (1) Insurance, $500.
  (2) Taxes, $2,000.
  (3) Maintenance, $650.
  (4) Straight-line depreciation and salvage value, $10,000.
(c) Discuss what should be presented in the balance sheet and income statement and related notes of both the lessee and the lessor at December 31, 2002.

P22-3 (Lessee-Lessor Entries, Balance Sheet Presentation; Sales-Type Lease) Cascade Industries and Barbara Hardy Inc. enter into an agreement that requires Barbara Hardy Inc. to build three diesel-electric engines to Cascade's specifications. Upon completion of the engines, Cascade has agreed to lease them for a period of 10 years and to assume all costs and risks of ownership. The lease is noncancelable, becomes effective on January 1, 2002, and requires annual rental payments of $620,956 each January 1, starting January 1, 2002.

Cascade's incremental borrowing rate is 10%, and the implicit interest rate used by Barbara Hardy Inc. and known to Cascade is 8%. The total cost of building the three engines is $3,900,000. The economic life of the engines is estimated to be 10 years with residual value set at zero. Cascade depreciates similar equipment on a straight-line basis. At the end of the lease, Cascade assumes title to the engines. Collectibility of the lease payments is reasonably certain and no uncertainties exist relative to unreimbursable lessor costs.

Instructions

(Round all numbers to the nearest dollar.)

(a) Discuss the nature of this lease transaction from the viewpoints of both lessee and lessor.
(b) Prepare the journal entry or entries to record the transaction on January 1, 2002, on the books of Cascade Industries.

(c) Prepare the journal entry or entries to record the transaction on January 1, 2002, on the books of Barbara Hardy Inc.
(d) Prepare the journal entries for both the lessee and lessor to record the first rental payment on January 1, 2002.
(e) Prepare the journal entries for both the lessee and lessor to record interest expense (revenue) at December 31, 2002. (Prepare a lease amortization schedule for 2 years.)
(f) Show the items and amounts that would be reported on the balance sheet (not notes) at December 31, 2002, for both the lessee and the lessor.

P22-4 (Balance Sheet and Income Statement Disclosure—Lessee) The following facts pertain to a noncancelable lease agreement between Ben Alschuler Leasing Company and John McKee Electronics, a lessee, for a computer system.

Inception date:	October 1, 2001
Lease term	6 years
Economic life of leased equipment	6 years
Fair value of asset at October 1, 2001	$200,255
Residual value at end of lease term	–0–
Lessor's implicit rate	10%
Lessee's incremental borrowing rate	10%
Annual lease payment due at the beginning of each year, beginning with October 1, 2001	$41,800

The collectibility of the lease payments is reasonably predictable, and there are no important uncertainties surrounding the costs yet to be incurred by the lessor. The lessee assumes responsibility for all executory costs, which amount to $5,500 per year and are to be paid each October 1, beginning October 1, 2001. (This $5,500 is not included in the rental payment of $41,800.) The asset will revert to the lessor at the end of the lease term. The straight-line depreciation method is used for all equipment.

The following amortization schedule has been prepared correctly for use by both the lessor and the lessee in accounting for this lease. The lease is to be accounted for properly as a capital lease by the lessee and as a direct financing lease by the lessor.

Date	Annual Lease Payment/ Receipt	Interest (10%) on Unpaid Obligation/ Net Investment	Reduction of Lease Obligation/ Net Investment	Balance of Lease Obligation/ Net Investment
10/01/01				$200,255
10/01/01	$ 41,800		$ 41,800	158,455
10/01/02	41,800	$15,846	25,954	132,501
10/01/03	41,800	13,250	28,550	103,951
10/01/04	41,800	10,395	31,405	72,546
10/01/05	41,800	7,255	34,545	38,001
10/01/06	41,800	3,799*	38,001	–0–
	$250,800	$50,545	$200,255	

*Rounding error is $1.

Instructions

(Round all numbers to the nearest cent.)

(a) Assuming the lessee's accounting period ends on September 30, answer the following questions with respect to this lease agreement:
  (1) What items and amounts will appear on the lessee's income statement for the year ending September 30, 2002?
  (2) What items and amounts will appear on the lessee's balance sheet at September 30, 2002?
  (3) What items and amounts will appear on the lessee's income statement for the year ending September 30, 2003?
  (4) What items and amounts will appear on the lessee's balance sheet at September 30, 2003?

(b) Assuming the lessee's accounting period ends on December 31, answer the following questions with respect to this lease agreement:
  (1) What items and amounts will appear on the lessee's income statement for the year ending December 31, 2001?
  (2) What items and amounts will appear on the lessee's balance sheet at December 31, 2001?

(3) What items and amounts will appear on the lessee's income statement for the year ending December 31, 2002?
(4) What items and amounts will appear on the lessee's balance sheet at December 31, 2002?

P22-5 (Balance Sheet and Income Statement Disclosure—Lessor) Assume the same information as in P22-4.

Instructions

(Round all numbers to the nearest cent.)

(a) Assuming the lessor's accounting period ends on September 30, answer the following questions with respect to this lease agreement:
(1) What items and amounts will appear on the lessor's income statement for the year ending September 30, 2002?
(2) What items and amounts will appear on the lessor's balance sheet at September 30, 2002?
(3) What items and amounts will appear on the lessor's income statement for the year ending September 30, 2003?
(4) What items and amounts will appear on the lessor's balance sheet at September 30, 2003?

(b) Assuming the lessor's accounting period ends on December 31, answer the following questions with respect to this lease agreement:
(1) What items and amounts will appear on the lessor's income statement for the year ending December 31, 2001?
(2) What items and amounts will appear on the lessor's balance sheet at December 31, 2001?
(3) What items and amounts will appear on the lessor's income statement for the year ending December 31, 2002?
(4) What items and amounts will appear on the lessor's balance sheet at December 31, 2002?

P22-6 (Lessee Entries with Residual Value) The following facts pertain to a noncancelable lease agreement between Frank Voris Leasing Company and Tom Zarle Company, a lessee.

Inception date:	January 1, 2001
Annual lease payment due at the beginning of each year, beginning with January 1, 2001	$81,365
Residual value of equipment at end of lease term, guaranteed by the lessee	$50,000
Lease term	6 years
Economic life of leased equipment	6 years
Fair value of asset at January 1, 2001	$400,000.00
Lessor's implicit rate	12%
Lessee's incremental borrowing rate	12%

The lessee assumes responsibility for all executory costs, which are expected to amount to $4,000 per year. The asset will revert to the lessor at the end of the lease term. The lessee has guaranteed the lessor a residual value of $50,000. The lessee uses the straight-line depreciation method for all equipment.

Instructions

(Round all numbers to the nearest cent.)

(a) Prepare an amortization schedule that would be suitable for the lessee for the lease term.
(b) Prepare all of the journal entries for the lessee for 2001 and 2002 to record the lease agreement, the lease payments, and all expenses related to this lease. Assume the lessee's annual accounting period ends on December 31 and reversing entries are used when appropriate.

P22-7 (Lessee Entries and Balance Sheet Presentation; Capital Lease) Hilary Brennan Steel Company as lessee signed a lease agreement for equipment for 5 years, beginning December 31, 2001. Annual rental payments of $32,000 are to be made at the beginning of each lease year (December 31). The taxes, insurance, and the maintenance costs are the obligation of the lessee. The interest rate used by the lessor in setting the payment schedule is 10%; Brennan's incremental borrowing rate is 12%. Brennan is unaware of the rate being used by the lessor. At the end of the lease, Brennan has the option to buy the equipment for $1, considerably below its estimated fair value at that time. The equipment has an estimated useful life of 7 years and no salvage value has been added. Brennan uses the straight-line method of depreciation on similar owned equipment.

Instructions

(Round all numbers to the nearest dollar.)

(a) Prepare the journal entry or entries, with explanations, that should be recorded on December 31, 2001, by Brennan. (Assume no residual value.)

(b) Prepare the journal entry or entries, with explanations, that should be recorded on December 31, 2002, by Brennan. (Prepare the lease amortization schedule for all five payments.)

(c) Prepare the journal entry or entries, with explanations, that should be recorded on December 31, 2003, by Brennan.

(d) What amounts would appear on Brennan's December 31, 2003, balance sheet relative to the lease arrangement?

P22-8 (Lessee Entries and Balance Sheet Presentation; Capital Lease) On January 1, 2002, Charlie Doss Company contracts to lease equipment for 5 years, agreeing to make a payment of $94,732 (including the executory costs of $6,000) at the beginning of each year, starting January 1, 2002. The taxes, the insurance, and the maintenance, estimated at $6,000 a year, are the obligations of the lessee. The leased equipment is to be capitalized at $370,000. The asset is to be amortized on a double-declining-balance basis and the obligation is to be reduced on an effective-interest basis. Doss's incremental borrowing rate is 12%, and the implicit rate in the lease is 10%, which is known by Doss. Title to the equipment transfers to Doss when the lease expires. The asset has an estimated useful life of 5 years and no residual value.

Instructions

(Round all numbers to the nearest dollar.)

(a) Explain the probable relationship of the $370,000 amount to the lease arrangement.

(b) Prepare the journal entry or entries that should be recorded on January 1, 2002, by Charlie Doss Company.

(c) Prepare the journal entry to record depreciation of the leased asset for the year 2002.

(d) Prepare the journal entry to record the interest expense for the year 2002.

(e) Prepare the journal entry to record the lease payment of January 1, 2003, assuming reversing entries are not made.

(f) What amounts will appear on the lessee's December 31, 2002, balance sheet relative to the lease contract?

P22-9 (Lessee Entries, Capital Lease with Monthly Payments) John Roesch Inc. was incorporated in 2000 to operate as a computer software service firm with an accounting fiscal year ending August 31. Roesch's primary product is a sophisticated on-line inventory-control system; its customers pay a fixed fee plus a usage charge for using the system.

Roesch has leased a large, Alpha-3 computer system from the manufacturer. The lease calls for a monthly rental of $50,000 for the 144 months (12 years) of the lease term. The estimated useful life of the computer is 15 years.

Each scheduled monthly rental payment includes $4,000 for full-service maintenance on the computer to be performed by the manufacturer. All rentals are payable on the first day of the month beginning with August 1, 2001, the date the computer was installed and the lease agreement was signed.

The lease is noncancelable for its 12-year term, and it is secured only by the manufacturer's chattel lien on the Alpha-3 system. Roesch can purchase the Alpha-3 system from the manufacturer at the end of the 12-year lease term for 75% of the computer's fair value at that time.

This lease is to be accounted for as a capital lease by Roesch, and it will be depreciated by the straight-line method with no expected salvage value. Borrowed funds for this type of transaction would cost Roesch 12% per year (1% per month). Following is a schedule of the present value of $1 for selected periods discounted at 1% per period when payments are made at the beginning of each period.

Periods (months)	Present Value of $1 per Period Discounted at 1% per Period
1	1.000
2	1.990
3	2.970
143	76.658
144	76.899

Instructions

Prepare, in general journal form, all entries Roesch should have made in its accounting records during August 2001 relating to this lease. Give full explanations and show supporting computations for each entry. Remember, August 31, 2001, is the end of Roesch's fiscal accounting period and it will be preparing financial statements on that date. Do not prepare closing entries.

(AICPA adapted)

P22-10 (Lessor Computations and Entries; Sales-Type Lease with Unguaranteed RV) Thomas Hanson Company manufactures a computer with an estimated economic life of 12 years and leases it to Flypaper Airlines for a period of 10 years. The normal selling price of the equipment is $210,482, and its unguaranteed residual value at the end of the lease term is estimated to be $20,000. Flypaper will pay annual payments of $30,000 at the beginning of each year and all maintenance, insurance, and taxes. Hanson incurred costs of $135,000 in manufacturing the equipment and $4,000 in negotiating and closing the lease. Hanson has determined that the collectibility of the lease payments is reasonably predictable, that no additional costs will be incurred, and that the implicit interest rate is 10%.

Instructions

(Round all numbers to the nearest dollar.)

(a) Discuss the nature of this lease in relation to the lessor and compute the amount of each of the following items:

  (1) Gross investment.

  (2) Unearned interest revenue.

  (3) Sales price.

  (4) Cost of sales.

(b) Prepare a 10-year lease amortization schedule.

(c) Prepare all of the lessor's journal entries for the first year.

P22-11 (Lessee Computations and Entries; Capital Lease with Unguaranteed Residual Value) Assume the same data as in P22-10 with Flypaper Airlines Co. having an incremental borrowing rate of 10%.

Instructions

(Round all numbers to the nearest dollar.)

(a) Discuss the nature of this lease in relation to the lessee and compute the amount of the initial obligation under capital leases.

(b) Prepare a 10-year lease amortization schedule.

(c) Prepare all of the lessee's journal entries for the first year.

P22-12 (Lessor Computations; Unearned Revenue Recognized Using Sum-of-Month's-Digits) During 2002, Frank Beals Robinson Leasing Co. began leasing equipment to small manufacturers. Below is information regarding leasing arrangement.

1. Frank Beals Robinson Leasing Co. leases equipment with terms from 3 to 5 years depending upon the useful life of the equipment. At the expiration of the lease, the equipment will be sold to the lessee at 10% of the lessor's cost, the expected salvage value of the equipment.
2. The amount of the lessee's monthly payment is computed by multiplying the lessor's cost of the equipment by the payment factor applicable to the term of lease.

Term of Lease	Payment Factor
3 years	3.32%
4 years	2.63%
5 years	2.22%

3. The excess of the gross contract receivable for equipment rentals over the cost (reduced by the estimated salvage value at the termination of the lease) is recognized as revenue over the term of the lease under the sum-of-the-year's-digits method computed on a monthly basis.
4. The following leases were entered into during 2002:

Machine	Dates of Lease	Period of Lease	Machine Cost
Die	7/1/02–6/30/06	4 years	$150,000
Press	9/1/02–8/31/05	3 years	$120,000

Instructions

(a) Prepare a schedule of gross contracts receivable for equipment rentals at the dates of the lease for the die and press machines.

(b) Prepare a schedule of unearned lease income at December 31, 2002, for each machine lease.

(c) Prepare a schedule computing the present dollar value of lease payments receivable (gross investment) for equipment rentals at December 31, 2002. (The present dollar value of the "lease receivables for equipment rentals" is the outstanding amount of the gross lease receivables less the unearned lease income included therein.) Without prejudice to your solution to part (b), assume that the unearned lease income at December 31, 2002, was $68,000.

(AICPA adapted)

P22-13 (Basic Lessee Accounting with Difficult PV Calculation) In 1999 Judy Yin Trucking Company negotiated and closed a long-term lease contract for newly constructed truck terminals and freight storage facilities. The buildings were erected to the company's specifications on land owned by the company. On January 1, 2000, Judy Yin Trucking Company took possession of the lease properties. On January 1, 2000 and 2001, the company made cash payments of $1,048,000 that were recorded as rental expenses.

Although the terminals have a composite useful life of 40 years, the noncancelable lease runs for 20 years from January 1, 2000, with a bargain purchase option available upon expiration of the lease.

The 20-year lease is effective for the period January 1, 2000, through December 31, 2019. Advance rental payments of $900,000 are payable to the lessor on January 1 of each of the first 10 years of the lease term. Advance rental payments of $320,000 are due on January 1 for each of the last 10 years of the lease. The company has an option to purchase all of these leased facilities for $1 on December 31, 2019. It also must make annual payments to the lessor of $125,000 for property taxes and $23,000 for insurance. The lease was negotiated to assure the lessor a 6% rate of return.

Instructions

(Round all numbers to the nearest dollar.)

(a) Prepare a schedule to compute for Judy Yin Trucking Company the discounted present value of the terminal facilities and related obligation at January 1, 2000.

(b) Assuming that the discounted present value of terminal facilities and related obligation at January 1, 2000, was $8,400,000, prepare journal entries for Judy Yin Trucking Company to record the:

(1) Cash payment to the lessor on January 1, 2002.

(2) Amortization of the cost of the leased properties for 2002 using the straight-line method and assuming a zero salvage value.

(3) Accrual of interest expense at December 31, 2002.

Selected present value factors are as follows:

Periods	For an Ordinary Annuity of $1 at 6%	For $1 at 6%
1	.943396	.943396
2	1.833393	.889996
8	6.209794	.627412
9	6.801692	.591898
10	7.360087	.558395
19	11.158117	.330513
20	11.469921	.311805

(AICPA adapted)

P22-14 (Lessor Computations and Entries; Sales-Type Lease with Guaranteed Residual Value) Laura Jennings Inc. manufactures an X-ray machine with an estimated life of 12 years and leases it to Craig Gocker Medical Center for a period of 10 years. The normal selling price of the machine is $343,734, and its guaranteed residual value at the end of the lease term is estimated to be $15,000. The hospital will pay rents of $50,000 at the beginning of each year and all maintenance, insurance, and taxes. Laura Jennings Inc. incurred costs of $210,000 in manufacturing the machine and $14,000 in negotiating and closing the lease. Laura Jennings Inc. has determined that the collectibility of the lease payments is reasonably predictable, that there will be no additional costs incurred, and that the implicit interest rate is 10%.

Instructions

(Round all numbers to the nearest dollar.)

(a) Discuss the nature of this lease in relation to the lessor and compute the amount of each of the following items:

(1) Gross investment.
(2) Unearned interest revenue.
(3) Sales price.
(4) Cost of sales.

(b) Prepare a 10-year lease amortization schedule.

(c) Prepare all of the lessor's journal entries for the first year.

P22-15 (Lessee Computations and Entries; Capital Lease with Guaranteed Residual Value) Assume the same data as in P22-14 and that Craig Gocker Medical Center has an incremental borrowing rate of 10%.

Instructions

(Round all numbers to the nearest dollar.)

(a) Discuss the nature of this lease in relation to the lessee and compute the amount of the initial obligation under capital leases.

(b) Prepare a 10-year lease amortization schedule.

(c) Prepare all of the lessee's journal entries for the first year.

P22-16 (Operating Lease vs. Capital Lease) You are auditing the December 31, 2000, financial statements of Sarah Shamess, Inc., manufacturer of novelties and party favors. During your inspection of the company garage, you discovered that a 1999 Shirk automobile not listed in the equipment subsidiary ledger is parked in the company garage. You ask Sally Straub, plant manager, about the vehicle, and she tells you that the company did not list the automobile because the company was only leasing it. The lease agreement was entered into on January 1, 2000, with Jack Hayes New and Used Cars.

You decide to review the lease agreement to ensure that the lease should be afforded operating lease treatment, and you discover the following lease terms:

1. Noncancelable term of 50 months.
2. Rental of $180 per month (at the end of each month; present value at 1% per month is $7,055).
3. Estimated residual value after 50 months is $1,100 (the present value at 1% per month is $699). Shamess guarantees the residual value of $1,100.
4. Estimated economic life of the automobile is 60 months.
5. Shamess's incremental borrowing rate is 12% per year (1% per month).

Instructions

You are a senior auditor writing a memo to your supervisor, the audit partner in charge of this audit, to discuss the above situation. Be sure to include (a) why you inspected the lease agreement, (b) what you determined about the lease, and (c) how you advised your client to account for this lease. Explain every journal entry that you believe is necessary to record this lease properly on the client's books. (It is also necessary to include the fact that you communicated this information to your client.)

P22-17 (Lessee-Lessor Accounting for Residual Values) Jodie Lanier Dairy leases its milking equipment from Steve Zeff Finance Company under the following lease terms:

1. The lease term is 10 years, noncancelable, and requires equal rental payments of $25,250 due at the beginning of each year starting January 1, 2001.
2. The equipment has a fair value and cost at the inception of the lease (January 1, 2001) of $185,078, an estimated economic life of 10 years, and a residual value (which is guaranteed by Lanier Dairy) of $20,000.
3. The lease contains no renewable options and the equipment reverts to Steve Zeff Finance Company upon termination of the lease.
4. Lanier Dairy's incremental borrowing rate is 9% per year; the implicit rate is also 9%.
5. Lanier Dairy depreciates similar equipment that it owns on a straight-line basis.
6. Collectibility of the payments is reasonably predictable, and there are no important uncertainties surrounding the costs yet to be incurred by the lessor.

Instructions

(a) Evaluate the criteria for classification of the lease and describe the nature of the lease. In general, discuss how the lessee and lessor should account for the lease transaction.

(b) Prepare the journal entries for the lessee and lessor at January 1, 2001, and December 31, 2001 (the lessee's and lessor's year-end). Assume no reversing entries.

(c) What would have been the amount capitalized by the lessee upon the inception of the lease if:
(1) The residual value of $20,000 had been guaranteed by a third party, not the lessee?
(2) The residual value of $20,000 had not been guaranteed at all?

(d) On the lessor's books, what would be the amount recorded as the Net Investment at the inception of the lease, assuming:
(1) The residual value of $20,000 had been guaranteed by a third party?
(2) The residual value of $20,000 had not been guaranteed at all?

(e) Suppose the useful life of the milking equipment is 20 years. How large would the residual value have to be at the end of 10 years in order for the lessee to qualify for the operating method? (Assume that the residual value would be guaranteed by a third party.) (*Hint:* The lessee's annual payments will be appropriately reduced as the residual value increases.)

CONCEPTUAL CASES

C22-1 (Lessee Accounting and Reporting) On January 1, 2002, Sandy Hayes Company entered into a noncancelable lease for a machine to be used in its manufacturing operations. The lease transfers ownership of the machine to Yen Quach by the end of the lease term. The term of the lease is 8 years. The minimum lease payment made by Yen Quach on January 1, 2002, was one of eight equal annual payments. At the inception of the lease, the criteria established for classification as a capital lease by the lessee were met.

Instructions

(a) What is the theoretical basis for the accounting standard that requires certain long-term leases to be capitalized by the lessee? Do not discuss the specific criteria for classifying a specific lease as a capital lease.

(b) How should Hayes account for this lease at its inception and determine the amount to be recorded?

(c) What expenses related to this lease will Hayes incur during the first year of the lease, and how will they be determined?

(d) How should Hayes report the lease transaction on its December 31, 2002, balance sheet?

C22-2 (Lessor and Lessee Accounting and Disclosure) Laurie Gocker Inc. entered into a lease arrangement with Nathan Morgan Leasing Corporation for a certain machine. Morgan's primary business is leasing and it is not a manufacturer or dealer. Gocker will lease the machine for a period of 3 years, which is 50% of the machine's economic life. Morgan will take possession of the machine at the end of the initial 3-year lease and lease it to another, smaller company that does not need the most current version of the machine. Gocker does not guarantee any residual value for the machine and will not purchase the machine at the end of the lease term.

Gocker's incremental borrowing rate is 15%, and the implicit rate in the lease is 14%. Gocker has no way of knowing the implicit rate used by Morgan. Using either rate, the present value of the minimum lease payments is between 90% and 100% of the fair value of the machine at the date of the lease agreement.

Gocker has agreed to pay all executory costs directly and no allowance for these costs is included in the lease payments.

Morgan is reasonably certain that Gocker will pay all lease payments, and, because Gocker has agreed to pay all executory costs, there are no important uncertainties regarding costs to be incurred by Morgan. Assume that no indirect costs are involved.

Instructions

(a) With respect to Gocker (the lessee), answer the following:

(1) What type of lease has been entered into? Explain the reason for your answer.

(2) How should Gocker compute the appropriate amount to be recorded for the lease or asset acquired?

(3) What accounts will be created or affected by this transaction and how will the lease or asset and other costs related to the transaction be matched with earnings?

(4) What disclosures must Gocker make regarding this leased asset?

(b) With respect to Morgan (the lessor), answer the following:

(1) What type of leasing arrangement has been entered into? Explain the reason for your answer.

(2) How should this lease be recorded by Morgan, and how are the appropriate amounts determined?

(3) How should Morgan determine the appropriate amount of earnings to be recognized from each lease payment?

(4) What disclosures must Morgan make regarding this lease?

(AICPA adapted)

C22-3 (Lessee Capitalization Criteria) On January 1, Melanie Shinault Company, a lessee, entered into three noncancelable leases for brand-new equipment, Lease L, Lease M, and Lease N. None of the three leases transfers ownership of the equipment to Melanie Shinault at the end of the lease term. For each of the three leases, the present value at the beginning of the lease term of the minimum lease payments, excluding that portion of the payments representing executory costs such as insurance, maintenance, and taxes to be paid by the lessor, is 75% of the fair value of the equipment.

The following information is peculiar to each lease:

1. Lease L does not contain a bargain purchase option; the lease term is equal to 80% of the estimated economic life of the equipment.
2. Lease M contains a bargain purchase option; the lease term is equal to 50% of the estimated economic life of the equipment.
3. Lease N does not contain a bargain purchase option; the lease term is equal to 50% of the estimated economic life of the equipment.

Instructions

(a) How should Melanie Shinault Company classify each of the three leases above, and why? Discuss the rationale for your answer.

(b) What amount, if any, should Melanie Shinault record as a liability at the inception of the lease for each of the three leases above?

(c) Assuming that the minimum lease payments are made on a straight-line basis, how should Melanie Shinault record each minimum lease payment for each of the three leases above?

(AICPA adapted)

C22-4 (Comparison of Different Types of Accounting by Lessee and Lessor)

Part 1

Capital leases and operating leases are the two classifications of leases described in FASB pronouncements from the standpoint of the **lessee**.

Instructions

(a) Describe how a capital lease would be accounted for by the lessee both at the inception of the lease and during the first year of the lease, assuming the lease transfers ownership of the property to the lessee by the end of the lease.

(b) Describe how an operating lease would be accounted for by the lessee both at the inception of the lease and during the first year of the lease, assuming equal monthly payments are made by the lessee at the beginning of each month of the lease. Describe the change in accounting, if any, when rental payments are not made on a straight-line basis.

Do **not** discuss the criteria for distinguishing between capital leases and operating leases.

Part 2

Sales-type leases and direct financing leases are two of the classifications of leases described in FASB pronouncements from the standpoint of the **lessor**.

Instructions

Compare and contrast a sales-type lease with a direct financing lease as follows:

(a) Gross investment in the lease.

(b) Amortization of unearned interest revenue.

(c) Manufacturer's or dealer's profit.

Do **not** discuss the criteria for distinguishing between the leases described above and operating leases.

(AICPA adapted)

C22-5 (Lessee Capitalization of Bargain Purchase Option) Brad Hayes Corporation is a diversified company with nationwide interests in commercial real estate developments, banking, copper mining, and metal fabrication. The company has offices and operating locations in major cities throughout the United States. Corporate headquarters for Brad Hayes Corporation is located in a metropolitan area of a midwestern state, and executives connected with various phases of company operations travel extensively. Corporate management is currently evaluating the feasibility of acquiring a business aircraft that can be used by company executives to expedite business travel to areas not adequately served by commercial airlines. Proposals for either leasing or purchasing a suitable aircraft have been analyzed, and the leasing proposal was considered to be more desirable.

The proposed lease agreement involves a twin-engine turboprop Viking that has a fair market value of $1,000,000. This plane would be leased for a period of 10 years beginning January 1, 2002. The lease agreement is cancelable only upon accidental destruction of the plane. An annual lease payment of $141,780 is due on January 1 of each year; the first payment is to be made on January 1, 2002. Maintenance operations are strictly scheduled by the lessor, and Brad Hayes Corporation will pay for these services as they are performed. Estimated annual maintenance costs are $6,900. The lessor will pay all insurance premiums and local property taxes, which amount to a combined total of $4,000 annually and are included in the annual lease payment of $141,780. Upon expiration of the 10-year lease, Brad Hayes Corporation can purchase the Viking for $44,440. The estimated useful life of the plane is 15 years, and its salvage value in the used plane market is estimated to be $100,000 after 10 years. The salvage value probably will never be less than $75,000 if the engines are overhauled and maintained as prescribed by the manufacturer. If the purchase option is not exercised, possession of the plane will revert to the lessor, and there is no provision for renewing the lease agreement beyond its termination on December 31, 2011.

Brad Hayes Corporation can borrow $1,000,000 under a 10-year term loan agreement at an annual interest rate of 12%. The lessor's implicit interest rate is not expressly stated in the lease agreement, but this rate appears to be approximately 8% based on ten net rental payments of $137,780 per year and the initial market value of $1,000,000 for the plane. On January 1, 2002, the present value of all net rental payments and the purchase option of $44,440 is $888,890 using the 12% interest rate. The present value of all net rental payments and the $44,440 purchase option on January 1, 2002, is $1,022,226 using the 8% interest rate implicit in the lease agreement. The financial vice-president of Brad Hayes Corporation has established that this lease agreement is a capital lease as defined in *Statement of Financial Accounting Standards No. 13,* "Accounting for Leases."

Instructions

(a) What is the appropriate amount that Brad Hayes Corporation should recognize for the leased aircraft on its balance sheet after the lease is signed?

(b) Without prejudice to your answer in part (a), assume that the annual lease payment is $141,780 as stated in the question, that the appropriate capitalized amount for the leased aircraft is $1,000,000 on January 1, 2002, and that the interest rate is 9%. How will the lease be reported in the December 31, 2002, balance sheet and related income statement? (Ignore any income tax implications.)

(CMA adapted)

***C22-6 (Sale-Leaseback)** On January 1, 2001, Laura Dwyer Company sold equipment for cash and leased it back. As seller-lessee, Laura Dwyer retained the right to substantially all of the remaining use of the equipment.

The term of the lease is 8 years. There is a gain on the sale portion of the transaction. The lease portion of the transaction is classified appropriately as a capital lease.

Instructions

(a) What is the theoretical basis for requiring lessees to capitalize certain long-term leases? **Do not discuss the specific criteria for classifying a lease as a capital lease.**

(b) (1) How should Laura Dwyer account for the sale portion of the sale-leaseback transaction at January 1, 2001?

(2) How should Laura Dwyer account for the leaseback portion of the sale-leaseback transaction at January 1, 2001?

(c) How should Laura Dwyer account for the gain on the sale portion of the sale-leaseback transaction during the first year of the lease? Why?

(AICPA adapted)

***C22-7 (Sale-Leaseback)** On December 31, 2001, Laura Truttman Co. sold 6-month old equipment at fair value and leased it back. There was a loss on the sale. Laura Truttman pays all insurance, maintenance, and taxes on the equipment. The lease provides for eight equal annual payments, beginning December 31, 2002, with a present value equal to 85% of the equipment's fair value and sales price. The lease's term is equal to 80% of the equipment's useful life. There is no provision for Laura Truttman to reacquire ownership of the equipment at the end of the lease term.

Instructions

(a) (1) Why is it important to compare an equipment's fair value to its lease payments' present value and its useful life to the lease term?

(2) Evaluate Laura Truttman's leaseback of the equipment in terms of each of the four criteria for determination of a capital lease.

(b) How should Laura Truttman account for the sale portion of the sale-leaseback transaction at December 31, 2001?

(c) How should Laura Truttman report the leaseback portion of the sale-leaseback transaction on its December 31, 2002, balance sheet?

USING YOUR JUDGMENT

FINANCIAL REPORTING PROBLEM: INTEL CORPORATION

Instructions

Refer to the financial statements and accompanying notes and discussion of Intel Corporation presented in Appendix 5B and answer the following questions.

(a) What types of leases are used for a portion of Intel's capital equipment and facilities rented?

(b) What amount of rental expense was reported by Intel in 1996, 1997, and 1998?

(c) What minimum annual rental commitments under all noncancelable leases at December 26, 1998, did Intel disclose?

FINANCIAL STATEMENT ANALYSIS CASE

Presented in Illustration 22-34 are the financial statement disclosures from the 1999 Annual Report of The Penn Traffic Company.

Instructions

Answer the following questions related to these disclosures.

(a) What are the total obligations under capital leases for the fiscal year-ended February 3, 1999, for Penn Traffic?

(b) What is the book value of the assets under capital lease at the year-ended February 3, 1999, for Penn Traffic? Explain why there is a difference between the amounts reported for assets and liabilities under capital leases.

(c) What is the total rental expense reported for leasing activity for the year-ended February 3, 1999, for Penn Traffic?

(d) Estimate the off-balance-sheet liability due to Penn Traffic's operating leases at fiscal year-end 1999.

COMPARATIVE ANALYSIS CASE

UAL, Inc., versus Southwest Airlines

Instructions

Go to the Digital Tool and using the UAL, Inc. and Southwest Airlines Annual Report Information, answer the following questions.

(a) What types of leases are used by Southwest and on what assets are these leases primarily used?

(b) How long-term are some of Southwest's leases? What are some of the characteristics or provisions of Southwest's (as lessee) leases?

(c) What did Southwest report in 1998 as its future minimum annual rental commitments under noncancelable leases?

(d) At year-end 1998, what was the present value of the minimum rental payments under Southwest's capital leases? How much imputed interest was deducted from the future minimum annual rental commitments to arrive at the present value?

(e) What were the amounts and details reported by Southwest for rental expense in 1998, 1997, and 1996?

(f) How does UAL's use of leases compare with Southwest's?

RESEARCH CASES

Case 1

The accounting for operating leases is a controversial issue. Many contend that firms employing operating leases are utilizing significantly more assets and are more highly leveraged than indicated by the balance sheet alone. As a result, analysts often use footnote disclosures to "constructively capitalize" operating lease obligations. One way to do so is to increase a firm's assets and liabilities by the present value of all future minimum rental payments.

Instructions

(a) Obtain the most recent annual report for a firm that relies heavily on operating leases (firms in the airline and retail industries are good candidates). The schedule of future minimum rental payments is usually included in the "Commitments and Contingencies" footnote. Use the schedule to determine the present value of future minimum rental payments, assuming a discount rate of 10%.

(b) Calculate the company's debt-to-total-assets ratio with and without the present value of operating lease payments. Is there a significant difference?

*Case 2

The December 1995 issue of *Management Accounting* includes an article by Renita Wolf entitled "Sale/Leasebacks of Corporate Real Estate Holdings."

Instructions

Read the article and answer the following questions.

(a) What are some advantages of a sale/leaseback?

(b) How does the cost of a lease compare to the cost of traditional long-term debt financing?

(c) What might a sale/leaseback signal to investors?

(d) Identify the types of investors engaging in sale/leasebacks.

INTERNATIONAL REPORTING CASE

As discussed in the chapter, U.S. GAAP accounting for leases allows companies to use off-balance-sheet financing for the purchase of operating assets. International accounting standards are similar to U.S. GAAP in that under these rules, companies can keep leased assets and obligations off their balance sheets. However, under *International Accounting Standard No. 17 (IAS 17),* leases are capitalized based on the subjective evaluation of whether the risks and rewards of ownership are transferred in the lease. In Japan, virtually all leases are treated as operating leases. Furthermore, unlike U.S. and IAS standards, the Japanese rules do not require disclosure of future minimum lease payments.

Presented below are recent financial data for three major airlines that lease some part of their aircraft fleet. **American Airlines** prepares its financial statements under U.S. GAAP and leases approximately 27% of its fleet. **KLM Royal Dutch Airlines** and **Japan Airlines (JAL)** present their statements in accordance with their home country GAAP (Netherlands and Japan respectively). KLM leases about 22% of its aircraft, and JAL leases approximately 50% of its fleet.

Financial Statement Data	American Airlines (millions of dollars)	KLM Royal Dutch Airlines (millions of guilders)	Japan Airlines (millions of yen)
As-reported			
Assets	20,915	19,205	2,042,761
Liabilities	14,699	13,837	1,857,800
Income	985	606	4,619
Estimated impact of capitalizing operating leases on:[1]			
Assets	5,897	1,812	244,063
Liabilities	6,886	1,776	265,103
Income	(143)	24	(9,598)

[1]Based on *Apples to Apples: Global Airlines: Flight to Quality* (New York: N.Y.: Morgan Stanley Dean Witter, October 1998).

Instructions

(a) Using the as-reported data for each of the airlines, compute the rate of return on assets and the debt to assets ratio. Compare these companies on the basis of this analysis.

(b) Adjust the as-reported numbers of the three companies for the effects of non-capitalization of leases and then redo the analysis in part (a).

(c) The following statement was overheard in the library: "Non-capitalization of operating leases is not that big a deal for profitability analysis based on rate of return on assets, since the operating lease payments (under operating lease accounting) are about the same as the sum of the interest and depreciation expense under capital lease treatment." Do you agree? Explain.

(d) Since the accounting for leases worldwide is similar, does your analysis above suggest there is a need for an improved accounting standard for leases? (*Hint:* Reflect on comparability of information about these companies' leasing activities, when leasing is more prevalent in one country than in others.)

ETHICS CASE

Cuby Corporation entered into a lease agreement for 10 photocopy machines for its corporate headquarters. The lease agreement qualifies as an operating lease in all terms except there is a bargain purchase option. After the 5-year lease term, the corporation can purchase each copier for $1,000, when the anticipated market value is $2,500.

Glenn Beckert, the financial vice president, thinks the financial statements must recognize the lease agreement as a capital lease because of the bargain purchase agreement. The controller, Donna Kessinger, disagrees: "Although I don't know much about the copiers themselves, there is a way to avoid recording the lease liability." She argues that the corporation might claim that copier technology advances rapidly and that by the end of the lease term the machines will most likely not be worth the $1,000 bargain price.

Instructions

Answer the following questions:

(a) What ethical issue is at stake?

(b) Should the controller's argument be accepted if she does not really know much about copier technology? Would it make a difference if the controller were knowledgeable about the pace of change in copier technology?

(c) What should Beckert do?

A visit with
Tracey Barber

Tracey Barber is a partner in the national office of Deloitte & Touche. After graduating from Georgetown University in 1984 with a major in business administration, she began her career on the audit staff in the firm's Washington, D.C., office. After ten years with the firm, she was appointed to serve two years as a Professional Accounting Fellow at the Securities & Exchange Commission, returning to Deloitte & Touche in 1996 as a partner.

PERSPECTIVES ON

A Career in Public Accounting

Describe your early years at the firm. When you first start working, you get audit assignments in a variety of industries. Some of the companies are publicly held. Others are small businesses. But the variety is very interesting. In the first few years as a new staff accountant, you are just trying to get a wide variety of experience so that you can see what interests you. One benefit of public accounting is that you get to see a lot of different businesses. My first assignment happened to be a water utility client, which was the luck of the draw.

While I was progressing up the ranks, I determined that I would specialize in financial institutions. In addition to their accounting issues, I was very interested in the impact that financial institutions have on the economy. And so, I was assigned to work with many of the office's financial institution clients.

Although you might think that working in Washington, D.C., would mean auditing the federal government, I saw very little of that. To be sure, the type of clients you have is dependent on the office in which you work. For instance, in New York, you'll probably work with a lot of Fortune 500 companies because so many are headquartered there, whereas if you work in the San Francisco Bay area, then you'll see a lot of technology companies.

Regardless of the type of clients you serve, your career can move very rapidly if you are ambitious and enthusiastic. Within eight years, I was promoted from staff accountant to senior accountant, then manager, and then senior manager with the firm. As a senior manager, you are preparing to become a partner, and you begin to really manage the relationship with the client. This means you will take part in discussions with company executives, giving you a much better understanding of the client's business concerns that you can then use to develop additional opportunities for the firm to serve the client.

How does one make partner at an accounting firm? In addition to being able to work with clients and bring in new business, it's important to develop a niche where the firm has a particular need. As I said, early on I decided to specialize in the financial services industry including insurance companies, investment companies, and mortgage banking. So, you look at what the firm needs, and what your developmental goals are, and you put those two together. In addition to an industry specialty, I decided that I wanted to become a consultation resource to deal with technical accounting issues, which helps us better serve our clients. I've always been very goal-oriented and knew that because I was in public accounting, I could go as far as I wanted, as long as I was willing to work to do that.

How did you happen to work for the SEC? To distinguish myself within the firm, and because of the intellectual challenge, I decided to apply to become a Professional Accounting Fellow at the Securities & Exchange Commission. You must be nominated by your firm, write a research paper, and go through an interviewing process with the SEC to be selected. I chose the SEC because I believed it would help me to develop expertise that would be valuable in furthering my career upon completion of that assignment. While at the SEC, I got to be part of the accounting standard-setting process, and I expanded my network of contacts particularly because I worked with all of the Big Five accounting firms, the Emerging Issues Task Force, and the Auditing Standards Board. In the Office of the Chief Accountant, some of the most difficult and complicated accounting issues are analyzed and resolved.

At the time, derivatives were a hot topic, as Orange County, California, faced bankruptcy because of adverse consequences associated with the use of financial instruments and the lack of disclosure to bondholders. In addition, Wall Street continued to invent more complicated instruments that corporations were employing to modify risks such as currency or interest rate movements. It became clear to the SEC and others in the standard-setting process that these financial instruments were no longer used by just a few companies, but rather were widespread. The existing hedge accounting rules did not require transparency in the accounting for these transactions or they allowed for too much discretion on the part of management to achieve desired accounting results. In fact, after many years of debate over the accounting, the FASB issued *Statement 133* which requires companies to recognize derivatives at fair value.

After you left the SEC, what did you do? After working with the SEC, I rejoined Deloitte & Touche as a partner in our national office where I consult with other partners at the firm on technical issues. For instance, a practice partner with a public client will call because he or she is concerned about the accounting for a particular transaction. My group researches, discusses, and concludes with respect to the issue, similar to the approach we used at the SEC. In addition, I might help a client communicate with the SEC about a proposed transaction.

For example, the SEC announced in late 1998 that the staff didn't like the way companies were valuing in-process research and development after a business combination. The SEC was concerned that companies were allocating too much of the purchase price to in-process research and development, which must be written off immediately rather than amortized like goodwill. A large number of companies were forced to restate their financial statements to reflect a lower allocation to in-process R & D.

In my role, I help our clients determine the appropriate response to the SEC's inquiries on topics such as this. My plan is to continue to be a technical resource for the firm, but soon I also will resume working directly with clients.

What accounting issues arise for Internet companies? We have a large number of clients that are either pure "dot-coms," or bricks and mortar companies that are entering into e-commerce in a significant way. A lot of questions that we're getting in that area have to do with revenue recognition. It's a big concern because their stock prices generally reflect revenue more than earnings. There are often no price-to-earnings multiples for investors to gauge, because many of the companies don't have earnings. One question is whether an Internet company can record gross sales or whether it should record only net commissions. For instance, let's say an Internet company sells clothes over the Internet. But it's really just an order processing facility, and never actually receives the clothes in inventory. There is diversity in that some companies record gross revenues, and some record only the fees or commissions on the sale. Another revenue recognition issue relates to barter transactions, where two companies trade advertising banners. Is this really revenue for each company? Right now, the Emerging Issues Task Force at the FASB is looking into these types of subjects and concluded at a recent meeting that barter transactions must meet certain criteria in order to be revenue.

What advice do you give college students? When I look back on college, it was very important to me to get a background that would allow me to do a variety of things after college. As a business major with a concentration in accounting, I was able to take finance, marketing, and management, and it was interesting to put all of these activities together in the financial statements. Similarly, public accounting is a great place to understand all the parts of a business and their economic impact through the financial reporting process. This broad background is why it's not surprising that many CEOs started out in public accounting.

CHAPTER 23

Accounting Changes and Error Analysis

An Art or a Science?

Is accounting an art or a science? One look at how many companies change accounting principles and estimates in a given year suggests that accounting is more art than science. For example, a recent survey of 600 large companies indicated that approximately one-third experienced some type of change in accounting in the past year.

Many of these changes are highlighted in the financial press, as indicated by the following headlines:

"Accounting Change at Mobil Makes First-Quarter Profit into $145 Million Loss"

"Westvaco Reports Three Accounting Changes"

"Flagstar Restates Financial Results"

"Aeronautical Company Revises Estimates of Service Lives of Boeing 747s"

"J.P. Stevens, Inc., Changes to the LIFO Method of Determining Inventory Cost"

Why do such changes in accounting occur? First, the accounting profession may **mandate** that a new accounting principle is to be used. For example, you have studied new standards on such topics as investments, stock options, earnings per share, income taxes, and pensions. To illustrate, Chrysler (now DaimlerChrysler) changed its method of revenue recognition on sales of vehicles to rental companies because of a recent accounting pronouncement.

Second, **changing economic conditions** may cause a company to change its method of accounting. Significant inflation often prompts companies to switch from FIFO to LIFO. As indicated in the above headlines, J.P. Stevens undoubtedly changed its method of accounting for inventories to minimize the impact of inflation on earnings and taxes.

Third, **changes in technology and in operations** may require a company to revise the service lives, depreciation method, or the expected salvage value of depreciable assets. AT&T changed its estimates and depreciation methods as a result of changes in its competitive environment and in telecommunications technology.

So, what do you think: Is accounting an art or a science?

LEARNING OBJECTIVES

After studying this chapter, you should be able to:

1. **Identify the types of accounting changes.**
2. **Describe the accounting for changes in accounting principles.**
3. **Understand how to account for cumulative-effect accounting changes.**
4. **Understand how to account for retroactive accounting changes.**
5. **Understand how to account for changes to LIFO.**
6. **Describe the accounting for changes in estimates.**
7. **Identify changes in a reporting entity.**
8. **Describe the accounting for correction of errors.**
9. **Identify economic motives for changing accounting methods.**
10. **Analyze the effect of errors.**

PREVIEW OF CHAPTER 23

As indicated in the opening story, accounting changes do occur. In addition, changes in accounting are needed when accounting errors are discovered. The purpose of this chapter is to discuss the various types of accounting changes and error corrections and how they are reported in the financial statements. The content and organization of the chapter are as follows:

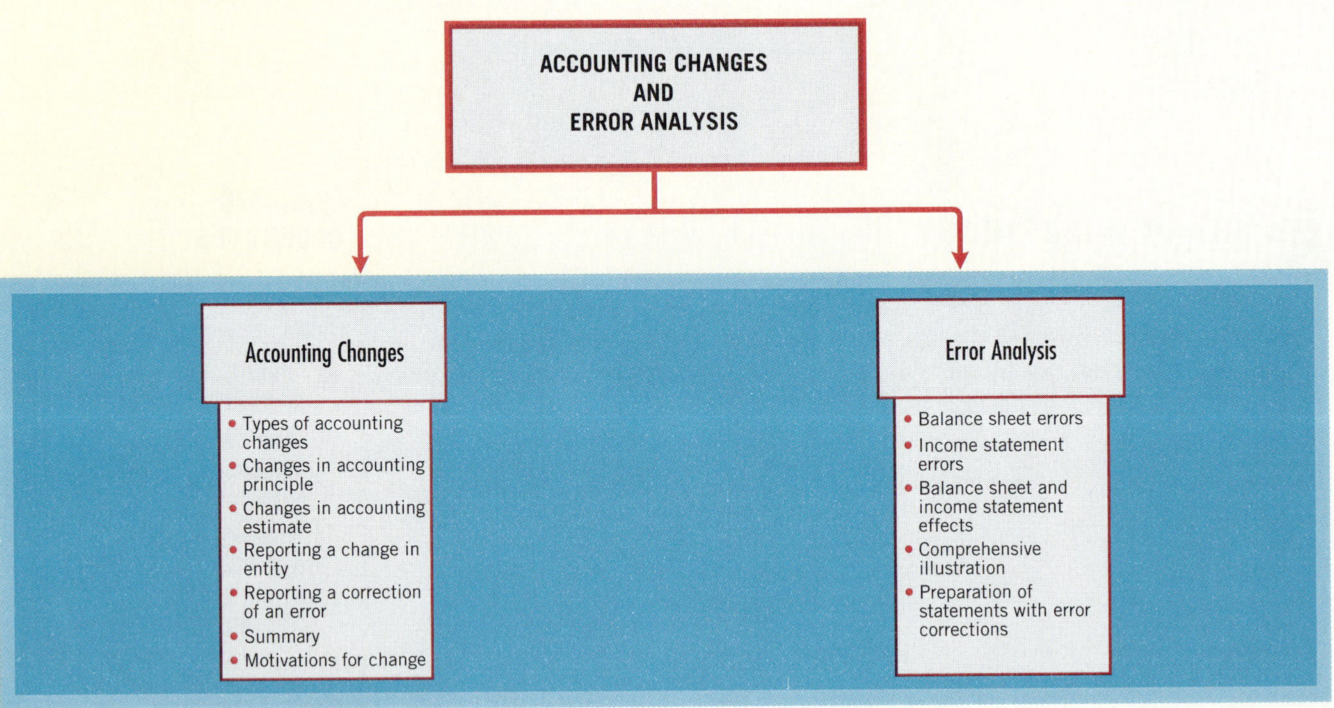

SECTION 1 ACCOUNTING CHANGES

Before the issuance of *APB Opinion No. 20,* "Accounting Changes," companies had considerable flexibility to use alternative accounting treatments for essentially equivalent situations. When steel companies changed their methods of depreciating plant assets from accelerated to straight-line depreciation, the effect of the change was presented in many different ways. The cumulative difference between the depreciation charges that had been recorded and what would have been recorded could have been reported in the income statement of the period of the change. Or, the change could have been ignored, and the undepreciated asset balance simply depreciated on a straight-line basis in the future. Or, companies could have restated the prior periods on the basis that the straight-line approach had always been used.

TYPES OF ACCOUNTING CHANGES

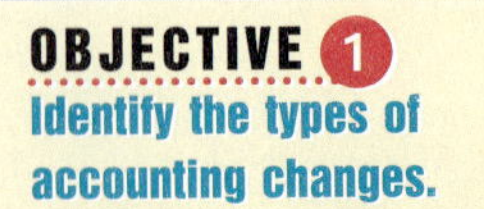
OBJECTIVE 1
Identify the types of accounting changes.

When accounting alternatives exist, comparability of the statements between periods and between companies is diminished and useful historical trend data are obscured. The profession's first step in this area, then, was to establish categories for the different types of changes and corrections that occur in practice.[1] The three types of accounting changes are:

1. ***Change in Accounting Principle.*** A change from one generally accepted accounting principle to another generally accepted accounting principle: for example, a change in the method of depreciation from double-declining to straight-line depreciation of plant assets.
2. ***Change in Accounting Estimate.*** A change that occurs as the result of new information or as additional experience is acquired. An example is a change in the estimate of the useful lives of depreciable assets.
3. ***Change in Reporting Entity.*** A change from reporting as one type of entity to another type of entity: for example, changing specific subsidiaries that constitute the group of companies for which consolidated financial statements are prepared.[2]

UNDERLYING CONCEPTS

While the qualitative characteristic of *usefulness* may be enhanced by changes in accounting, the characteristics of *comparability* and *consistency* may be adversely affected.

A fourth category necessitates changes in the accounting, though it is not classified as an accounting change.

4. ***Errors in Financial Statements.*** Errors occur as a result of mathematical mistakes, mistakes in the application of accounting principles, or oversight or misuse of facts that existed at the time financial statements were prepared. An example is the incorrect application of the retail inventory method for determining the final inventory value.

Changes are classified in these four categories because the individual characteristics of each category necessitate different methods of recognizing these changes in the financial statements. Each of these items is discussed separately to investigate its unusual characteristics and to determine how each item should be reported in the accounts and how the information should be disclosed in comparative statements.

CHANGES IN ACCOUNTING PRINCIPLE

OBJECTIVE 2
Describe the accounting for changes in accounting principles.

A change in accounting principle involves a change from one generally accepted accounting principle to another. For example, a company might change the basis of inventory pricing from average cost to LIFO. Or it might change the method of depreciation on plant assets from accelerated to straight-line, or vice versa. Yet another change might be from the completed-contract to percentage-of-completion method of accounting for construction contracts.

A careful examination must be made in each circumstance to ensure that a change in principle has actually occurred. **A change in accounting principle is not considered to result from the adoption of a new principle in recognition of events that have occurred for the first time or that were previously immaterial.** For example, when a depreciation method that is adopted for **newly** acquired plant assets is different from the method or methods used for **previously recorded** assets of a similar class, a change in accounting principle has **not occurred**. Certain marketing expenditures that were previously immaterial and expensed in the period incurred may become material and acceptably deferred and amortized without a change in accounting principle occurring.

Finally, **if the accounting principle previously followed was not acceptable, or if the principle was applied incorrectly, a change to a generally accepted accounting**

In some countries, changes in accounting principles are made by adjusting current period income and disclosing the effects on current and/or prior period income.

[1] "Accounting Changes," *Opinions of the Accounting Principles Board No. 20* (New York: AICPA, 1971).

[2] *Accounting Trends and Techniques—1999* in its survey of 600 annual reports identified the following specific types of accounting changes reported:

Software development costs	37	Software revenue recognition	4
Start-up costs	29	Impairment of long-lived assets	3
Business process reengineering costs	10	Reporting entity	2
Inventories	5	Other	13
Depreciable lives	4		

principle is considered a correction of an error. A switch from the cash or income tax basis of accounting to the accrual basis is considered a correction of an error. If the company deducted salvage value when computing double-declining depreciation on plant assets and later recomputed depreciation without deduction of estimated salvage value, an error is corrected.

Three approaches have been suggested for reporting changes in accounting principles in the accounts:

> **Retroactively.** The cumulative effect of the use of the new method on the financial statements at the beginning of the period is computed. A **retroactive adjustment** of the financial statements is then made, recasting the financial statements of prior years on a basis consistent with the newly adopted principle. Advocates of this position argue that only by restatement of prior periods can changes in accounting principles lead to comparable financial statements. If this approach is not used, the year previous to the change will be on the old method; the year of the change will report the entire cumulative adjustment in income; and the following year will present financial statements on the new basis without the cumulative effect of the change. Consistency is considered essential in providing meaningful earnings-trend data and other financial relationships necessary to evaluate the business.
>
> **Currently.** The cumulative effect of the use of the new method on the financial statements at the beginning of the period is computed. This adjustment is then reported in the current year's income statement as a **special item** between the captions "Extraordinary items" and "Net income." Advocates of this position argue that restating financial statements for prior years results in a loss of confidence by investors in financial reports. How will a present or prospective investor react when told that the earnings computed 5 years ago are now entirely different? Restatement, if permitted, also might upset many contractual and other arrangements that were based on the old figures. For example, profit-sharing arrangements computed on the old basis might have to be recomputed and completely new distributions made, which might create numerous legal problems. Many practical difficulties also exist; the cost of restatement may be excessive, or restatement may be impossible on the basis of data available.
>
> **Prospectively (in the future).** Previously reported results remain; no change is made. Opening balances are not adjusted, and no attempt is made to allocate charges or credits for prior events. Advocates of this position argue that once management presents financial statements based on acceptable accounting principles, they are final; management cannot change prior periods by adopting a new principle. According to this line of reasoning, the cumulative adjustment in the current year is not appropriate, because such an approach includes amounts that have little or no relationship to the current year's income or economic events.

Before the adoption of *APB Opinion No. 20,* all three of the approaches above were used. *APB Opinion No. 20,* however, settled this issue by establishing guidelines for changes depending on the type of change in accounting principle involved. We have classified these changes in accounting principle into three categories:

1. Cumulative-effect type accounting change.
2. Retroactive-effect type accounting change.
3. Change to the LIFO method of inventory.

Cumulative-Effect Type Accounting Change

OBJECTIVE 3
Understand how to account for cumulative-effect accounting changes.

The general requirement established by the profession was that the **current, or "catch-up," method should be used to account for changes in accounting principles**. The general requirements are as follows:

1. The current or catch-up approach should be employed. The cumulative effect of the adjustment should be reported in the income statement between the captions "extraordinary items" and "net income."
2. Financial statements for prior periods included for comparative purposes should not be restated.

3 Income before extraordinary items and net income, computed on a pro-forma **(as if)** basis should be shown on the face of the income statement for all periods. They are presented **as if the newly adopted principle had been applied during all periods affected**. Related earnings per share data should also be reported. The reader, then, has some understanding of how restated financial statements appear.[3]

INTERNATIONAL INSIGHT

In Canada, Hong Kong, and the United Kingdom, changes in accounting principles are accounted for retroactively. That is, the changes are accounted for as prior year adjustments.

Illustration

Assume that Lang Inc. decided at the beginning of 2002 to change from the sum-of-the-years'-digits method of depreciation to the straight-line method for financial reporting for its buildings. For tax purposes, the company has employed the straight-line method and will continue to do so. The assets originally cost $120,000 in 2000 and have an estimated useful life of 15 years. The data assumed for this illustration are:

ILLUSTRATION 23-1
Data for Change in Depreciation Method

Year	Sum-of-the-Years'-Digits Depreciation	Straight-Line Depreciation	Difference	Tax Effect 40%	Effect on Income (net of tax)
2000	$15,000[a]	$ 8,000[b]	$ 7,000	$2,800	$4,200
2001	14,000	8,000	6,000	2,400	3,600
	$29,000	$16,000	$13,000	$5,200	$7,800

[a]$120,000 × $\frac{15}{120}$ = $15,000 [b]$120,000 ÷ 15 = $8,000

Lang Inc. has income before extraordinary items and cumulative effect of changes in accounting principle of $130,000 in 2002 and $111,000 in 2001. Also, Lang Inc. has an extraordinary loss (net of tax) of $30,000 in 2002 and an extraordinary gain (net of tax) of $10,000 in 2001.

Journal Entry

Although the journal entry can be made any time during the year, it is effective **as of the beginning of the year**. The entry made to record this change to straight-line depreciation in 2002 should be:

Accumulated Depreciation	13,000	
Deferred Tax Asset		5,200
Cumulative Effect of Change in Accounting Principle—Depreciation		7,800

The debit of $13,000 to Accumulated Depreciation is the excess of the sum-of-the-years'-digits depreciation over the straight-line depreciation. The credit to the Deferred Tax Asset of $5,200 is recorded to eliminate this account from the financial statements. Prior to the change in accounting principle, sum-of-the-years'-digits was used for book but not tax purposes, which gave rise to a debit balance in the Deferred Tax Asset account of $5,200. The cumulative effect on income resulting from the difference between sum-of-the-years'-digits depreciation and straight-line depreciation is reduced by the tax effect on that difference. Now that the company intends to use the straight-line method for both tax and book purposes, no deferred income taxes related to depreciation should exist and the Deferred Tax Asset account should be eliminated.

Income Statement Presentation

The cumulative effect of the change in accounting principle should be reported on the income statement between the captions "Extraordinary items" and "Net income." The cumulative effect is not an extraordinary item but is reported on a net-of-tax basis similar to that used for extraordinary items. This information is shown in Illustration 23-2.

[3]Ibid., par. 21.

ILLUSTRATION 23-2
Income Statement without Pro-Forma Amounts

	2002	2001
Income before extraordinary item and cumulative effect of a change in accounting principles	$130,000	$111,000
Extraordinary item, net of tax	(30,000)	10,000
Cumulative effect on prior years of retroactive application of new depreciation method, net of tax	7,800	
Net income	$107,800	$121,000
Per share amounts		
Earnings per share (10,000 shares)		
Income before extraordinary item and cumulative effect of a change in accounting principle	$13.00	$11.10
Extraordinary item	(3.00)	1.00
Cumulative effect on prior years of retroactive application of new depreciation method	.78	
Net income	$10.78	$12.10

UNDERLYING CONCEPTS

The pro-forma treatment attempts to restore the comparability of the income statements.

Note that depreciation expense for 2002 is computed on the straight-line basis.

Pro-Forma Amounts

Pro-forma amounts permit financial statements users to determine the net income that would have been shown if the newly adopted principle had been in effect in earlier periods. In other words, how would Lang Inc.'s income be reported if the straight-line method had been used in 2001? To determine this amount, the prior year (2001) is restated, assuming that the straight-line method is used. The computation is as follows:

ILLUSTRATION 23-3
Computation of Pro-Forma Income, 2001

Income before extraordinary item (2001) not restated	$111,000
Excess of sum-of-the-years-digits depreciation over straight-line depreciation	3,600
Pro-forma income before extraordinary item (2001)	$114,600

This and other information is shown on the face of the income statement as follows:

ILLUSTRATION 23-4
Income Statement with Pro-Forma Amounts

Pro-forma (as if) amounts, assuming retroactive application of new depreciation method:

	2002	2001
Income before extraordinary item	$130,000	$114,600
Earnings per common share	$13.00	$11.46
Net income	$100,000[a]	$124,600[b]
Earnings per common share	$10.00	$12.46

[a]($130,000 − $30,000 = $100,000)
[b]($114,600 + $10,000 = $124,600)

The $130,000 of 2002 income before extraordinary item needs no restatement like the 2001 income because the new straight-line method of depreciation is used in 2002.

Pro-forma information is useful to individuals interested in assessing the trend of earnings over a period of time. Pro-forma information, which is only shown as supplementary information, may be reported in the income statement, in a separate schedule, or in the notes to the financial statements.

The pro-forma amounts should include both (1) the direct effects of a change and (2) nondiscretionary adjustments in items based on income before taxes or net income (such as profit-sharing expense and certain royalties) that would have been recognized if the newly adopted principle had been followed in prior periods; related income tax effects should be recognized for both (1) and (2). If an income statement is presented for the current period only, the actual and pro-forma amounts (including earnings per share) for the immediately preceding period should be disclosed.

Summary Illustration

Illustration 23-5 indicates how this information is presented on the income statement.[4] The appropriate note disclosure is also provided.

ILLUSTRATION 23-5
Cumulative-Effect Type Accounting Change

Cumulative-Effect Type Accounting Change
Reporting the Change in 2-Year Comparative Statements

	2002	2001
Income before extraordinary item and cumulative effect of a change in accounting principles	$130,000	$111,000
Extraordinary item, net of tax	(30,000)	10,000
Cumulative effect on prior years of retroactive application of new depreciation method, net of tax (Note A)	7,800	
Net income	$107,800	$121,000
Per share amounts		
Earnings per share (10,000 shares)		
Income before extraordinary item and cumulative effect of a change in accounting principle	$13.00	$11.10
Extraordinary item	(3.00)	1.00
Cumulative effect on prior years of rectroactive application of new depreciation method	.78	
Net income	$10.78	$12.10

Pro-forma (as if) amounts, assuming retroactive application of new depreciation method:

	2002	2001
Income before extraordinary item	$130,000	$114,600
Earnings per common share	$13.00	$11.46
Net income	$100,000	$124,600
Earnings per common share	$10.00	$12.46

Note A: Change in Depreciation Method for Plant Assets. In 2002 depreciation of plant assets is computed by use of the straight-line method. In prior years, beginning in 2000, depreciation of buildings was computed by the sum-of-the-years'-digits method. The new method of depreciation was adopted in recognition of . . . (state justification for the change of depreciation method) . . . and has been applied retroactively to building acquisitions of prior years to determine the cumulative effect. The effect of the change in 2002 was to increase income before extraordinary item by approximately $3,000 (or 30 cents per share). The adjustment necessary for retroactive application of the new method, amounting to $7,800, is included in income of 2002. The pro-forma amounts shown on the income statement have been adjusted for the effect of retroactive application on depreciation, and the pro-forma effect for related income taxes.

Retroactive-Effect Type Accounting Change

OBJECTIVE 4
Understand how to account for retroactive accounting changes.

In certain circumstances, a change in accounting principle may be handled retroactively. Under the retroactive treatment the cumulative effect of the new method on the financial statements at the beginning of the period is computed. A retroactive adjustment of the financial statements presented is made by **recasting the statements of prior**

[4]In practice, 3-year comparative income statements are prepared. For reasons of simplicity, we have presented 2-year comparatives.

years on a basis consistent with the newly adopted principle. Any part of the cumulative effect attributable to years prior to those presented is treated as an adjustment of beginning retained earnings of the earliest year presented. In such situations, the nature of and justification for the change and the effect on net income and related per share amounts should be disclosed for each period presented. The five situations that require the restatement of all prior period financial statements are:

1. A change from the LIFO inventory valuation method to another method.
2. A change in the method of accounting for long-term construction-type contracts.
3. A change to or from the "full-cost" method of accounting in the extractive industries.
4. Issuance of financial statements by a company for the first time to obtain additional equity capital, to effect a business combination, or to register securities. (This procedure may be used only by closely held companies and then only once.)
5. A professional pronouncement recommends that a change in accounting principle be treated retroactively. For example, *FASB No. 11* requires that retroactive treatment be given for changes in "Accounting for Contingencies" and *FASB Statement No. 73* requires retroactive treatment for a change from retirement-replacement-betterment accounting to depreciation accounting.[5]

IAS 8 generally requires restatement of prior years for accounting changes. However, IAS 8 permits the cumulative effect method or prospective method if the amounts to restate prior periods are not reasonably determinable.

Why did the profession provide for these exceptions? Though the reasons are varied, the major one is that reporting the cumulative adjustment in the period of the change might have such a large effect on net income that the income figure would be misleading. A perfect illustration is the experience of **Chrysler Corporation** (now **DaimlerChrysler**) when it changed its inventory accounting from LIFO to FIFO. If the change had been handled correctly, Chrysler would have had to report a $53,500,000 adjustment to net income, which would have resulted in net income of $45,900,000 instead of a net loss of $7,600,000.

As another illustration, in the early 1980s the railroad industry switched from the retirement-replacement method of depreciating railroad equipment to a more generally used method such as straight-line depreciation. Cumulative effect treatment meant that a substantial adjustment would be made to income in the period of change. Many in the railroad industry argued that the adjustment was so large that to include the cumulative effect in the current year instead of restating prior years would distort the information and make it less useful. Such situations lend support to restatement so that comparability is not seriously affected.

Illustration

To illustrate the retroactive method, assume that Denson Construction Co. has accounted for its income from long-term construction contracts using the completed-contract method. In 2002, the company changed to the percentage-of-completion method because management believes that this approach provides a more appropriate measure of the income earned. For tax purposes (assume a 40% enacted tax rate), the company has employed the completed-contract method and plans to continue using this method in the future.

Illustration 23-6 provides the information for analysis:

[5]"Accounting for Contingencies—Transition Method," *Statement of the Financial Accounting Standards Board No. 11* (Stamford, Conn.: FASB, 1975); "Reporting a Change in Accounting for Railroad Track Structures," *Statement of the Financial Accounting Standards Board No. 73* (Stamford, Conn.: FASB, 1983). Note that the FASB standard on "Accounting for Income Taxes" permits the company to use either the cumulative effect approach or the retroactive method in changing from the deferred method to the asset-liability method. In addition, if the company elects the cumulative effect approach, pro-forma amounts are not required because of the cost and difficulty of developing this information.

ILLUSTRATION 23-6
Data for Change in Accounting for Long-Term Construction Contracts

Year		Pretax Income from Percentage-of-Completion	Pretax Income from Completed-Contract	Difference	Difference in Income: Tax Effect 40%	Difference in Income: Income Effect (net of tax)
Prior to	2001	$600,000	$400,000	$200,000	$80,000	$120,000
In	2001	180,000	160,000	20,000	8,000	12,000
Total at beginning of	2002	$780,000	$560,000	$220,000	$88,000	$132,000
In	2002	$200,000	$190,000	$ 10,000	$ 4,000	$ 6,000

The entry to record the change in 2002 would be:

Construction in Process	220,000	
Deferred Tax Liability		88,000
Retained Earnings		132,000

The Construction in Process account is increased by $220,000, representing the adjustment in prior years' income of $132,000 and the adjustment in prior years' tax expense of $88,000. The Deferred Tax Liability account is used to recognize a tax liability for future taxable amounts. That is, in future periods taxable income will be higher than book income as a result of current temporary differences, and, therefore, a deferred tax liability must be reported in the current year.

Income Statement Presentation

The bottom portion of the income statement for Denson Construction Co., **before giving effect to the retroactive change in accounting principle**, would be as follows:

ILLUSTRATION 23-7
Income Statement before Retroactive Change

Income Statement	2002	2001
Net income	$114,000[a]	$96,000[a]
Per Share Amounts		
Earnings per share (100,000 shares)	$1.14	$.96

[a]The net income for the two periods is computed as follows:
2002 $190,000 − .40($190,000) = $114,000
2001 $160,000 − .40($160,000) = $96,000

The bottom portion of the income statement for Denson Construction Co., **after giving effect to the retroactive change in accounting principle**, would be as follows:

ILLUSTRATION 23-8
Income Statement after Retroactive Change

Income Statement	2002	2001
Net income	$120,000[a]	$108,000[a]
Per Share Amounts		
Earnings per share (100,000 shares)	$1.20	$1.08

[a]The net income for the two periods is computed as follows:
2002 $200,000 − .40($200,000) = $120,000
2001 $180,000 − .40($180,000) = $108,000

Note that the 2-year comparative income statement (Illustration 23-8) has a major difference from the earlier 2-year comparative income statement (Illustration 23-5). No pro-forma information is necessary when changes in accounting principles are handled retroactively, because the income numbers for previous periods are restated.

Retained Earnings Statement

Assuming a retained earnings balance of $1,600,000 at the beginning of 2001, the retained earnings statement **before giving effect to the retroactive change in accounting principle**, would appear as follows:

ILLUSTRATION 23-9
Retained Earnings Statement before Retroactive Change

Retained Earnings Statement

	2002	2001
Balance at beginning of year	$1,696,000	$1,600,000
Net income	114,000	96,000
Balance at end of year	$1,810,000	$1,696,000

A comparative retained earnings statement, **after giving effect to the retroactive change in accounting principle**, would be as follows:

ILLUSTRATION 23-10
Retained Earnings Statement after Retroactive Change

Retained Earnings Statement

	2002	2001
Balance at beginning of year, as previously reported	$1,696,000	$1,600,000
Add: Adjustment for the cumulative effect on prior years of applying retroactively the new method of accounting for long-term contracts (Note A)	132,000	120,000
Balance at beginning of year, as adjusted	1,828,000	1,720,000
Net income	120,000	108,000
Balance at end of year	$1,948,000	$1,828,000

Note A: Change in Method of Accounting for Long-Term Contracts. The company has accounted for revenue and costs for long-term construction contracts by the percentage-of-completion method in 2002, whereas in all prior years revenue and costs were determined by the completed-contract method. The new method of accounting for long-term contracts was adopted to recognize . . . (state justification for change in accounting principle) . . . and financial statements of prior years have been restated to apply the new method retroactively. For income tax purposes, the completed-contract method has been continued. The effect of the accounting change on income of 2002 was an increase of $6,000 net of related taxes and on income of 2001 as previously reported was an increase of $12,000 net of related taxes. The balances of retained earnings for 2001 and 2002 have been adjusted for the effect of applying retroactively the new method of accounting.

An expanded retained earnings statement is included in this 2-year comparative presentation to indicate the type of adjustment that is needed to restate the beginning balance of retained earnings. In 2001, the beginning balance was adjusted for the excess of the percentage-of-completion income over the completed-contract income prior to 2001 ($120,000). In 2002, the beginning balance was adjusted for the $120,000 cumulative difference plus the additional $12,000 for 2001.

No such adjustments are necessary when the current or catch-up method is employed, because the cumulative effect of the change on net income is reported in the income statement of the current year and no prior period reports are restated. It is ordinarily appropriate to prepare a retained earnings or stockholders' equity statement when presenting comparative statements regardless of what type of accounting change is involved; an illustration was provided for the retroactive method only to explain the additional computations required.

Change to LIFO Method

OBJECTIVE 5
Understand how to account for changes to LIFO.

As indicated, the cumulative effect of any accounting change should be shown in the income statement between "Extraordinary items" and "Net income," except for the conditions mentioned in the preceding section. In addition, this rule does not apply when a company changes to the LIFO method of inventory valuation. In such a situation, **the**

base-year inventory for all subsequent LIFO calculations is the opening inventory in the year the method is adopted. There is no restatement of prior years' income because it is just too impractical. A restatement to LIFO would be subject to assumptions as to the different years that the layers were established, and these assumptions would ordinarily result in the computation of a number of different earnings figures. The only adjustment necessary may be to restate the beginning inventory to a cost basis from a lower of cost or market approach.

Disclosure then is limited to showing the effect of the change on the results of operations in the period of change. Also the reasons for omitting the computations of the cumulative effect and the pro-forma amounts for prior years should be explained. Finally, the company should disclose the justification for the change to LIFO. The Annual Report of the Quaker Oats Company indicates the type of disclosure necessary.

ILLUSTRATION 23-11
Disclosure of Change to LIFO

THE QUAKER OATS COMPANY

Note 1 (In Part): Summary of Significant Accounting Policies

Inventories. Inventories are valued at the lower of cost or market, using various cost methods, and include the cost of raw materials, labor and overhead. The percentage of year-end inventories valued using each of the methods is as follows:

June 30	1989	1988	1987
Average quarterly cost	21%	54%	52%
Last-in, first-out (LIFO)	65%	29%	31%
First-in, first-out (FIFO)	14%	17%	17%

Effective July 1, 1988, the Company adopted the LIFO cost flow assumption for valuing the majority of remaining U.S. Grocery Products inventories. The Company believes that the use of the LIFO method better matches current costs with current revenues. The cumulative effect of this change on retained earnings at the beginning of the year is not determinable, nor are the pro-forma effects of retroactive application of LIFO to prior years. The effect of this change on fiscal 1989 was to decrease net income by $16.0 million, or $.20 per share.

If the LIFO method of valuing certain inventories were not used, total inventories would have been $60.1 million, $24.0 million and $14.6 million higher than reported at June 30, 1989, 1988, and 1987, respectively.

In practice, many companies defer the formal adoption of LIFO until year-end. Management thus has an opportunity to assess the impact that a change to LIFO will have on the financial statements and to evaluate the desirability of a change for tax purposes. As indicated in Chapter 8, many companies use LIFO because of the advantages of this inventory valuation method in a period of inflation.

CHANGES IN ACCOUNTING ESTIMATE

OBJECTIVE 6
Describe the accounting for changes in estimates.

The preparation of financial statements requires estimating the effects of future conditions and events. The following are examples of items that require estimates:

1. Uncollectible receivables.
2. Inventory obsolescence.
3. Useful lives and salvage values of assets.
4. Periods benefited by deferred costs.
5. Liabilities for warranty costs and income taxes.
6. Recoverable mineral reserves.

Future conditions and events and their effects cannot be perceived with certainty; therefore, estimating requires the exercise of judgment. Accounting estimates will change as new events occur, as more experience is acquired, or as additional information is obtained.

Changes in estimates must be handled prospectively. That is, no changes should be made in previously reported results. Opening balances are not adjusted, and no attempt is made to "catch-up" for prior periods. Financial statements of prior periods are not restated, and pro-forma amounts for prior periods are not reported. Instead, the effects of all changes in estimate are accounted for in (1) the period of change if the change affects that period only or (2) the period of change and future periods if the change affects both. As a result, changes in estimates are viewed as **normal recurring corrections and adjustments**, the natural result of the accounting process, and retroactive treatment is prohibited.

INTERNATIONAL INSIGHT

In most nations changes in accounting estimates are treated prospectively. International differences occur in the degree of disclosure required.

The circumstances related to a change in estimate are different from those surrounding a change in accounting principle. If changes in estimates were handled on a retroactive basis, or on a cumulative-effect basis, continual adjustments of prior years' income would occur. It seems proper to accept the view that because new conditions or circumstances exist, the revision fits the new situation and should be handled in the current and future periods.

To illustrate, Underwriters Labs Inc. purchased a building for $300,000 which was originally estimated to have a useful life of 15 years and no salvage value. Depreciation has been recorded for 5 years on a straight-line basis. On January 1, 2002, the estimate of the useful life is revised so that the asset is considered to have a total life of 25 years. Assume that the useful life for financial reporting and tax purposes is the same. The accounts at the beginning of the sixth year are as follows:

ILLUSTRATION 23-12
Book Value after 5 Years' Depreciation

Building	$300,000
Less: Accumulated depreciation—building (5 × $20,000)	100,000
Book value of building	$200,000

The entry to record depreciation for the year 2002 is:

Depreciation Expense	10,000	
Accumulated Depreciation—Building		10,000

The $10,000 depreciation charge is computed as follows:

ILLUSTRATION 23-13
Depreciation after Change in Estimate

$$\text{Depreciation charge} = \frac{\text{Book value of asset}}{\text{Remaining service live}} = \frac{\$200{,}000}{25 \text{ years} - 5 \text{ years}} = \$10{,}000$$

The disclosure of a change in estimated useful lives appeared in the Annual Report of **Ampco–Pittsburgh Corporation**.

ILLUSTRATION 23-14
Disclosure of Change in Estimated Useful Lives

AMPCO–PITTSBURGH CORPORATION

Note 11: Change in Accounting Estimate. The Corporation revised its estimate of the useful lives of certain machinery and equipment. Previously, all machinery and equipment, whether new when placed in use or not, were in one class and depreciated over 15 years. The change principally applies to assets purchased new when placed in use. Those lives are now extended to 20 years. These changes were made to better reflect the estimated periods during which such assets will remain in service. The change had the effect of reducing depreciation expense and increasing net income by approximately $991,000 ($.10 per share).

Differentiating between a change in an estimate and a change in an accounting principle is sometimes difficult. Is it a change in principle or a change in estimate when a company changes from deferring and amortizing certain marketing costs to recording them as an expense as incurred because future benefits of these costs have become doubtful? In such a case, **whenever it is impossible to determine whether a change in principle or a change in estimate has occurred, the change should be considered a change in estimate.**

A similar problem occurs in differentiating between a change in estimate and a correction of an error, although the answer is more clear cut. How do we determine whether the information was overlooked in earlier periods (an error) or whether the information is now available for the first time (change in estimate)? Proper classification is important because corrections of errors have a different accounting treatment from that given changes in estimates. The general rule is that **careful estimates that later prove to be incorrect should be considered changes in estimate.** Only when the estimate was obviously computed incorrectly because of lack of expertise or in bad faith should the adjustment be considered an error. There is no clear demarcation line here, and good judgment must be used in light of all the circumstances.[6]

REPORTING A CHANGE IN ENTITY

OBJECTIVE 7
Identify changes in a reporting entity.

An accounting change that results in financial statements that are actually the statements of a different entity should be reported by **restating the financial statements of all prior periods presented**, to show the financial information for the new reporting entity for all periods.

Examples of a change in reporting entity are:

1. Presenting consolidated statements in place of statements of individual companies.
2. Changing specific subsidiaries that constitute the group of companies for which consolidated financial statements are presented.
3. Changing the companies included in combined financial statements.
4. Accounting for a pooling of interests.
5. A change in the cost, equity, or consolidation method of accounting for subsidiaries and investments.[7] A change in the reporting entity does not result from creation, cessation, purchase, or disposition of a subsidiary or other business unit.

The financial statements of the year in which the change in reporting entity is made should disclose the nature of the change and the reason for it. The effect of the change on income before extraordinary items, net income, and earnings per share amounts should be reported for all periods presented. These disclosures need not be repeated in subsequent periods' financial statements. The Annual Report of **Hewlett-Packard Company** illustrates a note disclosing a change in reporting entity.

---

[6]In evaluating reasonableness, the auditor should use one or a combination of the following approaches:

(a) Review and test the process used by management to develop the estimate.
(b) Develop an independent expectation of the estimate to corroborate the reasonableness of management's estimate.
(c) Review subsequent events or transactions occurring prior to completion of fieldwork. "Auditing Accounting Estimates," *Statement on Auditing Standards No. 57* (New York: AICPA, 1988).

[7]An illustration of the accounting for a change from and to the equity method is provided in Appendix 23A.

ILLUSTRATION 23-15
Disclosure of Change in Reporting Entity

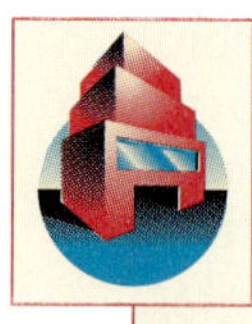

HEWLETT-PACKARD COMPANY

Note: Accounting and Reporting Changes (In Part)

Consolidation of Hewlett-Packard Finance Company. The company implemented *Statement of Financial Accounting Standards No. 94 (SFAS 94)*, "Consolidation of All Majority-owned Subsidiaries." With the adoption of *SFAS 94*, the company consolidated the accounts of Hewlett-Packard Finance Company (HPFC), a wholly owned subsidiary previously accounted for under the equity method, with those of the company. The change resulted in an increase in consolidated assets and liabilities but did not have a material effect on the company's financial position. Since HPFC was previously accounted for under the equity method, the change did not affect net earnings. Prior years' consolidated financial information has been restated to reflect this change for comparative purposes.

REPORTING A CORRECTION OF AN ERROR

OBJECTIVE 8
Describe the accounting for correction of errors.

APB Opinion No. 20 also discussed how a **correction of an error** should be handled in the financial statements. (No authoritative guidelines existed previously.) The conclusions of *APB Opinion No. 20* were reaffirmed in *FASB Statement No. 16.*[8] No business, large or small, is immune from errors. The risk of material errors, however, may be reduced through the installation of good internal control and the application of sound accounting procedures.

The following are examples of accounting errors:

1. A change from an accounting principle that is **not** generally accepted to an accounting principle that is acceptable. The rationale adopted is that the prior periods were incorrectly presented because of the application of an improper accounting principle. Example: a change from the cash or income tax basis of accounting to the accrual basis.
2. Mathematical mistakes that result from adding, subtracting, and so on. Example: the totaling of the inventory count sheets incorrectly in computing the inventory value.
3. Changes in estimate that occur because the estimates are not prepared in good faith. Example: the adoption of a clearly unrealistic depreciation rate.
4. An oversight, such as the failure to accrue or defer certain expenses and revenues at the end of the period.
5. A misuse of facts, such as the failure to use salvage value in computing the depreciation base for the straight-line approach.
6. The incorrect classification of a cost as an expense instead of an asset and vice versa.

As soon as they are discovered, errors must be corrected by proper entries in the accounts and reported in the financial statements. **The profession requires that corrections of errors be treated as prior period adjustments**, be recorded in the year in which the error was discovered, and be reported in the financial statements as an adjustment to the beginning balance of retained earnings. If comparative statements are presented, the prior statements affected should be restated to correct for the error. The disclosures need not be repeated in the financial statements of subsequent periods.

Illustration

To illustrate, in 2002 the bookkeeper for Selectric Company discovered that in 2001 the company failed to record in the accounts $20,000 of depreciation expense on a newly constructed building. The depreciation is correctly included in the tax return. Because of numerous temporary differences, reported net income for 2001 was $150,000 and

[8]"Prior Period Adjustments," *Statement of Financial Accounting Standards No. 16* (Stamford, Conn.: FASB, 1977), p. 5.

taxable income was $110,000. The following entry was made for income taxes (assume a 40% effective tax rate in 2001):

Income Tax Expense	60,000	
Income Tax Payable		44,000
Deferred Tax Liability		16,000

As a result of the $20,000 omission error in 2001:

Depreciation expense (2001) **was** understated	$20,000
Accumulated depreciation **is** understated	20,000
Income tax expense (2001) **was** overstated ($20,000 × 40%)	8,000
Net income (2001) **was** overstated	12,000
Deferred tax liability **is** overstated ($20,000 × 40%)	8,000

The entry made in 2002 to correct the omission of $20,000 of depreciation in 2001 would be:

2002 Correcting Entry

Retained Earnings	12,000	
Deferred Tax Liability	8,000	
Accumulated Depreciation—Buildings		20,000

The journal entry to record the correction of the error is the same whether single-period or comparative financial statements are prepared; however, presentation on the financial statements will differ. If single-period (noncomparative) statements are presented, the error should be reported as an adjustment to the opening balance of retained earnings of the period in which the error is discovered (see Illustration 23-16).

Retained earnings, January 1, 2002		
As previously reported		$350,000
Correction of an error (depreciation)	$20,000	
Less: Applicable income tax reduction	8,000	(12,000)
Adjusted balance of retained earnings, January 1, 2002		338,000
Add: Net income 2002		400,000
Retained earnings, December 31, 2002		$738,000

ILLUSTRATION 23-16
Reporting an Error—Single-Period Financial Statement

Comparative Statements

If comparative financial statements are prepared, adjustments should be made to correct the amounts for all affected accounts reported in the statements for all periods reported. The data for each year being presented should be restated to the correct basis, and any **catch-up adjustment should be shown as a prior period adjustment to retained earnings for the earliest period being reported**. For example, in the case of Selectric Company, the error of omitting the depreciation of $20,000 in 2001, which was discovered in 2002, results in the restatement of the 2001 financial statements when presented in comparison with those of 2002. The following accounts in the 2001 financial statements (presented in comparison with those of 2002) would have been restated:

In the balance sheet:	
Accumulated depreciation—buildings	$20,000 increase
Deferred tax liability	$ 8,000 decrease
Retained earnings, ending balance	$12,000 decrease
In the income statement:	
Depreciation expense—buildings	$20,000 increase
Tax expense	$ 8,000 decrease
Net income	$12,000 decrease
In the retained earnings statement:	
Retained earnings, ending balance (due to lower net income for the period)	$12,000 decrease

ILLUSTRATION 23-17
Reporting an Error—Comparative Financial Statements

The 2002 financial statements in comparative form with those of 2001 are prepared as if the error had not occurred. At a minimum, such comparative statements in 2002 would include a note in the financial statements calling attention to restatement of the 2001 statements and disclosing the effect of the correction on income before extraordinary items, net income, and the related per share amounts.

SUMMARY OF ACCOUNTING CHANGES AND CORRECTIONS OF ERRORS

The development of guidelines in reporting accounting changes and corrections has helped resolve several significant and long-standing accounting problems. Yet, because of diversity in situations and characteristics of the items encountered in practice, the application of professional judgment is of paramount importance. In applying these guidelines, the primary objective is to serve the user of the financial statements; achieving such service requires accuracy, full disclosure,[9] and an absence of misleading inferences. The principal distinction and treatments presented in the earlier discussion are summarized in Illustration 23-18 on the next page.

Changes in accounting principle are considered appropriate only when the enterprise demonstrates that the alternative generally accepted accounting principle that is adopted is **preferable** to the existing one. In applying the profession's guidelines, preferability among accounting principles should be determined on the basis of whether the new principle constitutes an **improvement in financial reporting**, not on the basis of the income tax effect alone. But it is not always easy to determine what is an improvement in financial reporting. **How does one measure preferability or improvement?** The Quaker Oats Company, for example argues that a change in accounting principle to LIFO inventory valuation "better matches current costs with current revenues" (see Illustration 23-11, page 1263). Conversely, another enterprise might change from LIFO to FIFO because it wishes to report a more realistic ending inventory. How do you determine which is the better of these two arguments? The auditor must have some "standard" or "objective" as a basis for determining the preferable method. Because no universal standard or objective is generally accepted, the problem of determining preferability continues to be a difficult one.

UNDERLYING CONCEPTS

This is an example of two widely accepted concepts conflicting. Which is more important, matching (emphasis on the income statement) or qualitative characteristic of representational faithfulness (emphasis on the balance sheet)?

Initially the SEC took the position that the auditor should indicate whether a change in accounting principle was preferable. The SEC has since modified this approach, noting that greater reliance may be placed on management's judgment in assessing preferability. Even though the criterion of preferability is difficult to apply, the general guidelines established have acted as a deterrent to capricious changes in accounting principles.[10] **If an FASB standard creates a new principle or expresses preference for or rejects a specific accounting principle, a change is considered clearly acceptable.** Similarly, other authoritative documents, such as AcSEC's statements of position and AICPA industry audit guides, are considered preferable accounting when a change in accounting principles is contemplated.

---

[9]A change in accounting principle, a change in the reporting entity (special type of change in accounting principle), and a correction of an error involving a change in accounting principle require an explanatory paragraph in the auditor's report discussing lack of consistency from one period to the next. A change in accounting estimate does not affect the auditor's opinion relative to consistency; however, if the change in estimate has a material effect on the financial statements, disclosure may still be required. Error correction not involving a change in accounting principle does not require disclosure relative to consistency.

[10]If management has not provided reasonable justification for the change in accounting principle, the auditor should express a qualified opinion or, if the effect of the change is sufficiently material, the auditor should express an adverse opinion on the financial statements. "Reports on Audited Financial Statements," *Statement on Auditing Standards No. 58* (New York: AICPA, 1988).

ILLUSTRATION 23-18
Summary of Guidelines for Accounting Changes and Errors

- **Changes in accounting principle.**

  General Rule:
  Employ the current or catch-up approach by:
  a. Reporting current results on the new basis.
  b. Reporting the cumulative effect of the adjustment in the current income statement between the captions "Extraordinary items" and "Net income."
  c. Presenting prior period financial statements as previously reported.
  d. Presenting pro-forma data on income and earnings per share for all prior periods presented.

  Exceptions:
  Employ the retroactive approach by:
  a. Restating the financial statements of all prior periods presented.
  b. Disclosing in the year of the change the effect on net income and earnings per share for all prior periods presented.
  c. Reporting an adjustment to the beginning retained earnings balance in the statement of retained earnings.

  Employ the change to LIFO approach by:
  a. Not restating prior years' income.
  b. Using opening inventory in the year the method is adopted as the base-year inventory for all subsequent LIFO computations.
  c. Disclosing the effect of the change on the current year, and the reasons for omitting the computation of the cumulative effect and pro-forma amounts for prior years.

- **Changes in accounting estimate.**

  Employ the current and prospective approach by:
  a. Reporting current and future financial statements on the new basis.
  b. Presenting prior period financial statements as previously reported.
  c. Making no adjustments to current period opening balances for purposes of catch-up, and making no pro-forma presentations.

- **Changes in reporting entity.**

  Employ the retroactive approach by:
  a. Restating the financial statements of all prior periods presented.
  b. Disclosing in the year of change the effect on net income and earnings per share data for all prior periods presented.

- **Changes due to error.**

  Employ the retroactive approach by:
  a. Correcting all prior period statements presented.
  b. Restating the beginning balance of retained earnings for the first period presented when the error effects occur in a period prior to that one.

MOTIVATIONS FOR CHANGE

OBJECTIVE 9
Identify economic motives for changing accounting methods.

Difficult as it is to determine which accounting standards have the strongest conceptual support, other complications make the process even more complex. These complications stem from the fact that managers (and others) have a self-interest in how the financial statements make the company look. Managers naturally wish to show their financial performance in the best light. A **favorable profit picture** can influence investors, and a strong liquidity position can influence creditors. **Too favorable a profit picture**, however, can provide union negotiators and government regulators with ammunition during bargaining talks. Hence, managers might have varying profit motives depending on economic times and whom they seek to impress.

Research has provided additional insight into why companies may prefer certain accounting methods. Some of these reasons are as follows:

1. *Political Costs.* As companies become larger and more politically visible, politicians and regulators devote more attention to them. Many suggest that these politicians and regulators can "feather their own nests" by imposing regulations on these organizations for the benefit of their own constituents. Thus the larger the firm, the more likely it is to become subject to regulation such as antitrust and the more

likely it is to be required to pay higher taxes. Therefore, companies that are politically visible may attempt to report income numbers that are low, to avoid the scrutiny of regulators. Companies thus hope to reduce their exposure to the perception of monopoly power. In addition, other constituents such as labor unions may be less willing to ask for wage increases if reported income is low. Researchers have found that the larger the company, the more likely it is to adopt income decreasing approaches in selecting accounting methods.[11]

2. ***Capital Structure.*** A number of studies have indicated that the capital structure of the company can affect the selection of accounting methods. For example, a company with a high debt-to-equity ratio is more likely to be constrained by debt covenants. That is, a company may have a debt covenant that indicates that it cannot pay any dividends if retained earnings fall below a certain level. As a result, this type of company is more likely to select accounting methods that will increase net income. For example, one group of writers indicated that a company's capital structure affected its decision whether to expense or capitalize interest.[12] Others indicated that full cost accounting was selected instead of successful efforts by companies that have high debt-to-equity ratios.[13]
3. ***Bonus Payments.*** If bonus payments paid to management are tied to income, it has been found that management will select accounting methods that maximize their bonus payments. Thus, in selecting accounting methods, management does concern itself with the effect of accounting income changes on their compensation plans.[14]
4. ***Smooth Earnings.*** Substantial increases in earnings attract the attention of politicians, regulators, and competitors. In addition, large increases in income create problems for management because the same results are difficult to achieve the following year. Executive compensation plans would use these higher numbers as a baseline and make it difficult for management to earn bonuses in subsequent years. Conversely, large decreases in earnings might be viewed as a signal that the company is in financial trouble. Furthermore, substantial decreases in income raise concerns on the part of stockholders, lenders, and other interested parties about the competency of management. Thus, companies have an incentive to "manage" or "smooth" earnings. Management therefore believes that a steady 10% growth a year is much better than a 30% growth one year and a 10% decline the next.[15] In other words, management usually prefers a gradually increasing income report (often referred to as income smoothers) and sometimes changes accounting methods to ensure such a result.

---

[11]Ross L. Watts and Jerold L. Zimmerman, "Positive Accounting Theory: A Ten-Year Perspective," *The Accounting Review,* January 1990.

[12]R. M. Bowen, E. W. Noreen, and J. M. Lacy, "Determinants of the Corporate Decision to Capitalize Interest," *Journal of Accounting and Economics,* August 1981.

[13]See, for example, Dan S. Dhaliwal, "The Effect of the Firm's Capital Structure on the Choice of Accounting Methods," *The Accounting Review,* January 1980; and W. Bruce Johnson and Ramachandran Ramanan, "Discretionary Accounting Changes from 'Successful Efforts' to 'Full Cost' Methods: 1970–1976," *The Accounting Review,* January 1988. The latter study found that firms that changed to full cost were more likely to exhibit higher levels of financial risk (leverage) than firms that retained successful efforts.

[14]See, for example, Mark Zmijewski and Robert Hagerman, "An Income Strategy Approach to the Positive Theory of Accounting Standard Setting/Choice," *Journal of Accounting and Economics,* 1985.

[15]O. Douglas Moses, "Income Smoothing and Incentives: Empirical Tests Using Accounting Changes," *The Accounting Review,* April 1987. Findings provide evidence that smoothers are associated with firm size, the existence of bonus plans, and the divergence of actual earnings from expectations.

Management pays careful attention to the accounting it follows and often changes accounting methods not for conceptual reasons, but rather for economic reasons. As indicated throughout this textbook, such arguments have come to be known as "economic consequences arguments," since they focus on the supposed impact of the accounting method on the behavior of investors, creditors, competitors, governments, or managers of the reporting companies themselves, rather than addressing the conceptual justification for accounting standards.[16]

To counter these pressures, standard setters such as the FASB have declared, as part of their conceptual framework, that they will assess the merits of proposed standards from a position of neutrality. That is, the soundness of standards should not be evaluated on the grounds of their possible impact on behavior. It is not the FASB's place to choose standards according to the kinds of behavior they wish to promote and the kinds they wish to discourage. At the same time, it must be admitted that some standards **will** often have the effect of influencing behavior. Yet their justification should be conceptual and not in terms of their impact.

ERROR ANALYSIS

SECTION 2

OBJECTIVE 10
Analyze the effect of errors.

As indicated earlier, material errors are unusual in large corporations because internal control procedures coupled with the diligence of the accounting staff are ordinarily sufficient to find any major errors in the system. Smaller businesses may face a different problem. These enterprises may not be able to afford an internal audit staff or to implement the necessary control procedures to ensure that accounting data are always recorded accurately.[17]

In practice, firms do not correct for errors discovered that do not have a significant effect on the presentation of the financial statements. For example, the failure to record accrued wages of $5,000 when the total payroll for the year is $1,750,000 and net income is $940,000 is not considered significant, and no correction is made. Obviously, defining materiality is difficult, and experience and judgment must be used to determine whether adjustment is necessary for a given error. **All errors discussed in this section are assumed to be material and to require adjustment.** Also, all tax effects are ignored in this section.

Three questions must be answered in error analysis:

1. What type of error is involved?
2. What entries are needed to correct for the error?
3. How are financial statements to be restated once the error is discovered?

As indicated earlier, errors are **treated as prior period adjustments and reported in the current year as adjustments to the beginning balance of Retained Earnings**. If comparative statements are presented, the prior statements affected should be restated to correct for the error.

Three types of errors can occur. Because each type has its own peculiarities, it is important to differentiate among them.

---

[16]Lobbyists use economic consequences arguments—and there are many of them—to put pressure on standard setters. We have seen examples of these arguments in the oil and gas industry about successful efforts versus full cost, in the technology area with the issue of mandatory expensing of research and developmental costs, and so on.

[17]See Mark L. DeFord and James Jiambalvo, "Incidence and Circumstances of Accounting Errors," *The Accounting Review*, July 1991, for examples of different types of errors and why these errors might have occurred.

BALANCE SHEET ERRORS

These errors affect only the presentation of an asset, liability, or stockholders' equity account. Examples are the classification of a short-term receivable as part of the investment section; the classification of a note payable as an account payable; and the classification of plant assets as inventory. Reclassification of the item to its proper position is needed when the error is discovered. If comparative statements that include the error year are prepared, the balance sheet for the error year is restated correctly.

INCOME STATEMENT ERRORS

These errors affect only the presentation of the nominal accounts in the income statement. Errors involve the improper classification of revenues or expenses, such as recording interest revenue as part of sales; purchases as bad debt expense; and depreciation expense as interest expense. An income statement classification error has no effect on the balance sheet and no effect on net income. A reclassification entry is needed when the error is discovered, if it is discovered in the year it is made. If the error occurred in prior periods, no entry is needed at the date of discovery because the accounts for the current year are correctly stated. If comparative statements that include the error year are prepared, the income statement for the error year is restated correctly.

BALANCE SHEET AND INCOME STATEMENT EFFECTS

The third type of error involves both the balance sheet and income statement. For example, assume that accrued wages payable were overlooked by the bookkeeper at the end of the accounting period. The effect of this error is to understate expenses, understate liabilities, and overstate net income for that period of time. This type of error affects both the balance sheet and the income statement and is classified in one of two ways—counterbalancing or noncounterbalancing.

Counterbalancing errors are errors that will be offset or corrected over two periods. In the previous illustration, the failure to record accrued wages is considered a counterbalancing error because over a 2-year period the error will no longer be present. In other words the failure to record accrued wages in the previous period means: (1) net income for the first period is overstated; (2) accrued wages payable (a liability) is understated, and (3) wages expense is understated. In the next period, net income is understated; accrued wages payable (a liability) is correctly stated; and wages expense is overstated. For the **2 years combined**: (1) net income is correct; (2) wages expense is correct; and (3) accrued wages payable at the end of the second year is correct. Most errors in accounting that affect both the balance sheet and income statement are counterbalancing errors.

Noncounterbalancing errors are errors that are not offset in the next accounting period, for example, the failure to capitalize equipment that has a useful life of 5 years. If we expense this asset immediately, expenses will be overstated in the first period but understated in the next four periods. At the end of the second period, the effect of the error is not fully offset. Net income is correct in the aggregate only at the end of 5 years, because the asset is fully depreciated at this point. Thus, **noncounterbalancing errors are those that take longer than two periods to correct themselves.**

Only in rare instances is an error never reversed, for example, when land is initially expensed. Because land is not depreciable, theoretically the error is never offset unless the land is sold.

Counterbalancing Errors

The usual types of counterbalancing errors are illustrated on the following pages. In studying these illustrations, a number of points should be remembered. First, determine whether or not the books have been closed for the period in which the error is found:

1. **If the books have been closed:**
   a. If the error is already counterbalanced, no entry is necessary.
   b. If the error is not yet counterbalanced, an entry is necessary to adjust the present balance of retained earnings.
2. **If the books have not been closed:**
   a. If the error is already counterbalanced and the company is in the second year, an entry is necessary to correct the current period and to adjust the beginning balance of Retained Earnings.
   b. If the error is not yet counterbalanced, an entry is necessary to adjust the beginning balance of Retained Earnings and correct the current period.

Second, if comparative statements are presented, restatement of the amounts for comparative purposes is necessary. **Restatement is necessary even if a correcting journal entry is not required.** To illustrate, assume that Sanford's Cement Co. failed to accrue revenue in 1999 when earned, but recorded the revenue in 2000 when received. The error was discovered in 2002. No entry is necessary to correct for this error because the effects have been counterbalanced by the time the error is discovered in 2002. However, if comparative financial statements for 1999 through 2002 are presented, the accounts and related amounts for the years 1999 and 2000 should be restated correctly for financial reporting purposes.

Failure to Record Accrued Wages

On December 31, 2001, Hurley Enterprises did not accrue wages in the amount of $1,500. The entry in 2002 to correct this error, assuming that the books have not been closed for 2002, is:

Retained Earnings	1,500	
Wages Expense		1,500

The rationale for this entry is as follows: (1) When the accrued wages of 2001 are paid in 2002 an additional debit of $1,500 is made to 2002 Wages Expense. (2) Wages Expense—2002 is overstated by $1,500. (3) Because 2001 accrued wages were not recorded as Wages Expense—2001, the net income for 2001 was overstated by $1,500. (4) Because 2001 net income is overstated by $1,500, the Retained Earnings account is overstated by $1,500 because net income is closed to Retained Earnings.

If the books have been closed for 2002, no entry is made because the error is counterbalanced.

Failure to Record Prepaid Expenses

In January 2001 Hurley Enterprises purchased a 2-year insurance policy costing $1,000; Insurance Expense was debited, and Cash was credited. No adjusting entries were made at the end of 2001.

The entry on December 31, 2002, to correct this error, assuming that the books have not been closed for 2002, is:

Insurance Expense	500	
Retained Earnings		500

If the books have been closed for 2002, no entry is made because the error is counterbalanced.

Understatement of Unearned Revenue

On December 31, 2001, Hurley Enterprises received $50,000 as a prepayment for renting certain office space for the following year. The entry made at the time of receipt of the rent payment was a debit to Cash and a credit to Rent Revenue. No adjusting entry was made as of December 31, 2001. The entry on December 31, 2002, to correct for this error, assuming that the books have not been closed for 2002, is:

Retained Earnings	50,000	
Rent Revenue		50,000

If the books have been closed for 2002, no entry is made because the error is counterbalanced.

Overstatement of Accrued Revenue

On December 31, 2001, Hurley Enterprises accrued as interest revenue $8,000 that applied to 2002. The entry made on December 31, 2001, was to debit Interest Receivable and credit Interest Revenue. The entry on December 31, 2002, to correct for this error, assuming that the books have not been closed for 2002, is:

Retained Earnings	8,000	
Interest Revenue		8,000

If the books have been closed for 2002, no entry is made because the error is counterbalanced.

Overstatement of Purchases

Hurley Enterprises' accountant recorded a purchase of merchandise for $9,000 in 2001 that applied to 2002. The physical inventory for 2001 was correctly stated. The company uses the periodic inventory method. The entry on December 31, 2002, to correct for this error, assuming that the books have not been closed for 2002, is:

Purchases	9,000	
Retained Earnings		9,000

If the books have been closed for 2002, no entry is made because the error is counterbalanced.

Noncounterbalancing Errors

Because such errors do not counterbalance over a 2-year period, the entries for noncounterbalancing errors are more complex and correcting entries are needed, even if the books have been closed.

Failure to Record Depreciation

Assume that on January 1, 2001, Hurley Enterprises purchased a machine for $10,000 that had an estimated useful life of 5 years. The accountant incorrectly expensed this machine in 2001. The error was discovered in 2002. If we assume that the company desires to use straight-line depreciation on this asset, the entry on December 31, 2002, to correct for this error, given that the books have not been closed, is:

Machinery	10,000	
Depreciation Expense	2,000	
Retained Earnings		8,000[a]
Accumulated Depreciation		4,000[a]

[a]Computations:

Retained Earnings	
Overstatement of expense in 2001	$10,000
Proper depreciation for 2001 (20% × $10,000)	(2,000)
Retained earnings understated as of Dec. 31, 2001	$ 8,000
Accumulated Depreciation	
Accumulated depreciation (20% × $10,000 × 2)	$ 4,000

If the books have been closed for 2002, the entry is:

Machinery	10,000	
Retained Earnings		6,000[a]
Accumulated Depreciation		4,000

[a]Computations:

Retained Earnings	
Retained earnings understated as of Dec. 31, 2001	$ 8,000
Proper depreciation for 2002 (20% × $10,000)	(2,000)
Retained earnings understated as of Dec. 31, 2002	$ 6,000

Failure to Adjust for Bad Debts

Companies sometimes use a specific charge-off method in accounting for bad debt expense when a percentage of sales is more appropriate. Adjustments are often made to change from the specific writeoff to some type of allowance method. For example, assume that Hurley Enterprises has recognized bad debt expense when the debts have actually become uncollectible as follows:

	2001	2002
From 2001 sales	$550	$690
From 2002 sales		700

Hurley estimates that an additional $1,400 will be charged off in 2003, of which $300 is applicable to 2001 sales and $1,100 to 2002 sales. The entry on December 31, 2002, assuming that the **books have not been closed for 2002**, is:

Bad Debt Expense	410[a]	
Retained Earnings	990[a]	
Allowance for Doubtful Accounts		1,400

[a]Computations:

Allowance for doubtful accounts—additional $300 for 2001 sales and $1,100 for 2002 sales.
Bad debts and retained earnings balance:

	2001	2002
Bad debts charged for	$1,240[b]	$ 700
Additional bad debts anticipated in 2003	300	1,100
Proper bad debt expense	1,540	1,800
Charges currently made to each period	(550)	(1,390)
Bad debt adjustment	$ 990	$ 410

[b]$550 + $690 = $1,240

If the **books have been closed for 2002**, the entry is:

Retained Earnings	1,400	
Allowance for Doubtful Accounts		1,400

COMPREHENSIVE ILLUSTRATION: NUMEROUS ERRORS

In some circumstances a combination of errors occurs. A work sheet is therefore prepared to facilitate the analysis. The following problem demonstrates the use of a work sheet. The mechanics of the work sheet preparation should be obvious from the solution format.

The income statements of the Hudson Company for the years ended December 31, 2000, 2001, and 2002 indicate the following net incomes.

2000	$17,400
2001	20,200
2002	11,300

An examination of the accounting records of the Hudson Company for these years indicates that several errors were made in arriving at the net income amounts reported. The following errors were discovered:

1. Wages earned by workers but not paid at December 31 were consistently omitted from the records. The amounts omitted were:

   December 31, 2000 $1,000
   December 31, 2001 $1,400
   December 31, 2002 $1,600

   These amounts were recorded as expenses when paid in the year following that in which they were earned.

2. The merchandise inventory on December 31, 2000, was overstated by $1,900 as the result of errors made in the footings and extensions on the inventory sheets.
3. Unexpired insurance of $1,200, applicable to 2002, was expensed on December 31, 2001.
4. Interest receivable in the amount of $240 was not recorded on December 31, 2001.
5. On January 2, 2001, a piece of equipment costing $3,900 was sold for $1,800. At the date of sale the equipment had accumulated depreciation of $2,400. The cash received was recorded as Miscellaneous Income in 2001. In addition, depreciation was recorded for this equipment in both 2001 and 2002 at the rate of 10% of cost.

The first step in preparing the work sheet is to prepare a schedule showing the corrected net income amounts for the years ended December 31, 2000, 2001, and 2002. Each correction of the amount originally reported is clearly labeled. The next step is to indicate the balance sheet accounts affected as of December 31, 2002. The completed work sheet for Hudson Company is as follows.

ILLUSTRATION 23-19
Work Sheet to Correct Income and Balance Sheet Errors

HUDSON COMPANY
Work Sheet to Correct Income and Balance Sheet Errors

	Work Sheet Analysis of Changes in Net Income				Balance Sheet Correction at December 31, 2002		
	2000	2001	2002	Totals	Debit	Credit	Account
Net income as reported	$17,400	$20,200	$11,300	$48,900			
Wages unpaid, 12/31/00	(1,000)	1,000		–0–			
Wages unpaid, 12/31/01		(1,400)	1,400	–0–			
Wages unpaid, 12/31/02			(1,600)	(1,600)		$1,600	Wages Payable
Inventory overstatement, 12/31/00	(1,900)	1,900		–0–			
Unexpired insurance, 12/31/01		1,200	(1,200)	–0–			
Interest receivable, 12/31/01		240	(240)	–0–			
Correction for entry made upon sale of equipment, 1/2/01		(1,500)		(1,500)	$2,400		Accumulated Depreciation
						3,900	Machinery
Overcharge of depreciation, 2001[a]		390		390	390		Accumulated Depreciation
Overcharge of depreciation, 2002			390	390	390		Accumulated Depreciation
Corrected net income	$14,500	$22,030	$10,050	$46,580			

[a]Cost	$ 3,900
Accumulated depreciation	2,400
Book value	1,500
Proceeds from sale	1,800
Gain on sale	300
Income reported	(1,800)
Adjustment	$ (1,500)

Correcting entries **if the books have not been closed** on December 31, 2002, are:

Account	Debit	Credit
Retained Earnings	1,400	
Wages Expense		1,400
(To correct improper charge to Wages Expense for 2002)		
Wages Expense	1,600	
Wages Payable		1,600
(To record proper wages expense for 2002)		
Insurance Expense	1,200	
Retained Earnings		1,200
(To record proper insurance expense for 2002)		
Interest Revenue	240	
Retained Earnings		240
(To correct improper credit to Interest Revenue in 2002)		
Retained Earnings	1,500	
Accumulated Depreciation	2,400	
Machinery		3,900
(To record writeoff of machinery in 2001 and adjustment of Retained Earnings)		
Accumulated Depreciation	780	
Depreciation Expense		390
Retained Earnings		390
(To correct improper charge for depreciation expense in 2001 and 2002)		

If the books have been closed for 2002, the correcting entries are:

Account	Debit	Credit
Retained Earnings	1,600	
Wages Payable		1,600
(To record proper wage expense for 2002)		
Retained Earnings	1,500	
Accumulated Depreciation	2,400	
Machinery		3,900
(To record writeoff of machinery in 2001 and adjustment of Retained Earnings)		
Accumulated Depreciation	780	
Retained Earnings		780
(To correct improper charge for depreciation expense in 2001 and 2002)		

PREPARATION OF FINANCIAL STATEMENTS WITH ERROR CORRECTIONS

Up to now, our discussion of error analysis has been concerned with the identification of the type of error involved and the accounting for its correction in the accounting records. The correction of the error should be presented on comparative financial statements. In addition, 5- or 10-year summaries are given for the interested financial reader. The following situation illustrates how a typical year's financial statements are restated given many different errors.

Dick & Wally's Outlet is a small retail outlet in the town of Holiday. Lacking expertise in accounting, they do not keep adequate records. As a result, numerous errors occurred in recording accounting information. The errors are listed below:

1. The bookkeeper inadvertently failed to record a cash receipt of $1,000 on the sale of merchandise in 2002.
2. Accrued wages expense at the end of 2001 was $2,500; at the end of 2002, $3,200. The company does not accrue for wages; all wages are charged to Administrative Expenses.
3. No allowance had been set up for estimated uncollectible receivables. Dick and Wally decided to set up such an allowance for the estimated probable losses as of

December 31, 2002 for 2001 accounts of $700, and for 2002 accounts of $1,500. It is also decided to correct the charge against each year so that it shows the losses (actual and estimated) relating to that year's sales. Accounts have been written off to bad debt expense (selling expense) as follows:

	In 2001	In 2002
2001 accounts	$400	$2,000
2002 accounts		1,600

4. Unexpired insurance not recorded at the end of 2001 was $600, and at the end of 2002, $400. All insurance is charged to Administrative Expenses.
5. An account payable of $6,000 should have been a note payable.
6. During 2001, an asset that cost $10,000 and had a book value of $4,000 was sold for $7,000. At the time of sale Cash was debited and Miscellaneous Income was credited for $7,000.
7. As a result of the last transaction, the company overstated depreciation expense (an administrative expense) in 2001 by $800 and in 2002 by $1,200.

ILLUSTRATION 23-20
Work Sheet to Analyze Effect of Errors in Financial Statements

A work sheet that begins with the unadjusted trial balance of Dick & Wally's Outlet is presented in Illustration 23-20. The correcting entries and their effect on the financial statements can be determined by examining the work sheet.

DICK & WALLY'S OUTLET
Work Sheet Analysis to Adjust Financial Statements for the Year 2002

	Trial Balance Unadjusted		Adjustments		Income Statement Adjusted		Balance Sheet Adjusted	
	Debit	Credit	Debit	Credit	Debit	Credit	Debit	Credit
Cash	3,100		(1) 1,000				4,100	
Accounts Receivable	17,600						17,600	
Notes Receivable	8,500						8,500	
Inventory	34,000						34,000	
Property, Plant and Equipment	112,000			(6) 10,000[a]			102,000	
Accumulated Depreciation		83,500	(6) 6,000[a] (7) 2,000					75,500
Investments	24,300						24,300	
Accounts Payable		14,500	(5) 6,000					8,500
Notes Payable		10,000		(5) 6,000				16,000
Capital Stock		43,500						43,500
Retained Earnings		20,000	(3) 2,700[b] (6) 4,000[a] (2) 2,500	(4) 600 (7) 800				12,200
Sales		94,000		(1) 1,000		95,000		
Cost of Goods Sold	21,000				21,000			
Selling Expenses	22,000			(3) 500[b]	21,500			
Administrative Expenses	23,000		(2) 700 (4) 600	(4) 400 (7) 1,200	22,700			
Totals	265,500	265,500						
Wages Payable				(2) 3,200				3,200
Allowance for Doubtful Accounts				(3) 2,200[b]				2,200
Unexpired Insurance			(4) 400				400	
Net Income					29,800			29,800
Totals			25,900	25,900	95,000	95,000	190,900	190,900

Computations:

[a]Machinery	
Proceeds from sale	$7,000
Book value of machinery	4,000
Gain on sale	3,000
Income credited	7,000
Retained earnings adjustment	$4,000

[b]Bad Debts	2001	2002
Bad debts charged for	$2,400	$1,600
Additional bad debts anticipated	700	1,500
	3,100	3,100
Charges currently made to each year	(400)	(3,600)
Bad debt adjustment	$2,700	$ (500)

SUMMARY OF LEARNING OBJECTIVES

1 Identify the types of accounting changes. The three different types of accounting changes are: (1) *Change in accounting principle:* a change from one generally accepted accounting principle to another generally accepted accounting principle. (2) *Change in accounting estimate:* a change that occurs as the result of new information or as additional experience is acquired. (3) *Change in reporting entity:* a change from reporting as one type of entity to another type of entity.

2 Describe the accounting for changes in accounting principles. A change in accounting principle involves a change from one generally accepted accounting principle to another. A change in accounting principle is not considered to result from the adoption of a new principle in recognition of events that have occurred for the first time or that were previously immaterial. If the accounting principle previously followed was not acceptable, or if the principle was applied incorrectly, a change to a generally accepted accounting principle is considered a correction of an error.

3 Understand how to account for cumulative-effect accounting changes. The general requirement for changes in accounting principle is that the cumulative effect of the change (net of tax) be shown at the bottom of the current year's income statement and that pro-forma net income and earnings per share amounts be reported for all prior periods presented.

4 Understand how to account for retroactive accounting changes. A number of accounting principle changes are handled in a retroactive manner; that is, prior years' financial statements are recast on a basis consistent with the newly adopted principle, and any part of the effect attributable to years prior to those presented is treated as an adjustment of the earliest retained earnings presented.

5 Understand how to account for changes to LIFO. In changing to LIFO, the base year inventory for all subsequent LIFO calculations is the opening inventory in the year the method is adopted. There is no restatement of prior years' income because it is just too impractical to do so.

6 Describe the accounting for changes in estimates. Changes in estimates must be handled prospectively; that is, no changes should be made in previously reported results. Opening balances are not adjusted, and no attempt is made to "catch up" for prior periods. Financial statements of prior periods are not restated, and pro-forma amounts for prior periods are not reported.

7 Identify changes in a reporting entity. An accounting change that results in financial statements that are actually the statements of a different entity should be reported by restating the financial statements of all prior periods presented, to show the financial information for the new reporting entity for all periods.

8 Describe the accounting for correction of errors. As soon as they are discovered, errors must be corrected by proper entries in the accounts and reported in the financial statements. The profession requires that corrections of errors be treated as prior period adjustments, be recorded in the year in which the error was discovered, and be reported in the financial statements as an adjustment to the beginning balance of retained earnings. If comparative statements are presented, the prior statements affected should be restated to correct for the error. The disclosures need not be repeated in the financial statements of subsequent periods.

9 Identify economic motives for changing accounting methods. Managers might have varying profit motives depending on economic times and whom they seek to impress. Some of the reasons for changing accounting methods are: (1) political costs, (2) capital structure, (3) bonus payments, and (4) smooth earnings.

KEY TERMS

- change in accounting estimate, *1255*
- change in accounting principle, *1255*
- change in reporting entity, *1255*
- correction of an error, *1266*
- counterbalancing errors, *1272*
- cumulative effect changes, *1256*
- current changes, *1256*
- noncounterbalancing errors, *1272*
- pro-forma, *1257*
- prospective changes, *1256*
- retroactive changes, *1256*

10 Analyze the effect of errors. Three types of errors can occur: (1) *Balance sheet errors:* affect only the presentation of an asset, liability, or stockholders' equity account. (2) *Income statement errors:* affect only the presentation of the nominal accounts in the income statement. (3) *Balance sheet and income statement effect:* involves both the balance sheet and income statement. Errors are classified into two types: (1) *Counterbalancing errors:* will be offset or corrected over two periods. (2) *Noncounterbalancing errors:* are not offset in the next accounting period and take longer than two periods to correct themselves.

APPENDIX 23A

Changing from and to the Equity Method

As noted in the chapter, an accounting change that results in financial statements for a different entity should be reported by **restating the financial statements of all prior periods presented**. An example of a change in reporting entity is when a company's level of ownership or influence changes, such that it should change from or to the equity method. We present illustrations for these changes in entity in the following two sections.

CHANGE FROM THE EQUITY METHOD

If the investor level of influence or ownership falls below that necessary for continued use of the equity method, a change must be made to the fair value method. The earnings or losses that were previously recognized by the investor under the equity method should **remain as part of the carrying amount** of the investment with no retroactive restatement to the new method.

OBJECTIVE 11
After studying Appendix 23A, you should be able to: Make the computations and prepare the entries necessary to record a change from or to the equity method of accounting.

When a change is made **from the equity method to the fair value method, the cost basis for accounting purposes is the carrying amount of the investment at the date of the change**. In addition, amortizing the excess of acquisition price over the proportionate share of book value acquired attributable to undervalued depreciable assets and unrecorded goodwill ceases when the change of methods occurs. In other words, the new method is applied in its entirety once the equity method is no longer appropriate. At the next reporting date, the investor should record the unrealized holding gain or loss to recognize the difference between the carrying amount and fair value.

Dividends in Excess of Earnings

To the extent that dividends received by the investor in subsequent periods exceed its share of the investee's earnings for such periods (all periods following the change in method), they should be accounted for as a **reduction of the investment carrying amount**, rather than as revenue.

To illustrate, assume that on January 1, 1999, Investor Company purchased 250,000 shares of Investee Company's 1,000,000 shares of outstanding stock for $8,500,000. Investor correctly accounted for this investment using the equity method. After accounting for dividends received, investee net income, and amortization of Investor's share of goodwill in 1999, Investor reported its investment in Investee Company at $8,780,000 at December 31, 1999. On January 2, 2000, Investee Company sold 1,500,000 additional shares of its own common stock to the public, thereby reducing Investor Company's ownership from 25% to 10%. The net income (or loss) and dividends of Investee Company for the years 2000 through 2002 are as shown below.

ILLUSTRATION 23A-1
Income Earned and Dividends Received

Year		Investor's Share of Investee Income (Loss)	Investee Dividends Received by Investor
2000		$600,000	$ 400,000
2001		350,000	400,000
2002		–0–	210,000
	Totals	$950,000	$1,010,000

Assuming a change from the equity method to the fair value method as of January 2, 2000, Investor Company's reported investment in Investee Company and its reported income would be as shown below.

ILLUSTRATION 23A-2
Impact on Investment Carrying Amount

Year	Dividend Revenue Recognized	Cumulative Excess of Share of Earnings Over Dividends Received	Investment at December 31
2000	$400,000	$200,000[a]	$8,780,000
2001	400,000	150,000[b]	8,780,000
2002	150,000	(60,000)[c]	8,780,000 – $60,000 = $8,720,000

[a]$600,000 – $400,000 = $200,000
[b]($350,000 – $400,000) + $200,000 = $150,000
[c]$150,000 – $210,000 = $(60,000)

The following entries would be recorded by Investor Company to recognize the above dividends and earnings data for the 3 years subsequent to the change in methods:

2000 and 2001

	Debit	Credit
Cash	400,000	
Dividend Revenue		400,000
(To record dividend received from Investee Company)		

2002

	Debit	Credit
Cash	210,000	
Available-for-Sale Securities		60,000
Dividend Revenue		150,000
(To record dividend revenue from Investee Company in 2002 and to recognize cumulative excess of dividends received over share of Investee earnings in periods subsequent to change from equity method)		

CHANGE TO THE EQUITY METHOD

When converting to the equity method, a retroactive adjustment is necessary. Such a change involves **adjusting retroactively the carrying amount of the investment, results of current and prior operations, and retained earnings of the investor as if the**

equity method has been in effect during all of the previous periods in which this investment was held.[1] When changing from the fair value method to the equity method, it is also necessary to eliminate any balances in the Unrealized Holding Gain or Loss—Equity account and the Securities Fair Value Adjustment account. In addition, the available-for-sale classification for this investment is eliminated, and the investment in stock under the equity method is recorded.

For example, on January 2, 2001, Amsted Corp. purchased for $500,000 cash 10% of the outstanding shares of Cable Company common stock. On that date, the net assets of Cable Company had a book value of $3,000,000. The excess of cost over the underlying equity in net assets of Cable Company is attributed to goodwill, which is amortized over 40 years. On January 2, 2003, Amsted Corp. purchased an additional 20% of Cable Company's stock for $1,200,000 cash when the book value of Cable's net assets was $4,000,000. Now having a 30% interest, Amsted Corp. must use the equity method. From January 2, 2001, to January 2, 2003, Amsted Corp. used the fair value method and categorized these securities as available-for-sale. At January 2, 2003, Amsted has a credit balance of $92,000 in its Unrealized Holding Gain or Loss—Equity account and a debit balance in its Securities Fair Value Adjustment account of the same amount. Assume that this adjustment was made on December 31, 2001. The net income reported by Cable Company and the Cable Company dividends received by Amsted during the period 2001 through 2003 were as follows:

ILLUSTRATION 23A-3
Income Earned and Dividends Received

Year	Cable Company Net Income	Cable Co. Dividends Paid to Amsted
2001	$ 500,000	$ 20,000
2002	1,000,000	30,000
2003	1,200,000	120,000

The journal entries recorded from January 2, 2001, through December 31, 2003, relative to Amsted Corp.'s investment in Cable Company, reflecting the data above and a change from the fair value method to the equity method, are as follows.[2]

	Debit	Credit
January 2, 2001		
Available-for-Sale Securities	500,000	
Cash		500,000
(To record the purchase of a 10% interest in Cable Company)		
December 31, 2001		
Cash	20,000	
Dividend Revenue		20,000
(To record the receipt of cash dividends from Cable Company)		
Securities Fair Value Adjustment (Available-for-Sale)	92,000	
Unrealized Holding Gain or Loss—Equity		92,000
(To record increase in fair value of securities)		
December 31, 2002		
Cash	30,000	
Dividend Revenue		30,000
(To record the receipt of cash dividends from Cable Company)		

[1] "The Equity Method of Accounting for Investments in Common Stock," *Opinions of the Accounting Principles Board No. 18* (New York: AICPA, 1971), par. 17.

[2] Adapted from Paul A. Pacter, "Applying APB Opinion No. 18—Equity Method," *Journal of Accountancy*, September 1971, pp. 59–60.

January 2, 2003

Investment in Cable Stock	1,290,000	
Cash		1,200,000
Retained Earnings		90,000
(To record the purchase of an additional interest in Cable Company and to reflect retroactively a change from the fair value method to the equity method of accounting for the investment. The $90,000 adjustment is computed as follows:		

	2001	2002	Total
Amsted Corp. equity in earnings of Cable Company (10%)	$50,000	$100,000	$150,000
Amortization of excess of acquisition price over underlying equity [$500,000 − (10% × $3,000,000)] ÷ 40 years = $5,000 per year	(5,000)	(5,000)	(10,000)
Dividend received	(20,000)	(30,000)	(50,000)
Prior period adjustment	$25,000	$ 65,000	$ 90,000)

January 2, 2003

Investment in Cable Stock	500,000	
Available-for-Sale Securities		500,000
(To reclassify initial 10% interest to equity method)		

January 2, 2003

Unrealized Holding Gain or Loss—Equity	92,000	
Securities Fair Value Adjustment (Available-for-Sale)		92,000
(To eliminate fair value accounts for change to equity method)		

December 31, 2003

Investment in Cable Stock	345,000	
Revenue from Investment		345,000
[To record equity in earnings of Cable Company (30% of $1,200,000) less $15,000 amortization of goodwill[a]]		

[a]Goodwill amortization includes $5,000 [$500,000 − (10% × $3,000,000) ÷ 40 years] from 2001 purchase of 10% interest plus $10,000 [$1,200,000 − (20% × $4,000,000) ÷ 40 years] from 2003 purchase of 20% interest.

Cash	120,000	
Investment in Cable Stock		120,000
(To record the receipt of cash dividends from Cable Company)		

Changing to the equity method is accomplished by placing the accounts related to and affected by the investment on the same basis as if the equity method had always been the basis of accounting for that investment. Thus, the effects of this accounting change are reported using the retroactive approach.

SUMMARY OF LEARNING OBJECTIVE FOR APPENDIX 23A

11 **Make the computations and prepare the entries necessary to record a change from or to the equity method of accounting.** When changing from the equity method to the fair value method, the cost basis for accounting purposes is the carrying amount used for the investment at the date of change. The new method is applied in its entirety once the equity method is no longer appropriate. When changing to the equity method, a retroactive adjustment of the carrying amount, of results of current and past operations, and of retained earnings is necessary to make the accounts as if the equity method has been in effect during all of the periods in which the investment was held.

Note: All **asterisked** Brief Exercises, Exercises, and Problems relate to material contained in the appendix to the chapter.

QUESTIONS

1 In recent years, *The Wall Street Journal* has indicated that many companies have changed their accounting principles. What are the major reasons why companies change accounting methods?

2 State how each of the following items is reflected in the financial statements:

(a) Change from straight-line method of depreciation to sum-of-the-years'-digits.

(b) Change from FIFO to LIFO method for inventory valuation purposes.

(c) Charge for failure to record depreciation in a previous period.

(d) Litigation won in current year, related to prior period.

(e) Change in the realizability of certain receivables.

(f) Writeoff of receivables.

(g) Change from the percentage-of-completion to the completed-contract method for reporting net income.

3 What are the advantages of employing the current or catch-up method for handling changes in accounting principle?

4 Explain when pro-forma amounts are reported and why these amounts are useful to financial statement readers.

5 Define a change in estimate and provide an illustration. When is a change in accounting estimate affected by a change in accounting principle?

6 Sandwich State Bank has followed the practice of capitalizing certain marketing costs and amortizing these costs over their expected life. In the current year, the bank determined that the future benefits from these costs were doubtful. Consequently, the bank adopted the policy of expensing these costs as incurred. How should this accounting change be reported in the comparative financial statements?

7 Indicate how the following items are recorded in the accounting records in the current year of Tami Agler Co.:

(a) Large writeoff of goodwill.

(b) A change in depreciating plant assets from accelerated to the straight-line method.

(c) Large writeoff of inventories because of obsolescence.

(d) Change from the cash basis to accrual basis of accounting.

(e) Change from LIFO to FIFO method for inventory valuation purposes.

(f) Change in the estimate of service lives for plant assets.

8 R. M. Andrews Construction Co. had followed the practice of expensing all materials assigned to a construction job without recognizing any salvage inventory. On December 31, 2001, it was determined that salvage inventory should be valued at $62,000. Of this amount, $29,000 arose during the current year. How does this information affect the financial statements to be prepared at the end of 2001?

9 E. A. Basler Inc. wishes to change from the sum-of-the-years'-digits to the straight-line depreciation method for financial reporting purposes. The auditor indicates that a change would be permitted only if it is to a preferable method. What difficulties develop in assessing preferability?

10 Discuss how a change to the LIFO method of inventory valuation is handled.

11 How should consolidated financial statements be reported this year when statements of individual companies were presented last year?

12 Karen Beers controlled four domestic subsidiaries and one foreign subsidiary. Prior to the current year, Beers had excluded the foreign subsidiary from consolidation. During the current year, the foreign subsidiary was included in the financial statements. How should this change in accounting principle be reflected in the financial statements?

13 Clara Beverage Co., a closely held corporation, is in the process of preparing financial statements to accompany an offering of its common stock. The company at this time has decided to switch from the accelerated depreciation method to the straight-line method of depreciation to better present its financial operations. How should this change in accounting principle be reported in the financial statements?

14 Distinguish between counterbalacing and non-counterbalancing errors. Give an example of each.

15 Discuss and illustrate how a correction of an error in previously issued financial statements should be handled.

16 Prior to 2002, Mary Boudreau Inc. excluded manufacturing overhead costs from work in process and finished goods inventory. These costs have been expensed as incurred. In 2002, the company decided to change its accounting methods for manufacturing inventories to full costing by including these costs as product costs. Assuming that these costs are material, how should this change be reflected in the financial statements for 2001 and 2002?

17 Lou Brady Corp. failed to record accrued salaries for 1999, $2,000; 2000, $2,100; and 2001, $3,900. What is the amount of the overstatement or understatement of Retained Earnings at December 31, 2002?

18 In January 2001, installation costs of $8,000 on new machinery were charged to Repair Expense. Other costs of this machinery of $30,000 were correctly recorded and have been depreciated using the straight-line method with an estimated life of 10 years and no salvage value. At December 31, 2002, it is decided that the machinery has a useful life of 20 years, starting with January 1, 2002. What entry(ies) should be made in 2002 to correctly record transactions related to machinery, assuming the machinery has no salvage value? The books have not been closed for 2002 and depreciation expense has not yet been recorded for 2002.

19 On January 2, 2001, $100,000 of 11%, 20-year bonds were issued for $97,000. The $3,000 discount was charged to Interest Expense. The bookkeeper, John Castle, records interest only on the interest payment dates of January 1 and July 1. What is the effect on reported net income for 2001 of this error, assuming straight-line amortization of the discount? What entry is necessary to correct for this error, assuming that the books are not closed for 2001?

20 An account payable of $13,000 for merchandise purchased on December 23, 2001, was recorded in January 2002. This merchandise was not included in inventory at December 31, 2001. What effect does this error have on reported net income for 2001? What entry should be made to correct for this error, assuming that the books are not closed for 2001?

21 Equipment was purchased on January 2, 2001, for $18,000, but no portion of the cost has been charged to depreciation. The corporation wishes to use the straight-line method for these assets, which have been estimated to have a life of 10 years and no salvage value. What effect does this error have on net income in 2001. What entry is necessary to correct for this error, assuming that the books are not closed for 2001?

BRIEF EXERCISES

BE23-1 Larry Beaty Corporation decided at the beginning of 2002 to change from double-declining balance depreciation to straight-line depreciation for financial reporting. The company will continue to use MACRS for tax purposes. For years prior to 2002, depreciation expense under the two methods was as follows: double-declining balance $128,000, and straight-line $80,000. The tax rate is 35%. Prepare Beaty's 2002 journal entry to record the change in accounting principle.

BE23-2 Bruce Bickner Company changed depreciation methods in 2002 from straight-line to double-declining balance, resulting in a cumulative-effect adjustment of $84,000. The 2002 income before the change was $250,000. Bickner had 10,000 shares of common stock outstanding all year. Prepare Bickner's 2002 income statement beginning with income before cumulative effect.

BE23-3 Robert Boey, Inc., changed from the LIFO cost flow assumption to the FIFO cost flow assumption in 2002. The increase in the prior year's income before taxes is $1,000,000. The tax rate is 40%. Prepare Boey's 2002 journal entry to record the change in accounting principle.

BE23-4 Nancy Castle Company purchased a computer system for $60,000 on January 1, 2000. It was depreciated based on a 7-year life and an $18,000 salvage value. On January 1, 2002, Castle revised these estimates to a total useful life of 4 years and a salvage value of $10,000. Prepare Castle's entry to record 2002 depreciation expense.

BE23-5 In 2002, John Hiatt Corporation discovered that equipment purchased on January 1, 2000, for $75,000 was expensed at that time. The equipment should have been depreciated over 5 years, with no salvage value. The effective tax rate is 30%. Prepare Hiatt's 2002 journal entry to correct the error.

BE23-6 At January 1, 2002, William R. Monat Company reported retained earnings of $2,000,000. In 2002, Monat discovered that 2001 depreciation expense was understated by $500,000. In 2002, net income was $900,000 and dividends declared were $250,000. The tax rate is 40%. Prepare a 2002 retained earnings statement for William R. Monat Company.

BE23-7 Indicate the effect—**U**nderstate, **O**verstate, **N**o **E**ffect—that each of the following errors has on 2001 net income and 2002 net income:

	2001	2002
(a) Wages payable were not recorded at 12/31/01.	____	____
(b) Equipment purchased in 2000 was expensed.	____	____
(c) Equipment purchased in 2001 was expensed.	____	____
(d) 2001 ending inventory was overstated.	____	____
(e) Goodwill amortization was not recorded in 2002.	____	____

***BE23-8** Robocop Corporation owns stock of Terminator, Inc. Prior to 2002, the investment was accounted for using the equity method. In early 2002, Robocop sold part of its investment in Terminator, and began using the fair value method. In 2002, Terminator earned net income of $80,000 and paid dividends of

$95,000. Prepare Robocop's entries related to Terminator's net income and dividends, assuming Robocop now owns 8% of Terminator's stock.

***BE23-9** Rocket Corporation has owned stock of Knight Corporation since 1998. At December 31, 2001, its balances related to this investment were:

Available-for-Sale Securities	$185,000
Securities Fair Value Adj (AFS)	34,000 Dr.
Unrealized Holding Gain or Loss—Equity	34,000 Cr.

On January 1, 2002, Rocket purchased additional stock of Knight Company for $445,000 and now has significant influence over Knight. If the equity method had been used in 1998–2001, income would have been $33,000 greater than dividends received. Prepare Rocket's journal entries to record the purchase of the investment and the change to the equity method.

EXERCISES

E23-1 (Error and Change in Principle—Depreciation) Joy Cunningham Co. purchased a machine on January 1, 1999, for $550,000. At that time it was estimated that the machine would have a 10-year life and no salvage value. On December 31, 2002, the firm's accountant found that the entry for depreciation expense had been omitted in 2000. In addition, management has informed the accountant that they plan to switch to straight-line depreciation, starting with the year 2002. At present, the company uses the sum-of-the-years'-digits method for depreciating equipment.

Instructions

Prepare the general journal entries the accountant should make at December 31, 2002 (ignore tax effects).

E23-2 (Change in Principle and Change in Estimate—Depreciation) Kathleen Cole Inc. acquired the following assets in January of 1999:

Equipment, estimated service life, 5 years; salvage value, $15,000	$525,000
Building, estimated service life, 30 years; no salvage value	$693,000

The equipment has been depreciated using the sum-of-the-years'-digits method for the first 3 years for financial reporting purposes. In 2002, the company decided to change the method of computing depreciation to the straight-line method for the equipment, but no change was made in the estimated service life or salvage value. It was also decided to change the total estimated service life of the building from 30 years to 40 years, with no change in the estimated salvage value. The building is depreciated on the straight-line method.

The company has 100,000 shares of capital stock outstanding. Results of operations for 2002 and 2001 are shown below:

	2002	2001
Income before cumulative effect of change in computing depreciation for 2002: depreciation for 2002 has been computed on the straight-line basis for both the equipment and building[a]	$385,000	$380,000
Income per share before cumulative effect of change in computing depreciation for 2002	$3.85	$3.80

[a]It should be noted that the computation for depreciation expense for 2002 and 2001 for the building was based on the original estimate of service life for 30 years.

Instructions

(a) Compute the cumulative effect of the change in accounting principle to be reported in the income statement for 2002, and prepare the journal entry to record the change. (Ignore tax effects.)

(b) Present comparative data for the years 2001 and 2002, starting with income before cumulative effect of accounting change. Prepare pro-forma data. Do not prepare the footnote. (Ignore tax effects.)

E23-3 (Change in Principle and Change in Estimated Depreciation) On January 1, 1998, Jackson Company purchased a building and equipment that have the following useful lives, salvage values, and costs:

Building, 40-year estimated useful life, $50,000 salvage value, $800,000 cost
Equipment, 12-year estimated useful life, $10,000 salvage value, $100,000 cost

The building has been depreciated under the double-declining balance method through 2001. In 2002, the company decided to switch to the straight-line method of depreciation. Jackson also decided to change the total useful life of the equipment to 9 years, with a salvage value of $5,000 at the end of that time. The equipment is depreciated using the straight-line method.

Instructions

(a) Compute the cumulative effect of the change in accounting principle for 2002.
(b) Prepare the journal entry(ies) necessary to record the changes made in 2002.
(c) Compute depreciation expense on the equipment for 2002.

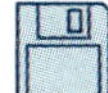

E23-4 (Change in Estimate—Depreciation) Peter M. Dell Co. purchased equipment for $510,000 which was estimated to have a useful life of 10 years with a salvage value of $10,000 at the end of that time. Depreciation has been entered for 7 years on a straight-line basis. In 2002, it is determined that the total estimated life should be 15 years with a salvage value of $5,000 at the end of that time.

Instructions

(a) Prepare the entry (if any) to correct the prior years' depreciation.
(b) Prepare the entry to record depreciation for 2002.

E23-5 (Change in Principle—Depreciation) Gerald Englehart Industries changed from the double-declining balance to the straight-line method in 2002 on all its plant assets. For tax purposes, assume that the amount of tax depreciation is higher than the double-declining balance depreciation for each of the 3 years. The appropriate information related to this change is as follows:

Year	Double-Declining Balance Depreciation	Straight-Line Depreciation	Difference
2000	$250,000	$125,000	$125,000
2001	225,000	125,000	100,000
2002	202,500	125,000	77,500

Net income for 2001 was reported at $270,000; net income for 2002 was reported at $300,000, excluding any adjustment for the cumulative effect of a change in depreciation methods. The straight-line method of depreciation was employed in computing net income for 2002.

Instructions

(a) Assuming a tax rate of 34%, what is the amount of the cumulative effect adjustment in 2002?
(b) Prepare the journal entry(ies) to record the cumulative effect adjustment in the accounting records.
(c) Starting with income before cumulative effect of change in accounting principle, prepare the remaining portion of the income statement for 2001 and 2002. Indicate the pro-forma net income that should be reported. Ignore per share computations and note disclosures.

E23-6 (Change in Principle—Depreciation) At the end of fiscal 2002, management of Carol Dilbeck Manufacturing Company has decided to change its depreciation method from the double-declining balance method to the straight-line method for financial reporting purposes. For federal income taxes the company will continue to use the MACRS method. The income tax rate for all years is 30%. At the end of fiscal 2002, the company has 200,000 common shares issued and outstanding. Information regarding depreciation expense and income after income taxes is as follows:

Depreciation expense to date under:

	MACRS	Straight-Line	Double-Declining Balance
Pre-2001	$1,000,000	$400,000	$950,000
2001	300,000	150,000	260,000
2002	280,000	140,000	250,000

Reported income after income taxes:

2001	$1,200,000
2002	1,400,000

Instructions

(a) Prepare the journal entries to record the change in accounting method in 2002 and indicate how the change in depreciation method would be reported in the income statement of 2002. Also indicate how earnings per share would be disclosed. (*Hint:* Adjust Deferred Tax Liability account.)
(b) Show the amount of depreciation expense to be reported in 2002.

E23-7 (Change in Principle—Long-term Contracts) Pam Erickson Construction Company changed from the completed-contract to the percentage-of-completion method of accounting for long-term construction contracts during 2002. For tax purposes, the company employs the completed-contract method and will continue this approach in the future. (*Hint:* Adjust all tax consequences through the Deferred Tax Liability account.) The appropriate information related to this change is as follows:

	Pretax Income from:		
	Percentage-of-Completion	Completed-Contract	Difference
2001	$780,000	$590,000	$190,000
2002	700,000	480,000	220,000

Instructions

(a) Assuming that the tax rate is 35%, what is the amount of net income that would be reported in 2002?

(b) What entry(ies) are necessary to adjust the accounting records for the change in accounting principle?

E23-8 (Various Changes in Principle—Inventory Methods) Below is the net income of Anita Ferreri Instrument Co., a private corporation, computed under the three inventory methods using a periodic system.

	FIFO	Average Cost	LIFO
1999	$26,000	$24,000	$20,000
2000	30,000	25,000	21,000
2001	28,000	27,000	24,000
2002	34,000	30,000	26,000

Instructions (Ignore tax considerations)

(a) Assume that in 2002 Ferreri decided to change from the FIFO method to the average cost method of pricing inventories. Prepare the journal entry necessary for the change that took place during 2002, and show all the appropriate information needed for reporting on a comparative basis.

(b) Assume that in 2002 Ferreri, which had been using the LIFO method since incorporation in 1999, changed to the FIFO method of pricing inventories. Prepare the journal entry necessary for the change, and show all the appropriate information needed for reporting on a comparative basis.

E23-9 (Change in Principle—Inventory Methods) Garner Company began operations on January 1, 1999, and uses the average cost method of pricing inventory. Management is contemplating a change in inventory methods for 2002. The following information is available for the years 1999–2001:

	Net Income Computed Using		
	Average Cost Method	FIFO Method	LIFO Method
1999	$15,000	$20,000	$12,000
2000	18,000	24,000	14,000
2001	20,000	27,000	17,000

Instructions

(a) Prepare the journal entry necessary to record a change from the average cost method to the FIFO method in 2002.

(b) Show the comparative income statements for 2001 and 2002, starting with income before the cumulative effect of change in accounting principle. Assume net income for 2002 was $32,000.

(c) Assume Garner Company used the LIFO method instead of the average cost method during the years 1999–2001. In 2002, Garner changed to the FIFO method. Prepare the journal entry necessary to record the change in principle.

E23-10 (Error Correction Entries) The first audit of the books of Bruce Gingrich Company was made for the year ended December 31, 2002. In examining the books, the auditor found that certain items had been overlooked or incorrectly handled in the last 3 years. These items are:

1. At the beginning of 2000, the company purchased a machine for $510,000 (salvage value of $51,000) that had a useful life of 6 years. The bookkeeper used straight-line depreciation, but failed to deduct the salvage value in computing the depreciation base for the 3 years.
2. At the end of 2001, the company failed to accrue sales salaries of $45,000.
3. A tax lawsuit that involved the year 2000 was settled late in 2002. It was determined that the company owed an additional $85,000 in taxes related to 2000. The company did not record a liability in 2000 or 2001 because the possibility of loss was considered remote, and charged the $85,000 to a loss account in 2002.
4. Gingrich Company purchased another company early in 2000 and recorded goodwill of $450,000. Gingrich had not amortized goodwill because its value had not diminished.

5. In 2002, the company changed its basis of inventory pricing from FIFO to LIFO. The cumulative effect of this change was to decrease net income by $71,000. The company debited this cumulative effect to Retained Earnings. LIFO was used in computing income for 2002.
6. In 2002, the company wrote off $87,000 of inventory considered to be obsolete; this loss was charged directly to Retained Earnings.

Instructions

Prepare the journal entries necessary in 2002 to correct the books, assuming that the books have not been closed. The proper amortization period for goodwill is 40 years. Disregard effects of corrections on income tax.

E23-11 (Change in Principle and Error; Financial Statements) Presented below are the comparative statements for Denise Habbe Inc.

	2002	2001
Sales	$340,000	$270,000
Cost of sales	200,000	142,000
Gross profit	140,000	128,000
Expenses	88,000	50,000
Net income	$ 52,000	$ 78,000
Retained earnings (Jan. 1)	$125,000	$ 72,000
Net income	52,000	78,000
Dividends	(30,000)	(25,000)
Retained earnings (Dec. 31)	$147,000	$125,000

The following additional information is provided:

1. In 2002, Denise Habbe Inc. decided to switch its depreciation method from sum-of-the-years'-digits to the straight-line method. The differences in the two depreciation methods for the assets involved are:

	2002	2001
Sum-of-the-years'-digits	$30,000[a]	$40,000
Straight-line	25,000	25,000

[a]The 2002 income statement contains depreciation expense of $30,000.

2. In 2002, the company discovered that the ending inventory for 2001 was overstated by $24,000; ending inventory for 2002 is correctly stated.

Instructions

(a) Prepare the revised income and retained earnings statement for 2001 and 2002, assuming comparative statements (ignore income tax effects). Do not prepare footnotes or pro-forma amounts.
(b) Prepare the revised income and retained earnings statement for 2002, assuming a noncomparative presentation (ignore income tax effects). Do not prepare footnotes or pro-forma amounts.

E23-12 (Error Analysis and Correcting Entry) You have been engaged to review the financial statements of Linette Gottschalk Corporation. In the course of your examination you conclude that the bookkeeper hired during the current year is not doing a good job. You notice a number of irregularities as follows:

1. Year-end wages payable of $3,400 were not recorded because the bookkeeper thought that "they were immaterial."
2. Accrued vacation pay for the year of $31,100 was not recorded because the bookkeeper "never heard that you had to do it."
3. Insurance for a 12-month period purchased on November 1 of this year was charged to insurance expense in the amount of $2,640 because "the amount of the check is about the same every year."
4. Reported sales revenue for the year is $2,120,000. This includes all sales taxes collected for the year. The sales tax rate is 6%. Because the sales tax is forwarded to the State Department of Revenue, the Sales Tax Expense account is debited because the bookkeeper thought that "the sales tax is a selling expense." At the end of the current year, the balance in the Sales Tax Expense account is $103,400.

Instructions

Prepare the necessary correcting entries, assuming that Gottschalk uses a calendar-year basis.

E23-13 (Error Analysis and Correcting Entry) The reported net incomes for the first 2 years of Sandra Gustafson Products, Inc., were as follows: 2001—$147,000; 2002—$185,000. Early in 2003, the following errors were discovered:

1. Depreciation of equipment for 2001 was overstated $17,000.
2. Depreciation of equipment for 2002 was understated $38,500.
3. December 31, 2001, inventory was understated $50,000.
4. December 31, 2002, inventory was overstated $16,200.

Instructions

Prepare the correcting entry necessary when these errors are discovered. Assume that the books are closed. Ignore income tax considerations.

E23-14 (Error Analysis) Peter Henning Tool Company's December 31 year-end financial statements contained the following errors:

	December 31, 2001	December 31, 2002
Ending inventory	$9,600 understated	$8,100 overstated
Depreciation expense	$2,300 understated	—

An insurance premium of $66,000 was prepaid in 2001 covering the years 2001, 2002, and 2003. The entire amount was charged to expense in 2001. In addition, on December 31, 2002, fully depreciated machinery was sold for $15,000 cash, but the entry was not recorded until 2003. There were no other errors during 2001 or 2002, and no corrections have been made for any of the errors. Ignore income tax considerations.

Instructions

(a) Compute the total effect of the errors on 2002 net income.

(b) Compute the total effect of the errors on the amount of Henning's working capital at December 31, 2002.

(c) Compute the total effect of the errors on the balance of Henning's retained earnings at December 31, 2002.

E23-15 (Error Analysis; Correcting Entries) A partial trial balance of Julie Hartsack Corporation is as follows on December 31, 2002:

	Dr.	Cr.
Supplies on hand	$ 2,700	
Accrued salaries and wages		$ 1,500
Interest receivable on investments	5,100	
Prepaid insurance	90,000	
Unearned rent		–0–
Accrued interest payable		15,000

Additional adjusting data:

1. A physical count of supplies on hand on December 31, 2002, totaled $1,100.
2. Through oversight, the Accrued Salaries and Wages account was not changed during 2002. Accrued salaries and wages on December 31, 2002, amounted to $4,400.
3. The Interest Receivable on Investments account was also left unchanged during 2002. Accrued interest on investments amounts to $4,350 on December 31, 2002.
4. The unexpired portions of the insurance policies totaled $65,000 as of December 31, 2002.
5. $28,000 was received on January 1, 2002 for the rent of a building for both 2002 and 2003. The entire amount was credited to rental income.
6. Depreciation for the year was erroneously recorded as $5,000 rather than the correct figure of $50,000.
7. A further review of depreciation calculations of prior years revealed that depreciation of $7,200 was not recorded. It was decided that this oversight should be corrected by a prior period adjustment.

Instructions

(a) Assuming that the books have not been closed, what are the adjusting entries necessary at December 31, 2002? Ignore income tax considerations.

(b) Assuming that the books have been closed, what are the adjusting entries necessary at December 31, 2002? Ignore income tax considerations.

E23-16 (Error Analysis) The before-tax income for Lonnie Holdiman Co. for 2001 was $101,000 and $77,400 for 2002. However, the accountant noted that the following errors had been made:

1. Sales for 2001 included amounts of $38,200 which had been received in cash during 2001, but for which the related products were delivered in 2002. Title did not pass to the purchaser until 2002.
2. The inventory on December 31, 2001, was understated by $8,640.

3. The bookkeeper in recording interest expense for both 2001 and 2002 on bonds payable made the following entry on an annual basis:

Interest Expense	15,000	
Cash		15,000

The bonds have a face value of $250,000 and pay a stated interest rate of 6%. They were issued at a discount of $15,000 on January 1, 2001, to yield an effective interest rate of 7%. (Assume that the effective yield method should be used.)

4. Ordinary repairs to equipment had been erroneously charged to the Equipment account during 2001 and 2002. Repairs in the amount of $8,500 in 2001 and $9,400 in 2002 were so charged. The company applies a rate of 10% to the balance in the Equipment account at the end of the year in its determination of depreciation charges.

Instructions

Prepare a schedule showing the determination of corrected income before taxes for 2001 and 2002.

E23-17 (Error Analysis) When the records of Debra Hanson Corporation were reviewed at the close of 2002, the errors listed below were discovered. For each item indicate by a check mark in the appropriate column whether the error resulted in an overstatement, an understatement, or had no effect on net income for the years 2001 and 2002.

	2001			2002		
Item	Over-statement	Under-statement	No Effect	Over-statement	Under-statement	No Effect
1. Failure to record amortization of patent in 2002.						
2. Failure to record the correct amount of ending 2001 inventory. The amount was understated because of an error in calculation.						
3. Failure to record merchandise purchased in 2001. Merchandise was also omitted from ending inventory in 2001 but was not yet sold.						
4. Failure to record accrued interest on notes payable in 2001; amount was recorded when paid in 2002.						
5. Failure to reflect supplies on hand on balance sheet at end of 2001.						

E23-18 (Accounting for Accounting Changes and Errors) Listed below are various types of accounting changes and errors.

____ 1. Change in a plant asset's salvage value.
____ 2. Change due to overstatement of inventory.
____ 3. Change from sum-of-the-years'-digits to straight-line method of depreciation.
____ 4. Change from presenting unconsolidated to consolidated financial statements.
____ 5. Change from LIFO to FIFO inventory method.
____ 6. Change in the rate used to compute warranty costs.
____ 7. Change from an unacceptable accounting principle to an acceptable accounting principle.
____ 8. Change in a patent's amortization period.
____ 9. Change from completed-contract to percentage-of-completion method on construction contracts.
____ 10. Change from FIFO to average-cost inventory method.

Instructions

For each change or error, indicate how it would be accounted for using the following code letters:

- **a.** Accounted for currently.
- **b.** Accounted for prospectively.
- **c.** Accounted for retroactively.
- **d.** None of the above.

***E23-19 (Change from Fair Value to Equity)** On January 1, 2001, Barbra Streisand Co. purchased 25,000 shares (a 10% interest) in Elton John Corp. for $1,400,000. At the time, the book value and the fair value of John's net assets were $13,000,000.

On July 1, 2002, Streisand paid $3,040,000 for 50,000 additional shares of John common stock, which represented a 20% investment in John. The fair value of John's identifiable assets net of liabilities was equal to their carrying amount of $14,200,000. As a result of this transaction, Streisand owns 30% of John and can exercise significant influence over John's operating and financial policies. Intangible assets are amortized over 10 years.

John reported the following net income and declared and paid the following dividends:

	Net Income	Dividend per Share
Year ended 12/31/01	$700,000	None
Six months ended 6/30/02	500,000	None
Six months ended 12/31/02	815,000	$1.55

Instructions

Determine the ending balance that Streisand Co. should report as its investment in John Corp. at the end of 2002.

***E23-20 (Change from Equity to Fair Value)** Dan Aykroyd Corp. was a 30% owner of John Belushi Company, holding 210,000 shares of Belushi's common stock on December 31, 2000. The investment account had the following entries:

Investment in Belushi

1/1/99 Cost	$3,180,000	12/6/99 Dividend received	$150,000
12/31/99 Share of income	390,000	12/31/99 Amortization of undervalued assets	30,000
12/31/00 Share of income	510,000	12/5/00 Dividend received	240,000
		12/31/00 Amortization of undervalued assets	30,000

On January 2, 2001, Aykroyd sold 126,000 shares of Belushi for $3,440,000, thereby losing its significant influence. During the year 2001 Belushi experienced the following results of operations and paid the following dividends to Aykroyd.

	Belushi Income (Loss)	Dividends Paid to Aykroyd
2001	$300,000	$50,400

At December 31, 2001, the fair value of Belushi shares held by Aykroyd is $1,570,000. This is the first reporting date since the January 2 sale.

Instructions

- **(a)** What effect does the January 2, 2001, transaction have upon Aykroyd's accounting treatment for its investment in Belushi?
- **(b)** Compute the carrying amount in Belushi as of December 31, 2001.
- **(c)** Prepare the adjusting entry on December 31, 2001, applying the fair value method to Aykroyd's long-term investment in Belushi Company securities.

PROBLEMS

P23-1 (Change in Estimate, Principle, and Error Correction) Roland Company is in the process of having its financial statements audited for the first time as of December 31, 2001. The auditor has found the following items that occurred in previous years:

1. Roland purchased equipment on January 2, 1998, for $65,000. At that time, the equipment had an estimated useful life of 10 years with a $5,000 salvage value. The equipment is depreciated on a

straight-line basis. On January 2, 2001, as a result of additional information, the company determined that the equipment had a total estimated useful life of 7 years with a $3,000 salvage value.

2. During 2001 Roland changed from the double-declining balance method for its building to the straight-line method. The auditor provided the following computations which present depreciation on both bases:

	2001	2000	1999
Straight-line	$27,000	$27,000	$27,000
Declining-balance	48,600	54,000	60,000

3. Roland purchased a machine on July 1, 1998, at a cost of $80,000. The machine has a salvage value of $8,000 and a useful life of 8 years. Roland's bookkeeper recorded straight-line depreciation during each year but failed to consider the salvage value.

Instructions

(a) Prepare the necessary journal entries to record each of the preceding changes or errors. The books for 2001 have not been closed.

(b) Compute the 2001 depreciation expense on the equipment.

(c) Show the comparative statements for 2000 and 2001, starting with income before the cumulative effect of change in accounting principle. Income before depreciation expense was $300,000 in 2001, and net income was $210,000 in 2000.

P23-2 (Comprehensive Accounting Change and Error Analysis Problem) On December 31, 2002, before the books were closed, the management and accountants of Eloise Keltner Inc. made the following determinations about three depreciable assets:

1. Depreciable asset A was purchased January 2, 1999. It originally cost $495,000 and, for depreciation purposes, the straight-line method was originally chosen. The asset was originally expected to be useful for 10 years and have a zero salvage value. In 2002, the decision was made to change the depreciation method from straight-line to sum-of-the-years'-digits, and the estimates relating to useful life and salvage value remained unchanged.
2. Depreciable asset B was purchased January 3, 1998. It originally cost $120,000 and, for depreciation purposes, the straight-line method was chosen. The asset was originally expected to be useful for 15 years and have a zero salvage value. In 2002, the decision was made to shorten the total life of this asset to 9 years and to estimate the salvage value at $3,000.
3. Depreciable asset C was purchased January 5, 1998. The asset's original cost was $140,000, and this amount was entirely expensed in 1998. This particular asset has a 10-year useful life and no salvage value. The straight-line method was chosen for depreciation purposes.

Additional data:

1. Income in 2002 before depreciation expense amount to $400,000.
2. Depreciation expense on assets other than A, B, and C totaled $55,000 in 2002.
3. Income in 2001 was reported at $370,000.
4. Ignore all income tax effects.
5. 100,000 shares of common stock were outstanding in 2001 and 2002.

Instructions

(a) Prepare all necessary entries in 2002 to record these determinations.

(b) Prepare comparative income statements for Eloise Keltner Inc. for 2001 and 2002, starting with income before the cumulative effects of any change in accounting principle.

(c) Prepare comparative retained earnings statements for Eloise Keltner Inc. for 2001 and 2002. The company had retained earnings of $200,000 at December 31, 2000.

P23-3 (Comprehensive Accounting Change and Error Analysis Problem) Larry Kingston Inc. was organized in late 1999 to manufacture and sell hosiery. At the end of its fourth year of operation, the company has been fairly successful, as indicated by the following reported net incomes.

1999	$140,000[a]	2001	$205,000
2000	160,000[b]	2002	276,000

[a]Includes a $12,000 increase because of change in bad debt experience rate.
[b]Includes extraordinary gain of $40,000.

The company has decided to expand operations and has applied for a sizable bank loan. The bank officer has indicated that the records should be audited and presented in comparative statements to facilitate analysis by the bank. Larry Kingston Inc., therefore, hired the auditing firm of Check & Doublecheck Co. and has provided the following additional information.

1. In early 2000, Larry Kingston Inc. changed its estimate from 2% to 1% on the amount of bad debt expense to be charged to operations. Bad debt expense for 1999, if a 1% rate had been used, would have been $12,000. The company, therefore, restated its net income for 1999.
2. In 2002, the auditor discovered that the company had changed its method of inventory pricing from LIFO to FIFO. The effect on the income statements for the previous years is as follows:

	1999	2000	2001	2002
Net income unadjusted—LIFO basis	$140,000	$160,000	$205,000	$276,000
Net income unadjusted—FIFO basis	155,000	165,000	215,000	260,000
	$ 15,000	$ 5,000	$ 10,000	($ 16,000)

3. In 2000, the company changed its method of depreciation from the accelerated method to the straight-line approach. The company used the straight-line method in 2000. The effect on the income statement for the previous year is as follows:

	1999
Net income unadjusted—accelerated method	$140,000
Net income unadjusted—straight-line method	147,000
	$ 7,000

4. In 2002, the auditor discovered that:
   a. The company incorrectly overstated the ending inventory by $11,000 in 2001.
   b. A dispute developed in 2000 with the Internal Revenue Service over the deductibility of entertainment expenses. In 1999, the company was not permitted these deductions, but a tax settlement was reached in 2002 that allowed these expenses. As a result of the court's finding, tax expenses in 2002 were reduced by $60,000.

Instructions

(a) Indicate how each of these changes or corrections should be handled in the accounting records. Ignore income tax considerations.

(b) Present comparative income statements for the years 1999 to 2002, starting with income before extraordinary items. Do not prepare pro-forma amounts. Ignore income tax considerations.

P23-4 (Change in Principle—LIFO to Average Cost; Income Statements—Periodic) The management of Scott Kreiter Instrument Company had concluded, with the concurrence of its independent auditors, that results of operations would be more fairly presented if Kreiter changed its method of pricing inventory from last-in, first-out (LIFO) to average cost in 2001. Given below is the 5-year summary of income and a schedule of what the inventories might have been if stated on the average cost method.

SCOTT KREITER INSTRUMENT COMPANY
Statement of Income and Retained Earnings
For the Years Ended May 31

	1997	1998	1999	2000	2001
Sales—net	$13,964	$15,506	$16,673	$18,221	$18,898
Cost of goods sold					
Beginning inventory	1,000	1,100	1,000	1,115	1,237
Purchases	13,000	13,900	15,000	15,900	17,100
Ending inventory	(1,100)	(1,000)	(1,115)	(1,237)	(1,369)
Total	12,900	14,000	14,885	15,778	16,968
Gross profit	1,064	1,506	1,788	2,443	1,930
Administrative expenses	700	763	832	907	989
Income before taxes	364	743	956	1,536	941
Income taxes (50%)	182	372	478	768	471
Net income	182	371	478	768	470
Retained earnings—beginning	1,206	1,388	1,759	2,237	3,005
Retained earnings—ending	$ 1,388	$ 1,759	$ 2,237	$ 3,005	$ 3,475
Earnings per share	$ 1.82	$ 3.71	$ 4.78	$ 7.68	$ 4.70

Schedule of Inventory Balances Using Average Cost Method
Year Ended May 31

1996	1997	1998	1999	2000	2001
$950	$1,124	$1,091	$1,270	$1,480	$1,699

Instructions

Prepare comparative statements for the 5 years, assuming that Kreiter changed its method of inventory pricing to average cost. Indicate the effects on net income and earnings per share for the years involved. (All amounts except EPS are rounded up to the nearest dollar.)

P23-5 (Financial Statement Effect of Changes in Principle and Estimate) James N. McInnes Corporation has decided that in the preparation of its 2002 financial statements two changes should be made from the methods used in prior years:

1. ***Depreciation.*** McInnes has always used an accelerated method for tax and financial reporting purposes but has decided to change during 2002 to the straight-line method for financial reporting only. Assume that the accelerated method for tax and reporting purposes has been the same in the past. The effect of this change is as follows:

	Excess of Accelerated Depreciation over Straight-line Depreciation
Prior to 2001	$1,365,000
2001	106,050
2002	103,950
	$1,575,000

   Depreciation is charged to cost of sales and to selling, general, and administrative expenses on the basis of 75% and 25%, respectively.

2. ***Bad debt expense.*** In the past, McInnes has recognized bad debt expense equal to 1.5% of net sales. After careful review it has been decided that a rate of 1.75% is more appropriate for 2002. Bad debt expense is charged to selling, general, and administrative expenses.

   The following information is taken from preliminary financial statements, prepared before giving effect to the two changes:

MCINNES CORPORATION
Condensed Balance Sheet
December 31, 2002
With Comparative Figures for 2001

	2002	2001
Assets		
Current assets	$43,561,000	$43,900,000
Plant assets, at cost	45,792,000	43,974,000
Less: Accumulated depreciation	23,761,000	22,946,000
	$65,592,000	$64,928,000
Liabilities and Stockholders' Equity		
Current liabilities	$21,124,000	$23,650,000
Long-term debt	15,154,000	14,097,000
Capital stock	11,620,000	11,620,000
Retained earnings	17,694,000	15,561,000
	$65,592,000	$64,928,000

MCINNES CORPORATION
Income Statement
For the Year Ended December 31, 2002
With Comparative Figures for 2001

	2002	2001
Net sales	$80,520,000	$78,920,000
Cost of goods sold	54,847,000	53,074,000
	25,673,000	25,846,000
Selling, general, and administrative expenses	19,540,000	18,411,000
	6,133,000	7,435,000
Other income (expense), net	(1,198,000)	(1,079,000)
Income before income taxes	4,935,000	6,356,000
Income taxes	2,220,750	2,860,200
Net income	$ 2,714,250	$ 3,495,800

There have been no temporary differences between any book and tax items prior to the changes above. The effective tax rate is 45%.

Instructions

For the items listed below compute the amounts that would appear on the comparative (2002 and 2001) financial statements of McInnes Corporation after adjustment for the two accounting changes. Show amounts for both 2002 and 2001, and prepare supporting schedules as necessary.

(a) Accumulated depreciation.
(b) Deferred tax liability (cumulative).
(c) Selling, general, and administrative expenses.
(d) Current portion of federal income tax expense.
(e) Deferred portion of federal income tax expense.
(f) Retained earnings.
(g) Pro-forma net income.

P23-6 (Error Corrections) You have been assigned to examine the financial statements of Vickie L. Lemke Company for the year ended December 31, 2002. You discover the following situations:

1. Depreciation of $3,200 for 2002 on delivery vehicles was not recorded.
2. The physical inventory count on December 31, 2001, improperly excluded merchandise costing $19,000 that had been temporarily stored in a public warehouse. Lemke uses a periodic inventory system.
3. The physical inventory count on December 31, 2002, improperly included merchandise with a cost of $8,500 that had been recorded as a sale on December 27, 2002, and held for the customer to pick up on January 4, 2003.
4. A collection of $5,600 on account from a customer received on December 31, 2002, was not recorded until January 2, 2003.
5. In 2002, the company sold for $3,700 fully depreciated equipment that originally cost $22,000. The company credited the proceeds from the sale to the Equipment account.
6. During November 2002, a competitor company filed a patent-infringement suit against Lemke claiming damages of $220,000. The company's legal counsel has indicated that an unfavorable verdict is probable and a reasonable estimate of the court's award to the competitor is $125,000. The company has not reflected or disclosed this situation in the financial statements.
7. Lemke has a portfolio of trading securities. No entry has been made to adjust to market. Information on cost and market value is as follows:

	Cost	Market
December 31, 2001	$95,000	$95,000
December 31, 2002	$84,000	$82,000

8. At December 31, 2002, an analysis of payroll information shows accrued salaries of $12,200. The Accrued Salaries Payable account had a balance of $16,000 at December 31, 2002, which was unchanged from its balance at December 31, 2001.

9. A large piece of equipment was purchased on January 3, 2002, for $32,000 and was charged to Repairs Expense. The equipment is estimated to have a service life of 8 years and no residual value. Lemke normally uses the straight-line depreciation method for this type of equipment.
10. A $15,000 insurance premium paid on July 1, 2001, for a policy that expires on June 30, 2004, was charged to insurance expense.
11. A trademark was acquired at the beginning of 2001 for $50,000. No amortization has been recorded since its acquisition. The maximum allowable amortization period is to be used.

Instructions

Assume the trial balance has been prepared but the books have not been closed for 2002. Assuming all amounts are material, prepare journal entries showing the adjustments that are required. Ignore income tax considerations.

P23-7 (Error Corrections and Changes in Principle) Patricia Voga Company is in the process of adjusting and correcting its books at the end of 2002. In reviewing its records, the following information is compiled.

1. Voga has failed to accrue sales commissions payable at the end of each of the last 2 years, as follows:

December 31, 2001	$4,000
December 31, 2002	$2,500

2. In reviewing the December 31, 2002, inventory, Voga discovered errors in its inventory-taking procedures that have caused inventories for the last 3 years to be incorrect, as follows:

December 31, 2000	Understated	$16,000
December 31, 2001	Understated	$21,000
December 31, 2002	Overstated	$ 6,700

Voga has already made an entry that established the incorrect December 31, 2002, inventory amount.

3. At December 31, 2002, Voga decided to change the depreciation method on its office equipment from double-declining balance to straight-line. Assume that tax depreciation is higher than the double-declining depreciation taken for each period. The following information is available (the tax rate is 40%):

	Double-Declining Balance	Straight-Line	Pretax Difference	Tax Effect	Difference, Net of Tax
Prior to 2002	$70,000	$40,000	$30,000	$12,000	$18,000
2002	12,000	10,000	2,000	800	1,200

Voga has already recorded the 2002 depreciation expense using the double-declining balance method.

4. Before 2002, Voga accounted for its income from long-term construction contracts on the completed contract basis. Early in 2002, Voga changed to the percentage-of-completion basis for both accounting and tax purposes. Income for 2002 has been recorded using the percentage-of-completion method. The income tax rate is 40%. The following information is available:

	Pretax Income	
	Percentage of Completion	Completed Contract
Prior to 2002	$150,000	$95,000
2002	60,000	20,000

Instructions

Prepare the journal entries necessary at December 31, 2002, to record the above corrections and changes. The books are still open for 2002. Voga has not yet recorded its 2002 income tax expense and payable amounts so current year tax effects may be ignored. Prior year tax effects must be considered in items 3 and 4.

P23-8 (Change in Principle) Plato Corporation performs year-end planning in November of each year before their calendar year ends in December. The preliminary estimated net income is $3 million. The CFO, Mary Sheets, meets with the company president, S. A. Plato, to review the projected numbers. She presents the following projected information:

PLATO CORPORATION
Projected Income Statement
For the Year Ended December 31, 2001

Sales		$29,000,000
Cost of goods sold	$14,000,000	
Depreciation	2,600,000	
Operating expenses	6,400,000	23,000,000
Income before income taxes		$ 6,000,000
Provision for income taxes		3,000,000
Net income		$ 3,000,000

PLATO CORPORATION
Selected Balance Sheet Information
at December 31, 2001

Estimated cash balance	$ 5,000,000
Available-for-sale securities (at cost)	10,000,000
Security fair value adjustment account (1/1/01)	200,000

Estimated market value at December 31, 2001:

Security	Cost	Estimated Market
A	$ 2,000,000	$ 2,200,000
B	4,000,000	3,900,000
C	3,000,000	3,000,000
D	1,000,000	2,800,000
Total	$10,000,000	$11,900,000

Equipment	$3,000,000
Accumulated depreciation (5-year SL)	1,200,000
New robotic equipment (purchased 1/1/01)	5,000,000
Accumulated depreciation (5-year DDB)	2,000,000

The corporation has never used robotic equipment before, and Sheets assumed an accelerated method because of the rapidly changing technology in robotic equipment. The company normally uses straight-line depreciation for production equipment.

Plato explains to Sheets that it is important for the corporation to show an $8,000,000 net income before taxes because Plato receives a $1,000,000 bonus if the income before taxes and bonus reaches $8,000,000. He also cautions that he will not pay more than $3,000,000 in income taxes to the government.

Instructions

(a) What can Sheets do within GAAP to accommodate the president's wishes to achieve $8,000,000 income before taxes and bonus? Present the revised income statement based on your decision.

(b) Are the actions ethical? Who are the stakeholders in this decision, and what effect does Sheets' actions have on their interests?

P23-9 (Comprehensive Error Analysis) On March 5, 2002, you were hired by Gretchen Hollenbeck Inc., a closely held company, as a staff member of its newly created internal auditing department. While reviewing the company's records for 2000 and 2001, you discover that no adjustments have yet been made for the items listed below.

Items

1. Interest income of $14,100 was not accrued at the end of 2000. It was recorded when received in February 2001.
2. A computer costing $8,000 was expensed when purchased on July 1, 2000. It is expected to have a 4-year life with no salvage value. The company typically uses straight-line depreciation for all fixed assets.
3. Research and development costs of $33,000 were incurred early in 2000. They were capitalized and were to be amortized over a 3-year period. Amortization of $11,000 was recorded for 2000 and $11,000 for 2001.

4. On January 2, 2000, Hollenbeck leased a building for 5 years at a monthly rental of $8,000. On that date, the company paid the following amounts, which were expensed when paid.

Security deposit	$25,000
First month's rent	8,000
Last month's rent	8,000
	$41,000

5. The company received $30,000 from a customer at the beginning of 2000 for services that it is to perform evenly over a 3-year period beginning in 2000. None of the amount received was reported as unearned revenue at the end of 2000.
6. Merchandise inventory costing $18,200 was in the warehouse at December 31, 2000, but was incorrectly omitted from the physical count at that date. The company uses the periodic inventory method.

Instructions

Indicate the effect of any errors on the net income figure reported on the income statement for the year ending December 31, 2000, and the retained earnings figure reported on the balance sheet at December 31, 2001. Assume all amounts are material and ignore income tax effects. Using the following format, enter the appropriate dollar amounts in the appropriate columns. Consider each item independent of the other items. It is not necessary to total the columns on the grid.

	Net Income for 2000		Retained Earnings at 12/31/01	
Item	Understated	Overstated	Understated	Overstated

(CIA adapted)

P23-10 (Error Analysis) Mary Keeton Corporation has used the accrual basis of accounting for several years. A review of the records, however, indicates that some expenses and revenues have been handled on a cash basis because of errors made by an inexperienced bookkeeper. Income statements prepared by the bookkeeper reported $29,000 net income for 2001 and $37,000 net income for 2002. Further examination of the records reveals that the following items were handled improperly.

1. Rent was received from a tenant in December 2001; the amount, $1,300, was recorded as income at that time even though the rental pertained to 2002.
2. Wages payable on December 31 have been consistently omitted from the records of that date and have been entered as expenses when paid in the following year. The amounts of the accruals recorded in this manner were:

December 31, 2000	$1,100
December 31, 2001	1,500
December 31, 2002	940

3. Invoices for office supplies purchased have been charged to expense accounts when received. Inventories of supplies on hand at the end of each year have been ignored, and no entry has been made for them.

December 31, 2000	$1,300
December 31, 2001	740
December 31, 2002	1,420

Instructions

Prepare a schedule that will show the corrected net income for the years 2001 and 2002. All items listed should be labeled clearly. Ignore income tax considerations.

P23-11 (Error Analysis and Correcting Entries) Sally Kolb Corporation is in the process of negotiating a loan for expansion purposes. Kolb's books and records have never been audited and the bank has requested that an audit be performed. Kolb has prepared the following comparative financial statements for the years ended December 31, 2002 and 2001:

SALLY KOLB CORPORATION
Balance Sheet
As of December 31, 2002 and 2001

	2002	2001
Assets		
Current assets		
Cash	$ 163,000	$ 82,000
Accounts receivable	392,000	296,000
Allowance for doubtful accounts	(37,000)	(18,000)
Available-for-sale securities, at cost	78,000	78,000
Merchandise inventory	207,000	202,000
Total current assets	803,000	640,000
Plant assets		
Property, plant, and equipment	167,000	169,500
Accumulated depreciation	(121,600)	(106,400)
Total fixed assets	45,400	63,100
Total assets	$ 848,400	$703,100
Liabilities and Stockholders' Equity		
Liabilities		
Accounts payable	$ 121,400	$196,100
Stockholders' equity		
Common stock, par value $10, authorized 50,000 shares, issued and outstanding 20,000 shares	260,000	260,000
Retained earnings	467,000	247,000
Total stockholders' equity	727,000	507,000
Total liabilities and stockholders' equity	$ 848,400	$703,100

SALLY KOLB CORPORATION
Statement of Income
For the Years Ended December 31, 2002 and 2001

	2002	2001
Sales	$1,000,000	$900,000
Cost of sales	430,000	395,000
Gross profit	570,000	505,000
Operating expenses	210,000	205,000
Administrative expenses	140,000	105,000
	350,000	310,000
Net income	$ 220,000	$195,000

During the course of the audit, the following additional facts were determined:

1. An analysis of collections and losses on accounts receivable during the past 2 years indicates a drop in anticipated losses due to bad debts. After consultation with management it was agreed that the loss experience rate on sales should be reduced from the recorded 2% to 1½%, beginning with the year ended December 31, 2002.
2. An analysis of available-for-sale securities revealed that the total market valuation for these investments as of the end of each year was as follows:

December 31, 2001	$82,000
December 31, 2002	$65,000

3. The merchandise inventory at December 31, 2001, was overstated by $8,900 and the merchandise inventory at December 31, 2002, was overstated by $13,600.
4. On January 2, 2001, equipment costing $30,000 (estimated useful life of 10 years and residual value of $5,000) was incorrectly charged to operating expenses. Kolb records depreciation on the straight-

line method. In 2002, fully depreciated equipment (with no residual value) that originally cost $17,500 was sold as scrap for $2,800. Kolb credited the proceeds of $2,800 to the equipment account.

5. An analysis of 2001 operating expenses revealed that Kolb charged to expense a 4-year insurance premium of $4,700 on January 15, 2001.

Instructions

(a) Prepare the journal entries to correct the books at December 31, 2002. The books for 2002 have not been closed. Ignore income taxes.

(b) Prepare a schedule showing the computation of corrected net income for the years ended December 31, 2002 and 2001, assuming that any adjustments are to be reported on comparative statements for the 2 years. The first items on your schedule should be the net income for each year. Ignore income taxes. (Do not prepare financial statements.)

(AICPA adapted)

P23-12 (Error Analysis and Correcting Entries) You have been asked by a client to review the records of Larry Landers Company, a small manufacturer of precision tools and machines. Your client is interested in buying the business, and arrangements have been made for you to review the accounting records.

Your examination reveals the following:

1. Landers Company commenced business on April 1, 1999, and has been reporting on a fiscal year ending March 31. The company has never been audited, but the annual statements prepared by the bookkeeper reflect the following income before closing and before deducting income taxes:

Year Ended March 31	Income Before Taxes
2000	$ 71,600
2001	111,400
2002	103,580

2. A relatively small number of machines have been shipped on consignment. These transactions have been recorded as ordinary sales and billed as such. On March 31 of each year, machines billed and in the hands of consignees amounted to:

2000	$6,500
2001	none
2002	5,590

Sales price was determined by adding 30% to cost. Assume that the consigned machines are sold the following year.

3. On March 30, 2001, two machines were shipped to a customer on a C.O.D. basis. The sale was not entered until April 5, 2001, when cash was received for $6,100. The machines were not included in the inventory at March 31, 2001. (Title passed on March 30, 2001.)
4. All machines are sold subject to a five-year warranty. It is estimated that the expense ultimately to be incurred in connection with the warranty will amount to 1/2 of 1% of sales. The company has charged an expense account for warranty costs incurred.

   Sales per books and warranty costs were:

Year Ended March 31	Sales	Warranty Expense for Sales Made In 2000	2001	2002	Total
2000	$ 940,000	$760			$ 760
2001	1,010,000	360	$1,310		1,670
2002	1,795,000	320	1,620	$1,910	3,850

5. A review of the corporate minutes reveals the manager is entitled to a bonus of 1/2 of 1% of the income before deducting income taxes and the bonus. The bonuses have never been recorded or paid.
6. Bad debts have been recorded on a direct writeoff basis. Experience of similar enterprises indicates that losses will approximate 1/4 of 1% of sales. Bad debts written off were:

	Bad Debts Incurred on Sales Made In 2000	2001	2002	Total
2000	$750			$ 750
2001	800	$ 520		1,320
2002	350	1,800	$1,700	3,850

7. The bank deducts 6% on all contracts financed. Of this amount, ½% is placed in a reserve to the credit of Landers Company that is refunded to Landers as finance contracts are paid in full. The reserve established by the bank has not been reflected in the books of Landers. The excess of credits over debits (net increase) to the reserve account with Landers on the books of the bank for each fiscal year were as follows:

2000	$ 3,000
2001	3,900
2002	5,100
	$12,000

8. Commissions on sales have been entered when paid. Commissions payable on March 31 of each year were:

2000	$1,400
2001	800
2002	1,120

Instructions

(a) Present a schedule showing the revised income before income taxes for each of the years ended March 31, 2000, 2001, and 2002. Make computations to the nearest whole dollar.

(b) Prepare the journal entry or entries you would give the bookkeeper to correct the books. Assume the books have not yet been closed for the fiscal year ended March 31, 2001. Disregard correction of income taxes.

(AICPA adapted)

***P23-13 (Fair Value to Equity Method with Goodwill)** On January 1, 2000, Latoya Inc. paid $700,000 for 10,000 shares of Jones Company's voting common stock, which was a 10% interest in Jones. At that date the net assets of Jones totaled $6,000,000. The fair values of all of Jones' identifiable assets and liabilities were equal to their book values. Latoya does not have the ability to exercise significant influence over the operating and financial policies of Jones. Latoya received dividends of $2.00 per share from Jones on October 1, 2000. Jones reported net income of $500,000 for the year ended December 31, 2000.

On July 1, 2001, Latoya paid $2,325,000 for 30,000 additional shares of Jones Company's voting common stock which represents a 30% investment in Jones. The fair values of all of Jones' identifiable assets net of liabilities were equal to their book values of $6,550,000. As a result of this transaction, Latoya has the ability to exercise significant influence over the operating and financial policies of Jones. Latoya received dividends of $2.00 per share from Jones on April 1, 2001, and $2.50 per share on October 1, 2001. Jones reported net income of $650,000 for the year ended December 31, 2001, and $400,000 for the 6 months ended December 31, 2001. Latoya amortizes goodwill over a 10-year period.

Instructions

(a) Prepare a schedule showing the income or loss before income taxes for the year ended December 31, 2000, that Latoya should report from its investment in Jones in its income statement issued in March 2001.

(b) During March 2002, Latoya issues comparative financial statements for 2000 and 2001. Prepare schedules showing the income or loss before income taxes for the years ended December 31, 2000 and 2001, that Latoya should report from its investment in Jones.

(AICPA adapted)

***P23-14 (Change from Fair Value to Equity Method)** On January 3, 1999, Calvin Company purchased for $500,000 cash a 10% interest in Coolidge Corp. On that date the net assets of Coolidge had a book value of $3,750,000. The excess of cost over the underlying equity in net assets is attributable to undervalued depreciable assets having a remaining life of 10 years from the date of Calvin's purchase.

The fair value of Calvin's investment in Coolidge securities is as follows: December 31, 1999, $570,000; December 31, 2000, $515,000.

On January 2, 2001, Calvin purchased an additional 30% of Coolidge's stock for $1,545,000 cash when the book value of Coolidge's net assets was $4,150,000. The excess was attributable to depreciable assets having a remaining life of 8 years.

During 1999, 2000, and 2001 the following occurred:

	Coolidge Net Income	Dividends Paid by Coolidge to Calvin
1999	$350,000	$15,000
2000	400,000	20,000
2001	550,000	70,000

Instructions

On the books of Calvin Company prepare all journal entries in 1999, 2000, and 2001 that relate to its investment in Coolidge Corp., reflecting the data above and a change from the fair value method to the equity method.

CONCEPTUAL CASES

C23-1 (Analysis of Various Accounting Changes and Errors) Erin Kramer Inc. has recently hired a new independent auditor, Jodie Larson, who says she wants "to get everything straightened out." Consequently, she has proposed the following accounting changes in connection with Erin Kramer Inc.'s 2002 financial statements:

1. At December 31, 2001, the client had a receivable of $820,000 from Holly Michael Inc. on its balance sheet. Holly Michael Inc. has gone bankrupt, and no recovery is expected. The client proposes to write off the receivable as a prior period item.
2. The client proposes the following changes in depreciation policies:
   (a) For office furniture and fixtures it proposes to change from a 10-year useful life to an 8-year life. If this change had been made in prior years, retained earnings at December 31, 2001, would have been $250,000 less. The effect of the change on 2002 income alone is a reduction of $60,000.
   (b) For its manufacturing assets the client proposes to change from double-declining balance depreciation to straight line. If straight-line depreciation had been used for all prior periods, retained earnings would have been $380,800 greater at December 31, 2001. The effect of the change on 2002 income alone is a reduction of $48,800.
   (c) For its equipment in the leasing division the client proposes to adopt the sum-of-the-years'-digits depreciation method. The client had never used SYD before. The first year the client operated a leasing division was 2002. If straight-line depreciation were used, 2002 income would be $110,000 greater.
3. In preparing its 2001 statements, one of the client's bookkeepers overstated ending inventory by $235,000 because of a mathematical error. The client proposes to treat this item as a prior period adjustment.
4. In the past, the client has spread preproduction costs in its furniture division over 5 years. Because its latest furniture is of the "fad" type, it appears that the largest volume of sales will occur during the first 2 years after introduction. Consequently, the client proposes to amortize preproduction costs on a per-unit basis, which will result in expensing most of such costs during the first 2 years after the furniture's introduction. If the new accounting method had been used prior to 2002, retained earnings at December 31, 2001, would have been $375,000 less.
5. For the nursery division the client proposes to switch from FIFO to LIFO inventories because it believes that LIFO will provide a better matching of current costs with revenues. The effect of making this change on 2002 earnings will be an increase of $320,000. The client says that the effect of the change on December 31, 2001, retained earnings cannot be determined.
6. To achieve a better matching of revenues and expenses in its building construction division, the client proposes to switch from the completed-contract method of accounting to the percentage-of-completion method. Had the percentage-of-completion method been employed in all prior years, retained earnings at December 31, 2001, would have been $1,175,000 greater.

Instructions

(a) For each of the changes described above decide whether:
   (1) The change involves an accounting principle, accounting estimate, or correction of an error.
   (2) Restatement of opening retained earnings is required.
(b) Do any of the changes require presentation of pro-forma amounts?
(c) What would be the proper adjustment to the December 31, 2001, retained earnings? What would be the "cumulative effect" shown separately in the 2002 income statement?

C23-2 (Analysis of Various Accounting Changes and Errors) Various types of accounting changes can affect the financial statements of a business enterprise differently. Assume that the following list describes changes that have a material effect on the financial statements for the current year of your business enterprise.

1. A change from the completed-contract method to the percentage-of-completion method of accounting for long-term construction-type contracts.
2. A change in the estimated useful life of previously recorded fixed assets as a result of newly acquired information.
3. A change from deferring and amortizing preproduction costs to recording such costs as an expense when incurred because future benefits of the costs have become doubtful. The new accounting method was adopted in recognition of the change in estimated future benefits.
4. A change from including the employer share of FICA taxes with Payroll Tax Expenses to including it with "Retirement benefits" on the income statement.
5. Correction of a mathematical error in inventory pricing made in a prior period.
6. A change from prime costing to full absorption costing for inventory valuation.
7. A change from presentation of statements of individual companies to presentation of consolidated statements.
8. A change in the method of accounting for leases for tax purposes to conform with the financial accounting method. As a result, both deferred and current taxes payable changed substantially.
9. A change from the FIFO method of inventory pricing to the LIFO method of inventory pricing.

Instructions

Identify the type of change that is described in each item above and indicate whether the prior year's financial statements should be restated when presented in comparative form with the current year's statements. Ignore possible pro-forma effects.

C23-3 (Analysis of Three Accounting Changes and Errors) Listed below are three independent, unrelated sets of facts relating to accounting changes.

Situation 1

Penelope Millhouse Company is in the process of having its first audit. The company's policy with regard to recognition of revenue is to use the installment method. However, *APB No. 10* states that the installment method of revenue recognition is not a generally accepted accounting principle except in certain circumstances, which are not present here. Millhouse president, A. G. Shumway, is willing to change to an acceptable method.

Situation 2

Cheri Nestor Co. decides in January 2002 to adopt the straight-line method of depreciation for plant equipment. The straight-line method will be used for new acquisitions as well as for previously acquired plant equipment for which depreciation had been provided on an accelerated basis.

Situation 3

Laura Osmund Co. determined that the depreciable lives of its fixed assets are too long at present to fairly match the cost of the fixed assets with the revenue produced. The company decided at the beginning of the current year to reduce the depreciable lives of all of its existing fixed assets by 5 years.

Instructions

For each of the situations described, provide the information indicated below.

(a) Type of accounting change.
(b) Manner of reporting the change under current generally accepted accounting principles including a discussion, where applicable, of how amounts are computed.
(c) Effect of the change on the balance sheet and income statement.

C23-4 (Analysis of Various Accounting Changes and Errors) Mischelle Reiners, controller of Lisa Terry Corp., is aware that an opinion on accounting changes has been issued. After reading the opinion, she is confused about what action should be taken on the following items related to Terry Corp. for the year 2001.

1. In 2001, Terry decided to change its policy on accounting for certain marketing costs. Previously, the company had chosen to defer and amortize all marketing costs over at least 5 years because Terry believed that a return on these expenditures did not occur immediately. Recently, however, the time differential has considerably shortened, and Terry is now expensing the marketing costs as incurred.
2. In 2001, the company examined its entire policy relating to the depreciation of plant equipment. Plant equipment had normally been depreciated over a 15-year period, but recent experience has indicated that the company was incorrect in its estimates and that the assets should be depreciated over a 20-year period.
3. One division of Terry Corp., Ralph Rosentiel Co., has consistently shown an increasing net income from period to period. On closer examination of their operating statement, it is noted that bad debt

expense and inventory obsolescence charges are much lower than in other divisions. In discussing this with the controller of this division, it has been learned that the controller has increased his net income each period by knowingly making low estimates related to the writeoff of receivables and inventory.

4. In 2001, the company purchased new machinery that should increase production dramatically. The company has decided to depreciate this machinery on an accelerated basis, even though other machinery is depreciated on a straight-line basis.
5. All equipment sold by Terry is subject to a 3-year warranty. It has been estimated that the expense ultimately to be incurred on these machines is 1% of sales. In 2001, because of a production breakthrough, it is now estimated that 1/2 of 1% of sales is sufficient. In 1999 and 2000, warranty expense was computed as $64,000 and $70,000, respectively. The company now believes that these warranty costs should be reduced by 50%.
6. In 2001, the company decided to change its method of inventory pricing from average cost to the FIFO method. The effect of this change on prior years is to increase 1999 income by $65,000 and increase 2000 income by $20,000.

Instructions

Mischelle Reiners has come to you, as her CPA, for advice about the situations above. Prepare a memorandum to Reiners, indicating the appropriate accounting treatment that should be given each of these situations.

C23-5 (Comprehensive Accounting Changes and Error Analysis) Charlene Rydell Manufacturing Co. is preparing its year-end financial statements. The controller, Kimbria Shumway, is confronted with several decisions about statement presentation with regard to the following items:

1. The vice president of sales had indicated that one product line has lost its customer appeal and will be phased out over the next 3 years. Therefore, a decision has been made to lower the estimated lives on related production equipment from the remaining 5 years to 3 years.
2. Estimating the lives of new products in the Leisure Products Division has become very difficult because of the highly competitive conditions in this market. Therefore, the practice of deferring and amortizing preproduction costs has been abandoned in favor of expensing such costs as they are incurred.
3. The Hightone Building was converted from a sales office to offices for the Accounting Department at the beginning of this year. Therefore, the expense related to this building will now appear as an administrative expense rather than a selling expense on the current year's income statement.
4. When the year-end physical inventory adjustment was made for the current year, the controller discovered that the prior year's physical inventory sheets for an entire warehouse were mislaid and excluded from last year's count.
5. The method of accounting used for financial reporting purposes for certain receivables has been approved for tax purposes during the current tax year by the Internal Revenue Service. This change for tax purposes will cause both deferred and current taxes payable to change substantially.
6. Management has decided to switch from the FIFO inventory valuation method to the LIFO inventory valuation method for all inventories.
7. Rydell's Custom Division manufactures large-scale, custom-designed machinery on a contract basis. Management decided to switch from the completed-contract method to the percentage-of-completion method of accounting for long-term contracts.

Instructions

(a) *APB Opinion No. 20,* "Accounting Changes," identifies four types of accounting changes—changes in accounting principle, changes in estimates, changes in entity, and changes due to error. For each of these four types of accounting changes:

  (1) Define the type of change.

  (2) Explain the general accounting treatment required according to *APB Opinion No. 20* with respect to the current year and prior years' financial statements.

(b) For each of the seven changes Rydell Manufacturing Co. has made in the current year, identify and explain whether the change is a change in accounting principle, in estimate, in entity, or due to error. If any of the changes is not one of these four types, explain why.

(CMA adapted)

C23-6 (Change in Principle, Estimate) As a certified public accountant, you have been contacted by Ben Thinken, CEO of Sports-Pro Athletics, Inc., a manufacturer of a variety of athletic equipment. He has asked you how to account for the following changes:

1. Sports-Pro appropriately changed its depreciation method for its production machinery from the double-declining balance method to the production method effective January 1, 2001.

2. Effective January 1, 2001, Sports-Pro appropriately changed the salvage values used in computing depreciation for its office equipment.
3. On December 31, 2001, Sports-Pro appropriately changed the specific subsidiaries constituting the group of companies for which consolidated financial statements are presented.

Instructions

Write a 1–1.5 page letter to Ben Thinken explaining how each of the above changes should be presented in the December 31, 2001, financial statements.

USING YOUR JUDGMENT

FINANCIAL REPORTING PROBLEM: INTEL CORPORATION

Instructions

Refer to the financial statements and accompanying notes and discussion of Intel Corporation presented in Appendix 5B and answer the following questions or instructions.

(a) Identify the changes in accounting principles reported by Intel during the three years covered by its income statements (1996–1998). Describe the nature of the change and the year of change.

(b) For each change in accounting principle, identify, if possible, the cumulative effect, the pro-forma effect of each change on prior years, and the effect on operating results in the year of change.

(c) Were any changes in estimates made by Intel in 1998?

(d) Why were the changes made?

COMPARATIVE ANALYSIS CASE

The Coca-Cola Company versus PepsiCo, Inc.

Instructions

Go to the Digital Tool and, using The Coca-Cola Company and PepsiCo, Inc. Annual Report information, answer the following questions or instructions.

(a) Identify the changes in accounting principles reported by Coca-Cola during the three years covered by its income statements (1996–1998). Describe the nature of the change and the year of change.

(b) Identify the changes in accounting principles reported by PepsiCo during the three years covered by its income statements (1996–1998). Describe the nature of the change and the year of change.

(c) For each change in accounting principle by Coca-Cola and PepsiCo, identify, if possible, the cumulative effect, the pro-forma effect of each change on prior years, and the effect on operating results in the year of change.

RESEARCH CASES

Case 1

Instructions

Use an appropriate source to identify two firms that recently reported a *voluntary* change in accounting principle. Answer the following questions with regard to each of the companies.

(a) What is the name of the company? What source did you use to identify the company?

(b) How did the change impact current earnings?

(c) How will the change impact future earnings?

(d) What rationale did the firm's management offer for the change? Do you agree with their stated reasons?

Case 2

Instructions

The March 25, 1996, issue of *Forbes* includes a brief article entitled "Super Slipup." Read the article and answer the following questions.

(a) What error was made with respect to the financial statements of Baby Superstore, Inc.?

(b) To what did the company attribute the error?

(c) What happened to the company's stock price upon discovery of the error?

(d) What negative effects did the error have on investors' perceptions of Baby Superstore? Are these concerns legitimate?

ETHICS CASE

Andy Frain is an audit senior of a large public accounting firm who has just been assigned to the Usher Corporation's annual audit engagement. Usher has been a client of Frain's firm for many years. Usher is a fast-growing business in the commercial construction industry. In reviewing the fixed asset ledger, Frain discovered a series of unusual accounting changes, in which the useful lives of assets, depreciated using the straight-line method, were substantially lowered near the midpoint of the original estimate. For example, the useful life of one dump truck was changed from 10 to 6 years during its fifth year of service. Upon further investigation, Andy was told by Vince Lloyd, Usher's accounting manager, "I don't really see your problem. After all, it's perfectly legal to change an accounting estimate. Besides, our CEO likes to see big earnings!"

Instructions

Answer the following questions:

(a) What are the ethical issues concerning Usher's practice of changing the useful lives of fixed assets?

(b) Who could be harmed by Usher's unusual accounting changes?

(c) What should Frain do in this situation?

CHAPTER 24

Statement of Cash Flows

Don't Take Cash Flow for Granted

Investors usually look to net income as a key indicator of a company's financial health and future prospects. The following graph shows the net income of one company over a 7-year period.

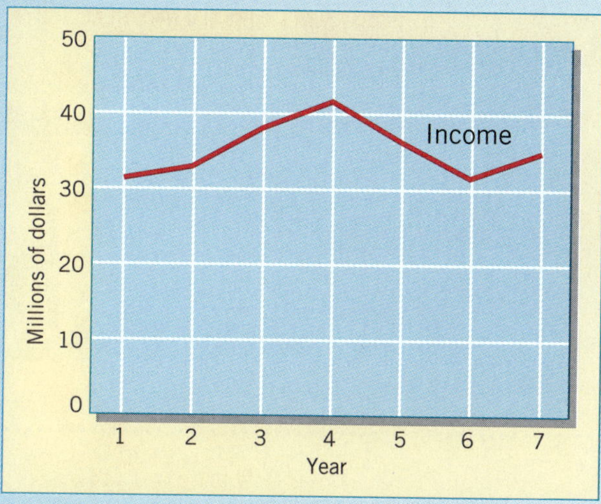

The company showed a pattern of consistent profitability and even some periods of income growth. Between years 1 and 4, net income for this company grew by 32 percent, from $31 million to $41 million. Does this company look like a good investment? Would you expect its profitability to continue? The company had consistently paid dividends and interest. Would you expect it to continue to do so? Investors answered "yes" to all three of these questions, by buying the company's stock.

Eighteen months later, this company—**W. T. Grant**—filed for bankruptcy, in what was then the largest bankruptcy filing in the United States. Closer examination of the company's financial statements revealed that the company had experienced several years of negative cash flow from its operations, even though it reported profits. How could this happen? It was partly because the sales that W. T. Grant reported on the income statement were made on credit and the company was having trouble collecting the receivables from the sales, causing cash flow to be less than the net income. Analysis of the cash flows would have provided an early warning signal of W. T. Grant's operating problems.[1]

[1]Adapted from James A. Largay III and Clyde P. Stickney, "Cash Flows, Ratio Analysis, and the W. T. Grant Company Bankruptcy," *Financial Analysts Journal,* July–August 1980, p. 51.

LEARNING OBJECTIVES

After studying this chapter, you should be able to:

1. **Describe the purpose of the statement of cash flows.**
2. **Identify the major classifications of cash flows.**
3. **Differentiate between net income and net cash flows from operating activities.**
4. **Contrast the direct and indirect methods of calculating net cash flow from operating activities.**
5. **Determine net cash flows from investing and financing activities.**
6. **Prepare a statement of cash flows.**
7. **Identify sources of information for a statement of cash flows.**
8. **Identify special problems in preparing a statement of cash flows.**
9. **Explain the use of a work sheet in preparing a statement of cash flows.**

PREVIEW OF CHAPTER 24

As indicated in the opening story, an examination of W. T. Grant's cash flow provided by operations would have shown the significant lack of liquidity and financial inflexibility that eventually caused the company's bankruptcy. The purpose of this chapter is to explain the main components of a statement of cash flows and the types of information it provides. The content and organization of the chapter are as follows:

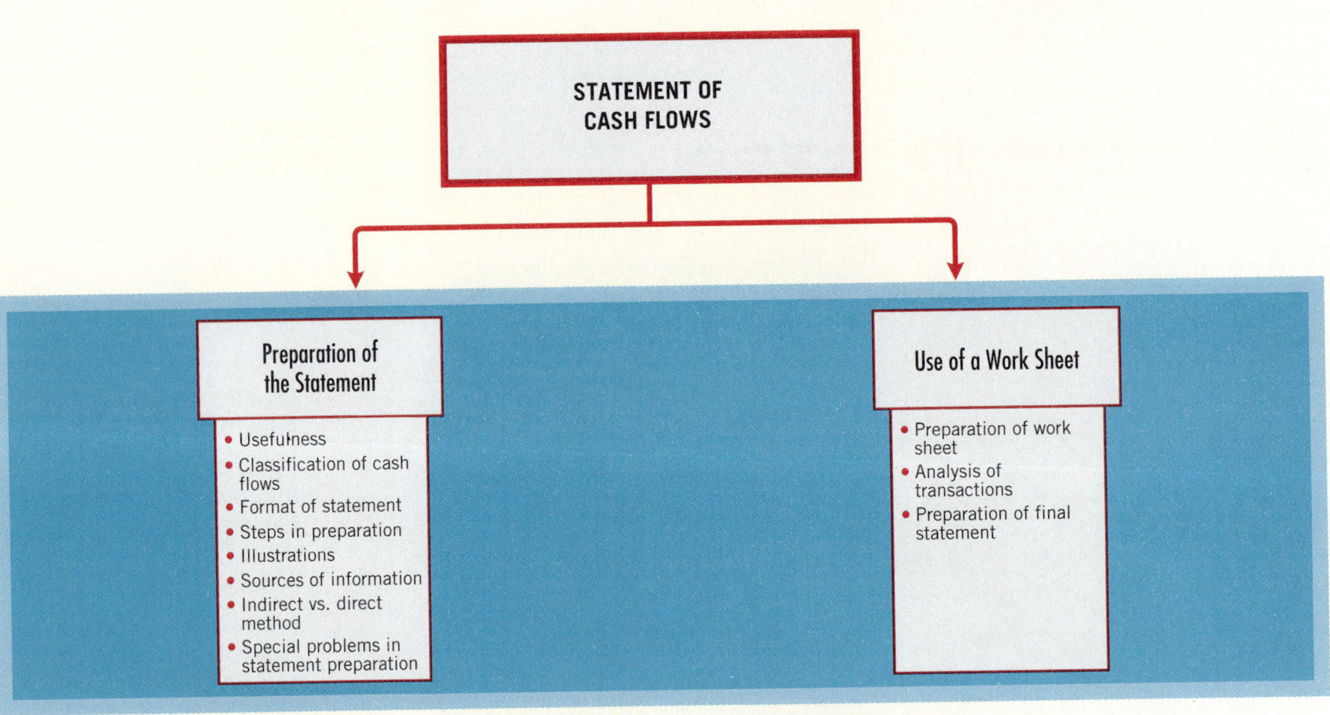

SECTION 1 PREPARATION OF THE STATEMENT OF CASH FLOWS

OBJECTIVE 1
Describe the purpose of the statement of cash flows.

The primary purpose of the **statement of cash flows** is to provide information about an entity's cash receipts and cash payments during a period. A secondary objective is to provide information on a cash basis about its operating, investing, and financing activities. **The statement of cash flows therefore reports cash receipts, cash payments, and net change in cash resulting from operating, investing, and financing activities of an enterprise during a period, in a format that reconciles the beginning and ending cash balances.**

USEFULNESS OF THE STATEMENT OF CASH FLOWS

The information in a statement of cash flows should help investors, creditors, and others assess the following:[2]

1. ***The entity's ability to generate future cash flows.*** A primary objective of financial reporting is to provide information that makes it possible to predict the amounts,

[2]"The Statement of Cash Flows," *Statement of Financial Accounting Standards No. 95* (Stamford, Conn.: FASB, 1987), pars. 4 and 5.

timing, and uncertainty of future cash flows. By examining relationships between items such as sales and net cash flow from operating activities, or net cash flow from operating activities and increases or decreases in cash, it is possible to make better predictions of the amounts, timing, and uncertainty of future cash flows than is possible using accrual basis data.

2. ***The entity's ability to pay dividends and meet obligations.*** Simply put, cash is essential. If a company does not have adequate cash, employees cannot be paid, debts cannot be settled, dividends cannot be paid, and equipment cannot be acquired. A statement of cash flows indicates how cash is used and where it comes from. Employees, creditors, stockholders, and customers should be particularly interested in this statement, because it alone shows the flows of cash in a business.

3. ***The reasons for the difference between net income and net cash flow from operating activities.*** The net income number is important, because it provides information on the success or failure of a business enterprise from one period to another. But some people are critical of accrual basis net income because estimates must be made to arrive at it. As a result, the reliability of the number is often challenged. Such is not the case with cash. Thus, as illustrated in the opening story, readers of the financial statements benefit from knowing the reasons for the difference between net income and net cash flow from operating activities. Then they can assess for themselves the reliability of the income number.

4. ***The cash and noncash investing and financing transactions during the period.*** By examining a company's investing activities (purchase and sales of assets other than its products) and its financing transactions (borrowings and repayments of borrowings, investments by owners and distributions to owners), a financial statement reader can better understand why assets and liabilities increased or decreased during the period. For example, the following questions might be answered:

    How did cash increase when there was a net loss for the period?

    How were the proceeds of the bond issue used?

    How was the expansion in plant and equipment financed?

    Why were dividends not increased?

    How was the retirement of debt accomplished?

    How much money was borrowed during the year?

    Is cash flow greater or less than net income?

CLASSIFICATION OF CASH FLOWS

OBJECTIVE 2
Identify the major classifications of cash flows.

The statement of cash flows classifies cash receipts and cash payments by operating, investing, and financing activities.[3] Transactions and other events characteristic of each kind of activity are as follows:

1. **Operating activities** involve the cash effects of transactions that enter into the determination of net income, such as cash receipts from sales of goods and services

[3]The basis recommended by the FASB for the statement of cash flows is actually "cash and cash equivalents." **Cash equivalents** are short-term, highly liquid investments that are both: (a) readily convertible to known amounts of cash, and (b) so near their maturity that they present insignificant risk of changes in interest rates. Generally, only investments with original maturities of three months or less qualify under this definition. Examples of cash equivalents are treasury bills, commercial paper, and money market funds purchased with cash that is in excess of immediate needs.

Although we use the term "cash" throughout our discussion and illustrations in this chapter, we mean cash and cash equivalents when reporting the cash flows and the net increase or decrease in cash.

and cash payments to suppliers and employees for acquisitions of inventory and expenses.

2. **Investing activities** generally involve long-term assets and include (a) making and collecting loans, and (b) acquiring and disposing of investments and productive long-lived assets.
3. **Financing activities** involve liability and stockholders' equity items and include (a) obtaining cash from creditors and repaying the amounts borrowed, and (b) obtaining capital from owners and providing them with a return on, and a return of, their investment.

Illustration 24-1 classifies the typical cash receipts and payments of a business enterprise that are classified according to operating, investing, and financing activities.

ILLUSTRATION 24-1
Classification of Typical Cash Inflows and Outflows

Operating Cash inflows From sales of goods or services. From returns on loans (interest) and on equity securities (dividends). Cash outflows To suppliers for inventory. To employees for services. To government for taxes. To lenders for interest. To others for expenses.	**Income Statement Items**
Investing Cash inflows From sale of property, plant, and equipment. From sale of debt or equity securities of other entities. From collection of principal on loans to other entities. Cash outflows To purchase property, plant, and equipment. To purchase debt or equity securities of other entities. To make loans to other entities.	**Generally Long-Term Asset Items**
Financing Cash inflows From sale of equity securities. From issuance of debt (bonds and notes). Cash outflows To stockholders as dividends. To redeem long-term debt or reacquire capital stock.	**Generally Long-Term Liability and Equity Items**

According to International Accounting Standards, "cash and cash equivalents" can be defined as "net monetary assets," that is, "cash and demand deposits and highly liquid investments less short-term borrowings."

Some cash flows relating to investing or financing activities are classified as operating activities.[4] For example, receipts of investment income (interest and dividends) and payments of interest to lenders are classified as operating activities. Conversely, some cash flows relating to operating activities are classified as investing or financing activities. For example, the cash received from the sale of property, plant, and equipment at a gain, although reported in the income statement, is classified as an investing activity, and the effects of the related gain would not be included in net cash flow from

[4]For exceptions to the treatment of purchases and sales of loans and securities by banks and brokers, see *Statement of Financial Accounting Standards No. 102* (February 1989) and "Relevance Gained: FASB Modifies Cash Flow Statement Requirements for Banks," James Don Edwards and Cynthia D. Heagy, *Journal of Accountancy,* June 1991. Banks and brokers are required to classify cash flows from purchases and sales of loans and securities specifically for resale and carried at market value **as operating activities.** This requirement recognizes that for these firms these assets are similar to inventory in other businesses.

operating activities. Likewise, a gain or loss on the payment (extinguishment) of debt would generally be part of the cash outflow related to the repayment of the amount borrowed and therefore is a financing activity.

FORMAT OF THE STATEMENT OF CASH FLOWS

The three activities discussed in the preceding paragraphs constitute the general format of the statement of cash flows. The cash flows from operating activities section always appears first, followed by the investing and financing activities sections. The individual inflows and outflows from investing and financing activities are reported separately, that is, they are reported gross, not netted against one another. Thus, cash outflow from the purchase of property is reported separately from the cash inflow from the sale of property. Similarly, the cash inflow from the issuance of debt is reported separately from the cash outflow from its retirement. The net increase or decrease in cash reported during the period should reconcile the beginning and ending cash balances as reported in the comparative balance sheets.

The skeleton format of the statement of cash flows is:

ILLUSTRATION 24-2
Format of the Statement of Cash Flows

COMPANY NAME
Statement of Cash Flows
Period Covered

Cash flows from operating activities		
Net income		XXX
Adjustments to reconcile net income to net cash provided by operating activities:		
(List of individual items)	XX	XX
Net cash flow from operating activities		XXX
Cash flows from investing activities		
(List of individual inflows and outflows)	XX	
Net cash provided (used) by investing activities		XXX
Cash flows from financing activities		
(List of individual inflows and outflows)	XX	
Net cash provided (used) by financing activities		XXX
Net increase (decrease) in cash		XXX
Cash at beginning of period		XXX
Cash at end of period		XXX

STEPS IN PREPARATION

Unlike the other major financial statements, the statement of cash flows is not prepared from the adjusted trial balance. The information to prepare this statement usually comes from three sources:

Comparative balance sheets provide the amount of the changes in assets, liabilities, and equities from the beginning to the end of the period.

Current income statement data help the reader determine the amount of cash provided by or used by operations during the period.

Selected transaction data from the general ledger provide additional detailed information needed to determine how cash was provided or used during the period.

Preparing the statement of cash flows from the data sources above involves three major steps:

Step 1. Determine the change in cash. This procedure is straightforward because the difference between the beginning and the ending cash balance can be easily computed from an examination of the comparative balance sheets.

Step 2. Determine the net cash flow from operating activities. This procedure is complex; it involves analyzing not only the current year's income statement but also comparative balance sheets as well as selected transaction data.

Step 3. Determine net cash flows from investing and financing activities. All other changes in the balance sheet accounts must be analyzed to determine their effects on cash.

On the following pages we work through these three steps in the process of preparing the statement of cash flows for a company over several years.

FIRST ILLUSTRATION—2000

To illustrate a statement of cash flows, we will use the **first year of operations** for Tax Consultants Inc. The company started on January 1, 2000, when it issued 60,000 shares of $1 par value common stock for $60,000 cash. The company rented its office space and furniture and equipment and performed tax consulting services throughout the first year. The comparative balance sheets at the beginning and end of the year 2000 appear as follows:

ILLUSTRATION 24-3
Comparative Balance Sheet, Tax Consultants Inc., Year 1

TAX CONSULTANTS INC.
Comparative Balance Sheet

Assets	Dec. 31, 2000	Jan. 1, 2000	Change Increase/Decrease
Cash	$49,000	$–0–	$49,000 Increase
Accounts receivable	36,000	–0–	36,000 Increase
Total	$85,000	$–0–	
Liabilities and Stockholders' Equity			
Accounts payable	$ 5,000	$–0–	5,000 Increase
Common stock ($1 par)	60,000	–0–	60,000 Increase
Retained earnings	20,000	–0–	20,000 Increase
Total	$85,000	$–0–	

The income statement and additional information for Tax Consultants Inc. are as follows:

ILLUSTRATION 24-4
Income Statement, Tax Consultants Inc., Year 1

TAX CONSULTANTS INC.
Income Statement
For the Year Ended December 31, 2000

Revenues	$125,000
Operating expenses	85,000
Income before income taxes	40,000
Income tax expense	6,000
Net income	$ 34,000

Additional Information
Examination of selected data indicates that a dividend of $14,000 was paid during the year.

Step 1: Determine the Change in Cash

To prepare a statement of cash flows, the first step, **determining the change in cash,** is a simple computation. Tax Consultants Inc. had no cash on hand at the beginning of the year 2000, but $49,000 was on hand at the end of 2000; thus, the change in cash for 2000 was an increase of $49,000. The other two steps are more complex and involve additional analysis.

Step 2: Determine Net Cash Flow from Operating Activities

OBJECTIVE 3
Differentiate between net income and net cash flows from operating activities.

A useful starting point in **determining net cash flow from operating activities**[5] is to understand why net income must be converted. Under generally accepted accounting principles, most companies must use the accrual basis of accounting requiring that revenue be recorded when earned and that expenses be recorded when incurred. Net income may include credit sales that have not been collected in cash and expenses incurred that may not have been paid in cash. Thus, under the accrual basis of accounting, net income will not indicate the net cash flow from operating activities.

To arrive at net cash flow from operating activities, it is necessary to report revenues and expenses on a **cash basis. This is done by eliminating the effects of income statement transactions that did not result in a corresponding increase or decrease in cash.** The relationship between net income and net cash flow from operating activities is graphically depicted as follows:

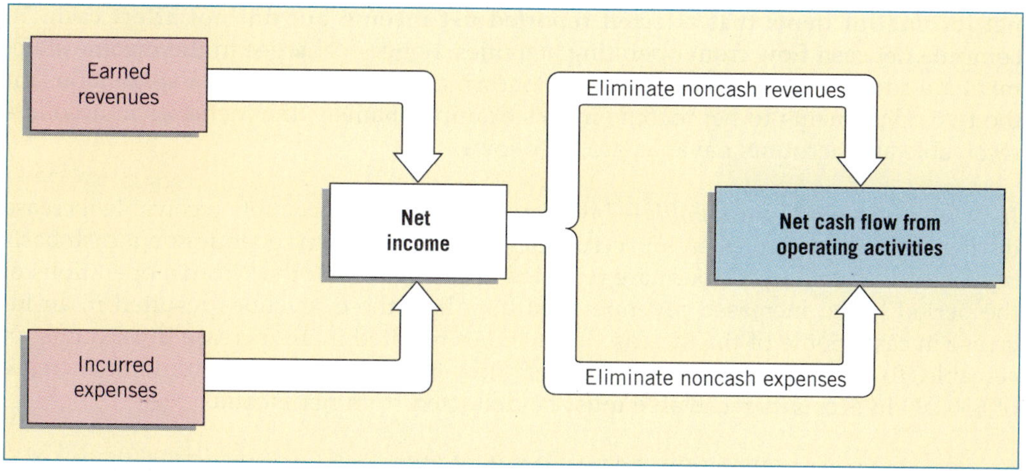

ILLUSTRATION 24-5
Net Income versus Net Cash Flow from Operating Activities

In this chapter, we use the term net income to refer to accrual-based net income. The conversion of net income to net cash flow from operating activities may be done through either a direct method or an indirect method as explained in the following discussion.

Direct Method

OBJECTIVE 4
Contrast the direct and indirect methods of calculating net cash flow from operating activities.

The **direct method** (also called the income statement method) reports cash receipts and cash disbursements from operating activities. The difference between these two amounts is the net cash flow from operating activities. In other words, the direct method deducts from operating cash receipts the operating cash disbursements. The direct method results in the presentation of a condensed cash receipts and cash disbursements statement.

As indicated from the accrual-based income statement, Tax Consultants Inc. reported revenues of $125,000. However, because the company's accounts receivable in-

[5]"Net cash flow from operating activities" is a generic phrase, which is replaced in the statement of cash flows with either "net cash **provided by** operating activities" if operations increase cash or "net cash **used by** operating activities" if operations decrease cash.

creased during 2000 by $36,000, only $89,000 ($125,000 – $36,000) in cash was collected on these revenues. Similarly, Tax Consultants Inc. reported operating expenses of $85,000, but accounts payable increased during the period of $5,000. Assuming that these payables related to operating expenses, cash operating expenses were $80,000 ($85,000 – $5,000). Because no taxes payable exist at the end of the year, the $6,000 income tax expense for 2000 must have been paid in cash during the year. Then the computation of net cash flow from operating activities is as follows:

ILLUSTRATION 24-6
Computation of Net Cash Flow from Operating Activities, Year 1—Direct Method

Cash collected from revenues	$89,000
Cash payments for expenses	80,000
Income before income taxes	9,000
Cash payments for income taxes	6,000
Net cash provided by operating activities	$ 3,000

"Net cash provided by operating activities" is the equivalent of cash basis net income ("net cash used by operating activities" would be equivalent to cash basis net loss).

Indirect Method

The **indirect method** (or reconciliation method) starts with net income and converts it to net cash flow from operating activities. In other words, **the indirect method adjusts net income for items that affected reported net income but did not affect cash**. To compute net cash flow from operating activities, noncash charges in the income statement are added back to net income and noncash credits are deducted. Explanations for the two adjustments to net income in this example, namely, the increases in accounts receivable and accounts payable, are as follows.

Increase in Accounts Receivable—Indirect Method. When accounts receivable increase during the year, revenues on an accrual basis are higher than revenues on a cash basis because goods sold on account are reported as revenues. In other words, operations of the period led to increased revenues, but not all of these revenues resulted in an increase in cash. Some of the increase in revenues resulted in an increase in accounts receivable. To convert net income to net cash flow from operating activities, the increase of $36,000 in accounts receivable must be deducted from net income.

Increase in Accounts Payable—Indirect Method. When accounts payable increase during the year, expenses on an accrual basis are higher than they are on a cash basis because expenses are incurred for which payment has not taken place. To convert net income to net cash flow from operating activities, the increase of $5,000 in accounts payable must be added to net income.

As a result of the accounts receivable and accounts payable adjustments, net cash provided by operating activities is determined to be $3,000 for the year 2000. This computation is shown as follows:

ILLUSTRATION 24-7
Computation of Net Cash Flow from Operating Activities, Year 1—Indirect Method

Net income		$34,000
Adjustments to reconcile net income to net cash provided by operating activities:		
Increase in accounts receivable	$(36,000)	
Increase in accounts payable	5,000	(31,000)
Net cash provided by operating activities		$ 3,000

Note that net cash provided by operating activities is the same whether the direct or the indirect method is used.

Step 3: Determine Net Cash Flows from Investing and Financing Activities

OBJECTIVE 5
Determine net cash flows from investing and financing activities.

Once the net cash flow from operating activities is computed, the next step is to determine whether any other changes in balance sheet accounts caused an increase or decrease in cash. For example, an examination of the remaining balance sheet accounts shows that both common stock and retained earnings have increased. The common stock increase of $60,000 resulted from the issuance of common stock for cash. The issuance of common stock is a receipt of cash from a financing activity and is reported as such in the statement of cash flows. The retained earnings increase of $20,000 is caused by two items:

1. Net income of $34,000 increased retained earnings.
2. Dividends declared of $14,000 decreased retained earnings.

Net income has been converted into net cash flow from operating activities as explained earlier. The additional data indicate that the dividend was paid. Thus, the dividend payment on common stock is reported as a cash outflow, classified as a financing activity.

Statement of Cash Flows—2000

OBJECTIVE 6
Prepare a statement of cash flows.

We are now ready to prepare the statement of cash flows. The statement starts with the operating activities section. Either the direct or indirect method may be used to report net cash flow from operating activities. The FASB **encourages** the use of the direct method over the indirect method. And, if the direct method of reporting net cash flow from operating activities is used, the FASB **requires** that the reconciliation of net income to net cash flow from operating activities be provided in a separate schedule. If the indirect method is used, the reconciliation may be either reported within the statement of cash flows or provided in a separate schedule, with the statement of cash flows reporting only the **net** cash flow from operating activities.[6] Therefore, the indirect method, which is also used more extensively in practice,[7] is used throughout this chapter. In doing homework assignments, you should follow instructions for use of either the direct or indirect method. The advantages and disadvantages of these two methods are discussed later in this chapter.

The statement of cash flows for Tax Consultants Inc. is as follows:

ILLUSTRATION 24-8
Statement of Cash Flows, Tax Consultants Inc., Year 1

TAX CONSULTANTS INC.
Statement of Cash Flows
For the Year Ended December 31, 2000
Increase (Decrease) in Cash

Cash flows from operating activities		
Net income		$34,000
Adjustments to reconcile net income to net cash provided by operating activities:		
Increase in accounts receivable	$(36,000)	
Increase in accounts payable	5,000	(31,000)
Net cash provided by operating activities		3,000
Cash flows from financing activities		
Issuance of common stock	60,000	
Payment of cash dividends	(14,000)	
Net cash provided by financing activities		46,000
Net increase in cash		49,000
Cash, January 1, 2000		–0–
Cash, December 31, 2000		$49,000

[6]"The Statement of Cash Flows," pars. 27 and 30.

[7]*Accounting Trends and Techniques—1999* reports that out of its 600 surveyed companies, 593 (approximately 99%) used the indirect method, while only 7 used the direct method.

As indicated, the $60,000 increase in common stock results in a cash inflow from a financing activity. The payment of $14,000 in cash dividends is classified as a use of cash from a financing activity. The $49,000 increase in cash reported in the statement of cash flows agrees with the increase of $49,000 shown as the change in the cash account in the comparative balance sheets.

SECOND ILLUSTRATION—2001

Tax Consultants Inc. continued to grow and prosper during its second year of operations. Land, building, and equipment were purchased, and revenues and earnings increased substantially over the first year. Information related to the second year of operations for Tax Consultants Inc. is presented in Illustrations 24-9 and 24-10.

ILLUSTRATION 24-9
Comparative Balance Sheet, Tax Consultants Inc., Year 2

TAX CONSULTANTS INC.
Comparative Balance Sheet
December 31

Assets	2001	2000	Change Increase/Decrease
Cash	$ 37,000	$49,000	$ 12,000 Decrease
Accounts receivable	26,000	36,000	10,000 Decrease
Prepaid expenses	6,000	–0–	6,000 Increase
Land	70,000	–0–	70,000 Increase
Building	200,000	–0–	200,000 Increase
Accumulated depreciation—building	(11,000)	–0–	11,000 Increase
Equipment	68,000	–0–	68,000 Increase
Accumulated depreciation—equipment	(10,000)	–0–	10,000 Increase
Total	$386,000	$85,000	
Liabilities and Stockholders' Equity			
Accounts payable	$ 40,000	$ 5,000	35,000 Increase
Bonds payable	150,000	–0–	150,000 Increase
Common stock ($1 par)	60,000	60,000	–0–
Retained earnings	136,000	20,000	116,000 Increase
Total	$386,000	$85,000	

ILLUSTRATION 24-10
Income Statement, Tax Consultants Inc., Year 2

TAX CONSULTANTS INC.
Income Statement
For the Year Ended December 31, 2001

Revenues		$492,000
Operating expenses (excluding depreciation)	$269,000	
Depreciation expense	21,000	290,000
Income from operations		202,000
Income tax expense		68,000
Net income		$134,000

Additional Information
(a) In 2001, the company paid an $18,000 cash dividend.
(b) The company obtained $150,000 cash through the issuance of long-term bonds.
(c) Land, building, and equipment were acquired for cash.

Step 1: Determine the Change in Cash

To prepare a statement of cash flows from the available information, the first step is to determine the change in cash. As indicated from the information presented, cash decreased $12,000 ($49,000 − $37,000).

Step 2: Determine Net Cash Flow from Operating Activities—Indirect Method

Using the indirect method, we adjust net income of $134,000 on an accrual basis to arrive at net cash flow from operating activities. Explanations for the adjustments to net income are as follows.

Decrease in Accounts Receivable

When accounts receivable decrease during the period, revenues on a cash basis are higher than revenues on an accrual basis, because cash collections are higher than revenues reported on an accrual basis. To convert net income to net cash flow from operating activities, the decrease of $10,000 in accounts receivable must be added to net income.

Increase in Prepaid Expenses

When prepaid expenses (assets) increase during a period, expenses on an accrual basis income statement are lower than they are on a cash basis income statement. Expenditures (cash payments) have been made in the current period, but expenses (as charges to the income statement) have been deferred to future periods. To convert net income to net cash flow from operating activities, the increase of $6,000 in prepaid expenses must be deducted from net income. An increase in prepaid expenses results in a decrease in cash during the period.

Increase in Accounts Payable

Like the increase in 2000, the 2001 increase of $35,000 in accounts payable must be added to net income to convert to net cash flow from operating activities. A greater amount of expense was incurred than cash disbursed.

Depreciation Expense (Increase in Accumulated Depreciation)

The purchase of depreciable assets is shown as a use of cash in the investing section in the year of acquisition. The depreciation expense of $21,000 (also represented by the increase in accumulated depreciation) is a noncash charge that is added back to net income to arrive at net cash flow from operating activities. The $21,000 is the sum of the depreciation on the building of $11,000 and the depreciation on the equipment of $10,000.

Other charges to expense for a period that do not require the use of cash, such as the amortization of intangible assets and depletion expense, are treated in the same manner as depreciation. Depreciation and similar noncash charges are frequently listed in the statement as the first adjustments to net income.

As a result of the foregoing items, net cash provided by operating activities is $194,000 as shown in Illustration 24-11.

Net income		$134,000
Adjustments to reconcile net income to		
net cash provided by operating activities:		
Depreciation expense	$21,000	
Decrease in accounts receivable	10,000	
Increase in prepaid expenses	(6,000)	
Increase in accounts payable	35,000	60,000
Net cash provided by operating activities		$194,000

ILLUSTRATION 24-11
Computation of Net Cash Flow from Operating Activities, Year 2—Indirect Method

Step 3: Determine Net Cash Flows from Investing and Financing Activities

After you have determined the items affecting net cash provided by operating activities, the next step involves analyzing the remaining changes in balance sheet accounts. The following accounts were analyzed:

Increase in Land

As indicated from the change in the land account, land of $70,000 was purchased during the period. This transaction is an investing activity that is reported as a use of cash.

Increase in Building and Related Accumulated Depreciation

As indicated in the additional data, and from the change in the building account, an office building was acquired using cash of $200,000. This transaction is a cash outflow reported in the investing section. The accumulated depreciation account increase of $11,000 is fully explained by the depreciation expense entry for the period. As indicated earlier, the reported depreciation expense has no effect on the amount of cash.

Increase in Equipment and Related Accumulated Depreciation

An increase in equipment of $68,000 resulted because equipment was purchased for cash. This transaction should be reported as an outflow of cash from an investing activity. The increase in Accumulated Depreciation—Equipment was explained by the depreciation expense entry for the period.

Increase in Bonds Payable

The bonds payable account increased $150,000. Cash received from the issuance of these bonds represents an inflow of cash from a financing activity.

Increase in Retained Earnings

Retained earnings increased $116,000 during the year. This increase can be explained by two factors: (1) net income of $134,000 increased retained earnings; (2) dividends of $18,000 decreased retained earnings. Payment of the dividends is a financing activity that involves a cash outflow.

Statement of Cash Flows—2001

Combining the foregoing items, we get a statement of cash flows for 2001 for Tax Consultants Inc., using the indirect method to compute net cash flow from operating activities.

ILLUSTRATION 24-12
Statement of Cash Flows, Tax Consultants Inc., Year 2

TAX CONSULTANTS INC.
Statement of Cash Flows
For the Year Ended December 31, 2001
Increase (Decrease) in Cash

Cash flows from operating activities		
Net income		$134,000
Adjustments to reconcile net income to net cash provided by operating activities:		
Depreciation expense	$ 21,000	
Decrease in accounts receivable	10,000	
Increase in prepaid expenses	(6,000)	
Increase in accounts payable	35,000	60,000
Net cash provided by operating activities		194,000
Cash flows from investing activities		
Purchase of land	(70,000)	
Purchase of building	(200,000)	
Purchase of equipment	(68,000)	
Net cash used by investing activities		(338,000)
Cash flows from financing activities		
Issuance of bonds	150,000	
Payment of cash dividends	(18,000)	
Net cash provided by financing activities		132,000
Net decrease in cash		(12,000)
Cash, January 1, 2001		49,000
Cash, December 31, 2001		$ 37,000

THIRD ILLUSTRATION—2002

Our third illustration covering the 2002 operations of Tax Consultants Inc. is slightly more complex; it again uses the indirect method to compute and present net cash flow from operating activities.

Tax Consultants Inc. experienced continued success in 2002 and expanded its operations to include the sale of selected lines of computer software that are used in tax return preparation and tax planning. Thus, inventories is one of the new assets appearing in its December 31, 2002, balance sheet. The comparative balance sheets, income statements, and selected data for 2002 are shown in Illustrations 24-13 and 24-14.

ILLUSTRATION 24-13
Comparative Balance Sheet, Tax Consultants Inc., Year 3

TAX CONSULTANTS INC.
Comparative Balance Sheet
December 31

Assets	2002	2001	Change Increase/Decrease
Cash	$ 54,000	$ 37,000	$ 17,000 Increase
Accounts receivable	68,000	26,000	42,000 Increase
Inventories	54,000	–0–	54,000 Increase
Prepaid expenses	4,000	6,000	2,000 Decrease
Land	45,000	70,000	25,000 Decrease
Buildings	200,000	200,000	–0–
Accumulated depreciation—buildings	(21,000)	(11,000)	10,000 Increase
Equipment	193,000	68,000	125,000 Increase
Accumulated depreciation—equipment	(28,000)	(10,000)	18,000 Increase
Totals	$569,000	$386,000	
Liabilities and Stockholders' Equity			
Accounts payable	$ 33,000	$ 40,000	7,000 Decrease
Bonds payable	110,000	150,000	40,000 Decrease
Common stock ($1 par)	220,000	60,000	160,000 Increase
Retained earnings	206,000	136,000	70,000 Increase
Totals	$569,000	$386,000	

ILLUSTRATION 24-14
Income Statement, Tax Consultants Inc., Year 3

TAX CONSULTANTS INC.
Income Statement
For the Year Ended December 31, 2002

Revenues		$890,000
Cost of goods sold	$465,000	
Operating expenses	221,000	
Interest expense	12,000	
Loss on sale of equipment	2,000	700,000
Income from operations		190,000
Income tax expense		65,000
Net income		$125,000

Additional Information

(a) Operating expenses include depreciation expense of $33,000 and amortization of prepaid expenses of $2,000.
(b) Land was sold at its book value for cash.
(c) Cash dividends of $55,000 were paid in 2002.
(d) Interest expense of $12,000 was paid in cash.
(e) Equipment with a cost of $166,000 was purchased for cash. Equipment with a cost of $41,000 and a book value of $36,000 was sold for $34,000 cash.
(f) Bonds were redeemed at their book value for cash.
(g) Common stock ($1 par) was issued for cash.

Step 1: Determine the Change in Cash

The first step in the preparation of the statement of cash flows is to determine the change in cash. As is shown in the comparative balance sheet, cash increased $17,000 in 2002. The second and third steps are discussed below and on the following pages.

Step 2: Determine Net Cash Flow from Operating Activities—Indirect Method

Explanations of the adjustments to net income of $125,000 are as follows.

Increase in Accounts Receivable

The increase in accounts receivable of $42,000 represents recorded accrual basis revenues in excess of cash collections in 2002; the increase is deducted from net income to convert from the accrual basis to the cash basis.

Increase in Inventories

The increase in inventories of $54,000 represents an operating use of cash for which an expense was not incurred. This amount is therefore deducted from net income to arrive at cash flow from operations. In other words, when inventory purchased exceeds inventory sold during a period, cost of goods sold on an accrual basis is lower than on a cash basis.

Decrease in Prepaid Expenses

The decrease in prepaid expenses of $2,000 represents a charge to the income statement for which there was no cash outflow in the current period. The decrease is added back to net income to arrive at net cash flow from operating activities.

Decrease in Accounts Payable

When accounts payable decrease during the year, cost of goods sold and expenses on a cash basis are higher than they are on an accrual basis, because on a cash basis the goods and expenses are recorded as expense when paid. To convert net income to net cash flow from operating activities, the decrease of $7,000 in accounts payable must be deducted from net income.

Depreciation Expense (Increase in Accumulated Depreciation)

Accumulated Depreciation—Buildings increased $10,000 ($21,000 − $11,000). The Buildings account did not change during the period, which means that $10,000 of depreciation was recorded in 2002.

Accumulated Depreciation—Equipment increased by $18,000 ($28,000 − $10,000) during the year. But Accumulated Depreciation—Equipment was decreased by $5,000 as a result of the sale during the year. Thus, depreciation for the year was $23,000. The reconciliation of Accumulated Depreciation—Equipment is as follows:

Beginning balance	$10,000
Add: Depreciation for 2002	23,000
	33,000
Deduct: Sale of equipment	5,000
Ending balance	$28,000

The total depreciation of $33,000 ($10,000 + $23,000) charged to the income statement must be added back to net income to determine net cash flow from operating activities.

Loss on Sale of Equipment

Equipment having a cost of $41,000 and a book value of $36,000 was sold for $34,000. As a result, the company reported a loss of $2,000 on its sale. To arrive at net cash flow from operating activities, it is necessary to add back to net income the loss on the sale of the equipment. The reason is that the loss is a noncash charge to the income statement; it did not reduce cash but it did reduce net income.

From the foregoing items, the operating activities section of the statement of cash flows is prepared as shown in Illustration 24-15.

Cash flows from operating activities		
Net income		$125,000
Adjustments to reconcile net income to net cash provided by operating activities:		
Depreciation expense	$33,000	
Increase in accounts receivable	(42,000)	
Increase in inventories	(54,000)	
Decrease in prepaid expenses	2,000	
Decrease in accounts payable	(7,000)	
Loss on sale of equipment	2,000	(66,000)
Net cash provided by operating activities		59,000

ILLUSTRATION 24-15
Operating Activities Section of Cash Flows Statement

Step 3: Determine Net Cash Flows from Investing and Financing Activities

By analyzing the remaining changes in the balance sheet accounts, we can identify cash flows from investing and financing activities.

Land

Land decreased $25,000 during the period. As indicated from the information presented, land was sold for cash at its book value. This transaction is an investing activity reported as a $25,000 source of cash.

Equipment

An analysis of the equipment account indicates the following:

Beginning balance	$ 68,000
Purchase of equipment	166,000
	234,000
Sale of equipment	41,000
Ending balance	$193,000

Equipment with a fair value of $166,000 was purchased for cash—an investing transaction reported as a cash outflow. The sale of the equipment for $34,000 is also an investing activity, but one that generates a cash inflow.

Bonds Payable

Bonds payable decreased $40,000 during the year. As indicated from the additional information, bonds were redeemed at their book value. This financing transaction used cash of $40,000.

Common Stock

The common stock account increased $160,000 during the year. As indicated from the additional information, common stock of $160,000 was issued at par. This is a financing transaction that provided cash of $160,000.

Retained Earnings

Retained earnings changed $70,000 ($206,000 − $136,000) during the year. The $70,000 change in retained earnings is the result of net income of $125,000 from operations and the financing activity of paying cash dividends of $55,000.

Statement of Cash Flows—2002

The statement of cash flows as shown in Illustration 24-16 is prepared by combining the foregoing items.

ILLUSTRATION 24-16
Statement of Cash Flows, Tax Consultants Inc., Year 3

TAX CONSULTANTS INC.
Statement of Cash Flows
For the Year Ended December 31, 2002
Increase (Decrease) in Cash

Cash flows from operating activities		
Net income		$125,000
Adjustments to reconcile net income to net cash provided by operating activities:		
Depreciation expense	$ 33,000	
Increase in accounts receivable	(42,000)	
Increase in inventories	(54,000)	
Decrease in prepaid expenses	2,000	
Decrease in accounts payable	(7,000)	
Loss on sale of equipment	2,000	(66,000)
Net cash provided by operating activities		59,000
Cash flows from investing activities		
Sale of land	25,000	
Sale of equipment	34,000	
Purchase of equipment	(166,000)	
Net cash used by investing activities		(107,000)
Cash flows from financing activities		
Redemption of bonds	(40,000)	
Sale of common stock	160,000	
Payment of dividends	(55,000)	
Net cash provided by financing activities		65,000
Net increase in cash		17,000
Cash, January 1, 2002		37,000
Cash, December 31, 2002		$ 54,000

SOURCES OF INFORMATION FOR THE STATEMENT OF CASH FLOWS

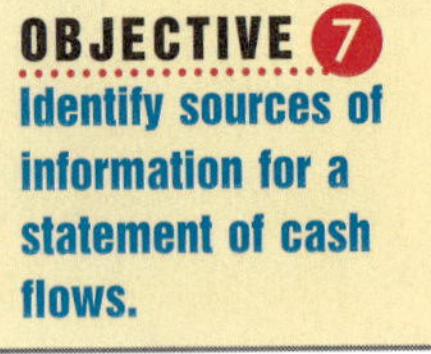

OBJECTIVE 7
Identify sources of information for a statement of cash flows.

Important points to remember in the preparation of the statement of cash flows are as follows:

1. Comparative balance sheets provide the basic information from which the report is prepared. Additional information obtained from analyses of specific accounts is also included.
2. An analysis of the Retained Earnings account is necessary. The net increase or decrease in Retained Earnings without any explanation is a meaningless amount in the statement, because it might represent the effect of net income, dividends declared, appropriations of retained earnings, or prior period adjustments.
3. The statement includes all changes that have passed through cash or have resulted in an increase or decrease in cash.
4. Writedowns, amortization charges, and similar "book" entries, such as depreciation of plant assets, are considered as neither inflows nor outflows of cash because

they have no effect on cash. To the extent that they have entered into the determination of net income, however, they must be added back to or subtracted from net income to arrive at net cash flow from operating activities.

NET CASH FLOW FROM OPERATING ACTIVITIES—INDIRECT VERSUS DIRECT METHOD

As we discussed previously, the two different methods available to adjust income from operations on an accrual basis to net cash flow from operating activities are the indirect (reconciliation) method and the direct (income statement) method.

The FASB encourages use of the direct method and permits use of the indirect method. Yet, if the direct method is used, the Board requires that a reconciliation of net income to net cash flow from operating activities be provided in a separate schedule. Therefore, under either method the indirect (reconciliation) method must be prepared and reported.

Indirect Method

For consistency and comparability and because it is the most widely used method in practice, we used the indirect method in the illustrations just presented. We determined net cash flows from operating activities by adding back to or deducting from net income those items that had no effect on cash. The following diagram presents more completely the common types of adjustments that are made to net income to arrive at net cash flow from operating activities.

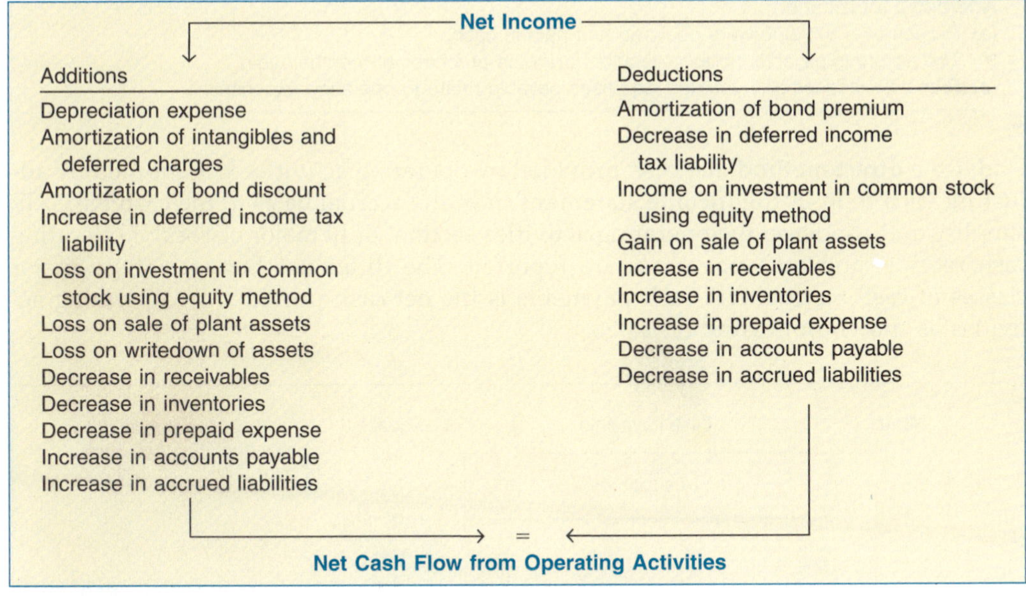

ILLUSTRATION 24-17
Adjustments Needed to Determine Net Cash Flow from Operating Activities—Indirect Method

The additions and deductions listed above reconcile net income to net cash flow from operating activities, illustrating the reason for referring to the indirect method as the reconciliation method.

Direct Method—An Illustration

Under the direct method the statement of cash flows reports net cash flow from operating activities as major classes of operating cash receipts (e.g., cash collected from customers and cash received from interest and dividends) and cash disbursements (e.g., cash paid to suppliers for goods, to employees for services, to creditors for interest, and to government authorities for taxes).

The direct method is illustrated here in more detail to help you understand the difference between accrual-based income and net cash flow from operating activities and to illustrate the data needed to apply the direct method. Emig Company, which began business on January 1, 2002, has the following selected balance sheet information:

ILLUSTRATION 24-18
Balance Sheet Accounts, Emig Co.

	December 31	
	2002	2001
Cash	$159,000	–0–
Accounts receivable	15,000	–0–
Inventory	160,000	–0–
Prepaid expenses	8,000	–0–
Property, plant, and equipment (net)	90,000	–0–
Accounts payable	60,000	–0–
Accrued expenses payable	20,000	–0–

Emig Company's December 31, 2002, income statement and additional information are:

ILLUSTRATION 24-19
Income Statement, Emig Co.

Revenues from sales		$780,000
Cost of goods sold		450,000
Gross profit		330,000
Operating expenses	$160,000	
Depreciation	10,000	170,000
Income before income taxes		160,000
Income tax expense		48,000
Net income		$112,000

Additional Information:
(a) Dividends of $70,000 were declared and paid in cash.
(b) The accounts payable increase resulted from the purchase of merchandise.
(c) Prepaid expenses and accrued expenses payable relate to operating expenses.

Under the **direct method**, net cash provided by operating activities is computed by **adjusting each item in the income statement** from the accrual basis to the cash basis. To simplify and condense the operating activities section, only major classes of operating cash receipts and cash payments are reported. The difference between these major classes of cash receipts and cash payments is the net cash provided by operating activities as shown in Illustration 24-20.

ILLUSTRATION 24-20
Major Classes of Cash Receipts and Payments

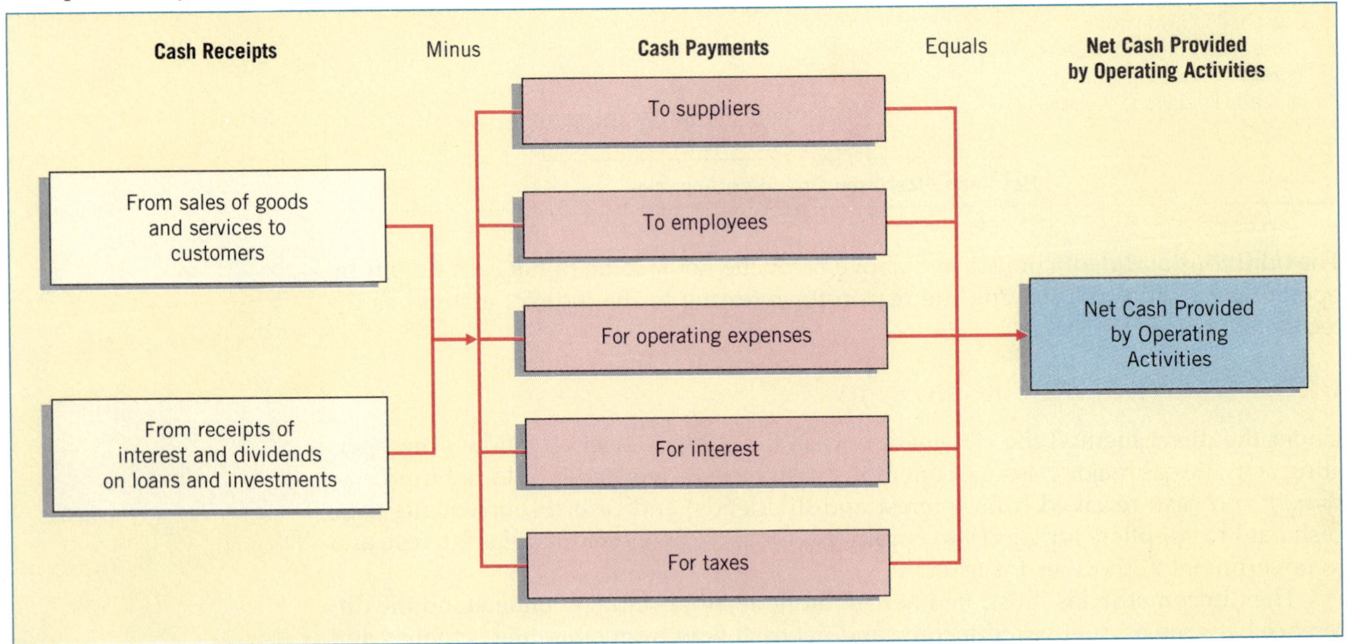

An efficient way to apply the direct method is to analyze the revenues and expenses reported in the income statement in the order in which they are listed. Cash receipts and cash payments related to these revenues and expenses should then be determined. The direct method adjustments for Emig Company in 2002 to determine net cash provided by operating activities are presented in the following sections.

Cash Receipts from Customers

The income statement for Emig Company reported revenues from customers of $780,000. To determine cash receipts from customers, it is necessary to consider the change in accounts receivable during the year. When accounts receivable increase during the year, revenues on an accrual basis are higher than cash receipts from customers. In other words, operations led to increased revenues, but not all of these revenues resulted in cash receipts. To determine the amount of increase in cash receipts, deduct the amount of the increase in accounts receivable from the total sales revenues. Conversely, a decrease in accounts receivable is added to sales revenues, because cash receipts from customers then exceed sales revenues.

For Emig Company, accounts receivable increased $15,000. Thus, cash receipts from customers were $765,000, computed as follows:

Revenues from sales	$780,000
Deduct: Increase in accounts receivable	15,000
Cash receipts from customers	$765,000

Cash receipts from customers may also be determined from an analysis of the Accounts Receivable account as shown below.

Accounts Receivable

1/1/02	Balance	–0–	Receipts from customers	765,000
	Revenue from sales	780,000		
12/31/02	Balance	15,000		

The relationships between cash receipts from customers, revenues from sales, and changes in accounts receivable are shown in Illustration 24-21.

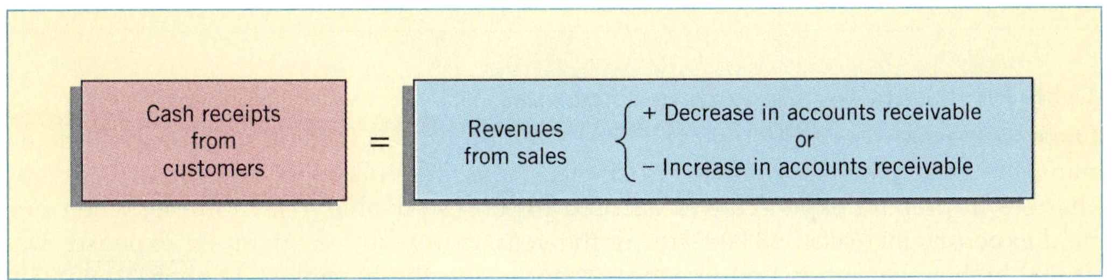

ILLUSTRATION 24-21
Formula to Compute Cash Receipts from Customers

Cash Payments to Suppliers

Emig Company reported cost of goods sold on its income statement of $450,000. To determine cash payments to suppliers, it is first necessary to find purchases for the year. To find purchases, cost of goods sold is adjusted for the change in inventory. When inventory increases during the year, it means that purchases this year exceed cost of goods sold. As a result, the increase in inventory is added to cost of goods sold to arrive at purchases.

In 2002, Emig Company's inventory increased $160,000. Purchases, therefore, are computed as follows:

Cost of goods sold	$450,000
Add: Increase in inventory	160,000
Purchases	$610,000

After purchases are computed, cash payments to suppliers are determined by adjusting purchases for the change in accounts payable. When accounts payable increase during the year, purchases on an accrual basis are higher than they are on a cash basis. As a result, an increase in accounts payable is deducted from purchases to arrive at cash payments to suppliers. Conversely, a decrease in accounts payable is added to purchases because cash payments to suppliers exceed purchases. Cash payments to suppliers were $550,000, computed as follows:

Purchases	$610,000
Deduct: Increase in accounts payable	60,000
Cash payments to suppliers	$550,000

Cash payments to suppliers may also be determined from an analysis of the Accounts Payable account as shown below.

Accounts Payable

Payments to suppliers	550,000	1/1/02	Balance	–0–
			Purchases	610,000
		12/31/02	Balance	60,000

The relationships between cash payments to customers, cost of goods sold, changes in inventory, and changes in accounts payable are shown in Illustration 24-22.

ILLUSTRATION 24-22
Formula to Compute Cash Payments to Suppliers

Cash payments to suppliers = Cost of goods sold { + Increase in inventory or − Decrease in inventory } { + Decrease in accounts payable or − Increase in accounts payable }

Cash Payments for Operating Expenses

Operating expenses of $160,000 were reported on Emig's income statement. To determine the cash paid for operating expenses, this amount must be adjusted for any changes in prepaid expenses and accrued expenses payable. For example, when prepaid expenses increased $8,000 during the year, cash paid for operating expenses was $8,000 higher than operating expenses reported on the income statement. To convert operating expenses to cash payments for operating expenses, the increase of $8,000 must be added to operating expenses. Conversely, if prepaid expenses decrease during the year, the decrease must be deducted from operating expenses.

Operating expenses must also be adjusted for changes in accrued expenses payable. When accrued expenses payable increase during the year, operating expenses on an accrual basis are higher than they are on a cash basis. As a result, an increase in accrued expenses payable is deducted from operating expenses to arrive at cash payments for operating expenses. Conversely, a decrease in accrued expenses payable is added to operating expenses because cash payments exceed operating expenses.

Emig Company's cash payments for operating expenses were $148,000, computed as follows:

Operating expenses	$160,000
Add: Increase in prepaid expenses	8,000
Deduct: Increase in accrued expenses payable	(20,000)
Cash payments for operating expenses	$148,000

The relationships among cash payments for operating expenses, changes in prepaid expenses, and changes in accrued expenses payable are shown in the following formula.

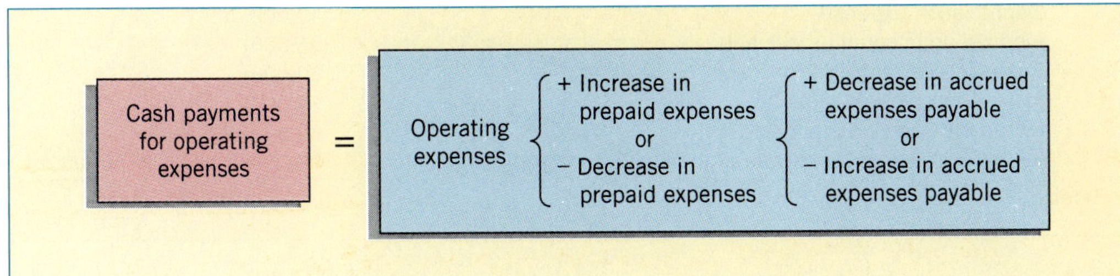

ILLUSTRATION 24-23
Formula to Compute Cash Payments for Operating Expenses

Note that depreciation expense was not considered because it is a noncash charge.

Cash Payments for Income Taxes

The income statement for Emig shows income tax expense of $48,000. This amount equals the cash paid because the comparative balance sheet indicated no income taxes payable at either the beginning or end of the year.

The computations illustrated above are summarized in the following schedule:

ILLUSTRATION 24-24
Accrual Basis to Cash Basis

Accrual Basis			Adjustment	Add (Subtract)	Cash Basis
Revenues from sales	$780,000	–	Increase in accounts receivable	$(15,000)	$765,000
Cost of goods sold	450,000	+	Increase in inventory	160,000	
		–	Increase in accounts payable	(60,000)	550,000
Operating expenses	160,000	+	Increase in prepaid expenses	8,000	
		–	Increase in accrued expenses payable	(20,000)	148,000
Depreciation expense	10,000	–	Depreciation expense	(10,000)	–0–
Income tax expense	48,000				48,000
Total expense	668,000				746,000
Net income	$112,000		Net cash provided by operating activities		$ 19,000

Presentation of the direct method for reporting net cash flow from operating activities takes the following form for the Emig Company illustration:

ILLUSTRATION 24-25
Operating Activities Section—Direct Method, 2002

EMIG COMPANY
Statement of Cash Flows (partial)

Cash flows from operating activities		
Cash received from customers		$765,000
Cash payments:		
To suppliers	$ 550,000	
For operating expenses	148,000	
For income taxes	48,000	746,000
Net cash provided by operating activities		$ 19,000

If Emig Company uses the direct method to present the net cash flows from operating activities, it must provide in a separate schedule the reconciliation of net income to net cash provided by operating activities. The reconciliation assumes the identical form and content of the indirect method of presentation as shown below:

ILLUSTRATION 24-26
Reconciliation of Net Income to Net Cash Provided by Operating Activities

Reconciliation		
Net income		$112,000
Adjustments to reconcile net income to net cash provided by operating activities:		
Depreciation expense	$ 10,000	
Increase in accounts receivable	(15,000)	
Increase in inventory	(160,000)	
Increase in prepaid expenses	(8,000)	
Increase in accounts payable	60,000	
Increase in accrued expense payable	20,000	(93,000)
Net cash provided by operating activities		$ 19,000

The reconciliation may be presented at the bottom of the statement of cash flows when the direct method is used or in a separate schedule.

Direct Versus Indirect Controversy

The most contentious decision that the FASB faced in issuing *Statement No. 95* was choosing between the direct method and the indirect method of determining net cash flow from operating activities. Companies lobbied against the direct method, urging adoption of the indirect method. Commercial lending officers expressed a strong preference to the FASB that the direct method be required.

In Favor of the Direct Method

The principal advantage of the direct method is that **it shows operating cash receipts and payments**. That is, it is more consistent with the objective of a statement of cash flows—to provide information about cash receipts and cash payments—than the indirect method, which does not report operating cash receipts and payments.

Supporters of the direct method contend that knowledge of the specific sources of operating cash receipts and the purposes for which operating cash payments were made in past periods is useful in estimating future operating cash flows. Furthermore, information about amounts of major classes of operating cash receipts and payments is more useful than information only about their arithmetic sum (the net cash flow from operating activities). Such information is more revealing of an enterprise's ability (1) to generate sufficient cash from operating activities to pay its debts, (2) to reinvest in its operations, and (3) to make distributions to its owners.[8]

Many corporate providers of financial statements say that they do not currently collect information in a manner that allows them to determine amounts such as cash received from customers or cash paid to suppliers directly from their accounting systems. But supporters of the direct method contend that the incremental cost of assimilating such operating cash receipts and payments data is not significant.

In Favor of the Indirect Method

The principal advantage of the indirect method is that **it focuses on the differences between net income and net cash flow from operating activities**. That is, it provides a useful link between the statement of cash flows and the income statement and balance sheet.

[8]"Statement of Cash Flows," pars. 107 and 111.

Many providers of financial statements contend that it is less costly to adjust net income to net cash flow from operating activities (indirect) than it is to report gross operating cash receipts and payments (direct). Supporters of the indirect method also state that the direct method, which effectively reports income statement information on a cash rather than an accrual basis, may erroneously suggest that net cash flow from operating activities is as good as, or better than, net income as a measure of performance.

Special Rules Applying to Direct and Indirect Methods

Companies that use the direct method are required, at a minimum, to report separately the following classes of operating cash receipts and payments:

Receipts

1. Cash collected from customers (including lessees, licensees, etc.).
2. Interest and dividends received.
3. Other operating cash receipts, if any.

Payments

1. Cash paid to employees and suppliers of goods or services (including suppliers of insurance, advertising, etc.).
2. Interest paid.
3. Income taxes paid.
4. Other operating cash payments, if any.

Companies are encouraged to provide further breakdowns of operating cash receipts and payments that they consider meaningful.

Consolidated statements of cash flows may be of limited use to analysts evaluating multinational companies. Without disaggregation, users of such statements are not able to determine "where in the world" the funds are sourced and used.

Companies using the indirect method are required to disclose separately changes in inventory, receivables, and payables to reconcile net income to net cash flow from operating activities. In addition, interest paid (net of amount capitalized) and income taxes paid must be disclosed elsewhere in the financial statements or accompanying notes.[9] The FASB requires these separate and additional disclosures so that users may approximate the direct method. Also, an acceptable alternative presentation of the indirect method is to report net cash flow from operating activities as a single line item in the statement of cash flows and to present the reconciliation details elsewhere in the financial statements.

SPECIAL PROBLEMS IN STATEMENT PREPARATION

OBJECTIVE 8
Identify special problems in preparing a statement of cash flows.

Some of the special problems related to preparing the statement of cash flows were discussed in connection with the preceding illustrations. Other problems that arise with some frequency in the preparation of this statement may be categorized as follows:

1. Adjustments similar to depreciation.
2. Accounts receivable (net).
3. Other working capital changes.
4. Net losses.
5. Gains.
6. Stock options.
7. Postretirement benefit costs.

[9] *Accounting Trends and Techniques — 1999* reports that of the 600 companies surveyed in 1998, 323 disclosed interest paid in notes to the financial statements, 251 disclosed interest at the bottom of the statement of cash flows, 8 disclosed interest within the statement of cash flows, and 18 reported no separate amount. Income taxes paid during the year were disclosed in a manner similar to interest payments.

8. Extraordinary items.
9. Significant noncash transactions.

Adjustments Similar to Depreciation

Depreciation expense is the most common adjustment to net income that is made to arrive at net cash flow from operating activities. But there are numerous other noncash expense or revenue items. Examples of expense items that must be added back to net income are the **amortization of intangible assets** such as goodwill and patents, and the **amortization of deferred costs** such as bond issue costs. These charges to expense involve expenditures made in prior periods that are being amortized currently and reduce net income without affecting cash in the current period.

Also, **amortization of bond discount or premium** on long-term bonds payable affects the amount of interest expense, but neither changes cash. As a result, amortization of these items should be added back to (discount) or subtracted from (premium) net income to arrive at net cash flow from operating activities. In a similar manner, **changes in deferred income taxes** affect net income but have no effect on cash. For example, Kroger Co. at one time experienced an increase in its liability for deferred taxes of approximately $42 million. Tax expense was increased and net income was decreased by this amount, but cash was not affected; therefore, $42 million would be added back to net income on a statement of cash flows. Conversely, General Electric Company at one time had a decrease in its liability for deferred taxes of $171 million. Tax expense decreased and net income increased by this amount, but cash flow was unaffected. Therefore, GE subtracted this amount from net income to arrive at net cash flow from operating activities.

Another common adjustment to net income is **a change related to an investment in common stock** when income or loss is accrued under the equity method. Recall that under the equity method, the investor (1) debits the investment account and credits revenue for its share of the investee's net income and (2) credits dividends received to the investment account. Therefore, the net increase in the investment account does not affect cash flow and must be deducted from net income in arriving at net cash flow from operating activities. To illustrate, assume that Victor Co. owns 40% of Milo Inc. and during the year Milo Inc. reports net income of $100,000 and pays a cash dividend of $30,000. This information is reported in Victor Co.'s statement of cash flows as a deduction from net income in the following manner—Equity in earnings of Milo Co., net of dividends, $28,000.

If the fair value method is used, income of the investee is not recognized and any cash dividend received is recorded as revenue. In this case, no adjustment to net income in the statement of cash flows is necessary for any cash dividend received.

Accounts Receivable (Net)

Up to this point, we have assumed that no allowance for doubtful accounts—a contra account—was needed to offset accounts receivable. However, if an allowance for doubtful accounts is needed, how does it affect the determination of net cash flow from operating activities? For example, assume that Redmark Co. reports net income of $40,000 and has the following balances related to accounts receivable:

ILLUSTRATION 24-27
Accounts Receivable Balances, Redmark Co.

	2002	2001	Change Increase/Decrease
Accounts receivable	$105,000	$90,000	$15,000 Increase
Allowance for doubtful accounts	10,000	4,000	6,000 Increase
Accounts receivable (net)	$ 95,000	$86,000	9,000 Increase

The proper reporting treatment using the indirect and direct methods is illustrated in the following sections.

Indirect Method

Because an increase in the Allowance for Doubtful Accounts is caused by a charge to bad debts expense, an increase in the Allowance for Doubtful Accounts should be added back to net income to arrive at net cash flow from operating activities. One method for presenting this information in a statement of cash flows is as follows:

ILLUSTRATION 24-28
Presentation of Allowance for Doubtful Accounts—Indirect Method

REDMARK CO. Statement of Cash Flows (partial) For the Year 2002		
Cash flows from operating activities		
Net income		$40,000
Adjustments to reconcile net income to net cash provided by operating activities:		
Increase in accounts receivable	$(15,000)	
Increase in allowance for doubtful accounts	6,000	(9,000)
		$31,000

As indicated, the increase in the Allowance for Doubtful Accounts balance is caused by a charge to bad debt expense for the year. Because bad debt expense is a noncash charge, it must be added back to net income in arriving at net cash flow from operating activities.

Instead of separately analyzing the allowance account, a short-cut approach is to net the allowance balance against the receivable balance and compare the change in accounts receivable on a net basis. This presentation would be as follows:

ILLUSTRATION 24-29
Net Approach to Allowance for Doubtful Accounts—Indirect Method

REDMARK CO. Statement of Cash Flows (partial) For the Year 2002	
Cash flows from operating activities	
Net income	$40,000
Adjustments to reconcile net income to net cash provided by operating activities:	
Increase in accounts receivable (net)	(9,000)
	$31,000

This short-cut procedure works also if the change in the allowance account was caused by a writeoff of accounts receivable. In this case, both the Accounts Receivable and the Allowance for Doubtful Accounts are reduced, and no effect on cash flows occurs. Because of its simplicity, you should use the net approach on your homework assignments.

Direct Method

If the direct method is used, the Allowance for Doubtful Accounts should **not be netted against the Accounts Receivable**. To illustrate, assume that Redmark Co.'s net income of $40,000 comprised the following items:

ILLUSTRATION 24-30
Income Statement, Redmark Co.

REDMARK CO. Income Statement For the Year 2002		
Sales		$100,000
Expenses:		
Salaries	$46,000	
Utilities	8,000	
Bad debts	6,000	60,000
Net income		$ 40,000

If the $9,000 increase in accounts receivable (net) is deducted from sales for the year, cash sales would be reported at $91,000 ($100,000 − $9,000) and cash payments for operating expenses at $60,000. Both items are misstated because cash sales should be reported at $85,000 ($100,000 − $15,000), and total cash payments for operating expenses should be reported at $54,000 ($60,000 − $6,000). The proper presentation is as follows:

ILLUSTRATION 24-31
Bad Debts—Direct Method

REDMARK CO. Statement of Cash Flows (partial) For the Year 2002		
Cash flows from operating activities		
Cash received from customers		$85,000
Salaries paid	$46,000	
Utilities paid	8,000	54,000
Net cash provided by operating activities		$31,000

An added complication develops when accounts receivable are written off. Simply adjusting sales for the change in accounts receivable will not provide the proper amount of cash sales. The reason is that the writeoff of the accounts receivable is not a cash collection. Thus an additional adjustment is necessary.

Other Working Capital Changes

Up to this point, all of the changes in working capital items (current asset and current liability items) have been handled as adjustments to net income in determining net cash flow from operating activities. You must be careful, however, because **some changes in working capital, although they affect cash, do not affect net income**. Generally, these are investing or financing activities of a current nature. For example, the purchase of **short-term available-for-sale securities** for $50,000 cash has no effect on net income but it does cause a $50,000 decrease in cash.[10] This transaction is reported as a cash flow from investing activities and reported gross as follows:[11]

Cash flows from investing activities	
Purchase of short-term available-for-sale securities	$(50,000)

Another example is the issuance of a $10,000 **short-term nontrade note payable** for cash. This change in a working capital item has no effect on income from operations but it increases cash $10,000. It is reported in the statement of cash flows as follows:

[10]If the basis of the statement of cash flows is cash **and cash equivalents** and the short-term investment is considered a cash equivalent, then nothing would be reported in the statement because the balance of cash and cash equivalents does not change as a result of this transaction.

[11]"Accounting for Certain Investments in Debt and Equity Securities," *Statement of Financial Accounting Standards No. 115* (Norwalk, CT: 1993), par. 118.

Cash flows from financing activities	
Issuance of short-term note	$10,000

Another change in a working capital item that has no effect on income from operations or on cash is a **cash dividend payable**. Although the cash dividends when paid will be reported as a financing activity, the declared but unpaid dividend is not reported on the statement of cash flows.

Because **trading securities** are bought and held principally for the purpose of selling them in the near term, the cash flows from purchases and sales of trading securities should be classified as cash flows from **operating activities.**[12]

Net Losses

If an enterprise reports a net loss instead of a net income, the net loss must be adjusted for those items that do not result in a cash inflow or outflow. The net loss after adjusting for the charges or credits not affecting cash may result in a negative **or** a positive cash flow from operating activities. For example, if the net loss was $50,000 and the total amount of charges to be added back was $60,000, then net cash provided by operating activities is $10,000, as shown in this computation:

Net loss		$(50,000)
Adjustments to reconcile net income to net cash provided by operating activities:		
Depreciation of plant assets	$55,000	
Amortization of patents	5,000	60,000
Net cash provided by operating activities		$ 10,000

ILLUSTRATION 24-32
Computation of Net Cash Flow from Operating Activities—Cash Inflow

If the company experiences a net loss of $80,000 and the total amount of the charges to be added back is $25,000, the presentation appears as follows:

Net loss	$(80,000)
Adjustments to reconcile net income to net cash used by operating activities:	
Depreciation of plant assets	25,000
Net cash used by operating activities	$(55,000)

ILLUSTRATION 24-33
Computation of Net Cash Flow from Operating Activities—Cash Outflow

Although it is not illustrated in this chapter, a negative cash flow may result even if the company reports a net income.

Gains

In the third illustration (2002) of Tax Consultants Inc., the company experiences a loss of $2,000 from the sale of equipment. This loss was added to net income to compute net cash flow from operating activities because **the loss is a noncash charge in the income statement.** If a gain from a sale of equipment is experienced, it too requires that net income be adjusted. Because the gain is reported in the statement of cash flows as part of the cash proceeds from the sale of equipment under investing activities, **the gain is deducted from net income to avoid double counting**—once as part of net income and again as part of the cash proceeds from the sale.

[12]Ibid., par. 118.

Stock Options

If a company has a stock option plan, compensation expense will be recorded during the period(s) in which the employee performs the services. Although compensation expense is debited, stockholders' equity (the paid-in capital accounts) is credited, and cash remains unaffected by the amount of the expense. **Therefore, net income has to be increased by the amount of compensation expense from stock options in computing net cash flow from operating activities.**

Postretirement Benefit Costs

If a company has postretirement costs such as an employee pension plan, chances are that the pension expense recorded during a period will either be higher than the cash funded (when there is an unfunded liability) or lower than the cash funded (when there is a deferred or prepaid pension cost). When the expense is higher or lower than the cash paid, **net income must be adjusted by the difference between cash paid and the expense reported** in computing net cash flow from operating activities.

Extraordinary Items

Cash flows from extraordinary transactions and other events whose effects are included in net income, but which are not related to operations, should be reported **either as investing activities or as financing activities**. For example, if Tax Consultants Inc. had extinguished its long-term bond debt of $40,000 by paying the bondholders $35,000 in cash, it would have recognized a $3,000 extraordinary gain ($5,000 gain less $2,000 of taxes). In the statement of cash flows (indirect method), the $5,000 gain would be deducted from net income in the operating activities section and the $35,000 cash outflow for debt extinguishment would be reported as a financing activity as follows:

Cash flows from financing activities	
Retirement of long-term bonds	$(35,000)

UNDERLYING CONCEPTS

By rejecting the requirement to allocate taxes to the various activities, the Board invoked the cost-benefit constraint. The information would be beneficial, but the cost of providing such information would exceed the benefits of providing the information.

Note that in this example the gain is handled at its gross amount ($5,000), not net of tax. The cash paid to retire the bonds is reported as a financing activity at $35,000, also exclusive of the tax effect. The FASB requires that **all income taxes paid be classified as operating cash outflows**. Some suggested that income taxes paid be allocated to investing and financing transactions. But, the Board decided that allocation of income taxes paid to operating, investing, and financing activities would be so complex and arbitrary that the benefits, if any, would not justify the costs involved. Under both the direct method and the indirect method the total amount of income taxes paid must be disclosed.[13]

Significant Noncash Transactions

Because the statement of cash flows reports only the effects of operating, investing, and financing activities in terms of cash flows, some **significant noncash transactions** and

[13]For an insightful article on some weaknesses and limitations in the statement of cash flows caused by implementation of *FASB Statement No. 95,* see Hugo Nurnberg, "Inconsistencies and Ambiguities in Cash Flow Statements Under *FASB Statement No. 95,*" *Accounting Horizons,* June 1993, pp. 60–73. Nurnberg identifies the inconsistencies caused by the three-way classification of all cash receipts and cash payments, gross versus net of tax, the ambiguous disclosure requirements for noncash investing and financing transactions, and the ambiguous presentation of third-party financing transactions. See also Paul R. Bahnson, Paul B. W. Miller, and Bruce P. Budge, "Nonarticulation in Cash Flow Statements and Implications for Education, Research, and Practice," *Accounting Horizons,* December 1996, pp. 1–15.

other events that are investing or financing activities are omitted from the body of the statement. Among the more common of these noncash transactions that should be reported or disclosed in some manner are the following:

Go to the Digital Tool for examples of cash flow statements, including disclosure of significant noncash transactions.

1. Acquisition of assets by assuming liabilities (including capital lease obligations) or by issuing equity securities.
2. Exchanges of nonmonetary assets.
3. Refinancing of long-term debt.
4. Conversion of debt or preferred stock to common stock.
5. Issuance of equity securities to retire debt.

These noncash items are not to be incorporated in the statement of cash flows. If material in amount, these disclosures may be either narrative or summarized in a separate schedule at the bottom of the statement, or they may appear in a separate note or supplementary schedule to the financial statements. The presentation of these significant noncash transactions or other events in a separate schedule at the bottom of the statement of cash flows is shown as follows:

ILLUSTRATION 24-34
Schedule Presentation of Noncash Investing and Financing Activities

Net increase in cash	$3,717,000
Cash at beginning of year	5,208,000
Cash at end of year	$8,925,000
Noncash investing and financing activities	
Purchase of land and building through issuance of 250,000 shares of common stock	$1,750,000
Exchange of Steadfast, NY, land for Bedford, PA, land	$2,000,000
Conversion of 12% bonds to 50,000 shares of common stock	$ 500,000

These noncash transactions might be presented in a separate note as follows:

ILLUSTRATION 24-35
Note Presentation of Noncash Investing and Financing Activities

Note G: Significant noncash transactions. During the year the company engaged in the following significant noncash investing and financing transactions:

Issued 250,000 shares of common stock to purchase land and building	$1,750,000
Exchanged land in Steadfast, NY, for land in Bedford, PA	$2,000,000
Converted 12% bonds due 2001 to 50,000 shares of common stock	$ 500,000

Certain other significant noncash transactions or other events are generally not reported in conjunction with the statement of cash flows. Examples of these types of transactions are **stock dividends, stock splits, and appropriations of retained earnings**. These items, neither financing nor investing activities, are generally reported in conjunction with the statement of stockholders' equity or schedules and notes pertaining to changes in capital accounts.

USE OF A WORK SHEET

SECTION 2

When numerous adjustments are necessary, or other complicating factors are present, **a work sheet is often used to assemble and classify the data that will appear on the statement of cash flows**. The work sheet (a **"spreadsheet"** when using computer software) is merely a device that aids in the preparation of the statement; its use is optional. The skeleton format of the work sheet for preparation of the statement of cash flows using the indirect method is shown in Illustration 24-36.

OBJECTIVE 9
Explain the use of a work sheet in preparing a statement of cash flows.

ILLUSTRATION 24-36
Format of Work Sheet for Preparation of Statement of Cash Flows

XYZ COMPANY
Statement of Cash Flows
For the Year Ended . . .

Balance Sheet Accounts	End of Prior Year Balances	Reconciling Items Debits	Reconciling Items Credits	End of Current Year Balances
Debit balance accounts	XX	XX	XX	XX
	XX	XX	XX	XX
Totals	XXX			XXX
Credit balance accounts	XX	XX	XX	XX
	XX	XX	XX	XX
Totals	XXX			XXX
Statement of Cash Flows Effects				
Operating activities				
Net income		XX		
Adjustments		XX	XX	
Investing activities				
Receipts and payments		XX	XX	
Financing activities				
Receipts and payments		XX	XX	
Totals		XXX	XXX	
Increase (decrease) in cash		(XX)	XX	
Totals		XXX	XXX	

The following guidelines are important in using a work sheet:

1. In the balance sheet accounts section, **accounts with debit balances are listed separately from those with credit balances**. This means, for example, that Accumulated Depreciation is listed under credit balances and not as a contra account under debit balances. The beginning and ending balances of each account are entered in the appropriate columns. The transactions that caused the change in the account balance during the year are entered as reconciling items in the two middle columns. After all reconciling items have been entered, each line pertaining to a balance sheet account should foot across. That is, the beginning balance plus or minus the reconciling item(s) must equal the ending balance. When this agreement exists for all balance sheet accounts, all changes in account balances have been reconciled.
2. The bottom portion of the work sheet consists of the operating, investing, and financing activities sections. Accordingly, it provides the information necessary to prepare the formal statement of cash flows. **Inflows of cash are entered as debits in the reconciling columns and outflows of cash are entered as credits in the reconciling columns.** Thus, in this section, the sale of equipment for cash at book value is entered as a debit under inflows of cash from investing activities. Similarly, the purchase of land for cash is entered as a credit under outflows of cash from investing activities.
3. **The reconciling items shown in the work sheet are not entered in any journal or posted to any account.** They do not represent either adjustments or corrections of the balance sheet accounts. They are used only to facilitate the preparation of the statement of cash flows.

PREPARATION OF THE WORK SHEET

The preparation of a work sheet involves a series of prescribed steps. The steps in this case are:

Step 1. Enter the balance sheet accounts and their beginning and ending balances in the balance sheet accounts section.

Step 2. Enter the data which explain the changes in the balance sheet accounts (other than cash) and their effects on the statement of cash flows in the reconciling columns of the work sheet.

Step 3. Enter the increase or decrease in cash on the cash line and at the bottom of the work sheet. This entry should enable the totals of the reconciling columns to be in agreement.

To illustrate the preparation and use of a work sheet and to illustrate the reporting of some of the special problems discussed in the prior section, the following comprehensive illustration is presented for Satellite Corporation. Again, the indirect method serves as the basis for the computation of net cash provided by operating activities. The financial statements and other data related to Satellite Corporation are presented with the balance sheet and the statement of income and retained earnings shown on the following pages. Additional explanations related to the preparation of the work sheet are provided throughout the discussion that follows the financial statements.

ILLUSTRATION 24-37
Comparative Balance Sheet, Satellite Corporation

SATELLITE CORPORATION
Comparative Balance Sheet
December 31, 2002 and 2001

	2002	2001	Difference Incr. or Decr.
Assets			
Cash	$ 59,000	$ 66,000	$ 7,000 Decr.
Accounts receivable (net)	104,000	51,000	53,000 Incr.
Inventories	493,000	341,000	152,000 Incr.
Prepaid expenses	16,500	17,000	500 Decr.
Investments in stock of Porter Co. (equity method)	18,500	15,000	3,500 Incr.
Land	131,500	82,000	49,500 Incr.
Equipment	187,000	142,000	45,000 Incr.
Accumulated depreciation—equipment	(29,000)	(31,000)	2,000 Decr.
Buildings	262,000	262,000	—
Accumulated depreciation—buildings	(74,100)	(71,000)	3,100 Incr.
Goodwill	7,600	10,000	2,400 Decr.
Total assets	$1,176,000	$884,000	
Liabilities			
Accounts payable	$ 132,000	$131,000	1,000 Incr.
Accrued liabilities	43,000	39,000	4,000 Incr.
Income tax payable	3,000	16,000	13,000 Decr.
Notes payable (long-term)	60,000	—	60,000 Incr.
Bonds payable	100,000	100,000	—
Premium on bonds payable	7,000	8,000	1,000 Decr.
Deferred tax liability (long-term)	9,000	6,000	3,000 Incr.
Total liabilities	354,000	300,000	
Stockholders' Equity			
Common stock ($1 par)	60,000	50,000	10,000 Incr.
Additional paid-in capital	187,000	38,000	149,000 Incr.
Retained earnings	592,000	496,000	96,000 Incr.
Treasury stock	(17,000)	—	17,000 Incr.
Total stockholders' equity	822,000	584,000	
Total liabilities and stockholders' equity	$1,176,000	$884,000	

ILLUSTRATION 24-38
Income and Retained Earnings Statements, Satellite Corporation

SATELLITE CORPORATION
Combined Statement of Income and Retained Earnings
For the Year Ended December 31, 2002

Net sales		$526,500
Other revenue		3,500
Total revenues		530,000
Expense		
Cost of goods sold		310,000
Selling and administrative expenses		47,000
Other expenses and losses		12,000
Total expenses		369,000
Income before income tax and extraordinary item		161,000
Income tax		
Current	$47,000	
Deferred	3,000	50,000
Income before extraordinary item		111,000
Gain on condemnation of land (net of $2,000 tax)		6,000
Net income		117,000
Retained earnings, January 1		496,000
Less:		
Cash dividends	6,000	
Stock dividend	15,000	21,000
Retained earnings, December 31		$592,000
Per share:		
Income before extraordinary item		$2.02
Extraordinary item		.11
Net income		$2.13

Additional Information

(a) Other income of $3,500 represents Satellite's equity share in the net income of Porter Co., an equity investee. Satellite owns 22% of Porter Co.

(b) An analysis of the equipment account and related accumulated depreciation indicates the following:

	Equipment Dr./(Cr.)	Accum. Dep. Dr./(Cr.)	Gain or (Loss)
Balance at end of 2001	$142,000	$(31,000)	
Purchases of equipment	53,000		
Sale of equipment	(8,000)	2,500	$(1,500)
Depreciation for the period		(11,500)	
Major repair charged to accumulated depreciation		11,000	
Balance at end of 2002	$187,000	$(29,000)	

(c) Land in the amount of $60,000 was purchased through the issuance of a long-term note; in addition, certain parcels of land costing $10,500 were condemned. The state government paid Satellite $18,500, resulting in an $8,000 gain which has a $2,000 tax effect.

(d) The change in the accumulated depreciation—buildings, goodwill, and premium on bonds payable accounts resulted from depreciation and amortization entries.

(e) An analysis of the paid-in capital accounts in stockholders' equity discloses the following:

	Common Stock	Additional Paid-In Capital
Balance at end of 2001	$50,000	$ 38,000
Issuance of 2% stock dividend	1,000	14,000
Sale of stock for cash	9,000	135,000
Balance at end of 2002	$60,000	$187,000

(f) Interest paid (net of amount capitalized) is $9,000; income taxes paid is $62,000.

ANALYSIS OF TRANSACTIONS

The following discussion provides an explanation of the individual adjustments that appear on the work sheet in Illustration 24-39 (page 1345). Because cash is the basis for the analysis, the cash account is reconciled last. Because income is the first item that appears on the statement of cash flows, it is handled first.

Change in Retained Earnings

Net income for the period is $117,000; the entry for it on the work sheet is as follows:

(1)

Operating—Net Income	117,000	
Retained Earnings		117,000

Net income is reported on the bottom section of the work sheet and **is the starting point for preparation of the statement of cash flows (under the indirect method).**

Retained earnings was also affected by a stock dividend and a cash dividend. The retained earnings statement reports a stock dividend of $15,000. The work sheet entry for this transaction is as follows:

(2)

Retained Earnings	15,000	
Common Stock		1,000
Additional Paid-in Capital		14,000

The issuance of stock dividends is not a cash operating, investing, or financing item; therefore, **although this transaction is entered on the work sheet for reconciling purposes, it is not reported in the statement of cash flows.**

The cash dividends paid of $6,000 represents a financing activity cash outflow. The following work sheet entry is made:

(3)

Retained Earnings	6,000	
Financing—Cash Dividends		6,000

The beginning and ending balances of retained earnings are reconciled by the entry of the three items above.

Accounts Receivable (Net)

The increase in accounts receivable (net) of $53,000 represents adjustments that did not result in cash inflows during 2002. As a result, the increase of $53,000 would be deducted from net income. The following work sheet entry is made:

(4)

Accounts Receivable (net)	53,000	
Operating—Increase in Accounts Receivable (net)		53,000

Inventories

The increase in inventories of $152,000 represents an operating use of cash. The incremental investment in inventories during the year reduces cash without increasing the cost of goods sold. The work sheet entry is made as follows:

(5)

Inventories	152,000	
Operating—Increase in Inventories		152,000

Prepaid Expense

The decrease in prepaid expenses of $500 represents a charge in the income statement for which there was no cash outflow in the current period. It should be added back to net income through the following entry:

(6)		
Operating—Decrease in Prepaid Expenses	500	
Prepaid Expenses		500

Investment in Stock

The investment in the stock of Porter Co. increased $3,500, which reflects Satellite's share of the income earned by its equity investee during the current year. Although revenue, and therefore income per the income statement, was increased $3,500 by the accounting entry that recorded Satellite's share of Porter Co.'s net income, no cash (dividend) was provided. The following work sheet entry is made:

(7)		
Investment in Stock of Porter Co.	3,500	
Operating—Equity in Earnings of Porter Co.		3,500

Land

Land in the amount of $60,000 was purchased through the issuance of a long-term note payable. This transaction did not affect cash; it is considered a significant noncash investing/financing transaction that would be disclosed either in a separate schedule below the statement of cash flows or in the accompanying notes. The following entry is made to reconcile the work sheet:

(8)		
Land	60,000	
Notes Payable		60,000

In addition to the noncash transaction involving the issuance of a note to purchase land, the Land account was decreased by the condemnation proceedings. The work sheet entry to record the receipt of $18,500 for land having a book value of $10,500 is as follows:

(9)		
Investing—Proceeds from Condemnation of Land	18,500	
Land		10,500
Operating—Gain on Condemnation of Land		8,000

The extraordinary gain of $8,000 is deducted from net income in reconciling net income to net cash flow from operating activities because the transaction that gave rise to the gain is an item whose cash effect is already classified as an investing cash inflow. The Land account is now reconciled.

Equipment and Accumulated Depreciation

An analysis of Equipment and Accumulated Depreciation shows that a number of transactions have affected these accounts. Equipment in the amount of $53,000 was purchased during the year. The entry to record this transaction on the work sheet is as follows:

(10)		
Equipment	53,000	
Investing—Purchase of Equipment		53,000

In addition, equipment with a book value of $5,500 was sold at a loss of $1,500. The entry to record this transaction on the work sheet is as follows:

(11)		
Investing—Sale of Equipment	4,000	
Operating—Loss on Sale of Equipment	1,500	
Accumulated Depreciation—Equipment	2,500	
Equipment		8,000

The proceeds from the sale of the equipment provided cash of $4,000. In addition, the loss on the sale of the equipment has reduced net income, but did not affect cash;

therefore, it is added back to net income to report accurately cash provided by operating activities.

Depreciation on the equipment was reported at $11,500 and is presented on the work sheet in the following manner:

(12)		
Operating—Depreciation Expense—Equipment	11,500	
Accumulated Depreciation—Equipment		11,500

The depreciation expense is added back to net income because it reduced income but did not affect cash.

Finally, a major repair to the equipment in the amount of $11,000 was charged to Accumulated Depreciation—Equipment. Because this expenditure required cash, the following work sheet entry is made:

(13)		
Accumulated Depreciation—Equipment	11,000	
Investing—Major Repairs of Equipment		11,000

The balances in the Equipment and related Accumulated Depreciation accounts are reconciled after adjustment for the foregoing items.

Building Depreciation and Amortization of Goodwill

Depreciation expense on the buildings of $3,100 and amortization of goodwill of $2,400 are both expenses in the income statement that reduced net income but did not require cash outflows in the current period. The following work sheet entry is made:

(14)		
Operating—Depreciation Expense—Buildings	3,100	
Operating—Amortization of Goodwill	2,400	
Accumulated Depreciation—Buildings		3,100
Goodwill		2,400

Other Noncash Charges or Credits

An analysis of the remaining accounts indicates that changes in the Accounts Payable, Accrued Liabilities, Income Tax Payable, Premium on Bonds Payable, and Deferred Tax Liability balances resulted from charges or credits to net income that did not affect cash. Each of these items should be individually analyzed and entered in the work sheet. We have summarized in the following compound entry to the work sheet these noncash, income-related items:

(15)		
Income Tax Payable	13,000	
Premium on Bonds Payable	1,000	
Operating—Increase in Accounts Payable	1,000	
Operating—Increase in Accrued Liabilities	4,000	
Operating—Increase in Deferred Tax Liability	3,000	
Operating—Decrease in Income Tax Payable		13,000
Operating—Amortization of Bond Premium		1,000
Accounts Payable		1,000
Accrued Liabilities		4,000
Deferred Tax Liability		3,000

Common Stock and Related Accounts

A comparison of the common stock balances and the additional paid-in capital balances shows that transactions during the year affected these accounts. First, a stock dividend of 2% was issued to stockholders. As indicated in the discussion of work sheet entry (2), no cash was provided or used by the stock dividend transaction. In addition to the shares issued via the stock dividend, Satellite sold shares of common stock at $16 per share. The work sheet entry to record this transaction is as follows:

(16)

Financing—Sale of Common Stock	144,000	
Common Stock		9,000
Additional Paid-in Capital		135,000

Also, the company purchased shares of its common stock in the amount of $17,000. The work sheet entry to record this transaction is as follows:

(17)

Treasury Stock	17,000	
Financing—Purchase of Treasury Stock		17,000

Final Reconciling Entry

The final entry to reconcile the change in cash and to balance the work sheet is shown below.

(18)

Decrease in Cash	7,000	
Cash		7,000

The $7,000 amount is the difference between the beginning and ending cash balance.

Once it has been determined that the differences between the beginning and ending balances per the work sheet columns have been accounted for, the reconciling transactions columns can be totaled, and they should balance. The statement of cash flows can be prepared entirely from the items and amounts that appear at the bottom of the work sheet under "Statement of Cash Flows Effects," as shown in Illustration 24-39 on the next page.

ILLUSTRATION 24-39
Completed Work Sheet for Preparation of Statement of Cash Flows, Satellite Corporation

SATELLITE CORPORATION
Work Sheet for Preparation of Statement of Cash Flows
For the Year Ended December 31, 2002

	Balance 12/31/01	Reconciling Items—2002 Debits	Credits	Balance 12/31/02
Debits				
Cash	$ 66,000		(18) $ 7,000	$ 59,000
Accounts receivable (net)	51,000	(4) $ 53,000		104,000
Inventories	341,000	(5) 152,000		493,000
Prepaid expenses	17,000		(6) 500	16,500
Investment (equity method)	15,000	(7) 3,500		18,500
Land	82,000	(8) 60,000	(9) 10,500	131,500
Equipment	142,000	(10) 53,000	(11) 8,000	187,000
Buildings	262,000			262,000
Goodwill	10,000		(14) 2,400	7,600
Treasury stock		(17) 17,000		17,000
Total debits	$986,000			$1,296,100
Credits		(11) 2,500		
Accum. depr.—equipment	$ 31,000	(13) 11,000	(12) 11,500	$ 29,000
Accum. depr.—buildings	71,000		(14) 3,100	74,100
Accounts payable	131,000		(15) 1,000	132,000
Accrued liabilities	39,000		(15) 4,000	43,000
Income tax payable	16,000	(15) 13,000		3,000
Notes payable	-0-		(8) 60,000	60,000
Bonds payable	100,000			100,000
Premium on bonds payable	8,000	(15) 1,000		7,000
Deferred tax liability	6,000		(15) 3,000	9,000
Common stock	50,000		(2) 1,000	
			(16) 9,000	60,000
Additional paid-in capital	38,000		(2) 14,000	
			(16) 135,000	187,000
Retained earnings	496,000	(2) 15,000	(1) 117,000	
		(3) 6,000		592,000
Total credits	$986,000			$1,296,100
Statement of Cash Flows Effects				
Operating activities				
Net income		(1) 117,000		
Increase in accounts receivable (net)			(4) 53,000	
Increase in inventories			(5) 152,000	
Decrease in prepaid expenses		(6) 500		
Equity in earnings of Porter Co.			(7) 3,500	
Gain on condemnation of land			(9) 8,000	
Loss on sale of equipment		(11) 1,500		
Depr. expense—equipment		(12) 11,500		
Depr. expense—buildings		(14) 3,100		
Amortization of goodwill		(14) 2,400		
Increase in accounts payable		(15) 1,000		
Increase in accrued liabilities		(15) 4,000		
Increase in deferred tax liability		(15) 3,000		
Decrease in income tax payable			(15) 13,000	
Amortization of bond premium			(15) 1,000	
Investing activities				
Proceeds from condemnation of land		(9) 18,500		
Purchase of equipment			(10) 53,000	
Sale of equipment		(11) 4,000		
Major repairs of equipment			(13) 11,000	
Financing activities				
Payment of cash dividend			(3) 6,000	
Issuance of common stock		(16) 144,000		
Purchase of treasury stock			(17) 17,000	
Totals		697,500	704,500	
Decrease in cash		(18) 7,000		
Totals		$704,500	$704,500	

PREPARATION OF FINAL STATEMENT

Presented below is a formal statement of cash flows prepared from the data compiled in the lower portion of the work sheet.

ILLUSTRATION 24-40
Statement of Cash Flows, Satellite Corporation

SATELLITE CORPORATION
Statement of Cash Flows
For the Year Ended December 31, 2002
Increase (Decrease) in Cash

Cash flows from operating activities		
Net income		$117,000
Adjustments to reconcile net income to net cash used by operating activities:		
Depreciation expense	$ 14,600	
Amortization of goodwill	2,400	
Amortization of bond premium	(1,000)	
Equity in earnings of Porter Co.	(3,500)	
Gain on condemnation of land	(8,000)	
Loss on sale of equipment	1,500	
Increase in deferred tax liability	3,000	
Increase in accounts receivable (net)	(53,000)	
Increase in inventories	(152,000)	
Decrease in prepaid expenses	500	
Increase in accounts payable	1,000	
Increase in accrued liabilities	4,000	
Decrease in income tax payable	(13,000)	(203,500)
Net cash used by operating activities		(86,500)
Cash flows from investing activities		
Proceeds from condemnation of land	18,500	
Purchase of equipment	(53,000)	
Sale of equipment	4,000	
Major repairs of equipment	(11,000)	
Net cash used by investing activities		(41,500)
Cash flows from financing activities		
Payment of cash dividend	(6,000)	
Issuance of common stock	144,000	
Purchase of treasury stock	(17,000)	
Net cash provided by financing activities		121,000
Net decrease in cash		(7,000)
Cash, January 1, 2002		66,000
Cash, December 31, 2002		$ 59,000

Supplemental Disclosures of Cash Flow Information:

Cash paid during the year for:		
Interest (net of amount capitalized)		$ 9,000
Income taxes		$ 62,000

Supplemental Schedule of Noncash Investing and Financing Activities:
Purchase of land for $60,000 in exchange for a $60,000 long-term note.

Go to the Digital Tool for discussion of the T-account approach to preparation of the statement of cash flows.

SUMMARY OF LEARNING OBJECTIVES

1 Describe the purpose of the statement of cash flows. The primary purpose of the statement of cash flows is to provide information about cash receipts and cash payments of an entity during a period. A secondary objective is to report the entity's operating, investing, and financing activities during the period.

2 Identify the major classifications of cash flows. The cash flows are classified as: (1) Operating activities—transactions that result in the revenues, expenses, gains, and losses that determine net income. (2) Investing activities—lending money and collecting on those loans, and acquiring and disposing of investments, plant assets, and intangible assets. (3) Financing activities—obtaining cash from creditors and repaying loans, issuing and reacquiring capital stock, and paying cash dividends.

3 Differentiate between net income and net cash flows from operating activities. Net income on an accrual basis must be adjusted to determine net cash flow from operating activities because some expenses and losses do not cause cash outflows and some revenues and gains do not provide cash inflows.

4 Contrast the direct and indirect methods of calculating net cash flow from operating activities. Under the direct approach, major classes of operating cash receipts and cash disbursements are calculated. The computations are summarized in a schedule of changes from the accrual to the cash basis income statement. Presentation of the direct approach of reporting net cash flow from operating activities takes the form of a condensed cash basis income statement. The indirect method adds back to net income the noncash expenses and losses and subtracts the noncash revenues and gains.

5 Determine net cash flows from investing and financing activities. Once the net cash flow from operating activities is computed, the next step is to determine whether any other changes in balance sheet accounts caused an increase or decrease in cash. Net cash flows from investing and financing activities can be determined by examining the changes in noncurrent balance sheet accounts.

6 Prepare a statement of cash flows. Preparing the statement involves three major steps: (1) determine the change in cash. This is the difference between the beginning and the ending cash balance shown on the comparative balance sheets. (2) determine the net cash flow from operating activities. This procedure is complex; it involves analyzing not only the current year's income statement but also the comparative balance sheets and the selected transaction data. (3) determine cash flows from investing and financing activities. All other changes in the balance sheet accounts must be analyzed to determine the effects on cash.

7 Identify sources of information for a statement of cash flows. The information to prepare the statement usually comes from three sources: (1) comparative balance sheets. Information in these statements indicate the amount of the changes in assets, liabilities, and equities during the period. (2) current income statement. Information in this statement is used in determining the cash provided by operations during the period. (3) selected transaction data. These data from the general ledger provide additional detailed information needed to determine how cash was provided or used during the period.

8 Identify special problems in preparing a statement of cash flows. These special problems are: (1) adjustments similar to depreciation; (2) accounts receivable (net); (3) other working capital changes; (4) net losses; (5) gains; (6) stock options; (7) postretirement benefit costs; (8) extraordinary items; and (9) significant noncash transactions.

9 Explain the use of a work sheet in preparing a statement of cash flows. When numerous adjustments are necessary, or other complicating factors are present, a work sheet is often used to assemble and classify the data that will appear on the statement of cash flows. The work sheet is merely a device that aids in the preparation of the statement; its use is optional.

KEY TERMS

FROM CLASSROOM TO CAREER

WILLIE SUTTON

is an accountant with Mutual Community Savings Bank in Durham, North Carolina. He has held this position since graduating Summa Cum Laude from North Carolina Central University in 1994. Prior to attending college, he served for three years in the United States Army. Currently, he is working on his MBA from NCCU.

Why did you join the Army after high school?

It was the only way that I could pay my way through college. Perhaps I could have financed college some other way, but I came from a poor family and was attracted to the college scholarships that the Army offered. For the most part, I enjoyed my experience in the Army, because it taught me discipline and hard work. It was probably one of the best decisions that I ever made, because without it, I probably wouldn't have been able to go to college and be where I am right now.

Did you find it advantageous to start college at an older age?

Perhaps it was because of age, but I can remember noticing that a lot of the students weren't as focused as I was. I knew a lot of students who would stay up all night getting their work done, but I was able to manage my time better. As a teenager, I watched my parents get up every day and not miss a day of work, and I learned discipline from that as well as my Army experience. Age is less of an issue in the MBA program that I have been attending at night, where there are some students who are much older than I am.

Describe Mutual Community Savings Bank.

This is a community bank with three branches, two in Durham and one in Greensboro, North Carolina. The bank is publicly held, which means management has to worry about the stock price (ticker symbol MTUC) as well as whether the bank is profitable and providing good customer service. I have found that working for a smaller institution provides me with a lot of exposure to many different areas of the bank that I wouldn't otherwise get with a larger bank.

What topic from Intermediate Accounting relates to your current position?

As you can imagine, the management and control of cash is very important in a bank. One of the most important things that I do is to go over the tellers' work at the end of the day after all the transactions have been calculated and closed out. There are usually some differences between what the system says and what the teller actually has in cash. In addition, working with the bank's Treasurer, I compile annual and quarterly financial statements and a variety of regulatory reports that generally draw on my accounting education. But my duties have broadened beyond accounting and into the bank's computer operations, where I have management duties. Many of our customers are elderly, and they tend to visit the bank a little bit more than young people, and some of them resist the new technology. But most have become accustomed to direct deposit of payroll checks and automatic payment of certain bills. In addition, we are in the process of converting to an online banking system, which will make us more competitive with some of the larger banks in the area.

QUESTIONS

1 What is the purpose of the statement of cash flows? What information does it provide?

2 Of what use is the statement of cash flows?

3 Differentiate between investing activities, financing activities, and operating activities.

4 What are the major sources of cash (inflows) in a statement of cash flows? What are the major uses (outflows) of cash?

5 Identify and explain the major steps involved in preparing the statement of cash flows.

6 Identify the following items as (1) operating, (2) investing, or (3) financing activities: purchase of land; payment of dividends; cash sales; and purchase of treasury stock.

7 Unlike the other major financial statements, the statement of cash flows is not prepared from the adjusted trial balance. From what sources does the information to prepare this statement come and what information does each source provide?

8 Why is it necessary to convert accrual-based net income to a cash basis when preparing a statement of cash flows?

9 Differentiate between the direct method and the indirect method by discussing each method.

10 Bonnie Raitt Company reported net income of $3.5 million in 2002. Depreciation for the year was $520,000; accounts receivable increased $500,000; and accounts payable increased $350,000. Compute net cash flow from operating activities using the indirect method.

11 Sophie B. Hawkins Co. reported sales on an accrual basis of $100,000. If accounts receivable increased $30,000, and the allowance for doubtful accounts increased $9,000 after a writeoff of $4,000, compute cash sales.

12 Your roommate is puzzled. During the last year, the company in which she is a stockholder reported a net loss of $675,000, yet its cash increased $321,000 during the same period of time. Explain to your roommate how this situation could occur.

13 The board of directors of Kenny G Corp. declared cash dividends of $260,000 during the current year. If dividends payable was $85,000 at the beginning of the year and $70,000 at the end of the year, how much cash was paid in dividends during the year?

14 Explain how the amount of cash payments to suppliers is computed under the direct method.

15 The net income for Silverchair Company for 2002 was $320,000. During 2002, depreciation on plant assets was $114,000, amortization of goodwill was $40,000, and the company incurred a loss on sale of plant assets of $21,000. Compute net cash flow from operating activities.

16 Each of the following items must be considered in preparing a statement of cash flows for Frogstomp Inc. for the year ended December 31, 2002. State where each item is to be shown in the statement, if at all.

- **(a)** Plant assets that had cost $20,000 6½ years before and were being depreciated on a straight-line basis over 10 years with no estimated scrap value were sold for $4,000.
- **(b)** During the year, 10,000 shares of common stock with a stated value of $20 a share were issued for $41 a share.
- **(c)** Uncollectible accounts receivable in the amount of $22,000 were written off against the Allowance for Doubtful Accounts.
- **(d)** The company sustained a net loss for the year of $50,000. Depreciation amounted to $22,000, and a gain of $9,000 was realized on the sale of available-for-sale securities for $38,000 cash.

17 Classify the following items as (1) operating, (2) investing, (3) financing, or (4) significant noncash investing and financing activities (using the direct method).

- **(a)** Purchase of equipment.
- **(b)** Redemption of bonds.
- **(c)** Sale of building.
- **(d)** Cash payments to suppliers.
- **(e)** Exchange of equipment for furniture.
- **(f)** Issuance of capital stock.
- **(g)** Cash received from customers.
- **(h)** Purchase of treasury stock.
- **(i)** Issuance of bonds for land.
- **(j)** Payment of dividends.
- **(k)** Cash payments to employees.
- **(l)** Cash payments for operating expenses.

18 Clay Walker and David Ball were discussing the presentation format of the statement of cash flows of Martina McBride Co. At the bottom of McBride's statement of cash flows was a separate section entitled "Noncash investing and financing activities." Give three examples of significant noncash transactions that would be reported in this section.

19 During 2002, Bryan Adams Company redeemed $2,000,000 of bonds payable for $1,780,000 cash. Indicate how this transaction would be reported on a statement of cash flows, if at all.

20 What are some of the arguments in favor of using the indirect (reconciliation) method as opposed to the direct method for reporting a statement of cash flows?

21 Why is it desirable to use a work sheet when preparing a statement of cash flows? Is a work sheet required to prepare a statement of cash flows?

BRIEF EXERCISES

BE24-1 American Gladhanders Corporation had the following activities in 2002:

Sale of land, $130,000
Purchase of inventory, $845,000
Purchase of treasury stock, $72,000
Purchase of equipment, $415,000
Issuance of common stock, $320,000
Purchase of available-for-sale securities, $59,000

Compute the amount American Gladhanders should report as net cash provided (used) by investing activities in its statement of cash flows.

BE24-2 Chrono Trigger Corporation had the following activities in 2002:

Payment of accounts payable, $770,000
Issuance of common stock, $250,000
Payment of dividends, $300,000
Collection of note receivable, $100,000
Issuance of bonds payable, $510,000
Purchase of treasury stock, $46,000

Compute the amount Chrono Trigger should report as net cash provided (used) by financing activities in its 2002 statement of cash flows.

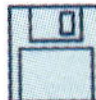

BE24-3 Ryker Corporation is preparing its 2002 statement of cash flows, using the indirect method. Presented below is a list of items that may affect the statement. Using the code below, indicate how each item will affect Ryker's 2002 statement of cash flows.

Code Letter	Effect
A	Added to net income in the operating section
D	Deducted from net income in the operating section
R-I	Cash receipt in investing section
P-I	Cash payment in investing section
R-F	Cash receipt in financing section
P-F	Cash payment in financing section
N	Noncash investing and/or financing activity

Items

____ (a) Increase in accounts receivable.
____ (b) Decrease in accounts receivable.
____ (c) Issuance of stock.
____ (d) Depreciation expense.
____ (e) Sale of land at book value.
____ (f) Sale of land at a gain.
____ (g) Payment of dividends.
____ (h) Purchase of land and building.
____ (i) Purchase of available-for-sale investment.
____ (j) Increase in accounts payable.
____ (k) Decrease in accounts payable.
____ (l) Loan from bank by signing note.
____ (m) Purchase of equipment using a note.
____ (n) Increase in inventory.
____ (o) Issuance of bonds.
____ (p) Retirement of bonds.
____ (q) Sale of equipment at a loss.
____ (r) Purchase of treasury stock.

BE24-4 Azure Corporation had the following 2002 income statement:

Sales	$200,000
Cost of goods sold	120,000
Gross profit	80,000

Operating expenses (includes depreciation of $21,000)	50,000
Net income	$ 30,000

The following accounts increased during 2002: accounts receivable, $17,000; inventory, $11,000; accounts payable, $13,000. Prepare the cash flows from operating activities section of Azure's 2002 statement of cash flows using the direct method.

BE24-5 Use the information from BE24-4 for Azure Corporation. Prepare the cash flows from operating activities section of Azure's 2002 statement of cash flows using the indirect method.

BE24-6 At January 1, 2002, Cyberslider Inc. had accounts receivable of $72,000. At December 31, 2002, accounts receivable is $59,000. Sales for 2002 is $420,000. Compute Cyberslider's 2002 cash receipts from customers.

BE24-7 Donkey Kong Corporation had January 1 and December 31 balances as follows:

	1/1/02	12/31/02
Inventory	$90,000	$113,000
Accounts payable	61,000	69,000

For 2002, cost of goods sold was $500,000. Compute Donkey Kong's 2002 cash payments to suppliers.

BE24-8 In 2002, Fieval Corporation had net cash provided by operating activities of $531,000; net cash used by investing activities of $963,000; and net cash provided by financing activities of $585,000. At January 1, 2002, the cash balance was $333,000. Compute December 31, 2002, cash.

BE24-9 Tool Time Corporation had the following 2002 income statement:

Revenues	$100,000
Expenses	60,000
	$ 40,000

In 2002, Tool Time had the following activity in selected accounts:

Accounts Receivable

	Debit	Credit	
1/1/02	20,000		
Revenues	100,000	1,000	Writeoffs
		90,000	Collections
12/31/02	29,000		

Allowance for Doubtful Accounts

	Debit	Credit	
		1,200	1/1/02
Writeoffs	1,000	1,540	Bad debt expense
		1,740	12/31/02

Prepare Tool Time's cash flows from operating activities section of the statement of cash flows using (a) the direct method and (b) the indirect method.

BE24-10 Red October Corporation reported net income of $50,000 in 2002. Depreciation expense was $17,000. The following working capital accounts changed:

Accounts receivable	$11,000	increase
Available-for-sale securities	16,000	increase
Inventory	7,400	increase
Nontrade note payable	15,000	decrease
Accounts payable	9,300	increase

Compute net cash provided by operating activities.

BE24-11 In 2002, Izzy Corporation reported a net loss of $70,000. Izzy's only net income adjustments were depreciation expense, $84,000, and increase in accounts receivable, $8,100. Compute Izzy's net cash provided (used) by operating activities.

BE24-12 In 2002, Mufosta Inc. issued 1,000 shares of $10 par value common stock for land worth $50,000.

(a) Prepare Mufosta's journal entry to record the transaction.
(b) Indicate the effect the transaction has on cash.
(c) Indicate how the transaction is reported on the statement of cash flows.

BE24-13 Indicate in general journal form how the items below would be entered in a work sheet for the preparation of the statement of cash flows.

(a) Net income is $317,000.
(b) Cash dividends declared and paid totaled $120,000.
(c) Equipment was purchased for $114,000.
(d) Equipment that originally cost $40,000 and had accumulated depreciation of $32,000 was sold for $13,000.

EXERCISES

E24-1 (Classification of Transactions) Red Hot Chili Peppers Co. had the following activity in its most recent year of operations:

(a) Purchase of equipment.
(b) Redemption of bonds.
(c) Sale of building.
(d) Depreciation.
(e) Exchange of equipment for furniture.
(f) Issuance of capital stock.
(g) Amortization of intangible assets.
(h) Purchase of treasury stock.
(i) Issuance of bonds for land.
(j) Payment of dividends.
(k) Increase in interest receivable on notes receivable.
(l) Pension expense exceeds amount funded.

Instructions

Classify the items as (1) operating—add to net income; (2) operating—deduct from net income; (3) investing; (4) financing; or (5) significant noncash investing and financing activities (use indirect method).

E24-2 (Statement Presentation of Transactions—Indirect Method) Each of the following items must be considered in preparing a statement of cash flows (indirect method) for Turbulent Indigo Inc. for the year ended December 31, 2001.

(a) Plant assets that had cost $20,000 6 years before and were being depreciated on a straight-line basis over 10 years with no estimated scrap value were sold for $5,300.
(b) During the year, 10,000 shares of common stock with a stated value of $10 a share were issued for $43 a share.
(c) Uncollectible accounts receivable in the amount of $27,000 were written off against the Allowance for Doubtful Accounts.
(d) The company sustained a net loss for the year of $50,000. Depreciation amounted to $22,000, and a gain of $9,000 was realized on the sale of land for $39,000 cash.
(e) A 3-month U.S. Treasury bill was purchased for $100,000. The company uses a cash and cash-equivalent basis for its cash flow statement.
(f) Goodwill amortized for the year was $20,000.
(g) The company exchanged common stock for a 70% interest in Tabasco Co. for $900,000.
(h) During the year, treasury stock costing $47,000 was purchased.

Instructions

State where each item is to be shown in the statement of cash flows, if at all.

E24-3 (Preparation of Operating Activities Section—Indirect Method, Periodic Inventory) The income statement of Vince Gill Company is shown below:

VINCE GILL COMPANY
Income Statement
For the Year Ended December 31, 2002

Sales		$6,900,000
Cost of goods sold		
Beginning inventory	$1,900,000	
Purchases	4,400,000	
Goods available for sale	6,300,000	
Ending inventory	1,600,000	
Cost of goods sold		4,700,000
Gross profit		2,200,000
Operating expenses		
Selling expenses	450,000	
Administrative expenses	700,000	1,150,000
Net income		$1,050,000

Additional information:

1. Accounts receivable decreased $360,000 during the year.
2. Prepaid expenses increased $170,000 during the year.
3. Accounts payable to suppliers of merchandise decreased $275,000 during the year.
4. Accrued expenses payable decreased $100,000 during the year.
5. Administrative expenses include depreciation expense of $60,000.

Instructions
Prepare the operating activities section of the statement of cash flows for the year ended December 31, 2002, for Vince Gill Company, using the indirect method.

E24-4 (Preparation of Operating Activities Section—Direct Method) Data for the Vince Gill Company are presented in E24-3.

Instructions
Prepare the operating activities section of the statement of cash flows using the direct method.

E24-5 (Preparation of Operating Activities Section—Direct Method) Alison Krauss Company's income statement for the year ended December 31, 2001, contained the following condensed information:

Revenue from fees		$840,000
Operating expenses (excluding depreciation)	$624,000	
Depreciation expense	60,000	
Loss on sale of equipment	26,000	710,000
Income before income taxes		130,000
Income tax expense		40,000
Net income		$ 90,000

Krauss's balance sheet contained the following comparative data at December 31:

	2001	2000
Accounts receivable	$37,000	$54,000
Accounts payable	41,000	31,000
Income taxes payable	4,000	8,500

(Accounts payable pertains to operating expenses.)

Instructions
Prepare the operating activities section of the statement of cash flows using the direct method.

E24-6 (Preparation of Operating Activities Section—Indirect Method) Data for Alison Krauss Company are presented in E24-5.

Instructions
Prepare the operating activities section of the statement of cash flows using the indirect method.

E24-7 (Computation of Operating Activities—Direct Method) Presented below are two independent situations:

Situation A:
Annie Lennox Co. reports revenues of $200,000 and operating expenses of $110,000 in its first year of operations, 2002. Accounts receivable and accounts payable at year-end were $71,000 and $29,000, respectively. Assume that the accounts payable related to operating expenses. Ignore income taxes.

Instructions
Using the direct method, compute net cash provided by operating activities.

Situation B:
The income statement for Blues Traveler Company shows cost of goods sold $310,000 and operating expenses (exclusive of depreciation) $230,000. The comparative balance sheet for the year shows that inventory increased $26,000, prepaid expenses decreased $8,000, accounts payable (related to merchandise) decreased $17,000, and accrued expenses payable increased $11,000.

Instructions
Compute (a) cash payments to suppliers and (b) cash payments for operating expenses.

E24-8 (Schedule of Net Cash Flow from Operating Activities—Indirect Method) Glen Ballard Co. reported $145,000 of net income for 2002. The accountant, in preparing the statement of cash flows, noted several items that might affect cash flows from operating activities. These items are listed below:

1. During 2002, Ballard purchased 100 shares of treasury stock at a cost of $20 per share. These shares were then resold at $25 per share.
2. During 2002, Ballard sold 100 shares of IBM common at $200 per share. The acquisition cost of these shares was $145 per share. This investment was shown on Ballard's December 31, 2001, balance sheet as an available-for-sale security.
3. During 2002, Ballard changed from the straight-line method to the double-declining balance method of depreciation for its machinery. The total cumulative effect was for $14,600.
4. During 2002, Ballard revised its estimate for bad debts. Before 2002, Ballard's bad debt expense was 1% of its net sales. In 2002, this percentage was increased to 2%. Net sales for 2002 were $500,000, and net accounts receivable decreased by $12,000 during 2002.
5. During 2002, Ballard issued 500 shares of its $10 par common stock for a patent. The market value of the shares on the date of the transaction was $23 per share.
6. Depreciation expense for 2002 is $39,000.
7. Ballard Co. holds 40% of the Nirvana Company's common stock as a long-term investment. Nirvana Company reported $27,000 of net income for 2002.
8. Nirvana Company paid a total of $2,000 of cash dividends to all investees in 2002.
9. During 2002, Ballard declared a 10% stock dividend. One thousand shares of $10 par common stock were distributed. The market price at date of issuance was $20 per share.

Instructions

Prepare a schedule that shows the net cash flow from operating activities using the indirect method. Assume no items other than those listed above affected the computation of 2002 net cash flow from operating activities.

E24-9 (SCF—Direct Method) Los Lobos Corp. uses the direct method to prepare its statement of cash flows. Los Lobos's trial balances at December 31, 2001 and 2000, are as follows:

	December 31	
	2001	2000
Debits		
Cash	$ 35,000	$ 32,000
Accounts receivable	33,000	30,000
Inventory	31,000	47,000
Property, plant, & equipment	100,000	95,000
Unamortized bond discount	4,500	5,000
Cost of goods sold	250,000	380,000
Selling expenses	141,500	172,000
General and administrative expenses	137,000	151,300
Interest expense	4,300	2,600
Income tax expense	20,400	61,200
	$756,700	$976,100
Credits		
Allowance for doubtful accounts	$ 1,300	$ 1,100
Accumulated depreciation	16,500	15,000
Trade accounts payable	25,000	15,500
Income taxes payable	21,000	29,100
Deferred income taxes	5,300	4,600
8% callable bonds payable	45,000	20,000
Common stock	50,000	40,000
Additional paid-in capital	9,100	7,500
Retained earnings	44,700	64,600
Sales	538,800	778,700
	$756,700	$976,100

Additional information:

1. Los Lobos purchased $5,000 in equipment during 2001.
2. Los Lobos allocated one-third of its depreciation expense to selling expenses and the remainder to general and administrative expenses.
3. Bad debt expense for 2001 was $5,000, and writeoffs of uncollectible accounts totaled $4,800.

Instructions

Determine what amounts Los Lobos should report in its statement of cash flows for the year ended December 31, 2001, for the following:

1. Cash collected from customers.
2. Cash paid to suppliers.
3. Cash paid for interest.
4. Cash paid for income taxes.
5. Cash paid for selling expenses.

E24-10 (Classification of Transactions) Following are selected balance sheet accounts of Allman Bros. Corp. at December 31, 2002 and 2001, and the increases or decreases in each account from 2001 to 2002. Also presented is selected income statement information for the year ended December 31, 2002, and additional information.

Selected balance sheet accounts	2002	2001	Increase (Decrease)
Assets			
Accounts receivable	$ 34,000	$ 24,000	$ 10,000
Property, plant, and equipment	277,000	247,000	30,000
Accumulated depreciation	(178,000)	(167,000)	(11,000)
Liabilities and stockholders' equity			
Bonds payable	49,000	46,000	3,000
Dividends payable	8,000	5,000	3,000
Common stock, $1 par	22,000	19,000	3,000
Additional paid-in capital	9,000	3,000	6,000
Retained earnings	104,000	91,000	13,000
Selected income statement information for the year ended December 31, 2002			
Sales revenue	$155,000		
Depreciation	33,000		
Gain on sale of equipment	14,500		
Net income	31,000		

Additional information:

1. During 2002, equipment costing $45,000 was sold for cash.
2. Accounts receivable relate to sales of merchandise.
3. During 2002, $20,000 of bonds payable were issued in exchange for property, plant, and equipment. There was no amortization of bond discount or premium.

Instructions

Determine the category (operating, investing, or financing) and the amount that should be reported in the statement of cash flows for the following items:

1. Payments for purchase of property, plant, and equipment.
2. Proceeds from the sale of equipment.
3. Cash dividends paid.
4. Redemption of bonds payable.

E24-11 (SCF—Indirect Method) Condensed financial data of Pat Metheny Company for 2002 and 2001 are presented below.

PAT METHENY COMPANY
Comparative Balance Sheet
As of December 31, 2002 and 2001

	2002	2001
Cash	$1,800	$1,150
Receivables	1,750	1,300
Inventory	1,600	1,900
Plant assets	1,900	1,700
Accumulated depreciation	(1,200)	(1,170)
Long-term investments (Held-to-maturity)	1,300	1,420
	$7,150	$6,300
Accounts payable	$1,200	$ 900
Accrued liabilities	200	250
Bonds payable	1,400	1,550
Capital stock	1,900	1,700
Retained earnings	2,450	1,900
	$7,150	$6,300

PAT METHENY COMPANY
Income Statement
For the Year Ended December 31, 2002

Sales	$6,900
Cost of goods sold	4,700
Gross margin	2,200
Selling and administrative expense	930
Income from operations	1,270
Other revenues and gains	
Gain on sale of investments	80
Income before tax	1,350
Income tax expense	540
Net income	810
Cash dividends	260
Income retained in business	$ 550

Additional information:

During the year, $70 of common stock was issued in exchange for plant assets. No plant assets were sold in 2002.

Instructions
Prepare a statement of cash flows using the indirect method.

E24-12 (SCF—Direct Method) Data for Pat Metheny Company are presented in E24-11.

Instructions
Prepare a statement of cash flows using the direct method. (Do not prepare a reconciliation schedule.)

E24-13 (SCF—Indirect Method) Condensed financial data of McCoy Tyner Company for the years ended December 31, 2002, and December 31, 2001, are presented below.

MCCOY TYNER COMPANY
Comparative Balance Sheet
As of December 31, 2002 and 2001

	2002	2001
Cash	$160,800	$ 38,400
Receivables	123,200	49,000
Inventories	112,500	57,900
Investments (Available-for-sale)	90,000	101,000
Plant assets	240,000	212,500
	$726,500	$458,800
Accounts payable	$100,000	$ 65,200
Mortgage payable	50,000	77,000
Accumulated depreciation	30,000	52,000
Common stock	175,000	131,100
Retained earnings	371,500	133,500
	$726,500	$458,800

MCCOY TYNER COMPANY
Income Statement
For the Year Ended December 31, 2002

Sales	$440,000	
Interest and other revenue (Includes gain on sale of investments of $5,000)	20,000	$460,000

Less:		
Cost of goods sold	130,000	
Selling and administrative expenses	10,000	
Depreciation	42,000	
Income taxes	5,000	
Interest charges	3,000	
Loss on sale of plant assets	12,000	202,000
Net income		258,000
Cash dividends		20,000
Income retained in business		$238,000

Additional information:
New plant assets costing $85,000 were purchased during the year. Common stock of $20,000 was issued in exchange for plant assets. Investments were sold during the year. No unrealized gains or losses have occurred in these securities.

Instructions
Prepare a statement of cash flows using the indirect method.

E24-14 (SCF—Direct Method) Data for McCoy Tyner Company are presented in E24-13.

Instructions
Prepare a statement of cash flows using the direct method. (Do not prepare a reconciliation schedule.)

E24-15 (SCF—Direct Method) Brecker Inc., a greeting card company, had the following statements prepared as of December 31, 2002.

BRECKER INC.
Comparative Balance Sheet
As of December 31, 2002 and 2001

	12/31/02	12/31/01
Cash	$ 6,000	$ 7,000
Accounts receivable	62,000	51,000
Short-term investments (Available-for-sale)	35,000	18,000
Inventories	40,000	60,000
Prepaid rent	5,000	4,000
Printing equipment	154,000	130,000
Accumulated depr.—equipment	(35,000)	(25,000)
Goodwill	46,000	50,000
Total assets	$313,000	$295,000
Accounts payable	$ 46,000	$ 40,000
Income taxes payable	4,000	6,000
Wages payable	8,000	4,000
Short-term loans payable	8,000	10,000
Long-term loans payable	60,000	69,000
Common stock, $10 par	100,000	100,000
Contributed capital, common stock	30,000	30,000
Retained earnings	57,000	36,000
Total liabilities & equity	$313,000	$295,000

BRECKER INC.
Income Statement
For the Year Ending December 31, 2002

Sales	$338,150
Cost of goods sold	175,000
Gross margin	163,150
Operating expenses	120,000
Operating income	43,150

Interest expense	$11,400	
Gain on sale of equipment	2,000	9,400
Income before tax		33,750
Income tax expense		6,750
Net income		$ 27,000

Additional information:

1. Dividends in the amount of $6,000 were declared and paid during 2002.
2. Depreciation expense and amortization expense are included in operating expenses.
3. No unrealized gains or losses have occurred on the investments during the year.
4. Equipment that had a cost of $20,000 and was 70% depreciated was sold during 2002.

Instructions

Prepare a statement of cash flows using the direct method. (Do not prepare a reconciliation schedule.)

E24-16 (SCF—Indirect Method) Data for Brecker Inc. are presented in E24-15.

Instructions

Prepare a statement of cash flows using the indirect method.

E24-17 (SCF—Indirect Method) Presented below are data taken from the records of Antonio Brasileiro Company.

	December 31, 2002	December 31, 2001
Cash	$ 15,000	$ 8,000
Current assets other than cash	85,000	60,000
Long-term investments	10,000	53,000
Plant assets	335,000	215,000
	$445,000	$336,000
Accumulated depreciation	$ 20,000	$ 40,000
Current liabilities	40,000	22,000
Bonds payable	75,000	–0–
Capital stock	254,000	254,000
Retained earnings	56,000	20,000
	$445,000	$336,000

Additional information:

1. Held-to-maturity securities carried at a cost of $43,000 on December 31, 2001, were sold in 2002 for $34,000. The loss (not extraordinary) was incorrectly charged directly to Retained Earnings.
2. Plant assets that cost $50,000 and were 80% depreciated were sold during 2002 for $8,000. The loss (not extraordinary) was incorrectly charged directly to Retained Earnings.
3. Net income as reported on the income statement for the year was $57,000.
4. Dividends paid amounted to $10,000.
5. Depreciation charged for the year was $20,000.

Instructions

Prepare a statement of cash flows for the year 2002 using the indirect method.

E24-18 (Cash Provided by Operating, Investing, and Financing Activities) The balance sheet data of Brown Company at the end of 2001 and 2000 follow:

	2001	2000
Cash	$ 30,000	$ 35,000
Accounts receivable (net)	55,000	45,000
Merchandise inventory	65,000	45,000
Prepaid expenses	15,000	25,000
Equipment	90,000	75,000
Accumulated depreciation—equipment	(18,000)	(8,000)
Land	70,000	40,000
Totals	$307,000	$257,000

Accounts payable	$ 65,000	$ 52,000
Accrued expenses	15,000	18,000
Notes payable—bank, long-term	–0–	23,000
Bonds payable	30,000	–0–
Common stock, $10 par	189,000	159,000
Retained earnings	8,000	5,000
	$307,000	$257,000

Land was acquired for $30,000 in exchange for common stock, par $30,000, during the year; all equipment purchased was for cash. Equipment costing $10,000 was sold for $3,000; book value of the equipment was $6,000. Cash dividends of $10,000 were declared and paid during the year.

Instructions

Compute net cash provided (used) by:

(a) operating activities.
(b) investing activities.
(c) financing activities.

E24-19 (SCF—Indirect Method and Balance Sheet) Jobim Inc., had the following condensed balance sheet at the end of operations for 2001.

JOBIM INC.
Balance Sheet
December 31, 2001

Cash	$ 8,500	Current liabilities	$ 15,000
Current assets other than cash	29,000	Long-term notes payable	25,500
Investments	20,000	Bonds payable	25,000
Plant assets (net)	67,500	Capital stock	75,000
Land	40,000	Retained earnings	24,500
	$165,000		$165,000

During 2002 the following occurred:

1. A tract of land was purchased for $9,000.
2. Bonds payable in the amount of $15,000 were retired at par.
3. An additional $10,000 in capital stock was issued at par.
4. Dividends totaling $9,375 were paid to stockholders.
5. Net income for 2002 was $35,250 after allowing depreciation of $13,500.
6. Land was purchased through the issuance of $22,500 in bonds.
7. Jobim Inc. sold part of its investment portfolio for $12,875. This transaction resulted in a gain of $2,000 for the firm. The company classifies the investments as available-for-sale.
8. Both current assets (other than cash) and current liabilities remained at the same amount.

Instructions

(a) Prepare a statement of cash flows for 2002 using the indirect method.
(b) Prepare the condensed balance sheet for Jobim Inc. as it would appear at December 31, 2002.

E24-20 (Partial SCF—Indirect Method) The accounts below appear in the ledger of Anita Baker Company.

	Retained Earnings	Dr.	Cr.	Bal.
Jan. 1, 2002	Credit Balance			$ 42,000
Aug. 15	Dividends (cash)	$15,000		27,000
Dec. 31	Net Income for 2002		$40,000	67,000

	Machinery	Dr.	Cr.	Bal.
Jan. 1, 2002	Debit Balance			$140,000
Aug. 3	Purchase of Machinery	$62,000		202,000
Sept. 10	Cost of Machinery Constructed	48,000		250,000
Nov. 15	Machinery Sold		$56,000	194,000

	Accumulated Depreciation—Machinery	Dr.	Cr.	Bal.
Jan. 1, 2002	Credit Balance			$ 84,000
Apr. 8	Extraordinary Repairs	$21,000		63,000
Nov. 15	Accum. Depreciation on Machinery Sold	25,200		37,800
Dec. 31	Depreciation for 2002		$16,800	54,600

Instructions

From the postings in the accounts above, indicate how the information is reported on a statement of cash flows by preparing a partial statement of cash flows using the indirect method. The loss on sale of equipment (November 15) was $5,800.

E24-21 (Work Sheet Analysis of Selected Accounts) Data for Anita Baker Company are presented in E24-20.

Instructions

Prepare entries in journal form for all adjustments that should be made on a work sheet for a statement of cash flows.

E24-22 (Work Sheet Analysis of Selected Transactions) The transactions below took place during the year 2002:

1. Convertible bonds payable with a par value of $300,000 were exchanged for unissued common stock with a par value of $300,000. The market price of both types of securities was par.
2. The net income for the year was $410,000.
3. Depreciation charged on the building was $90,000.
4. The Appropriations for Bond Indebtedness in the amount of $300,000 was returned to Retained Earnings during the year, because the bonds were retired during the year.
5. Some old office equipment was traded in on the purchase of some dissimilar office equipment and the following entry was made:

Office Equipment	50,000	
Accum. Depreciation—Office Equipment	30,000	
Office Equipment		40,000
Cash		34,000
Gain on Disposal of Plant Assets		6,000

The Gain on Disposal of Plant Assets was credited to current operations as ordinary income.

6. Dividends in the amount of $123,000 were declared. They are payable in January of next year.

Instructions

Show by journal entries the adjustments that would be made on a work sheet for a statement of cash flows.

E24-23 (Work Sheet Preparation) Below is the comparative balance sheet for Stevie Wonder Corporation.

	Dec. 31, 2002	Dec. 31, 2001
Cash	$ 16,500	$ 21,000
Short-term investments	25,000	19,000
Accounts receivable	43,000	45,000
Allowance for doubtful accounts	(1,800)	(2,000)
Prepaid expenses	4,200	2,500
Inventories	81,500	65,000
Land	50,000	50,000
Buildings	125,000	73,500
Accumulated depreciation—buildings	(30,000)	(23,000)
Equipment	53,000	46,000
Accumulated depreciation—equipment	(19,000)	(15,500)
Delivery equipment	39,000	39,000
Accumulated depreciation—delivery equipment	(22,000)	(20,500)
Patents	15,000	–0–
	$379,400	$300,000

Accounts payable	$ 26,000	$ 16,000
Short-term notes payable	4,000	6,000
Accrued payables	3,000	4,600
Mortgage payable	73,000	53,400
Bonds payable	50,000	62,500
Capital stock	140,000	102,000
Additional paid-in capital	10,000	4,000
Retained earnings	73,400	51,500
	$379,400	$300,000

Dividends in the amount of $15,000 were declared and paid in 2002.

Instructions

From this information, prepare a work sheet for a statement of cash flows. Make reasonable assumptions as appropriate. The short-term investments are considered available-for-sale and no unrealized gains or losses have occurred on these securities.

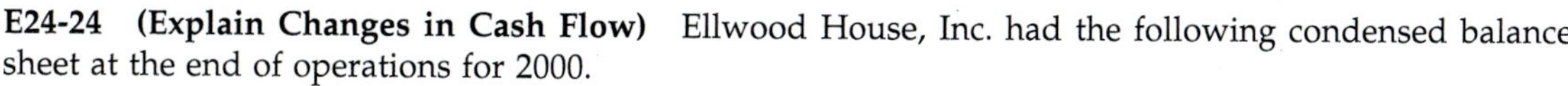

E24-24 (Explain Changes in Cash Flow) Ellwood House, Inc. had the following condensed balance sheet at the end of operations for 2000.

ELLWOOD HOUSE, INC.
Balance Sheet
December 31, 2000

Cash	$ 10,000	Current liabilities	$ 14,500
Current assets (noncash)	34,000	Long-term notes payable	30,000
Investments (available-for-sale)	40,000	Bonds payable	32,000
Plant assets	57,500	Capital stock	80,000
Land	38,500	Retained earnings	23,500
	$180,000		$180,000

During 2001 the following occurred:

1. Ellwood House, Inc., sold part of its investment portfolio for $15,500, resulting in a gain of $500 for the firm. The company often sells and buys securities of this nature.
2. Dividends totaling $19,000 were paid to stockholders.
3. A parcel of land was purchased for $5,500.
4. $20,000 of capital stock was issued at par.
5. $10,000 of bonds payable were retired at par.
6. Heavy equipment was purchased through the issuance of $32,000 of bonds.
7. Net income for 2001 was $42,000 after allowing depreciation of $13,550.
8. Both current assets (other than cash) and current liabilities remained at the same amount.

Instructions

(a) Prepare a statement of cash flows for 2001 using the indirect method.

(b) Draft a one-page letter to Mr. Gerald Brauer, president of Ellwood House, Inc., briefly explaining the changes within each major cash flow category. Refer to your cash flow statement whenever necessary.

PROBLEMS

P24-1 (SCF—Indirect Method) The following is Method Man Corp.'s comparative balance sheet accounts worksheet at December 31, 2002 and 2001, with a column showing the increase (decrease) from 2001 to 2002.

Comparative Balance Sheet

	2002	2001	Increase (Decrease)
Cash	$ 807,500	$ 700,000	$107,500
Accounts receivable	1,128,000	1,168,000	(40,000)
Inventories	1,850,000	1,715,000	135,000
Property, plant and equipment	3,307,000	2,967,000	340,000
Accumulated depreciation	(1,165,000)	(1,040,000)	(125,000)
Investment in Blige Co.	305,000	275,000	30,000
Loan receivable	262,500	—	262,500
Total assets	$6,495,000	$5,785,000	$710,000
Accounts payable	$1,015,000	$ 955,000	$ 60,000
Income taxes payable	30,000	50,000	(20,000)
Dividends payable	80,000	100,000	(20,000)
Capital lease obligation	400,000	—	400,000
Capital stock, common, $1 par	500,000	500,000	—
Additional paid-in capital	1,500,000	1,500,000	—
Retained earnings	2,970,000	2,680,000	290,000
Total liabilities and stockholders' equity	$6,495,000	$5,785,000	$710,000

Additional information:

1. On December 31, 2001, Method Man acquired 25% of Blige Co.'s common stock for $275,000. On that date, the carrying value of Blige's assets and liabilities, which approximated their fair values, was $1,100,000. Blige reported income of $120,000 for the year ended December 31, 2002. No dividend was paid on Blige's common stock during the year.
2. During 2002, Method Man loaned $300,000 to TLC Co., an unrelated company. TLC made the first semi-annual principal repayment of $37,500, plus interest at 10%, on December 31, 2002.
3. On January 2, 2002, Method Man sold equipment costing $60,000, with a carrying amount of $35,000, for $40,000 cash.
4. On December 31, 2002, Method Man entered into a capital lease for an office building. The present value of the annual rental payments is $400,000, which equals the fair value of the building. Method Man made the first rental payment of $60,000 when due on January 2, 2003.
5. Net income for 2002 was $370,000.
6. Method Man declared and paid cash dividends for 2002 and 2001 as follows:

	2002	2001
Declared	December 15, 2002	December 15, 2001
Paid	February 28, 2003	February 28, 2002
Amount	$80,000	$100,000

Instructions

Prepare a statement of cash flows for Method Man, Inc. for the year ended December 31, 2002, using the indirect method.

(AICPA adapted)

P24-2 (SCF—Indirect Method) The comparative balance sheets for Shenandoah Corporation show the following information:

	December 31 2002	2001
Cash	$ 38,500	$13,000
Accounts receivable	12,250	10,000
Inventory	12,000	9,000
Investments	–0–	3,000
Building	–0–	29,750
Equipment	40,000	20,000
Patent	5,000	6,250
Totals	$107,750	$91,000

Allowance for doubtful accounts	$3,000	$4,500
Accumulated depreciation on equipment	2,000	4,500
Accumulated depreciation on building	–0–	6,000
Accounts payable	5,000	3,000
Dividends payable	–0–	5,000
Notes payable, short-term (nontrade)	3,000	4,000
Long-term notes payable	31,000	25,000
Common stock	43,000	33,000
Retained earnings	20,750	6,000
	$107,750	$91,000

Additional data related to 2002 are as follows:

1. Equipment that had cost $11,000 and was 30% depreciated at time of disposal was sold for $2,500.
2. $10,000 of the long-term note payable was paid by issuing common stock.
3. Cash dividends paid were $5,000.
4. On January 1, 2002, the building was completely destroyed by a flood. Insurance proceeds on the building were $30,000 (net of $2,000 taxes).
5. Investments (available-for-sale) were sold at $3,700 above their cost. The company has made similar sales and investments in the past.
6. Cash of $15,000 was paid for the acquisition of equipment.
7. A long-term note for $16,000 was issued for the acquisition of equipment.
8. Interest of $2,000 and income taxes of $6,500 were paid in cash.

Instructions

Prepare a statement of cash flows using the indirect method. Flood damage is unusual and infrequent in that part of the country.

P24-3 (SCF—Direct Method) Mardi Gras Company has not yet prepared a formal statement of cash flows for the 2002 fiscal year. Comparative balance sheets as of December 31, 2001 and 2002, and a statement of income and retained earnings for the year ended December 31, 2002, are presented below.

MARDI GRAS COMPANY
Statement of Income and Retained Earnings
Year Ended December 31, 2002
($000 omitted)

Sales		$3,800
Expenses		
Cost of goods sold	$1,200	
Salaries and benefits	725	
Heat, light, and power	75	
Depreciation	80	
Property taxes	19	
Patent amortization	25	
Miscellaneous expenses	10	
Interest	30	2,164
Income before income taxes		1,636
Income taxes		818
Net income		818
Retained earnings—Jan. 1, 2002		310
		1,128
Stock dividend declared and issued		600
Retained earnings—Dec. 31, 2002		$ 528

MARDI GRAS COMPANY
Comparative Balance Sheet
December 31
($000 omitted)

Assets	2002	2001
Current assets		
Cash	$ 383	$ 100
U.S. Treasury notes (Available-for-sale)	–0–	50
Accounts receivable	740	500
Inventory	720	560
Total current assets	1,843	1,210
Long-term assets		
Land	150	70
Buildings and equipment	910	600
Accumulated depreciation	(200)	(120)
Patents (less amortization)	105	130
Total long-term assets	965	680
Total assets	$2,808	$1,890
Liabilities and Stockholders' Equity		
Current liabilities		
Accounts payable	$ 420	$ 340
Income taxes payable	40	20
Notes payable	320	320
Total current liabilities	780	680
Long-term notes payable—due 2004	200	200
Total liabilities	980	880
Stockholders' equity		
Common stock outstanding	1,300	700
Retained earnings	528	310
Total stockholders' equity	1,828	1,010
Total liabilities and stockholders' equity	$2,808	$1,890

Instructions

Prepare a statement of cash flows using the direct method. Changes in accounts receivable and accounts payable relate to sales and cost of sales. Do not prepare a reconciliation schedule.

(CMA adapted)

P24-4 (SCF—Direct Method) Ashley Cleveland Company had the following information available at the end of 2001:

ASHLEY CLEVELAND COMPANY
Comparative Balance Sheet
As of December 31, 2001 and 2000

	2001	2000
Cash	$ 15,000	$ 4,000
Accounts receivable	17,500	12,950
Short-term investments	20,000	30,000
Inventory	42,000	35,000
Prepaid rent	3,000	12,000
Prepaid insurance	2,100	900
Office supplies	1,000	750
Land	125,000	175,000
Building	350,000	350,000
Accumulated depreciation	(105,000)	(87,500)
Equipment	525,000	400,000
Accumulated depreciation	(130,000)	(112,000)
Patent	45,000	50,000
Total assets	$910,600	$871,100

Accounts payable	$ 27,000	$ 32,000
Taxes payable	5,000	4,000
Wages payable	5,000	3,000
Short-term notes payable	10,000	10,000
Long-term notes payable	60,000	70,000
Bonds payable	400,000	400,000
Premium on bonds payable	20,303	25,853
Common stock	240,000	220,000
Paid-in capital in excess of par	20,000	17,500
Retained earnings	123,297	88,747
Total liabilities and equity	$910,600	$871,100

ASHLEY CLEVELAND COMPANY
Income Statement
For the Year Ended December 31, 2001

Sales revenue		$1,160,000
Cost of goods sold		(748,000)
		412,000
Gross margin		
Operating expenses		
Selling expenses	$ 79,200	
Administrative expenses	156,700	
Depreciation/Amortization expense	40,500	
Total operating expenses		(276,400)
Income from operations		135,600
Other revenues/expenses		
Gain on sale of land	8,000	
Gain on sale of short-term investment	4,000	
Dividend revenue	2,400	
Interest expense	(51,750)	(37,350)
Income before taxes		98,250
Income tax expense		(39,400)
Net income		58,850
Dividends to common stockholders		(24,300)
To retained earnings		$ 34,550

Instructions

Prepare a statement of cash flows for Ashley Cleveland Company using the direct method accompanied by a reconciliation schedule. Assume the short-term investments are available-for-sale securities.

P24-5 (SCF—Indirect Method) Michael W. Smith Inc. had the following information available at the end of 2001:

MICHAEL W. SMITH INC.
Comparative Balance Sheet
As of December 31, 2001 and 2000

	2001	2000
Cash	$ 46,000	$ 30,000
Accounts receivable	330,000	296,000
Short-term investments (available-for-sale)	360,000	325,000
Prepaid insurance	16,000	22,000
Merchandise inventory	400,000	350,000
Office supplies	4,000	7,000
Long-term investments (equity)	775,000	700,000
Land	665,000	500,000
Building	1,300,000	1,300,000
Accumulated depreciation—building	(400,000)	(360,000)

Equipment	500,000	550,000
Accumulated depreciation—equipment	(155,000)	(135,000)
Goodwill	63,000	65,000
Total assets	$3,904,000	$3,650,000
Accounts payable	$ 95,000	$ 70,000
Taxes payable	26,000	15,000
Accrued liabilities	47,000	40,000
Dividends payable	–0–	80,000
Long-term notes payable	45,000	50,000
Bonds payable	1,000,000	1,000,000
Discount on bonds payable	(50,750)	(64,630)
Preferred stock	600,000	500,000
Contributed capital, preferred stock	135,000	100,000
Common stock	600,000	600,000
Contributed capital, common stock	550,000	550,000
Retained earnings	876,750	749,630
Treasury stock (common, at cost)	(20,000)	(40,000)
Total liabilities and equity	$3,904,000	$3,650,000

MICHAEL W. SMITH INC.
Income Statement
For the Year Ended December 31, 2001

Sales revenue		$1,007,500
Cost of goods sold		403,000
Gross profit		604,500
Selling/administrative expenses		222,087
Income from operations		382,413
Other revenues/expenses		
Long-term investment revenue	$115,000	
Short-term investment dividend	15,000	
Gain on sale of equipment	15,000	145,000
Interest expense		(98,880)
Income before taxes		428,533
Income tax expense		(171,413)
Net income		257,120
Dividends (current year)		(130,000)
Increase in retained earnings		$ 127,120

Additional information:

1. In early January, equipment with a book value of $45,000 was sold for a gain.
2. Long-term investments are carried under the equity method; Smith's share of investee income totaled $115,000 in 2001. Smith received dividends from its long-term investment totaling $40,000 during 2001.
3. No unrealized gains or losses on available-for-sale securities occurred during the year.

Instructions

Prepare a statement of cash flows using the indirect method.

P24-6 (SCF—Direct Method) Data for Michael W. Smith Inc. are presented in P24-5.

Instructions

Prepare a statement of cash flows using the direct method.

P24-7 (SCF—Indirect Method) You have completed the field work in connection with your audit of Shirley Caesar Corporation for the year ended December 31, 2002. The following schedule shows the balance sheet accounts at the beginning and end of the year.

	Dec. 31, 2002	Dec. 31, 2001	Increase or (Decrease)
Cash	$ 267,900	$ 298,000	($30,100)
Accounts receivable	479,424	353,000	126,424
Inventory	741,700	610,000	131,700
Prepaid expenses	12,000	8,000	4,000
Investment in subsidiary	110,500	–0–	110,500
Cash surrender value of life insurance	2,304	1,800	504
Machinery	207,000	190,000	17,000
Buildings	535,200	407,900	127,300
Land	52,500	52,500	–0–
Patents	69,000	64,000	5,000
Goodwill	40,000	50,000	(10,000)
Bond discount and expense	4,502	–0–	4,502
	$2,522,030	$2,035,200	$486,830
Accrued taxes payable	$ 90,250	$ 79,600	$ 10,650
Accounts payable	299,280	280,000	19,280
Dividends payable	70,000	–0–	70,000
Bonds payable—8%	125,000	–0–	125,000
Bonds payable—12%	–0–	100,000	(100,000)
Allowance for doubtful accounts	35,300	40,000	(4,700)
Accumulated depreciation—buildings	424,000	400,000	24,000
Accumulated depreciation—machinery	173,000	130,000	43,000
Premium on bonds payable	–0–	2,400	(2,400)
Capital stock—no par	1,176,200	1,453,200	(277,000)
Additional paid-in capital	109,000	–0–	109,000
Appropriation for plant expansion	10,000	–0–	10,000
Retained earnings—unappropriated	10,000	(450,000)	460,000
	$2,522,030	$2,035,200	$486,830

Statement of Retained Earnings

January 1, 2002	Balance (deficit)	$(450,000)
March 31, 2002	Net income for first quarter of 2002	25,000
April 1, 2002	Transfer from paid-in capital	425,000
	Balance	–0–
December 31, 2002	Net income for last three quarters of 2002	90,000
	Dividend declared—payable January 21, 2003	(70,000)
	Appropriation for plant expansion	(10,000)
	Balance	$ 10,000

Your working papers contain the following information:

1. On April 1, 2002, the existing deficit was written off against paid-in capital created by reducing the stated value of the no-par stock.
2. On November 1, 2002, 29,600 shares of no-par stock were sold for $257,000. The board of directors voted to regard $5 per share as stated capital.
3. A patent was purchased for $15,000.
4. During the year, machinery that had a cost basis of $16,400 and on which there was accumulated depreciation of $5,200 was sold for $7,000. No other plant assets were sold during the year.
5. The 12%, 20-year bonds were dated and issued on January 2, 1990. Interest was payable on June 30 and December 31. They were sold originally at 106. These bonds were retired at 102 (net of $100 tax) plus accrued interest on March 31, 2002.
6. The 8%, 40-year bonds were dated January 1, 2002, and were sold on March 31 at 97 plus accrued interest. Interest is payable semiannually on June 30 and December 31. Expense of issuance was $839.
7. Shirley Caesar Corporation acquired 70% control in Amarillo Company on January 2, 2002, for $100,000. The income statement of Amarillo Company for 2002 shows a net income of $15,000.
8. Extraordinary repairs to buildings of $7,200 were charged to Accumulated Depreciation—Buildings.
9. Interest paid in 2002 was $10,500 and income taxes paid were $34,000.

Instructions

From the information above prepare a statement of cash flows using the indirect method. A work sheet is not necessary, but the principal computations should be supported by schedules or skeleton ledger accounts.

P24-8 (SCF—Indirect Method) Presented below are the 2002 financial statements of Carol Cymbala Corporation.

CAROL CYMBALA CORPORATION
Comparative Balance Sheet

$ in millions	December 31, 2002	December 31, 2001
Assets		
Current assets:		
Cash	$ 20.4	$ 7.5
Receivables (net of allowance for doubtful accounts of $5.0 million in 2002 and $4.6 million in 2001)	241.6	213.2
Inventories		
Finished goods	83.7	84.7
Raw materials and supplies	115.7	123.8
Prepaid expenses	6.2	6.7
Total current assets	467.6	435.9
Property, plant, and equipment:		
Plant and equipment	2,361.8	2,217.7
Less: Accumulated depreciation	(993.4)	(890.1)
	1,368.4	1,327.6
Timberland—net	166.3	169.5
Total property, plant, and equipment—net	1,534.7	1,497.1
Other assets	74.7	34.7
Total assets	$2,077.0	$1,967.7
Liabilities and stockholders' investment		
Current liabilities:		
Current maturities of long-term debt	$ 13.2	$ 10.5
Bank overdrafts	25.5	20.2
Accounts payable	102.2	91.3
Accrued liabilities		
Payrolls and employee benefits	73.5	73.9
Interest and other expenses	44.3	29.4
Federal and state income taxes	17.4	12.7
Total current liabilities	276.1	238.0
Long-term liabilities:		
Deferred tax liability	333.6	280.0
4.75% to 11.25% revenue bonds with maturities to 2022	174.6	193.4
Other revenue bonds at variable rates with maturities to 2029	46.3	26.6
7⅞% sinking fund debentures due 2008	19.5	21.0
8.70% sinking fund debentures due 2018	75.0	75.0
9½% convertible subordinated debentures due 2023	–0–	38.9
9¾% notes due 2005	50.0	50.0
Promissory notes	–0–	60.2
Mortgage debt and miscellaneous obligations	25.7	21.7
Other long-term liabilities	21.8	–0–
Total long-term liabilities	746.5	766.8
Stockholders' equity:		
Common stock ($5 par value, 60,000,000 shares authorized, 26,661,770 and 25,265,921 shares outstanding as of December 31, 2002 and 2001)	133.3	126.3
Additional paid-in capital	111.1	70.6
Retained earnings	810.0	766.0
Total stockholders' equity	1,054.4	962.9
Total liabilities and stockholders' equity	$2,077.0	$1,967.7

Statement of Income and Retained Earnings	
$ in millions, except per share amounts	2002
Income	
Net sales	$2,044.2
Cost of sales	(1,637.8)
Gross margin	406.4
Selling, general, and administrative expense	(182.6)
Provision for reduced operations	(41.0)
Operating income	182.8
Interest on long-term debt	(33.5)
Other income—net	2.2
Pretax income	151.5
Income taxes	(61.2)
Net income	$ 90.3
Earnings per share	$ 3.39
Retained earnings	
Retained earnings at beginning of year	$ 766.0
Add: Net income	90.3
	856.3
Deduct: Dividends:	
Common stock ($1.76 a share in 2002)	46.3
Retained earnings at end of year	$ 810.0

Additional information:

1. Depreciation and cost of timberland harvested was $114.6 million.
2. The provision for reduced operations included a decrease in cash of $15.9 million.
3. Purchases of plant and equipment were $182.5 million, and purchases of other assets were $40 million.
4. Sales of plant and equipment resulted in cash inflows of $5.2 million. All sales were at book value.
5. The changes in long-term liabilities are summarized below:

Increase in deferred tax liability	$ 53.6
New borrowings	63.2
Debt retired by cash payments	(86.5)
Debt converted into stock	(37.4)
Reclassification of current maturities	(13.2)
Decrease in long-term liabilities	$(20.3)

6. The increase in common stock and additional paid-in capital results from the issuance of stock for debt conversion, $37.4 million, and stock issued for cash, $10.1 million.
7. Interest paid during 2002 was $21.2 and income tax paid was $7.6.

Instructions

Prepare a statement of cash flows for the Carol Cymbala Corporation using the indirect method.

P24-9 (SCF—Indirect Method, and Net Cash Flow from Operating Activities, Direct Method) Comparative balance sheet accounts of Jon Secada Inc. are presented below:

JON SECADA INC.
Comparative Balance Sheet Accounts
December 31, 2002 and 2001

	December 31	
Debit Accounts	2002	2001
Cash	$ 45,000	$ 33,750
Accounts Receivable	67,500	60,000
Merchandise Inventory	30,000	24,000

Investments (available-for-sale)	22,250	38,500
Machinery	30,000	18,750
Buildings	67,500	56,250
Land	7,500	7,500
Totals	$269,750	$238,750
Credit Accounts		
Allowance for Doubtful Accounts	$ 2,250	$ 1,500
Accumulated Depreciation—Machinery	5,625	2,250
Accumulated Depreciation—Buildings	13,500	9,000
Accounts Payable	30,000	24,750
Accrued Payables	3,375	2,625
Long-Term Note Payable	26,000	31,000
Common Stock, no par	150,000	125,000
Retained Earnings	39,000	42,625
Total	$269,750	$238,750

Additional data: (ignore taxes)

1. Net income for the year was $42,500.
2. Cash dividends declared during the year were $21,125.
3. A 20% stock dividend was declared during the year. $25,000 of retained earnings was capitalized.
4. Investments that cost $20,000 were sold during the year for $23,750.
5. Machinery that cost $3,750, on which $750 of depreciation had accumulated, was sold for $2,200.

Jon Secada's 2002 income statement follows (ignore taxes):

Sales		$540,000
Less cost of goods sold		380,000
Gross margin		160,000
Less: Operating expenses (includes $8,625 depreciation and $5,400 bad debts)		120,450
Income from operations		39,550
Other: Gain on sale of investments	$3,750	
Loss on sale of machinery	(800)	2,950
Net income		$ 42,500

Instructions

(a) Compute net cash flow from operating activities using the direct method.
(b) Prepare a statement of cash flows using the indirect method.

P24-10 (SCF—Direct and Indirect Methods from Comparative Financial Statements) George Winston Company, a major retailer of bicycles and accessories, operates several stores and is a publicly traded company. The comparative Statement of Financial Position and Income Statement for Winston as of May 31, 2002, are shown below and on the next page. The company is preparing its Statement of Cash Flows.

GEORGE WINSTON COMPANY
Comparative Statement of Financial Position
As of May 31, 2002 and May 31, 2001

	2002	2001
Current assets		
Cash	$ 33,250	$ 20,000
Accounts receivable	80,000	58,000
Merchandise inventory	210,000	250,000
Prepaid expenses	9,000	7,000
Total current assets	332,250	335,000
Plant assets		
Plant assets	600,000	502,000
Less: Accumulated depreciation	150,000	125,000
Net plant assets	450,000	377,000
Total assets	$782,250	$712,000

Current liabilities		
Accounts payable	$123,000	$115,000
Salaries payable	47,250	72,000
Interest payable	27,000	25,000
Total current liabilities	197,250	212,000
Long-term debt		
Bonds payable	70,000	100,000
Total liabilities	267,250	312,000
Shareholders' equity		
Common stock, $10 par	370,000	280,000
Retained earnings	145,000	120,000
Total shareholders' equity	515,000	400,000
Total liabilities and shareholders' equity	$782,250	$712,000

GEORGE WINSTON COMPANY
Income Statement
For the Year Ended May 31, 2002

Sales	$1,255,250
Cost of merchandise sold	722,000
Total contribution	533,250
Expenses	
Salary expense	252,100
Interest expense	75,000
Other expenses	8,150
Depreciation expense	25,000
Total expenses	360,250
Operating income	173,000
Income tax expense	43,000
Net income	$ 130,000

The following is additional information concerning Winston's transactions during the year ended May 31, 2002.

1. All sales during the year were made on account.
2. All merchandise was purchased on account, comprising the total accounts payable account.
3. Plant assets costing $98,000 were purchased by paying $48,000 in cash and issuing 5,000 shares of stock.
4. The "other expenses" are related to prepaid items.
5. All income taxes incurred during the year were paid during the year.
6. In order to supplement its cash, Winston issued 4,000 shares of common stock at par value.
7. There were no penalties assessed for the retirement of bonds.
8. Cash dividends of $105,000 were declared and paid at the end of the fiscal year.

Instructions

(a) Compare and contrast the direct method and the indirect method for reporting cash flows from operating activities.

(b) Prepare a statement of cash flows for Winston Company for the year ended May 31, 2002, using the direct method. Be sure to support the statement with appropriate calculations. (A reconciliation of net income to net cash is not required.)

(c) Using the indirect method, calculate only the net cash flow from operating activities for Winston Company for the year ended May 31, 2002.

P24-11 (SCF—Direct and Indirect Methods) Comparative balance sheet accounts of Jensen Company are presented below:

JENSEN COMPANY
Comparative Balance Sheet Accounts
December 31, 2001 and 2000

Debit Balances	2001	2000
Cash	$ 80,000	$ 51,000
Accounts Receivable	145,000	130,000
Merchandise Inventory	75,000	61,000
Investments (Available-for-sale)	55,000	85,000
Equipment	70,000	48,000
Buildings	145,000	145,000
Land	40,000	25,000
Totals	$610,000	$545,000
Credit Balances		
Allowance for Doubtful Accounts	$ 10,000	$ 8,000
Accumulated Depreciation—Equipment	21,000	14,000
Accumulated Depreciation—Building	37,000	28,000
Accounts Payable	70,000	60,000
Income Taxes Payable	12,000	10,000
Long-Term Notes Payable	62,000	70,000
Common Stock	310,000	260,000
Retained Earnings	88,000	95,000
Totals	$610,000	$545,000

Additional data:

1. Equipment that cost $10,000 and was 40% depreciated was sold in 2001.
2. Cash dividends were declared and paid during the year.
3. Common stock was issued in exchange for land.
4. Investments that cost $35,000 were sold during the year.

Jensen's 2001 income statement is as follows:

Sales		$950,000
Less: Cost of goods sold		600,000
Gross profit		350,000
Less: Operating expenses (includes depreciation and bad debt expense)		250,000
Income from operations		100,000
Other revenues and expenses		
Gain on sale of investments	$15,000	
Loss on sale of equipment	(3,000)	12,000
Income before taxes		112,000
Income taxes		45,000
Net income		$ 67,000

Instructions

(a) Compute net cash provided by operating activities under the direct method.
(b) Prepare a statement of cash flows using the indirect method.

P24-12 (Indirect SCF) Seneca Corporation has contracted with you to prepare a statement of cash flows. The controller has provided the following information:

	December 31	
	2001	2000
Cash	$ 38,500	$13,000
Accounts receivable	12,250	10,000
Inventory	12,000	9,000
Investments	–0–	3,000
Building	–0–	29,750
Equipment	40,000	20,000
Patent	5,000	6,250
Totals	$107,750	$91,000

Allowance for doubtful accounts	$ 3,000	$ 4,500
Accumulated depreciation on equipment	2,000	4,500
Accumulated depreciation on building	–0–	6,000
Accounts payable	5,000	3,000
Dividends payable	–0–	6,000
Notes payable, short-term (nontrade)	3,000	4,000
Long-term notes payable	31,000	25,000
Common stock	43,000	33,000
Retained earnings	20,750	5,000
	$107,750	$91,000

Additional data related to 2001 are as follows:

1. Equipment that had cost $11,000 and was 40% depreciated at time of disposal was sold for $2,500.
2. $10,000 of the long-term note payable was paid by issuing common stock.
3. Cash dividends paid were $6,000.
4. On January 1, 2001, the building was completely destroyed by a flood. Insurance proceeds on the building were $33,000 (net of $4,000 taxes).
5. Investments (available-for-sale) were sold at $2,500 above their cost. The company has made similar sales and investments in the past.
6. Cash of $15,000 was paid for the acquisition of equipment.
7. A long-term note for $16,000 was issued for the acquisition of equipment.
8. Interest of $2,000 and income taxes of $5,000 were paid in cash.

Instructions

(a) Use the indirect method to analyze the above information and prepare a statement of cash flows for Seneca. Flood damage is unusual and infrequent in that part of the country.

(b) What would you expect to observe in the operating, investing, and financing sections of a statement of cash flows of:

(1) a severely financially troubled firm?

(2) a recently formed firm which is experiencing rapid growth?

CONCEPTUAL CASES

C24-1 (Analysis of Improper SCF) The following statement was prepared by Abriendo Corporation's accountant:

ABRIENDO CORPORATION
Statement of Sources and Application of Cash
For the Year Ended September 30, 2002

Sources of cash	
Net income	$ 95,000
Depreciation and depletion	70,000
Increase in long-term debt	179,000
Common stock issued under employee option plans	16,000
Changes in current receivables and inventories, less current liabilities (excluding current maturities of long-term debt)	14,000
	$374,000
Application of cash	
Cash dividends	$ 60,000
Expenditure for property, plant, and equipment	214,000
Investments and other uses	20,000
Change in cash	80,000
	$374,000

The following additional information relating to Abriendo Corporation is available for the year ended September 30, 2002:

1. The corporation received $16,000 in cash from its employees on its employee stock option plans, and wage and salary expense attributable to the option plans was an additional $22,000.

2. Expenditures for property, plant, and equipment — $250,000
   Proceeds from retirements of property, plant, and equipment — 36,000
   Net expenditures — $214,000

3. A stock dividend of 10,000 shares of Abriendo Corporation common stock was distributed to common stockholders on April 1, 2002, when the per-share market price was $7 and par value was $1.
4. On July 1, 2002, when its market price was $6 per share, 16,000 shares of Abriendo Corporation common stock were issued in exchange for 4,000 shares of preferred stock.
5. Depreciation expense — $ 65,000
   Depletion expense — 5,000
   $ 70,000

6. Increase in long-term debt — $620,000
   Retirement of debt — 441,000
   Net increase — $179,000

Instructions

(a) In general, what are the objectives of a statement of the type shown above for the Abriendo Corporation? Explain.

(b) Identify the weaknesses in the form and format of the Abriendo Corporation's statement of cash flows without reference to the additional information (assume adoption of the indirect method).

(c) For each of the six items of additional information for the statement of cash flows indicate the preferable treatment and explain why the suggested treatment is preferable.

(AICPA adapted)

C24-2 (SCF Theory and Analysis of Improper SCF) Gloria Estefan and Flaco Jimenez are examining the following statement of cash flows for Tropical Clothing Store's first year of operations.

TROPICAL CLOTHING STORE
Statement of Cash Flows
For the Year Ended January 31, 2002

Sources of cash	
From sales of merchandise	$ 362,000
From sale of capital stock	400,000
From sale of investment	120,000
From depreciation	80,000
From issuance of note for truck	30,000
From interest on investments	8,000
Total sources of cash	1,000,000
Uses of cash	
For purchase of fixtures and equipment	340,000
For merchandise purchased for resale	253,000
For operating expenses (including depreciation)	170,000
For purchase of investment	85,000
For purchase of truck by issuance of note	30,000
For purchase of treasury stock	10,000
For interest on note	3,000
Total uses of cash	891,000
Net increase in cash	$ 109,000

Gloria claims that Tropical's statement of cash flows is an excellent portrayal of a superb first year with cash increasing $109,000. Flaco replies that it was not a superb first year, that the year was an operating failure, that the statement was incorrectly presented, and that $109,000 is not the actual increase in cash.

Instructions

(a) With whom do you agree, Gloria or Flaco? Explain your position.

(b) Using the data provided, prepare a statement of cash flows in proper indirect method form. The only noncash items in income are depreciation and the gain from the sale of the investment (purchase and sale are related).

C24-3 (SCF Theory and Analysis of Transactions) John Lee Hooker Company is a young and growing producer of electronic measuring instruments and technical equipment. You have been retained by Hooker to advise it in the preparation of a statement of cash flows using the indirect method. For the fiscal year ended October 31, 2002, you have obtained the following information concerning certain events and transactions of Hooker.

1. The amount of reported earnings for the fiscal year was $800,000, which included a deduction for an extraordinary loss of $110,000 (see item 5 below).
2. Depreciation expense of $315,000 was included in the earnings statement.
3. Uncollectible accounts receivable of $40,000 were written off against the allowance for doubtful accounts. Also, $51,000 of bad debt expense was included in determining income for the fiscal year, and the same amount was added to the allowance for doubtful accounts.
4. A gain of $9,000 was realized on the sale of a machine; it originally cost $75,000, of which $30,000 was undepreciated on the date of sale.
5. On April 1, 2002, lightning caused an uninsured building loss of $110,000 ($180,000 loss, less reduction in income taxes of $70,000). This extraordinary loss was included in determining income as indicated in 1 above.
6. On July 3, 2002, building and land were purchased for $700,000; Hooker gave in payment $75,000 cash, $200,000 market value of its unissued common stock, and signed a $425,000 mortgage note payable.
7. On August 3, 2002, $800,000 face value of Hooker's 10% convertible debentures were converted into $150,000 par value of its common stock. The bonds were originally issued at face value.

Instructions

Explain whether each of the seven numbered items above is a source or use of cash and explain how it should be disclosed in John Lee Hooker's statement of cash flows for the fiscal year ended October 31, 2002. If any item is neither a source nor a use of cash, explain why it is not and indicate the disclosure, if any, that should be made of the item in John Lee Hooker's statement of cash flows for the fiscal year ended October 31, 2002.

C24-4 (Analysis of Transactions' Effect on SCF) Each of the following items must be considered in preparing a statement of cash flows for Buddy Guy Fashions Inc. for the year ended December 31, 2002.

1. Fixed assets that had cost $20,000 $6^{1}/_{2}$ years before and were being depreciated on a 10-year basis, with no estimated scrap value, were sold for $5,250.
2. During the year, goodwill of $15,000 was completely written off to expense.
3. During the year, 500 shares of common stock with a stated value of $25 a share were issued for $34 a share.
4. The company sustained a net loss for the year of $2,100. Depreciation amounted to $2,000 and patent amortization was $400.
5. An Appropriation for Contingencies in the amount of $80,000 was created by a charge against Retained Earnings.
6. Uncollectible accounts receivable in the amount of $2,000 were written off against the Allowance for Doubtful Accounts.
7. Investments (available-for-sale) that cost $12,000 when purchased 4 years earlier were sold for $10,600. The loss was considered ordinary.
8. Bonds payable with a par value of $24,000 on which there was an unamortized bond premium of $2,000 were redeemed at 103. The gain was credited to income as an extraordinary item. Ignore income taxes.

Instructions

For each item, state where it is to be shown in the statement and then how you would present the necessary information, including the amount. Consider each item to be independent of the others. Assume that correct entries were made for all transactions as they took place.

C24-5 (Purpose and Elements of SCF) In 1961 the AICPA recognized the importance of the funds statement by publishing *Accounting Research Study No. 2,* "'Cash Flow' Analysis and the Funds Statement." Prior to this time, accountants had prepared funds statements primarily as management reports. The Accounting Principles Board responded by issuing *APB Opinion No. 3,* "The Statement of Source and Application of Funds," which recommended that a statement of source and application of funds be presented on a supplementary basis. Because of the favorable response of the business community to this pronouncement, the APB issued *Opinion No. 19,* "Reporting Changes in Financial Position" in 1971. This opinion required that a statement of changes in financial position be presented as a basic financial statement and be covered by the auditor's report.

In 1981 the Financial Accounting Standards Board reconsidered funds flow issues as part of the conceptual framework project. At this time, the Financial Accounting Standards Board decided that cash flow reporting issues should be considered at the standards level. Subsequent deliberations resulted in *Statement of Financial Accounting Standards (SFAS) No. 95,* "Statement of Cash Flows."

Instructions

(a) Explain the purposes of the statement of cash flows.

(b) List and describe the three categories of activities that must be reported in the statement of cash flows.

(c) Identify and describe the two methods that are allowed for reporting cash flows from operations.

(d) Describe the financial statement presentation of noncash investing and financing transactions. Include in your description an example of a noncash investing and financing transaction.

USING YOUR JUDGMENT

FINANCIAL REPORTING PROBLEM: INTEL CORPORATION

Instructions

Refer to the financial statements and accompanying notes and discussion of Intel Corporation presented in Appendix 5B and answer the following questions.

(a) Which method of computing net cash provided by operating activities does Intel use? What were the amounts of cash provided by operations for the years 1996, 1997, and 1998? Which two items were most responsible for the decrease in cash provided by operating activities in 1998?

(b) What was the most significant item in the cash flows used for the investing activities section in 1998? What was the most significant item in the cash flows used for the financing activities section in 1998?

(c) Where is the "net loss on retirements of property, plant and equipment" reported in Intel's statement of cash flows? How much is the loss in 1998 and why does it appear in that section of the statement of cash flows?

(d) Where is "deferred taxes" reported in Intel's statement of cash flows? Why does it appear in that section of the statement of cash flows?

(e) Where is depreciation reported in Intel's statement of cash flows? Why is depreciation added to net income in the statement of cash flows?

FINANCIAL STATEMENT ANALYSIS CASE

Vermont Teddy Bear Co.

Founded in the early 1980s, the Vermont Teddy Bear Co. designs and manufactures American-made teddy bears and markets them primarily as gifts called Bear-Grams or Teddy Bear-Grams. Bear-Grams are personalized teddy bears delivered directly to the recipient for special occasions such as birthdays and anniversaries. The Shelburne, Vermont, company's primary markets are New York, Boston, and Chicago. Sales have jumped dramatically in recent years. Such dramatic growth has significant implications for cash flows. Provided below are the cash flow statements for the current and prior years for the company.

	Current Year	Prior Year
Cash flows from operating activities:		
Net income	$ 17,523	$ 838,955
Adjustments to reconcile net income to net cash provided by operating activities		
Deferred income taxes	(69,524)	(146,590)
Depreciation and amortization	316,416	181,348
Changes in assets and liabilities:		
Accounts receivable, trade	(38,267)	(25,947)
Inventories	(1,599,014)	(1,289,293)
Prepaid and other current assets	(444,794)	(113,205)
Deposits and other assets	(24,240)	(83,044)
Accounts payable	2,017,059	(284,567)
Accrued expenses	61,321	170,755
Accrued interest payable, debentures	—	(58,219)
Other	—	(8,960)
Income taxes payable	—	117,810
Net cash provided by (used for) operating activities	236,480	(700,957)
Net cash used for investing activities	(2,102,892)	(4,422,953)
Net cash (used for) provided by financing activities	(315,353)	9,685,435
Net change in cash and cash equivalents	(2,181,765)	4,561,525

Other information

	Current Year	Prior Year
Current liabilities	$ 4,055,465	$ 1,995,600
Total liabilities	4,620,085	2,184,386
Net sales	20,560,566	17,025,856

Instructions

(a) Note that net income in the current year was only $17,523 compared to prior year income of $838,955, but cash flow from operations was $236,480 in the current year and a negative $700,957 in the prior year. Explain the causes of this apparent paradox.

(b) Evaluate Vermont Teddy Bear's liquidity, solvency, and profitability for the current year using cash flow-based ratios.

COMPARATIVE ANALYSIS CASE

The Coca-Cola Company versus PepsiCo, Inc.

Instructions

Go to the Digital Tool and, using The Coca-Cola Company and PepsiCo Annual Report information, answer the following questions:

(a) What method of computing net cash provided by operating activities does Coca-Cola use? What method does PepsiCo use? What were the amounts of cash provided by operating activities reported by Coca-Cola and PepsiCo in 1998?

(b) What was the most significant item reported by Coca-Cola and PepsiCo in 1998 in their investing activities sections? What is the most significant item reported by Coca-Cola and PepsiCo in 1998 in their financing activities sections?

(c) Where is "depreciation and amortization" reported by Coca-Cola and PepsiCo in their statement of cash flows? What is the amount and why does it appear in that section of the statement of cash flows?

(d) Based on the information contained in Coca-Cola's and PepsiCo's financial statements, compute the following 1998 ratios for each company. These ratios require the use of statement of cash flows data. (These ratios were covered in Chapter 5.)

(1) Current cash debt coverage ratio.

(2) Cash debt coverage ratio.

(e) What conclusions concerning the management of cash can be drawn from the ratios computed in (d)?

RESEARCH CASE

The March 25, 1996, issue of *Barron's* includes an article by Harry B. Ernst and Jeffrey D. Fotta entitled "Weary Bull."

Instructions

Read the article and answer the following questions.

(a) The article describes a cash flow-based model used by investors. Identify the model and briefly describe its purpose.

(b) How does the model classify a firm's cash flows?

(c) Identify one way in which the cash flow classifications described in the article differ from those under GAAP.

(d) How can the model be used to predict stock prices?

ETHICS CASE

Durocher Guitar Company is in the business of manufacturing top-quality, steel-string folk guitars. In recent years the company has experienced working capital problems resulting from the procurement of factory equipment, the unanticipated buildup of receivables and inventories, and the payoff of a balloon mortgage on a new manufacturing facility. The founder and president of the company, Laraine Durocher, has attempted to raise cash from various financial institutions, but to no avail because of the company's poor performance in recent years. In particular, the company's lead bank, First Financial, is especially concerned about Durocher's inability to maintain a positive cash position. The commercial loan officer from First Financial told Laraine, "I can't even consider your request for capital financing unless I see that your company is able to generate positive cash flows from operations."

Thinking about the banker's comment, Laraine came up with what she believes is a good plan: with a more attractive statement of cash flows, the bank might be willing to provide long-term financing. To "window dress" cash flows, the company can sell its accounts receivables to factors and liquidate its raw material inventories. These rather costly transactions would generate lots of cash. As the chief accountant for Durocher Guitar, it is your job to tell Laraine what you think of her plan.

Instructions

Answer the following questions:

(a) What are the ethical issues related to Laraine Durocher's idea?

(b) What would you tell Laraine Durocher?

CHAPTER 25

Full Disclosure in Financial Reporting

What Annual Reports Won't Tell You

Most stockholders receive their corporation's financial statements in the Annual Report, a glossy-covered booklet that sometimes gives a positive spin to even lackluster corporate performance. In addition to comprehending the GAAP-prepared financial statements and notes, you need to know how to translate the glowing nonaccounting phrases that accompany the financials. The following examples may help you make these translations:

Here's what happened: Performance was flat to abysmal for all segments, the company was named in several class-action suits, and the founder's messy divorce was all over the tabloids and TV shows.
Here's how it was described in the annual report: "The past year can be characterized by the words of the immortal Charles Dickens: 'It was the best of times, it was the worst of times.'"

Here's what happened: By every measure of corporate performance, the company dropped to or near the bottom of its industry.
Here's how it was described: "We are well positioned for future growth."

Here's what happened: The product launch and/or corporate acquisition that put the company's existence at risk fell flat on its face.
Here's how it was described: "This bold initiative reflects the competitive realities that await all companies in the 21st century."

Here's what happened: The company's stock price has languished for years while the major stock market indexes and competitors' share prices have rocketed to one new high after another.
Here's how it was described: "With perseverance the company's extraordinary performance in generating added value will be recognized in the marketplace."[1]

Clearly, you absolutely need to read and understand the audited financial statements and accompanying notes, in order to be able to read "between the lines" in management's presentation of the year's financial results.

LEARNING OBJECTIVES

After studying this chapter, you should be able to:

1. **Review the full disclosure principle and describe problems of implementation.**
2. **Explain the use of notes in financial statement preparation.**
3. **Describe the disclosure requirements for major segments of a business.**
4. **Describe the accounting problems associated with interim reporting.**
5. **Identify the major disclosures found in the auditor's report.**
6. **Understand management's responsibilities for financials.**
7. **Identify issues related to financial forecasts and projections.**
8. **Describe the profession's response to fraudulent financial reporting.**

[1]Adapted from David Stauffer, "Manager's Journal," *The Wall Street Journal,* April 7, 1997, p. A14.

PREVIEW OF CHAPTER 25

As the opening story indicates, you have to be careful when reading the annual report. That is why it is important to read not only the president's letter but also the financial statements and related information. In this chapter, we cover several disclosures that must accompany financial statements so that they are not misleading. The content and organization of this chapter are as follows:

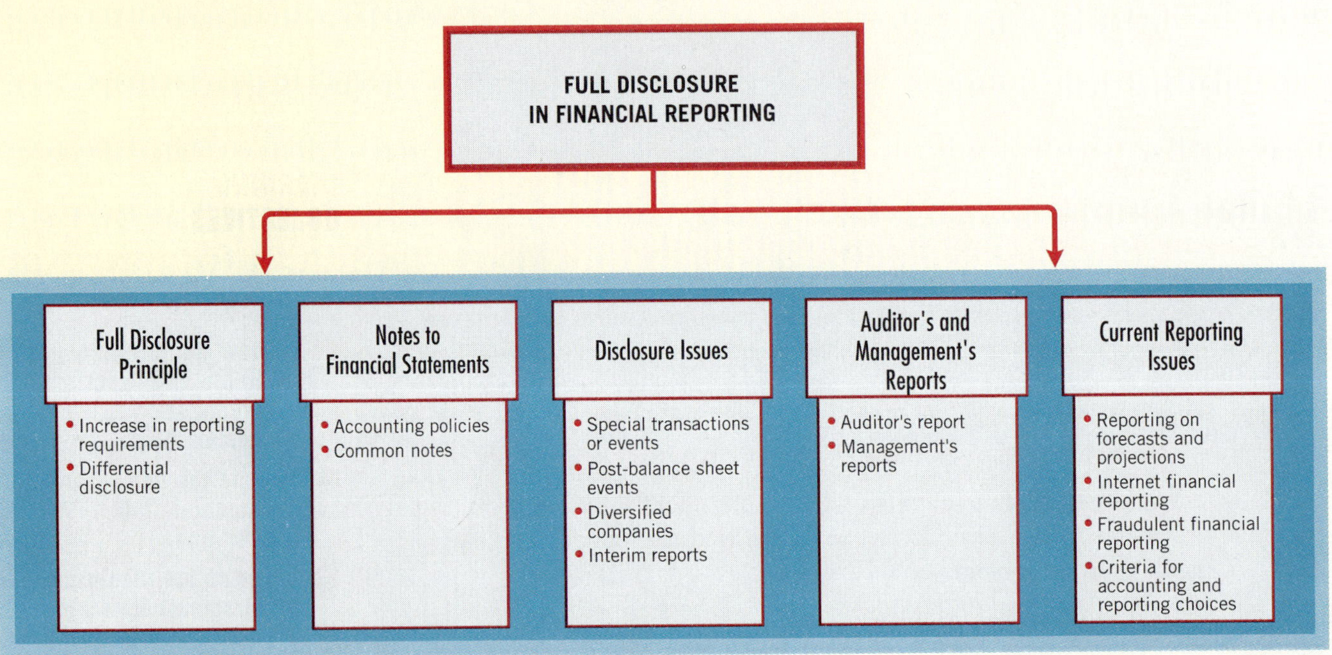

FULL DISCLOSURE PRINCIPLE

OBJECTIVE 1
Review the full disclosure principle and describe problems of implementation.

UNDERLYING CONCEPTS

Here is a good example of the trade-off between the cost/benefit constraint and the full disclosure principle.

FASB Concepts Statement No. 1 notes that some useful information is better provided in the financial statements, and some is better provided by means of financial reporting other than financial statements. For example, earnings and cash flows are readily available in financial statements—but investors might do better to look at comparisons to other companies in the same industry, found in news articles or brokerage house reports.

Financial statements, notes to the financial statements, and supplementary information are areas directly affected by FASB standards. Other types of information found in the annual report, such as management's discussion and analysis, are not subject to FASB standards. Illustration 25-1 indicates the types of financial information presented.

As indicated in Chapter 2, the profession has adopted a **full disclosure principle** that calls for financial reporting of **any financial facts significant enough to influence the judgment of an informed reader**. In some situations, the benefits of disclosure may be apparent but the costs uncertain, whereas in other instances the costs may be certain but the benefits of disclosure not as apparent.

For example, the SEC increased the amount of information financial institutions must disclose about their foreign lending practices. With some foreign countries in economic straits, the benefits of increased disclosure about the risk of uncollectibility are fairly obvious to the investing public. The exact costs of disclosure in these situations cannot be quantified, though they would appear to be relatively small.

On the other hand, the cost of disclosure can be substantial in some cases and the benefits difficult to assess. For example, *The Wall Street Journal* reported that, at one time, if segment reporting were adopted, a company like **Fruehauf** would have to in-

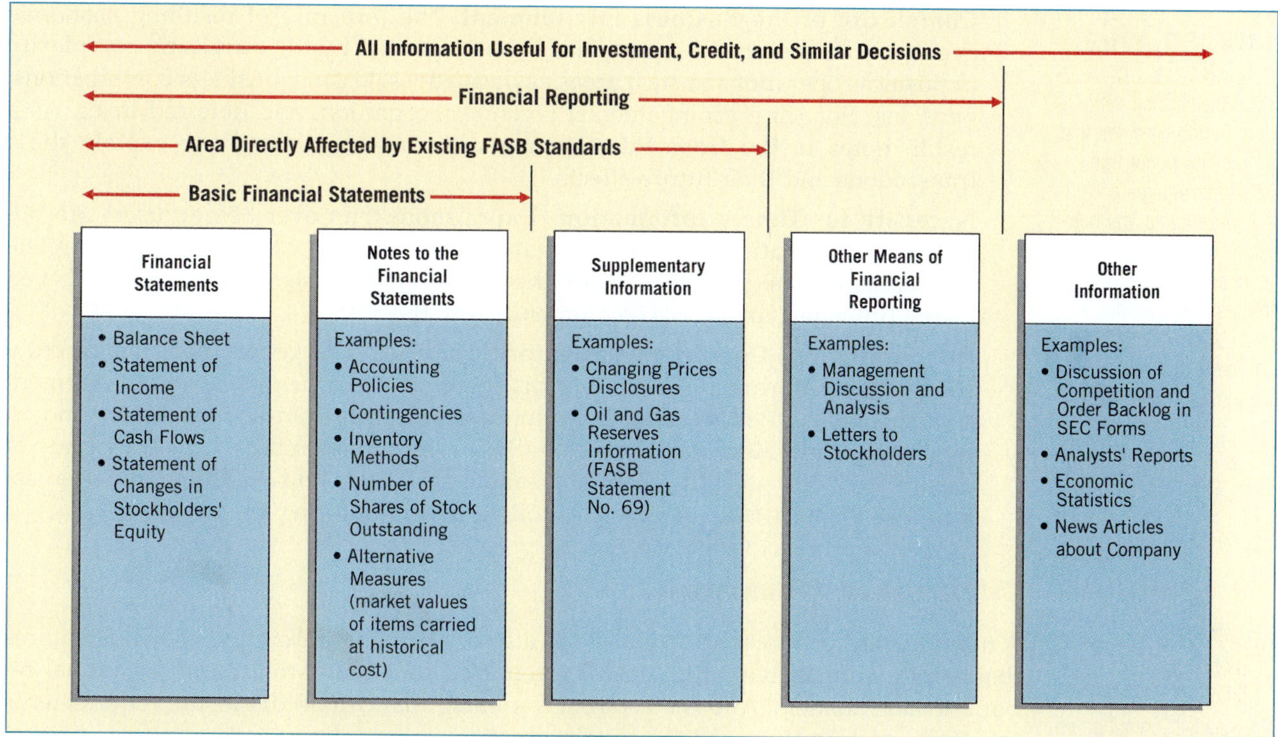

ILLUSTRATION 25-1
Types of Financial Information

crease its accounting staff 50%, from 300 to 450 individuals. In this case, the cost of disclosure is apparent but the benefits are less well defined. Some would even argue that the reporting requirements are so detailed and substantial that users will have a difficult time absorbing the information; they charge the profession with engaging in **information overload**.

The difficulty of implementing the full disclosure principle is highlighted by such financial disasters as **Phar-Mor**, **Miniscribe**, **Lincoln Savings and Loan**, and **BCCI**. Why were investors not aware of potential problems: Was the information presented about these companies not comprehensible? Was it buried? Was it too technical? Was it properly presented and fully disclosed as of the financial statement date—but the situation later deteriorated? Or was it simply not there? No easy answers are forthcoming.

One problem is that the profession is still in the process of developing the guidelines that tell whether a given transaction should be disclosed and what format this disclosure should take. Different users want different information, and it becomes exceedingly difficult to develop disclosure policies that meet their varied objectives.

Increase in Reporting Requirements

Disclosure requirements have increased substantially. One survey showed that in a sample of 25 large, well-known companies, the average number of pages of notes to the financial statements increased from 9 to 17 pages and the average number of pages for management's discussion and analysis from 7 to 12 pages over a recent 10-year period. This result is not surprising because as illustrated throughout this textbook, the FASB has issued many standards in the last 10 years that have substantial disclosure provisions.[2] The reasons for this increase in disclosure requirements are varied. Some of them are:

[2]As one writer has noted, rapid growth in additional financial reporting requirements and rapid changes in existing requirements are likely to be permanent features of the financial reporting environment. For the user, the result is a bewildering increase in financial data to interpret. William H. Beaver, *Financial Reporting: An Accounting Revolution*, 2d ed. (Englewood Cliffs, N.J.: Prentice-Hall, 1989), pp. 1–2. The survey results were taken from Ray J. Groves, "Financial Disclosure: When More Is Not Better," *Financial Executive*, May/June 1994.

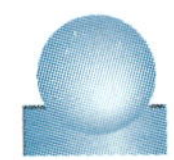

UNDERLYING CONCEPTS

The AICPA's Special Committee on Financial Reporting notes that business reporting is not free, and improving it requires considering the relative costs and benefits of information, just as costs and benefits are key to determining the features included in any product. Undisciplined expansion of mandated reporting could result in large and needless costs.

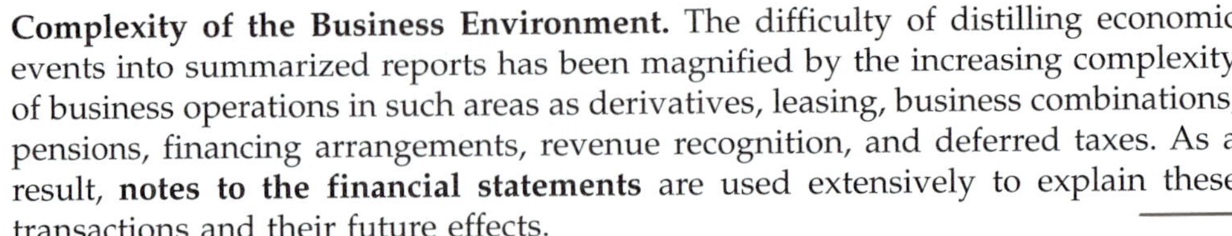

Complexity of the Business Environment. The difficulty of distilling economic events into summarized reports has been magnified by the increasing complexity of business operations in such areas as derivatives, leasing, business combinations, pensions, financing arrangements, revenue recognition, and deferred taxes. As a result, **notes to the financial statements** are used extensively to explain these transactions and their future effects.

Necessity for Timely Information. Today, more than ever before, users are demanding information that is current and predictive. For example, more complete **interim data** are required. And published financial forecasts, long avoided and even feared by management, are recommended by the SEC.

Accounting as a Control and Monitoring Device. The government has recently sought more information and public disclosure of such phenomena as management compensation, environmental pollution, related party transactions, errors and irregularities, and illegal activities. An "S&L crisis" concern is expressed in many of these newer disclosure requirements, and accountants and auditors have been selected as the agents to assist in controlling and monitoring these concerns.

Differential Disclosure

UNDERLYING CONCEPTS

The AICPA Special Committee on Financial Reporting indicated that users differ in their needs for information, and that not all companies should report all elements of information. Rather, companies should report only information that users and preparers agree is needed in the particular circumstances.

A trend toward **differential disclosure** is also occurring. For example, the SEC requires that certain substantive information be reported to it that is not found in annual reports to stockholders. And the FASB, recognizing that certain disclosure requirements are costly and unnecessary for certain companies, has eliminated reporting requirements for nonpublic enterprises in such areas as fair value of financial instruments and segment reporting.[3]

Some still complain that the FASB has not gone far enough. They note that certain types of companies (small or nonpublic) should not have to follow complex GAAP requirements such as deferred income taxes, leases, or pensions. This issue, often referred to as **Big GAAP versus Little GAAP**, continues to be controversial. The FASB takes the position that one set of GAAP should be used, except in unusual situations.

NOTES TO THE FINANCIAL STATEMENTS

OBJECTIVE 2
Explain the use of notes in financial statement preparation.

As you know from your study of this textbook, notes are an integral part of the financial statements of a business enterprise. However, they are often overlooked because they are highly technical and often appear in small print. **Notes are the accountant's means of amplifying or explaining the items presented in the main body of the statements.** Information pertinent to specific financial statement items can be explained in qualitative terms, and supplementary data of a quantitative nature can be provided to expand the information in the financial statements. Restrictions imposed by financial arrangements or basic contractual agreements also can be explained in notes. Although notes may be technical and difficult to understand, they provide meaningful information for the user of the financial statements.

Accounting Policies

Accounting policies of a given entity are the specific accounting principles and methods currently employed and considered most appropriate to present fairly the financial statements of the enterprise. *APB Opinion No. 22,* "Disclosure of Accounting Policies," concluded that information about the accounting policies adopted and followed by a reporting entity is essential for financial statement users in making economic de-

[3]Recently, the FASB has embarked on a disclosure effectiveness project. The revised pension and postretirement benefit disclosures discussed in Chapter 21 (*FASB Statement No. 132*) are one example of how disclosures can be streamlined and made more useful.

cisions. It recommended that a **statement identifying the accounting policies adopted and followed by the reporting entity should also be presented as an integral part of the financial statements**. The disclosure should be given as the initial note or in a separate Summary of Significant Accounting Policies section preceding the notes to the financial statements. The Summary of Significant Accounting Policies answers such questions as: What method of depreciation is used on plant assets? What valuation method is employed on inventories? What amortization policy is followed in regard to intangible assets? How are marketing costs handled for financial reporting purposes?

Refer to Appendix 5B, pages 216–242, for an illustration of note disclosure of accounting policies (Note 1) and other notes accompanying the audited financial statements of **Intel Corporation**. An illustration from **Campbell Soup Company** is provided below:

ILLUSTRATION 25-2
Note Disclosure of Accounting Policies

CAMPBELL SOUP COMPANY

Note 1: Summary of Significant Accounting Policies:

Consolidation

The consolidated financial statements include the accounts of the company and its majority-owned subsidiaries. Significant intercompany transactions are eliminated in consolidation. Investments of 20% or more in affiliates are accounted for by the equity method.

Fiscal Year

The company's fiscal year ends on the Sunday nearest July 31.

Cash and Cash Equivalents

All highly liquid debt instruments purchased with a maturity of three months or less are classified as cash equivalents.

Inventories

Substantially all domestic inventories are priced at the lower of cost or market, with cost determined by the last-in, first-out (LIFO) method. Other inventories are priced at the lower of average cost or market.

Plant Assets

Plant assets are stated at historical cost. Alterations and major overhauls which extend the lives or increase the capacity of plant assets are capitalized. The amounts for property disposals are removed from plant asset and accumulated depreciation accounts and any resultant gain or loss is included in earnings. Ordinary repairs and maintenance are charged to operating costs.

Depreciation

Depreciation provided in costs and expenses is calculated using the straight-line method. Buildings and machinery and equipment are depreciated over periods not exceeding 45 years and 15 years, respectively. Accelerated methods of depreciation are used for income tax purposes in certain jurisdictions.

Intangibles

Intangible assets consist principally of excess purchase price over net assets of businesses acquired and trademarks. Intangibles are amortized on a straight-line basis over periods not exceeding 40 years.

Asset Valuation

The company periodically reviews the recoverability of plant assets and intangibles based principally on an analysis of cash flows.

Pension and Retiree Benefit Plans

Costs are accrued over employees' careers based on plan benefit formulas.

Income Taxes

Deferred taxes are provided in accordance with Statement of Financial Accounting Standards (FAS) No. 109.

Use of Estimates

Generally accepted accounting principles require management to make estimates and assumptions that affect assets and liabilities, contingent assets and liabilities, and revenues and expenses. Actual results could differ from those estimates.

Reclassifications

Certain amounts in the prior years' financial statements and footnotes have been reclassified to conform to the current year presentation.

UNDERLYING CONCEPTS

The AICPA's Special Committee on Financial Reporting states that to meet users' changing needs, business reporting must: (1) Provide more forward-looking information about plans, opportunities, risks, and uncertainties; (2) Focus more on the factors that create longer-term value, including nonfinancial measures indicating how key business processes are performing; and (3) Better align information reported externally with the information reported internally.

Analysts examine carefully the summary of accounting policies section to determine whether the company is using conservative or liberal accounting practices. For example, amortizing intangible assets over 40 years (the maximum) or depreciating plant assets over an unusually long period of time is considered liberal. On the other hand, using LIFO inventory valuation in a period of inflation is generally viewed as following a conservative practice.

Common Notes

Many of the **notes to the financial statements** have been discussed throughout this textbook. Others will be discussed more fully in this chapter. The more common are as follows:

UNDERLYING CONCEPTS

The AICPA Special Committee on Financial Reporting notes that standard setters should address disclosures and accounting requirements for off-balance-sheet financial arrangements to ensure that business reporting faithfully reports the risks, opportunities, resources, and obligations that result from those arrangements, consistent with users' needs for information.

MAJOR DISCLOSURES

INVENTORY. The basis upon which inventory amounts are stated (lower of cost or market) and the method used in determining cost (LIFO, FIFO, average cost, etc.) should also be reported. Manufacturers should report the inventory composition (finished goods, work in process, raw materials) either in the balance sheet or in a separate schedule in the notes. Unusual or significant financing arrangements relating to inventories that may require disclosure include transactions with related parties, product financing arrangements, firm purchase commitments, involuntary liquidation of LIFO inventories, and pledging of inventories as collateral. Chapter 9 (pages 469–470) illustrates these disclosures.

PROPERTY, PLANT, AND EQUIPMENT. The basis of valuation for property, plant, and equipment should be stated: It is usually historical cost. Pledges, liens, and other commitments related to these assets should be disclosed. In the presentation of depreciation, the following disclosures should be made in the financial statements or in the notes: (1) depreciation expense for the period; (2) balances of major classes of depreciable assets, by nature and function, at the balance sheet date; (3) accumulated depreciation, either by major classes of depreciable assets or in total, at the balance sheet date; and (4) a general description of the method or methods used in computing depreciation with respect to major classes of depreciable assets. Chapter 11 (pages 570–571) illustrates these disclosures.

CREDIT CLAIMS. An investor normally finds it extremely useful to determine the nature and cost of creditorship claims. However, the liability section in the balance sheet can provide the major types of liabilities outstanding only in the aggregate. Note schedules regarding such obligations provide additional information about how the company is financing its operations, the costs that will have to be borne in future periods, and the timing of future cash outflows. Financial statements must disclose for each of the 5 years following the date of the financial statements the aggregate amount of maturities and sinking fund requirements for all long-term borrowings. Chapter 14 (pages 734–735) illustrates these disclosures.

EQUITY HOLDERS' CLAIMS. Many companies present in the body of the balance sheet the number of shares authorized, issued, and outstanding and the par value for each type of equity security. Such data may also be presented in a note. Beyond that, the most common type of equity note disclosure relates to contracts and senior securities outstanding that might affect the various claims of the residual equity holders; for example, the existence of outstanding stock options, outstanding convertible debt, redeemable preferred stock, and convertible preferred stock. In addition, it is necessary to disclose to equity claimants certain types of restrictions currently in force. Generally, these types of restrictions involve the amount of earnings available for dividend distribution. Examples of these types of disclosures are illustrated in Chapter 15 (pages 783, 788–790), Chapter 16 (page 827), and Chapter 17 (pages 870–871, 882–883).

CONTINGENCIES AND COMMITMENTS. An enterprise may have gain or loss contingencies that are not disclosed in the body of the financial statements. These contingencies include litigation, debt and other guarantees, possible tax assessments, renegotiation of government contracts, sales of receivables with recourse, and so on. In addition, commitments that relate to dividend restrictions, purchase agreements (through-put and take-or-pay), hedge contracts, and employment contracts are also disclosed. Disclosures of items of this nature are illustrated in Chapter 7 (pages 360–361), Chapter 9 (page 459), and Chapter 13 (pages 734–735).

DEFERRED TAXES, PENSIONS, AND LEASES. Extensive disclosure is required in these three areas. Chapter 20 (pages 1077–1081), Chapter 21 (pages 1143–1146), and Chapter 22 (pages 1219–1221) discuss each of these disclosures in detail. It should be emphasized that notes to the financial statements should be given a careful reading for information about off-balance-sheet commitments, future financing needs, and the quality of a company's earnings.

CHANGES IN ACCOUNTING PRINCIPLES. The profession defines various types of accounting changes and establishes guides for reporting each type. Either in the summary of significant accounting policies or in the other notes, changes in accounting principles (as well as material changes in estimates and corrections of errors) are discussed. See Chapter 23 (pages 1259–1263 and 1266–1267).

Go to the Digital Tool for additional examples of many of these disclosures.

The disclosures listed above have been discussed in earlier chapters. Four additional disclosures of significance—special transactions or events, subsequent events, segment reporting, and interim reporting—are illustrated in the following sections of this chapter.

DISCLOSURE ISSUES

Disclosure of Special Transactions or Events

Related party transactions, errors and irregularities, and illegal acts pose especially sensitive and difficult problems. The accountant/auditor who has responsibility for reporting on these types of transactions has to be extremely careful that the rights of the reporting company and the needs of users of the financial statements are properly balanced.

In Switzerland there are no requirements to disclose related party transactions. In Italy and Germany related parties do not include a company's directors.

Related party transactions arise when a business enterprise engages in transactions in which one of the transacting parties has the ability to influence significantly the policies of the other, or in which a nontransacting party has the ability to influence the policies of the two transacting parties.[4] Transactions involving related parties cannot be presumed to be carried out on an "arm's-length" basis because the requisite conditions of competitive, free-market dealings may not exist. Transactions such as borrowing or lending money at abnormally low or high interest rates, real estate sales at amounts that differ significantly from appraised value, exchanges of nonmonetary assets, and transactions involving enterprises that have no economic substance ("shell corporations") suggest that related parties may be involved.

[4]Examples of related party transactions include transactions between (a) a parent company and its subsidiaries; (b) subsidiaries of a common parent; (c) an enterprise and trusts for the benefit of employees (controlled or managed by the enterprise); and (d) an enterprise and its principal owners, management, or members of immediate families, and affiliates.

The accountant is expected to report the economic substance rather than the legal form of these transactions and to make adequate disclosures. *FASB Statement No. 57* requires the following disclosures of material related party transactions:

1. The nature of the relationship(s) involved.
2. A description of the transactions (including transactions to which no amounts or nominal amounts were ascribed) for each of the periods for which income statements are presented.
3. The dollar amounts of transactions for each of the periods for which income statements are presented.
4. Amounts due from or to related parties as of the date of each balance sheet presented.

Illustration 25-3 is an example of the disclosure of related party transactions taken from the annual report of **General Instrument Corporation**.

ILLUSTRATION 25-3
Disclosure of Related Party Transactions

GENERAL INSTRUMENT CORPORATION

19. Related Party Transactions
In connection with the asset purchase from TCI, which was consummated on July 17, 1998, TCI obtained approximately a 12% ownership interest in the Company, and at December 31, 1998, such ownership interest was 13%. TCI is also a significant customer of the Company. Sales to TCI represented 31% of total Company sales for the year ended December 31, 1998. Management believes the transactions with TCI are at arms length and are under terms no less favorable to the Company than those with other customers. At December 31, 1998 accounts receivable from TCI totaled $81 million.

Errors are defined as unintentional mistakes, whereas **irregularities** are intentional distortions of financial statements.[5] As indicated in this textbook, when errors are discovered, the financial statements should be corrected. The same treatment should be given irregularities. The discovery of irregularities, however, gives rise to a whole different set of suspicions, procedures, and responsibilities on the part of the accountant/auditor.[6]

Illegal acts encompass such items as illegal political contributions, bribes, kickbacks, and other violations of laws and regulations.[7] In these situations, the accountant/auditor must evaluate the adequacy of disclosure in the financial statements. For example, if revenue is derived from an illegal act that is considered material in relation to the financial statements, this information should be disclosed. To deter these illegal acts, Congress enacted the Foreign Corrupt Practices Act of 1977. In addition to affecting business practices, this Act has had a significant impact upon the accounting profession by encouraging increased disclosure and tighter controls.

Many companies are involved in related party transactions; errors and irregularities, and illegal acts, however, are the exception rather than the rule. Disclosure plays a very important role in these areas because the transaction or event is more qualitative than quantitative and involves more subjective than objective evaluation. The users

[5]"The Auditor's Responsibility to Detect and Report Errors and Irregularities," *Statement on Auditing Standards No. 53* (New York, AICPA, 1988).

[6]The profession became so concerned with certain management frauds that affect financial statements that it established a National Commission on Fraudulent Financial Reporting. The major purpose of this organization was to determine how fraudulent reporting practices can be constrained. Fraudulent financial reporting is discussed later in this chapter.

[7]"Illegal Acts by Clients," *Statement on Auditing Standards No. 54* (New York, AICPA, 1988).

of the financial statements must be provided with some indication of the existence and nature of these transactions, where material, through disclosures, modifications in the auditor's report, or reports of changes in auditors.

Post-Balance Sheet Events (Subsequent Events)

Notes to the financial statements should explain any significant financial events that took place after the formal balance sheet date, but before it is finally issued. These events are referred to as **post-balance sheet events**, events subsequent to the balance sheet date, or just plain **subsequent events**. The subsequent events period is time-diagrammed as shown in Illustration 25-4.

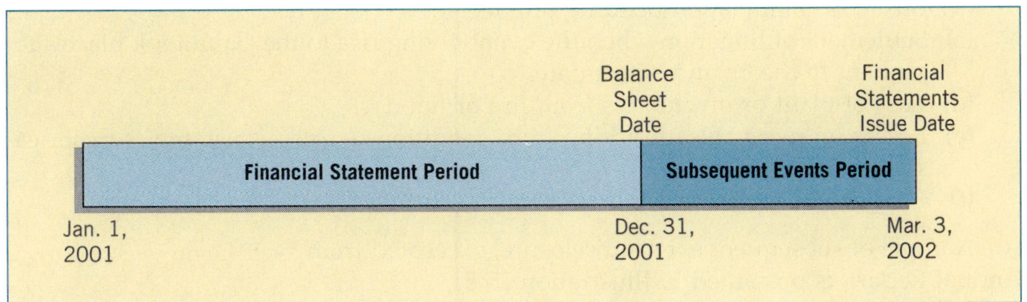

ILLUSTRATION 25-4
Time Periods for Subsequent Events

A period of several weeks, and sometimes months, may elapse after the end of the year before the financial statements are issued. Taking and pricing the inventory, reconciling subsidiary ledgers with controlling accounts, preparing necessary adjusting entries, assuring that all transactions for the period have been entered, obtaining an audit of the financial statements by independent certified public accountants, and printing the annual report all take time. During the period between the balance sheet date and its distribution to stockholders and creditors, important transactions or other events may occur that materially affect the company's financial position or operating situation.

Many who read a recent balance sheet believe the balance sheet condition is constant and project it into the future. However, readers must be told if the company has sold one of its plants, acquired a subsidiary, suffered extraordinary losses, settled significant litigation, or experienced any other important event in the post-balance sheet period. Without an explanation in a note, the reader might be misled and draw inappropriate conclusions.

Two types of events or transactions occurring after the balance sheet date may have a material effect on the financial statements or may need to be considered to interpret these statements accurately:

1. **Events that provide additional evidence about conditions that existed at the balance sheet date, affect the estimates used in preparing financial statements, and, therefore, result in needed adjustments:** All information available prior to the issuance of the financial statements is used to evaluate estimates previously made. To ignore these subsequent events is to pass up an opportunity to improve the accuracy of the financial statements. This first type encompasses information that would have been recorded in the accounts had it been known at the balance sheet date.

   For example, if a loss on an account receivable results from a customer's bankruptcy subsequent to the balance sheet date, the financial statements are adjusted before their issuance. The bankruptcy stems from the customer's poor financial health existing at the balance sheet date.

   The same criterion applies to settlements of litigation. The financial statements must be adjusted if the events that gave rise to the litigation, such as personal injury or patent infringement, took place prior to the balance sheet date. If the event

UNDERLYING CONCEPTS

The periodicity or time period assumption implies that economic activities of an enterprise can be divided into artificial time periods for purpose of analysis.

giving rise to the claim took place subsequent to the balance sheet date, no adjustment is necessary but disclosure is. To illustrate, a loss resulting from a customer's fire or flood after the balance sheet date is not indicative of conditions existing at that date. Thus, adjustment of the financial statements is not necessary.

2 **Events that provide evidence about conditions that did not exist at the balance sheet date but arise subsequent to that date and do not require adjustment of the financial statements:** Some of these events may have to be disclosed to keep the financial statements from being misleading. These disclosures take the form of notes, supplemental schedules, or even pro forma "as if" financial data prepared as if the event had occurred on the balance sheet date. Below are examples of such events that require disclosure (but do not result in adjustment):

(a) Sale of bonds or capital stock; stock splits or stock dividends.
(b) Business combination pending or effected.
(c) Settlement of litigation when the event giving rise to the claim took place subsequent to the balance sheet date.
(d) Loss of plant or inventories from fire or flood.
(e) Losses on receivables resulting from conditions (such as customer's major casualty) arising subsequent to the balance sheet date.
(f) Gains or losses on certain marketable securities.[8]

An example of subsequent events disclosure, excerpted from **Walt Disney Company's** Annual Report, is presented in Illustration 25-5.

ILLUSTRATION 25-5
Balance Sheet Disclosure of Subsequent Events

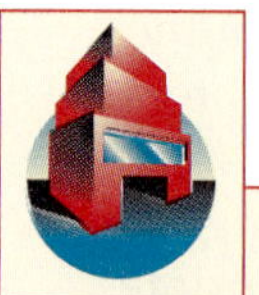

WALT DISNEY COMPANY

Note 14: Subsequent Event

In April 1997, the company purchased a significant equity stake in **Starwave Corporation** ("Starwave"), an internet technology company. On June 18, 1998, the company reached an agreement for the acquisition of Starwave by **Infoseek Corporation** ("Infoseek"), a publicly held Internet search company, pursuant to a merger. On November 18, 1998, the shareholders of both Infoseek and Starwave approved the merger. As a result of the merger and the company's purchase of additional shares of Infoseek common stock pursuant to the merger agreement, the company owns approximately 43% of Infoseek's outstanding common stock. In addition, pursuant to the merger agreement, the company purchased warrants enabling it, under certain circumstances, to achieve a majority stake in Infoseek. These warrants vest over a three-year period and expire in five years. Effective as of the November 18, 1998 closing date of the transaction, the company will record a significant noncash gain, a write-off for purchased in-process research and development costs and an increase in investments, reflecting the company's share of the fair value of Infoseek's intangible assets. The company is currently performing the necessary valuations to determine the gain, the research and development write-off and the amount of and amortization period for the intangible assets. Thereafter, the company will account for its investment in Infoseek under the equity method. The merger is not expected to have a material effect on the company's financial position.

Many subsequent events or developments are not likely to require either adjustment of or disclosure in the financial statements. Typically, these are nonaccounting events or conditions that managements normally communicate by other means. These events include legislation, product changes, management changes, strikes, unionization, marketing agreements, and loss of important customers.

[8]"Subsequent Events," *Statement on Auditing Standards No. 1* (New York: AICPA, 1973), pp. 123–124. *Accounting Trends and Techniques—1999* listed the following types of subsequent events and their frequency of occurrence among the 600 companies surveyed: debt incurred, reduced, or refinanced, 62; business combinations pending or effected, 81; discontinued operations, 46; litigation, 52; capital stock issued or repurchased, 25; employee benefit plans, 15; stock splits or dividends, stock rights, 26.

Reporting for Diversified (Conglomerate) Companies

OBJECTIVE 3
Describe the disclosure requirements for major segments of a business.

In the last several decades business enterprises have had, at times, a tendency to diversify their operations. Take the case of conglomerate GenCorp. whose products include tires, Penn tennis balls, parts for the MX missile, and linings for disposable diapers. Its RKO subsidiary owns radio and television stations, makes movies, bottles soda pop, runs hotels, and holds a big stake in an airline. As a result of such diversification efforts, investors and investment analysts have sought more information concerning the details behind conglomerate financial statements. Particularly, they want income statement, balance sheet, and cash flow information on the **individual** segments that compose the **total** business income figure.

An illustration of **segmented** (disaggregated) financial information is presented in the following example of an office equipment and auto parts company.

ILLUSTRATION 25-6
Segmented Income Statement

OFFICE EQUIPMENT AND AUTO PARTS COMPANY
Income Statement Data
(in millions)

	Consolidated	Office Equipment	Auto Parts
Net sales	$78.8	$18.0	$60.8
Manufacturing costs:			
Inventories, beginning	12.3	4.0	8.3
Materials and services	38.9	10.8	28.1
Wages	12.9	3.8	9.1
Inventories, ending	(13.3)	(3.9)	(9.4)
	50.8	14.7	36.1
Selling and administrative expense	12.1	1.6	10.5
Total operating expenses	62.9	16.3	46.6
Income before taxes	15.9	1.7	14.2
Income taxes	(9.3)	(1.0)	(8.3)
Net income	$ 6.6	$ 0.7	$ 5.9

If only the consolidated figures are available to the analyst, much information regarding the composition of these figures is hidden in aggregated totals. There is no way to tell from the consolidated data the extent to which the differing product lines **contribute to the company's profitability, risk, and growth potential**. For example, in Illustration 25-6 above, if the office equipment segment is deemed a risky venture, then segmented reporting provides useful information for purposes of making an informed investment decision regarding the whole company.

A classic situation that demonstrates the need for segmented data involved Caterpillar, Inc. Caterpillar was cited by the SEC because it failed to tell investors that nearly a quarter of its income in 1989 came from a Brazilian unit. This income was nonrecurring in nature. The company knew that different economic policies in the next year would probably greatly affect earnings of the Brazilian unit. But Caterpillar presented its financial results on a consolidated basis, not disclosing the Brazilian's operations. The SEC stated that Caterpillar's failure to include information about Brazil left investors with an incomplete picture of the company's financial results and denied investors the opportunity to see the company "through the eyes of management."

Companies have always been somewhat hesitant to disclose segmented data for the reasons listed below.

1. Without a thorough knowledge of the business and an understanding of such important factors as the competitive environment and capital investment requirements, the investor may find the segmented information meaningless or may even draw improper conclusions about the reported earnings of the segments.

2. Additional disclosure may harm reporting firms because it may be helpful to competitors, labor unions, suppliers, and certain government regulatory agencies.
3. Additional disclosure may discourage management from taking intelligent business risks because segments reporting losses or unsatisfactory earnings may cause stockholder dissatisfaction with management.
4. The wide variation among firms in the choice of segments, cost allocation, and other accounting problems limits the usefulness of segmented information.
5. The investor is investing in the company as a whole and not in the particular segments, and it should not matter how any single segment is performing if the overall performance is satisfactory.
6. Certain technical problems, such as classification of segments and allocation of segment revenues and costs (especially "common costs"), are formidable.

On the other hand, the advocates of segmented disclosures offer these reasons in support of the practice:

1. Segmented information is needed by the investor to make an intelligent investment decision regarding a diversified company.
   (a) Sales and earnings of individual segments are needed to forecast consolidated profits because of the differences between segments in growth rate, risk, and profitability.
   (b) Segmented reports disclose the nature of a company's businesses and the relative size of the components as an aid in evaluating the company's investment worth.
2. The absence of segmented reporting by a diversified company may put its unsegmented, single product-line competitors at a competitive disadvantage because the conglomerate may obscure information that its competitors must disclose.

The advocates of segmented disclosures appear to have a much stronger case. Many users indicate that segmented data are the most useful financial information provided, aside from the basic financial statements. As a result, the FASB has issued extensive reporting guidelines in this area.

Professional Pronouncements

The development of accounting standards for segmented financial information has been a continuing process during the past quarter century. Recognizing the need for guidelines in this area of reporting, the FASB in 1976 issued *FASB Statement No. 14,* "Financial Reporting for Segments of a Business Enterprise"; in 1993 it issued *Invitation to Comment,* "Reporting Disaggregated Information by Business Enterprises"; and in 1997 it issued *FASB Statement No. 131,* "Disclosures about Segments of an Enterprise and Related Information."[9] The basic reporting requirements related to the most recent pronouncement are discussed below.

Objective of Reporting Segmented Information

The objective of reporting segmented financial data is to provide information about the **different types of business activities** in which an enterprise engages and the **different economic environments** in which it operates, in order to help users of financial statements:

(a) Better understand the enterprise's performance.
(b) Better assess its prospects for future net cash flows.
(c) Make more informed judgments about the enterprise as a whole.

[9]"Disclosures about Segments of an Enterprise and Related Information," *Statement of Financial Accounting Standards No. 131* (Norwalk, Conn.: FASB, 1997).

Basic Principles

A company might meet the segmented reporting objective by providing complete sets of financial statements that are disaggregated in several ways, for example, by products or services, by geography, by legal entity, or by type of customer. However, it is not feasible to provide all of that information in every set of financial statements. *FASB Statement No. 131* requires that general purpose financial statements include selected information on a single basis of segmentation. The method chosen is referred to as the **management approach**. The management approach is based on the way the management segments the company for making operating decisions. Consequently, the segments are evident from the company's organization structure. It focuses on information about components of the business that management uses to make decisions about operating matters. These components are called **operating segments**.

Identifying Operating Segments

An **operating segment** is a component of an enterprise:

(a) That engages in business activities from which it earns revenues and incurs expenses.
(b) Whose operating results are regularly reviewed by the company's chief operating decision maker to assess segment performance and allocate resources to the segment.
(c) For which discrete financial information is available that is generated by or based on the internal financial reporting system.

Information about two or more operating segments may be aggregated only if the segments have the same basic characteristics in each of the following areas:

(a) The nature of the products and services provided.
(b) The nature of the production process.
(c) The type or class of customer.
(d) The methods of product or service distribution.
(e) If applicable, the nature of the regulatory environment.

After the company decides on the segments for possible disclosure, a quantitative materiality test is made to determine whether the segment is significant enough to warrant actual disclosure. An operating segment is regarded as significant and therefore identified as a reportable segment if it satisfies **one or more** of the following quantitative thresholds.

1. Its **revenue** (including both sales to external customers and intersegment sales or transfers) is 10% or more of the combined revenue of all the enterprise's operating segments.
2. The absolute amount of its **profit or loss** is 10% or more of the greater, in absolute amount, of
   (a) the combined operating profit of all operating segments that did not incur a loss, or
   (b) the combined loss of all operating segments that did report a loss.
3. Its **identifiable assets** are 10% or more of the combined assets of all operating segments.

In applying these tests, two additional factors must be considered. First, segment data must explain a significant portion of the company's business. Specifically, the segmented results must equal or exceed 75% of the combined sales to unaffiliated customers for the entire enterprise. This test prevents a company from providing limited information on only a few segments and lumping all the rest into one category.

Second, the profession recognizes that reporting too many segments may overwhelm users with detailed information. The FASB decided that 10 is a reasonable upper limit for the number of segments that a company should be required to disclose.

To illustrate these requirements, assume a company has identified six possible reporting segments (000 omitted):

ILLUSTRATION 25-7
Data for Different Possible Reporting Segments

Segments	Total Revenue (Unaffiliated)	Operating Profit (Loss)	Identifiable Assets
A	$ 100	$10	$ 60
B	50	2	30
C	700	40	390
D	300	20	160
E	900	18	280
F	100	(5)	50
	$2,150	$85	$970

The respective tests may be applied as follows:

Revenue test: 10% × $2,150 = $215; C, D, and E meet this test.

Operating profit (loss) test: 10% × $90 = $9 (note that the $5 loss is ignored); A, C, D, and E meet this test.

Identifiable assets tests: 10% × $970 = $97; C, D, and E meet this test.

The segments are therefore A, C, D, and E, assuming that these four segments have enough sales to meet the 75% of combined sales test. The 75% test is computed as follows:

75% of combined sales test: 75% × $2,150 = $1,612.50; the sales of A, C, D, and E total $2,000 ($100 + $700 + $300 + $900); therefore, the 75% test is met.

Measurement Principles

UNDERLYING CONCEPTS

The AICPA Special Committee on Financial Reporting notes that multi-segment companies operate diverse businesses that are subject to different opportunities and risks. Many users view business segments as the engines that generate future earnings or cash flows and, thereby, drive returns on investments. Segment information provides additional insight about the opportunities and risks of investments and sharpens predictions. Because of its predictive value, improving segment reporting is of the highest priority.

The accounting principles to be used for segment disclosure need not be the same as the principles used to prepare the consolidated statements. This flexibility may at first appear inconsistent. But, preparing segment information in accordance with generally accepted accounting principles would be difficult because some principles are not expected to apply at a segment level. Examples are accounting for the cost of company-wide employee benefit plans, accounting for income taxes in a company that files a consolidated tax return, and accounting for inventory on a LIFO basis if the pool includes items in more than one segment.

Allocations of joint, common, or company-wide costs solely for external reporting purposes are not required. **Common costs** are those incurred for the benefit of more than one segment and whose interrelated nature prevents a completely objective division of costs among segments. For example, the company president's salary is difficult to allocate to various segments. Allocations of common costs are inherently arbitrary and may not be meaningful if they are not used for internal management purposes. There is a presumption that allocations to segments are either directly attributable or reasonably allocable.

Segmented Information Reported

The FASB requires that an enterprise report:

1. ***General information about its operating segments.*** This includes factors that management considers most significant in determining the company's operating segments, and the types of products and services from which each operating segment derives its revenues.
2. ***Segment profit and loss and related information.*** Specifically, the following information about each operating segment must be reported if the amounts are included in the determination of segment profit or loss:
   - **(a)** Revenues from transactions with external customers.
   - **(b)** Revenues from transactions with other operating segments of the same enterprise.

(c) Interest revenue.
(d) Interest expense.
(e) Depreciation, depletion, and amortization expense.
(f) Unusual items.
(g) Equity in the net income of investees accounted for by the equity method.
(h) Income tax expense or benefit.
(i) Extraordinary items.
(j) Significant noncash items other than depreciation, depletion, and amortization expense.

3 ***Segment assets.*** An enterprise must report each operating segment's total assets.

4 ***Reconciliations.*** An enterprise must provide a reconciliation of the total of the segments' revenues to total revenues, a reconciliation of the total of the operating segments' profits and losses to its income before income taxes, and a reconciliation of the total of the operating segments' assets to total assets.

5 ***Information about products and services and geographic areas.*** For each operating segment that has not been determined based on geography, the enterprise must report (unless it is impracticable) [(a) in the enterprise's country of domicile and (b) in each other country if material]: (1) revenues from external customers, (2) long-lived assets, and (3) expenditures during the period for long-lived assets.

6 ***Major customers.*** If 10 percent or more of the revenues is derived from a single customer, the enterprise must disclose the total amount of revenues from each such customer by segment.

Illustration of Disaggregated Information

The segment disclosure for **Potlatch Corporation** is shown in Illustration 25-8.

ILLUSTRATION 25-8
Segment Disclosure, Potlatch Corporation

POTLATCH CORPORATION

13. Segment Information (in part)

The company has divided its operations into three reportable segments: wood products, printing papers and pulp and paper, based upon similarities in product lines, manufacturing processes, marketing and management of its businesses.

The reporting segments follow the same accounting policies used for the company's consolidated financial statements and described in the summary of significant accounting policies.

Following is a tabulation of business segment information for each of the past three years. Corporate information is included to reconcile segment data to the consolidated financial statements.

(Dollars in thousands)	1998	1997	1996
Segment sales:			
Wood products:			
Oriented strand board	$ 171,464	$ 106,807	$ 150,545
Lumber	225,668	247,232	201,022
Plywood	54,561	64,511	57,468
Particleboard	14,494	12,875	12,087
Logs, chips, etc.	124,536	119,435	111,118
	590,723	550,860	532,240
Printing papers	406,277	429,217	441,037
Pulp and paper:			
Pulp	12,467	11,183	12,346
Paperboard	390,708	420,054	404,136
Tissue	235,799	218,310	222,169
	638,974	649,547	638,651
	1,635,974	1,629,624	1,611,928
Elimination of intersegment sales	(70,096)	(60,754)	(57,479)
Total consolidated net sales	$1,565,878	$1,568,870	$1,554,449

(Dollars in thousands)	1998	1997	1996
Operating income:			
Wood products	$ 73,811	$ 47,674	$ 68,056
Printing papers	14,204	33,358	48,570
Pulp and paper	53,394	51,043	40,867
	141,409	132,075	157,493
Corporate items:			
Administration expense	(37,247)	(31,385)	(30,752)
Interest expense	(49,744)	(46,124)	(43,869)
Other, net	3,757	69	3,454
Consolidated earnings before taxes on income	$ 58,175	$ 54,635	$ 86,326

(Dollars in thousands)	1998	1997	1996
Depreciation, Amortization, and Cost of Fee Timber Harvested:			
Wood products	$ 54,245	$ 50,586	$ 49,072
Printing papers	41,618	39,436	35,318
Pulp and paper	53,525	58,689	56,092
	149,388	148,711	140,482
Corporate	890	1,074	1,039
Total	$ 150,278	$ 149,785	$ 141,521
Assets:			
Wood products	$ 671,381	$ 690,468	$ 698,151
Printing papers	685,743	644,457	592,228
Pulp and paper	825,547	842,337	850,612
	2,182,671	2,177,262	2,140,991
Corporate	194,635	187,874	124,688
Total consolidated assets	$2,377,306	$2,365,136	$2,265,679

(Dollars in thousands)	1998	1997	1996
Capital Expenditures:			
Wood products	$ 28,404	$ 31,578	$ 43,992
Printing papers	87,147	81,913	103,574
Pulp and paper	30,674	44,054	92,083
	146,225	157,545	239,649
Corporate	802	940	259
Total	$147,027	$158,485	$239,908

All of the company's manufacturing facilities and all other assets are located within the continental United States. However, the company sells and ships products to many foreign countries. Geographic information regarding the company's net sales is summarized as follows:

(Dollars in thousands)	1998	1997	1996
United States	$1,392,223	$1,382,674	$1,357,801
Japan	64,129	69,494	89,355
Australia	23,022	30,869	32,585
Canada	31,234	35,867	25,599
China	25,939	23,061	24,279
Italy	18,631	11,933	8,866
Other foreign countries	10,700	14,972	15,964
Total consolidated net sales	$1,565,878	$1,568,870	$1,554,449

ILLUSTRATION 25-8
Continued

Interim Reports

OBJECTIVE 4
Describe the accounting problems associated with interim reporting.

One further source of information for the investor is interim reports. As noted earlier, **interim reports** are those reports that cover periods of less than one year. At one time, interim reports were referred to as the "forgotten reports"; such is no longer the case. The stock exchanges, the SEC, and the accounting profession have taken an active role in developing guidelines for the presentation of interim information.

The SEC mandates that certain companies file a Form 10Q, which requires a company to disclose quarterly data similar to that disclosed in the annual report. It also requires those companies to disclose selected quarterly information in notes to the annual financial statements. Illustration 25-9 on page 1397 presents the disclosure of selected quarterly data for Tootsie Roll Industries, Inc. In addition to this requirement, the APB issued *Opinion No. 28,* which attempted to narrow the reporting alternatives related to interim reports.[10]

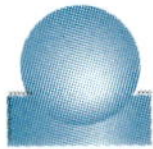

UNDERLYING CONCEPTS

For information to be relevant, it must be available to decision makers before it loses its capacity to influence their decisions (timeliness). Interim reporting is an excellent example of this concept.

Because of the short-term nature of the information in these reports, however, there is considerable controversy as to the general approach that should be employed. One group (which holds the **discrete view**) believes that each interim period should be treated as a separate accounting period; deferrals and accruals would therefore follow the principles employed for annual reports. Accounting transactions should be reported as they occur, and expense recognition should not change with the period of time covered. Another group (which holds the **integral view**) believes that the interim report is an integral part of the annual report and that deferrals and accruals should take into consideration what will happen for the entire year. In this approach, estimated expenses are assigned to parts of a year on the basis of sales volume or some other activity base. At present, many companies follow the discrete approach for certain types of expenses and the integral approach for others, because the standards currently employed in practice are vague and lead to differing interpretations.

[10]"Interim Financial Reporting," *Opinions of the Accounting Principles Board No. 28* (New York: AICPA, 1973).

ILLUSTRATION 25-9
Disclosure of Selected Quarterly Data

TOOTSIE ROLL INDUSTRIES, INC.

For the Year Ended December 31, 1998

(Thousands of dollars except per share data)

	First	Second	Third	Fourth
Net sales	$69,701	$85,931	$144,230	$88,797
Gross margin	36,966	45,133	73,251	45,692
Net earnings	11,217	13,910	27,216	15,183
Net earnings per share	.23	.29	.57	.32

	Stock Prices		
	High	Low	Dividends
1st Qtr	38–13/32	29–27/32	$.0401
2nd Qtr	40–3/4	34–31/32	$.0525
3rd Qtr	47–1/4	33–3/4	$.0525
4th Qtr	42–7/8	34–1/8	$.0525

Interim Reporting Requirements

The profession indicates that the same accounting principles used for annual reports should be employed for interim reports. Revenues should be recognized in interim periods on the same basis as they are for annual periods. For example, if the installment sales method is used as the basis for recognizing revenue on an annual basis, then the installment basis should be applied to interim reports as well. Also, costs directly associated with revenues (product costs), such as materials, labor and related fringe benefits, and manufacturing overhead should be treated in the same manner for interim reports as for annual reports.

Companies generally should use the same inventory pricing methods (FIFO, LIFO, etc.) for interim reports that they use for annual reports. However, the following exceptions are appropriate at interim reporting periods:

1. Companies may use the gross profit method for interim inventory pricing, but disclosure of the method and adjustments to reconcile with annual inventory are necessary.
2. When LIFO inventories are liquidated at an interim date and are expected to be replaced by year end, cost of goods sold should include the expected cost of replacing the liquidated LIFO base and not give effect to the interim liquidation.
3. Inventory market declines should not be deferred beyond the interim period unless they are temporary and no loss is expected for the fiscal year.
4. Planned variances under a standard cost system which are expected to be absorbed by year end ordinarily should be deferred.

Costs and expenses other than product costs, often referred to as **period costs**, are often charged to the interim period as incurred. But they may be allocated among interim periods on the basis of an estimate of time expired, benefit received, or activity associated with the periods. Considerable latitude is exercised in accounting for these costs in interim periods, and many believe more definitive guidelines are needed.

Regarding disclosure, the following interim data should be reported as a minimum:

1. Sales or gross revenues, provision for income taxes, extraordinary items, cumulative effect of a change in accounting principles or practices, and net income.
2. Basic and diluted earnings per share where appropriate.
3. Seasonal revenue, cost, or expenses.
4. Significant changes in estimates or provisions for income taxes.

5. Disposal of a segment of a business and extraordinary, unusual, or infrequently occurring items.
6. Contingent items.
7. Changes in accounting principles or estimates.
8. Significant changes in financial position.

The profession also encourages, but does not require, companies to publish a balance sheet and a statement of cash flows. When this information is not presented, significant changes in such items as liquid assets, net working capital, long-term liabilities, and stockholders' equity should be disclosed.

Unique Problems of Interim Reporting

In *APB Opinion No. 28,* the Board indicated that it favored the integral approach. However, within this broad guideline, a number of unique reporting problems develop related to the following items.

Advertising and Similar Costs. The general guidelines are that costs such as advertising should be **deferred in an interim period if the benefits extend beyond that period; otherwise they should be expensed as incurred**. But such a determination is difficult, and even if they are deferred, how should they be allocated between quarters? Because of the vague guidelines in this area, accounting for advertising varies widely. Some companies in the food industry, such as **RJR Nabisco** and **Pillsbury**, charge advertising costs as a percentage of sales and adjust to actual at year end, whereas **General Foods** and **Kellogg** expense these costs as incurred.

The same type of problem relates to such items as social security taxes, research and development costs, and major repairs. For example, should the company expense social security costs (payroll taxes) on highly paid personnel early in the year or allocate and spread them to subsequent quarters? Should a major repair that occurs later in the year be anticipated and allocated proportionately to earlier periods?

Expenses Subject to Year-End Adjustment. Bad debts, executive bonuses, pension costs, and inventory shrinkage are often not known with a great deal of certainty until year end. **These costs should be estimated and allocated in the best possible way to interim periods.** Companies use a variety of allocation techniques to accomplish this objective.

Income Taxes. Not every dollar of corporate taxable income is assessed at the same rate; the tax rate is progressive. This aspect of business income taxes poses a problem in preparing **interim financial statements**. Should the income to date be annualized and the proportionate income tax accrued for the period to date **(annualized approach)**? Or should the first amount of income earned be taxed at the lower rate of tax applicable to such income **(marginal principle approach)**? At one time, companies generally followed the latter approach and accrued the tax applicable to each additional dollar of income.

The marginal principle was especially applicable to businesses having a seasonal or uneven income pattern, because the interim accrual of tax was based on the actual results to date. The profession now, however, uses the annualized approach requiring that "at the end of each interim period the company should make its best estimate of the effective tax rate expected to be applicable for the full fiscal year. The rate so determined should be used in providing for income taxes on income for the quarter."[11]

[11]"Interim Financial Reporting," *Opinions of the Accounting Principles Board No. 28* (New York: AICPA, 1973), par. 19. The estimated annual effective tax rate should reflect anticipated tax credits, foreign tax rates, percentage depletion, capital gains rates, and other available tax planning alternatives.

Because businesses did not uniformly apply this guideline in accounting for similar situations, the FASB issued *Interpretation No. 18.* This interpretation requires that the **estimated annual effective tax rate** be applied to the year-to-date "ordinary" income at the end of each interim period to compute the year-to-date tax. Further, the **interim period tax** related to "ordinary" income shall be the difference between the amount so computed and the amounts reported for previous interim periods of the fiscal period.[12]

Extraordinary Items. Extraordinary items consist of unusual and nonrecurring material gains and losses. In the past, they were handled in interim reports in one of three ways: (1) absorbed entirely in the quarter in which they occurred; (2) prorated over the four quarters; or (3) disclosed only by note. **The required approach is to charge or credit the loss or gain in the quarter that it occurs instead of attempting some arbitrary multiple-period allocation.** This approach is consistent with the way in which extraordinary items are currently handled on an annual basis; no attempt is made to prorate the extraordinary items over several years.

Some favor the omission of extraordinary items from the quarterly net income. They believe that inclusion of extraordinary items that may be large in proportion to interim results distorts the predictive value of interim reports. Many accountants, however, consider such an omission inappropriate because it deviates from actual results.

Changes in Accounting. What happens if a company decides to change an accounting principle in the third quarter of a fiscal year? Should the cumulative effect adjustment be charged or credited to that quarter? Presentation of a cumulative effect in the third quarter may be misleading because of the inherent subjectivity associated with the first two quarters' reported income. In addition, a question arises as to whether such a change might not be used to manipulate a given quarter's income. As a result, *FASB Statement No. 3* was issued indicating that **if a cumulative effect change occurs in other than the first quarter, no cumulative effect should be recognized in those quarters.**[13] **Rather, the cumulative effect at the beginning of the year should be computed and the first quarter restated.** Subsequent quarters would not report a cumulative effect adjustment.

Earnings per Share. Interim reporting of earnings per share has all the problems inherent in computing and presenting annual earnings per share, and then some. If shares are issued in the third period, EPS for the first two periods will not be indicative of year-end EPS. If an extraordinary item is present in one period and new equity shares are sold in another period, the EPS figure for the extraordinary item will change for the year. On an annual basis only one EPS figure is associated with an extraordinary item and that figure does not change; the interim figure is subject to change. **For purposes of computing earnings per share and making the required disclosure determinations, each interim period should stand alone. That is, all applicable tests should be made for that single period.**

Seasonality. **Seasonality** occurs when sales are compressed into one short period of the year while certain costs are fairly evenly spread throughout the year. For example, the natural gas industry has its heavy sales in the winter months, as contrasted with the beverage industry, which has its heavy sales in the summer months.

---

[12]"Accounting for Income Taxes in Interim Periods," *FASB Interpretation No. 18* (Stamford, Conn.: FASB, March 1977), par. 9. "Ordinary" income (or loss) refers to "income (or loss) from continuing operations before income taxes (or benefits)" excluding extraordinary items, discontinued operations, and cumulative effects of changes in accounting principles.

[13]"Reporting Accounting Changes in Interim Financial Statements," *Statement of the Financial Accounting Standards Board No. 3* (Stamford, Conn.: FASB, 1974). This standard also provides guidance related to a LIFO change and accounting changes made in the fourth quarter of a fiscal year in which interim data are not presented.

The problem of seasonality is related to the matching concept in accounting. Expenses should be matched against the revenues they create. In a seasonal business, wide fluctuations in profits occur because off-season sales do not absorb the company's fixed costs (for example, manufacturing, selling, and administrative costs that tend to remain fairly constant regardless of sales or production).

To illustrate why seasonality is a problem, assume the following information:

ILLUSTRATION 25-10
Data for Seasonality Example

Selling price per unit	$1
Annual sales for the period (projected and actual)	
100,000 units @ $1.00	$100,000
Manufacturing costs:	
Variable	10¢ per unit
Fixed	20¢ per unit or $20,000 for the year
Nonmanufacturing costs:	
Variable	10¢ per unit
Fixed	30¢ per unit or $30,000 for the year

Sales for four quarters and the year (projected and actual) were:

ILLUSTRATION 25-11
Sales Data for Seasonality Example

		Percent of Sales
1st Quarter	$ 20,000	20%
2nd Quarter	5,000	5
3rd Quarter	10,000	10
4th Quarter	65,000	65
Total for the year	$100,000	100%

Under the present accounting framework, the income statements for the quarters might be presented as follows:

ILLUSTRATION 25-12
Interim Net Income for Seasonal Business—Discrete Approach

	1st Qtr	2nd Qtr	3rd Qtr	4th Qtr	Year
Sales	$20,000	$ 5,000	$10,000	$65,000	$100,000
Manufacturing costs					
Variable	(2,000)	(500)	(1,000)	(6,500)	(10,000)
Fixed[a]	(4,000)	(1,000)	(2,000)	(13,000)	(20,000)
	14,000	3,500	7,000	45,500	70,000
Nonmanufacturing costs					
Variable	(2,000)	(500)	(1,000)	(6,500)	(10,000)
Fixed[b]	(7,500)	(7,500)	(7,500)	(7,500)	(30,000)
Net income	$ 4,500	$ (4,500)	$ (1,500)	$31,500	$ 30,000

[a]The fixed manufacturing costs are inventoried, so that equal amounts of fixed costs do not appear during each quarter.
[b]The fixed nonmanufacturing costs are not inventoried so that equal amounts of fixed costs appear during each quarter.

An investor who uses the first quarter's results can be misled. If the first quarter's earnings are $4,500, should this figure be multiplied by four to predict annual earnings of $18,000? Or, as the analysis suggests, inasmuch as $20,000 in sales is 20% of the predicted sales for the year, net income for the year should be $22,500 ($4,500 × 5). Either figure is obviously wrong, and after the second quarter's results occur, the investor may become even more confused.

The problem with the conventional approach is that the fixed nonmanufacturing costs are not charged in proportion to sales. Some enterprises have adopted a way of avoiding this problem by making all fixed nonmanufacturing costs follow the sales pattern, as shown in Illustration 25-13.

	1st Qtr	2nd Qtr	3rd Qtr	4th Qtr	Year
Sales	$20,000	$ 5,000	$10,000	$65,000	$100,000
Manufacturing costs					
Variable	(2,000)	(500)	(1,000)	(6,500)	(10,000)
Fixed	(4,000)	(1,000)	(2,000)	(13,000)	(20,000)
	14,000	3,500	7,000	45,500	70,000
Nonmanufacturing costs					
Variable	(2,000)	(500)	(1,000)	(6,500)	(10,000)
Fixed	(6,000)	(1,500)	(3,000)	(19,500)	(30,000)
Net income	$ 6,000	$ 1,500	$ 3,000	$19,500	$ 30,000

ILLUSTRATION 25-13
Interim Net Income for Seasonal Business—Integral Approach

This approach solves some of the problems of interim reporting: sales in the first quarter are 20% of total sales for the year, and net income in the first quarter is 20% of total income. In this case, as in the previous example, the investor cannot rely on multiplying any given quarter by four, but can use comparative data or rely on some estimate of sales in relation to income for a given period.

The greater the degree of seasonality experienced by a company, the greater the possibility of distortion. Because no definitive guidelines are available for handling such items as the fixed nonmanufacturing costs, variability in income can be substantial. To alleviate this problem, the profession recommends that companies subject to material seasonal variations disclose the seasonal nature of their business and consider supplementing their interim reports with information for 12-month periods ended at the interim date for the current and preceding years.

The two illustrations above highlight the difference between the **discrete** and **integral** viewpoints. The fixed nonmanufacturing expenses are expensed as incurred under the discrete viewpoint. They are charged to expense on the basis of some measure of activity under the integral method.

Continuing Controversy. The profession has developed some standards for interim reporting; but much still has to be done. As yet, it is unclear whether the discrete, integral, or some combination of these two methods will be settled on.

Discussion also persists concerning the independent auditor's involvement in interim reports. Many auditors are reluctant to express an opinion on interim financial information, arguing that the data are too tentative and subjective. Conversely, an increasing number of individuals advocate some type of examination of interim reports. A compromise may be a limited review of interim reports that provides some assurance that an examination has been conducted by an outside party and that the published information appears to be in accord with generally accepted accounting principles.[14]

Analysts want financial information as soon as possible, before it's old news. We may not be far from a continuous database system in which corporate financial records can be accessed by microcomputer. Investors might be able to access a company's financial records via computer whenever they wish and put the information in the format they need. Thus, they could learn about sales slippage, cost increases, or earnings changes as they happen, rather than waiting until after the quarter has ended.[15]

A steady stream of information from the company to the investor could be very positive because it might alleviate management's continual concern with short-run

UNDERLYING CONCEPTS

The AICPA Special Committee on Financial Reporting indicates that users would benefit from separate fourth-quarter reporting, including management's analysis of fourth-quarter activities and events. Also, quarterly segment reporting was demanded. Under *FASB Statement No. 131*, companies now provide quarterly segment data.

[14]The AICPA has been involved in developing guidelines for the review of interim reports. "Limited Review of Interim Financial Statements," *Statement on Auditing Standards No. 24* (New York: AICPA, 1979) sets standards for the review of interim reports.

[15]A step in this direction is the SEC's mandate for companies to file their financial statements electronically with the SEC. The system, called EDGAR (electronic data gathering and retrieval) provides interested parties with computer access to financial information such as periodic filings, corporate prospectuses, and proxy materials.

interim numbers. Today many contend that U.S. management is too short-run oriented. The truth of this statement is echoed by the words of the president of a large company who decided to retire early: "I wanted to look forward to a year made up of four seasons rather than four quarters."

AUDITOR'S AND MANAGEMENT'S REPORTS

Auditor's Report

OBJECTIVE 5
Identify the major disclosures found in the auditor's report.

Another important source of information that is often overlooked is the **auditor's report**. An **auditor** is an accounting professional who conducts an independent examination of the accounting data presented by a business enterprise. If the auditor is satisfied that the financial statements present the financial position, results of operations, and cash flows fairly in accordance with generally accepted accounting principles, an unqualified opinion is expressed as shown in Illustration 25-14.[16]

ILLUSTRATION 25-14
Auditor's Report

UAL CORPORATION

Report of Independent Public Accountants

To the Stockholders and
Board of Directors, UAL Corporation:

We have audited, in accordance with generally accepted auditing standards, the statements of consolidated financial position of UAL Corporation (a Delaware corporation) and subsidiary companies as of December 31, 1998 and 1997, and the related statements of consolidated operations, consolidated cash flows, and consolidated stockholders' equity for each of the three years in the period ended December 31, 1998, appearing in the appendix to the proxy statement for the 1999 Annual Meeting of Stockholders of the Company (not presented herein). In our report dated February 24, 1999, also appearing in that proxy statement, we expressed an unqualified opinion on those consolidated financial statements.

In our opinion, the information set forth in the accompanying consolidated statements of financial position as of December 31, 1998 and 1997, and the related statements of consolidated operations, consolidated cash flows and consolidated stockholders' equity for each of the three years in the period ended December 31, 1998, is fairly stated, in all material respects, in relation to the consolidated financial statements from which it has been derived.

Arthur Andersen LLP

Chicago, Illinois
February 24, 1999

INTERNATIONAL INSIGHT
In Germany, auditor's opinions address whether the statements have been prepared in accordance with German law—a statutory audit.

In preparing this report, the auditor follows these reporting standards:

1. The report shall state whether the financial statements are presented in accordance with generally accepted accounting principles.
2. The report shall identify those circumstances in which such principles have not been consistently observed in the current period in relation to the preceding period.
3. Informative disclosures in the financial statements are to be regarded as reasonably adequate unless otherwise stated in the report.

[16] This auditor's report is in exact conformance with the specifications contained in "Reports on Audited Financial Statements," *Statement on Auditing Standards No. 58* (New York: AICPA, 1988).

4. The report shall contain either an expression of opinion regarding the financial statements taken as a whole or an assertion to the effect that an opinion cannot be expressed. When an overall opinion cannot be expressed, the reasons why should be stated. In all cases where an auditor's name is associated with financial statements, the report should contain a clear-cut indication of the character of the auditor's examination, if any, and the degree of responsibility being taken.

In most cases, the auditor issues a standard **unqualified** or **clean opinion**; that is, the auditor expresses the opinion that the financial statements present fairly, in all material respects, the financial position, results of operations, and cash flows of the entity in conformity with generally accepted accounting principles. Certain circumstances, although they do not affect the auditor's unqualified opinion, may require the auditor to add an explanatory paragraph to the audit report. Some of the more important circumstances are as follows:

1. ***Uncertainties.*** A matter involving an **uncertainty** is one that is expected to be resolved at a future date, at which time sufficient evidence concerning its outcome is expected to become available. In deciding whether an explanatory paragraph is needed, the auditor should consider the likelihood of a material loss resulting from the contingency. If, for example, the possibility that a loss will be incurred is remote, then an explanatory paragraph is not warranted. If the loss is probable but not estimable, or is reasonably possible and material, then an explanatory paragraph is warranted.
2. ***Lack of Consistency.*** If there has been a change in accounting principles or in the method of their application that has a material effect on the comparability of the company's financial statements, the auditor should refer to the change in an explanatory paragraph of the report. Such an explanatory paragraph should identify the nature of the change and refer the reader to the note in the financial statements that discusses the change in detail. The auditor's concurrence with a change is implicit unless exception to the change is taken in expressing the auditor's opinion as to fair presentation of the financial statements in conformity with generally accepted accounting principles.
3. ***Emphasis of a Matter.*** The auditor may wish to emphasize a matter regarding the financial statements, but nevertheless intends to express an unqualified opinion. For example, the auditor may wish to emphasize that the entity is a component of a larger business enterprise or that it has had significant transactions with related parties. Such explanatory information should be presented in a separate paragraph of the auditor's report.

In some situations, however, the auditor is required to (1) express a **qualified** opinion, (2) express an **adverse** opinion, or (3) **disclaim** an opinion. A **qualified opinion** contains an exception to the standard opinion. Ordinarily the exception is not of sufficient magnitude to invalidate the statements as a whole; if it were, an adverse opinion would be rendered. The usual circumstances in which the auditor may deviate from the standard unqualified short-form report on financial statements are as follows:

1. The scope of the examination is limited or affected by conditions or restrictions.
2. The statements do not fairly present financial position or results of operations because of:
   (a) Lack of conformity with generally accepted accounting principles and standards.
   (b) Inadequate disclosure.

If the auditor is confronted with one of the situations noted above, the opinion must be qualified. A qualified opinion states that, except for the effects of the matter to which the qualification relates, the financial statements present fairly, in all material respects, the financial position, results of operations, and cash flows in conformity with generally accepted accounting principles.

An **adverse opinion** is required in any report in which the exceptions to fair presentation are so material that in the independent auditor's judgment a qualified opinion is not justified. In such a case, the financial statements taken as a whole are not presented in accordance with generally accepted accounting principles. Adverse opinions are rare, because most enterprises change their accounting to conform with the auditor's desires.

A **disclaimer of an opinion** is appropriate when the auditor has gathered so little information on the financial statements that no opinion can be expressed.

An example of a report in which the opinion is qualified because of the use of an accounting principle at variance with generally accepted accounting principles is shown in Illustration 25-15 (assuming the effects are such that the auditor has concluded that an adverse opinion is not appropriate).

ILLUSTRATION 25-15
Qualified Auditor's Report

HELIO COMPANY

Independent Auditor's Report

(Same first paragraph as the standard report)

Helio Company has excluded, from property and debt in the accompanying balance sheets, certain lease obligations that, in our opinion, should be capitalized in order to conform with generally accepted accounting principles. If these lease obligations were capitalized, property would be increased by $1,500,000 and $1,300,000, long-term debt by $1,400,000 and $1,200,000, and retained earnings by $100,000 and $50,000 as of December 31, 1996 and 1995, respectively. Additionally, net income would be decreased by $40,000 and $30,000 and earnings per share would be decreased by $.06 and $.04, respectively, for the years then ended.

In our opinion, except for the effects of not capitalizing certain lease obligations as discussed in the preceding paragraph, the financial statements referred to above present fairly, in all material respects, the financial position of Helio Company as of December 31, 1996 and 1995, and the results of its operations and its cash flows for the years then ended in conformity with generally accepted accounting principles.

The profession also requires the auditor to evaluate whether there is substantial doubt about the entity's **ability to continue as a going concern** for a reasonable period of time (not to exceed one year beyond the date of the financial statements). If the auditor concludes that substantial doubt exists, an explanatory note to the auditor's report would be added describing the potential problem.[17]

INTERNATIONAL INSIGHT

In 1992, IOSCO agreed to accept international auditing standards for cross-border listings.

The audit report should provide useful information to the investor. One investment banker noted, "Probably the first item to check is the auditor's opinion to see whether or not it is a clean one—'in conformity with generally accepted accounting principles'—or is qualified in regard to differences between the auditor and company management in the accounting treatment of some major item, or in the outcome of some major litigation."

Management's Reports

Management's Discussion and Analysis

Management's discussion and analysis (MD&A) section covers three financial aspects of an enterprise's business—liquidity, capital resources, and results of operations. **It requires management to highlight favorable or unfavorable trends and to identify significant events and uncertainties that affect these three factors.** This approach obvi-

[17]"The Auditor's Consideration of an Entity's Ability to Continue as a Going Concern," *Statement on Auditing Standards No. 59* (New York: AICPA, 1988).

ously involves a number of subjective estimates, opinions, and soft data. However, the SEC, which has mandated this disclosure, believes the relevance of this information exceeds the potential lack of reliability.

The MD&A section (1999 outlook only) of **Kellogg Company**'s Annual Report is presented in Illustration 25-16.

ILLUSTRATION 25-16
Management's Discussion and Analysis

KELLOGG COMPANY

1999 Outlook

Management is not aware of any adverse trends that would materially affect the Company's strong financial position. Should suitable investment opportunities or working capital needs arise that would require additional financing, management believes that the Company's strong credit rating, balance sheet, and earnings history provide a base for obtaining additional financial resources at competitive rates and terms. Based on the expectation of cereal volume growth, and strong results from product innovation and the continued global roll-out of convenience foods, management believes the Company is well-positioned to deliver sales and earnings growth for the full year 1999. The Company will continue to identify and pursue streamlining and productivity initiatives to optimize its cost structure.

The Company is currently reviewing strategies related to the **Lender's Bagels** business, given its performance since acquisition. The Company has evaluated the recoverability of Lender's long-lived assets as of December 31, 1998, and although this evaluation has not resulted in the recognition of an impairment loss, management expects to update its assessment during 1999.

Additional expectations for 1999 include a gross profit margin of 51–52%, an SGA% of 36–37%, an effective income tax rate of 36–37%, and capital spending of approximately $270 million.

The foregoing projections concerning impact of future borrowing costs, accounting changes, volume growth, profitability, capital spending, and common stock repurchase activity are forward-looking statements that involve risks and uncertainties. Actual results may differ materially due to the impact of competitive conditions, marketing spending and/or incremental pricing actions on actual volumes and product mix; the levels of spending on system initiatives, properties, business opportunities, continued streamlining initiatives, and other general and administrative costs; raw material price and labor cost fluctuations; foreign currency exchange rate fluctuations; changes in statutory tax law; interest rates available on short-term financing; the impact of stock market conditions on common stock repurchase activity; and other items.

UNDERLYING CONCEPTS

FASB Concepts Statement No. 1 notes that management knows more about the enterprise than users and therefore can increase the usefulness of financial information by identifying significant transactions that affect the enterprise and by explaining their financial impact.

The MD&A section also must provide information concerning the effects of inflation and changing prices if material to financial statement trends. No specific numerical computations are specified, and companies have provided little analysis on changing prices.

How this section of the annual report can be made even more effective is the subject of continuing questions such as:

1. Is sufficient forward-looking information being disclosed under current MD&A requirements?
2. Should MD&A disclosures be changed to become more of a risk analysis?
3. Should the MD&A be audited by independent auditors?

www.wiley.com/college/kieso

Go to the Digital Tool for an expanded discussion of accounting for changing prices.

Management's Responsibilities for Financial Statements

The SEC has considered requiring companies to include a report on management's responsibilities including its responsibilities for, and assessment of, the internal control system. Some companies already present this type of information, although the SEC requirements would be more detailed about the internal control procedures used and their effectiveness. An example of the type of disclosure that some companies are now making is shown in Illustration 25-17.

OBJECTIVE 6
Understand management's responsibilities for financials.

ILLUSTRATION 25-17
Report on Management's Responsibilities

UAL CORPORATION

Management Statement on Accounting Controls

The integrity of UAL Corporation's financial records, from which the financial statements are prepared, is largely dependent on the Company's system of internal accounting controls. The purpose of the system is to provide reasonable assurance that transactions are executed in accordance with management's authorization; that transactions are appropriately recorded in order to permit preparation of financial statements which, in all material respects, are presented in conformity with generally accepted accounting principles consistently applied; and that assets are properly accounted for and safeguarded against loss from unauthorized use. Underlying this concept of reasonable assurance is the fact that limitations exist in any system of internal accounting controls based on the premise that the cost of such controls should not exceed the benefits derived therefrom.

To enhance the effective achievement of internal accounting controls, the Company carefully selects and trains its employees, gives due emphasis to appropriate division of clearly defined lines of responsibility and develops and communicates written policies and procedures. Based on a review and monitoring of internal accounting controls, augmented by an internal auditing function and the oversight responsibilities of the outside directors comprising the Audit Committee of the Company's Board of Directors, management believes that the Company's internal accounting control system is adequate and appropriately balances the relationship between the cost of the system and the benefits it provides.

Gerald Greenwald
Chairman and CEO

Douglas A. Hacker
Senior Vice President and CFO

CURRENT REPORTING ISSUES

Reporting on Financial Forecasts and Projections

In recent years, the investing public's demand for more and better information has focused on disclosure of corporate expectations for the future.[18] These disclosures take one of two forms:[19]

OBJECTIVE 7
Identify issues related to financial forecasts and projections.

Financial Forecast. Prospective financial statements that present, to the best of the responsible party's knowledge and belief, an entity's expected financial position, results of operations, and cash flows. A financial forecast is based on the responsible party's assumptions reflecting conditions it expects to exist and the course of action it expects to take.

Financial Projection. Prospective financial statements that present, to the best of the responsible party's knowledge and belief, given one or more hypothetical assumptions, an entity's expected financial position, results of operations, and cash flows. A financial projection is based on the responsible party's assumptions reflecting conditions it expects would

[18]Some areas in which companies are using financial information about the future are equipment lease-versus-buy analysis, analysis of a company's ability to successfully enter new markets, and examining merger and acquisition opportunities. In addition, forecasts and projections are also prepared for use by third parties in public offering documents (requiring financial forecasts), tax-oriented investments, and financial feasibility studies. Use of forward-looking data has been enhanced by the increased capability of the microcomputer to analyze, compare, and manipulate large quantities of data.

[19]"Financial Forecasts and Projections," *Statement of Standards for Accountants' Services on Prospective Financial Information* (New York: AICPA, October 1985), par. 6.

exist and the course of action it expects would be taken, given one or more hypothetical assumptions.

The difference between a financial forecast and a financial projection is that a forecast attempts to provide information on what is expected to happen, whereas a projection may provide information on what is not necessarily expected to happen, but **might** take place.

Financial forecasts are the subject of intensive discussion with journalists, corporate executives, the SEC, financial analysts, accountants, and others. Predictably, there are strong arguments on either side. Listed below are some of the arguments.

Arguments for requiring published forecasts:

1. Investment decisions are based on future expectations; therefore, information about the future facilitates better decisions.
2. Forecasts are already circulated informally, but are uncontrolled, frequently misleading, and not available equally to all investors. This confused situation should be brought under control.
3. Circumstances now change so rapidly that historical information is no longer adequate for prediction.

Arguments against requiring published forecasts:

1. No one can foretell the future. Therefore forecasts, while conveying an impression of precision about the future, will inevitably be wrong.
2. Organizations will strive only to meet their published forecasts, not to produce results that are in the stockholders' best interest.
3. When forecasts are not proved to be accurate, there will be recriminations and probably legal actions.[20]
4. Disclosure of forecasts will be detrimental to organizations, because it will fully inform not only investors, but also competitors (foreign and domestic).

The AICPA has issued a statement on standards for accountants' services on prospective financial information. This statement established procedures and reporting standards for presenting financial forecasts and projections. It requires accountants to provide (1) a summary of significant assumptions used in the forecast or projection and (2) guidelines for minimum presentation.[21]

To encourage management to disclose this type of information, the SEC has a **safe harbor rule**. This rule provides protection to an enterprise that presents an erroneous forecast as long as the forecast is prepared on a reasonable basis and is disclosed in good faith.[22] However, many companies note that the safe harbor rule does not work in practice, since it does not cover oral statements, nor has it kept them out of court.

UNDERLYING CONCEPTS

The AICPA's Special Committee on Financial Reporting indicates that the current legal environment discourages companies from disclosing forward-looking information. Companies should not have to expand reporting of forward-looking information until there are more effective deterrents to unwarranted litigation.

Experience in Great Britain

Great Britain has permitted financial forecasts for years, and the results have been fairly successful. Some significant differences exist between the English and the American business and legal environment,[23] but probably none that could not be overcome if

[20]The issue is serious. Over a recent 3-year period, 8 percent of the companies on the NYSE have been sued because of an alleged lack of financial disclosure. Companies complain that they are subject to lawsuits whenever the stock price drops. And as one executive noted: You can even be sued if the stock price goes up—because you did not disclose the good news fast enough.

[21]"Financial Forecasts and Projections," op. cit., 44 pages.

[22]"Safe-Harbor Rule for Projections," *Release No. 5993* (Washington: SEC, 1979). The Private Securities Litigation Reform Act of 1995 recognizes that some information that is useful to investors is inherently subject to less certainty or reliability than other information. By providing safe harbor for forward-looking statements, Congress has sought to facilitate access to this information by investors.

[23]The British system, for example, does not permit litigation on forecasted information, and the solicitor (lawyer) is not permitted to work on a contingent fee basis. See "A Case for Forecasting—The British Have Tried It and Find That It Works," *World* (New York: Peat, Marwick, Mitchell & Co., Autumn 1978), pp. 10–13.

influential interests in this country cooperated to produce an atmosphere conducive to quality forecasting. A typical British forecast adapted from a construction company's report to support a public offering of stock is as follows:

ILLUSTRATION 25-18
Financial Forecast of a British Company

> Profits have grown substantially over the past 10 years and directors are confident of being able to continue this expansion. . . . While the rate of expansion will be dependent on the level of economic activity in Ireland and England, the group is well structured to avail itself of opportunities as they arise, particularly in the field of property development, which is expected to play an increasingly important role in the group's future expansion.
>
> Profits before taxation for the half year ended 30th June 1999 were 402,000 pounds. On the basis of trading experiences since that date and the present level of sales and completions, the directors expect that in the absence of unforeseen circumstances, the group's profits before taxation for the year to 31st December 1999 will be not less than 960,000 pounds.
>
> No dividends will be paid in respect of the year December 31, 1999. In a full financial year, on the basis of above forecasts (not including full year profits) it would be the intention of the board, assuming current rates of tax, to recommend dividends totaling 40% (of after-tax profits), of which 15% payable would be as an interest dividend in November 2000 and 25% as a final dividend in June 2001.

A general narrative-type forecast issued by a U.S. corporation might appear as follows:

ILLUSTRATION 25-19
Financial Forecast for an American Company

> On the basis of promotions planned by the company for the second half of fiscal 1999, net earnings for that period are expected to be approximately the same as those for the first half of fiscal 1999, with net earnings for the third quarter expected to make the predominant contribution to net earnings for the second half of fiscal 1999.

Questions of Liability

What happens if a company does not meet its forecasts? Are the company and the auditor going to be sued? If a company, for example, projects an earnings increase of 15% and achieves only 5%, should the stockholder be permitted to have some judicial recourse against the company? One court case involving **Monsanto Chemical Corporation** has provided some guidelines. In this case, Monsanto predicted that sales would increase 8 to 9% and that earnings would rise 4 to 5%. In the last part of the year, the demand for Monsanto's products dropped as a result of a business turndown. Therefore, instead of increasing, the company's earnings declined. The company was sued because the projected earnings figure was erroneous, but the judge dismissed the suit because the forecasts were the best estimates of qualified people whose intents were honest.

As indicated earlier, the SEC's safe harbor rules are intended to protect enterprises that provide good-faith projections. However, much concern exists as to how the SEC and the courts will interpret such terms as "good faith" and "reasonable assumptions" when erroneous forecasts mislead users of this information.

Internet Financial Reporting

How can companies improve the usefulness of their financial reporting practices? Many companies are using the power and reach of the Internet to provide more useful information to financial statement readers. Recent surveys indicate that over 80% of large companies have Internet sites, and a large proportion of these companies' Web sites contain links to their financial statements and other disclosures.[24] The increased pop-

[24]The FASB has recently issued a report on electronic dissemination of financial reports. This report summarizes current practice and research conducted on Internet financial reporting. Business Reporting Research Project, "Electronic Distribution of Business Reporting Information" (Norwalk, Conn.: FASB, 2000).

ularity of such reporting is not surprising, since the costs of printing and dissemination of paper reports could be reduced with the use of Internet reporting.

How does Internet financial reporting improve the overall usefulness of a company's financial reports? First, dissemination of reports via the Web can allow firms **to communicate with more users** than is possible with traditional paper reports. In addition, **Internet reporting allows users to take advantage of tools** such as search engines and hyperlinks to quickly find information about the firm and, sometimes, to download the information for analysis, perhaps in computer spreadsheets. Finally, **Internet reporting can help make financial reports more relevant** by allowing companies to report expanded disaggregated data and more timely data than is possible through paper-based reporting. For example, some companies voluntarily report weekly sales data and segment operating data on their Web sites.

Given these benefits and ever-improving Internet tools, will it be long before electronic reporting replaces paper-based financial disclosure? The main obstacles to achieving complete electronic reporting are related to equality of access to electronic financial reporting and the reliability of the information distributed via the Internet. Although companies may practice Internet financial reporting, they must still prepare traditional paper reports because some investors may not have access to the Internet. These investors would receive differential (less) information relative to other "wired" investors if companies were to eliminate paper reports. In addition, at present, Internet financial reporting is a voluntary means of reporting. As a result, there are no standards as to the completeness of reports on the Internet, nor is there the requirement that these reports be audited. One concern in this regard is that computer "hackers" could invade a company's Web site and corrupt the financial information contained therein.

Thus, although Internet financial reporting is gaining in popularity, until issues related to differential access to the Internet and the reliability of information disseminated via the Web are addressed, we will continue to see traditional paper-based reporting.

Fraudulent Financial Reporting

OBJECTIVE 8
Describe the profession's response to fraudulent financial reporting.

The system of financial reporting in the United States is generally considered the finest in the world. The importance of an effective financial reporting system cannot be underestimated, because it provides the financial information that ensures the proper functioning of the capital and credit markets. Unfortunately, the system does not always work as planned. Evidence of the shortcomings of the system includes financial frauds such as E.S.M. Government Securities, Inc., Home-State Savings and Loan of Ohio, American Savings and Loan Association of Florida, Penn Square Bank, Continental Illinois Bank, Beverly Hills Savings and Loan Association, United American Bank, and Drysdale Government Securities as examples.

The case of **E.S.M. Government Securities, Inc. (E.S.M.)** exemplifies the seriousness of these frauds. E.S.M. was a Fort Lauderdale securities dealer entrusted with monies to invest by municipalities from Toledo, Ohio to Beaumont, Texas.[25] The cities provided the cash to E.S.M. which they thought was collateralized with government securities. Examination of E.S.M.'s balance sheet indicated that the company owed about as much as it expected to collect. Unfortunately, the amount it expected to collect was from insolvent affiliates which, in effect, meant that E.S.M. was bankrupt. In fact, E.S.M. had been bankrupt for more than 6 years, and the fraud was discovered only because a customer questioned a note to the balance sheet! More than $300 million of losses had been disguised.

Although frauds such as these are unusual, they do raise questions about the financial reporting process. As indicated in Chapter 1, Congress continues to examine

[25]For an expanded discussion of this case, see Robert J. Sack and Robert Tangreti, "ESM: Implications for the Profession," *Journal of Accountancy*, April 1987.

this process to determine whether improvements can be made. As this textbook is being written, for example, Congress is addressing basic issues such as the following:

1. How well are accounting practices and disclosures serving the public?
2. Are auditors meeting their obligations to the investing public?
3. What are the effects of the SEC's disclosure, compliance, and enforcement policies?
4. Could the effect of these regulatory accounting policies have contributed to these failures?
5. What legislative proposals, if any, are necessary to address perceived weaknesses in accounting and auditing standards and regulatory procedures?

Many other groups have been studying the financial reporting environment. One such group, the National Commission on Fraudulent Financial Reporting, chaired by James C. Treadway, Jr.—hereafter referred to as the **Treadway Commission**—identified causal factors that lead to fraudulent financial reporting and provided steps to reduce its incidence.[26]

The Commission defined **fraudulent financial reporting** **as "intentional or reckless conduct, whether act or omission, that results in materially misleading financial statements."** It also noted that fraudulent reporting can involve gross and deliberate distortion of corporate records (such as inventory count tags), or misapplication of accounting principles (failure to disclose material transactions).[27]

Causes of Fraudulent Financial Reporting

Fraudulent financial reporting usually occurs because of conditions in the internal or external environment.[28] Influences in the **internal environment** relate to poor systems of internal control, management's poor attitude toward ethics, or perhaps a company's liquidity or profitability. Those in the **external environment** may relate to industry conditions, overall business environment, or legal and regulatory considerations.

General incentives for fraudulent financial reporting are the desire to obtain a higher stock price or debt offering, to avoid default on a loan covenant, or to make a personal gain of some type (additional compensation, promotion). Situational pressures on the company or an individual manager also may lead to fraudulent financial reporting. Examples of these situational pressures include:

1. Sudden decreases in revenue or market share. A single company or an entire industry can experience these decreases.
2. Unrealistic budget pressures, particularly for short-term results. These pressures may occur when headquarters arbitrarily determines profit objectives and budgets without taking actual conditions into account.
3. Financial pressure resulting from bonus plans that depend on short-term economic performance. This pressure is particularly acute when the bonus is a significant component of the individual's total compensation.

Opportunities for fraudulent financial reporting are present in circumstances when the fraud is easy to commit and when detection is difficult. Frequently these opportunities arise from:

1. ***The absence of a Board of Directors or audit committee*** that vigilantly oversees the financial reporting process.

[26]"Report of the National Commission on Fraudulent Financial Reporting" (Washington, D.C., 1987).

[27]Ibid, page 2. Unintentional errors as well as corporate improprieties (such as tax fraud, employee embezzlements, and so on) which do not cause the financial statements to be misleading are excluded from the definition of fraudulent financial reporting.

[28]The discussion in this section is taken from the Report of the National Commission on Fraudulent Financial Reporting, pp. 23–24.

2. *Weak or nonexistent internal accounting controls.* This situation can occur, for example, when a company's revenue system is overloaded as a result of a rapid expansion of sales, an acquisition of a new division, or the entry into a new, unfamiliar line of business.
3. *Unusual or complex transactions* such as the consolidation of two companies, the divestiture or closing of a specific operation, and agreements to buy or sell government securities under a repurchase agreement.
4. *Accounting estimates, requiring significant subjective judgment* by company management, such as reserves for loan losses and the yearly provision for warranty expense.
5. *Ineffective internal audit staffs* resulting from inadequate staff size and severely limited audit scope.

A weak corporate ethical climate contributes to these situations. Opportunities for fraudulent financial reporting also increase dramatically when the accounting principles followed in reporting transactions are nonexistent, evolving, or subject to varying interpretations.

Response of the Profession

The profession is working to find solutions to the problem of fraudulent financial reporting. For example, the Auditing Standards Board of AICPA has issued numerous auditing standards in response not only to the Treadway Commission report, but also to the public's higher expectation of the auditor.[29] Recently the Board issued a new standard that "raises the bar" on the performance of financial statement audits by explicitly requiring auditors to assess the risk of material financial misstatement due to fraud.[30]

In addition, the SEC requires disclosure of a change in a company's independent auditor. Many observers have expressed concern about so-called "opinion shopping" in which companies attempt to find a more favorable accounting approach by asking various auditing firms how they would report a given transaction. Because a great deal of subjectivity may be involved, an auditing firm may provide a more favorable response to the prospective client and therefore eventually be engaged as the auditor. To increase public awareness of possible opinion-shopping situations, the SEC has adopted new disclosure requirements concerning certain consultations between a company and its newly engaged auditor during the company's two most recent fiscal years.

Criteria for Making Accounting and Reporting Choices

Throughout this textbook, we have stressed the need to provide information that is useful to predict the amounts, timing, and uncertainty of future cash flows. To achieve this objective, judicious choices between alternative accounting concepts, methods, and means of disclosure must be made. You are probably surprised by the large number of choices among acceptable alternatives that accountants are required to make.

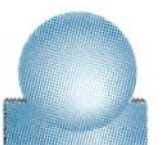

UNDERLYING CONCEPTS

The FASB concept statements on objectives of financial reporting, elements of financial statements, qualitative characteristics of accounting information, and recognition and measurement are important steps in the right direction.

You should recognize, however, as indicated in Chapter 1, that accounting is greatly influenced by its environment. Because it does not exist in a vacuum, it seems unrealistic to assume that alternative presentations of certain transactions and events will be eliminated entirely. Nevertheless, we are hopeful that the profession, through the development of a conceptual framework, will be able to focus on the needs of financial

[29]Because the profession believes that the role of the auditor is not well understood outside the profession, much attention has been focused on the expectation gap. The **expectation gap** is the gap between (1) the expectation of financial statement users concerning the level of assurance they believe the independent auditor provides and (2) the assurance that the independent auditor actually does provide under generally accepted auditing standards.

[30]"Consideration of Fraud in a Financial Statement Audit," *Statement on Auditing Standards No. 82* (New York: AICPA, 1996).

statement users and eliminate diversity where appropriate. The profession must continue its efforts to develop a sound foundation upon which financial standards and practice can be built. As Aristotle said: "The correct beginning is more than half the whole."

SUMMARY OF LEARNING OBJECTIVES

1 Review the full disclosure principle and describe problems of implementation. The full disclosure principle calls for financial reporting of any financial facts significant enough to influence the judgment of an informed reader. Implementing the full disclosure principle is difficult, because the cost of disclosure can be substantial and the benefits difficult to assess. Disclosure requirements have increased because of (1) the growing complexity of the business environment, (2) the necessity for timely information, and (3) the use of accounting as a control and monitoring device.

2 Explain the use of notes in financial statement preparation. Notes are the accountant's means of amplifying or explaining the items presented in the main body of the statements. Information pertinent to specific financial statement items can be explained in qualitative terms, and supplementary data of a quantitative nature can be provided to expand the information in the financial statements. Common note disclosures relate to such items as the following: accounting policies; inventories; property, plant, and equipment; credit claims; contingencies and commitments; and subsequent events.

3 Describe the disclosure requirements for major segments of a business. If only the consolidated figures are available to the analyst, much information regarding the composition of these figures is hidden in aggregated figures. There is no way to tell from the consolidated data the extent to which the differing product lines contribute to the company's profitability, risk, and growth potential. As a result, segment information is required by the profession in certain situations.

4 Describe the accounting problems associated with interim reporting. Interim reports cover periods of less than one year. Two viewpoints exist regarding interim reports. One view (discrete view) holds that each interim period should be treated as a separate accounting period. Another view (integral view) is that the interim report is an integral part of the annual report and that deferrals and accruals should take into consideration what will happen for the entire year.

The same accounting principles used for annual reports should be employed for interim reports. A number of unique reporting problems develop related to the following items: (1) advertising and similar costs; (2) expenses subject to year-end adjustment; (3) income taxes; (4) extraordinary items; (5) changes in accounting; (6) earnings per share; and (7) seasonality.

5 Identify the major disclosures found in the auditor's report. If the auditor is satisfied that the financial statements present the financial position, results of operations, and cash flows fairly in accordance with generally accepted accounting principles, an unqualified opinion is expressed. A qualified opinion contains an exception to the standard opinion; ordinarily the exception is not of sufficient magnitude to invalidate the statements as a whole.

An adverse opinion is required in any report in which the exceptions to fair presentation are so material that a qualified opinion is not justified. A disclaimer of an opinion is appropriate when the auditor has gathered so little information on the financial statements that no opinion can be expressed.

6 Understand management's responsibilities for financials. Management's discussion and analysis section covers three financial aspects of an enterprise's business: liquidity, capital resources, and results of operations. Management has primary responsibility for the financial statements and this responsibility is often indicated in a letter to stockholders in the annual report.

KEY TERMS

7 **Identify issues related to financial forecasts and projections.** The SEC has indicated that companies are permitted (not required) to include profit forecasts in reports filed with that agency. To encourage management to disclose this type of information, the SEC has issued a "safe harbor" rule. The safe harbor rule provides protection to an enterprise that presents an erroneous forecast as long as the projection was prepared on a reasonable basis and was disclosed in good faith. However, the safe harbor rule has not worked well in practice.

8 **Describe the profession's response to fraudulent financial reporting.** Fraudulent financial reporting is intentional or reckless conduct, whether act or omission, that results in materially misleading financial statements. Fraudulent financial reporting usually occurs because of poor internal control, management's poor attitude toward ethics, and so on. The profession is working to find solutions, and has issued a number of auditing standards that address part of the problem.

APPENDIX 25A

Basic Financial Statement Analysis

What would be important to you in studying a company's financial statements? The answer depends on your particular interest—whether you are a creditor, stockholder, potential investor, manager, government agency, or labor leader. For example, **short-term creditors**, such as banks, are primarily interested in the ability of the firm to pay its currently maturing obligations. In that case, you would examine the current assets and their relation to short-term liabilities to evaluate the short-run solvency of the firm. **Bondholders**, on the other hand, look more to long-term indicators, such as the enterprise's capital structure, past and projected earnings, and changes in financial position. **Stockholders**, present or prospective, also are interested in many of the features considered by a long-term creditor. As a stockholder, you would focus on the earnings picture, because changes in it greatly affect the market price of your investment. You also would be concerned with the financial position of the firm, because it affects indirectly the stability of earnings.

The **management** of a company is concerned about the composition of its capital structure and about the changes and trends in earnings. This financial information has a direct influence on the type, amount, and cost of external financing that the company can obtain. In addition, the company finds financial information useful on a day-to-day operating basis in such areas as capital budgeting, breakeven analysis, variance analysis, gross margin analysis, and for internal control purposes.

OBJECTIVE 9
After studying Appendix 25A, you should be able to: Understand the approach to financial statement analysis.

PERSPECTIVE ON FINANCIAL STATEMENT ANALYSIS

Information from financial statements can be gathered by examining relationships between items on the statements and identifying trends in these relationships. The relationships are expressed numerically in ratios and percentages, and trends are identified through comparative analysis. A problem with learning how to analyze statements is that the means may become an end in itself. There are thousands of possible relationships that could be calculated and trends that could be identified. If one knows only how to calculate ratios and trends without understanding how such information can be used, little is accomplished. Therefore, a logical approach to financial statement analysis is necessary. Such an approach may consist of the following steps:

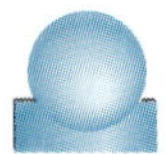

UNDERLYING CONCEPTS

Because financial statements report on the past, they emphasize the *qualitative characteristic of feedback value.* This feedback value is useful because it can be used to better achieve the *qualitative characteristic of predictive value.*

1. ***Know the questions for which you want to find answers.*** As indicated at the beginning of this chapter, various groups have different types of interest in a company.
2. ***Know the questions that particular ratios and comparisons are able to help answer.*** These will be discussed in the remainder of this chapter.
3. ***Match 1 and 2 above.*** By such a matching, the statement analysis will have a logical direction and purpose.

Several caveats must be mentioned. **Financial statements report on the past.** As such, analysis of these data is an examination of the past. Whenever such information is incorporated into a decision-making (future-oriented) process, a critical assumption is that the past is a reasonable basis for predicting the future. This is usually a reasonable approach, but the limitations associated with it should be recognized. Also, ratio and trend analyses will help identify present strengths and weaknesses of a company. They may serve as "red flags" indicating problem areas. In many cases, however, such analyses will not reveal **why** things are as they are. Finding answers about "why" usually requires an in-depth analysis and an awareness of many factors about a company that are not reported in the financial statements—for instance, the impact of inflation, actions of competitors, technological developments, a strike at a major supplier's or buyers operations, and so on.

INTERNATIONAL INSIGHT

Some firms outside the U.S. provide "convenience" financial statements for U.S. readers. These financial statements have been translated into English, and they may also translate the currency units into U.S. dollars. However, the statements are *not restated* using U.S. accounting principles, and financial statement analysis needs to take this fact into account.

Another point is that a **single ratio by itself is not likely to be very useful.** For example, a current ratio of 2 to 1 (current assets are twice current liabilities) may be viewed as satisfactory. However, if the industry average is 3 to 1, such a conclusion may be questioned. Even given this industry average, one may conclude that the particular company is doing well if the ratio last year was 1.5 to 1. Consequently, to derive meaning from ratios, some standard against which to compare them is needed. Such a standard may come from industry averages, past years' amounts, a particular competitor, or planned levels.

Finally, **awareness of the limitations of accounting numbers used in an analysis** is important. We will discuss some of these limitations and their consequences later in this appendix.

RATIO ANALYSIS

OBJECTIVE 10
Identify major analytic ratios and describe their calculation.

Various devices are used in the analysis of financial statement data to bring out the comparative and relative significance of the financial information presented. These devices include ratio analysis, comparative analysis, percentage analysis, and examination of related data. No one device is more useful than another. Every situation faced by the investment analyst is different, and the answers needed are often obtained only upon close examination of the interrelationships among all the data provided. Ratio analysis is the starting point in developing the information desired by the analyst.[1]

Ratios can be classified as follows:

[1]A fairly comprehensive list and explanation of ratios may be found in the AICPA's *CPA/MAS Technical Consulting Practice Aid No. 3,* "Financial Ratio Analysis," by Joseph E. Palmer (New York: AICPA, 1983), 28 pp.

MAJOR TYPES OF RATIOS

LIQUIDITY RATIOS. Measures of the enterprise's short-run ability to pay its maturing obligations.

ACTIVITY RATIOS. Measures of how effectively the enterprise is using the assets employed.

PROFITABILITY RATIOS. Measures of the degree of success or failure of a given enterprise or division for a given period of time.

COVERAGE RATIOS. Measures of the degree of protection for long-term creditors and investors.[2]

Discussions and illustrations about the computation and use of these financial ratios have been integrated throughout this book. Illustration 25A-1 summarizes all of the ratios presented in the book and identifies the specific chapters in which ratio coverage has been presented.

ILLUSTRATION 25A-1
Summary of Financial Ratios

Summary of Ratios Presented in Earlier Chapters

Ratio	Formula for Computation	Reference
I. Liquidity		
1. **Current ratio**	Current assets / Current liabilities	Chapter 13, p. 682
2. **Quick or acid-test ratio**	Cash, marketable securities, and receivables / Current liabilities	Chapter 13, p. 683
3. **Current cash debt ratio**	Net cash provided by operating activities / Average current liabilities	Chapter 5, p. 211
II. Activity		
4. **Receivables turnover**	Net sales / Average trade receivables (net)	Chapter 7, p. 361
5. **Inventory turnover**	Cost of goods sold / Average inventory	Chapter 9, p. 470
6. **Asset turnover**	Net sales / Average total assets	Chapter 11, p. 572
III. Profitability		
7. **Profit margin on sales**	Net income / Net sales	Chapter 11, p. 572
8. **Rate of return on assets**	Net income / Average total assets	Chapter 11, p. 572
9. **Rate of return on common stock equity**	Net income minus preferred dividends / Average common stockholders' equity	Chapter 16, p. 830
10. **Earnings per share**	Net income minus preferred dividends / Weighted shares outstanding	Chapter 17, p. 873
11. **Price earnings ratio**	Market price of stock / Earnings per share	Chapter 16, p. 831
12. **Payout ratio**	Cash dividends / Net income	Chapter 16, p. 831

[2]Other terms may be used to categorize these ratios. For example, liquidity ratios are sometimes referred to as solvency ratios; activity ratios as turnover or efficiency ratios; and coverage ratios as leverage or capital structure ratios.

ILLUSTRATION 25A-1
Continued

IV. Coverage		
13. **Debt to total assets ratio**	Debt / Total assets or equities	Chapter 14, p. 734
14. **Times interest earned**	Income before interest charges and taxes / Interest charges	Chapter 14, p. 736
15. **Cash debt coverage ratio**	Net cash provided by operating activities / Average total liabilities	Chapter 5, p. 211
16. **Book value per share**	Common stockholders' equity / Outstanding shares	Chapter 16, p. 831

Go to the Digital Tool for an expanded discussion of financial statement analysis techniques.

Supplemental coverage of these ratios, accompanied with assignment material, is contained at our Web site. This supplemental coverage takes the form of a comprehensive case adapted from the annual report of a large international chemical company that we have disguised under the name of Anetek Chemical Corporation.

Limitations of Ratio Analysis

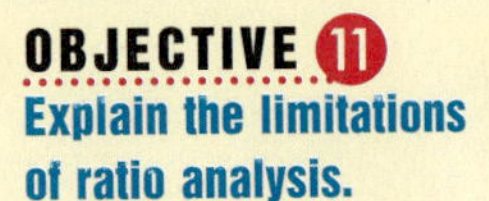
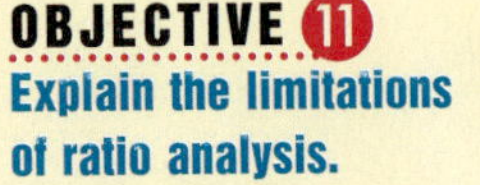
OBJECTIVE 11
Explain the limitations of ratio analysis.

The reader of financial statements must understand the basic limitations associated with ratio analysis. As analytical tools, ratios are attractive because they are simple and convenient. But too frequently, decisions are based on only these simple computations. The ratios are only as good as the data upon which they are based and the information with which they are compared.

One important limitation of ratios is that they are **based on historical cost, which can lead to distortions in measuring performance**. By failing to incorporate changing price information, many believe that inaccurate assessments of the enterprise's financial condition and performance result.

Also, investors must remember that **where estimated items (such as depreciation and amortization) are significant, income ratios lose some of their credibility**. Income recognized before the termination of the life of the business is an approximation. In analyzing the income statement, the user should be aware of the uncertainty surrounding the computation of net income. As one writer aptly noted, "The physicist has long since conceded that the location of an electron is best expressed by a probability curve. Surely an abstraction like earnings per share is even more subject to the rules of probability and risk."[3]

UNDERLYING CONCEPTS
Consistency and comparability are important concepts when financial statement analysis is performed. If the principles and assumptions used to prepare the financial statements are continually changing, it becomes difficult to make accurate assessments of a company's progress.

Probably the greatest criticism of ratio analysis is the **difficult problem of achieving comparability among firms in a given industry**. Achieving comparability among firms requires that the analyst (1) identify basic differences existing in their accounting principles and procedures and (2) adjust the balances to achieve comparability.

Basic differences in accounting usually involve one of the following areas:

1. Inventory valuation (FIFO, LIFO, average cost).
2. Depreciation methods, particularly the use of straight-line versus accelerated depreciation.
3. Capitalization versus expense of certain costs, particularly costs involved in developing natural resources.

[3]Richard E. Cheney, "How Dependable Is the Bottom Line?" *The Financial Executive,* January 1971, p. 12.

4. Pooling versus purchase in accounting for business combinations.
5. Capitalization of leases versus noncapitalization.
6. Investments in common stock carried at equity versus fair value.
7. Differing treatments of postretirement benefit costs.
8. Questionable practices of defining discontinued operations, impairments, and extraordinary items.

The use of these different alternatives can make quite a significant difference in the ratios computed. For example, in the brewing industry, at one time **Anheuser-Busch** noted that if it had used average cost for inventory valuation instead of LIFO, inventories would have increased approximately $33,000,000. Such an increase would have a substantive impact on the current ratio. Several studies have analyzed the impact of different accounting methods on financial statement analysis. The differences in income that can develop are staggering in some cases.[4] The average investor may find it difficult to grasp all these differences, but investors must be aware of the potential pitfalls if they are to be able to make the proper adjustments.

Finally, it must be recognized that a **substantial amount of important information** is not included in a company's financial statements. Events involving such things as industry changes, management changes, competitors' actions, technological developments, government actions, and union activities are often critical to a company's successful operation. These events occur continuously, and information about them must come from careful analysis of financial reports in the media and other sources. Indeed many argue, under what is known as the **efficient market hypothesis**, that financial statements contain "no surprises" to those engaged in market activities. They contend that the effect of these events is known in the marketplace—and the price of the company's stock adjusts accordingly—well before the issuance of such reports.

COMPARATIVE ANALYSIS

OBJECTIVE 12
Describe techniques of comparative analysis.

In **comparative analysis** the same information is presented for two or more different dates or periods so that like items may be compared. Ratio analysis provides only a single snapshot, the analysis being for one given point or period in time. In a comparative analysis, an investment analyst can concentrate on a given item and determine whether it appears to be growing or diminishing year by year and the proportion of such change to related items. Generally, companies present comparative financial statements.[5]

In addition, many companies include in their annual reports 5- or 10-year summaries of pertinent data that permit the reader to examine and analyze trends. *ARB No. 43* concluded that "the presentation of comparative financial statements in annual and other reports enhances the usefulness of such reports and brings out more clearly the nature and trends of current changes affecting the enterprise." An illustration of a 5-year condensed statement with additional supporting data as presented by Anetek Chemical Corporation is presented in Illustration 25A-2.

[4]An example of such a descriptive study is: Curtis L. Norton and Ralph E. Smith, "A Comparison of General Price Level and Historical Cost Financial Statements in the Prediction of Bankruptcy," *The Accounting Review,* January 1979, pp. 72–87.

[5]All 600 companies surveyed in *Accounting Trends and Techniques—1999* presented comparative 1997 amounts in their 1998 balance sheets and presented comparative 1996 and 1997 amounts in their 1998 income statements.

ANETEK CHEMICAL CORPORATION
Condensed Comparative Statements
(000,000 omitted)

	2001	2000	1999	1998	1997	10 Years Ago 1991	20 Years Ago 1981
Sales and other revenue:							
Net sales	$1,600.0	$1,350.0	$1,309.7	$1,176.2	$1,077.5	$636.2	$170.7
Other revenue	75.0	50.0	39.4	34.1	24.6	9.0	3.7
Total	1,675.0	1,400.0	1,349.1	1,210.3	1,102.1	645.2	174.4
Costs and other charges:							
Cost of sales	1,000.0	850.0	827.4	737.6	684.2	386.8	111.0
Depreciation and amortization	150.0	150.0	122.6	115.6	98.7	82.4	14.2
Selling and administrative expenses	225.0	150.0	144.2	133.7	126.7	66.7	10.7
Interest expense	50.0	25.0	28.5	20.7	9.4	8.9	1.8
Taxes on income	100.0	75.0	79.5	73.5	68.3	42.4	12.4
Total	1,525.0	1,250.0	1,202.2	1,081.1	987.3	587.2	150.1
Net income for the year	$ 150.0	$ 150.0	$ 146.9	$ 129.2	$ 114.8	$ 58.0	$ 24.3
Other Statistics							
Earnings per share on common stock (in dollars)[a]	$ 5.00	$ 5.00	$ 4.90	$ 3.58	$ 3.11	$ 1.66	$ 1.06
Cash dividends per share on common stock (in dollars)[a]	2.25	2.15	1.95	1.79	1.71	1.11	.25
Cash dividends declared on common stock	67.5	64.5	58.5	64.6	63.1	38.8	5.7
Stock dividend at approximate market value				46.8		27.3	
Taxes (major)	144.5	125.9	116.5	105.6	97.8	59.8	17.0
Wages paid	389.3	325.6	302.1	279.6	263.2	183.2	48.6
Cost of employee benefits	50.8	36.2	32.9	28.7	27.2	18.4	4.4
Number of employees at year end (thousands)	47.4	36.4	35.0	33.8	33.2	26.6	14.6
Additions to property	306.3	192.3	241.5	248.3	166.1	185.0	49.0

[a]Adjusted for stock splits and stock dividends.

ILLUSTRATION 25A-2
Condensed Comparative Financial Information

PERCENTAGE (COMMON-SIZE) ANALYSIS

OBJECTIVE 13
Describe techniques of percentage analysis.

Analysts also use percentage analysis to help them evaluate and compare companies. **Percentage analysis** consists of reducing a series of related amounts to a series of percentages of a given base. All items in an income statement are frequently expressed as a percentage of sales or sometimes as a percentage of cost of goods sold. A balance sheet may be analyzed on the basis of total assets. This analysis facilitates comparison and is helpful in evaluating the relative size of items or the relative change in items. A conversion of absolute dollar amounts to percentages may also facilitate comparison between companies of different size. To illustrate, here is a comparative analysis of the expense section of Anetek for the last 2 years.

ILLUSTRATION 25A-3
Horizontal Percentage Analysis

ANETEK CHEMICAL

	2001	2000	Difference	% Change Inc. (dec.)
Cost of sales	$1,000.0	$850.0	$150.0	17.6
Depreciation and amortization	150.0	150.0	0	0
Selling and administrative expenses	225.0	150.0	75.0	50.0
Interest expense	50.0	25.0	25.0	100.0
Taxes	100.0	75.0	25.0	33.3

This approach, normally called **horizontal analysis**, indicates the proportionate change over a period of time. It is especially useful in evaluating a trend situation, because absolute changes are often deceiving.

Another approach, called **vertical analysis**, is the proportional expression of each item on a financial statement in a given period to a base figure. For example, Anetek Chemical's income statement using this approach appears below.

ILLUSTRATION 25A-4
Vertical Percentage Analysis

ANETEK CHEMICAL
Income Statement
(000,000 omitted)

	Amount	Percentage of Total Revenue
Net sales	$1,600.0	96%
Other revenue	75.0	4
Total revenue	1,675.0	100
Less:		
Cost of goods sold	1,000.0	60
Depreciation and amortization	150.0	9
Selling and administrative expenses	225.0	13
Interest expense	50.0	3
Income tax	100.0	6
Total expenses	1,525.0	91
Net income	$ 150.0	9%

Reducing all the dollar amounts to a percentage of a base amount is frequently called **common-size analysis** because all of the statements and all of the years are reduced to a common size; that is, all of the elements within each statement are expressed in percentages of some common number and always add up to 100 percent. Common-size (percentage) analysis is the analysis of the composition of each of the financial statements.

In the analysis of the balance sheet, common-size analysis answers such questions as: What is the distribution of equities between current liabilities, long-term debt, and owners' equity? What is the mix of assets (percentage-wise) with which the enterprise has chosen to conduct its business? What percentage of current assets are in inventory, receivables, and so forth?

The income statement lends itself to common-size analysis because each item in it is related to a common amount, usually sales. It is instructive to know what proportion of each sales dollar is absorbed by various costs and expenses incurred by the enterprise.

Common-size statements may be used for comparing one company's statements from different years to detect trends not evident from the comparison of absolute amounts. Also, common-size statements provide intercompany comparisons regardless of size because the financial statements can be recast into a comparable common-size format.

KEY TERMS

acid-test ratio, *1415*
activity ratios, *1415*
asset turnover, *1415*
book value per share, *1416*
cash debt coverage ratio, *1416*
common-size analysis, *1419*
comparative analysis, *1417*
coverage ratios, *1415*
current cash debt ratio, *1415*
current ratio, *1415*
debt to total assets ratio, *1416*
earnings per share, *1415*
horizontal analysis, *1419*
inventory turnover, *1415*
liquidity ratios, *1415*
payout ratio, *1415*
percentage analysis, *1418*
price earnings ratio, *1415*
profit margin on sales, *1415*
profitability ratios, *1415*
quick ratio, *1415*
rate of return on assets, *1415*
rate of return on common stock equity, *1415*
receivables turnover, *1415*
times interest earned, *1416*
vertical analysis, *1419*

SUMMARY OF LEARNING OBJECTIVES FOR APPENDIX 25A

9 **Understand the approach to financial statement analysis.** Basic financial statement analysis involves examining relationships between items on the statements (ratio and percentage analysis) and identifying trends in these relationships (comparative analysis). Analysis is used to predict the future, but ratio analysis is limited because the data are from the past. Also, ratio analysis identifies present strengths and weaknesses of a company but it may not reveal why they are as they are. Although single ratios

are helpful, they are not conclusive; they must be compared with industry averages, past years, planned amounts, and the like for maximum usefulness.

10 **Identify major analytic ratios and describe their calculations.** Ratios are classified as liquidity ratios, activity ratios, profitability ratios, and coverage ratios: (1) *Liquidity ratio analysis* measures the short-run ability of the enterprise to pay its currently maturing obligations. (2) *Activity ratio analysis* measures how effectively the enterprise is using its assets. (3) *Profitability ratio analysis* measures the degree of success or failure of an enterprise to generate revenues adequate to cover its costs of operation and provide a return to the owners. (4) *Coverage ratio analysis* measures the degree of protection afforded long-term creditors and investors.

11 **Explain the limitations of ratio analysis.** One important limitation of ratios is that they are based on historical cost, which can lead to distortions in measuring performance. Also, where estimated items (such as depreciation and amortization) are significant, income ratios lose some of their credibility. In addition, difficult problems of comparability exist because firms use different accounting principles and procedures. Finally, it must be recognized that a substantial amount of important information is not included in a company's financial statements.

12 **Describe techniques of comparative analysis.** Companies present comparative data, which generally includes two years of balance sheet information and three years of income statement information. In addition, many companies include in their annual reports 5- to 10-year summaries of pertinent data that permit the reader to examine and analyze trends.

13 **Describe techniques of percentage analysis.** Percentage analysis consists of reducing a series of related amounts to a series of percentages of a given base. Two approaches are often used. The first, called horizontal analysis, indicates the proportionate change in financial statement items over a period of time; such analysis is most helpful in evaluating trends. Vertical analysis (common-size analysis) is a proportional expression of each item on the financial statements in a given period to a base amount. It analyzes the composition of each of the financial statements from different years (a) to detect trends not evident from the comparison of absolute amounts and (b) to make intercompany comparisons of different sized enterprises.

Note: All **asterisked** Questions, Brief Exercises, Exercises, Problems, and Conceptual Cases relate to materials contained in the appendix to the chapter.

QUESTIONS

1 What are the major advantages of notes to the financial statements? What types of items are usually reported in notes?

2 What is the full disclosure principle in accounting? Why has disclosure increased substantially in the last 10 years?

3 The FASB requires a reconciliation between the effective tax rate and the federal government's statutory rate. Of what benefit is such a disclosure requirement?

4 At the beginning of 2001, Beausoleil Inc. entered into an 8-year nonrenewable lease agreement. Provisions in the lease require the client to make substantial reconditioning and restoration expenditures at the end of the lease. What type of disclosure do you believe is necessary for this type of situation?

5 What type of disclosure or accounting do you believe is necessary for the following items:

(a) Because of a general increase in the number of labor disputes and strikes, both within and outside the industry, there is an increased likelihood that a company will suffer a costly strike in the near future.

(b) A company reports an extraordinary item (net of tax) correctly on the income statement. No other mention is made of this item in the annual report.

(c) A company expects to recover a substantial amount in connection with a pending refund claim for a prior year's taxes. Although the claim is being contested, counsel for the company has confirmed the client's expectation of recovery.

6 The following information was described in a note of Cebar Packing Co. "During August, A. Belew Products Corporation purchased 311,003 shares of the Company's common stock which constitutes approximately 35% of the stock outstanding. A. Belew has since obtained representation on the Board of Directors.

"An affiliate of A. Belew Products Corporation acts as a food broker for the Company in the greater New York City marketing area. The commissions for such services after August amounted to approximately $20,000." Why is this information disclosed?

7 What are the major types of subsequent events? Indicate how each of the following "subsequent events" would be reported.

(a) Collection of a note written off in a prior period.

(b) Issuance of a large preferred stock offering.

(c) Acquisition of a company in a different industry.

(d) Destruction of a major plant in a flood.

(e) Death of the company's chief executive officer (CEO).

(f) Settlement of a four-week strike at additional wage costs.

(g) Settlement of a federal income tax case at considerably more tax than anticipated at year-end.

(h) Change in the product mix from consumer goods to industrial goods.

8 What are diversified companies? What accounting problems are related to diversified companies?

9 What quantitative materiality test is applied to determine whether a segment is significant enough to warrant separate disclosure?

10 Identify the segment information that is required to be disclosed by *FASB Statement No. 131.*

11 What is an operating segment, and when can information about two operating segments be aggregated?

12 The controller for Fong Sai-Yuk Inc. recently commented: "If I have to disclose our segments individually, the only people who will gain are our competitors and the only people that will lose are our present stockholders." Evaluate this comment.

13 An article in the financial press entitled "Important Information in Annual Reports This Year" noted that annual reports include a discussion and analysis section. What would this section contain?

14 "The financial statements of a company are management's, not the accountant's." Discuss the implications of this statement.

15 Nancy Drew, a financial writer, noted recently: "There are substantial arguments for including earnings projections in annual reports and the like. The most compelling is that it would give anyone interested something now available to only a relatively select few—like large stockholders, creditors, and attentive bartenders." Identify some arguments against providing earnings projections.

16 The following recently appeared in the financial press: "Inadequate financial disclosure, particularly with respect to how management views the future and its role in the marketplace, has always been a stone in the shoe. After all, if you don't know how a company views the future, how can you judge the worth of its corporate strategy?" What are some arguments for reporting earnings forecasts?

17 What are interim reports? Why are balance sheets often not provided with interim data?

18 What are the accounting problems related to the presentation of interim data?

19 Mysteries Inc., a closely held corporation, has decided to go public. The controller, C. Keene, is concerned with presenting interim data when a LIFO inventory valuation is used. What problems are encountered with LIFO inventories when quarterly data are presented?

20 What approaches have been suggested to overcome the seasonal problem related to interim reporting?

21 What is the difference between a CPA's unqualified opinion or "clean" opinion and a qualified one?

22 Mary Beidler and Lee Pannebecker are discussing the recent fraud that occurred at Lowrental Leasing, Inc. The fraud involved the improper reporting of revenue to ensure that the company would have income in excess of $1 million. What is fraudulent financial reporting and how does it differ from an embezzlement of company funds?

***23** "The significance of financial statement data is not in the amount alone." Discuss the meaning of this statement.

***24** A close friend of yours, who is a history major and who has not had any college courses or any experience in business, is receiving the financial statements from companies in which he has minor investments (acquired for him by his now deceased father). He asks you what he needs to know to interpret and to evaluate the financial statement data that he is receiving. What would you tell him?

***25** Distinguish between ratio analysis and percentage analysis relative to the interpretation of financial statements. What is the value of these two types of analysis?

***26** In calculating inventory turnover, why is cost of goods sold used as the numerator? As the inventory turnover increases, what increasing risk does the business assume?

***27** What is the relationship of the asset turnover ratio to the rate of return on assets?

***28** Explain the meaning of the following terms: (a) common-size analysis, (b) vertical analysis, (c) horizontal analysis, (d) percentage analysis.

***29** Presently, the profession requires that earnings per share be disclosed on the face of the income statement. What are some disadvantages of reporting ratios on the financial statements?

BRIEF EXERCISES

BE25-1 An annual report of D. Robillard Industries states: "The company and its subsidiaries have long-term leases expiring on various dates after December 31, 2001. Amounts payable under such commitments, without reduction for related rental income, are expected to average approximately $5,711,000 annually for the next 3 years. Related rental income from certain subleases to others is estimated to average $3,094,000 annually for the next 3 years." What information is provided by this note?

BE25-2 An annual report of Ford Motor Corporation states: "Net income a share is computed based upon the average number of shares of capital stock of all classes outstanding. Additional shares of common stock may be issued or delivered in the future on conversion of outstanding convertible debentures, exercise of outstanding employee stock options, and for payment of defined supplemental compensation. Had such additional shares been outstanding, net income a share would have been reduced by 10¢ in the current year and 3¢ in the previous year.

"As a result of capital stock transactions by the company during the current year (primarily the purchase of Class A Stock from Ford Foundation), net income a share was increased by 6¢." What information is provided by this note?

BE25-3 Linden Corporation is preparing its December 31, 2000, financial statements. Two events that occurred between December 31, 2000, and March 10, 2001, when the statements were issued, are described below.

1. A liability, estimated at $150,000 at December 31, 2000, was settled on February 26, 2001, at $170,000.
2. A flood loss of $80,000 occurred on March 1, 2001.

What effect do these subsequent events have on 2000 net income?

BE25-4 Bess Marvin, a student of Intermediate Accounting, was heard to remark after a class discussion on diversified reporting: "All this is very confusing to me. First we are told that there is merit in presenting the consolidated results and now we are told that it is better to show segmental results. I wish they would make up their minds." Evaluate this comment.

BE25-5 Psuikoden Corporation has seven industry segments with total revenues as follows:

Genso	600	Sergei	225
Konami	650	Takuhi	200
RPG	250	Nippon	700
Red Moon	375		

Based only on the revenues test, which industry segments are reportable?

BE25-6 Operating profits and losses for the seven industry segments of Psuikoden Corporation are:

Genso	90	Sergei	(20)
Konami	(40)	Takuhi	34
RPG	25	Nippon	100
Red Moon	50		

Based only on the operating profit (loss) test, which industry segments are reportable?

BE25-7 Identifiable assets for the seven industry segments of Psuikoden Corporation are:

Genso	500	Sergei	200
Konami	550	Takuhi	150
RPG	400	Nippon	475
Red Moon	400		

Based only on the identifiable assets test, which industry segments are reportable?

***BE25-8** Answer each of the questions in the following unrelated situations:

(a) The current ratio of a company is 5 : 1 and its acid-test ratio is 1 : 1. If the inventories and prepaid items amount to $600,000, what is the amount of current liabilities?

(b) A company had an average inventory last year of $200,000 and its inventory turnover was 5. If sales volume and unit cost remain the same this year as last and inventory turnover is 8 this year, what will average inventory have to be during the current year?

(c) A company has current assets of $90,000 (of which $40,000 is inventory and prepaid items) and current liabilities of $30,000. What is the current ratio? What is the acid-test ratio? If the company borrows $15,000 cash from a bank on a 120-day loan, what will its current ratio be? What will the acid-test ratio be?

(d) A company has current assets of $600,000 and current liabilities of $240,000. The board of directors declares a cash dividend of $180,000. What is the current ratio after the declaration, but before payment? What is the current ratio after the payment of the dividend?

***BE25-9** Aston Martin Company's budgeted sales and budgeted cost of goods sold for the coming year are $144,000,000 and $90,000,000 respectively. Short-term interest rates are expected to average 10%. If Aston Martin can increase inventory turnover from its present level of nine times a year to a level of 12 times per year, compute its expected cost savings for the coming year.

***BE25-10** Ferrari Company's net accounts receivable were $1,000,000 at December 31, 2000, and $1,200,000 at December 31, 2001. Net cash sales for 2001 were $400,000. The accounts receivable turnover for 2001 was 5.0. Determine Ferrari's net sales for 2001.

EXERCISES

E25-1 (Post-Balance Sheet Events) Madrasah Corporation issued its financial statements for the year ended December 31, 2002, on March 10, 2003. The following events took place early in 2003.

(a) On January 10, 10,000 shares of $5 par value common stock were issued at $66 per share.
(b) On March 1, Madrasah determined after negotiations with the Internal Revenue Service that income taxes payable for 2002 should be $1,270,000. At December 31, 2002, income taxes payable were recorded at $1,100,000.

Instructions

Discuss how the preceding post-balance sheet events should be reflected in the 2002 financial statements.

E25-2 (Post-Balance Sheet Events) For each of the following subsequent (post-balance sheet) events, indicate whether a company should (a) adjust the financial statements, (b) disclose in notes to the financial statements, or (c) neither adjust nor disclose.

______ **1.** Settlement of federal tax case at a cost considerably in excess of the amount expected at year-end.
______ **2.** Introduction of a new product line.
______ **3.** Loss of assembly plant due to fire.
______ **4.** Sale of a significant portion of the company's assets.
______ **5.** Retirement of the company president.
______ **6.** Prolonged employee strike.
______ **7.** Loss of a significant customer.
______ **8.** Issuance of a significant number of shares of common stock.
______ **9.** Material loss on a year-end receivable because of a customer's bankruptcy.
______ **10.** Hiring of a new president.
______ **11.** Settlement of prior year's litigation against the company.
______ **12.** Merger with another company of comparable size.

E25-3 (Segmented Reporting) Carlton Company is involved in four separate industries. The following information is available for each of the four industries:

Operating Segment	Total Revenue	Operating Profit (Loss)	Identifiable Assets
W	$ 60,000	$15,000	$167,000
X	10,000	3,000	83,000
Y	23,000	(2,000)	21,000
Z	9,000	1,000	19,000
	$102,000	$17,000	$290,000

Instructions

Determine which of the operating segments are reportable based on the:

(a) Revenue test.
(b) Operating profit (loss) test.
(c) Identifiable assets test.

***E25-4 (Ratio Computation and Analysis; Liquidity)** As loan analyst for Utrillo Bank, you have been presented the following information:

	Toulouse Co.	Lautrec Co.
Assets		
Cash	$ 120,000	$ 320,000
Receivables	220,000	302,000
Inventories	570,000	518,000
Total current assets	910,000	1,140,000
Other assets	500,000	612,000
Total assets	$1,410,000	$1,752,000
Liabilities and Capital		
Current liabilities	$ 305,000	$ 350,000
Long-term liabilities	400,000	500,000
Capital stock and retained earnings	705,000	902,000
Total liabilities and capital	$1,410,000	$1,752,000
Annual sales	$ 930,000	$1,500,000
Rate of gross profit on sales	30%	40%

Each of these companies has requested a loan of $50,000 for 6 months with no collateral offered. Inasmuch as your bank has reached its quota for loans of this type, only one of these requests is to be granted.

Instructions

Which of the two companies, as judged by the information given above, would you recommend as the better risk and why? Assume that the ending account balances are representative of the entire year.

***E25-5 (Analysis of Given Ratios)** Picasso Company is a wholesale distributor of professional equipment and supplies. The company's sales have averaged about $900,000 annually for the 3-year period 2000–2002. The firm's total assets at the end of 2002 amounted to $850,000.

The president of Picasso Company has asked the controller to prepare a report that summarizes the financial aspects of the company's operations for the past 3 years. This report will be presented to the Board of Directors at their next meeting.

In addition to comparative financial statements, the controller has decided to present a number of relevant financial ratios which can assist in the identification and interpretation of trends. At the request of the controller, the accounting staff has calculated the following ratios for the 3-year period 2000–2002:

	2000	2001	2002
Current ratio	1.80	1.89	1.96
Acid-test (quick) ratio	1.04	0.99	0.87
Accounts receivable turnover	8.75	7.71	6.42
Inventory turnover	4.91	4.32	3.42
Percent of total debt to total assets	51	46	41
Percent of long-term debt to total assets	31	27	24
Sales to fixed assets (fixed asset turnover)	1.58	1.69	1.79
Sales as a percent of 2000 sales	1.00	1.03	1.07
Gross margin percentage	36.0	35.1	34.6
Net income to sales	6.9%	7.0%	7.2%
Return on total assets	7.7%	7.7%	7.8%
Return on stockholders' equity	13.6%	13.1%	12.7%

In preparation of the report, the controller has decided first to examine the financial ratios independently of any other data to determine if the ratios themselves reveal any significant trends over the 3-year period.

Instructions

(a) The current ratio is increasing while the acid-test (quick) ratio is decreasing. Using the ratios provided, identify and explain the contributing factor(s) for this apparently divergent trend.

(b) In terms of the ratios provided, what conclusion(s) can be drawn regarding the company's use of financial leverage during the 2000–2002 period?

(c) Using the ratios provided, what conclusion(s) can be drawn regarding the company's net investment in plant and equipment?

***E25-6 (Ratio Analysis)** Edna Millay Inc. is a manufacturer of electronic components and accessories with total assets of $20,000,000. Selected financial ratios for Millay and the industry averages for firms of similar size are presented below.

	Edna Millay			2001 Industry Average
	1999	2000	2001	
Current ratio	2.09	2.27	2.51	2.24
Quick ratio	1.15	1.12	1.19	1.22
Inventory turnover	2.40	2.18	2.02	3.50
Net sales to net worth	2.71	2.80	2.99	2.85
Net income to net worth	0.14	0.15	0.17	0.11
Total liabilities to net worth	1.41	1.37	1.44	0.95

Millay is being reviewed by several entities whose interests vary, and the company's financial ratios are a part of the data being considered. Each of the parties listed below must recommend an action based on its evaluation of Millay's financial position.

Archibald MacLeish Bank. The bank is processing Millay's application for a new 5-year term note. Archibald MacLeish has been Millay's banker for several years, but must reevaluate the company's financial position for each major transaction.

Robert Lowell Company. Lowell is a new supplier to Millay, and must decide on the appropriate credit terms to extend to the company.

Robert Penn Warren. A brokerage firm specializing in the stock of electronics firms that are sold over-the-counter, Robert Penn Warren must decide if it will include Millay in a new fund being established for sale to Robert Penn Warren's clients.

Working Capital Management Committee. This is a committee of Millay's management personnel chaired by the chief operating officer. The committee is charged with the responsibility of periodically reviewing the company's working capital position, comparing actual data against budgets, and recommending changes in strategy as needed.

Instructions

(a) Describe the analytical use of each of the six ratios presented above.

(b) For each of the four entities described above, identify two financial ratios, from those ratios presented, that would be most valuable as a basis for its decision regarding Millay.

(c) Discuss what the financial ratios presented in the question reveal about Millay. Support your answer by citing specific ratio levels and trends as well as the interrelationships between these ratios.

(CMA adapted)

PROBLEMS

P25-1 (Subsequent Events) Your firm has been engaged to examine the financial statements of Sabrina Corporation for the year 2002. The bookkeeper who maintains the financial records has prepared all the unaudited financial statements for the corporation since its organization on January 2, 1996. The client provides you with the information below.

SABRINA CORPORATION
Balance Sheet
As of December 31, 2002

Assets		Liabilities	
Current assets	$1,881,100	Current liabilities	$ 962,400
Other assets	5,171,400	Long-term liabilities	1,439,500
		Capital	4,650,600
	$7,052,500		$7,052,500

An analysis of current assets discloses the following:

Cash (restricted in the amount of $400,000 for plant expansion)	$ 571,000
Investments in land	185,000
Accounts receivable less allowance of $30,000	480,000
Inventories (LIFO flow assumption)	645,100
	$1,881,100

Other assets include:	
Prepaid expenses	$ 47,400
Plant and equipment less accumulated depreciation of $1,430,000	4,130,000
Cash surrender value of life insurance policy	84,000
Unamortized bond discount	49,500
Notes receivable (short-term)	162,300
Goodwill, at cost less amortization of $63,000	252,000
Land	446,200
	$5,171,400

Current liabilities include:	
Accounts payable	$ 510,000
Notes payable (due 2004)	157,400
Estimated income taxes payable	145,000
Premium on common stock	150,000
	$ 962,400

Long-term liabilities include:	
Unearned revenue	$ 489,500
Dividends payable (cash)	200,000
8% bonds payable (due May 1, 2007)	750,000
	$1,439,500

Capital includes:	
Retained earnings	$2,810,600
Capital stock, par value $10; authorized 200,000 shares, 184,000 shares issued	1,840,000
	$4,650,600

The supplementary information below is also provided.

1. On May 1, 2002, the corporation issued at 93.4, $750,000 of bonds to finance plant expansion. The long-term bond agreement provided for the annual payment of interest every May 1. The existing plant was pledged as security for the loan. Use straight-line method for discount amortization.
2. The bookkeeper made the following mistakes:
   - **(a)** In 2000, the ending inventory was overstated by $183,000. The ending inventories for 2001 and 2002 were correctly computed.
   - **(b)** In 2002, accrued wages in the amount of $275,000 were omitted from the balance sheet and these expenses were not charged on the income statement.
   - **(c)** In 2002, a gain of $175,000 (net of tax) on the sale of certain plant assets was credited directly to retained earnings.
3. A major competitor has introduced a line of products that will compete directly with Sabrina's primary line, now being produced in a specially designed new plant. Because of manufacturing innovations, the competitor's line will be of comparable quality but priced 50% below Sabrina's line. The competitor announced its new line on January 14, 2003. Sabrina indicates that the company will meet the lower prices that are high enough to cover variable manufacturing and selling expenses, but permit recovery of only a portion of fixed costs.
4. You learned on January 28, 2003, prior to completion of the audit, of heavy damage because of a recent fire to one of Sabrina's two plants; the loss will not be reimbursed by insurance. The newspapers described the event in detail.

Instructions

Analyze the above information to prepare a corrected balance sheet for Sabrina in accordance with proper accounting and reporting principles. Prepare a description of any notes that might need to be prepared. The books are closed and adjustments to income are to be made through retained earnings.

P25-2 (Segmented Reporting) Friendly Corporation is a diversified company that operates in five different industries: A, B, C, D, and E. The following information relating to each segment is available for 2001.

	A	B	C	D	E
Sales	$40,000	$ 80,000	$580,000	$35,000	$55,000
Cost of goods sold	19,000	50,000	270,000	19,000	30,000
Operating expenses	10,000	40,000	235,000	12,000	18,000
Total expenses	29,000	90,000	505,000	31,000	48,000
Operating profit (loss)	$11,000	$ (10,000)	$ 75,000	$ 4,000	$ 7,000
Identifiable assets	$35,000	$ 60,000	$500,000	$65,000	$50,000

Sales of segments B and C included intersegment sales of $20,000 and $100,000, respectively.

Instructions

(a) Determine which of the segments are reportable based on the:
  (1) Revenue test.
  (2) Operating profit (loss) test.
  (3) Identifiable assets test.

(b) Prepare the necessary disclosures required by *FASB No. 131.*

***P25-3 (Ratio Computations and Additional Analysis)** Carl Sandburg Corporation was formed 5 years ago through a public subscription of common stock. Robert Frost, who owns 15% of the common stock, was one of the organizers of Sandburg and is its current president. The company has been successful, but currently is experiencing a shortage of funds. On June 10, Robert Frost approached the Spokane National Bank, asking for a 24-month extension on two $35,000 notes, which are due on June 30, 2001, and September 30, 2001. Another note of $6,000 is due on December 31, 2002, but he expects no difficulty in paying this note on its due date. Frost explained that Sandburg's cash flow problems are due primarily to the company's desire to finance a $300,000 plant expansion over the next 2 fiscal years through internally generated funds.

The Commercial Loan Officer of Spokane National Bank requested financial reports for the last 2 fiscal years. These reports are reproduced below.

CARL SANDBURG CORPORATION
Statement of Financial Position
March 31

Assets	2000	2001
Cash	$ 12,500	$ 18,200
Notes receivable	132,000	148,000
Accounts receivable (net)	125,500	131,800
Inventories (at cost)	50,000	95,000
Plant & equipment (net of depreciation)	1,420,500	1,449,000
Total assets	$1,740,500	$1,842,000
Liabilities and Owners' Equity		
Accounts payable	$ 91,000	$ 69,000
Notes payable	61,500	76,000
Accrued liabilities	6,000	9,000
Common stock (130,000 shares, $10 par)	1,300,000	1,300,000
Retained earnings[a]	282,000	388,000
Total liabilities and owners' equity	$1,740,500	$1,842,000

[a]Cash dividends were paid at the rate of $1.00 per share in fiscal year 2000 and $2.00 per share in fiscal year 2001.

CARL SANDBURG CORPORATION
Income Statement
For the Fiscal Years Ended March 31

	2000	2001
Sales	$2,700,000	$3,000,000
Cost of goods sold[a]	1,425,000	1,530,000
Gross margin	$1,275,000	$1,470,000
Operating expenses	780,000	860,000
Income before income taxes	$ 495,000	$ 610,000
Income taxes (40%)	198,000	244,000
Net income	$ 297,000	$ 366,000

[a]Depreciation charges on the plant and equipment of $100,000 and $102,500 for fiscal years ended March 31, 2000 and 2001, respectively, are included in cost of goods sold.

Instructions

(a) Compute the following items for Carl Sandburg Corporation:
  (1) Current ratio for fiscal years 2000 and 2001.
  (2) Acid-test (quick) ratio for fiscal years 2000 and 2001.
  (3) Inventory turnover for fiscal year 2001.
  (4) Return on assets for fiscal years 2000 and 2001 (assume total assets were $1,688,500 at 3/31/99).
  (5) Percentage change in sales, cost of goods sold, gross margin, and net income after taxes from fiscal year 2000 to 2001.

(b) Identify and explain what other financial reports and/or financial analyses might be helpful to the commercial loan officer of Spokane National Bank in evaluating Robert Frost's request for a time extension on Sandburg's notes.

(c) Assume that the percentage changes experienced in fiscal year 2001 as compared with fiscal year 2000 for sales and cost of goods sold will be repeated in each of the next two years. Is Sandburg's desire to finance the planet expansion from internally generated funds realistic? Discuss.

(d) Should Spokane National Bank grant the extension on Sandburg's notes considering Robert Frost's statement about financing the plant expansion through internally generated funds? Discuss.

***P25-4 (Horizontal and Vertical Analysis)** Presented below are comparative balance sheets for the Eola Yevette Company.

EOLA YEVETTE COMPANY
Comparative Balance Sheet
December 31, 2001 and 2000

	December 31	
	2001	2000
Assets		
Cash	$ 180,000	$ 275,000
Accounts receivable (net)	220,000	155,000
Investments	270,000	150,000
Inventories	960,000	980,000
Prepaid expense	25,000	25,000
Fixed assets	2,685,000	1,950,000
Accumulated depreciation	(1,000,000)	(750,000)
	$3,340,000	$2,785,000
Liabilities and Stockholders' Equity		
Accounts payable	$ 50,000	$ 75,000
Accrued expenses	170,000	200,000
Bonds payable	500,000	190,000
Capital stock	2,100,000	1,770,000
Retained earnings	520,000	550,000
	$3,340,000	$2,785,000

Instructions

(a) Prepare a comparative balance sheet of Yevette Company showing the percent each item is of the total assets or total liabilities and stockholders' equity.
(b) Prepare a comparative balance sheet of Yevette Company showing the dollar change and the percent change for each item.
(c) Of what value is the additional information provided in part (a)?
(d) Of what value is the additional information provided in part (b)?

*P25-5 **(Dividend Policy Analysis)** Dawna Remmers Inc. went public 3 years ago. The board of directors will be meeting shortly after the end of the year to decide on a dividend policy. In the past, growth has been financed primarily through the retention of earnings. A stock or a cash dividend has never been declared. Presented below is a brief financial summary of Dawna Remmers Inc. operations.

			($000 omitted)		
	2001	2000	1999	1998	1997
Sales	$20,000	$16,000	$14,000	$6,000	$4,000
Net income	$ 2,900	$ 1,600	$ 800	$ 900	$ 250
Average total assets	$22,000	$19,000	$11,500	$4,200	$3,000
Current assets	$ 8,000	$ 6,000	$ 3,000	$1,200	$1,000
Working capital	$ 3,600	$ 3,200	$ 1,200	$ 500	$ 400
Common shares:					
Number of shares outstanding (000)	2,000	2,000	2,000	20	20
Average market price	$9	$6	$4	—	—

Instructions

(a) Suggest factors to be considered by the board of directors in establishing a dividend policy.
(b) Compute the rate of return on assets, profit margin on sales, earnings per share, price-earnings ratio, and current ratio for each of the 5 years for Dawna Remmers Inc.
(c) Comment on the appropriateness of declaring a cash dividend at this time, using the ratios computed in part (b) as a major factor in your analysis.

CONCEPTUAL CASES

C25-1 (General Disclosures, Inventories, Property, Plant, and Equipment) Dan D. Lion Corporation is in the process of preparing its annual financial statements for the fiscal year ended April 30, 2001. Because all of Lion's shares are traded intrastate, the company does not have to file any reports with the Securities and Exchange Commission. The company manufactures plastic, glass, and paper containers for sale to food and drink manufacturers and distributors.

Lion Corporation maintains separate control accounts for its raw materials, work-in-process, and finished goods inventories for each of the three types of containers. The inventories are valued at the lower of cost or market.

The company's property, plant, and equipment are classified in the following major categories: land, office buildings, furniture and fixtures, manufacturing facilities, manufacturing equipment, leasehold improvements. All fixed assets are carried at cost. The depreciation methods employed depend upon the type of asset (its classification) and when it was acquired.

Lion Corporation plans to present the inventory and fixed asset amounts in its April 30, 2001, balance sheet as shown below.

Inventories	$4,814,200
Property, plant, and equipment (net of depreciation)	$6,310,000

Instructions

What information regarding inventories and property, plant, and equipment must be disclosed by Dan D. Lion Corporation in the audited financial statements issued to stockholders, either in the body or the notes, for the 2000–2001 fiscal year?

(CMA adapted)

C25-2 (Disclosures Required in Various Situations) Rem Inc. produces electronic components for sale to manufacturers of radios, television sets, and digital sound systems. In connection with her examination of Rem's financial statements for the year ended December 31, 2001, Maggie Zeen, CPA, completed field work 2 weeks ago. Ms. Zeen now is evaluating the significance of the following items prior to preparing her auditor's report. Except as noted, none of these items have been disclosed in the financial statements or notes.

Item 1

A 10-year loan agreement, which the company entered into 3 years ago, provides that dividend payments may not exceed net income earned after taxes subsequent to the date of the agreement. The balance of retained earnings at the date of the loan agreement was $420,000. From that date through December 31, 2001, net income after taxes has totaled $570,000 and cash dividends have totaled $320,000. On the basis of these data the staff auditor assigned to this review concluded that there was no retained earnings restriction at December 31, 2001.

Item 2

Recently Rem interrupted its policy of paying cash dividends quarterly to its stockholders. Dividends were paid regularly through 2000, discontinued for all of 2001 to finance purchase of equipment for the company's new plant, and resumed in the first quarter of 2002. In the annual report dividend policy is to be discussed in the president's letter to stockholders.

Item 3

A major electronics firm has introduced a line of products that will compete directly with Rem's primary line, now being produced in the specially designed new plant. Because of manufacturing innovations, the competitor's line will be of comparable quality but priced 50% below Rem's line. The competitor announced its new line during the week following completion of field work. Ms. Zeen read the announcement in the newspaper and discussed the situation by telephone with Rem executives. Rem will meet the lower prices that are high enough to cover variable manufacturing and selling expenses but will permit recovery of only a portion of fixed costs.

Item 4

The company's new manufacturing plant building, which cost $2,400,000 and has an estimated life of 25 years, is leased from Ancient National Bank at an annual rental of $600,000. The company is obligated to pay property taxes, insurance, and maintenance. At the conclusion of its 10-year noncancellable lease, the company has the option of purchasing the property for $1.00. In Rem's income statement the rental payment is reported on a separate line.

Instructions

For each of the items above discuss any additional disclosures in the financial statements and notes that the auditor should recommend to her client. (The cumulative effect of the four items should not be considered.)

C25-3 (Disclosures Required in Various Situations) You have completed your audit of Keesha Inc. and its consolidated subsidiaries for the year ended December 31, 2001, and were satisfied with the results of your examination. You have examined the financial statements of Keesha for the past 3 years. The corporation is now preparing its annual report to stockholders. The report will include the consolidated financial statements of Keesha and its subsidiaries and your short-form auditor's report. During your audit the following matters came to your attention:

1. A vice-president who is also a stockholder resigned on December 31, 2001, after an argument with the president. The vice-president is soliciting proxies from stockholders and expects to obtain sufficient proxies to gain control of the board of directors so that a new president will be appointed. The president plans to have a note prepared that would include information of the pending proxy fight, management's accomplishments over the years, and an appeal by management for the support of stockholders.
2. The corporation decides in 2001 to adopt the straight-line method of depreciation for plant equipment. The straight-line method will be used for new acquisitions as well as for previously acquired plant equipment for which depreciation had been provided on an accelerated basis.
3. The Internal Revenue Service is currently examining the corporation's 1998 federal income tax return and is questioning the amount of a deduction claimed by the corporation's domestic subsidiary for a loss sustained in 1998. The examination is still in process, and any additional tax liability is indeterminable at this time. The corporation's tax counsel believes that there will be no substantial additional tax liability.

Instructions

(a) Prepare the notes, if any, that you would suggest for the items listed above.

(b) State your reasons for not making disclosure by note for each of the listed items for which you did not prepare a note.

(AICPA adapted)

C25-4 (Disclosures, Conditional and Contingent Liabilities) Presented below are three independent situations.

Situation 1

A company offers a one-year warranty for the product that it manufactures. A history of warranty claims has been compiled and the probable amounts of claims related to sales for a given period can be determined.

Situation 2

Subsequent to the date of a set of financial statements, but prior to the issuance of the financial statements, a company enters into a contract that will probably result in a significant loss to the company. The amount of the loss can be reasonably estimated.

Situation 3

A company has adopted a policy of recording self-insurance for any possible losses resulting from injury to others by the company's vehicles. The premium for an insurance policy for the same risk from an independent insurance company would have an annual cost of $4,000. During the period covered by the financial statements, there were no accidents involving the company's vehicles that resulted in injury to others.

Instructions

Discuss the accrual or type of disclosure necessary (if any) and the reason(s) why such disclosure is appropriate for each of the three independent sets of facts above.

(AICPA adapted)

C25-5 (Post-Balance Sheet Events) At December 31, 2001, Joni Brandt Corp. has assets of $10,000,000, liabilities of $6,000,000, common stock of $2,000,000 (representing 2,000,000 shares of $1.00 par common stock), and retained earnings of $2,000,000. Net sales for the year 2001 were $18,000,000, and net income was $800,000. As auditors of this company, you are making a review of subsequent events on February 13, 2002, and you find the following.

1. On February 3, 2002, one of Brandt's customers declared bankruptcy. At December 31, 2001, this company owed Brandt $300,000, of which $40,000 was paid in January, 2002.
2. On January 18, 2002, one of the three major plants of the client burned.
3. On January 23, 2002, a strike was called at one of Brandt's largest plants, which halted 30% of its production. As of today (February 13) the strike has not been settled.
4. A major electronics enterprise has introduced a line of products that would compete directly with Brandt's primary line, now being produced in a specially designed new plant. Because of manufacturing innovations, the competitor has been able to achieve quality similar to that of Brandt's products, but at a price 50% lower. Brandt officials say they will meet the lower prices, which are high enough to cover variable manufacturing and selling costs but which permit recovery of only a portion of fixed costs.
5. Merchandise traded in the open market is recorded in the company's records at $1.40 per unit on December 31, 2001. This price had prevailed for 2 weeks, after release of an official market report that predicted vastly enlarged supplies; however, no purchases were made at $1.40. The price throughout the preceding year had been about $2.00, which was the level experienced over several years. On January 18, 2002, the price returned to $2.00, after public disclosure of an error in the official calculations of the prior December, correction of which destroyed the expectations of excessive supplies. Inventory at December 31, 2001, was on a lower of cost or market basis.
6. On February 1, 2002, the board of directors adopted a resolution accepting the offer of an investment banker to guarantee the marketing of $1,200,000 of preferred stock.

Instructions

State in each case how the 2001 financial statements would be affected, if at all.

C25-6 (Segment Reporting) You are compiling the consolidated financial statements for Vender Corporation International. The corporation's accountant, Vincent Price, has provided you with the following segment information.

Note 7: Major Segments of Business

VCI conducts funeral service and cemetery operations in the United States and Canada. Substantially all revenues of VCI's major segments of business are from unaffiliated customers. Segment information for fiscal 2001, 2000, and 1999 follows:

(thousands)

	Funeral	Floral	Cemetery	Corporate	Dried Whey	Limousine	Consolidated
Revenues:							
2001	$302,000	$10,000	$ 83,000	$ —	$7,000	$14,000	$416,000
2000	245,000	6,000	61,000	—	4,000	8,000	324,000
1999	208,000	3,000	42,000	—	1,000	6,000	260,000
Operating Income:							
2001	$ 79,000	$ 1,500	$ 18,000	$(36,000)	$ 500	$ 2,000	$ 65,000
2000	64,000	200	12,000	(28,000)	200	400	48,800
1999	54,000	150	6,000	(21,000)	100	350	39,600
Capital Expenditures[a]:							
2001	$ 26,000	$ 1,000	$ 9,000	$ 400	$ 300	$ 1,000	$ 37,700
2000	28,000	2,000	60,000	1,500	100	700	92,300
1999	14,000	25	8,000	600	25	50	22,700
Depreciation and Amortization:							
2001	$ 13,000	$ 100	$ 2,400	$ 1,400	$ 100	$ 200	$ 17,200
2000	10,000	50	1,400	700	50	100	12,300
1999	8,000	25	1,000	600	25	50	9,700
Identifiable Assets:							
2001	$334,000	$ 1,500	$162,000	$114,000	$ 500	$ 8,000	$620,000
2000	322,000	1,000	144,000	52,000	1,000	6,000	526,000
1999	223,000	500	78,000	34,000	500	3,500	339,500

[a]Includes $4,520,000, $111,480,000, and $1,294,000 for the years ended April 30, 2001, 2000, and 1999, respectively, for purchases of businesses.

Instructions

Determine which of the above segments must be reported separately and which can be combined under the category "Other." Then, write a one-page memo to the company's accountant, Vincent Price, explaining the following:

(a) What segments must be reported separately and what segments can be combined.
(b) What criteria you used to determine reportable segments.
(c) What major items for each must be disclosed.

C25-7 (Segment Reporting—Theory) Presented below is an excerpt from the financial statements of **H. J. Heinz Company**

Segment and Geographic Data

The company is engaged principally in one line of business—processed food products—which represents over 90% of consolidated sales. Information about the business of the company by geographic area is presented in the table below.

There were no material amounts of sales or transfers between geographic areas or between affiliates, and no material amounts of United States export sales.

(in thousands of U.S. dollars)	Domestic	Foreign: United Kingdom	Canada	Western Europe	Other	Total	Worldwide
Sales	$2,381,054	$547,527	$216,726	$383,784	$209,354	$1,357,391	$3,738,445
Operating income	246,780	61,282	34,146	29,146	25,111	149,685	396,465
Identifiable assets	1,362,152	265,218	112,620	294,732	143,971	816,541	2,178,693
Capital expenditures	72,712	12,262	13,790	8,253	4,368	38,673	111,385
Depreciation expense	42,279	8,364	3,592	6,355	3,606	21,917	64,196

Instructions

(a) Why does H. J. Heinz not prepare segment information on its products or services?
(b) What are export sales, and when should they be disclosed?
(c) Why are sales by geographical area important to disclose?

 **C25-8 (Segment Reporting—Theory)** The following article appeared in *The Wall Street Journal:*

> WASHINGTON—The Securities and Exchange Commission staff issued guidelines for companies grappling with the problem of dividing up their business into industry segments for their annual reports.
>
> An industry segment is defined by the Financial Accounting Standards Board as a part of an enterprise engaged in providing a product or service or a group of related products or services primarily to unaffiliated customers for a profit.
>
> Although conceding that the process is a "subjective task" that "to a considerable extent, depends on the judgment of management," the SEC staff said companies should consider the nature of the products, the nature of their production and their markets and marketing methods to determine whether products and services should be grouped together or in separate industry segments.

Instructions

(a) What does financial reporting for segments of a business enterprise involve?
(b) Identify the reasons for requiring financial data to be reported by segments.
(c) Identify the possible disadvantages of requiring financial data to be reported by segments.
(d) Identify the accounting difficulties inherent in segment reporting.

C25-9 (Interim Reporting) J. J. Kersee Corporation, a publicly traded company, is preparing the interim financial data which it will issue to its stockholders and the Securities and Exchange Commission (SEC) at the end of the first quarter of the 2000–2001 fiscal year. Kersee's financial accounting department has compiled the following summarized revenue and expense data for the first quarter of the year:

Sales	$60,000,000
Cost of goods sold	36,000,000
Variable selling expenses	2,000,000
Fixed selling expenses	3,000,000

Included in the fixed selling expenses was the single lump sum payment of $2,000,000 for television advertisements for the entire year.

Instructions

(a) J. J. Kersee Corporation must issue its quarterly financial statements in accordance with generally accepted accounting principles regarding interim financial reporting.
  (1) Explain whether Kersee should report its operating results for the quarter as if the quarter were a separate reporting period in and of itself or as if the quarter were an integral part of the annual reporting period.
  (2) State how the sales, cost of goods sold, and fixed selling expenses would be reflected in Kersee Corporation's quarterly report prepared for the first quarter of the 2000–2001 fiscal year. Briefly justify your presentation.
(b) What financial information, as a minimum, must Kersee Corporation disclose to its stockholders in its quarterly reports?

(CMA adapted)

C25-10 (Treatment of Various Interim Reporting Situations) The following statement is an excerpt from Paragraphs 9 and 10 of *Accounting Principles Board (APB) Opinion No. 28,* "Interim Financial Reporting":

> Interim financial information is essential to provide investors and others with timely information as to the progress of the enterprise. The usefulness of such information rests on the relationship that it has to the annual results of operations. Accordingly, the Board has concluded that each interim period should be viewed primarily as an integral part of an annual period.
>
> In general, the results for each interim period should be based on the accounting principles and practices used by an enterprise in the preparation of its latest annual financial statements unless a change in an accounting practice or policy has been adopted in the current year. The Board has concluded, however, that certain accounting principles and practices followed for annual reporting purposes may require modification at interim reporting dates so that the reported results for the interim period may better relate to the results of operations for the annual period.

Instructions

Listed below are six independent cases on how accounting facts might be reported on an individual company's interim financial reports. For each of these cases, state whether the method proposed to be used for interim reporting would be acceptable under generally accepted accounting principles applicable to interim financial data. Support each answer with a brief explanation.

(a) B. J. King Company takes a physical inventory at year end for annual financial statement purposes. Inventory and cost of sales reported in the interim quarterly statements are based on estimated gross profit rates, because a physical inventory would result in a cessation of operations. King Company does have reliable perpetual inventory records.

(b) Florence Chadwick Company is planning to report one-fourth of its pension expense each quarter.

(c) N. Lopez Company wrote inventory down to reflect lower of cost or market in the first quarter. At year end the market exceeds the original acquisition cost of this inventory. Consequently, management plans to write the inventory back up to its original cost as a year-end adjustment.

(d) K. Witt Company realized a large gain on the sale of investments at the beginning of the second quarter. The company wants to report one-third of the gain in each of the remaining quarters.

(e) Alice Marble Company has estimated its annual audit fee. They plan to prorate this expense equally over all four quarters.

(f) Lori McNeil Company was reasonably certain it would have an employee strike in the third quarter. As a result, it shipped heavily during the second quarter but plans to defer the recognition of the sales in excess of the normal sales volume. The deferred sales will be recognized as sales in the third quarter when the strike is in progress. McNeil Company management thinks this is more nearly representative of normal second- and third-quarter operations.

C25-11 (Financial Forecasts) An article in *Barron's* noted:

> Okay. Last fall, someone with a long memory and an even longer arm reached into that bureau drawer and came out with a moldy cheese sandwich and the equally moldy notion of corporate forecasts. We tried to find out what happened to the cheese sandwich—but, rats!, even recourse to the Freedom of Information Act didn't help. However, the forecast proposal was dusted off, polished up and found quite serviceable. The SEC, indeed, lost no time in running it up the old flagpole—but no one was very eager to salute. Even after some of the more objectionable features—compulsory corrections and detailed explanations of why the estimates went awry—were peeled off the original proposal.
>
> Seemingly, despite the Commission's smiles and sweet talk, those craven corporations were still afraid that an honest mistake would lead down the primrose path to consent decrees and class action suits. To lay to rest such qualms, the Commission last week approved a "Safe Harbor" rule that, providing the forecasts were made on a reasonable basis and in good faith, protected corporations from litigation should the projections prove wide of the mark (as only about 99% are apt to do).

Instructions

(a) What are the arguments for preparing profit forecasts?

(b) What is the purpose of the "safe harbor" rule?

(c) Why are corporations concerned about presenting profit forecasts?

***C25-12 (Ratio Analysis and Limitations)** As the CPA for Packard Clipper, Inc., you have been requested to develop some key ratios from the comparative financial statements. This information is to be used to convince creditors that Packard Clipper, Inc. is solvent and to support the use of going-concern valuation procedures in the financial statements.

The data requested and the computations developed from the financial statements follow:

	2001	2000
Current ratio	2.6 times	2.1 times
Acid-test ratio	.8 times	1.3 times
Property, plant, and equipment to stockholders' equity	2.5 times	2.2 times
Sales to stockholders' equity	2.4 times	2.7 times
Net income	Up 32%	Down 9%
Earnings per share	$3.30	$2.50
Book value per share	Up 6%	Up 9%

Instructions

(a) Packard Clipper asks you to prepare a list of brief comments stating how each of these items supports the solvency and going concern potential of the business. The company wishes to use these comments to support its presentation of data to its creditors. You are to prepare the comments as requested, giving the implications and the limitations of each item separately, and then the collective inference that may be drawn from them about Packard Clipper's solvency and going-concern potential.

(b) Having done as the client requested in part (a), prepare a brief listing of additional ratio-analysis-type data for this client which you think its creditors are going to ask for to supplement the data provided in part (a). Explain why you think the additional data will be helpful to these creditors in evaluating the client's solvency.

(c) What warnings should you offer these creditors about the limitations of ratio analysis for the purposes stated here?

*C25-13 **(Effect of Transactions on Financial Statements and Ratios)** The transactions listed below relate to Botticelli Inc. You are to assume that on the date on which each of the transactions occurred the corporation's accounts showed only common stock ($100 par) outstanding, a current ratio of 2.7:1 and a substantial net income for the year to date (before giving effect to the transaction concerned). On that date the book value per share of stock was $151.53.

Each numbered transaction is to be considered completely independent of the others, and its related answer should be based on the effect(s) of that transaction alone. Assume that all numbered transactions occurred during 2001 and that the amount involved in each case is sufficiently material to distort reported net income if improperly included in the determination of net income. Assume further that each transaction was recorded in accordance with generally accepted accounting principles and, where applicable, in conformity with the all-inclusive concept of the income statement.

For each of the numbered transactions you are to decide whether it:

a. Increased the corporation's 2001 net income.
b. Decreased the corporation's 2001 net income.
c. Increased the corporation's total retained earnings directly (i.e., not via net income).
d. Decreased the corporation's total retained earnings directly.
e. Increased the corporation's current ratio.
f. Decreased the corporation's current ratio.
g. Increased each stockholder's proportionate share of total owner's equity.
h. Decreased each stockholder's proportionate share of total owner's equity.
i. Increased each stockholder's equity per share of stock (book value).
j. Decreased each stockholder's equity per share of stock (book value).
k. Had none of the foregoing effects.

Instructions

List the numbers 1 through 10. Select as many letters as you deem appropriate to reflect the effect(s) of each transaction as of the date of the transaction by printing beside the transaction number the letter(s) that identifies that transaction's effect(s).

Transactions

____ **1.** Treasury stock originally repurchased and carried at $127 per share was sold for cash at $153 per share.

____ **2.** The corporation sold at a profit land and a building that had been idle for some time. Under the terms of the sale, the corporation received a portion of the sales price in cash immediately, the balance maturing at six-month intervals.

____ **3.** In January the board directed the writeoff of certain patent rights that had suddenly and unexpectedly become worthless.

____ **4.** The corporation wrote off all of the unamortized discount and issue expense applicable to bonds that it refinanced in 2001.

____ **5.** The board of directors authorized the writeup of certain fixed assets to values established in a competent appraisal.

____ **6.** The corporation called in all its outstanding shares of stock and exchanged them for new shares on a 2-for-1 basis, reducing the par value at the same time to $50 per share.

____ **7.** The corporation paid a cash dividend which had been recorded in the accounts at time of declaration.

____ **8.** Litigation involving Botticelli Inc. as defendant was settled in the corporation's favor, with the plaintiff paying all court costs and legal fees. The corporation had appropriated retained earnings in 1998 as a special contingency appropriation for this court action, and the board directs abolition of the appropriation. (Indicate the effect of reversing the appropriation only.)

____ **9.** The corporation received a check for the proceeds of an insurance policy from the company with which it is insured against theft of trucks. No entries concerning the theft had been made previously, and the proceeds reduce but do not cover completely the loss.

____ **10.** Treasury stock, which had been repurchased at and carried at $127 per share, was issued as a stock dividend. In connection with this distribution, the board of directors of Botticelli Inc. had authorized a transfer from retained earnings to permanent capital of an amount equal to the aggregate market value ($153 per share) of the shares issued. No entries relating to this dividend had been made previously.

(AICPA adapted)

USING YOUR JUDGMENT

FINANCIAL REPORTING PROBLEM: INTEL CORPORATION

In response to the investing public's demand for greater disclosure of corporate expectations for the future, safe-harbor rules and legislation have been passed to encourage and protect corporations that issue financial forecasts and projections. Review Intel's Management Discussion and Analysis section in Appendix 5B.

Instructions

Refer to Intel's financial statements and accompanying notes to answer the following questions.

(a) What general expectation does Intel have for microprocessors and other semiconductor components in the next year, 1999? How is Intel reacting to this expectation?

(b) Give four examples of hard data forecasts Intel discloses for 1999.

(c) What caveats or other statements that temper its forecasts does Intel make?

(d) What is the difference between a financial forecast and a financial projection?

FINANCIAL STATEMENT ANALYSIS CASE

TRI Inc.

Twin Ricky Inc. (TRI) manufactures a variety of consumer products. The company's founders have run the company for thirty years and are now interested in retiring. Consequently, they are seeking a purchaser who will continue its operations, and a group of investors, Donna Inc., is looking into the acquisition of TRI. To evaluate its financial stability and operating efficiency, TRI was requested to provide the latest financial statements and selected financial ratios. Summary information provided by TRI is presented below.

Go to the Digital Tool for additional financial statement analysis problems.

TRI
Statement of Income
For the Year Ended November 30, 2001
(in thousands)

Sales (net)	$30,500
Interest income	500
Total revenue	31,000
Costs and expenses	
Cost of goods sold	17,600
Selling and administrative expense	3,550
Depreciation and amortization expense	1,890
Interest expense	900
Total costs and expenses	23,940
Income before taxes	7,060
Income taxes	2,900
Net income	$ 4,160

TRI
Statement of Financial Position
As of November 30
(in thousands)

	2001	2000
Cash	$ 400	$ 500
Marketable securities (at cost)	500	200
Accounts receivable (net)	3,200	2,900
Inventory	5,800	5,400
Total current assets	9,900	9,000
Property, plant, & equipment (net)	7,100	7,000
Total assets	$17,000	$16,000
Accounts payable	$ 3,700	$ 3,400
Income taxes payable	900	800
Accrued expenses	1,700	1,400
Total current liabilities	6,300	5,600
Long-term debt	2,000	1,800
Total liabilities	8,300	7,400
Common stock ($1 par value)	2,700	2,700
Paid-in capital in excess of par	1,000	1,000
Retained earnings	5,000	4,900
Total shareholders' equity	8,700	8,600
Total liabilities and shareholders' equity	$17,000	$16,000

Selected Financial Ratios

	TRI		Current Industry Average
	1999	2000	
Current ratio	1.62	1.61	1.63
Acid-test ratio	.63	.64	.68
Times interest earned	8.50	8.55	8.45
Net profit margin	12.1%	13.2%	13.0%
Total debt to net worth	1.02	.86	1.03
Total asset turnover	1.83	1.84	1.84
Inventory turnover	3.21	3.17	3.18

Instructions

(a) Calculate a new set of ratios for the fiscal year 2001 for TRI based on the financial statements presented.

(b) Explain the analytical use of each of the seven ratios presented, describing what the investors can learn about TRI's financial stability and operating efficiency.

(c) Identify two limitations of ratio analysis.

(CMA adapted)

COMPARATIVE ANALYSIS CASE

The Coca-Cola Company versus PepsiCo, Inc.

Instructions

Go to the Digital Tool and, using The Coca-Cola Company and PepsiCo, Inc. 1998 Annual Report information, answer the following questions.

(a) (1) What specific items does Coca-Cola discuss in its **Note 1—Accounting Policies** (prepare a list of the headings only)?

(2) What specific items does PepsiCo discuss in its **Note 1—Summary of Significant Accounting Policies** (prepare a list of the headings only)? Note the similarities and differences between Coca-Cola's and PepsiCo's lists.

(b) For what lines of business or segments do Coca-Cola and PepsiCo present segmented information?

(c) Note and comment on the similarities and differences between the auditors' reports submitted by the independent auditors of Coca-Cola and PepsiCo for the year 1998.

RESEARCH CASES

Case 1

The May/June 1994 issue of *Financial Executive* includes an article by Ray J. Groves, entitled "Financial Disclosure: When More Is Not Better."

Instructions

Read the article and answer the following questions.

(a) What is the author's professional background?

(b) What does the article assert regarding the quantity of disclosure presently required under GAAP?

(c) What specific disclosure requirements does the author find excessive?

(d) As of 1972, how many pages were devoted to the annual report, the footnotes to the financial statements, and the MD&A? What were these figures as of 1982?

(e) What were the author's two major suggestions?

Case 2

Companies registered with the Securities and Exchange Commission are required to file a quarterly report on Form 10-Q within 45 days of the end of the first three fiscal quarters.

Instructions

Use EDGAR or some other source to examine the most recent 10-Q for the company of your choice and answer the following questions.

(a) What financial information is included in Part I?

(b) Read the notes to the financial statements and identify any departures from the "integral approach."

(c) Does the 10-Q include any information under Part II? Describe the nature of the information.

ETHICS CASES

Case 1

Patty Gamble, the financial vice-president, and Victoria Maher, the controller, of Castle Manufacturing Company are reviewing the financial ratios of the company for the years 2000 and 2001. The financial vice-president notes that the profit margin on sales ratio has increased from 6% to 12%, a hefty gain for the 2-year period. Gamble is in the process of issuing a media release that emphasizes the efficiency of Castle Manufacturing in controlling cost. Victoria Maher knows that the difference in ratios is due primarily to an earlier company decision to reduce the estimates of warranty and bad debt expense for 2001. The controller, not sure of her supervisor's motives, hesitates to suggest to Gamble that the company's improvement is unrelated to efficiency in controlling cost. To complicate matters, the media release is scheduled in a few days.

Instructions

(a) What, if any, is the ethical dilemma in this situation?

(b) Should Maher, the controller, remain silent? Give reasons.

(c) What stakeholders might be affected by Gamble's media release?

(d) Give your opinion on the following statement and cite reasons: "Because Gamble, the vice-president, is most directly responsible for the media release, Maher has no real responsibility in this matter."

Case 2

In June 2001, the board of directors for Holtzman Enterprises Inc. authorized the sale of $10,000,000 of corporate bonds. Michelle Collins, treasurer for Holtzman Enterprises Inc., is concerned about the date when the bonds are issued. The company really needs the cash, but she is worried that if the bonds are issued before the company's year-end (December 31, 2001) the additional liability will have an adverse effect on a number of important ratios. In July, she explains to company president Kenneth Holtzman that if they delay issuing the bonds until after December 31 the bonds will not affect the ratios until December 31, 2002. They will have to report the issuance as a subsequent event which requires only footnote disclosure. Collins expects that with expected improved financial performance in 2002 ratios should be better.

Instructions

Answer the following questions:

(a) What are the ethical issues involved?

(b) Should Holtzman agree to the delay?

Index

OFFICIAL ACCOUNTING PRONOUNCEMENTS

The following list of official accounting pronouncements constitutes the major part of *generally accepted accounting principles* (GAAP) and represents the authoritative source documents for much of the discussion contained in this book.

Accounting Research Bulletins (ARB's), Committee on Accounting Procedures, AICPA (1953–1959)

Date Issued		No.	Title
June	1953	No. 43	Restatement and Revision of Accounting Research Bulletins Nos. 1–42, and Accounting Terminology Bulletin No. 1 (originally issued 1939–1953)
Oct.	1954	No. 44	Declining-Balance Depreciation; Revised July, 1958 (amended)
Oct.	1955	No. 45	Long-term Construction-type Contracts (unchanged)
Feb.	1956	No. 46	Discontinuance of Dating Earned Surplus (unchanged)
Sept.	1956	No. 47	Accounting for Costs of Pension Plans (superseded)
Jan.	1957	No. 48	Business Combinations (superseded)
April	1958	No. 49	Earnings Per Share (superseded)
Oct.	1958	No. 50	Contingencies (superseded)
Aug.	1959	No. 51	Consolidated Financial Statements (amended and partially superseded)

Accounting Terminology Bulletins, Committee on Terminology, AICPA

Aug.	1953	No. 1	Review and Résumé (of the eight original terminology bulletins) (amended)
Mar.	1955	No. 2	Proceeds, Revenue, Income, Profit, and Earnings (amended)
Aug.	1956	No. 3	Book Value (unchanged)
July	1957	No. 4	Cost, Expense, and Loss (amended)

Accounting Principles Board (APB) Opinions, AICPA (1962–1973)

Nov.	1962	No. 1	New Depreciation Guidelines and Rules (amended)
Dec.	1962	No. 2	Accounting for the "Investment Credit" (amended)
Oct.	1963	No. 3	The Statement of Source and Application of Funds (superseded)
Mar.	1964	No. 4	Accounting for the "Investment Credit" (Amending No. 2)
Sept.	1964	No. 5	Reporting of Leases in Financial Statements of Lessee (superseded)
Oct.	1965	No. 6	Status of Accounting Research Bulletins (partially superseded)
May	1966	No. 7	Accounting for Leases in Financial Statements of Lessors (superseded)
Nov.	1966	No. 8	Accounting for the Cost of Pension Plans (superseded)
Dec.	1966	No. 9	Reporting the Results of Operations (amended and partially superseded)
Dec.	1966	No. 10	Omnibus Opinion—1966 (amended and partially superseded)
Dec.	1967	No. 11	Accounting for Income Taxes (superseded)
Dec.	1967	No. 12	Omnibus Opinion—1967 (partially superseded)
Mar.	1969	No. 13	Amending Paragraph 6 of APB Opinion No. 9, Application to Commercial Banks (unchanged)
Mar.	1969	No. 14	Accounting for Convertible Debt and Debt Issued with Stock Purchase Warrants (unchanged)
May	1969	No. 15	Earnings per Share (superseded)
Aug.	1970	No. 16	Business Combinations (amended)
Aug.	1970	No. 17	Intangible Assets (amended)
Mar.	1971	No. 18	The Equity Method of Accounting for Investments in Common Stock (amended)
Mar.	1971	No. 19	Reporting Changes in Financial Position (amended)
July	1971	No. 20	Accounting Changes (amended)
Aug.	1971	No. 21	Interest on Receivables and Payables (amended)
April	1972	No. 22	Disclosure of Accounting Policies (amended)
April	1972	No. 23	Accounting for Income Taxes—Special Areas (superseded)
April	1972	No. 24	Accounting for Income Taxes—Equity Method Investments (unchanged)
Oct.	1972	No. 25	Accounting for Stock Issued to Employees (unchanged)
Oct.	1972	No. 26	Early Extinguishment of Debt (amended)
Nov.	1972	No. 27	Accounting for Lease Transactions by Manufacturer or Dealer Lessors (superseded)
May	1973	No. 28	Interim Financial Reporting (amended and partially superseded)
May	1973	No. 29	Accounting for Nonmonetary Transactions (unchanged)
June	1973	No. 30	Reporting the Results of Operations (amended)
June	1973	No. 31	Disclosure of Lease Commitments by Lessees (superseded)

Financial Accounting Standards Board (FASB), Statements of Financial Accounting Standards (1973–2000)

Dec.	1973	No. 1	Disclosure of Foreign Currency Translation Information (superseded)
Oct.	1974	No. 2	Accounting for Research and Development Costs
Dec.	1974	No. 3	Reporting Accounting Changes in Interim Financial Statements
Mar.	1975	No. 4	Reporting Gains and Losses from Extinguishment of Debt (amended)
Mar.	1975	No. 5	Accounting for Contingencies (amended)
May	1975	No. 6	Classification of Short-term Obligations Expected to be Refinanced
June	1975	No. 7	Accounting and Reporting by Development Stage Enterprises
Oct.	1975	No. 8	Accounting for the Translation of Foreign Currency Transactions and Foreign Financial Statements (superseded)

Date Issued		No.	Title
Oct.	1975	No. 9	Accounting for Income Taxes—Oil and Gas Producing Companies (superseded)
Oct.	1975	No. 10	Extension of "Grandfather" Provisions for Business Combinations
Dec.	1975	No. 11	Accounting for Contingencies—Transition Method
Dec.	1975	No. 12	Accounting for Certain Marketable Securities (superseded)
Nov.	1976	No. 13	Accounting for Leases (amended, interpreted, and partially superseded)
Dec.	1976	No. 14	Financial Reporting for Segments of a Business Enterprise (amended)
June	1977	No. 15	Accounting by Debtors and Creditors for Troubled Debt Restructurings (amended)
June	1977	No. 16	Prior Period Adjustments
Nov.	1977	No. 17	Accounting for Leases—Initial Direct Costs
Nov.	1977	No. 18	Financial Reporting for Segments of a Business Enterprise—Interim Financial Statements
Dec.	1977	No. 19	Financial Accounting and Reporting by Oil and Gas Producing Companies (amended)
Dec.	1977	No. 20	Accounting for Forward Exchange Contracts (superseded)
April	1978	No. 21	Suspension of the Reporting of Earnings per Share and Segment Information by Nonpublic Enterprises (amended)
June	1978	No. 22	Changes in the Provisions of Lease Agreements Resulting from Refundings of Tax-Exempt Debt
Aug.	1978	No. 23	Inception of the Lease
Dec.	1978	No. 24	Reporting Segment Information in Financial Statements That Are Presented in Another Enterprise's Financial Report
Feb.	1979	No. 25	Suspension of Certain Accounting Requirements for Oil and Gas Producing Companies
April	1979	No. 26	Profit Recognition on Sales-Type Leases of Real Estate
May	1979	No. 27	Classification of Renewals or Extensions of Existing Sales-Type or Direct Financing Leases
May	1979	No. 28	Accounting for Sales with Leasebacks
June	1979	No. 29	Determining Contingent Rentals
Aug.	1979	No. 30	Disclosure of Information about Major Customers
Sept.	1979	No. 31	Accounting for Tax Benefits Related to U.K. Tax Legislation Concerning Stock Relief
Sept.	1979	No. 32	Specialized Accounting and Reporting Principles and Practices in AICPA Statements of Position and Guides on Accounting and Auditing Matters (amended and partially superseded)
Sept.	1979	No. 33	Financial Reporting and Changing Prices (amended and partially superseded)
Oct.	1979	No. 34	Capitalization of Interest Cost (amended)
Mar.	1980	No. 35	Accounting and Reporting by Defined Benefit Pension Plans (amended)
May	1980	No. 36	Disclosure of Pension Information (superseded)
July	1980	No. 37	Balance Sheet Classification of Deferred Income Taxes (amended)
Sept.	1980	No. 38	Accounting for Preacquisition Contingencies of Purchased Enterprises
Oct.	1980	No. 39	Financial Reporting and Changing Prices: Specialized Assets—Mining and Oil and Gas
Nov.	1980	No. 40	Financial Reporting and Changing Prices: Specialized Assets—Timberlands and Growing Timber
Nov.	1980	No. 41	Financial Reporting and Changing Prices: Specialized Assets—Income-Producing Real Estate
Nov.	1980	No. 42	Determining Materiality for Capitalization of Interest Cost
Nov.	1980	No. 43	Accounting for Compensated Absences
Dec.	1980	No. 44	Accounting for Intangible Assets of Motor Carriers
Mar.	1981	No. 45	Accounting for Franchise Fee Revenue
Mar.	1981	No. 46	Financial Reporting and Changing Prices: Motion Picture Films
Mar.	1981	No. 47	Disclosure of Long-Term Obligations (amended)
June	1981	No. 48	Revenue Recognition When Right of Return Exists
June	1981	No. 49	Accounting for Product Financing Arrangements
Nov.	1981	No. 50	Financial Reporting in the Record and Music Industry
Nov.	1981	No. 51	Financial Reporting by Cable Television Companies
Dec.	1981	No. 52	Foreign Currency Translation (amended)
Dec.	1981	No. 53	Financial Reporting by Producers and Distributors of Motion Picture Films
Jan.	1982	No. 54	Financial Reporting and Changing Prices: Investment Companies (superseded)
Feb.	1982	No. 55	Determining Whether a Convertible Security is a Common Stock Equivalent (superseded)
Feb.	1982	No. 56	Designation of AICPA Guide and SOP 81-1 on Contractor Accounting and SOP 81-2 on Hospital-Related Organizations as Preferable for Applying APB Opinion 20 (superseded)
Mar.	1982	No. 57	Related Party Disclosures
April	1982	No. 58	Capitalization of Interest Cost in Financial Statements that Include Investments Accounted for by the Equity Method
April	1982	No. 59	Deferral of the Effective Date of Certain Accounting Requirements for Revision Plans of State and Local Governmental Units
June	1982	No. 60	Accounting and Reporting by Insurance Enterprises (amended)
June	1982	No. 61	Accounting for Title Plant
June	1982	No. 62	Capitalization of Interest Cost in Situations Involving Certain Tax-Exempt Borrowings and Certain Gifts and Grants
June	1982	No. 63	Financial Reporting by Broadcasters

Date Issued		No.	Title
Sept.	1982	No. 64	Extinguishment of Debt Made to Satisfy Sinking-Fund Requirements
Sept.	1982	No. 65	Accounting for Certain Mortgage Bank Activities (amended)
Oct.	1982	No. 66	Accounting for Sales of Real Estate
Oct.	1982	No. 67	Accounting for Costs and Initial Rental Operations of Real Estate Projects
Oct.	1982	No. 68	Research and Development Arrangements
Nov.	1982	No. 69	Disclosures about Oil and Gas Producing Activities
Dec.	1982	No. 70	Financial Reporting and Changing Prices: Foreign Currency Translation
Dec.	1982	No. 71	Accounting for the Effects of Certain Types of Regulation
Feb.	1983	No. 72	Accounting for Certain Acquisitions of Banking or Thrift Institutions
Aug.	1983	No. 73	Reporting a Change in Accounting for Railroad Track Structures
Aug.	1983	No. 74	Accounting for Special Termination Benefits Paid to Employees
Nov.	1983	No. 75	Deferral of the Effective Date of Certain Accounting Requirements for Pension Plans of State and Local Governmental Units (superseded)
Nov.	1983	No. 76	Extinguishment of Debt (superseded)
Dec.	1983	No. 77	Reporting by Transferors for Transfers of Receivables with Recourse (superseded)
Dec.	1983	No. 78	Classifications of Obligations that Are Callable by the Creditor
Feb.	1984	No. 79	Elimination of Certain Disclosures for Business Combinations by Nonpublic Enterprises
Aug.	1984	No. 80	Accounting for Futures Contracts (superseded)
Nov.	1984	No. 81	Disclosure of Postretirement Health Care and Life Insurance Benefits
Nov.	1984	No. 82	Financial Reporting and Changing Prices: Elimination of Certain Disclosures
Mar.	1985	No. 83	Designation of AICPA Guides and Statement of Position on Accounting by Brokers and Dealers in Securities, by Employee Benefit Plans, and by Banks as Preferable for Purposes of Applying APB Opinion 20
Mar.	1985	No. 84	Induced Conversions of Convertible Debt
Mar.	1985	No. 85	Yield Test for Determining Whether a Convertible Security Is a Common Stock Equivalent (superseded)
Aug.	1985	No. 86	Accounting for the Costs of Computer Software to be Sold, Leased, or Otherwise Marketed
Dec.	1985	No. 87	Employers' Accounting for Pensions (amended)
Dec.	1985	No. 88	Employers' Accounting for Settlements and Curtailments of Defined Benefit Pension Plans and for Termination Benefits
Dec.	1986	No. 89	Financial Reporting and Changing Prices
Dec.	1986	No. 90	Regulated Enterprises—Accounting for Abandonments and Disallowances of Plant Costs
Dec.	1986	No. 91	Accounting for Nonrefundable Fees and Costs Associated with Originating or Acquiring Loans and Initial Direct Costs of Leases
Aug.	1987	No. 92	Regulated Enterprises—Accounting for Phase-in Plans
Aug.	1987	No. 93	Recognition of Depreciation by Not-for-Profit Organizations
Oct.	1987	No. 94	Consolidation of All Majority-Owned Subsidiaries
Nov.	1987	No. 95	Statement of Cash Flows
Dec.	1987	No. 96	Accounting for Income Taxes (superseded)
Dec.	1987	No. 97	Accounting and Reporting by Insurance Enterprises for Certain Long-Duration Contracts and for Realized Gains and Losses from the Sale of Investments
June	1988	No. 98	Accounting for Leases; Sale-Leaseback Transactions Involving Real Estate; Sales-Type Leases of Real Estate; Definition of the Lease Term; Initial Direct Costs of Direct Financing Leases
Sept.	1988	No. 99	Deferral of the Effective Date of Recognition of Depreciation by Not-for-Profit Organizations
Dec.	1988	No. 100	Accounting for Income Taxes—Deferral of the Effective Date of FASB Statement No. 96
Dec.	1988	No. 101	Regulated Enterprises—Accounting for the Discontinuation of Application of FASB Statement No. 71
Feb.	1989	No. 102	Statement of Cash Flows—Exemption of Certain Enterprises and Classification of Cash Flows from Certain Securities Acquired for Resale
Dec.	1989	No. 103	Accounting for Income Taxes—Deferral of the Effective Date of FASB Statement No. 96
Dec.	1989	No. 104	Statement of Cash Flows—Net Reporting of Certain Cash Receipts and Cash Payments and Classification of Cash Flows from Hedging Transactions
Mar.	1990	No. 105	Disclosure of Information About Financial Instruments with Off-Balance-Sheet Risk and Financial Instruments with Concentrations of Credit Risk (superseded)
Dec.	1990	No. 106	Employers' Accounting for Postretirement Benefits Other Than Pensions (amended)
Dec.	1991	No. 107	Disclosures about Fair Value of Financial Instruments (amended)
Dec.	1991	No. 108	Accounting for Income Taxes—Deferral of the Effective Date of FASB Statement No. 96
Feb.	1992	No. 109	Accounting for Income Taxes
Aug.	1992	No. 110	Reporting by Defined Benefit Pension Plans of Investment Contracts
Nov.	1992	No. 111	Rescission of FASB Statement No. 32 and Technical Corrections
Nov.	1992	No. 112	Employers' Accounting for Postemployment Benefits
Dec.	1992	No. 113	Accounting and Reporting for Reinsurance of Short-Duration and Long-Duration Contracts
May	1993	No. 114	Accounting by Creditors for Impairment of a Loan (amended)
May	1993	No. 115	Accounting for Certain Investments in Debt and Equity Securities (amended)
June	1993	No. 116	Accounting for Contributions Received and Contributions Made

Date Issued		No.	Title
June	1993	No. 117	Financial Statements of Not-for-Profit Organizations
Oct.	1994	No. 118	Accounting by Creditors for Impairments of a Loan—Income Recognition and Disclosures
Oct.	1994	No. 119	Disclosure about Derivative Financial Instruments and Fair Value of Financial Instruments (superseded)
Jan.	1995	No. 120	Accounting and Reporting by Mutual Life Insurance Enterprises
Mar.	1995	No. 121	Accounting for the Impairment of Long-Lived Assets
May	1995	No. 122	Accounting for Mortgage Servicing Rights (superseded)
Oct.	1995	No. 123	Accounting for Stock-Based Compensation
Nov.	1995	No. 124	Accounting for Certain Investments Held by Not-for-Profit Organizations
June	1996	No. 125	Accounting for Transfers and Servicing of Financial Assets and Extinguishment of Liabilities (amended)
Dec.	1996	No. 126	Exemption from Certain Required Disclosures about Financial Instruments for Certain Nonpublic Entities
Dec.	1996	No. 127	Deferral of the Effective Date of Certain Provisions of FASB Statement No. 125
Feb.	1997	No. 128	Earnings per Share
Feb.	1997	No. 129	Disclosure of Information about Capital Structure
June	1997	No. 130	Reporting Comprehensive Income
June	1997	No. 131	Reporting Disaggregated Information about a Business Enterprise
Feb.	1998	No. 132	Employers' Disclosures about Pensions and Other Postretirement Benefits an amendment of FASB Statements No. 87, 88, and 106
June	1998	No. 133	Accounting for Derivative Instruments and Hedging Activities (amended)
Oct.	1998	No. 134	Accounting for Mortgage-Backed Securities Retained after the Securitization of Mortgage Loans Held for Sale by a Mortgage Banking Enterprise (an amendment of FASB Statement No. 65)
Feb.	1999	No. 135	Rescission of FASB Statement No. 75 and Technical Corrections
June	1999	No. 136	Transfers of Assets to a Not-for-Profit Organization or Charitable Trust That Raises or Holds Contributions for Others
June	1999	No. 137	Accounting for Derivative Instruments and Hedging Activities—Deferral of the Effective Date for FASB Statement No. 133 (an amendment of Statement No. 133)

Financial Accounting Standards Board (FASB), Interpretations (1974–2000)

June	1974	No. 1	Accounting Changes Related to the Cost of Inventory (APB Opinion No. 20)
June	1974	No. 2	Imputing Interest on Debt Arrangements Made Under the Federal Bankruptcy Act (APB Opinion No. 21) (superseded)
Dec.	1974	No. 3	Accounting for the Cost of Pension Plans Subject to the Employee Retirement Income Security Act of 1974 (APB Opinion No. 8)
Feb.	1975	No. 4	Applicability of FASB Statement No. 2 to Purchase Business Combinations
Feb.	1975	No. 5	Applicability of FASB St. No. 2 to Development Stage Enterprises (superseded)
Feb.	1975	No. 6	Applicability of FASB Statement No. 2 to Computer Software
Oct.	1975	No. 7	Applying FASB Statement No. 7 in Statements of Established Enterprises
Jan.	1976	No. 8	Classification of a Short-Term Obligation Repaid Prior to Being Replaced by a Long-Term Security (FASB Std. No. 6)
Feb.	1976	No. 9	Applying APB Opinion No. 16 and 17 when a Savings and Loan or Similar Institution is Acquired in a Purchase Business Combination (APB Op. No. 16 & 17)
Sept.	1976	No. 10	Application of FASB Statement No. 12 to Personal Financial Statements (FASB Std. No. 12)
Sept.	1976	No. 11	Changes in Market Value after the Balance Sheet Date (FASB Std. No. 12)
Sept.	1976	No. 12	Accounting for Previously Established Allowance Accounts (FASB Std. No. 12)
Sept.	1976	No. 13	Consolidation of a Parent and Its Subsidiaries Having Different Balance Sheet Dates (FASB Std. No. 12)
Sept.	1976	No. 14	Reasonable Estimation of the Amount of a Loss (FASB Std. No. 5)
Sept.	1976	No. 15	Translation of Unamortized Policy Acquisition Costs by Stock Life Insurance Company (FASB Std. No. 8) (amended and partially superseded)
Feb.	1977	No. 16	Clarification of Definitions and Accounting for Marketable Equity Securities That Become Nonmarketable (FASB Std. No. 12)
Feb.	1977	No. 17	Applying the Lower of Cost or Market Rule in Translated Financial Statements (FASB Std. No. 8) (superseded)
Mar.	1977	No. 18	Accounting for Income Taxes in Interim Periods (APB Op. No. 28)
Oct.	1977	No. 19	Lessee Guarantee of the Residual Value of Leased Property (FASB Std. No. 13)
Nov.	1977	No. 20	Reporting Accounting Changes under AICPA Statements of Position (APB Op. No. 20)
April	1978	No. 21	Accounting for Leases in a Business Combination (FASB Std. No. 13)
April	1978	No. 22	Applicability of Indefinite Reversal Criteria to Timing Differences (APB Op. No. 11 and 23)
Aug.	1978	No. 23	Leases of Certain Property Owned by a Governmental Unit or Authority (FASB Std. No. 13)
Sept.	1978	No. 24	Leases Involving Only Part of a Building (FASB Std. No. 13)
Sept.	1978	No. 25	Accounting for an Unused Investment Tax Credit (APB Op. No. 2, 4, 11, and 16)
Sept.	1978	No. 26	Accounting for Purchase of a Leased Asset by the Lessee During the Term of the Lease (FASB Std. No. 13)
Nov.	1978	No. 27	Accounting for a Loss on a Sublease (FASB Std. No. 13 and APB Op. No. 30)
Dec.	1978	No. 28	Accounting for Stock Appreciation Rights and Other Variable Stock Option or Award Plans (APB Op. No. 15 and 25) (amended)
Feb.	1979	No. 29	Reporting Tax Benefits Realized on Disposition of Investments in Certain Subsidiaries and Other Investees (APB Op. No. 23 and 24)

Date Issued		No.	Title
Sept.	1979	No. 30	Accounting for Involuntary Conversions of Nonmonetary Assets to Monetary Assets (APB Op. No. 29)
Feb.	1980	No. 31	Treatment of Stock Compensation Plans in EPS Computations (APB Op. No. 15 and Interp. 28) (superseded)
Mar.	1980	No. 32	Application of Percentage Limitations in Recognizing Investment Tax Credit (APB Op. No. 2, 4, and 11)
Aug.	1980	No. 33	Applying FASB Statement No. 34 to Oil and Gas Producing Operations (FASB Std. No. 34)
Mar.	1981	No. 34	Disclosure of Indirect Guarantees of Indebtedness of Others (FASB Std. No. 5)
May	1981	No. 35	Criteria for Applying the Equity Method of Accounting for Investments in Common Stock (APB Op. No. 18)
Oct.	1981	No. 36	Accounting for Exploratory Wells in Progress at the End of a Period
July	1983	No. 37	Accounting for Translation Adjustments upon Sale of Part of an Investment in a Foreign Entity (Interprets FASB Statement No. 52)
Aug.	1984	No. 38	Determining the Measurement Date for Stock Option, Purchase, and Award Plans Involving Junior Stock (Interprets APB Opinion No. 25)
Mar.	1992	No. 39	Offsetting of Amounts Related to Certain Contracts (Interprets APB Opinion No. 10 and FASB Statement No. 105)
Apr.	1993	No. 40	Applicability of Generally Accepted Accounting Principles to Mutual Life Insurance and Other Enterprises (Interprets FASB Statements No. 12, 60, 97, and 113)
Dec.	1994	No. 41	Offsetting of Amounts Related to Certain Repurchase and Reverse Repurchase Agreements
Sept.	1996	No. 42	Accounting for Transfers of Assets in Which a Not-for-Profit Organization is Granted Variance Power
June	1999	No. 43	Real Estate Sales (Interprets FASB Statement No. 66)

Financial Accounting Standards Board (FASB), Technical Bulletins (1979–2000)

Date Issued		No.	Title
Dec.	1979	No. 79-1	Purpose and Scope of FASB Technical Bulletins and Procedures for Issuance
Dec.	1979	No. 79-2	Computer Software Costs
Dec.	1979	No. 79-3	Subjective Acceleration Clauses in Long-Term Debt Agreements
Dec.	1979	No. 79-4	Segment Reporting of Puerto Rican Operations
Dec.	1979	No. 79-5	Meaning of the Term 'Customer' as it Applies to Health Care Facilities under FASB Statement No. 14
Dec.	1979	No. 79-6	Valuation Allowances Following Debt Restructuring
Dec.	1979	No. 79-7	Recoveries of a Previous Writedown under a Troubled Debt Restructuring Involving a Modification of Terms
Dec.	1979	No. 79-8	Applicability of FASB Statements 21 and 33 to Certain Brokers and Dealers in Securities
Dec.	1979	No. 79-9	Accounting in Interim Periods for Changes in Income Tax Rates
Dec.	1979	No. 79-10	Fiscal Funding Clauses in Lease Agreements
Dec.	1979	No. 79-11	Effect of a Penalty on the Term of a Lease
Dec.	1979	No. 79-12	Interest Rate Used in Calculating the Present Value of Minimum Lease Payments
Dec.	1979	No. 79-13	Applicability of FASB Statement No. 13 to Current Value Financial Statements
Dec.	1979	No. 79-14	Upward Adjustment of Guaranteed Residual Values
Dec.	1979	No. 79-15	Accounting for Loss on a Sublease Not Involving the Disposal of a Segment
Dec.	1979	No. 79-16	Effect on a Change in Income Tax Rate on the Accounting for Leveraged Leases
Dec.	1979	No. 79-17	Reporting Cumulative Effect Adjustment from Retroactive Application of FASB No. 13
Dec.	1979	No. 79-18	Transition Requirements of Certain FASB Amendments and Interpretations of FASB Statement No. 13
Dec.	1979	No. 79-19	Investor's Accounting for Unrealized Losses on Marketable Securities Owned by an Equity Method Investee
Dec.	1980	No. 80-1	Early Extinguishment of Debt through Exchange for Common or Preferred Stock
Dec.	1980	No. 80-2	Classification of Debt Restructuring by Debtors and Creditors
Feb.	1981	No. 81-1	Disclosure of Interest Rate Futures Contracts and Forward and Standby Contracts
Feb.	1981	No. 81-2	Accounting for Unused Investment Tax Credits Acquired in a Business Combination Accounted for by the Purchase Method
Feb.	1981	No. 81-3	Multiemployer Pension Plan Amendments Act of 1980
Feb.	1981	No. 81-4	Classification as Monetary or Nonmonetary Items
Feb.	1981	No. 81-5	Offsetting Interest Cost to be Capitalized with Interest Income
Nov.	1981	No. 81-6	Applicability of Statement 15 to Debtors in Bankruptcy Situations
Jan.	1982	No. 82-1	Disclosure of the Sale or Purchase of Tax Benefits through Tax Leases
Mar.	1982	No. 82-2	Accounting for the Conversion of Stock Options into Incentive Stock Options as a Result of the Economic Recovery Tax Act of 1981
July	1983	No. 83-1	Accounting for the Reduction in the Tax Basis of an Asset Caused by the Investment Tax Credit (ITC)
Mar.	1984	No. 84-1	Accounting for Stock Issued to Acquire the Results of a Research and Development Arrangement
June	1984	No. 79-1	Purpose and Scope of FASB Technical Bulletins and Procedures for Issuance (Revised)
Sept.	1984	No. 84-2	Accounting for the Effects of the Tax Reform Act of 1984 on Deferred Income Taxes Relating to Domestic International Sales Corporations
Sept.	1984	No. 84-3	Accounting for the Effects of the Tax Reform Act of 1984 on Deferred Income Taxes of Stock Life Insurance Enterprises
Oct.	1984	No. 84-4	In-Substance Defeasance of Debt

Date Issued		No.	Title
Mar.	1985	No. 85-1	Accounting for the Receipt of Federal Home Loan Mortgage Corporation Participating Preferred Stock
Mar.	1985	No. 85-2	Accounting for Collateralized Mortgage Obligations (CMOs)
Nov.	1985	No. 85-3	Accounting for Operating Leases with Scheduled Rent Increases
Nov.	1985	No. 85-4	Accounting for Purchases of Life Insurance
Dec.	1985	No. 85-5	Issues Relating to Accounting for Business Combinations
Dec.	1985	No. 85-6	Accounting for a Purchase of Treasury Shares
Oct.	1986	No. 86-1	Accounting for Certain Effects of the Tax Reform Act of 1986
Dec.	1986	No. 86-2	Accounting for an Interest in the Residual Value of a Leased Asset
April	1987	No. 87-1	Accounting for a Change in Method of Accounting for Certain Postretirement Benefits
Dec.	1987	No. 87-2	Computation of a Loss on an Abandonment
Dec.	1987	No. 87-3	Accounting for Mortgage Servicing Fees and Rights
Dec.	1988	No. 88-1	Issues Relating to Accounting for Leases
Dec.	1988	No. 88-2	Definition of a Right of Setoff
Dec.	1990	No. 90-1	Accounting for Separately Priced Extended Warranty and Product Maintenance Contracts
Apr.	1994	No. 94-1	Application of Statement 115 to Debt Securities Restructured in a Troubled Debt Restructuring
Dec.	1997	No. 97-1	Accounting under Statement 123 for Certain Employee Stock Purchase Plans with a Look-Back Option

Financial Accounting Standards Board (FASB), Statements of Financial Accounting Concepts (1978–2000)

Date Issued		No.	Title
Nov.	1978	No. 1	Objectives of Financial Reporting by Business Enterprises
May	1980	No. 2	Qualitative Characteristics of Accounting Information
Dec.	1980	No. 3	Elements of Financial Statements of Business Enterprises
Dec.	1980	No. 4	Objectives of Financial Reporting by Nonbusiness Organizations
Dec.	1984	No. 5	Recognition and Measurement in Financial Statements of Business Enterprises
Dec.	1985	No. 6	Elements of Financial Statements
Feb.	2000	No. 7	Using Cash Flow Information and Present Value in Accounting Measurements

NATIONAL ACCOUNTING BOARDS AND ORGANIZATIONS

American Accounting Association (AAA)
5717 Bessie Drive
Sarasota, FL 34233
(941) 921-7747
www.aaa-edu.org

American Institute of Certified Public Accountants (AICPA)
1211 Avenue of The Americas
New York, NY 10036
(212) 596-6200
www.aicpa.org

Association of Government Accountants (AGA)
2200 Mount Vernon Ave.
Alexandria, VA 22301
(703) 684-6931
www.rutgers.edu/accounting/raw/aga/home.htm

Financial Accounting Standards Board (FASB)
401 Merritt 7
P.O. Box 5116
Norwalk, CT 06856
(203) 847-0700
www.fasb.org

Financial Executives Institute (FEI)
10 Madison Ave.
P.O. Box 1938
Morristown, NJ 07962-1938
(201) 898-4609
www.ferf.org

Governmental Accounting Standards Board (GASB)
401 Merritt 7
P.O. Box 5116
Norwalk, CT 06856
(203) 847-0700
www.fasb.org

Institute of Certified Management Accountants
10 Paragon Drive
Montvale, NJ 07645-1760
(201) 573-9000
www.imanet.org

Institute of Internal Auditors (IIA)
249 Maitland Avenue, P.O. Box 1119
Altamonte Springs, FL 32701
(407) 830-7600
www.theiia.org

Institute of Management Accountants (IMA)
10 Paragon Drive
Montvale, NJ 07645-1760
(201) 573-9000
www.imanet.org

Securities and Exchange Commission (SEC)
450 Fifth Street NW
Washington, DC 20549
(202) 942-8088
www.sec.gov

CHAPTER 12

Intangible Assets

Trying to Grasp the Intangible

In 1494, a mathematically minded Venetian monk named Luca Pacioli published his *Summa de Arithmetica, Geometrica,* the first accounting textbook. It illustrated double-entry accounting, a system that makes the modern corporation manageable, even possible. Today, half a millennium later, Pacioli's process, still pretty much intact, is being challenged like never before.

Pacioli's accounting system lets businesses keep track of changes in their assets. But this system deals primarily with *tangible assets* such as cash, inventory, investments, receivables, and property, plant, and equipment. What go unrecorded are *intangible assets* such as quality of management, customer loyalty, information infrastructure, trade secrets, patents, goodwill, research, and, considered by some the ultimate intangible, *knowledge*—a company's intellectual capital. As present FASB chairman Edmund Jenkins attests, "The components of cost in a product today are largely R & D, intellectual assets, and services. The old accounting system, which tells us the cost of material and labor, isn't applicable." Argues Professor James Quinn of Dartmouth College, "Even in manufacturing, perhaps three-fourths of the value added derives from knowledge."[1]

This refrain is echoed by the managing editor of *Fortune* magazine, Walter Kiechel, who says, "To be sure, there are still industries in which the factory confers a competitive advantage. But this is changing fast, as more and more companies realize that their edge derives less from their machines, bricks, and mortar than from what we used to think of as the intangibles, like the brainpower resident in the corporation."[2]

In this emerging economy of knowledge, even some banks have concluded that "soft" assets (like computer programming know-how and information infrastructure) can be a better credit risk than "hard" assets (like buildings). But how should the "soft assets" be valued? Accountants get little solace from former FASB chairman Donald Kirk, who acknowledges, "There are arguments that balance sheets ignore certain intangibles, but the reporting issues of trying to recognize them are, in my mind, insurmountable."[3] It appears that the assets that really count are the ones accountants can't count—yet.

[1]Thomas Stewart, "Your Company's Most Valuable Asset: Intellectual Capital," *Fortune,* October 3, 1994, p. 68.

[2]"Searching for Nonfiction in Financial Statements," *Fortune,* December 23, 1996, p. 38.

[3]Ibid.

LEARNING OBJECTIVES

After studying this chapter, you should be able to:

1. **Describe the characteristics of intangible assets.**
2. **Identify the costs included in the initial valuation of intangible assets.**
3. **Explain the procedure for amortizing intangible assets.**
4. **Identify the types of intangible assets.**
5. **Explain the conceptual issues related to goodwill.**
6. **Describe the accounting procedures for recording goodwill.**
7. **Explain the accounting issues related to intangible asset impairments.**
8. **Identify the conceptual issues related to research and development costs.**
9. **Describe the accounting procedures for research and development costs and for other similar costs.**
10. **Indicate the presentation of intangible assets and related items.**

PREVIEW OF CHAPTER 12

As the opening story indicates, the accounting and reporting of intangibles is taking on increasing importance in this information age. The purpose of this chapter is to explain the basic conceptual and reporting issues related to intangible assets. The content and organization of the chapter are as follows:

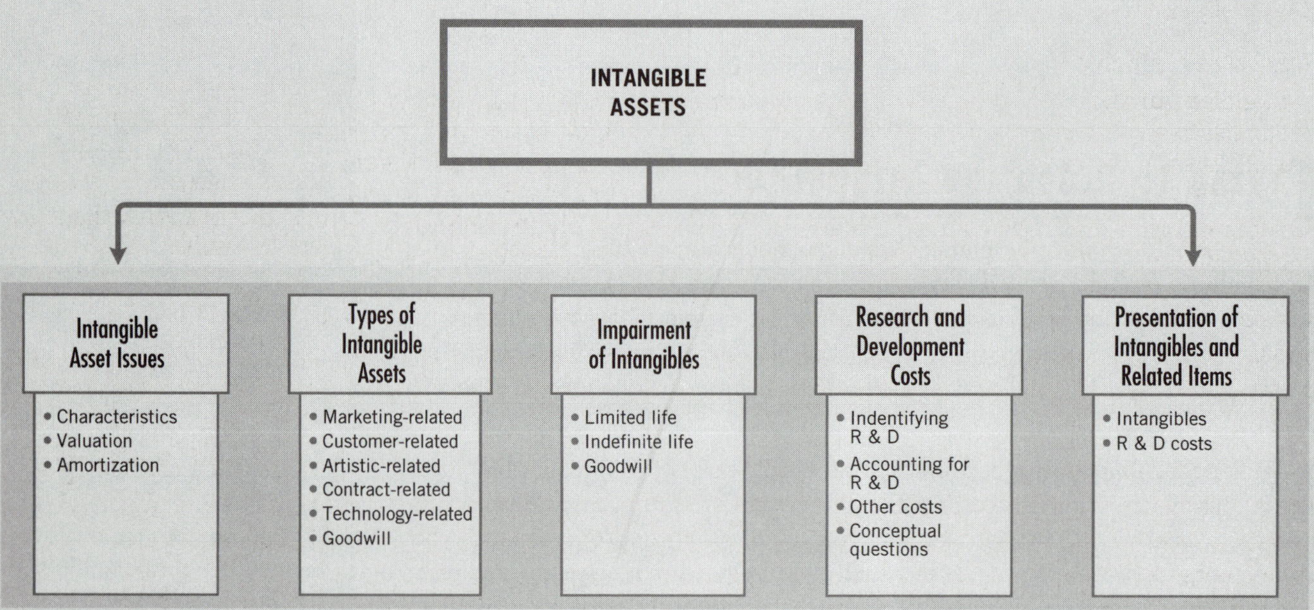

INTANGIBLE ASSET ISSUES

Characteristics

OBJECTIVE 1
Describe the characteristics of intangible assets.

Gap Inc.'s most important asset is not store fixtures—brand image is. The major asset of **Coca-Cola** is not its plant facilities—its secret formula for making Coke is. **America Online**'s most important asset is not its Internet connection equipment—its subscriber base is. As these examples show, we have an economy dominated today by information and service providers, and their major assets are often intangible in nature. Accounting for these intangibles is difficult, and as a result many intangibles are presently not reported on a company's balance sheet. **Intangible assets** have two main characteristics.[4]

1. **They lack physical existence.** Unlike tangible assets such as property, plant, and equipment, intangible assets derive their value from the rights and privileges granted to the company using them.
2. **They are not financial instruments.** Assets such as bank deposits, accounts receivable, and long-term investments in bonds and stocks lack physical substance, but are not classified as intangible assets. These assets are financial instruments and derive their value from the right (claim) to receive cash or cash equivalents in the future.

[4] "Goodwill and Other Intangible Assets," *Statement of Financial Accounting Standards No. 142* (Norwalk, Conn.: FASB, 2001).

In most cases, intangible assets provide services over a period of years. As a result, they are normally classified as long-term assets. The most common types of intangibles are patents, copyrights, franchises or licenses, trademarks or trade names, and goodwill.

Valuation

Purchased Intangibles

OBJECTIVE 2
Identify the costs included in the initial valuation of intangible assets.

Intangibles purchased from another party are **recorded at cost**. Cost includes all costs of acquisition and expenditures necessary to make the intangible asset ready for its intended use—for example, purchase price, legal fees, and other incidental expenses.

If intangibles are acquired for stock or in exchange for other assets, **the cost of the intangible is the fair value of the consideration given or the fair value of the intangible received, whichever is more clearly evident**. When several intangibles, or a combination of intangibles and tangibles, are bought in a "basket purchase," the cost should be allocated on the basis of fair values. Essentially the accounting treatment for purchased intangibles closely parallels that followed for purchased tangible assets.

UNDERLYING CONCEPTS

The basic attributes of intangibles, their uncertainty as to future benefits, and their uniqueness, have discouraged valuation in excess of cost.

Internally-Created Intangibles

Costs incurred internally to create intangibles are generally expensed as incurred. Thus, even though a company may incur substantial research and development costs to create an intangible, these costs are expensed. Various reasons are given for this approach. Some argue that the costs incurred internally to create intangibles bear no relationship to their real value; therefore, expensing these costs is appropriate. Others note that with a purchased intangible, a reliable number for the cost of the intangible can be determined; with internally developed intangibles, it is difficult to associate costs with specific intangible assets. And others argue that due to the underlying subjectivity related to intangibles, a conservative approach should be followed—that is, expense as incurred. As a result, the **only internal costs capitalized are direct costs** incurred in obtaining the intangible, such as legal costs.

INTERNATIONAL INSIGHT

In Japan the cost of intangibles can be capitalized whether they are externally purchased or internally developed.

Amortization of Intangibles

OBJECTIVE 3
Explain the procedure for amortizing intangible assets.

Intangibles have either a **limited (finite) useful life** or an **indefinite useful life**. An intangible asset with a **limited life is amortized**; an intangible asset with an **indefinite life is not amortized**.

Limited-Life Intangibles

As you learned in Chapter 11, the expiration of intangible assets is called **amortization**. Limited-life intangibles should be amortized by systematic charges to expense over their useful life. The useful life should reflect the periods over which these assets will contribute to cash flows. Factors considered in determining useful life are:

1. The expected use of the asset by the entity.
2. The expected useful life of another asset or a group of assets to which the useful life of the intangible asset may relate (such as mineral rights to depleting assets).
3. Any legal, regulatory, or contractual provisions that may limit the useful life.
4. Any legal, regulatory, or contractual provisions that enable renewal or extension of the asset's legal or contractual life without substantial cost. (This factor assumes that there is evidence to support renewal or extension and that renewal or extension can be accomplished without material modifications of the existing terms and conditions.)

5. The effects of obsolescence, demand, competition, and other economic factors. (Examples include the stability of the industry, known technological advances, legislative action that results in an uncertain or changing regulatory environment, and expected changes in distribution channels.)
6. The level of maintenance expenditure required to obtain the expected future cash flows from the asset. (For example, a material level of required maintenance in relation to the carrying amount of the asset may suggest a very limited useful life.)[5]

The amount of amortization expense for a limited-life intangible asset should reflect the pattern in which the asset is consumed or used up, if that pattern can be reliably determined. For example, assume that Second Wave, Inc. has purchased a license to provide a limited quantity of a gene product, called Mega. The cost of the license should be amortized following the pattern of use of Mega. If the pattern of production or consumption cannot be determined, the straight-line method of amortization should be used. For homework problems, assume the use of the straight-line method unless stated otherwise.

When intangible assets are amortized the charges should be shown as expenses, and the credits should be made either to the appropriate asset accounts or to separate accumulated amortization accounts.

The amount of an intangible asset to be amortized should be its cost less residual value. The residual value is assumed to be zero unless at the end of its useful life the intangible asset has value to another entity. For example, if U2D Co. has a commitment from Hardy Co. to purchase its intangible asset at the end of its useful life, U2D Co. should reduce the cost of its intangible asset by the residual value. Similarly, if market values for residual values can be reliably determined, market values should be considered.

What happens if a limited-life intangible asset's useful life is changed? In that case the remaining carrying amount should be amortized over the revised remaining useful life. Limited-life intangibles should be continually evaluated for impairment. Similar to property, plant, and equipment, an impairment loss should be recognized if the carrying amount of the intangible is not recoverable and its carrying amount exceeds its fair value. The accounting for impairments is discussed below.

Indefinite-Life Intangibles

If no legal, regulatory, contractual, competitive, or other factors limit the useful life of an intangible asset, the useful life is considered indefinite. **Indefinite** means that there is no foreseeable limit on the period of time over which the intangible asset is expected to provide cash flows. An intangible asset with an indefinite life is not amortized. To illustrate, assume that Double Clik, Inc. acquired a trademark that is used to distinguish a leading consumer product. The trademark is renewable every 10 years at minimal cost. All evidence indicates that this trademark product will generate cash flows for an indefinite period of time. In this case, the trademark has an indefinite life because it is expected to contribute to cash flows indefinitely.

Indefinite-life intangibles should be tested for impairment at least annually. The impairment test compares the fair value of an intangible asset with its carrying amount. This impairment test is different from the one used for a limited-life intangible. That is, there is no recoverability test related to indefinite-life intangibles, only the fair value test. The reason: Indefinite-life intangible assets might never fail the undiscounted cash flows recoverability test because cash flows could extend indefinitely into the future.

In summary, the accounting treatment for intangible assets is shown in Illustration 12-1.

---

[5]Ibid, par. 11.

ILLUSTRATION 12-1
Accounting Treatment for Intangibles

Type of Intangible	Manner Acquired: Purchased	Manner Acquired: Internally Created	Amortization	Impairment Test
Limited-life intangibles	Capitalize	Expense*	Over useful life	Recoverability test and then fair value test
Indefinite-life intangibles	Capitalize	Expense*	Do not amortize	Fair value test

*Except for direct costs, such as legal costs.

TYPES OF INTANGIBLE ASSETS

OBJECTIVE 4
Identify the types of intangible assets.

As indicated, the accounting for intangible assets depends on whether the intangible has a limited or an indefinite life. There are many different types of intangibles, and they are often classified into the following six major categories.[6]

1. Marketing-related intangible assets.
2. Customer-related intangible assets.
3. Artistic-related intangible assets.
4. Contract-related intangible assets.
5. Technology-related intangible assets.
6. Goodwill.

Marketing-Related Intangible Assets

Marketing-related intangible assets are those assets primarily used in the marketing or promotion of products or services. Examples are trademarks or trade names, newspaper mastheads, Internet domain names, and noncompetition agreements.

A very common form of a marketing-related intangible asset is a trademark or trade name. A **trademark** or **trade name** is a word, phrase, or symbol that distinguishes or identifies a particular enterprise or product. The right to use a trademark or trade name under common law, whether it is registered or not, rests exclusively with the original user as long as the original user continues to use it. Registration with the U.S. Patent and Trademark Office provides legal protection for an **indefinite number of renewals for periods of 10 years each**, so a business that uses an established trademark or trade name may properly consider it to have an indefinite life. Trade names like Kleenex, Pepsi-Cola, Oldsmobile, Excedrin, Wheaties, and Sunkist create immediate product identification in our minds, thereby enhancing marketability.

If a trademark or trade name is acquired, its capitalizable cost is the purchase price. If a trademark or trade name is developed by the enterprise itself, the capitalizable cost includes attorney fees, registration fees, design costs, consulting fees, successful legal defense costs, and other expenditures directly related to securing it (excluding research and development costs). When the total cost of a trademark or trade name is insignificant, it can be expensed rather than capitalized. In most cases, the life of a trademark or trade name is indefinite and therefore its cost is not amortized.

The value of a marketing-related intangible can be substantial. Consider Internet domain names as an example. The name **Drugs.com** recently sold for $800,000, and the bidding for the name **Loans.com** approached $500,000.

[6]This classification framework has been adopted from "Business Combinations," *Statement of Financial Accounting Standards No. 141* (Norwalk, Conn.: FASB, 2001).

Company names themselves identify qualities and characteristics that the companies have worked hard and spent much to develop. In a recent year an estimated 1,230 companies took on new names in an attempt to forge new identities and paid over $250 million to corporate-identity consultants. Among these were **Primerica** (formerly American Can), **Navistar** (formerly International Harvester), **Nissan** (formerly Datsun), and **USX** (U.S. Steel).[7]

Customer-Related Intangible Assets

Customer-related intangible assets occur as a result of interactions with outside parties. Examples are customer lists, order or production backlogs, and both contractual and noncontractual customer relationships.

To illustrate, assume that We-Market Inc. acquired the customer list of a large newspaper for $6,000,000 on January 1, 2003. The customer list is a database that includes name, contact information, order history, and demographic information for a list of customers. We-Market expects to benefit from the information on the acquired list for 3 years, and it believes that these benefits will be spread evenly over the 3 years. In this case, the customer list is a limited-life intangible that should be amortized on a straight-line basis over the 3-year period.

The entry to record the purchase of the customer list and the amortization of the customer list at the end of each year is as follows:

	Debit	Credit
January 1, 2003		
Customer List	6,000,000	
Cash		6,000,000
(To record purchase of customer list)		
December 31, 2003, 2004, 2005		
Customer List Amortization Expense	2,000,000	
Customer List (or Accumulated Customer List Amortization)		2,000,000
(To record amortization expense)		

In the preceding example it was assumed that the customer list had no residual value. If We-Market determined that it could sell the list for $60,000 to another company at the end of 3 years, this residual value should be subtracted from the cost in order to determine the proper amortization expense for each year. Amortization expense would therefore be $1,980,000 as shown below:

ILLUSTRATION 12-2
Calculation of Amortization Expense with Residual Value

Cost	$6,000,000
Residual value	60,000
Amortization base	$5,940,000
Amortization expense per period: $1,980,000 ($5,940,000 ÷ 3)	

The residual value should be assumed to be zero unless the asset's useful life is less than the economic life and reliable evidence is available concerning the residual value.[8]

[7]To illustrate how various intangibles might arise from a given product, consider what the creators of the highly successful game, Trivial Pursuit, did to protect their creation. First, they copyrighted the 6,000 questions that are at the heart of the game. Then they shielded the Trivial Pursuit name by applying for a registered trademark. As a third mode of protection, the creators obtained a design patent on the playing board's design because it represents a unique graphic creation.

[8]"Goodwill and Other Intangible Assets," *Statement of Financial Accounting Standards No. 142* (Norwalk, Conn.: FASB, 2001), par. B55.

Artistic-Related Intangible Assets

Artistic-related intangible assets involve ownership rights to plays, literary works, musical works, pictures, photographs, and video and audiovisual material. These ownership rights are protected by copyrights.

A **copyright** is a federally granted right that all authors, painters, musicians, sculptors, and other artists have in their creations and expressions. A copyright is granted for the **life of the creator plus 50 years**. It gives the owner, or heirs, the exclusive right to reproduce and sell an artistic or published work. Copyrights are not renewable. The costs of acquiring and defending a copyright may be capitalized, but the research and development costs involved must be expensed as incurred.

Generally, the useful life of the copyright is less than its legal life (life in being plus 50 years). The costs of the copyright should be allocated to the years in which the benefits are expected to be received. The difficulty of determining the number of years over which benefits will be received normally encourages the company to write these costs off over a fairly short period of time.

Copyrights can be valuable. **Really Useful Group** is a company that consists of copyrights on the musicals of Andrew Lloyd Webber—*Cats, Phantom of the Opera, Jesus Christ-Superstar,* and others. It has little in the way of hard assets, yet it has been valued at $300 million.

Contract-Related Intangible Assets

Contract-related intangible assets represent the value of rights that arise from contractual arrangements. Examples are franchise and licensing agreements, construction permits, broadcast rights, and service or supply contracts. A very common form of contract-based intangible asset is a franchise.

A **franchise** is a contractual arrangement under which the franchisor grants the franchisee the right to sell certain products or services, to use certain trademarks or trade names, or to perform certain functions, usually within a designated geographical area. For example, when you drive down the street in an automobile purchased from a **Toyota** dealer, fill your tank at the corner **Texaco** station, eat lunch at **McDonald's**, cool off with one of **Baskin-Robbins**' 31 flavors, work at a **Coca-Col**a bottling plant, live in a home purchased through a **Century 21** real estate broker, or vacation at a **Holiday Inn** resort, you are dealing with franchises.

The franchisor, having developed a unique concept or product, protects its concept or product through a patent, copyright, or trademark or trade name. The franchisee acquires the right to exploit the franchisor's idea or product by signing a franchise agreement.

Another type of franchise is the arrangement commonly entered into by a municipality (or other governmental body) and a business enterprise that uses public property. In such cases, a privately owned enterprise is permitted to use public property in performing its services. Examples are the use of public waterways for a ferry service, the use of public land for telephone or electric lines, the use of phone lines for cable TV, the use of city streets for a bus line, or the use of the airwaves for radio or TV broadcasting. Such operating rights, obtained through agreements with governmental units or agencies, are frequently referred to as **licenses** or **permits**.

Franchises and licenses may be for a definite period of time, for an indefinite period of time, or perpetual. The enterprise securing the franchise or license carries an intangible asset account entitled Franchise or License on its books only when there are costs (such as a lump sum payment in advance or legal fees and other expenditures) that are identified with the acquisition of the operating right. **The cost of a franchise (or license) with a limited life should be amortized as operating expense over the life of the franchise.** A franchise with an indefinite life, or a perpetual franchise, should be carried at cost and not be amortized.

Annual payments made under a franchise agreement should be entered as operating expenses in the period in which they are incurred. They do not represent an asset to the concern since they do not relate to future rights to use public property.

Technology-Related Intangible Assets

Technology-related intangible assets relate to innovations or technological advances. Examples are patented technology and trade secrets. To illustrate, patents are granted by the U.S. Patent and Trademark Office. The two principal kinds of patents are **product patents**, which cover actual physical products, and **process patents**, which govern the process by which products are made. A **patent** gives the holder exclusive right to use, manufacture, and sell a product or process **for a period of 20 years** without interference or infringement by others. With this exclusive right, fortunes can be made. For example, companies such as **Merck**, **Polaroid**, and **Xerox** were founded on patents.[9]

If a patent is purchased from an inventor (or other owner), the purchase price represents its cost. Other costs incurred in connection with securing a patent, as well as attorneys' fees and other unrecovered costs of a successful legal suit to protect the patent, can be capitalized as part of the patent cost. Research and development costs related to the **development** of the product, process, or idea that is subsequently patented **must be expensed as incurred**, however. See pages 15–19 for a more complete presentation of accounting for research and development costs.

The cost of a patent should be amortized over its legal life or its useful life (the period benefits are received), whichever is shorter. If a patent is owned from the date it is granted, and it is expected to be useful during its entire legal life, it should be amortized over 20 years. If it appears that the patent will be useful for a shorter period of time, say, for 5 years, its cost should be amortized to expense over 5 years. Changing demand, new inventions superseding old ones, inadequacy, and other factors often limit the useful life of a patent to less than the legal life. For example, the useful life of patents in the pharmaceutical and drug industry is frequently less than the legal life because of the testing and approval period that follows their issuance. A typical drug patent has 5 to 11 years knocked off its 20-year legal life because 1 to 4 years must be spent on tests on animals, 4 to 6 years on human tests, and 2 to 3 years for the Food and Drug Administration to review the tests—all after the patent is issued but before the product goes on a pharmacist's shelves.

From bioengineering to software design to the Internet,[10] battles over patents are heating up as global competition intensifies. For example, **Priceline.com** filed suit against **Microsoft** for launching Hotel Price Matcher, a service that operates pretty much like the name-your-own-price-system pioneered by Priceline. And **Amazon.com** filed a complaint against **Barnesandnoble.com**, its bitter rival in the Web-retailing wars. The suit alleges that Barnesandnoble.com is infringing on Amazon.com's patent for one-click shopping and asks the court to stop Barnesandnoble.com from using its own quick-checkout system, called ExpressLane.

Legal fees and other costs incurred in successfully defending a patent suit are debited to Patents, an asset account, because such a suit establishes the legal rights of the holder of the patent. Such costs should be amortized along with acquisition cost over the remaining useful life of the patent.

Amortization expense should reflect the pattern in which the patent is used up, if that pattern can be reliably determined. Amortization of patents may be credited directly to the Patent account, or it may be credited to an Accumulated Patent Amortization account. To illustrate, assume that Harcott Co. incurs $180,000 in legal costs on January 1, 2003, to successfully defend a patent. The patent has a useful life of 20 years, and is amortized on a straight-line basis. The entries to record the legal fees and the amortization at the end of each year are as follows:

---

[9]Consider the opposite result: Sir Alexander Fleming, who discovered penicillin, decided not to use a patent to protect his discovery. He hoped that companies would produce it more quickly to help save sufferers. Companies, however, refused to develop it because they did not have the patent shield and, therefore, were afraid to make the investment.

[10]"Battle over Patents Threatens to Damp Web's Innovative Spirit," *The Wall Street Journal*, November 8, 1999.

January 1, 2003		
Patents	180,000	
Cash		180,000
(To record legal fees related to patent)		
December 31, 2003		
Patent Amortization Expense	9,000	
Patents (or Accumulated Patent Amortization)		9,000
(To record amortization of patent)		

Amortization on a units-of-production basis would be computed in a manner similar to that described for depreciation on property, plant, and equipment in Chapter 11, page 553.

Although a patent's useful life should not extend beyond its legal life of 20 years, small modifications or additions may lead to a new patent. The effect may be to extend the life of the old patent. In that case it is permissible to apply the unamortized costs of the old patent to the new patent if the new patent provides essentially the same benefits.[11] Alternatively, if a patent becomes worthless (impaired) because demand drops for the product produced, the asset should be written down or written off immediately to expense.

Goodwill

OBJECTIVE 5
Explain the conceptual issues related to goodwill.

Although companies are permitted to capitalize certain costs to develop specifically identifiable assets such as patents and copyrights, the amounts capitalized are generally not significant. Material amounts of intangible assets are recorded when companies purchase intangible assets, particularly in situations involving the purchase of another business (often referred to as a business combination).

In a business combination, the cost (purchase price) is assigned where possible to the identifiable tangible and intangible net assets, and the remainder is recorded in an intangible asset account called **Goodwill**. Goodwill is often referred to as the most intangible of the intangibles because it can only be identified with the business as a whole. The only way it can be sold is to sell the business.

The problem of determining the proper cost to allocate to intangible assets in a business combination is complex because of the many different types of intangibles that might be considered. Many of these types of intangibles have been discussed earlier. It is extremely difficult not only to identify certain types of intangibles but also to assign a value to them in a business combination. As a result, the approach followed is to record identifiable intangible assets that can be reliably measured. Other intangible assets that are difficult to identify or measure are recorded as goodwill.[12]

Recording Goodwill

OBJECTIVE 6
Describe the accounting procedures for recording goodwill.

Internally Created Goodwill. **Goodwill generated internally should not be capitalized in the accounts,** because measuring the components of goodwill is simply too complex and associating any costs with future benefits too difficult. The future benefits of goodwill may have no relationship to the costs incurred in the development of that goodwill. To add to the mystery, goodwill may even exist in the absence of specific costs to develop it. In addition, because no objective transaction with outside parties has taken place, a great deal of subjectivity—even misrepresentation—might be involved.

[11] A good example is **Eli Lilly**'s drug Prozac (used to treat depression) which in 1998 accounted for 43% of its U.S. sales. The patent on Prozac is due to expire in 2001, but the company expects to get an additional 2 years of protection, to 2003, because the company has a second-use patent covering appetite disorders.

[12] The new business combination standard provides detailed guidance regarding the recognition of identifiable intangible assets in a business combination. Using this guidance, the expectation is that more identifiable intangible assets will be recognized in the financial statements as a result of business combinations. If this situation occurs, less goodwill will be recognized.

UNDERLYING CONCEPTS

Capitalizing goodwill only when it is purchased in an arm's-length transaction and not capitalizing any goodwill generated internally is another example of reliability winning out over relevance.

Purchased Goodwill. Goodwill is recorded only when an entire business is purchased, because goodwill is a "going concern" valuation and cannot be separated from the business as a whole. To record goodwill, the fair market value of the net tangible and identifiable intangible assets are compared with the purchase price of the acquired business. The difference is considered goodwill, which is why goodwill is sometimes referred to as a "plug," or "gap filler," or **"master valuation"** account. **Goodwill is the residual: the excess of cost over fair value of the identifiable net assets acquired.**

To illustrate, Multi-Diversified, Inc. decides that it needs a parts division to supplement its existing tractor distributorship. The president of Multi-Diversified is interested in buying a small concern in Chicago (Tractorling Company) that has an established reputation and is seeking a merger candidate. The balance sheet of Tractorling Company is presented in Illustration 12-3.

ILLUSTRATION 12-3
Tractorling Balance Sheet

TRACTORLING CO.
Balance Sheet
as of December 31, 2002

Assets		Equities	
Cash	$ 25,000	Current liabilities	$ 55,000
Receivables	35,000	Capital stock	100,000
Inventories	42,000	Retained earnings	100,000
Property, plant, and equipment, net	153,000		
Total assets	**$255,000**	**Total equities**	**$255,000**

After considerable negotiation, Tractorling Company decides to accept Multi-Diversified's offer of $400,000. What then is the value of the goodwill, if any?

The answer is not obvious. The fair market values of Tractorling's identifiable assets are not disclosed in its historical cost-based balance sheet. Suppose, though, that as the negotiations progressed, Multi-Diversified conducted an investigation of the underlying assets of Tractorling to determine the fair market value of the assets. Such an investigation may be accomplished either through a purchase audit undertaken by Multi-Diversified's auditors in order to estimate the values of the seller's assets, or by an independent appraisal from some other source. The following valuations are determined.

ILLUSTRATION 12-4
Fair Market Value of Tractorling's Net Assets

Fair Market Values	
Cash	$ 25,000
Receivables	35,000
Inventories	122,000
Property, plant, and equipment, net	205,000
Patents	18,000
Liabilities	(55,000)
Fair market value of net assets	**$350,000**

Normally, differences between current fair market value and book value are more common among long-term assets, although significant differences can also develop in the current asset category. Cash obviously poses no problems, and receivables normally are fairly close to current valuation, although at times certain adjustments need to be made because of inadequate bad debt provisions. Liabilities usually are stated at book value, although if interest rates have changed since the liabilities were incurred, a different valuation (such as present value) might be appropriate. Careful analysis must be made to determine that no unrecorded liabilities are present.

The $80,000 difference in inventories ($122,000 − $42,000) could result from a number of factors, the most likely being that Tractorling Company uses LIFO. Recall that during periods of inflation, LIFO better matches expenses against revenues, but in doing so creates a balance sheet distortion. Ending inventory is comprised of older layers costed at lower valuations.

In many cases, the values of long-term assets such as property, plant, and equipment, and intangibles may have increased substantially over the years. This difference could be due to inaccurate estimates of useful lives, continual expensing of small expenditures (say, less than $300), inaccurate estimates of salvage values, and the discovery of some unrecorded assets (as in Tractorling's case where Patents are discovered to have a fair value of $18,000). Or, replacement costs may have substantially increased.

Since the fair market value of net assets is now determined to be $350,000, why did Multi-Diversified pay $400,000? Undoubtedly, the seller pointed to an established reputation, good credit rating, top management team, well-trained employees, and so on, as factors that make the value of the business greater than $350,000. At the same time, Multi-Diversified placed a premium on the future earning power of these attributes as well as the basic asset structure of the enterprise today. At this point in the negotiations, price can be a function of many factors; the most important is probably sheer skill at the bargaining table.

The difference between the purchase price of $400,000 and the fair market value of $350,000 is labeled goodwill. Goodwill is viewed as one or a group of unidentifiable values (intangible assets) the cost of which "is measured by the difference between the cost of the group of assets or enterprise acquired and the sum of the assigned costs of individual tangible and identifiable intangible assets acquired less liabilities assumed."[13] This procedure for valuation is referred to as a **master valuation approach** because goodwill is assumed to cover all the values that cannot be specifically identified with any identifiable tangible or intangible asset; this approach is shown in Illustration 12-5.

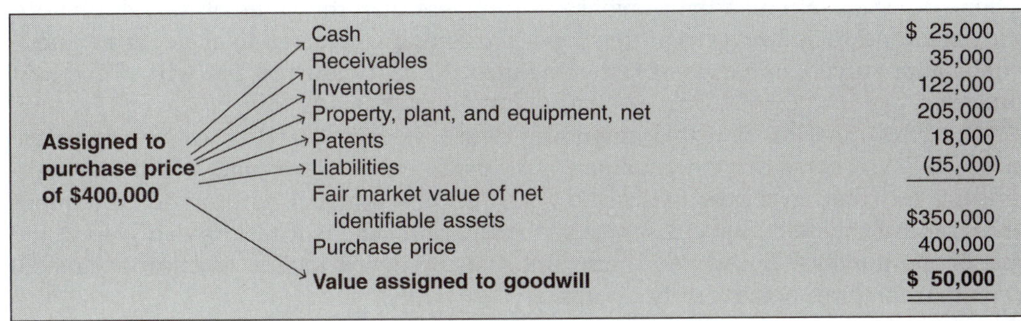

Assigned to purchase price of $400,000		
	Cash	$ 25,000
	Receivables	35,000
	Inventories	122,000
	Property, plant, and equipment, net	205,000
	Patents	18,000
	Liabilities	(55,000)
	Fair market value of net identifiable assets	$350,000
	Purchase price	400,000
	Value assigned to goodwill	**$ 50,000**

ILLUSTRATION 12-5
Determination of Goodwill—Master Valuation Approach

The entry to record this transaction would be as follows:

Cash	25,000	
Receivables	35,000	
Inventories	122,000	
Property, Plant, and Equipment	205,000	
Patents	18,000	
Goodwill	50,000	
Liabilities		55,000
Cash		400,000

Goodwill is often identified on the balance sheet as the **excess of cost over the fair value** of the net assets acquired.

[13]The Board expressed concern about measuring goodwill as a residual but noted that there is no real measurement alternative, since goodwill is not separable from the enterprise as a whole. "Business Combinations," *Statement of Financial Accounting Standards No. 141* (Norwalk, Conn.: FASB, 2001), par. B145.

Goodwill Write-off

Goodwill acquired in a business combination **is considered to have an indefinite life and therefore should not be amortized**. The Board's position is that investors find the amortization charge of little use in evaluating financial performance. In addition, although goodwill may decrease over time, predicting the actual life of goodwill and an appropriate pattern of amortization is extremely difficult.

On the other hand, knowing the amount invested in goodwill is important to the investment community. Therefore, **income statements are not charged unless goodwill has been impaired**. This approach will have a significant impact on the income statements of some companies because goodwill often is the largest intangible asset on a company's balance sheet. Prior to the new FASB standard, companies were required to amortize this intangible. For example, it is estimated that as a result of the new rules, earnings per share in 2001 will increase 21 percent for **International Paper**, 16 percent for **Johnson Controls**, and 30 percent for **Pepsi Bottling Group**.

Some believe that goodwill's value eventually disappears and therefore that goodwill should be charged to expense over the periods affected. Amortizing goodwill, they argue, provides a better matching of expense with revenues. Others note that the accounting treatment for purchased goodwill and goodwill created internally should be consistent. Goodwill created internally is immediately expensed and does not appear as an asset; the same treatment, they argue, should be accorded purchased goodwill. Even though these arguments may have some merit, the FASB decided that nonamortization of goodwill combined with an adequate impairment test provides the most useful financial information to the investment community.

Negative Goodwill—Badwill

Negative goodwill arises when the fair value of the assets acquired is higher than the purchase price of the assets. This situation is a result of market imperfection, because the seller would be better off to sell the assets individually than in total. However, situations do occur in which the purchase price is less than the value of the net identifiable assets and therefore a credit develops. This credit is referred to as **negative goodwill** or, alternatively, as **excess of fair value over the cost acquired**, **badwill**, or **bargain purchase**.

The FASB requires that this remaining excess be recognized as an extraordinary gain. The Board noted that extraordinary gain treatment is appropriate in order to highlight the fact that an excess exists and to reflect the unusual nature and infrequent occurrence of the item. Some disagree with the approach, as it results in a gain at the time of the purchase. However, it appears that the Board took a practical approach, given that this transaction rarely occurs.

IMPAIRMENT OF INTANGIBLE ASSETS

Limited-Life Intangibles

OBJECTIVE 7
Explain the accounting issues related to intangible asset impairments.

The rules that apply to **impairments of long-lived assets also apply to limited-life intangibles**. As indicated in Chapter 11, long-lived assets to be held and used by a company are to be reviewed for impairment whenever events or changes in circumstances indicate that **the carrying amount of the assets may not be recoverable** (recoverability test). In performing the review for recoverability, the company would estimate the future cash flows expected to result from the use of the asset and its eventual disposition. If the sum of the expected future net cash flows (undiscounted) is less than the carrying amount of the asset, an impairment loss would be measured and recognized. Otherwise, an impairment loss would not be recognized.[14] The impairment loss is the

[14]"Accounting for the Impairment of Long-Lived Assets," *Statement of Financial Accounting Standards No. 121* (Norwalk, Conn.: FASB, 1994).

amount by which the carrying amount of the asset exceeds the fair value of the impaired asset (fair value test).

To illustrate, assume that Lerch, Inc. has a patent on how to extract oil from shale rock. Unfortunately, reduced oil prices have made the shale oil technology somewhat unprofitable, and the patent has provided little income to date. As a result, a **recoverability test** is performed, and it is found that the expected net future cash flows from this patent are $35 million. Lerch's patent has a carrying amount of $60 million. Because the expected future net cash flows of $35 million are less than the carrying amount of $60 million, an impairment loss must be measured. Discounting the expected net future cash flows at its market rate of interest, Lerch determines the fair value of its patent to be $20 million. The impairment loss computation (fair value test) is shown in Illustration 12-6.

ILLUSTRATION 12-6
Computation of Loss on Impairment of Patent

Carrying amount of patent	$60,000,000
Fair value (based on present value computation)	20,000,000
Loss on impairment	**$40,000,000**

The journal entry to record this loss is:

Loss on Impairment	40,000,000	
Patents		40,000,000

After the impairment is recognized, the reduced carrying amount of the patents is its new cost basis. The patent's new cost should be amortized over its useful life or legal life, whichever is shorter. Even if oil prices increase in subsequent periods, and the value of the patent increases, **restoration of the previously recognized impairment loss is not permitted**.

Indefinite-Life Intangibles Other Than Goodwill

Indefinite-life intangibles other than goodwill should be tested for impairment at least annually. The impairment test for an indefinite-life asset other than goodwill is a fair value test. This test compares the fair value of the intangible asset with the asset's carrying amount. If the fair value of the intangible asset is less than the carrying amount, impairment is recognized. This one-step test is used because it would be relatively easy for many indefinite-life assets to meet the recoverability test because cash flows may extend many years into the future. As a result, the recoverability test is not used.

To illustrate, assume that Arcon Radio purchased a broadcast license for $2,000,000. The license is renewable every 10 years if the company provides appropriate service and does not violate Federal Communications Commission (FCC) rules and procedures. The license has been renewed with the FCC twice, at a minimal cost. Cash flows were expected to last indefinitely, and therefore Arcon reported the license as an indefinite-life intangible asset. Recently the FCC decided to no longer renew broadcast licenses, but to auction these licenses to the highest bidder. Arcon's existing license has 2 years remaining, and cash flows are expected for these 2 years. Arcon performs an impairment test and determines that the fair value of the intangible asset is $1,500,000. It therefore reports an impairment loss of $500,000 computed as follows.

ILLUSTRATION 12-7
Computation of Loss on Impairment of Broadcast License

Carrying amount of broadcast license	$2,000,000
Fair value of broadcast license	1,500,000
Loss on impairment	**$ 500,000**

The license would now be reported at $1,500,000, its fair value. Even if the value of the license increases in the remaining 2 years, restoration of the previously recognized impairment loss is not permitted.

Goodwill

The impairment rule for goodwill is a two-step process. First, the fair value of the reporting unit should be compared to its carrying amount including goodwill. If the fair value of the reporting unit is greater than the carrying amount, goodwill is considered not to be impaired, and the company does not have to do anything else.

To illustrate, assume that Kohlbuy Corporation has three divisions in its company. One division, Pritt Products, was purchased 4 years ago for $2 million. Unfortunately, it has experienced operating losses over the last 3 quarters, and management is reviewing the division for purposes of recognizing an impairment. The Pritt Division's net assets including the associated goodwill of $900,000 from purchase are listed in Illustration 12-8.

ILLUSTRATION 12-8
Net Assets of Pritt Division, Including Goodwill

Cash	$ 200,000
Receivables	300,000
Inventory	700,000
Property, plant, and equipment (net)	800,000
Goodwill	900,000
Less: Accounts and notes payable	(500,000)
Net assets	$2,400,000

It is determined that the fair value of Pritt Division is $2,800,000. As a result, no impairment is recognized because the fair value of the division is greater than the carrying amount of the net assets.

However, if the fair value of Pritt Division is less than the carrying amount of the net assets, then a second step must be performed to determine whether impairment has occurred. In the second step, the fair value of the goodwill must be determined (implied value of goodwill) and compared to its carrying amount. To illustrate, assume that the fair value of Pritt's Division was $1,900,000 instead of $2,800,000. The implied value of the goodwill in this case is computed in Illustration 12-9.

ILLUSTRATION 12-9
Determination of Implied Value of Goodwill

Fair value of Pritt Division	$1,900,000
Net identifiable assets (excluding goodwill) ($2,400,000 − $900,000)	1,500,000
Implied value of goodwill	**$ 400,000**

The implied value of the goodwill is then compared to the recorded goodwill to determine whether an impairment has occurred, as shown in Illustration 12-10.

ILLUSTRATION 12-10
Measurement of Goodwill Impairment

Carrying amount of goodwill	$900,000
Implied value of goodwill	400,000
Loss on impairment	**$500,000**

Illustration 12-11 summarizes the impairment tests for various intangible assets.

ILLUSTRATION 12-11
Summary of Intangible Asset Impairment Tests

Type of Intangible Asset	Impairment Test
Limited life	Recoverability test, then fair value test
Indefinite life	Fair value test
Goodwill	Fair value test on reporting unit, then fair value test on implied goodwill

RESEARCH AND DEVELOPMENT COSTS

OBJECTIVE 8
Identify the conceptual issues related to research and development costs.

Research and development (R & D) costs are not in themselves intangible assets. The accounting for R & D costs is presented here, however, because research and development activities frequently result in the development of something that is patented or copyrighted (such as a new product, process, idea, formula, composition, or literary work).

Many businesses spend considerable sums of money on research and development to create new products or processes, to improve present products, and to discover new knowledge that may be valuable at some future date. The following schedule shows the outlays for R & D made by selected U.S. companies:

ILLUSTRATION 12-12
R & D Outlays, as a Percentage of Sales and Profits

Company	R & D Dollars	% of Sales	% of Profits
Deere & Co.	$ 444,400,000	3.73%	43.51%
Dell Computer	272,000,000	1.49%	18.63%
General Mills	70,000,000	1.12%	13.10%
Johnson & Johnson	2,269,000,000	9.59%	74.17%
Kellogg	121,900,000	1.80%	24.25%
Merck	1,821,100,000	6.77%	34.70%

The difficulties in accounting for these research and development (R & D) expenditures are (1) identifying the costs associated with particular activities, projects, or achievements and (2) determining the magnitude of the future benefits and length of time over which such benefits may be realized. Because of these latter uncertainties, the accounting practice in this area has been simplified by requiring that **all research and development costs be charged to expense when incurred.**[15]

Contrary to U.S. practice, in most other nations (the Netherlands, Canada, and Japan, for example) the capitalization of research and development costs is allowed under specified circumstances.

Identifying R & D Activities

To differentiate research and development costs from similar costs, the following definitions are used for **research activities** and **development activities.**[16]

ILLUSTRATION 12-13
R & D Activities

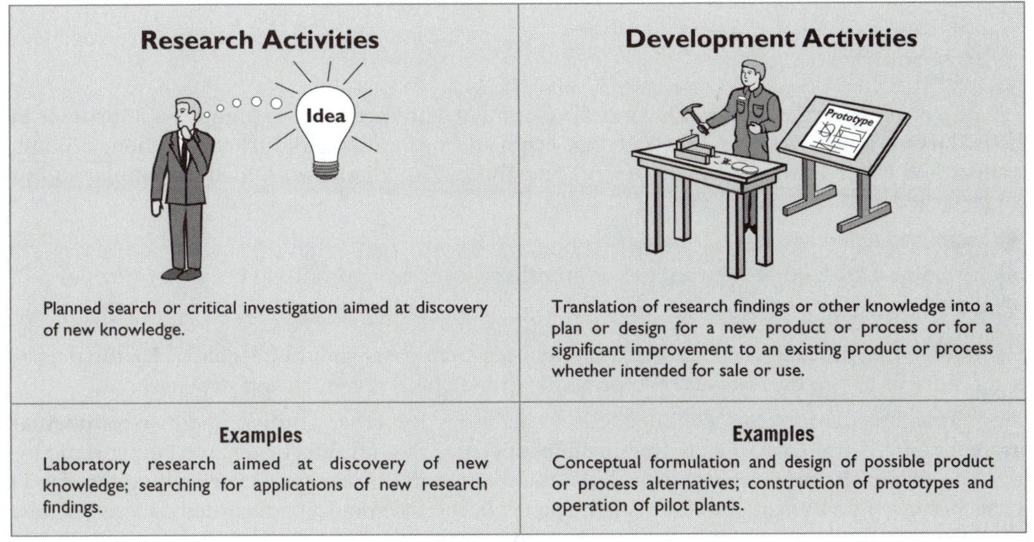

---

[15]"Accounting for Research and Development Costs," *Statement of Financial Accounting Standards No. 2* (Stamford, Conn.: FASB, 1974), par. 12.

[16]Ibid., par. 8.

It should be emphasized that R & D activities do not include routine or periodic alternatives to existing products, production lines, manufacturing processes, and other ongoing operations even though these alterations may represent improvements. For example, routine ongoing efforts to refine, enrich, or improve the qualities of an existing product are not considered R & D activities.

Accounting for R & D Activities

The costs associated with R & D activities and the accounting treatment accorded them are as follows:

OBJECTIVE 9
Describe the accounting procedures for research and development costs and for other similar costs.

1. *Materials, Equipment, and Facilities.* Expense the entire costs, **unless the items have alternative future uses** (in other R & D projects or otherwise), then carry as inventory and allocate as consumed; or capitalize and depreciate as used.
2. *Personnel.* Salaries, wages, and other related costs of personnel engaged in R & D should be expensed as incurred.
3. *Purchased Intangibles.* Expense the entire cost, **unless the items have alternative future uses** (in other R & D projects or otherwise), then capitalize and amortize.
4. *Contract Services.* The costs of services performed by others in connection with the reporting company's R & D should be expensed as incurred.
5. *Indirect Costs.* A reasonable allocation of indirect costs shall be included in R & D costs, except for general and administrative cost, which must be clearly related in order to be included and expensed.[17]

International accounting standards require the capitalization of appropriate development expenditures. This conflicts with U.S. GAAP.

Consistent with item 1 above, if an enterprise owns a research facility consisting of buildings, laboratories, and equipment that conducts R & D activities and that has alternative future uses (in other R & D projects or otherwise), the facility should be accounted for as a capitalized operational asset. The depreciation and other costs related to such research facilities are accounted for as R & D expenses.[18]

To illustrate the identification of R & D activities and the accounting treatment of related costs, assume that Next Century Incorporated develops, produces, and markets laser machines for medical, industrial, and defense uses.[19] The types of expenditures related to its laser machine activities, along with the recommended accounting treatment, are listed in Illustration 12-14.

---

[17]Ibid., par. 11.

[18]Costs of research, exploration, and development activities that are unique to companies in the **extractive industries** (e.g., prospecting, acquisition of mineral rights, exploration, drilling, mining, and related mineral development) and those costs discussed which are similar to but not classified as R & D costs may be:

1. expensed as incurred,
2. capitalized and either depreciated or amortized over an appropriate period of time, or
3. accumulated as part of inventoriable costs.

Choice of the appropriate accounting treatment for such costs should be guided by the degree of certainty of future benefits and the principle of matching revenues and expenses.

[19]Sometimes enterprises conduct R & D activities for other entities under a **contractual arrangement**. In this case, the contract usually specifies that all direct costs, certain specific indirect costs, plus a profit element, should be reimbursed to the enterprise performing the R & D work. Because reimbursement is expected, such R & D costs should be recorded as a receivable. It is the company for whom the work has been performed that reports these costs as R & D and expenses them as incurred.

For a more complete discussion of how an enterprise should account for its obligation under an arrangement for the funding of its research and development by others, see "Research and Development Arrangements," *Statement of Financial Accounting Standards No. 68* (Stamford, Conn.: FASB, 1982).

ILLUSTRATION 12-14
Sample R & D Expenditures and Their Accounting Treatment

Next Century Incorporated

Type of Expenditure	Accounting Treatment
1. Construction of long-range research facility for use in current and future projects (three-story, 400,000-square-foot building).	Capitalize and depreciate as R & D expense.
2. Acquisition of R & D equipment for use on current project only.	Expense immediately as R & D.
3. Acquisition of machinery to be used on current and future R & D projects.	Capitalize and depreciate as R & D expense.
4. Purchase of materials to be used on current and future R & D projects.	≈ and allocate to R & D projects; expense as consumed.
5. Salaries of research staff designing new laser bone scanner.	Expense immediately as R & D.
6. Research costs incurred under contract with New Horizon, Inc., and billable monthly.	Record as a receivable (reimbursable expenses).
7. Material, labor, and overhead costs of prototype laser scanner.	Expense immediately as R & D.
8. Costs of testing prototype and design modifications.	Expense immediately as R & D.
9. Legal fees to obtain patent on new laser scanner.	Capitalize as patent and amortize to overhead as part of cost of goods manufactured.
10. Executive salaries.	Expense as operating expense (general and administrative).
11. Cost of marketing research to promote new laser scanner.	Expense as operating expense (selling).
12. Engineering costs incurred to advance the laser scanner to full production stage.	Expense immediately as R & D.
13. Costs of successfully defending patent on laser scanner.	Capitalize as patent and amortize to overhead as part of cost of goods manufactured.
14. Commissions to sales staff marketing new laser scanner.	Expense as operating expense (selling).

Other Costs Similar to R & D Costs

Many costs have characteristics similar to research and development costs. Examples are:

1. Start-up costs for a new operation.
2. Initial operating losses.
3. Advertising costs.
4. Computer software costs.

For the most part, these costs are expensed as incurred, similar to the accounting for R & D costs. A brief explanation of these costs is provided below.

Start-up Costs

Start-up costs are costs incurred for one-time activities to start a new operation. Examples include opening a new plant, introducing a new product or service, or conducting business in a new territory or with a new class of customers. Start-up costs include **organizational costs**; these are costs incurred in the organizing of a new entity, such as legal and state fees of various types. The accounting for start-up costs is straightforward: **expense start-up costs as incurred**. The profession recognizes that these costs are incurred with the expectation that future revenues will occur or increased efficiencies will result. However, to determine the amount and timing of future benefits is so difficult that a conservative approach—expensing these costs as incurred—is required.[20]

[20]"Reporting on the Costs of Start-Up Activities," *Statement of Position 98-5* (New York: AICPA, 1998).

To illustrate the type of costs that should be expensed as start-up costs, assume that U.S.-based Hilo Beverage Company decides to construct a new plant in Brazil. This represents Hilo's first entry into the Brazilian market. As part of its overall strategy, Hilo plans to introduce the company's major U.S. brands into Brazil, on a locally produced basis. Following are some of the costs that might be involved with these start-up activities.

1. Travel-related costs, costs related to employee salaries, and costs related to feasibility studies, accounting, tax, and government affairs.
2. Training of local employees related to product, maintenance, computer systems, finance, and operations.
3. Recruiting, organizing, and training related to establishing a distribution network.

All of these costs are start-up costs and should be expensed as incurred.

It is not uncommon for start-up activities to occur at the same time as other activities, such as the acquisition or development of assets. For example, property, plant, and equipment or inventory used in Hilo's new plant should not be immediately expensed. These assets should be reported on the balance sheet and charged to operations using appropriate GAAP reporting guidelines.

Initial Operating Losses

Some contend that initial operating losses incurred in the start-up of a business should be capitalized, since they are unavoidable and are a cost of starting a business. For example, assume that Hilo lost money in its first year of operations and wished to capitalize this loss, arguing that as the company becomes profitable, it will offset these losses in future periods. What do you think? We believe that this approach is unsound, since losses have no future service potential and therefore cannot be considered an asset.

Our position that operating losses during the early years should not be capitalized is supported by *Statement of Financial Accounting Standards No. 7*, which clarifies the accounting and reporting practices for **development stage enterprises**. **The FASB concludes that the accounting practices and reporting standards should be no different for an enterprise trying to establish a new business than they are for other enterprises.** The same "generally accepted accounting principles that apply to established operating enterprises shall govern the recognition of revenue by a development stage enterprise and shall determine whether a cost incurred by a development stage enterprise is to be charged to expense when incurred or is to be capitalized or deferred."[21]

Advertising Costs

Recently, PepsiCo hired pop icon Britney Spears to advertise its products. How should these advertising costs related to Britney Spears be reported? These costs could be expensed in a variety of ways:

1. When she has completed her singing assignment.
2. The first time the advertising takes place.

[21]"Accounting and Reporting by Development Stage Enterprises," *Statement of Financial Accounting Standards No. 7* (Stamford, Conn.: FASB, 1975), par. 10. A company is considered to be in the developing stages when its efforts are directed toward establishing a new business and either the principal operations have not started or no significant revenue has been earned. To evaluate the economic impact of applying the same accounting principles to development stage enterprises that apply to established operating enterprises, the FASB interviewed officers of 15 venture capital companies. The consensus was that whether a development stage enterprise defers or expenses preoperating costs has little effect on the amount of, or the terms under which, venture capital is provided. According to these officers, venture capital investors instead rely on an evaluation of potential cash flows resulting from an investigation of the technological, marketing, management, and financial aspects of the enterprise.

❸ Over the estimated useful life of the advertising.
❹ In an appropriate fashion to each of the three periods identified above.
❺ Over the period revenues are expected to result.

After much discussion, the profession has concluded that future benefits from advertising generally are not sufficiently defined or measurable with a degree of reliability that is required to recognize these costs as an asset. **As a result, for the most part advertising costs must be expensed as incurred or the first time the advertising takes place.** These two alternatives are permitted because whichever approach is followed, the results are essentially the same. Tangible assets used in advertising, such as billboards or blimps, are recorded as assets because they do have alternative future use. Again the profession has taken a conservative approach to recording advertising costs because defining and measuring the future benefits are so difficult.[22]

Computer Software Costs

A special problem arises in distinguishing R & D costs from selling and administrative activities. The FASB's intent was that the acquisition, development, or improvement of a product or process by an enterprise **for use in its selling or administrative activities** be excluded from the definition of research and development activities. For example, the costs of software incurred by an airline in acquiring, developing, or improving its computerized reservation system, or the costs incurred during the development of a general management information system are not research and development costs. Accounting for computer software costs is a specialized and complicated accounting topic that is discussed and illustrated in an appendix (Appendix 12A, pages 623–626).

UNDERLYING CONCEPTS

The requirement that all R & D costs be expensed as incurred is an example of the conflict between relevance and reliability, with this requirement leaning strongly in support of reliability, as well as conservatism, consistency, and comparability. No attempt is made to match costs and revenues.

Conceptual Questions

The requirement that all R & D costs (and other costs mentioned in the previous section) incurred internally be expensed immediately is a conservative, practical solution that ensures consistency in practice and uniformity among companies. But the practice of immediately writing off expenditures made in the expectation of benefiting future periods cannot be justified on the grounds that it is good accounting theory.

Defendants of immediate expensing contend that from an income statement standpoint, long-run application of this standard frequently makes little difference. They contend that the amount of R & D cost charged to expense each accounting period would be about the same whether there is immediate expensing or capitalization and subsequent amortization because of the ongoing nature of most companies' R & D activities. Critics of this practice argue that the balance sheet should report an intangible asset related to expenditures that have future benefit. To preclude capitalization of all R & D expenditures removes from the balance sheet what may be a company's most valuable asset. This standard represents one of the many trade-offs made among relevance, reliability, and cost-benefit considerations.[23]

INTERNATIONAL INSIGHT

The International Accounting Standards Committee issued a standard that is in disagreement with the FASB's standard on accounting for R & D costs. The International Committee identified certain circumstances that justify the capitalization and deferral of development costs.

---

[22]"Reporting on Advertising Costs," *Statement of Position 93-7* (New York: AICPA, 1993). Note that there are some exceptions for immediate expensing of advertising costs when they relate to direct-response advertising, but this subject is beyond the scope of this book.

[23]Recent research suggests that capitalizing research and development costs may be helpful to investors. For example, one study showed that a significant relationship exists between R & D outlays and subsequent benefits in the form of increased productivity, earnings, and shareholder value for R & D – intensive companies. Baruch Lev and Theodore Sougiannis, "The Capitalization, Amortization, and Value-Relevance of R & D," *Journal of Accounting and Economics*, February 1996. In another study, it was found that there was a significant decline in earnings usefulness for companies that were forced to switch from capitalizing to expensing R & D costs and that the decline appears to persist over time. Martha L. Loudder and Bruce K. Behn, "Alternative Income Determination Rules and Earnings Usefulness: The Case of R & D Costs," *Contemporary Accounting Research*, Fall 1995.

PRESENTATION OF INTANGIBLES AND RELATED ITEMS

Intangible Assets

OBJECTIVE 10
Indicate the presentation of intangible assets and related items.

The reporting of intangible assets differs from the reporting of property, plant, and equipment in that contra accounts are not normally shown. On the balance sheet, all intangible assets other than goodwill should be reported as a separate item. If goodwill is present, it also should be reported as a separate item. The Board concluded that since goodwill and other intangible assets differ significantly from other types of assets, users of the balance sheet will benefit from this disclosure.

On the income statement, amortization expense and impairment losses for intangible assets other than goodwill should be presented as part of continuing operations. Goodwill impairment losses should also be presented as a separate line item in the continuing operations section, unless the goodwill impairment is associated with a discontinued operation.

The notes to the financial statements should include information about acquired intangible assets, including the aggregate amortization expense for each of the succeeding 5 years. The notes should include information about changes in the carrying amount of goodwill during the period. Illustration 12-15 on page 21 shows the type of disclosure made related to intangible assets in the financial statements and related notes for Harbaugh Company.

Research and Development Costs

Acceptable accounting practice requires that disclosure be made in the financial statements (generally in the notes) of the total R & D costs charged to expense each period for which an income statement is presented. **Merck & Co., Inc.**, a global research pharmaceutical company, reported both internal and acquired research and development in its recent income statement.

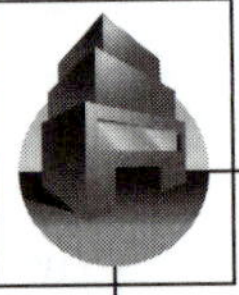

ILLUSTRATION 12-16
Income Statement Disclosure of R & D Costs

MERCK & CO., INC.
(in millions)

	Years Ended December 31		
	1998	1997	1996
Sales	$26,898.2	$23,636.9	$19,828.7
Costs, expenses, and other			
Materials and production	13,925.4	11,790.3	9,319.2
Marketing and administrative	4,511.4	4,299.2	3,841.3
Research and development	**1,821.1**	**1,683.7**	**1,487.3**
Acquired research	**1,039.5**	—	—
Equity income from affiliates	(884.3)	(727.9)	(600.7)
Gains on sales of businesses	(2,147.7)	(213.4)	—
Other (income) expense, net	499.7	342.7	240.8
	$18,765.1	$17,174.6	$14,287.9

Go to the Digital Tool for additional disclosures of intangibles and R & D costs.

In addition, Merck provides a discussion about R & D expenditures in its annual report, as shown in Illustration 12-17 on page 22.

ILLUSTRATION 12-15
Intangible Asset Disclosures

HARBAUGH COMPANY
Balance Sheet (partial)
(in thousands)

Intangible assets (Note C)	$3,840
Goodwill (Note D)	2,575

Income Statement (partial)
(in thousands)

as part of continuing operations	
Amortization expense	$380
Impairment losses (goodwill)	46

Note C: Acquired Intangible Assets

	As of December 31, 2003	
($000s)	Gross Carrying Amount	Accumulated Amortzation
Amortized intangible assets		
Trademark	$2,000	$(100)
Customer list	500	(310)
Other	60	(10)
Total	$2,560	$(420)
Unamortized intangible assets		
Licenses	$1,300	
Trademark	400	
Total	$1,700	

Aggregate Amortization Expense	
For year ended 12/31/03	$380
Estimated Amortization Expense	
For year ended 12/31/04	$200
For year ended 12/31/05	$ 90
For year ended 12/31/06	$ 70
For year ended 12/31/07	$ 60
For year ended 12/31/08	$ 50

Note D: Goodwill
The changes in the carrying amount of goodwill for the year ended December 31, 2003, are as follows:

($000s)	Technology Segment	Communications Segment	Total
Balance as of January 1, 2003	$1,413	$904	$2,317
Goodwill acquired during year	189	115	304
Impairment losses	—	(46)	(46)
Balance as of December 31, 2003	$1,602	$973	$2,575

The Communications segment is tested for impairment in the third quarter, after the annual forecasting process. Due to an increase in competition in the Texas and Louisiana cable industry, operating profits and cash flows were lower than expected in the fourth quarter of 2002 and the first and second quarters of 2003. Based on that trend, the earnings forecast for the next 5 years was revised. In September 2003, a goodwill impairment loss of $46 was recognized in the Communications reporting unit. The fair value of that reporting unit was estimated using the expected present value of future cash flows.

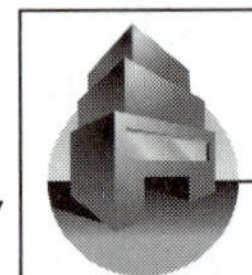

ILLUSTRATION 12-17
Merck's R & D Disclosure

MERCK & CO., INC.

Research and development in the pharmaceutical industry is inherently a long-term process. The following data show an unbroken trend of year-to-year increases in research and development spending. For the period 1989 to 1998, the compounded annual growth rate in research and development was 11%. Research and development expenses for 1999 are estimated to approximate $2.1 billion.

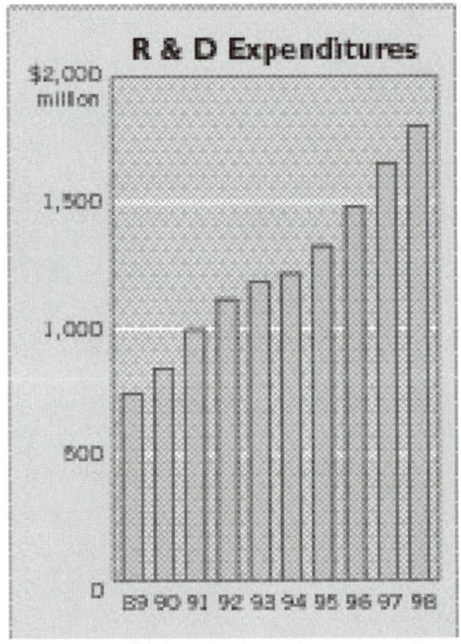

In 1998, in connection with the restructuring of AMI, the Company recorded a $1.04 billion charge for acquired research associated with 10 product candidates in Phase II or later stages of development and U.S. rights to future Astra products which have not yet entered Phase II, for which, at the acquisition date, commercial viability had not been established.

SUMMARY OF LEARNING OBJECTIVES

❶ **Describe the characteristics of intangible assets.** Intangible assets have two main characteristics: (1) They lack physical existence; and (2) they are not financial instruments. In most cases, intangible assets provide services over a period of years. As a result, they are normally classified as a long-term asset.

❷ **Identify the costs included in the initial valuation of intangible assets.** Intangibles are recorded at cost. Cost includes all costs of acquisition and expenditures necessary to make the intangible asset ready for its intended use. If intangibles are acquired for stock or in exchange for other assets, the cost of the intangible is the fair value of the consideration given or the fair value of the intangible received, whichever is more clearly evident. When several intangibles, or a combination of intangibles and tangibles, are bought in a "basket purchase," the cost should be allocated on the basis of fair values.

❸ **Explain the procedure for amortizing intangible assets.** Intangibles have either a limited useful life or an indefinite useful life. An intangible asset with a limited life is amortized; an intangible asset with an indefinite life is not amortized. Limited-life intangibles should be amortized by systematic charges to expense over their useful life. The useful life should reflect the period over which these assets will contribute to cash flows. The amount to report for amortization expense should reflect the pattern in which the asset is consumed or used up if that pattern can be reliably determined. Otherwise a straight-line approach should be used.

4 Identify the types of intangible assets. Major types of intangibles are: (1) marketing-related intangibles which are used in the marketing or promotion of products or services; (2) customer-related intangibles which are a result of interactions with outside parties; (3) artistic-related intangibles which involve ownership rights to such items as plays and literary works; (4) contract-related intangibles which represent the value of rights that arise from contractual arrangements; (5) technology-related intangible assets which relate to innovations or technological advances; and (6) goodwill which arises in business combinations.

5 Explain the conceptual issues related to goodwill. Goodwill is unique because unlike receivables, inventories, and patents that can be sold or exchanged individually in the marketplace, goodwill can be identified only with the business as a whole. Goodwill is a "going concern" valuation and is recorded only when an entire business is purchased. Goodwill generated internally should not be capitalized in the accounts, because measuring the components of goodwill is simply too complex and associating any costs with future benefits too difficult. The future benefits of goodwill may have no relationship to the costs incurred in the development of that goodwill. Goodwill may exist even in the absence of specific costs to develop it.

6 Describe the accounting procedures for recording goodwill. To record goodwill, the fair market value of the net tangible and identifiable intangible assets are compared with the purchase price of the acquired business. The difference is considered goodwill. Goodwill is the residual—the excess of cost over fair value of the identifiable net assets acquired. Goodwill is often identified on the balance sheet as the excess of cost over the fair value of the net assets acquired.

7 Explain the accounting issues related to intangible asset impairments. Impairments for limited-life intangible assets are based on a recoverability test and a fair value test. Indefinite-life intangibles use only a fair value test. Goodwill impairments use a two-step process: First, test the fair value of the reporting unit, then do the fair value test on implied goodwill.

8 Identify the conceptual issues related to research and development costs. R & D costs are not in themselves intangible assets, but research and development activities frequently result in the development of something that is patented or copyrighted. The difficulties in accounting for R & D expenditures are (1) identifying the costs associated with particular activities, projects, or achievements and (2) determining the magnitude of the future benefits and length of time over which such benefits may be realized. Because of these latter uncertainties, the FASB has standardized and simplified accounting practice by requiring that all research and development costs be charged to expense when incurred.

9 Describe the accounting procedures for research and development costs and for other similar costs. The costs associated with R & D activities and the accounting treatment accorded them are as follows: (1) *Materials, equipment, and facilities:* Expense the entire costs, unless the items have alternative future uses, then carry as inventory and allocate as consumed; or capitalize and depreciate as used. (2) *Personnel:* Salaries, wages, and other related costs of personnel engaged in R & D should be expensed as incurred. (3) *Purchased intangibles:* Expense the entire cost, unless the items have alternative future uses, then capitalize and amortize. (4) *Contract services:* The costs of services performed by others in connection with the reporting company's R & D should be expensed as incurred. (5) *Indirect costs:* A reasonable allocation of indirect costs shall be included in R & D costs, except for general and administrative costs, which must be related to be included and expensed. Many costs have characteristics similar to R & D costs. Examples are start-up costs, initial operating losses, advertising costs,

KEY TERMS

amortization, *3*
copyright, *7*
development activities, *15*
franchise, *7*
goodwill, *9*
indefinite-life intangibles, *3*
intangible assets, *2*
license, *7*
limited-life intangibles, *3*
master valuation approach, *11*
negative goodwill (badwill), *12*
organizational costs, *17*
patent, *8*
research activities, *15*
research and development (R & D) costs, *15*
start-up costs, *17*
trademark, trade name, *5*

and computer software costs. For the most part, these costs are expensed as incurred, similar to the accounting for R & D costs.

10 Indicate the presentation of intangible assets and related items. The reporting of intangibles differs from the reporting of property, plant, and equipment in that contra accounts are not normally shown. On the balance sheet, all intangible assets other than goodwill should be reported as a separate item. If goodwill is present, it too should be reported as a separate item. On the income statement, amortization expense and impairment losses should normally be reported in continuing operations. The notes to the financial statements have additional detailed information. Disclosure must be made in the financial statements for the total R & D costs charged to expense each period for which an income statement is presented.

EXERCISES

UE12-1 (Classification Issues—Intangibles) Presented below is a list of items that could be included in the intangible assets section of the balance sheet.

1. Investment in a subsidiary company.
2. Timberland.
3. Cost of engineering activity required to advance the design of a product to the manufacturing stage.
4. Lease prepayment (6 months' rent paid in advance).
5. Cost of equipment obtained.
6. Cost of searching for applications of new research findings.
7. Costs incurred in the formation of a corporation.
8. Operating losses incurred in the start-up of a business.
9. Training costs incurred in the start-up of new operation.
10. Purchase cost of a franchise.
11. Goodwill generated internally.
12. Cost of testing in search for product alternatives.
13. Goodwill acquired in the purchase of a business.
14. Cost of developing a patent.
15. Cost of purchasing a patent from an inventor.
16. Legal costs incurred in securing a patent.
17. Unrecovered costs of a successful legal suit to protect the patent.
18. Cost of conceptual formulation of possible product alternatives.
19. Cost of purchasing a copyright.
20. Research and development costs.
21. Long-term receivables.
22. Cost of developing a trademark.
23. Cost of purchasing a trademark.

Instructions

(a) Indicate which items on the list above would generally be reported as intangible assets in the balance sheet.

(b) Indicate how, if at all, the items not reportable as intangible assets would be reported in the financial statements.

UE12-2 (Classification Issues—Intangibles) Presented below is selected account information related to Martin Burke Inc. as of December 21, 2001. All these accounts have debit balances.

Cable television franchises
Music copyrights
Research and development costs
Goodwill
Cash
Discount on notes payable
Accounts receivable
Property, plant, and equipment
Internet domain name
Film contract rights
Customer lists
Prepaid expenses
Covenants not to compete
Brand names
Notes receivable
Investments in affiliated companies
Organization cost
Land

Instructions

Identify which items should be classified as an intangible asset. For those items not classified as an intangible asset, indicate where they would be reported in the financial statements.

UE12-3 (Classification Issues—Intangible Asset) Joni Hyde Inc. has the following amounts included in its general ledger at December 31, 2001:

Organization costs	$24,000
Trademarks	15,000
Discount on bonds payable	35,000
Deposits with advertising agency for ads to promote goodwill of company	10,000
Excess of cost over fair value of net identifiable assets of acquired subsidiary	75,000
Cost of equipment acquired for research and development projects; the equipment has an alternative future use	90,000
Costs of developing a secret formula for a product that is expected to be marketed for at least 20 years	80,000

Instructions

(a) On the basis of the information above, compute the total amount to be reported by Hyde for intangible assets on its balance sheet at December 31, 2001. Equipment has alternative future use.

(b) If an item is not to be included in intangible assets, explain its proper treatment for reporting purposes.

UE12-4 (Intangible Amortization) Presented below is selected information for Alatorre Company. Answer each of the factual situations.

1. Alatorre purchased a patent from Vania Co. for $1,000,000 on January 1, 2000. The patent is being amortized over its remaining legal life of 10 years, expiring on January 1, 2010. During 2002, Alatorre determined that the economic benefits of the patent would not last longer than 6 years from the date of acquisition. What amount should be reported in the balance sheet for the patent, net of accumulated amortization, at December 31, 2002?
2. Alatorre bought a franchise from Alexander Co. on January 1, 2001, for $400,000. The carrying amount of the franchise on Alexander's books on January 1, 2001, was $500,000. The franchise agreement had an estimated useful life of 30 years. Because Alatorre must enter a competitive bidding at the end of 2010, it is unlikely that the franchise will be retained beyond 2010. What amount should be amortized for the year ended December 31, 2002?
3. On January 1, 1998, Alatorre incurred organization costs of $275,000. Alatorre is amortizing these costs over 5 years. What amount, if any, should be reported as unamortized organization costs as of December 31, 2002?
4. Alatorre purchased the license for distribution of a popular consumer product on January 1, 2002, for $150,000. It is expected that this product will generate cash flows for an indefinite period of time. The license has an initial term of 5 years but by paying a nominal fee, Alatorre can renew the license indefinitely for successive 5-year terms. What amount should be amortized for the year ended December 31, 2002?

UE12-5 (Correct Intangible Asset Account) As the recently appointed auditor for William J. Bryan Corporation, you have been asked to examine selected accounts before the 6-month financial statements of June 30, 2001, are prepared. The controller for William J. Bryan Corporation mentions that only one account (shown below) is kept for Intangible Assets.

Intangible Assets

		Debit	Credit	Balance
January 4	Research and development costs	940,000		940,000
January 5	Legal costs to obtain patent	75,000		1,015,000
January 31	Payment of 7 months' rent on property leased by Bryan	91,000		1,106,000
February 11	Premium on common stock		250,000	856,000
March 31	Unamortized bond discount on bonds due March 31, 2021	84,000		940,000
April 30	Promotional expenses related to start-up of business	207,000		1,147,000
June 30	Operating losses for first 6 months	241,000		1,388,000

Instructions

Prepare the entry or entries necessary to correct this account. Assume that the patent has a useful life of 10 years.

UE12-6 (Recording and Amortization of Intangibles) Rolanda Marshall Company, organized in 2001, has set up a single account for all intangible assets. The following summary discloses the debit entries that have been recorded during 2002:

1/2/02	Purchased patent (8-year life)	$ 350,000
4/1/02	Purchased goodwill	360,000
7/1/02	Purchased franchise with 10-year life; expiration date 7/1/12	450,000
8/1/02	Payment of copyright (5-year life)	156,000
9/1/02	Research and development costs	215,000
		$1,531,000

Instructions

Prepare the necessary entries to clear the Intangible Assets account and to set up separate accounts for distinct types of intangibles. Make the entries as of December 31, 2002, recording any necessary amortization and reflecting all balances accurately as of that date (straight-line amortization).

UE12-7 (Accounting for Trade Name) In early January 2001, Gayle Crystal Corporation applied for a trade name, incurring legal costs of $16,000. In January 2002, Gayle Crystal incurred $7,800 of legal fees in a successful defense of its trade name.

Instructions

(a) Compute 2001 amortization, 12/31/01 book value, 2002 amortization, and 12/31/02 book value if the company amortizes the trade name over 10 years.

(b) Compute the 2002 amortization and the 12/31/02 book value, assuming that at the beginning of 2002, Crystal determines that the trade name will provide no future benefits beyond 12/31/05.

(c) Ignoring the response for part (b), compute the 2003 amortization and the 12/31/03 book value, assuming that at the beginning of 2003, based on new market research, Crystal determines that the fair value of the trade name is $15,000. Estimated total cash flow from the trade name is $16,000 on January 3, 2003.

UE12-8 (Accounting for Organization Costs) Horace Greeley Corporation was organized in 2000 and began operations at the beginning of 2001. The company is involved in interior design consulting services. The following costs were incurred prior to the start of operations:

Attorney's fees in connection with organization of the company	$15,000
Purchase of drafting and design equipment	10,000
Costs of meetings of incorporators to discuss organizational activities	7,000
State filing fees to incorporate	1,000
	$33,000

Instructions

(a) Compute the total amount of organization costs incurred by Greeley.

(b) Prepare the journal entry to record organization costs for 2001.

UE12-9 (Accounting for Patents, Franchises, and R & D) Jimmy Carter Company has provided information on intangible assets as follows:

A patent was purchased from Gerald Ford Company for $2,000,000 on January 1, 2001. Carter estimated the remaining useful life of the patent to be 10 years. The patent was carried in Ford's accounting records at a net book value of $2,000,000 when Ford sold it to Carter.

During 2002, a franchise was purchased from the Ronald Reagan Company for $480,000. In addition, 5% of revenue from the franchise must be paid to Reagan. Revenue from the franchise for 2002 was $2,500,000. Carter estimates the useful life of the franchise to be 10 years and takes a full year's amortization in the year of purchase.

Carter incurred research and development costs in 2002 as follows:

Materials and equipment	$142,000
Personnel	189,000
Indirect costs	102,000
	$433,000

Carter estimates that these costs will be recouped by December 31, 2005. The materials and equipment purchased have no alternative uses.

On January 1, 2002, because of recent events in the field, Carter estimates that the remaining life of the patent purchased on January 1, 2001, is only 5 years from January 1, 2002.

Instructions

(a) Prepare a schedule showing the intangibles section of Carter's balance sheet at December 31, 2002. Show supporting computations in good form.

(b) Prepare a schedule showing the income statement effect for the year ended December 31, 2002, as a result of the facts above. Show supporting computations in good form.

(AICPA adapted)

UE12-10 (Accounting for Patents) During 1998, George Winston Corporation spent $170,000 in research and development costs. As a result, a new product called the New Age Piano was patented. The patent was obtained on October 1, 1998, and had a legal life of 20 years and a useful life of 10 years. Legal costs of $18,000 related to the patent were incurred as of October 1, 1998.

Instructions

(a) Prepare all journal entries required in 1998 and 1999 as a result of the transactions above.

(b) On June 1, 2000, Winston spent $9,480 to successfully prosecute a patent infringement. As a result, the estimate of useful life was extended to 12 years from June 1, 2000. Prepare all journal entries required in 2000 and 2001.

(c) In 2002, Winston determined that a competitor's product would make the New Age Piano obsolete and the patent worthless by December 31, 2003. Prepare all journal entries required in 2002 and 2003.

UE12-11 (Accounting for Patents) Tones Industries has the following patents on its December 31, 2003, balance sheet:

Patent Item	Initial Cost	Date Acquired	Useful Life at Date Acquired
Patent A	$30,600	3/1/00	17 years
Patent B	$15,000	7/1/01	10 years
Patent C	$14,400	9/1/02	4 years

The following events occurred during the year ended December 31, 2004:

1. Research and development costs of $245,700 were incurred during the year.
2. Patent D was purchased on July 1 for $36,480. This patent has a useful life of 9½ years.
3. As a result of reduced demands for certain products protected by Patent B, a possible impairment of Patent B's value may have occurred at December 31, 2004. The controller for Tones estimates the future cash flows from Patent B will be as follows:

For the Year Ended	Future Cash Flows
December 31, 2005	$2,000
December 31, 2006	2,000
December 31, 2007	2,000

The proper discount rate to be used for these flows is 8%. (Assume that the cash flows occur at the end of the year.)

Instructions

(a) Compute the total carrying amount of Tones' patents on its December 31, 2003, balance sheet.

(b) Compute the total carrying amount of Tones' patents on its December 31, 2004, balance sheet.

UE12-12 (Accounting for Goodwill) Fred Moss, owner of Moss Interiors, is negotiating for the purchase of Zweifel Galleries. The condensed balance sheet of Zweifel is given in an abbreviated form at the top of the next page.

ZWEIFEL GALLERIES
Balance Sheet
As of December 31, 2002

Assets		**Liabilities and Stockholders' Equity**		
Cash	$100,000	Accounts payable		$ 50,000
Land	70,000	Long-term notes payable		300,000
Building (net)	200,000	Total liabilities		350,000
Equipment (net)	175,000	Common stock	$200,000	
Copyright (net)	30,000	Retained earnings	25,000	225,000
Total assets	$575,000	Total liabilities and stockholders' equity		$575,000

Moss and Zweifel agree that:

1. Land is undervalued by $30,000.
2. Equipment is overvalued by $5,000.

Zweifel agrees to sell the gallery to Moss for $350,000.

Instructions

Prepare the entry to record the purchase of Zweifel gallery on Moss's books.

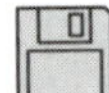

UE12-13 (Accounting for Goodwill) On July 1, 2001, Brigham Corporation purchased Young Company by paying $250,000 cash and issuing a $100,000 note payable to Steve Young. At July 1, 2001, the balance sheet of Young Company was as follows:

Cash	$ 50,000	Accounts payable	$200,000
Receivables	90,000	Young, capital	235,000
Inventory	100,000		$435,000
Land	40,000		
Buildings (net)	75,000		
Equipment (net)	70,000		
Trademarks	10,000		
	$435,000		

The recorded amounts all approximate current values except for land (worth $60,000), inventory (worth $125,000), and trademarks (worth $15,000).

Instructions

(a) Prepare the July 1 entry for Brigham Corporation to record the purchase.
(b) Prepare the December 31 entry for Brigham Corporation to record amortization of intangibles. The trademark has an estimated useful life of 4 years with a residual value of $3,000.

UE12-14 (Intangible Impairment) Presented below is information related to copyrights owned by Walter de la Mare Company at December 31, 2002.

Cost	$8,600,000
Carrying amount	4,300,000
Expected future net cash flows	4,000,000
Fair value	3,200,000

Assume that Walter de la Mare Company will continue to use this copyright in the future. As of December 31, 2002, the copyright is estimated to have a remaining useful life of 10 years.

Instructions

(a) Prepare the journal entry (if any) to record the impairment of the asset at December 31, 2002. The company does not use accumulated amortization accounts.
(b) Prepare the journal entry to record amortization expense for 2003 related to the copyrights.
(c) The fair value of the copyright at December 31, 2003, is $3,400,000. Prepare the journal entry (if any) necessary to record the increase in fair value.

UE12-15 (Goodwill Impairment) Presented below is net asset information (including associated goodwill of $200 million) related to the Carlos Division of Santana, Inc.

CARLOS DIVISION Net Assets as of December 31, 2002 (in millions)	
Cash	$ 50
Receivables	200
Property, plant, and equipment (net)	2,600
Goodwill	200
Less: Notes payable	(2,700)
Net assets	$ 350

The purpose of this division is to develop a nuclear-powered aircraft. If successful, traveling delays associated with refueling could be substantially reduced. Many other benefits would also occur. To date, management has not had much success and is deciding whether a writedown at this time is appropriate. Management estimated its future net cash flows from the project to be $400 million. Management has also received an offer to purchase the division for $335 million. All identifiable assets' and liabilities' book and fair value amounts are the same.

Instructions

(a) Prepare the journal entry (if any) to record the impairment at December 31, 2002.

(b) At December 31, 2003, it is estimated that the division's fair value increased to $345 million. Prepare the journal entry (if any) to record this increase in fair value.

UE12-16 (Accounting for R & D Costs) Leontyne Price Company from time to time embarks on a research program when a special project seems to offer possibilities. In 2001 the company expends $325,000 on a research project, but by the end of 2001 it is impossible to determine whether any benefit will be derived from it.

Instructions

(a) What account should be charged for the $325,000, and how should it be shown in the financial statements?

(b) The project is completed in 2002, and a successful patent is obtained. The R & D costs to complete the project are $110,000. The administrative and legal expenses incurred in obtaining patent number 472-1001-84 in 2002 total $16,000. The patent has an expected useful life of 5 years. Record these costs in journal entry form. Also, record patent amortization (full year) in 2002.

(c) In 2003, the company successfully defends the patent in extended litigation at a cost of $47,200, thereby extending the patent life to 12/31/10. What is the proper way to account for this cost? Also, record patent amortization (full year) in 2003.

(d) Additional engineering and consulting costs incurred in 2003 required to advance the design of a product to the manufacturing stage total $60,000. These costs enhance the design of the product considerably. Discuss the proper accounting treatment for this cost.

UE12-17 (Accounting for R & D Costs) Thomas More Company incurred the following costs during 2001 in connection with its research and development activities:

Cost of equipment acquired that will have alternative uses in future research and development projects over the next 5 years (uses straight-line depreciation)	$280,000
Materials consumed in research and development projects	59,000
Consulting fees paid to outsiders for research and development projects	100,000
Personnel costs of persons involved in research and development projects	128,000
Indirect costs reasonably allocable to research and development projects	50,000
Materials purchased for future research and development projects	34,000

Instructions

Compute the amount to be reported as research and development expense by More on its income statement for 2001. Assume equipment is purchased at beginning of year.

PROBLEMS

UP12-1 (Correct Intangible Asset Account) Esplanade Co., organized in 2000, has set up a single account for all intangible assets. The following summary discloses the debit entries that have been recorded during 2000 and 2001:

Intangible Assets

7/1/00	8-year franchise; expiration date 6/30/08	$ 42,000
10/1/00	Advance payment on laboratory space (2-year lease)	28,000
12/31/00	Net loss for 2000 including state incorporation fee, $1,000, and related legal fees of organizing, $5,000 (all fees incurred in 2000)	16,000
1/2/01	Patent purchased (10-year life)	74,000
3/1/01	Cost of developing a secret formula (indefinite life)	75,000
4/1/01	Goodwill purchased (indefinite life)	278,400
6/1/01	Legal fee for successful defense of patent purchased above	12,650
9/1/01	Research and development costs	160,000

Instructions

Prepare the necessary entries to clear the Intangible Assets account and to set up separate accounts for distinct types of intangibles. Make the entries as of December 31, 2001, recording any necessary amortization and reflecting all balances accurately as of that date. (Ignore income tax effects.)

UP12-2 (Accounting for Patents) Ankara Laboratories holds a valuable patent (No. 758-6002-1A) on a precipitator that prevents certain types of air pollution. Ankara does not manufacture or sell the products and processes it develops; it conducts research and develops products and processes which it patents, and then assigns the patents to manufacturers on a royalty basis. Occasionally it sells a patent. The history of Ankara patent number 758-6002-1A is as follows:

Date	Activity	Cost
1991–1992	Research conducted to develop precipitator	$384,000
Jan. 1993	Design and construction of a prototype	87,600
March 1993	Testing of models	42,000
Jan. 1994	Fees paid engineers and lawyers to prepare patent application; patent granted July 1, 1994	62,050
Nov. 1995	Engineering activity necessary to advance the design of the precipitator to the manufacturing stage	81,500
Dec. 1996	Legal fees paid to successfully defend precipitator patent	35,700
April 1997	Research aimed at modifying the design of the patented precipitator	43,000
July 2001	Legal fees paid in unsuccessful patent infringement suit against a competitor	34,000

Ankara assumed a useful life of 17 years when it received the initial precipitator patent. On January 1, 1999, it revised its useful life estimate downward to 5 remaining years. Amortization is computed for a full year if the cost is incurred prior to July 1, and no amortization for the year if the cost is incurred after June 30. The company's year ends December 31.

Instructions

Compute the carrying value of patent No. 758-6002-1A on each of the following dates:

(a) December 31, 1994.
(b) December 31, 1998.
(c) December 31, 2001.

UP12-3 (Accounting for Franchise, Patents, and Trade Name) Information concerning Haerhpin Corporation's intangible assets is as follows:

1. On January 1, 2002, Haerhpin signed an agreement to operate as a franchisee of Hsian Copy Service, Inc. for an initial franchise fee of $75,000. Of this amount, $15,000 was paid when the agreement was signed and the balance is payable in 4 annual payments of $15,000 each, beginning January 1, 2003. The agreement provides that the down payment is not refundable and no future services are required of the franchisor. The present value at January 1, 2002, of the 4 annual payments discounted at 14% (the implicit rate for a loan of this type) is $43,700. The agreement also provides that 5% of the revenue from the franchise must be paid to the franchisor annually. Haerhpin's

revenue from the franchise for 2002 was $950,000. Haerhpin estimates the useful life of the franchise to be 10 years. (*Hint:* You may refer to Appendix 19A to determine the proper accounting treatment for the franchise fee and payments.)

2. Haerhpin incurred $65,000 of experimental and development costs in its laboratory to develop a patent which was granted on January 2, 2002. Legal fees and other costs associated with registration of the patent totaled $13,600. Haerhpin estimates that the useful life of the patent will be 8 years.

3. A trademark was purchased from Shanghai Company for $32,000 on July 1, 1999. Expenditures for successful litigation in defense of the trademark totaling $8,160 were paid on July 1, 2002. Haerhpin estimates that the useful life of the trademark will be 20 years from the date of acquisition.

Instructions

(a) Prepare a schedule showing the intangible section of Haerhpin's balance sheet at December 31, 2002. Show supporting computations in good form.

(b) Prepare a schedule showing all expenses resulting from the transactions that would appear on Haerhpin's income statement for the year ended December 31, 2002. Show supporting computations in good form.

(AICPA adapted)

UP12-4 (Accounting for R & D Costs) During 1999, Florence Nightingale Tool Company purchased a building site for its proposed research and development laboratory at a cost of $60,000. Construction of the building was started in 1999. The building was completed on December 31, 2000, at a cost of $280,000 and was placed in service on January 2, 2001. The estimated useful life of the building for depreciation purposes was 20 years; the straight-line method of depreciation was to be employed and there was no estimated net salvage value.

Management estimates that about 50% of the projects of the research and development group will result in long-term benefits (i.e., at least 10 years) to the corporation. The remaining projects either benefit the current period or are abandoned before completion. A summary of the number of projects and the direct costs incurred in conjunction with the research and development activities for 2001 appears below.

Upon recommendation of the research and development group, Florence Nightingale Tool Company acquired a patent for manufacturing rights at a cost of $80,000. The patent was acquired on April 1, 2000, and has an economic life of 10 years.

	Number of Projects	Salaries and Employee Benefits	Other Expenses (excluding Building Depreciation Charges)
Completed projects with long-term benefits	15	$ 90,000	$50,000
Abandoned projects or projects that benefit the current period	10	65,000	15,000
Projects in process—results indeterminate	5	40,000	12,000
Total	30	$195,000	$77,000

Instructions

If generally accepted accounting principles were followed, how would the items above relating to research and development activities be reported on the company's

(a) Income statement for 2001?

(b) Balance sheet as of December 31, 2001?

Be sure to give account titles and amounts, and briefly justify your presentation.

(CMA adapted)

UP12-5 (Goodwill, Impairment) On July 31, 2003, Postera Company paid $3,000,000 to acquire all of the common stock of Mendota Incorporated, which became a division of Postera. Mendota reported the following balance sheet at the time of the acquisition.

Current assets	$ 800,000	Current liabilities	$ 600,000
Noncurrent assets	2,700,000	Long-term liabilities	500,000
		Stockholders' equity	2,400,000
Total assets	$3,500,000	Total liabilities and stockholders' equity	$3,500,000

It was determined at the date of the purchase that the fair value of the identifiable net assets of Mendota was $2,650,000. Over the next 6 months of operations, the newly purchased division experienced operating losses. In addition, it now appears that it will generate substantial losses for the foreseeable future. At December 31, 2003, Mendota reports the following balance sheet information.

Current assets	$ 450,000
Noncurrent assets (including goodwill recognized in purchase)	2,400,000
Current liabilities	(700,000)
Long-term liabilities	(500,000)
Net assets	$1,650,000

It is determined that the fair value of the Mendota Division is $1,850,000. The recorded amount for Mendota's net assets (excluding goodwill) is the same as fair value, except for property, plant, and equipment, which has a fair value $150,000 above the carrying value.

Instructions

(a) Compute the amount of goodwill recognized, if any, on July 31, 2003.
(b) Determine the impairment loss, if any, to be recorded on December 31, 2003.
(c) Assume that fair value of the Mendota Division is $1,500,000 instead of $1,850,000. Determine the impairment loss, if any, to be recorded on December 31, 2003.
(d) Prepare the journal entry to record the impairment loss, if any, and indicate where the loss would be reported in the income statement.

0-555-00073-7